OFFICIALLY LICENSED

OFFICIAL PUBLICATION

# The COMPLETE BASEBALL RECORD & FACT Book

2006 edition

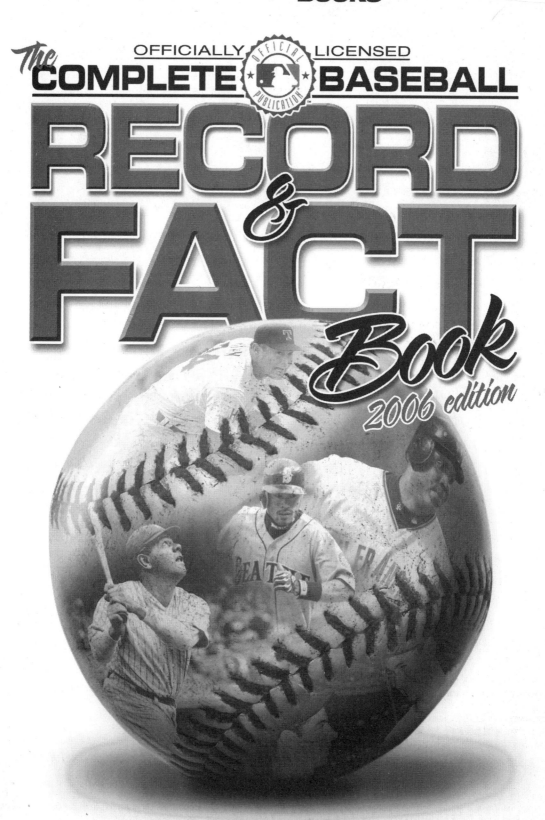

Compiled and Edited by
STEVE GIETSCHIER

**COVER DESIGN BY:** Chad Painter

**CONTRIBUTING PHOTOGRAPHERS**
**TSN Staff Photographers:** Albert Dickson, Bob Leverone, Robert Seale, Jay Drowns, TSN Archives.
**Other Photographers for TSN:** Dilip Vishwanat, Peter Newcomb, Scott Rovak, Doug Devoe, Steve Russel.

**Cover photo** of (clockwise from left) Babe Ruth, Nolan Ryan, Barry Bonds, Ted Williams, Joe DiMaggio, Ichiro Suzuki.
**Back cover photo** of (from left) Lou Gehrig, Tris Speaker, Ty Cobb, and Babe Ruth.

---



ISBN: 0-89204-815-8

10 9 8 7 6 5 4 3 2 1

# CONTENTS

## REGULAR SEASON



## DIVISION SERIES



## CHAMPIONSHIP SERIES



## WORLD SERIES



## ALL-STAR GAME

# FOREWORD

Welcome to the 2006 edition of the *Complete Baseball Record and Fact Book*. This edition combines material previously found in the *Complete Baseball Record Book* with material previously published in the *Official Major League Baseball Fact Book*.

The names of those who put together the first edition of the *Sporting News Record Book* after the 1908 season are lost to the mists of history. We can imagine without too much difficulty that they were all newspapermen with perhaps a secretary doing some typing and that their boss, Charles Spink, probably parted with no more than a few extra bucks to pay for work that went beyond their usual duties. The book they produced was, in truth, quite small. It measured only 3" by 5 1/4" and had but 36 pages. But it set a precedent that has endured for nearly a century.

That first edition, whose cover said it contained "Information of General Interest to Base Ball Enthusiasts," was not a record book at all. Then as now, major league baseball did not have an official record book, and this little volume did not fill this gap. In fact, there is much more interest now in baseball's early statistical history than there was in 1909. So, those three dozen pages contained the league leaders from 1908, a list of major league no-hitters, an abbreviated version of the *Sporting News* staple "Caught on the Fly," a bunch of miscellaneous notes, the 1909 schedules and the Ernest L. Thayer poem "Casey at the Bat."

The *Record Book* maintained this basic format through the 1940 edition. In that year, the company then known as C.C. Spink & Son introduced a second book, the *Baseball Register*. The following year, perhaps because the *Register* was such a success, the *Record Book* expanded greatly. Its first half, prepared by Ernest J. Lanigan, included some directory information, a review of the 1940 season and a long section summarizing every World Series. The second half, compiled by Leonard Gettelson, was a real record book. It contained 159 pages of fielding, batting, pitching and baserunning records covering individual players, clubs and leagues.

1942 saw the debut of three more titles. Much of Lanigan's work was transferred to the *Baseball Record Book*, and Gettelson's contributions were extended and published as the *Dope Book*. In addition, the right to publish the *Baseball Guide* came to the company when the American Sports Publishing Company, the publishing arm of the Spalding Sporting Goods Company, decided to give up a book it had produced every year since 1877.

The *Register* and the *Guide* have been published continually since their debuts, but the other two books introduced in 1942 immediately went on hiatus. The *Record Book*, which was really not a record book, reappeared in 1948, and was called the *Dope Book*. Gettelson's *Dope Book*, which really was a record book, re-emerged in 1949 and was called *One for the Book* and later, the *Baseball Record Book*.

In 1953, this quartet of titles became a quintet, as Gettelson produced the first edition of *World's Series Records*. And so things remained for more than three decades. In 1986, parts of the *Dope Book*, the *Baseball Record Book*, and *World's Series Records* were incorporated into a new title, the *Complete Baseball Record Book*, which appeared for the twentieth time in 2005.

Since 1941, editorial responsibility for these annuals has rested with only five individuals. Ernie Lanigan was a respected baseball statistician. Leonard Gettelson was a New Jersey grocer and a legendary recordkeeper. His reams of handwritten index cards, filling many, many file drawers, survive today in the Sporting News Research Center. In 1972, the editorship passed to Joe Marcin and in 1978 to Craig Carter, a man of unsurpassed perseverance and dedication.

The 2006 edition of this book is the third to bear my name on the title page, but it is, in many ways, still the product of the labors of those who have gone before. We have made some changes from last year, and we anticipate further changes next year. We hope you like what you see, and we would be pleased to hear from you. Most especially, we encourage communications that point out mistakes, typographical errors and omissions that are an inevitable part of the process. We plan to make next year's *Record and Fact Book* even better than this one, and we humbly ask for your assistance.

Steve Gietschier, Editor

Steve Gietschier

Sporting News
10176 Corporate Square Drive
Suite 200
St. Louis, MO 63132
sgietsch@sportingnews.com

# HOW TO USE THIS BOOK

Excluding the Season by Season Recaps, the 2006 edition of this book is divided into five sections:

**Regular Season**
**Division Series**
**Championship Series**
**World Series**
**All-Star Game**

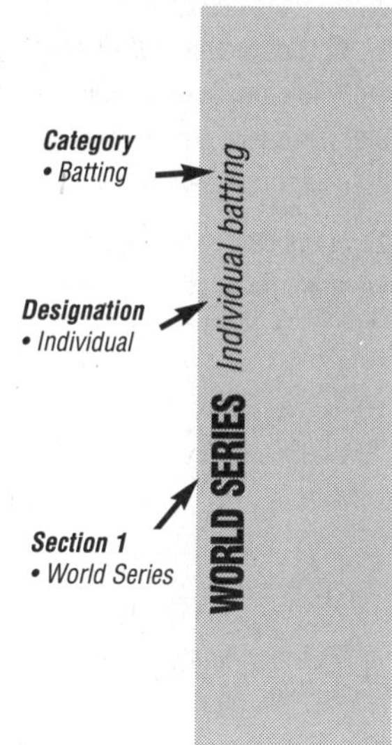


Each of these sections can be located by using the table of contents, the index or the vertical gray tabs on the side of each page.

Within these five sections, records are further divided into the following categories:

**Results**
**Service**
**Batting**
**Baserunning**
**Pitching**
**Fielding**
**Miscellaneous**
**Non-Playing Personnel**
**Career Milestones**
**General Reference**

The Regular Season section has the following additional categories:

- Yearly Leaders (year-by-year leaders in various offensive and defensive categories)
- American League Team Records (team-by-team records for each AL club)
- National League Team Records (team-by-team records for each NL club)

Finally, the Service, Batting, Baserunning, Pitching and Fielding categories are further designated as Individual, Club or (for the Regular Season) League records.

To look up a record, select the appropriate section, then the correct category and then the proper designation. For example, if you want to learn which players have hit the most home runs in a 7-game World Series, you would locate the World Series section, the Batting category and the Individual designation.

Use the vertical gray tabs on the sides of each page to navigate your way into one of the five sections. Use the tabs again to find the category and the designation you need. From this point, rely on the black and gray horizontal bars to locate the exact record you want. Black bars help narrow your search, and gray bars get even more specific.

Throughout the book, we have tried to arrange records in a sequence such as you would likely see in any standard statistical summary:

**Batting:** Games played, batting average, on-base percentage, slugging average, at-bats and plate appearances, runs, hits, singles, doubles, triples, home runs, grand slams, total bases, extra-base hits, runs batted in, bases on balls, strikeouts, sacrifice hits and flies, hit by pitch and grounding into double plays.

**Baserunning:** Stolen bases, caught stealing and left on bases.

**Pitching:** Games, games started, games relieved, complete games, innings, winning percentage, games won, saves, games lost, at-bats and plate appearances, runs, earned runs, ERA, shutouts and scoreless innings, 1-0 games, hits, home runs, total bases, extra-base hits, bases on balls, strikeouts, hit batsmen, wild pitches, sacrifice hits and flies, and balks.

**Fielding:** Games, average, putouts, assists, chances accepted, errors and double plays.

You can follow these sequences by using the black bars. Gray bars sub-divide records even further: records for rookies, righthanders, or switch-hitters, for example, or records for series, games and innings.

**Example:** To find the record for most regular season home runs by a rookie:

1. Determine which section you need (in this example it is Regular Season), which category within the Regular Season section you need (in this case it is Batting) and whether you are looking for an Individual, Club or League designation (in this case it is Individual).

2. Locate the vertical tab indicating you are in the Regular Season, Individual Batting section. This section runs from page 13 through page 31.

3. Find the horizontal black bar labeled "Home Runs," which can be found on page 20. Then find the horizontal gray bar labeled "Season," which can also be found on page 20. The record for most home runs by a rookie in the regular season can be found there.

## NOTES ON MAJOR LEAGUE RECORDS

**Here are some additional notes to help you use the Complete Baseball Record and Fact Book efficiently:**

1. Most of the records in this book refer to the following leagues: ML—major leagues, 1876 to date; NL—National League, 1876 to date; AL—American League, 1901 to date. Occasionally, National League records are divided in two with "NL since 1893" or "NL since 1900" identifying the second part. Other major leagues that appear in some places are: AA—American Association, 1882 to 1891; UA—Union Association, 1884; and PL—Players League, 1890; and in a few cases, FL—Federal League, 1914-1915.

2. In the categories called Service, Batting, Baserunning, Pitching and Fielding, some of the records designated as League records have separate listings depending upon the number of teams in a league. These listings conform to this scheme:

| | National League | American League |
|---|---|---|
| 8 clubs | 1900-1961 | 1901-1960 |
| 10 clubs | 1962-1968 | 1961-1968 |
| 12 clubs | 1969-1992 | 1969-1976 |
| 14 clubs | 1993-1997 | 1977-present |
| 16 clubs | 1998-present | |

3. Baseball has played two seasons shortened by World War I (1918 and 1919) and four shortened by labor-management difficulties (1972, 1981, 1994 and 1995). We have noted when play in these seasons affected some of the records beginning with the word "Fewest."

4. The category formerly called **long hits** is now called **extra-base hits.**

5. **Chances accepted** is the sum of putouts and assists. **Chances offered** is the sum of putouts, assists and errors. **Fielding percentage** is calculated by dividing **chances accepted** by **chances offered**.

7. Many of the records formerly listed separately as having occurred in **extra-inning games** have been consolidated with the same record for **nine-inning games.** The **extra-inning** records are enclosed within brackets.

8. In editions previous to 2004, records set during the special round of postseason play occasioned by baseball's split season in 1981 were incorporated in the Division Series section. Starting in 2004, these records were removed and placed in an addendum. Records in the Division Series section now commence with games played in 1995.

9. Records for two games in one day with separate admissions are included with doubleheader records.

# ACKNOWLEDGEMENTS

The 2006 edition of the *Complete Baseball Record and Fact Book* could not have been completed without considerable assistance from a number of people. Obviously, this year's book stands on the shoulders of every previous edition, so thanks are due to Ernie Lanigan, Leonard Gettelson and Joe Marcin, posthumously, and to Craig Carter. In addition, I thank my colleagues at the *Sporting News*, John Rawlings, Dale Bye and Joe Hoppel, for entrusting this assignment to me; Chad Painter, who redesigned the book and formatted the pages with skill and alacrity; and Zach Bodendieck and Sarah Gietschier, who provided crucial editing and proofreading assistance.

My extreme gratitude also goes to the following members of the Society for American Baseball Research, baseball experts, one and all, whose professionalism and willingness, even eagerness, to help were absolutely essential:

Mike McCormick of Major League Baseball Publishing for his support;

Trent McCotter, for his enthusiasm for baseball in the 19th century;

Pete Palmer, who compared the text of the entire book to his substantial statistical database, thereby generating hundreds of additions, changes and corrections;

Dave Smith and the volunteers of Retrosheet (www.retrosheet.org), whose database is an incomparable source of detail and accuracy;

Lyle Spatz, chairman of SABR's Records Committee, who shared his knowledge and his judgment even as the hurricane winds blew; and

David Vincent, custodian of SABR's Tattersall/McConnell Home Run Log, who embraced every home run query I could imagine.

Finally, I thank a group of volunteers who agreed to help revise and extend the "Team Records" section of the book: Bob Bogart, Nicole DiCicco, Steve Elsberry, Steve Ferenchick, Steve Friedman, Bill Gilbert, Steve Glassman, Ed Hartig, Paul Hirsch, Mike Hunssinger, Ron Kaplan, Francis Kinlaw, Henry Kirn, John Matthew IV, Wayne McElreavy, Brian Mohr, Darren Munk, David Marc Nieporent, Dwight Oxley, Scott Schleifer, Mark Schoen, Lyle Spatz, Mike Spatz, Tom Stillman, Bob Timmermann, Joel Tscherne, Mike Welch, Jim Wohlenhaus and Al Yellon.

Quite simply, there would be no book without them.

# REGULAR SEASON





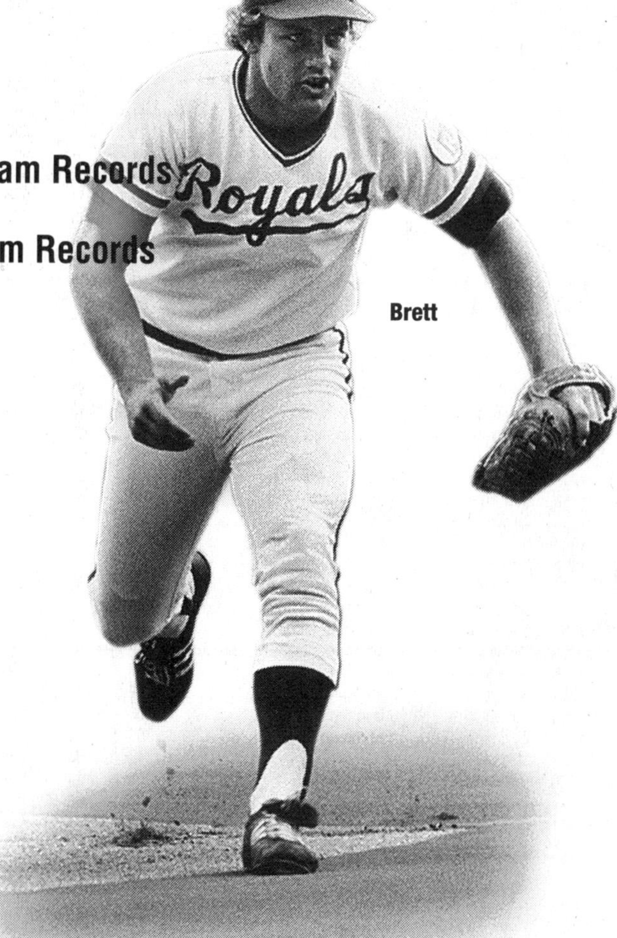


Brett

# RESULTS

## PENNANT AND DIVISION WINNERS

### AMERICAN LEAGUE

| Year | Club | Manager | W | L | Pct | GA |
|---|---|---|---|---|---|---|
| 1901 | Chicago | Clark Griffith | 83 | 53 | .610 | 4.0 |
| 1902 | Philadelphia | Connie Mack | 83 | 53 | .610 | 5.0 |
| 1903 | Boston | Jimmy Collins | 91 | 47 | .659 | 14.5 |
| 1904 | Boston | Jimmy Collins | 95 | 59 | .617 | 1.5 |
| 1905 | Philadelphia | Connie Mack | 92 | 56 | .622 | 2.0 |
| 1906 | Chicago | Fielder Jones | 93 | 58 | .616 | 3.0 |
| 1907 | Detroit | Hughey Jennings | 92 | 58 | .613 | 1.5 |
| 1908 | Detroit | Hughey Jennings | 90 | [illegible] | [illegible] | 0.5 |
| 1909 | Detroit | Hughey Jennings | 98 | 54 | .645 | 3.5 |
| 1910 | Philadelphia | Connie Mack | 102 | 48 | .680 | 14.5 |
| 1911 | Philadelphia | Connie Mack | 101 | 50 | .669 | 13.5 |
| 1912 | Boston | Jake Stahl | 105 | 47 | .691 | 14.0 |
| 1913 | Philadelphia | Connie Mack | 96 | 57 | .627 | 6.5 |
| 1914 | Philadelphia | Connie Mack | 99 | 53 | .651 | 8.5 |
| 1915 | Boston | Bill Carrigan | 101 | 50 | .669 | 2.5 |
| 1916 | Boston | Bill Carrigan | 91 | 63 | .591 | 2.0 |
| 1917 | Chicago | Pants Rowland | 100 | 54 | .649 | 9.0 |
| 1918 | Boston | Ed Barrow | 75 | 51 | .595 | 1.5 |
| 1919 | Chicago | Kid Gleason | 88 | 52 | .629 | 3.5 |
| 1920 | Cleveland | Tris Speaker | 98 | 56 | .636 | 2.0 |
| 1921 | New York | Miller Huggins | 98 | 55 | .641 | 4.5 |
| 1922 | New York | Miller Huggins | 94 | 60 | .610 | 1.0 |
| 1923 | New York | Miller Huggins | 98 | 54 | .645 | 16.0 |
| 1924 | Washington | Bucky Harris | 92 | 62 | .597 | 2.0 |
| 1925 | Washington | Bucky Harris | 96 | 55 | .636 | 8.5 |
| 1926 | New York | Miller Huggins | 91 | 63 | .591 | 3.0 |
| 1927 | New York | Miller Huggins | 110 | 44 | .714 | 19.0 |
| 1928 | New York | Miller Huggins | 101 | 53 | .656 | 2.5 |
| 1929 | Philadelphia | Connie Mack | 104 | 46 | .693 | 18.0 |
| 1930 | Philadelphia | Connie Mack | 102 | 52 | .662 | 8.0 |
| 1931 | Philadelphia | Connie Mack | 107 | 45 | .704 | 13.5 |
| 1932 | New York | Joe McCarthy | 107 | 47 | .695 | 13.0 |
| 1933 | Washington | Joe Cronin | 99 | 53 | .651 | 7.0 |
| 1934 | Detroit | Mickey Cochrane | 101 | 53 | .656 | 7.0 |
| 1935 | Detroit | Mickey Cochrane | 93 | 58 | .616 | 3.0 |
| 1936 | New York | Joe McCarthy | 102 | 51 | .667 | 19.5 |
| 1937 | New York | Joe McCarthy | 102 | 52 | .662 | 13.0 |
| 1938 | New York | Joe McCarthy | 99 | 53 | .651 | 9.5 |
| 1939 | New York | Joe McCarthy | 106 | 45 | .702 | 17.0 |
| 1940 | Detroit | Del Baker | 90 | 64 | .584 | 1.0 |
| 1941 | New York | Joe McCarthy | 101 | 53 | .656 | 17.0 |
| 1942 | New York | Joe McCarthy | 103 | 51 | .669 | 9.0 |
| 1943 | New York | Joe McCarthy | 98 | 56 | .636 | 13.5 |
| 1944 | St. Louis | Luke Sewell | 89 | 65 | .578 | 1.0 |
| 1945 | Detroit | Steve O'Neill | 88 | 65 | .575 | 1.5 |
| 1946 | Boston | Joe Cronin | 104 | 50 | .675 | 12.0 |
| 1947 | New York | Bucky Harris | 97 | 57 | .630 | 12.0 |
| 1948 | Cleveland† | Lou Boudreau | 97 | 58 | .626 | 1.0 |
| 1949 | New York | Casey Stengel | 97 | 57 | .630 | 1.0 |
| 1950 | New York | Casey Stengel | 98 | 56 | .636 | 3.0 |
| 1951 | New York | Casey Stengel | 98 | 56 | .636 | 5.0 |
| 1952 | New York | Casey Stengel | 95 | 59 | .617 | 2.0 |
| 1953 | New York | Casey Stengel | 99 | 52 | .656 | 8.5 |
| 1954 | Cleveland | Al Lopez | 111 | 43 | .721 | 8.0 |
| 1955 | New York | Casey Stengel | 96 | 58 | .623 | 3.0 |
| 1956 | New York | Casey Stengel | 97 | 57 | .630 | 9.0 |
| 1957 | New York | Casey Stengel | 98 | 56 | .636 | 8.0 |
| 1958 | New York | Casey Stengel | 92 | 62 | .597 | 10.0 |
| 1959 | Chicago | Al Lopez | 94 | 60 | .610 | 5.0 |
| 1960 | New York | Casey Stengel | 97 | 57 | .630 | 8.0 |
| 1961 | New York | Ralph Houk | 109 | 53 | .673 | 8.0 |
| 1962 | New York | Ralph Houk | 96 | 66 | .593 | 5.0 |
| 1963 | New York | Ralph Houk | 104 | 57 | .646 | 10.5 |
| 1964 | New York | Yogi Berra | 99 | 63 | .611 | 1.0 |
| 1965 | Minnesota | Sam Mele | 102 | 60 | .630 | 7.0 |
| 1966 | Baltimore | Hank Bauer | 97 | 63 | .606 | 9.0 |
| 1967 | Boston | Dick Williams | 92 | 70 | .568 | 1.0 |
| 1968 | Detroit | Mayo Smith | 103 | 59 | .636 | 12.0 |
| 1969 | Baltimore (E) | Earl Weaver | 109 | 53 | .673 | 19.0 |
| | Minnesota (W) | Billy Martin | 97 | 65 | .599 | 9.0 |
| 1970 | Baltimore (E) | Earl Weaver | 108 | 54 | .667 | 15.0 |
| | Minnesota (W) | Bill Rigney | 98 | 64 | .605 | 9.0 |
| 1971 | Baltimore (E) | Earl Weaver | 101 | 57 | .639 | 12.0 |
| | Oakland (W) | Dick Williams | 101 | 60 | .627 | 16.0 |
| 1972 | Detroit (E) | Billy Martin | 86 | 70 | .551 | 0.5 |
| | Oakland (W) | Dick Williams | 93 | 62 | .600 | 5.5 |
| 1973 | Baltimore (E) | Earl Weaver | 97 | 65 | .599 | 8.0 |
| | Oakland (W) | Dick Williams | 94 | 68 | .580 | 6.0 |
| 1974 | Baltimore (E) | Earl Weaver | 91 | 71 | .562 | 2.0 |
| | Oakland (W) | Alvin Dark | 90 | 72 | .556 | 5.0 |
| 1975 | Boston (E) | Darrell Johnson | 95 | 65 | .594 | 4.5 |
| | Oakland (W) | Al Dark | 98 | 64 | .605 | 7.0 |
| 1976 | New York (E) | Billy Martin | 97 | 62 | .610 | 10.5 |
| | Kansas City (W) | Whitey Herzog | 90 | 72 | .556 | 2.5 |
| 1977 | New York (E) | Billy Martin | 100 | 62 | .617 | 2.5 |
| | Kansas City (W) | Whitey Herzog | 102 | 60 | .630 | 8.0 |
| 1978 | New York (E)‡ | Billy Martin, Bob Lemon | 100 | 63 | .613 | 1.0 |
| | Kansas City (W) | Whitey Herzog | 92 | 70 | .568 | 5.0 |
| 1979 | Baltimore (E) | Earl Weaver | 102 | 57 | .642 | 8.0 |
| | California (W) | Jim Fregosi | 88 | 74 | .543 | 3.0 |
| 1980 | New York | Dick Howser | 103 | 59 | .636 | 3.0 |
| | Kansas City (W) | Jim Frey | 97 | 65 | .599 | 14.0 |
| 1981 | New York (E) | Gene Michael, Bob Lemon | 59 | 48 | .551 | § |
| | Oakland (W) | Billy Martin | 64 | 45 | .587 | §§ |
| 1982 | Milwaukee (E) | Buck Rodgers, Harvey Kuenn | 95 | 67 | .586 | 1.0 |
| | California (W) | Gene Mauch | 93 | 69 | .574 | 3.0 |
| 1983 | Baltimore (E) | Joe Altobelli | 98 | 64 | .605 | 6.0 |
| | Chicago (W) | Tony La Russa | 99 | 63 | .611 | 20.0 |
| 1984 | Detroit (E) | Sparky Anderson | 104 | 58 | .642 | 15.0 |
| | Kansas City (W) | Dick Howser | 84 | 78 | .519 | 3.0 |
| 1985 | Toronto (E) | Bobby Cox | 99 | 62 | .615 | 2.0 |
| | Kansas City (W) | Dick Howser | 91 | 71 | .562 | 1.0 |
| 1986 | Boston (E) | John McNamara | 95 | 66 | .590 | 5.5 |
| | California (W) | Gene Mauch | 92 | 70 | .568 | 5.0 |
| 1987 | Detroit (W) | Sparky Anderson | 98 | 64 | .605 | 2.0 |
| | Minnesota (W) | Tom Kelly | 85 | 77 | .525 | 2.0 |
| 1988 | Boston (E) | John McNamara, Joe Morgan | 89 | 73 | .549 | 1.0 |
| | Oakland (W) | Tony La Russa | 104 | 58 | .642 | 13.0 |
| 1989 | Toronto (E) | Jimy Williams, Cito Gaston | 89 | 73 | .549 | 2.0 |
| | Oakland (W) | Tony La Russa | 99 | 63 | .611 | 7.0 |
| 1990 | Boston (E) | Joe Morgan | 88 | 74 | .543 | 2.0 |
| | Oakland (W) | Tony La Russa | 103 | 59 | .636 | 9.0 |
| 1991 | Toronto (E) | Cito Gaston | 91 | 71 | .562 | 7.0 |
| | Minnesota (W) | Tom Kelly | 95 | 67 | .586 | 8.0 |
| 1992 | Toronto (E) | Cito Gaston | 96 | 66 | .593 | 4.0 |
| | Oakland (W) | Tony La Russa | 96 | 66 | .593 | 6.0 |
| 1993 | Toronto (E) | Cito Gaston | 95 | 67 | .586 | 7.0 |
| | Chicago (W) | Gene Lamont | 94 | 68 | .580 | 8.0 |
| 1994 | no division or pennant winners∞ | | | | | |
| 1995 | Boston (E) | Kevin Kennedy | 86 | 58 | .597 | 7.0 |
| | Cleveland (C) | Mike Hargrove | 100 | 44 | .694 | 30.0 |
| | Seattle (W)†† | Lou Piniella | 79 | 66 | .545 | 1.0 |
| 1996 | New York (E) | Joe Torre | 92 | 70 | .568 | 4.0 |
| | Cleveland (C) | Mike Hargrove | 99 | 62 | .615 | 14.5 |
| | Texas (W) | Johnny Oates | 90 | 72 | .556 | 4.5 |
| 1997 | Baltimore (E) | Davey Johnson | 98 | 64 | .605 | 2.0 |
| | Cleveland (C) | Mike Hargrove | 86 | 75 | .534 | 6.0 |
| | Seattle (W) | Lou Piniella | 90 | 72 | .556 | 6.0 |
| 1998 | New York (E) | Joe Torre | 114 | 48 | .704 | 22.0 |
| | Cleveland (C) | Mike Hargrove | 89 | 73 | .549 | 9.0 |
| | Texas (W) | Johnny Oates | 88 | 74 | .543 | 3.0 |
| 1999 | New York (E) | Joe Torre | 98 | 64 | .605 | 4.0 |
| | Cleveland (C) | Mike Hargrove | 97 | 65 | .599 | 21.5 |
| | Texas (W) | Johnny Oates | 95 | 67 | .586 | 8.0 |
| 2000 | New York (E) | Joe Torre | 87 | 74 | .540 | 2.5 |
| | Chicago (C) | Jerry Manuel | 95 | 67 | .586 | 5.0 |
| | Oakland (W) | Art Howe | 91 | 70 | .565 | 0.5 |
| 2001 | New York (E) | Joe Torre | 95 | 65 | .594 | 13.5 |
| | Cleveland (C) | Charlie Manuel | 91 | 71 | .562 | 6.0 |
| | Seattle (W) | Lou Piniella | 116 | 46 | .716 | 14.0 |
| 2002 | New York (E) | Joe Torre | 103 | 58 | .640 | 10.5 |
| | Minnesota (C) | Ron Gardenhire | 94 | 67 | .584 | 13.5 |
| | Oakland (W) | Art Howe | 103 | 59 | .636 | 4.0 |
| 2003 | New York (E) | Joe Torre | 101 | 61 | .623 | 6.0 |
| | Minnesota (C) | Ron Gardenhire | 90 | 72 | .556 | 4.0 |
| | Oakland (W) | Ken Macha | 96 | 66 | .593 | 3.0 |
| 2004 | New York (E) | Joe Torre | 101 | 61 | .623 | 3.0 |
| | Minnesota (C) | Ron Gardenhire | 92 | 70 | .568 | 9.0 |
| | Anaheim (W) | Mike Scioscia | 92 | 70 | .568 | 1.0 |
| 2005 | New York (E)* | Joe Torre | 95 | 67 | .586 | (tie) |
| | Chicago (C) | Ozzie Guillen | 99 | 63 | .611 | 6.0 |
| | Los Angeles (W) | Mike Scioscia | 95 | 67 | .586 | 7.0 |

†defeated Boston in 1-game playoff; ‡defeated Boston in 1-game playoff to win division; §first half 34-22, second half 25-26; §§first half 37-23, second half 27-22; ∞New York finished the strike-shortened season with the league's best record (70-43, .619); ††defeated California in 1-game playoff to win division; *awarded division title over Boston by tie-breaker

### NATIONAL LEAGUE

| Year | Club | Manager | W | L | Pct | GA |
|---|---|---|---|---|---|---|
| 1876 | Chicago | Al Spalding | 52 | 14 | .788 | 6.0 |
| 1877 | Boston | Harry Wright | 31 | 17 | .646 | 3.0 |
| 1878 | Boston | Harry Wright | 41 | 19 | .683 | 4.0 |
| 1879 | Providence | George Wright | 55 | 23 | .705 | 6.0 |
| 1880 | Chicago | Cap Anson | 67 | 17 | .798 | 15.0 |

| Year | Club | Manager | W | L | Pct | GA |
|---|---|---|---|---|---|---|
| 1881 | Chicago | Cap Anson | 56 | 28 | .667 | 9.0 |
| 1882 | Chicago | Cap Anson | 55 | 29 | .655 | 3.0 |
| 1883 | Boston | John Morrill | 63 | 35 | .643 | 4.0 |
| 1884 | Providence | Frank Bancroft | 84 | 28 | .750 | 10.5 |
| 1885 | Chicago | Cap Anson | 87 | 25 | .777 | 2.0 |
| 1886 | Chicago | Cap Anson | 90 | 34 | .726 | 2.5 |
| 1887 | Detroit | Bill Watkins | 79 | 45 | .637 | 3.5 |
| 1888 | New York | Jim Mutrie | 84 | 47 | .641 | 9.0 |
| 1889 | New York | Jim Mutrie | 83 | 43 | .659 | 1.0 |
| 1890 | Brooklyn | Bill McGunnigle | 86 | 43 | .667 | 6.5 |
| 1891 | Boston | Frank Selee | 87 | 51 | .630 | 3.5 |
| 1892 | Boston* | Frank Selee | 102 | 48 | .680 | 8.5 |
| 1893 | Boston | Frank Selee | 86 | 43 | .667 | 5.0 |
| 1894 | Baltimore | Ned Hanlon | 89 | 39 | .695 | 3.0 |
| 1895 | Baltimore | Ned Hanlon | 87 | 43 | .669 | 3.0 |
| 1896 | Baltimore | Ned Hanlon | 90 | 39 | .698 | 9.5 |
| 1897 | Boston | Frank Selee | 93 | 39 | .705 | 2.0 |
| 1898 | Boston | Frank Selee | 102 | 47 | .685 | 6.0 |
| 1899 | Brooklyn | Ned Hanlon | 88 | 42 | .677 | 4.0 |
| 1900 | Brooklyn | Ned Hanlon | 82 | 54 | .603 | 4.5 |
| 1901 | Pittsburgh | Fred Clarke | 90 | 49 | .647 | 7.5 |
| 1902 | Pittsburgh | Fred Clarke | 103 | 36 | .741 | 27.5 |
| 1903 | Pittsburgh | Fred Clarke | 91 | 49 | .650 | 6.5 |
| 1904 | New York | John McGraw | 106 | 47 | .693 | 13.0 |
| 1905 | New York | John McGraw | 105 | 48 | .686 | 9.0 |
| 1906 | Chicago | Frank Chance | 116 | 36 | .763 | 20.0 |
| 1907 | Chicago | Frank Chance | 107 | 45 | .704 | 17.0 |
| 1908 | Chicago | Frank Chance | 99 | 55 | .643 | 1.0 |
| 1909 | Pittsburgh | Fred Clarke | 110 | 42 | .724 | 6.5 |
| 1910 | Chicago | Frank Chance | 104 | 50 | .675 | 13.0 |
| 1911 | New York | John McGraw | 99 | 54 | .647 | 7.5 |
| 1912 | New York | John McGraw | 103 | 48 | .682 | 10.0 |
| 1913 | New York | John McGraw | 101 | 51 | .664 | 12.5 |
| 1914 | Boston | George Stallings | 94 | 59 | .614 | 10.5 |
| 1915 | Philadelphia | Pat Moran | 90 | 62 | .592 | 7.0 |
| 1916 | Brooklyn | Wilbert Robinson | 94 | 60 | .610 | 2.5 |
| 1917 | New York | John McGraw | 98 | 56 | .636 | 10.0 |
| 1918 | Chicago | Fred Mitchell | 84 | 45 | .651 | 10.5 |
| 1919 | Cincinnati | Pat Moran | 96 | 44 | .686 | 9.0 |
| 1920 | Brooklyn | Wilbert Robinson | 93 | 61 | .604 | 7.0 |
| 1921 | New York | John McGraw | 94 | 59 | .614 | 4.0 |
| 1922 | New York | John McGraw | 93 | 61 | .604 | 7.0 |
| 1923 | New York | John McGraw | 95 | 58 | .621 | 4.5 |
| 1924 | New York | John McGraw | 93 | 60 | .608 | 1.5 |
| 1925 | Pittsburgh | Bill McKechnie | 95 | 58 | .621 | 8.5 |
| 1926 | St. Louis | Rogers Hornsby | 89 | 65 | .578 | 2.0 |
| 1927 | Pittsburgh | Donie Bush | 94 | 60 | .610 | 1.5 |
| 1928 | St. Louis | Bill McKechnie | 95 | 59 | .617 | 2.0 |
| 1929 | Chicago | Joe McCarthy | 98 | 54 | .645 | 10.5 |
| 1930 | St. Louis | Gabby Street | 92 | 62 | .597 | 2.0 |
| 1931 | St. Louis | Gabby Street | 101 | 53 | .656 | 13.0 |
| 1932 | Chicago | Rogers Hornsby, Charlie Grimm | 90 | 64 | .584 | 4.0 |
| 1933 | New York | Bill Terry | 91 | 61 | .599 | 5.0 |
| 1934 | St. Louis | Frankie Frisch | 95 | 58 | .621 | 2.0 |
| 1935 | Chicago | Charlie Grimm | 100 | 54 | .649 | 4.0 |
| 1936 | New York | Bill Terry | 92 | 62 | .597 | 5.0 |
| 1937 | New York | Bill Terry | 95 | 57 | .625 | 3.0 |
| 1938 | Chicago | Charlie Grimm, Gabby Hartnett | 89 | 63 | .586 | 2.0 |
| 1939 | Cincinnati | Bill McKechnie | 97 | 57 | .630 | 4.5 |
| 1940 | Cincinnati | Bill McKechnie | 100 | 53 | .654 | 12.0 |
| 1941 | Brooklyn | Leo Durocher | 100 | 54 | .649 | 2.5 |
| 1942 | St. Louis | Billy Southworth | 106 | 48 | .688 | 2.0 |
| 1943 | St. Louis | Billy Southworth | 105 | 49 | .682 | 18.0 |
| 1944 | St. Louis | Billy Southworth | 105 | 49 | .682 | 14.5 |
| 1945 | Chicago | Charlie Grimm | 98 | 56 | .636 | 3.0 |
| 1946 | St. Louis† | Eddie Dyer | 98 | 58 | .628 | 2.0 |
| 1947 | Brooklyn | Burt Shotton | 94 | 60 | .610 | 5.0 |
| 1948 | Boston | Billy Southworth | 91 | 62 | .595 | 6.5 |
| 1949 | Brooklyn | Burt Shotton | 97 | 57 | .630 | 1.0 |
| 1950 | Philadelphia | Eddie Sawyer | 91 | 63 | .591 | 2.0 |
| 1951 | New York‡ | Leo Durocher | 98 | 59 | .624 | 1.0 |
| 1952 | Brooklyn | Charlie Dressen | 96 | 57 | .627 | 4.5 |
| 1953 | Brooklyn | Charlie Dressen | 105 | 49 | .682 | 13.0 |
| 1954 | New York | Leo Durocher | 97 | 57 | .630 | 5.0 |
| 1955 | Brooklyn | Walter Alston | 98 | 55 | .641 | 13.5 |
| 1956 | Brooklyn | Walter Alston | 93 | 61 | .604 | 1.0 |
| 1957 | Milwaukee | Fred Haney | 95 | 59 | .617 | 8.0 |
| 1958 | Milwaukee | Fred Haney | 92 | 62 | .597 | 8.0 |
| 1959 | Los Angeles†† | Walter Alston | 88 | 68 | .564 | 2.0 |
| 1960 | Pittsburgh | Danny Murtaugh | 95 | 59 | .617 | 7.0 |
| 1961 | Cincinnati | Fred Hutchinson | 93 | 61 | .604 | 4.0 |
| 1962 | San Francisco‡‡ | Alvin Dark | 103 | 62 | .624 | 1.0 |
| 1963 | Los Angeles | Walter Alston | 99 | 63 | .611 | 6.0 |
| 1964 | St. Louis | Johnny Keane | 93 | 69 | .574 | 1.0 |
| 1965 | Los Angeles | Walter Alston | 97 | 65 | .599 | 2.0 |
| 1966 | Los Angeles | Walter Alston | 95 | 67 | .586 | 1.5 |
| 1967 | St. Louis | Red Schoendienst | 101 | 60 | .627 | 10.5 |
| 1968 | St. Louis | Red Schoendienst | 97 | 65 | .599 | 9.0 |
| 1969 | New York (E) | Gil Hodges | 100 | 62 | .617 | 8.0 |
| | Atlanta (W) | Lum Harris | 93 | 69 | .574 | 3.0 |

| Year | Club | Manager | W | L | Pct | GA |
|---|---|---|---|---|---|---|
| 1970 | Pittsburgh (E) | Danny Murtaugh | 89 | 73 | .549 | 5.0 |
| | Cincinnati (W) | Sparky Anderson | 102 | 60 | .630 | 14.5 |
| 1971 | Pittsburgh (E) | Danny Murtaugh | 97 | 65 | .599 | 7.0 |
| | San Francisco (W) | Charlie Fox | 90 | 72 | .556 | 1.0 |
| 1972 | Pittsburgh (E) | Bill Virdon | 96 | 59 | .619 | 11.0 |
| | Cincinnati (W) | Sparky Anderson | 95 | 59 | .617 | 10.5 |
| 1973 | New York (E) | Yogi Berra | 82 | 79 | .509 | 1.5 |
| | Cincinnati (W) | Sparky Anderson | 99 | 63 | .611 | 3.5 |
| 1974 | Pittsburgh (E) | Danny Murtaugh | 88 | 74 | .543 | 1.5 |
| | Los Angeles (W) | Walter Alston | 102 | 60 | .630 | 4.0 |
| 1975 | Pittsburgh (E) | Danny Murtaugh | 92 | 69 | .571 | 6.5 |
| | Cincinnati (W) | Sparky Anderson | 108 | 54 | .667 | 20.0 |
| 1976 | Philadelphia (E) | Danny Ozark | 101 | 61 | .623 | 9.0 |
| | Cincinnati (W) | Sparky Anderson | 102 | 60 | .630 | 10.0 |
| 1977 | Philadelphia (E) | Danny Ozark | 101 | 61 | .623 | 5.0 |
| | Los Angeles (W) | Tommy Lasorda | 98 | 64 | .605 | 10.0 |
| 1978 | Philadelphia (E) | Danny Ozark | 90 | 72 | .556 | 1.5 |
| | Los Angeles (W) | Tommy Lasorda | 95 | 67 | .586 | 2.5 |
| 1979 | Pittsburgh (E) | Chuck Tanner | 98 | 64 | .605 | 2.0 |
| | Cincinnati (W) | John McNamara | 90 | 71 | .559 | 1.5 |
| 1980 | Philadelphia (E) | Dallas Green | 91 | 71 | .562 | 1.0 |
| | Houston (W)** | Bill Virdon | 93 | 70 | .571 | 1.0 |
| 1981 | Montreal (E) | Dick Williams, Jim Fanning | 60 | 48 | .556 | § |
| | Los Angeles (W) | Tommy Lasorda | 63 | 47 | .573 | §§ |
| 1982 | St. Louis (E) | Whitey Herzog | 92 | 70 | .568 | 3.0 |
| | Atlanta (W) | Joe Torre | 89 | 73 | .549 | 1.0 |
| 1983 | Philadelphia (E) | Pat Corrales, Paul Owens | 90 | 72 | .556 | 6.0 |
| | Los Angeles (W) | Tommy Lasorda | 91 | 71 | .562 | 3.0 |
| 1984 | Chicago (E) | Jim Frey | 96 | 65 | .596 | 6.5 |
| | San Diego (W) | Dick Williams | 92 | 70 | .568 | 12.0 |
| 1985 | St. Louis (E) | Whitey Herzog | 101 | 61 | .623 | 3.0 |
| | Los Angeles (W) | Tommy Lasorda | 95 | 67 | .586 | 5.5 |
| 1986 | New York (E) | Davey Johnson | 108 | 54 | .667 | 21.5 |
| | Houston (W) | Hal Lanier | 96 | 66 | .593 | 10.0 |
| 1987 | St. Louis (E) | Whitey Herzog | 95 | 67 | .586 | 3.0 |
| | San Francisco (W) | Roger Craig | 90 | 72 | .556 | 6.0 |
| 1988 | New York (E) | Davey Johnson | 100 | 60 | .625 | 15.0 |
| | Los Angeles (W) | Tommy Lasorda | 94 | 67 | .584 | 7.0 |
| 1989 | Chicago (E) | Don Zimmer | 93 | 69 | .571 | 6.0 |
| | San Francisco (W) | Roger Craig | 92 | 70 | .568 | 3.0 |
| 1990 | Pittsburgh (E) | Jim Leyland | 95 | 67 | .586 | 4.0 |
| | Cincinnati (W) | Lou Piniella | 91 | 71 | .562 | 5.0 |
| 1991 | Pittsburgh | Jim Leyland | 98 | 64 | .605 | 14.0 |
| | Atlanta (W) | Bobby Cox | 94 | 68 | .580 | 1.0 |
| 1992 | Pittsburgh (E) | Jim Leyland | 96 | 66 | .593 | 9.0 |
| | Atlanta (W) | Bobby Cox | 98 | 64 | .605 | 8.0 |
| 1993 | Philadelphia (E) | Jim Fregosi | 97 | 65 | .599 | 3.0 |
| | Atlanta (W) | Bobby Cox | 104 | 58 | .642 | 1.0 |
| 1994 | no division or pennant winners∞ | | | | | |
| 1995 | Atlanta (E) | Bobby Cox | 90 | 54 | .625 | 21.0 |
| | Cincinnati (C) | Davey Johnson | 85 | 59 | .590 | 9.0 |
| | Los Angeles (W) | Tommy Lasorda | 78 | 66 | .542 | 1.0 |
| 1996 | Atlanta (E) | Bobby Cox | 96 | 66 | .593 | 8.0 |
| | St. Louis (C) | Tony La Russa | 88 | 74 | .543 | 6.0 |
| | San Diego (W) | Bruce Bochy | 91 | 71 | .562 | 1.0 |
| 1997 | Atlanta (E) | Bobby Cox | 101 | 61 | .623 | 9.0 |
| | Houston (C) | Larry Dierker | 84 | 78 | .519 | 5.0 |
| | San Francisco (W) | Dusty Baker | 90 | 72 | .556 | 2.0 |
| 1998 | Atlanta (E) | Bobby Cox | 106 | 56 | .654 | 18.0 |
| | Houston (C) | Larry Dierker | 102 | 60 | .630 | 12.5 |
| | San Diego (W) | Bruce Bochy | 98 | 64 | .605 | 9.5 |
| 1999 | Atlanta (E) | Bobby Cox | 103 | 59 | .636 | 6.5 |
| | Houston (C) | Larry Dierker | 97 | 65 | .599 | 1.5 |
| | Arizona (W) | Buck Showalter | 100 | 62 | .617 | 14.0 |
| 2000 | Atlanta (E) | Bobby Cox | 95 | 67 | .586 | 1.0 |
| | St. Louis (C) | Tony La Russa | 95 | 67 | .586 | 10.0 |
| | San Francisco (W) | Dusty Baker | 97 | 65 | .599 | 11.0 |
| 2001 | Atlanta (E) | Bobby Cox | 88 | 74 | .543 | 2.0 |
| | Houston (C)*** | Larry Dierker | 93 | 69 | .574 | (tie) |
| | Arizona (W) | Bob Brenly | 92 | 70 | .568 | 2.0 |
| 2002 | Atlanta (E) | Bobby Cox | 101 | 59 | .631 | 19.0 |
| | St. Louis (C) | Tony La Russa | 97 | 65 | .599 | 13.0 |
| | Arizona (W) | Bob Brenly | 98 | 64 | .605 | 2.5 |
| 2003 | Atlanta (E) | Bobby Cox | 101 | 61 | .623 | 10.0 |
| | Chicago (C) | Dusty Baker | 88 | 74 | .543 | 1.0 |
| | San Francisco (W) | Felipe Alou | 100 | 61 | .621 | 15.5 |
| 2004 | Atlanta (E) | Bobby Cox | 96 | 66 | .593 | 10.0 |
| | St. Louis (C) | Tony La Russa | 105 | 57 | .648 | 13.0 |
| | Los Angeles (W) | Jim Tracy | 93 | 69 | .574 | 2.0 |
| 2005 | Atlanta (E) | Bobby Cox | 90 | 72 | .556 | 2.0 |
| | St. Louis (C) | Tony La Russa | 100 | 62 | .617 | 11.0 |
| | San Diego (W) | Bruce Bochy | 82 | 80 | .506 | 5.0 |

*Boston won first half, Cleveland won second half, and Boston won playoff, 5 games to none (1 tie); †defeated Brooklyn in playoff, 2 games to none; ‡defeated Brooklyn in playoff, 2 games to 1; ††defeated Milwaukee in playoff, 2 games to none; ‡‡defeated Los Angeles in playoff, 2 games to 1; **defeated Los Angeles in 1-game playoff to win division; §first half 30-25, second half 30-23; §§first half 36-21, second half 27-26; ∞Montreal finished the strike-shortened season with the league's best record (74-40, .649); ***awarded division title over St. Louis by tie-breaker

# INDIVIDUAL SERVICE

## YEARS

**Most years played**

ML—27—Nolan Ryan, New York NL, California AL, Houston NL, Texas AL; 1966-1993, except 1967 (14 in NL, 13 in AL), 807 G
AL—25—Eddie Collins, Philadelphia, Chicago, 1906-1930, 2,826 G
NL—24—Pete Rose, Cincinnati, Philadelphia, Montreal, 1963-1986, 3,562 G

**For complete lists of 20-year players and pitchers, see page 102.**

**Most consecutive years played**

ML—26—Nolan Ryan, New York NL, California AL, Houston NL, Texas AL; 1968-1993 (13 in NL, 13 in AL), 805 G
AL—25—Eddie Collins, Philadelphia, Chicago, 1906-1930, 2,826 G
NL—24—Pete Rose, Cincinnati, Philadelphia, Montreal, 1963-1986, 3,562 G

**Most years with one club**

AL—23—Brooks Robinson, Baltimore, 1955-1977, 2,896 G
Carl Yastrzemski, Boston, 1961-1983, 3,308 G
NL—22—Cap Anson, Chicago, 1876-1897, 2,253 G
Mel Ott, New York, 1926-1947, 2,730 G
Stan Musial, St. Louis, 1941-1963, except 1945 in military service, 3,026 G

**Most consecutive years with one club**

AL—23—Brooks Robinson, Baltimore, 1955-1977, 2,896 G
Carl Yastrzemski, Boston, 1961-1983, 3,308 G
NL—22—Cap Anson, Chicago, 1876-1897, 2,253 G
Mel Ott, New York, 1926-1947, 2,730 G
Stan Musial, St. Louis, 1941-1963 except 1945 in military service, 3,026 G

## BY POSITION (EXCEPT PITCHERS)

**Most seasons by first baseman**

NL—22—Willie McCovey, San Francisco, San Diego, 1959-1980, 2,045 G
AL—20—Joe Judge, Washington, Boston, 1915-1934, 2,056 G

**Most seasons by second baseman**

ML—22—Joe Morgan, Houston NL, Cincinnati NL, San Francisco NL, Philadelphia NL, Oakland AL, 1963-1984, 2,527 G
AL—21—Eddie Collins, Philadelphia, Chicago, 1908-1928, 2,651 G
NL—21—Joe Morgan, Houston, Cincinnati, San Francisco, Philadelphia, 1963-1983, 2,427 G

**Most years by third baseman**

AL—23—Brooks Robinson, Baltimore, 1955-1977, 2,870 G
NL—18—Mike Schmidt, Philadelphia, 1972-1989, 2,212 G

**Most years by shortstop**

ML—20—Bill Dahlen, Chicago NL, Brooklyn NL, New York NL, Boston NL, 1891-1911, except 1910, 2,139 G
Bobby Wallace, St. Louis NL, St. Louis AL, 1899-1918, 1,828 G
Luke Appling, Chicago AL, 1930-1950, except 1944 in military service, 2,218 G
Alan Trammell, Detroit, 1977-1996, 2,139 G
AL—20—Luke Appling, Chicago, 1930-1950, except 1944 in military service, 2,219 G
Alan Trammell, Detroit, 1977-1996, 2,139 G
NL—20—Bill Dahlen, Chicago, Brooklyn, New York, Boston, 1891-1911, except 1910, 2,139 G
NL since 1900—19—Rabbit Maranville, Boston, Pittsburgh, Chicago, Brooklyn, St. Louis, 1912-1931, except 1924, 2,153 G
Dave Concepcion, Cincinnati, 1970-1988, 2,178 G
Chris Speier, San Francisco, Montreal, St. Louis, Chicago, 1971-1989, 1,888 G
Ozzie Smith, San Diego, St. Louis, 1978-1996, 2,511 G

**Most years by outfielder**

ML—25—Rickey Henderson, Oakland AL, New York AL, Toronto AL, San Diego NL, Anaheim AL, New York NL, Seattle AL, Boston AL, Los Angeles NL, 1979-2003, 2,826 G
AL—24—Ty Cobb, Detroit, Philadelphia, 1905-1928, 2,938 G
NL—22—Willie Mays, New York Giants, San Francisco, New York Mets, 1951-1973, except 1953 in military service, 2,843 G

**Most years by catcher**

ML—25—Deacon McGuire, Toledo, Cleveland, Rochester, Washington AA; Detroit, Philadelphia, Washington, Brooklyn NL; Detroit, New York, Boston, Cleveland AL, 1884-1912, except 1889, 1908, 1909, 1911, 1,608 G
AL—24—Carlton Fisk, Boston, Chicago, 1969-1993, except 1970, 2,226 G
NL—21—Bob O'Farrell, Chicago, St. Louis, New York, Cincinnati, 1915-1935, 1,338 G

## YOUNGEST AND OLDEST PLAYERS

**Youngest player, game**

NL—15 years, 10 months, 11 days—Joe Nuxhall, Cincinnati, June 10, 1944 (pitcher)
AL—16 years, 8 months, 5 days—Carl Scheib, Philadelphia, Sept 6, 1943, second game (pitcher)

**Oldest player, game**

AL—59 years, 2 months, 18 days—Satchel Paige, Kansas City, Sept 25, 1965 (pitcher)
NL—54 years, 21 days—Jim O'Rourke, New York, Sept 22, 1904 (catcher)

## LEAGUES AND CLUBS

**Most leagues played for, career**

4—20 players; last—Lave Cross, AA, PL, NL, AL, 1887-1907, 21 seasons, 2,259 G

**Most leagues played for, season**

3—Willie Murphy, 1884, NL, AA, UA
Walter Prince, 1884, NL, AA, UA
George Strief, 1884, AA, UA, NL

**Most clubs played for, career**

ML—12—Deacon McGuire, Toledo AA, Detroit NL, Philadelphia NL, Cleveland AA, Rochester AA, Washington AA, Washington NL, Brooklyn NL, Detroit AL, New York AL, Boston AL, Cleveland AL, 1884-1912, except 1889, 1909, 1911, 26 seasons
Mike Morgan, Oakland AL, New York AL, Toronto AL, Seattle AL, Baltimore AL, Los Angeles NL, Chicago NL, St. Louis NL, Cincinnati NL, Minnesota AL, Texas AL, Arizona NL, 1978-2001, except 1980, 1981 and 1984, 21 seasons
NL—9—Dan Brouthers, Troy, Buffalo, Detroit, Boston, Brooklyn, Baltimore, Louisville, Philadelphia, New York, 1879-1889, 1892-1896, 1904, 17 seasons
NL since 1893—8—Chris Jones, Cincinnati, Houston, Colorado, New York, San Diego, Arizona, San Francisco, Milwaukee, 1991-2000, 10 seasons
Todd Zeile, St. Louis, Chicago, Philadelphia, Los Angeles, Florida, New York, Colorado, Montreal, 1989-1998, 2000-2004, 15 seasons
Lenny Harris, Cincinnati, Los Angeles, New York, Colorado, Arizona, Milwaukee, Chicago, Florida, 1988-2005, 18 seasons
AL—8—Juan Beniquez, Boston, Texas, New York, Seattle, California, Baltimore, Kansas City, Toronto, 1971-1988, except 1973, 17 seasons

**Most clubs played for, season**

ML—4—many players; last—Jose Bautista, Baltimore AL, Tampa Bay AL, Kansas City AL, Pittsburgh NL, 88 G, 2004
NL—4—Tom Dowse, Louisville, Cincinnati, Philadelphia, Washington, 63 G, 1892
AL—4—Frank Huelsman, Chicago, Detroit, St. Louis, Washington, 112 G, 1904
Paul Lehner, Philadelphia, Chicago, St. Louis, Cleveland, 65 G, 1951
Ted Gray, Chicago, Cleveland, New York, Baltimore, 14 G, 1955

**Most clubs played for, one day**

NL—2—Max Flack, Chicago, St. Louis, May 30 a.m., p.m., 1922
Cliff Heathcote, St. Louis, Chicago, May 30 a.m., p.m., 1922
Joel Youngblood, New York, Montreal, Aug 4, 1982

## POSITIONS

**Most positions played, season**

NL—9—Sport McAllister, Cleveland, 110 G, 1899
Jimmy M.T. Walsh, Philadelphia, 84 G, 1911
Gene Paulette, St. Louis, 125 G, 1918
Jose Oquendo, St. Louis, 148 G, 1988
AL—9—Sam Mertes, Chicago, 129 G, 1902
Jack Rothrock, Boston, 117 G, 1928
Bert Campaneris, Kansas City, 144 G, 1965
Cesar Tovar, Minnesota, 157 G, 1968
Scott Sheldon, Texas, 58 G, 2000
Shane Halter, Detroit, 105 G, 2000

**Most positions played, game**

AL—9—Bert Campaneris, Kansas City, Sept 8, 1965 (played 9 inn of 13-inn game)
Cesar Tovar, Minnesota, Sept 22, 1968
Scott Sheldon, Texas, Sept 6, 2000 (played 6 inn of 9-inn game)
Shane Halter, Detroit, October 1, 2000

## PITCHERS

### YEARS

**Most years pitched**

ML—27—Nolan Ryan, New York NL, California AL, Houston NL, Texas AL, 1966, 1968-1993, 807 G
AL—23—Early Wynn, Washington, Cleveland, Chicago, 1939, 1941-1963, except 1945 in military service, 691 G
NL—22—Steve Carlton, St. Louis, Philadelphia, San Francisco, 1965-1986, 695 G

**For a complete list of 20-year pitchers, see page 102.**

**Most consecutive years pitched**

ML—26—Nolan Ryan, New York NL, California AL, Houston NL, Texas AL, 1968-1993
AL—22—Samuel P. Jones, Cleveland, Boston, New York, St. Louis, Washington, Chicago, 1914-1935
Herb Pennock, Philadelphia, Boston, New York, 1912-1934 except 1918 in military service
Red Ruffing, Boston, New York, Chicago, 1924-1947 except 1943 and 1944 in military service
Early Wynn, Washington, Cleveland, Chicago, 1941-1963 except 1945 in military service

NL—22—Steve Carlton, St. Louis, Philadelphia, San Francisco, 1965-1986

**Most years pitched with one club**

AL—21—Walter Johnson, Washington, 1907-1927, 802 G
Ted Lyons, Chicago, 1923-1946, except 1943-1945 in military service, 594 G
NL—21—Phil Niekro, Milwaukee, Atlanta, 1964-1983, 1987, 740 G

**Most consecutive years pitched with one club**

AL—21—Walter Johnson, Washington, 1907-1927, 802 G
Ted Lyons, Chicago, 1923-1946 except 1943-1945 in military service, 594 G
NL—20—Phil Niekro, Milwaukee, Atlanta, 1964-1983, 739 G
Warren Spahn, Boston, Milwaukee, 1942-1964 except 1943-1945 in military service, 714 G

### YOUNGEST AND OLDEST PITCHERS

**Youngest pitcher, game**

NL—15 years, 10 months, 11 days—Joe Nuxhall, Cincinnati, June 10, 1944
AL—16 years, 8 months, 5 days—Carl Scheib, Philadelphia, Sept 6, 1943, 2nd game

**Oldest pitcher, game**

AL—59 years, 2 months, 18 days—Satchel Paige, Kansas City, Sept 25, 1965
NL—50 years, 2 days—Jack Quinn, Cincinnati, July 7, 1933

### LEAGUES AND CLUBS

**Most leagues pitched in**

4— Jersey Bakely, AA, UA, NL, PL
Ed Crane, UA, NL, PL, AA
Frank Foreman, UA, AA, NL, AL
Con Murphy, UA, NL, PL, AA

**Most clubs pitched on**

ML—12—Mike Morgan, Oakland AL, New York AL, Toronto AL, Seattle AL, Baltimore AL, Los Angeles NL, Chicago NL, St. Louis NL, Cincinnati NL, Minnesota AL, Texas AL, Arizona NL, 1978-2002, except 1980, 1981 and 1984, 22 seasons, 597 G
AL—7—Ken Sanders, Kansas City Athletics, Boston, Kansas City Athletics, Oakland, Milwaukee, Minnesota, Cleveland, California, Kansas City Royals, 1964, 1966, 1968, 1970-1974,1976, 9 seasons, 348 G (Kansas City Athletics and Oakland are same franchise.)
Ken Brett, Boston, Milwaukee, New York, Chicago, California, Minnesota, Kansas City, 1967, 1969-1972, 1976-1981, 11 seasons, 238 G
Mike Morgan, Oakland, New York, Toronto, Seattle, Baltimore, Minnesota, Texas, 1978, 1979, 1982, 1983, 1985-1988, 1998, 1999, 10 seasons, 209 G
NL—7—Mike Maddux, Philadelphia, Los Angeles, San Diego, New York, Pittsburgh, Montreal, Houston, 1986-1995, 1998-2000, 13 seasons, 407 G

**Most clubs pitched on, season**

ML—4—Willis Hudlin, Cleveland AL, Washington AL, St. Louis AL, New York NL, 19 G, 1940
Ted Gray, Chicago AL, Cleveland AL, New York AL, Baltimore AL, 14 G, 1955
Mike Kilkenny, Detroit AL, Oakland AL, San Diego NL, Cleveland AL, 29 G 1972
Dan Miceli, Colorado NL, Cleveland AL, New York AL, Houston NL, 57 G, 2003
AL—4—Ted Gray, Chicago, Cleveland, New York, Baltimore, 14 G, 1955
NL—3—many pitchers; last—Willie Banks, Chicago, Los Angeles, Florida, 25 G, 1995

# CLUB SERVICE

## PLAYERS USED

**Most players used, season**

AL—59—Cleveland, 2002
NL—59—San Diego, 2002

**Fewest players used, season**

NL—17—Boston, 1903
AL—18—Boston, 1904

**Most players used, game**

AL—27—Kansas City vs California, Sept 10, 1969
[30—Oakland vs Chicago, Sept 19, 1972, 15 inn]
NL—25—St. Louis vs Los Angeles, Apr 16, 1959
Milwaukee vs Philadelphia, Sept 26, 1964
Philadelphia vs Chicago, Sept 27, 1981, 2nd game
[27—Philadelphia vs St. Louis, Sept 13, 1974, 17 inn
Chicago vs Pittsburgh, Sept 21, 1978, 14 inn
Chicago vs Houston, Sept 2, finished Sept 3, 1986, 18 inn
Los Angeles vs San Francisco, Sept 28, 1986, 16 inn]

**Most players used by both clubs, game**

AL—46—New York 24, Boston 22, Oct 2, 2005
[54—Seattle 29, Texas 25, Sept 25, 1992, 16 inn]
NL—45—Chicago 24, Montreal 21, Sept 5, 1978
Atlanta 24, New York 21, Sept 29, 2002
[53—Chicago 27, Houston 26, Sept 2, finished Sept 3, 1986, 18 inn]

**Most players used, doubleheader**

AL—41—Chicago vs Oakland, Sept 7, 1970
NL—41—San Diego vs San Francisco, May 30, 1977
[42—St. Louis vs Brooklyn, Aug 29, 1948, 19 inn
Montreal vs Pittsburgh, Sept 5, 1975, 19 inn]

**Most players used by both clubs, doubleheader**

NL—74—San Diego 41, San Francisco 33, May 30, 1977
[74—Montreal 42, Pittsburgh 32, Sept 5, 1975, 19 inn]
AL—71—New York 39, Baltimore 32, Sept 26, 2003.
[73—Washington 37, Cleveland 36, Sept 14, finished Sept 20, 1971, 29 inn]

### PINCH-HITTERS

**Most pinch-hitters used, game**

NL—9—Los Angeles vs St. Louis, Sept 22, 1959
Montreal vs Pittsburgh, Sept 5, 1975, 2nd game
Atlanta vs Montreal, Sept 21, 1993
[9—San Francisco vs Los Angeles, Sept 28, 1986, 16 inn
St. Louis vs Cincinnati, Sept 25, 1997, 14 inn]
AL—8—Baltimore vs Chicago, May 28, 1954, 1st game
[10—Oakland vs Chicago, Sept 19, 1972, 15 inn]

**Most pinch-hitters used by both clubs, game**

NL—13—Atlanta 9, Montreal 4, Sept 21, 1993
[14—New York 7, Chicago 7, May 2, 1956, 17 inn
San Francisco 9, Los Angeles 5, Sept 28, 1986, 16 inn]
AL—10—Baltimore 6, New York 4, Apr 26, 1959, 2nd game
[14—Oakland 10, Chicago 4, Sept 19, 1972, 15 inn]

**Most pinch-hitters used, doubleheader**

AL—10—New York vs Boston, Sept 6, 1954
Baltimore vs Washington, Apr 19, 1959
NL—10—St. Louis vs Chicago, May 11, 1958
St. Louis vs Pittsburgh, July 13, 1958
[15—Montreal vs Pittsburgh, Sept 5, 1975, 19 inn]

**Most pinch-hitters used by both clubs, doubleheader**

NL—15—Milwaukee 8, San Francisco 7, Aug 30, 1964
[19—Montreal 15, Pittsburgh 4, Sept 5, 1975, 19 inn]
AL—14—New York 10, Boston 4, Sept 6, 1954
[17—New York 9, Washington 8, Aug 14, 1960, 24 inn]

**Most pinch-hitters used, inning**

NL—6—San Francisco vs Pittsburgh, May 5, 1958, 9th
San Diego vs San Francisco, Sept 16, 1986, 9th
Atlanta vs Montreal, Sept 21, 1993, 7th
Los Angeles vs Colorado, Sept 24, 2002, 6th
AL—6—Detroit vs New York, Sept 5, 1971, 7th

**Most consecutive pinch-hitters used, inning**

NL—5—many times; last—Chicago vs Pittsburgh, Sept 20, 1996, 8th
AL—5—many times; last—New York vs Milwaukee, Sept 22, 1987, 1st game, 8th

**Most pinch-hitters used by both clubs, inning**

AL—8—Chicago 5, Baltimore 3, May 18, 1957, 7th
NL—8—Philadelphia 5, St. Louis 3, Apr 30, 1961, 8th
New York 5, San Francisco 3, Sept 16, 1966, 9th

### PINCH-RUNNERS

**Most pinch-runners used, inning**

AL—4—Chicago vs Minnesota, Sept 16, 1967, 9th
Oakland vs Chicago, Sept 24, 1975, 7th
Texas vs California, Sept 10, 1987, 9th
Anaheim vs Texas, Sept 23, 2000, 7th
NL—4—Montreal vs St. Louis, Sept 26, 1977, 9th
San Diego vs Cincinnati, Aug 10, 1978, 7th

**Most pinch-runners used by both clubs, inning**

NL—5—Pittsburgh 3, New York 2, Sept 21, 1981, 9th
AL—5—Anaheim 4, Texas 1, Sept 23, 2000, 7th

## NUMBER OF PLAYERS USED BY POSITION

### INFIELDERS

**Most first basemen used, game**

AL—5—Chicago vs New York, June 25, 1953
NL—4—New York vs Arizona, May 11, 2004
New York vs Philadelphia, July 7, 2004

Los Angeles vs Arizona, July 17, 2004
San Diego vs Colorado, Sept 6, 2005
[4—Philadelphia vs Milwaukee, July 23, 1964, 10 inn
Cincinnati vs Chicago, May 28, 2001, 13 inn
Los Angeles vs Milwaukee, Apr 19, 2005, 10 inn
Houston vs St. Louis, Sept 2, 2005, 13 inn]

**Most first basemen used by both clubs, game**
AL—6—Chicago 5, New York 1, June 25, 1953
NL—6—Cincinnati 3, New York 3, July 1, 2004
New York 4, Philadelphia 2, July 7, 2004
[6—Cincinnati 4, Chicago 2, May 28, 2001, 13 inn]

**Most second basemen used, game**
AL—4—many times
[6—Oakland vs Chicago, Sept 19, 1972, 15 inn]
NL—4—many times
[5—New York vs Cincinnati, July 20, 1954, 13 inn]

**Most second basemen, both clubs, game**
AL—6—Oakland 4, Cleveland 2, May 5, 1973
Oakland 4, Cleveland 2, May 6, 1973, 1st game
Oakland 4, Cleveland 2, May 6, 1973, 2nd game
[8—Oakland 6, Chicago 2, Sept 19, 1972, 15 inn]
NL—5—many times
[7—New York 5, Cincinnati 2, July 20, 1954, 13 inn]

**Most third basemen used, game**
NL—5—Atlanta vs Philadelphia, Apr 21, 1966
Philadelphia vs Pittsburgh, Aug 6, 1971
AL—4—many clubs

**Most third basemen used by both clubs, game**
NL—7—Philadelphia 5, Pittsburgh 2, Aug 6, 1971
AL—6—Minnesota 3, Cleveland 3, July 27, 1969
Boston 3, Milwaukee 3, Sept 14, 1976
[6—Detroit 3, Cleveland 3, July 10, 1969, 11 inn]

**Most shortstops used, game**
AL—4—New York vs Washington, Sept 5, 1954
Minnesota vs Oakland, Sept 22, 1968
[4—Detroit vs New York, July 28, 1957, 2nd game, 15 inn
Baltimore vs New York, Sept 26, 1958, 12 inn
Texas vs Seattle, Sept 25, 1992, 16 inn]
NL—4—San Francisco vs Cincinnati, Sept 4, 1989
[5—Done by many teams in extra inn]

**Most shortstops used by both clubs, game**
AL—6—Detroit 3, Washington 3, Sept 21, 1968
Boston 3, New York 3, Oct 2, 2005
NL—5—Cincinnati 3, Houston 2, July 13, 1969
Montreal 3, Pittsburgh 2, Oct 1, 1969
San Francisco 4, Cincinnati 1, Sept 4, 1989

## OUTFIELDERS

**Most right fielders used, game**
AL—4—Baltimore vs Washington, Sept 25, 1955
[6—Kansas City vs California, Sept 8, 1965, 13 inn]
NL—4—many clubs
[5—New York vs Cincinnati, July 22, 1986, 14 inn]

**Most right fielders used by both clubs, game**
ML—5—Montreal NL 3, Anaheim AL 2, June 4, 2003
NL—6—Los Angeles 4, Houston 2, June 10, 1962, 1st game
Los Angeles 3, San Francisco 3, Apr 6, 2005
St. Louis 3, San Diego 3, May 8, 2005
St. Louis 4, Colorado 2, June 1, 2005
St. Louis 4, Milwaukee 2, Sept 24, 2005
[8—San Francisco 4, Los Angeles 4, Sept 28, 1986, 16 inn]
AL—5—many games
[7—Kansas City 6, California 1, Sept 8, 1965, 13 inn]

**Most center fielders used, game**
AL—5—Minnesota vs Oakland, Sept 22, 1968
NL—4—Cincinnati vs St. Louis, May 30, 1942, 2nd game
[4—Boston vs Brooklyn, Apr 25, 1917, 12 inn
Philadelphia vs St. Louis, Sept 25, 1966, 13 inn
Houston vs Chicago, Sept 2, finished Sept 3, 1986, 18 inn
Philadelphia vs Cincinnati, July 20, 1987, 11 inn]

**Most center fielders used by both clubs, game**
AL—7—Minnesota 5, Oakland 2, Sept 22, 1968
NL—6—Cincinnati 4, St. Louis 2, May 30, 1942, 2nd game
New York 3, St. Louis 3, Apr 30, 2003
[7—Houston 4, Chicago 3, Sept 2, finished Sept 3, 1986, 18 inn]

**Most left fielders used, game**
AL—5—Seattle vs Oakland, Sept 11, 1992
NL—4—Brooklyn vs Philadelphia, Sept 26, 1946
Los Angeles vs New York, June 4, 1966
Chicago vs Philadelphia, Sept 21, 1977
Atlanta vs Philadelphia, Sept 28, 2003
St. Louis vs Milwaukee, Oct 3, 2004
[5—Philadelphia vs Milwaukee, July 23, 1964, 10 inn]

**Most left fielders used by both clubs, game**
NL—6—New York 3, San Francisco 3, Sept 22, 1963
St. Louis 4, Milwaukee 2, Oct 3, 2004
[7—Los Angeles 4, St. Louis 3, May 12, 1962, 15 inn
Chicago 4, St. Louis 3, Sept 2, 2003, 1st game, 15 inn]
AL—6—Oakland 4, Cleveland 2, July 20, 1974
Seattle 5, Oakland 1, Sept 11, 1992
[6—Minnesota 3, Baltimore 3, Apr 16, 1961, 2nd game, 11 inn
Minnesota 3, Oakland 3, Sept 6, 1969, 18 inn]

## CATCHERS AND PITCHERS

**Most catchers used, game**
NL—4—Boston vs New York, Oct 6, 1929
Brooklyn vs St. Louis, May 5, 1940
New York vs St. Louis, Sept 12, 1962
AL—4—Minnesota vs California, Sept 27, 1967
[4—Kansas City vs Chicago, Sept 21, 1973, 12 inn]

**Most catchers used by both clubs, game**
AL—6—Chicago 3, Philadelphia 3, July 10, 1926
[6—Chicago 3, New York 3, Sept 10, 1955, 10 inn
California 3, Oakland 3, Sept 28, 1969, 11 inn
Kansas City 4, Chicago 2, Sept 21, 1972, 12 inn]
NL—6—Boston 4, New York 2, Oct 6, 1929
Brooklyn 4, St. Louis 2, May 5, 1940
New York 4, St. Louis 2, Sept 2, 1962
[6—New York 3, Chicago 3, May 2, 1956, 17 inn]

**Most pitchers used, season**
NL—37—San Diego, 2002
AL—32—Cleveland, 2000

**Fewest pitchers used, season**
AL—5—Boston, 1904
NL—5—Boston, 1901

**Most relief appearances, season**
NL—506—Colorado, 2002
AL—494—Texas, 2003

**Most pitchers used, game**
AL—10—Baltimore vs New York, Sept 12, 2004
[11—Seattle vs Texas, Sept 25, 1992, 16 inn]
NL—9—Montreal vs Chicago, Sept 10, 1996
St. Louis vs Los Angeles, Sept 8, 2001
St. Louis vs Cincinnati, Oct 2, 2005
[10—Chicago vs Pittsburgh, Apr 20, finished Aug 11, 1986, 17 inn
Colorado vs Atlanta, Aug 22, 2000, 12 inn
Atlanta vs Philadelphia, Sept 27, 2003, 10 inn
Philadelphia vs New York, Sept 11, 2004, 13 inn]

**Most pitchers used by both clubs, game**
NL—16—Houston 8, San Francisco 8, Sept 28, 2002
[18—Houston 10, Chicago 8, Sept 28, 1995, 11 inn
Philadelphia 10, New York 8, Sept 11, 2004, 13 inn]
AL—15—Detroit 8, Minnesota 7, Oct 1, 2000
Baltimore 10, New York 5, Sept 12, 2004
[18—Washington 9, Cleveland 9, Sept 14, finished Sept 20, 1971, 20 inn
Seattle 9, Oakland 9, Sept 20, 1997, 15 inn]

**Most pitchers used by winning club, shutout game**
AL—8—Boston vs Baltimore, Oct 3, 1999, 10 inn (won 1-0)
NL—6—Los Angeles vs Milwaukee, Oct 3, 1965 (won 3-0)
Florida vs Chicago, May 15, 1994 (won 3-0)
St. Louis vs Pittsburgh, May 17, 1994 (won 2-0)
St. Louis vs Philadelphia, Apr 19, 1996 (won 1-0)
Florida vs Philadelphia, June 4, 2002 (won 5-0)

**Most pitchers used by winning club, no-hit game**
NL—6—Houston vs New York AL, June 11, 2003 (won 8-0)
AL—4—Oakland vs California, Sept 28, 1975 (won 5-0)
Baltimore vs Oakland, July 13, 1991 (won 2-0)

**Most pitchers used, doubleheader**
NL—13—San Diego vs San Francisco, May 30, 1977
[13—Milwaukee vs Philadelphia, May 12, 1963, 23 inn]
AL—12—Cleveland vs Detroit, Sept 7, 1959
California vs Detroit, Sept 30, 1967
[13—Baltimore vs Texas, Aug 13, 1991, 21 inn]

**Most pitchers used by both clubs, doubleheader**
ML—24—Baltimore AL 12, San Francisco NL 12, June 12, 2004, 24 inn
NL—22—Milwaukee 11, New York 11, July 26, 1964
Chicago 12, Pittsburgh 11, Sept 19, 2003
AL—21—Detroit 11, Kansas City 10, July 23, 1961
[22—Washington 12, Cleveland 10, Sept 14, finished Sept 20, 1971, 29 inn]

**Most pitchers used, inning**
AL—6—Oakland vs Cleveland, Sept 3, 1983, 9th
NL—5—many times; last—Philadelphia vs Atlanta, Apr 8, 1999, 8th

**Most pitchers used by both clubs, inning**
NL—8—Los Angeles 5, New York 3, Aug 26, 1987, 8th
AL—7—Chicago 4, Baltimore 3, July 16, 1955, 9th
Baltimore 4, Boston 3, June 20, 1975, 9th
Oakland 6, Cleveland 1, Sept 3, 1983, 9th

## FRANCHISE LONGEVITY

**Most years in same city by a franchise**
NL—130—Chicago, 1876-2005 (consec)
AL—105—Boston, Chicago, Cleveland, Detroit, 1901-2005 (consec)

# LEAGUE SERVICE

## ALL PLAYERS

**Most players, season**
NL (16 clubs)—699 in 2000
NL (14 clubs)—588 in 1995, 1997
NL (12 clubs)—491 in 1990
NL (10 clubs)—373 in 1967
NL since 1900 (8 clubs)—333 in 1946
AL (14 clubs)—623 in 2004
AL (12 clubs)—440 in 1969
AL (10 clubs)—369 in 1962
AL (8 clubs )—323 in 1955

**Most players in 150 or more games, season**
AL (14 clubs)—46 in 1998
AL (12 clubs)—32 in 1976
AL (10 clubs)—30 in 1962
AL (8 clubs)—19 in 1921, 1936
NL (16 clubs)—42 in 1998, 2002
NL (14 clubs)—38 in 1997
NL (12 clubs)—40 in 1978, 1979
NL (10 clubs)—34 in 1965
NL since 1900 (8 clubs)—23 in 1953

**Fewest players, season**
AL (12 clubs)—412 in 1976
AL (8 clubs)—166 in 1904
NL (12 clubs)—420 in 1979
NL since 1900 (8 clubs)—188 in 1905

**Most players playing in all games, season**
NL since 1900—10 in 1932
AL—10 in 1933

**Fewest players playing in all games, season**
AL—0—1910, 1963
NL since 1900—0—1914

**Most players with two or more clubs, season**
NL since 1900—48 in 1998
AL—47 in 1952

**Fewest players with two or more clubs, season**
AL—2 in 1940
NL since 1900—5 in 1935

**Most players with three or more clubs, season**
AL—4 in 1952
NL since 1900—3 in 1919

## PITCHERS

**Most pitchers in league, season**
NL (16 clubs)—345 in 2003
NL (14 clubs)—290 in 1995
NL (12 clubs)—228 in 1990
NL (10 clubs)—167 in 1967
NL since 1900 (8 clubs)—152 in 1946
AL (14 clubs)—311 in 2004
AL (12 clubs)—189 in 1970
AL (10 clubs)—170 in 1962
AL (8 clubs)—141 in 1946, 1955

**Most pitchers in league, one day**
NL—72—Sept 7, 1964
AL—62—Aug 9, 1970

**Most pitchers in both leagues, one day**
121—Sept 7, 1964, 72 in NL (10 G), 49 in AL (8 G)

# INDIVIDUAL BATTING

## GAMES

**Most games, career**
NL—3,562—Pete Rose, Cincinnati, Philadelphia, Montreal, 24 seasons, 1963-1986
AL—3,308—Carl Yastrzemski, Boston, 23 seasons, 1961-1983

**For a complete list of players playing in 2,500 games in career, see page 102.**

**Most games with one club, career**
AL—3,308—Carl Yastrzemski, Boston, 23 seasons, 1961-1983
NL—3,076—Hank Aaron, Milwaukee/Atlanta, 21 seasons,1954-1974

**Most consecutive games, career**
AL—2,632—Cal Ripken Jr., Baltimore, May 30, 1982-Sept 19, 1998
NL—1,207—Steve Garvey, Los Angeles, San Diego, Sept 3, 1975-July 29, 1983, 1st game

**For a complete list of players playing in 500 consecutive games in career, see page 103.**

**Most consecutive games from start of career**
AL—487—Hideki Matsui, New York, Mar 31, 2003-Oct 2, 2005
NL—424—Ernie Banks, Chicago, Sept 17, 1953-Aug 10, 1957

**Most games, season**
NL—165—Maury Wills, Los Angeles, 1962
AL—164—Cesar Tovar, Minnesota, 1967

**Fewest games for leader, season**
NL—152—Stan Hack, Chicago, 1938
Billy Herman, Chicago, 1938
AL—154—many players

**Most games with two clubs, season**
NL—164—Frank Taveras, Pittsburgh, New York, 1979
AL—160—Julio Cruz, Seattle, Chicago, 1983
Cecil Fielder, Detroit, New York, 1996

**Most games by rookie, season**
AL—163—Hideki Matsui, New York, 2003
NL—162—Dick Allen, Philadelphia, 1964
Johnny Ray, Pittsburgh, 1982
Jeff Conine, Florida, 1993

**Most games by righthanded batter, season**
NL—164—Jose Pagan, San Francisco, 1962
Ron Santo, Chicago, 1965
Frank Taveras, Pittsburgh, New York, 1979
AL—164—Cesar Tovar, Minnesota, 1967

**Most games by lefthanded batter, season**
NL—164—Billy Williams, Chicago, 1965
AL—163—Leon Wagner, Cleveland, 1964
Al Oliver, Texas, 1980
Greg Walker, Chicago, 1985

**Most games by switch-hitter, season**
NL—165—Maury Wills, Los Angeles, 1962
AL—163—Don Buford, Chicago, 1966
Tony Fernandez, Toronto, 1986

**Most games by pinch-hitter, season**
NL—95—Lenny Harris, New York, 2001
AL—81—Elmer Valo, New York, Washington, 1960

**Most seasons leading league in games**
AL—9—Cal Ripken Jr., Baltimore, 1983 (tied), 1984 (tied), 1987, 1989 (tied), 1991 (tied),

1992, 1993, 1996, 1997 (tied)
NL—6—Ernie Banks, Chicago, 1954 (tied), 1955 (tied), 1957 (tied), 1958, 1959 (tied), 1960
Steve Garvey, Los Angeles, 1977 (tied), 1978 (tied), 1980, 1981 (tied), 1982 (tied), San Diego, 1985 (tied)

**Most seasons played all club's games**
AL—15—Cal Ripken Jr., Baltimore, 1983-1997
NL—10—Pete Rose, Cincinnati, 1965, 1972, 1974-1977, Philadelphia, 1979-1982

**Most seasons playing 150 or more games**
NL—17—Pete Rose, Cincinnati, Philadelphia, 1963-1983, except 1964, 1967, 1968, 1981
AL—15—Cal Ripken Jr., Baltimore, 1982-1998, except 1994 and 1995

**Most seasons playing 100 or more games**
NL—23—Pete Rose, Cincinnati, Philadelphia, Montreal, 1963-1985
AL—22—Carl Yastrzemski, Boston, 1961-1983, except 1981

## BATTING AVERAGE

**Highest average, career (1,500 or more hits)**
NL—.371—Willie Keeler, New York, Brooklyn, Baltimore, 12 seasons, 1892-1902, 1910 (5,278 AB, 1,958 H)
AL—.366—Ty Cobb, Detroit, Philadelphia, 24 seasons, 1905-1928 (11,434 AB, 4,189 H)

**For a complete list of players with .300 career batting averages and 1,500 or more hits, see page 103.**

**Highest average, season (400 or more at-bats)**
NL—.440—Hugh Duffy, Boston, 125 G, 1894
AA—.435—Tip O'Neill, St. Louis, 124 G, 1887
AL—.426—Nap Lajoie, Philadelphia, 131 G, 1901
NL since 1900—.424—Rogers Hornsby, St. Louis, 143 G, 1924

**Highest average for non-leader, season (400 or more at-bats)**
NL—.420—Dan Brouthers, Detroit, 123 G, 1887
NL since 1893—.415—Sam Thompson, Philadelphia, 102 G, 1894
AL—.408—Joe Jackson, Cleveland, 147 G, 1911
NL since 1900—.393—Babe Herman, Brooklyn, 153 G, 1930

**Lowest average for leader, season (400 or more at-bats)**
AL—.301—Carl Yastrzemski, Boston, 157 G, 1968
NL—.313—Tony Gwynn, San Diego, 133 G, 1988

**Highest average by rookie, season (400 or more at-bats)**
AL—.408—Joe Jackson, Cleveland, 147 G, 1911 (Jackson had 23 AB in 1908, 17 in 1909, and 75 in 1910.)
NL—.358—Bill Everitt, Chicago, 133 G, 1895 (George Watkins, St. Louis, 1930, batted .373; 119 G, 391 AB, 146 H)

**Highest average by righthander, season (400 or more at-bats)**
NL—.440—Hugh Duffy, Boston, 125 G, 1894
AA—.435—Tip O'Neill, St. Louis, 124 G, 1887
AL—.426—Nap Lajoie, Philadelphia, 131 G, 1910
NL since 1900—.424—Rogers Hornsby, St. Louis, 143 G, 1924

**Highest average by lefthander, season (400 or more at-bats)**
NL—.424—Willie Keeler, Baltimore, 129 G, 1897
AL—.41980—George Sisler, St. Louis, 142 G, 1922 (Ty Cobb, Detroit, 1911, batted 41963; 146 G)

**Highest average by switch-hitter, season (400 or more at-bats)**
AA—.372—Tommy Tucker, Baltimore, 134 G, 1889
AL—.365—Mickey Mantle, New York, 144 G, 1957
NL—.355—George Davis, New York, 133 G, 1893

**Highest average by first baseman, season (400 or more at-bats)**
AL—.420—George Sisler, St. Louis, 142 G, 1922; 141 G at 1B
NL—.401—Bill Terry, New York, 154 G, 1930; 154 G at 1B

**Highest average by second baseman, season (400 or more at-bats)**
AL—.426—Nap Lajoie, Philadelphia, 131 G, 1901; 119 G at 2B
NL—.424—Rogers Hornsby, St. Louis, 143 G, 1924; 143 G at 2B

**Highest average by third baseman, season (400 or more at-bats)**
NL—.391—John McGraw, Baltimore, 117 G, 1899; 117 G at 3B
AL—.390—George Brett, Kansas City, 117 G, 1980; 112 G at 3B

**Highest average by shortstop, season (400 or more at-bats)**
NL—.401—Hughie Jennings, Baltimore, 130 G, 1896; 130 G at SS
AL—.388—Luke Appling, Chicago, 138 G, 1936; 137 G at SS

**Highest average by outfielder, season (400 or more at-bats)**
NL—.440—Hugh Duffy, Boston, 125 G, 1894; 124 G in OF
AA—.435—Tip O'Neill, St. Louis, 124 G, 1887
AL—.420—Ty Cobb, Detroit, 146 G, 1911; 146 G in OF

**Highest average by catcher, season (400 or more at-bats)**
AL—.362—Bill Dickey, New York, 112 G, 1936; 107 G at C
NL—.362—Mike Piazza, Los Angeles, 152 G, 1997; 139 G at C

**Highest average by pitcher, season (only for games as a pitcher)**
AL—.440—Walter Johnson, Washington, 36 G, 1925; pitched 30 G
NL—.406—Jack Bentley, New York, 52 G, 1923; pitched 31 G

**Most seasons leading league in average**
AL—12—Ty Cobb, Detroit, 1907-1915, 1917-1919
NL—8—Honus Wagner, Pittsburgh, 1900, 1903, 1904, 1906-1909, 1911
Tony Gwynn, San Diego, 1984, 1987-1989, 1994-1997

**For a complete list of triple crown winners, see page 111.**

**Most consecutive seasons leading league in average**
AL—9—Ty Cobb, Detroit, 1907-1915
NL—6—Rogers Hornsby, St. Louis, 1920-1925

**Most seasons batting .400 or over (400 or more at-bats)**
NL—3—Ed Delahanty, Philadelphia, 1894, 1895, 1899
Rogers Hornsby, St. Louis, 1922, 1924, 1925
AL—3—Ty Cobb, Detroit, 1911, 1912, 1922

**For a complete list of .400 hitters, see page 111.**

**Most seasons batting .300 or over (400 or more at-bats)**
AL—23—Ty Cobb, Detroit, Philadelphia, 1906-1928
NL—19—Cap Anson, Chicago, 1876-1896, except 1891 and 1892
NL since 1893—18—Tony Gwynn, San Diego, 1983-1999, 2001

**Most seasons batting .300 or over by pitcher**
AL—8—Red Ruffing, Boston, 1928, 1929; Boston, New York, 1930; New York, 1931, 1932, 1935, 1939, 1941
NL—5—Red Lucas, Cincinnati, 1926-1928, 1930; Pittsburgh, 1935

**Highest average over two consecutive seasons (400 or more at-bats each season)**
AL—.415—Ty Cobb, Detroit, 1911, 1912
NL—.413—Rogers Hornsby, St. Louis, 1924, 1925

**Highest average over three consecutive seasons (400 or more at-bats each season)**
AL—.408—Ty Cobb, Detroit, 1911-1913
NL—.405—Rogers Hornsby, St. Louis, 1923-1925

**Highest average over four consecutive seasons (400 or more at-bats each season)**
NL—.404—Rogers Hornsby, St. Louis, 1922-1925
AL—.402—Ty Cobb, Detroit, 1910-1913

**Highest average over five consecutive seasons (400 or more at-bats each season)**
NL—.402—Rogers Hornsby, St. Louis, 1921-1925
AL—.397—Ty Cobb, Detroit, 1910-1914

**Lowest average, season (400 or more at-bats)**
AL—.182—Monte Cross, Philadelphia, 153 G, 1904
NL—.201—Dal Maxvill, St. Louis, 152 G, 1970

## ON-BASE PERCENTAGE

(official statistic since 1984; calculated from official statistics, 1931-1983, except for 1939 for which there is no official tabulation of sacrifice flies)

**Highest percentage, career (1,500 or more hits)**
AL—.482—Ted Williams, 18 seasons, 1940-1960, except 1943-1945
NL—.443—Barry Bonds, Pittsburgh, San Francisco, 19 seasons, 1986-2004

**Highest percentage, season (400 or more plate appearances)**
NL—.609—Barry Bonds, San Francisco, 147 G, 2004
AL—.553—Ted Williams, Boston, 143 G, 1941

**Lowest percentage for leader, season (400 or more plate appearances)**
NL—.391—Pete Rose, Cincinnati, 149 G, 1968
AL—.395—Carl Yastrzemski, Boston, 133 G, 1965

**Highest percentage by rookie, season (400 or more plate appearances)**
AL—.447—Charlie Keller, New York, 111 G, 1939 (If all Keller's 11 sacrifices were sacrifice flies, his OBP would be .437, still the record.)
NL—.454—Bernie Carbo, Cincinnati, 125 G, 1970

**Highest percentage by righthander, season (400 or more plate appearances)**
AL—.487—Frank E. Thomas, Chicago, 113 G, 1994
NL—.470—Mark McGwire, St. Louis, 155 G, 1998

**Highest percentage by lefthander, season (400 or more plate appearances)**
NL—.609—Barry Bonds, San Francisco, 147 G, 2004
AL—.553—Ted Williams, Boston, 143 G, 1941

**Highest percentage by switch-hitter, season (400 or more plate appearances)**
AL—.512—Mickey Mantle, New York, 144 G, 1957
NL—.449—Augie Galan, Cincinnati, 124 G, 1947

**Most seasons leading league in percentage**
AL—12—Ted Williams, Boston, 1940-1942, 1946-1949, 1951, 1954, 1956-1958
NL—8—Barry Bonds, Pittsburgh, San Francisco, 1991-1993, 1995, 2001-2004

**Lowest percentage, season (100 or more games)**
NL—.222—Hal Lanier, San Francisco, 151 G, 1968
AL—.201—Juan Bell, Baltimore, 100 G, 1991

## SLUGGING AVERAGE

**Highest average, career (2,500 or more total bases)**
ML—.690—Babe Ruth, Boston AL, New York AL, Boston NL, 22 seasons, 1914-1935
AL—.692—Babe Ruth, Boston, New York, 21 seasons, 1914-1934
NL—.611—Barry Bonds, Pittsburgh, San Francisco, 20 seasons, 1986-2005

For a complete list of players with .500 or more career slugging averages and 2,500 or more total bases, see page 103.

**Highest average, season (400 or more at-bats)**
NL—.863—Barry Bonds, San Francisco, 153 G, 2001
AL—.847—Babe Ruth, New York, 142 G, 1920

**Lowest average for leader, season (400 or more at-bats)**
NL—.436—Hy Myers, Brooklyn, 133 G, 1919
AL—.466—Elmer Flick, Cleveland, 131 G, 1905

**Highest average by rookie, season (400 or more at-bats)**
AL—.618—Mark McGwire, Oakland, 151 G, 1987
NL—.614—Wally Berger, Boston, 151 G, 1930

**Highest average by righthander, season (400 or more at-bats)**
NL—.756—Rogers Hornsby, St. Louis, 138 G, 1925
AL—.749—Jimmie Foxx, Philadelphia, 154 G, 1932

**Highest average by lefthander, season (400 or more at-bats)**
NL—.863—Barry Bonds, San Francisco, 153 G, 2001
AL—.847—Babe Ruth, New York, 142 G, 1920

**Highest average by switch-hitter, season (400 or more at-bats)**
AL—.705—Mickey Mantle, New York, 150 G, 1956
NL—.633—Chipper Jones, Atlanta, 157 G, 1999

**Most seasons leading league in average (400 or more at-bats)**
AL—13—Babe Ruth, Boston, New York, 1918-1931, except 1925 (only 317 AB in 1918, short season due to war)
NL—9—Rogers Hornsby, St. Louis, Boston, Chicago, 1917, 1920-1925, 1928, 1929

**Lowest average, season (400 or more at-bats)**
NL—.197—Jim Lillie, Kansas City, 114 G, 1886
NL since 1893—.206—Pete Childs, Philadelphia, 123 G, 1902
AL—.225—Charles Moran, Washington/St. Louis, 144 G, 1904

## PLATE APPEARANCES AND AT-BATS

### CAREER AND SEASON

**Most plate appearances, career**
NL—15,890—Pete Rose, Cincinnati, Philadelphia, Montreal, 24 seasons, 1963-1986
AL—13,990—Carl Yastrzemski, Boston, 23 seasons, 1961-1983

**Most plate appearances, season**
NL—773—Lenny Dykstra, Philadelphia, 161 G, 1993
AL—758—Wade Boggs, Boston, 161 G, 1985

**Most at-bats, career**
NL—14,053—Pete Rose, Cincinnati, Philadelphia, Montreal, 24 seasons, 1963-1986
AL—11,988—Carl Yastrzemski, Boston, 23 seasons, 1961-1983

For a complete list of players with 9,000 or more career at-bats, see page 103.

**Most at-bats, season**
AL—705—Willie Wilson, Kansas City, 161 G, 1980
NL—701—Juan Samuel, Philadelphia, 160 G, 1984

**Fewest at-bats for leader, season**
NL—585—Spike Shannon, New York, 155 G, 1907
AL—588—Ty Cobb, Detroit, 152 G, 1917

**Most at-bats by rookie, season**
NL—701—Juan Samuel, Philadelphia, 160 G, 1984
AL—692—Ichiro Suzuki, Seattle, 157 G, 2001

**Most at-bats by righthander, season**
NL—701—Juan Samuel, Philadelphia, 160 G, 1984
AL—696—Alfonso Soriano, New York, 156 G, 2002

**Most at-bats by lefthander, season**
NL—698—Matty Alou, Pittsburgh, 162 G, 1969
AL—704—Ichiro Suzuki, Seattle, 161 G, 2004

**Most at-bats by switch-hitter, season**
AL—705—Willie Wilson, Kansas City, 161 G, 1980
NL—696—Jose Reyes, New York, 161 G, 2005

**Most at-bats by pinch-hitter, season**
NL—83—Lenny Harris, New York, 95 G, 2001
AL—72—Dave Philley, Baltimore, 79 G, 1961

**Most seasons leading league in at-bats**
AL—7—Doc Cramer, Philadelphia, Boston, Washington, Detroit, 1933-1935, 1938, 1940-1942
NL—4—Abner Dalrymple, Chicago, 1880, 1882, 1884, 1885
NL since 1893—4—Pete Rose, Cincinnati, 1965, 1972, 1973, 1977

**Most consecutive seasons leading league in at-bats**
NL—3—Sparky Adams, Chicago, 1925-1927
Dave Cash, Philadelphia, 1974-1976
AL—3—Doc Cramer, Philadelphia, 1933-1935
Doc Cramer, Boston, Washington, Detroit, 1940-1942
Bobby Richardson, New York, 1962-1964

**Most seasons with 600 or more at-bats**
NL—17—Pete Rose, Cincinnati, Philadelphia, 1963-1982, except 1964, 1967, 1981
AL—13—Cal Ripken Jr., Baltimore, 1983-1998, except 1988, 1994, 1995

**Fewest at-bats, season (150 or more games)**
NL—362—Jim Eisenreich, Philadelphia, 153 G, 1993
AL—389—Tom McCraw, Chicago, 151 G, 1966

### GAME AND INNING

**Most plate appearances, game**
NL—8—many players
NL since 1894—8—Russ Wrightstone, Philadelphia, Aug 25, 1922
Frank Parkinson, Philadelphia, Aug 25, 1922
Taylor Douthit, St. Louis, July 6, 1929, 2nd game
Mike Cameron, Cincinnati, May 19, 1999
[12—Felix Millan, New York, Sept 11, 1974, 25 inn
John Milner, New York, Sept 11, 1974, 25 inn]
AL—8—Clyde Vollmer, Boston, June 8, 1950
Darryl Hamilton, Milwaukee, Aug 28, 1992
[12—Harold Baines, Carlton Fisk and Rudy Law, Chicago, May 8-9, 1984, 25 inn]

**Most plate appearances with no official at-bats, game**
NL—6—Pop Smith, Boston, Apr 17, 1890 (5 BB, 1 HP)
Walt Wilmot, Chicago, Aug 22, 1891 (6 BB)
Miller Huggins, St. Louis, June 1, 1910 (4 BB, 1 SH, 1 SF)
Billy Urbanski, Boston, June 13, 1934 (4 BB, 2 SH)
AL—6—Jimmie Foxx, Boston, June 16, 1938 (6 BB)

**Most plate appearances, inning**
AA—3—Larry Murphy, Washington, June 17, 1891, 1st
NL—3—many players
NL since 1893—3—Marty Callaghan, Chicago, Aug 25, 1922, 4th
Billy Cox, Pee Wee Reese and Duke Snider, Brooklyn, May 21, 1952, 1st
Gil Hodges, Brooklyn, Aug 8, 1954, 8th
Dusty Baker, Atlanta, Sept 20, 1972, 2nd
Mariano Duncan and Luis Quinones, Cincinnati, Aug 3, 1989, 1st
Stan Javier, San Francisco, July 15, 1997, 7th
AL—3—Ted Williams, Boston, July 4, 1948, 7th
Sammy White, Gene Stephens, Tom Umphlett, Johnny Lipon and George Kell, Boston, June 18, 1953, 7th
Darryl Hamilton, Texas, Apr 19, 1996, 8th
Johnny Damon, Boston, June 27, 2003, 1st

**Most at-bats, game**
NL—8—many players; last—Barry McCormick, Chicago, June 29, 1897
NL since 1893—7—many players
[11—Carson Bigbee, Pittsburgh, Aug 22, 1917, 22 inn
Charlie Pick and Tony Boekel, Boston, May 1, 1920, 26 inn
Ralph Garr, Atlanta, May 4, 1973, 20 inn
Dave Schneck, New York, Sept 11, 1974, 25 inn
Dave Cash, Montreal, May 21, 1977, 21 inn]
AL—7—many players
[11—Johnny Burnett, Cleveland, July 10, 1932, 18 inn
Ed Morgan, Cleveland, July 10, 1932, 18 inn
Irv Hall, Philadelphia, July 21, 1945, 24 inn
Bobby Richardson, New York, June 24, 1962, 22 inn
Cecil Cooper, Milwaukee, May 8-9, 1984, 25 inn
Julio Cruz, Carlton Fisk and Rudy Law, Chicago, May 8-9, 1984, 25 inn]

**Most at-bats, doubleheader**
NL—13—Rabbit Maranville, Pittsburgh, Aug 8, 1922
Billy Herman, Chicago, Aug 21, 1935
[14—many players; last—Al Oliver, Pittsburgh, June 7, 1972, 27 inn]
AL—13—Dave Philley, Chicago, May 30, 1950
[14—Rick Monday and Ramon Webster, Kansas City, June 17, 1967, 28 inn
Dick Billings, Washington, Sept 14, 1971, 29 inn (2nd game suspended; completed Sept 20)
Ted Uhlaender, Cleveland, Sept 14, 1971, 29 inn (2nd game suspended; completed Sept 20)]

## RUNS

### CAREER AND SEASON

**Most runs, career**
ML—2,295—Rickey Henderson, Oakland AL, New York AL, Toronto AL, San Diego NL, Anaheim AL, New York NL, Seattle AL, Boston AL, Los Angeles NL, 25 seasons, 1979-2003 (1,939 in AL, 356 in NL)
AL—2,246—Ty Cobb, Detroit, Philadelphia, 24 seasons, 1905-1928
NL—2,165—Pete Rose, Cincinnati, Philadelphia, Montreal, 24 seasons, 1963-1986

For a complete list of players with 1,500 or more career runs, see page 103.

**Most runs, season**
NL—198—Billy Hamilton, Philadelphia, 131 G, 1894
AL—177—Babe Ruth, New York, 152 G, 1921
NL since 1900—158—Chuck Klein, Philadelphia, 156 G, 1930

**Fewest runs for leader, season**
NL—89—Gavvy Cravath, Philadelphia, 150 G, 1915
AL—92—Harry H. Davis, Philadelphia, 149 G, 1905

**Most runs by rookie, season**
AA—142—Mike Griffin, Baltimore, 136 G, 1887

NL—135—Roy Thomas, Philadelphia, 148 G, 1899
NL since 1900—133—Lloyd Waner, Pittsburgh, 150 G, 1927
AL—132—Joe DiMaggio, New York, 138 G, 1936

**Most runs by righthander, season**
AA—167—Tip O'Neill, St. Louis, 124 G, 1887
NL—165—Joe Kelley, Baltimore, 129 G, 1894
NL since 1900—16—Rogers Hornsby, Chicago, 156 G, 1929
AL—152—Al Simmons, Philadelphia, 138 G, 1930

**Most runs by lefthander, season**
NL—198—Billy Hamilton, Philadelphia, 131 G, 1894
AL—177—Babe Ruth, New York, 152 G, 1921
NL since 1900—158—Chuck Klein, Philadelphia, 156 G, 1930

**Most runs by switch-hitter, season**
NL—140—Max Carey, Pittsburgh, 155 G, 1922
AL—138—Roberto Alomar, Cleveland, 159 G, 1999

**Most seasons leading league in runs**
AL—8—Babe Ruth, Boston, New York, 1919-1921, 1923, 1924, 1926-1928
NL—5—George J. Burns, New York, 1914, 1916, 1917, 1919, 1920
Rogers Hornsby, St. Louis, New York, Chicago, 1921, 1922, 1924 (tied), 1927 (tied), 1929
Stan Musial, St. Louis, 1946, 1948, 1951 (tied), 1952 (tied), 1954 (tied)

**Most consecutive seasons leading league in runs**
NL—3—King Kelly, Chicago, 1884, 1885, 1886
NL since 1893—3—Chuck Klein, Philadelphia, 1930, 1931 (tied), 1932
Duke Snider, Brooklyn, 1953, 1954 (tied), 1955
Pete Rose, Cincinnati, 1974-1976
AL—3—Ty Cobb, Detroit, 1909-1911
Eddie Collins, Philadelphia, 1912-1914
Babe Ruth, Boston, 1919, New York, 1920, 1921; and New York, 1926-1928
Ted Williams, Boston, 1940-1942 (Military service, 1943-1945, interrupted a 5-year streak by Williams who also led in 1946 and 1947.)
Mickey Mantle, New York, 1956-1958

**Most seasons with 150 or more runs**
AL—6—Babe Ruth, New York, 1920, 1921, 1923, 1927, 1928, 1930
NL—4—Billy Hamilton, Philadelphia, Boston, 1894-1897

**Most seasons with 100 or more runs**
NL—15—Hank Aaron, Milwaukee, Atlanta, 1955-1970, except 1968
AL—13—Lou Gehrig, New York, 1926-1938

**Most consecutive seasons with 100 or more runs**
AL—13—Lou Gehrig, New York, 1926-1938
NL—13—Hank Aaron, Milwaukee, Atlanta, 1955-1967

**Fewest runs, season (150 or more games)**
AL—25—Leo Cardenas, California, 150 G, 1972
NL—32—Mike Doolan, Philadelphia, 151 G, 1913

## GAME AND INNING

**Most runs, game**
AA—7—Guy Hecker, Louisville, Aug 15, 1886, 2nd game
NL—6—Jim Whitney, Boston, June 9, 1883
Cap Anson, Chicago, Aug 24, 1886
Mike Tiernan, New York, June 15, 1887
King Kelly, Boston, Aug 27, 1887
Ezra Sutton, Boston, Aug 27, 1887
NL since 1983—6—Jimmy Ryan, Chicago, July 25, 1894, 7 inn
Bobby Lowe, Boston, May 3, 1895
Ginger Beaumont, Pittsburgh, July 22, 1899
Mel Ott, New York, Aug 4, 1934, 2nd game; Apr 30, 1944, 1st game
Frank Torre, Milwaukee, Sept 2, 1957, 1st game
Edgardo Alfonzo, New York, Aug 30, 1999
Shawn Green, Los Angeles, May 23, 2002
AL—6—Johnny Pesky, Boston, May 8, 1946
Spike Owen, Boston, Aug 21, 1986
Joe Randa, Kansas City, Sept 9, 2004

**Most runs, doubleheader**
NL—9—Herman Long, Boston, May 30. 1894
AL—9—Mel Almada, Washington, July 25, 1937
NL since 1900—8—Chuck Klein, Chicago, Aug 21, 1935
[8—Frank Robinson, Cincinnati, July 8, 1962]

**Most consecutive games scoring one or more runs**
NL—24—Billy Hamilton, Philadelphia, July 6-Aug 2, 1894 (35 R)
AL—18—Red Rolfe, New York, Aug 9-25, 2nd game, 1939 (30 R)
Kenny Lofton, Cleveland, Aug 15-Sept 3, 2000 (26 R)

**Most times scoring five or more runs in one game, career**
ML—6—George Gore, Chicago NL, 1880, 1881, 1882 (2), 1883, New York PL, 1890
Jimmy Ryan, Chicago NL, 1887, 1889, 1891, 1894 (2), 1897
Willie Keeler, Baltimore NL, 1895 (2), 1897 (2), Brooklyn NL, 1901, 1902
NL—6—Jimmy Ryan, Chicago, 1887, 1889, 1891, 1894 (2), 1897
Willie Keeler, Baltimore, Brooklyn, 1895 (2), 1897 (2), 1901, 1902
AL—3—Lou Gehrig, New York, 1928, 1936 (2)
Jimmie Foxx, Philadelphia, Boston, 1932, 1935, 1939

**Most times with five or more runs in one game, season**
NL—2—many players; last—Craig Biggio, Houston, July 4, Sept 28, 1995
AL—2—Lou Gehrig, New York, May 3, July 28, 1936

**Most runs, inning**
AL—3—Sammy White, Boston, June 18, 1953, 7th
NL—3—Tommy Burns, Chicago, Sept 6, 1883, 7th
Ned Williamson, Chicago, Sept 6, 1883, 7th

# HITS

## CAREER AND SEASON

**Most hits, career**
NL—4,256—Pete Rose, Cincinnati, Philadelphia, Montreal, 24 seasons, 1963-1986
AL—4,189—Ty Cobb, Detroit, Philadelphia, 24 seasons, 1905-1928

**For a complete list of players with 2,500 or more career hits, see page 101.**

**Most hits by pinch-hitter, career**
NL—212—Lenny Harris, Cincinnati, Los Angeles, New York, Colorado, Arizona, Milwaukee, Chicago, Florida, 17 seasons, 1989-2005, 883 G
AL—107—Gates Brown, Detroit, 13 seasons, 1963-1975, 525 G

**Most hits, season (except 1887, when walks counted as hits)**
AL—262—Ichiro Suzuki, Seattle, 161 G, 2004
NL—254—Lefty O'Doul, Philadelphia, 154 G, 1929
Bill Terry, New York, 154 G, 1930

**Fewest hits for leader, season**
NL—171—Sherry Magee, Philadelphia, 146 G, 1914
AL—177—Bert Campaneris, Oakland, 159 G, 1968

**Most hits by rookie, season**
AL—242—Ichiro Suzuki, Seattle, 157 G, 2001
NL—223—Lloyd Waner, Pittsburgh, 150 G, 1927

**For a complete list of rookies with 200 or more hits, see page 111.**

**Most hits by righthander, season**
AL—253—Al Simmons, Philadelphia, 153 G, 1925
NL—250—Rogers Hornsby, St. Louis, 154 G, 1922

**Most hits by lefthander, season**
AL—262—Ichiro Suzuki, Seattle, 161 G, 2004
NL—254—Lefty O'Doul, Philadelphia, 154 G, 1929
Bill Terry, New York, 154 G, 1930

**Most hits by switch-hitter, season**
NL—230—Pete Rose, Cincinnati, 160 G, 1973
AL—230—Willie Wilson, Kansas City, 161 G, 1980

**Switch-hitters with 100 or more hits from each side of plate, season**
NL—Garry Templeton, St. Louis, 154 G, 1979 (111 lefthanded, 100 righthanded)
AL—Willie Wilson, Kansas City, 161 G, 1980 (130 lefthanded, 100 righthanded)

**Most hits by pinch-hitter, season**
NL—28—John Vander Wal, Colorado, 92 G, 1995
AL—24—Dave Philley, Baltimore, 79 G, 1961

**Most seasons leading league in hits**
AL—8—Ty Cobb, Detroit, 1907-1909, 1911, 1912, 1915, 1917, 1919 (tied)
NL—7—Pete Rose, Cincinnati, 1965, 1968 (tied), 1970 (tied), 1972, 1973, 1976; Philadelphia, 1981
Tony Gwynn, San Diego, 1984, 1986, 1987, 1989, 1994, 1995 (tied), 1997

**Most consecutive seasons leading league in hits**
NL—3—Ginger Beaumont, Pittsburgh, 1902-1904
Rogers Hornsby, St. Louis, 1920-1922
Frank McCormick, Cincinnati, 1938, 1939, 1940 (tied)
AL—3—Ty Cobb, Detroit, 1907-1909
Tony Oliva, Minnesota, 1964-1966
Kirby Puckett, Minnesota, 1987 (tied), 1988, 1989

**Most games with one or more hits, season**
NL—135—Rogers Hornsby, St. Louis, 154 G, 1922
Chuck Klein, Philadelphia, 156 G 1930
AL—135—Wade Boggs, Boston, 161 G, 1985
Derek Jeter, New York, 158 G, 1999
Ichiro Suzuki, Seattle, 157 G, 2001

**Most seasons with 200 or more hits, career**
NL—10—Pete Rose, Cincinnati, 1965, 1966, 1968-1970, 1973, 1975-1977; Philadelphia, 1979
AL—9—Ty Cobb, Detroit, 1907, 1909, 1911, 1912, 1915-1917, 1922, 1924

**For a complete list of players with 200 or more hits in a seson four or more times, see page 104.**

**Most consecutive years with 200 or more hits, career**
NL—8—Willie Keeler, Baltimore, Brooklyn, 1894-1901
AL—7—Wade Boggs, Boston, 1983-1989

**Most hits, two consecutive seasons**
NL—485—Rogers Hornsby, St. Louis, 235 in 1921, 250 in 1922
AL—474—Ty Cobb, Detroit, 248 in 1911, 227 in 1912
Ichiro Suzuki, Seattle, 212 in 2003, 262 in 2004

**Fewest hits, season (150 or more games)**
NL—80—Dal Maxvill, St. Louis, 152 G, 1970

AL—82—Eddie Brinkman, Washington, 154 G, 1965

**Most at-bats in hitless season**

NL—70—Bob Buhl, Milwaukee, Chicago, 35 G, 1962
AL—61—Bill Wight, Chicago, 30 G, 1950

## GAME AND DOUBLEHEADER

**Most hits, game**

NL—7—Wilbert Robinson, Baltimore, June 10, 1892, 1st game (6 singles, 1 double; consec)
Rennie Stennett, Pittsburgh, Sept 16, 1975 (4 singles, 2 doubles, 1 triple; consec)
AL—6—many players
[9—Johnny Burnett, Cleveland, July 10, 1932 (7 singles, 2 doubles), 18 inn]

**For a complete list of players with six or more hits in a game, see page 118.**

**Most times reached base safely, game (batting 1.000)**

NL—8—Piggy Ward, Cincinnati, June 18, 1893 (2 singles, 5 BB, 1 HP)
AA—7—Bill Gleason, St. Louis, Apr 30, 1887 (2 singles, 1 double, 4 BB)
Tip O'Neill, St. Louis, July 13, 1889 (3 singles, 1 HR, 3 BB)
NL since 1900—7—Cliff Heathcote, Chicago, Aug 25, 1922 (3 singles, 2 doubles, 2 BB)
Cookie Lavagetto, Brooklyn, Sept 23, 1939, 1st game (4 singles, 1 double, 1 triple, 1 BB)
Mel Ott, New York, Apr 30, 1944, 1st game (2 singles, 5 BB)
Rennie Stennett, Pittsburgh, Sept 16, 1975 (4 singles, 2 doubles, 1 triple)
Sean Casey, Cincinnati, May 19, 1999 (2 singles, 2 HR, 3 BB)
[9—Max Carey, Pittsburgh, July 7, 1922 (5 singles, 1 double, 3 BB), 18 inn]
AL—7—Joe Judge, Washington, July 27, 1920 (3 singles, 4 BB)
Ben Chapman, New York, May 24, 1936 (2 doubles, 5 BB)
[7—Cesar Gutierrez, Detroit, June 21, 1970, 2nd game (6 singles, 1 double), 12 inn
Dwight Evans, Boston, May 4, 1981 (3 singles, 4 BB), 12 inn
George Brett, Kansas City, June 27, 1985 (2 singles, 1 double, 4 BB), 14 inn
Tim Raines Sr., Chicago, Apr 20, 1994 (3 singles, 4 BB), 12 inn
Mark McGwire, Oakland, Apr 26, 1997 (1 double, 1 HR, 5 BB), 11 inn]

**Most hits with more than one club, one day**

NL—2—Joel Youngblood, New York, Montreal, Aug 4, 1982

**Most hits in first major league game**

NL—5—Fred Clarke, Louisville, June 30, 1894 (4 singles, 1 triple)
AL—4—Ray Jansen, St. Louis, Sept 30, 1910 (4 singles; only game in major league career)
Art Shires, Chicago, Aug 20, 1928 (3 singles, 1 triple)
Russ Van Atta, New York, Apr 25, 1933 (4 singles)
Spook Jacobs, Philadelphia, Apr 13, 1954 (4 singles)
Ted Cox, Boston, Sept 18, 1977 (3 singles, 1 double; consec)
Kirby Puckett, Minnesota, May 8, 1984 (4 singles)
Billy Bean, Detroit, Apr 25, 1987 (2 singles, 2 doubles)
[5—Cecil Travis, Washington, May 16, 1933 (5 singles), 12 inn]

**Most hits by pitcher, game**

AA—6—Guy Hecker, Louisville, Aug 15, 1886, 2nd game
NL—5—many pitchers; last—Pete Donohue, Cincinnati, May 22, 1925 (4 singles, 1 HR)
AL—5—many pitchers; last—Mel Stottlemyre, New York, Sept 26, 1964 (4 singles, 1 double)

**Most hits, club's first game of season**

NL—5—many players—last—Craig Biggio, Houston, Apr 3, 2001 (5 singles)
AL—5—many players; last—Harlond Clift, St. Louis, Apr 21, 1937 (2 singles, 2 doubles, 1 HR)
[5—Nellie Fox, Chicago, Apr 10, 1959 (3 singles, 1 double, 1 HR), 14 inn]

**Most hits accounting for all of club's hits, game**

AL—4—Kid Elberfeld, New York, Aug 1, 1903 (4 singles)
NL—4—Billy Williams, Chicago, Sept 5, 1969 (2 doubles, 2 HR)

**Most at-bats with no hits, extra-inning game**

NL—11—Charlie Pick, Boston, May 1, 1920, 26 inn
AL—10—George Kell, Philadelphia, July 21, 1945, 24 inn

**Most games with six hits in six at-bats, career**

ML—2—Ed Delahanty, Cleveland, PL, June 2, 1890; Philadelphia, NL, June 16, 1894
Jim Bottomley, St. Louis, Sept 16, 1924; Aug 5, 1931, 2nd game
Doc Cramer, Philadelphia, June 20, 1932; July 13, 1935
NL—2—Jim Bottomley, St. Louis, Sept 16, 1924; Aug 5, 1931, 2nd game
AL—2—Doc Cramer, Philadelphia, June 20, 1932; July 13, 1935

**Most games with five or more hits, career**

AL—14—Ty Cobb, Detroit, Philadelphia, 1908-1927
NL—12—Sam Thompson, Detroit, Philadelphia, 1886-1895
NL since 1893—10—Pete Rose, Cincinnati, Philadelphia, 1965-1986

**Most games with five hits by pitcher, career**

ML—3—Nixey Callahan, Chicago NL, 1897, Chicago AL, 1902, 1903

**Most games with five or more hits, season**

NL—5—Sam Thompson, Detroit, May 16, June 10, July 25, Aug 9, Sept 23, 1887
AA—4—Tip O'Neill, St. Louis, Apr 30, Aug 24, Sept 2, Sept 7, 1887
NL since 1893—4—Stan Musial, St. Louis, Apr 30, May 19, June 22, Sept 22, 1948
Tony Gwynn, San Diego, Apr 18, Apr 30, July 27, Aug 4, 1993
AL—4—Ty Cobb, Detroit, May 7, July 7 (2nd game), July 12, July 17, 1922
Ichiro Suzuki, Seattle, July 29 (13 inn), Aug 3, Sept 4, Sept 21, 2004

**Most hits, doubleheader**

AA—9—Fred Carroll, Pittsburgh, July 5, 1886
NL—9—Wilbert Robinson, Baltimore, June 10, 1892
NL since 1893—9—Joe Kelley, Baltimore, Sept 3, 18 94 (consec)
Fred Lindstrom, New York, June 25, 1928
Bill Terry, New York, June 18, 1929
AL—9—Ray Morehart, Chicago, Aug 31, 1926
George Case, Washington, July 4, 1940
Lee Thomas, Los Angeles, Sept 5, 1961
[9—Pete Runnels, Boston, Aug 30, 1960, 15 and 10 inn]

### HITTING FOR CYCLE
### (Single, double, triple, home run in game)

**Most times hitting for cycle, career**

ML—3—John Reilly, Cincinnati AA, 1883 (2), Cincinnati NL, 1890
Bob Meusel, New York AL, 1921, 1922, 1928
Babe Herman, Brooklyn NL, 1931 (2), Chicago NL, 1933
AL—3—Bob Meusel, New York, 1921, 1922, 1928
NL—3—Babe Herman, Brooklyn, 1931 (2), Chicago, 1933

**For a complete list of players hitting for cycle, see page 117.**

**Hitting for cycle in American and National Leagues**

Bob Watson, Houston NL, June 24, 1977; Boston AL, Sept 15, 1979
John Olerud, New York NL, Sept 11, 1997; Seattle AL, June 16, 2001

**Most times hitting for cycle, season**

AA—2—John Reilly, Cincinnati, 1883
Tip O'Neill, St. Louis, 1887
NL—2—Babe Herman, Brooklyn, 1931
AL—none more than one

## INNING

**Most hits, inning**

AL—3—Gene Stephens, Boston, June 18, 1953, 7th (2 singles, 1 double)
Johnny Damon, Boston, June 27, 2003, 1st (1 single, 1 double, 1 triple)
NL—3—Tommy Burns, Chicago, Sept 6, 1883, 7th (2 doubles, 1 HR)
Fred Pfeffer, Chicago, Sept 6, 1883, 7th (2 singles, 1 double)
Ned Williamson, Chicago, Sept 6, 1883, 7th (2 singles, 1 double)

**Most hits, inning, first major league game**

AL—2—Billy Martin, New York, Apr 18, 1950, 8th
Russ Morman, Chicago, Aug 3, 1986, 4th
Chad Kreuter, Texas, Sept 14, 1988, 5th
NL—2—Adam LaRoche, Atlanta, Apr 7, 2004, 4th

**Most times with two hits in one inning, game**

NL—2—Max Carey, Pittsburgh, June 22, 1925, 1st (2 singles), 8th (2 singles)
Rennie Stennett, Pittsburgh, Sept 16, 1975, 1st (single and double); 5th (1 double and 1 single)
AL—2—Johnny Hodapp, Cleveland, July 29, 1928, 2nd (2 singles), 6th (2 singles)
Sherm Lollar, Chicago, Apr 23, 1955, 2nd (single and HR), 6th (2 singles)

**Most times reached first base safely, inning**

NL—3—Ned Williamson, Chicago, Sept 6, 1883, 7th
Tommy Burns, Chicago, Sept 6, 1883, 7th
Fred Pfeffer, Chicago, Sept 6, 1883, 7th
NL since 1894—3—Herman Long, Boston, June 18, 1894, a.m. game, 1st
Bobby Lowe, Boston, June 18, 1894, a.m. game, 1st
Hugh Duffy, Boston, June 18, 1894, a.m. game, 1st
Pee Wee Reese, Brooklyn, May 21, 1952, 1st
AL—3—Sammy White, Boston, June 18, 1953, 7th
Gene Stephens, Boston, June 18, 1953, 7th
Tommy Umphlett, Boston, June 18, 1953, 7th
Johnny Damon, Boston, June 27, 2003, 1st

## BATTING STREAKS

**Most consecutive hits, season (walks shown in streak)**

AL—12—Pinky Higgins, Boston, June 19, 19, 21, 21, 1938 (2 BB)
Walt Dropo, Detroit, July 14, 15, 15, 1952
NL—10—Jake Stenzel, Pittsburgh, July 15, 17, 18, 1893 (3 BB)
Ed Delahanty, Philadelphia, July 13, 13, 14, 1897 (1 BB)
Jake Gettman, Washington, Sept 10, 11, 11, 1897
Ed Konetchy, Brooklyn, June 28, 2nd game, June 29, July 1, 1919
Kiki Cuyler, Pittsburgh, Sept 18, 19, 21, 1925 (1 BB)
Chick Hafey, St. Louis, July 6, 2nd game, July 8, 9, 1929 (2 BB)
Joe Medwick, St. Louis, July 19, 19, 21, 1936 (1 BB)
Buddy Hassett, Boston, June 9, 2nd game, June 10, 14, 1940 (1 BB)
Woody Williams, Cincinnati, Sept 5, 2nd game, Sept 6, 6, 1943 (1 BB)
Bip Roberts, Cincinnati, Sept 19, 20, 22, 2nd game, 23 1992 (1 BB)

**Most consecutive hits by pitcher, season**

NL—8—Livan Hernandez, San Francisco, July 31 (1), Aug 5 (3), 1 1 (4), 2001
AL—7—Don Larsen, St. Louis, July 24 (1), 28 (3), Aug 5 (3), 1953

**Most consecutive times reached base safely, season**

AL—16—Ted Williams, Boston, Sept 17 (1), 18 (1), 20 (1), 21 (4), 22 (4), 23 (5), 1957 (2 singles, 4 HR, 9 BB, 1 HP)
NL—15—Barry Bonds, San Francisco, Aug 31 (1), Sept 1 (5), 2 (4), 4 (5), 1998 (5 singles, 2 doubles, 2 HR, 6 BB)
John Olerud, New York, Sept 16 (1), 18 (5), 19 (4), 20 (4), 22 (1), 1998 (6 singles, 1 double, 2 HR, 6 BB)

**Most consecutive hits from start of career**
AL—6—Ted Cox, Boston, Sept 18, 19, 1977
NL—4—John Hale, Los Angeles, Oct 1, 2, 1974
Bob Dernier, Philadelphia, Sept 14, 30, Oct 5, 1980
Mike Piazza, Los Angeles, Sept 1, 4, 1992
Derrick Gibson, Colorado, Sept 8, 1988

**Most consecutive hits by pinch-hitter, career**
NL—9—Dave Philley, Philadelphia, Sept 9-28, 1958; Apr 16, 1959
AL—7—Bill Stein, Texas, Apr 14-May 25, 1981
Randy Bush, Minnesota, July 5-Aug 19, 1991

**Most consecutive hits by pinch-hitter, season**
NL—8—Dave Philley, Philadelphia, Sept 9-28, 1958
Rusty Staub, New York, June 11-26, 1st game, 1983 (1 HP during streak)
AL—7—Bill Stein, Texas, Apr 14-May 25, 1981
Randy Bush, Minnesota, July 5-Aug 19, 1991

**Most consecutive games reached base safely, season**
AL—84—Ted Williams, Boston, July 1-Sept 27, 1949
NL—58—Duke Snider, Brooklyn, May 13-July 11, 2nd game, 1954
Barry Bonds, San Francisco, June 27-Sept 20, 2003

**Most consecutive games batted safely, season**
AL—56—Joe DiMaggio, New York, May 15-July 16, 1941
NL—44—Willie Keeler, Baltimore, Apr 22-June 18, 1897
Pete Rose, Cincinnati, June 14-July 31, 1978

**Most consecutive games batted safely by rookie, season**
NL—34—Benito Santiago, San Diego, Aug 25-Oct 2, 1987
AL—30—Nomar Garciaparra, Boston, July 26-Aug 29, 1997

**Most consecutive games batted safely by righthander, season**
AL—56—Joe DiMaggio, New York, May 15-July 16, 1941
NL—42—Bill Dahlen, Chicago, June 20-Aug 6, 1894

**For a complete list of players with 30-game batting streaks, see page 112. For a detailed breakdown of Joe DiMaggio's 56-game hitting streak, see page 122.**

**Most consecutive games batted safely by lefthander, season**
NL—44—Willie Keeler, Baltimore, Apr 22-June 18, 1897
AL—41—George Sisler, St. Louis, July 27-Sept 17, 1922

**Most consecutive games batted safely by switch-hitter, season**
NL—44—Pete Rose, Cincinnati, June 14-July 31, 1978
AL—27—Jose Offerman, Kansas City, July 11-Aug 7, 1998

**Most consecutive games batted safely from start of season**
NL—44—Willie Keeler, Baltimore, Apr 22-June 18, 1897
AL—34—George Sisler, St. Louis, Apr 14-19, 1925

**Most 20-game batting streaks, career**
NL—8—Willie Keeler, Baltimore, Brooklyn, 1894, 1896, 1897, 1898 (2), 1899, 1900, 1902
NL since 1900—7—Pete Rose, Cincinnati, Philadelphia, 1967, 1968, 1977 (2), 1978, 1979, 1982
AL—7—Ty Cobb, Detroit, Philadelphia, 1911, 1912, 1917, 1918, 1920, 1926, 1927

**Most 20-game batting streaks, season**
AL—3—Tris Speaker, Boston, 1912
NL—2—many players; last—Steve Garvey, Los Angeles, 1978

**Most hits, two consecutive games**
NL—12—Cal McVey, Chicago, July 22 (6), 25 (6), 1876
NL since 1893—10—Rennie Stennett, Pittsburgh, Sept 16 (7), 17 (3), 1975
[10—Roberto Clemente, Pittsburgh, Aug 22 (5), 23 (5), 1970, 25 inn
Mike Benjamin, San Francisco, June 13 (4), 14 (6), 1995, 22 inn]
AL—10—Kirby Puckett, Minnesota, Aug 29 (4), 30 (6), 1987
[11—Johnny Burnett, Cleveland, July 9, 2nd game (2), 10 (9), 1932, 27 inn]

**Most hits by pitcher, two consecutive games**
AA—10—Guy Hecker, Louisville, Aug 12, 15, 2nd game, 1886
AL—8—George Earnshaw, Philadelphia, June 9, 12, 2nd game, 1931
NL since 1893—8—Kirby Higbe, Brooklyn, Aug 11, 17, 1st game, 1941

**Most consecutive games with three or more hits, season**
AL—6—George Brett, Kansas City, May 8, 9, 10, 11, 12, 13, 1976
NL—6—Sam Thompson, Philadelphia, June 11, 14, 14, 19, 20, 21, 1895

**Most consecutive games with four or more hits, season**
NL—4—Milt Stock, Brooklyn, June 30, July 1, 2, 3, 1925
AL—3—many players

## SINGLES

### CAREER AND SEASON

**Most singles, career**
NL—3,215—Pete Rose, Cincinnati, Philadelphia, Montreal, 24 seasons, 1963-1986
AL—3,053—Ty Cobb, Detroit, Philadelphia, 24 seasons, 1905-1928

**For a complete list of players with 2,000 or more career singles, see page 104.**

**Most singles, season**
AL—225—Ichiro Suzuki, Seattle, 161 G, 2004
NL—206—Willie Keeler, Baltimore, 129 G, 1898
NL since 1900—198—Lloyd Waner, Pittsburgh, 150 G, 1927

**Fewest singles by leader, season**
AL—129—Don Buford, Chicago, 155 G, 1965
NL—127—Enos Slaughter, St. Louis, 152 G, 1942

**Most singles by rookie, season**
NL—198—Lloyd Waner, Pittsburgh, 150 G, 1927
AL—192—Ichiro Suzuki, Seattle, 157 G, 2001

**Most singles by righthander, season**
NL—178—Curt Flood, St. Louis, 162 G, 1964
AL—174—Al Simmons, Philadelphia, 153 G, 1925

**Most singles by lefthander, season**
AL—225—Ichiro Suzuki, Seattle, 161 G, 2004
NL—206—Willie Keeler, Baltimore, 129 G, 1898
NL since 1900—198—Lloyd Waner, Pittsburgh, 150 G, 1927

**Most singles by switch-hitter, season**
AL—184—Willie Wilson, Kansas City, 161 G 1980
NL—181—Pete Rose, Cincinnati, 160 G, 1973

**Most seasons leading league in singles**
AL—8—Nellie Fox, Chicago, 1952, 1954-1960
NL—7—Tony Gwynn, San Diego, 1984, 1986 (tied), 1987, 1989, 1994, 1995, 1997

**Most consecutive seasons leading league in singles**
AL—7—Nellie Fox, Chicago, 1954-1960
NL—4—Brett Butler, San Francisco, 1990, Los Angeles, 1991-1993

**Fewest singles, season (150 or more games)**
NL—49—Barry Bonds, San Francisco, 153 G, 2001
AL—53—Mark McGwire, Oakland, 154 G, 1991

### GAME AND INNING

**Most singles, game**
NL—6—many players; last —Dave Bancroft, New York, June 28, 1920
[6—many players; last—Willie Davis, Los Angeles, May 24, 1973, 19 inn]
AL—6—Raul Ibanez, Seattle, Sept 22, 2004
[7—Johnny Burnett, Cleveland, July 10, 1932, 18 inn]

**Most singles, each batting in three runs, game**
NL—1—many players; last—Tim McCarver, Philadelphia, July 7, 1976, 1st game, 2nd inn
AL—1—many players; last—Ernest Riles, Milwaukee, June 5, 1985, 3rd inn

**Most singles, doubleheader**
NL—8—many players; last—Ken Hubbs, Chicago, May 20, 1962
AL—8—many players; last—Earl Averill, Cleveland, May 7, 1933

**Most singles, inning**
NL-AL—2—many players

## DOUBLES

### CAREER AND SEASON

**Most doubles, career**
AL—792—Tris Speaker, Boston, Cleveland, Washington, Philadelphia, 22 seasons, 1907-1928
NL—746—Pete Rose, Cincinnati, Philadelphia, Montreal, 24 seasons, 1963-1986

**For a complete list of players with 450 or more career doubles, see page 104.**

**Most doubles, season**
AL—67—Earl Webb, Boston, 151 G, 1931
NL since 1900—64—Joe Medwick, St. Louis, 155 G, 1936
NL—55—Ed Delahanty, Philadelphia, 146 G, 1899

**Fewest doubles for leader, season**
AL—32—Sal Bando, Oakland, 162 G, 1973
Pedro Garcia, Milwaukee, 160 G, 1973
NL—34—Hank Aaron, Milwaukee, 153 G, 1956

**Most doubles by rookie, season**
NL—52—Johnny Frederick, Brooklyn, 148 G, 1929
AL—47—Fred Lynn, Boston, 145 G, 1975

**Most doubles by righthander, season**
AL—64—George H. Burns, Cleveland, 151 G, 1926
NL—64—Joe Medwick, St. Louis, 155 G, 1936

**Most doubles by lefthander, season**
AL—67—Earl Webb, Boston, 151 G, 1931
NL—62—Paul Waner, Pittsburgh, 154 G, 1932

**Most doubles by switch-hitter, season**
NL—55—Lance Berkman, Houston, 156 G, 2001
AL—50—Brian Roberts, Baltimore, 159 G, 2004

**Most seasons leading league in doubles**
NL—8—Stan Musial, St. Louis, 1943, 1944, 1946, 1948, 1949, 1952-1954
AL—8—Tris Speaker, Boston, 1912, Cleveland, 1914, 1916 (tied), 1918, 1920-1923

**Most consecutive seasons leading league in doubles**
NL—4—Honus Wagner, Pittsburgh, 1906-1909

AL—4—Tris Speaker, Cleveland, 1920-1923

**Most seasons with 50 or more doubles, career**

AL—5—Tris Speaker, Boston, 1912, Cleveland, 1920, 1921, 1923, 1926
NL—3—Paul Waner, Pittsburgh, 1928, 1932, 1936
Stan Musial, St. Louis, 1944, 1946, 1953

**Fewest doubles, season (150 or more games)**

NL—5—Dal Maxvill, St. Louis, 152 G, 1970
AL—6—Billy Purtell, Chicago, Boston, 151 G, 1910

### GAME AND INNING

**Most doubles, game**

NL—4—22 times (by 22 players); last—Adam LaRoche, Atlanta, May 15, 2004
AL—4—22 times (by 21 players); last—Johnny Damon, Kansas City, July 18, 2000; Shannon Stewart, Toronto, July 18, 2000
AA—4—2 times (by 2 players)

**Most consecutive doubles, game**

NL—4—many players; last—Marcus Giles, Atlanta, July 27, 2003
AL—4—many players; last—Sandy Alomar Jr., Cleveland, June 6, 1997

**Most doubles by pitcher, game**

NL—3—George Hemming, Baltimore, Aug 1, 1895
Andy Messersmith, Los Angeles, Apr 25, 1975
AL—3—George Mullin, Detroit, Apr 27, 1903
Walter Johnson, Washington, July 29, 1917
George Uhle, Cleveland, June 1, 1923
Red Ruffing, Boston, May 25, 1929, 2nd game
Don Ferrarese, Cleveland, May 26, 1959
[3—Babe Ruth, Boston, May 9, 1918, 10 inn]

**Most doubles, each batting in three runs, game**

NL—2—Bob Gilks, Cleveland, Aug 5, 1890 (2nd and 8th)
Harry H. Davis, New York, June 27, 1896 (5th and 9th)
Klondike Douglass, Philadelphia, July 11, 1898 (2nd and 6th)
Gavvy Cravath, Philadelphia, Aug 8, 1915 (4th and 8th)
AL—1—many players
[2—Dan Wilson, Seattle, May 15, 2004 (6th and 13th)
Carlos Guillen, Detroit, Aug 21, 2004 (5th and 6th), 11 inn]

**Most doubles, doubleheader**

AL—6—Hank Majeski, Philadelphia, Aug 27, 1948
NL—5—Chick Hafey, Cincinnati, July 23, 1933
Joe Medwick, St. Louis, May 30, 1935
Red Schoendienst, St. Louis, June 6, 1948
Mike Ivie, San Diego, May 30, 1977

**Most doubles, inning**

NL—2—many players; last—Geoff Jenkins, Milwaukee, Sept 24, 2005, 2nd
AL—2—many players; last—Gary Sheffield, New York, Aug 28, 2004, 9th

**Most doubles by pitcher, inning**

NL—2—Fred Goldsmith, Chicago, Sept 6, 1883, 7th
Hank Borowy, Chicago, May 5, 1946, first game, 7th
AL—2—Smokey Joe Wood, Boston, July 4, 1913, a.m. game, 4th
Ted Lyons, Chicago, July 28, 1935, 1st game, 2nd

## TRIPLES

### CAREER AND SEASON

**Most triples, career**

ML—309—Sam Crawford, Cincinnati NL, Detroit AL, 19 seasons, 1899-1917 (60 in NL, 249 in AL)
AL—295—Ty Cobb, Detroit, Philadelphia, 24 seasons, 1905-1928
NL—252—Honus Wagner, Louisville, Pittsburgh, 21 seasons, 1897-1917

**For a complete list of players with 150 or more career triples, see page 104.**

**Most triples, season**

NL since 1900—36—Owen Wilson, Pittsburgh, 152 G, 1912
AA—31—Dave Orr, New York, 136 G, 1886
NL—31—Heinie Reitz, Baltimore, 108 G, 1894
AL—26—Joe Jackson, Cleveland, 152 G, 1912
Sam Crawford, Detroit, 157 G, 1914

**Fewest triples for leader, season**

AL—8—Del Unser, Washington, 153 G, 1969
NL—10—many players; last—Steve Finley, Arizona, 147 G, 2003; Rafael Furcal, Atlanta, 156 G, 2003

**Most triples by rookie, season**

NL—28—Jimmy Williams, Pittsburgh, 153 G, 1899
AL—19—Joe Cassidy, Washington, 152 G, 1904
(Home Run Baker had 19 triples in 148 G in 1909. He had 31 AB in 9 G in 1908 when there was no rookie qualification rule.)

**Most triples by righthander, season**

NL—29—Perry Werden, St. Louis, 124 G, 1893
AL—22—Bill Bradley, Cleveland, 136 G, 1903
Birdie Cree, New York, 137 G, 1911
George Stirnweiss, New York, 152 G, 1945

**Most triples by lefthander, season**

NL—36—Owen Wilson, Pittsburgh, 152 G, 1912
AL—26—Joe Jackson, Cleveland, 152 G, 1912
Sam Crawford, Detroit, 157 G, 1914

**Most triples by switch-hitter, season**

NL—27—George Davis, New York, 133 G, 1893
AL—21—Willie Wilson, Kansas City, 141 G, 1985

**Most seasons leading league in triples**

ML—6—Sam Crawford, Cincinnati NL, 1902; Detroit AL, 1903, 1910, 1913-1915
AL—5—Sam Crawford, Detroit, 1903, 1910, 1913-1915
Willie Wilson, Kansas City, 1980 (tied), 1982, 1985, 1987, 1988 (tied)
NL—5—Stan Musial, St. Louis, 1943, 1946, 1948, 1949 (tied), 1951 (tied)

**Most consecutive seasons leading league in triples**

AL—4—Lance Johnson, Chicago, 1991 (tied), 1992-1994
NL—3—Garry Templeton, St. Louis, 1977-1979

**Most seasons with 20 or more triples**

ML—5—Sam Crawford, Cincinnati NL, 1902, Detroit AL, 1903, 1912-1914
AL—4—Sam Crawford, Detroit, 1903, 1912-1914
Ty Cobb, Detroit, 1908, 1911, 1912, 1917
NL—3—Roger Connor, New York, 1886, 1887, St. Louis, 1894
Dan Brouthers, Detroit 1887, Brooklyn, 1892, Baltimore, 1894
Sam Thompson, Detroit, 1887, Philadelphia, 1894, 1895
NL since 1893—2—Sam Thompson, Philadelphia, 1894, 1895
Honus Wagner, Pittsburgh, 1900, 1912
Stan Musial, St. Louis, 1943, 1946

**Most triples with bases filled, career**

AL—8—Shano Collins, Chicago, Boston, 1910, 1915, 1916, 1918 (3), 1920 (2)
NL—7—Stan Musial, St. Louis, 1946, 1947 (2), 1948, 1949, 1951, 1954

**Most triples with bases filled, season**

NL—3—George J. Burns, New York, 154 G, 1914
Ted Sizemore, Los Angeles, 159 G, 1969
Manny Sanguillen, Pittsburgh, 138 G, 1971
Alfredo Griffin, Los Angeles, 95 G, 1988
AL—3—Shano Collins, Chicago, 103 G, 1918
Elmer Valo, Philadelphia, 150 G, 1949
Jackie Jensen, Boston, 151 G, 1956

**Most times with three triples in one game, career**

ML—2—Harry Stovey, Philadelphia AA, 1884, Baltimore NL, 1892
Billy Hamilton, Kansas City AA, 1889, Philadelphia NL, 1891
NL—2—John Reilly, Cincinnati, 1890, 1891
George Davis, Cleveland, New York, 1891, 1894
NL since 1893—2—Bill Dahlen, Chicago, 1896, 1898
Dave Brain, St. Louis, Pittsburgh, 1905 (2)
Jim Bottomley, St. Louis, 1923, 1927
AL—1—many players

**Most times with three triples in one game, season**

NL—2—Dave Brain, St. Louis, May 29, 1905; Pittsburgh, Aug 8, 1905
AL—1—many players

**Most at-bats without a triple, season**

AL—662—Miguel Tejada, Oakland, 162 G, 2002
NL—643—Sammy Sosa, Chicago, 159 G, 1998

### GAME AND INNING

**Most triples, game**

AA—4—George Strief, Philadelphia, June 25, 1885
NL—4—Bill Joyce, New York, May 18, 1897
AL—3—many players; last—Lance Johnson, Chicago, Sept 23, 1995

**Most consecutive triples, game**

NL—3—many players; last—Roberto Clemente, Pittsburgh, Sept 8, 1958
AL—3—many players; last—Ben Chapman, Cleveland, July 3, 1939

**Most triples by pitcher, game**

NL—3—Jouett Meekin, New York, July 4, 1894, 1st game
AL—2—many pitchers

**Most triples with bases filled, game**

NL—2—Sam Thompson, Detroit, May 7, 1887
NL since 1893—2—Heinie Reitz, Baltimore, June 4, 1894 (3rd and 7th)
Willie Clark, Pittsburgh, Sept 17, 1898, 2nd game (1st and 7th)
Bill Bruton, Milwaukee, Aug 2, 1959, 2nd game (1st and 6th)
AL—2—Elmer Valo, Philadelphia, May 1, 1949, 1st game (3rd and 7th)
Duane Kuiper, Cleveland, July 27, 1978, 2nd game (1st and 5th)

**Hitting triple and home run in first major league game**

AL—Hank Arft, St. Louis, July 27, 1948
NL—Lloyd Merriman, Cincinnati, Apr 24, 1949, 1st game
Frank Ernaga, Chicago, May 24, 1957
Ken Caminiti, Houston, July 16, 1987

**Hitting triple and home run with bases filled, game**

NL—Dan Brouthers, Detroit, May 17, 1887
Kid Nichols, Boston, Sept 19, 1892
NL since 1893—Jake Stenzel, Pittsburgh, July 15, 1893
Del Bissonette, Brooklyn, Apr 21, 1930
Eddie Phillips, Pittsburgh, May 28, 1931
Luis Olmo, Brooklyn, May 18, 1945
Robin Jennings, Cincinnati, Aug 31, 2001

AL—George Sisler, St. Louis, July 11, 1925
Harry Heilmann, Detroit, July 26, 1928, 2nd game

**Most triples, doubleheader**
AA—4—Billy Hamilton, Kansas City, June 28, 1889
NL—4—Mike Donlin, Cincinnati, Sept 22, 1903
AL—3—many players

**Most triples, inning**
NL—2—Joe Hornung, Boston, May 6, 1882, 8th
NL since 1893—2—Heinie Peitz, St. Louis, July 2, 1895, 1st
Frank Shugart, Louisville, July 30, 1895, 5th
Buck Freeman, Boston, July 25, 1900, 1st
Bill Dahlen, Brooklyn, Aug 30, 1900, 8th
Curt Walker, Cincinnati, July 22, 1926, 2nd
AA—2—Harry Wheeler, Cincinnati, June 28, 1882, 11th
Harry Stovey, Philadelphia, Aug 18, 1884, 8th
AL—2—Al Zarilla, St. Louis, July 13, 1946, 4th
Gil Coan, Washington, Apr 21, 1951, 6th

## HOME RUNS

### CAREER

**Most home runs, career**
ML—755—Hank Aaron, Milwaukee NL, Atlanta NL, Milwaukee AL, 23 seasons, 1954-1976 (733 in NL; 22 in AL)
NL—733—Hank Aaron, Milwaukee, Atlanta, 21 seasons, 1954-1974
AL—708—Babe Ruth, Boston, New York, 21 seasons, 1914-1934

**For a complete list of players with 300 or more career home runs, see page 104.**

**Most home runs with one club, career**
NL—733—Hank Aaron, Milwaukee, Atlanta, 21 seasons, 1954-1974
AL—659—Babe Ruth, New York, 15 seasons, 1920-1934

**Most home runs by righthander, career**
ML—755—Hank Aaron, Milwaukee NL, Atlanta NL, Milwaukee AL, 23 seasons, 1954-1976 (733 in NL; 22 in AL)
NL—733—Hank Aaron, Milwaukee, Atlanta, 21 seasons, 1954-1974
AL—573—Harmon Killebrew, Washington, Minnesota, Kansas City, 22 seasons, 1954-1975

**Most home runs by lefthander, career**
ML—714—Babe Ruth, Boston AL, New York AL, Boston NL, 22 seasons, 1914-1935 (708 in AL; 6 in NL)
AL—708—Babe Ruth, Boston, New York, 21 seasons, 1914-1934
NL—708—Barry Bonds, Pittsburgh, San Francisco, 20 seasons, 1986-2005

**Most home runs by switch-hitter, career**
AL—536—Mickey Mantle, New York, 18 seasons, 1951-1968
NL—331—Chipper Jones, Atlanta, 12 seasons, 1993-2005, except 1994

**Most home runs by pinch-hitter, career**
ML—20—Cliff Johnson, Houston NL, New York AL, Cleveland AL, Chicago NL, Oakland AL, Toronto AL, 1974 (5), 1975, 1976, 1977 (3), 1978 (2), 1979, 1980 (3), 1981, 1983, 1984, 1986
NL—18—Jerry Lynch, Cincinnati, Pittsburgh, 1957 (3), 1958, 1959, 1961 (5), 1962, 1963 (4), 1964, 1965, 1966
AL—16—Gates Brown, Detroit, 1963, 1964, 1965, 1966 (2), 1968 (3), 1970, 1971 (2), 1972, 1974 (3), 1975

**For a complete list of players with 10 or more career pinch-hit home runs, see page 105.**

**Most home runs leading off game, career**
ML—81—Rickey Henderson, Oakland AL, New York AL, Toronto AL, San Diego NL, Anaheim AL, New York NL, Seattle AL, Boston AL, Los Angeles NL, 25 seasons, 1979-2003 (73 in AL, 8 in NL)
AL—73—Rickey Henderson, Oakland, New York, Toronto, Anaheim, Seattle, Boston, 21 seasons, 1979-2002, except 1996, 1999 and 2001
NL—44—Craig Biggio, Houston, 18 seasons, 1988-2005

**Most home runs in extra innings, career**
NL—22—Willie Mays, New York/San Francisco Giants, New York Mets, 22 seasons, 1951-1973, except 1953 in military service
AL—16—Babe Ruth, Boston, New York, 21 seasons, 1914-1934

**Most home runs in opening games of season, career**
ML—8—Frank Robinson, Cincinnati NL, 1959, 1961, 1963; Baltimore AL, 1966, 1969, 1970; California AL, 1973; Cleveland AL, 1975 (5 in AL, 3 in NL)
NL—7—Eddie Mathews, Milwaukee, 1954 (2), 1958 (2), 1959, 1961, 1965
Willie Mays, New York, 1954; San Francisco, 1962, 1963, 1964 (2), 1966, 1971
AL—7—Ken Griffey Jr., Seattle, 1990, 1993, 1995, 1997 (2), 1998, 1999

**Most home runs by first baseman, career**
ML—566—Mark McGwire, Oakland AL, St. Louis NL, 16 seasons, 1986-2001 (349 in AL, 217 in NL)
AL—493—Lou Gehrig, New York, 17 seasons, 1923-1939
NL—439—Willie McCovey, San Francisco, San Diego, 22 seasons, 1959-1980

**Most home runs by second baseman, career**
ML—306—Jeff Kent, Toronto AL, New York NL, Cleveland AL, San Francisco NL, Houston NL, Los Angeles NL, 14 seasons, 1992-2005 (2 in AL, 304 in NL)
NL—277—Ryne Sandberg, Philadelphia, Chicago, 16 seasons, 1981-1997, except 1995
AL—246—Joe Gordon, New York, Cleveland, 11 seasons, 1938-1950, except 1944, 1945 in military service

**Most home runs by third baseman, career**
NL—509—Mike Schmidt, Philadelphia, 18 seasons, 1972-1989
AL—319—Graig Nettles, Minnesota, Cleveland, New York, 16 seasons, 1968-1983

**Most home runs by shortstop, career**
AL—345—Cal Ripken Jr., Baltimore, 16 seasons, 1981-1996
NL—277—Ernie Banks, Chicago, 9 seasons, 1953-1961

**Most home runs by outfielder, career**
ML—692—Babe Ruth, Boston AL, New York AL, Boston NL, 17 seasons, 1918-1935 (686 in AL; 6 in NL)
AL—686—Babe Ruth, Boston, New York, 17 seasons, 1918-1934
NL—661—Hank Aaron, Milwaukee, Atlanta, 21 seasons, 1954-1974

**Most home runs by catcher, career**
NL—376—Mike Piazza, Los Angeles, Florida, New York, 14 seasons, 1992-2005
AL—351—Carlton Fisk, Boston, Chicago, 24 seasons, 1969-1993, except 1970

**Most home runs by pitcher, career**
ML—37—Wes Ferrell, Cleveland AL, Boston AL, Washington AL, New York AL, Brooklyn NL, Boston NL, 15 seasons, 1927-1941 (also 1 HR as pinch-hitter, Boston AL, 1935)
AL—36—Wes Ferrell, Cleveland, Boston, Washington, New York, 13 seasons, 1927-1939 (also 1 HR as pinch-hitter, Boston, 1935)
NL—35—Warren Spahn, Boston, Milwaukee, New York, San Francisco, 21 seasons, 1942-1965, except 1943-1945 in military service

**Most major league ballparks, one or more home runs, career (since 1900)**
ML—43—Fred McGriff, Toronto AL, San Diego NL, Atlanta NL, Tampa Bay AL, Chicago NL, Los Angeles NL, 19 seasons, 1986-2004
AL—31—Rafael Palmeiro, Texas, Baltimore, 17 seasons, 1989-2005
NL—35—Mike Piazza, Los Angeles, Florida, New York, 14 seasons, 1992-2005 (includes one at Tokyo Dome)
Barry Bonds, Pittsburgh, San Francisco, 20 seasons, 1986-2005

**Most consecutive at-bats without hitting a home run, career**
NL—3,347—Tommy Thevenow, St. Louis, Philadelphia, Pittsburgh, Cincinnati, Boston, Sept 24, 1926-Oct 2, 1938 (end of career)
AL—3,278—Eddie Foster, Washington, Boston, St. Louis, Apr 20, 1916-Aug 5, 1923 (end of career)

### SEASON

**Most home runs, season**
NL since 1900—73—Barry Bonds, San Francisco, 153 G, 2001
AL—61—Roger Maris, New York, 161 G, 1961
NL—27—Ed Williamson, Chicago, 107 G, 1884
AA—19—Bug Holliday, Cincinnati, 135 G, 1889
Harry Stovey, Philadelphia, 137 G, 1889

**For a complete list of players with 40 or more home runs in a season, see page 112. For complete lists of players combining power and speed (40 HRs, 40 SBs; 30 HRs, 30 SBs; 50 HRs, 20 SBs and 20 HRs, 50 SBs) during a season, see page 116. For detailed breakdowns of Barry Bonds' 73-homer season, Mark McGwire's 70-homer season, Roger Maris' 61-homer season and Babe Ruth's 60-homer season, see page 119.**

**Most home runs for runner-up, season**
NL—66—Sammy Sosa, Chicago, 159 G, 1998
AL—54—Mickey Mantle, New York, 153 G, 1961

**Fewest home runs by leader, season**
NL—7—Red Murray, New York, 149 G, 1909
AL—7—Sam Crawford, Detroit, 152 G, 1908
Braggo Roth, Chicago, Cleveland, 109 G, 1915

**Most seasons leading league in home runs**
AL—12—Babe Ruth, Boston, New York, 1918 (tied), 1919-1921, 1923, 1924-1930, 1931 (tied)
NL—8—Mike Schmidt, Philadelphia, 1974-1976, 1980, 1981, 1983, 1984 (tied), 1986

**Most consecutive seasons leading league in home runs**
NL—7—Ralph Kiner, Pittsburgh, 1946, 1947 (tied), 1948 (tied), 1949-1951, 1952 (tied)
AL—6—Babe Ruth, New York, 1926-1930, 1931 (tied)

**Most home runs by rookie, season**
AL—49—Mark McGwire, Oakland, 151 G, 1987
NL—38—Wally Berger, Boston, 151 G, 1930
Frank Robinson, Cincinnati, 152 G, 1956

**Most home runs by righthander, season**
NL—70—Mark McGwire, St. Louis, 155 G, 1998
AL—58—Jimmie Foxx, Philadelphia, 154 G, 1932
Hank Greenberg, Detroit, 155 G, 1938

**Most home runs by lefthander, season**
NL—73—Barry Bonds, San Francisco, 153 G, 2001
AL—61—Roger Maris, New York, 161 G, 1961

**Most home runs by switch-hitter, season**
AL—54—Mickey Mantle, New York, 153 G, 1961
NL—45—Chipper Jones, Atlanta, 157 G, 1999

**Most home runs by pinch-hitter, season**
NL—7—Dave Hansen, Los Angeles, 2000

Craig Wilson, Pittsburgh, 2001
AL—5—Joe Cronin, Boston, 1943

**Most home runs leading off game, season**
AL—13—Alfonso Soriano, New York, 156 G, 2003 (38 HR for season)
NL—11—Bobby Bonds, San Francisco, 160 G, 1973 (39 HR for season)

**Most home runs by first baseman, season**
NL—69—Mark McGwire, St. Louis, 155 G, 1998, 151 G at 1B (also 1 HR as pinch-hitter)
AL—58—Hank Greenberg, Detroit, 155 G, 1938, 154 G at 1B

**Most home runs by second baseman, season**
NL—42—Rogers Hornsby, St. Louis, 154 G, 1922, 154 G at 2B
Dave Johnson, Atlanta, 157 G, 1973, 156 G at 2B (also 1 HR as pinch-hitter)
AL—39—Alfonso Soriano, New York, 156 G, 2002, 155 G at 2B

**Most home runs by third baseman, season**
NL—48—Mike Schmidt, Philadelphia, 150 G, 1980, 149 G at 3B
Adrian Beltre, Los Angeles, 156 G, 2004, 155 G at 3B
AL—46—Troy Glaus, Anaheim, 159 G, 2000, 156 G at 3B (also 1 HR as designated hitter)

**Most home runs by shortstop, season**
AL—57—Alex Rodriguez, Texas, 162 G, 2002, 162 G at SS
NL—47—Ernie Banks, Chicago, 154 G, 1958, 154 G at SS

**Most home runs by outfielder, season**
NL—71—Barry Bonds, San Francisco, 153 G, 2001, 143 G in OF (also 1 HR as pinch-hitter and 1 HR as designated hitter)
AL—61—Roger Maris, New York, 161 G, 1961, 160 G in OF

**Most home runs by catcher, season**
NL—42—Javy Lopez, Atlanta, 129 G, 2003, 120 G at C
(Johnny Bench, Cincinnati, 1970, had 38 HR in 139 G at C and 7 HR in OF and at 1B)
AL—35—Ivan Rodriguez, Texas, 144 G, 1999, 141 G at C
(Carlton Fisk, Chicago, 1985, had 33 HR in 130 G at C and 4 HR as designated hitter)

**Most home runs by pitcher, season**
AL—9—Wes Ferrell, Cleveland, 48 G, 1931, 40 G at P
NL—7—Don Newcombe, Brooklyn, 57 G, 1955, 34 G at P
Don Drysdale, Los Angeles, 47 G, 1958, 44 G at P
Don Drysdale, Los Angeles, 58 G, 1965, 44 G at P
Mike Hampton, Colorado, 43 G, 2001, 32 G at P

**Most home runs against one club, season**
AL—14—Lou Gehrig, New York vs Cleveland, 1936 (6 at New York, 8 at Cleveland)
NL—13—Hank Sauer, Chicago vs Pittsburgh, 1954 (8 at Chicago, 5 at Pittsburgh)
Joe Adcock, Milwaukee vs Brooklyn, 1956 (5 at Milwaukee, 7 at Brooklyn, 1 at Jersey City)

**Most at-bats without a home run, season**
NL—672—Rabbit Maranville, Pittsburgh, 155 G, 1922
AL—658—Doc Cramer, Boston, 148 G, 1938

**Fewest home runs, season (150 or more games)**
AL—many players; last—Lance Johnson, Chicago, 160 G, 1991
NL—many players; last—Ozzie Smith, St. Louis, 158 G, 1987

## HOME AND ROAD

**Most home runs at home, season**
AL—39—Hank Greenberg, Detroit, 1938
NL—38—Mark McGwire, St. Louis, 1998

**Most home runs at home by righthander, season**
AL—39—Hank Greenberg, Detroit, 1938
NL—38—Mark McGwire, St. Louis, 1998

**Most home runs at home by lefthander, season**
NL—37—Barry Bonds, San Francisco, 2001
AL—32—Babe Ruth, New York, 1921
Ken Williams, St. Louis, 1922

**Most home runs at home by switch-hitter, season**
AL—27—Mickey Mantle, New York, 1956
NL—25—Chipper Jones, Atlanta, 1999

**Most home runs at home against one club, season**
AL—10—Gus Zernial, Philadelphia vs St. Louis, 1951
NL—9—Stan Musial, St. Louis vs New York, 1954

**Most home runs on road, season**
NL—36—Barry Bonds, San Francisco, 2001
AL—32—Babe Ruth, New York, 1927

**Most home runs on road by righthander, season**
NL—32—Mark McGwire, St. Louis, 1998
AL—28—Harmon Killebrew, Minnesota, 1962
George Bell, Toronto, 1987
Mark McGwire, Oakland, 1987
Jose Canseco, Oakland, 1991
Mark McGwire, Oakland, 1996

**Most home runs on road by lefthander, season**
NL—36—Barry Bonds, San Francisco, 2001
AL—32—Babe Ruth, New York, 1927

**Most home runs on road by switch-hitter, season**
AL—30—Mickey Mantle, New York, 1961
NL—23—Howard Johnson, New York, 1987

**Most home runs on road against one club, season**
AL—10—Harry Heilmann, Detroit at Philadelphia, 1922
NL—9—Joe Adcock, Milwaukee at Brooklyn, 1954
Willie Mays, New York at Brooklyn, 1955

**Most major league ballparks, one or more home runs, season**
NL—18—Sammy Sosa, Chicago, 1998 (16 NL and 2 AL)
Mike Piazza, New York, 2000 (14 NL, 3 AL and 1 in Japan)
AL—16—Ken Griffey Jr., Seattle, 1998 (13 AL and 3 NL)
Juan Gonzalez, Texas, 1999 (13 AL and 3 NL)

**Most seasons hitting home runs in all parks, career**
AL—11—Babe Ruth, Boston, New York, 1919-1921, 1923, 1924, 1926-1931
NL—9—Hank Aaron, Milwaukee, Atlanta, 1954-1960, 1963, 1966

## 50, 40, 30 AND 20 IN SEASON

**Most seasons with 50 or more home runs**
ML—4—Babe Ruth, New York AL, 1920, 1921, 1927, 1928
Mark McGwire, Oakland AL, 1996; Oakland AL and St. Louis NL, 1997; St. Louis NL, 1998, 1999
Sammy Sosa, Chicago NL, 1998-2001
AL—4—Babe Ruth, New York, 1920, 1921, 1927, 1928
NL—4—Sammy Sosa, Chicago, 1998-2001

**Most consecutive seasons with 50 or more home runs**
ML—4—Mark McGwire, Oakland AL, 1996, Oakland AL and St. Louis NL, 1997, St. Louis NL, 1998, 1999
Sammy Sosa, Chicago, 1998-2001
NL—4—Sammy Sosa, Chicago, 1998-2001
AL—2—Babe Ruth, New York, 1920, 1921; and 1927, 1928
Ken Griffey Jr., Seattle, 1997, 1998
Alex Rodriguez, Texas, 2001, 2002

**Most seasons with 40 or more home runs**
AL—11—Babe Ruth, New York, 1920, 1921, 1923, 1924, 1926-1932
NL—8—Hank Aaron, Milwaukee, Atlanta, 1957, 1960, 1962, 1963, 1966, 1969, 1971, 1973
Barry Bonds, San Francisco, 1993, 1996, 1997, 2000-2004

**For a complete list of players with 40 or more home runs in a season, see page 112.**

**Most consecutive seasons with 40 or more home runs**
AL—7—Babe Ruth, New York, 1926-1932
NL—6—Sammy Sosa, Chicago, 1998-2003

**Most seasons with 30 or more home runs**
NL—15—Hank Aaron, Milwaukee, Atlanta, 1957-1973, except 1964, 1968
AL—13—Babe Ruth, New York, 1920-1933, except 1925

**Most consecutive seasons with 30 or more home runs**
NL—13—Barry Bonds, Pittsburgh, San Francisco, 1992-2004
AL—12—Jimmie Foxx, Philadelphia, Boston, 1929-1940

**Hitting 20 or more home runs for two leagues, season**
Mark McGwire, Oakland AL, 34, St. Louis NL, 24, 1997

**Most seasons with 20 or more home runs**
NL—20—Hank Aaron, Milwaukee, Atlanta, 1955-1974
AL—16—Babe Ruth, Boston, New York, 1919-1934
Ted Williams, Boston, 1939-1942, 1946-1951, 1954-1958, 1960
Reggie Jackson, Oakland, Baltimore, New York, California, 1968-1980, 1982, 1984, 1985

**Most consecutive seasons with 20 or more home runs**
NL—20—Hank Aaron, Milwaukee, Atlanta, 1955-1974
AL—16—Babe Ruth, Boston, New York, 1919-1934

## TWO CONSECUTIVE SEASONS

**Most home runs, two consecutive seasons**
NL—135—Mark McGwire, St. Louis, 70 in 1998, 65 in 1999
AL—114—Babe Ruth, New York, 60 in 1927, 54 in 1928

**Most home runs by righthander, two consecutive seasons**
NL—135—Mark McGwire, St. Louis, 70 in 1998, 65 in 1999
AL—109—Alex Rodriguez, Texas, 52 in 2001, 57 in 2002

**Most home runs by lefthander, two consecutive seasons**
NL—122—Barry Bonds, San Francisco, 49 in 2000, 73 in 2001
AL—114—Babe Ruth, New York, 60 in 1927, 54 in 1928

**Most home runs by switch-hitter, two consecutive seasons**
AL—94—Mickey Mantle, New York, 40 in 1960, 54 in 1961
NL—81—Chipper Jones, Atlanta, 45 in 1999, 36 in 2000

## MONTH AND WEEK

**Most home runs, one calendar month**
NL—20—Sammy Sosa, Chicago, June 1998
AL—18—Rudy York, Detroit, Aug 1937

**Most home runs by righthander, one month**
NL—20—Sammy Sosa, Chicago, June 1998
AL—18—Rudy York, Detroit, Aug 1937

**Most home runs by lefthander, one month**
AL—17—Babe Ruth, New York, Sept 1927
NL—17—Barry Bonds, San Francisco, May 2001

**Most home runs by switch-hitter, one month**
AL—16—Mickey Mantle, New York, May 1956
NL—14—Ken Caminiti, San Diego, Aug 1996

**Most home runs in March**
NL—2—Vinny Castilla, Colorado, 1998
AL—2—Jorge Posada, New York, 2004

**Most home runs in April**
AL—13—Ken Griffey Jr., Seattle, 1997
NL—13—Luis Gonzalez, Arizona, 2001

**Most home runs through April 30**
AL—13—Ken Griffey Jr., Seattle, 1997
NL—13—Luis Gonzalez, Arizona, 2001

**Most home runs in May**
NL—17—Barry Bonds, San Francisco, 2001
AL—16—Mickey Mantle, New York, 1956

**Most home runs through May 31**
NL—28—Barry Bonds, San Francisco, 2001
AL—24—Ken Griffey Jr., Seattle, 1997

**Most home runs in June**
NL—20—Sammy Sosa, Chicago, 1998
AL—15—Babe Ruth, New York, 1930
Bob Johnson, Philadelphia, 1934
Roger Maris, New York, 1961

**Most home runs through June 30**
NL—39—Barry Bonds, San Francisco, 2001
AL—32—Ken Griffey Jr., Seattle, 1994

**Most home runs in July**
AL—16—Albert Belle, Chicago, 1998
NL—16—Mark McGwire, St. Louis, 1999

**Most home runs through July 31**
NL—45—Mark McGwire, St. Louis, 1998
Barry Bonds, San Francisco, 2001
AL—41—Babe Ruth, New York, 1928
Jimmie Foxx, Philadelphia, 1932

**Most home runs in August**
AL—18—Rudy York, Detroit, Aug 1937
NL—17—Willie Mays, San Francisco, Aug 1965
Sammy Sosa, Chicago, Aug 2001

**Most home runs through August 31**
NL—57—Barry Bonds, San Francisco, 2001
AL—51—Roger Maris, New York, 1961

**Most home runs in September**
AL—17—Babe Ruth, New York, 1927
Albert Belle, Cleveland, 1995
NL—16—Ralph Kiner, Pittsburgh, 1949

**Most home runs through September 30**
NL—70—Mark McGwire, St. Louis, 1998
AL—60—Babe Ruth, New York, 1927
Roger Maris, New York, 1961

**Most home runs in October**
NL—5—Richie Sexson, Milwaukee, 2001
Sammy Sosa, Chicago, 2001
AA—4—John Milligan, St. Louis, 1889
AL—4—Gus Zernial, Chicago, 1950
George Brett, Kansas City, 1985
Ron Kittle, Chicago, 1985
Wally Joyner, California, 1987
Jose Cruz Jr., Toronto, 2001

**Most home runs in one week (Sunday through Saturday)**
AL—10—Frank Howard, Washington, May 12-18, 1968, 6 G
NL—9—Shawn Green, Los Angeles, May 19-25, 2002, 6 G

## GAME, DOUBLEHEADER, INNING

**Most home runs, game**
NL—4—Bobby Lowe, Boston, May 30, 1894, p.m. game (consec)
Ed Delahanty, Philadelphia, July 13, 1896
Gil Hodges, Brooklyn, Aug 31, 1950
Joe Adcock, Milwaukee, July 31, 1954
Willie Mays, San Francisco, Apr 30, 1961
Bob Horner, Atlanta, July 6, 1986
Mark Whiten, St. Louis, Sept 7, 1993, 2nd game
Shawn Green, Los Angeles, May 23, 2002
[4—Chuck Klein, Philadelphia, July 10, 1936, 10 inn
Mike Schmidt, Philadelphia, Apr 17, 1976, 10 inn (consec)]
AL—4—Lou Gehrig, New York, June 3, 1932 (consec)
Rocky Colavito, Cleveland, June 10, 1959 (consec)
Mike Cameron, Seattle, May 2, 2002 (consec)
Carlos Delgado, Toronto, Sept 25, 2003 (consec)
[4—Pat Seerey, Chicago, July 18, 1948, 1st game, 11 inn]

**For a complete list of players with three or more home runs in a game, see page 113.**

**Most home runs by pitcher, game**
AA—3—Guy Hecker, Louisville, Aug 15, 1886, 2nd game
NL—3—Jim Tobin, Boston, May 13, 1942
AL—2—many pitchers; last—Sonny Siebert, Boston, Sept 2, 1971

**Most home runs, first game in major leagues**
AA—2—Charlie Reilly, Columbus, Oct 9, 1889 (3rd and 5th AB)
AL—2—Bob Nieman, St. Louis, Sept 14, 1951 (1st and 2nd AB)
Bert Campaneris, Kansas City, July 23, 1964 (1st and 4th AB)
Mark Quinn, Kansas City, Sept 14, 1999, 2nd game (3rd and 4th AB)
NL—1—many players

**Most home runs, opening game of season**
AL—3—George Bell, Toronto, Apr 4, 1988
NL—3—Karl Rhodes, Chicago, Apr 4, 1994

**Most inside-the-park home runs, game**
NL—3—Tom McCreery, Louisville, July 12, 1897
AL—2—many players; last—Greg Gagne, Minnesota, Oct 4, 1986

**Most home runs in extra innings, game**
NL—2—Art Shamsky, Cincinnati, Aug 12, 1966, 10th and 11th inn (consec)
Ralph Garr, Atlanta, May 17, 1971, 10th and 12th inn (consec)
AL—2—Vern Stephens, St. Louis, Sept 29, 1943, 1st game, 11th and 13th inn (consec)
Willie Kirkland, Cleveland, June 14, 1963, 2nd game, 11th and 19th inn
Mike Young, Baltimore, May 28, 1987, 10th and 12th inn (consec)

**Home run winning longest extra-inning game**
AL—Harold Baines, Chicago, 25 inn, none on base, Chicago 7, Milwaukee 6, May 8-9, 1984
NL—Rick Dempsey, Los Angeles, 22 inn, none on base, Los Angeles 1, Montreal 0, Aug 23, 1989

**Home run winning longest 1-0 game**
NL—Rick Dempsey, Los Angeles, Aug 23, 1989, 22 inn
AL—Bill Skowron, New York, Apr 22, 1959, 14 inn

**Home run by pitcher winning 1-0 extra-inning complete game**
AL—Tom Hughes, Washington, Aug 3, 1906, 10 inn
Red Ruffing, New York, Aug 13, 1932, 10 inn
NL—none—(Johnny Klippstein, Cincinnati, Aug 6, 1962, hit HR in 13th inn after relieving Bob Purkey, who had pitched first 10 inn.)

**Home run in first major league at-bat**
***On first pitch †Not first plate appearance ‡Pitcher**

AA—George Tebeau, Cincinnati, Apr 16, 1887
Mike Griffin, Baltimore, Apr 16, 1887
**Total number of players: 2**

AL—Luke Stuart, St. Louis, Aug 8, 1921
Earl Averill, Cleveland, Apr 16, 1929
Ace Parker, Philadelphia, Apr 30, 1937
Gene Hasson, Philadelphia, Sept 9, 1937, 1st game
Bill Lefebvre, Boston, June 10, 1938*‡
Hack Miller, Detroit, Apr 23, 1944, 2nd game
Eddie Pellagrini, Boston, Apr 22, 1946
George Vico, Detroit, Apr 20, 1948*
Bob Nieman, St. Louis, Sept 14, 1951
Bob Tillman, Boston, May 19, 1962†
John Kennedy, Washington, Sept 5, 1962, 1st game
Buster Narum, Baltimore, May 3, 1963‡
Gates Brown, Detroit, June 19, 1963
Bert Campaneris, Kansas City, July 23, 1964*
Bill Roman, Detroit, Sept 30, 1964, 2nd game
Brant Alyea, Washington, Sept 12, 1965*
John Miller, New York, Sept 11, 1966
Rick Renick, Minnesota, July 11, 1968
Joe Keough, Oakland, Aug 7, 1968, 2nd game
Gene Lamont, Detroit, Sept 2, 1970, 2nd game
Don Rose, California, May 24, 1972*‡
Reggie J. Sanders, Detroit, Sept 1, 1974
Dave McKay, Minnesota, Aug 22, 1975
Al Woods, Toronto, Apr 7, 1977*
Dave Machemer, California, June 21, 1978
Gary Gaetti, Minnesota, Sept 20, 1981
Andre David, Minnesota, June 29, 1984, 1st game
Terry Steinbach, Oakland, Sept 12, 1986
Jay Bell, Cleveland, Sept 29, 1986*
Junior Felix, Toronto, May 4, 1989*
Jon Nunnally, Kansas City, Apr 29, 1995
Carlos Lee, Chicago, May 7, 1999
Esteban Yan, Tampa Bay, June 4, 2000*‡
Marcus Thames, New York, June 10, 2002*
Miguel Olivo, Chicago, Sept 15, 2002
Andy Phillips, New York, Sept 26, 2004
**Total number of players: 35**

NL—Joe Harrington, Boston, Sept 10, 1895
Bill Duggleby, Philadelphia, Apr 21, 1898 (grand slam)‡
Johnny Bates, Boston, Apr 12, 1906

Walter Mueller, Pittsburgh, May 7, 1922*
Clise Dudley, Brooklyn, Apr 27, 1929*‡
Gordon Slade, Brooklyn, May 24, 1930
Eddie Morgan, St. Louis, Apr 14, 1936*
Ernie Koy, Brooklyn, Apr 19, 1938
Emmett Mueller, Philadelphia, Apr 19, 1938
Clyde Vollmer, Cincinnati, May 31, 1942, 2nd game*
Paul Gillespie, Chicago, Sept 11, 1942
Buddy Kerr, New York, Sept 8, 1943
Whitey Lockman, New York, July 5, 1945
Dan Bankhead, Brooklyn, Aug 26, 1947‡
Les Layton, New York, May 21, 1948
Ed Sanicki, Philadelphia, Sept 14, 1949
Ted Tappe, Cincinnati, Sept 14, 1950, 1st game
Hoyt Wilhelm, New York, Apr 23, 1952‡
Wally Moon, St. Louis, Apr 13, 1954
Chuck Tanner, Milwaukee, Apr 12, 1955*
Bill White, New York, May 7, 1956
Frank Ernaga, Chicago, May 24, 1957
Don Leppert, Pittsburgh, June 18, 1961, 1st game
Cuno Barragan, Chicago, Sept 1, 1961
Benny Ayala, New York, Aug 27, 1974
John Montefusco, San Francisco, Sept 3, 1974†‡
Johnnie LeMaster, San Francisco, Sept 2, 1975
Tim Wallach, Montreal, Sept 6, 1980†
Carmelo Martinez, Chicago, Aug 22, 1983†
Mike Fitzgerald, New York, Sept 13, 1983
Will Clark, San Francisco, Apr 8, 1986
Ricky Jordan, Philadelphia, July 17, 1988†
Jose Offerman, Los Angeles, Aug 19, 1990
Dave Eiland, San Diego, Apr 10, 1992‡
Jim Bullinger, Chicago, June 8, 1992, 1st game*‡
Jay Gainer, Colorado, May 14, 1993*
Mitch Lyden, Florida, June 16, 1993
Garey Ingram, Los Angeles, May 19, 1994
Jermaine Dye, Atlanta, May 17, 1996
Dustin Hermanson, Montreal, Apr 16, 1997‡
Brad Fullmer, Montreal, Sept 2, 1997
Marlon Anderson, Philadelphia, Sept 8, 1998
Guillermo Mota, Montreal, June 9, 1999
Alex Cabrera, Arizona, June 26, 2000
Keith McDonald, St. Louis, July 4, 2000
Chris Richard, St. Louis, July 17, 2000*
Gene Stechschulte, St. Louis, Apr 17, 2001*‡ (pitcher as pinch-hitter)
Dave Matranga, Houston, June 27, 2003
Jeremy Hermida, Florida, Aug 31, 2005
Mike Jacobs, New York, Aug 21, 2005
**Total number of players: 49**

**Players hitting a pinch home run in first major league at-bat**
NL—Eddie Morgan, St. Louis, Apr 14, 1936, 7th
Les Layton, New York, May 21, 1948, 9th
Ted Tappe, Cincinnati, Sept 14, 1950, 1st game, 8th
Chuck Tanner, Milwaukee, Apr 12, 1955, 8th
Marlon Anderson, Philadelphia, Sept 8, 1998, 7th
Keith McDonald, St. Louis, July 4, 2000, 8th
Gene Stechschulte, St. Louis, Apr 17, 2001, 6th
AL—Ace Parker, Philadelphia, Apr 30, 1937, 9th
John Kennedy, Washington, Sept 5, 1962, 1st game, 6th
Gates Brown, Detroit, June 19, 1963, 5th
Bill Roman, Detroit, Sept 30, 1964, 2nd game, 7th
Brant Alyea, Washington, Sept 12, 1965, 6th
Joe Keough, Oakland, Aug 7, 1968, 2nd game, 8th
Al Woods, Toronto, Apr 7, 1977, 5th

**Home run in first two major league at-bats**
AL—Bob Nieman, St. Louis, Sept 14, 1951 (first 2 PA)
NL—Keith McDonald, St. Louis, July 4, July 6, 2000 (first 2 PA)

**Most home runs, doubleheader (homering in each game)**
NL—5—Stan Musial, St. Louis, May 2, 1954
Nate Colbert, San Diego, Aug 1, 1972
AL—4—Earl Averill, Cleveland, Sept 17, 1930
Jimmie Foxx, Philadelphia, July 2, 1933, 19 inn
Jim Tabor, Boston, July 4, 1939
Gus Zernial, Chicago, Oct 1, 1950
Charlie Maxwell, Detroit, May 3, 1959 (consec)
Roger Maris, New York, July 25, 1961
Rocky Colavito, Detroit, Aug 27, 1961
Harmon Killebrew, Minnesota, Sept 21, 1963
Bobby Murcer, New York, June 24, 1970 (consec)
Graig Nettles, New York, Apr 14, 1974
Otto Velez, Toronto, May 4, 1980, 19 inn
Al Oliver, Texas, Aug 17, 1980

**Players hitting home runs leading off both games of doubleheader**
AL—Harry Hooper, Boston, May 30, 1913
Rickey Henderson, Oakland, July 5, 1993
Brady Anderson, Baltimore, Aug 21, 1999
NL—none

**Most home runs by pinch-hitter, doubleheader**
AL—2—Joe Cronin, Boston, June 17, 1943
NL—2—Hal Breeden, Montreal, July 13, 1973

**Most home runs, inning**
AA—2—Ed Cartwright, St. Louis, Sept 23, 1890, 3rd
PL—2—Lou Bierbauer, Brooklyn, July 12, 1890, 3rd
AL—2—Ken Williams, St. Louis, Aug 7, 1922, 6th
Bill Regan, Boston, June 16, 1928, 4th
Joe DiMaggio, New York, June 24, 1936, 5th
Al Kaline, Detroit, Apr 17, 1955, 6th
Jim Lemon, Washington, Sept 5, 1959, 3rd
Joe Pepitone, New York, May 23, 1962, 8th
Rick Reichardt, California, Apr 30, 1966, 8th
Cliff Johnson, New York, June 30, 1977, 8th
Ellis Burks, Boston, Aug 27, 1990, 4th
Carlos Baerga, Cleveland, Apr 8, 1993, 7th
Joe Carter, Toronto, October 3, 1993, 2nd
Dave Nilsson, Milwaukee, May 17, 1996, 6th
Mark McGwire, Oakland, Sept 22, 1996, 5th
Bret Boone, Seattle, May 2, 2002, 1st
Mike Cameron, Seattle, May 2, 2002, 1st
Jared Sandberg, Tampa Bay, June 11, 2002, 5th
Nomar Garciaparra, Boston, July 23, 2002, a.m. game, 3rd
Carl Everett, Texas, July 26, 2002, 7th
NL—2—Charley Jones, Boston, June 10, 1880, 8th
Bobby Lowe, Boston, May 30, 1894, p.m. game, 3rd
Jake Stenzel, Pittsburgh, June 6, 1894, 3rd
Hack Wilson, New York, July 1, 1925, 2nd game, 3rd
Hank Leiber, New York, Aug 24, 1935, 2nd
Andy Seminick, Philadelphia, June 2, 1949, 8th
Sid Gordon, New York, July 31, 1949, 2nd game, 2nd
Willie McCovey, San Francisco, Apr 12, 1973, 4th, and June 27, 1977, 6th
John Boccabella, Montreal, July 6, 1973, 1st game, 6th
Lee May, Houston, Apr 29, 1974, 6th
Andre Dawson, Montreal, July 30, 1978, 3rd, and Sept 24, 1985, 5th
Ray Knight, Cincinnati, May 13, 1980, 5th
Von Hayes, Philadelphia, June 11, 1985, 1st
Dale Murphy, Atlanta, July 27, 1989, 6th
Jeff Bagwell, Houston, June 24, 1994, 6th
Jeff King, Pittsburgh, Aug 8, 1995, 2nd, and Apr 30, 1996, 4th
Sammy Sosa, Chicago, May 16, 1996, 7th
Mike Lansing, Montreal, May 7, 1997, 6th
Gary Sheffield, Florida, July 13, 1997, 4th
Fernando Tatis, St. Louis, Apr 23, 1999, 3rd
Eric Karros, Los Angeles, Aug 22, 2000, 6th
Aaron Boone, Cincinnati, Aug 9, 2002, 1st
Mark Bellhorn, Chicago, Aug 29, 2002, 4th
Reggie L. Sanders, Pittsburgh, Aug 20, 2003, 5th
Juan Rivera, Montreal, June 19, 2004, 2nd

**Most home runs, two consecutive innings (homering each inning)**
AL—3—Nomar Garciaparra, Boston, July 23, 2002, a.m. game, 3rd (2), 4th (1)
NL—2—many players

## THREE AND TWO IN GAME

**Most times hitting three or more home runs in a game, career**
ML—6—Johnny Mize, St. Louis NL, 1938 (2), 1940 (2), New York NL, 1947, New York AL, 1950
Sammy Sosa, Chicago NL, 1996, 1998, 2001 (3), 2002
NL—6—Sammy Sosa, Chicago, 1996, 1998, 2001 (3), 2002
AL—5—Joe Carter, Cleveland, 1986, 1987, 1989 (2), Toronto, 1993

**For a complete list of players with three or more home runs in a game, see page 113.**

**Most times hitting three or more home runs in a game, season**
NL—3—Sammy Sosa, Chicago, Aug 9, Aug 22, Sept 23, 2001
AL—2—Ted Williams, Boston, May 8, June 13, 1957
Doug DeCinces, California, Aug 3, Aug 8, 1982
Joe Carter, Cleveland, June 24, July 19, 1989
Cecil Fielder, Detroit, May 6, June 6, 1990
Geronimo Berroa, Oakland, May 22, Aug 12, 1996

**Most times hitting three home runs in a doubleheader, career (homering in both games)**
AL—7—Babe Ruth, New York, 1920, 1922, 1926, 1927, 1930, 1933 (2)
NL—5—Mel Ott, New York, 1929, 1931, 1932, 1933, 1944

**Most times hitting three or more consecutive home runs in a game, career**
ML—4—Johnny Mize, St. Louis NL, 1938, 1940, New York NL, 1947, New York AL, 1950
Sammy Sosa, Chicago NL, 1996, 2001 (2), 2002
NL—4—Sammy Sosa, Chicago, 1996, 2001 (2), 2002
AL—3—Cecil Fielder, Detroit, 1990 (2), 1996

**Most times hitting two or more home runs in a game, career**
ML—72—Babe Ruth, Boston AL, New York AL, Boston NL, 22 seasons, 1914-1935 (71 in AL, 1 in NL)
AL—71—Babe Ruth, Boston, New York, 21 seasons, 1914-1934
NL—68—Barry Bonds, Pittsburgh, San Francisco, 19 seasons, 1986-2004

**For a complete list of players with 25 or more multiple-home run games, see page 106.**

**Most times hitting two or more home runs in a game, season**
AL—11—Hank Greenberg, Detroit, 1938

NL—11—Sammy Sosa, Chicago, 1998

**Most times pitcher hitting two home runs in a game, career**

AL—5—Wes Ferrell, Cleveland, Boston, 1931, 1934 (2), 1935, 1936
NL—3—Don Newcombe, Brooklyn, 1955 (2), 1956

**Most times pitcher hitting two home runs in a game, season**

AL—2—Wes Ferrell, Boston, 1934
Jack Harshman, Baltimore, 1958
Dick Donovan, Cleveland, 1962
NL—2—Don Newcombe, Brooklyn, 1955
Tony Cloninger, Atlanta, 1966
Rick Wise, Philadelphia, 1971

**Most games hitting home runs from both sides of plate, career**

ML—11—Eddie Murray, Baltimore AL, 1977, 1979, 1981, 1982 (2), 1985, 1987 (2), Los Angeles NL, 1990 (2), Cleveland AL, 1994
AL—10—Mickey Mantle, New York, 1955 (2), 1956 (2), 1957, 1958, 1959, 1961, 1962, 1964
NL—10—Ken Caminiti, Houston, 1994; San Diego, 1995 (3), 1996 (4), 1998, Houston, 1999

**For a complete list of players hitting home runs from both sides of plate in a game, see page 115.**

**Most games hitting home runs from both sides of plate, season**

NL—4—Ken Caminiti, San Diego, 1996
AL—3—Tony Clark, Detroit, 1998

**Hitting home runs from both sides of plate, inning**

AL—Carlos Baerga, Cleveland, Apr 8, 1993, 7th
NL—Mark Bellhorn, Chicago, Aug 29, 2002, 4th

## CONSECUTIVE AND IN CONSECUTIVE GAMES

**Most consecutive home runs, game**

NL—4—Bobby Lowe, Boston, May 30, 1894, p.m. game
[4—Mike Schmidt, Philadelphia, Apr 17, 1976, 10 inn]
AL—4—Lou Gehrig, New York, June 3, 1932
Rocky Colavito, Cleveland, June 10, 1959
Mike Cameron, Seattle, May 2, 2002
Carlos Delgado, Toronto, Sept 25, 2003

**Most consecutive home runs, two games**

AL—4—Jimmie Foxx, Philadelphia, June 7 (1), 8 (3), 1933
Hank Greenberg, Detroit, July 26 (2), 27 (2), 1938
Charlie Maxwell, Detroit, May 3, 1st game (1), 3, 2nd game (3), 1959
Willie Kirkland, Cleveland, July 9, 2nd game (3), 13 (1), 1961 (inc. 2 BB and 1 SH)
Mickey Mantle, New York, July 4, 2nd game (2), 6 (2), 1962
Bobby Murcer, New York, June 24, 1st game (1), 24, 2nd game (3), 1970 (inc. 1 BB)
Mike Epstein, Oakland, June 15 (2), 16 (2), 1971
Don Baylor, Baltimore, July 1 (1), 2 (3), 1975 (inc. 1 BB)
Larry Herndon, Detroit, May 16 (1), 18 (3), 1982
Bo Jackson, Kansas City, July 17 (3), Aug 26 (1), 1990
Bobby Higginson, Detroit, June 30 (3), July 1 (1), 1997 (inc. 1 BB)
Manny Ramirez, Cleveland, Sept 15 (3), 16 (1), 1998
Troy Glaus, Anaheim, Sept 15 (3), 16 (1), 2002
NL—4—Bill Nicholson, Chicago, July 22 (1), 23, 1st game (3), 1944 (inc. 1 BB)
Ralph Kiner, Pittsburgh, Aug 15 (1), 16 (3), 1947 (inc. 1 BB)
Ralph Kiner, Pittsburgh, Sept 11 (2), 13 (2), 1949
Stan Musial, St. Louis, July 7, 2nd game (1), 8 (3), 1962 (inc. 1 BB)
Art Shamsky, Cincinnati, Aug 12 (3), 14 (1), 1966
Deron Johnson, Philadelphia, July 10, 2nd game (1), 11 (3), 1971
Johnny Bench, Cincinnati, May 8 (1), 9 (3), 1973 (inc. 1 BB)
Mike Schmidt, Philadelphia, July 6 (1), 7 (3), 1979
Benito Santiago, Philadelphia, Sept 14 (1), 15 (3), 1996 (inc 1 BB)
Barry Bonds, San Francisco, May 19 (2), 20 (2), 2001 (inc. 1 BB)
Shawn Green, Los Angeles, June 14 (2), 15 (2), 2002
Andruw Jones, Atlanta, Sept 7 (2), 10 (2), 2002 (inc. 1 HP)

**Most consecutive home runs, three games**

AL—4—Johnny Blanchard, New York, July 21 (1), 22 (1), 26 (2), 1961
Jeff Manto, Baltimore, June 8 (1), 9 (2), 10 (1), 1995 (inc. 1 BB)
NL—none

**Most consecutive home runs, four games**

AL—4—Ted Williams, Boston, Sept 17, 20, 21, 22, 1957 (inc. 4 BB)
NL—none

**Most home runs in consecutive at-bats as a pinch-hitter**

NL—3—Lee Lacy, Los Angeles, May 2, 6, 17, 1978 (inc. 1 BB)
Del Unser, Philadelphia, June 30, July 5, 10, 1979
AL—2—Ray Caldwell, New York, June 10, 11, 1915
Joe Cronin, Boston, June 17, 1st game, 17, 2nd game, 1943
Charlie Keller, New York, Sept 12, 14, 1948
Del Wilber, Boston, May 6, 10, 1953
Ted Williams, Boston, Sept 17, 20, 1957 (inc. 1 BB)
Johnny Blanchard, New York, July 21, 22, 1961
Chuck Schilling, Boston, Apr 30, May 1, 1965
Ray Barker, New York, June 20, 22, 1st game, 1965
Curt Motton, Baltimore, May 15, 17, 1968
Gates Brown, Detroit, Aug 9, 11, 1st game, 1968
Gary Alexander, Cleveland, July 5, 6, 1980
Daryl Sconiers, California, Apr 30, May 7, 1983
Alex Sanchez, Detroit, July 20, 23, 1985
Randy Bush, Minnesota, June 20, 23, 1986
Jeromy Burnitz, Milwaukee, Aug 2, 3, 1997

**Most consecutive games hitting home run in each game**

NL—8—Dale Long, Pittsburgh, May 19, 20, 20, 22, 23, 25, 26, 28, 1956 (8 HR)
AL—8—Don Mattingly, New York, July 8 (2), 9, 10, 11, 12, 16 (2), 17, 18, 1987 (10 HR)
Ken Griffey Jr., Seattle, July 20, 21, 22, 23, 24, 25, 27, 28, 1993 (8 HR)

**Most consecutive games hitting home runs from both sides of plate**

AL—2—Eddie Murray, Baltimore, May 8, 9, 1987
NL—2—Ken Caminiti, San Diego, Sept 16, 17, 1995

**Most consecutive games hitting home run by pitcher**

NL—4—Ken Brett, Philadelphia, June 9, 13, 18, 23, 1973
AL—2—many pitchers

**Most home runs, two consecutive days**

AL—6—Babe Ruth, New York, May 21 (3), 21 (0), 22 (2), 22, 1930, 4 G
Tony Lazzeri, New York, May 23, 23 (2), 24 (3), 1936, 3 G
NL—6—Ralph Kiner, Pittsburgh, Sept 11, 11 (3), 12 (2), 1947, 3 G

**Most home runs, first two major league games**

AA—3—Charlie Reilly, Columbus, October 9 (2), 10, 1889
NL—3—Joe Cunningham, St. Louis, June 30, July 1 (2), 1954
AL—2—Earl Averill, Cleveland, Apr 16, 17, 1929
Bob Nieman, St. Louis, Sept 14 (2), 15 (0), 1951
Bert Campaneris, Kansas City, July 23 (2), 24 (0), 1964
Curt Blefary, Baltimore, Apr 14 (0), 17 (2), 1965
Joe Lefebvre, New York, May 22, 23, 1980
Dave Stapleton, Boston, May 30 (0), 31 (2), 1980
Tim Laudner, Minnesota, Aug 28, 29, 1981
Alvin Davis, Seattle, Apr 11, 13, 1984
Sam Horn, Boston, July 25, 26, 1987
Mark Quinn, Kansas City, Sept 14 (2), 15 (0), 1999

**Most home runs in two straight games (homering in each game)**

NL—5—Cap Anson, Chicago, Aug 5 (2), 6 (3), 1884
Ralph Kiner, Pittsburgh, Aug 15 (2), 16 (3), 1947
Ralph Kiner, Pittsburgh, Sept 11 (3), 12 (2), 1947
Don Mueller, New York, Sept 1 (3), 2 (2), 1951
Stan Musial, St. Louis, May 2 (3), 2 (2), 1954
Joe Adcock, Milwaukee, July 30, 31 (4), 1954
Billy Williams, Chicago, Sept 8 (2), 10 (3), 1968
Nate Colbert, San Diego, Aug 1 (2), 1 (3), 1972
Mike Schmidt, Philadelphia, Apr 17 (4), 18, 1976
Dave Kingman, Chicago, July 27 (2), 28 (3), 1979
Gary Carter, New York, Sept 3 (3), 4 (2), 1985
Barry Larkin, Cincinnati, June 27 (2), 28 (3), 1991
Geoff Jenkins, Milwaukee, Apr 28 (3), 29 (2), 2001
Barry Bonds, San Francisco, May 19 (3), 20 (2), 2001
Shawn Green, Los Angeles, May 23 (4), 24 (1), 2002
AL—5—Ty Cobb, Detroit, May 5 (3), 6 (2), 1925
Tony Lazzeri, New York, May 23, 2nd game (2), 24 (3), 1936
Carl Yastrzemski, Boston, May 19 (3), 20 (2), 1976
Mark McGwire, Oakland, June 27 (3), 28 (2), 1987
Joe Carter, Cleveland, July 18 (2), 19 (3), 1989
Mark McGwire, Oakland, June 10 (2), 11 (3), 1995
Albert Belle, Cleveland, Sept 18 (2), 19 (3), 1995
Matt Williams, Cleveland, Apr 25 (3), 26 (2), 1997
Manny Ramirez, Cleveland, Sept 15 (3), 16 (2), 1998
Edgar Martinez, Seattle, May 17 (2), 18 (3), 1999
Nomar Garciaparra, Boston, July 21 (2), 23, a.m. game (3), 2002
Alex Rodriguez, Texas, Aug 17 (3), 18 (2), 2002
Travis Hafner, Cleveland, July 19 (2 in 10 inn), 20 (3), 2004

**Most home runs in three straight games (homering in each game)**

NL—7—Shawn Green, Los Angeles, May 23 (4), 24 (1), 25 (2), 2002
AL—6—Tony Lazzeri, New York, May 23, 23 (2), 24 (3), 1936
Gus Zernial, Philadelphia, May 13, 2nd game (2), 15 (2), 16 (2), 1951
Manny Ramirez, Cleveland, Sept 15 (3), 16 (2), 17, 1998
Alex Rodriguez, Texas, Aug 16 (1), 17 (3), 18 (2), 2002
Jeff DaVanon, Anaheim, June 1 (2), 3 (2), 4 (2), 2003

**Most home runs in four straight games (homering in each game)**

NL—8—Ralph Kiner, Pittsburgh, Sept 10 (2), 11, 11 (3), 12 (2), 1947
AL—7—Tony Lazzeri, New York, May 21, 23, 23 (2), 24 (3), 1936
Gus Zernial, Philadelphia, May 13, 2nd game (2), 15 (2), 16 (2), 17, 1951
Frank Howard, Washington, May 12 (2), 14 (2), 15, 16 (2), 1968

**Players hitting home runs in first four games of season**

NL—4—Willie Mays, San Francisco, Apr 6, 7, 8, 10, 1971
Mark McGwire, St. Louis, Mar 31, Apr 2, 3, 4, 1998
AL—none

**Most consecutive games with two or more home runs, start of season**

NL—2—Eddie Mathews, Milwaukee, Apr 15 (2), 17 (2), 1958
Barry Bonds, San Francisco, Apr 2 (2), 3 (2), 2002
AL—1—many players

**Most home runs in five straight games (homering in each game)**

AL—8—Frank Howard, Washington, May 12 (2), 14 (2), 15, 16 (2), 17, 1968
Frank Howard, Washington, May 14 (2), 15, 16 (2), 17, 18 (2), 1968
NL—8—Barry Bonds, San Francisco, May 17, 18, 19 (3), 20 (2), 21, 2001

Barry Bonds, San Francisco, May 18, 19 (3), 20 (2), 21, 22, 2001

**Most home runs in six straight games (homering in each game)**
AL—10—Frank Howard, Washington, May 12 (2), 14 (2), 15, 16 (2), 17, 18 (2), 1968
NL—9—Barry Bonds, San Francisco, May 17, 18, 19 (3), 20 (2), 21, 22, 2001

**Most home runs in seven straight games (homering in each game)**
AL—9—Don Mattingly, New York, July 8 (2), 9, 10, 11, 12, 16 (2), 17, 1987
NL—7—Dale Long, Pittsburgh, May 19, 20, 20, 22, 23, 25, 26, 1956

**Most homers in eight straight games (homering in each game)**
AL—10—Don Mattingly, New York, July 8 (2), 9, 10, 11, 12, 16 (2), 17, 18, 1987
NL—8—Dale Long, Pittsburgh, May 19, 20, 20, 22, 23, 25, 26, 28, 1956

## GRAND SLAMS

**Most grand slams, career**
AL—23—Lou Gehrig, New York, 17 seasons, 1923-1939
NL—18—Willie McCovey, San Francisco, San Diego, 22 seasons, 1959-1980

**For a complete list of players with 10 or more career grand slams, see page 105.**

**Most grand slams by pinch-hitter, career**
AL—3—Rich Reese, Minnesota, Aug 3, 1969; June 7, 1970; July 9, 1972
NL—3—Ron Northey, St. Louis, Sept 3, 1947; May 30, 1948, 2nd game; Chicago, Sept 18, 1950
Willie McCovey, San Francisco, June 12, 1960; Sept 10, 1965; San Diego, May 30, 1975

**Most grand slams, season**
AL—6—Don Mattingly, New York, 141 G, 1987
NL—5—Ernie Banks, Chicago, 154 G, 1955

**Most consecutive seasons hitting one or more grand slams**
NL—9—Willie McCovey, San Francisco, 1964-1972 (13 grand slams)
AL—8—Manny Ramirez, Cleveland, Boston, 1995-2002 (15 grand slams)

**Most grand slams by pinch-hitter, season**
NL—2—Dave Johnson, Philadelphia, Apr 30, June 3, 1978
Mike Ivie, San Francisco, May 28, June 30, 1st game, 1978
AL—2—Darryl Strawberry, New York, May 2, Aug 4, 1998
Ben Broussard, Cleveland, June 23, Aug 12, 2004

**Most grand slams, one month**
AL—3—Rudy York, Detroit, May 16, 22, 30, 1st game, 1938
Jim Northrup, Detroit, June 24 (2), 29, 1968
Larry Parrish, Texas, July 4, 7, 10, 1st game, 1982
Mike Blowers, Seattle, Aug 3, 14, 18, 1995
Shane Spencer, New York, Sept 18, 24, 27, 1998
NL—3—Eric Davis, Cincinnati, May 1, 3, 30, 1987
Mike Piazza, Los Angeles, Apr 9, 10, 24, 1998
Devon White, Milwaukee, May 10, 15, 20, 2001

**Most grand slams in one week (Sunday through Saturday)**
AL—3—Jim Northrup, Detroit, June 24 (2), 29, 1968 (Lou Gehrig, New York, hit grand slams on Saturday, Aug 29, Monday, Aug 31, Tuesday, Sept 1, 2nd game, 1931.)
Larry Parrish, Texas, July 4, 7, 10, 1st game, 1982.
NL—2—many players; last—Fernando Tatis, St. Louis, Apr 23 (2), 1999; Robin Ventura, New York, May 20, 1st and 2nd games, 1999

**Most grand slams, game**
AL—2—Tony Lazzeri, New York, May 24, 1936, 2nd and 5th
Jim Tabor, Boston, July 4, 1939, 2nd game, 3rd and 6th
Rudy York, Boston, July 27, 1946, 2nd and 5th
Jim Gentile, Baltimore, May 9, 1961, 1st and 2nd
Jim Northrup, Detroit, June 24, 1968, 5th and 6th
Frank Robinson, Baltimore, June 26, 1970, 5th and 6th
Robin Ventura, Chicago, Sept 4, 1995, 4th and 5th
Chris Hoiles, Baltimore, Aug 14, 1998, 3rd and 8th
Nomar Garciaparra, Boston, May 10, 1999, 1st and 8th
Bill Mueller, Boston, July 29, 2003, 7th and 8th (first time from both sides of the plate)
NL—2—Tony Cloninger, Atlanta, July 3, 1966, 1st and 4th
Fernando Tatis, St. Louis, Apr 23, 1999, both in 3rd

**Most grand slams in first major league game**
NL—1—Bill Duggleby, Philadelphia, Apr 21, 1898, 2nd (1st AB)
Bobby Bonds, San Francisco, June 25, 1968, 6th (3rd AB)
AL—none

**Most grand slams, two consecutive games (homering in each game)**
NL—2—Jimmy Bannon, Boston, Aug 6, 7, 1894
Jim Sheckard, Brooklyn, Sept 23, 24, 1901
Phil Garner, Pittsburgh, Sept 14, 15, 1978
Fred McGriff, San Diego, Aug 13, 14, 1991
Eric Davis, Cincinnati, May 4, 5, 1996
Mike Piazza, Los Angeles, Apr 9, 10, 1998
Sammy Sosa, Chicago, July 27, 28, 1998
Robin Ventura, New York, May 20, 1st and 2nd games, 1999
AL—2—Babe Ruth, New York, Sept 27, 29, 1927; also Aug 6, 2nd game, Aug 7, 1st game, 1929
Bill Dickey, New York, Aug 3, 2nd game, 4, 1937
Jimmie Foxx, Boston, May 20, 21, 1940
Jim Busby, Cleveland, July 5, 6, 1956
Brooks Robinson, Baltimore, May 6, 9, 1962
Willie Aikens, California, June 13, 2nd game, 14, 1979
Greg Luzinski, Chicago, June 8, 9, 1984
Rob Deer, Milwaukee, Aug 19, 20, 1987
Mike Blowers, Seattle, May 16, 17, 1993
Dan Gladden, Detroit, Aug 10, 11, 1993
Ken Griffey Jr., Seattle, Apr 29, 30, 1999
Albert Belle, Baltimore, June 14, 15, 2000
David Eckstein, Anaheim, Apr 27, 28, 2002; 2nd game 14 inn

**Hitting grand slam in both games of doubleheader**
NL—Robin Ventura, New York, May 20, 1999
AL—none

**Most grand slams, inning**
NL—2—Fernando Tatis, St. Louis, Apr 23, 1999, 3rd
AL—1—many players

## TOTAL BASES

### CAREER AND SEASON

**Most total bases, career**
ML—6,856—Hank Aaron, Milwaukee NL, Atlanta NL, Milwaukee AL, 23 seasons, 1954-1976 (6,591 in NL, 265 in AL)
NL—6,591—Hank Aaron, Milwaukee, Atlanta, 21 seasons, 1954-1974
AL—5,854—Ty Cobb, Detroit, Philadelphia, 24 seasons, 1905-1928

**For a complete list of players with 4,000 or more career total bases, see page 106.**

**Most total bases, season**
AL—457—Babe Ruth, New York, 152 G, 1921
NL—450—Rogers Hornsby, St. Louis, 154 G, 1922

**For a complete list of players with 400 or more total bases in a season, see page 116.**

**Fewest total bases for leader, season**
NL—237—Honus Wagner, Pittsburgh, 140 G, 1906
AL—260—George Stone, St. Louis, 154 G, 1905

**Most total bases by rookie, season**
AL—374—Hal Trosky, Cleveland, 154 G, 1934
Tony Oliva, Minnesota, 161 G, 1964
NL—360—Albert Pujols, St. Louis, 161 G, 2001

**Most total bases by righthander, season**
NL—450—Rogers Hornsby, St. Louis, 154 G, 1922
AL—438—Jimmie Foxx, Philadelphia, 154 G, 1932

**Most total bases by lefthander, season**
AL—457—Babe Ruth, New York, 152 G, 1921
NL—445—Chuck Klein, Philadelphia, 156 G, 1930

**Most total bases by switch-hitter, season**
AL—376—Mickey Mantle, New York, 150 G, 1956
NL—369—Rip Collins, St. Louis, 154 G, 1934

**Most seasons leading league in total bases**
NL—8—Hank Aaron, Milwaukee, 1956, 1957, 1959-1961, 1963; Atlanta, 1967, 1969
AL—6—Ty Cobb, Detroit, 1907-1909, 1911, 1915, 1917
Babe Ruth, Boston, 1919; New York, 1921, 1923, 1924, 1926, 1928
Ted Williams, Boston, 1939, 1942, 1946, 1947, 1949, 1951

**Most consecutive seasons leading league in total bases**
NL—4—Honus Wagner, Pittsburgh, 1906-1909
Chuck Klein, Philadelphia, 1930-1933
AL—3—Ty Cobb, Detroit, 1907-1909
Jim Rice, Boston, 1977-1979 (Ted Williams, Boston, led AL in 1942, 1946 and 1947 with military service from 1943 through 1945.)

**Most seasons with 400 or more total bases**
AL—5—Lou Gehrig, New York, 1927, 1930, 1931, 1934, 1936
NL—3—Chuck Klein, Philadelphia, 1929, 1930, 1932

**For a complete list of players with 400 or more total bases in a season, see page 116.**

**Most consecutive seasons with 400 or more total bases**
AL—2—Lou Gehrig, New York, 1930, 1931
Jimmie Foxx, Philadelphia, 1932, 1933
NL—2—Chuck Klein, Philadelphia, 1929, 1930
Todd Helton, Colorado, 2000, 2001

**Most seasons with 300 or more total bases**
NL—15—Hank Aaron, Milwaukee, Atlanta, 1955-1971, except 1964, 1970
AL—13—Lou Gehrig, New York, 1926-1938

**Most consecutive seasons with 300 or more total bases**
AL—13—Lou Gehrig, New York, 1926-1938
NL—13—Willie Mays, New York, San Francisco, 1954-1966

**Fewest total bases, season (150 or more games)**
NL—89—Dal Maxvill, St. Louis, 152 G, 1970
AL—114—Eddie Brinkman, Washington, 154 G, 1965

## GAME AND INNING

**Most total bases, game**

NL—19—Shawn Green, Los Angeles, May 23, 2002 (1 single, 1 double, 4 HR)
AL—16—Ty Cobb, Detroit, May 5, 1925 (2 singles, 1 double, 3 HR)
Lou Gehrig, New York, June 3, 1932 (4 HR)
Rocky Colavito, Cleveland, June 10, 1959 (4 HR)
Fred Lynn, Boston, June 18, 1975 (1 single, 1 triple, 3 HR)
Mike Cameron, Seattle, May 2, 2002 (4 HR)
Carlos Delgado, Toronto, Sept 25, 2003 (4 HR)
[16—Jimmie Foxx, Philadelphia, July 10, 1932, 18 inn (2 singles, 1 double, 3 HR)
Pat Seerey, Chicago, July 18, 1948, 1st game, 11 inn (4 HR)]

**Most total bases by pitcher, game**

AA—15—Guy Hecker, Louisville, Aug 15, 1886, 2nd game (3 singles, 3 HR)
NL—12—Jim Tobin, Boston, May 13, 1942 (3 HR)
AL—10—Snake Wiltse, Philadelphia, Aug 10, 1901, 2nd game (2 doubles, 2 triples)
Red Ruffing, New York, June 17, 1936, 1st game (2 singles, 2 HR)
Jack Harshman, Baltimore, Sept 23, 1958 (1 double, 2 HR)
[10—Babe Ruth, Boston, May 9, 1918, 10 inn (1 single, 3 doubles, 1 triple)]

**Most total bases, doubleheader**

NL—22—Nate Colbert, San Diego, Aug 1, 1972
AL—21—Jimmie Foxx, Philadelphia, July 2, 1933, 19 inn
Al Oliver, Texas, Aug 17, 1980

**Most total bases, inning**

NL-AL—8—many players

# EXTRA-BASE HITS

## CAREER AND SEASON

**Most extra-base hits, career**

ML—1,477—Hank Aaron, Milwaukee NL, Atlanta NL, Milwaukee AL, 23 seasons, 1954-1976 (1,429 in NL, 48 in AL; 624 doubles, 98 triples, 755 HR)
NL—1,429—Hank Aaron, Milwaukee, Atlanta, 21 seasons, 1954-1974 (600 doubles, 96 triples, 733 HR)
AL—1,350—Babe Ruth, Boston, New York, 21 seasons, 1914-1934 (506 doubles, 136 triples, 708 HR)

**For a complete list of players with 800 or more career extra-base hits, see page 106.**

**Most extra-base hits, season**

AL—119—Babe Ruth, New York, 152 G, 1921 (44 doubles, 16 triples, 59 HR)
NL—107—Chuck Klein, Philadelphia, 156 G, 1930 (59 doubles, 8 triples, 40 HR)
Barry Bonds, San Francisco, 153 G, 2001 (32 doubles, 2 triples, 73 HR)

**For a complete list of players with 100 or more extra-base hits in a season, see page 117.**

**Fewest extra-base hits for leader, season**

NL—50—Sherry Magee, Philadelphia, 154 G, 1906 (36 doubles, 8 triples, 6 HR)
AL—54—Sam Crawford, Detroit, 156 G, 1915 (31 doubles, 19 triples, 4 HR)

**Most extra-base hits by rookie, season**

AL—89—Hal Trosky, Cleveland, 154 G, 1934 (45 doubles, 9 triples, 35 HR)
NL—88—Albert Pujols, St. Louis, 161 G, 2001 (47 doubles, 4 triples, 37 HR)

**Most extra-base hits by righthander, season**

AL—103—Hank Greenberg, Detroit, 154 G, 1937 (49 doubles, 14 triples, 40 HR)
Albert Belle, Cleveland, 143 G, 1995 (52 doubles, 1 triple, 50 HR)
NL—103—Sammy Sosa, Chicago, 160 G, 2001 (34 doubles, 5 triples, 64 HR)

**Most extra-base hits by lefthander, season**

AL—119—Babe Ruth, New York, 152 G 1921 (44 doubles, 16 triples, 59 HR)
NL—107—Chuck Klein, Philadelphia, 156 G, 1930 (59 doubles, 8 triples, 40 HR)
Barry Bonds, San Francisco, 153 G, 2001 (32 doubles, 2 triples, 73 HR)

**Most extra-base hits by switch-hitter, season**

NL—94—Lance Berkman, Houston, 156 G, 2001 (55 doubles, 5 triples, 34 HR)
AL—80—Carlos Beltran, Kansas City, 162 G, 2002 (44 doubles, 7 triples, 29 HR)

**Most seasons leading league in extra-base hits**

NL—7—Honus Wagner, Pittsburgh, 1900, 1902-1904, 1907-1909
Stan Musial, St. Louis, 1943, 1944, 1946, 1948, 1949, 1950, 1953
AL—7—Babe Ruth, Boston, New York, 1918-1921, 1923, 1924, 1928

**Most consecutive seasons leading league in extra-base hits**

AL—4—Babe Ruth, Boston, New York, 1918-1921
NL—3—many players; last—Duke Snider, Brooklyn, 1954, 1955 (tied), 1956

**Twenty or more doubles, triples and homers in one season**

NL—Buck Freeman, Washington, 155 G, 1899 (20 doubles, 26 triples, 25 HR)
Frank Schulte, Chicago, 154 G, 1911 (30 doubles, 21 triples, 21 HR)
Jim Bottomley, St. Louis, 149 G, 1928 (42 doubles, 20 triples, 31 HR)
Willie Mays, New York, 152 G, 1957 (26 doubles, 20 triples, 35 HR)
AL—Jeff Heath, Cleveland, 151 G, 1941 (32 doubles, 20 triples, 24 HR)
George Brett, Kansas City, 154 G, 1979 (42 doubles, 20 triples, 23 HR)

**Fewest extra-base hits, season (150 or more games)**

NL—7—Dal Maxvill, St. Louis, 152 G, 1970 (5 doubles, 2 triples)
AL—10—Luis Gomez, Toronto, 153 G, 1978 (7 doubles, 3 triples)
Felix Fermin, Cleveland, 156 G, 1989 (9 doubles, 1 triple)

## GAME AND INNING

**Most extra-base hits, game**

AA—5—George Strief, Philadelphia, June 25, 1885 (1 double, 4 triples; consec)
NL—5—George Gore, Chicago, July 9, 1885 (3 doubles, 2 triples, consec)
Larry Twitchell, Cleveland, Aug 15, 1889 (1 double, 3 triples, 1 HR)
Joe Adcock, Milwaukee, July 31, 1954 (1 double, 4 HR; consec)
Willie Stargell, Pittsburgh, Aug 1, 1970 (3 doubles, 2 HR)
Steve Garvey, Los Angeles, Aug 28, 1977 (3 doubles, 2 HR; consec)
Shawn Green, Los Angeles, May 23, 2002 (1 double, 4 HR)
AL—5—Lou Boudreau, Cleveland, July 14, 1946, 1st game (4 doubles, 1 HR)

**Most extra-base hits by pitcher, game**

AA—4—Bob Caruthers, St. Louis, Aug 16, 1886 (1 double, 1 triple, 2 HR)
AL—4—Snake Wiltse, Philadelphia, Aug 10, 1901, 2nd game (2 doubles, 2 triples)
[4—Babe Ruth, Boston, May 9, 1918 (3 doubles, 1 triple), 10 inn]
NL—3—many players; last—Andy Messersmith, Los Angeles, Apr 25, 1975 (3 doubles)

**Most extra-base hits, opening game of season**

NL—4—George Myers, Indianapolis, Apr 20, 1888 (3 doubles, 1 HR)
Billy Herman, Chicago, Apr 14, 1936 (3 doubles, 1 HR)
Jim Greengrass, Cincinnati, Apr 13, 1954 (4 doubles)
AL—4—Frank Dillon, Detroit, Apr 25, 1901 (4 doubles)
Don Baylor, Baltimore, Apr 6, 1973 (2 doubles, 1 triple, 1 HR)

**Most consecutive games with one or more extra-base hits, season**

NL—14—Paul Waner, Pittsburgh, June 3-19, 1927 (12 doubles, 4 triples, 4 HR)
AL—11—Jesse Barfield, Toronto, Aug 17-27, 1985 (8 doubles, 3 triples, 1 HR)

**Most consecutive extra-base hits, season**

AL—7—Elmer Smith, Cleveland, Sept 4, 5, 5, 1921 (3 doubles, 4 HR; 2 BB in streak)
Earl Sheely, Chicago, May 20, 21, 1926 (6 doubles, 1 HR; 1 SH in streak)
NL—6—Larry Walker, Colorado, May 21, 22, 1996 (2 doubles, 3 triples, 1 HR)

**Most games with four or more extra-base hits, career**

AL—5—Lou Gehrig, New York, 1926, 1928, 1930, 1932, 1934
Joe DiMaggio, New York, 1936, 1937, 1941, 1948, 1950
NL—4—Willie Stargell, Pittsburgh, 1965, 1968, 1970, 1973

**Most games with four or more extra-base hits, season**

AA—2—Henry Larkin, Philadelphia, June 16, July 29, 1885
AL—2—George H. Burns, Cleveland, June 19, 1st game, July 23, 1924
Jimmie Foxx, Philadelphia, Apr 24, July 2, 2nd game, 1933
Albert Belle, Baltimore, Aug 29, Sept 23, 2nd game, 1999
NL—2—Joe Medwick, St. Louis, May 12, Aug 4, 1937
Billy Williams, Chicago, Apr 9, Sept 5, 1969

**Most extra-base hits, doubleheader**

NL—6—Joe Medwick, St. Louis, May 30, 1935 (5 doubles, 1 triple)
Red Schoendienst, St. Louis, June 6, 1948 (5 doubles, 1 HR)
[6—Chick Hafey, St. Louis, July 28, 1928 (4 doubles, 2 HR), 21 inn
Mel Ott, New York, June 19, 1929 (4 doubles, 2 HR), 20 inn
Dusty Rhodes, New York, Aug 29, 1954 (2 doubles, 2 triples, 2 HR), 20 inn]
AL—6—John Stone, Detroit, Apr 30, 1933 (4 doubles, 2 HR)
Hank Majeski, Philadelphia, Aug 27, 1948 (6 doubles)
Hal McRae, Kansas City, Aug 27, 1974 (5 doubles, 1 HR)
Al Oliver, Texas, Aug 17, 1980 (1 double, 1 triple, 1 HR)
[6—Jimmie Foxx, Philadelphia, July 2, 1933 (1 double, 1 triple, 4 HR), 19 inn]

**Most extra-base hits, inning**

NL—3—Tommy Burns, Chicago, Sept 6, 1883, 7th (2 doubles, 1 HR)
AL-NL since 1893—2—many players

**Most extra-base hits by pitcher, inning**

NL—2—Fred Goldsmith, Chicago, Sept 6, 1883, 7th (2 doubles)
Adonis Terry, Chicago, May 19, 1895, 3rd (1 double, 1 HR)
Hank Borowy, Chicago, May 5, 1946, 1st game, 7th (2 doubles)
AL—2—Smokey Joe Wood, Boston, July 4, 1913, a.m. game, 4th (2 doubles)
Bob Shawkey, New York, July 12, 1923, 3rd (1 double, 1 triple)
Ted Lyons, Chicago, July 28, 1935, 1st game, 2nd (2 doubles)

# RUNS BATTED IN

## CAREER AND SEASON

**Most runs batted in, career**

ML—2,297—Hank Aaron, Milwaukee NL, Atlanta NL, Milwaukee AL, 23 seasons, 1954-1976 (2,202 in NL, 95 in AL)
NL—2,202—Hank Aaron, Milwaukee, Atlanta, 21 seasons, 1954-1974
AL—2,192—Babe Ruth, Boston, New York, 21 seasons, 1914-1934

**For a complete list of players with 1,200 or more career runs batted in, see page 106.**

**Most runs batted in, season**

NL—191—Hack Wilson, Chicago, 155 G, 1930
AL—184—Lou Gehrig, New York, 155 G, 1931

**Fewest runs batted in by leader, season**

NL—94—George Kelly, New York, 155 G, 1920
Rogers Hornsby, St. Louis, 149 G, 1920
AL—105—Al Rosen, Cleveland, 148 G, 1952

**Most runs batted in by rookie, season**

AL—145—Ted Williams, Boston, 149 G, 1939
NL—130—Albert Pujols, St. Louis, 161 G, 2001

**Most runs batted in by righthander, season**
NL—191—Hack Wilson, Chicago, 155 G, 1930
AL—183—Hank Greenberg, Detroit, 154 G, 1937

**Most runs batted in by lefthander, season**
AL—184—Lou Gehrig, New York, 155 G, 1931
NL—170—Chuck Klein, Philadelphia, 156 G, 1930

**Most runs batted in by switch-hitter, season**
AL—144—Mark Teixeira, Texas, 162 G, 2005
NL—130—Ken Caminiti, San Diego, 146 G, 1996

**Most seasons leading league in runs batted in**
NL—8—Cap Anson, Chicago, 1880-1882, 1884-1886, 1888, 1891
AL—6—Babe Ruth, Boston, New York, 1919-1921, 1923, 1926, 1928 (tied)
NL since 1893—5—Honus Wagner, Pittsburgh, 1901, 1902, 1908, 1909, 1912

**For a complete list of triple crown winners, see page 111.**

**Most consecutive seasons leading league in runs batted in**
AL—3—Ty Cobb, Detroit, 1907-1909
Babe Ruth, Boston, New York, 1919-1921
Cecil Fielder, Detroit, 1990-1992
NL—3—Cap Anson, Chicago, 1880-1882 and 1884-1886
NL since 1893—3—Rogers Hornsby, St. Louis, 1920 (tied), 1921, 1922
Joe Medwick, St. Louis, 1936-1938
George Foster, Cincinnati, 1976-1978

**Most seasons with 150 or more runs batted in**
AL—7—Lou Gehrig, New York, 1927, 1930-1932, 1934, 1936, 1937
NL—2—Hack Wilson, Chicago, 1929, 1930
Sammy Sosa, Chicago, 1998, 2001

**Most consecutive seasons with 150 or more runs batted in**
AL—3—Babe Ruth, New York, 1929-1931
Lou Gehrig, New York, 1930-1932
NL—2—Hack Wilson, Chicago, 1929, 1930

**Most seasons with 100 or more runs batted in**
AL—13—Babe Ruth, Boston, New York, 1919-1933, except 1922 and 1925
Lou Gehrig, New York, 1926-1938
Jimmie Foxx, Philadelphia, Boston, 1929-1941
NL—12—Barry Bonds, Pittsburgh, San Francisco, 1990-1993, 1995-1998, 2000-2002, 2004

**Most consecutive seasons with 100 or more runs batted in**
AL—13—Lou Gehrig, New York, 1926-1938
Jimmie Foxx, Philadelphia, Boston, 1929-1941
NL—9—Sammy Sosa, Chicago, 1995-2003

**Fewest runs batted in, season (150 or more games)**
NL—20—Richie Ashburn, Philadelphia, 153 games, 1959
AL—19—Morrie Rath, Chicago, 157 games, 1912

## GAME AND INNING

**Most runs batted in, game**
NL—12—Jim Bottomley, St. Louis, Sept 16, 1924
Mark Whiten, St. Louis, Sept 7, 1993, 2nd game
AL—11—Tony Lazzeri, New York, May 24, 1936

**Most runs batted in by pitcher, game**
NL—9—Tony Cloninger, Atlanta, July 3, 1966
AL—7—Vic Raschi, New York, Aug 4, 1953

**Most consecutive games with one or more runs batted in, season**
NL—17—Oscar Grimes, Chicago, June 27-July 23, 1922 (27 RBI)
AL—13—Taffy Wright, Chicago, May 4-20, 1941 (22 RBI)
Mike Sweeney, Kansas City, June 23-July 4, 1999 (19 RBI)

**Most runs batted in accounting for all club's runs, game**
NL—8—George Kelly, New York vs Cincinnati, June 14, 1924 (won, 8-6)
AL—8—Bob Johnson, Philadelphia vs St. Louis, June 12, 1938 (won, 8-3)
[9—Mike Greenwell, Boston vs Seattle, Sept 2, 1996, 10 inn; (won, 9-8)]

**Most runs batted in, doubleheader**
NL—13—Nate Colbert, San Diego, Aug 1, 1972
Mark Whiten, St. Louis, Sept 7, 1993
AL—11—Earl Averill, Cleveland, Sept 17, 1930, 17 inn
Jim Tabor, Boston, July 4, 1939, 18 inn
Boog Powell, Baltimore, July 6, 1966, 20 inn

**Most runs batted in, inning**
NL—8—Fernando Tatis, St. Louis, Apr 23, 1999, 3rd
AL—6—Bob Johnson, Philadelphia, Aug 29, 1937, 1st game, 1st
Tom McBride, Boston, Aug 4, 1945, 2nd game, 4th
Joe Astroth, Philadelphia, Sept 23, 1950, 6th
Gil McDougald, New York, May 3, 1951, 9th
Sam Mele, Chicago, June 10, 1952, 4th
Jim Lemon, Washington, Sept 5, 1959, 3rd
Carlos Quintana, Boston, July 30, 1991, 3rd
Matt Stairs, Oakland, July 5, 1996, 1st
Matt Williams, Cleveland, Aug 27, 1997, 4th

## GAME-WINNING RBIs (1980-1988)

**Most game-winning RBIs, career**
NL—129—Keith Hernandez, St. Louis, New York, 1980-1988
AL—117—Eddie Murray, Baltimore, 1980-1988

**Most game-winning RBIs, season**
NL—24—Keith Hernandez, New York, 158 G, 1985
AL—23—Mike Greenwell, Boston, 158 G, 1988

**Most game-winning RBIs by pitcher, season**
NL—3—Rick Mahler, Atlanta, 39 G, 1985
Rick Rhoden, Pittsburgh, 35 G, 1985 (Tim Leary, Los Angeles, 1988, had 3, but 1 as a pinch-hitter.)
AL—none

**Most game-winning RBIs by rookie, season**
AL—14—Jose Canseco, Oakland, 157 G, 1986
Wally Joyner, California, 154 G, 1986
Mark McGwire, Oakland, 151 G, 1987
NL—13—Juan Samuel, Philadelphia, 160 G, 1984
Darryl Strawberry, New York, 122 g, 1983

**Fewest game-winning RBIs in a season (150 or more games)**
NL—0—Alan Wiggins, San Diego, 158 G, 1984
Rafael Palmeiro, Chicago, 152 G, 1988
AL—1—Jackie Gutierrez, Boston, 151 G, 1984
Tony Phillips, Oakland, 154 G, 1984
Steve Lombardozzi, Minnesota, 156 G, 1986
Dick Schofield, California, 155 G, 1988

**Most game-winning RBIs, doubleheader**
NL-AL—2—many players

**Most consecutive games with game-winning RBI, season**
AL—5—Kirk Gibson, Detroit, July 13-20, 1986
NL—4—Johnny Ray, Pittsburgh, Sept 18-21, 1984
Milt Thompson, Philadelphia, Aug 19-21, 2nd game, 1987
Ozzie Smith, St. Louis, Sept 8-11, 1988

**Most consecutive victories with game-winning RBI, season**
NL—6—Johnny Ray, Pittsburgh, Sept 13-21, 1984 (2 losses in streak)
AL—5—Kirk Gibson, Detroit, July 13-20, 1986 (no losses in streak)

## BASES ON BALLS

**Most bases on balls, career**
NL—2,311—Barry Bonds, Pittsburgh, San Francisco, 20 seasons, 1986-2005
AL—2,042—Babe Ruth, Boston, New York, 21 seasons, 1914-1934

**For a complete list of players with 1,000 or more career bases on balls, see page 107.**

**Most bases on balls, season**
NL—232—Barry Bonds, San Francisco, 147 G, 2004
AL—170—Babe Ruth, New York, 152 G, 1923

**Fewest bases on balls by leader, season**
NL—69—Hack Wilson, Chicago, 142 G, 1926
AL—89—Whitey Witt, New York, 140 G, 1922

**Most bases on balls by rookie, season**
AL—107—Ted Williams, Boston, 149 G, 1939
NL—100—Jim Gilliam, Brooklyn, 151 G, 1953

**Most bases on balls by righthander, season**
NL—162—Mark McGwire, St. Louis, 155 G, 1998
AL—151—Eddie Yost, Washington, 152 G, 1956

**Most bases on balls lefthander, season**
NL—232—Barry Bonds, San Francisco, 147 G, 2004
AL—170—Babe Ruth, New York, 152 G, 1923

**Most bases on balls by switch-hitter, season**
AL—146—Mickey Mantle, New York, 144 G, 1957
NL—126—Chipper Jones, Atlanta, 157 G, 1999

**Most bases on balls by pinch-hitter, season**
NL—20—Matt Franco, New York, 88 G, 1999
AL—18—Elmer Valo, New York, Washington, 81 G, 1960

**Most seasons leading league in bases on balls**
AL—11—Babe Ruth, New York, 1920-1924, 1926-1928, 1930-1933
NL—10—Barry Bonds, Pittsburgh, San Francisco, 1992, 1994-1997, 2000-2004

**Most consecutive seasons leading league in bases on balls**
NL—5—Barry Bonds, San Francisco, 2000-2004
AL—4—Babe Ruth, New York, 1930-1933
Ted Williams, Boston, 1946-1949 (Military service, 1943-1945, interrupted a 6-year streak, 1941-1949.)

**Most seasons with 100 or more bases on balls**
AL—13—Babe Ruth, Boston, New York, 1919-1934, except 1922, 1925 and 1929
NL—12—Barry Bonds, Pittsburgh, San Francisco, 1991-2004, except 1994 and 1999

**Most consecutive seasons with 100 or more bases on balls**
AL—8—Frank E. Thomas, Chicago, 1991-1998
NL—7—Mel Ott, New York, 1936-1942
Jeff Bagwell, Houston, 1996-2002

**Fewest bases on balls, season (150 or more games)**
AL—10—Ozzie Guillen, Chicago, 150 games, 1996
NL—12—Hal Lanier, San Francisco, 151 games, 1968

**Most consecutive bases on balls**
AL—7—Billy Rogell, Detroit, Aug 17, 2nd game, Aug 18, Aug 19, 1st game, 1938
Jose Canseco, Oakland, Aug 4, 5, 1992

NL—7—Mel Ott, New York, June 16-18, 1943
Eddie Stanky, New York, Aug 29, 30, 1950
Barry Bonds, San Francisco, Sept 24-26, 2004

**Most consecutive games with one or more bases on balls**
AL—22—Roy Cullenbine, Detroit, July 2-22, 1947 (34 BB)
NL—20—Barry Bonds, San Francisco, Sept 9, 2002- Apr 1, 2003 (37 BB)
AA—16—Yank Robinson, St. Louis, Sept 15-Oct 2, 1888 (23 BB)

**Most bases on balls, game**
NL—6—Walt Wilmot, Chicago, Aug 22, 1891 (consec)
AL—6—Jimmie Foxx, Boston, June 16, 1938 (consec)
[6—Andre Thornton, Cleveland, May 2, 1984, 16 inn]
NL since 1893—5—many players; last—Barry Bonds, Sept 25, 2004
[6—Jeff Bagwell, Houston, Aug 20, 1999, 16 inn]

**Most bases on balls, first major league game**
AL—4—Otto Saltzgaver, New York, Apr 12, 1932
Milt Galatzer, Cleveland, June 25, 1933, 1st game
NL—3—many players

**Most times receiving five bases on balls in one game, career**
NL—4—Mel Ott, New York, 1929, 1933, 1943, 1944
AL—2—Max Bishop, Philadelphia, 1929, 1930
Rickey Henderson, Oakland, 1982; Seattle, 2000
AA—2—Dan Brouthers, Boston, 1891

**Most bases on balls, doubleheader**
AL—8—Max Bishop, Philadelphia, May 21, 1930; Boston, July 8, 1934
NL—6—Mel Ott, New York, October 5, 1929
Johnny Mize, St. Louis, Aug 26, 1939
Mel Ott, New York, Apr 30, 1944
Cleon Jones, New York, June 25, 1971
Jim Wynn, Atlanta, July 31, 1976
Bobby Bonds, St. Louis, June 8, 1980
Mark Grace, Chicago, Aug 10, 1995
[6—Rusty Staub, Houston, Aug 9, 1963, 26 inn
Clay Dalrymple, Philadelphia, July 4, 1967, 19 inn
Jack Clark, St. Louis, July 8, 1987, 19 inn]

**Most bases on balls, inning**
NL-AL—2—many players

**Most times receiving two bases on balls in one inning, career**
AL—4—George Selkirk, New York, 1936 (2), 1938, 1940.
NL—2—Eddie Stanky, New York, 1950 (2).

**Most times receiving two bases on balls in one inning, season**
AL—2—George Selkirk, New York, June 24, Aug 28, 2nd game, 1936
Skeeter Webb, Chicago, July 30, Sept 3, 1940
NL—2—Eddie Stanky, New York, June 27, Aug 22, 1950

## INTENTIONAL (SINCE 1955)

**Most intentional bases on balls, career**
NL—606—Barry Bonds, Pittsburgh, San Francisco, 20 seasons, 1986-2005
AL—229—George Brett, Kansas City, 21 seasons, 1973-1993

**Most intentional bases on balls, season**
NL—120—Barry Bonds, San Francisco, 147 G, 2004
AL—33—Ted Williams, Boston, 132 G, 1957
John Olerud, Toronto, 158 G, 1993

**Most intentional bases on balls by rookie, season**
AL—16—Alvin Davis, Seattle, 152 G, 1984
NL—14—Willie Montanez, Philadelphia, 158 G, 1971

**Most intentional bases on balls by righthander, season**
NL—37—Sammy Sosa, Chicago, 160 G, 2001
AL—29—Frank Howard, Washington, 161 G, 1970
Frank E. Thomas, Chicago, 145 G, 1995

**Most intentional bases on balls by lefthander, season**
NL—120—Barry Bonds, San Francisco, 147 G, 2004
AL—33—Ted Williams, Boston, 132 G, 1957
John Olerud, Toronto, 158 G, 1993

**Most intentional bases on balls by switch-hitter, season**
NL—26—Tim Raines Sr., Montreal, 139 G, 1987
AL—25—Eddie Murray, Baltimore, 162 G, 1984

**Most seasons leading league in intentional bases on balls**
NL—10—Barry Bonds, Pittsburgh, San Francisco, 1992-1998, 2002-2004
AL—6—Wade Boggs, Boston, 1987, 1988 (tied), 1989-1992

**Most consecutive seasons leading league in intentional bases on balls**
NL—7—Barry Bonds, Pittsburgh, San Francisco, 1992-1998
AL—6—Wade Boggs, Boston, 1987, 1988 (tied), 1989-1992

**Most seasons with 10 or more intentional bases on balls**
NL—16—Hank Aaron, Milwaukee, Atlanta, 1957-1973, except 1964
AL—11—George Brett, Kansas City, 1979-1991, except 1981, 1984

**Most at-bats with no intentional bases on balls, season**
AL—691—Kirby Puckett, Minnesota, 161 G, 1985
NL—690—Neifi Perez, Colorado, 157 G, 1999

**Most bases on balls with no intentional bases on balls, season**
AL—118—Rickey Henderson, Oakland, 152 G, 1998
NL—94—Johnny Temple, Cincinnati, 145 G, 1957

**Most intentional bases on balls, game**
NL—4—Barry Bonds, San Francisco, May 1, 2004
Barry Bonds, San Francisco, Sept 22, 2004
[5—Andre Dawson, Chicago, May 22, 1990, 16 inn]
AL—3—many players
[4—Roger Maris, New York, May 22, 1962, 12 inn
Manny Ramirez, Boston, June 5, 2001, 18 inn]

# STRIKEOUTS

## CAREER AND SEASON

**Most strikeouts, career**
AL—2,597—Reggie Jackson, Kansas City, Oakland, Baltimore, New York, California, 21 seasons, 1967-1987
NL—1,936—Willie Stargell, Pittsburgh, 21 seasons, 1962-1982

**For a complete list of players with 1,200 or more career strikeouts, see page 107.**

**Most strikeouts, season**
NL—195—Adam Dunn, Cincinnati, 161 G, 2004
AL—188—Jose Hernandez, Milwaukee, 152 G, 2002

**Fewest strikeouts by leader, season**
NL—63—George Grantham, Chicago, 127 G, 1924
AL—66—Jimmie Foxx, Philadelphia, 153 G, 1930
Ed Morgan, Cleveland, 150 G, 1930

**Most strikeouts by rookie, season**
AL—185—Pete Incaviglia, Texas, 153 G, 1986
NL—168—Juan Samuel, Philadelphia, 160 G, 1984

**Most strikeouts by righthander, season**
NL—189—Bobby Bonds, San Francisco, 157 G, 1970
AL—188—Jose Hernandez, Milwaukee, 152 G, 2002

**Most strikeouts by lefthander, season**
NL—195—Adam Dunn, Cincinnati, 161 G, 2004
AL—185—Jim Thome, Cleveland, 156 G, 2001

**Most strikeouts by switch-hitter, season**
AL—177—Mark Bellhorn, Boston, 138 G, 2004
NL—146—Todd Hundley, New York, 153 G, 1996

**Most strikeouts by pitcher, season**
NL—80—Pud Galvin, Buffalo, 72 G, 1884
AL—65—Wilbur Wood, Chicago, 49 G, 1972
NL since 1893—62—Jerry Koosman, New York, 35 G, 1968

**Most seasons leading league in strikeouts**
AL—7—Jimmie Foxx, Philadelphia, Boston, 1929, 1930 (tied), 1931, 1933, 1935, 1936, 1941
NL—6—Vince DiMaggio, Boston, Pittsburgh, Philadelphia, 1937, 1938, 1942-1945

**Most consecutive seasons leading league in strikeouts**
AL—4—Reggie Jackson, Oakland, 1968-1971
NL—4—Hack Wilson, Chicago, 1927-1930
Vince DiMaggio, Pittsburgh, Philadelphia, 1942-1945
Juan Samuel, Philadelphia, 1984-1987

**Most seasons with 100 or more strikeouts**
AL—18—Reggie Jackson, Oakland, Baltimore, New York, California, 1968-1980, 1982-1986
NL—13—Willie Stargell, Pittsburgh, 1965-1976, 1979

**Most consecutive seasons with 100 or more strikeouts**
AL—13—Reggie Jackson, Oakland, Baltimore, New York, 1968-1980
NL—12—Willie Stargell, Pittsburgh, 1965-1976

**Fewest strikeouts, career (14 or more seasons; excludes pitchers)**
AL—113—Joe Sewell, Cleveland, New York, 14 seasons, 1920-1933, 1,903 G
NL—173—Lloyd Waner, Pittsburgh, Boston, Cincinnati, Philadelphia, Brooklyn, 18 seasons, 1927-1945, except 1943, 1,993 G

**Fewest strikeouts, season (150 or more games)**
AL—4—Joe Sewell, Cleveland, 155 G, 1925
Joe Sewell, Cleveland, 152 G, 1929
NL—5—Charlie Hollocher, Chicago, 152 G, 1922

**Fewest strikeouts by rookie, season (150 or more games)**
NL—17—Buddy Hassett, Brooklyn, 156 G, 1936
AL—25—Tom Oliver, Boston, 154 G, 1930

**Fewest strikeouts by righthander, season (150 or more games)**
NL—8—Emil Verban, Philadelphia, 155 G, 1947
AL—9—Stuffy McInnis, Boston, 152 G, 1921
Lou Boudreau, Cleveland, 152 G, 1948

**Fewest strikeouts by lefthander, season (150 or more games)**
AL—4—Joe Sewell, Cleveland, 155 G, 1925
Joe Sewell, Cleveland, 152 G, 1929
NL—5—Charlie Hollocher, Chicago, 152 G, 1922

**Fewest strikeouts by switch-hitter, season (150 or more games)**
NL—10—Frankie Frisch, St. Louis, 153 G, 1927
AL—23—Buck Weaver, Chicago, 151 G 1920

**Most seasons leading league in fewest strikeouts (150 or more games)**
AL—11—Nellie Fox, Chicago, 1952-1962
NL—4—Stan Musial, St. Louis, 1943, 1948, 1952, 1956 (tied)
Dick Groat, Pittsburgh, St. Louis, 1955, 1958, 1964, 1965 (tied)

## GAME AND INNING

**Most strikeouts, game (*consecutive)**
NL—5—Oscar Walker, Buffalo, June 20, 1879*
Pete Dowling, Louisville, Aug 15, 1899*
Floyd Young, Pittsburgh, Sept 29, 1935, 2nd game*
Bob Sadowski, Milwaukee, Apr 20, 1964*
Dick Allen, Philadelphia, June 28, 1964, 1st game*
Ron Swoboda, New York, June 22, 1969, 1st game*
Steve Whitaker, San Francisco, Apr 14, 1970*
Dick Allen, St. Louis, May 24, 1970*
Bill Russell, Los Angeles, June 9, 1971*
Jose Mangual, Montreal, Aug 11, 1975*
Frank Taveras, New York, May 1, 1979*
Bert Blyleven, Pittsburgh, July 27, 1979, 2nd game*
Dave Kingman, New York, May 28, 1982*
Darryl Strawberry, Los Angeles, May 1, 1991*
Delino DeShields, Montreal, Sept 17, 1991, 2nd game*
Scott Rolen, Philadelphia, Aug 23, 1999*
Richie Sexson, Milwaukee, May 29, 2001*
Adam Dunn, Cincinnati, Aug 20, 2002*
Tony Batista, Montreal, Aug 31, 2004*
[6—Don Hoak, Chicago, May 2, 1956, 17 inn
Geoff Jenkins, Milwaukee, June 8, 2004, 17 inn]
AL—5—Lefty Grove, Philadelphia, June 10, 1933, 1st game*
Johnny Broaca, New York, June 25, 1934*
Chet Laabs, Detroit, Oct 2, 1938, first game*
Larry Doby, Cleveland, Apr 25, 1948*
Jim Landis, Chicago, July 28, 1957*
Bob Allison, Minnesota, Sept 2, 1965*
Reggie Jackson, Oakland, Sept 27, 1968*
Ray Jarvis, Boston, Apr 20, 1969*
Rick Monday, Oakland, Apr 29, 1970*
Frank Howard, Washington, Sept 19, 1970, 1st game*
Don Buford, Baltimore, Aug 26, 1971*
Rick Manning, Cleveland, May 15, 1977*
Bo Jackson, Kansas City, Apr 18, 1987*
Rob Deer, Milwaukee, Aug 8, 1987, 1st game*
Jeffrey Leonard, Milwaukee, Aug 24, 1988*
Joey Meyer, Milwaukee, Sept 20, 1988*
Phil Bradley, Baltimore, Sept 7, 1989, 1st game
Bernie Williams, New York, Aug 21, 1991*
Phil Plantier, Boston, October 1, 1991*
Bob Hamelin, Kansas City, May 24, 1995*
Danny Bautista, Detroit, May 28, 1995
Jose Canseco, Oakland, July 16, 1997*
Jim Thome, Cleveland, Apr 9, 2000
John Jaha, Oakland, Apr 20, 2000*
Andy Phillips, New York, May 2, 2005
[6—Carl Weilman, St. Louis, July 25, 1913, 15 inn*
Rick Reichardt, California, May 31, 1966, 17 inn
Billy Cowan, California, July 9, 1971, 20 inn
Cecil Cooper, Boston, June 14, 1974, 15 inn
Sam Horn, Baltimore, July 17, 1991, 15 inn
Alex Gonzalez, Toronto, Sept 9, 1998, 13 inn*]

**Most games with four or more strikeouts, career**
AL—23—Reggie Jackson, Kansas City, Oakland, Baltimore, New York, California, 1967-1987
NL—16—Andres Galarraga, Montreal, St. Louis, Colorado, Atlanta, San Francisco, 1985-2004

**Most games with four or more strikeouts, season**
NL—7—Dick Allen, Philadelphia, Apr 13, May 1, 9, June 29, July 16, 21, Aug 19, 1968
AL—5—Reggie Jackson, Oakland, Apr 7, 2nd game, Apr 21, May 18, June 4, Sept 21, 1st game, 1971
Bobby Darwin, Minnesota, May 12, 13, June 23, July 14, Aug 6, 1st game, Aug 10, 1972

**Most consecutive games with no strikeouts, season**
AL—115—Joe Sewell, Cleveland, May 17-Sept 19, 1929 (437 AB)
NL—77—Lloyd Waner, Pittsburgh, Boston, Cincinnati, Apr 24-Sept 16, 1941 (219 AB)

**Most strikeouts, first major league game**
NL—4—Billy Sunday, Chicago, May 22, 1883
NL since 1893—4—Wes Bales, Atlanta, Aug 7, 1966
AA—4—Hercules Burnett, Louisville, June 26, 1888
George Goetz, Baltimore, June 17, 1889
AL—4—Rollie Naylor, Philadelphia, Sept 14, 1917
Sam Ewing, Chicago, Sept 11, 1973

**Most strikeouts, doubleheader**
NL—7—Mike Vail, New York, Sept 26, 1975, 24 inn
AL—7—Pat Seerey, Chicago, July 24, 1948, 19 inn
Dave Nicholson, Chicago, June 12, 1963, 17 inn
Frank Howard, Washington, July 9, 1965, 18 inn
Bill Melton, Chicago, July 24, 1970, 18 inn
Shea Hillenbrand, Toronto, Sept 27, 2005, 17 inn

**Ten or more consecutive strikeouts, season (consecutive plate appearances)**
NL—12—Sandy Koufax, Brooklyn, June 24-Sept 24, 2nd game, 1955 (12 AB for season, 12 K)
10—Tommie Sisk, Pittsburgh, July 27 (2), Aug 1 (3), 6 (4), 12 (1), 1966
AL—11—Dean Chance, Los Angeles, July 24 (1), 30 (2), Aug 4,1st game (3), 9 (4), 13 (1), 1965
10—Joe Grzenda, Washington, Apr 7 (2), 22 (1), May 26 (4), June 13 (1), 16 (1), Aug 3 (1), 1970

**Most consecutive strikeouts, season (not consecutive plate appearances)**
NL—14—Bill Hands, Chicago, June 9, 2nd game-July 11, 2nd game, 1968 (1 BB and 2 SH in streak)
Juan Eichelberger, San Diego, June 30-Aug 15, 1980 (1 SH in streak)
AL—13—Jim Hannan, Washington, July 24-Aug 13, 1968 (2 BB in streak)

**Most strikeouts, inning**
AL-NL—2—many players

## SACRIFICE HITS

**Most sacrifices, career**
AL—511—Eddie Collins, Philadelphia, Chicago, 25 seasons, 1906-1930
NL—392—Jake Daubert, Brooklyn, Cincinnati, 15 seasons, 1910-1924

**Most sacrifices, season (including sacrifice scoring flies)**
AL—67—Ray Chapman, Cleveland, 156 G, 1917
NL—46—Jim Sheckard, Chicago, 148 G, 1909

**Most sacrifices, season (excludes sacrifice flies)**
AL—46—Bill Bradley, Cleveland, 139 G, 1907
NL—43—Kid Gleason, Philadelphia, 155 G, 1905

**Fewest sacrifices for leader, season (excludes sacrifice flies)**
AL—13—Billy Martin, Detroit, 131 G, 1958
Tony Kubek, New York, 132 G, 1959
Jim Landis, Chicago, 149 G, 1959
Al Pilarcik, Baltimore, 130 G, 1959
Vic Power, Minnesota, 138 G, 1963
Paul Blair, Baltimore, 150 G, 1969
Denny McLain, Detroit, 42 G, 1969
NL—13—Maury Wills, Los Angeles, 148 G, 1961

**Most sacrifices by rookie, season (includes sacrifice scoring flies)**
AL—39—Emory Rigney, Detroit, 155 G, 1922
NL—31—Ozzie Smith, San Diego, 159 G, 1978

**Most sacrifices by rookie, season (since 1931; excludes sacrifice flies)**
AL—28—Joe Hoover, Detroit, 144 G, 1943
NL—28—Jackie Robinson, Brooklyn, 151 G, 1947
Ozzie Smith, San Diego, 159 G, 1978

**Most sacrifices by righthander, season**
AL—67—Ray Chapman, Cleveland, 156 G, 1917 (includes a few sacrifice scoring flies)
NL—42—Otto Knabe, Philadelphia, 151 G, 1908 (may include some sacrifice scoring flies)
Bob Fisher, Chicago, 147 G, 1915 (may include some sacrifice scoring flies)
Pie Traynor, Pittsburgh, 144 G, 1928 (may include some sacrifice scoring flies)

**Most sacrifices by lefthander, season**
AL—52—Bob Ganley, Washington, 150 G 1908 (includes a few sacrifice scoring flies)
NL—46—Jim Sheckard, Chicago, 148 G, 1909 (includes a few sacrifice scoring flies)

**Most sacrifices by switch-hitter, season**
AL—52—Donie Bush, Detroit, 157 G, 1909 (includes a few sacrifice scoring flies)
NL—43—Kid Gleason, Philadelphia, 155 G, 1905 (does not include sacrifice flies)

**Most seasons leading league in sacrifices**
AL—6—Mule Haas, Philadelphia, Chicago, 1930-1934, 1936
NL—4—Otto Knabe, Philadelphia, 1907, 1908, 1910, 1913

**Most consecutive seasons leading league in sacrifices**
AL—5—Mule Haas, Philadelphia, Chicago, 1930-1934
NL—2—many players; last—Jack Wilson, Pittsburgh, 2001 (tied), 2002

**Most at-bats with no sacrifice hits, season**
NL—701—Juan Samuel, Philadelphia, 160 G, 1984
AL—672—Garret Anderson, Anaheim, 161 G, 2001

**Most sacrifice hits, game**
AL—4—Red Killefer, Washington, Aug 27, 1910, 1st game
Jack Barry, Boston, Aug 21, 1916
Ray Chapman, Cleveland, Aug 31, 1919
[4—Felix Fermin, Cleveland, Aug 22, 1989, 10 inn]
NL—4—Jake Daubert, Brooklyn, Aug 15, 1914, 2nd game
Cy Seymour, Cincinnati, July 25, 1902
Kris Benson, Pittsburgh, Apr 18, 2004

**Most sacrifice hits, inning**
AL—2—Al Benton, Detroit, Aug 6, 1941, 3rd
NL—1—many players

## SACRIFICE FLIES

**Most sacrifice flies, career**
ML—128—Eddie Murray, Baltimore AL, Los Angeles NL, New York NL, Cleveland AL, Anaheim AL, 21 seasons, 1977-1997 (92 in AL, 36 in NL)
AL—127—Cal Ripken Jr., Baltimore, 21 seasons, 1981-2001
NL—113—Hank Aaron, Milwaukee, Atlanta, 21 seasons, 1954-1974

**Most sacrifice flies, season**
NL—19—Gil Hodges, Brooklyn, 154 G, 1954 (Pie Traynor, Pittsburgh, 144 G, 1928, had 31 SF, advancing runners to second base, third base and home.)
AL—17—Roy White, New York, 147 G, 1971
Bobby Bonilla, Baltimore, 159 G, 1996

**Most sacrifice flies by rookie, season**
NL—13—Willie Montanez, Philadelphia, 158 G, 1971
AL—13—Gary Gaetti, Minnesota, 145 G, 1982

**Most sacrifice flies by righthander, season**
NL—19—Gil Hodges, Brooklyn, 154 G, 1954
AL—16—Chick Gandil, Washington, 145 G, 1914
Juan Gonzalez, Cleveland, 140 G, 2001

**Most sacrifice flies by lefthander, season**
AL—16—Sam Crawford, Detroit, 157 G, 1914
NL—14—J.T. Snow, San Francisco, 155 G, 2000

**Most sacrifice flies by switch-hitter, season**
AL—17—Roy White, New York, 147 G, 1971
Bobby Bonilla, Baltimore, 159 G, 1996
NL—15—Bobby Bonilla, Pittsburgh, 160 G, 1990
Howard Johnson, New York, 156 G, 1991

**Most seasons leading league in sacrifice flies**
AL—4—Brooks Robinson, Baltimore, 1962 (tied), 1964, 1967 (tied), 1968 (tied)
NL—3—Ron Santo, Chicago, 1963, 1967, 1969
Johnny Bench, Cincinnati, 1970, 1972, 1973 (tied)

**Most at-bats with no sacrifice flies, season**
NL—680—Pete Rose, Cincinnati, 160 G, 1973
Frank Taveras, Pittsburgh, New York, 164 G, 1979
AL—680—Kirby Puckett, Minnesota, 161 G, 1986

**Most sacrifice flies, game**
NL—3—Harry Steinfeldt, Chicago, May 5, 1909
Ernie Banks, Chicago, June 2, 1961
Vince Coleman, St. Louis, May 1, 1986
Candy Maldonado, San Francisco, Aug 29, 1987
AL—3—Bob Meusel, New York, Sept 15, 1926
Russ Nixon, Boston, Aug 31, 1965, 2nd game
Don Mattingly, New York, May 3, 1986
George Bell, Toronto, Aug 14, 1990
Chad Kreuter, Detroit, July 30, 1994
Juan Gonzalez, Texas, July 3, 1999
Edgar Martinez, Seattle, Aug 3, 2002

## HIT BY PITCH

**Most hit by pitch, career**
ML—287—Hughie Jennings, Louisville AA, Louisville NL, Baltimore NL, Brooklyn NL, Philadelphia NL, Detroit AL, 17 seasons, 1891-1903, 1907, 1909, 1912, 1918 (9 in AA, 278 in NL, 0 in AL)
NL—278—Hughie Jennings, Louisville, Baltimore, Brooklyn, Philadelphia, 12 seasons, 1892-1903
NL since 1893—273—Craig Biggio, Houston, 18 seasons, 1988-2005
AL—267—Don Baylor, Baltimore, Oakland, California, New York, Boston, Minnesota, 19 seasons, 1970-1988

**Most hit by pitch, season**
NL—51—Hughie Jennings, Baltimore, 130 G, 1896
AL—35—Don Baylor, Boston, 160 G, 1986

**Most hit by pitch, rookie, season**
AA—29—Tommy Tucker, Baltimore, 136 G, 1887
AL—21—David Eckstein, Anaheim, 153 G, 2001
NL—20—Frank Robinson, Cincinnati, 152 G, 1956

**Most hit by pitch, righthander, season**
NL—51—Hughie Jennings, Baltimore, 130 G, 1896
AL—35—Don Baylor, Boston, 160 G, 1986

**Most hit by pitch, lefthander, season**
NL—31—Steve Evans, St. Louis, 151 G, 1910
AL—22—Brady Anderson, Baltimore, 149 G, 1996

**Most hit by pitch, switch-hitter, season**
NL—25—F.P. Santangelo, Montreal, 130 G, 1997
AL—15—Gene Larkin, Minnesota, 149 G, 1988

**Most seasons leading league in hit by pitch**
AL—10—Minnie Minoso, Cleveland, Chicago, 1951-1954, 1956-1961
NL—7—Ron Hunt, San Francisco, Montreal, St. Louis, 1968-1974

**Most consecutive seasons leading league in hit by pitch**
NL—7—Ron Hunt, San Francisco, Montreal, St. Louis, 1968-1974
AL—6—Minnie Minoso, Chicago, Cleveland, 1956-1961

**Fewest hit by pitch for leader, season**
AL—5—Frank Crosetti, New York, 138 G, 1934
Frank Pytlak, Cleveland, 91 G, 1934
NL—6—Buddy Blattner, New York, 126 G, 1946
Andre Dawson, Montreal, 151 G, 1980
Dan Driessen, Cincinnati, 154 G, 1980
Tim Foli, Pittsburgh, 127 G, 1980
Greg Luzinski, Philadelphia, 106 G, 1980
Elliott Maddox, New York, 130 G, 1980
Pete Rose, Philadelphia, 162 G, 1980

**Most at-bats with no hit by pitch, season**
AL—689—Sandy Alomar Sr., California, 162 G, 1971
NL—662—Hugh Critz, Cincinnati, New York, 152 G, 1930
Granny Hamner, Philadelphia, 154 G, 1949

**Most hit by pitch, game**
AA—3—5 times (by 5 players)
NL—3—15 times (by 12 players); last—Richard Hidalgo, Houston, Apr 19, 2000
[3—Ron Hunt, San Francisco, Apr 29, 1969, 13 inn]
AL—3—8 times (by 8 players); last—Jonny Gomes, Tampa Bay, Aug 15, 2005
[3—Jake Stahl, Washington, Apr 15, 1904, 10 inn
Craig Kusick, Minnesota, Aug 27, 1975, 11 inn]

**Most times hit by pitch three times in a game, career**
NL—3—Hughie Jennings, Baltimore, 1894, 1896, 1898
AL—1—five players

**Most hit by pitch, doubleheader**
NL—4—Frank Chance, Chicago, May 30, 1904
AL—3—Bert Daniels, New York, June 20, 1913
Al Smith, Chicago, June 21, 1961

**Most hit by pitch, inning**
NL—2—Willard Schmidt, Cincinnati, Apr 26, 1959, 3rd
Frank J. Thomas, New York, Apr 29, 1962, 1st game, 4th
Andres Galarraga, Colorado, July 12, 1996, 7th
AL—2—Brady Anderson, Baltimore, May 23, 1999, 1st

## GROUNDING INTO DOUBLE PLAYS

**Most grounding into double plays, career**
AL—350—Cal Ripken Jr., Baltimore, 21 seasons, 1981-2001
NL—305—Hank Aaron, Milwaukee, Atlanta, 21 seasons, 1954-1974

**Most grounding into double plays, season**
AL—36—Jim Rice, Boston, 159 G, 1984
NL—30—Ernie Lombardi, Cincinnati, 129 G, 1938
Brad Ausmus, Houston, 130 G, 2002

**Fewest grounding into double plays for leader, season**
NL—19—Andy Seminick, Philadelphia, 124 G, 1946
George Kurowski, St. Louis, 146 G, 1947
Andy Pafko, Chicago, 129 G, 1947
AL—21—Brooks Robinson, Baltimore, 158 G, 1967
John Olerud, Seattle, 159 G, 2001

**Most grounding into double plays by rookie, season**
AL—27—Billy Johnson, New York, 155 G, 1943
Al Rosen, Cleveland, 155 G, 1950
NL—21—Albert Pujols, St. Louis, 161 G, 2001

**Most grounding into double plays by righthander, season**
AL—36—Jim Rice, Boston, 159 G, 1984
NL—30—Ernie Lombardi, Cincinnati, 129 G, 1938
Brad Ausmus, Houston, 130 G, 2002

**Most grounding into double plays by lefthander, season**
AL—32—Ben Grieve, Oakland, 158 G, 2000
NL—27—A.J. Pierzynski, San Francisco, 131 G, 2004
Sean Casey, Cincinnati, 137 G, 2005

**Most grounding into double plays by switch-hitter, season**
AL—29—Dave Philley, Philadelphia, 151 G, 1952
NL—29—Ted Simmons, St. Louis, 161 G, 1973

**Most seasons leading league in grounding into double plays**
NL—4—Ernie Lombardi, Cincinnati, New York, 1933, 1934, 1938, 1944
AL—4—Jim Rice, Boston, 1982, 1983 (tied), 1984, 1985

**Fewest grounding into double plays, season (150 or more games)**
NL—0—Augie Galan, Chicago, 154 G, 1935
Craig Biggio, Houston, 162 G, 1997
AL—0—Dick McAuliffe, Detroit, 151 G, 1968

**Fewest grounding into double plays by rookie, season (150 or more games)**
NL—3—Vince Coleman, St. Louis, 151 G, 1985
AL—3—Ichiro Suzuki, Seattle, 157 G, 2001

**Fewest grounding into double plays by righthander, season (150 or more games)**
NL—0—Craig Biggio, Houston, 162 G, 1997
AL—2—Cesar Tovar, Minnesota, 157 G, 1968
Mark Belanger, Baltimore, 152 G, 1975

**Fewest grounding into double plays by lefthander, season (150 or more games)**
AL—0—Dick McAuliffe, Detroit, 151 G, 1968
NL—2—Lou Brock, St. Louis, 155 G, 1965
Lou Brock, St. Louis, 157 G, 1969
Will Clark, San Francisco, 150 G, 1987
Brett Butler, San Francisco, 157 G, 1988

**Fewest grounding into double plays by switch-hitter, season (150 or more games)**
NL—0—Augie Galan, Chicago, 154 G, 1935
AL—1—Willie Wilson, Kansas City, 154 G, 1979

**Most seasons leading league in fewest grounding into double plays (150 or more games)**
NL—6—Richie Ashburn, Philadelphia, Chicago, 1951, 1952, 1953, 1954, 1958, 1960 (tied)
AL—2—many players; last—Willie Wilson, Kansas City, 1979, 1980

**Most grounding into double plays, game**
AL—4—Goose Goslin, Detroit, Apr 28, 1934 (consec)

NL—4—Joe Torre, New York, July 21, 1975 (consec)

**Most grounding into infield triple plays, game or season**
NL-AL—1—many players

## REACHING ON ERRORS OR INTERFERENCE

**Most times reaching base on error, game (fair balls)**
PL—4—Mike Griffin, Philadelphia, June 23, 1890
NL—3—George Gore, New York, Aug 15, 1887
NL since 1893—3—Bill McKechnie, New York, May 9, 1916
Al Lopez, Boston, July 16, 1936
Jerry Grote, New York, Sept 5, 1975
AL—3—Phil Bradley, Baltimore, Aug 4, 1989
Ray Durham, Chicago, Apr 22, 1998

**Most times reaching base on error, inning (fair balls)**
AL—2—Emory Rigney, Detroit, Aug 21, 1922, 6th
Fred Spurgeon, Cleveland, Apr 14, 1925, 8th
Johnny Bassler, Detroit, June 17, 1925, 6th
Sam Rice, Washington, July 10, 1926, 8th
NL—2—Stu Martin, St. Louis, June 22, 1940, 6th

**Most times reaching base on catcher's interference, season**
AL—8—Roberto Kelly, New York, 152 G, 1992
NL—7—Dale Berra, Pittsburgh, 161 G, 1983

**Most times reaching base on catcher's interference, game**
NL—2—Ben Geraghty, Brooklyn, Apr 26, 1936
Pat Corrales, Philadelphia, Aug 15, 1965
Pat Corrales, Philadelphia, Sept 29, 1965
AL—2—Dan Meyer, Seattle, May 3, 1977
Bob Stinson, Seattle, July 24, 1979

# CLUB BATTING

## GAMES

**Most games, league**
NL—19,277—Chicago, 130 seasons, 1876-2005
AL—16,364—Detroit, 105 seasons, 1901-2005

**Most games, season**
NL—165—Los Angeles, 1962 (3-game playoff)
San Francisco, 1962 (3-game playoff)
AL—164—Cleveland, 1964 (2 ties)
New York, 1964, 1968 (2 ties)
Minnesota, 1967 (2 ties)
Detroit, 1968 (2 ties)

**Fewest games, season**
AL—147—Cleveland, 1945 (2 ties, 9 unplayed)
NL—149—Philadelphia, 1907 (2 ties, 7 unplayed), 1934 (5 unplayed)

**Three games, one day**
NL—Brooklyn and Pittsburgh, Sept 1, 1890 (Brooklyn won 3)
Baltimore and Louisville, Sept 7, 1896 (Baltimore won 3)
Pittsburgh and Cincinnati, Oct 2, 1920 (Cincinnati won 2)
AL—none

**Most doubleheaders, season**
AL—44—Chicago, 1943 (won 11, lost 10, split 23)
NL—43—Philadelphia, 1943 (won 11, lost 14, split 18)

**Fewest doubleheaders, season**
AL-NL—0—many clubs
Last in AL—Baltimore, Boston, Cleveland, Minnesota, New York, Oakland, Seattle, Tampa Bay, Toronto, 2005
Last in NL—Los Angeles, Milwaukee, St. Louis, 2005

**Most consecutive doubleheaders played, season**
NL—9—Boston, Sept 4-15, 1928
AL—8—Washington, July 27-Aug 5, 1909

**Most consecutive games between same clubs, season**
AL—11—Detroit vs St. Louis, Sept 8-14, 1904
NL—10—Chicago vs Philadelphia, Aug 7-16, 1907

**Most consecutive doubleheaders between same clubs, season**
AL—5—Philadelphia vs Washington, Aug 5, 7, 8, 9, 10, 1901
NL—4—New York vs Boston, Sept 10, 11, 13, 14, 1928

## BATTING AVERAGE

**Highest average, season**
NL—.350—Philadelphia, 132 G, 1894
NL since 1900—.319—New York, 154 G, 1930
AL—.316—Detroit, 154 G, 1921

**Lowest average, league leader, season**
AL—.240—Oakland, 163 G, 1968
NL—.254—St. Louis, 157 G, 1915

**Highest average, pennant winner, season**
NL—.343—Baltimore, 129 G, 1894
AL—.307—New York, 155 G, 1927

**Lowest average, pennant winner, season**
AL—.228—Chicago, 154 G, 1906; 8th in batting
NL—.242—New York, 162 G, 1969; 7th (tied) in batting

**Most seasons leading league in average (since 1900)**
NL—23—St. Louis, 1915, 1920, 1921, 1934, 1938, 1939, 1942-1944, 1946, 1949, 1952, 1954, 1956, 1957, 1963, 1971, 1975, 1979, 1980, 1985, 1992, 2004
AL—23—Boston, 1903, 1938, 1939, 1941, 1942, 1944, 1946, 1949, 1950, 1964, 1967, 1975, 1979, 1981, 1984, 1985, 1987-1990, 1997, 2003, 2005

**Most consecutive years leading league in average**
NL—8—Colorado, 1995-2002
AL—5—Philadelphia, 1910-1914

**Most players batting .400 or over, season (400 or more at-bats)**
NL—4—Philadelphia, 1894
AL—none more than one

**Most players batting .300 or over, season (400 or more at-bats)**
AL—10—Philadelphia, 1927
NL—10—St. Louis, 1930

**Lowest average, season**
NL—.207—Washington, 136 G, 1888
AL—.212—Chicago, 156 G, 1910
NL since 1894—.213—Brooklyn, 154 G, 1908

## ON-BASE PERCENTAGE

(official statistic since 1984; calculated from official statistics, 1931-1983, except for 1939 for which there is no official tabulation of sacrifice flies)

**Highest percentage, season**
AL—.385—Boston, 154 G, 1950
NL—.366—Brooklyn, 155 G, 1953

**Lowest percentage, season**
NL—.277—New York, 164 G, 1965
AL—.284—Chicago, 162 G, 1968

## SLUGGING AVERAGE

**Highest average, season**
AL—.491—Boston, 162 games, 2003
NL—.483—Colorado, 162 games, 2001

**Most years leading league in average (since 1900)**
AL—30—New York, 1901 (franchise in Baltimore), 1920, 1921, 1923, 1924, 1926, 1927, 1928, 1930, 1931, 1936, 1937, 1938, 1939, 1943, 1944, 1945, 1947, 1948, 1951, 1953, 1954, 1955, 1956, 1957, 1958, 1960, 1961, 1962, 1986
NL—21—New York/San Francisco, 1904, 1905, 1908, 1910, 1911, 1919, 1923, 1924, 1927, 1928, 1935, 1945, 1947, 1948, 1952, 1961, 1962, 1963, 1989, 1993, 2002 (15 NY, 6 SF)

**Most consecutive years leading in average (since 1900)**
AL—6—New York, 1953-1958
NL—5—Colorado, 1995-1999

**Lowest average, season (150 or more games)**
AL—.261—Chicago, 156 games, 1910
NL—.274—Boston, 155 games, 1909

## AT-BATS AND PLATE APPEARANCES

**Most at-bats, season**
AL—5,781—Boston, 162 G, 1997
NL—5,767—Cincinnati, 163 G, 1968

**Fewest at-bats, season**
NL—4,725—Philadelphia, 149 G, 1907
AL—4,827—Chicago, 153 G, 1913

**Most plate appearances, game**
NL—71—Chicago vs Louisville, June 29, 1897
[103—New York vs St. Louis, Sept 11, 1974, 25 inn]
AL—65—Milwaukee vs Toronto, Aug 28, 1992
[104—Chicago vs Milwaukee, May 8-9, 1984, 25 inn]

**Most plate appearances by both clubs, game**
NL—125—Philadelphia 66, Chicago 59, Aug 25, 1922
[202—New York 103, St. Louis 99, Sept 11, 1974, 25 inn]

AL—110—Tampa Bay 61, Toronto 49, June 24, 2004
[198—Chicago 104, Milwaukee 94, May 8-9, 1984, 25 inn]

**Most at-bats, game**
NL—66—Chicago vs Buffalo, July 3, 1883
NL since 1893—58—New York vs Philadelphia, Sept 2, 1925, 2nd game
New York vs Philadelphia, July 11, 1931, 1st game
[89—New York vs St. Louis, Sept 11, 1974, 25 inn]
AL—57—Milwaukee vs Toronto, Aug 28, 1992
[95—Chicago vs Milwaukee, May 8-9, 1984, 25 inn]

**Most at-bats by both clubs, game**
NL—106—Chicago 64, Louisville 42, July 22, 1876
NL since 1893—99—New York 56, Cincinnati 43, June 9, 1901
New York 58, Philadelphia 41, July 11, 1931, 1st game
Cincinnati 52, Philadelphia 47, Aug 3, 1960
[175—New York 89, St. Louis 86, Sept 11, 1974, 25 inn]
AL—96—Cleveland 51, Philadelphia 45, Apr 29, 1952
[175—Chicago 95, Milwaukee 80, May 8-9, 1984, 25 inn]

**Most at-bats, doubleheader**
AL—99—New York vs Philadelphia, June 28, 1939
NL—98—Pittsburgh vs Philadelphia, Aug 8, 1922

**Most at-bats by by both clubs, doubleheader**
NL—176—Pittsburgh 98, Philadelphia 78, Aug 8, 1922
[234—New York 119, San Francisco 115, May 31, 1964, 32 inn]
AL—172—Boston 89, Philadelphia 83, July 4, 1939
[215—Kansas City 112, Detroit 103, June 17, 1967, 28 inn]

**Fewest at-bats, game (batting eight times)**
AL—19—Baltimore vs Kansas City, Sept 12, 1964
NL—21—Pittsburgh vs St. Louis, Sept 8, 1908
Atlanta vs Pittsburgh, Sept 6, 1986

**Fewest at-bats, game (batting nine times)**
AL—23—Chicago vs St. Louis, May 6, 1917
Cleveland vs Chicago, May 9, 1961
Detroit vs Baltimore, May 6, 1968
NL—24—many times; last—Pittsburgh vs Tampa Bay AL, June 13, 2003

**Fewest at-bats by both clubs, game**
AL—46—Kansas City 27, Baltimore 19, Sept 12, 1964
NL—48—Boston 25, Philadelphia 23, Apr 22, 1910
Brooklyn 24, Cincinnati 24, July 22, 1911

**Fewest at-bats, doubleheader**
AL—50—Boston vs Chicago, Aug 28, 1912
NL—52—Brooklyn vs St. Louis, July 24, 1909
Philadelphia vs Chicago, Aug 23, 1961
St. Louis vs Montreal, Sept 29, 1987

**Fewest at-bats by both clubs, doubleheader**
AL—106—Boston 55, Baltimore 51, Sept 2, 1971
NL—109—St. Louis 57, Brooklyn 52, July 24, 1909

**Most plate appearances, inning**
AL—23—Boston vs Detroit, June 18, 1953, 7th
NL—23—Chicago vs Detroit, Sept 6, 1883, 7th
NL since 1893—21—Brooklyn vs Cincinnati, May 21, 1952, 1st

**Most batters with three plate appearances, inning**
NL—5—Chicago vs Detroit, Sept 6, 1883, 7th
AL—5—Boston vs Detroit, June 18, 1953, 7th
NL since 1893—3—Brooklyn vs Cincinnati, May 21, 1952, 1st

## RUNS

### SEASON

**Most runs, season**
NL—1,220—Boston, 133 G, 1894
AL—1,067—New York, 155 G, 1931
NL since 1900—1,004—St. Louis, 154 G, 1930

**Fewest runs scored by leader, season**
NL—590—St. Louis, 157 G, 1915
AL—622—Philadelphia, 152 G, 1905

**Most runs by pennant winner, season**
NL—1,170—Baltimore, 129 G, 1894
AL—1,065—New York, 155 G, 1936

**Fewest runs by pennant winner, season**
AL—550—Boston, 156 G, 1916
NL—571—Chicago, 155 G, 1907

**Most runs at home, season (since 1900)**
NL—658—Colorado, 81 G, 1996
AL—625—Boston, 77 G, 1950

**Most runs on road, season (since 1900)**
AL—591—New York, 78 G, 1930
NL—492—Chicago, 78 G, 1929

**Most runs against one club, season (since 1900)**
NL—218—Chicago vs Philadelphia, 24 G, 1930 (117 at home, 101 at Philadelphia)
AL—216—Boston vs St. Louis, 22 G, 1950 (118 at home, 98 at St. Louis)

**Most players scoring 100 or more runs, season**
NL—7—Boston, 1894
AL—6—New York, 1931

**Fewest runs, season**
NL—372—St. Louis, 154 G, 1908
AL—380—Washington, 156 G, 1909

### GAME AND DOUBLEHEADER—ONE CLUB

**Most runs, game**
NL—36—Chicago vs Louisville (7), June 29, 1897
AL—29—Boston vs St. Louis (4), June 8, 1950
Chicago vs Kansas City (6), Apr 23, 1955

**Most runs, opening game of season**
PL—23—Buffalo vs Cleveland (2), April 19, 1890
AL—21—Cleveland vs. St. Louis (14), Apr 14, 1925
NL—19—Philadelphia vs Boston (17), Apr 19, 1900, 10 inn

**Biggest run deficit overcome to win game**
AL—12—Detroit vs Chicago, June 18, 1911
Chicago ........................7 0 0 3 3 0 2 0 0—15
Detroit ..........................0 1 0 0 4 3 0 5 3—16

Philadelphia vs Cleveland, June 15, 1925
Cleveland......................0 4 2 2 4 2 1 0 0—15
Philadelphia..................0 1 1 0 0 1 1 13 x—17

Cleveland vs Seattle, Aug 5, 2001, 11 inn
Seattle.............0 4 8 0 2 0 0 0 0 0 0—14
Cleveland.........0 0 0 2 0 0 3 4 5 0 1—15

NL—11—St. Louis vs New York, June 15, 1952, 1st game
St. Louis.......................0 0 0 0 7 0 3 2 2—14
New York.....................0 5 6 0 0 0 0 0 1—12

Philadelphia vs Chicago, Apr 17, 1976, 10 inn
Philadelphia .....0 1 0 1 2 0 3 5 3 3—18
Chicago............0 7 5 1 0 0 0 0 2 1—16

Houston vs St. Louis, July 18, 1994
St. Louis.......................3 4 4 0 0 0 0 0 1—12
Houston........................0 0 0 2 2 11 0 0 x—15

**Most players scoring two or more runs, game**
NL—10—Chicago vs Louisville, June 29, 1897
AL—9—many teams; last—Minnesota vs Detroit, June 4, 1994

**Most players scoring one or more runs, game**
NL—15—Atlanta vs Florida, Oct 3, 1999
AL—14—Oakland vs Texas, Sept 30, 2000

**Most runs, doubleheader**
NL—43—Boston vs Cincinnati, Aug 21, 1894
AL—36—Detroit vs St. Louis, Aug 14, 1937

**Longest doubleheader without scoring a run**
NL—27 inn—St. Louis vs New York, July 2, 1933
New York vs Philadelphia, October 2, 1965
AL—18 inn—many clubs; last—Cleveland vs Boston, Sept 26, 1975

### GAME AND DOUBLEHEADER—BOTH CLUBS

**Most runs, game**
NL—49—Chicago 26, Philadelphia 23, Aug 25, 1922
AL—36—Boston 22, Philadelphia 14, June 29, 1950

**Most runs, opening game of season**
NL—36—Philadelphia 19, Boston 17, Apr 19, 1900, 10 inn
AL—35—Cleveland 21, St. Louis 14, Apr 14, 1925

**Most players scoring two or more runs, game**
NL—16—Chicago 9, Philadelphia 7, Aug 25, 1922
AL—13—Boston 9, Philadelphia 4, May 2, 1901
Boston 9, Philadelphia 4, June 29, 1950

**Most players scoring one or more runs, game**
NL—22—Philadelphia 13, Chicago 9, Aug 25, 1922
AL—19—Detroit 12, Baltimore 7, Aug 12, 1993

**Most runs, doubleheader**
AL—54—Boston 35, Philadelphia 19, July 4, 1939
NL—54—Boston 43, Cincinnati 11, Aug 21, 1894

**Fewest runs by both teams, doubleheader**
NL—1—Boston 1-0, Pittsburgh 0-0, Sept 4, 1902
Philadelphia 1-0, Boston 0-0, Sept 5, 1913
AL—2—Washington 1-0, St. Louis 0-1, Sept 25, 1904
Philadelphia 1-0, Boston 0-1, June 1, 1909
Philadelphia 1-0, Boston 0-1, Sept 11, 1909
Los Angeles 1-0, Detroit 0-1, Aug 18, 1964
Washington 1-0, Kansas City 0-1, May 2, 1967
Milwaukee 1-0, Chicago 0-1, July 11, 1971
Baltimore 1-1, Boston 0-0, Sept 2, 1974

### INNING

**Most runs, inning**
NL—18—Chicago vs Detroit, Sept 6, 1883, 7th
AL—17—Boston vs Detroit, June 18, 1953, 7th
NL since 1893—15—Brooklyn vs Cincinnati, May 21, 1952, 1st

**Most runs by both clubs, inning**
AA—19—Washington 14, Baltimore 5, June 17, 1891, 1st
AL—19—Cleveland 13, Boston 6, Apr 10, 1977, 8th
NL—18—Chicago 18, Detroit 0, Sept 6, 1883, 7th
NL since 1893—17—Boston 10, New York 7, June 20, 1912, 9th

**Most runs, extra inning**
AL—12—Texas vs Oakland, July 3, 1983, 15th
NL—10—Kansas City vs Detroit, July 21, 1886, 11th
Boston vs New York, June 17, 1887, a.m. game, 10th
NL since 1893—Cincinnati vs Brooklyn, May 15, 1919, 13th

**Most runs by both clubs, extra inning**
AL—12—Minnesota 11, Oakland 1, June 21, 1969, 10th
Texas 12, Oakland 0, July 3, 1983, 15th
NL—11—New York 8, Pittsburgh 3, June 15, 1929, 14th
New York 6, Brooklyn 5, Apr 24, 1955, 10th
New York 6, Chicago 5, June 30, 1979, 11th

**Most runs scored in 1st inning with none out**
AL—10—Boston vs Florida, June 27, 2003
NL—9—Philadelphia vs New York, Aug 13, 1948

**Most runs scored in any inning with none out**
NL—13—Chicago vs Detroit, Sept 6, 1883, 7th
AL—11—Detroit vs New York, June 17, 1925, 6th
NL since 1893—12—Brooklyn vs Philadelphia, May 24, 1953, 8th

**Most runs scored in any inning after two outs**
AL—13—Cleveland vs Boston, July 7, 1923, 1st game, 6th
Kansas City vs Chicago, Apr 21, 1956, 2nd
NL—12—Brooklyn vs Cincinnati, May 21, 1952, 1st
Brooklyn vs Cincinnati, Aug 8, 1954, 8th

**Most runs scored in any inning with none on base and two out**
NL—12—Brooklyn vs Cincinnati, Aug 8, 1954, 8th
AL—10—Chicago vs Detroit, Sept 2, 1959, 2nd game, 5th

**Most players scoring two or more runs in one inning**
NL—7—Chicago vs Detroit, Sept 6, 1883, 7th
NL since 1893—6—Brooklyn vs Cincinnati, May 21, 1952, 1st
Cincinnati vs Houston, Aug 3, 1989, 1st
AL—5—New York vs Washington, July 6, 1920, 5th
New York vs Boston, June 21, 1945, 5th
Boston vs Philadelphia, July 4, 1948, 7th
Cleveland vs Philadelphia, June 18, 1950, 2nd game, 1st
Boston vs Detroit, June 18, 1953, 7th
Boston vs Florida, June 27, 2003, 1st

**Clubs scoring in every inning of 9-inning game**
AA—9—Louisville vs Pittsburgh, Sept 22, 1882
Columbus vs Pittsburgh, June 14, 1883
Kansas City vs Brooklyn, May 20, 1889
NL—9—Cleveland vs Boston, Aug 15, 1889
NL since 1893—Washington vs Boston, June 22, 1894
Cleveland vs Philadelphia, July 12, 1894
Chicago vs Louisville, June 29, 1897
New York vs Philadelphia, June 1, 1923
St. Louis vs Chicago, Sept 13, 1964
Colorado vs Chicago, May 5, 1999
AL—8—Boston vs Cleveland, Sept 16, 1903, did not bat in 9th
Cleveland vs Boston, July 7, 1923, 1st game, did not bat in 9th
New York vs St. Louis, July 26, 1939, did not bat in 9th
Chicago vs Boston, May 11, 1949, did not bat in 9th
Kansas City vs Oakland, Sept 14, 1998, did not bat in 9th

**Most half-innings scored in by both clubs, 9-inning game**
NL—15—Philadelphia 8, Detroit 7, July 1, 1887
AA—15—Kansas City 9, Brooklyn 6, May 20, 1889
PL—15—New York 8, Chicago 7, May 23, 1890
NL since 1893—15—Washington 9, Boston 6, June 22, 1894
AL—14—Baltimore 8, Philadelphia 6, May 7, 1901
St. Louis 7, Detroit 7, Apr 23, 1927
Detroit 7, Chicago 7, July 2, 1940

**Most consecutive innings scoring runs**
AL—17—Boston, Sept 15 (last 3 inn), Sept 16 (8 inn), Sept 17 (first 6 inn), 1903, 3 G
NL—14—Pittsburgh, July 31 (last 5 inn), Aug 1 (8 inn), Aug 2 (1st inn), 1894, 3 G
New York, July 18 (last 3 innings), July 19 (8 inn), July 20 (first 3 inn), 1949, 3 G
Colorado, May 4 (last 4 inn), May 5 (9 inn), May 7 (1st inn), 1999, 3 G

## FIRST THROUGH 26TH INNINGS

**Most runs, 1st inning**
NL—16—Boston vs Baltimore, June 18, 1894, a.m. game
AL—14—Cleveland vs Philadelphia, June 18, 1950, 2nd game
Boston vs Florida NL, June 27, 2003

**Most runs by both clubs, 1st inning**
AA—19—Washington 14, Baltimore 5, June 17, 1891
AL—16—Oakland 13, California 3, July 5, 1996
NL—16—Boston 16, Baltimore 0, June 18, 1894, a.m. game

**Most runs, 2nd inning**
NL—13—Chicago vs Cincinnati, Aug 7, 1877
New York vs Cleveland, July 19, 1890, 1st game
NL since 1893—13—Atlanta vs Houston, Sept 20, 1972
San Diego vs Pittsburgh, May 31, 1994
AL—13—Kansas City vs Chicago, Apr 21, 1956
New York vs Tampa Bay, Apr 18, 2005

**Most runs by both clubs, 2nd inning**
AL—14—Philadelphia 10, Detroit 4, Sept 23, 1913
New York 11, Detroit 3, Aug 28, 1936, 2nd game
Chicago 8, Cleveland 6, Sept 2, 2001
NL—13—Chicago 13, Cincinnati 0, Aug 7, 1877
New York 13, Cleveland 0, July 19, 1890, 1st game
NL since 1983—13—Chicago 10, Philadelphia 3, Aug 25, 1922
Brooklyn 11, New York 2, Apr 29, 1930
Atlanta 13, Houston 0, Sept 20, 1972
San Diego 13, Pittsburgh 0, May 31, 1994

**Most runs, 3rd inning**
NL—14—Cleveland vs Washington, Aug 7, 1889
NL since 1893—13—San Francisco vs St. Louis, May 7, 1966
AL—12—New York vs Washington, Sept 11, 1949, 1st game

**Most runs by both clubs, 3rd inning**
NL—14—Cleveland 14, Washington 0, Aug 7, 1889
NL since 1893—13—San Francisco 13, St. Louis 0, May 7, 1966
St. Louis 7, Atlanta 6, Aug 21, 1973
AL—13—Boston 8, Detroit 5, July 2, 1995
ML—13—Cleveland AL 10, Arizona NL 3, June 15, 2005

**Most runs, 4th inning**
NL—15—Hartford vs New York, May 13, 1876
NL since 1893—14—Chicago vs Philadelphia, Aug 25, 1922
AL—13—Chicago vs Washington, Sept 26, 1943, 1st game

**Most runs by both clubs, 4th inning**
NL—15—Hartford 15, New York 0, May 13, 1876
NL since 1893—15—Chicago 14, Philadelphia 1, Aug 25, 1922
AL—14—Chicago 12, Philadelphia 2, June 10, 1952

**Most runs, 5th inning**
AL—14—New York vs Washington, July 6, 1920
NL—13—Chicago vs Pittsburgh, Aug 16, 1890
NL since 1893—12—New York vs Boston, Sept 3, 1926
Cincinnati vs Atlanta, Apr 25, 1977
Montreal vs Chicago, Sept 24, 1985

**Most runs by both clubs, 5th inning**
AL—18—Texas 10, Detroit 8, May 8, 2004
NL—16—Brooklyn 11, New York 5, June 3, 1890
NL since 1893—15—Brooklyn 10, Cincinnati 5, June 12, 1949
Philadelphia 9, Pittsburgh 6, Apr 16, 1953

**Most runs, 6th inning**
PL—14—Philadelphia vs Buffalo, June 26, 1890
AL—13—Cleveland vs Boston, July 7, 1923, 1st game
Detroit vs New York, June 17, 1925
NL—13—Montreal vs San Francisco, May 7, 1997

**Most runs by both clubs, 6th inning**
AL—15—Philadelphia 10, New York 5, Sept 5, 1912, 1st game
Detroit 10, Minnesota 5, June 13, 1967
NL—15—New York 10, Cincinnati 5, June 12, 1979

**Most runs, 7th inning**
NL—18—Chicago vs Detroit, Sept 6, 1883
NL since 1893—13—San Francisco vs San Diego, July 15, 1997
AL—17—Boston vs Detroit, June 18, 1953

**Most runs by both clubs, 7th inning**
NL—18—Chicago 18, Detroit 0, Sept 6, 1883
AL—17—Boston 17, Detroit 0, June 18, 1953

**Most runs, 8th inning**
AL—16—Texas vs Baltimore, Apr 19, 1996
NL—13—Brooklyn vs Cincinnati, Aug 8, 1954

**Most runs by both clubs, 8th inning**
AL—19—Cleveland 13, Boston 6, Apr 10, 1977
NL—14—New York 11, Pittsburgh 3, May 25, 1954
Brooklyn 13, Cincinnati 1, Aug 8, 1954
Atlanta 9, San Diego 5, Apr 27, 1975, 1st game
Colorado 8, Los Angeles 6, June 29, 1996

**Most runs, 9th inning**
NL—14—Baltimore vs Boston, Apr 24, 1894
AL—13—California vs Texas, Sept 14, 1978
Detroit vs Texas, Aug 8, 2001

**Most runs by both clubs, 9th inning**
NL—17—Boston 10, New York 7, June 20, 1912
AL—15—Toronto 11, Seattle 4, July 20, 1984

**Most runs in 9th inning after two out**
AL—9—Cleveland vs Washington, May 23, 1901 (won 14-13)
Boston vs Milwaukee, June 2, 1901 (won 13-2)
Cleveland vs New York, Aug 4, 1929, 2nd game (won 14-6)
NL—7—Chicago vs Cincinnati, June 29, 1952, 1st game (won 9-8)
San Francisco vs Pittsburgh, May 1, 1973 (won 8-7)
Pittsburgh vs Houston, July 28, 2001, a.m. game (won 9-8)

**Most runs in 9th inning with none on base and two out**
AL—9—Cleveland vs Washington, May 23, 1901 (won 14-13)
Boston vs Milwaukee, June 2, 1901 (won 13-2)
NL—7—Chicago vs Cincinnati, June 29, 1952, 1st game (won 9-8)
Pittsburgh vs Houston, July 28, 2001, a.m. game (won 9-8)

**inning**

ta vs Oakland, June 21, 1969
n vs New York, June 17, 1887, a.m. game
893—9—Cincinnati vs Philadelphia, Aug 24, 1947, 1st game
Diego vs Philadelphia, May 28, 1995

**Most runs by both clubs, 10th inning**

AL—12—Minnesota 11, Oakland 1, June 21, 1969
NL—11—New York 6, Brooklyn 5, Apr 24, 1955

**Most runs, 11th inning**

NL—10—Kansas City vs Detroit, July 21, 1886
NL since 1893—9—San Diego vs Colorado, June 28, 1994, 2nd game
AL—8—Philadelphia vs Detroit, May 1, 1951
Texas vs Seattle, Sept 23, 1991
Seattle vs Kansas City, Sept 8, 2002

**Most runs by both clubs, 11th inning**

AL—11—Seattle 6, Boston 5, May 16, 1969
NL—11—New York 6, Chicago 5, June 30, 1979
Pittsburgh 6, Chicago 5, Apr 21, 1991

**Most runs, 12th inning**

AL—11—New York vs Detroit, July 26, 1928, 1st game
NL—9—Chicago vs Pittsburgh, July 23, 1923

**Most runs by both clubs, 12th inning**

AL—11—New York 8, Detroit 3, May 14, 1923
New York 11, Detroit 0, July 26, 1928, 1st game
NL—9—Chicago 9, Pittsburgh 0, July 23, 1923
New York 8, Brooklyn 1, May 30, 1940, 2nd game
Houston 8, Cincinnati 1, June 2, 1966
San Diego 5, Houston 4, July 5, 1969

**Most runs, 13th inning**

NL—10—Cincinnati vs Brooklyn, May 15, 1919
AL—9—Cleveland vs Detroit, Aug 5, 1933, 1st game

**Most runs, 14th inning**

NL—8—New York vs Pittsburgh, June 15, 1929
AL—7—Cleveland vs St. Louis, June 3, 1935
Detroit vs Milwaukee, May 27, 1991

**Most runs, 15th inning**

AL—12—Texas vs Oakland, July 3, 1983
NL—7—St. Louis vs Boston, Sept 28, 1928

**Most runs, 16th inning**

AL—8—Chicago vs Washington, May 20, 1920
NL—5—Cincinnati vs New York, Aug 20, 1973
Houston vs Cincinnati, Apr 8, 1988

**Most runs, 17th inning**

NL—7—New York vs Pittsburgh, July 16, 1920
AL—6—New York vs Detroit, July 20, 1941

**Most runs, 18th inning**

NL—5—Chicago vs Boston, May 14, 1927
AL—4—Minnesota vs Seattle, July 19, 1969

**Most runs, 19th inning**

NL—5—New York vs Atlanta, July 4, 1985
AL—4—Cleveland vs Detroit, Apr 27, 1984

**Most runs by both clubs, 19th inning**

NL—7—New York 5, Atlanta 2, July 4, 1985
AL—5—Chicago 3, Boston 2, July 13, 1951

**Most runs, 20th inning**

NL—4—Brooklyn vs Boston, July 5, 1940
AL—3—Boston vs Seattle, July 27, 1969
Washington vs Cleveland, Sept 14, 2nd game, finished Sept 20, 1971

**Most runs by both clubs, 20th inning**

NL—4—Brooklyn 4, Boston 0, July 5, 1940
AL—4—Boston 3, Seattle 1, July 27, 1969
Washington 3, Cleveland 1, Sept 14, 2nd game, finished Sept 20, 1971

**Most runs, 21st inning**

AL—4—Chicago vs Cleveland, May 26, finished 28, 1973
NL—3—San Diego vs Montreal, May 21, 1977

**Most runs by both clubs, 21st inning**

AL—6—Milwaukee 3, Chicago 3, May 8, finished May 9, 1984
NL—3—San Diego 3, Montreal 0, May 21, 1977

**Most runs, 22nd inning**

AL—2—New York vs Detroit, June 24, 1962
NL—1—Brooklyn vs Pittsburgh, Aug 22, 1917
Chicago vs Boston, May 17, 1927

**Most runs, 23rd inning**

NL—2—San Francisco vs New York, May 31, 1964, 2nd game
AL—0—Boston vs Philadelphia, Sept 1, 1906
Philadelphia vs Boston, Sept 1, 1906
Detroit vs Philadelphia, July 21, 1945
Philadelphia vs Detroit, July 21, 1945

**Most runs, 24th inning**

AL—3—Philadelphia vs Boston, Sept 1, 1906
NL—1—Houston vs New York, Apr 15, 1968

**Most runs, 25th inning**

NL—1—St. Louis vs New York, Sept 11, 1974
AL—1—Chicago vs Milwaukee, May 8, finished May 9, 1984

**Most runs, 26th inning**

NL—0—Boston vs Brooklyn, May 1, 1920
Brooklyn vs Boston, May 1, 1920
AL—none

## GAMES BEING SHUT OUT

**Most games shut out, season**

NL—33—St. Louis, 1908
AL—30—Washington, 1909 (includes 1 tie)

**Most consecutive games shut out, season**

AL—4—Boston, Aug 2 through 6, 1906
Philadelphia, Sept 23 through 25, 1906
St. Louis, Aug 25 through 30, 1913
Washington, Sept 19, 20, 21, 22, 1958
Washington, Sept 1, 2, 4, 5, 1964
NL—4—Boston, May 19 through 23, 1906
Cincinnati, July 30 through Aug 3, 1908
Cincinnati, July 31 through Aug 3, 1931
Houston, June 20, 21, 22, 23, 1st game, 1963
Houston, Sept 9, 10, 11, 11, 1966
Chicago, June 16, 16, 19, 20, 1968

**Most consecutive innings shut out by opponent, season**

AL—48—Philadelphia, Sept 22 (last 7 inn)-Sept 26 (first 5 inn), 1906
NL—48—Chicago, June 15 (last 8 inn)-June 21 (first 2 inn), 1968

**Longest extra-inning game without a run**

NL—24 inn—New York vs Houston, Apr 15, 1968
AL—20 inn—California vs Oakland, July 9, 1971

**Most consecutive games without being shut out, league**

AL—308—New York, Aug 3, 1931-Aug 2, 1933
NL—208—Cincinnati, Apr 3, 2000-May 23, 2001

**Fewest games shut out, season (150 or more games)**

AL—0—New York, 156 games, 1932
NL—0—Cincinnati, 163 games, 2000

# HITS

## SEASON

**Most hits, season**

NL—1,783—Philadelphia, 156 G, 1930
AL—1,724—Detroit, 154 G, 1921

**Fewest hits, season**

NL—1,044—Brooklyn, 154 G, 1908
AL—1,061—Chicago, 156 G, 1910

**Most players with 200 or more hits, season**

NL—4—Philadelphia, 1929
AL—4—Detroit, 1937

**Most players with 100 or more hits, season**

NL—9—Pittsburgh, 1921, 1972, 1976; Philadelphia, 1923; New York, 1928; St. Louis, 1979; Arizona, 2001; Florida, 2001; San Francisco, 2004; Florida, 2005
AL—10—Detroit, 2004

**Fewest players with 100 or more hits, season**

NL—0—New York, 1972
AL—2—Washington, 1965

## GAME

**Most hits, game**

NL—36—Philadelphia vs Louisville, Aug 17, 1894
AL—31—Milwaukee vs Toronto, Aug 28, 1992
[33—Cleveland vs Philadelphia, July 10, 1932, 18 inn]

**Most hits by both clubs, game**

NL—51—Philadelphia 26, Chicago 25, Aug 25, 1922
[52—New York 28, Pittsburgh 24, June 15, 1929, 14 inn]
AL—45—Philadelphia 27, Boston 18, July 8, 1902
Detroit 28, New York 17, Sept 29, 1928
[58—Cleveland 33, Philadelphia 25, July 10, 1932, 18 inn]

**Most hits by pinch-hitters, game**

NL—6—Brooklyn vs Philadelphia, Sept 9, 1926
AL—4—many clubs

**Most hits in shutout loss**

NL—14—New York vs Chicago, Sept 14, 1913 (15 TB; lost 7-0)
[15—Boston vs Pittsburgh, July 10, 1901 (16 TB; lost 1-0), 12 inn
Boston vs Pittsburgh, Aug 1, 1918 (15 TB; lost 2-0), 21 inn]
AL—14—Cleveland vs Washington, July 10, 1928, 2nd game (16 TB; lost 9-0)
[15—Boston vs Washington, July 3, 1913 (19 TB; lost 1-0), 15 inn]

**Most consecutive hits, game**

NL—12—St. Louis vs Boston, Sept 17, 1920, 4th and 5th inn
Brooklyn vs Pittsburgh, June 23, 1930, 6th and 7th inn
AL—10—Boston vs Milwaukee, June 2, 1901, 9th
Detroit vs Baltimore, Sept 20, 1983, 1st (1 BB during streak)
Toronto vs Minnesota, Sept 4, 1992, 2nd

**Fewest hits, extra-inning game**
AA—0—Toledo vs Brooklyn, October 4, 1884, 10 inn
NL—0—Philadelphia vs New York, July 4, 1908, a.m. game, 10 inn
Chicago vs Cincinnati, May 2, 1917, 10 inn
Chicago vs Cincinnati, Aug 19, 1965, 1st game, 10 inn
AL—1—Cleveland vs Chicago, Sept 6, 1903, 10 inn
Boston vs St. Louis, Sept 18, 1934, 10 inn
Los Angeles vs New York, May 22, 1962, 12 inn

**Fewest hits by both clubs, game**
NL—1—Los Angeles 1, Chicago 0, Sept 9, 1965
AA—2—Philadelphia 1, Baltimore 1, Aug 20, 1886
AL—2—Cleveland 1, Washington 1, July 27, 1915
Cleveland 1, St. Louis 1, Apr 23, 1952
Chicago 1, Baltimore 1, June 21, 1956
Baltimore 1, Kansas City 1, Sept 12, 1964
Baltimore 2, Detroit 0, Apr 30, 1967, 1st game

**Most games held hitless, season**
AA—2—Pittsburgh 1884
NL—2—Providence 1885; Boston 1898; Philadelphia 1960; Chicago 1965; Cincinnati 1971; Colorado 1996; San Diego 2001
AL—2—Chicago 1917; Philadelphia 1923; Detroit 1967, 1973; California 1977

**Most consecutive seasons without being held hitless in a game**
AL—44—New York, 1959-2002
NL—40—St. Louis, 1920-1959

**Most players with six hits, game**
AA—2—Cincinnati vs Pittsburgh, Sept 12, 1883
NL—2—Baltimore vs St. Louis, Sept 3, 1897
AL—1—many clubs

**Most players with five or more hits, game**
NL—4—Philadelphia vs Louisville, Aug 17, 1894
AL—3—Detroit vs Washington, July 30, 1917
Chicago vs Philadelphia, Sept 11, 1936
[3—Cleveland vs Philadelphia, July 10, 1932, 18 inn
Washington vs Cleveland, May 16, 1933, 12 inn]

**Most players for both clubs with five or more hits, game**
NL—4—Philadelphia 4, Louisville 0, Aug 17, 1894
AL—3—Detroit 3, Washington 0, July 30, 1917
Chicago 3, Philadelphia 0, Sept 11, 1936
[5—Cleveland 3, Philadelphia 2, July 10, 1932, 18 inn]

**Most players with four or more hits, game**
NL—7—Chicago vs Cleveland, July 24, 1882
NL since 1893—5—San Francisco vs Los Angeles, May 13, 1958
AL—4—Detroit vs New York, Sept 29, 1928
Chicago vs Philadelphia, Sept 11, 1936
Boston vs St. Louis, June 8, 1950
Milwaukee vs Toronto, Aug 28, 1992
Minnesota vs Cleveland, June 4, 2002
Boston vs Tampa Bay, Sept 20, 2005

**Most players for both clubs with four or more hits, game**
NL—7—Chicago 7, Cleveland 0, July 24, 1882
NL since 1893—5—St. Louis 4, Philadelphia 1, July 6, 1929, 2nd game
San Francisco 5, Los Angeles 0, May 13, 1958
AL—4—Detroit 4, New York 0, Sept 29, 1928
Chicago 4, Philadelphia 0, Sept 11, 1936
Boston 4, St. Louis 0, June 8, 1950
Milwaukee 4, Toronto 0, Aug 28, 1992

**Most players with three or more hits, game**
NL—8—Chicago vs Detroit, Sept 6, 1883
NL since 1893—7—Cincinnati vs Philadelphia, May 13, 1902
Pittsburgh vs Philadelphia, June 12, 1928
Cincinnati vs Houston, Aug 3, 1989
Cincinnati vs Colorado, May 19, 1999
AL—7—New York vs Philadelphia, June 28, 1939, 1st game
Chicago vs Kansas City, Apr 23, 1955

**Most players with two or more hits, game**
AA—10—Brooklyn vs Philadelphia, June 25, 1885
NL—10—Pittsburgh vs Philadelphia, Aug 7, 1922
New York vs Philadelphia, Sept 2, 1925, 2nd game
AL—9—many clubs

**Most players with one or more hits, game**
NL—14—San Francisco vs San Diego, June 23, 1986
Chicago vs Colorado, Aug 18, 1995
Florida vs Atlanta, Sept 24, 1996
AL—14—Cleveland vs St. Louis, Aug 12, 1948, 2nd game

**Most players for both clubs with one or more hits, game**
NL—23—St. Louis 13, Philadelphia 10, May 11, 1923
AL—22—New York 12, Cleveland 10, July 18, 1934

**Most consecutive games with each player collecting one or more hits (including pitchers and substitutes)**
NL—5—Pittsburgh, Aug 5, 7, 8, 8, 10, 1922

## DOUBLEHEADER AND CONSECUTIVE GAMES

**Most hits, doubleheader**
NL—46—Pittsburgh vs Philadelphia, Aug 8, 1922
AL—43—New York vs Philadelphia, June 28, 1939

**Most hits by both clubs, doubleheader**
NL—73—Washington 41, Philadelphia 32, July 4, 1896
St. Louis 43, Philadelphia 30, July 6, 1929
AL—65—Boston 35, Philadelphia 30, July 4, 1939
[65—Baltimore 35, Kansas City 30, June 23, 1991, 1st game 10 inn, 2nd game 12 inn]

**Fewest hits, doubleheader**
AL—2—Cleveland vs Boston, Apr 12, 1992
NL—3—Brooklyn vs St. Louis, Sept 21, 1934
New York vs Philadelphia, June 21, 1964

## INNING

**Most hits, inning**
NL—18—Chicago vs Detroit, Sept 6, 1883, 7th
NL since 1893—16—Cincinnati vs Houston, Aug 3, 1989, 1st
AL—14—Boston vs Detroit, June 18, 1953, 7th

**Most hits by pinch-hitters, inning**
NL—4—Chicago vs Brooklyn, May 21, 1927, 2nd game, 9th
Philadelphia vs Pittsburgh, Sept 12, 1974, 8th
AL—4—Philadelphia vs Detroit, Sept 18, 1940, 2nd game, 9th
Texas vs Kansas City, June 8, 1995, 8th
Boston vs New York, Sept 8, 1995, 8th

**Most consecutive hits, inning**
NL—10—St. Louis vs Boston, Sept 17, 1920, 4th
St. Louis vs Philadelphia, June 12, 1922, 6th
Chicago vs Boston, Sept 7, 1929, 1st game, 4th
Brooklyn vs Pittsburgh, June 23, 1930, 6th
AL—10—Boston vs Milwaukee, June 2, 1901, 9th
Detroit vs Baltimore, Sept 20, 1983, 1st (1 BB during streak)
Toronto vs Minnesota, Sept 4, 1992, 2nd
Kansas City vs Detroit, Sept 9, 2004, 3rd

**Most hits by consecutive pinch-hitters, inning**
NL—3—many clubs; last—Pittsburgh vs San Francisco, July 2, 1961, 1st game, 8th
AL—3—many clubs; last—Boston vs New York, Sept 8, 1995, 8th

**Most consecutive hits before first out of game**
NL—8—Philadelphia vs Chicago, Aug 5, 1975 (4 singles, 2 doubles, 2 HR)
Pittsburgh vs Atlanta, Aug 26, 1975 (7 singles, 1 triple)
AL—8—Oakland vs Chicago, Sept 27, 1981, 1st game (8 singles)
New York vs Baltimore, Sept 25, 1990 (6 singles, 2 HR)

**Most batters reaching first base safely, inning**
AL—20—Boston vs Detroit, June 18, 1953, 7th
NL—20—Chicago vs Detroit, Sept 6, 1883, 7th
NL since 1893—19—Brooklyn vs Cincinnati, May 21, 1952, 1st

**Most consecutive batters reaching base safely, inning**
NL—19—Brooklyn vs Cincinnati, May 21, 1952, 1st
AL—13—Kansas City vs Chicago, Apr 21, 1956, 2nd
Kansas City vs Detroit, Sept 9, 2004, 3rd

**Most batters reaching base safely three times, inning**
NL—3—Chicago vs Detroit, Sept 6, 1883, 7th
NL since 1893—3—Boston vs Baltimore, June 18, 1894, a.m. game, 1st
AL—3—Boston vs Detroit, June 18, 1953, 7th

**Most players making two or more hits, inning**
NL—7—Cincinnati vs Houston, Aug 3, 1989, 1st
AL—5—Philadelphia vs Boston, July 8, 1902, 6th
New York vs Philadelphia, Sept 10, 1921, 9th

## SINGLES

**Most singles, season**
NL—1,338—Philadelphia, 132 G, 1894
AL—1,298—Detroit, 154 G, 1921
NL since 1900—1,297—Pittsburgh, 155 G, 1922

**Fewest singles, season**
AL—811—Baltimore, 162 G, 1968
NL—843—New York, 156 G, 1972

**Most singles, game**
NL—28—Philadelphia vs Louisville, Aug 17, 1894
Boston vs Baltimore, Apr 20, 1896
AL—26—Milwaukee vs Toronto, Aug 28, 1992

**Most singles by both clubs, game**
NL—37—Baltimore 21, Washington 16, Aug 8, 1896
[37—Los Angeles 19, New York 18, May 24, 1973, 19 inn]
AL—36—Chicago 21, Boston 15, Aug 15, 1922
[42—Oakland 25, Texas 17, July 1, 1979, 15 inn]

**Most singles, inning**
NL—12—Cincinnati vs Houston, Aug 3, 1989, 1st
AL—11—Boston vs Detroit, June 18, 1953, 7th

**Most consecutive singles, inning**
NL—10—St. Louis vs Boston, Sept 17, 1920, 4th
AL—8—Washington vs Cleveland, May 7, 1951, 4th
Oakland vs Chicago, Sept 27, 1981, 1st game, 1st
Baltimore vs Texas, May 18, 1990, 1st

## DOUBLES

**Most doubles, season**
NL—373—St. Louis, 154 G, 1930
AL—373—Boston, 162 G, 1997
Boston, 162 G, 2004

**Fewest doubles, season**
NL—110—Brooklyn, 154 G, 1908
AL—116—Chicago, 156 G, 1910

**Most doubles, game**
NL—14—Chicago vs Buffalo, July 3, 1883
NL since 1893—13—St. Louis vs Chicago, July 12, 1931, 2nd game
AL—12—Boston vs Detroit, July 29, 1990
Cleveland vs Minnesota, July 13, 1996

**Most doubles by both clubs, game**
NL—23—St. Louis 13, Chicago 10, July 12, 1931, 2nd game
AL—19—Kansas City 11, New York 8, Aug 11, 2003

**Most doubles, doubleheader**
NL—17—St. Louis vs Chicago, July 12, 1931
AL—14—Philadelphia vs Boston, July 8, 1905

**Most doubles by both clubs, doubleheader**
NL—32—St. Louis 17, Chicago 15, July 12, 1931
AL—26—Philadelphia 14, Boston 12, July 8, 1905

**Most doubles, inning**
NL—7—Boston vs St. Louis, Aug 25, 1936, 1st game, 1st
AL—6—Washington vs Boston, June 9, 1934, 8th
Texas vs New York, July 31, 2002, 2nd

**Most consecutive doubles, inning**
AL—5—Washington vs Boston, June 9, 1934, 8th
NL—4—many clubs; last—Philadelphia vs Cincinnati, May 4, 2000, 1st

## TRIPLES

**Most triples, season**
NL—153—Baltimore, 129 G, 1894
AL—112—Baltimore, 134 G, 1901
Boston, 141 G, 1903

**Fewest triples, season**
AL—11—Baltimore, 162 G, 1998
NL—14—Los Angeles, 162 G, 1986
New York, 163 G, 1999

**Most triples, game**
NL—9—Baltimore vs Cleveland, Sept 3, 1894, 1st game
AL—6—Chicago vs Milwaukee, Sept 15, 1901, 2nd game
Philadelphia vs Detroit, May 18, 1912
Chicago vs New York, Sept 17, 1920
Detroit vs New York, June 17, 1922

**Most triples by both clubs, game**
NL—11—Baltimore 9, Cleveland 2, Sept 3, 1894, 1st game
AL—9—Detroit 6, New York 3, June 17, 1922

**Most triples, doubleheader**
NL—9—Baltimore vs Cleveland, Sept 3, 1894
Cincinnati vs Chicago, May 27, 1922
AL—9—Chicago vs Milwaukee, Sept 15, 1901

**Most triples by both clubs, doubleheader**
AL—12—Detroit 7, St. Louis 5, July 4, 1907
NL—11—Baltimore 9, Cleveland 2, Sept 3, 1894

**Most triples, inning**
AL—5—Chicago vs Milwaukee, Sept 15, 1901, 2nd game, 8th
NL—4—many times; last—New York vs Pittsburgh, July 17, 1936, 1st

**Most consecutive triples, inning**
AL—4—Boston vs Detroit, May 6, 1934, 4th
NL—3—many times; last—Montreal vs San Diego, May 6, 1981, 9th

## HOME RUNS

### SEASON AND MONTH

**Most home runs, season**
AL—264—Seattle, 162 G, 1997 (131 at home, 133 on road)
NL—249—Houston, 162 G, 2000 (135 at home, 114 on road)

**For a complete list of home runs by club each year beginning in 1901, see page 123.**

**Fewest home runs, season**
NL—9—Pittsburgh, 157 G, 1917
AL—3—Chicago, 156 G, 1908

**Most home runs by pinch-hitters, season**
NL—14—Arizona, 2001
San Francisco, 2001
AL—11—Baltimore, 1982

**Most home runs at home, season**
AL—153—Texas, 2005, 81 G
NL—149—Colorado, 1996, 81 G

**Most home runs on road, season**
NL—138—San Francisco, 2001, 81 G
AL—136—Baltimore, 1996, 81 G

**Most home runs against one club, season**
AL—48—New York vs Kansas City, 1956
NL—44—Cincinnati vs Brooklyn, 1956

**Most years leading league in home runs**
AL—35—New York
NL since 1893—28—New York (24)/San Francisco (4)

**Most consecutive years leading league or tied in home runs**
AL—12—New York, 1936-1947
NL—7—Brooklyn, 1949-1955 (1954 tied)

**Most years with 200 or more home runs**
AL—8—New York, 1961 (240), 1998 (207), 2000 (205), 2001 (203), 2002 (223), 2003 (230), 2004 (242), 2005 (229)
NL—6—Colorado, 1995 (200), 1996 (221), 1997 (239), 1999 (223), 2001 (213), 2004 (202)

**Most consecutive years with 200 or more home runs**
AL—6—New York, 2000 (205), 2001 (203), 2002 (223), 2003 (230), 2004 (242), 2005 (229)
NL—3—Colorado, 1995 (200), 1996 (221), 1997 (239)

**Most years with 100 or more home runs**
AL—80—New York
NL since 1893—69—New York (26)/San Francisco (43)

**Most consecutive years with 100 or more home runs**
AL—35—Boston, 1946 through 1980
NL—29—New York, 1945-1957/San Francisco, 1958-1973
Cincinnati, 1952-1980

**Most home runs by two players, season**
AL—115—New York, 1961 (Maris 61, Mantle 54)
NL—110—San Francisco, 2001 (Bonds 73, Aurilia 37)

**Most home runs by three players, season**
AL—143—New York, 1961 (Maris 61, Mantle 54, Skowron 28)
NL—132—San Francisco, 2001 (Bonds 73, Aurilia 37, Kent 22)

**Most players with 50 or more home runs, season**
AL—2—New York, 1961 (Maris 61, Mantle 54)
NL—1—many clubs

**Most players with 40 or more home runs, season**
NL—3—Atlanta, 1973 (Johnson 43, Evans 41, Aaron 40)
Colorado, 1996 (Galarraga 47, Burks 40, Castilla 40)
Colorado, 1997 (Walker 49, Galarraga 41, Castilla 40)
AL—2—New York, 1927 (Ruth 60, Gehrig 47)
New York, 1930 (Ruth 49, Gehrig 41)
New York, 1931 (Ruth 46, Gehrig 46)
New York, 1961 (Maris 61, Mantle 54)
Detroit, 1961 (Colavito 45, Cash 41)
Boston, 1969 (Petrocelli 40, Yastrzemski 40)
Seattle, 1996 (Griffey 49, Buhner 44)
Seattle, 1997 (Griffey 56, Buhner 40)
Seattle, 1998 (Griffey 56, Rodriguez 42)
Seattle, 1999 (Griffey 48, Rodriguez 42)
Toronto, 1999 (Delgado 44, Green 42)
Toronto, 2000 (Delgado 41, Batista 41)
Texas, 2001 (A. Rodriguez 52, Palmeiro 47)
Texas, 2002 (A. Rodriguez 57, Palmeiro 43)

**Most players with 30 or more home runs, season**
NL—4—Los Angeles, 1977, 1997
Colorado, 1995, 1996, 1997, 1999
Atlanta, 1998
Chicago, 2004
AL—4—Anaheim, 2000
Toronto, 2000

**Most players with 20 or more home runs, season**
AL—7—Baltimore, 1996
Toronto, 2000
NL—6—Milwaukee, 1965

**Most home runs, one month**
AL—58—Baltimore, May 1987
NL—55—New York, July 1947
St. Louis, Apr 2000
Atlanta, May 2003

**Most times with five or more home runs in game, season**
AL—8—Boston, 1977
NL—6—New York, 1947

**Most players with three or more home runs in game, season**
NL—4—Brooklyn, 1950 (Snider, Campanella, Hodges, Brown)
Cincinnati, 1956 (Bell, Bailey, Kluszewski, Thurman)
Milwaukee, 2001 (Burnitz 2, Jenkins, Sexson)
AL—3—Cleveland, 1987 (Snyder, Carter, Jacoby)
Oakland, 1996 (Berroa 2, Young)

Seattle, 1996 (Wilson, Griffey, Martinez)

**Most times with two or more homers by one player in a game, season**
AL—24—New York, 1961
NL—24—Atlanta, 1966

## GAME

**Most home runs, game**
AL—10—Toronto vs Baltimore, Sept 14, 1987
NL—9—Cincinnati vs Philadelphia, Sept 4, 1999

**Most home runs by both clubs, game**
AL—12—Detroit 7, Chicago 5, May 28, 1995
Detroit 6, Chicago 6, July 2, 2002
NL—11—Chicago 7, New York 4, June 11, 1967, 2nd game
[11—Pittsburgh 6, Cincinnati 5, Aug 12, 1966, 13 inn
Chicago 6, Cincinnati 5, July 28, 1977, 13 inn
Chicago 6, Philadelphia 5, May 17, 1979, 10 inn]

**Most home runs, night game**
AL—10—Toronto vs Baltimore, Sept 14, 1987
NL—9—Cincinnati vs Philadelphia, Sept 4, 1999

**Most home runs by both clubs, night game**
AL—11—New York 6, Detroit 5, June 23, 1950
Toronto 10, Baltimore 1, Sept 14, 1987
Cleveland 8, Milwaukee 3, Apr 25, 1997
NL—10—Cincinnati 8, Milwaukee 2, Aug 18, 1956
Cincinnati 7, Atlanta 3, Apr 21, 1970
Cincinnati 9, Philadelphia 1, Sept 4, 1999

**Most home runs by pinch-hitters, game**
AL-NL—2—many clubs

**Most home runs by pinch-hitters for both clubs, game**
NL—3—Philadelphia 2, St. Louis 1, June 2, 1928
St. Louis 2, Brooklyn 1, July 21, 1930, 1st game
AL—2—many times; last—Cleveland 1, Minnesota 1, May 7, 1989, 1st game; New York 1, Chicago 1, June 22, 1989

**Most home runs, opening game of season**
NL—6—New York vs Montreal, Apr 4, 1988
AL—5—New York vs Philadelphia, Apr 12, 1932
Boston vs Washington, Apr 12, 1965
Milwaukee vs Boston, Apr 10, 1980
Cleveland vs Texas, Apr 27, 1995 (not Texas' opener)
Minnesota vs Kansas City, Apr 1, 2002

**Most home runs by both clubs, opening game of season**
AL—7—New York 5, Philadelphia 2, Apr 12, 1932
Boston 5, Washington 2, Apr 12, 1965
Milwaukee 5, Boston 2, Apr 10, 1980
Cleveland 5, Texas 2, Apr 27, 1995 (not Texas' opener)
Milwaukee 4, California 3, Apr 2, 1996
NL—7—New York 6, Montreal 1, Apr 4, 1988
Atlanta 4, Chicago 3, Apr 5, 1988
Atlanta 5, San Francisco 2, Apr 2, 1996

**Most home runs by first-game players for both clubs, game**
NL—2—Brooklyn 1 (Ernie Koy), Philadelphia 1 (Emmett Mueller), Apr 19, 1938 (each in 1st)

**Most runs, all scoring on solo home runs, club, game**
AL—6—Oakland vs Minnesota, Aug 3, 1991
NL—5—New York vs Chicago, June 16, 1930
St. Louis vs Brooklyn, Sept 1, 1953
Cincinnati vs Milwaukee, Apr 16, 1955
Chicago vs Pittsburgh, Apr 21, 1964
Pittsburgh vs Los Angeles, May 7, 1973
Colorado vs San Francisco, May 9, 1994
Atlanta vs Colorado, Apr 19, 1998, 1st game

**Most runs, all scoring on solo home runs, both clubs, game**
ML—5—Baltimore AL 3, Atlanta NL 2, June 5, 1998
NL—5—San Francisco 3, Milwaukee 2, Aug 30, 1962
Montreal 3, San Diego 2, May 16, 1986
AL—4—Cleveland 4, New York 0, Aug 2, 1956
New York 4, Baltimore 0, May 13, 1973, 1st game

**Most runs, all scoring on solo home runs, shutout game**
AL—4—Cleveland vs New York, Aug 2, 1956
New York vs Baltimore, May 13, 1973, 1st game
NL—3—St. Louis vs New York, July 19, 1923
Philadelphia vs Cincinnati, Aug 27, 1951, 2nd game
San Francisco vs Milwaukee, Aug 14, 1964
Cincinnati vs Pittsburgh, Sept 25, 1968
New York vs Philadelphia, June 29, 1971
New York vs Pittsburgh, Sept 17, 1971
New York vs Cincinnati, Aug 29, 1972
San Francisco vs Philadelphia, Sept 4, 2000

**Most home runs with none on bases, game**
AL—7—Boston vs Toronto, July 4, 1977 (8 HR by Boston)
NL—6—New York vs Philadelphia, Aug 13, 1939, 1st game (7 HR by New York)
New York vs Cincinnati, June 24, 1950 (7 HR by New York)
Atlanta vs Chicago, Aug 3, 1967 (7 HR by Atlanta)
Chicago vs San Diego, Aug 19, 1970 (7 HR by Chicago)

**Most home runs with none on bases, by both clubs, game**
AL—10—Detroit 5, Chicago 5, May 28, 1995
NL—7—Chicago 6, San Diego 1, Aug 19, 1970
Pittsburgh 4, Cincinnati 3, June 7, 1976
Philadelphia 5, Colorado 2, May 8, 1999

**Most players with three or more home runs, game**
NL—2—Milwaukee vs Arizona, Sept 25, 2001
AL—1—many clubs

**Most players with three or more home runs by both clubs, game**
NL—2—Milwaukee 2, Arizona 0, Sept 25, 2001
AL—1—many games

**Most players with two or more home runs, game**
NL—3—Pittsburgh vs St. Louis, Aug 16, 1947
New York vs Pittsburgh, July 8, 1956, 1st game
Cincinnati vs Milwaukee, Aug 18, 1956
Philadelphia vs New York, Sept 8, 1998
Colorado vs Montreal, Aug 14, 1999
Houston vs Chicago, Sept 9, 2000
San Francisco vs Colorado, July 2, 2002
[3—Chicago vs St. Louis, Apr 16, 1955, 14 inn]
AL—3—Boston vs St. Louis, June 8, 1950
New York vs Boston, May 30, 1961
Toronto vs Baltimore, Sept 14, 1987
Toronto vs California, July 14, 1990
Detroit vs Chicago, May 28, 1995
Seattle vs Milwaukee, July 31, 1996
Anaheim vs Tampa Bay, Apr 21, 2000
Minnesota vs Milwaukee NL, July 12, 2001

**Most players with two or more homers by both clubs, game**
NL—4—Pittsburgh 3, St. Louis 1, Aug 16, 1947
Colorado 3, Montreal 1, Aug 14, 1999
AL—4—Detroit 3, Chicago 1, May 28, 1995

**Most players with one or more home runs, game**
NL—8—Cincinnati vs Philadelphia, Sept 4, 1999 (9 HR by Cincinnati)
AL—7—Baltimore vs Boston, May 17, 1967 (7 HR by Baltimore)
Oakland vs California, June 27, 1996 (8 HR by Oakland)
Detroit vs Toronto, June 20, 2000 (8 HR by Detroit)

**Most players with one or more home runs by both clubs, game**
NL—9—New York 5, Brooklyn 4, Sept 2, 1939, 1st game
New York 6, Pittsburgh 3, July 11, 1954, 1st game
Chicago 5, Pittsburgh 4, Apr 21, 1964
Cincinnati 6, Atlanta 3, Apr 21, 1970
Los Angeles 5, Atlanta 4, Apr 24, 1977
Cincinnati 8, Philadelphia 1, Sept 4, 1999
[9—Cincinnati 5, Chicago 4, July 28, 1977, 13 inn]
AL—9—New York 5, Detroit 4, June 23, 1950
Minnesota 5, Boston 4, May 25, 1965
Baltimore 7, Boston 2, May 17, 1967
California 5, Cleveland 4, Aug 30, 1970
Boston 5, Milwaukee 4, May 22, 1977, 1st game
California 5, Oakland 4, Apr 23, 1985
Detroit 7, Toronto 2, June 20, 2000
Detroit 5, Chicago 4, July 2, 2002

**Longest extra-inning game without a home run by either club**
NL—26 inn—Boston 0, Brooklyn 0, May 1, 1920
AL—24 inn—Boston 0, Philadelphia 0, Sept 1, 1906
Detroit 0, Philadelphia 0, July 21, 1945

## DOUBLEHEADER AND CONSECUTIVE GAMES

**Most home runs, doubleheader**
AL—13—New York vs Philadelphia, June 28, 1939
NL—12—Milwaukee vs Pittsburgh, Aug 30, 1953

**Most home runs by both clubs, doubleheader**
NL—15—Milwaukee 9, Chicago 6, May 30, 1956
AL—14—New York 9, Philadelphia 5, May 22, 1930
[14—Chicago 7, Texas 7, Aug 28, 1998, 1st game 10 inn]

**Most home runs by pinch-hitters, doubleheader**
NL—3—Montreal vs Atlanta, July 13, 1973
AL—2—many doubleheaders

**Most home runs by pinch-hitters for both clubs, doubleheader**
NL—4—St. Louis 2, Brooklyn 2, July 21, 1930
AL—2—many doubleheaders

**Most consecutive games with one or more home runs**
AL—27—Texas, Aug 11-Sept 9, 2002 (55 HR)
NL—25—Atlanta, Apr 18-May 13, 1998 (45 HR)

**Most home runs in consecutive games in which homers were hit**
AL—55—Texas, Aug 11-Sept 9, 2002 (27 G)
NL—45—Atlanta, Apr 18-May 13, 1998 (25 G)

**Most consecutive games with one or more homers, start of season**
NL—13—Chicago, Apr 13-May 2 (2nd game), 1954 (28 HR)
AL—10—New York, Apr 5-16, 1999 (16 HR)

**Most consecutive games with two or more home runs, season**
AL—9—Cleveland, May 13 (1st game)-21, 1962 (28 HR)
Baltimore, May 8-16, 1987 (29 HR)
Baltimore, Aug 3-11, 1996 (23 HR)
NL—8—Milwaukee, July 19-26, 1956 (20 HR)

**Most home runs, two consecutive games (homering each game)**
NL—14—Cincinnati, Sept 4, 5, 1999
AL—13—New York, June 28, 28, 1939
Anaheim, June 3, 4, 2003

**Most home runs, three consecutive games**
AL—16—Boston, June 17-19, 1977
NL—15—Los Angeles, June 29, 30, July 1, 1996
Cincinnati, Sept 3-5, 1999
Cincinnati, Sept 4-6, 1999
Chicago, Aug 10-12, 2002

**Most home runs, four consecutive games**
NL—18—Houston, Aug 13-16, 2000
AL—18—Boston, June 16-19, 1977
Oakland, June 25-29, 1996

**Most home runs, five consecutive games**
AL—21—Boston, June 14-19, 1977
NL—19—New York, July 7-11 (1st game), 1954

**Most home runs, six consecutive games**
AL—24—Boston, June 17-22, 1977
NL—22—New York, July 6-July 11 (1st game), 1954

**Most home runs, seven consecutive games**
AL—26—Boston, June 16-22, 1977
NL—24—New York, July 5 (2nd game)-11 (1st game), 1954

**Most home runs, eight consecutive games**
AL—29—Boston, June 14-22, 1977
NL—26—New York, July 5 (1st game)-11 (1st game), 1954

**Most home runs, nine consecutive games**
AL—30—Boston June 14-23, 1977
Boston, June 16-24, 1977
NL—27—New York, July 4 (2nd game)-11 (1st game), 1954

**Most home runs, ten consecutive games**
AL—33—Boston, June 14-24, 1977
NL—28—New York, July 4 (1st game)-11 (1st game), 1954

## INNING

**Most home runs, inning**
AL—5—Minnesota vs Kansas City, June 9, 1966, 7th
NL—5—New York vs Cincinnati, June 6, 1939, 4th
Philadelphia vs Cincinnati, June 2, 1949, 8th
San Francisco vs Cincinnati, Aug 23, 1961, 9th

**For complete lists of clubs with four or more home runs in an inning and three or more consecutive home runs in an inning, see page 126.**

**Most home runs by pinch-hitters, inning (*consecutive)**
NL—2—New York vs St. Louis, June 20, 1954, 6th (Hofman, Rhodes)
San Francisco vs Milwaukee, June 4, 1958, 10th (Sauer, Schmidt)*
Los Angeles vs Chicago, Aug 8, 1963, 5th (Howard, Skowron)*
Los Angeles vs St. Louis, July 23, 1975, 9th (Crawford, Lacy)*
New York vs San Francisco, May 4, 1991, 9th (Sasser, Carreon)*
Cincinnati vs Atlanta, June 22, 1995, 8th (Anthony, Taubensee)
New York vs St. Louis, May 11, 1997, 9th (Everett, Huskey)*
AL—2—New York vs Kansas City, July 23, 1955, 9th (Cerv, Howard)
Baltimore vs Boston, Aug 26, 1966, 9th (Roznovsky, Powell)*
Seattle vs New York, Apr 27, 1979, 8th (Stinson, Meyer)
Minnesota vs Oakland, May 16, 1983, 9th (Engle, Hatcher)
Baltimore vs Cleveland, Aug 12, 1985, 9th (Gross, Sheets)*
Texas vs Boston, Sept 1, 1986, 9th (McDowell, Porter)*
Boston vs Chicago, Sept 19, 1997, 9th (Pride, Hatteberg)
Toronto vs Texas, Sept 11, 2004, 8th (Hinske, Gomez)

**Most home runs by both clubs, inning**
AL—5—St. Louis 3, Philadelphia 2, June 8, 1928, 9th
Detroit 4, New York 1, June 23, 1950, 4th
Minnesota 5, Kansas City 0, June 9, 1966, 7th
Baltimore 4, Boston 1, May 17, 1967, 7th
Minnesota 4, Oakland 1, May 16, 1983, 9th
Cleveland 3, Texas 2, June 29, 1984, 5th
Baltimore 3, Boston 2, Sept 10, 1985, 8th
Cleveland 3, Milwaukee 2, Apr 25, 1997, 4th
Detroit 3, Baltimore 2, Apr 7, 2000, 5th
Seattle 3, Kansas City 2, Aug 27, 2004, 5th
NL—5—New York 5, Cincinnati 0, June 6, 1939, 4th
Philadelphia 5, Cincinnati 0, June 2, 1949, 8th
New York 3, Boston 2, July 6, 1951, 3rd
Cincinnati 3, Brooklyn 2, June 11, 1954, 7th
San Francisco 5, Cincinnati 0, Aug 23, 1961, 9th
Philadelphia 3, Chicago 2, Apr 17, 1964, 5th
Chicago 3, Atlanta 2, July 3, 1967, 1st
Pittsburgh 3, Atlanta 2, Aug 1, 1970, 7th
Cincinnati 3, Chicago 2, July 28, 1977, 1st
San Francisco 3, Atlanta 2, May 25, 1979, 4th
Cincinnati 4, Atlanta 1, June 19, 1994, 1st
San Francisco 3, Pittsburgh 2, July 27, 1997, 9th
Colorado 3, St. Louis 2, July 31, 1999, 3rd
Atlanta 4, San Francisco 1, May 20, 2001, 7th

**Most consecutive home runs, inning**
NL—4—Milwaukee vs Cincinnati, June 8, 1961, 7th
AL—4—Cleveland vs Los Angeles, July 31, 1963, 2nd game, 6th
Minnesota vs Kansas City, May 2, 1964, 11th

**For a complete list of clubs with three or more consecutive home runs in an inning, see page 126.**

**Most times same players hitting back-to-back home runs, inning**
AL—2—Seattle vs Chicago, May 2, 2002, 1st (Boone, Cameron)
NL—1—many players

**Most home runs with two out, inning**
NL—5—New York vs Cincinnati, June 6, 1939, 4th
AL—4—Boston vs Detroit, July 18, 1998, 4th

**Most home runs with none on base, inning**
NL—4—New York vs Philadelphia, Aug 13, 1939, 1st game, 4th
AL—4—Cleveland vs Los Angeles, July 31, 1963, 2nd game, 6th (consec)
Minnesota vs Kansas City, May 2, 1964, 11th (consec)
Minnesota vs Kansas City, June 9, 1966, 7th (plus 1 HR with one on base)
Boston vs New York, June 17, 1977, 1st
Boston vs Toronto, July 4, 1977, 8th
Boston vs Milwaukee, May 31, 1980, 4th
Minnesota vs New York, May 2, 1992, 5th
Baltimore vs California, Sept 5, 1995, 2nd
Seattle vs Oakland, Sept 21, 1996, 3rd

**Most home runs, start of game**
NL—3—San Diego vs San Francisco, Apr 13, 1987 (Wynne, Gwynn, Kruk)
Atlanta vs Cincinnati, May 28, 2003 (Furcal, DeRosa, Sheffield)
AA—2—Boston vs Baltimore, June 25, 1891 (Brown, Joyce)
Philadelphia vs Boston, Aug 21, 1891 (McTamany, Larkin)
AL—2—many clubs; last—Detroit vs Boston, June 3, 2002 (Santiago, Easley); Cleveland vs Kansas City, July 21, 2002 (Magruder, Vizquel); Minnesota vs Chicago, Aug 19, 2002 (Jones, Guzman); Seattle vs Texas, Sept 9, 2002 (Suzuki, Relaford)

**Most times with three consecutive home runs in an inning (league)**
NL—17—New York/San Francisco, 1932, 1939 (2), 1948, 1949, 1953, 1954, 1956 in New York; 1963, 1969, 1982, 1998, 1999 (2), 2001, 2002, 2004 in San Francisco
AL—12—Detroit, 1947, 1956, 1961, 1971, 1972, 1974, 1986 (2), 1987, 1990, 1992, 2001

**For a complete list of clubs with three or more consecutive home runs in an inning, see page 126.**

**Most times with three or more home runs in an inning, season**
NL—5—New York, 1954
Chicago, 1955
AL—5—Baltimore, 1996

**Most times hitting two or more consecutive home runs, season**
AL—18—Seattle, 161 G, 1996
NL—15—Cincinnati, 155 G, 1956
St. Louis, 162 G, 2000

## GRAND SLAMS

**Most grand slams, season**
AL—14—Oakland, 2000
NL—12—Atlanta, 1997
St. Louis, 2000

**Most grand slams by pinch-hitters, season**
NL—3—San Francisco, 1973 (Arnold, Bonds, Goodson)
Chicago, 1975 (Summers, LaCock, Hosley)
San Francisco, 1978 (Ivie 2, Clark)
Philadelphia, 1978 (Johnson 2, McBride)
AL—3—Baltimore, 1982 (Ayala, Ford, Crowley)

**Most grand slams, game**
AL—2—Chicago vs Detroit, May 1, 1901 (Hoy, McFarland)
Boston vs Chicago, May 13, 1934 (Walters, Morgan)
New York vs Philadelphia, May 24, 1936 (Lazzeri 2)
Boston vs Philadelphia, July 4, 1939, 2nd game (Tabor 2)
Boston vs St. Louis, July 27, 1946 (York 2)
Detroit vs Philadelphia, June 11, 1954, 1st game (Boone, Kaline)
Baltimore vs New York, Apr 24, 1960 (Pearson, Klaus)
Boston vs Chicago, May 10, 1960 (Wertz, Repulski)
Baltimore vs Minnesota, May 9, 1961 (Gentile 2)
Minnesota vs Cleveland, July 18, 1962 (Allison, Killebrew)
Detroit vs Cleveland, June 24, 1968 (Northrup 2)
Baltimore vs Washington, June 26, 1970 (Frank Robinson 2)

Milwaukee vs Chicago, June 17, 1973 (Porter, Lahoud)
Milwaukee vs Boston, Apr 12, 1980 (Cooper, Money)
California vs Detroit, Apr 27, 1983 (Lynn, Sconiers)
Boston vs Detroit, Aug 7, 1984, 1st game (Buckner, Armas)
California vs Oakland, July 31, 1986 (Downing, Boone)
Baltimore vs Texas, Aug 6, 1986 (Sheets, Dwyer)
Boston vs Baltimore, June 10, 1987 (Burks, Barrett)
New York vs Toronto, June 29, 1987 (Mattingly, Winfield)
Cleveland vs Minnesota, Apr 22, 1988 (Snyder, Carter)
Boston vs New York, May 2, 1995 (Valentin, Vaughn)
Chicago vs Texas, Sept 4, 1995 (Ventura 2)
Chicago vs Detroit, May 19, 1996 (Ventura, Lewis)
Baltimore vs Cleveland, Aug 14, 1998 (Hoiles 2)
Boston vs Seattle, May 10, 1999 (Garciaparra 2)
New York vs Toronto, Sept 14, 1999 (Williams, O'Neill)
Cleveland vs Toronto, Sept 24, 1999 (Ramirez, Roberts)
Seattle vs Chicago, Aug 8, 2000, 1st game (Buhner, Martinez)
Boston vs Texas, July 29, 2003 (Mueller 2)
Oakland vs Toronto, Aug 24, 2003 (Hernandez, Tejada)
Texas vs Houston NL, July 4, 2004 (Blalock, Teixeira)
Kansas City vs Oakland, Aug 13, 2004 (Nunez, Buck)
Baltimore vs Detroit, Jun 4, 2005 (Palmeiro, Mora)
NL—2—Chicago vs Pittsburgh, Aug 16, 1890 (Burns, Kittredge)
Brooklyn vs Cincinnati, Sept 23, 1901 (Kelley, Sheckard)
Boston vs Chicago, Aug 12, 1903, 2nd game (Stanley, Moran)
Philadelphia vs Boston, Apr 28, 1921 (Miller, Meadows)
New York vs Philadelphia, Sept 5, 1924, 2nd game (Kelly, Jackson)
Pittsburgh vs St. Louis, June 22, 1925 (Grantham, Traynor)
St. Louis vs Philadelphia, July 6, 1929, 2nd game (Bottomley, Hafey)
Pittsburgh vs Philadelphia, May 1, 1933 (Vaughan, Grace)
Boston vs Philadelphia, Apr 30, 1938 (Moore, Maggert)
New York vs Brooklyn, July 4, 1938, 2nd game (Bartell, Mancuso)
New York vs St. Louis, July 13, 1951 (Westrum, Williams)
Cincinnati vs Pittsburgh, July 29, 1955 (Thurman, Burgess)
Atlanta vs San Francisco, July 3, 1966 (Cloninger 2)
Houston vs New York, July 30, 1969, 1st game (Menke, Wynn)
San Francisco vs Montreal, Apr 26, 1970, 1st game (McCovey, Dietz)
Pittsburgh vs Chicago, Sept 14, 1982 (Hebner, Madlock)
Los Angeles vs Montreal, Aug 23, 1985 (Guerrero, Duncan)
Atlanta vs Houston, May 2, 1987 (Nettles, James)
Chicago vs Houston, June 3, 1987 (Dayett, Moreland)
Cincinnati vs Chicago, Apr 24, 1993 (Sabo, Oliver)
Pittsburgh vs St. Louis, Apr 16, 1996 (Merced, Bell)
Montreal vs Colorado, Apr 28, 1996 (Fletcher, Segui)
Florida vs San Diego, Apr 28, 1997 (Alou, Sheffield)
Atlanta vs Philadelphia, July 14, 1997 (Spehr, Klesko)
Philadelphia vs San Francisco, Aug 18, 1997 (McMillon, Lieberthal)
San Francisco vs Los Angeles, Sept 19, 1998 (Mueller, Kent)
St. Louis vs Los Angeles, Apr 23, 1999 (Tatis 2)
Cincinnati vs Montreal, Aug 21, 1999 (Boone, Taubensee)
Los Angeles vs Florida, May 21, 2000 (Beltre, Green)
Milwaukee vs Chicago, May 12, 2002 (Casanova, Sexson)
Philadelphia vs Atlanta, Sept 9, 2003 (Perez, Michaels)

**Most grand slams by both clubs, game (each club homering)**
AL—3—Baltimore 2 (Sheets, Dwyer), Texas 1 (Harrah), Aug 6, 1986
NL—3—Chicago 2 (Dayett, Moreland), Houston 1 (Hatcher), June 3, 1987

**Most grand slams by pinch-hitters for both clubs, game**
NL—2—New York 1 (Crawford), Boston 1 (Bell), May 26, 1929
AL—1—many clubs

**Most grand slams, doubleheader**
NL—2—many times; last—New York vs Milwaukee, May 20, 1999
AL—2—many times; last—Baltimore vs Chicago, Aug 14, 1976

**Most grand slams by both clubs, doubleheader**
NL—3—Cincinnati 2, Atlanta 1, Sept 12, 1974
AL—2—many times; last—Seattle 2, Chicago 0, Aug 8, 2000
ML—2—Kansas City AL 1, Colorado NL 1, June 7, 2003

**Most consecutive games, one or more grand slams**
AL—3—Milwaukee, Apr 7, 8, 9, 1978 (1st three games of season)
Detroit, Aug 10, 11, 12, 1993
NL—2—many clubs

**Most grand slams, inning**
AL—2—Minnesota vs Cleveland, July 18, 1962, 1st (Allison, Killebrew)
Milwaukee vs Boston, Apr 12, 1980, 2nd (Cooper, Money)
Baltimore vs Texas, Aug 6, 1986, 4th (Sheets, Dwyer)
NL—2—Chicago vs Pittsburgh, Aug 16, 1890, 5th (Burns, Kittredge)
Houston vs New York, July 30, 1969, 1st game, 9th (Menke, Wynn)
St. Louis vs Los Angeles, Apr 23, 1999, 3rd (Tatis 2)

**Most grand slams by both clubs, inning**
NL—2—Chicago 2 (Burns, Kittredge), Pittsburgh 0, Aug 16, 1890, 5th
New York 1 (Irvin), Chicago 1 (Walker), May 18, 1950, 6th
Houston 2 (Menke, Wynn), New York 0, July 30, 1969, 1st game, 9th
Atlanta 1 (Evans), Cincinnati 1 (Geronimo), Sept 12, 1974, 1st game, 2nd
Chicago 1 (Sandberg), Pittsburgh 1 (King), Sept 9, 1992, 6th
St. Louis 2 (Tatis 2), Los Angeles 0, Apr 23, 1999, 3rd
Atlanta 1 (LaRoche), Los Angeles 1 (Bradley), May 13, 2005, 8th
AL—2—Washington 1 (Tasby), Boston 1 (Pagliaroni), June 18, 1961, 1st game, 9th
Minnesota 2 (Allison, Killebrew), Cleveland 0, July 18, 1962, 1st
Milwaukee 2 (Cooper, Money), Boston 0, Apr 12, 1980, 2nd
Cleveland 1 (Orta), Texas 1 (Sundberg), Apr 14, 1980, 1st
Baltimore 2 (Sheets, Dwyer), Texas 0, Aug 6, 1986, 4th
ML—2—Anaheim AL 1 (Fielder), Arizona NL 1 (Benitez), June 9, 1998, 3rd

## TOTAL BASES

**Most total bases, season**
AL—2,832—Boston, 162 G, 2003
NL—2,748—Colorado, 162 G, 2001

**Fewest total bases, season**
NL—1,358—Brooklyn, 154 G, 1908
AL—1,310—Chicago, 156 G, 1910

**Most total bases, game**
AL—60—Boston vs St. Louis, June 8, 1950
NL—58—Montreal vs Atlanta, July 30, 1978

**Most total bases by both clubs, game**
NL—81—Cincinnati 55, Colorado 26, May 19, 1999
[97—Chicago 49, Philadelphia 48, May 17, 1979, 10 inn]
AL—77—New York 50, Philadelphia 27, June 3, 1932
New York 47, Tampa Bay 30, Jun 21, 2005
[85—Cleveland 45, Philadelphia 40, July 10, 1932, 18 inn]

**Most total bases, doubleheader**
AL—87—New York vs Philadelphia, June 28, 1939
NL—73—Milwaukee vs Pittsburgh, Aug 30, 1953

**Most total bases by both clubs, doubleheader**
AL—114—New York 73, Philadelphia 41, May 22, 1930
NL—112—Milwaukee 63, New York 49, July 29, 1964
[112—Cincinnati 59, Houston 53, July 8, 1962, 22 inn]

**Most total bases, inning**
NL—29—Chicago vs Detroit, Sept 6, 1883, 7th
NL since 1893—27—San Francisco vs Cincinnati, Aug 23, 1961, 9th
AL—27—New York vs Tampa Bay, June 21, 2005, 8th

## EXTRA-BASE HITS

**Most extra-base hits, season**
AL—649—Boston, 162 G, 2003 (371 doubles, 40 triples, 238 HR)
NL—598—Colorado, 162 G, 2001 (324 doubles, 61 triples, 213 HR)

**Fewest extra-base hits, season**
AL—179—Chicago, 156 G, 1910 (116 doubles, 56 triples, 7 HR)
NL—182—Boston, 155 G, 1909 (124 doubles, 43 triples, 15 HR)

**Most extra-base hits, game**
AL—17—Boston vs St. Louis, June 8, 1950
NL—16—Chicago vs Buffalo, July 3, 1883
NL since 1893—15—Philadelphia vs Chicago, June 23, 1986
Cincinnati vs Colorado, May 19, 1999

**Most extra-base hits by both clubs, game**
NL—24—St. Louis 13, Chicago 11, July 12, 1931, 2nd game
AL—24—Cleveland 15, Minnesota 9, July 13, 1996

**Longest game without an extra-base hit**
NL—26 inn—Brooklyn vs Boston, May 1, 1920
AL—19 inn—Detroit vs New York, Aug 23, 1968, 2nd game

**Longest game without an extra-base by either club**
AL—18 inn—Chicago 0, New York 0, Aug 21, 1933
NL—17 inn—Boston 0, Chicago 0, Sept 21, 1901

**Most extra-base hits, doubleheader**
NL—21—Baltimore vs Cleveland, Sept 3, 1894
AL—18—New York vs Washington, July 4, 1927
New York vs Philadelphia, June 28, 1939

**Most extra-base hits by both clubs, doubleheader**
NL—35—Chicago 18, St. Louis 17, July 12, 1931
AL—28—Boston 16, Detroit 12, May 14, 1967

**Longest doubleheader without an extra-base hit**
AL—26—Cleveland vs Detroit, Aug 6, 1968

**Most extra-base hits, inning**
NL—8—Chicago vs Detroit, Sept 6, 1883, 7th
NL since 1893—7—Boston vs St. Louis, Aug 25, 1936, 1st game, 1st
Philadelphia vs Cincinnati, June 2, 1949, 8th
Philadelphia vs Cincinnati, July 6, 1986, 3rd
AL—7—St. Louis vs Washington, Aug 7, 1922, 6th
Boston vs Philadelphia, Sept 24, 1940, 1st game, 6th
New York vs St. Louis, May 3, 1951, 9th
Seattle vs Boston, Sept 3, 1982, 6th
Texas vs New York, July 31, 2002, 2nd

## RUNS BATTED IN

**Most runs batted in, season**
AL—995—New York, 155 G, 1936
NL—942—St. Louis, 154 G, 1930

**Fewest runs batted in, season**
NL—354—Philadelphia, 151 G, 1942

AL—424—Texas, 154 G, 1972

**Most players with 100 or more runs batted in, season**
AL—5—New York, 1936
NL—4—Pittsburgh, 1925; Chicago, 1929; Philadelphia, 1929; Colorado, 1996, 1997, 1999; Arizona, 1999, Atlanta, 2003

**Most runs batted in, game**
AL—29—Boston vs St. Louis, June 8, 1950
NL—26—New York vs Brooklyn, Apr 30, 1944, 1st game
Chicago vs Colorado, Aug 18, 1995

**Most runs batted in by both clubs, game**
NL—43—Chicago 24, Philadelphia 19, Aug 25, 1922
[45—Philadelphia 23, Chicago 22, May 17, 1979, 10 inn]
AL—35—Boston 21, Philadelphia 14, June 29, 1950

**Longest game without a run batted in by either club**
NL—19 inn—Cincinnati 0, Brooklyn 0, Sept 11, 1946
AL—18 inn—Washington 0, Detroit 0, July 16, 1909
Washington 0, Chicago 0, May 15, 1918

**Most runs batted in, doubleheader**
AL—34—Boston vs Philadelphia, July 4, 1939
NL—31—St. Louis vs Philadelphia, July 6, 1929

**Most runs batted in by both clubs, doubleheader**
AL—49—Boston 34, Philadelphia 15, July 4, 1939
NL—45—St. Louis 31, Philadelphia 14, July 6, 1929

**Most runs batted in, inning**
AL—17—Boston vs Detroit, June 18, 1953, 7th
NL—15—Chicago vs Detroit, Sept 6, 1883, 7th
Brooklyn vs Cincinnati, May 21, 1952, 1st

## GAME-WINNING RBIs (1980-1988)

**Most game-winning RBIs, season**
NL—102—New York, 1986 (108 wins)
AL—99—Oakland, 1988 (104 wins)

**Fewest game-winning RBIs, season**
AL—48—Baltimore, 1988 (54 wins)
NL—51—Atlanta, 1988 (54 wins)

**Most games won without game-winning RBIs, season**
AL—12—Detroit, 1980 (84 wins)
NL—12—Houston, 1980 (93 wins)

**Fewest games won without game-winning RBIs, season**
AL—0—New York, 1982 (79 wins)
NL—1—Pittsburgh, 1985 (57 wins)
Chicago, 1987 (76 wins)

## BASES ON BALLS

**Most bases on balls, season**
AL—835—Boston, 155 G, 1949
NL—732—Brooklyn, 155 G, 1947

**Fewest bases on balls, season**
NL—283—Philadelphia, 153 G, 1920
AL—356—Philadelphia, 156 G, 1920

**Most bases on balls, game**
AA—19—Louisville vs Cleveland, Sept 21, 1887
AL—18—Detroit vs Philadelphia, May 9, 1916
Cleveland vs Boston, May 20, 1948
[20—Boston vs Detroit, Sept 17, 1920, 12 inn]
NL—17—Chicago vs New York, May 30, 1887, a.m. game
NL since 1893—17—Brooklyn vs Philadelphia, Aug 27, 1903
New York vs Brooklyn, Apr 30, 1944, 1st game
[19—Philadelphia vs Baltimore AL, July 2, 2004, 16 inn]

**Most bases on balls by both clubs, game**
AL—30—Detroit 18, Philadelphia 12, May 9, 1916
[30—Washington 19, Cleveland 11, Sept 14, 1971, 2nd game, 20 inn, suspended, finished Sept 20]
NL—26—Houston 13, San Francisco 13, May 4, 1975, 2nd game

**Most bases on balls, game, being shut out**
AL—11—St. Louis vs New York, Aug 1, 1941
NL—9—Cincinnati vs St. Louis, Sept 1, 1958, 1st game
[10—Chicago vs Cincinnati, Aug 19, 1965, 1st game, 10 inn]

**Longest game without a base on balls**
NL—22 inn—Los Angeles vs Montreal, Aug 23, 1989
AL—20 inn—Philadelphia vs Boston, July 4, 1905, p.m. game

**Longest game without a base on balls by either club**
AL—13 inn—Washington 0, Detroit 0, July 22, 1904
Boston 0, Philadelphia 0, Sept 9, 1907
NL—12 inn—Chicago 0, Los Angeles 0, July 27, 1980

**Most bases on balls, doubleheader**
NL—25—New York vs Brooklyn, Apr 30, 1944
AL—23—Cleveland vs Philadelphia, June 18, 1950
[23—Washington vs Cleveland, Sept 14, 1971, 2nd game 20 innings, suspended, finished Sept 20]

**Most bases on balls by both clubs, doubleheader**
NL—42—Houston 21, San Francisco 21, May 4, 1975
AL—32—Baltimore 18, Chicago 14, May 28, 1954
Detroit 20, Kansas City 12, Aug 1, 1962
Texas 17, Chicago 15, May 24, 1995
[39—Washington 23, Cleveland 16, Sept 14, 1971, 2nd game 20 innings, suspended, finished Sept 20]

**Fewest bases on balls by both clubs, doubleheader**
NL—1—Cincinnati 1, Brooklyn 0, Aug 6, 1905
Cincinnati 1, Pittsburgh 0, Sept 7, 1924
Brooklyn 1, St. Louis 0, Sept 22, 1929
AL—2—Philadelphia 1, Chicago 1, July 12, 1912
Cleveland 2, Chicago 0, Sept 6, 1930
[2—Philadelphia 2, Detroit 0, Aug 28, 1908, 20 inn]

**Longest doubleheader without a base on balls**
NL—27 inn—St. Louis vs New York, July 2, 1933
AL—20 inn—Detroit vs Philadelphia, Aug 28, 1908

**Most bases on balls, inning**
AL—11—New York vs Washington, Sept 11, 1949, 1st game, 3rd
NL—9—Cincinnati vs Chicago, Apr 24, 1957, 5th

**Most consecutive bases on balls, inning**
AL—7—Chicago vs Washington, Aug 28, 1909, 1st game, 2nd
NL—7—Atlanta vs Pittsburgh, May 25, 1983, 3rd

**Most bases on balls by pinch-hitters, inning**
NL—3—Pittsburgh vs Philadelphia, June 3, 1911, 9th
Brooklyn vs New York, Apr 22, 1922, 7th
Boston vs Brooklyn, June 2, 1932, 1st game, 9th
Chicago vs Philadelphia, July 29, 1947, 7th
Philadelphia vs Pittsburgh, July 18, 1997, 6th
AL—3—Baltimore vs Washington, Apr 22, 1955, 7th
Washington vs Boston, May 14, 1961, 2nd game, 9th (consec)

**Most consecutive bases on balls by pinch-hitters, inning**
NL—3—Brooklyn vs New York, Apr 22, 1922, 7th
Boston vs Brooklyn, June 2, 1932, 1st game, 9th
AL—3—Washington vs Boston, May 14, 1961, 2nd game, 9th

**Most players with two bases on balls, inning**
AL—4—New York vs Washington, Sept 11, 1949, 1st game, 3rd
NL—2—many innings

**Most consecutive bases on balls at start of game**
NL—5—New York vs Cincinnati, June 16, 1941
AL—4—Philadelphia vs Boston, Apr 21, 1946
Toronto vs Texas, Apr 18, 1997
Kansas City vs Cleveland, June 29, 2000

## INTENTIONAL (SINCE 1955)

**Most intentional bases on balls, season**
NL—153—San Francisco, 162 G, 2004
AL—79—Minnesota, 162 G, 1965

**Fewest intentional bases on balls, season**
AL—10—Kansas City, 162 G, 1961
NL—22—Los Angeles, 154 G, 1958
Pittsburgh, 163 G, 1998

**Most intentional bases on balls, game**
NL—6—San Francisco vs St. Louis, July 19, 1975
[7—New York vs Chicago, May 2, 1956, 17 inn
Houston vs Philadelphia, July 15, 1984, 16 inn
Chicago vs Cincinnati, May 22, 1990, 16 inn
Cincinnati vs San Francisco, Apr 15, 1969, 12 inn]
AL—5—Minnesota vs Kansas City, Sept 14, 1965
California vs New York, May 10, 1967
Washington vs Cleveland, Sept 2, 1970
[7—New York vs Los Angeles, May 22, 1962, 12 inn]

**Most intentional bases on balls by both clubs, game**
ML—7—Philadelphia NL 4, Baltimore AL 3, July 2, 2004, 16 inn
NL—7—New York 4, Pittsburgh 3, June 27, 1979
[11—New York 7, Chicago 4, May 2, 1956, 17 inn]
AL—6—California 5, New York 1, May 10, 1967
[9—Boston 6, New York 1, Aug 29, 1967, 2nd game, 20 inn]

**Most intentional bases on balls, inning**
AL—4—Chicago vs Kansas City, Oct 1, 1965, 8th
NL—3—many innings

## STRIKEOUTS

**Most strikeouts, season**
NL—1,399—Milwaukee, 162 G, 2001
AL—1,268—Detroit, 162 G, 1996

**Fewest strikeouts, season**
NL—308—Cincinnati, 153 G, 1921
AL—326—Philadelphia, 155 G, 1927

**Most strikeouts, game**
AL—20—Seattle vs Boston, Apr 29, 1986

Detroit vs Boston, Sept 18, 1996
[26—California vs Oakland, July 9, 1971, 20 inn]
NL—20—Houston vs Chicago, May 6, 1998
[26—Milwaukee vs Anaheim, June 8, 2004, 17 inn]
UA—19—Boston vs Chicago, July 7, 1884

**Most strikeouts by both clubs, game**
AL—31—Texas 18, Seattle 13, July 13, 1997
[43—California 26, Oakland 17, July 9, 1971, 20 inn]
NL—30—Houston 20, Chicago 10, May 6, 1998
[40—San Francisco 20, San Diego 20, June 19, 2001, 15 inn]
UA—29—Boston 19, Chicago 10, July 7, 1884
St. Louis 18, Boston 11, July 19, 1884

**Most strikeouts by pinch-hitters, game**
AL—5—Detroit vs New York, Sept 8, 1979
NL—4—Brooklyn vs Philadelphia, Apr 27, 1950
Philadelphia vs Milwaukee, Sept 16, 1960
Chicago vs New York, Sept 21, 1962
Chicago vs New York, May 3, 1969
Cincinnati vs Houston, Sept 27, 1969
Montreal vs Philadelphia, June 24, 1972

**Most strikeouts by pinch-hitters from both clubs, game**
AL—5—New York 4, Boston 1, July 4, 1955, 1st game
Washington 4, Cleveland 1, May 1, 1957
Detroit 4, Cleveland 1, Aug 4, 1967
Detroit 5, New York 0, Sept 8, 1979
NL—4—many games; last—Montreal 4, Philadelphia 0, June 24, 1972

**Most consecutive strikeouts, game**
NL—10—San Diego vs New York, Apr 22, 1970 (1 in 6th, 3 in 7th, 3 in 8th, 3 in 9th)
AL—8—Boston vs California, July 9, 1972 (2 in 1st, 3 in 2nd, 3 in 3rd)
Milwaukee vs California, Aug 7, 1973 (1 in 1st, 3 in 2nd, 3 in 3rd, 1 in 4th)
Seattle vs Boston, Apr 29, 1986 (3 in 4th, 3 in 5th, 2 in 6th)
New York vs Houston, June 11, 2003 (2 in 7th, 4 in 8th, 2 in 9th)

**Most consecutive strikeouts at start of game**
NL—9—Cleveland vs New York, Aug 28, 1884
NL since 1893—8—Los Angeles vs Houston, Sept 23, 1986
AL—7—Texas vs Chicago, May 28, 1986

**Longest game without a strikeout**
NL—17 inn—New York vs Cincinnati, June 26, 1893
Cincinnati vs New York, Aug 27, 1920, 1st game
AL—16 inn—Cleveland vs New York, June 7, 1936

**Longest game without a strikeout, both clubs**
AL—12 inn—Chicago 0, St. Louis 0, July 7, 1931
NL—10 inn—Boston 0, New York 0, Apr 19, 1928

**Most strikeouts, inning (*consecutive)**
AA—4—Pittsburgh vs Philadelphia, Sept 30, 1885, 7th
NL—4—Chicago vs New York, October 4, 1888, 5th*
NL since 1893—4—Cincinnati vs New York, May 15, 1906, 5th*
St. Louis vs Chicago, May 27, 1956, 1st game, 6th*
Milwaukee vs Cincinnati, Aug 11, 1959, 1st game, 6th
Cincinnati vs Los Angeles, Apr 12, 1962, 3rd*
Philadelphia vs Los Angeles, Apr 17, 1965, 2nd*
Pittsburgh vs St. Louis, June 7, 1966, 4th
Houston vs St. Louis, July 18, 1972, 8th
Montreal vs Chicago, July 31, 1974, 1st game, 2nd*
Pittsburgh vs Atlanta, July 29, 1977, 6th
Chicago vs Cincinnati, May 17, 1984, 3rd*
Chicago vs Houston, Sept 3, 1986, 5th
St. Louis vs Atlanta, Aug 22, 1989, 5th
San Francisco vs Cincinnati, June 4, 1990, 7th
Chicago vs Atlanta, June 7, 1995, 9th
San Diego vs Colorado, Sept 19, 1995, 6th
Chicago vs Colorado, July 25, 1996, 9th
Atlanta vs New York, Sept 13, 1996, 9th
Montreal vs Florida, Sept 16, 1998, 4th*
Chicago vs Florida, Apr 28, 1999, 7th
San Diego vs San Francisco, July 22, 1999, 7th
San Francisco vs Montreal, Aug 17, 1999, 7th*
Milwaukee vs Montreal, May 5, 2000, 9th
Florida vs Cincinnati, July 22, 2001, 7th
New York vs Florida, July 5, 2002, 1st
Milwaukee vs Chicago, Sept 2, 2002, 4th*
Colorado vs Los Angeles, May 22, 2003, 2nd
Milwaukee vs Houston, June 13, 2004, 7th
Milwaukee vs New York, Aug 3, 2004, 8th
AL—4—Boston vs Washington, Apr 15, 1911, 5th
Philadelphia vs Cleveland, June 11, 1916, 6th*
Chicago vs Los Angeles, May 18, 1961, 7th
Washington vs Cleveland, Sept 2, 1964, 7th
California vs Baltimore, May 29, 1970, 4th*
Seattle vs Cleveland, July 21, 1978, 5th*
Baltimore vs Texas, Aug 2, 1987, 2nd*
New York vs Texas, July 4, 1988, 1st
Boston vs Detroit, Aug 13, 1988, 6th
Boston vs Seattle, Sept 9, 1990, 1st
California vs Cleveland, Apr 11, 1994, 9th
Detroit vs Cleveland, May 14, 1994, 9th
Toronto vs Kansas City, Sept 3, 1996, 4th
Detroit vs Chicago, July 21, 1997, 7th*
Tampa Bay vs Oakland, July 27, 1998, 4th
New York vs Anaheim, May 12, 1999, 3rd
Kansas City vs Boston, Aug 10, 1999, 9th
Detroit vs Anaheim, Aug 15, 1999, 1st*
Texas vs Cleveland, Apr 16, 2000, 3rd*
Texas vs Oakland, June 30, 2001, 7th
Texas vs Seattle, Apr 4, 2003, 9th*
New York vs Houston, June 11, 2003, 8th

**Most strikeouts by pinch-hitters, inning (*consecutive)**
AL—3—Philadelphia vs Washington, Sept 3, 1910, 8th*
Chicago vs Boston, June 5, 1911, 9th*
Detroit vs Cleveland, Sept 19, 1945, 8th*
Philadelphia vs Cleveland, Sept 9, 1952, 9th
Cleveland vs New York, May 12, 1953, 8th*
New York vs Philadelphia, Sept 24, 1954, 9th*
Detroit vs Cleveland, Aug 4, 1967, 8th
California vs Minnesota, May 17, 1971, 9th*
Cleveland vs Detroit, June 25, 1975, 9th
Detroit vs New York, Sept 8, 1979, 9th
NL—3—Pittsburgh vs Cincinnati, June 5, 1953, 9th*
Cincinnati vs Brooklyn, Aug 8, 1953, 9th
St. Louis vs Cincinnati, May 10, 1961, 9th
Cincinnati vs Houston, June 2, 1966, 8th*
Atlanta vs Houston, June 18, 1967, 8th*
Cincinnati vs Houston, Sept 27, 1969, 8th
St. Louis vs Montreal, July 4, 1970, 8th
Philadelphia vs Pittsburgh, July 6, 1970, 9th

**Most strikeouts, doubleheader**
NL—27—New York vs Arizona, Apr 27, 2003
[31—Pittsburgh vs Philadelphia, Sept 22, 1958, 23 inn
New York vs Philadelphia, October 2, 1965, 27 inn]
AL—25—Los Angeles vs Cleveland, July 31, 1963
[27—Cleveland vs Boston, Aug 25, 1963, 24 inn]

**Most strikeouts by both clubs, doubleheader**
NL—41—Philadelphia 26, New York 15, Sept 9, 1970
San Diego 26, New York 15, May 29, 1971
Chicago 21, New York 20, Sept 15, 1971
[51—New York 30, Philadelphia 21, Sept 26, 1975, 24 inn]
AL—44—Detroit 24, Baltimore 20, Sept 8, 1980
[48—Detroit 24, Kansas City 24, June 17, 1967, 28 inn]

**Longest doubleheader without a strikeout**
NL—21 inn—Pittsburgh vs Philadelphia, July 12, 1924
AL—20 inn—Boston vs St. Louis, July 28, 1917

**Fewest strikeouts by both clubs, doubleheader**
AL—1—Cleveland 1, Boston 0, Aug 28, 1926
NL—2—Brooklyn 2, New York 0, Aug 13, 1932
Pittsburgh 2, St. Louis 0, Sept 6, 1948

## SACRIFICE HITS

**Most sacrifice hits, season (includes sacrifice scoring flies)**
AL—310—Boston, 157 G, 1917
NL—270—Chicago, 158 G, 1908

**Most sacrifice hits, season (no sacrifice flies)**
NL—231—Chicago, 154 G, 1906
AL—207—Chicago, 154 G, 1906

**Fewest sacrifice hits, season (no sacrifice flies)**
AL—9—Texas, 162 G, 2005
NL—29—San Diego, 162 G, 2001

**Most sacrifices, game (includes sacrifice flies)**
AL—8—New York vs Boston, May 4, 1918 (2 sacrifice scoring flies)
Chicago vs Detroit, July 11, 1927
St. Louis vs Cleveland, July 23, 1928
Texas vs Chicago, Aug 1, 1977
NL—8—Cincinnati vs Philadelphia, May 6, 1926

**Most sacrifices by both clubs, game (includes sacrifice flies)**
AL—11—Washington 7, Boston 4, Sept 1, 1926
NL—9—New York 5, Chicago 4, Aug 29, 1921
Cincinnati 8, Philadelphia 1, May 6, 1926
[9—San Francisco 6, San Diego 3, May 23, 1970, 15 inn (no SF)]

**Longest extra-inning game without a sacrifice**
AL—24 inn—Detroit vs Philadelphia, July 21, 1945
NL—23 inn—Brooklyn vs Boston, June 27, 1939

**Longest extra-inning game without a sacrifice by either club**
NL—19 inn—Philadelphia 0, Cincinnati 0, Sept 15, 1950, 2nd game
AL—18 inn—Washington 0, St. Louis 0, June 20, 1952

**Most sacrifices, doubleheader (includes sacrifice flies)**
AL—10—Detroit vs Chicago, July 7, 1921
NL—9—many clubs

**Most sacrifices by both clubs, doubleheader (includes sacrifice flies)**
AL—13—Boston 9, Chicago 4, July 17, 1926

**Fewest sacrifices, doubleheader**
NL-AL—0—many doubleheaders

**Longest doubleheader without a sacrifice by either club**
NL—28 inn—Cincinnati 0, Philadelphia 0, Sept 15, 1950
AL—18 inn—many doubleheaders

**Most sacrifice hits, inning (no sacrifice flies)**
AL—3—Cleveland vs St. Louis, July 10, 1949, 5th
Los Angeles vs Cleveland, Aug 1, 1962, 2nd game
Los Angeles vs Chicago, Aug 8, 1962, 1st game
Detroit vs Baltimore, July 12, 1970, 1st game, 2nd (consec)
California vs Detroit, June 5, 1977, 8th
Oakland vs Kansas City, June 26, 1977, 1st game, 5th
Cleveland vs Chicago, June 8, 1980, 6th (consec)
Seattle vs California, Apr 29, 1984, 6th
Minnesota vs Milwaukee, July 26, 1991, 8th
NL—3—Milwaukee vs Pittsburgh, Sept 9, 1961
Chicago vs Milwaukee, Aug 26, 1962, 6th (consec)
Philadelphia vs Los Angeles, Sept 23, 1967, 7th (consec)
Los Angeles vs San Francisco, May 23, 1972, 6th
Houston vs San Diego, Apr 29, 1975, 7th
Houston vs Atlanta, July 6, 1975, 9th
Pittsburgh vs St. Louis, Sept 20, 1988, 8th

## SACRIFICE FLIES

**Most sacrifice flies, season**
AL—77—Oakland, 162 G, 1984
NL—75—Colorado, 162 G, 2000

**Fewest sacrifice flies, season**
NL—19—San Diego, 161 G, 1971
AL—23—California, 161 G, 1967

**Most sacrifice flies, game**
AL—5—Seattle vs Oakland, Aug 7, 1988
NL—4—many times; last—New York NL vs New York AL, June 24, 2005
[4—Montreal vs Chicago, May 28, 1980, 14 inn
Atlanta vs San Diego, May 23, 1991, 12 inn]

**Most sacrifice flies by both clubs, game**
AL—5—many games
NL—5—many games
[5—Los Angeles 3, San Francisco 2, Apr 15, 1984, 11 inn]

**Most sacrifice flies, inning**
AL—3—Chicago vs Cleveland, July 1, 1962, 2nd game, 5th
New York vs Detroit, June 29, 2000, 4th
New York vs Anaheim, Aug 19, 2000, 3rd
NL—3—New York NL vs New York AL, June 24, 2005, 2nd
Houston NL vs Texas AL, June 26, 2005, 7th

## HIT BY PITCH

**Most hit by pitch, season**
NL—148—Baltimore, 154 G, 1898
NL since 1900—100—Houston, 162 G, 1997
AL—92—Toronto, 162 G, 1996

**Fewest hit by pitch, season**
AL—5—Philadelphia, 154 G, 1937
NL—9—Philadelphia, 152 G, 1939
San Diego, 162 G, 1969

**Most hit by pitch, game**
AA—6—Brooklyn vs Baltimore, Apr 25, 1887
AL—6—New York vs Washington, June 20, 1913, 2nd game
NL—6—Louisville vs St. Louis, July 31, 1897, 1st game
[6—New York vs Chicago, June 16, 1893, 11 inn]

**Most hit by pitch by both clubs, game**
NL—8—Washington 5, Pittsburgh 3, May 9, 1896
Louisville 6, St. Louis 2, July 31, 1897, 1st game
AL—7—Detroit 4, Washington 3, Aug 24, 1914, 2nd game
Minnesota 4, Kansas City 3, Apr 13, 1971
Kansas City 5, Texas 2, Sept 3, 1989
Oakland 5, Anaheim 2, June 7, 2001

**Most hit by pitch, inning**
NL—4—Boston vs Pittsburgh, Aug 19, 1893, 1st game, 2nd
NL since 1900—3—New York vs Pittsburgh, Sept 25, 1905, 1st
Chicago vs Boston, Sept 17, 1928, 9th
Philadelphia vs Cincinnati, May 15, 1960, 1st game, 8th
Atlanta vs Cincinnati, July 2, 1969, 2nd
Cincinnati vs Pittsburgh, May 1, 1974, 1st (consec)
St. Louis vs Montreal, Aug 15, 1992, 1st
San Diego vs Colorado, June 28, 1994, 11th
Houston vs Los Angeles, Sept 13, 1997, 1st
Florida vs Houston, Aug 3, 1998, 8th
Atlanta vs San Diego, Aug 16, 2000, 8th
St. Louis vs San Diego, Sept 26, 2000, 8th
Chicago vs San Diego, Apr 22, 2003, 4th
Colorado vs Los Angeles, July 23, 2003, 4th
Pittsburgh vs, Chicago, May 28, 2004, 1st game, 5th
Milwaukee vs Colorado, June 22, 2004, 7th
Atlanta vs Los Angeles, Aug 21, 2004, 1st
Milwaukee vs San Francisco, July 31, 2005, 6th
AL—3—New York vs Washington, June 20, 1913, 2nd game, 1st
Cleveland vs New York, Aug 25, 1921, 8th
Boston vs New York, June 30, 1954, 3rd
Baltimore vs California, Aug 9, 1968, 7th
California vs Chicago, Sept 10, 1977, 1st (consec)
California vs Cleveland, July 8, 1988, 4th
Oakland vs Minnesota, Sept 28, 1988, 2nd
Oakland vs Seattle, Sept 22, 1996, 5th
Toronto vs Chicago, July 15, 1998, 7th
Tampa Bay vs Anaheim, May 22, 1999, 3rd
Boston vs Kansas City, Apr 30, 2003, 9th
Anaheim vs Baltimore, May 14, 2004, 2nd

## GROUNDING INTO DOUBLE PLAYS

**Most grounding into double plays, season**
AL—174—Boston, 162 G, 1990
NL—166—St. Louis, 154 G, 1958

**Fewest grounding into double plays, season**
NL—75—St. Louis, 155 G, 1945
AL—79—Kansas City, 161 G, 1967

**Most grounding into double plays, game**
NL—7—San Francisco vs Houston, May 4, 1969
AL—6—many teams
[6—Toronto vs Minnesota, Aug 29, 1977, 1st game, 10 inn]

**Most grounding into double plays by both clubs, game**
AL—9—Boston 6, California 3, May 1, 1966, 1st game
Boston 6, Minnesota 3, July 18, 1990
NL—8—Boston 5, Chicago 3, Sept 18, 1928
[10—New York 6, San Francisco 4, Aug 21, 2004, 12 inn]

## REACHING BASE ON ERRORS

**Most times reaching first base on error, game**
NL—10—Chicago vs Cleveland, July 24, 1882
AL—8—Detroit vs Chicago, May 6, 1903

**Most times reaching first base on error by both clubs, game**
NL—16—Chicago 10, Cleveland 6, July 24, 1882
AL—12—Detroit 8, Chicago 4, May 6, 1903

**Most times reaching first base on error, inning**
NL—4—St. Louis vs Pittsburgh, Aug 5, 1901, 8th
AL—4—St. Louis vs Boston, June 8, 1911, 4th

# LEAGUE BATTING

## GAMES

NL (8 clubs)—625 in 1914, 1917
NL (10 clubs)—813 in 1965, 1868
NL (12 clubs)—974 in 1983
NL (14 clubs)—1,135 in 1993
NL (16 clubs)—1,298 in 1998
AL (8 clubs)—631 in 1914
AL (10 clubs)—814 in 1964
AL (12 clubs)—973 in 1969, 1970, 1974
AL (14 clubs)—1,135 in 1982, 1983, 2003

## BATTING AVERAGE

**Highest batting average, season**
NL since 1900—.303 in 1930
AL—.292 in 1921

**Lowest batting average, season**
NL since 1900—.239 in 1908
AL—.230 in 1968

**Most .400 hitters, season (qualifiers for batting championship)**
NL—4 in 1894
NL since 1900—1 in 1922, 1924, 1925, 1930
AL—2 in 1911, 1922

**Most clubs batting .300 or over, season**
NL since 1900—6 in 1930
AL—4 in 1921

**Most .300 hitters, season (qualifiers for batting championship)**
NL since 1900—33 in 1930
AL—27 in 1924

**Fewest .300 hitters, season (qualifiers for batting title)**
NL since 1900—4 in 1907
AL—1 in 1968

## ON-BASE PERCENTAGE

**Highest on-base percentage, season**
NL since 1900—.360 in 1930
AL—.363 in 1936

**Lowest on-base percentage, season (since 1900)**
NL since 1900—.299 in 1908
AL—.295 in 1908

## SLUGGING AVERAGE

**Highest slugging average, season**
NL (since 1900)—.448 in 1930
AL—.445 in 1996

**Lowest slugging average, season**
NL since 1900—.306 in 1908
AL—.304 in 1908

## AT-BATS

**Most at-bats, season**
NL since 1900 (8 clubs)—43,891 in 1936
NL (10 clubs)—55,449 in 1962
NL (12 clubs)—66,700 in 1977
NL (14 clubs)—77,711 in 1996
NL (16 clubs)—89,011 in 1999
AL (8 clubs)—43,747 in 1930
AL (10 clubs)—55,239 in 1962
AL (12 clubs)—66,276 in 1973
AL (14 clubs)—79,090 in 1996

**Fewest at-bats, season**
NL since 1900 (8 clubs)—38,005 in 1903 (33,780 in shortened 1918 season)
NL (10 clubs)—54,803 in 1963
NL (12 clubs)—65,156 in 1978 (43,654 in shortened 1981 season)
NL (14 clubs)—77,203 in 1997 (55,068 in shortened 1994 season)
NL (16 clubs)—87,794 in 2002
AL (8 clubs)—37,434 in 1903 (33,535 in shortened 1918)
AL (10 clubs)—54,082 in 1966
AL (12 clubs)—64, 641 in 1971 (61,712 in shortened 1972 season)
AL (14 clubs)—76,411 in 1978 (50,813 in shortened 1981 season)

**Most players with 600 or more at-bats, season**
AL—24 in 2005
NL since 1900—19 in 1962

## RUNS

**Most runs, season**
NL since 1900 (8 clubs)—7,025 in 1930
NL (10 clubs)—7,278 in 1962
NL (12 clubs)—8,771 in 1970, 1987
NL (14 clubs)—10,623 in 1996
NL (16 clubs)—12,976 in 2000
AL (8 clubs)—7,009 in 1936
AL (10 clubs)—7,342 in 1961
AL (12 clubs)—8,314 in 1973
AL (14 clubs)—12,208 in 1996

**Fewest runs, season**
NL since 1900 (8 clubs)—4,136 in 1908
NL (10 clubs)—5,577 in 1968
NL (12 clubs)—7,522 in 1988 (5,035 in shortened 1981 season)
NL (14 clubs)—10,190 in 1993 (7,422 in shortened 1994 season)
NL (16 clubs)—11,516 in 2002
AL (8 clubs)—4,272 in 1909
AL (10 clubs)—5,532 in 1968
AL (12 clubs)—7,472 in 1971 (6,441 in shortened 1972 season)
AL (14 clubs)—9,509 in 1978 (6,112 in shortened 1981 season)

**Most players with 100 or more runs, season**
NL since 1900—31 in 1999
AL—29 in 1999

**Most runs in league, one day**
NL—159—Aug 7, 1894
NL since 1900—123—Aug 18, 1995
AL—128—May 30, 1932

**Most runs by both leagues, one day**
221 on July 3, 1999; 111 in NL (9 games); 110 in AL (8 games)

**Most players scoring five or more runs in a game, season**
NL since 1900—7 in 1930
AL—5 in 1939

**Total games with 20 or more runs by one club, league**
NL—1876 to date—264
NL —1900 to date—100
AL—1901 to date—107

**Most games with 20 or more runs by one club, season**
NL—32 in 1894
NL since 1900—5 in 1900, 1925
AL—5 in 1923, 1999, 2000

**Most games with 10 or more runs by one club, season**
NL—447 in 1894
NL since 1900—287 in 2000
AL—287 in 2000

**Most innings with 10 or more runs, season**
NL—12 in 1894
NL since 1900—6 in 1922
AL—7 in 1999

## HITS

**Most hits, season**
NL since 1900 (8 clubs)—13,260 in 1930
NL (10 clubs)—14,453 in 1962
NL (12 clubs)—17,465 in 1977
NL (14 clubs)—20,427 in 1993
NL (16 clubs)—23,880 in 1999
AL (8 clubs)—12,657 in 1962
AL (10 clubs)—14,068 in 1962
AL (12 clubs)—17,193 in 1973
AL (14 clubs)—21,922 in 1996

**Fewest hits, season**
NL since 1900 (8 clubs)—9,566 in 1907 (8,583 in shortened 1918 season)
NL (10 clubs)—13,351 in 1968
NL (12 clubs)—16,215 in 1989 (11,141 in shortened 1981 season)
NL (14 clubs)—20,300 in 1997 (14,695 in shortened 1994 season)
NL (16 clubs)—22,753 in 2002
AL (8 clubs)—9,553 in 1903 (8,502 in shortened 1918 season)
AL (10 clubs)—12,359 in 1968
AL (12 clubs)—15,957 in 1971 (14,751 in shortened 1972 season)
AL (14 clubs)—19,900 in 1990 (13,016 in shortened 1981 season)

**Most players with 200 or more hits, season**
NL—12 in 1929 and 1930
AL—9 in 1936 and 1937

**Most players with five or more hits in a game, season**
NL since 1900—27 in 1930
AL—22 in 1936

**Fewest players with five or more hits in a game, season**
NL since 1900—1 in 1914
AL—2 in 1913, 1914, 1963

**Most hits in league, one day**
AL—190, July 10, 1932
NL—183, July 21, 1963

**Most hits by both leagues, one day**
347 on July 3, 1999; 177 in NL (9 games); 170 in AL (8 games)

## SINGLES

**Most singles, season**
NL since 1900 (8 clubs)—9,476 in 1922
NL (10 clubs)—10,476 in 1962
NL (12 clubs)—12,564 in 1980
NL (14 clubs)—14,370 in 1993
NL (16 clubs)—15,856 in 1999
AL (8 clubs)—9,214 in 1921
AL (10 clubs)—9,878 in 1962
AL (12 clubs)—12,729 in 1974
AL (14 clubs)—15,072 in 1980

**Fewest singles, season**
NL since 1900 (8 clubs)—7,466 in 1956 (6,850 in shortened 1918 season)
NL (10 clubs)—9,796 in 1963
NL (12 clubs)—11,536 in 1989 (8,187 in shortened 1981 season)
NL (14 clubs)—13,745 in 1997 (10,002 in shortened 1994 season)
NL (16 clubs)—14,974 in 2001
AL (8 clubs)—7,202 in 1903 (6,792 in shortened 1918 season)
AL (10 clubs)—9,043 in 1968
AL (12 clubs)—11,696 in 1971 (11,000 in shortened 1972 season)
AL (14 clubs)—13,404 in 2002 (9,530 in shortened 1981 season)

## DOUBLES

**Most doubles, season**
NL since 1900 (8 clubs)—2,386 in 1930
NL (10 clubs)—2,161 in 1964
NL (12 clubs)—3,126 in 1987
NL (14 clubs)—3,907 in 1997
NL (16 clubs)—4,754 in 2005
AL (8 clubs)—2,400 in 1936
AL (10 clubs)—2,238 in 1962
AL (12 clubs)—2,662 in 1975

AL (14 clubs)—4,269 in 2000

**Fewest doubles, season**
NL since 1900 (8 clubs)—1,148 in 1907 (1,119 in shortened 1918 season)
NL (10 clubs)—1,984 in 1963
NL (12 clubs)—2,455 in 1969 (1,881 in shortened 1981 season)
NL (14 clubs)—3,588 in 1993 (2,784 in shortened 1994 season)
NL (16 clubs)—4,482 in 2002
AL (8 clubs)—1,272 in 1909 (1,204 in shortened 1918 season)
AL (10 clubs)—1,874 in 1968
AL (12 clubs)—2,385 in 1969 (2,260 in shortened 1972 season)
AL (14 clubs)—3,325 in 1978 (2,119 in shortened 1981 season)

**Most players with 40 or more doubles, season**
AL—15 in 2000
NL—12 in 1920

## TRIPLES

**Most triples, season**
NL since 1900 (8 clubs)—684 in 1912
NL (10 clubs)—453 in 1962
NL (12 clubs)—554 in 1970
NL (14 clubs)—513 in 1993
NL (16 clubs)—532 in 2000
AL (8 clubs)—694 in 1921
AL (10 clubs)—408 in 1966
AL (12 clubs)—467 in 1976
AL (14 clubs)—644 in 1977

**Fewest triples, season**
NL since 1900 (8 clubs)—323 in 1942
NL (10 clubs)—359 in 1968
NL (12 clubs)—386 in 1973 (354 in shortened 1981 season)
NL (14 clubs)—434 in 1996 (377 in shortened 1994 season)
NL (16 clubs)—468 in 2005
AL (8 clubs)—267 in 1959
AL (10 clubs)—333 in 1964
AL (12 clubs)—351 in 1971 (316 in shortened 1972 season)
AL (14 clubs)—386 in 1992 (305 in shortened 1981 season)

**Most players with 20 or more triples**
NL since 1900—3 in 1911, 1912
AL—4 in 1912

## HOME RUNS

### SEASON

**Most home runs, season**
NL since 1900 (8 clubs)—1,263 in 1955
NL (10 clubs)—1,449 in 1962
NL (12 clubs)—1,824 in 1987
NL (14 clubs)—2,220 in 1996
NL (16 clubs)—3,005 in 2000
AL (8 clubs)—1,091 in 1959
AL (10 clubs)—1,552 in 1962
AL (12 clubs)—1,746 in 1970
AL (14 clubs)—2,742 in 1996

**Most home runs by both leagues, season**
5,693 in 2000 (16-club NL, 14-club AL)—3,005 in NL, 2,688 in AL
4,962 in 1996 (14-club leagues)—2,742 in AL, 2,220 in NL
4,458 in 1987 (14-club AL, 12-club NL)—2,634 in AL, 1,824 in NL
3,429 in 1970 (12-club leagues)—1,746 in AL, 1,683 in NL
3,001 in 1962 (10-club leagues)—1,552 in AL, 1,449 in NL

**Fewest home runs, season**
NL since 1900 (8 clubs)—96 in 1902
NL (10 clubs)—891 in 1963
NL (12 clubs)—1,113 in 1976 (719 in shortened 1981 season)
NL (14 clubs)—1,956 in 1993 (1,532 in in shortened 1994 season)
NL (16 clubs)—2,565 in 1998
AL (8 clubs)—104 in 1907 (96 in shortened 1918 season)
AL (10 clubs)—1,104 in 1968
AL (12 clubs)—1,122 in 1976
AL (14 clubs)—1,680 in 1978 (1,062 in shortened 1981 season)

**Most home runs by pinch-hitters, season**
NL since 1900 (8 clubs)—42 in 1958
NL (10 clubs)—45 in 1962
NL (12 clubs)—57 in 1986
NL (14 clubs)—75 in 1995
NL (16 clubs)—95 in 2001
AL (8 clubs)—29 in 1953
AL (10 clubs)—50 in 1961
AL (12 clubs)—24 in 1975
AL (14 clubs)—53 in 1980

**Most home runs by pinch-hitters in both leagues, season**
133 in 2004 (16-club NL, 14-club AL)—93 in NL, 40 in AL
117 in 1996 (14-club leagues)—74 in NL, 43 in AL
95 in 1970 (12-club leagues)—49 in AL, 46 in NL
84 in 1962 (10-club leagues)—45 in NL, 39 in AL

**Most clubs with 100 or more home runs, season**
NL since 1900 (8 clubs)—8 in 1956, 1958, 1959, 1961
NL (10 clubs)—10 in 1962
NL (12 clubs)—11 in 1970, 1986, 1987
NL (14 clubs)—4 in 1996, 1997
NL (16 clubs)—16 in 1998-2005
AL (8 clubs)—8 in 1958, 1960
AL (10 clubs)—10 in 1964
AL (12 clubs)—11 in 1970, 1973
AL (14 clubs)—14 in 1977, 1982, 1985-1988, 1990, 1993, 1995-2005

**Most players with 50 or more home runs, season**
NL—3 in 1998, 2001
AL—2 in 1938, 1961, 1996, 2002

**Most players with 40 or more home runs, season**
NL (16-clubs)—9 in 2000
AL (14-clubs)—8 in 1996, 1998

**Most players with 30 or more home runs, season**
NL (16-clubs)—25 in 2001
AL (14-clubs)—23 in 2000

**Most players with 20 or more home runs, season**
NL (16-clubs)—54 in 1999
AL (14-clubs)—51 in 1987

**Most players hitting home runs in all parks, season (8-club league)**
NL—11 in 1956 (8 parks; 5 of 11 also hit home runs at Jersey City)
AL—7 in 1953 (8 parks)

**Most players hitting home runs in all parks, season (10-club league)**
AL—4 in 1962
NL—3 in 1963

**Most players hitting home runs in all parks, season (12-club league)**
NL—3 in 1970
AL—1 in 1975

### ONE DAY

**Most players with two or more home runs in a game, season**
NL (16-clubs)—201 in 1999
NL (14-clubs)—137 in 1996
NL (12-clubs)—110 in 1987
NL (8-clubs)—84 in 1955
AL (14-clubs)—180 in 1996
AL (10-clubs)—98 in 1964
AL (8-clubs)—62 in 1960

**Fewest players with two or more home runs in a game, season**
NL—0 in 1907, 1918
AL—0 in 1908, 1915

**Most players with two or more home runs in a game, one day**
AL (14-clubs)—6—Aug 2, 1983; May 8, 1987
AL (10-clubs)—5—June 11, 1961; May 20, 1962
AL (8-clubs)—4—Apr 30, 1933; May 30, 1956
NL (16-clubs)—6—July 31, 1999
NL (14-clubs)—5—July 14, 1996
NL (12-clubs)—5—May 8, 1970
NL (10-clubs)—5—June 5, 1966
NL (8-clubs)—5—Aug 16, 1947

**Most players with two home runs in a game, both leagues, one day**
9 on July 2, 2002; 5 in AL, 4 in NL

**Most players with three or more home runs in a game, season**
NL—16 in 2001
AL—11 in 1996

**Most players from both leagues with three homers in a game, season**
22 in 2001; 16 in NL, 6 in AL

**Most times with five or more home runs in a game, season (club)**
NL (16-club league)—30 in 1999
NL (8-club league)—15 in 1954
AL (14-club league)—27 in 1999
AL (12-club league)—8 in 1969
AL (8-club league)—8 in 1950

**Most times with three or more home runs in an inning, season**
AL (14-clubs)—24 in 2000
AL (10-clubs)—10 in 1961, 1962
AL (8-clubs)—5 in 1936, 1947, 1953, 1954, 1956, 1957, 1959
NL (16-clubs)—21 in 2000
NL (14-clubs)—18 in 1996
NL (8-clubs)—13 in 1954, 1955

**Most home runs by pitchers, one day**
AL—4—July 31, 1935
NL—3—June 3, 1892; May 13, 1942; July 2, 1961; June 23, 1971

**Most home runs by pinch-hitters, one day**
NL—4—June 2, 1928; July 21, 1930
AL—4—June 28, 1987

**Most home runs in league, one day**
AL—36—Apr 7, 2000 (7 games)
NL—34—May 21, 2000 (8 games)

**Most home runs by both leagues, one day**
62—July 2, 2002; 32 in NL (8 games), 30 in AL (8 games)

## GRAND SLAMS

**Most grand slams, season**
NL since 1900 (8 clubs)—35 in 1950
NL (10 clubs)—37 in 1962
NL (12 clubs)—49 in 1970
NL (14 clubs)—60 in 1996
NL (16 clubs)—87 in 2000
AL (8 clubs)—37 in 1938
AL (10 clubs)—48 in 1961
AL (12 clubs)—39 in 1970, 1973
AL (14 clubs)—89 in 2000

**Most grand slams by both leagues, season**
176 in 2000 (16-club NL, 14-club AL)—89 in AL; 87 in NL
141 in 1996 (14-club leagues)—81 in AL; 60 in NL
88 in 1970 (12-club leagues)—49 in NL; 39 in AL
77 in 1961 (10-club AL, 8-club NL)—48 in AL; 29 in NL

**Fewest grand slams, season**
N.L.(since 1900)—1 in 1920
AL—1 in 1907, 1909, 1915 (0 in shortened 1918 season)

**Fewest grand slams by both leagues, season**
3—1907 (2 in NL, 1 in AL)

**Most grand slams by pinch-hitters, season**
NL since 1900 (8-clubs)—4 in 1959
AL (14-clubs)—5 in 1982, 1988

**Most grand slams by pinch-hitters in both leagues, season**
(14-club AL; 12-club NL)—13 in 1978 (9 in NL; 4 in AL)
(12-club leagues)—9 in 1973 (6 in NL; 3 in AL)
(8-club leagues)—8 in 1953 (5 in AL; 3 in NL)

**Most grand slams, one day**
NL—4—May 21, 2000
AL—4—July 22, 2000

**Most grand slams by both leagues, one day**
6—May 21, 2000 (4 in NL, 2 in AL)

## TOTAL BASES

**Most total bases, season**
NL since 1900 (8 clubs)—19,572 in 1930
NL (10 clubs)—21,781 in 1962
NL (12 clubs)—26,743 in 1987
NL (14 clubs)—31,708 in 1996
NL (16 clubs)—38,305 in 2000
AL (8 clubs)—18,427 in 1936
AL (10 clubs)—21,762 in 1962
AL (12 clubs)—25,281 in 1973
AL (14 clubs)—35,195 in 1996

**Most players with 300 or more total bases, season**
NL since 1900—20 in 1999, 2001
AL—22 in 2000

**Most players with 400 or more total bases, season**
NL since 1900—4 in 2001
AL—2 in 1927, 1936

## EXTRA-BASE HITS

**Most extra-base hits, season**
NL since 1900 (8 clubs)—3,903 in 1930
NL (10 clubs)—3,977 in 1962
NL (12 clubs)—5,385 in 1987
NL (14 clubs)—6,555 in 1997
NL (16 clubs)—8,169 in 2000
AL (8 clubs)—3,706 in 1936
AL (10 clubs)—4,190 in 1962
AL (12 clubs)—4,611 in 1970
AL (14 clubs)—7,377 in 2000

## RUNS BATTED IN

**Most runs batted in, season**
NL since 1900 (8 clubs)—6,582 in 1930
NL (10 clubs)—6,760 in 1962
NL (12 clubs)—8,233 in 1987
NL (14 clubs)—9,987 in 1996
NL (16 clubs)—12,321 in 1999
AL (8 clubs)—6,520 in 1936
AL (10 clubs)—6,842 in 1961
AL (12 clubs)—7,769 in 1973
AL (14 clubs)—11,583 in 1996

**Most players with 100 or more runs batted in, season**
NL—27 in 1999
AL—32 in 1999

## BASES ON BALLS

**Most bases on balls, season**
NL since 1900 (8 clubs)—4,537 in 1950
NL (10 clubs)—5,265 in 1962
NL (12 clubs)—6,919 in 1970
NL (14 clubs)—7,704 in 1997
NL (16 clubs)—9,735 in 2000
AL (8 clubs)—5,627 in 1949
AL (10 clubs)—5,902 in 1961
AL (12 clubs)—7,032 in 1969
AL (14 clubs)—8,592 in 1996

**Fewest bases on balls, season (since 1900)**
NL since 1900 (8 clubs)—2,906 in 1921
NL (10 clubs)—4,275 in 1968
NL (12 clubs)—2,906 in 1921
NL (14 clubs)—7,104 in 1993 (5,193 in shortened 1994 season)
NL (16 clubs)—8,396 in 2005
AL (8 clubs)—3,797 in 1922
AL (10 clubs)—4,881 in 1968
AL (12 clubs)—6,128 in 1976
AL (14 clubs)—6,811 in 2005 (4,761 in shortened 1981 season)

**Most players with 100 or more bases on balls, season**
AL—10 in 2000
NL—8 in 2002

## INTENTIONAL (SINCE 1955)

**Most intentional bases on balls, season**
NL since 1900 (8 clubs)—504 in 1956
NL (10 clubs)—804 in 1967
NL (12 clubs)—862 in 1973
NL (14 clubs)—743 in 1993
NL (16 clubs)—964 in 2002
AL (8 clubs)—353 in 1957
AL (10 clubs)—534 in 1965
AL (12 clubs)—668 in 1969
AL (14 clubs)—734 in 1993

**Fewest intentional bases on balls, season**
NL since 1900 (8 clubs)—387 in 1957
NL (10 clubs)—452 in 1962
NL (12 clubs)—626 in 1991 (505 in shortened 1981 season)
NL (14 clubs)—629 in 1997 (559 in shortened 1994 season)
NL (16 clubs)—647 in 1998
AL (8 clubs)—257 in 1959
AL (10 clubs)—290 in 1961
AL (12 clubs)—471 in 1976
AL (14 clubs)—420 in 1998

## STRIKEOUTS

**Most strikeouts, season**
NL since 1900 (8 clubs)—6,824 in 1960
NL (10 clubs)—9,649 in 1965
NL (12 clubs)—11,657 in 1987
NL (14 clubs)—15,320 in 1997
NL (16 clubs)—17,908 in 2001
AL (8 clubs)—6,081 in 1959
AL (10 clubs)—9,956 in 1964
AL (12 clubs)—10,957 in 1970
AL (14 clubs)—14,617 in 1997

**Fewest strikeouts, season**
NL since 1900 (8 clubs)—3,359 in 1926
NL (10 clubs)—9,032 in 1962
NL (12 clubs)—9,602 in 1976
NL (14 clubs)—13,358 in 1993
NL (16 clubs)—16,880 in 2005
AL (8 clubs)—3,245 in 1924
AL (10 clubs)—8,330 in 1961
AL (12 clubs)—9,143 in 1976
AL (14 clubs)—10,115 in 1979 (6,905 in shortened 1981 season)

**Most players with 100 or more strikeouts, season**
NL—42 in 2001
AL—38 in 1997

## SACRIFICE HITS AND FLIES

**Most sacrifices including scoring flies, season**
AL—1,731 in 1917
NL since 1900—1,655 in 1908

**Most sacrifices with no sacrifice flies, season**
NL since 1900—1,349 in 1907
AL—1,401 in 1906

**Fewest sacrifices, season**
AL—469 in 2005

NL since 1900—510 in 1957

**Most sacrifice flies, season**

NL since 1900 (8 clubs)—425 in 1954
NL (10 clubs)—410 in 1962
NL (12 clubs)—589 in 1988
NL (14 clubs)—701 in 1993
NL (16 clubs)—809 in 2000
AL (8 clubs)—370 in 1954
AL (10 clubs)—448 in 1961
AL (12 clubs)—624 in 1976
AL (14 clubs)—765 in 1979

**Fewest sacrifice flies, season**

NL since 1900 (8 clubs)—304 in 1959
NL (10 clubs)—363 in 1966
NL (12 clubs)—430 in 1969
NL (14 clubs)—643 in 1997
NL (16 clubs)—660 in 2003
AL (8 clubs)—312 in 1959
AL (10 clubs)—348 in 1967
AL (12 clubs)—484 in 1969
AL (14 clubs)—629 in 1987

## HIT BY PITCH

**Most hit by pitch, season**

NL since 1900 (8 clubs)—415 in 1903
NL (10 clubs)—404 in 1965
NL (12 clubs)—43 in 1969
NL (14 clubs)—773 in 1997
NL (16 clubs)—980 in 2005
AL (8 clubs)—454 in 1911
AL (10 clubs)—426 in 1968
AL (12 clubs)—441 in 1969
AL (14 clubs)—921 in 2001

**Fewest hit by pitch, season**

NL since 1900 (8 clubs)—157 in 1943
NL (10 clubs)—327 in 1964
NL (12 clubs)—249 in 1984 (185 in shortened 1981 season)
NL (14 clubs)—567 in 1993 (451 in shortened 1994 season)
NL (16 clubs)—799 in 1999
AL (8 clubs)—132 in 1947
AL (10 clubs)—316 in 1965
AL (12 clubs)—374 in 1976
AL (14 clubs)—372 in 1982

## GROUNDING INTO DOUBLE PLAYS

**Most grounding into double plays, season**

NL since 1900 (8 clubs)—1,105 in 1958
NL (10 clubs)—1,251 in 1962
NL (12 clubs)—1,547 in 1971
NL (14 clubs)—1,699 in 1996
NL (16 clubs)—2,085 in 2002
AL (8 clubs)—1,181 in 1950
AL (10 clubs)—1,256 in 1961
AL (12 clubs)—1,608 in 1973
AL (14 clubs)—1,968 in 1980

**Fewest grounding into double plays, season**

NL since 1900 (8 clubs)—820 in 1945
NL (10 clubs)—1,117 in 1963
NL (12 clubs)—1,198 in 1991 (962 in shortened 1981 season)
NL (14 clubs)—1,638 in 1993 (1,206 in shortened 1994 season)
NL (16 clubs)—1,925 in 2001
AL (8 clubs)—890 in 1945
AL (10 clubs)—1,060 in 1967
AL (12 clubs)—1,442 in 1976
AL (14 clubs)—1,708 in 1978 (1,236 in shortened 1994 season)

# INDIVIDUAL BASERUNNING

## STOLEN BASES

**Most stolen bases, career**

ML—1,406—Rickey Henderson, Oakland AL, New York AL, Toronto AL, San Diego NL, Anaheim AL, New York NL, Seattle AL, Boston AL, Los Angeles NL, 25 seasons, 1979-2003 (1,270 in AL, 136 in NL)
AL—1,270—Rickey Henderson, Oakland, New York, Toronto, Anaheim, Seattle, Boston, 21 seasons, 1979-2002, except 1996, 1999 and 2001
NL—938—Lou Brock, Chicago, St. Louis, 19 seasons, 1961-1979

**For a complete list of players with 400 or more career stolen bases, see page 108.**

**Highest stolen base percentage, career (minimum 300 attempts)**

M.L.—.847—Tim Raines Sr., Montreal NL, Chicago AL, New York AL, Oakland AL, Baltimore AL, Florida NL, 1979-2002, except 2000
NL—.857—Tim Raines Sr., Montreal, Florida, 1979-1990, 2001, 2002
AL—.833—Willie Wilson, Kansas City, Oakland, 1976-1992

**Most consecutive stolen bases with no caught stealing, career**

NL—50—Vince Coleman, St. Louis, Sept 18, 1988-July 26, 1989
AL—40—Tim Raines Sr., Chicago, July 23, 1993-Aug 4, 1995

**Most stolen bases, season**

AA—138—Hugh Nicol, Cincinnati, 125 G, 1887
AL—130—Rickey Henderson, Oakland, 149 G, 1982 (42 CS)
NL—118—Lou Brock, St. Louis, 153 G, 1974 (33 CS)

**For complete lists of players combining power and speed (40 HRs, 40 SBs; 30 HRs, 30 SBs; 50 HRs, 20 SBs and 20 HRs, 50 SBs) during a season, see page 116.**

**Fewest stolen bases for leader, season**

AL—15—Dom DiMaggio, Boston, 141 G, 1950
NL—16—Stan Hack, Chicago, 152 G, 1938

**Most stolen bases by rookie, season**

NL—110—Vince Coleman, St. Louis, 151 G, 1985
AA—98—Mike Griffin, Baltimore, 136 G, 1887
AL—66—Kenny Lofton, Cleveland, 148 G, 1992

**Most stolen bases with no caught stealing, season**

NL—21—Kevin McReynolds, New York, 147 G, 1988
AL—20—Paul Molitor, Toronto, 115 G, 1994

**Most seasons leading league in stolen bases**

AL—12—Rickey Henderson, Oakland, New York, 1980-1986, 1988-1991, 1998
NL—10—Max Carey, Pittsburgh, 1913, 1915-1918, 1920, 1922-1925

**Most consecutive seasons leading league in stolen bases**

AL—9—Luis Aparicio, Chicago, Baltimore, 1956-1964
NL—6—Maury Wills, Los Angeles, 1960-1965
Vince Coleman, St. Louis, 1985-1990

**Most seasons with 50 or more stolen bases**

AL—13—Rickey Henderson, Oakland, New York, Toronto, 1980-1986, 1988-1991, 1993, 1998
NL—12—Lou Brock, St. Louis, 1965-1976

**Most consecutive seasons with 50 or more stolen bases**

NL—12—Lou Brock, St. Louis, 1965-1976
AL—7—Rickey Henderson, Oakland, New York, 1980-1986

**Most at-bats with no stolen bases, season**

AL—677—Don Mattingly, New York, 162 G, 1986 (0 CS)
NL—662—Pete Rose, Cincinnati, 162 G, 1975 (1 CS)

**Most seasons with no stolen bases (150 or more games)**

ML—5—John Olerud, Toronto AL, New York NL, Seattle AL, 1993, 1997, 2000, 2002, 2003 (4 in AL, 1 in NL)
AL—4—Ken Singleton, Baltimore, 1977, 1980, 1982, 1983
Cecil Fielder, Detroit, 1990-1993
John Olerud, Toronto, Seattle, 1993, 2000, 2002, 2003
NL—3—Dal Maxvill, St. Louis, 1967, 1968, 1970
Deron Johnson, Cincinnati, Philadelphia, 1965, 1970, 1971

**Most stolen bases, game**

NL—7—George Gore, Chicago, June 25, 1881*
Billy Hamilton, Philadelphia, Aug 31, 1894, 2nd game
AL—6—Eddie Collins, Philadelphia, Sept 11, 1912; also Sept 22, 1912, 1st game
*stolen bases not officially compiled until 1886

**Most stolen bases, inning**

NL—3—many players; last—Eric Young, Colorado, June 30, 1996, 3rd
AL—3—many players; last—Chris Stynes, Kansas City, May 12, 1996, 1st

**Most stolen bases by pinch-runner, inning**

NL—2—Bill O'Hara, New York, Sept 1, 1909, 6th
Bill O'Hara, New York, Sept 2, 1909, 9th
Sandy Piez, New York, July 6, 1914, 2nd game, 9th
Jake Pitler, Pittsburgh, May 24, 1918, 9th
Dave Concepcion, Cincinnati, July 7, 1974, 1st game, 7th
Rodney Scott, Montreal, Sept 19, 1976, 1st game, 8th
Ron LeFlore, Montreal, October 5, 1980, 8th
Jerry Royster, Atlanta, May 7, 1981, 8th
Bob Dernier, Philadelphia, July 30, 1983, 1st game, 9th
Gary Redus, Cincinnati, July 25, 1985, 8th

Eric Davis, Cincinnati, July 22, 1986, 10th
Chris Sabo, Cincinnati, Apr 12, 1988, 9th
Eric Davis, Cincinnati, May 6, 1988, 9th
AL—2—Ray Dowd, Philadelphia, July 9, 1919, 2nd game, 9th
Allan Lewis, Kansas City, July 15, 1967, 7th
Tommy Harper, Cleveland, Sept 27, 1968, 9th
Bert Campaneris, Oakland, October 4, 1972, 4th
Don Hopkins, Oakland, Apr 20, 1975, 2nd game, 7th
Claudell Washington, Oakland, June 13, 1976, 8th
Matt Alexander, Oakland, Aug 8, 1976, 2nd game, 8th
Bert Campaneris, Texas, Sept 3, 1978, 8th
Bert Campaneris, Texas, Sept 6, 1978, 1st game, 7th
Bert Campaneris, California, Aug 25, 1981, 8th
Billy Sample, Texas, Apr 29, 1984, 9th
Alfredo Griffin, Toronto, Aug 27, 1984, 9th
Otis Nixon, Cleveland, Aug 19, 1985, 8th
Otis Nixon, Cleveland, Aug 18, 1986, 7th
Gary Pettis, Detroit, June 28, 1989, 2nd
Sammy Sosa, Chicago, Sept 4, 1990, 8th

**Appearing as a pinch-runner and pinch-hitter in the same game (different innings)**
AL—Pat Collins, St. Louis, June 8, 1923 (courtesy PR in 3rd, PH in 9th)
NL—none

## STEALS OF HOME

**Most times stole home, career**
AL—50—Ty Cobb, Detroit, Philadelphia, 24 seasons, 1905-1928
NL—33—Max Carey, Pittsburgh, Brooklyn, 20 seasons, 1910-1929

**Most times stole home, season**
AL—8—Ty Cobb, Detroit, 140 G, 1912 (61 SB)
NL—7—Pete Reiser, Brooklyn, 122 G, 1946 (34 SB)

**Most times stole way from first to home in an inning, career**
AL—4—Ty Cobb, Detroit, 1909, 1911, 1912 (2)
NL—3—Honus Wagner, Pittsburgh, 1902, 1907, 1909
NL—last player—Eric Young, Colorado, June 30, 1996, 3rd
AL—last player—Chris Stynes, Kansas City, May 12, 1996, 1st

**Most times stole home, game**
NL—2—Honus Wagner, Pittsburgh, June 20, 1901
Ed Konetchy, St. Louis, Sept 30, 1907
Joe Tinker, Chicago, June 28, 1910
Larry Doyle, New York, Sept 18, 1911
Sherry Magee, Philadelphia, July 20, 1912
Doc Gautreau, Boston, Sept 3, 1927, 1st game
AL—2—Joe Jackson, Cleveland, Aug 11, 1912
Guy Zinn, New York, Aug 15, 1912
Eddie Collins, Philadelphia, Sept 6, 1913
Bill Barrett, Chicago, May 1, 1924
[2—Vic Power, Cleveland, Aug 14, 1958, 10 inn]

## CAUGHT STEALING

**Most caught stealing, career**
ML—335—Rickey Henderson, Oakland AL, New York AL, Toronto AL, San Diego NL, Anaheim AL, New York NL, Seattle AL, Boston AL, Los Angeles NL, 25 seasons, 1979-2003 (293 in AL, 42 in NL)
NL—307—Lou Brock, Chicago, St. Louis, 19 seasons, 1961-1979
AL—293—Rickey Henderson, Oakland, New York, Toronto, Anaheim, Seattle, Boston, 21 seasons, 1979-2002, except 1996, 1999 and 2001

**Most caught stealing, season**
AL—42—Rickey Henderson, Oakland, 149 G, 1982 (130 SB)
NL—36—Miller Huggins, St. Louis, 148 G, 1914 (32 SB)

**Fewest caught stealing for leader, season**
AL—9—Hoot Evers, Detroit, 143 G, 1950 (5 SB)
Jim Rivera, Chicago, 139 G, 1956 (20 SB)
NL—10—Willie Mays, New York, 152 G, 1956 (40 SB)

**Most caught stealing by rookie, season**
NL—25—Vince Coleman, St. Louis, 151 G, 1985 (110 SB)
AL—21—Mike Edwards, Oakland, 142 G, 1978 (27 SB)

**Most seasons leading league in caught stealing**
NL—7—Maury Wills, Los Angeles, Pittsburgh, Montreal, 1961, 1962 (tied), 1963, 1965, 1966, 1968, 1969
Lou Brock, Chicago, St. Louis, 1964, 1967, 1971, 1973, 1974, 1976, 1977 (tied)
AL—6—Minnie Minoso, Chicago, Cleveland, 1952-1954, 1957, 1958, 1960

**Fewest caught stealing with 50 or more stolen bases, season**
NL—2—Max Carey, Pittsburgh, 155 G, 1922 (51 SB)
AL—8—Luis Aparicio, Chicago, 153 G, 1960 (51 SB)
Bert Campaneris, Oakland, 135 G, 1969 (62 SB)
Amos Otis, Kansas City, 147 G, 1971 (52 SB)
Willie Wilson, Kansas City, 137 G, 1983 (59 SB)
Rickey Henderson, Oakland, Toronto, 134 G, 1993 (53 SB)
Vince Coleman, Kansas City, 104 G, 1994 (50 SB)

**Fewest caught stealing, season (150 or more games)**
NL-AL—0—many players

**Most consecutive games with no caught stealing, career**
ML—1,206—Gus Triandos, New York AL, Baltimore AL, Detroit AL, Philadelphia NL, Houston NL, Aug 3, 1953-Aug 15, 1965 (1 SB)
AL—1,079—Gus Triandos, New York, Baltimore, Detroit, Aug 3, 1953-Sept 28, 1963 (1 SB)
NL—592—Frank Torre, Milwaukee, Philadelphia, Apr 20, 1956-Aug 10, 1962 (4 SB)

**Most caught stealing, game**
NL—3—many players
[4—Robby Thompson, San Francisco, June 27, 1986, 12 inn]
AL—3—many players

**Most caught stealing, inning**
AL—2—Don Baylor, Baltimore, June 15, 1974, 9th
Roberto Kelly, New York, Apr 17, 1990, 2nd
NL—2—Jim Morrison, Pittsburgh, June 15, 1987, 8th
Paul Noce, Chicago, June 26, 1987, 3rd
Donell Nixon, San Francisco, July 6, 1988, 6th
Tony Fernandez, San Diego, June 26, 1992, 5th
Eric Young, Colorado, May 1, 1993, 8th
Phil Plantier, San Diego, Sept 25, 1993, 5th
Derek Bell, Houston, June 19, 1995, 4th
Larry Walker, Colorado, Apr 30, 1998, 8th

## LEFT ON BASE

**Most runners left on base, game**
NL—12—Glenn Beckert, Chicago, Sept 16, 1972
Todd Helton, Colorado, Apr 11, 1998
AL—11—Frank Isbell, Chicago, Aug 10, 1901
[11—John Donahue, Chicago, June 23, 1907, 12 inn
George Wright, Texas, Aug 12, 1984, 11 inn]

**Most times out for being hit by batted ball, game**
NL—2—Walt Wilmot, Chicago, Sept 30, 1890
AL—2—Ernie Shore, Boston, July 28, 1917, 2nd game

# CLUB BASERUNNING

## STOLEN BASES

**Most stolen bases, season**
AA—638—Philadelphia, 137 G, 1887
NL—426—New York, 136 G, 1893
NL since 1900—347—New York, 154 G, 1911
AL—341—Oakland, 161 G, 1976

**Most players with 50 or more stolen bases, season**
AL—3—Oakland, 161 G, 1976; Bill North (75), Bert Campaneris (54), Don Baylor (52)
NL—3—San Diego, 163 G, 1980; Gene Richards (61), Ozzie Smith (57), Jerry Mumphrey (52)

**Most seasons leading league in stolen bases**
AL—30—Chicago, 1901-1904, 1917, 1919, 1923, 1924, 1926, 1928, 1929, 1939, 1941-1943, 1946, 1947, 1949, 1951-1961, 1966
NL since 1886—24—Brooklyn/Los Angeles, 1890, 1892, 1900, 1903, 1938, 1942, 1946-1953, 1955, 1958-1965, 1970 (15 Brooklyn, 9 LA)

**Fewest stolen bases, season**
AL—13—Washington, 154 G, 1957
NL—17—St. Louis, 157 G, 1949

**Most stolen bases, game**
AA—19—Philadelphia vs Syracuse, Apr 22, 1890
NL—17—New York vs Pittsburgh, May 23, 1890
AL—15—New York vs St. Louis, Sept 28, 1911
NL since 1893—11—New York vs Boston, June 20, 1912
St. Louis vs Pittsburgh, Aug 13, 1916, 2nd game, 5 inn

**Most stolen bases by both clubs, game**
AA—21—Philadelphia 19, Syracuse 2, Apr 22, 1890
NL—20—New York 17, Pittsburgh 3, May 23, 1890
NL since 1893—14—New York 9, Boston 5, June 20, 1912
AL—15—New York 15, St. Louis 0, Sept 28, 1911
St. Louis 8, Detroit 7, October 1, 1916

**Most triple steals, game**
AL—2—Philadelphia vs Cleveland, July 25, 1930, 1st and 4th
NL—1—many games

**Most triples steals by both clubs, game**
AL—2—Philadelphia 2, Cleveland 0, July 25, 1930
NL—1—many games

**Longest game without a stolen base**
NL—26 inn—Boston vs Brooklyn, May 1, 1920
AL—24 inn—Detroit vs Philadelphia, July 21, 1945
Philadelphia vs Detroit, July 21, 1945

**Longest game without a stolen base by either club**
AL—24 inn—Detroit 0, Philadelphia 0, July 21, 1945
NL—23 inn—San Francisco 0, New York 0, May 31, 1964, 2nd game

**Most stolen bases, inning**
AL—8—Washington vs Cleveland, July 19, 1915, 1st
NL—8—Philadelphia vs New York, July 7, 1919, 1st game, 9th

## STEALS OF HOME

**Most times stole home, season**
AL—18—New York, 153 G, 1912 (245 SB)
NL—17—Chicago, 157 G, 1911 (214 SB)
New York, 154 G, 1912 (319 SB)

**Most times stole home, game**
NL—3—St. Louis vs Boston, Sept 30, 1907
Chicago vs Boston, Aug 23, 1909
New York vs Pittsburgh, Sept 18, 1911
AL—3—Chicago vs St. Louis, July 2, 1909
New York vs Philadelphia, Apr 17, 1915

**Most times stole home by both clubs, game**
AL—3—Chicago 3, St. Louis 0, July 2, 1909
New York 3, Philadelphia 0, Apr 17, 1915
Detroit 2, St. Louis 1, Apr 22, 1924
NL—3—St. Louis 3, Boston 0, Sept 30, 1907
Chicago 3, Boston 0, Aug 23, 1909
New York 3, Pittsburgh 0, Sept 18, 1911

**Most times stole home, inning**
NL—2—many times; last—St. Louis vs Brooklyn, Sept 19, 1925, 7th
AL—2—many times; last—Oakland vs Kansas City, May 28, 1980, 1st

## CAUGHT STEALING

**Most caught stealing, season (since 1920)**
NL—149—Chicago, 154 G, 1924
AL—123—Oakland, 161 G, 1976

**Fewest caught stealing, season**
NL—8—Milwaukee, 154 G, 1958 (26 SB)
AL—11—Kansas City, 155 G, 1960 (16 SB)
Cleveland, 161 G, 1961 (34 SB)

**Most caught stealing, game**
NL—8—Baltimore vs Washington, May 11, 1897
AL—6—St. Louis vs Philadelphia, May 12, 1915
Chicago vs Philadelphia, June 18, 1915

**Most caught stealing, inning**
AA—3—Cincinnati vs Philadelphia, July 26, 1887, 3rd
AL—3—Detroit vs New York, Aug 3, 1914, 2nd
NL—3—Los Angeles vs Atlanta, Aug 6, 1982, 5th

## LEFT ON BASE

**Most left on base, season**
AL—1,334—St. Louis, 157 G, 1941
NL—1,328—Cincinnati, 162 G, 1970

**Fewest left on base, season**
AL—925—Kansas City, 154 G, 1957
NL—964—Chicago, 154 G, 1924

**Most left on base, game**
AL—20—New York vs Boston, Sept 21, 1956
[25—Washington vs Cleveland, Sept 14, 1971; 20-inning suspended game completed Sept 20
Kansas City vs Texas, June 6, 1991, 18 inn]
AA—18—Baltimore vs Cincinnati, July 7, 1891
NL—18—many times; last—Atlanta vs Los Angeles, June 23, 1986
[27—Atlanta vs Philadelphia, May 4, 1973, 20 inn]

**Most left on base, shutout defeat**
NL—16—St. Louis vs Philadelphia, May 24, 1994.
[16—St. Louis vs Cincinnati, Aug 30, 1989, 13 inn]
AL—16—Seattle vs Toronto, May 7, 1998

**Most left on base by both clubs, game**
NL—30—Brooklyn 16, Pittsburgh 14, June 30, 1893
New York 17, Philadelphia 13, July 18, 1943, 1st game
[45—New York 25, St. Louis 20, Sept 11, 1974, 25 inn]
AL—30—New York 15, Chicago 15, Aug 27, 1935, 1st game
Los Angeles 15, Washington 15, July 21, 1961
[45—Kansas City 25, Texas 20, June 6, 1991, 18 inn]

**Fewest left on base, game**
AL—0—many games
[0—Philadelphia vs New York, June 22, 1929, 2nd game, 14 inn]
NL—0—many games

**Fewest left on base by both clubs, game**
NL—1—Los Angeles 1, Chicago 0, Sept 9, 1965
[3—Chicago 2, Cincinnati 1, May 2, 1917, 10 inn]
AL—2—many games; last—Cleveland 1, Oakland 1, July 19, 1974
[4—many games in extra innings]

# LEAGUE BASERUNNING

## STOLEN BASES

**Most stolen bases, season**
NL since 1900 (8 clubs)—1,691 in 1911
NL (10 clubs)—788 in 1962
NL (12 clubs)—1,851 in 1987
NL (14 clubs)—1,817 in 1997
NL (16-clubs)—1,959 in 1999
AL (8 clubs)—1,809 in 1912
AL (10 clubs)—811 in 1968
AL (12 clubs)—1,690 in 1976
AL (14 clubs)—1,734 in 1987

**Fewest stolen bases, season**
NL since 1900 (8 clubs)—37 in 1954
NL (10 clubs)—636 in 1964
NL (12 clubs)—817 in 1969
NL (14 clubs)—1,714 in 1993 (1,141 in shortened 1994 season)
NL (16-clubs)—1,294 in 2003
AL (8 clubs)—278 in 1950
AL (10 clubs)—540 in 1964
AL (12 clubs)—863 in 1970 (853 in shortened 1972 season)
AL (14 clubs)—1,216 in 2005

## CAUGHT STEALING

**Most caught stealing, season**
NL since 1900 (8 clubs)—1001 in 1915
NL (10 clubs)—494 in 1966
NL (12 clubs)—870 in 1983
NL (14 clubs)—841 in 1997
NL (16 clubs)—830 in 1999
AL (8 clubs)—1,372 in 1914
AL (10 clubs)—471 in 1968
AL (12 clubs)—867 in 1976
AL (14 clubs)—1,236 in 2002

**Fewest caught stealing, season**
NL since 1900 (8 clubs)—35 in 1944
NL (10 clubs)—409 in 1962
NL (12 clubs)—492 in 1971
NL (14 clubs)—709 in 1996 (529 in shortened 1994 season)
NL (16-clubs)—527 in 2004
AL (8 clubs)—231 in 1950
AL (10 clubs)—270 in 1963
AL (12 clubs)—547 in 1971 (539 in shortened 1972 season)
AL (14 clubs)—509 in 2005 (503 in shortened 1994 season)

## LEFT ON BASE

**Most left on bases, season**
NL since 1900 (8 clubs)—9,424 in 1945
NL (10 clubs)—11,416 in 1962
NL (12 clubs)—14,468 in 1975
NL (14 clubs)—16,195 in 1997
NL (16-clubs)—18,939 in 2000
AL (8 clubs)—9,628 in 1936
AL (10 clubs)—11,680 in 1961
AL (12 clubs)—13,925 in 1973
AL (14 clubs)—16,711 in 1996

**Fewest left on bases, season**
NL since 1900 (8 clubs)—8,254 in 1920
NL (10 clubs)—10,994 in 1966
NL (12 clubs)—13,295 in 1988
NL (14 clubs)—15,941 in 1993 (11,438 in shortened 1994 season)
NL (16-clubs)—18,034 in 2001
AL (8 clubs)—7,943 in 1914
AL (10 clubs)—10,668 in 1966
AL (12 clubs)—13,494 in 1976
AL (14 clubs)—15,580 in 1979 (10,377 in shortened 1981 season)

# INDIVIDUAL PITCHING



## GAMES

**Most games, career**

ML—1,252—Jesse Orosco, New York NL, Los Angeles, NL, Cleveland AL, Milwaukee AL, Baltimore AL, St. Louis NL, San Diego NL, New York AL, Minnesota AL, 24 seasons, 1979, 1981-2003 (686 in AL, 566 in NL)
NL—1,119—John Franco, Cincinnati, New York, Houston, 21 seasons, 1984-2001, 2003-2005
AL—869—Dennis Eckersley, Cleveland, Boston, Oakland, 20 seasons, 1975-1984, 1987-1995, 1998

**For a complete list of pitchers with 700 or more career games pitched, see page 108.**

**Most games with one club**

AL—802—Walter Johnson, Washington, 21 seasons, 1907-1927
NL—802—Roy Face, Pittsburgh, 15 seasons, 1953-1968, except 1954

**Most games, season**

NL since 1900—106—Mike G. Marshall, Los Angeles, 1974 (208 IP)
AL—90—Mike G. Marshall, Minnesota, 1979 (143 IP)
NL—76—Will White, Cincinnati, 1879 (680 IP)
Pud Galvin, Buffalo, 1883 (656.1 IP)
Hoss Radbourn, Providence, 1883 (632.1 IP)

**Fewest games pitched by leader, season**

AL—40—Joe Haynes, Chicago, 1942 (103 inn)
NL—41—Ray Kremer, Pittsburgh, 1924 (259 inn)
Johnny Morrison, Pittsburgh, 1924 (238 inn)

**Most seasons leading league in games**

ML—7—Joe McGinnity, Brooklyn NL, Baltimore AL, New York NL, 1900, 1901, 1903-1907
NL—6—Joe McGinnity, Brooklyn, New York, 1900, 1903-1907
AL—6—Fred Marberry, Washington, 1924-1926, 1928, 1929, 1932

**Most games by rookie, season**

AL—88—Sean Runyan, Detroit, 1998 (0 CG, 50.1 inn)
NL—86—Oscar Villarreal, Arizona, 2003 (0 CG, 98 inn)

## GAMES STARTED

**Most games started, career**

ML—815—Cy Young, Cleveland NL, St. Louis NL, Boston AL, Cleveland AL, Boston NL, 22 seasons, 1890-1911 (457 in NL, 358 in AL)
NL—677—Steve Carlton, St. Louis, Philadelphia, San Francisco, 22 seasons, 1965-1986
AL—666—Walter Johnson, Washington, 21 seasons, 1907-1927

**For a complete list of pitchers with 500 or more career games started, see page 108.**

**Most games started, season**

NL—75—Will White, Cincinnati, 1879 (pitched 76 G)
Pud Galvin, Buffalo, 1883 (pitched 76 G)
AL—51—Jack Chesbro, New York, 1904 (pitched 55 G)
NL since 1893—48—Joe McGinnity, New York, 1903 (pitched 55 G)

**Most seasons leading league in games started**

NL—6—Robin Roberts, Philadelphia, 1950 (tied), 1951-1955
Tom Glavine, Atlanta, 1993 (tied), 1996, 1999 (tied), 2000 (tied), 2001 (tied), 2002
Greg Maddux, Chicago, Atlanta, 1990 (tied), 1991, 1992 (tied), 1993 (tied), 2000 (tied), 2003
AL—5—Bob Feller, Cleveland, 1940, 1941, 1946-1948
Early Wynn, Washington, Cleveland, Chicago, 1943 (tied), 1951 (tied), 1954, 1957, 1959 (tied)

**Most opening games started**

ML—16—Tom Seaver, New York NL, Cincinnati NL, Chicago AL, 1968-1979, 1981, 1983, 1985, 1986 (14 in NL, 2 in AL)
AL—14—Walter Johnson, Washington, 1910-1926, except 1911, 1922, 1925
Jack Morris, Detroit, Minnesota, Toronto, 1980-1993
NL—14—Tom Seaver, New York, Cincinnati, 1968-1979, 1981, 1983
Steve Carlton, Philadelphia, 1972-1986, except 1976

**Most consecutive starting assignments, career (since 1900)**

ML—627—Roger Clemens, Boston AL, Toronto AL, New York AL, Houston NL, July 26, 1984-2004 (594 in AL, 33 in NL)
AL—594—Roger Clemens, Boston, Toronto, New York, July 26, 1984-2003
NL—576—Greg Maddux, Chicago, Atlanta, Sept 15, 1986-2004

**Most games started with none complete, season**

NL—37—Steve Bedrosian, Atlanta, 1985
AL—35—Wilson Alvarez, Chicago, 1996
Sterling Hitchcock, Seattle, 1996
Rick Helling, Texas, 2000
Rodrigo Lopez, Baltimore, 2005
Barry Zito, Oakland, 2005

**Most games taken out as starting pitcher, season**

NL—37—Steve Bedrosian, Atlanta, 1985 (started 37)
AL—36—Stan Bahnsen, Chicago, 1972 (started 41)

## GAMES RELIEVED

**Most games as relief pitcher, career**

ML—1,248—Jesse Orosco, New York NL, Los Angeles NL, Cleveland AL, Milwaukee AL, Baltimore AL, St. Louis NL, San Diego NL, New York AL, Minnesota AL, 24 seasons, 1979, 1981-2003 (686 in AL, 562 in NL)
NL—1,119—John Franco, Cincinnati, New York, Houston, 21 seasons, 1984-2001, 2003-2005
AL—807—Sparky Lyle, Boston, New York, Texas, Chicago, 15 seasons, 1967-1980, 1982

**Most consecutive appearances as relief pitcher, career**

ML—1,199—Jesse Orosco, New York NL, Los Angeles NL, Cleveland AL, Milwaukee AL, Baltimore AL, St. Louis NL, San Diego NL, New York AL, Minnesota AL, July 20, 1982-Sept 27, 2003
NL—1,119—John Franco, Cincinnati, New York, Houston, Apr 24, 1984-July 1, 2005
AL—807—Sparky Lyle, Boston, New York, Texas, Chicago, July 4, 1967-Sept 9, 1980; Aug 23, 1982-Sept 27, 2nd game, 1982

**Most games, none of which were starts, career**

NL—1,119—John Franco, Cincinnati, New York, Houston, 21 seasons, 1984-2001, 2002-2004
AL—807—Sparky Lyle, Boston, New York, Texas, Chicago, July 4, 1967-Sept 9, 1980; Aug 23, 1982-Sept 27, 2nd game, 1982

**Most games as relief pitcher, season**

NL—106—Mike G. Marshall, Los Angeles, 1974 (208 IP; no starts)
AL—89—Mike G. Marshall, Minnesota, 1979 (141 IP; 1 start)
Mark Eichhorn, Toronto, 1987, (127.2 inn; no starts)

**Most games, none of which were starts, season**

NL—106—Mike G. Marshall, Los Angeles, 1974 (finished 83, 208 inn)
AL—89—Mark Eichhorn, Toronto, 1987 (finished 27, 127.2 inn)

**Most consecutive games appearing as relief pitcher**

NL—13—Mike G. Marshall, Los Angeles, June 18-July 3, 1st game, 1974 (26.2 inn)
AL—13—Dale Mohorcic, Texas, Aug 6-20, 1986 (14 inn)

## COMPLETE GAMES

**Most complete games, career**

ML—749—Cy Young, Cleveland NL, St. Louis NL, Boston AL, Cleveland AL, Boston NL, 22 seasons, 1890-1911 (426 in NL, 323 in AL)
NL—558—Pud Galvin, Buffalo, Pittsburgh, St. Louis, 12 seasons, 1879-1892, except 1886, 1890
AL—531—Walter Johnson, Washington, 21 seasons, 1907-1927
NL since 1893—437—Grover Alexander, Philadelphia, Chicago, St. Louis, 20 seasons, 1911-1930

**For a complete list of pitchers with 300 or more career complete games, see page 108.**

**Most complete games by righthander, career**

ML—749—Cy Young, Cleveland NL, St. Louis NL, Boston AL, Cleveland AL, Boston NL, 22 seasons, 1890-1911 (426 in NL, 323 in AL)
NL—558—Pud Galvin, Buffalo, Pittsburgh, St. Louis,12 seasons, 1879-1892, except 1886, 1890
AL—531—Walter Johnson, Washington, 21 seasons, 1907-1927
NL since 1893—437—Grover Alexander, Philadelphia, Chicago, St. Louis, 20 seasons, 1911-1930

**Most complete games by lefthander, career**

AL—387—Eddie Plank, Philadelphia, St. Louis, 16 seasons, 1901-1917, except 1915
NL—382—Warren Spahn, Boston, Milwaukee, New York Mets, San Francisco, 21 seasons, 1942-1965, except 1943, 1944, 1945 in military service

**Most complete games, season**

NL—75—Will White, Cincinnati, 1879 (pitched in 76 G)
AL—48—Jack Chesbro, New York, 1904 (pitched in 55 G)
NL since 1893—45—Vic Willis, Boston, 1902 (pitched in 51 G)

**Fewest complete games for leader, season**

NL—6—Curt Schilling, Arizona, 2001
AL—5—Mark Mulder, Oakland, 2004
Sidney Ponson, Baltimore, 2004
Jake Westbrook, Cleveland, 2004
Roy Halladay, Toronto, 2005

**Most seasons leading league in complete games**

NL—9—Warren Spahn, Boston, Milwaukee, 1949, 1951, 1957-1959, 1960 (tied), 1961-1963
AL—6—Walter Johnson, Washington, 1910, 1911, 1913-1916

**Most consecutive complete games pitched, season (since 1900)**

NL—39—Jack W. Taylor, St. Louis, Apr 15-Oct 6, 1st game, 1904 (352 IP, including 2 games in relief)
AL—37—Bill Dinneen, Boston, Apr 16-Oct 10, 1st game, 1904 (337 IP)

**Most games, none of which were complete, season**

NL—106—Mike G. Marshall, Los Angeles, 1974 (208 IP; no starts)
AL—90—Mike G. Marshall, Minnesota, 1979 (143 IP; 1 start)

**Most complete games by rookie, season**

NL—67—Jim Devlin, Louisville, 1876 (67 G)
NL since 1900—41—Irv Young, Boston, 1905 (43 G)
AL—36—Roscoe Miller, Detroit, 1901 (38 G)

**Most complete doubleheaders, career**
ML—5—Joe McGinnity, Baltimore AL, 1901 (2); New York NL, 1903 (3)
NL—3—Joe McGinnity, New York, 1903
AL—2—many pitchers

**Most complete doubleheaders, season**
NL—3—Joe McGinnity, New York, Aug 1, 8, 31, 1903 (won 3)
AL—2—Joe McGinnity, Baltimore, 1901 (split 2)
Mule Watson, Philadelphia, 1918 (split 1; loss and tie in other DH)

## INNINGS

**Most innings pitched, career**
ML—7,356—Cy Young, Cleveland NL, St. Louis NL, Boston AL, Cleveland AL, Boston NL, 22 seasons, 1890-1911 (4,123.2 in NL, 3,232.1 in AL)
AL—5,914.2—Walter Johnson, Washington, 21 seasons, 1907-1927
NL—5,243.2—Warren Spahn, Boston, Milwaukee, New York Mets, San Francisco, 21 seasons, 1942-1965, except 1943-1945 in military service

**For a complete list of pitchers with 3,500 or more career innings, see page 108.**

**Most innings pitched, season**
NL—680—Will White, Cincinnati, 76 G, 1879
AL—464—Ed Walsh, Chicago, 66 G, 1908
NL since 1893—434—Joe McGinnity, New York, 55 G, 1903

**Fewest innings pitched by leader, season**
AL—231.2—David Wells, Toronto, 34 G, 1999
NL—233.1—Livan Hernandez, Montreal, 33 G, 2003

**Most seasons leading league in innings pitched**
NL—7—Grover Alexander, Philadelphia, Chicago, 1911, 1912 (tied), 1914-1917, 1920
AL—5—Walter Johnson, Washington, 1910, 1913-1916
Bob Feller, Cleveland, 1939-1941, 1946, 1947

**Most innings pitched by rookie, season (since 1900)**
NL—378—Irv Young, Boston, 43 G, 1905
AL—316—Reb Russell, Chicago, 43 G, 1913

**Most seasons with 200 or more innings pitched**
ML—20—Don Sutton, Los Angeles NL, Houston NL, Milwaukee AL, Oakland AL, California AL, 1966-1980, 1982-1986 (15 in NL, 4 in AL, 1 in NL/AL)
AL—18—Walter Johnson, Washington, 1908-1926, except 1920
NL—17—Warren Spahn, Boston, Milwaukee, 1947-1963
Greg Maddux, Chicago, Atlanta, 1988-2001, 2002-2005

**Most seasons with 300 or more innings pitched**
ML—16—Cy Young, Cleveland NL, St. Louis NL, Boston AL, 1891-1907, except 1906 (10 in NL, 6 in AL)
NL—12—Kid Nichols, Boston, 1890-1899, 1901, 1904
NL since 1893—11—Christy Mathewson, New York, 1901, 1903-1905, 1907, 1908, 1910-1914
AL—9—Walter Johnson, Washington, 1910-1918

**Most consecutive seasons with 300 or more innings (since 1900)**
AL—9—Walter Johnson, Washington, 1910-1918
NL—7—Grover Alexander, Philadelphia, 1911-1917

**Most seasons with 400 or more innings pitched (since 1900)**
NL—2—Joe McGinnity, New York, 1903 (434), 1904 (408)
AL—2—Ed Walsh, Chicago, 1907 (419), 1908 (464)

**Most consecutive innings without relief, career (since 1900)**
NL—1,729—Jack W. Taylor, Chicago, St. Louis, June 20, 2nd game, 1901-Aug 13, 1906 (204 G, 188 CG, 15 finished)

**Most consecutive innings without relief, season (since 1900)**
NL—352—Jack W. Taylor, St. Louis, Apr 15-Oct 6, 1st game, 1904 (complete season, 39 CG and 2 games finished)
AL—337—Bill Dinneen, Boston, Apr 16-Oct 10, 1st game, 1904 (complete season, 37 CG)

**Most innings pitched in relief, career**
ML—1,870—Hoyt Wilhelm, New York Giants NL, St. Louis NL, Cleveland AL, Baltimore AL, Chicago AL, California AL, Atlanta NL, Chicago NL, Los Angeles NL, 21 seasons, 1952-1972 (916 in NL, 954 in AL)
NL—1,436.1—Kent Tekulve, Pittsburgh, Philadelphia, Cincinnati, 16 seasons, 1974-1989
AL—1,265—Sparky Lyle, Boston, New York, Texas, Chicago, 15 seasons, 1967-1982, except 1981

**Most innings pitched in relief, season**
NL—208—Mike G. Marshall, Los Angeles, 1974 (106 games as relief pitcher)
AL—168.1—Bob Stanley, Boston, 1982 (48 games as relief pitcher) (Bill Campbell, Minnesota, 167.2 IP in relief, rounded to 168, in 1976)

**Most innings pitched, game**
NL—26—Leon Cadore, Brooklyn, May 1, 1920 (1-1 tie)
Joe Oeschger, Boston, May 1, 1920 (1-1 tie)
AL—24—Jack Coombs, Philadelphia, Sept 1, 1906 (won, 4-1)
Joe Harris, Boston, Sept 1, 1906 (lost, 4-1)

## WINNING PERCENTAGE

**Highest winning percentage, career (200 or more wins)**
AL—.690—Whitey Ford, New York, 16 seasons, 1950-1967, except 1951, 1952 in military service (won 236, lost 106)
NL—.665—Christy Mathewson, New York, Cincinnati, 17 seasons, 1900-1916 (won 373, lost 188)

**Highest winning percentage, season (70 or more decisions)**
NL—.833—Hoss Radbourn, Providence, 1884 (won 60, lost 12)
AL—none

**Highest winning percentage, season (34 or more decisions)**
AL—.886—Lefty Grove, Philadelphia, 1931 (won 31, lost 4)
NL—.824—Jack Chesbro, Pittsburgh, 1902 (won 28, lost 6)
Dazzy Vance, Brooklyn, 1924 (won 28, lost 6)

**Highest winning percentage, season (20 or more wins)**
AL—.893—Ron Guidry, New York, 1978 (won 25, lost 3)
NL since 1893—.880—Preacher Roe, Brooklyn, 1951 (won 22, lost 3)
NL—.875—Fred Goldsmith, Chicago, 1880 (won 22, lost 3)

**Highest winning percentage, season (16 or more decisions)**
NL—.947—Roy Face, Pittsburgh, 1959 (won 18, lost 1)
AL—.938—Johnny Allen, Cleveland, 1937 (won 15, lost 1)

**Most seasons leading league in winning percentage (15 or more wins)**
AL—5—Lefty Grove, Philadelphia, Boston, 1929-1931, 1933, 1939
NL—3—Ed Reulbach, Chicago, 1906-1908

## GAMES WON

### CAREER

**Most games won, career**
ML—511—Cy Young, Cleveland NL, St. Louis NL, Boston AL, Cleveland AL, Boston NL, 22 seasons, 1890-1911 (289 in NL, 222 in AL)
AL—417—Walter Johnson, Washington, 21 seasons, 1907-1927
NL—373—Christy Mathewson, New York, Cincinnati, 17 seasons, 1900-1916
Grover Alexander, Philadelphia, Chicago, St. Louis, 20 seasons, 1911-1930

**For a complete list of pitchers with 200 or more career victories, see page 109.**

**Most games won by righthander, career**
ML—511—Cy Young, Cleveland NL, St. Louis NL, Boston AL, Cleveland AL, Boston NL, 22 seasons, 1890-1911 (289 in NL, 222 in AL)
AL—417—Walter Johnson, Washington, 21 seasons, 1907-1927
NL—373—Christy Mathewson, New York, Cincinnati, 17 seasons, 1900-1916
Grover Alexander, Philadelphia, Chicago, St. Louis, 20 seasons, 1911-1930

**Most games won by lefthander, career**
NL—363—Warren Spahn, Boston, Milwaukee, New York, San Francisco, 21 seasons, 1942-1965, except 1943-1945 in military service
AL—305—Eddie Plank, Philadelphia, St. Louis, 16 seasons, 1901-1917, except 1915

**Most games won as relief pitcher, career**
ML—124—Hoyt Wilhelm, New York NL, St. Louis NL, Cleveland AL, California AL, Atlanta NL, Baltimore AL, Chicago AL, Chicago NL, Los Angeles NL, 21 seasons, 1952-1972 (73 in AL, 51 in NL)
NL—96—Roy Face, Pittsburgh, Montreal, 16 years, 1953 through 1969, except 1954 (lost 82)
AL—87—Sparky Lyle, Boston, New York, Texas, Chicago, 15 years, 1967 through 1982, except 1981 (lost 67)

**Most games won from one club, career**
NL—70—Grover Alexander, Philadelphia, Chicago, St. Louis, vs Cincinnati, 20 seasons, 1911-1930
AL—66—Walter Johnson, Washington, vs Detroit, 21 seasons, 1907-1927

**Most season-opening games won, career**
AL—9—Walter Johnson, Washington, 1910, 1913-1917, 1919, 1924, 1926 (all CG; 7 shutouts)
NL—8—Grover Alexander, Philadelphia, Chicago, St. Louis, 1914-1917, 1921, 1922, 1925, 1929 (7 CG; 1 shutout)

### SEASON AND MONTH

**Most games won by righthander, season**
NL—59—Hoss Radbourn, Providence, 1884 (lost 12)
AL—41—Jack Chesbro, New York, 1904 (lost 13)
NL since 1893—37—Christy Mathewson, New York, 1908 (lost 11)

**Most games won by lefthander, season**
AA—46—Matt Kilroy, Baltimore, 1887 (lost 20)
NL—42—Charles Baldwin, Detroit, 1886 (lost 14)
AL—31—Lefty Grove, Philadelphia, 1931 (lost 4)
NL since 1893—27—Sandy Koufax, Los Angeles, 1966 (lost 9)
Steve Carlton, Philadelphia, 1972 (lost 10)

**For a complete list of 20-game winners each season, see page 131.**

**Most games won as rookie, season**
NL—47—Al Spalding, Chicago, 1876 (lost 13)
NL since 1893—28—Grover Alexander, Philadelphia, 1911 (lost 13)
AL—26—Russ Ford, New York, 1910 (lost 6)

**Most games won as relief pitcher, season**
NL—18—Roy Face, Pittsburgh, 1959 (lost 1)
AL—17—John Hiller, Detroit, 1974 (lost 14)
Bill Campbell, Minnesota, 1976 (lost 5)

**Fewest games won by leader, season**
NL—18—Rick Sutcliffe, Chicago, 1987 (lost 10)
AL—18—Whitey Ford, New York, 1955 (lost 7)
Bob Lemon, Cleveland, 1955 (lost 10)
Frank Sullivan, Boston, 1955 (lost 13)

Chuck Estrada, Baltimore, 1960 (lost 11)
Jim Perry, Cleveland, 1960 (lost 10)

**Most seasons leading league in games won**
NL—8—Warren Spahn, Boston, Milwaukee, 1949, 1950, 1953 (tied), 1957, 1958 (tied), 1959 (tied), 1960 (tied), 1961 (tied)
AL—6—Walter Johnson, Washington, 1913-1916, 1918, 1924
Bob Feller, Cleveland, 1939-1941, 1946 (tied), 1947, 1951

**Most games won from one club, season**
NL—12—Hoss Radbourn, Providence, vs Cleveland, 1884 (lost 1)
NL since 1893—9—Ed Reulbach, Chicago, vs Brooklyn, 1908 (lost 0)
AL—9—Frank Smith, Chicago, vs Washington, 1904 (lost 1)
Ed Walsh, Chicago, vs New York, 1908 (lost 1), and vs Boston, 1908 (lost 0)
Walter Johnson, Washington, vs Chicago, 1912 (lost 1)

**Most games won, one month**
NL—15—John Clarkson, Chicago, June 1885 (lost 1)
NL since 1893—9—Christy Mathewson, New York, Aug 1903 (lost 1)
Christy Mathewson, New York, Aug 1904 (lost 1)
Grover Alexander, Chicago, May 1920 (lost 0)
AL—10—Rube Waddell, Philadelphia, July 1902 (lost 1, tied 1)

## 20- AND 30-WIN SEASONS

**Most seasons winning 30 or more games**
NL—7—Kid Nichols, Boston, 1891-1894, 1896-1898
AL—2—Cy Young, Boston, 1901, 1902
Walter Johnson, Washington, 1912, 1913

**For a complete list of pitchers with two or more 30-victory seasons, see page 109.**

**Most seasons winning 20 or more games**
ML—15—Cy Young, Cleveland NL, 1891-1898; St. Louis, NL, 1899; Boston AL, 1901-1904, 1907, 1908 (9 in NL, 6 in AL)
NL—13—Christy Mathewson, New York, 1901, 1903-1914
Warren Spahn, Boston, Milwaukee, 1947, 1949-1951, 1953, 1954, 1956-1961, 1963
AL—12—Walter Johnson, Washington, 1910-1919, 1924, 1925

**For a complete list of 20-game winners each season, see page 131.**
**For a complete list of pitchers with five or more 20-victory seasons, see page 109.**

**Most seasons winning 20 or more games by righthander**
ML—15—Cy Young, Cleveland NL, 1891-1898; St. Louis, NL, 1899; Boston AL, 1901-1904, 1907, 1908 (9 in NL, 6 in AL)
NL—13—Christy Mathewson, New York, 1901, 1903-1914
AL—12—Walter Johnson, Washington, 1910-1919, 1924, 1925

**Most seasons winning 20 or more games by lefthander**
NL—13—Warren Spahn, Boston, Milwaukee, 1947, 1949-1951, 1953, 1954, 1956-1961, 1963
AL—8—Lefty Grove, Philadelphia, Boston, 1927-1933, 1935

**Most consecutive seasons winning 20 or more games**
NL—12—Christy Mathewson, New York, 1903-1914
AL—10—Walter Johnson, Washington, 1910-1919

**Most consecutive seasons winning 20 or more games from start of career**
NL—10—Kid Nichols, Boston, 1890-1899
AL—3—Vean Gregg, Cleveland, 1911-1913

## DOUBLEHEADER

**Most complete-game doubleheaders won, career**
NL—3—Joe McGinnity, New York, 1903 (lost 0)
AL—2—Ed Walsh, Chicago, 1905, 1908 (lost 0)

**For a complete list of pitchers with two complete-game victories in one day, see page 129.**

**Most complete-game doubleheaders won, season**
NL—3—Joe McGinnity, New York, 1903
AL—1—many pitchers; last—Dutch Levsen, Cleveland vs Boston, Aug 28, 1926

## CONSECUTIVE

**Most consecutive games won, career**
NL—24—Carl Hubbell, New York, July 17, 1936-May 27, 1937 (16 in 1936, 8 in 1937)
AL—20—Roger Clemens, Toronto, New York, June 3, 1998-June 1, 1999 (15 with Toronto in 1998, 5 with New York in 1999)

**Most consecutive games won from start of career as starting pitcher**
NL—12—Hooks Wiltse, New York, May 29-Sept 15, 1904
AL—9—Whitey Ford, New York, July 17-Sept 24, 2nd game, 1950

**Most consecutive games won from start of career as relief pitcher**
NL—12—Butch Metzger, San Francisco, 1974 (1), San Diego, 1975 (1), 1976 (10), Sept 21, 1974-Aug 8, 1976
AL—11—Jesse Crain, Minnesota, Sept 1, 2004-July 1, 2005

**Most consecutive games won from one club, career**
NL—24—Christy Mathewson, New York, vs St. Louis, June 16, 1904-Sept 15, 1908
AL—24—Carl Mays, Boston, New York, vs Philadelphia, Aug 30, 1918-July 24, 1923

**Most consecutive games won, season**
NL—19—Tim Keefe, New York, June 23-Aug 10, 1888
Rube Marquard, New York, Apr 11-July 3, 1st game, 1912
AL—16—Walter Johnson, Washington, July 3, 2nd game-Aug 23, 1st game, 1912
Joe Wood, Boston, July 8-Sept 15, 2nd game, 1912
Lefty Grove, Philadelphia, June 8-Aug 19, 1931
Schoolboy Rowe, Detroit, June 15-Aug 25, 1934
Roger Clemens, New York, May 26-Sept 19, 2001

**For a complete list of pitchers with 12 consecutive victories in one season, see page 130.**

**Most consecutive games won from start of season**
NL—19—Rube Marquard, New York, Apr 11-July 3, 1st game, 1912
AL—15—Johnny Allen, Cleveland, Apr 23, 1937-Sept 30, 1st game, 1937
Dave McNally, Baltimore, Apr 12-July 30, 1969

**Most consecutive games won as relief pitcher, season**
NL—17—Roy Face, Pittsburgh, Apr 22-Aug 30, 2nd game, 1959
AL—12—Luis Arroyo, New York, July 1-Sept 9, 1961

**Most consecutive games won by rookie, season**
NL—17—Pat Luby, Chicago, Aug 6, 2nd game-Oct 3, 1890
NL since 1893—12—Hooks Wiltse, New York, May 29-Sept 15, 1904
AL—12—Atley Donald, New York, May 9-July 25, 1939
Russ Ford, New York, Aug 9-Oct 6, 1910

**Most consecutive games won by rookie as starting pitcher, season**
NL—17—Pat Luby, Chicago, Aug 6, 2nd game-Oct 3, 1890
NL since 1893—12—Hooks Wiltse, New York, May 29-Sept 15, 1904
AL—12—Atley Donald, New York, May 9-July 25, 1939

**Most consecutive games won by rookie as relief pitcher, season**
NL—10—Eddie Yuhas, St. Louis, June 5-Sept 25, 1952
Butch Metzger, San Diego, Apr 20-Aug 8, 1976
AL—9—Joe Pate, Philadelphia, Apr 15-Aug 10, 1926
Jeff Zimmerman, Texas, Apr 14-Aug 2, 1999

**Most consecutive games won as relief pitcher making consecutive appearances during club's winning streak**
AL—3—Hal White, Detroit, Sept 26, 2nd game, 27, 28, 1950 (5.1 IP)
Grant Jackson, Baltimore, Sept 29, 30, Oct 1, 1974 (5.1 IP)
Sparky Lyle, New York, Aug 29, 30, 31, 1977 (7.2 IP)
Chuck McElroy, California, June 10, 11, 12, 1996 (3.0 IP)
John Frascatore, Toronto, June 29, 30, July 1, 1999 (2.1 IP)
NL—3—Mike G. Marshall, Los Angeles, June 21, 22, 23, 1974 (7.0 IP)
Gene Garber, Philadelphia, May 15, 2nd game, 16, 17, 1975 (5.2 IP)
Al Hrabosky, St. Louis, July 12, 13, 17, 1975 (5.0 IP)
Kent Tekulve, Pittsburgh, May 6, 7, 9, 1980 (5.1 IP)
Mitch Williams, Philadelphia, Aug 4, 6, 7, 1991 (4.0 IP)

**Most consecutive games won, end of season**
NL—17—Pat Luby, Chicago, Aug 6, 2nd game-Oct 3, 1890
NL since 1893—16—Carl Hubbell, New York, July 17-Sept 23, 1936
AL—15—Alvin Crowder, Washington, Aug 2-Sept 25, 1932
Roger Clemens, Toronto, June 3-Sept 21, 1998

## SAVES (SINCE 1969)

**Most saves, career**
ML—478—Lee Smith, Chicago NL, Boston AL, St. Louis NL, New York AL, Baltimore AL, California AL, Cincinnati NL, Montreal NL, 18 seasons, 1980-1997 (347 in NL, 131 in AL)
NL—436—Trevor Hoffman, Florida, San Diego, 1993-2005, 13 seasons
AL—379—Mariano Rivera, New York, 11 seasons, 1995-2005

**For a complete list of pitchers with 150 or more career saves, see page 110.**

**Most saves, season**
AL—57—Bobby Thigpen, Chicago, 1990
NL—55—John Smoltz, Atlanta, 2002
Eric Gagne, Los Angeles, 2003

**Most saves by rookie, season**
AL—37—Kazuhiro Sasaki, Seattle, 2000
NL—36—Todd Worrell, St. Louis, 1986

## GAMES LOST

**Most games lost, career**
ML—316—Cy Young, Cleveland NL, St. Louis NL, Boston AL, Cleveland AL, Boston NL, 22 seasons, 1890-1911 (175 in NL, 141 in AL)
AL—279—Walter Johnson, Washington, 21 seasons, 1907-1927
NL—267—Pud Galvin, Buffalo, Pittsburgh, St. Louis, 12 seasons, 1879-1892, except 1886 and 1890
NL since 1893—251—Eppa Rixey, Philadelphia, Cincinnati, 21 seasons, 1912-1933, except 1918 in military service

**Most games lost by righthander, career**
ML—316—Cy Young, Cleveland NL, St. Louis NL, Boston AL, Cleveland AL, Boston NL, 22 seasons, 1890-1911 (175 in NL, 141 in AL)
AL—279—Walter Johnson, Washington, 21 seasons,1907-1927

NL—267—Pud Galvin, Buffalo, Pittsburgh, St. Louis,12 seasons, 1879-1892, except 1886 and 1890
NL since 1893—230—Phil Niekro, Milwaukee, Atlanta, 21 seasons, 1964-1983, 1987

**Most games lost by lefthander, career**
NL—251—Eppa Rixey, Philadelphia, Cincinnati, 21 seasons, 1912-1933, except 1918 in military service
AL—221—Frank Tanana, California, Boston, Texas, Detroit, New York, 21 seasons, 1973-1993

**Most consecutive games lost, career**
NL—27—Anthony Young, New York, May 6, 1992-July 24, 1993 (14 in 1992, 13 in 1993)
AL—19—Jack Nabors, Philadelphia, Apr 28-Sept 28, 1916

**Most consecutive games lost to one club, career**
NL—13—Don Sutton, Los Angeles vs Chicago, Apr 23, 1966-July 24, 1969 (start of career)
AL—10—Dave Morehead, Boston vs Los Angeles, July 28, 1963-Sept 20, 1965 (start of career)

**Most consecutive games lost from start of career**
AL—16—Terry Felton, Minnesota, Apr 18, 2nd game, 1980-Sept 12, 1982
AA—10—Charlie Stecher, Philadelphia, Sept 6-Oct 9, 1890

**Most games lost, season**
NL—48—John F. Coleman, Philadelphia, 1883 (won 12)
NL since 1893—29—Vic Willis, Boston, 1905 (won 12)
AL—26—Jack Townsend, Washington, 1904 (won 5)
Bob Groom, Washington, 1909 (won 6)

**Most games lost as relief pitcher, season**
NL—16—Gene Garber, Atlanta, 1979 (won 6
AL—14—Darold Knowles, Washington, 1970 (won 2)
John Hiller, Detroit, 1974 (won 17)
Mike G. Marshall, Minnesota, 1979 (won 10, also one loss as starter)

**Fewest games lost for leader, season**
AL—14—Ted Gray, Detroit, 1951 (won 7)
Alex Kellner, Philadelphia, 1951 (won 11)
Bob Lemon, Cleveland 1951 (won 17)
Billy Pierce, Chicago, 1951 (won 15)
Duane Pillette, St. Louis, 1951 (won 6)
Dizzy Trout, Detroit, 1951 (won 9)
NL—15—Don Carman, Philadelphia, 1989 (won 5)
Orel Hershiser, Los Angeles, 1989 (won 15)
Ken Hill, St. Louis, 1989 (won 7)
Tom Candiotti, Los Angeles, 1992 (won 11)
Orel Hershiser, Los Angeles, 1992 (won 10)

**Most seasons leading league in games lost**
NL—4—Phil Niekro, Atlanta, 1977 (tied), 1978-1980
AL—4—Bobo Newsom, St. Louis, Washington, Detroit, Philadelphia, 1934, 1935, 1941, 1945
Pedro Ramos, Washington, Minnesota, 1958-1961

**Most games lost by rookie, season**
NL—48—John F. Coleman, Philadelphia, 1883 (won 12)
NL since 1900—25—Harry McIntire, Brooklyn, 1906 (won 8)
AL—26—Bob Groom, Washington, 1909 (won 6)

**Most games lost to one club, season (since 1900)**
NL—7—7 pitchers; last—Cal McLish, Cincinnati vs Pittsburgh, 1960 (won 0)
AL—7—4 pitchers; last—Camilo Pascual, Washington vs New York, 1956 (won 0)

**Most consecutive games lost, season**
AL—19—Jack Nabors, Philadelphia, Apr 28-Sept 28, 1916
NL—18—Cliff Curtis, Boston, June 13, 1st game-Sept 20, 1st game, 1910
Roger Craig, New York, May 4-Aug 4, 1963

**For a complete list of pitchers with 12 consecutive games lost in one season, see page 130.**

**Most consecutive games lost from start of season**
AL—14—Joe Harris, Boston, May 10-July 25, 1906
Matt Keough, Oakland, Apr 15-Aug 8, 1979
NL—13—Anthony Young, New York, Apr 9-July 24, 1993

**Most consecutive games lost by rookie, season**
NL—16—Charles Dean, Cincinnati, July 11-Sept 12, 1876
NL since 1893—14—Anthony Young, New York, May 6-Sept 29, 1992
AL—13—Guy Morton, Cleveland, June 24-Sept 20, 1914
Terry Felton, Minnesota, Apr 17-Sept 12, 1982

**Most consecutive games lost at end of season**
AL—19—Jack Nabors, Philadelphia, Apr 28-Sept 28, 1916
NL—18—Cliff Curtis, Boston, June 13, 1st game-Sept 20, 1st game, 1910

## AT-BATS AND PLATE APPEARANCES

**Most opponents' at-bats, career (since 1900)**
AL—21,663—Walter Johnson, Washington, 21 seasons, 1907-1927
NL—19,778—Warren Spahn, Boston, Milwaukee, New York, San Francisco, 21 seasons, 1942-1965, except 1943-1945 in military service

**Most opponents' at-bats, season**
NL—2,808—Will White, Cincinnati, 75 G, 683 IP, 1879
NL since 1893—1,658—Joe McGinnity, New York, 55 G, 434 IP, 1903
AL—1,690—Ed Walsh, Chicago, 66 G, 464 IP, 1908

**Fewest opponents' at-bats for leader, season**
AL—942—Jim Bunning, Detroit, 250 IP, 1959
NL—890—Livan Hernandez, Montreal, 233.1 IP, 2003

**Most seasons leading league in opponents' at-bats**
NL—6—Grover Alexander, Philadelphia, Chicago, 1911, 1914-1917, 1920
AL—4—Ed Walsh, Chicago, 1908, 1910-1912
Walter Johnson, Washington, 1913-1916
Bob Lemon, Cleveland, 1948, 1950-1953

**Most consecutive seasons leading league in opponents' at-bats**
AL—4—Walter Johnson, Washington, 1913-1916
NL—4—Grover Alexander, Philadelphia, 1914-1917
Robin Roberts, Philadelphia, 1952-1955

**Most opponents' at-bats, game**
NL—66—George Derby, Buffalo, July 3, 1883
NL since 1900—49—Doc Parker, Cincinnati, June 21, 1901
Bill Phillips, Cincinnati, June 24, 1901, 2nd game
AL—53—Roy Patterson, Chicago, May 5, 1901

**Most batters facing pitcher, game**
NL—67—George Derby, Buffalo, July 3, 1883
NL since 1893—55—Bill Phillips, Cincinnati, June 24, 1901, 2nd game
AL—57—Roy Patterson, Chicago, May 5, 1901

**Most batters facing pitcher, inning**
NL—22—Tony Mullane, Baltimore, June 18, a.m. game, 1894, a.m. game, 1st
NL since 1893—16—Hal Kelleher, Philadelphia, May 5, 1938, 8th
AL—16—Merle Adkins, Boston, July 8, 1902, 6th
Lefty O'Doul, Boston, July 7, 1st game, 1923, 6th
Howard Ehmke, Boston, Sept 28, 1923, 6th

## RUNS

**Most runs allowed, career**
ML—3,315—Pud Galvin, Buffalo NL, Pittsburgh AA, Pittsburgh NL, Pittsburgh PL, St. Louis NL, 14 seasons, 1879-1892
AL—2,115—Red Ruffing, Boston, New York, Chicago, 22 seasons, 1924-1947, except 1943, 1944
NL—2,039—Burleigh Grimes, Pittsburgh, Brooklyn, New York, Boston, St. Louis, Chicago, 19 seasons, 1916-1934

**For a complete list of pitchers allowing 1,800 or more career runs, see page 110.**

**Most runs allowed, season**
NL—510—John F. Coleman, Philadelphia, 65 G, 538.1 IP, 1883
AL—226—Snake Wiltse, Philadelphia, Baltimore, 38 G, 302 IP, 1902
NL since 1893—224—Bill Carrick, New York, 45 G, 342 IP, 1900

**Fewest runs allowed for leader, season**
NL—102—George Smith, New York, Philadelphia, 196 IP, 1919
AL—108—Jim Bagby, Cleveland, 280 IP, 1918

**Most seasons leading league in runs allowed**
NL—3—Burleigh Grimes, Brooklyn, Pittsburgh, 1923, 1924, 1928
Robin Roberts, Philadelphia, 1955-1957
Phil Niekro, Atlanta, 1977-1979
Rick Mahler, Atlanta, Cincinnati, 1986, 1988, 1989
AL—3—Wilbur Wood, Chicago, 1972, 1973, 1975

**Most runs allowed, game**
NL—35—Dave Rowe, Cleveland, July 24, 1882
NL since 1893—21—Doc Parker, Cincinnati, June 21, 1901
AL—24—Al Travers, Detroit, May 18, 1912 (only ML game)

**Most runs allowed, inning**
NL—16—Tony Mullane, Baltimore, June 18, 1894, a.m. game, 1st
NL since 1893—12—Hal Kelleher, Philadelphia, May 5, 1938, 8th
AL—13—Lefty O'Doul, Boston, July 7, 1923, 1st game, 6th

## EARNED RUNS

**Most earned runs allowed, season (since 1900)**
AL—186—Bobo Newsom, St. Louis, 330 IP, 1938
NL—155—Guy Bush, Chicago, 225 IP, 1930

**Fewest earned runs for leader, season**
AL—83—Willie Adams, Philadelphia, 169 IP, 1918
Hooks Dauss, Detroit, 250 IP, 1918
NL—85—Pete Schneider, Cincinnati, 217 IP, 1918
Art Nehf, Boston, 284 IP, 1918
Wilbur Cooper, Pittsburgh, 287 IP, 1919

**Most seasons leading league in earned runs allowed**
NL—3—Burleigh Grimes, Brooklyn, 1922, 1924, 1925
Murry Dickson, St. Louis, Pittsburgh, 1948, 1951, 1952 (tied)
Robin Roberts, Philadelphia, 1955-1957
Jack Fisher, New York, 1964 (tied), 1965 (tied), 1967
AL—3—Bobo Newsom, St. Louis, Washington, Philadelphia, 1938, 1942, 1945
Wilbur Wood, Chicago, 1972, 1973, 1975

## EARNED-RUN AVERAGE

**Lowest earned-run average, career (3,000 or more IP)**
ML—2.06—Mordecai Brown, St. Louis NL, Chicago NL, St. Louis FL, Brooklyn FL, Chicago FL, 481 G, 14 seasons, 1903-1916
NL—2.13—Christy Mathewson, New York, Cincinnati, 636 G, 17 seasons, 1900-1916

AL—2.17—Walter Johnson, Washington, 802 G, 21 seasons, 1907-1927

**For a complete list of pitchers with career earned-run averages of 3.50 or lower with 3,000 or more innings, see page 110.**

**Lowest earned-run average, season (1 IP per team's games)**
NL—1.04—Mordecai Brown, Chicago, 277.1 IP, 1906
AL—1.14—Walter Johnson, Washington, 346 IP, 1913

**Lowest earned-run average by righthander, season (1 IP per team's games)**
NL—1.04—Mordecai Brown, Chicago, 277.1 IP, 1906
AL—1.14—Walter Johnson, Washington, 346 IP 1913

**Lowest earned-run average by lefthander, season (1 IP per team's games)**
NL—1.15—Jack Pfiester, Chicago, 195 IP, 1907
AL—0.96—Dutch Leonard, Boston, 224.2 IP, 1914

**Highest earned-run average for leader, season**
AL—3.20—Early Wynn, Cleveland, 214 IP, 1950
NL—3.08—Bill Walker, New York, 178 IP, 1929

**Most seasons leading league in lowest earned-run average**
AL—9—Lefty Grove, Philadelphia, Boston, 1926, 1929-1932, 1935, 1936, 1938, 1939
NL—5—Grover Alexander, Philadelphia, Chicago, 1915-1917, 1919, 1920
Sandy Koufax, Los Angeles, 1962-1966

**Most consecutive seasons leading league in lowest earned-run average**
NL—5—Sandy Koufax, Los Angeles, 1962-1966
AL—4—Lefty Grove, Philadelphia, 1929-1932

## SHUTOUTS

**Most shutouts won or tied, career**
AL—110—Walter Johnson, Washington, 21 seasons, 1907-1927
NL—90—Grover Alexander, Philadelphia, Chicago, St. Louis, 20 seasons, 1911-1930

**Most shutouts won or tied by righthander, career**
AL—110—Walter Johnson, Washington, 21 seasons, 1907-1927
NL—90—Grover Alexander, Philadelphia, Chicago, St. Louis, 20 seasons, 1911-1930

**Most shutouts won or tied by lefthander, career**
ML—69—Eddie Plank, Philadelphia AL, St. Louis FL, St. Louis AL, 17 seasons, 1901-1917
AL—64—Eddie Plank, Philadelphia, St. Louis, 16 seasons,1901-1917, except 1915
NL—63—Warren Spahn, Boston, Milwaukee, New York, San Francisco, 21 seasons, 1942-1965, except 1943-1945 in military service

**For a complete list of pitchers with 40 or more career shutouts, see page 110.**

**Most shutouts won from one club, career**
AL—23—Walter Johnson, Washington, vs Philadelphia, 21 seasons, 1907-1927
NL—20—Grover Alexander, Philadelphia, Chicago, St. Louis, vs Cincinnati, 20 seasons, 1911-1930

**Most shutouts won or tied, season**
NL—16—George Bradley, St. Louis, 1876
NL since 1893—16—Grover Alexander, Philadelphia, 1916
AL—13—Jack Coombs, Philadelphia, 1910

**Fewest shutouts pitched by leader, season**
AL-NL—3—many pitchers

**Most shutouts won or tied by rookie, season**
NL—16—George Bradley, St. Louis, 1876
NL since 1893—8—Fernando Valenzuela, Los Angeles, 1981
AL—8—Russ Ford, New York, 1910
Reb Russell, Chicago, 1913

**Most shutouts won or tied by righthander, season**
NL—16—George Bradley, St. Louis, 1876
NL since 1893—16—Grover Alexander, Philadelphia, 1916
AL—13—Jack Coombs, Philadelphia, 1910

**Most shutouts won or tied by lefthander, season**
AA—12—Ed Morris, Pittsburgh, 1886
NL—11—Sandy Koufax, Los Angeles, 1963
AL—9—Babe Ruth, Boston, 1916
Ron Guidry, New York, 1978

**Most seasons leading league in shutouts won or tied**
NL—7—Grover Alexander, Philadelphia, Chicago, 1911 (tied), 1913, 1915-1917, 1919, 1921 (tied)
AL—7—Walter Johnson, Washington, 1911 (tied), 1913-1915, 1918 (tied), 1919, 1924

**Most consecutive shutouts won or tied, season**
NL—6—Don Drysdale, Los Angeles, May 14, 18, 22, 26, 31, June 4, 1968
AL—5—Doc White, Chicago, Sept 12, 16, 19, 25, 30, 1904

**Most shutouts won or tied in season openers**
AL—7—Walter Johnson, Washington, 1910 . . . 1926
NL—3—Rip Sewell, Pittsburgh, 1943, 1947, 1949
Chris Short, Philadelphia, 1965, 1968, 1970
Rick Mahler, Atlanta, 1982, 1986, 1987

**Most shutouts participated in, season**
NL—20—Grover Alexander, Philadelphia, 1916 (won 16, lost 4)
AL—18—Ed Walsh, Chicago, 1908 (won 12, lost 6

**Pitching shutout in first major league game**
NL—39 pitchers; last—Jason Jennings, Colorado, Aug 23, 2001
AL—36 pitchers; last—Andy Van Hekken, Detroit, Sept 3, 2002

**Most seasons with 10 or more shutouts won or tied**
AL—2—Ed Walsh, Chicago, 1906, 1908
NL—2—Grover Alexander, Philadelphia, 1915, 1916

**Most clubs shut out (won or tied), season**
NL—8—Bob Gibson, St. Louis, 1968
AL—8—Nolan Ryan, California, 1972

**Most shutouts won from one club, season**
NL—5—Charles Baldwin, Detroit, vs Philadelphia, 1886
NL since 1893—5—Grover Alexander, Philadelphia, vs Cincinnati, 1916
Larry Jaster, St. Louis, vs Los Angeles, 1966, consec
AL—5—Tom Hughes, Washington, vs Cleveland, 1905
AA—5—Tony Mullane, Cincinnati, vs New York, 1887

**Most shutouts won or tied, one month**
AL—6—Doc White, Chicago, Sept 1904
Ed Walsh, Chicago, Aug, 1906; Sept 1908
NL—5—George Bradley, St. Louis, May 1876
Tommy Bond, Hartford, June 1876
Pud Galvin, Buffalo, Aug 1884
Ben Sanders, Philadelphia, Sept 1888
Jack Chesbro, Pittsburgh, July 1902.
Don Drysdale, Los Angeles, May, 1968
Bob Gibson, St. Louis, June 1968
Orel Hershiser, Los Angeles, Sept 1988

**Longest complete game shutout**
NL—18 inn—Monte Ward, Providence, Aug 17, 1882 (won 1-0)
Carl Hubbell, New York, July 2, 1933, 1st game (won 1-0)
AL—18 inn—Ed Summers, Detroit, July 16, 1909 (0-0 tie)
Walter Johnson, Washington, May 15, 1918 (won 1-0)

**Most shutouts lost, career**
AL—65—Walter Johnson, Washington, 21 seasons, 1907-1927 (won 109, tied 1)
NL—40—Christy Mathewson, New York, Cincinnati, 17 seasons, 1900-1916 (won 83)

**Most shutouts lost, season**
NL—14—Jim Devlin, Louisville, 1876 (won 5)
NL since 1893—11—Art Raymond, St. Louis, 1908 (won 5)
AL—10—Walter Johnson, Washington, 1909 (won 4)

**Most shutouts lost to one club, season**
NL—5—Jim Devlin, Louisville, vs Hartford, 1876
AL—5—Walter Johnson, Washington, vs Chicago, 1909
NL since 1893—4—Irv Young, Boston, vs Pittsburgh, 1906

**Most shutouts lost, one month**
AL—5—Walter Johnson, Washington, July 1909
NL—4—Jim Devlin, Louisville, June 1876
Fred Fitzsimmons, New York, Sept 1934
Jim McAndrew, New York, Aug 1968

**Most consecutive shutouts lost, season**
NL—4—Jim McAndrew, New York, July 21, 1st game; Aug 4, 2nd game; Aug 10, 2nd game; Aug 17, 1968
Randy Johnson, Arizona, June 25, 30, July 5, 10, 1999
AL—2—many pitchers

## CONSECUTIVE SCORELESS INNINGS

**Most consecutive scoreless innings by righthander, season**
NL—59—Orel Hershiser, Los Angeles, Aug 30 (6th)-Sept 28, (10th), 1988
AL—55.2—Walter Johnson, Washington, Apr 10 (2nd)-May 14 (3rd), 1913 (includes 2 relief appearances)

**Most consecutive scoreless innings by lefthander, season**
NL—45.1—Carl Hubbell, New York, July 13 (7th)-Aug 1 (5th), 1933 (includes 2 relief appearances)
AL—45—Doc White, Chicago, Sept 12-30, 1904

**Most consecutive scoreless innings from start of career**
NL—25—George McQuillan, Philadelphia, May 8 (1st)-Sept 29, 1st game (9th), 1907
AL—22—Dave Ferriss, Boston, Apr 29 (1st)-May 13 (4th), 1945

**Most consecutive scoreless innings, game**
NL—21—Joe Oeschger, Boston, May 1, 1920; 6th-26th
AL—20—Joe Harris, Boston, Sept 1, 1906; 4th-23rd

## 1-0 GAMES

**Most 1-0 games won, career**
AL—38—Walter Johnson, Washington, 21 seasons, 1907-1927
NL—17—Grover Alexander, Philadelphia, Chicago, St. Louis, 20 seasons, 1911-1930

**For a complete list of pitchers with 10 or more career 1-0 victories, see page 110.**

**Most 1-0 games won, season**
AL—5—Reb Russell, Chicago, 1913
Walter Johnson, Washington, 1913, 1919
Joe Bush, Boston, 1918
Dean Chance, Los Angeles, 1964 (also 1 incomplete game)
NL—5—Carl Hubbell, New York, 1933

**Most seasons leading league in 1-0 games won**
AL—8—Walter Johnson, Washington, 1913 (tied), 1914, 1915 (tied), 1919, 1920 (tied), 1922, 1923 (tied), 1926 (tied)

NL—4—Grover Alexander, Philadelphia, Chicago, 1913 (tied), 1916 (tied), 1917 (tied), 1922 (tied)
Bill C. Lee, Chicago, Philadelphia, Boston, 1934 (tied), 1936, 1944 (tied), 1945 (tied)

**Most 1-0 games won from one club, season**
AL—3—Stan Coveleski, Cleveland vs Detroit, 1917
Walter Johnson, Washington vs Philadelphia, 1919
Jim Bagby Jr., Cleveland vs Detroit, 1943
NL—2—many pitchers

**Most 1-0 games lost, career**
AL—26—Walter Johnson, Washington, 21 seasons, 1907-1927 (won 38)
NL—13—Lee Meadows, St. Louis, Philadelphia, Pittsburgh, 15 seasons, 1915-1929 (won 7)

**Most 1-0 games lost, season**
AL—5—Bill Donovan, Detroit, 1903 (won 1)
Jack Warhop, New York, 1914 (won 0)
NL—5—George McQuillan, Philadelphia, 1908 (won 2)
Roger Craig, New York, 1963 (won 0)
Jim Bunning, Philadelphia, 1967 (won 1)
Ferguson Jenkins, Chicago, 1968. (won 0)

**Most 1-0 games lost to one club, season**
AL—3—Jack Warhop, New York vs Washington, 1914
NL—2—many pitchers

## HITS

**Most hits allowed, career**
ML—7,092—Cy Young, Cleveland NL, St. Louis NL, Boston AL, Cleveland AL, Boston NL, 22 seasons, 1890-1911 (4,282 in NL, 2,796 in AL)
NL—5,523—Pud Galvin, Buffalo, Pittsburgh, St. Louis, 12 seasons, 1879-1892, except 1886, 1890
NL since 1893—4,868—Grover Alexander, Philadelphia, Chicago, St. Louis, 20 seasons, 1911-1930
AL—4,913—Walter Johnson, Washington, 21 seasons, 1907-1927

**For a complete list of pitchers with 4,000 or more career hits allowed, see page 110.**

**Most hits allowed, season**
NL—772—John F. Coleman, Philadelphia, 65 G, 538.1 IP, 1883
NL since 1893—415—Bill Carrick, New York, 45 G, 342 IP, 1900
AL—412—Joe McGinnity, Baltimore, 48 G, 382 IP, 1901

**Fewest hits allowed by leader, season**
NL—230—Andy Benes, San Diego, 231.1 IP, 1992
AL—243—Mel Stottlemyre, New York, 279 IP, 1968

**Most seasons leading league in hits allowed**
NL—5—Robin Roberts, Philadelphia, 1952-1956
AL—4—Jim Kaat, Minnesota, Chicago, 1965, 1966, 1967, 1975

**Most consecutive hitless innings, season**
AL—24—Cy Young, Boston, Apr 25 (7th inn)-May 11 (6th inn), 1904 (On Apr 30 Young relieved in 3rd after another pitcher had given up hits in that inning.)
NL—21—Johnny Vander Meer, Cincinnati, June 11 (1st inn)-June 19, first game (3rd inn), 1938

**Most consecutive batters retired, season**
NL—41—Jim Barr, San Francisco, Aug 23 (last 21), Aug 29 (first 20), 1972
AL—38—David Wells, New York, May 12 (last 10), May 17 (all 27), May 23 (first 1), 1998

**Most hits allowed, game**
NL—36—John Wadsworth, Louisville, Aug 17, 1894
NL since 1893—26—Harley Parker, Cincinnati, June 21, 1901
AL—26—Hod Lisenbee, Philadelphia, Sept 11, 1936
Al Travers, Detroit, May 18, 1912 (only ML game)
(29—Eddie Rommel, Philadelphia, July 10, 1932, pitched last 17 inn of 18-inn game)

**Most hits allowed, 9-inning shutout**
NL—14—Larry Cheney, Chicago vs New York, Sept 14, 1913 (won 7-0)
AL—14—Milt Gaston, Washington vs Cleveland, July 10, 1928, 2nd game (won 9-0)

**Most consecutive hits allowed, game**
AL—10—Bill Reidy, Milwaukee, June 2, 1901, 9th
NL—10—Heinie Meine, Pittsburgh, June 23, 1930, 6th

**Most consecutive hits allowed from start of game**
NL—7—Bill Bonham, Chicago, Aug 5, 1975 (3 singles, 2 doubles, 2 HR)
AL—7—Kenny Rogers, Minnesota, June 1, 2003 (6 singles, 1 triple)

**Fewest hits allowed, first major league game (9 inn)**
NL—0—Charles L. Jones, Cincinnati, October 15, 1892
NL since 1893—1—Juan Marichal, San Francisco, July 19, 1960 (single in 8th)
Jimmy Jones, San Diego, Sept 21, 1986 (triple in 3rd)
AL—1—Addie Joss, Cleveland, Apr 26, 1902 (single in 7th)
Mike Fornieles, Washington, Sept 2, 1952, 2nd game (single in 2nd)
Billy Rohr, Boston, Apr 14, 1967 (single with 2 out in 9th)

**Fewest hits allowed, opening game of season (9 inn)**
AL—0—Bob Feller, Cleveland, Apr 16, 1940
NL—1—many pitchers; last—Lon Warneke, Chicago, Apr 17, 1934 (Leon Ames, New York, allowed no hits in 9.1 inn on Apr 15, 1909, but lost on 7 hits in 13 inn.)

**Most hits allowed, inning**
NL—13—George Weidman, Detroit, Sept 6, 1883, 7th
AL—12—Merle Adkins, Boston, July 8, 1902, 6th
NL since 1893—11—Reggie Grabowski, Philadelphia, Aug 4, 1934, 2nd game, 9th

## NO-HIT AND ONE-HIT GAMES

**Most no-hitters pitched, career (9 or more inn)**
ML—7—Nolan Ryan, California AL, 1973 (2), 1974, 1975; Houston NL, 1981; Texas AL, 1990, 1991
AL—6—Nolan Ryan, California, 1973 (2), 1974, 1975; Texas, 1990, 1991
NL—4—Sandy Koufax, Los Angeles, 1962, 1963, 1964, 1965

**For a complete list of no-hitters, see page 127.**

**Most no-hit games, season**
NL—2—Johnny Vander Meer, Cincinnati, June 11, 15, 1938 (consec)
Jim Maloney, Cincinnati, June 14, first 10 inn of 11-inn game; Aug 19, 1965, 1st game, 10 inn
AL—2—Allie Reynolds, New York, July 12, Sept 28, 1st game, 1951
Virgil Trucks, Detroit, May 15, Aug 25, 1952
Nolan Ryan, California, May 15, July 15, 1973

**Most consecutive no-hit games**
NL—2—Johnny Vander Meer, Cincinnati, June 11, 15, 1938
AL—none

**Longest no-hit complete game**
AA—10 inn—Sam Kimber, Brooklyn vs Toledo, October 4, 1884
NL—10 inn—George Wiltse, New York vs Philadelphia, July 4, 1908, a.m. game
Fred Toney, Cincinnati vs Chicago, May 2, 1917
Jim Maloney, Cincinnati vs Chicago, Aug 19, 1965, 1st game
AL—none more than 9 inn

**Most low-hit (no-hit and one-hit) games (9 or more inn), career**
ML—19—Nolan Ryan, New York NL, California AL, Houston NL, Texas AL, 1966, 1968-1992 (6 no-hit, 9 one-hit in AL; 1 no-hit, 3 one-hit in NL)
AL—15—Nolan Ryan, California, Texas, 1972-1979, 1989-1992 (6 no-hit, 9 one-hit)
NL—8—Hoss Radbourn, Buffalo, Providence, Boston, Cincinnati, 1880-1889, 1891 (1 no-hit, 7 one-hit)
Jim Maloney, Cincinnati, 1960-1970 (3 no-hit, 5 one-hit)

**Most low-hit (no-hit and one-hit) games (9 or more inn), season**
UA—4—Hugh Daily, Chicago, 1884
NL—4—George Bradley, St. Louis, 1876
NL since 1893—4—Grover Alexander, Philadelphia, 1915
AL—3—Addie Joss, Cleveland, 1907
Bob Feller, Cleveland, 1946
Virgil Trucks, Detroit, 1952
Nolan Ryan, California, 1973
Dave Stieb, Toronto, 1988

**Longest one-hit complete game**
NL—12.2 inn—Harvey Haddix, Pittsburgh vs Milwaukee, May 26, 1959 (1 double)
AL—10—Doc White, Chicago vs Cleveland, Sept 6, 1903 (1 double)
Bobo Newsom, St. Louis vs Boston, Sept 18, 1934 (1 single)
Bert Blyleven, Texas vs Oakland, June 21, 1976 (1 single)

## SINGLES, DOUBLES AND TRIPLES

**Most singles allowed, game**
NL—28—John Wadsworth, Louisville, Aug 17, 1894
AL—23—Charles Baker, Cleveland, Apr 28, 1901

**Most singles allowed, inning**
NL—10—Reggie Grabowski, Philadelphia, Aug 4, 1934, 2nd game, 9th
AL—10—Eldon Auker, Detroit, Sept 29, 1935, 2nd game, 2nd

**Most doubles allowed, game**
NL—14—George Derby, Buffalo, July 3, 1883
AL—8—Ed LaFitte, Detroit, October 8, 1911, 1st game
Jim Abbott, New York, July 14, 1994

**Most doubles allowed, inning**
AL—6—Lefty Grove, Boston, June 9, 1934, 8th
Mike Mussina, New York, July 31, 2002, 2nd
NL—6—Dustin Hermanson, Montreal, July 22, 1999, 2nd

**Most triples allowed, game**
NL—9—Mike Sullivan, Cleveland, Sept 3, 1894, 1st game
AL—6—Al Travers, Detroit, May 18, 1912

**Most triples allowed, inning**
AL—4—Fred Marberry, Detroit, May 6, 1934, 4th
Al Travers, Detroit, May 18, 1912, 5th
NL—3—many pitchers

## HOME RUNS

**Most home runs allowed, career**
ML—505—Robin Roberts, Philadelphia NL, Baltimore AL, Houston NL, Chicago NL, 19 seasons, 1948-1966 (418 in NL, 87 in AL)
NL—434—Warren Spahn, Boston, Milwaukee, New York, San Francisco, 21 seasons, 1942-1965, except 1943-1945 in military service
AL—422—Frank Tanana, California, Boston, Texas, Detroit, New York, 21 seasons, 1973-1993

**Most home runs allowed, season**
AL—50—Bert Blyleven, Minnesota, 36 G, 271.2 IP, 1986

NL—48—Jose Lima, Houston, 33 G, 196.1 IP, 2000

**Most seasons leading league in home runs allowed**
ML—7—Ferguson Jenkins, Chicago NL, Texas AL, 1967, 1968 (tied), 1971-1973, 1975, 1979 (5 in NL, 2 in AL)
NL—5—Robin Roberts, Philadelphia, 1954-1957, 1960
Ferguson Jenkins, Chicago, 1967, 1968 (tied), 1971-1973
AL—3—Pedro Ramos, Washington, Minnesota, 1957, 1958, 1961
Denny McLain, Detroit, 1966-1968

**Most seasons allowing 30 or more home runs**
ML—9—Robin Roberts, Philadelphia NL, Baltimore AL, 1953-1960, 1963
NL—8—Robin Roberts, Philadelphia, 1953-1960
AL—4—Mudcat Grant, Cleveland, Minnesota, 1961, 1963-1965
Denny McLain, Detroit, Washington, 1966-1968, 1971
Jack Morris, Detroit, 1982, 1983, 1986, 1987

**Most home runs allowed to one club, season**
AL—15—Jim Perry, Cleveland vs New York, 1960
NL—13—Warren Hacker, Chicago vs Brooklyn, 1956
Warren Spahn, Milwaukee vs Chicago, 1958

**Fewest home runs allowed, season**
AL—0—many pitchers; most IP—Walter Johnson, Washington, 1916, 48 G, 369.2 IP
NL—0—many pitchers; most IP—Vic Willis, Pittsburgh, 1906, 41 G, 322 IP

**Most home runs allowed, game**
NL—7—Charlie Sweeney, St. Louis, June 12, 1886
NL since 1893—6—Larry Benton, New York, May 12, 1930
Hollis Thurston, Brooklyn, Aug 13, 1932, 1st game
Wayman Kerksieck, Philadelphia, Aug 13, 1939, 1st game
AL—6—Al Thomas, St. Louis, June 27, 1936
George Caster, Philadelphia, Sept 24, 1940, 1st game
Tim Wakefield, Boston, Aug 8, 2004

**Most home runs allowed, inning**
NL—4—Bill Lampe, Boston, June 6, 1894, 3rd
Larry Benton, New York, May 12, 1930, 7th
Wayman Kerksieck, Philadelphia, Aug 13, 1939, 1st game, 4th
Charlie Bicknell, Philadelphia, June 6, 1948, 1st game, 6th
Ben Wade, Brooklyn, May 28, 1954, 8th
Mario Soto, Cincinnati, Apr 29, 1986, 4th
John Smoltz, Atlanta, June 19, 1994, 1st
Jose Lima, Houston, Apr 27, 2000, 1st
Andy Benes, St. Louis, July 23, 2000, 2nd
Phil Norton, Chicago, Aug 8, 2000, 4th
Steve Trachsel, New York, May 17, 2001, 3rd
Alan Embree, San Francisco, May 20, 2001, 7th
Jeff Austin, Cincinnati, May 28, 2003, 1st
Jose Acevedo, Cincinnati, Sept 8, 2004, 1st
AL—4—George Caster, Philadelphia, Sept 24, 1940, 1st game, 6th
Cal McLish, Cleveland, May 22, 1957, 6th
Paul Foytack, Los Angeles, July 31, 1963, 2nd game, 6th (consec)
Catfish Hunter, New York, June 17, 1977, 1st
Mike Caldwell, Milwaukee, May 31, 1980, 4th
Scott Sanderson, New York, May 2, 1992, 5th
Brian Anderson, California, Sept 5, 1995, 2nd
Dave Telgheder, Oakland, Sept 21, 1996, 3rd
Dave Burba, Cleveland, June 29, 2001, 4th
Pat Mahomes, Texas, Aug 17, 2001, 6th
Travis Harper, Tampa Bay, June 21, 2005, 8th
Randy Johnson, New York, Aug 21, 2005, 4th

**Most consecutive home runs allowed, inning**
AL—4—Paul Foytack, Los Angeles, July 31, 1963, 2nd game, 6th
NL—3—many pitchers; last—Josh Beckett, Florida, Apr 28, 2002, 6th; Bruce Chen, Montreal, May 3, 2002, 1st; Jose Cabrera, Milwaukee, May 23, 2002, 9th; Kevin Jarvis, San Diego, July 2, 2002, 2nd; Todd Jones, Colorado, Sept 19, 2002, 8th

**Most grand slams allowed, career**
ML—10—Nolan Ryan, New York NL, California AL, Houston NL, Texas AL, 1970, 1972, 1973, 1977, 1984, 1985, 1988, 1990, 1992 (2) (6 in AL, 4 in NL)
AL—9—Ned Garver, St. Louis, Detroit, Kansas City, 1949, 1950 (2), 1951, 1952, 1954, 1955 (2), 1959
NL—9—Jerry Reuss, St. Louis, Houston, Pittsburgh, Los Angeles, 1971 (2), 1972-1974, 1976 (2), 1979, 1980

**For a complete list of pitchers with seven or more career grand slams allowed, see page 110.**

**Most grand slams allowed, season**
NL—4—Tug McGraw, Philadelphia, 1979
Chan Ho Park, Los Angeles, 1999
Matt Clement, San Diego, 2000
AL—4—Ray Narleski, Detroit, 1959
Mike Schooler, Seattle, 1992

## EXTRA-BASE HITS AND TOTAL BASES

**Most extra-base hits allowed, game**
NL—16—George Derby, Buffalo, July 3, 1883
AL—10—Dale Gear, Washington, Aug 10, 1901, 2nd game
Luis Tiant, Cleveland, Apr 18, 1969

**Most total bases allowed, game**
NL—55—Bill Rhodes, Louisville, June 18, 1893
AL—41—Dale Gear, Washington, Aug 10, 1901, 2nd game

**Most total bases allowed, inning**
NL—23—Bill Rhodes, Louisville, June 18, 1893, 1st
AL—23—Travis Harper, Tampa Bay, June 21, 2005, 8th

## BASES ON BALLS

**Most bases on balls, career**
ML—2,795—Nolan Ryan, New York NL, California AL, Houston NL, Texas AL, 27 seasons, 1966, 1968-1993 (1,655 in AL, 1,140 in NL)
AL—1,775—Early Wynn, Washington, Cleveland, Chicago, 23 seasons, 1939, 1941-1963, except 1945 in military service
NL—1,717—Steve Carlton, St. Louis, Philadelphia, San Francisco, 22 seasons, 1965-1986

**For a complete list of pitchers with 1,200 or more career bases on balls allowed, see page 110.**

**Most bases on balls, season**
NL—289—Amos Rusie, New York, 548.2 IP, 1890
AA—274—Mark Baldwin, Columbus, 513.2 IP, 1889
AL—208—Bob Feller, Cleveland, 278 IP, 1938
NL since 1893—185—Sam Jones, Chicago, 242 IP, 1955

**Most seasons leading league in bases on balls**
ML—8—Nolan Ryan, California AL, 1972-1978, except 1975; Houston NL, 1980, 1982
AL—6—Nolan Ryan, California, 1972-1974, 1976-1978
NL—5—Amos Rusie, New York, 1890-1894
NL since 1893—4—Jimmy Ring, Philadelphia, 1922-1925
Kirby Higbe, Chicago, Philadelphia, Pittsburgh, Brooklyn, 1939-1941, 1947
Sam Jones, Chicago, St. Louis, San Francisco, 1955, 1956, 1958, 1959
Bob Veale, Pittsburgh, 1964, 1965 (tied), 1967, 1968

**Most bases on balls, game**
NL—16—Bill George, New York, May 30, 1887, 1st game
George Van Haltren, Chicago, June 27, 1887
PL—16—Henry Gruber, Cleveland, Apr 19, 1890
AL—16—Bruno Haas, Philadelphia, June 23, 1915 (1st ML game)
[16—Tommy Byrne, St. Louis, Aug 22, 1951, 13 inn]
NL since 1893—14—Henry Mathewson, New York, Oct 5, 1906

**Most bases on balls, 9-inning shutout**
AL—11—Lefty Gomez, New York, Aug 1, 1941
Mel Stottlemyre, New York, May 21, 1970; pitched first 8.1 inn
NL—9—Vinegar Bend Mizell, St. Louis, Sept 1, 1958, 1st game
[10—Jim Maloney, Cincinnati, Aug 19, 1965, 1st game, 10 inn
J.R. Richard, Houston, July 6, 1976, 10 inn]

**Most bases on balls, inning**
AL—8—Bill Gray, Washington, Aug 28, 1909, 1st game, 2nd
NL—7—George Keefe, Washington, May 1, 1889, 5th
Tony Mullane, Baltimore, June 18, 1894, a.m. game, 1st
Bob Ewing, Cincinnati, Apr 19, 1902, 4th (1st ML game)

**Most consecutive bases on balls, inning**
AL—7—Bill Gray, Washington, Aug 28, 1909, 1st game, 2nd
NL—6—Bill Kennedy, Brooklyn, Aug 31, 1900, 2nd

**Most consecutive bases on balls from start of game**
NL—4—Johnny Vander Meer, Cincinnati, June 16, 1941
Don Warthen, Montreal, May 25, 1977
AL—4—Jim Bagby Jr., Boston, Apr 21, 1946, 2nd game
Brian Boehringer, New York, July 5, 1995
Roger Pavlik, Texas, Apr 18, 1997
Bartolo Colon, Cleveland, June 29, 2000

**Most consecutive innings with no bases on balls, season**
AL—84.1—Bill Fischer, Kansas City, Aug 3-Sept 30, 1962
NL—72.1—Greg Maddux, Atlanta, June 20 (3rd inn)-Aug 12 (2nd inn), 2001

**Most consecutive innings with no bases on balls from start of season**
NL—52—Grover Alexander, Chicago, Apr 18-May 17, 1923

**Longest game without a base on balls**
NL—21 inn—Babe Adams, Pittsburgh, July 17, 1914
AL—20 inn—Cy Young, Boston, July 4, 1905, p.m. game

**Fewest bases on balls, season (250 or more IP)**
NL—13—Tommy Bond, Hartford, 408 IP, 1876
NL since 1893—18—Babe Adams, Pittsburgh, 263 IP, 1920
AL—25—Cy Young, Boston, 287.2 IP, 1906

**Most intentional bases on balls, season**
NL—23—Mike Garman, St. Louis, 66 G, 79 IP, 1975
Dale Murray, Cincinnati, New York, 68 G, 119 IP, 1978
Kent Tekulve, Pittsburgh, 85 G, 128.2 IP, 1982
AL—19—John Hiller, Detroit, 59 G, 150 IP, 1974

## STRIKEOUTS

### CAREER

**Most strikeouts, career**
ML—5,714—Nolan Ryan, New York NL, California AL, Houston NL, Texas AL, 27 seasons, 1966, 1968-1993 (3,355 in AL, 2,359 in NL)
AL—4,099—Roger Clemens, Boston, Toronto, New York, 20 seasons, 1984-2003

NL—4,000—Steve Carlton, St. Louis, Philadelphia, San Francisco, 22 years, 1965-1986

**For a complete list of pitchers with 2,000 or more career strikeouts, see page 111.**

**Most strikeouts by righthander, career**
ML—5,714—Nolan Ryan, New York NL, California AL, Houston NL, Texas AL, 27 seasons, 1966, 1968-1993 (3,355 in AL, 2,359 in NL)
AL—4,099—Roger Clemens, Boston, Toronto, New York, 20 seasons, 1984-2003
NL—3,272—Tom Seaver, New York, Cincinnati, 17 seasons, 1967-1983

**Most strikeouts by lefthander, career**
ML—4,372—Randy Johnson, Montreal NL, Seattle AL, Houston NL, Arizona NL, New Yrok AL, 18 seasons, 1988-2005
NL—4,000—Steve Carlton, St. Louis, Philadelphia, San Francisco, 22 seasons, 1965-1986
AL—2,679—Mickey Lolich, Detroit, 13 seasons, 1963-1975

## SEASON

**Most strikeouts, season**
AA—513—Matt Kilroy, Baltimore, 68 G, 583 IP, 1886
NL—441—Hoss Radbourn, Providence, 75 G, 678.2 IP, 1884
AL—383—Nolan Ryan, California, 41 G, 326 IP, 1973
NL since 1893—382—Sandy Koufax, Los Angeles, 43 G, 336 IP, 1965

**Most strikeouts by righthander, season**
UA—483—Hugh Daily, Chicago, Pittsburgh, Washington, 56 G, 484.2 IP, 1884
NL—441—Hoss Radbourn, Providence, 75 G, 678.2 IP, 1884
NL since 1893—319—Curt Schilling, Philadelphia, 35 G, 254.1 IP, 1997
AL—383—Nolan Ryan, California, 41 G, 326 IP, 1973

**Most strikeouts by lefthander, season**
AA—513—Matt Kilroy, Baltimore, 68 G, 583 IP, 1886
NL—382—Sandy Koufax, Los Angeles, 43 G, 336 IP, 1965
AL—349—Rube Waddell, Philadelphia, 46 G, 383 IP, 1904

**Fewest strikeouts for leader, season**
AL—113—Cecil Hughson, Boston, 281 IP, 1942
Bobo Newsom, Washington, 214 IP, 1942
NL—133—Rube Waddell, Pittsburgh, 213 IP, 1900

**Most seasons leading league in strikeouts**
AL—12—Walter Johnson, Washington, 1910, 1912-1919, 1921, 1923, 1924
NL—7—Dazzy Vance, Brooklyn, 1922-1928

**Most consecutive seasons leading league in strikeouts**
AL—8—Walter Johnson, Washington, 1912-1919
NL—7—Dazzy Vance, Brooklyn, 1922-1928

**Most seasons with 400 or more strikeouts**
ML—1—Dupee Shaw, Detroit NL, Boston UA, 1884
AA—1—Matt Kilroy, Baltimore, 1886
Toad Ramsey, Louisville, 1886
UA—1—Hugh Daily, Chicago, Pittsburgh, Washington, 1884
NL—1—Hoss Radbourn, Providence, 1884
Charlie Buffinton, Boston, 1884

**Most seasons with 300 or more strikeouts**
ML—6—Nolan Ryan, California AL, 1972 (329), 1973 (383), 1974 (367), 1976 (327), 1977 (341); Texas AL, 1989 (301)
Randy Johnson, Seattle AL, 1993 (308); Seattle AL/Houston NL, 1998 (329—213 with Sea, 113 with Hou); Arizona NL, 1999 (364), 2000 (347), 2001 (372), 2002 (334)
AL—6—Nolan Ryan, California, 1972 (329), 1973 (383), 1974 (367), 1976 (327), 1977 (341); Texas, 1989 (301)
NL—4—Randy Johnson, Arizona, 1999 (364), 2000 (347), 2001 (372), 2002 (334)

**Most seasons with 200 or more strikeouts**
ML—15—Nolan Ryan, California AL, Houston NL, Texas AL, 1972-1974, 1976-1980, 1982, 1985, 1987-1991
AL—11—Roger Clemens, Boston, Toronto, New York, 1986-1992, 1996-1998, 2001
NL—10—Tom Seaver, New York, Cincinnati, 1968-1976, 1978

**Most consecutive seasons with 200 or more strikeouts**
NL—9—Tom Seaver, New York, 1968-1976
AL—7—Rube Waddell, Philadelphia, St. Louis, 1902-1908
Walter Johnson, Washington, 1910-1916
Roger Clemens, Boston, 1986-1992

**Most seasons with 100 or more strikeouts**
ML—24—Nolan Ryan, New York NL, California AL, Houston NL, Texas AL, 1968, 1970-1992 (12 in NL, 12 in AL)
AL—19—Roger Clemens, Boston, Toronto, New York, 1984, 1986-2003
NL—18—Steve Carlton, St. Louis, Philadelphia, 1967-1984

**Most consecutive years with 100 or more strikeouts**
ML—23—Nolan Ryan, New York NL, California AL, Houston NL, Texas AL, 1970-1992 (11 in NL, 12 in AL)
NL—18—Steve Carlton, St. Louis, Philadelphia, 1967-1984
AL—18—Roger Clemens, Boston, Toronto, New York, 1986-2003

**Most strikeouts by relief pitcher, season**
AL—181—Dick Radatz, Boston, 1964, 79 G, 157 IP
NL—153—Brad Lidge, Houston, 2004, 80 G, 94.2 IP

**Most strikeouts by rookie, season (since 1900)**
NL—276—Dwight Gooden, New York, 218 innings, 1984
AL—245—Herb Score, Cleveland, 227 innings, 1955

## GAME AND INNING

**Most strikeouts, game**
AL—20—Roger Clemens, Boston, Apr 29, 1986
Roger Clemens, Boston, Sept 18, 1996
[21—Tom Cheney, Washington, Sept 12, 1962, 16 inn]
NL—20—Kerry Wood, Chicago, May 6, 1998
[20—Randy Johnson, Arizona, May 8, 2001, pitched first 9 inn of 11-inn game]
UA—19—Hugh Daily, Chicago, July 7, 1884

**Most strikeouts by righthander, game**
AL—20—Roger Clemens, Boston, Apr 29, 1986
Roger Clemens, Boston, Sept 18, 1996
[21—Tom Cheney, Washington, Sept 12, 1962, 16 inn]
NL—20—Kerry Wood, Chicago, May 6, 1998

**Most strikeouts by lefthander, game**
NL—19—Steve Carlton, St. Louis, Sept 15, 1969
[20—Randy Johnson, Arizona, May 8, 2001, pitched first 9 inn of 11-inn game]
AL—19—Randy Johnson, Seattle, June 24, 1997
Randy Johnson, Seattle, Aug 8, 1997

**Most strikeouts, night game**
AL—20—Roger Clemens, Boston, Apr 29, 1986
Roger Clemens, Boston, Sept 18, 1996
NL—19—Steve Carlton, St. Louis, Sept 15, 1969

**Most strikeouts by losing pitcher, game**
NL—19—Steve Carlton, St. Louis, Sept 15, 1969 (lost 4-3)
AL—19—Randy Johnson, Seattle, June 24, 1997 (lost 4-1)
[19—Nolan Ryan, California, Aug 20, 1974, 11 inn (lost 1-0)]
UA—18—Fred Shaw, Boston, July 19, 1884 (lost 1-0)
Henry Porter, Milwaukee, October 3, 1884 (lost 5-4)
AA—17—Guy Hecker, Louisville, Aug 26, 1884 (lost 4-3)

**Most strikeouts, first major league game (since 1900)**
NL—15—Karl Spooner, Brooklyn, Sept 22, 1954
J.R. Richard, Houston, Sept 5, 1971, 2nd game
AL—12—Elmer Myers, Philadelphia, October 6, 1915, 2nd game
Steve Woodard, Milwaukee, July 28, 1997, 1st game

**Most strikeouts by relief pitcher, game**
NL—16—Randy Johnson, Arizona, July 18, finished July 19, 2001, I7 IP
AL—14—Denny McLain, Detroit, June 15, 1965, 6.2 IP
[15—Walter Johnson, Washington, July 25, 1913, 11.1 inn of 15-inn game]

**Most games with 15 or more strikeouts, career**
ML—29—Randy Johnson, Montreal NL, Seattle AL, Houston NL, Arizona NL, 17 seasons, 1988-2004 (17 in AL, 12 in NL)
AL—23—Nolan Ryan, California, 1972, 1973, 1974, 1976, 1977, 1978, 1979; Texas, 1989, 1990, 1991
NL—12—Randy Johnson, Houston, 1998, Arizona, 1999, 2001, 2002, 2004

**Most games with 10 or more strikeouts, career**
ML—215—Nolan Ryan, New York NL, California AL, Houston NL, Texas AL, 27 seasons, 1966-1993, except 1967 (148 in AL, 67 in NL)
AL—148—Nolan Ryan, California, Texas, 13 seasons, 1972-1979, 1989-1993
NL—97—Sandy Koufax, Brooklyn, Los Angeles, 12 seasons, 1955-1966

**Most games with 10 or more strikeouts, season**
AL—23—Nolan Ryan, California, 1973
NL—23—Randy Johnson, Arizona, 1999-2001

**Most strikeouts, inning (*consecutive)**
AA—4—Bobby Mathews, Philadelphia, Sept 30, 1885, 7th
NL—4—Ed Crane, New York, October 4, 1888, 5th*
Hooks Wiltse, New York, May 15, 1906, 5th*
Jim Davis, Chicago, May 27, 1956, 1st game, 6th*
Joe Nuxhall, Cincinnati, Aug 11, 1959, 1st game, 6th
Pete Richert, Los Angeles, Apr 12, 1962, 3rd*
Don Drysdale, Los Angeles, Apr 17, 1965, 2nd*
Bob Gibson, St. Louis, June 7, 1966, 4th
Bill Bonham, Chicago, July 31, 1974, 1st game, 2nd*
Phil Niekro, Atlanta, July 29, 1977, 6th
Mario Soto, Cincinnati, May 17, 1984, 3rd
Mike Scott, Houston, Sept 3, 1986, 5th
Paul Assenmacher, Atlanta, Aug 22, 1989, 5th
Tim Birtsas, Cincinnati, June 4, 1990, 7th
Mark Wohlers, Atlanta, June 7, 1995, 9th
Bruce Ruffin, Colorado, July 25, 1996, 9th
Derek Wallace, New York, Sept 13, 1996, 9th
Kirt Ojala, Florida, Sept 16, 1998, 4th*
Archie Corbin, Florida, Apr 28, 1999, 7th
Jerry Spradlin, San Francisco, July 22, 1999, 7th
Steve Kline, Montreal, Aug 17, 1999, 7th*
Frankie Rodriguez, Cincinnati, July 22, 2001, 7th
A.J. Burnett, Florida, July 5, 2002, 1st
Kerry Wood, Chicago, Sept 2, 2002, 4th*
Octavio Dotel, Houston, June 11, 2003, 8th*
Darren Dreifort, Los Angeles, May 22, 2003, 2nd
Brad Lidge, Houston, June 13, 2004, 7th
Mike Stanton, New York, Aug 3, 2004, 8th
AL—4—Walter Johnson, Washington, Apr 15, 1911, 5th
Guy Morton, Cleveland, June 11, 1916, 7th
Ryne Duren, Los Angeles, May 18, 1961, 7th
Lee Stange, Cleveland, Sept 2, 1964, 7th

Mike Cuellar, Baltimore, May 29, 1970, 4th*
Mike Paxton, Cleveland, July 21, 1978, 5th*
Bobby Witt, Texas, Aug 2, 1987, 2nd*
Charlie Hough, Texas, July 4, 1988, 1st
Matt Young, Seattle, Sept 9, 1990, 1st
Paul Shuey, Cleveland, May 14, 1994, 9th
Kevin Appier, Kansas City, Sept 3, 1996, 4th*
Wilson Alvarez, Chicago, July 21, 1997, 7th*
Blake Stein, Oakland, July 27, 1998, 4th
Chuck Finley, Anaheim, May 12, 1999, 3rd
Tim Wakefield, Boston, Aug 10, 1999, 9th
Chuck Finley, Anaheim, Aug 15, 1999, 1st*
Chuck Finley, Cleveland, Apr 16, 2000, 3rd*
Erik Hiljus, Oakland, June 30, 2001, 7th
Kazuhiro Sasaki, Seattle, Apr 4, 2003, 9th*

**Three strikeouts on nine pitched balls, inning**

AL—Rube Waddell, Philadelphia, July 1, 1902, 3rd
Hollis Thurston, Chicago, Aug 22, 1923, 12th
Lefty Grove, Philadelphia, Aug 23, 1928, 2nd
Lefty Grove, Philadelphia, Sept 27, 1928, 7th
Billy Hoeft, Detroit, Sept 7, 1953, 2nd game, 7th
Jim Bunning, Detroit, Aug 2, 1959, 9th
Al Downing, New York, Aug 11, 1967, 1st game, 2nd
Nolan Ryan, California, July 9, 1972, 2nd
Ron Guidry, New York, Aug 7, 1984, 2nd game, 9th
Jeff Montgomery, Kansas City, Apr 29, 1990, 8th
Pedro Martinez, Boston, May 18, 2002, 1st
NL—Pat Ragan, Brooklyn, October 5, 1914, 2nd game, 8th
Hod Eller, Cincinnati, Aug 21, 1917, 9th
Joe Oeschger, Boston, Sept 8, 1921, 1st game, 4th
Dazzy Vance, Brooklyn, Sept 14, 1924, 3rd
Warren Spahn, Boston, July 2, 1949, 2nd
Sandy Koufax, Los Angeles, June 30, 1962, 1st
Sandy Koufax, Los Angeles, Apr 18, 1964, 3rd
Bob Bruce, Houston, Apr 19, 1964, 8th
Nolan Ryan, New York, Apr 19, 1968, 3rd
Bob Gibson, St. Louis, May 12, 1969, 7th
Milt Pappas, Chicago, Sept 24, 1971, 4th
Bruce Sutter, Chicago, Sept 8, 1977, 9th
Jeff Robinson, Pittsburgh, Sept 7, 1987, 8th
Rob Dibble, Cincinnati, June 4, 1989, 8th
Andy Ashby, Philadelphia, June 15, 1991, 4th
David Cone, New York, Aug 30, 1991, 5th
Pete Harnisch, Houston, Sept 6, 1991, 7th
Trevor Wilson, San Francisco, June 7, 1992, 9th
Mel Rojas, Montreal, May 11, 1994, 9th
Mike Magnante, Houston, Aug 22, 1997, 9th
Randy Johnson, Arizona, Aug 23, 2001, 6th
Jason Isringhausen, St. Louis, Apr 13, 2002, 9th
Byung-Hyun Kim, Arizona, May 11, 2002, 8th
Brian Lawrence, San Diego, June 12, 2002, 3rd
Brandon Backe, Houston, Apr 15, 2004, 8th
Ben Sheets, Milwaukee, June 13, 2004, 3rd
LaTroy Hawkins, Chicago, Sept 11, 2004, 9th

## CONSECUTIVE AND IN CONSECUTIVE GAMES

**Most consecutive strikeouts, season**

NL—10—Tom Seaver, New York, Apr 22, 1970 (1 in 6th, 3 in 7th, 3 in 8th, 3 in 9th)
Eric Gagne, Los Angeles, May 17 (2), 18 (3), 20 (3), 21 (2), 2003
AL—9—Ron Davis, New York, May 4 (8), May 9 (1), 1981

**Most consecutive strikeouts, game**

NL—10—Tom Seaver, New York, Apr 22, 1970 (1 in 6th, 3 in 7th, 3 in 8th, 3 in 9th)
AL—8—Nolan Ryan, California, July 9, 1972 (2 in 1st, 3 in 2nd, 3 in 3rd)
Nolan Ryan, California, July 15, 1973 (1 in 1st, 3 in 2nd, 3 in 3rd, 1 in 4th)
Ron Davis, New York, May 4, 1981 (2 in 7th, 3 in 8th, 3 in 9th)
Roger Clemens, Boston, Apr 29, 1986 (3 in 4th, 3 in 5th, 2 in 6th)
Blake Stein, Kansas City, June 17, 2001 (1 in 1st, 3 in 2nd, 3 in 3rd, 1 in 4th)

**Most consecutive strikeouts, first major league game**

AL—7—Sammy Stewart, Baltimore, Sept 1, 1978, 2nd game (3 in 2nd, 3 in 3rd, 1 in 4th)
NL—6—Karl Spooner, Brooklyn, Sept 22, 1954 (3 in 7th, 3 in 8th)
Pete Richert, Los Angeles, Apr 12, 1962 (1 in 2nd, 4 in 3rd, 1 in 4th; first 6 batters faced in majors)

**Most consecutive strikeouts by relief pitcher, game**

AL—8—Ron Davis, New York, May 4, 1981 (2 in 7th, 3 in 8th, 3 in 9th)
NL—7—Randy Johnson, Arizona, July 18, finished July 19, 2001 (Johnson actually faced all his batters on July 19, 2 in 6th, 3 in 7th, 2 in 8th)

**Most consecutive strikeouts from start of game**

NL—9—Mickey Welch, New York, Aug 28, 1884
NL since 1893—8—Jim Deshaies, Houston, Sept 23, 1986
AL—7—Joe Cowley, Chicago, May 28, 1986

**Most strikeouts, two consecutive games**

UA—34—Fred Shaw, Boston, July 19 (18), 21 (16), 1884, 19 inn
NL—33—Kerry Wood, Chicago, May 6 (20), 11 (13), 1998, 16 inn
AL—32—Luis Tiant, Cleveland, June 29, first game (13), July 3 (19), 1968, 19 inn
Nolan Ryan, California, Aug 7 (13), 12 (19), 1974, 17.2 inn
Randy Johnson, Seattle, Aug 8 (19), 15 (13), 1997, 17 inn
Pedro Martinez, Boston, May 6 (17), 12 (15), 2000, 18 inn

## HIT BATTERS

**Most hit batters, career**

ML—278—Gus Weyhing, Philadelphia AA, Brooklyn PL, Pittsburgh NL, Louisville NL, Washington NL, St. Louis NL, Brooklyn NL, Cleveland AL, Cincinnati NL, 14 seasons, 1887-1901
AL—205—Walter Johnson, Washington, 21 seasons, 1907-1927
NL—201—Emerson Hawley, St. Louis, Pittsburgh, Cincinnati, New York, 9 seasons, 1892-1900
NL since 1893—190—Emerson Hawley, St. Louis, Pittsburgh, Cincinnati, New York, 8 seasons, 1893-1900
NL since 1900—154—Don Drysdale, Brooklyn, Los Angeles, 14 seasons, 1956-1969

**Most hit batters, season**

AA—54—Phil Knell, Columbus, 58 G, 1891
NL—40—Joe McGinnity, Brooklyn, 44 G, 1900
AL—32—Chick Fraser, Philadelphia, 40 G, 1901

**Fewest hit batters for leader, season**

AL—6—five pitchers; last—Spud Chandler, New York, 1940; Al Smith, Cleveland, 1940
NL—6—five pitchers; last—Rex Barney, Brooklyn, 1948; Sheldon Jones, New York, 1948; Kent Peterson, Cincinnati, 1948

**Most seasons leading league in hit batters**

AL—6—Howard Ehmke, Detroit, Boston, Philadelphia, 1920, 1921 (tied), 1922, 1923 (tied), 1925, 1927
NL—5—Don Drysdale, Los Angeles, 1958-1961, 1965 (tied)

**Most hit batters, game**

AA—6—Ed Knouff, Baltimore, Apr 25, 1887
NL—6—John Grimes, St. Louis, July 31, 1897, 1st game
AL—4—15 pitchers; last—Victor Zambrano, Tampa Bay, July 19, 2003

**Most hit batters, inning (*consecutive)**

AL—3—Bert Gallia, Washington, June 20, 1913, 2nd game, 1st
Harry Harper, New York, Aug 25, 1921, 8th
Tom Morgan, New York, June 30, 1954, 3rd
Wilbur Wood, Chicago, Sept 10, 1977, 1st*
Bud Black, Cleveland, July 8, 1988, 4th
Bert Blyleven, Minnesota, Sept 28, 1988, 2nd
Steve Sparks, Anaheim, May 22, 1999, 3rd*
NL—3—Pat Luby, Chicago, Sept 5, 1890, 6th
Emerson Hawley, St. Louis, July 4, 1894, 1st game, 1st*
Emerson Hawley, Pittsburgh, May 9, 1896, 7th
Walter Thornton, Chicago, May 18, 1898, 4th*
Deacon Phillippe, Pittsburgh, Sept 25, 1905, 1st
Ray Boggs, Boston, Sept 17, 1928, 9th
Raul Sanchez, Cincinnati, May 15, 1960, 1st game, 8th
Dock Ellis, Pittsburgh, May 1, 1974, 1st*
Mark Gardner, Montreal, Aug 15, 1992, 1st
Tom Candiotti, Los Angeles, Sept 13, 1997, 1st
C.J. Nitkowski, Houston, Aug 3, 1998, 8th*
Brian Lawrence, San Diego, Apr 22, 2003, 4th
Kazuhisa Ishii, Los Angeles, July 23, 2003, 4th
Pat Clement, Chicago, May 28, 2004, 5th
Jeff Weaver, Los Angeles, Aug 21, 2004, 1st*

**Longest game without a hit batter**

NL—26 inn—Leon Cadore, Brooklyn, May 1, 1920
Joe Oeschger, Boston, May 1, 1920
AL—21 inn—Ted Lyons, Chicago, May 24, 1929

**Most innings with no hit batters, season**

AL—327—Alvin Crowder, Washington, 50 G, 1932
NL—323—Sandy Koufax, Los Angeles, 41 G, 1966

## WILD PITCHES

**Most wild pitches, career**

ML—343—Tony Mullane, Detroit NL, Louisville AA, St. Louis AA, Toledo AA, Cincinnati AA, Cincinnati NL, Baltimore NL, Cleveland NL, 13 seasons, 1881-1894
ML since 1893—277—Nolan Ryan, New York NL, California AL, Houston NL, Texas AL, 27 seasons, 1966, 1968-1993
NL—274—Mickey Welch, Troy, New York, 13 seasons, 1880-1892
AL—206—Jack Morris, Detroit, Minnesota, Toronto, Cleveland, 18 seasons, 1977-1994
NL since 1894—200—Phil Niekro, Milwaukee, Atlanta, 21 seasons, 1964-1983, 1987

**Most wild pitches, season**

AA—Mark Baldwin, Columbus, 63 G, 1889
NL—63—Bill Stemmyer, Boston, 41 G, 1886
NL since 1900—30—Leon Ames, New York, 263 IP, 1905
AL—26—Juan Guzman, Toronto, 221 IP, 1993

**Fewest wild pitches by leader, season**

NL—6—Kirby Higbe, Brooklyn, 211 IP, 1946
Charley Schanz, Philadelphia, 116 IP, 1946
AL—7—8 pitchers; last—George Earnshaw, Philadelphia, 1928; Joe Shaute, Cleveland, 1928

**Most seasons leading league in wild pitches**

ML—6—Nolan Ryan, California AL, Houston NL, Texas AL, 1972, 1977, 1978, 1981, 1986, 1989
NL—6—Larry Cheney, Chicago, Brooklyn, 1912-1914, 1916, 1917 (tied), 1918
AL—6—Jack Morris, Detroit, Minnesota, Cleveland, 1983, 1984, 1985, 1987, 1991, 1994 (tied)

**Most wild pitches, game**
NL—10—Johnny Ryan, Louisville, July 22, 1876
NL since 1893—6—J.R. Richard, Houston, Apr 10, 1979
Phil Niekro, Atlanta, Aug 4, 1979, 2nd game
Bill Gullickson, Montreal, Apr 10, 1982
AL—5—Charlie Wheatley, Detroit, Sept 27, 1912
[5—Jack Morris, Detroit, Aug 3, 1987, 10 inn]

**Most wild pitches, first major league game**
AA—5—Tom Seymour, Pittsburgh, Sept 23, 1882 (only ML game)
NL—5—Mike Corcoran, Chicago, July 15, 1884 (only ML game)
George Winkelman, Washington, Aug 2, 1886

**Most wild pitches, opening game of season**
NL—4—Larry Cheney, Chicago, Apr 14, 1914

**Most wild pitches, inning**
PL—5—Bert Cunningham, Buffalo, Sept 15, 1890, 2nd game, 1st
AL—4—Walter Johnson, Washington, Sept 21, 1914, 4th
Kevin Gregg, Anaheim, July 25, 2004, 8th
NL—4—Phil Niekro, Atlanta, Aug 4, 1979, 2nd game, 5th

**Longest game without a wild pitch**
NL—26 inn—Leon Cadore, Brooklyn, May 1, 1920
AL—24 inn—Jack Coombs, Philadelphia, Sept 1, 1906
Joe Harris, Boston, Sept 1, 1906

**Most innings with no wild pitches, season**
NL—340—Joe McGinnity, New York, 1906
AL—327—Alvin Crowder, Washington, 1932

**Most innings with no wild pitches or hit batters, season**
AL—327—Alvin Crowder, Washington, 1932
NL—268—Jesse Barnes, Boston, 1924

## SACRIFICE HITS

**Most sacrifices allowed, season (sacrifice hits and sacrifice flies)**
AL—54—Stan Coveleski, Cleveland, 316 IP, 1921
Eddie Rommel, Philadelphia, 298 IP, 1923
NL—49—Eppa Rixey, Philadelphia, 284 IP, 1920
Jack Scott, Philadelphia, 233 IP, 1927

**Most sacrifice hits allowed, season (no sacrifice flies)**
NL—35—Ed Brandt, Boston, 283 IP, 1933
AL—28—Earl Whitehill, Detroit, 272 IP, 1931

**Fewest sacrifice hits allowed by leader, season (no sacrifice flies)**
AL—8—Hector Carrasco, Minnesota, Boston, 78.2 IP, 2000
Mike Mussina, Baltimore, 237.2 IP, 2000
NL—13—Johnny Antonelli, San Francisco, 242 IP, 1958
Dick Farrell, Philadelphia, 94 IP, 1958
Ron Kline, Pittsburgh, 237 IP, 1958

**Most seasons leading league in most sacrifices allowed**
NL—3—Eppa Rixey, Philadelphia, Cincinnati, 1920, 1921, 1928
AL—3—Earl Whitehill, Detroit, Washington, 1931, 1934, 1935

**Most innings by pitcher allowing no sacrifice hits, season**
AL—238.2—Dan Petry, Detroit, 34 G, 1985
NL—183—Carl Willey, New York, 30 G, 1963

## SACRIFICE FLIES

**Most sacrifice flies allowed, career**
ML—141—Jim Kaat, Washington AL, Minnesota AL, Chicago AL, Philadelphia NL, New York AL, St. Louis NL, 25 seasons, 1959-1983 (108 in AL, 33 in NL)
AL—108—Jim Kaat, Washington, Minnesota, Chicago, New York, 19 seasons, 1959-1975, 1979, 1980
NL—95—Bob Gibson, St. Louis, 17 seasons, 1959-1975

**Most sacrifice flies allowed, season**
AL—17—Larry Gura, Kansas City, 200.1 IP, 1983
Jaime Navarro, Milwaukee, 214.1 IP, 1993
NL—15—Randy Lerch, Philadelphia, 214 IP, 1979

**Most innings with no sacrifice flies allowed, season**
NL—284—Phil Niekro, Atlanta, 40 G, 1969
AL—258.1—Luis Tiant, Cleveland, 34 G, 1968

## BALKS

**Most balks, season**
AL—16—Dave Stewart, Oakland, 275.2 IP, 1988
NL—11—Steve Carlton, Philadelphia, 251 IP, 1979

**Most balks, game**
NL—5—Bob Shaw, Milwaukee, May 4, 1963
AL—4—Vic Raschi, New York, May 3, 1950
Bobby Witt, Texas, Apr 12, 1988
Rick Honeycutt, Oakland, Apr 13, 1988
Gene Walter, Seattle, July 18, 1988
John Dopson, Boston, June 13, 1989

**Most balks, inning**
AL—3—Milt Shoffner, Cleveland, May 12, 1930, 3rd
Don Heinkel, Detroit, May 3, 1988, 6th
NL—3—Jim Owens, Cincinnati, Apr 24, 1963, 2nd
Bob Shaw, Milwaukee, May 4, 1963, 3rd
Jim Gott, Pittsburgh, Aug 6, 1988, 8th

# CLUB PITCHING

## COMPLETE GAMES

**Most complete games, season**
AL—148—Boston, 157 G, 1904
NL—146—St. Louis, 155 G, 1904

**Fewest complete games, season**
AL—1—Tampa Bay, 162 G, 2001
New York, 162 G, 2004
Tampa Bay, 162 G, 2005
NL—1—Colorado, 162 G, 2002
Houston, 162 G, 2003

**Most consecutive games, none complete**
AL—194—Tampa Bay, Apr 14, 2001-May 19, 2002
NL—150—Cincinnati, July 29, 2001-July 14, 2002

## INNINGS

**Most innings, season**
AL—1,507—New York, 164 G, 1964
NL—1,493—Pittsburgh, 163 G, 1979

**Most pitchers with 300 or more innings, season**
NL—3—Boston, 1905, 1906
AL—3—Detroit, 1904

## GAMES WON

**Most games won by two pitchers on same club, season**
NL—77—Providence, 1884 (Hoss Radbourn, 60, Charlie Sweeney, 17)
NL since 1893—68—New York, 1904 (Joe McGinnity, 35, Christy Mathewson, 33)
AL—64—New York, 1904 (Jack Chesbro, 41, Jack Powell, 23)

**Most pitchers winning 20 or more games, season**
AL—4—Chicago, 1920
Baltimore, 1971
NL since 1893—3—Pittsburgh, 1902
Chicago, 1903
New York, 1904, 1905, 1913, 1920
Cincinnati, 1923

**Most consecutive years with pitcher winning 20 or more games**
AL—13—Baltimore, 1968-1980
NL—12—New York, 1903-1914

**Most consecutive years without pitcher winning 20 or more games**
NL—32—Philadelphia, 1918-1949
AL—29—California/Anaheim, 1975-2003
Cleveland, 1975-2003

## SAVES

**Most saves, season**
AL—68—Chicago, 162 games, 1990
NL—61—Montreal, 163 games, 1993

**Fewest saves, season**
AL—11—Toronto, 162 games, 1979
NL—13—Chicago, 162 games, 1971
St. Louis, 156 games, 1972

## GAMES LOST

**Most pitchers losing 20 or more games, season**
NL since 1900—4—Boston, 1905, 1906
AL—3—Washington, 1904
St. Louis, 1905
Philadelphia, 1916

## AT-BATS AND PLATE APPEARANCES

**Most opponents' at-bats, season**
AL—5,770—Oakland, 162 G, 1997
NL—5,763—Philadelphia, 156 G, 1930

**Fewest opponents' at-bats, season**
AL—4,845—Cleveland, 155 G, 1909
NL—4,875—Chicago, 155 G, 1907

**Most batters facing pitcher, season**
AL—6,713—Detroit, 162 G, 1996
NL—6,574—Colorado, 162 G, 1999

**Fewest batters facing pitcher, season**
NL—5,478—Philadelphia, 153 G, 1915
AL—6,189—Chicago, 162 G, 2004

## RUNS, EARNED RUNS AND ERA

**Most runs allowed, season**
NL—1,199—Philadelphia, 156 G, 1930
AL—1,103—Detroit, 162 G, 1996

**Fewest runs allowed, season**
NL—379—Chicago, 154 G, 1906
AL—408—Philadelphia, 153 G, 1909

**Most earned runs allowed, season**
NL—1,024—Philadelphia, 156 G, 1930
AL—1,015—Detroit, 162 G, 1996

**Fewest earned runs allowed, season**
NL—332—Philadelphia, 153 G, 1915
AL—343—Chicago, 156 G, 1917

**Lowest earned-run average, season**
NL—1.22—St. Louis, 64 G, 1876
NL since 1900—1.73—Chicago, 155 G, 1907
AL—1.79—Philadelphia, 155 G, 1910

**Highest earned-run average, season**
NL—6.72—Philadelphia, 156 G, 1930
AL—6.38—Detroit, 162 G, 1996

## SHUTOUTS

**Most shutouts, season**
AL—47—Chicago, 1910 (won 22, lost 24, tied 1)
NL—47—New York, 1968 (won 25, lost 22)

**Fewest shutouts, season**
AL—4—Texas, 2001 (won 3, lost 1)
NL—5—Colorado, 1999 (won 2, lost 3)
San Francisco, 1999 (won 3, lost 2)
Houston, 2000 (won 2, lost 3)

**Most shutouts won or tied, season**
NL—32—Chicago, 1907, 1909 (all wins)
AL—32—Chicago, 1906 (30 wins, 2 ties)

**Fewest shutouts won or tied, season (150 or more games)**
NL—0—Brooklyn, 1898; Washington, 1898; St. Louis, 1898; Cleveland, 1899; Colorado, 1993
AL—1—Chicago, 1924; Washington, 1956; Seattle, 1977; Baltimore, 1996; Oakland, 1997; Anaheim, 2001; Kansas City, 2001

**Most shutouts won from one club, season**
NL—10—Pittsburgh vs Boston, 1906 (lost 1)
AL—8—Chicago vs Boston, 1906 (lost 1)
Cleveland vs Washington, 1956 (lost 0)
Oakland vs Cleveland 1968 (lost 1)

**Most consecutive shutouts won, season**
NL—6—Pittsburgh, June 2-6, 1903 (51 inn)
AL—5—Baltimore, Sept 2-6, 1974 (45 inn)
Baltimore, Sept 26-Oct 1, 1995 (45 inn)

**Largest score, shutout day game**
NL—28-0—Providence vs Philadelphia, Aug 21, 1883
NL since 1893—22-0—Pittsburgh vs Chicago, Sept 16, 1975
AL—21-0—Detroit vs Cleveland, Sept 15, 1901, 8 inn
New York vs Philadelphia, Aug 13, 1939, 2nd game, 8 inn
AA—23-0—Cincinnati vs Baltimore, July 6, 1883

**Largest score, shutout night game**
NL—19-0—Pittsburgh vs St. Louis, Aug 3, 1961, at St. Louis
Los Angeles vs San Diego, June 28, 1969, at San Diego
AL—17-0—Los Angeles vs Washington, Aug 23, 1963, at Washington

**Most runs, doubleheader shutout**
AL—26—Detroit vs St. Louis, Sept 22, 1936 (12-0, 14-0)
NL—19—New York vs Cincinnati, July 31, 1949 (10-0, 9-0)

**Doubleheader shutouts since 1900**
NL—101 times; last—Sept 29, 1987, St. Louis vs Montreal (St. Louis won, 1-0 and 3-0)
AL—89 times; last—June 26, 1988, Minnesota vs Oakland (Minnesota won, 11-0 and 5-0)

**Most consecutive innings shut out opponent, season**
NL—56—Pittsburgh, June 1 (last 2 inn)-June 9 (1st 3 inn), 1903
AL—54—Baltimore, Sept 1, (last inn)-Sept 7 (1st 8 inn), 1974

## 1-0 GAMES

**Most 1-0 games won, season**
AL—11—Washington, 1914 (lost 4)
NL—10—Pittsburgh, 1908 (lost 1)

**Fewest 1-0 games won, season**
NL—0—many clubs; last—Arizona, Colorado, Florida, Los Angeles, Philadelphia, San Diego, 2004
AL—0—many clubs; last—Chicago, Detroit, Tampa Bay, 2004

**Most 1-0 games lost, season**
NL—10—Pittsburgh, 1914; Chicago, 1916; Philadelphia, 1967
AL—9—New York, 1914; Chicago, 1968

**Fewest 1-0 games lost, season**
NL—0—many clubs; last—Atlanta, Colorado, Houston, Los Angeles, Philadelphia, St. Louis, San Francisco, 2004
AL—0—many clubs; last—Baltimore, Boston, Kansas City, Tampa Bay, 2004

**Most consecutive 1-0 games won, season**
AL—3—Chicago, Apr 25-27, 1909
NL—3—St. Louis, Aug 31, 2nd game (5 inn), Sept 1, 1, 1917

**Most consecutive 1-0 games lost, season**
NL—3—Brooklyn, Sept 7, 7, 8 (11 inn), 1908
Pittsburgh, Aug 31, 2nd game (5 inn), Sept 1, 1, 1917
Philadelphia, May 11-13, 1960
AL—3—St. Louis, Apr 25-27, 1909
Washington, May 7, 8, 10 (11 inn), 1909

**Most 1-0 games won from one club, season**
NL—4—four clubs; last—Cincinnati vs Brooklyn, 1910
AL—4—four clubs; last—Detroit vs Boston, 1917

**Winning two 1-0 games in one day**
NL—12 times; last—Pittsburgh vs St. Louis, Oct 3, 1976
AL—1—Baltimore vs Boston, Sept 2, 1974

## HITS AND HOME RUNS

**Most hits allowed, season**
NL—1,993—Philadelphia, 156 G, 1930
AL—1,776—St. Louis, 155 G, 1936

**Fewest hits allowed, season**
AL—1,069—Philadelphia, 153 G, 1909
NL—1,018—Chicago, 155 G, 1906

**Most home runs allowed, season**
AL—241—Detroit, 162 G, 1996
NL—239—Colorado, 162 G, 2001

**Most home runs allowed at home, season**
NL—159—at Colorado, 81 G, 1999
AL—132—at Kansas City, 81 G, 1964

**Most grand slams allowed, season**
AL—14—Detroit, 162 G, 1996
NL—12—Montreal, 162 G, 2000

**Fewest grand slams allowed, season**
NL—0—many clubs; last—Cincinnati, 1999
AL—0—many clubs; last—Oakland, 2003

## NO-HIT AND ONE-HIT GAMES

**Most no-hit games, season**
AA—2—Louisville 1882; Columbus 1884; Philadelphia 1888
AL—2—Boston 1904; Cleveland 1908; Chicago 1914; Boston 1916; St. Louis 1917; New York 1951; Detroit 1952; Boston 1962; California 1973
NL—2—Brooklyn 1906; Cincinnati 1938; Brooklyn 1956; Milwaukee 1960; Cincinnati 1965; Chicago 1972

**Most consecutive years with at least one no-hit game**
NL—4—Los Angeles, 1962-1965
AL—3—Boston, 1916-1918; Cleveland, 1946-1948; Baltimore, 1967-1969; California, 1973-1975

**Most consecutive years without a no-hit game**
NL—57—Philadelphia, 1907-1963
AL—39—Detroit, 1913-1951

**Most one-hit games, season**
AL—5—Baltimore, 1964
NL—4—Chicago, 1906, 1909
Philadelphia, 1907, 1911, 1915, 1979

**Most consecutive one-hit games (9 or more inn)**
NL—2—Providence vs New York, June 17, 18, 1884
Brooklyn vs Cincinnati, July 5, 6, 1900
New York vs Boston, Sept 28, 2nd game, 30, 1st game, 1916
Milwaukee vs New York, Sept 10, 11, 1965
New York vs Chicago, Philadelphia, May 13, 15, 1970
Houston vs Philadelphia, New York, June 18, 19, 1972
Chicago vs Cincinnati, Milwaukee, May 24, 25, 2001
AL—2—Cleveland vs New York, Sept 25, 26, 1907
Washington vs Chicago, Aug 10, 11, 1917

Texas vs Detroit, May 3, 4, 1996

## BASES ON BALLS

**Most bases on balls, season**
AL—827—Philadelphia, 154 G, 1915
NL—737—Colorado, 162 G, 1999

**Fewest bases on balls, season**
NL—257—Cincinnati, 153 G, 1933
AL—284—Chicago, 156 G, 1908

**Most intentional bases on balls, season**
NL—116—San Diego, 162 G, 1974
AL—94—Seattle, 163 G, 1980

**Fewest intentional bases on balls, season**
NL—9—Los Angeles, 162 G, 1974
AL—16—Minnesota, 162 G, 1973
New York, 159 G, 1976
Minnesota, 162 G, 2001

## STRIKEOUTS

**Most strikeouts, season**
NL—1,404—Chicago, 162 G, 2003
AL—1,266—New York, 161 G, 2001

**Fewest strikeouts, season**
AL—310—Boston, 152 G, 1925
NL—357—New York, 153 G, 1921

## HIT BATTERS AND WILD PITCHES

**Most hit batters, season**
AL—95—Tampa Bay, 162 G, 2003
NL—85—Pittsburgh, 134 G, 1895

**Fewest hit batters, season**
AL—5—St. Louis, 154 G, 1945
NL—10—St. Louis, 155 G, 1948

**Most wild pitches, season**
NL—96—Cincinnati, 163 G, 2000
AL—94—Texas, 162 G, 1986

**Fewest wild pitches, season**
NL—8—Boston, 153 G, 1921
AL—10—Cleveland, 153 G, 1923
Cleveland, 152 G, 1929
St. Louis, 154 G, 1930
Cleveland, 153 G, 1943

## SACRIFICE HITS AND FLIES

**Most sacrifice hits allowed, season**
AL—127—Chicago, 154 G, 1944
Washington, 154 G, 1949
NL—142—Cincinnati, 154 G, 1931

**Fewest sacrifice hits allowed, season**
AL—20—Baltimore, 162 G, 2002
NL—44—Montreal, 156 G, 1972

**Most sacrifice flies allowed, season**
AL—80—Oakland, 162 G, 1997
NL—79—Pittsburgh, 154 G, 1954

**Fewest sacrifice flies allowed, season**
NL—17—San Francisco, 162 G, 1963
AL—17—Detroit, 164 G, 1968

## BALKS

**Most balks, season**
AL—76—Oakland, 162 G, 1988
NL—41—Montreal, 163 G, 1988

**Fewest balks season**
AL-NL—0—many clubs

**Most balks, game**
NL—6—Milwaukee vs Chicago, May 4, 1963
AL—5—Milwaukee vs New York, Apr 10, 1988
Oakland vs Seattle, Apr 13, 1988

**Most balks by both clubs, game**
NL—7—Pittsburgh 4, Cincinnati 3, Apr 13, 1963
Milwaukee 6, Chicago 1, May 4, 1963
AL—6—Milwaukee 5, New York 1, Apr 10, 1988
Chicago 4, California 2, Apr 12, 1988

# LEAGUE PITCHING

## COMPLETE GAMES AND INNINGS

**Most complete games, season**
NL since 1900 (8 clubs)—1,089 in 1904
NL (10 clubs)—471 in 1968
NL (12 clubs)—546 in 1972
NL (14 clubs)—162 in 1997
NL (16 clubs)—128 in 1999
AL (8 clubs)—1,097 in 1904
AL (12 clubs)—426 in 1968
AL (10 clubs)—650 in 1974
AL (14 clubs)—645 in 1978

**Fewest complete games, season**
NL since 1900 (8 clubs)—328 in 1961
NL (10 clubs)—402 in 1966
NL (12 clubs)—150 in 1991
NL (14 clubs)—127 in 1996 (102 in shortened 1994 season)
NL (16 clubs)—71 in 2004
AL (8 clubs)—312 in 1960
AL (12 clubs)—323 in 1965
AL (10 clubs)—382 in 1970
AL (14 clubs)—79 in 2004

**Most pitchers with 300 or more innings, season**
AL—12 in 1904
NL—10 in 1905

## GAMES WON AND LOST

**Most pitchers winning 20 or more games, season**
NL before 1900—22 in 1892
NL since 1900 (8 clubs)—9 in 1903
NL (10 clubs)—7 in 1965
NL (12 clubs)—9 in 1969
NL (14 clubs)—4 in 1993
NL (16 clubs)—4 in 2001
AA—12 in 1884, 1888
UA—9 in 1884
PL—9 in 1890
AL (8 clubs)—10 in 1907, 1920
AL (12 clubs)—5 in 1963
AL (10 clubs)—12 in 1973
AL (14 clubs)—6 in 1978

**Fewest pitchers winning 20 or more games, season**
NL since 1900—0 in 1931, 1983, 1987 (also the shortened seasons of 1981, 1994, 1995)
AL—0 in 1955, 1960, 1982 (also the shortened seasons of 1981, 1994, 1995)

**Most pitchers losing 20 or more games, season**
NL—8 in 1905
AL—7 in 1904

## SAVES (SINCE 1969)

**Most saves, season**
NL (12 clubs)—514 in 1991
NL (14 clubs)—599 in 1993
NL (16 clubs)—697 in 2004
AL (12 clubs)—467 in 1970
AL (14 clubs)—637 in 1990

## RUNS, EARNED RUNS AND ERA

**Most runs, season**
NL since 1900 (8 clubs)—7,025 in 1930
NL (10 clubs)—7,278 in 1962
NL (12 clubs)—8,771 in 1970, 1987
NL (14 clubs)—10,623 in 1996
NL (16 clubs)—13,021 in 2000
AL (8 clubs)—7,009 in 1936
AL (10 clubs)—7,342 in 1961
AL (12 clubs)—8,314 in 1973
AL (14 clubs)—12,208 in 1996

**Fewest runs, season**
NL since 1900 (8 clubs)—4,138 in 1908 (3,678 in shortened 1918 season)
NL (10 clubs)—5,577 in 1968
NL (12 clubs)—7,522 in 1988 (5,035 in shortened 1981 season)
NL (14 clubs)—10,190 in 1993 (7,422 in shortened 1993 season)

NL (16 clubs)—11,546 in 2002
AL (8 clubs)—4,272 in 1909 (3,702 in shortened 1918 season)
AL (12 clubs)—5,532 in 1968
AL (10 clubs)—7,472 in 1971 (6,441 in shortened 1972 season)
AL (14 clubs)—9,509 in 1978 (6,112 in shortened 1981 season)

**Most earned runs, season**
NL since 1900 (8 clubs)—6,049 in 1930
NL (10 clubs)—6,345 in 1962
NL (12 clubs)—7,878 in 1987
NL (14 clubs)—9,500 in 1996
NL (16 clubs)—11,884 in 2000
AL (8 clubs)—6,120 in 1936
AL (10 clubs)—6,451 in 1961
AL (12 clubs)—7,376 in 1973
AL (14 clubs)—11,241 in 1996

**Fewest earned runs, season**
NL since 1900 (8 clubs)—2,910 in 1908 (2,816 in shortened 1918 season)
NL (10 clubs)—4,870 in 1968
NL (12 clubs)—6,680 in 1988 (4,512 in shortened 1981 season)
NL (14 clubs)—9,057 in 1993 (6,717 in shortened 1994 season)
NL (16 clubs)—10,540 in 2002
AL (8 clubs)—3,320 in 1917 (2,840 in shortened 1918 season)
AL (12 clubs)—4,817 in 1968
AL (10 clubs)—6,662 in 1971 (5,682 in shortened 1972 season)
AL (14 clubs)—8,433 in 1978 (5,471 in shortened 1981 season)

**Lowest earned-run average, season**
NL—2.62 in 1916
AL—2.66 in 1917

**Highest earned-run average, season**
AL—5.04 in 1936
NL—4.97 in 1930

## SHUTOUTS

**(by one or more pitchers)**

**Most shutouts, season**
NL since 1900 (8 clubs)—164 in 1908
NL (10 clubs)—185 in 1968
NL (12 clubs)—166 in 1969
NL (14 clubs)—117 in 1996
NL (16 clubs)—153 in 2002
AL (8 clubs)—146 in 1909
AL (10 clubs)—154 in 1968
AL (12 clubs)—193 in 1972
AL (14 clubs)—161 in 1978

**Fewest shutouts, season**
NL since 1900 (8 clubs)—48 in 1925
NL (10 clubs)—95 in 1962
NL (12 clubs)—98 in 1987
NL (14 clubs)—110 in 1993 (78 in shortened 1994 season)
NL (16 clubs)—93 in 1999
AL (8 clubs)—41 in 1930
AL (10 clubs)—100 in 1962
AL (12 clubs)—110 in 1970
AL (14 clubs)—79 in 1999

**Most shutouts, one day**
NL—5 on July 13, 1888 (6 G)
June 24, 1892 (8 G)
July 21, 1896 (7 G)
July 8, 1907 (5 G)
Sept 7, 1908 (8 G)
Sept 9, 1916 (7 G)
May 31, 1943 (8 G)
June 17, 1969 (9 G)
Aug 9, 1984 (6 G)
AL—5 on Sept 7, 1903 (8 G)
Aug 5, 1909 (6 G)
May 6, 1945 (8 G)
June 4, 1972 (9 G)

**Most shutouts in both leagues, one day**
8—June 4, 1972, 5 in AL (9 G), 3 in NL (7 G)

## 1-0 GAMES

**Most 1-0 games, season**
NL since 1900 (8 clubs)—43 in 1907
NL (10 clubs)—44 in 1968
AL (8 clubs)—41 in 1908
AL (12 clubs)—42 in 1971

**Fewest 1-0 games, season**
NL since 1900 (8 clubs)—5 in 1932, 1956
NL (10 clubs)—13 in 1962
NL (12 clubs)—13 in 1983, 1990
NL (14 clubs)—22 in 1993
NL (16 clubs)—13 in 1999
AL (8 clubs)—4 in 1930, 1936
AL (14 clubs)—6 in 1996

**Most 1-0 games, one day**
AL—3—May 14, 1914; July 17, 1962
NL—3—July 4, 1918; Sept 12, 1969; Sept 1, 1976

## NO-HIT AND ONE-HIT GAMES

**Most no-hit games of nine or more innings, season**
ML—8—1884 (4 in AA, 2 in NL, 2 in UA); 1990 (6 in AL, 2 in NL)
NL since 1900 (8 clubs)—4 in 1880
NL (12 clubs)—5 in 1969
AL (8 clubs)—5 in 1917
AL (14 clubs)—6 in 1990

**Fewest no-hit games, season**
NL—0—many seasons; last—2005
AL—0—many seasons; last—2005

**Most no-hit games, one day**
NL—2—Apr 22, 1898
AL—1—many days

**Most one-hit games of nine or more innings, season**
NL since 1900 (8 clubs)—12 in 1906, 1910
NL (10 clubs)—13 in 1965
NL (16 clubs)—4 in 2001, 2002, 2003, 2004
AL (8 clubs)—12 in 1910, 1915
AL (14 clubs)—13 in 1979, 1988

**Fewest one-hit games of nine or more innings, season**
NL since 1900 (8 clubs)—0—1924, 1929, 1932, 1952
NL (12 clubs)—4—1980, 1987
NL (16 clubs)—2 in 1999, 2000
AL (8 clubs)—0—1922, 1926, 1927, 1930
AL (14 clubs)—0—2005

## HOME RUNS

**Most home runs allowed, season**
NL since 1900 (8 clubs)—1,263 in 1955
NL (10 clubs)—1,449 in 1962
NL (12 clubs)—1,824 in 1987
NL (14 clubs)—2,220 in 1996
NL (16 clubs)—2,997 in 2000
AL (8 clubs)—1,091 in 1959
AL (12 clubs)—1,552 in 1962
AL (10 clubs)—1,746 in 1970
AL (14 clubs)—2,742 in 1996

**Most pitchers allowing 30 or more home runs, season**
NL (16 clubs)—14 in 1999, 2000
AL (14 clubs)—18 in 1987

## BASES ON BALLS

**Most bases on balls, season**
NL since 1900 (8 clubs)—4,537 in 1950
NL (10 clubs)—5,265 in 1962
NL (12 clubs)—6,919 in 1970
NL (14 clubs)—7,807 in 1997
NL (16 clubs)—9,847 in 2000
AL (8 clubs)—5,627 in 1949
AL (10 clubs)—5,902 in 1961
AL (12 clubs)—7,032 in 1969
AL (14 clubs)—8,592 in 1996

**Fewest bases on balls, season**
NL since 1900 (8 clubs)—2,882 in 1921 (2,522 in shortened 1918 season)
NL (10 clubs)—4,275 in 1968
NL (12 clubs)—5,793 in 1988 (4,107 in shortened 1981 season)
NL (14 clubs)—7,104 in 1993 (5,193 in shortened 1993 season)
NL (16 clubs)—8,439 in 2005
AL (8 clubs)—2,266 in 1903
AL (12 clubs)—4,881 in 1968
AL (10 clubs)—6,128 in 1976 (5,742 in shortened 1972 season)
AL (14 clubs)—6,768 in 2005 (4,761 in shortened 1981 season)

**Most intentional bases on balls, season (since 1955)**
NL (8 clubs)—504 in 1956
NL (10 clubs)—804 in 1967
NL (12 clubs)—862 in 1973
NL (14 clubs)—743 in 1993
NL (16 clubs)—955 in 2002
AL (8 clubs)—353 in 1957
AL (10 clubs)—534 in 1965
AL (12 clubs)—668 in 1969
AL (14 clubs)—734 in 1993

## STRIKEOUTS

**Most strikeouts, season**
NL since 1900 (8 clubs)—6,824 in 1960
NL (10 clubs)—9,649 in 1965
NL (12 clubs)—11,657 in 1987
NL (14 clubs)—15,497 in 1997
NL (16 clubs)—17,930 in 2001
AL (8 clubs)—6,081 in 1959
AL (10 clubs)—9,956 in 1964
AL (12 clubs)—10,957 in 1970
AL (14 clubs)—14,474 in 2001

**Most pitchers with 300 or more strikeouts, season**
NL—4 in 1884
AA—6 in 1884
UA—3 in 1884
NL since 1900—2 in 1997, 2002
AL—2 in 1971

**Most pitchers with 200 or more strikeouts, season**
NL—12 in 1969
AL—7 in 1967, 1973, 1986

**Most pitchers with 100 or more strikeouts, season**
NL—59 in 1998
AL—44 in 1998

**Fewest strikeouts, season**
NL since 1900 (8 clubs)—2,697 in 1900
NL (10 clubs)—9,032 in 1962
NL (12 clubs)—9,602 in 1976 (6,332 in shortened 1981 season)
NL (14 clubs)—13,358 in 1993 (10,147 in shortened 1994 season)
NL (16 clubs)—16,830 in 2005
AL (8 clubs)—2,736 in 1901
AL (12 clubs)—8,330 in 1961
AL (10 clubs)—9,143 in 1976
AL (14 clubs)—10,115 in 1979

## HIT BATSMEN

**Most hit batsmen, season**
NL since 1900 (8 clubs)—415 in 1903
NL (10 clubs)—404 in 1965
NL (12 clubs)—443 in 1969
NL (14 clubs)—769 in 1997
NL (16 clubs)—956 in 2003
AL (8 clubs)—454 in 1911
AL (10 clubs)—426 in 1968
AL (12 clubs)—439 in 1969
AL (14 clubs)—937 in 2001

**Fewest hit batsmen, season**
NL since 1900 (8 clubs)—155 in 1943
NL (10 clubs)—327 in 1964
NL (12 clubs)—249 in 1984 (185 in shortened 1981 season)
NL (14 clubs)—1567 in 1993 (451 in shortened 1994 season)
NL (16 clubs)—784 in 1999
AL (8 clubs)—132 in 1947
AL (12 clubs)—316 in 1965
AL (10 clubs)—374 in 1976
AL (14 clubs)—372 in 1982 (279 in shortened 1981 season)

## WILD PITCHES AND BALKS

**Most wild pitches, season**
NL since 1900 (8 clubs)—356 in 1961
NL (10 clubs)—550 in 1965
NL (12 clubs)—648 in 1969
NL (14 clubs )—884 in 1999
NL (16 clubs)—953 in 2001
AL (8 clubs)—325 in 1936
AL (10 clubs)—513 in 1966
AL (12 clubs)—636 in 1969
AL (14 clubs)—785 in 1997

**Fewest wild pitches, season**
NL since 1900 (8 clubs)—148 in 1928 (147 in shortened 1918 season)
NL (10 clubs)—478 in 1967
NL (12 clubs)—443 in 1980 (355 in shortened 1981 season)
NL (14 clubs)—697 in 1997 (548 in shortened 1994 season)
NL (16 clubs)—718 in 2002
AL (8 clubs)—138 in 1928
AL (12 clubs)—404 in 1962
AL (10 clubs)—491 in 1976 (471 in shortened 1972 season)
AL (14 clubs)—553 in 1978 (359 in shortened 1981 season)

**Most balks, season**
NL since 1900 (8 clubs)—76 in 1950
NL (10 clubs)—147 in 1963
NL (12 clubs)—366 in 1988
NL (14 clubs)—195 in 1993
NL (16 clubs)—143 in 1998
AL (8 clubs)—47 in 1950
AL (10 clubs)—51 in 1966
AL (12 clubs)—60 in 1976
AL (14 clubs)—558 in 1988

**Fewest balks, season**
NL since 1900 (8 clubs)—6 in 1903
NL (10 clubs)—25 in 1965
NL (12 clubs)—52 in 1971, 1973
NL (14 clubs)—1112 in 1997 (106 in shortened 1994 season)
NL (16 clubs)—69 in 2004
AL (8 clubs)—5 in 1901
AL (12 clubs)—29 in 1964
AL (10 clubs)—43 in 1973 (29 in shortened 1972 season)
AL (14 clubs)—55 in 1979

# INDIVIDUAL FIELDING

## FIRST BASEMEN

### GAMES AND INNINGS

**Most games, career**
ML—2,413—Eddie Murray, Baltimore AL, Los Angeles NL, New York NL, Cleveland AL, 1977-1996, 20 seasons
NL—2,259—Jake Beckley, Pittsburgh, New York, Cincinnati, St. Louis, 1888-1907, except 1890, 19 seasons
NL since 1893—2,131—Charlie Grimm, St. Louis, Pittsburgh, Chicago, 1918-1936, 19 seasons
AL—2,227—Mickey Vernon, Washington, Cleveland, Boston, 1939-1958, except 1944, 1945 in military service, 18 seasons

**Most consecutive games, career**
AL—885—Lou Gehrig, New York, June 2, 1925-Sept 27, 1930
NL—652—Frank McCormick, Cincinnati, Apr 19, 1938-May 24, 1942, 2nd game

**Most games, season**
AL—162—Norm Siebern, Kansas City, 1962
Bill Buckner, Boston, 1985
Carlos Delgado, Toronto, 2000
NL—162—Bill White, St. Louis, 1963
Ernie Banks, Chicago, 1965
Steve Garvey, Los Angeles, 1976, 1979, 1980; San Diego, 1985
Pete Rose, Philadelphia, 1980, 1982
Jeff Bagwell, Houston, 1996
Eric Karros, Los Angeles, 1997
Derrek Lee, Florida, 2002
Richie Sexson, Milwaukee, 2003

**Fewest games for leader, season**
AL—121—Vic Power, Cleveland, 1959
NL—134—Ed Bouchee, Philadelphia, 1959

**Most seasons leading league in games**
NL—9—Steve Garvey, Los Angeles, 1975-1979, 1980 (tied), 1981; San Diego, 1984, 1985
AL—7—Lou Gehrig, New York, 1926, 1927, 1928 (tied), 1932, 1936-1938

**Most innings, game**
NL—26—Walter Holke, Boston, May 1, 1920
Ed Konetchy, Brooklyn, May 1, 1920
AL—25—Ted Simmons, Milwaukee, May 8, finished May 9, 1984 (fielded 24.1 inn)

### AVERAGE

**Highest average, career (1,000 or more games)**
NL—.9959—Steve Garvey, Los Angeles, San Diego, 1972-1987, 16 seasons, 2,059 G
AL—.9958—Don Mattingly, New York, 1983-1995, 13 seasons, 1,634 G

**Highest average, season (150 or more games)**
NL—1.000—Steve Garvey, San Diego, 159 G, 1984
AL—.9994—Stuffy McInnis, Boston, 152 G, 1921

**Highest average, season (100 or more games)**
NL—1.000—Steve Garvey, San Diego, 159 G, 1984
AL—.9994—Stuffy McInnis, Boston, 152 G, 1921

**Lowest average for leader, season (100 or more games)**
NL—.978—Alex McKinnon, St. Louis, 100 G, 1885
AL—.981—John Anderson, Milwaukee, 125 G, 1901
NL since 1893—.9836—Dan McGann, St. Louis, 103 G, 1901

**Most seasons leading league in average (100 or more games)**
NL—9—Charlie Grimm, Pittsburgh, Chicago, 1920, 1922 (tied), 1923, 1924, 1928 (tied), 1930, 1931, 1932 (tied), 1933
AL—6—Joe Judge, Washington, 1923, 1924 (tied), 1925, 1927, 1929, 1930
Don Mattingly, New York, 1984 (tied), 1985, 1986 (tied), 1987, 1992, 1993

**Most consecutive seasons leading league in average (100 or more games)**
NL—5—Ted Kluszewski, Cincinnati, 1951-1955
AL—4—Chick Gandil, Cleveland, Chicago, 1916-1919
Don Mattingly, New York, 1984 (tied), 1985, 1986 (tied), 1987

**Lowest fielding average, season (100 or more games)**
NL—.954—Alex McKinnon, New York, 112 G, 1884
NL since 1893—.970—Jack Doyle, New York, 130 G, 1900
AL—.9716—Pat Newnam, St. Louis, 103 G, 1910

### PUTOUTS

**Most putouts, career**
ML—23,696—Jake Beckley, Pittsburgh NL, Pittsburgh PL, New York NL, Cincinnati NL,

St. Louis NL, 1888-1907, 20 seasons
NL—22,438—Jake Beckley, New York, Pittsburgh, Cincinnati, St. Louis, 1888-1907, except 1890, 19 seasons
NL since 1893—20,700—Charlie Grimm, St. Louis, Pittsburgh, Chicago, 1918-1936, 19 seasons
AL—19,754—Mickey Vernon, Washington, Cleveland, Boston, 1939-1958, except 1944, 1945 in military service, 18 seasons

**Most putouts, season**
AL—1,846—Jiggs Donahue, Chicago, 157 G, 1907
NL—1,759—George Kelly, New York, 155 G, 1920

**Fewest putouts for leader, season**
AL—971—Vic Wertz, Cleveland, 133 G, 1956
NL—1,127—Ed Bouchee, Philadelphia, 134 G, 1959

**Most seasons leading league in putouts**
NL—6—Jake Beckley, Pittsburgh, Cincinnati, St. Louis, 1892, 1894, 1895, 1900, 1902, 1904
Frank McCormick, Cincinnati, 1939-1942, 1944, 1945
Steve Garvey, Los Angeles, San Diego, 1974-1978, 1985
AL—4—Wally Pipp, New York, 1915, 1919, 1920, 1922

**Fewest putouts, season (150 or more games)**
AL—1,154—Tino Martinez, New York, 154 G, 2000
NL—1,162—Gordy Coleman, Cincinnati, 150 G, 1961

**Most putouts, game**
AL—22—Tom Jones, St. Louis, May 11, 1906
Hal Chase, New York, Sept 21, 1906, 1st game
Don Mattingly, New York, July 20, 1987
Alvin Davis, Seattle, May 28, 1988
[32—Mike Epstein, Washington, June 12, 1967, 22 inn
Rod Carew, California, Apr 13, finished Apr 14, 1982, 20 inn]
NL—22—Ernie Banks, Chicago, May 9, 1963
[42—Walter Holke, Boston, May 1, 1920, 26 inn]

## ASSISTS

**Most assists, career**
ML—1,865—Eddie Murray, Baltimore AL, Los Angeles NL, New York NL, Cleveland AL, 1977-1996, 20 seasons
NL—1,704—Jeff Bagwell, Houston, 1991-2005, 15 seasons
AL—1,444—Mickey Vernon, Washington, Cleveland, Washington, Boston, 1939-1958, except 1944, 1945 in military service, 18 seasons

**Most assists, season**
AL—184—Bill Buckner, Boston, 162 G, 1985
NL—180—Mark Grace, Chicago, 153 G, 1990

**Fewest assists for leader, season**
NL—83—Herm Reich, Chicago, 85 G, 1949
AL—85—Wally Pipp, New York, 134 G, 1915

**Most seasons leading league in assists**
NL—8—Fred Tenney, Boston, 1899, 1901-1907
AL—6—George Sisler, St. Louis, 1919, 1920, 1922, 1924, 1925, 1927
Vic Power, Kansas City, Cleveland, Minnesota, 1955, 1957, 1959-1962
Rafael Palmeiro, Texas, Baltimore, 1989, 1992, 1993, 1995, 1996, 1998

**Fewest assists, season (150 or more games)**
NL—54—Jim Bottomley, St. Louis, 154 G, 1926
AL—58—Lou Gehrig, New York, 154 G, 1931

**Most assists, game**
NL—8—Bob Robertson, Pittsburgh, June 21, 1971
[8—Bob Skinner, Pittsburgh, July 22, 1954, 14 inn]
AL—7—George Stovall, St. Louis, Aug 7, 1912
[7—Ferris Fain, Philadelphia, June 9, 1949, 12 inn]

## CHANCES ACCEPTED AND OFFERED

**Most chances accepted, career**
ML—25,000—Jake Beckley, Pittsburgh NL, Pittsburgh PL, New York NL, Cincinnati NL, St. Louis NL, 1888-1907, 20 seasons
NL—23,687—Jake Beckley, Pittsburgh, New York, Cincinnati, St. Louis, 1888-1907, except 1890, 19 seasons
NL since 1893—21,914—Charlie Grimm, St. Louis, Pittsburgh, Chicago, 1918-1936, 19 seasons
AL—21,198—Mickey Vernon, Washington, Cleveland, Boston, 1939-1958, except 1944, 1945 in military service, 18 seasons

**Most chances accepted, season**
AL—1,986—Jiggs Donahue, Chicago, 157 G, 1907
NL—1,862—George Kelly, New York, 155 G, 1920

**Fewest chances accepted by leader, season**
AL—1,048—Bill Skowron, New York, 120 G, 1956
Vic Wertz, Cleveland, 133 G, 1956
NL—1,222—Ed Bouchee, Philadelphia, 134 G, 1959

**Most seasons leading league in chances accepted**
NL—6—Jake Beckley, Pittsburgh, Cincinnati, St. Louis, 1892, 1894, 1895, 1900, 1902, 1904
Bill Terry, New York, 1927 (tied), 1928-1930, 1932, 1934
AL—4—Wally Pipp, New York, 1915, 1919, 1920, 1922

**Fewest chances accepted, season (150 or more games)**
AL—1,242—Tino Martinez, New York, 154 G, 2000
NL—1,251—Deron Johnson, Philadelphia, 154 G, 1970

**Most chances accepted, game**
AL—22—many first basemen; last—Alvin Davis, Seattle, May 28, 1988 (22 PO)
[34—Rudy York, Detroit, July 21, 1945, 24 inn
Mike Epstein, Washington, June 12, 1967, 22 inn
Rod Carew, California, Apr 13, finished Apr 14, 1982, 20 inn]
NL—22—many first basemen; last—Ernie Banks, Chicago, May 9, 1963 (22 PO)
[43—Walter Holke, Boston, May 1, 1920, 26 inn]

**Longest game with no chances offered**
AA—9 inn—Al McCauley, Washington, Aug 6, 1891
AL—9 inn—Bud Clancy, Chicago, Apr 27, 1930
Gene Tenace, Oakland, Sept 1, 1974
NL—9 inn—Rip Collins, Chicago, June 29, 1937
Fred McGriff, Chicago, Aug 15, 2002

## ERRORS

**Most errors, career**
NL—568—Cap Anson, Chicago, 1879-1897, 19 seasons
AL—285—Hal Chase, New York, Chicago, 1905-1914, 10 seasons
NL since 1893—347—Jake Beckley, Pittsburgh, New York, Cincinnati, St. Louis, 1893-1907, 15 seasons

**Most errors, season**
UA—62—Joe Quinn, St. Louis, 100 G, 1884
NL—58—Cap Anson, Chicago, 108 G, 1884
NL since 1893—47—Bill Joyce, New York, 130 G, 1898
Bill Everitt, Chicago, 136 G, 1899
AL—41—Jerry Freeman, Washington, 154 G, 1908

**Fewest errors for leader, season**
AL—10—Vic Power, Kansas City, 144 G, 1955
Gus Triandos, Baltimore, 103 G, 1955
NL—12—Fred McGriff, San Diego, 151 G, 1992
Eddie Murray, New York, 154 G, 1992

**Most seasons leading league in errors**
ML—7—Dick Stuart, Pittsburgh NL, 1958 (tied), 1959, 1960 (tied), 1961, 1962 (tied); Boston, AL, 1963, 1964
Mo Vaughn, Boston AL, 1992, 1993, 1994 (tied), 1996, 1997; Anaheim AL, 2000; New York NL, 2002
AL—6—Mo Vaughn, Boston, 1992, 1993, 1994 (tied), 1996, 1997; Anaheim, 2000
NL—5—Cap Anson, Chicago, 1882, 1884-1886, 1892
Dick Stuart, Pittsburgh, 1958 (tied), 1959, 1960 (tied), 1961, 1962 (tied)
Willie McCovey, San Francisco, 1967 (tied), 1968, 1970, 1971, 1977

**Fewest errors, season (150 or more games)**
NL—0—Steve Garvey, San Diego, 159 G, 1984
AL—1—Stuffy McInnis, Boston, 152 G, 1921

**Most consecutive errorless games, career**
NL—193—Steve Garvey, San Diego, June 26, 2nd game, 1983-Apr 14, 1985 (1,623 CA)
AL—178—Mike Hegan, Milwaukee, Oakland, Sept 24, 1970-May 20, 1973 (758 CA)

**Most consecutive errorless games, season**
NL—159—Steve Garvey, San Diego, Apr 3-Sept 29, 1984 (entire season; 1,319 CA)
AL—121—Travis Lee, Tampa Bay, May 9-Sept 28, 2003 (1,104 CA)

**Most consecutive chances accepted without an error, career**
AL—1,700—Stuffy McInnis, Boston, Cleveland, May 31, 1st game, 1921-June 2, 1922, 163 G (1,300 in 1921, 400 in 1922)
NL—1,633—Steve Garvey, San Diego, June 26, first game, 1983-Apr 15, 1985 (255 in 1983, 1,319 in 1984, 59 in 1985)

**Most consecutive chances accepted without an error, season**
NL—1,319—Steve Garvey, San Diego, Apr 3-Sept 29, 1984 (entire season; 159 G)
AL—1,300—Stuffy McInnis, Boston, May 31, first game-Oct 2, 1921 (119 G)

**Most errors, game**
AA—5—Lew Brown, Louisville, Sept 10, 1883
UA—5—John Gorman, Kansas City, June 28, 1884
Joe Quinn, St. Louis, July 4, 1884
NL—5—John Carbine, Louisville, Apr 29, 1876
George Zettlein, Philadelphia, June 22, 1876
Everett Mills, Hartford, October 7, 1876
Tom Esterbrook, Buffalo, July 27, 1880
Roger Connor, Troy City, May 27, 1882
NL since 1893—4—John Menefee, Chicago, Oct 6, 1901
Johnny Lush, Philadelphia, June 11, 1904
Johnny Lush, Philadelphia, Sept 15, 1904, 2nd game
Fred Tenney, Boston, July 12, 1905, 1st game
Todd Zeile, Philadelphia, Aug 7, 1996
AL—4—Hal Chase, Chicago, July 23, 1913
George Sisler, St. Louis, Apr 14, 1925
Jimmy Wasdell, Washington, May 3, 1939
[4—Glenn Davis, Baltimore, Apr 18, 1991, 10.2 inn]

**Longest game with no errors**
NL—26 inn—Walter Holke, Boston, May 1, 1920
Ed Konetchy, Brooklyn, May 1, 1920
AL—25 inn—Ted Simmons, Milwaukee, May 8, finished May 9, 1984 (fielded 24.1 inn)

**Most errors, inning**
NL—3—Dolph Camilli, Philadelphia, Aug 2, 1935, 1st
Al Oliver, Pittsburgh, May 23, 1969, 4th
Jack Clark, St. Louis, May 25, 1987, 2nd
AL—3—George Metkovich, Boston, Apr 17, 1945, 7th
Tom McCraw, Chicago, May 3, 1968, 3rd

Willie Upshaw, Toronto, July 1, 1986, 5th

## DOUBLE PLAYS

**Most double plays, career**
ML—2,044—Mickey Vernon, Washington AL, Cleveland AL, Boston AL, Milwaukee NL, 1939-1959, except 1944, 1945 in military service, 19 seasons, 2,237 G (2,041 in AL, 3 in NL)
AL—2,041—Mickey Vernon, Washington, Cleveland, Boston, 1939-1958, except 1944, 1945 in military service, 18 seasons, 2,227 G
NL—1,733—Charlie Grimm, St. Louis, Pittsburgh, Chicago, 1918-1936, 19 seasons, 2,131 G

**Most double plays, season**
AL—194—Ferris Fain, Philadelphia, 150 G, 1949
NL—182—Donn Clendenon, Pittsburgh, 152 G, 1966

**Fewest double plays for leader, season**
AL—98—Vic Power, Cleveland, 121 G, 1959
NL—109—Bill White, St. Louis, 123 G, 1960

**Most seasons leading league in double plays**
NL—6—Keith Hernandez, St. Louis, New York, 1977, 1979-1981, 1983, 1984
AL—4—Stuffy McInnis, Philadelphia, Boston, 1912, 1914, 1919, 1920 (tied)
Wally Pipp, New York, 1915, 1916, 1917 (tied), 1920 (tied)
Cecil Cooper, Milwaukee, 1980-1983

**Fewest double plays, season (150 or more games)**
NL—82—Mark Grace, Chicago, 156 G, 1998
AL—87—Lou Gehrig, New York, 155 G, 1926

**Most double plays, game**
NL—7—Curt Blefary, Houston, May 4, 1969
AL—6—many first basemen
[6—Jimmie Foxx, Philadelphia, Aug 24, 1935, 15 inn
Rod Carew, Minnesota, Aug 29, 1977, 1st game, 10 inn]

**Most double plays started, game**
AL—3—Lu Blue, Detroit, Sept 8, 1922
Walt Judnich, St. Louis, Sept 6, 1947
Vic Power, Philadelphia, Sept 26, 1954
Pete O'Brien, Texas, May 22, 1984
Pat Tabler, Cleveland, Apr 27, 1985
[3—Vic Power, Cleveland, Sept 30, 1960, 13 inn
Kent Hrbek, Minnesota, Aug 12, 1986, 12 inn]
NL—3—Frank Hurst, Philadelphia, Sept 17, 1930
Tommie Aaron, Milwaukee, May 27, 1962
Ernie Banks, Chicago, July 13, 1964
Keith Hernandez, St. Louis, Aug 6, 1976

**Most unassisted double plays, season**
AL—8—Jim Bottomley, St. Louis, 140 G, 1936
NL—8—Bill White, St. Louis, 151 G, 1961

**Most unassisted double plays, game**
NL—2—many first basemen; last—Richie Sexson, Milwaukee, Sept 11, 2002
AL—2—many first basemen; last—Jason Giambi, Oakland, Aug 2, 2000

---

**For a complete list of players turning unassisted triple plays, see page 138.**

---

# SECOND BASEMEN

## GAMES AND INNINGS

**Most games, career**
AL—2,650—Eddie Collins, Philadelphia, Chicago, 1908-1928, 21 seasons
NL—2,427—Joe Morgan, Houston, Cincinnati, San Francisco, Philadelphia, 1963-1983, 21 seasons

**Most consecutive games, career**
AL—798—Nellie Fox, Chicago, Aug 7, 1955-Sept 3, 1960
NL—443—Dave Cash, Pittsburgh, Philadelphia, Sept 20, 1973-Aug 5, 1976

**Most games, season**
AL—162—Jake Wood, Detroit, 1961
Bobby Grich, Baltimore, 1973
NL—163—Bill Mazeroski, Pittsburgh, 1967

**Fewest games for leader, season**
AL—133—Frank LaPorte, St. Louis, 1911
NL—134—George Cutshaw, Pittsburgh, 1917

**Most seasons leading league in games**
AL—8—Nellie Fox, Chicago, 1952-1959
NL—8—Craig Biggio, Houston, 1992-1998, 2001

**Most innings, game**
NL—26—Charlie Pick, Boston, May 1, 1920
Ivy Olson, Brooklyn, May 1, 1920
AL—25—Julio Cruz, Chicago, May 8, finished May 9, 1984
Jim Gantner, Milwaukee, May 8, finished May 9, 1984 (fielded 24.1 inn)

## AVERAGE

**Highest average, career (1,000 or more games)**
NL—.989—Ryne Sandberg, Philadelphia, Chicago, 1981-1997, except 1995, 16 seasons, 1,995 G
AL—.987—Roberto Alomar, Toronto, Baltimore, Cleveland, Chicago, 1991-2001, 2003, 2004, 13 seasons, 1,637 G

**Highest average, season (150 or more games)**
NL—.996—Jose Oquendo, St. Louis, 150 G, 1990
AL—.995—Bobby Grich, Baltimore, 162 G, 1973

**Highest average, season (100 or more games)**
AL—.997—Bobby Grich, California, 116 G, 1985
NL—.997—Bret Boone, Cincinnati, 136 G, 1997

**Lowest average for leader, season (100 or more games)**
NL—.928—Charley Bassett, Indianapolis, 119 G, 1887
NL since 1893—.953—John Miller, Pittsburgh, 150 G, 1909
AL—.960—Jimmy Williams, New York, 132 G, 1903

**Most seasons leading league in average (100 or more games)**
AL—9—Eddie Collins, Philadelphia, Chicago, 1909, 1910, 1914-1916, 1920-1922, 1924
NL—7—Red Schoendienst, St. Louis, New York, Milwaukee, 1946, 1949, 1953, 1955, 1956, 1957 (tied), 1958

**Most consecutive seasons leading league in average (100 or more games)**
NL—6—Claude Ritchey, Pittsburgh, 1902, 1903, 1904 (tied), 1905-1907
AL—4—Charlie Gehringer, Detroit, 1934 (tied), 1935-1937

**Lowest fielding average, season (100 or more games)**
NL—.893—Fred Pfeffer, Chicago, 109 G, 1885
AL—.914—Frank Truesdale, St. Louis, 122 G, 1910
NL since 1893—.927—John Farrell, St. Louis, 118 G, 1903

## PUTOUTS

**Most putouts, career**
AL—6,526—Eddie Collins, Philadelphia, Chicago, 1908-1928, 21 seasons
NL—5,541—Joe Morgan, Houston, Cincinnati, San Francisco, Philadelphia, 1963-1983, 21 seasons

**Most putouts, season**
AA—525—John McPhee, Cincinnati, 140 G, 1886
AL—484—Bobby Grich, Baltimore 160 G, 1974
NL—466—Billy Herman, Chicago, 153 G, 1933

**Fewest putouts for leader, season**
AL—285—Damion Easley, Detroit, 140 G, 1998
NL—292—Larry Doyle, New York, 144 G, 1909

**Most seasons leading league in putouts**
AL—10—Nellie Fox, Chicago, 1952-1961
NL—7—Fred Pfeffer, Chicago, 1884-1889, 1891
Billy Herman, Chicago, Brooklyn, 1933, 1935, 1936, 1938, 1939, 1940 (tied), 1942

**Fewest putouts, season (150 or more games)**
AL—230—Luis Rivas, Minnesota, 150 G, 2001
NL—260—John Miller, Pittsburgh, 150 G, 1909
Jose Vidro, Montreal, 153 G, 2000

**Most putouts, game**
AA—12—Lou Bierbauer, Philadelphia, June 22, 1888
AL—12—Bobby Knoop, California, Aug 30, 1966
[14—Roy Hughes, Cleveland, May 10, 1936, 15 inn]
NL—11—Sam Wise, Washington, Aug 29, 1893
John McPhee, Cincinnati, Apr 21, 1894
Nap Lajoie, Philadelphia, Apr 25, 1899
Billy Herman, Chicago, June 28, 1933, 1st game
Gene Baker, Chicago, May 27, 1955
Charlie Neal, Los Angeles, July 2, 1959
Julian Javier, St. Louis, June 27, 1964
[15—Jake Pitler, Pittsburgh, Aug 22, 1917, 22 inn]

## ASSISTS

**Most assists, career**
AL—7,630—Eddie Collins, Philadelphia, Chicago, 1908-1928, 21 seasons
NL—6,738—Joe Morgan, Houston, Cincinnati, San Francisco, Philadelphia, 1963-1983, 21 seasons

**Most assists, season**
NL—641—Frankie Frisch, St. Louis, 153 G, 1927
AL—572—Oscar Melillo, St. Louis, 148 G, 1930

**Fewest assists for leader, season**
NL—381—Emil Verban, Philadelphia, 138 G, 1946
AL—396—Nellie Fox, Chicago, 154 G, 1956

**Most seasons leading league in assists**
NL—9—Bill Mazeroski, Pittsburgh, 1958, 1960-1964, 1966-1968
AL—7—Charlie Gehringer, Detroit, 1927, 1928, 1933-1936, 1938

**Fewest assists, season (150 or more games)**
AL—310—Joey Cora, Seattle, Cleveland, 151 G, 1998
NL—358—Tony Taylor, Philadelphia, 150 G, 1964

**Most assists, game**
NL—12—Fred Dunlap, Cleveland, July 24, 1882
Monte Ward, Brooklyn, June 10, 1892, 1st game
NL since 1893—12—Jim Gilliam, Brooklyn, July 21, 1956

Ryne Sandberg, Chicago, June 12, 1983
Glenn Hubbard, Atlanta, Apr 14, 1985
Juan Samuel, Philadelphia, Apr 20, 1985
[15—Lave Cross, Philadelphia, Aug 5, 1897, 12 inn]
AL—12—Don Money, Milwaukee, June 24, 1977
Tony Phillips, Oakland, July 6, 1986
Harold Reynolds, Seattle, Aug 27, 1986
[13—Bobby Avila, Cleveland, July 1, 1952, 19 inn
Willie Randolph, New York, Aug 25, 1976, 19 inn]

## CHANCES ACCEPTED AND OFFERED

**Most chances accepted, career**
AL—14,156—Eddie Collins, Philadelphia, Chicago, 1908-1928, 21 seasons
NL—12,279—Joe Morgan, Houston, Cincinnati, San Francisco, Philadelphia, 1963-1983, 21 seasons

**Most chances accepted, season**
NL—1,037—Frankie Frisch, St. Louis, 153 G, 1927
AL—988—Nap Lajoie, Cleveland, 156 G, 1908

**Fewest chances accepted by leader, season**
NL—686—John Miller, Pittsburgh, 150 G, 1909
AL—697—Eddie Collins, Philadelphia, 132 G, 1911

**Most seasons leading league in chances accepted**
AL—9—Nellie Fox, Chicago, 1952-1960
NL—8—Bill Mazeroski, Pittsburgh, 1958, 1960-1964, 1966, 1967

**Fewest chances accepted, season (150 or more games)**
AL—553—Joey Cora, Seattle, Cleveland, 151 G, 1998
AL—671—Mickey Morandini, Chicago, 151 G, 1998

**Most chances accepted, game**
AA—18—Clarence Childs, Syracuse, June 1, 1890
NL—18—Fred Dunlap, Cleveland, July 24, 1882
NL since 1893—18—Terry Harmon, Philadelphia, June 12, 1971
[21—Eddie Moore, Boston vs Chicago, May 17, 1927, 22 inn]
AL—17—Jimmie Dykes, Philadelphia, Aug 28, 1921
Nellie Fox, Chicago, June 12, 1952
[20—Willie Randolph, New York, Aug 25, 1976, 19 inn]

**Longest game with no chances offered**
AL—15 inn—Steve Yerkes, Boston, June 11, 1919
NL—12 inn—Ken Boswell, New York, Aug 7, 1972

## ERRORS

**Most errors, career**
ML—828—Fred Pfeffer, Troy NL, Chicago NL, Chicago PL, Louisville NL, New York NL, 1882-1897, 16 seasons (654 in NL, 74 in PL)
NL—754—Fred Pfeffer, Troy, Chicago, Louisville, New York, 1882-1897, except 1890, 15 seasons
NL since 1893—443—Larry Doyle, New York, Chicago, 1907-1920, 14 seasons
AL—435—Eddie Collins, Philadelphia, Chicago, 1908-1928, 21 seasons

**Most errors, season**
AA—105—Bill McClellan, Brooklyn, 136 G, 1887
NL—96—Al Myers, Washington, Philadelphia, 121 G, 1889
AL—61—Kid Gleason, Detroit, 136 G, 1901
Hobe Ferris, Boston, 138 G, 1901
NL since 1893—55—George Grantham, Chicago, 150 G, 1923

**Fewest errors for leader, season**
NL—13—Luis Castillo, Florida, 133 G, 2001
AL—14—Hector Lopez, Kansas City, 96 G, 1958

**Most seasons leading league in errors**
NL—5—Fred Pfeffer, Chicago, 1884-1888
NL since 1893—4—Billy Herman, Chicago, 1932, 1933, 1937, 1939
Glenn Beckert, Chicago, 1966, 1967, 1969, 1970 (tied)
ML since 1900—4—Tito Fuentes, San Francisco NL, 1971, 1972; San Diego NL, 1976; Detroit AL, 1977
AL—4—Bill Wambsganss, Cleveland, Boston, 1917, 1919, 1920, 1924
Joe Gordon, New York, 1938, 1941, 1942, 1943 (tied)
Harold Reynolds, Seattle, 1987-989, 1990 (tied)

**Fewest errors, season (150 or more games)**
NL—3—Jose Oquendo, St. Louis, 150 G, 1990
AL—5—Jerry Adair, Baltimore, 153 G, 1964
Bobby Grich, Baltimore, 162 G, 1973
Roberto Alomar, Toronto, 150 G, 1992
Roberto Alomar, Cleveland, 157 G, 2001

**Most consecutive errorless games, career**
NL—123—Ryne Sandberg, Chicago, June 21, 1989-May 17, 1990 (577 CA)
AL—104—Roberto Alomar, Toronto, June 21, 1994-July 3, 1995 (482 CA)

**Most consecutive errorless games, season**
NL—90—Ryne Sandberg, Chicago, June 21-Oct 1, 1989 (430 CA)
AL—86—Rich Dauer, Baltimore, Apr 10-Sept 29, 1978 (418 CA)

**Most consecutive chances accepted without an error, season**
NL—479—Manny Trillo, Philadelphia, Apr 8 (part)-July 31 (part), 1982, 91 G
AL—425—Rich Dauer, Baltimore, Apr 10-Sept 30 (part), 1978, 87 G

**Most errors, game**
NL—9—Andy Leonard, Boston, June 14, 1876
NL since 1893—4—six second basemen; last—Casey Wise, Chicago, May 3, 1957
AL—5—Charles Hickman, Washington, Sept 29, 1905
Nap Lajoie, Philadelphia, Apr 22, 1915

**Longest game with no errors**
NL—25 inn—Felix Millan, New York, Sept 11, 1974
Ted Sizemore, St. Louis, Sept 11, 1974
AL—25 inn—Julio Cruz, Chicago, May 8, finished May 9, 1984
Jim Gantner, Milwaukee, May 8, finished May 9, 1984 (fielded 24.1 inn)

**Most errors, inning**
NL—3—Bid McPhee, Cincinnati, Sept 23, 1894, 1st game, 2nd
Claude Ritchey, Pittsburgh, Sept 22, 1900, 6th
Bama Rowell, Boston, Sept 25, 1941, 3rd
Eddie Stanky, Chicago, June 20, 1943, 1st game, 8th
George Hausmann, New York, Aug 13, 1944, 2nd game, 4th
Kermit Wahl, Cincinnati, Sept 18, 1945, 1st game, 11th
Davey Lopes, Los Angeles, June 2, 1973, 1st
Ted Sizemore, St. Louis, Apr 17, 1975, 6th
AL—3—Del Pratt, St. Louis, Sept 1, 1914, 2nd game, 4th
Bill Wambsganss, Cleveland, May 15, 1923, 4th
Bobby Doerr, Boston, May 11, 1949, 2nd
Tim Cullen, Washington, Aug 30, 1969, 8th (consec)

## DOUBLE PLAYS

**Most double plays, career**
NL—1,706—Bill Mazeroski, Pittsburgh, 17 seasons, 1956-1972
AL—1,568—Nellie Fox, Philadelphia, Chicago, 17 seasons, 1947-1963

**Most double plays, season**
NL—161—Bill Mazeroski, Pittsburgh, 162 G, 1966
AL—150—Gerry Priddy, Detroit, 157 G, 1950

**Fewest double plays for leader, season**
NL—81—Rogers Hornsby, St. Louis, 154 G, 1922
AL—84—Charlie Gehringer, Detroit, 121 G, 1927

**Most seasons leading league in double plays**
NL—8—Bill Mazeroski, Pittsburgh, 1960-1967
AL—5—Nap Lajoie, Cleveland, 1903, 1906-1908, 1909 (tied)
Eddie Collins, Philadelphia, Chicago, 1909 (tied), 1910, 1912, 1916, 1919
Bucky Harris, Washington, 1921-1923, 1924 (tied), 1925
Bobby Doerr, Boston, 1938, 1940, 1943, 1946, 1947
Nellie Fox, Chicago, 1954, 1956-1958, 1960

**Fewest double plays, season (150 or more games)**
NL—65—George Hausmann, New York, 154 G, 1945
Jose Oquendo, St. Louis, 150 G, 1990
AL—65—Luis Rivas, Minnesota, 150 G, 2001

**Most double plays, game**
AL—6—Bobby Knoop, California, May 1, 1966, 1st game
Alfonso Soriano, New York, June 17, 2003
[6—Joe Gordon, Cleveland, Aug 31, 1949, 1st game, 14 inn]
NL—6—Bill Doran, Houston, May 8, 1988
[6—Felix Millan, Atlanta, Aug 5, 1971, 17 inn]

**Most double plays started, game**
AL—5—Gerry Priddy, Detroit, May 20, 1950
NL—5—Juan Samuel, Philadelphia, June 14, 1988, 1st game
[6—Felix Millan, Atlanta, Aug 5, 1971, 17 inn]

**Most unassisted double plays, game**
NL—2—Dave Force, Buffalo, Sept 15, 1881
Claude Ritchey, Louisville, July 9, 1899, 1st game
AL—2—Mike Edwards, Oakland, Aug 10, 1978
Luis Alicea, Anaheim, Aug 8, 1997

**For a complete list of players turning unassisted triple plays, see page 138.**

# THIRD BASEMEN

## GAMES AND INNINGS

**Most games, career**
AL—2,870—Brooks Robinson, Baltimore, 1955-1977, 23 seasons
NL—2,212—Mike Schmidt, Philadelphia, 1972-1989, 18 seasons

**Most consecutive games, career**
AL—576—Eddie Yost, Washington, July 3, 1951-May 11, 1955
NL—364—Ron Santo, Chicago, Apr 19, 1964-May 31, 1966

**Most games, season**
NL—164—Ron Santo, Chicago, 1965
AL—163—Brooks Robinson, Baltimore, 1961, 1964

**Fewest games for leader, season**
NL—111—Art Whitney, Boston, 1934
AL—131—George Kell, Philadelphia, Detroit, 1946

**Most seasons leading league in games**

AL—8—Brooks Robinson, Baltimore, 1960-1964, 1966 (tied), 1968 (tied), 1970
NL—7—Ron Santo, Chicago, 1961 (tied), 1963, 1965-1968, 1969 (tied)

**Most innings, game**

NL—26—Tony Boeckel, Boston, May 1, 1920
Jimmy Johnston, Brooklyn, May 1, 1920
AL—25—Vance Law, Chicago, May 8, finished May 9, 1984
Randy Ready, Milwaukee, May 8, finished May 9, 1984 (fielded 24.1 inn)

## AVERAGE

**Highest average, career (1,000 or more games)**

AL—.971—Brooks Robinson, Baltimore, 1955-1977, 23 seasons, 2,870 G
NL—.970—Ken Reitz, St. Louis, San Francisco, Chicago, Pittsburgh, 1972-1982, 11 seasons, 1,321 G

**Highest average, season (150 or more games)**

AL—.989—Don Money, Milwaukee, 157 G, 1974
NL—.982—Mike Lowell, Florida, 154 G, 2004

**Highest average, season (100 or more games)**

AL—.991—Steve Buechele, Texas, 111 G, 1991
NL—.987—Vinny Castilla, New York, 148 G, 1924

**Lowest average for leader, season (100 or more games)**

NL—.891—Ned Williamson, Chicago, 111 G, 1885
NL since 1893—.912—Bobby Lowe, Boston, 111 G, 1901
AL—.936—Bill Bradley, Cleveland, 133 G, 1901

**Most seasons leading league in average (100 or more games)**

AL—11—Brooks Robinson, Baltimore, 1960-1964, 1966-1968, 1969 (tied), 1972, 1975
NL—6—Heinie Groh, Cincinnati, New York, 1915 (tied), 1917, 1918, 1922-1924
Ken Reitz, St. Louis, Chicago, 1973, 1974, 1977, 1978, 1980, 1981

**Most consecutive seasons leading league in average (100 or more games)**

AL—6—Willie Kamm, Chicago, 1924-1929
NL—4—Willie Jones, Philadelphia, 1953-1956

**Lowest fielding average, season (100 or more games)**

NL—.836—Charles Hickman, New York, 118 G, 1900
AL—.860—Hunter Hill, Washington, 135 G, 1904

## PUTOUTS

**Most putouts, career**

AL—2,697—Brooks Robinson, Baltimore, 1955-1977, 23 seasons
NL—2,288—Pie Traynor, Pittsburgh, 1921-1937, except 1936, 16 seasons

**Most putouts, season**

AA—252—Denny Lyons, Philadelphia, 137 G, 1887
NL—252—Jimmy Collins, Boston, 142 G, 1900
AL—243—Willie Kamm, Chicago, 155 G, 1928

**Fewest putouts for leader, season**

NL—107—Mike Lowell, Florida, 144 G, 2001
AL—111—Joe Randa, Kansas City, 137 G, 2001

**Most seasons leading league in putouts**

AL—8—Eddie Yost, Washington, Detroit, 1948, 1950-1953, 1954 (tied), 1956, 1959
NL—7—Pie Traynor, Pittsburgh, 1923, 1925-1927, 1931, 1933, 1934
Willie Jones, Philadelphia, 1949, 1950, 1952-1956
Ron Santo, Chicago, 1962-1967, 1969

**Fewest putouts, season (150 or more games)**

NL—77—Chipper Jones, Atlanta, 152 G, 1997
AL—79—Travis Fryman, Cleveland, 154 G, 2000

**Most putouts, game**

NL—10—Willie Kuehne, Pittsburgh, May 24, 1889
NL since 1893—9—Pat Dillard, St. Louis, June 18, 1900
AL—7—Bill Bradley, Cleveland, Sept 21, 1901, 1st game
Bill Bradley, Cleveland, May 13, 1909
Harry Riconda, Philadelphia, July 5, 1924, 2nd game
Ossie Bluege, Washington, June 18, 1927
Ray Boone, Detroit, Apr 24, 1954

## ASSISTS

**Most assists, career**

AL—6,205—Brooks Robinson, Baltimore, 1955-1977, 23 seasons
NL—5,045—Mike Schmidt, Philadelphia, 1972-1989, 18 seasons

**Most assists, season**

AL—412—Graig Nettles, Cleveland, 158 G, 1971
NL—404—Mike Schmidt, Philadelphia, 162 G, 1974

**Fewest assists for leader, season**

NL—227—Art Whitney, Boston, 111 G, 1934
AL—258—Ossie Bluege, Washington, 134 G, 1930

**Most seasons leading league in assists**

AL—8—Brooks Robinson, Baltimore, 1960, 1963, 1964, 1966-1969, 1974
NL—7—Ron Santo, Chicago, 1962-1968
Mike Schmidt, Philadelphia, 1974, 1976, 1977, 1980-1983

**Fewest assists, season (150 or more games)**

AL—221—Harry Lord, Chicago, 150 G, 1913
Dean Palmer, Texas, 154 G, 1996
NL—238—Chipper Jones, Atlanta, 156 G, 1999

**Most assists, game**

NL—11—Deacon White, Buffalo, May 16, 1884
Jerry Denny, New York, May 29, 1890
NL since 1893—11—Damon Phillips, Boston, Aug 29, 1944
Chris Sabo, Cincinnati, Apr 7, 1988
Kevin Young, Pittsburgh, June 25, 1995
[12—Bobby Byrne, Pittsburgh, June 8, 1910, 2nd game, 11 inn]
AL—11—Ken McMullen, Washington, Sept 26, 1966, 1st game
Mike Ferraro, New York, Sept 14, 1968
[11—Home Run Baker, New York, May 24, 1918, 19 inn
Doug DeCinces, California, May 7, 1983, 12 inn]

## CHANCES ACCEPTED AND OFFERED

**Most chances accepted, career**

AL—8,902—Brooks Robinson, Baltimore, 1955-1977, 23 seasons
NL—6,636—Mike Schmidt, Philadelphia, 1972-1989, 18 seasons

**Most chances accepted, season**

AL—603—Harlond Clift, St. Louis, 155 G, 1937
NL—593—Jimmy Collins, Boston, 151 G, 1899

**Fewest chances accepted for leader, season**

NL—332—Art Whitney, Boston, 111 G, 1934
AL—372—Robin Ventura, Chicago, 150 G, 1996

**Most seasons leading league in chances accepted**

NL—9—Ron Santo, Chicago, 1961-1968, 1969 (tied)
AL—8—Home Run Baker, Philadelphia, New York, 1909, 1910, 1912-1914, 1917-1919
Brooks Robinson, Baltimore, 1960, 1963, 1964-1969, 1974

**Fewest chances accepted, season (150 or more games)**

NL—318—Chipper Jones, Atlanta, 152 G, 1997
AL—326—Dean Palmer, Texas, 154 G, 1996

**Most chances accepted, game**

AL—13—Wid Conroy, Washington, Sept 25, 1911
[14—Jimmy Collins, Boston, June 21, 1902, 15 inn
Ben Dyer, Detroit, July 16, 1919, 14 inn]
NL—13—Bill Kuehne, Pittsburgh, May 24, 1889
Jerry Denny, New York, May 19, 1890
[16—Jerry Denny, Providence, Aug 17, 1882, 18 inn]
NL since 1893—13—Bill Shindle, Baltimore, Sept 28, 1893
Bill Joyce, Washington, May 26, 1894
Art Devlin, New York, May 23, 1908, 1st game
Tony Cuccinello, Brooklyn, July 12, 1934, 1st game
Roy Hughes, Chicago, Aug 29, 1944, 2nd game
[14—Don Hoak, Cincinnati, May 4, 1958, 2nd game, 14 inn]

**Longest game with no chances offered**

NL—20 inn—Jeff Hamilton, Los Angeles, June 3, 1989
AL—15 inn—Toby Harrah, Cleveland, June 20, 1980

## ERRORS

**Most errors, career**

ML—780—Arlie Latham, St. Louis AA, Chicago PL, Cincinnati NL, St. Louis NL, 1883-1896, 14 seasons
NL—533—Jerry Denny, Providence, St. Louis, Indianapolis, New York, Cleveland, Philadelphia, Louisville, 1881-1894, except 1892, 13 seasons
NL since 1893—324—Pie Traynor, Pittsburgh, 1921-1935, 1937, 16 seasons, 1,864 G
AL—359—Jimmy Austin, New York, St. Louis, 1909-1922, 1925, 1926, 1929, 17 seasons, 1,433 G

**Most errors, season**

PL—107—Bill Joyce, Brooklyn, 133 G, 1890
NL—91—Charles Hickman, New York, 118 G, 1900
AL—64—Sammy Strang, Chicago, 137 G, 1902

**Fewest errors for leader, season**

NL—16—Eddie Mathews, Milwaukee, 147 G, 1957
Gene Freese, Pittsburgh, 74 G, 1957
AL—17—Cecil Travis, Washington, 56 G, 1946

**Most seasons leading league in errors**

NL—5—Pie Traynor, Pittsburgh, 1926, 1928 (tied), 1931-1933
AL—5—Jim Tabor, Boston, 1939, 1940 (tied), 1941, 1942, 1943 (tied)

**Fewest errors, season (150 or more games)**

AL—5—Don Money, Milwaukee, 157 G, 1974
NL—8—Ken Reitz, St. Louis, 150 G, 1980

**Most consecutive errorless games, career**

ML—99—John Wehner, Pittsburgh NL, Aug 2, 1992-Sept 29, 2000 (202 CA; played other positions during streak)
Jeff Cirillo, Colorado NL, Seattle AL, June 20, 2001-Apr 19, 2002 (255 CA)
NL—99—John Wehner, Pittsburgh, Aug 2, 1992-Sept 29, 2000 (202 CA; played other positions during streak)
AL—88—Don Money, Milwaukee, Sept 28, 2nd game,1973-July 16, 1974 (261 CA)

**Most consecutive errorless games, season**

AL—86—Don Money, Milwaukee, Apr 5-July 16, 1974 (257 CA)
NL—85—Jeff Cirillo, Colorado, June 20-Oct 7, 2001 (228 CA)

**Most consecutive chances accepted without an error, career**

AL—261—Don Money, Milwaukee, Sept 28, 1st game, 1973-July 16, 1974, 88 G
NL—246—Jeff Cirillo, Colorado, June 20-Oct 7, 2001; San Diego, May 19-July 21, 2004, 96 G

**Most consecutive chances accepted without an error, season**
AL—257—Don Money, Milwaukee, Apr 5-July 16, 1974, 88 G
NL—230—Vinny Castilla, Colorado, July 5-Oct 3, 2004, 75 G

**Most errors, game**
UA—6—Jim Donnelly, Kansas City, July 16, 1884
AA—6—Joe Moffett, Toledo, Aug 2, 1884
Joe Werrick, Louisville, July 28, 1888
Billy Alvord, Toledo, May 22, 1890
NL—6—Joe Mulvey, Philadelphia, July 30, 1884
NL since 1893—5—Dave Brain, Boston, June 11, 1906
AL—4—22 third basemen; last—Edgar Martinez, Seattle, May 6, 1990

**Longest game with no errors**
NL—26 inn—Tony Boeckel, Boston, May 1, 1920
Jimmy Johnston, Brooklyn, May 1, 1920
AL—25 inn—Vance Law, Chicago, May 8, finished May 9, 1984

**Most errors, inning**
NL—4—Lew Whistler, New York, June 19, 1891, 4th
Bob Brenly, San Francisco, Sept 14, 1986, 4th
AL—4—Jimmy Burke, Milwaukee, May 27, 1901, 4th

## DOUBLE PLAYS

**Most double plays, career**
AL—618—Brooks Robinson, Baltimore, 23 seasons, 1955-1977
NL—450—Mike Schmidt, Philadelphia, 18 seasons, 1972-1989

**Most double plays, season**
AL—54—Graig Nettles, Cleveland, 158 G, 1971
NL—45—Darrell Evans, Atlanta, 160 G, 1974
Jeff Cirillo, Milwaukee, 149 G, 1998

**Fewest double plays for leader, season**
NL—17—Joe Stripp, Brooklyn, 140 G, 1933
Johnny Vergez, New York, 123 G, 1933
Whitey Kurowski, St. Louis, 138 G, 1946
Jim Tabor, Philadelphia, 124 G, 1946
AL—23—Marty McManus, Detroit, 130 G, 1930

**Most seasons leading league in double plays**
NL—6—Heinie Groh, Cincinnati, New York, 1915, 1916, 1918, 1919, 1920 (tied), 1922
Ron Santo, Chicago, 1961, 1964, 1966, 1967, 1968 (tied), 1971
Mike Schmidt, Philadelphia, 1978-1980, 1982 (tied), 1983, 1987
AL—5—Jimmy Austin, New York, St. Louis, 1909, 1911, 1913, 1915, 1917
Ken Keltner, Cleveland, 1939, 1941, 1942, 1944, 1947
Frank Malzone, Boston, 1957-1961

**Fewest double plays, season (150 or more games)**
NL—10—Bob Aspromonte, Houston, 155 G, 1964
Chipper Jones, Atlanta, 156 G, 1999
AL—17—Max Alvis, Cleveland, 156 G, 1965
Wade Boggs, Boston, 151 G, 1988
Dean Palmer, Texas, 154 G, 1996

**Most double plays, game**
NL—4—Pie Traynor, Pittsburgh, July 9, 1925, 1st game
Johnny Vergez, Philadelphia, Aug 15, 1935
Dennis Walling, Houston, May 8, 1988
Edgardo Alfonzo, New York, May 14, 1997
Shane Andrews, Chicago, Sept 23, 2000
AL—4—Andy Carey, New York, July 31, 1955, 2nd game
Felix Torres, Los Angeles, Aug 23, 1963
Ken McMullen, Washington, Aug 13, 1965
Wade Boggs, Boston, Aug 9, 1985
Jack Howell, California, May 17, 1989
Scott Brosius, New York, July 6, 2000

**Most double plays started, game**
NL—5—Dennis Walling, Houston, May 8, 1988
AL—4—Felix Torres, Los Angeles, Aug 23, 1963
Ken McMullen, Washington, Aug 13, 1965
Jack Howell, California, May 17, 1989
Scott Brosius, New York, July 6, 2000

**Most unassisted double plays, season**
AL—4—Joe Dugan, New York, 148 G, 1924
NL—3—Harry Wolverton, Philadelphia, 34 G, 1902
Heinie Groh, Cincinnati, 131 G, 1915

**Most unassisted double plays, game**
AL-NL—1—many third basemen

# SHORTSTOPS

## GAMES AND INNINGS

**Most games, career**
AL—2,581—Luis Aparicio, Chicago, Baltimore, Boston, 1956-1973, 18 seasons
NL—2,511—Ozzie Smith, San Diego, St. Louis, 1978-1996, 19 seasons

**Most consecutive games, career**
AL—2,216—Cal Ripken Jr., Baltimore, July 1, 1982-July 14, 1996
NL—584—Roy McMillan, Cincinnati, Sept 16, 1951, 1st game-Aug 6, 1955

**Most games, season**
NL—165—Maury Wills, Los Angeles, 1962
AL—163—Tony Fernandez, Toronto, 1986

**Most games by lefthander, season**
NL—73—Billy Hulen, Philadelphia, 1896

**Fewest games for leader, season**
NL—141—Rabbit Maranville, Pittsburgh, 1923
AL—142—Luis Aparicio, Chicago, 1957

**Most seasons leading league in games**
AL—12—Cal Ripken Jr., Baltimore, 1983, 1984, 1987-1996
NL—6—Mickey Doolan, Philadelphia, 1906, 1909-1913
Arky Vaughan, Pittsburgh, 1933 (tied), 1934, 1936, 1938-1940
Roy McMillan, Cincinnati, Milwaukee, 1952, 1953, 1954 (tied), 1956, 1957, 1961

**Most innings, game**
NL—26—Chuck Ward, Brooklyn, May 1, 1920
Rabbit Maranville, Boston, May 1, 1920
AL—25—Robin Yount, Milwaukee, May 8, finished May 9, 1984 (fielded 24.1 inn)

## AVERAGE

**Highest average, career (1,000 or more games)**
ML—.984—Omar Vizquel, Seattle AL, Cleveland AL, San Francisco NL, 1989-2005, 17 seasons, 2,275 G
AL—.983—Omar Vizquel, Seattle, Cleveland, 1989-2004, 16 seasons, 2,125 G
NL—.980—Larry Bowa, Philadelphia, Chicago, 1970-1985, 16 seasons, 2,222 G

**Highest average, season (150 or more games)**
AL—.996—Cal Ripken Jr., Baltimore, 161 G, 1990
NL—.994—Rey Ordonez, New York, 154 G, 1999

**Highest average, season (100 or more games)**
AL—.998—Mike Bordick, Baltimore, 117 G, 2002
NL—.994—Rey Ordonez, New York, 154 G, 1999

**Lowest average for leader (100 or more games)**
NL—.9003—Arthur Irwin, Philadelphia, 121 G, 1888
NL since 1893—.936—Tommy Corcoran, Cincinnati, 150 G, 1904
AL—.930—Freddy Parent, Boston, 139 G, 1903

**Most seasons leading league in average (100 or more games)**
AL—8—Everett Scott, Boston, New York, 1916-1923
Lou Boudreau, Cleveland, 1940-1944, 1946-1948
Luis Aparicio, Chicago, Baltimore, 1959-1966
NL—7—Ozzie Smith, San Diego, St. Louis, 1981, 1982, 1984-1987, 1991 (also led in the shortened 1994 season when he played 96 G)

**Most consecutive seasons leading league in average (100 or more games)**
AL—8—Everett Scott, Boston, New York, 1916-1923
Luis Aparicio, Chicago, Baltimore, 1959-1966
NL—5—Hughie Jennings, Baltimore, 1894-1898

**Lowest fielding average, season (100 or more games)**
AL—.851—Bill Keister, Baltimore, 112 G, 1901
NL—.884—Tom Burns, Chicago, 111 G, 1885
NL since 1893—.891—Otto Krueger, St. Louis, 107 G, 1902

## PUTOUTS

**Most putouts, career**
NL—5,133—Rabbit Maranville, Boston, Pittsburgh, Chicago, Brooklyn, St. Louis, 1912-1931, except 1924, 19 seasons
AL—4,548—Luis Aparicio, Chicago, Baltimore, Boston, 1956-1973, 18 seasons

**Most putouts, season**
NL—425—Hughie Jennings, Baltimore, 131 G, 1895
AL—425—Donie Bush, Detroit, 157 G, 1914
NL since 1893—407—Rabbit Maranville, Boston, 156 G, 1914

**Fewest putouts for leader, season**
NL—230—Barry Larkin, Cincinnati, 151 G, 1996
AL—248—Joe DeMaestri, Kansas City, 134 G, 1957

**Most seasons leading league in putouts**
NL—6—Rabbit Maranville, Boston, Pittsburgh, 1914, 1915 (tied), 1916, 1917, 1919, 1923
AL—6—Cal Ripken, Baltimore, 1984, 1985, 1988, 1989, 1991, 1992

**Fewest putouts, season (150 or more games)**
NL—180—Larry Bowa, Philadelphia, 156 G, 1976
Mark Grudzielanek, Montreal, 153 G, 1996
AL—212—Gary DiSarcina, California, 150 G, 1996
Derek Jeter, New York, 150 G, 2001

**Most putouts, game**
NL—11—Shorty Fuller, New York, Aug 20, 1895
Hod Ford, Cincinnati, Sept 18, 1929
[14—Monte Cross, Philadelphia, July 7, 1899, 11 inn]
AL—11—John Cassidy, Washington, Aug 30, 1904, 1st game

## ASSISTS

**Most assists, career**
NL—8,375—Ozzie Smith, San Diego, St. Louis, 1978-1996, 19 seasons
AL—8,016—Luis Aparicio, Chicago, Baltimore, Boston, 1956-1973, 18 seasons

**Most assists, season**
NL—621—Ozzie Smith, San Diego, 158 G, 1980
AL—583—Cal Ripken Jr., Baltimore, 162 G, 1984

**Fewest assists for leader, season**
AL—438—Joe Sewell, Cleveland, 137 G, 1928
NL—440—Johnny Logan, Milwaukee, 129 G, 1957

**Most seasons leading league in assists**
NL—8—Ozzie Smith, San Diego, 1979-1981; St. Louis, 1982, 1985, 1987-1989
AL—7—Luke Appling, Chicago, 1933, 1935, 1937, 1939, 1941, 1943, 1946
Luis Aparicio, Chicago, 1956-1961, 1968
Cal Ripken Jr., Baltimore, 1983, 1984, 1986, 1987, 1989, 1991, 1993

**Fewest assists, season (150 or more games)**
AL—343—Derek Jeter, New York, 150 G, 2001
NL—374—Kevin Elster, New York, 150 G, 1989

**Most assists, game**
NL—14—Tommy Corcoran, Cincinnati, Aug 7, 1903
[14—Herman Long, Boston, May 6, 1892, 14 inn
Bud Harrelson, New York, May 24, 1973, 19 inn]
AL—13—Bobby Reeves, Washington, Aug 7, 1927
Alex Gonzalez, Toronto, Apr 26, 1996
[15—Rick Burleson, California, Apr 13, finished Apr 14, 1982, 20 inn]

## CHANCES ACCEPTED AND OFFERED

**Most chances accepted, career**
NL—12,624—Ozzie Smith, San Diego, St. Louis, 1978-1996, 19 seasons
AL—12,564—Luis Aparicio, Chicago, Baltimore, Boston, 1956-1973, 18 seasons

**Most chances accepted, season**
NL—984—Dave Bancroft, New York, 156 G, 1922
AL—969—Donie Bush, Detroit, 157 G, 1914

**Fewest chances accepted by leader, season**
NL—683—Mark Grudzielanek, Montreal, 156 G, 1997
AL—695—Luis Aparicio, Chicago, 142 G, 1957

**Most seasons leading league in chances accepted**
NL—8—Ozzie Smith, San Diego, St. Louis, 1978, 1980, 1981, 1983, 1985, 1987-1989
AL—7—Luis Aparicio, Chicago, 1956-1961, 1968

**Fewest chances accepted, season (150 or more games)**
AL—555—Derek Jeter, New York, 150 G, 2001
NL—609—Kevin Elster, New York, 150 G, 1989

**Most chances accepted, game**
NL—19—Danny Richardson, Washington, June 20, 1892, 1st game
NL since 1983—19—Eddie Joost, Cincinnati, May 7, 1941
[21—Eddie R. Miller, Boston, June 27, 1939, 23 inn]
AL—17—Bobby Wallace, St. Louis, June 10, 1902
[20—Roy Smalley, Minnesota, Aug 25, 1976, 18.2 inn]

**Longest game with no chances offered**
AL—12 inn—John Gochnauer, Cleveland, July 14, 1903
Billy Rogell, Detroit, June 16, 1937, fielded 11.2 inn
NL—12 inn—Irv Ray, Boston, Aug 15, 1888
NL since 1893—12 inn—Khalil Greene, San Diego, Aug 1, 2004

## ERRORS

**Most errors, career**
ML—1,037—Herman Long, Kansas City AA, Boston NL, New York AL, Detroit AL, 1889-1903, 15 seasons
NL—972—Bill Dahlen, Chicago, Brooklyn, New York, Boston, 1891-1909, 1911, 20 seasons, 2,139 G
NL since 1893—676—Bill Dahlen, Chicago, Brooklyn, New York, Boston, 1893-1909, 1911, 18 seasons, 2,045 G
AL—689—Donie Bush, Detroit, Washington, 1908-1921, 14 seasons, 1,866 G

**Most errors, season**
PL—115—Bill Shindle, Philadelphia, 132 G, 1890
NL—106—Joe Sullivan, Washington, 127 G, 1893
NL since 1893—81—Rudy Hulswitt, Philadelphia, 138 G, 1903
AL—95—John Gochnauer, Cleveland, 128 G, 1903

**Fewest errors for leader, season**
NL—21—Mariano Duncan, Los Angeles, 67 G, 1987
AL—21—Cristian Guzman, Minnesota, 118 G, 2001

**Most seasons leading league in errors**
NL—6—Dick Groat, Pittsburgh, St. Louis, 1955, 1956, 1959, 1961, 1962, 1964
Rafael Ramirez, Atlanta, 1981-1983, 1984 (tied), 1985, Houston, 1989
AL—5—Luke Appling, Chicago, 1933, 1935, 1937, 1939, 1946

**Fewest errors, season (150 or more games)**
AL—3—Cal Ripken Jr., Baltimore, 161 G, 1990
Omar Vizquel, Cleveland, 156 G, 2000
NL—4—Rey Ordonez, New York, 154 G, 1999

**Most consecutive errorless games, career**
AL—110—Mike Bordick, Baltimore, Apr 11-Sept 29, 2002 (541 CA)
NL—101—Rey Ordonez, New York, June 14, 1999-Mar 29, 2000 (418 CA)

**Most consecutive errorless games, season**
AL—110—Mike Bordick, Baltimore, Apr 11-Sept 29, 2002 (541 CA)
NL—100—Rey Ordonez, New York, June 14-Oct 4, 1999 (411 CA)

**Most consecutive chances accepted without an error, career**
AL—543—Mike Bordick, Baltimore, Apr 10 (part)-Sept 29, 2002
NL—419—Rey Ordonez, New York, June 13, 1999 (part)-Mar 29, 2000

**Most consecutive chances accepted without an error, season**
AL—543—Mike Bordick, Baltimore, Apr 10 (part)-Sept 29, 2002
NL—412—Rey Ordonez, New York, June 13 (part)-Oct 4, 1999

**Most errors, game**
NL—7—Jimmy Hallinan, New York, July 29, 1876
AA—7—Germany Smith, Brooklyn, June 17, 1885
NL since 1893—5—Charlie Babb, New York, Aug 24, 1903, 1st game
Charlie Babb, Brooklyn, June 20, 1904
Phil Lewis, Brooklyn, July 20, 1905
[5—many shortstops in extra innings]
AL—5—Donie Bush, Detroit, Aug 25, 1911, 1st game
[6—Bill O'Neill, Boston, May 21, 1904, 13 inn]

**Longest game with no errors**
NL—26 inn—Rabbit Maranville, Boston, May 1, 1920
AL—25 inn—Robin Yount, Milwaukee, May 8, finished May 9, 1984 (fielded 24.1 inn)

**Most errors, inning**
NL—4—Shorty Fuller, Washington, Aug 17, 1888, 2nd
Lennie Merullo, Chicago, Sept 13, 1942, 2nd game, 2nd
AL—4—Ray Chapman, Cleveland, June 20, 1914, 5th

## DOUBLE PLAYS

**Most double plays, career**
NL—1,590—Ozzie Smith, San Diego, St. Louis, 19 seasons, 1978-1996
AL—1,565—Cal Ripken Jr., Baltimore, 16 seasons, 1981-1996

**Most double plays, season**
AL—147—Rick Burleson, Boston, 155 G, 1980
NL—137—Bobby Wine, Montreal, 159 G, 1970

**Fewest double plays for leader, season**
NL—79—Ozzie Smith, St. Louis, 150 G, 1991
AL—81—Roger Peckinpaugh, Washington, 155 G, 1924

**Most seasons leading league in double plays**
AL—8—Cal Ripken Jr., Baltimore, 1983-1985, 1989, 1991, 1992, 1994, 1995
NL—5—Mickey Doolan, Philadelphia, 1907, 1909 (tied), 1910, 1911, 1913
Dick Groat, Pittsburgh, St. Louis, 1958, 1959, 1961, 1962, 1964
Ozzie Smith, San Diego, St. Louis, 1980, 1984 (tied), 1986 (tied), 1987, 1991

**Fewest double plays, season (150 or more games)**
AL—60—Jackie Gutierrez, Boston, 150 G, 1984
NL—63—Kevin Elster, New York, 150 G, 1989

**Most double plays, game**
AL—5—29 times by 26 shortstops; last—Alex Rodriguez, Texas, July 26, 2002
[6—Bert Campaneris, Oakland, Sept 13, 1970, 1st game, 11 inn]
NL—5—19 times by 19 shortstops; last—David Eckstein, St. Louis, Aug 18, 2005
[6—Ozzie Smith, San Diego, Aug 25, 1979, 19 inn
Rafael Ramirez, Atlanta, June 27, 1982, 14 inn]

**Most double plays started, game**
AL—5—Charley O'Leary, Detroit, July 23, 1905
John P. Sullivan, Washington, Aug 13, 1944, 2nd game
Jim Fregosi, California, May 1, 1966, 1st game
NL—4—many players
[5—Ozzie Smith, San Diego, Aug 25, 1979, 19 inn]

**Most unassisted double plays, game**
AL—2—Lee Tannehill, Chicago, Aug 4, 1911, 1st game
NL—1—many shortstops

---

**For a complete list of players turning unassisted triple plays, see page 138.**

---

# OUTFIELDERS

## GAMES AND INNINGS

**Most games, career**
AL—2,934—Ty Cobb, Detroit, Philadelphia, 1905-1928, 24 seasons
NL—2,842—Willie Mays, New York Giants, San Francisco, New York Mets, 1951-1973, except 1943 in military service, 22 seasons

**Most consecutive games, career**
NL—897—Billy Williams, Chicago, Sept 22, 1963-June 13, 1969
AL—511—Clyde Milan, Washington, Aug 12, 1910-Oct 3, 1913, 2nd game

**Most games, season**
AL—163—Leon Wagner, Cleveland, 1964
NL—164—Billy Williams, Chicago, 1965

**Fewest games for leader, season**
AL—147—Ted Williams, Boston, 1951
NL—149—Max Carey, Pittsburgh, 1924
Chet Ross, Boston, 1940

**Most seasons leading league in games**
NL—6—George J. Burns, New York, Cincinnati, 1914 (tied), 1916 (tied), 1919, 1920 (tied), 1922, 1923 (tied)
Billy Williams, Chicago, 1964 (tied), 1965-1968, 1970 (tied)

Dale Murphy, Atlanta, 1982 (tied), 1983 (tied), 1984 (tied), 1985, 1987, 1988
AL—5—Rocky Colavito, Cleveland, Detroit, 1959, 1961-1963, 1965

**Most innings, game**
NL—26—Walt Cruise, Boston, May 1, 1920
Les Mann, Boston, May 1, 1920
Bernie Neis, Brooklyn, May 1, 1920
Ray Powell, Boston, May 1, 1920
Zack Wheat, Brooklyn, May 1, 1920
AL—25—Harold Baines, Chicago, May 8, finished May 9, 1984
Rudy Law, Chicago, May 8, finished May 9, 1984
Ben Oglivie, Milwaukee, May 8, finished May 9, 1984 (fielded 24.1 inn)

## AVERAGE

**Highest average, career (1,000 or more games)**
ML—.995—Darryl Hamilton, Milwaukee AL, Texas AL, San Francisco NL, Colorado NL, New York NL, 1988, 1990-2001,13 seasons, 1,233 G
NL—.993—Terry Puhl, Houston, 1977-1990, 14 seasons, 1,299 G
AL—.991—Amos Otis, Kansas City, 1970-1983, 14 seasons, 1,845 G

**Highest average, season (150 or more games)**
NL—1.000—Danny Litwhiler, Philadelphia, 151 G, 1942
Curt Flood, St. Louis, 159 G, 1966
Terry Puhl, Houston, 152 G, 1979
Brett Butler, Los Angeles, 161 G, 1991
Brett Butler, Los Angeles, 155 G, 1993
Luis Gonzalez, Arizona, 161 G, 2001
Juan Encarnacion, Florida, 155 G, 2003
AL—1.000—Rocky Colavito, Cleveland, 162 G, 1965
Brian Downing, California, 158 G, 1982

**Highest average, season (100 or more games)**
NL—1.000—many players
AL—1.000—many players

**Lowest average for leader (100 or more games)**
NL—.941—Pete Gillespie, New York, 102 G, 1885
NL since 1893—.96753—Zack Wheat, Brooklyn, 120 G, 1912
AL—.959—Chick Stahl, Boston, 130 G, 1901

**Most seasons leading league in average (100 or more games)**
AL—5—Amos Strunk, Philadelphia, Boston, Chicago, 1912, 1914, 1917 (tied), 1918, 1920
NL—4—Joe Hornung, Boston, 1881, 1882, 1883, 1887
NL since 19893—3—Stan Musial, St. Louis, 1949, 1954, 1961
Tony Gonzalez, Philadelphia, 1962, 1964, 1967
Pete Rose, Cincinnati, 1970, 1971 (tied), 1974

**Most consecutive seasons leading league in average (100 or more games)**
AL—3—Gene Woodling, New York, 1951 (tied), 1952, 1953 (tied)
NL—3—Joe Hornung, Boston, 1881-1883
NL since 1893—2—many players; last—Pete Rose, Cincinnati, 1970, 1971 (tied)

**Lowest fielding average, season (100 or more games)**
NL—.843—Jack Manning, Philadelphia, 103 G, 1884
NL since 1893—.900—Mike Donlin, Cincinnati, 118 G, 1903
AL—.872—Bill O'Neill, Washington, 112 G, 1904

## PUTOUTS

**Most putouts, career**
NL—7,095—Willie Mays, New York Giants, San Francisco, New York Mets, 1951-1973, except 1953 in military service, 22 seasons
AL—6,794—Tris Speaker, Boston, Cleveland, Washington, Philadelphia, 1907-1928, 22 seasons

**Most putouts, season**
NL—547—Taylor Douthit, St. Louis, 154 G, 1928
AL—512—Chet Lemon, Chicago, 149 G, 1977

**Fewest putouts for leader, season**
AL—319—Tris Speaker, Boston, 142 G, 1909
NL—321—Roy Thomas, Philadelphia, 139 G, 1904

**Most seasons leading league in putouts**
NL—9—Max Carey, Pittsburgh, 1912, 1913, 1916-1918, 1921-1924
Richie Ashburn, Philadelphia, 1949-1954, 1956-1958
AL—7—Tris Speaker, Boston, Cleveland, 1909, 1910, 1913-1915, 1918, 1919

**Fewest putouts, season (150 or more games)**
AL—182—Ed Hahn, Chicago, 156 G, 1907
NL—210—Sam Thompson, Philadelphia, 151 G, 1892
NL since 1900—217—Al Martin, Pittsburgh, 152 G, 1996

**Most putouts by left fielder, game**
NL—11—Dick Harley, St. Louis, June 30, 1898
Topsy Hartsel, Chicago, Sept 10, 1901
[12—Fred Treacy, New York, July 10, 1876, 16 inn]
AL—11—Paul Lehner, Philadelphia, June 25, 1950, 2nd game
Willie Horton, Detroit, July 18, 1969
[12—Tom McBride, Washington, July 2, 1948, 12 inn
Rickey Henderson, New York, Sept 11, 1988, 18 inn
Darin Erstad, Anaheim, July 24, 2000, 12 inn]

**Most putouts by center fielder, game**
NL—12—Earl Clark, Boston, May 10, 1929
[12—Carden Gillenwater, Boston, Sept 11, 1946, 17 inn
Lloyd Merriman, Cincinnati, Sept 7, 1951, 18 inn
Garry Maddox, Philadelphia, June 10, 1984, 12 inn]
AL—12—Lyman Bostock, Minnesota, May 25, 1977, 2nd game
[12—Harry Bay, Cleveland, July 19, 1904, 12 inn
Ruppert Jones, Seattle, May 16, 1978, 16 inn
Rick Manning, Milwaukee, July 11, 1983, 15 inn
Gary Pettis, California, June 4, 1985, 15 inn
Oddibe McDowell, Texas, July 20, 1985, 15 inn
Claudell Washington, New York, May 30, 1988, 13 inn]

**Most putouts by right fielder, game**
AL—11—Tony Armas, Oakland, June 12, 1982
NL—10—Bill Nicholson, Chicago, Sept 17, 1945
[12—Rolando Roomes, Cincinnati, July 28, 1989, 17 inn]

## ASSISTS

**Most assists, career**
AL—450—Tris Speaker, Boston, Cleveland, Washington, Philadelphia, 1907-1928, 22 seasons
NL—356—Jimmy Ryan, Chicago, 1885-1889, 1891-1900, 15 seasons
NL since 1893—339—Max Carey, Pittsburgh, Brooklyn, 1910-1929, 20 seasons

**Most assists, season**
NL—45—Hardy Richardson, Buffalo, 78 G, 1881
NL since 1893—44—Chuck Klein, Philadelphia, 156 G, 1930
AL—35—Sam Mertes, Chicago, 123 G, 1902
Tris Speaker, Boston, 142 G, 1909
Tris Speaker, Boston, 153 G, 1912

**Fewest assists for leader, season**
AL—13—Ken Berry, California, 116 G, 1972
Carlos May, Chicago, 145 G, 1972
NL—14—Bill Bruton, Milwaukee, 141 G, 1954
Don Mueller, New York, 153 G, 1954
Frank J. Thomas, Pittsburgh, 153 G, 1954
Barry Bonds, Pittsburgh, 150 G, 1990
Kevin McReynolds, New York, 144 G, 1990
Vladimir Guerrero, Montreal, 161 G, 2002
Larry Walker, Colorado, 123 G, 2002

**Most seasons leading league in assists**
AL—7—Carl Yastrzemski, Boston, 1962, 1963, 1964 (tied), 1966, 1969, 1971, 1977
NL—5—Roberto Clemente, Pittsburgh, 1958, 1960, 1961, 1966, 1967

**Fewest assists, season (150 or more games)**
AL—1—Harmon Killebrew, Minnesota, 157 G, 1964
Albert Belle, Chicago, 154 G, 1997
NL—2—Lenny Dykstra, Philadelphia, 160 G, 1993
Brian McRae, Chicago, 155 G, 1996
Barry Bonds, San Francisco, 155 G, 1998

**Most assists, game**
NL—4—Harry Schafer, Boston, Sept 26, 1877
Bill Crowley, Buffalo, May 24, 1880
Bill Crowley, Buffalo, Aug 27, 1880
NL since 1893—4—Mike Griffin, Brooklyn, July 17, 1893
Fred Clarke, Pittsburgh, Aug 23, 1910
[4—Dusty Miller, May 30, 1895, 2nd game, 11 inn]
AL—4—James W. Holmes, Chicago, Aug 21, 1903
Lee Magee, New York, June 28, 1916
Happy Felsch, Chicago, Aug 14, 1919
Bob Meusel, New York, Sept 5, 1921, 2nd game
Sam Langford, Cleveland, May 1, 1928

**Most assists, outfielder to catcher, game**
NL—3—Dummy Hoy, Washington, June 19, 1889
Jim Jones, New York, June 30, 1902
Jack McCarthy, Chicago, Apr 26, 1905
AL—2—many outfielders.

**Most assists, inning**
AL-NL—2—many outfielders

## CHANCES ACCEPTED AND OFFERED

**Most chances accepted, career**
NL—7,290—Willie Mays, New York Giants, San Francisco, New York Mets, 1951-1973, except 1953 in military service, 22 seasons
AL—7,244—Tris Speaker, Boston, Cleveland, Washington, Philadelphia, 1907-1928, 22 seasons

**Most chances accepted, season**
NL—557—Taylor Douthit, St. Louis, 154 G, 1928
AL—524—Chet Lemon, Chicago, 149 G, 1977

**Fewest chances accepted for leader, season**
AL—333—Sam Crawford, Detroit, 144 G, 1907
NL—342—Roy Thomas, Philadelphia, 139 G, 1904

**Most seasons leading league in chances accepted**
NL—9—Max Carey, Pittsburgh, 1912, 1913, 1916-1918, 1921-1924
Richie Ashburn, Philadelphia, 1949-1954, 1956-1958
AL—8—Tris Speaker, Boston, Cleveland, 1909, 1910, 1912-1915, 1918, 1919

**Fewest chances accepted, season (150 or more games)**
AL—206—Ed Hahn, Chicago, 156 G, 1907

NL—222—Al Martin, Pittsburgh, 152 G, 1996

**Most chances accepted by left fielder, game**
NL—12—Ducky Holmes, Baltimore, Sept 12, 1899
[12—Fred Treacy, New York, July 10, 1876, 16 inn]
AL—11—Paul Lehner, Philadelphia, June 25, 1950, 2nd game
Willie Horton, Detroit, July 18, 1969
[12—Tom McBride, Washington, July 2, 1948, 12 inn
Darin Erstad, Anaheim, July 24, 2000, 12 inn]

**Most chances accepted by center fielder, game**
NL—13—Earl Clark, Boston, May 10, 1929
AL—12—Happy Felsch, Chicago, June 23, 1919
Johnny Mostil, Chicago, May 22, 1928
Lyman Bostock, Minnesota, May 25, 1977, 2nd game
[12—Harry Bay, Cleveland, July 19, 1904, 12 inn
Ruppert Jones, Seattle, May 16, 1978, 16 inn
Rick Manning, Milwaukee, July 11, 1983, 15 inn
Gary Pettis, California, June 4, 1985, 15 inn
Oddibe McDowell, Texas, July 20, 1985, 15 inn]

**Most chances accepted by right fielder, game**
AL—12—Tony Armas, Oakland, June 12, 1982
NL—10—Greasy Neale, Cincinnati, July 13, 1920
Casey Stengel, Philadelphia, July 30, 1920
Bill Nicholson, Chicago, Sept 17, 1945
Bake McBride, Philadelphia, Sept 8, 1978, 2nd game
Raul Mondesi, Los Angeles, Sept 25, 1995
Jeromy Burnitz, Milwaukee, Sept 17, 2001

**Longest game with no chances offered, left fielder**
AL—18 inn—Chuck Hinton, Washington, June 14, 1963, 2nd game
NL—16.1 inn—Larry Stahl, San Diego, July 15, 1971

**Longest game with no chances offered, center fielder**
AL—22 inn—Bill Bruton, Detroit, June 24, 1962
NL—17.1 inn—Ernie Orsatti, St. Louis, July 2, 1933, 1st game

**Longest game with no chances offered, right fielder**
AL—22 inn—Cap Peterson, Washington, June 12, 1967
NL—18 inn—Lance Richbourg, Boston, May 14, 1927
Art Shamsky, Cincinnati, July 19, 1966

## ERRORS

**Most errors, career**
ML—384—Dummy Hoy, Washington NL, Buffalo PL, St. Louis AA, Cincinnati NL, Louisville NL, Chicago AL, 1888-1902, except 1900, 14 seasons
NL—347—George Gore, Chicago, New York, St. Louis, 1879-1889, 1891, 1892, 13 seasons
NL since 1893—235—Max Carey, Pittsburgh, Brooklyn, 1910-1929, 20 seasons
AL—271—Ty Cobb, Detroit, Philadelphia, 1905-1928, 24 seasons

**Most errors, season**
PL—52—Ed Beecher, Buffalo, 125 G, 1890
NL—49—Fred Clarke, Louisville, 132 G, 1895
AL—31—Roy C. Johnson, Detroit, 146 G, 1929

**Fewest errors for leader, season**
NL—8—David Justice, Atlanta, 140 G, 1992
AL—8—Albert Belle, Chicago, 159 G, 1998
Kenny Lofton, Cleveland, 154 G, 1998

**Most seasons leading league in errors**
NL—7—Lou Brock, Chicago, St. Louis, 1964-1967, 1968 (tied), 1972, 1973 (tied)
AL—5—Burt Shotton, St. Louis, Washington, 1912 (tied), 1914, 1915 (tied), 1916, 1918
Reggie Jackson, Oakland, Baltimore, 1968, 1970, 1972, 1975, 1976 (tied)

**Fewest errors, season (150 or more games)**
NL—0—Danny Litwhiler, Philadelphia, 151 G, 1942
Curt Flood, St. Louis, 159 G, 1966
Terry Puhl, Houston, 152 G, 1979
Brett Butler, Los Angeles, 161 G, 1991
Brett Butler, Los Angeles, 155 G, 1993
Luis Gonzalez, Arizona, 161 G, 2001
AL—0—Rocky Colavito, Cleveland, 162 G, 1965
Brian Downing, California, 158 G, 1982

**Most consecutive errorless games, career**
ML—392—Darren Lewis, Oakland AL, San Francisco NL, Aug 21, 1990-June 29, 1994 (938 CA)
NL—369—Darren Lewis, San Francisco, July 13, 1991-June 29, 1994 (905 CA)
AL—336—Rich Amaral, Seattle, Baltimore, Apr 30, 1995-June 14, 2000 (531 CA)

**Most consecutive errorless games, season**
AL—162—Rocky Colavito, Cleveland, Apr 13-Oct 3, 1965 (274 CA)
NL—161—Brett Butler, Los Angeles, Apr 10-Oct 6, 1991 (380 CA)
Luis Gonzalez, Arizona, Apr 3-Oct 7, 2001 (288 CA)

**Most consecutive chances accepted without an error, career**
ML—938—Darren Lewis, Oakland AL, San Francisco NL, Aug 21, 1990-June 29, 1994, 392 G
NL—905—Darren Lewis, San Francisco, July 13, 1991-June 29, 1994, 369 G
AL—723—Darin Erstad, Anaheim, May 30, 2001-Sept 22, 2002, 238 G

**Most errors, game**
AA—5—Jim Clinton, Baltimore, May 3, 1884
UA—5—Fred Tenney, Washington, May 29, 1884
AL—5—Kip Selbach, Baltimore, Aug 19, 1902
NL—5—Jack Manning, Boston, May 1, 1876
Pop Snyder, Louisville, July 29, 1876
Jim O'Rourke, Boston, June 21, 1877
Charlie Bennett, Milwaukee, June 15, 1878
Mike Dorgan, New York, May 24, 1884
Mike Tiernan, New York, May 16, 1887
Marty Sullivan, Chicago, May 18, 1887
NL since 1893—4—Fred Nicholson, Boston, June 16, 1922

**Longest game with no errors**
NL—26 inn—Walt Cruise, Boston, May 1, 1920
Les Mann, Boston, May 1, 1920
Dornic Neis, Brooklyn, May 1, 1920
Ray Powell, Boston, May 1, 1920
Zack Wheat, Brooklyn, May 1, 1920
AL—25 inn—Harold Baines, Chicago, May 8, finished May 9, 1984
Rudy Law, Chicago, May 8, finished May 9, 1984
Ben Oglivie, Milwaukee, May 8, finished May 9, 1984 (fielded 24.1 inn)

**Most errors, inning**
NL—3—George Gore, Chicago, Aug 8, 1883, 1st
NL since 1893—3—Larry Herndon, San Francisco, Sept 6, 1980, 4th
AA—3—Jim Donahue, Kansas City, July 4, 1889, p.m. game, 1st
AL—3—Kip Selbach, Washington, June 23, 1904, 8th
Harry Bay, Cleveland, June 29, 1905, 2nd game, 9th
Harry Heilmann, Detroit, May 22, 1914, 1st
Herschel Bennett, St. Louis, Apr 14, 1925, 8th
Scott Lusader, Detroit, Sept 9, 1989, 1st

## DOUBLE PLAYS

**Most double plays, career**
AL—136—Tris Speaker, Boston, Cleveland, Washington, Philadelphia, 22 seasons, 1907-1928
NL—86—Max Carey, Pittsburgh, Brooklyn, 20 seasons, 1910-1929

**Most double plays, season**
AL—15—Happy Felsch, Chicago, 125 G, 1919
NL—14—Jimmy Sheckard, Baltimore, 147 G, 1899

**Fewest double plays for leader, season**
NL—3—Brett Butler, Los Angeles, 161 G, 1991
Willie McGee, San Francisco, 128 G, 1991
AL—4—many outfielders; last—Tony Armas, Oakland, 112 G, 1977; Roy White, New York, 135 G, 1977

**Most seasons leading league in double plays**
AL—5—Tris Speaker, Boston, Cleveland, 1909, 1912, 1914-1916
NL—4—Willie Mays, New York Giants, San Francisco, 1954-1956, 1965

**Fewest double plays, seasons (150 or more games)**
NL—0—many outfielders; last—Bobby Abreu, Philadelphia, 158 G, 2003; Lance Berkman, Houston, 153 G, 2003
AL—0—many outfielders; last—Jose Cruz Jr., Tampa Bay, 152 G, 2004

**Most double plays started, game**
AA—3—Candy Nelson, New York, June 9, 1887
NL—3—Jack McCarthy, Chicago, Apr 26, 1905
AL—3—Ira Flagstead, Boston, Apr 19, 1926, p.m. game

**Most unassisted double plays, career**
AL—6—Tris Speaker, Boston, Cleveland, 1909 (1), 1910 (1), 1914 (2), 1918 (2)
NL—2—many outfielders

**Most unassisted double plays, season**
AL—2—Socks Seybold, Philadelphia, Aug 15, Sept 10, 1st game, 1907
Tris Speaker, Boston, Apr 21, Aug 8, 1914
Tris Speaker, Cleveland, Apr 18, Apr 29, 1918
Jose Cardenal, Cleveland, June 8, July 16, 1968
NL—2—Adam Comorosky, Pittsburgh, May 31, June 13, 1931

**Most unassisted double plays, game**
NL—1—many outfielders; last—Jose Guillen, Washington, May 8, 2005
AL—1—many outfielders; last—Mike Cameron, Seattle, May 23, 2003

**Most triple plays started, season**
AL—2—Charlie Jamieson, Cleveland, May 23, June 9, 1928
NL—1—many outfielders

# CATCHERS

## GAMES AND INNINGS

**Most games, career**
AL—2,226—Carlton Fisk, Boston, Chicago, 1969, 1971-1993, 24 seasons
NL—2,056—Gary Carter, Montreal, New York, San Francisco, Los Angeles, 1974-1992, 19 seasons

**Most consecutive games, career**
AL—312—Frankie Hayes, St. Louis, Philadelphia, Cleveland, October 2, 2nd game, 1943-Apr 21, 1946
NL—233—Ray Mueller, Cincinnati, July 31, 1943-May 5, 1946, except 1945 in military service

**Most games, season**
NL—160—Randy Hundley, Chicago, 1968
AL—155—Jim Sundberg, Texas, 1975
Frankie Hayes, Philadelphia, 1944

**Most games, lefthanded catcher, season**
NL—105—Jack Clements, Philadelphia, 1891
AL—23—Jiggs Donahue, St. Louis, 1902

**Most games catching all club's games, season**
NL—155—Ray Mueller, Cincinnati, 1944 (135 CG)
AL—155—Frankie Hayes, Philadelphia, 1944 (135 CG)

**Fewest games for leader, season**
NL—96—Ernie Lombardi, New York, 1945
AL—98—Jake Early, Washington, 1942

**Most seasons leading league in games**
AL—8—Yogi Berra, New York, 1950-1957
NL—6—Gary Carter, Montreal, 1977-1982

**Most seasons, 100 or more games**
ML—15—Bob Boone, Philadelphia NL, California AL, Kansas City AL, 1973, 1974, 1976-1980, 1982-1989
AL—13—Bill Dickey, New York, 1929-1941
NL—13—Johnny Bench, Cincinnati, 1968-1980

**Most consecutive seasons, 100 or more games**
AL—13—Bill Dickey, New York, 1929-1941
NL—13—Johnny Bench, Cincinnati, 1968-1980

**Most innings caught, game**
AL—25—Carlton Fisk, Chicago, May 8, finished May 9, 1984
NL—24—Hal King, Houston, Apr 15, 1968
Jerry Grote, New York, Apr 15, 1968 (caught 23.1 inn)

## AVERAGE

**Highest average, career (1,000 or more games)**
AL—.995—Dan Wilson, Seattle, 1994-2005, 12 seasons, 1,237 G
NL—.994—Brad Ausmus, San Diego, Houston, 1993-1998, 2001-2005, 11 seasons, 1,208 G

**Highest average, season (150 or more games)**
NL—.996—Randy Hundley, Chicago, 152 G, 1967
AL—.995—Jim Sundberg, Texas, 150 G, 1979

**Highest average, season (100 or more games)**
AL—1.000—Buddy Rosar, Philadelphia, 117 G, 1946
NL—1.000—Charles Johnson, Florida, 123 G, 1997
Mike Matheny, St. Louis, 138 G, 2003

**Lowest average for leader, season (100 or more games)**
AL—.954—Mike Powers, Philadelphia, 111 G, 1901
NL—.958—Gabby Hartnett, Chicago, 110 G, 1925

**Most seasons leading league in average (100 or more games)**
AL—8—Ray Schalk, Chicago, 1913-1917, 1920-1922
NL—7—Gabby Hartnett, Chicago, 1925, 1928, 1930, 1934-1937

**Most consecutive seasons leading league in average (100 or more games)**
AL—6—Bill Freehan, Detroit, 1965, 1966, 1967 (tied), 1968, 1969 (tied), 1970
NL—4—Johnny Kling, Chicago, 1902-1905
Gabby Hartnett, Chicago, 1934-1937

**Lowest fielding average, season (100 or more games)**
AL—.934—Sam Agnew, St. Louis, 102 G, 1915
NL since 1893—.947—Red Dooin, Philadelphia, 140 G, 1909

## PUTOUTS

**Most putouts, career**
NL—11,785—Gary Carter, Montreal, New York, San Francisco, Los Angeles, 1974-1992, 19 seasons
AL—11,369—Carlton Fisk, Boston, Chicago, 1969-1993, except 1970, 24 seasons

**Most putouts, season**
NL—1,135—Johnny Edwards, Houston, 151 G, 1969
AL—1,051—Dan Wilson, Seattle, 144 G, 1997

**Fewest putouts for leader, season**
NL—409—Gabby Hartnett, Chicago, 110 G, 1925
AL—446—Birdie Tebbetts, Detroit, 97 G, 1942

**Most seasons leading league in putouts**
AL—9—Ray Schalk, Chicago, 1913-1920, 1922
NL—8—Gary Carter, Montreal, 1977-1982; New York, 1985, 1988

**Fewest putouts, season (150 or more games)**
NL—471—Ray Mueller, Cincinnati, 155 G, 1944
AL—575—Mike Tresh, Chicago, 150 G, 1945

**Most putouts, game**
NL—20—Jerry Grote, New York, Apr 22, 1970 (19 K)
Sandy Martinez, Chicago, May 6, 1998 (20 K)
[24—Damian Miller, Chicago, May 15, 2003 (24 K), 17 inn]
AL—20—Rich Gedman, Boston, Apr 29, 1986 (20 K)
Dan Wilson, Seattle, Aug 8, 1997 (19 K)
[26—Jose Molina, Anaheim, June 8, 2004 (26 K), 17 inn]

**Most fouls caught, game**
NL—6—Wes Westrum, New York, Aug 24, 1949
AL—6—Sherm Lollar, Chicago, Apr 10, 1962

**Most fouls caught, inning**
NL—3—Mickey Owen, Brooklyn, Aug 4, 1941, 3rd
Wes Westrum, New York, Aug 24, 1949, 9th
Wes Westrum, New York, Sept 23, 1956, 5th
AL—3—Matt Batts, Detroit, Aug 2, 1953, 2nd game, 4th

## ASSISTS

**Most assists, career**
ML—1,835—Deacon McGuire, Toledo AA, Detroit NL, Philadelphia NL, Cleveland AA, Rochester AA, Washington AA, Washington NL, Brooklyn NL, Detroit AL, New York AL, Boston AL, Cleveland AL, 1884-1912, except 1889, 1908, 1909, 1911, 25 seasons
AL—1,810—Ray Schalk, Chicago, 1912-1928, 17 seasons
NL—1,593—Red Dooin, Philadelphia, Cincinnati, New York, 1902-1916, 15 seasons

**Most assists, season**
NL—214—Pat Moran, Boston, 107 G, 1903
AL—212—Oscar Stanage, Detroit, 141 G, 1911

**Fewest assists for leader, season**
NL—52—Phil Masi, Boston, 95 G, 1945
AL—58—Terry Kennedy, Baltimore, 142 G, 1987

**Most seasons leading league in assists**
NL—6—Gabby Hartnett, Chicago, 1925, 1927, 1928 (tied), 1930, 1934, 1935
Del Crandall, Milwaukee, 1953, 1954, 1957-1960
AL—6—Jim Sundberg, Texas, 1975-1978, 1980, 1981

**Fewest assists, season (150 or more games)**
NL—59—Randy Hundley, Chicago, 152 G, 1967
AL—68—Brad Ausmus, Detroit, 150 G, 2000

**Most assists, game**
NL—9—Mike Hines, Boston, May 1, 1883
AL—8—Wally Schang, Boston, May 12, 1920
NL since 1893—7—Ed McFarland, Philadelphia, May 7, 1901
Fred Jacklitsch, Brooklyn, Apr 21, 1903
Bill Bergen, Brooklyn, Aug 23, 1909, 2nd game
Jimmy Archer, Pittsburgh, May 24, 1918
Bert Adams, Philadelphia, Aug 21, 1919

**Most assists, inning**
AA—3—Jocko Milligan, Philadelphia, July 26, 1887, 3rd
AL—3—Les Nunamaker, New York, Aug 3, 1914, 2nd
Ray Schalk, Chicago, Sept 30, 1921, 8th
Bill Dickey, New York, May 13, 1929, 6th
Joe Azcue, Cleveland, Sept 20, 1967, 5th
Jim Sundberg, Texas, Sept 3, 1976, 5th
Sal Butera, Minnesota, Sept 7, 1981, 3rd
Bob Boone, California, Aug 29, 1986, 5th
NL—3—Bruce Edwards, Brooklyn, Aug 15, 1946, 4th
Clay Dalrymple, Philadelphia, May 31, 1961, 4th
Jim Campbell, Houston, June 16, 1963, 2nd game, 3rd
Vic Correll, Atlanta, Sept 17, 1976, 2nd game, 5th
Bruce Benedict, Atlanta, Aug 6, 1982, 5th
Alan Ashby, Houston, July 28, 1987, 8th

## CHANCES ACCEPTED AND OFFERED

**Most chances accepted, career**
NL—12,988—Gary Carter, Montreal, New York, San Francisco, Los Angeles, 1974-1992, 19 seasons
AL—12,417—Carlton Fisk, Boston, Chicago, 1969-1993, except 1970, 24 seasons

**Most chances accepted, season**
NL—1,214—Johnny Edwards, Houston, 151 G, 1969
AL—1,044—Bill Freehan, Detroit, 138 G, 1968

**Fewest chances accepted by leader, season**
NL—474—Ernie Lombardi, New York, 96 G, 1945
AL—515—Birdie Tebbetts, Detroit, 97 G, 1942

**Most seasons leading league in chances accepted**
AL—8—Ray Schalk, Chicago, 1913-1917, 1919, 1920, 1922
Yogi Berra, New York, 1950-1952, 1954-1957, 1959
NL—8—Gary Carter, Montreal, 1977-1982, New York, 1985, 1988

**Fewest chances accepted, season (150 or more games)**
NL—536—Ray Mueller, Cincinnati, 155 G, 1944
AL—677—Mike Tresh, Chicago, 150 G, 1945

**Most chances accepted, game**
UA—23—George Bignell, Milwaukee, October 3, 1884 (18 K)
NL—22—Sandy Nava, Providence, June 7, 1884 (19 K)
NL since 1893—20—Jerry Grote, New York, Apr 22, 1970 (19 K)
Sandy Martinez, Chicago, May 6, 1998 (20 K)
[25—Damian Miller, Chicago, May 15, 2003 (24 K), 17 inn]
AL—20—Ellie Rodriguez, California, Aug 12, 1974 (19 K)
Rich Gedman, Boston, Apr 29, 1986 (20 K)
Bill Haselman, Boston, Sept 18, 1996 (20 K)
Dan Wilson, Seattle, Aug 8, 1997 (19 K)
[27—Jose Molina, Anaheim, June 8, 2004 (26 K), 17 inn]

**Longest game with no chances offered**
AL—14 inn—Gene Desautels, Cleveland, Aug 11, 1942, 1st game
NL—13 inn—Jimmie Wilson, Philadelphia, Aug 31, 1927, 1st game

## ERRORS

**Most errors, career (since 1900)**
NL—234—Ivy Wingo, St. Louis, Cincinnati, 1911-1926, 1929, 17 seasons
AL—218—Wally Schang, Philadelphia, Boston, New York, St. Louis, Detroit, 1913-1931, 19 seasons

**Most errors, season**
NL—94—Nat Hicks, New York, 45 G, 1876
AA—85—Ed Whiting, Baltimore, 72 G, 1882
AL—41—Oscar Stanage, Detroit, 141 G, 1911
NL since 1893—40—Red Dooin, Philadelphia, 140 G, 1909

**Fewest errors for leader, season**
AL—7—Rick Ferrell, St. Louis, 137 G, 1933
NL—9—Hank Foiles, Pittsburgh, 109 G, 1957

**Most seasons leading league in errors**
NL—7—Ivy Wingo, St. Louis, Cincinnati, 1912 (tied), 1913, 1916-1918, 1920, 1921
AL—6—Birdie Tebbetts, Detroit, Boston, 1939, 1940 (tied), 1942 (tied), 1947-1949

**Fewest errors, season (150 or more games)**
NL—4—Randy Hundley, Chicago, 152 G, 1967
AL—4—Jim Sundberg, Texas, 150 G, 1979

**Fewest errors, season (100 or more games)**
AL—0—Buddy Rosar, Philadelphia, 117 G, 1946
NL—0—Charles Johnson, Florida, 123 G, 1997
Mike Matheny, St. Louis, 138 G, 2003

**Most consecutive errorless games, career**
NL—252—Mike Matheny, St. Louis, Aug 2, 2002-Aug 1, 2004 (1,565 CA)
AL—159—Rick Cerone, New York, Boston, July 5, 1987-May 8, 1989 (896 CA)

**Most consecutive errorless games, season**
NL—138—Mike Matheny, St. Louis, March 31-Sept 28, 2003 (entire season; 823 CA)
AL—117—Buddy Rosar, Philadelphia, Apr 16-Sept 29, 1946, 1st game (605 CA)
A.J. Pierzynski, Chicago, Apr 19-Oct 2, 2005 (772 CA)

**Most consecutive chances accepted without an error, career**
NL—1,565—Mike Matheny, St. Louis, 252 G, Aug 2, 2002-Aug 1, 2004
AL—950—Yogi Berra, New York, 148 G, July 28, 1957, 2nd game-May 10, 1959, 2nd game

**Most consecutive chances accepted without an error, season**
NL—973—Charles Johnson, Florida, 123 G, Apr 1-Sept 28, 1997
AL—777—A.J. Pierzynski, Chicago, 118 G, Apr 18-Oct 2, 2005

**Most errors, game (all fielding errors)**
NL—7—Jack Rowe, Buffalo, May 16, 1883
Dickie Lowe, Detroit, June 26, 1884
AA—7—Billy Taylor, Baltimore, May 29, 1886, a.m. game
NL since 1893—4—Gabby Street, Boston, June 7, 1905
AL—4—John Peters, Cleveland, May 16, 1918
Lena Styles, Philadelphia, July 29, 1921
Bill Moore, Boston, Sept 26, 1927, 2nd game

**Longest game with no errors**
AL—24 inn—Mike R. Powers, Philadelphia, Sept 1, 1906
Buddy Rosar, Philadelphia, July 21, 1945
Bob Swift, Detroit, July 21, 1945
NL—24 inn—Hal King, Houston, Apr 15, 1968
Jerry Grote, New York, Apr 15, 1968 (caught 23.1 inn)

**Most errors, inning**
NL—4—Doggie Miller, St. Louis, May 24, 1895, 2nd
AL—3—Jeff Sweeney, New York, July 10, 1912, 1st
John Peters, Cleveland, May 16, 1918, 1st

## PASSED BALLS

**Most passed balls, career**
ML—647—Pop Snyder, Louisville NL, Boston NL, Cincinnati AA, Cleveland AA, Cleveland NL, Cleveland PL, Washington AA, 1876-1891 except 1880, 15 seasons
NL—602—Silver Flint, Indianapolis, Chicago, 1878-1889, 12 seasons
NL since 1893—167—Ted Simmons, St. Louis, Atlanta, 1968-1980, 1986-1988, 16 seasons
AL—158—Lance Parrish, Detroit, California, Seattle, Cleveland, Toronto, 1977-1986, 1989-1993, 1995, 16 seasons

**Most passed balls, season**
NL—99—Pop Snyder, Boston, 58 G, 1881
Michael P. Hines, Boston, 56 G, 1883
NL since 1893—29—Frank Bowerman, New York, 73 G, 1900
AL—35—Geno Petralli, Texas, 63 G, 1987

**Fewest passed balls for leader, season**
AL—6—Mickey Cochrane, Philadelphia, 117 G, 1931
Charlie F. Berry, Boston, 102 G, 1931
Rick Ferrell, St. Louis, 108 G, 1931
NL—7—5 catchers

**Most seasons leading league in passed balls**
NL—9—Ernie Lombardi, Cincinnati, Boston, New York, 1932, 1935, 1936 (tied), 1937-1939, 1940 (tied), 1941, 1945
AL—5—Rick Ferrell, St. Louis, Washington, 1931 (tied), 1939, 1940, 1944, 1945

**Fewest passed balls, season (150 or more games)**
NL—1—Gary Carter, Montreal, 152 G, 1978
AL—3—Brad Ausmus, Detroit, 150 G, 2000

**Fewest passed balls, season (100 or more games)**
NL—0—Al Todd, Pittsburgh, 128 G, 1937
Al Lopez, Pittsburgh, 114 G, 1941
Johnny Bench, Cincinnati, 121 G, 1975
Benito Santiago, San Diego, 103 G, 1992
AL—0—Bill Dickey, New York, 125 G, 1931

**Most passed balls, game**
AA—12—Alex Gardner, Washington, May 10, 1884
NL—10—Alamazoo Jennings, Milwaukee, Aug 15, 1878
Pat Dealey, Boston, May 1886
NL since 1893—6—Harry Vickers, Cincinnati, October 4, 1902
Jerry Goff, Houston, May 12, 1996
AL—6—Geno Petralli, Texas, Aug 30, 1987

**Longest game with no passed balls**
AL—25 inn—Carlton Fisk, Chicago, May 8, finished May 9, 1984
NL—24 inn—Hal King, Houston, Apr 15, 1968
Jerry Grote, New York, Apr 15, 1968 (caught 23.1 inn)

**Most passed balls, inning**
AA—5—Dan Sullivan, St. Louis, Aug 9, 1885, 3rd
NL—4—Ray Katt, New York, Sept 10, 1954, 8th
AL—4—Geno Petralli, Texas, Aug 22, 1987, 7th

## DOUBLE PLAYS

**Most double plays, career**
AL—226—Ray Schalk, Chicago, 17 seasons, 1912-1928
NL—163—Gabby Hartnett, Chicago, New York, 20 seasons, 1922-1941

**Most double plays, season**
AL—36—Steve O'Neill, Cleveland, 128 G, 1916
NL—23—Tom Haller, Los Angeles, 139 G, 1968

**Fewest double plays for leader, season**
NL—8—Phil Masi, Boston/Pittsburgh, 81 G, 1949
Clyde McCullough, Pittsburgh, 90 G, 1949
AL—8—Mike DiFelice, Tampa Bay, 84 G, 1998
A.J. Hinch, Oakland, 118 G, 1998

**Most seasons leading league in double plays**
NL—6—Gabby Hartnett, Chicago, 1925 (tied), 1927, 1930 (tied), 1931, 1934, 1935
AL—6—Yogi Berra, New York, 1949-1952, 1954, 1956

**Most double plays, game**
NL—3—Jack O'Neill, Chicago, Apr 26, 1905
Shanty Hogan, New York, Aug 19, 1931
Ebba St. Claire, Boston, Aug 9, 1951
Eddie Taubensee, Cincinnati, Apr 23, 1999
Damian Miller, Arizona, May 25, 1999
Brian Schneider, Montreal, June 11, 2004 (fielded 8.2 inn)
[3—Bob O'Farrell, Chicago, July 9, 1919, 2nd game, 10.1 inn
Ron Hodges, New York, Apr 23, 1978, 11.2 inn]
AL—4—Chris Hoiles, Baltimore, Apr 9, 1998

**Most double plays started, game**
NL—3—J. Shanty Hogan, New York, Aug 19, 1931
Damian Miller, Arizona, May 25, 1999
AL—3—Rick Dempsey, Baltimore, June 1, 1977
Bengie Molina, Anaheim, July 29, 2003
[3—Lance Parrish, California, June 29, 1991, 13 inn]

**Most unassisted double plays, career**
AL—2—many catchers

**Most unassisted double plays, season**
AL—2—Frank Crossin, St. Louis, 1914
Jorge Posada, New York, 2000
NL—1—many catchers

**Most unassisted double plays, game**
AL-NL—1—many catchers

## BASERUNNERS VS CATCHERS

**Most stolen bases off catcher, game**
AA—19—Grant Briggs, Syracuse, Apr 22, 1890
NL—17—Doggie Miller, Pittsburgh, May 23, 1890
NL since 1893—11—Bill Fischer, St. Louis, Aug 13, 1916, 2nd game, 5 inn
AL—13—Branch Rickey, New York, June 28, 1907

**Most stolen bases off catcher, inning**
AL—8—Steve O'Neill, Cleveland, July 19, 1915, 1st
NL—8—Mike Gonzalez, New York, July 7, 1919, 1st game, 9th

**Most runners caught stealing, game**
NL—8—Duke Farrell, Washington, May 11, 1897
AL—6—Wally Schang, Philadelphia, May 12, 1915

**Most runners caught stealing, inning**
AA—3—Jocko Milligan, Philadelphia, July 26, 1887, 3rd

AL—3—Les Nunamaker, New York, Aug 3, 1914, 2nd
NL—2—many catchers

## NO-HITTERS CAUGHT

**Most no-hit victories caught, career (entire game; 9 or more innings)**

ML—3—Jeff Torborg, Los Angeles NL, 1965, 1970; California AL, 1973
NL—3—Roy Campanella, Brooklyn, 1952, 1956 (2)
Del Crandall, Milwaukee, 1954, 1960 (2)
Alan Ashby, Houston, 1979, 1981, 1986
Charles Johnson, Florida, 1996, 1997, 2001
AL—3—Bill Carrigan, Boston, 1911, 1916 (2)
Ray Schalk, Chicago, 1914, 1917, 1922 (caught a no-hitter broken up in the 10th inn, 1914)
Val Picinich, Philadelphia, 1916, Washington, 1920, Boston, 1923
Luke Sewell, Cleveland, 1931, Chicago, 1935, 1937
Jim Hegan, Cleveland, 1947, 1948, 1951

# PITCHERS

## GAMES AND INNINGS

**Most games, career**

ML—1,252—Jesse Orosco, New York NL, Los Angeles NL, Cleveland AL, Milwaukee AL, Baltimore AL, St. Louis NL, San Diego NL, New York AL, Minnesota AL, 1979-2003, except 1980 (686 in AL, 566 in NL), 24 seasons
NL—1,119—John Franco, Cincinnati, New York, Houston, 1984-2005, except 2002, 21 seasons
AL—869—Dennis Eckersley, Cleveland, Boston, Oakland, 1975-1984, 1987-1995, 1998, 20 seasons

**Most games, season**

NL—106—Mike Marshall, Los Angeles, 208 inn, 1974
AL—90—Mike Marshall, Minnesota, 143 inn, 1979

**Fewest games for leader, season**

AL—40—Joe Haynes, Chicago, 103 inn, 1942
NL—41—Ray Kremer, Pittsburgh, 259 inn, 1924
Johnny Morrison, Pittsburgh, 238 inn, 1924

**Most seasons leading league in games**

ML—7—Joe McGinnity, Brooklyn NL, Baltimore AL, New York NL, 1900, 1901, 1903-1907
NL—6—Joe McGinnity, Brooklyn, New York, 1900, 1903-1907
AL—6—Firpo Marberry, Washington, 1924-1926, 1928, 1929, 1932

**Most innings, game**

NL—26—Leon Cadore, Brooklyn, May 1, 1920
Joe Oeschger, Boston, May 1, 1920
AL—24—Jack Coombs, Philadelphia, Sept 1, 1906
Joe Harris, Boston, Sept 1, 1906

## AVERAGE

**Highest average with most chances accepted, season**

NL—1.000—Randy Jones, San Diego, 1976, 40 G; 31 PO, 81 A, 112 CA
AL—1.000—Walter Johnson, Washington, 1913, 48 G; 21 PO, 82 A, 103 CA

**Most seasons leading league in average with most chances accepted**

NL—4—Claude Passeau, Philadelphia, Chicago, 1939, 1942, 1943, 1945
Larry Jackson, St. Louis, Chicago, Philadelphia, 1957, 1964, 1965, 1968
AL—3—Walter Johnson, Washington, 1913, 1917, 1922 (tied)

## PUTOUTS

**Most putouts, career**

NL since 1893—477—Greg Maddux, Chicago, Atlanta, 1986-2004, 19 seasons
AL—387—Jack Morris, Detroit, Minnesota, Toronto, Cleveland, 1977-1994, 18 seasons

**Most putouts, season**

NL—50—George Bradley, St. Louis, 64 G, 1876
AL—49—Nick Altrock, Chicago, 38 G, 1904
Mike Boddicker, Baltimore, 34 G, 1984
NL since 1893—41—Kevin Brown, Los Angeles, 35 G, 1999

**Fewest putouts for leader, season**

NL—14—Howie Camnitz, Pittsburgh, 38 G, 1910
Art Nehf, New York, 37 G, 1922
Tony Kaufmann, Chicago, 37 G, 1922
AL—16—Roxie Lawson, Detroit, 27 G, 1937

**Most seasons leading league in putouts**

NL—8—Greg Maddux, Chicago, 1989-1992, 2004 (tied); Atlanta, 1993, 1996, 1998 (tied)
AL—5—Bob Lemon, Cleveland, 1948, 1949, 1952-1954

**Most putouts, game**

NL—7—Greg Maddux, Chicago, Apr 29, 1990
AL—6—Bert Blyleven, Cleveland, June 24, 1984
Eric King, Detroit, July 8, 1986
Kirk Saarloos, Oakland, Apr 22, 2005
[7—Dick Fowler, Philadelphia, June 9, 1949, 12 inn]

## ASSISTS

**Most assists, career (since 1900)**

NL—1,489—Christy Mathewson, New York, Cincinnati, 1900-1916, 17 seasons
AL—1,337—Walter Johnson, Washington, 1907-1927, 21 seasons

**Most assists, season**

AL—227—Ed Walsh, Chicago, 56 G, 1907
NL—168—John Clarkson, Boston, 72 G, 1889
NL since 1893—141—Christy Mathewson, New York, 56 G, 1908

**Fewest assists for leader, season**

AL—42—Mark Langston, California, 33 G, 1990
NL—47—Ron Darling, New York, 36 G, 1985
Ron Darling, New York, 34 G, 1986
Bob Knepper, Houston, 40 G, 1986
Fernando Valenzuela, Los Angeles, 34 G, 1986

**Most seasons leading league in assists**

NL—9—Greg Maddux, Chicago, Atlanta, 1990, 1992, 1993, 1995, 1996, 1998, 2000, 2001, 2003
AL—6—Bob Lemon, Cleveland, 1948, 1949, 1951-1953, 1956

**Most assists, game**

NL—11—Rip Sewell, Pittsburgh, June 6, 1941, 2nd game
[12—Leon Cadore, Brooklyn, May 1, 1920, 26 inn]
AL—11—Al Orth, New York, Aug 12, 1906
Ed Walsh, Chicago, Apr 19, 1907
Ed Walsh, Chicago, Aug 12, 1907
George McConnell, New York, Sept 2, 1912, 2nd game
Mellie Wolfgang, Chicago, Aug 29, 1914
[12—Nick Altrock, Chicago, June 7, 1908, 10 inn
Ed Walsh, Chicago, July 16, 1907, 13 inn]

## CHANCES ACCEPTED AND OFFERED

**Most chances accepted, career (since 1900)**

NL—1,761—Christy Mathewson, New York, Cincinnati, 1900-1916, 17 seasons
AL—1,606—Walter Johnson, Washington, 1907-1927, 21 seasons

**Most chances accepted, season**

AL—262—Ed Walsh, Chicago, 56 G, 1907
NL—206—John Clarkson, Boston, 72 G, 1889
NL since 1893—168—Christy Mathewson, New York, 56 G, 1908

**Fewest chances accepted for leader, season**

AL—61—Charles Nagy, Cleveland, 34 G, 1997
NL—67—Paul Minner, Chicago, 31 G, 1953
Robin Roberts, Philadelphia, 44 G, 1953
Jim Hearn, New York, 39 G, 1955

**Most seasons leading league in chances accepted**

NL—13—Greg Maddux, Chicago, Atlanta, 1989-1996, 1998, 1999 (tied), 2000, 2001, 2003
AL—8—Bob Lemon, Cleveland, 1948-1956, except 1955

**Most chances accepted, game**

AL—13—Nick Altrock, Chicago, Aug 6, 1904 (3 PO, 10 A)
Ed Walsh, Chicago, Apr 19, 1907 (2 PO, 11 A)
[15—Ed Walsh, Chicago, July 16, 1907, 13 inn]
NL—12—Rip Sewell, Pittsburgh, June 6, 1941, 2nd game (1 PO, 11 A)
[13—Leon Cadore, Brooklyn, May 1, 1920, 26 inn]

**Longest game with no chances offered**

NL—20 inn—Milt Watson, Philadelphia, July 17, 1918
AL—15 inn—Red Ruffing, New York, July 23, 1932, 1st game

## ERRORS

**Most errors, career (since 1900)**

NL—64—Hippo Vaughn, Chicago, 1913-1921, 9 seasons
AL—55—Ed Walsh, Chicago, 1904-1916, 13 seasons

**Most errors, season**

AA—63—Tim Keefe, New York, 68 G, 1883
NL—28—Jim Whitney, Boston, 63 G, 1881
NL since 1893—17—Doc Newton, Cincinnati, Brooklyn, 33 G, 1901
AL—15—Jack Chesbro, New York, 55 G, 1904
Rube Waddell, Philadelphia, 46 G, 1905
Ed Walsh, Chicago, 62 G, 1912

**Fewest errors for leader, season**

NL-AL—4—many pitchers

**Most seasons leading league in errors**

NL—5—Hippo Vaughn, Chicago, 1914, 1915 (tied), 1917 (tied), 1919, 1920
Warren Spahn, Boston, Milwaukee, 1949 (tied), 1950, 1952 (tied), 1954 (tied), 1964 (tied)
AL—4—Allen Sothoron, St. Louis, 1917, 1918 (tied), 1919, 1920
Nolan Ryan, California, 1975, 1976, 1977 (tied), 1978

**Most consecutive errorless games, career**

NL—546—Lee Smith, Chicago, St. Louis, July 5, 1982-Sept 22, 1992 (93 CA)
AL—470—Dennis Eckersley, Oakland, May 1, 1987-May 4, 1995 (76 CA)

**Most consecutive errorless games, season**

AL—88—Wilbur Wood, Chicago, Apr 10-Sept 29, 1968 (32 CA)
NL—89—Steve Kline, St. Louis, Apr 4-October 7, 2001 (entire season; 13 CA)
Paul Quantrill, Los Angeles, Apr 1-Sept 28, 2003 (entire season; 21 CA)

**Most consecutive chances accepted without an error, career**

NL—273—Claude Passeau, Chicago, Sept 21, first game, 1941-May 20, 1946, 145 G
AL—230—Rick Langford, Oakland, Apr 13, 1977-October 2, 1980, 142 G

**Most errors, game**
NL—5—Ed Doheny, New York, Aug 15, 1899
AL—4—Buster Ross, Boston, May 17, 1925

**Longest game with no errors**
NL—26 inn—Leon Cadore, Brooklyn, May 1, 1920
Joe Oeschger, Boston, May 1, 1920
AL—24 inn—Jack Coombs, Philadelphia, Sept 1, 1906
Joe Harris, Boston, Sept 1, 1906

**Most errors, inning**
NL—3—Cy Seymour, New York, May 21, 1898, 6th
Jaime Navarro, Chicago, Aug 18, 1996, 3rd
AL—3—Tommy John, New York, July 27, 1988, 4th
Mike Sirotka, Chicago, Apr 9, 1999, 5th

## DOUBLE PLAYS

**Most double plays, career**
ML—83—Phil Niekro, Milwaukee NL, Atlanta NL, New York AL, Clevelan AL, Toronto AL, 1964-1987, 24 seasons
NL—82—Warren Spahn, Boston Milwaukee, New York, San Francisco, 1942-1965, except 1943-1945 in military service, 21 seasons
AL—78—Bob Lemon, Cleveland, 1946-1958, 13 seasons

**Most double plays, season**
AL—15—Bob Lemon, Cleveland, 41 G, 1953
NL—12—Curt Davis, Philadelphia, 51 G, 1934
Randy Jones, San Diego, 40 G, 1976

**Fewest double plays for leader, season**
NL—4—Bud Black, San Francisco, 1992
Doug Drabek, Pittsburgh, 1992
Omar Olivares, St. Louis, 1992
AL—5—many pitchers

**Most seasons leading league in double plays**
N—5—Bucky Walters, Philadelphia, Cincinnati, 1937, 1939, 1941 (tied), 1943 (tied), 1944 (tied)
Warren Spahn, Milwaukee, 1953 (tied), 1956, 1960 (tied), 1961 (tied), 1963
Greg Maddux, Chicago, Atlanta, 1987, 1990, 1991 (tied), 1994 (tied), 1996
AL—4—Willis Hudlin, Cleveland, 1929-1931, 1934

**Most double plays, game**
AL—4—Milt Gaston, Chicago, May 17, 1932
Hal Newhouser, Detroit, May 19, 1948
NL—3—6 pitchers; last—Wandy Rodriguez, Houston, June 15, 2005

**Most unassisted double plays, career**
NL—2—Tex Carleton, Chicago, Brooklyn, 1935, 1940
Claude Passeau, Philadelphia, Chicago, 1938, 1945
AL—1—many pitchers

**Most unassisted double plays, game**
NL—1—many pitchers; last—Jason Isringhausen, New York, July 31, 1999
AL—1—many pitchers; last—Jason Boyd, Cleveland, Aug 9, 2003, 2nd game

**Most triple plays started, season**
NL—2—Wilbur Cooper, Pittsburgh, July 7, Aug 21, 1920
AL—1—many pitchers

# CLUB FIELDING

## AVERAGE

**Highest fielding average, season**
NL—.989—New York, 163 G, 1999
AL—.989—Seattle, 162 G, 2003

**Lowest fielding average, season (since 1900)**
AL—.928—Detroit, 136 G, 1901
NL—.936—Philadelphia, 155 G, 1904

**Most consecutive seasons leading league in fielding**
AL—6—Boston, 1916-1921
NL—6—St. Louis, 1984-1989

## PUTOUTS

**Most putouts, season**
AL—4,520—New York, 164 G, 1964
NL—4,480—Pittsburgh, 163 G, 1979

**Fewest putouts, season**
NL—3,887—Philadelphia, 149 G, 1907
AL—3,907—Cleveland, 147 G, 1945

**Most putouts by infield, game**
AL—26—Seattle vs New York, May 28, 1988
NL—25—Chicago vs Philadelphia, Sept 24, 1927
Pittsburgh vs New York, June 6, 1941, 2nd game
St. Louis vs Boston, July 17, 1947
Chicago vs Pittsburgh, May 9, 1963

**Most putouts by infielders from both clubs, game**
NL—46—Cincinnati 24, New York 22, May 7, 1941
St. Louis 25, Boston 21, July 17, 1947
AL—45—Detroit 24, Washington 21, Sept 15, 1945, 2nd game
Boston 24, Cleveland 21, July 11, 1977

**Fewest putouts by infield, game**
AL—3—St. Louis vs New York, July 20, 1945, 2nd game
Boston vs Seattle, Apr 29, 1986
Boston vs Toronto, June 1, 2003 (fielded 8 inn)
Anaheim vs Boston, Aug 6, 2003 (fielded 8 inn)
Cleveland vs Boston, June 29, 2005 (fielded 8 inn)
NL—3—New York vs San Diego, Apr 22, 1970

**Most putouts by outfield, game**
NL—19—Pittsburgh vs Cincinnati, July 5, 1948, 2nd game
[23—Brooklyn vs Boston, May 1, 1920, 26 inn
Chicago vs Boston, May 17, 1927, 22 inn
Florida vs St. Louis, Apr 27, 2003, 20 inn]
AL—19—Minnesota vs Toronto, July 7, 1994
[22—Chicago vs Washington, May 15, 1918, 18 inn]

**Most putouts by outfielders from both clubs, game**
NL—30—Chicago 16, Philadelphia 14, Aug 7, 1953
[42—New York 21, Pittsburgh 21, July 17, 1914, 21 inn]
AL—29—Washington 17, St. Louis 12, May 3, 1939
[38—Washington 20, St. Louis 18, July 19, 1924, 16 inn]

**Longest game with no putouts by outfield**
NL—13 inn—New York vs Brooklyn, Apr 15, 1909
St. Louis vs Philadelphia, Aug 13, 1987
AL—11 inn—St. Louis vs Cleveland, Apr 23, 1905

**Fewest putouts by outfielders from both clubs, game**
AA—1—St. Louis 1, New York 0, June 30, 1886
NL—1—Pittsburgh 1, Brooklyn 0, Aug 26, 1910
AL—2—New York 2, Detroit 0, May 9, 1930

**Most putouts by outfield, doubleheader**
NL—27—Pittsburgh vs Cincinnati, July 5, 1948
[29—Boston vs New York, Sept 3, 1933, 23 inn]
AL—24—Detroit vs Philadelphia, June 28, 1931

**Most putouts by outfielders from both clubs, doubleheader**
NL—47—Pittsburgh 26, Boston 21, June 26, 1935
AL—43—Detroit 24, Philadelphia 19, June 28, 1931

## ASSISTS

**Most assists, season**
AL—2,446—Chicago, 157 G, 1907
NL—2,293—St. Louis, 154 G, 1917

**Fewest assists, season**
AL—1,422—Minnesota, 161 G, 2002
NL—1,437—Philadelphia, 156 G, 1957

**Most consecutive seasons leading league in assists**
AL—6—Chicago, 1905-1910
NL—6—New York, 1933-1938

**Most assists, game**
NL—28—Pittsburgh vs New York, June 7, 1911
[41—Boston vs Brooklyn, May 1, 1920, 26 inn]
AL—27—St. Louis vs Philadelphia, Aug 16, 1919
[38—Detroit vs Philadelphia, July 21, 1945, 24 inn
Washington vs Chicago, June 12, 1967, 22 inn]

**Most assists by both clubs, game**
AL—44—Cleveland 22, St. Louis 22, May 27, 1909
[72—Detroit 38, Philadelphia 34, July 21, 1945, 24 inn]
NL—43—Brooklyn 24, New York 19, Apr 21, 1903
[72—Boston 41, Brooklyn 31, May 1, 1920, 26 inn]

**Fewest assists, game**
AL—0—St. Louis vs Cleveland, Aug 8, 1943, 2nd game (fielded 8 inn)
Cleveland vs New York, July 4, 1945, 1st game
New York vs Cleveland, Sept 11, 1995
Baltimore vs Oakland, June 20, 2000 (fielded 8 inn)
Tampa Bay vs Minnesota, May 1, 2002 (fielded 8 inn)

Tampa Bay vs Baltimore, May 17, 2003 (fielded 8 inn)
NL—0—New York vs Philadelphia, June 25, 1989
Cincinnati vs Colorado, Aug 20, 1997
Milwaukee vs St. Louis, July 22, 2004 (fielded 8 inn)

**Fewest assists by both clubs, game**
AL—5—Baltimore 3, Cleveland 2, Aug 31, 1955
Boston 4, New York 1, Aug 9, 1992
NL—6—Chicago 5, Philadelphia 1, May 2, 1957
San Francisco 3, Philadelphia 3, May 13, 1959

**Most assists, doubleheader**
NL—42—New York vs Boston, Sept 30, 1914
AL—41—Boston vs Detroit, Sept 20, 1927
Boston vs Washington, Sept 26, 1927

**Most assists by both clubs, doubleheader**
NL—70—Brooklyn 36, Philadelphia 34, Sept 5, 1922
AL—68—Detroit 34, Philadelphia 34, Sept 5, 1901
Cleveland 35, Boston 33, Sept 7, 1935
St. Louis 39, Boston 29, July 23, 1939

**Fewest assists, doubleheader**
AL—8—Philadelphia vs New York, July 7, 1946
[8—Minnesota vs Los Angeles, July 19, 1961, 17.2 inn]
NL—7—New York vs San Diego, May 29, 1971

**Fewest assists by both clubs, doubleheader**
NL—22—Milwaukee 14, Philadelphia 8, Sept 12, 1954
AL—25—Washington 13, New York 12, July 4, 1931

**Most assists by infield, game**
AL—22—Seattle vs New York, May 28, 1988
NL—21—New York vs Pittsburgh, July 13, 1919
Philadelphia vs Boston, May 30, 1931, p.m. game
Brooklyn vs Pittsburgh, Aug 18, 1935, 2nd game

**Most assists by infielders from both clubs, game**
NL—38—Brooklyn 20, Cincinnati 18, June 10, 1917
AL—35—Detroit 19, Cleveland 16, Apr 18, 1924
Chicago 18, Boston 17, Sept 17, 1945, 2nd game

**Fewest assists by infield, game**
NL—0—Pittsburgh vs Chicago, July 19, 1902
New York vs Philadelphia, July 29, 1934, 1st game
Chicago vs Cincinnati, Apr 26, 1935
Cincinnati vs Brooklyn, Aug 6, 1938
Boston vs Pittsburgh, June 17, 1940, 1st game
New York vs Chicago, May 6, 1953
Philadelphia, vs Chicago, May 2, 1957
Houston vs Cincinnati, Sept 10, 1968, 1st game
Pittsburgh vs Montreal, Sept 17, 1977
New York vs Philadelphia, June 25, 1989
AL—0—Boston vs Chicago, Aug 13, 1924, 1st game
Cleveland vs New York, July 4, 1945, 1st game
St. Louis vs New York, July 20, 1945, 2nd game
Washington vs St. Louis, May 20, 1952
New York vs Cleveland, Sept 11, 1995
Tampa Bay vs Baltimore, May 17, 2003 (fielded 8 inn)

**Fewest assists by infielders from both clubs, game**
AL—2—Philadelphia 2, Washington 0, May 5, 1910 (Washington fielded 8 inn)
NL—2—Chicago 2, Philadelphia 0, May 2, 1957

**Most assists by outfield, game**
NL—5—Pittsburgh vs Philadelphia, Aug 23, 1910
AL—5—New York vs Boston, Sept 5, 1921, 2nd game
Cleveland vs St. Louis, May 1, 1928

**Most assists, outfielder to catcher, runner thrown out, game**
NL—3—Washington vs Indianapolis, June 19, 1889
New York vs Boston, June 30, 1902
Chicago vs Pittsburgh, Apr 26, 1905
St. Louis vs San Francisco, July 7, 1975
AL—2—many games

**Longest game with no outfield assists**
NL—26 inn—Boston vs Brooklyn, May 1, 1920
AL—24 inn—Boston vs Philadelphia, Sept 1, 1906
Philadelphia vs Detroit, July 21, 1945

**Longest game with no outfield assists by either club**
NL—24 inn—Houston 0, New York 0, Apr 15, 1968
AL—22 inn—Chicago 0, Washington 0, June 12, 1967

**Most assists, inning**
AL—10—Cleveland vs Philadelphia, Aug 17, 1921, 1st
Boston vs New York, May 10, 1952, 5th
NL—8—Boston vs Philadelphia, May 1, 1911, 4th

## CHANCES ACCEPTED AND OFFERED

**Most chances accepted, season**
AL—6,655—Chicago, 157 G, 1907
NL—6,508—Chicago, 162 G, 1977

**Fewest chances accepted, season**
AL—5,470—Cleveland, 147 G, 1945
NL—5,545—Philadelphia, 154 G, 1955

**Most chances accepted, game**
NL—55—Pittsburgh vs New York, June 7, 1911
[119—Boston vs Brooklyn, May 1, 1920, 26 inn]
AL—54—St. Louis vs Philadelphia, Aug 16, 1919
[110—Detroit vs Philadelphia, July 21, 1945, 24 inn]

**Most chances accepted by both clubs, game**
NL—98—Brooklyn 50, New York 48, Apr 21, 1903
New York 52, Cincinnati 46, May 15, 1909
AL—98—Cleveland 49, St. Louis 49, May 7, 1909

**Most chances accepted by infield, game**
AL—48—Seattle vs New York, May 28, 1988
NL—45—New York vs Pittsburgh, July 13, 1919
Chicago vs Philadelphia, Sept 24, 1927
Chicago vs Pittsburgh, May 9, 1963

**Most chances accepted by infielders from both clubs, game**
NL—78—Cincinnati 41, New York 37, May 7, 1941
AL—76—Boston 43, Cleveland 33, June 24, 1931

**Fewest chances offered to infield, game**
AL—3—St. Louis vs New York, July 20, 1945, 2nd game
NL—4—New York vs San Diego, Apr 22, 1970

**Fewest chances offered to infielders from both clubs, game**
AL—17—Chicago 10, Cleveland 9, Sept 6, 2003
NL—18—Houston 13, Chicago 5, Aug 14, 2003

**Most chances accepted by outfield, game**
NL—20—Pittsburgh vs Cincinnati, July 5, 1948, 2nd game
[25—Florida vs St. Louis, Apr 27, 2003, 20 inn]
AL—18—Cleveland vs St. Louis, Sept 28, 1929
New York vs Boston, October 1, 1933
Philadelphia vs Boston, May 27, 1941, 2nd game
New York vs Cleveland, June 26, 1955, 2nd game
[22—Chicago vs Washington, May 15, 1918, 18 inn]

**Most chances accepted by outfielders from both clubs, game**
AL—30—Washington 17, St. Louis 13, May 3, 1939
[40—Washington 21, St. Louis 19, July 19, 1924, 16 inn]
NL—30—Chicago 16, Philadelphia 14, Aug 7, 1953
[43—New York 22, Pittsburgh 21, July 17, 1914, 21 inn]

**Fewest chances offered to outfield, game**
NL—0—many games
AL—0—many games

**Fewest chances offered to outfielders from both clubs, game**
AA—2—St. Louis 2, New York 0, June 30, 1886
NL—2—Pittsburgh 1, Brooklyn 1, Aug 26, 1910
Cincinnati 1, New York 1, May 7, 1941
AL—3—St. Louis 2, Chicago 1, Apr 24, 1908
New York 2, Boston 1, May 4, 1911
New York 2, Detroit 1, May 9, 1930

**Longest game with no outfield chances offered**
NL—13 inn—St. Louis vs Philadelphia, Aug 13, 1987
AL—11 inn—St. Louis vs Cleveland, Apr 23, 1905

**Most chances accepted by outfield, doubleheader**
NL—28—Pittsburgh vs Cincinnati, July 5, 1948
AL—24—Detroit vs Philadelphia, June 28, 1931
Philadelphia vs Boston, May 27, 1941

**Most chances accepted by outfielders from both clubs, doubleheader**
NL—48—Pittsburgh 26, Boston 22, June 26, 1935
AL—44—Detroit 24, Philadelphia 20, June 28, 1931

## ERRORS

**Most errors, season**
NL—867—Washington, 122 G, 1886
AL—425—Detroit, 136 G, 1901
NL since 1893—408—Brooklyn, 155 G, 1905

**Fewest errors, season**
AL—65—Seattle, 162 G, 2003
NL—68—New York, 163 G, 1999

**Most seasons leading league with fewest errors**
NL since 1893—25—Cincinnati
AL—19—St. Louis/Baltimore (St. Louis 2; Baltimore 17)

**Most consecutive seasons leading league in errors**
NL—7—Philadelphia, 1930-1936
AL—6—Philadelphia, 1936-1941
St. Louis, 1948-1953

**Most errorless games, season**
AL—104—Baltimore, 162 G, 1998
NL—104—New York, 163 G, 199

**Most errors, game**
NL—24—Boston vs St. Louis, June 14, 1876
NL since 1893—11—St. Louis vs Pittsburgh, Apr 19, 1902
Boston vs St. Louis, June 11, 1906
St. Louis vs Cincinnati, July 3, 1909, 2nd game
AL—12—Detroit vs Chicago, May 1, 1901
Chicago vs Detroit, May 6, 1903

**Most errors by both clubs, game**
NL—40—Boston 24, St. Louis 16, June 14, 1876
NL since 1893—15—St. Louis 11, Pittsburgh 4, Apr 19, 1902
Boston 10, Chicago 5, October 3, 1904
AL—18—Chicago 12, Detroit 6, May 6, 1903

**Longest game with no errors**
AL—22 innings—Chicago vs Washington, June 12, 1967
Washington vs Chicago, June 12, 1967
NL—21 innings—Boston vs Pittsburgh, Aug 1, 1918
Chicago vs Philadelphia, July 17, 1918
Philadelphia vs Chicago, July 17, 1918 (fielded 20 inn, Chicago winning with none out in 21st inn)
San Francisco vs Cincinnati, Sept 1, 1967
San Diego vs Montreal, May 21, 1977

**Longest game with no errors by either club**
AL—22—Chicago 0, Washington 0, June 12, 1967
NL—21—Chicago 0, Philadelphia 0, July 17, 1918 (Philadelphia fielded 20 inn; Chicago winning with none out in 21st inn)

**Most consecutive errorless games, season**
NL—16—St. Louis, July 30 through Aug 16, 1992
AL—15—Texas, Aug 4, through 19, 1996

**Most errors by infield, game**
NL—17—Boston vs St. Louis, June 14, 1876
AL—10—Detroit vs Chicago, May 1, 1901

**Most errors by infielders from both clubs, game**
NL—22—Boston 17, St. Louis 5, June 14, 1876
AL—13—Chicago 8, Detroit 5, May 6, 1903

**Longest game without an error by infield**
AL—25—Chicago vs Milwaukee, May 8, finished May 9, 1984
NL—24—Houston vs New York, Apr 15, 1968

**Most errors by outfield, game**
NL—11—Boston vs Hartford, May 1, 1876
AL—5—Baltimore vs St. Louis, Aug 19, 1902
NL since 1893—4—many games; last—San Francisco vs Los Angeles, July 4, 1971

**Most errors, inning (since 1900)**
AL—7—Cleveland vs Chicago, Sept 20, 1905, 8th
NL—6—Pittsburgh vs New York, Aug 20, 1903, 1st game, 1st

**Most errors, doubleheader (since 1900)**
NL—17—Cincinnati vs Brooklyn, Sept 13, 1900
Chicago vs Cincinnati, Oct 8, 1900
St. Louis vs Cincinnati, July 3, 1909
AL—16—Cleveland vs Washington, Sept 21, 1901

**Most errors by both clubs, doubleheader (since 1900)**
NL—25—Chicago 17, Cincinnati 8, Oct 8, 1900
AL—22—Cleveland 16, Washington 6, Sept 21, 1901

## PASSED BALLS

**Most passed balls, season**
NL—167—Boston, 98 G, 1883
AL—73—Texas, 162 G, 1987
NL since 1900—42—Boston, 156 G, 1905
Atlanta, 162 G, 1967

**Fewest passed balls, season**
AL—0—New York, 155 G, 1931
NL—2—Boston, 153 G, 1943
New York, 162 G, 1980
San Diego, 162 G, 1992

**Most passed balls, game**
AA—12—Washington vs New York, May 10, 1884
NL—10—Boston vs Washington, May 3, 1886
NL since 1893—6—Cincinnati vs Pittsburgh, October 4, 1902
Houston vs Montreal, May 12, 1996
AL—6—Texas vs Detroit, Aug 30, 1987

**Most passed balls by both clubs, game**
AA—14—Washington 12, New York 2, May 10, 1884
NL—11—Troy 7, Cleveland 4, June 16, 1880
NL since 1893—6—Cincinnati 6, Pittsburgh 0, October 4, 1902
Houston 6, Montreal 0, May 12, 1996
AL—6—Texas 6, Detroit 0, Aug 30, 1987

**Longest game with no passed balls**
NL—26 inn—Boston vs Brooklyn, May 1, 1920
Brooklyn vs Boston, May 1, 1920
AL—25 inn—Chicago vs Milwaukee, May 8, finished May 9, 1984
Milwaukee vs Chicago, May 8, finished May 9, 1984 (fielded 24.1 inn)

**Longest game with no passed balls by either club**
NL—26 inn—Boston 0, Brooklyn 0, May 1, 1920
AL—25 inn—Chicago 0, Milwaukee 0, May 8, finished May 9, 1984 (Milwaukee fielded 24.1 inn)

## DOUBLE PLAYS

**Most double plays, season**
AL—217—Philadelphia, 154 G, 1949
NL—215—Pittsburgh, 162 G, 1966

**Fewest double plays, season (AL since 1912; NL since 1919)**
AL—74—Boston, 151 G, 1913
NL—94—Pittsburgh, 153 G, 1935

**Most seasons with 200 or more double plays**
AL—3—Philadelphia, 1949 (217), 1950 (208), 1951 (204)
NL—1—Pittsburgh, 1966 (215)
Colorado, 1997 (202)

**Most double plays, game**
AL—7—New York vs Philadelphia, Aug 14, 1942
NL—7—Houston vs San Francisco, May 4, 1969
Atlanta vs Cincinnati, June 27, 1982, 14 inn
St. Louis vs Pittsburgh, June 16, 1994, 10 inn

**Most double plays by both clubs, game**
AL—10—Minnesota 6, Boston 4, July 18, 1990
NL—9—Chicago 5, Cincinnati 4, July 3, 1929
Los Angeles 5, Pittsburgh 4, Apr 15, 1961
[10—Boston 5, Cincinnati 5, June 7, 1925, 12 inn
Cincinnati 6, New York 4, May 1, 1955, 16 inn
San Francisco 6, New York, 4, Aug 21, 2004, 12 inn]

**Most games with five or more double plays, season**
NL—3—New York, 1950
AL—3—Cleveland, 1970
Kansas City, 1971

**Most consecutive games with one or more double plays**
AL—25—Boston, May 7-June 4, 2nd game, 1951 (38 DP)
Cleveland, Aug 21, 2nd game-Sept 12, 1953 (38 DP)
NL—23—Brooklyn, Aug 7, 2nd game-Aug 27, 1952 (36 DP)

**Most consecutive games with one or more double or triple plays**
NL—26—New York, Aug 21-Sept 16, 2nd game, 1951 (44 DP, 1 TP)
AL—25—Boston, May 7-June 4, 2nd game, 1951 (38 DP)
Cleveland, Aug 21, 2nd game-Sept 12, 1953 (38 DP)

**Most unassisted double plays, game**
NL-AL—2—many games

**Most unassisted double plays by both clubs, game**
NL-AL—2—many games

**Most double plays, doubleheader**
AL—10—Washington vs Chicago, Aug 18, 1943, 22.1 inn
NL—9—St. Louis vs Cincinnati, June 11, 1944, 18 inn

**Most double plays by both clubs, doubleheader**
NL—13—New York 7, Philadelphia 6, Sept 28, 1939
Pittsburgh 8, St. Louis 5, Sept 6, 1948
AL—12—Philadelphia 9, Cleveland 3, Sept 14, 1931
Boston 7, Chicago 5, Sept 15, 1947
New York 7, Kansas City 5, July 31, 1955
California 8, Boston 4, May 1, 1966
[12—California 7, Baltimore 5, May 19, 1988, 19 inn]

## TRIPLE PLAYS

**Most triple plays, season**
AA—3—Cincinnati, 1882
Rochester, 1890
AL—3—Detroit, 1911
Boston, 1924
Boston, 1979
Oakland, 1979
NL—3—Philadelphia, 1964
Chicago, 1965

**Most triple plays, game**
AL—2—Minnesota vs Boston, July 17, 1990, 4th and 8th
NL—1—many clubs

**Most triple plays by both clubs, game**
AL—2—Minnesota 2, Boston 0, July 17, 1990
NL—1—many games

**Most consecutive games with triple play**
AL—2—Detroit vs Boston, June 6, 7, 1908
NL—none

# LEAGUE FIELDING

## AVERAGE

**Highest fielding percentage, season**
NL—.9834 in 2005
AL—.9831 in 2005

**Lowest fielding percentage, season (since 1900)**
AL—.937 in 1901
NL—.949 in 1903

## PUTOUTS

**Most putouts, season**
NL since 1900 (8 clubs)—33,724 in 1917
NL (10 clubs)—44,042 in 1968
NL (12 clubs)—52,630 in 1982
NL (14 clubs)—60,867 in 1996
NL (16 clubs)—69,720 in 1998
AL (8 clubs)—33,830 in 1916
AL (10 clubs)—43,847 in 1964
AL (12 clubs)—52,510 in 1969
AL (14 clubs)—61,146 in 1991

**Fewest putouts, season**
NL since 1900 (8 clubs)—32,296 in 1906
NL (10 clubs)—43,470 in 1962
NL (12 clubs)—52,000 in 1978
NL (14 clubs)—60,767 in 1997
NL (16 clubs)—69,157 in 2005
AL (8 clubs)—32,235 in 1938
AL (10 clubs)—43,281 in 1961
AL (12 clubs)—51,821 in 1975
AL (14 clubs)—60,155 in 1979

## ASSISTS

**Most assists, season**
NL since 1900 (8 clubs)—16,759 in 1920
NL (10 clubs)—18,205 in 1968
NL (12 clubs)—22,341 in 1980
NL (14 clubs)—24,442 in 1993
NL (16 clubs)—27,513 in 1998
AL (8 clubs)—17,167 in 1910
AL (10 clubs)—17,269 in 1961
AL (12 clubs)—21,786 in 1976
AL (14 clubs)—25,626 in 1980

**Fewest assists, season**
NL since 1900 (8 clubs)—13,345 in 1956
NL (10 clubs)—17,681 in 1963
NL (12 clubs)—20,351 in 1990
NL (14 clubs)—24,198 in 1997
NL (16 clubs)—26,279 in 2001
AL (8 clubs)—13,219 in 1958
AL (10 clubs)—16,999 in 1963
AL (12 clubs)—21,001 in 1971
AL (14 clubs)—22,740 in 2002

## CHANCES ACCEPTED

**(Chances accepted equals putouts plus assists)**

**Most chances accepted, season**
NL since 1900 (8 clubs)—50,419 in 1920
NL (10 clubs)—62,247 in 1968
NL (12 clubs)—74,930 in 1980
NL (14 clubs)—85,296 in 1993
NL (16 clubs)—97,233 in 1998
AL (8 clubs)—50,870 in 1910
AL (10 clubs)—60,997 in 1964
AL (12 clubs)—74,191 in 1976
AL (14 clubs)—86,621 in 1980

**Fewest chances accepted, season**
NL since 1900 (8 clubs)—46,404 in 1955
NL (10 clubs)—61,302 in 1962
NL (12 clubs)—72,495 in 1970
NL (14 clubs)—84,965 in 1997
NL (16 clubs)—95,502 in 2001
AL (8 clubs)—46,086 in 1938
AL (10 clubs)—60,450 in 1961
AL (12 clubs)—72,875 in 1971
AL (14 clubs)—83, 232 in 2002 (57,511 in shortened 1981 season)

## ERRORS

**Most errors, season**
NL since 1900 (8 clubs)—2,757 in 1900
NL (10 clubs)—1,586 in 1964
NL (12 clubs)—1,859 in 1975
NL (14 clubs)—1,876 in 1993
NL (16 clubs)—1,915 in 1999
AL (8 clubs)—2,870 in 1901
AL (10 clubs)—1,385 in 1966
AL (12 clubs)—1,851 in 1975
AL (14 clubs)—1,986 in 1977

**Fewest errors, season**
NL since 1900 (8 clubs)—1,082 in 1956
NL (10 clubs)—1,389 in 1968
NL (12 clubs)—1,401 in 1992 (1,138 in shortened 1981 season)
NL (14 clubs)—1,677 in 1997 (1,205 in shortened 1994 season)
NL (16 clubs)—1,624 in 2005
AL (8 clubs)—1,002 in 1958
AL (10 clubs)—1,261 in 1964
AL (12 clubs)—1,512 in 1971
AL (14 clubs)—1,436 in 2005

## PASSED BALLS

**Most passed balls, season**
NL since 1900 (8 clubs)—202 in 1905
NL (10 clubs)—216 in 1962
NL (12 clubs)—217 in 1969
NL (14 clubs)—199 in 1993
NL (16 clubs)—192 in 2002
AL (8 clubs)—197 in 1911
AL (10 clubs)—211 in 1965
AL (12 clubs)—247 in 1969
AL (14 clubs)—267 in 1987

**Fewest passed balls, season**
NL since 1900 (8 clubs)—65 in 1936
NL (10 clubs)—148 in 1968
NL (12 clubs)—122 in 1980
NL (14 clubs)—154 in 1997 (147 in shortened 1994 season)
NL (16 clubs)—149 in 2005
AL (8 clubs)—53 in 1949
AL (10 clubs)—147 in 1963, 1966
AL (12 clubs)—127 in 1976
AL (14 clubs)—128 in 1977

## DOUBLE PLAYS

**Most double plays, season**
NL since 1900 (8 clubs)—1,337 in 1951
NL (10 clubs)—1,596 in 1962
NL (12 clubs)—1,888 in 1971
NL (14 clubs)—2,075 in 1997
NL (16 clubs)—2,484 in 2002
AL (8 clubs)—1,487 in 1949
AL (10 clubs)—1,585 in 1961
AL (12 clubs)—1,994 in 1973
AL (14 clubs)—2,368 in 1980

**Fewest double plays, season**
NL since 1900 (8 clubs)—600 in 1908
NL (10 clubs)—1,431 in 1963
NL (12 clubs)—1,527 in 1991 (1,177 in shortened 1981 season)
NL (14 clubs)—2,028 in 1993
NL (16 clubs)—2,340 in 2001
AL (8 clubs)—640 in 1905
AL (10 clubs)—1,388 in 1967, 1968
AL (12 clubs)—1,821 in 1976 (1,770 in shortened 1972 season)
AL (14 clubs)—2,081 in 2001

**Most double plays, one day**
NL—29—July 23, 1972
AL—28—July 24, 1976

## TRIPLE PLAYS

**Most triple plays, season**
AL (14-club league)—10 in 1979
AL (8-club league)—7 in 1922, 1936
NL—7 in 1891, 1905, 1910, 1929
AA—7 in 1890
PL—7 in 1890

**Fewest triple plays, season**
NL—0 in 1928, 1938, 1941, 1943, 1945, 1946, 1959, 1961, 1974, 1984, 1994, 2001
AL—0 in 1904, 1933, 1942, 1956, 1961, 1962, 1974, 1975, 1987, 1993, 1998, 2003, 2005

**Fewest triple plays by both leagues, season**
0 in 1961, 1974

**Most triple plays, one day**
NL—2—May 29, 1897; Aug 30, 1921
AL—2—July 17, 1990

# INDIVIDUAL MISCELLANEOUS



## HISTORIC FIRSTS

**First player with two clubs in one season**
NL—Neal Phelps, New York, Philadelphia, 1876
AL—Harry Lockhead, Detroit, Philadelphia, 1901

**First player with three clubs in one season**
NL—Gus Krock, Chicago, Indianapolis, Washington, 1889
AL—Pat Donahue, Boston, Cleveland, Philadelphia, 1910
(See next entry: Frank Huelsman played with four clubs in 1904.)

**First player with four clubs in one season**
NL—Tom Dowse, Louisville, Cincinnati, Philadelphia, Washington, 63 G, 1892
AL—Frank Huelsman, Chicago, Detroit, St. Louis, Washington, 112 G, 1904

**First pitcher with two clubs in one season**
NL—Tom Healey, Providence, Indianapolis, 1878
AL—Charles Baker, Cleveland, Philadelphia, 1901

**First pitcher with three clubs in one season**
NL—Gus Krock, Chicago, Indianapolis, Washington, 1889
AL—Bill James, Detroit, Boston, Chicago, 1919

**First player to enter military service in World War I**
Hank Gowdy, Boston NL, June 27, 1917

**First player to enter military service in World War II**
Hugh Mulcahy, Philadelphia NL, March 8, 1941

**First player to come to bat three times in one inning**
NL—Tom Carey, Hartford, May 13, 1876, 4th
AL—Ted Williams, Boston, July 4, 1948, 7th

**First player with seven at-bats in 9-inning game**
NL—Jack Burdock, Hartford, May 13, 1876
AL—Billy Gilbert, Milwaukee, May 5, 1901

**First player with eight at-bats in 9-inning game**
NL—Ross Barnes, Chicago, July 22, 1876

**First player to score five runs in 9-inning game**
NL—George Hall, Philadelphia, June 17, 1876
AL—Mike Donlin, Baltimore, June 24, 1901

**First player to score six runs in 9-inning game**
NL—Jim Whitney, Boston, June 9, 1883
AL—Johnny Pesky, Boston, May 8, 1946

**First player with five hits in 9-inning game**
NL—Joe Battin, St. Louis, May 13, 1876
Jack Burdock, Hartford, May 13, 1876
Tom Carey, Hartford, May 13, 1876
AL—Irv Waldron, Milwaukee, Apr 28, 1901

**First player with six hits in 9-inning game**
NL—Dave Force, Philadelphia, June 27, 1876 (6 AB)
AL—Mike Donlin, Baltimore, June 24, 1901 (6 AB)

**First player with eight hits in a doubleheader**
AA—Henry Simon, Syracuse, October 11, 1890
(See next entry: Fred Carroll had 9 H in DH hits in 1886.)
NL—Joe Quinn, St. Louis, Sept 30, 1893
(See next entry: Wilbert Robinson had 9 H in DH in 1892.)
AL—Charles Hickman, Washington, Sept 7, 1905

**First player with nine hits in a doubleheader**
AA—Fred Carroll, Pittsburgh, July 5, 1886
NL—Wilbert Robinson, Baltimore, June 10, 1892
AL—Ray Morehart, Chicago, Aug 31, 1926

**First player with four extra-base hits in 9-inning game**
NL—George Hall, Philadelphia, June 14, 1876 (3 triples, 1 HR)
AL—Frank Dillon, Detroit, Apr 25, 1901 (4 doubles)

**First player with five extra-base hits in 9-inning game**
AA—George Strief, Philadelphia, June 25, 1885 (4 triples, 1 double)
NL—George Gore, Chicago, July 9, 1885 (2 triples, 3 doubles)
AL—Lou Boudreau, Cleveland, July 14, 1946, 1st game (1 HR, 4 doubles)

**First player with four doubles in 9-inning game**
NL—John O'Rourke, Boston, Sept 15, 1880
AL—Frank Dillon, Detroit, Apr 25, 1901

**First player with three triples in 9-inning game**
NL—George Hall, Philadelphia, June 14, 1876
Ezra Sutton, Philadelphia, June 14, 1876.
AL—Elmer Flick, Cleveland, July 6, 1902

**First player with four triples in 9-inning game**
AA—George Strief, Philadelphia, June 25, 1885
NL—Bill Joyce, New York, May 18, 1897
AL—none

**First player to hit home run**
NL—Ross Barnes, Chicago, May 2, 1876
Charley Jones, Cincinnati, May 2, 1876
AL—Erve Beck, Cleveland, Apr 25, 1901

**First player to hit two homers in 9-inning game**
NL—George Hall, Philadelphia, June 17, 1876
AL—Buck Freeman, Boston, June 1, 1901

**First player to hit three homers in 9-inning game**
NL—Ned Williamson, Chicago, May 30, 1884, p.m. game
AL—Kenny Williams, St. Louis, Apr 22, 1922

**First player to hit four homers in 9-inning game**
NL—Bobby Lowe, Boston, May 30, 1894, p.m. game
AL—Lou Gehrig, New York, June 3, 1932

**First player to hit two homers in one inning**
NL—Charley Jones, Boston, June 10, 1880, 8th
AL—Ken Williams, St. Louis, Aug 7, 1922, 6th

**First player to hit grand slam**
NL—Roger Connor, Troy, Sept 10, 1881
AL—Herm McFarland, Chicago, May 1, 1901

**First player to hit grand slam as pinch-hitter**
NL—Mike O'Neill, St. Louis, June 3, 1902, 9th
AL—Marty Kavanagh, Cleveland, Sept 24, 1916, 5th

**First player to hit home run in night game**
NL—Babe Herman, Cincinnati, July 10, 1935
AL—Frankie Hayes, Philadelphia, May 16, 1939

**First player to hit for cycle**
NL—Curry Foley, Buffalo, May 25, 1882
AL—Harry Davis, Philadelphia, July 10, 1901

**First player to receive five bases on balls in 9-inning game**
AA—Henry Larkin, Philadelphia, May 2, 1887
NL—Fred Carroll, Pittsburgh, July 4, 1889, am game
AL—Sammy Strang, Chicago, Apr 27, 1902

**First player to receive six bases on balls in 9-inning game**
NL—Walt Wilmot, Chicago, Aug 22, 1891
AL—Jimmie Foxx, Boston, June 16, 1938

**First player to receive two bases on balls in one inning**
NL—Elmer Smith, Pittsburgh, Apr 22, 1892, 1st
AL—Donie Bush, Detroit, Aug 27, 1909, 4th

**First player to strike out four times in 9-inning game**
NL—George Derby, Detroit, Aug 6, 1881
(See next item: Oscar Walker had 5 K in game in 1879.)
AL—Emmett Heidrick, St. Louis, May 16, 1902

**First player to strike out five times in 9-inning game**
NL—Oscar Walker, Buffalo, June 20, 1879
AL—Lefty Grove, Philadelphia, June 10, 1933, 1st game

**First player to strike out twice in one inning**
AL—Billy Purtell, Chicago, May 10, 1910, 6th
NL—Edd Roush, Cincinnati, July 22, 1916, 6th

**First pinch-hitter**
NL—Mickey Welch, New York, Aug 10, 1889 (struck out)
AL—Larry McLean, Boston, Apr 26, 1901 (doubled)

**First hit by pinch-hitter**
NL—Tom Daly, Brooklyn, May 14, 1892 (homered)
AL—Larry McLean, Boston, Apr 26, 1901 (doubled)

**First pitcher to lose doubleheader (two complete games)**
NL—Dave Anderson, Pittsburgh vs Brooklyn, Sept 1, 1890; lost 3-2, 8-4
(pitched 2 games of tripleheader)

**First player to be intentionally walked with bases filled**
AL—Nap Lajoie, Philadelphia, May 23, 1901, 9th

**First manager ejected from two games in one day by umpires**
NL—Mel Ott, New York vs Pittsburgh, June 9, 1946
AL—Jimmie Dykes, Baltimore vs New York, June 6, 1954

**First lefthanded catcher**
Bill Harbidge, Hartford NL, May 6, 1876

**First lefthanded pitcher**
Bobby Mitchell, Cincinnati NL, 1877

**First pitcher to wear glasses**
Will White, Boston NL, 1877

**First infielder to wear glasses**
George Toporcer, St. Louis NL, 1921

**First catcher to wear glasses**
Clint Courtney, New York AL, 1951

# CLUB MISCELLANEOUS



## HISTORIC FIRSTS

**First shutout game**
NL—Apr 25, 1876, Chicago 4, Louisville 0
AL—May 15, 1901, Washington 4, Boston 0

**First 1-0 game**
NL—May 5, 1876, St. Louis 1, Chicago 0
AL—July 27, 1901, Detroit 1, Baltimore 0

**First tie game**
NL—May 25, 1876, Philadelphia 2, Louisville 2, 14 inn (darkness)
AL—May 31, 1901, Washington 3, Milwaukee 3, 7 inn (darkness)

**First extra-inning game**
NL—Apr 29, 1876, Hartford 3, Boston 2, 10 inn
AL—Apr 30, 1901, Boston 8, Philadelphia 6, 10 inn

**First extra-inning shutout game**
NL—May 25, 1876, Boston 4, Cincinnati 0, 10 inn
AL—Aug 11, 1902, Philadelphia 1, Detroit 0, 13 inn

**First extra-inning 1-0 game**
NL—June 10, 1876, New York Mutuals 1, Cincinnati 0, 10 inn
AL—Aug 11, 1902, Philadelphia 1, Detroit 0, 13 inn

**First extra-inning tie game**
NL—May 25, 1876, Philadelphia 2, Louisville 2, 14 inn (darkness)
AL—Aug 27, 1901, Milwaukee 5, Baltimore 5, 11 inn (darkness)

**First time two games played in one day**
NL—Sept 9, 1876, Hartford 14, Cincinnati 6; Hartford 8, Cincinnati 3
AL—May 30, 1901, Baltimore 10, Detroit 7; Detroit 4, Baltimore 1
Chicago 8, Boston 3; Chicago 5, Boston 3
Milwaukee 5, Washington 2; Milwaukee 14, Washington 3
Philadelphia 3, Cleveland 1; Philadelphia 8, Cleveland 2, 8 inn

**First doubleheader**
NL—Sept 25, 1882, Worcester 4, Providence 3; Providence 8, Worcester 6
AL—July 15, 1901, Washington 3, Baltimore 2; Baltimore 7, Washington 3

**First doubleheader shutout victory**
NL—July 13, 1888, Pittsburgh 4, Boston 0; Pittsburgh 6, Boston 0
AL—Sept 3, 1901, Cleveland 1, Boston 0; Cleveland 4, Boston 0

**First forfeited game**
NL—Aug 21, 1876, St. Louis 7, Chicago 6, at St. Louis; forfeited to St. Louis
AL—May 2, 1901, Detroit 7, Chicago 5, at Chicago; forfeited to Detroit

**Last forfeited game**
NL—Aug 10, 1995, St. Louis 2, Los Angeles 1, at Los Angeles; forfeited to St. Louis
AL—July 12, 1979, 2nd game, Detroit 9, Chicago 0, at Chicago; forfeited to Detroit

**First game played by**
Boston NL—Apr 22, 1876—Boston 6, Philadelphia Athletics 5 (A)
Philadelphia Athletics NL—Apr 22, 1876—Boston 6, Philadelphia 5 (H)
New York Mutuals NL—Apr 25, 1876—Boston 7, New York Mutuals 6 (H)
Chicago NL—Apr 25, 1876—Chicago 4, Louisville 0 (A)
Cincinnati NL—Apr 25, 1876—Cincinnati 2, St. Louis 1 (H)
St. Louis NL—Apr 25, 1876—Cincinnati 2, St. Louis 1 (A)
Philadelphia NL—May 1, 1883—Providence 4, Philadelphia 3 (H)
New York NL (original club)—May 1, 1883—New York 7, Boston 5 (H)
Pittsburgh NL—Apr 30, 1887—Pittsburgh 6, Chicago 2 (H)
Brooklyn NL—Apr 19, 1890—Boston 15, Brooklyn 9 (A)
Chicago AL—Apr 24, 1901—Chicago 8, Cleveland 2 (H)
Cleveland AL—Apr 24, 1901—Chicago 8, Cleveland 2 (A)
Detroit AL—Apr 25, 1901—Detroit 14, Milwaukee 13 (H)
Baltimore AL—Apr 26, 1901—Baltimore 10, Boston 6 (H)
Boston AL—Apr 26, 1901—Baltimore 10, Boston 6 (A)
Philadelphia AL—Apr 26, 1901—Washington 5, Philadelphia 1 (H)
Washington AL (original club)—Apr 26, 1901—Washington 5, Philadelphia 1 (A)
Milwaukee AL—Apr 25, 1901—Detroit 14, Milwaukee 13 (A)
St. Louis AL—Apr 23, 1902—St. Louis 5, Cleveland 2 (H)
New York AL—Apr 22, 1903—Washington 3, New York 1 (A)
Milwaukee NL since 1900—Apr 13, 1953—Milwaukee 2, Cincinnati 0 (A)
Baltimore AL (present Club)—Apr 13, 1954—Detroit 3, Baltimore 0 (A)
Kansas City AL—Apr 12, 1955—Kansas City 6, Detroit 2 (H)
Los Angeles NL—Apr 15, 1958—San Francisco 8, Los Angeles 0 (A)
San Francisco NL—Apr 15, 1958—San Francisco 8, Los Angeles 0 (H)
Los Angeles AL—Apr 11, 1961—Los Angeles 7, Baltimore 2 (A)
Minnesota AL—Apr 11, 1961—Minnesota 6, New York 0 (A)
Washington AL (second club)—Apr 10, 1961—Chicago 4, Washington 3 (H)
Houston NL—Apr 10, 1962—Houston 11, Chicago 2 (H)
New York NL (present club)—Apr 11, 1962—St. Louis 11, New York 4 (A)
Atlanta NL—Apr 12, 1966—Pittsburgh 3, Atlanta 2, 13 inn (H)
Oakland AL—Apr 10, 1968—Baltimore 3, Oakland 1 (A)
San Diego NL—Apr 8, 1969—San Diego 2, Houston 1 (H)
Seattle AL (original club)—Apr 8, 1969—Seattle 4, California 3 (A)
Montreal NL—Apr 8, 1969—Montreal 11, New York 10 (A)
Kansas City AL (present club)—Apr 8, 1969—Kansas City 4, Minnesota 3, 12 inn (H)
Milwaukee AL (present club)—Apr 7, 1970—California 12, Milwaukee 0 (H)
Texas AL—Apr 15, 1972—California 1, Texas 0 (A)
Seattle AL (present club)—Apr 6, 1977—California 7, Seattle 0 (H)
Toronto AL—Apr 7, 1977—Toronto 9, Chicago 5 (H)
Florida NL—Apr 5, 1993—Florida 6, Los Angeles 3 (H)
Colorado NL—Apr 5, 1993—New York 3, Colorado 0 (A)
Tampa Bay AL—Mar 31, 1998—Detroit 11, Tampa Bay 6 (H)
Arizona NL—Mar 31, 1998—Colorado 9, Arizona 2 (H)
Washington NL—Apr 4, 2005—Philadelphia 8, Washington 4 (A)

**First game played**
At Sportsman's Park, St. Louis—May 5, 1876—St. Louis NL 1, Chicago 0
by St. Louis AL—Apr 23, 1902—St. Louis 5, Cleveland 2
by St. Louis NL (since 1900)—July 1, 1920—Pittsburgh 6, St. Louis 2, 10 inn
At Shibe Park, Philadelphia—Apr 12, 1909—Philadelphia AL 8, Boston 1
At Shibe Park, Philadelphia—May 16, 1927—St. Louis NL 2, Philadelphia NL
At Forbes Field, Pittsburgh—June 30, 1909—Chicago NL 3, Pittsburgh 2
At Comiskey Park (old), Chicago—July 1, 1910—St. Louis AL 2, Chicago 0
At League Park, Cleveland—Apr 21, 1910—Detroit AL 5, Cleveland 0
At Griffith Stadium, Washington—Apr 12, 1911—Washington AL 8, Boston 5
At Polo Grounds, NY(1st game after fire)—June 28, 1911—New York NL 3, Boston 0
formal opening—Apr 19, 1912—New York NL 6, Brooklyn 2
At Redland Field, Cincinnati—Apr 11, 1912—Cincinnati NL 10, Chicago 6
At Navin Field, Detroit—Apr 20, 1912—Detroit AL 6, Cleveland 5, 11 inn
At Fenway Park, Boston—Apr 20, 1912—Boston AL 7, New York 6, 11 inn
formal opening—May 17, 1912—Chicago AL 5, Boston 2
At Ebbets Field, Brooklyn—Apr 9, 1913—Philadelphia NL 1, Brooklyn 0
At Wrigley Field, Chicago—Apr 23, 1914—Chicago FL 9, Kansas City 1
by Chicago NL—Apr 20, 1916—Chicago 7, Cincinnati 6, 11 inn
At Braves Field, Boston—Aug 18, 1915—Boston NL 3, St. Louis 1
At Yankee Stadium, New York—Apr 18, 1923, New York AL 4, Boston 1
At Municipal Stadium, Cleveland—July 31, 1932, Philadelphia AL 1, Cleveland 0
At Milwaukee County Stadium—Apr 14, 1953, Milwaukee NL 3, St. Louis 2, 10 inn
At Memorial Stadium, Baltimore—Apr 15, 1954, Baltimore AL 3, Chicago 1
At Municipal Stadium, Kansas City—Apr 12, 1955, Kansas City AL 6, Detroit 2
At Roosevelt Stadium, Jersey City—Apr 19, 1956, Brooklyn NL 5, Philadelphia 4, 10 inn
At Seals Stadium, San Francisco—Apr 15, 1958—San Francisco NL 8, Los Angeles 0
At Memorial Coliseum, Los Angeles—Apr 18, 1958—Los Angeles NL 6, San Francisco 5
At Candlestick Park, San Francisco—Apr 12, 1960—San Francisco NL 3, St. Louis 1
At Metropolitan Stadium, Minnesota—Apr 21, 1961—Washington AL 5, Minnesota 3
At Wrigley Field, Los Angeles—Apr 27, 1961—Minnesota AL 4, Los Angeles 2
At Dodger Stadium, Los Angeles—Apr 10, 1962—Cincinnati NL 6, Los Angeles 3
At Colt Stadium, Houston—Apr 10, 1962—Houston NL 11, Chicago 2
At District of Columbia Stadium, Washington—Apr 9, 1962, Washington AL 4, Detroit 1
by Washington NL—Apr 14, 2005—Washington NL 5, Arizona 3
At Shea Stadium, New York—Apr 17, 1964—Pittsburgh NL 4, New York 3
At Astrodome, Houston—Apr 12, 1965—Philadelphia NL 2, Houston 0
At Atlanta Stadium, Atlanta—Apr 12, 1966—Pittsburgh NL 3, Atlanta 2, 13 inn
At Anaheim Stadium, California—Apr 19, 1966—Chicago AL 3, California 1
At Busch Memorial Stadium, St. Louis—May 12, 1966—St. Louis NL 4, Atlanta 3, 12 inn
At Oakland-Alameda County Coliseum—Apr 17, 1968—Baltimore AL 4, Oakland 1
At San Diego Stadium—Apr 8, 1969—San Diego NL 2, Houston 1
At Sicks' Stadium, Seattle—Apr 11, 1969—Seattle AL 7, Chicago 0
At Jarry Park, Montreal—Apr 14, 1969—Montreal NL 8, St. Louis 7
At Riverfront Stadium, Cincinnati—June 30, 1970—Atlanta NL 8, Cincinnati 2
At Three Rivers Stadium, Pittsburgh—July 16, 1970—Cincinnati NL 3, Pittsburgh 2
At Veterans Stadium, Philadelphia—Apr 10, 1971—Philadelphia NL 4, Montreal 1
At Arlington Stadium, Texas—Apr 21, 1972—Texas AL 7, California 6
At Royals Stadium, Kansas City—Apr 10, 1973—Kansas City AL 12, Texas 1
At Kingdome, Seattle—Apr 6, 1977—California AL 7, Seattle 0
At Exhibition Stadium, Toronto—Apr 7, 1977—Toronto AL 9, Chicago 5
At Olympic Stadium, Montreal—Apr 15, 1977—Philadelphia NL 7, Montreal 2
At Metrodome, Minnesota—Apr 6, 1982—Seattle AL 11, Minnesota 7
At SkyDome, Toronto—June 5, 1989—Milwaukee AL 5, Toronto 3
At Comiskey Park (new), Chicago—Apr 18, 1991—Detroit AL 16, Chicago 0
At Oriole Park at Camden Yards, Baltimore—Apr 6, 1992—Baltimore AL 2, Cleveland 0
At Joe Robbie Stadium, Florida—Apr 5, 1993—Florida NL 6, Los Angeles 3
At Mile High Stadium, Colorado—Apr 9, 1993—Colorado NL 11, Montreal 4
At Jacobs Field, Cleveland—Apr 4, 1994—Cleveland AL 4, Seattle 3, 11 inn
At The Ballpark in Arlington, Texas—Apr 11, 1994—Milwaukee AL 4, Texas 3
At Coors Field, Colorado—Apr 26, 1995—Colorado NL 11, New York 9 (11 inn)
At Cashman Field, Las Vegas—Apr 1, 1996—Toronto AL 9, Oakland 6
At Monterrey Stadium, Mexico—Aug 16, 1996—San Diego NL 15, New York 10
At Turner Field, Atlanta—Apr 4, 1997—Atlanta NL 5, Chicago 4
At Aloha Stadium, Honolulu—Apr 19, 1997, 1st game, St. Louis NL 1, San Diego 0
At Tropicana Field, Tampa Bay—Mar 31, 1998—Detroit AL 11, Tampa Bay 6
At Bank One Ballpark, Arizona—Mar 31, 1998—Colorado NL 9, Arizona 2
At Safeco Field, Seattle—July 15, 1999—San Diego NL 3, Seattle AL 2
At Tokyo Dome, Japan—Mar 29, 2000—Chicago NL 5, New York NL 3
At Enron Field, Houston—Apr 7, 2000—Philadelphia NL 4, Houston 1
At Pacific Bell Park, San Francisco—Apr 11, 2000—Los Angeles NL 6, San Francisco 5
At Comerica Park, Detroit—Apr 11, 2000—Detroit AL 5, Seattle 2
At Hiram Bithorn Stadium, San Juan, Puerto Rico—Apr 1, 2001—Toronto AL 8, Texas 1
At Miller Park, Milwaukee—Apr 6, 2001—Milwaukee NL 5, Cincinnati 4
At PNC Park, Pittsburgh—Apr 9, 2001—Cincinnati NL 8, Pittsburgh 2
At Great American Ball Park, Cincinnati—March 31, 2003—Pittsburgh NL 10, Cincinnati 1
At Petco Field, San Diego—Apr 8, 2004—San Diego NL 4, San Francisco 3, 10 inn
At Citizens Bank Park, Philadelphia—Apr 12, 2004—Cincinnati NL 4, Philadelphia 1

**First Sunday game**
AA—At Louisville—May 7, 1882, Louisville 10, St. Louis 3
NL—At St. Louis—Apr 17, 1892, Cincinnati 5, St. Louis 1
AL—At Detroit—Apr 28, 1901, Detroit 12, Milwaukee 11
At Chicago AL—Apr 28, 1901, Chicago 13, Cleveland 1

**First night game**
At Cincinnati—May 24, 1935, Cincinnati 2, Philadelphia 1
By Pittsburgh (at Cincinnati)—May 31, 1935, Pittsburgh 4, Cincinnati 1
By Chicago NL (at Cincinnati)—July 1, 1935, Chicago 8, Cincinnati 4

By Brooklyn (at Cincinnati)—July 10, 1935, Cincinnati 15, Brooklyn 2
By Boston NL (at Cincinnati)—July 24, 1935, Cincinnati 5, Boston 4
By St. Louis NL (at Cincinnati)—July 31, 1935, Cincinnati 4, St. Louis 3, 10 inn
At Brooklyn—June 15, 1938, Cincinnati 6, Brooklyn 0
At Philadelphia AL—May 16, 1939, Cleveland 8, Philadelphia 3, 10 inn
By Chicago AL (at Philadelphia)—May 24, 1939, Chicago 4, Philadelphia 1
At Philadelphia NL—June 1, 1939, Pittsburgh 5, Philadelphia 2
By St. Louis AL (at Philadelphia)—June 14, 1939, St. Louis 6, Philadelphia 0
By Detroit (at Philadelphia)—June 20, 1939, Detroit 5, Philadelphia 0
By New York AL (at Philadelphia)—June 26, 1939, Philadelphia 3, New York 2
At Cleveland—June 27, 1939, Cleveland 5, Detroit 0
By Washington (at Philadelphia)—July 6, 1939, Philadelphia 9, Washington 3
At Chicago AL—Aug 14, 1939, Chicago 5, St. Louis 2
By Boston AL (at Cleveland)—July 13, 1939, Boston 6, Cleveland 5, 10 inn
At New York NL—May 24, 1940, New York 8, Boston 1
By New York NL—May 24, 1940, New York 8, Boston 1
At St. Louis AL—May 24, 1940, Cleveland 3, St. Louis 2
At Pittsburgh—June 4, 1940, Pittsburgh 14, Boston 2
At St. Louis NL—June 4, 1940, Brooklyn 10, St. Louis 1
At Washington—May 28, 1941, New York 6, Washington 5.
At Boston NL—May 11, 1946, New York 5, Boston 1
At New York AL—May 28, 1946, Washington 2, New York 1
At Boston AL—June 13, 1947, Boston 5, Chicago 3
At Detroit—June 15, 1948, Detroit 4, Philadelphia 1
By Milwaukee NL (at St. Louis)—Apr 20, 1953, St. Louis 9, Milwaukee 4
At Milwaukee NL—May 8, 1953, Milwaukee 2, Chicago 0
At Baltimore—Apr 21, 1954, Cleveland 2, Baltimore 1
At Kansas City—Apr 18, 1955, Cleveland 11, Kansas City 9
At San Francisco—Apr 16, 1958, Los Angeles 13, San Francisco 1
At Los Angeles NL—Apr 22, 1958, Los Angeles 4, Chicago 2
By Minnesota—Apr 14, 1961, Minnesota 3, Baltimore 2
At Minnesota—May 18, 1961, Kansas City 4, Minnesota 3
At Los Angeles AL—Apr 28, 1961, Los Angeles 6, Minnesota 5, 12 inn
At Houston—Apr 11, 1962, Houston 2, Chicago 0
At Atlanta—Apr 12, 1966, Pittsburgh 3, Atlanta 2, 13 inn
At Oakland—Apr 17, 1968, Baltimore 4, Oakland 1
At San Diego—Apr 8, 1969, San Diego 2, Houston 1
By Seattle—Apr 8, 1969, Seattle 4, California 3
By Montreal—Apr 17, 1969, Montreal 7, Philadelphia 0
At Seattle—Apr 12, 1969, Seattle 5, Chicago 1
At Montreal—Apr 30, 1969, New York 2, Montreal 1
By Milwaukee AL—Apr 13, 1970, Oakland 2, Milwaukee 1
At Milwaukee AL—May 5, 1970, Boston 6, Milwaukee 0
At Texas—Apr 21, 1972, Texas 7, California 6
At Toronto—May 2, 1977, Milwaukee 3, Toronto 1
At Chicago NL—Aug 9, 1988, Chicago 6, New York 4
At Florida—Apr 6, 1993, Los Angeles 4, Florida 2
At Colorado—Apr 13, 1993, New York 8, Colorado 4
At Tampa Bay—Mar 31, 1998, Detroit 11, Tampa Bay 6
At Arizona—Mar 31, 1998, Colorado 9, Arizona 2
By Washington NL (at Philadelphia)—Apr 6, 2005, Washington 7, Philadelphia 3
At Washington NL—Apr 14, 2005, Washington 5, Arizona 3

**First night opening game**
NL—At St. Louis—Apr 18, 1950, St. Louis 4, Pittsburgh 2
AL—At Philadelphia—Apr 17, 1951, Washington 6, Philadelphia 1

**First ladies day**
NL—At Cincinnati, 1876 season
AL—At St. Louis, 1912 season

**First ladies night**
NL—At New York, June 27, 1941, New York 7, Philadelphia 4
AL—At Boston, Aug 17, 1950, Boston 10, Philadelphia 6

**First day games completed with lights**
NL—At Boston, Apr 23, 1950, second game, Philadelphia 6, Boston 5
AL—At New York, Aug 29, 1950, New York 6, Cleveland 5

**First time all games played at night**
(8-club leagues)—Aug 9, 1946 (4 in NL, 4 in AL)
(12-club leagues)—Apr 25, 1969 (6 in NL, 6 in AL)

**First time all games were twi-night doubleheaders**
NL—Aug 25, 1953

**First time uniforms were numbered**
NL—Cincinnati, 1883 season
AL—New York, 1929 season, complete (Cleveland vs Chicago at Cleveland, June 26, 1916, wore numbers on the sleeves of their uniforms.)

**First team with 1,000,000 home attendance**
AL—New York, 1920 (1,289,422)
NL—Chicago, 1927 (1,159,168)

**First team with 2,000,000 home attendance**
AL—New York, 1946 (2,265,512)
NL—Milwaukee, 1954 (2,131,388)

**First team with 3,000,000 home attendance**
NL—Los Angeles, 1978 (3,347,845)
AL—Minnesota, 1988 (3,030,672)

**First team with 4,000,000 home attendance**
AL—Toronto, 1991 (4,001,527)
NL—Colorado, 1993 (4,483,350)

## NIGHT GAMES AND POSTPONEMENTS

**Most night games, season (includes twilight games)**
NL—134—Houston, 1984 (won 68, lost 66)
AL—133—Texas, 1979 (won 67, lost 66)
Seattle, 1982 (won 62, lost 71)
Texas, 1989 (won 67, lost 66)
Texas, 1990 (won 70, lost 63)

**Most games postponed at start of season**
AL—5—Chicago, Apr 6-10, 1982
New York, Apr 6-10, 1982
NL—4—New York, Apr 12-15, 1933

**Most consecutive games postponed, season**
NL—9—Philadelphia, Aug 10-19, 1903
AL—7—Detroit, May 14-18, 1945
Philadelphia, May 14-18, 1945
Washington, Apr 23-29, 1952

## TIES AND ONE-RUN DECISIONS

**Most tie games, season**
AL—10—Detroit, 1904
NL—9—St. Louis, 1911

**Fewest tie games, season**
AL-NL—0—all clubs in many seasons
Last AL season—2005
Last NL season—2004

**Most games decided by one run, season**
AL—74—Chicago, 1968 (won 30, lost 44)
NL—75—Houston, 1971 (won 32, lost 43)

**Fewest games decided by one run, season**
AL—27—Cleveland, 1948 (won 9, lost 18)
NL—28—Brooklyn, 1949 (won 16, lost 12)

## LENGTH OF GAMES

### BY INNINGS

**Longest game**
NL—26 inn—Brooklyn 1, Boston 1, May 1, 1920, at Boston
AL—25 inn—Chicago 7, Milwaukee 6, May 8, finished May 9, 1984, at Chicago

**For a complete list of games of 18 or more innings, see page 143.**

**Longest night game**
NL—25 inn—St. Louis 4, New York 3, Sept 11, 1974, at New York
AL—25 inn—Chicago 7, Milwaukee 6, May 8, finished May 9, 1984, at Chicago

**Longest opening game**
AL—15 inn—Washington 1, Philadelphia 0, Apr 13, 1926 at Washington
Detroit 4, Cleveland 2, Apr 19, 1960, at Cleveland
NL—14 inn—Philadelphia 5, Brooklyn 5, Apr 17, 1923, at Brooklyn
New York 1, Brooklyn 1, Apr 16, 1933, at Brooklyn (opener for New York only)
Pittsburgh 4, Milwaukee 3, Apr 15, 1958, at Milwaukee
Pittsburgh 6, St. Louis 2, Apr 8, 1969, at St. Louis
Cincinnati 2, Los Angeles 1, Apr 7, 1975, at Cincinnati
New York 1, Philadelphia 0, Mar 31, 1998, at New York

**Longest 0-0 game**
NL—19 inn—Brooklyn vs Cincinnati, Sept 11, 1946, at Brooklyn
AL—18 inn—Detroit vs Washington, July 16, 1909, at Detroit

**Longest 0-0 night game**
NL—18 inn—Philadelphia vs New York, October 2, 1965, 2nd game, at New York
AL—none

**Longest 1-0 day game**
NL—18 inn—Providence 1, Detroit 0, Aug 17, 1882, at Providence
New York 1, St. Louis 0, July 2, 1933, 1st game, at New York
AL—18 inn—Washington 1, Chicago 0, May 15, 1918, at Washington
Washington 1, Chicago 0, June 8, 1947, 1st game, at Chicago

**Longest 1-0 night game**
NL—24 inn—Houston 1, New York 0, Apr 15, 1968, at Houston
AL—20 inn—Oakland 1, California 0, July 9, 1971, at Oakland

**Longest shutout game**
NL—24 inn—Houston 1, New York 0, Apr 15, 1968, at Houston
AL—20 inn—Oakland 1, California 0, July 9, 1971, at Oakland

**Longest tie game**
NL—26 inn—Boston 1, Brooklyn 1, May 1, 1920, at Boston
AL—24 inn—Detroit 1, Philadelphia 1, July 21, 1945, at Philadelphia

**Most innings, one day**
NL—32—San Francisco at New York, May 31, 1964
AL—29—Boston at Philadelphia, July 4, 1905
Boston at New York, Aug 29, 1967

**Most extra-inning games, season**
AL—31—Boston, 1943 (won 15, lost 14, tied 2)

NL—27—Boston, 1943 (won 14, lost 13)
Los Angeles, 1967 (won 10, lost 17)

**Most consecutive extra-inning games, one club**
AL—5—Detroit, Sept 9-13, 1908 (54 inn)
NL—4—Pittsburgh, Aug 18-22, 1917 (59 inn)
San Francisco, July 7-10, 1987 (49 inn)

**Most consecutive extra-inning games between same clubs**
AL—4—Chicago and Detroit, Sept 9-12, 1908 (43 inn)
Cleveland and St. Louis, May 1, 2, 4, 5, 1910 (46 inn)
Boston and St. Louis, May 31, first game, to June 2, 2nd game, 1943 (45 inn)
NL—4—New York and Pittsburgh, May 24, 25, June 23, 24, 1978 (44 inn; both clubs played other teams between these contests)
NL—3—Brooklyn and Pittsburgh, Aug 20, 21, 22, 1917 (45 inn)
Chicago and Pittsburgh, Aug 18, 19, 20, 1961 (33 inn)
Cincinnati and New York, May 5, 6, 7, 1980 (36 inn)

**Most innings, two consecutive extra-inning games**
NL—45—Boston, May 1 (26), 3 (19), 1920
AL—37—Minnesota vs Milwaukee May 12 (22), May 13 (15), 1972

**Most innings between same clubs, two consecutive extra-inning games**
NL—40—Boston and Chicago, May 14 (18), May 17 (22), 1927
AL—37—Minnesota and Milwaukee, May 12 (22), May 13 (15), 1972

**Most innings, three consecutive extra-inning games**
NL—58—Brooklyn, May 1-3, 1920
AL—41—Cleveland, Apr 16-21, 1935
Boston, Apr 8-11, 1969

**Most innings between same clubs, three consecutive extra-inning games**
NL—45—Brooklyn and Pittsburgh, Aug 20-22, 1917
AL—40—Chicago and Washington, Aug 24-26, 1915
Detroit and Philadelphia, May 12-14, 1943

**Most innings, four consecutive extra-inning games**
NL—59—Pittsburgh, Aug 18-22, 1917
AL—51—Chicago, Aug 23-26, 1915
Detroit, May 9, 2nd game-May 14, 1943

**Most innings between same clubs, four consecutive extra-inning games**
AL—46—Cleveland and St. Louis, May 1, 2, 4, 5, 1910
NL—none

## BY TIME

**Longest 9-inning game**
NL—4 hrs, 27 min—Los Angeles 11, San Francisco 10, Oct 5, 2001
AL—4 hrs, 22 min—Baltimore 13, New York 9, Sept 5, 1997

**Longest extra-inning game**
AL—8 hrs, 6 min—Chicago 7, Milwaukee 6, May 8, finished May 9, 1984, 25 inn
NL—7 hrs, 23 min—San Francisco 8, New York 6, May 31, 1964, 2nd game, 23 inn

**Longest 9-inning 1-0 game**
AL—3 hrs, 20 min—Milwaukee 1, Oakland 0, May 7, 1997
ML—3 hrs, 16 min—Anaheim AL 1, Los Angeles NL 0, June 8, 2001
NL—3 hrs, 7 min—New York 1, San Diego 0, May 17, 1988

**Longest extra-inning 1-0 game**
NL—6 hrs, 14 min—Los Angeles 1, Montreal 0, Aug 23, 1989, 22 inn
AL—5 hrs, 5 min—Oakland 1, California 0, July 9, 1971, 20 inn

**Longest extra-inning 1-0 night game**
NL—6 hrs, 14 min—Los Angeles 1, Montreal 0, Aug 23, 1989, 22 inn
AL—5 hrs, 5 min—Oakland 1, California 0, July 9, 1971, 20 inn

**Longest 9-inning night game**
NL—4 hrs, 27 min—Los Angeles 11, San Francisco 10, Oct 5, 2001
AL—4 hrs, 22 min—Baltimore 13, New York 9, Sept 5, 1997

**Longest extra-inning night game**
AL—8 hrs, 6 min—Chicago 7, Milwaukee 6, at Chicago, May 8, finished May 9, 1984, 25 inn
NL—7 hrs, 14 min—Houston 5, Los Angeles 4, at Houston, June 3, 1989, 22 inn

**Longest doubleheader (18 innings)**
AL—7 hrs, 39 min—Texas at Chicago, May 24, 1995
NL—6 hrs, 46 min—Brooklyn at New York, Aug 7, 1952

**Longest doubleheader (more than 18 innings)**
NL—9 hrs, 52 min—San Francisco at New York, May 31, 1964, 32 inn
AL—9 hrs, 5 min—Kansas City at Detroit, June 17, 1967, 28 inn

**Shortest official game, less than 9 innings**
AL—48 min—Baltimore 1, Kansas City 0, July 30, 1971, 4.5 inn
NL—50 min—Brooklyn, 4, Cincinnati 0, Sept 21, 1911, 2nd game, 5 innFax

**Shortest 9-inning game**
NL—50 min—Philadelphia 2, New York 0, Apr 12, 1911
AL—55 min—St. Louis 6, New York 2, Sept 26, 2nd game, 1926

**Shortest 9-inning night game**
NL—1 hr, 15 min—Boston 2, Cincinnati 0, Aug 10, 1944
AL—1 hr, 29 min—Chicago 1, Washington 0, May 21, 1943

**Shortest 1-0 game**
NL—57 min—New York 1, Brooklyn 0, Aug 30, 1918
AL—1 hour, 13 min—Detroit 1, New York 0, Aug 8, 1920

**Shortest doubleheader (18 innings)**
AL—2 hrs, 7 min—New York at St. Louis, Sept 26, 1926
NL—2 hrs, 20 min—Chicago at Brooklyn, Aug 14, 1919

## GAMES WON

**Most games won, league**
NL—9,834—Chicago, 1230 years, 1876-2005
AL—9,074—New York, 103 years, 1903-2005

**For a complete list of franchise won-lost records, see page 139.**

**Most games won, season**
NL—116—Chicago, 1906 (lost 36)
AL—116—Seattle, 2001 (lost 46)

**For a complete list of clubs with 100 or more victories in a season, see page 140.**

**Fewest games won, season**
NL—20—Cleveland, 1899 (lost 134)
NL since 1900—38—Boston, 1935 (lost 115)
AL—36—Philadelphia, 1916 (lost 117)

**Most games won, two consecutive seasons**
NL—223—Chicago, 1906, 1907 (lost 81)
AL—217—Baltimore, 1969, 1970 (lost 107)

**Most games won, three consecutive seasons**
NL—322—Chicago, 1906, 1907, 1908 (lost 130)
AL—318—Baltimore, 1969, 1970, 1971 (lost 164)

**Most years winning 100 or more games**
AL—18—New York, 1927, 1928, 1932, 1936, 1937, 1939, 1941, 1942, 1954, 1961, 1963, 1977, 1978, 1980, 1998, 2002-2004
NL—8—Boston/Milwaukee/Atlanta, 1892, 1898 in Boston; none in Milwaukee; 1993, 1997-1999, 2002, 2003 in Atlanta

**Most consecutive years winning 100 or more games**
AL—3—Philadelphia, 1929-1931
Baltimore, 1969-1971
New York, 2002-2004
NL—3—St. Louis, 1942-1944
Atlanta, 1997-1999

**Most games won at home, season**
AL—65—New York, 1961 (lost 16)
NL—64—Cincinnati, 1975 (lost 17)

**Most games won on road, season**
NL—60—Chicago, 1906 (lost 15)
AL—59—Seattle, 2001 (lost 22)

**Most games won from one club, season**
NL (8 clubs)—21—Chicago vs Boston, 1909 (lost 1)
Pittsburgh vs Cincinnati, 1937 (lost 1)
Chicago vs Cincinnati, 1945 (lost 1)
NL (12 clubs)—17—Atlanta vs San Diego, 1974 (lost 1)
New York vs Pittsburgh, 1986 (lost 1)
AL (8 clubs)—21—New York vs St. Louis, 1927 (lost 1)
AL (12 clubs)—15—Baltimore vs Milwaukee, 1973 (lost 3)

**Most games won from one club at home**
NL—16—Brooklyn vs Pittsburgh, 1890 (lost 2)
Philadelphia vs Pittsburgh, 1890 (lost 1)
NL since 1900—13—New York vs Philadelphia, 1904 (lost 2)
AL—12—Chicago vs St. Louis, 1915 (lost 0)

**Most games won from one club on road**
NL (8 clubs)—11—Pittsburgh vs St. Louis, 1908 (lost 0)
Chicago vs Boston, 1909 (lost 0)
Brooklyn vs Philadelphia, 1945 (lost 0)
AL (8 clubs)—11—Chicago vs Philadelphia, 1915 (lost 0)
New York vs St. Louis, 1927 (lost 0)
New York vs St. Louis, 1939 (lost 0)
Cleveland vs Boston, 1954 (lost 0)

**Most games won by one run, season**
NL—42—San Francisco, 1978 (lost 26)
AL—40—Baltimore, 1970 (lost 15)
Baltimore, 1974 (lost 21)

**Fewest games won by one run, season**
AL—9—Cleveland, 1948 (lost 18)
NL—9—New York, 1953 (lost 24)

**Most games won from league champions, season**
NL—16—St. Louis vs Chicago, 1945 (lost 6)
AL—14—Philadelphia vs Detroit, 1909 (lost 8)
Minnesota vs Oakland, 1973 (lost 4)

**Most games won from one club, two consecutive seasons**
NL (8 clubs)—40—Pittsburgh vs St. Louis, 1907, 1908
AL (8 clubs)—37—Philadelphia vs St. Louis, 1910, 1911
Chicago vs Philadelphia, 1915, 1916
New York vs Philadelphia, 1919, 1920
New York vs St. Louis, 1926, 1927

**Fewest games won from one club, season (excludes interleague games)**
NL-AL—0—many clubs

**Most times winning two games in one day, season**
NL—20—Chicago, 1945 (lost 3)
AL—15—Chicago, 1961 (lost 7)

**Most times winning two games in one day, from one club, season**
AL—7—Chicago vs Philadelphia, 1943 (lost 0)
NL—7—Chicago vs Cincinnati, 1945 (lost 0)

**Fewest times winning two games in one day, season**
AL-NL—0—many clubs

**Most games won, one month**
NL—29—New York, Sept, 1916 (lost 5)
AL—28—New York, Aug, 1938 (lost 8)

**Most games won, two consecutive days**
NL—5—Baltimore, Sept 7 (3), Sept 8 (2), 1896
AL—4—many days

## CONSECUTIVE

**Most consecutive games won, season**
NL—26—New York, Sept 7-30, first game, 1916 (1 tie)
AL—20—Oakland, Aug 13-Sept 4, 2002

**For a complete list of clubs with 13 or more consecutive victories in a season, see page 141.**

**Most consecutive games won with no tie games, season**
NL—21—Chicago, June 2-July 8, 1880
Chicago, Sept 4-27, second game, 1935
AL—20—Oakland, Aug 13-Sept 4, 2002

**Most consecutive games won at start of season**
UA—20—St. Louis, Apr 20-May 22, 1884
NL—13—Atlanta, Apr 6-21, 1982
AL—13—Milwaukee, Apr 6-20, 1987

**For a complete list of clubs with eight or more consecutive victories at the start of a season, see page 143.**

**Most consecutive home games won, season**
AA—27—St. Louis, Apr 26-July 16, 1885
NL—26—New York, Sept 7-30, first game, 1916 (1 tie)
AL—24—Boston, June 25-Aug 13, 1988

**Most consecutive road games won, season**
NL—17—New York, May 9-29, 1916
AL—17—Detroit, Apr 3-May 24, 1984 (start of season)

**Most consecutive games won from one club, league**
AL (12 clubs)—23—Baltimore vs Kansas City, May 10, 1969-Aug 2, 1970 (last 11 in 1969, all 12 in 1970)
NL (8 clubs)—22—Boston vs Philadelphia, May 4, 1883-June 3, 1884 (all 14 in 1883, first 8 in 1884)
NL since 1900 (8 clubs)—20—Pittsburgh vs Cincinnati, May 31, 2nd game, 1937-Apr 24, 1938 (last 17 in 1937, first 3 in 1938)
AL (8 clubs)—22—Boston vs Washington, Aug 31, 1903-Sept 6, 1st game, 1904 (last 6 in 1903, first 16 in 1904)

**Most consecutive games won from one club at home, league**
NL—32—Baltimore vs Louisville, June 7, 1894-July 11, 1899 (last 6 in 1894, all 6 in 1895, 1896 and 1897, all 7 in 1898, first 1 in 1899)
NL since 1900—25—St. Louis vs Cincinnati, Apr 27, 1929, 2nd game-May 31, 1931, 1st game (last 9 in 1929, all 11 in 1930, first 5 in 1931)
AL—27—Cleveland vs St. Louis/Baltimore, Aug 13, 1952, 2nd game-Aug 15, 1954, 2nd game (last 5 in 1952, all 11 in 1953 and 1954)

**Most consecutive games won from one club on road, league**
NL—18—Brooklyn vs Philadelphia, May 5, 1st game, 1945-Aug 10, 1946 (all 11 in 1945; first 7 in 1946)
St. Louis vs Pittsburgh, May 7, 1964-Apr 15, 1966 (last 8 in 1964, all 9 in 1965, first in 1966)
AL—18—Boston vs New York, October 3, 1st game, 1911-June 2, 2nd game, 1913 (last 3 in 1911; all 10 in 1912; first 6, excluding one tie, in 1913)

**Most consecutive doubleheaders won, season (no other games between)**
AL—5—New York, Aug 30-Sept 4, 1906
NL—4—Brooklyn, Sept 1-4, 1924
New York, Sept 10-14, 1928

## GAMES LOST

**Most games lost, league**
NL—9,878—Philadelphia, 123 years, 1883-2005
AL—8,050—Detroit, 105 years, 1901-2005

**For a complete list of franchise won-lost records, see page 139.**

**Most games lost, season**
NL—134—Cleveland, 1899 (won 20)
NL since 1900—120—New York, 1962 (won 40)
AL—119—Detroit, 2003 (won 43)

**For a complete list of clubs with 100 or more games lost in a season, see page 141.**

**Most games lost, two consecutive seasons**
NL—231—New York, 1962, 1963 (won 91)
AL—226—Philadelphia, 1915, 1916 (won 79)

**Most games lost, three consecutive seasons**
NL—340—New York, 1962-1964 (won 144)
AL—324—Philadelphia, 1915-1917 (won 134)

**Most years losing 100 or more games**
AL—15—Philadelphia/Kansas City, 1915, 1916, 1919, 1920, 1921, 1936, 1940, 1943, 1946, 1950, 1954 in Philadelphia, 1956, 1961, 1964, 1965 in Kansas City
NL—14—Philadelphia, 1904, 1921, 1923, 1927, 1928, 1930, 1936, 1938, 1939, 1940, 1941, 1942, 1945, 1961

**Most consecutive years losing 100 or more games**
NL—5—Philadelphia, 1938-1942
AL—4—Washington, 1961-1964

**Most night games lost, season**
AL—83—Seattle, 1980 (won 44)
NL—82—Atlanta, 1977 (won 43)

**Most games lost at home, season**
AL—59—St. Louis, 1939 (won 18)
NL—58—New York, 1962 (won 22)

**Most games lost on road, season**
NL—102—Cleveland, 1899 (won 11)
NL since 1900—65—Boston, 1935 (won 13)
AL—64—Philadelphia, 1916 (won 13)

**Most games lost by one run, season**
AL—44—Chicago, 1968 (won 30)
NL—43—Houston, 1971 (won 32)

**Fewest games lost by one run, season**
AL—10—Boston, 1986 (won 24)
New York, 1998 (won 21)
NL—12—Brooklyn, 1949 (won 16)
San Francisco, 2003 (won 28)

**Most times losing two games in one day, season**
NL—19—Chicago, 1950 (won 4)
AL—18—Philadelphia, 1943 (won 4)

**Fewest times losing two games in one day, season**
NL-AL—0—many clubs

**Most games lost, one month**
AL—29—Washington, July, 1909 (won 5)
NL—27—Pittsburgh, Aug, 1890 (won 1)
Cleveland, Sept, 1899 (won 1)
St. Louis, Sept, 1908 (won 7)
Brooklyn, Sept, 1908 (won 6)
Philadelphia, Sept, 1939 (won 6)

**Most games lost, two consecutive days**
NL—5—Louisville, Sept 7 (3), Sept 8 (2), 1896
AL—4—many days

## CONSECUTIVE

**Most consecutive games lost, season**
AA—26—Louisville, May 22-June 22, 2nd game, 1889
NL—24—Cleveland, Aug 26-Sept 16, 1899
NL since 1900—23—Philadelphia, July 29-Aug 20, 1st game, 1961
AL—21—Baltimore, Apr 4-28, 1988

**For a complete list of clubs with 13 or more consecutive games lost in a season, see page 142.**

**Most consecutive games lost at start of season**
AL—21—Baltimore, Apr 4-28, 1988
NL—14—Chicago, Apr 1-20, first game, 1997

**For a complete list of clubs with eight or more consecutive games lost at the start of a season, see page 143.**

**Most consecutive home games lost, season**
AL—20—St. Louis, June 3-July 7, 1953
NL—14—Boston, May 8-24, 1911

**Most consecutive road games lost, season**
NL—41—Pittsburgh, July 18-Sept 12, 2nd game, 1890
NL since 1900—22—New York, June 16, 1st game,-July 28, 1963
AL—19—Philadelphia, July 25-Aug 8, 1916

**Most consecutive games lost to one club, league**

AL (12 clubs)—23—Kansas City vs Baltimore, May 9, 1969-Aug 2, 1970; last 11 in 1969, all 12 in 1970

AL (8 clubs)—22—Washington vs Boston, Aug 31, 1903-Sept 6, first game, 1904; last 6 in 1903, first 16 in 1904

NL (8 clubs)—22—Philadelphia vs Boston, May 4, 1883-June 3, 1884; all 14 in 1883, first 8 in 1884

NL since 1900 (8 clubs)—20—Cincinnati vs Pittsburgh, May 31, second game, 1937-Apr 24, 1938; last 17 in 1937, first 3 in 1938

**Most consecutive doubleheaders lost, season (no other games between)**

NL—5—Boston, Sept 8-14, 1928
AL—4—Boston, June 29-July 5, 1921

## WINNING PERCENTAGE

### HIGHEST

**Highest percentage games won, season**

UA—.850—St. Louis, 1884 (won 91, lost 16)
NL—.798—Chicago, 1880 (won 67, lost 17)
NL since 1900—.763—Chicago, 1906 (won 116, lost 36)
AL—.721—Cleveland, 1954 (won 111, lost 43)

**Highest percentage games won, season, for league champions since 1969**

AL—.704—New York, 1998 (won 114, lost 48)
NL—.667—Cincinnati, 1975 (won 108, lost 54)
New York, 1986 (won 108, lost 54)

### LOWEST

**Lowest percentage games won, season**

NL—.130—Cleveland, 1899 (won 20, lost 134)
NL since 1900—.248—Boston, 1935 (won 38, lost 115)
AL—.235—Philadelphia, 1916 (won 36, lost 117)

**Lowest percentage games won, pennant winner, through 1968**

NL—.564—Los Angeles, 1959 (won 88, lost 68)
AL—.568—Boston, 1967 (won 92, lost 70)

**Lowest percentage games won, league champion, since 1969**

NL—.509—New York, 1973 (won 82, lost 79)
AL—.525—Minnesota, 1987 (won 85, lost 77)

## CHAMPIONSHIPS

**Most championships won, club**

AL—39—New York, 1921-1923, 1926-1928, 1932, 1936-1939, 1941-1943, 1947, 1949-1953, 1955-1958, 1960-1964, 1976-1978, 1981, 1996, 1998-2001, 2003

NL—21—Brooklyn/Los Angeles, 1890, 1899, 1900, 1916, 1920, 1941, 1947, 1949, 1952, 1953, 1955, 1956 in Brooklyn; 1959, 1963, 1965, 1966, 1974, 1977, 1978, 1981, 1988 in Los Angeles

NL since 1900—19—Brooklyn/Los Angeles, 1900, 1916, 1920, 1941, 1947, 1949, 1952, 1953, 1955, 1956 in Brooklyn; 1959, 1963, 1965, 1966, 1974, 1977, 1978, 1981, 1988 in Los Angeles

**Most consecutive championships won, club**

AL—5—New York, 1949-1953
New York, 1960-1964
AA—4—St. Louis, 1885-1888
NL—4—New York, 1921-1924

**Most consecutive years without winning championship, league**

NL—60—Chicago, 1946-2005
AL—45—Chicago, 1960-2004

**Most consecutive years with first-division finishes, through 1968**

AL—39—New York, 1926-1964
NL—14—Chicago, 1878-1891
Pittsburgh, 1900-1913
Chicago, 1926-1939

## LAST-PLACE AND SECOND-DIVISION FINISHES

**Most times finished in overall last place, league**

AL—26—Philadelphia/Kansas City/Oakland, 1915-1921, 1935, 1936, 1938, 1940-1943, 1945, 1946, 1950, 1954 in Philadelphia; 1956, 1960, 1961 (tied), 1964, 1965, 1967 in Kansas City; 1993, 1997 in Oakland

NL—27—Philadelphia, 1883, 1904, 1919-1921, 1923, 1926-1928, 1930, 1936, 1938-1942, 1944, 1945, 1947 (tied), 1958-1961, 1972, 1996, 1997, 2000 (tied)

**Most consecutive last-place finishes, through 1968**

AL—7—Philadelphia, 1915-1921
NL—5—Philadelphia, 1938-1942

**Most consecutive times with lowest winning percentage, through 1968**

AL—7—Philadelphia, 1915-1921
NL—5—Philadelphia, 1938-1942

**Most consecutive years with second-division finishes, through 1968**

NL—20—Chicago, 1947-1966
AL—16—Philadelphia/Kansas City/Oakland, 1953-1968

**Most consecutive years without lowest winning percentage, season**

NL—87—St. Louis, 1919-2005
AL—73—Boston, 1933-2005

## GAMES FINISHED AHEAD AND BEHIND

**Best gain in games from previous season, pennant winner**

AA—64 games—Louisville, 1889 to 1890
1889—won 27, lost 111, .196, 8th place
1890—won 88, lost 44, .667
NL—41.5 games—Brooklyn, 1898 to 1899*
1898—won 54, lost 91, .372, 10th place
1899—won 88, lost 42, .677 (*some sources list 1899 record as 101-47, but NL president threw out 18 Brooklyn games for using an illegal player)
NL (12 clubs)—29 games—Atlanta, 1990 to 1991
1990—won 65, lost 97, .401, 6th place
1991—won 94, lost 68, .580
NL (8-clubs)—27 games—New York, 1953 to 1954
1953—won 70, lost 84, .455, 5th place
1954—won 97, lost 57, .630
AL (8-clubs)—33 games—Boston, 1945 to 1946
1945—won 71, lost 83, .461, 7th place
1946—won 104, lost 50, .675

**Best gain in games by any club from previous season**

AA—64—Louisville, 1889 to 1890
1889—won 27, lost 111, .196, 8th place
1890—won 88, lost 44, .667, 1st place
NL—41.5—Brooklyn, 1898 to 1899*
1898—won 54, lost 91, .372, 10th place
1899—won 88, lost 42, .677, 1st place (*some sources list 1899 record as 101-47, but NL president threw out 18 Brooklyn games for using an illegal player)
NL since 1900 (8-clubs)—34.5—New York, 1902 to 1903
1902—won 48, lost 88, .353, 8th place
1903—won 84, lost 55, .604, 2nd place
NL (10-clubs)—27.5—Chicago, 1966 to 1967
1966—won 59, lost 103, .364, 10th place
1967—won 87, lost 74, .540, 3rd place
NL (12-clubs)—29—Atlanta, 1990 to 1991
1990—won 65, lost 97, .401, 6th place
1991—won 94, lost 68, .580, 1st place
NL (14-clubs)—31—San Francisco, 1992 to 1993
1992—won 72, lost 90, .444, 5th place
1993—won 103, lost 59, .636, 2nd place
NL (16-clubs)—35—Arizona, 1998 to 1999
1998—won 65, lost 97, .401, 5th place
1999—won 100, lost 62, .617, 1st place
AL—33—Boston, 1945 to 1946
1945—won 71, lost 83, .461, 7th place
1946—won 104, lost 50, .675, 1st place

**Best gain in position from previous season, any club, through 1968**

NL—10th to 1st—Brooklyn, 1898 to 1899*
1898—won 54, lost 91, .372, 41.5 games behind
1899—won 88, lost 42, .677 (*some sources list 1899 record as 101-47, but NL president threw out 18 Brooklyn games for using an illegal player)
NL since 1900 (8-clubs)—7th to 1st—Los Angeles, 1958 to 1959
1958—won 71, lost 83, .461, 16 games behind
1959—won 88, lost 68, .564
NL (12-clubs)—9th to 1st—New York, 1968 to 1969
1968—won 73, lost 89, .451, 27 games behind
1969—won 100, lost 62, .617
AA—8th to 1st—Louisville, 1889 to 1890
1889—won 27, lost 111, .196, 64 games behind
1890—won 88, lost 44, .667
AL (8-clubs)—7th to 1st—New York, 1925 to 1926
1925—won 69, lost 85, .448, 22 games behind
1926—won 91, lost 63, .591
Boston, 1945 to 1946
1945—won 71, lost 83, .461, 33 games behind
1946—won 104, lost 50, .675
AL (10-clubs)—9th to 1st—Boston, 1966 to 1967
1966—won 72, lost 90, .444, 20 games behind
1967—won 92, lost 70, .568

**Most games leading league or division at end of season**

AL—30—Cleveland, 1995
NL—27.5—Pittsburgh, 1902

**Fewest games leading league or division at end of season (before any playoff)**

NL—0—St. Louis and Brooklyn, 1946 (8-club league)
New York and Brooklyn, 1951 (8-club league)
Los Angeles and Milwaukee, 1959 (8-club league)
San Francisco and Los Angeles, 1962 (10-club league)
Houston and Los Angeles, 1980 (12-club league)
Houston and St. Louis, 2001 (16-club league)
AL—0—Cleveland and Boston, 1948 (8-club league)
New York and Boston, 1978 (14-club league)
Oakland and Seattle, 2000 (14-club league)

Boston and New York, 2005 (14-club league)

**Largest lead (in games) for pennant winner on July 4, p.m., through 1968**
NL—14.5—New York, 1912
AL—12—New York, 1928

**Most games behind, eventual pennant winner, on July 4, p.m., through 1968**
NL—15—Boston, 1914 (8th place)
AL—6.5—Detroit, 1907 (4th place)

**Most games behind pennant winner, last-place club, through 1968**
NL (12-club league)—80—Cleveland, 1899
NL since 1900 (8-club league)—66.5—Boston, 1906
AL (8-club league)—64.5—St. Louis, 1939

**Fewest games behind pennant winner, last-place club, through 1968**
NL (8-club league)—21—New York, 1915
AL (8-club league)—25—Washington, 1944 (24—Philadelphia in shortened 1918 season)

**Most games behind Eastern Division leader, last-place club, since 1969**
NL—52—Florida, 1998
AL—51—Tampa Bay, 1998

**Most games behind Central Division leader, last-place club, since 1994**
AL—47—Detroit, 2003
NL—41—Milwaukee, 2002

**Most games behind Western Division leader, last-place club, since 1969**
NL—43.5—Houston, 1975
AL—43—Texas, 2001

**Fewest games behind Eastern Division leader, last-place club, since 1969**
NL—9—Washington, 2005
AL—17—Toronto, 1982
Cleveland, 1982

**Fewest games behind Central Division leader, last-place club, since 1994**
NL—15—Pittsburgh, 1996
AL—19—Kansas City, 1997 (15—Milwaukee in shortened 1994 season)

**Western Division leader, last-place club, since 1969**
AL—10—California, 1987
Texas, 1987
NL—15—Colorado, 2005

## PENNANT-CLINCHING DATES

**Fewest games played before clinching pennant**
AL—136—New York, Sept 4, 1941 (won 91, lost 45, .669)
NL—137—New York, Sept 22, 1904 (won 100, lost 37, .730)

**Earliest date for pennant clinching, through 1968**
AL—Sept 4, 1941—New York (won 91, lost 45, .669, 136th game)
NL—Sept 8, 1955—Brooklyn (won 92, lost 46, .667, 138th game)

**Earliest date for Western Division pennant clinching, since 1969**
AL—Sept 15, 1971, 1st game—Oakland (won 94, lost 55, .631, 148th game)
NL—Sept 7, 1975—Cincinnati (won 95, lost 47, .669, 142nd game)

**Earliest date for Eastern Division pennant clinching, since 1969**
AL—Sept 13, 1969—Baltimore (won 101, lost 45, .690, 146th game)
NL—Sept 17, 1986—New York (won 95, lost 50, .655, 145th game)

## DAYS IN FIRST PLACE

**Leading or tied for first place for entire season**
AL—New York, 1927
Detroit (East), 1984
Baltimore (East), 1997
Cleveland (Central), 1998
Seattle (West), 2001
NL—New York, 1923
Brooklyn Dodgers, 1955
Cincinnati Reds (West), 1990
San Francisco (West), 2003

**Fewest days in first place, season, for pennant winner, through 1968**
NL—3—New York, 1951 (before playoff)
AL—20—Boston, 1967 (6 days alone)

## ATTENDANCE

**Highest home attendance, season**
NL—4,483,350—Colorado, 1993
AL—4,090,696—New York, 2005

**For a complete list of clubs with 3,200,000 or higher home attendance, see page 144.**

**Highest road attendance, season**
NL—3,016,074—Cincinnati, 2000
AL—3,308,666—New York, 2004

**Largest crowd, day game**
NL—80,227—Montreal at Colorado, Apr 9, 1993 (opener)
AL—74,420—Detroit at Cleveland, Apr 7, 1973 (opener)

**Largest crowd, night game**
AL—78,382—Chicago at Cleveland, Aug 20, 1948
NL—72,208—San Francisco at Colorado, July 31, 1993

**Largest crowd, doubleheader**
AL—84,587—New York at Cleveland, Sept 12, 1954
NL—72,140—Cincinnati at Los Angeles, Aug 16, 1961

**Largest crowd, opening day**
NL—80,227—Montreal at Colorado, Apr 9, 1993
AL—74,420—Detroit at Cleveland, Apr 7, 1973

# LEAGUE MISCELLANEOUS

## NIGHT GAMES

**Most night games, season (through 1996)**
AL (14-club league)—830 in 1982
AL (12-club league)—652 in 1975
AL (10-club league)—484 in 1968
NL (14-club league)—761 in 1993
NL (12-club league)—674 in 1990
NL (10-club league)—487 in 1968

**Most night games in both leagues, season (1997- )**
1,677 in 1998 (875 in 16-club NL; 802 in 14-club AL; includes interleague games)

## CANCELED AND POSTPONED GAMES

**Most unplayed games, season (since 1900, except 1918)**
AL—19 in 1901
NL—14 in 1938

**Fewest unplayed scheduled games, season (since 1900)**
NL-AL—0—many years

**Fewest unplayed games in both leagues, season**
0 in 1930, 1947, 1949, 1951, 1954, 1956, 1959, 1960, 1964, 1972, 1982, 1983, 1992, 1993, 1998, 2005 (16 years)

**Most postponed games, season**
AL (8-club league)—97 in 1935
NL (10-club league)—49 in 1967
NL (8-club league)—49 in 1956

**Fewest postponed dates, season**
NL—12 in 1987
AL—15 in 1987

**Most postponed doubleheaders, season**
AL—14 in 1945
NL—5 in 1959

**Fewest postponed doubleheaders, season**
AL—0 in 1914, 1957
NL—0 in 1961, 1966, 1970

## TIE GAMES

**Most tie games, season**
AL—19 in 1910
NL—16 in 1913

**Most tie games, one day**
NL—3, Apr 6, 1897
AL—2—many days

**Fewest tie games, season**
NL—0 in 1925, 1954, 1958, 1970, 1976-1978, 1982, 1984, 1986, 1987, 1990-1992, 1995-1997, 1999, 2001, 2003-2005 (22 seasons)
AL—0 in 1930, 1963, 1965, 1971-1973, 1975-1979, 1987-1994, 1997, 2000, 2002, 2004, 2005 (24 seasons)

**Most 0-0 games, season**
AL—6 in 1904
NL—3 in 1917

## EXTRA-INNING GAMES

**Most extra-inning games, season (through 1996)**
AL (14-club league)—117 in 1991
AL (12-club league)—115 in 1976
AL (10-club league)—91 in 1965
AL (8-club league)—91 in 1943
NL (14-club league)—108 in 1976
NL (12-club league)—116 in 1986
NL (10-club league)—93 in 1967
NL (8-club league)—86 in 1916

**Most extra-inning games in both leagues, season (1997- )**
218 in 2004 (119 in 16-club NL; 99 in 14-club AL; includes interleague games)

**Most extra-inning games, one day**
NL—5—May 30, 1892, May 11, 1988
AL—4—June 11, 1969, June 4, 1976

**Most extra-inning games in both leagues, one day**
6 on Aug 22, 1951; 3 in NL (5 G), 3 in AL (5 G)
6 on May 12, 1963; 4 in NL (8 G), 2 in AL (7 G)
6 on May 11, 1988; 5 in NL (6 G), 1 in AL (6 G)

## 100- AND 90-WIN AND LOSS SEASONS

**Most clubs winning 100 or more games, season**
AL (14-club league)—2 in 1977, 1980, 2001, 2002
AL (12-club league)—2 in 1971
AL (10-club league)—2 in 1961
AL (8-club league)—2 in 1915, 1954
NL (16-club league)—2 in 1998, 1999, 2003
NL (14-club league)—2 in 1993
NL (12-club league)—2 in 1976
NL (10-club league)—2 in 1962
NL (8-club league)—2 in 1909, 1942

**For a complete list of clubs with 100 or more victories in a season, see page 140.**

**Most clubs winning 90 or more games, season**
AL (14-club league)—6 in 1977, 2002
AL (12-club league)—4 in 1975
AL (8-club league)—4 in 1950
NL (16-club league)—5 in 1999, 2002, 2004
NL (14-club league)—4 in 1993
NL (12-club league)—4 in 1969, 1976, 1980, 1987
NL (10-club league)—4 in 1962, 1964
NL (8-club league)—3—many seasons

**Most clubs losing 100 or more games, season**
AL (14-club league)—3 in 2002
AL (10-club league)—2 in 1961, 1964, 1965
AL (8-club league)—2 in 1912, 1932, 1949, 1954
NL (16-club league)—1 in 2001, 2002, 2004
NL (14-club league)—2 in 1993
NL (12-club league)—2 in 1969, 1985
NL (10-club league)—2 in 1962
NL (8-club league)—2 in 1898, 1905, 1908, 1923, 1938

**For a complete list of clubs with 100 or more games lost in a season, see page 141.**

## HOME AND ROAD VICTORIES

**Most games won by home clubs, season**
NL (16-club league)—720 in 2003 (lost 575)
NL (14-club league)—641 in 1996 (lost 493)
NL (12-club league)—556 in 1978 (lost 415), 1980 (lost 416)
NL (10-club league)—464 in 1967 (lost 345)
NL (8-club league)—358 in 1931 (lost 256), 1955 (lost 257)
AL (14-club league)—649 in 1978 (lost 482)
AL (12-club league)—540 in 1969 (lost 431)
AL (10-club league)—454 in 1961 (lost 353)
AL (8-club league)—360 in 1945 (lost 244), 1949 (lost 256)

**Most games won by home clubs, one day**
NL-AL (8-club leagues)—8—many days

**Most games won by home clubs in both leagues, one day**
14 on May 30, 1903 (AL won 8, lost 0; NL won 6, lost 2)

**Most games won by visiting clubs, season**
NL (16-club league)—622 in 1999 (lost 674); 622 in 2004 (lost 673)
NL (14-club league)—532 in 1993 (lost 602)
NL (12-club league)—473 in 1982 (lost 499)
NL (10-club league)—400 in 1968 (lost 410)
NL (8-club league)—307 in 1948 (lost 308)
AL (14-club league)—547 in 1980 (lost 582)
AL (12-club league)—469 in 1971 (lost 497)
AL (10-club league)—391 in 1968 (lost 418)
AL (8-club league)—312 in 1953 (lost 301)

**Most games won by visiting clubs, one day**
NL-AL (8-club league)—8—many days

**Most games won by visiting clubs in both leagues, one day**
(8-club leagues)—12 on July 4, 1935 (N.L. won 7, lost 1; AL won 5, lost 3)
12 on Aug 5, 1951 (N.L. won 7, lost 0; AL won 5, lost 2)
12 on June 15, 1958 (AL won 8, lost 0; NL won 4, lost 1)

## ONE-RUN DECISIONS

**Most games won by one run, season (through 1996)**
NL (14-club league)—356 in 1993
NL (12-club league)—346 in 1986
NL (10-club league)—294 in 1968
NL (8-club league)—223 in 1946
AL (14-club league)—368 in 1978
AL (12-club league)—332 in 1969
AL (10-club league)—281 in 1967, 1968
AL (8-club league)—217 in 1943

**Fewest games won by one run, season (through 1996)**
AL (14-club league)—300 in 1996
AL (12-club league)—279 in 1973
AL (10-club league)—242 in 1963
AL (8-club league)—157 in 1938
NL (14-club league)—351 in 1996
NL (12-club league)—286 in 1990
NL (10-club league)—242 in 1962
NL (8-club league)—170 in 1949

**Most games won by one run, one day (through 1996)**
AL—6—May 30, 1967 (10 G); Aug 22, 1967 (9 G)
NL—6—June 6, 1967 (7 G); June 8, 1969 (6 G)

**Most games won by one run both leagues, one day (through 1996)**
10 on May 30, 1967, AL 6 (10 G), NL 4 (7 G)

## ATTENDANCE

**Highest attendance, season**
NL (16-club league)—41,643,985 in 2005
NL (14-club league)—36,923,856 in 1993
NL (12-club league)—25,323,834 in 1989
NL (10-club league)—15,015,471 in 1966
NL (8-club league)—10,684,963 in 1960
AL (14-club league)—33,332,603 in 1993
AL (12-club league)—14,657,802 in 1976
AL (10-club league)—11,336,923 in 1967
AL (8-club league)—11,150,099 in 1948

# NON-PLAYING PERSONNEL

## MANAGERS

### INDIVIDUAL

**Most years as manager**
ML—53—Connie Mack, Pittsburgh NL (1894-1896), Philadelphia AL (1901-1950)
AL—50—Connie Mack, Philadelphia, 1901-1950
NL—32—John McGraw, Baltimore, 1899; New York, 1902-1932

**Most clubs managed, career**
ML—7—Frank Bancroft, Worcester NL, Detroit NL, Cleveland NL, Providence NL, Philadelphia AA, Indianapolis NL, Cincinnati NL
ML since 1900—6—Rogers Hornsby, St. Louis NL, New York NL, Boston NL, Chicago NL, St. Louis AL, Cincinnati NL
Jimmie Dykes, Chicago AL, Philadelphia AL, Baltimore AL, Cincinnati NL, Detroit AL, Cleveland AL
Dick Williams, Boston AL, Oakland AL, California AL, Montreal NL, San Diego NL, Seattle AL
John McNamara, Oakland AL, San Diego NL, Cincinnati NL, California AL, Boston AL, Cleveland AL
NL—6—Frank Bancroft, Worcester, Detroit, Cleveland, Providence, Indianapolis, Cincinnati
NL since 1900—5—Rogers Hornsby, St. Louis, New York, Boston, Chicago, Cincinnati

AL—5—Jimmie Dykes, Chicago, Philadelphia, Baltimore, Detroit, Cleveland
Billy Martin, Minnesota, Detroit, Texas, New York, Oakland

**Most clubs managed in one season**

UA—2—Ted Sullivan, St. Louis, Kansas City, 1884
AA—2—Billy Barnie, Baltimore, Philadelphia, 1891
NL—2—Leo Durocher, Brooklyn, New York, 1948
Leo Durocher, Chicago, Houston, 1972
AL—2—Jimmie Dykes, Detroit, Cleveland, 1960
Joe Gordon, Cleveland, Detroit, 1960
Billy Martin, Detroit, Texas, 1973
Billy Martin, Texas, New York, 1975
Bob Lemon, Chicago, New York, 1978
Tony La Russa, Chicago, Oakland, 1986

**Most clubs managed in different major leagues, season**

2—Joe Battin, 1884 (Pittsburgh AA, Pittsburgh UA)
Bill Watkins, 1888 (Detroit NL, Kansas City AA)
Gus Schmelz, 1890 (Cleveland NL, Columbus AA)
John McGraw, 1902 (Baltimore AL, New York NL)
Rogers Hornsby, 1952 (St. Louis AL, Cincinnati NL)
Bill Virdon, 1975 (New York AL, Houston NL)
Pat Corrales, 1983 (Philadelphia NL, Cleveland AL)
Buck Rodgers, 1991 (Montreal NL, California AL)

**Most different times as manager for one major league club**

AL—5—Billy Martin, New York, 1975 (part)-1978 (part), 1979 (part), 1983, 1985 (part), 1988 (part)
NL—4—Danny Murtaugh, Pittsburgh, 1957 (part)-1964; 1967 (part), 1970-1971, 1973 (part)-1976

**Most years managing championship club, league**

NL—10—John McGraw, New York, 1904, 1905, 1911-1913, 1917, 1921-1923, 1924
AL—10—Casey Stengel, New York, 1949-1953, 1955-1958, 1960

**Most consecutive years as championship manager**

AL—5—Casey Stengel, New York, 1949-1953 (first 5 seasons as New York manager)
AA—4—Charlie Comiskey, St. Louis, 1885-1888
NL—4—John McGraw, New York, 1921-1924

**Most years managed without winning championship, career**

ML—26—Gene Mauch, Philadelphia NL, 1960 to 1968; Montreal NL, 1969-1975; Minnesota AL, 1976-1980; California AL, 1981-1982, 1985-1987
AL—20—Jimmie Dykes, Chicago, 1934-1946, Philadelphia, 1951-1953, Baltimore, 1954, Detroit, 1959, 1960, Cleveland, 1960, 1961
NL—16—Gene Mauch, Philadelphia, 1960-1968; Montreal, 1969-1975

**Most consecutive years managed without winning championship**

ML—23—Gene Mauch, Philadelphia NL, 1960-1968; Montreal NL, 1969-1975; Minnesota AL, 1976-1980; California AL, 1981-1982
AL—19—Connie Mack, Philadelphia, 1932-1950
NL—16—Gene Mauch, Philadelphia, 1960-1968; Montreal, 1969-1975

**Youngest manager to start season**

Lou Boudreau, Cleveland AL, appointed Nov 25, 1941; 24 years, 4 months, 8 days

**Youngest manager to finish season**

Roger Peckinpaugh, New York AL, appointed Sept 16, 1914; 23 years, 7 months, 11 days

**Oldest to make debut as manager**

Tom Sheehan, San Francisco NL, appointed June 18, 1960; 66 years, 2 months, 18 days

## CLUB

**Most managers on one club, season**

AA—7—Louisville, 1889
NL—4—Washington, 1892, 1898
St. Louis, 1895, 1896, 1897, 1980
Chicago, 1961
AL—4—Texas, 1977

## LEAGUE

**Most managers, season (since 1900)**

AL (14-club league)—19—1977, 1981, 1986 (Tony La Russa, Chicago, Oakland, counted as one), 1988
AL (12-club league)—16—1969, 1975
AL (10-club league)—15—1966
AL (8-club league)—12—1933, 1946
NL (12-club league)—16—1972, 1991 (Leo Durocher, Chicago, Houston, counted as one in 1972)
NL (14-club league)—16—1993
NL (16-club league)—18—2001, 2003, 2004, 2005
NL (8-club league)—12—1902, 1948 (Leo Durocher, Brooklyn, New York, counted as one in 1948)
NL (10-club league)—12—1965, 1966, 1967, 1968

**Most player/managers in both leagues, season**

10—1934, 6 in NL, 4 in AL (both 8-club leagues)

**Most managerial changes, start of season**

AL—6—1955
NL—5—2001

## UMPIRES

**Most years umpired**

NL—37—Bill Klem, 1905-1941
AL—31—Tommy Connolly, 1901-1931 (also NL, 1898-1900)

**Longest game, plate umpire by time**

AL—8 hrs, 6 min—Jim Evans, Milwaukee at Chicago, May 8, 1984, finished May 9, 25 inn (Chicago won 7-6.)
NL—7 hrs, 23 min—Ed Sudol, San Francisco at New York, May 31, 1964, 2nd game, 23 inn (San Francisco won 8-6.)

# YEARLY LEADERS

## BATTING

## BATTING AVERAGE

### AMERICAN LEAGUE

| Year | Player, Club | BA |
|---|---|---|
| 1901 | Nap Lajoie, Philadelphia | .426 |
| 1902 | Nap Lajoie, Philadelphia | .378 |
| 1903 | Nap Lajoie, Cleveland | .344 |
| 1904 | Nap Lajoie, Cleveland | .376 |
| 1905 | Elmer Flick, Cleveland | .308 |
| 1906 | George Stone, St. Louis | .358 |
| 1907 | Ty Cobb, Detroit | .350 |
| 1908 | Ty Cobb, Detroit | .324 |
| 1909 | Ty Cobb, Detroit | .377 |
| 1910 | Ty Cobb, Detroit | .383 |
| 1911 | Ty Cobb, Detroit | .420 |
| 1912 | Ty Cobb, Detroit | .409 |
| 1913 | Ty Cobb, Detroit | .390 |
| 1914 | Ty Cobb, Detroit | .368 |
| 1915 | Ty Cobb, Detroit | .369 |
| 1916 | Tris Speaker, Cleveland | .386 |
| 1917 | Ty Cobb, Detroit | .383 |
| 1918 | Ty Cobb, Detroit | .382 |
| 1919 | Ty Cobb, Detroit | .384 |
| 1920 | George Sisler, St. Louis | .407 |
| 1921 | Harry Heilmann, Detroit | .394 |
| 1922 | George Sisler, St. Louis | .420 |
| 1923 | Harry Heilmann, Detroit | .403 |
| 1924 | Babe Ruth, New York | .378 |
| 1925 | Harry Heilmann, Detroit | .393 |
| 1926 | Heinie Manush, Detroit | .378 |
| 1927 | Harry Heilmann, Detroit | .398 |
| 1928 | Goose Goslin, Washington | .379 |
| 1929 | Lew Fonseca, Cleveland | .369 |
| 1930 | Al Simmons, Philadelphia | .381 |
| 1931 | Al Simmons, Philadelphia | .390 |
| 1932 | Dale Alexander, Detroit/Boston | .367 |
| 1933 | Jimmie Foxx, Philadelphia | .356 |
| 1934 | Lou Gehrig, New York | .363 |
| 1935 | Buddy Myer, Washington | .349 |
| 1936 | Luke Appling, Chicago | .388 |
| 1937 | Charlie Gehringer, Detroit | .371 |
| 1938 | Jimmie Foxx, Boston | .349 |
| 1939 | Joe DiMaggio, New York | .381 |
| 1940 | Joe DiMaggio, New York | .352 |
| 1941 | Ted Williams, Boston | .406 |
| 1942 | Ted Williams, Boston | .356 |
| 1943 | Luke Appling, Chicago | .328 |
| 1944 | Lou Boudreau, Cleveland | .327 |
| 1945 | George Stirnweiss, New York | .309 |
| 1946 | Mickey Vernon, Washington | .353 |
| 1947 | Ted Williams, Boston | .343 |
| 1948 | Ted Williams, Boston | .369 |
| 1949 | George Kell, Detroit | .343 |
| 1950 | Billy Goodman, Boston | .354 |
| 1951 | Ferris Fain, Philadelphia | .344 |
| 1952 | Ferris Fain, Philadelphia | .327 |
| 1953 | Mickey Vernon, Washington | .337 |
| 1954 | Bobby Avila, Cleveland | .341 |
| 1955 | Al Kaline, Detroit | .340 |
| 1956 | Mickey Mantle, New York | .353 |
| 1957 | Ted Williams, Boston | .388 |
| 1958 | Ted Williams, Boston | .328 |
| 1959 | Harvey Kuenn, Detroit | .353 |
| 1960 | Pete Runnels, Boston | .320 |
| 1961 | Norm Cash, Detroit | .361 |
| 1962 | Pete Runnels, Boston | .326 |
| 1963 | Carl Yastrzemski, Boston | .321 |
| 1964 | Tony Oliva, Minnesota | .323 |
| 1965 | Tony Oliva, Minnesota | .321 |
| 1966 | Frank Robinson, Baltimore | .316 |
| 1967 | Carl Yastrzemski, Boston | .326 |
| 1968 | Carl Yastrzemski, Boston | .301 |
| 1969 | Rod Carew, Minnesota | .332 |
| 1970 | Alex Johnson, California | .329 |
| 1971 | Tony Oliva, Minnesota | .337 |
| 1972 | Rod Carew, Minnesota | .318 |
| 1973 | Rod Carew, Minnesota | .350 |
| 1974 | Rod Carew, Minnesota | .364 |
| 1975 | Rod Carew, Minnesota | .359 |
| 1976 | George Brett, Kansas City | .333 |
| 1977 | Rod Carew, Minnesota | .388 |
| 1978 | Rod Carew, Minnesota | .333 |
| 1979 | Fred Lynn, Boston | .333 |
| 1980 | George Brett, Kansas City | .390 |
| 1981 | Carney Lansford, Boston | .336 |
| 1982 | Willie Wilson, Kansas City | .332 |
| 1983 | Wade Boggs, Boston | .361 |
| 1984 | Don Mattingly, New York | .343 |
| 1985 | Wade Boggs, Boston | .368 |
| 1986 | Wade Boggs, Boston | .357 |
| 1987 | Wade Boggs, Boston | .363 |
| 1988 | Wade Boggs, Boston | .366 |
| 1989 | Kirby Puckett, Minnesota | .339 |

| Year | Player, Club | BA |
|---|---|---|
| 1990 | George Brett, Kansas City | .329 |
| 1991 | Julio Franco, Texas | .341 |
| 1992 | Edgar Martinez, Seattle | .343 |
| 1993 | John Olerud, Toronto | .363 |
| 1994 | Paul O'Neill, New York | .359 |
| 1995 | Edgar Martinez, Seattle | .356 |
| 1996 | Alex Rodriguez, Seattle | .358 |
| 1997 | Frank E. Thomas, Chicago | .347 |
| 1998 | Bernie Williams, New York | .339 |
| 1999 | Nomar Garciaparra, Boston | .357 |
| 2000 | Nomar Garciaparra, Boston | .372 |
| 2001 | Ichiro Suzuki, Seattle | .350 |
| 2002 | Manny Ramirez, Boston | .349 |
| 2003 | Bill Mueller, Boston | .326 |
| 2004 | Ichiro Suzuki, Seattle | .372 |
| 2005 | Michael Young, Texas | .331 |

## NATIONAL LEAGUE

| Year | Player, Club | BA |
|---|---|---|
| 1876 | Ross Barnes, Chicago | .429 |
| 1877 | Deacon White, Boston | .387 |
| 1878 | Paul Hines, Providence | .358 |
| 1879 | Paul Hines, Providence | .357 |
| 1880 | George Gore, Chicago | .360 |
| 1881 | Cap Anson, Chicago | .399 |
| 1882 | Dan Brouthers, Buffalo | .368 |
| 1883 | Dan Brouthers, Buffalo | .374 |
| 1884 | King Kelly, Chicago | .354 |
| 1885 | Roger Connor, New York | .371 |
| 1886 | King Kelly, Chicago | .388 |
| 1887 | Sam Thompson, Detroit | .372 |
| 1888 | Cap Anson, Chicago | .344 |
| 1889 | Dan Brouthers, Boston | .373 |
| 1890 | Jack Glasscock, New York | .336 |
| 1891 | Billy Hamilton, Philadelphia | .340 |
| 1892 | Dan Brouthers, Brooklyn | .335 |
| 1893 | Billy Hamilton, Philadelphia | .380 |
| 1894 | Hugh Duffy, Boston | .440 |
| 1895 | Jesse Burkett, Cleveland | .405 |
| 1896 | Jesse Burkett, Cleveland | .410 |
| 1897 | Willie Keeler, Baltimore | .424 |
| 1898 | Willie Keeler, Baltimore | .385 |
| 1899 | Ed Delahanty, Philadelphia | .410 |
| 1900 | Honus Wagner, Pittsburgh | .381 |
| 1901 | Jesse Burkett, St. Louis | .376 |
| 1902 | Ginger Beaumont, Pittsburgh | .357 |
| 1903 | Honus Wagner, Pittsburgh | .355 |
| 1904 | Honus Wagner, Pittsburgh | .349 |
| 1905 | Cy Seymour, Cincinnati | .377 |
| 1906 | Honus Wagner, Pittsburgh | .339 |
| 1907 | Honus Wagner, Pittsburgh | .350 |
| 1908 | Honus Wagner, Pittsburgh | .354 |
| 1909 | Honus Wagner, Pittsburgh | .339 |
| 1910 | Sherry Magee, Philadelphia | .331 |
| 1911 | Honus Wagner, Pittsburgh | .334 |
| 1912 | Heinie Zimmerman, Chicago | .372 |
| 1913 | Jake Daubert, Brooklyn | .350 |
| 1914 | Jake Daubert, Brooklyn | .329 |
| 1915 | Larry Doyle, New York | .320 |
| 1916 | Hal Chase, Cincinnati | .339 |
| 1917 | Edd Roush, Cincinnati | .341 |
| 1918 | Zack Wheat, Brooklyn | .335 |
| 1919 | Edd Roush, Cincinnati | .321 |
| 1920 | Rogers Hornsby, St. Louis | .370 |
| 1921 | Rogers Hornsby, St. Louis | .397 |
| 1922 | Rogers Hornsby, St. Louis | .401 |
| 1923 | Rogers Hornsby, St. Louis | .384 |
| 1924 | Rogers Hornsby, St. Louis | .424 |
| 1925 | Rogers Hornsby, St. Louis | .403 |
| 1926 | Bubbles Hargrave, Cincinnati | .353 |
| 1927 | Paul Waner, Pittsburgh | .380 |
| 1928 | Rogers Hornsby, Boston | .387 |
| 1929 | Lefty O'Doul, Philadelphia | .398 |
| 1930 | Bill Terry, New York | .401 |
| 1931 | Chick Hafey, St. Louis | .349 |
| 1932 | Lefty O'Doul, Brooklyn | .368 |
| 1933 | Chuck Klein, Philadelphia | .368 |
| 1934 | Paul Waner, Pittsburgh | .362 |
| 1935 | Arky Vaughan, Pittsburgh | .385 |
| 1936 | Paul Waner, Pittsburgh | .373 |
| 1937 | Joe Medwick, St. Louis | .374 |
| 1938 | Ernie Lombardi, Cincinnati | .342 |
| 1939 | Johnny Mize, St. Louis | .349 |
| 1940 | Debs Garms, Pittsburgh | .355 |
| 1941 | Pete Reiser, Brooklyn | .343 |
| 1942 | Ernie Lombardi, Boston | .330 |
| 1943 | Stan Musial, St. Louis | .357 |
| 1944 | Dixie Walker, Brooklyn | .357 |
| 1945 | Phil Cavarretta, Chicago | .355 |
| 1946 | Stan Musial, St. Louis | .365 |
| 1947 | Harry Walker, St. Louis/Philadelphia | .363 |
| 1948 | Stan Musial, St. Louis | .376 |
| 1949 | Jackie Robinson, Brooklyn | .342 |
| 1950 | Stan Musial, St. Louis | .346 |
| 1951 | Stan Musial, St. Louis | .355 |
| 1952 | Stan Musial, St. Louis | .336 |
| 1953 | Carl Furillo, Brooklyn | .344 |
| 1954 | Willie Mays, New York | .345 |
| 1955 | Richie Ashburn, Philadelphia | .338 |
| 1956 | Hank Aaron, Milwaukee | .328 |
| 1957 | Stan Musial, St. Louis | .351 |
| 1958 | Richie Ashburn, Philadelphia | .350 |
| 1959 | Hank Aaron, Milwaukee | .355 |
| 1960 | Dick Groat, Pittsburgh | .325 |
| 1961 | Roberto Clemente, Pittsburgh | .351 |
| 1962 | Tommy Davis, Los Angeles | .346 |
| 1963 | Tommy Davis, Los Angeles | .326 |
| 1964 | Roberto Clemente, Pittsburgh | .339 |
| 1965 | Roberto Clemente, Pittsburgh | .329 |
| 1966 | Matty Alou, Pittsburgh | .342 |
| 1967 | Roberto Clemente, Pittsburgh | .357 |
| 1968 | Pete Rose, Cincinnati | .335 |
| 1969 | Pete Rose, Cincinnati | .348 |
| 1970 | Rico Carty, Atlanta | .366 |
| 1971 | Joe Torre, St. Louis | .363 |
| 1972 | Billy Williams, Chicago | .333 |
| 1973 | Pete Rose, Cincinnati | .338 |
| 1974 | Ralph Garr, Atlanta | .353 |
| 1975 | Bill Madlock, Chicago | .354 |
| 1976 | Bill Madlock, Chicago | .339 |
| 1977 | Dave Parker, Pittsburgh | .338 |
| 1978 | Dave Parker, Pittsburgh | .334 |
| 1979 | Keith Hernandez, St. Louis | .344 |
| 1980 | Bill Buckner, Chicago | .324 |
| 1981 | Bill Madlock, Pittsburgh | .341 |
| 1982 | Al Oliver, Montreal | .331 |
| 1983 | Bill Madlock, Pittsburgh | .323 |
| 1984 | Tony Gwynn, San Diego | .351 |
| 1985 | Willie McGee, St. Louis | .353 |
| 1986 | Tim Raines Sr., Montreal | .334 |
| 1987 | Tony Gwynn, San Diego | .370 |
| 1988 | Tony Gwynn, San Diego | .313 |
| 1989 | Tony Gwynn, San Diego | .336 |
| 1990 | Willie McGee, St. Louis | *.335 |
| 1991 | Terry Pendleton, Atlanta | .319 |
| 1992 | Gary Sheffield, San Diego | .330 |
| 1993 | Andres Galarraga, Colorado | .370 |
| 1994 | Tony Gwynn, San Diego | .394 |
| 1995 | Tony Gwynn, San Diego | .368 |
| 1996 | Tony Gwynn, San Diego | †.353 |
| 1997 | Tony Gwynn, San Diego | .372 |
| 1998 | Larry Walker, Colorado | .363 |
| 1999 | Larry Walker, Colorado | .379 |
| 2000 | Todd Helton, Colorado | .372 |
| 2001 | Larry Walker, Colorado | .350 |
| 2002 | Barry Bonds, San Francisco | .370 |
| 2003 | Albert Pujols, St. Louis | .359 |
| 2004 | Barry Bonds, San Francisco | .362 |
| 2005 | Derrek Lee, Chicago | .335 |

Note—bases on balls not counted as outs in 1876 or as hits in 1887

*Eddie Murray of Los Angeles hit .330 in 1990, the highest batting average in the majors. McGee won the NL title, but was traded to Oakland on August 29 and finished the season with a combined .324 in for both leagues.

†Gwynn's 498 plate appearances were four short of the qualifying mark. Under Rule 10.23 (a), if Gwynn were charged with four more at-bats, his subsequent batting average of .349 would still be higher than the next-highest mark of .344, achieved by Ellis Burks of Colorado.

# SLUGGING AVERAGE

## AMERICAN LEAGUE

| Year | Player, Club | SLG |
|---|---|---|
| 1901 | Nap Lajoie, Philadelphia | .643 |
| 1902 | Ed Delahanty, Washington | .590 |
| 1903 | Nap Lajoie, Cleveland | .518 |
| 1904 | Nap Lajoie, Cleveland | .546 |
| 1905 | Elmer Flick, Cleveland | .462 |
| 1906 | George Stone, St. Louis | .501 |
| 1907 | Ty Cobb, Detroit | .468 |
| 1908 | Ty Cobb, Detroit | .475 |
| 1909 | Ty Cobb, Detroit | .517 |
| 1910 | Ty Cobb, Detroit | .551 |
| 1911 | Ty Cobb, Detroit | .621 |
| 1912 | Ty Cobb, Detroit | .584 |
| 1913 | Joe Jackson, Cleveland | .551 |
| 1914 | Ty Cobb, Detroit | .513 |
| 1915 | Jack Fournier, Chicago | .491 |
| 1916 | Tris Speaker, Cleveland | .502 |
| 1917 | Ty Cobb, Detroit | .570 |
| 1918 | Babe Ruth, Boston | .555 |
| 1919 | Babe Ruth, Boston | .657 |
| 1920 | Babe Ruth, New York | .847 |
| 1921 | Babe Ruth, New York | .846 |
| 1922 | Babe Ruth, New York | .672 |
| 1923 | Babe Ruth, New York | .764 |
| 1924 | Babe Ruth, New York | .739 |
| 1925 | Ken Williams, St. Louis | .613 |
| 1926 | Babe Ruth, New York | .737 |
| 1927 | Babe Ruth, New York | .772 |
| 1928 | Babe Ruth, New York | .709 |
| 1929 | Babe Ruth, New York | .697 |
| 1930 | Babe Ruth, New York | .732 |
| 1931 | Babe Ruth, New York | .700 |
| 1932 | Jimmie Foxx, Philadelphia | .749 |
| 1933 | Jimmie Foxx, Philadelphia | .703 |
| 1934 | Lou Gehrig, New York | .706 |
| 1935 | Jimmie Foxx, Philadelphia | .636 |
| 1936 | Lou Gehrig, New York | .696 |
| 1937 | Joe DiMaggio, New York | .673 |
| 1938 | Jimmie Foxx, Boston | .704 |
| 1939 | Jimmie Foxx, Boston | .694 |
| 1940 | Hank Greenberg, Detroit | .670 |
| 1941 | Ted Williams, Boston | .735 |
| 1942 | Ted Williams, Boston | .648 |
| 1943 | Rudy York, Detroit | .527 |
| 1944 | Bobby Doerr, Boston | .528 |
| 1945 | George Stirnweiss, New York | .476 |
| 1946 | Ted Williams, Boston | .667 |
| 1947 | Ted Williams, Boston | .634 |
| 1948 | Ted Williams, Boston | .615 |
| 1949 | Ted Williams, Boston | .650 |
| 1950 | Joe DiMaggio, New York | .585 |
| 1951 | Ted Williams, Boston | .556 |
| 1952 | Larry Doby, Cleveland | .541 |
| 1953 | Al Rosen, Cleveland | .613 |
| 1954 | Ted Williams, Boston | .635 |
| 1955 | Mickey Mantle, New York | .611 |
| 1956 | Mickey Mantle, New York | .705 |
| 1957 | Ted Williams, Boston | .731 |
| 1958 | Rocky Colavito, Cleveland | .620 |
| 1959 | Al Kaline, Detroit | .530 |
| 1960 | Roger Maris, New York | .581 |
| 1961 | Mickey Mantle, New York | .687 |
| 1962 | Mickey Mantle, New York | .605 |
| 1963 | Harmon Killebrew, Minnesota | .555 |
| 1964 | Boog Powell, Baltimore | .606 |
| 1965 | Carl Yastrzemski, Boston | .536 |
| 1966 | Frank Robinson, Baltimore | .637 |
| 1967 | Carl Yastrzemski, Boston | .622 |
| 1968 | Frank Howard, Washington | .552 |
| 1969 | Reggie Jackson, Oakland | .608 |
| 1970 | Carl Yastrzemski, Boston | .592 |
| 1971 | Tony Oliva, Minnesota | .546 |
| 1972 | Dick Allen, Chicago | .603 |
| 1973 | Reggie Jackson, Oakland | .531 |
| 1974 | Dick Allen, Chicago | .563 |
| 1975 | Fred Lynn, Boston | .566 |
| 1976 | Reggie Jackson, Baltimore | .502 |
| 1977 | Jim Rice, Boston | .593 |
| 1978 | Jim Rice, Boston | .600 |
| 1979 | Fred Lynn, Boston | .637 |
| 1980 | George Brett, Kansas City | .664 |
| 1981 | Bobby Grich, California | .543 |
| 1982 | Robin Yount, Milwaukee | .578 |
| 1983 | George Brett, Kansas City | .563 |
| 1984 | Harold Baines, Chicago | .541 |
| 1985 | George Brett, Kansas City | .585 |
| 1986 | Don Mattingly, New York | .573 |
| 1987 | Mark McGwire, Oakland | .618 |
| 1988 | Jose Canseco, Oakland | .569 |
| 1989 | Ruben Sierra, Texas | .543 |
| 1990 | Cecil Fielder, Detroit | .592 |
| 1991 | Danny Tartabull, Kansas City | .593 |
| 1992 | Mark McGwire, Oakland | .585 |
| 1993 | Juan Gonzalez, Texas | .632 |
| 1994 | Frank E. Thomas, Chicago | .729 |
| 1995 | Albert Belle, Cleveland | .690 |
| 1996 | Mark McGwire, Oakland | .730 |
| 1997 | Ken Griffey Jr., Seattle | .646 |
| 1998 | Albert Belle, Chicago | .655 |
| 1999 | Manny Ramirez, Cleveland | .663 |
| 2000 | Manny Ramirez, Cleveland | .697 |
| 2001 | Jason Giambi, Oakland | .660 |
| 2002 | Jim Thome, Cleveland | .677 |
| 2003 | Alex Rodriguez, Texas | .600 |
| 2004 | Manny Ramirez, Boston | .613 |
| 2005 | Alex Rodriguez, New York | .610 |

## NATIONAL LEAGUE

| Year | Player, Club | SLG |
|---|---|---|
| 1900 | Honus Wagner, Pittsburgh | .573 |
| 1901 | Jimmy Sheckard, Brooklyn | .534 |
| 1902 | Honus Wagner, Pittsburgh | .463 |
| 1903 | Fred Clarke, Pittsburgh | .532 |
| 1904 | Honus Wagner, Pittsburgh | .520 |
| 1905 | Cy Seymour, Cincinnati | .559 |
| 1906 | Harry Lumley, Brooklyn | .477 |
| 1907 | Honus Wagner, Pittsburgh | .513 |
| 1908 | Honus Wagner, Pittsburgh | .542 |
| 1909 | Honus Wagner, Pittsburgh | .489 |
| 1910 | Sherry Magee, Philadelphia | .507 |
| 1911 | Frank Schulte, Chicago | .534 |
| 1912 | Heinie Zimmerman, Chicago | .571 |
| 1913 | Gavvy Cravath, Philadelphia | .568 |
| 1914 | Sherry Magee, Philadelphia | .509 |
| 1915 | Gavvy Cravath, Philadelphia | .510 |
| 1916 | Zack Wheat, Brooklyn | .461 |
| 1917 | Rogers Hornsby, St. Louis | .484 |
| 1918 | Edd Roush, Cincinnati | .455 |

| Year | Player, Club | SLG |
|---|---|---|
| 1919 | Hy Myers, Brooklyn | .436 |
| 1920 | Rogers Hornsby, St. Louis | .559 |
| 1921 | Rogers Hornsby, St. Louis | .659 |
| 1922 | Rogers Hornsby, St. Louis | .722 |
| 1923 | Rogers Hornsby, St. Louis | .627 |
| 1924 | Rogers Hornsby, St. Louis | .696 |
| 1925 | Rogers Hornsby, St. Louis | .756 |
| 1926 | Cy Williams, Philadelphia | .569 |
| 1927 | Chick Hafey, St. Louis | .590 |
| 1928 | Rogers Hornsby, Boston | .632 |
| 1929 | Rogers Hornsby, Chicago | .679 |
| 1930 | Hack Wilson, Chicago | .723 |
| 1931 | Chuck Klein, Philadelphia | .584 |
| 1932 | Chuck Klein, Philadelphia | .646 |
| 1933 | Chuck Klein, Philadelphia | .602 |
| 1934 | Rip Collins, St. Louis | .615 |
| 1935 | Arky Vaughan, Pittsburgh | .607 |
| 1936 | Mel Ott, New York | .588 |
| 1937 | Joe Medwick, St. Louis | .641 |
| 1938 | Johnny Mize, St. Louis | .614 |
| 1939 | Johnny Mize, St. Louis | .626 |
| 1940 | Johnny Mize, St. Louis | .636 |
| 1941 | Pete Reiser, Brooklyn | .558 |
| 1942 | Johnny Mize, New York | .521 |
| 1943 | Stan Musial, St. Louis | .562 |
| 1944 | Stan Musial, St. Louis | .549 |
| 1945 | Tommy Holmes, Boston | .577 |
| 1946 | Stan Musial, St. Louis | .587 |
| 1947 | Ralph Kiner, Pittsburgh | .639 |
| 1948 | Stan Musial, St. Louis | .702 |
| 1949 | Ralph Kiner, Pittsburgh | .658 |
| 1950 | Stan Musial, St. Louis | .596 |
| 1951 | Ralph Kiner, Pittsburgh | .627 |
| 1952 | Stan Musial, St. Louis | .538 |
| 1953 | Duke Snider, Brooklyn | .627 |
| 1954 | Willie Mays, New York | .667 |
| 1955 | Willie Mays, New York | .659 |
| 1956 | Duke Snider, Brooklyn | .598 |
| 1957 | Willie Mays, New York | .626 |
| 1958 | Ernie Banks, Chicago | .614 |
| 1959 | Hank Aaron, Milwaukee | .636 |
| 1960 | Frank Robinson, Cincinnati | .595 |
| 1961 | Frank Robinson, Cincinnati | .611 |
| 1962 | Frank Robinson, Cincinnati | .624 |
| 1963 | Hank Aaron, Milwaukee | .586 |
| 1964 | Willie Mays, San Francisco | .607 |
| 1965 | Willie Mays, San Francisco | .645 |
| 1966 | Dick Allen, Philadelphia | .632 |
| 1967 | Hank Aaron, Atlanta | .573 |
| 1968 | Willie McCovey, San Francisco | .545 |
| 1969 | Willie McCovey, San Francisco | .656 |
| 1970 | Willie McCovey, San Francisco | .612 |
| 1971 | Hank Aaron, Atlanta | .669 |
| 1972 | Billy Williams, Chicago | .606 |
| 1973 | Willie Stargell, Pittsburgh | .646 |
| 1974 | Mike Schmidt, Philadelphia | .546 |
| 1975 | Dave Parker, Pittsburgh | .541 |
| 1976 | Joe Morgan, Cincinnati | .576 |
| 1977 | George Foster, Cincinnati | .631 |
| 1978 | Dave Parker, Pittsburgh | .585 |
| 1979 | Dave Kingman, Chicago | .613 |
| 1980 | Mike Schmidt, Philadelphia | .624 |
| 1981 | Mike Schmidt, Philadelphia | .644 |
| 1982 | Mike Schmidt, Philadelphia | .547 |
| 1983 | Dale Murphy, Atlanta | .540 |
| 1984 | Dale Murphy, Atlanta | .547 |
| 1985 | Pedro Guerrero, Los Angeles | .577 |
| 1986 | Mike Schmidt, Philadelphia | .547 |
| 1987 | Jack Clark, St. Louis | .597 |
| 1988 | Darryl Strawberry, New York | .545 |
| 1989 | Kevin Mitchell, San Francisco | .635 |
| 1990 | Barry Bonds, Pittsburgh | .565 |
| 1991 | Will Clark, San Francisco | .536 |
| 1992 | Barry Bonds, Pittsburgh | .624 |
| 1993 | Barry Bonds, San Francisco | .677 |
| 1994 | Jeff Bagwell, Houston | .750 |
| 1995 | Dante Bichette, Colorado | .620 |
| 1996 | Ellis Burks, Colorado | .639 |
| 1997 | Larry Walker, Colorado | .720 |
| 1998 | Mark McGwire, St. Louis | .752 |
| 1999 | Larry Walker, Colorado | .710 |
| 2000 | Todd Helton, Colorado | .698 |
| 2001 | Barry Bonds, San Francisco | .863 |
| 2002 | Barry Bonds, San Francisco | .799 |
| 2003 | Barry Bonds, San Francisco | .749 |
| 2004 | Barry Bonds, San Francisco | .812 |
| 2005 | Derrek Lee, Chicago | .662 |

## ON-BASE PERCENTAGE

### AMERICAN LEAGUE

| Year | Player, Club | OBP |
|---|---|---|
| 1931 | Babe Ruth, New York | .495 |
| 1932 | Babe Ruth, New York | .489 |
| 1933 | Mickey Cochrane, Philadelphia | .459 |
| 1934 | Lou Gehrig, New York | .465 |
| 1935 | Lou Gehrig, New York | .466 |
| 1936 | Lou Gehrig, New York | .478 |
| 1937 | Lou Gehrig, New York | .473 |
| 1938 | Jimmie Foxx, Boston | .462 |
| 1939 | none | |
| 1940 | Ted Williams, Boston | .442 |
| 1941 | Ted Williams, Boston | .553 |
| 1942 | Ted Williams, Boston | .499 |
| 1943 | Luke Appling, Chicago | .419 |
| 1944 | Bob Johnson, Boston | .431 |
| 1945 | Eddie Lake, Boston | .412 |
| 1946 | Ted Williams, Boston | .497 |
| 1947 | Ted Williams, Boston | .499 |
| 1948 | Ted Williams, Boston | .497 |
| 1949 | Ted Williams, Boston | .490 |
| 1950 | Larry Doby, Cleveland | .442 |
| 1951 | Ted Williams, Boston | .464 |
| 1952 | Ferris Fain, Philadelphia | .438 |
| 1953 | Gene Woodling, New York | .429 |
| 1954 | Ted Williams, Boston | .513 |
| 1955 | Mickey Mantle, New York | .431 |
| 1956 | Ted Williams, Boston | .479 |
| 1957 | Ted Williams, Boston | .526 |
| 1958 | Ted Williams, Boston | .458 |
| 1959 | Eddie Yost, Detroit | .435 |
| 1960 | Eddie Yost, Detroit | .414 |
| 1961 | Norm Cash, Detroit | .487 |
| 1962 | Mickey Mantle, New York | .486 |
| 1963 | Carl Yastrzemski, Boston | .418 |
| 1964 | Mickey Mantle, Boston | .423 |
| 1965 | Carl Yastrzemski, Boston | .395 |
| 1966 | Frank Robinson, Baltimore | .410 |
| 1967 | Carl Yastrzemski, Boston | .418 |
| 1968 | Carl Yastrzemski, Boston | .426 |
| 1969 | Harmon Killebrew, Minnesota | .427 |
| 1970 | Carl Yastrzemski, Boston | .452 |
| 1971 | Bobby Murcer, New York | .427 |
| 1972 | Dick Allen, Chicago | .420 |
| 1973 | John Mayberry, Kansas City | .417 |
| 1974 | Rod Carew, Minnesota | .433 |
| 1975 | Rod Carew, Minnesota | .421 |
| 1976 | Hal McRae, Kansas City | .407 |
| 1977 | Rod Carew, Minnesota | .449 |
| 1978 | Rod Carew, Minnesota | .411 |
| 1979 | Fred Lynn, Boston | .423 |
| 1980 | George Brett, Kansas City | .454 |
| 1981 | Mike Hargrove, Cleveland | .424 |
| 1982 | Dwight Evans, Boston | .402 |
| 1983 | Wade Boggs, Boston | .444 |
| 1984 | Eddie Murray, Baltimore | .410 |
| 1985 | Wade Boggs, Boston | .450 |
| 1986 | Wade Boggs, Boston | .453 |
| 1987 | Wade Boggs, Boston | .461 |
| 1988 | Wade Boggs, Boston | .476 |
| 1989 | Wade Boggs, Boston | .430 |
| 1990 | Rickey Henderson, Oakland | .439 |
| 1991 | Frank Thomas, Chicago | .453 |
| 1992 | Frank Thomas, Chicago | .439 |
| 1993 | John Olerud, Toronto | .473 |
| 1994 | Frank Thomas, Chicago | .487 |
| 1995 | Edgar Martinez, Seattle | .479 |
| 1996 | Mark McGwire, Oakland | .467 |
| 1997 | Frank Thomas, Chicago | .456 |
| 1998 | Edgar Martinez, Seattle | .429 |
| 1999 | Edgar Martinez, Seattle | .447 |
| 2000 | Jason Giambi, Oakland | .476 |
| 2001 | Jason Giambi, Oakland | .477 |
| 2002 | Manny Ramirez, Boston | .450 |
| 2003 | Manny Ramirez, Boston | .427 |
| 2004 | Melvin Mora, Baltimore | .419 |
| 2005 | Jason Giambi, New York | .440 |

### NATIONAL LEAGUE

| Year | Player, Club | OBP |
|---|---|---|
| 1931 | Chick Hafey, St. Louis | .404 |
| 1932 | Mel Ott, New York | .424 |
| 1933 | Chuck Klein, Philadelphia | .422 |
| 1934 | Arky Vaughan, Pittburgh | .431 |
| 1935 | Arky Vaughan, Pittsburgh | .491 |
| 1936 | Arky Vaughan, Pittsburgh | .453 |
| 1937 | Dolf Camilli, Philadelphia | .446 |
| 1938 | Mel Ott, New York | .462 |
| 1939 | none | |
| 1940 | Elbie Fletcher, Pittsburgh | .418 |
| 1941 | Elbie Fletcher Pittsburgh | .421 |
| 1942 | Elbie Fletcher, Pittsburgh | .417 |
| 1943 | Stan Musial, St. Louis | .425 |
| 1944 | Stan Musial, St. Louis | .440 |
| 1945 | Phil Cavaretta, Chicago | .449 |
| 1946 | Eddie Stanky, Brooklyn | .436 |
| 1947 | Augie Galan, Cincinnati | .449 |
| 1948 | Stan Musial, St. Louis | .450 |
| 1949 | Stan Musial, St. Louis | .438 |
| 1950 | Eddie Stanky, New York | .460 |
| 1951 | Ralph Kiner, Pittsburgh | .452 |
| 1952 | Jackie Robinson, Brooklyn | .440 |
| 1953 | Stan Musial, St. Louis | .437 |
| 1954 | Richie Ashburn, Philadelphia | .441 |
| 1955 | Richie Ashburn, Philadelphia | .449 |
| 1956 | Duke Snider, Brooklyn | .399 |
| 1957 | Stan Musial, St. Louis | .422 |
| 1958 | Richie Ashburn, Philadelphia | .440 |
| 1959 | Joe Cunningham, St. Louis | .453 |
| 1960 | Richie Ashburn, Chicago | .415 |
| 1961 | Wally Moon, Los Angeles | .434 |
| 1962 | Frank Robinson, Cincinnati | .421 |
| 1963 | Eddie Mathews, Milwaukee | .399 |
| 1964 | Ron Santo, Chicago | .398 |
| 1965 | Willie Mays, San Francisco | .398 |
| 1966 | Ron Santo, Chicago | .412 |
| 1967 | Dick Allen, Philadelphia | .404 |
| 1968 | Pete Rose, Cincinnati | .391 |
| 1969 | Willie McCovey, San Francisco | .453 |
| 1970 | Rico Carty, Atlanta | .454 |
| 1971 | Willie Mays, San Francisco | .425 |
| 1972 | Joe Morgan, Cincinnati | .417 |
| 1973 | Ken Singleton, Montreal | .425 |
| 1974 | Joe Morgan, Cincinnati | .427 |
| 1975 | Joe Morgan, Cincinnati | .466 |
| 1976 | Joe Morgan, Cincinnati | .444 |
| 1977 | Reggie Smith, Los Angeles | .427 |
| 1978 | Jeff Burroughs, Atlanta | .432 |
| 1979 | Pete Rose, Philadelphia | .418 |
| 1980 | Keith Hernandez, St. Louis | .408 |
| 1981 | Mike Schmidt, Philadelphia | .435 |
| 1982 | Mike Schmidt, Philadelphia | .403 |
| 1983 | Mike Schmidt, Philadelphia | .399 |
| 1984 | Gary Matthews, Chicago | .410 |
| 1985 | Pedro Guerrero, Los Angeles | .422 |
| 1986 | Tim Raines, Montreal | .413 |
| 1987 | Jack Clark, St. Louis | .459 |
| 1988 | Kal Daniels, Cincinnati | .397 |
| 1989 | Lonnie Smith, Atlanta | .415 |
| 1990 | Lennie Dykstra, Philadelphia | .418 |
| 1991 | Barry Bonds, Pittsburgh | .410 |
| 1992 | Barry Bonds, Pittsburgh | .456 |
| 1993 | Barry Bonds, San Francisco | .458 |
| 1994 | Tony Gwynn, San Diego | .454 |
| 1995 | Barry Bonds, San Francisco | .431 |
| 1996 | Gary Sheffield, Florida | .465 |
| 1997 | Larry Walker, Colorado | .452 |
| 1998 | Mark McGwire, St. Louis | .470 |
| 1999 | Larry Walker, Colorado | .458 |
| 2000 | Todd Helton, Colorado | .463 |
| 2001 | Barry Bonds, San Francisco | .515 |
| 2002 | Barry Bonds, San Francisco | .582 |
| 2003 | Barry Bonds, San Francisco | .529 |
| 2004 | Barry Bonds, San Francisco | .609 |
| 2005 | Todd Helton, Colorado | .445 |

Note—calculated from official statistics, 1931-1983, except for 1939 for which there is no official tabulation of sacrifice flies; official statistic since 1984

## RUNS

### AMERICAN LEAGUE

| Year | Player, Club | Runs |
|---|---|---|
| 1901 | Nap Lajoie, Philadelphia | 145 |
| 1902 | Dave Fultz, Philadelphia | 109 |
| | Topsy Hartsel, Philadelphia | 109 |
| 1903 | Patsy Dougherty, Boston | 107 |
| 1904 | Patsy Dougherty, Boston/New York | 113 |
| 1905 | Harry Davis, Philadelphia | 93 |
| 1906 | Elmer Flick, Cleveland | 98 |
| 1907 | Sam Crawford, Detroit | 102 |
| 1908 | Matty McIntyre, Detroit | 105 |
| 1909 | Ty Cobb, Detroit | 116 |
| 1910 | Ty Cobb, Detroit | 106 |
| 1911 | Ty Cobb, Detroit | 147 |
| 1912 | Eddie Collins, Philadelphia | 137 |
| 1913 | Eddie Collins, Philadelphia | 125 |
| 1914 | Eddie Collins, Philadelphia | 122 |
| 1915 | Ty Cobb, Detroit | 144 |
| 1916 | Ty Cobb, Detroit | 113 |
| 1917 | Donie Bush, Detroit | 112 |
| 1918 | Ray Chapman, Cleveland | 84 |
| 1919 | Babe Ruth, Boston | 103 |
| 1920 | Babe Ruth, New York | 158 |
| 1921 | Babe Ruth, New York | 177 |
| 1922 | George Sisler, St. Louis | 134 |
| 1923 | Babe Ruth, New York | 151 |
| 1924 | Babe Ruth, New York | 143 |
| 1925 | Johnny Mostil, Chicago | 135 |
| 1926 | Babe Ruth, New York | 139 |
| 1927 | Babe Ruth, New York | 158 |
| 1928 | Babe Ruth, New York | 163 |
| 1929 | Charlie Gehringer, Detroit | 131 |
| 1930 | Al Simmons, Philadelphia | 152 |
| 1931 | Lou Gehrig, New York | 163 |
| 1932 | Jimmie Foxx, Philadelphia | 151 |
| 1933 | Lou Gehrig, New York | 138 |
| 1934 | Charlie Gehringer, Detroit | 134 |
| 1935 | Lou Gehrig, New York | 125 |
| 1936 | Lou Gehrig, New York | 167 |

| Year | Player, Club | Runs |
|---|---|---|
| 1937 | Joe DiMaggio, New York | 151 |
| 1938 | Hank Greenberg, Detroit | 144 |
| 1939 | Red Rolfe, New York | 139 |
| 1940 | Ted Williams, Boston | 134 |
| 1941 | Ted Williams, Boston | 135 |
| 1942 | Ted Williams, Boston | 141 |
| 1943 | George Case, Washington | 102 |
| 1944 | George Stirnweiss, New York | 125 |
| 1945 | George Stirnweiss, New York | 107 |
| 1946 | Ted Williams, Boston | 142 |
| 1947 | Ted Williams, Boston | 125 |
| 1948 | Tommy Henrich, New York | 138 |
| 1949 | Ted Williams, Boston | 150 |
| 1950 | Dom DiMaggio, Boston | 131 |
| 1951 | Dom DiMaggio, Boston | 113 |
| 1952 | Larry Doby, Cleveland | 104 |
| 1953 | Al Rosen, Cleveland | 115 |
| 1954 | Mickey Mantle, New York | 129 |
| 1955 | Al Smith, Cleveland | 123 |
| 1956 | Mickey Mantle, New York | 132 |
| 1957 | Mickey Mantle, New York | 121 |
| 1958 | Mickey Mantle, New York | 127 |
| 1959 | Eddie Yost, Detroit | 115 |
| 1960 | Mickey Mantle, New York | 119 |
| 1961 | Mickey Mantle, New York | 132 |
| | Roger Maris, New York | 132 |
| 1962 | Albie Pearson, Los Angeles | 115 |
| 1963 | Bob Allison, Minnesota | 99 |
| 1964 | Tony Oliva, Minnesota | 109 |
| 1965 | Zoilo Versalles, Minnesota | 126 |
| 1966 | Frank Robinson, Baltimore | 122 |
| 1967 | Carl Yastrzemski, Boston | 112 |
| 1968 | Dick McAuliffe, Detroit | 95 |
| 1969 | Reggie Jackson, Oakland | 123 |
| 1970 | Carl Yastrzemski, Boston | 125 |
| 1971 | Don Buford, Baltimore | 99 |
| 1972 | Bobby Murcer, New York | 102 |
| 1973 | Reggie Jackson, Oakland | 99 |
| 1974 | Carl Yastrzemski, Boston | 93 |
| 1975 | Fred Lynn, Boston | 103 |
| 1976 | Roy White, New York | 104 |
| 1977 | Rod Carew, Minnesota | 128 |
| 1978 | Ron LeFlore, Detroit | 126 |
| 1979 | Don Baylor, California | 120 |
| 1980 | Willie Wilson, Kansas City | 133 |
| 1981 | Rickey Henderson, Oakland | 89 |
| 1982 | Paul Molitor, Milwaukee | 136 |
| 1983 | Cal Ripken, Baltimore | 121 |
| 1984 | Dwight Evans, Boston | 121 |
| 1985 | Rickey Henderson, New York | 146 |
| 1986 | Rickey Henderson, New York | 130 |
| 1987 | Paul Molitor, Milwaukee | 114 |
| 1988 | Wade Boggs, Boston | 128 |
| 1989 | Wade Boggs, Boston | 113 |
| | Rickey Henderson, New York/Oakland | 113 |
| 1990 | Rickey Henderson, Oakland | 119 |
| 1991 | Paul Molitor, Milwaukee | 133 |
| 1992 | Tony Phillips, Detroit | 114 |
| 1993 | Rafael Palmeiro, Texas | 124 |
| 1994 | Frank E. Thomas, Chicago | 106 |
| 1995 | Albert Belle, Cleveland | 121 |
| | Edgar Martinez, Seattle | 121 |
| 1996 | Alex Rodriguez, Seattle | 141 |
| 1997 | Ken Griffey Jr., Seattle | 125 |
| 1998 | Derek Jeter, New York | 127 |
| 1999 | Roberto Alomar, Cleveland | 138 |
| 2000 | Johnny Damon, Kansas City | 136 |
| 2001 | Alex Rodriguez, Texas | 133 |
| 2002 | Alfonso Soriano, New York | 128 |
| 2003 | Alex Rodriguez, Texas | 124 |
| 2004 | Vladimir Guerrero, Anaheim | 124 |
| 2005 | Alex Rodriguez, New York | 124 |

## NATIONAL LEAGUE

| Year | Player, Club | Runs |
|---|---|---|
| 1900 | Roy Thomas, Philadelphia | 132 |
| 1901 | Jesse Burkett, St. Louis | 142 |
| 1902 | Honus Wagner, Pittsburgh | 105 |
| 1903 | Ginger Beaumont, Pittsburgh | 137 |
| 1904 | George Browne, New York | 99 |
| 1905 | Mike Donlin, New York | 124 |
| 1906 | Frank Chance, Chicago | 103 |
| | Honus Wagner, Pittsburgh | 103 |
| 1907 | Spike Shannon, New York | 104 |
| 1908 | Fred Tenney, New York | 101 |
| 1909 | Tommy Leach, Pittsburgh | 126 |
| 1910 | Sherry Magee, Philadelphia | 110 |
| 1911 | Jimmy Sheckard, Chicago | 121 |
| 1912 | Bob Bescher, Cincinnati | 120 |
| 1913 | Max Carey, Pittsburgh | 99 |
| | Tommy Leach, Chicago | 99 |
| 1914 | George J. Burns, New York | 100 |
| 1915 | Gavvy Cravath, Philadelphia | 89 |
| 1916 | George J. Burns, New York | 105 |
| 1917 | George J. Burns, New York | 103 |
| 1918 | Heinie Groh, Cincinnati | 88 |
| 1919 | George J. Burns, New York | 86 |
| 1920 | George J. Burns, New York | 115 |
| 1921 | Rogers Hornsby, St. Louis | 131 |
| 1922 | Rogers Hornsby, St. Louis | 141 |
| 1923 | Ross Youngs, New York | 121 |
| 1924 | Frankie Frisch, New York | 121 |
| | Rogers Hornsby, St. Louis | 121 |
| 1925 | Kiki Cuyler, Pittsburgh | 144 |
| 1926 | Kiki Cuyler, Pittsburgh | 113 |
| 1927 | Lloyd Waner, Pittsburgh | 133 |
| | Rogers Hornsby, New York | 133 |
| 1928 | Paul Waner, Pittsburgh | 142 |
| 1929 | Rogers Hornsby, Chicago | 156 |
| 1930 | Chuck Klein, Philadelphia | 158 |
| 1931 | Bill Terry, New York | 121 |
| | Chuck Klein, Philadelphia | 121 |
| 1932 | Chuck Klein, Philadelphia | 152 |
| 1933 | Pepper Martin, St. Louis | 122 |
| 1934 | Paul Waner, Pittsburgh | 122 |
| 1935 | Augie Galan, Chicago | 133 |
| 1936 | Arky Vaughan, Pittsburgh | 122 |
| 1937 | Joe Medwick, St. Louis | 111 |
| 1938 | Mel Ott, New York | 116 |
| 1939 | Bill Werber, Cincinnati | 115 |
| 1940 | Arky Vaughan, Pittsburgh | 113 |
| 1941 | Pete Reiser, Brooklyn | 117 |
| 1942 | Mel Ott, New York | 118 |
| 1943 | Arky Vaughan, Brooklyn | 112 |
| 1944 | Bill Nicholson, Chicago | 116 |
| 1945 | Eddie Stanky, Brooklyn | 128 |
| 1946 | Stan Musial, St. Louis | 124 |
| 1947 | Johnny Mize, New York | 137 |
| 1948 | Stan Musial, St. Louis | 135 |
| 1949 | Pee Wee Reese, Brooklyn | 132 |
| 1950 | Earl Torgeson, Boston | 120 |
| 1951 | Stan Musial, St. Louis | 124 |
| | Ralph Kiner, Pittsburgh | 124 |
| 1952 | Stan Musial, St. Louis | 105 |
| | Solly Hemus, St. Louis | 105 |
| 1953 | Duke Snider, Brooklyn | 132 |
| 1954 | Stan Musial, St. Louis | 120 |
| | Duke Snider, Brooklyn | 120 |
| 1955 | Duke Snider, Brooklyn | 126 |
| 1956 | Frank Robinson, Cincinnati | 122 |
| 1957 | Hank Aaron, Milwaukee | 118 |
| 1958 | Willie Mays, San Francisco | 121 |
| 1959 | Vada Pinson, Cincinnati | 131 |
| 1960 | Billy Bruton, Milwaukee | 112 |
| 1961 | Willie Mays, San Francisco | 129 |
| 1962 | Frank Robinson, Cincinnati | 134 |
| 1963 | Hank Aaron, Milwaukee | 121 |
| 1964 | Dick Allen, Philadelphia | 125 |
| 1965 | Tommy Harper, Cincinnati | 126 |
| 1966 | Felipe Alou, Atlanta | 122 |
| 1967 | Hank Aaron, Atlanta | 113 |
| | Lou Brock, St. Louis | 113 |
| 1968 | Glenn Beckert, Chicago | 98 |
| 1969 | Bobby Bonds, San Francisco | 120 |
| | Pete Rose, Cincinnati | 120 |
| 1970 | Billy Williams, Chicago | 137 |
| 1971 | Lou Brock, St. Louis | 126 |
| 1972 | Joe Morgan, Cincinnati | 122 |
| 1973 | Bobby Bonds, San Francisco | 131 |
| 1974 | Pete Rose, Cincinnati | 110 |
| 1975 | Pete Rose, Cincinnati | 112 |
| 1976 | Pete Rose, Cincinnati | 130 |
| 1977 | George Foster, Cincinnati | 124 |
| 1978 | Ivan DeJesus, Chicago | 104 |
| 1979 | Keith Hernandez, St. Louis | 116 |
| 1980 | Keith Hernandez, St. Louis | 111 |
| 1981 | Mike Schmidt, Philadelphia | 78 |
| 1982 | Lonnie Smith, St. Louis | 120 |
| 1983 | Tim Raines Sr., Montreal | 133 |
| 1984 | Ryne Sandberg, Chicago | 114 |
| 1985 | Dale Murphy, Atlanta | 118 |
| 1986 | Tony Gwynn, San Diego | 107 |
| | Von Hayes, Philadelphia | 107 |
| 1987 | Tim Raines Sr., Montreal | 123 |
| 1988 | Brett Butler, San Francisco | 109 |
| 1989 | Will Clark, San Francisco | 104 |
| | Howard Johnson, New York | 104 |
| | Ryne Sandberg, Chicago | 104 |
| 1990 | Ryne Sandberg, Chicago | 116 |
| 1991 | Brett Butler, Los Angeles | 112 |
| 1992 | Barry Bonds, Pittsburgh | 109 |
| 1993 | Lenny Dykstra, Philadelphia | 143 |
| 1994 | Jeff Bagwell, Houston | 104 |
| 1995 | Craig Biggio, Houston | 123 |
| 1996 | Ellis Burks, Colorado | 142 |
| 1997 | Craig Biggio, Houston | 146 |
| 1998 | Sammy Sosa, Chicago | 134 |
| 1999 | Jeff Bagwell, Houston | 143 |
| 2000 | Jeff Bagwell, Houston | 152 |
| 2001 | Sammy Sosa, Chicago | 146 |
| 2002 | Sammy Sosa, Chicago | 122 |
| 2003 | Albert Pujols, St. Louis | 137 |
| 2004 | Albert Pujols, St. Louis | 133 |
| 2005 | Albert Pujols, St. Louis | 129 |

# HITS

## AMERICAN LEAGUE

| Year | Player, Club | Hits |
|---|---|---|
| 1901 | Nap Lajoie, Philadelphia | 232 |
| 1902 | Charles Hickman, Boston/Cleveland | 193 |
| 1903 | Patsy Dougherty, Boston | 195 |
| 1904 | Nap Lajoie, Cleveland | 208 |
| 1905 | George Stone, St. Louis | 187 |
| 1906 | Nap Lajoie, Cleveland | 214 |
| 1907 | Ty Cobb, Detroit | 212 |
| 1908 | Ty Cobb, Detroit | 188 |
| 1909 | Ty Cobb, Detroit | 216 |
| 1910 | Nap Lajoie, Cleveland | 227 |
| 1911 | Ty Cobb, Detroit | 248 |
| 1912 | Ty Cobb, Detroit | 226 |
| | Joe Jackson, Cleveland | 226 |
| 1913 | Joe Jackson, Cleveland | 197 |
| 1914 | Tris Speaker, Boston | 193 |
| 1915 | Ty Cobb, Detroit | 208 |
| 1916 | Tris Speaker, Cleveland | 211 |
| 1917 | Ty Cobb, Detroit | 225 |
| 1918 | George H. Burns, Philadelphia | 178 |
| 1919 | Ty Cobb, Detroit | 191 |
| | Bobby Veach, Detroit | 191 |
| 1920 | George Sisler, St. Louis | 257 |
| 1921 | Harry Heilmann, Detroit | 237 |
| 1922 | George Sisler, St. Louis | 246 |
| 1923 | Charlie Jamieson, Cleveland | 222 |
| 1924 | Sam Rice, Washington | 216 |
| 1925 | Al Simmons, Philadelphia | 253 |
| 1926 | George H. Burns, Cleveland | 216 |
| | Sam Rice, Washington | 216 |
| 1927 | Earle Combs, New York | 231 |
| 1928 | Heinie Manush, St. Louis | 241 |
| 1929 | Dale Alexander, Detroit | 215 |
| | Charlie Gehringer, Detroit | 215 |
| 1930 | Johnny Hodapp, Cleveland | 225 |
| 1931 | Lou Gehrig, New York | 211 |
| 1932 | Al Simmons, Philadelphia | 216 |
| 1933 | Heinie Manush, Washington | 221 |
| 1934 | Charlie Gehringer, Detroit | 214 |
| 1935 | Joe Vosmik, Cleveland | 216 |
| 1936 | Earl Averill Sr., Cleveland | 232 |
| 1937 | Beau Bell, St. Louis | 218 |
| 1938 | Joe Vosmik, Boston | 201 |
| 1939 | Red Rolfe, New York | 213 |
| 1940 | Rip Radcliff, St. Louis | 200 |
| | Barney McCosky, Detroit | 200 |
| | Doc Cramer, Boston | 200 |
| 1941 | Cecil Travis, Washington | 218 |
| 1942 | Johnny Pesky, Boston | 205 |
| 1943 | Dick Wakefield, Detroit | 200 |
| 1944 | George Stirnweiss, New York | 205 |
| 1945 | George Stirnweiss, New York | 195 |
| 1946 | Johnny Pesky, Boston | 208 |
| 1947 | Johnny Pesky, Boston | 207 |
| 1948 | Bob Dillinger, St. Louis | 207 |
| 1949 | Dale Mitchell, Cleveland | 203 |
| 1950 | George Kell, Detroit | 218 |
| 1951 | George Kell, Detroit | 191 |
| 1952 | Nellie Fox, Chicago | 192 |
| 1953 | Harvey Kuenn, Detroit | 209 |
| 1954 | Nellie Fox, Chicago | 201 |
| | Harvey Kuenn, Detroit | 201 |
| 1955 | Al Kaline, Detroit | 200 |
| 1956 | Harvey Kuenn, Detroit | 196 |
| 1957 | Nellie Fox, Chicago | 196 |
| 1958 | Nellie Fox, Chicago | 187 |
| 1959 | Harvey Kuenn, Detroit | 198 |
| 1960 | Minnie Minoso, Chicago | 184 |
| 1961 | Norm Cash, Detroit | 193 |
| 1962 | Bobby Richardson, New York | 209 |
| 1963 | Carl Yastrzemski, Boston | 183 |
| 1964 | Tony Oliva, Minnesota | 217 |
| 1965 | Tony Oliva, Minnesota | 185 |
| 1966 | Tony Oliva, Minnesota | 191 |
| 1967 | Carl Yastrzemski, Boston | 189 |
| 1968 | Bert Campaneris, Oakland | 177 |
| 1969 | Tony Oliva, Minnesota | 197 |
| 1970 | Tony Oliva, Minnesota | 204 |
| 1971 | Cesar Tovar, Minnesota | 204 |
| 1972 | Joe Rudi, Oakland | 181 |
| 1973 | Rod Carew, Minnesota | 203 |
| 1974 | Rod Carew, Minnesota | 218 |
| 1975 | George Brett, Kansas City | 195 |
| 1976 | George Brett, Kansas City | 215 |
| 1977 | Rod Carew, Minnesota | 239 |
| 1978 | Jim Rice, Boston | 213 |
| 1979 | George Brett, Kansas City | 212 |
| 1980 | Willie Wilson, Kansas City | 230 |
| 1981 | Rickey Henderson, Oakland | 135 |
| 1982 | Robin Yount, Milwaukee | 210 |
| 1983 | Cal Ripken, Baltimore | 211 |
| 1984 | Don Mattingly, New York | 207 |
| 1985 | Wade Boggs, Boston | 240 |
| 1986 | Don Mattingly, New York | 238 |
| 1987 | Kirby Puckett, Minnesota | 207 |

| Year | Player, Club | Hits |
|---|---|---|
| | Kevin Seitzer, Kansas City | 207 |
| 1988 | Kirby Puckett, Minnesota | 234 |
| 1989 | Kirby Puckett, Minnesota | 215 |
| 1990 | Rafael Palmeiro, Texas | *191 |
| 1991 | Paul Molitor, Milwaukee | 216 |
| 1992 | Kirby Puckett, Minnesota | 210 |
| 1993 | Paul Molitor, Toronto | 211 |
| 1994 | Kenny Lofton, Cleveland | 160 |
| 1995 | Lance Johnson, Chicago | 186 |
| 1996 | Paul Molitor, Minnesota | 225 |
| 1997 | Nomar Garciaparra, Boston | 209 |
| 1998 | Alex Rodriguez, Seattle | 213 |
| 1999 | Derek Jeter, New York | 219 |
| 2000 | Darin Erstad, Anaheim | 240 |
| 2001 | Ichiro Suzuki, Seattle | 242 |
| 2002 | Alfonso Soriano, New York | 209 |
| 2003 | Vernon Wells, Toronto | 215 |
| 2004 | Ichiro Suzuki, Seattle | 262 |
| 2005 | Michael Young, Texas | 221 |

## NATIONAL LEAGUE

| Year | Player, Club | Hits |
|---|---|---|
| 1900 | Willie Keeler, Brooklyn | 204 |
| 1901 | Jesse Burkett, St. Louis | 226 |
| 1902 | Ginger Beaumont, Pittsburgh | 193 |
| 1903 | Ginger Beaumont, Pittsburgh | 209 |
| 1904 | Ginger Beaumont, Pittsburgh | 185 |
| 1905 | Cy Seymour, Cincinnati | 219 |
| 1906 | Harry Steinfeldt, Chicago | 176 |
| 1907 | Ginger Beaumont, Boston | 187 |
| 1908 | Honus Wagner, Pittsburgh | 201 |
| 1909 | Larry Doyle, New York | 172 |
| 1910 | Honus Wagner, Pittsburgh | 178 |
| | Bobby Byrne, Pittsburgh | 178 |
| 1911 | Doc Miller, Boston | 192 |
| 1912 | Heinie Zimmerman, Chicago | 207 |
| 1913 | Gavvy Cravath, Philadelphia | 179 |
| 1914 | Sherry Magee, Philadelphia | 171 |
| 1915 | Larry Doyle, New York | 189 |
| 1916 | Hal Chase, Cincinnati | 184 |
| 1917 | Heinie Groh, Cincinnati | 182 |
| 1918 | Charlie Hollocher, Chicago | 161 |
| 1919 | Ivy Olson, Brooklyn | 164 |
| 1920 | Rogers Hornsby, St. Louis | 218 |
| 1921 | Rogers Hornsby, St. Louis | 235 |
| 1922 | Rogers Hornsby, St. Louis | 250 |
| 1923 | Frankie Frisch, New York | 223 |
| 1924 | Rogers Hornsby, St. Louis | 227 |
| 1925 | Jim Bottomley, St. Louis | 227 |
| 1926 | Eddie Brown, Boston | 201 |
| 1927 | Paul Waner, Pittsburgh | 237 |
| 1928 | Fred Lindstrom, New York | 231 |
| 1929 | Lefty O'Doul, Philadelphia | 254 |
| 1930 | Bill Terry, New York | 254 |
| 1931 | Lloyd Waner, Pittsburgh | 214 |
| 1932 | Chuck Klein, Philadelphia | 226 |
| 1933 | Chuck Klein, Philadelphia | 223 |
| 1934 | Paul Waner, Pittsburgh | 217 |
| 1935 | Billy Herman, Chicago | 227 |
| 1936 | Joe Medwick, St. Louis | 223 |
| 1937 | Joe Medwick, St. Louis | 237 |
| 1938 | Frank McCormick, Cincinnati | 209 |
| 1939 | Frank McCormick, Cincinnati | 209 |
| 1940 | Stan Hack, Chicago | 191 |
| | Frank McCormick, Cincinnati | 191 |
| 1941 | Stan Hack, Chicago | 186 |
| 1942 | Enos Slaughter, St. Louis | 188 |
| 1943 | Stan Musial, St. Louis | 220 |
| 1944 | Stan Musial, St. Louis | 197 |
| | Phil Cavarretta, Chicago | 197 |
| 1945 | Tommy Holmes, Boston | 224 |
| 1946 | Stan Musial, St. Louis | 228 |
| 1947 | Tommy Holmes, Boston | 191 |
| 1948 | Stan Musial, St. Louis | 230 |
| 1949 | Stan Musial, St. Louis | 207 |
| 1950 | Duke Snider, Brooklyn | 199 |
| 1951 | Richie Ashburn, Philadelphia | 221 |
| 1952 | Stan Musial, St. Louis | 194 |
| 1953 | Richie Ashburn, Philadelphia | 205 |
| 1954 | Don Mueller, New York | 212 |
| 1955 | Ted Kluszewski, Cincinnati | 192 |
| 1956 | Hank Aaron, Milwaukee | 200 |
| 1957 | Red Schoendienst, New York/Milwaukee | 200 |
| 1958 | Richie Ashburn, Philadelphia | 215 |
| 1959 | Hank Aaron, Milwaukee | 223 |
| 1960 | Willie Mays, San Francisco | 190 |
| 1961 | Vada Pinson, Cincinnati | 208 |
| 1962 | Tommy Davis, Los Angeles | 230 |
| 1963 | Vada Pinson, Cincinnati | 204 |
| 1964 | Roberto Clemente, Pittsburgh | 211 |
| | Curt Flood, St. Louis | 211 |
| 1965 | Pete Rose, Cincinnati | 209 |
| 1966 | Felipe Alou, Atlanta | 218 |
| 1967 | Roberto Clemente, Pittsburgh | 209 |
| 1968 | Felipe Alou, Atlanta | 210 |
| | Pete Rose, Cincinnati | 210 |
| 1969 | Matty Alou, Pittsburgh | 205 |
| 1970 | Billy Williams, Chicago | 205 |
| 1971 | Joe Torre, St. Louis | 230 |
| 1972 | Pete Rose, Cincinnati | 198 |
| 1973 | Pete Rose, Cincinnati | 230 |
| 1974 | Ralph Garr, Atlanta | 214 |
| 1975 | Dave Cash, Philadelphia | 213 |
| 1976 | Pete Rose, Cincinnati | 215 |
| 1977 | Dave Parker, Pittsburgh | 215 |
| 1978 | Steve Garvey, Los Angeles | 202 |
| 1979 | Garry Templeton, St. Louis | 211 |
| 1980 | Steve Garvey, Los Angeles | 200 |
| 1981 | Pete Rose, Philadelphia | 140 |
| 1982 | Al Oliver, Montreal | 204 |
| 1983 | Jose Cruz, Houston | 189 |
| | Andre Dawson, Montreal | 189 |
| 1984 | Tony Gwynn, San Diego | 213 |
| 1985 | Willie McGee, St. Louis | 216 |
| 1986 | Tony Gwynn, San Diego | 211 |
| 1987 | Tony Gwynn, San Diego | 218 |
| 1988 | Andres Galarraga, Montreal | 184 |
| 1989 | Tony Gwynn, San Diego | 203 |
| 1990 | Brett Butler, San Francisco | *192 |
| | Lenny Dykstra, Philadelphia | *192 |
| 1991 | Terry Pendleton, Atlanta | 187 |
| 1992 | Terry Pendleton, Atlanta | 199 |
| | Andy Van Slyke, Pittsburgh | 199 |
| 1993 | Lenny Dykstra, Philadelphia | 194 |
| 1994 | Tony Gwynn, San Diego | 165 |
| 1995 | Dante Bichette, Colorado | 197 |
| | Tony Gwynn, San Diego | 197 |
| 1996 | Lance Johnson, New York | 227 |
| 1997 | Tony Gwynn, San Diego | 220 |
| 1998 | Dante Bichette, Colorado | 219 |
| 1999 | Luis Gonzalez, Arizona | 206 |
| 2000 | Todd Helton, Colorado | 216 |
| 2001 | Rich Aurilia, San Francisco | 206 |
| 2002 | Vladimir Guerrero, Montreal | 206 |
| 2003 | Albert Pujols, St. Louis | 212 |
| 2004 | Juan Pierre, Florida | 221 |
| 2005 | Derrek Lee, Chicago | 199 |

*Willie McGee led the majors with 199 hits in 1990, collecting 168 with St. Louis (NL) and another 31 with Oakland (AL) following an August 29 trade.

# SINGLES

## AMERICAN LEAGUE

| Year | Player, Club | Singles |
|---|---|---|
| 1901 | Nap Lajoie, Philadelphia | 156 |
| 1902 | Fielder Jones, Chicago | 150 |
| 1903 | Patsy Dougherty, Boston | 160 |
| 1904 | Willie Keeler, New York | 162 |
| 1905 | Willie Keeler, New York | 147 |
| 1906 | Willie Keeler, New York | 167 |
| 1907 | Ty Cobb, Detroit | 163 |
| 1908 | Matty McIntyre, Detroit | 131 |
| | George Stone, St. Louis | 131 |
| 1909 | Ty Cobb, Detroit | 164 |
| 1910 | Nap Lajoie, Cleveland | 165 |
| 1911 | Ty Cobb, Detroit | 169 |
| 1912 | Ty Cobb, Detroit | 167 |
| 1913 | Eddie Collins, Philadelphia | 145 |
| 1914 | Stuffy McInnis, Philadelphia | 160 |
| 1915 | Ty Cobb, Detroit | 161 |
| 1916 | Tris Speaker, Cleveland | 160 |
| 1917 | Ty Cobb, Detroit | 151 |
| | Clyde Milan, Washington | 151 |
| 1918 | George H. Burns, Philadelphia | 141 |
| 1919 | Sam Rice, Washington | 144 |
| 1920 | George Sisler, St. Louis | 171 |
| 1921 | Jack Tobin, St. Louis | 179 |
| 1922 | George Sisler, St. Louis | 178 |
| 1923 | Charlie Jamieson, Cleveland | 172 |
| 1924 | Charlie Jamieson, Cleveland | 168 |
| 1925 | Sam Rice, Washington | 182 |
| 1926 | Sam Rice, Washington | 167 |
| 1927 | Earle Combs, New York | 166 |
| 1928 | Heinie Manush, St. Louis | 161 |
| 1929 | Earle Combs, New York | 151 |
| 1930 | Sam Rice, Washington | 158 |
| 1931 | Oscar Melillo, St. Louis | 142 |
| | John Stone, Detroit | 142 |
| 1932 | Heinie Manush, Washington | 145 |
| 1933 | Heinie Manush, Washington | 167 |
| 1934 | Doc Cramer, Philadelphia | 158 |
| 1935 | Doc Cramer, Philadelphia | 170 |
| 1936 | Rip Radcliff, Chicago | 161 |
| 1937 | Buddy Lewis, Washington | 162 |
| 1938 | Mel Almada, Washington/St. Louis | 158 |
| 1939 | Doc Cramer, Boston | 147 |
| 1940 | Doc Cramer, Boston | 160 |
| 1941 | Cecil Travis, Washington | 153 |
| 1942 | Johnny Pesky, Boston | 165 |
| 1943 | Doc Cramer, Detroit | 159 |
| 1944 | George Stirnweiss, New York | 146 |
| 1945 | Irv Hall, Philadelphia | 139 |
| 1946 | Johnny Pesky, Boston | 159 |
| 1947 | Johnny Pesky, Boston | 172 |
| 1948 | Dale Mitchell, Cleveland | 162 |
| 1949 | Dale Mitchell, Cleveland | 161 |
| 1950 | Phil Rizzuto, New York | 150 |
| 1951 | George Kell, Detroit | 150 |
| 1952 | Nellie Fox, Chicago | 157 |
| 1953 | Harvey Kuenn, Detroit | 167 |
| 1954 | Nellie Fox, Chicago | 167 |
| 1955 | Nellie Fox, Chicago | 157 |
| 1956 | Nellie Fox, Chicago | 158 |
| 1957 | Nellie Fox, Chicago | 155 |
| 1958 | Nellie Fox, Chicago | 160 |
| 1959 | Nellie Fox, Chicago | 149 |
| 1960 | Nellie Fox, Chicago | 139 |
| 1961 | Bobby Richardson, New York | 148 |
| 1962 | Bobby Richardson, New York | 158 |
| 1963 | Albie Pearson, Los Angeles | 139 |
| 1964 | Bobby Richardson, New York | 148 |
| 1965 | Don Buford, Chicago | 129 |
| 1966 | Luis Aparicio, Baltimore | 143 |
| 1967 | Horace Clarke, New York | 140 |
| 1968 | Bert Campaneris, Oakland | 139 |
| 1969 | Horace Clarke, New York | 146 |
| 1970 | Alex Johnson, California | 156 |
| 1971 | Cesar Tovar, Minnesota | 171 |
| 1972 | Rod Carew, Minnesota | 143 |
| 1973 | Rod Carew, Minnesota | 156 |
| 1974 | Rod Carew, Minnesota | 180 |
| 1975 | Thurman Munson, New York | 151 |
| 1976 | George Brett, Kansas City | 160 |
| 1977 | Rod Carew, Minnesota | 171 |
| 1978 | Ron LeFlore, Detroit | 153 |
| 1979 | Willie Wilson, Kansas City | 148 |
| 1980 | Willie Wilson, Kansas City | 184 |
| 1981 | Willie Wilson, Kansas City | 115 |
| 1982 | Willie Wilson, Kansas City | 157 |
| 1983 | Wade Boggs, Boston | 154 |
| 1984 | Wade Boggs, Boston | 162 |
| 1985 | Wade Boggs, Boston | 187 |
| 1986 | Tony Fernandez, Toronto | 161 |
| 1987 | Kevin Seitzer, Kansas City | 151 |
| 1988 | Kirby Puckett, Minnesota | 163 |
| 1989 | Steve Sax, New York | 171 |
| 1990 | Rafael Palmeiro, Texas | 136 |
| 1991 | Julio Franco, Texas | 156 |
| 1992 | Carlos Baerga, Cleveland | 152 |
| 1993 | Kenny Lofton, Cleveland | 148 |
| 1994 | Kenny Lofton, Cleveland | 107 |
| | Paul Molitor, Toronto | 107 |
| 1995 | Otis Nixon, Texas | 151 |
| 1996 | Paul Molitor, Minnesota | 167 |
| 1997 | Garret Anderson, Anaheim | 142 |
| | Derek Jeter, New York | 142 |
| 1998 | Derek Jeter, New York | 151 |
| 1999 | Randy Velarde, Anaheim/Oakland | 152 |
| 2000 | Darin Erstad, Anaheim | 170 |
| 2001 | Ichiro Suzuki, Seattle | 192 |
| 2002 | Ichiro Suzuki, Seattle | 165 |
| 2003 | Ichiro Suzuki, Seattle | 162 |
| 2004 | Ichiro Suzuki, Seattle | 225 |
| 2005 | Ichiro Suzuki, Seattle | 158 |

## NATIONAL LEAGUE

| Year | Player, Club | Singles |
|---|---|---|
| 1900 | Willie Keeler, Brooklyn | 175 |
| 1901 | Jesse Burkett, St. Louis | 181 |
| 1902 | Ginger Beaumont, Pittsburgh | 166 |
| 1903 | Ginger Beaumont, Pittsburgh | 166 |
| 1904 | Ginger Beaumont, Pittsburgh | 158 |
| 1905 | Mike Donlin, New York | 162 |
| 1906 | Miller Huggins, Cincinnati | 141 |
| | Spike Shannon, St. Louis/New York | 141 |
| 1907 | Ginger Beaumont, Pittsburgh | 150 |
| 1908 | Mike Donlin, New York | 153 |
| 1909 | Eddie Grant, Philadelphia | 147 |
| 1910 | Eddie Grant, Philadelphia | 134 |
| 1911 | Jake Daubert, Brooklyn | 146 |
| | Doc Miller, Boston | 146 |
| 1912 | Bill Sweeney, Boston | 159 |
| 1913 | Jake Daubert, Brooklyn | 152 |
| 1914 | Beals Becker, Philadelphia | 128 |
| 1915 | Larry Doyle, New York | 135 |
| 1916 | Dave Robertson, New York | 142 |
| 1917 | Benny Kauff, New York | 141 |
| | Edd Roush, Cincinnati | 141 |
| 1918 | Charlie Hollocher, Chicago | 130 |
| 1919 | Ivy Olson, Brooklyn | 140 |
| 1920 | Milt Stock, St. Louis | 170 |
| 1921 | Carson Bigbee, Pittsburgh | 161 |
| 1922 | Carson Bigbee, Pittsburgh | 166 |
| 1923 | Frankie Frisch, New York | 169 |
| 1924 | Zack Wheat, Brooklyn | 149 |
| 1925 | Milt Stock, Brooklyn | 164 |
| 1926 | Eddie Brown, Boston | 160 |
| 1927 | Lloyd Waner, Pittsburgh | 198 |
| 1928 | Lloyd Waner, Pittsburgh | 180 |

| Year | Player, Club | Singles |
|---|---|---|
| 1929 | Lefty O'Doul, Philadelphia | 181 |
| | Lloyd Waner, Pittsburgh | 181 |
| 1930 | Bill Terry, New York | 177 |
| 1931 | Lloyd Waner, Pittsburgh | 172 |
| 1932 | Lefty O'Doul, Brooklyn | 158 |
| 1933 | Chick Fullis, Philadelphia | 162 |
| 1934 | Bill Terry, New York | 169 |
| 1935 | Woody Jensen, Pittsburgh | 160 |
| 1936 | Joe Moore, New York | 160 |
| 1937 | Paul Waner, Pittsburgh | 178 |
| 1938 | Frank McCormick, Cincinnati | 160 |
| 1939 | Buddy Hassett, Boston | 162 |
| 1940 | Burgess Whitehead, New York | 141 |
| 1941 | Stan Hack, Chicago | 141 |
| 1942 | Enos Slaughter, St. Louis | 127 |
| 1943 | Mickey Witek, New York | 172 |
| 1944 | Phil Cavarretta, Chicago | 142 |
| 1945 | Stan Hack, Chicago | 155 |
| 1946 | Stan Musial, St. Louis | 142 |
| 1947 | Tommy Holmes, Boston | 146 |
| 1948 | Stan Rojek, Pittsburgh | 150 |
| 1949 | Red Schoendienst, St. Louis | 160 |
| 1950 | Eddie Waitkus, Philadelphia | 143 |
| 1951 | Richie Ashburn, Philadelphia | 181 |
| 1952 | Bobby Adams, Cincinnati | 145 |
| 1953 | Richie Ashburn, Philadelphia | 169 |
| 1954 | Don Mueller, New York | 165 |
| 1955 | Don Mueller, New York | 152 |
| 1956 | Johnny Temple, Cincinnati | 157 |
| 1957 | Richie Ashburn, Philadelphia | 152 |
| 1958 | Richie Ashburn, Philadelphia | 176 |
| 1959 | Don Blasingame, St. Louis | 144 |
| 1960 | Dick Groat, Pittsburgh | 154 |
| 1961 | Vada Pinson, Cincinnati | 150 |
| | Maury Wills, Los Angeles | 150 |
| 1962 | Maury Wills, Los Angeles | 179 |
| 1963 | Curt Flood, St. Louis | 152 |
| 1964 | Curt Flood, St. Louis | 178 |
| 1965 | Maury Wills, Los Angeles | 165 |
| 1966 | Sonny Jackson, Houston | 160 |
| 1967 | Maury Wills, Pittsburgh | 162 |
| 1968 | Curt Flood, St. Louis | 160 |
| 1969 | Matty Alou, Pittsburgh | 183 |
| 1970 | Matty Alou, Pittsburgh | 171 |
| 1971 | Ralph Garr, Atlanta | 180 |
| 1972 | Lou Brock, St. Louis | 156 |
| 1973 | Pete Rose, Cincinnati | 181 |
| 1974 | Dave Cash, Philadelphia | 167 |
| 1975 | Dave Cash, Philadelphia | 166 |
| 1976 | Willie Montanez, San Francisco/Atlanta | 164 |
| 1977 | Garry Templeton, St. Louis | 155 |
| 1978 | Larry Bowa, Philadelphia | 153 |
| 1979 | Pete Rose, Philadelphia | 159 |
| 1980 | Gene Richards, San Diego | 155 |
| 1981 | Pete Rose, Philadelphia | 117 |
| 1982 | Bill Buckner, Chicago | 147 |
| 1983 | Rafael Ramirez, Atlanta | 160 |
| 1984 | Tony Gwynn, San Diego | 177 |
| 1985 | Willie McGee, St. Louis | 162 |
| 1986 | Tony Gwynn, San Diego | 157 |
| | Steve Sax, Los Angeles | 157 |
| 1987 | Tony Gwynn, San Diego | 162 |
| 1988 | Steve Sax, Los Angeles | 147 |
| 1989 | Tony Gwynn, San Diego | 165 |
| 1990 | Brett Butler, San Francisco | 160 |
| 1991 | Brett Butler, Los Angeles | 162 |
| 1992 | Brett Butler, Los Angeles | 143 |
| 1993 | Brett Butler, Los Angeles | 149 |
| 1994 | Tony Gwynn, San Diego | 117 |
| 1995 | Tony Gwynn, San Diego | 154 |
| 1996 | Lance Johnson, New York | 166 |
| 1997 | Tony Gwynn, San Diego | 152 |
| 1998 | Tony Womack, Pittsburgh | 149 |
| 1999 | Doug Glanville, Philadelphia | 149 |
| 2000 | Luis Castillo, Florida | 158 |
| 2001 | Juan Pierre, Colorado | 163 |
| 2002 | Luis Castillo, Florida | 160 |
| 2003 | Juan Pierre, Florida | 168 |
| 2004 | Juan Pierre, Florida | 184 |
| 2005 | Willy Taveras, Houston | 152 |

## DOUBLES

### AMERICAN LEAGUE

| Year | Player, Club | Doubles |
|---|---|---|
| 1901 | Nap Lajoie, Philadelphia | 48 |
| 1902 | Harry Davis, Philadelphia | 43 |
| | Ed Delahanty, Washington | 43 |
| 1903 | Socks Seybold, Philadelphia | 45 |
| 1904 | Nap Lajoie, Cleveland | 49 |
| 1905 | Harry Davis, Philadelphia | 47 |
| 1906 | Nap Lajoie, Cleveland | 48 |
| 1907 | Harry Davis, Philadelphia | 35 |
| 1908 | Ty Cobb, Detroit | 36 |
| 1909 | Sam Crawford, Detroit | 35 |
| 1910 | Nap Lajoie, Cleveland | 51 |

| Year | Player, Club | Doubles |
|---|---|---|
| 1911 | Ty Cobb, Detroit | 47 |
| 1912 | Tris Speaker, Boston | 53 |
| 1913 | Joe Jackson, Cleveland | 39 |
| 1914 | Tris Speaker, Boston | 46 |
| 1915 | Bobby Veach, Detroit | 40 |
| 1916 | Jack Graney, Cleveland | 41 |
| | Tris Speaker, Cleveland | 41 |
| 1917 | Ty Cobb, Detroit | 44 |
| 1918 | Tris Speaker, Cleveland | 33 |
| 1919 | Bobby Veach, Detroit | 45 |
| 1920 | Tris Speaker, Cleveland | 50 |
| 1921 | Tris Speaker, Cleveland | 52 |
| 1922 | Tris Speaker, Cleveland | 48 |
| 1923 | Tris Speaker, Cleveland | 59 |
| 1924 | Joe Sewell, Cleveland | 45 |
| | Harry Heilmann, Detroit | 45 |
| 1925 | Marty McManus, St. Louis | 44 |
| 1926 | George H. Burns, Cleveland | 64 |
| 1927 | Lou Gehrig, New York | 52 |
| 1928 | Heinie Manush, St. Louis | 47 |
| | Lou Gehrig, New York | 47 |
| 1929 | Heinie Manush, St. Louis | 45 |
| | Roy Johnson, Detroit | 45 |
| | Charlie Gehringer, Detroit | 45 |
| 1930 | Johnny Hodapp, Cleveland | 51 |
| 1931 | Earl Webb, Boston | 67 |
| 1932 | Eric McNair, Philadelphia | 47 |
| 1933 | Joe Cronin, Washington | 45 |
| 1934 | Hank Greenberg, Detroit | 63 |
| 1935 | Joe Vosmik, Cleveland | 47 |
| 1936 | Charlie Gehringer, Detroit | 60 |
| 1937 | Beau Bell, St. Louis | 51 |
| 1938 | Joe Cronin, Boston | 51 |
| 1939 | Red Rolfe, New York | 46 |
| 1940 | Hank Greenberg, Detroit | 50 |
| 1941 | Lou Boudreau, Cleveland | 45 |
| 1942 | Don Kolloway, Chicago | 40 |
| 1943 | Dick Wakefield, Detroit | 38 |
| 1944 | Lou Boudreau, Cleveland | 45 |
| 1945 | Wally Moses, Chicago | 35 |
| 1946 | Mickey Vernon, Washington | 51 |
| 1947 | Lou Boudreau, Cleveland | 45 |
| 1948 | Ted Williams, Boston | 44 |
| 1949 | Ted Williams, Boston | 39 |
| 1950 | George Kell, Detroit | 56 |
| 1951 | George Kell, Detroit | 36 |
| | Eddie Yost, Washington | 36 |
| | Sam Mele, Washington | 36 |
| 1952 | Ferris Fain, Philadelphia | 43 |
| 1953 | Mickey Vernon, Washington | 43 |
| 1954 | Mickey Vernon, Washington | 33 |
| 1955 | Harvey Kuenn, Detroit | 38 |
| 1956 | Jimmy Piersall, Boston | 40 |
| 1957 | Minnie Minoso, Chicago | 36 |
| | Billy Gardner, Baltimore | 36 |
| 1958 | Harvey Kuenn, Detroit | 39 |
| 1959 | Harvey Kuenn, Detroit | 42 |
| 1960 | Tito Francona, Cleveland | 36 |
| 1961 | Al Kaline, Detroit | 41 |
| 1962 | Floyd Robinson, Chicago | 45 |
| 1963 | Carl Yastrzemski, Boston | 40 |
| 1964 | Tony Oliva, Minnesota | 43 |
| 1965 | Zoilo Versalles, Minnesota | 45 |
| | Carl Yastrzemski, Boston | 45 |
| 1966 | Carl Yastrzemski, Boston | 39 |
| 1967 | Tony Oliva, Minnesota | 34 |
| 1968 | Reggie Smith, Boston | 37 |
| 1969 | Tony Oliva, Minnesota | 39 |
| 1970 | Tony Oliva, Minnesota | 36 |
| | Amos Otis, Kansas City | 36 |
| | Cesar Tovar, Minnesota | 36 |
| 1971 | Reggie Smith, Boston | 33 |
| 1972 | Lou Piniella, Kansas City | 33 |
| 1973 | Sal Bando, Oakland | 32 |
| | Pedro Garcia, Milwaukee | 32 |
| 1974 | Joe Rudi, Oakland | 39 |
| 1975 | Fred Lynn, Boston | 47 |
| 1976 | Amos Otis, Kansas City | 40 |
| 1977 | Hal McRae, Kansas City | 54 |
| 1978 | George Brett, Kansas City | 45 |
| 1979 | Chet Lemon, Chicago | 44 |
| | Cecil Cooper, Milwaukee | 44 |
| 1980 | Robin Yount, Milwaukee | 49 |
| 1981 | Cecil Cooper, Milwaukee | 35 |
| 1982 | Hal McRae, Kansas City | 46 |
| | Robin Yount, Milwaukee | 46 |
| 1983 | Cal Ripken, Baltimore | 47 |
| 1984 | Don Mattingly, New York | 44 |
| 1985 | Don Mattingly, New York | 48 |
| 1986 | Don Mattingly, New York | 53 |
| 1987 | Paul Molitor, Milwaukee | 41 |
| 1988 | Wade Boggs, Boston | 45 |
| 1989 | Wade Boggs, Boston | 51 |
| 1990 | George Brett, Kansas City | 45 |
| | Jody Reed, Boston | 45 |
| 1991 | Rafael Palmeiro, Texas | 49 |
| 1992 | Edgar Martinez, Seattle | 46 |

| Year | Player, Club | Doubles |
|---|---|---|
| | Frank Thomas, Chicago | 46 |
| 1993 | John Olerud, Toronto | 54 |
| 1994 | Chuck Knoblauch, Minnesota | 45 |
| 1995 | Albert Belle, Cleveland | 52 |
| | Edgar Martinez, Seattle | 52 |
| 1996 | Alex Rodriguez, Seattle | 54 |
| 1997 | John Valentin, Boston | 47 |
| 1998 | Juan Gonzalez, Texas | 50 |
| 1999 | Shawn Green, Toronto | 45 |
| 2000 | Carlos Delgado, Toronto | 57 |
| 2001 | Jason Giambi, Oakland | 47 |
| 2002 | Garret Anderson, Anaheim | 56 |
| | Nomar Garciaparra, Boston | 56 |
| 2003 | Garret Anderson, Anaheim | 49 |
| | Vernon Wells, Toronto | 49 |
| 2004 | Brian Roberts, Baltimore | 50 |
| 2005 | Miguel Tejada, Baltimore | 50 |

### NATIONAL LEAGUE

| Year | Player, Club | Doubles |
|---|---|---|
| 1876 | Ross Barnes, Chicago | 21 |
| | Dick Higham, Hartford | 21 |
| | Paul Hines, Chicago | 21 |
| 1877 | Cap Anson, Chicago | 19 |
| 1878 | Dick Higham, Providence | 22 |
| 1879 | Charlie Eden, Cleveland | 31 |
| 1880 | Fred Dunlap, Cleveland | 27 |
| 1881 | Paul Hines, Providenc | 27 |
| | King Kelly, Chicago | 27 |
| 1882 | King Kelly, Chicago | 37 |
| 1883 | Ned Williamson, Chicago | 49 |
| 1884 | Paul Hines, Providence | 36 |
| 1885 | Cap Anson, Chicago | 35 |
| 1886 | Dan Brouthers, Detroit | 40 |
| 1887 | Dan Brouthers, Detroit | 36 |
| 1888 | Dan Brouthers, Detroit | 33 |
| | Jimmy Ryan, Chicago | 33 |
| 1889 | King Kelly, Boston | 41 |
| 1890 | Sam Thompson, Philadelphia | 41 |
| 1891 | Mike Griffin, Brooklyn | 36 |
| 1892 | Roger Connor, Philadelphia | 37 |
| 1893 | Sam Thompson, Philadelphia | 37 |
| 1894 | Hugh Duffy, Boston | 51 |
| 1895 | Ed Delahanty, Philadelphia | 49 |
| 1896 | Ed Delahanty, Philadelphia | 44 |
| 1897 | Jake Stenzel, Baltimore | 43 |
| 1898 | Nap Lajoie, Philadelphia | 43 |
| 1899 | Ed Delahanty, Philadelphia | 55 |
| 1900 | Honus Wagner, Pittsburgh | 45 |
| 1901 | Tom Daly, Brooklyn | 38 |
| | Ed Delahanty, Philadelphia | 38 |
| 1902 | Honus Wagner, Pittsburgh | 30 |
| 1903 | Fred Clarke, Pittsburgh | 32 |
| | Sam Mertes, New York | 32 |
| | Harry Steinfeldt, Cincinnati | 32 |
| 1904 | Honus Wagner, Pittsburgh | 44 |
| 1905 | Cy Seymour, Cincinnati | 40 |
| 1906 | Honus Wagner, Pittsburgh | 38 |
| 1907 | Honus Wagner, Pittsburgh | 38 |
| 1908 | Honus Wagner, Pittsburgh | 39 |
| 1909 | Honus Wagner, Pittsburgh | 39 |
| 1910 | Bobby Byrne, Pittsburgh | 43 |
| 1911 | Ed Konetchy, St. Louis | 38 |
| 1912 | Heinie Zimmerman, Chicago | 41 |
| 1913 | Red Smith, Brooklyn | 40 |
| 1914 | Sherry Magee, Philadelphia | 39 |
| 1915 | Larry Doyle, New York | 40 |
| 1916 | Bert Niehoff, Philadelphia | 42 |
| 1917 | Heinie Groh, Cincinnati | 39 |
| 1918 | Heinie Groh, Cincinnati | 28 |
| 1919 | Ross Youngs, New York | 31 |
| 1920 | Rogers Hornsby, St. Louis | 44 |
| 1921 | Rogers Hornsby, St. Louis | 44 |
| 1922 | Rogers Hornsby, St. Louis | 46 |
| 1923 | Edd Roush, Cincinnati | 41 |
| 1924 | Rogers Hornsby, St. Louis | 43 |
| 1925 | Jim Bottomley, St. Louis | 44 |
| 1926 | Jim Bottomley, St. Louis | 40 |
| 1927 | Riggs Stephenson, Chicago | 46 |
| 1928 | Paul Waner, Pittsburgh | 50 |
| 1929 | Johnny Frederick, Brooklyn | 52 |
| 1930 | Chuck Klein, Philadelphia | 59 |
| 1931 | Sparky Adams, St. Louis | 46 |
| 1932 | Paul Waner, Pittsburgh | 62 |
| 1933 | Chuck Klein, Philadelphia | 44 |
| 1934 | Kiki Cuyler, Chicago | 42 |
| | Ethan Allen, Philadelphia | 42 |
| 1935 | Billy Herman, Chicago | 57 |
| 1936 | Joe Medwick, St. Louis | 64 |
| 1937 | Joe Medwick, St. Louis | 56 |
| 1938 | Joe Medwick, St. Louis | 47 |
| 1939 | Enos Slaughter, St. Louis | 52 |
| 1940 | Frank McCormick, Cincinnati | 44 |
| 1941 | Pete Reiser, Brooklyn | 39 |
| | Johnny Mize, St. Louis | 39 |
| 1942 | Marty Marion, St. Louis | 38 |
| 1943 | Stan Musial, St. Louis | 48 |

| Year | Player, Club | Doubles |
|---|---|---|
| 1944 | Stan Musial, St. Louis | 51 |
| 1945 | Tommy Holmes, Boston | 47 |
| 1946 | Stan Musial, St. Louis | 50 |
| 1947 | Eddie Miller, Cincinnati | 38 |
| 1948 | Stan Musial, St. Louis | 46 |
| 1949 | Stan Musial, St. Louis | 41 |
| 1950 | Red Schoendienst, St. Louis | 43 |
| 1951 | Alvin Dark, New York | 41 |
| 1952 | Stan Musial, St. Louis | 42 |
| 1953 | Stan Musial, St. Louis | 53 |
| 1954 | Stan Musial, St. Louis | 41 |
| 1955 | Johnny Logan, Milwaukee | 37 |
| | Hank Aaron, Milwaukee | 37 |
| 1956 | Hank Aaron, Milwaukee | 34 |
| 1957 | Don Hoak, Cincinnati | 39 |
| 1958 | Orlando Cepeda, San Francisco | 38 |
| 1959 | Vada Pinson, Cincinnati | 47 |
| 1960 | Vada Pinson, Cincinnati | 37 |
| 1961 | Hank Aaron, Milwaukee | 39 |
| 1962 | Frank Robinson, Cincinnati | 51 |
| 1963 | Dick Groat, St. Louis | 43 |
| 1964 | Lee Maye, Milwaukee | 44 |
| 1965 | Hank Aaron, Milwaukee | 40 |
| 1966 | Johnny Callison, Philadelphia | 40 |
| 1967 | Rusty Staub, Houston | 44 |
| 1968 | Lou Brock, St. Louis | 46 |
| 1969 | Matty Alou, Pittsburgh | 41 |
| 1970 | Wes Parker, Los Angeles | 47 |
| 1971 | Cesar Cedeno, Houston | 40 |
| 1972 | Cesar Cedeno, Houston | 39 |
| | Willie Montanez, Philadelphia | 39 |
| 1973 | Willie Stargell, Pittsburgh | 43 |
| 1974 | Pete Rose, Cincinnati | 45 |
| 1975 | Pete Rose, Cincinnati | 47 |
| 1976 | Pete Rose, Cincinnati | 42 |
| 1977 | Dave Parker, Pittsburgh | 44 |
| 1978 | Pete Rose, Cincinnati | 51 |
| 1979 | Keith Hernandez, St. Louis | 48 |
| 1980 | Pete Rose, Philadelphia | 42 |
| 1981 | Bill Buckner, Chicago | 35 |
| 1982 | Al Oliver, Montreal | 43 |
| 1983 | Bill Buckner, Chicago | 38 |
| | Al Oliver, Montreal | 38 |
| | Johnny Ray, Pittsburgh | 38 |
| 1984 | Tim Raines Sr., Montreal | 38 |
| | Johnny Ray, Pittsburgh | 38 |
| 1985 | Dave Parker, Cincinnati | 42 |
| 1986 | Von Hayes, Philadelphia | 46 |
| 1987 | Tim Wallach, Montreal | 42 |
| 1988 | Andres Galarraga, Montreal | 42 |
| 1989 | Pedro Guerrero, St. Louis | 42 |
| | Tim Wallach, Montreal | 42 |
| 1990 | Gregg Jefferies, New York | 40 |
| 1991 | Bobby Bonilla, Pittsburgh | 44 |
| 1992 | Andy Van Slyke, Pittsburgh | 45 |
| 1993 | Charlie Hayes, Colorado | 45 |
| 1994 | Craig Biggio, Houston | 44 |
| | Larry Walker, Montreal | 44 |
| 1995 | Mark Grace, Chicago | 51 |
| 1996 | Jeff Bagwell, Houston | 48 |
| 1997 | Mark Grudzielanek, Montreal | 54 |
| 1998 | Craig Biggio, Houston | 51 |
| 1999 | Craig Biggio, Houston | 56 |
| 2000 | Todd Helton, Colorado | 59 |
| 2001 | Lance Berkman, Houston | 55 |
| 2002 | Bobby Abreu, Philadelphia | 50 |
| 2003 | Albert Pujols, St. Louis | 51 |
| 2004 | Lyle Overbay, Milwaukee | 53 |
| 2005 | Derrek Lee, Chicago | 50 |

## TRIPLES

### AMERICAN LEAGUE

| Year | Player, Club | Triples |
|---|---|---|
| 1901 | Bill Keister, Baltimore | 21 |
| | Jimmy Williams, Baltimore | 21 |
| 1902 | Jimmy Williams, Baltimore | 21 |
| 1903 | Sam Crawford, Detroit | 25 |
| 1904 | Joe Cassidy, Washington | 19 |
| | Buck Freeman, Boston | 19 |
| | Chick Stahl, Boston | 19 |
| 1905 | Elmer Flick, Cleveland | 18 |
| 1906 | Elmer Flick, Cleveland | 22 |
| 1907 | Elmer Flick, Cleveland | 18 |
| 1908 | Ty Cobb, Detroit | 20 |
| 1909 | Home Run Baker, Philadelphia | 19 |
| 1910 | Sam Crawford, Detroit | 19 |
| 1911 | Ty Cobb, Detroit | 24 |
| 1912 | Joe Jackson, Cleveland | 26 |
| 1913 | Sam Crawford, Detroit | 23 |
| 1914 | Sam Crawford, Detroit | 26 |
| 1915 | Sam Crawford, Detroit | 19 |
| 1916 | Joe Jackson, Chicago | 21 |
| 1917 | Ty Cobb, Detroit | 24 |
| 1918 | Ty Cobb, Detroit | 14 |
| 1919 | Bobby Veach, Detroit | 17 |
| 1920 | Joe Jackson, Chicago | 20 |
| 1921 | Howard Shanks, Washington | 18 |
| | George Sisler, St. Louis | 18 |
| | Jack Tobin, St. Louis | 18 |
| 1922 | George Sisler, St. Louis | 18 |
| 1923 | Sam Rice, Washington | 18 |
| | Goose Goslin, Washington | 18 |
| 1924 | Wally Pipp, New York | 19 |
| 1925 | Goose Goslin, Washington | 20 |
| 1926 | Lou Gehrig, New York | 20 |
| 1927 | Earle Combs, New York | 23 |
| 1928 | Earle Combs, New York | 21 |
| 1929 | Charlie Gehringer, Detroit | 19 |
| 1930 | Earle Combs, New York | 22 |
| 1931 | Roy Johnson, Detroit | 19 |
| 1932 | Joe Cronin, Washington | 18 |
| 1933 | Heinie Manush, Washington | 17 |
| 1934 | Ben Chapman, New York | 13 |
| 1935 | Joe Vosmik, Cleveland | 20 |
| 1936 | Earl Averill Sr., Cleveland | 15 |
| | Joe DiMaggio, New York | 15 |
| | Red Rolfe, New York | 15 |
| 1937 | Dixie Walker, Chicago | 16 |
| | Mike Kreevich, Chicago | 16 |
| 1938 | Jeff Heath, Cleveland | 18 |
| 1939 | Buddy Lewis, Washington | 16 |
| 1940 | Barney McCosky, Detroit | 19 |
| 1941 | Jeff Heath, Cleveland | 20 |
| 1942 | Stan Spence, Washington | 15 |
| 1943 | Johnny Lindell, New York | 12 |
| | Wally Moses, Chicago | 12 |
| 1944 | Johnny Lindell, New York | 16 |
| | George Stirnweiss, New York | 16 |
| 1945 | George Stirnweiss, New York | 22 |
| 1946 | Hank Edwards, Cleveland | 16 |
| 1947 | Tommy Henrich, New York | 13 |
| 1948 | Tommy Henrich, New York | 14 |
| 1949 | Dale Mitchell, Cleveland | 23 |
| 1950 | Dom DiMaggio, Boston | 11 |
| | Bobby Doerr, Boston | 11 |
| | Hoot Evers, Detroit | 11 |
| 1951 | Minnie Minoso, Cleveland/Chicago | 14 |
| 1952 | Bobby Avila, Cleveland | 11 |
| 1953 | Jim Rivera, Chicago | 16 |
| 1954 | Minnie Minoso, Chicago | 18 |
| 1955 | Mickey Mantle, New York | 11 |
| | Andy Carey, New York | 11 |
| 1956 | Minnie Minoso, Chicago | 11 |
| | Jackie Jensen, Boston | 11 |
| | Harry Simpson, Kansas City | 11 |
| | Jim Lemon, Washington | 11 |
| 1957 | Gil McDougald, New York | 9 |
| | Hank Bauer, New York | 9 |
| | Harry Simpson, New York | 9 |
| 1958 | Vic Power, Kansas City/Cleveland | 10 |
| 1959 | Bob Allison, Washington | 9 |
| 1960 | Nellie Fox, Chicago | 10 |
| 1961 | Jake Wood, Detroit | 14 |
| 1962 | Gino Cimoli, Kansas City | 15 |
| 1963 | Zoilo Versalles, Minnesota | 13 |
| 1964 | Rich Rollins, Minnesota | 10 |
| | Zoilo Versalles, Minnesota | 10 |
| 1965 | Bert Campaneris, Kansas City | 12 |
| | Zoilo Versalles, Minnesota | 12 |
| 1966 | Bobby Knoop, California | 11 |
| 1967 | Paul Blair, Baltimore | 12 |
| 1968 | Jim Fregosi, California | 13 |
| 1969 | Del Unser, Washington | 8 |
| 1970 | Cesar Tovar, Minnesota | 13 |
| 1971 | Fred Patek, Kansas City | 11 |
| 1972 | Carlton Fisk, Boston | 9 |
| | Joe Rudi, Oakland | 9 |
| 1973 | Al Bumbry, Baltimore | 11 |
| | Rod Carew, Minnesota | 11 |
| 1974 | Mickey Rivers, California | 11 |
| 1975 | George Brett, Kansas City | 13 |
| | Mickey Rivers, California | 13 |
| 1976 | George Brett, Kansas City | 14 |
| 1977 | Rod Carew, Minnesota | 16 |
| 1978 | Jim Rice, Boston | 15 |
| 1979 | George Brett, Kansas City | 20 |
| 1980 | Alfredo Griffin, Toronto | 15 |
| | Willie Wilson, Kansas City | 15 |
| 1981 | John Castino, Minnesota | 9 |
| 1982 | Willie Wilson, Kansas City | 15 |
| 1983 | Robin Yount, Milwaukee | 10 |
| 1984 | Dave Collins, Toronto | 15 |
| | Lloyd Moseby, Toronto | 15 |
| 1985 | Willie Wilson, Kansas City | 21 |
| 1986 | Brett Butler, Cleveland | 14 |
| 1987 | Willie Wilson, Kansas City | 15 |
| 1988 | Harold Reynolds, Seattle | 11 |
| | Willie Wilson, Kansas City | 11 |
| | Robin Yount, Milwaukee | 11 |
| 1989 | Ruben Sierra, Texas | 14 |
| 1990 | Tony Fernandez, Toronto | 17 |
| 1991 | Lance Johnson, Chicago | 13 |
| | Paul Molitor, Milwaukee | 13 |
| 1992 | Lance Johnson, Chicago | 12 |
| 1993 | Lance Johnson, Chicago | 14 |
| 1994 | Lance Johnson, Chicago | 14 |
| 1995 | Kenny Lofton, Cleveland | 13 |
| 1996 | Chuck Knoblauch, Minnesota | 14 |
| 1997 | Nomar Garciaparra, Boston | 11 |
| 1998 | Jose Offerman, Kansas City | 13 |
| 1999 | Jose Offerman, Boston | 11 |
| 2000 | Cristian Guzman, Minnesota | 20 |
| 2001 | Cristian Guzman, Minnesota | 14 |
| 2002 | Johnny Damon, Boston | 11 |
| 2003 | Cristian Guzman, Minnesota | 14 |
| 2004 | Carl Crawford, Tampa Bay | 19 |
| 2005 | Carl Crawford, Tampa Bay | 15 |

### NATIONAL LEAGUE

| Year | Player, Club | Triples |
|---|---|---|
| 1876 | Ross Barnes, Chicago | 14 |
| 1877 | Deacon White, Boston | 11 |
| 1878 | Tom York, Providence | 10 |
| 1879 | Buttercup Dickerson, Cincinnati | 14 |
| 1880 | Harry Stovey, Worcester | 14 |
| 1881 | Jack Rowe, Buffalo | 11 |
| 1882 | Roger Connor, Troy | 18 |
| 1883 | Dan Brouthers, Buffalo | 17 |
| 1884 | Buck Ewing, New York | 20 |
| 1885 | Jim O'Rourke, New York | 16 |
| 1886 | Roger Connor, New York | 20 |
| 1887 | Sam Thompson, Detroit | 23 |
| 1888 | Dick Johnston, Boston | 18 |
| 1889 | Walt Wilmot, Washington | 19 |
| 1890 | John Reilly, Cincinnati | 26 |
| 1891 | Harry Stovey, Boston | 20 |
| 1892 | Ed Delahanty, Philadelphia | 21 |
| 1893 | Perry Werden, St. Louis | 29 |
| 1894 | Heinie Reitz, Baltimore | 31 |
| 1895 | Kip Selbach, Washington | 22 |
| 1896 | Tom McCreery, Louisville | 21 |
| | George Van Haltren, New York | 21 |
| 1897 | Harry Davis, Pittsburgh | 28 |
| 1898 | John Anderson, Brooklyn/Washington | 22 |
| 1899 | Jimmy Williams, Pittsburgh | 27 |
| 1900 | Honus Wagner, Pittsburgh | 22 |
| 1901 | Jimmy Sheckard, Brooklyn | 19 |
| 1902 | Sam Crawford, Cincinnati | 22 |
| | Tommy Leach, Pittsburgh | 22 |
| 1903 | Honus Wagner, Pittsburgh | 19 |
| 1904 | Harry Lumley, Brooklyn | 18 |
| 1905 | Cy Seymour, Cincinnati | 21 |
| 1906 | Fred Clarke, Pittsburgh | 13 |
| | Frank Schulte, Chicago | 13 |
| 1907 | John Ganzel, Cincinnati | 16 |
| | Whitey Alperman, Brooklyn | 16 |
| 1908 | Honus Wagner, Pittsburgh | 19 |
| 1909 | Mike Mitchell, Cincinnati | 17 |
| 1910 | Mike Mitchell, Cincinnati | 18 |
| 1911 | Larry Doyle, New York | 25 |
| 1912 | Chief Wilson, Pittsburgh | 36 |
| 1913 | Vic Saier, Chicago | 21 |
| 1914 | Max Carey, Pittsburgh | 17 |
| 1915 | Tommy Long, St. Louis | 25 |
| 1916 | Bill Hinchman, Pittsburgh | 16 |
| 1917 | Rogers Hornsby, St. Louis | 17 |
| 1918 | Jake Daubert, Brooklyn | 15 |
| 1919 | Hy Myers, Brooklyn | 14 |
| | Billy Southworth, Pittsburgh | 14 |
| 1920 | Hy Myers, Brooklyn | 22 |
| 1921 | Rogers Hornsby, St. Louis | 18 |
| | Ray Powell, Boston | 18 |
| 1922 | Jake Daubert, Cincinnati | 22 |
| 1923 | Max Carey, Pittsburgh | 19 |
| | Pie Traynor, Pittsburgh | 19 |
| 1924 | Edd Roush, Cincinnati | 21 |
| 1925 | Kiki Cuyler, Pittsburgh | 26 |
| 1926 | Paul Waner, Pittsburgh | 22 |
| 1927 | Paul Waner, Pittsburgh | 18 |
| 1928 | Jim Bottomley, St. Louis | 20 |
| 1929 | Lloyd Waner, Pittsburgh | 20 |
| 1930 | Adam Comorosky, Pittsburgh | 23 |
| 1931 | Bill Terry, New York | 20 |
| 1932 | Babe Herman, Cincinnati | 19 |
| 1933 | Arky Vaughan, Pittsburgh | 19 |
| 1934 | Joe Medwick, St. Louis | 18 |
| 1935 | Ival Goodman, Cincinnati | 18 |
| 1936 | Ival Goodman, Cincinnati | 14 |
| 1937 | Arky Vaughan, Pittsburgh | 17 |
| 1938 | Johnny Mize, St. Louis | 16 |
| 1939 | Billy Herman, Chicago | 18 |
| 1940 | Arky Vaughan, Pittsburgh | 15 |
| 1941 | Pete Reiser, Brooklyn | 17 |
| 1942 | Enos Slaughter, St. Louis | 17 |
| 1943 | Stan Musial, St. Louis | 20 |
| 1944 | Johnny Barrett, Pittsburgh | 19 |
| 1945 | Luis Olmo, Brooklyn | 13 |

| Year | Player, Club | Triples |
|---|---|---|
| 1946 | Stan Musial, St. Louis | 20 |
| 1947 | Harry Walker, St. Louis/Philadelphia | 16 |
| 1948 | Stan Musial, St. Louis | 18 |
| 1949 | Stan Musial, St. Louis | 13 |
| | Enos Slaughter, St. Louis | 13 |
| 1950 | Richie Ashburn, Philadelphia | 14 |
| 1951 | Stan Musial, St. Louis | 12 |
| | Gus Bell, Pittsburgh | 12 |
| 1952 | Bobby Thomson, New York | 14 |
| 1953 | Jim Gilliam, Brooklyn | 17 |
| 1954 | Willie Mays, New York | 13 |
| 1955 | Willie Mays, New York | 13 |
| | Dale Long, Pittsburgh | 13 |
| 1956 | Billy Bruton, Milwaukee | 15 |
| 1957 | Willie Mays, New York | 20 |
| 1958 | Richie Ashburn, Philadelphia | 13 |
| 1959 | Wally Moon, Los Angeles | 11 |
| | Charlie Neal, Los Angeles | 11 |
| 1960 | Billy Bruton, Milwaukee | 13 |
| 1961 | George Altman, Chicago | 12 |
| 1962 | Johnny Callison, Philadelphia | 10 |
| | Bill Virdon, Pittsburgh | 10 |
| | Willie Davis, Los Angeles | 10 |
| | Maury Wills, Los Angeles | 10 |
| 1963 | Vada Pinson, Cincinnati | 14 |
| 1964 | Dick Allen, Philadelphia | 13 |
| | Ron Santo, Chicago | 13 |
| 1965 | Johnny Callison, Philadelphia | 16 |
| 1966 | Tim McCarver, St. Louis | 13 |
| 1967 | Vada Pinson, Cincinnati | 13 |
| 1968 | Lou Brock, St. Louis | 14 |
| 1969 | Roberto Clemente, Pittsburgh | 12 |
| 1970 | Willie Davis, Los Angeles | 16 |
| 1971 | Joe Morgan, Houston | 11 |
| | Roger Metzger, Houston | 11 |
| 1972 | Larry Bowa, Philadelphia | 13 |
| 1973 | Roger Metzger, Houston | 14 |
| 1974 | Ralph Garr, Atlanta | 17 |
| 1975 | Ralph Garr, Atlanta | 11 |
| 1976 | Dave Cash, Philadelphia | 12 |
| 1977 | Garry Templeton, St. Louis | 18 |
| 1978 | Garry Templeton, St. Louis | 13 |
| 1979 | Garry Templeton, St. Louis | 19 |
| 1980 | Omar Moreno, Pittsburgh | 13 |
| | Rodney Scott, Montreal | 13 |
| 1981 | Craig Reynolds, Houston | 12 |
| | Gene Richards, San Diego | 12 |
| 1982 | Dickie Thon, Houston | 10 |
| 1983 | Brett Butler, Atlanta | 13 |
| 1984 | Juan Samuel, Philadelphia | 19 |
| | Ryne Sandberg, Chicago | 19 |
| 1985 | Willie McGee, St. Louis | 18 |
| 1986 | Mitch Webster, Montreal | 13 |
| 1987 | Juan Samuel, Philadelphia | 15 |
| 1988 | Andy Van Slyke, Pittsburgh | 15 |
| 1989 | Robby Thompson, San Francisco | 11 |
| 1990 | Mariano Duncan, Cincinnati | 11 |
| 1991 | Ray Lankford, St. Louis | 15 |
| 1992 | Deion Sanders, Atlanta | 14 |
| 1993 | Steve Finley, Houston | 13 |
| 1994 | Brett Butler, Los Angeles | 9 |
| | Darren Lewis, San Francisco | 9 |
| 1995 | Brett Butler, New York/Los Angeles | 9 |
| | Eric Young, Colorado | 9 |
| 1996 | Lance Johnson, New York | 21 |
| 1997 | Delino DeShields, St. Louis | 14 |
| 1998 | David Dellucci, Arizona | 12 |
| 1999 | Bobby Abreu, Philadelphia | 11 |
| | Neifi Perez, Colorado | 11 |
| 2000 | Tony Womack, Arizona | 14 |
| 2001 | Jimmy Rollins, Philadelphia | 12 |
| 2002 | Jimmy Rollins, Philadelphia | 10 |
| 2003 | Steve Finley, Arizona | 10 |
| | Rafael Furcal, Atlanta | 10 |
| 2004 | Juan Pierre, Florida | 12 |
| | Jimmy Rollins, Philadelphia | 12 |
| | Jack Wilson, Pittsburgh | 12 |
| 2005 | Jose Reyes, New York | 17 |

## HOME RUNS

### AMERICAN LEAGUE

| Year | Player, Club | HRs |
|---|---|---|
| 1901 | Nap Lajoie, Philadelphia | 14 |
| 1902 | Socks Seybold, Philadelphia | 16 |
| 1903 | Buck Freeman, Boston | 13 |
| 1904 | Harry Davis, Philadelphia | 10 |
| 1905 | Harry Davis, Philadelphia | 8 |
| 1906 | Harry Davis, Philadelphia | 12 |
| 1907 | Harry Davis, Philadelphia | 8 |
| 1908 | Sam Crawford, Detroit | 7 |
| 1909 | Ty Cobb, Detroit | 9 |
| 1910 | Jake Stahl, Boston | 10 |
| 1911 | Home Run Baker, Philadelphia | 11 |
| 1912 | Home Run Baker, Philadelphia | 10 |
| | Tris Speaker, Boston | 10 |
| 1913 | Home Run Baker, Philadelphia | 12 |
| 1914 | Home Run Baker, Philadelphia | 9 |
| 1915 | Braggo Roth, Chicago/Cleveland | 7 |
| 1916 | Wally Pipp, New York | 12 |
| 1917 | Wally Pipp, New York | 9 |
| 1918 | Babe Ruth, Boston | 11 |
| | Tilly Walker, Philadelphia | 11 |
| 1919 | Babe Ruth, Boston | 29 |
| 1920 | Babe Ruth, New York | 54 |
| 1921 | Babe Ruth, New York | 59 |
| 1922 | Ken Williams, St. Louis | 39 |
| 1923 | Babe Ruth, New York | 41 |
| 1924 | Babe Ruth, New York | 46 |
| 1925 | Bob Meusel, New York | 33 |
| 1926 | Babe Ruth, New York | 47 |
| 1927 | Babe Ruth, New York | 60 |
| 1928 | Babe Ruth, New York | 54 |
| 1929 | Babe Ruth, New York | 46 |
| 1930 | Babe Ruth, New York | 49 |
| 1931 | Babe Ruth, New York | 46 |
| | Lou Gehrig, New York | 46 |
| 1932 | Jimmie Foxx, Philadelphia | 58 |
| 1933 | Jimmie Foxx, Philadelphia | 48 |
| 1934 | Lou Gehrig, New York | 49 |
| 1935 | Jimmie Foxx, Philadelphia | 36 |
| | Hank Greenberg, Detroit | 36 |
| 1936 | Lou Gehrig, New York | 49 |
| 1937 | Joe DiMaggio, New York | 46 |
| 1938 | Hank Greenberg, Detroit | 58 |
| 1939 | Jimmie Foxx, Boston | 35 |
| 1940 | Hank Greenberg, Detroit | 41 |
| 1941 | Ted Williams, Boston | 37 |
| 1942 | Ted Williams, Boston | 36 |
| 1943 | Rudy York, Detroit | 34 |
| 1944 | Nick Etten, New York | 22 |
| 1945 | Vern Stephens, St. Louis | 24 |
| 1946 | Hank Greenberg, Detroit | 44 |
| 1947 | Ted Williams, Boston | 32 |
| 1948 | Joe DiMaggio, New York | 39 |
| 1949 | Ted Williams, Boston | 43 |
| 1950 | Al Rosen, Cleveland | 37 |
| 1951 | Gus Zernial, Chicago/Philadelphia | 33 |
| 1952 | Larry Doby, Cleveland | 32 |
| 1953 | Al Rosen, Cleveland | 43 |
| 1954 | Larry Doby, Cleveland | 32 |
| 1955 | Mickey Mantle, New York | 37 |
| 1956 | Mickey Mantle, New York | 52 |
| 1957 | Roy Sievers, Washington | 42 |
| 1958 | Mickey Mantle, New York | 42 |
| 1959 | Rocky Colavito, Cleveland | 42 |
| | Harmon Killebrew, Washington | 42 |
| 1960 | Mickey Mantle, New York | 40 |
| 1961 | Roger Maris, New York | 61 |
| 1962 | Harmon Killebrew, Minnesota | 48 |
| 1963 | Harmon Killebrew, Minnesota | 45 |
| 1964 | Harmon Killebrew, Minnesota | 49 |
| 1965 | Tony Conigilaro, Boston | 32 |
| 1966 | Frank Robinson, Baltimore | 49 |
| 1967 | Harmon Killebrew, Minnesota | 44 |
| | Carl Yastrzemski, Boston | 44 |
| 1968 | Frank Howard, Washington | 44 |
| 1969 | Harmon Killebrew, Minnesota | 49 |
| 1970 | Frank Howard, Washington | 44 |
| 1971 | Bill Melton, Chicago | 33 |
| 1972 | Dick Allen, Chicago | 37 |
| 1973 | Reggie Jackson, Oakland | 32 |
| 1974 | Dick Allen, Chicago | 32 |
| 1975 | Reggie Jackson, Oakland | 36 |
| | George Scott, Milwaukee | 36 |
| 1976 | Graig Nettles, New York | 32 |
| 1977 | Jim Rice, Boston | 39 |
| 1978 | Jim Rice, Boston | 46 |
| 1979 | Gorman Thomas, Milwaukee | 45 |
| 1980 | Reggie Jackson, New York | 41 |
| | Ben Oglivie, Milwaukee | 41 |
| 1981 | Tony Armas, Oakland | 22 |
| | Dwight Evans, Boston | 22 |
| | Bobby Grich, California | 22 |
| | Eddie Murray, Baltimore | 22 |
| 1982 | Reggie Jackson, California | 39 |
| | Gorman Thomas, Milwaukee | 39 |
| 1983 | Jim Rice, Boston | 39 |
| 1984 | Tony Armas, Boston | 43 |
| 1985 | Darrell Evans, Detroit | 40 |
| 1986 | Jesse Barfield, Toronto | 40 |
| 1987 | Mark McGwire, Oakland | 49 |
| 1988 | Jose Canseco, Oakland | 42 |
| 1989 | Fred McGriff, Toronto | 36 |
| 1990 | Cecil Fielder, Detroit | 51 |
| 1991 | Jose Canseco, Oakland | 44 |
| | Cecil Fielder, Detroit | 44 |
| 1992 | Juan Gonzalez, Texas | 43 |
| 1993 | Juan Gonzalez, Texas | 46 |
| 1994 | Ken Griffey Jr., Seattle | 40 |
| 1995 | Albert Belle, Cleveland | 50 |
| 1996 | Mark McGwire, Oakland | 52 |
| 1997 | Ken Griffey Jr., Seattle | *56 |
| 1998 | Ken Griffey Jr., Seattle | 56 |
| 1999 | Ken Griffey Jr., Seattle | 48 |
| 2000 | Troy Glaus, Anaheim | 47 |
| 2001 | Alex Rodriguez, Texas | 52 |
| 2002 | Alex Rodriguez, Texas | 57 |
| 2003 | Alex Rodriguez, Texas | 47 |
| 2004 | Manny Ramirez, Boston | 43 |
| 2005 | Alex Rodriguez, New York | 48 |

### NATIONAL LEAGUE

| Year | Player, Club | HRs |
|---|---|---|
| 1876 | George Hall, Philadelphia | 5 |
| 1877 | Lipman Pike, Cincinnati | 4 |
| 1878 | Paul Hines, Providence | 4 |
| 1879 | Charley Jones, Boston | 9 |
| 1880 | Jim O'Rourke, Boston | 6 |
| | Harry Stovey, Worcester | 6 |
| 1881 | Dan Brouthers, Buffalo | 8 |
| 1882 | George Wood, Detroit | 7 |
| 1883 | Buck Ewing, New York | 10 |
| 1884 | Ned Williamson, Chicago | 27 |
| 1885 | Abner Dalrymple, Chicago | 11 |
| 1886 | Dan Brouthers, Detroit | 11 |
| | Hardy Richardson, Detroit | 11 |
| 1887 | Billy O'Brien, Washington | 19 |
| 1888 | Jimmy Ryan, Chicago | 16 |
| 1889 | Sam Thompson, Philadelphia | 20 |
| 1890 | Walt Wilmot, Chicago | 13 |
| 1891 | Harry Stovey, Boston | 16 |
| | Mike Tiernan, New York | 16 |
| 1892 | Bug Holliday, Cincinnati | 13 |
| 1893 | Ed Delahanty, Philadelphia | 19 |
| 1894 | Hugh Duffy, Boston | 18 |
| 1895 | Sam Thompson, Philadelphia | 18 |
| 1896 | Ed Delahanty, Philadelphia | 13 |
| | Bill Joyce, Washington/New York | 13 |
| 1897 | Hugh Duffy, Boston | 11 |
| 1898 | Jimmy Collins, Boston | 15 |
| 1899 | Buck Freeman, Washington | 25 |
| 1900 | Herman Long, Boston | 12 |
| 1901 | Sam Crawford, Cincinnati | 16 |
| 1902 | Tommy Leach, Pittsburgh | 6 |
| 1903 | Jimmy Sheckard, Brooklyn | 9 |
| 1904 | Harry Lumley, Brooklyn | 9 |
| 1905 | Fred Odwell, Cincinnati | 9 |
| 1906 | Tim Jordan, Brooklyn | 12 |
| 1907 | Dave Brain, Boston | 10 |
| 1908 | Tim Jordan, Brooklyn | 12 |
| 1909 | Red Murray, New York | 7 |
| 1910 | Fred Beck, Boston | 10 |
| | Frank Schulte, Chicago | 10 |
| 1911 | Frank Schulte, Chicago | 21 |
| 1912 | Heinie Zimmerman, Chicago | 14 |
| 1913 | Gavvy Cravath, Philadelphia | 19 |
| 1914 | Gavvy Cravath, Philadelphia | 19 |
| 1915 | Gavvy Cravath, Philadelphia | 24 |
| 1916 | Dave Robertson, New York | 12 |
| | Cy Williams, Chicago | 12 |
| 1917 | Dave Robertson, New York | 12 |
| | Gavvy Cravath, Philadelphia | 12 |
| 1918 | Gavvy Cravath, Philadelphia | 8 |
| 1919 | Gavvy Cravath, Philadelphia | 12 |
| 1920 | Cy Williams, Philadelphia | 15 |
| 1921 | George Kelly, New York | 23 |
| 1922 | Rogers Hornsby, St. Louis | 42 |
| 1923 | Cy Williams, Philadelphia | 41 |
| 1924 | Jack Fournier, Brooklyn | 27 |
| 1925 | Rogers Hornsby, St. Louis | 39 |
| 1926 | Hack Wilson, Chicago | 21 |
| 1927 | Hack Wilson, Chicago | 30 |
| | Cy Williams, Philadelphia | 30 |
| 1928 | Hack Wilson, Chicago | 31 |
| | Jim Bottomley, St. Louis | 31 |
| 1929 | Chuck Klein, Philadelphia | 43 |
| 1930 | Hack Wilson, Chicago | 56 |
| 1931 | Chuck Klein, Philadelphia | 31 |
| 1932 | Chuck Klein, Philadelphia | 38 |
| | Mel Ott, New York | 38 |
| 1933 | Chuck Klein, Philadelphia | 28 |
| 1934 | Rip Collins, St. Louis | 35 |
| | Mel Ott, New York | 35 |
| 1935 | Wally Berger, Boston | 34 |
| 1936 | Mel Ott, New York | 33 |
| 1937 | Mel Ott, New York | 31 |
| | Joe Medwick, St. Louis | 31 |
| 1938 | Mel Ott, New York | 36 |
| 1939 | Johnny Mize, St. Louis | 28 |
| 1940 | Johnny Mize, St. Louis | 43 |
| 1941 | Dolf Camilli, Brooklyn | 34 |
| 1942 | Mel Ott, New York | 30 |
| 1943 | Bill Nicholson, Chicago | 29 |
| 1944 | Bill Nicholson, Chicago | 33 |
| 1945 | Tommy Holmes, Boston | 28 |
| 1946 | Ralph Kiner, Pittsburgh | 23 |
| 1947 | Ralph Kiner, Pittsburgh | 51 |
| | Johnny Mize, New York | 51 |
| 1948 | Ralph Kiner, Pittsburgh | 40 |
| | Johnny Mize, New York | 40 |

| Year | Player, Club | HRs |
|---|---|---|
| 1949 | Ralph Kiner, Pittsburgh | 54 |
| 1950 | Ralph Kiner, Pittsburgh | 47 |
| 1951 | Ralph Kiner, Pittsburgh | 42 |
| 1952 | Ralph Kiner, Pittsburgh | 37 |
| | Hank Sauer, Chicago | 37 |
| 1953 | Eddie Mathews, Milwaukee | 47 |
| 1954 | Ted Kluszewski, Cincinnati | 49 |
| 1955 | Willie Mays, New York | 51 |
| 1956 | Duke Snider, Brooklyn | 43 |
| 1957 | Hank Aaron, Milwaukee | 44 |
| 1958 | Ernie Banks, Chicago | 47 |
| 1959 | Eddie Mathews, Milwaukee | 46 |
| 1960 | Ernie Banks, Chicago | 41 |
| 1961 | Orlando Cepeda, San Francisco | 46 |
| 1962 | Willie Mays, San Francisco | 49 |
| 1963 | Hank Aaron, Milwaukee | 44 |
| | Willie McCovey, San Francisco | 44 |
| 1964 | Willie Mays, San Francisco | 47 |
| 1965 | Willie Mays, San Francisco | 52 |
| 1966 | Hank Aaron, Atlanta | 44 |
| 1967 | Hank Aaron, Atlanta | 39 |
| 1968 | Willie McCovey, San Francisco | 36 |
| 1969 | Willie McCovey, San Francisco | 45 |
| 1970 | Johnny Bench, Cincinnati | 45 |
| 1971 | Willie Stargell, Pittsburgh | 48 |
| 1972 | Johnny Bench, Cincinnati | 40 |
| 1973 | Willie Stargell, Pittsburgh | 44 |
| 1974 | Mike Schmidt, Philadelphia | 36 |
| 1975 | Mike Schmidt, Philadelphia | 38 |
| 1976 | Mike Schmidt, Philadelphia | 38 |
| 1977 | George Foster, Cincinnati | 52 |
| 1978 | George Foster, Cincinnati | 40 |
| 1979 | Dave Kingman, Chicago | 48 |
| 1980 | Mike Schmidt, Philadelphia | 48 |
| 1981 | Mike Schmidt, Philadelphia | 31 |
| 1982 | Dave Kingman, New York | 37 |
| 1983 | Mike Schmidt, Philadelphia | 40 |
| 1984 | Dale Murphy, Atlanta | 36 |
| | Mike Schmidt, Philadelphia | 36 |
| 1985 | Dale Murphy, Atlanta | 37 |
| 1986 | Mike Schmidt, Philadelphia | 37 |
| 1987 | Andre Dawson, Chicago | 49 |
| 1988 | Darryl Strawberry, New York | 39 |
| 1989 | Kevin Mitchell, San Francisco | 47 |
| 1990 | Ryne Sandberg, Chicago | 40 |
| 1991 | Howard Johnson, New York | 38 |
| 1992 | Fred McGriff, San Diego | 35 |
| 1993 | Barry Bonds, San Francisco | 46 |
| 1994 | Matt Williams, San Francisco | 43 |
| 1995 | Dante Bichette, Colorado | 40 |
| 1996 | Andres Galarraga, Colorado | 47 |
| 1997 | Larry Walker, Colorado | *49 |
| 1998 | Mark McGwire, St. Louis | 70 |
| 1999 | Mark McGwire, St. Louis | 65 |
| 2000 | Sammy Sosa, Chicago | 50 |
| 2001 | Barry Bonds, San Francisco | 73 |
| 2002 | Sammy Sosa, Chicago | 49 |
| 2003 | Jim Thome, Philadelphia | 47 |
| 2004 | Adrian Beltre, Los Angeles | 48 |
| 2005 | Andruw Jones, Atlanta | 51 |

*Mark McGwire led the majors with 58 home runs in 1997, 34 with Oakland AL and 24 with St. Louis NL following a July 31 trade.

## TOTAL BASES

### AMERICAN LEAGUE

| Year | Player, Club | TB |
|---|---|---|
| 1901 | Nap Lajoie, Philadelphia | 350 |
| 1902 | Charlie Hickman, Boston/Cleveland | 288 |
| 1903 | Buck Freeman, Boston | 281 |
| 1904 | Nap Lajoie, Cleveland | 302 |
| 1905 | George Stone, St. Louis | 259 |
| 1906 | George Stone, St. Louis | 291 |
| 1907 | Ty Cobb, Detroit | 283 |
| 1908 | Ty Cobb, Detroit | 276 |
| 1909 | Ty Cobb, Detroit | 296 |
| 1910 | Nap Lajoie, Cleveland | 304 |
| 1911 | Ty Cobb, Detroit | 367 |
| 1912 | Joe Jackson, Cleveland | 331 |
| 1913 | Sam Crawford, Detroit | 298 |
| 1914 | Tris Speaker, Boston | 287 |
| 1915 | Ty Cobb, Detroit | 274 |
| 1916 | Joe Jackson, Chicago | 293 |
| 1917 | Ty Cobb, Detroit | 335 |
| 1918 | George H. Burns, Philadelphia | 236 |
| 1919 | Babe Ruth, Boston | 284 |
| 1920 | George Sisler, St. Louis | 399 |
| 1921 | Babe Ruth, New York | 457 |
| 1922 | Ken Williams, St. Louis | 367 |
| 1923 | Babe Ruth, New York | 399 |
| 1924 | Babe Ruth, New York | 391 |
| 1925 | Al Simmons, Philadelphia | 392 |
| 1926 | Babe Ruth, New York | 365 |
| 1927 | Lou Gehrig, New York | 447 |
| 1928 | Babe Ruth, New York | 380 |
| 1929 | Al Simmons, Philadelphia | 373 |
| 1930 | Lou Gehrig, New York | 419 |
| 1931 | Lou Gehrig, New York | 410 |
| 1932 | Jimmie Foxx, Philadelphia | 438 |
| 1933 | Jimmie Foxx, Philadelphia | 403 |
| 1934 | Lou Gehrig, New York | 409 |
| 1935 | Hank Greenberg, Detroit | 389 |
| 1936 | Hal Trosky, Cleveland | 405 |
| 1937 | Joe DiMaggio, New York | 418 |
| 1938 | Jimmie Foxx, Boston | 398 |
| 1939 | Ted Williams, Boston | 344 |
| 1940 | Hank Greenberg, Detroit | 384 |
| 1941 | Joe DiMaggio, New York | 348 |
| 1942 | Ted Williams, Boston | 338 |
| 1943 | Rudy York, Detroit | 301 |
| 1944 | Johnny Lindell, New York | 297 |
| 1945 | George Stirnweiss, New York | 301 |
| 1946 | Ted Williams, Boston | 343 |
| 1947 | Ted Williams, Boston | 335 |
| 1948 | Joe DiMaggio, New York | 355 |
| 1949 | Ted Williams, Boston | 368 |
| 1950 | Walt Dropo, Boston | 326 |
| 1951 | Ted Williams, Boston | 295 |
| 1952 | Al Rosen, Cleveland | 297 |
| 1953 | Al Rosen, Cleveland | 367 |
| 1954 | Minnie Minoso, Chicago | 304 |
| 1955 | Al Kaline, Detroit | 321 |
| 1956 | Mickey Mantle, New York | 376 |
| 1957 | Roy Sievers, Washington | 331 |
| 1958 | Mickey Mantle, New York | 307 |
| 1959 | Rocky Colavito, Cleveland | 301 |
| 1960 | Mickey Mantle, New York | 294 |
| 1961 | Roger Maris, New York | 366 |
| 1962 | Rocky Colavito, Detroit | 309 |
| 1963 | Dick Stuart, Boston | 319 |
| 1964 | Tony Oliva, Minnesota | 374 |
| 1965 | Zoilo Versalles, Minnesota | 308 |
| 1966 | Frank Robinson, Baltimore | 367 |
| 1967 | Carl Yastrzemski, Boston | 360 |
| 1968 | Frank Howard, Washington | 330 |
| 1969 | Frank Howard, Washington | 340 |
| 1970 | Carl Yastrzemski, Boston | 335 |
| 1971 | Reggie Smith, Boston | 302 |
| 1972 | Bobby Murcer, New York | 314 |
| 1973 | Dave May, Milwaukee | 295 |
| | George Scott, Milwaukee | 295 |
| | Sal Bando, Oakland | 295 |
| 1974 | Joe Rudi, Oakland | 287 |
| 1975 | George Scott, Milwaukee | 318 |
| 1976 | George Brett, Kansas City | 298 |
| 1977 | Jim Rice, Boston | 382 |
| 1978 | Jim Rice, Boston | 406 |
| 1979 | Jim Rice, Boston | 369 |
| 1980 | Cecil Cooper, Milwaukee | 335 |
| 1981 | Dwight Evans, Boston | 215 |
| 1982 | Robin Yount, Milwaukee | 367 |
| 1983 | Jim Rice, Boston | 344 |
| 1984 | Tony Armas, Boston | 339 |
| 1985 | Don Mattingly, New York | 370 |
| 1986 | Don Mattingly, New York | 388 |
| 1987 | George Bell, Toronto | 369 |
| 1988 | Kirby Puckett, Minnesota | 358 |
| 1989 | Ruben Sierra, Texas | 344 |
| 1990 | Cecil Fielder, Detroit | 339 |
| 1991 | Cal Ripken, Baltimore | 368 |
| 1992 | Kirby Puckett, Minnesota | 313 |
| 1993 | Ken Griffey Jr., Seattle | 359 |
| 1994 | Albert Belle, Cleveland | 294 |
| 1995 | Albert Belle, Cleveland | 377 |
| 1996 | Alex Rodriguez, Seattle | 379 |
| 1997 | Ken Griffey Jr., Seattle | 393 |
| 1998 | Albert Belle, Chicago | 399 |
| 1999 | Shawn Green, Toronto | 361 |
| 2000 | Carlos Delgado, Toronto | 378 |
| 2001 | Alex Rodriguez, Texas | 393 |
| 2002 | Alex Rodriguez, Texas | 389 |
| 2003 | Vernon Wells, Toronto | 373 |
| 2004 | Vladimir Guerrero, Anaheim | 366 |
| 2005 | Mark Teixeira, Texas | 370 |

### NATIONAL LEAGUE

| Year | Player, Club | TB |
|---|---|---|
| 1900 | Elmer Flick, Philadelphia | 302 |
| 1901 | Jesse Burkett, St. Louis | 306 |
| 1902 | Sam Crawford, Cincinnati | 256 |
| 1903 | Ginger Beaumont, Pittsburgh | 272 |
| 1904 | Honus Wagner, Pittsburgh | 255 |
| 1905 | Cy Seymour, Cincinnati | 325 |
| 1906 | Honus Wagner, Pittsburgh | 237 |
| 1907 | Honus Wagner, Pittsburgh | 264 |
| 1908 | Honus Wagner, Pittsburgh | 308 |
| 1909 | Honus Wagner, Pittsburgh | 242 |
| 1910 | Sherry Magee, Philadelphia | 263 |
| 1911 | Frank Schulte, Chicago | 308 |
| 1912 | Heinie Zimmerman, Chicago | 318 |
| 1913 | Gavvy Cravath, Philadelphia | 298 |
| 1914 | Sherry Magee, Philadelphia | 277 |
| 1915 | Gavvy Cravath, Philadelphia | 266 |
| 1916 | Zack Wheat, Brooklyn | 262 |
| 1917 | Rogers Hornsby, St. Louis | 253 |
| 1918 | Charlie Hollocher, Chicago | 202 |
| 1919 | Hy Myers, Brooklyn | 223 |
| 1920 | Rogers Hornsby, St. Louis | 329 |
| 1921 | Rogers Hornsby, St. Louis | 378 |
| 1922 | Rogers Hornsby, St. Louis | 450 |
| 1923 | Frankie Frisch, New York | 311 |
| 1924 | Rogers Hornsby, St. Louis | 373 |
| 1925 | Rogers Hornsby, St. Louis | 381 |
| 1926 | Jim Bottomley, St. Louis | 305 |
| 1927 | Paul Waner, Pittsburgh | 342 |
| 1928 | Jim Bottomley, St. Louis | 362 |
| 1929 | Rogers Hornsby, Chicago | 409 |
| 1930 | Chuck Klein, Philadelphia | 445 |
| 1931 | Chuck Klein, Philadelphia | 347 |
| 1932 | Chuck Klein, Philadelphia | 420 |
| 1933 | Chuck Klein, Philadelphia | 365 |
| 1934 | Rip Collins, St. Louis | 369 |
| 1935 | Joe Medwick, St. Louis | 365 |
| 1936 | Joe Medwick, St. Louis | 367 |
| 1937 | Joe Medwick, St. Louis | 406 |
| 1938 | Johnny Mize, St. Louis | 326 |
| 1939 | Johnny Mize, St. Louis | 353 |
| 1940 | Johnny Mize, St. Louis | 368 |
| 1941 | Pete Reiser, Brooklyn | 299 |
| 1942 | Enos Slaughter, St. Louis | 292 |
| 1943 | Stan Musial, St. Louis | 347 |
| 1944 | Bill Nicholson, Chicago | 317 |
| 1945 | Tommy Holmes, Boston | 367 |
| 1946 | Stan Musial, St. Louis | 366 |
| 1947 | Ralph Kiner, Pittsburgh | 361 |
| 1948 | Stan Musial, St. Louis | 429 |
| 1949 | Stan Musial, St. Louis | 382 |
| 1950 | Duke Snider, Brooklyn | 343 |
| 1951 | Stan Musial, St. Louis | 355 |
| 1952 | Stan Musial, St. Louis | 311 |
| 1953 | Duke Snider, Brooklyn | 370 |
| 1954 | Duke Snider, Brooklyn | 378 |
| 1955 | Willie Mays, New York | 382 |
| 1956 | Hank Aaron, Milwaukee | 340 |
| 1957 | Hank Aaron, Milwaukee | 369 |
| 1958 | Ernie Banks, Chicago | 379 |
| 1959 | Hank Aaron, Milwaukee | 400 |
| 1960 | Hank Aaron, Milwaukee | 334 |
| 1961 | Hank Aaron, Milwaukee | 358 |
| 1962 | Willie Mays, San Francisco | 382 |
| 1963 | Hank Aaron, Milwaukee | 370 |
| 1964 | Dick Allen, Philadelphia | 352 |
| 1965 | Willie Mays, San Francisco | 360 |
| 1966 | Felipe Alou, Atlanta | 355 |
| 1967 | Hank Aaron, Atlanta | 344 |
| 1968 | Billy Williams, Chicago | 321 |
| 1969 | Hank Aaron, Atlanta | 332 |
| 1970 | Billy Williams, Chicago | 373 |
| 1971 | Joe Torre, St. Louis | 352 |
| 1972 | Billy Williams, Chicago | 348 |
| 1973 | Bobby Bonds, San Francisco | 341 |
| 1974 | Johnny Bench, Cincinnati | 315 |
| 1975 | Greg Luzinski, Philadelphia | 322 |
| 1976 | Mike Schmidt, Philadelphia | 306 |
| 1977 | George Foster, Cincinnati | 388 |
| 1978 | Dave Parker, Pittsburgh | 340 |
| 1979 | Dave Winfield, San Diego | 333 |
| 1980 | Mike Schmidt, Philadelphia | 342 |
| 1981 | Mike Schmidt, Philadelphia | 228 |
| 1982 | Al Oliver, Montreal | 317 |
| 1983 | Andre Dawson, Montreal | 341 |
| 1984 | Dale Murphy, Atlanta | 332 |
| 1985 | Dave Parker, Cincinnati | 350 |
| 1986 | Dave Parker, Cincinnati | 304 |
| 1987 | Andre Dawson, Chicago | 353 |
| 1988 | Andres Galarraga, Montreal | 329 |
| 1989 | Kevin Mitchell, San Francisco | 345 |
| 1990 | Ryne Sandberg, Chicago | 344 |
| 1991 | Will Clark, San Francisco | 303 |
| | Terry Pendleton, Atlanta | 303 |
| 1992 | Gary Sheffield, San Diego | 323 |
| 1993 | Barry Bonds, San Francisco | 365 |
| 1994 | Jeff Bagwell, Houston | 300 |
| 1995 | Dante Bichette, Colorado | 359 |
| 1996 | Ellis Burks, Colorado | 392 |
| 1997 | Larry Walker, Colorado | 409 |
| 1998 | Sammy Sosa, Chicago | 416 |
| 1999 | Sammy Sosa, Chicago | 397 |
| 2000 | Todd Helton, Colorado | 405 |
| 2001 | Sammy Sosa, Chicago | 425 |
| 2002 | Vladimir Guerrero, Montreal | 364 |
| 2003 | Albert Pujols, St. Louis | 394 |
| 2004 | Albert Pujols, St. Louis | 389 |
| 2005 | Derrek Lee, Chicago | 393 |

## RUNS BATTED IN

### AMERICAN LEAGUE

| Year | Player, Club | RBIs |
|---|---|---|
| 1907 | Ty Cobb, Detroit | 119 |
| 1908 | Ty Cobb, Detroit | 108 |
| 1909 | Ty Cobb, Detroit | 107 |
| 1910 | Sam Crawford, Detroit | 120 |
| 1911 | Ty Cobb, Detroit | 127 |
| 1912 | Home Run Baker, Philadelphia | 130 |
| 1913 | Home Run Baker, Philadelphia | 117 |
| 1914 | Sam Crawford, Detroit | 104 |
| 1915 | Sam Crawford, Detroit | 112 |
| | Bobby Veach, Detroit | 112 |
| 1916 | Del Pratt, St. Louis | 103 |
| 1917 | Bobby Veach, Detroit | 103 |
| 1918 | Bobby Veach, Detroit | 78 |
| 1919 | Babe Ruth, Boston | 114 |
| 1920 | Babe Ruth, New York | 137 |
| 1921 | Babe Ruth, New York | 171 |
| 1922 | Ken Williams, St. Louis | 155 |
| 1923 | Babe Ruth, New York | 131 |
| 1924 | Goose Goslin, Washington | 129 |
| 1925 | Bob Meusel, New York | 138 |
| 1926 | Babe Ruth, New York | 146 |
| 1927 | Lou Gehrig, New York | 175 |
| 1928 | Babe Ruth, New York | 142 |
| | Lou Gehrig, New York | 142 |
| 1929 | Al Simmons, Philadelphia | 157 |
| 1930 | Lou Gehrig, New York | 174 |
| 1931 | Lou Gehrig, New York | 184 |
| 1932 | Jimmie Foxx, Philadelphia | 169 |
| 1933 | Jimmie Foxx, Philadelphia | 163 |
| 1934 | Lou Gehrig, New York | 165 |
| 1935 | Hank Greenberg, Detroit | 170 |
| 1936 | Hal Trosky, Cleveland | 162 |
| 1937 | Hank Greenberg, Detroit | 183 |
| 1938 | Jimmie Foxx, Boston | 175 |
| 1939 | Ted Williams, Boston | 145 |
| 1940 | Hank Greenberg, Detroit | 150 |
| 1941 | Joe DiMaggio, New York | 125 |
| 1942 | Ted Williams, Boston | 137 |
| 1943 | Rudy York, Detroit | 118 |
| 1944 | Vern Stephens, St. Louis | 109 |
| 1945 | Nick Etten, New York | 111 |
| 1946 | Hank Greenberg, Detroit | 127 |
| 1947 | Ted Williams, Boston | 114 |
| 1948 | Joe DiMaggio, New York | 155 |
| 1949 | Ted Williams, Boston | 159 |
| | Vern Stephens, Boston | 159 |
| 1950 | Walt Dropo, Boston | 144 |
| | Vern Stephens, Boston | 144 |
| 1951 | Gus Zernial, Chicago-Philadelphia | 129 |
| 1952 | Al Rosen, Cleveland | 105 |
| 1953 | Al Rosen, Cleveland | 145 |
| 1954 | Larry Doby, Cleveland | 126 |
| 1955 | Ray Boone, Detroit | 116 |
| | Jackie Jensen, Boston | 116 |
| 1956 | Mickey Mantle, New York | 130 |
| 1957 | Roy Sievers, Washington | 114 |
| 1958 | Jackie Jensen, Boston | 122 |
| 1959 | Jackie Jensen, Boston | 112 |
| 1960 | Roger Maris, New York | 112 |
| 1961 | Roger Maris, New York | 142 |
| 1962 | Harmon Killebrew, Minnesota | 126 |
| 1963 | Dick Stuart, Boston | 118 |
| 1964 | Brooks Robinson, Baltimore | 118 |
| 1965 | Rocky Colavito, Cleveland | 108 |
| 1966 | Frank Robinson, Baltimore | 122 |
| 1967 | Carl Yastrzemski, Boston | 121 |
| 1968 | Ken Harrelson, Boston | 109 |
| 1969 | Harmon Killebrew, Minnesota | 140 |
| 1970 | Frank Howard, Washington | 126 |
| 1971 | Harmon Killebrew, Minnesota | 119 |
| 1972 | Dick Allen, Chicago | 113 |
| 1973 | Reggie Jackson, Oakland | 117 |
| 1974 | Jeff Burroughs, Texas | 118 |
| 1975 | George Scott, Milwaukee | 109 |
| 1976 | Lee May, Baltimore | 109 |
| 1977 | Larry Hisle, Minnesota | 119 |
| 1978 | Jim Rice, Boston | 139 |
| 1979 | Don Baylor, California | 139 |
| 1980 | Cecil Cooper, Milwaukee | 122 |
| 1981 | Eddie Murray, Baltimore | 78 |
| 1982 | Hal McRae, Kansas City | 133 |
| 1983 | Cecil Cooper, Milwaukee | 126 |
| | Jim Rice, Boston | 126 |
| 1984 | Tony Armas, Boston | 123 |
| 1985 | Don Mattingly, New York | 145 |
| 1986 | Joe Carter, Cleveland | 121 |
| 1987 | George Bell, Toronto | 134 |
| 1988 | Jose Canseco, Oakland | 124 |
| 1989 | Ruben Sierra, Texas | 119 |
| 1990 | Cecil Fielder, Detroit | 132 |
| 1991 | Cecil Fielder, Detroit | 133 |
| 1992 | Cecil Fielder, Detroit | 124 |
| 1993 | Albert Belle, Cleveland | 129 |
| 1994 | Kirby Puckett, Minnesota | 112 |
| 1995 | Albert Belle, Cleveland | 126 |
| | Mo Vaughn, Boston | 126 |
| 1996 | Albert Belle, Cleveland | 148 |
| 1997 | Ken Griffey Jr., Seattle | 147 |
| 1998 | Juan Gonzalez, Texas | 157 |
| 1999 | Manny Ramirez, Cleveland | 165 |
| 2000 | Edgar Martinez, Seattle | 145 |
| 2001 | Bret Boone, Seattle | 141 |
| 2002 | Alex Rodriguez, Texas | 142 |
| 2003 | Carlos Delgado, Toronto | 145 |
| 2004 | Miguel Tejada, Baltimore | 150 |
| 2005 | David Ortiz, Boston | 148 |

### NATIONAL LEAGUE

| Year | Player, Club | RBIs |
|---|---|---|
| 1907 | Sherry Magee, Philadelphia | 85 |
| 1908 | Honus Wagner, Pittsburgh | 109 |
| 1909 | Honus Wagner, Pittsburgh | 100 |
| 1910 | Sherry Magee, Philadelphia | 123 |
| 1911 | Frank Schulte, Chicago | 107 |
| | Chief Wilson, Pittsburgh | 107 |
| 1912 | Honus Wagner, Pittsburgh | 102 |
| 1913 | Gavvy Cravath, Philadelphia | 128 |
| 1914 | Sherry Magee, Philadelphia | 103 |
| 1915 | Gavvy Cravath, Philadelphia | 115 |
| 1916 | Heinie Zimmerman, Chicago/New York | 83 |
| 1917 | Heinie Zimmerman, New York | 102 |
| 1918 | Sherry Magee, Cincinnati | 76 |
| 1919 | Hy Myers, Brooklyn | 73 |
| 1920 | George Kelly, New York | 94 |
| | Rogers Hornsby, St. Louis | 94 |
| 1921 | Rogers Hornsby, St. Louis | 126 |
| 1922 | Rogers Hornsby, St. Louis | 152 |
| 1923 | Irish Meusel, New York | 125 |
| 1924 | George Kelly, New York | 136 |
| 1925 | Rogers Hornsby, St. Louis | 143 |
| 1926 | Jim Bottomley, St. Louis | 120 |
| 1927 | Paul Waner, Pittsburgh | 131 |
| 1928 | Jim Bottomley, St. Louis | 136 |
| 1929 | Hack Wilson, Chicago | 159 |
| 1930 | Hack Wilson, Chicago | 191 |
| 1931 | Chuck Klein, Philadelphia | 121 |
| 1932 | Don Hurst, Philadelphia | 143 |
| 1933 | Chuck Klein, Philadelphia | 120 |
| 1934 | Mel Ott, New York | 135 |
| 1935 | Wally Berger, Boston | 130 |
| 1936 | Joe Medwick, St. Louis | 138 |
| 1937 | Joe Medwick, St. Louis | 154 |
| 1938 | Joe Medwick, St. Louis | 122 |
| 1939 | Frank McCormick, Cincinnati | 128 |
| 1940 | Johnny Mize, St. Louis | 137 |
| 1941 | Dolf Camilli, Brooklyn | 120 |
| 1942 | Johnny Mize, New York | 110 |
| 1943 | Bill Nicholson, Chicago | 128 |
| 1944 | Bill Nicholson, Chicago | 122 |
| 1945 | Dixie Walker, Brooklyn | 124 |
| 1946 | Enos Slaughter, St. Louis | 130 |
| 1947 | Johnny Mize, New York | 138 |
| 1948 | Stan Musial, St. Louis | 131 |
| 1949 | Ralph Kiner, Pittsburgh | 127 |
| 1950 | Del Ennis, Philadelphia | 126 |
| 1951 | Monte Irvin, New York | 121 |
| 1952 | Hank Sauer, Chicago | 121 |
| 1953 | Roy Campanella, Brooklyn | 142 |
| 1954 | Ted Kluszewski, Cincinnati | 141 |
| 1955 | Duke Snider, Brooklyn | 136 |
| 1956 | Stan Musial, St. Louis | 109 |
| 1957 | Hank Aaron, Milwaukee | 132 |
| 1958 | Ernie Banks, Chicago | 129 |
| 1959 | Ernie Banks, Chicago | 143 |
| 1960 | Hank Aaron, Milwaukee | 126 |
| 1961 | Orlando Cepeda, San Francisco | 142 |
| 1962 | Tommy Davis, Los Angeles | 153 |
| 1963 | Hank Aaron, Milwaukee | 130 |
| 1964 | Ken Boyer, St. Louis | 119 |
| 1965 | Deron Johnson, Cincinnati | 130 |
| 1966 | Hank Aaron, Atlanta | 127 |
| 1967 | Orlando Cepeda, St. Louis | 111 |
| 1968 | Willie McCovey, San Francisco | 105 |
| 1969 | Willie McCovey, San Francisco | 126 |
| 1970 | Johnny Bench, Cincinnati | 148 |
| 1971 | Joe Torre, St. Louis | 137 |
| 1972 | Johnny Bench, Cincinnati | 125 |
| 1973 | Willie Stargell, Pittsburgh | 119 |
| 1974 | Johnny Bench, Cincinnati | 129 |
| 1975 | Greg Luzinski, Philadelphia | 120 |
| 1976 | George Foster, Cincinnati | 121 |
| 1977 | George Foster, Cincinnati | 149 |
| 1978 | George Foster, Cincinnati | 120 |
| 1979 | Dave Winfield, San Diego | 118 |
| 1980 | Mike Schmidt, Philadelphia | 121 |
| 1981 | Mike Schmidt, Philadelphia | 91 |
| 1982 | Dale Murphy, Atlanta | 109 |
| | Al Oliver, Montreal | 109 |
| 1983 | Dale Murphy, Atlanta | 121 |
| 1984 | Gary Carter, Montreal | 106 |
| | Mike Schmidt, Philadelphia | 106 |
| 1985 | Dave Parker, Cincinnati | 125 |
| 1986 | Mike Schmidt, Philadelphia | 119 |
| 1987 | Andre Dawson, Chicago | 137 |
| 1988 | Will Clark, San Francisco | 109 |
| 1989 | Kevin Mitchell, San Francisco | 125 |
| 1990 | Matt Williams, San Francisco | 122 |
| 1991 | Howard Johnson, New York | 117 |
| 1992 | Darren Daulton, Philadelphia | 109 |
| 1993 | Barry Bonds, San Francisco | 123 |
| 1994 | Jeff Bagwell, Houston | 116 |
| 1995 | Dante Bichette, Colorado | 128 |
| 1996 | Andres Galarraga, Colorado | 150 |
| 1997 | Andres Galarraga, Colorado | 140 |
| 1998 | Sammy Sosa, Chicago | 158 |
| 1999 | Mark McGwire, St. Louis | 147 |
| 2000 | Todd Helton, Colorado | 147 |
| 2001 | Sammy Sosa, Chicago | 160 |
| 2002 | Lance Berkman, Houston | 128 |
| 2003 | Preston Wilson, Colorado | 141 |
| 2004 | Vinnie Castilla, Colorado | 131 |
| 2005 | Andruw Jones, Atlanta | 128 |

Note—official statistic since 1920

## BASES ON BALLS

### AMERICAN LEAGUE

| Year | Player, Club | BB |
|---|---|---|
| 1913 | Burt Shotton, St. Louis | 99 |
| 1914 | Donie Bush, Detroit | 112 |
| 1915 | Eddie Collins, Chicago | 119 |
| 1916 | Burt Shotton, St. Louis | 110 |
| 1917 | Jack Graney, Cleveland | 94 |
| 1918 | Ray Chapman, Cleveland | 84 |
| 1919 | Jack Graney, Cleveland | 105 |
| 1920 | Babe Ruth, New York | 150 |
| 1921 | Babe Ruth, New York | 145 |
| 1922 | Whitey Witt, New York | 89 |
| 1923 | Babe Ruth, New York | 170 |
| 1924 | Babe Ruth, New York | 142 |
| 1925 | Willie Kamm, Chicago | 90 |
| | Johnny Mostil, Chicago | 90 |
| 1926 | Babe Ruth, New York | 144 |
| 1927 | Babe Ruth, New York | 138 |
| 1928 | Babe Ruth, New York | 135 |
| 1929 | Max Bishop, Philadelphia | 128 |
| 1930 | Babe Ruth, New York | 136 |
| 1931 | Babe Ruth, New York | 128 |
| 1932 | Babe Ruth, New York | 130 |
| 1933 | Babe Ruth, New York | 114 |
| 1934 | Jimmie Foxx, Philadelphia | 111 |
| 1935 | Lou Gehrig, New York | 132 |
| 1936 | Lou Gehrig, New York | 130 |
| 1937 | Lou Gehrig, New York | 127 |
| 1938 | Jimmie Foxx, Boston | 119 |
| | Hank Greenberg, Detroit | 119 |
| 1939 | Harlond Clift, St. Louis | 111 |
| 1940 | Charlie Keller, New York | 106 |
| 1941 | Ted Williams, Boston | 147 |
| 1942 | Ted Williams, Boston | 145 |
| 1943 | Charlie Keller, New York | 106 |
| 1944 | Nick Etten, New York | 97 |
| 1945 | Roy Cullenbine, Cleveland/Detroit | 112 |
| 1946 | Ted Williams, Boston | 156 |
| 1947 | Ted Williams, Boston | 162 |
| 1948 | Ted Williams, Boston | 126 |
| 1949 | Ted Williams, Boston | 162 |
| 1950 | Eddie Yost, Washington | 141 |
| 1951 | Ted Williams, Boston | 144 |
| 1952 | Eddie Yost, Washington | 129 |
| 1953 | Eddie Yost, Washington | 123 |
| 1954 | Ted Williams, Boston | 136 |
| 1955 | Mickey Mantle, New York | 113 |
| 1956 | Eddie Yost, Washington | 151 |
| 1957 | Mickey Mantle, New York | 146 |
| 1958 | Mickey Mantle, New York | 129 |
| 1959 | Eddie Yost, Detroit | 135 |
| 1960 | Eddie Yost, Detroit | 125 |
| 1961 | Mickey Mantle, New York | 126 |
| 1962 | Mickey Mantle, New York | 122 |
| 1963 | Carl Yastrzemski, Boston | 95 |
| 1964 | Norm Siebern, Baltimore | 106 |
| 1965 | Rocky Colavito, Cleveland | 93 |
| 1966 | Harmon Killebrew, Minnesota | 103 |
| 1967 | Harmon Killebrew, Minnesota | 131 |
| 1968 | Carl Yastrzemski, Boston | 119 |
| 1969 | Harmon Killebrew, Minnesota | 145 |
| 1970 | Frank Howard, Washington | 132 |
| 1971 | Harmon Killebrew, Minnesota | 114 |
| 1972 | Dick Allen, Chicago | 99 |
| | Roy White, New York | 99 |
| 1973 | John Mayberry, Kansas City | 122 |
| 1974 | Gene Tenace, Oakland | 110 |
| 1975 | John Mayberry, Kansas City | 119 |
| 1976 | Mike Hargrove, Texas | 97 |
| 1977 | Toby Harrah, Texas | 109 |
| 1978 | Mike Hargrove, Texas | 107 |

| Year | Player, Club | BB |
|---|---|---|
| 1979 | Darrell Porter, Kansas City | 121 |
| 1980 | Willie Randolph, New York | 119 |
| 1981 | Dwight Evans, Boston | 85 |
| 1982 | Rickey Henderson, Oakland | 116 |
| 1983 | Rickey Henderson, Oakland | 103 |
| 1984 | Eddie Murray, Baltimore | 107 |
| 1985 | Dwight Evans, Boston | 114 |
| 1986 | Wade Boggs, Boston | 105 |
| 1987 | Brian Downing, California | 106 |
| | Dwight Evans, Boston | 106 |
| 1988 | Wade Boggs, Boston | 125 |
| 1989 | Rickey Henderson, New York/Oakland | 126 |
| 1990 | Mark McGwire, Oakland | 110 |
| 1991 | Frank Thomas, Chicago | 138 |
| 1992 | Mickey Tettleton, Detroit | 122 |
| | Frank Thomas, Chicago | 122 |
| 1993 | Tony Phillips, Detroit | 132 |
| 1994 | Frank Thomas, Chicago | 109 |
| 1995 | Frank Thomas, Chicago | 136 |
| 1996 | Tony Phillips, Chicago | 125 |
| 1997 | Jim Thome, Cleveland | 120 |
| 1998 | Rickey Henderson, Oakland | 118 |
| 1999 | Jim Thome, Cleveland | 127 |
| 2000 | Jason Giambi, Oakland | 137 |
| 2001 | Jason Giambi, Oakland | 129 |
| 2002 | Jim Thome, Cleveland | 122 |
| 2003 | Jason Giambi, New York | 129 |
| 2004 | Eric Chavez, Oakland | 95 |
| 2005 | Jason Giambi, New York | 108 |

## NATIONAL LEAGUE

| Year | Player, Club | BB |
|---|---|---|
| 1910 | Miller Huggins, St. Louis | 116 |
| 1911 | Jimmy Sheckard, Chicago | 147 |
| 1912 | Jimmy Sheckard, Chicago | 122 |
| 1913 | Bob Bescher, Cincinnati | 94 |
| 1914 | Miller Huggins, St. Louis | 105 |
| 1915 | Gavvy Cravath, Philadelphia | 86 |
| 1916 | Heinie Groh, Cincinnati | 84 |
| 1917 | George J. Burns, New York | 75 |
| 1918 | Max Carey, Pittsburgh | 62 |
| 1919 | George J. Burns, New York | 82 |
| 1920 | George J. Burns, New York | 76 |
| 1921 | George J. Burns, New York | 80 |
| 1922 | Max Carey, Pittsburgh | 80 |
| 1923 | George J. Burns, New York | 101 |
| 1924 | Rogers Hornsby, St. Louis | 89 |
| 1925 | Jack Fournier, Brooklyn | 86 |
| 1926 | Hack Wilson, Chicago | 69 |
| 1927 | Rogers Hornsby, New York | 86 |
| 1928 | Rogers Hornsby, Boston | 107 |
| 1929 | Mel Ott, New York | 113 |
| 1930 | Hack Wilson, Chicago | 105 |
| 1931 | Mel Ott, New York | 80 |
| 1932 | Mel Ott, New York | 100 |
| 1933 | Mel Ott, New York | 75 |
| 1934 | Arky Vaughan, Pittsburgh | 94 |
| 1935 | Arky Vaughan, Pittsburgh | 97 |
| 1936 | Arky Vaughan, Pittsburgh | 118 |
| 1937 | Mel Ott, New York | 102 |
| 1938 | Dolf Camilli, Brooklyn | 119 |
| 1939 | Dolf Camilli, Brooklyn | 110 |
| 1940 | Elbie Fletcher, Pittsburgh | 119 |
| 1941 | Elbie Fletcher, Pittsburgh | 118 |
| 1942 | Mel Ott, New York | 109 |
| 1943 | Augie Galan, Brooklyn | 103 |
| 1944 | Augie Galan, Brooklyn | 101 |
| 1945 | Eddie Stanky, Brooklyn | 148 |
| 1946 | Eddie Stanky, Brooklyn | 137 |
| 1947 | Hank Greenberg, Pittsburgh | 104 |
| | Pee Wee Reese, Brooklyn | 104 |
| 1948 | Bob Elliott, Boston | 131 |
| 1949 | Ralph Kiner, Pittsburgh | 117 |
| 1950 | Eddie Stanky, New York | 144 |
| 1951 | Ralph Kiner, Pittsburgh | 137 |
| 1952 | Ralph Kiner, Pittsburgh | 110 |
| 1953 | Stan Musial, St. Louis | 105 |
| 1954 | Richie Ashburn, Philadelphia | 125 |
| 1955 | Eddie Mathews, Milwaukee | 109 |
| 1956 | Duke Snider, Brooklyn | 99 |
| 1957 | Richie Ashburn, Philadelphia | 94 |
| | Johnny Temple, Cincinnati | 94 |
| 1958 | Richie Ashburn, Philadelphia | 97 |
| 1959 | Jim Gilliam, Los Angeles | 96 |
| 1960 | Richie Ashburn, Chicago | 116 |
| 1961 | Eddie Mathews, Milwaukee | 93 |
| 1962 | Eddie Mathews, Milwaukee | 101 |
| 1963 | Eddie Mathews, Milwaukee | 124 |
| 1964 | Ron Santo, Chicago | 86 |
| 1965 | Joe Morgan, Houston | 97 |
| 1966 | Ron Santo, Chicago | 95 |
| 1967 | Ron Santo, Chicago | 96 |
| 1968 | Ron Santo, Chicago | 96 |
| 1969 | Jim Wynn, Houston | 148 |
| 1970 | Willie McCovey, San Francisco | 137 |
| 1971 | Willie Mays, San Francisco | 112 |
| 1972 | Joe Morgan, Cincinnati | 115 |
| 1973 | Darrell Evans, Atlanta | 124 |
| 1974 | Darrell Evans, Atlanta | 126 |
| 1975 | Joe Morgan, Cincinnati | 132 |
| 1976 | Jim Wynn, Atlanta | 127 |
| 1977 | Gene Tenace, San Diego | 125 |
| 1978 | Jeff Burroughs, Atlanta | 117 |
| 1979 | Mike Schmidt, Philadelphia | 120 |
| 1980 | Dan Driessen, Cincinnati | 93 |
| | Joe Morgan, Houston | 93 |
| 1981 | Mike Schmidt, Philadelphia | 73 |
| 1982 | Mike Schmidt, Philadelphia | 107 |
| 1983 | Mike Schmidt, Philadelphia | 128 |
| 1984 | Gary Matthews, Chicago | 103 |
| 1985 | Dale Murphy, Atlanta | 90 |
| 1986 | Keith Hernandez, New York | 94 |
| 1987 | Jack Clark, St. Louis | 136 |
| 1988 | Will Clark, San Francisco | 100 |
| 1989 | Jack Clark, San Diego | 132 |
| 1990 | Jack Clark, San Diego | 104 |
| 1991 | Brett Butler, Los Angeles | 108 |
| 1992 | Barry Bonds, Pittsburgh | 127 |
| 1993 | Lenny Dykstra, Philadelphia | 129 |
| 1994 | Barry Bonds, San Francisco | 74 |
| 1995 | Barry Bonds, San Francisco | 120 |
| 1996 | Barry Bonds, San Francisco | 151 |
| 1997 | Barry Bonds, San Francisco | 145 |
| 1998 | Mark McGwire, St. Louis | 162 |
| 1999 | Jeff Bagwell, Houston | 149 |
| 2000 | Barry Bonds, San Francisco | 117 |
| 2001 | Barry Bonds, San Francisco | 177 |
| 2002 | Barry Bonds, San Francisco | 198 |
| 2003 | Barry Bonds, San Francisco | 148 |
| 2004 | Barry Bonds, San Francisco | 232 |
| 2005 | Brian Giles, San Diego | 119 |

Note—not included in batting records in AL prior to 1913 and NL prior to 1910

## STRIKEOUTS

### AMERICAN LEAGUE

| Year | Player, Club | Ks |
|---|---|---|
| 1913 | Danny Moeller, Washington | 103 |
| 1914 | Gus Williams, St. Louis | 120 |
| 1915 | Doc Lavan, St. Louis | 83 |
| 1916 | Wally Pipp, New York | 82 |
| 1917 | Braggo Roth, Cleveland | 73 |
| 1918 | Babe Ruth, Boston | 58 |
| 1919 | Red Shannon, Philadelphia/Boston | 70 |
| 1920 | Aaron Ward, New York | 84 |
| 1921 | Bob Meusel, New York | 88 |
| 1922 | Jimmie Dykes, Philadelphia | 98 |
| 1923 | Babe Ruth, New York | 93 |
| 1924 | Babe Ruth, New York | 81 |
| 1925 | Marty McManus, St. Louis | 69 |
| 1926 | Tony Lazzeri, New York | 96 |
| 1927 | Babe Ruth, New York | 89 |
| 1928 | Babe Ruth, New York | 87 |
| 1929 | Jimmie Foxx, Philadelphia | 70 |
| 1930 | Jimmie Foxx, Philadelphia | 66 |
| | Ed Morgan, Cleveland | 66 |
| 1931 | Jimmie Foxx, Philadelphia | 84 |
| 1932 | Bruce Campbell, Chicago/St. Louis | 104 |
| 1933 | Jimmie Foxx, Philadelphia | 93 |
| 1934 | Harlond Clift, St. Louis | 100 |
| 1935 | Jimmie Foxx, Philadelphia | 99 |
| 1936 | Jimmie Foxx, Boston | 119 |
| 1937 | Frank Crosetti, New York | 105 |
| 1938 | Frank Crosetti, New York | 97 |
| 1939 | Hank Greenberg, Detroit | 95 |
| 1940 | Sam Chapman, Philadelphia | 96 |
| 1941 | Jimmie Foxx, Boston | 103 |
| 1942 | Joe Gordon, New York | 95 |
| 1943 | Chet Laabs, St. Louis | 105 |
| 1944 | Pat Seerey, Cleveland | 99 |
| 1945 | Pat Seerey, Cleveland | 97 |
| 1946 | Charlie Keller, New York | 101 |
| | Pat Seerey, Cleveland | 101 |
| 1947 | Eddie Joost, Philadelphia | 110 |
| 1948 | Pat Seerey, Cleveland/Chicago | 102 |
| 1949 | Dick Kokos, St. Louis | 91 |
| 1950 | Gus Zernial, Chicago | 110 |
| 1951 | Gus Zernial, Chicago/Philadelphia | 101 |
| 1952 | Larry Doby, Cleveland | 111 |
| | Mickey Mantle, New York | 111 |
| 1953 | Larry Doby, Cleveland | 121 |
| 1954 | Mickey Mantle, New York | 107 |
| 1955 | Norm Zauchin, Boston | 105 |
| 1956 | Jim Lemon, Washington | 138 |
| 1957 | Jim Lemon, Washington | 94 |
| 1958 | Jim Lemon, Washington | 120 |
| | Mickey Mantle, New York | 120 |
| 1959 | Mickey Mantle, New York | 126 |
| 1960 | Mickey Mantle, New York | 125 |
| 1961 | Jake Wood, Detroit | 141 |
| 1962 | Harmon Killebrew, Minnesota | 142 |
| 1963 | Dave Nicholson, Chicago | 175 |
| 1964 | Nelson Mathews, Kansas City | 143 |
| 1965 | Zoilo Versalles, Minnesota | 122 |
| 1966 | George Scott, Boston | 152 |
| 1967 | Frank Howard, Washington | 155 |
| 1968 | Reggie Jackson, Oakland | 171 |
| 1969 | Reggie Jackson, Oakland | 142 |
| 1970 | Reggie Jackson, Oakland | 135 |
| 1971 | Reggie Jackson, Oakland | 161 |
| 1972 | Bobby Darwin, Minnesota | 145 |
| 1973 | Bobby Darwin, Minnesota | 137 |
| 1974 | Bobby Darwin, Minnesota | 127 |
| 1975 | Jeff Burroughs, Texas | 155 |
| 1976 | Jim Rice, Boston | 123 |
| 1977 | Butch Hobson, Boston | 162 |
| 1978 | Gary Alexander, Oakland/Cleveland | 166 |
| 1979 | Gorman Thomas, Milwaukee | 175 |
| 1980 | Gorman Thomas, Milwaukee | 170 |
| 1981 | Tony Armas, Oakland | 115 |
| 1982 | Reggie Jackson, California | 156 |
| 1983 | Ron Kittle, Chicago | 150 |
| 1984 | Tony Armas, Boston | 156 |
| 1985 | Steve Balboni, Kansas City | 166 |
| 1986 | Pete Incaviglia, Texas | 185 |
| 1987 | Rob Deer, Milwaukee | 186 |
| 1988 | Rob Deer, Milwaukee | 153 |
| | Pete Incaviglia, Texas | 153 |
| 1989 | Bo Jackson, Kansas City | 172 |
| 1990 | Cecil Fielder, Detroit | 182 |
| 1991 | Rob Deer, Detroit | 175 |
| 1992 | Dean Palmer, Texas | 154 |
| 1993 | Rob Deer, Detroit/Boston | 169 |
| 1994 | Travis Fryman, Detroit | 128 |
| 1995 | Mo Vaughn, Boston | 150 |
| 1996 | Jay Buhner, Seattle | 159 |
| 1997 | Jay Buhner, Seattle | 175 |
| 1998 | Jose Canseco, Toronto | 159 |
| 1999 | Jim Thome, Cleveland | 171 |
| 2000 | Mo Vaughn, Anaheim | 181 |
| 2001 | Jim Thome, Cleveland | 185 |
| 2002 | Mike Cameron, Seattle | 176 |
| 2003 | Jason Giambi, New York | 140 |
| 2004 | Mark Bellhorn, Boston | 177 |
| 2005 | Richie Sexson, Seattle | 167 |

### NATIONAL LEAGUE

| Year | Player, Club | Ks |
|---|---|---|
| 1910 | John Hummel, Brooklyn | 81 |
| 1911 | Bob Bescher, Cincinnati | 78 |
| | Bob Coulson, Brooklyn | 78 |
| 1912 | Ed McDonald, Boston | 91 |
| 1913 | George J. Burns, New York | 74 |
| 1914 | Fred Merkle, New York | 80 |
| 1915 | Doug Baird, Pittsburgh | 88 |
| 1916 | Gavvy Cravath, Philadelphia | 89 |
| 1917 | Cy Williams, Chicago | 78 |
| 1918 | Ross Youngs, New York | 49 |
| | Dode Paskert, Chicago | 49 |
| 1919 | Ray Powell, Boston | 79 |
| 1920 | George Kelly, New York | 92 |
| 1921 | Ray Powell, Boston | 85 |
| 1922 | Frank Parkinson, Philadelphia | 93 |
| 1923 | George Grantham, Chicago | 92 |
| 1924 | George Grantham, Chicago | 63 |
| 1925 | Gabby Hartnett, Chicago | 77 |
| 1926 | Barney Friberg, Philadelphia | 77 |
| 1927 | Hack Wilson, Chicago | 70 |
| 1928 | Hack Wilson, Chicago | 94 |
| 1929 | Hack Wilson, Chicago | 83 |
| 1930 | Hack Wilson, Chicago | 84 |
| 1931 | Nick Cullop, Cincinnati | 86 |
| 1932 | Hack Wilson, Brooklyn | 85 |
| 1933 | Wally Berger, Boston | 77 |
| 1934 | Dolf Camilli, Chicago/Philadelphia | 94 |
| 1935 | Dolf Camilli, Philadelphia | 113 |
| 1936 | Bill Brubaker, Pittsburgh | 96 |
| 1937 | Vince DiMaggio, Boston | 111 |
| 1938 | Vince DiMaggio, Boston | 134 |
| 1939 | Dolf Camilli, Brooklyn | 107 |
| 1940 | Chet Ross, Boston | 128 |
| 1941 | Dolf Camilli, Brooklyn | 115 |
| 1942 | Vince DiMaggio, Pittsburgh | 87 |
| 1943 | Vince DiMaggio, Pittsburgh | 126 |
| 1944 | Vince DiMaggio, Pittsburgh | 83 |
| 1945 | Vince DiMaggio, Philadelphia | 91 |
| 1946 | Ralph Kiner, Pittsburgh | 109 |
| 1947 | Bill Nicholson, Chicago | 83 |
| 1948 | Hank Sauer, Cincinnati | 85 |
| 1949 | Duke Snider, Brooklyn | 92 |
| 1950 | Roy Smalley, Chicago | 114 |
| 1951 | Gil Hodges, Brooklyn | 99 |
| 1952 | Eddie Mathews, Boston | 115 |
| 1953 | Steve Bilko, St. Louis | 125 |
| 1954 | Duke Snider, Brooklyn | 96 |
| 1955 | Wally Post, Cincinnati | 102 |
| 1956 | Wally Post, Cincinnati | 124 |
| 1957 | Duke Snider, Brooklyn | 104 |
| 1958 | Harry Anderson, Philadelphia | 95 |
| 1959 | Wally Post, Philadelphia | 101 |
| 1960 | Frank Herrera, Philadelphia | 136 |

| Year | Player, Club | Ks |
|---|---|---|
| 1961 | Dick Stuart, Pittsburgh | 121 |
| 1962 | Ken Hubbs, Chicago | 129 |
| 1963 | Donn Clendenon, Pittsburgh | 136 |
| 1964 | Dick Allen, Philadelphia | 138 |
| 1965 | Dick Allen, Philadelphia | 150 |
| 1966 | Byron Browne, Chicago | 143 |
| 1967 | Jim Wynn, Houston | 137 |
| 1968 | Donn Clendenon, Pittsburgh | 163 |
| 1969 | Bobby Bonds, San Francisco | 187 |
| 1970 | Bobby Bonds, San Francisco | 189 |
| 1971 | Willie Stargell, Pittsburgh | 154 |
| 1972 | Lee May, Houston | 145 |
| 1973 | Bobby Bonds, San Francisco | 148 |
| 1974 | Mike Schmidt, Philadelphia | 138 |
| 1975 | Mike Schmidt, Philadelphia | 180 |
| 1976 | Mike Schmidt, Philadelphia | 149 |
| 1977 | Greg Luzinski, Philadelphia | 140 |
| 1978 | Dale Murphy, Atlanta | 145 |
| 1979 | Dave Kingman, Chicago | 131 |
| 1980 | Dale Murphy, Atlanta | 133 |
| 1981 | Dave Kingman, New York | 105 |
| 1982 | Dave Kingman, New York | 156 |
| 1983 | Mike Schmidt, Philadelphia | 148 |
| 1984 | Juan Samuel, Philadelphia | 168 |
| 1985 | Dale Murphy, Atlanta | 141 |
| | Juan Samuel, Philadelphia | 141 |
| 1986 | Juan Samuel, Philadelphia | 142 |
| 1987 | Juan Samuel, Philadelphia | 162 |
| 1988 | Andres Galarraga, Montreal | 153 |
| 1989 | Andres Galarraga, Montreal | 158 |
| 1990 | Andres Galarraga, Montreal | 169 |
| 1991 | Delino DeShields, Montreal | 151 |
| 1992 | Ray Lankford, St. Louis | 147 |
| 1993 | Cory Snyder, Los Angeles | 147 |
| 1994 | Reggie Sanders, Cincinnati | 114 |
| 1995 | Andres Galarraga, Colorado | 146 |
| 1996 | Henry Rodriguez, Montreal | 160 |
| 1997 | Sammy Sosa, Chicago | 174 |
| 1998 | Sammy Sosa, Chicago | 171 |
| 1999 | Sammy Sosa, Chicago | 171 |
| 2000 | Preston Wilson, Florida | 187 |
| 2001 | Jose Hernandez, Milwaukee | 185 |
| 2002 | Jose Hernandez, Milwaukee | 188 |
| 2003 | Jim Thome, Philadelphia | 162 |
| 2004 | Adam Dunn, Cincinnati | 195 |
| 2005 | Adam Dunn, Cincinnati | 168 |

Note—not included in batting records in AL prior to 1913 and NL prior to 1910

## BASERUNNING

### STOLEN BASES

### AMERICAN LEAGUE

| Year | Player, Club | SB |
|---|---|---|
| 1901 | Frank Isbell, Chicago | 52 |
| 1902 | Topsy Hartsel, Philadelphia | 47 |
| 1903 | Harry Bay, Cleveland | 45 |
| 1904 | Harry Bay, Cleveland | 38 |
| | Elmer Flick, Cleveland | 38 |
| 1905 | Danny Hoffman, Philadelphia | 46 |
| 1906 | Elmer Flick, Cleveland | 39 |
| | John Anderson, Washington | 39 |
| 1907 | Ty Cobb, Detroit | 53 |
| 1908 | Patsy Dougherty, Chicago | 47 |
| 1909 | Ty Cobb, Detroit | 76 |
| 1910 | Eddie Collins, Philadelphia | 81 |
| 1911 | Ty Cobb, Detroit | 83 |
| 1912 | Clyde Milan, Washington | 88 |
| 1913 | Clyde Milan, Washington | 75 |
| 1914 | Fritz Maisel, New York | 74 |
| 1915 | Ty Cobb, Detroit | 96 |
| 1916 | Ty Cobb, Detroit | 68 |
| 1917 | Ty Cobb, Detroit | 55 |
| 1918 | George Sisler, St. Louis | 45 |
| 1919 | Eddie Collins, Chicago | 33 |
| 1920 | Sam Rice, Washington | 63 |
| 1921 | George Sisler, St. Louis | 35 |
| 1922 | George Sisler, St. Louis | 51 |
| 1923 | Eddie Collins, Chicago | 48 |
| 1924 | Eddie Collins, Chicago | 42 |
| 1925 | Johnny Mostil, Chicago | 43 |
| 1926 | Johnny Mostil, Chicago | 35 |
| 1927 | George Sisler, St. Louis | 27 |
| 1928 | Buddy Myer, Boston | 30 |
| 1929 | Charlie Gehringer, Detroit | 27 |
| 1930 | Marty McManus, Detroit | 23 |
| 1931 | Ben Chapman, New York | 61 |
| 1932 | Ben Chapman, New York | 38 |
| 1933 | Ben Chapman, New York | 27 |
| 1934 | Bill Werber, Boston | 40 |
| 1935 | Bill Werber, Boston | 29 |
| 1936 | Lyn Lary, St. Louis | 37 |
| 1937 | Bill Werber, Philadelphia | 35 |
| | Ben Chapman, Washington/Boston | 35 |
| 1938 | Frank Crosetti, New York | 27 |
| 1939 | George Case, Washington | 51 |
| 1940 | George Case, Washington | 35 |
| 1941 | George Case, Washington | 33 |
| 1942 | George Case, Washington | 44 |
| 1943 | George Case, Washington | 61 |
| 1944 | George Stirnweiss, New York | 55 |
| 1945 | George Stirnweiss, New York | 33 |
| 1946 | George Case, Cleveland | 28 |
| 1947 | Bob Dillinger, St. Louis | 34 |
| 1948 | Bob Dillinger, St. Louis | 28 |
| 1949 | Bob Dillinger, St. Louis | 20 |
| 1950 | Dom DiMaggio, Boston | 15 |
| 1951 | Minnie Minoso, Cleveland/Chicago | 31 |
| 1952 | Minnie Minoso, Chicago | 22 |
| 1953 | Minnie Minoso, Chicago | 25 |
| 1954 | Jackie Jensen, Boston | 22 |
| 1955 | Jim Rivera, Chicago | 25 |
| 1956 | Luis Aparicio, Chicago | 21 |
| 1957 | Luis Aparicio, Chicago | 28 |
| 1958 | Luis Aparicio, Chicago | 29 |
| 1959 | Luis Aparicio, Chicago | 56 |
| 1960 | Luis Aparicio, Chicago | 51 |
| 1961 | Luis Aparicio, Chicago | 53 |
| 1962 | Luis Aparicio, Chicago | 31 |
| 1963 | Luis Aparicio, Baltimore | 40 |
| 1964 | Luis Aparicio, Baltimore | 57 |
| 1965 | Bert Campaneris, Kansas City | 51 |
| 1966 | Bert Campaneris, Kansas City | 52 |
| 1967 | Bert Campaneris, Kansas City | 55 |
| 1968 | Bert Campaneris, Oakland | 62 |
| 1969 | Tommy Harper, Seattle | 73 |
| 1970 | Bert Campaneris, Oakland | 42 |
| 1971 | Amos Otis, Kansas City | 52 |
| 1972 | Bert Campaneris, Oakland | 52 |
| 1973 | Tommy Harper, Boston | 54 |
| 1974 | Billy North, Oakland | 54 |
| 1975 | Mickey Rivers, California | 70 |
| 1976 | Billy North, Oakland | 75 |
| 1977 | Fred Patek, Kansas City | 53 |
| 1978 | Ron LeFlore, Detroit | 68 |
| 1979 | Willie Wilson, Kansas City | 83 |
| 1980 | Rickey Henderson, Oakland | 100 |
| 1981 | Rickey Henderson, Oakland | 56 |
| 1982 | Rickey Henderson, Oakland | 130 |
| 1983 | Rickey Henderson, Oakland | 108 |
| 1984 | Rickey Henderson, Oakland | 66 |
| 1985 | Rickey Henderson, New York | 80 |
| 1986 | Rickey Henderson, New York | 87 |
| 1987 | Harold Reynolds, Seattle | 60 |
| 1988 | Rickey Henderson, New York | 93 |
| 1989 | Rickey Henderson, New York/Oakland | 77 |
| 1990 | Rickey Henderson, Oakland | 65 |
| 1991 | Rickey Henderson, Oakland | 58 |
| 1992 | Kenny Lofton, Cleveland | 66 |
| 1993 | Kenny Lofton, Cleveland | 70 |
| 1994 | Kenny Lofton, Cleveland | 60 |
| 1995 | Kenny Lofton, Cleveland | 54 |
| 1996 | Kenny Lofton, Cleveland | 75 |
| 1997 | Brian L. Hunter, Detroit | 74 |
| 1998 | Rickey Henderson, Oakland | 66 |
| 1999 | Brian L. Hunter, Detroit/Seattle | 44 |
| 2000 | Johnny Damon, Kansas City | 46 |
| 2001 | Ichiro Suzuki, Seattle | 56 |
| 2002 | Alfonso Soriano, New York | 41 |
| 2003 | Carl Crawford, Tampa Bay | 55 |
| 2004 | Carl Crawford, Tampa Bay | 59 |
| 2005 | Chone Figgins, Los Angeles | 62 |

### NATIONAL LEAGUE

| Year | Player, Club | SB |
|---|---|---|
| 1886 | Ed Andrews, Philadelphia | 56 |
| 1887 | Monte Ward, New York | 111 |
| 1888 | Dummy Hoy, Washington | 82 |
| 1889 | Jim Fogarty, Philadelphia | 99 |
| 1890 | Billy Hamilton, Philadelphia | 102 |
| 1891 | Billy Hamilton, Philadelphia | 111 |
| 1892 | Monte Ward, Brooklyn | 88 |
| 1893 | Tom Brown, Louisville | 66 |
| 1894 | Billy Hamilton, Philadelphia | 100 |
| 1895 | Billy Hamilton, Philadelphia | 97 |
| 1896 | Joe Kelley, Baltimore | 87 |
| 1897 | Bill Lange, Chicago | 73 |
| 1898 | Ed Delahanty, Philadelphia | 58 |
| 1899 | Jimmy Sheckard, Baltimore | 77 |
| 1900 | Patsy Donovan, St. Louis | 45 |
| | George Van Haltren, New York | 45 |
| 1901 | Honus Wagner, Pittsburgh | 49 |
| 1902 | Honus Wagner, Pittsburgh | 42 |
| 1903 | Jimmy Sheckard, Brooklyn | 67 |
| | Frank Chance, Chicago | 67 |
| 1904 | Honus Wagner, Pittsburgh | 53 |
| 1905 | Billy Maloney, Chicago | 59 |
| | Art Devlin, New York | 59 |
| 1906 | Frank Chance, Chicago | 57 |
| 1907 | Honus Wagner, Pittsburgh | 61 |
| 1908 | Honus Wagner, Pittsburgh | 53 |
| 1909 | Bob Bescher, Cincinnati | 54 |
| 1910 | Bob Bescher, Cincinnati | 70 |
| 1911 | Bob Bescher, Cincinnati | 81 |
| 1912 | Bob Bescher, Cincinnati | 67 |
| 1913 | Max Carey, Pittsburgh | 61 |
| 1914 | George J. Burns, New York | 62 |
| 1915 | Max Carey, Pittsburgh | 36 |
| 1916 | Max Carey, Pittsburgh | 63 |
| 1917 | Max Carey, Pittsburgh | 46 |
| 1918 | Max Carey, Pittsburgh | 58 |
| 1919 | George J. Burns, New York | 40 |
| 1920 | Max Carey, Pittsburgh | 52 |
| 1921 | Frankie Frisch, New York | 49 |
| 1922 | Max Carey, Pittsburgh | 51 |
| 1923 | Max Carey, Pittsburgh | 51 |
| 1924 | Max Carey, Pittsburgh | 49 |
| 1925 | Max Carey, Pittsburgh | 46 |
| 1926 | Kiki Cuyler, Pittsburgh | 35 |
| 1927 | Frankie Frisch, St. Louis | 48 |
| 1928 | Kiki Cuyler, Chicago | 37 |
| 1929 | Kiki Cuyler, Chicago | 43 |
| 1930 | Kiki Cuyler, Chicago | 37 |
| 1931 | Frankie Frisch, St. Louis | 28 |
| 1932 | Chuck Klein, Philadelphia | 20 |
| 1933 | Pepper Martin, St. Louis | 26 |
| 1934 | Pepper Martin, St. Louis | 23 |
| 1935 | Augie Galan, Chicago | 22 |
| 1936 | Pepper Martin, St. Louis | 23 |
| 1937 | Augie Galan, Chicago | 23 |
| 1938 | Stan Hack, Chicago | 16 |
| 1939 | Stan Hack, Chicago | 17 |
| | Lee Handley, Pittsburgh | 17 |
| 1940 | Lonny Frey, Cincinnati | 22 |
| 1941 | Danny Murtaugh, Philadelphia | 18 |
| 1942 | Pete Reiser, Brooklyn | 20 |
| 1943 | Arky Vaughan, Brooklyn | 20 |
| 1944 | Johnny Barrett, Pittsburgh | 28 |
| 1945 | Red Schoendienst, St. Louis | 26 |
| 1946 | Pete Reiser, Brooklyn | 34 |
| 1947 | Jackie Robinson, Brooklyn | 29 |
| 1948 | Richie Ashburn, Philadelphia | 32 |
| 1949 | Jackie Robinson, Brooklyn | 37 |
| 1950 | Sam Jethroe, Boston | 35 |
| 1951 | Sam Jethroe, Boston | 35 |
| 1952 | Pee Wee Reese, Brooklyn | 30 |
| 1953 | Billy Bruton, Milwaukee | 26 |
| 1954 | Billy Bruton, Milwaukee | 34 |
| 1955 | Billy Bruton, Milwaukee | 25 |
| 1956 | Willie Mays, New York | 40 |
| 1957 | Willie Mays, New York | 38 |
| 1958 | Willie Mays, San Francisco | 31 |
| 1959 | Willie Mays, San Francisco | 27 |
| 1960 | Maury Wills, Los Angeles | 50 |
| 1961 | Maury Wills, Los Angeles | 35 |
| 1962 | Maury Wills, Los Angeles | 104 |
| 1963 | Maury Wills, Los Angeles | 40 |
| 1964 | Maury Wills, Los Angeles | 53 |
| 1965 | Maury Wills, Los Angeles | 94 |
| 1966 | Lou Brock, St. Louis | 74 |
| 1967 | Lou Brock, St. Louis | 52 |
| 1968 | Lou Brock, St. Louis | 62 |
| 1969 | Lou Brock, St. Louis | 53 |
| 1970 | Bobby Tolan, Cincinnati | 57 |
| 1971 | Lou Brock, St. Louis | 64 |
| 1972 | Lou Brock, St. Louis | 63 |
| 1973 | Lou Brock, St. Louis | 70 |
| 1974 | Lou Brock, St. Louis | 118 |
| 1975 | Dave Lopes, Los Angeles | 77 |
| 1976 | Dave Lopes, Los Angeles | 63 |
| 1977 | Frank Taveras, Pittsburgh | 70 |
| 1978 | Omar Moreno, Pittsburgh | 71 |
| 1979 | Omar Moreno, Pittsburgh | 77 |
| 1980 | Ron LeFlore, Montreal | 97 |
| 1981 | Tim Raines Sr., Montreal | 71 |
| 1982 | Tim Raines Sr., Montreal | 78 |
| 1983 | Tim Raines Sr., Montreal | 90 |
| 1984 | Tim Raines Sr., Montreal | 75 |
| 1985 | Vince Coleman, St. Louis | 110 |
| 1986 | Vince Coleman, St. Louis | 107 |
| 1987 | Vince Coleman, St. Louis | 109 |
| 1988 | Vince Coleman, St. Louis | 81 |
| 1989 | Vince Coleman, St. Louis | 65 |
| 1990 | Vince Coleman, St. Louis | 77 |
| 1991 | Marquis Grissom, Montreal | 76 |
| 1992 | Marquis Grissom, Montreal | 78 |
| 1993 | Chuck Carr, Florida | 58 |
| 1994 | Craig Biggio, Houston | 39 |
| 1995 | Quilvio Veras, Florida | 56 |
| 1996 | Eric Young, Colorado | 53 |
| 1997 | Tony Womack, Pittsburgh | 60 |
| 1998 | Tony Womack, Pittsburgh | 58 |
| 1999 | Tony Womack, Arizona | 72 |
| 2000 | Luis Castillo, Florida | 62 |
| 2001 | Juan Pierre, Colorado | 46 |
| | Jimmy Rollins, Philadelphia | 46 |
| 2002 | Luis Castillo, Florida | 48 |
| 2003 | Juan Pierre, Florida | 65 |
| 2004 | Scott Podsednik, Milwaukee | 70 |
| 2005 | Jose Reyes, New York | 60 |

Note—not compiled prior to 1886

# PITCHING

## WINNING PERCENTAGE

### AMERICAN LEAGUE

| Year | Pitcher, Club | W | L | Pct. |
|---|---|---|---|---|
| 1901 | Clark Griffith, Chicago | 24 | 7 | .774 |
| 1902 | Bill Bernhard, Philadelphia/Cleveland | 18 | 5 | .783 |
| 1903 | Cy Young, Boston | 28 | 9 | .757 |
| 1904 | Jack Chesbro, New York | 41 | 12 | .774 |
| 1905 | Rube Waddell, Philadelphia | 27 | 10 | .730 |
| 1906 | Eddie Plank, Philadelphia | 19 | 6 | .760 |
| 1907 | Bill Donovan, Detroit | 25 | 4 | .862 |
| 1908 | Ed Walsh Sr., Chicago | 40 | 15 | .727 |
| 1909 | George Mullin, Detroit | 29 | 8 | .784 |
| 1910 | Chief Bender, Philadelphia | 23 | 5 | .821 |
| 1911 | Chief Bender, Philadelphia | 17 | 5 | .773 |
| 1912 | Joe Wood, Boston | 34 | 5 | .872 |
| 1913 | Walter Johnson, Washington | 36 | 7 | .837 |
| 1914 | Chief Bender, Philadelphia | 17 | 3 | .850 |
| 1915 | Joe Wood, Boston | 15 | 5 | .750 |
| 1916 | Ed Cicotte, Chicago | 15 | 7 | .682 |
| 1917 | Reb Russell, Chicago | 15 | 5 | .750 |
| 1918 | Sam Jones, Boston | 16 | 5 | .762 |
| 1919 | Ed Cicotte, Chicago | 29 | 7 | .806 |
| 1920 | Jim Bagby Sr., Cleveland | 31 | 12 | .721 |
| 1921 | Carl Mays, New York | 27 | 9 | .750 |
| 1922 | Joe Bush, New York | 26 | 7 | .788 |
| 1923 | Herb Pennock, New York | 19 | 6 | .760 |
| 1924 | Walter Johnson, Washington | 23 | 7 | .767 |
| 1925 | Stan Coveleski, Washington | 20 | 5 | .800 |
| 1926 | George Uhle, Cleveland | 27 | 11 | .711 |
| 1927 | Waite Hoyt, New York | 22 | 7 | .759 |
| 1928 | Alvin Crowder, St. Louis | 21 | 5 | .808 |
| 1929 | Lefty Grove, Philadelphia | 20 | 6 | .769 |
| 1930 | Lefty Grove, Philadelphia | 28 | 5 | .848 |
| 1931 | Lefty Grove, Philadelphia | 31 | 4 | .886 |
| 1932 | Johnny Allen, New York | 17 | 4 | .810 |
| 1933 | Lefty Grove, Philadelphia | 24 | 8 | .750 |
| 1934 | Lefty Gomez, New York | 26 | 5 | .839 |
| 1935 | Eldon Auker, Detroit | 18 | 7 | .720 |
| 1936 | Monte Pearson, New York | 19 | 7 | .731 |
| 1937 | Johnny Allen, Cleveland | 15 | 1 | .938 |
| 1938 | Red Ruffing, New York | 21 | 7 | .750 |
| 1939 | Lefty Grove, Boston | 15 | 4 | .789 |
| 1940 | Schoolboy Rowe, Detroit | 16 | 3 | .842 |
| 1941 | Lefty Gomez, New York | 15 | 5 | .750 |
| 1942 | Tiny Bonham, New York | 21 | 5 | .808 |
| 1943 | Spud Chandler, New York | 20 | 4 | .833 |
| 1944 | Tex Hughson, Boston | 18 | 5 | .783 |
| 1945 | Hal Newhouser, Detroit | 25 | 9 | .735 |
| 1946 | Boo Ferriss, Boston | 25 | 6 | .806 |
| 1947 | Allie Reynolds, New York | 19 | 8 | .704 |
| 1948 | Jack Kramer, Boston | 18 | 5 | .783 |
| 1949 | Ellis Kinder, Boston | 23 | 6 | .793 |
| 1950 | Vic Raschi, New York | 21 | 8 | .724 |
| 1951 | Bob Feller, Cleveland | 22 | 8 | .733 |
| 1952 | Bobby Shantz, Philadelphia | 24 | 7 | .774 |
| 1953 | Eddie Lopat, New York | 16 | 4 | .800 |
| 1954 | Sandy Consuegra, Chicago | 16 | 3 | .842 |
| 1955 | Tommy Byrne, New York | 16 | 5 | .762 |
| 1956 | Whitey Ford, New York | 19 | 6 | .760 |
| 1957 | Dick Donovan, Chicago | 16 | 6 | .727 |
|  | Tom Sturdivant, New York | 16 | 6 | .727 |
| 1958 | Bob Turley, New York | 21 | 7 | .750 |
| 1959 | Bob Shaw, Chicago | 18 | 6 | .750 |
| 1960 | Jim Perry, Cleveland | 18 | 10 | .643 |
| 1961 | Whitey Ford, New York | 25 | 4 | .862 |
| 1962 | Ray Herbert, Chicago | 20 | 9 | .690 |
| 1963 | Whitey Ford, New York | 24 | 7 | .774 |
| 1964 | Wally Bunker, Baltimore | 19 | 5 | .792 |
| 1965 | Mudcat Grant, Minnesota | 21 | 7 | .750 |
| 1966 | Sonny Siebert, Cleveland | 16 | 8 | .667 |
| 1967 | Joe Horlen, Chicago | 19 | 7 | .731 |
| 1968 | Denny McLain, Detroit | 31 | 6 | .838 |
| 1969 | Jim Palmer, Baltimore | 16 | 4 | .800 |
| 1970 | Mike Cuellar, Baltimore | 24 | 8 | .750 |
| 1971 | Dave McNally, Baltimore | 21 | 5 | .808 |
| 1972 | Catfish Hunter, Oakland | 21 | 7 | .750 |
| 1973 | Catfish Hunter, Oakland | 21 | 5 | .808 |
| 1974 | Mike Cuellar, Baltimore | 22 | 10 | .688 |
| 1975 | Mike Torrez, Baltimore | 20 | 9 | .690 |
| 1976 | Bill Campbell, Minnesota | 17 | 5 | .773 |
| 1977 | Paul Splittorff, Kansas City | 16 | 6 | .727 |
| 1978 | Ron Guidry, New York | 25 | 3 | .893 |
| 1979 | Mike Caldwell, Milwaukee | 16 | 6 | .727 |
| 1980 | Steve Stone, Baltimore | 25 | 7 | .781 |
| 1981 | Pete Vuckovich, Milwaukee | 14 | 4 | .778 |
| 1982 | Pete Vuckovich, Milwaukee | 18 | 6 | .750 |
| 1983 | Rich Dotson, Chicago | 22 | 7 | .759 |
| 1984 | Doyle Alexander, Toronto | 17 | 6 | .739 |
| 1985 | Ron Guidry, New York | 22 | 6 | .786 |
| 1986 | Roger Clemens, Boston | 24 | 4 | .857 |
| 1987 | Roger Clemens, Boston | 20 | 9 | .690 |
| 1988 | Frank Viola, Minnesota | 24 | 7 | .774 |
| 1989 | Bret Saberhagen, Kansas City | 23 | 6 | .793 |
| 1990 | Bob Welch, Oakland | 27 | 6 | .818 |
| 1991 | Scott Erickson, Minnesota | 20 | 8 | .714 |
| 1992 | Mike Mussina, Baltimore | 18 | 5 | .783 |
| 1993 | Jimmy Key, New York | 18 | 6 | .750 |
| 1994 | Jason Bere, Chicago | 12 | 2 | .857 |
| 1995 | Randy Johnson, Seattle | 18 | 2 | .900 |
| 1996 | Charles Nagy, Cleveland | 17 | 5 | .773 |
| 1997 | Randy Johnson, Seattle | 20 | 4 | .833 |
| 1998 | David Wells, New York | 18 | 4 | .818 |
| 1999 | Pedro Martinez, Boston | 23 | 4 | .852 |
| 2000 | Tim Hudson, Oakland | 20 | 6 | .769 |
| 2001 | Roger Clemens, New York | 20 | 3 | .870 |
| 2002 | Pedro Martinez, Boston | 20 | 4 | .833 |
| 2003 | Roy Halladay, Toronto | 22 | 7 | .759 |
| 2004 | Curt Schilling, Boston | 21 | 6 | .778 |
| 2005 | Cliff Lee, Cleveland | 18 | 5 | .783 |

### NATIONAL LEAGUE

| Year | Pitcher, Club | W | L | Pct. |
|---|---|---|---|---|
| 1876 | Al Spalding, Chicago | 47 | 12 | .797 |
| 1877 | Tommy Bond, Boston | 40 | 17 | .702 |
| 1878 | Tommy Bond, Boston | 40 | 19 | .678 |
| 1879 | Monte Ward, Providence | 47 | 19 | .712 |
| 1880 | Fred Goldsmith, Chicago | 21 | 3 | .875 |
| 1881 | Hoss Radbourn, Providence | 25 | 11 | .694 |
| 1882 | Larry Corcoran, Chicago | 27 | 12 | .692 |
| 1883 | Jim McCormick, Cleveland | 28 | 12 | .700 |
| 1884 | Hoss Radbourn, Providence | 59 | 12 | .831 |
| 1885 | Mickey Welch, New York | 44 | 11 | .800 |
| 1886 | Jocko Flynn, Chicago | 23 | 6 | .793 |
| 1887 | Charlie Getzien, Detroit | 29 | 13 | .690 |
| 1888 | Tim Keefe, New York | 35 | 12 | .745 |
| 1889 | John Clarkson, Boston | 49 | 19 | .721 |
| 1890 | Tom Lovett, Brooklyn | 30 | 11 | .732 |
| 1891 | John Ewing, New York | 21 | 8 | .724 |
| 1892 | Cy Young, Cleveland | 36 | 12 | .750 |
| 1893 | Hank Gastright, Pittsburgh/Boston | 15 | 5 | .750 |
| 1894 | Jouett Meekin, New York | 33 | 9 | .786 |
| 1895 | Bill Hoffer, Baltimore | 31 | 6 | .838 |
| 1896 | Bill Hoffer, Baltimore | 25 | 7 | .781 |
| 1897 | Fred Klobedanz, Boston | 26 | 7 | .788 |
| 1898 | Ted Lewis, Boston | 26 | 8 | .765 |
| 1899 | Jim Hughes, Brooklyn | 28 | 6 | .824 |
| 1900 | Joe McGinnity, Brooklyn | 28 | 8 | .778 |
| 1901 | Jack Chesbro, Pittsburgh | 21 | 10 | .677 |
| 1902 | Jack Chesbro, Pittsburgh | 28 | 6 | .824 |
| 1903 | Sam Leever, Pittsburgh | 25 | 7 | .781 |
| 1904 | Joe McGinnity, New York | 35 | 8 | .814 |
| 1905 | Sam Leever, Pittsburgh | 20 | 5 | .800 |
| 1906 | Ed Reulbach, Chicago | 19 | 4 | .826 |
| 1907 | Ed Reulbach, Chicago | 17 | 4 | .810 |
| 1908 | Ed Reulbach, Chicago | 24 | 7 | .774 |
| 1909 | Christy Mathewson, New York | 25 | 6 | .806 |
|  | Howie Camnitz, Pittsburgh | 25 | 6 | .806 |
| 1910 | King Cole, Chicago | 20 | 4 | .833 |
| 1911 | Rube Marquard, New York | 24 | 7 | .774 |
| 1912 | Claude Hendrix, Pittsburgh | 24 | 9 | .727 |
| 1913 | Bert Humphries, Chicago | 16 | 4 | .800 |
| 1914 | Bill James, Boston | 26 | 7 | .788 |
| 1915 | Grover Alexander, Philadelphia | 31 | 10 | .756 |
| 1916 | Tom Hughes, Boston | 16 | 3 | .842 |
| 1917 | Ferdie Schupp, New York | 21 | 7 | .750 |
| 1918 | Claude Hendrix, Chicago | 20 | 7 | .741 |
| 1919 | Dutch Ruether, Cincinnati | 19 | 6 | .760 |
| 1920 | Burleigh Grimes, Brooklyn | 23 | 11 | .676 |
| 1921 | Bill Doak, St. Louis | 15 | 6 | .714 |
| 1922 | Pete Donohue, Cincinnati | 18 | 9 | .667 |
| 1923 | Dolf Luque, Cincinnati | 27 | 8 | .771 |
| 1924 | Emil Yde, Pittsburgh | 16 | 3 | .842 |
| 1925 | Willie Sherdel, St. Louis | 15 | 6 | .714 |
| 1926 | Ray Kremer, Pittsburgh | 20 | 6 | .769 |
| 1927 | Larry Benton, Boston/New York | 17 | 7 | .708 |
| 1928 | Larry Benton, New York | 25 | 9 | .735 |
| 1929 | Charlie Root, Chicago | 19 | 6 | .760 |
| 1930 | Freddie Fitzsimmons, New York | 19 | 7 | .731 |
| 1931 | Paul Derringer, St. Louis | 18 | 8 | .692 |
| 1932 | Lon Warneke, Chicago | 22 | 6 | .786 |
| 1933 | Ben Cantwell, Boston | 20 | 10 | .667 |
| 1934 | Dizzy Dean, St. Louis | 30 | 7 | .811 |
| 1935 | Bill Lee, Chicago | 20 | 6 | .769 |
| 1936 | Carl Hubbell, New York | 26 | 6 | .813 |
| 1937 | Carl Hubbell, New York | 22 | 8 | .733 |
| 1938 | Bill Lee, Chicago | 22 | 9 | .710 |
| 1939 | Paul Derringer, Cincinnati | 25 | 7 | .781 |
| 1940 | Freddie Fitzsimmons, Brooklyn | 16 | 2 | .889 |
| 1941 | Elmer Riddle, Cincinnati | 19 | 4 | .826 |
| 1942 | Larry French, Brooklyn | 15 | 4 | .789 |
| 1943 | Mort Cooper, St. Louis | 21 | 8 | .724 |
| 1944 | Ted Wilks, St. Louis | 17 | 4 | .810 |
| 1945 | Harry Brecheen, St. Louis | 15 | 4 | .789 |
| 1946 | Murry Dickson, St. Louis | 15 | 6 | .714 |
| 1947 | Larry Jansen, New York | 21 | 5 | .808 |
| 1948 | Harry Brecheen, St. Louis | 20 | 7 | .741 |
| 1949 | Preacher Roe, Brooklyn | 15 | 6 | .714 |
| 1950 | Sal Maglie, New York | 18 | 4 | .818 |
| 1951 | Preacher Roe, Brooklyn | 22 | 3 | .880 |
| 1952 | Hoyt Wilhelm, New York | 15 | 3 | .833 |
| 1953 | Carl Erskine, Brooklyn | 20 | 6 | .769 |
| 1954 | Johnny Antonelli, New York | 21 | 7 | .750 |
| 1955 | Don Newcombe, Brooklyn | 20 | 5 | .800 |
| 1956 | Don Newcombe, Brooklyn | 27 | 7 | .794 |
| 1957 | Bob Buhl, Milwaukee | 18 | 7 | .720 |
| 1958 | Warren Spahn, Milwaukee | 22 | 11 | .667 |
|  | Lew Burdette, Milwaukee | 20 | 10 | .667 |
| 1959 | Roy Face, Pittsburgh | 18 | 1 | .947 |
| 1960 | Ernie Broglio, St. Louis | 21 | 9 | .700 |
| 1961 | Johnny Podres, Los Angeles | 18 | 5 | .783 |
| 1962 | Bob Purkey, Cincinnati | 23 | 5 | .821 |
| 1963 | Ron Perranoski, Los Angeles | 16 | 3 | .842 |
| 1964 | Sandy Koufax, Los Angeles | 19 | 5 | .792 |
| 1965 | Sandy Koufax, Los Angeles | 26 | 8 | .765 |
| 1966 | Juan Marichal, San Francisco | 25 | 6 | .806 |
| 1967 | Dick Hughes, St. Louis | 16 | 6 | .727 |
| 1968 | Steve Blass, Pittsburgh | 18 | 6 | .750 |
| 1969 | Tom Seaver, New York | 25 | 7 | .781 |
| 1970 | Bob Gibson, St. Louis | 23 | 7 | .767 |
| 1971 | Don Gullett, Cincinnati | 16 | 6 | .727 |
| 1972 | Gary Nolan, Cincinnati | 15 | 5 | .750 |
| 1973 | Tommy John, Los Angeles | 16 | 7 | .696 |
| 1974 | Andy Messersmith, Los Angeles | 20 | 6 | .769 |
| 1975 | Don Gullett, Cincinnati | 15 | 4 | .789 |
| 1976 | Steve Carlton, Philadelphia | 20 | 7 | .741 |
| 1977 | John Candelaria, Pittsburgh | 20 | 5 | .800 |
| 1978 | Gaylord Perry, San Diego | 21 | 6 | .778 |
| 1979 | Tom Seaver, Cincinnati | 16 | 6 | .727 |
| 1980 | Jim Bibby, Pittsburgh | 19 | 6 | .760 |
| 1981 | Tom Seaver, Cincinnati | 14 | 2 | .875 |
| 1982 | Phil Niekro, Atlanta | 17 | 4 | .810 |
| 1983 | John Denny, Philadelphia | 19 | 6 | .760 |
| 1984 | Rick Sutcliffe, Chicago | 16 | 1 | .941 |
| 1985 | Orel Hershiser, Los Angeles | 19 | 3 | .864 |
| 1986 | Bob Ojeda, New York | 18 | 5 | .783 |
| 1987 | Dwight Gooden, New York | 15 | 7 | .682 |
| 1988 | David Cone, New York | 20 | 3 | .870 |
| 1989 | Mike Bielecki, Chicago | 18 | 7 | .720 |
| 1990 | Doug Drabek, Pittsburgh | 22 | 6 | .786 |
| 1991 | John Smiley, Pittsburgh | 20 | 8 | .714 |
|  | Jose Rijo, Cincinnati | 15 | 6 | .714 |
| 1992 | Bob Tewksbury, St. Louis | 16 | 5 | .762 |
| 1993 | Mark Portugal, Houston | 18 | 4 | .818 |
| 1994 | Marvin Freeman, Colorado | 10 | 2 | .833 |
| 1995 | Greg Maddux, Atlanta | 19 | 2 | .905 |
| 1996 | John Smoltz, Atlanta | 24 | 8 | .750 |
| 1997 | Greg Maddux, Atlanta | 19 | 4 | .826 |
| 1998 | John Smoltz, Atlanta | 17 | 3 | .850 |
| 1999 | Mike Hampton, Houston | 22 | 4 | .846 |
| 2000 | Randy Johnson, Arizona | 19 | 7 | .731 |
| 2001 | Curt Schilling, Arizona | 22 | 6 | .786 |
| 2002 | Randy Johnson, Arizona | 24 | 5 | .828 |
| 2003 | Jason Schmidt, San Francisco | 17 | 5 | .773 |
| 2004 | Roger Clemens, Houston | 18 | 4 | .818 |
| 2005 | Chris Carpenter, St. Louis | 21 | 5 | .808 |

Note—based on 15 or more wins, except for 1981 and 1994, based on 10 or more wins

## EARNED RUN AVERAGE

### AMERICAN LEAGUE

| Year | Pitcher, Club | G | IP | ERA |
|---|---|---|---|---|
| 1913 | Walter Johnson, Washington | 48 | 346 | 1.14 |
| 1914 | Dutch Leonard, Boston | 36 | 225 | 0.96 |
| 1915 | Joe Wood, Boston | 25 | 157 | 1.49 |
| 1916 | Babe Ruth, Boston | 44 | 324 | 1.75 |
| 1917 | Ed Cicotte, Chicago | 49 | 346 | 1.53 |
| 1918 | Walter Johnson, Washington | 39 | 325 | 1.27 |
| 1919 | Walter Johnson, Washington | 39 | 290 | 1.49 |
| 1920 | Bob Shawkey, New York | 38 | 267 | 2.45 |
| 1921 | Red Faber, Chicago | 43 | 331 | 2.48 |
| 1922 | Red Faber, Chicago | 43 | 352 | 2.81 |
| 1923 | Stan Coveleski, Cleveland | 33 | 228 | 2.76 |
| 1924 | Walter Johnson, Washington | 38 | 278 | 2.72 |
| 1925 | Stan Coveleski, Washington | 32 | 241 | 2.84 |
| 1926 | Lefty Grove, Philadelphia | 45 | 258 | 2.51 |
| 1927 | Wilcy Moore, New York | 50 | 213 | 2.28 |
| 1928 | Garland Braxton, Washington | 38 | 218 | 2.51 |
| 1929 | Lefty Grove, Philadelphia | 42 | 275 | 2.81 |
| 1930 | Lefty Grove, Philadelphia | 50 | 291 | 2.54 |
| 1931 | Lefty Grove, Philadelphia | 41 | 289 | 2.06 |
| 1932 | Lefty Grove, Philadelphia | 44 | 292 | 2.84 |
| 1933 | Monte Pearson, Cleveland | 19 | 135 | 2.33 |
| 1934 | Lefty Gomez, New York | 38 | 282 | 2.33 |
| 1935 | Lefty Grove, Boston | 35 | 273 | 2.70 |
| 1936 | Lefty Grove, Boston | 35 | 253 | 2.81 |
| 1937 | Lefty Gomez, New York | 34 | 278 | 2.33 |
| 1938 | Lefty Grove, Boston | 24 | 164 | 3.07 |
| 1939 | Lefty Grove, Boston | 23 | 191 | 2.54 |
| 1940 | Bob Feller, Cleveland | 43 | 320 | 2.62 |
| 1941 | Thornton Lee, Chicago | 35 | 300 | 2.37 |
| 1942 | Ted Lyons, Chicago | 20 | 180 | 2.10 |
| 1943 | Spud Chandler, New York | 30 | 253 | 1.64 |
| 1944 | Dizzy Trout, Detroit | 49 | 352 | 2.12 |
| 1945 | Hal Newhouser, Detroit | 40 | 313 | 1.81 |
| 1946 | Hal Newhouser, Detroit | 37 | 293 | 1.94 |
| 1947 | Spud Chandler, New York | 17 | 128 | 2.46 |

| Year | Pitcher, Club | G | IP | ERA |
|---|---|---|---|---|
| 1948 | Gene Bearden, Cleveland | 37 | 230 | 2.43 |
| 1949 | Mel Parnell, Boston | 39 | 295 | 2.78 |
| 1950 | Early Wynn, Cleveland | 32 | 214 | 3.20 |
| 1951 | Saul Rogovin, Detroit/Chicago | 27 | 217 | 2.78 |
| 1952 | Allie Reynolds, New York | 35 | 244 | 2.07 |
| 1953 | Eddie Lopat, New York | 25 | 178 | 2.43 |
| 1954 | Mike Garcia, Cleveland | 45 | 259 | 2.64 |
| 1955 | Billy Pierce, Chicago | 33 | 206 | 1.97 |
| 1956 | Whitey Ford, New York | 31 | 226 | 2.47 |
| 1957 | Bobby Shantz, New York | 30 | 173 | 2.45 |
| 1958 | Whitey Ford, New York | 30 | 219 | 2.01 |
| 1959 | Hoyt Wilhelm, Baltimore | 32 | 226 | 2.19 |
| 1960 | Frank Baumann, Chicago | 47 | 185 | 2.68 |
| 1961 | Dick Donovan, Washington | 23 | 169 | 2.40 |
| 1962 | Hank Aguirre, Detroit | 42 | 216 | 2.21 |
| 1963 | Gary Peters, Chicago | 41 | 243 | 2.33 |
| 1964 | Dean Chance, Los Angeles | 46 | 278 | 1.65 |
| 1965 | Sam McDowell, Cleveland | 42 | 273 | 2.18 |
| 1966 | Gary Peters, Chicago | 30 | 205 | 1.98 |
| 1967 | Joe Horlen, Chicago | 35 | 258 | 2.06 |
| 1968 | Luis Tiant, Cleveland | 34 | 258 | 1.60 |
| 1969 | Dick Bosman, Washington | 31 | 193 | 2.19 |
| 1970 | Diego Segui, Oakland | 47 | 162 | 2.56 |
| 1971 | Vida Blue, Oakland | 39 | 312 | 1.82 |
| 1972 | Luis Tiant, Boston | 43 | 179 | 1.91 |
| 1973 | Jim Palmer, Baltimore | 38 | 296 | 2.40 |
| 1974 | Catfish Hunter, Oakland | 41 | 318 | 2.49 |
| 1975 | Jim Palmer, Baltimore | 39 | 323 | 2.09 |
| 1976 | Mark Fidrych, Detroit | 31 | 250 | 2.34 |
| 1977 | Frank Tanana, California | 31 | 241 | 2.54 |
| 1978 | Ron Guidry, New York | 35 | 274 | 1.74 |
| 1979 | Ron Guidry, New York | 33 | 236 | 2.78 |
| 1980 | Rudy May, New York | 41 | 175 | 2.47 |
| 1981 | Steve McCatty, Oakland | 22 | 186 | 2.32 |
| 1982 | Rick Sutcliffe, Cleveland | 34 | 216 | 2.96 |
| 1983 | Rick Honeycutt, Texas | 25 | 174.2 | 2.42 |
| 1984 | Mike Boddicker, Baltimore | 34 | 261.1 | 2.79 |
| 1985 | Dave Stieb, Toronto | 36 | 265.0 | 2.48 |
| 1986 | Roger Clemens, Boston | 33 | 254.0 | 2.48 |
| 1987 | Jimmy Key, Toronto | 36 | 261.0 | 2.76 |
| 1988 | Allan Anderson, Minnesota | 30 | 202.1 | 2.45 |
| 1989 | Bret Saberhagen, Kansas City | 36 | 262.1 | 2.16 |
| 1990 | Roger Clemens, Boston | 31 | 228.1 | 1.93 |
| 1991 | Roger Clemens, Boston | 35 | 271.1 | 2.62 |
| 1992 | Roger Clemens, Boston | 32 | 246.2 | 2.41 |
| 1993 | Kevin Appier, Kansas City | 34 | 238.2 | 2.56 |
| 1994 | Steve Ontiveros, Oakland | 27 | 115.1 | 2.65 |
| 1995 | Randy Johnson, Seattle | 30 | 214.1 | 2.48 |
| 1996 | Juan Guzman, Toronto | 27 | 187.2 | 2.93 |
| 1997 | Roger Clemens, Toronto | 34 | 264.0 | 2.05 |
| 1998 | Roger Clemens, Toronto | 33 | 234.2 | 2.65 |
| 1999 | Pedro Martinez, Boston | 31 | 213.1 | 2.07 |
| 2000 | Pedro Martinez, Boston | 29 | 217.0 | 1.74 |
| 2001 | Freddy Garcia, Seattle | 34 | 238.2 | 3.05 |
| 2002 | Pedro Martinez, Boston | 30 | 199.1 | 2.26 |
| 2003 | Pedro Martinez, Boston | 29 | 186.2 | 2.22 |
| 2004 | Johan Santana, Minnesota | 34 | 228.0 | 2.61 |
| 2005 | Kevin Millwood, Cleveland | 30 | 192.0 | 2.86 |

## NATIONAL LEAGUE

| Year | Pitcher, Club | G | IP | ERA |
|---|---|---|---|---|
| 1912 | Jeff Tesreau, New York | 36 | 243 | 1.96 |
| 1913 | Christy Mathewson, New York | 40 | 306 | 2.06 |
| 1914 | Bill Doak, St. Louis | 36 | 256 | 1.72 |
| 1915 | Grover Alexander, Philadelphia | 49 | 376 | 1.22 |
| 1916 | Grover Alexander, Philadelphia | 48 | 390 | 1.55 |
| 1917 | Grover Alexander, Philadelphia | 45 | 388 | 1.83 |
| 1918 | Hippo Vaughn, Chicago | 35 | 290 | 1.74 |
| 1919 | Grover Alexander, Chicago | 30 | 235 | 1.72 |
| 1920 | Grover Alexander, Chicago | 46 | 363 | 1.91 |
| 1921 | Bill Doak, St. Louis | 32 | 209 | 2.59 |
| 1922 | Phil Douglas, New York | 24 | 158 | 2.63 |
| 1923 | Dolf Luque, Cincinnati | 41 | 322 | 1.93 |
| 1924 | Dazzy Vance, Brooklyn | 35 | 309 | 2.16 |
| 1925 | Dolf Luque, Cincinnati | 36 | 291 | 2.63 |
| 1926 | Ray Kremer, Pittsburgh | 37 | 231 | 2.61 |
| 1927 | Ray Kremer, Pittsburgh | 35 | 226 | 2.47 |
| 1928 | Dazzy Vance, Brooklyn | 38 | 280 | 2.09 |
| 1929 | Bill Walker, New York | 29 | 178 | 3.09 |
| 1930 | Dazzy Vance, Brooklyn | 35 | 259 | 2.61 |
| 1931 | Bill Walker, New York | 37 | 239 | 2.26 |
| 1932 | Lon Warneke, Chicago | 35 | 277 | 2.37 |
| 1933 | Carl Hubbell, New York | 45 | 309 | 1.66 |
| 1934 | Carl Hubbell, New York | 49 | 313 | 2.30 |
| 1935 | Cy Blanton, Pittsburgh | 35 | 254 | 2.59 |
| 1936 | Carl Hubbell, New York | 42 | 304 | 2.31 |
| 1937 | Jim Turner, Boston | 33 | 257 | 2.38 |
| 1938 | Bill Lee, Chicago | 44 | 291 | 2.66 |
| 1939 | Bucky Walters, Cincinnati | 39 | 319 | 2.29 |
| 1940 | Bucky Walters, Cincinnati | 36 | 305 | 2.48 |
| 1941 | Elmer Riddle, Cincinnati | 33 | 217 | 2.24 |
| 1942 | Mort Cooper, St. Louis | 37 | 279 | 1.77 |
| 1943 | Howie Pollet, St. Louis | 16 | 118 | 1.75 |
| 1944 | Ed Heusser, Cincinnati | 30 | 193 | 2.38 |
| 1945 | Hank Borowy, Chicago | 15 | 122 | 2.14 |
| 1946 | Howie Pollet, St. Louis | 40 | 266 | 2.10 |
| 1947 | Warren Spahn, Boston | 40 | 290 | 2.33 |
| 1948 | Harry Brecheen, St. Louis | 33 | 233 | 2.24 |
| 1949 | Dave Koslo, New York | 38 | 212 | 2.50 |
| 1950 | Jim Hearn, St. Louis/New York | 22 | 134 | 2.49 |
| 1951 | Chet Nichols, Boston | 33 | 156 | 2.88 |
| 1952 | Hoyt Wilhelm, New York | 71 | 159 | 2.43 |
| 1953 | Warren Spahn, Milwaukee | 35 | 266 | 2.10 |
| 1954 | Johnny Antonelli, New York | 39 | 259 | 2.29 |
| 1955 | Bob Friend, Pittsburgh | 44 | 200 | 2.84 |
| 1956 | Lew Burdette, Milwaukee | 39 | 256 | 2.71 |
| 1957 | Johnny Podres, Brooklyn | 31 | 196 | 2.66 |
| 1958 | Stu Miller, San Francisco | 41 | 182 | 2.47 |
| 1959 | Sam Jones, San Francisco | 50 | 271 | 2.82 |
| 1960 | Mike McCormick, San Francisco | 40 | 253 | 2.70 |
| 1961 | Warren Spahn, Milwaukee | 38 | 263 | 3.01 |
| 1962 | Sandy Koufax, Los Angeles | 28 | 184 | 2.54 |
| 1963 | Sandy Koufax, Los Angeles | 40 | 311 | 1.88 |
| 1964 | Sandy Koufax, Los Angeles | 29 | 223 | 1.74 |
| 1965 | Sandy Koufax, Los Angeles | 43 | 336 | 2.04 |
| 1966 | Sandy Koufax, Los Angeles | 41 | 323 | 1.73 |
| 1967 | Phil Niekro, Atlanta | 46 | 207 | 1.87 |
| 1968 | Bob Gibson, St. Louis | 34 | 305 | 1.12 |
| 1969 | Juan Marichal, San Francisco | 37 | 300 | 2.10 |
| 1970 | Tom Seaver, New York | 37 | 291 | 2.81 |
| 1971 | Tom Seaver, New York | 36 | 286 | 1.76 |
| 1972 | Steve Carlton, Philadelphia | 41 | 346 | 1.98 |
| 1973 | Tom Seaver, New York | 36 | 290 | 2.08 |
| 1974 | Buzz Capra, Atlanta | 39 | 217 | 2.28 |
| 1975 | Randy Jones, San Diego | 37 | 285 | 2.24 |
| 1976 | John Denny, St. Louis | 30 | 207 | 2.52 |
| 1977 | John Candelaria, Pittsburgh | 33 | 231 | 2.34 |
| 1978 | Craig Swan, New York | 29 | 207 | 2.43 |
| 1979 | J.R. Richard, Houston | 38 | 292 | 2.71 |
| 1980 | Don Sutton, Los Angeles | 32 | 212 | 2.21 |
| 1981 | Nolan Ryan, Houston | 21 | 149 | 1.69 |
| 1982 | Steve Rogers, Montreal | 35 | 277 | 2.40 |
| 1983 | Atlee Hammaker, San Francisco | 23 | 172.1 | 2.25 |
| 1984 | Alejandro Pena, Los Angeles | 28 | 199.1 | 2.48 |
| 1985 | Dwight Gooden, New York | 35 | 276.2 | 1.53 |
| 1986 | Mike Scott, Houston | 37 | 275.1 | 2.22 |
| 1987 | Nolan Ryan, Houston | 34 | 211.2 | 2.76 |
| 1988 | Joe Magrane, St. Louis | 24 | 165.1 | 2.18 |
| 1989 | Scott Garrelts, San Francisco | 30 | 193.1 | 2.28 |
| 1990 | Danny Darwin, Houston | 48 | 162.2 | 2.21 |
| 1991 | Dennis Martinez, Montreal | 31 | 222.0 | 2.39 |
| 1992 | Bill Swift, San Francisco | 30 | 164.2 | 2.08 |
| 1993 | Greg Maddux, Atlanta | 36 | 267.0 | 2.36 |
| 1994 | Greg Maddux, Atlanta | 25 | 202.0 | 1.56 |
| 1995 | Greg Maddux, Atlanta | 28 | 209.2 | 1.63 |
| 1996 | Kevin Brown, Florida | 32 | 233.0 | 1.89 |
| 1997 | Pedro J. Martinez, Montreal | 31 | 241.1 | 1.90 |
| 1998 | Greg Maddux, Atlanta | 34 | 251.0 | 2.22 |
| 1999 | Randy Johnson, Arizona | 35 | 271.2 | 2.48 |
| 2000 | Kevin Brown, Los Angeles | 33 | 230.0 | 2.58 |
| 2001 | Randy Johnson, Arizona | 35 | 249.2 | 2.49 |
| 2002 | Randy Johnson, Arizona | 35 | 260.0 | 2.32 |
| 2003 | Jason Schmidt, San Francisco | 29 | 207.2 | 2.34 |
| 2004 | Jake Peavy, San Diego | 27 | 166.1 | 2.27 |
| 2005 | Roger Clemens, Houston | 32 | 211.1 | 1.87 |

Note—not tabulated in NL prior to 1912 and in AL prior to 1913; based on 10 CG through 1950; 154 IP until 1961 in AL and 1962 in NL; 162 IP since 1962, except 1981 based on one IP per game played by team

Note—In 1916, Ferdie Schupp, New York NL, appeared in 30 games and had a 0.90 ERA, but pitched only 8 CG. He was recognized as the league leader at the time.

Note—In 1927, Wilcy Moore, New York AL, appeared in 50 games but had only 6 CG. He is recognized as the leader because he had 213 IP.

Note—In 1940, Tiny Bonham, New York AL, had 10 complete games and a 1.91 ERA, but he appeared in only 12 games and had only 99.1 IP. Bob Feller is recognized as the leader.

## WINS

For the list of pitchers who led each league in wins, see page 131.

## SHUTOUTS

### AMERICAN LEAGUE

| Year | Pitcher, Club | Shutouts |
|---|---|---|
| 1901 | Clark Griffith, Chicago | 5 |
| | Cy Young, Boston | 5 |
| 1902 | Addie Joss, Cleveland | 5 |
| 1903 | Cy Young, Boston | 7 |
| 1904 | Cy Young, Boston | 10 |
| 1905 | Ed Killian, Detroit | 8 |
| 1906 | Ed Walsh Sr., Chicago | 10 |
| 1907 | Eddie Plank, Philadelphia | 8 |
| 1908 | Ed Walsh Sr., Chicago | 11 |
| 1909 | Ed Walsh Sr., Chicago | 8 |
| 1910 | Jack Coombs, Philadelphia | 13 |
| 1911 | Walter Johnson, Washington | 6 |
| | Eddie Plank, Philadelphia | 6 |
| 1912 | Joe Wood, Boston | 10 |
| 1913 | Walter Johnson, Washington | 11 |
| 1914 | Walter Johnson, Washington | 9 |
| 1915 | Walter Johnson, Washington | 7 |
| | Jim Scott, Chicago | 7 |
| 1916 | Babe Ruth, Boston | 9 |
| 1917 | Stan Coveleski, Cleveland | 9 |
| 1918 | Walter Johnson, Washington | 8 |
| | Carl Mays, Boston | 8 |
| 1919 | Walter Johnson, Washington | 7 |
| 1920 | Carl Mays, New York | 6 |
| 1921 | Sam P. Jones, Boston | 5 |
| 1922 | George Uhle, Cleveland | 5 |
| 1923 | Stan Coveleski, Cleveland | 5 |
| 1924 | Walter Johnson, Washington | 6 |
| 1925 | Ted Lyons, Chicago | 5 |
| 1926 | Ed Wells, Detroit | 4 |
| 1927 | Hod Lisenbee, Washington | 4 |
| 1928 | Herb Pennock, New York | 5 |
| 1929 | George Blaeholder, St. Louis | 4 |
| | Alvin Crowder, St. Louis | 4 |
| | Sam Gray, St. Louis | 4 |
| | Danny MacFayden, Boston | 4 |
| 1930 | Clint Brown, Cleveland | 3 |
| | George Earnshaw, Philadelphia | 3 |
| | George Pipgras, New York | 3 |
| 1931 | Lefty Grove, Philadelphia | 4 |
| | Vic Sorrell, Detroit | 4 |
| 1932 | Tommy Bridges, Detroit | 4 |
| | Lefty Grove, Philadelphia | 4 |
| 1933 | Oral Hildebrand, Cleveland | 6 |
| 1934 | Lefty Gomez, New York | 6 |
| | Mel Harder, Cleveland | 6 |
| 1935 | Schoolboy Rowe, Detroit | 6 |
| 1936 | Lefty Grove, Boston | 6 |
| 1937 | Lefty Gomez, New York | 6 |
| 1938 | Lefty Gomez, New York | 4 |
| 1939 | Red Ruffing, New York | 5 |
| 1940 | Bob Feller, Cleveland | 4 |
| | Ted Lyons, Chicago | 4 |
| | Al Milnar, Cleveland | 4 |
| 1941 | Bob Feller, Cleveland | 6 |
| 1942 | Tiny Bonham, New York | 6 |
| 1943 | Spud Chandler, New York | 5 |
| | Dizzy Trout, Detroit | 5 |
| 1944 | Dizzy Trout, Detroit | 7 |
| 1945 | Hal Newhouser, Detroit | 8 |
| 1946 | Bob Feller, Cleveland | 10 |
| 1947 | Bob Feller, Cleveland | 5 |
| 1948 | Bob Lemon, Cleveland | 10 |
| 1949 | Mike Garcia, Cleveland | 6 |
| | Ellis Kinder, Boston | 6 |
| | Virgil Trucks, Detroit | 6 |
| 1950 | Art Houtteman, Detroit | 4 |
| 1951 | Allie Reynolds, New York | 7 |
| 1952 | Mike Garcia, Cleveland | 6 |
| | Allie Reynolds, New York | 6 |
| 1953 | Bob Porterfield, Washington | 9 |
| 1954 | Mike Garcia, Cleveland | 5 |

| Year | Pitcher, Club | Shutouts |
|---|---|---|
| | Virgil Trucks, Chicago | 5 |
| 1955 | Billy Hoeft, Detroit | 7 |
| 1956 | Herb Score, Cleveland | 5 |
| 1957 | Jim Wilson, Chicago | 5 |
| 1958 | Whitey Ford, New York | 7 |
| 1959 | Camilo Pascual, Washington | 6 |
| 1960 | Whitey Ford, New York | 4 |
| | Jim Perry, Cleveland | 4 |
| | Early Wynn, Chicago | 4 |
| 1961 | Steve Barber, Baltimore | 8 |
| | Camilo Pascual, Minnesota | 8 |
| 1962 | Dick Donovan, Cleveland | 5 |
| | Jim Kaat, Minnesota | 5 |
| | Camilo Pascual, Minnesota | 5 |
| 1963 | Ray Herbert, Chicago | 7 |
| 1964 | Dean Chance, Los Angeles | 11 |
| 1965 | Mudcat Grant, Minnesota | 6 |
| 1966 | Tommy John, Chicago | 5 |
| | Sam McDowell, Cleveland | 5 |
| | Luis Tiant, Cleveland | 5 |
| 1967 | Steve Hargan, Cleveland | 6 |
| | Joe Horlen, Chicago | 6 |
| | Tommy John, Chicago | 6 |
| | Mickey Lolich, Detroit | 6 |
| | Jim McGlothlin, California | 6 |
| 1968 | Luis Tiant, Cleveland | 9 |
| 1969 | Denny McLain, Detroit | 9 |
| 1970 | Chuck Dobson, Oakland | 5 |
| | Jim Palmer, Baltimore | 5 |
| 1971 | Vida Blue, Oakland | 8 |
| 1972 | Nolan Ryan, California | 9 |
| 1973 | Bert Blyleven, Minnesota | 9 |
| 1974 | Luis Tiant, Boston | 7 |
| 1975 | Jim Palmer, Baltimore | 10 |
| 1976 | Nolan Ryan, California | 7 |
| 1977 | Frank Tanana, California | 7 |
| 1978 | Ron Guidry, New York | 9 |
| 1979 | Nolan Ryan, California | 5 |
| | Mike Flanagan, Baltimore | 5 |
| | Dennis Leonard, Kansas City | 5 |
| 1980 | Tommy John, New York | 6 |
| 1981 | Rich Dotson, Chicago | 4 |
| | Ken Forsch, California | 4 |
| | Steve McCatty, Oakland | 4 |
| | Doc Medich, Texas | 4 |
| 1982 | Dave Stieb, Toronto | 5 |
| 1983 | Mike Boddicker, Baltimore | 5 |
| 1984 | Bob Ojeda, Boston | 5 |
| | Geoff Zahn, California | 5 |
| 1985 | Bert Blyleven, Cleveland/Minnesota | 5 |
| 1986 | Jack Morris, Detroit | 6 |
| 1987 | Roger Clemens, Boston | 7 |
| 1988 | Roger Clemens, Boston | 8 |
| 1989 | Bert Blyleven, California | 5 |
| 1990 | Roger Clemens, Boston | 4 |
| | Dave Stewart, Oakland | 4 |
| 1991 | Roger Clemens, Boston | 4 |
| 1992 | Roger Clemens, Boston | 5 |
| 1993 | Jack McDowell, Chicago | 4 |
| 1994 | Randy Johnson, Seattle | 4 |
| 1995 | Mike Mussina, Baltimore | 4 |
| 1996 | Pat Hentgen, Toronto | 3 |
| | Ken Hill, Texas | 3 |
| | Rich Robertson, Minnesota | 3 |
| 1997 | Roger Clemens, Toronto | 3 |
| | Pat Hentgen, Toronto | 3 |
| 1998 | David Wells, New York | 5 |
| 1999 | Scott Erickson, Baltimore | 3 |
| 2000 | Pedro Martinez, Boston | 4 |
| 2001 | Mark Mulder, Oakland | 4 |
| 2002 | Jeff Weaver, Detroit/New York | 3 |
| 2003 | Roy Halladay, Toronto | 2 |
| | Tim Hudson, Oakland. | 2 |
| | John Lackey, Anaheim | 2 |
| | Mark Mulder, Oakland | 2 |
| | Joel Pineiro, Seattle | 2 |
| 2004 | Jeremy Bonderman, Detroit | 2 |
| | Tim Hudson, Oakland | 2 |
| | Sidney Ponson, Baltimore | 2 |
| 2005 | Jon Garland, Chicago | 3 |

## NATIONAL LEAGUE

| Year | Pitcher, Club | Shutouts |
|---|---|---|
| 1900 | Clark Griffith, Chicago | 4 |
| | Noodles Hahn, Cincinnati | 4 |
| | Kid Nichols, Boston | 4 |
| | Cy Young, St. Louis | 4 |
| 1901 | Jack Chesbro, Pittsburgh | 6 |
| | Al Orth, Philadelphia | 6 |
| | Vic Willis, Boston | 6 |
| 1902 | Jack Chesbro, Pittsburgh | 8 |
| | Christy Mathewson, New York | 8 |
| 1903 | Sam Leever, Pittsburgh | 7 |
| 1904 | Joe McGinnity, New York | 9 |
| 1905 | Christy Mathewson, New York | 8 |
| 1906 | Mordecai Brown, Chicago | 9 |
| 1907 | Christy Mathewson, New York | 8 |
| | Orval Overall, Chicago | 8 |
| 1908 | Christy Mathewson, New York | 11 |
| 1909 | Orval Overall, Chicago | 9 |
| 1910 | Mordecai Brown, Chicago | 6 |
| | Al Mattern, Boston | 6 |
| | Earl Moore, Philadelphia | 6 |
| | Nap Rucker, Brooklyn | 6 |
| 1911 | Grover Alexander, Philadelphia | 7 |
| 1912 | Nap Rucker, Brooklyn | 6 |
| 1913 | Grover Alexander, Philadelphia | 9 |
| 1914 | Jeff Tesreau, New York | 8 |
| 1915 | Grover Alexander, Philadelphia | 12 |
| 1916 | Grover Alexander, Philadelphia | 16 |
| 1917 | Grover Alexander, Philadelphia | 8 |
| 1918 | Lefty Tyler, Chicago | 8 |
| | Hippo Vaughn, Chicago | 8 |
| 1919 | Grover Alexander, Chicago | 9 |
| 1920 | Babe Adams, Pittsburgh | 8 |
| 1921 | Grover Alexander, Chicago | 3 |
| | Phil Douglas, New York | 3 |
| | Dana Fillingim, Boston | 3 |
| | Dolf Luque, Cincinnati | 3 |
| | Clarence Mitchell, Brooklyn | 3 |
| | Johnny Morrison, Pittsburgh | 3 |
| | Joe Oeschger, Boston | 3 |
| | Jesse Haines, St. Louis | 3 |
| 1922 | Dazzy Vance, Brooklyn | 6 |
| 1923 | Dolf Luque, Cincinnati | 6 |
| 1924 | Jesse Barnes, Boston | 4 |
| | Wilbur Cooper, Pittsburgh | 4 |
| | Ray Kremer, Pittsburgh | 4 |
| | Eppa Rixey, Cincinnati | 4 |
| | Allen Sothoron, St. Louis | 4 |
| | Emil Yde, Pittsburgh | 4 |
| 1925 | Hal Carlson, Philadelphia | 4 |
| | Dolf Luque, Cincinnati | 4 |
| | Dazzy Vance, Brooklyn | 4 |
| 1926 | Pete Donohue, Cincinnati | 5 |
| 1927 | Jesse Haines, St. Louis | 6 |
| 1928 | Sheriff Blake, Chicago | 4 |
| | Burleigh Grimes, Pittsburgh | 4 |
| | Red Lucas, Cincinnati | 4 |
| | Doug McWeeny, Brooklyn | 4 |
| | Dazzy Vance, Brooklyn | 4 |
| 1929 | Pat Malone, Chicago | 5 |
| 1930 | Charlie Root, Chicago | 4 |
| | Dazzy Vance, Brooklyn | 4 |
| 1931 | Bill Walker, New York | 6 |
| 1932 | Lon Warneke, Chicago | 4 |
| | Dizzy Dean, St. Louis | 4 |
| | Steve Swetonic, Pittsburgh | 4 |
| 1933 | Carl Hubbell, New York | 10 |
| 1934 | Dizzy Dean, St. Louis | 7 |
| 1935 | Cy Blanton, Pittsburgh | 4 |
| | Freddie Fitzsimmons, New York | 4 |
| | Larry French, Chicago | 4 |
| | Van Lingle Mungo, Brooklyn | 4 |
| | Jim Weaver, Pittsburgh | 4 |
| 1936 | Cy Blanton, Pittsburgh | 4 |
| | Tex Carleton, Chicago | 4 |
| | Larry French, Chicago | 4 |
| | Bill Lee, Chicago | 4 |
| | Al Smith, New York | 4 |
| | Bucky Walters, Philadelphia | 4 |
| | Lon Warneke, Chicago | 4 |
| 1937 | Lou Fette, Boston | 5 |
| | Lee Grissom, Cincinnati | 5 |
| | Jim Turner, Boston | 5 |
| 1938 | Bill Lee, Chicago | 9 |
| 1939 | Lou Fette, Boston | 6 |
| 1940 | Bill Lohrman, New York | 5 |
| | Manny Salvo, Boston | 5 |
| | Whitlow Wyatt, Brooklyn | 5 |
| 1941 | Whitlow Wyatt, Brooklyn | 7 |
| 1942 | Mort Cooper, St. Louis | 10 |
| 1943 | Hi Bithorn, Chicago | 7 |
| 1944 | Mort Cooper, St. Louis | 7 |
| 1945 | Claude Passeau, Chicago | 5 |
| 1946 | Ewell Blackwell, Cincinnati | 6 |
| 1947 | Warren Spahn, Boston | 7 |
| 1948 | Harry Brecheen, St. Louis | 7 |
| 1949 | Ken Heintzelman, Philadelphia | 5 |
| | Don Newcombe, Brooklyn | 5 |
| | Howie Pollet, St. Louis | 5 |
| | Ken Raffensberger, Cincinnati | 5 |
| 1950 | Jim Hearn, New York | 5 |
| | Larry Jansen, New York | 5 |
| | Sal Maglie, New York | 5 |
| | Robin Roberts, Philadelphia | 5 |
| 1951 | Warren Spahn, Boston | 7 |
| 1952 | Ken Raffensberger, Cincinnati | 6 |
| | Curt Simmons, Philadelphia | 6 |
| 1953 | Harvey Haddix, St. Louis | 6 |
| 1954 | Johnny Antonelli, New York | 6 |
| 1955 | Joe Nuxhall, Cincinnati | 5 |
| 1956 | Johnny Antonelli, New York | 6 |
| | Lew Burdette, Milwaukee | 6 |
| 1957 | Johnny Podres, Brooklyn | 6 |
| 1958 | Carl Willey, Milwaukee | 4 |
| 1959 | Johnny Antonelli, San Francisco | 4 |
| | Bob Buhl, Milwaukee | 4 |
| | Lew Burdette, Milwaukee | 4 |
| | Roger Craig, Los Angeles | 4 |
| | Don Drysdale, Los Angeles | 4 |
| | Sam Jones, San Francisco | 4 |
| | Warren Spahn, Milwaukee | 4 |
| 1960 | Jack Sanford, San Francisco | 6 |
| 1961 | Joey Jay, Cincinnati | 4 |
| | Warren Spahn, Milwaukee | 4 |
| 1962 | Bob Friend, Pittsburgh | 5 |
| | Bob Gibson, St. Louis | 5 |
| 1963 | Sandy Koufax, Los Angeles | 11 |
| 1964 | Sandy Koufax, Los Angeles | 7 |
| 1965 | Juan Marichal, San Francisco | 10 |
| 1966 | Jim Bunning, Philadelphia | 5 |
| | Bob Gibson, St. Louis | 5 |
| | Larry Jackson, Philadelphia | 5 |
| | Larry Jaster, St. Louis | 5 |
| | Sandy Koufax, Los Angeles | 5 |
| | Jim Maloney, Cincinnati | 5 |
| 1967 | Jim Bunning, Philadelphia | 6 |
| 1968 | Bob Gibson, St. Louis | 13 |
| 1969 | Juan Marichal, San Francisco | 8 |
| 1970 | Gaylord Perry, San Francisco | 5 |
| 1971 | Steve Blass, Pittsburgh | 5 |
| | Al Downing, Los Angeles | 5 |
| | Bob Gibson, St. Louis | 5 |
| | Milt Pappas, Chicago | 5 |
| 1972 | Don Sutton, Los Angeles | 9 |
| 1973 | Jack Billingham, Cincinnati | 7 |
| 1974 | Jon Matlack, New York | 7 |
| 1975 | Andy Messersmith, Los Angeles | 7 |
| 1976 | Jon Matlack, New York | 6 |
| | John Montefusco, San Francisco | 6 |
| 1977 | Tom Seaver, New York/Cincinnati | 7 |
| 1978 | Bob Knepper, San Francisco | 6 |
| 1979 | Tom Seaver, Cincinnati | 5 |
| | Joe Niekro, Houston | 5 |
| | Steve Rogers, Montreal | 5 |
| 1980 | Jerry Reuss, Los Angeles | 6 |
| 1981 | Fernando Valenzuela, Los Angeles | 8 |
| 1982 | Steve Carlton, Philadelphia | 6 |
| 1983 | Steve Rogers, Montreal | 5 |
| 1984 | Joaquin Andujar, St. Louis | 4 |
| | Orel Hershiser, Los Angeles | 4 |
| | Alejandro Pena, Los Angeles | 4 |
| 1985 | John Tudor, St. Louis | 10 |
| 1986 | Bob Knepper, Houston | 5 |
| | Mike Scott, Houston | 5 |
| 1987 | Rick Reuschel, Pittsburgh/San Francisco | 4 |
| | Bob Welch, Los Angeles | 4 |
| 1988 | Orel Hershiser, Los Angeles | 8 |
| 1989 | Tim Belcher, Los Angeles | 8 |
| 1990 | Bruce Hurst, San Diego | 4 |

| Year | Pitcher, Club | Shutouts |
|---|---|---|
| | Mike Morgan, Los Angeles | 4 |
| 1991 | Dennis Martinez, Montreal | 5 |
| 1992 | David Cone, New York | 5 |
| | Tom Glavine, Atlanta | 5 |
| 1993 | Pete Harnisch, Houston | 4 |
| 1994 | Greg Maddux, Atlanta | 3 |
| | Ramon Martinez, Los Angeles | 3 |
| 1995 | Greg Maddux, Atlanta | 3 |
| | Hideo Nomo, Los Angeles | 3 |
| 1996 | Kevin Brown, Florida | 3 |
| 1997 | Carlos Perez, Montreal | 5 |
| 1998 | Greg Maddux, Atlanta | 5 |
| 1999 | Andy Ashby, San Diego | 3 |
| 2000 | Randy Johnson, Arizona | 3 |
| | Greg Maddux, Atlanta | 3 |
| 2001 | Greg Maddux, Atlanta | 3 |
| | Javier Vazquez, Montreal | 3 |
| 2002 | A.J. Burnett, Florida | 5 |
| 2003 | Kevin Millwood, Philadelphia | 3 |
| | Matt Morris, St. Louis | 3 |
| | Jason Schmidt, San Francisco | 3 |
| 2004 | Cory Lidle, Philadelphia | 3 |
| | Jason Schmidt, San Francisco | 3 |
| 2005 | Dontrelle Willis, Florida | 5 |

## SAVES

### AMERICAN LEAGUE

| Year | Pitcher, Club | Saves |
|---|---|---|
| 1969 | Ron Perranoski, Minnesota | 31 |
| 1970 | Ron Perranoski, Minnesota | 34 |
| 1971 | Ken Sanders, Milwaukee | 31 |
| 1972 | Sparky Lyle, New York | 35 |
| 1973 | John Hiller, Detroit | 38 |
| 1974 | Terry Forster, Chicago | 24 |
| 1975 | Rich Gossage, Chicago | 26 |
| 1976 | Sparky Lyle, New York | 23 |
| 1977 | Bill Campbell, Boston | 31 |
| 1978 | Rich Gossage, New York | 27 |
| 1979 | Mike Marshall, Minnesota | 32 |
| 1980 | Rich Gossage, New York | 33 |
| | Dan Quisenberry, Kansas City | 33 |
| 1981 | Rollie Fingers, Milwaukee | 28 |
| 1982 | Dan Quisenberry, Kansas City | 35 |
| 1983 | Dan Quisenberry, Kansas City | 45 |
| 1984 | Dan Quisenberry, Kansas City | 44 |
| 1985 | Dan Quisenberry, Kansas City | 37 |
| 1986 | Dave Righetti, New York | 46 |
| 1987 | Tom Henke, Toronto | 34 |
| 1988 | Dennis Eckersley, Oakland | 45 |
| 1989 | Jeff Russell, Texas | 38 |
| 1990 | Bobby Thigpen, Chicago | 57 |
| 1991 | Bryan Harvey, California | 46 |
| 1992 | Dennis Eckersley, Oakland | 51 |
| 1993 | Jeff Montgomery, Kansas City | 45 |
| | Duane Ward, Toronto | 45 |
| 1994 | Lee Smith, Baltimore | 33 |
| 1995 | Jose Mesa, Cleveland | 46 |
| 1996 | John Wetteland, New York | 43 |
| 1997 | Randy Myers, Baltimore | 45 |
| 1998 | Tom Gordon, Boston | 46 |
| 1999 | Mariano Rivera, New York | 45 |
| 2000 | Todd Jones, Detroit | 42 |
| | Derek Lowe, Boston | 42 |
| 2001 | Mariano Rivera, New York | 50 |
| 2002 | Eddie Guardado, Minnesota | 45 |
| 2003 | Keith Foulke, Oakland | 43 |
| 2004 | Mariano Rivera, New York | 53 |
| 2005 | Francisco Rodriguez, Los Angeles | 45 |
| | Bob Wickman, Cleveland | 45 |

### NATIONAL LEAGUE

| Year | Pitcher, Club | Saves |
|---|---|---|
| 1969 | Fred Gladding, Houston | 29 |
| 1970 | Wayne Granger, Cincinnati | 35 |
| 1971 | Dave Giusti, Pittsburgh | 30 |
| 1972 | Clay Carroll, Cincinnati | 37 |
| 1973 | Mike Marshall, Montreal | 31 |
| 1974 | Mike Marshall, Los Angeles | 21 |
| 1975 | Rawly Eastwick, Cincinnati | 22 |
| | Al Hrabosky, St. Louis | 22 |
| 1976 | Rawly Eastwick, Cincinnati | 26 |
| 1977 | Rollie Fingers, San Diego | 35 |
| 1978 | Rollie Fingers, San Diego | 37 |
| 1979 | Bruce Sutter, Chicago | 37 |
| 1980 | Bruce Sutter, Chicago | 28 |
| 1981 | Bruce Sutter, St. Louis | 25 |
| 1982 | Bruce Sutter, St. Louis | 36 |
| 1983 | Lee Smith, Chicago | 29 |
| 1984 | Bruce Sutter, St. Louis | 45 |
| 1985 | Jeff Reardon, Montreal | 41 |
| 1986 | Todd Worrell, St. Louis | 36 |
| 1987 | Steve Bedrosian, Philadelphia | 40 |
| 1988 | John Franco, Cincinnati | 39 |
| 1989 | Mark Davis, San Diego | 44 |
| 1990 | John Franco, New York | 33 |
| 1991 | Lee Smith, St. Louis | 47 |
| 1992 | Lee Smith, St. Louis | 43 |
| 1993 | Randy Myers, Chicago | 53 |
| 1994 | John Franco, New York | 30 |
| 1995 | Randy Myers, Chicago | 38 |
| 1996 | Jeff Brantley, Cincinnati | 44 |
| | Todd Worrell, Los Angeles | 44 |
| 1997 | Jeff Shaw, Cincinnati | 42 |
| 1998 | Trevor Hoffman, San Diego | 53 |
| 1999 | Ugueth Urbina, Montreal | 41 |
| 2000 | Antonio Alfonseca, Florida | 45 |
| 2001 | Robb Nen, San Francisco | 45 |
| 2002 | John Smoltz, Atlanta | 55 |
| 2003 | Eric Gagne, Los Angeles | 55 |
| 2004 | Armando Benitez, Florida | 47 |
| | Jason Isringhausen, St. Louis | 47 |
| 2005 | Chad Cordero, Washington | 47 |

## STRIKEOUTS

### AMERICAN LEAGUE

| Year | Pitcher, Club | Ks |
|---|---|---|
| 1901 | Cy Young, Boston | 158 |
| 1902 | Rube Waddell, Philadelphia | 210 |
| 1903 | Rube Waddell, Philadelphia | 302 |
| 1904 | Rube Waddell, Philadelphia | 349 |
| 1905 | Rube Waddell, Philadelphia | 287 |
| 1906 | Rube Waddell, Philadelphia | 196 |
| 1907 | Rube Waddell, Philadelphia | 232 |
| 1908 | Ed Walsh, Chicago | 269 |
| 1909 | Frank Smith, Chicago | 177 |
| 1910 | Walter Johnson, Washington | 313 |
| 1911 | Ed Walsh, Chicago | 255 |
| 1912 | Walter Johnson, Washington | 303 |
| 1913 | Walter Johnson, Washington | 243 |
| 1914 | Walter Johnson, Washington | 225 |
| 1915 | Walter Johnson, Washington | 203 |
| 1916 | Walter Johnson, Washington | 228 |
| 1917 | Walter Johnson, Washington | 188 |
| 1918 | Walter Johnson, Washington | 162 |
| 1919 | Walter Johnson, Washington | 147 |
| 1920 | Stan Coveleski, Cleveland | 133 |
| 1921 | Walter Johnson, Washington | 143 |
| 1922 | Urban Shocker, St. Louis | 149 |
| 1923 | Walter Johnson, Washington | 130 |
| 1924 | Walter Johnson, Washington | 158 |
| 1925 | Lefty Grove, Philadelphia | 116 |
| 1926 | Lefty Grove, Philadelphia | 194 |
| 1927 | Lefty Grove, Philadelphia | 174 |
| 1928 | Lefty Grove, Philadelphia | 183 |
| 1929 | Lefty Grove, Philadelphia | 170 |
| 1930 | Lefty Grove, Philadelphia | 209 |
| 1931 | Lefty Grove, Philadelphia | 175 |
| 1932 | Red Ruffing, New York | 190 |
| 1933 | Lefty Gomez, New York | 163 |
| 1934 | Lefty Gomez, New York | 158 |
| 1935 | Tommy Bridges, Detroit | 163 |
| 1936 | Tommy Bridges, Detroit | 175 |
| 1937 | Lefty Gomez, New York | 194 |
| 1938 | Bob Feller, Cleveland | 240 |
| 1939 | Bob Feller, Cleveland | 246 |
| 1940 | Bob Feller, Cleveland | 261 |
| 1941 | Bob Feller, Cleveland | 260 |
| 1942 | Bobo Newsom, Washington | 113 |
| | Tex Hughson, Boston | 113 |
| 1943 | Allie Reynolds, Cleveland | 151 |
| 1944 | Hal Newhouser, Detroit | 187 |
| 1945 | Hal Newhouser, Detroit | 212 |
| 1946 | Bob Feller, Cleveland | 348 |
| 1947 | Bob Feller, Cleveland | 196 |
| 1948 | Bob Feller, Cleveland | 164 |
| 1949 | Virgil Trucks, Detroit | 153 |
| 1950 | Bob Lemon, Cleveland | 170 |
| 1951 | Vic Raschi, New York | 164 |
| 1952 | Allie Reynolds, New York | 160 |
| 1953 | Billy Pierce, Chicago | 186 |
| 1954 | Bob Turley, Baltimore | 185 |
| 1955 | Herb Score, Cleveland | 245 |
| 1956 | Herb Score, Cleveland | 263 |
| 1957 | Early Wynn, Cleveland | 184 |
| 1958 | Early Wynn, Chicago | 179 |
| 1959 | Jim Bunning, Detroit | 201 |
| 1960 | Jim Bunning, Detroit | 201 |
| 1961 | Camilo Pascual, Minnesota | 221 |
| 1962 | Camilo Pascual, Minnesota | 206 |
| 1963 | Camilo Pascual, Minnesota | 202 |
| 1964 | Al Downing, New York | 217 |
| 1965 | Sam McDowell, Cleveland | 325 |
| 1966 | Sam McDowell, Cleveland | 225 |
| 1967 | Jim Lonborg, Boston | 246 |
| 1968 | Sam McDowell, Cleveland | 283 |
| 1969 | Sam McDowell, Cleveland | 279 |
| 1970 | Sam McDowell, Cleveland | 304 |
| 1971 | Mickey Lolich, Detroit | 308 |
| 1972 | Nolan Ryan, California | 329 |
| 1973 | Nolan Ryan, California | 383 |
| 1974 | Nolan Ryan, California | 367 |
| 1975 | Frank Tanana, California | 269 |
| 1976 | Nolan Ryan, California | 327 |
| 1977 | Nolan Ryan, California | 341 |
| 1978 | Nolan Ryan, California | 260 |
| 1979 | Nolan Ryan, California | 223 |
| 1980 | Len Barker, Cleveland | 187 |
| 1981 | Len Barker, Cleveland | 127 |
| 1982 | Floyd Bannister, Seattle | 209 |
| 1983 | Jack Morris, Detroit | 232 |
| 1984 | Mark Langston, Seattle | 204 |
| 1985 | Bert Blyleven, Cleveland/Minnesota | 206 |
| 1986 | Mark Langston, Seattle | 245 |
| 1987 | Mark Langston, Seattle | 262 |
| 1988 | Roger Clemens, Boston | 291 |
| 1989 | Nolan Ryan, Texas | 301 |
| 1990 | Nolan Ryan, Texas | 232 |
| 1991 | Roger Clemens, Boston | 241 |
| 1992 | Randy Johnson, Seattle | *241 |
| 1993 | Randy Johnson, Seattle | 308 |
| 1994 | Randy Johnson, Seattle | 204 |
| 1995 | Randy Johnson, Seattle | 294 |
| 1996 | Roger Clemens, Boston | 257 |
| 1997 | Roger Clemens, Toronto | 292 |
| 1998 | Roger Clemens, Toronto | †271 |
| 1999 | Pedro Martinez, Boston | 313 |
| 2000 | Pedro Martinez, Boston | 284 |
| 2001 | Hideo Nomo, Boston | 220 |
| 2002 | Pedro Martinez, Boston | 239 |
| 2003 | Esteban Loaiza, Chicago | 207 |
| 2004 | Johan Santana, Minnesota | 265 |
| 2005 | Johan Santana, Minnesota | 238 |

### NATIONAL LEAGUE

| Year | Pitcher, Club | Ks |
|---|---|---|
| 1900 | Noodles Hahn, Cincinnati | 132 |
| 1901 | Noodles Hahn, Cincinnati | 239 |
| 1902 | Vic Willis, Boston | 225 |
| 1903 | Christy Mathewson, New York | 267 |
| 1904 | Christy Mathewson, New York | 212 |
| 1905 | Christy Mathewson, New York | 206 |
| 1906 | Fred Beebe, Chicago/St. Louis | 171 |
| 1907 | Christy Mathewson, New York | 178 |
| 1908 | Christy Mathewson, New York | 259 |
| 1909 | Orval Overall, Chicago | 205 |
| 1910 | Earl Moore, Philadelphia | 185 |
| 1911 | Rube Marquard, New York | 237 |
| 1912 | Grover Alexander, Philadelphia | 195 |
| 1913 | Tom Seaton, Philadelphia | 168 |
| 1914 | Grover Alexander, Philadelphia | 214 |
| 1915 | Grover Alexander, Philadelphia | 241 |
| 1916 | Grover Alexander, Philadelphia | 167 |
| 1917 | Grover Alexander, Philadelphia | 200 |
| 1918 | Hippo Vaughn, Chicago | 148 |
| 1919 | Hippo Vaughn, Chicago | 141 |
| 1920 | Grover Alexander, Chicago | 173 |
| 1921 | Burleigh Grimes, Brooklyn | 136 |
| 1922 | Dazzy Vance, Brooklyn | 134 |
| 1923 | Dazzy Vance, Brooklyn | 197 |

| Year | Pitcher, Club | Ks |
|---|---|---|
| 1924 | Dazzy Vance, Brooklyn | 262 |
| 1925 | Dazzy Vance, Brooklyn | 221 |
| 1925 | Dazzy Vance, Brooklyn | 140 |
| 1927 | Dazzy Vance, Brooklyn | 184 |
| 1928 | Dazzy Vance, Brooklyn | 200 |
| 1929 | Pat Malone, Chicago | 166 |
| 1930 | Bill Hallahan, St. Louis | 177 |
| 1931 | Bill Hallahan, St. Louis | 159 |
| 1932 | Dizzy Dean, St. Louis | 191 |
| 1933 | Dizzy Dean, St. Louis | 199 |
| 1934 | Dizzy Dean, St. Louis | 195 |
| 1935 | Dizzy Dean, St. Louis | 182 |
| 1936 | Van Lingle Mungo, Brooklyn | 238 |
| 1937 | Carl Hubbell, New York | 159 |
| 1938 | Clay Bryant, Chicago | 135 |
| 1939 | Claude Passeau, Philadelphia/Chicago | 137 |
| | Bucky Walters, Cincinnati | 137 |
| 1940 | Kirby Higbe, Philadelphia | 137 |
| 1941 | Johnny Vander Meer, Cincinnati | 202 |
| 1942 | Johnny Vander Meer, Cincinnati | 186 |
| 1943 | Johnny Vander Meer, Cincinnati | 174 |
| 1944 | Bill Voiselle, New York | 161 |
| 1945 | Preacher Roe, Pittsburgh | 148 |
| 1946 | Johnny Schmitz, Chicago | 135 |
| 1947 | Ewell Blackwell, Cincinnati | 193 |
| 1948 | Harry Brecheen, St. Louis | 149 |
| 1949 | Warren Spahn, Boston | 151 |
| 1950 | Warren Spahn, Boston | 191 |
| 1951 | Warren Spahn, Boston | 164 |
| | Don Newcombe, Brooklyn | 164 |
| 1952 | Warren Spahn, Boston | 183 |
| 1953 | Robin Roberts, Philadelphia | 198 |
| 1954 | Robin Roberts, Philadelphia | 185 |
| 1955 | Sam Jones, Chicago | 198 |
| 1956 | Sam Jones, Chicago | 176 |
| 1957 | Jack Sanford, Philadelphia | 188 |
| 1958 | Sam Jones, St. Louis | 225 |
| 1959 | Don Drysdale, Los Angeles | 242 |
| 1960 | Don Drysdale, Los Angeles | 246 |
| 1961 | Sandy Koufax, Los Angeles | 269 |
| 1962 | Don Drysdale, Los Angeles | 232 |
| 1963 | Sandy Koufax, Los Angeles | 306 |
| 1964 | Bob Veale, Pittsburgh | 250 |
| 1965 | Sandy Koufax, Los Angeles | 382 |
| 1966 | Sandy Koufax, Los Angeles | 317 |
| 1967 | Jim Bunning, Philadelphia | 253 |
| 1968 | Bob Gibson, St. Louis | 268 |
| 1969 | Ferguson Jenkins, Chicago | 273 |
| 1970 | Tom Seaver, New York | 283 |
| 1971 | Tom Seaver, New York | 289 |
| 1972 | Steve Carlton, Philadelphia | 310 |
| 1973 | Tom Seaver, New York | 251 |
| 1974 | Steve Carlton, Philadelphia | 240 |
| 1975 | Tom Seaver, New York | 243 |
| 1976 | Tom Seaver, New York | 235 |
| 1977 | Phil Niekro, Atlanta | 262 |
| 1978 | J.R. Richard, Houston | 303 |
| 1979 | J.R. Richard, Houston | 313 |
| 1980 | Steve Carlton, Philadelphia | 286 |
| 1981 | Fernando Valenzuela, Los Angeles | 180 |
| 1982 | Steve Carlton, Philadelphia | 286 |
| 1983 | Steve Carlton, Philadelphia | 275 |
| 1984 | Dwight Gooden, New York | 276 |
| 1985 | Dwight Gooden, New York | 268 |
| 1986 | Mike Scott, Houston | 306 |
| 1987 | Nolan Ryan, Houston | 270 |
| 1988 | Nolan Ryan, Houston | 228 |
| 1989 | Jose DeLeon, St. Louis | 201 |
| 1990 | David Cone, New York | 233 |
| 1991 | David Cone, New York | 241 |
| 1992 | John Smoltz, Atlanta | *215 |
| 1993 | Jose Rijo, Cincinnati | 227 |
| 1994 | Andy Benes, San Diego | 189 |
| 1995 | Hideo Nomo, Los Angeles | 236 |
| 1996 | John Smoltz, Atlanta | 276 |
| 1997 | Curt Schilling, Philadelphia | 319 |
| 1998 | Curt Schilling, Philadelphia | †300 |
| 1999 | Randy Johnson, Arizona | 364 |
| 2000 | Randy Johnson, Arizona | 347 |
| 2001 | Randy Johnson, Arizona | 372 |
| 2002 | Randy Johnson, Arizona | 334 |
| 2003 | Kerry Wood, Chicago | 266 |
| 2004 | Randy Johnson, Arizona | 290 |
| 2005 | Jake Peavy, San Diego | 216 |

*David Cone led the majors with 261 strikeouts in 1992, compiling 214 with New York NL and another 47 with Toronto AL following an August 27 trade.

†Randy Johnson led the majors with 329 strikeouts in 1998, compiling 213 with Seattle AL and another 116 with Houston NL following a July 31 trade.

# CAREER MILESTONES

**(Players active in the major leagues in 2005 are in boldface.)**

## SERVICE

### 20-SEASON PLAYERS

**(does not include pitchers)**

| | Player | Seasons | Games |
|---|---|---|---|
| 1. | Deacon McGuire | 26 | 1,782 |
| 2. | Rickey Henderson | 25 | 3,081 |
| 3. | Eddie Collins | 25 | 2,826 |
| | Bobby Wallace | 25 | 2,383 |
| 5. | Pete Rose | 24 | 3,562 |
| | Ty Cobb | 24 | 3,035 |
| | Carlton Fisk | 24 | 2,499 |
| | Rick Dempsey | 24 | 1,766 |
| 9. | Carl Yastrzemski | 23 | 3,308 |
| | Hank Aaron | 23 | 3,298 |
| | Rusty Staub | 23 | 2,951 |
| | Brooks Robinson | 23 | 2,896 |
| | Tony Perez | 23 | 2,777 |
| | Rabbit Maranville | 23 | 2,670 |
| | Tim Raines Sr. | 23 | 2,502 |
| | Rogers Hornsby | 23 | 2,259 |
| 17. | Stan Musial | 22 | 3,026 |
| | Willie Mays | 22 | 2,992 |
| | Dave Winfield | 22 | 2,973 |
| | Al Kaline | 22 | 2,834 |
| | Harold Baines | 22 | 2,830 |
| | Tris Speaker | 22 | 2,789 |
| | Mel Ott | 22 | 2,730 |
| | Graig Nettles | 22 | 2,700 |
| | Joe Morgan | 22 | 2,649 |
| | Willie McCovey | 22 | 2,588 |
| | Bill Buckner | 22 | 2,517 |
| | Babe Ruth | 22 | 2,503 |
| | Harmon Killebrew | 22 | 2,435 |
| | Jimmie Dykes | 22 | 2,282 |
| | Cap Anson | 22 | 2,277 |
| | Phil Cavarretta | 22 | 2,030 |
| | Kid Gleason | 22 | 1,968 |
| | Harry H. Davis | 22 | 1,755 |
| 35. | Eddie Murray | 21 | 3,026 |
| | Cal Ripken Jr. | 21 | 3,001 |
| | Reggie Jackson | 21 | 2,820 |
| | Frank Robinson | 21 | 2,808 |
| | Honus Wagner | 21 | 2,794 |
| | George Brett | 21 | 2,707 |
| | Darrell Evans | 21 | 2,687 |
| | Paul Molitor | 21 | 2,683 |
| | Andre Dawson | 21 | 2,627 |
| | Nap Lajoie | 21 | 2,480 |
| | Ted Simmons | 21 | 2,456 |
| | Bill Dahlen | 21 | 2,444 |
| | Ron Fairly | 21 | 2,442 |
| | **Julio Franco** | **21** | **2,377** |
| | Willie Stargell | 21 | 2,360 |
| | Lave Cross | 21 | 2,278 |
| | Fred Clarke | 21 | 2,246 |
| | Tim McCarver | 21 | 1,909 |
| | Bob O'Farrell | 21 | 1,492 |
| | Jack O'Connor | 21 | 1,452 |
| 55. | Robin Yount | 20 | 2,856 |
| | **Rafael Palmeiro** | **20** | **2,831** |
| | **Barry Bonds** | **20** | **2,730** |
| | Dwight Evans | 20 | 2,606 |
| | Paul Waner | 20 | 2,549 |
| | Gary Gaetti | 20 | 2,507 |
| | Max Carey | 20 | 2,476 |
| | Tony Gwynn | 20 | 2,440 |
| | Luke Appling | 20 | 2,422 |
| | Mickey Vernon | 20 | 2,409 |
| | Sam Rice | 20 | 2,404 |
| | Jake Beckley | 20 | 2,389 |
| | George Davis | 20 | 2,372 |
| | Brian Downing | 20 | 2,344 |
| | Jimmie Foxx | 20 | 2,317 |
| | Alan Trammell | 20 | 2,293 |
| | Doc Cramer | 20 | 2,239 |
| | Al Simmons | 20 | 2,215 |
| | Joe Judge | 20 | 2,171 |
| | Charlie Grimm | 20 | 2,166 |
| | Joe Cronin | 20 | 2,124 |
| | Gabby Hartnett | 20 | 1,990 |
| | **Benito Santiago** | **20** | **1,978** |
| | Elmer Valo | 20 | 1,806 |
| | Jay Johnstone | 20 | 1,748 |
| | Luke Sewell | 20 | 1,630 |
| | Manny Mota | 20 | 1,536 |
| | Johnny Cooney | 20 | 1,172 |

### 20-SEASONS, ONE CLUB

**(does not include pitchers)**

| | Player | Seasons |
|---|---|---|
| 1. | Brooks Robinson, Orioles | 23 |
| | Carl Yastrzemski, Red Sox | 23 |
| 3. | Cap Anson, Cubs | 22 |
| | Ty Cobb, Tigers | 22 |
| | Al Kaline, Tigers | 22 |
| | Stan Musial, Cardinals | 22 |
| | Mel Ott, Giants | 22 |
| 8. | Hank Aaron, Braves | 21 |
| | George Brett, A's | 21 |
| | Harmon Killebrew, Senators/Twins | 21 |
| | Willie Mays, Giants | 21 |
| | Cal Ripken, Orioles | 21 |
| | Willie Stargell, Pirates | 21 |
| 14. | Luke Appling, White Sox | 20 |
| | Phil Cavarretta, Cubs | 20 |
| | Tony Gwynn, Padres | 20 |
| | Alan Trammell, Tigers | 20 |
| | Robin Yount, Braves | 20 |

### 20-SEASON PITCHERS

| | Pitcher | Seasons | Games |
|---|---|---|---|
| 1. | Nolan Ryan | 27 | 807 |
| 2. | Tommy John | 26 | 760 |
| 3. | Jim Kaat | 25 | 898 |
| | Charlie Hough | 25 | 858 |
| 5. | Jesse Orosco | 24 | 1,252 |
| | Dennis Eckersley | 24 | 1,071 |
| | Phil Niekro | 24 | 864 |
| | Steve Carlton | 24 | 741 |
| 9. | Don Sutton | 23 | 774 |
| | Jack Quinn | 23 | 756 |
| | Dennis Martinez | 23 | 692 |
| | Early Wynn | 23 | 691 |
| 13. | Rich Gossage | 22 | 1,002 |
| | Cy Young | 22 | 906 |
| | Gaylord Perry | 22 | 777 |
| | Joe Niekro | 22 | 702 |
| | Bert Blyleven | 22 | 692 |
| | **Roger Clemens** | **22** | **672** |
| | Sam Jones | 22 | 647 |
| | Jerry Reuss | 22 | 628 |
| | Red Ruffing | 22 | 624 |
| | Herb Pennock | 22 | 617 |
| | Mike Morgan | 22 | 597 |
| **24.** | **John Franco** | **21** | **1,119** |
| | Hoyt Wilhelm | 21 | 1,070 |
| | Lindy McDaniel | 21 | 987 |
| | Walter Johnson | 21 | 802 |
| | Rick Honeycutt | 21 | 797 |
| | Warren Spahn | 21 | 750 |
| | Danny Darwin | 21 | 716 |
| | Eppa Rixey | 21 | 692 |
| | Waite Hoyt | 21 | 674 |
| | Frank Tanana | 21 | 638 |
| | Ted Lyons | 21 | 594 |
| 35. | Grover Alexander | 20 | 696 |
| | Red Faber | 20 | 669 |
| | Tom Seaver | 20 | 656 |
| | **Greg Maddux** | **20** | **643** |
| | Dutch Leonard | 20 | 640 |
| | Bobo Newsom | 20 | 600 |
| | Mel Harder | 20 | 582 |
| | Curt Simmons | 20 | 569 |
| | Dolf Luque | 20 | 550 |
| | Clark Griffith | 20 | 453 |

### 20-SEASONS, ONE CLUB

**(pitchers only )**

| | Player | Seasons |
|---|---|---|
| 1. | Walter Johnson, Senators | 21 |
| | Ted Lyons, White Sox | 21 |
| | Phil Niekro, Braves | 21 |
| 4. | Red Faber, White Sox | 20 |
| | Mel Harder, Indians | 20 |
| | Warren Spahn, Braves | 20 |

## BATTING

### 2,500 GAMES

**(does not include pitchers)**

| | Player | Games |
|---|---|---|
| 1. | Pete Rose | 3,562 |
| 2. | Carl Yastrzemski | 3,308 |
| 3. | Hank Aaron | 3,298 |
| 4. | Rickey Henderson | 3,081 |
| 5. | Ty Cobb | 3,035 |
| 6. | Eddie Murray | 3,026 |
| | Stan Musial | 3,026 |
| 8. | Cal Ripken Jr. | 3,001 |
| 9. | Willie Mays | 2,992 |
| 10. | Dave Winfield | 2,973 |
| 11. | Rusty Staub | 2,951 |
| 12. | Brooks Robinson | 2,896 |
| 13. | Robin Yount | 2,856 |
| 14. | Al Kaline | 2,834 |
| **15.** | **Rafael Palmeiro** | **2,831** |
| 16. | Harold Baines | 2,830 |
| 17. | Eddie Collins | 2,826 |
| 18. | Reggie Jackson | 2,820 |
| 19. | Frank Robinson | 2,808 |
| 20. | Honus Wagner | 2,794 |
| 21. | Tris Speaker | 2,789 |
| 22. | Tony Perez | 2,777 |
| **23.** | **Barry Bonds** | **2,730** |
| | Mel Ott | 2,730 |
| 25. | George Brett | 2,707 |
| 26. | Graig Nettles | 2,700 |
| 27. | Darrell Evans | 2,687 |
| 28. | Paul Molitor | 2,683 |
| 29. | Rabbit Maranville | 2,670 |
| 30. | Joe Morgan | 2,649 |
| 31. | Andre Dawson | 2,627 |
| 32. | Lou Brock | 2,616 |
| 33. | Dwight Evans | 2,606 |
| 34. | Luis Aparicio | 2,599 |
| 35. | Willie McCovey | 2,588 |
| 36. | Ozzie Smith | 2,573 |
| **37.** | **Craig Biggio** | **2,564** |

| | Player | Games |
|---|---|---|
| 38. | Paul Waner | 2,549 |
| 39. | Ernie Banks | 2,528 |
| 40. | Bill Buckner | 2,517 |
| | Sam Crawford | 2,517 |
| 42. | Gary Gaetti | 2,507 |
| 43. | Babe Ruth | 2,503 |
| 44. | Tim Raines Sr. | 2,502 |

## 500 CONSECUTIVE GAMES

| | Player | No. |
|---|---|---|
| 1. | Cal Ripken Jr. | 2,632 |
| 2. | Lou Gehrig | 2,130 |
| 3. | Everett Scott | 1,307 |
| 4. | Steve Garvey | 1,207 |
| 5. | Billy Williams | 1,117 |
| 6. | Joe Sewell | 1,103 |
| **7.** | **Miguel Tejada** | ****918** |
| 8. | Stan Musial | 895 |
| 9. | Eddie Yost | 829 |
| 10. | Gus Suhr | 822 |
| 11. | Nellie Fox | 798 |
| 12. | Pete Rose* | 745 |
| 13. | Dale Murphy | 740 |
| 14. | Richie Ashburn | 730 |
| 15. | Ernie Banks | 717 |
| 16. | Pete Rose* | 678 |
| 17. | Earl Averill | 673 |
| 18. | Frank McCormick | 652 |
| 19. | Sandy Alomar Sr. | 648 |
| 20. | Eddie Brown | 618 |
| 21. | Roy McMillan | 585 |
| 22. | George Pinckney | 577 |
| 23. | Steve Brodie | 574 |
| 24. | Aaron Ward | 565 |
| 25. | Alex Rodriguez | 546 |
| 26. | Candy LaChance | 540 |
| 27. | Buck Freeman | 535 |
| 28. | Fred Luderus | 533 |
| 29. | Charlie Gehringer* | 511 |
| | Clyde Milan | 511 |
| 31. | Vada Pinson | 508 |
| 32. | Joe Carter | 507 |
| 33. | Tony Cuccinello | 504 |
| | Charlie Gehringer* | 504 |
| 35. | Omar Moreno | 503 |

*only players with two streaks
**ongoing streak

## .300 BATTING AVERAGE

(1,500 or more hits)

| | Player | Hits | Avg. |
|---|---|---|---|
| 1. | Ty Cobb | 4,189 | .366 |
| 2. | Rogers Hornsby | 2,930 | .358 |
| 3. | Joe Jackson | 1,772 | .356 |
| 4. | Ed Delahanty | 2,597 | .346 |
| 5. | Tris Speaker | 3,514 | .345 |
| 6. | Billy Hamilton | 2,164 | .344 |
| 7. | Ted Williams | 2,654 | .344 |
| 8. | Dan Brouthers | 2,296 | .342 |
| 9. | Babe Ruth | 2,873 | .342 |
| 10. | Harry Heilmann | 2,660 | .342 |
| 11. | Pete Browning | 1,646 | .341 |
| 12. | Willie Keeler | 2,932 | .341 |
| 13. | Bill Terry | 2,193 | .341 |
| 14. | George Sisler | 2,812 | .340 |
| 15. | Lou Gehrig | 2,721 | .340 |
| 16. | Jesse Burkett | 2,850 | .338 |
| 17. | Tony Gwynn | 3,141 | .338 |
| 18. | Nap Lajoie | 3,242 | .338 |
| **19.** | **Todd Helton** | **1,535** | **.337** |
| 20. | Riggs Stephenson | 1,515 | .336 |
| 21. | Al Simmons | 2,927 | .334 |
| 22. | Paul Waner | 3,152 | .333 |
| 23. | Eddie Collins | 3,315 | .333 |
| 24. | Sam Thompson | 1,988 | .331 |
| 25. | Cap Anson | 3,012 | .331 |
| 26. | Stan Musial | 3,630 | .331 |
| 27. | Heinie Manush | 2,524 | .330 |
| 28. | Wade Boggs | 3,010 | .328 |
| 29. | Rod Carew | 3,053 | .328 |
| 30. | Honus Wagner | 3,420 | .328 |
| 31. | Hugh Duffy | 2,293 | .326 |
| 32. | Jimmie Foxx | 2,646 | .325 |
| 33. | Earle Combs | 1,866 | .325 |
| 34. | Joe DiMaggio | 2,214 | .325 |
| 35. | Babe Herman | 1,818 | .324 |
| **36.** | **Vlad Guerrero** | **1,586** | **.324** |
| 37. | Joe Medwick | 2,471 | .324 |
| 38. | Edd Roush | 2,376 | .323 |
| 39. | Sam Rice | 2,987 | .322 |
| 40. | Kiki Cuyler | 2,299 | .321 |
| 41. | Charlie Gehringer | 2,839 | .320 |
| 42. | Chuck Klein | 2,076 | .320 |
| 43. | Pie Traynor | 2,416 | .320 |
| 44. | Mickey Cochrane | 1,652 | .320 |
| 45. | Kenny Williams | 1,552 | .319 |
| 46. | Kirby Puckett | 2,304 | .318 |
| 47. | Earl Averill | 2,019 | .318 |
| 48. | Arky Vaughan | 2,103 | .318 |
| 49. | Roberto Clemente | 3,000 | .317 |
| 50. | Joe Kelley | 2,220 | .317 |
| 51. | Zack Wheat | 2,884 | .317 |
| 52. | Roger Connor | 2,467 | .316 |
| 53. | Lloyd Waner | 2,459 | .316 |
| 54. | George Van Haltren | 2,544 | .316 |
| 55. | Frankie Frisch | 2,880 | .316 |
| 56. | Goose Goslin | 2,735 | .316 |
| 57. | Elmer Flick | 1,767 | .315 |
| 58. | Cecil Travis | 1,544 | .314 |
| **59.** | **Derek Jeter** | **1,936** | **.314** |
| **60.** | **Manny Ramirez** | **1,922** | **.314** |
| 61. | Hank Greenberg | 1,628 | .313 |
| 62. | Jack Fournier | 1,631 | .313 |
| **63.** | **Larry Walker** | **2,160** | **.313** |
| 64. | Bill Dickey | 1,969 | .313 |
| 65. | Johnny Mize | 2,011 | .312 |
| 66. | Joe Sewell | 2,226 | .312 |
| 67. | Fred Clarke | 2,678 | .312 |
| 68. | Hughey Jennings | 1,526 | .312 |
| 69. | Edgar Martinez | 2,247 | .312 |
| 70. | Fred Lindstrom | 1,747 | .311 |
| 71. | Bing Miller | 1,934 | .311 |
| 72. | Jackie Robinson | 1,518 | .311 |
| 73. | Baby Doll Jacobson | 1,714 | .311 |
| **74.** | **Mike Piazza** | **1,929** | **.311** |
| 75. | Ginger Beaumont | 1,759 | .311 |
| 76. | Mike Tiernan | 1,838 | .311 |
| 77. | Luke Appling | 2,749 | .310 |
| 78. | Irish Meusel | 1,521 | .310 |
| 79. | Bobby Veach | 2,063 | .310 |
| 80. | Jim O'Rourke | 2,304 | .310 |
| 81. | Jim Bottomley | 2,313 | .310 |
| 82. | Sam Crawford | 2,961 | .309 |
| 83. | Bob Meusel | 1,693 | .309 |
| 84. | Jack Tobin | 1,906 | .309 |
| 85. | Richie Ashburn | 2,574 | .308 |
| 86. | Jake Beckley | 2,934 | .308 |
| 87. | King Kelly | 1,813 | .308 |
| 88. | Jim Ryan | 2,513 | .308 |
| 89. | Stuffy McInnis | 2,405 | .307 |
| 90. | Don Mattingly | 2,153 | .307 |
| 91. | Joe Vosmik | 1,682 | .307 |
| 92. | Home Run Baker | 1,838 | .307 |
| **93.** | **Frank Thomas** | **2,136** | **.307** |
| 94. | George Burns | 2,018 | .307 |
| 95. | Matty Alou | 1,777 | .307 |
| **96.** | **Alex Rodriguez** | **1,901** | **.307** |
| 97. | George Kell | 2,054 | .306 |
| 98. | Paul Molitor | 3,319 | .306 |
| 99. | Dixie Walker | 2,064 | .306 |
| 100. | Cupid Childs | 1,721 | .306 |
| 101. | Ernie Lombardi | 1,792 | .306 |
| 102. | Ralph Garr | 1,562 | .306 |
| 103. | Hank Aaron | 3,771 | .305 |
| 104. | Chick Stahl | 1,546 | .305 |
| 105. | George Brett | 3,154 | .305 |
| 106. | Bill Madlock | 2,008 | .305 |
| 107. | Billy Herman | 2,345 | .304 |
| **108.** | **Ivan Rodriguez** | **2,190** | **.304** |
| 109. | Tony Oliva | 1,917 | .304 |
| 110. | Mel Ott | 2,876 | .304 |
| 111. | Deacon White | 1,619 | .303 |
| 112. | Will Clark | 2,176 | .303 |
| 113. | Charlie Jamieson | 1,990 | .303 |
| 114. | Cy Seymour | 1,724 | .303 |
| 115. | Mark Grace | 2,445 | .303 |
| **116.** | **Chipper Jones** | **1,811** | **.303** |
| 117. | Jake Daubert | 2,326 | .303 |
| 118. | Al Oliver | 2,743 | .303 |
| 119. | Buck Ewing | 1,625 | .303 |
| 120. | Steve Brodie | 1,728 | .303 |
| 121. | Pete Rose | 4,256 | .303 |
| 122. | Buddy Myer | 2,131 | .303 |
| 123. | Harvey Kuenn | 2,092 | .303 |
| 124. | Hal Trosky | 1,561 | .302 |
| 125. | Ed McKean | 2,084 | .302 |
| 126. | George Grantham | 1,508 | .302 |
| 127. | Ben Chapman | 1,958 | .302 |
| **128.** | **Jason Kendall** | **1,572** | **.302** |
| 129. | Tommy Holmes | 1,507 | .302 |
| 130. | Willie Mays | 3,283 | .302 |
| 131. | Joe Cronin | 2,285 | .301 |
| 132. | Stan Hack | 2,193 | .301 |
| **133.** | **Moises Alou** | **1,764** | **.301** |
| 134. | George Gore | 1,612 | .301 |
| 135. | Paul Hines | 1,881 | .301 |
| 136. | Patsy Donovan | 2,256 | .301 |
| 137. | Roberto Alomar | 1,508 | .300 |
| 138. | Wally Berger | 1,550 | .300 |
| 139. | Pedro Guerrero | 1,618 | .300 |
| **140.** | **Barry Bonds** | **2,730** | **.300** |
| 141. | Enos Slaughter | 2,383 | .300 |
| 142. | Billy Goodman | 1,691 | .300 |

(in strict numerical order rounded to three places)

## LEADING LEAGUE IN BATTING, 5 TIMES

| | Player | Seasons |
|---|---|---|
| 1. | Ty Cobb | 12 |
| 2. | Tony Gwynn | 8 |
| | Honus Wagner | 8 |
| 4. | Rod Carew | 7 |
| | Rogers Hornsby | 7 |
| | Stan Musial | 7 |
| 7. | Ted Williams | 6 |
| 8. | Wade Boggs | 5 |
| | Dan Brouthers | *5 |

*1891 in AA

## .500 SLUGGING AVERAGE

(2,500 or more total bases)

| | Player | TB | Slg. |
|---|---|---|---|
| 1. | Babe Ruth | 5,793 | .690 |
| 2. | Ted Williams | 4,884 | .634 |
| 3. | Lou Gehrig | 5,060 | .632 |
| **4.** | **Barry Bonds** | **5,584** | **.611** |
| 5. | Jimmie Foxx | 4,956 | .609 |
| **6.** | **Todd Helton** | **2,769** | **.607** |
| 7. | Hank Greenberg | 3,142 | .605 |
| **8.** | **Manny Ramirez** | **3,668** | **.599** |
| 9. | Mark McGwire | 3,639 | .588 |
| **10.** | **Vlad Guerrero** | **2,871** | **.587** |
| 11. | Joe DiMaggio | 3,948 | .579 |
| **12.** | **Alex Rodriguez** | **3,576** | **.577** |
| 13. | Rogers Hornsby | 4,712 | .577 |
| **14.** | **Frank Thomas** | **3,949** | **.568** |
| **15.** | **Larry Walker** | **3,904** | **.565** |
| 16. | Albert Belle | 3,300 | .564 |
| **17.** | **Jim Thome** | **3,327** | **.562** |
| 18. | Johnny Mize | 3,621 | .562 |
| **19.** | **Ken Griffey Jr.** | **4,414** | **.561** |
| **20.** | **Juan Gonzalez** | **3,676** | **.561** |
| 21. | Stan Musial | 6,134 | .559 |
| **22.** | **Carlos Delgado** | **3,089** | **.559** |
| 23. | Willie Mays | 6,066 | .557 |
| 24. | Mickey Mantle | 4,511 | .557 |
| **25.** | **Mike Piazza** | **3,440** | **.555** |
| 26. | Hank Aaron | 6,856 | .555 |
| 27. | Ralph Kiner | 2,852 | .548 |
| 28. | Hack Wilson | 2,593 | .545 |
| 29. | Chuck Klein | 3,522 | .543 |
| **30.** | **Jim Edmonds** | **3,016** | **.543** |
| **31.** | **Brian Giles** | **2,522** | **.542** |
| **32.** | **Jeff Bagwell** | **4,213** | **.540** |
| 33. | Duke Snider | 3,865 | .540 |
| **34.** | **Jason Giambi** | **2,791** | **.539** |
| **35.** | **Chipper Jones** | **3,213** | **.538** |
| 36. | Frank Robinson | 5,373 | .537 |
| **37.** | **Sammy Sosa** | **4,511** | **.537** |
| 38. | Al Simmons | 4,685 | .535 |
| 39. | Dick Allen | 3,379 | .534 |
| 40. | Earl Averill | 3,390 | .534 |
| 41. | Mel Ott | 5,041 | .533 |
| 42. | Babe Herman | 2,980 | .532 |
| 43. | Ken Williams | 2,579 | .530 |
| 44. | Willie Stargell | 4,190 | .529 |
| 45. | Mike Schmidt | 4,404 | .527 |
| **46.** | **Gary Sheffield** | **4,153** | **.527** |
| 47. | Mo Vaughn | 2,894 | .523 |
| 48. | Hal Trosky | 2,692 | .522 |
| 49. | Wally Berger | 2,693 | .522 |
| 50. | Harry Heilmann | 4,053 | .520 |
| 51. | Dan Brouthers | 3,484 | .519 |
| 52. | Joe Jackson | 2,577 | .517 |
| 53. | Edgar Martinez | 3,718 | .515 |
| 54. | Willie McCovey | 4,219 | .515 |
| 55. | Jose Canseco | 3,361 | .515 |
| **56.** | **Rafael Palmeiro** | **5,388** | **.515** |
| **57.** | **Moises Alou** | **3,241** | **.513** |
| 58. | Ty Cobb | 5,854 | .512 |
| 59. | Ellis Burks | 3,691 | .510 |
| 60. | Eddie Mathews | 4,349 | .509 |
| 61. | Fred McGriff | 4,458 | .509 |
| 62. | Jeff Heath | 2,512 | .509 |
| 63. | Harmon Killebrew | 4,143 | .509 |
| **64.** | **Ryan Klesko** | **2,658** | **.507** |
| **65.** | **Jeff Kent** | **3,621** | **.506** |
| 66. | Bob Johnson | 3,501 | .506 |
| 67. | Bill Terry | 3,252 | .506 |
| 68. | Darryl Strawberry | 2,738 | .505 |
| 69. | Sam Thompson | 3,031 | .505 |
| 70. | Ed Delahanty | 3,794 | .505 |
| **71.** | **Shawn Green** | **3,081** | **.505** |
| 72. | Joe Medwick | 3,852 | .505 |
| **73.** | **Andruw Jones** | **2,649** | **.503** |
| 74. | Jim Rice | 4,129 | .502 |
| 75. | Tris Speaker | 5,101 | .500 |
| 76. | David Justice | 2,814 | .500 |
| **77.** | **Tim Salmon** | **2,863** | **.500** |
| 74. | Jim Bottomley | 3,737 | .500 |
| 75. | Goose Goslin | 4,325 | .500 |
| 76. | Ernie Banks | 4,706 | .500 |

(in strict numerical order rounded to three places)

## 9,000 AT-BATS

| | Player | AB |
|---|---|---|
| 1. | Pete Rose | 14,053 |
| 2. | Hank Aaron | 12,364 |
| 3. | Carl Yastrzemski | 11,988 |
| 4. | Cal Ripken Jr. | 11,551 |
| 5. | Ty Cobb | 11,434 |
| 6. | Eddie Murray | 11,336 |
| 7. | Robin Yount | 11,008 |
| 8. | Dave Winfield | 11,003 |
| 9. | Stan Musial | 10,972 |
| 10. | Rickey Henderson | 10,961 |
| 11. | Willie Mays | 10,881 |
| 12. | Paul Molitor | 10,835 |
| 13. | Brooks Robinson | 10,654 |
| **14.** | **Rafael Palmeiro** | **10,472** |
| 15. | Honus Wagner | 10,439 |
| 16. | George Brett | 10,349 |
| 17. | Lou Brock | 10,332 |
| 18. | Luis Aparicio | 10,230 |
| 19. | Tris Speaker | 10,195 |
| 20. | Al Kaline | 10,116 |
| 21. | Rabbit Maranville | 10,078 |
| 22. | Frank Robinson | 10,006 |
| 23. | Eddie Collins | 9,949 |
| 24. | Andre Dawson | 9,927 |
| 25. | Harold Baines | 9,908 |
| 26. | Reggie Jackson | 9,864 |
| **27.** | **Craig Biggio** | **9,811** |
| 28. | Tony Perez | 9,778 |
| 29. | Rusty Staub | 9,720 |
| 30. | Vada Pinson | 9,645 |
| 31. | Nap Lajoie | 9,589 |
| 32. | Sam Crawford | 9,570 |
| 33. | Jake Beckley | 9,538 |
| 34. | Paul Waner | 9,459 |
| 35. | Mel Ott | 9,456 |
| 36. | Roberto Clemente | 9,454 |
| 37. | Ernie Banks | 9,421 |
| 38. | Bill Buckner | 9,397 |
| 39. | Ozzie Smith | 9,396 |
| 40. | Max Carey | 9,363 |
| 41. | Dave Parker | 9,358 |
| 42. | Billy Williams | 9,350 |
| 43. | Rod Carew | 9,315 |
| 44. | Tony Gwynn | 9,288 |
| 45. | Joe Morgan | 9,277 |
| 46. | Sam Rice | 9,269 |
| 47. | Nellie Fox | 9,232 |
| 48. | Wade Boggs | 9,180 |
| 49. | Willie Davis | 9,174 |
| **50.** | **Barry Bonds** | **9,140** |
| | Roger Cramer | 9,140 |
| 52. | Frankie Frisch | 9,112 |
| 53. | Zack Wheat | 9,106 |
| 54. | Cap Anson | 9,104 |
| 55. | Lave Cross | 9,085 |
| 56. | Roberto Alomar | 9,073 |
| 57. | Al Oliver | 9,049 |
| 58. | George Davis | 9,045 |
| 59. | Bill Dahlen | 9,036 |

## 1,500 RUNS

| | Player | Runs |
|---|---|---|
| 1. | Rickey Henderson | 2,295 |
| 2. | Ty Cobb | 2,246 |
| 3. | Hank Aaron | 2,174 |
| | Babe Ruth | 2,174 |
| 5. | Pete Rose | 2,165 |
| **6.** | **Barry Bonds** | **2,078** |
| 7. | Willie Mays | 2,062 |
| 8. | Stan Musial | 1,949 |
| 9. | Lou Gehrig | 1,888 |
| 10. | Tris Speaker | 1,882 |
| 11. | Mel Ott | 1,859 |
| 12. | Frank Robinson | 1,829 |
| 13. | Eddie Collins | 1,821 |
| 14. | Carl Yastrzemski | 1,816 |
| 15. | Ted Williams | 1,798 |
| 16. | Paul Molitor | 1,782 |
| 17. | Charlie Gehringer | 1,774 |
| 18. | Jimmie Foxx | 1,751 |
| 19. | Honus Wagner | 1,739 |
| 20. | Cap Anson | 1,722 |
| 21. | Jesse Burkett | 1,720 |
| 22. | Willie Keeler | 1,719 |
| **23.** | **Craig Biggio** | **1,697** |
| 24. | Billy Hamilton | 1,697 |
| 25. | Bid McPhee | 1,684 |
| 26. | Mickey Mantle | 1,677 |
| 27. | Dave Winfield | 1,669 |
| **28.** | **Rafael Palmeiro** | **1,663** |
| 29. | Joe Morgan | 1,650 |
| 30. | Cal Ripken Jr. | 1,647 |
| 31. | Jim Ryan | 1,643 |
| 32. | George Van Haltren | 1,642 |
| 33. | Robin Yount | 1,632 |
| 34. | Eddie Murray | 1,627 |
| | Paul Waner | 1,627 |

| | Player | Runs |
|---|---|---|
| 36. | Fred Clarke | 1,622 |
| | Al Kaline | 1,622 |
| 38. | Roger Connor | 1,620 |
| 39. | Lou Brock | 1,610 |
| 40. | Jake Beckley | 1,602 |
| 41. | Ed Delahanty | 1,600 |
| 42. | Bill Dahlen | 1,590 |
| 43. | George Brett | 1,583 |
| 44. | Rogers Hornsby | 1,579 |
| 45. | Tim Raines Sr. | 1,571 |
| 46. | Hugh Duffy | 1,554 |
| 47. | Reggie Jackson | 1,551 |
| 48. | Max Carey | 1,545 |
| | George Davis | 1,545 |
| 50. | Frankie Frisch | 1,532 |
| 51. | Dan Brouthers | 1,523 |
| | Tom Brown | 1,523 |
| **53.** | **Jeff Bagwell** | **1,517** |
| 54. | Sam Rice | 1,514 |
| 55. | Wade Boggs | 1,513 |
| 56. | Eddie Mathews | 1,509 |
| 57. | Roberto Alomar | 1,508 |
| 58. | Al Simmons | 1,507 |
| | Mike Schmidt | 1,506 |
| 60. | Nap Lajoie | 1,504 |

## LEADING LEAGUE IN RUNS, 5 TIMES

| | Player | Seasons |
|---|---|---|
| 1. | Babe Ruth | 8 |
| 2. | Mickey Mantle | 6 |
| | Ted Williams | 6 |
| 4. | George Burns | 5 |
| | Ty Cobb | 5 |
| | Rickey Henderson | 5 |
| | Rogers Hornsby | 5 |
| | Stan Musial | 5 |

## 2,500 HITS

| | Player | Hits |
|---|---|---|
| 1. | Pete Rose | 4,256 |
| 2. | Ty Cobb | 4,189 |
| 3. | Hank Aaron | 3,771 |
| 4. | Stan Musial | 3,630 |
| 5. | Tris Speaker | 3,514 |
| 6. | Honus Wagner | 3,420 |
| 7. | Carl Yastrzemski | 3,419 |
| 8. | Paul Molitor | 3,319 |
| 9. | Eddie Collins | 3,315 |
| 10. | Willie Mays | 3,283 |
| 11. | Eddie Murray | 3,255 |
| 12. | Nap Lajoie | 3,242 |
| 13. | Cal Ripken Jr. | 3,184 |
| 14. | George Brett | 3,154 |
| 15. | Paul Waner | 3,152 |
| 16. | Robin Yount | 3,142 |
| 17. | Tony Gwynn | 3,141 |
| 18. | Dave Winfield | 3,110 |
| 19. | Rickey Henderson | 3,055 |
| 20. | Rod Carew | 3,053 |
| 21. | Lou Brock | 3,023 |
| **22.** | **Rafael Palmeiro** | **3,020** |
| 23. | Cap Anson | 3,012 |
| 24. | Wade Boggs | 3,010 |
| 25. | Al Kaline | 3,007 |
| 26. | Roberto Clemente | 3,000 |
| 27. | Sam Rice | 2,987 |
| 28. | Sam Crawford | 2,961 |
| 29. | Frank Robinson | 2,943 |
| 30. | Jake Beckley | 2,934 |
| 31. | Willie Keeler | 2,932 |
| 32. | Rogers Hornsby | 2,930 |
| 33. | Al Simmons | 2,927 |
| 34. | Zack Wheat | 2,884 |
| 35. | Frankie Frisch | 2,880 |
| 36. | Mel Ott | 2,876 |
| 37. | Babe Ruth | 2,873 |
| 38. | Harold Baines | 2,866 |
| 39. | Jesse Burkett | 2,850 |
| 40. | Brooks Robinson | 2,848 |
| 41. | Charlie Gehringer | 2,839 |
| 42. | George Sisler | 2,812 |
| **43.** | **Craig Biggio** | **2,795** |
| 44. | Andre Dawson | 2,774 |
| 45. | Vada Pinson | 2,757 |
| 46. | Luke Appling | 2,749 |
| 47. | Al Oliver | 2,743 |
| **48.** | **Barry Bonds** | **2,742** |
| 49. | Goose Goslin | 2,735 |
| 50. | Tony Perez | 2,732 |
| 51. | Roberto Alomar | 2,724 |
| 52. | Lou Gehrig | 2,721 |
| 53. | Rusty Staub | 2,716 |
| 54. | Bill Buckner | 2,715 |
| 55. | Dave Parker | 2,712 |
| 56. | Billy Williams | 2,711 |
| 57. | Roger Cramer | 2,705 |
| 58. | Fred Clarke | 2,678 |
| 59. | Luis Aparicio | 2,677 |
| 60. | Max Carey | 2,665 |
| | George Davis | 2,665 |
| 62. | Nellie Fox | 2,663 |
| 63. | Harry Heilmann | 2,660 |
| 64. | Lave Cross | 2,651 |
| 65. | Ted Williams | 2,654 |
| 66. | Jimmie Foxx | 2,646 |
| 67. | Rabbit Maranville | 2,605 |
| | Tim Raines Sr. | 2,605 |
| 69. | Steve Garvey | 2,597 |
| 70. | Ed Delahanty | 2,593 |
| 71. | Reggie Jackson | 2,584 |
| 72. | Ernie Banks | 2,583 |
| 73. | Richie Ashburn | 2,574 |
| 74. | Willie Davis | 2,561 |
| 75. | George Van Haltren | 2,544 |
| 76. | Heinie Manush | 2,524 |
| **77.** | **Julio Franco** | **2,521** |
| 78. | Joe Morgan | 2,517 |
| 79. | Buddy Bell | 2,514 |
| 80. | Jim Ryan | 2,513 |

## LEADING LEAGUE IN HITS , 5 TIMES

| | Player | Seasons |
|---|---|---|
| 1. | Ty Cobb | 8 |
| 2. | Tony Gwynn | 7 |
| | Pete Rose | 7 |
| 4. | Stan Musial | 6 |
| 5. | Tony Oliva | 5 |

## 200 HITS, 4 TIMES

| | Player | Seasons |
|---|---|---|
| 1. | Pete Rose | 10 |
| 2. | Ty Cobb | 9 |
| 3. | Lou Gehrig | 8 |
| | Willie Keeler | 8 |
| | Paul Waner | 8 |
| 6. | Wade Boggs | 7 |
| | Charlie Gehringer | 7 |
| | Rogers Hornsby | 7 |
| 9. | Jesse Burkett | 6 |
| | Steve Garvey | 6 |
| | Stan Musial | 6 |
| | Sam Rice | 6 |
| | Al Simmons | 6 |
| | George Sisler | 6 |
| | Bill Terry | 6 |
| 16. | Tony Gwynn | 5 |
| | Chuck Klein | 5 |
| | Kirby Puckett | 5 |
| | **Ichiro Suzuki** | **5** |
| 20. | Lou Brock | 4 |
| | Rod Carew | 4 |
| | Roberto Clemente | 4 |
| | Ed Delahanty | 4 |
| | Harry Heilmann | 4 |
| | Joe Jackson | 4 |
| | Nap Lajoie | 4 |
| | Heinie Manush | 4 |
| | Joe Medwick | 4 |
| | Paul Molitor | 4 |
| | Vada Pinson | 4 |
| | Jim Rice | 4 |
| | Tris Speaker | 4 |
| | Jack Tobin | 4 |
| | Lloyd Waner | 4 |

## 100 PINCH HITS

| | Player | Hits |
|---|---|---|
| **1.** | **Lenny Harris** | **212** |
| 2. | Manny Mota | 150 |
| 3. | Smoky Burgess | 145 |
| 4. | Greg Gross | 143 |
| **5.** | **Dave Hansen** | **139** |
| **6.** | **Mark Sweeney** | **131** |
| 7. | John Vander Wal | 126 |
| 8. | Jose Morales | 123 |
| 9. | Jerry Lynch | 116 |
| 10. | Red Lucas | 114 |
| 11. | Steve Braun | 113 |
| 12. | Terry Crowley | 108 |
| 13. | Denny Walling | 108 |
| 14. | Gates Brown | 107 |
| 15. | Mike Lum | 103 |
| 16. | Jim Dwyer | 102 |
| 17. | Rusty Staub | 100 |

## 2,000 SINGLES

| | Player | Singles |
|---|---|---|
| 1. | Pete Rose | 3,215 |
| 2. | Ty Cobb | 2,643 |
| | Eddie Collins | 2,643 |
| 4. | Willie Keeler | 2,513 |
| 5. | Honus Wagner | 2,424 |
| 6. | Rod Carew | 2,404 |
| 7. | Tris Speaker | 2,383 |
| 8. | Tony Gwynn | 2,378 |
| 9. | Paul Molitor | 2,366 |
| 10. | Nap Lajoie | 2,340 |
| 11. | Hank Aaron | 2,294 |
| 12. | Jesse Burkett | 2,273 |
| 13. | Sam Rice | 2,271 |
| 14. | Cap Anson | 2,262 |
| | Carl Yastrzemski | 2,262 |
| 16. | Wade Boggs | 2,253 |
| | Stan Musial | 2,253 |
| 18. | Lou Brock | 2,247 |
| 19. | Paul Waner | 2,243 |
| 20. | Rickey Henderson | 2,182 |
| | Robin Yount | 2,182 |
| 22. | Frankie Frisch | 2,171 |
| 23. | Roger Cramer | 2,163 |
| 24. | Luke Appling | 2,162 |
| 25. | Nellie Fox | 2,161 |
| 26. | Eddie Murray | 2,156 |
| 27. | Roberto Clemente | 2,154 |
| 28. | Jake Beckley | 2,130 |
| 29. | George Sisler | 2,121 |
| 30. | Richie Ashburn | 2,119 |
| 31. | Luis Aparicio | 2,108 |
| 32. | Cal Ripken | 2,106 |
| 33. | Zack Wheat | 2,104 |
| 34. | Sam Crawford | 2,097 |
| 35. | Lave Cross | 2,056 |
| 36. | George Brett | 2,035 |
| 37. | Al Kaline | 2,035 |
| 38. | Lloyd Waner | 2,033 |
| 39. | Brooks Robinson | 2,030 |
| | Fred Clarke | 2,030 |
| 41. | George Van Haltren | 2,028 |
| 42. | Rabbit Maranville | 2,020 |
| 43. | Max Carey | 2,017 |
| 44. | Dave Winfield | 2,017 |

## 450 DOUBLES

| | Player | Doubles |
|---|---|---|
| 1. | Tris Speaker | 792 |
| 2. | Pete Rose | 746 |
| 3. | Stan Musial | 725 |
| 4. | Ty Cobb | 724 |
| 5. | George Brett | 665 |
| 6. | Nap Lajoie | 657 |
| 7. | Carl Yastrzemski | 646 |
| 8. | Honus Wagner | 643 |
| 9. | Hank Aaron | 624 |
| 10. | Paul Molitor | 605 |
| | Paul Waner | 605 |
| **12.** | **Craig Biggio** | **604** |
| 13. | Cal Ripken Jr. | 603 |
| **14.** | **Rafael Palmeiro** | **585** |
| 15. | Robin Yount | 583 |
| 16. | Wade Boggs | 578 |
| 17. | Charlie Gehringer | 574 |
| **18.** | **Barry Bonds** | **564** |
| 19. | Eddie Murray | 560 |
| 20. | Tony Gwynn | 543 |
| 21. | Harry Heilmann | 542 |
| 22. | Rogers Hornsby | 541 |
| 23. | Joe Medwick | 540 |
| | Dave Winfield | 540 |
| 25. | Al Simmons | 539 |
| 26. | Lou Gehrig | 534 |
| 27. | Cap Anson | 529 |
| | Al Oliver | 529 |
| 29. | Frank Robinson | 528 |
| 30. | Dave Parker | 526 |
| 31. | Ted Williams | 525 |
| 32. | Willie Mays | 523 |
| 33. | Ed Delahanty | 522 |
| 34. | Joe Cronin | 515 |
| 35. | Edgar Martinez | 514 |
| 36. | Mark Grace | 511 |
| 37. | Rickey Henderson | 510 |
| 38. | Babe Ruth | 506 |
| 39. | Tony Perez | 505 |
| 40. | Roberto Alomar | 504 |
| 41. | Andre Dawson | 503 |
| **42.** | **John Olerud** | **500** |
| 43. | Goose Goslin | 500 |
| 44. | Rusty Staub | 499 |
| 45. | Bill Buckner | 498 |
| | Al Kaline | 498 |
| | Sam Rice | 498 |
| **48.** | **Luis Gonzalez** | **495** |
| 49. | Heinie Manush | 491 |
| 50. | Mickey Vernon | 490 |
| **51.** | **Jeff Bagwell** | **488** |
| 52. | Harold Baines | 488 |
| | Mel Ott | 488 |
| 54. | Lou Brock | 486 |
| | Billy Herman | 486 |
| 56. | Vada Pinson | 485 |
| | Hal McRae | 484 |
| 58. | Dwight Evans | 483 |
| | Ted Simmons | 483 |
| 60. | Brooks Robinson | 482 |
| 61. | Zack Wheat | 476 |
| **62.** | **Jeff Kent** | **474** |
| 63. | Jake Beckley | 473 |
| **64.** | **Larry Walker** | **471** |
| 65. | Frankie Frisch | 466 |
| 66. | Jim Bottomley | 465 |
| 67. | Reggie Jackson | 463 |
| 68. | Dan Brouthers | 460 |
| 69. | Sam Crawford | 458 |
| | Jimmie Foxx | 458 |
| 71. | George Davis | 453 |
| | Jimmie Dykes | 453 |
| 73. | Paul O'Neill | 451 |
| | Jimmy Ryan | 451 |

## 150 TRIPLES

| | Player | Triples |
|---|---|---|
| 1. | Sam Crawford | 309 |
| 2. | Ty Cobb | 295 |
| 3. | Honus Wagner | 252 |
| 4. | Jake Beckley | 244 |
| 5. | Roger Connor | 233 |
| 6. | Tris Speaker | 222 |
| 7. | Fred Clarke | 220 |
| 8. | Dan Brouthers | 205 |
| 9. | Joe Kelley | 194 |
| 10. | Paul Waner | 191 |
| 11. | Bid McPhee | 189 |
| 12. | Eddie Collins | 187 |
| 13. | Ed Delahanty | 186 |
| 14. | Sam Rice | 184 |
| 15. | Jesse Burkett | 182 |
| | Ed Konetchy | 182 |
| | Edd Roush | 182 |
| 18. | Buck Ewing | 178 |
| 19. | Rabbit Maranville | 177 |
| | Stan Musial | 177 |
| 21. | Harry Stovey | 174 |
| 22. | Goose Goslin | 173 |
| 23. | Zack Wheat | 172 |
| | Tommy Leach | 172 |
| 25. | Rogers Hornsby | 169 |
| 26. | Joe Jackson | 168 |
| 27. | Roberto Clemente | 166 |
| | Sherry Magee | 166 |
| 29. | Jake Daubert | 165 |
| 30. | Elmer Flick | 164 |
| | George Sisler | 164 |
| | Pie Traynor | 164 |
| 33. | Bill Dahlen | 163 |
| | George Davis | 163 |
| | Lou Gehrig | 163 |
| | Nap Lajoie | 163 |
| 37. | Mike Tiernan | 162 |
| 38. | Sam Thompson | 161 |
| | George Van Haltren | 161 |
| 40. | Harry Hooper | 160 |
| | Heinie Manush | 160 |
| 42. | Max Carey | 159 |
| | Joe Judge | 159 |
| 44. | Ed McKean | 158 |
| 45. | Kiki Cuyler | 157 |
| | Jim Ryan | 157 |
| 47. | Tommy Corcoran | 155 |
| 48. | Earle Combs | 154 |
| 49. | Jim Bottomley | 151 |
| | Harry Heilmann | 151 |

## 300 HOME RUNS

| | Player | HRs |
|---|---|---|
| 1. | Hank Aaron | 755 |
| 2. | Babe Ruth | 714 |
| **3.** | **Barry Bonds** | **708** |
| 4. | Willie Mays | 660 |
| **5.** | **Sammy Sosa** | **588** |
| 6. | Frank Robinson | 586 |
| 7. | Mark McGwire | 583 |
| 8. | Harmon Killebrew | 573 |
| **9.** | **Rafael Palmeiro** | **569** |
| 10. | Reggie Jackson | 563 |
| 11. | Mike Schmidt | 548 |
| **12.** | **Ken Griffey Jr.** | **536** |
| | Mickey Mantle | 536 |
| 14. | Jimmie Foxx | 534 |
| 15. | Willie McCovey | 521 |
| | Ted Williams | 521 |
| 17. | Ernie Banks | 512 |
| | Eddie Mathews | 512 |
| 19. | Mel Ott | 511 |
| 20. | Eddie Murray | 504 |
| 21. | Lou Gehrig | 493 |
| | Fred McGriff | 493 |
| 23. | Stan Musial | 475 |
| | Willie Stargell | 475 |

| | Player | HRs |
|---|---|---|
| 25. | Dave Winfield | 465 |
| 26. | Jose Canseco | 462 |
| 27. | Carl Yastrzemski | 452 |
| **28.** | **Jeff Bagwell** | **449** |
| **29.** | **Gary Sheffield** | **449** |
| **30.** | **Frank Thomas** | **448** |
| 31. | Dave Kingman | 442 |
| 32. | Andre Dawson | 438 |
| **33.** | **Manny Ramirez** | **435** |
| **34.** | **Juan Gonzalez** | **434** |
| 35. | Cal Ripken Jr. | 431 |
| **36.** | **Jim Thome** | **430** |
| **37.** | **Alex Rodriguez** | **429** |
| 38. | Billy Williams | 426 |
| 39. | Darrell Evans | 414 |
| 40. | Duke Snider | 407 |
| 41. | Andres Galarraga | 399 |
| | Al Kaline | 399 |
| 43. | Dale Murphy | 398 |
| **44.** | **Mike Piazza** | **397** |
| 45. | Joe Carter | 396 |
| 46. | Graig Nettles | 390 |
| 47. | Johnny Bench | 389 |
| 48. | Dwight Evans | 385 |
| 49. | Harold Baines | 384 |
| **50.** | **Larry Walker** | **383** |
| 51. | Frank Howard | 382 |
| | Jim Rice | 382 |
| 53. | Albert Belle | 381 |
| 54. | Orlando Cepeda | 379 |
| | Tony Perez | 379 |
| 56. | Matt Williams | 378 |
| 57. | Norm Cash | 377 |
| 58. | Carlton Fisk | 376 |
| 59. | Rocky Colavito | 374 |
| 60. | Gil Hodges | 370 |
| **61.** | **Carlos Delgado** | **369** |
| | Ralph Kiner | 369 |
| 63. | Joe DiMaggio | 361 |
| 64. | Gary Gaetti | 360 |
| 65. | Johnny Mize | 359 |
| 66. | Yogi Berra | 358 |
| 67. | Greg Vaughn | 355 |
| 68. | Lee May | 354 |
| 69. | Ellis Burks | 352 |
| 70. | Dick Allen | 351 |
| 71. | Chili Davis | 350 |
| 72. | George Foster | 348 |
| 73. | Ron Santo | 342 |
| 74. | Jack Clark | 340 |
| **75.** | **Tino Martinez** | **339** |
| | Dave Parker | 339 |
| | Boog Powell | 339 |
| 78. | Don Baylor | 338 |
| 79. | Joe Adcock | 336 |
| 80. | Darryl Strawberry | 335 |
| 81. | Bobby Bonds | 332 |
| **82.** | **Jim Edmonds** | **331** |
| | **Chipper Jones** | **331** |
| | **Jeff Kent** | **331** |
| | Hank Greenberg | 331 |
| 86. | Mo Vaughn | 328 |
| 87. | Willie Horton | 325 |
| 88. | Gary Carter | 324 |
| | Lance Parrish | 324 |
| 90. | Ron Gant | 321 |
| 91. | Cecil Fielder | 319 |
| 92. | Roy Sievers | 318 |
| 93. | George Brett | 317 |
| **94.** | **Luis Gonzalez** | **316** |
| | Ron Cey | 316 |
| **96.** | **Vinny Castilla** | **315** |
| 97. | Reggie Smith | 314 |
| **98.** | **Jason Giambi** | **313** |
| 99. | Jay Buhner | 310 |
| 100. | Edgar Martinez | 309 |
| 101. | Greg Luzinski | 307 |
| | Al Simmons | 307 |
| **103.** | **Ruben Sierra** | **306** |
| | Fred Lynn | 306 |
| **105.** | **Vlad Guerrero** | **305** |
| | David Justice | 305 |
| **107.** | **Shawn Green** | **303** |
| **108.** | **Andruw Jones** | **301** |
| | Rogers Hornsby | 301 |
| 110. | Chuck Klein | 300 |

## 400 HOME RUNS, AL

| | Player | HRs |
|---|---|---|
| 1. | Babe Ruth | 708 |
| 2. | Harmon Killebrew | 573 |
| 3. | Reggie Jackson | 563 |
| **4.** | **Rafael Palmeiro** | **544** |
| 5. | Mickey Mantle | 536 |
| 6. | Jimmie Foxx | 524 |
| 7. | Ted Williams | 521 |
| 8. | Lou Gehrig | 493 |
| 9. | Jose Canseco | 462 |
| 10. | Carl Yastrzemski | 452 |
| **11.** | **Frank Thomas** | **448** |
| **12.** | **Manny Ramirez** | **435** |
| **13.** | **Juan Gonzalez** | **434** |
| 14. | Cal Ripken | 431 |
| **15.** | **Alex Rodriguez** | **429** |

## 400 HOME RUNS, NL

| | Player | HRs |
|---|---|---|
| 1. | Hank Aaron | 733 |
| **2.** | **Barry Bonds** | **708** |
| 3. | Willie Mays | 660 |
| 4. | Mike Schmidt | 548 |
| 5. | Sammy Sosa | 545 |
| 5. | Willie McCovey | 521 |
| 6. | Ernie Banks | 512 |
| 7. | Mel Ott | 511 |
| 9. | Eddie Mathews | 503 |
| 10. | Stan Musial | 475 |
| 11. | Willie Stargell | 475 |
| **12.** | **Jeff Bagwell** | **449** |
| 13. | Andre Dawson | 409 |
| 14. | Duke Snider | 407 |

## 350 HOME RUNS, ONE CLUB

| | Player | HRs |
|---|---|---|
| 1. | Hank Aaron, Braves | 733 |
| 2. | Babe Ruth, Yankees | 659 |
| 3. | Willie Mays, Giants | 646 |
| 4. | Harmon Killebrew, Senators/Twins | 559 |
| 5. | Mike Schmidt, Phillies | 548 |
| 6. | Sammy Sosa, Cubs | 545 |
| 7. | Mickey Mantle, Yankees | 536 |
| **8.** | **Barry Bonds, Giants** | **532** |
| 9. | Ted Williams, Red Sox | 521 |
| 10. | Ernie Banks, Cubs | 512 |
| 11. | Mel Ott, Giants | 511 |
| 12. | Lou Gehrig, Yankees | 493 |
| 13. | Eddie Mathews, Braves | 493 |
| 14. | Stan Musial, Cardinals | 475 |
| 15. | Willie Stargell, Pirates | 475 |
| 16. | Willie McCovey, Giants | 469 |
| 17. | Carl Yastrzemski, Red Sox | 452 |
| **18.** | **Jeff Bagwell, Astros** | **449** |
| **19.** | **Frank Thomas, White Sox** | **448** |
| 20. | Cal Ripken Jr., Orioles | 431 |
| 21. | Al Kaline, Tigers | 399 |
| 22. | Ken Griffey Jr., Mariners | 398 |
| 23. | Billy Williams, Cubs | 392 |
| 24. | Johnny Bench, Reds | 389 |
| 25. | Duke Snider, Dodgers | 389 |
| 26. | Jim Rice, Red Sox | 382 |
| 27. | Dwight Evans, Red Sox | 379 |
| 28. | Norm Cash, Tigers | 373 |
| 29. | Juan Gonzalez, Rangers | 372 |
| 30. | Dale Murphy, Braves | 371 |
| 31. | Mark McGwire, Athletics | 363 |
| 32. | Joe DiMaggio, Yankees | 361 |
| 33. | Gil Hodges, Dodgers | 361 |
| 34. | Yogi Berra, Yankees | 358 |

## 400 HOME RUNS, RIGHTHANDER

| | Player | HRs |
|---|---|---|
| 1. | Hank Aaron | 755 |
| 2. | Willie Mays | 660 |
| **3.** | **Sammy Sosa** | **588** |
| 4. | Frank Robinson | 586 |
| 5. | Mark McGwire | 583 |
| 6. | Harmon Killebrew | 573 |
| 7. | Mike Schmidt | 548 |
| 8. | Jimmie Foxx | 534 |
| 9. | Ernie Banks | 512 |
| 10. | Dave Winfield | 465 |
| 11. | Jose Canseco | 462 |
| **12.** | **Jeff Bagwell** | **449** |
| | **Gary Sheffield** | **449** |
| **14.** | **Frank Thomas** | **448** |
| 15. | Dave Kingman | 442 |
| 16. | Andre Dawson | 438 |
| **17.** | **Manny Ramirez** | **435** |
| **18.** | **Juan Gonzalez** | **434** |
| 19. | Cal Ripken | 431 |
| **20.** | **Alex Rodriguez** | **429** |

## 400 HOME RUNS, LEFTHANDER

| | Player | HRs |
|---|---|---|
| 1. | Babe Ruth | 714 |
| **2.** | **Barry Bonds** | **708** |
| **3.** | **Rafael Palmeiro** | **569** |
| 4. | Reggie Jackson | 563 |
| **5.** | **Ken Griffey, Jr.** | **536** |
| 6. | Willie McCovey | 521 |
| | Ted Williams | 521 |
| 8. | Eddie Mathews | 512 |
| 9. | Mel Ott | 511 |
| 10. | Lou Gehrig | 493 |
| 11. | Fred McGriff | 493 |
| 12. | Stan Musial | 475 |
| 11. | Willie Stargell | 475 |
| 14. | Carl Yastrzemski | 452 |
| **15.** | **Jim Thome** | **430** |
| 16. | Billy Williams | 426 |
| 17. | Darrell Evans | 414 |
| 18. | Duke Snider | 407 |

## 300 HOME RUNS, SWITCH HITTER

| | Player | HRs |
|---|---|---|
| 1. | Mickey Mantle | 536 |
| 2. | Eddie Murray | 504 |
| 3. | Chili Davis | 350 |
| **4.** | **Chipper Jones** | **331** |
| 5. | Reggie Smith | 314 |
| **6.** | **Ruben Sierra** | **306** |

## 300 HOME RUNS, FIRST BASEMAN

| | Player | HRs |
|---|---|---|
| 1. | Mark McGwire | 566 |
| 2. | Lou Gehrig | 493 |
| 3. | Jimmie Foxx | 480 |
| 4. | Fred McGriff | 462 |
| **5.** | **Jeff Bagwell** | **446** |
| **6.** | **Rafael Palmeiro** | **440** |
| 7. | Willie McCovey | 439 |
| 8. | Eddie Murray | 409 |
| 9. | Andres Galarraga | 387 |
| 10. | Norm Cash | 367 |
| **11.** | **Carlos Delgado** | **324** |
| **12.** | **Tino Martinez** | **316** |
| 13. | Jim Thome | 309 |

## 200 HOME RUNS, SECOND BASEMAN

| | Player | HRs |
|---|---|---|
| **1.** | **Jeff Kent** | **306** |
| 2. | Ryne Sandberg | 275 |
| 3. | Joe Morgan | 266 |
| 4. | Rogers Hornsby | 264 |
| **5.** | **Bret Boone** | **251** |
| 6. | Joe Gordon | 246 |
| 7. | Lou Whitaker | 239 |
| 8. | Bobby Doerr | 223 |
| 9. | Roberto Alomar | 207 |

## 300 HOME RUNS, THIRD BASEMAN

| | Player | HRs |
|---|---|---|
| 1. | Mike Schmidt | 509 |
| 2. | Eddie Mathews | 486 |
| 3. | Graig Nettles | 368 |
| 4. | Matt Williams | 359 |
| 5. | Ron Santo | 337 |
| 6. | Gary Gaetti | 333 |
| 7. | Ron Cey | 312 |
| **8.** | **Vinny Castilla** | **303** |

## 200 HOME RUNS, SHORTSTOP

| | Player | HRs |
|---|---|---|
| 1. | Cal Ripken | 345 |
| **2.** | **Alex Rodriguez** | **344** |
| 3. | Ernie Banks | 277 |
| **4.** | **Miguel Tejada** | **216** |
| 5. | Vern Stephens | 213 |

## 350 HOME RUNS, OUTFIELDER

| | Player | HRs |
|---|---|---|
| **1.** | **Barry Bonds** | **697** |
| 2. | Babe Ruth | 692 |
| 3. | Hank Aaron | 661 |
| 4. | Willie Mays | 642 |
| **5.** | **Sammy Sosa** | **581** |
| **6.** | **Ken Griffey Jr.** | **517** |
| 7. | Ted Williams | 514 |
| 8. | Mickey Mantle | 490 |
| 9. | Frank Robinson | 463 |
| 10. | Reggie Jackson | 458 |
| 11. | Andre Dawson | 404 |
| 12. | Dave Winfield | 399 |
| **13.** | **Manny Ramirez** | **377** |
| **14.** | **Gary Sheffield** | **361** |

## 200 HOME RUNS, CATCHER

| | Player | HRs |
|---|---|---|
| **1.** | **Mike Piazza** | **376** |
| 2. | Carlton Fisk | 351 |
| 3. | Johnny Bench | 327 |
| 4. | Yogi Berra | 306 |
| 5. | Gary Carter | 298 |
| 6. | Lance Parrish | 295 |
| **7.** | **Ivan Rodriguez** | **258** |
| **8.** | **Javy Lopez** | **240** |
| 9. | Roy Campenella | 239 |
| 10. | Gabby Hartnett | 232 |
| **11.** | **Benito Santiago** | **213** |
| 12. | Bill Dickey | 200 |

## 20 HOME RUNS, PITCHER

| | Player | HRs |
|---|---|---|
| 1. | Wes Ferrell | 37 |
| 2. | Bob Lemon | 35 |
| 3. | Warren Spahn | 35 |
| 4. | Red Ruffing | 34 |
| 5. | Earl Wilson | 33 |
| 6. | Don Drysdale | 29 |
| 7. | John Clarkson | 24 |
| 8. | Bob Gibson | 24 |
| 9. | Walter Johnson | 23 |
| 10. | Jack Stivetts | 20 |
| 11. | Dizzy Trout | 20 |

## 200 HOME RUNS, DESIGNATED HITTER

| | Player | HRs |
|---|---|---|
| 1. | Edgar Martinez | 243 |
| 2. | Harold Baines | 235 |
| 3. | Don Baylor | 219 |
| 4. | Jose Canseco | 208 |
| 5. | Chili Davis | 200 |

## 20 LEADOFF HOME RUNS

| | Player | HRs |
|---|---|---|
| 1. | Rickey Henderson | 81 |
| **2.** | **Craig Biggio** | **44** |
| 3. | Brady Anderson | 43 |
| 4. | Bobby Bonds | 35 |
| **5.** | **Ray Durham** | **34** |
| 6. | Devon White | 34 |
| 7. | Paul Molitor | 33 |
| 8. | Chuck Knoblauch | 31 |
| 9. | Tony Phillips | 30 |
| **10.** | **Kenny Lofton** | **28** |
| 11. | Davey Lopes | 28 |
| 12. | Eddie Yost | 27 |
| 13. | Brian Downing | 25 |
| 14. | Lou Brock | 24 |
| **15.** | **Alfonso Soriano** | **23** |
| **16.** | Tommy Harper | 23 |
| 17. | Lou Whitaker | 23 |
| **18.** | **Shannon Stewart** | **22** |
| 19. | Jimmy Ryan | 22 |
| **20.** | **Barry Bonds** | **20** |
| **21.** | **Jacque Jones** | **20** |
| **22.** | **Eric Young** | **20** |
| 23. | Felipe Alou | 20 |
| 24. | Lenny Dykstra | 20 |

## 10 PINCH HOME RUNS

| | Player | HRs |
|---|---|---|
| 1. | Cliff Johnson | 20 |
| 2. | Jerry Lynch | 18 |
| 3. | John Vander Wal | 17 |
| 4. | Gates Brown | 16 |
| | Smoky Burgess | 16 |
| | Willie McCovey | 16 |
| **7.** | **Dave Hansen** | **15** |
| 8. | George Crowe | 14 |
| **9.** | **Mark Sweeney** | **13** |
| 10. | Glenallen Hill | 13 |
| 11. | Joe Adcock | 12 |
| | Bob Cerv | 12 |
| | Jose Morales | 12 |
| | Graig Nettles | 12 |
| **15.** | **Craig Wilson** | **11** |
| | Jeff Burroughs | 11 |
| | Jay Johnstone | 11 |
| | Candy Maldonado | 11 |
| | Orlando Merced | 11 |
| | Fred Whitfield | 11 |
| | Cy Williams | 11 |
| 22. | Mark Carreon | 10 |
| | Dave Clark | 10 |
| | Jim Dwyer | 10 |
| | Mike Lum | 10 |
| | Ken McMullen | 10 |
| | Don Mincher | 10 |
| | Wally Post | 10 |
| | Champ Summers | 10 |
| | Jerry Turner | 10 |
| | Gus Zernial | 10 |

## 10 GRAND SLAMS

| | Player | HRs |
|---|---|---|
| 1. | Lou Gehrig | 23 |
| **2.** | **Manny Ramirez** | **20** |

| | Player | HRs |
|---|---|---|
| 3. | Eddie Murray | 19 |
| 4. | Willie McCovey | 18 |
| | Robin Ventura | 18 |
| 6. | Jimmie Foxx | 17 |
| | Ted Williams | 17 |
| 8. | Hank Aaron | 16 |
| | Dave Kingman | 16 |
| | Babe Ruth | 16 |
| **11.** | **Ken Griffey Jr.** | **14** |
| | **Mike Piazza** | **14** |
| | Gil Hodges | 14 |
| | Mark McGwire | 14 |
| 15. | **Jeff Kent** | **13** |
| | Harold Baines | 13 |
| | Albert Belle | 13 |
| | Joe DiMaggio | 13 |
| | George Foster | 13 |
| | Ralph Kiner | 13 |
| 20. | **Rafael Palmeiro** | **12** |
| | Ernie Banks | 12 |
| | Don Baylor | 12 |
| | Rogers Hornsby | 12 |
| | Joe Rudi | 12 |
| | Matt Williams | 12 |
| | Rudy York | 12 |
| **27.** | **Barry Bonds** | **11** |
| | **Tino Martinez** | **11** |
| | **Alex Rodriguez** | **11** |
| | **Gary Sheffield** | **11** |
| | **Bernie Williams** | **11** |
| | Johnny Bench | 11 |
| | Gary Carter | 11 |
| | Eric Davis | 11 |
| | Cecil Fielder | 11 |
| | Gary Gaetti | 11 |
| | Hank Greenberg | 11 |
| | Reggie Jackson | 11 |
| | Harmon Killebrew | 11 |
| | Lee May | 11 |
| | Willie Stargell | 11 |
| | Danny Tartabull | 11 |
| | Devon White | 11 |
| | Dave Winfield | 11 |
| **45.** | **Carlos Delgado** | **10** |
| | **Steve Finley** | **10** |
| | **Jason Giambi** | **10** |
| | Joe Adcock | 10 |
| | George Bell | 10 |
| | Jay Buhner | 10 |
| | Ellis Burks | 10 |
| | Jeff Burroughs | 10 |
| | Joe Carter | 10 |
| | Darrell Evans | 10 |
| | Andres Galarraga | 10 |
| | John Milner | 10 |
| | Roy Sievers | 10 |
| | Al Simmons | 10 |
| | Vern Stephens | 10 |
| | Mo Vaughn | 10 |
| | Vic Wertz | 10 |

## 25 MULTIPLE-HR GAMES

| | Player | Games |
|---|---|---|
| 1. | Babe Ruth | 72 |
| **2.** | **Barry Bonds** | **68** |
| | **Sammy Sosa** | **68** |
| 4. | Mark McGwire | 67 |
| 5. | Willie Mays | 63 |
| 6. | Hank Aaron | 62 |
| 7. | Jimmie Foxx | 55 |
| 8. | Frank Robinson | 54 |
| **9.** | **Ken Griffey Jr.** | **52** |
| 10. | Eddie Mathews | 49 |
| | Mel Ott | 49 |
| **12.** | **Juan Gonzalez** | **48** |
| 13. | Harmon Killebrew | 46 |
| | Mickey Mantle | 46 |
| 15. | Willie McCovey | 44 |
| | Mike Schmidt | 44 |
| **17.** | **Manny Ramirez** | **43** |
| | Lou Gehrig | 43 |
| | Dave Kingman | 43 |
| 20. | Ernie Banks | 42 |
| | Reggie Jackson | 42 |
| **22.** | **Alex Rodriguez** | **40** |
| 23. | Fred McGriff | 40 |
| | Ralph Kiner | 40 |
| 25. | Albert Belle | 39 |
| | Andre Dawson | 39 |
| **27.** | **Carlos Delgado** | **37** |
| | Stan Musial | 37 |
| | Ted Williams | 37 |
| **30.** | **Mike Piazza** | **36** |
| | Jose Canseco | 36 |
| | Willie Stargell | 36 |
| **33.** | **Jim Thome** | **35** |
| | Joe DiMaggio | 35 |
| | Hank Greenberg | 35 |
| | Lee May | 35 |
| | Jim Rice | 35 |

| | Player | Games |
|---|---|---|
| **38.** | **Rafael Palmeiro** | **34** |
| | Joe Carter | 34 |
| | Cecil Fielder | 34 |
| | Duke Snider | 34 |
| **42.** | **Gary Sheffield** | **33** |
| **43.** | **Vinny Castilla** | **32** |
| | **Chipper Jones** | **32** |
| | **Larry Walker** | **32** |
| | Dick Allen | 32 |
| | Rocky Colavito | 32 |
| | Dale Murphy | 32 |
| | Billy Williams | 32 |
| | Gus Zernial | 32 |
| **51.** | **Jeff Bagwell** | **31** |
| | Eddie Murray | 31 |
| | Hank Sauer | 31 |
| | Greg Vaughn | 31 |
| | Matt Williams | 31 |
| 56. | Andres Galarraga | 30 |
| | Gil Hodges | 30 |
| | Willie Horton | 30 |
| | Johnny Mize | 30 |
| | Darryl Strawberry | 30 |
| | Mo Vaughn | 30 |
| | Dave Winfield | 30 |
| **63.** | **Shawn Green** | **29** |
| **64.** | **Moises Alou** | **28** |
| | Joe Adcock | 28 |
| | Gary Carter | 28 |
| | Chili Davis | 28 |
| | Chuck Klein | 28 |
| **68.** | **Vlad Guerrero** | **27** |
| | Graig Nettles | 27 |
| | Roy Sievers | 27 |
| | Hack Wilson | 27 |
| | Carl Yastrzemski | 27 |
| **73.** | **Reggie Sanders** | **26** |
| | **Frank Thomas** | **26** |
| | Bob Horner | 26 |
| | Frank Howard | 26 |
| | Ron Santo | 26 |
| **78.** | **Jim Edmonds** | **25** |
| | **Luis Gonzalez** | **25** |
| | **Todd Helton** | **25** |
| | Norm Cash | 25 |
| | Roger Maris | 25 |
| | Ryne Sandberg | 25 |
| | Hal Trosky | 25 |

## 20 HOME RUNS, 15 TIMES

| | Player | Seasons |
|---|---|---|
| 1. | Hank Aaron | 20 |
| **2.** | **Barry Bonds** | **17** |
| | Willie Mays | 17 |
| | Frank Robinson | 17 |
| 5. | Reggie Jackson | 16 |
| | Eddie Murray | 16 |
| | Babe Ruth | 16 |
| | Ted Williams | 16 |
| 9. | Fred McGriff | 15 |
| | Mel Ott | 15 |
| | Willie Stargell | 15 |
| | Dave Winfield | 15 |

## 30 HOME RUNS, 10 TIMES

| | Player | Seasons |
|---|---|---|
| 1. | Hank Aaron | 15 |
| **2.** | **Barry Bonds** | **14** |
| 3. | Babe Ruth | 13 |
| | Mike Schmidt | 13 |
| 5. | Jimmie Foxx | 12 |
| 6. | Willie Mays | 11 |
| | Mark McGwire | 11 |
| | Frank Robinson | 11 |
| | **Sammy Sosa** | **11** |
| **10.** | **Rafael Palmeiro** | **10** |
| | **Manny Ramirez** | **10** |
| | Lou Gehrig | 10 |
| | Harmon Killebrew | 10 |
| | Eddie Mathews | 10 |
| | Fred McGriff | 10 |

## LESS THAN 15 AB/HR

| | Player | AB/HR |
|---|---|---|
| 1. | Mark McGwire | 10.61 |
| 2. | Babe Ruth | 11.76 |
| **3.** | **Barry Bonds** | **12.91** |
| **4.** | **Jim Thome** | **13.77** |
| **5.** | **Manny Ramirez** | **14.08** |
| 6. | Ralph Kiner | 14.11 |
| 7. | Harmon Killebrew | 14.22 |
| **8.** | **Sammy Sosa** | **14.29** |
| **9.** | **Alex Rodriguez** | **14.44** |
| **10.** | **Ken Griffey, Jr** | **14.68** |
| **11.** | **Albert Pujols** | **14.70** |
| 12. | Ted Williams | 14.79 |
| **13.** | **Carlos Delgado** | **14.98** |

## 4,000 TOTAL BASES

| | Player | TB |
|---|---|---|
| 1. | Hank Aaron | 6,856 |
| 2. | Stan Musial | 6,134 |
| 3. | Willie Mays | 6,066 |
| 4. | Ty Cobb | 5,854 |
| 5. | Babe Ruth | 5,793 |
| 6. | Pete Rose | 5,752 |
| **7.** | **Barry Bonds** | **5,584** |
| 8. | Carl Yastrzemski | 5,539 |
| 9. | Eddie Murray | 5,397 |
| **10.** | **Rafael Palmeiro** | **5,388** |
| 11. | Frank Robinson | 5,373 |
| 12. | Dave Winfield | 5,221 |
| 13. | Cal Ripken Jr. | 5,168 |
| 14. | Tris Speaker | 5,101 |
| 15. | Lou Gehrig | 5,060 |
| 16. | George Brett | 5,044 |
| 17. | Mel Ott | 5,041 |
| 18. | Jimmie Foxx | 4,956 |
| 19. | Ted Williams | 4,884 |
| 20. | Honus Wagner | 4,870 |
| 21. | Paul Molitor | 4,854 |
| 22. | Al Kaline | 4,852 |
| 23. | Reggie Jackson | 4,834 |
| 24. | Andre Dawson | 4,787 |
| 25. | Robin Yount | 4,730 |
| 26. | Rogers Hornsby | 4,712 |
| 27. | Ernie Banks | 4,706 |
| 28. | Al Simmons | 4,685 |
| 29. | Harold Baines | 4,604 |
| 30. | Billy Williams | 4,599 |
| 31. | Rickey Henderson | 4,588 |
| 32. | Tony Perez | 4,532 |
| **33.** | **Sammy Sosa** | **4,511** |
| | Mickey Mantle | 4,511 |
| 35. | Roberto Clemente | 4,492 |
| 36. | Paul Waner | 4,478 |
| 37. | Nap Lajoie | 4,471 |
| 38. | Fred McGriff | 4,458 |
| **39.** | **Ken Griffey Jr.** | **4,414** |
| 40. | Dave Parker | 4,405 |
| 41. | Mike Schmidt | 4,404 |
| 42. | Eddie Mathews | 4,349 |
| 43. | Sam Crawford | 4,328 |
| 44. | Goose Goslin | 4,325 |
| **45.** | **Craig Biggio** | **4,283** |
| 46. | Brooks Robinson | 4,270 |
| 47. | Eddie Collins | 4,268 |
| 48. | Vada Pinson | 4,264 |
| 49. | Tony Gwynn | 4,259 |
| 50. | Charlie Gehringer | 4,257 |
| 51. | Lou Brock | 4,238 |
| 52. | Dwight Evans | 4,230 |
| 53. | Willie McCovey | 4,219 |
| **54.** | **Jeff Bagwell** | **4,213** |
| 55. | Willie Stargell | 4,190 |
| 56. | Rusty Staub | 4,185 |
| 57. | Jake Beckley | 4,156 |
| **58.** | **Gary Sheffield** | **4,153** |
| 59. | Harmon Killebrew | 4,143 |
| 60. | Jim Rice | 4,129 |
| 61. | Zack Wheat | 4,100 |
| 62. | Al Oliver | 4,083 |
| 63. | Cap Anson | 4,080 |
| 64. | Wade Boggs | 4,064 |
| 65. | Harry Heilmann | 4,053 |
| 66. | Andres Galarraga | 4,038 |
| 67. | Roberto Alomar | 4,018 |

## 300 TOTAL BASES, 10 TIMES

| | Player | Seasons |
|---|---|---|
| 1. | Hank Aaron | 15 |
| 2. | Lou Gehrig | 13 |
| | Willie Mays | 13 |
| | Stan Musial | 13 |
| 5. | Babe Ruth | 11 |
| 6. | Jimmie Foxx | 10 |

## 800 EXTRA-BASE HITS

| | Player | EBH |
|---|---|---|
| 1. | Hank Aaron | 1,477 |
| 2. | Stan Musial | 1,377 |
| 3. | Babe Ruth | 1,356 |
| **4.** | **Barry Bonds** | **1,349** |
| 5. | Willie Mays | 1,323 |
| **6.** | **Rafael Palmeiro** | **1,192** |
| 7. | Lou Gehrig | 1,190 |
| 8. | Frank Robinson | 1,186 |
| 9. | Carl Yastrzemski | 1,157 |
| 10. | Ty Cobb | 1,136 |
| 11. | Tris Speaker | 1,131 |
| 12. | George Brett | 1,119 |
| 13. | Jimmie Foxx | 1,117 |
| | Ted Williams | 1,117 |
| 15. | Eddie Murray | 1,099 |
| 16. | Dave Winfield | 1,093 |
| 17. | Cal Ripken Jr. | 1,078 |
| 18. | Reggie Jackson | 1,075 |
| 19. | Mel Ott | 1,071 |
| 20. | Pete Rose | 1,041 |
| 21. | Andre Dawson | 1,039 |
| 22. | Mike Schmidt | 1,015 |
| 23. | Rogers Hornsby | 1,011 |
| 24. | Ernie Banks | 1,009 |
| **25.** | **Ken Griffey Jr.** | **1,002** |
| 26. | Honus Wagner | 996 |
| 27. | Al Simmons | 995 |
| **28.** | **Sammy Sosa** | **987** |
| 29. | Al Kaline | 972 |
| **30.** | **Jeff Bagwell** | **969** |
| 31. | Tony Perez | 963 |
| 32. | Robin Yount | 960 |
| 33. | Fred McGriff | 958 |
| 34. | Paul Molitor | 953 |
| | Willie Stargell | 953 |
| 36. | Mickey Mantle | 952 |
| 37. | Billy Williams | 948 |
| 38. | Dwight Evans | 941 |
| 39. | Dave Parker | 940 |
| 40. | Eddie Mathews | 938 |
| 41. | Harold Baines | 921 |
| | Goose Goslin | 921 |
| 43. | Willie McCovey | 920 |
| **44.** | **Craig Biggio** | **916** |
| | **Larry Walker** | **916** |
| 46. | Paul Waner | 909 |
| **47.** | **Frank Thomas** | **906** |
| 48. | Charlie Gehringer | 904 |
| 49. | Nap Lajoie | 902 |
| 50. | Harmon Killebrew | 887 |
| **51.** | **Gary Sheffield** | **886** |
| 52. | Joe Carter | 881 |
| | Joe DiMaggio | 881 |
| 54. | Harry Heilmann | 876 |
| 55. | Andres Galarraga | 875 |
| **56.** | **Luis Gonzalez** | **874** |
| 57. | Rickey Henderson | 873 |
| 58. | Vada Pinson | 868 |
| 59. | Sam Crawford | 864 |
| **60.** | **Manny Ramirez** | **861** |
| 61. | Joe Medwick | 858 |
| 62. | Duke Snider | 850 |
| **63.** | **Juan Gonzalez** | **847** |
| | **Jeff Kent** | **847** |
| 65. | Roberto Clemente | 846 |
| 66. | Carlton Fisk | 844 |
| 67. | Gary Gaetti | 842 |
| 68. | Mark McGwire | 841 |
| 69. | Edgar Martinez | 838 |
| | Rusty Staub | 838 |
| 71. | Jim Bottomley | 835 |
| **72.** | **Steve Finley** | **834** |
| | Jim Rice | 834 |
| 74. | Al Oliver | 825 |
| 75. | Orlando Cepeda | 823 |
| 76. | Brooks Robinson | 818 |
| 77. | Ellis Burks | 817 |
| 78. | Jose Canseco | 816 |
| 79. | Joe Morgan | 813 |
| 80. | Roger Connor | 812 |
| 81. | Ed Delahanty | 809 |
| | Johnny Mize | 809 |
| 83. | Jake Beckley | 804 |
| | Chili Davis | 804 |
| 85. | Joe Cronin | 803 |

## 1,200 RUNS BATTED IN

| | Player | RBIs |
|---|---|---|
| 1. | Hank Aaron | 2,297 |
| 2. | Babe Ruth | 2,213 |
| 3. | Lou Gehrig | 1,995 |
| 4. | Stan Musial | 1,951 |
| 5. | Ty Cobb | 1,938 |
| 6. | Jimmie Foxx | 1,922 |
| 7. | Eddie Murray | 1,917 |
| 8. | Willie Mays | 1,903 |
| 9. | Cap Anson | 1,880 |
| 10. | Mel Ott | 1,860 |
| **11.** | **Barry Bonds** | **1,853** |
| 12. | Carl Yastrzemski | 1,844 |
| 13. | Ted Williams | 1,839 |
| **14.** | **Rafael Palmeiro** | **1,835** |
| 15. | Dave Winfield | 1,833 |
| 16. | Al Simmons | 1,827 |
| 17. | Frank Robinson | 1,812 |
| 18. | Honus Wagner | 1,733 |
| 19. | Reggie Jackson | 1,702 |
| 20. | Cal Ripken Jr. | 1,695 |
| 21. | Tony Perez | 1,652 |
| 22. | Ernie Banks | 1,636 |
| 23. | Harold Baines | 1,628 |
| 24. | Goose Goslin | 1,609 |

| | Player | RBIs |
|---|---|---|
| 25. | Nap Lajoie | 1,599 |
| 26. | George Brett | 1,595 |
| | Mike Schmidt | 1,595 |
| 28. | Andre Dawson | 1,591 |
| 29. | Harmon Killebrew | 1,584 |
| | Rogers Hornsby | 1,584 |
| 31. | Al Kaline | 1,583 |
| 32. | Jake Beckley | 1,578 |
| **33.** | **Sammy Sosa** | **1,575** |
| 34. | Willie McCovey | 1,555 |
| 35. | Fred McGriff | 1,550 |
| 36. | Willie Stargell | 1,540 |
| 37. | Harry Heilmann | 1,539 |
| 38. | Joe DiMaggio | 1,537 |
| **39.** | **Ken Griffey Jr.** | **1,536** |
| **40.** | **Jeff Bagwell** | **1,529** |
| | Tris Speaker | 1,529 |
| 42. | Sam Crawford | 1,525 |
| 43. | Mickey Mantle | 1,509 |
| 44. | Dave Parker | 1,493 |
| **45.** | **Gary Sheffield** | **1,476** |
| 46. | Billy Williams | 1,475 |
| 47. | Ed Delahanty | 1,466 |
| | Rusty Staub | 1,466 |
| **49.** | **Frank Thomas** | **1,465** |
| 50. | Eddie Mathews | 1,453 |
| 51. | Jim Rice | 1,451 |
| 52. | Joe Carter | 1,445 |
| 53. | George Davis | 1,440 |
| 54. | Yogi Berra | 1,430 |
| 55. | Charlie Gehringer | 1,427 |
| 56. | Andres Galaragga | 1,425 |
| 57. | Joe Cronin | 1,424 |
| 58. | Jim Bottomley | 1,422 |
| **59.** | **Manny Ramirez** | **1,414** |
| | Mark McGwire | 1,414 |
| 61. | Jose Canseco | 1,407 |
| 62. | Robin Yount | 1,406 |
| **63.** | **Juan Gonzalez** | **1,404** |
| 64. | Ted Simmons | 1,389 |
| 65. | Dwight Evans | 1,384 |
| 66. | Joe Medwick | 1,383 |
| 67. | Lave Cross | 1,378 |
| 68. | Johnny Bench | 1,376 |
| 69. | Chili Davis | 1,372 |
| 70. | Orlando Cepeda | 1,365 |
| 71. | Brooks Robinson | 1,357 |
| 72. | Darrell Evans | 1,354 |
| 73. | Gary Gaetti | 1,341 |
| 74. | Johnny Mize | 1,337 |
| 75. | Duke Snider | 1,333 |
| 76. | Ron Santo | 1,331 |
| 77. | Carlton Fisk | 1,330 |
| 78. | Al Oliver | 1,326 |
| 79. | Roger Connor | 1,323 |
| **80.** | **RubenSierra** | **1,318** |
| 81. | Graig Nettles | 1,314 |
| | Pete Rose | 1,314 |
| **83.** | **Jeff Kent** | **1,312** |
| **84.** | **Larry Walker** | **1,311** |
| | Mickey Vernon | 1,311 |
| 86. | Paul Waner | 1,309 |
| 87. | Steve Garvey | 1,308 |
| 88. | Paul Molitor | 1,307 |
| 89. | Roberto Clemente | 1,305 |
| | Sam Thompson | 1,305 |
| 91. | Enos Slaughter | 1,304 |
| 92. | Hugh Duffy | 1,302 |
| 93. | Eddie Collins | 1,300 |
| 94. | Dan Brouthers | 1,296 |
| 95. | Del Ennis | 1,284 |
| 96. | Bob Johnson | 1,283 |
| 97. | Don Baylor | 1,276 |
| | Hank Greenberg | 1,276 |
| 99. | Gil Hodges | 1,274 |
| 100. | Pie Traynor | 1,273 |
| **101.** | **Tino Martinez** | **1,271** |
| 102. | Paul O'Neill | 1,269 |
| 103. | Dale Murphy | 1,266 |
| 104. | Edgar Martinez | 1,261 |
| **105.** | **Luis Gonzalez** | **1,251** |
| 106. | Ty Cobb | 1,249 |
| 107. | Zack Wheat | 1,248 |
| 108. | Bobby Doerr | 1,247 |
| 109. | Frankie Frisch | 1,244 |
| | Lee May | 1,244 |
| 111. | Albert Belle | 1,239 |
| | George Foster | 1,239 |
| 113. | Bill Dahlen | 1,234 |
| **114.** | **John Olerud** | **1,230** |
| **115.** | **Alex Rodriguez** | **1,226** |
| 115. | Gary Carter | 1,225 |
| **117.** | **Mike Piazza** | **1,223** |
| 118. | Matt Williams | 1,218 |
| 119. | Dave Kingman | 1,210 |
| 120. | Bill Dickey | 1,209 |
| 121. | Bill Buckner | 1,208 |
| 122. | Ellis Burks | 1,206 |
| 123. | Will Clark | 1,205 |
| 124. | Chuck Klein | 1,201 |

## 1,500 RBIs, RIGHTHANDER

| | Player | RBIs |
|---|---|---|
| 1. | Hank Aaron | 2297 |
| 2. | Jimmie Foxx | 1922 |
| 3. | Willie Mays | 1903 |
| 4. | Cap Anson | 1880 |
| 5. | Dave Winfield | 1833 |
| 6. | Al Simmons | 1827 |
| 7. | Frank Robinson | 1812 |
| 8. | Honus Wagner | 1733 |
| 9. | Cal Ripken | 1695 |
| 10. | Tony Perez | 1652 |
| 11. | Ernie Banks | 1636 |
| 12. | Nap Lajoie | 1599 |
| 13. | Mike Schmidt | 1595 |
| 14. | Andre Dawson | 1591 |
| 15. | Rogers Hornsby | 1584 |
| | Harmon Killebrew | 1584 |
| 17. | Al Kaline | 1583 |
| **18.** | **Sammy Sosa** | **1575** |
| 19. | Harry Heilmann | 1,539 |
| 20. | Joe DiMaggio | 1,537 |
| **21.** | **Jeff Bagwell** | **1,529** |

## 1,500 RBIs, LEFTHANDER

| | Player | RBIs |
|---|---|---|
| 1. | Babe Ruth | 2213 |
| 2. | Lou Gehrig | 1995 |
| 3. | Stan Musial | 1951 |
| 4. | Ty Cobb | 1938 |
| 5. | Mel Ott | 1860 |
| **6.** | **Barry Bonds** | **1853** |
| 7. | Carl Yastrzemski | 1844 |
| 8. | Ted Williams | 1839 |
| **9.** | **Rafael Palmeiro** | **1,835** |
| 10. | Reggie Jackson | 1702 |
| 11. | Harold Baines | 1628 |
| 12. | Goose Goslin | 1609 |
| 13. | George Brett | 1595 |
| 14. | Jake Beckley | 1578 |
| 15. | Willie McCovey | 1555 |
| 16. | Fred McGriff | 1550 |
| 17. | Willie Stargell | 1540 |
| 18. | Tris Speaker | 1529 |
| 19. | Sam Crawford | 1525 |

## 1,500 RBIs, SWITCH HITTER

| | Player | RBIs |
|---|---|---|
| 1. | Eddie Murray | 1917 |
| 2. | Mickey Mantle | 1509 |

## 100 RBIs, 10 TIMES

| | Player | Seasons |
|---|---|---|
| 1. | Jimmie Foxx | 13 |
| | Lou Gehrig | 13 |
| | Babe Ruth | 13 |
| **4.** | **Barry Bonds** | **12** |
| | Al Simmons | 12 |
| 6. | Hank Aaron | 11 |
| | Goose Goslin | 11 |
| **8.** | **Rafael Palmeiro** | **10** |
| | **Manny Ramirez** | **10** |
| | **Frank Thomas** | **10** |
| 11. | Joe Carter | 10 |
| | Willie Mays | 10 |
| | Stan Musial | 10 |

## 1,000 BASES ON BALLS

| | Player | BBs |
|---|---|---|
| **1.** | **Barry Bonds** | **2,311** |
| 2. | Rickey Henderson | 2,190 |
| 3. | Babe Ruth | 2,062 |
| 4. | Ted Williams | 2,021 |
| 5. | Joe Morgan | 1,865 |
| 6. | Carl Yastrzemski | 1,845 |
| 7. | Mickey Mantle | 1,733 |
| 8. | Mel Ott | 1,708 |
| 9. | Eddie Yost | 1,614 |
| 10. | Darrell Evans | 1,605 |
| 11. | Stan Musial | 1,599 |
| 12. | Pete Rose | 1,566 |
| 13. | Harmon Killebrew | 1,559 |
| 14. | Lou Gehrig | 1,508 |
| 15. | Mike Schmidt | 1,507 |
| 16. | Eddie Collins | 1,499 |
| **17.** | **Frank Thomas** | **1,466** |
| 18. | Willie Mays | 1,464 |
| 19. | Jimmie Foxx | 1,452 |
| 20. | Eddie Mathews | 1,444 |
| 21. | Frank Robinson | 1,420 |
| 22. | Wade Boggs | 1,412 |
| 23. | Hank Aaron | 1,402 |
| **24.** | **Jeff Bagwell** | **1,401** |
| 25. | Dwight Evans | 1,391 |
| 26. | Tris Speaker | 1,381 |
| 27. | Reggie Jackson | 1,375 |
| **28.** | **Rafael Palmeiro** | **1,353** |
| 29. | Willie McCovey | 1,345 |
| 30. | Eddie Murray | 1,333 |
| 31. | Tim Raines, Sr., | 1,330 |
| 32. | Tony Phillips | 1,319 |
| 33. | Mark McGwire | 1,317 |
| 34. | Fred McGriff | 1,305 |
| 35. | Luke Appling | 1,302 |
| | Edgar Martinez | 1,283 |
| **37.** | **Gary Sheffield** | **1,280** |
| 38. | Al Kaline | 1,277 |
| **39.** | **John Olerud** | **1,275** |
| 40. | Ken Singleton | 1,263 |
| 41. | Jack Clark | 1,262 |
| **42.** | **Jim Thome** | **1,257** |
| 43. | Rusty Staub | 1,255 |
| 44. | Ty Cobb | 1,249 |
| 45. | Willie Randolph | 1,243 |
| 46. | Jim Wynn | 1,224 |
| 47. | Dave Winfield | 1,216 |
| 48. | Pee Wee Reese | 1,210 |
| 49. | Richie Ashburn | 1,198 |
| 50. | Brian Downing | 1,197 |
| | Lou Whitaker | 1,197 |
| 52. | Chili Davis | 1,194 |
| 53. | Billy Hamilton | 1,189 |
| 54. | Charlie Gehringer | 1,186 |
| 55. | Donie Bush | 1,158 |
| 56. | Max Bishop | 1,156 |
| 57. | Toby Harrah | 1,153 |
| 58. | Harry Hooper | 1,136 |
| 59. | Jimmy Sheckard | 1,135 |
| 60. | Brett Butler | 1,129 |
| | Cal Ripken Jr. | 1,129 |
| 62. | Ron Santo | 1,108 |
| **63.** | **Craig Biggio** | **1,097** |
| 64. | George Brett | 1,096 |
| 65. | Paul Molitor | 1,094 |
| 66. | Lu Blue | 1,092 |
| | Stan Hack | 1,092 |
| 68. | Paul Waner | 1,091 |
| 69. | Graig Nettles | 1,088 |
| 70. | Bobby Grich | 1,087 |
| 71. | Mark Grace | 1,075 |
| | Bob Johnson | 1,075 |
| | Robin Ventura | 1,075 |
| 74. | Ozzie Smith | 1,072 |
| 75. | Harlond Clift | 1,070 |
| | Keith Hernandez | 1,070 |
| 77. | Bill Dahlen | 1,064 |
| 78. | Harold Baines | 1,062 |
| 79. | Joe Cronin | 1,059 |
| 80. | Ron Fairly | 1,052 |
| 81. | Billy Williams | 1,045 |
| 82. | Norm Cash | 1,043 |
| | Eddie Joost | 1,043 |
| 84. | Roy Thomas | 1,042 |
| 85. | Max Carey | 1,040 |
| **86.** | **Ken Griffey Jr.** | **1,038** |
| | Rogers Hornsby | 1,038 |
| **88.** | **Bernie Williams** | **1,036** |
| | Jim Gilliam | 1,036 |
| 90. | Roberto Alomar | 1,032 |
| 91. | Sal Bando | 1,031 |
| 92. | Jesse Burkett | 1,029 |
| 93. | Rod Carew | 1,018 |
| | Enos Slaughter | 1,018 |
| 95. | Ron Cey | 1,012 |
| 96. | Ralph Kiner | 1,011 |
| **97.** | **Chipper Jones** | **1,009** |
| 98. | Dummy Hoy | 1,006 |
| 99. | Miller Huggins | 1,003 |
| 100. | Roger Connor | 1,002 |
| 101. | Boog Powell | 1,001 |

## 200 INTENTIONAL WALKS

| | Player | IBBs |
|---|---|---|
| **1.** | **Barry Bonds** | **607** |
| 2. | Hank Aaron | 293 |
| 3. | Willie McCovey | 260 |
| 4. | George Brett | 229 |
| 5. | Willie Stargell | 227 |
| 6. | Eddie Murray | 222 |
| 7. | Frank Robinson | 218 |
| **8.** | **Ken Griffey Jr** | **210** |
| 9. | Ken Griffey | 207 |
| 10. | Tony Gwynn | 203 |
| 11. | Mike Schmidt | 201 |

## 1,200 STRIKEOUTS

| | Player | Ks |
|---|---|---|
| 1. | Reggie Jackson | 2,597 |
| **2.** | **Sammy Sosa** | **2,194** |
| 3. | Andres Galarraga | 2,003 |
| 4. | Jose Canseco | 1,942 |
| 5. | Willie Stargell | 1,936 |
| 6. | Mike Schmidt | 1,883 |
| 7. | Fred McGriff | 1,882 |
| 8. | Tony Perez | 1,867 |
| 9. | Dave Kingman | 1,816 |
| **10.** | **Jim Thome** | **1,762** |
| 11. | Bobby Bonds | 1,757 |
| 12. | Dale Murphy | 1,748 |
| 13. | Lou Brock | 1,730 |
| 14. | Mickey Mantle | 1,710 |
| 15. | Harmon Killebrew | 1,699 |
| 16. | Chili Davis | 1,698 |
| 17. | Dwight Evans | 1,697 |
| 18. | Rickey Henderson | 1,694 |
| 19. | Dave Winfield | 1,686 |
| 20. | Gary Gaetti | 1,602 |
| 21. | Mark McGwire | 1,596 |
| 22. | Lee May | 1,570 |
| **23.** | **Jeff Bagwell** | **1,558** |
| **24.** | **Craig Biggio** | **1,557** |
| 25. | Dick Allen | 1,556 |
| 26. | Ray Lankford | 1,550 |
| | Willie McCovey | 1,550 |
| 28. | Dave Parker | 1,537 |
| 29. | Frank Robinson | 1,532 |
| 30. | Lance Parrish | 1,527 |
| 31. | Willie Mays | 1,526 |
| | Devon White | 1,526 |
| 33. | Eddie Murray | 1,516 |
| **34.** | **Reggie Sanders** | **1,513** |
| 35. | Rick Monday | 1,513 |
| | Greg Vaughn | 1,513 |
| 37. | Andre Dawson | 1,509 |
| 38. | Tony Phillips | 1,499 |
| 39. | Greg Luzinski | 1,495 |
| 40. | Eddie Mathews | 1,487 |
| 41. | Frank Howard | 1,460 |
| 42. | Jay Bell | 1,443 |
| 43. | Juan Samuel | 1,442 |
| 44. | Harold Baines | 1,441 |
| | Jack Clark | 1,441 |
| **46.** | **Barry Bonds** | **1,434** |
| 47. | Mo Vaughn | 1,429 |
| 48. | Jim Wynn | 1,427 |
| 49. | Jim Rice | 1,423 |
| 50. | George Foster | 1,419 |
| 51. | George Scott | 1,418 |
| **52.** | **Ken Griffey Jr.** | **1,416** |
| **53.** | **Jim Edmonds** | **1,411** |
| | Ron Gant | 1,411 |
| 55. | Darrell Evans | 1,410 |
| 56. | Rob Deer | 1,409 |
| 57. | Jay Buhner | 1,406 |
| 58. | Eric Davis | 1,398 |
| 59. | Carl Yastrzemski | 1,393 |
| 60. | Joe Carter | 1,387 |
| 61. | Carlton Fisk | 1,386 |
| 62. | Hank Aaron | 1,383 |
| 63. | Travis Fryman | 1,369 |
| **64.** | **Carlos Delgado** | **1,363** |
| | Matt Williams | 1,363 |
| 66. | Danny Tartabull | 1,362 |
| 67. | Larry Parrish | 1,359 |
| 68. | Darryl Strawberry | 1,352 |
| **69.** | **Jose Hernandez** | **1,351** |
| 70. | Robin Yount | 1,350 |
| **71.** | **Manny Ramirez** | **1,349** |
| **72.** | **Rafael Palmeiro** | **1,348** |
| 73. | Ron Santo | 1,343 |
| **74.** | **Jeff Kent** | **1,340** |
| | Ellis Burks | 1,340 |
| 76. | Gorman Thomas | 1,339 |
| 77. | Dean Palmer | 1,332 |
| 78. | Babe Ruth | 1,330 |
| 79. | Deron Johnson | 1,318 |
| **80.** | **Tim Salmon** | **1,316** |
| | Cecil Fielder | 1,316 |
| 82. | Willie Horton | 1,313 |
| 83. | Jimmie Foxx | 1,311 |
| 84. | Mickey Tettleton | 1,307 |
| | Tim Wallach | 1,307 |
| 86. | Cal Ripken Jr. | 1,305 |
| **87.** | **Jeromy Burnitz** | **1,302** |
| **88.** | **Bret Boone** | **1,295** |
| 89. | Kirk Gibson | 1,285 |
| 90. | Todd Zeile | 1,279 |
| 91. | Johnny Bench | 1,278 |
| | Bobby Grich | 1,278 |
| **93.** | **Royce Clayton** | **1,277** |
| | Pete Incaviglia | 1,277 |
| **95.** | **Juan Gonzalez** | **1,273** |
| **96.** | **Benito Santiago** | **1,270** |
| **97.** | **Julio Franco** | **1,269** |
| 98. | Claudell Washington | 1,266 |
| **99.** | **Alex Rodriguez** | **1,265** |
| 100. | Ryne Sandberg | 1,260 |
| 101. | Ken Singleton | 1,246 |
| 102. | Paul Molitor | 1,244 |
| **103.** | **Steve Finley** | **1,240** |
| | **Marquis Grissom** | **1,240** |
| 105. | Willie McGee | 1,238 |
| 106. | Duke Snider | 1,237 |

| | Player | Ks |
|---|---|---|
| 107. | Ernie Banks | 1,236 |
| 108. | Ron Cey | 1,235 |
| 109. | Jesse Barfield | 1,234 |
| **110.** | **Ruben Sierra** | **1,232** |
| **111.** | **Larry Walker** | **1,231** |
| 112. | Roberto Clemente | 1,230 |
| 113. | Boog Powell | 1,226 |
| 114. | Graig Nettles | 1,209 |
| 115. | Bobby Bonilla | 1,204 |
| 116. | Edgar Martinez | 1,202 |
| 117. | Tony Armas | 1,201 |

### 150 HIT BY PITCH

| | Player | HPs |
|---|---|---|
| 1. | Hughie Jennings | 287 |
| **2.** | **Craig Biggio** | **273** |
| 3. | Tommy Tucker | 272 |
| 4. | Don Baylor | 267 |
| 5. | Ron Hunt | 243 |
| 6. | Dan McGann | 230 |
| 7. | Frank Robinson | 198 |
| **8.** | **Jason Kendall** | **197** |
| 9. | Minnie Minoso | 192 |
| 10. | Jake Beckley | 183 |
| 11. | Andres Galarraga | 178 |
| 12. | Curt Welch | 173 |
| 13. | Kid Elberfeld | 165 |
| **14.** | **Fernando Vina** | **157** |
| 15. | Brady Anderson | 154 |
| | Fred Clarke | 154 |
| 17. | Chet Lemon | 151 |

## BASERUNNING

### 400 STOLEN BASES

| | Player | SBs |
|---|---|---|
| 1. | Rickey Henderson | 1,406 |
| 2. | Lou Brock | 938 |
| 3. | Billy Hamilton | 914 |
| 4. | Ty Cobb | 897 |
| 5. | Tim Raines, Sr. | 808 |
| 6. | Vince Coleman | 752 |
| 7. | Arlie Latham | 742 |
| 8. | Eddie Collins | 741 |
| 9. | Max Carey | 738 |
| 10. | Honus Wagner | 723 |
| 11. | Joe Morgan | 689 |
| 12. | Willie Wilson | 668 |
| 13. | Tom Brown | 657 |
| 14. | Bert Campaneris | 649 |
| 15. | Otis Nixon | 620 |
| 16. | George Davis | 619 |
| 17. | Dummy Hoy | 596 |
| 18. | Maury Wills | 586 |
| 19. | George Van Haltren | 583 |
| 20. | Ozzie Smith | 580 |
| 21. | Hugh Duffy | 574 |
| 22. | Bid McPhee | 568 |
| **23.** | **Kenny Lofton** | **567** |
| 24. | Brett Butler | 558 |
| 25. | Dave Lopes | 557 |
| 26. | Cesar Cedeno | 550 |
| 27. | Bill Dahlen | 548 |
| 28. | Monte Ward | 540 |
| 29. | Herman Long | 537 |
| 30. | Patsy Donovan | 518 |
| | Jack Doyle | 518 |
| 32. | Fred Clarke | 509 |
| | Harry Stovey | 509 |
| **34.** | **Barry Bonds** | **506** |
| | Luis Aparicio | 506 |
| 36. | Paul Molitor | 504 |
| 37. | Willie Keeler | 495 |
| | Clyde Milan | 495 |
| 39. | Omar Moreno | 487 |
| 40. | Roberto Alomar | 474 |
| 41. | Mike Griffin | 473 |
| 42. | Tom McCarthy | 468 |
| 43. | Jim Sheckard | 465 |
| 44. | Delino DeShields | 463 |
| 45. | Bobby Bonds | 461 |
| **46.** | **Eric Young** | **457** |
| 47. | Ed Delahanty | 455 |
| | Ron LeFlore | 455 |
| 49. | Curt Welch | 453 |
| 50. | Steve Sax | 444 |
| 51. | Joe Kelley | 443 |
| 52. | Sherry Magee | 441 |
| 53. | John McGraw | 436 |
| | Tris Speaker | 436 |
| **55.** | **Marquis Grissom** | **429** |
| | Bob Bescher | 428 |
| | Mike Tiernan | 428 |
| 58. | Frankie Frisch | 419 |
| | Jim Ryan | 419 |
| 60. | Charlie Comiskey | 416 |
| 61. | Tommy Harper | 408 |
| **62.** | **Craig Biggio** | **407** |
| | Chuck Knoblauch | 407 |
| 64. | Donie Bush | 406 |
| 65. | Frank Chance | 403 |
| 66. | Bill Lange | 400 |

### 150 CAUGHT STEALING

| | Player | CSs |
|---|---|---|
| 1. | Rickey Henderson | 335 |
| 2. | Lou Brock | 307 |
| 3. | Brett Butler | 257 |
| 4. | Maury Wills | 208 |
| 5. | Bert Campaneris | 199 |
| 6. | Rod Carew | 187 |
| 7. | Otis Nixon | 186 |
| 8. | Omar Moreno | 182 |
| 9. | Cesar Cedeno | 179 |
| 10. | Ty Cobb | 178 |
| | Steve Sax | 178 |
| 12. | Vince Coleman | 177 |
| 13. | George Burns | 174 |
| 14. | Eddie Collins | 173 |
| 15. | Bobby Bonds | 169 |
| **16.** | **Eric Young** | **166** |
| 17. | Joe Morgan | 162 |
| | Billy North | 162 |

## PITCHING

### 700 GAMES

| | Pitcher | Seasons | Games |
|---|---|---|---|
| 1. | Jesse Orosco | 24 | 1,252 |
| **2.** | **John Franco** | **21** | **1,119** |
| 3. | Dennis Eckersley | 24 | 1,071 |
| 4. | Hoyt Wilhelm | 21 | 1,070 |
| 5. | Dan Plesac | 18 | 1,064 |
| 6. | Kent Tekulve | 16 | 1,050 |
| **7.** | **Mike Stanton** | **17** | **1,027** |
| 8. | Lee Smith | 18 | 1,022 |
| 9. | Mike Jackson | 17 | 1,005 |
| 10. | Rich Gossage | 22 | 1,002 |
| 11. | Lindy McDaniel | 21 | 987 |
| 12. | Rollie Fingers | 17 | 944 |
| 13. | Gene Garber | 19 | 931 |
| 14. | Cy Young | 22 | 906 |
| 15. | Sparky Lyle | 16 | 899 |
| 16. | Jim Kaat | 25 | 898 |
| **17.** | **Mike Timlin** | **15** | **893** |
| **18.** | **Roberto Hernandez** | **15** | **892** |
| **19.** | **Jose Mesa** | **17** | **887** |
| 20. | Paul Assenmacher | 14 | 884 |
| 21. | Jeff Reardon | 16 | 880 |
| 22. | Don McMahon | 18 | 874 |
| 23. | Phil Niekro | 24 | 864 |
| 24. | Charlie Hough | 25 | 858 |
| 25. | Roy Face | 16 | 848 |
| 26. | Doug Jones | 16 | 846 |
| **27.** | **Paul Quantrill** | **14** | **841** |
| **28.** | **Steve Reed** | **14** | **833** |
| 29. | Tug McGraw | 19 | 824 |
| **30.** | **Todd Jones** | **13** | **812** |
| 31. | Nolan Ryan | 27 | 807 |
| 32. | Walter Johnson | 21 | 802 |
| 33. | Rick Honeycutt | 21 | 797 |
| **34.** | **Jeff Nelson** | **14** | **792** |
| **35.** | **Buddy Groom** | **14** | **786** |
| 36. | Gaylord Perry | 22 | 777 |
| 37. | Don Sutton | 23 | 774 |
| 38. | Mark Guthrie | 15 | 765 |
| | Darold Knowles | 16 | 765 |
| 40. | Tommy John | 26 | 760 |
| **41.** | **Trevor Hoffman** | **13** | **756** |
| | John Quinn | 23 | 756 |
| 43. | Ron Reed | 19 | 751 |
| **44.** | **Tom Gordon** | **17** | **750** |
| | Warren Spahn | 21 | 750 |
| **46.** | **Mike Myers** | **11** | **749** |
| 47. | Tom Burgmeier | 17 | 745 |
| | Gary Lavelle | 13 | 745 |
| 49. | Willie Hernandez | 13 | 744 |
| 50. | Steve Carlton | 24 | 741 |
| **51.** | **Eddie Guardado** | **13** | **738** |
| 52. | Ron Perranoski | 13 | 737 |
| 53. | Ron Kline | 17 | 736 |
| 54. | Rick Aguilera | 16 | 732 |
| | Steve Bedrosian | 14 | 732 |
| 56. | Clay Carroll | 15 | 731 |
| 57. | Randy Myers | 14 | 728 |
| 58. | Mike G. Marshall | 14 | 723 |
| | Roger McDowell | 12 | 723 |
| **60.** | **Bob Wickman** | **13** | **721** |
| 61. | Dave Righetti | 16 | 718 |
| 62. | Danny Darwin | 21 | 716 |
| 63. | Eric Plunk | 14 | 714 |
| 64. | Johnny Klippstein | 18 | 711 |
| **65.** | **Jeff Fassero** | **15** | **710** |
| | Greg Minton | 16 | 710 |
| 67. | Rod Beck | 13 | 704 |
| | Stu Miller | 16 | 704 |
| 69. | Greg A. Harris | 15 | 703 |
| 70. | Joe Niekro | 22 | 702 |
| 71. | Bill Campbell | 15 | 700 |
| | Jeff Montgomery | 13 | 700 |

### 500 GAMES STARTED

| | Pitcher | Games |
|---|---|---|
| 1. | Cy Young | 815 |
| 2. | Nolan Ryan | 773 |
| 3. | Don Sutton | 756 |
| 4. | Phil Niekro | 716 |
| 5. | Steve Carlton | 709 |
| 6. | Tommy John | 700 |
| 7. | Gaylord Perry | 690 |
| 8. | Bert Blyleven | 685 |
| 9. | Pud Galvin | 681 |
| **10.** | **Roger Clemens** | **671** |
| 11. | Walter Johnson | 666 |
| 12. | Warren Spahn | 665 |
| 13. | Tom Seaver | 647 |
| **14.** | **Greg Maddux** | **639** |
| 15. | Jim Kaat | 625 |
| 16. | Frank Tanana | 616 |
| 17. | Early Wynn | 612 |
| 18. | Robin Roberts | 609 |
| **19.** | **Tom Glavine** | **603** |
| 20. | Grover Alexander | 600 |
| 21. | Ferguson Jenkins | 594 |
| | Tim Keefe | 594 |
| 23. | Kid Nichols | 562 |
| | Dennis Martinez | 562 |
| 25. | Eppa Rixey | 554 |
| 26. | Christy Mathewson | 552 |
| 27. | Mickey Welch | 549 |
| 28. | Jerry Reuss | 547 |
| 29. | Red Ruffing | 538 |
| 30. | Eddie Plank | 529 |
| | Rick Reuschel | 529 |
| 32. | Jerry Koosman | 527 |
| | Jack Morris | 527 |
| 34. | Jim Palmer | 521 |
| 35. | Jim Bunning | 519 |
| 36. | John Clarkson | 518 |
| 37. | Jack Powell | 516 |
| **38.** | **Randy Johnson** | **513** |
| 39. | Gus Weyhing | 505 |
| 40 | Tony Mullane | 504 |
| 41. | Hoss Radbourn | 502 |
| 42. | Joe Niekro | 500 |

### 300 COMPLETE GAMES

| | Pitcher | CGs |
|---|---|---|
| 1. | Cy Young | 749 |
| 2. | Pud Galvin | 639 |
| 3. | Tim Keefe | 554 |
| 4. | Kid Nichols | 532 |
| 5. | Walter Johnson | 531 |
| 6. | Mickey Welch | 525 |
| 7. | Hoss Radbourn | 488 |
| 8. | John Clarkson | 485 |
| 9. | Tony Mullane | 468 |
| 10. | Jim McCormick | 466 |
| 11. | Gus Weyhing | 449 |
| 12. | Grover Alexander | 437 |
| 13. | Christy Mathewson | 435 |
| 14. | Jack Powell | 422 |
| 15. | Eddie Plank | 410 |
| 16. | Will White | 394 |
| 17. | Amos Rusie | 393 |
| 18. | Vic Willis | 388 |
| 19. | Warren Spahn | 382 |
| 20. | Jim Whitney | 377 |
| 21. | Adonis Terry | 367 |
| 22. | Ted Lyons | 356 |
| 23. | George Mullin | 353 |
| 24. | Charlie Buffinton | 351 |
| 25. | Chick Fraser | 342 |
| 26. | Clark Griffith | 337 |
| 27. | Red Ruffing | 335 |
| 28. | Silver King | 328 |
| 29. | Al Orth | 324 |
| 30. | Bill Hutchinson | 321 |
| 31. | Burleigh Grimes | 314 |
| | Joe McGinnity | 314 |
| 33. | Red Donahue | 312 |
| | Guy Hecker | 312 |
| 35. | Bill Dinneen | 306 |
| 36. | Robin Roberts | 305 |
| 37. | Gaylord Perry | 303 |
| 38. | Ted Breitenstein | 301 |

### 10 OPENING DAY STARTS

| | Pitcher | Starts |
|---|---|---|
| 1. | Tom Seaver | 16 |
| 2. | Steve Carlton | 14 |
| | Walter Johnson | 14 |
| | Jack Morris | 14 |
| **5.** | **Roger Clemens** | **13** |
| | **Randy Johnson** | **13** |
| | Robin Roberts | 13 |
| | Cy Young | 13 |
| 9. | Grover Cleveland Alexander | 12 |
| | Bert Blyleven | 12 |
| 11. | Ferguson Jenkins | 11 |
| | Dennis Martinez | 11 |
| 13. | Bob Gibson | 10 |
| | Juan Marichal | 10 |
| | George Mullin | 10 |
| | Warren Spahn | 10 |

### 3,500 INNINGS

| | Pitcher | IP |
|---|---|---|
| 1. | Cy Young | 7,356.0 |
| 2. | Pud Galvin | 5,941.1 |
| 3. | Walter Johnson | 5,914.1 |
| 4. | Phil Niekro | 5,404.1 |
| 5. | Nolan Ryan | 5,386.0 |
| 6. | Gaylord Perry | 5,350.1 |
| 7. | Don Sutton | [illegible] |
| 8. | Warren Spahn | 5,243.2 |
| 9. | Steve Carlton | 5,217.1 |
| 10. | Grover Alexander | 5,190.0 |
| 11. | Kid Nichols | 5,067.1 |
| 12. | Tim Keefe | 5,049.2 |
| 13. | Bert Blyleven | 4,970.0 |
| 14. | Mickey Welch | 4,802.0 |
| 15. | Christy Mathewson | 4,788.2 |
| 16. | Tom Seaver | 4,782.2 |
| 17. | Tommy John | 4,710.1 |
| **18.** | **Roger Clemens** | **4,704.1** |
| 19. | Robin Roberts | 4,688.2 |
| 20. | Early Wynn | 4,564.0 |
| 21. | John Clarkson | 4,536.1 |
| 22. | Tony Mullane | 4,531.1 |
| 23. | Jim Kaat | 4,530.1 |
| 24. | Hoss Radbourn | 4,527.1 |
| **25.** | **Greg Maddux** | **4,406.1** |
| 26. | Ferguson Jenkins | 4,400.2 |
| 27. | Eddie Plank | 4,495.2 |
| 28. | Eppa Rixey | 4,494.2 |
| 29. | Jack Powell | 4,389.0 |
| 30. | Red Ruffing | 4,344.0 |
| 31. | Gus Weyhing | 4,337.0 |
| 32. | Jim McCormick | 4,275.2 |
| 33. | Frank Tanana | 4,188.1 |
| 34. | Burleigh Grimes | 4,179.2 |
| 35. | Ted Lyons | 4,161.0 |
| 36. | Red Faber | 4,086.2 |
| 37. | Dennis Martinez | 3,999.2 |
| 38. | Vic Willis | 3,996.0 |
| **39.** | **Tom Glavine** | **3,951.2** |
| 40. | Jim Palmer | 3,947.1 |
| 41. | Lefty Grove | 3,940.2 |
| 42. | Jack Quinn | 3,920.1 |
| 43. | Bob Gibson | 3,884.1 |
| 44. | Sam Jones | 3,883.0 |
| 45. | Jerry Koosman | 3,839.1 |
| 46. | Bob Feller | 3,827.0 |
| 47. | Jack Morris | 3,824.0 |
| 48. | Charlie Hough | 3,801.1 |
| 49. | Amos Rusie | 3,778.2 |
| 50. | Waite Hoyt | 3,762.1 |
| 51. | Jim Bunning | 3,760.1 |
| 52. | Bobo Newsom | 3,759.1 |
| 53. | George Mullin | 3,686.2 |
| 54. | Jerry Reuss | 3,669.2 |
| 55. | Paul Derringer | 3,645.0 |
| 56. | Mickey Lolich | 3,638.1 |
| 57. | Bob Friend | 3,611.0 |
| **58.** | **Randy Johnson** | **3,593.2** |
| 59. | Carl Hubbell | 3,590.1 |
| 60. | Joe Niekro | 3,584.0 |
| 61. | Herb Pennock | 3,571.2 |
| 62. | Earl Whitehill | 3,564.2 |
| 63. | Rick Reuschel | 3,548.1 |
| 64. | Will White | 3,542.2 |
| 65. | Adonis Terry | 3,514.1 |
| 66. | Juan Marichal | 3,507.1 |

### 4,500 IP, STARTER

| | Pitcher | IP |
|---|---|---|
| 1. | Cy Young | 7,034.2 |
| 2. | Pud Galvin | 5,872.2 |
| 3. | Walter Johnson | 5,550.1 |
| 4. | Nolan Ryan | 5,326.0 |
| 5. | Don Sutton | 5,248.1 |
| 6. | Steve Carlton | 5,165.0 |
| 7. | Gaylord Perry | 5,161.2 |
| 8. | Phil Niekro | 5,149.1 |
| 9. | Warren Spahn | 5,106.2 |
| 10. | Tim Keefe | 5,021.1 |
| 11. | Grover Cleveland Alexander | 4,983.1 |
| 12. | Bert Blyleven | 4,957.1 |
| 13. | Kid Nichols | 4,891.1 |
| 14. | Tom Seaver | 4,776.0 |
| 15. | Christy Mathewson | 4,753.1 |
| 16. | Mickey Welch | 4,749.0 |
| **17.** | **Roger Clemens** | **4,702.1** |
| 18. | Tommy John | 4,622.0 |
| 19. | Robin Roberts | 4,567.1 |

### 1,200 IP, RELIEVER

| | Pitcher | IP |
|---|---|---|
| 1. | Hoyt Wilhelm | 1871.0 |
| 2. | Lindy McDaniel | 1694.0 |

| | Pitcher | IP |
|---|---|---|
| 3. | Rich Gossage | 1556.2 |
| 4. | Rollie Fingers | 1500.1 |
| 5. | Gene Garber | 1452.2 |
| 6. | Kent Tekulve | 1436.1 |
| 7. | Sparky Lyle | 1390.1 |
| 8. | Tug McGraw | 1301.1 |
| 9. | Don McMahon | 1297.0 |
| 10. | Jesse Orosco | 1277.0 |
| 11. | Mike Marshall | 1259.1 |
| 12. | Lee Smith | 1252.1 |
| 13. | Tom Burgmeier | 1248.2 |
| **14.** | **John Franco** | **1245.2** |
| 15. | Roy Face | 1212.1 |
| 16. | Clay Carroll | 1204.2 |

## 200 INNINGS, 15 TIMES

| | Pitcher | Seasons |
|---|---|---|
| 1. | Don Sutton | 20 |
| 2. | Phil Niekro | 19 |
| | Cy Young | 19 |
| 4. | Walter Johnson | 18 |
| 5. | Gaylord Perry | 17 |
| | Warren Spahn | 17 |
| 7. | Grover Alexander | 16 |
| | Bert Blyleven | 16 |
| | Steve Carlton | 16 |
| | Greg Maddux | 16 |
| | Tom Seaver | 16 |
| **12.** | **Roger Clemens** | **15** |
| | Eddie Plank | 15 |
| | Jack Powell | 15 |

## 300 INNINGS, 8 TIMES

| | Pitcher | Seasons |
|---|---|---|
| 1. | Cy Young | 16 |
| 2. | Kid Nichols | 12 |
| 3. | Pud Galvin | 11 |
| | Christy Mathewson | 11 |
| 5. | Tim Keefe | 10 |
| 6. | Grover Alexander | 9 |
| | Walter Johnson | 9 |
| | Joe McGinnity | 9 |
| | Mickey Welch | 9 |
| | Gus Weyhing | 9 |
| 11. | John Clarkson | 8 |
| | Jim McCormick | 8 |
| | Tony Mullane | 8 |
| | Charles Radbourn | 8 |
| | Amos Rusie | 8 |
| | Jim Whitney | 8 |
| | Vic Willis | 8 |

## 200 VICTORIES

| | Pitcher | W | L |
|---|---|---|---|
| 1. | Cy Young | 511 | 316 |
| 2. | Walter Johnson | 417 | 279 |
| 3. | Christy Mathewson | 373 | 188 |
| | Grover Alexander | 373 | 208 |
| 5. | Warren Spahn | 363 | 245 |
| 6. | Kid Nichols | 361 | 208 |
| | Pud Galvin | 361 | 308 |
| 8. | Tim Keefe | 342 | 225 |
| **9.** | **Roger Clemens** | **341** | **172** |
| 10. | Steve Carlton | 329 | 244 |
| 11. | John Clarkson | 328 | 178 |
| 12. | Eddie Plank | 326 | 194 |
| 13. | Don Sutton | 324 | 256 |
| | Nolan Ryan | 324 | 292 |
| **15.** | **Greg Maddux** | **318** | **189** |
| | Phil Niekro | 318 | 274 |
| 17. | Gaylord Perry | 314 | 265 |
| 18. | Tom Seaver | 311 | 205 |
| 19. | Hoss Radbourn | 309 | 194 |
| 20. | Mickey Welch | 307 | 210 |
| 21. | Lefty Grove | 300 | 141 |
| | Early Wynn | 300 | 244 |
| 23. | Tommy John | 288 | 231 |
| 24. | Bert Blyleven | 287 | 250 |
| 25. | Robin Roberts | 286 | 245 |
| 26. | Tony Mullane | 284 | 220 |
| | Ferguson Jenkins | 284 | 226 |
| 28. | Jim Kaat | 283 | 237 |
| **29.** | **Tom Glavine** | **275** | **184** |
| 30. | Red Ruffing | 273 | 225 |
| 31. | Burleigh Grimes | 270 | 212 |
| 32. | Jim Palmer | 268 | 152 |
| 33. | Bob Feller | 266 | 162 |
| | Eppa Rixey | 266 | 251 |
| 35. | Jim McCormick | 265 | 214 |
| 36. | Gus Weyhing | 264 | 232 |
| **37.** | **Randy Johnson** | **263** | **136** |
| 38. | Ted Lyons | 260 | 230 |
| 39. | Jack Morris | 254 | 186 |
| | Red Faber | 254 | 213 |
| 41. | Carl Hubbell | 253 | 154 |
| 42. | Bob Gibson | 251 | 174 |
| 43. | Vic Willis | 249 | 205 |
| 44. | Jack Quinn | 247 | 218 |
| 45. | Joe McGinnity | 246 | 142 |
| | Amos Rusie | 246 | 174 |
| 47. | Dennis Martinez | 245 | 193 |
| | Jack Powell | 245 | 254 |
| 49. | Juan Marichal | 243 | 142 |
| 50. | Herb Pennock | 241 | 162 |
| 51. | Frank Tanana | 240 | 236 |
| 52. | Mordecai Brown | 239 | 130 |
| 53. | Clark Griffith | 237 | 146 |
| | Waite Hoyt | 237 | 182 |
| 55. | Whitey Ford | 236 | 106 |
| 56. | Charlie Buffinton | 233 | 152 |
| 57. | Will White | 229 | 166 |
| | Luis Tiant | 229 | 172 |
| | Sam Jones | 229 | 217 |
| 60. | George Mullin | 228 | 196 |
| **61.** | **David Wells** | **227** | **143** |
| **62.** | **Mike Mussina** | **224** | **127** |
| | Catfish Hunter | 224 | 166 |
| | Jim Bunning | 224 | 184 |
| 65. | Hooks Dauss | 223 | 182 |
| | Mel Harder | 223 | 186 |
| | Paul Derringer | 223 | 212 |
| 68. | Jerry Koosman | 222 | 209 |
| 69. | Joe Niekro | 221 | 204 |
| 70. | Jerry Reuss | 220 | 191 |
| 71. | Bob Caruthers | 218 | 99 |
| | Earl Whitehill | 218 | 185 |
| 73. | Fred Fitzsimmons | 217 | 146 |
| | Mickey Lolich | 217 | 191 |
| 75. | Wilbur Cooper | 216 | 178 |
| | Charlie Hough | 216 | 216 |
| 77. | Stan Coveleski | 215 | 142 |
| | Jim Perry | 215 | 174 |
| 79. | Rick Reuschel | 214 | 191 |
| 80. | Chief Bender | 212 | 127 |
| **81.** | **Kevin Brown** | **211** | **144** |
| | Bob Welch | 211 | 146 |
| | Billy Pierce | 211 | 169 |
| | Bobo Newsom | 211 | 222 |
| 85. | Jesse Haines | 210 | 158 |
| 86. | Ed Cicotte | 209 | 148 |
| | Vida Blue | 209 | 161 |
| | Milt Pappas | 209 | 164 |
| | Don Drysdale | 209 | 166 |
| 90. | Carl Mays | 208 | 126 |
| 91. | Bob Lemon | 207 | 128 |
| | Hal Newhouser | 207 | 150 |
| **93.** | **Jamie Moyer** | **205** | **152** |
| 94. | Orel Hershiser | 204 | 150 |
| | Al Orth | 204 | 189 |
| 96. | Jack Stivetts | 203 | 132 |
| | Silver King | 203 | 154 |
| | Lew Burdette | 203 | 144 |
| 99. | Charlie Root | 201 | 160 |
| | Rube Marquard | 201 | 177 |
| 101. | George Uhle | 200 | 166 |
| | Chuck Finley | 200 | 173 |

## 300 VICTORIES, RIGHTHANDER

| | Pitcher | Wins |
|---|---|---|
| 1. | Cy Young | 511 |
| 2. | Walter Johnson | 417 |
| 3. | Grover Alexander | 373 |
| | Christy Mathewson | 373 |
| 5. | Warren Spahn | 363 |
| 6. | Jim Galvin | 361 |
| | Kid Nichols | 361 |
| 8. | Tim Keefe | 342 |
| **9.** | **Roger Clemens** | **341** |
| 10. | Steve Carlton | 329 |
| 11. | John Clarkson | 328 |
| 12. | Eddie Plank | 326 |
| 13. | Nolan Ryan | 324 |
| | Don Sutton | 324 |
| **15.** | **Greg Maddux** | **318** |
| 16. | Phil Niekro | 318 |
| 17. | Gaylord Perry | 314 |
| 18. | Tom Seaver | 311 |
| 19. | Charley Radbourn | 309 |
| 20. | Mickey Welch | 307 |
| 21. | Early Wynn | 300 |

## 300 VICTORIES, LEFTHANDER

| | Pitcher | Wins |
|---|---|---|
| 1. | Warren Spahn | 363 |
| 2. | Steve Carlton | 329 |
| 3. | Eddie Plank | 326 |
| 4. | Lefty Grove | 300 |

## 80 VICTORIES, RELIEVER

| | Pitcher | Wins |
|---|---|---|
| 1. | Hoyt Wilhelm | 124 |
| 2. | Lindy McDaniel | 119 |
| 3. | Rich Gossage | 115 |
| 4. | Rollie Fingers | 107 |
| 5. | Sparky Lyle | 99 |
| 6. | Roy Face | 96 |
| 7. | Gene Garber | 94 |
| | Kent Tekulve | 94 |
| 9. | Mike Marshall | 92 |
| **10.** | **John Franco** | **90** |
| | Don McMahon | 90 |
| 12. | Tug McGraw | 89 |
| 13. | Clay Carroll | 88 |
| 14. | Jesse Orosco | 87 |
| 15. | Bob Stanley | 85 |
| 16. | Bill Campbell | 80 |
| | Gary Lavelle | 80 |

## 5 OPENING DAY VICTORIES

| | Pitcher | Wins |
|---|---|---|
| 1. | Walter Johnson | 9 |
| 2. | Grover Cleveland Alexander | 8 |
| | Jack Morris | 8 |
| 4. | Jimmy Key | 7 |
| | Tom Seaver | 7 |
| **6.** | **Roger Clemens** | **6** |
| | **Randy Johnson** | **6** |
| | **Greg Maddux** | **6** |
| | John Clarkson | 6 |
| | Wes Ferrell | 6 |
| | Dwight Gooden | 6 |
| | Mickey Lolich | 6 |
| | Juan Marichal | 6 |
| | Kid Nichols | 6 |
| 15. | Don Drysdale | 5 |
| | George Mullin | 5 |
| | Jim Palmer | 5 |
| | Robin Roberts | 5 |
| | Nolan Ryan | 5 |
| | Rick Sutcliffe | 5 |
| | Lon Warneke | 5 |
| | Cy Young | 5 |

## 20 VICTORIES, 5 TIMES

| | Pitcher | Seasons |
|---|---|---|
| 1. | Cy Young | 16 |
| 2. | Christy Mathewson | 13 |
| | Warren Spahn | 13 |
| 4. | Walter Johnson | 12 |
| 5. | Kid Nichols | 11 |
| 6. | Pud Galvin | 10 |
| 7. | Grover Alexander | 9 |
| | Hoss Radbourn | 9 |
| | Mickey Welch | 9 |
| 10. | John Clarkson | 8 |
| | Lefty Grove | 8 |
| | Jim McCormick | 8 |
| | Joe McGinnity | 8 |
| | Tony Mullane | 8 |
| | Jim Palmer | 8 |
| | Amos Rusie | 8 |
| 17. | Charlie Buffinton | 7 |
| | Clark Griffith | 7 |
| | Ferguson Jenkins | 7 |
| | Tim Keefe | 7 |
| | Bob Lemon | 7 |
| | Eddie Plank | 7 |
| | Gus Weyhing | 7 |
| | Vic Willis | 7 |
| **25.** | **Roger Clemens** | **6** |
| | Mordecai Brown | 6 |
| | Steve Carlton | 6 |
| | Bob Caruthers | 6 |
| | Bob Feller | 6 |
| | Wes Ferrell | 6 |
| | Juan Marichal | 6 |
| | Robin Roberts | 6 |
| | Jack Stivetts | 6 |
| | Jesse Tannehill | 6 |
| **35.** | **Tom Glavine** | **5** |
| | Tommy Bond | 5 |
| | Jack Chesbro | 5 |
| | Larry Corcoran | 5 |
| | Stan Coveleski | 5 |
| | Bob Gibson | 5 |
| | Burleigh Grimes | 5 |
| | Carl Hubbell | 5 |
| | Catfish Hunter | 5 |
| | Charles King | 5 |
| | Carl Mays | 5 |
| | John McMahon | 5 |
| | George Mullin | 5 |
| | Gaylord Perry | 5 |
| | Deacon Phillippe | 5 |
| | Tom Seaver | 5 |
| | Hippo Vaughn | 5 |
| | Will White | 5 |
| | Jim Whitney | 5 |
| | Early Wynn | 5 |

## 30 VICTORIES, 2 TIMES

| | Pitcher | Seasons |
|---|---|---|
| 1. | Kid Nichols | 7 |
| 2. | John Clarkson | 6 |
| | Tim Keefe | 6 |
| 4. | Tony Mullane | 5 |
| | Cy Young | 5 |
| 6. | Tommy Bond | 4 |
| | Larry Corcoran | 4 |
| | Silver King | 4 |
| | Christy Mathewson | 4 |
| | Jim McCormick | 4 |
| | Mickey Welch | 4 |
| | Will White | 4 |
| 13. | Grover Alexander | 3 |
| | Bob Caruthers | 3 |
| | Pud Galvin | 3 |
| | Bill Hutchison | 3 |
| | Bobby Mathews | 3 |
| | Ed Morris | 3 |
| | Hoss Radbourn | 3 |
| | Amos Rusie | 3 |
| 21. | Dave Foutz | 2 |
| | George Haddock | 2 |
| | Guy Hecker | 2 |
| | Walter Johnson | 2 |
| | Frank Killen | 2 |
| | Joe McGinnity | 2 |
| | John McMahon | 2 |
| | Tom Ramsey | 2 |
| | Jack Stivetts | 2 |
| | Monte Ward | 2 |
| | Gus Weyhing | 2 |
| | Jim Whitney | 2 |

## .600 WINNING PERCENTAGE

**(200 or more wins)**

| | Pitcher | Pct. |
|---|---|---|
| 1. | Whitey Ford | .690 |
| 2. | Bob Caruthers | .688 |
| 3. | Lefty Grove | .680 |
| 4. | Christy Mathewson | .665 |
| **5.** | **Roger Clemens** | **.665** |
| **6.** | **Randy Johnson** | **.659** |
| 7. | John Clarkson | .649 |
| 8. | Mordecai Brown | .648 |
| 9. | Grover Alexander | .642 |
| **10.** | **Mike Mussina** | **.638** |
| 11. | Jim Palmer | .638 |
| 12. | Kid Nichols | .637 |
| 13. | Joe McGinnity | .636 |
| 14. | Juan Marichal | .631 |
| **15.** | **Greg Maddux** | **.627** |
| 16. | Eddie Plank | .627 |
| 17. | Chief Bender | .625 |
| 18. | Clark Griffith | .623 |
| 19. | Carl Mays | .622 |
| 20. | Carl Hubbell | .622 |
| 21. | Bob Feller | .621 |
| 22. | Cy Young | .619 |
| 23. | Bob Lemon | .618 |
| **24.** | **David Wells** | **.614** |
| 25. | Hoss Radbourn | .613 |
| 26. | Charlie Buffinton | .607 |
| 27. | Jack Stivetts | .606 |
| 28. | Tim Keefe | .605 |
| 29. | Tom Seaver | .603 |
| 30. | Stan Coveleski | .602 |

(in strict numerical order rounded to three places)

## 200 LOSSES

| | Pitcher | Losses |
|---|---|---|
| 1. | Cy Young | 316 |
| 2. | Jim Galvin | 308 |
| 3. | Nolan Ryan | 292 |
| 4. | Walter Johnson | 279 |
| 5. | Phil Niekro | 274 |
| 6. | Gaylord Perry | 265 |
| 7. | Don Sutton | 256 |
| 8. | Jack Powell | 254 |
| 9. | Eppa Rixey | 251 |
| 10. | Bert Blyleven | 250 |
| 11. | Robin Roberts | 245 |
| 16. | Warren Spahn | 245 |
| 13. | Steve Carlton | 244 |
| 14. | Early Wynn | 244 |
| 15. | Jim Kaat | 237 |
| 16. | Frank Tanana | 236 |
| 17. | Gus Weyhing | 232 |
| 18. | Tommy John | 231 |
| 19. | Bob Friend | 230 |
| 15. | Ted Lyons | 230 |
| 21. | Ferguson Jenkins | 226 |
| 22. | Red Ruffing | 225 |
| 23. | Tim Keefe | 223 |

| Pitcher | Losses |
|---|---|
| 24. Bobo Newsom | 222 |
| 25. Jack Quinn | 218 |
| 26. Sam Jones | 217 |
| 27. Chick Fraser | 216 |
| 28. Charlie Hough | 216 |
| 29. Jim McCormick | 214 |
| 30. Tony Mullane | 214 |
| 31. Red Faber | 213 |
| 32. Paul Derringer | 212 |
| 33. Burleigh Grimes | 212 |
| 34. Mickey Welch | 212 |
| 35. Jerry Koosman | 209 |
| 36. Grover Alexander | 208 |
| 37. Vic Willis | 207 |
| 38. Kid Nichols | 205 |
| 39. Tom Seaver | 205 |
| 40. Joe Niekro | 204 |
| 41. Jim Whitney | 204 |
| 42. Adonis Terry | 202 |

## 150 SAVES

(Since 1969)

| Pitcher | Saves |
|---|---|
| 1. Lee Smith | 478 |
| **2. Trevor Hoffman** | **436** |
| **3. John Franco** | **424** |
| 4. Dennis Eckersley | 390 |
| **5. Mariano Rivera** | **379** |
| 6. Jeff Reardon | 367 |
| 7. Randy Myers | 347 |
| 8. Rollie Fingers | 341 |
| **9. Roberto Hernandez** | **324** |
| **Troy Percival** | **324** |
| 11. John Wetteland | 330 |
| **12. Jose Mesa** | **319** |
| 13. Rick Aguilera | 318 |
| 14. Robb Nen | 314 |
| 15. Tom Henke | 311 |
| 16. Rich Gossage | 310 |
| 17. Jeff Montgomery | 304 |
| 18. Doug Jones | 303 |
| 19. Bruce Sutter | 300 |
| 20. Rod Beck | 286 |
| **21. Billy Wagner** | **284** |
| **22. Armando Benitez** | **263** |
| 23. Todd Worrell | 256 |
| 24. Dave Righetti | 252 |
| 25. Dan Quisenberry | 244 |
| **26. Ugueth Urbina** | **237** |
| **27. Todd Jones** | **226** |
| 28. Sparky Lyle | 222 |
| 29. Gene Garber | 218 |
| 30. Gregg Olson | 217 |
| **31. Jason Isringhausen** | **216** |
| Dave Smith | 216 |
| **33. Bob Wickman** | **214** |
| 34. Jeff Shaw | 203 |
| 35. Bobby Thigpen | 201 |
| 36. Mike Henneman | 193 |
| 37. Mitch Williams | 192 |
| **38. Keith Foulke** | **190** |
| 39. Jeff Russell | 186 |
| 40. Steve Bedrosian | 184 |
| Kent Tekulve | 184 |
| **42. Danny Graves** | **182** |
| 43. Tug McGraw | 179 |
| 44. Mike G. Marshall | 178 |
| 45. Bryan Harvey | 177 |
| 46. Jeff Brantley | 172 |
| **47. Eddie Guardado** | **170** |
| 48. Bill Koch | 163 |
| **49. Eric Gagne** | **160** |
| 50. Roger McDowell | 159 |
| 51. Dan Plesac | 158 |
| 52. Jay Howell | 155 |
| **53. John Smoltz** | **154** |
| 54. Greg Minton | 150 |

## 1,800 RUNS ALLOWED

| Pitcher | Runs |
|---|---|
| 1. Pud Galvin | 3,315 |
| 2. Cy Young | 3,167 |
| 3. Gus Weyhing | 2,796 |
| 4. Mickey Welch | 2,556 |
| 5. Tony Mullane | 2,523 |
| 6. Kid Nichols | 2,480 |
| 7. Tim Keefe | 2,471 |
| 8. John Clarkson | 2,384 |
| 9. Phil Niekro | 2,337 |
| 10. Adonis Terry | 2,303 |
| 11. Hoss Radbourn | 2,273 |
| 12. Nolan Ryan | 2,178 |
| 13. Steve Carlton | 2,130 |
| 14. Gaylord Perry | 2,128 |
| 15. Red Ruffing | 2,115 |
| 16. Don Sutton | 2,104 |
| 17. Jim McCormick | 2,095 |
| 18. Amos Rusie | 2,068 |
| 19. Ted Lyons | 2,056 |
| 20. Burleigh Grimes | 2,050 |
| 21. Jim Kaat | 2,038 |
| 22. Early Wynn | 2,037 |
| 23. Bert Blyleven | 2,029 |
| 24. Jim Whitney | 2,026 |
| 25. Earl Whitehill | 2,018 |
| 26. Tommy John | 2,017 |
| 27. Warren Spahn | 2,016 |
| 28. Sam Jones | 2,008 |
| 29. Chick Fraser | 1,995 |
| 30. Jack Powell | 1,991 |
| 31. Eppa Rixey | 1,986 |
| 32. Robin Roberts | 1,962 |
| 33. Bert Cunningham | 1,942 |
| 34. Pink Hawley | 1,927 |
| 35. Bill Hutchinson | 1,913 |
| 36. Frank Tanana | 1,910 |
| 37. Bobo Newsom | 1,908 |
| 38. Walter Johnson | 1,902 |
| 39. Red Ehret | 1,881 |
| 40. Brickyard Kennedy | 1,863 |
| 41. Ferguson Jenkins | 1,853 |
| 42. Grover Alexander | 1,852 |
| Clark Griffith | 1,852 |
| 44. Ted Breitenstein | 1,848 |
| 45. Will White | 1,844 |
| 46. Jack Quinn | 1,837 |
| 47. Jack Stivetts | 1,836 |
| 48. Dennis Martinez | 1,835 |
| 49. Charlie Buffinton | 1,824 |
| 50. Mark Baldwin | 1,816 |
| 51. Jack Morris | 1,815 |
| 52. Red Faber | 1,813 |
| 53. Charlie Hough | 1,807 |
| 54. Silver King | 1,803 |

## 3.50 OR UNDER ERA

(Pitchers with 3,000 or more IP)

| Pitcher | IP | ERA |
|---|---|---|
| 1. Mordecai Brown | 3,172.1 | 2.06 |
| 2. Christy Mathewson | 4,788.2 | 2.13 |
| 3. Walter Johnson | 5,914.0 | 2.17 |
| 4. Will White | 3,542.2 | 2.28 |
| 5. Eddie Plank | 4,495.2 | 2.35 |
| 6. Eddie Cicotte | 3,226.0 | 2.38 |
| 7. Doc White | 3,041.0 | 2.39 |
| 8. Jim McCormick | 4,275.2 | 2.43 |
| 9. Chief Bender | 3,017.0 | 2.46 |
| 10. Grover Alexander | 5,190.0 | 2.56 |
| 11. Tim Keefe | 5,049.2 | 2.63 |
| 12. Cy Young | 7,356.0 | 2.63 |
| 13. Vic Willis | 3,996.0 | 2.63 |
| 14. Red Ames | 3,198.0 | 2.63 |
| 15. Joe McGinnity | 3,441.1 | 2.66 |
| 16. Hoss Radbourn | 4,527.1 | 2.68 |
| 17. Mickey Welch | 4,802.0 | 2.71 |
| 18. Whitey Ford | 3,171.1 | 2.75 |
| 19. John Clarkson | 4,536.1 | 2.81 |
| 20. George Mullin | 3,686.2 | 2.82 |
| 21. Jim Palmer | 3,948.0 | 2.86 |
| 22. Tom Seaver | 4,782.2 | 2.86 |
| 23. Pud Galvin | 5,941.1 | 2.87 |
| 24. Juan Marichal | 3,507.1 | 2.89 |
| 25. Stan Coveleski | 3,082.0 | 2.89 |
| 26. Wilbur Cooper | 3,480.0 | 2.89 |
| 27. Bob Gibson | 3,884.1 | 2.91 |
| 28. Carl Mays | 3,021.1 | 2.92 |
| 29. Don Drysdale | 3,432.0 | 2.95 |
| 30. Kid Nichols | 5,067.1 | 2.96 |
| 31. Charlie Buffinton | 3,404.0 | 2.96 |
| 32. Jim Whitney | 3,496.1 | 2.97 |
| 33. Jack Powell | 4,389.0 | 2.97 |
| 34. Carl Hubbell | 3,590.1 | 2.98 |
| 35. Bill Dinneen | 3,074.2 | 3.01 |
| **36. Greg Maddux** | **4,406.1** | **3.01** |
| 37. Tony Mullane | 4,531.1 | 3.05 |
| 38. Lefty Grove | 3,940.2 | 3.06 |
| 39. Amos Rusie | 3,778.2 | 3.07 |
| 40. Rube Marquard | 3,306.2 | 3.08 |
| 41. Warren Spahn | 5,243.2 | 3.09 |
| 42. Gaylord Perry | 5,350.1 | 3.11 |
| **43. Randy Johnson** | **3,593.2** | **3.11** |
| **44. Roger Clemens** | **4,704.1** | **3.12** |
| 45. Eppa Rixey | 4,494.2 | 3.15 |
| 46. Red Faber | 4,086.2 | 3.15 |
| 47. Silver King | 3,180.2 | 3.18 |
| 48. Nolan Ryan | 5,386.0 | 3.19 |
| 49. Steve Carlton | 5,217.1 | 3.22 |
| 50. Dolf Luque | 3,220.1 | 3.24 |
| 51. Dutch Leonard | 3,218.1 | 3.25 |
| 52. Bob Feller | 3,827.0 | 3.25 |
| 53. Catfish Hunter | 3,449.1 | 3.26 |
| 54. Vida Blue | 3,343.1 | 3.26 |
| 55. Don Sutton | 5,282.1 | 3.26 |
| 56. Billy Pierce | 3,306.2 | 3.27 |
| 57. Jim Bunning | 3,760.1 | 3.27 |
| **58. Kevin Brown** | **3,256.1** | **3.28** |
| 59. Jack Quinn | 3,920.1 | 3.29 |
| 60. Claude Osteen | 3,460.1 | 3.30 |
| 61. Bucky Walters | 3,104.2 | 3.30 |
| 62. Luis Tiant | 3,486.1 | 3.30 |
| 63. Hooks Dauss | 3,390.2 | 3.30 |
| 64. Clark Griffith | 3,385.2 | 3.31 |
| 65. Bert Blyleven | 4,970.0 | 3.31 |
| 66. Ferguson Jenkins | 4,500.2 | 3.34 |
| 67. Tommy John | 4,710.1 | 3.34 |
| 68. Phil Niekro | 5,404.1 | 3.35 |
| 69. Jerry Koosman | 3,839.1 | 3.36 |
| 70. Al Orth | 3,354.2 | 3.37 |
| 71. Rick Reuschel | 3,548.1 | 3.37 |
| 72. Lee Meadows | 3,160.2 | 3.37 |
| 73. Milt Pappas | 3,186.0 | 3.40 |
| 74. Larry Jackson | 3,262.0 | 3.40 |
| 75. Robin Roberts | 4,688.2 | 3.41 |
| 76. Mickey Lolich | 3,638.1 | 3.44 |
| 77. Larry French | 3,152.0 | 3.44 |
| **78. Tom Glavine** | **3,951.2** | **3.44** |
| 79. Jim Perry | 3,285.2 | 3.45 |
| 80. Jim Kaat | 4,530.1 | 3.45 |
| 81. Paul Derringer | 3,645.0 | 3.46 |
| 82. Bob Welch | 3,092.0 | 3.47 |
| 83. Orel Hershiser | 3,130.1 | 3.48 |
| 84. Dennis Eckersley | 3,285.2 | 3.50 |

(in strict numerical order rounded to three places)

## 40 SHUTOUTS

| Pitcher | No. |
|---|---|
| 1. Walter Johnson | 110 |
| 2. Grover Alexander | 90 |
| 3. Christy Mathewson | 79 |
| 4. Cy Young | 76 |
| 5. Eddie Plank | 69 |
| 6. Warren Spahn | 63 |
| 7. Nolan Ryan | 61 |
| Tom Seaver | 61 |
| 9. Bert Blyleven | 60 |
| 10. Don Sutton | 58 |
| 11. Pud Galvin | 57 |
| Ed Walsh | 57 |
| 13. Bob Gibson | 56 |
| 14. Mordecai Brown | 55 |
| Steve Carlton | 55 |
| 16. Jim Palmer | 53 |
| Gaylord Perry | 53 |
| 18. Juan Marichal | 52 |
| 19. Rube Waddell | 50 |
| Vic Willis | 50 |
| 21. Don Drysdale | 49 |
| Ferguson Jenkins | 49 |
| Luis Tiant | 49 |
| Early Wynn | 49 |
| 25. Kid Nichols | 48 |
| **26. Roger Clemens** | **46** |
| Tommy John | 46 |
| Jack Powell | 46 |
| 29. Whitey Ford | 45 |
| Addie Joss | 45 |
| Phil Niekro | 45 |
| Robin Roberts | 45 |
| Red Ruffing | 45 |
| Doc White | 45 |
| 35. Babe Adams | 44 |
| Bob Feller | 44 |
| 37. Milt Pappas | 43 |
| 38. Catfish Hunter | 42 |
| Bucky Walters | 42 |
| 40. Mickey Lolich | 41 |
| Hippo Vaughn | 41 |
| Mickey Welch | 41 |
| 43. Chief Bender | 40 |
| Jim Bunning | 40 |
| Larry French | 40 |
| Sandy Koufax | 40 |
| Claude Osteen | 40 |
| Ed Reulbach | 40 |
| Mel Stottlemyre | 40 |

## TEN 1-0 VICTORIES

(complete games)

| Pitcher | Wins |
|---|---|
| 1. Walter Johnson | 38 |
| 2. Grover Alexander | 17 |
| 3. Bert Blyleven | 15 |
| 4. Christy Mathewson | 14 |
| 5. Dean Chance | 13 |
| Ed Au. Walsh | 13 |
| Doc White | 13 |
| Cy Young | 13 |
| 9. Steve Carlton | 12 |
| Stan Coveleski | 12 |
| Gaylord Perry | 12 |
| Eddie Plank | 12 |
| **13. Greg Maddux** | **11** |
| Mordecai Brown | 11 |
| Ferguson Jenkins | 11 |
| Kid Nichols | 11 |
| Nap Rucker | 11 |
| Nolan Ryan | 11 |
| 18. Joe Bush | 10 |
| Paul Derringer | 10 |
| Bill Doak | 10 |
| Addie Joss | 10 |
| Sandy Koufax | 10 |
| Dick Rudolph | 10 |
| Warren Spahn | 10 |
| Virgil Trucks | 10 |
| Hippo Vaughn | 10 |

## THREE NO-HIT GAMES

| Pitcher | Games |
|---|---|
| 1. Nolan Ryan | 7 |
| 2. Sandy Koufax | 4 |
| 3. Larry Corcoran | 3 |
| Bob Feller | 3 |
| Cy Young | 3 |

## 4,000 HITS ALLOWED

| Pitcher | Hits |
|---|---|
| 1. Cy Young | 7,092 |
| 2. Pud Galvin | 6,352 |
| 3. Phil Niekro | 5,044 |
| 4. Gaylord Perry | 4,938 |
| 5. Kid Nichols | 4,929 |
| 6. Walter Johnson | 4,913 |
| 7. Grover Alexander | 4,868 |
| 8. Warren Spahn | 4,830 |
| 9. Tommy John | 4,783 |
| 10. Don Sutton | 4,692 |
| 11. Steve Carlton | 4,672 |
| 12. Eppa Rixey | 4,633 |
| 13. Bert Blyleven | 4,632 |
| 14. Jim Kaat | 4,620 |
| 15. Mickey Welch | 4,588 |
| 16. Robin Roberts | 4,582 |
| 17. Gus Weyhing | 4,576 |
| 18. Ted Lyons | 4,489 |
| 19. Tim Keefe | 4,438 |
| 20. Burleigh Grimes | 4,412 |
| 21. Hoss Radbourn | 4,328 |
| 22. Jack Powell | 4,319 |
| 23. John Clarkson | 4,295 |
| 24. Early Wynn | 4,291 |
| 25. Red Ruffing | 4,284 |
| 26. Jack Quinn | 4,238 |
| 27. Christy Mathewson | 4,219 |
| 28. Tony Mullane | 4,195 |
| 29. Ferguson Jenkins | 4,142 |
| 30. Red Faber | 4,106 |
| 31. Jim McCormick | 4,092 |
| 32. Sam Jones | 4,084 |
| **33. Greg Maddux** | **4,082** |
| 33. Frank Tanana | 4,063 |
| 34. Waite Hoyt | 4,037 |

## 7 GRAND SLAMS ALLOWED

| Pitcher | GS |
|---|---|
| 1. Mike Jackson | 10 |
| Nolan Ryan | 10 |
| 3. Ned Garver | 9 |
| Milt Pappas | 9 |
| Jerry Reuss | 9 |
| Lee Smith | 9 |
| Frank Viola | 9 |
| **8. Tom Gordon** | **8** |
| **Al Leiter** | **8** |
| **Kenny Rogers** | **8** |
| Willie Blair | 8 |
| Bert Blyleven | 8 |
| Brian Boehringer | 8 |
| Jim Brewer | 8 |
| Roy Face | 8 |
| Bob Feller | 8 |
| Alex Fernandez | 8 |
| Jimmy Haynes | 8 |
| Mike Jackson | 8 |
| Jim Kaat. | 8 |
| Johnny Klippstein | 8 |
| Lindy McDaniel | 8 |
| Tug McGraw | 8 |
| Jesse Orosco | 8 |
| Gaylord Perry | 8 |
| Frank Tanana | 8 |
| Early Wynn | 8 |

## 1,200 BASES ON BALLS

| Pitcher | BBs |
|---|---|
| 1. Nolan Ryan | 2,795 |
| 2. Steve Carlton | 1,833 |
| 3. Phil Niekro | 1,809 |
| 4. Early Wynn | 1,775 |
| 5. Bob Feller | 1,764 |
| 6. Bobo Newsom | 1,732 |
| 7. Amos Rusie | 1,707 |
| 8. Charlie Hough | 1,665 |
| 9. Gus Weyhing | 1,570 |
| 10. Red Ruffing | 1,541 |
| **11. Roger Clemens** | **1,520** |

| Pitcher | BBs |
|---|---|
| 12. Bump Hadley | 1,442 |
| 13. Warren Spahn | 1,434 |
| 14. Earl Whitehill | 1,431 |
| 15. Tony Mullane | 1,408 |
| 16. Sam Jones | 1,396 |
| 17. Jack Morris | 1,390 |
| Tom Seaver | 1,390 |
| 19. Gaylord Perry | 1,379 |
| 20. Bobby Witt | 1,375 |
| 21. Mike Torrez | 1,371 |
| 22. Walter Johnson | 1,363 |
| **23. Randy Johnson** | **1,349** |
| 24. Don Sutton | 1,343 |
| 25. Chick Fraser | 1,338 |
| **26. Tom Glavine** | **1,337** |
| 27. Bob Gibson | 1,336 |
| 28. Chuck Finley | 1,332 |
| 29. Bert Blyleven | 1,322 |
| 30. Sam McDowell | 1,312 |
| 31. Jim Palmer | 1,311 |
| 32. Mark Baldwin | 1,307 |
| 33. Adonis Terry | 1,298 |
| 34. Mickey Welch | 1,297 |
| 35. Burleigh Grimes | 1,295 |
| 36. Mark Langston | 1,289 |
| 37. Kid Nichols | 1,272 |
| 38. Joe Bush | 1,263 |
| 39. Joe Niekro | 1,262 |
| 40. Allie Reynolds | 1,261 |
| 41. Tommy John | 1,259 |
| 42. Frank Tanana | 1,255 |
| 43. Bob Lemon | 1,251 |
| 44. Hal Newhouser | 1,249 |
| 45. George Mullin | 1,238 |
| 46. Tim Keefe | 1,233 |
| 47. Cy Young | 1,217 |
| 48. Red Faber | 1,213 |
| 49. Vic Willis | 1,212 |
| 50. Ted Breitenstein | 1,207 |
| 51. Brickyard Kennedy | 1,203 |

### 2,000 STRIKEOUTS

| Pitcher | Ks |
|---|---|
| 1. Nolan Ryan | 5,714 |
| **2. Roger Clemens** | **4,502** |
| **3. Randy Johnson** | **4,372** |
| 4. Steve Carlton | 4,136 |
| 5. Bert Blyleven | 3,701 |
| 6. Tom Seaver | 3,640 |
| 7. Don Sutton | 3,574 |
| 8. Gaylord Perry | 3,534 |
| 9. Walter Johnson | 3,509 |
| 10. Phil Niekro | 3,342 |
| 11. Ferguson Jenkins | 3,192 |
| 12. Bob Gibson | 3,117 |
| **13. Greg Maddux** | **3,052** |
| **14. Pedro Martinez** | **2,861** |
| 15. Jim Bunning | 2,855 |
| **16. Curt Schilling** | **2,832** |
| Mickey Lolich | 2,832 |
| 18. Cy Young | 2,803 |
| 19. Frank Tanana | 2,773 |
| 20. David Cone | 2,668 |
| 21. Chuck Finley | 2,610 |
| 22. Warren Spahn | 2,583 |
| 23. Bob Feller | 2,581 |
| **24. John Smoltz** | **2,567** |
| 25. Tim Keefe | 2,564 |
| 26. Jerry Koosman | 2,556 |
| 27. Christy Mathewson | 2,507 |
| 28. Don Drysdale | 2,486 |
| 29. Jack Morris | 2,478 |
| 30. Mark Langston | 2,464 |
| 31. Jim Kaat | 2,461 |
| 32. Sam McDowell | 2,453 |
| 33. Luis Tiant | 2,416 |
| 34. Dennis Eckersley | 2,401 |
| **35. Mike Mussina** | **2,400** |
| **36. Kevin Brown** | **2,397** |
| 37. Sandy Koufax | 2,396 |
| 38. Charlie Hough | 2,362 |
| 39. Robin Roberts | 2,357 |
| **40. Tom Glavine** | **2,350** |
| 41. Early Wynn | 2,334 |
| 42. Rube Waddell | 2,316 |
| 43. Juan Marichal | 2,303 |
| 44. Dwight Gooden | 2,293 |
| 45. Lefty Grove | 2,266 |
| 46. Eddie Plank | 2,246 |
| 47. Tommy John | 2,245 |
| 48. Jim Palmer | 2,212 |
| 49. Grover Alexander | 2,198 |
| 50. Vida Blue | 2,175 |
| 51. Camilo Pascual | 2,167 |
| 52. Dennis Martinez | 2,149 |
| 53. Bobo Newsom | 2,082 |
| **54. David Wells** | **2,081** |
| 55. Fernando Valenzuela | 2,074 |
| 56. Dazzy Vance | 2,045 |
| 57. Rick Reuschel | 2,015 |
| 58. Orel Hershiser | 2,014 |
| 59. Catfish Hunter | 2,012 |
| 60. Andy Benes | 2,000 |

### 150 HIT BATSMEN

| Pitcher | HB |
|---|---|
| 1. Gus Weyhing | 278 |
| 2. Chick Fraser | 219 |
| 3. Pink Hawley | 210 |
| 4. Walter Johnson | 205 |
| 5. Eddie Plank | 190 |
| 6. Tony Mullane | 185 |
| 7. Joe McGinnity | 179 |
| 8. Charlie Hough | 174 |
| 9. Clark Griffith | 171 |
| 10. Cy Young | 163 |
| 11. Jim Bunning | 160 |
| 12. Nolan Ryan | 158 |
| 13. Randy Johnson | 156 |
| 12. Vic Willis | 156 |
| 15. Bert Blyleven | 155 |
| 16. Don Drysdale | 154 |
| **17. Roger Clemens** | **150** |
| 18. Bert Cunningham | 148 |
| 19. Adonis Terry | 148 |

### 200 WILD PITCHES

| Pitcher | WP |
|---|---|
| 1. Tony Mullane | 343 |
| 2. Nolan Ryan | 277 |
| 3. Mickey Welch | 274 |
| 4. Tim Keefe | 240 |
| Gus Weyhing | 240 |
| 6. Phil Niekro | 226 |
| 7. Mark Baldwin | 221 |
| Will White | 221 |
| 9. Jim Galvin | 220 |
| 10. Charley Radbourn | 214 |
| Jim Whitney | 214 |
| 12. Jack Morris | 206 |
| Adonis Terry | 206 |
| 14. Matt Kilroy | 203 |

## MANAGERIAL

### 20 SEASONS AS MANAGER

| Manager | Seasons |
|---|---|
| 1. Connie Mack | 53 |
| 2. John McGraw | 33 |
| 3. Bucky Harris | 29 |
| **4. Tony La Russa** | **27** |
| 5. Sparky Anderson | 26 |
| Gene Mauch | 26 |
| 7. Bill McKechnie | 25 |
| Casey Stengel | 25 |
| **9. Bobby Cox** | **24** |
| **Joe Torre** | **24** |
| 11. Leo Durocher | 24 |
| Joe McCarthy | 24 |
| 13. Walter Alston | 23 |
| 14. Jimmy Dykes | 21 |
| Tom Lasorda | 21 |
| Dick Williams | 21 |
| 17. Cap Anson | 20 |
| Clark Griffith | 20 |
| Ralph Houk | 20 |

### 1,500 WINS AS MANAGER

| Manager | Wins |
|---|---|
| 1. Connie Mack | 3,731 |
| 2. John McGraw | 2,763 |
| **3. Tony La Russa** | **2,214** |
| 4. Sparky Anderson | 2,194 |
| 5. Bucky Harris | 2,157 |
| 6. Joe McCarthy | 2,125 |
| **7. Bobby Cox** | **2,092** |
| 8. Walter Alston | 2,040 |
| 9. Leo Durocher | 2,008 |
| 10. Casey Stengel | 1,905 |
| 11. Gene Mauch | 1,902 |
| 12. Bill McKechnie | 1,896 |
| **13. Joe Torre** | **1,855** |
| 14. Ralph Houk | 1,619 |
| 15. Fred Clarke | 1,602 |
| 16. Tom Lasorda | 1,599 |
| 17. Dick Williams | 1,571 |
| **18. Lou Piniella** | **1,519** |
| 19. Clark Griffith | 1,491 |
| 20. Earl Weaver | 1,480 |

### 4 PENNANTS WON AS MANAGER

| Manager | Pennants |
|---|---|
| 1. John McGraw | 10 |
| Casey Stengel | 10 |
| 3. Connie Mack | 9 |
| Joe McCarthy | 9 |
| 5. Walter Alston | 7 |
| 6. Miller Huggins | 6 |
| **7. Bobby Cox** | **5** |
| **Joe Torre** | **5** |
| Sparky Anderson | 5 |
| Cap Anson | 5 |
| Ned Hanlon | 5 |
| Frank Selee | 5 |
| **13. Tony La Russa** | **4** |
| 14. Frank Chance | 4 |
| Fred Clarke | 4 |
| Charlie Comiskey | 4 |
| Tom Lasorda | 4 |
| Bill McKechnie | 4 |
| Billy Southworth | 4 |
| Earl Weaver | 4 |
| Dick Williams | 4 |

# GENERAL REFERENCE

## BATTING

### TRIPLE CROWN HITTERS

#### AMERICAN LEAGUE

| Year | Player, Club | Avg. | HR | RBI |
|---|---|---|---|---|
| 1901 | Napoleon Lajoie, Philadelphia | .426 | 14 | 125 |
| 1909 | Ty Cobb, Detroit | .377 | 9 | 107 |
| 1933 | Jimmie Foxx, Philadelphia | .356 | 48 | 163 |
| 1934 | Lou Gehrig, New York | .363 | 49 | 165 |
| 1942 | Ted Williams, Boston | .356 | 36 | 137 |
| 1947 | Ted Williams, Boston | .343 | 32 | 114 |
| 1956 | Mickey Mantle, New York | .353 | 52 | 130 |
| 1966 | Frank Robinson, Baltimore | .316 | 49 | 122 |
| 1967 | Carl Yastrzemski, Boston | .326 | 44 | 121 |

**Total number of occurrences: 9**

#### NATIONAL LEAGUE

| Year | Player, Club | Avg. | HR | RBI |
|---|---|---|---|---|
| 1922 | Rogers Hornsby, St. Louis | .401 | 42 | 152 |
| 1925 | Rogers Hornsby, St. Louis | .403 | 39 | 143 |
| 1933 | Chuck Klein, Philadelphia | .368 | 28 | 120 |
| 1937 | Joe Medwick, St. Louis | .374 | 31 | 154 |

**Total number of occurrences: 4**

### .400 HITTERS

| Year | Player, Club | Avg. |
|---|---|---|
| 1894 | Hugh Duffy, Boston NL | .440 |
| 1887 | Tip O'Neill, St. Louis AA. | .435 |
| 1876 | Ross Barnes, Chicago NL | .429 |
| 1901 | Nap Lajoie, Philadelphia AL | .426 |
| 1897 | Willie Keeler, Baltimore NL | .424 |
| 1924 | Rogers Hornsby, St. Louis NL | .424 |
| 1911 | Ty Cobb, Detroit AL | .420 |
| 1922 | George Sisler, St. Louis AL | .420 |
| 1894 | Sam Thompson, Philadelphia NL | .415 |
| 1884 | Fred Dunlap, St. Louis UA. | .412 |
| 1896 | Jesse Burkett, Cleveland NL | .410 |
| 1899 | Ed Delahanty, Philadelphia NL | .410 |
| 1912 | Ty Cobb, Detroit AL | .409 |
| 1911 | Joe Jackson, Cleveland AL | .408 |
| 1920 | George Sisler, St. Louis AL | .407 |
| 1941 | Ted Williams, Boston AL | .406 |
| 1895 | Jesse Burkett, Cleveland NL | .405 |
| 1894 | Ed Delahanty, Philadelphia NL | .404 |
| 1895 | Ed Delahanty, Philadelphia NL | .404 |
| 1894 | Billy Hamilton, Philadelphia NL | .403 |
| 1923 | Harry Heilmann, Detroit AL | .403 |
| 1925 | Rogers Hornsby, St. Louis NL | .403 |
| 1887 | Pete Browning, Louisville AA | .402 |
| 1896 | Hughie Jennings, Baltimore NL | .401 |
| 1922 | Ty Cobb, Detroit AL | .401 |
| 1922 | Rogers Hornsby, St. Louis NL | .401 |
| 1930 | Bill Terry, New York NL | .401 |

**Total number of occurrences: 27**

### 200 HITS BY ROOKIES IN SEASON

#### AMERICAN LEAGUE

| Year | Player, Club | G | H |
|---|---|---|---|
| 2001 | Ichiro Suzuki, Seattle | 157 | 242 |
| 1964 | Tony Oliva, Minnesota | 161 | 217 |

| | | | |
|---|---|---|---|
| 1929 | Dale Alexander, Detroit | 155 | 215 |
| 1997 | Nomar Garciaparra, Boston | 153 | 209 |
| 1953 | Harvey Kuenn, Detroit | 155 | 209 |
| 1987 | Kevin Seitzer, Kansas City | 161 | 207 |
| 1936 | Joe DiMaggio, New York | 138 | 206 |
| 1934 | Hal Trosky, Cleveland | 154 | 206 |
| 1942 | Johnny Pesky, Boston | 147 | 205 |
| 1929 | Roy Johnson, Detroit | 148 | 201 |
| 1943 | Dick Wakefield, Detroit | 155 | 200 |

### NATIONAL LEAGUE

| Year | Player, Club | G | H |
|---|---|---|---|
| 1927 | Lloyd Waner, Pittsburgh | 150 | 223 |
| 1899 | Jimmy Williams, Pittsburgh | 153 | 219 |
| 1929 | Johnny Frederick, Brooklyn | 148 | 206 |
| 1964 | Dick Allen, Philadelphia | 162 | 201 |

## 30-GAME BATTING STREAKS

| Year | Player, Club | G |
|---|---|---|
| 1941 | Joe DiMaggio, New York AL | 56 |
| 1897 | Willie Keeler, Baltimore NL* | 44 |
| 1978 | Pete Rose, Cincinnati NL | 44 |
| 1894 | Bill Dahlen, Chicago NL | 42 |
| 1922 | George Sisler, St. Louis AL | 41 |
| 1911 | Ty Cobb, Detroit AL | 40 |
| 1987 | Paul Molitor, Milwaukee AL | 39 |
| 1945 | Tommy Holmes, Boston NL | 37 |
| 2005 | Jimmy Rollins, Philadelphia NL | 36 |
| 1895 | Fred Clarke, Louisville NL | 35 |
| 1917 | Ty Cobb, Detroit AL | 35 |
| 2002 | Luis Castillo, Florida NL | 35 |
| 1925 | George Sisler, St. Louis AL* | 34 |
| 1938 | George McQuinn, St. Louis AL | 34 |
| 1949 | Dom DiMaggio, Boston AL | 34 |
| 1987 | Benito Santiago, San Diego NL | 34 |
| 1893 | George Davis, New York NL | 33 |
| 1907 | Hal Chase, New York AL | 33 |
| 1922 | Rogers Hornsby, St. Louis NL | 33 |
| 1933 | Heinie Manush, Washington AL | 33 |
| 1899 | Ed Delahanty, Philadelphia NL | 31 |
| 1906 | Nap Lajoie, Cleveland AL | 31 |
| 1924 | Sam Rice, Washington AL | 31 |
| 1969 | Willie Davis, Los Angeles NL | 31 |
| 1970 | Rico Carty, Atlanta NL | 31 |
| 1980 | Ken Landreaux, Minnesota AL | 31 |
| 1999 | Vladimir Guerrero, Montreal NL | 31 |
| 1876 | Cal McVey, Chicago NL | 30 |
| 1898 | Elmer E. Smith, Cincinnati NL | 30 |
| 1912 | Tris Speaker, Boston AL | 30 |
| 1934 | Goose Goslin, Detroit AL | 30 |
| 1950 | Stan Musial, St. Louis NL | 30 |
| 1976 | Ron LeFlore, Detroit AL* | 30 |
| 1980 | George Brett, Kansas City AL | 30 |
| 1989 | Jerome Walton, Chicago NL | 30 |
| 1997 | Sandy Alomar Jr., Cleveland AL | 30 |
| 1997 | Nomar Garciaparra, Boston AL | 30 |
| 1998 | Eric Davis, Baltimore AL | 30 |
| 1999 | Luis Gonzalez, Arizona NL | 30 |
| 2003 | Albert Pujols, St. Louis NL | 30 |

*From start of season.

**Total number of occurrences: 39**

## 40 HOME RUNS IN SEASON

### AMERICAN LEAGUE

| Year | Player, Club | HR |
|---|---|---|
| 1961 | Roger Maris, New York | 61 |
| 1927 | Babe Ruth, New York | 60 |
| 1921 | Babe Ruth, New York | 59 |
| 1932 | Jimmie Foxx, Philadelphia | 58 |
| 1938 | Hank Greenberg, Detroit | 58 |
| 2002 | Alex Rodriguez, Texas | 57 |
| 1997 | Ken Griffey Jr., Seattle | 56 |
| 1998 | Ken Griffey Jr., Seattle | 56 |
| 1920 | Babe Ruth, New York | 54 |
| 1928 | Babe Ruth, New York | 54 |
| 1961 | Mickey Mantle, New York | 54 |
| 1956 | Mickey Mantle, New York | 52 |
| 1996 | Mark McGwire, Oakland | 52 |
| 2001 | Alex Rodriguez, Texas | 52 |
| 2002 | Jim Thome, Cleveland | 52 |
| 1990 | Cecil Fielder, Detroit | 51 |
| 1938 | Jimmie Foxx, Boston | 50 |
| 1995 | Albert Belle, Cleveland | 50 |
| 1996 | Brady Anderson, Baltimore | 50 |
| 1930 | Babe Ruth, New York | 49 |
| 1934 | Lou Gehrig, New York | 49 |
| 1936 | Lou Gehrig, New York | 49 |
| 1964 | Harmon Killebrew, Minnesota | 49 |
| 1966 | Frank Robinson, Baltimore | 49 |
| 1969 | Harmon Killebrew, Minnesota | 49 |
| 1987 | Mark McGwire, Oakland | 49 |
| 1996 | Ken Griffey Jr., Seattle | 49 |
| 1998 | Albert Belle, Chicago | 49 |
| 2001 | Jim Thome, Cleveland | 49 |
| 1933 | Jimmie Foxx, Philadelphia | 48 |
| 1962 | Harmon Killebrew, Minnesota | 48 |
| 1969 | Frank Howard, Washington | 48 |
| 1996 | Albert Belle, Cleveland | 48 |
| 1999 | Ken Griffey Jr., Seattle | 48 |
| 2005 | Alex Rodriguez, New York | 48 |
| 1926 | Babe Ruth, New York | 47 |
| 1927 | Lou Gehrig, New York | 47 |
| 1969 | Reggie Jackson, Oakland | 47 |
| 1987 | George Bell, Toronto | 47 |
| 1996 | Juan Gonzalez, Texas | 47 |
| 1999 | Rafael Palmeiro, Texas | 47 |
| 2000 | Troy Glaus, Anaheim | 47 |
| 2001 | Rafael Palmeiro, Texas | 47 |
| 2003 | Alex Rodriguez, Texas | 47 |
| 2005 | David Ortiz, Boston | 47 |
| 1924 | Babe Ruth, New York | 46 |
| 1929 | Babe Ruth, New York | 46 |
| 1931 | Lou Gehrig, New York | 46 |
| 1931 | Babe Ruth, New York | 46 |
| 1937 | Joe DiMaggio, New York | 46 |
| 1961 | Jim Gentile, Baltimore | 46 |
| 1961 | Harmon Killebrew, Minnesota | 46 |
| 1978 | Jim Rice, Boston | 46 |
| 1993 | Juan Gonzalez, Texas | 46 |
| 1998 | Jose Canseco, Toronto | 46 |
| 1961 | Rocky Colavito, Detroit | 45 |
| 1963 | Harmon Killebrew, Minnesota | 45 |
| 1979 | Gorman Thomas, Milwaukee | 45 |
| 1993 | Ken Griffey Jr., Seattle | 45 |
| 1998 | Juan Gonzalez, Texas | 45 |
| 1998 | Manny Ramirez, Cleveland | 45 |
| 2005 | Manny Ramirez, Boston | 45 |
| 1934 | Jimmie Foxx, Philadelphia | 44 |
| 1946 | Hank Greenberg, Detroit | 44 |
| 1967 | Harmon Killebrew, Minnesota | 44 |
| 1967 | Carl Yastrzemski, Boston | 44 |
| 1968 | Frank Howard, Washington | 44 |
| 1970 | Frank Howard, Washington | 44 |
| 1991 | Jose Canseco, Oakland | 44 |
| 1991 | Cecil Fielder, Detroit | 44 |
| 1996 | Jay Buhner, Seattle | 44 |
| 1996 | Mo Vaughn, Boston | 44 |
| 1997 | Tino Martinez, New York | 44 |
| 1999 | Carlos Delgado, Toronto | 44 |
| 1999 | Manny Ramirez, Cleveland | 44 |
| 1949 | Ted Williams, Boston | 43 |
| 1953 | Al Rosen, Cleveland | 43 |
| 1984 | Tony Armas, Boston | 43 |
| 1992 | Juan Gonzalez, Texas | 43 |
| 1998 | Rafael Palmeiro, Baltimore | 43 |
| 2000 | Jason Giambi, Oakland | 43 |
| 2000 | Frank Thomas, Chicago | 43 |
| 2002 | Rafael Palmeiro, Texas | 43 |
| 2004 | Manny Ramirez, Boston | 43 |
| 2005 | Mark Teixeira, Texas | 43 |
| 1936 | Hal Trosky, Cleveland | 42 |
| 1953 | Gus Zernial, Philadelphia | 42 |
| 1957 | Roy Sievers, Washington | 42 |
| 1958 | Mickey Mantle, New York | 42 |
| 1959 | Rocky Colavito, Cleveland | 42 |
| 1959 | Harmon Killebrew, Washington | 42 |
| 1963 | Dick Stuart, Boston | 42 |
| 1988 | Jose Canseco, Oakland | 42 |
| 1992 | Mark McGwire, Oakland | 42 |
| 1997 | Juan Gonzalez, Texas | 42 |
| 1998 | Alex Rodriguez, Seattle | 42 |
| 1999 | Shawn Green, Toronto | 42 |
| 1999 | Alex Rodriguez, Seattle | 42 |
| 2003 | Carlos Delgado, Toronto | 42 |
| 2003 | Frank Thomas, Chicago | 42 |
| 1923 | Babe Ruth, New York | 41 |
| 1930 | Lou Gehrig, New York | 41 |
| 1932 | Babe Ruth, New York | 41 |
| 1936 | Jimmie Foxx, Boston | 41 |
| 1940 | Hank Greenberg, Detroit | 41 |
| 1958 | Rocky Colavito, Cleveland | 41 |
| 1961 | Norm Cash, Detroit | 41 |
| 1970 | Harmon Killebrew, Minnesota | 41 |
| 1980 | Reggie Jackson, New York | 41 |
| 1980 | Ben Oglivie, Milwaukee | 41 |
| 1993 | Frank Thomas, Chicago | 41 |
| 2000 | Tony Batista, Toronto | 41 |
| 2000 | Carlos Delgado, Toronto | 41 |
| 2000 | David Justice, Cleveland-New York | 41 |
| 2000 | Alex Rodriguez, Seattle | 41 |
| 2001 | Troy Glaus, Anaheim | 41 |
| 2001 | Manny Ramirez, Boston | 41 |
| 2002 | Jason Giambi, New York | 41 |
| 2003 | Jason Giambi, New York | 41 |
| 2004 | Paul Konerko, Chicago | 41 |
| 2004 | David Ortiz, Boston | 41 |
| 1937 | Hank Greenberg, Detroit | 40 |
| 1960 | Mickey Mantle, New York | 40 |
| 1969 | Rico Petrocelli, Boston | 40 |
| 1969 | Carl Yastrzemski, Boston | 40 |
| 1970 | Carl Yastrzemski, Boston | 40 |
| 1985 | Darrell Evans, Detroit | 40 |
| 1986 | Jesse Barfield, Toronto | 40 |
| 1994 | Ken Griffey Jr., Seattle | 40 |
| 1995 | Jay Buhner, Seattle | 40 |
| 1995 | Frank Thomas, Chicago | 40 |
| 1996 | Frank Thomas, Chicago | 40 |
| 1997 | Jay Buhner, Seattle | 40 |

| Year | Player, Club | HR |
|---|---|---|
| 1997 | Jim Thome, Cleveland | 40 |
| 1998 | Mo Vaughn, Boston | 40 |
| 2005 | Paul Konerko, Chicago | 40 |

**Total number of occurrences: 136**

## NATIONAL LEAGUE

| Year | Player, Club | HR |
|---|---|---|
| 2001 | Barry Bonds, San Francisco | 73 |
| 1998 | Mark McGwire, St. Louis | 70 |
| 1998 | Sammy Sosa, Chicago | 66 |
| 1999 | Mark McGwire, St. Louis | 65 |
| 2001 | Sammy Sosa, Chicago | 64 |
| 1999 | Sammy Sosa, Chicago | 63 |
| 2001 | Luis Gonzalez, Arizona | 57 |
| 1930 | Hack Wilson, Chicago | 56 |
| 1949 | Ralph Kiner, Pittsburgh | 54 |
| 1965 | Willie Mays, San Francisco | 52 |
| 1977 | George Foster, Cincinnati | 52 |
| 1947 | Ralph Kiner, Pittsburgh | 51 |
| 1947 | Johnny Mize, New York | 51 |
| 1955 | Willie Mays, New York | 51 |
| 2005 | Andruw Jones, Atlanta | 51 |
| 1998 | Greg Vaughn, San Diego | 50 |
| 2000 | Sammy Sosa, Chicago | 50 |
| 1954 | Ted Kluszewski, Cincinnati | 49 |
| 1962 | Willie Mays, San Francisco | 49 |
| 1987 | Andre Dawson, Chicago | 49 |
| 1997 | Larry Walker, Colorado | 49 |
| 2000 | Barry Bonds, San Francisco | 49 |
| 2001 | Todd Helton, Colorado | 49 |
| 2001 | Shawn Green, Los Angeles | 49 |
| 2002 | Sammy Sosa, Chicago | 49 |
| 1971 | Willie Stargell, Pittsburgh | 48 |
| 1979 | Dave Kingman, Chicago | 48 |
| 1980 | Mike Schmidt, Philadelphia | 48 |
| 2004 | Adrian Beltre, Los Angeles | 48 |
| 1950 | Ralph Kiner, Pittsburgh | 47 |
| 1953 | Eddie Mathews, Milwaukee | 47 |
| 1955 | Ted Kluszewski, Cincinnati | 47 |
| 1958 | Ernie Banks, Chicago | 47 |
| 1964 | Willie Mays, San Francisco | 47 |
| 1971 | Hank Aaron, Atlanta | 47 |
| 1989 | Kevin Mitchell, San Francisco | 47 |
| 1996 | Andres Galarraga, Colorado | 47 |
| 2000 | Jeff Bagwell, Houston | 47 |
| 2003 | Jim Thome, Philadelphia | 47 |
| 1959 | Eddie Mathews, Milwaukee | 46 |
| 1961 | Orlando Cepeda, San Francisco | 46 |
| 1993 | Barry Bonds, San Francisco | 46 |
| 1998 | Vinny Castilla, Colorado | 46 |
| 2002 | Barry Bonds, San Francisco | 46 |
| 2004 | Adam Dunn, Cincinnati | 46 |
| 2004 | Albert Pujols, St. Louis | 46 |
| 2005 | Derrek Lee, Chicago | 46 |
| 1959 | Ernie Banks, Chicago | 45 |
| 1962 | Hank Aaron, Milwaukee | 45 |
| 1969 | Willie McCovey, San Francisco | 45 |
| 1970 | Johnny Bench, Cincinnati | 45 |
| 1979 | Mike Schmidt, Philadelphia | 45 |
| 1999 | Chipper Jones, Atlanta | 45 |
| 1999 | Greg Vaughn, Cincinnati | 45 |
| 2001 | Richie Sexson, Milwaukee | 45 |
| 2003 | Barry Bonds, San Francisco | 45 |
| 2003 | Richie Sexson, Milwaukee | 45 |
| 2004 | Barry Bonds, San Francisco | 45 |
| 1955 | Ernie Banks, Chicago | 44 |
| 1957 | Hank Aaron, Milwaukee | 44 |
| 1963 | Hank Aaron, Milwaukee | 44 |
| 1963 | Willie McCovey, San Francisco | 44 |
| 1966 | Hank Aaron, Atlanta | 44 |
| 1969 | Hank Aaron, Atlanta | 44 |
| 1973 | Willie Stargell, Pittsburgh | 44 |
| 1987 | Dale Murphy, Atlanta | 44 |
| 1998 | Andres Galarraga, Atlanta | 44 |
| 2000 | Vladimir Guerrero, Montreal | 44 |
| 2000 | Richard Hidalgo, Houston | 44 |
| 1929 | Chuck Klein, Philadelphia | 43 |
| 1940 | Johnny Mize, St. Louis | 43 |
| 1956 | Duke Snider, Brooklyn | 43 |
| 1957 | Ernie Banks, Chicago | 43 |
| 1973 | Dave Johnson, Atlanta | 43 |
| 1994 | Matt Williams, San Francisco | 43 |
| 1997 | Jeff Bagwell, Houston | 43 |
| 2000 | Gary Sheffield, Los Angeles | 43 |
| 2003 | Javier Lopez, Atlanta | 43 |
| 2003 | Albert Pujols, St. Louis | 43 |
| 1922 | Rogers Hornsby, St. Louis | 42 |
| 1929 | Mel Ott, New York | 42 |
| 1951 | Ralph Kiner, Pittsburgh | 42 |
| 1953 | Duke Snider, Brooklyn | 42 |
| 1954 | Gil Hodges, Brooklyn | 42 |
| 1955 | Duke Snider, Brooklyn | 42 |
| 1970 | Billy Williams, Chicago | 42 |
| 1996 | Barry Bonds, San Francisco | 42 |
| 1996 | Gary Sheffield, Florida | 42 |
| 1999 | Jeff Bagwell, Houston | 42 |
| 1999 | Vladimir Guerrero, Montreal | 42 |
| 2000 | Jim Edmonds, St. Louis | 42 |
| 2000 | Todd Helton, Colorado | 42 |
| 2002 | Lance Berkman, Houston | 42 |
| 2002 | Shawn Green, Los Angeles | 42 |
| 2004 | Jim Edmonds, St. Louis | 42 |
| 2004 | Jim Thome, Philadelphia | 42 |
| 1923 | Fred Williams, Philadelphia | 41 |
| 1953 | Roy Campanella, Brooklyn | 41 |
| 1954 | Hank Sauer, Chicago | 41 |
| 1954 | Willie Mays, New York | 41 |
| 1955 | Eddie Mathews, Milwaukee | 41 |
| 1960 | Ernie Banks, Chicago | 41 |
| 1973 | Darrell Evans, Atlanta | 41 |
| 1977 | Jeff Burroughs, Atlanta | 41 |
| 1996 | Todd Hundley, New York | 41 |
| 1997 | Andres Galarraga, Colorado | 41 |
| 2001 | Phil Nevin, San Diego | 41 |
| 2005 | Albert Pujols, St. Louis | 41 |
| 1930 | Chuck Klein, Philadelphia | 40 |
| 1948 | Ralph Kiner, Pittsburgh | 40 |
| 1948 | Johnny Mize, New York | 40 |
| 1951 | Gil Hodges, Brooklyn | 40 |
| 1953 | Ted Kluszewski, Cincinnati | 40 |
| 1954 | Duke Snider, Brooklyn | 40 |
| 1954 | Eddie Mathews, Milwaukee | 40 |
| 1955 | Wally Post, Cincinnati | 40 |
| 1957 | Duke Snider, Brooklyn | 40 |
| 1960 | Hank Aaron, Milwaukee | 40 |
| 1961 | Willie Mays, San Francisco | 40 |
| 1966 | Dick Allen, Philadelphia | 40 |
| 1970 | Tony Perez, Cincinnati | 40 |
| 1972 | Johnny Bench, Cincinnati | 40 |
| 1973 | Hank Aaron, Atlanta | 40 |
| 1978 | George Foster, Cincinnati | 40 |
| 1983 | Mike Schmidt, Philadelphia | 40 |
| 1990 | Ryne Sandberg, Chicago | 40 |
| 1993 | David Justice, Atlanta | 40 |
| 1995 | Dante Bichette, Colorado | 40 |
| 1996 | Ellis Burks, Colorado | 40 |
| 1996 | Vinny Castilla, Colorado | 40 |
| 1996 | Ken Caminiti, San Diego | 40 |
| 1996 | Sammy Sosa, Chicago | 40 |
| 1997 | Barry Bonds, San Francisco | 40 |
| 1997 | Vinny Castilla, Colorado | 40 |
| 1997 | Mike Piazza, Los Angeles | 40 |
| 1999 | Mike Piazza, New York | 40 |
| 2000 | Ken Griffey Jr., Cincinnati | 40 |
| 2003 | Sammy Sosa, Chicago | 40 |
| 2005 | Adam Dunn, Cincinnati | 40 |

**Total number of occurences: 133**

## TWO LEAGUES IN SEASON

| Year | Player, Club | HR |
|---|---|---|
| 1997 | Mark McGwire, Oak AL (34), St. L, NL (24) | 58 |
| 1996 | Greg Vaughn, Mil AL (31), SD NL (10) | 41 |

**Total number of occurrences: 2**

## PLAYERS WITH FOUR HOMERS IN GAME

### NATIONAL LEAGUE

BOBBY LOWE, Boston, May 30, 1894, 2nd game (H)
Ed Delahanty, Philadelphia, July 13, 1896 (A) (3 consec)
Chuck Klein, Philadelphia, July 10, 1936, 10 inn (A) (3 consec)
Gil Hodges, Brooklyn, Aug 31, 1950 (H)
Joe Adcock, Milwaukee, July 31, 1954 (A) (3 consec)
Willie Mays, San Francisco, Apr 30, 1961 (A)
MIKE SCHMIDT, Philadelphia, Apr 17, 1976, 10 inn (A)
Bob Horner, Atlanta, July 6, 1986 (H)
Mark Whiten, St. Louis, Sept 7, 1993 (A) (3 consec)
Shawn Green, Los Angeles, May 23, 2002 (A) (3 consec)
**Total number of occurrences: 10**

### AMERICAN LEAGUE

LOU GEHRIG, New York, June 3, 1932 (A)
Pat Seerey, Chicago, July 18, 1948, 1st game, 11 inn (A) (3 consec)
ROCKY COLAVITO, Cleveland, June 10, 1959 (A)
MIKE CAMERON, Seattle, May 2, 2002 (A)
CARLOS DELGADO, Toronto, Sept 25, 2003 (H)
**Total number of occurrences: 5**
Note—Capitalized name denotes 4 consecutive homers (bases on balls excluded); parentheses denotes home or away games.

## PLAYERS WITH THREE HOMERS IN GAME

### AMERICAN ASSOCIATION

Guy Hecker, Louisville, Aug 15, 1886, 2nd game (H)
**Total number of occurrences: 1**

### AMERICAN LEAGUE

Ken Williams, St. Louis, Apr 22, 1922 (H)
Joe Hauser, Philadelphia, Aug 2, 1924 (A)
Goose Goslin, Washington, June 19, 1925, 12 inn (A)
Ty Cobb, Detroit, May 5, 1925 (A)
Mickey Cochrane, Philadelphia, May 21, 1925 (A)
Tony Lazzeri, New York, June 8, 1927 (H)
Lou Gehrig, New York, June 23, 1927 (A)
Lou Gehrig, New York, May 4, 1929 (A)
Babe Ruth, New York, May 21, 1930, 1st game (A)
Lou Gehrig, New York, May 22, 1930, 2nd game (A)
CARL REYNOLDS, Chicago, July 2, 1930, 2nd game (A)
GOOSE GOSLIN, St. Louis, Aug 19, 1930 (A)
EARL AVERILL, Cleveland, Sept 17, 1930, 1st game (H)
Goose Goslin, St. Louis, June 23, 1932 (H)
Ben Chapman, New York, July 9, 1932, 2nd game (H)
Jimmie Foxx, Philadelphia, July 10, 1932, 18 inn (A)
Al Simmons, Philadelphia, July 15, 1932 (H)
JIMMIE FOXX, Philadelphia, June 8, 1933 (H)
HAL TROSKY, Cleveland, May 30, 1934, 2nd game (H)
ED COLEMAN, Philadelphia, Aug 17, 1934, 1st game (H)
FRANK HIGGINS, Philadelphia, June 27, 1935 (H)
MOOSE SOLTERS, St. Louis, July 7, 1935 (A)
Tony Lazzeri, New York, May 24, 1936 (A)

JOE DiMAGGIO, New York, June 13, 1937, 2nd game, 11 inn (A)
Hal Trosky, Cleveland, July 5, 1937, 1st game (A)
MERV CONNORS, Chicago, Sept 17, 1938, 2nd game (H)
KEN KELTNER, Cleveland, May 25, 1939 (A)
Jim Tabor, Boston, July 4, 1939, 2nd game (A)
BILL DICKEY, New York, July 26, 1939 (H)
FRANK HIGGINS, Detroit, May 20, 1940 (H)
Charlie Keller, New York, July 28, 1940, 1st game (A)
Rudy York, Detroit, Sept 1, 1941, 1st game (H)
Pat Seerey, Cleveland, July 13, 1945 (A)
Ted Williams, Boston, July 14, 1946, 1st game (H)
Sam Chapman, Philadelphia, Aug 15, 1946 (H)
JOE DiMAGGIO, New York, May 23, 1948, 1st game (A)
Pat Mullin, Detroit, June 26, 1949, 2nd game (A)
Bobby Doerr, Boston, June 8, 1950 (H)
LARRY DOBY, Cleveland, Aug 2, 1950 (H)
Joe DiMaggio, New York, Sept 10, 1950 (A)
JOHNNY MIZE, New York, Sept 15, 1950 (A)
Gus Zernial, Chicago, October 1, 1950, 2nd game (H)
Bobby Avila, Cleveland, June 20, 1951 (A)
Clyde Vollmer, Boston, July 26, 1951 (H)
Al Rosen, Cleveland, Apr 29, 1952 (A)
BILL GLYNN, Cleveland, July 5, 1954, 1st game (A)
Al Kaline, Detroit, Apr 17, 1955 (H)
Mickey Mantle, New York, May 13, 1955 (H)
Norm Zauchin, Boston, May 27, 1955 (H)
JIM LEMON, Washington, Aug 31, 1956 (H)
Ted Williams, Boston, May 8, 1957 (A)
Ted Williams, Boston, June 13, 1957 (A)
Hector Lopez, Kansas City, June 26, 1958 (H)
PRESTON WARD, Kansas City, Sept 9, 1958 (H)
CHARLIE MAXWELL, Detroit, May 3, 1959, 2nd game (H)
Bob Cerv, Kansas City, Aug 20, 1959 (H)
WILLIE KIRKLAND, Cleveland, July 9, 1961, 2nd game (H)
Rocky Colavito, Detroit, Aug 27, 1961, 2nd game (A)
Lee Thomas, Los Angeles, Sept 5, 1961, 2nd game (A)
ROCKY COLAVITO, Detroit, July 5, 1962 (A)
Steve Boros, Detroit, Aug 6, 1962 (A)
DON LEPPERT, Washington, Apr 11, 1963 (H)
BOB ALLISON, Minnesota, May 17, 1963 (A)
BOOG POWELL, Baltimore, Aug 10, 1963 (A)
Harmon Killebrew, Minnesota, Sept 21, 1963, 1st game (A)
Jim King, Washington, June 8, 1964 (H)
Boog Powell, Baltimore, June 27, 1964 (A)
MANNY JIMENEZ, Kansas City, July 4, 1964 (A)
TOM TRESH, New York, June 6, 1965, 2nd game (H)
Boog Powell, Baltimore, Aug 15, 1966 (A)
Tom McGraw, Chicago, May 24, 1967 (A)
Curt Blefary, Baltimore, June 6, 1967, 1st game (A)
KEN HARRELSON, Boston, June 14, 1968 (A)
Mike Epstein, Washington, May 16, 1969 (A)
Joe Lahoud, Boston, June 11, 1969 (A)
BILL MELTON, Chicago, June 24, 1969, 2nd game (A)
Reggie Jackson, Oakland, July 2, 1969 (H)
Paul Blair, Baltimore, Apr 29, 1970 (A)
Tony Horton, Cleveland, May 24, 1970, 2nd game (H)
Willie Horton, Detroit, June 9, 1970 (H)
BOBBY MURCER, New York, June 24, 1970, 2nd game (H)
Bill Freehan, Detroit, Aug 9, 1971 (A)
GEORGE HENDRICK, Cleveland, June 19, 1973 (H)
Tony Oliva, Minnesota, July 3, 1973 (A)
Leroy Stanton, California, July 10, 1973, 10 inn (A)
Bobby Murcer, New York, July 13, 1973 (H)
BOBBY GRICH, Baltimore, June 18, 1974 (H)
Fred Lynn, Boston, June 18, 1975 (A)
John Mayberry, Kansas City, July 1, 1975 (A)
DON BAYLOR, Baltimore, July 2, 1975 (A)
TONY SOLAITA, Kansas City, Sept 7, 1975, 11 inn (A)
Carl Yastrzemski, Boston, May 19, 1976 (A)
Willie Horton, Texas, May 15, 1977 (A)
JOHN MAYBERRY, Kansas City, June 1, 1977 (A)
CLIFF JOHNSON, New York, June 30, 1977 (A)
Jim Rice, Boston, Aug 29, 1977 (H)
Al Oliver, Texas, May 23, 1979 (H)
Ben Oglivie, Milwaukee, July 8, 1979, 1st game (H)
Claudell Washington, Chicago, July 14, 1979 (H)
George Brett, Kansas City, July 22, 1979 (A)
Cecil Cooper, Milwaukee, July 27, 1979 (H)
EDDIE MURRAY, Baltimore, Aug 29, 1979, 2nd game (A)
CARNEY LANSFORD, California, Sept 1, 1979 (A)
Otto Velez, Toronto, May 4, 1980, 1st game, 10 inn (H)
Fred Patek, California, June 20, 1980 (A)
AL OLIVER, Texas, Aug 17, 1980, 2nd game (A)
Eddie Murray, Baltimore, Sept 14, 1980, 13 inn (A)
Jeff Burroughs, Seattle, Aug 14, 1981, 2nd game (A)
Paul Molitor, Milwaukee, May 12, 1982 (A)
LARRY HERNDON, Detroit, May 18, 1982 (H)
BEN OGLIVIE, Milwaukee, June 20, 1982 (A)
HAROLD BAINES, Chicago, July 7, 1982 (H)
DOUG DeCINCES, California, Aug 3, 1982 (H)
Doug DeCinces, California, Aug 8, 1982 (A)
George Brett, Kansas City, Apr 20, 1983 (A)
Ben Oglivie, Milwaukee, May 14, 1983 (H)
Dan Ford, Baltimore, July 20, 1983 (A)
Jim Rice, Boston, Aug 29, 1983, 2nd game (A)
DAVE KINGMAN, Oakland, Apr 16, 1984 (A)
Harold Baines, Chicago, Sept 17, 1984 (A)
GORMAN THOMAS, Seattle, Apr 11, 1985 (H)
LARRY PARRISH, Texas, Apr 29, 1985 (H)
Eddie Murray, Baltimore, Aug 26, 1985 (A)
Leon Lacy, Baltimore, June 8, 1986 (A)
JUAN BENIQUEZ, Baltimore, June 12, 1986 (H)
Joe Carter, Cleveland, Aug 29, 1986 (A)
Jim Presley, Seattle, Sept 1, 1986 (H)
Reggie Jackson, California, Sept 18, 1986 (H)
Cory Snyder, Cleveland, May 21, 1987 (H)
Joe Carter, Cleveland, May 28, 1987 (A)
Mark McGwire, Oakland, June 27, 1987 (A)
Bill Madlock, Detroit, June 28, 1987, 11 inn (H)
BROOK JACOBY, Cleveland, July 3, 1987 (H)
Dale Sveum, Milwaukee, July 17, 1987 (H)
Mike Brantley, Seattle, Sept 14, 1987 (H)
Ernie Whitt, Toronto, Sept 14, 1987 (H)
Wally Joyner, California, October 3, 1987 (H)
George Bell, Toronto, Apr 4, 1988 (A)
Jose Canseco, Oakland, July 3, 1988 (A)
JOE CARTER, Cleveland, June 24, 1989 (A)
Joe Carter, Cleveland, July 19, 1989 (A)
CECIL FIELDER, Detroit, May 6, 1990 (A)
CECIL FIELDER, Detroit, June 6, 1990 (A)
RANDY MILLIGAN, Baltimore, June 9, 1990 (H)
BO JACKSON, Kansas City, July 17, 1990 (A)
TOM BRUNANSKY, Boston, Sept 29, 1990 (H)
DAVE WINFIELD, California, Apr 13, 1991 (A)
Harold Baines, Oakland, May 7, 1991 (H)
Danny Tartabull, Kansas City, July 6, 1991 (H)
Jack Clark, Boston, July 31, 1991 (H)
DAVE HENDERSON, Oakland, Aug 3, 1991 (H)
Juan Gonzalez, Texas, June 7, 1992 (H)
Albert Belle, Cleveland, Sept 6, 1992 (H)
Carlos Baerga, Cleveland, June 17, 1993 (A)
Joe Carter, Toronto, Aug 23, 1993 (H)
Juan Gonzalez, Texas, Aug 28, 1993 (H)
Tim Raines Sr., Chicago, Apr 18, 1994 (A)
Jose Canseco, Texas, June 13, 1994 (H)
Darnell Coles, Toronto, July 5, 1994 (A)
JIM THOME, Cleveland, July 22, 1994 (H)
John Valentin, Boston, June 2, 1995 (H)
MARK McGWIRE, Oakland, June 11, 1995 (A)
MIKE STANLEY, New York, Aug 10, 1995, 1st game (H)
PAUL O'NEILL, New York, Aug 31, 1995 (H)
ALBERT BELLE, Cleveland, Sept 19, 1995 (A)
Dan Wilson, Seattle, Apr 11, 1996 (A)
CECIL FIELDER, Detroit, Apr 16, 1996 (A)
Ernie Young, Oakland, May 10, 1996 (H)
Geronimo Berroa, Oakland, May 22, 1996 (A)
KEN GRIFFEY JR., Seattle, May 24, 1996 (H)
Cal Ripken Jr., Baltimore, May 28, 1996 (A)
EDGAR MARTINEZ, Seattle, July 6, 1996 (A)
DARRYL STRAWBERRY, New York, Aug 6, 1996 (H)
Geronimo Berroa, Oakland, Aug 12, 1996 (H)
FRANK THOMAS, Chicago, Sept 15, 1996 (A)
MO VAUGHN, Boston, Sept 24, 1996 (H)
TINO MARTINEZ, New York, Apr 2, 1997 (A)
Matt Williams, Cleveland, Apr 25, 1997 (A)
Ken Griffey Jr., Seattle, Apr 25, 1997 (A)
ROBERTO ALOMAR, Baltimore, Apr 26, 1997 (A)
MO VAUGHN, Boston, May 30, 1997 (H)
BOB HIGGINSON, Detroit, June 30, 1997 (H)
IVAN RODRIGUEZ, Texas, Sept 11, 1997 (H)
Lee Stevens, Texas, Apr 13, 1998 (H)
CARLOS DELGADO, Toronto, Aug 4, 1998 (A)
MANNY RAMIREZ, Cleveland, Sept 15, 1998 (H)
Nomar Garciaparra, Boston, May 10, 1999 (H)
EDGAR MARTINEZ, Seattle, May 18, 1999 (H)
Miguel Tejada, Oakland, June 11, 1999 (H)
Trot Nixon, Boston, July 24, 1999 (A)
Albert Belle, Baltimore, July 25, 1999 (H)
Carlos Delgado, Toronto, Aug 6, 1999 (A)
Manny Ramirez, Cleveland, Aug 25, 1999 (A)
JUAN GONZALEZ, Texas, Sept 24, 1999 (H)
Alex Rodriguez, Seattle, Apr 16, 2000 (A)
BOBBY HIGGINSON, Detroit, June 24, 2000 (A)
Darrin Fletcher, Toronto, Aug 27, 2000 (A)
CARLOS DELGADO, Toronto, Apr 4, 2001 (A)
Carlos Delgado, Toronto, Apr 20, 2001 (A)
Jason Varitek, Boston, May 20, 2001 (A)
Ellis Burks, Cleveland, June 19, 2001 (H)
Miguel Tejada, Oakland, June 30, 2001 (A)
Jim Thome, Cleveland, July 6, 2001 (H)
NOMAR GARCIAPARRA, Boston, July 23, 2002, a.m. game (H)
CHRIS WOODWARD, Toronto, Aug 7, 2002 (H)
Alex Rodriguez, Texas, Aug 17, 2002 (H)
TROY GLAUS, Anaheim, Sept 15, 2002 (H)
CARLOS PENA, Detroit, May 19, 2003 (A)
Garret Anderson, Anaheim, July 4, 2003 (A)
Bill Mueller, Boston, July 29, 2003 (A)
JOSE VALENTIN, Chicago, July 30, 2003 (A)
Victor Martinez, Cleveland, July 16, 2004 (A)
TRAVIS HAFNER, Cleveland, July 20, 2004 (H)
KEVIN MILLAR, Boston, July 23, 2004 (H)
ERUBIEL DURAZO, Oakland, Aug 18, 2004 (A)
TONY CLARK, New York, Aug 28, 2004 (A)
Dmitri Young, Detroit, Apr 4, 2005 (H)
ALEX RODRIGUEZ, New York, Apr 26, 2005 (H)
KEVIN MENCH, Texas, June 30, 2005 (H)
JOHNNY GOMES, Tampa Bay, July 30, 2005 (H)
**Total number of occurrences: 220**

## NATIONAL LEAGUE

Ned Williamson, Chicago, May 30, 1884, 2nd game (H)
CAP ANSON, Chicago, Aug 6, 1884 (H)
JACK MANNING, Philadelphia, October 9, 1884 (A)
Dennis Brouthers, Detroit, Sept 10, 1886 (A)
Roger Connor, New York, May 9, 1888 (A)
Frank Shugart, St. Louis, May 10, 1894 (A)
BILL JOYCE, Washington, Aug 20, 1894 (H)
Tom McCreery, Louisville, July 12, 1897 (A)
Jake Beckley, Cincinnati, Sept 26, 1897, 1st game (A)
Butch Henline, Philadelphia, Sept 15, 1922 (H)
Fred Williams, Philadelphia, May 11, 1923 (H)
GEORGE KELLY, New York, Sept 17, 1923 (A)
George Kelly, New York, June 14, 1924 (H)
Jack Fournier, Brooklyn, July 13, 1926 (A)
Les Bell, Boston, June 2, 1928 (H)
GEORGE HARPER, St. Louis, Sept 20, 1928, 1st game (A)
Hack Wilson, Chicago, July 26, 1930 (A)
MEL OTT, New York, Aug 31, 1930, 2nd game (H)
ROGERS HORNSBY, Chicago, Apr 24, 1931 (A)
GEORGE WATKINS, St. Louis, June 24, 1931, 2nd game (A)
Bill Terry, New York, Aug 13, 1932, 1st game (H)
Babe Herman, Chicago, July 20, 1933 (H)
Hal Lee, Boston, July 6, 1934 (A)
Babe Ruth, Boston, May 25, 1935 (A)
JOHNNY MOORE, Philadelphia, July 22, 1936 (H)
Alex Kampouris, Cincinnati, May 9, 1937 (A)
JOHNNY MIZE, St. Louis, July 13, 1938 (H)
Johnny Mize, St. Louis, July 20, 1938, 2nd game (H)
HANK LEIBER, Chicago, July 4, 1939, 1st game (H)
Johnny Mize, St. Louis, May 13, 1940, 14 inn (A)
JOHNNY MIZE, St. Louis, Sept 8, 1940, 1st game (H)
JIM TOBIN, Boston, May 13, 1942 (H)
CLYDE McCULLOUGH, Chicago, July 26, 1942, 1st game (A)
BILL NICHOLSON, Chicago, July 23, 1944, 1st game (A)
JOHNNY MIZE, New York, Apr 24, 1947 (A)
WILLARD MARSHALL, New York, July 18, 1947 (H)
RALPH KINER, Pittsburgh, Aug 16, 1947 (H)
RALPH KINER, Pittsburgh, Sept 11, 1947, 2nd game (H)
Ralph Kiner, Pittsburgh, July 5, 1948, 1st game (H)
GENE HERMANSKI, Brooklyn, Aug 5, 1948 (H)
Andy Seminick, Philadelphia, June 2, 1949 (H)
Walker Cooper, Cincinnati, July 6, 1949 (H)
BOB ELLIOTT, Boston, Sept 24, 1949 (A)
DUKE SNIDER, Brooklyn, May 30, 1950, 2nd game (H)
Wes Westrum, New York, June 24, 1950 (H)
ANDY PAFKO, Chicago, Aug 2, 1950, 2nd game (A)
ROY CAMPANELLA, Brooklyn, Aug 26, 1950 (A)
HANK SAUER, Chicago, Aug 28, 1950, 1st game (H)
TOMMY BROWN, Brooklyn, Sept 18, 1950 (H)
Ralph Kiner, Pittsburgh, July 18, 1951 (A)
DEL WILBER, Philadelphia, Aug 27, 1951, 2nd game (H)
Don Mueller, New York, Sept 1, 1951 (H)
Hank Sauer, Chicago, June 11, 1952 (H)
EDDIE MATHEWS, Boston, Sept 27, 1952 (A)
DUSTY RHODES, New York, Aug 26, 1953 (H)
Jim Pendleton, Milwaukee, Aug 30, 1953, 1st game (A)
Stan Musial, St. Louis, May 2, 1954, 1st game (H)
HANK THOMPSON, New York, June 3, 1954 (A)
DUSTY RHODES, New York, July 28, 1954 (H)
Duke Snider, Brooklyn, June 1, 1955 (H)
GUS BELL, Cincinnati, July 21, 1955 (H)
Del Ennis, Philadelphia, July 23, 1955 (H)
Smoky Burgess, Cincinnati, July 29, 1955 (H)
Ernie Banks, Chicago, Aug 4, 1955 (H)
GUS BELL, Cincinnati, May 29, 1956 (A)
Ed Bailey, Cincinnati, June 24, 1956, 1st game (A)
Ted Kluszewski, Cincinnati, July 1, 1956, 1st game, 10 inn (A)
BOB THURMAN, Cincinnati, Aug 18, 1956 (H)
ERNIE BANKS, Chicago, Sept 14, 1957, 2nd game (H)
Lee Walls, Chicago, Apr 24, 1958 (A)
Roman Mejias, Pittsburgh, May 4, 1958, 1st game (A)
Walt Moryn, Chicago, May 30, 1958, 2nd game (H)
FRANK THOMAS, Pittsburgh, Aug 16, 1958 (A)
Don Demeter, Los Angeles, Apr 21, 1959, 11 inn (H)
Hank Aaron, Milwaukee, June 21, 1959 (A)
FRANK ROBINSON, Cincinnati, Aug 22, 1959 (H)
DICK STUART, Pittsburgh, June 30, 1960, 2nd game (H)
Willie Mays, San Francisco, June 29, 1961, 10 inn (A)
BILL WHITE, St. Louis, July 5, 1961 (A)
Don Demeter, Philadelphia, Sept 12, 1961 (A)
ERNIE BANKS, Chicago, May 29, 1962 (H)
STAN MUSIAL, St. Louis, July 8, 1962 (A)
Willie Mays, San Francisco, June 2, 1963 (A)
Ernie Banks, Chicago, June 9, 1963 (H)
WILLIE McCOVEY, San Francisco, Sept 22, 1963, (H)
WILLIE McCOVEY, San Francisco, Apr 22, 1964 (A)
JOHNNY CALLISON, Philadelphia, Sept 27, 1964 (H)
Johnny Callison, Philadelphia, June 6, 1965, 2nd game (A)
Willie Stargell, Pittsburgh, June 24, 1965 (A)
JIM HICKMAN, New York, Sept 3, 1965 (A)
Gene Oliver, Atlanta, July 30, 1966, 2nd game (H)
ART SHAMSKY, Cincinnati, Aug 12, 1966, 13 inn (H)
Willie McCovey, San Francisco, Sept 17, 1966, 10 inn (H)
Roberto Clemente, Pittsburgh, May 15, 1967, 10 inn (A)
ADOLFO PHILLIPS, Chicago, June 11, 1967, 2nd game (H)

JIM WYNN, Houston, June 15, 1967 (H)
Willie Stargell, Pittsburgh, May 22, 1968 (A)
Billy Williams, Chicago, Sept 10, 1968 (H)
DICK ALLEN, Philadelphia, Sept 29, 1968 (A)
BOB TILLMAN, Atlanta, July 30, 1969, 1st game (A)
ROBERTO CLEMENTE, Pittsburgh, Aug 13, 1969 (A)
Rico Carty, Atlanta, May 31, 1970 (H)
Mike Lum, Atlanta, July 3, 1970, 1st game (H)
JOHNNY BENCH, Cincinnati, July 26, 1970 (H)
ORLANDO CEPEDA, Atlanta, July 26, 1970, 1st game (A)
Willie Stargell, Pittsburgh, Apr 10, 1971, 12 inn (A)
WILLIE STARGELL, Pittsburgh, Apr 21, 1971 (H)
DERON JOHNSON, Philadelphia, July 11, 1971 (H)
RICK MONDAY, Chicago, May 16, 1972 (A)
Nate Colbert, San Diego, Aug 1, 1972, 2nd game (A)
Johnny Bench, Cincinnati, May 9, 1973 (A)
Lee May, Houston, June 21, 1973 (A)
George Mitterwald, Chicago, Apr 17, 1974 (H)
Jim Wynn, Los Angeles, May 11, 1974 (A)
Dave Lopes, Los Angeles, Aug 20, 1974 (A)
Reggie Smith, St. Louis, May 22, 1976 (A)
Dave Kingman, New York, June 4, 1976 (A)
Bill Robinson, Pittsburgh, June 5, 1976, 15 inn (H)
Gary Matthews, San Francisco, Sept 25, 1976 (H)
GARY CARTER, Montreal, Apr 20, 1977 (H)
LARRY PARRISH, Montreal, May 29, 1977 (A)
GEORGE FOSTER, Cincinnati, July 14, 1977 (H)
Pete Rose, Cincinnati, Apr 29, 1978 (A)
Dave Kingman, Chicago, May 14, 1978 (A)
LARRY PARRISH, Montreal, July 30, 1978 (A)
Dave Kingman, Chicago, May 17, 1979 (H)
Dale Murphy, Altanta, May 18, 1979 (H)
MIKE SCHMIDT, Philadelphia, July 7, 1979 (H)
DAVE KINGMAN, Chicago, July 28, 1979 (A)
Larry Parrish, Montreal, Apr 25, 1980 (A)
Johnny Bench, Cincinnati, May 29, 1980 (A)
Claudell Washington, New York, June 22, 1980 (A)
Darrell Evans, San Francisco, June 15, 1983 (H)
DARRYL STRAWBERRY, New York, Aug 5, 1985 (A)
GARY CARTER, New York, Sept 3, 1985 (A)
Andre Dawson, Montreal, Sept 24, 1985 (A)
Ken Griffey Sr., Atlanta, July 22, 1986, 11 inn (H)
Eric Davis, Cincinnati, Sept 10, 1986 (A)
ERIC DAVIS, Cincinnati, May 3, 1987 (A)
Tim Wallach, Montreal, May 4, 1987 (A)
MIKE SCHMIDT, Philadelphia, June 14, 1987 (A)
Andre Dawson, Chicago, Aug 1, 1987 (H)
GLENN DAVIS, Houston, Sept 10, 1987 (A)
Darnell Coles, Pittsburgh, Sept 30, 1987, 2nd game (H)
Von Hayes, Philadelphia, Aug 29, 1989 (A)
KEVIN MITCHELL, San Francisco, May 25, 1990 (A)
Jeff Treadway, Atlanta, May 26, 1990 (A)
GLENN DAVIS, Houston, June 1, 1990 (A)
BARRY LARKIN, Cincinnati, June 28, 1991 (H)
Jeff Blauser, Atlanta, July 12, 1992, 10 inn (A)
KARL RHODES, Chicago, Apr 4, 1994 (H)
Cory Snyder, Los Angeles, Apr 17, 1994 (A)
JEFF BAGWELL, Houston, June 24, 1994 (H)
Barry Bonds, San Francisco, Aug 2, 1994 (H)
ANDRES GALARRAGA, Colorado, June 25, 1995 (A)
REGGIE SANDERS, Cincinnati, Aug 15, 1995 (H)
SAMMY SOSA, Chicago, June 5, 1996 (H)
Mike Piazza, Los Angeles, June 29, 1996 (A)
BENITO SANTIAGO, Philadelphia, Sept 15, 1996 (A)
Willie Greene, Cincinnati, Sept 24, 1996 (H)
LARRY WALKER, Colorado, Apr 5, 1997 (A)
Steve Finley, San Diego, May 19, 1997 (A)
Steve Finley, San Diego, June 23, 1997 (A)
Bobby Estalella, Philadelphia, Sept 4, 1997 (A)
JOSE VALENTIN, Milwaukee, Apr 3, 1998 (A)
MARK McGWIRE, St. Louis, Apr 14, 1998 (H)
Mark McGwire, St. Louis, May 19, 1998 (A)
Sammy Sosa, Chicago, June 15, 1998 (H)
Brant Brown, Chicago, June 18, 1998 (H)
Ken Caminiti, San Diego, July 12, 1998 (A)
BRET BOONE, Cincinnati, Sept 20, 1998 (A)
Mike Lansing, Colorado, Sept 22, 1998 (H)
Jeff Bagwell, Houston, Apr 21, 1999 (A)
Larry Walker, Colorado, Apr 28, 1999 (A)
Jeffrey Hammonds, Cincinnati, May 19, 1999 (A)
Vinny Castilla, Colorado, June 5, 1999 (H)
JEFF BAGWELL, Houston, June 9, 1999 (A)
Edgardo Alfonzo, New York, Aug 30, 1999 (A)
GREG VAUGHN, Cincinnati, Sept 7, 1999, 2nd game (A)
STEVE FINLEY, Arizona, Sept 8, 1999 (A)
Kevin Elster, Los Angeles, Apr 11, 2000 (A)
Todd Helton, Colorado, May 1, 2000 (H)
Mark McGwire, St. Louis, May 18, 2000 (A)
BRET BOONE, San Diego, June 23, 2000 (A)
Jeff Cirillo, Colorado, June 28, 2000 (H)
TYLER HOUSTON, Milwaukee, July 9, 2000 (H)
ARAMIS RAMIREZ, Pittsburgh, Apr 8, 2001 (A)
TODD HOLLANDSWORTH, Colorado, Apr 15, 2001 (H)
GEOFF JENKINS, Milwaukee, Apl 28, 2001 (H)
Jeromy Burnitz, Milwaukee, May 10, 2001 (H)
Barry Bonds, San Francisco, May 19, 2001 (A)
Luis Gonzalez, Arizona, June 8, 2001 (A)
Vinny Castilla, Houston, July 28, 2001, 1st game (A)
SAMMY SOSA, Chicago, Aug 9, 2001 (H)
Shawn Green, Los Angeles, Aug 15, 2001 (H)
JOSE ORTIZ, Colorado, Aug 17, 2001 (H)
Sammy Sosa, Chicago, Aug 22, 2001 (H)
Barry Bonds, San Francisco, Sept 9, 2001 (A)
SAMMY SOSA, Chicago, Sept 23, 2001 (A)
RICHIE SEXSON, Milwaukee, Sept 25, 2001 (A)
JEROMY BURNITZ, Milwaukee, Sept 25, 2001 (A)
Phil Nevin, San Diego, Oct 6, 2001 (H)
LANCE BERKMAN, Houston, Apr 16, 2002 (A)
Erubiel Durazo, Colorado, May 17, 2002 (H)
Russell Branyan, Cincinnati, Aug 4, 2002 (A)
AARON BOONE, Cincinnati, Aug 9, 2002 (H)
MIKE LIEBERTHAL, Philadelphia, Aug 10, 2002 (A)
SAMMY SOSA, Chicago, Aug 10, 2002 (A)
BARRY BONDS, San Francisco, Aug 27, 2002 (A)
Andruw Jones, Atlanta, Sept 25, 2002 (A)
Richie Sexson, Milwaukee, Apr 25, 2003 (A)
Aaron Boone, Cincinnati, May 8, 2003 (H)
GEOFF JENKINS, Milwaukee, May 21, 2003 (H)
Todd Helton, Colorado, May 29, 2003 (H)
Moises Alou, Chicago, July 4, 2003 (H)
SHEA HILLENBRAND, Arizona, July 7, 2003 (H)
RICHARD HIDALGO, Houston, Sept 16, 2003 (A)
Mike Lowell, Florida, Apr 21, 2004 (A)
Steve Finley, Arizona, Apr 28, 2004 (H)
LUIS GONZALEZ, Arizona, May 10, 2004 (H)
Larry Walker, Colorado, June 25, 2004 (A)
Albert Pujols, St. Louis, July 20, 2004 (A)
Aramis Ramirez, Chicago, July 30, 2004 (H)
J.T. SNOW, San Francisco, Aug 13, 2004 (A)
Aramis Ramirez, Chicago, Sept 16, 2004 (A)
Morgan Ensberg, Houston, May 15, 2005 (H)
HEE-SEOP CHOI, Los Angeles, June 12, 2005 (H)

**Total number of occurrences: 227**

Note—Capitalized name denotes three consecutive homers (bases on balls excluded);
parentheses denotes home or away games.

## SWITCH-HIT HOME RUNS IN GAME

**(players hitting home runs from both sides of plate in game)**

AL—Wally Schang, Philadelphia, Sept 8, 1916
Johnny Lucadello, St. Louis, Sept 16, 1940
Mickey Mantle, New York, May 13, 1955 (1 RH, 2 LH)
Mickey Mantle, New York, Aug 15, 1955, 2nd game
Mickey Mantle, New York, May 18, 1956
Mickey Mantle, New York, July 1, 1956, 2nd game
Mickey Mantle, New York, June 12, 1957
Mickey Mantle, New York, July 28, 1958
Mickey Mantle, New York, Sept 15, 1959
Mickey Mantle, New York, Apr 26, 1961
Mickey Mantle, New York, May 6, 1962, 2nd game
Tom Tresh, New York, Sept 1, 1963
Tom Tresh, New York, July 13, 1964
Mickey Mantle, New York, Aug 12, 1964
Tom Tresh, New York, June 6, 1965, 2nd game (1 RH, 2 LH)
Reggie Smith, Boston, Aug 20, 1967, 1st game
Reggie Smith, Boston, Aug 11, 1968, 2nd game
Don Buford, Baltimore, Apr 9, 1970
Roy White, New York, May 7, 1970
Reggie Smith, Boston, July 2, 1972, 1st game
Reggie Smith, Boston, Apr 16, 1973
Roy White, New York, Aug 13, 1973
Roy White, New York, Apr 23, 1975
Ken Henderson, Chicago, Aug 29, 1975
Roy White, New York, Aug 18, 1976
Eddie Murray, Baltimore, Aug 3, 1977
Roy White, New York, June 13, 1978
Larry Milbourne, Seattle, July 15, 1978
Willie Wilson, Kansas City, June 15, 1979
Eddie Murray, Baltimore, Aug 29, 1979, 2nd game (2 RH, 1 LH)
U.L. Washington, Kansas City, Sept 21, 1979
Eddie Murray, Baltimore, Aug 16, 1981
Eddie Murray, Baltimore, Apr 24, 1982
Ted Simmons, Milwaukee, May 2, 1982
Eddie Murray, Baltimore, Aug 26, 1982
Roy Smalley, New York, Sept 5, 1982
Donnie Scott, Seattle, Apr 29, 1985
Mike Young, Baltimore, Aug 13, 1985
Eddie Murray, Baltimore, Aug 26, 1985 (1 RH, 2 LH)
Nelson Simmons, Detroit, Sept 16, 1985
Roy Smalley, Minnesota, May 30, 1986
Tony Bernazard, Cleveland, July 1, 1986
Ruben Sierra, Texas, Sept 13, 1986
Eddie Murray, Baltimore, May 8, 1987
Eddie Murray, Baltimore, May 9, 1987
Devon White, California, June 23, 1987
Dale Sveum, Milwaukee, July 17, 1987 (1 RH, 2 LH)
Dale Sveum, Milwaukee, June 12, 1988
Mickey Tettleton, Baltimore, June 13, 1988
Chili Davis, California, July 30, 198
Ruben Sierra, Texas, Aug 27, 1988
Ruben Sierra, Texas, June 8, 1989
Chili Davis, California, July 1, 1989
Devon White, California, June 29, 1990
Roberto Alomar, Toronto, May 10, 1991
Devon White, Toronto, June 1, 1992
Chili Davis, Minnesota, Oct 2, 1992
Carlos Baerga, Cleveland, Apr 8, 1993
Mickey Tettleton, Detroit, May 7, 1993, 12 inn
Tim Raines Sr., Chicago, Aug 31, 1993
Chad Kreuter, Detroit, Sept 7, 1993
Eddie Murray, Cleveland, Apr 21, 1994
Chili Davis, California, May 11, 1994
Bernie Williams, New York, June 6, 1994
Ruben Sierra, Oakland, June 7, 1994
Chili Davis, California, July 30, 1994
Mickey Tettleton, Texas, Apr 28, 1995
Roberto Alomar, Toronto, May 3, 1995, 10 inn
Luis Alicea, Boston, July 28, 1995
Raul Casanova, Detroit, June 6, 1996
J.T. Snow, California, June 9, 1996, 13 inn
Ruben Sierra, New York, June 22, 1996
Melvin Nieves, Detroit, July 15, 1996
Roberto Alomar, Baltimore, July 25, 1996
Roberto Alomar, Baltimore, Aug 14, 1996
Melvin Nieves, Detroit, Aug 20, 1996
Chili Davis, California, Aug 21, 1996
Bernie Williams, New York, Sept 12, 1996
Tony Clark, Detroit, Apr 5, 1997
Chili Davis, Kansas City, June 7, 1997
Jose Cruz Jr., Toronto, Aug 24, 1997, 13 inn
David Segui, Seattle, Apr 1, 1998
Tony Clark, Detroit, June 17, 1998
Tony Clark, Detroit, July 26, 1998
Tony Clark, Detroit, Aug 1, 1998
Jorge Posada, New York, Aug 23, 1998
Bernie Williams, New York, Sept 4, 1998
Brian Simmons, Chicago, Sept 26, 1998
Bernie Williams, New York, May 4, 1999
Jorge Posada, New York, July 10, 1999
Tony Clark, Detroit, July 18, 1999
Tony Clark, Detroit, July 25, 1999
Carl Everett, Boston, Apr 11, 2000
Bernie Williams, New York, Apr 23, 2000
Jorge Posada, New York, Apr 23, 2000
Bernie Williams, New York, May 17, 2000
Carlos Beltran, Kansas City, June 29, 2000
Carl Everett, Boston, Aug 29, 2000
Jose Valentin, Chicago, Sept 30, 2000
Ruben Sierra, Texas, June 13, 2001
Bernie Williams, New York, June 30, 2001
Roberto Alomar, Cleveland, July 16, 2001
Bernie Williams, New York, May 17, 2002, 14 inn
Jorge Posada, New York, June 28, 2002
Jose Valentin, Chicago, Aug 13, 2002
Carlos Beltran, Kansas City, Sept 6, 2002
Jeff DaVanon, Anaheim, June 3, 2003
Jeff DaVanon, Anaheim, June 4, 2003
Bill Mueller, Boston, July 4, 2003
Bill Mueller, Boston, July 29, 2003
Jose Valentin, Chicago, July 29, 2003
Jorge Posada, New York, March 31, 2004
Geoff Blum, Tampa Bay, May 4, 2004
Carlos Guillen, Detroit, May 31, 2004
Mark Texeira, Texas, July 4, 2004
Victor Martinez, Cleveland, July 16, 2004 (2 RH, 1 LH)
Carlos Guillen, Detroit, July 24, 2004
Tony Clark, New York, Aug 28, 2004 (2 LH, 1 RH)
Dmitri Young, Detroit, Sept 18, 2004, 12 inn
Jorge Posada, New York, May 24, 2005
Nick Swisher, Oakland, June 26, 2005
Gary Matthews Jr., Texas, July 27, 2005
Jason Varitek, Boston, Aug 16, 2005
Mark Teixeira, Texas, Sept 18, 2005

**Total number of occurrences: 124**

NL—Augie Galan, Chicago, June 25, 1937
Jim Russell, Boston, June 7, 1948
Jim Russell, Brooklyn, July 26, 1950
Red Schoendienst, St. Louis, July 8, 1951, 2nd game
Maury Wills, Los Angeles, May 30, 1962, 1st game
Ellis Burton, Chicago, Aug 1, 1963
Ellis Burton, Chicago, Sept 7, 1964, 1st game
Jim Lefebvre, Los Angeles, May 7, 1966
Wes Parker, Los Angeles, June 5, 1966, 1st game
Pete Rose, Cincinnati, Aug 30, 1966
Pete Rose, Cincinnati, Aug 2, 1967
Ted Simmons, St. Louis, Apr 17, 1975
Reggie Smith, St. Louis, May 4, 1975
Reggie Smith, St. Louis, May 22, 1976 (2 RH, 1 LH)
Lee Mazzilli, New York, Sept 3, 1978
Ted Simmons, St. Louis, June 11, 1979
Alan Ashby, Houston, Sept 27, 1982
Chili Davis, San Francisco, June 5, 1983
Mark Bailey, Houston, Sept 16, 1984
Chili Davis, San Francisco, June 27, 1987
Bobby Bonilla, Pittsburgh, July 3, 1987
Kevin Bass, Houston, Aug 3, 1987, 13 inn
Kevin Bass, Houston, Sept 2, 1987
Chili Davis, San Francisco, Sept 15, 1987
Bobby Bonilla, Pittsburgh, Apr 6, 1988, 14 inn
Tim Raines Sr, Montreal, July 16, 1988
Steve Jeltz, Philadelphia, June 8, 1989
Kevin Bass, Houston, Aug 20, 1989
Eddie Murray, Los Angeles, Apr 18, 1990
Eddie Murray, Los Angeles, June 9, 1990

Bret Barberie, Montreal, Aug 2, 1991
Howard Johnson, New York, Aug 31, 1991
Kevin Bass, San Francisco, Aug 2, 1992, 2nd game
Bobby Bonilla, New York, Apr 23, 1993
Bobby Bonilla, New York, June 10, 1993
Todd Benzinger, San Francisco, Aug 30, 1993
Mark Whiten, St. Louis, Sept 14, 1993
Geronimo Pena, St. Louis, Apr 17, 1994
Bobby Bonilla, New York, May 4, 1994
Todd Hundley, New York, June 18, 1994
Ken Caminiti, Houston, July 3, 1994
Bobby Bonilla, New York, May 12, 1995
Ken Caminiti, San Diego, Sept 16, 1995
Ken Caminiti, San Diego, Sept 17, 1995
Ken Caminiti, San Diego, Sept 19, 1995
Todd Hundley, New York, May 18, 1996
Todd Hundley, New York, June 10, 1996
Ken Caminiti, San Diego, Aug 1, 1996
Ken Caminiti, San Diego, Aug 21, 1996
Ken Caminiti, San Diego, Aug 28, 1996, 12 inn
Ken Caminiti, San Diego, Sept 11, 1996
Carl Everett, New York, Apr 20, 1997, 1st game
Todd Hundley, New York, May 5, 1997
F.P. Santangelo, Montreal, June 7, 1997
Todd Hundley, New York, July 20, 1997
Carl Everett, Houston, Apr 24, 1998
Ken Caminiti, San Diego, July 12, 1998
Chipper Jones, Atlanta, May 1, 1999
Jose Valentin, Milwaukee, July 1, 1999
Chipper Jones, Atlanta, Aug 1, 1999
Carl Everett, Houston, Aug 7, 1999
Dale Sveum, Pittsburgh, Aug 18, 1999
Ken Caminiti, Houston, Aug 20, 1999
Chipper Jones, Atlanta, Sept 21, 1999
Chipper Jones, Atlanta, May 14, 2000
Jose Vidro, Montreal, July 3, 2000
Chipper Jones, Atlanta, July 5, 2000
Geoff Blum, Montreal, July 5, 2001
Tomas Perez, Philadelphia, July 24, 2001
Mark Bellhorn, Chicago, June 30, 2002
Mark Bellhorn, Chicago, Aug 29, 2002
Tony Clark, New York, Aug 3, 2003
Jose Reyes, New York, Aug 28, 2003
Aaron Miles, Colorado, Apr 14, 2004
Carlos Beltran, Houston, July 1, 2004, 10 inn
Alex Citron, Arizona, July 8, 2004
Geoff Blum, San Diego, Apr 13, 2005
Rafael Furcal, Atlanta, Apr 15, 2005
Milton Bradley, Los Angeles, Apr 18, 2005
Milton Bradley, Los Angeles, May 13, 2005
Javier Valentin, Cincinnati, July 17, 2005
Rafael Furcal, Atlanta, July 31, 2005
Jose Cruz, Los Angeles, Sept 7, 2005
Tony Clark, Arizona, Sept 17, 2005

**Total number of occurrences: 84**

## 40 STOLEN BASES AND 40 HOMERS IN SEASON

### AMERICAN LEAGUE

| Player, Club | Year | G | SB | HR |
|---|---|---|---|---|
| Jose Canseco, Oakland | 1988 | 158 | 40 | 42 |
| Alex Rodriguez, Seattle | 1998 | 161 | 46 | 42 |

**Total number of occurrences: 2**

### NATIONAL LEAGUE

| Player, Club | Year | G | SB | HR |
|---|---|---|---|---|
| Barry Bonds, San Francisco | 1996 | 158 | 40 | 42 |

**Total number of occurrences: 1**

## 30 STOLEN BASES AND 30 HOMERS IN SEASON

### AMERICAN LEAGUE

| Player, Club | Year | G | SB | HR |
|---|---|---|---|---|
| Kenny Williams, St. Louis | 1922 | 153 | 37 | 39 |
| Tommy Harper, Milwaukee | 1970 | 154 | 38 | 31 |
| Bobby Bonds, New York | 1975 | 145 | 30 | 32 |
| Bobby Bonds, California | 1977 | 158 | 41 | 37 |
| Bobby Bonds, Chicago/Texas | 1978 | 156 | 43 | 31 |
| Joe Carter, Cleveland | 1987 | 149 | 31 | 32 |
| Jose Canseco, Oakland | 1988 | 158 | 40 | 42 |
| Alex Rodriguez, Seattle | 1998 | 161 | 46 | 42 |
| Shawn Green, Toronto | 1998 | 158 | 35 | 35 |
| Jose Cruz Jr., Toronto | 2001 | 146 | 32 | 34 |
| Alfonso Soriano, New York | 2002 | 156 | 41 | 39 |
| Alfonso Soriano, New York | 2003 | 156 | 35 | 38 |
| Alfonso Soriano, Texas | 2005 | 156 | 30 | 36 |

**Total number of occurrences: 13**

### NATIONAL LEAGUE

| Player, Club | Year | G | SB | HR |
|---|---|---|---|---|
| Willie Mays, New York | 1956 | 152 | 40 | 36 |
| Willie Mays, New York | 1957 | 152 | 38 | 35 |
| Hank Aaron, Milwaukee | 1963 | 161 | 31 | 44 |
| Bobby Bonds, San Francisco | 1969 | 158 | 45 | 32 |
| Bobby Bonds, San Francisco | 1973 | 160 | 43 | 39 |
| Dale Murphy, Atlanta | 1983 | 162 | 30 | 36 |
| Eric Davis, Cincinnati | 1987 | 129 | 50 | 37 |
| Howard Johnson, New York | 1987 | 157 | 32 | 36 |
| Darryl Strawberry, New York | 1987 | 154 | 36 | 39 |
| Howard Johnson, New York | 1989 | 153 | 41 | 36 |
| Ron Gant, Atlanta | 1990 | 152 | 33 | 32 |
| Barry Bonds, Pittsburgh | 1990 | 151 | 52 | 33 |
| Ron Gant, Atlanta | 1991 | 154 | 34 | 32 |
| Howard Johnson, New York | 1991 | 156 | 30 | 38 |
| Barry Bonds, Pittsburgh | 1992 | 140 | 39 | 34 |
| Sammy Sosa, Chicago | 1993 | 159 | 36 | 33 |
| Sammy Sosa, Chicago | 1995 | 144 | 34 | 36 |
| Barry Bonds, San Francisco | 1995 | 144 | 31 | 33 |
| Dante Bichette, Colorado | 1996 | 159 | 31 | 31 |
| Barry Bonds, San Francisco | 1996 | 158 | 40 | 42 |
| Ellis Burks, Colorado | 1996 | 156 | 32 | 40 |
| Barry Larkin, Cincinnati | 1996 | 152 | 36 | 33 |
| Larry Walker, Colorado | 1997 | 153 | 33 | 49 |
| Jeff Bagwell, Houston | 1997 | 162 | 31 | 43 |
| Barry Bonds, San Francisco | 1997 | 159 | 37 | 40 |
| Raul Mondesi, Los Angeles | 1997 | 159 | 32 | 30 |
| Jeff Bagwell, Houston | 1999 | 162 | 30 | 42 |
| Raul Mondesi, Los Angeles | 1999 | 159 | 36 | 33 |
| Preston Wilson, Florida | 2000 | 161 | 36 | 31 |
| Vladimir Guerrero, Montreal | 2001 | 159 | 37 | 34 |
| Bobby Abreu, Philadelphia | 2001 | 162 | 36 | 31 |
| Vladimir Guerrero, Montreal | 2002 | 161 | 40 | 39 |
| Bobby Abreu, Philadelphia | 2004 | 159 | 40 | 30 |

**Total number of occurrences: 33**

### BOTH LEAGUES

| Player, Club | Year | G | SB | HR |
|---|---|---|---|---|
| Carlos Beltran, KC/Hou<br>KC 14/15, Hou 28/23 | 2004 | 159 | 42 | 38 |

## 20 STOLEN BASES AND 50 HOMERS IN SEASON

### AMERICAN LEAGUE

| Player, Club | Year | G | SB | HR |
|---|---|---|---|---|
| Brady Anderson, Baltimore | 1996 | 149 | 21 | 50 |
| Ken Griffey Jr., Seattle | 1998 | 161 | 20 | 56 |

**Total number of occurrences: 2**

### NATIONAL LEAGUE

| Player, Club | Year | G | SB | HR |
|---|---|---|---|---|
| Willie Mays, New York | 1955 | 152 | 24 | 51 |

**Total number of occurrences: 1**

## 50 STOLEN BASES AND 20 HOMERS IN SEASON

### AMERICAN LEAGUE

| Player, Club | Year | G | SB | HR |
|---|---|---|---|---|
| Rickey Henderson, New York | 1985 | 143 | 80 | 24 |
| Rickey Henderson, New York | 1986 | 153 | 87 | 28 |
| Rickey Henderson, Oakland | 1990 | 136 | 65 | 28 |
| Brady Anderson, Baltimore | 1992 | 159 | 53 | 21 |
| Rickey Henderson, Oak-Tor | 1993 | 134 | 53 | 21 |

**Total number of occurrences: 5**

### NATIONAL LEAGUE

| Player, Club | Year | G | SB | HR |
|---|---|---|---|---|
| Lou Brock, St. Louis | 1967 | 159 | 52 | 21 |
| Cesar Cedeno, Houston | 1972 | 139 | 55 | 22 |
| Cesar Cedeno, Houston | 1973 | 139 | 56 | 25 |
| Joe Morgan, Cincinnati | 1973 | 157 | 67 | 26 |
| Cesar Cedeno, Houston | 1974 | 160 | 57 | 26 |
| Joe Morgan, Cincinnati | 1974 | 149 | 58 | 22 |
| Joe Morgan, Cincinnati | 1976 | 141 | 60 | 27 |
| Ryne Sandberg, Chicago | 1985 | 153 | 54 | 26 |
| Eric Davis, Cincinnati | 1986 | 132 | 80 | 27 |
| Eric Davis, Cincinnati | 1987 | 129 | 50 | 37 |
| Barry Bonds, Pittsburgh | 1990 | 151 | 52 | 33 |
| Craig Biggio, Houston | 1998 | 160 | 50 | 20 |

**Total number of occurrences: 12**

## 400 TOTAL BASES IN SEASON

### AMERICAN LEAGUE

| Year | Player, Club | TB |
|---|---|---|
| 1921 | Babe Ruth, New York | 457 |
| 1927 | Lou Gehrig, New York | 447 |
| 1932 | Jimmie Foxx, Philadelphia | 438 |
| 1930 | Lou Gehrig, New York | 419 |
| 1937 | Joe DiMaggio, New York | 418 |
| 1927 | Babe Ruth, New York | 417 |
| 1931 | Lou Gehrig, New York | 410 |
| 1934 | Lou Gehrig, New York | 409 |
| 1978 | Jim Rice, Boston | 406 |
| 1936 | Hal Trosky, Cleveland | 405 |
| 1936 | Lou Gehrig, New York | 403 |
| 1933 | Jimmie Foxx, Philadelphia | 403 |

**Total number of occurrences: 12**

### NATIONAL LEAGUE

| Year | Player, Club | TB |
|---|---|---|
| 1922 | Rogers Hornsby, St. Louis | 450 |
| 1930 | Chuck Klein, Philadelphia | 445 |
| 1948 | Stan Musial, St. Louis | 429 |
| 2001 | Sammy Sosa, Chicago | 425 |
| 1930 | Hack Wilson, Chicago | 423 |
| 1932 | Chuck Klein, Philadelphia | 420 |
| 2001 | Luis Gonzalez, Arizona | 419 |
| 1930 | Babe Herman, Brooklyn | 416 |
| 1998 | Sammy Sosa, Chicago | 416 |
| 2001 | Barry Bonds, San Francisco | 411 |
| 1929 | Rogers Hornsby, Chicago | 409 |
| 1997 | Larry Walker, Colorado | 409 |
| 1937 | Joe Medwick, St. Louis | 406 |
| 1929 | Chuck Klein, Philadelphia | 405 |
| 2000 | Todd Helton, Colorado | 405 |

| Year | Player, Club | TB |
|---|---|---|
| 2001 | Todd Helton, Colorado | 402 |
| 1959 | Hank Aaron, Milwaukee | 400 |

**Total number of occurrences: 17**

## 100 EXTRA-BASE HITS IN SEASON

### AMERICAN LEAGUE

| Year | Player, Club | 2B | 3B | HR | EBH |
|---|---|---|---|---|---|
| 1921 | Babe Ruth, New York | 44 | 16 | 59 | 119 |
| 1927 | Lou Gehrig, New York | 52 | 18 | 47 | 117 |
| 1937 | Hank Greenberg, Detroit | 49 | 14 | 40 | 103 |
| 1995 | Albert Belle, Cleveland | 52 | 1 | 50 | 103 |
| 1930 | Lou Gehrig, New York | 42 | 17 | 41 | 100 |
| 1932 | Jimmie Foxx, Philadelphia | 33 | 9 | 58 | 100 |

**Total number of occurrences: 6**

### NATIONAL LEAGUE

| Year | Player, Club | 2B | 3B | HR | EBH |
|---|---|---|---|---|---|
| 1930 | Chuck Klein, Philadelphia | 59 | 8 | 40 | 107 |
| 2001 | Barry Bonds, San Francisco | 32 | 2 | 73 | 107 |
| 2001 | Todd Helton, Colorado | 54 | 2 | 49 | 105 |
| 1932 | Chuck Klein, Philadelphia | 50 | 15 | 38 | 103 |
| 1948 | Stan Musial, St. Louis | 46 | 18 | 39 | 103 |
| 2000 | Todd Helton, Colorado | 59 | 2 | 42 | 103 |
| 2001 | Sammy Sosa, Chicago | 34 | 5 | 64 | 103 |
| 1922 | Rogers Hornsby, St. Louis | 46 | 14 | 42 | 102 |
| 2001 | Luis Gonzalez, Arizona | 36 | 7 | 57 | 100 |

**Total number of occurrences: 9**

## PLAYERS HITTING FOR CYCLE

**(single, double, triple and home run in game)**

### AMERICAN ASSOCIATION

Al Knight, Philadelphia, July 30, 1883
John Reilly, Cincinnati, Sept 12, 1883
John Reilly, Cincinnati, Sept 19, 1883
Dave Orr, New York, June 12, 1885
Henry Larkin, Philadelphia, June 16 ,1885
Pete Browning, Louisville, Aug 8, 1886
Jim McGarr, Philadelphia, Sept 23, 1886
Tip O'Neill, St. Louis, Apr 30, 1887
Tip O'Neill, St. Louis, May 7 ,1887
Dave Orr, New York, Aug 10, 1887
Bid McPhee, Cincinnati, Aug 26, 1887
Harry Stovey, Philadelphia, May 15, 1888
Sam Barkley, Kansas City, June 13, 1888
Pete Browning, Louisville, June 7, 1889
Bill Van Dyke, Toledo, July 5, 1890
Jim Davis, Brooklyn, July 18, 1890
Bill Weaver, Louisville, Aug 12, 1890
Abner Dalrymple, Milwaukee, Sept 12, 1891
**Total number of occurrences: 18**

### PLAYERS LEAGUE

Roger Conner, New York, July 21, 1890
**Total number of occurrences: 1**

### AMERICAN LEAGUE

Harry Davis, Philadelphia, July 10, 1901
Nap Lajoie, Philadelphia, July 30, 1901
Patsy Dougherty, Boston, July 29, 1903
Bill Bradley, Cleveland, Sept 24, 1903
Otis Clymer, Washington, Oct 2, 1908
Danny Murphy, Philadelphia, Aug 25, 1910
Home Run Baker, Philadelphia, July 3, 1911, 2nd game
Tris Speaker, Boston, June 9, 1912
Bert Daniels, New York, July 25, 1912
George Sisler, St. Louis, Aug 8, 1920, 2nd game
Bobby Veach, Detroit, Sept 17, 1920, 12 inn
Bob Meusel, New York, May 7, 1921
George Sisler, St. Louis, Aug 13, 1921, 10 inn
Ray Schalk, Chicago, June 27, 1922
Bob Meusel, New York, July 3, 1922
Bill Jacobson, St. Louis, Apr 17, 1924
Goose Goslin, Washington, Aug 28, 1924
Roy Carlyle, Boston, July 21, 1925, 1st game
Bob Fothergill, Detroit, Sept 26, 1926, 1st game
Bob Meusel, New York, July 26, 1928, 1st game, 12 inn
Oscar Melillo, St. Louis, May 23, 1929, 2nd game
Joe Cronin, Washington, Sept 2, 1929, 1st game
Tony Lazzeri, New York, June 3, 1932
Mickey Cochrane, Philadelphia, July 22, 1932
Mickey Cochrane, Philadelphia, Aug 2, 1933
Pinky Higgins, Philadelphia, Aug 6, 1933
Jimmie Foxx, Philadelphia, Aug 14, 1933
Earl Averill, Cleveland, Aug 17, 1933
Doc Cramer, Philadelphia, June 10, 1934
Lou Gehrig, New York, June 25, 1934
Moose Solters, Boston, Aug 19, 1934, 1st game
Gee Walker, Detroit, Apr 20, 1937
Joe DiMaggio, New York, July 9, 1937
Lou Gehrig, New York, Aug 1, 1937
Odell Hale, Cleveland, July 12, 1938
Sam Chapman, Philadelphia, May 5, 1939
Charlie Gehringer, Detroit, May 27, 1939
Buddy Rosar, New York, July 19, 1940
Joe Cronin, Boston, Augt 2, 1940
Joe Gordon, New York, Sept 8, 1940
George McQuinn, St. Louis, July 19, 1941, 1st game
Leon Culberson, Boston, July 3, 1943
Bobby Doerr, Boston, May 17, 1944, 2nd game
Bob Johnson, Boston, July 6, 1944
Mickey Vernon, Washington, May 19, 1946, 2nd game
Ted Williams, Boston, July 21, 1946, 2nd game
Bobby Doerr, Boston, May 13, 1947
Vic Wertz , Detroit, Sept 14, 1947, 1st game
Joe DiMaggio, New York, May 20, 1948
George Kell, Detroit, June 2, 1950, 2nd game
Elmer Valo, Philadelphia, Aug 2, 1950
Hoot Evers, Detroit, Sept 7, 1950, 10 inn
Larry Doby, Cleveland, June 4, 1952
Mickey Mantle, New York, July 23, 1957
Brooks Robinson, Baltimore, July 15, 1960
Lu Clinton, Boston, July 13, 1962, 15 inn
Jim King, Washington, May 26, 1964
Jim Fregosi, Los Angeles, July 28, 1964
Carl Yastrzemski, Boston, May 14, 1965, 10 inn
Jim Fregosi, California, May 20, 1968, 11 inn
Rod Carew, Minnesota, May 20, 1970
Tony Horton, Cleveland, July 2, 1970
Fred Patek, Kansas City, July 9, 1971
Bobby Murcer, New York, Aug 29, 1972, 1st game, 11 inn
Cesar Tovar, Minnesota, Sept 19, 1972
Larry Hisle, Minnesota, June 4, 1976, 10 inn
Lyman Bostock, Minnesota, July 24, 1976
Mike Hegan, Milwaukee, Sept 3, 1976
John Mayberry, Kansas City, Aug 5, 1977
Jack Brohamer, Chicago, Sept 24, 1977
Andre Thornton, Cleveland, Apr 22, 1978
Mike Cubbage, Minnesota, July 27, 1978
George Brett, Kansas City, May 28, 1979, 16 inn
Dan Ford, California, Aug 10, 1979, 14 inn
Bob Watson, Boston, Sept 15, 1979
Frank White, Kansas City, Sept 26, 1979
Fred Lynn, Boston, May 13, 1980
Gary Ward, Minnesota, Sept 18, 1980, 1st game
Charlie Moore, Milwaukee, Oct 1, 1980
Frank White, Kansas City, Aug 3, 1982
Cal Ripken Jr., Baltimore, May 6, 1984
Carlton Fisk, Chicago, May 16, 1984
Dwight Evans, Boston, June 28, 1984, 11 inn
Oddibe McDowell, Texas, July 23, 1985
Rich Gedman, Boston, Sept 18, 1985
Tony Phillips, Oakland, May 16, 1986
Kirby Puckett, Minnesota, Aug 1, 1986
Robin Yount, Milwaukee, June 12, 1988
Mike Greenwell, Boston, Sept 14, 1988
Kelly Gruber, Toronto, Apr 16, 1989
George Brett, Kansas City, July 25, 1990
Paul Molitor, Milwaukee, May 15, 1991
Dave Winfield, California, June 24, 1991
Jay Buhner, Seattle, June 23, 1993, 14 inn
Travis Fryman, Detroit, July 28, 1993
Scott Cooper, Boston, Apr 12, 1994
Tony Fernandez, New York, Sept 3, 1995, 10 inn
John Valentin, Boston, June 6, 1996
Alex Rodriguez, Seattle, June 5, 1997
Mike Blowers, Oakland, May 18, 1998
Chris Singleton, Chicago, July 6, 1999, 10 inn
Jose Valentin, Chicago, Apr 27, 2000
Eric Chavez, Oakland, June 21, 2000
Damion Easley, Detroit, June 8, 2001
John Olerud, Seattle, June 16, 2001
Jeff Frye, Toronto, Aug 17, 2001
Miguel Tejada, Oakland, Sept 29, 2001
Eric Byrnes, Oakland, June 29, 2003
Travis Hafner, Cleveland, Aug 14, 2003
Mark Teixeira, Texas, Aug 17, 2004
Jeff DaVanon, Anaheim, Aug 25, 2004
**Total number of occurrences: 111**

### NATIONAL LEAGUE

Charles Foley, Buffalo, May 25, 1882
Jim O'Rourke, Buffalo, June 16, 1884
George Wood, Detroit, June 13, 1885
Bill McQuery, Detroit, Sept 28, 1885
Fred Dunlap, St. Louis, May 24, 1886
John Rowe, Detroit, Aug 21, 1886
Fred Carroll, Pittsburgh, May 2, 1887
Jimmy Ryan, Chicago, July 28, 1888
Mike Tiernan, New York, Aug 25, 1888
John Glasscock, Indianapolis, Aug 8, 1889
Larry Twitchell, Cleveland, Aug 15, 1889
Tom Burns, Brooklyn, Aug 1, 1890, 2nd game
John Reilly, Cincinnati, Aug6, 1890
Jimmy Ryan, Chicago, July 1, 1891
Lave Cross, Philadelphia, Apr 24, 1894
Bill Hassamaer, Washington, June 13, 1894
Sam Thompson, Philadelphia, Aug 17, 1894
Tom Parrott, Cincinnati, Sept 28, 1894
Tom Dowd, St. Louis, Aug 16,1895
Ed Cartwright, Washington, Sept 30, 1895, 1st game
Herman Long, Boston, May 9, 1896
Bill Joyce, Washington, May 30, 1896, 1st game
Fred Clarke, Pittsburgh, July 23, 1901
Fred Clarke, Pittsburgh, May 7, 1903
Rich Cooley, Boston, June 20, 1904, 2nd game
Sam Mertes, New York, Oct 4, 1904, 1st game
John Bates, Boston, Apr 26, 1907
Chief Wilson, Pittsburgh, July 3, 1910
Bill Collins, Boston, Oct 6, 1910
Mike Mitchell, Cincinnati, Aug 19, 1911, 2nd game
Chief Meyers, New York, June 10, 1912
Honus Wagner, Pittsburgh, Aug 22, 1912, 2nd game
Heinie Groh, Cincinnati, July 5, 1915, 2nd game
Cliff Heathcote, St. Louis, June 13, 1918, 19 inn
George Burns, New York, Sept 17, 1920, 10 inn
Dave Bancroft, New York, June 1, 1921, 2nd game
Dave Robertson, Pittsburgh, Aug 30, 1921
Ross Youngs, New York, Apr 29, 1922
Jimmy Johnston, Brooklyn, May 25, 1922, 1st game
Pie Traynor, Pittsburgh, July 7, 1923
Kiki Cuyler, Pittsburgh, June 4, 1925
Max Carey, Pittsburgh, June 20, 1925.
Jim Bottomley, St. Louis, July 15, 1927
Cy Williams, Philadelphia, Aug 5, 1927
Bill Terry, New York, May 29, 1928
Mel Ott, New York, May 16, 1929, 2nd game
Fred Lindstrom, New York, May 8, 1930
Hack Wilson, Chicago, June 23, 1930
Chick Hafey, St. Louis, Aug 21, 1930
Babe Herman, Brooklyn, May 18, 1931
Chuck Klein, Philadelphia, July 1, 1931
Babe Herman, Brooklyn, July 24, 1931
Pepper Martin, St. Louis, May 5, 1933
Chuck Klein, Philadelphia, May 26, 1933, 14 inn
Arky Vaughan, Pittsburgh, June 24, 1933
Babe Herman, Chicago, Sept 30, 1933
Joe Medwick, St. Louis, June 29, 1935
Sam Leslie, New York, May 24, 1936
Arky Vaughan, Pittsburgh, July 19, 1939
Harry Craft, Cincinnati, June 8, 1940
Harry Danning, New York, June 15, 1940
Johnny Mize, St. Louis, July 13, 1940, 1st game
Dixie Walker, Brooklyn, Sept 2, 1944
Bob Elliott, Pittsburgh, July 15, 1945, 2nd game
Bill Salkeld, Pittsburgh, Aug 4, 1945
Wally Westlake, Pittsburgh, July 30, 1948
Jackie Robinson, Brooklyn, Aug 29, 1948, 1st game
Wally Westlake, Pittsburgh, June 14, 1949
Gil Hodges, Brooklyn, June 25, 1949
Stan Musial, St. Louis, July 24, 1949
Ralph Kiner, Pittsburgh, June 25, 1950
Roy Smalley, Chicago, June 28, 1950
Gus Bell, Pittsburgh, June 4, 1951
Don Mueller, New York, July 11, 1954, 1st game
Lee Walls, Chicago, July 2, 1957, 10 inn
Frank Robinson, Cincinnati, May 2, 1959
Bill White, St. Louis, Aug 14, 1960, 1st game
Ken Boyer, St. Louis, Sept 14, 1961, 2nd game, 11 inn
Johnny Callison, Philadelphia, June 27, 1963
Jim Hickman, New York, Aug 7, 1963
Ken Boyer, St. Louis, June 16, 1964
Willie Stargell, Pittsburgh, July 22, 1964
Billy Williams, Chicago, July 17, 1966, 2nd game
Randy Hundley, Chicago, Aug 11, 1966, 1st game, 11 inn
Wes Parker, Los Angeles, May 7, 1970, 10 inn
Tommie Agee, New York, July 6, 1970
Jim Hart, San Francisco, July 8, 1970
Dave Kingman, San Francisco, Apr 16, 1972
Cesar Cedeno, Houston, Aug 2, 1972
Joe Torre, St. Louis, June 27, 1973
Richie Zisk, Pittsburgh, June 9, 1974
Lou Brock, St. Louis, May 27, 1975
Tim Foli, Montreal, Apr 21, 1976, suspended game completed Apr 22
Mike Phillips, New York, June 25, 1976
Cesar Cedeno, Houston, Aug 9, 1976
Bob Watson, Houston, June 24, 1977, 11 inn
Chris Speier, Montreal, July 20, 1978
Ivan DeJesus, Chicago, Apr 22, 1980
Mike Easler, Pittsburgh, June 12, 1980
Willie McGee, St. Louis, June 23, 1984, 11 inn
Jeff Leonard, San Francisco, June 27, 1985
Keith Hernandez, New York, July 4, 1985, 19 inn
Andre Dawson, Chicago, Apr 29, 1987

Candy Maldonado, San Francisco, May 4, 1987
Tim Raines Sr., Montreal, Aug 16, 1987
Albert Hall, Atlanta, Sept 23, 1987
Chris Speier, San Francisco, July 9, 1988
Eric Davis, Cincinnati, June 2, 1989
Kevin McReynolds, New York, Aug 1, 1989
Gary Redus, Pittsburgh, Aug 25, 1989
Robby Thompson, San Francisco, Apr 22, 1991
Ray Lankford, St. Louis, Sept 15, 1991
Andujar Cedeno, Houston, Aug 25, 1992
Mark Grace, Chicago, May 9, 1993
Rondell White, Montreal, June 11, 1995, 13 inn
Gregg Jefferies, Philadelphia, Aug 25, 1995
John Mabry, St. Louis, May 18, 1996
Alex Ochoa, New York, July 3, 1996
John Olerud, New York, Sept 11, 1997
Dante Bichette, Colorado, June 10, 1998
Neifi Perez, Colorado, July 25, 1998
Jeff Kent, San Francisco, May 3, 1999
Todd Helton, Colorado, June 19, 1999
Jason Kendall, Pittsburgh, May 19, 2000
Mike Lansing, Colorado, June 18, 2000
Luis Gonzalez, Arizona, July 5, 2000
Jeff Bagwell, Houston, July 18, 2000
Craig Biggio, Houston, Apr 8, 2002
Greg Colbrunn, Arizona, Sept 18, 2002
Brad Wilkerson, Montreal, June 24, 2003
Vladimir Guerrero, Montreal, Sept 14, 2003
Chad Moeller, Milwaukee, Apr 27, 2004
David Bell, Philadelphia, June 28, 2004
Daryle Ward, Pittsburgh, May 26, 2004
Eric Valent, New York, July 29, 2004
Brad Wilkerson, Washington, Apr 6, 2005
Mark Grudzielanek, St. Louis, Apr 27, 2005
Randy Winn, San Francisco, Aug 15, 2005
**Total number of occurrences: 138**

## SIX HITS IN ONE GAME

### AMERICAN ASSOCIATION

| Player | Club, Date | Place | AB | R | H | 2B | 3B | HR |
|---|---|---|---|---|---|---|---|---|
| Hick Carpenter | Cincinnati, Sept 12, 1883 | H | 7 | 5 | 6 | 0 | 0 | 0 |
| John Reilly | Cincinnati, Sept12, 1883 | H | 7 | 6 | 6 | 1 | 1 | 1 |
| Oscar Walker | Brooklyn, May 31, 1884 | H | 6 | 2 | 6 | 1 | 1 | 0 |
| Lon Knight | Philadelphia, July 30, 1884 | H | 6 | 5 | 6 | 0 | 1 | 0 |
| Dave Orr | New York, June 12, 1885 | H | 6 | 4 | 6 | 2 | 1 | 1 |
| Henry Larkin | Philadelphia, June 16, 1885 | H | 6 | 4 | 6 | 2 | 1 | 1 |
| George Pinckney | Brooklyn, June 25, 1885 | H | 6 | 5 | 6 | 0 | 0 | 0 |
| Arlie Latham | St. Louis, Apr 24, 1886 | H | 6 | 5 | 6 | 0 | 1 | 0 |
| Guy Hecker | Louisville, Aug 15, 1886† | H | 7 | 7 | 6 | 0 | 0 | 3 |
| Denny Lyons | Philadelphia, Apr 26, 1887 | H | 6 | 4 | 6 | 2 | 1 | 0 |
| Pete Hotaling | Cleveland, June 6, 1888 | H | 7 | 5 | 6 | 0 | 1 | 0 |
| Jim McTamany | Kansas City, June 15, 1888 | H | 6 | 3 | 6 | 0 | 0 | 1 |
| Darby O'Brien | Brooklyn, Aug 8, 1889 | A | 6 | 1 | 6 | 3 | 0 | 0 |
| Farmer Weaver | Louisville, Aug 12, 1890 | H | 6 | 3 | 6 | 1 | 2 | 1 |
| Frank Sheibeck | Toledo, Sept 27, 1890 | H | 6 | 4 | 6 | 1 | 1 | 0 |
| Reddy Mack | Louisville, May 26, 1887 | H | 6 | 5 | 6 | 0 | 0 | 0 |

†pitcher
**Total number of occurrences: 16**

### PLAYERS LEAGUE

| Player | Club, Date | Place | AB | R | H | 2B | 3B | HR |
|---|---|---|---|---|---|---|---|---|
| Ed Delahanty | Cleveland, June 2, 1890 | H | 6 | 4 | 6 | 1 | 1 | 0 |
| Bill Shindle | Philadelphia, Aug 26, 1890 | H | 6 | 3 | 6 | 2 | 1 | 0 |

**Total number of occurrences: 2**

### AMERICAN LEAGUE

| Player | Club, Date | Place | AB | R | H | 2B | 3B | HR |
|---|---|---|---|---|---|---|---|---|
| Mike Donlin | Baltimore, June 24, 1901 | H | 6 | 5 | 6 | 2 | 2 | 0 |
| Doc Nance | Detroit, July 13, 1901 | H | 6 | 3 | 6 | 1 | 0 | 0 |
| Erwin Harvey | Cleveland, Apr 25, 1902 | A | 6 | 3 | 6 | 0 | 0 | 0 |
| Danny Murphy | Philadelphia, July 8, 1902 | A | 6 | 3 | 6 | 0 | 0 | 1 |
| Jimmy Williams | Baltimore, Aug 25, 1902 | H | 6 | 1 | 6 | 1 | 1 | 0 |
| Bobby Veach | Detroit, Sept 17, 1920, 12 inn | H | 6 | 2 | 6 | 1 | 1 | 1 |
| George Sisler | St. Louis, Aug 9, 1921, 19 inn | A | 9 | 2 | 6 | 0 | 1 | 0 |
| Frank Brower | Cleveland, Aug 7, 1923 | A | 6 | 3 | 6 | 1 | 0 | 0 |
| George Burns | Cleveland, June 19, 1924, 1st game | A | 6 | 2 | 6 | 3 | 1 | 0 |
| Ty Cobb | Detroit, May 5, 1925 | A | 6 | 4 | 6 | 1 | 0 | 3 |
| Jimmie Foxx | Philadelphia, May 30, 1930, 1st game, 13 inn | H | 7 | 0 | 6 | 2 | 1 | 0 |
| Roger Cramer | Philadelphia, June 20, 1932 | A | 6 | 3 | 6 | 0 | 0 | 0 |
| Jimmie Foxx | Philadelphia, July 10, 1932, 18 inn | A | 9 | 4 | 6 | 1 | 0 | 3 |
| Johnny Burnett | Cleveland, July 10, 1932, 18 inn | H | 11 | 4 | 9 | 2 | 0 | 0 |
| Sam West | St. Louis, Apr 13, 1933, 11 inn | H | 6 | 2 | 6 | 1 | 0 | 0 |
| Myril Hoag | New York, June 6, 1934, 1st game | A | 6 | 3 | 6 | 0 | 0 | 0 |
| Bob Johnson | Philadelphia, June 16, 1934, 2nd game, 11 inn | H | 6 | 3 | 6 | 1 | 0 | 2 |
| Roger Cramer | Philadelphia, July 13, 1935, 1st game | H | 6 | 3 | 6 | 1 | 0 | 0 |
| Bruce Campbell | Cleveland, July 2, 1936, 1st game | A | 6 | 1 | 6 | 1 | 0 | 0 |
| Ray Radcliff | Chicago, July 18, 1936, 2nd game | A | 7 | 4 | 6 | 2 | 0 | 0 |
| Henry Steinbacher | Chicago, June 22, 1938 | H | 6 | 3 | 6 | 1 | 0 | 0 |
| George Myatt | Washington, May 1, 1944 | A | 6 | 3 | 6 | 1 | 0 | 0 |
| Stan Spence | Washington, June 1, 1944 | A | 6 | 2 | 6 | 0 | 0 | 1 |
| George Kell | Detroit, Sept 20, 1946 | A | 7 | 4 | 6 | 1 | 0 | 0 |
| Jim Fridley | Cleveland, Apr 29, 1952 | A | 6 | 4 | 6 | 0 | 0 | 0 |
| Jimmy Piersall | Boston, June 10, 1953, 1st game | A | 6 | 2 | 6 | 1 | 0 | 0 |
| Joe DeMaestri | Kansas City, July 8, 1955, 11 inn | A | 6 | 2 | 6 | 0 | 0 | 0 |
| Pete Runnels | Boston, Aug 30, 1960, 1st game, 15 inn | H | 7 | 1 | 6 | 1 | 0 | 0 |
| Rocky Colavito | Detroit, June 24, 1962, 22 inn | H | 10 | 1 | 7 | 0 | 1 | 0 |
| Floyd Robinson | Chicago, July 22, 1962 | A | 6 | 1 | 6 | 0 | 0 | 0 |
| Bob Oliver | Kansas City, May 4, 1969 | A | 6 | 2 | 6 | 1 | 0 | 1 |
| Jim Northrup | Detroit, Aug 28, 1969, 13 inn | H | 6 | 2 | 6 | 0 | 0 | 2 |
| Cesar Gutierrez | Detroit, June 21, 1970, 2nd game, 12 inn | A | 7 | 3 | 7 | 1 | 0 | 0 |
| John Briggs | Milwaukee, Aug 4, 1973 | A | 6 | 2 | 6 | 2 | 0 | 0 |
| Jorge Orta | Cleveland, June 15, 1980 | H | 6 | 4 | 6 | 1 | 0 | 0 |
| Jerry Remy | Boston, Sept 3, 1981, 20 inn | H | 10 | 2 | 6 | 0 | 0 | 0 |
| Kevin Seitzer | Kansas City, Aug 2, 1987 | H | 6 | 4 | 6 | 1 | 0 | 2 |
| Kirby Puckett | Minnesota, Aug 30, 1987 | A | 6 | 4 | 6 | 2 | 0 | 2 |
| Kirby Puckett | Minnesota, May 23, 1991, 11 inn | H | 7 | 2 | 6 | 0 | 1 | 0 |
| Carlos Baerga | Cleveland, Apr 11, 1992, 19 inn | H | 9 | 1 | 6 | 0 | 0 | 0 |
| Kevin Reimer | Milwaukee, Aug 24, 1993, 2nd game | H | 6 | 4 | 6 | 2 | 0 | 0 |
| Lance Johnson | Chicago, Sept 23, 1995 | A | 6 | 4 | 6 | 0 | 3 | 0 |
| Gerald Williams | New York, May 1, 1996, 15 inn | A | 8 | 1 | 6 | 0 | 0 | 1 |
| Garret Anderson | California, Sept 27, 1996, 15 inn | A | 7 | 0 | 6 | 0 | 0 | 0 |
| Cal Ripken Jr. | Baltimore, June 13, 1999 | A | 6 | 5 | 6 | 1 | 0 | 2 |
| Damion Easley | Detroit, Aug 8, 2001 | A | 6 | 3 | 6 | 0 | 0 | 1 |
| Nomar Garciaparra | Boston, June 21, 2003, 13 inn | A | 6 | 1 | 6 | 0 | 0 | 0 |
| Frank Catalanotto | Toronto, May 1, 2004 | A | 6 | 2 | 6 | 1 | 0 | 0 |
| Alfonso Soriano | Texas, May 8, 2004, 10 inn | H | 6 | 1 | 6 | 2 | 0 | 0 |
| Carlos Pena | Detroit, May 27, 2004 | A | 6 | 4 | 6 | 1 | 0 | 2 |
| Omar Vizquel | Cleveland, Aug 31, 2004 | A | 7 | 3 | 6 | 2 | 0 | 0 |
| Joe Randa | Kansas City, Sept 9, 2004 | A | 7 | 6 | 6 | 1 | 0 | 0 |
| Raul Ibanez | Seattle, Sept 22, 2004 | A | 6 | 1 | 6 | 0 | 0 | 0 |

**Total number of occurrences: 53**

## NATIONAL LEAGUE

| Player | Club, Date | Place | AB | R | H | 2B | 3B | HR |
|---|---|---|---|---|---|---|---|---|
| David Force | Philadelphia, June 27, 1876 | H | 6 | 3 | 6 | 1 | 0 | 0 |
| Cal McVey | Chicago, July 22, 1876 | H | 7 | 4 | 6 | 1 | 0 | 0 |
| Cal McVey | Chicago, July 25, 1876 | H | 7 | 4 | 6 | 1 | 0 | 0 |
| Ross Barnes | Chicago, July 27, 1876 | H | 6 | 3 | 6 | 1 | 1 | 0 |
| Paul Hines | Providence, Aug 26, 1879, 10 inn | H | 6 | 1 | 6 | 0 | 0 | 0 |
| George Gore | Chicago, May 7, 1880 | H | 6 | 5 | 6 | 0 | 0 | 0 |
| Lew Dickerson | Worcester, June 16, 1881 | H | 6 | 3 | 6 | 0 | 1 | 0 |
| Sam Wise | Boston, June 20, 1883 | H | 7 | 5 | 6 | 1 | 1 | 0 |
| Dennis Brouthers | Buffalo, July 19, 1883 | H | 6 | 3 | 6 | 2 | 0 | 0 |
| Danny Richardson | New York, June 11, 1887 | H | 7 | 2 | 6 | 0 | 0 | 0 |
| King Kelly | Boston, Aug 27, 1887 | H | 7 | 6 | 6 | 1 | 0 | 1 |
| Jerry Denny | Indianapolis, May 4, 1889 | H | 6 | 3 | 6 | 1 | 0 | 1 |
| Larry Twitchell | Cleveland, Aug 15, 1889 | H | 6 | 5 | 6 | 1 | 3 | 1 |
| John Glasscock | New York, Sept 27, 1890 | A | 6 | 2 | 6 | 0 | 0 | 0 |
| Bobby Lowe | Boston, June 11, 1891 | H | 6 | 4 | 6 | 1 | 0 | 1 |
| Henry Larkin | Washington, June 7, 1892 | H | 7 | 3 | 6 | 0 | 1 | 0 |
| Wilbert Robinson | Baltimore, June 10, 1892, 1st game | H | 7 | 1 | 7 | 1 | 0 | 0 |
| John Boyle | Philadelphia, July 6, 1893, 11 inn | A | 6 | 1 | 6 | 1 | 0 | 0 |
| Duff Cooley | St. Louis, Sept 30, 1893, 2nd game | A | 6 | 1 | 6 | 1 | 1 | 0 |
| Ed Delahanty | Philadelphia, June 16, 1894 | H | 6 | 4 | 6 | 1 | 0 | 0 |
| Steve Brodie | Baltimore, July 9, 1894 | H | 6 | 2 | 6 | 2 | 1 | 0 |
| Chief Zimmer | Cleveland, July 11, 1894, 10 inn | H | 6 | 3 | 6 | 2 | 0 | 0 |
| Sam Thompson | Philadelphia, Aug 17, 1894 | H | 7 | 4 | 6 | 1 | 1 | 1 |
| Roger Connor | St. Louis, June 1, 1895 | A | 6 | 4 | 6 | 2 | 1 | 0 |
| George Davis | New York, Aug 15, 1895 | A | 6 | 3 | 6 | 2 | 1 | 0 |
| Jacob Stenzel | Pittsburgh, May 14, 1896 | H | 6 | 3 | 6 | 0 | 0 | 0 |
| Fred Tenney | Boston, May 31, 1897 | H | 8 | 3 | 6 | 1 | 0 | 0 |
| Dick Harley | St. Louis, June 24, 1897, 12 inn | A | 6 | 2 | 6 | 1 | 0 | 0 |
| Barry McCormick | Chicago, June 29, 1897 | H | 8 | 5 | 6 | 0 | 1 | 1 |
| Tommy Tucker | Washington, July 15, 1897 | A | 6 | 1 | 6 | 1 | 0 | 0 |
| Willie Keeler | Baltimore, Sept 3, 1897 | H | 6 | 5 | 6 | 0 | 1 | 0 |
| Jack Doyle | Baltimore, Sept 3, 1897 | H | 6 | 2 | 6 | 2 | 0 | 0 |
| Chick Stahl | Boston, May 31, 1899 | H | 6 | 4 | 6 | 0 | 0 | 0 |
| Ginger Beaumont | Pittsburgh, July 22, 1899 | H | 6 | 6 | 6 | 0 | 0 | 0 |
| Kip Selbach | New York, June 9, 1901 | A | 7 | 4 | 6 | 2 | 0 | 0 |
| George Cutshaw | Brooklyn, Aug 9, 1915 | A | 6 | 2 | 6 | 0 | 0 | 0 |
| Carson Bigbee | Pittsburgh, Aug 22, 1917, 22 inn | A | 11 | 0 | 6 | 0 | 0 | 0 |
| Dave Bancroft | New York, June 28, 1920 | A | 6 | 2 | 6 | 0 | 0 | 0 |
| Johnny Gooch | Pittsburgh, July 7, 1922, 18 inn | H | 8 | 1 | 6 | 1 | 0 | 0 |
| Max Carey | Pittsburgh, July 7, 1922, 18 inn | H | 6 | 3 | 6 | 1 | 0 | 0 |
| Jack Fournier | Brooklyn, June 29, 1923 | A | 6 | 1 | 6 | 2 | 0 | 1 |
| Kiki Cuyler | Pittsburgh, Aug 9, 1924, 1st game | A | 6 | 3 | 6 | 3 | 1 | 0 |
| Frankie Frisch | New York, Sept 10, 1924, 1st game | H | 7 | 3 | 6 | 0 | 0 | 1 |
| Jim Bottomley | St. Louis, Sept 16, 1924 | A | 6 | 3 | 6 | 1 | 0 | 2 |
| Paul Waner | Pittsburgh, Aug 26, 1926 | H | 6 | 1 | 6 | 2 | 1 | 0 |
| Lloyd Waner | Pittsburgh, June 15, 1929, 14 inn | H | 8 | 2 | 6 | 1 | 1 | 0 |
| Hank DeBerry | Brooklyn, June 23, 1929, 14 inn | H | 7 | 0 | 6 | 0 | 0 | 0 |
| Wally Gilbert | Brooklyn, May 30, 1931, 2nd game | A | 7 | 3 | 6 | 1 | 0 | 0 |
| Jim Bottomley | St. Louis, Aug 5, 1931, 2nd game | A | 6 | 2 | 6 | 1 | 0 | 0 |
| Tony Cuccinello | Cincinnati, Aug 13, 1931, 1st game | A | 6 | 4 | 6 | 2 | 1 | 0 |
| Terry Moore | St. Louis, Sept 5, 1935 | H | 6 | 2 | 6 | 1 | 0 | 0 |
| Ernie Lombardi | Cincinnati, May 9, 1937 | A | 6 | 3 | 6 | 1 | 0 | 0 |
| Frank Demaree | Chicago, July 5, 1937, 1st game, 14 inn | H | 7 | 2 | 6 | 3 | 0 | 0 |
| Cookie Lavagetto | Brooklyn, Sept 23, 1939, 1st game | A | 6 | 4 | 6 | 1 | 1 | 0 |
| Walker Cooper | Cincinnati, July 6, 1949 | H | 7 | 5 | 6 | 0 | 0 | 3 |
| Johnny Hopp | Pittsburgh, May 14, 1950, 2nd game | A | 6 | 3 | 6 | 0 | 0 | 2 |
| Connie Ryan | Philadelphia, Apr 16, 1953 | A | 6 | 3 | 6 | 2 | 0 | 0 |
| Dick Groat | Pittsburgh, May 13, 1960 | A | 6 | 2 | 6 | 3 | 0 | 0 |
| Jesus Alou | San Francisco, July 10, 1964 | A | 6 | 1 | 6 | 0 | 0 | 1 |
| Joe Morgan | Houston, July 8, 1965, 12 inn | A | 6 | 4 | 6 | 0 | 1 | 2 |
| Felix Millan | Atlanta, July 6, 1970 | H | 6 | 2 | 6 | 1 | 1 | 0 |
| Don Kessinger | Chicago, June 17, 1971, 10 inn | H | 6 | 3 | 6 | 1 | 0 | 0 |
| Willie Davis | Los Angeles, May 24, 1973, 19 inn | H | 9 | 1 | 6 | 0 | 0 | 0 |
| Bill Madlock | Chicago, July 26, 1975, 10 inn | H | 6 | 1 | 6 | 0 | 1 | 0 |
| Rennie Stennett | Pittsburgh, Sept 16, 1975 | A | 7 | 5 | 7 | 2 | 1 | 0 |
| Jose Cardenal | Chicago, May 2, 1976, 1st game, 14 inn | A | 7 | 2 | 6 | 1 | 0 | 1 |
| Gene Richards | San Diego, July 26, 1977, 2nd game, 15 inn | H | 7 | 1 | 6 | 1 | 0 | 0 |
| Joe Lefebvre | San Diego, Sept 13, 1982, 16 inn | A | 8 | 1 | 6 | 1 | 0 | 1 |
| Wally Backman | Pittsburgh, Apr 27, 1990 | A | 6 | 1 | 6 | 1 | 0 | 0 |
| Sammy Sosa | Chicago, July 2, 1993 | A | 6 | 2 | 6 | 1 | 0 | 0 |
| Tony Gwynn | San Diego, Aug 4, 1993, 12 inn | H | 7 | 2 | 6 | 2 | 0 | 0 |
| Rondell White | Montreal, June 11, 1995, 13 inn | A | 7 | 5 | 6 | 2 | 1 | 1 |
| Mike Benjamin | San Francisco, June 14, 1995, 13 inn | A | 7 | 0 | 6 | 1 | 0 | 0 |
| Andres Galarraga | Colorado, July 3, 1995 | H | 6 | 4 | 6 | 1 | 0 | 2 |
| Edgardo Alfonzo | New York, Aug 30, 1999 | A | 6 | 6 | 6 | 1 | 0 | 3 |
| Paul Lo Duca | Los Angeles, May 28, 2001, 11 inn | H | 6 | 3 | 6 | 0 | 0 | 1 |
| Shawn Green | Los Angeles, May 23, 2002 | A | 6 | 6 | 6 | 1 | 0 | 4 |

**Total number of occurrences: 77**

## BARRY BONDS' 73 HOME RUNS—2001

| HR No. | Team game No. | Date | Opposing pitcher, Club | Place | Inning | On base |
|---|---|---|---|---|---|---|
| 1 | 1 | Apr 2 | Woody Williams (RH), San Diego | H | 5 | 0 |
| 2 | 9 | Apr 12 | Adam Eaton (RH), San Diego | A | 4 | 0 |
| 3 | 10 | Apr 13 | Jamey Wright (RH), Milwaukee | A | 1 | 1 |
| 4 | 11 | Apr 14 | Jimmy Haynes (RH), Milwaukee | A | 5 | 2 |
| 5 | 12 | Apr 15 | Dave Weathers (RH), Milwaukee | A | 8 | 0 |
| 6 | 13 | Apr 17 | Terry Adams (RH), Los Angeles | H | 8 | 1 |
| 7 | 14 | Apr 18 | Chan Ho Park (RH), Los Angeles | H | 7 | 0 |
| 8 | 16 | Apr 20 | Jimmy Haynes (RH), Milwaukee | H | 4 | 1 |
| 9 | 19 | Apr 24 | Jim Brower (RH), Cincinnati | H | 3 | 1 |
| 10 | 21 | Apr 26 | Scott Sullivan (RH), Cincinnati | H | 8 | 1 |
| 11 | 24 | Apr 29 | Manny Aybar (RH), Chicago NL | H | 4 | 0 |
| 12 | 26 | May 2 | Todd Ritchie (RH), Pittsburgh | A | 5 | 1 |
| 13 | 27 | May 3 | Jimmy Anderson (LH), Pittsburgh | A | 1 | 1 |
| 14 | 28 | May 4 | Bruce Chen (LH), Philadelphia | A | 6 | 1 |

| HR No. | Team game No. | Date | Opposing pitcher, Club | Place | Inning | On base |
|---|---|---|---|---|---|---|
| 15 | 35 | May 11 | Steve Trachsel (RH), New York NL | H | 4 | 0 |
| 16 | 40 | May 17 | Chuck Smith (RH), Florida | A | 3 | 1 |
| 17 | 41 | May 18 | Mike Remlinger (LH), Atlanta | A | 8 | 0 |
| 18 | 42 | May 19 | Odalis Perez (LH), Atlanta | A | 3 | 0 |
| 19 | 42 | May 19 | Jose Cabrera (RH), Atlanta | A | 7 | 0 |
| 20 | 42 | May 19 | Jason Marquis (RH), Atlanta | A | 8 | 0 |
| 21 | 43 | May 20 | John Burkett (RH), Atlanta | A | 1 | 0 |
| 22 | 43 | May 20 | Mike Remlinger (LH), Atlanta | A | 7 | 0 |
| 23 | 44 | May 21 | Curt Schilling (RH), Arizona | A | 4 | 0 |
| 24 | 45 | May 22 | Russ Springer (RH), Arizona | A | 9 | 1 |
| 25 | 47 | May 24 | John Thomson (RH), Colorado | H | 3 | 0 |
| 26 | 50 | May 27 | Denny Neagle (LH), Colorado | H | 1 | 1 |
| 27 | 53 | May 30 | Robert Ellis (RH), Arizona | H | 2 | 0 |
| 28 | 53 | May 30 | Robert Ellis (RH), Arizona | H | 6 | 1 |
| 29 | 54 | June 1 | Shawn Chacon (RH), Colorado | A | 0 | 1 |
| 30 | 57 | June 4 | Bobby J. Jones (RH), San Diego | H | 4 | 0 |
| 31 | 58 | June 5 | Wascar Serrano (RH), San Diego | H | 3 | 1 |
| 32 | 60 | June 7 | Brian Lawrence (RH), San Diego | H | 7 | 1 |
| 33 | 64 | June 12 | Pat Rapp (RH), Anaheim | H | 1 | 0 |
| 34 | 66 | June 14 | Lou Pote (RH), Anaheim | H | 6 | 0 |
| 35 | 67 | June 15 | Mark Mulder (LH), Oakland | H | 1 | 0 |
| 36 | 67 | June 15 | Mark Mulder (LH), Oakland | H | 6 | 0 |
| 37 | 70 | June 19 | Adam Eaton (RH), San Diego | A | 5 | 0 |
| 38 | 71 | June 20 | Rodney Myers (RH), San Diego | A | 8 | 1 |
| 39 | 74 | June 23 | Darryl Kile (RH), St Louis | A | 1 | 1 |
| 40 | 89 | July 12 | Paul Abbott (RH), Seattle | A | 1 | 0 |
| 41 | 95 | July 18 | Mike Hampton (LH), Colorado | H | 4 | 0 |
| 42 | 95 | July 18 | Mike Hampton (LH), Colorado | H | 5 | 1 |
| 43 | 103 | July 26 | Curt Schilling (RH), Arizona | A | 4 | 0 |
| 44 | 103 | July 26 | Curt Schilling (RH), Arizona | A | 5 | 3 |
| 45 | 104 | July 27 | Brian Anderson (LH), Arizona | A | 4 | 0 |
| 46 | 108 | Aug 1 | Joe Beimel (LH), Pittsburgh | H | 1 | 0 |
| 47 | 111 | Aug 4 | Nelson Figueroa (RH), Philadelphia | H | 6 | 1 |
| 48 | 113 | Aug 7 | Danny Graves (RH), Cincinnati | A | 11 | 0 |
| 49 | 115 | Aug 9 | Scott Winchester (RH), Cincinnati | A | 3 | 0 |
| 50 | 117 | Aug 11 | Joe Borowski (RH), Chicago NL | A | 2 | 2 |
| 51 | 119 | Aug 14 | Ricky Bones (RH), Florida | H | 6 | 3 |
| 52 | 121 | Aug 16 | A.J. Burnett (RH), Florida | H | 4 | 0 |
| 53 | 121 | Aug 16 | Vic Darensbourg (LH), Florida | H | 8 | 2 |
| 54 | 123 | Aug 18 | Jason Marquis (RH), Atlanta | H | 8 | 0 |
| 55 | 127 | Aug 23 | Graeme Lloyd (LH), Montreal | A | 9 | 0 |
| 56 | 131 | Aug 27 | Kevin Appier (RH), New York NL | A | 5 | 0 |
| 57 | 135 | Aug 31 | John Thomson (RH), Colorado | A | 8 | 1 |
| 58 | 138 | Sept 3 | Jason Jennings (RH), Colorado | H | 4 | 0 |
| 59 | 139 | Sept 4 | Miguel Batista (RH), Arizona | H | 7 | 0 |
| 60 | 141 | Sept 6 | Albie Lopez (RH), Arizona | H | 2 | 0 |
| 61 | 144 | Sept 9 | Scott Elarton (RH), Colorado | A | 1 | 0 |
| 62 | 144 | Sept 9 | Scott Elarton (RH), Colorado | A | 5 | 0 |
| 63 | 144 | Sept 9 | Todd Belitz (LH), Colorado | A | 11 | 2 |
| 64 | 147 | Sept 20 | Wade Miller (RH), Houston | H | 5 | 1 |
| 65 | 150 | Sept 23 | Jason Middlebrook (RH), San Diego | A | 2 | 0 |
| 66 | 150 | Sept 23 | Jason Middlebrook (RH), San Diego | A | 4 | 0 |
| 67 | 151 | Sept 24 | James Baldwin (RH), Los Angeles | A | 7 | 0 |
| 68 | 154 | Sept 28 | Jason Middlebrook (RH), San Diego | H | 2 | 0 |
| 69 | 155 | Sept 29 | Chuck McElroy (LH), San Diego | H | 6 | 0 |
| 70 | 159 | Oct 4 | Wilfredo Rodriguez (LH), Houston | A | 9 | 0 |
| 71 | 160 | Oct 5 | Chan Ho Park (RH), Los Angeles | H | 1 | 0 |
| 72 | 160 | Oct 5 | Chan Ho Park (RH), Los Angeles | H | 3 | 0 |
| 73 | 162 | Oct 7 | Dennis Springer (RH), Los Angeles | H | 1 | 0 |

Bonds played 153 games.

## MARK McGWIRE'S 70 HOME RUNS—1998

| HR No. | Team game No. | Date | Opposing pitcher, Club | Place | Inning | On base |
|---|---|---|---|---|---|---|
| 1 | 1 | Mar 31 | Ramon Martinez (RH), Los Angeles | H | 5 | 3 |
| 2 | 2 | Apr 2 | Frank Lankford (RH), Los Angeles | H | 12 | 2 |
| 3 | 3 | Apr 3 | Mark Langston (LH), San Diego | H | 5 | 1 |
| 4 | 4 | Apr 4 | Don Wengert (RH), San Diego | H | 6 | 2 |
| 5 | 13 | Apr 14 | Jeff Suppan (RH), Arizona | H | 3 | 1 |
| 6 | 13 | Apr 14 | Jeff Suppan (RH), Arizona | H | 5 | 0 |
| 7 | 13 | Apr 14 | Barry Manuel (RH), Arizona | H | 8 | 1 |
| 8 | 16 | Apr 17 | Matt Whiteside (RH), Philadelphia | H | 4 | 1 |
| 9 | 19 | Apr 21 | Trey Moore (LH), Montreal | A | 3 | 1 |
| 10 | 23 | Apr 25 | Jerry Spradlin (RH), Philadelphia | A | 7 | 1 |
| 11 | 27 | Apr 30 | Marc Pisciotta (RH), Chicago NL | A | 8 | 1 |
| 12 | 28 | May 1 | Rod Beck (RH), Chicago NL | A | 9 | 1 |
| 13 | 34 | May 8 | Rick Reed (RH), New York NL | A | 3 | 1 |
| 14 | 36 | May 12 | Paul Wagner (RH), Milwaukee | H | 5 | 2 |
| 15 | 38 | May 14 | Kevin Millwood (RH), Atlanta | H | 4 | 0 |
| 16 | 40 | May 16 | Livan Hernandez (RH), Florida | H | 4 | 0 |
| 17 | 42 | May 18 | Jesus Sanchez (LH), Florida | H | 4 | 0 |
| 18 | 43 | May 19 | Tyler Green (RH), Philadelphia | A | 3 | 1 |
| 19 | 43 | May 19 | Tyler Green (RH), Philadelphia | A | 5 | 1 |
| 20 | 43 | May 19 | Wayne Gomes (RH), Philadelphia | A | 8 | 1 |
| 21 | 46 | May 22 | Mark Gardner (RH), San Francisco | H | 6 | 1 |
| 22 | 47 | May 23 | Rich Rodriguez (LH), San Francisco | H | 4 | 0 |
| 23 | 47 | May 23 | John Johnstone (RH), San Francisco | H | 5 | 2 |
| 24 | 48 | May 24 | Robb Nen (RH), San Francisco | H | 12 | 1 |
| 25 | 49 | May 25 | John Thomson (RH), Colorado | H | 1 | 0 |
| 26 | 52 | May 29 | Dan Miceli (RH), San Diego | A | 9 | 1 |
| 27 | 53 | May 30 | Andy Ashby (RH), San Diego | A | 1 | 0 |
| 28 | 59 | June 5 | Orel Hershiser (RH), San Francisco | H | 1 | 1 |
| 29 | 62 | June 8 | Jason Bere (RH), Chicago AL | A | 4 | 1 |
| 30 | 64 | June 10 | Jim Parque (LH), Chicago AL | A | 3 | 2 |

| HR No. | Team game No. | Date | Opposing pitcher, Club | Place | Inning | On base |
|---|---|---|---|---|---|---|
| 31 | 65 | June 12 | Andy Benes (RH), Arizona | A | 3 | 3 |
| 32 | 69 | June 17 | Jose Lima (RH), Houston | A | 3 | 0 |
| 33 | 70 | June 18 | Shane Reynolds (RH), Houston | A | 5 | 0 |
| 34 | 76 | June 24 | Jaret Wright (RH), Cleveland | A | 4 | 0 |
| 35 | 77 | June 25 | Dave Burba (RH), Cleveland | A | 1 | 0 |
| 36 | 79 | June 27 | Mike Trombley (RH), Minnesota | A | 7 | 1 |
| 37 | 81 | June 30 | Glendon Rusch (LH), Kansas City | H | 7 | 0 |
| 38 | 89 | July 11 | Billy Wagner (LH), Houston | H | 11 | 1 |
| 39 | 90 | July 12 | Sean Bergman (RH), Houston | H | 1 | 0 |
| 40 | 90 | July 12 | Scott Elarton (RH), Houston | H | 7 | 0 |
| 41 | 95 | July 17 | Brian Bohanon (LH), Los Angeles | H | 1 | 0 |
| 42 | 95 | July 17 | Antonio Osuna (RH), Los Angeles | H | 8 | 0 |
| 43 | 98 | July 20 | Brian Boehringer (RH), San Diego | A | 5 | 1 |
| 44 | 104 | July 26 | John Thomson (RH), Colorado | A | 4 | 0 |
| 45 | 105 | July 28 | Mike Myers (LH), Milwaukee | H | 8 | 0 |
| 46 | 115 | Aug 8 | Mark Clark (RH), Chicago NL | H | 4 | 0 |
| 47 | 118 | Aug 11 | Bobby J. Jones (RH), New York NL | H | 4 | 0 |
| 48 | 124 | Aug 19 | Matt Karchner (RH), Chicago NL | A | 8 | 0 |
| 49 | 124 | Aug 19 | Terry Mulholland (LH), Chicago NL | A | 10 | 0 |
| 50 | 125 | Aug *20 | Willie Blair (RH), New York NL | A | 7 | 0 |
| 51 | 126 | Aug †20 | Rick Reed (RH), New York NL | A | 1 | 0 |
| 52 | 129 | Aug 22 | Francisco Cordova (RH), Pittsburgh | A | 1 | 0 |
| 53 | 130 | Aug 23 | Ricardo Rincon (LH), Pittsburgh | A | 8 | 0 |
| 54 | 133 | Aug 26 | Justin Speier (RH), Florida | H | 8 | 1 |
| 55 | 137 | Aug 30 | Dennis Martinez (RH), Atlanta | H | 7 | 2 |
| 56 | 139 | Sept 1 | Livan Hernandez (RH), Florida | A | 7 | 0 |
| 57 | 139 | Sept 1 | Donn Pall (RH), Florida | A | 9 | 0 |
| 58 | 140 | Sept 2 | Brian Edmondson (RH), Florida | A | 7 | 1 |
| 59 | 140 | Sept 2 | Rob Stanifer (RH), Florida | A | 8 | 1 |
| 60 | 142 | Sept 5 | Dennis Reyes (LH), Cincinnati | H | 1 | 1 |
| 61 | 144 | Sept 7 | Mike Morgan (RH), Chicago NL | H | 1 | 0 |
| 62 | 145 | Sept 8 | Steve Trachsel (RH), Chicago NL | H | 4 | 0 |
| 63 | 153 | Sept *15 | Jason Christiansen (LH), Pittsburgh | H | 9 | 0 |
| 64 | 155 | Sept 18 | Rafael Roque (LH), Milwaukee | A | 4 | 1 |
| 65 | 157 | Sept 20 | Scott Karl (LH), Milwaukee | A | 1 | 1 |
| 66 | 161 | Sept 25 | Shayne Bennett (RH), Montreal | H | 5 | 1 |
| 67 | 162 | Sept 26 | Dustin Hermanson (RH), Montreal | H | 4 | 0 |
| 68 | 162 | Sept 26 | Kirk Bullinger (RH), Montreal | H | 7 | 1 |
| 69 | 163 | Sept 27 | Mike Thurman (RH), Montreal | H | 3 | 0 |
| 70 | 163 | Sept 27 | Carl Pavano (RH), Montreal | H | 7 | 2 |

*1st game of doubleheader; †2nd game of doubleheader; St. Louis played 163 games in 1998 (one tie on Aug 24). McGwire did not play in this game. McGwire played 155 games.

## ROGER MARIS' 61 HOME RUNS—1961

| HR No. | Team game No. | Date | Opposing pitcher, Club | Place | Inning | On base |
|---|---|---|---|---|---|---|
| 1 | 11 | Apr 26 | Paul Foytack (RH), Detroit | A | 5 | 0 |
| 2 | 17 | May 3 | Pedro Ramos (RH), Minnesota | A | 7 | 2 |
| 3 | 20 | May 6 | Eli Grba (RH), Los Angeles | A | 5 | 0 |
| 4 | 29 | May 17 | Pete Burnside (LH), Washington | H | 8 | 1 |
| 5 | 30 | May 19 | Jim Perry (RH), Cleveland | A | 1 | 1 |
| 6 | 31 | May 20 | Gary Bell (RH), Cleveland | A | 3 | 0 |
| 7 | 32 | May 21 | Chuck Estrada (RH), Baltimore | H | 1 | 0 |
| 8 | 35 | May 24 | Gene Conley (RH), Boston | H | 4 | 1 |
| 9 | 38 | May †28 | Cal McLish (RH), Chicago | H | 2 | 1 |
| 10 | 40 | May 30 | Gene Conley (RH), Boston | A | 3 | 0 |
| 11 | 40 | May 30 | Mike Fornieles (RH), Boston | A | 8 | 2 |
| 12 | 41 | May 31 | Billy Muffett (RH), Boston | A | 3 | 0 |
| 13 | 43 | June 2 | Cal McLish (RH), Chicago | A | 3 | 2 |
| 14 | 44 | June 3 | Bob Shaw (RH), Chicago | A | 8 | 2 |
| 15 | 45 | June 4 | Russ Kemmerer (RH), Chicago | A | 3 | 0 |
| 16 | 48 | June 6 | Ed Palmquist (RH), Minnesota | H | 6 | 2 |
| 17 | 49 | June 7 | Pedro Ramos (RH), Minnesota | H | 3 | 2 |
| 18 | 52 | June 9 | Ray Herbert (RH), Kansas City | H | 7 | 1 |
| 19 | 55 | June †11 | Eli Grba (RH), Los Angeles | H | 3 | 0 |
| 20 | 55 | June †11 | Johnny James (RH), Los Angeles | H | 7 | 0 |
| 21 | 57 | June 13 | Jim Perry (RH), Cleveland | A | 6 | 0 |
| 22 | 58 | June 14 | Gary Bell (RH), Cleveland | A | 4 | 1 |
| 23 | 61 | June 17 | Don Mossi (LH), Detroit | A | 4 | 0 |
| 24 | 62 | June 18 | Jerry Casale (RH), Detroit | A | 8 | 1 |
| 25 | 63 | June 19 | Jim Archer (LH), Kansas City | A | 9 | 0 |
| 26 | 64 | June 20 | Joe Nuxhall (LH), Kansas City | A | 1 | 0 |
| 27 | 66 | June 22 | Norm Bass (RH), Kansas City | A | 2 | 1 |
| 28 | 74 | July 1 | Dave Sisler (RH), Washington | H | 9 | 1 |
| 29 | 75 | July 2 | Pete Burnside (LH), Washington | H | 3 | 2 |
| 30 | 75 | July 2 | Johnny Klippstein (RH), Washington | H | 7 | 1 |
| 31 | 77 | July †4 | Frank Lary (RH), Detroit | H | 8 | 1 |
| 32 | 78 | July 5 | Frank Funk (RH), Cleveland | H | 7 | 0 |
| 33 | 82 | July*9 | Bill Monbouquette (RH), Boston | H | 7 | 0 |
| 34 | 84 | July 13 | Early Wynn (RH), Chicago | A | 1 | 1 |
| 35 | 86 | July 15 | Ray Herbert (RH), Chicago | A | 3 | 0 |
| 36 | 92 | July 21 | Bill Monbouquette (RH), Boston | A | 1 | 0 |
| 37 | 95 | July *25 | Frank Baumann (LH), Chicago | H | 4 | 1 |
| 38 | 95 | July *25 | Don Larsen (RH), Chicago | H | 8 | 0 |
| 39 | 96 | July †25 | Russ Kemmerer (RH), Chicago | H | 4 | 0 |
| 40 | 96 | July †25 | Warren Hacker (RH), Chicago | H | 6 | 2 |
| 41 | 106 | Aug 4 | Camilo Pascual (RH), Minnesota | H | 1 | 2 |
| 42 | 114 | Aug 11 | Pete Burnside (LH), Washington | A | 5 | 0 |
| 43 | 115 | Aug 12 | Dick Donovan (RH), Washington | A | 4 | 0 |
| 44 | 116 | Aug *13 | Bennie Daniels (RH), Washington | A | 4 | 0 |
| 45 | 117 | Aug †13 | Marty Kutyna (RH), Washington | A | 1 | 1 |
| 46 | 118 | Aug 15 | Juan Pizarro (LH), Chicago | H | 4 | 0 |
| 47 | 119 | Aug 16 | Billy Pierce (LH), Chicago | H | 1 | 1 |
| 48 | 119 | Aug 16 | Billy Pierce (LH), Chicago | H | 3 | 1 |
| 49 | 124 | Aug *20 | Jim Perry (RH), Cleveland | A | 3 | 1 |

| HR No. | Team game No. | Date | Opposing pitcher, Club | Place | Inning | On base |
|---|---|---|---|---|---|---|
| 50 | 125 | Aug 22 | Ken McBride (RH), Los Angeles | A | 6 | 1 |
| 51 | 129 | Aug 26 | Jerry Walker (RH), Kansas City | A | 6 | 0 |
| 52 | 135 | Sept 2 | Frank Lary (RH), Detroit | H | 6 | 0 |
| 53 | 135 | Sept 2 | Hank Aguirre (LH), Detroit | H | 8 | 1 |
| 54 | 140 | Sept 6 | Tom Cheney (RH), Washington | H | 4 | 0 |
| 55 | 141 | Sept 7 | Dick Stigman (LH), Cleveland | H | 3 | 0 |
| 56 | 143 | Sept 9 | Mudcat Grant (RH), Cleveland | H | 7 | 0 |
| 57 | 151 | Sept 16 | Frank Lary (RH), Detroit | A | 3 | 1 |
| 58 | 152 | Sept 17 | Terry Fox (RH), Detroit | A | 12 | 1 |
| 59 | 155 | Sept 20 | Milt Pappas (RH), Baltimore | A | 3 | 0 |
| 60 | 159 | Sept 26 | Jack Fisher (RH), Baltimore | H | 3 | 0 |
| 61 | 163 | Oct. 1 | Tracy Stallard (RH), Boston | H | 4 | 0 |

*1st game of doubleheader; †2nd game of doubleheader; New York played 163 games in 1961 (one tie on Apr 22). Maris did not hit a home run in this game. Maris played 161 games.

## BABE RUTH'S 60 HOME RUNS—1927

| HR No. | Team game No. | Date | Opposing pitcher, Club | Place | Inning | On base |
|---|---|---|---|---|---|---|
| 1 | 4 | Apr 15 | Howard Ehmke (RH), Philadelphia | H | 1 | 0 |
| 2 | 11 | Apr 23 | Rube Walberg (LH), Philadelphia | A | 1 | 0 |
| 3 | 12 | Apr 24 | Sloppy Thurston (RH), Washington | A | 6 | 0 |
| 4 | 14 | Apr 29 | Slim Harriss (RH), Boston | A | 5 | 0 |
| 5 | 16 | May 1 | Jack Quinn (RH), Philadelphia | H | 1 | 1 |
| 6 | 16 | May 1 | Rube Walberg (LH), Philadelphia | H | 8 | 0 |
| 7 | 24 | May 10 | Milt Gaston (RH), St. Louis | A | 1 | 2 |
| 8 | 25 | May 11 | Ernie Nevers (RH), St. Louis | A | 1 | 1 |
| 9 | 29 | May 17 | Rip H Collins (RH), Detroit | A | 8 | 0 |
| 10 | 33 | May 22 | Benn Karr (RH), Cleveland | A | 6 | 1 |
| 11 | 34 | May 23 | Sloppy Thurston (RH), Washington | A | 1 | 0 |
| 12 | 37 | May *28 | Sloppy Thurston (RH), Washington | H | 7 | 2 |
| 13 | 39 | May 29 | Danny MacFayden (RH), Boston | H | 8 | 0 |
| 14 | 41 | May ‡30 | Rube Walberg (LH), Philadelphia | A | 11 | 0 |
| 15 | 42 | May *31 | Jack Quinn (RH), Philadelphia | A | 1 | 1 |
| 16 | 43 | May †31 | Howard Ehmke (RH), Philadelphia | A | 5 | 1 |
| 17 | 47 | June 5 | Earl Whitehill (LH), Detroit | H | 6 | 0 |
| 18 | 48 | June 7 | Tommy Thomas (RH), Chicago | H | 4 | 0 |
| 19 | 52 | June 11 | Garland Buckeye (LH), Cleveland | H | 3 | 1 |
| 20 | 52 | June 11 | Garland Buckeye (LH), Cleveland | H | 5 | 0 |
| 21 | 53 | June 12 | George Uhle (RH), Cleveland | H | 7 | 0 |
| 22 | 55 | June 16 | Tom Zachary (LH), St. Louis | H | 1 | 1 |
| 23 | 60 | June *22 | Hal Wiltse (LH), Boston | A | 5 | 0 |
| 24 | 60 | June *22 | Hal Wiltse (LH), Boston | A | 7 | 1 |
| 25 | 70 | June 30 | Slim Harriss (RH), Boston | H | 4 | 1 |
| 26 | 73 | July 3 | Hod Lisenbee (RH), Washington | A | 1 | 0 |
| 27 | 78 | July †8 | Don Hankins (RH), Detroit | A | 2 | 2 |
| 28 | 79 | July *9 | Ken Holloway (RH), Detroit | A | 1 | 1 |
| 29 | 79 | July *9 | Ken Holloway (RH), Detroit | A | 4 | 2 |
| 30 | 83 | July 12 | Joe Shaute (LH), Cleveland | A | 9 | 1 |
| 31 | 94 | July 24 | Tommy Thomas (RH), Chicago | A | 3 | 0 |
| 32 | 95 | July *26 | Milt Gaston (RH), St. Louis | H | 1 | 1 |
| 33 | 95 | July *26 | Milt Gaston (RH), St. Louis | H | 6 | 0 |
| 34 | 98 | July 28 | Lefty Stewart (LH), St. Louis | H | 8 | 1 |
| 35 | 106 | Aug 5 | George S Smith (RH), Detroit | H | 8 | 0 |
| 36 | 110 | Aug 10 | Tom Zachary (LH), Washington | A | 3 | 2 |
| 37 | 114 | Aug 16 | Tommy Thomas (RH), Chicago | A | 5 | 0 |
| 38 | 115 | Aug 17 | Sarge Connally (RH), Chicago | A | 11 | 0 |
| 39 | 118 | Aug 20 | Jake Miller (LH), Cleveland | A | 1 | 1 |
| 40 | 120 | Aug 22 | Joe Shaute (LH), Cleveland | A | 6 | 0 |
| 41 | 124 | Aug 27 | Ernie Nevers (RH), St. Louis | A | 8 | 1 |
| 42 | 125 | Aug 28 | Ernie Wingard (LH), St. Louis | A | 1 | 1 |
| 43 | 127 | Aug 31 | Tony Welzer (RH), Boston | H | 8 | 0 |
| 44 | 128 | Sept 2 | Rube Walberg (LH), Philadelphia | A | 1 | 0 |
| 45 | 132 | Sept *6 | Tony Welzer (RH), Boston | A | 6 | 2 |
| 46 | 132 | Sept *6 | Tony Welzer (RH), Boston | A | 7 | 1 |
| 47 | 133 | Sept †6 | Jack Russell (RH), Boston | A | 9 | 0 |
| 48 | 134 | Sept 7 | Danny MacFayden (RH), Boston | A | 1 | 0 |
| 49 | 134 | Sept 7 | Slim Harriss (RH), Boston | A | 8 | 1 |
| 50 | 138 | Sept 11 | Milt Gaston (RH), St. Louis | H | 4 | 0 |
| 51 | 139 | Sept *13 | Willis Hudlin (RH), Cleveland | H | 7 | 1 |
| 52 | 140 | Sept †13 | Joe Shaute (LH), Cleveland | H | 4 | 0 |
| 53 | 143 | Sept 16 | Ted Blankenship (RH), Chicago | H | 3 | 0 |
| 54 | 147 | Sept †18 | Ted Lyons (RH), Chicago | H | 5 | 1 |
| 55 | 148 | Sept 21 | Sam Gibson (RH), Detroit | H | 9 | 0 |
| 56 | 149 | Sept 22 | Ken Holloway (RH), Detroit | H | 9 | 1 |
| 57 | 152 | Sept 27 | Lefty Grove (LH), Philadelphia | H | 6 | 3 |
| 58 | 153 | Sept 29 | Hod Lisenbee (RH), Washington | H | 1 | 0 |
| 59 | 153 | Sept 29 | Paul Hopkins (RH), Washington | H | 5 | 3 |
| 60 | 154 | Sept 30 | Tom Zachary (LH), Washington | H | 8 | 1 |

*1st game of doubleheader; †2nd game of doubleheader; ‡afternoon game of split doubleheader; New York played 155 games in 1927 (one tie on Apr 14). Ruth played 151 games. He did not hit a home run in game No. 155 on October 1.

## JOE DIMAGGIO'S 56-GAME HITTING STREAK—1941

| Date | | Opposing pitcher(s), Club | AB | R | H | 2B | 3B | HR | RBI |
|---|---|---|---|---|---|---|---|---|---|
| May | 15 | Eddie Smith, Chicago | 4 | 0 | 1 | 0 | 0 | 0 | 1 |
| | 16 | Thornton Lee, Chicago | 4 | 2 | 2 | 0 | 1 | 1 | 1 |
| | 17 | Johnny Rigney, Chicago | 3 | 1 | 1 | 0 | 0 | 0 | 0 |
| | 18 | Bob Harris (2), Johnny Niggeling (1), St. Louis | 3 | 3 | 3 | 1 | 0 | 0 | 1 |
| | 19 | Denny Galehouse, St. Louis | 3 | 0 | 1 | 1 | 0 | 0 | 0 |
| | 20 | Eldon Auker, St. Louis | 5 | 1 | 1 | 0 | 0 | 0 | 1 |
| | 21 | Schoolboy Rowe (1), Al Benton (1), Detroit | 5 | 0 | 2 | 0 | 0 | 0 | 1 |
| | 22 | Archie McKain, Detroit | 4 | 0 | 1 | 0 | 0 | 0 | 1 |
| | 23 | Dick Newsome, Boston | 5 | 0 | 1 | 0 | 0 | 0 | 2 |
| | 24 | Earl Johnson, Boston | 4 | 2 | 1 | 0 | 0 | 0 | 2 |

| Date | Opposing pitcher(s), Club | AB | R | H | 2B | 3B | HR | RBI |
|---|---|---|---|---|---|---|---|---|
| 25 | Lefty Grove, Boston | 4 | 0 | 1 | 0 | 0 | 0 | 0 |
| 27 | Ken Chase (1), Red Anderson (2), Alex Carrasquel (1), Washington | 5 | 3 | 4 | 0 | 0 | 1 | 3 |
| 28 | Sid Hudson, Washington | 4 | 1 | 1 | 0 | 1 | 0 | 0 |
| 29 | Steve Sundra, Washington | 3 | 1 | 1 | 0 | 0 | 0 | 0 |
| 30 | Earl Johnson, Boston | 2 | 1 | 1 | 0 | 0 | 0 | 0 |
| 30 | Mickey Harris, Boston | 3 | 0 | 1 | 1 | 0 | 0 | 0 |
| June 1 | Al Milnar, Cleveland | 4 | 1 | 1 | 0 | 0 | 0 | 0 |
| 1 | Mel Harder, Cleveland | 4 | 0 | 1 | 0 | 0 | 0 | 0 |
| 2 | Bob Feller, Cleveland | 4 | 2 | 2 | 1 | 0 | 0 | 0 |
| 3 | Dizzy Trout, Detroit | 4 | 1 | 1 | 0 | 0 | 1 | 1 |
| 5 | Hal Newhouser, Detroit | 5 | 1 | 1 | 0 | 1 | 0 | 1 |
| 7 | Bob Muncrief (1), Johnny Allen (1), George Caster (1), St. Louis | 5 | 2 | 3 | 0 | 0 | 0 | 1 |
| 8 | Elden Auker, St. Louis | 4 | 3 | 2 | 0 | 0 | 2 | 4 |
| 8 | George Caster (1), Jack Kramer (1), St. Louis | 4 | 1 | 2 | 1 | 0 | 1 | 3 |
| 10 | Johnny Rigney, Chicago | 5 | 1 | 1 | 0 | 0 | 0 | 0 |
| 12 | Thornton Lee, Chicago | 4 | 1 | 2 | 0 | 0 | 1 | 1 |
| 14 | Bob Feller, Cleveland | 2 | 0 | 1 | 1 | 0 | 0 | 1 |
| 15 | Jim Bagby, Cleveland | 3 | 1 | 1 | 0 | 0 | 1 | 1 |
| 16 | Al Milnar, Cleveland | 5 | 0 | 1 | 1 | 0 | 0 | 0 |
| 17 | Johnny Rigney, Chicago | 4 | 1 | 1 | 0 | 0 | 0 | 0 |
| 18 | Thornton Lee, Chicago | 3 | 0 | 1 | 0 | 0 | 0 | 0 |
| 19 | Eddie Smith (1), Buck Ross (2), Chicago | 3 | 2 | 3 | 0 | 0 | 1 | 2 |
| 20 | Bobo Newsom (2), Archie McKain (2), Detroit | 5 | 3 | 4 | 1 | 0 | 0 | 1 |
| 21 | Dizzy Trout, Detroit | 4 | 0 | 1 | 0 | 0 | 0 | 1 |
| 22 | Hal Newhouser (1), Bobo Newsom (1), Detroit | 5 | 1 | 2 | 1 | 0 | 1 | 2 |
| 24 | Bob Muncrief, St. Louis | 4 | 1 | 1 | 0 | 0 | 0 | 0 |
| 25 | Denny Galehouse, St. Louis | 4 | 1 | 1 | 0 | 0 | 1 | 3 |
| 26 | Elden Auker, St. Louis | 4 | 0 | 1 | 1 | 0 | 0 | 1 |
| 27 | Chubby Dean, Philadelphia | 3 | 1 | 2 | 0 | 0 | 1 | 2 |
| 28 | Johnny Babich (1), Lum Harris (1), Philadelphia | 5 | 1 | 2 | 1 | 0 | 0 | 0 |
| 29 | Dutch E. Leonard, Washington | 4 | 1 | 1 | 1 | 0 | 0 | 0 |
| 29 | Red Anderson, Washington | 5 | 1 | 1 | 0 | 0 | 0 | 1 |
| July 1 | Mickey Harris (1), Mike Ryba (1), Boston | 4 | 0 | 2 | 0 | 0 | 0 | 1 |
| 1 | Jack Wilson, Boston | 3 | 1 | 1 | 0 | 0 | 0 | 1 |
| 2 | Dick Newsome, Boston | 5 | 1 | 1 | 0 | 0 | 1 | 3 |
| 5 | Phil Marchildon, Philadelphia | 4 | 2 | 1 | 0 | 0 | 1 | 2 |
| 6 | Johnny Babich (1), Bump Hadley (3), Philadelphia | 5 | 2 | 4 | 1 | 0 | 0 | 2 |
| 6 | Jack Knott, Philadelphia | 4 | 0 | 2 | 0 | 1 | 0 | 2 |
| 10 | Johnny Niggeling, St. Louis | 2 | 0 | 1 | 0 | 0 | 0 | 0 |
| 11 | Bob Harris (3), Jack Kramer (1), St. Louis | 5 | 1 | 4 | 0 | 0 | 1 | 2 |
| 12 | Elden Auker (1), Bob Muncrief (1), St. Louis | 5 | 1 | 2 | 1 | 0 | 0 | 1 |
| July 13 | Ted Lyons (2), Jack Hallett (1), Chicago | 4 | 2 | 3 | 0 | 0 | 0 | 0 |
| 13 | Thornton Lee, Chicago | 4 | 0 | 1 | 0 | 0 | 0 | 0 |
| 14 | Johnny Rigney, Chicago | 3 | 0 | 1 | 0 | 0 | 0 | 0 |
| 15 | Eddie Smith, Chicago | 4 | 1 | 2 | 1 | 0 | 0 | 2 |
| 16 | Al Milnar (2), Joe Krakauskas (1), Cleveland | 4 | 3 | 3 | 1 | 0 | 0 | 0 |
| **Totals for 56 games** | | **223** | **56** | **91** | **16** | **4** | **15** | **55** |

Note—Numbers in parentheses refer to hits off each pitcher. Streak stopped July 17 at Cleveland, New York won, 4-3. 1st inning, Al Smith pitching, thrown out by Ken Keltner; 4th inning, Smith pitching, walked; 7th inning, Smith pitching, thrown out by Keltner; 8th inning, Jim Bagby Jr., pitching, grounded into double play.

## HOME RUNS BY CLUBS, EACH YEAR

### AMERICAN LEAGUE (1901-2005)

| Year | Bal | Bos | Chi | Cle | Det | KC | LA | Mil | Min | NY | Oak | Sea | TB | Tex | Tor | Total |
|---|---|---|---|---|---|---|---|---|---|---|---|---|---|---|---|---|
| 1901 | 26 | *37 | 32 | 12 | 29 | .. | .. | .. | 33 | 24 | 35 | .. | .. | .. | .. | 228 |
| 1902 | 29 | 42 | 14 | 33 | 22 | .. | .. | .. | *47 | 33 | 38 | .. | .. | .. | .. | 258 |
| 1903 | 12 | *48 | 14 | 31 | 12 | .. | .. | .. | 17 | 18 | 32 | .. | .. | .. | .. | 184 |
| 1904 | 10 | 26 | 14 | 27 | 11 | .. | .. | .. | 10 | 27 | *31 | .. | .. | .. | .. | 156 |
| 1905 | 16 | *29 | 11 | 18 | 13 | .. | .. | .. | 22 | 23 | 24 | .. | .. | .. | .. | 156 |
| 1906 | 20 | 13 | 7 | 12 | 10 | .. | .. | .. | 26 | 17 | *32 | .. | .. | .. | .. | 137 |
| 1907 | 10 | 18 | 5 | 11 | 11 | .. | .. | .. | 12 | 15 | *22 | .. | .. | .. | .. | 104 |
| 1908 | *20 | 14 | 3 | 18 | 19 | .. | .. | .. | 8 | 13 | 21 | .. | .. | .. | .. | 116 |
| 1909 | 10 | *20 | 4 | 10 | 19 | .. | .. | .. | 9 | 16 | 21 | .. | .. | .. | .. | 109 |
| 1910 | 12 | *43 | 7 | 9 | 28 | .. | .. | .. | 9 | 20 | 19 | .. | .. | .. | .. | 147 |
| 1911 | 17 | *35 | 20 | 20 | 30 | .. | .. | .. | 16 | 25 | *35 | .. | .. | .. | .. | 198 |
| 1912 | 19 | *29 | 17 | 12 | 19 | .. | .. | .. | 20 | 18 | 22 | .. | .. | .. | .. | 156 |
| 1913 | 18 | 17 | 24 | 16 | 24 | .. | .. | .. | 19 | 8 | *33 | .. | .. | .. | .. | 159 |
| 1914 | 17 | 18 | 19 | 10 | 25 | .. | .. | .. | 18 | 12 | *29 | .. | .. | .. | .. | 148 |
| 1915 | 19 | 14 | 25 | 20 | 23 | .. | .. | .. | 12 | *31 | 16 | .. | .. | .. | .. | 160 |
| 1916 | 14 | 14 | 17 | 16 | 17 | .. | .. | .. | 12 | *35 | 19 | .. | .. | .. | .. | 144 |
| 1917 | 15 | 14 | 18 | 13 | 25 | .. | .. | .. | 4 | *27 | 17 | .. | .. | .. | .. | 133 |
| 1918 | 5 | 15 | 8 | 9 | 13 | .. | .. | .. | 4 | 20 | *22 | .. | .. | .. | .. | 96 |
| 1919 | 31 | 33 | 25 | 24 | 23 | .. | .. | .. | 24 | *45 | 35 | .. | .. | .. | .. | 240 |
| 1920 | 50 | 22 | 37 | 35 | 30 | .. | .. | .. | 36 | *115 | 44 | .. | .. | .. | .. | 369 |
| 1921 | 67 | 17 | 35 | 42 | 58 | .. | .. | .. | 42 | *134 | 82 | .. | .. | .. | .. | 477 |
| 1922 | 98 | 45 | 45 | 32 | 54 | .. | .. | .. | 45 | 95 | *111 | .. | .. | .. | .. | 525 |
| 1923 | 82 | 34 | 42 | 59 | 41 | .. | .. | .. | 26 | *105 | 53 | .. | .. | .. | .. | 442 |
| 1924 | 67 | 30 | 41 | 41 | 35 | .. | .. | .. | 22 | *98 | 63 | .. | .. | .. | .. | 397 |
| 1925 | *110 | 41 | 38 | 52 | 50 | .. | .. | .. | 56 | *110 | 76 | .. | .. | .. | .. | 533 |
| 1926 | 72 | 32 | 32 | 27 | 36 | .. | .. | .. | 43 | *121 | 61 | .. | .. | .. | .. | 424 |
| 1927 | 55 | 28 | 36 | 26 | 51 | .. | .. | .. | 29 | *158 | 56 | .. | .. | .. | .. | 439 |
| 1928 | 63 | 38 | 24 | 34 | 62 | .. | .. | .. | 40 | *133 | 89 | .. | .. | .. | .. | 483 |
| 1929 | 46 | 28 | 37 | 62 | 110 | .. | .. | .. | 48 | *142 | 122 | .. | .. | .. | .. | 595 |
| 1930 | 75 | 47 | 63 | 72 | 82 | .. | .. | .. | 57 | *152 | 125 | .. | .. | .. | .. | 673 |
| 1931 | 76 | 37 | 27 | 71 | 43 | .. | .. | .. | 49 | *155 | 118 | .. | .. | .. | .. | 576 |
| 1932 | 67 | 53 | 36 | 78 | 80 | .. | .. | .. | 61 | 160 | *172 | .. | .. | .. | .. | 707 |
| 1933 | 64 | 50 | 43 | 50 | 57 | .. | .. | .. | 60 | *144 | 139 | .. | .. | .. | .. | 607 |
| 1934 | 62 | 51 | 71 | 100 | 74 | .. | .. | .. | 51 | 135 | *144 | .. | .. | .. | .. | 688 |
| 1935 | 73 | 69 | 74 | 93 | 106 | .. | .. | .. | 32 | 104 | *112 | .. | .. | .. | .. | 663 |
| 1936 | 79 | 86 | 60 | 123 | 94 | .. | .. | .. | 62 | *182 | 72 | .. | .. | .. | .. | 758 |
| 1937 | 71 | 100 | 67 | 103 | 150 | .. | .. | .. | 47 | *174 | 94 | .. | .. | .. | .. | 806 |
| 1938 | 92 | 98 | 67 | 113 | 137 | .. | .. | .. | 85 | *174 | 98 | .. | .. | .. | .. | 864 |
| 1939 | 91 | 124 | 64 | 85 | 124 | .. | .. | .. | 44 | *166 | 98 | .. | .. | .. | .. | 796 |
| 1940 | 118 | 145 | 73 | 101 | 134 | .. | .. | .. | 52 | *155 | 105 | .. | .. | .. | .. | 883 |
| 1941 | 91 | 124 | 47 | 103 | 81 | .. | .. | .. | 52 | *151 | 85 | .. | .. | .. | .. | 734 |

| Year | Bal | Bos | Chi | Cle | Det | KC | LA | Mil | Min | NY | Oak | Sea | TB | Tex | Tor | Total |
|---|---|---|---|---|---|---|---|---|---|---|---|---|---|---|---|---|
| 1942 | 98 | 103 | 25 | 50 | 76 | .. | .. | .. | 40 | *108 | 33 | .. | .. | .. | .. | 533 |
| 1943 | 78 | 57 | 33 | 55 | 77 | .. | .. | .. | 47 | *100 | 26 | .. | .. | .. | .. | 473 |
| 1944 | 72 | 69 | 23 | 70 | 60 | .. | .. | .. | 33 | *96 | 36 | .. | .. | .. | .. | 459 |
| 1945 | 63 | 50 | 22 | 65 | 77 | .. | .. | .. | 27 | *93 | 33 | .. | .. | .. | .. | 430 |
| 1946 | 84 | 109 | 37 | 79 | 108 | .. | .. | .. | 60 | *136 | 40 | .. | .. | .. | .. | 653 |
| 1947 | 90 | 103 | 53 | 112 | 103 | .. | .. | .. | 42 | *115 | 61 | .. | .. | .. | .. | 679 |
| 1948 | 63 | 121 | 55 | *155 | 78 | .. | .. | .. | 31 | 139 | 68 | .. | .. | .. | .. | 710 |
| 1949 | 117 | *131 | 43 | 112 | 88 | .. | .. | .. | 81 | 115 | 82 | .. | .. | .. | .. | 769 |
| 1950 | 106 | 161 | 93 | *164 | 114 | .. | .. | .. | 76 | 159 | 100 | .. | .. | .. | .. | 973 |
| 1951 | 86 | 127 | 86 | *140 | 104 | .. | .. | .. | 54 | *140 | 102 | .. | .. | .. | .. | 839 |
| 1952 | 82 | 113 | 80 | *148 | 103 | .. | .. | .. | 50 | 129 | 89 | .. | .. | .. | .. | 794 |
| 1953 | 112 | 101 | 74 | *160 | 108 | .. | .. | .. | 69 | 139 | 116 | .. | .. | .. | .. | 879 |
| 1954 | 52 | 123 | 94 | *156 | 90 | .. | .. | .. | 81 | 133 | 94 | .. | .. | .. | .. | 823 |
| 1955 | 54 | 137 | 116 | 148 | 130 | .. | .. | .. | 80 | *175 | 121 | .. | .. | .. | .. | 961 |
| 1956 | 91 | 139 | 128 | 153 | 150 | .. | .. | .. | 112 | *190 | 112 | .. | .. | .. | .. | 1,075 |
| 1957 | 87 | 153 | 106 | 140 | 110 | .. | .. | .. | 111 | 145 | *166 | .. | .. | .. | .. | 1,024 |
| 1958 | 108 | 155 | 101 | 161 | 109 | .. | .. | .. | 121 | *164 | 138 | .. | .. | .. | .. | 1,057 |
| 1959 | 109 | 125 | 97 | *167 | 160 | .. | .. | .. | 163 | 153 | 117 | .. | .. | .. | .. | 1,091 |
| 1960 | 123 | 124 | 112 | 127 | 150 | .. | .. | .. | 147 | *193 | 110 | .. | .. | .. | .. | 1,086 |
| 1961 | 149 | 112 | 138 | 150 | 180 | .. | 189 | .. | 167 | *240 | 90 | .. | .. | 119 | .. | 1,534 |
| 1962 | 156 | 146 | 92 | 180 | *209 | .. | 137 | .. | 185 | 199 | 116 | .. | .. | 132 | .. | 1,552 |
| 1963 | 95 | 146 | 171 | 114 | 169 | .. | 95 | .. | *225 | 188 | 95 | .. | .. | 138 | .. | 1,489 |
| 1964 | 162 | 186 | 106 | 164 | 157 | .. | 102 | .. | *221 | 162 | 166 | .. | .. | 125 | .. | 1,551 |
| 1965 | 125 | *165 | 125 | 156 | 162 | .. | 92 | .. | 150 | 149 | 110 | .. | .. | 136 | .. | 1,370 |
| 1966 | 175 | 145 | 87 | 155 | *179 | .. | 122 | .. | 144 | 162 | 70 | .. | .. | 126 | .. | 1,365 |
| 1967 | 138 | *158 | 89 | 131 | 152 | .. | 114 | .. | 131 | 100 | 69 | .. | .. | 115 | .. | 1,197 |
| 1968 | 133 | 125 | 71 | 75 | *185 | .. | 83 | .. | 105 | 109 | 94 | .. | .. | 124 | .. | 1,104 |
| 1969 | 175 | *197 | 112 | 119 | 182 | 98 | 88 | 125 | 163 | 94 | 148 | .. | .. | 148 | .. | 1,649 |
| 1970 | 179 | *203 | 123 | 183 | 148 | 97 | 114 | 126 | 153 | 111 | 171 | .. | .. | 138 | .. | 1,746 |
| 1971 | 158 | 161 | 138 | 109 | *179 | 80 | 96 | 104 | 116 | 97 | 160 | .. | .. | 86 | .. | 1,484 |
| 1972 | 100 | 124 | 108 | 91 | 122 | 78 | 78 | 88 | 93 | 103 | *134 | .. | .. | 56 | .. | 1,175 |
| 1973 | 119 | 147 | 111 | *158 | 157 | 114 | 93 | 145 | 120 | 131 | 147 | .. | .. | 110 | .. | 1,552 |
| 1974 | 116 | 109 | *135 | 131 | 131 | 89 | 95 | 120 | 111 | 101 | 132 | .. | .. | 99 | .. | 1,369 |
| 1975 | 124 | 134 | 94 | *153 | 125 | 118 | 55 | 146 | 121 | 110 | 151 | .. | .. | 134 | .. | 1,465 |
| 1976 | 119 | *134 | 73 | 85 | 101 | 65 | 63 | 88 | 81 | 120 | 113 | .. | .. | 80 | .. | 1,122 |
| 1977 | 148 | *213 | 192 | 100 | 166 | 146 | 131 | 125 | 123 | 184 | 117 | 133 | .. | 135 | 100 | 2,013 |
| 1978 | 154 | 172 | 106 | 106 | 129 | 98 | 108 | *173 | 82 | 125 | 100 | 97 | .. | 132 | 98 | 1,680 |
| 1979 | 181 | *194 | 127 | 138 | 164 | 116 | 164 | 185 | 112 | 150 | 108 | 132 | .. | 140 | 95 | 2,006 |
| 1980 | 156 | 162 | 91 | 89 | 143 | 115 | 106 | *203 | 99 | 189 | 137 | 104 | .. | 124 | 126 | 1,844 |
| 1981 | 88 | 90 | 76 | 39 | 65 | 61 | 97 | 96 | 47 | 100 | *104 | 89 | .. | 49 | 61 | 1,062 |
| 1982 | 179 | 136 | 136 | 109 | 177 | 132 | 186 | *216 | 148 | 161 | 149 | 130 | .. | 115 | 106 | 2,080 |
| 1983 | *168 | 142 | 157 | 86 | 156 | 109 | 154 | 132 | 141 | 153 | 121 | 111 | .. | 106 | 167 | 1,903 |
| 1984 | 160 | 181 | 172 | 123 | *187 | 117 | 150 | 96 | 114 | 130 | 158 | 129 | .. | 120 | 143 | 1,980 |
| 1985 | *214 | 162 | 146 | 116 | 202 | 154 | 153 | 101 | 141 | 176 | 155 | 171 | .. | 129 | 158 | 2,178 |
| 1986 | 169 | 144 | 121 | 157 | *198 | 137 | 167 | 127 | 196 | 188 | 163 | 158 | .. | 184 | 181 | 2,290 |
| 1987 | 211 | 174 | 173 | 187 | *225 | 168 | 172 | 163 | 196 | 196 | 199 | 161 | .. | 194 | 215 | 2,634 |
| 1988 | 137 | 124 | 132 | 134 | 143 | 121 | 124 | 113 | 151 | 148 | 156 | 148 | .. | 112 | *158 | 1,901 |
| 1989 | 129 | 108 | 94 | 127 | 116 | 101 | *145 | 126 | 117 | 130 | 127 | 134 | .. | 122 | 142 | 1,718 |
| 1990 | 132 | 106 | 106 | 110 | *172 | 100 | 147 | 128 | 100 | 147 | 164 | 107 | .. | 110 | 167 | 1,796 |
| 1991 | 170 | 126 | 139 | 79 | *209 | 117 | 115 | 116 | 140 | 147 | 159 | 126 | .. | 177 | 133 | 1,953 |
| 1992 | 148 | 84 | 110 | 127 | *182 | 75 | 88 | 82 | 104 | 163 | 142 | 149 | .. | 159 | 163 | 1,776 |
| 1993 | 157 | 114 | 162 | 141 | 178 | 125 | 114 | 125 | 121 | 178 | 158 | 161 | .. | *181 | 159 | 2,074 |
| 1994 | 139 | 120 | 121 | *167 | 161 | 100 | 120 | 99 | 103 | 139 | 113 | 153 | .. | 124 | 115 | 1,774 |
| 1995 | 173 | 175 | 146 | *207 | 159 | 119 | 186 | 128 | 120 | 122 | 169 | 182 | .. | 138 | 140 | 2,164 |
| 1996 | *257 | 209 | 195 | 218 | 204 | 123 | 192 | 178 | 118 | 162 | 243 | 245 | .. | 221 | 177 | 2,742 |
| 1997 | 196 | 185 | 158 | 220 | 176 | 158 | 161 | 135 | 132 | 161 | 197 | *264 | .. | 187 | 147 | 2,477 |
| 1998 | 214 | 205 | 198 | 198 | 165 | 134 | 147 | .. | 115 | 207 | 149 | *234 | 111 | 201 | 221 | 2,499 |
| 1999 | 203 | 176 | 162 | 209 | 212 | 151 | 158 | .. | 105 | 193 | 235 | *244 | 145 | 230 | 212 | 2,635 |
| 2000 | 184 | 167 | 216 | 221 | 177 | 150 | 236 | .. | 116 | 205 | 239 | 198 | 162 | 173 | *244 | 2,688 |
| 2001 | 136 | 198 | 214 | 212 | 139 | 152 | 158 | .. | 164 | 203 | 199 | 169 | 121 | *246 | 195 | 2,506 |
| 2002 | 165 | 177 | 217 | 192 | 124 | 140 | 152 | .. | 167 | 223 | 205 | 152 | 133 | *230 | 187 | 2,464 |
| 2003 | 152 | 238 | 220 | 158 | 153 | 162 | 150 | .. | 155 | 230 | 176 | 139 | 137 | *239 | 190 | 2,499 |
| 2004 | 169 | 222 | *242 | 184 | 201 | 150 | 162 | .. | 191 | *242 | 189 | 136 | 145 | 227 | 145 | 2,605 |
| 2005 | 189 | 199 | 200 | 207 | 168 | 126 | 147 | .. | 134 | 229 | 155 | 130 | 157 | *260 | 136 | 2,437 |
| **Totals** | **10,816** | **11,099** | **8,966** | **10,755** | **11,431** | **4,396** | **5,906** | **3,789** | **8,824** | **13,212** | **10,918** | **4,486** | **1,111** | **6,631** | **4,481** | **116,878** |

*led league or tied; Note: Baltimore column includes Milwaukee, 1901, and St. Louis, 1902-1953 (3,014). Los Angeles column includes Los Angeles Angels, California Angels and Anaheim Angels. Milwaukee column includes Seattle, 1969. Minnesota column includes Washington, 1901-1960 (2,786). New York column includes Baltimore, 1901-1902 (57). Oakland column includes Philadelphia, 1901-1954 (3,502), and Kansas City, 1955-1967 (1,480). Texas column includes Washington, 1961-1971 (1,387).

## NATIONAL LEAGUE (1900-2005)

| Year | Ari | Atl | Chi | Cin | Col | Fla | Hou | LA | Mil | NY | Phi | Pit | StL | SD | SF | Was | Total |
|---|---|---|---|---|---|---|---|---|---|---|---|---|---|---|---|---|---|
| 1900 | .. | *48 | 33 | 33 | .. | .. | .. | 26 | .. | .. | 29 | 26 | 36 | .. | 23 | .. | 254 |
| 1901 | .. | 28 | 18 | 38 | .. | .. | .. | 32 | .. | .. | 24 | 29 | *39 | .. | 19 | .. | 227 |
| 1902 | .. | 14 | 6 | 18 | .. | .. | .. | *19 | .. | .. | 5 | 18 | 10 | .. | 6 | .. | 96 |
| 1903 | .. | 25 | 9 | 28 | .. | .. | .. | 15 | .. | .. | 12 | *34 | 8 | .. | 20 | .. | 151 |
| 1904 | .. | 24 | 22 | 21 | .. | .. | .. | 15 | .. | .. | 23 | 15 | 24 | .. | *31 | .. | 175 |
| 1905 | .. | 17 | 12 | 27 | .. | .. | .. | 29 | .. | .. | 16 | 22 | 20 | .. | *39 | .. | 182 |
| 1906 | .. | 16 | 20 | 16 | .. | .. | .. | *25 | .. | .. | 12 | 12 | 10 | .. | 15 | .. | 126 |
| 1907 | .. | 22 | 13 | 15 | .. | .. | .. | 18 | .. | .. | 12 | 19 | 18 | .. | *23 | .. | 140 |
| 1908 | .. | 17 | 19 | 14 | .. | .. | .. | *28 | .. | .. | 11 | 25 | 17 | .. | 20 | .. | 151 |
| 1909 | .. | 14 | 20 | 22 | .. | .. | .. | 16 | .. | .. | 12 | 25 | 15 | .. | *26 | .. | 150 |
| 1910 | .. | 31 | *34 | 23 | .. | .. | .. | 25 | .. | .. | 22 | 33 | 15 | .. | 31 | .. | 214 |
| 1911 | .. | 37 | 54 | 21 | .. | .. | .. | 28 | .. | .. | *60 | 49 | 26 | .. | 41 | .. | 316 |
| 1912 | .. | 35 | 42 | 21 | .. | .. | .. | 32 | .. | .. | 43 | 39 | 27 | .. | *47 | .. | 286 |
| 1913 | .. | 32 | 59 | 27 | .. | .. | .. | 39 | .. | .. | *73 | 35 | 15 | .. | 30 | .. | 310 |
| 1914 | .. | 35 | 42 | 16 | .. | .. | .. | 31 | .. | .. | *62 | 18 | 33 | .. | 30 | .. | 267 |
| 1915 | .. | 17 | 53 | 15 | .. | .. | .. | 14 | .. | .. | *58 | 24 | 20 | .. | 24 | .. | 225 |
| 1916 | .. | 22 | *46 | 14 | .. | .. | .. | 28 | .. | .. | 42 | 20 | 25 | .. | 42 | .. | 239 |
| 1917 | .. | 22 | 17 | 26 | .. | .. | .. | 25 | .. | .. | 38 | 9 | 26 | .. | *39 | .. | 202 |
| 1918 | .. | 13 | 21 | 15 | .. | .. | .. | 10 | .. | .. | 25 | 15 | *27 | .. | 13 | .. | 139 |
| 1919 | .. | 24 | 21 | 20 | .. | .. | .. | 25 | .. | .. | *42 | 17 | 18 | .. | 40 | .. | 207 |
| 1920 | .. | 23 | 34 | 18 | .. | .. | .. | 28 | .. | .. | *64 | 16 | 32 | .. | 46 | .. | 261 |
| 1921 | .. | 61 | 37 | 20 | .. | .. | .. | 59 | .. | .. | *88 | 37 | 83 | .. | 75 | .. | 460 |

| Year | Ari | Atl | Chi | Cin | Col | Fla | Hou | LA | Mil | NY | Phi | Pit | StL | SD | SF | Was | Total |
|---|---|---|---|---|---|---|---|---|---|---|---|---|---|---|---|---|---|
| 1922 | .. | 32 | 42 | 45 | .. | .. | .. | 56 | .. | .. | *116 | 52 | 107 | .. | 80 | .. | 530 |
| 1923 | .. | 32 | 90 | 45 | .. | .. | .. | 62 | .. | .. | *112 | 49 | 63 | .. | 85 | .. | 538 |
| 1924 | .. | 25 | 66 | 36 | .. | .. | .. | 72 | .. | .. | 94 | 44 | 67 | .. | *95 | .. | 499 |
| 1925 | .. | 41 | 86 | 44 | .. | .. | .. | 64 | .. | .. | 100 | 78 | 109 | .. | *114 | .. | 636 |
| 1926 | .. | 16 | 66 | 35 | .. | .. | .. | 40 | .. | .. | 75 | 44 | *90 | .. | 73 | .. | 439 |
| 1927 | .. | 37 | 74 | 29 | .. | .. | .. | 39 | .. | .. | 57 | 54 | 84 | .. | *109 | .. | 483 |
| 1928 | .. | 52 | 92 | 32 | .. | .. | .. | 66 | .. | .. | 85 | 52 | 113 | .. | *118 | .. | 610 |
| 1929 | .. | 33 | 139 | 34 | .. | .. | .. | 99 | .. | .. | *153 | 60 | 100 | .. | 136 | .. | 754 |
| 1930 | .. | 66 | *171 | 74 | .. | .. | .. | 122 | .. | .. | 126 | 86 | 104 | .. | 143 | .. | 892 |
| 1931 | .. | 34 | 84 | 21 | .. | .. | .. | 71 | .. | .. | 81 | 41 | 60 | .. | *101 | .. | 493 |
| 1932 | .. | 63 | 69 | 47 | .. | .. | .. | 110 | .. | .. | *122 | 48 | 76 | .. | 116 | .. | 651 |
| 1933 | .. | 54 | 72 | 34 | .. | .. | .. | 62 | .. | .. | 60 | 39 | 57 | .. | *82 | .. | 460 |
| 1934 | .. | 83 | 101 | 55 | .. | .. | .. | 79 | .. | .. | 56 | 52 | 104 | .. | *126 | .. | 656 |
| 1935 | .. | 75 | 88 | 73 | .. | .. | .. | 59 | .. | .. | 92 | 66 | 86 | .. | *123 | .. | 662 |
| 1936 | .. | 67 | 76 | 82 | .. | .. | .. | 33 | .. | .. | *103 | 60 | 88 | .. | 97 | .. | 606 |
| 1937 | .. | 63 | 96 | 73 | .. | .. | .. | 37 | .. | .. | 103 | 47 | 94 | .. | *111 | .. | 624 |
| 1938 | .. | 54 | 65 | 110 | .. | .. | .. | 61 | .. | .. | 40 | 65 | 91 | .. | *125 | .. | 611 |
| 1939 | .. | 56 | 91 | 98 | .. | .. | .. | 78 | .. | .. | 49 | 63 | 98 | .. | *116 | .. | 649 |
| 1940 | .. | 59 | 86 | 89 | .. | .. | .. | 93 | .. | .. | 75 | 76 | *119 | .. | 91 | .. | 688 |
| 1941 | .. | 48 | 99 | 64 | .. | .. | .. | *101 | .. | .. | 64 | 56 | 70 | .. | 95 | .. | 597 |
| 1942 | .. | 68 | 75 | 66 | .. | .. | .. | 62 | .. | .. | 44 | 54 | 60 | .. | *109 | .. | 538 |
| 1943 | .. | 39 | 52 | 43 | .. | .. | .. | 39 | .. | .. | 66 | 42 | 70 | .. | *81 | .. | 432 |
| 1944 | .. | 79 | 71 | 51 | .. | .. | .. | 56 | .. | .. | 55 | 70 | *100 | .. | 93 | .. | 575 |
| 1945 | .. | 101 | 57 | 56 | .. | .. | .. | 57 | .. | .. | 56 | 72 | 64 | .. | *114 | .. | 577 |
| 1946 | .. | 44 | 56 | 65 | .. | .. | .. | 55 | .. | .. | 80 | 60 | 81 | .. | *121 | .. | 562 |
| 1947 | .. | 85 | 71 | 95 | .. | .. | .. | 83 | .. | .. | 60 | 156 | 115 | .. | *221 | .. | 886 |
| 1948 | .. | 95 | 87 | 104 | .. | .. | .. | 91 | .. | .. | 91 | 108 | 105 | .. | *164 | .. | 845 |
| 1949 | .. | 103 | 97 | 86 | .. | .. | .. | *152 | .. | .. | 122 | 126 | 102 | .. | 147 | .. | 935 |
| 1950 | .. | 148 | 161 | 99 | .. | .. | .. | *194 | .. | .. | 125 | 138 | 102 | .. | 133 | .. | 1,100 |
| 1951 | .. | 130 | 103 | 88 | .. | .. | .. | *184 | .. | .. | 108 | 137 | 95 | .. | 179 | .. | 1,024 |
| 1952 | .. | 110 | 107 | 104 | .. | .. | .. | *153 | .. | .. | 93 | 92 | 97 | .. | 151 | .. | 907 |
| 1953 | .. | 156 | 137 | 166 | .. | .. | .. | *208 | .. | .. | 115 | 99 | 140 | .. | 176 | .. | 1,197 |
| 1954 | .. | 139 | 159 | 147 | .. | .. | .. | *186 | .. | .. | 102 | 76 | 119 | .. | *186 | .. | 1,114 |
| 1955 | .. | 182 | 164 | 181 | .. | .. | .. | *201 | .. | .. | 132 | 91 | 143 | .. | 169 | .. | 1,263 |
| 1956 | .. | 177 | 142 | *221 | .. | .. | .. | 179 | .. | .. | 121 | 110 | 124 | .. | 145 | .. | 1,219 |
| 1957 | .. | *199 | 147 | 187 | .. | .. | .. | 147 | .. | .. | 117 | 92 | 132 | .. | 157 | .. | 1,178 |
| 1958 | .. | 167 | *182 | 123 | .. | .. | .. | 172 | .. | .. | 124 | 134 | 111 | .. | 170 | .. | 1,183 |
| 1959 | .. | *177 | 163 | 161 | .. | .. | .. | 148 | .. | .. | 113 | 112 | 118 | .. | 167 | .. | 1,159 |
| 1960 | .. | *170 | 119 | 140 | .. | .. | .. | 126 | .. | .. | 99 | 120 | 138 | .. | 130 | .. | 1,042 |
| 1961 | .. | *188 | 176 | 158 | .. | .. | .. | 157 | .. | .. | 103 | 128 | 103 | .. | 183 | .. | 1,196 |
| 1962 | .. | 181 | 126 | 167 | .. | .. | 105 | 140 | .. | 139 | 142 | 108 | 137 | .. | *204 | .. | 1,449 |
| 1963 | .. | 139 | 127 | 122 | .. | .. | 62 | 110 | .. | 96 | 126 | 108 | 128 | .. | *197 | .. | 1,215 |
| 1964 | .. | 159 | 145 | 130 | .. | .. | 70 | 79 | .. | 103 | 130 | 121 | 109 | .. | *165 | .. | 1,211 |
| 1965 | .. | *196 | 134 | 183 | .. | .. | 97 | 78 | .. | 107 | 144 | 111 | 109 | .. | 159 | .. | 1,318 |
| 1966 | .. | *207 | 140 | 149 | .. | .. | 112 | 108 | .. | 98 | 117 | 158 | 108 | .. | 181 | .. | 1,378 |
| 1967 | .. | *158 | 128 | 109 | .. | .. | 93 | 82 | .. | 83 | 103 | 91 | 115 | .. | 140 | .. | 1,102 |
| 1968 | .. | 80 | *130 | 106 | .. | .. | 66 | 67 | .. | 81 | 100 | 80 | 73 | .. | 108 | .. | 891 |
| 1969 | .. | 141 | 142 | *171 | .. | .. | 104 | 97 | .. | 109 | 137 | 119 | 90 | 99 | 136 | 125 | 1,470 |
| 1970 | .. | 160 | 179 | *191 | .. | .. | 129 | 87 | .. | 120 | 101 | 130 | 113 | 172 | 165 | 136 | 1,683 |
| 1971 | .. | 153 | 128 | 138 | .. | .. | 71 | 95 | .. | 98 | 123 | *154 | 95 | 96 | 140 | 88 | 1,379 |
| 1972 | .. | 144 | 133 | 124 | .. | .. | 134 | 98 | .. | 105 | 98 | 110 | 70 | 102 | *150 | 91 | 1,359 |
| 1973 | .. | *206 | 117 | 137 | .. | .. | 134 | 110 | .. | 85 | 134 | 154 | 75 | 112 | 161 | 125 | 1,550 |
| 1974 | .. | 120 | 110 | 135 | .. | .. | 110 | *139 | .. | 96 | 95 | 114 | 83 | 99 | 93 | 86 | 1,280 |
| 1975 | .. | 107 | 95 | 124 | .. | .. | 84 | 118 | .. | 101 | 125 | *138 | 81 | 78 | 84 | 98 | 1,233 |
| 1976 | .. | 82 | 105 | *141 | .. | .. | 66 | 91 | .. | 102 | 110 | 110 | 63 | 64 | 85 | 94 | 1,113 |
| 1977 | .. | 139 | 111 | 181 | .. | .. | 114 | *191 | .. | 188 | 186 | 133 | 96 | 120 | 134 | 138 | 1,631 |
| 1978 | .. | 123 | 72 | 136 | .. | .. | 70 | *149 | .. | 86 | 133 | 115 | 79 | 75 | 117 | 121 | 1,276 |
| 1979 | .. | 126 | 135 | 132 | .. | .. | 49 | *183 | .. | 74 | 119 | 148 | 100 | 93 | 125 | 143 | 1,427 |
| 1980 | .. | 144 | 107 | 113 | .. | .. | 75 | *148 | .. | 61 | 117 | 116 | 101 | 67 | 80 | 114 | 1,243 |
| 1981 | .. | 64 | 57 | 64 | .. | .. | 45 | *82 | .. | 57 | 69 | 55 | 50 | 32 | 63 | 81 | 719 |
| 1982 | .. | *146 | 102 | 82 | .. | .. | 74 | 138 | .. | 97 | 112 | 134 | 67 | 81 | 133 | 133 | 1,299 |
| 1983 | .. | 130 | 140 | 107 | .. | .. | 97 | *146 | .. | 112 | 125 | 121 | 83 | 93 | 142 | 102 | 1,398 |
| 1984 | .. | 111 | 136 | 106 | .. | .. | 79 | 102 | .. | 107 | *147 | 98 | 75 | 109 | 112 | 96 | 1,278 |
| 1985 | .. | 126 | *150 | 114 | .. | .. | 121 | 129 | .. | 134 | 141 | 80 | 87 | 109 | 115 | 118 | 1,424 |
| 1986 | .. | 138 | *155 | 144 | .. | .. | 125 | 130 | .. | 148 | 154 | 111 | 58 | 136 | 114 | 110 | 1,523 |
| 1987 | .. | 152 | *209 | 192 | .. | .. | 122 | 125 | .. | 192 | 169 | 131 | 94 | 113 | 205 | 120 | 1,824 |
| 1988 | .. | 96 | 113 | 122 | .. | .. | 96 | 99 | .. | *152 | 106 | 110 | 71 | 94 | 113 | 107 | 1,279 |
| 1989 | .. | 128 | 124 | 128 | .. | .. | 97 | 89 | .. | *147 | 123 | 95 | 73 | 120 | 141 | 100 | 1,365 |
| 1990 | .. | 162 | 136 | 125 | .. | .. | 94 | 129 | .. | *172 | 103 | 138 | 73 | 123 | 152 | 114 | 1,521 |
| 1991 | .. | 141 | 159 | *164 | .. | .. | 79 | 108 | .. | 117 | 111 | 126 | 68 | 121 | 141 | 95 | 1,430 |
| 1992 | .. | *138 | 104 | 99 | .. | .. | 96 | 72 | .. | 93 | 118 | 106 | 94 | 135 | 105 | 102 | 1,262 |
| 1993 | .. | *169 | 161 | 137 | 142 | 94 | 138 | 130 | .. | 158 | 156 | 110 | 118 | 153 | 168 | 122 | 1,956 |
| 1994 | .. | *137 | 109 | 124 | 125 | 94 | 120 | 115 | .. | 117 | 80 | 80 | 108 | 92 | 123 | 108 | 1,532 |
| 1995 | .. | 168 | 158 | 161 | *200 | 144 | 109 | 140 | .. | 125 | 94 | 125 | 107 | 116 | 152 | 118 | 1,917 |
| 1996 | .. | 197 | 175 | 191 | *221 | 150 | 129 | 150 | .. | 147 | 132 | 138 | 142 | 147 | 153 | 148 | 2,220 |
| 1997 | .. | 174 | 127 | 142 | *239 | 136 | 133 | 174 | .. | 153 | 116 | 129 | 144 | 152 | 172 | 172 | 2,163 |
| 1998 | 159 | 215 | 212 | 138 | 183 | 114 | 166 | 159 | 152 | 136 | 126 | 107 | *223 | 167 | 161 | 147 | 2,565 |
| 1999 | 216 | 197 | 189 | 209 | *223 | 128 | 168 | 187 | 165 | 181 | 161 | 171 | 194 | 153 | 188 | 163 | 2,893 |
| 2000 | 179 | 179 | 183 | 200 | 161 | 160 | 249 | 211 | 177 | 198 | 144 | 168 | 235 | 157 | 226 | 178 | 3,005 |
| 2001 | 208 | 174 | 194 | 176 | 213 | 166 | 208 | 206 | 209 | 147 | 164 | 161 | 199 | 161 | *235 | 131 | 2,952 |
| 2002 | 165 | 164 | *200 | 169 | 152 | 146 | 167 | 155 | 139 | 160 | 165 | 142 | 175 | 136 | 198 | 162 | 2,595 |
| 2003 | 152 | *235 | 172 | 182 | 198 | 157 | 191 | 124 | 196 | 124 | 166 | 163 | 196 | 128 | 180 | 144 | 2,708 |
| 2004 | 135 | 178 | *235 | 194 | 202 | 148 | 187 | 203 | 135 | 185 | 215 | 142 | 214 | 139 | 183 | 151 | 2,846 |
| 2005 | 191 | 184 | 194 | *222 | 150 | 128 | 161 | 149 | 175 | 175 | 167 | 139 | 170 | 130 | 128 | 117 | 2,580 |
| **Totals** | **1,405** | **10,792** | **10,969** | **10,310** | **2,409** | **1,765** | **4,996** | **10,243** | **1,348** | **5,366** | **10,166** | **8 9,084** | **9,386** | **4,274** | **12,239** | **4,498** | **109,250** |

*led league or tied; Note: Atlanta column includes Boston, 1900-1952 (2,569), and Milwaukee, 1953-1965 (2,230). Los Angeles column includes Brooklyn, 1900-1957 (4,018). San Francisco column includes New York, 1900-1957 (5,162). Washington column includes Montreal, 1969-2004 (4,281).

## CLUBS WITH FIVE HOME RUNS IN INNING

### AMERICAN LEAGUE

| Date | Inn | Club (Players) |
|---|---|---|
| June 9, 1966 | 7 | Minnesota (Rollins, Versalles, OLIVA, MINCHER, KILLEBREW) |

**Total number of clubs: 1**

### NATIONAL LEAGUE

| Date | Inn | Club (Players) |
|---|---|---|
| June 6, 1939 | 4 | New York (Danning, Demaree, WHITEHEAD, SALVO, MOORE) |
| June 2, 1949 | 8 | Philadelphia (Ennis, Seminick, Jones, Rowe, Seminick) |
| Aug 23, 1961 | 9 | San Francisco (Cepeda, F. Alou, Davenport, Mays, Orsino) |

**Total number of clubs: 3**

Note—Capitalized letters denote three or more consecutive homers.

## CLUBS WITH FOUR HOME RUNS IN INNING

### AMERICAN LEAGUE

| Date | Inn | Club (Players) |
|---|---|---|
| Sept 24, 1940* | 6 | Boston (WILLIAMS, FOXX, CRONIN, Tabor) |
| June 23, 1950 | 4 | Detroit (Trout, Priddy, Wertz, Evers) |
| May 22, 1957 | 6 | Boston (Mauch, Williams, Gernert, Malzone) |
| Aug 26, 1957 | 7 | Boston (Zauchin, Lepcio, Piersall, Malzone) |
| July 31, 1963† | 6 | Cleveland (HELD, RAMOS, FRANCONA, BROWN) |
| May 2, 1964 | 11 | Minnesota (OLIVA, ALLISON, HALL, KILLEBREW) |
| May 17, 1967 | 7 | Baltimore (Etchebarren, Bowens, Powell, D. Johnson) |
| July 29, 1974 | 1 | Detroit (KALINE, FREEHAN, STANLEY, Brinkman) |
| June 17, 1977 | 1 | Boston (Burleson, Lynn, Fisk, Scott) |
| June 30, 1977 | 8 | New York (Johnson, Piniella, Munson, Johnson) |
| July 4, 1977 | 8 | Boston (LYNN, RICE, YASTRZEMSKI, Scott) |
| May 31, 1980 | 4 | Boston (Stapleton, PEREZ, FISK, HOBSON) |
| May 16, 1983 | 9 | Minnesota (Engle, Mitchell, Gaetti, Hatcher) |
| Sept 10, 1986 | 4 | Detroit (Lemon, Heath, Gibson, Coles) |
| May 2, 1992 | 5 | Minnesota (Mack, Puckett, Hrbek, Bush) |
| Sept 5, 1995 | 2 | Baltimore (Hoiles, MANTO, SMITH, ANDERSON) |
| May 26, 1996 | 8 | Chicago (THOMAS, BAINES, VENTURA, Kreuter) |
| Sept 21, 1996 | 3 | Seattle (RODRIGUEZ, GRIFFEY, MARTINEZ, Sorrento) |
| Aug 21, 1997 | 3 | Oakland (Giambi, Young, McDonald, Canseco) |
| July 18, 1998 | 4 | Boston (Sadler, Lewis, Garciaparra, Vaughn) |
| Aug 1, 1999 | 4 | Oakland (Tejada, Chavez, Giambi, Jaha) |
| May 3, 2000 | 6 | Chicago (Johnson, VALENTIN, THOMAS, KONERKO) |
| May 26, 2000 | 6 | Kansas City (Dye, Quinn, Johnson, Febles) |
| May 28, 2000 | 5 | Anaheim (Erstad, VAUGHN, SALMON, ANDERSON) |
| July 3, 2000 | 4 | Boston (Everett, O'Leary, Varitek, Burkhart) |
| June 29, 2001 | 4 | Kansas City (Sweeney, DYE, IBANEZ, BELTRAN) |
| Aug 17, 2001 | 6 | Toronto (Frye, Cruz, Stewart, Delgado) |
| Apr 27, 2002 | 3 | Oakland (Hatteberg, Long, Pena, Menechino) |
| May 2, 2002 | 1 | Seattle (Boone 2, Cameron 2) |
| July 23, 2002‡ | 3 | Boston (Damon, Garciaparra 2, Ramirez) |
| July 16, 2004 | 9 | Cleveland (Broussard, Martinez, Hafner, Gerut) |
| May 21, 2005 | 3 | Texas (Barajas, Teixeira, Blalock, Nix) |
| June 21, 2005 | 8 | New York (Posada, SHEFFIELD, RODRIGUEZ, MATSUI) |
| Aug 21, 2005 | 4 | Chicago (IGUCHI, ROWAND, KONERKO, Widger) |

**Total number of clubs: 34**

### NATIONAL LEAGUE

| Date | Inn | Club (Players) |
|---|---|---|
| June 6, 1894 | 3 | Pittsburgh (Stenzel, Lyons, Bierbauer, Stenzel) |
| May 12, 1930 | 7 | Chicago (Heathcote, Wilson, Grimm, Beck) |
| Aug 13, 1939* | 4 | New York (Bonura, KAMPOURIS, LOHRMAN, MOORE) |
| June 6, 1948* | 6 | St. Louis (Dusak, Schoendienst, Slaughter, Jones) |
| May 28, 1954 | 8 | New York (Williams, Dark, Irvin, Gardner) |
| July 8, 1956* | 4 | New York (Mays, THOMPSON, SPENCER, WESTRUM) |
| June 8, 1961 | 7 | Milwaukee (MATHEWS, AARON, ADCOCK, THOMAS) |
| June 8, 1965 | 10 | Milwaukee (Torre, Mathews, Aaron, Oliver) |
| July 10, 1970 | 9 | San Diego (Murrell, Spiezio, Campbell, Gaston) |
| June 21, 1971* | 8 | Atlanta (Lum, King, H. Aaron, Evans) |
| July 30, 1978 | 3 | Montreal (Dawson, Parrish, Cash, Dawson) |
| Aug 17, 1985 | 7 | Philadelphia (SAMUEL, WILSON, SCHMIDT, Daulton) |
| Apr 29, 1986 | 4 | Montreal (Dawson, Brooks, Wallach, Fitzgerald) |
| Sept 20, 1992 | 6 | Atlanta (JUSTICE, HUNTER, GANT, Lemke) |
| June 19, 1994 | 1 | Cincinnati (Morris, Mitchell, Branson, Taubensee) |
| Aug 8, 1995 | 2 | Pittsburgh (King, Merced, King, Cummings) |
| Aug 17, 1996 | 8 | Cincinnati (Taubensee, Sanders, Branson, Larkin) |
| June 22, 1997 | 3 | Atlanta (Blauser, C. Jones, McGriff, Tucker) |
| Aug 26, 1998 | 9 | Florida (LEE, FLOYD, ORIE, Kotsay) |
| June 6, 1999 | 7 | Colorado (Blanco, Perez, Bichette, Echevarria) |
| Apr 27, 2000 | 1 | Chicago (Young, Gutierrez, Rodriguez, Buford) |
| July 23, 2000 | 2 | Houston (Spiers, Bagwell, Berkman, Hidalgo) |
| Aug 8, 2000 | 4 | Los Angeles (Elster, Dreifort, Sheffield, Green) |
| May 17, 2001 | 3 | San Diego (Arias, Henderson, Klesko, Trammell) |
| May 20, 2001 | 7 | Atlanta (A. Jones, Jordan, Lopez, Helms) |
| May 28, 2003 | 1 | Atlanta (FURCAL, DEROSA, SHEFFIELD, Lopez) |
| Aug 20, 2003 | 5 | Pittsburgh (KENDALL, GILES, SANDERS, Sanders) |
| Sept 8, 2004 | 1 | Houston (Biggio, Bagwell, Berkman, Lamb) |

**Total number of clubs: 28**

Note—Capitalized letters denote three or more consecutive homers.
*1st game; †2nd game; ‡a.m. game

## CLUBS WITH THREE CONSECUTIVE HOME RUNS IN INNING

### PLAYERS LEAGUE

| Date | Inn | Club (Players) |
|---|---|---|
| May 31, 1890 | 8 | New York (GORE, EWING, CONNOR) |

**Total number of clubs: 1**

### AMERICAN LEAGUE

| Date | Inn | Club (Players) |
|---|---|---|
| June 30, 1902* | 6 | Cleveland (LAJOIE, HICKMAN, BRADLEY) |
| May 2, 1922 | 4 | Philadelphia (WALKER, PERKINS, MILLER) |
| Sept 10, 1925* | 4 | New York (MEUSEL, RUTH, GEHRIG) |
| May 4, 1929 | 7 | New York (RUTH, GEHRIG, MEUSEL) |
| June 18, 1930 | 5 | Philadelphia (SIMMONS, FOXX, MILLER) |
| July 17, 1934 | 4 | Philadelphia (JOHNSON, FOXX, HIGGINS) |
| June 25, 1939* | 7 | Cleveland (CHAPMAN, TROSKY, HEATH) |
| Sept 24, 1940*‡ | 6 | Boston (WILLIAMS, FOXX, CRONIN) |
| May 23, 1946 | 5 | New York (DiMAGGIO, ETTEN, GORDON) |
| Apr 23, 1947 | 8 | Detroit (CULLENBINE, WAKEFIELD, EVERS) |
| May 13, 1947 | 6 | New York (KELLER, DiMAGGIO, LINDELL) |
| Apr 19, 1948* | 2 | Boston (SPENCE, STEPHENS, DOERR) |
| June 6, 1948† | 6 | Boston (WILLIAMS, SPENCE, STEPHENS) |
| July 28, 1950 | 3 | Cleveland (DOBY, ROSEN, EASTER) |
| Sept 2, 1951 | 1 | Cleveland (SIMPSON, ROSEN, EASTER) |
| July 16, 1953† | 5 | St. Louis (COURTNEY, KRYHOSKI, DYCK) |
| July 7, 1956 | 7 | Detroit (KUENN, TORGESON, MAXWELL) |
| Sept 7, 1959 | 2 | Boston (BUDDIN, CASALE, GREEN) |
| Apr 30, 1961† | 7 | Baltimore (GENTILE, TRIANDOS, HANSEN) |
| May 23, 1961 | 9 | Detroit (CASH, BOROS, BROWN) |
| June 27, 1961 | 1 | Washington (GREEN, TASBY, LONG) |
| June 17, 1962* | 2 | Cleveland (KINDALL, PHILLIPS, MAHONEY) |
| Aug 19, 1962 | 7 | Kansas City (CIMOLI, CAUSEY, BRYAN) |
| Aug 28, 1962 | 4 | Los Angeles (J. L. THOMAS, WAGNER, RODGERS) |
| July 31, 1963†‡ | 6 | Cleveland (HELD, RAMOS, FRANCONA, BROWN) |
| May 2, 1964‡ | 11 | Minnesota (OLIVA, ALLISON, HALL, KILLEBREW) |
| Sept 10, 1965 | 8 | Baltimore (ROBINSON, BLEFARY, ADAIR) |
| June 9, 1966‡ | 7 | Minnesota (OLIVA, MINCHER, KILLEBREW) |
| June 29, 1966 | 3 | New York (RICHARDSON, MANTLE, PEPITONE) |
| July 2, 1966 | 6 | Washington (HOWARD, LOCK, McMULLEN) |
| June 22, 1969* | 3 | Oakland (KUBIAK, JACKSON, BANDO) |
| Aug 10, 1969 | 6 | New York (MURCER, MUNSON, MICHAEL) |
| Sept 4, 1969 | 9 | Baltimore (F. ROBINSON, POWELL, B. C. ROBINSON) |
| Aug 22, 1970 | 6 | Cleveland (SIMS, NETTLES, LEON) |
| Apr 17, 1971 | 7 | Detroit (NORTHRUP, CASH, HORTON) |
| June 27, 1972 | 1 | Detroit (RODRIGUEZ, KALINE, HORTON) |
| July 15, 1973 | 8 | Minnesota (MITTERWALD, LIS, HOLT) |
| July 29, 1974‡ | 1 | Detroit (KALINE, FREEHAN, STANLEY) |
| May 11, 1977 | 2 | California (BONDS, BAYLOR, JACKSON) |
| July 4, 1977‡ | 8 | Boston (LYNN, RICE, YASTRZEMSKI) |
| Aug 13, 1977 | 6 | Boston (SCOTT, HOBSON, EVANS) |
| May 8, 1979 | 6 | Baltimore (MURRAY, MAY, ROENICKE) |
| June 19, 1979 | 4 | Oakland (GROSS, REVERING, HEATH) |
| May 31, 1980‡ | 4 | Boston (PEREZ, FISK, HOBSON) |
| June 3, 1980 | 9 | Oakland (REVERING, PAGE, ARMAS) |
| May 28, 1982 | 6 | Milwaukee (COOPER, MONEY, THOMAS) |
| June 5, 1982 | 7 | Milwaukee (YOUNT, COOPER, OGLIVIE) |
| June 7, 1982 | 8 | Minnesota (WASHINGTON, BRUNANSKY, HRBEK) |
| Sept 12, 1982 | 3 | Milwaukee (COOPER, SIMMONS, OGLIVIE) |
| Aug 2, 1983 | 3 | Seattle (S. HENDERSON, D. HENDERSON, RAMOS) |
| Sept 9, 1983 | 1 | Chicago (FISK, PACIOREK, LUZINSKI) |
| Apr 24, 1984 | 4 | California (R.M. JACKSON, DOWNING, GRICH) |
| Apr 26, 1984 | 6 | Toronto (UPSHAW, BELL, BARFIELD) |
| May 29, 1984 | 6 | New York (MATTINGLY, BAYLOR, WINFIELD) |
| June 3, 1984 | 4 | New York (GAMBLE, KEMP, HARRAH) |
| June 29, 1984 | 5 | Cleveland (THORNTON, HALL, WILLARD) |
| Aug 19, 1984 | 7 | Kansas City (MOTLEY, WHITE, BALBONI) |
| Aug 24, 1985 | 9 | Chicago (LAW, LITTLE, BAINES) |
| Sept 16, 1985 | 8 | Baltimore (RIPKEN, MURRAY, LYNN) |
| July 8, 1986 | 4 | Detroit (GIBSON, PARRISH, EVANS) |
| July 31, 1986 | 5 | Detroit (TRAMMELL, GIBSON, GRUBB) |
| Sept 28, 1986 | 4 | Kansas City (BRETT, WHITE, QUIRK) |
| June 28, 1987 | 9 | Detroit (GRUBB, NOKES, MADLOCK) |
| Sept 12, 1987 | 8 | Toronto (WHITT, BARFIELD, GRUBER) |
| July 9, 1988* | 4 | Chicago (PASQUA, WALKER, BOSTON) |
| May 16, 1990 | 4 | Oakland (CANSECO, McGWIRE, HASSEY) |
| June 17, 1990 | 7 | Cleveland (MALDONADO, JACOBY, SNYDER) |
| July 6, 1990† | 3 | Oakland (R. HENDERSON, LANSFORD, CANSECO) |
| Aug 7, 1990 | 9 | Detroit (TRAMMELL, FIELDER, WARD) |
| Apr 20, 1992 | 3 | Detroit (TRAMMELL, FIELDER, TETTLETON) |
| May 8, 1994 | 6 | New York (TARTABULL, STANLEY, G. WILLIAMS) |
| May 28, 1995 | 4 | Chicago (DURHAM, KARKOVICE, GREBECK) |
| Sept 5, 1995‡ | 2 | Baltimore (MANTO, SMITH, ANDERSON) |
| May 26, 1996‡ | 8 | Chicago (THOMAS, BAINES, VENTURA) |
| Sept 12, 1996 | 7 | Cleveland (THOME, BELLE, FRANCO) |
| Sept 21, 1996‡ | 3 | Seattle (RODRIGUEZ, GRIFFEY, MARTINEZ) |
| Aug 28, 1998 | 4 | Texas (GONZALEZ, CLARK, RODRIGUEZ) |
| May 19, 1999 | 5 | Texas (RODRIGUEZ, PALMEIRO, ZEILE) |
| May 28, 1999 | 1 | Texas (GONZALEZ, PALMEIRO, RODRIGUEZ) |
| Apr 9, 2000 | 6 | Minnesota (COOMER, JONES, LeCROY) |
| Apr 9, 2000 | 8 | Kansas City (BELTRAN, DYE, SWEENEY) |
| Apr 18, 2000 | 6 | Toronto (GREBECK, MONDESI, DELGADO) |
| May 3, 2000 | 6 | Chicago (VALENTIN, THOMAS, KONERKO) |
| May 28, 2000 | 5 | Anaheim (VAUGHN, SALMON, ANDERSON) |
| June 16, 2000 | 8 | Oakland (CHAVEZ, TEJADA, HERNANDEZ) |
| June 23, 2000 | 2 | Oakland (VELARDE, JA. GIAMBI, GRIEVE) |
| June 24, 2000 | 2 | Anaheim (ANDERSON, GLAUS, SPIEZIO) |
| June 24, 2001 | 2 | Detroit (FICK, ENCARNACION, HALTER) |
| June 29, 2001 | 4 | Kansas City (DYE, IBANEZ, BELTRAN) |
| July 12, 2001 | 3 | Minnesota (MIENTKIEWICZ, KOSKIE, HUNTER) |
| July 26, 2001 | 1 | Anaheim (GLAUS, ERSTAD, ANDERSON) |
| Aug 21, 2001 | 6 | Toronto (STEWART, DELGADO, MONDESI) |
| May 31, 2002 | 11 | Kansas City (BELTRAN, SWEENEY, RANDA) |
| Apr 18, 2004 | 6 | Texas (NIX, BARAJAS, GONZALEZ) |
| May 24, 2004 | 3 | Anaheim (GUERRERO, GUILLEN, DaVANON) |
| July 16, 2004 | 3 | Cleveland (LAWTON, MARTINEZ, BLAKE) |
| Aug 27, 2004 | 5 | Seattle (OLIVO, LOPEZ, BOCACHICA) |
| Apr 9, 2005 | 3 | Toronto (WELLS, KOSKIE, HILLENBRAND) |

| Date | Inn | Club (Players) |
|---|---|---|
| June 21, 2005 | 8 | New York (SHEFFIELD, RODRIGUEZ, MATSUI) |
| Aug 21, 2005 | 4 | Chicago (IGUCHI, ROWAND, KONERKO) |

**Total number of clubs: 100**

## NATIONAL LEAGUE

| Date | Inn | Club (Players) |
|---|---|---|
| May 10, 1894 | 7 | St. Louis (SHUGART, MILLER, PEITZ) |
| Aug 13, 1932* | 4 | New York (TERRY, OTT, LINDSTROM) |
| June 10, 1935 | 8 | Pittsburgh (P. WANER, VAUGHAN, YOUNG) |
| July 9, 1938 | 3 | Boston (CUCCINELLO, WEST, FLETCHER) |
| June 6, 1939‡ | 4 | New York (WHITEHEAD, SALVO, MOORE) |
| Aug 13, 1939*‡ | 4 | New York (KAMPOURIS, LOHRMAN, MOORE) |
| Aug 11, 1941 | 5 | Chicago (CAVARRETTA, HACK, NICHOLSON) |
| June 11, 1944† | 8 | St. Louis (W. COOPER, KUROWSKI, LITWHILER) |
| Aug 11, 1946* | 8 | Cincinnati (HATTON, WEST, MUELLER) |
| June 20, 1948† | 8 | New York (MIZE, MARSHALL, GORDON) |
| June 4, 1949 | 6 | New York (LOCKMAN, GORDON, MARSHALL) |
| Apr 19, 1952 | 7 | Brooklyn (CAMPANELLA, PAFKO, SNIDER) |
| Sept 27, 1952 | 7 | Pittsburgh (KINER, GARAGIOLA, BELL) |
| Sept. 4, 1953 | 4 | New York (WESTRUM, CORWIN, LOCKMAN) |
| June 20, 1954 | 6 | New York (HOFMAN, WESTRUM, RHODES) |
| Aug 15, 1954 | 9 | Cincinnati (BELL, KLUSZEWSKI, GREENGRASS) |
| Apr 16, 1955 | 2 | Chicago (JACKSON, BANKS, FONDY) |
| July 6, 1955* | 6 | Pittsburgh (LYNCH, THOMAS, LONG) |
| May 30, 1956* | 1 | Milwaukee (MATHEWS, AARON, THOMSON) |
| May 31, 1956 | 9 | Cincinnati (BELL, KLUSZEWSKI, ROBINSON) |
| June 29, 1956 | 9 | Brooklyn (SNIDER, JACKSON, HODGES) |
| July 8, 1956*‡ | 4 | New York (THOMPSON, SPENCER, WESTRUM) |
| Apr 21, 1957* | 3 | Pittsburgh (THOMAS, SMITH, GROAT) |
| June 26, 1957 | 5 | Milwaukee (AARON, MATHEWS, COVINGTON) |
| May 7, 1958 | 5 | Pittsburgh (SKINNER, KLUSZEWSKI, THOMAS) |
| May 31, 1958 | 1 | Milwaukee (AARON, MATHEWS, COVINGTON) |
| June 8, 1961‡ | 7 | Milwaukee (MATHEWS, AARON, ADCOCK, THOMAS) |
| June 18, 1961 | 3 | Milwaukee (AARON, ADCOCK, THOMAS) |
| Apr 28, 1962 | 6 | New York (THOMAS, NEAL, HODGES) |
| Aug 27, 1963 | 3 | San Francisco (MAYS, CEPEDA, F. ALOU) |
| July 18, 1964 | 8 | St. Louis (BOYER, WHITE, McCARVER) |
| Aug 5, 1969* | 5 | San Francisco (MARSHALL, HUNT, BONDS) |
| May 18, 1970 | 8 | New York (MARSHALL, FOY, GROTE) |
| Aug 1, 1970 | 7 | Pittsburgh (ROBERTSON, STARGELL, PAGAN) |
| July 16, 1974 | 9 | San Diego (COLBERT, McCOVEY, WINFIELD) |
| July 20, 1974 | 5 | New York (THEODORE, STAUB, JONES) |
| May 17, 1977 | 5 | Chicago (BIITTNER, MURCER, MORALES) |
| Sept 30, 1977 | 2 | Philadelphia (LUZINSKI, HEBNER, MADDOX) |
| Aug 14, 1978 | 3 | Atlanta (MATTHEWS, BURROUGHS, HORNER) |
| June 17, 1979 | 4 | Montreal (PEREZ, CARTER, VALENTINE) |
| July 11, 1979 | 1 | San Diego (TURNER, WINFIELD, TENACE) |
| May 27, 1980 | 3 | Cincinnati (GRIFFEY, FOSTER, DRIESSEN) |
| Aug 31, 1980† | 2 | Los Angeles (CEY, MONDAY, FERGUSON) |
| July 11, 1982 | 2 | San Francisco (SMITH, MAY, SUMMERS) |
| June 24, 1984 | 5 | Houston (CABELL, GARNER, CRUZ) |
| Aug 17, 1985‡ | 7 | Philadelphia (SAMUEL, WILSON, SCHMIDT) |
| July 27, 1986 | 3 | New York (CARTER, STRAWBERRY, MITCHELL) |
| Apr 13, 1987 | 1 | San Diego (WYNNE, GWYNN, KRUK) |
| July 26, 1987 | 8 | Philadelphia (THOMPSON, HAYES, SCHMIDT) |
| May 1, 1988 | 5 | New York (TEUFEL, HERNANDEZ, STRAWBERRY) |
| Apr 17, 1989 | 3 | New York (STRAWBERRY, McREYNOLDS, HERNANDEZ) |
| June 16, 1990 | 5 | Cincinnati (SABO, LARKIN, DAVIS) |
| Sept 14, 1991 | 4 | Cincinnati (DUNCAN, MORRIS, O'NEILL) |
| Sept 20, 1992‡ | 6 | Atlanta (JUSTICE, HUNTER, GANT) |
| Sept 6, 1993 | 6 | Chicago (BUECHELE, WILSON, LAKE) |
| Apr 15, 1994 | 1 | Atlanta (McGRIFF, PENDLETON, TARASCO) |
| Apr 18, 1994 | 1 | Atlanta (KLESKO, McGRIFF, JUSTICE) |
| July 7, 1995 | 2 | Colorado (WALKER, GALARRAGA, CASTILLA) |
| Aug 8, 1995‡ | 2 | Pittsburgh (MERCED, KING, CUMMINGS) |
| Apr 19, 1996 | 6 | Chicago (McRAE, SANDBERG, GRACE) |
| June 30, 1996 | 3 | Los Angeles (PIAZZA, KARROS, MONDESI) |
| July 23, 1996 | 1 | Colorado (BICHETTE, GALARRAGA, CASTILLA) |
| Apr 1, 1997 | 6 | San Diego (GOMEZ, HENDERSON, VERAS) |
| Apr 9, 1997 | 6 | Cincinnati (LARKIN, GREENE, SANDERS) |
| May 29, 1997 | 6 | Colorado (WALKER, GALARRAGA, BICHETTE) |
| June 1, 1997 | 4 | Los Angeles (PIAZZA, KARROS, ZEILE) |
| June 7, 1997* | 1 | Colorado (WALKER, GALARRAGA, BICHETTE) |
| Aug 23, 1997 | 9 | Montreal (STANKIEWICZ, GRUDZIELANEK, LANSING) |
| Aug 2, 1998 | 2 | San Francisco (BURKS, BONDS, KENT) |
| Aug 10, 1998 | 5 | Chicago (SOSA, GRACE, RODRIGUEZ) |
| Aug 26, 1998‡ | 9 | Florida (LEE, FLOYD, ORIE) |
| Apr 28, 1999 | 1 | Philadelphia (ROLEN, BROGNA, GANT) |
| June 18, 1999 | 8 | Chicago (SOSA, GRACE, RODRIGUEZ) |
| Aug 20, 1999 | 4 | San Francisco (MARTINEZ, BONDS, BURKS) |
| Aug 22, 1999 | 1 | San Francisco (BONDS, KENT, BURKS) |
| Aug 22, 1999 | 1 | Arizona (GONZALEZ, WILLIAMS, DURAZO) |
| Sept 17, 1999 | 4 | St. Louis (McGWIRE, T. HOWARD, TATIS) |
| Apr 6, 2000 | 3 | St. Louis (TATIS, DREW, MATHENY) |
| May 13, 2000 | 8 | Cincinnati (TUCKER, GRIFFEY, YOUNG) |
| June 14, 2000 | 8 | Houston (ALOU, HIDALGO, EUSEBIO) |
| July 22, 2001 | 5 | San Francisco (KENT, DAVIS, SANTIAGO) |
| Aug 3, 2001 | 6 | Cincinnati (YOUNG, LaRUE, REESE) |
| Sept 29, 2001 | 1 | Chicago (McGRIFF, WHITE, HUNDLEY) |
| Apr 28, 2002 | 6 | Arizona (FINLEY, MILLER, GRACE) |
| May 3, 2002 | 1 | Arizona (BAUTISTA, FINLEY, MILLER) |
| May 23, 2002 | 9 | Los Angeles (BELTRE, GREEN, HANSEN) |
| June 11, 2002 | 5 | Atlanta (A. JONES, CASTILLA, M. FRANCO) |
| June 22, 2002 | 5 | Colorado (BUTLER, WALKER, HELTON) |
| July 2, 2002 | 2 | St. Louis (POLANCO, EDMONDS, PUJOLS) |
| Aug 4, 2002 | 6 | San Francisco (SNOW, SANDERS, BELL) |
| Sept 19, 2002 | 8 | St. Louis (MARRERO, EDMONDS, PUJOLS) |
| Apr 7, 2003 | 6 | Atlanta (SHEFFIELD, C. JONES, A. JONES) |
| May 28, 2003‡ | 1 | Atlanta (FURCAL, DEROSA, SHEFFIELD) |
| June 24, 2003 | 6 | Chicago (WOOD, GRUDZIELANEK, GONZALEZ) |
| July 19, 2003 | 1 | Houston (BERKMAN, HIDALGO, ENSBERG) |
| Aug 20, 2003‡ | 5 | Pittsburgh (KENDALL, GILES, SANDERS) |
| Sept 21, 2003 | 4 | Los Angeles (VENTURA, BELTRE, BURNITZ) |
| Apr 18, 2004 | 5 | Los Angeles (BELTRE, ENCARNACION, ROSS) |
| Apr 27, 2004 | 4 | Colorado (BURNITZ, JOHNSON, HOLLIDAY) |
| May 4, 2004 | 5 | Philadelphia (ABREU, THOME, BURRELL) |
| May 18, 2004 | 4 | Philadelphia (ABREU, BURRELL, THOME) |
| Aug 3, 2004 | 7 | San Francisco (SNOW, BONDS, FELIZ) |
| Aug 5, 2004 | 1 | Los Angeles (WERTH, BRADLEY, BELTRE) |
| Aug 31, 2004 | 5 | Houston (BELTRAN, BAGWELL, BERKMAN) |
| Sept 15, 2004 | 1 | Chicago (LEE, SOSA, BARRETT) |
| Oct 2, 2005 | 3 | Cincinnati (LOPEZ, DUNN, KEARNS) |

**Total number of clubs: 106**

*1st game; †2nd game; ‡Club had more than three homers in inning.



# PITCHING

## NO-HIT GAMES

### PERFECT GAMES OF NINE OR MORE INNINGS

#### AMERICAN LEAGUE

| Year | | Score |
|---|---|---|
| 1904 | Cy Young, Boston vs. Philadelphia, May 5 | 3-0 |
| 1908 | Addie Joss, Cleveland vs. Chicago, Oct 2 | 1-0 |
| 1922 | Charlie Robertson, Chicago at Detroit, Apr 30 | 2-0 |
| 1968 | Catfish Hunter, Oakland vs. Minnesota, May 8 | 4-0 |
| 1981 | Len Barker, Cleveland vs. Toronto, May 15 | 3-0 |
| 1984 | Mike Witt, California at Texas, Sept 30 | 1-0 |
| 1994 | Kenny Rogers, Texas vs. California, July 28 | 4-0 |
| 1998 | David Wells, New York vs. Minnesota, May 17 | 4-0 |
| 1999 | David Cone, New York vs. Montreal NL, July 18 | 6-0 |

Note: Ernie Shore of Boston is often included in the list of perfect game pitchers. In the 1st game of a June 23, 1917 doubleheader at Boston, Babe Ruth, the starting Red Sox pitcher, was removed for arguing with umpire Brick Owens after giving a base on balls to Washington's Ray Morgan, the 1st batter. Shore, without warming up, took Ruth's place. Morgan was retired trying to steal 2nd. From then on, Shore faced 26 batters, with none reaching base. Shore won the game, 4-0. He and Ruth are listed under the category "No-hit games of nine or more inn."

Note: Don Larsen of the New York Yankees pitched a perfect game in the World Series, defeating the Brooklyn Dodgers, 2-0, at Yankee Stadium on Oct 8, 1956.

**Total number of games (excluding Shore's and Larsen's): 9**

#### NATIONAL LEAGUE

| Year | | Score |
|---|---|---|
| 1880 | Lee Richmond, Worcester vs. Cleveland, June 12 | 1-0 |
| | Monte Ward, Providence vs. Buffalo, June 17 | 5-0 |
| 1964 | Jim Bunning, Philadelphia at New York, June 21, 1st game | 6-0 |
| 1965 | Sandy Koufax, Los Angeles vs. Chicago, Sept 9 | 1-0 |
| 1988 | Tom Browning, Cincinnati vs. Los Angeles, Sept 16 | 1-0 |
| 1991 | Dennis Martinez, Montreal at Los Angeles, July 28 | 2-0 |
| 2004 | Randy Johnson, Arizona at Atlanta, May 18 | 2-0 |

**Total number of games: 7**

### PERFECT GAMES FOR NINE INNINGS THAT WERE BROKEN UP IN EXTRA INNINGS

#### NATIONAL LEAGUE

1959—Harvey Haddix, Pittsburgh at Milwaukee, May 26 (Haddix pitched 12 perfect innings before Felix Mantilla, leading off the 13th, reached base on third baseman Don Hoak's throwing error. After Eddie Mathews sacrificed and Hank Aaron was walked intentionally, Joe Adcock doubled to score Mantilla, ending the game.) **Score: 0-1**

1995—Pedro J. Martinez, Montreal at San Diego, June 3 (Martinez pitched nine perfect innings before Bip Roberts doubled leading off the 10th. Mel Rojas then relieved and retired the game's final three batters.) **Score: 1-0**

**Total number of games: 2**

### PERFECT GAMES OF LESS THAN NINE INNINGS

#### AMERICAN LEAGUE

| Year | | Score |
|---|---|---|
| 1907 | Rube Vickers, Philadelphia at Washington, October 5, 2nd game, 5 inn | 4-0 |
| 1967 | Dean Chance, Minnesota vs. Boston, Aug 6, 5 inn | 2-0 |

**Total number of games: 2**

#### NATIONAL LEAGUE

| Year | | Score |
|---|---|---|
| 1907 | Ed Karger, St. Louis vs. Boston, Aug 11, 2nd game, seven inn | 4-0 |
| 1984 | David Palmer, Montreal at St. Louis, Apr 21, 2nd game, five inn | 4-0 |

**Total number of games: 2**

### NO-HIT GAMES OF NINE OR MORE INNINGS

#### AMERICAN ASSOCIATION

| Year | | Score |
|---|---|---|
| 1882 | Tony Mullane, Louisville at Cincinnati, Sept 11 (1st no-hitter at 50-foot distance) | 2-0 |
| | Guy Hecker, Louisville at Pittsburgh, Sept 19 | 3-1 |
| 1884 | Al Atkinson, Philadelphia vs. Pittsburgh, May 24 | 10-1 |
| | Ed Morris, Columbus at Pittsburgh, May 29 | 5-0 |
| | Frank Mountain, Columbus at Washington, June 5 | 12-0 |
| | Sam Kimber, Brooklyn vs. Toledo, October 4, 10 inn | 0-0 |
| 1886 | Al Atkinson, Philadelphia vs. New York, May 1 | 3-2 |
| | Adonis Terry, Brooklyn vs. St. Louis, July 24 | 1-0 |
| | Matt Kilroy, Baltimore at Pittsburgh, Oct 6 | 6-0 |
| 1888 | Adonis Terry, Brooklyn vs. Louisville, May 27 | 4-0 |
| | Henry Porter, Kansas City at Baltimore, June 6 | 4-0 |
| | Ed Seward, Philadelphia vs. Cincinnati, July 26 | 12-2 |

| Year | | Score |
|---|---|---|
| | Gus Weyhing, Philadelphia vs. Kansas City, July 31 | 4-0 |
| 1890 | Cannonball Titcomb, Rochester vs. Syracuse, Sept 15 | 7-0 |
| 1891 | Ted Breitenstein, St. Louis vs. Louisville, Oct 4, 1st game (1st major league start) | 8-0 |

**Total number of games: 15**

## UNION ASSOCIATION

| Year | | Score |
|---|---|---|
| 1884 | Dick Burns, Cincinnati at Kansas City, Aug 26 | 3-1 |
| 1884 | Ed Cushman, Milwaukee vs. Washington, Sept 28 | 5-0 |

**Total number of games: 2**

## AMERICAN LEAGUE

| Year | | Score |
|---|---|---|
| 1902 | Nixey Callahan, Chicago vs. Detroit, Sept 20, 1st game | 3-0 |
| 1904 | Jesse Tannehill, Boston at Chicago, Aug 17 | 6-0 |
| 1905 | Weldon Henley, Philadelphia at St. Louis, July 22, 1st game | 6-0 |
| | Frank E. Smith, Chicago at Detroit, Sept 6, 2nd game | 15-0 |
| | Bill Dinneen, Boston vs. Chicago, Sept 27, 1st game | 2-0 |
| 1908 | Cy Young, Boston at New York, June 30 | 8-0 |
| | Bob Rhoads, Cleveland vs. Boston, Sept 18 | 2-1 |
| | Frank Smith, Chicago vs. Philadelphia, Sept 20 | 1-0 |
| 1910 | Addie Joss, Cleveland at Chicago, Apr 20 | 1-0 |
| | Chief Bender, Philadelphia vs. Cleveland, May 12 | 4-0 |
| 1911 | Joe Wood, Boston vs. St. Louis, July 29, 1st game | 5-0 |
| | Ed Walsh Sr., Chicago vs. Boston, Aug 27 | 5-0 |
| 1912 | George Mullin, Detroit vs. St. Louis, July 4, 2nd game | 7-0 |
| | Earl Hamilton, St. Louis at Detroit, Aug 30 | 5-1 |
| 1914 | Joe Benz, Chicago vs. Cleveland, May 31 | 6-1 |
| 1916 | Rube Foster, Boston vs. New York, June 21 | 2-0 |
| | Bullet Joe Bush, Philadelphia vs. Cleveland, Aug 26 | 5-0 |
| | Dutch H. Leonard, Boston vs. St. Louis, Aug 30 | 4-0 |
| 1917 | Eddie Cicotte, Chicago at St. Louis, Apr 14 | 11-0 |
| | George Mogridge, New York at Boston, Apr 24 | 2-1 |
| | Ernie Koob, St. Louis vs. Chicago, May 5 | 1-0 |
| | Bob Groom, St. Louis vs. Chicago, May 6, 2nd game | 3-0 |
| | Babe Ruth (0 inn) and Ernie Shore (9 inn), Boston vs. Washington, June 23, 1st game (see note under American League "perfect games of nine or more inn") | 4-0 |
| 1918 | Dutch H. Leonard, Boston at Detroit, June 3 | 5-0 |
| 1919 | Ray Caldwell, Cleveland at New York, Sept 10, 1st game | 3-0 |
| 1920 | Walter Johnson, Washington at Boston, July 1 | 1-0 |
| 1923 | Sad Sam Jones, New York at Philadelphia, Sept 4 | 2-0 |
| | Howard Ehmke, Boston at Philadelphia, Sept 7 | 4-0 |
| 1926 | Ted Lyons, Chicago at Boston, Aug 21 | 6-0 |
| 1931 | Wes Ferrell, Cleveland vs. St. Louis, Apr 29 | 9-0 |
| | Bobby Burke, Washington vs. Boston, Aug 8 | 5-0 |
| 1935 | Vern Kennedy, Chicago vs. Cleveland, Aug 31 | 5-0 |
| 1937 | Bill Dietrich, Chicago vs. St. Louis, June 1 | 8-0 |
| 1938 | Monte Pearson, New York vs. Cleveland, Aug 27, 2nd game | 13-0 |
| 1940 | Bob Feller, Cleveland at Chicago, Apr 16 (season opener for both clubs) | 1-0 |
| 1945 | Dick Fowler, Philadelphia vs. St. Louis, Sept 9, 2nd game | 1-0 |
| 1946 | Bob Feller, Cleveland at New York, Apr 30 | 1-0 |
| 1947 | Don Black, Cleveland vs. Philadelphia, July 10, 1st game | 3-0 |
| | Bill McCahan, Philadelphia vs. Washington, Sept 3 | 3-0 |
| 1948 | Bob Lemon, Cleveland at Detroit, June 30 | 2-0 |
| 1951 | Bob Feller, Cleveland vs. Detroit, July 1, 1st game | 2-1 |
| | Allie Reynolds, New York at Cleveland, July 12 | 1-0 |
| | Allie Reynolds, New York vs. Boston, Sept 28, 1st game | 8-0 |
| 1952 | Virgil Trucks, Detroit vs. Washington, May 15 | 1-0 |
| | Virgil Trucks, Detroit at New York, Aug 25 | 1-0 |
| 1953 | Bobo Holloman, St. Louis vs. Philadelphia, May 6 (1st major league start) | 6-0 |
| 1956 | Mel Parnell, Boston vs. Chicago, July 14 | 4-0 |
| 1957 | Bob Keegan, Chicago vs. Washington, Aug 20, 2nd game | 6-0 |
| 1958 | Jim Bunning, Detroit at Boston, July 20, 1st game | 3-0 |
| | Hoyt Wilhelm, Baltimore vs. New York, Sept 20 | 1-0 |
| 1962 | Bo Belinsky, Los Angeles vs. Baltimore, May 5 | 2-0 |
| | Earl Wilson, Boston vs. Los Angeles, June 26 | 2-0 |
| | Bill Monbouquette, Boston at Chicago, Aug 1 | 1-0 |
| | Jack Kralick, Minnesota vs. Kansas City, Aug 26 | 1-0 |
| 1965 | Dave Morehead, Boston vs. Cleveland, Sept 16 | 2-0 |
| 1966 | Sonny Siebert, Cleveland vs. Washington, June 10 | 2-0 |
| 1967 | Steve Barber (8.2 IP) and Stu Miller (.1 IP), Baltimore vs. Detroit, Apr 30, 1st game | 1-2 |
| | Dean Chance, Minnesota at Cleveland, Aug 25, 2nd game | 2-1 |
| | Joel Horlen, Chicago vs. Detroit, Sept 10, 1st game | 6-0 |
| 1968 | Tom Phoebus, Baltimore vs. Boston, Apr 27 | 6-0 |
| 1969 | Jim Palmer, Baltimore vs. Oakland, Aug 13 | 8-0 |
| 1970 | Clyde Wright, California vs. Oakland, July 3 | 4-0 |
| | Vida Blue, Oakland vs. Minnesota, Sept 21 | 6-0 |
| 1973 | Steve Busby, Kansas City at Detroit, Apr 27 | 3-0 |
| | Nolan Ryan, California at Kansas City, May 15 | 3-0 |
| | Nolan Ryan, California at Detroit, July 15 | 6-0 |
| | Jim Bibby, Texas at Oakland, July 30 | 6-0 |
| 1974 | Steve Busby, Kansas City at Milwaukee, June 19 | 2-0 |
| | Dick Bosman, Cleveland vs. Oakland, July 19 | 4-0 |
| | Nolan Ryan, California vs. Minnesota, Sept 28 | 4-0 |
| 1975 | Nolan Ryan, California vs. Baltimore, June 1 | 1-0 |
| | Vida Blue (5 IP), Glenn Abbott (1 IP), Paul Lindblad (1 IP) and Rollie Fingers (2 IP), Oakland vs. California, Sept 28 | 5-0 |
| 1976 | Blue Moon Odom (5 IP) and Francisco Barrios (4 IP), Chicago at Oakland, July 28 | 2-1 |
| 1977 | Jim Colborn, Kansas City vs. Texas, May 14 | 6-0 |
| | Dennis Eckersley, Cleveland vs. California, May 30 | 1-0 |
| | Bert Blyleven, Texas at California, Sept 22 | 6-0 |
| 1983 | Dave Righetti, New York vs. Boston, July 4 | 4-0 |
| | Mike Warren, Oakland vs. Chicago, Sept 29 | 3-0 |
| 1984 | Jack Morris, Detroit at Chicago, Apr 7 | 4-0 |
| 1986 | Joe Cowley, Chicago at California, Sept 19 | 7-1 |
| 1987 | Juan Nieves, Milwaukee at Baltimore, Apr 15 | 7-0 |
| 1990 | Mark Langston (7 IP) and Mike Witt (2 IP), California vs. Seattle, Apr 11 | 1-0 |
| | Randy Johnson, Seattle vs. Detroit, June 2 | 2-0 |
| | Nolan Ryan, Texas at Oakland, June 11 | 5-0 |
| | Dave Stewart, Oakland at Toronto, June 29 | 5-0 |
| | Dave Stieb, Toronto at Cleveland, Sept 2 | 3-0 |
| 1991 | Nolan Ryan, Texas vs. Toronto, May 1 | 3-0 |
| | Bob Milacki (6 IP), Mike Flanagan (1 IP), Mark Williamson (1 IP) and Gregg Olson (1 IP), Baltimore at Oakland, July 13 | 2-0 |
| | Wilson Alvarez, Chicago at Baltimore, Aug 11 | 7-0 |
| | Bret Saberhagen, Kansas City vs. Chicago, Aug 26 | 7-0 |
| 1993 | Chris Bosio, Seattle vs. Boston, Apr 22 | 2-0 |
| | Jim Abbott, New York vs. Cleveland, Sept 4 | 4-0 |
| 1994 | Scott Erickson, Minnesota vs. Milwaukee, Apr 27 | 6-0 |
| 1996 | Dwight Gooden, New York vs. Seattle, May 14 | 2-0 |
| 1999 | Eric Milton, Minnesota vs. Anaheim, Sept 11 | 7-0 |
| 2001 | Hideo Nomo, Boston at Baltimore, Apr 4 | 3-0 |
| 2002 | Derek Lowe, Boston vs. Tampa Bay, Apr 27 | 10-0 |

Note—Andy Hawkins (1990) and Matt Young (1992), as visiting teams' pitchers, pitched all eight inn of nine-inning, no-hit losses. Both are listed under the category "No-hit games of less than nine inn."

**Total number of games (excluding Hawkins and M. Young): 97**

## NATIONAL LEAGUE

| Year | | Score |
|---|---|---|
| 1876 | George Bradley, St. Louis vs. Hartford, July 15 | 2-0 |
| 1880 | Larry Corcoran, Chicago vs. Boston, Aug 19 | 6-0 |
| | Pud Galvin, Buffalo at Worcester, Aug 20 | 1-0 |
| 1882 | Larry Corcoran, Chicago vs. Worcester, Sept 20 | 5-0 |
| 1883 | Hoss Radbourn, Providence at Cleveland, July 25 | 8-0 |
| | Hugh Daily, Cleveland at Philadelphia, Sept 13 | 1-0 |
| 1884 | Larry Corcoran, Chicago vs. Providence, June 27 | 6-0 |
| | Pud Galvin, Buffalo at Detroit, Aug 4 | 18-0 |
| 1885 | John Clarkson, Chicago at Providence, July 27 | 4-0 |
| | Charlie J. Ferguson, Philadelphia vs. Providence, Aug 29 | 1-0 |
| 1891 | Tom Lovett, Brooklyn vs. New York, June 22 | 4-0 |
| | Amos Rusie, New York vs. Brooklyn, July 31 | 6-0 |
| 1892 | Jack Stivetts, Boston vs. Brooklyn, Aug 6 | 11-0 |
| | Ben Sanders, Louisville vs. Baltimore, Aug 22 | 6-2 |
| | Bumpus Jones, Cincinnati vs. Pittsburgh, October 15 (1st major league game) | 7-1 |
| 1893 | Bill Hawke, Baltimore vs. Washington, Aug 16 (1st no-hitter at 60-foot, 6-inch distance) | 5-0 |
| 1897 | Cy Young, Cleveland vs. Cincinnati, Sept 18, 1st game | 6-0 |
| 1898 | Ted Breitenstein, Cincinnati vs. Pittsburgh, Apr 22 | 11-0 |
| | Jim J. Hughes, Baltimore vs. Boston, Apr 22 | 8-0 |
| | Frank Donahue, Philadelphia vs. Boston, July 8 | 5-0 |
| | Walter Thornton, Chicago vs. Brooklyn, Aug 21, 2nd game | 2-0 |
| 1899 | Deacon Phillippe, Louisville vs. New York, May 25 | 7-0 |
| | Vic Willis, Boston vs. Washington, Aug 7 | 7-1 |
| 1900 | Noodles Hahn, Cincinnati vs. Philadelphia, July 12 | 4-0 |
| 1901 | Christy Mathewson, New York at St. Louis, July 15 | 5-0 |
| 1903 | Chick Fraser, Philadelphia at Chicago, Sept 18, 2nd game | 10-0 |
| 1905 | Christy Mathewson, New York at Chicago, June 13 | 1-0 |
| 1906 | Johnny Lush, Philadelphia at Brooklyn, May 1 | 6-0 |
| | Mal Eason, Brooklyn at St. Louis, July 20 | 2-0 |
| 1907 | Frank Pfeffer, Boston vs. Cincinnati, May 8 | 6-0 |
| | Nick Maddox, Pittsburgh vs. Brooklyn, Sept 20 | 2-1 |
| 1908 | Hooks Wiltse, New York vs. Philadelphia, July 4, 1st game, 10 inn | 1-0 |
| | Nap Rucker, Brooklyn vs. Boston, Sept 5, 2nd game | 6-0 |
| 1912 | Jeff Tesreau, New York at Philadelphia, Sept 6, 1st game | 3-0 |
| 1914 | George A. Davis, Boston vs. Philadelphia, Sept 9, 2nd game | 7-0 |
| 1915 | Rube Marquard, New York vs. Brooklyn, Apr 15 | 2-0 |
| | Jimmy Lavender, Chicago at New York, Aug 31, 1st game | 2-0 |
| 1916 | Tom L. Hughes, Boston vs. Pittsburgh, June 16 | 2-0 |
| 1917 | Fred Toney, Cincinnati at Chicago, May 2, 10 inn (Hippo Vaughn of Chicago pitched 9.1 hitless inn in the same game before his no-hitter was spoiled.) | 1-0 |
| 1919 | Hod Eller, Cincinnati vs. St. Louis, May 11 | 6-0 |
| 1922 | Jesse Barnes, New York vs. Philadelphia, May 7 | 6-0 |
| 1924 | Jesse Haines, St. Louis vs. Boston, July 17 | 5-0 |
| 1925 | Dazzy Vance, Brooklyn vs. Philadelphia, Sept 13, 1st game | 10-1 |
| 1929 | Carl Hubbell, New York vs. Pittsburgh, May 8 | 11-0 |
| 1934 | Paul Dean, St. Louis at Brooklyn, Sept 21, 2nd game | 3-0 |
| 1938 | Johnny Vander Meer, Cincinnati vs. Boston, June 11 | 3-0 |
| | Johnny Vander Meer, Cincinnati at Brooklyn, June 15 (His two no-hitters were consecutive.) | 6-0 |
| 1940 | Tex Carleton, Brooklyn at Cincinnati, Apr 30 | 3-0 |
| 1941 | Lon Warneke, St. Louis at Cincinnati, Aug 30 | 2-0 |
| 1944 | Jim Tobin, Boston vs. Brooklyn, Apr 27 | 2-0 |
| | Clyde Shoun, Cincinnati vs. Boston, May 15 | 1-0 |
| 1946 | Ed Head, Brooklyn vs. Boston, Apr 23 | 5-0 |
| 1947 | Ewell Blackwell, Cincinnati vs. Boston, June 18 | 6-0 |
| 1948 | Rex Barney, Brooklyn at New York, Sept 9 | 2-0 |
| 1950 | Vern Bickford, Boston vs. Brooklyn, Aug 11 | 7-0 |
| 1951 | Cliff Chambers, Pittsburgh at Boston, May 6, 2nd game | 3-0 |
| 1952 | Carl Erskine, Brooklyn vs. Chicago, June 19 | 5-0 |
| 1954 | Jim Wilson, Milwaukee vs. Philadelphia, June 12 | 2-0 |
| 1955 | Sam Jones, Chicago vs. Pittsburgh, May 12 | 4-0 |
| 1956 | Carl Erskine, Brooklyn vs. New York, May 12 | 3-0 |
| | Sal Maglie, Brooklyn vs. Philadelphia, Sept 25 | 5-0 |

| Year | | Score |
|---|---|---|
| 1960 | Don Cardwell, Chicago vs. St. Louis, May 15, 2nd game | 4-0 |
| | Lew Burdette, Milwaukee vs. Philadelphia, Aug 18 | 1-0 |
| | Warren Spahn, Milwaukee vs. Philadelphia, Sept 16 | 4-0 |
| 1961 | Warren Spahn, Milwaukee vs. San Francisco, Apr 28 | 1-0 |
| 1962 | Sandy Koufax, Los Angeles vs. New York, June 30 | 5-0 |
| 1963 | Sandy Koufax, Los Angeles vs. San Francisco, May 11 | 8-0 |
| | Don Nottebart, Houston vs. Philadelphia, May 17 | 4-1 |
| | Juan Marichal, San Francisco vs. Houston, June 15 | 1-0 |
| 1964 | Ken Johnson, Houston vs. Cincinnati, Apr 23 | 0-1 |
| | Sandy Koufax, Los Angeles at Philadelphia, June 4 | 3-0 |
| 1965 | Jim Maloney, Cincinnati at Chicago, Aug 19, 1st game, 10 inn | 1-0 |
| 1967 | Don Wilson, Houston vs. Atlanta, June 18 | 2-0 |
| 1968 | George Culver, Cincinnati at Philadelphia, July 29, 2nd game | 6-1 |
| | Gaylord Perry, San Francisco vs. St. Louis, Sept 17 | 1-0 |
| | Ray Washburn, St. Louis at San Francisco, Sept 18 | 2-0 |
| 1969 | Bill Stoneman, Montreal at Philadelphia, Apr 17 | 7-0 |
| | Jim Maloney, Cincinnati vs. Houston, Apr 30 | 10-0 |
| | Don Wilson, Houston at Cincinnati, May 1 | 4-0 |
| | Ken Holtzman, Chicago vs. Atlanta, Aug 19 | 3-0 |
| | Bob Moose, Pittsburgh at New York, Sept 20 | 4-0 |
| 1970 | Dock Ellis, Pittsburgh at San Diego, June 12, 1st game | 2-0 |
| | Bill Singer, Los Angeles vs. Philadelphia, July 20 | 5-0 |
| 1971 | Ken Holtzman, Chicago at Cincinnati, June 3 | 1-0 |
| | Rick Wise, Philadelphia at Cincinnati, June 23 | 4-0 |
| | Bob Gibson, St. Louis at Pittsburgh, Aug 14 | 11-0 |
| 1972 | Burt Hooton, Chicago vs. Philadelphia, Apr 16 | 4-0 |
| | Milt Pappas, Chicago vs. San Diego, Sept 2 | 8-0 |
| | Bill Stoneman, Montreal vs. New York, Oct 2, 1st game | 7-0 |
| 1973 | Phil Niekro, Atlanta vs. San Diego, Aug 5 | 9-0 |
| 1975 | Ed Halicki, San Francisco vs. New York, Aug 24, 2nd game | 6-0 |
| 1976 | Larry Dierker, Houston vs. Montreal, July 9 | 6-0 |
| | John Candelaria, Pittsburgh vs. Los Angeles, Aug 9 | 2-0 |
| | John Montefusco, San Francisco at Atlanta, Sept 29 | 9-0 |
| 1978 | Bob Forsch, St. Louis vs. Philadelphia, Apr 16 | 5-0 |
| | Tom Seaver, Cincinnati vs. St. Louis, June 16 | 4-0 |
| 1979 | Ken Forsch, Houston vs. Atlanta, Apr 7 | 6-0 |
| 1980 | Jerry Reuss, Los Angeles at San Francisco, June 27 | 8-0 |
| 1981 | Charlie Lea, Montreal vs. San Francisco, May 10, 2nd game | 4-0 |
| | Nolan Ryan, Houston vs. Los Angeles, Sept 26 | 5-0 |
| 1983 | Bob Forsch, St. Louis vs. Montreal, Sept 26 | 3-0 |
| 1986 | Mike Scott, Houston vs. San Francisco, Sept 25 | 2-0 |
| 1990 | Fernando Valenzuela, Los Angeles vs. St. Louis, June 29 | 6-0 |
| | Terry Mulholland, Philadelphia vs. San Francisco, Aug 15 | 6-0 |
| 1991 | Tommy Greene, Philadelphia at Montreal, May 23 | 2-0 |
| | Kent Mercker (6 IP), Mark Wohlers (2 IP) and Alejandro Pena (1 IP), Atlanta vs. San Diego, Sept 11 | 1-0 |
| 1992 | Kevin Gross, Los Angeles vs. San Francisco, Aug 17 | 2-0 |
| 1993 | Darryl Kile, Houston vs. New York, Sept 8 | 7-1 |
| 1994 | Kent Mercker, Atlanta vs. Los Angeles, Apr 8 | 6-0 |
| 1995 | Ramon Martinez, Los Angeles vs. Florida, July 14 | 7-0 |
| 1996 | Al Leiter, Florida vs. Colorado, May 11 | 11-0 |
| | Hideo Nomo, Los Angeles at Colorado, Sept 17 | 9-0 |
| 1997 | Kevin Brown, Florida at San Francisco, June 10 | 9-0 |
| | Francisco Cordova (9 IP) and Ricardo Rincon (1 IP), Pittsburgh vs. Houston, July 12, 10 inn | 3-0 |
| 1999 | Jose Jimenez, St. Louis at Arizona, June 25 | 1-0 |
| 2001 | A.J. Burnett, Florida at San Diego, May 12 | 3-0 |
| | Bud Smith, St. Louis at San Diego, Sept 3 | 4-0 |
| 2003 | Kevin Millwood, Philadelphia vs. San Francisco, Apr 27 | 1-0 |
| | Roy Oswalt (1 IP), Peter Munro (2 IP), Kirk Saarloos (1 IP), Brad Lidge (2 IP), Octavio Dotel (1 IP) and Billy Wagner (1 IP), Houston at New York AL, June 11 | 8-0 |

**Total number of games: 119**

## NO-HIT GAMES FOR NINE OR MORE INNINGS THAT WERE BROKEN UP IN EXTRA INNINGS

### AMERICAN LEAGUE

| Year | | Score |
|---|---|---|
| 1901 | Earl Moore, Cleveland vs. Chicago, May 9 (Moore pitched nine hitless inn before Sam Mertes singled; lost on two hits in 10 inn.) | 2-4 |
| 1910 | Tom L. Hughes, New York vs. Cleveland, Aug 30, 2nd game (Hughes pitched 9.1 hitless inn before Harry Niles singled; lost on seven hits in 11 inn.) | 0-5 |
| 1914 | Jim Scott, Chicago at Washington, May 14 (Scott pitched nine hitless inn before Chick Gandil singled; lost on two hits in 10 inn) | 0-1 |
| 1934 | Bobo Newsom, St. Louis vs. Boston, Sept 18 (Newsom pitched 9.2 hitless inn before Roy Johnson singled; lost on one hit in 10 inn.) | 1-2 |

**Total number of games: 4**

### NATIONAL LEAGUE

| Year | | Score |
|---|---|---|
| 1904 | Bob Wicker, Chicago at New York, June 11 (pitched 9.1 hitless inn before Sam Mertes singled; won on one hit in 12 inn.) | 1-0 |
| 1906 | Harry McIntire, Brooklyn vs. Pittsburgh, Aug 1 (pitched 10.2 hitless inn before Claude Ritchey singled; lost on four hits in 13 inn.) | 0-1 |
| 1909 | Red Ames, New York vs. Brooklyn, Apr 15 (pitched 9.1 hitless inn before Whitey Alperman singled; lost on seven hits in 13 inn. The game was both teams' season opener.) | 0-3 |
| 1917 | Hippo Vaughn, Chicago vs. Cincinnati, May 2 (pitched 9.1 hitless inn before Larry Kopf singled; lost on two hits in 10 inn. Fred Toney of Cincinnati pitched 10 no-hit inn in the same game.) | 0-1 |
| 1956 | Johnny Klippstein (7 IP), Hershell Freeman (1 IP) and Joe Black (3 IP), Cincinnati at Milwaukee, May 26 (Jack Dittmer doubled for the 1st hit with two outs in the 10th, and Black lost on three hits in the 11th.) | 1-2 |
| 1965 | Jim Maloney, Cincinnati vs. New York, June 14 (pitched 10 hitless inn before Johnny Lewis homered; lost on two hits in the 11th) | 0-1 |
| 1991 | Mark Gardner (9 IP) and Jeff Fassero (0 IP), Montreal at Los Angeles, July 26 (Lenny Harris singled off Gardner in the 10th inning; Gardner allowed another hit and Fassero allowed one hit; Gardner lost the game in the 10th.) | 0-1 |

**Total number of games: 7**

## NO-HIT GAMES OF LESS THAN NINE INNINGS

### AMERICAN ASSOCIATION

| Year | | Score |
|---|---|---|
| 1884 | Larry McKeon, Indianapolis at Cincinnati, May 6, 6 IP | 0-0 |
| 1889 | Matt Kilroy, Baltimore vs. St. Louis, July 29, 2nd game, 7 IP | 0-0 |
| 1890 | George Nicol, St. Louis vs. Philadelphia, Sept 23, 7 IP | 21-2 |
| | Hank Gastright, Columbus vs. Toledo, October 12, 8 IP | 6-0 |

**Total number of games: 4**

### PLAYERS LEAGUE

| Year | | Score |
|---|---|---|
| 1890 | Charles King, Chicago vs. Brooklyn, June 21, 8 IP | 0-1 |

**Total number of games: 1**

### UNION ASSOCIATION

| Year | | Score |
|---|---|---|
| 1884 | Charlie Geggus, Washington vs. Wilmington, Aug 21, 8 IP | 12-1 |
| | Charlie Sweeney (2 IP) and Henry Boyle (3 IP), St. Louis vs. St. Paul, October 5, 5 IP | 0-1 |

**Total number of games: 2**

### AMERICAN LEAGUE

| Year | | Score |
|---|---|---|
| 1905 | Rube Waddell, Philadelphia vs. St. Louis, Aug 15, 5 IP | 2-0 |
| 1907 | Ed Walsh Sr., Chicago vs. New York, May 26, 5 IP | 8-1 |
| 1912 | Jay Cashion, Washington vs. Cleveland, Aug 20, 2nd game, 6 IP | 2-0 |
| 1924 | Walter Johnson, Washington vs. St. Louis, Aug 25, 7 IP | 2-0 |
| 1940 | John Whitehead, St. Louis vs. Detroit, Aug 5, 2nd game, 6 IP | 4-0 |
| 1990 | Andy Hawkins, New York at Chicago, July 1 (As a visiting team's pitcher, he pitched all 8 inn of a 9-inning, no-hit loss.) | 0-4 |
| | Melido Perez, Chicago at New York, July 12, 6 IP | 8-0 |
| 1992 | Matt Young, Boston at Cleveland, Apr 12 (As a visiting team's pitcher, he pitched all 8 inn of a 9-inning, no-hit loss.) | 1-2 |

**Total number of games: 8**

### NATIONAL LEAGUE

| Year | | Score |
|---|---|---|
| 1884 | Charlie Getzien, Detroit vs. Philadelphia, October 1, 6 IP | 1-0 |
| 1885 | Fred Shaw, Providence at Buffalo, October 7, 1st game, 5 IP | 4-0 |
| 1888 | George Van Haltren, Chicago vs. Pittsburgh, June 21, 6 IP | 1-0 |
| | Cannonball Crane, New York vs. Washington, Sept 27, 7 IP | 3-0 |
| 1892 | Jack Stivetts, Boston at Washington, October 15, 2nd game, 5 IP | 4-0 |
| 1893 | Elton Chamberlain, Cincinnati vs. Boston, Sept 23, 2nd game, 7 IP | 6-0 |
| 1894 | Ed Stein, Brooklyn vs. Chicago, June 2, 6 IP | 1-0 |
| 1903 | Red Ames, New York at St. Louis, Sept 14, 2nd game, 5 IP (1st major league game) | 5-0 |
| 1906 | Jake Weimer, Cincinnati vs. Brooklyn, Aug 24, 2nd game, 7 IP | 1-0 |
| | Stoney McGlynn, St. Louis at Brooklyn, Sept 24, 2nd game, 7 IP | 1-1 |
| | Lefty Leifield, Pittsburgh at Philadelphia, Sept 26, 2nd game, 6 IP | 8-0 |
| 1907 | Howie Camnitz, Pittsburgh at New York, Aug 23, 2nd game, 5 IP | 1-0 |
| 1908 | Johnny Lush, St. Louis at Brooklyn, Aug 6, 6 IP | 2-0 |
| 1910 | King Cole, Chicago at St. Louis, July 31, 2nd game, 7 IP | 4-0 |
| 1937 | Fred Frankhouse, Brooklyn vs. Cincinnati, Aug 27, 8 IP | 5-0 |
| 1944 | Jim Tobin, Boston vs. Philadelphia, June 22, 2nd game, 5 IP | 7-0 |
| 1959 | Mike McCormick, San Francisco at Philadelphia, June 12, 5 IP (McCormick allowed a single to Richie Ashburn in the 6th, but the game was halted because of rain before completion of the inning. The hit was erased because, under existing rules, records reverted to the last completed inning.) | 3-0 |
| | Sam Jones, San Francisco at St. Louis, Sept 26, 7 IP | 4-0 |
| 1988 | Pascual Perez, Montreal at Philadelphia, Sept 24, 5 IP | 1-0 |

**Total number of games: 19**

## TWO COMPLETE-GAME VICTORIES IN ONE DAY

### PLAYERS LEAGUE

| | | Scores | |
|---|---|---|---|
| July 26, 1890 | Henry Gruber, Cleveland | 6-1 | 8-7 |
| Aug 20, 1890 | Bert Cunningham, Buffalo | 6-2 | 7-0 |
| Sept 27, 1890 | Ed Crane, New York | 9-8 | 8-3 |

**Total number of occurrences: 3**

### AMERICAN ASSOCIATION

| | | Scores | |
|---|---|---|---|
| July 4, 1883 | Tim Keefe, New York | 9-1 | 3-0 |
| July 4, 1884 | Guy Hecker, Louisville | 5-4 | 8-2 |
| July 26, 1887 | Matt Kilroy, Baltimore | ‡8-0 | 9-1 |
| Oct 1, 1887 | Matt Kilroy, Baltimore | 5-2 | ‡8-1 |
| Sept 20, 1888 | Tony Mullane, Cincinnati | 1-0 | 2-1 |

**Total number of occurrences: 5**

### AMERICAN LEAGUE

| | | Scores | |
|---|---|---|---|
| July 1, 1905 | Frank Owen, Chicago | 3-2 | 2-0 |
| Sept 26, 1905 | Ed Walsh, Chicago | 10-5 | §3-1 |

| | | Scores | |
|---|---|---|---|
| Sept 22, 1906 | George Mullin, Detroit | 5-3 | 4-3 |
| Sept 25, 1908 | Ed Summers, Detroit | 7-2 | ∞1-0 |
| Sept 29, 1908 | Ed Walsh, Chicago | 5-1 | 2-0 |
| Sept 22, 1914 | Ray Collins, Boston | 5-3 | §5-0 |
| July 29, 1916 | Dave Davenport, St. Louis | 3-1 | 3-2 |
| Aug 30, 1918 | Carl Mays, Boston | 12-0 | 4-1 |
| Sept 6, 1924 | Urban Shocker, St. Louis | 6-2 | 6-2 |
| Aug 28, 1926 | Dutch Levsen, Cleveland | 6-1 | 5-1 |

**Total number of occurrences: 10**

## NATIONAL LEAGUE

| | | Scores | |
|---|---|---|---|
| Sept 19, 1876 | Candy Cummings, Hartford | 14-4 | 8-4 |
| Aug 9, 1878 | Monte Ward, Providence | 12-6 | 8-5 |
| July 12, 1879 | Pud Galvin, Buffalo | 4-2 | ◆5-1 |
| July 4, 1881 | Mickey Welch, Troy | 8-0 | 12-3 |
| July 4, 1882 | Pud Galvin, Buffalo | 9-5 | 18-8 |
| May 30, 1884 | Hoss Radbourn, Providence | 12-9 | 9-2 |
| Oct 7, 1885 | Fred Shaw, Providence | *4-0 | *6-1 |
| Oct 10, 1885 | Fred Shaw, Providence | †3-0 | *7-3 |
| Oct 9, 1886 | Charlie Ferguson, Philadelphia | 5-1 | †6-1 |
| Aug 20, 1887 | Jim Whitney, Washington | 3-1 | 4-3 |
| Sept 12, 1889 | John Clarkson, Boston | 3-2 | 5-0 |
| May 30, 1890 | Bill Hutchinson, Chicago | 6-4 | 11-7 |
| Oct 4, 1890 | Cy Young, Cleveland | 5-1 | 7-3 |
| Sept 12, 1891 | Mark Baldwin, Pittsburgh | 13-3 | 8-4 |
| Sept 28, 1891 | Amos Rusie, New York | 10-4 | †13-5 |
| May 30, 1892 | Mark Baldwin, Pittsburgh | 11-1 | 4-3 |
| Sept 5, 1892 | Jack Stivetts, Boston | ▲2-1 | 5-2 |
| Oct 4, 1892 | Amos Rusie, New York | 6-4 | 9-5 |
| May 30, 1893 | William Kennedy, Brooklyn | 3-0 | 6-2 |
| June 3, 1897 | Cy Seymour, New York | 6-1 | ‡10-6 |
| Oct 13, 1898 | Al Orth, Philadelphia | 5-1 | *9-6 |
| Aug 1, 1903 | Joe McGinnity, New York | 4-1 | 5-2 |
| Aug 8, 1903 | Joe McGinnity, New York | 6-1 | 4-3 |
| Aug 31, 1903 | Joe McGinnity, New York | 4-1 | 9-2 |
| Oct 3, 1905 | Doc Scanlan, Brooklyn | 4-0 | 3-2 |
| Sept 26, 1908 | Ed Reulbach, Chicago | 5-0 | 3-0 |
| Sept 9, 1916 | Pol Perritt, New York | 3-1 | 3-0 |
| Sept 20, 1916 | Al Demaree, Philadelphia | 7-0 | 3-2 |
| Sept 23, 1916 | Grover Alexander, Philadelphia | 7-3 | 4-0 |
| July 1, 1917 | Fred Toney, Cincinnati | 4-1 | 5-1 |
| Sept 3, 1917 | Grover Alexander, Philadelphia | 5-0 | 9-3 |
| Sept 18, 1917 | Bill Doak, St. Louis | 2-0 | 12-4 |
| Aug 13, 1921 | Mule Watson, Boston | 4-3 | 8-0 |
| July 10, 1923 | Johnny Stuart, St. Louis | 11-1 | 6-3 |
| July 19, 1924 | Herman Bell, St. Louis | 6-1 | 2-1 |

*5 inn; †6 inn; ‡7 inn; §8 inn; ∞10 inn; ▲11 inn; ◆12 inn

**Total number of occurrences: 35**

## PITCHERS WITH 12 STRAIGHT VICTORIES IN SEASON

### AMERICAN ASSOCIATION

| Year | Pitcher | Won |
|---|---|---|
| 1890 | Scott Stratton, Louisville | 15 |
| 1884 | John Lynch, New York | 14 |
| 1882 | Will White, Cincinnati | 12 |

**Total number of occurrences: 3**

### UNION ASSOCIATION

| Year | Pitcher | Won |
|---|---|---|
| 1884 | Jim McCormick, Cincinnati | 14 |

**Total number of occurrences: 1**

### AMERICAN LEAGUE

| Year | Pitcher | Won |
|---|---|---|
| 1912 | Walter Johnson, Washington | 16 |
| 1912 | Joe Wood, Boston | 16 |
| 1931 | Lefty Grove, Philadelphia | 16 |
| 1934 | Schoolboy Rowe, Detroit | 16 |
| 2001 | Roger Clemens, New York | 16 |
| 1932 | Alvin Crowder, Washington | 15 |
| 1937 | Johnny Allen, Cleveland | 15 |
| 1969 | Dave McNally, Baltimore | 15 |
| 1974 | Gaylord Perry, Cleveland | 15 |
| 1998 | Roger Clemens, Toronto | 15 |
| 2003 | Roy Halladay, Toronto | 15 |
| 1904 | Jack Chesbro, New York | 14 |
| 1913 | Walter Johnson, Washington | 14 |
| 1914 | Chief Bender, Philadelphia | 14 |
| 1928 | Lefty Grove, Philadelphia | 14 |
| 1961 | Whitey Ford, New York | 14 |
| 1980 | Steve Stone, Baltimore | 14 |
| 1986 | Roger Clemens, Boston | 14 |
| 1924 | Walter Johnson, Washington | 13 |
| 1925 | Stan Coveleski, Washington | 13 |
| 1930 | Wes Ferrell, Cleveland | 13 |
| 1940 | Bobo Newsom, Detroit | 13 |
| 1949 | Ellis Kinder, Boston | 13 |
| 1971 | Dave McNally, Baltimore | 13 |
| 1973 | Catfish Hunter, Oakland | 13 |
| 1978 | Ron Guidry, New York | 13 |
| 1983 | LaMarr Hoyt, Chicago | 13 |
| 1901 | Cy Young, Boston | 12 |
| 1910 | Russ Ford, New York | 12 |
| 1914 | Dutch H. Leonard, Boston | 12 |
| 1929 | Tom Zachary, New York | 12 |
| 1931 | George Earnshaw, Philadelphia | 12 |
| 1938 | Johnny Allen, Cleveland | 12 |
| 1939 | Atley Donald, New York | 12 |
| 1946 | Dave Ferriss, Boston | 12 |
| 1961 | Luis Arroyo, New York | 12 |
| 1963 | Whitey Ford, New York | 12 |
| 1968 | Dave McNally, Baltimore | 12 |
| 1971 | Pat Dobson, Baltimore | 12 |
| 1985 | Ron Guidry, New York | 12 |
| 1990 | Bobby Witt, Texas | 12 |
| 1991 | Scott Erickson, Minnesota | 12 |
| 1997 | Brad Radke, Minnesota | 12 |
| 2002 | Jarrod Washburn, Anaheim | 12 |
| 2004 | Johan Santana, Minnesota | 12 |

**Total number of occurrences: 45**

### NATIONAL LEAGUE

| Year | Pitcher | Won |
|---|---|---|
| 1888 | Tim Keefe, New York | 19 |
| 1912 | Rube Marquard, New York | 19 |
| 1884 | Hoss Radbourn, Providence | 18 |
| 1885 | Mickey Welch, New York | 17 |
| 1890 | Pat Luby, Chicago | 17 |
| 1959 | Elroy Face, Pittsburgh | 17 |
| 1886 | Jim McCormick, Chicago | 16 |
| 1936 | Carl Hubbell, New York | 16 |
| 1947 | Ewell Blackwell, Cincinnati | 16 |
| 1962 | Jack Sanford, San Francisco | 16 |
| 1924 | Dazzy Vance, Brooklyn | 15 |
| 1968 | Bob Gibson, St. Louis | 15 |
| 1972 | Steve Carlton, Philadelphia | 15 |
| 1885 | Jim McCormick, Chicago | 14 |
| 1886 | John Flynn, Chicago | 14 |
| 1904 | Joe McGinnity, New York | 14 |
| 1909 | Ed Reulbach, Chicago | 14 |
| 1984 | Rick Sutcliffe, Chicago | 14 |
| 1985 | Dwight Gooden, New York | 14 |
| 1996 | John Smoltz, Atlanta | 14 |
| 1880 | Larry Corcoran, Chicago | 13 |
| 1884 | Charlie Buffinton, Boston | 13 |
| 1885 | John Clarkson, Chicago | 13 |
| 1892 | Cy Young, Cleveland | 13 |
| 1893 | Frank Killen, Pittsburgh | 13 |
| 1896 | Frank Dwyer, Cincinnati | 13 |
| 1897 | Fred Klobedanz, Boston | 13 |
| 1898 | Ted Lewis, Boston | 13 |
| 1909 | Christy Mathewson, New York | 13 |
| 1910 | Deacon Phillippe, Pittsburgh | 13 |
| 1927 | Burleigh Grimes, New York | 13 |
| 1956 | Brooks Lawrence, Cincinnati | 13 |
| 1966 | Phil Regan, Los Angeles | 13 |
| 1971 | Dock Ellis, Pittsburgh | 13 |
| 1992 | Tom Glavine, Atlanta | 13 |
| 1886 | Charlie Ferguson, Philadelphia | 12 |
| 1902 | Jack Chesbro, Pittsburgh | 12 |
| 1904 | George Wiltse, New York | 12 |
| 1906 | Ed Reulbach, Chicago | 12 |
| 1975 | Burt Hooton, Los Angeles | 12 |
| 1993 | Mark Portugal, Houston | 12 |
| 2002 | Wade Miller, Houston | 12 |

**Total number of occurrences: 42**

## PITCHERS WITH 12 STRAIGHT LOSSES IN SEASON

### AMERICAN ASSOCIATION

| Year | Pitcher | Lost |
|---|---|---|
| 1882 | Fred Nichols, Baltimore | 12 |
| 1887 | Billy Crowell, Cleveland | 12 |

**Total number of occurrences: 2**

### AMERICAN LEAGUE

| Year | Pitcher | Lost |
|---|---|---|
| 1916 | John Nabors, Philadelphia | 19 |
| 1980 | Mike Parrott, Seattle | 16 |
| 1909 | Bob Groom, Washington | 15 |
| 1906 | Joe Harris, Boston | 14 |
| 1949 | Howard Judson, Chicago | 14 |
| 1949 | Paul Calvert, Washington | 14 |
| 1979 | Matt Keough, Oakland | 14 |
| 1914 | Guy Morton, Cleveland | 13 |
| 1920 | Roy Moore, Philadelphia | 13 |
| 1930 | Frank Henry, Chicago | 13 |
| 1943 | Luman Harris, Philadelphia | 13 |
| 1982 | Terry Felton, Minnesota | 13 |
| 1901 | Bill Carrick, Washington | 12 |

| Year | Pitcher | Lost |
|---|---|---|
| 1929 | Red Ruffing, Boston | 12 |
| 1940 | Walt Masterson, Washington | 12 |
| 1945 | Bobo Newsom, Philadelphia | 12 |
| 1945 | Steve Gerkin, Philadelphia | 12 |
| 1953 | Charlie Bishop, Philadelphia | 12 |

**Total number of occurrences: 18**

## NATIONAL LEAGUE

| Year | Pitcher | Lost |
|---|---|---|
| 1910 | Cliff Curtis, Boston | 18 |
| 1963 | Roger Craig, New York | 18 |
| 1876 | Dory Dean, Cincinnati | 16 |
| 1899 | Jim Hughey, Cleveland | 16 |
| 1962 | Craig Anderson, New York | 16 |
| 1887 | Frank Gilmore, Washington | 14 |
| 1899 | Fred Bates, Cleveland | 14 |
| 1908 | Jim Pastorius, Brooklyn | 14 |
| 1911 | Buster Brown, Boston | 14 |
| 1992 | Anthony Young, New York | 14 |
| 1884 | Sam Moffett, Cleveland | 13 |
| 1917 | Burleigh Grimes, Pittsburgh | 13 |
| 1922 | Joe Oeschger, Boston | 13 |
| 1935 | Ben Cantwell, Boston | 13 |
| 1948 | Bob McCall, Chicago | 13 |
| 1993 | Anthony Young, New York | 13 |
| 2000 | Jose Lima, Houston | 13 |
| 1880 | William Purcell, Cincinnati | 12 |
| 1883 | John Coleman, Philadelphia | 12 |
| 1897 | Bill Hart, St. Louis | 12 |
| 1902 | Henry Thielman, Cincinnati | 12 |
| 1905 | Mal Eason, Brooklyn | 12 |
| 1914 | Rube Marquard, New York | 12 |
| 1914 | Pete Schneider, Cincinnati | 12 |
| 1928 | Russ Miller, Philadelphia | 12 |
| 1933 | Silas Johnson, Cincinnati | 12 |
| 1939 | Max Butcher, Philadelphia-Pittsburgh | 12 |
| 1940 | Hugh Mulcahy, Philadelphia | 12 |
| 1962 | Bob Miller, New York | 12 |
| 1972 | Ken Reynolds, Philadelphia | 12 |

**Total number of occurrences: 30**

# 20-GAME WINNERS

**(Numbers in parentheses after club denote position of team at close of season)**

## AMERICAN ASSOCIATION

| | W | L |
|---|---|---|
| **1882 (5)** | | |
| Will White, Cincinnati (1) | 40 | 12 |
| Tony Mullane, Louisville (2) | 30 | 24 |
| Sam Weaver, Philadelphia (3) | 26 | 15 |
| George McGinnis, St. Louis (5) | 25 | 21 |
| Harry Salisbury, Pittsburgh (5) | 20 | 19 |
| **1883 (8)** | | |
| Will White, Cincinnati (3) | 43 | 22 |
| Tim Keefe, New York (4) | 41 | 27 |
| Tony Mullane, St. Louis (2) | 35 | 15 |
| Bobby Mathews, Philadelphia (1) | 30 | 14 |
| George McGinnis, St. Louis (2) | 29 | 15 |
| Guy Hecker, Louisville (5) | 28 | 25 |
| Frank Mountain, Columbus (6) | 26 | 33 |
| Sam Weaver, Louisville (5) | 24 | 20 |
| **1884 (12)** | | |
| Guy Hecker, Louisville (3) | 52 | 20 |
| Jack Lynch, New York (1) | 37 | 15 |
| Tim Keefe, New York (1) | 37 | 17 |
| Ed Morris, Columbus (2) | 35 | 13 |
| Tony Mullane, Toledo (8) | 35 | 25 |
| Will White, Cincinnati (5) | 34 | 18 |
| Bob Emslie, Baltimore (6) | 32 | 18 |
| Bobby Mathews, Philadelphia (7) | 30 | 18 |
| Hardie Henderson, Baltimore (6) | 27 | 22 |
| George McGinnis, St. Louis (4) | 24 | 16 |
| Frank Mountain, Columbus (2) | 24 | 17 |
| Billy Mountjoy, Cincinnati (5) | 20 | 12 |
| **1885 (9)** | | |
| Bob Caruthers, St. Louis (1) | 40 | 13 |
| Ed Morris, Pittsburgh (3) | 39 | 24 |
| Dave Foutz, St. Louis (1) | 33 | 14 |
| Henry Porter, Brooklyn (5T) | 33 | 21 |
| Bobby Mathews, Philadelphia (4) | 30 | 17 |
| Guy Hecker, Louisville (5T) | 30 | 24 |
| Hardie Henderson, Baltimore (8) | 26 | 35 |
| Jack Lynch, New York (7) | 23 | 21 |
| Larry McKeon, Cincinnati (2) | 20 | 15 |
| **1886 (11)** | | |
| Dave Foutz, St. Louis (1) | 41 | 16 |
| Ed Morris, Pittsburgh (2) | 41 | 20 |
| Tom Ramsey, Louisville (4) | 37 | 27 |
| Tony Mullane, Cincinnati (5) | 31 | 27 |

| | W | L |
|---|---|---|
| **1886 (11)** | | |
| Bob Caruthers, St. Louis (1) | 30 | 14 |
| Pud Galvin, Pittsburgh (2) | 29 | 21 |
| Matt Kilroy, Baltimore (8) | 29 | 34 |
| Henry Porter, Brooklyn (3) | 28 | 20 |
| Guy Hecker, Louisville (4) | 27 | 23 |
| Al Atkinson, Philadelphia (6) | 25 | 17 |
| Jack Lynch, New York (7) | 20 | 20 |
| **1887 (10)** | | |
| Matt Kilroy, Baltimore (3) | 46 | 20 |
| Tom Ramsey, Louisville (4) | 39 | 27 |
| Charles King, St. Louis (1) | 34 | 11 |
| Elmer Smith, Cincinnati (2) | 33 | 18 |
| Tony Mullane, Cincinnati (2) | 31 | 17 |
| Bob Caruthers, St. Louis (1) | 29 | 9 |
| John Smith, Baltimore (3) | 29 | 29 |
| Gus Weyhing, Philadelphia (5) | 26 | 25 |
| Ed Seward, Philadelphia (5) | 25 | 24 |
| Dave Foutz, St. Louis (1) | 24 | 12 |
| **1888 (12)** | | |
| Charles King, St. Louis (1) | 45 | 21 |
| Ed Seward, Philadelphia (3) | 34 | 19 |
| Bob Caruthers, Brooklyn (2) | 29 | 15 |
| Gus Weyhing, Philadelphia (3) | 29 | 19 |
| Lee Viau, Cincinnati (4) | 27 | 14 |
| Tony Mullane, Cincinnati (4) | 26 | 16 |
| Nat Hudson, St. Louis (1) | 25 | 11 |
| Elton Chamberlain, 9-8 Louisville (7), 16-4 St. L (1) | 25 | 12 |
| Mickey Hughes, Brooklyn (2) | 25 | 13 |
| Ed Bakely, Cleveland (6) | 25 | 33 |
| Elmer Smith, Cincinnati (4) | 22 | 17 |
| Bert Cunningham, Baltimore (5) | 22 | 29 |
| **1889 (11)** | | |
| Bob Caruthers, Brooklyn (1) | 40 | 12 |
| Elton Chamberlain, St. Louis (2) | 35 | 15 |
| Charles King, St. Louis (2) | 33 | 17 |
| Jesse Duryea, Cincinnati (4) | 32 | 21 |
| Gus Weyhing, Philadelphia (3) | 28 | 19 |
| Matt Kilroy, Baltimore (5) | 28 | 25 |
| Mark Baldwin, Columbus (6) | 26 | 24 |
| Frank Foreman, Baltimore (5) | 25 | 21 |
| Adonis Terry, Brooklyn (1) | 21 | 16 |
| Ed Seward, Philadelphia (3) | 21 | 16 |
| Lee Viau, Cincinnati (4) | 21 | 19 |
| **1890 (8)** | | |
| John McMahon, 29-19 Phi (8), 7-2 Bal (6) | 36 | 21 |
| Scott Stratton, Louisville (1) | 34 | 13 |
| Hank Gastright, Columbus (2) | 29 | 13 |
| Bob Barr, Rochester (5) | 28 | 25 |
| Jack Stivetts, St. Louis (3) | 27 | 21 |
| Tom Ramsey, St. Louis (3) | 26 | 16 |
| Red Ehret, Louisville (1) | 25 | 14 |
| Egyptian Healy, Toledo (4) | 22 | 23 |
| **1891 (8)** | | |
| John McMahon, Baltimore (3) | 35 | 24 |
| George Haddock, Boston (1) | 34 | 11 |
| Jack Stivetts, St. Louis (2) | 33 | 22 |
| Gus Weyhing, Philadelphia (4) | 31 | 20 |
| Charlie Buffinton, Boston (1) | 29 | 9 |
| Phil Knell, Columbus (5) | 27 | 26 |
| Elton Chamberlain, Philadelphia (4) | 23 | 23 |
| Willie McGill, 2-5 Cincinnati (5), 19-10 St. L (2) | 21 | 15 |

## PLAYERS LEAGUE

| | W | L |
|---|---|---|
| **1890 (9)** | | |
| Mark Baldwin, Chicago (4) | 32 | 24 |
| Gus Weyhing, Brooklyn (2) | 30 | 16 |
| Charles King, Chicago (4) | 30 | 22 |
| Hoss Radbourn, Boston (1) | 27 | 12 |
| Adison Gumbert, Boston (1) | 23 | 12 |
| Hank O'Day, New York (3) | 22 | 13 |
| Henry Gruber, Cleveland (7) | 22 | 23 |
| Phil Knell, Philadelphia (5) | 21 | 10 |
| Harry Staley, Pittsburgh (6) | 21 | 23 |

## UNION ASSOCIATION

| | W | L |
|---|---|---|
| **1884 (9)** | | |
| Bill Sweeney, Baltimore (3) | 40 | 21 |
| Hugh Daily, 22-25 Chi (6), 1-1 Was (5), 5-4 Pit (8) | 28 | 30 |
| Billy Taylor, St. Louis (1) | 25 | 4 |
| Dick Burns, Cincinnati (2) | 25 | 15 |
| Charlie Sweeney, St. Louis (1) | 24 | 8 |
| Bill Wise, Washington (5) | 23 | 20 |
| Jim McCormick, Cincinnati (2) | 22 | 4 |
| Fred Shaw, Boston (4) | 22 | 15 |
| George Bradley, Cincinnati (2) | 21 | 13 |

## AMERICAN LEAGUE

| | W | L |
|---|---|---|
| **1901 (5)** | | |
| Cy Young, Boston (2) | 33 | 10 |
| Joe McGinnity, Baltimore (5) | 26 | 21 |
| Clark Griffith, Chicago (1) | 24 | 7 |
| Roscoe Miller, Detroit (3) | 23 | 13 |
| Chick Fraser, Philadelphia (4) | 20 | 15 |
| **1902 (7)** | | |
| Cy Young, Boston (3) | 32 | 11 |
| Rube Waddell, Philadelphia (1) | 23 | 7 |

| | W | L |
|---|---|---|
| **1902 (7)** | | |
| Frank Donahue, St. Louis (2) | 22 | 11 |
| Jack Powell, St. Louis (2) | 22 | 17 |
| Bill Dinneen, Boston (3) | 21 | 21 |
| Roy Patterson, Chicago (4) | 20 | 12 |
| Eddie Plank, Philadelphia (1) | 20 | 15 |
| **1903 (7)** | | |
| Cy Young, Boston (1) | 28 | 9 |
| Eddie Plank, Philadelphia (2) | 23 | 16 |
| Bill Dinneen, Boston (1) | 21 | 13 |
| Willie Sudhoff, St. Louis (6) | 21 | 15 |
| Jack Chesbro, New York (4) | 21 | 15 |
| Rube Waddell, Philadelphia (2) | 21 | 16 |
| Tom Hughes, Boston (1) | 20 | 7 |
| **1904 (9)** | | |
| Jack Chesbro, New York (2) | 41 | 13 |
| Cy Young, Boston (1) | 26 | 16 |
| Eddie Plank, Philadelphia (5) | 26 | 17 |
| Rube Waddell, Philadelphia (5) | 25 | 19 |
| Bill Bernhard, Cleveland (4) | 23 | 13 |
| Bill Dinneen, Boston (1) | 23 | 14 |
| Jack Powell, New York (2) | 23 | 19 |
| Jesse Tannehill, Boston (1) | 21 | 11 |
| Frank Owen, Chicago (3) | 21 | 15 |
| **1905 (9)** | | |
| Rube Waddell, Philadelphia (1) | 26 | 11 |
| Eddie Plank, Philadelphia (1) | 25 | 12 |
| Nick Altrock, Chicago (2) | 24 | 12 |
| Ed Killian, Detroit (3) | 23 | 13 |
| Jesse Tannehill, Boston (4) | 22 | 9 |
| Frank Owen, Chicago (2) | 21 | 13 |
| George Mullin, Detroit (3) | 21 | 20 |
| Addie Joss, Cleveland (5) | 20 | 11 |
| Frank Smith, Chicago (2) | 20 | 14 |
| **1906 (8)** | | |
| Al Orth, New York (2) | 27 | 17 |
| Jack Chesbro, New York (2) | 24 | 16 |
| Bob Rhoads, Cleveland (3) | 22 | 10 |
| Frank Owen, Chicago (1) | 22 | 13 |
| Addie Joss, Cleveland (3) | 21 | 9 |
| George Mullin, Detroit (6) | 21 | 18 |
| Nick Altrock, Chicago (1) | 20 | 13 |
| Otto Hess, Cleveland (3) | 20 | 17 |
| **1907 (10)** | | |
| Addie Joss, Cleveland (4) | 27 | 10 |
| Guy White, Chicago (3) | 27 | 13 |
| Bill Donovan, Detroit (1) | 25 | 4 |
| Ed Killian, Detroit (1) | 25 | 13 |
| Eddie Plank, Philadelphia (2) | 24 | 16 |
| Ed Walsh, Chicago (3) | 24 | 18 |
| Frank Smith, Chicago (3) | 22 | 11 |
| Cy Young, Boston (7) | 22 | 15 |
| Jimmy Dygert, Philadelphia (2) | 20 | 9 |
| George Mullin, Detroit (1) | 20 | 20 |
| **1908 (4)** | | |
| Ed Walsh, Chicago (3) | 40 | 15 |
| Addie Joss, Cleveland (2) | 24 | 11 |
| Ed Summers, Detroit (1) | 24 | 12 |
| Cy Young, Boston (5) | 21 | 11 |
| **1909 (3)** | | |
| George Mullin, Detroit (1) | 29 | 8 |
| Frank Smith, Chicago (4) | 25 | 17 |
| Ed Willett, Detroit (1) | 22 | 9 |
| **1910 (5)** | | |
| Jack Coombs, Philadelphia (1) | 31 | 9 |
| Russ Ford, New York (2) | 26 | 6 |
| Walter Johnson, Washington (7) | 25 | 17 |
| Chief Bender, Philadelphia (1) | 23 | 5 |
| George Mullin, Detroit (3) | 21 | 12 |
| **1911 (7)** | | |
| Jack Coombs, Philadelphia (1) | 28 | 12 |
| Ed Walsh, Chicago (4) | 27 | 18 |
| Walter Johnson, Washington (7) | 25 | 13 |
| Vean Gregg, Cleveland (3) | 23 | 7 |
| Joe Wood, Boston (5) | 23 | 17 |
| Eddie Plank, Philadelphia (1) | 22 | 8 |
| Russ Ford, New York (6) | 22 | 11 |
| **1912 (9)** | | |
| Joe Wood, Boston (1) | 34 | 5 |
| Walter Johnson, Washington (2) | 33 | 12 |
| Ed Walsh, Chicago (4) | 27 | 17 |
| Eddie Plank, Philadelphia (3) | 26 | 6 |
| Bob Groom, Washington (2) | 24 | 13 |
| Jack Coombs, Philadelphia (3) | 21 | 10 |
| Hugh Bedient, Boston (1) | 20 | 9 |
| Vean Gregg, Cleveland (5) | 20 | 13 |
| Tom O'Brien, Boston (1) | 20 | 13 |
| **1913 (6)** | | |
| Walter Johnson, Washington (2) | 36 | 7 |
| Fred Falkenberg, Cleveland (3) | 23 | 10 |
| Ewell Russell, Chicago (5) | 22 | 16 |
| Chief Bender, Philadelphia (1) | 21 | 10 |
| Vean Gregg, Cleveland (3) | 20 | 13 |
| Jim Scott, Chicago (5) | 20 | 20 |

| | W | L |
|---|---|---|
| **1914 (3)** | | |
| Walter Johnson, Washington (3) | 28 | 18 |
| Harry Coveleski, Detroit (4) | 22 | 12 |
| Ray Collins, Boston (2) | 20 | 13 |
| **1915 (5)** | | |
| Walter Johnson, Washington (4) | 27 | 13 |
| Jim Scott, Chicago (3) | 24 | 11 |
| Hooks Dauss, Detroit (2) | 24 | 13 |
| Red Faber, Chicago (3) | 24 | 14 |
| Harry Coveleski, Detroit (2) | 22 | 13 |
| **1916 (4)** | | |
| Walter Johnson, Washington (7) | 25 | 20 |
| Bob Shawkey, New York (4) | 24 | 14 |
| Babe Ruth, Boston (1) | 23 | 12 |
| Harry Coveleski, Detroit (3) | 21 | 11 |
| **1917 (5)** | | |
| Ed Cicotte, Chicago (1) | 28 | 12 |
| Babe Ruth, Boston (2) | 24 | 13 |
| Jim Bagby, Cleveland (3) | 23 | 13 |
| Walter Johnson, Washington (5) | 23 | 16 |
| Carl Mays, Boston (2) | 22 | 9 |
| **1918 (4)** | | |
| Walter Johnson, Washington (3) | 23 | 13 |
| Stan Coveleski, Cleveland (2) | 22 | 13 |
| Carl Mays, Boston (1) | 21 | 13 |
| Scott Perry, Philadelphia (8) | 20 | 19 |
| **1919 (7)** | | |
| Ed Cicotte, Chicago (1) | 29 | 7 |
| Lefty Williams, Chicago (1) | 23 | 11 |
| Stan Coveleski, Cleveland (2) | 23 | 12 |
| Hooks Dauss, Detroit (4) | 21 | 9 |
| Allen Sothoron, St. Louis (5) | 21 | 11 |
| Bob Shawkey, New York (3) | 20 | 13 |
| Walter Johnson, Washington (7) | 20 | 14 |
| **1920 (10)** | | |
| Jim Bagby, Cleveland (1) | 31 | 12 |
| Carl Mays, New York (3) | 26 | 11 |
| Stan Coveleski, Cleveland (1) | 24 | 14 |
| Red Faber, Chicago (2) | 23 | 13 |
| Lefty Williams, Chicago (2) | 22 | 14 |
| Dickie Kerr, Chicago (2) | 21 | 9 |
| Ed Cicotte, Chicago (2) | 21 | 10 |
| Ray Caldwell, Cleveland (1) | 20 | 10 |
| Urban Shocker, St. Louis (4) | 20 | 10 |
| Bob Shawkey, New York (3) | 20 | 13 |
| **1921 (5)** | | |
| Carl Mays, New York (1) | 27 | 9 |
| Urban Shocker, St. Louis (3) | 27 | 12 |
| Red Faber, Chicago (7) | 25 | 15 |
| Stan Coveleski, Cleveland (2) | 23 | 13 |
| Sam Jones, Boston (5) | 23 | 16 |
| **1922 (6)** | | |
| Eddie Rommel, Philadelphia (7) | 27 | 13 |
| Joe Bush, New York (1) | 26 | 7 |
| Urban Shocker, St. Louis (2) | 24 | 17 |
| George Uhle, Cleveland (4) | 22 | 16 |
| Red Faber, Chicago (5) | 21 | 17 |
| Bob Shawkey, New York (1) | 20 | 12 |
| **1923 (5)** | | |
| George Uhle, Cleveland (3) | 26 | 16 |
| Sam Jones, New York (1) | 21 | 8 |
| Hooks Dauss, Detroit (2) | 21 | 13 |
| Urban Shocker, St. Louis (5) | 20 | 12 |
| Howard Ehmke, Boston (8) | 20 | 17 |
| **1924 (4)** | | |
| Walter Johnson, Washington (1) | 23 | 7 |
| Herb Pennock, New York (2) | 21 | 9 |
| Sloppy Thurston, Chicago (8) | 20 | 14 |
| Joe Shaute, Cleveland (6) | 20 | 17 |
| **1925 (4)** | | |
| Eddie Rommel, Philadelphia (2) | 21 | 10 |
| Ted Lyons, Chicago (5) | 21 | 11 |
| Stan Coveleski, Washington (1) | 20 | 5 |
| Walter Johnson, Washington (1) | 20 | 7 |
| **1926 (2)** | | |
| George Uhle, Cleveland (2) | 27 | 11 |
| Herb Pennock, New York (1) | 23 | 11 |
| **1927 (3)** | | |
| Waite Hoyt, New York (1) | 22 | 7 |
| Ted Lyons, Chicago (5) | 22 | 14 |
| Lefty Grove, Philadelphia (2) | 20 | 13 |
| **1928 (5)** | | |
| Lefty Grove, Philadelphia (2) | 24 | 8 |
| George Pipgras, New York (1) | 24 | 13 |
| Waite Hoyt, New York (1) | 23 | 7 |
| Alvin Crowder, St. Louis (3) | 21 | 5 |
| Sam Gray, St. Louis (3) | 20 | 12 |
| **1929 (3)** | | |
| George Earnshaw, Philadelphia (1) | 24 | 8 |
| Wes Ferrell, Cleveland (3) | 21 | 10 |
| Lefty Grove, Philadelphia (1) | 20 | 6 |
| **1930 (5)** | | |
| Lefty Grove, Philadelphia (1) | 28 | 5 |
| Wes Ferrell, Cleveland (4) | 25 | 13 |
| George Earnshaw, Philadelphia (1) | 22 | 13 |

| | W | L |
|---|---|---|
| **1930 (5)** | | |
| Ted Lyons, Chicago (7) | 22 | 15 |
| Walter Stewart, St. Louis (6) | 20 | 12 |
| **1931 (5)** | | |
| Lefty Grove, Philadelphia (1) | 31 | 4 |
| Wes Ferrell, Cleveland (4) | 22 | 12 |
| George Earnshaw, Philadelphia (1) | 21 | 7 |
| Lefty Gomez, New York (2) | 21 | 9 |
| Rube Walberg, Philadelphia (1) | 20 | 12 |
| **1932 (5)** | | |
| Alvin Crowder, Washington (3) | 26 | 13 |
| Lefty Grove, Philadelphia (2) | 25 | 10 |
| Lefty Gomez, New York (1) | 24 | 7 |
| Wes Ferrell, Cleveland (4) | 23 | 13 |
| Monte Weaver, Washington (3) | 22 | 10 |
| **1933 (3)** | | |
| Lefty Grove, Philadelphia (3) | 24 | 8 |
| Alvin Crowder, Washington (1) | 24 | 15 |
| Earl Whitehill, Washington (1) | 22 | 8 |
| **1934 (4)** | | |
| Lefty Gomez, New York (2) | 26 | 5 |
| Schoolboy Rowe, Detroit (1) | 24 | 8 |
| Tommy Bridges, Detroit (1) | 22 | 11 |
| Mel Harder, Cleveland (3) | 20 | 12 |
| **1935 (4)** | | |
| Wes Ferrell, Boston (4) | 25 | 14 |
| Mel Harder, Cleveland (3) | 22 | 11 |
| Tommy Bridges, Detroit (1) | 21 | 10 |
| Lefty Grove, Boston (4) | 20 | 12 |
| **1936 (5)** | | |
| Tommy Bridges, Detroit (2) | 23 | 11 |
| Vern Kennedy, Chicago (3) | 21 | 9 |
| Johnny Allen, Cleveland (5) | 20 | 10 |
| Red Ruffing, New York (1) | 20 | 12 |
| Wes Ferrell, Boston (6) | 20 | 15 |
| **1937 (2)** | | |
| Lefty Gomez, New York (1) | 21 | 11 |
| Red Ruffing, New York (1) | 20 | 7 |
| **1938 (2)** | | |
| Red Ruffing, New York (1) | 21 | 7 |
| Bobo Newsom, St. Louis (7) | 20 | 16 |
| **1939 (4)** | | |
| Bob Feller, Cleveland (3) | 24 | 9 |
| Red Ruffing, New York (1) | 21 | 7 |
| Dutch E. Leonard, Washington (6) | 20 | 8 |
| Bobo Newsom, 3-1 St. Louis (8), 17-10 Detroit (5) | 20 | 11 |
| **1940 (2)** | | |
| Bob Feller, Cleveland (2) | 27 | 11 |
| Bobo Newsom, Detroit (1) | 21 | 5 |
| **1941 (2)** | | |
| Bob Feller, Cleveland (4T) | 25 | 13 |
| Thornton Lee, Chicago (3) | 22 | 11 |
| **1942 (2)** | | |
| Cecil Hughson, Boston (2) | 22 | 6 |
| Ernie Bonham, New York (1) | 21 | 5 |
| **1943 (2)** | | |
| Spud Chandler, New York (1) | 20 | 4 |
| Dizzy Trout, Detroit (5) | 20 | 12 |
| **1944 (2)** | | |
| Hal Newhouser, Detroit (2) | 29 | 9 |
| Dizzy Trout, Detroit (2) | 27 | 14 |
| **1945 (3)** | | |
| Hal Newhouser, Detroit (1) | 25 | 9 |
| Dave Ferriss, Boston (7) | 21 | 10 |
| Roger Wolff, Washington (2) | 20 | 10 |
| **1946 (5)** | | |
| Hal Newhouser, Detroit (2) | 26 | 9 |
| Bob Feller, Cleveland (6) | 26 | 15 |
| Dave Ferriss, Boston (1) | 25 | 6 |
| Spud Chandler, New York (3) | 20 | 8 |
| Cecil Hughson, Boston (1) | 20 | 11 |
| **1947 (1)** | | |
| Bob Feller, Cleveland (4) | 20 | 11 |
| **1948 (3)** | | |
| Hal Newhouser, Detroit (5) | 21 | 12 |
| Gene Bearden, Cleveland (1) | 20 | 7 |
| Bob Lemon, Cleveland (1) | 20 | 14 |
| **1949 (5)** | | |
| Mel Parnell, Boston (2) | 25 | 7 |
| Ellis Kinder, Boston (2) | 23 | 6 |
| Bob Lemon, Cleveland (3) | 22 | 10 |
| Vic Raschi, New York (1) | 21 | 10 |
| Alex Kellner, Philadelphia (5) | 20 | 12 |
| **1950 (2)** | | |
| Bob Lemon, Cleveland (4) | 23 | 11 |
| Vic Raschi, New York (1) | 21 | 8 |
| **1951 (6)** | | |
| Bob Feller, Cleveland (2) | 22 | 8 |
| Eddie Lopat, New York (1) | 21 | 9 |
| Vic Raschi, New York (1) | 21 | 10 |
| Ned Garver, St. Louis (8) | 20 | 12 |
| Mike Garcia, Cleveland (2) | 20 | 13 |
| Early Wynn, Cleveland (2) | 20 | 13 |
| **1952 (5)** | | |
| Bobby Shantz, Philadelphia (4) | 24 | 7 |
| **1952 (5)** | | |
| Early Wynn, Cleveland (2) | 23 | 12 |
| Mike Garcia, Cleveland (2) | 22 | 11 |
| Bob Lemon, Cleveland (2) | 22 | 11 |
| Allie Reynolds, New York (1) | 20 | 8 |
| **1953 (4)** | | |
| Bob Porterfield, Washington (5) | 22 | 10 |
| Mel Parnell, Boston (4) | 21 | 8 |
| Bob Lemon, Cleveland (2) | 21 | 15 |
| Virgil Trucks, 5-4 St. Louis (8), 15-6 Chicago (3) | 20 | 10 |
| **1954 (3)** | | |
| Bob Lemon, Cleveland (1) | 23 | 7 |
| Early Wynn, Cleveland (1) | 23 | 11 |
| Bob Grim, New York (2) | 20 | 6 |
| **1955 (0)** | | |
| Whitey Ford, New York, Bob Lemon, Cleveland, and Frank Sullivan, Boston, each had 18 wins. | | |
| **1956 (6)** | | |
| Frank Lary, Detroit (5) | 21 | 13 |
| Herb Score, Cleveland (2) | 20 | 9 |
| Early Wynn, Cleveland (2) | 20 | 9 |
| Billy Pierce, Chicago (3) | 20 | 9 |
| Bob Lemon, Cleveland (2) | 20 | 14 |
| Billy Hoeft, Detroit (5) | 20 | 14 |
| **1957 (2)** | | |
| Jim Bunning, Detroit (4) | 20 | 8 |
| Billy Pierce, Chicago (2) | 20 | 12 |
| **1958 (1)** | | |
| Bob Turley, New York (1) | 21 | 7 |
| **1959 (1)** | | |
| Early Wynn, Chicago (1) | 22 | 10 |
| **1960 (0)** | | |
| Chuck Estrada, Baltimore, and Jim Perry, Cleveland, each had 18 wins. | | |
| **1961 (2)** | | |
| Whitey Ford, New York (1) | 25 | 4 |
| Frank Lary, Detroit (2) | 23 | 9 |
| **1962 (4)** | | |
| Ralph Terry, New York (1) | 23 | 12 |
| Ray Herbert, Chicago (5) | 20 | 9 |
| Dick Donovan, Cleveland (6) | 20 | 10 |
| Camilo Pascual, Minnesota (2) | 20 | 11 |
| **1963 (5)** | | |
| Whitey Ford, New York (1) | 24 | 7 |
| Jim Bouton, New York (1) | 21 | 7 |
| Camilo Pascual, Minnesota (3) | 21 | 9 |
| Bill Monbouquette, Boston (7) | 20 | 10 |
| Steve Barber, Baltimore (4) | 20 | 13 |
| **1964 (2)** | | |
| Dean Chance, Los Angeles (5) | 20 | 9 |
| Gary Peters, Chicago (2) | 20 | 8 |
| **1965 (2)** | | |
| Mudcat Grant, Minnesota (1) | 21 | 7 |
| Mel Stottlemyre, New York (6) | 20 | 9 |
| **1966 (2)** | | |
| Jim Kaat, Minnesota (2) | 25 | 13 |
| Denny McLain, Detroit (3) | 20 | 14 |
| **1967 (3)** | | |
| Jim Lonborg, Boston (1) | 22 | 9 |
| Earl Wilson, Detroit (2T) | 22 | 11 |
| Dean Chance, Minnesota (2T) | 20 | 14 |
| **1968 (4)** | | |
| Denny McLain, Detroit (1) | 31 | 6 |
| Dave McNally, Baltimore (2) | 22 | 10 |
| Luis Tiant, Cleveland (3) | 21 | 9 |
| Mel Stottlemyre, New York (5) | 21 | 12 |
| **1969 (6)** | | |
| Denny McLain, Detroit (2E) | 24 | 9 |
| Mike Cuellar, Baltimore (1E) | 23 | 11 |
| Jim Perry, Minnesota (1W) | 20 | 6 |
| Dave McNally, Baltimore (1E) | 20 | 7 |
| Dave Boswell, Minnesota (1W) | 20 | 12 |
| Mel Stottlemyre, New York (5E) | 20 | 14 |
| **1970 (7)** | | |
| Mike Cuellar, Baltimore (1E) | 24 | 8 |
| Dave McNally, Baltimore (1E) | 24 | 9 |
| Jim Perry, Minnesota (1W) | 24 | 12 |
| Clyde Wright, California (3W) | 22 | 12 |
| Jim Palmer, Baltimore (1E) | 20 | 10 |
| Fritz Peterson, New York (2E) | 20 | 11 |
| Sam McDowell, Cleveland (5E) | 20 | 12 |
| **1971 (10)** | | |
| Mickey Lolich, Detroit (2E) | 25 | 14 |
| Vida Blue, Oakland (1W) | 24 | 8 |
| Wilbur Wood, Chicago (3W) | 22 | 13 |
| Dave McNally, Baltimore (1E) | 21 | 5 |
| Catfish Hunter, Oakland (1W) | 21 | 11 |
| Pat Dobson, Baltimore (1E) | 20 | 8 |
| Jim Palmer, Baltimore (1E) | 20 | 9 |
| Mike Cuellar, Baltimore (1E) | 20 | 9 |
| Joe Coleman, Detroit (2E) | 20 | 9 |
| Andy Messersmith, California (4W) | 20 | 13 |
| **1972 (6)** | | |
| Gaylord Perry, Cleveland (5W) | 24 | 16 |
| Wilbur Wood, Chicago (2W) | 24 | 17 |

| | W | L |
|---|---|---|
| **1972 (6)** | | |
| Mickey Lolich, Detroit (1E) | 22 | 14 |
| Catfish Hunter, Oakland (1W) | 21 | 7 |
| Jim Palmer, Baltimore (3E) | 21 | 10 |
| Stan Bahnsen, Chicago (2W) | 21 | 16 |
| **1973 (12)** | | |
| Wilbur Wood, Chicago (5W) | 24 | 20 |
| Joe Coleman, Detroit (3E) | 23 | 15 |
| Jim Palmer, Baltimore (1E) | 22 | 9 |
| Catfish Hunter, Oakland (1W) | 21 | 5 |
| Ken Holtzman, Oakland (1W) | 21 | 13 |
| Nolan Ryan, California (4W) | 21 | 16 |
| Vida Blue, Oakland (1W) | 20 | 9 |
| Paul Splittorff, Kansas City (2W) | 20 | 11 |
| Jim Colborn, Milwaukee (5E) | 20 | 12 |
| Luis Tiant, Boston (2E) | 20 | 13 |
| Bill Singer, California (4W) | 20 | 14 |
| Bert Blyleven, Minnesota (3W) | 20 | 17 |
| **1974 (9)** | | |
| Catfish Hunter, Oakland (1W) | 25 | 12 |
| Ferguson Jenkins, Texas (2W) | 25 | 12 |
| Mike Cuellar, Baltimore (1E) | 22 | 10 |
| Luis Tiant, Boston (3E) | 22 | 13 |
| Steve Busby, Kansas City (5W) | 22 | 14 |
| Nolan Ryan, California (6W) | 22 | 16 |
| Jim Kaat, Chicago (4W) | 21 | 13 |
| Gaylord Perry, Cleveland (4E) | 21 | 13 |
| Wilbur Wood, Chicago (4W) | 20 | 19 |
| **1975 (5)** | | |
| Jim Palmer, Baltimore (2E) | 23 | 11 |
| Catfish Hunter, New York (3E) | 23 | 14 |
| Vida Blue, Oakland (1W) | 22 | 11 |
| Mike Torrez, Baltimore (2E) | 20 | 9 |
| Jim Kaat, Chicago (5W) | 20 | 14 |
| **1976 (3)** | | |
| Jim Palmer, Baltimore (2E) | 22 | 13 |
| Luis Tiant, Boston (3E) | 21 | 12 |
| Wayne Garland, Baltimore (2E) | 20 | 7 |
| **1977 (3)** | | |
| Jim Palmer, Baltimore (2TE) | 20 | 11 |
| Dave Goltz, Minnesota (4W) | 20 | 11 |
| Dennis Leonard, Kansas City (1W) | 20 | 12 |
| **1978 (6)** | | |
| Ron Guidry, New York (1E) | 25 | 3 |
| Mike Caldwell, Milwaukee (3E) | 22 | 9 |
| Jim Palmer, Baltimore (4E) | 21 | 12 |
| Dennis Leonard, Kansas City (1W) | 21 | 17 |
| Dennis Eckersley, Boston (2E) | 20 | 8 |
| Ed Figueroa, New York (1E) | 20 | 9 |
| **1979 (3)** | | |
| Mike Flanagan, Baltimore (1E) | 23 | 9 |
| Tommy John, New York (4E) | 21 | 9 |
| Jerry Koosman, Minnesota (4W) | 20 | 13 |
| **1980 (5)** | | |
| Steve Stone, Baltimore (2E) | 25 | 7 |
| Tommy John, New York (1E) | 22 | 9 |
| Mike Norris, Oakland (2W) | 22 | 9 |
| Scott McGregor, Baltimore (2E) | 20 | 8 |
| Dennis Leonard, Kansas City (1W) | 20 | 11 |
| **1981 (0)** | | |
| Dennis Martinez, Baltimore, Steve McCatty, Oakland, Jack Morris, Detroit, and Pete Vukovich, Milwaukee, each had 14 wins. | | |
| **1982 (0)** | | |
| La Marr Hoyt, Chicago, had 19 wins. | | |
| **1983 (4)** | | |
| LaMarr Hoyt, Chicago (1W) | 24 | 10 |
| Rich Dotson, Chicago (1W) | 22 | 7 |
| Ron Guidry, New York (3E) | 21 | 9 |
| Jack Morris, Detroit (2E) | 20 | 13 |
| **1984 (1)** | | |
| Mike Boddicker, Baltimore (5E) | 20 | 11 |
| **1985 (2)** | | |
| Ron Guidry, New York (2E) | 22 | 6 |
| Bret Saberhagen, Kansas City (1W) | 20 | 6 |
| **1986 (3)** | | |
| Roger Clemens, Boston (1E) | 24 | 4 |
| Jack Morris, Detroit (3E) | 21 | 8 |
| Ted Higuera, Milwaukee (6E) | 20 | 11 |
| **1987 (2)** | | |
| Roger Clemens, Boston (5E) | 20 | 9 |
| Dave Stewart, Oakland (3W) | 20 | 13 |
| **1988 (3)** | | |
| Frank Viola, Minnesota (2W) | 24 | 7 |
| Dave Stewart, Oakland (1W) | 21 | 12 |
| Mark Gubicza, Kansas City (3W) | 20 | 8 |
| **1989 (2)** | | |
| Bret Saberhagen, Kansas City (2W) | 23 | 6 |
| Dave Stewart, Oakland (1W) | 21 | 9 |
| **1990 (3)** | | |
| Bob Welch, Oakland (1W) | 27 | 6 |
| Dave Stewart, Oakland (1W) | 22 | 11 |
| Roger Clemens, Boston (1E) | 21 | 6 |
| **1991 (2)** | | |
| Scott Erickson, Minnesota (1W) | 20 | 8 |
| Bill Gullickson, Detroit (2TE) | 20 | 9 |
| **1992 (3)** | | |
| Jack Morris, Toronto (1E) | 21 | 6 |
| Kevin Brown, Texas (4W) | 21 | 11 |
| Jack McDowell, Chicago (3W) | 20 | 10 |
| **1993 (1)** | | |
| Jack McDowell, Chicago (1W) | 22 | 10 |
| **1994 (0)** | | |
| Jimmy Key, New York, had 17 wins. | | |
| **1995 (0)** | | |
| Mike Mussina, Baltimore, had 19 wins. | | |
| **1996 (2)** | | |
| Andy Pettitte, New York (1E) | 21 | 8 |
| Pat Hentgen, Toronto (4E) | 20 | 10 |
| **1997 (3)** | | |
| Roger Clemens, Toronto (5E) | 21 | 7 |
| Randy Johnson, Seattle (1W) | 20 | 4 |
| Brad Radke, Minnesota (4C) | 20 | 10 |
| **1998 (3)** | | |
| Roger Clemens, Toronto (3E) | 20 | 6 |
| David Cone, New York (1E) | 20 | 7 |
| Rick Helling, Texas (1W) | 20 | 7 |
| **1999 (1)** | | |
| Pedro Martinez, Boston (2E) | 23 | 4 |
| **2000 (2)** | | |
| Tim Hudson, Oakland (1W) | 20 | 6 |
| David Wells, Toronto (3E) | 20 | 8 |
| **2001 (3)** | | |
| Mark Mulder, Oakland (2W) | 21 | 8 |
| Roger Clemens, New York (1E) | 20 | 3 |
| Jamie Moyer, Seattle (1W) | 20 | 6 |
| **2002 (3)** | | |
| Barry Zito, Oakland (1W) | 23 | 5 |
| Derek Lowe, Boston (2E) | 21 | 8 |
| Pedro Martinez, Boston (2E) | 20 | 4 |
| **2003 (4)** | | |
| Roy Halladay, Toronto (3E) | 22 | 7 |
| Esteban Loaiza, Chicago (2C) | 21 | 9 |
| Jamie Moyer, Seattle (2W) | 21 | 7 |
| Andy Pettitte, New York (1E) | 21 | 8 |
| **2004 (2)** | | |
| Curt Schilling, Boston (2E) | 21 | 6 |
| Johan Santana, Minnesota (1C) | 20 | 6 |
| **2005 (1)** | | |
| Bartolo Colon, Los Angeles (1W) | 21 | 8 |

## NATIONAL LEAGUE

| | W | L |
|---|---|---|
| **1876 (5)** | | |
| Al Spalding, Chicago (1) | 47 | 13 |
| George Bradley, St. Louis (2) | 45 | 19 |
| Tommy Bond, Hartford (3) | 32 | 13 |
| Jim Devlin, Louisville (5) | 30 | 34 |
| Bobby Mathews, New York (6) | 21 | 34 |
| **1877 (3)** | | |
| Tommy Bond, Boston (1) | 31 | 17 |
| Jim Devlin, Louisville (2) | 28 | 20 |
| Terry Larkin, Hartford (3) | 22 | 21 |
| **1878 (4)** | | |
| Tommy Bond, Boston (1) | 40 | 19 |
| Will White, Cincinnati (2) | 29 | 21 |
| Terry Larkin, Chicago (4) | 29 | 26 |
| Monte Ward, Providence (3) | 22 | 13 |
| **1879 (6)** | | |
| Monte Ward, Providence (1) | 44 | 18 |
| Tommy Bond, Boston (2) | 43 | 19 |
| Will White, Cincinnati (5) | 43 | 31 |
| Pud Galvin, Buffalo (3T) | 37 | 27 |
| Terry Larkin, Chicago (3T) | 30 | 23 |
| Jim McCormick, Cleveland (6) | 20 | 40 |
| **1880 (8)** | | |
| Jim McCormick, Cleveland (3) | 45 | 28 |
| Larry Corcoran, Chicago (1) | 43 | 14 |
| Monte Ward, Providence (2) | 40 | 23 |
| Mickey Welch, Troy (4) | 34 | 30 |
| Lee Richmond, Worcester (5) | 31 | 33 |
| Tommy Bond, Boston (6) | 26 | 29 |
| Fred Goldsmith, Chicago (1) | 22 | 3 |
| Pud Galvin, Buffalo (7) | 20 | 37 |
| **1881 (9)** | | |
| Larry Corcoran, Chicago (1) | 31 | 14 |
| Jim Whitney, Boston (6) | 31 | 33 |
| Pud Galvin, Buffalo (3) | 29 | 24 |
| George Derby, Detroit (4) | 29 | 26 |
| Jim McCormick, Cleveland (7) | 26 | 30 |
| Hoss Radbourn, Providence (2) | 25 | 11 |
| Fred Goldsmith, Chicago (1) | 25 | 13 |
| Lee Richmond, Worcester (8) | 25 | 27 |
| Mickey Welch, Troy (5) | 21 | 18 |
| **1882 (7)** | | |
| Jim McCormick, Cleveland (5) | 36 | 29 |
| Hoss Radbourn, Providence (2) | 31 | 19 |
| Pud Galvin, Buffalo (3T) | 28 | 22 |
| Fred Goldsmith, Chicago (1) | 28 | 16 |
| Larry Corcoran, Chicago (1) | 27 | 13 |
| George Weidman, Detroit (6) | 26 | 20 |
| Jim Whitney, Boston (3T) | 24 | 22 |

| 1883 (9) | W | L |
|---|---|---|
| Hoss Radbourn, Providence (3) | 49 | 25 |
| Pud Galvin, Buffalo (5) | 46 | 29 |
| Jim Whitney, Boston (1) | 37 | 21 |
| Larry Corcoran, Chicago (2) | 31 | 21 |
| Fred Goldsmith, Chicago (2) | 28 | 18 |
| Jim McCormick, Cleveland (4) | 27 | 13 |
| Charlie Buffinton, Boston (1) | 25 | 14 |
| Mickey Welch, New York (6) | 25 | 23 |
| Hugh Daily, Cleveland (4) | 24 | 18 |
| **1884 (7)** | | |
| Hoss Radbourn, Providence (1) | 60 | 12 |
| Charlie Buffinton, Boston (2) | 48 | 16 |
| Pud Galvin, Buffalo (3) | 46 | 22 |
| Mickey Welch, New York (4T) | 39 | 21 |
| Larry Corcoran, Chicago (4T) | 35 | 23 |
| Jim Whitney, Boston (2) | 23 | 14 |
| Charlie Ferguson, Philadelphia (6) | 21 | 24 |
| **1885 (9)** | | |
| John Clarkson, Chicago (1) | 53 | 16 |
| Mickey Welch, New York (2) | 44 | 11 |
| Tim Keefe, New York (2) | 32 | 13 |
| Charlie Ferguson, Philadelphia (3) | 26 | 19 |
| Hoss Radbourn, Providence (4) | 26 | 20 |
| Ed Daily, Philadelphia (3) | 26 | 22 |
| Fred Shaw, Providence (4) | 23 | 26 |
| Charlie Buffinton, Boston (5) | 22 | 27 |
| Jim McCormick, 1-3 Providence (4), 20-4 Chicago (1) | 21 | 7 |
| **1886 (11)** | | |
| Charles Baldwin, Detroit (2) | 42 | 13 |
| Tim Keefe, New York (3) | 42 | 20 |
| John Clarkson, Chicago (1) | 35 | 17 |
| Mickey Welch, New York (3) | 33 | 22 |
| Charlie Ferguson, Philadelphia (4) | 32 | 9 |
| Charlie Getzien, Detroit (2) | 31 | 11 |
| Jim McCormick, Chicago (1) | 31 | 11 |
| Hoss Radbourn, Boston (5) | 27 | 30 |
| Dan Casey, Philadelphia (4) | 25 | 19 |
| John Flynn, Chicago (1) | 24 | 6 |
| Bill Stemmeyer, Boston (5) | 22 | 18 |
| **1887 (11)** | | |
| John Clarkson, Chicago (3) | 38 | 21 |
| Tim Keefe, New York (4) | 35 | 19 |
| Charlie Getzien, Detroit (1) | 29 | 13 |
| Dan Casey, Philadelphia (2) | 28 | 13 |
| Pud Galvin, Pittsburgh (6) | 28 | 21 |
| Jim Whitney, Washington (7) | 24 | 21 |
| Hoss Radbourn, Boston (5) | 24 | 23 |
| Mickey Welch, New York (4) | 22 | 15 |
| Michael Madden, Boston (5) | 22 | 14 |
| Charlie Ferguson, Philadelphia (2) | 21 | 10 |
| Charlie Buffinton, Philadelphia (2) | 21 | 17 |
| **1888 (8)** | | |
| Tim Keefe, New York (1) | 35 | 12 |
| John Clarkson, Boston (4) | 33 | 20 |
| Pete Conway, Detroit (5) | 30 | 14 |
| Ed Morris, Pittsburgh (6) | 29 | 23 |
| Charlie Buffinton, Philadelphia (3) | 28 | 17 |
| Mickey Welch, New York (1) | 26 | 19 |
| Gus Krock, Chicago (2) | 25 | 14 |
| Pud Galvin, Pittsburgh (6) | 23 | 25 |
| **1889 (10)** | | |
| John Clarkson, Boston (2) | 49 | 19 |
| Tim Keefe, New York (1) | 28 | 13 |
| Mickey Welch, New York (1) | 27 | 12 |
| Charlie Buffinton, Philadelphia (4) | 26 | 17 |
| Pud Galvin, Pittsburgh (5) | 23 | 16 |
| John O'Brien, Cleveland (6) | 22 | 17 |
| Harry Staley, Pittsburgh (5) | 21 | 26 |
| Hoss Radbourn, Boston (2) | 20 | 11 |
| Ed Beatin, Cleveland (6) | 20 | 14 |
| Henry Boyle, Indianapolis (7) | 20 | 23 |
| **1890 (13)** | | |
| Bill Hutchison, Chicago (2) | 42 | 25 |
| Kid Gleason, Philadelphia (3) | 38 | 16 |
| Tom Lovett, Brooklyn (1) | 32 | 11 |
| Amos Rusie, New York (6) | 29 | 30 |
| Billy Rhines, Cincinnati (4) | 28 | 17 |
| Kid Nichols, Boston (5) | 27 | 19 |
| John Clarkson, Boston (5) | 26 | 18 |
| Adonis Terry, Brooklyn (1) | 25 | 16 |
| Bob Caruthers, Brooklyn (1) | 23 | 11 |
| Charlie Getzien, Boston (5) | 23 | 17 |
| Tom Vickery, Philadelphia (3) | 22 | 23 |
| Ed Beatin, Cleveland (7) | 22 | 31 |
| Pat Luby, Chicago (2) | 21 | 9 |
| **1891 (12)** | | |
| Bill Hutchison, Chicago (2) | 43 | 19 |
| John Clarkson, Boston (1) | 33 | 19 |
| Amos Rusie, New York (3) | 32 | 19 |
| Kid Nichols, Boston (1) | 30 | 17 |
| Cy Young, Cleveland (5) | 27 | 20 |
| Harry Staley, 4-5 Pittsburgh (8), 20-8 Boston (1) | 24 | 13 |
| Kid Gleason, Philadelphia (4) | 24 | 19 |
| Tony Mullane, Cincinnati (7) | 24 | 25 |
| John Ewing, New York (3) | 22 | 8 |
| Tom Lovett, Brooklyn (6) | 21 | 20 |
| Mark Baldwin, Pittsburgh (8) | 21 | 27 |
| Charles Esper, Philadelphia (4) | 20 | 14 |

| 1892 (22) | W | L |
|---|---|---|
| Bill Hutchison, Chicago (7) | 37 | 34 |
| Cy Young, Cleveland (2) | 36 | 11 |
| Kid Nichols, Boston (1) | 35 | 16 |
| Jack Stivetts, Boston (1) | 35 | 16 |
| George Haddock, Brooklyn (3) | 31 | 13 |
| Amos Rusie, New York (8) | 31 | 28 |
| Frank Killen, Washington (10) | 30 | 23 |
| George Cuppy, Cleveland (2) | 28 | 12 |
| Gus Weyhing, Philadelphia (4) | 28 | 18 |
| Mark Baldwin, Pittsburgh (6) | 27 | 20 |
| Ed Stein, Brooklyn (3) | 26 | 16 |
| John Clarkson, 8-6 Boston (1), 17-10 Cleveland (2) | 25 | 16 |
| Ad Gumbert, Chicago (7) | 23 | 21 |
| Harry Staley, Boston (1) | 22 | 10 |
| Charles King, New York (8) | 22 | 24 |
| Tony Mullane, Cincinnati (5) | 21 | 10 |
| Adonis Terry 2-4, Baltimore (12), 19-6 Pittsburgh (6) | 21 | 10 |
| Frank Dwyer 3-11, St. Louis (11), 18-8 Cincinnati (5) | 21 | 19 |
| Scott Stratton, Louisville (9) | 21 | 19 |
| Elton Chamberlain, Cincinnati (5) | 20 | 22 |
| Kid Gleason, St. Louis (11) | 20 | 24 |
| John McMahon, Baltimore (12) | 20 | 25 |
| **1893 (8)** | | |
| Frank Killen, Pittsburgh (2) | 36 | 14 |
| Kid Nichols, Boston (1) | 34 | 14 |
| Cy Young, Cleveland (3) | 32 | 16 |
| Amos Rusie, New York (5) | 29 | 18 |
| William Kennedy, Brooklyn (6T) | 26 | 19 |
| John McMahon, Baltimore (8) | 24 | 16 |
| Gus Weyhing, Philadelphia (4) | 24 | 16 |
| Jack Stivetts, Boston (1) | 20 | 12 |
| **1894 (13)** | | |
| Amos Rusie, New York (2) | 36 | 13 |
| Jouett Meekin, New York (2) | 34 | 9 |
| Kid Nichols, Boston (3) | 32 | 13 |
| Ted Breitenstein, St. Louis (9) | 27 | 22 |
| Jack Stivetts, Boston (3) | 26 | 14 |
| John McMahon, Baltimore (1) | 25 | 8 |
| Ed Stein, Brooklyn (5) | 25 | 15 |
| Cy Young, Cleveland (6) | 25 | 22 |
| George Cuppy, Cleveland (6) | 23 | 17 |
| John B. Taylor, Philadelphia (4) | 22 | 11 |
| William Kennedy, Brooklyn (5) | 22 | 20 |
| Clark Griffith, Chicago (8) | 21 | 11 |
| Frank Dwyer, Cincinnati (10) | 20 | 18 |
| **1895 (13)** | | |
| Cy Young, Cleveland (2) | 35 | 10 |
| Emerson Hawley, Pittsburgh (7) | 32 | 21 |
| Bill Hoffer, Baltimore (1) | 30 | 7 |
| John B. Taylor, Philadelphia (3) | 26 | 13 |
| Kid Carsey, Philadelphia (3) | 26 | 15 |
| Kid Nichols, Boston (5T) | 26 | 16 |
| Clark Griffith, Chicago (4) | 25 | 13 |
| George Cuppy, Cleveland (2) | 25 | 15 |
| Adonis Terry, Chicago (4) | 23 | 13 |
| Amos Rusie, New York (9) | 22 | 21 |
| George Hemming, Baltimore (1) | 20 | 10 |
| Billy Rhines, Cincinnati (8) | 20 | 10 |
| Ted Breitenstein, St. Louis (11) | 20 | 29 |
| **1896 (12)** | | |
| Kid Nichols, Boston (4) | 30 | 14 |
| Frank Killen, Pittsburgh (6) | 29 | 15 |
| Cy Young, Cleveland (2) | 29 | 16 |
| Bill Hoffer, Baltimore (1) | 26 | 7 |
| Jouett Meekin, New York (7) | 26 | 13 |
| Frank Dwyer, Cincinnati (3) | 25 | 10 |
| George Cuppy, Cleveland (2) | 25 | 15 |
| George Mercer, Washington (9T) | 25 | 19 |
| Clark Griffith, Chicago (5) | 22 | 13 |
| Jack Stivetts, Boston (4) | 22 | 14 |
| John B. Taylor, Philadelphia (8) | 21 | 20 |
| Emerson Hawley, Pittsburgh (6) | 21 | 21 |
| **1897 (13)** | | |
| Kid Nichols, Boston (1) | 31 | 11 |
| Amos Rusie, New York (3) | 29 | 8 |
| Fred Klobedanz, Boston (1) | 26 | 7 |
| Joe Corbett, Baltimore (2) | 24 | 8 |
| George Mercer, Washington (6T) | 24 | 21 |
| Ted Breitenstein, Cincinnati (4) | 23 | 12 |
| Bill Hoffer, Baltimore (2) | 22 | 10 |
| Ed Lewis, Boston (1) | 21 | 12 |
| Cy Young, Cleveland (5) | 21 | 18 |
| Clark Griffith, Chicago (9) | 21 | 19 |
| Jerry Nops, Baltimore (2) | 20 | 7 |
| Jouett Meekin, New York (3) | 20 | 11 |
| Cy Seymour, New York (3) | 20 | 14 |
| **1898 (17)** | | |
| Kid Nichols, Boston (1) | 31 | 12 |
| Bert Cunningham, Louisville (9) | 28 | 15 |
| James McJames, Baltimore (2) | 27 | 14 |
| Ed Lewis, Boston (1) | 26 | 8 |
| Clark Griffith, Chicago (4) | 26 | 10 |
| Emerson Hawley, Cincinnati (3) | 26 | 12 |
| Vic Willis, Boston (1) | 25 | 13 |
| Cy Young, Cleveland (5) | 25 | 14 |
| Cy Seymour, New York (7) | 25 | 17 |
| Wiley Piatt, Philadelphia (6) | 24 | 14 |

| | W | L |
|---|---|---|
| **1898 (17)** | | |
| Jesse Tannehill, Pittsburgh (8) | 24 | 14 |
| Jack Powell, Cleveland (5) | 24 | 15 |
| Jim Hughes, Baltimore (2) | 21 | 11 |
| Ted Breitenstein, Cincinnati (3) | 21 | 14 |
| Al Maul, Baltimore (2) | 20 | 7 |
| Amos Rusie, New York (7) | 20 | 10 |
| Jim Callahan, Chicago (4) | 20 | 11 |
| **1899 (17)** | | |
| Jim Hughes, Brooklyn (1) | 28 | 6 |
| Joe McGinnity, Baltimore (4) | 28 | 17 |
| Vic Willis, Boston (2) | 27 | 8 |
| Cy Young, St. Louis (5) | 26 | 15 |
| Frank Hahn, Cincinnati (6) | 23 | 7 |
| Jim Callahan, Chicago (8) | 23 | 12 |
| Jesse Tannehill, Pittsburgh (7) | 20 | 11 |
| Wiley Piatt, Philadelphia (3) | 23 | 15 |
| Jack Powell, St. Louis (5) | 23 | 21 |
| Frank Donahue, Philadelphia (3) | 22 | 7 |
| Clark Griffith, Chicago (8) | 22 | 13 |
| Jack Dunn, Brooklyn (1) | 21 | 12 |
| Charles Fraser, Philadelphia (3) | 21 | 13 |
| Kid Nichols, Boston (2) | 21 | 19 |
| Frank Kitson, Baltimore (4) | 20 | 16 |
| Deacon Phillippe, Louisville (9) | 20 | 17 |
| Sam Leever, Pittsburgh (7) | 20 | 23 |
| **1900 (5)** | | |
| Joe McGinnity, Brooklyn (1) | 29 | 9 |
| William Kennedy, Brooklyn (1) | 22 | 15 |
| Bill Dinneen, Boston (4) | 21 | 15 |
| Jesse Tannehill, Pittsburgh (2) | 20 | 7 |
| Cy Young, St. Louis (5T) | 20 | 18 |
| **1901 (9)** | | |
| Bill Donovan, Brooklyn (3) | 25 | 15 |
| Deacon Phillippe, Pittsburgh (1) | 22 | 12 |
| Frank Hahn, Cincinnati (8) | 22 | 19 |
| Jack Chesbro, Pittsburgh (1) | 21 | 9 |
| Al Orth, Philadelphia (2) | 20 | 12 |
| Jack Harper, St. Louis (4) | 20 | 12 |
| Frank Donahue, Philadelphia (2) | 20 | 13 |
| Christy Mathewson, New York (7) | 20 | 17 |
| Vic Willis, Boston (5) | 20 | 17 |
| **1902 (7)** | | |
| Jack Chesbro, Pittsburgh (1) | 28 | 6 |
| Charlie Pittinger, Boston (3) | 27 | 16 |
| Vic Willis, Boston (3) | 27 | 20 |
| John W. Taylor, Chicago (5) | 22 | 10 |
| Frank Hahn, Cincinnati (4) | 22 | 12 |
| Jesse Tannehill, Pittsburgh (1) | 20 | 6 |
| Deacon Phillippe, Pittsburgh (1) | 20 | 9 |
| **1903 (9)** | | |
| Joe McGinnity, New York (2) | 31 | 20 |
| Christy Mathewson, New York (2) | 30 | 13 |
| Sam Leever, Pittsburgh (1) | 25 | 7 |
| Deacon Phillippe, Pittsburgh (1) | 25 | 9 |
| Frank Hahn, Cincinnati (4) | 22 | 12 |
| Henry Schmidt, Brooklyn (5) | 22 | 13 |
| John W. Taylor, Chicago (3) | 21 | 14 |
| Jacob Weimer, Chicago (3) | 20 | 8 |
| Bob Wicker, 0-0 St. Louis (8), 20-9 Chicago (3) | 20 | 9 |
| **1904 (7)** | | |
| Joe McGinnity, New York (1) | 35 | 8 |
| Christy Mathewson, New York (1) | 33 | 12 |
| Jack Harper, Cincinnati (3) | 23 | 9 |
| Kid Nichols, St. Louis (5) | 21 | 13 |
| Luther Taylor, New York (1) | 21 | 15 |
| Jacob Weimer, Chicago (2) | 20 | 14 |
| John W. Taylor, St. Louis (5) | 20 | 19 |
| **1905 (8)** | | |
| Christy Mathewson, New York(1) | 31 | 9 |
| Charlie Pittinger, Philadelphia (4) | 23 | 14 |
| Leon Ames, New York (1) | 22 | 8 |
| Joe McGinnity, New York (1) | 21 | 15 |
| Sam Leever, Pittsburgh (2) | 20 | 5 |
| Bob Ewing, Cincinnati (5) | 20 | 11 |
| Deacon Phillippe, Pittsburgh (2) | 20 | 13 |
| Irv Young, Boston (7) | 20 | 21 |
| **1906 (8)** | | |
| Joe McGinnity, New York (2) | 27 | 12 |
| Mordecai Brown, Chicago (1) | 26 | 6 |
| Vic Willis, Pittsburgh (3) | 23 | 13 |
| Sam Leever, Pittsburgh (3) | 22 | 7 |
| Christy Mathewson, New York (2) | 22 | 12 |
| Jack Pfiester, Chicago (1) | 20 | 8 |
| John W. Taylor, 8-9 St. Louis (7), 12-3 Chicago (1) | 20 | 12 |
| Jacob Weimer, Cincinnati (6) | 20 | 14 |
| **1907 (6)** | | |
| Christy Mathewson, New York (4) | 24 | 12 |
| Orval Overall, Chicago (1) | 23 | 8 |
| Frank Sparks, Philadelphia (3) | 22 | 8 |
| Vic Willis, Pittsburgh (2) | 21 | 11 |
| Mordecai Brown, Chicago (1) | 20 | 6 |
| Lefty Leifield, Pittsburgh (2) | 20 | 16 |
| **1908 (7)** | | |
| Christy Mathewson, New York (2T) | 37 | 11 |
| **1908 (7)** | | |
| Mordecai Brown, Chicago (1) | 29 | 9 |
| Ed Reulbach, Chicago (1) | 24 | 7 |
| Nick Maddox, Pittsburgh (2T) | 23 | 8 |
| Vic Willis, Pittsburgh (2T) | 23 | 11 |
| George Wiltse, New York (2T) | 23 | 14 |
| George McQuillan, Philadelphia (4) | 23 | 17 |
| **1909 (6)** | | |
| Mordecai Brown, Chicago (2) | 27 | 9 |
| Howie Camnitz, Pittsburgh (1) | 25 | 6 |
| Christy Mathewson, New York (3) | 25 | 6 |
| Vic Willis, Pittsburgh (1) | 22 | 11 |
| George Wiltse, New York (3) | 20 | 11 |
| Orval Overall, Chicago (2) | 20 | 11 |
| **1910 (5)** | | |
| Christy Mathewson, New York (2) | 27 | 9 |
| Mordecai Brown, Chicago (1) | 25 | 14 |
| Earl Moore, Philadelphia (4) | 22 | 15 |
| Leonard Cole, Chicago (1) | 20 | 4 |
| George Suggs, Cincinnati (5) | 20 | 12 |
| **1911 (8)** | | |
| Grover Alexander, Philadelphia (4) | 28 | 13 |
| Christy Mathewson, New York (1) | 26 | 13 |
| Rube Marquard, New York (1) | 24 | 7 |
| Bob Harmon, St. Louis (5) | 23 | 16 |
| Babe Adams, Pittsburgh (3) | 22 | 12 |
| George Rucker, Brooklyn (7) | 22 | 18 |
| Mordecai Brown, Chicago (2) | 21 | 11 |
| Howie Camnitz, Pittsburgh (3) | 20 | 15 |
| **1912 (5)** | | |
| Larry Cheney, Chicago (3) | 26 | 10 |
| Rube Marquard, New York (1) | 26 | 11 |
| Claude Hendrix, Pittsburgh (2) | 24 | 9 |
| Christy Mathewson, New York (1) | 23 | 12 |
| Howie Camnitz, Pittsburgh (2) | 22 | 12 |
| **1913 (7)** | | |
| Tom Seaton, Philadelphia (2) | 27 | 12 |
| Christy Mathewson, New York (1) | 25 | 11 |
| Rube Marquard, New York (1) | 23 | 10 |
| Grover Alexander, Philadelphia (2) | 22 | 8 |
| Jeff Tesreau, New York (1) | 22 | 13 |
| Babe Adams, Pittsburgh (4) | 21 | 10 |
| Larry Cheney, Chicago (3) | 21 | 14 |
| **1914 (9)** | | |
| Grover Alexander, Philadelphia (6) | 27 | 15 |
| Dick Rudolph, Boston (1) | 26 | 10 |
| Bill James, Boston (1) | 26 | 7 |
| Jeff Tesreau, New York (2) | 26 | 10 |
| Christy Mathewson, New York (2) | 24 | 13 |
| Jeff Pfeffer, Brooklyn (5) | 23 | 12 |
| Hippo Vaughn, Chicago (4) | 21 | 13 |
| Erskine Mayer, Philadelphia (6) | 21 | 19 |
| Larry Cheney, Chicago (4) | 20 | 18 |
| **1915 (5)** | | |
| Grover Alexander, Philadelphia (1) | 31 | 10 |
| Dick Rudolph, Boston (2) | 22 | 19 |
| Al Mamaux, Pittsburgh (5) | 21 | 8 |
| Erskine Mayer, Philadelphia (1) | 21 | 15 |
| Hippo Vaughn, Chicago (4) | 20 | 12 |
| **1916 (4)** | | |
| Grover Alexander, Philadelphia (2) | 33 | 12 |
| Jeff Pfeffer, Brooklyn (1) | 25 | 11 |
| Eppa Rixey, Philadelphia (2) | 22 | 10 |
| Al Mamaux, Pittsburgh (6) | 21 | 15 |
| **1917 (5)** | | |
| Grover Alexander, Philadelphia (2) | 30 | 13 |
| Fred Toney, Cincinnati (4) | 24 | 16 |
| Hippo Vaughn, Chicago (5) | 23 | 13 |
| Ferdie Schupp, New York (1) | 21 | 7 |
| Pete Schneider, Cincinnati (4) | 20 | 19 |
| **1918 (2)** | | |
| Hippo Vaughn, Chicago (1) | 22 | 10 |
| Claude Hendrix, Chicago (1) | 20 | 7 |
| **1919 (3)** | | |
| Jesse Barnes, New York (2) | 25 | 9 |
| Harry Sallee, Cincinnati (1) | 21 | 7 |
| Hippo Vaughn, Chicago (3) | 21 | 14 |
| **1920 (7)** | | |
| Grover Alexander, Chicago (5T) | 27 | 14 |
| Wilbur Cooper, Pittsburgh (4) | 24 | 15 |
| Burleigh Grimes, Brooklyn (1) | 23 | 11 |
| Fred Toney, New York (2) | 21 | 11 |
| Art Nehf, New York (2) | 21 | 12 |
| Bill Doak, St. Louis (5T) | 20 | 12 |
| Jesse Barnes, New York (2) | 20 | 15 |
| **1921 (4)** | | |
| Burleigh Grimes, Brooklyn (5) | 22 | 13 |
| Wilbur Cooper, Pittsburgh (2) | 22 | 14 |
| Art Nehf, New York (1) | 20 | 10 |
| Joe Oeschger, Boston (4) | 20 | 14 |
| **1922 (3)** | | |
| Eppa Rixey, Cincinnati (2) | 25 | 13 |
| Wilbur Cooper, Pittsburgh (3T) | 23 | 14 |

| | W | L |
|---|---|---|
| **1922 (3)** | | |
| Walt Ruether, Brooklyn (6) | 21 | 12 |
| **1923 (7)** | | |
| Dolf Luque, Cincinnati (2) | 27 | 8 |
| Johnny Morrison, Pittsburgh (3) | 25 | 13 |
| Grover Alexander, Chicago (4) | 22 | 12 |
| Pete Donohue, Cincinnati (2) | 21 | 15 |
| Burleigh Grimes, Brooklyn (6) | 21 | 18 |
| Jesse Haines, St. Louis (5) | 20 | 13 |
| Eppa Rixey, Cincinnati (2) | 20 | 15 |
| **1924 (4)** | | |
| Dazzy Vance, Brooklyn (2) | 28 | 6 |
| Burleigh Grimes, Brooklyn (2) | 22 | 13 |
| Carl Mays, Cincinnati (4) | 20 | 9 |
| Wilbur Cooper, Pittsburgh (3) | 20 | 14 |
| **1925 (3)** | | |
| Dazzy Vance, Brooklyn (6T) | 22 | 9 |
| Eppa Rixey, Cincinnati (3) | 21 | 11 |
| Pete Donohue, Cincinnati (3) | 21 | 14 |
| **1926 (4)** | | |
| Remy Kremer, Pittsburgh (3) | 20 | 6 |
| Flint Rhem, St. Louis (1) | 20 | 7 |
| Lee Meadows, Pittsburgh (3) | 20 | 9 |
| Pete Donohue, Cincinnati (2) | 20 | 14 |
| **1927 (4)** | | |
| Charlie Root, Chicago (4) | 26 | 15 |
| Jesse Haines, St. Louis (2) | 24 | 10 |
| Carmen Hill, Pittsburgh (1) | 22 | 11 |
| Grover Alexander, St. Louis (2) | 21 | 10 |
| **1928 (6)** | | |
| Larry Benton, New York (2) | 25 | 9 |
| Burleigh Grimes, Pittsbrugh (4) | 25 | 14 |
| Dazzy Vance, Brooklyn (6) | 22 | 10 |
| Bill Sherdel, St. Louis (1) | 21 | 10 |
| Jesse Haines, St. Louis (1) | 20 | 8 |
| Fred Fitzsimmons, New York (2) | 20 | 9 |
| **1929 (1)** | | |
| Pat Malone, Chicago (1) | 22 | 10 |
| **1930 (2)** | | |
| Pat Malone, Chicago (2) | 20 | 9 |
| Remy Kremer, Pittsburgh (5) | 20 | 12 |
| **1931 (0)** | | |
| Jumbo Elliott, Philadelphia, Bill Hallahan, St. Louis, and Heinie Meine, Pittsburgh, each had 19 wins. | | |
| **1932 (2)** | | |
| Lon Warneke, Chicago (1) | 22 | 6 |
| Watty Clark, Brooklyn (3) | 20 | 12 |
| **1933 (4)** | | |
| Carl Hubbell, New York (1) | 23 | 12 |
| Ben Cantwell, Boston (4) | 20 | 10 |
| Guy Bush, Chicago (3) | 20 | 12 |
| Dizzy Dean, St. Louis (5) | 20 | 18 |
| **1934 (4)** | | |
| Dizzy Dean, St. Louis (1) | 30 | 7 |
| Hal Schumacher, New York (2) | 23 | 10 |
| Lon Warneke, Chicago (3) | 22 | 10 |
| Carl Hubbell, New York (2) | 21 | 12 |
| **1935 (5)** | | |
| Dizzy Dean, St. Louis (2) | 28 | 12 |
| Carl Hubbell, New York (3) | 23 | 12 |
| Paul Derringer, Cincinnati (6) | 22 | 13 |
| Bill Lee, Chicago (1) | 20 | 6 |
| Lon Warneke, Chicago (1) | 20 | 13 |
| **1936 (2)** | | |
| Carl Hubbell, New York (1) | 26 | 6 |
| Dizzy Dean, St. Louis (2T) | 24 | 13 |
| **1937 (4)** | | |
| Carl Hubbell, New York (1) | 22 | 8 |
| Cliff Melton, New York (1) | 20 | 9 |
| Lou Fette, Boston (5) | 20 | 10 |
| Jim Turner, Boston (5) | 20 | 11 |
| **1938 (2)** | | |
| Bill Lee, Chicago (1) | 22 | 9 |
| Paul Derringer, Cincinnati (4) | 21 | 14 |
| **1939 (4)** | | |
| Bucky Walters, Cincinnati (1) | 27 | 11 |
| Paul Derringer, Cincinnati (1) | 25 | 7 |
| Curt Davis, St. Louis (2) | 22 | 16 |
| Luke Hamlin, Brooklyn (3) | 20 | 13 |
| **1940 (3)** | | |
| Bucky Walters, Cincinnati (1) | 22 | 10 |
| Paul Derringer, Cincinnati (1) | 20 | 12 |
| Claude Passeau, Chicago (5) | 20 | 13 |
| **1941 (2)** | | |
| Kirby Higbe, Brooklyn (1) | 22 | 9 |
| Whit Wyatt, Brooklyn (1) | 22 | 10 |
| **1942 (2)** | | |
| Mort Cooper, St. Louis (1) | 22 | 7 |
| Johnny Beazley, St. Louis (1) | 21 | 6 |
| **1943 (3)** | | |
| Mort Cooper, St. Louis (1) | 21 | 8 |
| Rip Sewell, Pittsburgh (4) | 21 | 9 |
| Elmer Riddle, Cincinnati (2) | 21 | 11 |
| **1944 (4)** | | |
| Bucky Walters, Cincinnati (3) | 23 | 8 |
| Mort Cooper, St. Louis (1) | 22 | 7 |
| **1944 (4)** | | |
| Rip Sewell, Pittsburgh (2) | 21 | 12 |
| Bill Voiselle, New York (5) | 21 | 16 |
| **1945 (2)** | | |
| Red Barrett, 2-3 Boston (6), 21-9 St. Louis (2) | 23 | 12 |
| Hank Wyse, Chicago (1) | 22 | 10 |
| **1946 (2)** | | |
| Howie Pollet, St. Louis (1) | 21 | 10 |
| Johnny Sain, Boston (4) | 20 | 14 |
| **1947 (5)** | | |
| Ewell Blackwell, Cincinnati (5) | 22 | 8 |
| Larry Jansen, New York (4) | 21 | 5 |
| Warren Spahn, Boston (3) | 21 | 10 |
| Ralph Branca, Brooklyn (1) | 21 | 12 |
| Johnny Sain, Boston (3) | 21 | 12 |
| **1948 (2)** | | |
| Johnny Sain, Boston (1) | 24 | 15 |
| Harry Brecheen, St. Louis (2) | 20 | 7 |
| **1949 (2)** | | |
| Warren Spahn, Boston (4) | 21 | 14 |
| Howie Pollet, St. Louis (2) | 20 | 9 |
| **1950 (3)** | | |
| Warren Spahn, Boston (4) | 21 | 17 |
| Robin Roberts, Philadelphia (1) | 20 | 11 |
| Johnny Sain, Boston (4) | 20 | 13 |
| **1951 (7)** | | |
| Sal Maglie, New York (1) | 23 | 6 |
| Larry Jansen, New York (1) | 23 | 11 |
| Preacher Roe, Brooklyn (2) | 22 | 3 |
| Warren Spahn, Boston (4) | 22 | 14 |
| Robin Roberts, Philadelphia (5) | 21 | 15 |
| Don Newcombe, Brooklyn (2) | 20 | 9 |
| Murry Dickson, Pittsburgh (7) | 20 | 16 |
| **1952 (1)** | | |
| Robin Roberts, Philadelphia (4) | 28 | 7 |
| **1953 (4)** | | |
| Warren Spahn, Milwaukee (2) | 23 | 7 |
| Robin Roberts, Philadelphia (3T) | 23 | 16 |
| Carl Erskine, Brooklyn (1) | 20 | 6 |
| Harvey Haddix, St. Louis (3T) | 20 | 9 |
| **1954 (3)** | | |
| Robin Roberts, Philadelphia (4) | 23 | 15 |
| Johnny Antonelli, New York (1) | 21 | 7 |
| Warren Spahn, Milwaukee (3) | 21 | 12 |
| **1955 (2)** | | |
| Robin Roberts, Philadelphia (4) | 23 | 14 |
| Don Newcombe, Brooklyn (1) | 20 | 5 |
| **1956 (3)** | | |
| Don Newcombe, Brooklyn (1) | 27 | 7 |
| Warren Spahn, Milwaukee (2) | 20 | 11 |
| Johnny Antonelli, New York (6) | 20 | 13 |
| **1957 (1)** | | |
| Warren Spahn, Milwaukee (1) | 21 | 11 |
| **1958 (3)** | | |
| Warren Spahn, Milwaukee (1) | 22 | 11 |
| Bob Friend, Pittsburgh (2) | 22 | 14 |
| Lew Burdette, Milwaukee (1) | 20 | 10 |
| **1959 (3)** | | |
| Lew Burdette, Milwaukee (2) | 21 | 15 |
| Warren Spahn, Milwaukee (2) | 21 | 15 |
| Sam Jones, San Francisco (3) | 21 | 15 |
| **1960 (3)** | | |
| Ernie Broglio, St. Louis (3) | 21 | 9 |
| Warren Spahn, Milwaukee (2) | 21 | 10 |
| Vernon Law, Pittsburgh (1) | 20 | 9 |
| **1961 (2)** | | |
| Joey Jay, Cincinnati (1) | 21 | 10 |
| Warren Spahn, Milwaukee (4) | 21 | 13 |
| **1962 (4)** | | |
| Don Drysdale, Los Angeles (2) | 25 | 9 |
| Jack Sanford, San Francisco (1) | 24 | 7 |
| Bob Purkey, Cincinnati (3) | 23 | 5 |
| Joey Jay, Cincinnati (3) | 21 | 14 |
| **1963 (5)** | | |
| Sandy Koufax, Los Angeles (1) | 25 | 5 |
| Juan Marichal, San Francisco (3) | 25 | 8 |
| Jim Maloney, Cincinnati (5) | 23 | 7 |
| Warren Spahn, Milwaukee (6) | 23 | 7 |
| Dick Ellsworth, Chicago (7) | 22 | 10 |
| **1964 (3)** | | |
| Larry Jackson, Chicago (8) | 24 | 11 |
| Juan Marichal, San Francisco (4) | 21 | 8 |
| Ray Sadecki, St. Louis (1) | 20 | 11 |
| **1965 (7)** | | |
| Sandy Koufax, Los Angeles (1) | 26 | 8 |
| Tony Cloninger, Milwaukee (5) | 24 | 11 |
| Don Drysdale, Los Angeles (1) | 23 | 12 |
| Sammy Ellis, Cincinnati (4) | 22 | 10 |
| Juan Marichal, San Francisco (2) | 22 | 13 |
| Jim Maloney, Cincinnati (4) | 20 | 9 |
| Bob Gibson, St. Louis (7) | 20 | 12 |
| **1966 (5)** | | |
| Sandy Koufax, Los Angeles (1) | 27 | 9 |
| Juan Marichal, San Francisco (2) | 25 | 6 |
| Gaylord Perry, San Francisco (2) | 21 | 8 |

| | W | L |
|---|---|---|
| **1966 (5)** | | |
| Bob Gibson, St. Louis (6) | 21 | 12 |
| Chris Short, Philadelphia (4) | 20 | 10 |
| **1967 (2)** | | |
| Mike McCormick, San Francisco (2) | 22 | 10 |
| Ferguson Jenkins, Chicago (3) | 20 | 13 |
| **1968 (3)** | | |
| Juan Marichal, San Francisco (2) | 26 | 9 |
| Bob Gibson, St. Louis (1) | 22 | 9 |
| Ferguson Jenkins, Chicago (3) | 20 | 15 |
| **1969 (9)** | | |
| Tom Seaver, New York (1E) | 25 | 7 |
| Phil Niekro, Atlanta (1W) | 23 | 13 |
| Juan Marichal, San Francisco (2W) | 21 | 11 |
| Ferguson Jenkins, Chicago (2E) | 21 | 15 |
| Bill Singer, Los Angeles (4W) | 20 | 12 |
| Larry Dierker, Houston (5W) | 20 | 13 |
| Bob Gibson, St. Louis (4E) | 20 | 13 |
| Bill Hands, Chicago (2E) | 20 | 14 |
| Claude Osteen, Los Angeles (4W) | 20 | 15 |
| **1970 (4)** | | |
| Bob Gibson, St. Louis (4E) | 23 | 7 |
| Gaylord Perry, San Francisco (3W) | 23 | 13 |
| Ferguson Jenkins, Chicago (2E) | 22 | 16 |
| Jim Merritt, Cincinnati (1W) | 20 | 12 |
| **1971 (4)** | | |
| Ferguson Jenkins, Chicago (3ET) | 24 | 13 |
| Al Downing, Los Angeles (2W) | 20 | 9 |
| Steve Carlton, St. Louis (2E) | 20 | 9 |
| Tom Seaver, New York (3ET) | 20 | 10 |
| **1972 (4)** | | |
| Steve Carlton, Philadelphia (6E) | 27 | 10 |
| Tom Seaver, New York (3E) | 21 | 12 |
| Claude Osteen, Los Angeles (3W) | 20 | 11 |
| Ferguson Jenkins, Chicago (2E) | 20 | 12 |
| **1973 (1)** | | |
| Ron Bryant, San Francisco (3W) | 24 | 12 |
| **1974 (2)** | | |
| Andy Messersmith, Los Angeles (1W) | 20 | 6 |
| Phil Niekro, Atlanta (3W) | 20 | 13 |
| **1975 (2)** | | |
| Tom Seaver, New York (3ET) | 22 | 9 |
| Randy Jones, San Diego (4W) | 20 | 12 |
| **1976 (5)** | | |
| Randy Jones, San Diego (5W) | 22 | 14 |
| Jerry Koosman, New York (3E) | 21 | 10 |
| Don Sutton, Los Angeles (2W) | 21 | 10 |
| Steve Carlton, Philadelphia (1E) | 20 | 7 |
| J.R. Richard, Houston (3W) | 20 | 15 |
| **1977 (6)** | | |
| Steve Carlton, Philadelphia (1E) | 23 | 10 |
| Tom Seaver, 7-3, New York (6E), 14-3, Cin (2W) | 21 | 6 |
| John Candelaria, Pittsburgh (2E) | 20 | 5 |
| Bob Forsch, St. Louis (3E) | 20 | 7 |
| Tommy John, Los Angeles (1W) | 20 | 7 |
| Rick Reuschel, Chicago (4E) | 20 | 10 |
| **1978 (2)** | | |
| Gaylord Perry, San Diego (3W) | 21 | 6 |
| Ross Grimsley, Montreal (4E) | 20 | 11 |
| **1979 (2)** | | |
| Joe Niekro, Houston (2W) | 21 | 11 |
| Phil Niekro, Atlanta (6W) | 21 | 20 |
| **1980 (2)** | | |
| Steve Carlton, Philadelphia (1E) | 24 | 9 |
| Joe Niekro, Houston (1W) | 20 | 12 |
| **1981 (0)** | | |
| Tom Seaver, Cincinnati, had 14 wins. | | |
| **1982 (1)** | | |
| Steve Carlton, Philadelphia (2E) | 23 | 11 |
| **1983 (0)** | | |
| John Denny, Philadelphia, had 19 wins. | | |
| **1984 (1)** | | |
| Joaquin Andujar, St. Louis (3E) | 20 | 14 |
| **1985 (4)** | | |
| Dwight Gooden, New York (2E) | 24 | 4 |
| John Tudor, St. Louis (1E) | 21 | 8 |
| Joaquin Andujar, St. Louis (1E) | 21 | 12 |
| Tom Browning, Cincinnati (2W) | 20 | 9 |
| **1986 (2)** | | |
| Fernando Valenzuela, Los Angeles (5W) | 21 | 11 |
| Mike Krukow, San Francisco (3W) | 20 | 9 |
| **1987 (0)** | | |
| Rick Sutcliffe, Chicago, had 18 wins. | | |
| **1988 (3)** | | |
| Orel Hershiser, Los Angeles (1W) | 23 | 8 |
| Danny Jackson, Cincinnati (2W) | 23 | 8 |
| David Cone, New York (1E) | 20 | 3 |
| **1989 (1)** | | |
| Mike Scott, Houston (3W) | 20 | 10 |
| **1990 (3)** | | |
| Doug Drabek, Pittsburgh (1E) | 22 | 6 |
| Ramon Martinez, Los Angeles (2W) | 20 | 6 |
| Frank Viola, New York (2E) | 20 | 12 |
| **1991 (2)** | | |
| John Smiley, Pittsburgh (1E) | 20 | 8 |
| Tom Glavine, Atlanta (1W) | 20 | 11 |
| **1992 (2)** | | |
| Tom Glavine, Atlanta (1W) | 20 | 8 |
| Greg Maddux, Chicago (4E) | 20 | 11 |
| **1993 (4)** | | |
| Tom Glavine, Atlanta (1W) | 22 | 6 |
| John Burkett, San Francisco (2W) | 22 | 7 |
| Bill Swift, San Francisco (2W) | 21 | 8 |
| Greg Maddux, Atlanta (1W) | 20 | 10 |
| **1994 (0)** | | |
| Ken Hill, Montreal, and Greg Maddux, Atlanta, each had 16 wins. | | |
| **1995 (0)** | | |
| Greg Maddux, Atlanta, had 19 wins. | | |
| **1996 (1)** | | |
| John Smoltz, Atlanta (1E) | 24 | 8 |
| **1997 (1)** | | |
| Denny Neagle, Atlanta (1E) | 20 | 5 |
| **1998 (1)** | | |
| Tom Glavine, Atlanta (1E) | 20 | 6 |
| **1999 (2)** | | |
| Mike Hampton, Houston (1C) | 22 | 4 |
| Jose Lima, Houston (1C) | 21 | 10 |
| **2000 (2)** | | |
| Tom Glavine, Atlanta (1E) | 21 | 9 |
| Darryl Kile, St. Louis (1C) | 20 | 9 |
| **2001 (4)** | | |
| Curt Schilling, Arizona (1W) | 22 | 6 |
| Matt Morris, St. Louis (2C) | 22 | 8 |
| Randy Johnson, Arizona (1W) | 21 | 6 |
| Jon Lieber, Chicago (3C) | 20 | 6 |
| **2002 (2)** | | |
| Randy Johnson, Arizona (1W) | 24 | 5 |
| Curt Schilling, Arizona (1W) | 23 | 7 |
| **2003 (1)** | | |
| Russ Ortiz, Atlanta (1E) | 21 | 7 |
| **2004 (1)** | | |
| Roy Oswalt, Houston (2C) | 20 | 10 |
| **2005 (3)** | | |
| Dontrelle Willis, Florida (3E) | 22 | 10 |
| Chris Carpenter, St. Louis (1C) | 21 | 5 |
| Roy Oswalt, Houston (2C) | 20 | 12 |

## TWO LEAGUES IN SEASON

| | W | L |
|---|---|---|
| **1884 (4)** | | |
| Billy Taylor, 25-4 St. L UA (1), 18-12 Phil AA (7) | 43 | 16 |
| Charlie Sweeney, 17-7 Prov NL (1), 24-8 St. L UA (1) | 41 | 15 |
| Jim McCormick, 19-22 Clev NL (7), 22-4 Cin UA (2) | 41 | 26 |
| Fred Shaw, 8-18 Detroit NL (8), 22-15 Boston UA (4) | 30 | 33 |
| **1902 (1)** | | |
| Joe McGinnity, 13-10 Bal AL (8), 8-8 NY NL (8) | 21 | 18 |
| **1904 (1)** | | |
| Patsy Flaherty, 2-2 Chi AL (3), 19-9 Pit NL (4) | 21 | 11 |
| **1945 (1)** | | |
| Hank Borowy, 10-5 NY AL (4), 11-2 Chi NL (1) | 21 | 7 |
| **1984 (1)** | | |
| Rick Sutcliffe, 4-5 Clev AL (6E), 16-1 Chi NL (1E) | 20 | 6 |
| **2002 (1)** | | |
| Bartolo Colon, 10-4 Clev AL (3C), 10-4 Mon NL (2E) | 20 | 8 |

# FIELDING

## UNASSISTED TRIPLE PLAYS

Neal Ball, SS, Cleveland AL vs. Boston at Cleveland, July 19, 1909, 1st game, 2nd. Ball caught McConnell's liner, touched 2B, retiring Wagner, who was on his way to 3B, and then tagged Stahl as he came up to 2B.

George H. Burns, 1B, Boston AL vs. Cleveland at Boston, Sept 14, 1923, 2nd. Burns caught Brower's liner, tagged Lutzke off 1B and then ran to 2B and reached that bag before Stephenson could return from 3B.

Ernie Padgett, SS, Boston NL vs. Philadelphia at Boston, October 6, 1923, 2nd game, 4th. Padgett caught Holke's liner, ran to 2B to retire Tierney, then tagged Lee before he could return to 1B.

Glenn Wright, SS, Pittsburgh NL vs. St. Louis at Pittsburgh, May 7, 1925, 9th. Wright caught Bottomley's liner, ran to 2B to retire Cooney and then tagged Hornsby, who was on his way to 2B.

Jimmy E. Cooney, SS Chicago NL vs. Pittsburgh at Pittsburgh, May 30, 1927, a.m. game, 4th. Cooney caught Paul Waner's liner, stepped on 2B to retire Lloyd Waner, then tagged Barnhart off 1B

Johnny Neun, 1B, Detroit AL vs. Cleveland at Detroit, May 31, 1927, 9th. Neun caught Summa's liner, ran over and tagged Jamieson between 1B and 2B and then touched 2B before Myatt could return.

Ron Hansen, SS, Washington AL vs. Cleveland at Cleveland, July 30, 1968, 1st. With the count 3-and-2 on Azcue, Nelson broke for 3B. Hansen caught Azcue's liner, stepped on 2B to double Nelson and then tagged Snyder going into 2B.

Mickey Morandini, 2B, Philadelphia NL vs. Pittsburgh at Pittsburgh, Sept 20, 1992, 6th. Morandini caught King's liner, stepped on 2B to retire Van Slyke, then tagged Bonds coming from 1B.

John Valentin, SS, Boston AL vs. Seattle at Boston, July 8, 1994, 6th. Valentin caught Newfield's line drive, stepped on 2B to retire Blowers, then tagged Mitchell coming from 1B.

Randy Velarde, 2B, Oakland AL vs. New York AL at New York, May 29, 2000, 6th. Velarde caught Spencer's line drive, tagged Posada off 1B, then stepped on 2B to retire Martinez.

Rafael Furcal, SS, Atlanta NL vs. St. Louis at St. Louis, Aug 10, 2003, 5th. Furcal caught Williams' line drive, stepped on 2B to retire Matheny, then tagged Palmeiro coming from 1B

(Note: All above unassisted triple plays made with runners on 1B and 2B bases only. In addition to the 11 regular-season unassisted triple plays, Bill Wambsganss turned one in the 1920 World Series. For details see World Series General Reference section.)

**Total number of occurrences (excluding Wambsganss): 11**



# CLUB MISCELLANEOUS

## ALL-TIME FRANCHISE WON-LOST RECORDS

### CURRENT AMERICAN LEAGUE CLUBS (1901 THROUGH 2005)

| Present franchise | Years | Total Games | Won | Lost | Tied | Pct. |
|---|---|---|---|---|---|---|
| Baltimore | 1954-2005 | 8,225 | 4,280 | 3,933 | 12 | .520 |
| Boston | 1901-2005 | 16,325 | 8,358 | 7,884 | 83 | .515 |
| Chicago | 1901-2005 | 16,333 | 8,210 | 8,020 | 103 | .506 |
| Cleveland | 1901-2005 | 16,339 | 8,302 | 7,946 | 91 | .511 |
| Detroit | 1901-2005 | 16,364 | 8,221 | 8,050 | 93 | .505 |
| Kansas City | 1969-2005 | 5,857 | 2,872 | 2,983 | 2 | .491 |
| Los Angeles (previously California and Anaheim) | 1961-2005 | 7,163 | 3,507 | 3,653 | 3 | .490 |
| Minnesota | 1961-2005 | 7,157 | 3,565 | 3,584 | 8 | .499 |
| New York | 1903-2005 | 16,038 | 9,074 | 6,876 | 88 | .569 |
| Oakland | 1968-2005 | 6,027 | 3,155 | 2,871 | 1 | .524 |
| Seattle | 1977-2005 | 4,575 | 2,149 | 2,424 | 2 | .470 |
| Tampa Bay | 1998-2005 | 1,293 | 518 | 775 | 0 | .401 |
| Texas | 1972-2005 | 5,376 | 2,596 | 2,775 | 5 | .483 |
| Toronto | 1977-2005 | 4,576 | 2,258 | 2,315 | 3 | .494 |
| **Present Totals** | | **131,648** | **67,065** | **64,089** | **494** | **.511** |

### DEFUNCT AMERICAN LEAGUE CLUBS (1901 THROUGH 1997)

| Extinct franchise | Years | Total Games | Won | Lost | Tied | Pct. |
|---|---|---|---|---|---|---|
| Baltimore | 1901-1902 | 276 | 118 | 153 | 5 | .435 |
| Kansas City | 1955-1967 | 2,060 | 829 | 1,224 | 7 | .404 |
| Milwaukee (original club) | 1901 | 139 | 48 | 89 | 2 | .350 |
| Milwaukee (second club) | 1970-1997 | 4,407 | 2,136 | 2,269 | 2 | .485 |
| Philadelphia | 1901-1954 | 8,213 | 3,886 | 4,248 | 79 | .478 |
| St. Louis | 1902-1953 | 7,975 | 3,414 | 4,465 | 96 | .433 |
| Seattle | 1969 | 163 | 64 | 98 | 1 | .395 |
| Washington (original club) | 1901-1960 | 9,188 | 4,223 | 4,864 | 101 | .465 |
| Washington (second club) | 1961-1971 | 1,773 | 740 | 1,032 | 1 | .418 |
| **Extinct totals** | | **34,194** | **15,458** | **18,442** | **294** | **.456** |
| **American League totals** | | **165,842** | **82,523** | **82,531** | **789** | **.500** |

### CURRENT NATIONAL LEAGUE CLUBS (1876 THROUGH 2005)

| Present franchise | Years | Total Games | Won | Lost | Tied | Pct. |
|---|---|---|---|---|---|---|
| Arizona | 1998-2005 | 1,296 | 652 | 644 | 0 | .503 |
| Atlanta | 1966-2005 | 6,345 | 3,269 | 3,068 | 8 | .516 |
| Chicago | 1876-2005 | 19,277 | 9,834 | 9,286 | 157 | .514 |
| Cincinnati | 1890-2005 | 17,906 | 8,971 | 8,808 | 127 | .505 |
| Colorado | 1993-2005 | 2,043 | 949 | 1,094 | 0 | .465 |
| Florida | 1993-2005 | 2,039 | 963 | 1,076 | 0 | .472 |
| Houston | 1962-2005 | 7,005 | 3,497 | 3,503 | 5 | .500 |
| Los Angeles | 1958-2005 | 7,626 | 4,082 | 3,538 | 6 | .536 |
| Milwaukee | 1998-2005 | 1,295 | 561 | 733 | 1 | .434 |
| New York | 1962-2005 | 6,996 | 3,311 | 3,677 | 8 | .474 |
| Philadelphia | 1883-2005 | 18,671 | 8,679 | 9,878 | 114 | .468 |
| Pittsburgh | 1887-2005 | 18,286 | 9,253 | 8,900 | 133 | .510 |
| St. Louis | 1892-2005 | 17,633 | 8,901 | 8,601 | 131 | .509 |
| San Diego | 1969-2005 | 5,869 | 2,693 | 3,174 | 2 | .459 |
| San Francisco | 1958-2005 | 7,626 | 3,970 | 3,650 | 6 | .521 |
| Washington | 2005 | 162 | 81 | 81 | 0 | .500 |
| **Present Totals** | | **140,076** | **69,666** | **69,711** | **698** | **.500** |

NOTE: Totals for the current Milwaukee Brewers franchise include its American League totals in the Extinct American League Clubs chart and its National League totals in the Current National League Clubs.

### DEFUNCT NATIONAL LEAGUE CLUBS (1876 THROUGH 2005)

| Extinct franchise | Years | Total Games | Won | Lost | Tied | Pct. |
|---|---|---|---|---|---|---|
| Baltimore | 1892-1899 | 1,117 | 644 | 447 | 26 | .590 |
| Boston | 1876-1952 | 10,854 | 5,118 | 5,598 | 138 | .478 |
| Brooklyn | 1890-1957 | 10,254 | 5,214 | 4,926 | 114 | .514 |
| Buffalo | 1879-1885 | 656 | 314 | 333 | 9 | .485 |
| Cincinnati | 1876-1880 | 348 | 125 | 217 | 6 | .365 |
| Cleveland | 1879-1884 | 549 | 242 | 299 | 8 | .447 |
| Cleveland | 1889-1899 | 1,534 | 738 | 764 | 32 | .491 |
| Detroit | 1881-1888 | 880 | 426 | 437 | 17 | .494 |
| Hartford | 1876-1877 | 129 | 78 | 48 | 3 | .619 |
| Indianapolis | 1878 | 63 | 24 | 36 | 3 | .400 |
| Indianapolis | 1887-1889 | 398 | 146 | 249 | 3 | .370 |
| Kansas City | 1886 | 126 | 30 | 91 | 5 | .250 |
| Louisville | 1876-1877 | 130 | 65 | 61 | 4 | .516 |
| Louisville | 1892-1899 | 1,124 | 419 | 683 | 22 | .380 |
| Milwaukee | 1878 | 61 | 15 | 45 | 1 | .250 |
| Milwaukee | 1953-1965 | 2,044 | 1,146 | 890 | 8 | .563 |
| Montreal | 1969-2004 | 5,702 | 2,755 | 2,943 | 4 | .484 |
| New York | 1876 | 57 | 21 | 35 | 1 | .375 |
| New York | 1883-1957 | 11,120 | 6,067 | 4,898 | 155 | .553 |

| Extinct franchise | Years | Total Games | Won | Lost | Tied | Pct. |
|---|---|---|---|---|---|---|
| Philadelphia | 1876 | 60 | 14 | 45 | 1 | .237 |
| Providence | 1878-1885 | 725 | 438 | 278 | 9 | .612 |
| St. Louis | 1876-1877 | 124 | 73 | 51 | 0 | .589 |
| St. Louis | 1885-1886 | 237 | 79 | 151 | 7 | .343 |
| Syracuse | 1879 | 71 | 22 | 48 | 1 | .314 |
| Troy | 1879-1882 | 330 | 134 | 191 | 5 | .412 |
| Washington | 1886-1889 | 514 | 163 | 337 | 14 | .326 |
| Washington | 1892-1899 | 1,126 | 410 | 697 | 19 | .370 |
| Worcester | 1880-1882 | 252 | 90 | 159 | 3 | .361 |
| **Extinct totals** | | **50,585** | **25,010** | **24,957** | **618** | **.501** |
| **National League totals** | | **190,662** | **94,677** | **94,669** | **1,316** | **.500** |

## AMERICAN ASSOCIATION CLUBS (1882 THROUGH 1891)

| Franchise | Years | Total Games | Won | Lost | Tied | Pct. |
|---|---|---|---|---|---|---|
| Baltimore | 1882-1891 | 1,121 | 489 | 602 | 30 | .448 |
| Boston | 1891 | 139 | 93 | 42 | 4 | .689 |
| Brooklyn | 1884-1889 | 783 | 410 | 354 | 19 | .537 |
| Brooklyn | 1890 | 100 | 26 | 72 | 2 | .265 |
| Cincinnati | 1882-1889 | 957 | 549 | 396 | 12 | .581 |
| Cincinnati | 1891 | 102 | 43 | 57 | 2 | .430 |
| Cleveland | 1887-1888 | 268 | 89 | 174 | 5 | .338 |
| Columbus | 1883-1884 | 207 | 101 | 104 | 2 | .493 |
| Columbus | 1889-1891 | 418 | 200 | 209 | 9 | .489 |
| Indianapolis | 1884 | 110 | 29 | 78 | 3 | .271 |
| Kansas City | 1888-1889 | 271 | 98 | 171 | 2 | .364 |
| Louisville | 1882-1891 | 1,231 | 574 | 637 | 20 | .474 |
| Milwaukee | 1891 | 36 | 21 | 15 | 0 | .583 |
| New York | 1883-1887 | 592 | 270 | 309 | 13 | .466 |
| Philadelphia | 1882-1890 | 1,076 | 560 | 498 | 18 | .529 |
| Philadelphia | 1891 | 143 | 73 | 66 | 4 | .525 |
| Pittsburgh | 1882-1886 | 538 | 236 | 296 | 6 | .444 |
| Richmond | 1884 | 46 | 12 | 30 | 4 | .286 |
| Rochester | 1890 | 133 | 63 | 63 | 7 | .500 |
| St. Louis | 1882-1891 | 1,233 | 780 | 432 | 21 | .644 |
| Syracuse | 1890 | 128 | 55 | 72 | 1 | .433 |
| Toledo | 1884 | 110 | 46 | 58 | 6 | .442 |
| Toledo | 1890 | 134 | 68 | 64 | 2 | .515 |
| Washington | 1884 | 63 | 12 | 51 | 0 | .190 |
| Washington | 1891 | 139 | 44 | 91 | 4 | .326 |
| **American Association totals** | | **10,078** | **4,941** | **4,941** | **196** | **.500** |

## CLUBS WITH 100 VICTORIES IN SEASON

### AMERICAN LEAGUE

| Year | Club | Won | Lost | Pct. |
|---|---|---|---|---|
| 2001 | Seattle | 116 | 46 | .716 |
| 1998 | New York | 114 | 48 | .704 |
| 1954 | Cleveland | 111 | 43 | .721 |
| 1927 | New York | 110 | 44 | .714 |
| 1961 | New York | 109 | 53 | .673 |
| 1969 | Baltimore | 109 | 53 | .673 |
| 1970 | Baltimore | 108 | 54 | .667 |
| 1931 | Philadelphia | 107 | 45 | .704 |
| 1932 | New York | 107 | 47 | .695 |
| 1939 | New York | 106 | 45 | .702 |
| 1912 | Boston | 105 | 47 | .691 |
| 1929 | Philadelphia | 104 | 46 | .693 |
| 1946 | Boston | 104 | 50 | .675 |
| 1963 | New York | 104 | 57 | .646 |
| 1984 | Detroit | 104 | 58 | .642 |
| 1988 | Oakland | 104 | 58 | .642 |
| 1942 | New York | 103 | 51 | .669 |
| 1954 | New York | 103 | 51 | .669 |
| 2002 | New York | 103 | 58 | .640 |
| 1968 | Detroit | 103 | 59 | .636 |
| 1980 | New York | 103 | 59 | .636 |
| 1990 | Oakland | 103 | 59 | .636 |
| 2002 | Oakland | 103 | 59 | .636 |
| 1910 | Philadelphia | 102 | 48 | .680 |
| 1936 | New York | 102 | 51 | .667 |
| 1930 | Philadelphia | 102 | 52 | .662 |
| 1937 | New York | 102 | 52 | .662 |
| 1979 | Baltimore | 102 | 57 | .642 |
| 1965 | Minnesota | 102 | 60 | .630 |
| 1977 | Kansas City | 102 | 60 | .630 |
| 2001 | Oakland | 102 | 60 | .630 |
| 1911 | Philadelphia | 101 | 50 | .669 |
| 1915 | Boston | 101 | 50 | .669 |
| 1928 | New York | 101 | 53 | .656 |
| 1934 | Detroit | 101 | 53 | .656 |
| 1941 | New York | 101 | 53 | .656 |
| 1971 | Baltimore | 101 | 57 | .639 |
| 1971 | Oakland | 101 | 60 | .627 |
| 1961 | Detroit | 101 | 61 | .623 |
| 2003 | New York | 101 | 61 | .623 |
| 2004 | New York | 101 | 61 | .623 |
| 1995 | Cleveland | 100 | 44 | .694 |
| 1915 | Detroit | 100 | 54 | .649 |
| 1917 | Chicago | 100 | 54 | .649 |
| 1977 | New York | 100 | 62 | .617 |
| 1980 | Baltimore | 100 | 62 | .617 |
| 1978 | New York | 100 | 63 | .613 |

### NATIONAL LEAGUE

| Year | Club | Won | Lost | Pct. |
|---|---|---|---|---|
| 1906 | Chicago | 116 | 36 | .763 |
| 1909 | Pittsburgh | 110 | 42 | .724 |
| 1975 | Cincinnati | 108 | 54 | .667 |
| 1986 | New York | 108 | 54 | .667 |
| 1907 | Chicago | 107 | 45 | .704 |
| 1904 | New York | 106 | 47 | .693 |
| 1942 | St. Louis | 106 | 48 | .688 |
| 1998 | Atlanta | 106 | 56 | .654 |
| 1905 | New York | 105 | 48 | .686 |
| 1943 | St. Louis | 105 | 49 | .682 |
| 1944 | St. Louis | 105 | 49 | .682 |
| 1953 | Brooklyn | 105 | 49 | .682 |
| 2004 | St. Louis | 105 | 47 | .648 |
| 1909 | Chicago | 104 | 49 | .680 |
| 1910 | Chicago | 104 | 50 | .675 |
| 1942 | Brooklyn | 104 | 50 | .675 |
| 1993 | Atlanta | 104 | 58 | .642 |
| 1902 | Pittsburgh | 103 | 36 | .741 |
| 1912 | New York | 103 | 48 | .682 |
| 1993 | San Francisco | 103 | 59 | .636 |
| 1999 | Atlanta | 103 | 59 | .636 |
| 1962 | San Francisco | 103 | 62 | .624 |
| 1898 | Boston | 102 | 47 | .685 |
| 1892 | Boston | 102 | 48 | .680 |
| 1970 | Cincinnati | 102 | 60 | .630 |
| 1998 | Houston | 102 | 60 | .630 |
| 1974 | Los Angeles | 102 | 60 | .630 |
| 1976 | Cincinnati | 102 | 60 | .630 |
| 1962 | Los Angeles | 102 | 63 | .618 |
| 1899 | Brooklyn | 101 | 47 | .682 |
| 1913 | New York | 101 | 51 | .664 |
| 1931 | St. Louis | 101 | 53 | .656 |

| Year | Club | Won | Lost | Pct. |
|---|---|---|---|---|
| 2002 | Atlanta | 101 | 59 | .631 |
| 1967 | St. Louis | 101 | 60 | .627 |
| 1976 | Philadelphia | 101 | 61 | .623 |
| 1977 | Philadelphia | 101 | 61 | .623 |
| 1985 | St. Louis | 101 | 61 | .623 |
| 1997 | Atlanta | 101 | 61 | .623 |
| 2003 | Atlanta | 101 | 61 | .623 |
| 1940 | Cincinnati | 100 | 53 | .654 |
| 1935 | Chicago | 100 | 54 | .649 |
| 1941 | Brooklyn | 100 | 54 | .649 |
| 1988 | New York | 100 | 60 | .625 |
| 2003 | San Francisco | 100 | 61 | .621 |
| 1969 | New York | 100 | 62 | .617 |
| 1999 | Arizona | 100 | 62 | .617 |
| 2005 | St. Louis | 100 | 62 | .617 |

## CLUBS WITH 100 LOSSES IN SEASON

### AMERICAN ASSOCIATION

| Year | Club | Won | Lost | Pct. |
|---|---|---|---|---|
| 1890 | Pittsburgh | 23 | 113 | .169 |
| 1889 | Louisville | 27 | 111 | .196 |

### AMERICAN LEAGUE

| Year | Club | Won | Lost | Pct. |
|---|---|---|---|---|
| 1916 | Philadelphia | 36 | 117 | .235 |
| 1904 | Washington | 38 | 113 | .251 |
| 2003 | Detroit | 43 | 119 | .265 |
| 1932 | Boston | 43 | 111 | .279 |
| 1939 | St. Louis | 43 | 111 | .279 |
| 1909 | Washington | 42 | 110 | .276 |
| 1915 | Philadelphia | 43 | 109 | .283 |
| 1996 | Detroit | 53 | 109 | .327 |
| 1979 | Toronto | 53 | 109 | .327 |
| 1937 | St. Louis | 46 | 108 | .299 |
| 1979 | Oakland | 54 | 108 | .333 |
| 1911 | St. Louis | 45 | 107 | .296 |
| 1926 | Boston | 46 | 107 | .301 |
| 1910 | St. Louis | 47 | 107 | .305 |
| 1988 | Baltimore | 54 | 107 | .335 |
| 1977 | Toronto | 54 | 107 | .335 |
| 1920 | Philadelphia | 48 | 106 | .312 |
| 2002 | Tampa Bay | 55 | 106 | .342 |
| 2002 | Detroit | 55 | 106 | .342 |
| 1970 | Chicago | 56 | 106 | .346 |
| 1963 | Washington | 56 | 106 | .346 |
| 2005 | Kansas City | 56 | 106 | .346 |
| 1925 | Boston | 47 | 105 | .309 |
| 1906 | Boston | 49 | 105 | .318 |
| 1943 | Philadelphia | 49 | 105 | .318 |
| 1946 | Philadelphia | 49 | 105 | .318 |
| 1991 | Cleveland | 57 | 105 | .352 |
| 1964 | Kansas City | 57 | 105 | .352 |
| 1973 | Texas | 57 | 105 | .352 |
| 1919 | Philadelphia | 36 | 104 | .257 |
| 1952 | Detroit | 50 | 104 | .325 |
| 1949 | Washington | 50 | 104 | .325 |
| 1978 | Seattle | 56 | 104 | .350 |
| 2004 | Kansas City | 58 | 104 | .358 |
| 1927 | Boston | 51 | 103 | .331 |
| 1908 | New York | 51 | 103 | .331 |
| 1954 | Philadelphia | 51 | 103 | .331 |
| 1989 | Detroit | 59 | 103 | .364 |
| 1965 | Kansas City | 59 | 103 | .364 |
| 1980 | Seattle | 59 | 103 | .364 |
| 1932 | Chicago | 49 | 102 | .325 |
| 1907 | Washington | 49 | 102 | .325 |
| 1912 | New York | 50 | 102 | .329 |
| 1914 | Cleveland | 51 | 102 | .333 |
| 1930 | Boston | 52 | 102 | .338 |
| 1956 | Kansas City | 52 | 102 | .338 |
| 1950 | Philadelphia | 52 | 102 | .338 |
| 1951 | St. Louis | 52 | 102 | .338 |
| 1975 | Detroit | 57 | 102 | .358 |
| 1978 | Toronto | 59 | 102 | .366 |
| 1971 | Cleveland | 60 | 102 | .370 |
| 1985 | Cleveland | 60 | 102 | .370 |
| 1982 | Minnesota | 60 | 102 | .370 |
| 1983 | Seattle | 60 | 102 | .370 |
| 1948 | Chicago | 51 | 101 | .336 |
| 1912 | St. Louis | 53 | 101 | .344 |
| 1949 | St. Louis | 53 | 101 | .344 |
| 1955 | Washington | 53 | 101 | .344 |
| 1962 | Washington | 60 | 101 | .373 |
| 1987 | Cleveland | 61 | 101 | .377 |
| 1921 | Philadelphia | 53 | 100 | .346 |
| 1936 | Philadelphia | 53 | 100 | .346 |
| 1954 | Baltimore | 54 | 100 | .351 |
| 1940 | Philadelphia | 54 | 100 | .351 |
| 1953 | St. Louis | 54 | 100 | .351 |
| 1972 | Texas | 54 | 100 | .351 |
| 1961 | Kansas City | 61 | 100 | .379 |
| 1961 | Washington | 61 | 100 | .379 |
| 1965 | Boston | 62 | 100 | .383 |
| 1964 | Washington | 62 | 100 | .383 |
| 2001 | Tampa Bay | 62 | 100 | .383 |
| 2002 | Kansas City | 62 | 100 | .383 |

### NATIONAL LEAGUE

| Year | Club | Won | Lost | Pct. |
|---|---|---|---|---|
| 1899 | Cleveland | 20 | 134 | .130 |
| 1962 | New York | 40 | 120 | .250 |
| 1935 | Boston | 38 | 115 | .248 |
| 1952 | Pittsburgh | 42 | 112 | .273 |
| 1965 | New York | 50 | 112 | .309 |
| 1898 | St. Louis | 39 | 111 | .260 |
| 1941 | Philadelphia | 43 | 111 | .279 |
| 1963 | New York | 51 | 111 | .315 |
| 2004 | Arizona | 51 | 111 | .315 |
| 1969 | Montreal | 52 | 110 | .321 |
| 1969 | San Diego | 52 | 110 | .321 |
| 1942 | Philadelphia | 42 | 109 | .278 |
| 1928 | Philadelphia | 43 | 109 | .283 |
| 1964 | New York | 53 | 109 | .327 |
| 1909 | Boston | 45 | 108 | .294 |
| 1945 | Philadelphia | 46 | 108 | .299 |
| 1998 | Florida | 54 | 108 | .333 |
| 1911 | Boston | 44 | 107 | .291 |
| 1961 | Philadelphia | 47 | 107 | .305 |
| 1976 | Montreal | 55 | 107 | .340 |
| 1939 | Philadelphia | 45 | 106 | .298 |
| 1988 | Atlanta | 54 | 106 | .338 |
| 2002 | Milwaukee | 56 | 106 | .346 |
| 1938 | Philadelphia | 45 | 105 | .300 |
| 1908 | St. Louis | 49 | 105 | .318 |
| 1905 | Brooklyn | 48 | 104 | .316 |
| 1923 | Philadelphia | 50 | 104 | .325 |
| 1953 | Pittsburgh | 50 | 104 | .325 |
| 1985 | Pittsburgh | 57 | 104 | .354 |
| 1928 | Boston | 50 | 103 | .327 |
| 1940 | Philadelphia | 50 | 103 | .327 |
| 1905 | Boston | 51 | 103 | .331 |
| 1921 | Philadelphia | 51 | 103 | .331 |
| 1927 | Philadelphia | 51 | 103 | .331 |
| 1917 | Pittsburgh | 51 | 103 | .331 |
| 1962 | Chicago | 59 | 103 | .364 |
| 1966 | Chicago | 59 | 103 | .364 |
| 1993 | New York | 59 | 103 | .364 |
| 1897 | St. Louis | 29 | 102 | .221 |
| 1906 | Boston | 49 | 102 | .325 |
| 1930 | Philadelphia | 52 | 102 | .338 |
| 1973 | San Diego | 60 | 102 | .370 |
| 1974 | San Diego | 60 | 102 | .370 |
| 1892 | Baltimore | 46 | 101 | .313 |
| 1898 | Washington | 51 | 101 | .336 |
| 1912 | Boston | 52 | 101 | .340 |
| 1907 | St. Louis | 52 | 101 | .340 |
| 1908 | Brooklyn | 53 | 101 | .344 |
| 1954 | Pittsburgh | 53 | 101 | .344 |
| 1977 | Atlanta | 61 | 101 | .377 |
| 1982 | Cincinnati | 61 | 101 | .377 |
| 1967 | New York | 61 | 101 | .377 |
| 1993 | San Diego | 61 | 101 | .377 |
| 1904 | Philadelphia | 52 | 100 | .342 |
| 1910 | Boston | 53 | 100 | .346 |
| 1922 | Boston | 53 | 100 | .346 |
| 1924 | Boston | 53 | 100 | .346 |
| 1923 | Boston | 54 | 100 | .351 |
| 1936 | Philadelphia | 54 | 100 | .351 |
| 1971 | San Diego | 61 | 100 | .379 |
| 1985 | San Francisco | 62 | 100 | .383 |
| 2001 | Pittsburgh | 62 | 100 | .383 |

## CLUBS WITH 13 STRAIGHT VICTORIES IN SEASON

### AMERICAN ASSOCIATION

| Year | Club | G | Home | Away |
|---|---|---|---|---|
| 1885 | St. Louis | 17 | 14 | 3 |
| 1887 | St. Louis | 15 | 15 | 0 |
| 1889 | Philadelphia (1 tie) | 14 | 13 | 1 |

### UNION ASSOCIATION

| Year | Club | G | Home | Away |
|---|---|---|---|---|
| 1884 | St. Louis | 20 | 16 | 4 |
| 1884 | Baltimore | 16 | 7 | 9 |

## AMERICAN LEAGUE

| Year | Club | G | Home | Away |
|---|---|---|---|---|
| 2002 | Oakland | 20 | 10 | 10 |
| 1906 | Chicago (1 tie) | 19 | 11 | 8 |
| 1947 | New York | 19 | 6 | 13 |
| 1953 | New York | 18 | 3 | 15 |
| 1912 | Washington | 17 | 1 | 16 |
| 1931 | Philadelphia | 17 | 5 | 12 |
| 1926 | New York | 16 | 12 | 4 |
| 1977 | Kansas City | 16 | 9 | 7 |
| 1906 | New York | 15 | 12 | 3 |
| 1913 | Philadelphia | 15 | 13 | 2 |
| 1946 | Boston | 15 | 11 | 4 |
| 1960 | New York | 15 | 9 | 6 |
| 1991 | Minnesota | 15 | 10 | 5 |
| 2001 | Seattle | 15 | 10 | 5 |
| 1909 | Detroit | 14 | 14 | 0 |
| 1916 | St. Louis | 14 | 13 | 1 |
| 1934 | Detroit | 14 | 9 | 5 |
| 1941 | New York | 14 | 6 | 8 |
| 1951 | Chicago | 14 | 3 | 11 |
| 1973 | Baltimore | 14 | 10 | 4 |
| 1988 | Oakland | 14 | 5 | 9 |
| 1991 | Texas | 14 | 7 | 7 |
| 1994 | Kansas City | 14 | 12 | 2 |
| 1908 | Chicago | 13 | 12 | 1 |
| 1910 | Philadelphia (1 tie) | 13 | 12 | 1 |
| 1927 | Detroit (1 tie) | 13 | 13 | 0 |
| 1931 | Philadelphia | 13 | 13 | 0 |
| 1933 | Washington | 13 | 1 | 12 |
| 1942 | Cleveland | 13 | 4 | 9 |
| 1948 | Boston | 13 | 12 | 1 |
| 1951 | Cleveland | 13 | 7 | 6 |
| 1954 | New York | 13 | 8 | 5 |
| 1961 | New York | 13 | 12 | 1 |
| 1978 | Baltimore | 13 | 3 | 10 |
| 1987 | Milwaukee | 13 | 6 | 7 |
| 1999 | Baltimore | 13 | 5 | 8 |

## NATIONAL LEAGUE

| Year | Club | G | Home | Away |
|---|---|---|---|---|
| 1916 | New York (1 tie) | 26 | 26 | 0 |
| 1880 | Chicago (1 tie) | 21 | 11 | 10 |
| 1935 | Chicago | 21 | 18 | 3 |
| 1884 | Providence | 20 | 16 | 4 |
| 1885 | Chicago | 18 | 14 | 4 |
| 1891 | Boston (1 tie) | 18 | 16 | 2 |
| 1894 | Baltimore | 18 | 13 | 5 |
| 1904 | New York | 18 | 13 | 5 |
| 1897 | Boston | 17 | 16 | 1 |
| 1907 | New York | 17 | 14 | 3 |
| 1916 | New York | 17 | 0 | 17 |
| 1887 | Philadelphia (1 tie) | 16 | 5 | 11 |
| 1890 | Philadelphia | 16 | 14 | 2 |
| 1892 | Philadelphia | 16 | 11 | 5 |
| 1909 | Pittsburgh | 16 | 12 | 4 |
| 1912 | New York | 16 | 11 | 5 |
| 1951 | New York | 16 | 13 | 3 |
| 1886 | Detroit | 15 | 12 | 3 |
| 1903 | Pittsburgh | 15 | 11 | 4 |
| 1924 | Brooklyn | 15 | 3 | 12 |
| 1936 | Chicago | 15 | 11 | 4 |
| 1936 | New York | 15 | 7 | 8 |
| 2000 | Atlanta | 15 | 9 | 6 |
| 1886 | Chicago | 14 | 13 | 1 |
| 1895 | Baltimore | 14 | 13 | 1 |
| 1899 | Cincinnati | 14 | 10 | 4 |
| 1903 | Pittsburgh (1 tie) | 14 | 7 | 7 |
| 1906 | Chicago | 14 | 14 | 0 |
| 1909 | Pittsburgh | 14 | 12 | 2 |
| 1913 | New York | 14 | 6 | 8 |
| 1932 | Chicago | 14 | 14 | 0 |
| 1935 | St. Louis | 14 | 12 | 2 |
| 1965 | San Francisco | 14 | 6 | 8 |
| 1999 | San Diego | 14 | 10 | 4 |
| 1880 | Chicago | 13 | 9 | 4 |
| 1890 | Cincinnati | 13 | 13 | 0 |
| 1892 | Chicago | 13 | 11 | 2 |
| 1905 | New York | 13 | 8 | 5 |
| 1911 | Pittsburgh | 13 | 9 | 4 |
| 1922 | Pittsburgh | 13 | 2 | 11 |
| 1928 | Chicago | 13 | 13 | 0 |
| 1938 | Pittsburgh | 13 | 5 | 8 |
| 1947 | Brooklyn | 13 | 2 | 11 |
| 1953 | Brooklyn | 13 | 7 | 6 |
| 1962 | Los Angeles | 13 | 8 | 5 |
| 1965 | Los Angeles | 13 | 7 | 6 |
| 1977 | Philadelphia | 13 | 8 | 5 |
| 1982 | Atlanta | 13 | 5 | 8 |
| 1991 | Philadelphia | 13 | 9 | 4 |
| 1992 | Atlanta | 13 | 3 | 10 |

## CLUBS WITH 13 STRAIGHT LOSSES IN SEASON

### AMERICAN ASSOCIATION

| Year | Club | G | Home | Away |
|---|---|---|---|---|
| 1889 | Louisville | 26 | 5 | 21 |
| 1890 | Philadelphia | 22 | 6 | 16 |
| 1882 | Baltimore | 15 | 0 | 15 |
| 1884 | Washington | 15 | 0 | 15 |
| 1891 | Louisville | 15 | 0 | 15 |
| 1889 | Louisville | 14 | 14 | 0 |
| 1886 | Louisville | 13 | 0 | 13 |
| 1890 | Brooklyn | 13 | 0 | 13 |

### UNION ASSOCIATION

| Year | Club | G | Home | Away |
|---|---|---|---|---|
| 1884 | Kansas City (1 tie) | 15 | 3 | 12 |
| 1884 | Kansas City | 14 | 0 | 14 |

### AMERICAN LEAGUE

| Year | Club | G | Home | Away |
|---|---|---|---|---|
| 1988 | Baltimore | 21 | 8 | 13 |
| 1906 | Boston | 20 | 19 | 1 |
| 1916 | Philadelphia | 20 | 1 | 19 |
| 1943 | Philadelphia | 20 | 3 | 17 |
| 1975 | Detroit | 19 | 9 | 10 |
| 1920 | Philadelphia | 18 | 0 | 18 |
| 1948 | Washington | 18 | 8 | 10 |
| 1959 | Washington | 18 | 3 | 15 |
| 1926 | Boston | 17 | 14 | 3 |
| 1907 | Boston (2 ties) | 16 | 9 | 7 |
| 1927 | Boston | 15 | 10 | 5 |
| 1937 | Philadelphia (1 tie) | 15 | 10 | 5 |
| 1972 | Texas | 15 | 5 | 10 |
| 2002 | Tampa Bay | 15 | 9 | 6 |
| 2005 | Kansas City | 15 | 8 | 7 |
| 1911 | St. Louis | 14 | 6 | 8 |
| 1930 | Boston | 14 | 3 | 11 |
| 1940 | St. Louis | 14 | 0 | 14 |
| 1945 | Philadelphia | 14 | 0 | 14 |
| 1953 | St. Louis | 14 | 14 | 0 |
| 1954 | Baltimore | 14 | 7 | 7 |
| 1961 | Washington | 14 | 11 | 3 |
| 1970 | Washington | 14 | 4 | 10 |
| 1977 | Oakland | 14 | 9 | 5 |
| 1982 | Minnesota | 14 | 6 | 8 |
| 1992 | Seattle | 14 | 4 | 10 |
| 1994 | Milwaukee | 14 | 6 | 8 |
| 1904 | Washington (1 tie) | 13 | 7 | 6 |
| 1913 | New York | 13 | 7 | 6 |
| 1920 | Detroit | 13 | 5 | 8 |
| 1924 | Chicago | 13 | 2 | 11 |
| 1935 | Philadelphia | 13 | 10 | 3 |
| 1936 | St. Louis | 13 | 2 | 11 |
| 1953 | Detroit (2 ties) | 13 | 12 | 1 |
| 1958 | Washington | 13 | 4 | 9 |
| 1959 | Kansas City | 13 | 4 | 9 |
| 1961 | Minnesota | 13 | 0 | 13 |
| 1962 | Washington | 13 | 7 | 6 |

### NATIONAL LEAGUE

| Year | Club | G | Home | Away |
|---|---|---|---|---|
| 1899 | Cleveland | 24 | 5 | 19 |
| 1890 | Pittsburgh | 23 | 1 | 22 |
| 1961 | Philadelphia | 23 | 6 | 17 |
| 1894 | Louisville | 20 | 0 | 20 |
| 1969 | Montreal | 20 | 12 | 8 |
| 1906 | Boston | 19 | 3 | 16 |
| 1914 | Cincinnati | 19 | 6 | 13 |
| 1876 | Cincinnati | 18 | 9 | 9 |
| 1894 | Louisville | 18 | 0 | 18 |
| 1897 | St. Louis | 18 | 4 | 14 |
| 1894 | Washington | 17 | 4 | 13 |
| 1962 | New York | 17 | 7 | 10 |
| 1977 | Atlanta | 17 | 8 | 9 |
| 1882 | Troy (1 tie) | 16 | 5 | 11 |
| 1885 | Buffalo | 16 | 12 | 4 |
| 1888 | Detroit | 16 | 5 | 11 |
| 1899 | Cleveland | 16 | 0 | 16 |
| 1907 | Boston | 16 | 5 | 11 |
| 1911 | Boston | 16 | 8 | 8 |
| 1944 | Brooklyn | 16 | 0 | 16 |
| 1895 | Louisville | 15 | 10 | 5 |
| 1909 | Boston | 15 | 0 | 15 |
| 1909 | St. Louis | 15 | 11 | 4 |

| Year | Club | G | Home | Away |
|---|---|---|---|---|
| 1927 | Boston | 15 | 0 | 15 |
| 1935 | Boston | 15 | 0 | 15 |
| 1963 | New York | 15 | 8 | 7 |
| 1982 | New York | 15 | 6 | 9 |
| 1878 | Milwaukee | 14 | 9 | 5 |
| 1882 | Worcester | 14 | 2 | 12 |
| 1883 | Philadelphia | 14 | 4 | 10 |
| 1896 | St. Louis (1 tie) | 14 | 9 | 5 |
| 1898 | Washington | 14 | 3 | 11 |
| 1899 | Cleveland | 14 | 1 | 13 |
| 1905 | St. Louis | 14 | 9 | 5 |
| 1911 | Boston | 14 | 14 | 0 |
| 1916 | St. Louis | 14 | 0 | 14 |
| 1927 | Philadelphia | 14 | 1 | 13 |
| 1935 | Boston | 14 | 4 | 10 |
| 1936 | Philadelphia | 14 | 10 | 4 |
| 1937 | Brooklyn | 14 | 0 | 14 |
| 1937 | Cincinnati | 14 | 10 | 4 |
| 1997 | Chicago | 14 | 6 | 8 |
| 2004 | Arizona | 14 | 11 | 3 |
| 1876 | Cincinnati | 13 | 6 | 7 |
| 1877 | Cincinnati | 13 | 3 | 10 |
| 1884 | Cleveland | 13 | 1 | 12 |
| 1885 | Detroit | 13 | 1 | 12 |
| 1885 | Providence | 13 | 2 | 11 |
| 1886 | Washington | 13 | 13 | 0 |
| 1886 | Kansas City (2 ties) | 13 | 0 | 13 |
| 1888 | Indianapolis | 13 | 0 | 13 |
| 1890 | Pittsburgh | 13 | 2 | 11 |
| 1892 | Baltimore | 13 | 2 | 11 |
| 1899 | Cleveland | 13 | 3 | 10 |
| 1902 | New York | 13 | 4 | 9 |
| 1909 | Boston | 13 | 13 | 0 |
| 1910 | St. Louis | 13 | 5 | 8 |
| 1919 | Philadelphia | 13 | 0 | 13 |
| 1919 | Philadelphia | 13 | 7 | 6 |
| 1930 | Cincinnati | 13 | 1 | 12 |
| 1942 | Philadelphia | 13 | 4 | 9 |
| 1944 | Chicago | 13 | 7 | 6 |
| 1944 | New York | 13 | 0 | 13 |
| 1945 | Cincinnati | 13 | 2 | 11 |
| 1955 | Philadelphia | 13 | 9 | 4 |
| 1962 | New York | 13 | 9 | 4 |
| 1976 | Atlanta | 13 | 6 | 7 |
| 1980 | New York | 13 | 3 | 10 |
| 1982 | Chicago | 13 | 7 | 6 |
| 1985 | Chicago | 13 | 4 | 9 |
| 1993 | Colorado | 13 | 7 | 6 |
| 1994 | San Diego | 13 | 4 | 9 |

## CLUBS WINNING FIRST EIGHT GAMES OF SEASON

### AMERICAN ASSOCIATION

Never accomplished

### UNION ASSOCIATION

| Year | Club | G | Home | Away |
|---|---|---|---|---|
| 1884 | St. Louis | 20 | 16 | 4 |

### AMERICAN LEAGUE

| Year | Club | G | Home | Away |
|---|---|---|---|---|
| 1987 | Milwaukee | 13 | 6 | 7 |
| 1981 | Oakland | 11 | 3 | 8 |
| 1966 | Cleveland | 10 | 8 | 2 |
| 1944 | St. Louis | 9 | 5 | 4 |
| 1984 | Detroit | 9 | 3 | 6 |
| 2003 | Kansas City | 9 | 5 | 4 |
| 1982 | Chicago | 8 | 3 | 5 |

### NATIONAL LEAGUE

| Year | Club | G | Home | Away |
|---|---|---|---|---|
| 1982 | Atlanta | 13 | 5 | 8 |
| 1884 | New York | 12 | 12 | 0 |
| 1955 | Brooklyn | 10 | 3 | 7 |
| 1962 | Pittsburgh | 10 | 3 | 7 |
| 1888 | Boston | 9 | 0 | 9 |
| 1918 | New York | 9 | 6 | 3 |
| 1940 | Brooklyn | 9 | 3 | 6 |
| 1990 | Cincinnati | 9 | 3 | 6 |
| 1881 | Worcester | 8 | 3 | 5 |
| 1915 | Philadelphia | 8 | 2 | 6 |
| 1980 | Cincinnati | 8 | 1 | 7 |

## CLUBS LOSING FIRST EIGHT GAMES OF SEASON

### AMERICAN ASSOCIATION

| Year | Club | G | Home | Away |
|---|---|---|---|---|
| 1884 | Toledo | 8 | 0 | 8 |
| 1887 | New York | 10 | 0 | 10 |

### UNION ASSOCIATION

| Year | Club | G | Home | Away |
|---|---|---|---|---|
| 1884 | Altoona | 11 | 4 | 7 |

### AMERICAN LEAGUE

| Year | Club | G | Home | Away |
|---|---|---|---|---|
| 1988 | Baltimore | 21 | 8 | 13 |
| 1904 | Washington (1 tie) | 13 | 7 | 6 |
| 1920 | Detroit | 13 | 5 | 8 |
| 2002 | Detroit | 11 | 5 | 6 |
| 1968 | Chicago | 10 | 4 | 6 |
| 2003 | Detroit | 9 | 6 | 3 |
| 1914 | Cleveland | 8 | 1 | 7 |
| 1945 | Boston | 8 | 3 | 5 |
| 1952 | Detroit | 8 | 3 | 5 |

### NATIONAL LEAGUE

| Year | Club | G | Home | Away |
|---|---|---|---|---|
| 1997 | Chicago | 14 | 6 | 8 |
| 1884 | Detroit | 11 | 0 | 11 |
| 1988 | Atlanta | 10 | 8 | 2 |
| 1918 | Brooklyn | 9 | 3 | 6 |
| 1919 | Boston | 9 | 5 | 4 |
| 1962 | New York | 9 | 6 | 3 |
| 1983 | Houston | 9 | 6 | 3 |
| 1883 | Philadelphia | 8 | 6 | 2 |
| 1889 | Washington | 8 | 4 | 4 |
| 1955 | Pittsburgh | 8 | 4 | 4 |
| 1963 | New York | 8 | 2 | 6 |

## GAMES OF 18 OR MORE INN

### AMERICAN LEAGUE

**25 Inn—(1)**
Chicago 7 vs. Milwaukee 6, May 8, finished May 9, 1984

**24 Inn—(2)**
Philadelphia 4 at Boston 1, Sept 1, 1906
Detroit 1 at Philadelphia 1 (tie), July 21, 1945

**22 Inn—(4)**
New York 9 at Detroit 7, June 24, 1962
Washington 6 vs Chicago 5, June 12, 1967
Milwaukee 4 at Minnesota 3, May 12, finished May 13, 1972
Minnesota 5 vs Cleveland 4, Aug 31, 1993

**21 inn—(3)**
Detroit 6 at Chicago 5, May 24, 1929
Oakland 5 at Washington 3, June 4, 1971
Chicago 6 vs Cleveland 3, May 26, finished May 28, 1973

**20 Inn—(8)**
Philadelphia 4 at Boston 2, July 4, 1905, p.m. game
Washington 9 at Minnesota 7, Aug 9, 1967
New York 4 vs Boston 3, Aug 29, 1967, 2nd game
Boston 5 at Seattle 3, July 27, 1969
Oakland 1 vs California 0, July 9, 1971
Washington 8 at Cleveland 6, Sept 14, 2nd game, finished Sept 20, 1971
(game completed at Washington)
Seattle 8 at Boston 7, Sept 3, finished Sept 4, 1981
California 4 vs Seattle 3, Apr 13, finished Apr 14, 1982

**19 Inn—(15)**
Washington 5 at Philadelphia 4, Sept 27, 1912
Chicago 5 at Cleveland 4, June 24, 1915
Cleveland 3 at New York 2, May 24, 1918
St. Louis 8 at Washington 6, Aug 9, 1921
Chicago 5 vs Boston 4, July 13, 1951
Cleveland 4 vs St. Louis 3, July 1, 1952
Cleveland 3 vs Washington 2, June 14, 1963, 2nd game
Baltimore 7 vs Washington 5, June 4, 1967
Kansas City 6 at Detroit 5, June 17, 1967, 2nd game
Detroit 3 at New York 3 (tie), Aug 23, 1968, 2nd game
Oakland 5 vs Chicago 3, Aug 10, finished Aug 11, 1972
New York 5 vs Minnesota 4, Aug 25, 1976
Cleveland 8 at Detroit 4, Apr 27, 1984
Milwaukee 10 vs Chicago 9, May 1, 1991
Boston 7 at Cleveland 5, Apr 11, 1992
Seattle 5 vs Boston 4, Aug 1, 2000

**18 Inn—(26)**
Chicago 6 vs New York 6 (tie), June 25, 1903
Washington 0 at Detroit 0 (tie), July 16, 1909
Washington 1 vs Chicago 0, May 15, 1918
Detroit 7 vs Washington 6, Aug 4, 1918
Boston 12 vs New York 11, Sept 5, 1927, 1st game
Philadelphia 18 at Cleveland 17, July 10, 1932
New York 3 at Chicago 3 (tie), Aug 21, 1933
Washington 1 at Chicago 0, June 8, 1947, 1st game
Washington 5 at St. Louis 5 (tie), June 20, 1952
Chicago 1 at Baltimore 1 (tie), Aug 6, 1959
New York 7 vs Boston 6, Apr 16, 1967
Minnesota 3 at New York 2, July 26, 1967, 2nd game
Baltimore 3 vs Boston 2, Aug 25, 1968
Minnesota 11 at Seattle 7, July 19, finished July 20, 1969
Oakland 9 vs Baltimore 8, Aug 24, 1969, 2nd game
Minnesota 8 at Oakland 6, Sept 6, 1969
Washington 2 vs New York 1, Apr 22, 1970
Texas 4 at Kansas City 3, May 17, 1972
Detroit 4 vs Cleveland 3, June 9, finished Sept 24, 1982
New York 5 vs Detroit 4, Sept 11, 1988
Kansas City 4 vs Texas 3, June 6, 1991
Boston 4 vs Detroit 3, June 5, 2001
Texas 8 vs Boston 7, Aug 25, 2001
Texas 9 vs Seattle 7, June 24, 2004
Oakland 6 at Minnesota 5, Aug 8, 2004
Los Angeles 1 at Toronto 2, July 28, 2005

### NATIONAL LEAGUE

**26 Inn—(1)**
Brooklyn 1 at Boston 1 (tie), May 1, 1920

**25 Inn—(1)**
St Louis 4 at New York 3, Sept 11, 1974

**24 Inn—(1)**
Houston 1 vs New York 0, Apr 15, 1968

**23 Inn—(2)**
- Brooklyn 2 at Boston 2 (tie), June 27, 1939
- San Francisco 8 at New York 6, May 31, 1964, 2nd game

**22 Inn—(4)**
- Brooklyn 6 vs Pittsburgh 5, Aug 22, 1917
- Chicago 4 at Boston 3, May 17, 1927
- Houston 5 vs Los Angeles 4, June 3, 1989
- Los Angeles 1 at Montreal 0, Aug 23, 1989

**21 Inn—(7)**
- New York 3 at Pittsburgh 1, July 17, 1914
- Chicago 2 vs Philadelphia 1, July 17, 1918
- Pittsburgh 2 at Boston 0, Aug 1, 1918
- San Francisco 1 at Cincinnati 0, Sept 1, 1967
- Houston 2 at San Diego 1, Sept 24, 1971, 1st game
- San Diego 11 at Montreal 8, May 21, 1977
- Los Angeles 2 at Chicago 1, Aug 17, finished Aug 18, 1982

**20 Inn—(10)**
- Chicago 7 at Cincinnati 7 (tie), June 30, 1892
- Chicago 2 at Philadelphia 1, Aug 24, 1905
- Brooklyn 9 at Philadelphia 9 (tie), Apr 30, 1919
- St. Louis 8 at Chicago 7, Aug 28, 1930
- Brooklyn 6 at Boston 2, July 5, 1940
- Philadelphia 5 vs Atlanta 4, May 4, 1973
- Pittsburgh 5 vs Chicago 4, July 6, 1980
- Houston 3 at San Diego 1, Aug 15, 1980
- Philadelphia 7 vs Los Angeles 6, July 7, 1993
- St. Louis 7 at Florida 6, Apr 27, 2003

**19 Inn—(16)**
- Chicago 3 vs Pittsburgh 2, June 22, 1902
- Pittsburgh 7 at Boston 6, July 31, 1912
- Chicago 4 vs Brooklyn 3, June 17, 1915
- St. Louis 8 at Philadelphia 8 (tie), June 13, 1918
- Boston 2 vs Brooklyn 1, May 3, 1920
- Chicago 3 vs Boston 2, Aug 17, 1932
- Brooklyn 9 at Chicago 9 (tie), May 17, 1939
- Cincinnati 0 at Brooklyn 0 (tie), Sept 11, 1946
- Philadelphia 8 vs Cincinnati 7, Sept 15, 1950, 2nd game
- Pittsburgh 4 vs Milwaukee 3, July 19, 1955
- Cincinnati 2 vs Los Angeles 1, Aug 8, 1972
- New York 7 at Los Angeles 3, May 24, 1973
- Pittsburgh 4 at San Diego 3, Aug 25, 1979
- New York 16 at Atlanta 13, July 4, 1985
- Montreal 6 at Houston 3, July 7, 1985
- Atlanta 7 at St. Louis 5, May 14, 1988

**18 Inn—(33)**
- Providence 1 vs Detroit 0, Aug 17, 1882
- Brooklyn 7 at St. Louis 7 (tie), Aug 17, 1902
- Chicago 2 at St. Louis 1, June 24, 1905
- Pittsburgh 3 at Chicago 2, June 28, 1916, 2nd game
- Philadelphia 10 at Brooklyn 9, June 1, 1919
- New York 9 at Pittsburgh 8, July 7, 1922
- Chicago 7 at Boston 2, May 14, 1927
- New York 1 vs St Louis 0, July 2, 1933, 1st game
- St. Louis 8 at Cincinnati 6, July 1, 1934, 1st game
- Chicago 10 at Cincinnati 8, Aug 9, 1942, 1st game
- Philadelphia 4 vs Pittsburgh 3, June 9, 1949
- Cincinnati 7 vs Chicago 6, Sept 7, 1951
- Philadelphia 0 at New York 0 (tie), October 2, 1965, 2nd game
- Cincinnati 3 at Chicago 2, July 19, 1966
- Philadelphia 2 vs Cincinnati 1, May 21, 1967
- Pittsburgh 1 at San Diego 0, June 7, 1972, 2nd game
- New York 3 vs Philadelphia 2, Aug 1, 1972, 1st game
- Montreal 5 at Chicago 4, June 27, 1973, finished June 28, 1973
- Chicago 8 at Montreal 7, June 28, 1974, 1st game
- New York 4 vs Montreal 3, Sept 16, 1975
- Pittsburgh 2 vs Chicago 1, Aug 10, 1977
- Chicago 9 vs Cincinnati 8, May 10, finished July 23, 1979
- Houston 3 vs New York 2, June 18, 1979
- San Diego 8 at New York 6, Aug 26, 1980
- St. Louis 3 at Houston 1, May 27, 1983
- Pittsburgh 4 vs San Francisco 3, July 13, 1984, 2nd game
- Atlanta 3 at Los Angeles 2, Sept 6, 1984
- New York 5 vs Pittsburgh 4, Apr 28, 1985
- San Francisco 5 at Atlanta 4, June 11, 1985
- Houston 8 at Chicago 7, Sept 2, finished Sept 3, 1986
- Pittsburgh 5 vs Chicago 4, Aug 6, 1989
- Atlanta 5 at Los Angeles 3, Aug 3, 1996
- Arizona 1 at San Francisco 0, May 29, 2001

## CLUBS WITH 3,200,000 HOME ATTENDANCE

### AMERICAN LEAGUE

| Year | Club | Attendance |
|---|---|---|
| 2005 | New York Yankees | 4,090,692 |
| 1993 | Toronto Blue Jays | 4,057,947 |
| 1992 | Toronto Blue Jays | 4,028,318 |
| 1991 | Toronto Blue Jays | 4,001,527 |
| 1990 | Toronto Blue Jays | 3,885,284 |
| 2004 | New York Yankees | 3,775,292 |
| 2005 | Los Angeles Angels | 3,404,686 |
| 2004 | Anaheim Angels | 3,375,677 |
| 1997 | Baltimore Orioles | 3,711,132 |
| 1998 | Baltimore Orioles | 3,685,194 |
| 1996 | Baltimore Orioles | 3,646,950 |
| 1993 | Baltimore Orioles | 3,644,965 |
| 1992 | Baltimore Orioles | 3,567,819 |
| 2002 | Seattle Mariners | 3,540,482 |
| 2001 | Seattle Mariners | 3,507,975 |
| 1999 | Cleveland Indians | 3,468,456 |
| 1998 | Cleveland Indians | 3,467,299 |
| 2002 | New York Yankees | 3,461,644 |
| 2000 | Cleveland Indians | 3,456,278 |
| 1999 | Baltimore Orioles | 3,433,150 |
| 1997 | Cleveland Indians | 3,404,750 |
| 1989 | Toronto Blue Jays | 3,375,883 |
| 2003 | New York Yankees | 3,335,293 |
| 1996 | Cleveland Indians | 3,318,174 |
| 2000 | Baltimore Orioles | 3,295,128 |
| 1999 | New York Yankees | 3,292,736 |
| 2003 | Seattle Mariners | 3,268,509 |
| 2001 | New York Yankees | 3,264,777 |
| 2000 | New York Yankees | 3,227,657 |

### NATIONAL LEAGUE

| Year | Club | Attendance |
|---|---|---|
| 1993 | Colorado Rockies | 4,483,350 |
| 1996 | Colorado Rockies | 3,891,014 |
| 1997 | Colorado Rockies | 3,888,453 |
| 1993 | Atlanta Braves | 3,884,725 |
| 1998 | Colorado Rockies | 3,789,347 |
| 1982 | Los Angeles Dodgers | 3,608,881 |
| 2005 | Los Angeles Dodgers | 3,603,646 |
| 1998 | Arizona Diamondbacks | 3,600,412 |
| 2005 | St. Louis Cardinals | 3,538,948 |
| 1983 | Los Angeles Dodgers | 3,510,313 |
| 2004 | Los Angeles Dodgers | 3,488,283 |
| 1999 | Colorado Rockies | 3,481,065 |
| 1997 | Atlanta Braves | 3,464,488 |
| 1995 | Colorado Rockies | 3,390,037 |
| 1998 | Atlanta Braves | 3,361,350 |
| 1991 | Los Angeles Dodgers | 3,348,170 |
| 1978 | Los Angeles Dodgers | 3,347,845 |
| 2000 | St. Louis Cardinals | 3,336,493 |
| 1997 | Los Angeles Dodgers | 3,319,504 |
| 2000 | San Francisco Giants | 3,315,330 |
| 2000 | Colorado Rockies | 3,285,710 |
| 1999 | Atlanta Braves | 3,284,897 |
| 1994 | Colorado Rockies | 3,281,511 |
| 2001 | San Francisco Giants | 3,277,244 |
| 1985 | Los Angeles Dodgers | 3,264,593 |
| 2004 | San Francisco Giants | 3,258,864 |
| 2002 | San Francisco Giants | 3,253,205 |
| 1980 | Los Angeles Dodgers | 3,249,287 |
| 2000 | Atlanta Braves | 3,234,301 |
| 1999 | St. Louis Cardinals | 3,225,334 |
| 2003 | San Francisco Giants | 3,222,706 |
| 2004 | Philadelphia Phillies | 3,206,532 |
| 2002 | Arizona Diamondbacks | 3,200,725 |

## NON-PLAYING PERSONNEL

### COMMISSIONERS

- Kenesaw Landis, Jan 12, 1921-Nov 25, 1944
- Happy Chandler, Apr 24, 1945-July 15, 1951
- Ford Frick, Oct 8, 1951-Dec 14, 1965
- William Eckert, Dec 15, 1965-Feb 4, 1969
- Bowie Kuhn, Feb 4, 1969-Sept 30, 1984
- Peter Ueberroth, Oct 1, 1984-Mar 31, 1989
- Bart Giamatti, Apr 1-Sept 1, 1989
- Fay Vincent, Sept 2, 1989-Sept 7, 1992
- Bud Selig, Sept 9, 1992-July 9, 1998, acting; July 9, 1998 to present

### PRESIDENTS

#### NATIONAL LEAGUE

- Morgan Bulkeley, 1876
- William Hulbert, 1876-882
- Arthur Soden, 1882
- A. G. Mills, 1882-1884
- Nicholas Young, 1884-1902
- Harry Pulliam, 1902-July 29, 1909
- John Heydler, July 30, 1909-Dec 15, 1909
- Thomas Lynch, Dec 15, 1909-Dec 9, 1913
- John Tener, Dec 9, 1913-Aug 6, 1918
- John Heydler, Dec 10, 1918-Dec 11, 1934
- Ford Frick, Dec 11, 1934-Oct 8, 1951
- Warren Giles, Oct 8, 1951-Dec 31, 1969
- Chub Feeney, Jan 1, 1970-Dec 11, 1986
- Bart Giamatti, Dec 11, 1986-Mar 31, 1989
- Bill White, Apr 1, 1989-Feb 28, 1994
- Leonard Coleman Jr, Mar 1, 1994-Oct 31, 1999

#### AMERICAN LEAGUE

- Byron Bancroft Johnson, 1901-Oct 17, 1927
- Ernest Barnard, Oct 31, 1927-Mar 27, 1931
- Will Harridge, May 27, 1931-Jan 31, 1959
- Joe Cronin, Feb 1, 1959-Dec 31, 1973
- Lee MacPhail Jr., Jan 1, 1974-1983
- Bobby Brown, 1984-July 31, 1994
- Gene Budig, Aug 1, 1994-Dec 31, 1999

Ichiro Suzuki

# AMERICAN LEAGUE TEAM RECORDS

## BALTIMORE ORIOLES (1901-1902)

### YEARLY FINISHES

(Original American League franchise moved to New York after the 1902 season)

| Year | Position | W | L | Pct. | GB | Manager | Attendance |
|---|---|---|---|---|---|---|---|
| 1901 | 5th | 68 | 65 | .511 | 13.5 | John McGraw | 141,952 |
| 1902 | 8th | 50 | 88 | .362 | 34.0 | John McGraw, Wilbert Robinson | 174,606 |

### INDIVIDUAL AND CLUB RECORDS

#### BATTING

| | Individual Season | Individual Career | Club Season |
|---|---|---|---|
| Games | 134—Cy Seymour, 1901 | 255—Jimmy Williams | 141 (1902) |
| At-bats | 547—Cy Seymour, 134 G, 1901 | 999—Jimmy Williams | 4,760 (1902) |
| Runs | 113—Jimmy Williams, 130 G, 1901 | 196—Jimmy Williams | 760 (1901) |
| | | | Fewest—715 (1902) |
| Hits | 166—Cy Seymour, 134 G, 1901 | 315—Jimmy Williams | 1,348 (1901) |
| | | | Fewest—1,318 (1902) |
| Hitting streak | unknown | | |
| Singles | 138—Cy Seymour, 134 G, 1901 | 205—Jimmy Williams | 1,034 (1901) |
| Doubles | 27—Kip Selbach, 128 G, 1902 | 53—Jimmy Williams | 202 (1902) |
| | Jimmy Williams, 125 G, 1902 | | |
| Triples | 21—Bill Keisler, 115 G, 1901 | 42—Jimmy Williams | 111 (1901) |
| | Jimmy Williams, 130 G, 1901 | | |
| | Jimmy Williams, 125 G, 1902 | | |
| **HOME RUNS** | | | 33 (1902) |
| | | | Fewest—24 (1901) |
| Righthander | 8—Jimmy Williams, 125 G, 1902 | 15—Jimmy Williams | |
| Lefthander | 5—Mike Donlin, 121 G, 1901 | 5—Mike Donlin | |
| Switch-hitter | none | none | |
| Rookie | 2—Harry Arndt, 68 G, 1902 | | |
| | Frank Foutz, 20 G, 1901 | | |
| | Jim Jackson, 99 G, 1901 | | |
| | Snake Wiltse, 19 G, 1902 | | |
| Home | 3—Mike Donlin, 1901 | 6—Jimmy Williams | 16 (1902) |
| | Cy Seymour, 1902 | | |
| | Jimmy Williams, 1901 | | |
| | Jimmy Williams, 1902 | | |
| Road | 5—Jimmy Williams, 1902 | 9—Jimmy Williams | 17 (1902) |
| Month | 3—Mike Donlin, May 1901 | | 10 (Sept 1902) |
| | Jimmy Williams, July 1901 | | |
| | Jimmy Williams, July 1902 | | |
| Pinch | 0 | 0 | 0 |
| Grand slams | 1—Herm McFarland, 61 G, 1902 | 1—Herm McFarland | 2 (1902) |
| | Jimmy Williams, 125 G, 1901 | Jimmy Williams | |
| | Snake Wiltse, 19 G, 1902 | Snake Wiltse | |
| Home runs at American League Park, all teams | | | 34 (1902) |
| Total bases | 249—Jimmy Williams, 125 G, 1902 | 497—Jimmy Williams | 1,833 (1902) |
| Extra-base hits | 56—Jimmy Williams, 125 G, 1902 | 110—Jimmy Williams | 342 (1902) |
| Sacrifice hits | 20—Billy Gilbert, 129 G, 1902 | 21—Cy Seymour | 115 (1902) |
| Bases on balls | 61—John McGraw, 73 G, 1901 | 92—Jimmy Williams | 417 (1902) |
| | | | Fewest—369 (1901) |
| Strikeouts | unknown | unknown | 429 (1902) |
| | Fewest-unknown | | Fewest—377 (1901) |
| Hit by pitch | 14—John McGraw, 73 G, 1901 | 16—John McGraw | 54 (1902) |
| | | | Fewest—52 (1901) |
| Runs batted in | 96—Jimmy Williams, 130 G, 1901 | 179—Jimmy Williams | 633 (1901) |
| | | | Fewest—598 (1902) |
| Grounded into double plays | unknown | unknown | unknown |
| | Fewest-unknown | Fewest-unknown | |
| Left on base | | | unknown |
| Batting average | .340—Mike Donlin, 121 G, 1901 | .315—Jimmy Williams | 294 (1901) |
| | | | Lowest—.277 (1902) |
| Most .300 hitters | | | 4 (1901) |
| Slugging average | .500—Jimmy Williams, 125 G, 1901 | .497—Jimmy Williams | .397 (1901) |
| | | | Lowest—.385 (1902) |

| | Individual Season | Individual Career | Club Season |
|---|---|---|---|
| **On-base percentage** | .409—Mike Donlin, 121 G, 1901 | .375—Jimmy Williams | .353 (1901)<br>Lowest—.342 (1902) |

## BASERUNNING

| | Individual Season | Individual Career | Club Season |
|---|---|---|---|
| **Stolen bases** | 38—Cy Seymour, 134 G, 1901<br>Billy Gilbert, 129 G, 1902 | 50—Cy Seymour | 207 (1901) |
| **Caught stealing** | unknown | unknown | unknown |

## PITCHING

| | Individual Season | Individual Career | Club Season |
|---|---|---|---|
| **Games** | 48—Joe McGinnity, 1901 | 73—Joe McGinnity | |
| **Games started** | 43—Joe McGinnity, 1901 | 66—Joe McGinnity, 1901 | |
| **Complete games** | 39—Joe McGinnity, 1901 | 58—Joe McGinnity, 1901 | 119 (1902) |
| **Wins** | 26—Joe McGinnity, 1901 | 39—Joe McGinnity, 1901 | |
| **Percentage** | .565—Joe McGinnity, (26-20), 1901 | .565—Joe McGinnity | |
| **Winning streak** | unknown | | |
| **20-win seasons** | | 1—Joe McGinnity | |
| **Losses** | 21—Harry Howell, 1901 | 36—Harry Howell | |
| **Losing streak** | unknown | | |
| **Innings** | 382—Joe McGinnity, 1901 | 580.2—Joe McGinnity | 1,210.1 (1902) |
| **Hits** | 412—Joe McGinnity, 1901 | 631—Joe McGinnity | 1,531 (1902) |
| **Runs** | 219—Joe McGinnity, 1901 | 324—Harry Howell | 848 (1902) |
| **Earned runs** | 151—Joe McGinnity, 1901 | 227—Joe McGinnity | 582 (1902) |
| **Bases on balls** | 96—Joe McGinnity, 1901 | 142—Joe McGinnity | 354 (1902) |
| **Strikeouts** | 93—Harry Howell, 1901 | 126—Harry Howell | 271 (1901) |
| **Strikeouts, game** | unknown | | |
| **Hit batsmen** | 21—Joe McGinnity, 1901 | 29—Joe McGinnity | 48 (1901) |
| **Wild pitches** | 10—Jerry Nops, 1901 | 10—Jerry Nops | 29 (1901) |
| **Home runs** | 7—Joe McGinnity, 1901<br>Charlie Shields, 1902 | 10—Joe McGinnity<br>Harry Howell | 30 (1902) |
| **Sacrifice hits** | 28—Harry Howell, 1901 | 41—Joe McGinnity | unknown |
| **Earned run average** | 3.44—Joe McGinnity, 198.2 inn, 1902 | 3.52—Joe McGinnity | 3.73 (1901) |
| **Shutouts** | 1—held by many players | 2—Harry Howell | 4 (1901)<br>Lost—7 (1902) |
| **1-0 games won** | 1—Frank Foreman, 1901 | 1—Frank Foreman | 1 (1901)<br>Lost—1 (1901, 1902) |

## TEAM FIELDING

| | | | |
|---|---|---|---|
| **Putouts** | 3,622 (1902)<br>Fewest—3,472 (1901) | **Assists** | 1,763 (1902)<br>Fewest—1,560 (1901) |
| **Chances accepted** | 5,385 (1902)<br>Fewest—5,032 (1901) | **Errors** | 401 (1901)<br>Fewest—357 (1902) |
| **Double plays** | 109 (1902)<br>Fewest—76 (1901) | **Passed balls** | 26 (1902)<br>Fewest—20 (1901) |
| **Errorless games** | 14 (1902)<br>Consecutive—1—many times | **Fielding average** | .947 (1902)<br>Lowest—.935 (1901) |

## MISCELLANEOUS

**Most players, season** 39 (1902)
**Fewest players, season** 23 (1901)
**Games won** 68 (1901)
**Month** 16 (July 1901)
**Consecutive** 11 (1901)
**Winning percentage** .511 (1901), 68-65
**Lowest** .362 (1902), 50-88
**Number of league championships** 0
**Most recent** ---
**Runs, game** 21 vs Chicago, Aug 25, 1902
**Opponents'** 23 by Cleveland, Sept 2, 1902
**Hits, game** 28 vs Chicago, Aug 25, 1902
**Home runs, game** 2, many times
**Runs, shutout** 13 vs Washington, July 7, 1902
**Opponents'** 12 by Chicago, June 13, 1901
**Longest 1-0 win** none over 9 inn

**Most seasons, non-pitcher** 2—many players
**Most seasons, pitcher** 2—many players
**Games lost** 88 (1902)
**Month** 23 (Sept 1902)
**Consecutive** 9 (1902)
**Overall record** 118-153 (2 seasons)

**Number of times worst record in league** 1
**Most recent** 1902
**Runs, inning** 9 vs Cleveland, June 2, 1902, 3rd

**Total bases, game** 39 vs Chicago, Aug 25, 1902
**Consecutive games with one or more home runs** 3 (4 HRs), 1901
**Longest shutout** none over 9 inn

**Longest 1-0 loss** 10 inn vs St. Louis, Aug 28, 1902

## ATTENDANCE

| | |
|---|---|
| **Highest home attendance** | 174,606 (1901) |
| **Highest road attendance** | 293,242 (1902) |

**Largest crowds**

| | |
|---|---|
| **Day** | 12,726 vs Philadelphia, Apr 23, 1902 |
| **Doubleheader** | 13,041 vs Cleveland, May 30, 1902 |
| **Home opener** | 12,726 vs Philadelphia, Apr 23, 1902 |

# BALTIMORE ORIOLES (1954-Present)

## YEARLY FINISHES

**(Original American League franchise moved from Milwaukee to St. Louis after the 1901 season and to Baltimore after the 1953 season)**

| Year | Position | W | L | Pct. | GB | Manager | Attendance |
|---|---|---|---|---|---|---|---|
| 1954 | 7th | 54 | 100 | .351 | 57.0 | Jimmie Dykes | 1,060,910 |
| 1955 | 7th | 57 | 97 | .370 | 39.0 | Paul Richards | 852,039 |
| 1956 | 6th | 69 | 85 | .448 | 28.0 | Paul Richards | 901,201 |
| 1957 | 5th | 76 | 76 | .500 | 21.0 | Paul Richards | 1,029,581 |
| 1958 | 6th | 74 | 79 | .484 | 17.5 | Paul Richards | 829,991 |
| 1959 | 6th | 74 | 80 | .481 | 20.0 | Paul Richards | 891,926 |
| 1960 | 2nd | 89 | 65 | .578 | 8.0 | Paul Richards | 1,187,849 |
| 1961 | 3rd | 95 | 67 | .586 | 14.0 | Paul Richards, Luman Harris | 951,089 |
| 1962 | 7th | 77 | 85 | .475 | 19.0 | Billy Hitchcock | 790,254 |
| 1963 | 4th | 86 | 76 | .531 | 18.5 | Billy Hitchcock | 774,343 |
| 1964 | 3rd | 97 | 65 | .599 | 2.0 | Hank Bauer | 1,116,215 |
| 1965 | 3rd | 94 | 68 | .580 | 8.0 | Hank Bauer | 781,649 |
| 1966 | 1st (S) | 97 | 63 | .606 | +9.0 | Hank Bauer | 1,203,366 |
| 1967 | 6th (tied) | 76 | 85 | .472 | 15.5 | Hank Bauer | 955,053 |
| 1968 | 2nd | 91 | 71 | .562 | 12.0 | Hank Bauer, Earl Weaver | 943,977 |

## EAST DIVISION

| Year | Position | W | L | Pct. | GB | Manager | Attendance |
|---|---|---|---|---|---|---|---|
| 1969 | 1st (C,s) | 109 | 53 | .673 | +19.0 | Earl Weaver | 1,058,168 |
| 1970 | 1st (C,S) | 108 | 54 | .667 | +15.0 | Earl Weaver | 1,057,069 |
| 1971 | 1st (C,s) | 101 | 57 | .639 | +12.0 | Earl Weaver | 1,023,037 |
| 1972 | 3rd | 80 | 74 | .519 | 5.0 | Earl Weaver | 899,950 |
| 1973 | 1st (c) | 97 | 65 | .599 | +8.0 | Earl Weaver | 958,667 |
| 1974 | 1st (c) | 91 | 71 | .562 | +2.0 | Earl Weaver | 962,572 |
| 1975 | 2nd | 90 | 69 | .566 | 4.5 | Earl Weaver | 1,002,157 |
| 1976 | 2nd | 88 | 74 | .543 | 10.5 | Earl Weaver | 1,058,609 |
| 1977 | 2nd (tied) | 97 | 64 | .602 | 2.5 | Earl Weaver | 1,195,769 |
| 1978 | 4th | 90 | 71 | .559 | 9.0 | Earl Weaver | 1,051,724 |
| 1979 | 1st (C,s) | 102 | 57 | .642 | +8.0 | Earl Weaver | 1,681,009 |
| 1980 | 2nd | 100 | 62 | .617 | 3.0 | Earl Weaver | 1,797,438 |
| 1981 | 2nd/4th | 59 | 46 | .562 | * | Earl Weaver | 1,024,652 |
| 1982 | 2nd | 94 | 68 | .580 | 1.0 | Earl Weaver | 1,613,031 |
| 1983 | 1st (C,S) | 98 | 64 | .605 | +6.0 | Joe Altobelli | 2,042,071 |
| 1984 | 5th | 85 | 77 | .525 | 19.0 | Joe Altobelli | 2,045,784 |
| 1985 | 4th | 83 | 78 | .516 | 16.0 | Joe Altobelli, Earl Weaver | 2,132,387 |
| 1986 | 7th | 73 | 89 | .451 | 22.5 | Earl Weaver | 1,973,176 |
| 1987 | 6th | 67 | 95 | .414 | 31.0 | Cal Ripken Sr. | 1,835,692 |
| 1988 | 7th | 54 | 107 | .335 | 34.5 | Cal Ripken Sr., Frank Robinson | 1,660,738 |
| 1989 | 2nd | 87 | 75 | .537 | 2.0 | Frank Robinson | 2,535,208 |
| 1990 | 5th | 76 | 85 | .472 | 11.5 | Frank Robinson | 2,415,189 |
| 1991 | 6th | 67 | 95 | .414 | 24.0 | Frank Robinson, Johnny Oates | 2,552,753 |
| 1992 | 3rd | 89 | 73 | .549 | 7.0 | Johnny Oates | 3,567,819 |
| 1993 | 3rd (tied) | 85 | 77 | .525 | 10.0 | Johnny Oates | 3,644,965 |
| 1994 | 2nd | 63 | 49 | .563 | 6.5 | Johnny Oates | 2,535,359 |
| 1995 | 3rd | 71 | 73 | .493 | 15.0 | Phil Regan | 3,098,475 |
| 1996 | 2nd (D,c) | 88 | 74 | .543 | 4.0 | Dave Johnson | 3,646,950 |
| 1997 | 1st (D,c) | 98 | 64 | .605 | +2.0 | Dave Johnson | 3,711,132 |
| 1998 | 4th | 79 | 83 | .488 | 35.0 | Ray Miller | 3,685,194 |
| 1999 | 4th | 78 | 84 | .481 | 20.0 | Ray Miller | 3,433,150 |
| 2000 | 4th | 74 | 88 | .457 | 13.5 | Mike Hargrove | 3,295,128 |
| 2001 | 4th | 63 | 98 | .391 | 32.5 | Mike Hargrove | 3,094,841 |
| 2002 | 4th | 67 | 95 | .414 | 36.5 | Mike Hargrove | 2,682,917 |
| 2003 | 4th | 71 | 91 | .438 | 30.0 | Mike Hargrove | 2,454,523 |
| 2004 | 3rd | 78 | 84 | .481 | 23.0 | Lee Mazzilli | 2,744,013 |
| 2005 | 4th | 74 | 88 | .457 | 21.0 | Lee Mazzilli, Sam Perlozzo | 2,624,740 |

(S) won World Series; (C) won League Championship Series; (s) lost World Series; *first half 31-23, second 28-23; (D) won Division Series; (c) lost League Championship Series

## INDIVIDUAL AND CLUB RECORDS

### BATTING

| | Individual Season | Individual Career | Club Season |
|---|---|---|---|
| **Games** | 163—Brooks Robinson, 1961, 1964<br>Cal Ripken Jr., 1996 | 3,001—Cal Ripken Jr. | 163 (1961, 1964, 1982, 1996, 2003) |
| **At-bats** | 673—B.J. Surhoff, 162 G, 1999 | 11,551—Cal Ripken Jr. | 5,736 (2004) |
| **Runs** | 132—Roberto Alomar, 153 G, 1996 | 1,647—Cal Ripken Jr. | 949 (1996)<br>Fewest—483 (1954) |
| **Hits** | 211—Cal Ripken Jr., 162 G, 1983 | 3,184—Cal Ripken Jr. | 1,614 (2004)<br>Fewest—1,187 (1968) |
| **Hitting streak** | 30 G—Eric Davis, 1998 | | |
| **Singles** | 158—Al Bumbry, 160 G, 1980 | 2,106—Cal Ripken Jr. | 1,108 (2004) |
| **Doubles** | 50—Brian Roberts, 159 G, 2004<br>Miguel Tejada, 162 G, 2005 | 603—Cal Ripken Jr. | 319 (2004) |
| **Triples** | 12—Paul Blair, 151 G, 1967 | 68—Brooks Robinson | 49 (1954) |
| **HOME RUNS** | | | 257 (1996)<br>Fewest—52 (1954) |
| **Righthander** | 49—Frank Robinson, 155 G, 1966 | 431—Cal Ripken Jr. | |
| **Lefthander** | 50—Brady Anderson, 149 G, 1996 | 303—Boog Powell | |
| **Switch-hitter** | 35—Ken Singleton, 159 G, 1979 | 343—Eddie Murray | |
| **Rookie** | 28—Cal Ripken Jr., 160 G, 1982 | | |
| **Home** | 27—Frank Robinson, 1966 | 214—Cal Ripken Jr. | 121(1996) |
| **Road** | 31—Brady Anderson, 1996 | 217—Cal Ripken Jr. | 136 (1996) |

| | Individual Season | Career | Club Season |
|---|---|---|---|
| Month | 15—Jim Gentile, Aug 1961 | | 58 (May 1987) |
| Pinch | 3—Sam Bowens, 1967<br>Jim Dwyer, 1986<br>Whitey Herzog, 1962<br>Sam Horn, 1991<br>Pat Kelly, 1979 | 9—Jim Dwyer | 11 (1982) |
| Grand slams | 5—Jim Gentile, 148 G, 1961 | 16—Eddie Murray | 11 (1996) |
| Home runs at Memorial Stadium, all teams | | | 235 (1987) |
| Home runs at Oriole Park at Camden Yards, all teams | | | 229 (1996) |
| Total bases | 369—Brady Anderson, 149 G, 1996 | 5,168—Cal Ripken Jr. | 2,685 (1996) |
| Extra-base hits | 92—Brady Anderson, 149 G, 1996 | 1,078—Cal Ripken Jr. | 585 (1996) |
| Sacrifice hits | 23—Mark Belanger, 152 G, 1975 | 153—Mark Belanger | 110 (1957) |
| Sacrifice flies | 17—Bobby Bonilla, 159 G, 1996 | 127—Cal Ripken Jr. | 67 (1996) |
| Bases on balls | 118—Ken Singleton, 155 G, 1975 | 1,129—Cal Ripken Jr. | 717 (1970)<br>Fewest—431 (2003) |
| Strikeouts | 160—Mickey Tettleton, 135 G, 1990<br>Fewest—19—Rick Dauer, 152 G, 1980 | 1,305—Cal Ripken Jr. | 1,019 (1964, 1968)<br>Fewest—634 (1954) |
| Hit by pitch | 24—Brady Anderson, 150 G, 1999 | 148—Brady Anderson | 77 (2001)<br>Fewest—19 (1955, 1985) |
| Runs batted in | 150—Miguel Tejada, 162 G, 2004 | 1,695—Cal Ripken Jr. | 914 (1996)<br>Fewest—451 (1954) |
| Grounded into double plays | 32—Cal Ripken Jr., 161 G, 1985<br>Fewest—1—Brady Anderson, 151 G, 1997 | 350—Cal Ripken Jr. | 159 (1986)<br>Fewest—102 (1968) |
| Left on base | | | 1,262 (1970)<br>Fewest—1,037 (2002) |
| Batting average | .340—Melvin Mora, 140 G, 2004 | .294—Eddie Murray | .281 (2004)<br>Lowest—.225 (1968) |
| Most .300 hitters | | | 3 (1980, 2004) |
| Slugging average | .646—Jim Gentile, 148 G, 1961 | .520—Rafael Palmeiro | .472 (1996)<br>Lowest—.320 (1955) |
| On-base percentage | .442—Bob Nieman, 114 G, 1956 | .401—Frank Robinson | .353 (1999) |

## BASERUNNING

| | Individual Season | Career | Club Season |
|---|---|---|---|
| Stolen bases | 57—Luis Aparicio, 146 G, 1964 | 307—Brady Anderson | 150 (1976) |
| Caught stealing | 18—Don Buford, 144 G, 1969 | 98—Brady Anderson | 65 (2000) |

## PITCHING

| | Individual Season | Career | Club Season |
|---|---|---|---|
| Games | 76—Tippy Martinez, 1982<br>B.J. Ryan, 2003, 2004 | 558—Jim Palmer | |
| Games started | 40—Dave McNally, 1969<br>Mike Cuellar, 1970<br>Dave McNally, 1970<br>Jim Palmer, 1976<br>Mike Flanagan, 1978 | 521—Jim Palmer | |
| Complete games | 25—Jim Palmer, 1975 | 211—Jim Palmer | 71 (1971) |
| Wins | 25—Steve Stone, 1980 | 268—Jim Palmer | |
| Percentage | .808—Dave McNally (21-5), 1971 | .645—Mike Mussina | |
| Winning streak | 15—Dave McNally, 1969 | | |
| Winning streak, two seasons | 17—Dave McNally, 1968 (2), 1969 (15) | | |
| 20-win seasons | | 8—Jim Palmer | |
| Losses | 21—Don Larsen, 1954 | 152—Jim Palmer | |
| Losing streak | 10—Jay Tibbs, 1988 | | |
| Saves | 45—Randy Myers, 1997 | 160—Gregg Olson | 59 (1997) |
| Innings | 323—Jim Palmer, 1975 | 3,948—Jim Palmer | 1,478.2 (1970) |
| Hits | 284—Scott Erickson, 1996 | 3,349—Jim Palmer | 1,604 (1996) |
| Runs | 137—Scott Erickson, 1996<br>Mike Mussina, 1996 | 1,395—Jim Palmer | 913 (2000) |
| Earned runs | 130—Mike Mussina, 1996 | 1,253—Jim Palmer | 855 (2000) |
| Bases on balls | 181—Bob Turley, 1954 | 1,311—Jim Palmer | 688 (1954) |
| Strikeouts | 218—Mike Mussina, 1997 | 2,212—Jim Palmer | 1,139 (1997) |
| Strikeouts, game | 15—Mike Mussina, Aug 1, 2000<br>Mike Mussina, Sept 24, 2000 | | |
| Hit batsmen | 15—Chuck Estrada, 1960 | 68—Dave McNally | 80 (2003) |
| Wild pitches | 14—Milt Pappas, 1959 | 85—Jim Palmer | 70 (2005) |
| Home runs | 35—Robin Roberts, 1963<br>Scott McGregor, 1986<br>Sidney Ponson, 1999 | 303—Jim Palmer | 226 (1987) |
| Sacrifice hits | 20—Mike Cuellar, 1975 | 133—Jim Palmer | 100 (1955) |
| Sacrifice flies | 14—Jim Palmer, 1976<br>David Wells, 1996 | 84—Jim Palmer | 63 (1955, 1976) |
| Earned run average | 1.95—Dave McNally, 273 inn, 1968 | 2.86—Jim Palmer | 2.53 (1972) |

| | Individual Season | Individual Career | Club Season |
|---|---|---|---|
| **Shutouts** | 10—Jim Palmer, 1975 | 53—Jim Palmer | 21 (1961)<br>Lost—22 (1955) |
| **1-0 games won** | 3—Mike Cuellar, 1974<br>Ross Grimsley, 1974<br>Jim Palmer, 1975, 1978 | 9—Jim Palmer | 8 (1974)<br>Lost—5 (1973) |

## TEAM FIELDING

| | | | |
|---|---|---|---|
| **Putouts** | 4,436 (1970)<br>Fewest—4,082 (1956) | **Assists** | 1,974 (1975)<br>Fewest—1,516 (1958) |
| **Chances accepted** | 6,344 (1974)<br>Fewest—5,625 (1958) | **Errors** | 167 (1955)<br>Fewest—81 (1998) |
| **Double plays** | 191 (1999)<br>Fewest—131 (1968) | **Passed balls** | 10 (1960)<br>Fewest—4 (1985) |
| **Errorless games** | 104 (1998)<br>Consecutive—13 (1991) | **Fielding average** | .987 (1998)<br>Lowest—.972 (1955) |

## MISCELLANEOUS

**Most players, season** 54 (1955)
**Fewest players, season** 30 (1969)
**Games won** 109 (1969)
**Month** 25 (June 1966)
**Consecutive** 14 (1973)
**Winning percentage** .673 (1969), 109-53
**Lowest** .335 (1988), 54-107
**Number of league championships** 6
**Most recent** 1983
**Runs, game** 23 vs Toronto, Sept 28, 2000
**Opponents'** 26 by Texas, Apr 19, 1996
**Hits, game** 26 vs California, Aug 28, 1980
**Home runs, game** 7 vs Boston, May 17, 1967
vs California, Aug 26, 1985
**Runs, shutout** 17 vs Chicago, July 27, 1969
**Opponents'** 16 by New York, Apr 30, 1960
**Longest 1-0 win** 17 inn, vs Milwaukee, Sept 27, 1974

**Most seasons, non-pitcher** 23—Brooks Robinson
**Most seasons, pitcher** 19—Jim Palmer
**Games lost** 107 (1988)
**Month** 25 (Aug 1954)
**Consecutive** 21 (1988)
**Overall record** 4,280-3,933 (52 seasons)
**Interleague play** 64-93
**Number of times worst record in league** 1
**Most recent** 1988
**Runs, inning** 12 vs Tampa Bay, April 11, 2002, 6th
vs Chicago, May 12, 1997, 7th
**Total bases, game** 44 vs Atlanta NL, June 13, 1999
**Consecutive games with one or more home runs** 20 (38 HRs), 1998

**Longest shutout** unknown

**Longest 1-0 loss** 15 inn, vs Cleveland, May 14, 1961, 1st game

## ATTENDANCE

**Highest home attendance**
**Memorial Stadium** 2,552,753 (1991)
**Oriole Park at Camden Yards** 3,711,132 (1997)

**Highest road attendance** 2,333,664 (2001)

**Largest crowds**
**Day** 52,395 vs Milwaukee, Apr 4, 1988
**Night** 52,159 vs Boston, June 27, 1986
**Doubleheader** 51,883 vs Milwaukee, Oct 1, 1982
**Home opener** 52,395 vs Milwaukee, Apr 4, 1988

# BOSTON RED SOX

## YEARLY FINISHES

**(Original American League franchise)**

| Year | Position | W | L | Pct. | GB | Manager | Attendance |
|---|---|---|---|---|---|---|---|
| 1901 | 2nd | 79 | 57 | .581 | 4.0 | Jimmy Collins | 289,448 |
| 1902 | 3rd | 77 | 60 | .562 | 6.5 | Jimmy Collins | 348,567 |
| 1903 | 1st (S) | 91 | 47 | .659 | +14.5 | Jimmy Collins | 379,338 |
| 1904 | 1st (n) | 95 | 59 | .617 | +1.5 | Jimmy Collins | 623,295 |
| 1905 | 4th | 78 | 74 | .513 | 16.0 | Jimmy Collins | 468,828 |
| 1906 | 8th | 49 | 105 | .318 | 45.5 | Jimmy Collins, Chick Stahl | 410,209 |
| 1907 | 7th | 59 | 90 | .396 | 32.5 | George Huff, Bob Unglaub, Deacon McGuire | 436,777 |
| 1908 | 5th | 75 | 79 | .487 | 15.5 | Deacon McGuire, Fred Lake | 473,048 |
| 1909 | 3rd | 88 | 63 | .583 | 9.5 | Fred Lake | 668,965 |
| 1910 | 4th | 81 | 72 | .529 | 22.5 | Patsy Donovan | 584,619 |
| 1911 | 5th | 78 | 75 | .510 | 24.0 | Patsy Donovan | 503,961 |
| 1912 | 1st (S) | 105 | 47 | .691 | +14.0 | Jake Stahl | 597,096 |
| 1913 | 4th | 79 | 71 | .527 | 15.5 | Jake Stahl, Bill Carrigan | 437,194 |
| 1914 | 2nd | 91 | 62 | .595 | 8.5 | Bill Carrigan | 481,359 |
| 1915 | 1st (S) | 101 | 50 | .669 | +2.5 | Bill Carrigan | 539,885 |
| 1916 | 1st (S) | 91 | 63 | .591 | +2.0 | Bill Carrigan | 496,397 |
| 1917 | 2nd | 90 | 62 | .592 | 9.0 | Jack Barry | 387,856 |
| 1918 | 1st (S) | 75 | 51 | .595 | +2.5 | Ed Barrow | 249,513 |
| 1919 | 6th | 66 | 71 | .482 | 20.5 | Ed Barrow | 417,291 |
| 1920 | 5th | 72 | 81 | .471 | 25.5 | Ed Barrow | 402,445 |
| 1921 | 5th | 75 | 79 | .487 | 23.5 | Hugh Duffy | 279,273 |
| 1922 | 8th | 61 | 93 | .396 | 33.0 | Hugh Duffy | 259,184 |
| 1923 | 8th | 61 | 91 | .401 | 37.0 | Frank Chance | 229,668 |
| 1924 | 7th | 67 | 87 | .435 | 25.0 | Lee Fohl | 448,556 |
| 1925 | 8th | 47 | 105 | .309 | 49.5 | Lee Fohl | 267,782 |
| 1926 | 8th | 46 | 107 | .301 | 44.5 | Lee Fohl | 285,155 |
| 1927 | 8th | 51 | 103 | .331 | 59.0 | Bill Carrigan | 305,275 |
| 1928 | 8th | 57 | 96 | .373 | 43.5 | Bill Carrigan | 396,920 |
| 1929 | 8th | 58 | 96 | .377 | 48.0 | Bill Carrigan | 394,620 |
| 1930 | 8th | 52 | 102 | .338 | 50.0 | Heinie Wagner | 444,045 |
| 1931 | 6th | 62 | 90 | .408 | 45.0 | Shano Collins | 350,975 |
| 1932 | 8th | 43 | 111 | .279 | 64.0 | Shano Collins, Marty McManus | 182,150 |
| 1933 | 7th | 63 | 86 | .423 | 34.5 | Marty McManus | 268,715 |
| 1934 | 4th | 76 | 76 | .500 | 24.0 | Bucky Harris | 610,640 |
| 1935 | 4th | 78 | 75 | .510 | 16.0 | Joseph Cronin | 558,568 |

| Year | Position | W | L | Pct. | GB | Manager | Attendance |
|---|---|---|---|---|---|---|---|
| 1936 | 6th | 74 | 80 | .481 | 28.5 | Joe Cronin | 626,895 |
| 1937 | 5th | 80 | 72 | .526 | 21.0 | Joe Cronin | 559,659 |
| 1938 | 2nd | 88 | 61 | .591 | 9.5 | Joe Cronin | 646,459 |
| 1939 | 2nd | 89 | 62 | .589 | 17.0 | Joe Cronin | 573,070 |
| 1940 | 4th (tied) | 82 | 72 | .532 | 8.0 | Joe Cronin | 716,234 |
| 1941 | 2nd | 84 | 70 | .545 | 17.0 | Joe Cronin | 718,497 |
| 1942 | 2nd | 93 | 59 | .612 | 9.0 | Joe Cronin | 730,340 |
| 1943 | 7th | 68 | 84 | .447 | 29.0 | Joe Cronin | 358,275 |
| 1944 | 4th | 77 | 77 | .500 | 12.0 | Joe Cronin | 506,975 |
| 1945 | 7th | 71 | 83 | .461 | 17.5 | Joe Cronin | 603,794 |
| 1946 | 1st (s) | 104 | 50 | .675 | +12.0 | Joe Cronin | 1,416,944 |
| 1947 | 3rd | 83 | 71 | .539 | 14.0 | Joe Cronin | 1,427,315 |
| 1948 | 2nd (l) | 96 | 59 | .619 | 1.0 | Joe McCarthy | 1,558,798 |
| 1949 | 2nd | 96 | 58 | .623 | 1.0 | Joe McCarthy | 1,596,650 |
| 1950 | 3rd | 94 | 60 | .610 | 4.0 | Joe McCarthy, Steve O'Neill | 1,344,080 |
| 1951 | 3rd | 87 | 67 | .565 | 11.0 | Steve O'Neill | 1,312,282 |
| 1952 | 6th | 76 | 78 | .494 | 19.0 | Lou Boudreau | 1,115,750 |
| 1953 | 4th | 84 | 69 | .549 | 16.0 | Lou Boudreau | 1,026,133 |
| 1954 | 4th | 69 | 85 | .448 | 42.0 | Lou Boudreau | 931,127 |
| 1955 | 4th | 84 | 70 | .545 | 12.0 | Pinky Higgins | 1,203,200 |
| 1956 | 4th | 84 | 70 | .545 | 13.0 | Pinky Higgins | 1,137,158 |
| 1957 | 3rd | 82 | 72 | .532 | 16.0 | Pinky Higgins | 1,181,087 |
| 1958 | 3rd | 79 | 75 | .513 | 13.0 | Pinky Higgins | 1,077,047 |
| 1959 | 5th | 75 | 79 | .487 | 19.0 | Pinky Higgins, Billy Jurges | 984,102 |
| 1960 | 7th | 65 | 89 | .422 | 32.0 | Billy Jurges, Pinky Higgins | 1,129,866 |
| 1961 | 6th | 76 | 86 | .469 | 33.0 | Pinky Higgins | 850,589 |
| 1962 | 8th | 76 | 84 | .475 | 19.0 | Pinky Higgins | 733,080 |
| 1963 | 7th | 76 | 85 | .472 | 28.0 | Johnny Pesky | 942,642 |
| 1964 | 8th | 72 | 90 | .444 | 27.0 | Johnny Pesky, Billy Herman | 883,276 |
| 1965 | 9th | 62 | 100 | .383 | 40.0 | Billy Herman | 652,201 |
| 1966 | 9th | 72 | 90 | .444 | 26.0 | Billy Herman, Pete Runnels | 811,172 |
| 1967 | 1st (s) | 92 | 70 | .568 | +1.0 | Dick Williams | 1,727,832 |
| 1968 | 4th | 86 | 76 | .531 | 17.0 | Dick Williams | 1,940,788 |

## EAST DIVISION

| Year | Position | W | L | Pct. | GB | Manager | Attendance |
|---|---|---|---|---|---|---|---|
| 1969 | 3rd | 87 | 75 | .537 | 22.0 | Dick Williams, Eddie Popowski | 1,833,246 |
| 1970 | 3rd | 87 | 75 | .537 | 21.0 | Eddie Kasko | 1,595,278 |
| 1971 | 3rd | 85 | 77 | .525 | 18.0 | Eddie Kasko | 1,678,732 |
| 1972 | 2nd | 85 | 70 | .548 | 0.5 | Eddie Kasko | 1,441,718 |
| 1973 | 2nd | 89 | 73 | .549 | 8.0 | Eddie Kasko | 1,481,002 |
| 1974 | 3rd | 84 | 78 | .519 | 7.0 | Darrell Johnson | 1,556,411 |
| 1975 | 1st (C,s) | 95 | 65 | .594 | +4.5 | Darrell Johnson | 1,748,587 |
| 1976 | 3rd | 83 | 79 | .512 | 15.5 | Darrell Johnson, Don Zimmer | 1,895,846 |
| 1977 | 2nd (tied) | 97 | 64 | .602 | 2.5 | Don Zimmer | 2,074,549 |
| 1978 | 2nd (p) | 99 | 64 | .607 | 1.0 | Don Zimmer | 2,320,643 |
| 1979 | 3rd | 91 | 69 | .569 | 11.5 | Don Zimmer | 2,353,114 |
| 1980 | 4th | 83 | 77 | .519 | 19.0 | Don Zimmer, Johnny Pesky | 1,956,092 |
| 1981 | 5th/2nd (tied) | 59 | 49 | .546 | * | Ralph Houk | 1,060,379 |
| 1982 | 3rd | 89 | 73 | .549 | 6.0 | Ralph Houk | 1,950,124 |
| 1983 | 6th | 78 | 84 | .481 | 20.0 | Ralph Houk | 1,782,285 |
| 1984 | 4th | 86 | 76 | .531 | 18.0 | Ralph Houk | 1,661,618 |
| 1985 | 5th | 81 | 81 | .500 | 18.5 | John McNamara | 1,786,633 |
| 1986 | 1st (C,s) | 95 | 66 | .590 | +5.5 | John McNamara | 2,147,641 |
| 1987 | 5th | 78 | 84 | .481 | 20.0 | John McNamara | 2,231,551 |
| 1988 | 1st (c) | 89 | 73 | .549 | +1.0 | John McNamara, Joe Morgan | 2,464,851 |
| 1989 | 3rd | 83 | 79 | .512 | 6.0 | Joe Morgan | 2,510,012 |
| 1990 | 1st (c) | 88 | 74 | .543 | +2.0 | Joe Morgan | 2,528,986 |
| 1991 | 2nd (tied) | 84 | 78 | .519 | 7.0 | Joe Morgan | 2,562,435 |
| 1992 | 7th | 73 | 89 | .451 | 23.0 | Butch Hobson | 2,468,574 |
| 1993 | 5th | 80 | 82 | .494 | 15.0 | Butch Hobson | 2,422,021 |
| 1994 | 4th | 54 | 61 | .470 | 17.0 | Butch Hobson | 1,775,818 |
| 1995 | 1st (d) | 86 | 58 | .597 | +7.0 | Kevin Kennedy | 2,164,410 |
| 1996 | 3rd | 85 | 77 | .525 | 7.0 | Kevin Kennedy | 2,315,231 |
| 1997 | 4th | 78 | 84 | .481 | 20.0 | Jimy Williams | 2,226,136 |
| 1998 | 2nd (d) | 92 | 70 | .568 | 22.0 | Jimy Williams | 2,343,947 |
| 1999 | 2nd (D,c) | 94 | 68 | .580 | 4.0 | Jimy Williams | 2,446,162 |
| 2000 | 2nd | 85 | 77 | .525 | 2.5 | Jimy Williams | 2,586,032 |
| 2001 | 2nd | 82 | 79 | .509 | 13.5 | Jimy Williams, Joe Kerrigan | 2,625,333 |
| 2002 | 2nd | 93 | 69 | .574 | 10.5 | Grady Little | 2,650,063 |
| 2003 | 2nd (D,c) | 95 | 67 | .586 | 6.0 | Grady Little | 2,724,165 |
| 2004 | 2nd (D,C,S) | 98 | 64 | .605 | 3.0 | Terry Francona | 2,837,304 |
| 2005 | 1st (tied) (d) | 95 | 67 | .586 | 0.0 | Terry Francona | 2,847,898 |

(S) won World Series; (n) no World Series; (s) lost World Series; (l) lost league playoff; (C) won League Championship Series; (p) lost division playoff; *first half 30-26, second half 29-23; (c) lost League Championship Series; (d) lost Division Series; (D) won Division Series

## INDIVIDUAL AND CLUB RECORDS

### BATTING

| | Individual Season | Individual Career | Club Season |
|---|---|---|---|
| **Games** | 163—Jim Rice, 1978 | 3,308—Carl Yastrzemski | 163 (1961, 1978, 1985) |
| **At-bats** | 684—Nomar Garciaparra, 153 G, 1997 | 11,988—Carl Yastrzemski | 5,781 (1997) |
| **Runs** | 150—Ted Williams, 155 G, 1949 | 1,816—Carl Yastrzemski | 1,027 (1950)<br>Fewest—463 (1906) |
| **Hits** | 240—Wade Boggs, 161 G, 1985 | 3,419—Carl Yastrzemski | 1,684 (1997)<br>Fewest—1,175 (1905) |
| **Hitting streak** | 34 G—Dom DiMaggio, 1949 | | |
| **Singles** | 187—Wade Boggs, 161 G, 1985 | 2,262—Carl Yastrzemski | 1,156 (1950) |
| **Doubles** | 67—Earl Webb, 151 G, 1931 | 646—Carl Yastrzemski | 373 (1997, 2004) |
| **Triples** | 22—Tris Speaker, 141 G, 1913 | 130—Harry Hooper | 112 (1903) |

| | Individual Season | Individual Career | Club Season |
|---|---|---|---|
| **HOME RUNS** | | | 238 (2003)<br>Fewest—13 (1906) |
| **Righthander** | 50—Jimmie Foxx, 149 G, 1938 | 382—Jim Rice | |
| **Lefthander** | 47—David Ortiz, 159 G, 2005 | 521—Ted Williams | |
| **Switch-hitter** | 34—Carl Everett, 137 G, 2000 | 149—Reggie Smith | |
| **Rookie** | 34—Walt Dropo, 136 G, 1950 | | |
| **Home** | 35—Jimmie Foxx, 1938 | 248—Ted Williams | 124 (1977) |
| **Road** | 27—David Ortiz, 2005 | 273—Ted Williams | 127 (2003) |
| **Month** | 14—Jackie Jensen, June 1958 | | 55 (July 2003) |
| **Pinch** | 5—Joe Cronin, 1943 | 7—Ted Williams | 6 (1953) |
| **Grand slams** | 4—Babe Ruth, 130 G, 1919 | 17—Ted Williams | 9 (1941, 1950, 1987, 2001) |
| **Home runs at Huntington Avenue Grounds, all teams** | | | 53 (1910) |
| **Home runs at Fenway Park, all teams** | | | 219 (1977) |
| **Total bases** | 406—Jim Rice, 163 G, 1978 | 5,539—Carl Yastrzemski | 2,832 (2003) |
| **Extra-base hits** | 92—Jimmie Foxx, 149 G, 1938 | 1,157—Carl Yastrzemski | 649 (2003) |
| **Sacrifice hits** | 35—Freddy Parent, 153 G, 1905 | 218—Duffy Lewis | 142 (1906) |
| **Sacrifice flies** | 12—Jackie Jensen, 152 G, 1955<br>Jimmy Piersall, 155 G, 1956<br>Jackie Jensen, 148 G, 1959 | 105—Carl Yastrzemski | 64 (2003) |
| **Bases on balls** | 162—Ted Williams, 156 G, 1947<br>Ted Williams, 155 G, 1949 | 2,021—Ted Williams | 835 (1949)<br>Fewest—262 (1903) |
| **Strikeouts** | 177—Mark Bellhorn, 138 G, 2004<br>Fewest—9—Stuffy McInnis, 152 G, 1921 | 1,643—Dwight Evans | 1,189 (2004)<br>Fewest—282 (1901) |
| **Hit by pitch** | 35—Don Baylor, 160 G, 1986 | 71—Mo Vaughn | 72 (2002)<br>Fewest—11 (1934) |
| **Runs batted in** | 175—Jimmie Foxx, 149 G, 1938 | 1,844—Carl Yastrzemski | 974 (1950)<br>Fewest—405 (1907) |
| **Grounded into double plays** | 36—Jim Rice, 159 G, 1984<br>Fewest—3—Tony Lupien, 154 G, 1943 | 323—Carl Yastrzemski | 174 (1990)<br>Fewest—94 (1942) |
| **Left on base** | | | 1,308 (1989)<br>Fewest—1,015 (1929) |
| **Batting average** | .406—Ted Williams, 143 G, 1941 | .344—Ted Williams | .302 (1950)<br>Lowest—.234 (1905, 1907) |
| **Most .300 hitters** | | | 9 (1950) |
| **Slugging average** | .735—Ted Williams, 143 G, 1941 | .634—Ted Williams | .491 (2003)<br>Lowest—.318 (1916, 1917) |
| **On-base percentage** | .553—Ted Williams, 143 G, 1941 | .482—Ted Williams | .385 (1950)<br>Lowest—.281 (1907) |

## BASERUNNING

| | Individual Season | Individual Career | Club Season |
|---|---|---|---|
| **Stolen bases** | 54—Tommy Harper, 147 G, 1973 | 300—Harry Hooper | 215 (1909) |
| **Caught stealing** | 31—Duffy Lewis, 146 G, 1914 | 116—Carl Yastrzemski | 176 (1914) |

## PITCHING

| | Individual Season | Individual Career | Club Season |
|---|---|---|---|
| **Games** | 81—Mike Timlin, 2005 | 637—Bob Stanley | |
| **Games started** | 43—Cy Young, 1902 | 382—Roger Clemens | |
| **Complete games** | 41—Cy Young, 1902 | 275—Cy Young | 148 (1904) |
| **Wins** | 34—Joe Wood, 1912 | 192—Cy Young<br>Roger Clemens | |
| **Percentage** | .882—Bob Stanley (15-2), 1978 | .760—Pedro Martinez | |
| **Winning streak** | 16—Joe Wood, 1912 | | |
| **20-win seasons** | | 6—Cy Young | |
| **Losses** | 25—Red Ruffing, 1928 | 112—Cy Young | |
| **Losing streak** | 14—Joe W. Harris, 1906 | | |
| **Saves** | 46—Tom Gordon, 1998 | 132—Bob Stanley | 53 (1998) |
| **Innings** | 384.2—Cy Young, 1902 | 2,776—Roger Clemens | 1,472.2 (1978) |
| **Hits** | 350—Cy Young, 1902 | 2,359—Roger Clemens | 1,615 (1925) |
| **Runs** | 162—Red Ruffing, 1929<br>Jack Russell, 1930 | 1,140—Tim Wakefield | 922 (1925) |
| **Earned runs** | 140—Wes Ferrell, 1936 | 988—Tim Wakefield | 807 (1996) |
| **Bases on balls** | 134—Mel Parnell, 1949 | 856—Roger Clemens | 748 (1950) |
| **Strikeouts** | 313—Pedro Martinez, 1999 | 2,590—Roger Clemens | 1,259 (2001) |
| **Strikeouts, game** | 20—Roger Clemens, Apr 29, 1986<br>Roger Clemens, Sept 18, 1996 | | |
| **Hit batsmen** | 20—Howard Ehmke, 1923<br>Bronson Arroyo, 2004 | 126—Tim Wakefield | 93 (2001) |
| **Wild pitches** | 21—Earl Wilson, 1963 | 72—Roger Clemens | 73 (1968) |
| **Home runs** | 38—Tim Wakefield, 1996 | 279—Tim Wakefield | 190 (1987) |
| **Sacrifice hits** | 24—Tex Hughson, 1943<br>Gordon Rhodes, 1934 | 208—Cy Young | 288 (1926) |
| **Sacrifice Flies** | 14—Dave Morehead, 1964 | 74—Tim Wakefield | 67 (1996) |

| | Individual Season | Career | Club Season |
|---|---|---|---|
| **Earned run average** | 0.96—Dutch Leonard, 224.2 inn, 1914 | 2.00—Cy Young | 2.12 (1904) |
| **Shutouts** | 10—Cy Young, 1904<br>Joe Wood, 1912 | 38—Cy Young<br>Roger Clemens | 26 (1918)<br>Lost—28 (1906) |
| **1-0 games won** | 5—Joe Bush, 1918 | 7—Tex Hughson | 8 (1918)<br>Lost—7 (1909, 1914) |

## TEAM FIELDING

| | | | |
|---|---|---|---|
| **Putouts** | 4,418 (1978)<br>Fewest—3,949 (1938) | **Assists** | 2,195 (1907)<br>Fewest—1,542 (1988) |
| **Chances accepted** | 6,425 (1907)<br>Fewest—5,667 (1938) | **Errors** | 337 (1901)<br>Fewest—93 (1988) |
| **Double plays** | 207 (1949)<br>Fewest—74 (1913) | **Passed balls** | 36 (1997)<br>Fewest—3 (1933, 1975) |
| **Errorless games** | 92 (1988, 1998)<br>Consecutive—10 (1986) | **Fielding average** | .984 (1988)<br>Lowest—.943 (1901) |

## MISCELLANEOUS

**Most players, season** 55 (1996)
**Fewest players, season** 18 (1904)

**Games won** 105 (1912)
**Month** 25 (July 1948)
**Consecutive** 15 (1946)
**Winning percentage** .691 (1912), 105-47
**Lowest** .279 (1932), 43-111
**Number of league championships** 11
**Most recent** 2004
**Runs, game** 29 vs St. Louis, June 8, 1950
**Opponents'** 27 by Cleveland, July 7, 1923, 1st game
**Hits, game** 28 vs St. Louis, June 8, 1950
vs Florida, June 27, 2003
**Home runs, game** 8 vs Toronto, July 4, 1977
**Runs, shutout** 19 vs Philadelphia, Apr 30, 1950, 1st game
**Opponents'** 19 by Cleveland, Aug 21, 1920
**Longest 1-0 win** 15 inn, vs Detroit, May 11, 1904

**Most seasons, non-pitcher** 23—Carl Yastrzemski
**Most seasons, pitcher** 13—Bob Stanley
Roger Clemens

**Games lost** 111 (1932)
**Month** 24 (July 1925, June 1927, July 1928)
**Consecutive** 20 (1906)
**Overall record** 8,358-7,884 (105 seasons)
**Interleague play** 77-80
**Number of times worst record in league** 10
**Most recent** 1932
**Runs, inning** 17 vs Detroit, June 18, 1953, 7th

**Total bases, game** 60 vs St. Louis, June 8, 1950

**Consecutive games with one or more home runs** 19 (30 HRs), 1996
**Longest shutout** 15 inn, 1-0, vs Detroit, May 11, 1904

**Longest 1-0 loss** 15 inn, vs Washington, July 3, 1915

## ATTENDANCE

**Highest home attendance**
**Huntington Avenue Grounds** 668,965 (1909)
**Fenway Park** 2,847,888 (2005)

**Highest road attendance** 3,056,551 (2005)

**Largest crowds**
**Day** 36,388 vs Cleveland, Apr 22, 1978
**Night** 36,228 vs New York, June 28, 1949
**Doubleheader** 47,627 vs New York, Sept 22, 1935
**Home opener** 35,343 vs Baltimore, Apr 14, 1969

# CHICAGO WHITE SOX

## YEARLY FINISHES

**(Original American League franchise)**

| Year | Position | W | L | Pct. | GB | Manager | Attendance |
|---|---|---|---|---|---|---|---|
| 1901 | 1st | 83 | 53 | .610 | +4.0 | Clark Griffith | 354,350 |
| 1902 | 4th | 74 | 60 | .552 | 8.0 | Clark Griffith | 337,898 |
| 1903 | 7th | 60 | 77 | .438 | 30.5 | Nixey Callahan | 286,183 |
| 1904 | 3rd | 89 | 65 | .578 | 6.0 | Nixey Callahan, Fielder Jones | 557,123 |
| 1905 | 2nd | 92 | 60 | .605 | 2.0 | Fielder Jones | 687,419 |
| 1906 | 1st (S) | 93 | 58 | .616 | +3.0 | Fielder Jones | 585,202 |
| 1907 | 3rd | 87 | 64 | .576 | 5.5 | Fielder Jones | 666,307 |
| 1908 | 3rd | 88 | 64 | .579 | 1.5 | Fielder Jones | 636,096 |
| 1909 | 4th | 78 | 74 | .513 | 20.0 | Billy Sullivan | 478,400 |
| 1910 | 6th | 68 | 85 | .444 | 35.5 | Hugh Duffy | 552,084 |
| 1911 | 4th | 77 | 74 | .510 | 24.0 | Hugh Duffy | 583,208 |
| 1912 | 4th | 78 | 76 | .506 | 28.0 | Nixey Callahan | 602,241 |
| 1913 | 5th | 78 | 74 | .513 | 17.5 | Nixey Callahan | 644,501 |
| 1914 | 6th (tied) | 70 | 84 | .455 | 30.0 | Nixey Callahan | 469,290 |
| 1915 | 3rd | 93 | 61 | .604 | 9.5 | Pants Rowland | 539,461 |
| 1916 | 2nd | 89 | 65 | .578 | 2.0 | Pants Rowland | 679,923 |
| 1917 | 1st (S) | 100 | 54 | .649 | +9.0 | Pants Rowland | 684,521 |
| 1918 | 6th | 57 | 67 | .460 | 17.0 | Pants Rowland | 195,081 |
| 1919 | 1st (s) | 88 | 52 | .629 | +3.5 | Kid Gleason | 627,186 |
| 1920 | 2nd | 96 | 58 | .623 | 2.0 | Kid Gleason | 833,492 |
| 1921 | 7th | 62 | 92 | .403 | 36.5 | Kid Gleason | 543,650 |
| 1922 | 5th | 77 | 77 | .500 | 17.0 | Kid Gleason | 602,860 |
| 1923 | 7th | 69 | 85 | .448 | 30.0 | Kid Gleason | 573,778 |
| 1924 | 8th | 66 | 87 | .431 | 25.5 | Johnny Evers | 606,658 |
| 1925 | 5th | 79 | 75 | .513 | 18.5 | Eddie Collins | 832,231 |
| 1926 | 5th | 81 | 72 | .529 | 9.5 | Eddie Collins | 710,339 |
| 1927 | 5th | 70 | 83 | .458 | 29.5 | Ray Schalk | 614,423 |
| 1928 | 5th | 72 | 82 | .468 | 29.0 | Ray Schalk, Lena Blackburne | 494,152 |
| 1929 | 7th | 59 | 93 | .388 | 46.0 | Lena Blackburne | 426,795 |
| 1930 | 7th | 62 | 92 | .403 | 40.0 | Donie Bush | 406,123 |
| 1931 | 8th | 56 | 97 | .366 | 51.0 | Donie Bush | 403,550 |
| 1932 | 7th | 49 | 102 | .325 | 56.5 | Lew Fonseca | 233,198 |
| 1933 | 6th | 67 | 83 | .447 | 31.0 | Lew Fonseca | 397,789 |
| 1934 | 8th | 53 | 99 | .349 | 47.0 | Lew Fonseca, Jimmie Dykes | 236,559 |
| 1935 | 5th | 74 | 78 | .487 | 19.5 | Jimmie Dykes | 470,281 |
| 1936 | 3rd | 81 | 70 | .536 | 20.0 | Jimmie Dykes | 440,810 |
| 1937 | 3rd | 86 | 68 | .558 | 16.0 | Jimmie Dykes | 589,245 |
| 1938 | 6th | 65 | 83 | .439 | 32.0 | Jimmie Dykes | 338,278 |

| Year | Position | W | L | Pct. | GB | Manager | Attendance |
|---|---|---|---|---|---|---|---|
| 1939 | 4th | 85 | 69 | .552 | 22.5 | Jimmie Dykes | 594,104 |
| 1940 | 4th (tied) | 82 | 72 | .532 | 8.0 | Jimmie Dykes | 660,336 |
| 1941 | 3rd | 77 | 77 | .500 | 24.0 | Jimmie Dykes | 677,077 |
| 1942 | 6th | 66 | 82 | .446 | 34.0 | Jimmie Dykes | 425,734 |
| 1943 | 4th | 82 | 72 | .532 | 16.0 | Jimmie Dykes | 508,962 |
| 1944 | 7th | 71 | 83 | .461 | 18.0 | Jimmie Dykes | 563,539 |
| 1945 | 6th | 71 | 78 | .477 | 15.0 | Jimmie Dykes | 657,981 |
| 1946 | 5th | 74 | 80 | .481 | 30.0 | Jimmie Dykes, Ted Lyons | 983,403 |
| 1947 | 6th | 70 | 84 | .455 | 27.0 | Ted Lyons | 876,948 |
| 1948 | 8th | 51 | 101 | .336 | 44.5 | Ted Lyons | 777,844 |
| 1949 | 6th | 63 | 91 | .409 | 34.0 | Jack Onslow | 937,151 |
| 1950 | 6th | 60 | 94 | .390 | 38.0 | Jack Onslow, Red Corriden | 781,330 |
| 1951 | 4th | 81 | 73 | .526 | 17.0 | Paul Richards | 1,328,234 |
| 1952 | 3rd | 81 | 73 | .526 | 14.0 | Paul Richards | 1,231,675 |
| 1953 | 3rd | 89 | 65 | .578 | 11.5 | Paul Richards | 1,191,353 |
| 1954 | 3rd | 94 | 60 | .610 | 17.0 | Paul Richards, Marty Marion | 1,231,629 |
| 1955 | 3rd | 91 | 63 | .591 | 5.0 | Marty Marion | 1,175,684 |
| 1956 | 3rd | 85 | 69 | .552 | 12.0 | Marty Marion | 1,000,090 |
| 1957 | 2nd | 90 | 64 | .584 | 8.0 | Al Lopez | 1,135,668 |
| 1958 | 2nd | 82 | 72 | .532 | 10.0 | Al Lopez | 797,451 |
| 1959 | 1st (s) | 94 | 60 | .610 | +5.0 | Al Lopez | 1,423,144 |
| 1960 | 3rd | 87 | 67 | .565 | 10.0 | Al Lopez | 1,644,460 |
| 1961 | 4th | 86 | 76 | .531 | 23.0 | Al Lopez | 1,146,019 |
| 1962 | 5th | 85 | 77 | .525 | 11.0 | Al Lopez | 1,131,562 |
| 1963 | 2nd | 94 | 68 | .580 | 10.5 | Al Lopez | 1,158,848 |
| 1964 | 2nd | 98 | 64 | .605 | 1.0 | Al Lopez | 1,250,053 |
| 1965 | 2nd | 95 | 67 | .586 | 7.0 | Al Lopez | 1,130,519 |
| 1966 | 4th | 83 | 79 | .512 | 15.0 | Eddie Stanky | 990,016 |
| 1967 | 4th | 89 | 73 | .549 | 3.0 | Eddie Stanky | 985,634 |
| 1968 | 8th (tied) | 67 | 95 | .414 | 36.0 | Eddie Stanky, Al Lopez | 803,775 |

## WEST DIVISION

| Year | Position | W | L | Pct. | GB | Manager | Attendance |
|---|---|---|---|---|---|---|---|
| 1969 | 5th | 68 | 94 | .420 | 29.0 | Al Lopez, Don Gutteridge | 589,546 |
| 1970 | 6th | 56 | 106 | .346 | 42.0 | Don Gutteridge, Chuck Tanner | 495,355 |
| 1971 | 3rd | 79 | 83 | .488 | 22.5 | Chuck Tanner | 833,891 |
| 1972 | 2nd | 87 | 67 | .565 | 5.5 | Chuck Tanner | 1,177,318 |
| 1973 | 5th | 77 | 85 | .475 | 17.0 | Chuck Tanner | 1,302,527 |
| 1974 | 4th | 80 | 80 | .500 | 9.0 | Chuck Tanner | 1,149,596 |
| 1975 | 5th | 75 | 86 | .466 | 22.5 | Chuck Tanner | 750,802 |
| 1976 | 6th | 64 | 97 | .398 | 25.5 | Paul Richards | 914,945 |
| 1977 | 3rd | 90 | 72 | .556 | 12.0 | Bob Lemon | 1,657,135 |
| 1978 | 5th | 71 | 90 | .441 | 20.5 | Bob Lemon, Larry Doby | 1,491,100 |
| 1979 | 5th | 73 | 87 | .456 | 14.0 | Don Kessinger, Tony La Russa | 1,280,702 |
| 1980 | 5th | 70 | 90 | .438 | 26.0 | Tony La Russa | 1,200,365 |
| 1981 | 3rd/6th | 54 | 52 | .509 | * | Tony La Russa | 946,651 |
| 1982 | 3rd | 87 | 75 | .537 | 6.0 | Tony La Russa | 1,567,787 |
| 1983 | 1st (c) | 99 | 63 | .611 | +20.0 | Tony La Russa | 2,132,821 |
| 1984 | 5th (tied) | 74 | 88 | .457 | 10.0 | Tony La Russa | 2,136,988 |
| 1985 | 3rd | 85 | 77 | .525 | 6.0 | Tony La Russa | 1,669,888 |
| 1986 | 5th | 72 | 90 | .444 | 20.0 | Tony La Russa, Jim Fregosi | 1,424,313 |
| 1987 | 5th | 77 | 85 | .475 | 8.0 | Jim Fregosi | 1,208,060 |
| 1988 | 5th | 71 | 90 | .441 | 32.5 | Jim Fregosi | 1,115,749 |
| 1989 | 7th | 69 | 92 | .429 | 29.5 | Jeff Torborg | 1,045,651 |
| 1990 | 2nd | 94 | 68 | .580 | 9.0 | Jeff Torborg | 2,002,357 |
| 1991 | 2nd | 87 | 75 | .537 | 8.0 | Jeff Torborg | 2,934,154 |
| 1992 | 3rd | 86 | 76 | .531 | 10.0 | Gene Lamont | 2,681,156 |
| 1993 | 1st (c) | 94 | 68 | .580 | +8.0 | Gene Lamont | 2,581,091 |

## CENTRAL DIVISION

| Year | Position | W | L | Pct. | GB | Manager | Attendance |
|---|---|---|---|---|---|---|---|
| 1994 | 1st | 67 | 46 | .593 | +1.0 | Gene Lamont | 1,697,398 |
| 1995 | 3rd | 68 | 76 | .472 | 32.0 | Gene Lamont, Terry Bevington | 1,609,773 |
| 1996 | 2nd | 85 | 77 | .525 | 14.5 | Terry Bevington | 1,676,403 |
| 1997 | 2nd | 80 | 81 | .497 | 6.0 | Terry Bevington | 1,864,782 |
| 1998 | 2nd | 80 | 82 | .494 | 9.0 | Jerry Manuel | 1,391,146 |
| 1999 | 2nd | 75 | 86 | .466 | 21.5 | Jerry Manuel | 1,338,851 |
| 2000 | 1st (d) | 95 | 67 | .586 | +5.0 | Jerry Manuel | 1,947,799 |
| 2001 | 3rd | 83 | 79 | .512 | 8.0 | Jerry Manuel | 1,766,172 |
| 2002 | 2nd | 81 | 81 | .500 | 13.5 | Jerry Manuel | 1,676,804 |
| 2003 | 2nd | 86 | 76 | .531 | 4.0 | Jerry Manuel | 1,939,611 |
| 2004 | 2nd | 83 | 79 | .512 | 9.0 | Ozzie Guillen | 1,930,537 |
| 2005 | 1st (D,C,S) | 99 | 63 | .611 | +6.0 | Ozzie Guillen | 2,342,833 |

(S) won World Series; (s) lost World Series; *first half 31-22, second half 23-30; (c) lost League Championship Series; (d) lost Division Series, (D) won Division Series, (C) won League Championship Series

## INDIVIDUAL AND CLUB RECORDS

### BATTING

| | Individual Season | Individual Career | Club Season |
|---|---|---|---|
| **Games** | 163—Don Buford, 1966<br>Greg Walker, 1985<br>Albert Belle, 1998 | 2,422—Luke Appling | 163 (1961, 1966, 1974, 1985, 1998) |
| **At-bats** | 649—Nellie Fox, 154 G, 1956 | 8,856—Luke Appling | 5,646 (2000) |
| **Runs** | 135—Johnny Mostil, 153 G, 1925 | 1,327—Frank Thomas | 978 (2000)<br>Fewest—457 (1910) |

| | Individual Season | Career | Club Season |
|---|---|---|---|
| **Hits** | 224—Eddie Collins, 153 G, 1920 | 2,749—Luke Appling | 1,615 (2000)<br>Fewest—1,061 (1910) |
| **Hitting streak** | 28 G—Carlos Lee, 2004 | | |
| **Singles** | 170—Eddie Collins, 153 G, 1920 | 2,162—Luke Appling | 1,199 (1936) |
| **Doubles** | 48—Albert Belle, 163 G, 1998 | 447—Frank Thomas | 325 (2000) |
| **Triples** | 21—Joe Jackson, 153 G, 1916 | 104—Shano Collins<br>Nellie Fox | 102 (1915) |
| **HOME RUNS** | | | 242 (2004)<br>Fewest—3 (1908) |
| **Righthander** | 49—Albert Belle, 163 G, 1998 | 448—Frank Thomas | |
| **Lefthander** | 34—Robin Ventura, 158 G, 1996 | 221—Harold Baines | |
| **Switch-hitter** | 28—Jose Valentin, 124 G, 2001<br>Jose Valentin, 144 G, 2003 | 106—Ray Durham<br>106—Jose Valentin | |
| **Rookie** | 35—Ron Kittle, 145 G, 1983 | | |
| **Home** | 30—Frank Thomas, 2000 | 263—Frank Thomas | 145 (2004) |
| **Road** | 25—Frank Thomas, 1995 | 185—Frank Thomas | 119 (1996) |
| **Month** | 16—Albert Belle, July 1998 | | 51 (Aug 2001, July 2003) |
| **Pinch** | 3—Oscar Gamble, 1977<br>Ron Northey, 1956<br>John Romano, 1959 | 7—Jerry Hairston | 9 (1984) |
| **Grand slams** | 4—Albert Belle, 161 G, 1997 | 10—Robin Ventura | 8 (1996, 2002) |
| **Home runs at South Side Park, all teams** | | | 25 (1901) |
| **Home runs at Comiskey Park, all teams** | | | 175 (1970) |
| **Home runs at U.S. Cellular Field, all teams** | | | 277 (2004) |
| **Total bases** | 399—Albert Belle, 163 G, 1998 | 3,949—Frank Thomas | 2,654 (2000) |
| **Extra-base hits** | 99—Albert Belle, 163 G, 1998 | 906—Frank Thomas | 574 (2000) |
| **Sacrifice hits** | 40—George Davis, 151 G, 1905 | 342—Eddie Collins | 207 (1906) |
| **Sacrifice flies** | 15—Albert Belle, 163 G, 1998<br>Magglio Ordonez, 153 G, 2000 | 106—Frank Thomas | 69 (1992) |
| **Bases on balls** | 138—Frank Thomas, 158 G, 1991 | 1,466—Frank Thomas | 702 (1949)<br>Fewest—325 (1903) |
| **Strikeouts** | 175—Dave Nicholson, 126 G, 1963<br>Fewest—11—Nellie Fox, 155 G, 1958 | 1,165—Frank Thomas | 1,030 (2004)<br>Fewest—355 (1920) |
| **Hit by pitch** | 23—Minnie Minoso, 151 G, 1956 | 145—Minnie Minoso | 79 (2005)<br>Fewest—10 (1940) |
| **Runs batted in** | 152—Albert Belle, 163 G, 1998 | 1,465—Frank Thomas | 926 (2000)<br>Fewest—351 (1910) |
| **Grounded into double plays** | 29—George Bell, 155 G, 1992<br>Fewest—3—Tony Lupien, 154 G, 1948<br>Don Buford, 163 G, 1966<br>Don Buford, 156 G, 1967 | 188—Frank Thomas | 156 (1950, 1974)<br>Fewest—94 (1966) |
| **Left on base** | | | 1,279 (1936)<br>Fewest—1,009 (1985) |
| **Batting average** | .388—Luke Appling, 138 G, 1936 | .340—Joe Jackson | .295 (1920)<br>Lowest—.212 (1910) |
| **Most .300 hitters** | | | 8 (1924) |
| **Slugging average** | .729—Frank Thomas, 113 G, 1994 | .568—Frank Thomas | .470 (2000)<br>Lowest—.261 (1910) |
| **On-base percentage** | .487—Frank Thomas, 113 G, 1994 | .429—Frank Thomas | .373 (1936)<br>Lowest—.275 (1910) |

## BASERUNNING

| | Individual Season | Career | Club Season |
|---|---|---|---|
| **Stolen bases** | 77—Rudy Law, 141 G, 1983 | 368—Eddie Collins | 275 (1901) |
| **Caught stealing** | 29—Eddie Collins, 145 G, 1923 | 141—Eddie Collins | 119 (1923) |

## PITCHING

| | Individual Season | Career | Club Season |
|---|---|---|---|
| **Games** | 88—Wilbur Wood, 1968 | 669—Red Faber | |
| **Games started** | 49—Ed Au. Walsh, 1908<br>Wilbur Wood, 1972 | 484—Ted Lyons | |
| **Complete games** | 42—Ed Au. Walsh, 1908 | 356—Ted Lyons | 134 (1904) |
| **Wins** | 40—Ed Au. Walsh, 1908 | 260—Ted Lyons | |
| **Percentage** | .842—Sandy Consuegra (16-3), 1954 | .609—Ed Au. Walsh | |
| **Winning streak** | 13—LaMarr Hoyt, 1983 | | |
| **20-win seasons** | | 4—Ed Au. Walsh<br>Red Faber<br>Wilbur Wood | |
| **Losses** | 25—Patrick Flaherty, 1903 | 230—Ted Lyons | |
| **Losing streak** | 14—Howard Judson, 1949 | | |

| | Individual Season | Career | Club Season |
|---|---|---|---|
| Saves | 57—Bobby Thigpen, 1990 | 201—Bobby Thigpen | 68 (1990) |
| Innings | 464—Ed Au. Walsh, 1908 | 4,161—Ted Lyons | 1,490.1 (1967) |
| Hits | 381—Wilbur Wood, 1973 | 4,489—Ted Lyons | 1,635 (1924) |
| Runs | 182—Dick Kerr, 1921 | 2,056—Ted Lyons | 946 (1934) |
| Earned runs | 162—Dick Kerr, 1921 | 1,696—Ted Lyons | 835 (1998) |
| Bases on balls | 147—Vern Kennedy, 1936 | 1,213—Red Faber | 734 (1950) |
| Strikeouts | 269—Ed A. Walsh, 1908 | 1,796—Billy Pierce | 1,056 (2003) |
| Strikeouts, game | 16—Jack Harshman, July 25, 1954, 1st game | | |
| Hit batsmen | 16—Jim Scott, 1909 | 103—Red Faber | 88 (2001) |
| Wild pitches | 20—Jose Contreras, 2005<br>Freddy Garcia, 2005 | 83—Ed Au. Walsh | 71 (1997) |
| Home runs | 38—Floyd Bannister, 1987 | 241—Billy Pierce | 224 (2004) |
| Sacrifice hits | 27—Bill Dietrich, 1944 | 519—Red Faber | 232 (1923) |
| Sacrifice flies | 16—Charlie Hough, 1991 | 64—Wilbur Wood | 61 (1976, 1988) |
| Earned run average | 1.53—Ed Cicotte, 346 inn, 1917 | 1.81—Ed Au. Walsh | 1.99 (1905) |
| Shutouts | 12—Ed Au. Walsh, 1908 | 58—Ed Au. Walsh | 32 (1906)<br>Lost—24 (1910) |
| 1-0 games won | 5—Reb Russell, 1913 | 13—Doc White<br>Ed Au. Walsh | 9 (1909, 1967)<br>Lost—9 (1968) |

## TEAM FIELDING

| | | | |
|---|---|---|---|
| **Putouts** | 4,471 (1967)<br>Fewest—3,943 (1942) | **Assists** | 2,446 (1907)<br>Fewest—1,439 (1997) |
| **Chances accepted** | 6,655 (1907)<br>Fewest—5,670 (1942) | **Errors** | 358 (1901)<br>Fewest—93 (2003) |
| **Double plays** | 190 (2000)<br>Fewest—94 (1915) | **Passed balls** | 45 (1965)<br>Fewest—3 (1922) |
| **Errorless games** | 97 (2005)<br>Consecutive—9 (1955, 1964, 1995) | **Fielding average** | .985 (2005)<br>Lowest—.938 (1901) |

## MISCELLANEOUS

**Most players, season** 50 (1932)
**Fewest players, season** 19 (1905)
**Games won** 100 (1917)
**Month** 23 (Sept 1905)
**Consecutive** 19 (1906)
**Winning percentage** .649 (1917), 100-54
**Lowest** .325 (1932), 49-102
**Number of league championships** 6
**Most recent** 2005
**Runs, game** 29 vs Kansas City, Apr 23, 1955
**Opponents'** 22 by New York, July 26, 1931, 2nd game
**Total bases, game** 55 vs Kansas City, Apr 23, 1955
**Home runs, game** 7 vs Kansas City, Apr 23, 1955
**Runs, shutout** 17 vs Washington, Sept 19, 1925, 2nd game
vs Cleveland, July 5, 1987
**Opponents'** 19 by Anaheim, May 10, 2002
**Longest 1-0 win** 15 inn, vs Chicago, Apr 13, 1963

**Most seasons, non-pitcher** 20—Luke Appling
**Most seasons, pitcher** 21—Ted Lyons
**Games lost** 106 (1970)
**Month** 24 (June 1934, Aug 1968)
**Consecutive** 13 (1924)
**Overall record** 8,210-8,020 (105 seasons)
**Interleague play** 86-71
**Number of times worst record in league** 6
**Most recent** 1976
**Runs, inning** 13 vs Washington, Sept 26, 1943, 1st game, 4th
**Hits, game** 29 vs Kansas City, Apr 23, 1955

**Consecutive games with one or more home runs** 17 (28 HRs), 2000
**Longest shutout** 17 inn, 1-0, vs Cleveland, Sept 13, 1967

**Longest 1-0 loss** 18 inn, vs Washington, May 15, 1918
vs Washington, June 8, 1947, 1st game

## ATTENDANCE

**Highest home attendance**

| | |
|---|---|
| **South Side Park** | 687,419 (1905) |
| **Comiskey Park** | 2,136,988 (1984) |
| **U.S. Cellular Field** | 2,934,154 (1991) |

**Highest road attendance** 2,571,969 (1993)

**Largest crowds**

| | |
|---|---|
| **Day** | 51,560 vs Milwaukee, Apr 14, 1981 |
| **Night** | 53,940 vs New York, June 8, 1951 |
| **Doubleheader** | 55,555 vs Minnesota, May 20, 1973 |
| **Home opener** | 51,560 vs Milwaukee, Apr 14, 1981 |

# CLEVELAND INDIANS

## YEARLY FINISHES

(Original American League franchise)

| Year | Position | W | L | Pct. | GB | Manager | Attendance |
|---|---|---|---|---|---|---|---|
| 1901 | 7th | 54 | 82 | .397 | 29.0 | James McAleer | 131,380 |
| 1902 | 5th | 69 | 67 | .507 | 14.0 | Bill Armour | 275,395 |
| 1903 | 3rd | 77 | 63 | .550 | 15.0 | Bill Armour | 311,280 |
| 1904 | 4th | 86 | 65 | .570 | 7.5 | Bill Armour | 264,749 |
| 1905 | 5th | 76 | 78 | .494 | 19.0 | Nap Lajoie | 316,306 |
| 1906 | 3rd | 89 | 64 | .582 | 5.0 | Nap Lajoie | 325,733 |
| 1907 | 4th | 85 | 67 | .559 | 8.0 | Nap Lajoie | 382,046 |
| 1908 | 2nd | 90 | 64 | .584 | 0.5 | Nap Lajoie | 422,242 |
| 1909 | 6th | 71 | 82 | .464 | 27.5 | Nap Lajoie, Deacon McGuire | 354,627 |
| 1910 | 5th | 71 | 81 | .467 | 32.0 | Deacon McGuire | 293,456 |

| Year | Position | W | L | Pct. | GB | Manager | Attendance |
|---|---|---|---|---|---|---|---|
| 1911 | 3rd | 80 | 73 | .523 | 22.0 | Deacon McGuire, George Stovall | 406,296 |
| 1912 | 5th | 75 | 78 | .490 | 30.5 | Harry Davis, J.L. Birmingham | 336,844 |
| 1913 | 3rd | 86 | 66 | .566 | 9.5 | J.L. Birmingham | 541,000 |
| 1914 | 8th | 51 | 102 | .333 | 48.5 | J.L. Birmingham | 185,997 |
| 1915 | 7th | 57 | 95 | .375 | 44.5 | J.L. Birmingham, Lee Fohl | 159,285 |
| 1916 | 6th | 77 | 77 | .500 | 14.0 | Lee Fohl | 492,106 |
| 1917 | 3rd | 88 | 66 | .571 | 12.0 | Lee Fohl | 477,298 |
| 1918 | 2nd | 73 | 54 | .575 | 2.5 | Lee Fohl | 295,515 |
| 1919 | 2nd | 84 | 55 | .604 | 3.5 | Lee Fohl, Tris Speaker | 538,135 |
| 1920 | 1st (S) | 98 | 56 | .636 | +2.0 | Tris Speaker | 912,832 |
| 1921 | 2nd | 94 | 60 | .610 | 4.5 | Tris Speaker | 748,705 |
| 1922 | 4th | 78 | 76 | .506 | 16.0 | Tris Speaker | 528,145 |
| 1923 | 3rd | 82 | 71 | .536 | 16.5 | Tris Speaker | 558,856 |
| 1924 | 6th | 67 | 86 | .438 | 24.5 | Tris Speaker | 481,905 |
| 1925 | 6th | 70 | 84 | .455 | 27.5 | Tris Speaker | 419,005 |
| 1926 | 2nd | 88 | 66 | .571 | 3.0 | Tris Speaker | 627,426 |
| 1927 | 6th | 66 | 87 | .431 | 43.5 | Jack McAllister | 373,138 |
| 1928 | 7th | 62 | 92 | .403 | 39.0 | Roger Peckinpaugh | 375,907 |
| 1929 | 3rd | 81 | 71 | .533 | 24.0 | Roger Peckinpaugh | 536,210 |
| 1930 | 4th | 81 | 73 | .526 | 21.0 | Roger Peckinpaugh | 528,657 |
| 1931 | 4th | 78 | 76 | .506 | 30.0 | Roger Peckinpaugh | 483,027 |
| 1932 | 4th | 87 | 65 | .572 | 19.0 | Roger Peckinpaugh | 468,953 |
| 1933 | 4th | 75 | 76 | .497 | 23.5 | Roger Peckinpaugh, Walter Johnson | 387,936 |
| 1934 | 3rd | 85 | 69 | .552 | 16.0 | Walter Johnson | 391,338 |
| 1935 | 3rd | 82 | 71 | .536 | 12.0 | Walter Johnson, Steve O'Neill | 397,615 |
| 1936 | 5th | 80 | 74 | .519 | 22.5 | Steve O'Neill | 500,391 |
| 1937 | 4th | 83 | 71 | .539 | 19.0 | Steve O'Neill | 564,849 |
| 1938 | 3rd | 86 | 66 | .566 | 13.0 | Ossie Vitt | 652,006 |
| 1939 | 3rd | 87 | 67 | .565 | 20.5 | Ossie Vitt | 563,926 |
| 1940 | 2nd | 89 | 65 | .578 | 1.0 | Ossie Vitt | 902,576 |
| 1941 | 4th (tied) | 75 | 79 | .487 | 26.0 | Roger Peckinpaugh | 745,948 |
| 1942 | 4th | 75 | 79 | .487 | 28.0 | Lou Boudreau | 459,447 |
| 1943 | 3rd | 82 | 71 | .536 | 15.5 | Lou Boudreau | 438,894 |
| 1944 | 5th (tied) | 72 | 82 | .468 | 17.0 | Lou Boudreau | 475,272 |
| 1945 | 5th | 73 | 72 | .503 | 11.0 | Lou Boudreau | 558,182 |
| 1946 | 6th | 68 | 86 | .442 | 36.0 | Lou Boudreau | 1,057,289 |
| 1947 | 4th | 80 | 74 | .519 | 17.0 | Lou Boudreau | 1,521,978 |
| 1948 | 1st (L,S) | 97 | 58 | .626 | +1.0 | Lou Boudreau | 2,620,627 |
| 1949 | 3rd | 89 | 65 | .578 | 8.0 | Lou Boudreau | 2,233,771 |
| 1950 | 4th | 92 | 62 | .597 | 6.0 | Lou Boudreau | 1,727,464 |
| 1951 | 2nd | 93 | 61 | .604 | 5.0 | Al Lopez | 1,704,984 |
| 1952 | 2nd | 93 | 61 | .604 | 2.0 | Al Lopez | 1,444,607 |
| 1953 | 2nd | 92 | 62 | .597 | 8.5 | Al Lopez | 1,069,176 |
| 1954 | 1st (s) | 111 | 43 | .721 | +8.0 | Al Lopez | 1,335,472 |
| 1955 | 2nd | 93 | 61 | .604 | 3.0 | Al Lopez | 1,221,780 |
| 1956 | 2nd | 88 | 66 | .571 | 9.0 | Al Lopez | 865,467 |
| 1957 | 6th | 76 | 77 | .497 | 21.5 | Kerby Farrell | 722,256 |
| 1958 | 4th | 77 | 76 | .503 | 14.5 | Bobby Bragan, Joe Gordon | 663,805 |
| 1959 | 2nd | 89 | 65 | .578 | 5.0 | Joe Gordon | 1,497,976 |
| 1960 | 4th | 76 | 78 | .494 | 21.0 | Joe Gordon, Jimmie Dykes | 950,985 |
| 1961 | 5th | 78 | 83 | .484 | 30.5 | Jimmie Dykes | 725,547 |
| 1962 | 6th | 80 | 82 | .494 | 16.0 | Mel McGaha | 716,076 |
| 1963 | 5th (tied) | 79 | 83 | .488 | 25.5 | Birdie Tebbetts | 562,507 |
| 1964 | 6th (tied) | 79 | 83 | .488 | 20.0 | Birdie Tebbetts | 653,293 |
| 1965 | 5th | 87 | 75 | .537 | 15.0 | Birdie Tebbetts | 934,786 |
| 1966 | 5th | 81 | 81 | .500 | 17.0 | Birdie Tebbetts, George Strickland | 903,359 |
| 1967 | 8th | 75 | 87 | .463 | 17.0 | Joe Adcock | 662,980 |
| 1968 | 3rd | 86 | 75 | .534 | 16.5 | Alvin Dark | 857,994 |

## EAST DIVISION

| Year | Position | W | L | Pct. | GB | Manager | Attendance |
|---|---|---|---|---|---|---|---|
| 1969 | 6th | 62 | 99 | .385 | 46.5 | Alvin Dark | 619,970 |
| 1970 | 5th | 76 | 86 | .469 | 32.0 | Alvin Dark | 729,752 |
| 1971 | 6th | 60 | 102 | .370 | 43.0 | Alvin Dark, John Lipon | 591,361 |
| 1972 | 5th | 72 | 84 | .462 | 14.0 | Ken Aspromonte | 626,354 |
| 1973 | 6th | 71 | 91 | .438 | 26.0 | Ken Aspromonte | 615,107 |
| 1974 | 4th | 77 | 85 | .475 | 14.0 | Ken Aspromonte | 1,114,262 |
| 1975 | 4th | 79 | 80 | .497 | 15.5 | Frank Robinson | 977,039 |
| 1976 | 4th | 81 | 78 | .509 | 16.0 | Frank Robinson | 948,776 |
| 1977 | 5th | 71 | 90 | .441 | 28.5 | Frank Robinson, Jeff Torborg | 900,365 |
| 1978 | 6th | 69 | 90 | .434 | 29.0 | Jeff Torborg | 800,584 |
| 1979 | 6th | 81 | 80 | .503 | 22.0 | Jeff Torborg, Dave Garcia | 1,011,644 |
| 1980 | 6th | 79 | 81 | .494 | 23.0 | Dave Garcia | 1,033,827 |
| 1981 | 6th/5th | 52 | 51 | .505 | * | Dave Garcia | 661,395 |
| 1982 | 6th (tied) | 78 | 84 | .481 | 17.0 | Dave Garcia | 1,044,021 |
| 1983 | 7th | 70 | 92 | .432 | 28.0 | Mike Ferraro, Pat Corrales | 768,941 |
| 1984 | 6th | 75 | 87 | .463 | 29.0 | Pat Corrales | 734,079 |
| 1985 | 7th | 60 | 102 | .370 | 39.5 | Pat Corrales | 655,181 |
| 1986 | 5th | 84 | 78 | .519 | 11.5 | Pat Corrales | 1,471,805 |
| 1987 | 7th | 61 | 101 | .377 | 37.0 | Pat Corrales, Doc Edwards | 1,077,898 |
| 1988 | 6th | 78 | 84 | .481 | 11.0 | Doc Edwards | 1,411,610 |
| 1989 | 6th | 73 | 89 | .451 | 16.0 | Doc Edwards, John Hart | 1,285,542 |
| 1990 | 4th | 77 | 85 | .475 | 11.0 | John McNamara | 1,225,240 |
| 1991 | 7th | 57 | 105 | .352 | 34.0 | John McNamara, Mike Hargrove | 1,051,863 |
| 1992 | 4th (tied) | 76 | 86 | .469 | 20.0 | Mike Hargrove | 1,224,274 |
| 1993 | 6th | 76 | 86 | .469 | 19.0 | Mike Hargrove | 2,177,908 |

## CENTRAL DIVISION

| Year | Position | W | L | Pct. | GB | Manager | Attendance |
|---|---|---|---|---|---|---|---|
| 1994 | 2nd | 66 | 47 | .584 | 1.0 | Mike Hargrove | 1,995,174 |
| 1995 | 1st (D,C,s) | 100 | 44 | .694 | +30.0 | Mike Hargrove | 2,842,745 |

| Year | Position | W | L | Pct. | GB | Manager | Attendance |
|---|---|---|---|---|---|---|---|
| 1996 | 1st (d) | 99 | 62 | .615 | +14.5 | Mike Hargrove | 3,318,174 |
| 1997 | 1st (D,C,s) | 86 | 75 | .534 | +6.0 | Mike Hargrove | 3,404,750 |
| 1998 | 1st (D,c) | 89 | 73 | .549 | +9.0 | Mike Hargrove | 3,467,299 |
| 1999 | 1st (d) | 97 | 65 | .599 | +21.5 | Mike Hargrove | 3,468,456 |
| 2000 | 2nd | 90 | 72 | .556 | 5.0 | Charlie Manuel | 3,456,278 |
| 2001 | 1st (d) | 91 | 71 | .562 | +6.0 | Charlie Manuel | 3,175,523 |
| 2002 | 3rd | 74 | 88 | .457 | 20.5 | Charlie Manuel, Joel Skinner | 2,616,940 |
| 2003 | 4th | 68 | 94 | .420 | 22.0 | Eric Wedge | 1,730,001 |
| 2004 | 3rd | 80 | 82 | .494 | 12.0 | Eric Wedge | 1,814,401 |
| 2005 | 2nd | 93 | 69 | .574 | 6.0 | Eric Wedge | 2,013,763 |

(S) won World Series; (L) won league playoff; (s) lost World Series; *first half 26-24, second half 26-27; (D) won Division Series; (C) won League Championship Series; (d) lost Division Series; (c) lost League Championship Series

## INDIVIDUAL AND CLUB RECORDS

### BATTING

| | Individual Season | Individual Career | Club Season |
|---|---|---|---|
| **Games** | 163—Leon Wagner, 1964 | 1,626—Terry Turner | 164 (1964) |
| **At-bats** | 663—Joe Carter, 162 G, 1986 | 6,034—Nap Lajoie | 5,702 (1986) |
| **Runs** | 140—Earl Averill, 155 G, 1931 | 1,154—Earl Averill | 1,009 (1999)<br>Fewest—493 (1909) |
| **Hits** | 233—Joe Jackson, 147 G, 1911 | 2,046—Nap Lajoie | 1,715 (1936)<br>Fewest—1,210 (1915) |
| **Hitting streak** | 31 G—Nap Lajoie, 1906 | | |
| **Singles** | 172—Charlie Jamieson, 152 G, 1923 | 1,511—Nap Lajoie | 1,218 (1925) |
| **Doubles** | 64—George Burns, 151 G, 1926 | 486—Tris Speaker | 358 (1930) |
| **Triples** | 26—Joe Jackson, 152 G, 1912 | 121—Earl Averill | 95 (1920) |
| **HOME RUNS** | | | 221 (2000)<br>Fewest—9 (1910) |
| **Righthander** | 50—Albert Belle, 143 G, 1995 | 242—Albert Belle | |
| **Lefthander** | 52—Jim Thome, 147 G, 2002 | 334—Jim Thome | |
| **Switch-hitter** | 24—Roberto Alomar, 159 G, 1999 | 104—Carlos Baerga | |
| **Rookie** | 37—Al Rosen, 155 G, 1950 | | |
| **Home** | 30—Hal Trosky, 1936<br>Jim Thome, 2001, 2002 | 182—Jim Thome | 133 (1970) |
| **Road** | 26—Albert Belle, 1996 | 152—Jim Thome | 124 (1997) |
| **Month** | 17—Albert Belle, Sept 1995 | | 50 (June 1950, Aug 1997) |
| **Pinch** | 3—Gene Green, 1962<br>Ron Kittle, 1988<br>Ted Uhlaender, 1970<br>Fred Whitfield, 1965 | 8—Fred Whitfield | 9 (1965, 1970) |
| **Grand slams** | 4—Al Rosen, 154 G, 1951 | 13—Manny Ramirez | 12 (1999) |
| **Home runs at Municipal Stadium, all teams** | | | 236 (1970) |
| **Home runs at Jacobs Field, all teams** | | | 219 (1999) |
| **Total bases** | 405—Hal Trosky, 151 G, 1936 | 3,200—Earl Averill | 2,700 (1996) |
| **Extra-base hits** | 103—Albert Belle, 143 G, 1995 | 724—Earl Averill | 576 (1996) |
| **Sacrifice hits** | 46—Bill Bradley, 139 G, 1907 | 340—Ray Chapman | 195 (1906) |
| **Sacrifice flies** | 16—Juan Gonzalez, 140 G, 2001 | 62—Omar Vizquel | 74 (1980) |
| **Bases on balls** | 127—Jim Thome, 146 G, 1999 | 997—Jim Thome | 743 (1999)<br>Fewest—243 (1901) |
| **Strikeouts** | 185—Jim Thome, 156 G, 2001<br>Fewest—4—Joe Sewell, 155 G, 1925<br>Joe Sewell, 152 G, 1929 | 1,377—Jim Thome | 1,102 (1963)<br>Fewest—331 (1922, 1926) |
| **Hit by pitch** | 17—Minnie Minoso, 148 G, 1959<br>Travis Hafner, 140 G, 2004 | 79—Nap Lajoie | 78 (2004)<br>Fewest—11 (1943, 1976) |
| **Runs batted in** | 165—Manny Ramirez, 147 G, 1999 | 1,084—Earl Averill | 960 (1999)<br>Fewest—407 (1909) |
| **Grounded into double plays** | 28—Julio Franco, 149 G, 1986<br>Fewest—3—Jose Cardenal, 157 G, 1986<br>Cory Snyder, 157 G, 1987 | 165—Julio Franco | 165 (1980)<br>Fewest—94 (1941) |
| **Left on base** | | | 1,260 (2000)<br>Fewest—995 (1959) |
| **Batting average** | .408—Joe Jackson, 147 G, 1911 | .375—Joe Jackson | .308 (1921)<br>Lowest—.234 (1968, 1972) |
| **Most .300 hitters** | | | 9 (1921) |
| **Slugging average** | .697—Manny Ramirez, 118 G, 2000 | .592—Manny Ramirez | .484 (1994)<br>Lowest—.305 (1910) |
| **On-base percentage** | .483—Tris Speaker, 150 G, 1920 | .444—Tris Speaker | .383 (1921)<br>Lowest—.288 (1909) |

### BASERUNNING

| | Individual Season | Individual Career | Club Season |
|---|---|---|---|
| **Stolen bases** | 75—Kenny Lofton, 154 G, 1996 | 450—Kenny Lofton | 210 (1917) |
| **Caught stealing** | 23—Bobby Bonds, 146 G, 1979 | 109—Charlie Jamieson | 92 (1920) |

## PITCHING

| | Individual Season | Individual Career | Club Season |
|---|---|---|---|
| **Games** | 81—Bobby Howry, 2005 | 582—Mel Harder | |
| **Games started** | 44—George Uhle, 1923 | 484—Bob Feller | |
| **Complete games** | 36—Bob Feller, 1946 | 279—Bob Feller | 141 (1904) |
| **Wins** | 31—Jim Bagby Sr., 1920 | 266—Bob Feller | |
| **Percentage** | .938—Johnny Allen (15-1), 1937 | .623—Addie Joss | |
| **Winning streak** | 15—Johnny Allen, 1937<br>Gaylord Perry, 1974 | | |
| **Winning streak, two seasons** | 17—Johnny Allen 1936 (2), 1937 (15) | | |
| **20-win seasons** | | 7—Bob Lemon | |
| **Losses** | 22—Pete Dowling, 1901 | 186—Mel Harder | |
| **Losing streak** | 13—Guy Morton, 1914 | | |
| **Saves** | 46—Jose Mesa, 1995 | 129—Doug Jones | 50 (1995) |
| **Innings** | 371—Bob Feller, 1946 | 3,827—Bob Feller | 1,487.2 (1964) |
| **Hits** | 378—George Uhle, 1923 | 3,706—Mel Harder | 1,663 (1930) |
| **Runs** | 167—George Uhle, 1923 | 1,714—Mel Harder | 957 (1987) |
| **Earned runs** | 150—George Uhle, 1923 | 1,447—Mel Harder | 835 (1987) |
| **Bases on balls** | 208—Bob Feller, 1938 | 1,764—Bob Feller | 770 (1971) |
| **Strikeouts** | 348—Bob Feller, 1946 | 2,581—Bob Feller | 1,218 (2001) |
| **Strikeouts, game** | 18—Bob Feller, Oct 2, 1938, 1st game<br>(19—Luis Tiant, July 3, 1968, 10 inn) | | |
| **Hit batsmen** | 20—Otto Hess, 1906 | 95—George Uhle | 73 (1901) |
| **Wild pitches** | 18—Sam McDowell, 1967 | 114—Sam McDowell | 87 (1973) |
| **Home runs** | 37—Luis Tiant, 1969 | 224—Bob Feller | 219 (1987) |
| **Sacrifice hits** | 25—Bob Feller, 1946 | 301—George Uhle | 216 (1927) |
| **Sacrifice flies** | 13—Bob Lemon, 1954 | 55—Charles Nagy | 73 (1984) |
| **Earned run average** | 1.60—Luis Tiant, 258 inn, 1968 | 1.89—Addie Joss | 2.02 (1908) |
| **Shutouts** | 10—Bob Feller, 1946<br>Bob Lemon, 1948 | 45—Addie Joss | 27 (1906)<br>Lost—24 (1914) |
| **1-0 games won** | 3—Addie Joss, 1908<br>Stan Coveleski, 1917<br>Jim Bagby Jr., 1943<br>Bob Feller, 1946<br>Steve Hargan, 1967 | 10—Addie Joss | 7 (1989)<br>Lost—7 (1918, 1955) |

## TEAM FIELDING

| | | | |
|---|---|---|---|
| **Putouts** | 4,463 (1964)<br>Fewest—3,907 (1945) | **Assists** | 2,267 (1907)<br>Fewest—1,468 (1968) |
| **Chances accepted** | 6,663 (1910)<br>Fewest—5,470 (1945) | **Errors** | 329 (1901)<br>Fewest—72 (2000) |
| **Double plays** | 197 (1953)<br>Fewest—77 (1915) | **Passed balls** | 35 (1958)<br>Fewest—3 (1943) |
| **Errorless games** | 99 (2000)<br>Consecutive—11 (1967) | **Fielding average** | .988 (2000)<br>Lowest—.941 (1901) |

## MISCELLANEOUS

**Most players, season** 59 (2002)
**Fewest players, season** 24 (1904)
**Games won** 111 (1954)
**Month** 26 (Aug 1954)
**Consecutive** 13 (1942, 1951)
**Winning percentage** .721 (1954), 111-43
**Lowest** .333 (1914), 51-102
**Number of league championships** 5
**Most recent** 1997
**Runs, game** 27 vs Boston, July 7, 1923
**Opponents'** 24 by Boston, Aug 21, 1986
**Hits, game** 29 vs St. Louis, Aug 12, 1948, 2nd game
vs Boston, June 20, 1980
**Home runs, game** 8 vs Milwaukee, Apr 25, 1997
vs Seattle, July 16, 2004
**Runs, shutout** 22 vs New York, Aug 31, 2004
**Opponents'** 21 by Detroit, Sept 15, 1901, 8 inn
**Longest 1-0 win** 15 inn, vs Baltimore, May 14, 1961, 1st game

**Most seasons, non-pitcher** 15—Terry Turner
**Most seasons, pitcher** 20—Mel Harder
**Games lost** 105 (1991)
**Month** 24 (July 1914)
**Consecutive** 12 (1931)
**Overall record** 8,209-7,877 (104 seasons)
**Interleague play** 70-69
**Number of times worst record in league** 6
**Most recent** 1991
**Runs, inning** 14 vs Philadelphia, June 18, 1950, 2nd game, 1st
**Total bases, game** 50 vs Seattle, July 16, 2004
**Consecutive games with one or more home runs** 19 (40 HRs), 2000
**Longest shutout** 16 inn, 3-0 vs Chicago, Sept 22, 1975
**Longest 1-0 loss** 17 inn, vs Chicago, Sept 13, 1967

## ATTENDANCE

| **Highest home attendance** | |
|---|---|
| **League Park** | 912,832 (1920) |
| **Municipal Stadium** | 2,620,627 (1948) |
| **Jacobs Field** | 3,468,456 (1999) |
| **Highest road attendance** | 2,449,537 (1999) |

| **Largest crowds** | |
|---|---|
| **Day** | 74,420 vs Detroit, Apr 7, 1973 |
| **Night** | 78,382 vs Chicago, Aug 20, 1948 |
| **Doubleheader** | 84,587 vs New York, Sept 12, 1954 |
| **Home opener** | 74,420 vs Detroit, Apr 7, 1973 |

# DETROIT TIGERS

## YEARLY FINISHES

(Original American League franchise)

| Year | Position | W | L | Pct. | GB | Manager | Attendance |
|---|---|---|---|---|---|---|---|
| 1901 | 3rd | 74 | 61 | .548 | 8.5 | George Stallings | 259,430 |
| 1902 | 7th | 52 | 83 | .385 | 30.5 | Frank Dwyer | 189,469 |
| 1903 | 5th | 65 | 71 | .478 | 25.0 | Ed Barrow | 224,523 |
| 1904 | 7th | 62 | 90 | .408 | 32.0 | Ed Barrow, Bobby Lowe | 177,796 |
| 1905 | 3rd | 79 | 74 | .516 | 15.5 | Bill Armour | 193,384 |
| 1906 | 6th | 71 | 78 | .477 | 21.0 | Bill Armour | 174,043 |
| 1907 | 1st (s) | 92 | 58 | .613 | +1.5 | Hughey Jennings | 297,079 |
| 1908 | 1st (s) | 90 | 63 | .588 | +.5 | Hughey Jennings | 436,199 |
| 1909 | 1st (s) | 98 | 54 | .645 | +3.5 | Hughey Jennings | 490,490 |
| 1910 | 3rd | 86 | 68 | .558 | 18.0 | Hughey Jennings | 391,288 |
| 1911 | 2nd | 89 | 65 | .578 | 1.5 | Hughey Jennings | 404,000 |
| 1912 | 6th | 69 | 84 | .451 | 36.5 | Hughey Jennings | 402,870 |
| 1913 | 6th | 66 | 87 | .431 | 30.0 | Hughey Jennings | 398,502 |
| 1914 | 4th | 80 | 73 | .523 | 19.5 | Hughey Jennings | 416,225 |
| 1915 | 2nd | 100 | 54 | .649 | 2.5 | Hughey Jennings | 476,105 |
| 1916 | 3rd | 87 | 67 | .565 | 4.0 | Hughey Jennings | 616,772 |
| 1917 | 4th | 78 | 75 | .510 | 21.5 | Hughey Jennings | 457,289 |
| 1918 | 7th | 55 | 71 | .437 | 20.0 | Hughey Jennings | 203,719 |
| 1919 | 4th | 80 | 60 | .571 | 8.0 | Hughey Jennings | 643,805 |
| 1920 | 7th | 61 | 93 | .396 | 37.0 | Hughey Jennings | 579,650 |
| 1921 | 6th | 71 | 82 | .464 | 27.0 | Ty Cobb | 661,527 |
| 1922 | 3rd | 79 | 75 | .513 | 15.0 | Ty Cobb | 861,206 |
| 1923 | 2nd | 83 | 71 | .539 | 16.0 | Ty Cobb | 911,377 |
| 1924 | 3rd | 86 | 68 | .558 | 6.0 | Ty Cobb | 1,015,136 |
| 1925 | 4th | 81 | 73 | .526 | 16.5 | Ty Cobb | 820,766 |
| 1926 | 6th | 79 | 75 | .513 | 12.0 | Ty Cobb | 711,914 |
| 1927 | 4th | 82 | 71 | .536 | 27.5 | George Moriarty | 773,716 |
| 1928 | 6th | 68 | 86 | .442 | 3.0 | George Moriarty | 474,323 |
| 1929 | 6th | 70 | 84 | .455 | 36.0 | Bucky Harris | 869,318 |
| 1930 | 5th | 75 | 79 | .487 | 27.0 | Bucky Harris | 649,450 |
| 1931 | 7th | 61 | 93 | .396 | 47.0 | Bucky Harris | 434,056 |
| 1932 | 5th | 76 | 75 | .503 | 29.5 | Bucky Harris | 397,157 |
| 1933 | 5th | 75 | 79 | .487 | 25.0 | Del Baker | 320,972 |
| 1934 | 1st (s) | 101 | 53 | .656 | +7.0 | Mickey Cochrane | 919,161 |
| 1935 | 1st (S) | 93 | 58 | .616 | +3.0 | Mickey Cochrane | 1,034,929 |
| 1936 | 2nd | 83 | 71 | .539 | 19.5 | Mickey Cochrane | 875,948 |
| 1937 | 2nd | 89 | 65 | .578 | 13.0 | Mickey Cochrane | 1,072,276 |
| 1938 | 4th | 84 | 70 | .545 | 16.0 | Mickey Cochrane, Del Baker | 799,557 |
| 1939 | 5th | 81 | 73 | .526 | 26.5 | Del Baker | 836,279 |
| 1940 | 1st (s) | 90 | 64 | .584 | +1.0 | Del Baker | 1,112,693 |
| 1941 | 4th (tied) | 75 | 79 | .487 | 26.0 | Del Baker | 684,915 |
| 1942 | 5th | 73 | 81 | .474 | 30.0 | Del Baker | 580,087 |
| 1943 | 5th | 78 | 76 | .506 | 20.0 | Steve O'Neill | 606,287 |
| 1944 | 2nd | 88 | 66 | .571 | 1.0 | Steve O'Neill | 923,176 |
| 1945 | 1st (S) | 88 | 65 | .575 | +1.5 | Steve O'Neill | 1,280,341 |
| 1946 | 2nd | 92 | 62 | .597 | 12.0 | Steve O'Neill | 1,722,590 |
| 1947 | 2nd | 85 | 69 | .552 | 12.0 | Steve O'Neill | 1,398,093 |
| 1948 | 5th | 78 | 76 | .506 | 18.5 | Steve O'Neill | 1,743,035 |
| 1949 | 4th | 87 | 67 | .565 | 10.0 | Red Rolfe | 1,821,204 |
| 1950 | 2nd | 95 | 59 | .617 | 3.0 | Red Rolfe | 1,951,474 |
| 1951 | 5th | 73 | 81 | .474 | 25.0 | Red Rolfe | 1,132,641 |
| 1952 | 8th | 50 | 104 | .325 | 45.0 | Red Rolfe, Fred Hutchinson | 1,026,846 |
| 1953 | 6th | 60 | 94 | .390 | 40.5 | Fred Hutchinson | 884,658 |
| 1954 | 5th | 68 | 86 | .442 | 43.0 | Fred Hutchinson | 1,079,847 |
| 1955 | 5th | 79 | 75 | .513 | 17.0 | Bucky Harris | 1,181,838 |
| 1956 | 5th | 82 | 72 | .532 | 15.0 | Bucky Harris | 1,051,182 |
| 1957 | 4th | 78 | 76 | .506 | 20.0 | Jack Tighe | 1,272,346 |
| 1958 | 5th | 77 | 77 | .500 | 15.0 | Jack Tighe, Bill Norman | 1,098,924 |
| 1959 | 4th | 76 | 78 | .494 | 18.0 | Bill Norman, Jimmie Dykes | 1,221,221 |
| 1960 | 6th | 71 | 83 | .461 | 26.0 | Jimmie Dykes, Billy Hitchcock, Joe Gordon | 1,167,669 |
| 1961 | 2nd | 101 | 61 | .623 | 8.0 | Bob Scheffing | 1,600,710 |
| 1962 | 4th | 85 | 76 | .528 | 10.5 | Bob Scheffing | 1,207,881 |
| 1963 | 5th (tied) | 79 | 83 | .488 | 25.5 | Bob Scheffing, Charlie Dressen | 821,952 |
| 1964 | 4th | 85 | 77 | .525 | 14.0 | Charlie Dressen | 816,139 |
| 1965 | 4th | 89 | 73 | .549 | 13.0 | Charlie Dressen, Bob Swift | 1,029,645 |
| 1966 | 3rd | 88 | 74 | .543 | 10.0 | Charlie Dressen, Bob Swift, Frank Skaff | 1,124,293 |
| 1967 | 2nd (tied) | 91 | 71 | .562 | 1.0 | Mayo Smith | 1,447,143 |
| 1968 | 1st (S) | 103 | 59 | .636 | +12.0 | Mayo Smith | 2,031,847 |

## EAST DIVISION

| Year | Position | W | L | Pct. | GB | Manager | Attendance |
|---|---|---|---|---|---|---|---|
| 1969 | 2nd | 90 | 72 | .556 | 19.0 | Mayo Smith | 1,577,481 |
| 1970 | 4th | 79 | 83 | .488 | 29.0 | Mayo Smith | 1,501,293 |
| 1971 | 2nd | 91 | 71 | .562 | 12.0 | Billy Martin | 1,591,073 |
| 1972 | 1st (c) | 86 | 70 | .551 | +0.5 | Billy Martin | 1,892,386 |
| 1973 | 3rd | 85 | 77 | .525 | 12.0 | Billy Martin, Joe Schultz | 1,724,146 |
| 1974 | 6th | 72 | 90 | .444 | 19.0 | Ralph Houk | 1,243,080 |
| 1975 | 6th | 57 | 102 | .358 | 37.5 | Ralph Houk | 1,058,836 |
| 1976 | 5th | 74 | 87 | .460 | 24.0 | Ralph Houk | 1,467,020 |
| 1977 | 4th | 74 | 88 | .457 | 26.0 | Ralph Houk | 1,359,856 |
| 1978 | 5th | 86 | 76 | .531 | 13.5 | Ralph Houk | 1,714,893 |
| 1979 | 5th | 85 | 76 | .528 | 18.0 | Les Moss, Dick Tracewski, Sparky Anderson | 1,630,929 |
| 1980 | 5th | 84 | 78 | .519 | 19.0 | Sparky Anderson | 1,785,293 |
| 1981 | 4th/2nd (tied) | 60 | 49 | .550 | * | Sparky Anderson | 1,149,144 |
| 1982 | 4th | 83 | 79 | .512 | 12.0 | Sparky Anderson | 1,636,058 |
| 1983 | 2nd | 92 | 70 | .568 | 6.0 | Sparky Anderson | 1,829,636 |
| 1984 | 1st (C,S) | 104 | 58 | .642 | +15.0 | Sparky Anderson | 2,704,794 |
| 1985 | 3rd | 84 | 77 | .522 | 15.0 | Sparky Anderson | 2,286,609 |

| Year | Position | W | L | Pct. | GB | Manager | Attendance |
|---|---|---|---|---|---|---|---|
| 1986 | 3rd | 87 | 75 | .537 | 8.5 | Sparky Anderson | 1,899,437 |
| 1987 | 1st (c) | 98 | 64 | .605 | +2.0 | Sparky Anderson | 2,061,830 |
| 1988 | 2nd | 88 | 74 | .543 | 1.0 | Sparky Anderson | 2,081,162 |
| 1989 | 7th | 59 | 103 | .364 | 30.0 | Sparky Anderson | 1,543,656 |
| 1990 | 3rd | 79 | 83 | .488 | 9.0 | Sparky Anderson | 1,495,785 |
| 1991 | 2nd | 84 | 78 | .519 | 7.0 | Sparky Anderson | 1,641,661 |
| 1992 | 6th | 75 | 87 | .463 | 21.0 | Sparky Anderson | 1,423,963 |
| 1993 | 3rd (tied) | 85 | 77 | .525 | 10.0 | Sparky Anderson | 1,971,421 |
| 1994 | 5th | 53 | 62 | .461 | 18.0 | Sparky Anderson | 1,184,783 |
| 1995 | 4th | 60 | 84 | .417 | 26.0 | Sparky Anderson | 1,180,979 |
| 1996 | 5th | 53 | 109 | .327 | 39.0 | Buddy Bell | 1,168,610 |
| 1997 | 3rd | 79 | 83 | .488 | 19.0 | Buddy Bell | 1,365,157 |

## CENTRAL DIVISION

| Year | Position | W | L | Pct. | GB | Manager | Attendance |
|---|---|---|---|---|---|---|---|
| 1998 | 5th | 65 | 97 | .401 | 24.0 | Buddy Bell, Larry Parrish | 1,409,391 |
| 1999 | 3rd | 69 | 92 | .429 | 27.5 | Larry Parrish | 2,026,441 |
| 2000 | 3rd | 79 | 83 | .488 | 16.0 | Phil Garner | 2,533,753 |
| 2001 | 4th | 66 | 96 | .407 | 25.0 | Phil Garner | 1,921,305 |
| 2002 | 4th | 55 | 106 | .342 | 39.0 | Phil Garner, Luis Pujols | 1,503,623 |
| 2003 | 5th | 43 | 119 | .265 | 47.0 | Alan Trammell | 1,368,285 |
| 2004 | 4th | 72 | 90 | .444 | 20.0 | Alan Trammell | 1,917,004 |
| 2005 | 4th | 71 | 91 | .438 | 28.0 | Alan Trammell | 2,024,485 |

(s) lost World Series; (S) won World Series; (c) lost League Championship Series; *first half 31-26, second half 29-23; (C) won League Championship Series

## INDIVIDUAL AND CLUB RECORDS

### BATTING

| | Individual Season | Individual Career | Club Season |
|---|---|---|---|
| **Games** | 163—Rocky Colavito, 1961 | 2,834—Al Kaline | 164 (1968) |
| **At-bats** | 679—Harvey Kuenn, 155 G, 1953 | 10,586—Ty Cobb | 5,664 (1998) |
| **Runs** | 147—Ty Cobb, 146 G, 1911 | 2,087—Ty Cobb | 958 (1934)<br>Fewest—499 (1904) |
| **Hits** | 248—Ty Cobb, 146 G, 1911 | 3,902—Ty Cobb | 1,724 (1921)<br>Fewest—1,204 (1905) |
| **Hitting streak** | 40 G—Ty Cobb, 1911 | | |
| **Singles** | 169—Ty Cobb, 146 G, 1911 | 2,839—Ty Cobb | 1,298 (1921) |
| **Doubles** | 63—Hank Greenberg, 153 G, 1934 | 665—Ty Cobb | 349 (1934) |
| **Triples** | 26—Sam Crawford, 157 G, 1914 | 286—Ty Cobb | 102 (1913) |
| **HOME RUNS** | | | 225 (1987)<br>Fewest—9 (1906) |
| **Righthander** | 58—Hank Greenberg, 155 G, 1938 | 399—Al Kaline | |
| **Lefthander** | 41—Norm Cash, 159 G, 1961 | 373—Norm Cash | |
| **Switch-hitter** | 34—Tony Clark, 157 G, 1998 | 156—Tony Clark | |
| **Rookie** | 35—Rudy York, 104 G, 1937 | | |
| **Home** | 39—Hank Greenberg, 1938 | 226—Al Kaline | 125 (1987) |
| **Road** | 27—Rocky Colavito, 1961 | 173—Al Kaline | 108 (2000) |
| **Month** | 18—Rudy York, Aug 1937 | | 49 (Aug 1937) |
| **Pinch** | 3—many players | 16—Gates Brown | 8 (1971) |
| **Grand slams** | 4—Rudy York, 135 G, 1938<br>Jim Northrup,155 G, 1968 | 10—Rudy York<br>Hank Greenberg<br>Cecil Fielder | 10 (1938) |
| **Home runs at Tiger Stadium, all teams** | | | 235 (1999) |
| **Home runs at Comerica Park, all teams** | | | 175 (2005) |
| **Total bases** | 397—Hank Greenberg, 154 G, 1937 | 5,475—Ty Cobb | 2,548 (1987) |
| **Extra-base hits** | 103—Hank Greenberg, 154 G, 1937 | 1,063—Ty Cobb | 546 (1929) |
| **Sacrifice hits** | 36—Bill Coughlin, 147 G, 1906 | 327—Donie Bush | 182 (1906) |
| **Sacrifice flies** | 16—Sam Crawford, 157 G, 1914 | 104—Al Kaline | 59 (1983) |
| **Bases on balls** | 137—Roy Cullenbine, 142 G, 1947 | 1,277—Al Kaline | 765 (1993)<br>Fewest—292 (1903) |
| **Strikeouts** | 182—Cecil Fielder, 159 G, 1990<br>Fewest—13—Charlie Gehringer, 154 G, 1936<br>Harvey Kuenn, 155 G, 1954 | 1,099—Lou Whitaker | 1,268 (1996)<br>Fewest—376 (1921) |
| **Hit by pitch** | 24—Bill Freehan, 155 G, 1968 | 114—Bill Freehan | 82 (1999)<br>Fewest—9 (1945) |
| **Runs batted in** | 183—Hank Greenberg, 154 G, 1937 | 1,828—Ty Cobb | 873 (1937)<br>Fewest—404 (1906) |
| **Grounded into double plays** | 29—Jimmy Bloodworth, 129 G, 1943<br>Fewest—0—Dick McAuliffe, 151 G, 1968 | 271—Al Kaline | 164 (1949)<br>Fewest—81 (1985) |
| **Left on base** | | | 1,312 (1993)<br>Fewest—1,021 (1917) |
| **Batting average** | .420—Ty Cobb, 146 G, 1911 | .367—Ty Cobb | .316 (1921)<br>Lowest—.231 (1904) |
| **Most .300 hitters** | | | 8 (1922, 1924, 1934) |
| **Slugging average** | .683—Hank Greenberg, 155 G, 1938 | .616—Hank Greenberg | .454 (1994)<br>Lowest—.321 (1918) |
| **On-base percentage** | .487—Norm Cash, 159 G, 1961 | .434—Ty Cobb | .385 (1921)<br>Lowest—.282 (1904) |

## BASERUNNING

| | Individual Season | Career | Club Season |
|---|---|---|---|
| Stolen bases | 96—Ty Cobb, 156 G, 1915 | 865—Ty Cobb | 281 (1909) |
| Caught stealing | 38—Ty Cobb, 156 G, 1915 | 188—Ty Cobb | 92 (1921) |

## PITCHING

| | Individual Season | Career | Club Season |
|---|---|---|---|
| Games | 88—Mike Myers, 1997<br>Sean Runyan, 1998 | 545—John Hiller | |
| Games started | 45—Mickey Lolich, 1971 | 459—Mickey Lolich | |
| Complete games | 42—George Mullin, 1904 | 336—George Mullin | 143 (1904) |
| Wins | 31—Denny McLain, 1968 | 222—Hooks Dauss | |
| Percentage | .862—Bill Donovan (25-4), 1907 | .654—Denny McLain | |
| Winning streak | 16—Schoolboy Rowe, 1934 | | |
| Winning streak, two seasons | 16—Bill Donovan, 1907 (8), 1908 (8) | | |
| 20-win seasons | | 5—George Mullin | |
| Losses | 23—George Mullin, 1904 | 182—Hooks Dauss | |
| Losing streak | 10—Mickey Lolich, 1967<br>Mike Moore, 1995 | | |
| Saves | 42—Todd Jones, 2000 | 154—Mike Henneman | 51 (1984) |
| Innings | 382—George Mullin, 1904 | 3,394—George Mullin | 1,489.2 (1968) |
| Hits | 346—George Mullin, 1904 | 3,407—Hooks Dauss | 1,699 (1996) |
| Runs | 160—Joe Coleman Jr., 1974 | 1,594—Hooks Dauss | 1,103 (1996) |
| Earned runs | 142—Mickey Lolich, 1974 | 1,289—Mickey Lolich | 1,015 (1996) |
| Bases on balls | 158—Joe Coleman Jr., 1974 | 1,227—Hal Newhouser | 784 (1996) |
| Strikeouts | 308—Mickey Lolich, 1971 | 2,679—Mickey Lolich | 1,115 (1968) |
| Strikeouts, game | 16—Mickey Lolich, May 23, 1969<br>Mickey Lolich, June 9, 1969 (pitched first 9 inn of 10-inn game) | | |
| Hit batsmen | 23—Howard Ehmke, 1922 | 121—Hooks Dauss | 84 (1922) |
| Wild pitches | 24—Jack Morris, 1987 | 155—Jack Morris | 82 (1996) |
| Home runs | 42—Denny McLain, 1966 | 329—Mickey Lolich | 241 (1996) |
| Sacrifice hits | 28—Earl Whitehill, 1931 | 423—George Mullin | 222 (1927) |
| Sacrifice flies | 13—Jack Morris, 1980 | 90—Jack Morris | 72 (1996) |
| Earned run average | 1.81—Hal Newhouser, 313 inn, 1945 | 2.38—Ed Killian | 2.26 (1909) |
| Shutouts | 9—Denny McLain, 1969 | 39—Mickey Lolich | 20 (1917, 1944, 1969)<br>Lost—22 (1904) |
| 1-0 games won | 4—Ed Summers, 1908 | 9—Bill Donovan | 9 (1908)<br>Lost—7 (1903, 1943) |

## TEAM FIELDING

| | | | |
|---|---|---|---|
| **Putouts** | 4,469 (1968)<br>Fewest—4,006 (1906) | **Assists** | 2,272 (1914)<br>Fewest—1,443 (1962) |
| **Chances accepted** | 6,504 (1914)<br>Fewest—5,594 (1959) | **Errors** | 425 (1901)<br>Fewest—92 (1997) |
| **Double plays** | 194 (1950, 2003)<br>Fewest—94 (1912, 1917) | **Passed balls** | 30 (2001)<br>Fewest—4 (1924, 2005) |
| **Errorless games** | 92 (1997)<br>Consecutive—12 (1963) | **Fielding average** | .985 (1997)<br>Lowest—.922 (1901) |

## MISCELLANEOUS

**Most players, season** 57 (2002)

**Fewest players, season** 24 (1906, 1907)
**Games won** 104 (1984)
**Month** 23 (July 1908, Aug 1915, Aug 1934, Aug 1935)
**Consecutive** 14 (1909, 1934)
**Winning percentage** .656 (1934), 101-53
**Lowest** .265 (2003), 43-119
**Number of league championships** 9
**Most recent** 1984
**Runs, game** 21 vs Cleveland, Sept 15, 1901, 8 inn
vs Philadelphia, July 17, 1908
vs St. Louis, July 25, 1920
vs Chicago, July 1, 1936
**Opponents'** 26 by Kansas City, Sept 9, 2004
**Hits, game** 27 vs New York, Sept 29, 1928
vs Kansas City, May 27, 2004
**Home runs, game** 8 vs Toronto, June 20, 2000
**Runs, shutout** 21 vs Cleveland, Sept 15, 1901, 8 inn
**Opponents'** 16 by St. Louis, Sept 9, 1922
**Longest 1-0 win** 12 inn, vs St. Louis, Sept 8, 1917
vs Cleveland, June 26, 1919
vs Chicago, Sept 10, 1950, 1st game

**Most seasons, non-pitcher** 22—Ty Cobb
Al Kaline
**Most seasons, pitcher** 16—Tommy Bridges
**Games lost** 119 (2003)
**Month** 24 (June 1975)
**Consecutive** 19 (1975)
**Overall record** 8,221-8,050 (105 seasons)
**Interleague play** 71-86
**Number of times worst record in league** 6 (inc. 1 tie)
**Most recent** 2003
**Runs, inning** 13 vs New York, Sept 22, 1936, 6th
vs Texas, Aug 8, 2001, 9th

**Total bases, game** 47 vs Toronto, June 20, 2000

**Consecutive games with one or more home runs** 25 (46 HRs), 1994
**Longest shutout** 16 inn, 3-0 vs Chicago, Sept 22, 1975

**Longest 1-0 loss** 16 inn, vs Chicago, Aug 14, 1954

## ATTENDANCE

| | | | |
|---|---|---|---|
| **Highest home attendance** | | **Largest crowds** | |
| **Tiger Stadium** | 2,704,794 (1984) | **Day** | 57,888 vs Cleveland, Sept 26, 1948 |
| **Comerica Park** | 2,533,752 (2000) | **Night** | 56,586 vs Cleveland, Aug 9, 1948 |
| | | **Doubleheader** | 58,369 vs New York, July 20, 1947 |
| **Highest road attendance** | 2,396,528 (1991) | **Home opener** | 54,089 vs Cleveland, Apr 6, 1971 |

# KANSAS CITY ATHLETICS

## YEARLY FINISHES

**(Original American League franchise moved from Philadelphia to Kansas City after the 1954 season and to Oakland after the 1967 season)**

| Year | Position | W | L | Pct. | GB | Manager | Attendance |
|---|---|---|---|---|---|---|---|
| 1955 | 6th | 63 | 91 | .409 | 33.0 | Lou Boudreau | 1,393,054 |
| 1956 | 8th | 52 | 102 | .338 | 45.0 | Lou Boudreau | 1,015,154 |
| 1957 | 7th | 59 | 94 | .386 | 38.5 | Lou Boudreau, Harry Craft | 901,067 |
| 1958 | 7th | 73 | 81 | .474 | 19.0 | Harry Craft | 925,090 |
| 1959 | 7th | 66 | 88 | .429 | 28.0 | Harry Craft | 963,683 |
| 1960 | 8th | 58 | 96 | .377 | 39.0 | Bob Elliott | 774,944 |
| 1961 | 9th (tied) | 61 | 100 | .379 | 47.5 | Joe Gordon, Hank Bauer | 683,817 |
| 1962 | 9th | 72 | 90 | .444 | 24.0 | Hank Bauer | 635,675 |
| 1963 | 8th | 73 | 89 | .451 | 31.5 | Ed Lopat | 762,364 |
| 1964 | 10th | 57 | 105 | .352 | 42.0 | Ed Lopat, Mel McGaha | 642,478 |
| 1965 | 10th | 59 | 103 | .364 | 43.0 | Mel McGaha, Haywood Sullivan | 528,344 |
| 1966 | 7th | 74 | 86 | .463 | 23.0 | Alvin Dark | 773,929 |
| 1967 | 10th | 62 | 99 | .385 | 29.5 | Alvin Dark, Luke Appling | 726,639 |

## INDIVIDUAL AND CLUB RECORDS

### BATTING

| | Individual | | Club |
|---|---|---|---|
| | **Season** | **Career** | **Season** |
| **Games** | 162—Norm Siebern, 1962 | 726—Ed Charles | 163 (1964) |
| **At-bats** | 641—Jerry Lumpe, 156 G, 1962 | 2,782—Jerry Lumpe | 5,576 (1962) |
| **Runs** | 114—Norm Siebern, 162 G, 1962 | 361—Jerry Lumpe | 745 (1962)<br>Fewest—533 (1967) |
| **Hits** | 193—Jerry Lumpe, 156 G, 1962 | 775—Jerry Lumpe | 1,467 (1962)<br>Fewest—1,244 (1967) |
| **Hitting streak** | 22 G—Hector Lopez, 1957<br>Vic Power, 1958 | | |
| **Singles** | 139—Jerry Lumpe, 156 G, 1962 | 593—Jerry Lumpe | 1,073 (1962) |
| **Doubles** | 36—Norm Siebern, 153 G, 1961 | 119—Jerry Lumpe | 231 (1959) |
| **Triples** | 15—Gino Cimoli, 152 G, 1962 | 34—Jerry Lumpe | 59 (1965) |
| **HOME RUNS** | | | 138 (1958)<br>Fewest—70 (1966) |
| **Righthander** | 38—Bob Cerv, 141 G, 1958 | 75—Bob Cerv | |
| **Lefthander** | 28—Jim Gentile, 136 G, 1964 | 78—Norm Siebern | |
| **Switch-hitter** | 3—Jerry Walker, 36 G, 1962 | 3—Jerry Walker<br>Tommie Reynolds | |
| **Rookie** | 20—Woodie Held, 92 G, 1957 | | |
| **Home** | 22—Rocky Colavito, 1964 | 44—Bob Cerv<br>Hector Lopez | 107 (1964) |
| **Road** | 17—Bob Cerv, 1958 | 43—Norm Siebern | 75 (1957) |
| **Month** | 10—Rocky Colavito, May 1964 | | 38 (June 1957) |
| **Pinch** | 3—Bob Cerv, 1957 | 4—George Alusik<br>Bob Cerv | 7 (1964) |
| **Grand slams** | 2—Gus Zernial, 120 G, 1955<br>Harry Simpson, 141 G, 1956<br>Roger Maris, 99 G, 1958<br>Marv Throneberry, 104 G, 1960<br>Nelson Mathews, 157 G, 1964 | 3—Marv Throneberry<br>Roger Maris | 4 (1958, 1959, 1960) |
| **Home runs at Municipal Stadium, all teams** | | | 239 (1964) |
| **Total bases** | 305—Bob Cerv, 141 G, 1958 | 1,065—Ed Charles | 2,151 (1962) |
| **Extra-base hits** | 67—Rocky Colavito, 160 G, 1964 | 214—Norm Siebern | 411 (1964) |
| **Sacrifice hits** | 11—Dick Williams, 130 G, 1959 | 27—Wayne Causey | 89 (1961) |
| **Sacrifice flies** | 12—Leo Posada, 116 G, 1961 | 25—Norm Siebern | 50 (1962) |
| **Bases on balls** | 110—Norm Siebern, 162 G, 1962 | 343—Norm Siebern | 580 (1961)<br>Fewest—364 (1957) |
| **Strikeouts** | 143—Nelson Mathews, 157 G, 1964<br>Fewest—16—Vic Power, 127 G, 1956 | 379—Ed Charles | 1,104 (1964)<br>Fewest—725 (1955) |
| **Hit by pitch** | 13—Bobby Del Greco, 132 G, 1962 | 25—Bert Campaneris | 42 (1962, 1964, 1967)<br>Fewest—12 (1960) |
| **Runs batted in** | 117—Norm Siebern, 162 G, 1962 | 367—Norm Siebern | 691 (1962)<br>Fewest—481 (1967) |

| | Individual Season | Individual Career | Club Season |
|---|---|---|---|
| **Grounded into double plays** | 23—Hector Lopez, 151 G, 1958<br>Fewest—4—Norm Siebern, 153 G, 1961 | 73—Ed Charles | 154 (1960)<br>Fewest—79 (1967) |
| **Left on base** | | | 1,224 (1962)<br>Fewest—925 (1957) |
| **Batting average** | .319—Vic Power, 147 G, 1955 | .289—Norm Siebern | .263 (1959, 1962)<br>Lowest—.233 (1967) |
| **Most .300 hitters** | | | 4 (1955) |
| **Slugging average** | .592—Bob Cerv, 148 G, 1958 | .463—Norm Siebern | .394 (1957)<br>Lowest—.330 (1967) |
| **On-base percentage** | .412—Norm Siebern, 162 G, 1962 | .381—Norm Siebern | .332 (1962)<br>Lowest—.294 (1966) |

## BASERUNNING

| | Season | Career | Club Season |
|---|---|---|---|
| **Stolen bases** | 55—Bert Campaneris, 147 G, 1967 | 168—Bert Campaneris | 132 (1966, 1967) |
| **Caught stealing** | 19—Bert Campaneris, 144 G, 1965 | 47—Bert Campaneris | 59 (1967) |

## PITCHING

| | Season | Career | Club Season |
|---|---|---|---|
| **Games** | 81—John Wyatt, 1964 | 292—John Wyatt | |
| **Games started** | 35—Bud Daley, 1960<br>Ed Rakow, 1962<br>Diego Segui, 1964<br>Catfish Hunter, 1967 | 99—Diego Segui | |
| **Complete games** | 14—Art Ditmar, 1956<br>Ray Herbert, 1960 | 32—Ray Herbert | 44 (1959, 1960) |
| **Wins** | 16—Bud Daley, 1959, 1960 | 39—Bud Daley | |
| **Percentage** | .552—Bud Daley (16-13), 1959 | none with 1,500 inn | |
| **Winning streak** | 9—Bud Daley, 1960 | | |
| **20-win seasons** | | none | |
| **Losses** | 22—Art Ditmar, 1956 | 48—Ray Herbert | |
| **Losing streak** | 11—Troy Herriage, 1956 | | |
| **Innings** | 259.2—Catfish Hunter, 1967 | 782.2—Ray Herbert | 1458 (1963) |
| **Hits** | 256—Ray Herbert, 1960 | 815—Ray Herbert | 1519 (1961) |
| **Runs** | 141—Art Ditmar, 1956 | 411—Ray Herbert | 911 (1955) |
| **Earned runs** | 125—Art Ditmar, 1956 | 370—Ray Herbert | 822 (1955) |
| **Bases on balls** | 108—Art Ditmar, 1956 | 311—Diego Segui | 707 (1955) |
| **Strikeouts** | 196—Catfish Hunter, 1967 | 513—Diego Segui | 990 (1967) |
| **Strikeouts, game** | 12—Jim Nash, July 13, 1967<br>Jim Nash, July 23, 1967, 2nd game<br>Catfish Hunter, Sept 12, 1967 | | |
| **Hit batsmen** | 12—Johnny Kucks, 1959 | 32—Bud Daley | 54 (1964) |
| **Wild pitches** | 13—John Wyatt, 1965 | 35—John Wyatt | 67 (1965) |
| **Home runs** | 40—Orlando Pena, 1964 | 85—Diego Segui | 220 (1964) |
| **Sacrifice hits** | 16—Ray Herbert, 1960<br>Jim Archer, 1961 | 48—Ray Herbert | 110 (1960) |
| **Sacrifice flies** | 10—Ray Herbert, 1959, 1960<br>Dave Wickersham, 1963<br>Jim Nash, 1967 | 36—Ray Herbert | 64 (1961) |
| **Earned run average** | 2.80—Catfish Hunter, 260 inn, 1967 | none with 1,500 inn | 3.56 (1966) |
| **Shutouts** | 5—Catfish Hunter, 1967 | 8—Ned Garver | 11 (1963, 1966)<br>Lost—19 (1967) |
| **1-0 games won** | 2—Alex Kellner, 1955<br>Ed Rakow, 1962<br>Catfish Hunter, 1967 | 2—Catfish Hunter<br>Alex Kellner<br>John O'Donoghue<br>Ed Rakow<br>Ralph Terry | 4 (1966)<br>Lost—5 (1967) |

## TEAM FIELDING

| | | | |
|---|---|---|---|
| **Putouts** | 4,374 (1963)<br>Fewest—4,086 (1959) | **Assists** | 1,785 (1956)<br>Fewest—1,533 (1967) |
| **Chances accepted** | 6,095 (1963)<br>Fewest—5,755 (1959) | **Errors** | 175 (1961)<br>Fewest—125 (1957, 1958) |
| **Double plays** | 187 (1956)<br>Fewest—120 (1967) | **Passed balls** | 34 (1958)<br>Fewest—11 (1963) |
| **Errorless games** | 78 (1963)<br>Consecutive—8 (1960, 1964) | **Fielding average** | .980 (1963)<br>Lowest—.972 (1961) |

## MISCELLANEOUS

**Most players, season** 52 (1955, 1961)

**Fewest players, season** 38 (1957)
**Games won** 74 (1966)
**Month** 19 (July 1959)
**Consecutive** 11 (1959)
**Winning percentage** .474 (1958), 73-81
**Lowest** .338 (1956), 52-102

**Most seasons, non-pitcher** 6—Billy Bryan
Ed Charles
Wayne Causey
**Most seasons, pitcher** 6—John Wyatt
**Games lost** 105 (1964)
**Month** 26 (Aug 1961)
**Consecutive** 13 (1959)
**Overall record** 829-1,224 (13 seasons)

**Number of league championships** 0
**Most recent** ---
**Runs, game** 20 vs Minnesota, Apr 25, 1961
**Opponents'** 29 by Chicago, Apr 23, 1955
**Total bases, game** vs Washington, June 13, 1956
vs Chicago, May 23, 1959
vs Cleveland, May 5, 1962, 1st game
(vs New York, July 27, 1956, 14 inn)
**Home runs, game** 5 vs Cleveland, Apr 18, 1955
vs Cleveland, Apr 24, 1957
vs Baltimore, Sept 9, 1958
**Runs, shutout** 16 vs Chicago, May 23, 1959
**Opponents'** 16 by Detroit, Apr 17, 1955
by Boston, Aug 26, 1957
**Longest 1-0 win** 11 inn, vs Cleveland, Sept 15, 1966

**Number of times worst record in league** 6 (inc. 1 tie)
**Most recent** 1967
**Runs, inning** 13 vs Chicago, Apr 21, 1956, 2nd
**Hits, game** 21 vs Washington, June 13, 1956
vs Chicago, May 23, 1959
vs Cleveland, May 5, 1962, 1st game
(26 vs New York, July 27, 1956, 14 inn)
**Consecutive games with one or more home runs** 11 (13 HRs), 1964
**Longest shutout** unknown
**Longest 1-0 loss** none over 9 innings

### ATTENDANCE

**Highest home attendance** 1,393,054 (1955)

**Highest road attendance** 938,214 (1967)

**Largest crowds**

| | |
|---|---|
| **Day** | 34,065 vs New York, Aug 27, 1961 |
| **Night** | 33,471 vs New York, Apr 29, 1955 |
| **Doubleheader** | 35,147 vs New York, Aug 18, 1962 |
| **Home opener** | 32,147 vs Detroit, Apr 12, 1955 |

## KANSAS CITY ROYALS

### YEARLY FINISHES

(American League expansion franchise)

### WEST DIVISION

| Year | Position | W | L | Pct. | GB | Manager | Attendance |
|---|---|---|---|---|---|---|---|
| 1969 | 4th | 69 | 93 | .426 | 28.0 | Joe Gordon | 902,414 |
| 1970 | 4th (tied) | 65 | 97 | .401 | 33.0 | Charlie Metro, Bob Lemon | 693,047 |
| 1971 | 2nd | 85 | 76 | .528 | 16.0 | Bob Lemon | 910,784 |
| 1972 | 4th | 76 | 78 | .494 | 16.5 | Bob Lemon | 707,656 |
| 1973 | 2nd | 88 | 74 | .543 | 6.0 | Jack McKeon | 1,345,341 |
| 1974 | 5th | 77 | 85 | .475 | 13.0 | Jack McKeon | 1,173,292 |
| 1975 | 2nd | 91 | 71 | .562 | 7.0 | Jack McKeon, Whitey Herzog | 1,151,836 |
| 1976 | 1st (c) | 90 | 72 | .556 | +2.5 | Whitey Herzog | 1,680,265 |
| 1977 | 1st (c) | 102 | 60 | .630 | +8.0 | Whitey Herzog | 1,852,603 |
| 1978 | 1st (c) | 92 | 70 | .568 | +5.0 | Whitey Herzog | 2,255,493 |
| 1979 | 2nd | 85 | 77 | .525 | 3.0 | Whitey Herzog | 2,261,845 |
| 1980 | 1st (C,s) | 97 | 65 | .599 | +14.0 | Jim Frey | 2,288,714 |
| 1981 | 5th/1st (i) | 50 | 53 | .485 | * | Jim Frey, Dick Howser | 1,279,403 |
| 1982 | 2nd | 90 | 72 | .556 | 3.0 | Dick Howser | 2,284,464 |
| 1983 | 2nd | 79 | 83 | .488 | 20.0 | Dick Howser | 1,963,875 |
| 1984 | 1st (c) | 84 | 78 | .519 | +3.0 | Dick Howser | 1,810,018 |
| 1985 | 1st (C,S) | 91 | 71 | .562 | +1.0 | Dick Howser | 2,162,717 |
| 1986 | 3rd (tied) | 76 | 86 | .469 | 16.0 | Dick Howser, Mike Ferraro | 2,320,794 |
| 1987 | 2nd | 83 | 79 | .512 | 2.0 | Billy Gardner, John Wathan | 2,392,471 |
| 1988 | 3rd | 84 | 77 | .522 | 19.5 | John Wathan | 2,350,181 |
| 1989 | 2nd | 92 | 70 | .568 | 7.0 | John Wathan | 2,477,700 |
| 1990 | 6th | 75 | 86 | .466 | 27.5 | John Wathan | 2,244,956 |
| 1991 | 6th | 82 | 80 | .506 | 13.0 | John Wathan, Hal McRae | 2,161,537 |
| 1992 | 5th (tied) | 72 | 90 | .444 | 24.0 | Hal McRae | 1,867,689 |
| 1993 | 3rd | 84 | 78 | .519 | 10.0 | Hal McRae | 1,934,578 |

### CENTRAL DIVISION

| Year | Position | W | L | Pct. | GB | Manager | Attendance |
|---|---|---|---|---|---|---|---|
| 1994 | 3rd | 64 | 51 | .557 | 4.0 | Hal McRae | 1,400,494 |
| 1995 | 2nd | 70 | 74 | .486 | 30.0 | Bob Boone | 1,233,530 |
| 1996 | 5th | 75 | 86 | .466 | 24.0 | Bob Boone | 1,435,997 |
| 1997 | 5th | 67 | 94 | .416 | 19.0 | Bob Boone, Tony Muser | 1,517,638 |
| 1998 | 3rd | 72 | 89 | .447 | 16.5 | Tony Muser | 1,494,875 |
| 1999 | 4th | 64 | 97 | .398 | 32.5 | Tony Muser | 1,506,068 |
| 2000 | 4th | 77 | 85 | .475 | 18.0 | Tony Muser | 1,677,915 |
| 2001 | 5th | 65 | 97 | .401 | 26.0 | Tony Muser | 1,536,371 |
| 2002 | 4th | 62 | 100 | .383 | 32.5 | Tony Muser, Tony Pena | 1,323,034 |
| 2003 | 3rd | 83 | 79 | .512 | 7.0 | Tony Pena | 1,779,895 |
| 2004 | 5th | 58 | 104 | .358 | 34.0 | Tony Pena | 1,661,478 |
| 2005 | 5th | 56 | 106 | .346 | 43.0 | Tony Pena, Bob Schaefer, Buddy Bell | 1,371,181 |

(c) lost League Championship Series; (C) won League Championship Series; (s) lost World Series; (i) lost intra-divisional playoff; *first half 20-30, second half 30-23; (S) won World Series

### INDIVIDUAL AND CLUB RECORDS

#### BATTING

| | Individual | | Club |
|---|---|---|---|
| | **Season** | **Career** | **Season** |
| **Games** | 162—Al Cowens, 1977<br>Hal McRae, 1977<br>Carlos Beltran, 2002 | 2,707—George Brett | 163 (1969, 1983) |

| | Individual Season | Individual Career | Club Season |
|---|---|---|---|
| At-bats | 705—Willie Wilson, 161 G, 1980 | 10,349—George Brett | 5,714 (1980) |
| Runs | 136—Johnny Damon, 159 G, 2000 | 1,583—George Brett | 879 (2000)<br>Fewest—586 (1969) |
| Hits | 230—Willie Wilson, 161 G, 1980 | 3,154—George Brett | 1,644 (2000)<br>Fewest—1,311 (1969) |
| Hitting streak | 30 G—George Brett, 1980 | | |
| Singles | 184—Willie Wilson, 161 G, 1980 | 2,035—George Brett | 1,193 (1980) |
| Doubles | 54—Hal McRae, 162 G, 1977 | 665—George Brett | 316 (1990) |
| Triples | 21—Willie Wilson, 141 G, 1985 | 137—George Brett | 79 (1979) |
| **HOME RUNS** | | | 168 (1987)<br>Fewest—65 (1976) |
| Righthander | 36—Steve Balboni, 160 G, 1985 | 193—Amos Otis | |
| Lefthander | 34—John Mayberry, 156 G, 1975 | 317—George Brett | |
| Switch-hitter | 30—Chili Davis, 140 G, 1997 | 123—Carlos Beltran | |
| Rookie | 24—Bob Hamelin, 101 G, 1994 | | |
| Home | 21—Chili Davis, 1997<br>Dean Palmer, 1998 | 136—George Brett | 88 (1997, 2002) |
| Road | 23—John Mayberry, 1975 | 181—George Brett | 95 (1987) |
| Month | 12—John Mayberry, July 1975<br>Chili Davis, Aug 1997 | | 43 (Aug 1987, Aug 1997) |
| Pinch | 2—Steve Balboni, 1987<br>Carmelo Martinez, 1991 | 2—many players | 6 (1995) |
| Grand slams | 3—Danny Tartabull, 146 G, 1988 | 6—Frank White | 7 (1991) |
| Home runs at Municipal Stadium, all teams | | | 102 (1969) |
| Home runs at Royals Stadium, all teams | | | 209 (2002) |
| Total bases | 363—George Brett, 154 G, 1979 | 5,044—George Brett | 2,440 (1977) |
| Extra-base hits | 86—Hal McRae, 162 G, 1977 | 1,119—George Brett | 522 (1977) |
| Sacrifice hits | 21—Tom Goodwin, 143 G, 1996 | 101—Frank White | 72 (1972) |
| Sacrifice flies | 13—Darrell Porter, 157 G, 1979<br>Dean Palmer, 152 G, 1998<br>Mike Sweeney, 159 G, 2000 | 120—George Brett | 76 (1979) |
| Bases on balls | 122—John Mayberry, 152 G, 1973 | 1,096—George Brett | 644 (1973)<br>Fewest—397 (1983) |
| Strikeouts | 172—Bo Jackson, 135 G, 1989<br>Fewest—29—Gregg Jefferies, 152 G, 1992 | 1,035—Frank White | 1,061 (1997)<br>Fewest—644 (1997) |
| Hit by pitch | 18—Mike Macfarlane, 92 G, 1994<br>Angel Berroa, 158 G, 2003 | 78—Mike Macfarlane | 76 (2004)<br>Fewest—21 (1970) |
| Runs batted in | 144—Mike Sweeney, 159 G, 2000 | 1,595—George Brett | 831 (2000)<br>Fewest—538 (1969) |
| Grounded into double plays | 26—John Wathan, 121 G, 1982<br>Fewest—1—Willie Wilson, 154 G, 1979 | 235—George Brett | 156 (1999)<br>Fewest—95 (1978) |
| Left on base | | | 1,209 (1980)<br>Fewest—1,057 (1985) |
| Batting average | .390—George Brett, 117 G, 1980 | .305—George Brett<br>Mike Sweeney | .288 (2000)<br>Lowest—.240 (1969) |
| Most .300 hitters | | | 4 (2000) |
| Slugging average | .664—George Brett, 117 G, 1980 | .518—Danny Tartabull | .436 (1977)<br>Lowest—.338 (1969) |
| On-base percentage | .454—George Brett, 117 G, 1980 | .377—Mike Sweeney | .348 (1999, 2000)<br>Lowest—.309 (1969, 1970) |

## BASERUNNING

| | Individual Season | Individual Career | Club Season |
|---|---|---|---|
| Stolen bases | 83—Willie Wilson, 154 G, 1979 | 612—Willie Wilson | 218 (1976) |
| Caught stealing | 22—Tom Goodwin, 143 G, 1996 | 119—Willie Wilson | 106 (1976) |

## PITCHING

| | Individual Season | Individual Career | Club Season |
|---|---|---|---|
| Games | 84—Dan Quisenberry, 1985 | 686—Jeff Montgomery | |
| Games started | 40—Dennis Leonard, 1978 | 392—Paul Splittorff | |
| Complete games | 21—Dennis Leonard, 1977 | 103—Dennis Leonard | 54 (1974) |
| Wins | 23—Bret Saberhagen, 1989 | 166—Paul Splittorff | |
| Percentage | .800—Larry Gura (16-4), 1978 | .587—Larry Gura | |
| Winning streak | 11—Rich Gale, 1980 | | |
| Winning streak, two seasons | 11—Paul Splittorff, 1977 (7), 1978 (4) | | |
| 20-win seasons | | 3—Dennis Leonard | |
| Losses | 19—Paul Splittorff, 1974<br>Darrell May, 2004 | 143—Paul Splittorff | |
| Losing streak | 9—Jeff Suppan, 2002<br>Brian Anderson, 2004 | | |

| | Individual Season | Career | Club Season |
|---|---|---|---|
| **Saves** | 45—Dan Quisenberry, 1983<br>Jeff Montgomery, 1993 | 304—Jeff Montgomery | 50 (1984) |
| **Innings** | 294.2—Dennis Leonard, 1978 | 2,554.2—Paul Splittorff | 1,472.1 (1976) |
| **Hits** | 284—Steve Busby, 1974 | 2,644—Paul Splittorff | 1,640 (2005) |
| **Runs** | 140—Jose Lima, 2005 | 1,243—Paul Splittorff | 935 (2005) |
| **Earned runs** | 131—Jose Lima, 2005 | 1,082—Paul Splittorff | 876 (2000) |
| **Bases on balls** | 120—Mark Gublcza, 1987 | 783—Mark Gubicza | 694 (2000) |
| **Strikeouts** | 244—Dennis Leonard, 1977 | 1,458—Kevin Appier | 1,006 (1990) |
| **Strikeouts, game** | 14—Mark Gubicza, Aug 27, 1988 | | |
| **Hit batsmen** | 13—Jim Colborn, 1977<br>Mike Boddicker, 1991<br>Zack Greinke, 2005 | 58—Mark Gubicza | 74 (2005) |
| **Wild pitches** | 18—Dan Reichert, 2000 | 107—Mark Gubicza | 77 (2000) |
| **Home runs** | 38—Darrell May, 2004 | 202—Dennis Leonard | 239 (2000) |
| **Sacrifice hits** | 18—Larry Gura, 1978 | 122—Paul Splittorff | 92 (1970) |
| **Sacrifice flies** | 17—Larry Gura, 1983 | 92—Paul Splittorff | 69 (2002) |
| **Earned run average** | 2.08—Roger Nelson, 173 inn, 1972 | 3.21—Bret Saberhagen | 3.21 (1976) |
| **Shutouts** | 6—Roger Nelson, 1972 | 23—Dennis Leonard | 16 (1972)<br>Lost—18 (1971, 1989) |
| **1-0 games won** | 2—Dick Drago, 1971<br>Roger Nelson, 1972<br>Al Fitzmorris, 1974<br>Dennis Leonard, 1979<br>Larry Gura, 1982 | 4—Dennis Leonard | 5 (1972)<br>Lost—4 (1971, 1989, 1992) |

## TEAM FIELDING

**Putouts** 4,417 (1976)
Fewest—4,144 (1972)
**Chances accepted** 6,290 (1974, 1985)
Fewest—5,860 (1990)
**Double plays** 204 (2001)
Fewest—114 (1969)
**Errorless games** 95 (1993)
Consecutive—11 (1997)

**Assists** 1,912 (1973)
Fewest—1,598 (1990)
**Errors** 167 (1973)
Fewest—91 (1997)
**Passed balls** 29 (1974)
Fewest—3 (1984)
**Fielding average** .985 (1997)
Lowest—.974 (1973, 1983)

## MISCELLANEOUS

**Most players, season** 58 (2004)
**Fewest players, season** 32 (1975)
**Games won** 102 (1977)
**Month** 25 (Sept 1977)
**Consecutive** 16 (1977)
**Winning percentage** .630 (1977), 102-60
**Lowest** .346 (2005), 56-106
**Number of league championships** 2
**Most recent** 1985
**Runs, game** 26 vs Detroit, Sept 9, 2004, 1st game
**Opponents'** 22 by Boston, Apr 12, 1994
**Hits, game** 26 vs Detroit, Sept 9, 2004, 1st game
**Home runs, game** 6 vs Detroit, July 14, 1991
**Runs, shutout** 16 vs Oakland, June 25, 1984
**Opponents'** 17 by Detroit, July 19, 1991
**Longest 1-0 win** 15 inn, vs Minnesota, May 23, 1981

**Most seasons, non-pitcher** 21—George Brett
**Most seasons, pitcher** 15—Paul Splittorff
**Games lost** 106 (2005)
**Month** 21 (Aug 1999, Aug 2005)
**Consecutive** 19 (2005)
**Overall record** 2,872-2,983 (37 seasons)
**Interleague play** 66-91
**Number of times worst record in league** 2
**Most recent** 2005
**Runs, inning** 12 vs Minnesota, June 17, 2003, 6th
**Total bases, game** 37 vs Chicago, July 18, 2000
**Consecutive games with one or more home runs** 12 (19 HRs), 1985
**Longest shutout** 16 inn, 3-0 vs Chicago, Sept 22, 1975
**Longest 1-0 loss** 14 inn, vs Cleveland, July 23, 1992

## ATTENDANCE

**Highest home attendance**
**Municipal Stadium** 910,784 (1971)
**Kauffman Stadium** 2,477,700 (1989)
**Highest road attendance** 2,378,624 (1993)

**Largest crowds**
**Day** 41,788 vs Seattle, Apr 11, 2005
**Night** 41,860 vs New York, July 26, 1980
**Doubleheader** 42,039 vs Milwaukee, Aug 8, 1983
**Home opener** 41,788 vs Seattle, Apr 11, 2005

# LOS ANGELES ANGELS OF ANAHEIM

## YEARLY FINISHES

**(American League expansion franchise known as Los Angeles Angels until September 1965, California Angels from September 1965 to 1996 and Anaheim Angels from 1997 to 2004)**

| Year | Position | W | L | Pct. | GB | Manager | Attendance |
|---|---|---|---|---|---|---|---|
| 1961 | 8th | 70 | 91 | .435 | 38.5 | Bill Rigney | 603,510 |
| 1962 | 3rd | 86 | 76 | .531 | 10.0 | Bill Rigney | 1,144,063 |
| 1963 | 9th | 70 | 91 | .435 | 34.0 | Bill Rigney | 821,015 |
| 1964 | 5th | 82 | 80 | .506 | 1.0 | Bill Rigney | 760,439 |
| 1965 | 7th | 75 | 87 | .463 | 27.0 | Bill Rigney | 566,727 |
| 1966 | 6th | 80 | 82 | .494 | 18.0 | Bill Rigney | 1,400,321 |
| 1967 | 5th | 84 | 77 | .522 | 7.5 | Bill Rigney | 1,317,713 |
| 1968 | 8th | 67 | 95 | .414 | 36.0 | Bill Rigney | 1,025,956 |

## WEST DIVISION

| Year | Position | W | L | Pct. | GB | Manager | Attendance |
|---|---|---|---|---|---|---|---|
| 1969 | 3rd | 71 | 91 | .438 | 26.0 | Bill Rigney, Lefty Phillips | 758,388 |
| 1970 | 3rd | 86 | 76 | .531 | 12.0 | Lefty Phillips | 1,077,741 |
| 1971 | 4th | 76 | 86 | .469 | 25.5 | Lefty Phillips | 926,373 |
| 1972 | 5th | 75 | 80 | .484 | 18.0 | Del Rice | 744,190 |

| Year | Position | W | L | Pct. | GB | Manager | Attendance |
|---|---|---|---|---|---|---|---|
| 1973 | 4th | 79 | 83 | .488 | 15.0 | Bobby Winkles | 1,058,206 |
| 1974 | 6th | 68 | 94 | .420 | 22.0 | Bobby Winkles, Dick Williams | 917,269 |
| 1975 | 6th | 72 | 89 | .447 | 25.5 | Dick Williams | 1,058,163 |
| 1976 | 4th (tied) | 76 | 86 | .469 | 14.0 | Dick Williams, Norm Sherry | 1,006,774 |
| 1977 | 5th | 74 | 88 | .457 | 28.0 | Norm Sherry, Dave Garcia | 1,432,633 |
| 1978 | 2nd (tied) | 87 | 75 | .537 | 5.0 | Dave Garcia, Jim Fregosi | 1,755,386 |
| 1979 | 1st (c) | 88 | 74 | .543 | +3.0 | Jim Fregosi | 2,523,575 |
| 1980 | 6th | 65 | 95 | .406 | 31.0 | Jim Fregosi | 2,297,327 |
| 1981 | 4th/7th | 51 | 59 | .464 | * | Jim Fregosi, Gene Mauch | 1,441,545 |
| 1982 | 1st (c) | 93 | 69 | .574 | +3.0 | Gene Mauch | 2,807,360 |
| 1983 | 5th (tied) | 70 | 92 | .432 | 29.0 | John McNamara | 2,555,016 |
| 1984 | 2nd (tied) | 81 | 81 | .500 | 3.0 | John McNamara | 2,402,997 |
| 1985 | 2nd | 90 | 72 | .556 | 1.0 | Gene Mauch | 2,567,427 |
| 1986 | 1st (c) | 92 | 70 | .568 | +5.0 | Gene Mauch | 2,655,872 |
| 1987 | 6th (tied) | 75 | 87 | .463 | 10.0 | Gene Mauch | 2,696,299 |
| 1988 | 4th | 75 | 87 | .463 | 29.0 | Cookie Rojas | 2,340,925 |
| 1989 | 3rd | 91 | 71 | .562 | 8.0 | Doug Rader | 2,647,291 |
| 1990 | 4th | 80 | 82 | .494 | 23.0 | Doug Rader | 2,555,688 |
| 1991 | 7th | 81 | 81 | .500 | 14.0 | Doug Rader, Buck Rodgers | 2,416,236 |
| 1992 | 5th (tied) | 72 | 90 | .444 | 24.0 | Buck Rodgers | 2,065,444 |
| 1993 | 5th (tied) | 71 | 91 | .438 | 23.0 | Buck Rodgers | 2,057,460 |
| 1994 | 4th | 47 | 68 | .409 | 5.5 | Buck Rodgers, Marcel Lachemann | 1,512,622 |
| 1995 | 2nd (p) | 78 | 67 | .538 | 1.0 | Marcel Lachemann | 1,748,680 |
| 1996 | 4th | 70 | 91 | .435 | 19.5 | Marcel Lachemann, John McNamara, Joe Maddon | 1,820,521 |
| 1997 | 2nd | 84 | 78 | .519 | 6.0 | Terry Collins | 1,767,330 |
| 1998 | 2nd | 85 | 77 | .525 | 3.0 | Terry Collins | 2,519,210 |
| 1999 | 4th | 70 | 92 | .432 | 25.0 | Terry Collins, Joe Maddon | 2,253,123 |
| 2000 | 3rd | 82 | 80 | .506 | 9.5 | Mike Scioscia | 2,066,977 |
| 2001 | 3rd | 75 | 87 | .463 | 41.0 | Mike Scioscia | 2,000,917 |
| 2002 | 2nd (D,C,S) | 99 | 63 | .611 | 4.0 | Mike Scioscia | 2,305,565 |
| 2003 | 3rd | 77 | 85 | .475 | 19.0 | Mike Scioscia | 3,061,090 |
| 2004 | 1st (d) | 92 | 70 | .568 | +1.0 | Mike Scioscia | 3,375,677 |
| 2005 | 1st (D, c) | 95 | 67 | .586 | +7.0 | Mike Scioscia | 3,404,686 |

(c) lost League Championship Series; *first half 31-29, second half 20-30; (p) lost division playoff; (D) won Division Series; (C) won League Championship Series; (S) won World Series; (d) lost Division Series

## INDIVIDUAL AND CLUB RECORDS

### BATTING

| | Individual | | Club |
|---|---|---|---|
| | **Season** | **Career** | **Season** |
| **Games** | 162—Bobby Knoop, 1964 | 1,661—Brian Downing | 163 (1969, 1974) |
| | Jim Fregosi, 1966 | | |
| | Sandy Alomar, 1970, 1971 | | |
| | Don Baylor, 1979 | | |
| **At-bats** | 689—Sandy Alomar, 162 G, 1971 | 6,472—Garret Anderson | 5,686 (1996) |
| **Runs** | 124—Vlad Guerrero, 157 G, 2004 | 956—Tim Salmon | 866 (1979) |
| | | | Fewest—498 (1968) |
| **Hits** | 240—Darin Erstad, 157 G, 2000 | 1,929—Garret Anderson | 1,603 (2002, 2004) |
| | | | Fewest—1,209 (1968) |
| **Hitting streak** | 28 G—Garret Anderson, 1998 | | |
| **Singles** | 170—Darin Erstad, 157 G, 2000 | 1,273—Garret Anderson | 1,132 (2004) |
| **Doubles** | 56—Garret Anderson, 158 G, 2002 | 403—Garret Anderson | 333 (2002) |
| **Triples** | 17—Chone Figgins, 148 G, 2004 | 70—Jim Fregosi | 54 (1966) |
| **HOME RUNS** | | | 236 (2000) |
| | | | Fewest—55 (1975) |
| **Righthander** | 47—Troy Glaus, 159 G, 2000 | 290—Tim Salmon | |
| **Lefthander** | 39—Reggie Jackson, 153 G, 1982 | 224—Garret Anderson | |
| **Switch-hitter** | 28—Chili Davis, 145 G, 1996 | 156—Chili Davis | |
| **Rookie** | 31—Tim Salmon, 142 G, 1993 | | |
| **Home** | 24—Troy Glaus, 2000 | 155—Tim Salmon | 130 (2000) |
| **Road** | 24—Leon Wagner, 1962, 1963 | 135—Tim Salmon | 106 (2000) |
| **Month** | 13—Tim Salmon, Jun 1996 | | 50 (May 2000) |
| | Mo Vaughn, May 2000 | | |
| **Pinch** | 4—Jack Howell, 1996 | 7—Jack Howell | 9 (1987) |
| **Grand slams** | 3—Joe Rudi, 133 G, 1978 | 7—Joe Rudi | 8 (1979, 1983) |
| | Joe Rudi, 90 G, 1979 | | |
| | David Eckstein, 152 G, 2002 | | |
| **Home runs at Wrigley Field, all teams** | | | 248 (1961) |
| **Home runs at Chavez Ravine, all teams** | | | 102 (1964) |
| **Home runs at Angel Field, all teams** | | | 243 (2000) |
| **Total bases** | 366—Darin Erstad, 157 G, 2000 | 3,062—Garrett Anderson | 2,659 (2000) |
| | Vlad Guerrero, 156 G, 2004 | | |
| **Extra-base hits** | 88—Garret Anderson, 158 G, 2002 | 656—Garrett Anderson | 579 (2000) |
| **Sacrifice hits** | 26—Tim Foli, 150 G, 1982 | 90—Bob Boone | 114 (1982) |
| **Sacrifice flies** | 13—Dan Ford, 142 G, 1979 | 67—Tim Salmon | 64 (2002) |
| **Bases on balls** | 113—Tony Phillips, 139 G, 1995 | 941—Tim Salmon | 681 (1961) |
| | | | Fewest—416 (1992) |

| | Individual Season | Individual Career | Club Season |
|---|---|---|---|
| **Strikeouts** | 181—Mo Vaughn, 161 G, 2000 | 1,316—Tim Salmon | 1,080 (1968) |
| | Fewest—22—Tim Foli, 150 G, 1982 | | Fewest—682 (1978) |
| **Hit by pitch** | 27—David Eckstein, 152 G, 2002 | 105—Brian Downing | 77 (2001) |
| | | | Fewest—22 (1965) |
| **Runs batted in** | 139—Don Baylor, 162 G, 1982 | 1,043—Garret Anderson | 837 (2000) |
| | | | Fewest—453 (1968) |
| **Grounded into double plays** | 26—Lyman Bostock, 147 G, 1978 | 152—Brian Downing | 148 (1966) |
| | Fewest—5—Leon Wagner, 160 G, 1962 | | Fewest—98 (1975) |
| | Albie Pearson, 154 G, 1963 | | |
| | Dick Schofield, 155 G, 1988 | | |
| **Left on base** | | | 1,209 (1966) |
| | | | Fewest—975 (1992) |
| **Batting average** | .355—Darin Erstad, 157 G, 2000 | .314—Rod Carew | .282 (2002, 2004) |
| | | | Lowest—.227 (1968) |
| **Most .300 hitters** | | | 2 (1963, 1964, 1979, 1982, 1995, 1998, 2002) |
| **Slugging average** | .604—Troy Glaus, 159 G, 2000 | .506—Tim Salmon | .472 (2000) |
| | | | Lowest—.318 (1968, 1976) |
| **On-base percentage** | .429—Tim Salmon, 143 G, 1995 | .393—Rod Carew | .352 (2000) |
| | Chili Davis, 119 G, 1995 | | Lowest—.290 (1971) |

## BASERUNNING

| | Individual Season | Individual Career | Club Season |
|---|---|---|---|
| **Stolen bases** | 70—Mickey Rivers, 155 G, 1975 | 186—Gary Pettis | 220 (1975) |
| **Caught stealing** | 24—Chad Curtis, 152 G, 1993 | 82—Luis Polonia | 108 (1975) |

## PITCHING

| | Individual Season | Individual Career | Club Season |
|---|---|---|---|
| **Games** | 78—Scot Shields, 2005 | 579—Troy Percival | |
| **Games started** | 41—Nolan Ryan, 1974 | 379—Chuck Finley | |
| **Complete games** | 26—Nolan Ryan, 1973, 1974 | 156—Nolan Ryan | 72 (1973) |
| **Wins** | 22—Clyde Wright, 1970 | 165—Chuck Finley | |
| | Nolan Ryan, 1974 | | |
| **Percentage** | .773—Bert Blyleven (17-5), 1989 | .567—Frank Tanana | |
| **Winning streak** | 12—Jarrod Washburn, 2002 | | |
| **20-win seasons** | | 2—Nolan Ryan | |
| **Losses** | 19—George Brunet, 1967 | 140—Chuck Finley | |
| | Clyde Wright, 1973 | | |
| | Frank Tanana, 1974 | | |
| | Kirk McCaskill, 1991 | | |
| **Losing streak** | 11—Andy Hassler, 1975 | | |
| | Jim Abbott, 1996 | | |
| **Saves** | 46—Bryan Harvey, 1991 | 316—Troy Percival | 54 (2002) |
| **Innings** | 333—Nolan Ryan, 1974 | 2,675—Chuck Finley | 1,481 (1971) |
| **Hits** | 287—Tommy John, 1983 | 2,544—Chuck Finley | 1,636 (1983) |
| **Runs** | 130—Mike Witt, 1988 | 1,234—Chuck Finley | 943 (1996) |
| **Earned runs** | 118—Jim Abbott, 1996 | 1,107—Chuck Finley | 847 (1996) |
| **Bases on balls** | 204—Nolan Ryan, 1977 | 1,302—Nolan Ryan | 713 (1961) |
| **Strikeouts** | 383—Nolan Ryan, 1973 | 2,416—Nolan Ryan | 1,091 (1998) |
| **Strikeouts, game** | 19—Nolan Ryan, Aug 12, 1974 | | |
| | Nolan Ryan, June 14, 1974 (pitched first 13 inn of 15-inn game) | | |
| | Nolan Ryan, Aug 20, 1974, 11 inn | | |
| | Nolan Ryan, June 8, 1977 (pitched first 11 inn of 13-inn game) | | |
| **Hit batsmen** | 21—Tom Murphy, 1969 | 71—Chuck Finley | 84 (1996) |
| **Wild pitches** | 21—Nolan Ryan, 1977 | 117—Chuck Finley | 80 (1996) |
| **Home runs** | 40—Shawn Boskie, 1996 | 254—Chuck Finley | 228 (2000) |
| | Ramon Ortiz, 2002 | | |
| **Sacrifice hits** | 22—Nolan Ryan, 1977 | 90—Chuck Finley | 89 (1965) |
| **Sacrifice flies** | 14—Nolan Ryan, 1978 | 70—Chuck Finley | 67 (1988) |
| **Earned run average** | 1.65—Dean Chance, 278 inn, 1964 | 3.07—Nolan Ryan | 2.91 (1964) |
| **Shutouts** | 11—Dean Chance, 1964 | 40—Nolan Ryan | 28 (1964) |
| | | | Lost—23 (1971) |
| **1-0 games won** | 5—Dean Chance, 1964 | 9—Dean Chance | 10 (1964) |
| | | | Lost—5 (1968) |

## TEAM FIELDING

| | |
|---|---|
| **Putouts** | 4,443 (1971) |
| | Fewest—4,133 (1972) |
| **Chances accepted** | 6,499 (1983) |
| | Fewest—5,740 (1972) |
| **Double plays** | 202 (1985) |
| | Fewest—126 (2004) |
| **Errorless games** | 96 (2005) |
| | Consecutive—14 (1991, 2005) |
| **Assists** | 2,077 (1983) |
| | Fewest—1,511 (2004) |
| **Errors** | 192 (1961) |
| | Fewest—87 (2002, 2005) |
| **Passed balls** | 30 (1969) |
| | Fewest—4 (1982, 1984) |
| **Fielding average** | .986 (2002, 2005) |
| | Lowest—.969 (1961) |

## MISCELLANEOUS

**Most players, season** 52 (1996)

**Fewest players, season** 33 (1963)

**Games won** 99 (2002)
**Month** 22 (June 1998)
**Consecutive** 11 (1964)

**Winning percentage** .611 (2002), 99-63
**Lowest** .406 (1980), 65-95

**Number of league championships** 1
**Most recent** 2002

**Runs, game** 24 vs Toronto, Aug 25, 1979
**Opponents'** 21 by Seattle, Sept 30, 2000

**Hits, game** 26 vs Toronto, Aug 25, 1979
vs Boston, June 20, 1980

**Home runs, game** 7 vs Montreal, June 4, 2003

**Runs, shutout** 19 vs Chicago, May 10, 2003
**Opponents'** 14 by Seattle, Aug 7, 1987

**Longest 1-0 win** 15 inn, vs Chicago, Apr 13, 1963

**Most seasons, non-pitcher** 13—Brian Downing
Tim Salmon

**Most seasons, pitcher** 14—Chuck Finley

**Games lost** 95 (1968, 1980)
**Month** 22 (June 1961, May 1964, Aug 1968)
**Consecutive** 12 (1988)

**Overall record** 3,507-3,653 (45 seasons)
**Interleague play** 83-75

**Number of times worst record in league** 2
**Most recent** 1994

**Runs, inning** 13 vs Texas, Sept 14, 1978, 9th
vs Chicago, May 12, 1997, 7th

**Total bases, game** 52 vs Boston, June 20, 1980

**Consecutive games with one or more home runs** 18 (30 HRs), 1982

**Longest shutout** 16 inn, 3-0 vs Chicago, Sept 22, 1975

**Longest 1-0 loss** 20 inn, vs Oakland, July 9, 1971

## ATTENDANCE

| **Highest home attendance** | |
|---|---|
| **Wrigley Field** | 605,510 (1961) |
| **Chavez Ravine** | 1,400,321 (1965) |
| **Angel Field** | 3,404,686 (2005) |
| **Highest road attendance** | 2,491,562 (2001) |

| **Largest crowds** | |
|---|---|
| **Day** | 63,132 vs Kansas City, July 4, 1983 |
| **Night** | 63,073 vs Baltimore, Apr 23, 1983 |
| **Doubleheader** | 43,461 vs Chicago, Aug 5, 1988 |
| **Home opener** | 51,145 vs Detroit, Apr 26, 1995 |

# MILWAUKEE BREWERS (1901)

## YEARLY FINISH

(Original American League franchise moved from Milwaukee to St. Louis after the 1901 season)

| Year | Position | W | L | Pct. | GB | Manager | Attendance |
|---|---|---|---|---|---|---|---|
| 1901 | 8th | 48 | 89 | .350 | 35.5 | Hugh Duffy | 139,034 |

## INDIVIDUAL AND CLUB RECORDS

### BATTING

| | Individual Season | Club Season |
|---|---|---|
| **Games** | 139—Bill Hallman | 139 |
| **At-bats** | 576—John Anderson, 138 G | 4,795 |
| **Runs** | 90—John Anderson, 138 G | 641 |
| **Hits** | 190—John Anderson, 138 G | 1,250 |
| **Hitting streak** | unknown | |
| **Singles** | 129—John Anderson, 138 G | 966 |
| **Doubles** | 46—John Anderson, 138 G | 192 |
| **Triples** | 9—Hugh Duffy, 79 G | 66 |
| **HOME RUNS** | | 26 |
| **Righthander** | 5—Wid Conroy, 131 G | |
| **Lefthander** | 4—Bill Friel, 106 G | |
| **Switch-hitter** | 8—John Anderson, 138 G | |
| **Rookie** | 5—Wid Conroy, 131 G | |
| **Home** | 6—John Anderson | 15 |
| **Road** | 3—Davy Jones | 11 |
| **Month** | 3—John Anderson, July<br>John Anderson, Sept<br>Davy Jones, Sept | 9 (Sept) |
| **Pinch** | 0 | 0 |
| **Grand slams** | 0 | 0 |
| **Home runs at Milwaukee Park (Lloyd Street Grounds), all teams** | | 29 |
| **Total bases** | 274—John Anderson, 138 G | 1,652 |
| **Extra-base hits** | 61—John Anderson, 138 G | 284 |
| **Sacrifice hits** | 15—Billy Gilbert, 127 G | 122 |
| **Bases on balls** | 41—Bill Hallman, 139 G | 325 |
| **Strikeouts** | unknown | 385 |
| **Hit by pitch** | 8—Wid Conroy, 131 G<br>Billy Maloney, 86 G | 46 |
| **Runs batted in** | 99—John Anderson, 138 G | 513 |
| **Grounded into double plays** | unknown | unknown |
| **Left on base** | | unknown |
| **Batting average** | .330—John Anderson, 138 G | .261 |
| **Most .300 hitters** | | 1 |
| **SluggingG average** | .476—John Anderson, 138 G | .345 |
| **On-base percentage** | .360—John Anderson, 138 G | .314 |

## BASERUNNING

| | Individual Season | Club Season |
|---|---|---|
| **Stolen bases** | 35—John Anderson, 138 G | 176 |
| **Caught stealing** | unknown | unknown |

## PITCHING

| | Individual Season | Club Season |
|---|---|---|
| **Games** | 37—Ned Garvin<br>Bill Reidy | |
| **Games started** | 33—Bill Reidy | |
| **Complete games** | 28—Bill Reidy | 107 |
| **Wins** | 16—Bill Reidy | |
| **Percentage** | .444—Bill Reidy (16-20) | |
| **Winning streak** | unknown | |
| **20-win seasons** | | none |
| **Losses** | 20—Ned Garvin<br>Bill Reidy | |
| **Losing streak** | unknown | |
| **Innings** | 301.1—Bill Reidy | 1,218 |
| **Hits** | 364—Bill Reidy | 1,383 |
| **Runs** | 183—Bill Reidy | 828 |
| **Earned runs** | 141—Bill Reidy | 549 |
| **Bases on balls** | 95—Bert Husting | 395 |
| **Strikeouts** | 122—Ned Garvin | 376 |
| **Strikeouts, game** | unknown | |
| **Hit batsmen** | 14—Ned Garvin<br>Tully Sparks | 63 |
| **Wild pitches** | 13—Ned Garvin | 34 |
| **Home runs** | 14—Bill Reidy | 32 |
| **Sacrifice hits** | unknown | unknown |
| **Earned run average** | 3.46—Ned Garvin, 257.1 inn | 4.06 |
| **Shutouts** | 2—Bill Reidy | 3<br>Lost—13 |
| **1-0 games won** | 1—Ned Garvin<br>Bill Reidy | 2<br>Lost—0 |

## TEAM FIELDING

| | | | |
|---|---|---|---|
| **Putouts** | 3,650 | **Assists** | 1,886 |
| **Chances accepted** | 5,536 | **Errors** | 393 |
| **Double plays** | 106 | **Passed balls** | 30 |
| **Errorless games** | 13<br>Consecutive—3 | **Fielding average** | .934 |

## MISCELLANEOUS

**Most players, season** 17
**Games won** 48
**Month** 11 (May, July)
**Consecutive** 4
**Winning percentage** .350, 48-89
**Number of league championships** 0
**Runs, game** 21 vs Chicago, May 5
**Opponents'** 20 by Washington, Sept 7
**Hits, game** 25 vs Chicago, May 5
**Home runs, game** 2 vs Detroit, Aug 5
vs Washington, Sept 8, 1st game
vs Boston, Sept 28
**Runs, shutout** 2 vs Cleveland, July 7
**Opponents'** 10 by Baltimore, Sept 3
**Longest 1-0 win** 9 inn vs Washington, July 28
vs Washington, Aug 24

**Games lost** 89
**Month** 18 (June, July, Sept)
**Consecutive** 8
**Overall record** 48-89 (1 season)
**Number of times worst record in league** 1
**Runs, inning** 10 vs Detroit, Aug 4, 4th
**Total bases, game** 36 vs Chicago, May 5
**Consecutive games with one or more home runs** 4 (5 HRs)
**Longest shutout** none more than 9 inn
**Longest 1-0 loss** none

## ATTENDANCE

**Highest home attendance** 139,034
**Highest road attendance** 219,921

**Largest crowds**
**Day** 10,000 vs Philadelphia, May 26
**Doubleheader** 6,500 vs Boston, July 21
**Home opener** 4,000 vs Chicago, May 3

# MINNESOTA TWINS

## YEARLY FINISHES

**(Original American League franchise moved from Washington to Minnesota after the 1960 season)**

| Year | Position | W | L | Pct. | GB | Manager | Attendance |
|---|---|---|---|---|---|---|---|
| 1961 | 7th | 70 | 90 | .438 | 38.0 | Cookie Lavagetto, Sam Mele | 1,256,723 |
| 1962 | 2nd | 91 | 71 | .562 | 5.0 | Sam Mele | 1,433,116 |
| 1963 | 3rd | 91 | 70 | .565 | 13.0 | Sam Mele | 1,406,652 |
| 1964 | 6th (tied) | 79 | 83 | .488 | 20.0 | Sam Mele | 1,207,514 |
| 1965 | 1st (s) | 102 | 60 | .630 | +7.0 | Sam Mele | 1,463,258 |
| 1966 | 2nd | 89 | 73 | .549 | 9.0 | Sam Mele | 1,259,374 |
| 1967 | 2nd (tied) | 91 | 71 | .562 | 1.0 | Sam Mele, Cal Ermer | 1,483,547 |
| 1968 | 7th | 79 | 83 | .488 | 24.0 | Cal Ermer | 1,143,257 |

## WEST DIVISION

| Year | Position | W | L | Pct. | GB | Manager | Attendance |
|---|---|---|---|---|---|---|---|
| 1969 | 1st (c) | 97 | 65 | .599 | +9.0 | Billy Martin | 1,349,328 |
| 1970 | 1st (c) | 98 | 64 | .605 | +9.0 | Bill Rigney | 1,261,887 |
| 1971 | 5th | 74 | 86 | .463 | 26.5 | Bill Rigney | 940,858 |
| 1972 | 3rd | 77 | 77 | .500 | 15.5 | Bill Rigney, Frank Quilici | 797,901 |
| 1973 | 3rd | 81 | 81 | .500 | 13.0 | Frank Quilici | 907,499 |
| 1974 | 3rd | 82 | 80 | .506 | 8.0 | Frank Quilici | 662,401 |
| 1975 | 4th | 76 | 83 | .478 | 20.5 | Frank Quilici | 737,156 |
| 1976 | 3rd | 85 | 77 | .525 | 5.0 | Gene Mauch | 715,394 |
| 1977 | 4th | 84 | 77 | .522 | 17.5 | Gene Mauch | 1,162,727 |
| 1978 | 4th | 73 | 89 | .451 | 19.0 | Gene Mauch | 787,878 |
| 1979 | 4th | 82 | 80 | .506 | 6.0 | Gene Mauch | 1,070,521 |
| 1980 | 3rd | 77 | 84 | .478 | 19.5 | Gene Mauch, Johnny Goryl | 769,206 |
| 1981 | 7th/4th | 41 | 68 | .376 | * | Johnny Goryl, Billy Gardner | 469,090 |
| 1982 | 7th | 60 | 102 | .370 | 33.0 | Billy Gardner | 921,186 |
| 1983 | 5th (tied) | 70 | 92 | .432 | 29.0 | Billy Gardner | 858,939 |
| 1984 | 2nd (tied) | 81 | 81 | .500 | 3.0 | Billy Gardner | 1,598,422 |
| 1985 | 4th (tied) | 77 | 85 | .475 | 14.0 | Billy Gardner, Ray Miller | 1,651,814 |
| 1986 | 6th | 71 | 91 | .438 | 21.0 | Ray Miller, Tom Kelly | 1,255,453 |
| 1987 | 1st (C,S) | 85 | 77 | .525 | +2.0 | Tom Kelly | 2,081,976 |
| 1988 | 2nd | 91 | 71 | .562 | 13.0 | Tom Kelly | 3,030,672 |
| 1989 | 5th | 80 | 82 | .494 | 19.0 | Tom Kelly | 2,277,438 |
| 1990 | 7th | 74 | 88 | .457 | 29.0 | Tom Kelly | 1,751,584 |
| 1991 | 1st (C,S) | 95 | 67 | .586 | +8.0 | Tom Kelly | 2,293,842 |
| 1992 | 2nd | 90 | 72 | .556 | 6.0 | Tom Kelly | 2,482,428 |
| 1993 | 5th (tied) | 71 | 91 | .438 | 23.0 | Tom Kelly | 2,048,673 |

## CENTRAL DIVISION

| Year | Position | W | L | Pct. | GB | Manager | Attendance |
|---|---|---|---|---|---|---|---|
| 1994 | 4th | 53 | 60 | .469 | 14.0 | Tom Kelly | 1,398,565 |
| 1995 | 5th | 56 | 88 | .389 | 44.0 | Tom Kelly | 1,057,667 |
| 1996 | 4th | 78 | 84 | .481 | 21.5 | Tom Kelly | 1,437,352 |
| 1997 | 4th | 68 | 94 | .420 | 18.5 | Tom Kelly | 1,411,064 |
| 1998 | 4th | 70 | 92 | .432 | 19.0 | Tom Kelly | 1,165,980 |
| 1999 | 5th | 63 | 97 | .394 | 33.0 | Tom Kelly | 1,202,829 |
| 2000 | 5th | 69 | 93 | .426 | 26.0 | Tom Kelly | 1,059,715 |
| 2001 | 2nd | 85 | 77 | .525 | 6.0 | Tom Kelly | 1,782,926 |
| 2002 | 1st (D,c) | 94 | 67 | .584 | +13.5 | Ron Gardenhire | 1,924,473 |
| 2003 | 1st (d) | 90 | 72 | .556 | +4.0 | Ron Gardenhire | 1,946,011 |
| 2004 | 1st (d) | 92 | 70 | .568 | +9.0 | Ron Gardenhire | 1,879,222 |
| 2005 | 3rd | 83 | 79 | .512 | 16.0 | Ron Gardenhire | 2,034,243 |

(s) lost World Series; (c) lost League Championship Series; *first half 17-39, second half 24-29; (C) won League Championship Series; (S) won World Series; (D) won Division Series; (d) lost Division Series

## INDIVIDUAL AND CLUB RECORDS

### BATTING

| | Individual: Season | Individual: Career | Club: Season |
|---|---|---|---|
| **Games** | 164—Cesar Tovar, 1967 | 1,939—Harmon Killebrew | 164 (1967) |
| **At-bats** | 691—Kirby Puckett, 161 G, 1985 | 7,244—Kirby Puckett | 5,837 (2005) |
| **Runs** | 140—Chuck Knoblauch, 153 G, 1996 | 1,071—Kirby Puckett | 877 (1996)<br>Fewest—562 (1968) |
| **Hits** | 239—Rod Carew, 155 G, 1977 | 2,304—Kirby Puckett | 1,633 (1966)<br>Fewest—1,274 (1968) |
| **Hitting streak** | 31 G—Ken Landreaux, 1980 | | |
| **Singles** | 180—Rod Carew, 153 G, 1974 | 1,626—Kirby Puckett | 1,192 (1974) |
| **Doubles** | 46—Marty Cordova, 145 G, 1996 | 414—Kirby Puckett | 348 (2002) |
| **Triples** | 20—Christian Guzman, 156 G, 2000 | 90—Rod Carew | 60 (1977) |
| **HOME RUNS** | | | 225 (1963)<br>Fewest—81 (1976) |
| **Righthander** | 49—Harmon Killebrew, 158 G, 1964<br>Harmon Killebrew, 162 G, 1969 | 475—Harmon Killebrew | |
| **Lefthander** | 34—Kent Hrbek, 143 G, 1987 | 293—Kent Hrbek | |
| **Switch-hitter** | 29—Chili Davis, 153 G, 1991 | 110—Roy Smalley | |
| **Rookie** | 33—Jimmie Hall, 156 G, 1963 | | |
| **Home** | 29—Harmon Killebrew, 1961 | 244—Harmon Killebrew | 116 (1986) |
| **Road** | 28—Harmon Killebrew, 1962 | 231—Harmon Killebrew | 113 (1963) |
| **Month** | 14—Harmon Killebrew, June 1964 | | 55 (May 1964) |
| **Pinch** | 4—Don Mincher, 1964<br>Matt LeCroy, 2004 | 8—Bob Allison | 7 (1964, 1967) |
| **Grand slams** | 3—Bob Allison, 159 G, 1961<br>Rod Carew, 156 G, 1976<br>Kent Hrbek, 158 G, 1985<br>Kirby Puckett, 160 G, 1992 | 10—Harmon Killebrew | 8 (1961) |
| **Home runs at Metropolitan Stadium, all teams** | | | 211 (1963) |
| **Home runs at Metrodome, all teams** | | | 223 (1986) |

| | Individual | | Club |
|---|---|---|---|
| | **Season** | **Career** | **Season** |
| **Total bases** | 374—Tony Oliva, 161 G, 1964 | 3,453—Kirby Puckett | 2,440 (2003) |
| **Extra-base hits** | 84—Tony Oliva, 161 G, 1964 | 728—Harmon Killebrew | 551 (2002) |
| **Sacrifice hits** | 25—Rob Wilfong, 140 G, 1979 | 79—Roy Smalley | 142 (1979) |
| **Sacrifice flies** | 13—Gary Gaetti, 145 G, 1982 | 66—Kent Hrbek | 63 (1996) |
| | Tom Brunansky, 157 G, 1985 | Harmon Killebrew | |
| **Bases on balls** | 145—Harmon Killebrew, 162 G, 1969 | 1,321—Harmon Killebrew | 649 (1962) |
| | | | Fewest—436 (1980) |
| **Strikeouts** | 145—Bobby Darwin, 145 G, 1972 | 1,314—Harmon Killebrew | 1,121 (1997) |
| | Fewest—22—Brian Harper, 140 G, 1992 | | Fewest—684 (1978) |
| **Hit by pitch** | 19—Chuck Knoblauch, 153 G, 1996 | 74—Chuck Knoblauch | 65 (1996) |
| | | | Fewest—21 (1980) |
| **Runs batted in** | 140—Harmon Killebrew, 162 G, 1969 | 1,325—Harmon Killebrew | 812 (1996) |
| | | | Fewest—522 (1968) |
| **Grounded into double plays** | 28—Harmon Killebrew, 157 G, 1970 | 210—Harmon Killebrew | 172 (1996) |
| | Fewest—2—Cesar Tovar, 157 G, 1968 | | Fewest—93 (1965) |
| **Left on base** | | | 1,263 (1974) |
| | | | Fewest—1,041 (1987) |
| **Batting average** | .388—Rod Carew, 155 G, 1977 | .334—Rod Carew | .288 (1996) |
| | | | Lowest—.237 (1968) |
| **Most .300 hitters** | | | 3 (1977, 1988, 1992, 1996, 2003) |
| **Slugging average** | .606—Harmon Killebrew, 150 G, 1961 | .518—Harmon Killebrew | .437 (2002) |
| | | | Lowest—.338 (1981) |
| **On-base percentage** | .449—Rod Carew, 155 G, 1977 | .393—Rod Carew | .357 (1996) |
| | | | Lowest—.293 (1981) |

## BASERUNNING

| | Season | Career | Club Season |
|---|---|---|---|
| **Stolen bases** | 62—Chuck Knoblauch, 156 G, 1997 | 276—Chuck Knoblauch | 151 (1997) |
| **Caught stealing** | 22—Rod Carew, 156 G, 1976 | 123—Rod Carew | 75 (1976) |

## PITCHING

| | Season | Career | Club Season |
|---|---|---|---|
| **Games** | 90—Mike Marshall, 1979 | 639—Eddie Guardado | |
| **Games started** | 42—Jim Kaat, 1965 | 422—Jim Kaat | |
| **Complete games** | 25—Bert Blyleven, 1973 | 141—Bert Blyleven | 58 (1963, 1967) |
| **Wins** | 25—Jim Kaat, 1966 | 189—Jim Kaat | |
| **Percentage** | .774—Frank Viola (24-7), 1988 | .587—Jim Perry | |
| **Winning streak** | 13—Johan Santana, 2004 | | |
| **Winning streak, two seasons** | 17—Johan Santana, 2004 (13), 2005 (4) | | |
| **20-win seasons** | | 2—Camilo Pascual, Jim Perry | |
| **Losses** | 20—Pedro Ramos, 1961 | 152—Jim Kaat | |
| **Losing streak** | 13—Terry Felton, 1982 | | |
| **Saves** | 45—Eddie Guardado, 2002 | 254—Rick Aguilera | 58 (1970) |
| **Innings** | 325—Bert Blyleven, 1973 | 2,959.1—Jim Kaat | 1,497.2 (1969) |
| **Hits** | 296—Bert Blyleven, 1973 | 2,927—Jim Kaat | 1,634 (2000) |
| **Runs** | 141—Frank Viola, 1983 | 1,295—Jim Kaat | 900 (1996) |
| **Earned runs** | 129—LaTroy Hawkins, 1999 | 1,080—Jim Kaat | 844 (1996) |
| **Bases on balls** | 127—Jim Hughes, 1975 | 694—Jim Kaat | 643 (1982) |
| **Strikeouts** | 265—Johan Santana, 2004 | 2,035—Bert Blyleven | 1,123 (2004) |
| **Strikeouts, game** | 15—Camilo Pascual, July 19, 1961, 1st game | | |
| | Joe Decker, June 26, 1973 | | |
| | Jerry Koosman, June 23, 1980 | | |
| | Bert Blyleven, Aug 1, 1986 | | |
| **Hit batsmen** | 18—Jim Katt, 1962 | 89—Jim Kaat | 56 (2001) |
| **Wild pitches** | 15—Dave Goltz, 1976 | 104—Jim Kaat | 73 (1964) |
| | Mike Smithson, 1986 | | |
| | Jack Morris, 1991 | | |
| | Johan Santana, 2002 | | |
| **Home runs** | 50—Bert Blyleven, 1986 | 302—Brad Radke | 233 (1996) |
| **Sacrifice hits** | 17—Dean Chance, 1968 | 104—Jim Kaat | 76 (1964, 1978) |
| | Jerry Koosman, 1980 | | |
| **Sacrifice flies** | 13—Bert Blyleven, 1973 | 79—Jim Kaat | 68 (1998) |
| | Scott Erickson, 1993 | | |
| **Earned run average** | 2.45—Allan Anderson, 202.1 inn, 1988 | 3.15—Jim Perry | 2.84 (1972) |
| **Shutouts** | 9—Bert Blyleven, 1973 | 29—Bert Blyleven | 18 (1967, 1973) |
| | | | Lost—14 (1964, 1972, 1990) |
| **1-0 games won** | 3—Bert Blyleven, 1971 | 8—Bert Blyleven | 5 (1966) |
| | | | Lost—5 (1974) |

## TEAM FIELDING

**Putouts** 4,493 (1969)
Fewest—4,198 (1972)

**Chances accepted** 6,349 (1969)
Fewest—5,756 (2002)

**Double plays** 203 (1979)
Fewest—114 (2003)

**Errorless games** 103 (2002)
Consecutive—12 (2002)

**Assists** 2,007 (1979)
Fewest—1,422 (2002)

**Errors** 174 (1961)
Fewest—74 (2002)

**Passed balls** 21 (1987, 1993)
Fewest—4 (1984, 2001)

**Fielding average** .987 (2002)
Lowest—.972 (1961)

## MISCELLANEOUS

**Most players, season** 46 (1995)
**Fewest players, season** 31 (1970)
**Games won** 102 (1965)
**Month** 23 (July 1969)
**Consecutive** 15 (1991)
**Winning percentage** .630 (1965), 102-60
**Lowest** .370 (1982), 60-102
**Number of league championships** 3
**Most recent** 1991
**Runs, game** 24 vs Detroit, Apr 24, 1996
**Opponents'** 23 by Kansas City, Apr 6, 1974

**Hits, game** 25 vs Cleveland, June 4, 2002
**Home runs, game** 8 vs Washington, Aug 29, 1963, 1st game
**Runs, shutout** 16 vs Boston, May 25, 1990
**Opponents'** 17 by California, Apr 23, 1980
**Longest 1-0 win** 13 inn, vs Texas, Sept 22, 1992

**Most seasons, non-pitcher** 15—Tony Oliva
**Most seasons, pitcher** 13—Jim Kaat
**Games lost** 102 (1982)
**Month** 26 (May 1982)
**Consecutive** 14 (1982)
**Overall record** 3,482-3,505 (44 seasons)
**Interleague play** 71-67
**Number of times worst record in league** 4 (inc. 1 tie)
**Most recent** 2000
**Runs, inning** 11 vs Cleveland, July 18, 1962, 1st
vs Oakland, June 21, 1969, 10th
vs Cleveland, Aug 5, 1977, 4th
vs Boston, May 20, 1994, 5th
**Total bases, game** 47 vs Washington, Aug 29, 1963, 1st game
**Consecutive games with one or more home runs** 16 (28 HRs), 1979
**Longest shutout** 13 inn, 1-0 vs Texas, Sept 22, 1992

**Longest 1-0 loss** 15 inn, vs Kansas City, May 23, 1981

## ATTENDANCE

**Highest home attendance**
**Metropolitan Stadium** 1,483,547 (1967)
**Metrodome** 3,030,672 (1988)

**Highest road attendance** 2,332,786 (1988)

**Largest crowds**
**Day** 53,106 vs Kansas City, Sept 27, 1987
**Night** 53,067 vs Toronto, Apr 8, 1988
**Doubleheader** 51,017 vs Oakland, July 28, 1990
**Home opener** 53,067 vs Toronto, Apr 8, 1988

# NEW YORK YANKEES

## YEARLY FINISHES

**(Original American League franchise moved from Baltimore to New York after the 1902 season)**

| Year | Position | W | L | Pct. | GB | Manager | Attendance |
|---|---|---|---|---|---|---|---|
| 1903 | 4th | 72 | 62 | .537 | 17.0 | Clark Griffith | 211,808 |
| 1904 | 2nd | 92 | 59 | .609 | 1.5 | Clark Griffith | 438,919 |
| 1905 | 6th | 71 | 78 | .477 | 21.5 | Clark Griffith | 309,100 |
| 1906 | 2nd | 90 | 61 | .596 | 3.0 | Clark Griffith | 434,709 |
| 1907 | 5th | 70 | 78 | .473 | 21.0 | Clark Griffith | 350,020 |
| 1908 | 8th | 51 | 103 | .331 | 39.5 | Clark Griffith, Kid Elberfeld | 305,500 |
| 1909 | 5th | 74 | 77 | .490 | 23.5 | George Stallings | 501,000 |
| 1910 | 2nd | 88 | 63 | .583 | 14.5 | George Stallings, Hal Chase | 355,857 |
| 1911 | 6th | 76 | 76 | .500 | 25.5 | Hal Chase | 302,444 |
| 1912 | 8th | 50 | 102 | .329 | 55.0 | Harry Wolverton | 242,194 |
| 1913 | 7th | 57 | 94 | .377 | 38.0 | Frank Chance | 357,551 |
| 1914 | 6th (tied) | 70 | 84 | .455 | 30.0 | Frank Chance, Roger Peckinpaugh | 359,477 |
| 1915 | 5th | 69 | 83 | .454 | 32.5 | Bill Donovan | 256,035 |
| 1916 | 4th | 80 | 74 | .519 | 11.0 | Bill Donovan | 469,211 |
| 1917 | 6th | 71 | 82 | .464 | 28.5 | Bill Donovan | 330,294 |
| 1918 | 4th | 60 | 63 | .488 | 13.5 | Miller Huggins | 282,047 |
| 1919 | 3rd | 80 | 59 | .576 | 7.5 | Miller Huggins | 619,164 |
| 1920 | 3rd | 95 | 59 | .617 | 3.0 | Miller Huggins | 1,289,422 |
| 1921 | 1st (s) | 98 | 55 | .641 | +4.5 | Miller Huggins | 1,230,696 |
| 1922 | 1st (s) | 94 | 60 | .610 | +1.0 | Miller Huggins | 1,026,134 |
| 1923 | 1st (S) | 98 | 54 | .645 | +16.0 | Miller Huggins | 1,007,066 |
| 1924 | 2nd | 89 | 63 | .586 | 2.0 | Miller Huggins | 1,053,533 |
| 1925 | 7th | 69 | 85 | .448 | 30.0 | Miller Huggins | 697,267 |
| 1926 | 1st (s) | 91 | 63 | .591 | +3.0 | Miller Huggins | 1,027,095 |
| 1927 | 1st (S) | 110 | 44 | .714 | +19.0 | Miller Huggins | 1,164,015 |
| 1928 | 1st (S) | 101 | 53 | .656 | +2.5 | Miller Huggins | 1,072,132 |
| 1929 | 2nd | 88 | 66 | .571 | 18.0 | Miller Huggins, Art Fletcher | 960,148 |
| 1930 | 3rd | 86 | 68 | .558 | 16.0 | Bob Shawkey | 1,169,230 |
| 1931 | 2nd | 94 | 59 | .614 | 13.5 | Joe McCarthy | 912,437 |
| 1932 | 1st (S) | 107 | 47 | .695 | +13.0 | Joe McCarthy | 962,320 |
| 1933 | 2nd | 91 | 59 | .607 | 7.0 | Joe McCarthy | 728,014 |
| 1934 | 2nd | 94 | 60 | .610 | 7.0 | Joe McCarthy | 854,682 |

| Year | Position | W | L | Pct. | GB | Manager | Attendance |
|---|---|---|---|---|---|---|---|
| 1935 | 2nd | 89 | 60 | .597 | 3.0 | Joe McCarthy | 657,508 |
| 1936 | 1st (S) | 102 | 51 | .667 | +19.5 | Joe McCarthy | 976,913 |
| 1937 | 1st (S) | 102 | 52 | .662 | +13.0 | Joe McCarthy | 998,148 |
| 1938 | 1st (S) | 99 | 53 | .651 | +9.5 | Joe McCarthy | 970,916 |
| 1939 | 1st (S) | 106 | 45 | .702 | +17.0 | Joe McCarthy | 859,785 |
| 1940 | 3rd | 88 | 66 | .571 | 2.0 | Joe McCarthy | 988,975 |
| 1941 | 1st (S) | 101 | 53 | .656 | +17.0 | Joe McCarthy | 964,722 |
| 1942 | 1st (s) | 103 | 51 | .669 | +9.0 | Joe McCarthy | 988,251 |
| 1943 | 1st (S) | 98 | 56 | .636 | +13.5 | Joe McCarthy | 645,006 |
| 1944 | 3rd | 83 | 71 | .539 | 6.0 | Joe McCarthy | 822,864 |
| 1945 | 4th | 81 | 71 | .533 | 6.5 | Joe McCarthy | 881,846 |
| 1946 | 3rd | 87 | 67 | .565 | 17.0 | Joe McCarthy, Bill Dickey, Johnny Neun | 2,265,512 |
| 1947 | 1st (S) | 97 | 57 | .630 | +12.0 | Bucky Harris | 2,178,937 |
| 1948 | 3rd | 94 | 60 | .610 | 2.5 | Bucky Harris | 2,373,901 |
| 1949 | 1st (S) | 97 | 57 | .630 | +1.0 | Casey Stengel | 2,281,676 |
| 1950 | 1st (S) | 98 | 56 | .636 | +3.0 | Casey Stengel | 2,081,380 |
| 1951 | 1st (S) | 98 | 56 | .636 | +5.0 | Casey Stengel | 1,950,107 |
| 1952 | 1st (S) | 95 | 59 | .617 | +2.0 | Casey Stengel | 1,629,665 |
| 1953 | 1st (S) | 99 | 52 | .656 | +8.5 | Casey Stengel | 1,537,811 |
| 1954 | 2nd | 103 | 51 | .669 | 8.0 | Casey Stengel | 1,475,171 |
| 1955 | 1st (s) | 96 | 58 | .623 | +3.0 | Casey Stengel | 1,490,138 |
| 1956 | 1st (S) | 97 | 57 | .630 | +9.0 | Casey Stengel | 1,491,784 |
| 1957 | 1st (s) | 98 | 56 | .636 | +8.0 | Casey Stengel | 1,497,134 |
| 1958 | 1st (S) | 92 | 62 | .597 | +10.0 | Casey Stengel | 1,428,438 |
| 1959 | 3rd | 79 | 75 | .513 | 15.0 | Casey Stengel | 1,552,030 |
| 1960 | 1st (s) | 97 | 57 | .630 | +8.0 | Casey Stengel | 1,627,349 |
| 1961 | 1st (S) | 109 | 53 | .673 | +8.0 | Ralph Houk | 1,747,725 |
| 1962 | 1st (S) | 96 | 66 | .593 | +5.0 | Ralph Houk | 1,493,574 |
| 1963 | 1st (s) | 104 | 57 | .646 | +10.5 | Ralph Houk | 1,308,920 |
| 1964 | 1st (s) | 99 | 63 | .611 | +1.0 | Yogi Berra | 1,305,638 |
| 1965 | 6th | 77 | 85 | .475 | 25.0 | Johnny Keane | 1,213,552 |
| 1966 | 10th | 70 | 89 | .440 | 26.5 | Johnny Keane, Ralph Houk | 1,124,648 |
| 1967 | 9th | 72 | 90 | .444 | 20.0 | Ralph Houk | 1,259,514 |
| 1968 | 5th | 83 | 79 | .512 | 20.0 | Ralph Houk | 1,185,666 |

## EAST DIVISION

| Year | Position | W | L | Pct. | GB | Manager | Attendance |
|---|---|---|---|---|---|---|---|
| 1969 | 5th | 80 | 81 | .497 | 28.5 | Ralph Houk | 1,067,996 |
| 1970 | 2nd | 93 | 69 | .574 | 15.0 | Ralph Houk | 1,136,879 |
| 1971 | 4th | 82 | 80 | .506 | 21.0 | Ralph Houk | 1,070,771 |
| 1972 | 4th | 79 | 76 | .510 | 6.5 | Ralph Houk | 966,328 |
| 1973 | 4th | 80 | 82 | .494 | 17.0 | Ralph Houk | 1,262,103 |
| 1974 | 2nd | 89 | 73 | .549 | 2.0 | Bill Virdon | 1,273,075 |
| 1975 | 3rd | 83 | 77 | .519 | 12.0 | Bill Virdon, Billy Martin | 1,288,048 |
| 1976 | 1st (C,s) | 97 | 62 | .610 | +10.5 | Billy Martin | 2,012,434 |
| 1977 | 1st (C,S) | 100 | 62 | .617 | +2.5 | Billy Martin | 2,103,092 |
| 1978 | 1st (P,C,S) | 100 | 63 | .613 | +1.0 | Billy Martin, Bob Lemon | 2,335,871 |
| 1979 | 4th | 89 | 71 | .556 | 13.5 | Bob Lemon, Billy Martin | 2,537,765 |
| 1980 | 1st (c) | 103 | 59 | .636 | +3.0 | Dick Howser | 2,627,417 |
| 1981 | 1st/6th (I,C,s) | 59 | 48 | .551 | * | Gene Michael, Bob Lemon | 1,614,533 |
| 1982 | 5th | 79 | 83 | .488 | 16.0 | Bob Lemon, Gene Michael, Clyde King | 2,041,219 |
| 1983 | 3rd | 91 | 71 | .562 | 7.0 | Billy Martin | 2,257,976 |
| 1984 | 3rd | 87 | 75 | .537 | 17.0 | Yogi Berra | 1,821,815 |
| 1985 | 2nd | 97 | 64 | .602 | 2.0 | Yogi Berra, Billy Martin | 2,214,587 |
| 1986 | 2nd | 90 | 72 | .556 | 5.5 | Lou Piniella | 2,268,030 |
| 1987 | 4th | 89 | 73 | .549 | 9.0 | Lou Piniella | 2,427,672 |
| 1988 | 5th | 85 | 76 | .528 | 3.5 | Billy Martin, Lou Piniella | 2,633,701 |
| 1989 | 5th | 74 | 87 | .460 | 14.5 | Dallas Green, Bucky Dent | 2,170,485 |
| 1990 | 7th | 67 | 95 | .414 | 21.0 | Bucky Dent, Stump Merrill | 2,006,436 |
| 1991 | 5th | 71 | 91 | .438 | 20.0 | Stump Merrill | 1,863,733 |
| 1992 | 4th (tied) | 76 | 86 | .469 | 20.0 | Buck Showalter | 1,748,733 |
| 1993 | 2nd | 88 | 74 | .543 | 7.0 | Buck Showalter | 2,416,965 |
| 1994 | 1st (n) | 70 | 43 | .619 | +6.5 | Buck Showalter | 1,675,556 |
| 1995 | 2nd (d) | 79 | 65 | .549 | 7.0 | Buck Showalter | 1,705,263 |
| 1996 | 1st (D,C,S) | 92 | 70 | .568 | +4.0 | Joe Torre | 2,250,877 |
| 1997 | 2nd (d) | 96 | 66 | .593 | 2.0 | Joe Torre | 2,580,325 |
| 1998 | 1st (D,C,S) | 114 | 48 | .704 | +22.0 | Joe Torre | 2,949,734 |
| 1999 | 1st (D,C,S) | 98 | 64 | .605 | +4.0 | Joe Torre | 3,292,736 |
| 2000 | 1st (D,C,S) | 87 | 74 | .540 | +2.5 | Joe Torre | 3,227,657 |
| 2001 | 1st (D,C,s) | 95 | 65 | .594 | +13.5 | Joe Torre | 3,264,777 |
| 2002 | 1st (d) | 103 | 58 | .640 | +10.5 | Joe Torre | 3,461,644 |
| 2003 | 1st (D,C,s) | 101 | 61 | .623 | +6.0 | Joe Torre | 3,465,585 |
| 2004 | 1st (D,c) | 101 | 61 | .623 | +3.0 | Joe Torre | 3,775,292 |
| 2005 | 1st (tied) (d) | 95 | 67 | .586 | 0.0 | Joe Torre | 4,090,692 |

(s) lost World Series; (S) won World Series; (C) won League Championship Series; (P) won division playoff; (c) lost League Championship Series; (I) won intra-divisional playoff;
*first half 34-22, second half 25-26; (n) no World Series; (d) lost Division Series; (D) won Division Series

## INDIVIDUAL AND CLUB RECORDS

### BATTING

| | Individual: Season | Individual: Career | Club: Season |
|---|---|---|---|
| **Games** | 163—Hideki Matsui, 2003 | 2,401—Mickey Mantle | 164 (1964, 1968) |
| **At-bats** | 696—Alfonso Soriano, 156 G, 2002 | 8,102—Mickey Mantle | 5,710 (1997) |
| **Runs** | 177—Babe Ruth, 152 G, 1921 | 1,959—Babe Ruth | 1,067 (1931) |
| | | | Fewest—459 (1908) |
| **Hits** | 238—Don Mattingly, 162 G, 1986 | 2,721—Lou Gehrig | 1,683 (1930) |
| | | | Fewest—1,137 (1968) |
| **Hitting streak** | 56 G—Joe DiMaggio, 1941 | | |
| **Singles** | 171—Steve Sax, 158 G, 1989 | 1,531—Lou Gehrig | 1,157 (1931) |
| **Doubles** | 53—Don Mattingly, 162 G, 1986 | 534—Lou Gehrig | 325 (1997) |
| **Triples** | 23—Earle Combs, 152 G, 1927 | 163—Lou Gehrig | 110 (1930) |
| **HOME RUNS** | | | 242 (2004) |
| | | | Fewest—8 (1913) |
| **Righthander** | 48—Alex Rodriguez, 162 G, 2005 | 361—Joe DiMaggio | |
| **Lefthander** | 61—Roger Maris, 161 G, 1961 | 659—Babe Ruth | |
| **Switch-hitter** | 54—Mickey Mantle, 153 G, 1961 | 536—Mickey Mantle | |
| **Rookie** | 29—Joe DiMaggio, 138 G, 1936 | | |
| **Home** | 32—Babe Ruth, 1921 | 334—Babe Ruth | 117 (2000) |
| **Road** | 32—Babe Ruth, 1927 | 325—Babe Ruth | 128 (1961) |
| **Month** | 17—Babe Ruth, Sept 1927 | | 54 (July 1940, Aug 1998) |
| **Pinch** | 4—Johnny Blanchard, 1961 | 9—Yogi Berra | 10 (1961) |
| **Grand slams** | 6—Don Mattingly, 141 G, 1987 | 23—Lou Gehrig | 10 (1987) |
| **Home runs at Hilltop Park, all teams** | | | 48 (1904) |
| **Home runs at the Polo Grounds, all teams** | | | 117 (1921) |
| **Home runs at Yankee Stadium, all teams** | | | 209 (2000) |
| **Total bases** | 457—Babe Ruth, 152 G, 1921 | 5,131—Babe Ruth | 2,703 (1936) |
| **Extra-base hits** | 119—Babe Ruth, 152 G, 1921 | 1,190—Lou Gehrig | 580 (1936) |
| **Sacrifice hits** | 42—Willie Keeler, 149 G, 1905 | 225—Wally Pipp | 178 (1906) |
| **Sacrifice flies** | 17—Roy White, 147 G, 1971 | 96—Don Mattingly | 72 (1974, 1996) |
| **Bases on balls** | 170—Babe Ruth, 152 G, 1923 | 1,852—Babe Ruth | 766 (1932) |
| | | | Fewest—288 (1908) |
| **Strikeouts** | 157—Alfonso Soriano, 156 G, 2002 | 1,710—Mickey Mantle | 1,171 (2002) |
| | Fewest—12—Yogi Berra, 151 G, 1950 | | Fewest—420 (1924) |
| **Hit by pitch** | 24—Don Baylor, 142 G, 1985 | 114—Frankie Crosetti | 81 (2003) |
| | | | Fewest—14 (1969) |
| **Runs batted in** | 184—Lou Gehrig, 155 G, 1931 | 1,995—Lou Gehrig | 995 (1936) |
| | | | Fewest—372 (1908) |
| **Grounded into double plays** | 30—Dave Winfield, 152 G, 1983 | 209—Bernie Williams | 157 (2004) |
| | Fewest—2—Mickey Mantle, 153 G, 1961 | | Fewest—91 (1963) |
| **Left on base** | | | 1,276 (1997) |
| | | | Fewest—1,010 (1920) |
| **Batting average** | .393—Babe Ruth, 152 G, 1923 | .349—Babe Ruth | .309 (1930) |
| | | | Lowest—.214 (1968) |
| **Most .300 hitters** | | | 9 (1930) |
| **Slugging average** | .847—Babe Ruth, 142 G, 1920 | .711—Babe Ruth | .489 (1927) |
| | | | Lowest—.287 (1914) |
| **On-base percentage** | .545—Babe Ruth, 152 G, 1923 | .484—Babe Ruth | .384 (1930) |
| | | | Lowest—.283 (1908) |

### BASERUNNING

| | Individual: Season | Individual: Career | Club: Season |
|---|---|---|---|
| **Stolen bases** | 93—Rickey Henderson, 140 G, 1988 | 326—Rickey Henderson | 289 (1910) |
| **Caught stealing** | 23—Ben Chapman, 149 G, 1931 | 117—Babe Ruth | 82 (1920) |

### PITCHING

| | Individual: Season | Individual: Career | Club: Season |
|---|---|---|---|
| **Games** | 86—Paul Quantrill, 2004 | 657—Mariano Rivera | |
| **Games started** | 51—Jack Chesbro, 1904 | 438—Whitey Ford | |
| **Complete games** | 48—Jack Chesbro, 1904 | 261—Red Ruffing | 123 (1904) |
| **Wins** | 41—Jack Chesbro, 1904 | 236—Whitey Ford | |
| **Percentage** | .893—Ron Guidry (25-3), 1978 | .717—Spud Chandler | |
| **Winning streak** | 16—Roger Clemens, 2001 | | |
| **20-win seasons** | | 4—Bob Shawkey<br>Lefty Gomez<br>Red Ruffing | |

| | Individual Season | Career | Club Season |
|---|---|---|---|
| **Losses** | 21—Al Orth, 1907<br>Sam Jones, 1925<br>Joe Lake, 1908<br>Russ Ford, 1912 | 139—Mel Stottlemyre Sr. | |
| **Losing streak** | 11—George Mogridge, 1916 | | |
| **Saves** | 50—Mariano Rivera, 2001 | 379—Mariano Rivera | 59 (2004) |
| **Innings** | 454—Jack Chesbro, 1904 | 3,170.1—Whitey Ford | 1,506.2 (1964) |
| **Hits** | 340—Jack Powell, 1904 | 2,995—Red Ruffing | 1,566 (1930) |
| **Runs** | 165—Russ Ford, 1912 | 1,406—Red Ruffing | 898 (1930) |
| **Earned runs** | 127—Sam Jones, 1925 | 1,222—Red Ruffing | 753 (2000) |
| **Bases on balls** | 179—Tommy Byrne, 1949 | 1,090—Lefty Gomez | 812 (1949) |
| **Strikeouts** | 248—Ron Guidry, 1978 | 1,956—Whitey Ford | 1,266 (2001) |
| **Strikeouts, game** | 18—Ron Guidry, June 17, 1978 | | |
| **Hit batsmen** | 26—Jack Warhop, 1909 | 114—Jack Warhop | 84 (2005) |
| **Wild pitches** | 23—Tim Leary, 1990 | 75—Whitey Ford | 83 (1990) |
| **Home runs** | 40—Ralph Terry, 1962 | 228—Whitey Ford | 179 (1987) |
| **Sacrifice hits** | 23—Ed Lopat, 1948 | 239—Waite Hoyt | 202 (1926) |
| **Sacrifice flies** | 15—Doc Medich, 1975 | 65—Ron Guidry | 59 (1982, 1983) |
| **Earned run average** | 1.64—Spud Chandler, 253 inn, 1943 | 2.58—Jack Chesbro | 2.57 (1904) |
| **Shutouts** | 9—Ron Guidry, 1978 | 45—Whitey Ford | 24 (1951)<br>Lost—27 (1914) |
| **1-0 games won** | 2—many pitchers | 7—Whitey Ford<br>Bob Shawkey | 6 (1908, 1968)<br>Lost—9 (1914) |

## TEAM FIELDING

**Putouts** 4,520 (1964)
Fewest—3,993 (1935)

**Chances accepted** 6,377 (1968)
Fewest—5,551 (1935)

**Double plays** 214 (1956)
Fewest—81 (1912)

**Errorless games** 94 (1996)
Consecutive—10 (1977, 1993, 1995)

**Assists** 2,086 (1904)
Fewest—1,487 (2000)

**Errors** 386 (1912)
Fewest—91 (1996)

**Passed balls** 32 (1913)
Fewest—0 (1931)

**Fielding average** .986 (1995)
Lowest—.939 (1912)

## MISCELLANEOUS

**Most players, season** 51 (2005)
**Fewest players, season** 25 (1923, 1927)
**Games won** 114 (1998)
**Month** 28 (Aug 1938)
**Consecutive** 19 (1947)
**Winning percentage** .714 (1927), 110-44
**Lowest** .329 (1912), 50-102
**Number of league championships** 39
**Most recent** 2003
**Runs, game** 25 vs Philadelphia, May 24, 1936
**Opponents'** 24 by Cleveland, July 29, 1928
**Hits, game** 30 vs Boston, Sept 28, 1923
**Home runs, game** 8 vs Philadelphia, June 28, 1939, 1st game
**Runs, shutout** 21 vs Philadelphia, Aug 13, 1939, 2nd game, 8 inn
**Opponents'** 22 by Cleveland, Aug 31, 2004
**Longest 1-0 win** 15 inn, vs Philadelphia, July 4, 1925, 1st game

**Most seasons, non-pitcher** 18—Yogi Berra
Mickey Mantle
**Most seasons, pitcher** 16—Whitey Ford
**Games lost** 103 (1908)
**Month** 24 (July 1908)
**Consecutive** 13 (1913)
**Overall record** 9,074-6,876 (103 seasons)
**Interleague play** 93-63
**Number of times worst record in league** 5
**Most recent** 1990
**Runs, inning** 14 vs Washington, July 6, 1920, 5th
**Total bases, game** 53 vs Philadelphia, June 28, 1939, 1st game
**Consecutive games with one or more home runs** 25 (40 HRs), 1941
**Longest shutout** unknown
**Longest 1-0 loss** 14 inn, vs Boston, Sept 24, 1969

## ATTENDANCE

**Highest home attendance**

| | |
|---|---|
| **Hilltop Park** | 501,000 (1909) |
| **Polo Grounds** | 1,289,422 (1920) |
| **Yankee Stadium** | 3,775,292 (2004) |
| **Highest road attendance** | 3,308,666 (2004) |

**Largest crowds**

| | |
|---|---|
| **Day** | 73,205 vs Philadelphia, Apr 19, 1931 |
| **Night** | 74,747 vs Boston, May 26, 1947 |
| **Doubleheader** | 81,841 vs Boston, May 30, 1938 |
| **Home opener** | 55,814 vs Kansas City, Apr 2, 2001 |

# OAKLAND ATHLETICS

## YEARLY FINISHES

**(Original American League franchise moved from Philadelphia to Kansas City after the 1954 season and to Oakland after the 1967 season)**

| Year | Position | W | L | Pct. | GB | Manager | Attendance |
|---|---|---|---|---|---|---|---|
| 1968 | 6th | 82 | 80 | .506 | 21.0 | Bob Kennedy | 837,466 |

## WEST DIVISION

| Year | Position | W | L | Pct. | GB | Manager | Attendance |
|---|---|---|---|---|---|---|---|
| 1969 | 2nd | 88 | 74 | .543 | 9.0 | Hank Bauer, John McNamara | 778,232 |
| 1970 | 2nd | 89 | 73 | .549 | 9.0 | John McNamara | 778,355 |
| 1971 | 1st (c) | 101 | 60 | .627 | +16.0 | Dick Williams | 914,993 |
| 1972 | 1st (C,S) | 93 | 62 | .600 | +5.5 | Dick Williams | 921,323 |

| Year | Position | W | L | Pct. | GB | Manager | Attendance |
|---|---|---|---|---|---|---|---|
| 1973 | 1st (C,S) | 94 | 68 | .580 | +6.0 | Dick Williams | 1,000,763 |
| 1974 | 1st (C,S) | 90 | 72 | .556 | +5.0 | Alvin Dark | 845,693 |
| 1975 | 1st (c) | 98 | 64 | .605 | +7.0 | Alvin Dark | 1,075,518 |
| 1976 | 2nd | 87 | 74 | .540 | 2.5 | Chuck Tanner | 780,593 |
| 1977 | 7th | 63 | 98 | .391 | 38.5 | Jack McKeon, Bobby Winkles | 495,599 |
| 1978 | 6th | 69 | 93 | .426 | 23.0 | Bobby Winkles, Jack McKeon | 526,999 |
| 1979 | 7th | 54 | 108 | .333 | 34.0 | Jim Marshall | 306,763 |
| 1980 | 2nd | 83 | 79 | .512 | 14.0 | Billy Martin | 842,259 |
| 1981 | 1st/2nd (I,c) | 64 | 45 | .587 | * | Billy Martin | 1,304,054 |
| 1982 | 5th | 68 | 94 | .420 | 25.0 | Billy Martin | 1,735,489 |
| 1983 | 4th | 74 | 88 | .457 | 25.0 | Steve Boros | 1,294,941 |
| 1984 | 4th | 77 | 85 | .475 | 7.0 | Steve Boros, Jackie Moore | 1,353,281 |
| 1985 | 4th (tied) | 77 | 85 | .475 | 14.0 | Jackie Moore | 1,334,599 |
| 1986 | 3rd (tied) | 76 | 86 | .469 | 16.0 | Jackie Moore, Tony La Russa | 1,314,646 |
| 1987 | 3rd | 81 | 81 | .500 | 4.0 | Tony La Russa | 1,678,921 |
| 1988 | 1st (C,s) | 104 | 58 | .642 | +13.0 | Tony La Russa | 2,287,335 |
| 1989 | 1st (C,S) | 99 | 63 | .611 | +7.0 | Tony La Russa | 2,667,225 |
| 1990 | 1st (C,s) | 103 | 59 | .636 | +9.0 | Tony La Russa | 2,900,217 |
| 1991 | 4th | 84 | 78 | .519 | 11.0 | Tony La Russa | 2,713,493 |
| 1992 | 1st (c) | 96 | 66 | .593 | +6.0 | Tony La Russa | 2,494,160 |
| 1993 | 7th | 68 | 94 | .420 | 26.0 | Tony La Russa | 2,035,025 |
| 1994 | 2nd | 51 | 63 | .447 | 1.0 | Tony La Russa | 1,242,692 |
| 1995 | 4th | 67 | 77 | .465 | 11.5 | Tony La Russa | 1,174,310 |
| 1996 | 3rd | 78 | 84 | .481 | 12.0 | Art Howe | 1,148,380 |
| 1997 | 4th | 65 | 97 | .401 | 25.0 | Art Howe | 1,264,218 |
| 1998 | 4th | 74 | 88 | .457 | 14.0 | Art Howe | 1,232,339 |
| 1999 | 2nd | 87 | 75 | .537 | 8.0 | Art Howe | 1,434,610 |
| 2000 | 1st (d) | 91 | 70 | .565 | +0.5 | Art Howe | 1,728,888 |
| 2001 | 2nd (d) | 102 | 60 | .630 | 14.0 | Art Howe | 2,133,277 |
| 2002 | 1st (d) | 103 | 59 | .636 | +4.0 | Art Howe | 2,169,811 |
| 2003 | 1st (d) | 96 | 66 | .593 | +3.0 | Ken Macha | 2,216,596 |
| 2004 | 2nd | 91 | 71 | .562 | 1.0 | Ken Macha | 2,201,516 |
| 2005 | 2nd | 88 | 74 | .543 | 7.0 | Ken Macha | 2,109,118 |

(c) lost League Championship Series; (C) won League Championship Series; (S) won World Series; (I) won intra-divisional playoff; *first half 37-23, second 27-22;
(d) lost Division Series

## INDIVIDUAL AND CLUB RECORDS

### BATTING

| | Individual | | Club |
|---|---|---|---|
| | Season | Career | Season |
| Games | 162—Sal Bando, 1968, 1969, 1973<br>Alfredo Griffin, 1985, 1986<br>Terrence Long, 2001, 2002<br>Miguel Tejada, 2001, 2002, 2003 | 1,704—Rickey Henderson | 163 (1968) |
| At-bats | 662—Miguel Tejada, 162 G, 2002 | 6,140—Rickey Henderson | 5,728 (2004) |
| Runs | 123—Reggie Jackson, 152 G, 1969 | 1,270—Rickey Henderson<br>Fewest—532 (1978) | 947 (2000) |
| Hits | 204—Miguel Tejada, 162 G, 2002 | 1,768—Rickey Henderson | 1,545 (2004)<br>Fewest—1,276 (1979) |
| Hitting streak | 25 G—Jason Giambi, 1997 | | |
| Singles | 153—Carney Lansford, 148 G, 1989 | 1,271—Rickey Henderson | 1,061 (1983) |
| Doubles | 47—Jason Giambi, 154 G, 2001 | 289—Rickey Henderson | 336 (2004) |
| Triples | 12—Phil Garner, 159 G, 1976 | 41—Rickey Henderson | 40 (1968) |
| **HOME RUNS** | | | 243 (1996)<br>Fewest—94 (1968) |
| Righthander | 52—Mark McGwire, 130 G, 1996 | 363—Mark McGwire | |
| Lefthander | 47—Reggie Jackson, 152 G, 1969 | 268—Reggie Jackson | |
| Switch-hitter | 23—Ruben Sierra, 110 G, 1994 | 60—Ruben Sierra | |
| Rookie | 49—Mark McGwire, 151 G, 1987 | | |
| Home | 27—Jason Giambi, 2001 | 166—Mark McGwire | 126 (2000) |
| Road | 28—Mark McGwire, 1987, 1996<br>Jose Canseco, 1991 | 197—Mark McGwire | 130 (1996) |
| Month | 15—Mark McGwire, May 1987 | | 55 (June 1996, Aug 1999) |
| Pinch | 4—Jeff Burroughs, 1982 | 5—Mike Aldrete<br>Jeff Burroughs<br>Mark McGwire<br>Terry Steinbach | 8 (1970) |
| Grand slams | 4—Jason Giambi, 152 G, 2000 | 9—Mark McGwire | 14 (2000) |
| Home runs at Network Associates Coliseum, all teams | | | 215 (1996)<br>(inc. 23 at Las Vegas) |
| Total bases | 347—Jose Canseco, 158 G, 1988 | 2,640—Reggie Jackson | 2,546 (1996) |
| Extra-base hits | 87—Jason Giambi, 154 G, 2001 | 563—Mark McGwire | 555 (2001) |
| Sacrifice hits | 22—Dwayne Murphy, 159 G, 1980 | 101—Bert Campaneris | 108 (1978) |
| Sacrifice flies | 14—Dave Kingman, 147 G, 1984 | 59—Mark McGwire | 77 (1984) |
| Bases on balls | 137—Jason Giambi, 152 G, 2000 | 1,227—Rickey Henderson | 770 (1999)<br>Fewest—433 (1978) |
| Strikeouts | 175—Jose Canseco, 157 G, 1986<br>Fewest—31—Felipe Alou, 154 G, 1970 | 1,180—Reggie Jackson | 1,181 (1997)<br>Fewest—751 (1979) |
| Hit by pitch | 20—Don Baylor, 157 G, 1976<br>Jason Kendall, 150 G, 2005 | 59—Sal Bando | 88 (2001)<br>Fewest—16 (1985) |

| | Individual Season | Career | Club Season |
|---|---|---|---|
| **Runs batted in** | 137—Jason Giambi, 152 G, 2000 | 941—Mark McGwire | 908 (2000)<br>Fewest—492 (1978) |
| **Grounded into double plays** | 32—Ben Grieve, 158 G, 2000<br>Fewest—3—Reggie Jackson, 154 G, 1968 | 137—Terry Steinbach | 163 (1989)<br>Fewest—87 (1968) |
| **Left on base** | | | 1,274 (2004)<br>Fewest—1,030 (1979) |
| **Batting average** | .342—Jason Giambi, 154 G, 2001 | .308—Jason Giambi | 270 (2000, 2004)<br>Lowest—.236 (1982) |
| **Most .300 hitters** | | | 2 (1988) |
| **Slugging average** | .730—Mark McGwire, 130 G, 1996 | .551—Mark McGwire | .458 (2000)<br>Lowest—.343 (1968) |
| **On-base percentage** | .477—Jason Giambi, 154 G, 2001 | .409—Rickey Henderson | .360 (2000)<br>Lowest—.302 (1979) |

## BASERUNNING

| | Individual Season | Career | Club Season |
|---|---|---|---|
| **Stolen bases** | 130—Rickey Henderson, 149 G, 1982 | 867—Rickey Henderson | 341 (1976) |
| **Caught stealing** | 42—Rickey Henderson, 149 G, 1982 | 219—Rickey Henderson | 123 (1976) |

## PITCHING

| | Individual Season | Career | Club Season |
|---|---|---|---|
| **Games** | 84—Billy Koch, 2002 | 525—Dennis Eckersley | |
| **Games started** | 41—Catfish Hunter, 1974 | 262—Vida Blue | |
| **Complete games** | 28—Rick Langford, 1980 | 105—Vida Blue | 94 (1980) |
| **Wins** | 27—Bob Welch, 1990 | 131—Catfish Hunter | |
| **Percentage** | .821—Barry Zito (23-5), 2002 | .630—Catfish Hunter | |
| **Winning streak** | 13—Catfish Hunter, 1973 | | |
| **20-win seasons** | | 4—Catfish Hunter<br>Dave Stewart | |
| **Losses** | 20—Brian Kingman, 1980 | 105—Rick Langford | |
| **Losing streak** | 14—Matt Keough, 1979 | | |
| **Saves** | 51—Dennis Eckersley, 1992 | 320—Dennis Eckersley | 64 (1988, 1990) |
| **Innings** | 318—Catfish Hunter, 1974 | 1,946—Vida Blue | 1,489.1 (1988) |
| **Hits** | 284—Vida Blue, 1977 | 1,650—Vida Blue | 1,734 (1997) |
| **Runs** | 144—Matt Keough, 1982 | 784—Dave Stewart | 943 (1996) |
| **Earned runs** | 133—Matt Keough, 1982 | 712—Dave Stewart | 880 (1997) |
| **Bases on balls** | 112—John Odom, 1969 | 655—Dave Stewart | 680 (1993) |
| **Strikeouts** | 301—Vida Blue, 1971 | 1,315—Vida Blue | 1,117 (2001) |
| **Strikeouts, game** | 17—Vida Blue, July 9, 1971 (pitched first 11 inn of 20-inn game)<br>16—Jose Rijo, Apr 19, 1986 (pitched first 8 inn of 9-inn game) | | |
| **Hit batsmen** | 13—Barry Zito, 2001, 2005 | 52—Barry Zito | 64 (1997) |
| **Wild pitches** | 22—Mike Moore, 1992 | 78—Dave Stewart | 72 (1979) |
| **Home runs** | 39—Catfish Hunter, 1973 | 207—Catfish Hunter | 205 (1996) |
| **Sacrifice hits** | 17—Bob Lacey, 1977 | 77—Vida Blue | 92 (1978) |
| **Sacrifice flies** | 15—Dave Stewart, 1991 | 64—Dave Stewart | 80 (1997) |
| **Earned run average** | 1.82—Vida Blue, 312 inn, 1971 | 2.94—Vida Blue | 2.58 (1972) |
| **Shutouts** | 8—Vida Blue, 1971 | 28—Vida Blue | 23 (1972)<br>Lost—19 (1978) |
| **1-0 games won** | 2—Vida Blue, 1971<br>Catfish Hunter, 1971<br>Mike Torrez, 1976 | 3—Vida Blue | 5 (1971, 1978)<br>Lost—5 (1971, 1978) |

## TEAM FIELDING

**Putouts** 4,468 (1988)
Fewest—4,288 (1979)
**Chances accepted** 6,230 (1969)
Fewest—5,798 (1984)
**Double plays** 195 (1997)
Fewest—115 (1980)
**Errorless games** 97 (2004)
Consecutive—12 (2002)

**Assists** 1,821 (1976)
Fewest—1,508 (1984)
**Errors** 190 (1977)
Fewest—87 (1990)
**Passed balls** 26 (1969)
Fewest—4 (2001)
**Fielding average** .986 (1990, 2004, 2005)
Lowest—.970 (1977)

## MISCELLANEOUS

**Most players, season** 49 (1997)
**Fewest players, season** 34 (1968, 1980)

**Games won** 104 (1988)
**Month** 24 (Aug 2002)
**Consecutive** 20 (2002)
**Winning percentage** .642 (1988), 104-58
**Lowest** .333 (1979), 54-108
**Number of league championships** 6
**Most recent** 1990
**Runs, game** 23 vs Texas, Sept 30, 2000
**Opponents'** 20 by Minnesota, Apr 27, 1980
by Cleveland, May 4, 1991
by Detroit, Apr 13, 1993

**Most seasons, non-pitcher** 14—Rickey Henderson
**Most seasons, pitcher** 10—Rick Langford
Mike Norris
Curt Young

**Games lost** 108 (1979)
**Month** 24 (June 1979)
**Consecutive** 14 (1977)
**Overall record** 3,155-2,871 (38 seasons)
**Interleague play** 95-63
**Number of times worst record in league** 2
**Most recent** 1997
**Runs, inning** 13 vs California, July 5, 1996, 1st
vs Chicago, May 12, 1997, 7th

**Hits, game** 25 vs Boston, June 14, 1969
[29 vs Texas, July 1, 1979, 15 inn]
**Home runs, game** 8 vs California, June 27, 1996
**Runs, shutout** 16 vs San Francisco, June 26, 2005
**Opponents'** 16 by Kansas City, June 25, 1984
**Longest 1-0 win** 20 inn, vs California, July 9, 1971

**Total bases, game** 44 vs California, June 27, 1996

**Consecutive games with one or more home runs** 23 (50 HRs), 1996
**Longest shutout** 16 inn, 3-0 vs Chicago, Sept 22, 1975

**Longest 1-0 loss** 13 inn, vs Detroit, May 25, 1973

## ATTENDANCE

**Highest home attendance** 2,900,217 (1990)

**Highest road attendance** 2,636,157 (1991)

**Largest crowds**
- **Day** 55,413 vs San Francisco NL, June 22, 2003
- **Night** 55,989 vs San Francisco NL, June 26, 2004
- **Doubleheader** 48,592 vs New York, May 3, 1981
- **Home opener** 53,498 vs Detroit, Apr 3, 2000

# PHILADELPHIA ATHLETICS

## YEARLY FINISHES

**(Original American League franchise moved to Kansas City after the 1954 season)**

| Year | Position | W | L | Pct. | GB | Manager | Attendance |
|---|---|---|---|---|---|---|---|
| 1901 | 4th | 74 | 62 | .544 | 9.0 | Connie Mack | 206,329 |
| 1902 | 1st | 83 | 53 | .610 | +5.0 | Connie Mack | 442,473 |
| 1903 | 2nd | 75 | 60 | .556 | 14.5 | Connie Mack | 420,078 |
| 1904 | 5th | 81 | 70 | .536 | 12.5 | Connie Mack | 512,294 |
| 1905 | 1st (s) | 92 | 56 | .622 | +2.0 | Connie Mack | 554,576 |
| 1906 | 4th | 78 | 67 | .538 | 12.0 | Connie Mack | 489,129 |
| 1907 | 2nd | 88 | 57 | .607 | 1.5 | Connie Mack | 625,581 |
| 1908 | 6th | 68 | 85 | .444 | 22.0 | Connie Mack | 455,062 |
| 1909 | 2nd | 95 | 58 | .621 | 3.5 | Connie Mack | 674,915 |
| 1910 | 1st (S) | 102 | 48 | .680 | +14.5 | Connie Mack | 588,905 |
| 1911 | 1st (S) | 101 | 50 | .669 | +13.5 | Connie Mack | 605,749 |
| 1912 | 3rd | 90 | 62 | .592 | 15.0 | Connie Mack | 517,653 |
| 1913 | 1st (S) | 96 | 57 | .627 | +6.5 | Connie Mack | 571,896 |
| 1914 | 1st (s) | 99 | 53 | .651 | +8.5 | Connie Mack | 346,641 |
| 1915 | 8th | 43 | 109 | .283 | 58.5 | Connie Mack | 146,223 |
| 1916 | 8th | 36 | 117 | .235 | 54.5 | Connie Mack | 184,471 |
| 1917 | 8th | 55 | 98 | .359 | 44.5 | Connie Mack | 221,432 |
| 1918 | 8th | 52 | 76 | .406 | 24.0 | Connie Mack | 177,926 |
| 1919 | 8th | 36 | 104 | .257 | 52.0 | Connie Mack | 225,209 |
| 1920 | 8th | 48 | 106 | .312 | 50.0 | Connie Mack | 287,888 |
| 1921 | 8th | 53 | 100 | .346 | 45.0 | Connie Mack | 344,430 |
| 1922 | 7th | 65 | 89 | .422 | 29.0 | Connie Mack | 425,356 |
| 1923 | 6th | 69 | 83 | .454 | 29.0 | Connie Mack | 534,122 |
| 1924 | 5th | 71 | 81 | .467 | 20.0 | Connie Mack | 531,992 |
| 1925 | 2nd | 88 | 64 | .579 | 8.5 | Connie Mack | 869,703 |
| 1926 | 3rd | 83 | 67 | .553 | 6.0 | Connie Mack | 714,308 |
| 1927 | 2nd | 91 | 63 | .591 | 19.0 | Connie Mack | 605,529 |
| 1928 | 2nd | 98 | 55 | .641 | 2.5 | Connie Mack | 689,756 |
| 1929 | 1st (S) | 104 | 46 | .693 | +18.0 | Connie Mack | 839,176 |
| 1930 | 1st (S) | 102 | 52 | .662 | +8.0 | Connie Mack | 721,663 |
| 1931 | 1st (s) | 107 | 45 | .704 | +13.5 | Connie Mack | 627,464 |
| 1932 | 2nd | 94 | 60 | .610 | 13.0 | Connie Mack | 405,500 |
| 1933 | 3rd | 79 | 72 | .523 | 19.5 | Connie Mack | 297,138 |
| 1934 | 5th | 68 | 82 | .453 | 31.0 | Connie Mack | 305,847 |
| 1935 | 8th | 58 | 91 | .389 | 34.0 | Connie Mack | 233,173 |
| 1936 | 8th | 53 | 100 | .346 | 49.0 | Connie Mack | 285,173 |
| 1937 | 7th | 54 | 97 | .358 | 46.5 | Connie Mack | 430,733 |
| 1938 | 8th | 53 | 99 | .349 | 46.0 | Connie Mack | 385,357 |
| 1939 | 7th | 55 | 97 | .362 | 51.5 | Connie Mack | 395,022 |
| 1940 | 8th | 54 | 100 | .351 | 36.0 | Connie Mack | 432,145 |
| 1941 | 8th | 64 | 90 | .416 | 37.0 | Connie Mack | 528,894 |
| 1942 | 8th | 55 | 99 | .357 | 48.0 | Connie Mack | 423,487 |
| 1943 | 8th | 49 | 105 | .318 | 49.0 | Connie Mack | 376,735 |
| 1944 | 5th (tied) | 72 | 82 | .468 | 17.0 | Connie Mack | 505,322 |
| 1945 | 8th | 52 | 98 | .347 | 34.5 | Connie Mack | 462,631 |
| 1946 | 8th | 49 | 105 | .318 | 55.0 | Connie Mack | 621,793 |
| 1947 | 5th | 78 | 76 | .506 | 19.0 | Connie Mack | 911,566 |
| 1948 | 4th | 84 | 70 | .545 | 12.5 | Connie Mack | 945,076 |
| 1949 | 5th | 81 | 73 | .526 | 16.0 | Connie Mack | 816,514 |
| 1950 | 8th | 52 | 102 | .338 | 46.0 | Connie Mack | 309,805 |
| 1951 | 6th | 70 | 84 | .455 | 28.0 | Jimmie Dykes | 465,469 |
| 1952 | 4th | 79 | 75 | .513 | 16.0 | Jimmie Dykes | 627,100 |
| 1953 | 7th | 59 | 95 | .383 | 41.5 | Jimmie Dykes | 362,113 |
| 1954 | 8th | 51 | 103 | .331 | 60.0 | Ed Joost | 304,666 |

(s) lost World Series; (S) won World Series

## INDIVIDUAL AND CLUB RECORDS

### BATTING

| | Individual Season | Career | Club Season |
|---|---|---|---|
| **Games** | 157—Dave Philley, 1953 | 1,702—Jimmie Dykes | 158 (1914) |
| **At-bats** | 670—Al Simmons, 154 G, 1932 | 6,023—Jimmie Dykes | 5,537 (1932) |
| **Runs** | 152—Al Simmons, 138 G, 1930 | 997—Bob Johnson | 981 (1932)<br>Fewest—447 (1916) |
| **Hits** | 253—Al Simmons, 153 G, 1925 | 1,827—Al Simmons | 1,659 (1925)<br>Fewest—1,131 (1908) |

| | Individual Season | Individual Career | Club Season |
|---|---|---|---|
| Hitting streak | 29 G—Bill Lamar, 1925 | | |
| Singles | 174—Al Simmons, 153 G, 1925 | 1,181—Jimmie Dykes | 1,206 (1925) |
| Doubles | 53—Al Simmons, 147 G, 1926 | 365—Jimmie Dykes | 323 (1928) |
| Triples | 21—Home Run Baker, 149 G, 1912 | 102—Danny Murphy | 108 (1912) |
| **HOME RUNS** | | | 172 (1932)<br>Fewest—76 (1925) |
| Righthander | 58—Jimmie Foxx, 154 G, 1932 | 302—Jimmie Foxx | |
| Lefthander | 27—Joe Hauser, 149 G, 1924 | 108—Mickey Cochrane | |
| Switch-hitter | 9—Dave Philley, 157 G, 1953 | 23—Dave Philley | |
| Rookie | 21—Bob Johnson, 142 G, 1933 | | |
| Home | 31—Jimmie Foxx, 1932<br>Jimmie Foxx, 1933 | 169—Jimmie Foxx | 109 (1932) |
| Road | 27—Jimmie Foxx, 1932 | 133—Jimmie Foxx | 67 (1953) |
| Month | 15—Bob Johnson, June 1934 | | 34 (June 1932, July 1932, June 1934) |
| Pinch | 3—Allie Clark, 1952<br>Kite Thomas, 1952 | 3—Allie Clark<br>Frankie Hayes<br>Kite Thomas<br>Tilly Walker | 6 (1952) |
| Grand slams | 3—Jimmie Foxx, 154 G, 1932<br>Jimmie Foxx, 150 G, 1934<br>Bob Johnson, 152 G, 1938<br>Gus Zernial, 145 G, 1952 | 9—Jimmie Foxx<br>Sam Chapman | 8 (1932) |
| Home runs at Columbia Park, all teams | | | 34 (1902) |
| Home runs at Shibe Park, all teams | | | 189 (1932) |
| Total bases | 438—Jimmie Foxx, 154 G, 1932 | 2,998—Al Simmons | 2,529 (1932) |
| Extra-base hits | 100—Jimmie Foxx, 154 G, 1932 | 655—Al Simmons | 527 (1932) |
| Sacrifice hits | 43—Roy Grover, 141 G, 1917 | 188—Jimmie Dykes | 248 (1909) |
| Sacrifice flies | 7—Joe DeMaestri, 146 G, 1954 | 7—Joe DeMaestri | 31 (1954) |
| Bases on balls | 149—Ed Joost, 144 G, 1949 | 1,043—Max Bishop | 783 (1949)<br>Fewest—268 (1903) |
| Strikeouts | 110—Ed Joost, 151 G, 1947<br>Fewest—7—Mickey Cochrane, 126 G, 1927 | 706—Jimmie Dykes | 677 (1954)<br>Fewest—293 (1902) |
| Hit by pitch | 15—Eddie Collins, 132 G, 1911 | 87—Jimmie Dykes | 65 (1911, 1913)<br>Fewest—5 (1937) |
| Runs batted in | 169—Jimmie Foxx, 154 G, 1932 | 1,178—Al Simmons | 923 (1932)<br>Fewest—380 (1916) |
| Grounded into double plays | 29—Dave Philley, 151 G, 1952<br>Fewest—4—Wally Moses, 142 G, 1938<br>Wally Moses, 142 G, 1940<br>Eddie Joost, 135 G, 1948<br>Dave Philley, 125 G, 1951 | 157—Pete Suder | 170 (1950)<br>Fewest—105 (1945) |
| Left on base | | | 1,235 (1949)<br>Fewest—999 (1924) |
| Batting average | .426—Nap Lajoie, 131 G, 1901 | .356—Al Simmons | .307 (1925)<br>Lowest—.223 (1908) |
| Most .300 hitters | | | 11 (1927) |
| Slugging average | .749—Jimmie Foxx, 154 G, 1932 | .640—Jimmie Foxx | .457 (1932)<br>Lowest—.292 (1908) |
| On-base percentage | .469—Jimmie Foxx, 154 G, 1932 | .440—Jimmie Foxx | .372 (1927)<br>Lowest—.281 (1908) |
| **BASERUNNING** | | | |
| Stolen bases | 81—Eddie Collins, 153 G, 1910 | 376—Eddie Collins | 258 (1912) |
| Caught stealing | 32—Eddie Murphy, 148 G, 1914 | 70—Amos Strunk | 188 (1914) |
| **PITCHING** | | | |
| Games | 58—Morrie Martin, 1953 | 524—Eddie Plank | |
| Games started | 46—Rube Waddell, 1904 | 459—Eddie Plank | |
| Complete games | 39—Rube Waddell, 1904 | 362—Eddie Plank | 136 (1904) |
| Wins | 31—Jack Coombs, 1910<br>Lefty Grove, 1931 | 284—Eddie Plank | |
| Percentage | .886—Lefty Grove (31-4), 1931 | .712—Lefty Grove | |
| Winning streak | 16—Lefty Grove, 1931 | | |
| 20-win seasons | | 7—Eddie Plank<br>Lefty Grove | |
| Losses | 25—Scott Perry, 1920 | 162—Eddie Plank | |
| Losing streak | 19—Jack Nabors, 1916 | | |
| Innings | 383—Rube Waddell, 1904 | 3,860.2—Eddie Plank | 1,421.2 (1910) |
| Hits | 360—Jack Coombs, 1911 | 3,438—Eddie Plank | 1,687 (1939) |
| Runs | 210—Chick Fraser, 1901 | 1,374—Eddie Plank | 1,045 (1936) |
| Earned runs | 146—George Earnshaw, 1930 | 1,025—Eddie Plank | 913 (1936) |

| | Individual Season | Career | Club Season |
|---|---|---|---|
| **Bases on balls** | 168—Elmer Myers, 1916 | 913—Eddie Plank | 827 (1915) |
| **Strikeouts** | 349—Rube Waddell, 1904 | 1,985—Eddie Plank | 895 (1905) |
| **Strikeouts, game** | 14—Rube Waddell, July 14, 1903<br>Rube Waddell, Sept 6, 1904, 1st game<br>Rube Waddell, Aug 2, 1905<br>[18—Jack Coombs, Sept 1, 1906, 24 inn<br>Jack Coombs, Aug 4, 1910, 16 inn] | | |
| **Hit batsmen** | 32—Chick Fraser, 1901 | 185—Eddie Plank | 81 (1911) |
| **Wild pitches** | 16—Stu Flythe, 1936 | 80—Eddie Plank | 68 (1915) |
| **Home runs** | 29—Lynn Nelson, 1938 | 138—Eddie Rommel | 148 (1939) |
| **Sacrifice hits** | 54—Eddie Rommel, 1923 | 343—Eddie Plank | 217 (1921) |
| **Sacrifice flies** | 17—Arnie Portocarrero, 1954 | 17—Arnie Portocarrero | 69 (1954) |
| **Earned run average** | 1.30—Jack Coombs, 353 inn, 1910 | 1.97—Rube Waddell | 1.79 (1910) |
| **Shutouts** | 13—Jack Coombs, 1910 | 59—Eddie Plank | 27 (1907, 1909-plus 1 tie)<br>Lost—24 (1943) |
| **1-0 games won** | 4—Harry Krause, 1909 | 12—Eddie Plank | 9 (1909)<br>Lost—7 (1908, 1909) |

## TEAM FIELDING

**Putouts** 4,255 (1910)
Fewest—3,600 (1901)

**Chances accepted** 6,293 (1920)
Fewest—5,601 (1938)

**Double plays** 217 (1949)
Fewest—64 (1905)

**Errorless games** unknown
Consecutive—7 (1951)

**Assists** 2,173 (1920)
Fewest—1,594 (1946)

**Errors** 338 (1915)
Fewest—113 (1948)

**Passed balls** 25 (1914)
Fewest—5 (1947)

**Fielding average** .981 (1948)
Lowest—.942 (1901)

## MISCELLANEOUS

**Most players, season** 56 (1915)
**Fewest players, season** 19 (1905)
**Games won** 107 (1931)
**Month** 26 (July 1931)
**Consecutive** 17 (1931)
**Winning percentage** .704 (1931), 107-45
**Lowest** .235 (1916), 36-117
**Number of league championships** 9
**Most recent** 1931
**Runs, game** 24 vs Detroit, May 18, 1912
vs Boston, May 1, 1929
**Opponents'** 25 by Cleveland, May 11, 1930
by New York, May 24, 1936
**Hits, game** 29 vs Boston, May 1, 1929
**Home runs, game** 7 vs Detroit, June 3, 1921
**Runs, shutout** 16 vs Chicago, July 25, 1928, 1st game
vs Chicago, Aug 29, 1937, 1st game
**Opponents'** 21 by New York, Aug 13, 1939, 2nd game, 8 inn
**Longest 1-0 win** 13 inn, vs Detroit, Aug 11, 1902
vs Boston, Sept 10, 1904
vs Chicago, May 16, 1909
vs Cleveland, May 14, 1914

**Most seasons, non-pitcher** 16—Harry Davis
**Most seasons, pitcher** 14—Eddie Plank
**Games lost** 117 (1916)
**Month** 28 (July 1916)
**Consecutive** 20 (1916, 1943)
**Overall record** 3,886-4,248 (54 seasons)

**Number of times worst record in league** 18
**Most recent** 1954
**Runs, inning** 13 vs Cleveland, June 15, 1925, 8th

**Total bases, game** 44 vs Boston, May 1, 1929
**Consecutive games with one or more home runs** 12 (20 HRs), 1951
**Longest shutout** unknown

**Longest 1-0 loss** 16 inn, vs St. Louis, June 5, 1942

## ATTENDANCE

**Highest home attendance**

| | |
|---|---|
| **Columbia Park** | 625,076 (1907) |
| **Shibe Park** | 945,076 (1948) |

**Highest road attendance** 1,562,360 (1948)

**Largest crowds**

| | |
|---|---|
| **Day** | 37,534 vs New York, May 16, 1937 |
| **Night** | 37,383 vs New York, June 27, 1947 |
| **Doubleheader** | 38,800 vs New York, July 13, 1931 |
| **Home opener** | 32,825 vs New York, Apr 20, 1927 |

# ST. LOUIS BROWNS

## YEARLY FINISHES

**(Original American League franchise moved from Milwaukee to St. Louis after the 1901 season and to Baltimore after the 1953 season)**

| Year | Position | W | L | Pct. | GB | Manager | Attendance |
|---|---|---|---|---|---|---|---|
| 1902 | 2nd | 78 | 58 | .574 | 5.0 | Jimmy McAleer | 272,283 |
| 1903 | 6th | 65 | 74 | .468 | 26.5 | Jimmy McAleer | 380,405 |
| 1904 | 6th | 65 | 87 | .428 | 29.0 | Jimmy McAleer | 318,108 |
| 1905 | 8th | 54 | 99 | .353 | 40.5 | Jimmy McAleer | 339,112 |
| 1906 | 5th | 76 | 73 | .510 | 16.0 | Jimmy McAleer | 389,157 |
| 1907 | 6th | 69 | 83 | .454 | 24.0 | Jimmy McAleer | 419,025 |
| 1908 | 4th | 83 | 69 | .546 | 6.5 | Jimmy McAleer | 618,947 |
| 1909 | 7th | 61 | 89 | .407 | 36.0 | Jimmy McAleer | 366,274 |
| 1910 | 8th | 47 | 107 | .305 | 57.0 | Jack O'Connor | 249,889 |
| 1911 | 8th | 45 | 107 | .296 | 56.5 | Bobby Wallace | 207,984 |
| 1912 | 7th | 53 | 101 | .344 | 53.0 | Bobby Wallace, George Stovall | 214,070 |

| Year | Position | W | L | Pct. | GB | Manager | Attendance |
|---|---|---|---|---|---|---|---|
| 1913 | 8th | 57 | 96 | .373 | 39.0 | George Stovall, Branch Rickey | 250,330 |
| 1914 | 5th | 71 | 82 | .464 | 28.5 | Branch Rickey | 244,714 |
| 1915 | 6th | 63 | 91 | .409 | 39.5 | Branch Rickey | 150,358 |
| 1916 | 5th | 79 | 75 | .513 | 12.0 | Fielder Jones | 335,740 |
| 1917 | 7th | 57 | 97 | .370 | 43.0 | Fielder Jones | 210,486 |
| 1918 | 5th | 58 | 64 | .475 | 15.0 | Fielder Jones, Jimmy Austin, Jimmy Burke | 122,076 |
| 1919 | 5th | 67 | 72 | .482 | 20.5 | Jimmy Burke | 349,350 |
| 1920 | 4th | 76 | 77 | .497 | 21.5 | Jimmy Burke | 419,311 |
| 1921 | 3rd | 81 | 73 | .526 | 17.5 | Lee Fohl | 355,978 |
| 1922 | 2nd | 93 | 61 | .604 | 1.0 | Lee Fohl | 712,918 |
| 1923 | 5th | 74 | 78 | .487 | 24.0 | Lee Fohl, Jimmy Austin | 430,296 |
| 1924 | 4th | 74 | 78 | .487 | 17.0 | George Sisler | 533,349 |
| 1925 | 3rd | 82 | 71 | .536 | 15.0 | George Sisler | 462,898 |
| 1926 | 7th | 62 | 92 | .403 | 29.0 | George Sisler | 283,986 |
| 1927 | 7th | 59 | 94 | .386 | 50.5 | Dan Howley | 247,879 |
| 1928 | 3rd | 82 | 72 | .532 | 19.0 | Dan Howley | 339,497 |
| 1929 | 4th | 79 | 73 | .520 | 26.0 | Dan Howley | 280,697 |
| 1930 | 6th | 64 | 90 | .416 | 38.0 | Bill Killefer | 152,088 |
| 1931 | 5th | 63 | 91 | .409 | 45.0 | Bill Killefer | 179,126 |
| 1932 | 6th | 63 | 91 | .409 | 44.0 | Bill Killefer | 112,558 |
| 1933 | 8th | 55 | 96 | .364 | 43.5 | Bill Killefer, Allen Sothoron, Rogers Hornsby | 88,113 |
| 1934 | 6th | 67 | 85 | .441 | 33.0 | Rogers Hornsby | 115,305 |
| 1935 | 7th | 65 | 87 | .428 | 28.5 | Rogers Hornsby | 80,922 |
| 1936 | 7th | 57 | 95 | .375 | 44.5 | Rogers Hornsby | 93,267 |
| 1937 | 8th | 46 | 108 | .299 | 56.0 | Rogers Hornsby, Jim Bottomley | 123,121 |
| 1938 | 7th | 55 | 97 | .362 | 44.0 | Gabby Street | 130,417 |
| 1939 | 8th | 43 | 111 | .279 | 64.5 | Fred Haney | 109,159 |
| 1940 | 6th | 67 | 87 | .435 | 23.0 | Fred Haney | 239,591 |
| 1941 | 6th (tied) | 70 | 84 | .455 | 31.0 | Fred Haney, Luke Sewell | 176,240 |
| 1942 | 3rd | 82 | 69 | .543 | 19.5 | Luke Sewell | 255,617 |
| 1943 | 6th | 72 | 80 | .474 | 25.0 | Luke Sewell | 214,392 |
| 1944 | 1st (s) | 89 | 65 | .578 | +1.0 | Luke Sewell | 508,644 |
| 1945 | 3rd | 81 | 70 | .536 | 6.0 | Luke Sewell | 482,986 |
| 1946 | 7th | 66 | 88 | .429 | 38.0 | Luke Sewell, Zack Taylor | 526,435 |
| 1947 | 8th | 59 | 95 | .383 | 38.0 | Muddy Ruel | 320,474 |
| 1948 | 6th | 59 | 94 | .386 | 37.0 | Zack Taylor | 335,546 |
| 1949 | 7th | 53 | 101 | .344 | 44.0 | Zack Taylor | 270,936 |
| 1950 | 7th | 58 | 96 | .377 | 40.0 | Zack Taylor | 247,131 |
| 1951 | 8th | 52 | 102 | .338 | 46.0 | Zack Taylor | 293,790 |
| 1952 | 7th | 64 | 90 | .416 | 31.0 | Rogers Hornsby, Marty Marion | 518,796 |
| 1953 | 8th | 54 | 100 | .351 | 46.5 | Marty Marion | 297,238 |

(s) lost World Series

## INDIVIDUAL AND CLUB RECORDS

### BATTING

| | Individual Season | Individual Career | Club Season |
|---|---|---|---|
| **Games** | 159—Del Pratt, 1915 | 1,647—George Sisler | 159 (1914, 1915) |
| **At-bats** | 671—Jack Tobin, 150 G, 1921 | 6,667—George Sisler | 5,510 (1937) |
| **Runs** | 145—Harlond Clift, 152 G, 1936 | 1,091—George Sisler | 900 (1925)<br>Fewest—441 (1909) |
| **Hits** | 257—George Sisler, 154 G, 1920 | 2,295—George Sisler | 1,693 (1922)<br>Fewest—1,105 (1910) |
| **Hitting streak** | 41 G—George Sisler, 1922 | | |
| **Singles** | 179—Jack Tobin, 150 G, 1921 | 1,714—George Sisler | 1,239 (1920) |
| **Doubles** | 51—Beau Bell, 156 G, 1937 | 343—George Sisler | 327 (1937) |
| **Triples** | 20—Heinie Manush, 154 G, 1928<br>George Stone, 154 G, 1906 | 145—George Sisler | 106 (1921) |

| **HOME RUNS** | | | 98 (1922)<br>Fewest—10 (1904, 1907, 1909) |
|---|---|---|---|
| **Righthander** | 34—Harlond Clift, 149 G, 1938 | 170—Harlond Clift | |
| **Lefthander** | 39—Ken Williams, 153 G, 1922 | 185—Ken Williams | |
| **Switch-hitter** | 14—Lu Blue, 154 G, 1928 | 24—Lu Blue | |
| **Rookie** | 24—Wally Judnich, 137 G, 1940 | | |
| **Home** | 32—Ken Williams, 1922 | 137—Ken Williams | 73 (1925) |
| **Road** | 16—Goose Goslin, 1930 | 82—Harlond Clift | 54 (1950, 1953) |
| **Month** | 15—Harlond Clift, Aug 1938 | | 36 (June 1940) |
| **Pinch** | 2—Hank Arft, 1951<br>Pat Collins, 1922<br>Pat Collins, 1923<br>Les Moss, 1950 | 4—Pat Collins | 4 (1950, 1951) |
| **Grand slams** | 2—many players | 5—Ken Williams<br>Harlond Clift<br>Vern Stephens | 5 (1922, 1940, 1950) |
| **Home runs at Sportsman's Park, all teams** | | | 146 (1925) |

| | Individual Season | Career | Club Season |
|---|---|---|---|
| Total bases | 399—George Sisler, 154 G, 1920 | 3,207—George Sisler | 2,466 (1922) |
| Extra-base hits | 86—George Sisler, 154 G, 1920 | 581—George Sisler | 482 (1922, 1925) |
| Sacrifice hits | 48—Joe Gedeon, 153 G, 1920 | 222—Jimmy Austin | 223 (1908) |
| Bases on balls | 126—Lu Blue, 151 G, 1929 | 986—Harlond Clift | 775 (1941)<br>Fewest—271 (1903) |
| Strikeouts | 120—Gus Williams, 143 G, 1914<br>Fewest—9—Hank Severeid, 143 G, 1921 | 649—Harlond Clift | 863 (1914)<br>Fewest—339 (1920) |
| Hit by pitch | 18—Dick Padden, 132 G, 1904 | 40—George Sisler | 56 (190-4)<br>Fewest—12 (1931) |
| Runs batted in | 155—Ken Williams, 153 G, 1922 | 959—George Sisler | 708 (1925)<br>Fewest—347 (1910) |
| Grounded into double plays | 21—Glenn McQuillen, 100 G, 1942<br>Fewest—1—George McQuinn, 146 G, 1944 | 66—John Berardino | 151 (1951)<br>Fewest—93 (1944) |
| Left on base | | | 1,334 (1941)<br>Fewest—1,055 (1951) |
| Batting average | .420—George Sisler, 142 G, 1922 | .344—George Sisler | .313 (1922)<br>Lowest—.218 (1910) |
| Most .300 hitters | | | 8 (1922) |
| Slugging average | .632—George Sisler, 154 G, 1920 | .558—Ken Williams | .455 (1922)<br>Lowest—.274 (1910) |
| On-base percentage | .467—George Sisler, 142 G, 1922 | .403—Ken Williams | .372 (1922)<br>Lowest—.281 (1910) |

## BASERUNNING

| | Individual Season | Career | Club Season |
|---|---|---|---|
| Stolen bases | 51—George Sisler, 142 G, 1922 | 351—George Sisler | 234 (1916) |
| Caught stealing | 32—Burt Shotton, 156 G, 1915 | 126—George Sisler | 189 (1914) |

## PITCHING

| | Individual Season | Career | Club Season |
|---|---|---|---|
| Games | 60—Marlin Stuart, 1953 | 323—Elam Vangilder | |
| Games started | 40—Bobo Newsom, 1938 | 264—Jack Powell | |
| Complete games | 36—Jack Powell, 1902 | 210—Jack Powell | 135 (1904) |
| Wins | 27—Urban Shocker, 1922 | 126—Urban Shocker | |
| Percentage | .808—Alvin Crowder (21-5), 1928 | .612—Urban Shocker | |
| Winning streak | 10—Alvin Crowder, 1928 | | |
| Winning streak, two seasons | 10—Bill Dinneen, 1907 (1), 1908 (9) | | |
| 20-win seasons | | 4—Urban Shocker | |
| Losses | 25—Fred Glade, 1905 | 142—Jack Powell | |
| Losing streak | 9—Walter Leverenz, 1913, 1914<br>Earl Hamilton, 1917 | | |
| Losing streak, two seasons | 12—Earl Hamilton, 1916 (3), 1917 (9) | | |
| Innings | 348—Urban Shocker, 1922 | 2,229.2—Jack Powell | 1,443.2 (1916) |
| Hits | 365—Urban Shocker, 1922 | 2,083—Jack Powell | 1,776 (1936) |
| Runs | 205—Bobo Newsom, 1938 | 958—George Blaeholder | 1,064 (1936) |
| Earned runs | 186—Bobo Newsom, 1938 | 824—George Blaeholder | 935 (1936) |
| Bases on balls | 192—Bobo Newsom, 1938 | 640—Dixie Davis | 801 (1951) |
| Strikeouts | 232—Rube Waddell, 1908 | 884—Jack Powell | 639 (1953) |
| Strikeouts, game | 16—Rube Waddell, July 29, 1908<br>[17—Rube Waddell, Sept 20, 1908, 10 inn] | | |
| Hit batsmen | 20—Barney Pelty, 1904 | 103—Barney Pelty | 64 (1915) |
| Wild pitches | 11—Dave Davenport, 1917<br>Bill James, 1914<br>Jack Knott, 1936<br>Carl Weilman, 1913 | 42—Barney Pelty | 47 (1948) |
| Home runs | 30—Bobo Newsom, 1938 | 142—George Blaeholder | 143 (1937) |
| Sacrifice hits | 53—Tom Zachary, 1926 | 224—Elam Vangilder | 258 (1926) |
| Earned run average | 1.59—Barney Pelty, 260.2 inn, 1906 | 2.06—Harry Howell | 2.15 (1908) |
| Shutouts | 6—Fred Glade, 1904<br>Harry Howell, 1906 | 27—Jack Powell | 21 (1909)<br>Lost—25 (1904, 1906, 1910) |
| 1-0 games won | 3—Fred Glade, 1904 | 6—Jack Powell | 6 (1909)<br>Lost—7 (1907) |

## TEAM FIELDING

| | | | |
|---|---|---|---|
| Putouts | 4,328 (1916)<br>Fewest—3,993 (1911) | Assists | 2,189 (1910)<br>Fewest—1,584 (1938) |
| Chances accepted | 6,516 (1916)<br>Fewest—5,618 (1972) | Errors | 378 (1910)<br>Fewest—134 (1947) |
| Double plays | 190 (1948)<br>Fewest—116 (1914) | Passed balls | 30 (1914, 1915)<br>Fewest—4 (1930, 1933) |
| Errorless games | unknown<br>Consecutive—8 (1928) | Fielding average | .977 (1947)<br>Lowest—.943 (1910) |

## MISCELLANEOUS

**Most players, season** 52 (1951)
**Fewest players, season** 19 (1906)

**Games won** 93 (1922)
**Month** 23 (Aug 1945)
**Consecutive** 14 (1916)
**Winning percentage** .604 (1922), 93-61
**Lowest** .279 (1939), 43-111
**Number of league championships** 1
**Most recent** 1944
**Runs, game** 20 vs Detroit, Aug 18, 1951
**Opponents'** 29 by Boston, June 8, 1950
**Hits, game** 24 vs Philadelphia, Sept 17, 1920
vs Washington, June 14, 1932
**Home runs, game** 5 vs New York, Sept 16, 1940
**Runs, shutout** 16 vs Detroit, Sept 9, 1922
**Opponents'** 18 by Detroit, Apr 29, 1935
**Longest 1-0 win** 16 inn, vs Philadelphia, June 5, 1942

**Most seasons, non-pitcher** 16—Jimmy Austin
**Most seasons, pitcher** 10—George Blaeholder
Barney Pelty
Jack Powell
**Games lost** 111 (1939)
**Month** 24 (Sept 1939, July 1952)
**Consecutive** 14 (1911, 1953)
**Overall record** 3,414-4,465 (52 seasons)

**Number of times worst record in league** 11
**Most recent** 1953
**Runs, inning** 11 vs Philadelphia, July 21, 1949, 1st game, 6th
vs Detroit, Aug 18, 1951, 7th
**Total bases, game** 40 vs Chicago, May 31, 1925

**Consecutive games with one or more home runs** 11 (20 HRs), 1922
**Longest shutout** unknown

**Longest 1-0 loss** 15 inn, vs Washington, Aug 14, 1903, 1st game
vs Washington, July 25, 1918

## ATTENDANCE

**Highest home attendance** 712,918 (1922)

**Highest road attendance** 1,170,349 (1948)

**Largest crowds**
**Day** 34,625 vs New York, Oct 1, 1944
**Night** 22,847 vs Cleveland, May 24, 1940
**Doubleheader** 31,932 vs New York, June 17, 1928
**Home opener** 19,561 vs Detroit, Apr 18, 1923

# SEATTLE MARINERS

## YEARLY FINISHES

(American League expansion franchise)

### WEST DIVISION

| Year | Position | W | L | Pct. | GB | Manager | Attendance |
|---|---|---|---|---|---|---|---|
| 1977 | 6th | 64 | 98 | .395 | 38.0 | Darrell Johnson | 1,338,511 |
| 1978 | 7th | 56 | 104 | .350 | 35.0 | Darrell Johnson | 877,440 |
| 1979 | 6th | 67 | 95 | .414 | 21.0 | Darrell Johnson | 844,447 |
| 1980 | 7th | 59 | 103 | .364 | 38.0 | Darrell Johnson, Maury Wills | 836,204 |
| 1981 | 6th/5th | 44 | 65 | .404 | * | Maury Wills, Rene Lachemann | 636,276 |
| 1982 | 4th | 76 | 86 | .469 | 17.0 | Rene Lachemann | 1,070,404 |
| 1983 | 7th | 60 | 102 | .370 | 39.0 | Rene Lachemann, Del Crandall | 813,537 |
| 1984 | 5th (tied) | 74 | 88 | .457 | 10.0 | Del Crandall, Chuck Cottier | 870,372 |
| 1985 | 6th | 74 | 88 | .457 | 17.0 | Chuck Cottier | 1,128,696 |
| 1986 | 7th | 67 | 95 | .414 | 25.0 | Chuck Cottier, Marty Martinez, Dick Williams | 1,029,045 |
| 1987 | 4th | 78 | 84 | .481 | 7.0 | Dick Williams | 1,134,255 |
| 1988 | 7th | 68 | 93 | .422 | 35.5 | Dick Williams, Jim Snyder | 1,022,398 |
| 1989 | 6th | 73 | 89 | .451 | 26.0 | Jim Lefebvre | 1,298,443 |
| 1990 | 5th | 77 | 85 | .475 | 26.0 | Jim Lefebvre | 1,509,727 |
| 1991 | 5th | 83 | 79 | .512 | 12.0 | Jim Lefebvre | 2,147,905 |
| 1992 | 7th | 64 | 98 | .395 | 32.0 | Bill Plummer | 1,651,398 |
| 1993 | 4th | 82 | 80 | .506 | 12.0 | Lou Piniella | 2,051,853 |
| 1994 | 3rd | 49 | 63 | .438 | 2.0 | Lou Piniella | 1,104,206 |
| 1995 | 1st (P,D,c) | 79 | 66 | .545 | +1.0 | Lou Piniella | 1,643,203 |
| 1996 | 2nd | 85 | 76 | .528 | 4.5 | Lou Piniella | 2,723,850 |
| 1997 | 1st (d) | 90 | 72 | .556 | +6.0 | Lou Piniella | 3,192,237 |
| 1998 | 3rd | 76 | 85 | .472 | 11.5 | Lou Piniella | 2,644,166 |
| 1999 | 3rd | 79 | 83 | .488 | 16.0 | Lou Piniella | 2,916,346 |
| 2000 | 2nd (D,c) | 91 | 71 | .562 | 0.5 | Lou Piniella | 3,148,317 |
| 2001 | 1st (D,c) | 116 | 46 | .716 | +14.0 | Lou Piniella | 3,507,975 |
| 2002 | 3rd | 93 | 69 | .574 | 10.0 | Lou Piniella | 3,540,482 |
| 2003 | 2nd | 93 | 69 | .574 | 3.0 | Bob Melvin | 3,268,864 |
| 2004 | 4th | 63 | 99 | .389 | 29.0 | Bob Melvin | 2,940,731 |
| 2005 | 4th | 69 | 93 | .426 | 26.0 | Mike Hargrove | 2,725,549 |

*first half 21-36, second half 23-29; (P) won division playoff; (D) won Division Series; (c) lost League Championship Series; (d) lost Division Series

## INDIVIDUAL AND CLUB RECORDS

### BATTING

| | Individual Season | Individual Career | Club Season |
|---|---|---|---|
| **Games** | 162—Ruppert Jones, 1979<br>Willie Horton, 1979<br>Ichiro Suzuki, 2005<br>Raul Ibanez, 2005 | 2,055—Edgar Martinez | 163 (1980) |
| **At-bats** | 704—Ichiro Suzuki, 161 G, 2004 | 7,213—Edgar Martinez | 5,722 (2004) |
| **Runs** | 141—Alex Rodriguez, 146 G, 1996 | 1,219—Edgar Martinez | 993 (1996)<br>Fewest—558 (1983) |
| **Hits** | 262—Ichiro Suzuki, 161 G, 2004 | 2,247—Edgar Martinez | 1,637 (2001)<br>Fewest—1,280 (1983) |
| **Hitting streak** | 24 G—Joey Cora, 1997 | | |

| | Individual Season | Career | Club Season |
|---|---|---|---|
| Singles | 225—Ichiro Suzuki, 161 G, 2004 | 1,409—Edgar Martinez | 1,120 (2001) |
| Doubles | 54—Alex Rodriguez, 146 G, 1996 | 514—Edgar Martinez | 343 (1996) |
| Triples | 12—Ichiro Suzuki, 162 G, 2005 | 48—Harold Reynolds | 52 (1979) |
| **HOME RUNS** | | | 264 (1997)<br>Fewest—97 (1978) |
| Righthander | 44—Jay Buhner, 150 G, 1996 | 309—Edgar Martinez | |
| Lefthander | 56—Ken Griffey Jr., 157 G, 1997<br>Ken Griffey Jr., 161 G, 1998 | 398—Ken Griffey Jr. | |
| Switch-hitter | 19—David Segui, 143 G, 1998 | 31—Randy Winn | |
| Rookie | 27—Alvin Davis, 152 G, 1984 | | |
| Home | 30—Ken Griffey Jr., 1998 | 212—Ken Griffey Jr. | 131 (1997) |
| Road | 29—Ken Griffey Jr., 1997 | 186—Ken Griffey Jr. | 133 (1997) |
| Month | 15—Ken Griffey Jr., May 1994 | | 58 (May 1999) |
| Pinch | 2—Greg Briley, 1992<br>Gary Gray, 1981<br>Ken Phelps, 1986<br>Leon Roberts, 1978<br>Paul Sorrento, 1997 | 4—Ken Phelps | 5 (1994, 1996) |
| Grand slams | 4—Edgar Martinez, 153 G, 2000 | 12—Ken Griffey Jr. | 11 (1996, 2000) |
| Home runs at Kingdome, all teams | | | 237 (1996) |
| Home runs at Safeco Field, all teams | | | 179 (2004) |
| Total bases | 393—Ken Griffey Jr., 157 G, 1997 | 3,718—Edgar Martinez | 2,741 (1996) |
| Extra-base hits | 93—Ken Griffey Jr., 157 G, 1997 | 838—Edgar Martinez | 607 (1996) |
| Sacrifice hits | 15—Craig Reynolds, 135 G, 1977<br>Larry Milbourne, 106 G, 1980 | 85—Dan Wilson | 106 (1980) |
| Sacrifice flies | 13—Bret Boone, 158 G, 2001<br>Mike Cameron, 150 G, 2001 | 77—Edgar Martinez | 72 (2002) |
| Bases on balls | 123—Edgar Martinez, 139 G, 1996 | 1,283—Edgar Martinez | 775 (2000)<br>Fewest—426 (1977) |
| Strikeouts | 176—Mike Cameron, 158 G, 2002<br>Fewest—34—Harold Reynolds, 160 G, 1987 | 1,375—Jay Buhner | 1,148 (1986)<br>Fewest—702 (1978) |
| Hit by pitch | 17—Dave Valle, 135 G, 1993 | 89—Edgar Martinez | 75 (1996)<br>Fewest—19 (1980) |
| Runs batted in | 147—Ken Griffey Jr., 157 G, 1997 | 1,261—Edgar Martinez | 954 (1996)<br>Fewest—536 (1983) |
| Grounded into double plays | 29—Jim Presley, 155 G, 1985<br>Fewest—3—Ichiro Suzuki, 157 G, 2001<br>Ichiro Suzuki, 159 G, 2003 | 190—Edgar Martinez | 158 (1979)<br>Fewest—101 (1984) |
| Left on base | | | 1,257 (2001)<br>Fewest—1,034 (1983) |
| Batting average | .372—Ichiro Suzuki, 161 G, 2004 | .332—Ichiro Suzuki | .288 (2001)<br>Lowest—.240 (1983) |
| Most .300 hitters | | | 4 (1997, 2001) |
| Slugging average | .646—Ken Griffey Jr., 157 G, 1997 | .569—Ken Griffey Jr. | .485 (1997)<br>Lowest—.356 (1980) |
| On-base percentage | .479—Edgar Martinez, 145 G, 1995 | .418—Edgar Martinez | .366 (1996)<br>Lowest—.301 (1983) |

## BASERUNNING

| | Individual Season | Career | Club Season |
|---|---|---|---|
| Stolen bases | 60—Harold Reynolds, 160 G, 1987 | 290—Julio Cruz | 174 (1987, 2001) |
| Caught stealing | 29—Harold Reynolds, 158 G, 1988 | 120—Harold Reynolds | 82 (1982) |

## PITCHING

| | Individual Season | Career | Club Season |
|---|---|---|---|
| Games | 78—Ed Vande Berg, 1982 | 432—Jeff Nelson | |
| Games started | 37—Mike Moore, 1986 | 298—Jamie Moyer | |
| Complete games | 14—Mike Moore, 1985<br>Mark Langston, 1987 | 56—Mike Moore | 39 (1987) |
| Wins | 21—Jamie Moyer, 2003 | 139—Jamie Moyer | |
| Percentage | .900—Randy Johnson (18-2), 1995 | .650—Jamie Moyer | |
| Winning streak | 10—Paul Abbott, 2001<br>Jamie Moyer, 2001 | | |
| Winning streak, two seasons | 12—Randy Johnson, 1995 (7), 1996 (5) | | |
| Winning streak, three seasons | 16—Randy Johnson, 1995 (7), 1996 (5), 1997 (4) | | |
| 20-win seasons | | 2—Jamie Moyer | |
| Losses | 19—Matt Young, 1985<br>Mike Moore, 1987 | 96—Mike Moore | |
| Losing streak | 16—Mike Parrott, 1980 | | |

| | Individual | | Club |
|---|---|---|---|
| | **Season** | **Career** | **Season** |
| **Saves** | 45—Kazuhiro Sasaki, 1991 | 129—Kazuhiro Sasaki | 56 (2001) |
| **Innings** | 272—Mark Langston, 1987 | 1,933—Jamie Moyer | 1,476.1 (1982) |
| **Hits** | 279—Mike Moore, 1986 | 1,696—Jamie Moyer | 1,613 (1999) |
| **Runs** | 145—Mike Moore, 1987 | 910—Jamie Moyer | 943 (1996) |
| **Earned runs** | 129—Mark Langston, 1986 | 846—Jamie Moyer | 834 (1999) |
| **Bases on balls** | 152—Randy Johnson, 1991 | 884—Randy Johnson | 684 (1999) |
| **Strikeouts** | 308—Randy Johnson, 1993 | 2,162—Randy Johnson | 1,207 (1997) |
| **Strikeouts, game** | 19—Randy Johnson, June 24, 1997<br>Randy Johnson, Aug 8, 1997 | | |
| **Hit batsmen** | 18—Randy Johnson, 1992 | 89—Randy Johnson | 72 (2004) |
| **Wild pitches** | 16—Matt Young, 1990 | 66—Randy Johnson | 82 (1991) |
| **Home runs** | 44—Jamie Moyer, 2004 | 236—Jamie Moyer | 216 (1996) |
| **Sacrifice hits** | 15—Shane Rawley, 1980 | 54—Jamie Moyer | 75 (1979, 1980) |
| **Sacrifice flies** | 14—Rich DeLucia, 1991 | 48—Jamie Moyer | 64 (1978) |
| **Earned run average** | 2.28—Randy Johnson, 213 inn, 1997 | 3.42—Randy Johnson | 3.54 (2001) |
| **Shutouts** | 4—Dave Fleming, 1992<br>Randy Johnson, 1992 | 19—Randy Johnson | 15 (2003)<br>Lost—15 (1978, 1983, 1990) |
| **1-0 games won** | 1—many pitchers | 3—Mark Langston | 3 (1979, 2002)<br>Lost—4 (1980, 1989, 1990) |

## TEAM FIELDING

| | | | |
|---|---|---|---|
| **Putouts** | 4,429 (1982)<br>Fewest—4,255 (1982) | **Assists** | 1930 (1980)<br>Fewest—1,450 (2003) |
| **Chances accepted** | 6,302 (1980)<br>Fewest—5,773 (2003) | **Errors** | 156 (1986)<br>Fewest—65 (2003) |
| **Double plays** | 191 (1986)<br>Fewest—134 (2002) | **Passed balls** | 24 (1991)<br>Fewest—3 (1997) |
| **Errorless games** | 112 (2003)<br>Consecutive—11 (1993) | **Fielding average** | .989 (2003)<br>Lowest—.975 (1986) |

## MISCELLANEOUS

**Most players, season** 51 (1999)
**Fewest players, season** 34 (1978, 1980)

**Games won** 116 (2001)
**Month** 20 (June 1997, Apr 2001, May 2001, Aug 2001)
**Consecutive** 15 (2001)
**Winning percentage** .716 (2001), 116-46
**Lowest** .350 (1978), 56-104
**Number of league championships** 0
**Most recent** ---
**Runs, game** 22 vs Detroit, Apr 29, 1999
**Opponents** 20 by Detroit, Apr 17, 1993
**Hits, game** 24 vs Minnesota, June 11, 1996
Anaheim, Sept 22, 2004
[24 vs Boston, Sept 3, 1981, 20 inn]
**Home runs, game** 7 vs Oakland, Apr 11, 1985
vs Milwaukee, July 31, 1996
vs Anaheim, July 5, 1999
vs Chicago, May 2, 2002
**Runs, shutout** 14 vs California, Aug 7, 1987
vs Minnesota, May 15, 2000
vs Baltimore, Sept 16, 2000
**Opponents'** 15 by Minnesota, July 10, 1977
**Longest 1-0 win** none over 9 inn

**Most seasons, non-pitcher** 18—Edgar Martinez
**Most seasons, pitcher** 10—Randy Johnson
Jamie Moyer

**Games lost** 104 (1978)
**Month** 22 (Aug 1977)
**Consecutive** 14 (1992)
**Overall record** 2,149-2,424 (29 seasons)
**Interleague play** 84-74
**Number of times worst record in league** 5
**Most recent** 1992
**Runs, inning** 11 vs Detroit, Apr 29, 1999, 5th
vs Chicago, May 12, 1997, 7th
**Total bases, game** 44 vs Toronto, Apr 16, 2000

**Consecutive games with one or more home runs** 19 (29 HRs), 1999

**Longest shutout** unknown

**Longest 1-0 loss** 12 inn, vs Texas, June 29, 1988

## ATTENDANCE

| | | | |
|---|---|---|---|
| **Highest home attendance** | | **Largest crowds** | |
| **Kingdome** | 3,192,237 (1997) | **Day** | 57,822 vs Cleveland, Mar 31, 1998 |
| **Safeco Field** | 3,540,482 (2002) | **Night** | 57,806 vs Minnesota, Apr 11, 1994 |
| | | **Doubleheader** | 32,597 vs California, Aug 12, 1985 |
| **Highest road attendance** | 2,572,882 (2001) | **Home opener** | 57,822 vs Cleveland, Mar 31, 1998 |

# SEATTLE PILOTS

## YEARLY FINISH

**(American League expansion franchise moved to Milwaukee after the 1969 season)**

### WEST DIVISION

| Year | Position | W | L | Pct. | GB | Manager | Attendance |
|---|---|---|---|---|---|---|---|
| 1969 | 6th | 64 | 98 | .395 | 33 | Joe Schultz | 677,944 |

## INDIVIDUAL AND CLUB RECORDS

### BATTING

| | Individual Season | Club Season |
|---|---|---|
| **Games** | 148—Tommy Harper | 163 |
| **At-bats** | 537—Tommy Harper, 148 G | 5,444 |
| **Runs** | 88—Wayne Comer, 147 G | 639 |
| **Hits** | 126—Tommy Harper, 148 G | 1,276 |
| **HittinG streak** | 18 G—Tommy Davis | |
| **Singles** | 105—Tommy Harper, 148 G | 945 |
| **Doubles** | [illegible]—Tommy Davis, 123 G | 179 |
| **Triples** | 6—Mike Hegan, 95 G | 27 |
| **HOME RUNS** | | 125 |
| **Righthander** | 15—Wayne Comer, 147 G | |
| **Lefthander** | 25—Don Mincher, 140 | |
| **Switch-hitter** | none | |
| **Rookie** | 15—Wayne Comer | |
| **Home** | 13—Don Mincher | 74 |
| **Road** | 12—Don Mincher | 51 |
| **Month** | 8—Don Mincher, July | 28 (May) |
| **Pinch** | 1—Greg Goossen<br>Mike Hegan<br>Don Mincher<br>Jim Pagliaroni | 4 |
| **Grand slams** | 1—Don Mincher, 140 G<br>Rich Rollins, 58 G<br>Fred Talbot, 27 G | 3 |
| **Home runs at Sicks' Stadium, all teams** | | 167 |
| **Total bases** | 194—Don Mincher, 140 G | 1,884 |
| **Extra-base hits** | 39—Don Mincher, 140 G | 331 |
| **Sacrifice hits** | 9—Jerry McNertney, 128 G | 72 |
| **Sacrifice flies** | 5—Tommy Davis, 123 G | 29 |
| **Bases on balls** | 95—Tommy Harper, 148 G | 626 |
| **Strikeouts** | 90—Tommy Harper, 148 G<br>Fewest—46—Tommy Davis, 123 G | 1,015 |
| **Hit by pitch** | 5—Don Mincher, 140 G<br>Rich Rollins, 58 G | 34 |
| **Runs batted in** | 80—Tommy Davis, 123 G | 583 |
| **Grounded into double plays** | 17—Tommy Davis, 123 G<br>Fewest—8—Tommy Harper, 148 G | 111 |
| **Left on base** | | 1,130 |
| **Batting average** | .271—Tommy Davis, 123 G | .234 |
| **Most .300 hitters** | | none |
| **Slugging average** | .454—Don Mincher, 140 G | .346 |
| **On-base percentage** | .366—Don Mincher, 140 G | .316 |

### BASERUNNING

| | Individual | Club |
|---|---|---|
| **Stolen bases** | 73—Tommy Harper, 148 G | 167 |
| **Caught stealing** | 18—Tommy Harper, 148 G | 59 |

### PITCHING

| | Individual | Club |
|---|---|---|
| **Games** | 66—Diego Segui | |
| **Games started** | 29—Gene Brabender | |
| **Complete games** | 7—Gene Brabender | 21 |
| **Wins** | 13—Gene Brabender | |
| **Percentage** | .667—Diego Segui (12-6) | |
| **Winning streak** | 5—Diego Segui | |
| **20-win seasons** | none | |
| **Losses** | 14—Gene Brabender | |
| **Losing streak** | 9—John Gelnar | |
| **Saves** | 12—Diego Segui | 33 |
| **Innings** | 202—Gene Brabender | 1,463.2 |
| **Hits** | 193—Gene Brabender | 1,490 |
| **Runs** | 111—Gene Brabender | 799 |
| **Earned runs** | 99—Marty Pattin | 707 |
| **Bases on balls** | 103—Gene Brabender | 653 |
| **Strikeouts** | 139—Gene Brabender | 963 |
| **Strikeouts, game** | 11—Marty Pattin, Apr 29 | |
| **Hit batsmen** | 13—Gene Brabender | 47 |

| | Individual Season | Club Season |
|---|---|---|
| **Wild pitches** | 8—Jim Bouton | 61 |
| **Home runs** | 29—Marty Pattin | 172 |
| **Sacrifice hits** | 10—Diego Segui | 60 |
| **Sacrifice flies** | 6—Gene Brabender | 40 |
| **Earned run average** | 3.36—Diego Segui, 142 inn | 4.35 |
| **Shutouts** | 1—held by 5 pitchers | 6 |
| **1-0 games won** | 1—Gene Brabender<br>Marty Pattin | 2<br>Lost—0 |

## TEAM FIELDING

| | | | |
|---|---|---|---|
| **Putouts** | 4,391 | **Assists** | 1,763 |
| **Chances accepted** | 6,154 | **Errors** | 167 |
| **Double plays** | 14 | **Passed balls** | 21 |
| **Errorless games** | 65<br>Consecutive—4 | **Fielding average** | .974 |

## MISCELLANEOUS

**Players, season** 53
**Games won** 64
**Month** 14 (June, Sept)
**Consecutive** 5
**Winning percentage** .395, 64-98
**Number of league championships** 0
**Runs, game** 16 vs Washington, May 10
**Opponents'** 15 by Baltimore, Aug 16
**Hits, game** 16 vs Oakland, Sept 10
**Hits, extra inn** 20 vs Minnesota, July 19, 18 inn
**Home runs, game** 4 vs Boston, May 16, 11 inn
**Runs, shutout** 8 vs California, July 9, 1st game
**Opponents'** 10 by Baltimore, June 7
**Longest 1-0 win** none over 9 inn

**Games lost** 98
**Month** 22 (Aug)
**Consecutive** 10
**Overall record** 64-98 (1 season)
**Number of times worst record in league** 0
**Runs, inning** 6 vs Boston, May 16, 11th
**Total bases, game** 31 vs Boston, May 16, 11 inn
**Consecutive games with one or more home runs** 5 (8 HRs)
**Longest shutout** none over 9 inn
**Longest 1-0 loss** none

## ATTENDANCE

| | | | |
|---|---|---|---|
| **Highest home attendance** | 677,944 | **Largest crowds** | |
| | | **Day** | 23,657 vs New York, Aug 3 |
| **Highest road attendance** | 889,578 | **Night** | 20,490 vs Baltimore, May 28 |
| | | **Doubleheader** | 18,413 vs Kansas City, June 20 |
| | | **Home opener** | 14,993 vs Chicago, Apr 11 |

# TAMPA BAY DEVIL RAYS

## YEARLY FINISHES

**(American League expansion franchise)**

### EAST DIVISION

| Year | Position | W | L | Pct. | GB | Manager | Attendance |
|---|---|---|---|---|---|---|---|
| 1998 | 5th | 63 | 99 | .389 | 51.0 | Larry Rothschild | 2,506,023 |
| 1999 | 5th | 69 | 93 | .426 | 29.0 | Larry Rothschild | 1,562,827 |
| 2000 | 5th | 69 | 92 | .429 | 18.0 | Larry Rothschild | 1,549,052 |
| 2001 | 5th | 62 | 100 | .383 | 34.0 | Larry Rothschild, Hal McRae | 1,227,673 |
| 2002 | 5th | 55 | 106 | .342 | 48.0 | Hal McRae | 1,065,762 |
| 2003 | 5th | 63 | 99 | .389 | 38.0 | Lou Piniella | 1,058,622 |
| 2004 | 4th | 70 | 91 | .435 | 30.5 | Lou Piniella | 1,275,011 |
| 2005 | 5th | 67 | 95 | .414 | 28.0 | Lou Piniella | 1,152,793 |

## INDIVIDUAL AND CLUB RECORDS

### BATTING

| | Individual Season | Individual Career | Club Season |
|---|---|---|---|
| **Games** | 162—Aubrey Huff, 2003 | 736—Aubrey Huff | 162 (1998, 1999, 2001, 2003, 2005) |
| **At-bats** | 644—Carl Crawford, 156 G, 2005 | 2,798—Aubrey Huff | 5,654 (2003) |
| **Runs** | 104—Carl Crawford, 152 G, 2004 | 374—Aubrey Huff | 772 (1999)<br>Fewest—620 (1998) |
| **Hits** | 198—Aubrey Huff, 162 G, 2003 | 805—Aubrey Huff | 1,531 (1999)<br>Fewest—1,414 (2000) |
| **Hitting streak** | 18 G—Quinton McCracken, 1998 | | |
| **Singles** | 145—Carl Crawford, 151 G, 2003 | 520—Aubrey Huff | 1,085 (1999) |
| **Doubles** | 47—Aubrey Huff, 162 G, 2003 | 157—Aubrey Huff | 333 (2002) |
| **Triples** | 19—Carl Crawford, 152 G, 2004 | 49—Carl Crawford | 46 (2004) |

| | Individual Season | Career | Club Season |
|---|---|---|---|
| **HOME RUNS** | | | 162 (2000)<br>Fewest—111 (1998) |
| **Righthander** | 34—Jose Canseco, 113 G, 1999 | 60—Greg Vaughn | |
| **Lefthander** | 34—Aubrey Huff, 162 G, 2003 | 120—Aubrey Huff | |
| **Switch-hitter** | 21—Jose Cruz Jr, 153 G, 2004 | 24—Randy Winn | |
| **Rookie** | 21—Jonny Gomes, 101 G, 2005 | | |
| **Home** | 18—Fred McGriff, 1999 | 65—Aubrey Huff | 76 (2000) |
| **Road** | 22—Jose Canseco, 1999 | 55—Aubrey Huff | 86 (2000, 2005) |
| **Month** | 10—Jose Canseco, April 1999<br>Aubrey Huff, May 2003 | | 38 (Aug 2005) |
| **Pinch** | 3—Bubba Trammell, 2000 | 4—Bubba Trammell | 4 (2000) |
| **Grand slams** | 2—Paul Sorrento, 137 G, 1998<br>Fred McGriff, 158 G, 2000<br>Ben Grieve, 154 G, 2001<br>Greg Vaughn, 136 G, 2001<br>Aubrey Huff, 154 G, 2005 | 2—Paul Sorrento<br>Fred McGriff<br>Ben Grieve<br>Greg Vaughn<br>Randy Winn<br>Aubrey Huff | 4 (2000, 2001) |
| **Home runs at Tropicana Field, all teams** | | | 185 (2000) |
| **Total bases** | 353—Aubrey Huff, 162 G, 2003 | 1,338—Aubrey Huff | 2,359 (2005) |
| **Extra-base hits** | 84—Aubrey Huff, 162 G, 2003 | 285—Aubrey Huff | 486 (2005) |
| **Sacrifice hits** | 12—Felix Martinez, 106 G, 2000 | 24—Miguel Cairo | 53 (1998) |
| **Sacrifice flies** | 10—John Flaherty, 117 G, 1999 | 24—Aubrey Huff | 56 (2004) |
| **Bases on balls** | 91—Fred McGriff, 158 G, 2000 | 305—Fred McGriff | 558 (2000)<br>Fewest—412 (2005) |
| **Strikeouts** | 159—Ben Grieve, 154 G, 2001<br>Fewest—44—Miguel Cairo, 150 G, 1998 | 433—Fred McGriff | 1,116 (2001)<br>Fewest—944 (2004) |
| **Hit by pitch** | 14—Jonny Gomes, 101 G, 2005 | 23—Jose Guillen | 69 (2005)<br>Fewest—37 (1998) |
| **Runs batted in** | 117—Jorge Cantu, 150 G, 2005 | 421—Aubrey Huff | 728 (1999)<br>Fewest—579 (1998) |
| **Grounded into double plays** | 24—Jorge Cantu, 150 G, 2005<br>Fewest—2—Carl Crawford, 152 G, 2004 | 81—Aubrey Huff | 157 (1999)<br>Fewest—97 (2004) |
| **Left on base** | | | 1,169 (1999)<br>Fewest—1,065 (2005) |
| **Batting average** | .311—Aubrey Huff, 162 G, 2003 | .288—Aubrey Huff | .274 (1999, 2005)<br>Lowest—.253 (2002) |
| **Most .300 hitters** | | | 1 (1999, 2003, 2005) |
| **Slugging average** | .563—Jose Canseco, 113 G, 1999 | .478—Aubrey Huff | .425 (2005)<br>Lowest—.385 (1998) |
| **On-base percentage** | .405—Fred McGriff, 144 G, 1999 | .342—Aubrey Huff | .343 (1999)<br>Lowest—.314 (2002) |

## BASERUNNING

| | Individual Season | Career | Club Season |
|---|---|---|---|
| **Stolen bases** | 59—Carl Crawford, 152 G, 2004 | 169—Carl Crawford | 151 (2005) |
| **Caught stealing** | 15—Carl Crawford, 152 G, 2004 | 46—Randy Winn | 73 (1998) |

## PITCHING

| | Individual Season | Career | Club Season |
|---|---|---|---|
| **Games** | 72—Roberto Hernandez, 1999 | 266—Esteban Yan | |
| **Games started** | 33—Tanyon Sturtze, 2002 | 83—Ryan Rupe | |
| **Complete games** | 5—Joe Kennedy, 2002 | 6—Joe Kennedy | 12 (2002) |
| **Wins** | 14—Rolando Arrojo, 1998 | 35—Victor Zambrano | |
| **Percentage** | .579—Mark Hendrickson (11-8), 2005<br>(no pitcher with 15 wins in any season) | none with 1,500 inn | |
| **Winning streak** | 6—Victor Zambrano, 2004 | | |
| **20-win seasons** | | none | |
| **Losses** | 18—Tanyon Sturtze, 2002 | 37—Bryan Rekar<br>Ryan Rupe | |
| **Losing streak** | 10—Albie Lopez, 2001 | | |
| **Saves** | 43—Roberto Hernandez, 1999 | 101—Roberto Hernandez | 45 (1999) |
| **Innings** | 224.0—Tanyon Sturtze, 2002 | 495.1—Bryan Rekar | 1,443 (1998) |
| **Hits** | 271—Tanyon Sturtze, 2002 | 583—Bryan Rekar | 1,606 (1999) |
| **Runs** | 141—Tanyon Sturtze, 2002 | 327—Ryan Rupe | 936 (2005) |
| **Earned runs** | 129—Tanyon Sturtze, 2002 | 303—Ryan Rupe | 851 (2005) |
| **Bases on balls** | 111—Tony Saunders, 1998 | 288—Victor Zambrano | 695 (1999) |
| **Strikeouts** | 174—Scott Kazmir, 2005 | 372—Victor Zambrano | 1,055 (1999) |
| **Strikeouts, game** | 12—Dan Wheeler, Sept 12, 1999 | | |
| **Hit batsmen** | 20—Victor Zambrano, 2003 | 43—Victor Zambrano | 95 (2003) |
| **Wild pitches** | 15—Victor Zambrano, 2003 | 34—Victor Zambrano | 75 (2001) |
| **Home runs** | 33—Tanyon Sturtze, 2002 | 77—Ryan Rupe | 215 (2002) |
| **Sacrifice hits** | 8—Mark Hendrickson, 2005 | 21—Travis Harper | 47 (2005) |
| **Sacrifice flies** | 12—Paul Wilson, 2001 | 28—Victor Zambrano | 65 (2003) |
| **Earned run average** | 3.56—Rolando Arrojo, 202 inn, 1998 | none with 1,500 inn | 4.35 (1998) |
| **Shutouts** | 2—Rolando Arrojo, 1998<br>Bobby Witt, 1999 | 2—Rolando Arrojo<br>Albie Lopez<br>Joe Kennedy<br>Bobby Witt | 8 (2000)<br>Lost—17 (1998) |

| | Individual Season | Career | Club Season |
|---|---|---|---|
| **1-0 games won** | 1—Steve Trachsel, 2000<br>Joe Kennedy, 2003<br>Jorge Sosa, 2003 | 1—Steve Trachsel<br>Joe Kennedy<br>Jorge Sosa | 3 (2000, 2005)<br>Lost—2 (2003) |

## TEAM FIELDING

**Putouts** 4,329 (1998)
Fewest—4,251 (2004)
**Chances accepted** 6,108 (2000)
Fewest—5,711 (2005)
**Double plays** 198 (1999)
Fewest—139 (2005)
**Errorless games** 91 (2003)
Consecutive—8 (2003)

**Assists** 1,814 (2000)
Fewest—1,446 (2005)
**Errors** 139 (2001)
Fewest—94 (1998)
**Passed balls** 19 (1998)
Fewest—8 (2001, 2004)
**Fielding average** .985 (1998)
Lowest—.977 (2001)

## MISCELLANEOUS

**Most players, season** 51 (2003)
**Fewest players, season** 42 (1998)
**Games won** 70 (2004)
**Month** 20 (June 2004)
**Consecutive** 12 (2004)
**Winning percentage** .435 (2004), 70-91
**Lowest** .342 (2002), 55-106
**Number of league championships** 0
**Most recent** ---
**Runs, game** 19 vs Toronto, June 24, 2004
**Opponents** 22 by Boston, July 23, 2002, a.m. game
**Hits, game** 24 vs Toronto, June 24, 2004
**Home runs, game** 6 vs Kansas City, Aug 10, 2002
**Runs, shutout** 10 vs Seattle, Sept 8, 1998
vs Montreal NL, July 12, 2001
**Opponents'** 14 by Toronto, July 1, 2004
**Longest 1-0 win** none over 9 inn

**Most seasons, non-pitcher** 6—Toby Hall
Aubrey Huff
**Most seasons, pitcher** 6—Travis Harper
**Games lost** 106 (2002)
**Month** 21 (June 2003)
**Consecutive** 15 (2002)
**Overall record** 518-775 (8 seasons)
**Interleague play** 56-86
**Number of times worst record in league** 3 (inc. 1 tie)
**Most recent** 2002 (tie)
**Runs, inning** 11 vs Seattle, May 28, 2000, 8th
**Total bases, game** 37 vs Toronto, June 24, 2004
vs Kansas City, Aug 10, 2002
**Consecutive games with one or more home runs** 12 (21 HRs), 2003
**Longest shutout** none over 9 inn
**Longest 1-0 loss** 12 inn, vs New York, June 18, 2003

## ATTENDANCE

**Highest home attendance** 2,261,158 (1998)
**Highest road attendance** 2,289,235 (2001)

**Largest crowds**
**Day** 43,373 vs New York, July 12, 1998
**Night** 45,369 vs Detroit, Mar 31, 1998
**Doubleheader** 10,309 vs Detroit, Sept 30, 2004
**Home opener** 45,369 vs Detroit, Mar 31, 1998
(Devil Rays drew 55,000 to 2004 "home opener" in Tokyo, Mar 30.)

# TEXAS RANGERS

## YEARLY FINISHES

**(American League expansion franchise moved from Washington to Texas after the 1971 season)**

### WEST DIVISION

| Year | Position | W | L | Pct. | GB | Manager | Attendance |
|---|---|---|---|---|---|---|---|
| 1972 | 6th | 54 | 100 | .351 | 38.5 | Ted Williams | 662,974 |
| 1973 | 6th | 57 | 105 | .352 | 37.0 | Whitey Herzog, Del Wilber, Billy Martin | 686,085 |
| 1974 | 2nd | 84 | 76 | .525 | 5.0 | Billy Martin | 1,193,902 |
| 1975 | 3rd | 79 | 83 | .488 | 19.0 | Billy Martin, Frank Lucchesi | 1,127,924 |
| 1976 | 4th (tied) | 76 | 86 | .469 | 14.0 | Frank Lucchesi | 1,164,982 |
| 1977 | 2nd | 94 | 68 | .580 | 8.0 | Frank Lucchesi, Eddie Stanky, Connie Ryan, Billy Hunter | 1,250,722 |
| 1978 | 2nd (tied) | 87 | 75 | .537 | 5.0 | Billy Hunter, Pat Corrales | 1,447,963 |
| 1979 | 3rd | 83 | 79 | .512 | 5.0 | Pat Corrales | 1,519,671 |
| 1980 | 4th | 76 | 85 | .472 | 20.5 | Pat Corrales | 1,198,175 |
| 1981 | 2nd/3rd | 57 | 48 | .543 | * | Don Zimmer | 850,076 |
| 1982 | 6th | 64 | 98 | .395 | 29.0 | Don Zimmer, Darrell Johnson | 1,154,432 |
| 1983 | 3rd | 77 | 85 | .475 | 22.0 | Doug Rader | 1,363,469 |
| 1984 | 7th | 69 | 92 | .429 | 14.5 | Doug Rader | 1,102,471 |
| 1985 | 7th | 62 | 99 | .385 | 28.5 | Doug Rader, Bobby Valentine | 1,112,497 |
| 1986 | 2nd | 87 | 75 | .537 | 5.0 | Bobby Valentine | 1,692,002 |
| 1987 | 6th (tied) | 75 | 87 | .463 | 10.0 | Bobby Valentine | 1,763,053 |
| 1988 | 6th | 70 | 91 | .435 | 33.5 | Bobby Valentine | 1,581,901 |
| 1989 | 4th | 83 | 79 | .512 | 16.0 | Bobby Valentine | 2,043,993 |
| 1990 | 3rd | 83 | 79 | .512 | 20.0 | Bobby Valentine | 2,057,911 |
| 1991 | 3rd | 85 | 77 | .525 | 10.0 | Bobby Valentine | 2,297,720 |
| 1992 | 4th | 77 | 85 | .475 | 19.0 | Bobby Valentine, Toby Harrah | 2,198,231 |
| 1993 | 2nd | 86 | 76 | .531 | 8.0 | Kevin Kennedy | 2,244,616 |
| 1994 | 1st (n) | 52 | 62 | .456 | +1.0 | Kevin Kennedy | 2,503,198 |
| 1995 | 3rd | 74 | 70 | .514 | 4.5 | Johnny Oates | 1,985,910 |
| 1996 | 1st (d) | 90 | 72 | .556 | +4.5 | Johnny Oates | 2,889,020 |
| 1997 | 3rd | 77 | 85 | .475 | 13.0 | Johnny Oates | 2,945,228 |
| 1998 | 1st (d) | 88 | 74 | .543 | +3.0 | Johnny Oates | 2,927,409 |
| 1999 | 1st (d) | 95 | 67 | .586 | +8.0 | Johnny Oates | 2,771,469 |
| 2000 | 4th | 71 | 91 | .438 | 20.5 | Johnny Oates | 2,800,147 |
| 2001 | 4th | 73 | 89 | .451 | 43.0 | Johnny Oates, Jerry Narron | 2,831,111 |
| 2002 | 4th | 72 | 90 | .444 | 31.0 | Jerry Narron | 2,352,447 |
| 2003 | 4th | 71 | 91 | .438 | 25.0 | Buck Showalter | 2,095,132 |
| 2004 | 3rd | 89 | 73 | .549 | 3.0 | Buck Showalter | 2,513,685 |
| 2005 | 3rd | 79 | 83 | .488 | 16.0 | Buck Showalter | 2,525,231 |

*first half 33-22, second half 24-26; (n) no World Series; (d) lost Division Series

## INDIVIDUAL AND CLUB RECORDS

### BATTING

| | Individual Season | Individual Career | Club Season |
|---|---|---|---|
| **Games** | 163—Al Oliver, 1980 | 1,573—Rafael Palmeiro | 163 (1980, 1983, 1996) |
| **At-bats** | 690—Michael Young, 160 G, 2004 | 5,830—Rafael Palmeiro | 5,716 (2005) |
| **Runs** | 133—Alex Rodriguez, 162 G, 2001 | 958—Rafael Palmeiro | 945 (1999)<br>Fewest—590 (1982) |
| **Hits** | 221—Michael Young, 159 G, 2005 | 1,723—Ivan Rodriguez | 1,653 (1999)<br>Fewest—1,353 (1978) |
| **Hitting streak** | 28 G—Gabe Kapler, 2000 | | |
| **Singles** | 165—Mickey Rivers, 147 G, 1980 | 1,136—Ivan Rodriguez | 1,202 (1980) |
| **Doubles** | 50—Juan Gonzalez, 154 G, 1998 | 344—Ivan Rodriguez | 330 (2000) |
| **Triples** | 14—Ruben Sierra, 162 G, 1989 | 44—Ruben Sierra | 46 (1989) |
| **HOME RUNS** | | | 260 (2005)<br>Fewest—80 (1976) |
| **Righthander** | 57—Alex Rodriguez, 162 G, 2002 | 372—Juan Gonzalez | |
| **Lefthander** | 47—Rafael Palmeiro, 158 G, 1999<br>Rafael Palmeiro, 160 G, 2001 | 321—Rafael Palmeiro | |
| **Switch-hitter** | 43—Mark Texeira, 162 G, 2005 | 180—Ruben Sierra | |
| **Rookie** | 30—Pete Incaviglia, 153 G, 1986 | | |
| **Home** | 34—Alex Rodriguez, 2002 | 176—Rafael Palmeiro | 153 (2005) |
| **Road** | 26—Alex Rodriguez, 2001 | 206—Juan Gonzalez | 127 (1999) |
| **Month** | 15—Juan Gonzalez, July 1996<br>Rafael Palmeiro, Aug 1999<br>Alex Rodriguez, Aug 2003 | | 55 (Aug 1999) |
| **Pinch** | 3—Darrell Porter, 1987 | 6—Geno Petralli | 7 (1980) |
| **Grand slams** | 3—Jeff Burroughs, 151 G, 1973<br>Larry Parrish, 128 G, 1982<br>Rafael Palmeiro, 158 G, 1999<br>Hank Blalock, 159 G, 2004 | 7—Juan Gonzalez<br>Rafael Palmeiro | 8 (1999) |
| **Home runs at Arlington Stadium, all teams** | | | 204 (1987) |
| **Home runs at Ameriquest Field in Arlington, all teams** | | | 245 (2002, 2003) |
| **Total bases** | 393—Alex Rodriguez, 162 G, 2001 | 3,073—Juan Gonzalez | 2,705 (1999) |
| **Extra-base hits** | 97—Juan Gonzalez, 154 G, 1998 | 713—Juan Gonzalez | 600 (2005) |
| **Sacrifice hits** | 40—Bert Campaneris, 150 G, 1977 | 102—Jim Sundberg | 116 (1977) |
| **Sacrifice flies** | 12—Jeff Burroughs, 152 G, 1974<br>Ruben Sierra, 158 G, 1987<br>Juan Gonzalez, 144 G, 1999 | 66—Ruben Sierra | 69 (1979) |
| **Bases on balls** | 113—Toby Harrah, 126 G, 1985 | 805—Rafael Palmeiro | 660 (1996)<br>Fewest—420 (1984) |
| **Strikeouts** | 185—Pete Incaviglia, 153 G, 1986<br>Fewest—33—Cesar Tovar, 138 G, 1974 | 1,076—Juan Gonzalez | 1,116 (1997)<br>Fewest—589 (1980) |
| **Hit by pitch** | 16—Alex Rodriguez, 162 G, 2001 | 54—Rafael Palmeiro | 75 (2001, 2003)<br>Fewest—20 (1984) |
| **Runs batted in** | 157—Juan Gonzalez, 154 G, 1998 | 1,180—Juan Gonzalez | 897 (1999)<br>Fewest—558 (1982) |
| **Grounded into double plays** | 31—Ivan Rodriguez, 144 G, 1999<br>Fewest—2—Cecil Espy, 142 G, 1989<br>Tom Goodwin, 154 G, 1998 | 187—Ivan Rodriguez | 161 (2000)<br>Fewest—91 (2004) |
| **Left on base** | | | 1,253 (1996)<br>Fewest—1,034 (1993) |
| **Batting average** | .341—Julio Franco, 146 G, 1983 | .3046—Ivan Rodriguez<br>.3045—Rusty Greer | .293 (1999)<br>Lowest—.249 (1982) |
| **Most .300 hitters** | | | 4 (1998, 1999) |
| **Slugging average** | .643—Juan Gonzalez, 134 G, 1996 | .565—Juan Gonzalez | .479 (1999)<br>Lowest—.290 (1972) |
| **On-base percentage** | .432—Toby Harrah, 126 G, 1985 | .399—Mike Hargrove | .361 (1999)<br>Lowest—.290 (1972) |

### BASERUNNING

| | Individual Season | Individual Career | Club Season |
|---|---|---|---|
| **Stolen bases** | 52—Bump Wills, 157 G, 1978 | 161—Bump Wills | 196 (1978) |
| **Caught stealing** | 21—Otis Nixon, 139 G, 1995 | 60—Toby Harrah | 91 (1978) |

### PITCHING

| | Individual Season | Individual Career | Club Season |
|---|---|---|---|
| **Games** | 85—Mitch Williams, 1987 | 528—Kenny Rogers | |
| **Games started** | 41—Jim Bibby, 1974<br>Ferguson Jenkins, 1974 | 313—Charlie Hough | |
| **Complete games** | 29—Ferguson Jenkins, 1974 | 98—Charlie Hough | 63 (1976) |
| **Wins** | 25—Ferguson Jenkins, 1974 | 139—Charlie Hough | |

| | Individual Season | Individual Career | Club Season |
|---|---|---|---|
| **Percentage** | .741—Rick Helling (20-7), 1998 | .575—Kenny Rogers | |
| **Winning streak** | 12—Bobby Witt, 1990 | | |
| **20-win seasons** | | 1—Ferguson Jenkins<br>Kevin Brown<br>Rick Helling | |
| **Losses** | 19—Jim Bibby, 1974 | 123—Charlie Hough | |
| **Losing streak** | 9—David Clyde, 1974 | | |
| **Saves** | 49—Francisco Cordero, 2004 | 150—John Wetteland | 52 (2004) |
| **Innings** | 328.1—Ferguson Jenkins, 1974 | 2,308—Charlie Hough | 1,479 (1991) |
| **Hits** | 286—Ferguson Jenkins, 1974 | 1,995—Charlie Hough | 1,683 (2000) |
| **Runs** | 159—Charlie Hough, 1987 | 1,086—Charlie Hough | 974 (2000) |
| **Earned runs** | 139—Jim Bibby, 1974 | 943—Charlie Hough | 913 (2001) |
| **Bases on balls** | 143—Bobby Witt, 1986 | 1,001—Bobby Witt | 760 (1987) |
| **Strikeouts** | 301—Nolan Ryan, 1989 | 1,452—Charlie Hough | 1,112 (1989) |
| **Strikeouts, game** | 16—Nolan Ryan, Apr 26, 1990<br>Nolan Ryan, May 1, 1991 | | |
| **Hit batsmen** | 19—Charlie Hough, 1987 | 89—Charlie Hough | 81 (2004) |
| **Wild pitches** | 22—Bobby Witt, 1986 | 99—Charlie Hough | 94 (1986) |
| **Home runs** | 41—Rick Helling, 1999 | 238—Charlie Hough | 222 (2001) |
| **Sacrifice hits** | 16—Jim Umbarger, 1976 | 53—Kenny Rogers | 90 (1976) |
| **Sacrifice flies** | 14—Charlie Hough, 1987 | 66—Bobby Witt | 73 (2001) |
| **Earned run average** | 2.17—Mike Paul, 162 inn, 1972 | 3.68—Charlie Hough | 3.31 (2001) |
| **Shutouts** | 6—Ferguson Jenkins, 1974<br>Bert Blyleven, 1976 | 17—Ferguson Jenkins | 17 (1977)<br>Lost—27 (1972) |
| **1-0 games won** | 4—Ferguson Jenkins, 1974<br>Bert Blyleven, 1976 | 7—Ferguson Jenkins | 5 (1974, 1975, 1976, 1990)<br>Lost—7 (1976) |

## TEAM FIELDING

**Putouts** 4,437 (1991)
Fewest—4,235 (1985)

**Chances accepted** 6,377 (1975)
Fewest—5,874 (1998)

**Double plays** 173 (1975)
Fewest—137 (1989)

**Errorless games** 95 (1996)
Consecutive—15 (1996)

**Assists** 1,980 (1975)
Fewest—1,580 (1998)

**Errors** 191 (1975)
Fewest—87 (1996)

**Passed balls** 73 (1987)
Fewest—2 (1999, 2001)

**Fielding average** .986 (1996)
Lowest—.971 (1975)

## MISCELLANEOUS

**Most players, season** 52 (1992, 2003, 2004)
**Fewest players, season** 35 (1984)
**Games won** 95 (1999)
**Month** 21 (Sept 1978)
**Consecutive** 14 (1991)
**Winning percentage** .586 (1999), 95-67
**Lowest** .351 (1972), 54-100
**Number of league championships** 0
**Most recent** ---
**Runs, game** 26 vs Baltimore, Apr 19, 1996
**Opponents'** 23 by Oakland, Sept 30, 2000
**Hits, game** 23 vs Chicago, Apr 2, 1998
vs Seattle, June 24, 2004
**Home runs, game** 8 vs Houston NL, May 21, 2005
vs Los Angeles AL, June 30, 2005
**Runs, shutout** 14 vs Oakland, July 26, 1977
**Opponents'** 14 by Chicago, Apr 18, 1972
by Chicago, Sept 4, 1973
**Longest 1-0 win** 14 inn, vs Boston, Apr 17, 1983

**Most seasons, non-pitcher** 13—Juan Gonzalez
**Most seasons, pitcher** 12—Kenny Rogers
**Games lost** 105 (1973)
**Month** 24 (Aug 1973)
**Consecutive** 15 (1972)
**Overall record** 2,517-2,692 (33 seasons)
**Interleague play** 66-74
**Number of times worst record in league** 2
**Most recent** 1973
**Runs, inning** 16 vs Baltimore, Apr 19, 1996, 8th
**Total bases, game** 44 vs Houston NL, May 21, 2005
**Consecutive games with one or more home runs** 27 (55 HRs), 2002
**Longest shutout** 16 inn, 3-0 vs Chicago, Sept 22, 1975
**Longest 1-0 loss** 13 inn, vs Minnesota, Sept 22, 1992

## ATTENDANCE

**Highest home attendance**

| | |
|---|---|
| **Arlington Stadium** | 2,297,720 (1991) |
| **Ameriquest Field in Arlington** | 2,945,228 (1997) |
| **Highest road attendance** | 2,406,986 (2000) |

**Largest crowds**

| | |
|---|---|
| **Day** | 50,054 vs Los Angeles AL, Apr 11, 2005 |
| **Night** | 50,708 vs Oakland, July 31, 2004 |
| **Doubleheader** | 44,598 vs Boston, May 1, 2004 |
| **Home opener** | 50,054 vs Los Angeles AL, Apr 11, 2005 |

# TORONTO BLUE JAYS

## YEARLY FINISHES

**(American League expansion franchise)**

### EAST DIVISION

| Year | Position | W | L | Pct. | GB | Manager | Attendance |
|---|---|---|---|---|---|---|---|
| 1977 | 7th | 54 | 107 | .335 | 45.5 | Roy Hartsfield | 1,701,052 |
| 1978 | 7th | 59 | 102 | .366 | 40.0 | Roy Hartsfield | 1,562,585 |
| 1979 | 7th | 53 | 109 | .327 | 50.5 | Roy Hartsfield | 1,431,651 |

| Year | Position | W | L | Pct. | GB | Manager | Attendance |
|---|---|---|---|---|---|---|---|
| 1980 | 7th | 67 | 95 | .414 | 36.0 | Bobby Mattick | 1,400,327 |
| 1981 | 7th/7th | 37 | 69 | .349 | * | Bobby Mattick | 755,083 |
| 1982 | 6th (tied) | 78 | 84 | .481 | 17.0 | Bobby Cox | 1,275,978 |
| 1983 | 4th | 89 | 73 | .549 | 9.0 | Bobby Cox | 1,930,415 |
| 1984 | 2nd | 89 | 73 | .549 | 15.0 | Bobby Cox | 2,110,009 |
| 1985 | 1st (c) | 99 | 62 | .615 | +2.0 | Bobby Cox | 2,468,925 |
| 1986 | 4th | 86 | 76 | .531 | 9.5 | Jimy Williams | 2,455,477 |
| 1987 | 2nd | 96 | 66 | .593 | 2.0 | Jimy Williams | 2,778,429 |
| 1988 | 3rd (tied) | 87 | 75 | .537 | 2.0 | Jimy Williams | 2,595,175 |
| 1989 | 1st (c) | 89 | 73 | .549 | +2.0 | Jimy Williams, Cito Gaston | 3,375,883 |
| 1990 | 2nd | 86 | 76 | .531 | 2.0 | Cito Gaston | 3,885,284 |
| 1991 | 1st (c) | 91 | 71 | .562 | +7.0 | Cito Gaston | 4,001,527 |
| 1992 | 1st (C,S) | 96 | 66 | .593 | +4.0 | Cito Gaston | 4,028,318 |
| 1993 | 1st (C,S) | 95 | 67 | .586 | +7.0 | Cito Gaston | 4,057,947 |
| 1994 | 3rd | 55 | 60 | .478 | 16.0 | Cito Gaston | 2,907,933 |
| 1995 | 5th | 56 | 88 | .389 | 30.0 | Cito Gaston | 2,826,483 |
| 1996 | 4th | 74 | 88 | .457 | 18.0 | Cito Gaston | 2,559,573 |
| 1997 | 5th | 76 | 86 | .469 | 22.0 | Cito Gaston, Mel Queen | 2,589,297 |
| 1998 | 3rd | 88 | 74 | .543 | 26.0 | Tim Johnson | 2,454,183 |
| 1999 | 3rd | 84 | 78 | .519 | 14.0 | Jim Fregosi | 2,163,464 |
| 2000 | 3rd | 83 | 79 | .512 | 4.5 | Jim Fregosi | 1,819,886 |
| 2001 | 3rd | 80 | 82 | .494 | 16.0 | Buck Martinez | 1,915,438 |
| 2002 | 3rd | 78 | 84 | .481 | 25.5 | Buck Martinez, Carlos Tosca | 1,636,904 |
| 2003 | 3rd | 86 | 76 | .531 | 15.0 | Carlos Tosca | 1,799,458 |
| 2004 | 5th | 67 | 94 | .416 | 33.5 | Carlos Tosca, John Gibbons | 1,900,041 |
| 2005 | 3rd | 80 | 82 | .494 | 15.0 | John Gibbons | 2,014,987 |

*first half 16-42, second half 21-27; (c) lost League Championship Series; (C) won League Championship Series; (S) won World Series

## INDIVIDUAL AND CLUB RECORDS

### BATTING

| | Individual Season | Individual Career | Club Season |
|---|---|---|---|
| **Games** | 163—Tony Fernandez, 1986 | 1,450—Tony Fernandez | 163 (1984, 1986, 1998) |
| **At-bats** | 687—Tony Fernandez, 163 G, 1986 | 5,335—Tony Fernandez | 5,716 (1986) |
| **Runs** | 134—Shawn Green, 153 G, 1999 | 889—Carlos Delgado | 894 (2003)<br>Fewest—590 (1978) |
| **Hits** | 215—Vernon Wells, 161 G, 2003 | 1,583—Tony Fernandez | 1,580 (1999, 2003)<br>Fewest—1,333 (1997) |
| **Hitting streak** | 28 G—Shawn Green, 1999 | | |
| **Singles** | 161—Tony Fernandez, 163 G, 1986 | 1,160—Tony Fernandez | 1,069 (1984) |
| **Doubles** | 57—Carlos Delgado, 162 G, 2000 | 343—Carlos Delgado | 357 (2003) |
| **Triples** | 17—Tony Fernandez, 161 G, 1990 | 72—Tony Fernandez | 68 (1984) |
| **HOME RUNS** | | | 244 (2000)<br>Fewest—95 (1979) |
| **Righthander** | 47—George Bell, 156 G, 1987 | 203—Joe Carter | |
| **Lefthander** | 44—Carlos Delgado, 152 G, 1999 | 336—Carlos Delgado | |
| **Switch-hitter** | 34—Jose Cruz Jr., 146 G, 2001 | 122—Jose Cruz Jr. | |
| **Rookie** | 24—Eric Hinske, 151 G, 2002 | | |
| **Home** | 30—Carlos Delgado, 2000 | 175—Carlos Delgado | 134 (2000) |
| **Road** | 28—George Bell, 1987 | 161—Carlos Delgado | 116 (1999) |
| **Month** | 12—Carlos Delgado, Aug 1999<br>Jose Cruz Jr., Aug 2001 | | 48 (June 2000) |
| **Pinch** | 3—Willie Greene, 1999 | 4—Jesse Barfield<br>Ernie Whitt | 6 (1984) |
| **Grand slams** | 3—Carlos Delgado, 153 G, 1997<br>Darrin Fletcher, 122 G, 2000 | 9—Carlos Delgado | 9 (2000) |
| **Home runs at Exhibition Stadium, all teams** | | | 185 (1983) |
| **Home runs at SkyDome, all teams** | | | 226 (2000) |
| **Total bases** | 378—Carlos Delgado, 162 G, 2000 | 2,786—Carlos Delgado | 2,664 (2000) |
| **Extra-base hits** | 99—Carlos Delgado, 162 G, 2000 | 690—Carlos Delgado | 593 (2000) |
| **Sacrifice hits** | 19—Luis Gomez, 153 G, 1978 | 74—Alfredo Griffin | 81 (1977) |
| **Sacrifice flies** | 14—George Bell, 153 G, 1989 | 65—Joe Carter | 65 (1991) |
| **Bases on balls** | 123—Carlos Delgado, 162 G, 2000 | 827—Carlos Delgado | 588 (1993)<br>Fewest—415 (1982) |
| **Strikeouts** | 159—Jose Canseco, 151 G, 1998<br>Fewest—21—Bob Bailor, 154 G, 1978 | 1,242—Carlos Delgado | 1,142 (2002)<br>Fewest—645 (1978) |
| **Hit by pitch** | 22—Shea Hillenbrand, 152 G, 2005 | 122—Carlos Delgado | 92 (1996)<br>Fewest—23 (1977, 1978) |
| **Runs batted in** | 145—Carlos Delgado, 161 G, 2003 | 1,058—Carlos Delgado | 856 (1999)<br>Fewest—551 (1978) |
| **Grounded into double plays** | 23—Ed Sprague, 150 G, 1993<br>Fewest—5—Alfredo Griffin, 162 G, 1983<br>Willie Upshaw, 155 G, 1986<br>Roberto Alomar, 161 G, 1991<br>Russ Adams, 139 G, 2005 | 112—George Bell | 156 (1977)<br>Fewest—91 (1984) |
| **Left on base** | | | 1,187 (1993)<br>Fewest—1,064 (1979) |

| | Individual | | Club |
|---|---|---|---|
| | **Season** | **Career** | **Season** |
| **Batting average** | .363—John Olerud, 158 G, 1993 | .307—Roberto Alomar | .280 (1999)<br>Lowest—.244 (1997) |
| **Most .300 hitters** | | | 4 (1999) |
| **Slugging average** | .558—Carlos Delgado, 162 G, 2000 | .556—Carlos Delgado | .469 (2000)<br>Lowest—.359 (1978) |
| **On-base percentage** | .473—John Olerud, 158 G, 1993 | .392—Carlos Delgado | .352 (1999)<br>Lowest—.286 (1981) |

## BASERUNNING

| | | | |
|---|---|---|---|
| **Stolen bases** | 60—Dave Collins, 128 G, 1984 | 255—Lloyd Moseby | 193 (1984) |
| **Caught stealing** | 23—Alfredo Griffin, 155 G, 1980 | 86—Tony Fernandez<br>Damaso Garcia<br>Lloyd Moseby | 81 (1982, 1998) |

## PITCHING

| | | | |
|---|---|---|---|
| **Games** | 89—Mark Eichhorn, 1987 | 452—Duane Ward | |
| **Games started** | 40—Jim Clancy, 1982 | 408—Dave Stieb | |
| **Complete games** | 19—Dave Stieb, 1982 | 103—Dave Stieb | 44 (1979) |
| **Wins** | 22—Roy Halladay, 2003 | 175—Dave Stieb | |
| **Percentage** | .778—Jack Morris (21-6), 1992 | .589—Jimmy Key | |
| **Winning streak** | 15—Roger Clemens, 1998<br>Roy Halladay, 2003 | | |
| **20-win seasons** | | 2—Roger Clemens | |
| **Losses** | 18—Jerry Garvin, 1977<br>Phil Huffman, 1979 | 140—Jim Clancy | |
| **Losing streak** | 10—Jerry Garvin, 1977, 1978<br>Paul Mirabella, 1980 | | |
| **Saves** | 45—Duane Ward, 1993 | 217—Tom Henke | 60 (1991) |
| **Innings** | 288.1—Dave Stieb, 1982 | 2,873—Dave Stieb | 1,476 (1986) |
| **Hits** | 278—Dave Lemanczyk, 1977 | 2,545—Dave Stieb | 1,615 (2000) |
| **Runs** | 143—Dave Lemanczyk, 1977<br>Erik Hanson, 1996 | 1,208—Dave Stieb | 908 (2000) |
| **Earned runs** | 129—Erik Hanson, 1996 | 1,091—Dave Stieb | 821 (2000) |
| **Bases on balls** | 128—Jim Clancy, 1980 | 1,020—Dave Stieb | 654 (1995) |
| **Strikeouts** | 292—Roger Clemens, 1997 | 1,658—Dave Stieb | 1,154 (1998) |
| **Strikeouts, game** | 18—Roger Clemens, Aug 25, 1998 | | |
| **Hit batsmen** | 16—Chris Carpenter, 2001 | 129—Dave Stieb | 76 (2001) |
| **Wild pitches** | 26—Juan Guzman, 1993 | 88—Juan Guzman | 83 (1993) |
| **Home runs** | 36—Woody Williams, 1998 | 224—Dave Stieb | 195 (2000) |
| **Sacrifice hits** | 16—Jerry Garvin, 1977 | 96—Dave Stieb | 92 (1980) |
| **Sacrifice flies** | 12—Jim Clancy, 1983<br>Doyle Alexander, 1984 | 72—Jim Clancy | 70 (1977) |
| **Earned run average** | 2.05—Roger Clemens, 264 inn, 1997 | 3.42—Jimmy Key<br>Dave Stieb | 3.31 (1985) |
| **Shutouts** | 5—Dave Stieb, 1982 | 30—Dave Stieb | 17 (1988)<br>Lost—20 (1981) |
| **1-0 games won** | 2—Jim Clancy, 1980<br>Jimmy Key, 1988 | 3—Pat Hentgen<br>Jimmy Key<br>Dave Stieb | 5 (1980)<br>Lost—3 (1979, 1992) |

## TEAM FIELDING

| | | | |
|---|---|---|---|
| **Putouts** | 4,428 (1986)<br>Fewest—4,251 (1979) | **Assists** | 1,939 (1980)<br>Fewest—1,532 (1998) |
| **Chances accepted** | 6,337 (1980)<br>Fewest—5,864 (1997) | **Errors** | 164 (1977)<br>Fewest—86 (1990) |
| **Double plays** | 206 (1980)<br>Fewest—109 (1992) | **Passed balls** | 31 (1995)<br>Fewest—3 (1985) |
| **Errorless games** | 103 (1990)<br>Consecutive—11 (1986) | **Fielding average** | .986 (1990)<br>Lowest—.974 (1977) |

## MISCELLANEOUS

**Most players, season** 53 (1999)
**Fewest players, season** 33 (1983)
**Games won** 99 (1985)
**Month** 21 (May 2003)
**Consecutive** 11 (1987, 1998)
**Winning percentage** .615 (1985), 99-62
**Lowest** .327 (1979), 53-109
**Number of league championships** 2
**Most recent** 1993

**Most seasons, non-pitcher** 12—Carlos Delgado
Tony Fernandez
Ernie Whitt
**Most seasons, pitcher** 15—Dave Stieb
**Games lost** 109 (1979)
**Month** 23 (May 1979)
**Consecutive** 12 (1981)
**Overall record** 2,258-2,315 (29 seasons)
**Interleague play** 74-83
**Number of times worst record in league** 4 (inc. 1 tie)
**Most recent** 1995 (tie)

**Runs, game** 24 vs Baltimore, June 26, 1978
**Opponents'** 24 by California, Aug 25, 1979
**Hits, game** 25 vs Texas, Aug 9, 1999
vs Boston, June 20, 1980
**Home runs, game** 10 vs Baltimore, Sept 14, 1987
**Runs, shutout** 15 vs Detroit, July 6, 1996
**Opponents'** 15 by New York, Sept 25, 1977, 1st game
**Longest 1-0 win** 12 inn, vs Boston, Sept 26, 1986

**Runs, inning** 11 vs Seattle, July 20, 1984, 9th
vs Chicago, May 12, 1997, 7th
**Total bases, game** 53 vs Baltimore, Sept 14, 1987

**Consecutive games with one or more home runs** 23 (44 HRs), 2000
**Longest shutout** 14 inn, 5-0 vs Milwaukee, Apr 29, 1981

**Longest 1-0 loss** 15 inn, vs Oakland, July 27, 1986

## ATTENDANCE

**Highest home attendance**
**Exhibition Stadium** 2,778,429 (1987)
**Skydome** 4,057,947 (1993)

**Highest road attendance** 2,549,898 (1993)

**Largest crowds**
**Day** 50,533 vs Cleveland, Apr 9, 1993
**Night** 50,560 vs Boston, Apr 8, 2005
**Doubleheader** 48,641 vs California, July 17, 1989
**Home opener** 50,560 vs Boston, Apr 8, 2005

# WASHINGTON SENATORS (1901-1960)

## YEARLY FINISHES

**(Original American League franchise moved to Minnesota after the 1960 season)**

| Year | Position | W | L | Pct. | GB | Manager | Attendance |
|---|---|---|---|---|---|---|---|
| 1901 | 6th | 61 | 72 | .459 | 20.5 | Jimmy Manning | 161,661 |
| 1902 | 6th | 61 | 75 | .449 | 22.0 | Tom Loftus | 188,158 |
| 1903 | 8th | 43 | 94 | .314 | 47.5 | Tom Loftus | 128,878 |
| 1904 | 8th | 38 | 113 | .252 | 55.5 | Patsy Donovan | 131,744 |
| 1905 | 7th | 64 | 87 | .424 | 29.5 | Jake Stahl | 252,027 |
| 1906 | 7th | 55 | 95 | .367 | 37.5 | Jake Stahl | 129,903 |
| 1907 | 8th | 49 | 102 | .325 | 43.5 | Joe Cantillon | 221,929 |
| 1908 | 7th | 67 | 85 | .441 | 22.5 | Joe Cantillon | 264,252 |
| 1909 | 8th | 42 | 110 | .276 | 56.0 | Joe Cantillon | 205,199 |
| 1910 | 7th | 66 | 85 | .437 | 36.5 | Jimmy McAleer | 254,591 |
| 1911 | 7th | 64 | 90 | .416 | 38.5 | Jimmy McAleer | 244,884 |
| 1912 | 2nd | 91 | 61 | .599 | 14.0 | Clark Griffith | 350,663 |
| 1913 | 2nd | 90 | 64 | .584 | 6.5 | Clark Griffith | 325,831 |
| 1914 | 3rd | 81 | 73 | .526 | 19.0 | Clark Griffith | 243,888 |
| 1915 | 4th | 85 | 68 | .556 | 17.0 | Clark Griffith | 167,332 |
| 1916 | 7th | 76 | 77 | .497 | 14.5 | Clark Griffith | 177,265 |
| 1917 | 5th | 74 | 79 | .484 | 25.5 | Clark Griffith | 89,682 |
| 1918 | 3rd | 72 | 56 | .563 | 4.0 | Clark Griffith | 182,122 |
| 1919 | 7th | 56 | 84 | .400 | 32.0 | Clark Griffith | 234,096 |
| 1920 | 6th | 68 | 84 | .447 | 29.0 | Clark Griffith | 359,260 |
| 1921 | 4th | 80 | 73 | .523 | 18.0 | George McBride | 456,069 |
| 1922 | 6th | 69 | 85 | .448 | 25.0 | Clyde Milan | 458,552 |
| 1923 | 4th | 75 | 78 | .490 | 23.5 | Donie Bush | 357,406 |
| 1924 | 1st (S) | 92 | 62 | .597 | +2.0 | Bucky Harris | 534,310 |
| 1925 | 1st (s) | 96 | 55 | .636 | +8.5 | Bucky Harris | 817,199 |
| 1926 | 4th | 81 | 69 | .540 | 8.0 | Bucky Harris | 551,580 |
| 1927 | 3rd | 85 | 69 | .552 | 25.0 | Bucky Harris | 528,976 |
| 1928 | 4th | 75 | 79 | .487 | 26.0 | Bucky Harris | 378,501 |
| 1929 | 5th | 71 | 81 | .467 | 34.0 | Walter Johnson | 355,506 |
| 1930 | 2nd | 94 | 60 | .610 | 8.0 | Walter Johnson | 614,474 |
| 1931 | 3rd | 92 | 62 | .597 | 16.0 | Walter Johnson | 492,657 |
| 1932 | 3rd | 93 | 61 | .604 | 14.0 | Walter Johnson | 371,396 |
| 1933 | 1st (s) | 99 | 53 | .651 | +7.0 | Joe Cronin | 437,533 |
| 1934 | 7th | 66 | 86 | .434 | 34.0 | Joe Cronin | 330,074 |
| 1935 | 6th | 67 | 86 | .438 | 27.0 | Bucky Harris | 255,011 |
| 1936 | 4th | 82 | 71 | .536 | 20.0 | Bucky Harris | 379,525 |
| 1937 | 6th | 73 | 80 | .477 | 28.5 | Bucky Harris | 397,799 |
| 1938 | 5th | 75 | 76 | .497 | 23.5 | Bucky Harris | 522,694 |
| 1939 | 6th | 65 | 87 | .428 | 41.5 | Bucky Harris | 339,257 |
| 1940 | 7th | 64 | 90 | .416 | 26.0 | Bucky Harris | 381,241 |
| 1941 | 6th (tied) | 70 | 84 | .455 | 31.0 | Bucky Harris | 415,663 |
| 1942 | 7th | 62 | 89 | .411 | 39.5 | Bucky Harris | 403,493 |
| 1943 | 2nd | 84 | 69 | .549 | 13.5 | Ossie Bluege | 574,694 |
| 1944 | 8th | 64 | 90 | .416 | 25.0 | Ossie Bluege | 525,235 |
| 1945 | 2nd | 87 | 67 | .565 | 1.5 | Ossie Bluege | 652,660 |
| 1946 | 4th | 76 | 78 | .494 | 28.0 | Ossie Bluege | 1,027,216 |
| 1947 | 7th | 64 | 90 | .416 | 33.0 | Ossie Bluege | 850,758 |
| 1948 | 7th | 56 | 97 | .366 | 40.0 | Joe Kuhel | 795,254 |
| 1949 | 8th | 50 | 104 | .325 | 47.0 | Joe Kuhel | 770,745 |
| 1950 | 5th | 67 | 87 | .435 | 31.0 | Bucky Harris | 699,697 |
| 1951 | 7th | 62 | 92 | .403 | 36.0 | Bucky Harris | 695,167 |
| 1952 | 5th | 78 | 76 | .506 | 17.0 | Bucky Harris | 699,457 |
| 1953 | 5th | 76 | 76 | .500 | 23.5 | Bucky Harris | 595,594 |
| 1954 | 6th | 66 | 88 | .429 | 45.0 | Bucky Harris | 503,542 |
| 1955 | 8th | 53 | 101 | .344 | 43.0 | Chuck Dressen | 425,238 |
| 1956 | 7th | 59 | 95 | .383 | 38.0 | Chuck Dressen | 431,647 |
| 1957 | 8th | 55 | 99 | .357 | 43.0 | Chuck Dressen, Cookie Lavagetto | 457,079 |
| 1958 | 8th | 61 | 93 | .396 | 31.0 | Cookie Lavagetto | 475,288 |
| 1959 | 8th | 63 | 91 | .409 | 31.0 | Cookie Lavagetto | 615,372 |
| 1960 | 5th | 73 | 81 | .474 | 24.0 | Cookie Lavagetto | 743,404 |

(S) won World Series; (s) lost World Series

# INDIVIDUAL AND CLUB RECORDS

## BATTING

| | Individual Season | Individual Career | Club Season |
|---|---|---|---|
| Games | 158—Eddie Foster, 1916 | 2,307—Sam Rice | 159 (1916) |
| At-bats | 668—Buddy Lewis, 156 G, 1937 | 8,934—Sam Rice | 5,592 (1935) |
| Runs | 127—Joe Cronin, 154 G, 1930 | 1,466—Sam Rice | 892 (1930)<br>Fewest—380 (1909) |
| Hits | 227—Sam Rice, 152 G, 1925 | 2,889—Sam Rice | 1,620 (1930)<br>Fewest—1,112 (1909) |
| Hitting streak | 33 G—Heinie Manush, 1933 | | |
| Singles | 182—Sam Rice, 152 G, 1925 | 2,195—Sam Rice | 1,209 (1935) |
| Doubles | 51—Mickey Vernon, 148 G, 1946 | 479—Sam Rice | 308 (1931) |
| Triples | 20—Goose Goslin, 150 G, 1925 | 183—Sam Rice | 100 (1932) |
| **HOME RUNS** | | | 85 (1938)<br>Fewest—42 (1947) |
| Righthander | 42—Roy Sievers, 152 G, 1957<br>Harmon Killebrew, 153, 1959 | 180—Roy Sievers | |
| Lefthander | 20—Mickey Vernon, 151 G, 1954 | 127—Goose Goslin | |
| Switch-hitter | 6—Danny Moeller, 132 G, 1912 | 15—Danny Moeller | |
| Rookie | 30—Bob Allison, 150 G, 1959 | | |
| Home | 26—Roy Sievers, 1957 | 88—Jim Lemon | 83 (1959) |
| Road | 21—Roy Sievers, 1958 | 100—Roy Sievers | 80 (1959) |
| Month | 15—Harmon Killebrew, May 1959 | | 38 (May 1959, June 1959) |
| Pinch | 2—Carlos Paula, 1955 | 3—Clint Courtney<br>Goose Goslin<br>Carlos Paula<br>Roy Sievers | 4 (1955, 1957) |
| Grand slams | 2—many players | 4—Roy Sievers | 8 (1938) |
| Home runs at American League Park, all teams | | | 74 (1902) |
| Home runs at Griffith Stadium, all teams | | | 158 (1956) |
| Total bases | 331—Roy Sievers, 152 G, 1957 | 3,833—Sam Rice | 2,287 (1930) |
| Extra-base hits | 76—Stan Spence, 152 G, 1946 | 694—Sam Rice | 464 (1932) |
| Sacrifice hits | 36—Hunter Hill, 103 G, 1905 | 249—Joe Judge | 135 (1906) |
| Sacrifice flies | 11—Roy Sievers, 145 G, 1954 | 33—Roy Sievers | 42 (1954) |
| Bases on balls | 151—Eddie Yost, 152 G, 1956 | 927—Tim Salmon | 690 (1956)<br>Fewest—257 (1903) |
| Strikeouts | 138—Jim Lemon, 146 G, 1956<br>Fewest—9—Sam Rice, 150 G, 1929 | 1,274—Eddie Yost | 883 (1960)<br>Fewest—359 (1927) |
| Hit by pitch | 24—Kid Elberfeld, 127 G, 1911 | 99—Bucky Harris | 80 (1911)<br>Fewest—8 (1947) |
| Runs batted in | 129—Goose Goslin, 154 G, 1924 | 1,044—Sam Rice | 822 (1936)<br>Fewest—306 (1909) |
| Grounded into double plays | 25—Sam Dente, 155 G, 1950<br>Fewest—5—George Case, 154 G, 1940<br>George Case, 153 G, 1941<br>Stan Spence, 153 G, 1944<br>Eddie Yost, 155 G, 1954 | 144—Mickey Vernon | 145 (1951)<br>Fewest—94 (1943) |
| Left on base | | | 1,305 (1935)<br>Fewest—998 (1959) |
| Batting average | .379—Goose Goslin, 135 G, 1923 | .328—Heinie Manush | .303 (1925)<br>Lowest—.223 (1909) |
| Most .300 hitters | | | 9 (1925) |
| Slugging average | .614—Goose Goslin, 135 G, 1928 | .502—Goose Goslin | .426 (1930)<br>Lowest—.287 (1910) |
| On-base percentage | .454—Buddy Myer, 127 G, 1938 | .392—Buddy Myer | .372 (1925)<br>Lowest—.274 (1905) |

## BASERUNNING

| | Individual Season | Individual Career | Club Season |
|---|---|---|---|
| Stolen bases | 88—Clyde Milan, 154 G, 1912 | 494—Clyde Milan | 291 (1913) |
| Caught stealing | 30—Sam Rice, 153 G, 1920 | 142—Sam Rice | 56 (1975) |

## PITCHING

| | Individual Season | Individual Career | Club Season |
|---|---|---|---|
| Games | 64—Firpo Marberry, 1926 | 802—Walter Johnson | |
| Games started | 42—Walter Johnson, 1910 | 666—Walter Johnson | |
| Complete games | 38—Walter Johnson, 1910 | 531—Walter Johnson | 137 (1904) |
| Wins | 36—Walter Johnson, 1913 | 417—Walter Johnson | |

| | Individual | | Club |
|---|---|---|---|
| | Season | Career | Season |
| Percentage | .837—Walter Johnson (36-7), 1913 | .622—Firpo Marberry | |
| Winning streak | 16—Walter Johnson, 1912 | | |
| Winning streak, two seasons | 16—Alvin Crowder, 1932 (15), 1933 (1) | | |
| 20-win seasons | | 12—Walter Johnson | |
| Losses | 26—Jack Townsend, 1904 | 279—Walter Johnson | |
| | Bob Groom, 1909 | | |
| Losing streak | 15—Bob Groom, 1909 | | |
| Innings | 374—Walter Johnson, 1910 | 5,923—Walter Johnson | 1,430.2 (1916) |
| Hits | 367—Bill Carrick, 1901 | 4,021—Walter Johnson | 1,672 (1935) |
| | Al Orth, 1902 | | |
| | Case Patten, 1904 | | |
| Runs | 172—Al Orth, 1903 | 1,902—Walter Johnson | 943 (1996) |
| Earned runs | 144—Jimmie DeShong, 1937 | 1,424—Walter Johnson | 811 (1956) |
| Bases on balls | 146—Bobo Newsom, 1936 | 1,353—Walter Johnson | 779 (1949) |
| Strikeouts | 313—Walter Johnson, 1910 | 3,508—Walter Johnson | 828 (1912) |
| Strikeouts, game | 15—Camilo Pascual, Apr 18, 1960 | | |
| Hit batsmen | 20—Walter Johnson, 1923 | 203—Walter Johnson | 69 (1913) |
| Wild pitches | 21—Walter Johnson, 1910 | 155—Walter Johnson | 57 (1911) |
| Home runs | 43—Pedro Ramos, 1957 | 170—Pedro Ramos | 171 (1956) |
| Sacrifice hits | 42—Beany Jacobson, 1904 | 534—Walter Johnson | 218 (1926) |
| | Jack Townsend, 1904 | | |
| Sacrifice flies | 12—Camilo Pascual, 1957 | 42—Pedro Ramos | 60 (1955) |
| Earned run average | 1.14—Walter Johnson, 346 inn, 1913 | 2.16—Walter Johnson | 2.14 (1918) |
| Shutouts | 12—Walter Johnson, 1913 | 110—Walter Johnson | 25 (1914) |
| | | | Lost—29 (1909) |
| 1-0 games won | 5—Walter Johnson, 1913, 1919 | 38—Walter Johnson | 11 (1914) |
| | | | Lost—7 (1915) |

## TEAM FIELDING

| | | | |
|---|---|---|---|
| **Putouts** | 4,291 (1916)<br>Fewest—3,944 (1906) | **Assists** | 2,232 (1911)<br>Fewest—1,587 (1951) |
| **Chances accepted** | 6,363 (1910)<br>Fewest—5,672 (1953) | **Errors** | 325 (1901)<br>Fewest—118 (1958) |
| **Double plays** | 186 (1935)<br>Fewest—93 (1912) | **Passed balls** | 40 (1945)<br>Fewest—3 (1927) |
| **Errorless games** | unknown<br>Consecutive—9 (1952) | **Fielding average** | .980 (1958)<br>Lowest—.936 (1902) |

## MISCELLANEOUS

**Most players, season** 44 (1909)
**Fewest players, season** 25 (1908, 1917)
**Games won** 99 (1933)
**Month** 24 (Aug 1945)
**Consecutive** 17 (1912)
**Winning percentage** .651 (1933), 99-53
**Lowest** .252 (1904), 38-113
**Number of league championships** 3
**Most recent** 1933
**Runs, game** 21 vs Detroit, Aug 5, 1929
**Opponents'** 24 by Boston, Sept 27, 1940
**Hits, game** 24 vs Detroit, July 9, 1903
vs Cleveland, July 18, 1925
**Home runs, game** 5 vs Detroit, May 2, 1959
[7 vs Chicago, May 3, 1949, 10 inn]

**Runs, shutout** 14 vs Boston, Sept 11, 1905, 2nd game, 7 inn
vs Chicago, Sept 3, 1942, 2nd game
**Opponents'** 17 by New York, Apr 24, 1909
by New York, July 6, 1920
by Chicago, Sept 19, 1925, 2nd game
**Longest 1-0 win** 18 inn, vs Chicago, May 15, 1918
vs Chicago, June 8, 1947, 1st game

**Most seasons, non-pitcher** 19—Sam Rice
**Most seasons, pitcher** 21—Walter Johnson
**Games lost** 113 (1904)
**Month** 29 (July 1909)
**Consecutive** 18 (1948, 1959)
**Overall record** 4,223-4,864 (60 seasons)

**Number of times worst record in league** 10
**Most recent** 1959
**Runs, inning** 12 vs St. Louis, July 10, 1926, 8th
vs Chicago, May 12, 1997, 7th
**Total bases, game** 41 vs Detroit, July 9, 1904

**Consecutive games with one or more home runs** 8 (14 HRs), 1959

**Longest shutout** 16 inn, 3-0 vs Chicago, Sept 22, 1975

**Longest 1-0 loss** 13 inn, vs Boston, Aug 15, 1916
vs Chicago, July 29, 1918

## ATTENDANCE

**Highest home attendance** 1,027,216 (1946)

**Highest road attendance** 1,055,171 (1948)

**Largest crowds**

| | |
|---|---|
| **Day** | 31,728 vs New York, Apr 19, 1948 |
| **Night** | 30,701 vs Cleveland, June 17, 1947 |
| **Doubleheader** | 35,563 vs New York, July 4, 1936 |
| **Home opener** | 31,728 vs New York, Apr 19, 1948 |

# WASHINGTON SENATORS (1961-1971)

## YEARLY FINISHES

**(American League expansion club moved to Texas after the 1971 season)**

| Year | Position | W | L | Pct. | GB | Manager | Attendance |
|---|---|---|---|---|---|---|---|
| 1961 | 9th (tied) | 61 | 100 | .379 | 47.5 | Mickey Vernon | 597,287 |
| 1962 | 10th | 60 | 101 | .373 | 35.5 | Mickey Vernon | 729,775 |
| 1963 | 10th | 56 | 106 | .346 | 48.5 | Mickey Vernon, Gil Hodges | 535,604 |

| Year | Position | W | L | Pct. | GB | Manager | Attendance |
|---|---|---|---|---|---|---|---|
| 1964 | 9th | 62 | 100 | .383 | 37.0 | Gil Hodges | 600,106 |
| 1965 | 8th | 70 | 92 | .432 | 32.0 | Gil Hodges | 560,083 |
| 1966 | 8th | 71 | 88 | .447 | 25.5 | Gil Hodges | 576,260 |
| 1967 | 6th (tied) | 76 | 85 | .472 | 15.5 | Gil Hodges | 770,863 |
| 1968 | 10th | 65 | 96 | .404 | 37.5 | Jim Lemon | 546,661 |

## EAST DIVISION

| Year | Position | W | L | Pct. | GB | Manager | Attendance |
|---|---|---|---|---|---|---|---|
| 1969 | 4th | 86 | 76 | .531 | 23.0 | Ted Williams | 918,106 |
| 1970 | 6th | 70 | 92 | .432 | 38.0 | Ted Williams | 824,789 |
| 1971 | 5th | 63 | 96 | .396 | 38.5 | Ted Williams | 655,156 |

## INDIVIDUAL AND CLUB RECORDS

### BATTING

| | Individual Season | Individual Career | Club Season |
|---|---|---|---|
| **Games** | 161—Frank Howard, 1969, 1970 | 1,142—Eddie Brinkman | 162 (1962-64, 1966, 1969, 1970) |
| **At-bats** | 635—Del Unser, 156 G, 1968 | 3,845—Eddie Brinkman | 5,484 (1962) |
| **Runs** | 111—Frank Howard, 161 G, 1969 | 516—Frank Howard | 694 (1969)<br>Fewest—524 (1968) |
| **Hits** | 175—Frank Howard, 161 G, 1969 | 1,071—Frank Howard | 1,370 (1962)<br>Fewest—1,209 (1968) |
| **Hitting streak** | 19 G—Ken McMullen, 1967 | | |
| **Singles** | 144—Eddie Brinkman, 158 G, 1970 | 685—Eddie Brinkman | 1,006 (1969) |
| **Doubles** | 31—Aurelio Rodriguez, 142 G, 1970 | 146—Frank Howard | 217 (1961) |
| **Triples** | 12—Chuck Hinton, 150 G, 1963 | 30—Chuck Hinton | 44 (1961) |
| **HOME RUNS** | | | 119 (1961)<br>Fewest—124 (1968) |
| **Righthander** | 48—Frank Howard, 161 G, 1969 | 237—Frank Howard | |
| **Lefthander** | 30—Mike Epstein, 131 G, 1969 | 89—Jim King | |
| **Switch-hitter** | 16—Fred Valentine, 146 G, 1966 | 34—Fred Valentine | |
| **Rookie** | 13—Paul Casanova, 122 G, 1966 | | |
| **Home** | 27—Frank Howard, 1969 | 116—Frank Howard | 77 (1969) |
| **Road** | 26—Frank Howard, 1968 | 121—Frank Howard | 85 (1961) |
| **Month** | 15—Frank Howard, May 1968 | | 37 (May 1965) |
| **Pinch** | 3—Brant Alyea, 1969<br>Don Lock, 1966<br>Tommy McCraw, 1971<br>Rick Reichardt, 1970 | 6—Brant Alyea | 8 (1965, 1966) |
| **Grand slams** | 2—Don Zimmer, 121 G, 1963 | 3—Mike Epstein<br>Don Zimmer | 4 (1961, 1963, 1967) |
| **Home runs at Griffith Stadium, all teams** | | | 87 (1961) |
| **Home runs at Robert F. Kennedy Memorial Stadium, all teams** | | | 166 (1964) |
| **Total bases** | 340—Frank Howard, 161 G, 1969 | 1,968—Frank Howard | 2,060 (1969) |
| **Extra-base hits** | 75—Frank Howard, 158 G, 1968 | 403—Frank Howard | 380 (1961) |
| **Sacrifice hits** | 15—Danny O'Connell, 138 G, 1961 | 34—Eddie Brinkman | 84 (1966) |
| **Sacrifice flies** | 8—Ken McMullen, 158 G, 1969 | 26—Ken McMullen | 44 (1961) |
| **Bases on balls** | 132—Frank Howard, 161 G, 1970 | 533—Frank Howard | 635 (1970)<br>Fewest—450 (1966) |
| **Strikeouts** | 155—Frank Howard, 149 G, 1967<br>Fewest—41—Eddie Brinkman, 158 G, 1970 | 854—Frank Howard | 1,125 (1965)<br>Fewest—789 (1962) |
| **Hit by pitch** | 13—Mike Epstein, 123 G, 1968 | 42—Mike Epstein | 46 (1970)<br>Fewest—15 (1962) |
| **Runs batted in** | 126—Frank Howard, 161 G, 1970 | 670—Frank Howard | 640 (1969)<br>Fewest—489 (1968) |
| **Grounded into double plays** | 29—Frank Howard, 161 G, 1969<br>Frank Howard, 153 G, 1971<br>Fewest—4—Del Unser, 153 G, 1971 | 131—Frank Howard | 148 (1966)<br>Fewest—98 (1975) |
| **Left on base** | | | 1,196 (1970)<br>Fewest—1,054 (1966) |
| **Batting average** | .310—Chuck Hinton, 151 G, 1962 | .280—Chuck Hinton | .251 (1969)<br>Lowest—.223 (1967) |
| **Most .300 hitters** | | | 1 (1961, 1962) |
| **Slugging average** | .574—Frank Howard, 161 G, 1969 | .513—Frank Howard | .378 (1969)<br>Lowest—.326 (1967, 1971) |
| **On-base percentage** | .416—Frank Howard, 161 G, 1970 | .369—Frank Howard | .330 (1969)<br>Lowest—.287 (1968) |

### BASERUNNING

| | Individual Season | Individual Career | Club Season |
|---|---|---|---|
| **Stolen bases** | 29—Ed Stroud, 129 G, 1970 | 92—Chuck Hinton | 99 (1962) |
| **Caught stealing** | 10—Willie Tasby, 141 G, 1961<br>Chuck Hinton, 150 G, 1962<br>Fred Valentine, 146 G, 1966<br>Del Unser, 153 G, 1969 | 30—Eddie Brinkman<br>Chuck Hinton | 53 (1962) |

## PITCHING

| | Individual Season | Individual Career | Club Season |
|---|---|---|---|
| Games | 74—Ron Kline, 1965 | 267—Casey Cox | |
| Games started | 36—Claude Osteen, 1964<br>Joe Coleman, 1969 | 123—Joe Coleman | |
| Complete games | 13—Claude Osteen, 1964 | 36—Joe Coleman | 39 (1961) |
| Wins | 16—Dick Bosman, 1970 | 49—Dick Bosman | |
| Percentage | .571—Dick Bosman (16-12), 1970 | none over 1,500 inn | |
| Winning streak | 8—Dick Bosman, 1969 | | |
| 20-win seasons | | none | |
| Losses | 22—Denny McLain, 1971 | 60—Bennie Daniels | |
| Losing streak | 10—Bennie Daniels, 1962 | | |
| Saves | 27—Darold Knowles, 1970 | 40—Darold Knowles | 41 (1969) |
| Innings | 257—Claude Osteen, 1964 | 889.2—Dick Bosman | 1,473.1 (1967) |
| Hits | 256—Claude Osteen, 1964 | 850—Dick Bosman | 1,486 (1963) |
| Runs | 115—Denny McLain, 1971 | 428—Bennie Daniels | 812 (1963) |
| Earned runs | 103—Denny McLain, 1971 | 378—Bennie Daniels | 710 (1963) |
| Bases on balls | 100—Joe Coleman, 1969 | 378—Jim Hannan | 656 (1969) |
| Strikeouts | 195—Pete Richert, 1966 | 561—Joe Coleman | 878 (1967) |
| Strikeouts, game | 13—Jim Duckworth, Sept 25, 1965, 2nd game<br>[21—Tom Cheney, Sept 12, 1962, 16 inn] | | |
| Hit batsmen | 12—Joe Coleman, 1968 | 31—Joe Coleman | 45 (1971) |
| Wild pitches | 17—Frank Bertaina, 1968 | 43—Joe Coleman | 61 (1968) |
| Home runs | 36—Pete Richert, 1966 | 90—Phil Ortega | 176 (1963) |
| Sacrifice hits | 20—Buster Narum, 1965 | 51—Jim Hannan | 97 (1968) |
| Sacrifice flies | 12—Casey Cox, 1970<br>Joe McClain, 1961<br>Denny McLain, 1971 | 29—Joe Coleman<br>Casey Cox | 59 (1963) |
| Earned run average | 2.19—Dick Bosman, 193 inn, 1969 | none with 1,500 inn | 3.38 (1967) |
| Shutouts | 4—Tom Cheney, 1963<br>Frank Bertaina, 1967<br>Camilo Pascual, 1968<br>Joe Coleman, 1969 | 7—Tom Cheney | 14 (1967)<br>Lost—22 (1964) |
| 1-0 games won | 2—Dick Donovan, 1961<br>Dave Stenhouse, 1962 | 3—Phil Ortega | 4 (1962, 1967, 1968)<br>Lost—5 (1963, 1971) |

## TEAM FIELDING

**Putouts** 4,420 (1967)
Fewest—4,1256 (1971)

**Chances accepted** 6,319 (1970)
Fewest—5,949 (1966)

**Double plays** 173 (1970)
Fewest—139 (1966)

**Errorless games** 83 (1964)
Consecutive—6 (1970)

**Assists** 1,946 (1970)
Fewest—1,647 (1965)

**Errors** 182 (1963)
Fewest—116 (1970)

**Passed balls** 23 (1961, 1971)
Fewest—12 (1970)

**Fielding average** .982 (1970)
Lowest—.971 (1963)

## MISCELLANEOUS

**Most players, season** 43 (1963)
**Fewest players, season** 36 (1969)
**Games won** 86 (1969)
**Month** 19 (July 1967)
**Consecutive** 8 (1967)
**Winning percentage** .531 (1969), 86-76
**Lowest** .346 (1963), 56-106
**Number of league championships** 0
**Most recent** ---
**Runs, game** 15 vs Detroit, May 18, 1965
vs Cleveland, July 5, 1971
**Opponents'** 18 by Baltimore, Apr 22, 1965
**Hits, game** 20 vs Boston, July 27, 1962, 2nd game

**Home runs, game** 5 vs Detroit, May 20, 1965
vs Chicago, May 16, 1969
vs Chicago, June 13, 1970
**Runs, shutout** 13 vs Los Angeles, June 2, 1965, 1st game
**Opponents'** 17 by Los Angeles, Aug 23, 1963
**Longest 1-0 win** 10 inn, vs Chicago, June 9, 1961, 1st game
vs Chicago, Sept 19, 1964

**Most seasons, non-pitcher** 10—Eddie Brinkman
**Most seasons, pitcher** 9—Jim Hannan
**Games lost** 106 (1963)
**Month** 24 (Aug 1961)
**Consecutive** 14 (1961, 1970)
**Overall record** 740-1,032 (11 seasons)

**Number of times worst record in league** 4 (inc. 1 tie)
**Most recent** 1968
**Runs, inning** 11 vs Baltimore, May 11, 1962, 6th

**Total bases, game** 32 vs Boston, July 27, 1962, 2nd game
vs Chicago, June 13, 1970
**Consecutive games with one or more home runs** 10 (16 HRs), 1970

**Longest shutout** 16 inn, 3-0 vs Chicago, Sept 22, 1975

**Longest 1-0 loss** 10 inn, vs Chicago, Sept 9, 1966

## ATTENDANCE

**Highest home attendance** 918,106 (1969)
**Griffith Stadium** 597,287 (1961)
**Robert F. Kennedy Stadium** 918, 106 (1969)

**Highest road attendance** 1,042,638 (1968)

**Largest crowds**
**Day** 45,125 vs New York, Apr 7, 1969
**Night** 30,421 vs New York, July 31, 1962
**Doubleheader** 40,359 vs Minnesota, June 14, 1964
**Home opener** 45,125 vs New York, Apr 7, 1969

# NATIONAL LEAGUE TEAM RECORDS

## ARIZONA DIAMONDBACKS

### YEARLY FINISHES

(National League expansion franchise)

#### WEST DIVISION

| Year | Position | W | L | Pct. | GB | Manager | Attendance |
|---|---|---|---|---|---|---|---|
| 1998 | 5th | 65 | 97 | .401 | 33.0 | Buck Showalter | 3,600,412 |
| 1999 | 1st (d) | 100 | 62 | .617 | +14.0 | Buck Showalter | 3,019,654 |
| 2000 | 3rd | 85 | 77 | .525 | 12.0 | Buck Showalter | 2,942,516 |
| 2001 | 1st (D,C,S) | 92 | 70 | .556 | 2.0 | Bob Brenly | 2,740,554 |
| 2002 | 1st (d) | 98 | 64 | .605 | +2.5 | Bob Brenly | 3,200,725 |
| 2003 | 3rd | 84 | 78 | .519 | 16.5 | Bob Brenly | 2,805,202 |
| 2004 | 5th | 51 | 111 | .315 | 42.0 | Bob Brenly, Al Pedrique | 2,519,560 |
| 2005 | 2nd | 77 | 85 | .475 | 5.0 | Bob Melvin | 2,058,741 |

(d) lost Division Series; (D) won Division Series; (C) won League Championship Series; (S) won World Series

### INDIVIDUAL AND CLUB RECORDS

#### BATTING

| | Individual Season | Individual Career | Club Season |
|---|---|---|---|
| **Games** | 162—Luis Gonzalez, 2000, 2001 | 1,041—Luis Gonzalez | 162 (1998-2005) |
| **At-bats** | 627—Matt Williams, 154 G, 1999 | 3,902—Luis Gonzalez | 5,658 (1999) |
| **Runs** | 132—Jay Bell, 151 G, 1999 | 687—Luis Gonzalez | 908 (1999)<br>Fewest—615 (2004) |
| **Hits** | 206—Luis Gonzalez, 153 G, 1999 | 1,178—Luis Gonzalez | 1,566 (1999)<br>Fewest—1,353 (1998) |
| **Hitting streak** | 30 G—Luis Gonzalez, 1999 | | |
| **Singles** | 131—Luis Gonzalez, 153 G, 1999<br>Tony Womack, 144 G, 1999 | 686—Luis Gonzalez | 1,015 (1999) |
| **Doubles** | 47—Luis Gonzalez, 162 G, 2000 | 258—Luis Gonzalez | 303 (2003) |
| **Triples** | 14—Tony Womack, 146 G, 2000 | 37—Tony Womack | 47 (2003) |
| **HOME RUNS** | | | 216 (1999)<br>Fewest—135 (2004) |
| **Righthander** | 38—Jay Bell, 151 G, 1999 | 99—Matt Williams | |
| **Lefthander** | 57—Luis Gonzalez, 162 G, 2001 | 209—Luis Gonzalez | |
| **Switch-hitter** | 30—Tony Clark, 130 G, 2005 | 30—Tony Clark | |
| **Rookie** | 22—Travis Lee, 146 G, 1998 | | |
| **Home** | 26—Luis Gonzalez, 2001 | 87—Luis Gonzalez | 107 (2001) |
| **Road** | 31—Luis Gonzalez, 2001 | 122—Luis Gonzalez | 115 (1999) |
| **Month** | 13—Luis Gonzalez, April 2001 | | 44 (Apr 2000, Apr 2001) |
| **Pinch** | 5—David Dellucci, 2001<br>Erubiel Durazo, 2001 | 6—David Dellucci<br>Erubiel Durazo | 14 (2001) |
| **Grand slams** | 2—Matt Williams, 135 G, 1998<br>Travis Lee, 120 G, 1999<br>Matt Williams, 154 G, 1999<br>Luis Gonzalez, 162 G, 2001 | 7—Matt Williams | 9 (2001) |
| **Home runs at Chase Field, all teams** | | | 228 (2001) |
| **Total bases** | 419—Luis Gonzalez, 162 G, 2001 | 2,113—Luis Gonzalez | 2,595 (1999) |
| **Extra-base hits** | 100—Luis Gonzalez, 162 G, 2001 | 492—Luis Gonzalez | 551 (1999) |
| **Sacrifice hits** | 14—Curt Schilling, 35 G, 2001 | 33—Curt Schilling | 71 (2001, 2005) |
| **Sacrifice flies** | 12—Luis Gonzalez, 162 G, 2000 | 38—Luis Gonzalez | 60 (1999) |
| **Bases on balls** | 100—Luis Gonzalez, 162 G, 2001 | 581—Luis Gonzalez | 643 (2002)<br>Fewest—441 (2004) |
| **Strikeouts** | 145—Troy Glaus, 149 G, 2005<br>Fewest—49—Shea Hillenbrand, 148 G, 2004 | 522—Luis Gonzalez | 1,239 (1998)<br>Fewest—975 (2000) |
| **Hit by pitch** | 18—Andy Fox, 139 G, 1998 | 54—Luis Gonzalez | 64 (1998)<br>Fewest—35 (2004) |
| **Runs batted in** | 142—Matt Williams, 154 G, 1999<br>Luis Gonzalez, 162 G, 2001 | 701—Luis Gonzalez | 865 (1999)<br>Fewest—582 (2004) |
| **Grounded into double plays** | 20—Danny Bautista, 141 G, 2004<br>Fewest—4—Steve Finley, 156 G, 1999 | 93—Luis Gonzalez | 137 (2004)<br>Fewest—94 (1999) |
| **Left on base** | | | 1,247 (2005)<br>Fewest—1,104 (1998) |
| **Batting average** | .336—Luis Gonzalez, 153 G, 1999 | .302—Luis Gonzalez | 277 (1999)<br>Lowest—.246 (1998) |
| **Most .300 hitters** | | | 2 (1999) |
| **Slugging average** | .688—Luis Gonzalez, 162 G, 2001 | .542—Luis Gonzalez | .459 (1999)<br>Lowest—.393 (1998, 2004) |
| **On-base percentage** | .429—Luis Gonzalez, 162 G, 2001 | .396—Luis Gonzalez | .347 (1999)<br>Lowest—.310 (2004) |

## BASERUNNING

| | Individual Season | Career | Club Season |
|---|---|---|---|
| Stolen bases | 72—Tony Womack, 144 G, 1999 | 182—Tony Womack | 137 (1999) |
| Caught stealing | 13—Tony Womack, 144 G, 1999 | 46—Tony Womack | 46 (2002) |

## PITCHING

| | Individual Season | Career | Club Season |
|---|---|---|---|
| Games | 86—Oscar Villarreal, 2003 | 243—Byung-Hyun Kim | |
| Games started | 35—Randy Johnson, 1999, 2000, 2002, 2004<br>Curt Schilling, 2001, 2002<br>Brandon Webb, 2004 | 192—Randy Johnson | |
| Complete games | 12—Randy Johnson, 1999 | 36—Randy Johnson | 16 (1999, 2000) |
| Wins | 24—Randy Johnson, 2002 | 103—Randy Johnson | |
| Percentage | .828—Randy Johnson (24-5), 2002 | .678—Randy Johnson | |
| Winning streak | 9—Curt Schilling, 2002 | | |
| 20-win seasons | | 2—Randy Johnson<br>Curt Schilling | |
| Losses | 16—Brandon Webb, 2004 | 49—Randy Johnson | |
| Losing streak | 9—Edgar Gonzalez, 2004 | | |
| Saves | 36—Byung-Hyun Kim, 2002 | 74—Matt Mantei | 46 (2005) |
| Innings | 271.2—Randy Johnson, 1999 | 1,389.2—Randy Johnson | 1,467.1 (1999) |
| Hits | 237—Curt Schilling, 2001 | 1,089—Randy Johnson | 1,480 (2004) |
| Runs | 117—Andy Benes, 1999 | 476—Randy Johnson | 899 (2004) |
| Earned runs | 113—Javier Vazquez, 2005 | 422—Brian Johnson | 794 (2004) |
| Bases on balls | 119—Brandon Webb, 2004 | 359—Randy Johnson | 668 (2004) |
| Strikeouts | 372—Randy Johnson, 2001 | 1,832—Randy Johnson | 1,303 (2002) |
| Strikeouts, game | 20—Randy Johnson, May 8, 2001 (pitched first 9 inn of 11-inn game)<br>17—Randy Johnson, June 30, 1999<br>Curt Schilling, Apr 7, 2002<br>Randy Johnson, Apr 21, 2002<br>Randy Johnson, Sept 14, 2002 | | |
| Hit batsmen | 18—Randy Johnson, 2001 | 64—Randy Johnson | 75 (2004) |
| Wild pitches | 17—Brandon Webb, 2004 | 43—Brandon Webb | 71 (2004) |
| Home runs | 39—Brian Anderson, 1998 | 143—Brian Anderson | 197 (2004) |
| Sacrifice hits | 14—Randy Johnson, 2000<br>Brandon Webb, 2004 | 43—Randy Johnson | 81 (2003) |
| Sacrifice flies | 8—Andy Benes, 1998<br>Brian Anderson, 2002<br>Miguel Batista, 2002<br>Russ Ortiz, 2005 | 23—Randy Johnson | 47 (2004) |
| Earned run average | 2.32—Randy Johnson, 260 inn, 2002 | 2.65—Randy Johnson | 3.77 (1999) |
| Shutouts | 4—Randy Johnson, 2002 | 14—Randy Johnson | 13 (2001)<br>Lost—16 (1998) |
| 1-0 games won | 1—Brian Anderson, 1998<br>Randy Johnson, 2000 | 1—Brian Anderson<br>Randy Johnson | 2 (2003)<br>Lost—3 (1998, 2001, 2002) |

## TEAM FIELDING

| | | | |
|---|---|---|---|
| Putouts | 4,402 (1999)<br>Fewest—4,297 (1998) | Assists | 1,794 (2005)<br>Fewest—1,506 (2002) |
| Chances accepted | 6,163 (2005)<br>Fewest—5,846 (2002) | Errors | 139 (2004)<br>Fewest—84 (2001) |
| Double plays | 159 (2005)<br>Fewest—116 (2002) | Passed balls | 18 (2004)<br>Fewest—4 (2000) |
| Errorless games | 94 (2001, 2005)<br>Consecutive—9 (1999) | Fielding average | .986 (2001)<br>Lowest—.977 (2004) |

## MISCELLANEOUS

**Most players, season** 52 (2004)
**Fewest players, season** 41 (2000)

**Games won** 100 (1999)
**Month** 22 (Aug 1998)
**Consecutive** 12 (2003)
**Winning percentage** .617 (1999), 100-62
**Lowest** .315 (2004), 51-111
**Number of league championships** 1
**Most recent** 2001
**Runs, game** 17 vs St. Louis, July 4, 1999
vs St. Louis, July 27, 2000
vs St. Louis, Apr 17, 2001
vs Colorado, Sept 28, 2002
**Opponents'** 20 by Colorado, Sept 23, 2003
**Hits, game** 20 vs Montreal, June 2, 1999
vs Los Angeles, May 8, 2000
vs Milwaukee, Apr 22, 2004
vs Kansas City AL, June 10, 2005
[21 vs Los Angeles, Apr 13, 1999, 16 inn]
**Home runs, game** 5, many times
**Runs, shutout** 12 vs San Diego, July 26, 2002
**Opponents'** 12 by San Diego, Sept 3, 2003
**Longest 1-0 win** 18 inn, vs San Francisco, May 29, 2001

**Most seasons, non-pitcher** 7—Luis Gonzalez
**Most seasons, pitcher** 6—Randy Johnson
Matt Mantei

**Games lost** 111 (2004)
**Month** 23 (Jul 2004)
**Consecutive** 14 (2004)
**Overall record** 652-644 (8 seasons)
**Interleague play** 61-66
**Number of times worst record in league** 1
**Most recent** 2004
**Runs, inning** 8 vs Florida, Aug 26, 1999, 9th
vs Chicago, Aug 19, 2000, 3rd
vs Kansas City AL, June 10, 2001, 4th
vs Atlanta, Apr 25, 2002, 5th

**Total bases, game** 40 vs St. Louis, Apr 17, 2001

**Consecutive games with one or more home runs** 13 (21 HRs), 1999
**Longest shutout** 18 inn, vs. San Francisco, May 29, 2001

**Longest 1-0 loss** 13 inn, by San Diego, Sept 2, 2001

## ATTENDANCE

| | | | |
|---|---|---|---|
| **Highest home attendance** | 3,600,412 (1998) | **Largest crowds** | |
| | | **Day** | 48,277 vs Los Angeles, May 24, 1998 |
| **Highest road attendance** | 2,689,308 (2002) | **Night** | 48,389 vs Seattle, June 27, 1998 |
| | | **Doubleheader** | none |
| | | **Home opener** | 47,465 vs Colorado, Mar 31, 1998 |

# ATLANTA BRAVES

## YEARLY FINISHES

**(Original National League franchise moved from Boston to Milwaukee after the 1952 season and to Atlanta after the 1965 season)**

| Year | Position | W | L | Pct. | GB | Manager | Attendance |
|---|---|---|---|---|---|---|---|
| 1966 | 5th | 85 | 77 | .525 | 10.0 | Bobby Bragan, Billy Hitchcock | 1,539,801 |
| 1967 | 7th | 77 | 85 | .475 | 24.5 | Billy Hitchcock, Ken Silvestri | 1,389,222 |
| 1968 | 5th | 81 | 81 | .500 | 16.0 | Lum Harris | 1,126,540 |

### WEST DIVISION

| Year | Position | W | L | Pct. | GB | Manager | Attendance |
|---|---|---|---|---|---|---|---|
| 1969 | 1st (c) | 93 | 69 | .574 | +3.0 | Lum Harris | 1,458,320 |
| 1970 | 5th | 76 | 86 | .469 | 26.0 | Lum Harris | 1,078,848 |
| 1971 | 3rd | 82 | 80 | .506 | 8.0 | Lum Harris | 1,006,320 |
| 1972 | 4th | 70 | 84 | .455 | 25.0 | Lum Harris, Eddie Mathews | 752,973 |
| 1973 | 5th | 76 | 85 | .472 | 22.5 | Eddie Mathews | 800,655 |
| 1974 | 3rd | 88 | 74 | .543 | 14.0 | Eddie Mathews, Clyde King | 981,085 |
| 1975 | 5th | 67 | 94 | .416 | 40.5 | Clyde King, Connie Ryan | 534,672 |
| 1976 | 6th | 70 | 92 | .432 | 32.0 | Dave Bristol | 818,179 |
| 1977 | 6th | 61 | 101 | .377 | 37.0 | Dave Bristol, Ted Turner | 872,464 |
| 1978 | 6th | 69 | 93 | .426 | 26.0 | Bobby Cox | 904,494 |
| 1979 | 6th | 66 | 94 | .413 | 23.5 | Bobby Cox | 769,465 |
| 1980 | 4th | 81 | 80 | .503 | 11.0 | Bobby Cox | 1,048,411 |
| 1981 | 4th/5th | 50 | 56 | .472 | * | Bobby Cox | 535,418 |
| 1982 | 1st (c) | 89 | 73 | .549 | +1.0 | Joe Torre | 1,801,985 |
| 1983 | 2nd | 88 | 74 | .543 | 3.0 | Joe Torre | 2,119,935 |
| 1984 | 2nd (tied) | 80 | 82 | .494 | 12.0 | Joe Torre | 1,724,892 |
| 1985 | 5th | 66 | 96 | .407 | 29.0 | Eddie Haas, Bobby Wine | 1,350,137 |
| 1986 | 6th | 72 | 89 | .447 | 23.5 | Chuck Tanner | 1,387,181 |
| 1987 | 5th | 69 | 92 | .429 | 20.5 | Chuck Tanner | 1,217,402 |
| 1988 | 6th | 54 | 106 | .338 | 39.5 | Chuck Tanner, Russ Nixon | 848,089 |
| 1989 | 6th | 63 | 97 | .394 | 28.0 | Russ Nixon | 984,930 |
| 1990 | 6th | 65 | 97 | .401 | 26.0 | Russ Nixon, Bobby Cox | 980,129 |
| 1991 | 1st (C,s) | 94 | 68 | .580 | +1.0 | Bobby Cox | 2,140,217 |
| 1992 | 1st (C,s) | 98 | 64 | .605 | +8.0 | Bobby Cox | 3,077,400 |
| 1993 | 1st (c) | 104 | 58 | .642 | +1.0 | Bobby Cox | 3,884,725 |

### EAST DIVISION

| Year | Position | W | L | Pct. | GB | Manager | Attendance |
|---|---|---|---|---|---|---|---|
| 1994 | 2nd | 68 | 46 | .596 | 6.0 | Bobby Cox | 2,539,240 |
| 1995 | 1st (D,C,S) | 90 | 54 | .625 | +21.0 | Bobby Cox | 2,561,831 |
| 1996 | 1st (D,C,s) | 96 | 66 | .593 | +8.0 | Bobby Cox | 2,901,242 |
| 1997 | 1st (D,c) | 101 | 61 | .623 | +9.0 | Bobby Cox | 3,464,488 |
| 1998 | 1st (D,c) | 106 | 56 | .654 | +18.0 | Bobby Cox | 3,361,350 |
| 1999 | 1st(D,C,s) | 103 | 59 | .636 | +6.5 | Bobby Cox | 3,284,897 |
| 2000 | 1st (d) | 95 | 67 | .586 | +1.0 | Bobby Cox | 3,234,301 |
| 2001 | 1st (D,c) | 88 | 74 | .543 | +2.0 | Bobby Cox | 2,823,494 |
| 2002 | 1st (d) | 101 | 59 | .631 | +19.0 | Bobby Cox | 2,603,482 |
| 2003 | 1st (d) | 101 | 61 | .623 | +10.0 | Bobby Cox | 2,401,082 |
| 2004 | 1st (d) | 96 | 66 | .593 | +10.0 | Bobby Cox | 2,322,565 |
| 2005 | 1st (d) | 90 | 72 | .556 | +2.0 | Bobby Cox | 2,521,527 |

(c) lost League Championship Series; *first half 25-29, second half 25-27; (C) won League Championship Series; (s) lost World Series; (D) won Division Series; (S) won World Series; (d) lost Division Series

## INDIVIDUAL AND CLUB RECORDS

### BATTING

| | Individual — Season | Individual — Career | Club — Season |
|---|---|---|---|
| **Games** | 162—Felix Millan, 1969<br>Dale Murphy, 1982, 1983, 1984, 1985<br>Andruw Jones, 1999 | 1,926—Dale Murphy | 163 (1966, 1968, 1974) |
| **At-bats** | 671—Marquis Grissom, 158 G, 1996 | 7,098—Dale Murphy | 5,670 (2003) |
| **Runs** | 131—Dale Murphy, 162 G, 1983 | 1,103—Dale Murphy | 907 (2003)<br>Fewest—514 (1968) |
| **Hits** | 219—Ralph Garr, 154 G, 1971 | 1,901—Dale Murphy | 1,608 (2003)<br>Fewest—1,281 (1989) |
| **Hitting streak** | 31 G—Rico Carty, 1970 | | |
| **Singles** | 180—Ralph Garr, 154 G, 1971 | 1,187—Dale Murphy | 1,109 (1968) |
| **Doubles** | 49—Marcus Giles, 145 G, 2003 | 355—Chipper Jones | 321 (2003) |
| **Triples** | 17—Ralph Garr, 143 G, 1974 | 40—Ralph Garr | 48 (1992) |

| | Individual Season | Career | Club Season |
|---|---|---|---|
| **HOME RUNS** | | | 235 (2003) |
| | | Fewest—80 (1968) | |
| Righthander | 51—Andruw Jones, 160 G, 2005 | 371—Dale Murphy | |
| Lefthander | 41—Darrell Evans, 161 G, 1973 | 160—David Justice | |
| Switch-hitter | 45—Chipper Jones, 157 G, 1999 | 331—Chipper Jones | |
| Rookie | 33—Earl Williams, 145 G, 1971 | | |
| Home | 31—Hank Aaron, 1971 | 205—Dale Murphy | 119 (1966) |
| Road | 28—Andres Galarraga, 1998 | 166—Dale Murphy | 124 (2003) |
| Month | 14—Bob Horner, July 1980 | | 55 (May 2003) |
| Pinch | 4—Tommy Gregg, 1990 | 6—Tommy Gregg<br>Mike Lum | 9 (1992) |
| Grand slams | 3—Chipper Jones, 157 G, 1997 | 7—Hank Aaron<br>Javy Lopez | 12 (1997) |
| Home runs at Atlanta-Fulton County Stadium, all teams | | | 211 (1970) |
| Home runs at Turner Field, all teams | | | 179 (2003) |
| Total bases | 359—Chipper Jones, 157 G, 1999 | 3,394—Dale Murphy | 2,696 (2003) |
| Extra-base hits | 87—Chipper Jones, 157 G, 1999 | 714—Dale Murphy | 587 (2003) |
| Sacrifice hits | 20—Rod Gilbreath, 116 G, 1976<br>Glenn Hubbard, 145 G, 1982 | 168—Tom Glavine | 109 (1974) |
| Sacrifice flies | 10—Bob Horner, 141 G, 1986<br>Gerald Perry, 141 G, 1988<br>Chipper Jones, 156 G, 2000 | 66—Chipper Jones | 52 (1997, 2001) |
| Bases on balls | 127—Jimmy Wynn, 148 G, 1976 | 1,009—Chipper Jones | 641 (1987)<br>Fewest—414 (1968) |
| Strikeouts | 147—Andruw Jones, 154 G, 2004<br>Fewest—35—Felix Millan, 162 G, 1969 | 1,581—Dale Murphy | 1,160 (1997)<br>Fewest—665 (1969) |
| Hit by pitch | 25—Andres Galarraga, 153 G, 1998 | 75—Jeff Blauser | 61 (1998)<br>Fewest—17 (1977, 1983) |
| Runs batted in | 132—Gary Sheffield, 155 G, 2003 | 1,143—Dale Murphy | 872 (2003)<br>Fewest—480 (1968) |
| Grounded into double plays | 24—Dale Murphy, 156 G, 1988<br>Andruw Jones, 154 G, 2004<br>Fewest—1—Rafael Furcal, 156 G, 2003 | 170—Dale Murphy | 154 (1985)<br>Fewest—82 (1992) |
| Left on base | | | 1,213 (1974)<br>Fewest—1,038 (1988) |
| Batting average | .366—Rico Carty, 136 G, 1970 | .317—Ralph Garr | .284 (2003)<br>Lowest—.234 (1989) |
| Most .300 hitters | | | 4 (2003) |
| Slugging average | .669—Hank Aaron, 139 G, 1971 | .567—Hank Aaron | .475 (2003)<br>Lowest—.334 (1976) |
| On-base percentage | .454—Rico Carty, 136 G, 1970 | .401—Chipper Jones | .349 (2003)<br>Lowest—.298 (1989) |

## BASERUNNING

| | Individual Season | Career | Club Season |
|---|---|---|---|
| Stolen bases | 72—Otis Nixon, 124 G, 1991 | 189—Rafael Furcal | 165 (1991) |
| Caught stealing | 23—Brett Butler, 151 G, 1983 | 83—Jerry Royster | 88 (1983) |

## PITCHING

| | Individual Season | Career | Club Season |
|---|---|---|---|
| Games | 84—Chris Reitsma, 2004 | 689—Phil Niekro | |
| Games started | 44—Phil Niekro, 1979 | 594—Phil Niekro | |
| Complete games | 23—Phil Niekro, 1979 | 226—Phil Niekro | 46 (1974) |
| Wins | 24—John Smoltz, 1996 | 266—Phil Niekro | |
| Percentage | .905—Greg Maddux (19-2), 1995 | .688—Greg Maddux | |
| Winning streak | 14—John Smoltz, 1996 | | |
| 20-win seasons | | 5—Tom Glavine | |
| Losses | 20—Phil Niekro, 1977, 1979 | 227—Phil Niekro | |
| Losing streak | 9—Tommy Boggs, 1981<br>Marty Clary, 1990 | | |
| Losing streak, two seasons | 11—Jim Acker, 1986 (6), 1987 (5) | | |
| Saves | 55—John Smoltz, 2002 | 154—John Smoltz | 57 (2002) |
| Innings | 342—Phil Niekro, 1979 | 4,533—Phil Niekro | 1,474.2 (1968, 1971) |
| Hits | 315—Phil Niekro, 1977 | 4,136—Phil Niekro | 1,581 (1977) |
| Runs | 166—Phil Niekro, 1977 | 1,880—Phil Niekro | 895 (1977) |
| Earned runs | 148—Phil Niekro, 1977 | 1,613—Phil Niekro | 779 (1977) |
| Bases on balls | 164—Phil Niekro, 1977 | 1,425—Phil Niekro | 701 (1977) |
| Strikeouts | 276—John Smoltz, 1996 | 2,855—Phil Niekro | 1,245 (1996) |
| Strikeouts, game | 15—John Smoltz, May 24, 1992<br>John Smoltz, Apr 10, 2005 | | |
| Hit batsmen | 13—Phil Niekro, 1978 | 104—Phil Niekro | 45 (1979) |
| Wild pitches | 27—Tony Cloninger, 1966 | 190—Phil Niekro | 83 (1966) |
| Home runs | 41—Phil Niekro, 1979 | 386—Phil Niekro | 185 (1970) |

| | Individual | | Club |
|---|---|---|---|
| | Season | Career | Season |
| **Sacrifice hits** | 22—Tom Glavine, 1999 | 193—Phil Niekro | 107 (1975) |
| **Sacrifice flies** | 12—Tony Cloninger, 1966<br>Carl Morton, 1974 | 84—Tom Glavine | 60 (1973) |
| **Earned run average** | 1.56—Greg Maddux, 202 inn, 1994 | 2.63—Greg Maddux | 2.92 (1968) |
| **Shutouts** | 6—Phil Niekro, 1974 | 43—Phil Niekro | 24 (1992)<br>Lost—24 (1978) |
| **1-0 games won** | 2—Phil Niekro, 1969<br>Greg Maddux, 1995, 2001 | 6—Greg Maddux<br>Phil Niekro | 7 (1974)<br>Lost—4 (1988, 1989) |

## TEAM FIELDING

**Putouts** 4,424 (1971)
Fewest—4,223 (1979)
**Chances accepted** 6,400 (1985)
Fewest—5,970 (1969)
**Double plays** 197 (1985)
Fewest—114 (1969)
**Errorless games** 97 (1998, 2005)
Consecutive—11 (2005)

**Assists** 2,028 (1985)
Fewest—1,635 (1969)
**Errors** 183 (1979)
Fewest—86 (2005)
**Passed balls** 42 (1967)
Fewest—6 (1983)
**Fielding average** .986 (2005)
Lowest—.970 (1979)

## MISCELLANEOUS

**Most players, season** 47 (2000, 2001)
**Fewest players, season** 32 (1980)
**Games won** 106 (1998)
**Month** 21 (May 1988, Aug 1999, June 2002)
**Consecutive** 15 (2000)
**Winning percentage** .654 (1998), 106-56
**Lowest** .338 (1988), 54-106
**Number of league championships** 5
**Most recent** 1999
**Runs, game** 20 vs Colorado, Apr 18, 1999
vs Florida, Oct 5, 2001
**Opponents'** 23 by Cincinnati, Apr 25, 1977
by San Francisco, June 8, 1990
**Hits, game** 25 vs Cincinnati, May 1, 1985
**Home runs, game** 7 vs Chicago, Aug 3, 1967
**Runs, shutout** 18 vs Florida, Oct 3, 1999
**Opponents'** 19 by Montreal, July 30, 1978
**Longest 1-0 win** 13 inn, vs St. Louis, May 16, 1997

**Most seasons, non-pitcher** 15—Dale Murphy
**Most seasons, pitcher** 19—Phil Niekro
**Games lost** 106 (1988)
**Month** 21 (May 1976)
**Consecutive** 17 (1977)
**Overall record** 3,269-3,068 (40 seasons)
**Interleague play** 86-65
**Number of times worst record in league** 4
**Most recent** 1990
**Runs, inning** 13 vs Houston, Sept 20, 1972, 2nd

**Total bases, game** 46 vs Chicago, Apr 15, 1994
**Consecutive games with one or more home runs** 25 (45 HRs), 1998
**Longest shutout** 16 inn, 3-0 vs Chicago, Sept 22, 1975

**Longest 1-0 loss** 13 inn, vs Los Angeles, May 18, 1974
13 inn, vs St. Louis, May 20, 1989

## ATTENDANCE

**Highest home attendance**
**Atlanta-Fulton County Stadium** 3,884,725 (1993)
**Turner Field** 3,464,488 (1997)

**Highest road attendance** 2,944,157 (1993)

**Largest crowds**
**Day** 51,638 vs Philadelphia, Apr 1, 2002
**Night** 53,775 vs Los Angeles, Apr 8, 1974
**Doubleheader** 50,597 vs Chicago, July 4, 1972
**Home opener** 53,775 vs Los Angeles, Apr 8, 1974

# BOSTON BRAVES

## YEARLY FINISHES

**(Original National League franchise moved to Milwaukee after the 1952 season)**

| Year | Position | W | L | Pct. | GB | Manager | Attendance |
|---|---|---|---|---|---|---|---|
| 1876 | 4th | 39 | 31 | .557 | 15.0 | Harry Wright | 51,000 |
| 1877 | 1st | 42 | 18 | .700 | +7.0 | Harry Wright | 55,240 |
| 1878 | 1st | 41 | 19 | .683 | +4.0 | Harry Wright | 48,915 |
| 1879 | 2nd | 54 | 30 | .643 | 5.0 | Harry Wright | 36,501 |
| 1880 | 6th | 40 | 44 | .476 | 27.0 | Harry Wright | 34,000 |
| 1881 | 6th | 38 | 45 | .458 | 17.5 | Harry Wright | 34,343 |
| 1882 | 3rd (tied) | 45 | 39 | .536 | 10.0 | John Morrill | 50,971 |
| 1883 | 1st | 63 | 35 | .643 | +4.0 | Jack Burdock, John Morrill | 128,968 |
| 1884 | 2nd | 73 | 38 | .658 | 10.5 | John Morrill | 146,777 |
| 1885 | 5th | 46 | 66 | .411 | 41.0 | John Morrill | 110,290 |
| 1886 | 5th | 56 | 61 | .479 | 30.5 | John Morrill | 133,683 |
| 1887 | 5th | 61 | 06 | .504 | 16.5 | John Morrill | 261,000 |
| 1888 | 4th | 70 | 64 | .522 | 15.5 | John Morrill | 265,015 |
| 1889 | 2nd | 83 | 45 | .648 | 1.0 | Jim Hart | 283,257 |
| 1890 | 5th | 76 | 57 | .571 | 12.0 | Frank Selee | 147,539 |
| 1891 | 1st | 87 | 51 | .630 | +3.5 | Frank Selee | 184,472 |
| 1892 | 1st/2nd (C) | 102 | 48 | .680 | ** | Frank Selee | 146,421 |
| 1893 | 1st | 86 | 43 | .667 | +5.0 | Frank Selee | 193,300 |
| 1894 | 3rd | 83 | 49 | .629 | 8.0 | Frank Selee | 152,800 |
| 1895 | 5th (tied) | 71 | 60 | .542 | 16.5 | Frank Selee | 242,000 |
| 1896 | 4th | 74 | 57 | .565 | 17.0 | Frank Selee | 240,000 |
| 1897 | 1st (T) | 93 | 39 | .705 | +2.0 | Frank Selee | 334,800 |
| 1898 | 1st | 102 | 47 | .685 | +6.0 | Frank Selee | 229,275 |
| 1899 | 2nd | 95 | 57 | .625 | 8.0 | Frank Selee | 200,384 |
| 1900 | 4th | 66 | 72 | .478 | 17.0 | Frank Selee | 190,000 |
| 1901 | 5th | 69 | 69 | .500 | 20.5 | Frank Selee | 146,502 |
| 1902 | 3rd | 73 | 64 | .533 | 29.0 | Al Buckenberger | 116,960 |
| 1903 | 6th | 58 | 80 | .420 | 32.0 | Al Buckenberger | 143,155 |

| Year | Position | W | L | Pct. | GB | Manager | Attendance |
|---|---|---|---|---|---|---|---|
| 1904 | 7th | 55 | 98 | .359 | 51.0 | Al Buckenberger | 140,694 |
| 1905 | 7th | 51 | 103 | .331 | 54.5 | Fred Tenney | 150,003 |
| 1906 | 8th | 49 | 102 | .325 | 66.5 | Fred Tenney | 143,280 |
| 1907 | 7th | 58 | 90 | .392 | 47.0 | Fred Tenney | 203,221 |
| 1908 | 6th | 63 | 91 | .409 | 36.0 | Joe Kelley | 253,750 |
| 1909 | 8th | 45 | 108 | .294 | 65.5 | Frank Bowerman, Harry Smith | 195,188 |
| 1910 | 8th | 53 | 100 | .346 | 50.5 | Fred Lake | 149,027 |
| 1911 | 8th | 44 | 107 | .291 | 54.0 | Fred Tenney | 116,000 |
| 1912 | 8th | 52 | 101 | .340 | 52.0 | Johnny Kling | 121,000 |
| 1913 | 5th | 69 | 82 | .457 | 31.5 | George Stallings | 208,000 |
| 1914 | 1st (S) | 94 | 59 | .614 | +10.5 | George Stallings | 382,913 |
| 1915 | 2nd | 83 | 69 | .546 | 7.0 | George Stallings | 376,283 |
| 1916 | 3rd | 89 | 63 | .586 | 4.0 | George Stallings | 313,495 |
| 1917 | 6th | 72 | 81 | .471 | 25.5 | George Stallings | 174,253 |
| 1918 | 7th | 53 | 71 | .427 | 28.5 | George Stallings | 84,938 |
| 1919 | 6th | 57 | 82 | .410 | 38.5 | George Stallings | 167,401 |
| 1920 | 7th | 62 | 90 | .408 | 30.0 | George Stallings | 162,483 |
| 1921 | 4th | 79 | 74 | .516 | 15.0 | Fred Mitchell | 318,627 |
| 1922 | 8th | 53 | 100 | .346 | 39.5 | Fred Mitchell | 167,965 |
| 1923 | 7th | 54 | 100 | .351 | 41.5 | Fred Mitchell | 227,802 |
| 1924 | 8th | 53 | 100 | .346 | 40.0 | Dave Bancroft | 117,478 |
| 1925 | 5th | 70 | 83 | .458 | 25.0 | Dave Bancroft | 313,528 |
| 1926 | 7th | 66 | 86 | .434 | 22.0 | Dave Bancroft | 303,598 |
| 1927 | 7th | 60 | 94 | .390 | 34.0 | Dave Bancroft | 288,685 |
| 1928 | 7th | 50 | 103 | .327 | 44.5 | Jack Slattery, Rogers Hornsby | 227,001 |
| 1929 | 8th | 56 | 98 | .364 | 43.0 | Emil Fuchs | 372,351 |
| 1930 | 6th | 70 | 84 | .455 | 22.0 | Bill McKechnie | 464,835 |
| 1931 | 7th | 64 | 90 | .416 | 37.0 | Bill McKechnie | 515,005 |
| 1932 | 5th | 77 | 77 | .500 | 13.0 | Bill McKechnie | 507,606 |
| 1933 | 4th | 83 | 71 | .539 | 9.0 | Bill McKechnie | 517,803 |
| 1934 | 4th | 78 | 73 | .517 | 16.0 | Bill McKechnie | 303,205 |
| 1935 | 8th | 38 | 115 | .248 | 61.5 | Bill McKechnie | 232,754 |
| 1936 | 6th | 71 | 83 | .461 | 21.0 | Bill McKechnie | 340,585 |
| 1937 | 5th | 79 | 73 | .520 | 16.0 | Bill McKechnie | 385,339 |
| 1938 | 5th | 77 | 75 | .507 | 12.0 | Casey Stengel | 341,149 |
| 1939 | 7th | 63 | 88 | .417 | 32.5 | Casey Stengel | 285,994 |
| 1940 | 7th | 65 | 87 | .428 | 34.5 | Casey Stengel | 241,616 |
| 1941 | 7th | 62 | 92 | .403 | 38.0 | Casey Stengel | 263,680 |
| 1942 | 7th | 59 | 89 | .399 | 44.0 | Casey Stengel | 285,332 |
| 1943 | 6th | 68 | 85 | .444 | 36.5 | Casey Stengel | 271,289 |
| 1944 | 6th | 65 | 89 | .422 | 40.0 | Bob Coleman | 208,691 |
| 1945 | 6th | 67 | 85 | .441 | 30.0 | Bob Coleman, Del Bissonette | 374,178 |
| 1946 | 4th | 81 | 72 | .529 | 15.5 | Billy Southworth | 969,673 |
| 1947 | 3rd | 86 | 68 | .558 | 8.0 | Billy Southworth | 1,277,361 |
| 1948 | 1st (s) | 91 | 62 | .595 | +6.5 | Billy Southworth | 1,455,439 |
| 1949 | 4th | 75 | 79 | .487 | 22.0 | Billy Southworth | 1,081,795 |
| 1950 | 4th | 83 | 71 | .539 | 8.0 | Billy Southworth | 944,391 |
| 1951 | 4th | 76 | 78 | .494 | 20.5 | Billy Southworth, Tommy Holmes | 487,475 |
| 1952 | 7th | 64 | 89 | .418 | 32.0 | Tommy Holmes, Charlie Grimm | 281,278 |

**first half 52-22; second half 50-26; (C) won championship series; (T) won Temple Cup; (S) won World Series; (s) lost World Series

## INDIVIDUAL AND CLUB RECORDS

### BATTING

| | Individual Season | Individual Career | Club Season |
|---|---|---|---|
| **Games** | 158—Ed Konetchy, 1916 | 1,795—Rabbit Maranville | 158 (1914, 1916) |
| **At-bats** | 647—Herman Long, 151 G, 1892<br>*637—Gene Moore, 151 G, 1936 | 6,764—Herman Long<br>*6,724—Rabbit Maranville | 5,506 (1932) |
| **Runs** | 160—Hugh Duffy, 125 G, 1894<br>*125—Tommy Holmes, 154 G, 1945 | 1,294—Herman Long<br>*801—Rabbit Maranville<br>Fewest—408 (1906) | 1,220 (1894)<br>*785 (1950) |
| **Hits** | 236—Hugh Duffy, 125 G, 1894<br>*224—Tommy Holmes, 154 G, 1945 | 2,002—Fred Tenney<br>*1,696—Rabbit Maranville | 1,567 (1925)<br>Fewest—1,115 (1906) |
| **Hitting streak** | 37 G—Tommy Holmes, 1945 | | |
| **Singles** | 172—Fred Tenney, 150 G, 1899<br>*166—Lance Richbourg, 148 G, 1928 | 1,661—Fred Tenney<br>*1,326—Rabbit Maranville | 1,196 (1925) |
| **Doubles** | 50—Hugh Duffy, 125 G, 1894<br>*47—Tommy Holmes, 154 G, 1945 | 295—Herman Long<br>*291—Tommy Holmes | 272 (1948) |
| **Triples** | 20—Dick Johnston, 124 G, 1887<br>*18—Ray Powell, 149 G, 1921 | 103—Rabbit Maranville | 100 (1921) |

### HOME RUNS

| | Individual Season | Individual Career | Club Season |
|---|---|---|---|
| | | | 148 (1950)<br>Fewest—2 (1878) *14 (1902, 1909) |
| **Righthander** | 38—Wally Berger, 151 G, 1930 | 199—Wally Berger | |
| **Lefthander** | 28—Tommy Holmes, 154 G, 1945 | 88—Herman Long<br>Tommy Holmes | |
| **Switch-hitter** | 18—Sam Jethroe, 141 G, 1950<br>Sam Jethroe, 148 G, 1951 | 49—Sam Jethroe | |
| **Rookie** | 38—Wally Berger, 151 G, 1930 | | |
| **Home** | 19—Chuck Workman, 1945 | 103—Wally Berger | 77 (1894) *69 (1945) |
| **Road** | 22—Sid Gordon, 1950 | 96—Wally Berger | 89 (1950) |
| **Month** | 11—Wally Berger, May 1930 | | 33 (June 1950) |
| **Pinch** | 5—Butch Nieman, 1945 | 5—Butch Nieman | 6 (1945) |

| | Individual Season | Individual Career | Club Season |
|---|---|---|---|
| Grand slams | 4—Sid Gordon, 134 G, 1950 | 6—Wally Berger | 7 (1950) |
| Home runs at South End Grounds, all teams | | | 147 (1894) |
| Home runs at Braves Field, all teams | | | 131 (1945) |
| Total bases | 374—Hugh Duffy, 125 G, 1894<br>*367—Tommy Holmes, 154 G, 1945 | 2,629—Herman Long<br>*2,215—Rabbit Maranville | 2,173 (1950) |
| Extra-base hits | 81—Hugh Duffy, 125 G, 1894<br>Tommy Holmes, 154 G, 1945 | 499—Wally Berger | 430 (1950) |
| Sacrifice hits | 31—Freddie Maguire, 148 G, 1931 | 244—Fred Tenney<br>*220—Rabbit Maranville | 140 (1948) |
| Bases on balls | 131—Bob Elliott, 151 G, 1948 | 750—Fred Tenney<br>*561—Rabbit Maranville | 684 (1949)<br>Fewest—35 (1878) *302 (1905) |
| Strikeouts | 134—Vince DiMaggio, 150 G, 1938<br>Fewest—9—Tommy Holmes, 154 G, 1945 | 632—John Morrill<br>*544—Wally Berger | 711 (1952)<br>Fewest—348 (1926) |
| Hit by pitch | 11—Sam Jethroe, 148 G, 1951 | 150—Tommy Tucker<br>*45—Fred Tenney | 45 (1917)<br>Fewest—13 (1941) |
| Runs batted in | 130—Wally Berger, 150 G, 1935 | 746—Wally Berger | 1,043 (1894) *726 (1950)<br>Fewest—330 (1906) |
| Grounded into double plays | 28—Sid Gordon, 150 G, 1951<br>Fewest—4—Vince DiMaggio, 150 G, 1938 | 95—Tommy Holmes | 146 (1936)<br>Fewest—93 (1944) |
| Left on base | | | 1,255 (1948)<br>Fewest—1,003 (1933) |
| Batting average | .438—Hugh Duffy, 125 G, 1894<br>*.387—Rogers Hornsby, 140 G, 1928 | .338—Billy Hamilton<br>*.311—Lance Richbourg | .292 (1925)<br>Lowest—.223 (1909) |
| Most .300 hitters | | | 8 (1931) |
| Slugging average | .694—Hugh Duffy, 125 G, 1894<br>*.632—Rogers Hornsby, 140 G, 1928 | .533—Wally Berger | .405 (1950)<br>Lowest—.274 (1909) |
| On-base percentage | .502—Hugh Duffy, 125 G, 1894<br>*.498—Rogers Hornsby, 140 G, 1928 | unknown | .401 (1894) *.359 (1948)<br>Lowest—.253 (1878) *.284 (1905) |

## BASERUNNING

| | Individual Season | Individual Career | Club Season |
|---|---|---|---|
| Stolen bases | 93—Billy Hamilton, 131 G, 1896<br>*57—Hap Myers, 140 G, 1913 | 431—Herman Long<br>*194—Rabbit Maranville | 189 (1902) |
| Caught stealing | 20—Billy Southworth, 141 G, 1921 | unknown | 100 (1921) |

## PITCHING

| | Individual Season | Individual Career | Club Season |
|---|---|---|---|
| Games | 73—John Clarkson, 1889<br>*57—Johnny Hutchings, 1945 | 557—Kid Nichols<br>*349—Bob Smith | |
| Games started | 72—John Clarkson, 1889<br>*46—Vic Willis, 1902 | 502—Kid Nichols<br>*239—Dick Rudolph | |
| Complete games | 68—John Clarkson, 1889<br>*45—Vic Willis, 1902 | 477—Kid Nichols<br>*204—Vic Willis | 142 (1892) *139 (1905) |
| Wins | 49—John Clarkson, 1889<br>*27—Togie Pittinger, 1902<br>Vic Willis, 1902 | 329—Kid Nichols<br>*122—Warren Spahn | |
| Percentage | .842—Tom Hughes (16-3), 1916 | .647—John Clarkson<br>*.573—Warren Spahn | |
| Winning streak | 13—Charlie Buffinton, 1884<br>Fred Klobedanz, 1897<br>Ted Lewis, 1898<br>*11—Dick Rudolph, 1914 | | |
| Winning streak, two seasons | 13—Charlie Buffinton, 1883 (5), 1884 (8)<br>Harry Staley, 1891 (5), 1892 (8)<br>Bill James, 1914 (10), 1915 (3) | | |
| 20-win seasons | | 4—Johnny Sain<br>Warren Spahn | |
| Losses | 33—Jim Whitney, 1881<br>*29—Vic Willis, 1905 | 180—Kid Nichols<br>*129—Vic Willis | |
| Losing streak | 18—Cliff Curtis, 1910 | | |
| Innings | 620—John Clarkson, 1889<br>*410—Vic Willis, 1902 | 4,538—Kid Nichols<br>*2,035—Dick Rudolph | 1,424.2 (1917) |
| Hits | 628—Hoss Radbourn, 1887<br>*396—Togie Pittinger, 1903 | 4,434—Kid Nichols<br>*2,010—Bob Smith | 1,662 (1923) |
| Runs | 308—Kid Nichols, 1894<br>*205—Togie Pittinger, 1903 | 2,270—Kid Nichols<br>*947—Bob Smith | 1,021 (1911) |
| Earned runs | 215—Hoss Radbourn, 1887<br>Kid Nichols, 1894<br>*136—Togie Pittinger, 1903 | 1,511—Kid Nichols<br>*818—Bob Smith | 776 (1911) |
| Bases on balls | 203—John Clarkson, 1889<br>*149—Chick Fraser, 1905 | 1,159—Kid Nichols<br>*678—Lefty Tyler | 672 (1911) |

| | Individual Season | Career | Club Season |
|---|---|---|---|
| **Strikeouts** | 417—Charlie Buffinton, 1884<br>*225—Vic Willis, 1902 | 1,672—Kid Nichols<br>*1,000—Warren Spahn | 742 (1884) *687 (1952) |
| **Strikeouts, game** | 13—Vic Willis, May 28, 1902<br>Warren Spahn, Sept 13, 1952<br>[18—Warren Spahn, June 14, 1952, 15 inn] | | |
| **Hit batsmen** | 30—Vic Willis, 1898, 1899<br>*17—Togie Pittinger, 1903 | 134—Vic Willis<br>*74—Vic Willis | 69 (1899) *68 (1907) |
| **Wild pitches** | 63—Bill Stemmeyer, 1886<br>*14—Togie Pittinger, 1903 | 162—Jim Whitney<br>*53—Vic Willis | 95 (1886) *50 (1904) |
| **Home runs** | 34—Johnny Sain, 1950 | 151—Kid Nichols<br>*128—Warren Spahn | 129 (1950) |
| **Sacrifice hits** | 45—Bob Smith, 1927 | 227—Dick Rudolph | 239 (1927) |
| **Earned run average** | 1.90—Bill James, 332.1 inn, 1914 | 2.21—Tommy Bond<br>*2.62—Dick Rudolph | 2.15 (1877) *2.19 (1916) |
| **Shutouts** | 11—Tommy Bond, 1879<br>*7—Togie Pittinger, 1902<br>Irv Young, 1905<br>Warren Spahn, 1947, 1951 | 44—Kid Nichols<br>*27—Dick Rudolph<br>Warren Spahn | 23 (1916)<br>Lost—28 (1906) |
| **1-0 games won** | 4—Dick Rudolph, 1916<br>Joe Oeschger, 1920 | 10—Kid Nichols<br>*10—Dick Rudolph | 9 (1916)<br>Lost—6 (1906, 1933) |

## TEAM FIELDING

**Putouts** 4,262 (1914)
Fewest—3,975 (1906)

**Chances accepted** 6,424 (1914)
Fewest—5,750 (1935)

**Double plays** 178 (1939)
Fewest—101 (1935)

**Errorless games** unknown
Consecutive—5 (1933, twice)

**Assists** 2,225 (1908)
Fewest—1,665 (1946)

**Errors** 353 (1904)
Fewest—138 (1933)

**Passed balls** 167 (1883) *42 (1905)
Fewest—2 (1943)

**Fielding average** .978 (1933)
Lowest—.945 (1904)

## MISCELLANEOUS

**Most players, season** 48 (1946)

**Fewest players, season** 23 (1905)

**Games won** 102 (1892, 1898) *94 (1914)
**Month** 26 (Sept 1914)
**Consecutive** 18 (1891) *9 (1902, 1914 twice, 1945)

**Winning percentage** .705 (1897), 93-39 *.614 (1914), 94-59
**Lowest** .248 (1935), 38-115

**Number of league championships** 10
**Most recent** 1948

**Runs, game** 30 vs Detroit, June 9, 1883
*20 vs Philadelphia, June 25, 1900
vs Philadelphia, Oct 6, 1910
vs St. Louis, Sept 18, 1915, 1st game
vs St. Louis, Aug 25, 1936, 1st game

**Opponents'** 27 by Pittsburgh, June 6, 1894
*26 by Cincinnati, June 4, 1911

**Hits, game** 32 vs St. Louis, Sept 3, 1896, 1st game
*25 vs St. Louis, Aug 25, 1936, 1st game

**Home runs, game** 5 vs Cincinnati, May 30, 1894, p.m. game
vs Chicago, May 13, 1942
vs Cincinnati, May 6, 1950

**Runs, shutout** 18 vs Buffalo, Oct 3, 1885
*16 vs Brooklyn, May 7, 1918
vs Pittsburgh, Sept 12, 1952, 2nd game

**Opponents'** 17 by Chicago, Sept 16, 1884
*15, seven times; last by St. Louis, May 7, 1950

**Longest 1-0 win** 13 inn, six times; last vs Brooklyn, May 4, 1923

**Most seasons, non-pitcher** 15—Fred Tenney
Rabbit Maranville
Johnny Cooney

**Most seasons, pitcher** 12—Kid Nichols *11—Dick Rudolph

**Games lost** 115 (1935)
**Month** 25 (Sept 1928, Sept 1935)
**Consecutive** 19 (1906)

**Overall record** 5,118-5,598 (77 seasons)

**Number of times worst record in league** 9
**Most recent** 1935

**Runs, inning** 16 vs Baltimore, June 18, 1894, a.m. game, 1st
*13 vs St. Louis, July 25, 1900, 1st

**Total bases, game** 46 vs Detroit, June 9, 1883
vs Cleveland, July 5, 1984
*37 vs Philadelphia, July 6, 1934
vs Cincinnati, May 6, 1950

**Consecutive games with one or more home runs** unknown

**Longest shutout** unknown

**Longest 1-0 loss** 17 inn vs Chicago, Sept 21, 1901

## ATTENDANCE

**Highest home attendance**
**South End Grounds** 334,800 (1897)
**Braves Field** 1,455,439 (1948)

**Highest road attendance** 1,308,175 (1947)

**Largest crowds**
**Day** 41,527 vs Chicago, Aug 8, 1948
**Night** 39,549 vs Brooklyn, Aug 5, 1946
**Doubleheader** 47,123 vs Philadelphia, May 22, 1932
**Home opener** 25,000 vs New York, Apr 16, 1935

*records made since 1900 that do not exceed pre-1900 records

# BROOKLYN DODGERS

## YEARLY FINISHES

(American Association franchise moved to the National League after the 1889 season)

| Year | Position | W | L | Pct. | GB | Manager | Attendance |
|---|---|---|---|---|---|---|---|
| 1890 | 1st | 86 | 43 | .667 | +6.0 | Bill McGunnigle | 121,412 |
| 1891 | 6th | 71 | 76 | .445 | 25.5 | John Montgomery Ward | 181,477 |
| 1892 | 2nd/3rd | 95 | 59 | .617 | ** | John Montgomery Ward | 183,727 |
| 1893 | 6th (tied) | 65 | 63 | .508 | 20.5 | Dave Foutz | 235,000 |
| 1894 | 5th | 70 | 61 | .534 | 20.5 | Dave Foutz | 214,000 |
| 1895 | 5th (tied) | 71 | 60 | .542 | 16.5 | Dave Foutz | 230,000 |
| 1896 | 9th (tied) | 58 | 73 | .443 | 33.0 | Dave Foutz | 201,000 |
| 1897 | 6th (tied) | 61 | 71 | .462 | 32.0 | Billy Barnie | 220,831 |
| 1898 | 10th | 54 | 91 | .372 | 46.0 | Billy Barnie, Mike Griffin, Charlie Ebbets | 122,514 |
| 1899 | 1st | 101 | 47 | .682 | +8.0 | Ned Hanlon | 269,641 |
| 1900 | 1st (C) | 82 | 54 | .603 | +4.5 | Ned Hanlon | 170,000 |
| 1901 | 3rd | 79 | 57 | .581 | 9.5 | Ned Hanlon | 189,200 |
| 1902 | 2nd | 75 | 63 | .543 | 27.5 | Ned Hanlon | 199,868 |
| 1903 | 5th | 70 | 66 | .515 | 19.0 | Ned Hanlon | 224,670 |
| 1904 | 6th | 56 | 97 | .366 | 50.0 | Ned Hanlon | 214,600 |
| 1905 | 8th | 48 | 104 | .316 | 56.5 | Ned Hanlon | 227,924 |
| 1906 | 5th | 66 | 86 | .434 | 50.0 | Patsy Donovan | 227,400 |
| 1907 | 5th | 65 | 83 | .439 | 40.0 | Patsy Donovan | 312,500 |
| 1908 | 7th | 53 | 101 | .344 | 46.0 | Patsy Donovan | 275,600 |
| 1909 | 6th | 55 | 98 | .359 | 55.5 | Harry Lumley | 321,300 |
| 1910 | 6th | 64 | 90 | .416 | 40.0 | Bill Dahlen | 279,321 |
| 1911 | 7th | 64 | 86 | .427 | 33.5 | Bill Dahlen | 269,000 |
| 1912 | 7th | 58 | 95 | .379 | 46.0 | Bill Dahlen | 243,000 |
| 1913 | 6th | 65 | 84 | .436 | 34.5 | Bill Dahlen | 347,000 |
| 1914 | 5th | 75 | 79 | .487 | 19.5 | Wilbert Robinson | 122,671 |
| 1915 | 3rd | 80 | 72 | .526 | 10.0 | Wilbert Robinson | 297,766 |
| 1916 | 1st | 94 | 60 | .610 | +2.5 | Wilbert Robinson | 447,747 |
| 1917 | 7th | 70 | 81 | .464 | 26.5 | Wilbert Robinson | 221,619 |
| 1918 | 5th | 57 | 69 | .452 | 25.5 | Wilbert Robinson | 83,831 |
| 1919 | 5th | 69 | 71 | .493 | 27.0 | Wilbert Robinson | 360,721 |
| 1920 | 1st (s) | 93 | 61 | .604 | +7.0 | Wilbert Robinson | 808,722 |
| 1921 | 5th | 77 | 75 | .507 | 16.5 | Wilbert Robinson | 613,245 |
| 1922 | 6th | 76 | 78 | .494 | 17.0 | Wilbert Robinson | 498,856 |
| 1923 | 6th | 76 | 78 | .494 | 19.5 | Wilbert Robinson | 564,666 |
| 1924 | 2nd | 92 | 62 | .597 | 1.5 | Wilbert Robinson | 818,883 |
| 1925 | 6th (tied) | 68 | 85 | .444 | 27.0 | Wilbert Robinson | 659,435 |
| 1926 | 6th | 71 | 82 | .464 | 17.5 | Wilbert Robinson | 650,819 |
| 1927 | 6th | 65 | 88 | .425 | 28.5 | Wilbert Robinson | 637,230 |
| 1928 | 6th | 77 | 76 | .503 | 17.5 | Wilbert Robinson | 664,863 |
| 1929 | 6th | 70 | 83 | .458 | 28.5 | Wilbert Robinson | 731,886 |
| 1930 | 4th | 86 | 68 | .558 | 6.0 | Wilbert Robinson | 1,097,339 |
| 1931 | 4th | 79 | 73 | .520 | 21.0 | Wilbert Robinson | 753,133 |
| 1932 | 3rd | 81 | 73 | .526 | 9.0 | Max Carey | 681,827 |
| 1933 | 6th | 65 | 88 | .425 | 26.5 | Max Carey | 526,815 |
| 1934 | 6th | 71 | 81 | .467 | 23.5 | Casey Stengel | 434,188 |
| 1935 | 5th | 70 | 83 | .458 | 29.5 | Casey Stengel | 470,517 |
| 1936 | 7th | 67 | 87 | .435 | 25.0 | Casey Stengel | 489,618 |
| 1937 | 6th | 62 | 91 | .405 | 33.5 | Burleigh Grimes | 482,481 |
| 1938 | 7th | 69 | 80 | .463 | 18.5 | Burleigh Grimes | 663,087 |
| 1939 | 3rd | 84 | 69 | .549 | 12.5 | Leo Durocher | 955,668 |
| 1940 | 2nd | 88 | 65 | .575 | 12.0 | Leo Durocher | 975,978 |
| 1941 | 1st (s) | 100 | 54 | .649 | +2.5 | Leo Durocher | 1,214,910 |
| 1942 | 2nd | 104 | 50 | .675 | 2.0 | Leo Durocher | 1,037,765 |
| 1943 | 3rd | 81 | 72 | .529 | 23.5 | Leo Durocher | 661,739 |
| 1944 | 7th | 63 | 91 | .409 | 42.0 | Leo Durocher | 605,905 |
| 1945 | 3rd | 87 | 67 | .565 | 11.0 | Leo Durocher | 1,059,220 |
| 1946 | 2nd (l) | 96 | 60 | .615 | 2.0 | Leo Durocher | 1,796,824 |
| 1947 | 1st (s) | 94 | 60 | .610 | +5.0 | Clyde Sukeforth, Burt Shotton | 1,807,526 |
| 1948 | 3rd | 84 | 70 | .545 | 7.5 | Leo Durocher, Burt Shotton | 1,398,967 |
| 1949 | 1st (s) | 97 | 57 | .630 | +1.0 | Burt Shotton | 1,633,747 |
| 1950 | 2nd | 89 | 65 | .578 | 2.0 | Burt Shotton | 1,185,896 |
| 1951 | 2nd (l) | 97 | 60 | .618 | 1.0 | Chuck Dressen | 1,282,628 |
| 1952 | 1st (s) | 96 | 57 | .627 | +4.5 | Chuck Dressen | 1,088,704 |
| 1953 | 1st (s) | 105 | 49 | .682 | +13.0 | Chuck Dressen | 1,163,419 |
| 1954 | 2nd | 92 | 62 | .597 | 5.0 | Walter Alston | 1,020,531 |
| 1955 | 1st (S) | 98 | 55 | .641 | +13.5 | Walter Alston | 1,033,589 |
| 1956 | 1st (s) | 93 | 61 | .604 | +1.0 | Walter Alston | 1,213,562 |
| 1957 | 3rd | 84 | 70 | .545 | 11.0 | Walter Alston | 1,028,258 |

**first half 51-26, second half 44-33; (C) won Chronicle-Telegraph Cup; (s) lost World Series; (l) lost league playoff; (S) won World Series

## INDIVIDUAL AND CLUB RECORDS

### BATTING

| | Individual Season | Individual Career | Club Season |
|---|---|---|---|
| Games | 158—Carl Furillo, 1951<br>Gil Hodges, 1951 | 2,318—Zack Wheat | 158 (1892, 1951) |
| At-bats | 667—Carl Furillo, 158 G, 1951 | 8,859—Zack Wheat | 5,574 (1936) |
| Runs | 148—Hub Collins, 129 G, 1890<br>*143—Babe Herman, 153 G, 1930 | 1,317—Pee Wee Reese | 1,021 (1894) *955 (1953)<br>Fewest—375 (1908) |
| Hits | 241—Babe Herman, 153 G, 1930 | 2,804—Zack Wheat | 1,654 (1930)<br>Fewest—1,044 (1908) |

| | Individual Season | Career | Club Season |
|---|---|---|---|
| Hitting streak | 29 G—Zack Wheat, 1916 | | |
| Singles | 188—Willie Keeler, 141 G, 1899<br>*179—Willie Keeler, 137 G, 1900 | 2,038—Zack Wheat | 1,223 (1925) |
| Doubles | 52—Johnny Frederick, 148 G, 1929 | 464—Zack Wheat | 303 (1930) |
| Triples | 26—George Treadway, 124 G, 1894<br>*22—Hy Myers, 154 G, 1920 | 171—Zack Wheat | 130 (1894) *99 (1920) |
| **HOME RUNS** | | | 208 (1953)<br>Fewest—14 (1915) |
| Righthander | 42—Gil Hodges, 154 G, 1954 | 298—Gil Hodges | |
| Lefthander | 43—Duke Snider, 151 G, 1956 | 316—Duke Snider | |
| Switch-hitter | 13—Jim Gilliam, 146 G, 1954 | 44—Tom Daly | |
| Rookie | 25—Del Bissonette, 155 G, 1928 | | |
| Home | 25—Gil Hodges, 1954<br>Duke Snider (inc. 2 at Jersey City), 1956 | 177—Duke Snider | 119 (1955) |
| Road | 24—Gil Hodges, 1951 | 139—Duke Snider | 98 (1953) |
| Month | 15—Duke Snider, Aug 1953 | | 49 (July 1953, Aug 1953) |
| Pinch | 6—Johnny Frederick, 1932 | 8—Johnny Frederick | 7 (1932) |
| Grand slams | 2—many players | 13—Gil Hodges | 8 (1952) |
| Home runs at Ebbets Field, all teams | | | 206 (1950) |
| Total bases | 416—Babe Herman, 153 G, 1930 | 4,003—Zack Wheat | 2,545 (1953) |
| Extra-base hits | 94—Babe Herman, 153 G, 1930 | 766—Zack Wheat | 541 (1953) |
| Sacrifice hits | 39—Jake Daubert, 150 G, 1915 | 237—Jake Daubert | 197 (1907) |
| Sacrifice flies | 19—Gil Hodges, 154 G, 1954 | 37—Gil Hodges | 59 (1954) |
| Bases on balls | 148—Eddie Stanky, 153 G, 1945 | 1,184—Pee Wee Reese | 732 (1947)<br>Fewest—179 (1884) *312 (1901) |
| Strikeouts | 115—Dolf Camilli, 149 G, 1941<br>Fewest—15—Jimmy Johnston, 151 G, 1923 | 875—Pee Wee Reese | 848 (1957)<br>Fewest—255 (1897) *272 (1900) |
| Hit by pitch | 20—Hughie Jennings, 115 G, 1900 | 72—Jackie Robinson | 125 (1899) *81 (1900)<br>Fewest—14 (1942, 1944) |
| Runs batted in | 142—Roy Campanella, 144 G, 1953 | 1,227—Zack Wheat | 887 (1953)<br>Fewest—306 (1908) |
| Grounded into double plays | 27—Carl Furillo, 149 G, 1956<br>Fewest—5—Jackie Robinson, 151 G, 1947<br>Pee Wee Reese, 155 G, 1949<br>Jim Gilliam, 153 G, 1956 | 187—Carl Furillo | 151 (1952)<br>Fewest—87 (1947) |
| Left on base | | | 1,278 (1947)<br>Fewest—1,012 (1921) |
| Batting average | .393—Babe Herman, 153 G, 1930 | .352—Willie Keeler<br>*.339—Babe Herman | .313 (1894) *.304 (1930)<br>Lowest—.213 (1908) |
| Most .300 hitters | | | 6 (1900, 1922, 1925, 1930, 1943, 1953) |
| Slugging average | .678—Babe Herman, 153 G, 1930 | .560—Duke Snider | .474 (1953)<br>Lowest—.277 (1908) |
| On-base percentage | .467—Mike Griffin, 107 G, 1894<br>*.455—Babe Herman, 153 G, 1930 | .409—Jackie Robinson | .378 (1894) *.366 (1953)<br>Lowest—.263 (1884) *.266 (1908) |

## BASERUNNING

| | Individual Season | Career | Club Season |
|---|---|---|---|
| Stolen bases | 91—Darby O'Brien, 136 G, 1889<br>*67—Jimmy Sheckard, 139 G, 1903 | 298—Tom Daly<br>*231—Pee Wee Reese | 409 (1882, 1987)<br>*274 (1900) |
| Caught stealing | 23—George Cutshaw, 154 G, 1915 | 83—Jimmy Johnston | 126 (1915) |

## PITCHING

| | Individual Season | Career | Club Season |
|---|---|---|---|
| Games | 62—Clem Labine, 1956 | 382—Brickyard Kennedy<br>*378—Dazzy Vance | |
| Games started | 56—Adonis Terry, 1884<br>*41—Oscar Jones, 1904 | 333—Brickyard Kennedy<br>*328—Dazzy Vance | |
| Complete games | 55—Adonis Terry, 1884<br>*38—Oscar Jones, 1904 | 280—Brickyard Kennedy<br>*212—Dazzy Vance | 138 (1886, 1888)<br>*135 (1904) |
| Wins | 40—Bob Caruthers, 1889<br>*28—Joe McGinnity, 1900 | 190—Dazzy Vance | |
| Percentage | .889—Freddie Fitzsimmons (16-2), 1940 | .677—Bob Caruthers<br>*672—Don Newcombe | |
| Winning streak | 15—Dazzy Vance, 1924 | | |
| 20-win seasons | | 4—Burleigh Grimes | |
| Losses | 35—Adonis Terry, 1884<br>*27—George Bell, 1910 | 144—Brickyard Kennedy<br>*134—Nap Rucker | |
| Losing streak | 14—Jim Pastorius, 1908 | | |
| Innings | 485—Adonis Terry, 1884<br>*377—Oscar Jones, 1904 | 2,857—Brickyard Kennedy<br>*2,757.2—Dazzy Vance | 1,433 (1940) |
| Hits | 512—Henry Porter, 1887<br>*387—Oscar Jones, 1904 | 3,102—Brickyard Kennedy<br>*2,579—Dazzy Vance | 1,608 (1925) |

| | Individual Season | | Club Season |
|---|---|---|---|
| Runs | 308—Adonis Terry, 1884<br>*188—Harry McIntire, 1905 | 1,772—Brickyard Kennedy<br>*1,175—Burleigh Grimes | 1,007 (1894) *888 (1929) |
| Earned runs | 197—Brickyard Kennedy, 1894<br>*138—Burleigh Grimes, 1925 | 1,264—Brickyard Kennedy<br>*972—Dazzy Vance | 743 (1929) |
| Bases on balls | 171—Ed Stein, 1894<br>*152—Bill Donovan, 1901 | 1,128—Brickyard Kennedy<br>*764—Dazzy Vance | 671 (1946) |
| Strikeouts | 262—Dazzy Vance, 1924 | 1,918—Dazzy Vance | 891 (1957) |
| Strikeouts, game | 17—Dazzy Vance, July 20, 1925, 10 inn<br>[16—Nap Rucker, July 24, 1909] | | |
| Hit batsmen | 41—Joe McGinnity, 1900 | 82—Harry McIntire | 72 (1900) |
| Wild pitches | 39—John Harkins, 1885<br>*15—Larry Cheney, 1916 | 107—Adonis Terry<br>*62—Burleigh Grimes | 80 (1885) *42 (1956) |
| Home runs | 35—Don Newcombe, 1955 | 180—Carl Erskine | 171 (1956) |
| Sacrifice hits | 54—Nap Rucker, 1908 | 272—Burleigh Grimes | 216 (1926) |
| Sacrifice flies | 8—Roger Craig, 1956<br>Clem Labine, 1957 | 15—Carl Erskine | 44 (1954) |
| Earned run average | 1.58—Rube Marquard, 205 inn, 1916 | 2.31—Jeff Pfeffer | 2.12 (1916) |
| Shutouts | 7—Bob Caruthers, 1889<br>Burleigh Grimes, 1918<br>Whit Wyatt, 1941 | 38—Nap Rucker | 22 (1906, 1916)<br>Lost—26 (1907) |
| 1-0 games won | 3—Nap Rucker, 1911 | 11—Nap Rucker | 7 (1907, 1909)<br>Lost—9 (1910, 1913) |

## TEAM FIELDING

**Putouts** 4,286 (1940)
Fewest—2,840 (1884) *3,636 (1901)
**Chances accepted** 6,334 (1920)
Fewest—5,672 (1944)
**Double plays** 192 (1951)
Fewest—56 (1885) *73 (1906)
**Errorless games** unknown
Consecutive—10 (1942)

**Assists** 2,132 (1921)
Fewest—1,340 (1884) *1,577 (1944)
**Errors** 610 (1886) *408 (1905)
Fewest—106 (1952)
**Passed balls** 169 (1884) *31 (1901)
Fewest—4 (1933, 1951, 1953, 1954)
**Fielding average** .993 (1952)
Lowest—.864 (1887) *.947 (1900)

## MISCELLANEOUS

**Most players, season** 53 (1944)
**Fewest players, season** 23 (1905)
**Games won** 105 (1953)
**Month** 25 (July 1947, Aug 1953)
**Consecutive** 15 (1924)
**Winning percentage** .682 (1899), 101-47 and (1953), 105-49
**Lowest** .316 (1905), 48-104
**Number of league championships** 13
**Most recent** 1956
**Runs, game** 25 vs Pittsburgh, May 20, 1896
*25 vs Cincinnati, Sept 23, 1901
**Opponents'** 28 by Chicago, Aug 25, 1891
*26 by New York, Apr 30, 1944, 1st game
**Hits, game** 28 vs Pittsburgh, June 23, 1930
**Home runs, game** 6 vs Milwaukee, June 1, 1955
**Runs, shutout** 15 vs Philadelphia, Aug 16, 1952, 6 inn
**Opponents'** 17 by St. Louis, Aug 24, 1924, 2nd game
**Longest 1-0 win** 13 inn vs St. Louis, Aug 21, 1909
vs Boston, May 29, 1938

**Most seasons, non-pitcher** 18—Zack Wheat
**Most seasons, pitcher** 12—Dazzy Vance
**Games lost** 104 (1905)
**Month** 27 (Sept 1908)
**Consecutive** 16 (1944)
**Overall record** 5,214-4,926 (68 seasons)

**Number of times worst record in league** 1
**Most recent** 1905
**Runs, inning** 15 vs Cincinnati, May 21, 1952, 1st

**Total bases, game** 46 vs Philadelphia, Sept 23, 1939, 1st game
**Consecutive games with one or more home runs** 24 (39 HRs), 1953
**Longest shutout** unknown

**Longest 1-0 loss** 15 inn vs Cincinnati, June 11, 1915

## ATTENDANCE

**Highest home attendance**
**Washington Park I** 121,412 (1890)
**Eastern Park** 235,000 (1893)
**Washington Park II** 321,300 (1909)
**Ebbets Field** 1,807,526 (1947)
**Highest road attendance** 1,863,542 (1947)
*records made since 1900 that do not exceed pre-1900 records

**Largest crowds**
**Day** 37,512 vs New York, Aug 30, 1947
**Night** 35,583 vs Philadelphia, Sept 24, 1949
**Doubleheader** 41,209 vs New York, May 30, 1934
**Home opener** 34,530 vs New York, Apr 19, 1949

# CHICAGO CUBS

## YEARLY FINISHES

**(Original National League franchise)**

| Year | Position | W | L | Pct. | GB | Manager | Attendance |
|---|---|---|---|---|---|---|---|
| 1876 | 1st | 52 | 14 | .788 | +6.0 | Albert Spalding | 65,441 |
| 1877 | 5th | 26 | 33 | .441 | 15.5 | Albert Spalding | 46,454 |
| 1878 | 4th | 30 | 30 | .500 | 11.0 | Bob Ferguson | 58,691 |
| 1879 | 4th | 46 | 33 | .582 | 10.5 | Cap Anson | 67,687 |
| 1880 | 1st | 67 | 17 | .798 | +15.0 | Cap Anson | 66,708 |
| 1881 | 1st | 56 | 28 | .667 | +9.0 | Cap Anson | 82,000 |
| 1882 | 1st | 55 | 29 | .665 | +3.0 | Cap Anson | 125,452 |
| 1883 | 2nd | 59 | 39 | .602 | 4.0 | Cap Anson | 124,880 |
| 1884 | 4th (tied) | 62 | 50 | .554 | 22.0 | Cap Anson | 87,667 |
| 1885 | 1st | 87 | 25 | .777 | +2.0 | Cap Anson | 117,519 |
| 1886 | 1st | 90 | 34 | .726 | +2.5 | Cap Anson | 142,438 |
| 1887 | 3rd | 71 | 50 | .587 | 6.5 | Cap Anson | 217,070 |
| 1888 | 2nd | 77 | 58 | .570 | 9.0 | Cap Anson | 228,906 |

| Year | Position | W | L | Pct. | GB | Manager | Attendance |
|---|---|---|---|---|---|---|---|
| 1889 | 3rd | 67 | 65 | .508 | 19.0 | Cap Anson | 149,175 |
| 1890 | 2nd | 83 | 53 | .610 | 6.5 | Cap Anson | 102,536 |
| 1891 | 2nd | 82 | 53 | .607 | 3.5 | Cap Anson | 201,188 |
| 1892 | 8th/7th | 70 | 76 | .479 | ** | Cap Anson | 109,067 |
| 1893 | 9th | 56 | 71 | .441 | 29.0 | Cap Anson | 223,500 |
| 1894 | 8th | 57 | 75 | .432 | 34.0 | Cap Anson | 239,000 |
| 1895 | 4th | 72 | 58 | .554 | 15.0 | Cap Anson | 382,300 |
| 1896 | 5th | 71 | 57 | .555 | 18.5 | Cap Anson | 317,500 |
| 1897 | 9th | 59 | 73 | .447 | 34.0 | Cap Anson | 327,160 |
| 1898 | 4th | 85 | 65 | .567 | 17.5 | Tom Burns | 424,352 |
| 1899 | 8th | 75 | 73 | .507 | 26.0 | Tom Burns | 352,130 |
| 1900 | 5th (tied) | 65 | 75 | .464 | 19.0 | Tom Loftus | 248,577 |
| 1901 | 6th | 53 | 86 | .381 | 37.0 | Tom Loftus | 205,071 |
| 1902 | 5th | 68 | 69 | .496 | 34.0 | Frank Selee | 263,700 |
| 1903 | 3rd | 82 | 56 | .594 | 8.0 | Frank Selee | 386,205 |
| 1904 | 2nd | 93 | 60 | .608 | 13.0 | Frank Selee | 439,100 |
| 1905 | 3rd | 92 | 61 | .601 | 13.0 | Frank Selee, Frank Chance | 509,900 |
| 1906 | 1st (s) | 116 | 36 | .763 | +20.0 | Frank Chance | 654,300 |
| 1907 | 1st (S) | 107 | 45 | .704 | +17.0 | Frank Chance | 422,550 |
| 1908 | 1st (S) | 99 | 55 | .643 | +1.0 | Frank Chance | 665,325 |
| 1909 | 2nd | 104 | 49 | .680 | 6.5 | Frank Chance | 633,480 |
| 1910 | 1st (s) | 104 | 50 | .675 | +13.0 | Frank Chance | 526,152 |
| 1911 | 2nd | 92 | 62 | .597 | 7.5 | Frank Chance | 576,000 |
| 1912 | 3rd | 91 | 59 | .607 | 11.5 | Frank Chance | 514,000 |
| 1913 | 3rd | 88 | 65 | .575 | 13.5 | Johnny Evers | 419,000 |
| 1914 | 4th | 78 | 76 | .506 | 16.5 | Hank O'Day | 202,516 |
| 1915 | 4th | 73 | 80 | .477 | 17.5 | Roger Bresnahan | 217,058 |
| 1916 | 5th | 67 | 86 | .438 | 26.5 | Joe Tinker | 453,685 |
| 1917 | 5th | 74 | 80 | .481 | 24.0 | Fred Mitchell | 360,218 |
| 1918 | 1st (s) | 84 | 45 | .651 | +10.5 | Fred Mitchell | 337,256 |
| 1919 | 3rd | 75 | 65 | .536 | 21.0 | Fred Mitchell | 424,430 |
| 1920 | 5th (tied) | 75 | 79 | .487 | 18.0 | Fred Mitchell | 480,783 |
| 1921 | 7th | 64 | 89 | .418 | 30.0 | Johnny Evers, Bill Killefer | 410,107 |
| 1922 | 5th | 80 | 74 | .519 | 13.0 | Bill Killefer | 542,283 |
| 1923 | 4th | 83 | 71 | .539 | 12.5 | Bill Killefer | 703,705 |
| 1924 | 5th | 81 | 72 | .529 | 12.0 | Bill Killefer | 716,922 |
| 1925 | 8th | 68 | 86 | .442 | 27.5 | Bill Killefer, Rabbit Maranville, George Gibson | 622,610 |
| 1926 | 4th | 82 | 72 | .532 | 7.0 | Joe McCarthy | 885,063 |
| 1927 | 4th | 85 | 68 | .556 | 8.5 | Joe McCarthy | 1,159,168 |
| 1928 | 3rd | 91 | 63 | .591 | 4.0 | Joe McCarthy | 1,143,740 |
| 1929 | 1st (s) | 98 | 54 | .645 | +10.5 | Joe McCarthy | 1,485,166 |
| 1930 | 2nd | 90 | 64 | .584 | 2.0 | Joe McCarthy, Rogers Hornsby | 1,463,624 |
| 1931 | 3rd | 84 | 70 | .545 | 17.0 | Rogers Hornsby | 1,086,422 |
| 1932 | 1st (s) | 90 | 64 | .584 | +4.0 | Rogers Hornsby, Charlie Grimm | 974,688 |
| 1933 | 3rd | 86 | 68 | .558 | 6.0 | Charlie Grimm | 594,112 |
| 1934 | 3rd | 86 | 65 | .570 | 8.0 | Charlie Grimm | 707,525 |
| 1935 | 1st (s) | 100 | 54 | .649 | +4.0 | Charlie Grimm | 692,604 |
| 1936 | 2nd (tied) | 87 | 67 | .565 | 5.0 | Charlie Grimm | 699,370 |
| 1937 | 2nd | 93 | 61 | .604 | 3.0 | Charlie Grimm | 895,020 |
| 1938 | 1st | 89 | 63 | .586 | +2.0 | Charlie Grimm, Gabby Hartnett | 951,640 |
| 1939 | 4th | 84 | 70 | .545 | 13.0 | Gabby Hartnett | 726,663 |
| 1940 | 5th | 75 | 79 | .487 | 25.5 | Gabby Hartnett | 534,878 |
| 1941 | 6th | 70 | 84 | .455 | 30.0 | Jimmy Wilson | 545,159 |
| 1942 | 6th | 68 | 86 | .442 | 38.0 | Jimmy Wilson | 590,872 |
| 1943 | 5th | 74 | 79 | .484 | 30.5 | Jimmy Wilson | 508,247 |
| 1944 | 4th | 75 | 79 | .487 | 30.0 | Jimmy Wilson, Charlie Grimm | 640,110 |
| 1945 | 1st (s) | 98 | 56 | .636 | +3.0 | Charlie Grimm | 1,036,386 |
| 1946 | 3rd | 82 | 71 | .536 | 14.5 | Charlie Grimm | 1,342,970 |
| 1947 | 6th | 69 | 85 | .448 | 25.0 | Charlie Grimm | 1,364,039 |
| 1948 | 8th | 64 | 90 | .416 | 27.5 | Charlie Grimm | 1,237,792 |
| 1949 | 8th | 61 | 93 | .396 | 36.0 | Charlie Grimm, Frankie Frisch | 1,143,139 |
| 1950 | 7th | 64 | 89 | .418 | 26.5 | Frankie Frisch | 1,165,944 |
| 1951 | 8th | 62 | 92 | .403 | 34.5 | Frankie Frisch, Phil Cavarretta | 894,415 |
| 1952 | 5th | 77 | 77 | .500 | 19.5 | Phil Cavarretta | 1,024,826 |
| 1953 | 7th | 65 | 89 | .422 | 40.0 | Phil Cavarretta | 763,658 |
| 1954 | 7th | 64 | 90 | .416 | 33.0 | Stan Hack | 748,183 |
| 1955 | 6th | 72 | 81 | .471 | 26.0 | Stan Hack | 875,800 |
| 1956 | 8th | 60 | 94 | .390 | 33.0 | Stan Hack | 720,118 |
| 1957 | 7th (tied) | 62 | 92 | .403 | 33.0 | Bob Scheffing | 670,629 |
| 1958 | 5th (tied) | 72 | 82 | .468 | 20.0 | Bob Scheffing | 979,904 |
| 1959 | 5th (tied) | 74 | 80 | .481 | 13.0 | Bob Scheffing | 858,255 |
| 1960 | 7th | 60 | 94 | .390 | 35.0 | Charlie Grimm, Lou Boudreau | 809,770 |
| 1961 | 7th | 64 | 90 | .416 | 29.0 | Vedie Himsl, Harry Craft, Elvin Tappe, Lou Klein | 673,057 |
| 1962 | 9th | 59 | 103 | .364 | 42.5 | Charlie Metro, Elvin Tappe, Lou Klein | 609,802 |
| 1963 | 7th | 82 | 80 | .506 | 17.0 | Bob Kennedy | 979,551 |
| 1964 | 8th | 76 | 86 | .469 | 17.0 | Bob Kennedy | 751,647 |
| 1965 | 8th | 72 | 90 | .444 | 25.0 | Bob Kennedy, Lou Klein | 641,361 |
| 1966 | 10th | 59 | 103 | .364 | 36.0 | Leo Durocher | 635,891 |
| 1967 | 3rd | 87 | 74 | .540 | 14.0 | Leo Durocher | 977,226 |
| 1968 | 3rd | 84 | 78 | .519 | 13.0 | Leo Durocher | 1,043,409 |

## EAST DIVISION

| Year | Position | W | L | Pct. | GB | Manager | Attendance |
|---|---|---|---|---|---|---|---|
| 1969 | 2nd | 92 | 70 | .568 | 8.0 | Leo Durocher | 1,674,993 |
| 1970 | 2nd | 84 | 78 | .519 | 5.0 | Leo Durocher | 1,642,705 |
| 1971 | 3rd (tied) | 83 | 79 | .512 | 14.0 | Leo Durocher | 1,653,007 |
| 1972 | 2nd | 85 | 70 | .548 | 11.0 | Leo Durocher, Whitey Lockman | 1,299,163 |
| 1973 | 5th | 77 | 84 | .478 | 5.0 | Whitey Lockman | 1,351,705 |
| 1974 | 6th | 66 | 96 | .407 | 22.0 | Whitey Lockman, Jim Marshall | 1,015,378 |
| 1975 | 5th (tied) | 75 | 87 | .463 | 17.5 | Jim Marshall | 1,034,819 |

| Year | Position | W | L | Pct. | GB | Manager | Attendance |
|---|---|---|---|---|---|---|---|
| 1976 | 4th | 75 | 87 | .463 | 26.0 | Jim Marshall | 1,026,217 |
| 1977 | 4th | 81 | 81 | .500 | 20.0 | Herman Franks | 1,439,834 |
| 1978 | 3rd | 79 | 83 | .488 | 11.0 | Herman Franks | 1,525,311 |
| 1979 | 5th | 80 | 82 | .494 | 18.0 | Herman Franks, Joe Amalfitano | 1,648,587 |
| 1980 | 6th | 64 | 98 | .395 | 27.0 | Preston Gomez, Joe Amalfitano | 1,206,776 |
| 1981 | 6th/5th | 38 | 65 | .369 | * | Joe Amalfitano | 565,637 |
| 1982 | 5th | 73 | 89 | .451 | 19.0 | Lee Elia | 1,249,278 |
| 1983 | 5th | 71 | 91 | .438 | 19.0 | Lee Elia, Charlie Fox | 1,479,717 |
| 1984 | 1st (c) | 96 | 65 | .596 | +6.5 | Jim Frey | 2,104,219 |
| 1985 | 4th | 77 | 84 | .478 | 23.5 | Jim Frey | 2,161,534 |
| 1986 | 5th | 70 | 90 | .438 | 37.0 | Jim Frey, John Vukovich, Gene Michael | 1,859,102 |
| 1987 | 6th | 76 | 85 | .472 | 18.5 | Gene Michael, Frank Lucchesi | 2,035,130 |
| 1988 | 4th | 77 | 85 | .475 | 24.0 | Don Zimmer | 2,089,034 |
| 1989 | 1st (c) | 93 | 69 | .574 | +6.0 | Don Zimmer | 2,491,942 |
| 1990 | 4th | 77 | 85 | .475 | 18.0 | Don Zimmer | 2,243,791 |
| 1991 | 4th | 77 | 83 | .481 | 20.0 | Don Zimmer, Joe Altobelli, Jim Essian | 2,314,250 |
| 1992 | 4th | 78 | 84 | .481 | 18.0 | Jim Lefebvre | 2,126,720 |
| 1993 | 4th | 84 | 78 | .519 | 13.0 | Jim Lefebvre | 2,653,763 |

## CENTRAL DIVISION

| Year | Position | W | L | Pct. | GB | Manager | Attendance |
|---|---|---|---|---|---|---|---|
| 1994 | 5th | 49 | 64 | .434 | 16.5 | Tom Trebelhorn | 1,845,208 |
| 1995 | 3rd | 73 | 71 | .507 | 12.0 | Jim Riggleman | 1,918,265 |
| 1996 | 4th | 76 | 86 | .469 | 12.0 | Jim Riggleman | 2,219,110 |
| 1997 | 5th | 68 | 94 | .420 | 16.0 | Jim Riggleman | 2,190,308 |
| 1998 | 2nd (W,d) | 90 | 73 | .552 | 12.5 | Jim Riggleman | 2,623,000 |
| 1999 | 6th | 67 | 95 | .414 | 30.0 | Jim Riggleman | 2,813,854 |
| 2000 | 6th | 65 | 97 | .401 | 30.0 | Don Baylor | 2,789,511 |
| 2001 | 3rd | 88 | 74 | .543 | 5.0 | Don Baylor | 2,779,456 |
| 2002 | 5th | 67 | 95 | .414 | 30.0 | Don Baylor, Bruce Kimm | 2,693,071 |
| 2003 | 1st (D,c) | 88 | 74 | .543 | +1.0 | Dusty Baker | 2,962,630 |
| 2004 | 3rd | 89 | 73 | .549 | 16.0 | Dusty Baker | 3,170,184 |
| 2005 | 4th | 79 | 83 | .488 | 21.0 | Dusty Baker | 3,099,992 |

**first half 31-39, second half 39-37; (s) lost World Series; (S) won World Series; *first half 15-37, second half 23-28; (c) lost League Championship Series; (W) won wild card playoff; (d) lost Division Series; (D) won Division Series

## INDIVIDUAL AND CLUB RECORDS

### BATTING

| | Individual Season | Individual Career | Club Season |
|---|---|---|---|
| **Games** | 164—Ron Santo, 1965<br>Billy Williams, 1965 | 2,528—Ernie Banks | 164 (1965) |
| **At-bats** | 666—Billy Herman, 154 G, 1935 | 9,421—Ernie Banks | 5,675 (1988) |
| **Runs** | 156—Rogers Hornsby, 156 G, 1929 | 1,445—Cap Anson<br>*1,316—Ryne Sandberg | 1,041 (1894), *998 (1930)<br>Fewest—366 (1877) *520 (1916) |
| **Hits** | 229—Rogers Hornsby, 156 G, 1929 | 3,012—Cap Anson<br>*2,583—Ernie Banks | 1,722 (1930)<br>Fewest—633 (1877) *1,200 (1902) |
| **Hitting streak** | 42 G—Bill Dahlen, 1894<br>*30 G—Jerome Walton, 1989 | | |
| **Singles** | 165—Sparky Adams, 146 G, 1927 | 1,910—Cap Anson<br>*1,692—Stan Hack | 1,230 (1887), *1,226 (1921) |
| **Doubles** | 57—Billy Herman, 154 G, 1935<br>Billy Herman, 153 G, 1936 | 476—Cap Anson<br>*456—Mark Grace | 340 (1931) |
| **Triples** | 21—Wildfire Schulte, 154 G, 1911<br>Vic Saier, 149 G, 1913 | 142—Jimmy Ryan | 101 (1911) |
| **HOME RUNS** | | | 235 (2004)<br>Fewest—6 (1902) |
| **Righthander** | 66—Sammy Sosa, 159 G, 1998 | 545—Sammy Sosa | |
| **Lefthander** | 42—Billy Williams, 161 G, 1970 | 392—Billy Williams | |
| **Switch-hitter** | 27—Mark Bellhorn, 146 G, 2002 | 59—Augie Galan | |
| **Rookie** | 25—Billy Williams, 146 G, 1961 | | |
| **Home** | 35—Sammy Sosa, 1998 | 293—Sammy Sosa | 131 (1884) |
| **Road** | 31—Sammy Sosa, 1998 | 242—Sammy Sosa | 101 (1998, 2002) |
| **Month** | 20—Sammy Sosa, June 1998 | 47 (Aug 1987, June 1998) | |
| **Pinch** | 4—Glenallen Hill, 1999 | 9—Glenallen Hill | 10 (1998) |
| **Grand slams** | 5—Ernie Banks, 154 G, 1955 | 12—Ernie Banks | 9 (1929) |
| **Home runs at Wrigley Field, all teams** | | 233 (2004) | |
| **Total bases** | 425—Sammy Sosa, 160 G, 2001 | 4,706—Ernie Banks | 2,684 (1930) |
| **Extra-base hits** | 103—Sammy Sosa, 160 G, 2001 | 1,009—Ernie Banks | 572 (1904) |
| **Sacrifice hits** | 40—Jimmy Sheckard, 149 G, 1906 | 263—Wildfire Schulte | 270 (1908) |
| **Sacrifice flies** | 14—Ron Santo, 1969 | 96—Ernie Banks | 66 (1975) |
| **Bases on balls** | 147—Jimmy Sheckard, 156 G, 1911 | 1,092—Stan Hack | 650 (1975)<br>Fewest—57 (1877) *298 (1904) |
| **Strikeouts** | 174—Sammy Sosa, 162 G, 1997<br>Fewest—5—Charlie Hollocher, 152 G, 1922 | 1,815—Sammy Sosa | 1,269 (2002)<br>Fewest—45 (1876) *374 (1921) |
| **Hit by pitch** | 23—Bill Dahlen, 142 G, 1898<br>*14—Scott Servais, 129 G, 1996 | 137—Frank Chance<br>*70—Ernie Banks | 66 (2001)<br>Fewest— 13 (1956) |
| **Runs batted in** | 191—Hack Wilson, 155 G, 1930 | 1,879—Cap Anson<br>*1,636—Ernie Banks | 940 (1930)<br>Fewest—248 (1877) *423 (1902) |

| | Individual Season | Individual Career | Club Season |
|---|---|---|---|
| Grounded into double plays | 27—Ron Santo, 149 G, 1973<br>Fewest—0—Augie Galan, 154 G, 1935 | 240—Ron Santo | 161 (1933)<br>Fewest—87 (1991) |
| Left on base | | | 1,262 (1975)<br>Fewest—964 (1924) |
| Batting average | .429—Ross Barnes, 66 G, 1876<br>*.380—Rogers Hornsby, 156 G, 1929 | .331—Cap Anson<br>*.309—Billy Herman | .333 (1887), *.309 (1930)<br>Lowest—.235 (1892) *.238 (1963, 1965) |
| Most .300 hitters | | | 8 (1921) |
| Slugging average | .737—Sammy Sosa, 160 G, 2001 | .569—Sammy Sosa | .481 (1930)<br>Lowest—.298 (1902) |
| On-base percentage | .483—King Kelly, 118 G, 1886<br>*.460—Rogers Hornsby, 156 G, 1929 | .398—Cap Anson<br>*.394—Stan Hack | .388 (1887), *.378 (1930)<br>Lowest—.276 (1879) *.295 (1904) |

## BASERUNNING

| | Individual Season | Individual Career | Club Season |
|---|---|---|---|
| Stolen bases | 100—Bill Lange, 123 G, 1896<br>*67—Frank Chance, 123 G, 1903 | 404—Frank Chance | 382 (1887) *283 (1906) |
| Caught stealing | 29—Charlie Hollocher, 152 G, 1922 | 385—Frank Chance<br>*107—Ryne Sandberg | 149 (1924) |

## PITCHING

| | Individual Season | Individual Career | Club Season |
|---|---|---|---|
| Games | 84—Ted Abernathy, 1965<br>Dick Tidrow, 1980 | 605—Charlie Root | |
| Games started | 70—John Clarkson, 1885<br>Bill Hutchison, 1892<br>*42—Ferguson Jenkins, 1969 | 347—Ferguson Jenkins | |
| Complete games | 68—John Clarkson, 1885<br>*34—Jack Taylor, 1902 | 317—Bill Hutchison<br>*206—Mordecai Brown | 147 (1889) *139 (1904) |
| Wins | 53—John Clarkson, 1885<br>*29—Mordecai Brown, 1908 | 201—Charlie Root | |
| Percentage | .941—Rick Sutcliffe (16-1), 1984 | .706—John Clarkson<br>*.686—Mordecai Brown | |
| Winning streak | 17—John Luby, 1890<br>*14—Ed Reulbach, 1909<br>Rick Sutcliffe, 1984 | | |
| 20-win seasons | | 6—Mordecai Brown<br>Ferguson Jenkins<br>Clark Griffith | |
| Losses | 36—Bill Hutchison, 1892<br>*23—Tom Hughes, 1901 | 156—Charlie Root | |
| Losing streak | 13—Dutch McCall, 1948 | | |
| Saves | 53—Randy Myers, 1993 | 180—Lee Smith | 56 (1993, 1998) |
| Innings | 623—John Clarkson, 1885<br>*363.1—Grover Alexander, 1920 | 3,137.1—Charlie Root | 1,479 (1980) |
| Hits | 605—John Clarkson, 1887<br>*347—Nixey Callahan, 1900 | 3,184—Charlie Root | 1,642 (1930) |
| Runs | 316—Bill Hutchison, 1892<br>*195—Nixey Callahan, 1900 | 1,861—Bill Hutchison<br>*1,422—Charlie Root | 1,080 (1894) *920 (1999) |
| Earned runs | 191—Bill Hutchison, 1892<br>*155—Guy Bush, 1930 | 1,236—Charlie Root | 849 (2000) |
| Bases on balls | 199—Bill Hutchison, 1890<br>*185—Sam Jones, 1955 | 1,109—Bill Hutchison<br>*871—Charlie Root | 658 (2000) |
| Strikeouts | 314—Bill Hutchison, 1892<br>*274—Ferguson Jenkins, 1970 | 2,038—Ferguson Jenkins | 1,404 (2001) |
| Strikeouts, game | 20—Kerry Wood, May 6, 1998 | | |
| Hit batsmen | 39—Danny Friend, 1896<br>*22—Nixey Callahan, 1900 | 116—Clark Griffith<br>*85—Ed Reulbach | 82 (1898, 1899) *81 (1900) |
| Wild pitches | 41—Mark Baldwin, 1887<br>*26—Larry Cheney, 1914 | 120—Bill Hutchison<br>*71—Larry Cheney | 86 (1887) *68 (1992) |
| Home runs | 38—Warren Hacker, 1955 | 271—Ferguson Jenkins | 231 (2000) |
| Sacrifice hits | 23—Bill Bonham, 1974 | 117—Rick Reuschel | 107 (1990) |
| Sacrifice flies | 14—Rick Reuschel, 1980<br>Steve Trachsel, 1999 | 73—Ferguson Jenkins | 74 (1954) |
| Earned run average | 1.04—Mordecai Brown, 277.1 inn, 1906 | 1.80—Mordecai Brown | 1.73 (1907) |
| Shutouts | 10—John Clarkson, 1885<br>*9—Mordecai Brown, 1906, 1908<br>Orval Overall, 1909<br>Grover Alexander, 1919<br>Bill Lee, 1938 | 48—Hippo Vaughn | 32 (1907, 1909)<br>Lost—22 (1915, 1968) |
| 1-0 games won | 3—many pitchers | 10—Hippo Vaughn | 9 (1906)<br>Lost—10 (1916) |

## TEAM FIELDING

| | | | |
|---|---|---|---|
| Putouts | 4,437 (1980)<br>Fewest—1,602 (1877) *3,693 (1903) | Assists | 2,178 (1899) *2,155 (1916)<br>Fewest—731 (1876) *1,493 (2001) |

**Chances accepted** 6,508 (1977)
Fewest—2,356 (1877) *5,468 (1903)
**Double plays** 176 (1928)
Fewest—33 (1876) *76 (1908)
**Errorless games** 99 (2004)
Consecutive—10 (1984, 1998)

**Errors** 595 (1884) *418 (1900)
Fewest—86 (2004)
**Passed balls** 144 (1886) *38 (1900)
Fewest—4 (1967)
**Fielding average** .986 (2004)
Lowest—.879 (1883) *.933 (1900)

## MISCELLANEOUS

**Most players, season** 51 (2000)
**Fewest players, season** 11 (1876, 1883), 20* (1905)
**Games won** 116 (1906)
**Month** 26 (Aug 1906, July 1935, July 1945)
**Consecutive** 21 (1880, 1935)
**Winning percentage** .798 (1880), 67-17
*.763 (1906), 116-36
**Lowest** .364 (1962, 1966), 59-103
**Number of league championships** 16
**Most recent** 1945
**Runs, game** 36 vs Louisville, June 29, 1897
*26 vs Philadelphia, Aug 25, 1922
vs Colorado, Aug 18, 1995
**Opponents'** 25 by Boston, Sept 10, 1894
*23 five times, last by New York, Aug 16, 1987
**Hits, game** 32 vs Buffalo, July 3, 1883
vs Louisville, June 29, 1897
*28 vs Boston, July 3, 1945
**Home runs, game** 7 vs New York, June 11, 1967, 2nd game
vs San Diego, Aug 19, 1970
vs San Diego, May 17, 1977
**Runs, shutout** 20 vs Washington, May 28, 1886
*19 vs New York, June 7, 1906
vs San Diego, May 13, 1969
**Opponents'** 22 by Pittsburgh, Sept 16, 1975
**Longest 1-0 win** 17 inn, vs Boston, Apr 13, 1901

**Most seasons, non-pitcher** 22—Cap Anson
*20—Phil Cavarretta
**Most seasons, pitcher** 16—Charlie Root
**Games lost** 103 (1962, 1966)
**Month** 24 (July 1957, Aug 1999)
**Consecutive** 14 (1997)
**Overall record** 9,834-9,286 (130 seasons)
**Interleague play** 66-64
**Number of times worst record in league** 11
**Most recent** 2000
**Runs, inning** 18 vs Detroit, Sept 6, 1883, 7th
*14 vs Philadelphia, Aug 25, 1922, 4th
**Total bases, game** 54 vs Brooklyn, Aug 25, 1891
*45 vs New York, June 11, 1967, 2nd game
vs Colorado, Aug 18, 1995
[49 vs Philadelphia, May 17, 1979, 10 inn]
**Consecutive games with one or more home runs** 17 (28 HRs), 1998
**Longest shutout** 17 inn, vs. Boston, Sept 21, 1901
**Longest 1-0 loss** 17 inn, vs Houston, Aug 23, 1980

## ATTENDANCE

**Highest home attendance**
**23rd Street Grounds** 65,441 (1876)
**Lake Front Park** 125,452 (1882)
**West Side Park** 228,906 (1888)
**West Side Grounds** 665,325 (1908)
**Wrigley Field** 3,170,184 (2004)
**Highest road attendance** 2,953,637 (2005)
*records made since 1900 that do not exceed pre-1900 records

**Largest crowds**
**Day** 51,556 vs Brooklyn, June 27, 1930
**Night** 40,656 vs Milwaukee, Aug 20, 2001
**Doubleheader** 46,965 vs Pittsburgh, May 31, 1948
**Home opener** 45,777 vs Pittsburgh, Apr 14, 1978
(Cubs drew 55,000 to 2000 "home opener" in Tokyo, Japan, March 30.)

# CINCINNATI REDS

## YEARLY FINISHES

**(American Association franchise moved to the National League after the 1889 season)**

| Year | Position | W | L | Pct. | GB | Manager | Attendance |
|---|---|---|---|---|---|---|---|
| 1890 | 4th | 77 | 55 | .583 | 10.5 | Tom Loftus | 97,500 |
| 1891 | 7th | 56 | 81 | .409 | 30.5 | Tom Loftus | 196,473 |
| 1892 | 4th/8th | 82 | 68 | .547 | ** | Charlie Comiskey | 194,250 |
| 1893 | 6th (tied) | 65 | 63 | .508 | 20.5 | Charlie Comiskey | 158,000 |
| 1894 | 10th | 55 | 75 | .423 | 35.0 | Charlie Comiskey | 281,000 |
| 1895 | 8th | 66 | 64 | .508 | 21.0 | Buck Ewing | 373,000 |
| 1896 | 3rd | 77 | 50 | .606 | 12.0 | Buck Ewing | 336,800 |
| 1897 | 4th | 76 | 56 | .576 | 17.0 | Buck Ewing | 336,800 |
| 1898 | 3rd | 92 | 60 | .605 | 11.5 | Buck Ewing | 336,378 |
| 1899 | 6th | 83 | 67 | .553 | 19.0 | Buck Ewing | 259,536 |
| 1900 | 7th | 62 | 77 | .446 | 21.5 | Bob Allen | 155,000 |
| 1901 | 8th | 52 | 87 | .374 | 38.0 | Bid McPhee | 205,728 |
| 1902 | 4th | 70 | 70 | .500 | 33.5 | Bid McPhee, Frank Bancroft, Joe Kelley | 217,300 |
| 1903 | 4th | 74 | 65 | .532 | 16.5 | Joe Kelley | 351,680 |
| 1904 | 3rd | 88 | 65 | .575 | 18.0 | Joe Kelley | 391,915 |
| 1905 | 5th | 79 | 74 | .516 | 26.0 | Joe Kelley | 313,927 |
| 1906 | 6th | 64 | 87 | .424 | 51.5 | Ned Hanlon | 330,056 |
| 1907 | 6th | 66 | 87 | .431 | 41.5 | Ned Hanlon | 317,500 |
| 1908 | 5th | 73 | 81 | .474 | 26.0 | John Ganzel | 399,200 |
| 1909 | 4th | 77 | 76 | .503 | 33.5 | Clark Griffith | 424,643 |
| 1910 | 5th | 75 | 79 | .487 | 29.0 | Clark Griffith | 380,622 |
| 1911 | 6th | 70 | 83 | .458 | 29.0 | Clark Griffith | 300,000 |
| 1912 | 4th | 75 | 78 | .490 | 29.0 | Hank O'Day | 344,000 |
| 1913 | 7th | 64 | 89 | .418 | 37.5 | Joe Tinker | 258,000 |
| 1914 | 8th | 60 | 94 | .390 | 34.5 | Buck Herzog | 100,791 |
| 1915 | 7th | 71 | 83 | .461 | 20.0 | Buck Herzog | 218,878 |
| 1916 | 7th (tied) | 60 | 93 | .392 | 33.5 | Buck Herzog, Christy Mathewson | 255,846 |
| 1917 | 4th | 78 | 76 | .506 | 20.0 | Christy Mathewson | 269,056 |
| 1918 | 3rd | 68 | 60 | .531 | 15.5 | Christy Mathewson, Heinie Groh | 163,009 |
| 1919 | 1st (S) | 96 | 44 | .686 | +9.0 | Pat Moran | 532,501 |

| Year | Position | W | L | Pct. | GB | Manager | Attendance |
|---|---|---|---|---|---|---|---|
| 1920 | 3rd | 82 | 71 | .536 | 10.5 | Pat Moran | 568,107 |
| 1921 | 6th | 70 | 83 | .458 | 24.0 | Pat Moran | 311,227 |
| 1922 | 2nd | 86 | 68 | .558 | 7.0 | Pat Moran | 493,754 |
| 1923 | 2nd | 91 | 63 | .591 | 4.5 | Pat Moran | 575,063 |
| 1924 | 4th | 83 | 70 | .542 | 10.0 | Jack Hendricks | 437,707 |
| 1925 | 3rd | 80 | 73 | .523 | 15.0 | Jack Hendricks | 464,920 |
| 1926 | 2nd | 87 | 67 | .565 | 2.0 | Jack Hendricks | 672,987 |
| 1927 | 5th | 75 | 78 | .490 | 18.5 | Jack Hendricks | 442,164 |
| 1928 | 5th | 78 | 74 | .513 | 16.0 | Jack Hendricks | 490,490 |
| 1929 | 7th | 66 | 88 | .429 | 33.0 | Jack Hendricks | 295,040 |
| 1930 | 7th | 59 | 95 | .383 | 33.0 | Dan Howley | 386,727 |
| 1931 | 8th | 58 | 96 | .377 | 43.0 | Dan Howley | 263,316 |
| 1932 | 8th | 60 | 94 | .390 | 30.0 | Dan Howley | 356,950 |
| 1933 | 8th | 58 | 94 | .382 | 33.0 | Donie Bush | 218,281 |
| 1934 | 8th | 52 | 99 | .344 | 42.0 | Bob O'Farrell, Chuck Dressen | 206,773 |
| 1935 | 6th | 68 | 85 | .444 | 31.5 | Chuck Dressen | 448,247 |
| 1936 | 5th | 74 | 80 | .481 | 18.0 | Chuck Dressen | 466,245 |
| 1937 | 8th | 56 | 98 | .364 | 40.0 | Chuck Dressen, Bobby Wallace | 411,221 |
| 1938 | 4th | 82 | 68 | .547 | 6.0 | Bill McKechnie | 706,756 |
| 1939 | 1st (s) | 97 | 57 | .630 | +4.5 | Bill McKechnie | 981,443 |
| 1940 | 1st (S) | 100 | 53 | .654 | +12.0 | Bill McKechnie | 850,180 |
| 1941 | 3rd | 88 | 66 | .571 | 12.0 | Bill McKechnie | 643,513 |
| 1942 | 4th | 76 | 76 | .500 | 29.0 | Bill McKechnie | 427,031 |
| 1943 | 2nd | 87 | 67 | .565 | 18.0 | Bill McKechnie | 379,122 |
| 1944 | 3rd | 89 | 65 | .578 | 16.0 | Bill McKechnie | 409,567 |
| 1945 | 7th | 61 | 93 | .396 | 37.0 | Bill McKechnie | 290,070 |
| 1946 | 6th | 67 | 87 | .435 | 30.0 | Bill McKechnie | 715,751 |
| 1947 | 5th | 73 | 81 | .474 | 21.0 | Johnny Neun | 899,975 |
| 1948 | 7th | 64 | 89 | .418 | 27.0 | Johnny Neun, Bucky Walters | 823,386 |
| 1949 | 7th | 62 | 92 | .403 | 35.0 | Bucky Walters | 707,782 |
| 1950 | 6th | 66 | 87 | .431 | 24.5 | Luke Sewell | 538,794 |
| 1951 | 6th | 68 | 86 | .442 | 28.5 | Luke Sewell | 588,268 |
| 1952 | 6th | 69 | 85 | .448 | 27.5 | Luke Sewell, Rogers Hornsby | 604,197 |
| 1953 | 6th | 68 | 86 | .442 | 37.0 | Rogers Hornsby, Buster Mills | 548,086 |
| 1954 | 5th | 74 | 80 | .481 | 23.0 | Birdie Tebbetts | 704,167 |
| 1955 | 5th | 75 | 79 | .487 | 23.5 | Birdie Tebbetts | 693,662 |
| 1956 | 3rd | 91 | 63 | .591 | 2.0 | Birdie Tebbetts | 1,125,928 |
| 1957 | 4th | 80 | 74 | .519 | 15.0 | Birdie Tebbetts | 1,070,850 |
| 1958 | 4th | 76 | 78 | .494 | 16.0 | Birdie Tebbetts, Jimmie Dykes | 788,582 |
| 1959 | 5th (tied) | 74 | 80 | .481 | 13.0 | Mayo Smith, Fred Hutchinson | 801,289 |
| 1960 | 6th | 67 | 87 | .435 | 28.0 | Fred Hutchinson | 663,486 |
| 1961 | 1st (s) | 93 | 61 | .604 | +4.0 | Fred Hutchinson | 1,117,603 |
| 1962 | 3rd | 98 | 64 | .605 | 3.5 | Fred Hutchinson | 982,085 |
| 1963 | 5th | 86 | 76 | .531 | 13.0 | Fred Hutchinson | 858,805 |
| 1964 | 2nd (tied) | 92 | 70 | .568 | 1.0 | Fred Hutchinson, Dick Sisler | 862,466 |
| 1965 | 4th | 89 | 73 | .549 | 8.0 | Dick Sisler | 1,047,824 |
| 1966 | 7th | 76 | 84 | .475 | 18.0 | Don Heffner, Dave Bristol | 742,958 |
| 1967 | 4th | 87 | 75 | .537 | 14.5 | Dave Bristol | 958,300 |
| 1968 | 4th | 83 | 79 | .512 | 14.0 | Dave Bristol | 733,354 |

## WEST DIVISION

| Year | Position | W | L | Pct. | GB | Manager | Attendance |
|---|---|---|---|---|---|---|---|
| 1969 | 3rd | 89 | 73 | .549 | 4.0 | Dave Bristol | 987,991 |
| 1970 | 1st (C,s) | 102 | 60 | .630 | +14.5 | Sparky Anderson | 1,803,568 |
| 1971 | 4th (tied) | 79 | 83 | .488 | 11.0 | Sparky Anderson | 1,501,122 |
| 1972 | 1st (C,s) | 95 | 59 | .617 | +10.5 | Sparky Anderson | 1,611,459 |
| 1973 | 1st (c) | 99 | 63 | .611 | +3.5 | Sparky Anderson | 2,017,601 |
| 1974 | 2nd | 98 | 64 | .605 | 4.0 | Sparky Anderson | 2,164,307 |
| 1975 | 1st (C,S) | 108 | 54 | .667 | +20.0 | Sparky Anderson | 2,315,603 |
| 1976 | 1st (C,S) | 102 | 60 | .630 | +10.0 | Sparky Anderson | 2,629,708 |
| 1977 | 2nd | 88 | 74 | .543 | 10.0 | Sparky Anderson | 2,519,670 |
| 1978 | 2nd | 92 | 69 | .571 | 2.5 | Sparky Anderson | 2,532,497 |
| 1979 | 1st (c) | 90 | 71 | .559 | +1.5 | John McNamara | 2,356,933 |
| 1980 | 3rd | 89 | 73 | .549 | 3.5 | John McNamara | 2,022,450 |
| 1981 | 2nd/2nd | 66 | 42 | .611 | * | John McNamara | 1,093,730 |
| 1982 | 6th | 61 | 101 | .377 | 28.0 | John McNamara, Russ Nixon | 1,326,528 |
| 1983 | 6th | 74 | 88 | .457 | 17.0 | Russ Nixon | 1,190,419 |
| 1984 | 5th | 70 | 92 | .432 | 22.0 | Vern Rapp, Pete Rose | 1,275,887 |
| 1985 | 2nd | 89 | 72 | .553 | 5.5 | Pete Rose | 1,834,619 |
| 1986 | 2nd | 86 | 76 | .531 | 10.0 | Pete Rose | 1,692,432 |
| 1987 | 2nd | 84 | 78 | .519 | 6.0 | Pete Rose | 2,185,205 |
| 1988 | 2nd | 87 | 74 | .540 | 7.0 | Pete Rose | 2,072,528 |
| 1989 | 5th | 75 | 87 | .463 | 17.0 | Pete Rose, Tommy Helms | 1,979,320 |
| 1990 | 1st (C,S) | 91 | 71 | .562 | +5.0 | Lou Piniella | 2,400,892 |
| 1991 | 5th | 74 | 88 | .457 | 20.0 | Lou Piniella | 2,372,377 |
| 1992 | 2nd | 90 | 72 | .556 | 8.0 | Lou Piniella | 2,315,946 |
| 1993 | 5th | 73 | 89 | .451 | 31.0 | Tony Perez, Dave Johnson | 2,453,232 |

## CENTRAL DIVISION

| Year | Position | W | L | Pct. | GB | Manager | Attendance |
|---|---|---|---|---|---|---|---|
| 1994 | 1st | 66 | 48 | .579 | +0.5 | Dave Johnson | 1,897,681 |
| 1995 | 1st (D,c) | 85 | 59 | .590 | +9.0 | Dave Johnson | 1,837,649 |
| 1996 | 3rd | 81 | 81 | .500 | 7.0 | Ray Knight | 1,861,428 |
| 1997 | 3rd | 76 | 86 | .469 | 8.0 | Ray Knight, Jack McKeon | 1,785,788 |
| 1998 | 4th | 77 | 85 | .475 | 25.0 | Jack McKeon | 1,793,679 |
| 1999 | 2nd (w) | 96 | 67 | .589 | 1.5 | Jack McKeon | 2,061,222 |
| 2000 | 2nd | 85 | 77 | .525 | 10.0 | Jack McKeon | 2,577,351 |
| 2001 | 5th | 66 | 96 | .407 | 27.0 | Bob Boone | 1,882,732 |
| 2002 | 3rd | 78 | 84 | .481 | 19.0 | Bob Boone | 1,855,973 |
| 2003 | 5th | 69 | 93 | .426 | 19.0 | Bob Boone, Dave Miley | 2,355,160 |
| 2004 | 4th | 76 | 86 | .469 | 29.0 | Dave Miley | 2,287,250 |
| 2005 | 5th | 73 | 89 | .451 | 27.0 | Dave Miley, Jerry Narron | 1,943,068 |

(S) won World Series; (s) lost World Series; (C) won League Championship Series; (c) lost League Championship Series; *first half 35-21, second half 31-21; (D) won Division Series; (w) lost wild card playoff

# INDIVIDUAL AND CLUB RECORDS

## BATTING

| | Individual Season | Career | Club Season |
|---|---|---|---|
| Games | 163—Leo Cardenas, 1964 | 2,722—Pete Rose | 163 (1964, 1968, 1969, 1974, 1980, 1999, 2000, 2005) |
| At-bats | 680—Pete Rose, 160 G, 1973 | 10,934—Pete Rose | 5,767 (1968) |
| Runs | 134—Frank Robinson, 162 G, 1962 | 1,741—Pete Rose | 865 (1999)<br>Fewest—488 (1908) |
| Hits | 230—Pete Rose, 160 G, 1973 | 3,358—Pete Rose | 1,599 (1976)<br>Fewest—1,108 (1908) |
| Hitting streak | 44 G—Pete Rose, 1978 | | |
| Singles | 181—Pete Rose, 160 G, 1973 | 2,490—Pete Rose | 1,191 (1922) |
| Doubles | 51—Frank Robinson, 162 G, 1962<br>Pete Rose, 159 G, 1978 | 601—Pete Rose | 335 (2005) |
| Triples | 25—Bid McPhee, 132 G, 1890<br>*23—Sam Crawford, 140 G, 1902 | 152—Edd Roush | 120 (1926) |
| **HOME RUNS** | | | 222 (2005)<br>Fewest—14 (1908, 1916) |
| Righthander | 52—George Foster, 158 G, 1977 | 389—Johnny Bench | |
| Lefthander | 49—Ted Kluszewski, 149 G, 1954 | 251—Ted Kluszewski | |
| Switch-hitter | 23—Felipe Lopez, 148 G, 2005 | 152—Pete Rose | |
| Rookie | 38—Frank Robinson, 152 G, 1956 | | |
| Home | 34—Ted Kluszewski, 1954 | 195—Johnny Bench | 128 (1956) |
| Road | 31—George Foster, 1977 | 194—Johnny Bench | 112 (1999) |
| Month | 14—Frank Robinson, Aug 1962<br>Greg Vaughn, Sept 1999 | | 51 (Sept 1999) |
| Pinch | 5—Jerry Lynch, 1961 | 13—Jerry Lynch | 12 (1957) |
| Grand slams | 3—Frank Robinson, 162 G, 1962<br>Lee May, 153 G, 1970<br>Ray Knight, 162 G, 1980<br>Eric Davis, 129 G, 1987<br>Chris Sabo, 148 G, 1993 | 11—Johnny Bench | 9 (2002) |
| Home runs at Crosley Field, all teams | | | 219 (1957) |
| Home runs at Riverfront Stadium, all teams | | | 213 (1999) |
| Home runs at Great American Ball Park, all teams | | | 246 (2005) |
| Total bases | 388—George Foster, 158 G, 1977 | 4,645—Pete Rose | 2,549 (1999) |
| Extra-base hits | 92—Frank Robinson, 162 G, 1962 | 868—Pete Rose | 572 (2005) |
| Sacrifice hits | 33—Dummy Hoy, 1896<br>*31—Roy McMillan, 154 G, 1954 | 186—Edd Roush | 195 (1907) |
| Sacrifice flies | 13—Johnny Temple, 149 G, 1959 | 90—Johnny Bench | 66 (1993) |
| Bases on balls | 132—Joe Morgan, 146 G, 1975 | 1,210—Pete Rose | 693 (1974)<br>Fewest—297 (1902) |
| Strikeouts | 195—Adam Dunn, 161 G, 2004<br>Fewest—13—Frank McCormick, 154 G, 1941 | 1,306—Tony Perez | 1,335 (2004)<br>Fewest—308 (1921) |
| Hit by pitch | 24—Jason LaRue, 114 G, 2004 | 118—Frank Robinson | 81 (2004)<br>Fewest—11 (1951) |
| Runs batted in | 149—George Foster, 158 G, 1977 | 1,376—Johnny Bench | 820 (1999)<br>Fewest—398 (1908) |
| Grounded into double plays | 30—Ernie Lombardi, 129 G, 1938<br>Fewest—3—Billy Myers, 151 G, 1939 | 266—Dave Concepcion | 161 (1933)<br>Fewest—85 (1991) |
| Left on base | | | 1,328 (1976)<br>Fewest—984 (1920) |
| Batting average | .377—Cy Seymour, 149 G, 1905 | .332—Cy Seymour | .296 (1922)<br>Lowest—.227 (1968) |
| Most .300 hitters | | | 8 (1926) |
| Slugging average | .642—Ted Kluszewski, 149 G, 1954 | .554—Frank Robinson | .451 (1999)<br>Lowest—.304 (1906) |
| On-base percentage | .466—Joe Morgan, 146 G, 1975 | .415—Joe Morgan | .368 (1894) *.357 (1976)<br>Lowest—.288 (1908) |

## BASERUNNING

| | Individual Season | Career | Club Season |
|---|---|---|---|
| Stolen bases | 93—Arlie Latham, 135 G, 1891<br>*81—Bob Bescher, 153 G, 1911 | 406—Joe Morgan | 310 (1910) |
| Caught stealing | 28—Pat Duncan, 151 G, 1922 | 110—Pete Rose | 136 (1922) |

## PITCHING

| | Individual Season | Career | Club Season |
|---|---|---|---|
| Games | 90—Wayne Granger, 1969 | 531—Pedro Borbon Sr. | |
| Games started | 42—Noodles Hahn, 1901<br>Pete Schneider, 1917<br>Fred Toney, 1917 | 357—Eppa Rixey | |
| Complete games | 41—Noodles Hahn, 1901 | 195—Bucky Walters | 142 (1904) |

| | Individual Season | Individual Career | Club Season |
|---|---|---|---|
| **Wins** | 27—Dolf Luque, 1923<br>Bucky Walters, 1939 | 179—Eppa Rixey | |
| **Percentage** | .826—Elmer Riddle (19-4), 1941 | .663—Will White<br>*.623—Jim Maloney | |
| **Winning streak** | 16—Ewell Blackwell, 1947 | | |
| **20-win seasons** | | 4—Paul Derringer | |
| **Losses** | 25—Paul Derringer, 1933 | 152—Dolf Luque | |
| **Losing streak** | 12—Henry Thielman, 1902<br>Pete Schneider, 1914<br>Si Johnson, 1933 | | |
| **Saves** | 44—Jeff Brantley, 1996 | 182—Danny Graves | 60 (1970, 1972) |
| **Innings** | 375—Noodles Hahn, 1901 | 2,890.2—Eppa Rixey | 1,490 (1968) |
| **Hits** | 370—Noodles Hahn, 1901 | 3,115—Eppa Rixey | 1,657 (2005) |
| **Runs** | 159—Noodles Hahn, 1901 | 1,442—Tony Mullane<br>*1,304—Eppa Rixey | 907 (2004) |
| **Earned runs** | 145—Herm Wehmeier, 1950 | 1,068—Eppa Rixey | 832 (2004) |
| **Bases on balls** | 162—Johnny Vander Meer, 1943 | 1,072—Johnny Vander Meer | 659 (2000) |
| **Strikeouts** | 274—Mario Soto, 1982 | 1,592—Jim Maloney | 1,159 (1997) |
| **Strikeouts, game** | 16—Noodles Hahn, May 22, 1901<br>Jim Maloney, May 1, 1963<br>Ron Villone, Sept 29, 2000<br>[18—Jim Maloney, June 14, 1965, 11 inn] | | |
| **Hit batsmen** | 23—Jake Weimer, 1907 | 139—Tony Mullane<br>*66—Rube Benton | 80 (2005) |
| **Wild pitches** | 21—Scott Williamson, 2000 | 184—Tony Mullane<br>*121—Jim Maloney | 96 (2000) |
| **Home runs** | 40—Eric Milton, 2005 | 234—Tom Browning | 236 (2004) |
| **Sacrifice hits** | 26—Si Johnson, 1933 | 354—Eppa Rixey | 205 (1928) |
| **Sacrifice flies** | 13—Bill Gullickson, 1986 | 62—Tom Browning | 60 (1986) |
| **Earned run average** | 1.57—Fred Toney, 223 inn, 1915 | 2.37—Bob Ewing | 1.65 (1882) *2.23 (1919) |
| **Shutouts** | 7—Jake Weimer, 1906<br>Fred Toney, 1917<br>Hod Eller, 1919<br>Jack Billingham, 1973 | 32—Bucky Walters | 23 (1919)<br>Lost—24 (1908) |
| **1-0 games won** | 4—Jake Weimer, 1906 | 7—Johnny Vander Meer | 7 (1910, 1943, 1963)<br>Lost—7 (1907, 1916) |

## TEAM FIELDING

| | | | |
|---|---|---|---|
| **Putouts** | 4,471 (1968)<br>Fewest—4,006 (1930) | **Assists** | 2,151 (1905)<br>Fewest—1,534 (1966) |
| **Chances accepted** | 6,399 (1915)<br>Fewest—5,655 (1950) | **Errors** | 314 (1914)<br>Fewest—95 (1977) |
| **Double plays** | 194 (1928, 1931, 1954)<br>Fewest—108 (1989) | **Passed balls** | 39 (1914)<br>Fewest—3 (1975) |
| **Errorless games** | 99 (1992)<br>Consecutive—15 (1975) | **Fielding average** | .985 (1995)<br>Lowest—.952 (1914) |

## MISCELLANEOUS

**Most players, season** 57 (2003)

**Fewest players, season** 21 (1904)
**Games won** 108 (1975)
**Month** 24 (Aug 1918, July 1973)
**Consecutive** 14 (1899) *12 (1939, 1957)
**Winning percentage** .686 (1919), 96-44
**Lowest** .344 (1934), 52-99
**Number of league championships** 9
**Most recent** 1990
**Runs, game** 30 vs Louisville, June 18, 1893
*26 vs Boston, June 4, 1911
**Opponents'** 26 by Philadelphia, July 26, 1892
*25 by New York, June 9, 1901
by Brooklyn, Sept 23, 1901
**Hits, game** 32 vs Louisville, June 18, 1893
*28 vs Philadelphia, May 13, 1902
vs Colorado, May 19, 1999
vs Boston, June 20, 1980
**Home runs, game** 9 vs Philadelphia, Sept 4, 1999
**Runs, shutout** 18 vs Los Angeles, Aug 8, 1965
**Opponents'** 18 by Philadelphia, Aug 10, 1930, 1st game
by Philadelphia, July 14, 1934, 1st game
by St. Louis, June 10, 1944
**Longest 1-0 win** 15 inn vs New York, July 16, 1933, 1st game
vs Brooklyn, June 11, 1915

**Most seasons, non-pitcher** 19—Dave Concepcion
Barry Larkin
Pete Rose
**Most seasons, pitcher** 15—Joe Nuxhall
**Games lost** 101 (1982)
**Month** 26 (Sept 1914)
**Consecutive** 19 (1914)
**Overall record** 8,971-8,808 (116 seasons)
**Interleague play** 55-69
**Number of times worst record in league** 11 (tied in 1916)
**Most recent** 1982
**Runs, inning** 14 vs Louisville, June 18, 1893, 1st
*14 vs Houston, Aug 3, 1989, 1st

**Total bases, game** 55 vs Louisville, June 18, 1893
*55 vs Colorado, May 19, 1999

**Consecutive games with one or more home runs** 21 (41 HRs), 1956
**Longest shutout** 16 inn 3-0 vs Chicago, Sept 22, 1975

**Longest 1-0 loss** 21 inn vs San Francisco, Sept 1, 1967

## ATTENDANCE

| Highest home attendance | |
|---|---|
| League Park I | 196,473 (1892) |
| League Park II | 373,000 (1896) |
| Palace of the Fans | 424,643 (1909) |
| Crosley Field | 1,125,928 (1956) |
| Cinergy Field | 2,629,708 (1976) |
| Great American Ball Park | 2,355,160 (2003) |
| Highest road attendance | 3,016,074 (2000) |

*records made since 1900 that do not exceed pre-1900 records

| Largest crowds | |
|---|---|
| Day | 55,596 vs Milwaukee, Apr 3, 2000 |
| Night | 54,621 vs New York, Oct 4, 1999 |
| Doubleheader | 53,328 vs Pittsburgh, July 9, 1976 |
| Home opener | 55,596 vs Milwaukee, Apr 3, 2000 |

# COLORADO ROCKIES

## YEARLY FINISHES

(National League expansion franchise)

### WEST DIVISION

| Year | Position | W | L | Pct. | GB | Manager | Attendance |
|---|---|---|---|---|---|---|---|
| 1993 | 6th | 67 | 95 | .414 | 37.0 | Don Baylor | 4,483,350 |
| 1994 | 3rd | 53 | 64 | .453 | 6.5 | Don Baylor | 3,281,511 |
| 1995 | 2nd (d) | 77 | 67 | .535 | 1.0 | Don Baylor | 3,390,037 |
| 1996 | 3rd | 83 | 79 | .512 | 8.0 | Don Baylor | 3,891,014 |
| 1997 | 3rd | 83 | 79 | .512 | 7.0 | Don Baylor | 3,888,453 |
| 1998 | 4th | 77 | 85 | .475 | 21.0 | Don Baylor | 3,789,347 |
| 1999 | 5th | 72 | 90 | .444 | 28.0 | Jim Leyland | 3,481,065 |
| 2000 | 4th | 82 | 80 | .506 | 15.0 | Buddy Bell | 3,285,710 |
| 2001 | 5th | 73 | 89 | .451 | 19.0 | Buddy Bell | 3,159,385 |
| 2002 | 4th | 73 | 89 | .451 | 25.0 | Buddy Bell, Clint Hurdle | 2,737,918 |
| 2003 | 4th | 74 | 88 | .457 | 26.5 | Clint Hurdle | 2,334,085 |
| 2004 | 4th | 68 | 94 | .420 | 25.0 | Clint Hurdle | 2,338,069 |
| 2005 | 5th | 67 | 95 | .414 | 15.0 | Clint Hurdle | 1,914,389 |

(d) lost Division Series

## INDIVIDUAL AND CLUB RECORDS

### BATTING

| | Individual Season | Individual Career | Club Season |
|---|---|---|---|
| Games | 162—Vinny Castilla, 1998<br>Neifi Perez, 1998, 2000 | 1,279—Todd Helton | 162 (1993, 1996-2005) |
| At-bats | 690—Neifi Perez, 157 G, 1999 | 4,560—Todd Helton | 5,717 (1999) |
| Runs | 143—Larry Walker, 153 G, 1997 | 924—Todd Helton | 968 (2000)<br>Fewest—740 (2005) |
| Hits | 219—Dante Bichette, 161 G, 1998 | 1,535—Todd Helton | 1,664 (2000)<br>Fewest—1,472 (2003) |
| Hitting streak | 23 G—Dante Bichette, 1995 | | |
| Singles | 163—Juan Pierre, 156 G, 2001 | 867—Todd Helton | 1,130 (2000) |
| Doubles | 59—Todd Helton, 160 G, 2000 | 373—Todd Helton | 333 (1998) |
| Triples | 11—Neifi Perez, 157 G, 1999<br>Neifi Perez, 162 G, 2000<br>Juan Pierre, 156 G, 2001<br>Juan Uribe, 72 G, 2001 | 49—Neifi Perez | 61 (2001) |
| **HOME RUNS** | | | 239 (1997)<br>Fewest—142 (1993) |
| Righthander | 47—Andres Galarraga, 159 G, 1996 | 238—Vinny Castilla | |
| Lefthander | 49—Larry Walker, 153 G, 1997<br>Todd Helton, 159 G, 2001 | 271—Todd Helton | |
| Switch-hitter | 13—Greg Norton, 117 G, 2001 | 43—Neifi Perez | |
| Rookie | 25—Todd Helton, 152 G, 1998 | | |
| Home | 32—Andres Galarraga, 1996 | 168—Todd Helton | 149 (1996) |
| Road | 29—Larry Walker, 1997 | 104—Larry Walker | 115 (1997) |
| Month | 12—Dante Bichette, Aug 1995<br>Vinny Castilla, June 1996<br>Andres Galarraga, Aug 1996<br>Vinny Castilla, July 1998 | | 53 (Aug 1996) |
| Pinch | 5—Mark Sweeney, 2004 | 12—John Vander Wal | 11 (1995, 2004) |
| Grand slams | 2—many players | 6—Andres Galarraga<br>Dante Bichette | 5 (1994, 1998, 2000, 2002) |
| Home runs at Mile High Stadium, all teams | | | 184 (1993) |
| Home runs at Coors Field, all teams | | | 303 (1999) |
| Total bases | 409—Larry Walker, 153 G, 1997 | 2,769—Todd Helton | 2,748 (2001) |
| Extra-base hits | 105—Todd Helton, 159 G, 2001 | 668—Todd Helton | 598 (2001) |
| Sacrifice hits | 24—Royce Clayton, 146 G, 2004 | 48—Neifi Perez | 98 (1998) |
| Sacrifice flies | 12—Jeff Cirillo, 157 G, 2000 | 48—Dante Bichette<br>Todd Helton | 75 (2000) |
| Bases on balls | 127—Todd Helton, 154 G, 2004 | 773—Todd Helton | 619 (2003)<br>Fewest—388 (1993) |

| | Individual Season | Career | Club Season |
|---|---|---|---|
| **Strikeouts** | 157—Andres Galarraga, 159 G, 1996<br>Fewest—29—Juan Pierre, 156 G, 2001 | 659—Larry Walker | 1,181 (2004)<br>Fewest—863 (1999) |
| **Hit by pitch** | 21—Eric Young, 141 G, 1996 | 98—Larry Walker | 82 (1996)<br>Fewest—37 (1998) |
| **Runs batted in** | 150—Andres Galarraga, 159 G, 1996 | 915—Todd Helton | 909 (1996)<br>Fewest—704 (1993, 2005) |
| **Grounded into double plays** | 27—Todd Zeile, 144 G, 2002<br>Jay Payton, 157 G, 2003<br>Fewest—4—Neifi Perez, 157 G, 1999 | 126—Vinny Castilla | 148 (1998)<br>Fewest—116 (2001) |
| **Left on base** | | | 1,244 (2005)<br>Fewest—978 (1993) |
| **Batting average** | .379—Larry Walker, 127 G, 1999 | .337—Todd Helton | .294 (2000)<br>Lowest—.267 (2003, 2005) |
| **Most .300 hitters** | | | 5 (1996) |
| **Slugging average** | .720—Larry Walker, 153 G, 1997 | .618—Larry Walker | .483 (2001)<br>Lowest—.411 (2005) |
| **On-base percentage** | .469—Todd Helton, 154 G, 2004 | .433—Todd Helton | .362 (2000)<br>Lowest—.323 (1993) |

## BASERUNNING

| | Individual Season | Career | Club Season |
|---|---|---|---|
| **Stolen bases** | 53—Eric Young, 141 G, 1996 | 180—Eric Young | 201 (1996) |
| **Caught stealing** | 19—Eric Young, 144 G, 1993<br>Eric Young, 141 G, 1996 | 69—Eric Young | 90 (1993) |

## PITCHING

| | Individual Season | Career | Club Season |
|---|---|---|---|
| **Games** | 79—Todd Jones, 2002 | 461—Steve Reed | |
| **Games started** | 35—Kevin Ritz, 1996<br>Darryl Kile, 1998 | 132—Jamey Wright | |
| **Complete games** | 7—Pedro Astacio, 1999 | 14—Pedro Astacio | 12 (1999) |
| **Wins** | 17—Kevin Ritz, 1996<br>Pedro Astacio, 1999 | 53—Pedro Astacio | |
| **Percentage** | .667—Jason Jennings (16-8), 2002 | none over 1,500 inn. | |
| **Winning streak** | 9—Julian Tavarez, 2000 | | |
| **20-win seasons** | | none | |
| **Losses** | 17—Darryl Kile, 1998 | 52—Jamey Wright | |
| **Losing streak** | 8—Greg Harris, 1994<br>Darryl Kile, 1998 | | |
| **Losing streak, two seasons** | 12—Jose Jimenez, 2002 (6), 2003 (6) | | |
| **Saves** | 41—Jose Jimenez, 2002 | 102—Jose Jimenez | 43 (1995, 2002) |
| **Innings** | 232.0—Pedro Astacio,1999 | 827.1—Pedro Astacio | 1,435.1 (2004) |
| **Hits** | 258—Pedro Astacio, 1998 | 931—Jamey Wright | 1,700 (1999) |
| **Runs** | 160—Pedro Astacio, 1998 | 533—Pedro Astacio | 1,028 (1999) |
| **Earned runs** | 145—Pedro Astacio, 1998 | 499—Pedro Astacio | 955 (1999) |
| **Bases on balls** | 109—Darryl Kile, 1999 | 387—Jamey Wright | 737 (1999) |
| **Strikeouts** | 210—Pedro Astacio, 1999 | 749—Pedro Astacio | 1,058 (2001) |
| **Strikeouts, game** | 14—Darryl Kile, Aug 20, 1998 | | |
| **Hit batsmen** | 17—Pedro Astacio, 1998 | 58—Pedro Astacio | 84 (2003, 2005) |
| **Wild pitches** | 13—Marvin Freeman, 1996<br>Darryl Kile, 1999 | 34—Curtis Leskanic | 82 (1993) |
| **Home runs** | 39—Pedro Astacio, 1998 | 139—Pedro Astacio | 239 (2001) |
| **Sacrifice hits** | 18—Brian Bohanon, 1999 | 32—John Thomson | 82 (1993) |
| **Sacrifice flies** | 10—Pedro Astacio, 1999<br>Jeff Francis, 2005 | 23—Pedro Astacio | 78 (1993) |
| **Earned run average** | 3.66—Joe Kennedy, 162.1 inn, 2004 | none with 1,500 inn | 4.97 (1995) |
| **Shutouts** | 2—Roger Bailey, 1997 | 2—Roger Bailey<br>Brian Bohanon<br>John Thomson | 8 (2001, 2002)<br>Lost—13 (1993) |
| **1-0 games won** | none | none | 2 (1994, 1998, 2002)<br>Lost—2 (2003) |

## TEAM FIELDING

| | | | |
|---|---|---|---|
| **Putouts** | 4,306 (2004)<br>Fewest—4,256 (2005) | **Assists** | 1,946 (1997)<br>Fewest—1,694 (2001) |
| **Chances accepted** | 6,244 (1997)<br>Fewest—5,962 (2005) | **Errors** | 167 (1993)<br>Fewest—89 (2004) |
| **Double plays** | 202 (1997)<br>Fewest—149 (1993) | **Passed balls** | 19 (1996)<br>Fewest—5 (1997) |
| **Errorless games** | 93 (2001)<br>Consecutive—13 (1998) | **Fielding average** | .986 (2004)<br>Lowest—.973 (1993) |

## MISCELLANEOUS

**Most players, season** 54 (2005)
**Fewest players, season** 42 (1998)

**Games won** 83 (1996, 1997)
**Month** 19 (May 2002)
**Consecutive** 9 (1997)
**Winning percentage** .535 (1995, 1997), 77-67
**Lowest** .414 (1993, 2005), 67-95
**Number of league championships** 0
**Most recent** ---
**Runs, game** 20 vs Arizona, Sept 23, 2003
vs San Diego, Sept 20, 2005
**Opponents'** 26 by Chicago, Aug 18, 1995
**Total bases, game** 43 vs Pittsburgh, Aug 3, 2003
**Home runs, game** 7 vs Montreal, Apr 5, 1997

**Runs, shutout** 11 vs Florida, Aug 6, 1996
vs San Diego, Sept 13, 2000
**Opponents'** 17 by Florida, Sept 17, 1995
**Longest 1-0 win** 11 inn, vs San Diego, Sept 20, 1998

**Most seasons, non-pitcher** 10—Larry Walker
**Most seasons, pitcher** 7—Curtis Leskanic
Steve Reed
**Games lost** 95 (1993, 2005)
**Month** 22 (July 2000)
**Consecutive** 13 (1993)
**Overall record** 949-1,094 (13 seasons)
**Interleague play** 55-75
**Number of times worst record in league** 1
**Most recent** (2005, tied)
**Runs, inning** 11 vs San Diego, July 12, 1996, 7th

**Hits, game** 24 vs Montreal, May 3, 2000
vs Pittsburgh, Aug 3, 2003
**Consecutive games with one or more home runs** 17 (24 HRs), 1993
(36 HRs), 1996
**Longest shutout** 11 inn, 1-0 vs San Diego, Sept 20, 1998

**Longest 1-0 loss** 11 inn, vs Los Angeles, July 24, 2003

## ATTENDANCE

| | |
|---|---|
| **Highest home attendance** | |
| **Mile High Stadium** | 4,483,350 (1993) |
| **Coors Field** | 3,891,014 (1996) |
| **Highest road attendance** | 2,695,071 (1993) |

| | |
|---|---|
| **Largest crowds** | |
| **Day** | 80,227 vs Montreal, Apr 9, 1993 |
| **Night** | 73,957 vs San Francisco, June 24, 1994 |
| **Doubleheader** | 60,613 vs New York, Aug 21, 1993 |
| **Home opener** | 80,227 vs Montreal, Apr 9, 1993 |

# FLORIDA MARLINS

## YEARLY FINISHES

(National League expansion franchise)

### EAST DIVISION

| Year | Position | W | L | Pct. | GB | Manager | Attendance |
|---|---|---|---|---|---|---|---|
| 1993 | 6th | 64 | 98 | .395 | 33.0 | Rene Lachemann | 3,064,847 |
| 1994 | 5th | 51 | 64 | .443 | 23.5 | Rene Lachemann | 1,937,467 |
| 1995 | 4th | 67 | 76 | .469 | 22.5 | Rene Lachemann | 1,700,466 |
| 1996 | 3rd | 80 | 82 | .494 | 16.0 | Rene Lachemann, John Boles | 1,746,767 |
| 1997 | 2nd (D,C,S) | 92 | 70 | .568 | 9.0 | Jim Leyland | 2,364,387 |
| 1998 | 5th | 54 | 108 | .333 | 52.0 | Jim Leyland | 1,750,395 |
| 1999 | 5th | 64 | 98 | .395 | 39.0 | John Boles | 1,369,421 |
| 2000 | 3rd | 79 | 82 | .491 | 15.5 | John Boles | 1,218,326 |
| 2001 | 4th | 76 | 86 | .469 | 12.0 | John Boles, Tony Perez | 1,261,220 |
| 2002 | 4th | 79 | 83 | .488 | 23.0 | Jeff Torborg | 813,111 |
| 2003 | 2nd (D,C,S) | 91 | 71 | .562 | 10.0 | Jeff Torborg, Jack McKeon | 1,303,214 |
| 2004 | 3rd | 83 | 79 | .512 | 13.0 | Jack McKeon | 1,723,105 |
| 2005 | 3rd | 83 | 79 | .512 | 7.0 | Jack McKeon | 1,852,608 |

(D) won Division Series; (C) won League Championship Series; (S) won World Series

## INDIVIDUAL AND CLUB RECORDS

### BATTING

| | Individual Season | Individual Career | Club Season |
|---|---|---|---|
| **Games** | 162—Jeff Conine, 1993<br>Derrek Lee, 2002<br>Juan Pierre, 2003-2005 | 1,128—Luis Castillo | 162 (1993, 1996-1999, 2001-2005) |
| **At-bats** | 678—Juan Pierre, 162 G, 2004 | 4,347—Luis Castillo | 5,578 (1999) |
| **Runs** | 123—Cliff Floyd, 149 G, 2001 | 675—Luis Castillo | 751 (2003)<br>Fewest—581 (1993) |
| **Hits** | 221—Juan Pierre, 162 G, 2004 | 1,273—Luis Castillo | 1,499 (2005)<br>Fewest—1,356 (1993) |
| **Hitting streak** | 35 G—Luis Castillo, 2002 | | |
| **Singles** | 184—Juan Pierre, 162 G, 2004 | 1,081—Luis Castillo | 1,034 (1993) |
| **Doubles** | 45—Cliff Floyd, 153 G, 1998 | 241—Mike Lowell | 325 (2001) |
| **Triples** | 13—Juan Pierre, 161 G, 2005 | 42—Luis Castillo | 44 (1999, 2003) |
| **HOME RUNS** | | | 166 (2001)<br>Fewest—94 (1993) |
| **Righthander** | 42—Gary Sheffield, 161 G, 1996 | 143—Mike Lowell | |
| **Lefthander** | 33—Carlos Delgado, 133 G, 2005 | 110—Cliff Floyd | |
| **Switch-hitter** | 20—Orestes Destrade, 153 G, 1993 | 25—Orestes Destrade | |
| **Rookie** | 26—Preston Wilson, 149 G, 1999 | | |
| **Home** | 19—Gary Shefflield, 1996 | 61—Gary Sheffield | 84 (2001) |
| **Road** | 23—Gary Sheffield, 1996 | 88—Derrek Lee | 89 (2000) |
| **Month** | 11—Gary Sheffield, Apr 1996 | | 35 (Apr 2001) |
| **Pinch** | 3—Preston Wilson, 1999 | 3—Preston Wilson | 8 (1999) |

| | Individual | | Club |
|---|---|---|---|
| | **Season** | **Career** | **Season** |
| **Grand slams** | 3—Bobby Bonilla, 153 G, 1997 | 4—Derrek Lee | 9 (1997) |
| **Home runs at Pro Player Stadium, all teams** | | | 153 (2001) |
| **Total bases** | 344—Miguel Cabrera, 158 G, 2005 | 1,641—Mike Lowell | 2,344 (2001) |
| **Extra-base hits** | 79—Cliff Floyd, 149 G, 2001 | 387—Mike Lowell | 521 (2001) |
| **Sacrifice hits** | 19—Edgar Renteria, 154 G, 1997 | 65—Luis Castillo | 82 (2003, 2005) |
| **Sacrifice flies** | 12—Jeff Conine, 133 G, 1995 | 55—Mike Lowell | 56 (1999) |
| **Bases on balls** | 142—Gary Sheffield, 161 G, 1996 | 533—Luis Castillo | 686 (1997)<br>Fewest—470 (2001) |
| **Strikeouts** | 187—Preston Wilson, 161 G, 2000<br>Fewest—35—Juan Pierre, 162 G, 2003<br>Juan Pierre, 162 G, 2004 | 734—Derrek Lee | 1,184 (2000)<br>Fewest—918 (2005) |
| **Hit by pitch** | 17—Carlos Delgado, 133 G, 2005 | 51—Alex Gonzalez | 67 (2001, 2005)<br>Fewest—45 (1998) |
| **Runs batted in** | 121—Preston Wilson, 161 G, 2000 | 578—Mike Lowell | 713 (2001)<br>Fewest—542 (1993) |
| **Grounded into double plays** | 22—Greg Colbrunn, 141 G, 1996<br>Fewest—5—Walt Weiss, 158 G, 1993 | 92—Jeff Conine | 144 (2005)<br>Fewest—100 (2000) |
| **Left on base** | | | 1,248 (1997)<br>Fewest—1,114 (2003) |
| **Batting average** | .334—Luis Castillo, 136 G, 2000 | .293—Luis Castillo | .272 (2005)<br>Lowest—.248 (1993, 1998) |
| **Most .300 hitters** | | | 3 (2005) |
| **Slugging average** | .624—Gary Sheffield, 161 G, 1996 | .543—Gary Sheffield | .423 (2001)<br>Lowest—.346 (1993) |
| **On-base percentage** | .465—Gary Sheffield, 161 G, 1996 | .368—Luis Castillo | .346 (1997)<br>Lowest—.314 (1993) |

## BASERUNNING

| | Season | Career | Club Season |
|---|---|---|---|
| **Stolen bases** | 65—Juan Pierre, 162 G, 2003 | 281—Luis Castillo | 177 (2002) |
| **Caught stealing** | 24—Juan Pierre, 162 G, 2004 | 114—Luis Castillo | 74 (2003) |

## PITCHING

| | Season | Career | Club Season |
|---|---|---|---|
| **Games** | 78—Braden Looper, 2002 | 368—Braden Looper | |
| **Games started** | 34—Charlie Hough, 1993<br>Ryan Dempster, 2001<br>Dontrelle Willis, 2005 | 131—A.J. Burnett | |
| **Complete games** | 9—Livan Hernandez, 1998 | 14—A.J. Burnett | 14 (2005) |
| **Wins** | 22—Dontrelle Willis, 2005 | 49—A.J. Burnett | |
| **Percentage** | .692—Carl Pavano (18-8), 2004 | none with 1,500 inn | |
| **Winning streak** | 9—Pat Rapp, 1995<br>Livan Hernandez, 1997 | | |
| **20-win seasons** | | 1—Dontrelle Willis | |
| **Losses** | 17—Jack Armstrong, 1993 | 50—A.J. Burnett | |
| **Losing streak** | 8—Reid Cornelius, 2000<br>Brad Penny, 2001 | | |
| **Saves** | 47—Armando Benitez, 2004 | 108—Robb Nen | 53 (2004) |
| **Innings** | 237.1—Kevin Brown, 1997 | 853.2—A.J. Burnett | 1,456.1 (2002) |
| **Hits** | 265—Livan Hernandez, 1998 | 772—Ryan Dempster | 1,617 (1998) |
| **Runs** | 133—Livan Hernandez, 1998 | 415—Ryan Dempster | 923 (1998) |
| **Earned runs** | 123—Livan Hernandez, 1998 | 392—Ryan Dempster | 834 (1998) |
| **Bases on balls** | 119—Al Leiter, 1996 | 395—Ryan Dempster | 715 (1998) |
| **Strikeouts** | 209—Ryan Dempster, 2000 | 753—A.J. Burnett | 1,188 (1997) |
| **Strikeouts, game** | 14—A.J. Burnett, Aug 29, 2004 | | |
| **Hit batsmen** | 16—Kevin Brown, 1996 | 37—Ryan Dempster | 70 (2001) |
| **Wild pitches** | 15—Matt Clement, 2001 | 44—A.J. Burnett | 85 (1993) |
| **Home runs** | 37—Livan Hernandez, 1998 | 90—Ryan Dempster | 182 (1998) |
| **Sacrifice hits** | 16—Brian Meadows, 1999 | 43—Pat Rapp | 95 (1998) |
| **Sacrifice flies** | 12—Jesus Sanchez, 2000 | 27—Ryan Dempster<br>A.J. Burnett | 69 (1999) |
| **Earned run average** | 1.89—Kevin Brown, 233 inn, 1996 | none with 1,500 inn | 3.83 (1997) |
| **Shutouts** | 5—A.J. Burnett, 2002<br>Dontrelle Willis, 2005 | 8—A.J. Burnett | 15 (2005)<br>Lost—14 (1993, 1996) |
| **1-0 games won** | 1—Alex Fernandez, 1997<br>Brad Penny, 2002<br>Dontrelle Willis, 2003<br>A.J. Burnett, 2005 | 1—Alex Fernandez<br>Brad Penny<br>Dontrelle Willis<br>A.J. Burnett | 3 (2001, 2002)<br>Lost—4 (1993) |

## TEAM FIELDING

| | | | |
|---|---|---|---|
| **Putouts** | 4,369 (2002)<br>Fewest—4,289 (2000) | **Assists** | 1,796 (1996)<br>Fewest—1,590 (2003) |
| **Chances accepted** | 6,125 (1996)<br>Fewest—5,920 (2004) | **Errors** | 129 (1998)<br>Fewest—78 (2003) |

| | | | |
|---|---|---|---|
| **Double plays** | 187 (1996)<br>Fewest—130 (1993) | **Passed balls** | 29 (1993)<br>Fewest—6 (2002) |
| **Errorless games** | 100 (2003)<br>Consecutive—9 (2003) | **Fielding average** | .987 (2003)<br>Lowest—.979 (1998, 1999) |

## MISCELLANEOUS

**Most players, season** 49 (1998)
**Fewest players, season** 40 (2000, 2003)
**Games won** 92 (1997)
**Month** 19 (Aug 1997)
**Consecutive** 9 (1996)
**Winning percentage** .568 (1997), 92-70
**Lowest** .333 (1998), 54-108
**Number of league championships** 2
**Most recent** 2003
**Runs, game** 20 vs Atlanta, July 1, 2003
**Opponents'** 25 by Boston, June 27, 2003
**Hits, game** 25 vs Atlanta, July 1, 2003
**Home runs, game** 4, many times
**Runs, shutout** 17 vs Colorado, Sept 17, 1995
**Opponents'** 18 by Atlanta, Oct 3, 1999
**Longest 1-0 win** 13 inn, vs Philadelphia, Sept 26, 1998

**Most seasons, non-pitcher** 10—Luis Castillo
**Most seasons, pitcher** 7—A. J. Burnett
**Games lost** 108 (1998)
**Month** 20 (May 1995, May 1998, Aug 1998, Aug 2001)
**Consecutive** 11 (1998)
**Overall record** 963-1,076 (13 seasons)
**Interleague play** 87-63
**Number of times worst record in league** 2
**Most recent** 1999
**Runs, inning** 8, many times

**Total bases, game** 43 vs Atlanta, July 1, 2003
**Consecutive games with one or more home runs** 11 (18 HRs), 1995
**Longest shutout** 16 inn, 3-0 vs Chicago, Sept 22, 1975

**Longest 1-0 loss** none over 9 innings

## ATTENDANCE

| | |
|---|---|
| **Highest home attendance** | 3,064,847 (1993) |
| **Highest road attendance** | 2,701,068 (1993) |

**Largest crowds**

| | |
|---|---|
| **Day** | 57,405 vs Atlanta, Apr 5, 2005 |
| **Night** | 45,796 vs San Francisco, Aug 27, 1993 |
| **Doubleheader** | 37,007 vs Philadelphia, Sept 27, 1998 |
| **Home opener** | 57,405 vs Atlanta, Apr 5, 2005 |

# HOUSTON ASTROS

## YEARLY FINISHES

**(National League expansion franchise known as Houston Colt .45s through 1964)**

| Year | Position | W | L | Pct. | GB | Manager | Attendance |
|---|---|---|---|---|---|---|---|
| 1962 | 8th | 64 | 96 | .400 | 36.5 | Harry Craft | 924,456 |
| 1963 | 9th | 66 | 96 | .407 | 33.0 | Harry Craft | 719,502 |
| 1964 | 9th | 66 | 96 | .407 | 27.0 | Harry Craft, Luman Harris | 725,773 |
| 1965 | 9th | 65 | 97 | .401 | 32.0 | Luman Harris | 2,151,470 |
| 1966 | 8th | 72 | 90 | .444 | 23.0 | Grady Hatton | 1,872,108 |
| 1967 | 9th | 69 | 93 | .426 | 32.5 | Grady Hatton | 1,348,303 |
| 1968 | 10th | 72 | 90 | .444 | 25.0 | Grady Hatton, Harry Walker | 1,312,887 |

## WEST DIVISION

| Year | Position | W | L | Pct. | GB | Manager | Attendance |
|---|---|---|---|---|---|---|---|
| 1969 | 5th | 81 | 81 | .500 | 12.0 | Harry Walker | 1,442,995 |
| 1970 | 4th | 79 | 83 | .488 | 23.0 | Harry Walker | 1,253,444 |
| 1971 | 4th (tied) | 79 | 83 | .488 | 11.0 | Harry Walker | 1,261,589 |
| 1972 | 2nd | 84 | 69 | .549 | 10.5 | Harry Walker, Salty Parker, Leo Durocher | 1,469,247 |
| 1973 | 4th | 82 | 80 | .506 | 17.0 | Leo Durocher, Preston Gomez | 1,394,004 |
| 1974 | 4th | 81 | 81 | .500 | 21.0 | Preston Gomez | 1,090,728 |
| 1975 | 6th | 64 | 97 | .398 | 43.5 | Preston Gomez, Bill Virdon | 858,002 |
| 1976 | 3rd | 80 | 82 | .494 | 22.0 | Bill Virdon | 886,146 |
| 1977 | 3rd | 81 | 81 | .500 | 17.0 | Bill Virdon | 1,109,560 |
| 1978 | 5th | 74 | 88 | .457 | 21.0 | Bill Virdon | 1,126,145 |
| 1979 | 2nd | 89 | 73 | .549 | 1.5 | Bill Virdon | 1,900,312 |
| 1980 | 1st (P,c) | 93 | 70 | .571 | +1.0 | Bill Virdon | 2,278,217 |
| 1981 | 3rd/1st (i) | 61 | 49 | .555 | * | Bill Virdon | 1,321,282 |
| 1982 | 5th | 77 | 85 | .475 | 12.0 | Bill Virdon, Bob Lillis | 1,558,555 |
| 1983 | 3rd | 85 | 77 | .525 | 6.0 | Bob Lillis | 1,351,962 |
| 1984 | 2nd (tied) | 80 | 82 | .494 | 12.0 | Bob Lillis | 1,229,862 |
| 1985 | 3rd (tied) | 83 | 79 | .512 | 12.0 | Bob Lillis | 1,184,314 |
| 1986 | 1st (c) | 96 | 66 | .593 | +10.0 | Hal Lanier | 1,734,276 |
| 1987 | 3rd | 76 | 86 | .469 | 14.0 | Hal Lanier | 1,909,902 |
| 1988 | 5th | 82 | 80 | .506 | 12.5 | Hal Lanier | 1,933,505 |
| 1989 | 3rd | 86 | 76 | .531 | 6.0 | Art Howe | 1,834,908 |
| 1990 | 4th (tied) | 75 | 87 | .463 | 16.0 | Art Howe | 1,310,927 |
| 1991 | 6th | 65 | 97 | .401 | 29.0 | Art Howe | 1,196,152 |
| 1992 | 4th | 81 | 81 | .500 | 17.0 | Art Howe | 1,211,412 |
| 1993 | 3rd | 85 | 77 | .525 | 19.0 | Art Howe | 2,084,546 |

## CENTRAL DIVISION

| Year | Position | W | L | Pct. | GB | Manager | Attendance |
|---|---|---|---|---|---|---|---|
| 1994 | 2nd | 66 | 49 | .574 | 0.5 | Terry Collins | 1,561,136 |
| 1995 | 2nd | 76 | 68 | .528 | 9.0 | Terry Collins | 1,363,801 |
| 1996 | 2nd | 82 | 80 | .506 | 6.0 | Terry Collins | 1,975,888 |
| 1997 | 1st (d) | 84 | 78 | .519 | +5.0 | Larry Dierker | 2,046,781 |
| 1998 | 1st (d) | 102 | 60 | .630 | +12.5 | Larry Dierker | 2,450,451 |
| 1999 | 1st (d) | 97 | 65 | .599 | +1.5 | Larry Dierker | 2,706,017 |
| 2000 | 4th | 72 | 90 | .444 | 23.0 | Larry Dierker | 3,056,139 |
| 2001 | 1st (tied) (d) | 93 | 69 | .574 | 0.0 | Larry Dierker | 2,904,280 |
| 2002 | 2nd | 84 | 78 | .519 | 13.0 | Jimy Williams | 2,517,407 |

| Year | Position | W | L | Pct. | GB | Manager | Attendance |
|---|---|---|---|---|---|---|---|
| 2003 | 2nd | 87 | 75 | .537 | 1.0 | Jimy Williams | 2,454,038 |
| 2004 | 2nd (D,c) | 92 | 70 | .568 | 13.0 | Jimy Williams, Phil Garner | 3,087,872 |
| 2005 | 2nd (D,C,s) | 89 | 73 | .549 | 11.0 | Phil Garner | 2,804,760 |

(P) won division playoff; (c) lost League Championship Series; (i) lost intra-divisional playoff; *first half 28-29, second half 33-20; (d) lost Division Series; (D) won Division Series; (C) won League Championship Series; (s) lost World Series

## INDIVIDUAL AND CLUB RECORDS

### BATTING

| | Individual Season | Career | Club Season |
|---|---|---|---|
| **Games** | 102—Enos Cabell, 1978<br>Bill Doran, 1987<br>Jeff Bagwell, 1992, 1996, 1997, 1999<br>Craig Biggio, 1992, 1996, 1997<br>Steve Finley, 1992 | 2,564—Craig Biggio | 163 (1966, 1980, 2005) |
| **At-bats** | 660—Enos Cabell, 162 G, 1978 | 9,811—Craig Biggio | 5,641 (1998) |
| **Runs** | 152—Jeff Bagwell, 159 G, 2000 | 1,697—Craig Biggio | 938 (2000)<br>Fewest—464 (1963) |
| **Hits** | 210—Craig Biggio, 160 G, 1998 | 2,795—Craig Biggio | 1,578 (1998)<br>Fewest—1,184 (1963) |
| **Hitting streak** | 25 G—Jeff Kent, 2004 | | |
| **Singles** | 160—Sonny Jackson, 150 G, 1966 | 1,879—Craig Biggio | 1,097 (1984) |
| **Doubles** | 56—Craig Biggio, 160 G, 1999 | 604—Craig Biggio | 326 (1998) |
| **Triples** | 14—Roger Metzger, 154 G, 1973 | 80—Jose Cruz | 67 (1980, 1984) |
| **HOME RUNS** | | | 249 (2000)<br>Fewest—49 (1979) |
| **Righthander** | 47—Jeff Bagwell, 159 G, 2000 | 449—Jeff Bagwell | |
| **Lefthander** | 23—Franklin Stubbs, 146 G, 1990 | 138—Jose Cruz | |
| **Switch-hitter** | 42—Lance Berkman, 158 G, 2002 | 180—Lance Berkman | |
| **Rookie** | 21—Lance Berkman, 114 G, 2000 | | |
| **Home** | 28—Jeff Bagwell, 2000 | 234—Jeff Bagwell | 135 (2000) |
| **Road** | 30—Jeff Bagwell, 1999 | 215—Jeff Bagwell | 114 (2000) |
| **Month** | 13—Jeff Bagwell, June 1994 | | 49 (June 2001) |
| **Pinch** | 5—Cliff Johnson, 1974 | 9—Cliff Johnson | 9 (1995) |
| **Grand slams** | 2—many players | 6—Bob Aspromonte<br>Jeff Bagwell | 7 (2001) |
| **Home runs at Colt Stadium, all teams** | | | 85 (1962) |
| **Home runs at Astrodome, all teams** | | | 153 (1998) |
| **Home runs at Minute Maid Park, all teams** | | | 266 (2000) |
| **Total bases** | 363—Jeff Bagwell, 159 G, 2000 | 4,283—Jeff Bagwell | 2,655 (2000) |
| **Extra-base hits** | 94—Lance Berkman, 156 G, 2001 | 969—Jeff Bagwell | 574 (2000) |
| **Sacrifice hits** | 34—Craig Reynolds, 146 G, 1979 | 100—Joe Niekro | 109 (1979) |
| **Sacrifice flies** | 13—Ray Knight, 158 G, 1982<br>Jeff Bagwell, 162 G, 1999 | 102—Jeff Bagwell | 61 (2000) |
| **Bases on balls** | 149—Jeff Bagwell, 162 G, 1999 | 1,401—Jeff Bagwell | 728 (1999)<br>Fewest—381 (1964) |
| **Strikeouts** | 145—Lee May, 148 G, 1972<br>Fewest—39—Greg Gross, 156 G, 1974 | 1,558—Jeff Bagwell | 1,138 (1999)<br>Fewest—719 (1976) |
| **Hit by pitch** | 34—Craig Biggio, 162 G, 1997 | 273—Craig Biggio | 100 (1997)<br>Fewest—13 (1980) |
| **Runs batted in** | 135—Jeff Bagwell, 162 G, 1997 | 1,529—Jeff Bagwell | 900 (2000)<br>Fewest—420 (1963) |
| **Grounded into double plays** | 30—Brad Ausmus, 130 G, 2002<br>Fewest—0—Craig Biggio, 162 G, 1997 | 221—Jeff Bagwell | 154 (2000)<br>Fewest—76 (1983) |
| **Left on base** | | | 1,252 (1999)<br>Fewest—1,040 (1964) |
| **Batting average** | .368—Jeff Bagwell, 110 G, 1994 | .302—Lance Berkman | .280 (1998)<br>Lowest—.220 (1963) |
| **Most .300 hitters** | | | 4 (1998) |
| **Slugging average** | .750—Jeff Bagwell, 110 G, 1994 | .557—Lance Berkman | .477 (2000)<br>Lowest—.301 (1963) |
| **On-base percentage** | .454—Jeff Bagwell, 162 G, 1999 | .416—Lance Berkman | .361 (2000)<br>Lowest—.283 (1963) |

### BASERUNNING

| | Individual Season | Career | Club Season |
|---|---|---|---|
| **Stolen bases** | 65—Gerald Young, 149 G, 1988 | 487—Cesar Cedeno | 198 (1988) |
| **Caught stealing** | 27—Gerald Young, 149 G, 1988 | 149—Cesar Cedeno | 95 (1979, 1983) |

### PITCHING

| | Individual Season | Career | Club Season |
|---|---|---|---|
| **Games** | 83—Octavio Dotel, 2002 | 563—Dave Smith | |
| **Games started** | 40—Jerry Reuss, 1973 | 320—Larry Dierker | |
| **Complete games** | 20—Lary Dierker, 1969 | 106—Larry Dierker | 55 (1979) |
| **Wins** | 22—Mike Hampton, 1999 | 144—Joe Niekro | |

| | Individual Season | Career | Club Season |
|---|---|---|---|
| **Percentage** | .846—Mike Hampton (22-4), 1999 | .601—J.R. Richard | |
| **Winning streak** | 12—Mark Portugal, 1993<br>Wade Miller, 2002 | | |
| **20-win seasons** | | 2—Joe Niekro<br>Roy Oswalt | |
| **Losses** | 20—Dick Farrell, 1962 | 117—Larry Dierker | |
| **Losing streak** | 13—Jose Lima, 2000 | | |
| **Saves** | 44—Billy Wagner, 2003 | 225—Billy Wagner | 51 (1986) |
| **Innings** | 305—Larry Dierker, 1969 | 2,294.1—Larry Dierker | 1,482.2 (2000) |
| **Hits** | 271—Jerry Reuss, 1973 | 2,090—Larry Dierker | 1,596 (2000) |
| **Runs** | 152—Jose Lima, 2000 | 934—Joe Niekro | 944 (2000) |
| **Earned runs** | 145—Jose Lima, 2000<br>Jerry Reuss, 1973 | 837—Larry Dierker | 864 (2000) |
| **Bases on balls** | 151—J.R. Richard, 1976 | 818—Joe Niekro | 679 (1975) |
| **Strikeouts** | 313—J.R. Richard, 1979 | 1,866—Nolan Ryan | 1,228 (2001) |
| **Strikeouts, game** | 18—Don Wilson, July 14, 1968, 2nd game | | |
| **Hit batsmen** | 16—Jack Billingham, 1971<br>Darryl Kile, 1996 | 72—Darryl Kile | 74 (2003) |
| **Wild pitches** | 21—Joe Niekro, 1985 | 128—Joe Niekro | 91 (1970) |
| **Home runs** | 48—Jose Lima, 2000 | 177—Larry Dierker | 234 (2000) |
| **Sacrifice hits** | 22—Bob Knepper, 1986 | 91—Bob Knepper | 99 (1964) |
| **Sacrifice flies** | 13—Mark Lemongello, 1978<br>Jim Deshaies, 1988 | 78—Joe Niekro | 64 (2000) |
| **Earned run average** | 1.87—Roger Clemens, 211.1 inn, 2005 | 3.13—Nolan Ryan | 2.66 (1981) |
| **Shutouts** | 6—Dave A. Roberts, 1973 | 25—Larry Dierker | 19 (1979, 1981, 1986)<br>Lost—23 (1963) |
| **1-0 games won** | 3—Bob Bruce, 1964<br>J.R. Richard, 1976<br>Bob Knepper, 1981 | 5—Mike Scott | 9 (1976)<br>Lost—6 (1964, 1969) |

## TEAM FIELDING

**Putouts** 4,448 (1980)
Fewest—4,284 (1964)

**Chances accepted** 6,255 (1975)
Fewest—5,827 (1972)

**Double plays** 175 (1999)
Fewest—100 (1963)

**Errorless games** 96 (2002)
Consecutive—14 (2005)

**Assists** 1,880 (1975)
Fewest—1,561 (2000)

**Errors** 174 (1966)
Fewest—83 (2002)

**Passed balls** 38 (1984)
Fewest—4 (2001, 2003, 2004)

**Fielding average** .986 (2002)
Lowest—.972 (1966)

## MISCELLANEOUS

**Most players, season** 48 (1965)
**Fewest players, season** 32 (1972)
**Games won** 102 (1998)
**Month** 22 (Aug 1998)
(July 2005)
**Consecutive** 12 (1999, 2004)
**Winning percentage** .630 (1998), 102-60
**Lowest** .398 (1975), 64-97
**Number of league championships** 1
**Most recent** 2005
**Runs, game** 19 vs Chicago, June 25, 1995
vs Pittsburgh, May 11, 1999
**Opponents'** 22 by Chicago, June 3, 1987
**Hits, game** 25 vs Atlanta, May 30, 1976, 2nd game
(25 vs Cincinnati, July 2, 1976, 1st game, 14 inn)
**Home runs, game** 7 vs Chicago, Sept 9, 2000
**Runs, shutout** 15 vs Montreal, Apr 26, 1998
**Opponents'** 16 by Philadelphia, Sept 10, 1963
by Atlanta, May 8, 2005
**Longest 1-0 win** 24 inn, vs New York, Apr 15, 1968

**Most seasons, non-pitcher** 18—Craig Biggio
**Most seasons, pitcher** 13—Larry Dierker
**Games lost** 97 (1965, 1975, 1991)
**Month** 24 (July 1962)
**Consecutive** 11 (1995)
**Overall record** 3,497-3,503 (44 seasons)
**Interleague play** 71-60
**Number of times worst record in league** 3
**Most recent** 1991
**Runs, inning** 12 vs Philadelphia, May 31, 1975, 8th
vs Chicago, May 12, 1997, 7th
**Total bases, game** 44 vs Chicago, Sept 9, 2000
**Consecutive games with one or more home runs** 18 (33 HRs), 2000
**Longest shutout** 24 inn, 1-0 vs New York, Apr 15, 1968
**Longest 1-0 loss** 16 inn, vs Chicago, May 31, 2003

## ATTENDANCE

**Highest home attendance**

| | |
|---|---|
| **Colt Stadium** | 924,456 (1962) |
| **Astrodome** | 2,706,017 (1999) |
| **Minute Maid Park** | 3,087,872 (2004) |
| **Highest road attendance** | 2,461,031 (2004) |

**Largest crowds**

| | |
|---|---|
| **Day** | 52,199 vs Chicago, Aug 16, 1998 |
| **Night** | 54,037 vs Cincinnati, Sept 28, 1999 |
| **Doubleheader** | 45,115 vs Atlanta, Aug 4, 1979 |
| **Home opener** | 51,668 vs Chicago, Apr 6, 1999 |

# LOS ANGELES DODGERS

## YEARLY FINISHES

**(American Association franchise moved to the National League after the 1889 season and from Brooklyn to Los Angeles after the 1957 season)**

| Year | Position | W | L | Pct. | GB | Manager | Attendance |
|---|---|---|---|---|---|---|---|
| 1958 | 7th | 71 | 83 | .461 | 21.0 | Walter Alston | 1,845,556 |
| 1959 | 1st (L,S) | 88 | 68 | .564 | +2.0 | Walter Alston | 2,071,045 |
| 1960 | 4th | 82 | 72 | .532 | 13.0 | Walter Alston | 2,253,887 |

| Year | Position | W | L | Pct. | GB | Manager | Attendance |
|---|---|---|---|---|---|---|---|
| 1961 | 2nd | 89 | 65 | .578 | 4.0 | Walter Alston | 1,804,250 |
| 1962 | 2nd (l) | 102 | 63 | .618 | 1.0 | Walter Alston | 2,755,184 |
| 1963 | 1st (S) | 99 | 63 | .611 | +6.0 | Walter Alston | 2,538,602 |
| 1964 | 6th (tied) | 80 | 82 | .494 | 13.0 | Walter Alston | 2,228,751 |
| 1965 | 1st (S) | 97 | 65 | .599 | +2.0 | Walter Alston | 2,553,577 |
| 1966 | 1st (s) | 95 | 67 | .586 | +1.5 | Walter Alston | 2,617,029 |
| 1967 | 8th | 73 | 89 | .451 | 28.5 | Walter Alston | 1,664,362 |
| 1968 | 7th | 76 | 86 | .469 | 21.0 | Walter Alston | 1,581,093 |

## WEST DIVISION

| Year | Position | W | L | Pct. | GB | Manager | Attendance |
|---|---|---|---|---|---|---|---|
| 1969 | 4th | 85 | 77 | .525 | 8.0 | Walter Alston | 1,784,527 |
| 1970 | 2nd | 87 | 74 | .540 | 14.5 | Walter Alston | 1,697,142 |
| 1971 | 2nd | 89 | 73 | .549 | 1.0 | Walter Alston | 2,064,594 |
| 1972 | 3rd | 85 | 70 | .548 | 10.5 | Walter Alston | 1,860,858 |
| 1973 | 2nd | 95 | 66 | .590 | 3.5 | Walter Alston | 2,136,192 |
| 1974 | 1st (C,s) | 102 | 60 | .630 | +4.0 | Walter Alston | 2,632,474 |
| 1975 | 2nd | 88 | 74 | .543 | 20.0 | Walter Alston | 2,539,349 |
| 1976 | 2nd | 92 | 70 | .568 | 10.0 | Walter Alston, Tommy Lasorda | 2,386,301 |
| 1977 | 1st (C,s) | 98 | 64 | .605 | +10.0 | Tommy Lasorda | 2,955,087 |
| 1978 | 1st (C,s) | 95 | 67 | .586 | +2.5 | Tommy Lasorda | 3,347,845 |
| 1979 | 3rd | 79 | 83 | .488 | 11.5 | Tommy Lasorda | 2,860,954 |
| 1980 | 2nd (p) | 92 | 71 | .564 | 1.0 | Tommy Lasorda | 3,249,287 |
| 1981 | 1st/4th (M,C,S) | 63 | 47 | .573 | * | Tommy Lasorda | 2,381,292 |
| 1982 | 2nd | 88 | 74 | .543 | 1.0 | Tommy Lasorda | 3,608,881 |
| 1983 | 1st (c) | 91 | 71 | .562 | +3.0 | Tommy Lasorda | 3,510,313 |
| 1984 | 4th | 79 | 83 | .488 | 13.0 | Tommy Lasorda | 3,134,824 |
| 1985 | 1st (c) | 95 | 67 | .586 | +5.5 | Tommy Lasorda | 3,264,593 |
| 1986 | 5th | 73 | 89 | .451 | 23.0 | Tommy Lasorda | 3,023,208 |
| 1987 | 4th | 73 | 89 | .451 | 17.0 | Tommy Lasorda | 2,797,409 |
| 1988 | 1st (C,S) | 94 | 67 | .584 | +7.0 | Tommy Lasorda | 2,980,262 |
| 1989 | 4th | 77 | 83 | .481 | 14.0 | Tommy Lasorda | 2,944,653 |
| 1990 | 2nd | 86 | 76 | .531 | 5.0 | Tommy Lasorda | 3,002,396 |
| 1991 | 2nd | 93 | 69 | .574 | 1.0 | Tommy Lasorda | 3,348,170 |
| 1992 | 6th | 63 | 99 | .389 | 35.0 | Tommy Lasorda | 2,473,266 |
| 1993 | 4th | 81 | 81 | .500 | 23.0 | Tommy Lasorda | 3,170,392 |
| 1994 | 1st | 58 | 56 | .509 | +3.5 | Tommy Lasorda | 2,279,355 |
| 1995 | 1st (d) | 78 | 66 | .542 | +1.0 | Tommy Lasorda | 2,766,251 |
| 1996 | 2nd (d) | 90 | 72 | .556 | 1.0 | Tommy Lasorda, Bill Russell | 3,188,454 |
| 1997 | 2nd | 88 | 74 | .543 | 2.0 | Bill Russell | 3,319,504 |
| 1998 | 3rd | 83 | 79 | .512 | 15.0 | Bill Russell, Glenn Hoffman | 3,089,201 |
| 1999 | 3rd | 77 | 85 | .475 | 23.0 | Dave Johnson | 3,095,346 |
| 2000 | 2nd | 86 | 76 | .531 | 11.0 | Dave Johnson | 3,010,819 |
| 2001 | 3rd | 86 | 76 | .531 | 6.0 | Jim Tracy | 3,017,502 |
| 2002 | 3rd | 92 | 70 | .568 | 6.0 | Jim Tracy | 3,131,077 |
| 2003 | 2nd | 85 | 77 | .525 | 15.5 | Jim Tracy | 3,138,626 |
| 2004 | 1st (d) | 93 | 69 | .574 | +2.0 | Jim Tracy | 3,448,283 |
| 2005 | 4th | 71 | 91 | .458 | 11.0 | Jim Tracy | 3,603,646 |

(L) won league playoff; (S) won World Series; (l) lost league playoff; (s) lost World Series; (C) won League Championship Series; (p) lost division playoff; (M) won intra-divisional playoff; *first half 36-21, second half 27-26; (c) lost League Championship Series; (d) lost division series

## INDIVIDUAL AND CLUB RECORDS

### BATTING

| | Individual Season | Individual Career | Club Season |
|---|---|---|---|
| Games | 165—Maury Wills, 1962 | 2,181—Bill Russell | 165 (1962) |
| At-bats | 695—Maury Wills, 165 G, 1962 | 7,495—Willie Davis | 5,642 (1982) |
| Runs | 130—Maury Wills, 165 G, 1962 | 1,004—Willie Davis | 842 (1962)<br>Fewest—470 (1968) |
| Hits | 230—Tommy Davis, 163 G, 1962 | 2,091—Willie Davis | 1,515 (1970)<br>Fewest—1,234 (1968) |
| Hitting streak | 31 G—Willie Davis, 1969 | | |
| Singles | 179—Maury Wills, 165 G, 1962 | 1,530—Bill Russell | 1,128 (1970) |
| Doubles | 49—Shawn Green, 160 G, 2003 | 333—Steve Garvey | 286 (2002) |
| Triples | 16—Willie Davis, 146 G, 1970 | 110—Willie Davis | 67 (1970) |
| **HOME RUNS** | | | 211 (2000)<br>Fewest—67 (1968) |
| Righthander | 48—Adrian Beltre, 156 G, 2004 | 270—Eric Karros | |
| Lefthander | 49—Shawn Green, 161 G, 2001 | 162—Shawn Green | |
| Switch-hitter | 32—Reggie Smith, 148 G, 1977 | 97—Reggie Smith | |
| Rookie | 35—Mike Piazza, 149 G, 1993 | | |
| Home | 23—Gary Sheffield, 2000<br>Adrian Beltre, 2004 | 130—Eric Karros | 108 (2000) |
| Road | 30—Shawn Green, 2001 | 140—Eric Karros | 112 (2001) |
| Month | 15—Pedro Guerrero, June 1985 | | 43 (May 1979) |
| Pinch | 7—Dave Hansen, 2000 | 13—Dave Hansen | 12 (2000) |
| Grand slams | 3—Kal Daniels, 130 G, 1990<br>Mike Piazza, 37 G, 1998<br>Adrian Beltre, 156 G, 2004 | 8—Mike Piazza | 9 (2000) |
| Home runs at Los Angeles Coliseum, all teams | | | 193 (1958) |
| Home runs at Dodger Stadium, all teams | | | 194 (1999) |

## BATTING

| | Individual Season | Career | Club Season |
|---|---|---|---|
| Total bases | 376—Adrian Beltre, 156 G, 2004 | 3,094—Willie Davis | 2,362 (2000) |
| Extra-base hits | 84—Shawn Green, 161 G, 2001 | 585—Willie Davis | 504 (2000) |
| Sacrifice hits | 25—Jose Offerman, 158 G, 1993 | 132—Bill Russell | 120 (1964) |
| Sacrifice flies | 13—Reggie Smith, 128 G, 1978 | 74—Eric Karros | 64 (1974) |
| Bases on balls | 110—Jimmy Wynn, 130 G, 1975 | 765—Ron Cey | 668 (2000)<br>Fewest—407 (2003) |
| Strikeouts | 149—Bill Grabarkewitz, 156 G, 1970<br>Fewest—26—Bill Buckner, 154 G, 1976 | 1,105—Eric Karros | 1,190 (1996)<br>Fewest—744 (1976) |
| Hit by pitch | 18—Alex Cora, 138 G, 2004 | 52—Alex Cora | 72 (2003)<br>Fewest—14 (1984) |
| Runs batted in | 153—Tommy Davis, 163 G, 1962 | 992—Steve Garvey | 781 (1962)<br>Fewest—434 (1968) |
| Grounded into double plays | 27—Eric Karros, 154 G, 1996<br>Fewest—2—Todd Hollandsworth, 149 G, 1996 | 174—Bill Russell | 145 (1979)<br>Fewest—79 (1965) |
| Left on base | | | 1,223 (1982)<br>Fewest—1,012 (1958) |
| Batting average | .362—Mike Piazza, 152 G, 1997 | .309—Pedro Guerrero | .272 (1974)<br>Lowest—.230 (1968) |
| Most .300 hitters | | | 4 (1970) |
| Slugging average | .643—Gary Sheffield, 141 G, 2000 | .512—Pedro Guerrero | .431 (2000)<br>Lowest—.319 (1968) |
| On-base percentage | .438—Gary Sheffield, 141 G, 2000 | .381—Pedro Guerrero | .342 (1974)<br>Lowest—.289 (1968) |

## BASERUNNING

| | Individual Season | Career | Club Season |
|---|---|---|---|
| Stolen bases | 104—Maury Wills, 165 G, 1962 | 490—Maury Wills | 198 (1962) |
| Caught stealing | 31—Maury Wills, 158 G, 1965 | 171—Maury Wills | 78 (1992) |

## PITCHING

| | Individual Season | Career | Club Season |
|---|---|---|---|
| Games | 106—Mike G. Marshall, 1974 | 550—Don Sutton | |
| Games started | 42—Don Drysdale, 1963, 1965 | 533—Don Sutton | |
| Complete games | 27—Sandy Koufax, 1965, 1966 | 156—Don Drysdale<br>Don Sutton | 58 (1965) |
| Wins | 27—Sandy Koufax, 1966 | 233—Don Sutton | |
| Percentage | .864—Orel Hershiser (19-3), 1985 | .670—Sandy Koufax | |
| Winning streak | 13—Phil Regan, 1966 | | |
| Winning streak, two seasons | 15—Phil Regan, 1966 (13), 1967 (2) | | |
| 20-win seasons | | 3—Sandy Koufax | |
| Losses | 18—Claude Osteen, 1968<br>Don Sutton, 1969 | 181—Don Sutton | |
| Losing streak | 11—Rick Honeycutt, 1987 | | |
| Saves | 55—Eric Gagne, 2003 | 160—Eric Gagne | 58 (2003) |
| Innings | 336—Sandy Koufax, 1965 | 3,816.1—Don Sutton | 1,491 (1973) |
| Hits | 298—Claude Osteen, 1967 | 3,291—Don Sutton | 1,438 (1999) |
| Runs | 127—Don Sutton, 1970 | 1,450—Don Sutton | 787 (1999) |
| Earned runs | 118—Don Sutton, 1970 | 1,311—Don Sutton | 718 (1999) |
| Bases on balls | 124—Fernando Valenzuela, 1987<br>Chan Ho Park, 2000 | 996—Don Sutton | 614 (1959) |
| Strikeouts | 382—Sandy Koufax, 1965 | 2,696—Don Sutton | 1,289 (2003) |
| Strikeouts, game | 18—Sandy Koufax, Aug 31, 1959<br>Sandy Koufax, Apr 24, 1962<br>Ramon Martinez, June, 1990 | | |
| Hit batsmen | 20—Don Drysdale, 1961<br>Chan Ho Park, 2001 | 144—Don Drysdale | 75 (2000) |
| Wild pitches | 19—Hideo Nomo, 1995 | 94—Fernando Valenzuela | 70 (1958) |
| Home runs | 38—Don Sutton, 1970 | 309—Don Sutton | 192 (1999) |
| Sacrifice hits | 27—Fernando Valenzuela, 1983 | 169—Don Sutton | 109 (1992) |
| Sacrifice flies | 11—Burt Hooton, 1979 | 85—Don Sutton | 50 (1979) |
| Earned run average | 1.73—Sandy Koufax, 323 inn, 1966 | 2.64—Sandy Koufax | 2.62 (1966) |
| Shutouts | 11—Sandy Koufax, 1963 | 52—Don Sutton | 24 (1963, 1988)<br>Lost—23 (1968) |
| 1-0 games won | 4—Don Drysdale, 1968 | 10—Sandy Koufax | 7 (1963, 1984)<br>Lost—7 (1989) |

## TEAM FIELDING

| | | | |
|---|---|---|---|
| Putouts | 4,473 (1973)<br>Fewest—4,105 (1958) | Assists | 1,946 (1982)<br>Fewest—1,563 (1997) |
| Chances accepted | 6,411 (1982)<br>Fewest—5,708 (1961) | Errors | 193 (1962)<br>Fewest—73 (2004) |

**Double plays** 198 (1958)
Fewest—104 (1997)
**Errorless games** 102 (2004)
Consecutive—11 (1979)

**Passed balls** 24 (1973)
Fewest—6 (1958)
**Fielding average** .988 (2004)
Lowest—.970 (1962)

## MISCELLANEOUS

**Most players, season** 53 (1998)
**Fewest players, season** 30 (1962)
**Games won** 102 (1962, 1974)
**Month** 21 (May 1962, July 1963, June 1973, July 2004)
**Consecutive** 13 (1962, 1965)
**Winning percentage** .630 (1974), 102-60
**Lowest** .389 (1992), 63-99
**Number of league championships** 9
**Most recent** 1988
**Runs, game** 22 vs Colorado, July 21, 2001
**Opponents'** 20 by Chicago, May 20, 1967
by Chicago, May 5, 2001

**Hits, game** 24 vs Chicago, Aug 20, 1974
vs Arizona, Sept 2, 2002
**Home runs, game** 8 vs Milwaukee, May 23, 2002
**Runs, shutout** 19 vs San Diego, June 28, 1969
**Opponents'** 18 by Cincinnati, Aug 8, 1965
**Longest 1-0 win** 22 inn, vs Montreal, Aug 23, 1989

**Most seasons, non-pitcher** 18—Bill Russell
**Most seasons, pitcher** 16—Don Sutton
**Games lost** 99 (1992)
**Month** 20 (July 1968, June 1979)
**Consecutive** 10 (1961, 1992)
**Overall record** 4,082-3,538 (48 seasons)
**Interleague play** 75-71
**Number of times worst record in league** 1
**Most recent** 1992
**Runs, inning** 10 vs San Diego, June 28, 1969, 3rd
vs San Francisco, July 4, 1971, 8th
vs San Diego, Sept 13, 1977, 2nd
vs. Cincinnati, May 6, 2005, 1st
**Total bases, game** 48 vs Chicago, Aug 20, 1974

**Consecutive games with one or more home runs** 15 (23 HRs), 1977
**Longest shutout** 16 inn, 3-0 vs Chicago, Sept 22, 1975

**Longest 1-0 loss** 16 inn, vs Houston, Apr 21, 1976

## ATTENDANCE

**Highest home attendance**
**Los Angeles Coliseum** 2,253,887 (1960)
**Dodger Stadium** 3,608,881 (1982)

**Highest road attendance** 2,678,742 (2000)

**Largest crowds**
**Day** 78,672 vs San Francisco, Apr 18, 1958
**Night** 67,550 vs Chicago, Apr 12, 1960
**Doubleheader** 72,140 vs Cincinnati, Aug 16, 1961
**Home opener** 78,672 vs San Francisco, Apr 18, 1958

# MILWAUKEE BRAVES

## YEARLY FINISHES

**(Original National League franchise moved from Boston to Milwaukee after the 1952 season and to Atlanta after the 1965 season)**

| Year | Position | W | L | Pct. | GB | Manager | Attendance |
|---|---|---|---|---|---|---|---|
| 1953 | 2nd | 92 | 62 | .597 | 13.0 | Charlie Grimm | 1,826,397 |
| 1954 | 3rd | 89 | 65 | .578 | 8.0 | Charlie Grimm | 2,131,388 |
| 1955 | 2nd | 85 | 69 | .552 | 13.5 | Charlie Grimm | 2,005,836 |
| 1956 | 2nd | 92 | 62 | .597 | 1.0 | Charlie Grimm, Fred Haney | 2,046,331 |
| 1957 | 1st (S) | 95 | 59 | .617 | +8.0 | Fred Haney | 2,215,404 |
| 1958 | 1st (s) | 92 | 62 | .597 | +8.0 | Fred Haney | 1,971,101 |
| 1959 | 2nd (l) | 86 | 70 | .551 | 2.0 | Fred Haney | 1,749,112 |
| 1960 | 2nd | 88 | 66 | .571 | 7.0 | Chuck Dressen | 1,497,799 |
| 1961 | 4th | 83 | 71 | .539 | 10.0 | Chuck Dressen, Birdie Tebbetts | 1,101,441 |
| 1962 | 5th | 86 | 76 | .531 | 15.5 | Birdie Tebbetts | 766,921 |
| 1963 | 6th | 84 | 78 | .519 | 15.0 | Bobby Bragan | 773,018 |
| 1964 | 5th | 88 | 74 | .543 | 5.0 | Bobby Bragan | 910,911 |
| 1965 | 5th | 86 | 76 | .531 | 11.0 | Bobby Bragan | 555,584 |

(S) won World Series; (s) lost World Series; (l) lost pennant playoff

## INDIVIDUAL AND CLUB RECORDS

### BATTING

| | Individual | | Club |
|---|---|---|---|
| | Season | Career | Season |
| Games | 161—Hank Aaron, 1963 | 1,944—Eddie Mathews | 163 (1963) |
| At-bats | 636—Bill Bruton, 149 G, 1955 | 7,080—Hank Aaron | 5,591 (1964) |
| Runs | 127—Hank Aaron, 156 G, 1962 | 1,300—Eddie Mathews | 803 (1964)<br>Fewest—670 (1954) |
| Hits | 223—Hank Aaron, 154 G, 1959 | 2,266—Hank Aaron | 1,522 (1964)<br>Fewest—1,345 (1963) |
| Hitting streak | 25 G—Hank Aaron, 1956<br>Hank Aaron, 1962 | | |
| Singles | 132—Joe Torre, 154 G, 1964 | 1,397—Hank Aaron | 1,057 (1964) |
| Doubles | 46—Hank Aaron, 154 G, 1959 | 391—Hank Aaron | 274 (1964) |
| Triples | 15—Bill Bruton, 147 G, 1956 | 80—Hank Aaron | 62 (1957) |
| **HOME RUNS** | | | 181 (1962)<br>Fewest—170 (1960) |
| Righthander | 45—Hank Aaron, 156 G, 1962 | 398—Hank Aaron | |
| Lefthander | 47—Eddie Mathews, 157 G, 1953 | 452—Eddie Mathews | |
| Switch-hitter | 6—Red Schoendienst, 93 G, 1957 | 8—Red Schoendienst | |
| Rookie | 22—Rico Carty, 133 G, 1964 | | |

| | Individual Season | Career | Club Season |
|---|---|---|---|
| Home | 23—Joe Adcock, 1956 | 211—Eddie Mathews | 98 (1965) |
| | Eddie Mathews, 1960 | | |
| Road | 30—Eddie Mathews, 1953 | 241—Eddie Mathews | 124 (1957) |
| Month | 15—Joe Adcock, July 1956 | | 52 (June 1961) |
| Pinch | 2—many players | 7—Joe Adcock | 7 (1965) |
| Grand slams | 3—Del Crandall, 133 G, 1955 | 9—Hank Aaron | 8 (1962) |
| | Hank Aaron, 156 G, 1962 | Joe Adcock | |
| Home runs at County Stadium, all teams | | | 173 (1965) |
| Total bases | 400—Hank Aaron, 154 G, 1959 | 4,011—Hank Aaron | 2,411 (1957) |
| Extra-base hits | 92—Hank Aaron, 154 G, 1959 | 869—Hank Aaron | 482 (1957) |
| Sacrifice hits | 31—Johnny Logan, 148 G, 1956 | 107—Johnny Logan | 142 (1956) |
| Sacrifice flies | 12—Hank Aaron, 153 G, 1960 | 72—Hank Aaron | 60 (1960) |
| | Del Crandall, 142 G, 1960 | | |
| Bases on balls | 124—Eddie Mathews, 158 G, 1963 | 1,254—Eddie Mathews | 581 (1962) |
| | | | Fewest—408 (1965) |
| Strikeouts | 122—Mack Jones, 122 G, 1965 | 1,190—Eddie Mathews | 976 (1965) |
| | Fewest—33—Johnny Logan, 150 G, 1953 | | Fewest—619 (1954) |
| Hit by pitch | 9—Frank Torre, 129 G, 1957 | 36—Johnny Logan | 43 (1963) |
| | Mack Jones, 122 G, 1965 | | Fewest—20 (1956) |
| Runs batted in | 135—Eddie Mathews, 157 G, 1953 | 1,305—Hank Aaron | 755 (1964) |
| | | | Fewest—624 (1963) |
| Grounded into double plays | 26—Joe Torre, 154 G, 1964 | 193—Hank Aaron | 134 (1964) |
| | Fewest—4—Eddie Mathews, 151 G, 1956 | | Fewest—99 (1956) |
| | Bill Bruton, 151 G, 1960 | | |
| Left on base | | | 1,138 (1962, 1963) |
| | | | Fewest—1,021 (1953) |
| Batting average | .355—Hank Aaron, 154 G, 1959 | .320—Hank Aaron | .272 (1964) |
| | | | Lowest—.244 (1963) |
| Most .300 hitters | | | 5 (1964) |
| Slugging average | .636—Hank Aaron, 154 G, 1959 | .567—Hank Aaron | .442 (1957) |
| | | | Lowest—.370 (1963) |
| On-base percentage | .423—Eddie Mathews, 138 G, 1954 | .385—Eddie Mathews | .333 (1964) |
| | | | Lowest—.310 (1965) |

## BASERUNNING

| | Individual Season | Career | Club Season |
|---|---|---|---|
| Stolen bases | 34—Bill Bruton, 142 G, 1954 | 149—Hank Aaron | 75 (1963) |
| Caught stealing | 13—Bill Bruton, 142 G, 1954 | 64—Bill Bruton | 52 (1963) |
| | Bill Bruton, 151 G, 1960 | | |

## PITCHING

| | Individual Season | Career | Club Season |
|---|---|---|---|
| Games | 62—Billy O'Dell, 1965 | 452—Warren Spahn | |
| Games started | 39—Lew Burdette, 1959 | 399—Warren Spahn | |
| Complete games | 24—Warren Spahn, 1953 | 232—Warren Spahn | 72 (1953, 1958) |
| Wins | 24—Tony Cloninger, 1965 | 234—Warren Spahn | |
| Percentage | .767—Warren Spahn (23-7), 1953, 1963 | .629—Warren Spahn | |
| Winning streak | 11—Warren Spahn, 1954 | | |
| 20-win seasons | | 9—Warren Spahn | |
| Losses | 15—Lew Burdette, 1959 | 138—Warren Spahn | |
| | Warren Spahn, 1959 | | |
| Losing streak | unknown | | |
| Innings | 292—Warren Spahn, 1959 | 3,162—Warren Spahn | 1,471.2 (1963) |
| Hits | 312—Lew Burdette, 1959 | 2,934—Warren Spahn | 1,443 (1962) |
| Runs | 144—Lew Burdette, 1959 | 1,181—Warren Spahn | 744 (1964) |
| Earned runs | 131—Lew Burdette, 1959 | 1,073—Warren Spahn | 656 (1964) |
| Bases on balls | 121—Bob Buhl, 1957 | 791—Warren Spahn | 591 (1955) |
| Strikeouts | 211—Tony Cloninger, 1965 | 1,493—Warren Spahn | 966 (1965) |
| Strikeouts, game | 15—Warren Spahn, Sept 16, 1960 | | |
| Hit batsmen | 12—Bob Shaw, 1962 | 37—Lew Burdette | 35 (1960) |
| Wild pitches | 22—Tony Cloninger, 1965 | 58—Tony Cloninger | 71 (1964) |
| Home runs | 38—Lew Burdette, 1959 | 280—Warren Spahn | 160 (1964) |
| Sacrifice hits | 20—Warren Spahn, 1961 | 134—Warren Spahn | 87 (1961) |
| Sacrifice flies | 11—Lew Burdette, 1957 | 67—Warren Spahn | 43 (1957) |
| Earned run average | 2.10—Warren Spahn, 266 inn, 1953 | 3.05—Warren Spahn | 3.11 (1956) |
| Shutouts | 7—Warren Spahn, 1963 | 36—Warren Spahn | 18 (1959, 1963) |
| | | | Lost—13 (1963) |
| 1-0 games won | 2—Bob Buhl, 1960 | 6—Lew Burdette | 4 (1957, 1963) |
| | Warren Spahn, 1961, 1963 | Warren Spahn | Lost—unknown |

## TEAM FIELDING

| | | | |
|---|---|---|---|
| Putouts | 4,416 (1963) | Assists | 1,848 (1961, 1963) |
| | Fewest—4,128 (1958) | | Fewest—1,665 (1960) |
| Chances accepted | 6,264 (1963) | Errors | 152 (1955) |
| | Fewest—5,827 (1960) | | Fewest—111 (1961) |

**Double plays** 173 (1957)
Fewest—137 (1960)

**Errorless games** unknown
Consecutive—7 (1954, 1956, 1964)

**Passed balls** 28 (1965)
Fewest—5 (1956, 1959)

**Fielding average** .982 (1961)
Lowest—.975 (1955)

## MISCELLANEOUS

**Most players, season** 42 (1964)
**Fewest players, season** 31 (1953, 1954)
**Games won** 95 (1957)
**Month** 23 (Aug 1953, Aug 1958)
**Consecutive** 11 (1956)
**Winning percentage** .617 (1957), 95-59
**Lowest** .519 (1963), 84-78
**Number of league championships** 2
**Most recent** 1958
**Runs, game** 23 vs Chicago, Sept 2, 1957, 1st game
**Opponents'** unknown
**Hits, game** 26 vs Chicago, Sept 2, 1957, 1st game
**Home runs, game** 8 vs Pittsburgh, Aug 30, 1953, 1st game
**Runs, shutout** 15 vs Cincinnati, May 13, 1956, 1st game
**Opponents'** 10 by Philadelphia, July 21, 1953, 1st game
**Longest 1-0 win** 15 inn, vs Chicago, Apr 13, 1963

**Most seasons, non-pitcher** 13—Eddie Mathews
**Most seasons, pitcher** 12—Warren Spahn
**Games lost** 78 (1963)
**Month** 18 (June 1954)
**Consecutive** 8 (1961)
**Overall record** 1,146-890 (13 seasons)

**Number of times worst record in league** 0
**Most recent** ---
**Runs, inning** 10 vs Pittsburgh, June 12, 1953, 2nd game, 1st

**Total bases, game** 47 vs Pittsburgh, Aug 30, 1953, 1st game
**Consecutive games with one or more home runs** 22 (39 HRs), 1956
**Longest shutout** unknown

**Longest 1-0 loss** 16 inn, vs San Francisco, July 2, 1963

## ATTENDANCE

**Highest home attendance** 2,215,404 (1957)

**Highest road attendance** 1,633,569 (1959)

**Largest crowds**
**Day** 48,642 vs Philadelphia, Sept 27, 1959
**Night** 46,944 vs New York, Aug 27, 1954
**Doubleheader** 47,604 vs Cincinnati, Sept 3, 1956
**Home opener** 43,640 vs Cincinnati, Apr 12, 1955

# MILWAUKEE BREWERS

## YEARLY FINISHES

**(American League expansion franchise moved from Seattle to Milwaukee after the 1969 season and from the American League to the National League after the 1997 season)**

### AMERICAN LEAGUE WEST DIVISION

| Year | Position | W | L | Pct. | GB | Manager | Attendance |
|---|---|---|---|---|---|---|---|
| 1970 | 4th | 65 | 97 | .401 | 33.0 | Dave Bristol | 933,690 |
| 1971 | 6th | 69 | 92 | .429 | 32.0 | Dave Bristol | 731,531 |

### AMERICAN LEAGUE EAST DIVISION

| Year | Position | W | L | Pct. | GB | Manager | Attendance |
|---|---|---|---|---|---|---|---|
| 1972 | 6th | 65 | 91 | .417 | 21.0 | Dave Bristol, Del Crandall | 600,440 |
| 1973 | 5th | 74 | 88 | .457 | 23.0 | Del Crandall | 1,092,158 |
| 1974 | 5th | 76 | 86 | .469 | 15.0 | Del Crandall | 955,741 |
| 1975 | 5th | 68 | 94 | .420 | 28.0 | Del Crandall | 1,213,357 |
| 1976 | 6th | 66 | 95 | .410 | 32.0 | Alex Grammas | 1,012,164 |
| 1977 | 6th | 67 | 95 | .414 | 33.0 | Alex Grammas | 1,114,938 |
| 1978 | 3rd | 93 | 69 | .574 | 6.5 | George Bamberger | 1,601,406 |
| 1979 | 2nd | 95 | 66 | .590 | 8.0 | George Bamberger | 1,918,343 |
| 1980 | 3rd | 86 | 76 | .531 | 17.0 | George Bamberger, Buck Rodgers | 1,857,408 |
| 1981 | 3rd/1st (i) | 62 | 47 | .569 | * | Buck Rodgers | 878,432 |
| 1982 | 1st (C,s) | 95 | 67 | .586 | +1.0 | Buck Rodgers, Harvey Kuenn | 1,978,896 |
| 1983 | 5th | 87 | 75 | .537 | 11.0 | Harvey Kuenn | 2,397,131 |
| 1984 | 7th | 67 | 94 | .416 | 36.5 | Rene Lachemann | 1,608,509 |
| 1985 | 6th | 71 | 90 | .441 | 28.0 | George Bamberger | 1,360,265 |
| 1986 | 6th | 77 | 84 | .478 | 18.0 | George Bamberger, Tom Trebelhorn | 1,265,041 |
| 1987 | 3rd | 91 | 71 | .562 | 7.0 | Tom Trebelhorn | 1,909,244 |
| 1988 | 3rd (tied) | 87 | 75 | .537 | 2.0 | Tom Trebelhorn | 1,923,238 |
| 1989 | 4th | 81 | 81 | .500 | 8.0 | Tom Trebelhorn | 1,970,735 |
| 1990 | 6th | 74 | 88 | .457 | 14.0 | Tom Trebelhorn | 1,752,900 |
| 1991 | 4th | 83 | 79 | .512 | 8.0 | Tom Trebelhorn | 1,478,729 |
| 1992 | 2nd | 92 | 70 | .568 | 4.0 | Phil Garner | 1,857,314 |
| 1993 | 7th | 69 | 93 | .426 | 26.0 | Phil Garner | 1,688,080 |

### AMERICAN LEAGUE CENTRAL DIVISION

| Year | Position | W | L | Pct. | GB | Manager | Attendance |
|---|---|---|---|---|---|---|---|
| 1994 | 5th | 53 | 62 | .461 | 15.0 | Phil Garner | 1,268,399 |
| 1995 | 4th | 65 | 79 | .451 | 35.0 | Phil Garner | 1,087,560 |
| 1996 | 3rd | 80 | 82 | .494 | 19.5 | Phil Garner | 1,327,155 |
| 1997 | 3rd | 78 | 83 | .484 | 8.0 | Phil Garner | 1,444,027 |

### NATIONAL LEAGUE CENTRAL DIVISION

| Year | Position | W | L | Pct. | GB | Manager | Attendance |
|---|---|---|---|---|---|---|---|
| 1998 | 5th | 74 | 88 | .457 | 28.0 | Phil Garner | 1,811,548 |
| 1999 | 5th | 74 | 87 | .460 | 22.5 | Phil Garner, Jim Lefebvre | 1,701,796 |
| 2000 | 3rd | 73 | 89 | .451 | 22.0 | Davey Lopes | 1,573,621 |
| 2001 | 4th | 68 | 94 | .420 | 25.0 | Davey Lopes | 2,811,041 |
| 2002 | 6th | 56 | 106 | .346 | 41.0 | Davey Lopes, Jerry Royster | 1,969,693 |
| 2003 | 6th | 68 | 94 | .420 | 20.0 | Ned Yost | 1,685,049 |
| 2004 | 6th | 67 | 94 | .416 | 37.5 | Ned Yost | 2,062,382 |
| 2005 | 3rd | 81 | 81 | .500 | 19.0 | Ned Yost | 2,211,023 |

(i) lost intra-divisional series; *first half 31-25, second half 31-22; (C) won League Championship Series; (s) lost World Series

## INDIVIDUAL AND CLUB RECORDS

**Note: All records prior to 1998 are as an American League club.**

### BATTING

| | Individual Season | Individual Career | Club Season |
|---|---|---|---|
| **Games** | 162—Gorman Thomas, 1980<br>Robin Yount, 1988<br>Richie Sexson, 2003<br>Carlos Lee, 2005 | 2,856—Robin Yount | 163 (1970, 1982, 2000) |
| **At-bats** | 666—Paul Molitor, 160 G, 1982 | 11,008—Robin Yount | 5,733 (1982) |
| **Runs** | 136—Paul Molitor, 160 G, 1982 | 1,632—Robin Yount | 894 (1996)<br>Fewest—534 (1971) |
| **Hits** | 219—Cecil Cooper, 153 G, 1980 | 3,142—Robin Yount | 1,599 (1982)<br>Fewest—1,188 (1971) |
| **Hitting streak** | 39 G—Paul Molitor, 1987 | | |
| **Singles** | 157—Cecil Cooper, 153 G, 1980 | 2,182—Robin Yount | 1,107 (1991) |
| **Doubles** | 53—Lyle Overbay, 159 G, 2004 | 583—Robin Yount | 327 (2005) |
| **Triples** | 16—Paul Molitor, 140 G, 1979 | 126—Robin Yount | 57 (1983) |
| **HOME RUNS** | | | 216 (1982)<br>Fewest—82 (1992) |
| **Righthander** | 45—Gorman Thomas, 156 G, 1979<br>Richie Sexson, 158 G, 2001<br>Richie Sexson, 162 G, 2003 | 251—Robin Yount | |
| **Lefthander** | 41—Ben Oglivie, 156 G, 1980 | 201—Cecil Cooper | |
| **Switch-hitter** | 25—Dale Sveum, 153 G, 1987 | 90—Jose Valentin | |
| **Rookie** | 17—Greg Vaughn, 120 G, 1990<br>Danny Walton, 117 G, 1970 | | |
| **Home** | 28—Richie Sexson, 2001 | 124—Robin Yount | 108 (2003) |
| **Road** | 26—Ben Oglivie, 1980 | 127—Robin Yount | 127 (1982) |
| **Month** | 12—Gorman Thomas, Aug 1979<br>Greg Vaughn, June 1996<br>Jeromy Burnitz, June 1999 | | 47 (June 1982) |
| **Pinch** | 4—Bob Hamelin, 1998 | 4—Bob Hamelin | 8 (2002) |
| **Grand slams** | 3—John Jaha, 88 G, 1995<br>Devon White, 126 G, 2001<br>John Vander Wal, 117 G, 2003 | 5—Cecil Cooper<br>John Jaha<br>Jeromy Burnitz | 10 (1995) |
| **Home runs at County Stadium, all teams** | | | 187 (1999) |
| **Home runs at Miller Park, all teams** | | | 232 (2003) |
| **Total bases** | 367—Robin Yount, 156 G, 1982 | 4,730—Robin Yount | 2,606 (1982) |
| **Extra-base hits** | 87—Robin Yount, 156 G, 1982 | 960—Robin Yount | 537 (1980) |
| **Sacrifice hits** | 19—Ron Theobald, 126 G, 1971 | 106—Jim Gantner | 115 (1970) |
| **Sacrifice flies** | 14—Dave Parker, 157 G, 1990 | 123—Robin Yount | 72 (1992) |
| **Bases on balls** | 99—Jeromy Burnitz, 161 G, 2000 | 966—Robin Yount | 658 (1999)<br>Fewest—432 (1984) |
| **Strikeouts** | 188—Jose Hernandez, 152 G, 2002<br>Fewest—42—Cecil Cooper, 153 G, 1980<br>Charlie Moore, 151 G, 1983 | 1,350—Robin Yount | 1,399 (2001)<br>Fewest—665 (1983) |
| **Hit by pitch** | 25—Fernando Vina, 159 G, 1998 | 75—Geoff Jenkins | 73 (2005)<br>Fewest—18 (1982) |
| **Runs batted in** | 126—Cecil Cooper, 160 G, 1983 | 1,406—Robin Yount | 845 (1996)<br>Fewest—496 (1971) |
| **Grounded into double plays** | 26—George Scott, 158 G, 1975<br>Jeff Cirillo, 156 G, 1998<br>Fewest—2—Jose Valentin, 151 G, 1998 | 217—Robin Yount | 158 (2003)<br>Fewest—94 (1978) |
| **Left on base** | | | 1,276 (1999)<br>Fewest—1,031 (1972) |
| **Batting average** | .353—Paul Molitor, 118 G, 1987 | .303—Paul Molitor | .280 (1979)<br>Lowest—.229 (1971) |
| **Most .300 hitters** | | | 3 (1979, 1980, 1982, 1983, 1986) |
| **Slugging average** | .588—Geoff Jenkins, 135 G, 2000 | .470—Cecil Cooper | .455 (1982)<br>Lowest—.329 (1971) |
| **On-base percentage** | .438—Paul Molitor, 118 G, 1987 | .367—Paul Molitor | .353 (1996, 1999)<br>Lowest—.302 (1972) |

### BASERUNNING

| | Individual Season | Individual Career | Club Season |
|---|---|---|---|
| **Stolen bases** | 70—Scott Podsednik, 154 G, 2004 | 412—Paul Molitor | 256 (1992) |
| **Caught stealing** | 18—Pat Listach, 149 G, 1992 | 115—Paul Molitor | 115 (1992) |

### PITCHING

| | Individual Season | Individual Career | Club Season |
|---|---|---|---|
| **Games** | 83—Ken Sanders, 1971 | 365—Dan Plesac | |

| | Individual Season | Career | Club Season |
|---|---|---|---|
| **Games started** | 38—Jim Slaton, 1973, 1976 | 268—Jim Slaton | |
| **Complete games** | 23—Mike Caldwell, 1978 | 81—Mike Caldwell | 62 (1978) |
| **Wins** | 22—Mike Caldwell, 1978 | 117—Jim Slaton | |
| **Percentage** | .750—Pete Vuckovich (18-6), 1982 | .560—Mike Caldwell | |
| **Winning streak** | 10—Chris Bosio, 1992<br>Cal Eldred, 1992 | | |
| **20-win seasons** | | 1—Jim Colborn<br>Mike Caldwell<br>Teddy Higuera | |
| **Losses** | 20—Clyde Wright, 1974 | 121—Jim Slaton | |
| **Losing streak** | 10—Danny Darwin, 1985 | | |
| **Saves** | 39—Danny Kolb, 2004<br>Derrick Turnbow, 2005 | 133—Dan Plesac | 51 (1988) |
| **Innings** | 314—Jim Colborn, 1973 | 2,025.1—Jim Slaton | 1,467.1 (1982) |
| **Hits** | 297—Jim Colborn, 1973 | 2,054—Jim Slaton | 1,618 (1999) |
| **Runs** | 135—Jaime Navarro, 1993 | 971—Jim Slaton | 899 (1996) |
| **Earned runs** | 127—Jaime Navarro, 1993 | 869—Jim Slaton | 826 (1996) |
| **Bases on balls** | 106—Pete Broberg, 1975 | 760—Jim Slaton | 728 (2000) |
| **Strikeouts** | 264—Ben Sheets, 2004 | 1,081—Teddy Higuera | 1,173 (2005) |
| **Strikeouts, game** | 18—Ben Sheets, May 16, 2004 | | |
| **Hit batsmen** | 20—Jamey Wright, 2001 | 49—Jamey Wright | 72 (2001) |
| **Wild pitches** | 14—Jim Slaton, 1974<br>Chris Bosio, 1987 | 71—Jim Slaton | 66 (2005) |
| **Home runs** | 36—Wayne Franklin, 2003 | 192—Jim Slaton | 219 (2003) |
| **Sacrifice hits** | 15—Jim Slaton, 1976 | 76—Jim Slaton | 93 (2002) |
| **Sacrifice flies** | 17—Jaime Navarro, 1993 | 74—Jim Slaton | 76 (1993) |
| **Earned run average** | 2.37—Mike Caldwell, 293 inn, 1978 | 3.74—Mike Caldwell | 3.38 (1971) |
| **Shutouts** | 6—Mike Caldwell, 1978 | 19—Jim Slaton | 23 (1971)<br>Lost—20 (1972) |
| **1-0 games won** | 1—many pitchers | 5—Teddy Higuera | 5 (1971)<br>Lost—5 (2001) |

## TEAM FIELDING

**Putouts** 4,402 (1982)
Fewest—4,175 (1972)
**Chances accepted** 6,284 (1978)
Fewest—5,784 (1972)
**Double plays** 192 (1998)
Fewest—132 (2004)
**Errorless games** 90 (1992)
Consecutive—10 (1970, 1979)

**Assists** 1,976 (1978)
Fewest—1,482 (2005)
**Errors** 180 (1975)
Fewest—89 (1992)
**Passed balls** 34 (1995)
Fewest—4 (1978)
**Fielding average** .986 (1992)
Lowest—.971 (1975)

## MISCELLANEOUS

**Most players, season** 49 (2002)
**Fewest players, season** 31 (1979)
**Games won** 95 (1979, 1982)
**Month** 21 (June 1978)
**Consecutive** 13 (1987)
**Winning percentage** .590 (1979), 95-66
**Lowest** .346 (2002), 56-106
**Number of league championships** 1
**Most recent** 1982
**Runs, game** 22 vs Toronto, Aug 28, 1992
**Opponents'** 20 by Boston, Sept 6, 1975
by Chicago, May 15, 1996
**Hits, game** 31 vs Toronto, Aug 28, 1992
**Home runs, game** 7 vs Cleveland, Apr 29, 1980
**Runs, shutout** 18 vs Boston, Apr 16, 1990
**Opponents'** 17 by Cincinnati, Aug 7, 1998
**Longest 1-0 win** 17 inn, vs Anaheim AL, June 8, 2004

**Most seasons, non-pitcher** 20—Robin Yount
**Most seasons, pitcher** 12—Jim Slaton
**Games lost** 106 (2002)
**Month** 23 (Aug 1977)
**Consecutive** 14 (1994)
**Overall record** 2,697-3,002 (36 seasons)
**Interleague play** 58-65
**Number of times worst record in league** 2
**Most recent** 2002
**Runs, inning** 13 vs California, July 8, 1990, 5th
**Total bases, game** 38 vs Toronto, Aug 28, 1992
vs New York, Apr 26, 2001
[40 vs Philadelphia, May 15, 2001, 10 inn]
**Consecutive games with one or more home runs** 19 (35 HRs), 1996
**Longest shutout** 17 inn, 1-0 vs Anaheim AL, June 8, 2004
**Longest 1-0 loss** 17 inn, vs Baltimore, Sept 27, 1974

## ATTENDANCE

**Highest home attendance**
**County Stadium** 2,397,131 (1983)
**Miller Park** 2,811,041 (2001)
**Highest road attendance** 2,376,690 (2005)

**Largest crowds**
**Day** 56,354 vs Cincinnati, Sept 28, 2000
**Night** 55,716 vs Boston, July 3, 1982
**Doubleheader** 54,630 vs Detroit, July 6, 1979
**Home opener** 55,887 vs New York, Apr 15, 1988

# MONTREAL EXPOS

## YEARLY FINISHES

**(National League expansion franchise moved to Washington after the 2004 season)**

### EAST DIVISION

| Year | Position | W | L | Pct. | GB | Manager | Attendance |
|---|---|---|---|---|---|---|---|
| 1969 | 6th | 52 | 110 | .321 | 48.0 | Gene Mauch | 1,212,608 |
| 1970 | 6th | 73 | 89 | .451 | 16.0 | Gene Mauch | 1,424,683 |
| 1971 | 5th | 71 | 90 | .441 | 25.5 | Gene Mauch | 1,290,963 |

| Year | Position | W | L | Pct. | GB | Manager | Attendance |
|---|---|---|---|---|---|---|---|
| 1972 | 5th | 70 | 86 | .449 | 26.5 | Gene Mauch | 1,142,145 |
| 1973 | 4th | 79 | 83 | .488 | 3.5 | Gene Mauch | 1,246,863 |
| 1974 | 4th | 79 | 82 | .491 | 8.5 | Gene Mauch | 1,019,134 |
| 1975 | 5th (tied) | 75 | 87 | .463 | 17.5 | Gene Mauch | 908,292 |
| 1976 | 6th | 55 | 107 | .340 | 46.0 | Karl Kuehl, Charlie Fox | 646,704 |
| 1977 | 5th | 75 | 87 | .463 | 26.0 | Dick Williams | 1,433,757 |
| 1978 | 4th | 76 | 86 | .469 | 14.0 | Dick Williams | 1,427,007 |
| 1979 | 2nd | 95 | 65 | .594 | 2.0 | Dick Williams | 2,102,173 |
| 1980 | 2nd | 90 | 72 | .556 | 1.0 | Dick Williams | 2,208,175 |
| 1981 | 3rd/1st (I,c) | 60 | 48 | .556 | * | Dick Williams, Jim Fanning | 1,534,564 |
| 1982 | 3rd | 86 | 76 | .531 | 6.0 | Jim Fanning | 2,318,292 |
| 1983 | 3rd | 82 | 80 | .506 | 8.0 | Bill Virdon | 2,320,651 |
| 1984 | 5th | 78 | 83 | .484 | 18.0 | Bill Virdon, Jim Fanning | 1,606,531 |
| 1985 | 3rd | 84 | 77 | .522 | 16.5 | Buck Rodgers | 1,502,494 |
| 1986 | 4th | 78 | 83 | .484 | 29.5 | Buck Rodgers | 1,128,981 |
| 1987 | 3rd | 91 | 71 | .562 | 4.0 | Buck Rodgers | 1,850,324 |
| 1988 | 3rd | 81 | 81 | .500 | 20.0 | Buck Rodgers | 1,478,659 |
| 1989 | 4th | 81 | 81 | .500 | 12.0 | Buck Rodgers | 1,783,533 |
| 1990 | 3rd | 85 | 77 | .525 | 10.0 | Buck Rodgers | 1,373,087 |
| 1991 | 6th | 71 | 90 | .441 | 26.5 | Buck Rodgers, Tom Runnells | 934,742 |
| 1992 | 2nd | 87 | 75 | .537 | 9.0 | Tom Runnells, Felipe Alou | 1,669,077 |
| 1993 | 2nd | 94 | 68 | .580 | 3.0 | Felipe Alou | 1,641,437 |
| 1994 | 1st (n) | 74 | 40 | .649 | +6.0 | Felipe Alou | 1,276,250 |
| 1995 | 5th | 66 | 78 | .458 | 24.0 | Felipe Alou | 1,309,618 |
| 1996 | 2nd | 88 | 74 | .543 | 8.0 | Felipe Alou | 1,616,709 |
| 1997 | 4th | 78 | 84 | .481 | 23.0 | Felipe Alou | 1,497,609 |
| 1998 | 4th | 65 | 97 | .401 | 41.0 | Felipe Alou | 914,717 |
| 1999 | 4th | 68 | 94 | .420 | 35.0 | Felipe Alou | 773,277 |
| 2000 | 4th | 67 | 95 | .414 | 28.0 | Felipe Alou | 926,263 |
| 2001 | 5th | 68 | 94 | .420 | 20.0 | Felipe Alou, Jeff Torborg | 609,473 |
| 2002 | 2nd | 83 | 79 | .512 | 19.0 | Frank Robinson | 732,901 |
| 2003 | 4th | 83 | 79 | .512 | 18.0 | Frank Robinson | 1,023,680 |
| 2004 | 5th | 67 | 95 | .414 | 29.0 | Frank Robinson | 748,550 |

(I) won intra-divisional playoff; (c) lost League Championship Series; *first half 30-25, second half 30-23; (n) no World Series

## INDIVIDUAL AND CLUB RECORDS

### BATTING

| | Individual Season | Individual Career | Club Season |
|---|---|---|---|
| **Games** | 162—Rusty Staub, 1971<br>Ken Singleton, 1973<br>Warren Cromartie, 1980<br>Orlando Cabrera, 2001, 2003 | 1,767—Tim Wallach | 163 (1983, 1988, 1993) |
| **At-bats** | 659—Warren Cromartie, 158 G, 1979 | 6,529—Tim Wallach | 5,675 (1977) |
| **Runs** | 133—Tim Raines Sr., 156 G, 1983 | 947—Tim Raines Sr. | 741 (1987, 1996)<br>Fewest—531 (1976) |
| **Hits** | 206—Vlad Guerrero, 161 G, 2002 | 1,694—Tim Wallach | 1,482 (1983)<br>Fewest—1,275 (1976) |
| **Hitting streak** | 31 G—Vlad Guerrero, 1999 | | |
| **Singles** | 157—Mark Grudzielanek, 153 G, 1996 | 1,163—Tim Raines Sr. | 1,042 (1983) |
| **Doubles** | 54—Mark Grudzielanek, 156 G, 1997 | 360—Tim Wallach | 339 (1997) |
| **Triples** | 13—Rodney Scott, 154 G, 1980<br>Tim Raines Sr., 150 G, 1985<br>Mitch Webster, 151 G, 1986 | 82—Tim Raines Sr. | 61 (1980) |
| **HOME RUNS** | | | 178 (2000)<br>Fewest—86 (1974) |
| **Righthander** | 44—Vlad Guerrero, 154 G, 2000 | 234—Vlad Guerrero | |
| **Lefthander** | 36—Henry Rodriguez, 145 G, 1996 | 99—Larry Walker | |
| **Switch-hitter** | 24—Jose Vidro, 153 G, 2000 | 101—Jose Vidro | |
| **Rookie** | 20—Brad Wilkerson, 153 G, 2002 | | |
| **Home** | 25—Vlad Guerrero, 2000 | 128—Vlad Guerrero | 88 (2000) |
| **Road** | 22—Andre Dawson, 1983 | 130—Andre Dawson | 91 (1997) |
| **Month** | 13—Vlad Guerrero, Sept 2000 | | 48 (Aug 1999) |
| **Pinch** | 4—Hal Breeden, 1973 | 5—Jose Morales | 9 (1973, 2002) |
| **Grand slams** | 2—many players | 7—Gary Carter | 9 (1996) |
| **Home runs at Jarry Park, all teams** | | | 168 (1970) |
| **Home runs at Olympic Stadium, all teams** | | | 190 (2000) |
| **Total bases** | 379—Vlad Guerrero, 154 G, 2000 | 2,728—Tim Wallach | 2,389 (2000) |
| **Extra-base hits** | 84—Vlad Guerrero, 160 G, 1999 | 595—Tim Wallach | 545 (1997) |
| **Sacrifice hits** | 23—Larry Lintz, 113 G, 1974 | 101—Steve Rogers | 115 (1973) |
| **Sacrifice flies** | 18—Andre Dawson, 159 G, 1983 | 71—Andre Dawson | 57 (1983) |
| **Bases on balls** | 123—Ken Singleton, 162 G, 1973 | 793—Tim Raines Sr. | 695 (1973)<br>Fewest—396 (1978) |
| **Strikeouts** | 169—Andres Galarraga, 155 G, 1990<br>Fewest—29—Dave Cash, 159 G, 1978 | 1,009—Tim Wallach | 1,104 (2002)<br>Fewest—733 (1983) |
| **Hit by pitch** | 50—Ron Hunt, 152 G, 1971 | 114—Ron Hunt | 78 (1971)<br>Fewest—16 (1976) |
| **Runs batted in** | 131—Vlad Guerrero, 160 G, 1999 | 905—Tim Wallach | 705 (2000)<br>Fewest—507 (1976) |
| **Grounded into double plays** | 27—John Bateman, 139 G, 1971<br>Ken Singleton, 162 G, 1973<br>Fewest—1—Ron Hunt, 152 G, 1971 | 152—Tim Wallach | 151 (2001)<br>Fewest—95 (1993, 1997) |

| | Individual Season | Career | Club Season |
|---|---|---|---|
| **Left on base** | | | 1,232 (1973)<br>Fewest—1,024 (2001) |
| **Batting average** | .345—Vlad Guerrero, 154 G, 2000 | .323—Vlad Guerrero | .278 (1994)<br>Lowest—.235 (1976) |
| **Most .300 hitters** | | | 3 (1999) |
| **Slugging average** | .664—Vlad Guerrero, 154 G, 2000 | .588—Vlad Guerrero | .435 (1994)<br>Lowest—.340 (1976) |
| **On-base percentage** | .429—Tim Raines Sr., 139 G, 1987 | .391—Tim Raines Sr. | .343 (1994)<br>Lowest—.291 (1976) |

## BASERUNNING

| | | | |
|---|---|---|---|
| **Stolen bases** | 97—Ron LeFlore, 139 G, 1980 | 635—Tim Raines Sr. | 237 (1980) |
| **Caught stealing** | 23—Delino DeShields, 151 G, 1991 | 106—Tim Raines Sr. | 100 (1991) |

## PITCHING

| | | | |
|---|---|---|---|
| **Games** | 92—Mike Marshall, 1973 | 425—Tim Burke | |
| **Games started** | 40—Steve Rogers, 1977 | 393—Steve Rogers | |
| **Complete games** | 20—Bill Stoneman, 1971 | 129—Steve Rogers | 49 (1971) |
| **Wins** | 20—Ross Grimsley, 1978 | 158—Steve Rogers | |
| **Percentage** | .783—Bryn Smith (18-5), 1985 | .581—Dennis Martinez | |
| **Winning streak** | 11—Dennis Martinez, 1989 | | |
| **20-win seasons** | | 1—Ross Grimsley | |
| **Losses** | 22—Steve Rogers, 1974 | 152—Steve Rogers | |
| **Losing streak** | 10—Steve Renko, 1972 | | |
| **Saves** | 43—John Wetteland, 1993 | 152—Jeff Reardon | 61 (1993) |
| **Innings** | 302—Steve Rogers, 1977 | 2,837.2—Steve Rogers | 1,482.2 (1988) |
| **Hits** | 281—Carl Morton, 1970 | 2,619—Steve Rogers | 1,575 (2000) |
| **Runs** | 139—Steve Rogers, 1974 | 1,122—Steve Rogers | 902 (2000) |
| **Earned runs** | 126—Steve Rogers, 1974 | 1,001—Steve Rogers | 812 (2000) |
| **Bases on balls** | 146—Bill Stoneman, 1971 | 876—Steve Rogers | 716 (1970) |
| **Strikeouts** | 305—Pedro Martinez, 1997 | 1,621—Steve Rogers | 1,206 (1996) |
| **Strikeouts, game** | 18—Bill Gullickson, Sept 10, 1980 | | |
| **Hit batsmen** | 14—Bill Stoneman, 1970 | 52—Dennis Martinez | 79 (2004) |
| **Wild pitches** | 19—Steve Renko, 1974 | 87—Steve Rogers | 71 (2003) |
| **Home runs** | 31—Javier Vazquez, 1998 | 155—Javier Vasquez | 191 (2004) |
| **Sacrifice hits** | 21—Steve Rogers, 1979 | 153—Steve Rogers | 106 (1976) |
| **Sacrifice flies** | 11—Woodie Fryman, 1976<br>Miguel Batista, 1999 | 70—Steve Rogers | 58 (2000) |
| **Earned run average** | 1.90—Pedro Martinez, 241.1 inn, 1997 | 3.06—Dennis Martinez | 3.08 (1988) |
| **Shutouts** | 5—Bill Stoneman, 1969<br>Steve Rogers, 1979, 1983<br>Dennis Martinez, 1991<br>Carlos Perez, 1997 | 37—Steve Rogers | 18 (1979)<br>Lost—20 (1972) |
| **1-0 games won** | 2—Carl Morton, 1970<br>Bill Stoneman, 1972<br>Woodie Fryman, 1976<br>Scott Sanderson, 1980<br>Pascual Perez, 1988<br>Carlos Perez, 1997 | 3—Woodie Fryman<br>Carl Morton<br>Scott Sanderson<br>Bill Stoneman | 4 (1972, 1988, 1991)<br>Lost—5 (1982, 1986) |

## TEAM FIELDING

| | | | |
|---|---|---|---|
| **Putouts** | 4,448 (1988)<br>Fewest—4,204 (1972) | **Assists** | 1,956 (1976)<br>Fewest—1,618 (1999) |
| **Chances accepted** | 6,393 (1975)<br>Fewest—5,915 (2001) | **Errors** | 184 (1969)<br>Fewest—99 (2004) |
| **Double plays** | 193 (1970)<br>Fewest—113 (1992) | **Passed balls** | 24 (1973)<br>Fewest—3 (1978) |
| **Errorless games** | 93 (2003)<br>Consecutive—10 (1977, 2004) | **Fielding average** | .984 (2004)<br>Lowest—.971 (1969) |

## MISCELLANEOUS

**Most players, season** 49 (2000)

**Fewest players, season** 30 (1972)

**Games won** 95 (1979)
**Month** 23 (Sept 1979)
**Consecutive** 10 (1979, 1980, 1997)

**Winning percentage** .649 (1994), 74-40
**Lowest** .321 (1969), 52-110

**Number of league championships** 0
**Most recent** ----

**Runs, game** 21 vs Colorado, Apr 28, 1996
**Opponents'** 20 by San Diego, May 19, 2001

**Hits, game** 28 vs Atlanta, July 30, 1978

**Home runs, game** 8 vs Atlanta, July 30, 1978

**Runs, shutout** 19 vs Atlanta, July 30, 1978
**Opponents'** 18 by San Francisco, May 24, 2000

**Longest 1-0 win** 17 inn, vs Philadelphia, Sept 21, 1981

**Most seasons, non-pitcher** 13—Tim Wallach
Tim Raines Sr.

**Most seasons, pitcher** 13—Steve Rogers

**Games lost** 110 (1969)
**Month** 23 (Aug 1969, Sept 1976)
**Consecutive** 20 (1969)

**Overall record** 2,755-2,943 (36 seasons)
**Interleague play** 69-70

**Number of times worst record in league** 3 (inc. 1 tie)
**Most recent** 2001

**Runs, inning** 13 vs San Francisco, May 7, 1997, 6th

**Total bases, game** 58 vs Atlanta, July 30, 1978

**Consecutive games with one or more home runs** 16 (29 HRs), 1999

**Longest shutout** 16 inn, 3-0 vs Chicago, Sept 22, 1975

**Longest 1-0 loss** 22 inn, vs Los Angeles, Aug 23, 1989

## ATTENDANCE

| | | | |
|---|---|---|---|
| **Highest home attendance** | | **Largest crowds** | |
| **Jarry Park** | 1,424,683 (1970) | **Day** | 57,694 vs Philadelphia, Aug 15, 1982 |
| **Olympic Stadium** | 2,320,651 (1983) | **Night** | 57,121 vs Philadelphia, Oct 3, 1980 |
| | | **Doubleheader** | 59,282 vs St. Louis, Sept 16, 1979 |
| **Highest road attendance** | 2,620,064 (1993) | **Home opener** | 57,592 vs Philadelphia, Apr 15, 1977 |

# NEW YORK GIANTS

## YEARLY FINISHES

**(National League franchise established in 1883 moved from New York to San Francisco after the 1957 season)**

| Year | Position | W | L | Pct. | GB | Manager | Attendance |
|---|---|---|---|---|---|---|---|
| 1883 | 6th | 46 | 50 | .479 | 16.0 | John Clapp | 75,000 |
| 1884 | 4th (tied) | 62 | 50 | .554 | 22.0 | Jim Pierce, John Montgomery Ward | 105,000 |
| 1885 | 2nd | 85 | 27 | .759 | 2.0 | Jim Mutrie | 185,000 |
| 1886 | 3rd | 75 | 44 | .630 | 12.5 | Jim Mutrie | 189,000 |
| 1887 | 4th | 68 | 55 | .553 | 10.5 | Jim Mutrie | 270,945 |
| 1888 | 1st | 84 | 47 | .641 | +9.0 | Jim Mutrie | 305,455 |
| 1889 | 1st | 83 | 43 | .659 | +1.0 | Jim Mutrie | 201,989 |
| 1890 | 6th | 63 | 68 | .481 | 24.0 | Jim Mutrie | 60,667 |
| 1891 | 3rd | 71 | 61 | .538 | 13.0 | Jim Mutrie | 210,568 |
| 1892 | 10th/6th | 71 | 80 | | ** | Pat Powers | 130,566 |
| 1893 | 5th | 68 | 64 | .515 | 19.5 | John Montgomery Ward | 290,000 |
| 1894 | 2nd (t) | 88 | 44 | .667 | 3.0 | John Montgomery Ward | 387,000 |
| 1895 | 9th | 6 | 65 | .504 | 21.5 | George Davis, Jack Doyle, Harvey Watkins | 240,000 |
| 1896 | 7th | 64 | 67 | .489 | 27.0 | Art Irwin, Bill Joyce | 274,000 |
| 1897 | 3rd | 83 | 48 | .634 | 9.5 | Bill Joyce | 390,340 |
| 1898 | 7th | 77 | 73 | .513 | 25.5 | Bill Joyce, Cap Anson, Bill Joyce | 206,700 |
| 1899 | 10th | 60 | 90 | .400 | 42.0 | John Day, Fred Hoey | 121,384 |
| 1900 | 8th | 60 | 78 | .435 | 23.0 | Buck Ewing, George Davis | 175,000 |
| 1901 | 7th | 52 | 85 | .380 | 37.0 | George Davis | 297,650 |
| 1902 | 8th | 48 | 88 | .353 | 53.5 | Horace Fogel, Heinie Smith, John McGraw | 302,875 |
| 1903 | 2nd | 84 | 55 | .604 | 6.5 | John McGraw | 579,530 |
| 1904 | 1st (n) | 106 | 47 | .693 | +13.0 | John McGraw | 609,826 |
| 1905 | 1st (S) | 105 | 48 | .686 | +9.0 | John McGraw | 552,700 |
| 1906 | 2nd | 96 | 56 | .632 | 20.0 | John McGraw | 402,850 |
| 1907 | 4th | 82 | 71 | .536 | 25.5 | John McGraw | 538,350 |
| 1908 | 2nd (tied) | 98 | 56 | .636 | 1.0 | John McGraw | 910,000 |
| 1909 | 3rd | 92 | 61 | .601 | 18.5 | John McGraw | 783,700 |
| 1910 | 2nd | 91 | 63 | .591 | 13.0 | John McGraw | 511,785 |
| 1911 | 1st (s) | 99 | 54 | .647 | +7.5 | John McGraw | 675,000 |
| 1912 | 1st (s) | 103 | 48 | .682 | +10.0 | John McGraw | 638,000 |
| 1913 | 1st (s) | 101 | 51 | .664 | +12.5 | John McGraw | 630,000 |
| 1914 | 2nd | 84 | 70 | .545 | 10.5 | John McGraw | 364,313 |
| 1915 | 8th | 69 | 83 | .454 | 21.0 | John McGraw | 391,850 |
| 1916 | 4th | 86 | 66 | .566 | 7.0 | John McGraw | 552,056 |
| 1917 | 1st (s) | 98 | 56 | .636 | +10.0 | John McGraw | 500,264 |
| 1918 | 2nd | 71 | 53 | .573 | 10.5 | John McGraw | 256,618 |
| 1919 | 2nd | 87 | 53 | .621 | 9.0 | John McGraw | 708,857 |
| 1920 | 2nd | 86 | 68 | .558 | 7.0 | John McGraw | 929,609 |
| 1921 | 1st (S) | 94 | 59 | .614 | +4.0 | John McGraw | 773,477 |
| 1922 | 1st (S) | 93 | 61 | .604 | +7.0 | John McGraw | 945,809 |
| 1923 | 1st (s) | 95 | 58 | .621 | +4.5 | John McGraw | 820,780 |
| 1924 | 1st (s) | 93 | 60 | .608 | +1.5 | John McGraw | 844,068 |
| 1925 | 2nd | 86 | 66 | .566 | 8.5 | John McGraw | 778,993 |
| 1926 | 5th | 74 | 77 | .490 | 13.5 | John McGraw | 700,362 |
| 1927 | 3rd | 92 | 62 | .597 | 2.0 | John McGraw, Rogers Hornsby | 858,190 |
| 1928 | 2nd | 93 | 61 | .604 | 2.0 | John McGraw | 916,191 |
| 1929 | 3rd | 84 | 67 | .556 | 13.5 | John McGraw | 868,806 |
| 1930 | 3rd | 87 | 67 | .565 | 5.0 | John McGraw | 868,714 |
| 1931 | 2nd | 87 | 65 | .572 | 13.0 | John McGraw | 812,163 |
| 1932 | 6th (tied) | 72 | 82 | .468 | 18.0 | John McGraw, Bill Terry | 484,868 |
| 1933 | 1st (S) | 91 | 61 | .599 | +5.0 | Bill Terry | 604,471 |
| 1934 | 2nd | 93 | 60 | .608 | 2.0 | Bill Terry | 730,851 |
| 1935 | 3rd | 91 | 62 | .595 | 8.5 | Bill Terry | 748,748 |
| 1936 | 1st (s) | 92 | 62 | .597 | +5.0 | Bill Terry | 837,952 |
| 1937 | 1st (s) | 95 | 57 | .625 | +3.0 | Bill Terry | 926,887 |
| 1938 | 3rd | 83 | 67 | .553 | 5.0 | Bill Terry | 799,633 |
| 1939 | 5th | 77 | 74 | .510 | 18.5 | Bill Terry | 702,457 |
| 1940 | 6th | 72 | 80 | .474 | 27.5 | Bill Terry | 747,852 |
| 1941 | 5th | 74 | 79 | .484 | 25.5 | Bill Terry | 763,098 |
| 1942 | 3rd | 85 | 67 | .559 | 20.0 | Mel Ott | 779,621 |
| 1943 | 8th | 55 | 98 | .359 | 49.5 | Mel Ott | 466,095 |
| 1944 | 5th | 67 | 87 | .435 | 38.0 | Mel Ott | 674,083 |
| 1945 | 5th | 78 | 74 | .513 | 19.0 | Mel Ott | 1,016,468 |
| 1946 | 8th | 61 | 93 | .396 | 36.0 | Mel Ott | 1,219,873 |
| 1947 | 4th | 81 | 73 | .526 | 13.0 | Mel Ott | 1,600,793 |
| 1948 | 5th | 78 | 76 | .506 | 13.5 | Mel Ott, Leo Durocher | 1,459,269 |
| 1949 | 5th | 73 | 81 | .474 | 24.0 | Leo Durocher | 1,218,446 |
| 1950 | 3rd | 86 | 68 | .558 | 5.0 | Leo Durocher | 1,008,876 |
| 1951 | 1st (L,s) | 98 | 59 | .624 | +1.0 | Leo Durocher | 1,059,539 |
| 1952 | 2nd | 92 | 62 | .597 | 4.5 | Leo Durocher | 984,940 |
| 1953 | 5th | 70 | 84 | .455 | 35.0 | Leo Durocher | 811,518 |
| 1954 | 1st (S) | 97 | 57 | .630 | +5.0 | Leo Durocher | 1,155,067 |

| Year | Position | W | L | Pct. | GB | Manager | Attendance |
|---|---|---|---|---|---|---|---|
| 1955 | 3rd | 80 | 74 | .519 | 18.5 | Leo Durocher | 824,112 |
| 1956 | 6th | 67 | 87 | .435 | 26.0 | Bill Rigney | 629,179 |
| 1957 | 6th | 69 | 85 | .448 | 26.0 | Bill Rigney | 653,923 |

**first half 31-43, second half 40-37; (t) lost Temple Cup; (S) won World Series; (s) lost World Series; (L) won league playoff

## INDIVIDUAL AND CLUB RECORDS

### BATTING

| | Individual Season | Individual Career | Club Season |
|---|---|---|---|
| **Games** | 157—Art Devlin, 1908 | 2,730—Mel Ott | 158 (1904, 1909, 1917) |
| **At-bats** | 681—Joe Moore, 155 G, 1935 | 9,456—Mel Ott | 5,623 (1935) |
| **Runs** | 147—Mike Tiernan, 122 G, 1889 | 1,859—Mel Ott | 959 (1930) |
| | *139—Bill Terry, 154 G, 1930 | | Fewest—540 (1956) |
| **Hits** | 254—Bill Terry, 154 G, 1930 | 2,876—Mel Ott | 1,769 (1930) |
| | | | Fewest—1,217 (1906) |
| **Hitting streak** | 33 G—George Davis, 1893 | | |
| | *24 G—Freddie Lindstrom, 1930 | | |
| | Don Mueller, 1955 | | |
| **Singles** | 177—Bill Terry, 154 G, 1930 | 1,805—Mel Ott | 1,279 (1930) |
| **Doubles** | 43—Bill Terry, 153 G, 1931 | 488—Mel Ott | 276 (1928) |
| **Triples** | 27—George Davis, 133 G, 1893 | 162—Mike Tiernan | 103 (1911) |
| | *25—Larry Doyle, 141 G, 1911 | *117—Larry Doyle | |
| **HOME RUNS** | | | 179 (1951) |
| | | | Fewest—145 (1956) |
| **Righthander** | 51—Willie Mays, 152 G, 1955 | 189—Bobby Thomson | |
| **Lefthander** | 51—Johnny Mize, 154 G, 1947 | 511—Mel Ott | |
| **Switch-hitter** | 12—Frankie Frisch, 151 G, 1923 | 54—Frankie Frisch | |
| **Rookie** | 29—Bobby Thomson, 138 G, 1947 | | |
| **Home** | 29—Johnny Mize, 1947 | 323—Mel Ott | 131 (1947) |
| **Road** | 29—Willie Mays, 1955 | 188—Mel Ott | 90 (1947) |
| **Month** | 13—Walker Cooper, June 1947 | | 55 (July 1947) |
| | Johnny Mize, Aug 1947 | | |
| | Willie Mays, July 1955 | | |
| **Pinch** | 4—Ernie Lombardi, 1946 | 9—Bobby Hofman | 10 (1954) |
| | Bill Taylor, 1955 | | |
| **Grand slams** | 3—George Kelly, 149 G, 1921 | 7—George Kelly | 8 (1951) |
| | Sid Gordon, 142 G, 1948 | Mel Ott | |
| | Wes Westrum, 124 G, 1951 | | |
| **Home runs at Polo Grounds V, all teams** | | | 206 (1947) |
| **Total bases** | 392—Bill Terry, 154 G, 1930 | 5,041—Mel Ott | 2,628 (1930) |
| **Extra-base hits** | 87—Willie Mays, 151 G, 1954 | 1,071—Mel Ott | 490 (1930) |
| **Sacrifice hits** | 36—Art Devlin, 143 G, 1907 | 171—Travis Jackson | 250 (1908) |
| **Sacrifice flies** | 8—Don Mueller, 153 G, 1954 | 23—Willie Mays | 52 (1954) |
| | Hank Thompson, 135 G, 1955 | | |
| | Ray Jablonski, 107 G, 1957 | | |
| **Bases on balls** | 144—Eddie Stanky, 152 G, 1950 | 1,708—Mel Ott | 671 (1951) |
| | | | Fewest—127 (1883) *252 (1902) |
| **Strikeouts** | 93—Wes Westrum, 124 G, 1951 | 896—Mel Ott | 672 (1952) |
| | Fewest—12—Frankie Frisch, 151 G, 1917 | | Fewest—376 (1928) |
| **Hit by pitch** | 25—Eddie Burke, 135 G, 1893 | 132—Art Fletcher | 91 (1903) |
| | *22—Charlie Bass, 121 G, 1903 | | Fewest—15 (1933) |
| **Runs batted in** | 151—Mel Ott, 150 G, 1929 | 1,860—Mel Ott | 880 (1930) |
| | | | Fewest—336 (1902) |
| **Grounded into double plays** | 26—Bill Jurges, 138 G, 1939 | 106—Bobby Thomson | 153 (1939) |
| | Sid Gordon, 131 G, 1943 | | Fewest—96 (1952) |
| | Fewest—3—Joe Moore, 152 G, 1936 | | |
| **Left on base** | | | 1,214 (1935) |
| | | | Fewest—975 (1926) |
| **Batting average** | .401—Bill Terry, 154 G, 1930 | .341—Bill Terry | .319 (1930) |
| | | | Lowest—.238 (1902) |
| **Most .300 hitters** | | | 8 (1921, 1922, 1924, 1930, 1931) |
| **Slugging average** | .667—Willie Mays, 151 G, 1954 | .593—Willie Mays | .473 (1930) |
| | | | Lowest—.290 (1902) |
| **On-base percentage** | .464—Roger Connor, 127 G, 1887 | .414—Mel Ott | .384 (1887) *.369 (1930) |
| | *.460—Eddie Stanky, 152 G, 1950 | | Lowest—.281 (1883) *.283 (1902) |

### BASERUNNING

| | Individual Season | Individual Career | Club Season |
|---|---|---|---|
| **Stolen bases** | 111—Monte Ward, 129 G, 1887 | 428—Mike Tiernan | 347 (1911) |
| | *62—George J. Burns, 154 G, 1914 | *334—George J. Burns | |
| **Caught stealing** | 35—George J. Burns, 150 G, 1913 | 123—George J. Burns | 114 (1915) |

## PITCHING

| | Individual Season | Career | Club Season |
|---|---|---|---|
| **Games** | 71—Hoyt Wilhelm, 1952 | 634—Christy Mathewson | |
| **Games started** | 48—Joe McGinnity, 1903 | 550—Christy Mathewson | |
| **Complete games** | 44—Joe McGinnity, 1903 | 433—Christy Mathewson | 140 (1898) *127 (1904) |
| **Wins** | 37—Christy Mathewson, 1908 | 372—Christy Mathewson | |
| **Percentage** | .833—Hoyt Wilhelm (15-3), 1952 | .682—Tim Keefe<br>*.664—Christy Mathewson | |
| **Winning streak** | 19—Rube Marquard, 1912 | | |
| **Winning streak, two seasons** | 24—Carl Hubbell, 1936 (16), 1937 (8) | | |
| **20-win seasons** | | 13—Christy Mathewson | |
| **Losses** | 27—Dummy Taylor, 1901 | 188—Christy Mathewson | |
| **Losing streak** | 12—Rube Marquard, 1914 | | |
| **Innings** | 434—Joe McGinnity, 1903 | 4,771.2—Christy Mathewson | 1,440.2 (1909) |
| **Hits** | 415—Bill Carrick, 1900 | 4,203—Christy Mathewson | 1,546 (1930) |
| **Runs** | 224—Bill Carrick, 1900 | 1,860—Amos Rusie<br>*1,609—Christy Mathewson | 814 (1930) |
| **Earned runs** | 117—Freddie Fitzsimmons, 1932 | 1,188— Carl Hubbell | 699 (1930) |
| **Bases on balls** | 128—Jeff Tesreau, 1914 | 902—Hal Schumacher | 660 (1946) |
| **Strikeouts** | 267—Christy Mathewson, 1903 | 2,504—Christy Mathewson | 771 (1911) |
| **Strikeouts, game** | 16—Christy Mathewson, Oct 3, 1904 | | |
| **Hit batsmen** | 36—Ed Doheny, 1889<br>*22—Ed Doheny, 1990 | 93—Ed Doheny<br>*84—Joe McGinnity | 100 (1899) *94 (1900) |
| **Wild pitches** | 30—Red Ames, 1905 | 222—Mickey Welch<br>*113—Christy Mathewson | 101 (1884) *58 (1905) |
| **Home runs** | 36—Larry Jensen, 1949 | 227—Carl Hubbell | 155 (1955) |
| **Sacrifice hits** | 45—Jesse Barnes, 1920 | 396—Christy Mathewson | 185 (1921) |
| **Sacrifice flies** | 9—Ruben Gomez, 1957 | 26—Ruben Gomez | 47 (1957) |
| **Earned run average** | 1.66—Carl Hubbell, 309 inn, 1933 | 2.12—Christy Mathewson | 1,72 (1885) *2.14 (1908) |
| **Shutouts** | 11—Christy Mathewson, 1908 | 79—Christy Mathewson | 25 (1908)<br>Lost—20 (1915) |
| **1-0 games won** | 5—Carl Hubbell, 1933 | 14—Christy Mathewson | 6 (1907, 1933)<br>Lost—8 (1907) |

## TEAM FIELDING

| | | | |
|---|---|---|---|
| **Putouts** | 4,306 (1909)<br>Fewest—3,964 (1939) | **Assists** | 2,240 (1920)<br>Fewest—1,660 (1956) |
| **Chances accepted** | 6,472 (1920)<br>Fewest—5,794 (1956) | **Errors** | 307 (1909)<br>Fewest—137 (1942, 1950) |
| **Double plays** | 181 (1950)<br>Fewest—75 (1907) | **Passed balls** | 26 (1906)<br>Fewest—4 (1928) |
| **Errorless games** | unknown<br>Consecutive—8 (1950) | **Fielding average** | .977 (1940, 1942, 1950)<br>Lowest—.954 (1909) |

## MISCELLANEOUS

**Most players, season** 49 (1946)
**Fewest players, season** 21 (1905)
**Games won** 106 (1904)
**Month** 29 (Sept 1916)
**Consecutive** 26 (1916)
**Winning percentage** .759 (1885), 85-27
*.693 (1904), 106-47
**Lowest** .353 (1902), 48-88
**Number of league championships** 17
**Most recent** 1954
**Runs, game** 29 vs Philadelphia, June 15, 1887
*26 vs Brooklyn, Apr 30, 1944, 1st game
**Opponents'** 28 by Hartford, May 13, 1876
*16 vs Brooklyn, Aug 2, 1948
**Hits, game** 31 vs Cincinnati, June 9, 1901
**Home runs, game** 7 vs Indianapolis, May 9, 1888
vs Cincinnati, June 6, 1939
vs Philadelphia, Aug 13, 1939, 1st game
vs Cincinnati, June 24, 1950
vs Pittsburgh, July 8, 1956, 1st game
**Runs, shutout** 24 vs Buffalo, May 27, 1885
*16 vs Brooklyn, July 3, 1949
**Opponents'** 19 by Chicago, June 7, 1906
**Longest 1-0 win** 18 inn vs St. Louis, July 2, 1933, 1st game

**Most seasons, non-pitcher** 22—Mel Ott
**Most seasons, pitcher** 17—Christy Mathewson
**Games lost** 98 (1943)
**Month** 25 (Aug 1953)
**Consecutive** 13 (1902, 1944)
**Overall record** 6,067-4,898 (75 seasons)

**Number of times worst record in league** 5
**Most recent** 1946
**Runs, inning** 13 vs Philadelphia, Sept 8, 1883, 3rd
vs Cleveland, July 19, 1890, 1st game, 2nd
vs St. Louis, May 13, 1911, 1st

**Total bases, game** 47 vs Philadelphia, July 11, 1931, 1st game
**Consecutive games with one or more home runs** 19 (33 HRs), 1947

**Longest shutout** 16 inn, 3-0 vs Chicago, Sept 22, 1975

**Longest 1-0 loss** 15 inn vs Cincinnati, July 16, 1933, 1st game

## ATTENDANCE

**Highest home attendance** 1,600,793 (1947)

**Largest crowds**

| | |
|---|---|
| **Day** | 54,922 vs Brooklyn, Apr 20, 1941 |
| **Night** | 51,790 vs Brooklyn, May 27, 1947 |
| **Doubleheader** | 60,747 vs Brooklyn, May 31, 1937 |
| **Home opener** | 54,392 vs Brooklyn, Apr 14, 1936 |

*records made since 1900 that do not exceed pre-1900 records

# NEW YORK METS

## YEARLY FINISHES

(National League expansion franchise)

| Year | Position | W | L | Pct. | GB | Manager | Attendance |
|---|---|---|---|---|---|---|---|
| 1962 | 10th | 40 | 120 | .250 | 60.5 | Casey Stengel | 922,530 |
| 1963 | 10th | 51 | 111 | .315 | 48.0 | Casey Stengel | 1,080,108 |
| 1964 | 10th | 53 | 109 | .327 | 40.0 | Casey Stengel | 1,732,597 |
| 1965 | 10th | 50 | 112 | .309 | 47.0 | Casey Stengel, Wes Westrum | 1,768,389 |
| 1966 | 9th | 66 | 95 | .410 | 28.5 | Wes Westrum | 1,932,693 |
| 1967 | 10th | 61 | 101 | .377 | 40.5 | Wes Westrum, Salty Parker | 1,565,492 |
| 1968 | 9th | 73 | 89 | .451 | 24.0 | Gil Hodges | 1,781,657 |

## EAST DIVISION

| Year | Position | W | L | Pct. | GB | Manager | Attendance |
|---|---|---|---|---|---|---|---|
| 1969 | 1st (C,S) | 100 | 62 | .617 | +8.0 | Gil Hodges | 2,175,373 |
| 1970 | 3rd | 83 | 79 | .512 | 6.0 | Gil Hodges | 2,697,479 |
| 1971 | 3rd (tied) | 83 | 79 | .512 | 14.0 | Gil Hodges | 2,266,680 |
| 1972 | 3rd | 83 | 73 | .532 | 13.5 | Yogi Berra | 2,134,185 |
| 1973 | 1st (C,s) | 82 | 79 | .509 | +1.5 | Yogi Berra | 1,912,390 |
| 1974 | 5th | 71 | 91 | .438 | 17.0 | Yogi Berra | 1,722,209 |
| 1975 | 3rd (tied) | 82 | 80 | .506 | 10.5 | Yogi Berra, Roy McMillan | 1,730,566 |
| 1976 | 3rd | 86 | 76 | .531 | 15.0 | Joe Frazier | 1,468,754 |
| 1977 | 6th | 64 | 98 | .395 | 37.0 | Joe Frazier, Joe Torre | 1,066,825 |
| 1978 | 6th | 66 | 96 | .407 | 24.0 | Joe Torre | 1,007,328 |
| 1979 | 6th | 63 | 99 | .389 | 35.0 | Joe Torre | 788,905 |
| 1980 | 5th | 67 | 95 | .414 | 24.0 | Joe Torre | 1,192,073 |
| 1981 | 5th/4th | 41 | 62 | .398 | * | Joe Torre | 704,244 |
| 1982 | 6th | 65 | 97 | .401 | 27.0 | George Bamberger | 1,323,036 |
| 1983 | 6th | 68 | 94 | .420 | 22.0 | George Bamberger, Frank Howard | 1,112,774 |
| 1984 | 2nd | 90 | 72 | .556 | 6.5 | Dave Johnson | 1,842,695 |
| 1985 | 2nd | 98 | 64 | .605 | 3.0 | Dave Johnson | 2,761,601 |
| 1986 | 1st (C,S) | 108 | 54 | .667 | +21.5 | Dave Johnson | 2,767,601 |
| 1987 | 2nd | 92 | 70 | .568 | 3.0 | Dave Johnson | 3,034,129 |
| 1988 | 1st (c) | 100 | 60 | .625 | +15.0 | Dave Johnson | 3,055,445 |
| 1989 | 2nd | 87 | 75 | .537 | 6.0 | Dave Johnson | 2,918,710 |
| 1990 | 2nd | 91 | 71 | .562 | 4.0 | Dave Johnson, Bud Harrelson | 2,732,745 |
| 1991 | 5th | 77 | 84 | .478 | 20.5 | Bud Harrelson, Mike Cubbage | 2,284,484 |
| 1992 | 5th | 72 | 90 | .444 | 24.0 | Jeff Torborg | 1,779,534 |
| 1993 | 7th | 59 | 103 | .364 | 38.0 | Jeff Torborg, Dallas Green | 1,873,183 |
| 1994 | 3rd | 55 | 58 | .487 | 18.5 | Dallas Green | 1,151,471 |
| 1995 | 2nd (tied) | 69 | 75 | .479 | 21.0 | Dallas Green | 1,273,183 |
| 1996 | 4th | 71 | 91 | .438 | 25.0 | Dallas Green, Bobby Valentine | 1,588,323 |
| 1997 | 3rd | 88 | 74 | .543 | 13.0 | Bobby Valentine | 1,766,174 |
| 1998 | 2nd | 88 | 74 | .543 | 18.0 | Bobby Valentine | 2,287,942 |
| 1999 | 2nd (W,D,c) | 97 | 66 | .595 | 6.5 | Bobby Valentine | 2,725,668 |
| 2000 | 2nd (D,C,s) | 94 | 68 | .580 | 1.0 | Bobby Valentine | 2,800,221 |
| 2001 | 3rd | 82 | 80 | .506 | 6.0 | Bobby Valentine | 2,658,279 |
| 2002 | 5th | 75 | 86 | .466 | 26.5 | Bobby Valentine | 2,804,838 |
| 2003 | 5th | 66 | 95 | .410 | 34.5 | Art Howe | 2,132,341 |
| 2004 | 4th | 71 | 91 | .438 | 29.0 | Art Howe | 2,318,321 |
| 2005 | 3rd (tied) | 83 | 79 | .512 | 7.0 | Willie Randolph | 2,829,931 |

(C) won League Championship Series; (S) won World Series; (s) lost World Series; *first half 17-34, second half 24-28; (c) lost League Championship Series; (W) won wild card playoff; (D) won Division Series

## INDIVIDUAL AND CLUB RECORDS

### BATTING

| | Individual Season | Individual Career | Club Season |
|---|---|---|---|
| Games | 162—Felix Millan, 1975<br>John Olerud, 1999 | 1,853—Ed Kranepool | 164 (1965) |
| At-bats | 696—Jose Reyes, 161 G, 2005 | 5,436—Ed Kranepool | 5,618 (1996) |
| Runs | 123—Edgardo Alfonso, 158 G, 1999 | 662—Darryl Strawberry | 853 (1999)<br>Fewest—473 (1968) |
| Hits | 227—Lance Johnson, 160 G, 1996 | 1,418—Ed Kranepool | 1,553 (1999)<br>Fewest—1,168 (1963) |
| Hitting streak | 24 G—Hubie Brooks, 1984<br>Mike Piazza, 1999 | | |
| Singles | 166—Lance Johnson, 160 G, 1996 | 1,050—Ed Kranepool | 1,087 (1980) |
| Doubles | 44—Bernard Gilkey, 153 G, 1996 | 225—Ed Kranepool | 297 (1999) |
| Triples | 21—Lance Johnson, 160 G, 1996 | 62—Mookie Wilson | 47 (1978, 1996) |
| **HOME RUNS** | | | 198 (2000)<br>Fewest—61 (1980) |
| Righthander | 40—Mike Piazza, 141 G, 1999 | 220—Mike Piazza | |
| Lefthander | 39—Darryl Strawberry, 154 G, 1987<br>Darryl Strawberry, 153 G, 1988 | 252—Darryl Strawberry | |
| Switch-hitter | 41—Todd Hundley, 153 G, 1996 | 192—Howard Johnson | |
| Rookie | 26—Darryl Strawberry, 122 G, 1983 | | |
| Home | 24—Darryl Strawberry, 1990 | 123—Darryl Strawberry | 93 (1962, 1987, 2000) |
| Road | 23—Howard Johnson, 1987 | 129—Darryl Strawberry | 105 (2000) |
| Month | 13—Dave Kingman, Julyy 1975 | | 39 (June 1990, May 1999, Sept 2002) |

| | Individual Season | Career | Club Season |
|---|---|---|---|
| | Gary Carter, Sep 1985 | | |
| Pinch | 4—Mark Carreon, 1989<br>Danny Heep, 1983 | 8—Mark Carreon | 12 (1983) |
| Grand slams | 3—John Milner, 127 G, 1976<br>Robin Ventura, 161 G, 1999<br>Mike Piazza, 136 G, 2000 | 6—Mike Piazza | 8 (1999, 2000) |
| **Home runs at Polo Grounds, all teams** | | | 213 (1962) |
| **Home runs at Shea Stadium, all teams** | | | 165 (2000) (inc. 3 at Tokyo Dome) |
| **Total bases** | 327—Lance Johnson, 160 G, 1996 | 2,047—Ed Kranepool | 2,430 (1987) |
| **Extra-base hits** | 80—Howard Johnson, 153 G, 1989 | 469—Darryl Strawberry | 513 (1987) |
| **Sacrifice hits** | 24—Feliz Millan, 136 G, 1974 | 85—Dwight Gooden | 108 (1973) |
| **Sacrifice flies** | 15—Gary Carter, 132 G, 1986<br>Howard Johnson, 156 G, 1991 | 58—Ed Kranepool | 59 (1997) |
| **Bases on balls** | 125—John Olerud, 162 G, 1999 | 580—Darryl Strawberry | 717 (1999)<br>Fewest—353 (1964) |
| **Strikeouts** | 156—Tommie Agee, 153 G, 1970<br>Dave Kingman, 149 G, 1982<br>Fewest—22—Felix Millan, 153 G, 1973 | 960—Darryl Strawberry | 1,203 (1968)<br>Fewest—735 (1974) |
| **Hit by pitch** | 13—Ron Hunt, 143 G, 1963<br>John Olerud, 154 G, 1997 | 41—Ron Hunt | 65 (2001)<br>Fewest—20 (1984, 1985) |
| **Runs batted in** | 124—Mike Piazza, 141 G, 1999 | 733—Darryl Strawberry | 814 (1999)<br>Fewest—434 (1968) |
| **Grounded into double plays** | 27—Mike Piazza, 141 G, 1999<br>Fewest—3—Wally Backman, 145 G, 1985<br>Kaz Matsui, 114 G, 2004 | 138—Ed Kranepool | 149 (1999)<br>Fewest—87 (1989) |
| **Left on base** | | | 1,267 (1999)<br>Fewest—1,011 (1993) |
| **Batting average** | .354—John Olerud, 160 G, 1998 | .307—Mike Piazza | .279 (1999)<br>Lowest—.219 (963) |
| **Most .300 hitters** | | | 5 (1999) |
| **Slugging average** | .614—Mike Piazza, 136 G, 2000 | .573—Mike Piazza | .434 (1987, 1999)<br>Lowest—.315 (1963, 1968) |
| **On-base percentage** | .447—John Olerud, 160 G, 1998 | .387—Keith Hernandez | .363 (1999)<br>Lowest—.277 (1965) |

## BASERUNNING

| | Individual Season | Career | Club Season |
|---|---|---|---|
| **Stolen bases** | 66—Roger Cedeno, 155 G, 1999 | 281—Mookie Wilson | 159 (1987) |
| **Caught stealing** | 21—Lenny Randle, 136 G, 1977 | 90—Mookie Wilson | 99 (1980) |

## PITCHING

| | Individual Season | Career | Club Season |
|---|---|---|---|
| **Games** | 83—Mike Stanton, 2004 | 695—John Franco | |
| **Games started** | 36—Jack Fisher, 1965<br>Tom Seaver, 1970, 1973, 1975 | 395—Tom Seaver | |
| **Complete games** | 21—Tom Seaver, 1971 | 171—Tom Seaver | 53 (1976) |
| **Wins** | 25—Tom Seaver, 1969 | 198—Tom Seaver | |
| **Percentage** | .870—David Cone (20-3), 1988 | .649—Dwight Gooden | |
| **Winning streak** | 14—Dwight Gooden, 1985 | | |
| **20-win seasons** | | 4—Tom Seaver | |
| **Losses** | 24—Roger Craig, 1962<br>Jack Fisher, 1965 | 137—Jerry Koosman | |
| **Losing streak** | 18—Roger Craig, 1963 | | |
| **Losing streak, two seasons** | 27—Anthony Young, 1992 (14), 1993 (13) | | |
| **Saves** | 43—Armando Benitez, 2001 | 276—John Franco | 51 (1987) |
| **Innings** | 291—Tom Seaver, 1970 | 3,045.1—Tom Seaver | 1,488 (1985) |
| **Hits** | 261—Roger Craig, 1962 | 2,431—Tom Seaver | 1,577 (1962) |
| **Runs** | 137—Jay Hook, 1962 | 994—Jerry Koosman | 948 (1962) |
| **Earned runs** | 117—Roger Craig, 1962 | 875—Jerry Koosman | 801 (1962) |
| **Bases on balls** | 116—Nolan Ryan, 1971 | 847—Tom Seaver | 617 (1999) |
| **Strikeouts** | 289—Tom Seaver, 1971 | 2,541—Tom Seaver | 1,217 (1990) |
| **Strikeouts, game** | 19—Tom Seaver, Apr 22, 1970<br>David Cone, Oct 6, 1991 | | |
| **Hit batsmen** | 16—Pedro Astacio, 2002 | 63—Al Leiter | 68 (1998) |
| **Wild pitches** | 18—Jack Hamilton, 1966 | 81—Tom Seaver | 76 (1966) |
| **Home runs** | 35—Roger Craig, 1962 | 212—Tom Seaver | 192 (1962) |
| **Sacrifice hits** | 21—Mike Scott, 1982 | 130—Jerry Koosman | 96 (1980) |
| **Sacrifice flies** | 13—Ron Darling, 1989 | 75—Jerry Koosman | 59 (1978) |

| | Individual Season | Career | Club Season |
|---|---|---|---|
| **Earned run average** | 1.53—Dwight Gooden, 276.2 inn, 1985 | 2.57—Tom Seaver | 2.72 (1968) |
| **Shutouts** | 8—Dwight Gooden, 1985 | 44—Tom Seaver | 28 (1969)<br>Lost—30 (1963) |
| **1-0 games won** | 3—Bob Ojeda, 1988 | 8—Jerry Koosman | 9 (1969)<br>Lost—8 (1963) |

## TEAM FIELDING

**Putouts** 4,464 (1985)
Fewest—4,240 (2003)

**Chances accepted** 6,000 (1905)
Fewest—5,825 (1989)

**Double plays** 171 (1966, 1983)
Fewest—107 (1990)

**Errorless games** 104 (1999)
Consecutive—12 (1999)

**Assists** 1,995 (1966)
Fewest—1,462 (1989)

**Errors** 210 (1962, 1963)
Fewest—68 (1999)

**Passed balls** 32 (1964)
Fewest—2 (1980)

**Fielding average** .989 (1999)
Lowest—.967 (1962, 1963)

## MISCELLANEOUS

**Most players, season** 54 (1967)
**Fewest players, season** 32 (1988)
**Games won** 108 (1986)
**Month** 23 (Sept 1969)
**Consecutive** 11 (1969, 1972, 1986, 1990)
**Winning percentage** .667 (1986), 108-54
**Lowest** .250 (1962), 40-120
**Number of league championships** 4
**Most recent** 2000
**Runs, game** 23 vs Chicago, Aug 16, 1987
**Opponents'** 26 by Philadelphia, June 11, 1985
**Hits, game** 23 vs Chicago, May 26, 1964
vs Colorado, Apr 29, 2000
(28 vs Atlanta, July 4, 1985, 19 inn)
**Home runs, game** 7 vs Philadelphia, Apr 19, 2005
**Runs, shutout** 14 vs Chicago, July 29, 1965, 1st game
vs Cincinnati, Apr 19, 1998
**Opponents'** 16 by Atlanta, July 2, 1999
**Longest 1-0 win** 15 inn, vs Los Angeles, July 4, 1969

**Most seasons, non-pitcher** 18—Ed Kranepool
**Most seasons, pitcher** 14—John Franco
**Games lost** 120 (1962)
**Month** 26 (Aug 1962)
**Consecutive** 17 (1962)
**Overall record** 3,228-3,598 (43 seasons)
**Interleague play** 72-64
**Number of times worst record in league** 9
**Most recent** 1993
**Runs, inning** 10 vs Cincinnati, June 12, 1979, 6th
vs Atlanta, June 30, 2000, 8th
**Total bases, game** 44 vs Arizona, August 24, 2005

**Consecutive games with one or more home runs** 21 (29 HRs), 1996
**Longest shutout** 16 inn, 3-0 vs Chicago, Sept 22, 1975

**Longest 1-0 loss** 24 inn, vs Houston, Apr 15, 1968

## ATTENDANCE

**Highest home attendance** 3,055,445 (1988)
**Polo Grounds** 1,080,108 (1963)
**Shea Stadium** 3,055,445 (1988)

**Highest road attendance** 2,660,426 (1993)

**Largest crowds**
**Day** 56,738 vs Los Angeles, June 23, 1968
**Night** 56,658 vs San Francisco, May 13, 1966
**Doubleheader** 57,175 vs Los Angeles, Junee 13, 1965
**Home opener** 53,734 vs Pittsburgh, Apr 1, 2002
(Mets drew 55,000 to "home opener" in Tokyo, Mar 29, 2000.)

# PHILADELPHIA PHILLIES

## YEARLY FINISHES

(National League franchise established in 1883)

| Year | Position | W | L | Pct. | GB | Manager | Attendance |
|---|---|---|---|---|---|---|---|
| 1883 | 8th | 17 | 81 | .173 | 46.0 | Bob Ferguson, Blondie Purcell | 55,992 |
| 1884 | 6th | 39 | 73 | .348 | 45.0 | Harry Wright | 100,475 |
| 1885 | 3rd | 56 | 54 | .509 | 30.0 | Harry Wright | 150,698 |
| 1886 | 4th | 71 | 43 | .623 | 14.0 | Harry Wright | 175,623 |
| 1887 | 2nd | 75 | 48 | .610 | 3.5 | Harry Wright | 253,671 |
| 1888 | 3rd | 69 | 61 | .531 | 14.5 | Harry Wright | 151,804 |
| 1889 | 4th | 63 | 64 | .496 | 20.5 | Harry Wright | 281,869 |
| 1890 | 3rd | 78 | 53 | .595 | 9.0 | Harry Wright | 148,366 |
| 1891 | 4th | 68 | 69 | .496 | 18.5 | Harry Wright | 217,282 |
| 1892 | 3rd/4th | 87 | 66 | .569 | ** | Harry Wright | 193,731 |
| 1893 | 4th | 72 | 57 | .558 | 14.0 | Harry Wright | 293,019 |
| 1894 | 4th | 71 | 57 | .555 | 18.0 | Art Irwin | 352,773 |
| 1895 | 3rd | 78 | 53 | .595 | 9.5 | Art Irwin | 474,971 |
| 1896 | 8th | 62 | 68 | .477 | 28.5 | Billy Nash | 357,025 |
| 1897 | 10th | 55 | 77 | .417 | 38.0 | George Stallings | 288,816 |
| 1898 | 6th | 78 | 71 | .523 | 24.0 | George Stallings, Bill Shettsline | 265,414 |
| 1899 | 3rd | 94 | 58 | .618 | 9.0 | Bill Shettsline | 388,933 |
| 1900 | 3rd | 75 | 63 | .543 | 8.0 | Bill Shettsline | 301,913 |
| 1901 | 2nd | 83 | 57 | .593 | 7.5 | Bill Shettsline | 234,937 |
| 1902 | 7th | 56 | 81 | .409 | 46.0 | Bill Shettsline | 112,066 |
| 1903 | 7th | 49 | 86 | .363 | 39.5 | Chief Zimmer | 151,729 |
| 1904 | 8th | 52 | 100 | .342 | 53.5 | Hugh Duffy | 140,771 |
| 1905 | 4th | 83 | 69 | .546 | 21.5 | Hugh Duffy | 317,932 |
| 1906 | 4th | 71 | 82 | .464 | 45.5 | Hugh Duffy | 294,680 |
| 1907 | 3rd | 83 | 64 | .565 | 21.5 | Bill Murray | 341,216 |
| 1908 | 4th | 83 | 71 | .539 | 16.0 | Bill Murray | 420,660 |
| 1909 | 5th | 74 | 79 | .484 | 36.5 | Bill Murray | 303,177 |
| 1910 | 4th | 78 | 75 | .510 | 25.5 | Red Dooin | 296,597 |
| 1911 | 4th | 79 | 73 | .520 | 19.5 | Red Dooin | 416,000 |
| 1912 | 5th | 73 | 79 | .480 | 30.5 | Red Dooin | 250,000 |
| 1913 | 2nd | 88 | 63 | .583 | 12.5 | Red Dooin | 470,000 |

| Year | Position | W | L | Pct. | GB | Manager | Attendance |
|---|---|---|---|---|---|---|---|
| 1914 | 6th | 74 | 80 | .481 | 20.5 | Red Dooin | 138,474 |
| 1915 | 1st (s) | 90 | 62 | .592 | +7.0 | Pat Moran | 449,898 |
| 1916 | 2nd | 91 | 62 | .595 | 2.5 | Pat Moran | 515,365 |
| 1917 | 2nd | 87 | 65 | .572 | 10.0 | Pat Moran | 354,428 |
| 1918 | 6th | 55 | 68 | .447 | 26.0 | Pat Moran | 122,266 |
| 1919 | 8th | 47 | 90 | .343 | 47.5 | Jack Coombs, Gavvy Cravath | 240,424 |
| 1920 | 8th | 62 | 91 | .405 | 30.5 | Gavvy Cravath | 330,998 |
| 1921 | 8th | 51 | 103 | .331 | 43.5 | Bill Donovan, Kaiser Wilhelm | 273,961 |
| 1922 | 7th | 57 | 96 | .373 | 35.5 | Kaiser Wilhelm | 232,471 |
| 1923 | 8th | 50 | 104 | .325 | 45.5 | Art Fletcher | 228,168 |
| 1924 | 7th | 55 | 96 | .364 | 37.0 | Art Fletcher | 299,818 |
| 1925 | 6th (tied) | 68 | 85 | .444 | 27.0 | Art Fletcher | 304,905 |
| 1926 | 8th | 58 | 93 | .384 | 29.5 | Art Fletcher | 240,600 |
| 1927 | 8th | 51 | 103 | .331 | 43.0 | Stuffy McInnis | 305,420 |
| 1928 | 8th | 43 | 109 | .283 | 51.0 | Burt Shotton | 182,168 |
| 1929 | 5th | 71 | 82 | .464 | 27.5 | Burt Shotton | 281,200 |
| 1930 | 8th | 52 | 102 | .338 | 40.0 | Burt Shotton | 299,007 |
| 1931 | 6th | 66 | 88 | .429 | 35.0 | Burt Shotton | 284,849 |
| 1932 | 4th | 78 | 76 | .506 | 12.0 | Burt Shotton | 268,914 |
| 1933 | 7th | 60 | 92 | .395 | 31.0 | Burt Shotton | 156,421 |
| 1934 | 7th | 56 | 93 | .376 | 37.0 | Jimmy Wilson | 169,885 |
| 1935 | 7th | 64 | 89 | .418 | 35.5 | Jimmy Wilson | 205,470 |
| 1936 | 8th | 54 | 100 | .351 | 38.0 | Jimmy Wilson | 249,219 |
| 1937 | 7th | 61 | 92 | .399 | 34.5 | Jimmy Wilson | 212,790 |
| 1938 | 8th | 45 | 105 | .300 | 43.0 | Jimmy Wilson, Hans Lobert | 166,111 |
| 1939 | 8th | 45 | 106 | .298 | 50.5 | Doc Prothro | 277,973 |
| 1940 | 8th | 50 | 103 | .327 | 50.0 | Doc Prothro | 207,177 |
| 1941 | 8th | 43 | 111 | .279 | 57.0 | Doc Prothro | 231,401 |
| 1942 | 8th | 42 | 109 | .278 | 62.5 | Hans Lobert | 230,183 |
| 1943 | 7th | 64 | 90 | .416 | 41.0 | Bucky Harris, Fred Fitzsimmons | 466,975 |
| 1944 | 8th | 61 | 92 | .399 | 43.5 | Fred Fitzsimmons | 369,586 |
| 1945 | 8th | 46 | 108 | .299 | 52.0 | Fred Fitzsimmons, Ben Chapman | 285,057 |
| 1946 | 5th | 69 | 85 | .448 | 28.0 | Ben Chapman | 1,045,247 |
| 1947 | 7th (tied) | 62 | 92 | .403 | 32.0 | Ben Chapman | 907,332 |
| 1948 | 6th | 66 | 88 | .429 | 25.5 | Ben Chapman, Dusty Cooke, Eddie Sawyer | 767,429 |
| 1949 | 3rd | 81 | 73 | .526 | 16.0 | Eddie Sawyer | 819,698 |
| 1950 | 1st (s) | 91 | 63 | .591 | +2.0 | Eddie Sawyer | 1,217,035 |
| 1951 | 5th | 73 | 81 | .474 | 23.5 | Eddie Sawyer | 937,658 |
| 1952 | 4th | 87 | 67 | .565 | 9.5 | Eddie Sawyer, Steve O'Neill | 775,417 |
| 1953 | 3rd (tied) | 83 | 71 | .539 | 22.0 | Steve O'Neill | 853,644 |
| 1954 | 4th | 75 | 79 | .487 | 22.0 | Steve O'Neill, Terry Moore | 738,991 |
| 1955 | 4th | 77 | 77 | .500 | 21.5 | Mayo Smith | 922,886 |
| 1956 | 5th | 71 | 83 | .461 | 22.0 | Mayo Smith | 934,798 |
| 1957 | 5th | 77 | 77 | .500 | 19.0 | Mayo Smith | 1,146,230 |
| 1958 | 8th | 69 | 85 | .448 | 23.0 | Mayo Smith, Eddie Sawyer | 931,110 |
| 1959 | 8th | 64 | 90 | .416 | 23.0 | Eddie Sawyer | 802,815 |
| 1960 | 8th | 59 | 95 | .383 | 36.0 | Eddie Sawyer, Andy Cohen, Gene Mauch | 862,205 |
| 1961 | 8th | 47 | 107 | .305 | 46.0 | Gene Mauch | 590,039 |
| 1962 | 7th | 81 | 80 | .503 | 20.0 | Gene Mauch | 762,034 |
| 1963 | 4th | 87 | 75 | .537 | 12.0 | Gene Mauch | 907,141 |
| 1964 | 2nd (tied) | 92 | 70 | .568 | 1.0 | Gene Mauch | 1,425,891 |
| 1965 | 6th | 85 | 76 | .528 | 11.5 | Gene Mauch | 1,166,376 |
| 1966 | 4th | 87 | 75 | .537 | 8.0 | Gene Mauch | 1,108,201 |
| 1967 | 5th | 82 | 80 | .506 | 19.5 | Gene Mauch | 828,888 |
| 1968 | 7th (tied) | 76 | 86 | .469 | 21.0 | Gene Mauch, George Myatt, Bob Skinner | 664,546 |

## EAST DIVISION

| Year | Position | W | L | Pct. | GB | Manager | Attendance |
|---|---|---|---|---|---|---|---|
| 1969 | 5th | 63 | 99 | .389 | 37.0 | Bob Skinner, George Myatt | 519,414 |
| 1970 | 5th | 73 | 88 | .453 | 15.5 | Frank Lucchesi | 708,247 |
| 1971 | 6th | 67 | 95 | .414 | 30.0 | Frank Lucchesi | 1,511,223 |
| 1972 | 6th | 59 | 97 | .378 | 37.5 | Frank Lucchesi, Paul Owens | 1,343,329 |
| 1973 | 6th | 71 | 91 | .438 | 11.5 | Danny Ozark | 1,475,934 |
| 1974 | 3rd | 80 | 82 | .494 | 8.0 | Danny Ozark | 1,808,648 |
| 1975 | 2nd | 86 | 76 | .531 | 6.5 | Danny Ozark | 1,909,233 |
| 1976 | 1st (c) | 101 | 61 | .623 | +9.0 | Danny Ozark | 2,480,150 |
| 1977 | 1st (c) | 101 | 61 | .623 | +5.0 | Danny Ozark | 2,700,070 |
| 1978 | 1st (c) | 90 | 72 | .556 | +1.5 | Danny Ozark | 2,583,389 |
| 1979 | 4th | 84 | 78 | .519 | 14.0 | Danny Ozark, Dallas Green | 2,775,011 |
| 1980 | 1st (C,S) | 91 | 71 | .562 | +1.0 | Dallas Green | 2,651,650 |
| 1981 | 1st/3rd (i) | 59 | 48 | .551 | * | Dallas Green | 1,638,752 |
| 1982 | 2nd | 89 | 73 | .549 | 3.0 | Pat Corrales | 2,376,394 |
| 1983 | 1st (C,s) | 90 | 72 | .556 | +6.0 | Pat Corrales, Paul Owens | 2,128,339 |
| 1984 | 4th | 81 | 81 | .500 | 15.5 | Paul Owens | 2,062,693 |
| 1985 | 5th | 75 | 87 | .463 | 26.0 | John Felske | 1,830,350 |
| 1986 | 2nd | 86 | 75 | .534 | 21.5 | John Felske | 1,933,335 |
| 1987 | 4th (tied) | 80 | 82 | .494 | 15.0 | John Felske, Lee Elia | 2,100,110 |
| 1988 | 6th | 65 | 96 | .404 | 35.5 | Lee Elia, John Vukovich | 1,990,041 |
| 1989 | 6th | 67 | 95 | .414 | 26.0 | Nick Leyva | 1,861,985 |
| 1990 | 4th (tied) | 77 | 85 | .475 | 18.0 | Nick Leyva | 1,992,484 |
| 1991 | 3rd | 78 | 84 | .481 | 20.0 | Nick Leyva, Jim Fregosi | 2,050,012 |
| 1992 | 6th | 70 | 92 | .432 | 26.0 | Jim Fregosi | 1,927,448 |
| 1993 | 1st (C,s) | 97 | 65 | .599 | +3.0 | Jim Fregosi | 3,137,674 |
| 1994 | 4th | 54 | 61 | .470 | 20.5 | Jim Fregosi | 2,290,971 |
| 1995 | 2nd (tied) | 69 | 75 | .479 | 21.0 | Jim Fregosi | 2,043,598 |
| 1996 | 5th | 67 | 95 | .414 | 29.0 | Jim Fregosi | 1,801,677 |
| 1997 | 5th | 68 | 94 | .420 | 33.0 | Terry Francona | 1,490,638 |
| 1998 | 3rd | 75 | 87 | .463 | 31.0 | Terry Francona | 1,715,702 |
| 1999 | 3rd | 77 | 85 | .475 | 26.0 | Terry Francona | 1,825,337 |
| 2000 | 5th | 65 | 97 | .401 | 30.0 | Terry Francona | 1,612,769 |
| 2001 | 2nd | 86 | 76 | .531 | 2.0 | Larry Bowa | 1,782,460 |
| 2002 | 3rd | 80 | 81 | .497 | 21.5 | Larry Bowa | 1,618,141 |
| 2003 | 3rd | 86 | 76 | .531 | 15.0 | Larry Bowa | 2,223,353 |
| 2004 | 2nd | 86 | 76 | .531 | 10.0 | Larry Bowa, Gary Varsho | 3,206,532 |
| 2005 | 2nd | 88 | 74 | .543 | 2.0 | Charlie Manuel | 2,665,304 |

(s) lost World Series; (c) lost League Championship Series; (C) won League Championship Series; (S) won World Series; (i) lost intra-divisional playoff; *first half 34-21, second half 25-27

# INDIVIDUAL AND CLUB RECORDS

## BATTING

| | Individual Season | Individual Career | Club Season |
|---|---|---|---|
| Games | 163—Pete Rose, 1979 | 2,404—Mike Schmidt | 163 (1979, 1983, 1989) |
| At-bats | 701—Juan Samuel, 160 G, 1984 | 8,352—Mike Schmidt | 5,685 (1993) |
| Runs | 196—Billy Hamilton, 131 G, 1894<br>*158—Chuck Klein, 156 G, 1930 | 1,506—Mike Schmidt | 944 (1930)<br>Fewest—394 (1942) |
| Hits | 254—Lefty O'Doul, 154 G, 1929 | 2,234—Mike Schmidt | 1,783 (1930)<br>Fewest—1,110 (1907) |
| Hitting streak | 36 G—Jimmy Rollins, 2005 | | |
| Singles | 183—Billy Hamilton, 1894<br>*181—Lefty O'Doul, 154 G, 1929<br>Richie Ashburn, 154 G, 1951 | 1,811—Richie Ashburn | 1,338 (1894) *1,268 (1930) |
| Doubles | 59—Chuck Klein, 156 G, 1930 | 442—Ed Delahanty<br>*408—Mike Schmidt | 345 (1930) |
| Triples | 26—Sam Thompson, 102 G, 1894<br>*19—Juan Samuel, 160 G, 1984 | 158—Ed Delahanty<br>*127—Sherry Magee | 148 (1894) *82 (1905) |
| **HOME RUNS** | | | 215 (2004)<br>Fewest—11 (1908) |
| Righthander | 48—Mike Schmidt, 150 G, 1980 | 548—Mike Schmidt | |
| Lefthander | 47—Jim Thome, 159 G, 2003 | 243—Chuck Klein | |
| Switch-hitter | 27—Dave Hollins, 156 G, 1992 | 67—Dave Hollins | |
| Rookie | 30—Willie Montanez, 158 G, 1971 | | |
| Home | 29—Chuck Klein, 1932 | 265—Mike Schmidt | 113 (2004) |
| Road | 29—Mike Schmidt, 1979 | 283—Mike Schmidt | 89 (1987) |
| Month | 15—Cy Williams, May 1923<br>Jim Thome, June 2004 | | 44 (June 2004) |
| Pinch | 5—Gene Freese, 1959 | 9—Cy Williams | 11 (1958) |
| Grand slams | 4—Vince DiMaggio, 127 G, 1945 | 7—Mike Schmidt | 8 (1993, 2005) |
| Home runs at Baker Bowl, all teams | | | 160 (1929) |
| Home runs at Connie Mack Stadium, all teams | | | 154 (1955) |
| Home runs at Veterans Stadium, all teams | | | 185 (1999) |
| Home runs at Citizens Bank Park, all teams | | | 228 (2004) |
| Total bases | 445—Chuck Klein, 156 G, 1930 | 4,404—Mike Schmidt | 2,594 (1930) |
| Extra-base hits | 107—Chuck Klein, 156 G, 1930 | 1,015—Mike Schmidt | 541 (2004) |
| Sacrifice hits | 43—Kid Gleason, 155 G, 1905 | 216—Otto Knabe | 174 (1905) |
| Sacrifice flies | 13—Willie Montanez, 158 G, 1971<br>Mike Schmidt, 150 G, 1980 | 108—Mike Schmidt | 74 (1977) |
| Bases on balls | 129—Lenny Dykstra, 161 G, 1993 | 1,507—Mike Schmidt | 665 (1993) |
| Strikeouts | 182—Jim Thome, 159 G, 2003<br>Fewest—8—Emil Verban, 155 G, 1947 | 1,883—Mike Schmidt | 1,155 (2003)<br>Fewest—452 (1924) |
| Hit by pitch | 19—Dave Hollins, 156 G, 1992 | 80—Ed Delahanty<br>*79—Mike Schmidt | 58 (2004)<br>Fewest—9 (1939) |
| Runs batted in | 170—Chuck Klein, 154 G, 1930 | 1,595—Mike Schmidt | 884 (1930)<br>Fewest—298 (1883) *356 (1942) |
| Grounded into double plays | 25—Del Ennis, 153 G, 1950<br>Ted Sizemore, 152 G, 1977<br>Fewest—1—Richie Ashburn, 117 G, 1948 | 171—Del Ennis<br>Granny Hamner | 144 (1950)<br>Fewest—91 (1935, 1973) |
| Left on base | | | 1,281 (1993)<br>Fewest—991 (1920) |
| Batting average | .408—Ed Delahanty, 145 G, 1899<br>*.398—Lefty O'Doul, 154 G, 1929 | .362—Billy Hamilton<br>*.326—Chuck Klein | .343 (1894) *.315 (1930)<br>Lowest—.225 (1888) *.232 (1942) |
| Most .300 hitters | | | 6 (1929, 1932) |
| Slugging average | .687—Chuck Klein, 156 G, 1930 | .553—Chuck Klein | .467 (1929)<br>Lowest—.305 (1907) |
| On-base percentage | .523—Billy Hamilton, 1894<br>*.465—Lefty O'Doul, 1929 | .468—Billy Hamilton<br>*.460—Lefty O'Doul | .414 (1894) *.377 (1929)<br>Lowest—.269 (1883) *.289 (1942) |

## BASERUNNING

| | Individual Season | Individual Career | Club Season |
|---|---|---|---|
| Stolen bases | 115—Billy Hamilton, 133 G, 1891<br>*72—Juan Samuel, 160 G, 1984 | 508—Billy Hamilton<br>*387—Sherry Magee | 200 (1908) |
| Caught stealing | 19—Juan Samuel, 161 G, 1985 | 94—Larry Bowa | 83 (1920) |

## PITCHING

| | Individual Season | Individual Career | Club Season |
|---|---|---|---|
| Games | 90—Kent Tekulve, 1987 | 529—Robin Roberts | |
| Games started | 45—Grover Alexander, 1916 | 499—Steve Carlton | |
| Complete games | 38—Grover Alexander, 1916 | 272—Robin Roberts | 131 (1904) |
| Wins | 33—Grover Alexander, 1916 | 241—Steve Carlton | |

| | Individual Season | Individual Career | Club Season |
|---|---|---|---|
| **Percentage** | .800—Robin Roberts (28-7), 1952<br>Tommy Greene (16-4), 1993 | .676—Grover Alexander | |
| **Winning streak** | 15—Steve Carlton, 1972 | | |
| **20-win seasons** | | 6—Grover Alexander<br>Robin Roberts | |
| **Losses** | 24—Chick Fraser, 1904 | 199—Robin Roberts | |
| **Losing streak** | 12—Russ Miller, 1928<br>Hugh Mulcahy, 1940<br>Ken Reynolds, 1972 | | |
| **Saves** | 45—Jose Mesa, 2002 | 111—Jose Mesa | 48 (1987) |
| **Innings** | 389—Grover Alexander, 1916 | 3,739.1—Robin Roberts | 1,480 (1980) |
| **Hits** | 348—Claude Passeau, 1937 | 3,661—Robin Roberts | 1,993 (1930) |
| **Runs** | 178—Ray Benge, 1930 | 1,501—Robin Roberts | 1,199 (1930) |
| **Earned runs** | 147—Robin Roberts, 1956 | 1,437—Robin Roberts | 1,024 (1930) |
| **Bases on balls** | 164—Earl Moore, 1911 | 1,252—Steve Carlton | 682 (1974) |
| **Strikeouts** | 319—Curt Schilling, 1997 | 3,031—Steve Carlton | 1,209 (1997) |
| **Strikeouts, game** | 17—Art Mahaffey, Apr 23, 1961, 2nd game<br>[18—Chris Short, Oct 2, 1965, 2nd game, pitched first 15 inn of 18-inn game] | | |
| **Hit batsmen** | 19—Fred Mitchell, 1903<br>Jim Bunning, 1966 | 82—Bill Duggleby | 77 (2003) |
| **Wild pitches** | 22—Jack Hamilton, 1962 | 120—Steve Carlton | 91 (1989) |
| **Home runs** | 46—Robin Roberts, 1956 | 402—Robin Roberts | 212 (1999) |
| **Sacrifice hits** | 27—Tommy Hughes, 1942 | 221—Grover Alexander | 221 (1928) |
| **Sacrifice flies** | 15—Randy Lerch, 1979 | 82—Steve Carlton | 63 (1960, 1997) |
| **Earned run average** | 1.22—Grover Alexander, 376 inn, 1915 | 1.79—George McQuillan | 2.18 (1915) |
| **Shutouts** | 16—Grover Alexander, 1916 | 61—Grover Alexander | 24 (1916)<br>Lost—23 (1908, 1909) |
| **1-0 games won** | 4—Grover Alexander, 1916 | 13—Grover Alexander | 7 (1913)<br>Lost—10 (1967) |

## TEAM FIELDING

**Putouts** 4,440 (1980)
Fewest—3,887 (1907)
**Chances accepted** 6,440 (1913)
Fewest—5,545 (1955)
**Double plays** 179 (1961, 1973)
Fewest—111 (1991)
**Errorless games** 103 (2004)
Consecutive—11 (1967, 1998)

**Assists** 2,176 (1921)
Fewest—1,437 (1957)
**Errors** 403 (1904)
Fewest—81 (2004)
**Passed balls** 27 (1947, 1971)
Fewest—3 (1952, 1956)
**Fielding average** .987 (2004)
Lowest—.936 (1904)

## MISCELLANEOUS

**Most players, season** 54 (1996)
**Fewest players, season** 23 (1915)
**Games won** 101 (1976, 1977)
**Month** 22 (Sept 1916, July 1950, July 1952, May 1976, Aug 1977, Sep 1983)
**Consecutive** 16 (1887, 1890, 1892) *13 (1977, 1991)
**Winning percentage** .623 (1886), 71-43 *.623 )1976, 1977), 101-61
**Lowest** .173 (1883), 17-81 *.278 (1942) 42-109
**Number of league championships** 5
**Most recent** 1993
**Runs, game** 29 vs Louisville, Aug 17, 1894
*26 vs New York, June 11, 1985
**Opponents'** 29 by Boston, June 20, 1883
by New York, June 15, 1887
*28 by St. Louis, July 6, 1929, 2nd game
**Hits, game** 36 vs Louisville, Aug 17, 1894
*27 vs New York, June 11, 1985
**Home runs, game** 7 vs New York, Sept 8,1998
**Runs, shutout** 24 vs Indianapolis, June 28, 1887
*18 vs Pittsburgh, July 11, 1910
vs Cincinnati, Aug 10, 1930, 1st game
vs Cincinnati, July 14, 1934, 1st game
**Opponents'** 28 by Providence, Aug 21, 1883
*16 by Chicago, May 4, 1929, 1st game
**Longest 1-0 win** 16 inn vs Chicago, May 17, 1991

**Most seasons, non-pitcher** 18—Mike Schmidt
**Most seasons, pitcher** 15—Steve Carlton
**Games lost** 111 (1941)
**Month** 27 (Sept 1939)
**Consecutive** 23 (1961)
**Overall record** 8,679-9,879 (123 seasons)
**Interleague play** 73-78
**Number of times worst record in league** 27 (tied in 1947, 1997, 2000)
**Most recent** 2000
**Runs, inning** 13 vs Cincinnati, Apr 13, 2003, 4th
**Total bases, game** 49 vs Louisville, Aug 17, 1894
*47 vs New York, June 11, 1985
[48 vs Pittsburgh, July 23, 1930, 2nd game, 13 inn
vs Chicago, May 17, 1979, 10 inn]
**Consecutive games with one or more home runs** 16 (24 HRs), 2002
**Longest shutout** 16 inn, 3-0 vs Chicago, Sept 22, 1975
16 inn, 1-0 vs Chicago, May 17, 1991
**Longest 1-0 loss** 17 inn vs Montreal, Sept 21, 1981

## ATTENDANCE

| **Highest home attendance** | |
|---|---|
| **Baker Bowl** | 515,365 (1916) |
| **Connie Mack Stadium** | 1,425,891 (1964) |
| **Veterans Stadium** | 3,137,674 (1993) |
| **Citizens Bank Park** | 3,250,092 (2004) |
| **Highest road attendance** | 2,666,219 (1993) |

*records made since 1900 that do not exceed pre-1900 records

| **Largest crowds** | |
|---|---|
| **Day** | 61,068 vs Boston, Sept 1, 2003 |
| **Night** | 63,816 vs Cincinnati, July 3, 1984 |
| **Doubleheader** | 63,346 vs Pittsburgh, Aug 10, 1979 |
| **Home opener** | 60,985 vs Chicago, Apr 9, 1993 |

# PITTSBURGH PIRATES

## YEARLY FINISHES

(American Association franchise moved to the National League after the 1886 season)

| Year | Position | W | L | Pct. | GB | Manager | Attendance |
|---|---|---|---|---|---|---|---|
| 1887 | 6th | 55 | 69 | .444 | 24.0 | Horace Phillips | 140,000 |
| 1888 | 6th | 66 | 68 | .493 | 19.5 | Horace Phillips | 112,000 |
| 1889 | 5th | 61 | 71 | .462 | 25.0 | Horace Phillips, Fred Dunlap, Ned Hanlon | 117,338 |
| 1890 | 8th | 23 | 113 | .169 | 66.5 | Guy Hecker | 16,064 |
| 1891 | 8th | 55 | 80 | .407 | 30.5 | Ned Hanlon, Bill McGunnigle | 128,000 |
| 1892 | 6th/4th | 80 | 73 | .523 | ** | Al Buckenberger, Tom Burns, Al Buckenberger | 177,205 |
| 1893 | 2nd | 81 | 48 | .628 | 5.0 | Al Buckenberger | 184,000 |
| 1894 | 7th | 65 | 65 | .500 | 25.0 | Al Buckenberger, Connie Mack | 159,000 |
| 1895 | 7th | 71 | 61 | .538 | 17.0 | Connie Mack | 188,000 |
| 1896 | 6th | 66 | 63 | .512 | 24.0 | Connie Mack | 197,000 |
| 1897 | 8th | 60 | 71 | .458 | 32.5 | Patsy Donovan | 165,950 |
| 1898 | 8th | 72 | 76 | .486 | 29.5 | Bill Watkins | 150,900 |
| 1899 | 7th | 76 | 73 | .510 | 25.5 | Bill Watkins, Patsy Donovan | 251,834 |
| 1900 | 2nd (t) | 79 | 60 | .568 | 4.5 | Fred Clarke | 250,000 |
| 1901 | 1st | 90 | 49 | .647 | +7.5 | Fred Clarke | 251,955 |
| 1902 | 1st | 103 | 36 | .741 | +27.5 | Fred Clarke | 243,826 |
| 1903 | 1st (s) | 91 | 49 | .650 | +6.5 | Fred Clarke | 326,855 |
| 1904 | 4th | 87 | 66 | .569 | 19.0 | Fred Clarke | 340,615 |
| 1905 | 2nd | 96 | 57 | .627 | 9.0 | Fred Clarke | 369,124 |
| 1906 | 3rd | 93 | 60 | .608 | 23.5 | Fred Clarke | 394,877 |
| 1907 | 2nd | 91 | 63 | .591 | 17.0 | Fred Clarke | 319,506 |
| 1908 | 2nd | 98 | 56 | .636 | 1.0 | Fred Clarke | 382,444 |
| 1909 | 1st (S) | 110 | 42 | .724 | +6.5 | Fred Clarke | 534,950 |
| 1910 | 3rd | 86 | 67 | .562 | 17.5 | Fred Clarke | 436,586 |
| 1911 | 3rd | 85 | 69 | .552 | 14.5 | Fred Clarke | 432,000 |
| 1912 | 2nd | 93 | 58 | .616 | 10.0 | Fred Clarke | 384,000 |
| 1913 | 4th | 78 | 71 | .523 | 21.5 | Fred Clarke | 296,000 |
| 1914 | 7th | 69 | 85 | .448 | 25.5 | Fred Clarke | 139,620 |
| 1915 | 5th | 73 | 81 | .474 | 18.0 | Fred Clarke | 225,743 |
| 1916 | 6th | 65 | 89 | .422 | 29.0 | Jimmy Callahan | 289,132 |
| 1917 | 8th | 51 | 103 | .331 | 47.0 | Jimmy Callahan, Honus Wagner, Hugo Bezdek | 192,807 |
| 1918 | 4th | 65 | 60 | .520 | 17.0 | Hugo Bezdek | 213,610 |
| 1919 | 4th | 71 | 68 | .511 | 24.5 | Hugo Bezdek | 276,810 |
| 1920 | 4th | 79 | 75 | .513 | 14.0 | George Gibson | 429,037 |
| 1921 | 2nd | 90 | 63 | .588 | 4.0 | George Gibson | 701,567 |
| 1922 | 3rd (tied) | 85 | 69 | .552 | 8.0 | George Gibson, Bill McKechnie | 523,675 |
| 1923 | 3rd | 87 | 67 | .565 | 8.5 | Bill McKechnie | 611,082 |
| 1924 | 3rd | 90 | 63 | .588 | 3.0 | Bill McKechnie | 736,883 |
| 1925 | 1st (S) | 95 | 58 | .621 | +8.5 | Bill McKechnie | 804,354 |
| 1926 | 3rd | 84 | 69 | .549 | 4.5 | Bill McKechnie | 798,542 |
| 1927 | 1st (s) | 94 | 60 | .610 | +1.5 | Donie Bush | 869,720 |
| 1928 | 4th | 85 | 67 | .559 | 9.0 | Donie Bush | 495,070 |
| 1929 | 2nd | 88 | 65 | .575 | 10.5 | Donie Bush, Jewel Ens | 491,377 |
| 1930 | 5th | 80 | 74 | .519 | 12.0 | Jewel Ens | 357,795 |
| 1931 | 5th | 75 | 79 | .487 | 26.0 | Jewel Ens | 260,392 |
| 1932 | 2nd | 86 | 68 | .558 | 4.0 | George Gibson | 287,262 |
| 1933 | 2nd | 87 | 67 | .565 | 5.0 | George Gibson | 288,747 |
| 1934 | 5th | 74 | 76 | .493 | 19.5 | George Gibson, Pie Traynor | 322,622 |
| 1935 | 4th | 86 | 67 | .562 | 13.5 | Pie Traynor | 352,885 |
| 1936 | 4th | 84 | 70 | .545 | 8.0 | Pie Traynor | 372,524 |
| 1937 | 3rd | 86 | 68 | .558 | 10.0 | Pie Traynor | 459,679 |
| 1938 | 2nd | 86 | 64 | .573 | 2.0 | Pie Traynor | 641,033 |
| 1939 | 6th | 68 | 85 | .444 | 28.5 | Pie Traynor | 376,734 |
| 1940 | 4th | 78 | 76 | .506 | 22.5 | Frankie Frisch | 507,934 |
| 1941 | 4th | 81 | 73 | .526 | 19.0 | Frankie Frisch | 482,241 |
| 1942 | 5th | 66 | 81 | .449 | 36.5 | Frankie Frisch | 448,897 |
| 1943 | 4th | 80 | 74 | .519 | 25.0 | Frankie Frisch | 604,278 |
| 1944 | 2nd | 90 | 63 | .588 | 14.5 | Frankie Frisch | 498,740 |
| 1945 | 4th | 82 | 72 | .532 | 16.0 | Frankie Frisch | 604,694 |
| 1946 | 7th | 63 | 91 | .409 | 34.0 | Frankie Frisch, Spud Davis | 749,962 |
| 1947 | 7th (tied) | 62 | 92 | .403 | 32.0 | Billy Herman, Bill Burwell | 1,283,531 |
| 1948 | 4th | 83 | 71 | .539 | 8.5 | Billy Meyer | 1,517,021 |
| 1949 | 6th | 71 | 83 | .461 | 26.0 | Billy Meyer | 1,499,435 |
| 1950 | 8th | 57 | 96 | .373 | 33.5 | Billy Meyer | 1,166,267 |
| 1951 | 7th | 64 | 90 | .416 | 32.5 | Billy Meyer | 980,590 |
| 1952 | 8th | 42 | 112 | .273 | 54.5 | Billy Meyer | 686,673 |
| 1953 | 8th | 50 | 104 | .325 | 55.0 | Fred Haney | 572,757 |
| 1954 | 8th | 53 | 101 | .344 | 44.0 | Fred Haney | 475,494 |
| 1955 | 8th | 60 | 94 | .390 | 38.5 | Fred Haney | 469,397 |
| 1956 | 7th | 66 | 88 | .429 | 27.0 | Bobby Bragan | 949,878 |
| 1957 | 7th (tied) | 62 | 92 | .403 | 33.0 | Bobby Bragan, Danny Murtaugh | 850,732 |
| 1958 | 2nd | 84 | 70 | .545 | 8.0 | Danny Murtaugh | 1,311,988 |
| 1959 | 4th | 78 | 76 | .506 | 9.0 | Danny Murtaugh | 1,359,917 |
| 1960 | 1st (S) | 95 | 59 | .617 | +7.0 | Danny Murtaugh | 1,705,828 |
| 1961 | 6th | 75 | 79 | .487 | 18.0 | Danny Murtaugh | 1,199,128 |
| 1962 | 4th | 93 | 68 | .578 | 8.0 | Danny Murtaugh | 1,090,648 |
| 1963 | 8th | 74 | 88 | .457 | 25.0 | Danny Murtaugh | 783,648 |
| 1964 | 6th (tied) | 80 | 82 | .494 | 13.0 | Danny Murtaugh | 759,496 |
| 1965 | 3rd | 90 | 72 | .556 | 7.0 | Harry Walker | 909,279 |
| 1966 | 3rd | 92 | 70 | .568 | 3.0 | Harry Walker | 1,196,618 |
| 1967 | 6th | 81 | 81 | .500 | 20.5 | Harry Walker, Danny Murtaugh | 907,012 |
| 1968 | 6th | 80 | 82 | .494 | 17.0 | Larry Shepard | 693,485 |

## EAST DIVISION

| Year | Position | W | L | Pct. | GB | Manager | Attendance |
|---|---|---|---|---|---|---|---|
| 1969 | 3rd | 88 | 74 | .543 | 12.0 | Larry Shepard, Alex Grammas | 769,369 |
| 1970 | 1st (c) | 89 | 73 | .549 | +5.0 | Danny Murtaugh | 1,341,947 |
| 1971 | 1st (C,S) | 97 | 65 | .599 | +7.0 | Danny Murtaugh | 1,501,132 |
| 1972 | 1st (c) | 96 | 59 | .619 | +11.0 | Bill Virdon | 1,427,460 |
| 1973 | 3rd | 80 | 82 | .494 | 2.5 | Bill Virdon, Danny Murtaugh | 1,319,913 |
| 1974 | 1st (c) | 88 | 74 | .543 | +1.5 | Danny Murtaugh | 1,110,552 |
| 1975 | 1st (c) | 92 | 69 | .571 | +6.5 | Danny Murtaugh | 1,270,018 |
| 1976 | 2nd | 92 | 70 | .568 | 9.0 | Danny Murtaugh | 1,025,945 |
| 1977 | 2nd | 96 | 66 | .593 | 5.0 | Chuck Tanner | 1,237,349 |
| 1978 | 2nd | 88 | 73 | .547 | 1.5 | Chuck Tanner | 964,106 |
| 1979 | 1st (C,S) | 98 | 64 | .605 | +2.0 | Chuck Tanner | 1,435,454 |
| 1980 | 3rd | 83 | 79 | .512 | 8.0 | Chuck Tanner | 1,646,757 |
| 1981 | 4th/6th | 46 | 56 | .451 | * | Chuck Tanner | 541,789 |
| 1982 | 4th | 84 | 78 | .519 | 8.0 | Chuck Tanner | 1,024,106 |
| 1983 | 2nd | 84 | 78 | .519 | 6.0 | Chuck Tanner | 1,225,916 |
| 1984 | 6th | 75 | 87 | .463 | 21.5 | Chuck Tanner | 773,500 |
| 1985 | 6th | 57 | 104 | .354 | 43.5 | Chuck Tanner | 735,900 |
| 1986 | 6th | 64 | 98 | .395 | 44.0 | Jim Leyland | 1,000,917 |
| 1987 | 4th (tied) | 80 | 82 | .494 | 15.0 | Jim Leyland | 1,161,193 |
| 1988 | 2nd | 85 | 75 | .531 | 15.0 | Jim Leyland | 1,866,713 |
| 1989 | 5th | 74 | 88 | .457 | 19.0 | Jim Leyland | 1,374,141 |
| 1990 | 1st (c) | 95 | 67 | .586 | +4.0 | Jim Leyland | 2,049,908 |
| 1991 | 1st (c) | 98 | 64 | .605 | +14.0 | Jim Leyland | 2,065,302 |
| 1992 | 1st (c) | 96 | 66 | .593 | +9.0 | Jim Leyland | 1,829,395 |
| 1993 | 5th | 75 | 87 | .463 | 22.0 | Jim Leyland | 1,650,593 |

## CENTRAL DIVISION

| Year | Position | W | L | Pct. | GB | Manager | Attendance |
|---|---|---|---|---|---|---|---|
| 1994 | 3rd (tied) | 53 | 61 | .465 | 13.0 | Jim Leyland | 1,222,520 |
| 1995 | 5th | 58 | 86 | .403 | 27.0 | Jim Leyland | 905,517 |
| 1996 | 5th | 73 | 89 | .451 | 15.0 | Jim Leyland | 1,332,150 |
| 1997 | 2nd | 79 | 83 | .488 | 5.0 | Gene Lamont | 1,657,022 |
| 1998 | 6th | 69 | 93 | .426 | 33.0 | Gene Lamont | 1,560,950 |
| 1999 | 3rd | 78 | 83 | .484 | 18.5 | Gene Lamont | 1,638,023 |
| 2000 | 5th | 69 | 93 | .426 | 26.0 | Gene Lamont | 1,748,908 |
| 2001 | 6th | 62 | 100 | .383 | 31.0 | Lloyd McClendon | 2,436,126 |
| 2002 | 4th | 72 | 89 | .447 | 24.5 | Lloyd McClendon | 1,784,993 |
| 2003 | 4th | 75 | 87 | .463 | 13.0 | Lloyd McClendon | 1,636,761 |
| 2004 | 5th | 72 | 89 | .447 | 32.5 | Lloyd McClendon | 1,583,031 |
| 2005 | 6th | 67 | 95 | .414 | 33.0 | Lloyd McClendon, Pete Mackanin | 1,817,245 |

**first half 37-39, second half 43-34; (t) lost Chronicle-Telegraph Cup; (s) lost World Series; (S) won World Series; (c) lost League Championship Series; (C) won League Championship Series; *first half 25-23, second half 21-33

## INDIVIDUAL AND CLUB RECORDS

### BATTING

| | Individual Season | Career | Club Season |
|---|---|---|---|
| **Games** | 163—Bill Mazeroski, 1967<br>Bobby Bonilla, 1989 | 2,433—Roberto Clemente | 164 (1989) |
| **At-bats** | 698—Matty Alou, 162 G, 1969 | 9,454—Roberto Clemente | 5,724 (1967) |
| **Runs** | 148—Jake Stenzel, 131 G, 1894<br>*144—Kiki Cuyler, 153 G, 1925 | 1,521—Honus Wagner | 912 (1925)<br>Fewest—464 (1917) |
| **Hits** | 237—Paul Waner, 155 G, 1927 | 3,000—Roberto Clemente | 1,698 (1922)<br>Fewest—1,197 (1914) |
| **Hitting streak** | 27 G—Jimmy Williams, 1899<br>*26 G—Danny O'Connell, 1953 | | |
| **Hitting streak, two seasons** | 30 G—Charlie Grimm, 1922 (5), 1923 (25) | | |
| **Singles** | 198—Lloyd Waner, 150 G, 1927 | 2,154—Roberto Clemente | 1,297 (1922) |
| **Doubles** | 62—Paul Waner, 154 G, 1932 | 558—Paul Waner | 320 (2000) |
| **Triples** | 36—Owen Wilson, 152 G, 1912 | 232—Honus Wagner | 129 (1912) |

### HOME RUNS

| | Individual Season | Career | Club Season |
|---|---|---|---|
| | | | 171 (1999)<br>Fewest—9 (1917) |
| **Righthander** | 54—Ralph Kiner, 152 G, 1949 | 301—Ralph Kiner | |
| **Lefthander** | 48—Willie Stargell,141 G, 1971 | 475—Willie Stargell | |
| **Switch-hitter** | 32—Bobby Bonilla, 1460 G, 1990 | 114—Bobby Bonilla | |
| **Rookie** | 26—Jason Bay, 120 G, 2004 | | |
| **Home** | 31—Ralph Kiner, 1948 | 221—Willie Stargell | 95 (1947) |
| **Road** | 27—Willie Stargell, 1971 | 254—Willie Stargell | 110 (1966) |
| **Month** | 16—Ralph Kiner, Sep 1949 | | 43 (Aug 1947) |
| **Pinch** | 7—Craig Wilson, 2001 | 9—Craig Wilson | 10 (1996, 2001) |
| **Grand slams** | 4—Ralph Kiner, 152 G, 1949 | 11—Ralph Kiner<br>Willie Stargell | 7 (1978, 1996) |
| **Home runs at Forbes Field, all teams** | | | 182 (1947) |
| **Home runs at Three Rivers Stadium, all teams** | | | 172 (2000) |
| **Home runs at PNC Park, all teams** | | | 161 (2003) |

| | Individual Season | Individual Career | Club Season |
|---|---|---|---|
| Total bases | 369—Kiki Cuyler, 153 G, 1925 | 4,492—Roberto Clemente | 2,430 (1966) |
| Extra-base hits | 90—Willie Stargell, 148 G, 1973 | 953—Willie Stargell | 519 (2000) |
| Sacrifice hits | 39—Jay Bell, 159 G, 1990 | 257—Max Carey | 190 (1906) |
| Sacrifice flies | 15—Bobby Bonilla, 160 G, 1990 | 75—Willie Stargell | 67 (1982) |
| Bases on balls | 137—Ralph Kiner, 151 G, 1951<br>Fewest—194 (1888) *327 (1900) | 937—Willie Stargell | 620 (1991) |
| Strikeouts | 169—Craig Wilson, 155 G, 2004<br>Fewest—13—Carson Bigbee, 150 G, 1922<br>Lloyd Waner, 152 G, 1928 | 1,936—Willie Stargell | 1,197 (1999)<br>Fewest—326 (1922) |
| Hit by pitch | 31—Jason Kendall, 144 G, 1997<br>Jason Kendall, 149 G, 1998 | 177—Jason Kendall | 95 (2004, 2005)<br>Fewest—11 (1937) |
| Runs batted in | 131—Paul Waner, 155 G, 1927 | 1,540—Willie Stargell | 844 (1930)<br>Fewest—392 (1888) *396 (1917) |
| Grounded into double plays | 25—Al Todd, 133 G, 1938<br>Fewest—3—Rob Mackowiak, 155 G, 2004 | 275—Roberto Clemente | 142 (1950)<br>Fewest—95 (1978) |
| Left on base | | | 1,241 (1936)<br>Fewest—992 (1924) |
| Batting average | .385—Arky Vaughan, 137 G, 1935 | .340—Paul Waner | .309 (1928)<br>Lowest—.231 (1952) |
| Most .300 hitters | | | 9 (1928) |
| Slugging average | .658—Ralph Kiner, 152 G, 1949 | .591—Brian Giles | .449 (1930)<br>Lowest—.298 (1917) |
| On-base percentage | .491—Arky Vaughan, 137 G, 1935 | .415—Arky Vaughan | .379 (1894) *.369 (1925)<br>Lowest—.264 (1888) *.295 (1914) |

## BASERUNNING

| | Individual Season | Individual Career | Club Season |
|---|---|---|---|
| Stolen bases | 96—Omar Moreno, 162 G, 1980 | 688—Max Carey | 264 (1907) |
| Caught stealing | 33—Omar Moreno, 162 G, 1980 | 137—Omar Moreno | 120 (1977) |

## PITCHING

| | Individual Season | Individual Career | Club Season |
|---|---|---|---|
| Games | 94—Kent Tekulve, 1979 | 802—Roy Face | |
| Games started | 42—Bob Friend, 1956 | 477—Bob Friend | |
| Complete games | 32—Vic Willis, 1906 | 263—Wilbur Cooper | 133 (1904) |
| Wins | 28—Jack Chesbro, 1902 | 202—Wilbur Cooper | |
| Percentage | .947—Roy Face (18-1), 1959 | .661—Sam Leever | |
| Winning streak | 17—Roy Face, 1959 | | |
| Winning streak, two seasons | 22—Roy Face, 1958 (5), 1959 (17) | | |
| 20-win seasons | | 4—Deacon Phillipe<br>Vic Willis<br>Wilbur Cooper | |
| Losses | 21—Murry Dickson, 1952 | 218—Bob Friend | |
| Losing streak | 13—Burleigh Grimes, 1917 | | |
| Saves | 46—Mike Williams, 2002 | 158—Kent Tekulve | 52 (1979) |
| Innings | 331—Burleigh Grimes, 1928 | 3,480.1—Bob Friend | 1,493 (1979) |
| Hits | 366—Ray Kremer, 1930 | 3,610—Bob Friend | 1,730 (1930) |
| Runs | 181—Ray Kremer, 1930 | 1,575—Bob Friend | 928 (1930) |
| Earned runs | 154—Ray Kremer, 1930 | 1,372—Bob Friend | 792 (1930) |
| Bases on balls | 159—Marty O'Toole, 1912 | 869—Bob Friend | 711 (2000) |
| Strikeouts | 276—Bob Veale, 1965 | 1,682—Bob Friend | 1,124 (1969) |
| Strikeouts, game | 16—Bob Veale, June 1, 1965 | | |
| Hit batsmen | 21—Jack Chesbro, 1902 | 93—Wilbur Cooper | 80 (2001) |
| Wild pitches | 18—Bob Veale, 1964 | 90—Bob Veale | 67 (2000) |
| Home runs | 32—Murry Dickson, 1951<br>Ramon Ortiz, 2002 | 273—Bob Friend | 183 (1996) |
| Sacrifice hits | 24—Cy Blanton, 1935 | 354—Wilbur Cooper | 207 (1917) |
| Sacrifice flies | 12—Vern Law, 1954<br>George O'Donnell, 1954<br>John Candelaria, 1974 | 73—Vernon Law | 79 (1954) |
| Earned run average | 1.87—Wilbur Cooper, 246 inn, 1916 | 2.38—Lefty Leifield | 2.07 (1909) |
| Shutouts | 8—Jack Chesbro, 1902<br>Lefty Leifield, 1906<br>Al Mamaux, 1915<br>Babe Adams, 1920 | 44—Babe Adams | 26 (1906)<br>Lost—27 (1916) |
| 1-0 games won | 3—Vic Willis, 1908<br>Claude Hendrix, 1912<br>Wilbur Cooper, 1917 | 8—Babe Adams<br>Wilbur Cooper | 10 (1908)<br>Lost—10 (1914) |

## TEAM FIELDING

| | | | |
|---|---|---|---|
| Putouts | 4,480 (1979)<br>Fewest—3,983 (1934) | Assists | 2,089 (1905)<br>Fewest—1,584 (1934) |

**Chances accepted** 6,462 (1968)
Fewest—5,567 (1934)
**Double plays** 215 (1966)
Fewest—94 (1935)
**Errorless games** 87 (1992)
Consecutive—10 (2001, 2004, 2005)

**Errors** 291 (1904)
Fewest—101 (1992)
**Passed balls** 32 (1953)
Fewest—2 (2004)
**Fielding average** .984 (1992)
Lowest—.955 (1904)

## MISCELLANEOUS

**Most players, season** 49 (1987, 2001)
**Fewest players, season** 25 (1938)
**Games won** 110 (1909)
**Month** 25 (Sept 1901, Sept 1908, July 1932)
**Consecutive** 16 (1909)
**Winning percentage** .741 (1902), 103-36
**Lowest** .169 (1890), 23-113 *.273 (1952), 42-112
**Number of league championships** 9
**Most recent** 1979
**Runs, game** 27 vs Boston, June 6, 1894
*24 vs St. Louis, June 22, 1925
**Opponents'** 28 by Boston, Aug 27, 1887
*23 by Philadelphia, July 13, 1900, 8 inn
by Brooklyn, July 10, 1943
**Total bases, game** 47 vs Atlanta, Aug 1, 1970
**Home runs, game** 7 vs Boston, June 8, 1894
vs St. Louis, Aug 16, 1947
vs St. Louis, Aug 20, 2003
**Runs, shutout** 22 vs Chicago, Sept 16, 1975
**Opponents'** 18 by Philadelphia, July 11, 1910
**Longest 1-0 win** 18 inn vs San Diego, June 7, 1972, 2nd game

**Most seasons, non-pitcher** 21—Willie Stargell
**Most seasons, pitcher** 18—Babe Adams
**Games lost** 113 (1890) *112 (1952)
**Month** 24 (Sept 1916)
**Consecutive** 23 (1890) *12 (1939)
**Overall record** 9,253-8,900 (119 seasons)
**Interleague play** 49-72
**Number of times worst record in league** 12 (tied in 1947, 1957, 2005)
**Most recent** 2005 (tied)
**Runs, inning** 12 vs St. Louis, Apr 22, 1892, 1st
vs Boston, June 6, 1894, 3rd
*11 vs St. Louis, Sept 7, 1942, 1st game, 6th inn
vs Cincinnati, May 4, 1992, 6th
**Hits, game** 27 vs Philadelphia, Aug 8, 1922, 1st game
**Consecutive games with one or more home runs** 13 (21 HRs), 1994
**Longest shutout** 16 inn, 3-0 vs Chicago, Sept 22, 1975
**Longest 1-0 loss** 14 inn vs Cincinnati, June 18, 1943

## ATTENDANCE

**Highest home attendance**

| | |
|---|---|
| **Exposition Park** | 394,877 (1906) |
| **Forbes Field** | 1,705,828 (1960) |
| **Three Rivers Stadium** | 2,065,302 (1991) |
| **PNC Park** | 2,436,139 (2001) |
| **Highest road attendance** | 2,674,131 (2005) |

*records made since 1900 that do not exceed pre-1900 records

**Largest crowds**

| | |
|---|---|
| **Day** | 55,351 vs Chicago, Oct 1, 2000 |
| **Night** | 54,274 vs Montreal, Apr 8, 1991 |
| **Doubleheader** | 49,886 vs New York, July 27, 1972 |
| **Home opener** | 54,274 vs Montreal, Apr 8, 1991 |

# ST. LOUIS CARDINALS

## YEARLY FINISHES

(American Association franchise moved to the National League after the 1891 season)

| Year | Position | W | L | Pct. | GB | Manager | Attendance |
|---|---|---|---|---|---|---|---|
| 1892 | 9th/11th | 56 | 94 | .373 | ** | Chris von der Ahe | 192,442 |
| 1893 | 10th | 57 | 75 | .432 | 30.5 | Bill Watkins | 195,000 |
| 1894 | 9th | 56 | 76 | .424 | 35.0 | George Miller | 155,000 |
| 1895 | 11th | 39 | 92 | .298 | 48.5 | Al Buckenberger, Chris von der Ahe, Joe Quinn, Lew Phelan | 170,000 |
| 1896 | 11th | 40 | 90 | .308 | 50.5 | Harry Diddlebock, Arlie Latham, Chris von der Ahe, Roger Connor, Tommy Dowd | 184,000 |
| 1897 | 12th | 29 | 102 | .221 | 63.5 | Tommy Dowd, Hugh Nicol, Bill Hallman, Chris von der Ahe | 136,400 |
| 1898 | 12th | 39 | 111 | .260 | 63.5 | Tim Hurst | 151,700 |
| 1899 | 5th | 84 | 67 | .556 | 18.5 | Patsy Tebeau | 373,909 |
| 1900 | 5th (tied) | 65 | 75 | .464 | 19.0 | Patsy Tebeau, Louis Heilbroner | 255,000 |
| 1901 | 4th | 76 | 64 | .543 | 14.5 | Patsy Donovan | 379,988 |
| 1902 | 6th | 56 | 78 | .418 | 44.5 | Patsy Donovan | 226,417 |
| 1903 | 8th | 43 | 94 | .314 | 46.5 | Patsy Donovan | 226,538 |
| 1904 | 5th | 75 | 79 | .487 | 31.5 | Kid Nichols | 386,750 |
| 1905 | 6th | 58 | 96 | .377 | 47.5 | Kid Nichols, Jimmy Burke, Matt Robison | 292,800 |
| 1906 | 7th | 52 | 98 | .347 | 63.0 | John McCloskey | 283,770 |
| 1907 | 8th | 52 | 101 | .340 | 55.5 | John McCloskey | 185,377 |
| 1908 | 8th | 49 | 105 | .318 | 50.0 | John McCloskey | 205,129 |
| 1909 | 7th | 54 | 98 | .355 | 56.0 | Roger Bresnahan | 299,982 |
| 1910 | 7th | 63 | 90 | .412 | 40.5 | Roger Bresnahan | 355,668 |
| 1911 | 5th | 75 | 74 | .503 | 22.0 | Roger Bresnahan | 447,768 |
| 1912 | 6th | 63 | 90 | .412 | 41.0 | Roger Bresnahan | 241,759 |
| 1913 | 8th | 51 | 99 | .340 | 49.0 | Miller Huggins | 203,531 |
| 1914 | 3rd | 81 | 72 | .529 | 13.0 | Miller Huggins | 256,099 |
| 1915 | 6th | 72 | 81 | .471 | 18.5 | Miller Huggins | 252,666 |
| 1916 | 7th (tied) | 60 | 93 | .392 | 33.5 | Miller Huggins | 224,308 |
| 1917 | 3rd | 82 | 70 | .539 | 15.0 | Miller Huggins | 288,491 |
| 1918 | 8th | 51 | 78 | .395 | 33.0 | Jack Hendricks | 110,599 |
| 1919 | 7th | 54 | 83 | .394 | 40.5 | Branch Rickey | 167,059 |
| 1920 | 5th (tied) | 75 | 79 | .487 | 18.0 | Branch Rickey | 326,836 |
| 1921 | 3rd | 87 | 66 | .569 | 7.0 | Branch Rickey | 384,773 |
| 1922 | 3rd (tied) | 85 | 69 | .552 | 8.0 | Branch Rickey | 536,998 |
| 1923 | 5th | 79 | 74 | .516 | 16.0 | Branch Rickey | 338,551 |
| 1924 | 6th | 65 | 89 | .422 | 28.5 | Branch Rickey | 272,885 |
| 1925 | 4th | 77 | 76 | .503 | 18.0 | Branch Rickey, Rogers Hornsby | 404,959 |
| 1926 | 1st (S) | 89 | 65 | .578 | +2.0 | Rogers Hornsby | 668,428 |
| 1927 | 2nd | 92 | 61 | .601 | 1.5 | Bob O'Farrell | 749,340 |
| 1928 | 1st (s) | 95 | 59 | .617 | +2.0 | Bill McKechnie | 761,574 |

| Year | Position | W | L | Pct. | GB | Manager | Attendance |
|---|---|---|---|---|---|---|---|
| 1929 | 4th | 78 | 74 | .513 | 20.0 | Bill McKechnie, Billy Southworth | 399,887 |
| 1930 | 1st (s) | 92 | 62 | .597 | +2.0 | Gabby Street | 508,501 |
| 1931 | 1st (S) | 101 | 53 | .656 | +13.0 | Gabby Street | 608,535 |
| 1932 | 6th (tied) | 72 | 82 | .468 | 18.0 | Gabby Street | 279,219 |
| 1933 | 5th | 82 | 71 | .536 | 9.5 | Gabby Street, Frankie Frisch | 256,171 |
| 1934 | 1st (S) | 95 | 58 | .621 | +2.0 | Frankie Frisch | 325,056 |
| 1935 | 2nd | 96 | 58 | .623 | 4.0 | Frankie Frisch | 506,084 |
| 1936 | 2nd (tied) | 87 | 67 | .565 | 5.0 | Frankie Frisch | 448,078 |
| 1937 | 4th | 81 | 73 | .526 | 15.0 | Frankie Frisch | 430,811 |
| 1938 | 6th | 71 | 80 | .470 | 17.5 | Frankie Frisch, Mike Gonzalez | 291,418 |
| 1939 | 2nd | 92 | 61 | .601 | 4.5 | Ray Blades | 400,245 |
| 1940 | 3rd | 84 | 69 | .549 | 16.0 | Ray Blades, Mike Gonzalez, Billy Southworth | 324,078 |
| 1941 | 2nd | 97 | 56 | .634 | 2.5 | Billy Southworth | 633,645 |
| 1942 | 1st (S) | 106 | 48 | .688 | +2.0 | Billy Southworth | 553,552 |
| 1943 | 1st (s) | 105 | 49 | .682 | +18.0 | Billy Southworth | 517,135 |
| 1944 | 1st (S) | 105 | 49 | .682 | +14.5 | Billy Southworth | 461,968 |
| 1945 | 2nd | 95 | 59 | .617 | 3.0 | Billy Southworth | 594,630 |
| 1946 | 1st (L,S) | 98 | 58 | .628 | +2.0 | Eddie Dyer | 1,061,807 |
| 1947 | 2nd | 89 | 65 | .578 | 5.0 | Eddie Dyer | 1,247,913 |
| 1948 | 2nd | 85 | 69 | .552 | 6.5 | Eddie Dyer | 1,111,440 |
| 1949 | 2nd | 96 | 58 | .623 | 1.0 | Eddie Dyer | 1,430,676 |
| 1950 | 5th | 78 | 75 | .510 | 12.5 | Eddie Dyer | 1,093,411 |
| 1951 | 3rd | 81 | 73 | .526 | 15.5 | Marty Marion | 1,013,429 |
| 1952 | 3rd | 88 | 66 | .571 | 8.5 | Eddie Stanky | 913,113 |
| 1953 | 3rd (tied) | 83 | 71 | .539 | 22.0 | Eddie Stanky | 880,242 |
| 1954 | 6th | 72 | 82 | .468 | 25.0 | Eddie Stanky | 1,039,698 |
| 1955 | 7th | 68 | 86 | .442 | 30.5 | Eddie Stanky, Harry Walker | 849,130 |
| 1956 | 4th | 76 | 78 | .494 | 17.0 | Fred Hutchinson | 1,029,773 |
| 1957 | 2nd | 87 | 67 | .565 | 8.0 | Fred Hutchinson | 1,183,575 |
| 1958 | 5th (tied) | 72 | 82 | .468 | 20.0 | Fred Hutchinson, Stan Hack | 1,063,730 |
| 1959 | 7th | 71 | 83 | .461 | 16.0 | Solly Hemus | 929,953 |
| 1960 | 3rd | 86 | 68 | .558 | 9.0 | Solly Hemus | 1,096,632 |
| 1961 | 5th | 80 | 74 | .519 | 13.0 | Solly Hemus, Johnny Keane | 855,305 |
| 1962 | 6th | 84 | 78 | .519 | 17.5 | Johnny Keane | 953,895 |
| 1963 | 2nd | 93 | 69 | .574 | 6.0 | Johnny Keane | 1,170,546 |
| 1964 | 1st (S) | 93 | 69 | .574 | +1.0 | Johnny Keane | 1,143,294 |
| 1965 | 7th | 80 | 81 | .497 | 16.5 | Red Schoendienst | 1,241,201 |
| 1966 | 6th | 83 | 79 | .512 | 12.0 | Red Schoendienst | 1,712,980 |
| 1967 | 1st (S) | 101 | 60 | .627 | +10.5 | Red Schoendienst | 2,090,145 |
| 1968 | 1st (s) | 97 | 65 | .599 | +9.0 | Red Schoendienst | 2,011,167 |

## EAST DIVISION

| Year | Position | W | L | Pct. | GB | Manager | Attendance |
|---|---|---|---|---|---|---|---|
| 1969 | 4th | 87 | 75 | .537 | 13.0 | Red Schoendienst | 1,682,783 |
| 1970 | 4th | 76 | 86 | .469 | 13.0 | Red Schoendienst | 1,629,736 |
| 1971 | 2nd | 90 | 72 | .556 | 7.0 | Red Schoendienst | 1,604,671 |
| 1972 | 4th | 75 | 81 | .481 | 21.5 | Red Schoendienst | 1,196,894 |
| 1973 | 2nd | 81 | 81 | .500 | 1.5 | Red Schoendienst | 1,574,046 |
| 1974 | 2nd | 86 | 75 | .534 | 1.5 | Red Schoendienst | 1,838,413 |
| 1975 | 3rd (tied) | 82 | 80 | .506 | 10.5 | Red Schoendienst | 1,695,270 |
| 1976 | 5th | 72 | 90 | .444 | 29.0 | Red Schoendienst | 1,207,079 |
| 1977 | 3rd | 83 | 79 | .512 | 18.0 | Vern Rapp | 1,659,287 |
| 1978 | 5th | 69 | 93 | .426 | 21.0 | Vern Rapp, Jack Krol, Ken Boyer | 1,278,215 |
| 1979 | 3rd | 86 | 76 | .531 | 12.0 | Ken Boyer | 1,627,256 |
| 1980 | 4th | 74 | 88 | .457 | 17.0 | Ken Boyer, Jack Krol, Whitey Herzog, Red Schoendienst | 1,385,147 |
| 1981 | 2nd/2nd | 59 | 43 | .578 | * | Whitey Herzog | 1,010,247 |
| 1982 | 1st (L,S) | 92 | 70 | .568 | +3.0 | Whitey Herzog | 2,111,906 |
| 1983 | 4th | 79 | 83 | .488 | 11.0 | Whitey Herzog | 2,317,914 |
| 1984 | 3rd | 84 | 78 | .519 | 12.5 | Whitey Herzog | 2,037,448 |
| 1985 | 1st (L,s) | 101 | 61 | .623 | +3.0 | Whitey Herzog | 2,637,563 |
| 1986 | 3rd | 79 | 82 | .491 | 28.5 | Whitey Herzog | 2,471,974 |
| 1987 | 1st (L,s) | 95 | 67 | .586 | +3.0 | Whitey Herzog | 3,072,122 |
| 1988 | 5th | 76 | 86 | .469 | 25.0 | Whitey Herzog | 2,892,799 |
| 1989 | 3rd | 86 | 76 | .531 | 7.0 | Whitey Herzog | 3,080,980 |
| 1990 | 6th | 70 | 92 | .432 | 25.0 | Whitey Herzog, Red Schoendienst, Joe Torre | 2,573,225 |
| 1991 | 2nd | 84 | 78 | .519 | 14.0 | Joe Torre | 2,448,699 |
| 1992 | 3rd | 83 | 79 | .512 | 13.0 | Joe Torre | 2,418,483 |
| 1993 | 3rd | 87 | 75 | .537 | 10.0 | Joe Torre | 2,844,328 |

## CENTRAL DIVISION

| Year | Position | W | L | Pct. | GB | Manager | Attendance |
|---|---|---|---|---|---|---|---|
| 1994 | 3rd (tied) | 53 | 61 | .465 | 13.0 | Joe Torre | 1,866,544 |
| 1995 | 4th | 62 | 81 | .434 | 22.5 | Joe Torre, Mike Jorgensen | 1,756,727 |
| 1996 | 1st (D,c) | 88 | 74 | .543 | +6.0 | Tony La Russa | 2,654,718 |
| 1997 | 4th | 73 | 89 | .451 | 11.0 | Tony La Russa | 2,634,014 |
| 1998 | 3rd | 83 | 79 | .512 | 19.0 | Tony La Russa | 3,194,092 |
| 1999 | 4th | 75 | 86 | .466 | 21.5 | Tony La Russa | 3,225,334 |
| 2000 | 1st (D,c) | 95 | 67 | .586 | +10.0 | Tony La Russa | 3,336,493 |
| 2001 | 1st (tied) (d) | 93 | 69 | .574 | 0.0 | Tony La Russa | 3,113,091 |
| 2002 | 1st (D,c) | 97 | 65 | .599 | +13.0 | Tony La Russa | 3,011,756 |
| 2003 | 3rd | 85 | 77 | .525 | 3.0 | Tony La Russa | 2,910,371 |
| 2004 | 1st (D,C,s) | 105 | 57 | .648 | +13.0 | Tony La Russa | 3,048,427 |
| 2005 | 1st (D,c) | 100 | 62 | .617 | +11.0 | Tony La Russa | 3,538,948 |

**first half 31-42, second half 25-52; (S) won World Series; (s) lost World Sereies; (L) won league playoff; *first half 30-20, second half 29-23; (L) won League Championship Series; (D) won Division Series; (c) lost League Championship Series; (d) lost Division Series

## INDIVIDUAL AND CLUB RECORDS

### BATTING

| | Individual | | Club |
|---|---|---|---|
| | Season | Career | Season |
| **Games** | 163—Jose Oquendo, 1989 | 3,026—Stan Musial | 164 (1989) |

| | Individual Season | Career | Club Season |
|---|---|---|---|
| **At-bats** | 689—Lou Brock, 159 G, 1967 | 10,972—Stan Musial | 5,734 (1979) |
| **Runs** | 141—Rogers Hornsby, 154 G, 1922 | 1,949—Stan Musial | 1,004 (1930)<br>Fewest—372 (1908) |
| **Hits** | 250—Rogers Hornsby, 154 G, 1922 | 3,630—Stan Musial | 1,732 (1930)<br>Fewest—1,105 (1908) |
| **Hitting streak** | 33 G—Rogers Hornsby, 1922 | | |
| **Singles** | 194—Jesse Burkett, 141 G, 1901 | 2,253—Stan Musial | 1,223 (1920) |
| **Doubles** | 64—Joe Medwick, 155 G, 1936 | 725—Stan Musial | 373 (1939) |
| **Triples** | 33—Perry Werden, 124 G, 1893<br>*25—Tommy Long, 140 G, 1915 | 177—Stan Musial | 96 (1920) |
| **HOME RUNS** | | | 235 (2000)<br>Fewest—10 (1906) |
| **Righthander** | 70—Mark McGwire,155 G, 1998 | 255—Ken Boyer | |
| **Lefthander** | 43—Johnny Mize, 155 G, 1940 | 475—Stan Musial | |
| **Switch-hitter** | 35—Rip Collins, 154 G, 1934 | 172—Ted Simmons | |
| **Rookie** | 37—Albert Pujols, 161 G, 2001 | | |
| **Home** | 38—Mark McGwire, 1998 | 252—Stan Musial | 124 (2000) |
| **Road** | 32—Mark McGwire, 1998 | 223—Stan Musial | 111 (2000, 2003) |
| **Month** | 16—Mark McGwire, May 1998<br>Mark McGwire, July 1999 | | 55 (Apr 2000) |
| **Pinch** | 4—George Crowe, 1959<br>George Crowe, 1960<br>Carl Sawatski, 1961 | 8—George Crowe | 10 (1998) |
| **Grand slams** | 3—Jim Bottomley, 153 G, 1925<br>Keith Hernandez, 161 G, 1977<br>Fernando Tatis, 149 G, 1999 | 9—Stan Musial | 12 (2000) |
| **Home runs at Sportsman's Park, all teams** | | | 176 (1955) |
| **Home runs at Busch Stadium, all teams** | | | 229 (2000) |
| **Total bases** | 450—Rogers Hornsby, 154 G, 1922 | 6,134—Stan Musial | 2,595 (1930) |
| **Extra-base hits** | 103—Stan Musial, 155 G, 1948 | 1,377—Stan Musial | 570 (2003) |
| **Sacrifice hits** | 36—Harry Walker, 148 G, 1943 | 154—Jim Bottomley | 172 (1943) |
| **Sacrifice flies** | 14—George Hendrick, 136 G, 1982 | 67—Ted Simmons | 70 (2004) |
| **Bases on balls** | 162—Mark McGwire, 155 G, 1998 | 1,599—Stan Musial | 676 (1998)<br>Fewest—273 (1902) |
| **Strikeouts** | 167—Jim Edmonds, 152 G, 2000<br>Fewest—10—Frankie Frisch, 153 G, 1927 | 1,469—Lou Brock | 1,253 (2000)<br>Fewest—414 (1925) |
| **Hit by pitch** | 31—Steve Evans, 151 G, 1910 | 87—Steve Evans | 84 (2000)<br>Fewest—15 (1925) |
| **Runs batted in** | 154—Joe Medwick, 156 G, 1937 | 1,951—Stan Musial | 942 (1930)<br>Fewest—301 (1908) |
| **Grounded into double plays** | 29—Ted Simmons, 161 G, 1973<br>Fewest—2—Lou Brock, 155 G, 1965<br>Lou Brock, 157 G, 1969 | 243—Stan Musial | 166 (1958)<br>Fewest—75 (1945) |
| **Left on base** | | | 1,251 (1939)<br>Fewest—968 (1924) |
| **Batting average** | .424—Rogers Hornsby, 143 G, 1924 | .359—Rogers Hornsby | .314 (1930)<br>Lowest—.223 (1908) |
| **Most .300 hitters** | | | 11 (1930) |
| **Slugging average** | .756—Rogers Hornsby, 138 G, 1925 | .683—Mark McGwire | .471 (1930)<br>Lowest—.288 (1908) |
| **On-base percentage** | .507—Rogers Hornsby, 143 G, 1924 | .427—Mark McGwire | .372 (1930)<br>Lowest—.271 (1908) |

## BASERUNNING

| | Individual Season | Career | Club Season |
|---|---|---|---|
| **Stolen bases** | 118—Lou Brock, 153 G, 1974 | 888—Lou Brock | 314 (1985) |
| **Caught stealing** | 36—Miller Huggins, 148 G, 1914 | 285—Lou Brock | 118 (1992) |

## PITCHING

| | Individual Season | Career | Club Season |
|---|---|---|---|
| **Games** | 89—Steve Kline, 2001 | 554—Jesse Haines | |
| **Games started** | 41—Bob Harmon, 1911 | 482—Bob Gibson | |
| **Complete games** | 39—Jack W. Taylor, 1904 | 255—Bob Gibson | 146 (1904) |
| **Wins** | 30—Dizzy Dean, 1934 | 251—Bob Gibson | |
| **Percentage** | .811—Dizzy Dean (30-7), 1934 | .705—John Tudor | |
| **Winning streak** | 15—Bob Gibson, 1968 | | |
| **20-win seasons** | | 5—Bob Gibson | |
| **Losses** | 25—Stoney McGlynn, 1907<br>Bugs Raymond, 1908 | 174—Bob Gibson | |
| **Losing streak** | 12—Bill Hart, 1897<br>*9—Bill McGee, 1938<br>Tom Poholsky, 1951<br>Bob Forsch, 1978<br>Danny Jackson, 1995 | | |

| | Individual Season | Individual Career | Club Season |
|---|---|---|---|
| **Saves** | 47—Lee Smith, 1991<br>Jason Isringhausen, 2004 | 160—Lee Smith | 57 (2004) |
| **Innings** | 352—Jack Taylor, 1904<br>Stoney McGlynn, 1907 | 3,884.1—Bob Gibson | 1,486 (1979) |
| **Hits** | 353—Jack Powell, 1901 | 3,455—Jesse Haines | 1,553 (1993) |
| **Runs** | 194—Jack Powell, 1900 | 1,555—Jesse Haines | 838 (1999) |
| **Earned runs** | 129—Bill Sherdel, 1929 | 1,297—Jesse Haines | 778 (1897) *761 (1999) |
| **Bases on balls** | 181—Bob Harmon, 1911 | 1,336—Bob Gibson | 667 (1999) |
| **Strikeouts** | 274—Bob Gibson, 1970 | 3,117—Bob Gibson | 1,130 (1997) |
| **Strikeouts, game** | 19—Steve Carlton, Sept 15, 1969 | | |
| **Hit batsmen** | 17—Gerry Staley, 1953 | 102—Bob Gibson | 86 (1898) *72 (2001) |
| **Wild pitches** | 15—Fred Beebe, 1907, 1909<br>Dave LaPoint, 1984 | 108—Bob Gibson | 66 (1970) |
| **Home runs** | 39—Murry Dickson, 1948 | 257—Bob Gibson | 210 (2003) |
| **Sacrifice hits** | 21—Bill Hallahan, 1933 | 337—Jesse Haines | 221 (1914) |
| **Sacrifice flies** | 13—Bob Forsch, 1979 | 95—Bob Gibson | 64 (1990) |
| **Earned run average** | 1.12—Bob Gibson, 305 inn, 1968 | 2,67—Slim Sallee | 2.49 (1968) |
| **Shutouts** | 13—Bob Gibson, 1968 | 56—Bob Gibson | 30 (1968)<br>Lost—33 (1908) |
| **1-0 games won** | 4—Bob Gibson, 1968 | 9—Bob Gibson | 8 (1907, 1968)<br>Lost—8 (1918) |

## TEAM FIELDING

**Putouts** 4,460 (1979)
Fewest—3,952 (1906)
**Chances accepted** 6,459 (1917)
Fewest—5,742 (1960)
**Double plays** 196 (2005)
Fewest—114 (1990)
**Errorless games** 105 (2003)
Consecutive—16 (1992)

**Assists** 2,293 (1917)
Fewest—1,524 (2000)
**Errors** 348 (1908)
Fewest—77 (2003)
**Passed balls** 38 (1906)
Fewest—4 (1925)
**Fielding average** .987 (2003)
Lowest—.946 (1908)

## MISCELLANEOUS

**Most players, season** 51 (1997)
**Fewest players, season** 25 (1904)
**Games won** 106 (1942)
**Month** 26 (July 1944)
**Consecutive** 14 (1935)
**Winning percentage** .688 (1942), 106-48
**Lowest** .221 (1897), 29-102
*.314 (1903), 43-94
**Number of league championships** 16
**Most recent** 2004
**Runs, game** 28 vs Philadelphia, July 6, 1929, 2nd game
**Opponents'** 28 by Boston, Sept 3, 1896, 1st game
*24 by Pittsburgh, June 22, 1925
**Hits, game** 30 vs New York, June 1, 1895
*28 vs Philadelphia, July 6, 1929, 2nd game
**Home runs, game** 7 vs Brooklyn, May 7, 1940
vs Chicago, July 12, 1996
**Runs, shutout** 18 vs Cincinnati, June 10, 1944
**Opponents'** 19 by Pittsburgh, Aug 3, 1961
**Longest 1-0 win** 14 inn vs Boston, June 15, 1939

**Most seasons, non-pitcher** 22—Stan Musial
**Most seasons, pitcher** 18—Jesse Haines
**Games lost** 111 (1898) *105 (1908)
**Month** 27 (Sept 1908)
**Consecutive** 18 (1897) *15 (1909)
**Overall record** 8,901-8,601 (114 seasons)
**Interleague play** 73-57

**Number of times worst record in league** 8 (tied in 1916)
**Most recent** 1918
**Runs, inning** 12 vs Philadelphia, Sept 16, 1926, 1st game, 3rd

**Total bases, game** 49 vs Brooklyn, May 7, 1940

**Consecutive games with one or more home runs** 17 (34 HRs), 1998

**Longest shutout** 16 inn 3-0 vs Chicago, Sept 22, 1975

**Longest 1-0 loss** 18 inn vs New York, July 2, 1933, 1st game

## ATTENDANCE

| | |
|---|---|
| **Highest home attendance** | 3,336,493 (2000) |
| **League Park** | 447,768 (1911) |
| **Sportsman's Park** | 1,430,676 (1949) |
| **Busch Stadium** | 3,336,493 (2000) |
| **Highest road attendance** | 2,820,564 (1999) |

**Largest crowds**

| | |
|---|---|
| **Day** | 52,876 vs Cincinnati, Sept 28, 1996 |
| **Night** | 53,415 vs Chicago, July 30, 1994 |
| **Doubleheader** | 52,657 vs Atlanta, July 22, 1994 |
| **Home opener** | 52,841 vs Montreal, Apr 8, 1996 |

*records made since 1900 that do not exceed pre-1900 records

# SAN DIEGO PADRES

## YEARLY FINISHES

(National League expansion franchise)

### WEST DIVISION

| Year | Position | W | L | Pct. | GB | Manager | Attendance |
|---|---|---|---|---|---|---|---|
| 1969 | 6th | 52 | 110 | .321 | 41.0 | Preston Gomez | 512,970 |
| 1970 | 6th | 63 | 99 | .389 | 39.0 | Preston Gomez | 643,679 |
| 1971 | 6th | 61 | 100 | .379 | 28.5 | Preston Gomez | 557,513 |
| 1972 | 6th | 58 | 95 | .379 | 36.5 | Preston Gomez, Don Zimmer | 644,273 |
| 1973 | 6th | 60 | 102 | .370 | 39.0 | Don Zimmer | 611,826 |
| 1974 | 6th | 60 | 102 | .370 | 42.0 | John McNamara | 1,075,399 |
| 1975 | 4th | 71 | 91 | .438 | 37.0 | John McNamara | 1,281,747 |
| 1976 | 5th | 73 | 89 | .451 | 29.0 | John McNamara | 1,458,478 |
| 1977 | 5th | 69 | 93 | .426 | 29.0 | John McNamara, Bob Skinner, Alvin Dark | 1,376,269 |
| 1978 | 4th | 84 | 78 | .519 | 11.0 | Roger Craig | 1,670,107 |

| Year | Position | W | L | Pct. | GB | Manager | Attendance |
|---|---|---|---|---|---|---|---|
| 1979 | 5th | 68 | 93 | .422 | 22.0 | Roger Craig | 1,456,967 |
| 1980 | 6th | 73 | 89 | .451 | 19.5 | Jerry Coleman | 1,139,026 |
| 1981 | 6th/6th | 41 | 69 | .373 | * | Frank Howard | 519,161 |
| 1982 | 4th | 81 | 81 | .500 | 8.0 | Dick Williams | 1,607,516 |
| 1983 | 4th | 81 | 81 | .500 | 10.0 | Dick Williams | 1,539,815 |
| 1984 | 1st (C,s) | 92 | 70 | .568 | +12.0 | Dick Williams | 1,983,904 |
| 1985 | 3rd (tied) | 83 | 79 | .512 | 12.0 | Dick Williams | 2,210,352 |
| 1986 | 4th | 74 | 88 | .457 | 22.0 | Steve Boros | 1,805,716 |
| 1987 | 6th | 65 | 97 | .401 | 25.0 | Larry Bowa | 1,454,061 |
| 1988 | 3rd | 83 | 78 | .516 | 11.0 | Larry Bowa, Jack McKeon | 1,506,896 |
| 1989 | 2nd | 89 | 73 | .549 | 3.0 | Jack McKeon | 2,009,031 |
| 1990 | 4th (tied) | 75 | 87 | .463 | 16.0 | Jack McKeon, Greg Riddoch | 1,856,396 |
| 1991 | 3rd | 84 | 78 | .519 | 10.0 | Greg Riddoch | 1,804,289 |
| 1992 | 3rd | 82 | 80 | .506 | 16.0 | Greg Riddoch, Jim Riggleman | 1,722,102 |
| 1993 | 7th | 61 | 101 | .377 | 43.0 | Jim Riggleman | 1,375,432 |
| 1994 | 4th | 47 | 70 | .402 | 12.5 | Jim Riggleman | 953,857 |
| 1995 | 3rd | 70 | 74 | .486 | 8.0 | Bruce Bochy | 1,041,805 |
| 1996 | 1st (d) | 91 | 71 | .562 | +1.0 | Bruce Bochy | 2,187,886 |
| 1997 | 4th | 76 | 86 | .469 | 14.0 | Bruce Bochy | 2,089,333 |
| 1998 | 1st (D,C,s) | 98 | 64 | .605 | +9.5 | Bruce Bochy | 2,555,901 |
| 1999 | 4th | 74 | 88 | .457 | 26.0 | Bruce Bochy | 2,523,538 |
| 2000 | 5th | 76 | 86 | .469 | 21.0 | Bruce Bochy | 2,423,149 |
| 2001 | 4th | 79 | 83 | .488 | 13.0 | Bruce Bochy | 2,377,969 |
| 2002 | 5th | 66 | 96 | .407 | 32.0 | Bruce Bochy | 2,220,416 |
| 2003 | 5th | 64 | 98 | .395 | 36.5 | Bruce Bochy | 2,030,064 |
| 2004 | 3rd | 87 | 75 | .537 | 6.0 | Bruce Bochy | 3,040,046 |
| 2005 | 1st (d) | 82 | 80 | .506 | +5.0 | Bruce Bochy | 2,869,787 |

*first half 23-33, second half 18-36; (C) won League Championship Series; (s) lost World Series; (d) lost Division Series; (D) won Division Series

## INDIVIDUAL AND CLUB RECORDS

### BATTING

| | Individual Season | Individual Career | Club Season |
|---|---|---|---|
| **Games** | 162—Dave Winfield, 1980<br>Steve Garvey, 1985<br>Joe Carter, 1990 | 2,440—Tony Gwynn | 163 (1980, 1983) |
| **At-bats** | 655—Steve Finley, 161 G, 1996 | 9,288—Tony Gwynn | 5,655 (1996) |
| **Runs** | 126—Steve Finley, 161 G, 1996 | 1,383—Tony Gwynn | 795 (1997)<br>Fewest—468 (1969) |
| **Hits** | 220—Tony Gwynn, 149 G, 1997 | 3,141—Tony Gwynn | 1,521 (2004)<br>Fewest—1,203 (1969) |
| **Hitting streak** | 34 G—Benito Santiago, 1987 | | |
| **Singles** | 177—Tony Gwynn, 158 G, 1984 | 2,378—Tony Gwynn | 1,105 (1980) |
| **Doubles** | 49—Tony Gwynn, 149 G, 1997 | 543—Tony Gwynn | 304 (2004) |
| **Triples** | 13—Tony Gwynn, 157 G, 1987 | 85—Tony Gwynn | 53 (1979) |
| **HOME RUNS** | | | 172 (1970)<br>Fewest—64 (1976) |
| **Righthander** | 50—Greg Vaughn, 158 G, 1998 | 163—Nate Colbert | |
| **Lefthander** | 35—Fred McGriff, 152 G, 1992 | 135—Tony Gwynn | |
| **Switch-hitter** | 40—Ken Caminiti, 146 G, 1996 | 121—Ken Caminiti | |
| **Rookie** | 24—Nate Colbert, 139 G, 1969 | | |
| **Home** | 23—Greg Vaughn, 1998<br>Gary Sheffield, 1992 | 72—Nate Colbert | 87 (1992, 1993) |
| **Road** | 27—Greg Vaughn, 1998 | 91—Nate Colbert | 104 (1970) |
| **Month** | 14—Ken Caminiti, Aug 1996 | | 47 (May 1970) |
| **Pinch** | 5—Jerry Turner, 1978 | 9—Jerry Turner | 10 (1995) |
| **Grand slams** | 4—Phil Nevin, 149 G, 2001 | 6—Phil Nevin | 10 (2001) |
| **Home runs at Qualcomm Stadium, all teams** | | | 178 (2001) |
| **Home runs at Petco Park, all teams** | | | 132 (2004) |
| **Total bases** | 348—Steve Finley, 161 G, 1996 | 4,259—Tony Gwynn | 2,306 (2004) |
| **Extra-base hits** | 84—Steve Finley, 161 G, 1996 | 763—Tony Gwynn | 489 (1998) |
| **Sacrifice hits** | 28—Ozzie Smith, 159 G, 1978 | 83—Enzo Hernandez<br>Ozzie Smith | 133 (1975) |
| **Sacrifice flies** | 16—Mark Loretta, 154 G, 2004 | 85—Tony Gwynn | 66 (2004) |
| **Bases on balls** | 132—Jack Clark, 142 G, 1989 | 790—Tony Gwynn | 678 (2001)<br>Fewest—401 (1973) |
| **Strikeouts** | 150—Nate Colbert, 156 G, 1970<br>Fewest—23—Tony Gwynn, 158 G, 1984 | 773—Nate Colbert | 1,273 (2001)<br>Fewest—716 (1976) |
| **Hit by pitch** | 13—Gene Tenace, 147 G, 1977 | 35—Gene Tenace | 59 (1993)<br>Fewest—9 (1989) |
| **Runs batted in** | 130—Ken Caminiti, 146 G, 1996 | 1,138—Tony Gwynn | 761 (1997)<br>Fewest—431 (1969) |
| **Grounded into double plays** | 25—Steve Garvey, 161 G, 1984<br>Steve Garvey, 162 G, 1985<br>Fewest—2—Alan Wiggins, 158 G, 1984 | 260—Tony Gwynn | 146 (1996)<br>Fewest—81 (1978) |
| **Left on base** | | | 1,239 (1980)<br>Fewest—1,006 (1972) |

| | Individual | | Club |
|---|---|---|---|
| | Season | | Season |
| **Batting average** | .372—Tony Gwynn, 149 G, 1997 | .338—Tony Gwynn | .275 (1994)<br>Lowest—.225 (1969) |
| **Most .300 hitters** | | | 3 (1987) |
| **Slugging average** | .621—Ken Caminiti, 146 G, 1996 | .540—Ken Caminiti | .414 (2004)<br>Lowest—.329 (1969) |
| **On-base percentage** | .454—Tony Gwynn, 110 G, 1994 | .388—Tony Gwynn | .343 (2004)<br>Lowest—.283 (1972) |

## BASERUNNING

| | Individual Season | Individual | Club Season |
|---|---|---|---|
| **Stolen bases** | 70—Alan Wiggins, 158 G, 1984 | 319—Tony Gwynn | 239 (1980) |
| **Caught stealing** | 21—Alan Wiggins, 158 G, 1984 | 125—Tony Gwynn | 91 (1987) |

## PITCHING

| | Individual Season | Individual | Club Season |
|---|---|---|---|
| **Games** | 83—Craig Lefferts, 1986 | 728—Trevor Hoffman | |
| **Games started** | 40—Randy Jones, 1976 | 253—Randy Jones | |
| **Complete games** | 25—Randy Jones, 1976 | 71—Randy Jones | 47 (1971, 1976) |
| **Wins** | 22—Randy Jones, 1976 | 100—Eric Show | |
| **Percentage** | .778—Gaylord Perry (21-6), 1978 | .535—Eric Show | |
| **Winning streak** | 11—Andy Hawkins, 1985<br>LaMarr Hoyt, 1985<br>Kevin Brown, 1998 | | |
| **20-win seasons** | | 2—Randy Jones | |
| **Losses** | 22—Randy Jones, 1974 | 105—Randy Jones | |
| **Losing streak** | 11—Gary Ross, 1969 | | |
| **Saves** | 53—Trevor Hoffman, 1998 | 434—Trevor Hoffman | 59 (1998) |
| **Innings** | 315—Randy Jones, 1976 | 1,766—Randy Jones | 1,489 (1996) |
| **Hits** | 274—Randy Jones, 1986 | 1,720—Randy Jones | 1,581 (1997) |
| **Runs** | 137—Bobby J. Jones, 2001 | 759—Randy Jones | 891 (1997) |
| **Earned runs** | 117—Bill Greif, 1974<br>Matt Clement, 2000 | 648—Randy Jones | 802 (1997) |
| **Bases on balls** | 125—Matt Clement, 2000 | 593—Eric Show | 715 (1974) |
| **Strikeouts** | 257—Kevin Brown, 1998 | 1,036—Andy Benes | 1,217 (1998) |
| **Strikeouts, game** | 15—Fred Norman, Sept 15, 1972<br>Sterling Hitchcock, Aug 29, 1998 (pitched first 13 inn of 15-inn game) | | |
| **Hit batsmen** | 16—Matt Clement, 2000 | 46—Joey Hamilton<br>Eric Show | 68 (2000) |
| **Wild pitches** | 23—Matt Clement, 2000 | 48—Clay Kirby | 73 (1999) |
| **Home runs** | 37—Kevin Jarvis, 2001<br>Bobby J. Jones, 2001 | 166—Eric Show | 219 (2001) |
| **Sacrifice hits** | 23—Randy Jones, 1979 | 109—Randy Jones | 112 (1975) |
| **Sacrifice flies** | 12—Dave A. Roberts, 1971<br>Andy Hawkins, 1985 | 48—Randy Jones | 62 (1993) |
| **Earned run average** | 2.10—David Roberts, 270 inn, 1971 | 3.30—Randy Jones | 3.22 (1971) |
| **Shutouts** | 6—Fred Norman, 1972<br>Randy Jones, 1975 | 18—Randy Jones | 19 (1985)<br>Lost—23 (1969, 1976) |
| **1-0 games won** | 2—Joe Niekro, 1969<br>Randy Jones, 1975, 1978<br>Greg W. Harris, 1991 | 5—Randy Jones | 6 (1985)<br>Lost—5 (1976, 1996) |

## TEAM FIELDING

**Putouts** 4,467 (1996)
Fewest—4,211 (1972)

**Chances accepted** 6,411 (1980)
Fewest—5,832 (1972)

**Double plays** 171 (1978)
Fewest—126 (1974)

**Errorless games** 89 (2003)
Consecutive—10 (2005)

**Assists** 2,012 (1980)
Fewest—1,529 (2005)

**Errors** 189 (1977)
Fewest—102 (2003)

**Passed balls** 22 (1987)
Fewest—2 (1992)

**Fielding average** .983 (1998, 2003)
Lowest—.971 (1975, 1977)

## MISCELLANEOUS

**Most players, season** 59 (2002)
**Fewest players, season** 31 (1984)
**Games won** 98 (1998)
**Month** 22 (May, 2005)
**Consecutive** 14 (1999)
**Winning percentage** .605 (1998), 98-64
**Lowest** .321 (1969), 52-110
**Number of league championships** 2
**Most recent** 1998
**Runs, game** 20 vs Florida, July 27, 1996
vs Montreal, May 19, 2001
**Opponents'** 23 by Chicago, May 17, 1977

**Most seasons, non-pitcher** 20—Tony Gwynn
**Most seasons, pitcher** 13—Trevor Hoffman
**Games lost** 110 (1969)
**Month** 23 (May 2003)
**Consecutive** 13 (1994)
**Overall record** 2,693-3,174 (37 seasons)
**Interleague play** 66-77
**Number of times worst record in league** 9 (inc. one tie)
**Most recent** 2003
**Runs, inning** 13 vs St. Louis, Aug 24, 1993, 1st
vs Pittsburgh, May 31, 1994, 2nd

**Hits, game** 24 vs San Francisco, Apr 19, 1982
vs Atlanta, Aug 12, 2003
**Home runs, game** 6 vs Cincinnati, July 17, 1998
**Runs, shutout** 13 vs Cincinnati, Aug 11, 1991
**Opponents'** 19 by Chicago, May 13, 1969
by Los Angeles, June 28, 1969
**Longest 1-0 win** 14 inn, vs New York, June 6, 1972
14 inn, vs Cincinnati, Aug 4, 1972, 2nd game

**Total bases, game** 38 vs Philadelphia, Aug 10, 2000
(39 vs San Francisco, May 23, 1970, 15 inn)
**Consecutive games with one or more home runs** 14 (23 HRs), 1998
**Longest shutout** 14 inn, 1-0 vs New York, June 6, 1972
14 inn, 1-0 vs Cincinnati, Aug 4, 1974, 2nd game

**Longest 1-0 loss** 18 inn, vs Pittsburgh, June 7, 1972, 2nd game

### ATTENDANCE

**Highest home attendance**

| | |
|---|---|
| **Qualcomm Stadium** | 2,555,901 (1998) |
| **Petco Park** | 3,040,046 (2004) |
| **Highest road attendance** | 2,587,940 (2004) |

**Largest crowds**

| | |
|---|---|
| **Day** | 61,707 vs San Francisco, Mar 31, 2003 |
| **Night** | 61,674 vs Arizona, Apr 24, 1999 |
| **Doubleheader** | 43,473 vs Philadelphia, June 13, 1976 |
| **Home opener** | 61,707 vs San Francisco, Mar 31, 2003 |

## SAN FRANCISCO GIANTS

### YEARLY FINISHES

**(National League franchise established in 1883 moved from New York to San Francisco after the 1957 season)**

| Year | Position | W | L | Pct. | GB | Manager | Attendance |
|---|---|---|---|---|---|---|---|
| 1958 | 3rd | 80 | 74 | .519 | 12.0 | Bill Rigney | 1,272,625 |
| 1959 | 3rd | 83 | 71 | .539 | 4.0 | Bill Rigney | 1,422,130 |
| 1960 | 5th | 79 | 75 | .513 | 16.0 | Bill Rigney, Tom Sheehan | 1,795,356 |
| 1961 | 3rd | 85 | 69 | .552 | 8.0 | Alvin Dark | 1,390,679 |
| 1962 | 1st (L,s) | 103 | 62 | .624 | +1.0 | Alvin Dark | 1,592,594 |
| 1963 | 3rd | 88 | 74 | .543 | 11.0 | Alvin Dark | 1,571,306 |
| 1964 | 4th | 90 | 72 | .556 | 3.0 | Alvin Dark | 1,504,364 |
| 1965 | 2nd | 95 | 67 | .586 | 2.0 | Herman Franks | 1,546,075 |
| 1966 | 2nd | 93 | 68 | .578 | 1.5 | Herman Franks | 1,657,192 |
| 1967 | 2nd | 91 | 71 | .562 | 10.5 | Herman Franks | 1,242,480 |
| 1968 | 2nd | 88 | 74 | .543 | 9.0 | Herman Franks | 837,220 |

### WEST DIVISION

| Year | Position | W | L | Pct. | GB | Manager | Attendance |
|---|---|---|---|---|---|---|---|
| 1969 | 2nd | 90 | 72 | .556 | 3.0 | Clyde King | 873,603 |
| 1970 | 3rd | 86 | 76 | .531 | 16.0 | Clyde King, Charlie Fox | 740,720 |
| 1971 | 1st (c) | 90 | 72 | .556 | +1.0 | Charlie Fox | 1,106,043 |
| 1972 | 5th | 69 | 86 | .445 | 26.5 | Charlie Fox | 647,744 |
| 1973 | 3rd | 88 | 74 | .543 | 11.0 | Charlie Fox | 834,193 |
| 1974 | 5th | 72 | 90 | .444 | 30.0 | Charlie Fox, Wes Westrum | 519,987 |
| 1975 | 3rd | 80 | 81 | .497 | 27.5 | Wes Westrum | 522,919 |
| 1976 | 4th | 74 | 88 | .457 | 28.0 | Bill Rigney | 626,868 |
| 1977 | 4th | 75 | 87 | .463 | 23.0 | Joe Altobelli | 700,056 |
| 1978 | 3rd | 89 | 73 | .549 | 6.0 | Joe Altobelli | 1,740,477 |
| 1979 | 4th | 71 | 91 | .438 | 19.5 | Joe Altobelli, Dave Bristol | 1,456,402 |
| 1980 | 5th | 75 | 86 | .466 | 17.0 | Dave Bristol | 1,096,115 |
| 1981 | 5th/3rd | 56 | 55 | .505 | * | Frank Robinson | 632,274 |
| 1982 | 3rd | 87 | 75 | .537 | 2.0 | Frank Robinson | 1,200,948 |
| 1983 | 5th | 79 | 83 | .488 | 12.0 | Frank Robinson | 1,251,530 |
| 1984 | 6th | 66 | 96 | .407 | 26.0 | Frank Robinson, Danny Ozark | 1,001,545 |
| 1985 | 6th | 62 | 100 | .383 | 33.0 | Jim Davenport, Roger Craig | 818,697 |
| 1986 | 3rd | 83 | 79 | .512 | 13.0 | Roger Craig | 1,528,748 |
| 1987 | 1st (c) | 90 | 72 | .556 | +6.0 | Roger Craig | 1,917,168 |
| 1988 | 4th | 83 | 79 | .512 | 11.5 | Roger Craig | 1,785,297 |
| 1989 | 1st (C,s) | 92 | 70 | .568 | +3.0 | Roger Craig | 2,059,701 |
| 1990 | 3rd | 85 | 77 | .525 | 6.0 | Roger Craig | 1,975,528 |
| 1991 | 4th | 75 | 87 | .463 | 19.0 | Roger Craig | 1,737,478 |
| 1992 | 5th | 72 | 90 | .444 | 26.0 | Roger Craig | 1,561,987 |
| 1993 | 2nd | 103 | 59 | .636 | 1.0 | Dusty Baker | 2,606,354 |
| 1994 | 2nd | 55 | 60 | .478 | 3.5 | Dusty Baker | 1,704,608 |
| 1995 | 4th | 67 | 77 | .465 | 11.0 | Dusty Baker | 1,241,500 |
| 1996 | 4th | 68 | 94 | .420 | 23.0 | Dusty Baker | 1,413,922 |
| 1997 | 1st (d) | 90 | 72 | .556 | +2.0 | Dusty Baker | 1,690,869 |
| 1998 | 2nd (w) | 89 | 74 | .546 | 9.5 | Dusty Baker | 1,925,634 |
| 1999 | 2nd | 86 | 76 | .531 | 14.0 | Dusty Baker | 2,078,399 |
| 2000 | 1st (d) | 97 | 65 | .599 | +11.0 | Dusty Baker | 3,315,330 |
| 2001 | 2nd | 90 | 72 | .556 | 2.0 | Dusty Baker | 3,277,244 |
| 2002 | 2nd (D,C,s) | 95 | 66 | .590 | 2.5 | Dusty Baker | 3,253,205 |
| 2003 | 1st (d) | 100 | 61 | .621 | +15.5 | Felipe Alou | 3,264,903 |
| 2004 | 2nd | 91 | 71 | .562 | 2.0 | Felipe Alou | 3,258,864 |
| 2005 | 3rd | 75 | 87 | .463 | 7.0 | Felipe Alou | 3,181,023 |

(L) won league playoff; (s) lost World Series; (c) lost League Championship Series; *first half 27-32, second half 29-23; (C) won League Championship Series; (d) lost Division Series; (w) lost wild card playoff; (D) won Division Series

### INDIVIDUAL AND CLUB RECORDS

#### BATTING

| | Individual Season | Individual Career | Club Season |
|---|---|---|---|
| **Games** | 164—Jose Pagan, 1962 | 2,256—Willie McCovey | 165 (1962) |
| **At-bats** | 663—Bobby Bonds, 157 G, 1970 | 7,578—Willie Mays | 5,650 (1984) |
| **Runs** | 134—Bobby Bonds, 157 G, 1970 | 1,480—Willie Mays | 925 (2000)<br>Fewest—556 (1985) |
| **Hits** | 208—Willie Mays, 152 G, 1958 | 2,284—Willie Mays | 1,552 (1962)<br>Fewest—1,263 (1985) |

| | Individual Season | Individual Career | Club Season |
|---|---|---|---|
| **Hitting streak** | 26 G—Jack Clark, 1978 | | |
| **Singles** | 160—Brett Butler, 160 G, 1990 | 1,373—Willie Mays | 1,132 (1984) |
| **Doubles** | 49—Jeff Kent, 159 G, 2001 | 376—Willie Mays | 314 (2004) |
| **Triples** | 12—Willie Mays, 153 G, 1960 | 76—Willie Mays | 62 (1960) |
| **HOME RUNS** | | | 235 (2001)<br>Fewest—80 (1980) |
| **Righthander** | 52—Willie Mays, 157 G, 1965 | 459—Willie Mays | |
| **Lefthander** | 73—Barry Bonds, 153 G, 2001 | 532—Barry Bonds | |
| **Switch-hitter** | 28—J.T. Snow, 157 G, 1997 | 120—J.T. Snow | |
| **Rookie** | 31—Jim Hart, 153 G, 1964 | | |
| **Home** | 37—Barry Bonds, 2001 | 268—Barry Bonds | 118 (1987) |
| **Road** | 36—Barry Bonds, 2001 | 264—Barry Bonds | 138 (2001) |
| **Month** | 17—Willie Mays, Aug 1965<br>Barry Bonds, May 2001 | | 45 (Aug 1999, May 2001) |
| **Pinch** | 4—Mike Ivie, 1978<br>Candy Maldonado, 1986<br>Ernest Riles, 1990 | 13—Willie McCovey | 14 (2001) |
| **Grand slams** | 3—Willie McCovey, 135 G, 1967<br>Jeff Kent, 155 G, 1997 | 16—Willie McCovey | 7 (1970, 1998, 2000) |
| **Home runs at Seals Stadium, all teams** | | | 173 (1958) |
| **Home runs at Candlestick Park, all teams** | | | 190 (1987) |
| **Home runs at SBC Park, all teams** | | | 171 (2000) |
| **Total bases** | 411—Barry Bonds, 153 G, 2001 | 4,189—Willie Mays | 2,605 (2000) |
| **Extra-base hits** | 107—Barry Bonds, 153 G, 2001 | 917—Barry Bonds | 579 (2001) |
| **Sacrifice hits** | 20—Omar Vizquel, 152 G, 2005 | 111—Jim Davenport | 127 (1978) |
| **Sacrifice flies** | 14—J.T. Snow, 155 G, 2000 | 67—Willie Mays<br>Willie McCovey | 66 (2000) |
| **Bases on balls** | 232—Barry Bonds, 147 G, 2004 | 1,700—Barry Bonds | 729 (1970)<br>Fewest—414 (1966) |
| **Strikeouts** | 189—Bobby Bonds, 157 G, 1970<br>Fewest—22—Dave Rader, 148 G, 1973 | 1,351—Willie McCovey | 1,189 (1996)<br>Fewest—764 (1961) |
| **Hit by pitch** | 26—Ron Hunt, 117 G, 1970 | 76—Ron Hunt | 72 (2004)<br>Fewest—14 (1980) |
| **Runs batted in** | 142—Orlando Cepeda, 152 G, 1961 | 1,388—Willie McCovey | 889 (2000)<br>Fewest—517 (1985) |
| **Grounded into double plays** | 27—A.J. Pierzynski, 131 G, 2004<br>Fewest—2—Jose Uribe, 157 G, 1986<br>Will Clark, 150 G, 1987<br>Brett Butler, 157 G, 1988 | 172—Willie Mays | 149 (1961)<br>Fewest—83 (1986, 1990) |
| **Left on base** | | | 1,289 (2004)<br>Fewest—983 (1961) |
| **Batting average** | .370—Barry Bonds, 143 G, 2002 | .316—Barry Bonds | .278 (1962, 2000)<br>Lowest—.233 (1985) |
| **Most .300 hitters** | | | 4 (1962) |
| **Slugging average** | .863—Barry Bonds, 153 G, 2001 | .680—Barry Bonds | .472 (2000)<br>Lowest—.341 (1968) |
| **On-base percentage** | .609—Barry Bonds, 147 G, 2004 | .478—Barry Bonds | .362 (2000)<br>Lowest—.299 (1985) |

## BASERUNNING

| | Individual Season | Individual Career | Club Season |
|---|---|---|---|
| **Stolen bases** | 58—Bill North, 142 G, 1979 | 263—Bobby Bonds | 148 (1986) |
| **Caught stealing** | 24—Bill North, 142 G, 1979 | 69—Barry Bonds | 97 (1987) |

## PITCHING

| | Individual Season | Individual Career | Club Season |
|---|---|---|---|
| **Games** | 89—Julian Tavarez, 1997<br>Jim Brower, 2004 | 647—Gary Lavelle | |
| **Games started** | 42—Jack Sanford, 1963 | 446—Juan Marichal | |
| **Complete games** | 30—Juan Marichal, 1968 | 244—Juan Marichal | 77 (1968) |
| **Wins** | 26—Juan Marichal, 1968 | 238—Juan Marichal | |
| **Percentage** | .806—Juan Marichal (25-6), 1966 | .630—Juan Marichal | |
| **Winning streak** | 16—Jack Sanford, 1962 | | |
| **20-win seasons** | | 6—Juan Marichal | |
| **Losses** | 18—Ray Sadecki, 1968 | 140—Juan Marichal | |
| **Losing streak** | 9—Mark Davis, 1984<br>Terry Mulholland, 1995<br>Rod Beck, 1996 | | |
| **Saves** | 48—Rod Beck, 1993 | 206—Robb Nen | 50 (1993) |
| **Innings** | 328.2—Gaylord Perry, 1970 | 3,444—Juan Marichal | 1,477 (1998) |
| **Hits** | 295—Juan Marichal, 1968 | 3,081—Juan Marichal | 1,589 (1984) |
| **Runs** | 143—Vida Blue, 1979<br>Livan Hernandez, 2001 | 1,288—Juan Marichal | 862 (1996) |

| | Individual Season | Career | Club Season |
|---|---|---|---|
| **Earned runs** | 132—Vida Blue, 1979<br>Livan Hernandez, 2001 | 1,086—Juan Marichal | 762 (1999) |
| **Bases on balls** | 125—Russ Ortiz, 1999 | 690—Juan Marichal | 655 (1999) |
| **Strikeouts** | 251—Jason Schmidt, 2004 | 2,281—Juan Marichal | 1,089 (1998) |
| **Strikeouts, game** | 15—Gaylord Perry, July 22, 1966 | | |
| **Hit batsmen** | 17—Mark Leiter, 1995<br>Jerome Williams, 2004 | 53—Bobby Bolin | 67 (1996) |
| **Wild pitches** | 18—Rich Robertson, 1970 | 81—Gaylord Perry | 76 (1970) |
| **Home runs** | 34—Juan Marichal, 1962 | 315—Juan Marichal | 194 (1996, 1999) |
| **Sacrifice hits** | 19—Kirk Rueter, 2000 | 122—Juan Marichal | 99 (1975, 1976) |
| **Sacrifice flies** | 14—Rick Reuschel, 1988 | 64—Jim Barr<br>Juan Marichal | 64 (1984) |
| **Earned run average** | 1.98—Bobby Bolin, 177 inn, 1968 | 2,84—Juan Marichal | 2.71 (1968) |
| **Shutouts** | 10—Juan Marichal, 1965 | 52—Juan Marichal | 20 (1968)<br>Lost—18 (1992) |
| **1-0 games won** | 2—many pitchers | 7—Juan Marichal | 6 (1968)<br>Lost—4 (1972, 1976, 1978, 1985, 1989, 1996) |

## TEAM FIELDING

**Putouts** 4,431 (1998)
Fewest—4,129 (1959)
**Chances accepted** 6,349 (1969)
Fewest—5,677 (1961)
**Double plays** 183 (1987)
Fewest—109 (1983)
**Errorless games** 96 (2000)
Consecutive—11 (1999, 2000)

**Assists** 1,940 (1976)
Fewest—1,513 (1961)
**Errors** 186 (1976)
Fewest—80 (2003)
**Passed balls** 30 (1970)
Fewest—6 (1978, 1994, 2005)
**Fielding average** .987 (2003)
Lowest—.971 (1976)

## MISCELLANEOUS

**Most players, season** 51 (1990)
**Fewest players, season** 31 (1962, 1968)
**Games won** 103 (1962, 1993)
**Month** 21 (Sept 1965, Aug 1968)
**Consecutive** 14 (1965)
**Winning percentage** .636 (1993), 103-59
**Lowest** .383 (1985), 62-100
**Number of league championships** 3
**Most recent** 2002
**Runs, game** 23 vs Atlanta, June 8, 1990
**Opponents'** 20 by Chicago, Aug 13, 1959
**Hits, game** 27 vs Atlanta, June 8, 1990
**Home runs, game** 8 vs Milwaukee Apr 30, 1961
**Runs, shutout** 18 vs Montreal, May 24, 2000
**Opponents'** 16 by Oakland AL, Jun 26, 2005
**Longest 1-0 win** 21 inn, vs Cincinnati, Sept 1, 1967

**Most seasons, non-pitcher** 19—Willie McCovey
**Most seasons, pitcher** 14—Juan Marichal
**Games lost** 100 (1985)
**Month** 21 (May 1972)
**Consecutive** 10 (1985, 1996)
**Overall record** 3,970-3,650 (48 seasons)
**Interleague play** 78-68
**Number of times worst record in league** 1
**Most recent** 1984
**Runs, inning** 13 vs St. Louis, May 7, 1966, 3rd
vs San Diego, July 15, 1997, 7th
**Total bases, game** 50 vs Los Angeles, May 13, 1958
**Consecutive games with one or more home runs** 16 (22 HRs), 1962
(30 HRs), 1963
**Longest shutout** 21 inn, 1-0 vs Cincinnati, Sept 1, 1967
**Longest 1-0 loss** 18 inn, vs Arizona, May 29, 2001

## ATTENDANCE

**Highest home attendance**
**Seals Stadium** 1,442,130 (1959)
**Candlestick Park** 2,606,354 (1993)
**SBC Park** 3,315,330 (2000)
**Highest road attendance** 2,895,206 (2004)

**Largest crowds**
**Day** 61,389 vs Los Angeles, Sept 30, 1999
**Night** 55,920 vs Cincinnati, June 20, 1978
**Doubleheader** 53,178 vs Los Angeles, July 31, 1983
**Home opener** 58,077 vs Pittsburgh, April 4, 1994

# WASHINGTON NATIONALS

## YEARLY FINISH

**(National League expansion franchise moved from Montreal to Washington after the 2004 season)**

### WEST DIVISION

| Year | Position | W | L | Pct. | GB | Manager | Attendance |
|---|---|---|---|---|---|---|---|
| 2005 | 5th | 81 | 81 | .500 | 9.0 | Frank Robinson | 2,731,993 |

## INDIVIDUAL AND CLUB RECORDS

### BATTING

| | Individual Season | Club Season |
|---|---|---|
| **Games** | 148—Jose Guillen<br>Brad Wilkerson | 162 |
| **At-bats** | 565—Brad Wilkerson, 148 G | 5,426 |
| **Runs** | 81—Jose Guillen, 148 G | 639 |
| **Hits** | 156—Jose Guillen, 148 G | 1,367 |

| | Individual Season | Club Season |
|---|---|---|
| Hitting streak | 16 G—Nick Johnson | |
| Singles | 98—Jose Guillen, 148 G | 907 |
| Doubles | 42—Brad Wilkerson, 148 G | 311 |
| Triples | 7—Brad Wilkerson, 148 G | 32 |
| **HOME RUNS** | | 117 |
| Righthander | 24—Jose Guillen, 148 G | |
| Lefthander | 15—Nick Johnson, 131 G | |
| Switch-hitter | 7—Jose Vidro, 87 G | |
| Rookie | 9—Ryan Church, 102 G | |
| Home | 8—Vinny Castilla | 46 |
| Road | 21—Jose Guillen | 71 |
| Month | 6—Jose Guillen, April | 26, August |
| Pinch | 1—Brendan Harris<br>Carlos Baerga | 2 |
| Grand slams | 1—Brad Wilkerson, 148 G | 1 |
| Home runs at RFK Stadium, all teams | | 112 |
| Total bases | 264—Jose Guillen, 148 G | 2,093 |
| Extra-base hits | 60—Brad Wilkerson, 148 G | 460 |
| Sacrifice hits | 14—Livan Hernandez, 35 G | 91 |
| Sacrifice flies | 9—Jose Guillen, 148 G | 45 |
| Bases on balls | 84—Brad Wilkerson, 148 G | 491 |
| Strikeouts | 147—Brad Wilkerson, 148 G<br>Fewest—82—Vinny Castilla, 142 G | 1,090 |
| Hit by pitch | 19—Jose Guillen, 148 G | 89 |
| Runs batted in | 76—Jose Guillen, 148 G | 615 |
| Grounded into double plays | 16—Vinny Castilla, 142 G<br>Fewest—6—Brad Wilkerson, 148 G | 130 |
| Left on base | | 1,137 |
| Batting average | .289—Nick Johnson, 131 G | .252 |
| Most .300 hitters | | none |
| Slugging average | .479—Nick Johnson, 131 G<br>Jose Guillen, 148 G | .386 |
| On-base percentage | .408—Nick Johnson, 131 G | .322 |

## BASERUNNING

| | Individual Season | Club Season |
|---|---|---|
| Stolen bases | 8—Brad Wilkerson, 148 G | 45 |
| Caught stealing | 10—Brad Wilkerson, 148 G | 45 |

## PITCHING

| | Individual Season | Club Season |
|---|---|---|
| Games | 79—Gary Majewski | |
| Games started | 35—Livan Hernandez | |
| Complete games | 2—Livan Hernandez<br>John Patterson | 4 |
| Wins | 15—Livan Hernandez | |
| Percentage | .600—Livan Hernandez (15-10) | |
| Winning streak | 11—Livan Hernandez | |
| 20-win seasons | | none |
| Losses | 10—Livan Hernandez<br>Esteban Loaiza | |
| Losing streak | 5—Ryan Drese | |
| Saves | 47—Chad Cordero | 51 |
| Innings | 246.1—Livan Hernandez | 1,458 |
| Hits | 268—Livan Hernandez | 1,456 |
| Runs | 116—Livan Hernandez | 673 |
| Earned runs | 109—Livan Hernandez | 627 |
| Bases on balls | 84—Livan Hernandez | 539 |
| Strikeouts | 185—John Patterson | 997 |
| Strikeouts, game | 13—John Patterson, Aug 4 | |
| Hit batsmen | 13—Livan Hernandez | 72 |
| Wild pitches | 9—John Patterson | 49 |
| Home runs | 25—Livan Hernandez | 140 |
| Sacrifice hits | 15— Livan Hernandez | 79 |
| Sacrifice flies | 9—Livan Hernandez | 46 |
| Earned run average | 3.13—John Patterson, 198.1 inn | 3.87 |
| Shutouts | 1—John Patterson | 9 |
| 1-0 games won | None | 2<br>Lost—2 |

## TEAM FIELDING

| | | | |
|---|---|---|---|
| Putouts | 4,374 | Assists | 1,548 |
| Chances accepted | 5,922 | Errors | 92 |

**Double plays** 156
**Errorless games** 91
Consecutive—9

**Passed balls** 7
**Fielding average** .985

## MISCELLANEOUS

**Players, season** 55
**Games won** 81
**Month** 20 (June)
**Consecutive** 10
**Winning percentage** .500 (2005), 81-81

**Number of league championships** 0
**Runs, game** 11, 5 times
**Opponents'** 14 by Houston, July 22
**Hits, game** 17 vs New York Mets, April 24
**Home runs, game** 4 vs Houston, Aug 9
vs. Philadelphia, Aug 15
**Runs, shutout** 8 vs Colorado, Aug 13
**Opponents'** 9 by Florida, April 8
**Longest 1-0 win** none over 9 inn

**Games lost** 81
**Month** 18 (July)
**Consecutive** 7
**Overall record** 81-81 (1 season)
**Interleague** 12-6
**Number of times worst record in league** 0
**Runs, inning** 7, many times

**Total bases, game** 29 vs Philadelphia, April 6
**Consecutive games with one or more home runs** 5, twice (6 HRs and 5 HRs)

**Longest shutout** none over 9 inn

**Longest 1-0 loss** none over 9 inn

## ATTENDANCE

**Highest home attendance** 2,731,993

**Highest road attendance** 2,564,178

**Largest crowds**
**Day** 44,492 vs New York Mets, July 7
**Night** 43,861 vs. Arizona, April 14
**Doubleheader** none
**Home opener** 43,861 vs Arizona, April 14

Stan Musial

# DIVISION SERIES

Ramirez

# SERIES WINNERS

## AMERICAN LEAGUE

| Year | Winner | Loser | Games |
|---|---|---|---|
| 1995 | Cleveland (Central) | Boston (East) | 3-0 |
| | Seattle (West) | New York (East)* | 3-2 |
| 1996 | New York (East) | Texas (West) | 3-1 |
| | Baltimore (East)* | Cleveland (Central) | 3-1 |
| 1997 | Baltimore (East) | Seattle (West) | 3-1 |
| | Cleveland (Central) | New York (East)* | 3-2 |
| 1998 | New York (East) | Texas (West) | 3-0 |
| | Cleveland (Central) | Boston (East)* | 3-1 |
| 1999 | New York (East) | Texas (West) | 3-0 |
| | Boston (East)* | Cleveland (Central) | 3-2 |
| 2000 | New York (East) | Oakland (West) | 3-2 |
| | Seattle (West)* | Chicago (Central) | 3-0 |
| 2001 | New York (East) | Oakland (West)* | 3-2 |
| | Seattle (West) | Cleveland (Central) | 3-2 |
| 2002 | Anaheim (West)* | New York (East) | 3-1 |
| | Minnesota (Central) | Oakland (West) | 3-2 |
| 2003 | New York (East) | Minnesota (Central) | 3-1 |
| | Boston (East)* | Oakland (West) | 3-2 |
| 2004 | New York (East) | Minnesota (Central) | 3-1 |
| | Boston (East)* | Anaheim (West) | 3-0 |
| 2005 | Los Angeles (West) | New York (East) | 3-2 |
| | Chicago (Central) | Boston (East)* | 3-0 |

*wild-card team

## NATIONAL LEAGUE

| Year | Winner | Loser | Games |
|---|---|---|---|
| 1995 | Atlanta (East) | Colorado (West)* | 3-1 |
| | Cincinnati (Central) | Los Angelese (West) | 3-0 |
| 1996 | Atlanta (East) | Los Angeles (West)* | 3-0 |
| | St. Louis (Central) | San Diego (West) | 3-0 |
| 1997 | Atlanta (East) | Houston (Central) | 3-0 |
| | Florida (East)* | San Francisco (West) | 3-0 |
| 1998 | Atlanta (East) | Chicago (Central)* | 3-0 |
| | San Diego (West) | Houston (Central) | 3-1 |
| 1999 | Atlanta (East) | Houston (Central) | 3-1 |
| | New York (East)* | Arizona (West) | 3-1 |
| 2000 | St. Louis (Central) | Atlanta (East) | 3-0 |
| | New York (East)* | San Francisco (West) | 3-1 |
| 2001 | Atlanta (East) | Houston (Central) | 3-0 |
| | Arizona (West) | St. Louis (Central)* | 3-2 |
| 2002 | San Francisco (West)* | Atlanta (East) | 3-2 |
| | St. Louis (Central) | Arizona (West) | 3-0 |
| 2003 | Chicago (Central) | Atlanta (East) | 3-2 |
| | Florida (East)* | San Francisco (West) | 3-1 |
| 2004 | Houston (Central)* | Atlanta (East) | 3-2 |
| | St. Louis (Central) | Los Angeles (West) | 3-1 |
| 2005 | Houston (Central)* | Atlanta (East) | 3-1 |
| | St. Louis (Central) | San Diego (West) | 3-0 |

*wild-card team

# INDIVIDUAL SERVICE

## ALL PLAYERS

### SERIES AND CLUBS

**Most series played**
AL—11—Bernie Williams, New York, 1995-2005
Mariano Rivera, New York, 1995-2005
NL—11—Chipper Jones, Atlanta, 1995-2005

**Most clubs, career**
ML—5—Kenny Lofton, Cleveland AL, 1995, 1996, 1998-2001; Atlanta NL, 1997; San Francisco NL, 2002; Chicago NL, 2003; New York AL, 2004
NL—5—Reggie Sanders, Cincinnati, 1995; Atlanta, 2000; Arizona, 2001; San Francisco, 2002; St. Louis, 2004, 2005
AL—3—Harold Baines, Baltimore, 1997; Cleveland, 1999; Chicago, 2000
Keith Foulke, Chicago, 2000; Oakland, 2003; Boston, 2004
Mike Stanton, Boston, 1995; Texas, 1996; New York, 1997, 2001, 2002

### BY POSITION (EXCEPT PITCHERS)

**Most series by first baseman**
ML—9—Tino Martinez, Seattle AL, 1995; New York AL, 1996-2001, 2005; St. Louis, 2002; 37 G
AL—7—Tino Martinez, Seattle, 1995; New York, 1996-2001, 2005; 34 G
NL—5—Jeff Bagwell, Houston, 1997-1999, 2001, 2004; 19 G
Julio Franco, Atlanta, 2001-2005; 15 G

**Most series by second baseman**
NL—6—Keith Lockhart, Atlanta, 1997-2002; 15 G
AL—4—Mark McLemore, Texas, 1996, 1998, 1999; Seattle, 2000; 13 G
Roberto Alomar, Baltimore, 1996, 1997; Cleveland, 1999, 2001; 18 G

**Most series by third baseman**
NL—9—Chipper Jones, Atlanta, 1995-2001, 2004, 2005; 32 G
AL—4—Scott Brosius, New York, 1998-2001; 16 G
Eric Chavez, Oakland, 2000-2003; 20 G

**Most series by shortstop**
AL—10—Derek Jeter, New York, 1996-2005; 42 G
NL—5—Edgar Renteria, Florida, 1997; St. Louis, 2000-2002, 2004; 18 G
Rafael Furcal, Atlanta, 2001-2005; 22 G

**Most series by outfielder**
AL—11—Bernie Williams, New York, 1995-2005; 45 G
NL—10—Andruw Jones, Atlanta, 1996-2005; 38 G

**Most series by catcher**
AL—9—Jorge Posada, New York, 1997-2005; 31 G
NL—7—Javy Lopez, Atlanta, 1995-1998, 2000, 2003; 21 G

### YOUNGEST AND OLDEST NON-PITCHERS

**Youngest player, non-pitcher**
NL—19 years, 5 months, 9 days—Andruw Jones, Atlanta, Oct 2, 1996
AL—20 years, 2 months, 11 days—Alex Rodriguez, Seattle, Oct 8, 1995

**Oldest player, non-pitcher**
NL—47 years, 1 month, 16 days—Julio Franco, Atlanta, Oct 9, 2005
AL—41 years, 10 months, 12 days—Rickey Henderson, Seattle, Oct 6, 2000

### YEARS BETWEEN SERIES (INCLUDES PITCHERS)

**Most years between first and second series**
NL—9—Larry Walker, Colorado, 1995; St. Louis, 2004
AL—8—Ruben Sierra, New York, 1995; New York, 2003

**Most years between first and last series**
AL—10—Mariano Rivera, New York, 1995; New York, 2005
Ruben Sierra, New York, 1995; New York, 2005
Bernie Williams, New York, 1995; New York, 2005
NL—10—Chipper Jones, Atlanta, 1995; Atlanta, 2005
Larry Walker, Colorado, 1995; St. Louis, 2005

### POSITIONS

**Most positions played, career**
AL—4—Randy Velarde, New York, 1995; Oakland, 2000, 2002 (2B, 3B, LF, 1B)
NL—3—many players

**Most positions played, series**
AL—3—Randy Velarde, New York, 1995 (2B, 3B, LF)
Jeff Kent, Cleveland, 1996 (2B, 1B, 3B)
NL—3—Craig Paquette, St. Louis, 2001 (RF, LF, 3B)
Albert Pujols, St. Louis, 2002 (LF, 3B, 1B)
Eric Bruntlett, Houston, 2005 (CF, 2B, SS)
Jose Vizcaino, Houston, 2005 (1B, 2B, SS)

## PITCHERS

### SERIES

**Most series pitched**
AL—11—Mariano Rivera, New York, 1995-2005; 27 G
NL—10—John Smoltz, Atlanta, 1995-1999, 2001-2005; 15 G

**Most series pitched by relief pitcher**
AL—11—Mariano Rivera, New York, 1995-2005; 27 G
NL—5—Mike Remlinger, Atlanta, 1999-2002; Chicago, 2003; 11 G

### YOUNGEST AND OLDEST PITCHERS

**Youngest pitcher**
NL—21 years, 2 months, 15 days—Rick Ankiel, St. Louis, Oct 3, 2000
AL—20 years, 8 months, 25 days—Francisco Rodriguez, Anaheim, Oct 2, 2002

**Oldest division series pitcher**
AL—43 years, 11 months, 29 days—Dennis Eckersley, Boston, Oct 2, 1998
NL—43 years, 2 months, 5 days—Roger Clemens, Houston, Oct 9, 2005

# CLUB SERVICE

## PLAYERS USED

**Most players, series**
AL-NL—25—many clubs

**For a list of players and pitchers used each series, see page 298.**

**Most players used by both clubs, series**
AL—50—Boston 25, Cleveland 25, 1999 (5-game series)
Minnesota 25, Oakland 25, 2002 (5-game series)
NL—49—San Francisco 25, New York 24, 2000 (4-game series)
Atlanta 25, Houston 24, 2004 (5-game series)
Houston 25, Atlanta 24, 2005 (4-game series)

**Fewest players, series**
AL—17—Texas vs New York, 1998 (3-game series)
NL—18—Cincinnati vs Los Angeles, 1995 (3-game series)
Atlanta vs Houston, 1997 (3-game series)

**Fewest players used by both clubs, series**
AL—36—New York 19, Texas 17, 1998 (3-game series)
NL—40—Los Angeles 22, Cincinnati 18, 1995 (3-game series)
San Francisco 21, Florida 19, 1997 (3-game series)

**Most times one club using only nine players in game, series**
NL—1—Arizona vs St. Louis, 2001 (5-game series)
Los Angeles vs St. Louis, 2004 (4-game series)
AL—none

**Most players, game**
NL—20—Colorado vs Atlanta, Oct 3, 1995
[23—Houston vs Atlanta, Oct 9, 2005, 18 inn]
AL—20—Texas vs New York, Oct 5, 1996
[20—New York vs Texas, Oct 2, 1996, 12 inn]

**Most players used by both clubs, game**
AL—39—Texas 20, New York 19, Oct 5, 1996
NL—37—Colorado 20, Atlanta 17, Oct 3, 1995
Florida 19, San Francisco 18, Oct 1, 2003
[42—Houston 23, Atlanta 19, Oct 9, 2005, 18 inn]

## PINCH-HITTERS

**Most pinch-hitters, series**
NL—15—San Diego vs St. Louis, 2005 (3-game series)
AL—10—Oakland vs New York, 2001 (5-game series)

**Most pinch-hitters used by both clubs, series**
NL—22—Atlanta 12, Colorado 10, 1995 (4-game series)
AL—14—Oakland 8, Minnesota 6, 2002 (5-game series)

**Fewest pinch-hitters, series**
AL—0—Texas vs New York, 1999 (3-game series)
Boston vs Anaheim, 2004 (3-game series)
New York vs Minnesota, 2004 (4-game series)
NL—1—Atlanta vs Houston, 1997 (3-game series)

**Fewest pinch-hitters used by both clubs, series**
AL—2—Texas 1, New York 1, 1998 (3-game series)
New York 2, Texas 0, 1999 (3-game series)
NL—8—Houston 7, Atlanta 1, 1997 (3-game series)

**Most pinch-hitters, game**
NL—6—San Diego vs St. Louis, Oct 4, 2005
AL—4—many clubs

**Most pinch-hitters used by both clubs, game**
NL—7—Atlanta 4, Colorado 3, Oct 4, 1995
Atlanta 4, San Francisco 3, Oct 7, 2002
[8—Atlanta 4, Houston 4, Oct 9, 2005, 18 inn]
AL—5—Seattle 4, Cleveland 1, Oct 13, 2001
Oakland 4, New York 1, Oct 14, 2001
[5—Boston 3, Oakland 2, Oct 1, 2003, 12 inn]

**Most pinch-hitters, inning**
NL—4—Arizona vs St. Louis, Oct 10, 2001, 8th
AL—4—Anaheim vs Boston, Oct 8, 2004, 7th

## PINCH-RUNNERS

**Most pinch-runners, series**
AL—7—Baltimore vs Cleveland, 1996 (4-game series)
NL—3—San Diego vs Houston, 1998 (4-game series)
New York vs San Francisco, 2000 (4-game series)
Arizona vs St. Louis, 2001 (5-game series)
Atlanta vs Houston, 2004 (5-game series)

**Most pinch-runners used by both clubs, series**
AL—9—Baltimore 7, Cleveland 2, 1996 (4-game series)
NL—4—Atlanta 3, Houston 1, 2004 (5-game series)

**Fewest pinch-runners used, series**
AL-NL—0—many clubs

**Fewest pinch-runners used by both clubs, series**
NL—0—many series
AL—0—Minnesota 0, Oakland 0, 2002 (5-game series)

**Most pinch-runners, game**
AL—3—Baltimore vs Cleveland, Oct 2, 1996
NL—2—Arizona vs St. Louis, Oct 14, 2001
Atlanta vs Chicago, Oct 1, 2003
[2—Atlanta vs Houston, Oct 7, 2004, 11 inn]

**Most pinch-runners used by both clubs, game**
AL—4—Baltimore 3, Cleveland 1, Oct 2, 1996
NL—3—Atlanta 2, Chicago 1, Oct 1, 2003

**Most pinch-runners, inning**
AL—3—Baltimore vs Cleveland, Oct 2, 1996, 8th
NL—2—Arizona vs St. Louis, Oct 14, 2001, 9th
Atlanta vs Houston, Oct 7, 2004, 8th

## NUMBER OF PLAYERS USED BY POSITION

### FIRST BASEMEN

**Most first basemen, series**
AL—4—Oakland vs Minnesota, 2002 (5-game series)
NL—5—Houston vs Atlanta, 2005 (4-game series)

**Most first basemen used by both clubs, series**
AL—5—Oakland 4, Minnesota 1, 2002 (5-game series)
Minnesota 3, New York 2, 2004 (4-game series)
NL—7—Houston 5, Atlanta 2, 2005 (4-game series)

**Most first basemen, game**
AL—3—Oakland vs Minnesota, Oct 1, 2002
[3—Minnesota vs New York, Oct 6, 2004, 12 inn]
NL—2—many games
[5—Houston vs Atlanta, Oct 9, 2005, 18 inn]

**Most first basemen used by both clubs, game**
NL—4—St. Louis 2, Arizona 2, Oct 3, 2002
Chicago 2, Atlanta 2, Oct 1, 2003
[7—Houston 5, Atlanta 2, Oct 9, 2005, 18 inn]
AL—3—many games
[4—Minnesota 3, New York 1, Oct 6, 2004, 12 inn]

### SECOND BASEMEN

**Most second basemen, series**
AL—3—New York vs Cleveland, 1997 (5-game series)
Minnesota vs New York, 2003 (4-game series)
NL—3—Atlanta vs Chicago, 2003 (5-game series)
Houston vs Atlanta, 2005 (4-game series)

**Most second basemen used by both clubs, series**
AL—5—New York 3, Cleveland 2, 1997 (5-game series)
NL—4—Florida 2, San Francisco 2, 1997 (3-game series)
Atlanta 3, Chicago 1, 2003 (5-games series)
Houston 3, Atlanta 1, 2005 (4-game series)

**Most second basemen, game**
AL—3—New York vs Cleveland, Oct 6, 1997
Minnesota vs New York, Oct 4, 2003
NL—3—Atlanta vs Chicago, Sept 30, 2003

**Most second basemen used by both clubs, game**
AL—4—New York 3, Cleveland 1, Oct 6, 1997
Minnesota 3, New York 1, Oct 4, 2003
Oakland 2, Boston 2, Oct 6, 2003
Anaheim 2, Boston 2, Oct 5, 2004
[4—New York 2, Seattle 2, Oct 4, 1995, 15 inn]
NL—4—Atlanta 3, Chicago 1, Sept 30, 2003

### THIRD BASEMEN

**Most third basemen, series**
AL—3—Seattle vs Baltimore, 1997 (4-game series)
NL—3—St. Louis vs Arizona, 2002 (3-game series)

**Most third basemen used by both clubs, series**
NL—5—St. Louis 3, Arizona 2, 2002 (3-game series)
AL—4—New York 2, Seattle 2, 1995 (5-game series)
Seattle 3, Baltimore 1, 1997 (4-game series)
Anaheim 2, Boston 2, 2004 (3-game series)

**Most third basemen, game**
NL—3—St. Louis vs Arizona, Oct 3, 2002
AL—2—many clubs

**Most third basemen used by both clubs, game**
NL—4—St. Louis 3, Arizona 1, Oct 3, 2002
AL—3—many games

## SHORTSTOPS

**Most shortstops, series**
AL—3—Seattle vs New York, 1995 (5-game series)
NL—3—Atlanta vs Colorado, 1995 (3-game series)
Houston vs Atlanta, 2004 (5-game series)
Houston vs Atlanta, 2005 (4-game series)

**Most shortstops used by both clubs, series**
AL—4—Seattle 3, New York 1, 1995 (5-game series)
NL—4—many series

**Most shortstops, game**
NL—2—many clubs
[3—Atlanta vs Colorado, Oct 6, 1995, 10 inn
Houston vs Atlanta, Oct 9, 2005, 18 inn]
AL—2—many clubs

**Most shortstops used by both clubs, game**
NL—4—Atlanta 2, Houston 2, Oct 9, 2001
[4—Atlanta 3, Colorado 1, Oct 6, 1995, 10 inn
New York 2, San Francisco 2, Oct 7, 2000, 13 inn
Houston 3, Atlanta 1, Oct 9, 2005, 18 inn]
AL—3—many games

## LEFT FIELDERS

**Most left fielders, series**
AL—4—Cleveland vs Seattle, 2001 (5-game series)
Oakland vs Boston, 2003 (5-game series)
NL—4—Houston vs Atlanta, 1999 (4-game series)
St. Louis vs Arizona, 2001 (5-game series)
Houston vs Atlanta, 2005 (4-game series)

**Most left fielders used by both clubs, series**
AL—7—Cleveland 4, Seattle 3, 2001 (5-game series)
NL—6—Houston 4, Atlanta 2, 1999 (4-game series)
Atlanta 3, Houston 3, 2004 (5-game series)
Houston 4, Atlanta 2, 2005 (4-game series)

**Most left fielders, game**
AL—3—Seattle vs Chicago, Oct 4, 2000
[3—New York vs Seattle, Oct 4, 1995, 15 inn
Oakland vs Boston, Oct 1, 2003, 12 inn]
NL—3—New York vs San Francisco, Oct 4, 2000
St. Louis vs Arizona, Oct 10, 2001
St. Louis vs San Diego, Oct 4, 2005
[3—Houston vs Atlanta, Oct 8, 1999, 12 inn
New York vs San Francisco, Oct 5, 2000, 10 inn
Houston vs Atlanta, Oct 9, 2005, 18 inn]

**Most left fielders used by both clubs, game**
AL—4—many games
[5—New York 3, Seattle 2, Oct 4, 1995, 15 inn]
NL—4—many games
[5—Houston 3, Atlanta 2, Oct 8, 1999, 12 inn]

## CENTER FIELDERS

**Most center fielders, series**
NL—4—New York vs Arizona, 1999 (4-game series)
San Diego vs St. Louis, 2005 (3-game series)
AL—3—Boston vs Cleveland, 1995 (3-game series)
New York vs Los Angeles, 2005 (5-game series)

**Most center fielders used by both clubs, series**
NL—5—New York 4, Arizona 1, 1999 (4-game series)
San Diego 3, St. Louis 2, 2005 (3-game series)
AL—5—New York 3, Los Angeles 2, 2005 (5-game series)

**Most center fielders, game**
NL—3—New York vs Arizona, Oct 5, 1999
[3—Houston vs Atlanta, Oct 9, 2005, 18 inn]
AL—2—many clubs

**Most center fielders used by both clubs, game**
NL—4—New York 3, Arizona 1, Oct 5, 1999
[4—Houston 3, Atlanta 1, Oct 9, 2005, 18 inn]
AL—3—many games

## RIGHT FIELDERS

**Most right fielders, series**
AL—5—Oakland vs New York, 2000 (5-game series)
NL—4—Houston vs Atlanta, 1999 (4-game series)

**Most right fielders used by both clubs, series**
NL—5—Houston 4, Atlanta 1, 1999 (4-game series)
New York 3, San Francisco 2, 2000 (4-game series)
AL—6—Oakland 5, New York 1, 2000 (5-game series)

**Most right fielders, game**
AL—3—Baltimore vs Seattle, Oct 2, 1997
Oakland vs New York, Oct 7, 2000
Minnesota vs Oakland, Oct 2, 2002
Minnesota vs Oakland, Oct 5, 2002
[3—Boston vs Oakland, Oct 1, 2003, 12 inn]
NL—3—St. Louis vs San Diego, Oct 8, 2005

**Most right fielders used by both clubs, game**
AL—4—Baltimore 3, Seattle 1, Oct 2, 1997
Oakland 3, New York 1, Oct 7, 2000
Minnesota 3, Oakland 1, Oct 2, 2002
Minnesota 3, Oakland 1, Oct 5, 2002
[5—Boston 3, Oakland 2, Oct 1, 2003, 12 inn]
NL—4—many games

## CATCHERS

**Most catchers, series**
AL—3—Minnesota vs New York, 2004 (4-game series)
NL—3—Chicago vs Atlanta, 1998 (3-game series)
Arizona vs St. Louis, 2002 (3-game series)
Los Angeles vs St. Louis, 2004 (4-game series)

**Most catchers used by both clubs, series**
NL—5—Houston 3, Atlanta 2, 1997 (3-game series)
Chicago 3, Atlanta 2, 1998 (3-game series)
AL—4—many series

**Most catchers, game**
NL—3—Los Angeles vs St. Louis, Oct 10, 2004
[3—Houston vs Atlanta, Oct 9, 2005, 18 inn]
AL—2—many clubs

**Most catchers used by both clubs, game**
AL-NL—4—many games

## PITCHERS

**Most pitchers, series**
3-game series
AL—10—Boston vs Cleveland, 1995
Chicago vs Seattle, 2000
NL—10—Los Angeles vs Atlanta, 1996
Arizona vs St. Louis, 2002
4-game series
NL—12—San Francisco vs Florida, 2003
AL—11—Texas vs New York, 1996
Cleveland vs Boston, 1998
5-game series
AL—11—Boston vs Cleveland, 1999
Cleveland vs Boston, 1999
Oakland vs New York, 2001
Minnesota vs Oakland, 2002
NL—11—San Francisco vs Atlanta, 2002
Chicago vs Atlanta, 2003
Atlanta vs Houston, 2004

**For a list of players and pitchers used each series, see page 298.**

**Most pitchers used by both clubs, series**
3-game series
AL—19—Boston 10, Cleveland 9, 1995
NL—18—St. Louis 9, Atlanta 9, 2000
Arizona 10, St. Louis 8, 2002
4-game series
NL—21—Colorado 11, Atlanta 10, 1995
New York 11, Arizona 10, 1999
San Francisco 11, New York 10, 2000
San Francisco 12, Florida 9, 2003
St. Louis 11, Los Angeles 10, 2004
AL—21—Texas 11, New York 10, 1996
Cleveland 11, Boston 10, 1998
5-game series
AL—22—Boston 11, Cleveland 11, 1999
NL—21—San Francisco 11, Atlanta 10, 2002
Chicago 11, Atlanta 10, 2003
Atlanta 11, Houston 10, 2004

**Fewest pitchers, series**
NL—5—Atlanta vs Houston, 1997 (3-game series)
AL—5—Texas vs New York, 1998 (3-game series)
New York vs Texas, 1999 (3-game series)

**Fewest pitchers used by both clubs, series**
AL—11—New York 6, Texas 5, 1998 (3-game series)
NL—14—Los Angeles 8, Cincinnati 6, 1995 (3-game series)
Houston 9, Atlanta 5, 1997 (3-game series)
San Francisco 8, Florida 6, 1997 (3-game series)

**Most pitchers used by winning club, game**
AL—6—Seattle vs New York, Oct 7, 1995
Cleveland vs Baltimore, Oct 4, 1996
Cleveland vs Boston, Oct 3, 1998
Boston vs Cleveland, Oct 10, 1999
[7—Cleveland vs Boston, Oct 3, 1995, 13 inn
New York vs Texas, Oct 2, 1996, 12 inn]

NL—6—St. Louis vs Los Angeles, Oct 7, 2004
[8—Houston vs Atlanta, Oct 9, 2005, 18 inn]

**Most pitchers used by losing club, game**
AL—8—Texas vs New York, Oct 5, 1996
NL—8—San Francisco vs Atlanta, Oct 5, 2002

**Most pitchers used by both clubs, game**
NL—14—San Francisco 7, Florida 7, Oct 1, 2003
[14—Houston 8, Atlanta 6, Oct 9, 2005, 18 inn]
AL—13—Texas 8, New York 5, Oct 5, 1996
[14—Boston 7, Cleveland 7, Oct 3, 1995, 13 inn]

**Most pitchers, inning**
NL—4—Los Angeles vs Cincinnati, Oct 6, 1995, 6th
Colorado vs Atlanta, Oct 6, 1995, 7th
Atlanta vs Houston, Oct 9, 1999, 8th
San Francisco vs Atlanta, Oct 5, 2002, 9th
AL—4—New York vs Texas, Oct 2, 1996, 12th
Boston vs Cleveland, Oct 10, 1999, 5th
Boston vs Anaheim, Oct 8, 2004, 7th

## SERIES

**Most series played**
AL—11—New York, 1995-2005; won 7, lost 4
NL—11—Atlanta, 1995-2005; won 6, lost 5

**For a complete list of series won and lost by teams, see page 295.**

# INDIVIDUAL BATTING



## GAMES

**Most games, career**
AL—47—Bernie Williams, New York, 1995-2005; 11 series
NL—42—Chipper Jones, Atlanta, 1995-2005; 11 series

**Most games with one club, career**
AL—47—Bernie Williams, New York, 1995-2005; 11 series
NL—42—Chipper Jones, Atlanta, 1995-2005; 11 series

**Most games by pinch-hitter, career**
ML—9—John Vander Wal, Colorado NL, 1995; San Diego NL, 1998; New York AL, 2002 (9 PA, 9 AB)
NL—7—John Vander Wal, Colorado, 1995; San Diego, 1998 (7 PA, 7 AB)
AL—4—Olmedo Saenz, Oakland, 2000, 2001 (4 PA, 4 AB)

**Most games by pinch-hitter, series**
NL—5—Orlando Palmeiro, Houston, 2004 (5-game series)
Dewayne Wise, Atlanta, 2004 (5-games series)
AL—3—Midre Cummings, Boston, 1998 (4-game series)
Olmedo Saenz, Oakland, 2001 (5-game series)
Randy Velarde, Oakland, 2002 (5-game series)
Matthew LeCroy, Minnesota, 2004 (4-game series)
Jose Offerman, Minnesota, 2004 (4-game series)

**Most games by pinch-runner, career**
AL—4—Andy Fox, New York, 1996, 1997; 2 series
Damon Buford, Texas, 1996; Boston, 1998; 2 series
NL—3—Joe McEwing, New York, 2000; 1 series

**Most games by pinch-runner, series**
NL—4—Mike Lamb, Houston, 2004 (5-game series)
AL—3—Pat Kelly, New York, 1995 (5-game series)
Manny Alexander, Baltimore, 1996 (4-game series)
Mike Devereaux, Baltimore, 1996 (4-game series)
Jose Offerman, Minnesota, 2004 (4-game series)

## BATTING AVERAGE

**Highest batting average, career (50 or more at-bats)**
AL—.400—Mike Stanley, New York, 1995, 1997; Boston, 1998, 1999; 4 series, 15 G, 55 AB, 22 H
NL—.353—Edgardo Alfonzo, New York, 1999, 2000; San Francisco, 2003; 3 series, 12 G, 51 AB, 18 H
(Fernando Vina, St. Louis, 2000-2002, batted .404 in 3 series, 11 G, 47 AB, 19 H, 2 BB, 2 HP.)

**For a list of batting leaders each series and a complete list of .500 hitters, see page 296.**

**Highest batting average, series (10 or more at-bats)**
3-game series
AL—.600—Luis Alicea, Boston, 1995
NL—.600—Fernando Vina, St. Louis, 2002
4-game series
NL—.588—Dante Bichette, Colorado, 1995
AL—.500—Derek Jeter, New York, 2002
5-game series
AL—.600—Ichiro Suzuki, Seattle, 2001
NL—.526—Andruw Jones, Atlanta, 2004

## ON-BASE PERCENTAGE

**Highest percentage, career (50 or more plate appearances)**
AL—.481—Edgar Martinez, Seattle, 1995, 1997, 2000, 2001; 4 series, 17 G, 64 AB, 24 H, 2 BB
NL—.451—Fernando Vina, St. Louis, 2000-2002; 3 series, 11 G, 47 AB, 19 H, 2 BB, 2 HP, 1 SH

**Highest percentage, series (10 or more plate appearances)**
3-game series
NL—.714—Gary Sheffield, Florida, 1997
AL—.688—David Ortiz, Boston, 2004
4-game series
NL—.611—Dante Bichette, Colorado, 1995
AL—.571—Mike Bordick, Baltimore, 1997
5-game series
AL—.667—Edgar Martinez, Seattle, 1995
NL—.571—Andruw Jones, Atlanta, 2004

## SLUGGING AVERAGE

**Highest average, career (50 or more PA)**
AL—.781—Edgar Martinez, Seattle, 1995, 1997, 2000, 2001; 4 series, 17 G, 64 AB, 24 H, 5 doubles, 7 HR, 50 TB
NL—.750—Jim Edmonds, St. Louis, 1999, 2000, 2001, 2004, 2005; 5 series, 18 G, 68 AB, 23 H, 7 doubles, 7 HR, 51 TB

**Highest average, series (10 or more PA)**
3-game series
AL—1.333—A.J. Pierzynski, Chicago, 2005
NL—1.286—Jim Edmonds, St. Louis, 2000
4-game series
AL—1.375—Juan Gonzalez, Texas, 1996
NL—1.300—Jim Leyritz, San Diego, 1998
5-game series
NL—1.091—Carlos Beltran, Houston, 2004
AL—1.083—Nomar Garciaparra, Boston, 1999

## PLATE APPEARANCES AND AT-BATS

**Most plate appearances, career**
AL—212—Bernie Williams, New York, 1995-2005; 11 series, 47 G
NL—189—Chipper Jones, Atlanta, 1995-2005; 11 series, 42 G

**Most plate appearances by pinch-hitter, career**
ML—9—John Vander Wal, Colorado NL, 1995; San Diego NL, 1998; New York AL, 2002; 3 series, 9 G
NL—7—John Vander Wal, Colorado, 1995; San Diego, 1998; 2 series, 7 G
Orlando Palmeiro, Houston, 2004, 2005; 2 series, 7 G
AL—4—Olmedo Saenz, Oakland, 2000, 2001; 2 series, 4 G

**Most plate appearances, series**
3-game series
AL—16—Mark Bellhorn, Boston, 2004
Johnny Damon, Boston, 2004
David Ortiz, Boston, 2004
Manny Ramirez, Boston, 2004
NL—16—Fernando Vina, St. Louis, 2002
4-game series
NL—24—Rafael Furcal, Atlanta, 2005
AL—21—many players
5-game series
AL—28—Bernie Williams, New York, 1995
NL—26—Rafael Furcal, Atlanta, 2004

**Most plate appearances, inning**
AL-NL—2—many players

**Most at-bats, career**
AL—180—Bernie Williams, New York, 1995-2005; 11 series, 47 G
NL—151—Chipper Jones, Atlanta, 1995-2005; 11 series, 42 G

**Most at-bats by pinch-hitter, career**
ML—9—John Vander Wal, Colorado NL, 1995; San Diego NL, 1998; New York AL, 2002; 3 series, 9 G
NL—7—John Vander Wal, Colorado, 1995; San Diego, 1998; 2 series, 7 G
AL—4—Olmedo Saenz, Oakland, 2000, 2001; 2 series, 4 G

**Most at-bats, series**
3-game series
AL—15—Mike Greenwell, Boston, 1995
Johnny Damon, Boston, 2004

NL—15—Brett Butler, Los Angeles, 1995
Fernando Vina, St. Louis, 2002
Mark Loretta, San Diego, 2005

4-game series
NL—21—Marquis Grissom, Atlanta, 1995
AL—20—Jacque Jones, Minnesota, 2004
Shannon Stewart, Minnesota, 2004

5-game series
AL—24—Jay Buhner, Seattle, 1995
Don Mattingly, New York, 1995
NL—24—Rafael Furcal, Atlanta, 2002
Marcus Giles, Atlanta, 2004

**Most at-bats by pinch-hitter, series**
NL—5—Dewayne Wise, Atlanta, 2004 (5-game series)
AL—3—many players

**Most consecutive at-bats without a hit, career**
AL—19—Joey Cora, Seattle, 1997 (last 9 AB); Cleveland, 1998 (all 10 AB)
NL—17—Tim Wallach, Los Angeles, 1995 (last 6 AB), 1996 (all 11 AB)

**Most at-bats by player with no hits, series**
AL—13—Jose Canseco, Boston, 1995
NL—11—Tino Martinez, St. Louis, 2002
Jose Cruz Jr., San Francisco, 2003
Robert Fick, Atlanta, 2003

**Most at-bats, game**
NL—6—Marquis Grissom, Atlanta, Oct 4, 1995
Fernando Vina, St. Louis, Oct 1, 2002
[8—Brian McCann, Atlanta, Oct 9, 2005, 18 inn]
AL—6—Brian Daubach, Boston, Oct 10, 1999
Mike Stanley, Boston, Oct 10, 1999
Juan Gonzalez, Cleveland, Oct 13, 2001
Jim Thome, Cleveland, Oct 13, 2001
Omar Vizquel, Cleveland, Oct 13, 2001
Chone Figgins, Los Angeles, Oct 9, 2005
[7—Luis Sojo, Seattle, Oct 4, 1995, 15 inn
Tino Martinez, Seattle, Oct 4, 1995, 15 inn
Ruben Sierra, New York, Oct 4, 1995, 15 inn]

**Most at-bats by player with no hits, game**
AL—6—Brian Daubach, Boston, Oct 10, 1999
NL—5—many players
[7—Craig Biggio, Houston, Oct 9, 2005, 18 inn]

**Most at-bats, inning**
AL-NL—2—many players

## RUNS

**Most runs, career**
AL—36—Bernie Williams, New York, 1995-2005; 11 series, 47 G
NL—30—Chipper Jones, Atlanta, 1995-2005; 11 series, 42 G

**Most runs by pinch-hitter, career**
NL—2—Turner Ward, Arizona, 1999; 1 series, 2 G
AL—1—many players

**Most runs by pinch-runner, career**
AL—2—Pat Kelly, New York, 1995; 1 series, 3 G
NL—1—many players

**Most runs, series**
3-game series
NL—5—Hal Morris, Cincinnati, 1995
Charles Johnson, Florida, 1997
Jim Edmonds, St. Louis, 2000, 2005
Edgar Renteria, St. Louis, 2000
AL—5—A.J. Pierzynski, Chicago, 2005

4-game series
NL—6—Dante Bichette, Colorado, 1995
Edgardo Alfonzo, New York, 1999
Larry Walker, St. Louis, 2004
Craig Biggio, Houston, 2005
AL—6—Derek Jeter, New York, 2002

5-game series
AL—9—Ken Griffey Jr., Seattle, 1995
NL—9—Carlos Beltran, Houston, 2004

**Most runs by pinch-hitter, series**
NL—2—Eric Young, San Diego, 2005
AL—1—many players

**Most runs by pinch-runner, series**
AL—2—Pat Kelly, New York, 1995 (5-game series)
NL—1—many players

**Most runs, game**
AL—5—Jason Varitek, Boston, Oct 10, 1999
NL—3—many players

**Most runs, inning**
AL—2—Shawn Wooten, Anaheim, Oct 5, 2002, 5th
NL—1—many players

## HITS

### CAREER AND SERIES

**Most hits, career**
AL—59—Derek Jeter, New York, 1996-2005; 10 series, 42 G
NL—41—Chipper Jones, Atlanta, 1995-2005; 11 series, 42 G

**Most hits by pinch-hitter, career**
NL—3—Greg Colbrunn, Atlanta, 1997, 1998; Arizona, 2001; 3 series, 6 G
AL—2—Randy Velarde, Oakland, 2002; 1 series, 3 G

**Most hits, series**
3-game series
NL—9—Fernando Vina, St. Louis, 2002
AL—7—Johnny Damon, Boston, 2004

4-game series
NL—11—Marquis Grissom, Atlanta, 1995
AL—8—Cal Ripken, Baltimore, 1996
Darin Erstad, Anaheim, 2002
Derek Jeter, New York, 2002
Alex Rodriguez, New York, 2004

5-game series
AL—12—Edgar Martinez, Seattle, 1995
Ichiro Suzuki, Seattle, 2001
NL—10—Moises Alou, Chicago, 2003
Carlos Beltran, Houston, 2004
Andruw Jones, Atlanta, 2004

**Most hits by pinch-hitter, series**
NL—2—many players
AL—2—Randy Velarde, Oakland, 2002

**Most series with one or more hits**
NL—8—Chipper Jones, Atlanta, 1995-2002
AL—7—Tino Martinez, Seattle, 1995; New York, 1996-2001
Paul O'Neill, New York, 1995-2001
Bernie Williams, New York, 1995-1997, 1999-2002
Derek Jeter, New York, 1996-2002

**Most consecutive hits, career**
AL—5—Derek Jeter, New York, Oct 1 (2), 2 (3), 2002 (2 BB during streak)
NL—5—Marquis Grissom, Atlanta, Oct 7 (5), 1995
Chad Fonville, Los Angeles, Oct 3 (1), 4 (4), 1995 (1 SH during streak)
Andruw Jones, Atlanta, Oct 9 (2), 10 (3), 2001
Moises Alou, Chicago, Oct 3 (2), 4 (3), 2003

**Most consecutive hits by pinch-hitter, career**
NL—2—Chris Gwynn, San Diego, Oct 1, 3, 1996
Darryl Hamilton, New York, Oct 5, 7, 2000
Greg Colbrunn, Arizona, Oct 10, 12, 2001
Damian Jackson, San Diego, Oct 4, 6, 2005
Eric Young, San Diego, Oct 4, 8, 2005
AL—2—Randy Velarde, Oakland, Oct 1, 4, 2002

**Most consecutive hits, series**
AL—5—Derek Jeter, New York, Oct 1 (2), 2 (3), 2002 (2 BB during streak)
NL—5—Marquis Grissom, Atlanta, Oct 7 (5), 1995
Chad Fonville, Los Angeles, Oct 3 (1), 4 (4), 1995 (1 SH during streak)
Andruw Jones, Atlanta, Oct 9 (2), 10 (3), 2001
Moises Alou, Chicago, Oct 3 (2), 4 (3), 2003

### GAME AND INNING

**Most hits, game**
NL—5—Marquis Grissom, Atlanta, Oct 7, 1995
AL—5—Mike Stanley, Boston, Oct 10, 1999

**Most times reached base safely, game (batting 1.000)**
NL—5—Marquis Grissom, Atlanta, Oct 7, 1995 (4 singles, 1 double)
AL—5—Johnny Damon, Oakland, Oct 10, 2001 (4 singles, 1 BB)

**Most hits accounting for all of club's hits, game**
AL—2—Ivan Rodriguez, Texas, Oct 5, 1999
NL—1—Ken Caminiti, Houston, Oct 6, 1999
Jeff Kent, San Francisco, Oct 8, 2000

**Most consecutive games with one or more hits, career**
AL—15—Derek Jeter, New York, 2001 (last 2), 2002 (all 4), 2003 (all 4), 2004 (all 4), 2005 (first)
NL—10—Edgardo Alfonzo, New York, 1999 (last 2), 2000 (all 4); San Francisco, 2003 (all 4)

**Most hits, inning**
AL—2—Chuck Knoblauch, New York, Oct 8, 2000, 1st
Doug Mientkiewicz, Minnesota, Oct 5, 2002, 4th
Shawn Wooten, Anaheim, Oct 5, 2002, 5th
Benji Gil, Anaheim, Oct 5, 2002, 5th
NL—none more than one

## SINGLES

**Most singles, career**
AL—45—Derek Jeter, New York, 1996-2005; 10 series, 42 G
NL—27—Chipper Jones, Atlanta, 1995-2005; 11 series, 42 G

**Most singles by pinch-hitter, career**
NL—3—Greg Colbrunn, Atlanta, 1997, 1998; Arizona, 2001; 3 series, 6 G
AL—1—many players

**Most singles, series**
3-game series
NL—9—Fernando Vina, St. Louis, 2002
AL—6—Johnny Damon, Boston, 2004
4-game series
NL—8—Bret Boone, Atlanta, 1999
AL—7—Michael Cuddyer, Minnesota, 2004
5-game series
AL—11—Ichiro Suzuki, Seattle, 2001
NL—9—Moises Alou, Chicago, 2003

**Most singles by pinch-hitter, series**
NL—2—Dave Hansen, Los Angeles, 1995 (3-game series)
Chris Gwynn, San Diego, 1996 (3-game series)
Greg Colbrunn, Arizona, 2001 (5-game series)
Damian Jackson, San Diego, 2005 (3-game series)
AL—1—many players

**Most singles, game**
NL—4—Chad Fonville, Los Angeles, Oct 4, 1995
Marquis Grissom, Atlanta, Oct 7, 1995
Fernando Vina, St. Louis, Oct 3, 2002
AL—4—Johnny Damon, Oakland, Oct 10, 2001
Jason Giambi, Oakland, Oct 15, 2001

**Most singles, inning**
AL—2—Chuck Knoblauch, New York, Oct 8, 2000, 1st
Doug Mientkiewicz, Minnesota, Oct 5, 2002, 4th
Benji Gil, Anaheim, Oct 5, 2002, 5th
NL—1—many players

## DOUBLES

**Most doubles, career**
AL—16—Bernie Williams, New York, 1995-2005; 11 series, 47 G
NL—7—Edgardo Alfonzo, New York, 1999, 2000; San Francisco, 2003; 3 series, 12 G
Craig Biggio, Houston, 1997-1999, 2001, 2004, 2005; 6 series, 23 G
Jim Edmonds, St. Louis, 2000-2002, 2004, 2005; 5 series, 18 G
Andruw Jones, Atlanta, 1996-2005; 10 series, 38 G

**Most doubles by pinch-hitter, career**
AL-NL—1—many players

**Most doubles, series**
3-game series
NL—4—Jim Edmonds, St. Louis, 2000
AL—2—many players
4-game series
AL—4—David Justice, Cleveland, 1998
NL—4—Edgardo Alfonzo, San Francisco, 2003
Craig Biggio, Houston, 2005
5-game series
AL—4—Don Mattingly, New York, 1995
Roberto Alomar, Cleveland, 1999
Torii Hunter, Minnesota, 2002
NL—3—Jeff Kent, Houston, 2004

**Most doubles, game**
NL—3—Jim Edmonds, St. Louis, Oct 5, 2000
Craig Biggio, Houston, Oct 8, 2005
AL—2—many players

**Most doubles, inning**
AL-NL—1—many players

## TRIPLES

**Most triples, career**
AL—2—Omar Vizquel, Cleveland, 1995-1999, 2001; 6 series, 26 G
David Justice, Cleveland, 1997-1999; New York, 2000, 2001; Oakland, 2002; 6 series, 26 G
NL—2—Rafael Furcal, Atlanta, 2000, 2002-2005; 5 series, 22 G
Tony Womack, Arizona, 1999, 2001, 2002; St. Louis, 2004; 4 series, 16 G

**Most triples by pinch-hitter, career**
NL—1—John Vander Wal, Colorado, 1995; San Diego, 1998; 2 series, 7 G
AL—none

**Most triples, series and game**
AL-NL—1—many players

**Most bases-loaded triples, game**
AL—1—David Justice, Oakland, Oct 2, 2002, 4th inn
NL—none

## HOME RUNS

### CAREER AND SERIES

**Most home runs, career**
NL—9—Chipper Jones, Atlanta, 1995-2005; 11 series, 42 G
AL—8—Juan Gonzalez, Texas, 1996, 1998, 1999; Cleveland, 2001; 4 series, 15 G
Derek Jeter, New York, 1996-2005; 10 series, 42 G
Manny Ramirez, Cleveland, 1995-1999; Boston, 2003-2005; 8 series; 32 G
Jim Thome, Cleveland, 1995-1999, 2001; 6 series, 25 G
Bernie Williams, New York, 1995-2005; 11 series, 47 G

**For a list of all home runs each series, and a complete list of players with four or more career home runs, see page 296.**

**Most home runs, series**
3-game series
NL—3—Ken Caminiti, San Diego, 1996
AL—2—Shane Spencer, New York, 1998
Troy Glaus, Anaheim, 2004
Paul Konerko, Chicago, 2005
A.J. Pierzynski, Chicago, 2005
Manny Ramirez, Boston, 2005
4-game series
AL—5—Juan Gonzalez, Texas, 1995
NL—3—many players
5-game series
AL—5—Ken Griffey Jr., Seattle, 1995
NL—4—Carlos Beltran, Houston, 2004

**Most series with one or more home runs**
NL—6—Chipper Jones, Atlanta, 1995 (2), 1996 (1), 1997 (1), 2001 (2), 2003 (2), 2005 (1)
AL—5—Bernie Williams, New York, 1995 (2), 1996 (3), 1999 (1), 2002 (1), 2004 (1)

**Most series with two or more home runs**
AL—3—Edgar Martinez, Seattle, 1995 (2), 1997 (2), 2001 (2)
NL—3—Chipper Jones, Atlanta, 1995 (2), 2001 (2), 2003 (2)

### GAME AND INNING

**Most home runs, game**
NL—2—Chipper Jones, Atlanta, Oct 3, 1995
Eric Karros, Los Angeles, Oct 4, 1995
Marquis Grissom, Atlanta, Oct 4, 1995
Fred McGriff, Atlanta, Oct 7, 1995
Ken Caminiti, San Diego, Oct 5, 1996
Jeff Kent, San Francisco, Oct 3, 1997
Edgardo Alfonzo, New York, Oct 5, 1999
Chipper Jones, Atlanta, Oct 4, 2003
Eric Karros, Chicago, Oct 4, 2003
Larry Walker, St. Louis, Oct 5, 2004
Shawn Green, Los Angeles, Oct 9, 2004
Carlos Beltran, Houston, Oct 11, 2004
AL—2—Ken Griffey Jr., Seattle, Oct 3, 1995
Bernie Williams, New York, Oct 6, 1995
Edgar Martinez, Seattle, Oct 7, 1995
B.J. Surhoff, Baltimore, Oct 1, 1996
Juan Gonzalez, Texas, Oct 2, 1996
Bernie Williams, New York, Oct 5, 1996
Mo Vaughn, Boston, Sept 29, 1998
Manny Ramirez, Cleveland, Oct 2, 1998
John Valentin, Boston, Oct 10, 1999
Jim Thome, Cleveland, Oct 11, 1999
Troy O'Leary, Boston, Oct 11, 1999
Terrence Long, Oakland, Oct 10, 2001
Troy Glaus, Anaheim, Oct 1, 2002
Todd Walker, Boston, Oct 1, 2003
A.J. Pierzynski, Chicago, Oct 4, 2005
Manny Ramirez, Boston, Oct 7, 2005

**Most grand slams, game**
AL—1—Edgar Martinez, Seattle, Oct 7, 1995, 8th
Bobby Bonilla, Baltimore, Oct 1, 1996, 6th
Albert Belle, Cleveland, Oct 4, 1996, 7th
Paul O'Neill, New York, Oct 4, 1997, 4th
Jim Thome, Cleveland, Oct 7, 1999, 4th
Troy O'Leary, Boston, Oct 11, 1999, 3rd
Vlad Guerrero, Anaheim, Oct 9, 2004, 7th
NL—1—Mark Lewis, Cincinnati, Oct 6, 1995, 6th
Devon White, Florida, Oct 3, 1997, 6th
Ryan Klesko, Atlanta, Sept 30, 1998, 7th
Eddie Perez, Atlanta, Oct 3, 1998, 8th
Edgardo Alfonzo, New York, Oct 5, 1999, 9th
Reggie Sanders, St. Louis, Oct 4, 2005, 5th
Adam LaRoche, Atlanta, Oct 9, 2005, 3rd
Lance Berkman, Houston, Oct 9, 2005, 8th

**Inside-the-park home runs**
AL—Ray Durham, Oakland, Oct 4, 2002, 1st
NL—none

**Home runs by pinch-hitter, game**
NL—Mark Lewis, Cincinnati, Oct 6, 1995, 6th
Jim Leyritz, San Diego, Oct 1, 1998, 9th
Turner Ward, Arizona, Oct 8, 1999, 5th
Mark McGwire, St. Louis, Oct 5, 2000, 8th
J.T. Snow, San Francisco, Oct 5, 2000, 9th
Daryle Ward, Houston, Oct 12, 2001, 7th
Eric Young, San Diego, Oct 4, 2005, 8th
AL—David Justice, New York, Oct 15, 2001, 6th

**Home runs by leadoff batter, start of game**
NL—Marquis Grissom, Atlanta, Oct 4, 1995 (at Colorado)
Fernando Vina, St. Louis, Oct 7, 2000 (at Atlanta)
AL—Brady Anderson, Baltimore, Oct 1, 1996 (at Baltimore)
Ray Durham, Oakland, Oct 4, 2002 (at Minnesota)
Derek Jeter, New York, Oct 6, 2004 (at New York)

**Home runs winning 1-0 games**
AL—Jorge Posada, New York, Oct 13, 2001, 5th
NL—none

**Most home runs by pitcher, game**
AL-NL—none

**Most home runs by rookie, game**
NL—2—Chipper Jones, Atlanta, Oct 3, 1995
AL—1—Shane Spencer, New York, Sept 30, 1998
Shane Spencer, New York, Oct 2, 1998
Brian Daubach, Boston, Oct 9, 1999
Terrence Long, Oakland, Oct 6, 2000
Mark Ellis, Oakland, Oct 6, 2002
Hideki Matsui, New York, Oct 4, 2003
Tadahito Iguchi, Chicago, Oct 5, 2005

**Hitting home runs from both sides of plate, game**
AL—Bernie Williams, New York, Oct 6, 1995
Bernie Williams, New York, Oct 5, 1996
NL—none

**Most consecutive games hitting one or more home runs, career**
AL—4—Juan Gonzalez, Texas, Oct 1, 2 (2 in 12 inn), 4, 5, 1996
NL—3—Jim Leyritz, San Diego, Oct 1, 3, 4, 1998
Vinny Castilla, Colorado, Oct 6, 7, 1995; Atlanta, Oct 9, 2001

**Most consecutive games hitting one or more home runs, series**
AL—4—Juan Gonzalez, Texas, Oct 1, 2 (2 in 12 inn), 4, 5, 1996
NL—3—Jim Leyritz, San Diego, Oct 1, 3, 4, 1998

**Most home runs in two consecutive games, series (homering each game)**
AL—3—Ken Griffey, Jr., Seattle, Oct 3 (2), 4 (1 in 15 inn), 1995
Juan Gonzalez, Texas, Oct 1 (1), 2 (2 in 12 inn), 1996
Juan Gonzalez, Texas, Oct 2 (2 in 12 inn), 4 (1), 1996
Bernie Williams, New York, Oct 4 (1), 5 (2), 1996
John Valentin, Boston, Oct 9 (1), 10 (2), 1999
Troy Glaus, Anaheim, Oct 1 (2), 2 (1), 2002
NL—3—Marquis Grissom, Atlanta, Oct 3 (1), 4 (2), 1995
Ken Caminiti, San Diego, Oct 3 (1), 5 (2), 1996
Shawn Green, Los Angeles, Oct 7 (1), 9 (2), 2004

**Most home runs in three consecutive games, series (homering each game)**
AL—4—Juan Gonzalez, Texas, Oct 1 (1), 2 (2 in 12 inn), 4 (1), 1996
NL—3—Jim Leyritz, San Diego, Oct 1, 3, 4, 1998

**Most home runs in four consecutive games, series (homering each game)**
AL—5—Juan Gonzalez, Texas, Oct 1 (1), 2 (2 in 12 inn), 4 (1), 5 (1), 1996
NL—none

**Hitting home run in first division series at-bat (*not first plate appearance)**
NL—Benito Santiago, Cincinnati, Oct 3, 1995, 1st
Edgardo Alfonzo, New York, Oct 5, 1999, 1st
Mark McGwire, St. Louis, Oct 5, 2000, 8th*
Brian McCann, Atlanta, Oct 6, 2005, 2nd
AL—Brady Anderson, Baltimore, Oct 1, 1996, 1st
Harold Baines, Baltimore, Oct 2, 1997, 2nd
Shane Spencer, New York, Sept 30, 1998, 2nd
Todd Walker, Boston, Oct 1, 2003, 1st

**Hitting home runs in first two division series at-bats**
AL-NL—none

**Most home runs, inning**
AL-NL—1—many players

**Most home runs, two consecutive innings**
AL—2—Juan Gonzalez, Texas, Oct 2, 1996, 2nd and 3rd
NL—none

## TOTAL BASES

**Most total bases, career**
AL—91—Bernie Williams, New York, 1995-2005; 11 series, 47 G
NL—73—Chipper Jones, Atlanta, 1995-2005; 11 series, 42 G

**Most total bases by pinch-hitter, career**
NL—5—Eric Young, San Diego, 2005; 1 series, 2 G
AL—4—David Justice, New York, 2001; 1 series, 1 G
Trot Nixon, Boston, 2003; 1 series, 1 G

**Most total bases, series**
3-game series
NL—18—Jim Edmonds, St. Louis, 2000
AL—12—Troy Glaus, Anaheim, 2004
A.J. Pierzynski, Chicago, 2005
4-game series
AL—22—Juan Gonzalez, Texas, 1996
NL—22—Marquis Grissom, Atlanta, 1995
5-game series
AL—24—Ken Griffey Jr., Seattle, 1995
NL—24—Carlos Beltran, 2004

**Most total bases by pinch-hitter, series**
NL—6—many players
AL—4—David Justice, New York, 2001, 1 G
Trot Nixon, Boston, 2003, 1G

**Most total bases, game**
AL—11—John Valentin, Boston, Oct 10, 1999 (1 single, 1 double, 2 HR)
NL—10—Eric Karros, Los Angeles, Oct 4, 1995 (1 double, 2 HR)
Carlos Beltran, Houston, Oct 11, 2004 (2 singles, 2 HR)

**Most total bases, inning**
AL—5—Shawn Wooten, Anaheim, Oct 5, 2002, 5th inn (1 single, 1 HR)
NL—4—many players

## EXTRA-BASE HITS

**Most extra-base hits, career**
AL—24—Bernie Williams, New York, 1995-2005; 11 series, 47 G
NL—14—Chipper Jones, Atlanta, 1995-2005; 11 series, 42 G
Jim Edmonds, St. Louis, 1999-2001, 2004, 2005; 5 series; 18 G

**Most extra-base hits, series**
3-game series
NL—6—Jim Edmonds, St. Louis, 2000
AL—4—Troy Glaus, Anaheim, 2004
A.J. Pierzynski, Chicago, 2005
4-game series
AL—5—Juan Gonzalez, Texas, 1996
David Justice, Cleveland, 1998
NL—5—Marquis Grissom, Atlanta, 1995
5-game series
NL—6—Carlos Beltran, Houston, 2004
AL—5—many players

**Most extra-base hits, game**
NL—3—Eric Karros, Los Angeles, Oct 4, 1995 (1 double, 2 HR)
Jim Edmonds, St. Louis, Oct 5, 2000 (3 doubles)
Craig Biggio, Houston, Oct 8, 2005 (3 doubles)
AL—3—Mo Vaughn, Boston, Sept 29, 1998 (1 double, 2 HR)
John Valentin, Boston, Oct 10, 1999 (1 double, 2 HR)
Jason Varitek, Boston, Oct 10, 1999 (2 doubles, 1 HR)
Juan Gonzalez, Cleveland, Oct 13, 2001 (2 doubles, 1 HR)
Troy Glaus, Anaheim, Oct 5, 2004 (2 doubles, 1 HR)
David Ortiz, Boston, Oct 8, 2004 (2 doubles, 1 HR)
A.J. Pierzynski, Chicago, Oct 4, 2005 (1 double, 2 HR)

**Most extra-base hits, inning**
AL-NL—1—many players

## RUNS BATTED IN

**Most runs batted in, career**
AL—33—Bernie Williams, New York, 1995-2005; 11 series, 47 G
NL—26—Chipper Jones, Atlanta, 1995-2005; 11 series, 42 G

**Most runs batted in by pinch-hitter, career**
NL—5—Mark Lewis, Cincinnati, 1995; 1 series, 2 G
AL—2—B.J. Surhoff, Baltimore, 1996, 1997; 2 series, 2 G

**Most runs batted in, series**
3-game series
NL—10—Reggie Sanders, St. Louis, 2005
AL—7—Manny Ramirez, Boston, 2004
4-game series
AL—11—Nomar Garciaparra, Boston, 1998
NL—8—Ken Caminiti, Houston, 1999
5-game series
AL—12—John Valentin, Boston, 1999
NL—9—Carlos Beltran, Houston, 2004

**Most runs batted in by pinch-hitter, series**
NL—5—Mark Lewis, Cincinnati, 1995; 2 G
AL—2—B.J. Surhoff, Baltimore, 1997; 1 G

**Most runs batted in, game**
AL—7—Edgar Martinez, Seattle, Oct 7, 1995
Mo Vaughn, Boston, Sept 29, 1998
John Valentin, Boston, Oct 10, 1999
Troy O'Leary, Boston, Oct 11, 1999
NL—6—Reggie Sanders, St. Louis, Oct 4, 2005

**Most runs batted in by pinch-hitter, game**
NL—4—Mark Lewis, Cincinnati, Oct 6, 1995
AL—2—B.J. Surhoff, Baltimore, Oct 1, 1997

**Most consecutive games with one or more runs batted in, career**
NL—7—Edgardo Alfonzo, Oct 5, 2000-Oct 4, 2003
AL—5—Nomar Garciaparra, Boston, Sept 29, 1998-Oct 6, 1999

**Most runs batted in accounting for all club's runs, game**
NL—5—Brian Jordan, Oct 8, 1999, 12 inn
AL—4—Juan Gonzalez, Texas, Oct 2, 1996, 12 inn

**Most runs batted in, inning**
AL—4—many players
NL—4—many players

## BASES ON BALLS

**Most bases on balls, career**
NL—36—Chipper Jones, Atlanta, 1995-2005; 11 series, 42 G
AL—26—Bernie Williams, New York, 1995-2005; 11 series, 47 G

**Most bases on balls, series**
3-game series
NL—5—Gary Sheffield, Florida, 1997
Jeff Bagwell, Houston, 2001
AL—5—Mark Bellhorn, Boston, 2004
David Ortiz, Boston, 2004
4-game series
NL—8—Barry Bonds, San Francisco, 2003
AL—5—Mickey Tettleton, Texas, 1996

5-game series
AL—7—Bernie Williams, New York, 1995
Jose Offerman, Boston, 1999
Jason Giambi, Oakland, 2000
NL—7—Gary Sheffield, Atlanta, 2002

**Most consecutive bases on balls, series**
AL—4—Edgar Martinez, Seattle, Oct 6 (3), 7 (1), 1995
NL—3—Chipper Jones, Atlanta, Oct 1, 1997
Richard Hidalgo, Houston, Oct 9, 2001
Gary Sheffield, Atlanta, Oct 5, 2002
[3—Jeff Bagwell, Houston, Oct 8, 1999, 12 inn]

**Most bases on balls, game**
AL—3—many players
[4—Bernie Williams, New York, Oct 8, 1995, 11 inn]
NL—3—many players
[3—Jeff Bagwell, Houston, Oct 8, 1999, 12 inn
Chipper Jones, Atlanta, Oct 9, 2005, 18 inn]

**Most bases on balls with bases filled, game**
AL-NL—1—many players

**Bases on balls with bases filled, pinch-hitter, game**
AL—Jim Leyritz, New York, Oct 7, 1999, 8th
NL—none

**Most bases on balls, inning**
AL-NL—1—many players

## STRIKEOUTS

**Most strikeouts, career**
AL—34—Jim Thome, Cleveland, 1995-1999, 2001; 6 series, 25 G
NL—30—Chipper Jones, Atlanta, 1995-2005; 11 series, 42 G

**Most strikeouts, series**
3-game series
NL—9—Reggie Sanders, Cincinnati, 1995
AL—7—Mo Vaughn, Boston, 1995
4-game series
AL—9—Dan Wilson, Seattle, 1997
NL—9—Jim Edmonds, St. Louis, 2004
5-game series
AL—11—Bret Boone, Seattle, 2001
NL— 7—Jeff Kent, San Francisco, 2002
Andruw Jones, Atlanta, 2003
J.D. Drew, Atlanta, 2004

**Most strikeouts by pinch-hitter, series**
NL—2—John Vander Wal, Colorado, 1995; 4 G
Dave Clark, Los Angeles, 1996; 2 G
Billy Ashley, Los Angeles, 1996; 2 G
Bob Abreu, Houston, 1997; 2 G
Tom Goodwin, San Francisco, 2002; 2 G
AL—1—many players

**Most consecutive strikeouts, series (consecutive at-bats)**
AL—6—Dan Wilson, Seattle, Oct 1 (1), Oct 2 (4), Oct 4 (1), 1997
NL—5—Reggie Sanders, Cincinnati, Oct 6 (5), 1995

**Most strikeouts, game**
NL—5—Reggie Sanders, Cincinnati, Oct 6, 1995
AL—4—Dan Wilson, Seattle, Oct 2, 1997
Brady Anderson, Baltimore, Oct 5, 1997
Ben Grieve, Oakland, Oct 8, 2000
Bret Boone, Seattle, Oct 13, 2001
[4—Rafael Palmeiro, Baltimore, Oct 5, 1996, 12 inn
Bobby Bonilla, Baltimore, Oct 5, 1996, 12 inn
Pete Incaviglia, Baltimore, Oct 5, 1996, 12 inn
Derek Jeter, New York, Oct 9, 2004, 11 inn]

**Most strikeouts, inning**
AL-NL—1—many players

## SACRIFICE HITS

**Most sacrifice hits, career**
AL—4—Omar Vizquel, Cleveland, 1995-1999, 2001; 6 series, 26 G
Steve Finley, Los Angeles AL, 2005; 1 series, 5 G
NL—4—John Smoltz, Atlanta, 1995-1999, 2001-2005; 10 series, 15 G

**Most sacrifice hits, series**
AL—4—Steve Finley, Los Angeles, 2005; 5 G
NL—3—Placido Polanco, St. Louis, 2001; 5 G

**Most sacrifice hits, game**
NL—3—Placido Polanco, St. Louis, Oct 13, 2001
AL—2—Stan Javier, Seattle, Oct 15, 2001

## SACRIFICE FLIES

**Most sacrifice flies, career**
AL—4—Bernie Williams, New York, 1995-2005; 11 series, 47 G
NL—3—Barry Bonds, San Francisco, 1997, 2000, 2002, 2003; 4 series, 16 G

**Most sacrifice flies, series**
AL—2—Luis Sojo, Seattle, 1995; 5 G
Nomar Garciaparra, Boston, 1998; 4 G
Trot Nixon, Boston, 1999; 5 G
Adam Kennedy, Anaheim, 2002; 4 G
Manny Ramirez, Boston, 2004; 3 G
NL—1—many players

**Most sacrifice flies, game**
AL-NL—1—many players

## HIT BY PITCH

**Most hit by pitch, career**
AL—4—Manny Ramirez, Cleveland, 1995-1999; Boston, 2003-2005; 8 series, 32 G
NL—3—Larry Walker, Colorado, 1995; St. Louis, 2004, 2005; 3 series; 11 G

**Most hit by pitch, series**
AL—2—many players
NL—2—Craig Biggio, Houston, 1998; 4 G
Mike Bordick, New York, 2000; 4 G
Derrek Lee, Florida, 2003; 4 G
Xavier Nady, San Diego, 2005; 2 G

**Most hit by pitch, game**
AL—2—Manny Ramirez, Cleveland, Sept 30, 1998
NL—2—Xavier Nady, San Diego, Oct 6, 2005

## GROUNDING INTO DOUBLE PLAYS

**Most grounding into double plays, career**
AL—11—Bernie Williams, New York, 1995-2005; 11 series, 47 G
NL—7—Chipper Jones, Atlanta, 1995-2005; 11 series, 42 G

**Most grounding into double plays, series**
AL—4—Bernie Williams, New York, 2004 (4-game series)
NL—2—many players

**Most grounding into double plays, game**
NL—2—Chipper Jones, Atlanta, Oct 3, 1995
Lance Berkman, Houston, Oct 10, 2001
Jeff Kent, Houston, Oct 10, 2004
AL—2—Paul O'Neill, New York, Oct 4, 1996
Sandy Alomar Jr., Cleveland, Sept 30, 1998
Roberto Alomar, Cleveland, Oct 15, 2001
Darin Erstad, Anaheim, Oct 5, 2002
Bernie Williams, New York, Oct 8, 2004

## REACHING BASE ON INTERFERENCE

**Most times awarded first base on catcher's interference, game**
AL-NL—none

# CLUB BATTING

## GAMES

**Most games, total series**
AL—47—New York; 11 series (won 28, lost 19)
NL—42—Atlanta; 11 series (won 25, lost 17)

**For summaries of series won and lost, games won and lost, and home and road games played, see page 295. For a list of batting statistics by teams each series, see page 297.**

## BATTING AVERAGE

**Highest average, series**
3-game series
NL—.314—St. Louis vs Arizona, 2002
AL—.302—Boston vs Anaheim, 2004
4-game series
AL—.376—Anaheim vs New York, 2002
NL—.331—Atlanta vs Colorado, 1995
5-game series
NL—.322—Houston vs Atlanta, 2004

AL—.318—Boston vs Cleveland, 1999

**Highest average, both clubs, series**

3-game series
NL—.293—San Diego .302, St. Louis .284, 2005
AL—.266—Boston .302, Anaheim .226, 2004
4-game series
AL—.331—Anaheim .376, New York .281, 2002
NL—.310—Atlanta .331, Colorado .287, 1995
5-game series
AL—.289—Minnesota .291, Oakland .288, 2002
NL—.253—Atlanta .259, San Francisco .247, 2002

**Highest average, losing club, series**

NL—.302—San Diego vs St. Louis, 2005 (4-game series)
AL—.281—New York vs Anaheim, 2002 (4-game series)

**Lowest average, series**

3-game series
AL—.141—Texas vs New York, 1998
NL—.147—Los Angeles vs Atlanta, 1996
4-game series
NL—.182—Houston vs San Diego, 1998
AL—.198—Minnesota vs New York, 2003
5-game series
NL—.191—St. Louis vs Arizona, 2001
AL—.211—Boston vs Oakland, 2003

**Lowest average, both clubs, series**

3-game series
NL—.163—Atlanta .180, Los Angeles .147, 1996
AL—.195—New York .235, Texas .152, 1999
4-game series
NL—.199—San Diego .216, Houston .182, 1998
AL—.230—Boston .252, Cleveland .206, 1998
5-game series
AL—.212—Oakland .213, Boston .211, 2003
NL—.214—Arizona .237, St. Louis .191, 2001

**Lowest average, winning club, series**

NL—.180—Atlanta vs Los Angeles, 1996 (3-game series)
AL—.206—Cleveland vs Boston, 1998 (4-game series)

## ON-BASE PERCENTAGE

**Highest percentage, series**

3-game series
AL—.403—Boston vs Anaheim, 2004
NL—.395—Florida vs San Francisco, 1997
4-game series
AL—.406—Anaheim vs New York, 2002
NL—.381—Atlanta vs Colorado, 1995
5-game series
AL—.391—Seattle vs New York, 1995
NL—.390—Houston vs Atlanta, 2004

**Highest percentage, both clubs, series**

3-game series
NL—.373—San Diego .375, St. Louis .371, 2005
AL—.360—Boston .403, Anaheim .311, 2004
4-game series
AL—.387—Anaheim .406, New York .367, 2002
NL—.360—Atlanta .381, Colorado .338, 1995
5-game series
AL—.378—Seattle .391, New York .365, 1995
NL—.366—Houston .390, Atlanta .342, 2004

**Lowest percentage, series**

3-game series
AL—.177—Texas vs New York, 1998
NL—.204—Los Angeles vs Atlanta, 1996
4-game series
AL—.248—Minnesota vs New York, 2003
NL—.277—Houston vs San Diego, 1998
5-game series
NL—.253—St. Louis vs Arizona, 2001
AL—.290—Boston vs Oakland, 2003

**Lowest percentage, both clubs, series**

3-game series
NL—.242—Atlanta .282, Los Angeles .204, 1996
AL—.246—New York .313, Texas .177, 1998
4-game series
NL—.277—Houston .277, San Diego .277, 1998
AL—.298—New York .344, Minnesota .248, 2003
5-game series
NL—.287—Arizona .320, St. Louis .253, 2001
AL—.300—Oakland .310, Boston .290, 2003

## SLUGGING AVERAGE

**Highest average, series**

3-game series
AL—.567—Chicago vs Boston, 2005
NL—.545—Atlanta vs Houston, 2001
4-game series
AL—.624—Anaheim vs New York, 2002
NL—.519—Atlanta vs Colorado, 1995
5-game series
AL—.597—Boston vs Cleveland, 1999
NL—.572—Houston vs Atlanta, 2004

**Highest average, both clubs, series**

3-game series
AL—.488—Chicago .567, Boston .413, 2005
NL—.433—St. Louis .441, San Diego .425, 2005
4-game series
NL—.492—Atlanta .519, Colorado .462, 1995
AL—.549—Anaheim .624, New York .467, 2002
5-game series
AL—.510—Boston .597, Cleveland .417, 1999
NL—.494—Houston .572, Atlanta .417, 2004

**Lowest average, series**

3-game series
AL—.174—Texas vs New York, 1998
NL—.208—Houston vs Atlanta, 1997
4-game series
NL—.248—Houston vs San Diego, 1998
AL—.282—Minnesota vs New York, 2003
5-game series
AL—.287—Oakland vs Boston, 2003
NL—.301—Atlanta vs Chicago, 2003

**Lowest average, both clubs, series**

3-game series
NL—.282—Atlanta .359, Houston .208, 1997
AL—.295—New York .378, Texas .207, 1999
4-game series
NL—.317—San Diego .384, Houston .248, 1998
AL—.335—New York .384, Minnesota .282, 2003
5-game series
NL—.328—St. Louis .329, Arizona .327, 2001
AL—.332—Boston .378, Oakland .287, 2003

## AT-BATS AND PLATE APPEARANCES

**Most at-bats, total series**

AL—1,615—New York; 11 series, 47 G
NL—1,452—Atlanta; 11 series, 42 G

**Most at-bats, series**

3-game series
AL—116—Boston vs Anaheim, 2004
NL—111—Los Angeles vs Cincinnati, 1995
4-game series
NL—161—Atlanta vs Houston, 2005
AL—154—New York vs Minnesota, 2004
5-game series
AL—200—Seattle vs New York, 1995
NL—180—Atlanta vs Houston, 2004
Houston vs Atlanta, 2004

**Most at-bats by both clubs, series**

3-game series
AL—228—Boston 114, Cleveland 114, 1995
NL—215—Los Angeles 111, Cincinnati 104, 1995
4-game series
NL—316—Atlanta 161, Houston 155, 2005
AL—306—New York 154, Minnesota 152, 2004
5-game series
AL—393—Seattle 200, New York 193, 1995
NL—360—Atlanta 180, Houston 180, 2004

**Most at-bats by pinch-hitters, series**

NL—11—Atlanta vs Colorado, 1995 (4-game series)
Atlanta vs San Francisco, 2002 (5-game series)
San Diego vs St. Louis, 2005 (3-game series)
AL—9—Oakland vs New York, 2001 (5-game series)

**Most at-bats by pinch-hitters on both clubs, series**

NL—20—Atlanta 11, Colorado 9, 1995 (4-game series)
AL—13—Oakland 7, Minnesota 6, 2002 (5-game series)

**Most plate appearances by pinch-hitters, series**

NL—15—San Diego vs St. Louis, 2005 (3-game series)
AL—9—Oakland vs New York, 2001 (5-game series)

**Most plate appearances by pinch-hitters on both clubs, series**

NL—21—Atlanta 11, Colorado 10, 1995 (4-game series)
AL—14—Oakland 8, Minnesota 6, 2002 (5-game series)

**Fewest at-bats, series**

3-game series
NL—89—Atlanta vs Los Angeles, 1996
AL—91—New York vs Texas, 1998
4-game series
NL—121—Houston vs San Diego, 1998
AL—126—Cleveland vs Boston, 1998
5-game series
NL—152—St. Louis vs Arizona, 2001
AL—158—Seattle vs Cleveland, 2001

**Fewest at-bats by both clubs, series**
3-game series
AL—183—Texas 92, New York 91, 1998
NL—184—Los Angeles 95, Atlanta 89, 1996
4-game series
NL—246—San Diego 125, Houston 121, 1998
AL—261—Boston 135, Cleveland 126, 1998
5-game series
NL—308—Arizona 156, St. Louis 152, 2001
AL—331—Cleveland 173, Seattle 158, 2001

**Most at-bats by club, game**
AL—48—Boston vs Cleveland, Oct 10, 1999
[56—Seattle vs New York, Oct 4, 1995, 15 inn]
NL—42—Florida vs San Francisco, Oct 1, 2003
[62—Atlanta vs Houston, Oct 9, 2005, 18 inn]

**Most at-bats by both clubs, game**
AL—81—Los Angeles 43, New York 38, Oct 7, 2005
[107—Seattle 56, New York 51, Oct 4, 1995, 15 inn]
NL—77—Atlanta 41, Colorado 36, Oct 4, 1995
[120—Atlanta 62, Houston 58, Oct 9, 2005, 18 inn]

**Most at-bats by pinch-hitters, game**
NL—5—San Diego vs St. Louis, Oct 6, 2005
AL—4—Seattle vs Cleveland, Oct 13, 2001
Oakland vs New York, Oct 14, 2001

**Most at-bats by pinch-hitters on both clubs, game**
NL—7—Atlanta 4, Colorado 3, Oct 4, 1995
AL—5—Seattle 4, Cleveland 1, Oct 13, 2001

**Most plate appearances by pinch-hitters, game**
NL—5—San Diego vs St. Louis, Oct 6, 2005
AL—4—Seattle vs Cleveland, Oct 13, 2001
Oakland vs New York, Oct 14, 2001

**Most plate appearances by pinch-hitters on both clubs, game**
NL—7—Atlanta 4, Colorado 3, Oct 4, 1995
[8—Atlanta 4, Houston 4, Oct 9, 2005, 18 inn]
AL—5—Seattle 4, Cleveland 1, Oct 13, 2001
Oakland 4, New York 1, Oct 14, 2001

**Fewest at-bats, game**
NL—24—San Diego vs Houston, Oct 3, 1998 (batted 8 inn)
AL—25—New York vs Texas, Sept 29, 1998 (batted 8 inn)
Chicago vs Seattle, Oct 6, 2000

**Fewest at-bats by both clubs, game**
NL—52—Houston 28, San Diego 24, Oct 3, 1998 (San Diego batted 8 inn)
AL—53—Seattle 28, Chicago 25, Oct 6, 2000

**Most at-bats, inning**
AL—13—Anaheim vs New York, Oct 5, 2002, 5th
NL—9—Atlanta vs Houston, Oct 9, 1999, 6th
San Diego vs St. Louis, Oct 4, 2005, 9th

**Most at-bats by both clubs, inning**
AL—17—Anaheim 13, New York 4, Oct 5, 2002, 5th
NL—13—Atlanta 7, Colorado 6, Oct 7, 1995, 3rd
Atlanta 7, Chicago 6, Oct 3, 1998, 8th
San Francisco 7, Atlanta 6, Oct 2, 2002, 2nd
Houston 7, Atlanta 6, Oct 10, 2004, 2nd

**Most plate appearances, inning**
AL—13—Anaheim vs New York, Oct 5, 2002, 5th
NL—11—St. Louis vs Arizona, Oct 1, 2002, 7th
Houston vs Atlanta, Oct 5, 2005, 8th

**Most plate appearances by both clubs, inning**
AL—18—Anaheim 13, New York 5, Oct 5, 2002, 5th
New York, 12, Minnesota 6, Oct 5, 2003, 4th
NL—17—Houston 11, Atlanta 6, Oct 5, 2005, 8th

## RUNS

### SERIES AND GAMES

**Most runs, total series**
AL—215—New York; 11 series, 47 G
NL—196—Atlanta; 11 series, 42 G

**Most runs, series**
3-game series
AL—25—Boston vs Anaheim, 2004
NL—24—St. Louis vs Atlanta, 2000
4-game series
AL—31—Anaheim vs New York, 2002
NL—27—Atlanta vs Colorado, 1995
5-game series
AL—47—Boston vs Cleveland, 1999
NL—36—Houston vs Atlanta, 2004

**Most runs by both clubs, series**
3-game series
AL—37—Boston 25, Anaheim 12, 2004
NL—34—St. Louis 24, Atlanta 10, 2000
4-game series
AL—56—Anaheim 31, New York 25, 2002
NL—46—Atlanta 27, Colorado 19, 1995
Houston 25, Atlanta 21, 2005
5-game series
AL—79—Boston 47, Cleveland 32, 1999
NL—57—Houston 36, Atlanta 21, 2004

**Most runs by losing club, series**
AL—33—New York vs Seattle, 1995 (5-game series)
NL—26—Atlanta vs San Francisco, 2002 (5-game series)

**Fewest runs, series**
3-game series
AL—1—Texas vs New York, 1998
Texas vs New York, 1999
NL—4—Chicago vs Atlanta, 1998
4-game series
AL—6—Minnesota vs New York, 2003
NL—8—Houston vs San Diego, 1998
5-game series
NL—10—Arizona vs St. Louis, 2001
AL—12—Oakland vs New York, 2001

**Fewest runs by both clubs, series**
3-game series
AL—10—New York 9, Texas 1, 1998
NL—15—Atlanta 10, Los Angeles 5, 1996
4-game series
NL—22—San Diego 14, Houston 8, 1998
AL—22—New York 16, Minnesota 6, 2003
5-game series
NL—22—St. Louis 12, Arizona 10, 2001
AL—30—New York 18, Oakland 12, 2001

**Most runs, game**
AL—23—Boston vs Cleveland, Oct 10, 1999
NL—13—Atlanta vs Houston, Oct 1, 1997

**Most earned runs, game**
AL—23—Boston vs Cleveland, Oct 10, 1999
NL—12—Houston vs Atlanta, Oct 11, 2004

**Most runs by both clubs, game**
AL—30—Boston 23, Cleveland 7, Oct 10, 1999
NL—16—Atlanta 13, Houston 3, Oct 1, 1997

**Largest score, shutout game**
AL—New York 8, Texas 0, Oct 5, 1999
NL—New York 4, San Francisco 0, Oct 8, 2000
Los Angeles 4, St. Louis 0, Oct 9, 2004

**Most players scoring one or more runs, game**
AL—10—Cleveland vs Seattle, Oct 13, 2001
NL—8—St. Louis vs Arizona, Oct 1, 2002
San Francisco vs Atlanta, Oct 2, 2002
Houston vs Atlanta, Oct 11, 2004

**Most players from both clubs scoring one or more runs, game**
AL—15—Boston 9, Cleveland 6, Oct 10, 1999
NL—12—San Francisco 8, Atlanta 4, Oct 2, 2002
Houston 7, Atlanta 5, Oct 5, 2005
[Houston 7, Atlanta 5, Oct 9, 2005, 18 inn]

### INNING

**Most runs, inning**
AL—8—Anaheim vs New York, Oct 5, 2002, 5th
NL—6—New York vs Arizona, Oct 8, 1999, 6th
St. Louis vs Atlanta, Oct 3, 2000, 1st
St. Louis vs Arizona, Oct 1, 2002, 7th

**Most runs by both clubs, inning**
AL—9—Anaheim 8, New York 1, Oct 5, 2002, 5th
NL—7—Atlanta 4, Colorado 3, Oct 7, 1995, 3rd
Atlanta 5, Chicago 2, Oct 3, 1998, 8th
Houston 5, Atlanta 2, Oct 10, 2004, 2nd

**Most runs, extra inning**
AL—3—Seattle vs Chicago, Oct 3, 2000, 10th
NL—2—Colorado vs Atlanta, Oct 6, 1995, 10th
Atlanta vs Houston, Oct 8, 1999, 12th
Florida vs San Francisco, Oct 3, 2003 11th
Atlanta vs Houston, Oct 7, 2004, 11th

**Most runs by both clubs, extra inning**
AL—3—Seattle 2, New York 1, Oct 8, 1995, 11th
Seattle 3, Chicago 0, Oct 3, 2000, 10th
New York 2, Minnesota 1, Oct 6, 2004, 12th
NL—3—Florida 2, San Francisco 1, Oct 3, 2003, 11th

**Most innings scored, game**
AL—7—Boston vs Cleveland, Oct 10, 1999
NL—6—San Francisco vs Florida, Oct 1, 1997
St. Louis vs Atlanta, Oct 5, 2000

**Most innings scored by both clubs, game**
NL—11—San Francisco 6, Florida 5, Oct 1, 1997
AL—11—Boston 7, Cleveland 4, Oct 10, 1999

**Most runs, 1st inning**
AL—6—New York vs Oakland, Oct 8, 2000
NL—6—St. Louis vs Atlanta, Oct 3, 2000

**Most runs, 2nd inning**
AL—5—Cleveland vs Boston, Sept 30, 1998
Boston vs Cleveland, Oct 10, 1999
Oakland vs Boston, Oct 2, 2003
NL—5—Houston vs Atlanta, Oct 10, 2004

**Most runs, 3rd inning**
AL—6—Cleveland vs Boston, Oct 7, 1999
NL—5—St. Louis vs Los Angeles, Oct 6, 2004

**Most runs, 4th inning**
AL—7—Minnesota vs Oakland, Oct 6, 2002
Boston vs Anaheim, Oct 5, 2004
NL—4—Atlanta vs Los Angeles, Oct 5, 1996

**Most runs, 5th inning**
AL—8—Anaheim vs New York, Oct 5, 2002
NL—4—St. Louis vs San Diego, Oct 4, 2005

**Most runs, 6th inning**
NL—6—New York vs Arizona, Oct 8, 1999
Atlanta vs San Francisco, Oct 5, 2002
AL—5—Cleveland vs Boston, Oct 6, 1995
Baltimore vs Cleveland, Oct 1, 1996
New York vs Cleveland, Sept 30, 1997

**Most runs, 7th inning**
AL—6—Boston vs Cleveland, Oct 9, 1999
NL—6—St. Louis vs Arizona, Oct 1, 2002

**Most runs, 8th inning**
AL—5—Seattle vs New York, Oct 7, 1995
Cleveland vs Seattle, Oct 13, 2001
NL—5—Atlanta vs Chicago, Oct 3, 1998
Houston vs Atlanta, Oct 5, 2005

**Most runs, 9th inning**
NL—4—Atlanta vs Colorado, Oct 4, 1995
New York vs Arizona, Oct 5, 1999
Houston vs Atlanta, Oct 5, 1999
Atlanta vs San Francisco, Oct 5, 2002
AL—4—Oakland vs New York, Oct 7, 2000
Boston vs Anaheim, Oct 6, 2004

**Most runs, 10th inning**
AL—3—Seattle vs Chicago, Oct 3, 2000
NL—2—Colorado vs Atlanta, Oct 6, 1995

**Most runs, 11th inning**
AL—2—Seattle vs New York, Oct 8, 1995
Boston vs Oakland, Oct 4, 2003
NL—2—Florida vs San Francisco, Oct 3, 2003
Atlanta vs Houston, Oct 7, 2004

**Most runs, 12th inning**
NL—2—Atlanta vs Houston, Oct 8, 1999
AL—2—New York vs Minnesota, Oct 6, 2004

**Most runs, 13th inning**
AL—1—Cleveland vs Boston, Oct 3, 1995
NL—1—New York vs San Francisco, Oct 7, 2000

**Most runs, 14th inning**
AL-NL—none

**Most runs, 15th inning**
AL—2—New York vs Seattle, Oct 4, 1995
NL—none

**Most runs, 16th inning**
AL-NL—none

**Most runs, 17th inning**
AL-NL—none

**Most runs, 18th inning**
NL—1—Houston vs Atlanta, Oct 9, 2005
AL—none

## GAMES BEING SHUT OUT

**Most times being shut out, total series**
AL—4—Texas; 3 series, 10 G
NL—1—many times

**Most consecutive games without being shut out, total series**
NL—42—Atlanta, Oct 3, 1995-Oct 9, 2005
AL—26—New York, Oct 3, 1995-Oct 10, 2001
Cleveland, Oct 3, 1995-Oct 15, 2001

## HITS

### SERIES

**Most hits, total series**
AL—418—New York; 11 series, 47 G
NL—371—Atlanta; 11 series, 42 G

**Most hits, series**
3-game series
AL—35—Boston vs Anaheim, 2004
NL—33—St. Louis vs Arizona, 2002
4-game series
AL—56—Anaheim vs New York, 2002
NL—51—Atlanta vs Colorado, 1995
5-game series
AL—63—Seattle vs New York, 1995
NL—58—Houston vs Atlanta, 2004

**Most hits by both clubs, series**
3-game series
NL—61—San Diego 32, St. Louis 29, 2005
AL—60—Boston 36, Anaheim 24, 2004
4-game series
AL—94—Anaheim 56, New York 38, 2002
NL—92—Atlanta 51, Colorado 41, 1995
5-game series
AL—113—Seattle 63, New York 50, 1995
NL—106—Houston 58, Atlanta 48, 2004

**Fewest hits, series**
3-game series
AL—13—Texas vs New York, 1998
NL—14—Los Angeles vs Atlanta, 1996
4-game series
NL—22—Houston vs San Diego, 1998
AL—26—Cleveland vs Boston, 1998
Minnesota vs New York, 2003
5-game series
NL—29—St. Louis vs Arizona, 2001
AL—38—Boston vs Oakland, 2003
Oakland vs Boston, 2003

**Fewest hits by both clubs, series**
3-game series
NL—30—Atlanta 16, Los Angeles 14, 1996
AL—37—New York 23, Texas 14, 1999
4-game series
NL—49—San Diego 27, Houston 22, 1998
AL—60—Boston 34, Cleveland 26, 1998
5-game series
NL—66—Arizona 37, St. Louis 29, 2001
AL—76—Boston 38, Oakland 38, 2003

**Most hits by pinch-hitters, series**
NL—5—Atlanta vs Colorado, 1995 (4-game series)
AL—2—Oakland vs Minnesota, 2002 (5-game series)

**Most hits by pinch-hitters on both clubs, series**
NL—6—Atlanta 5, Colorado 1, 1995 (4-game series)
AL—2—many games

### GAME AND INNING

**Most hits, game**
AL—24—Boston vs Cleveland, Oct 10, 1999
NL—17—Houston vs Atlanta, Oct 11, 2004

**Most hits by both clubs, game**
AL—32—Boston 24, Cleveland 8, Oct 10, 1999
NL—26—Atlanta 15, Colorado 11, Oct 7, 1995
Houston 17, Atlanta 9, Oct 11, 2004

**Most hits by pinch-hitters, game**
NL—2—Atlanta vs Colorado, Oct 4, 1995
Arizona vs St. Louis, Oct 10, 2001
St. Louis vs Arizona, Oct 12, 2001
San Diego vs St. Louis, Oct 4, 2005
[2—Atlanta vs Colorado, Oct 6, 1995, 10 inn
Houston vs Atlanta, Oct 8, 1999, 12 inn
San Francisco vs New York, Oct 5, 2000, 10 inn]
AL—1—many clubs

**Most hits by pinch-hitters on both clubs, game**
NL—3—Atlanta 2, Colorado 1, Oct 4, 1995
St. Louis 2, Arizona 1, Oct 12, 2001
[3—San Francisco 2, New York 1, Oct 5, 2000, 10 inn]
AL—2—Boston 1, Chicago 1, Oct 4, 2005

**Fewest hits, game**
NL—1—Houston vs Atlanta, Oct 6, 1999
San Francisco vs New York, Oct 8, 2000
AL—2—Seattle vs Baltimore, Oct 5, 1997
Texas vs New York, Oct 5, 1999
New York vs Oakland, Oct 13, 2001

**Fewest hits by both clubs, game**
AL—7—Cleveland 4, Boston 3, Oct 4, 1995
NL—6—Florida 3, San Francisco 3, Sept 30, 2003

**Most players with one or more hits, game**
NL—10—Atlanta vs Colorado, Oct 4, 1995
Florida vs San Francisco, Oct 1, 2003
San Diego vs St. Louis, Oct 4, 2005
[10—Atlanta vs Houston, Oct 7, 2004, 11 inn

Atlanta vs Houston, Oct 9, 2005, 18 inn]
AL—10—Boston vs Anaheim, Oct 6, 2004
Los Angeles vs New York, Oct 7, 2005

**Most players with one or more hits by both clubs, game**
AL—17—Anaheim 9, New York 8, Oct 2, 2002
NL—17—San Francisco 9, Atlanta 8, Oct 2, 2002
Florida 10, San Francisco 7, Oct 1, 2003
San Diego 10, St. Louis 7, Oct 4, 2005
[17—Atlanta 10, Houston 7, Oct 9, 2005, 18 inn]

**Most hits, inning**
AL—10—Anaheim vs New York, Oct 5, 2002, 5th
NL—7—Atlanta vs Houston, Oct 9, 1999, 6th

**Most hits by pinch-hitters, inning**
NL—2—Houston vs Atlanta, Oct 8, 1999, 7th
Arizona vs St. Louis, Oct 10, 2001, 8th
AL—1—many clubs

**Most hits by both clubs, inning**
AL—11—Anaheim 10, New York 1, Oct 5, 2002, 5th
NL—9—Houston 5, Atlanta 4, Oct 10, 2004, 8th

**Most consecutive hits, inning (consecutive at-bats)**
AL—6—Boston vs Cleveland, Oct 10, 1999, 2nd
NL—6—Atlanta vs Houston, Oct 9, 1999, 6th (1 SH during streak)

**Most consecutive hits, inning (consecutive plate appearances)**
AL—6—Boston vs Cleveland, Oct 10, 1999, 2nd
NL—5—Atlanta vs Houston, Oct 9, 1999, 6th
Houston vs Atlanta, Oct 11, 2004, 7th

## SINGLES

**Most singles, total series**
AL—277—New York; 11 series, 47 G
NL—263—Atlanta; 11 series, 42 G

**Most singles, series**
3-game series
NL—27—St. Louis vs Arizona, 2002
AL—25—Boston vs Anaheim, 2004
4-game series
AL—37—Anaheim vs New York, 2002
NL—36—Atlanta vs Colorado, 1995
5-game series
AL—45—Seattle vs New York, 1995
NL—36—Houston vs Atlanta, 2004

**Most singles by both clubs, series**
3-game series
NL—44—Los Angeles 26, Cincinnati 18, 1995
San Diego 25, St. Louis 19, 2005
AL—42—Boston 25, Anaheim 17, 2004
4-game series
NL—64—Atlanta 36, Colorado 28, 1995
AL—64—Anaheim 37, New York 27, 2002
5-game series
AL—72—Seattle 45, New York 27, 1995
NL—71—Atlanta 36, Houston 35, 2004

**Fewest singles, series**
3-game series
NL—7—Los Angeles vs Atlanta, 1996
AL—8—Chicago vs Seattle, 2000
4-game series
AL—7—Cleveland vs Boston, 1998
NL—13—Los Angeles vs St. Louis, 2004
5-game series
NL—20—St. Louis vs Arizona, 2001
AL—23—Cleveland vs Boston, 1999

**Fewest singles by both clubs, series**
3-game series
NL—15—Atlanta 8, Los Angeles 7, 1996
AL—23—New York 13, Texas 10, 1998
4-game series
AL—30—Boston 23, Cleveland 7, 1998
NL—33—San Diego 17, Houston 16, 1998
5-game series
NL—49—Arizona 29, St. Louis 20, 2001
AL—51—Boston 28, Cleveland 23, 1999

**Most singles by pinch-hitters, series**
NL—3—Atlanta vs Colorado, 1995 (4-game series)
San Diego vs St. Louis, 1996 (3-game series)
Arizona vs St. Louis, 2001 (5-game series)
San Diego vs St. Louis, 2005 (3-game series)
AL—1—many clubs

**Most singles by pinch-hitters on both clubs, series**
NL—5—Arizona 3, St. Louis 2, 2001 (5-game series)
AL—1—many times

**Most singles, game**
NL—13—Atlanta vs Houston, Oct 9, 1999
AL—12—Seattle vs New York, Oct 7, 1995
Boston vs Cleveland, Oct 10, 1999
Anaheim vs New York, Oct 2, 2002
Anaheim vs New York, Oct 5, 2002
Los Angeles vs New York, Oct 7, 2005

**Most singles by both clubs, game**
AL—22—Anaheim 12, New York 10, Oct 2, 2002
NL—19—Atlanta 10, Colorado 9, Oct 7, 1995

**Fewest singles, game**
NL—0—Atlanta vs Houston, Sept 30, 1997
Houston vs Atlanta, Oct 6, 1999
San Francisco vs New York, Oct 8, 2000
AL—0—New York vs Oakland, Oct 13, 2001

**Fewest singles by both clubs, game**
NL—2—New York 2, San Francisco 0, Oct 8, 2000
AL—4—Boston 3, Cleveland 1, Oct 4, 1995
Boston 2, Cleveland 2, Oct 3, 1998
Boston 3, Cleveland 1, Oct 11, 1999
Oakland 4, New York 0, Oct 13, 2001

**Most singles, inning**
AL—8—Anaheim vs New York, Oct 5, 2002, 5th
NL—7—Atlanta vs Houston, Oct 9, 1999, 6th

**Most singles by both clubs, inning**
AL—8—Anaheim 8, New York 0, Oct 5, 2002, 5th
NL—7—Atlanta 7, Houston 0, Oct 9, 1999, 6th
Atlanta 4, Houston 3, Oct 10, 2004, 2nd

## DOUBLES

**Most doubles, total series**
AL—89—New York; 11 series, 47 G
NL—57—Atlanta; 11 series, 42 G

**Most doubles, series**
3-game series
AL—9—Boston vs Chicago, 2005
NL—7—Los Angeles vs Atlanta, 1996
St. Louis vs San Diego, 2005
4-game series
AL—12—Boston vs Cleveland, 1998
NL—12—Houston vs Atlanta, 2005
5-game series
AL—17—Boston vs Cleveland, 1999
NL—12—Houston vs Atlanta, 2004

**Most doubles by both clubs, series**
3-game series
AL—15—Boston 9, Chicago 6, 2005
NL—11—St. Louis 7, San Diego 4, 2005
4-game series
NL—23—Houston 12, Atlanta 11, 2005
AL—18—Cleveland 12, Boston 6, 1998
5-game series
AL—28—Minnesota 15, Oakland 13, 2002
NL—16—Houston 12, Atlanta 4, 2004

**Fewest doubles, series**
3-game series
AL—2—Texas vs New York, 1999
NL—1—Houston vs Atlanta, 1997
4-game series
NL—2—Houston vs Atlanta, 1999
AL—3—Minnesota vs New York, 2003
5-game series
NL—3—St. Louis vs Arizona, 2001
AL—6—Seattle vs New York, 1995
Cleveland vs New York, 1997
Boston vs Oakland, 2003

**Fewest doubles by both clubs, series**
3-game series
NL—4—Atlanta 2, Chicago 2, 1998
St. Louis 2, Arizona 2, 2002
AL—6—Cleveland 4, Boston 2, 1995
4-game series
NL—7—Atlanta 5, Houston 2, 1999
Los Angeles 4, St. Louis 3, 2004
AL—8—New York 4, Texas 4, 1996
5-game series
NL—8—Arizona 5, St. Louis 3, 2001
AL—13—New York 7, Cleveland 6, 1997

**Most doubles by pinch-hitters, series**
NL—2—Atlanta vs Colorado, 1995 (4-game series)
AL—1—Baltimore vs Seattle, 1997 (4-game series)
Boston vs Cleveland, 1999 (5-game series)
Oakland vs New York, 2000 (5-game series)
Oakland vs Minnesota, 2002 (5-game series)
Boston vs Chicago, 2005 (3-game series)

**Most doubles by pinch-hitters on both clubs, series**
NL—2—Atlanta 2, Colorado 0, 1995 (4-game series)
Atlanta 1, Chicago 1, 2003 (5-game series)
Atlanta 1, Houston 1, 2005 (4-game series)
AL—1—Baltimore 1, Seattle 0, 1997 (4-game series)
Boston 1, Cleveland 0, 1999 (5-game series)
Oakland 1, New York 0, 2000 (5-game series)
Oakland 1, Minnesota 0, 2002 (5-game series)
Boston 1, Chicago 0, 2005 (3-game series)

**Most doubles, game**
AL—7—Boston vs Cleveland, Oct 10, 1999
NL—7—Houston vs Atlanta, Oct 8, 2005

**Most doubles by both clubs, game**
AL—9—Cleveland 5, Seattle 4, Oct 10, 2001
NL—9—Houston 7, Atlanta 2, Oct 8, 2005

**Most doubles, inning**
NL—3—Cincinnati vs Los Angeles, Oct 3, 1995, 5th
AL—4—New York vs Minnesota, Oct 5, 2003, 4th

## TRIPLES

**Most triples, total series**
AL—4—Cleveland; 6 series, 26 G
NL—4—Atlanta; 11 series, 42 G

**Most triples, series**
AL—3—Los Angeles vs New York, 2005 (5-game series)
NL—2—Atlanta vs San Francisco, 2002 (5-game series)

**Most triples by both clubs, series**
3-game series
AL—2—Chicago 2, Seattle 0, 2000
NL—1—St. Louis 1, San Diego 0, 1996
St. Louis 1, Arizona 0, 2002
4-game series
NL—2—Florida 1, San Francisco 1, 2003
Los Angeles 1, St. Louis 1, 2004
AL—none
5-game series
AL—3—Minnesota 2, Oakland 1, 2002
Los Angeles 3, New York 0, 2005
NL—2—Atlanta 2, San Francisco 0, 2002

**Fewest triples, series**
AL-NL—0—many clubs

**Fewest triples by both clubs, series**
AL-NL—0—many series

**Most triples by pinch-hitters, series**
NL—1—San Diego vs Houston, 1998 (4-game series)
San Francisco vs Florida, 2003 (4-game series)
AL—none

**Most triples, game**
AL—2—Los Angeles vs New York, Oct 7, 2005
[2—Chicago vs Seattle, Oct 3, 2000, 10 inn]
NL—1—many clubs
[1—many clubs in extra inn]

**Most triples by both clubs, game**
NL—1—many games
AL—2—Los Angeles 2, New York 0, 2005
[2—Chicago 2, Seattle 0, Oct 3, 2000, 10 inn]

**Most triples, inning**
AL-NL—1—many clubs

## HOME RUNS

### SERIES

**Most home runs, total series**
AL—50—New York; 11 series, 47 G
NL—47—Atlanta; 11 series, 42 G

**Most grand slams, total series**
NL—3—Atlanta; 11 series, 42 G
AL—2—Cleveland; 6 series; 26 G

**Most home runs, series**
3-game series
AL—7—Chicago vs Boston, 2005
NL—6—St. Louis vs Atlanta, 2000
Atlanta vs Houston, 2001
4-game series
AL—9—Baltimore vs Cleveland, 1996
Anaheim vs New York, 2002
NL—7—Atlanta vs Colorado, 1995
Los Angeles vs St. Louis, 2004
St. Louis vs Los Angeles, 2004
5-game series
AL—11—New York vs Seattle, 1995
Seattle vs New York, 1995
NL—11—Houston vs Atlanta, 2004

**Most home runs by both clubs, series**
3-game series
AL—10—Chicago 7, Boston 3, 2005
NL—9—Atlanta 6, Houston 3, 2001
4-game series
AL—16—Anaheim 9, New York 7, 2002
NL—14—Los Angeles 7, St. Louis 7, 2004
5-game series
AL—22—New York 11, Seattle 11, 1995
NL—18—Houston 11, Atlanta 7, 2004

**Fewest home runs, series**
3-game series
AL—0—Texas vs New York, 1998
NL—0—Los Angeles vs Atlanta, 1996
4-game series
NL—0—San Francisco vs Florida, 2003
AL—2—Minnesota vs New York, 2003
New York vs Minnesota, 2003
5-game series
AL—1—New York vs Oakland, 2000
Oakland vs Boston, 2003
NL—3—Arizona vs St. Louis, 2001
Atlanta vs Chicago, 2003

**Fewest home runs by both clubs, series**
3-game series
AL—3—New York 2, Texas 1, 1999
NL—5—Atlanta 5, Los Angeles 0, 1996
Atlanta 4, Chicago 1, 1998
St. Louis 3, Arizona 2, 2002
4-game series
NL—2—Florida 2, San Francisco 0, 2003
AL—4—Minnesota 2, New York 2, 2003
5-game series
AL—3—Oakland 2, New York 1, 2000
NL—7—Chicago 4, Atlanta 3, 2003

**Most grand slams, series**
NL—2—Atlanta vs Chicago, 1998
AL—1—many clubs

**Most home runs by pinch-hitters, series**
AL—1—New York vs Oakland, 2001 (5-game series)
Boston vs Oakland, 2003 (5-game series)
NL—1—many clubs

### GAME AND INNING

**Most home runs, game**
AL—5—Chicago vs Boston, Oct 4, 2005
NL—5—St. Louis vs Los Angeles, Oct 5, 2004

**Most home runs by both clubs, game**
AL—6—New York 4, Anaheim 2, Oct 1, 2002
Anaheim 4, New York 2, Oct 2, 2002
[6—New York 4, Seattle 2, Oct 4, 1995, 15 inn]
NL—7—St. Louis 5, Los Angeles 1, Oct 5, 2004

**Most grand slams, game**
AL-NL—many clubs

**Most grand slams by both teams, game**
AL—1—many games
NL—1—many games
[2—Atlanta 1, Houston 1, Oct 9, 2005]

**Most consecutive games with one or more home runs, total series**
NL—10—Atlanta, last G vs Colorado, 1995 (2 HR), all 3 G vs Los Angeles, 1996 (5 HR), all 3 G vs Houston, 1997 (3 HR), all 3 G vs Chicago, 1998 (4 HR)
AL—6—Cleveland, all 3 G vs Boston, 1995 (4 HR), first 3 G vs Baltimore, 1996 (4 HR)
New York, last 3 G vs Texas, 1996 (4 HR), first 3 G vs Cleveland, 1997 (6 HR)

**Most consecutive games with one or more home runs, series**
AL—5—New York vs Seattle, Oct 3, 4, 6, 7, 8, 1995 (11 HR)
Seattle vs New York, Oct 3, 4, 6, 7, 8, 1995 (11 HR)
NL—4—Colorado vs Atlanta, Oct 3, 4, 6, 7, 1995 (6 HR)
San Diego vs Houston, Sept 29, Oct 1, 3, 4, 1998 (5 HR)
St. Louis vs Arizona, Oct 10, 12, 13, 14, 2001 (6 HR)
San Francisco vs Atlanta, Oct 3, 5, 6, 7, 2002 (6 HR)

**Most home runs, inning**
AL—3—New York vs Cleveland, Sept 30, 1997, 6th (consec)
NL—2—many clubs

**Most home runs by both clubs, inning**
AL—3—New York 3, Cleveland 0, Sept 30, 1997, 6th
Boston 2, Anaheim 1, Oct 5, 2004, 4th
NL—3—Atlanta 2, San Francisco 1, Oct 3, 2002, 2nd

**Most consecutive home runs, inning**
AL—3—New York (Raines Sr., Jeter, O'Neill) vs Cleveland, Sept 30, 1997, 6th
NL—2—Atlanta (Lopez, Castilla) vs San Francisco, Oct 3, 2002, 2nd
Los Angeles (Green, Bradley) vs St. Louis, Oct 7, 2004, 4th

## TOTAL BASES

**Most total bases, total series**
AL—661—New York; 11 series, 47 G
NL—577—Atlanta; 11 series, 42 G

**Most total bases, series**
3-game series
AL—55—Chicago vs Boston, 2005
NL—54—Atlanta vs Houston, 2001
4-game series
AL—93—Anaheim vs New York, 2002
NL—80—Atlanta vs Colorado, 1995
5-game series
AL—105—Boston vs Cleveland, 1999
NL—103—Houston vs Atlanta, 2004

**Most total bases by both clubs, series**
3-game series
AL—98—Chicago 55, Boston 43, 2005
NL—92—Cincinnati 50, Los Angeles 42, 1995
4-game series
AL—156—Anaheim 93, New York 63, 2002
NL—146—Atlanta 80, Colorado 66, 1995
5-game series
AL—199—Seattle 104, New York 95, 1995
NL—178—Houston 103, Atlanta 75, 2004

**Fewest total bases, series**
3-game series
AL—16—Texas vs New York, 1998
NL—20—Houston vs Atlanta, 1997
4-game series
NL—30—Houston vs San Diego, 1998
AL—37—Minnesota vs New York, 2003
5-game series
NL—49—Atlanta vs Chicago, 2003
AL—51—Oakland vs Boston, 2003

**Fewest total bases by both clubs, series**
3-game series
NL—53—Atlanta 33, Houston 20, 1997
AL—56—New York 37, Texas 19, 1999
4-game series
NL—78—San Diego 48, Houston 30, 1998
AL—90—New York 53, Minnesota 37, 2003
5-game series
NL—101—Arizona 51, St. Louis 50, 2001
AL—115—Oakland 59, New York 56, 2000

**Most total bases, game**
AL—45—Boston vs Cleveland, Oct 10, 1999
NL—30—Houston vs Atlanta, Oct 11, 2004

**Most total bases by both clubs, game**
AL—57—Boston 45, Cleveland 12, Oct 10, 1999
NL—45—Houston 30, Atlanta 15, Oct 11, 2004
[45—Atlanta 25, Houston 20, Oct 9, 2005, 18 inn]

**Fewest total bases, game**
NL—2—San Francisco vs New York, Oct 8, 2000
AL—3—Boston vs Cleveland, Oct 4, 1995
Texas vs New York, Oct 2, 1998
Texas vs New York, Oct 5, 1999

**Fewest total bases by both clubs, game**
NL—7—San Francisco 4, Florida 3, Sept 30, 2003
AL—10—Seattle 6, Chicago 4, Oct 6, 2000

**Most total bases, inning**
AL—14—New York vs Cleveland, Sept 30, 1997, 6th
Anaheim vs New York, Oct 5, 2002, 5th
NL—11—St. Louis vs Los Angeles, Oct 5, 2004, 3rd
Houston vs Atlanta, Oct 6, 2004, 3rd

**Most total bases by both clubs, inning**
AL—16—Anaheim 14, New York 2, Oct 5, 2002, 5th
NL—14—Atlanta 8, Colorado 6, Oct 7, 1995, 3rd

## EXTRA-BASE HITS

**Most extra-base hits, total series**
AL—141—New York; 11 series, 47 G
NL—108—Atlanta; 11 series, 42 G

**Most extra-base hits, series**
3-game series
AL—13—Chicago vs Boston, 2005
NL—12—Atlanta vs Houston, 2001
4-game series
AL—19—Cleveland vs Boston, 1998
Anaheim vs New York, 2002
NL—17—Atlanta vs Houston, 2005
5-game series
AL—28—Boston vs Cleveland, 1999
NL—23—Houston vs Atlanta, 2004

**Most extra-base hits by both clubs, series**
3-game series
AL—25—Chicago 13, Boston 12, 2005
NL—17—Florida 9, San Francisco 8, 1997
St. Louis 11, Atlanta 6, 2000
Atlanta 12, Houston 5, 2001
St. Louis 10, San Diego 7, 2005
4-game series
NL—33—Atlanta 17, Houston 16, 2005
AL—30—Cleveland 19, Boston 11, 1998
Oakland 18, New York 12, 2001
Anaheim 19, New York 11, 2002
5-game series
AL—43—Boston 28, Cleveland 15, 1999
NL—35—Houston 23, Atlanta 12, 2004

**Fewest extra-base hits, series**
3-game series
AL—3—Texas vs New York, 1998
Texas vs New.York, 1999
NL—2—Houston vs Atlanta, 1997
4-game series
NL—6—Houston vs San Diego, 1998
Atlanta vs Houston, 1999
AL—6—Minnesota vs New York, 2003
5-game series
NL—8—Arizona vs St. Louis, 2001
Atlanta vs Chicago, 2003
AL—10—Oakland vs Boston, 2003

**Fewest extra-base hits by both clubs, series**
3-game series
NL—9—Atlanta 7, Houston 2, 1997
Atlanta 6, Chicago 3, 1998
AL—12—New York 9, Texas 3, 1999
4-game series
NL—13—Houston 7, Atlanta 6, 1999
AL—17—New York 11, Minnesota 6, 2003
5-game series
NL—17—St. Louis 9, Arizona 8, 2001
AL—24—New York 13, Cleveland 11, 1997
New York 13, Oakland 11, 2000
Boston 14, Oakland 10, 2003

**Most extra-base hits, game**
AL—12—Boston vs Cleveland, Oct 10, 1999 (7 doubles, 1 triple, 4 HR)
NL—8—Houston vs Atlanta, Oct 8, 2005 (7 doubles, 1 HR)
[8—Atlanta vs Houston, Oct 9, 2005, 18 inn (6 doubles, 2 HR)]

**Most extra-base hits by both clubs, game**
AL—14—Boston 12 (7 doubles, 1 triple, 4 HR), Cleveland 2 (1 double, 1 HR), Oct 10, 1999
NL—10—St. Louis 7 (4 doubles, 3 HR), Atlanta 3 (2 doubles, 1 HR), Oct 5, 2000
St. Louis 6 (1 double, 5 HR), Los Angeles 4 (2 doubles, 1 triple, 1 HR), Oct 5, 2004
Houston 8 (7 doubles, 1 HR), Atlanta 2 (2 doubles), Oct 8, 2005
[12—Atlanta 8 (6 doubles, 2 HR), Houston 4 (1 double, 3 HR), Oct 9, 2005, 18 inn]

## RUNS BATTED IN

**Most runs batted in, total series**
AL—206—New York; 11 series, 47 G
NL—184—Atlanta; 11 series, 42 G

**Most runs batted in, series**
3-game series
AL—24—Chicago vs Boston, 2005
NL—23—St. Louis vs Atlanta, 2000
4-game series
AL—31—Anaheim vs New York, 2002
NL—24—Atlanta vs Colorado, 1995
Houston vs Atlanta, 2005
5-game series
AL—47—Boston vs Cleveland, 1999
NL—36—Houston vs Atlanta, 2004

**Most runs batted in by both clubs, series**
3-game series
AL—35—Boston 23, Anaheim 12, 2004
NL—32—St. Louis 23, Atlanta 9, 2000
4-game series
AL—55—Anaheim 31, New York 24, 2002
NL—45—Houston 24, Atlanta 21, 2005
5-game series
AL—78—Boston 47, Cleveland 31, 1999
NL—56—Houston 36, Atlanta 20, 2004

**Fewest runs batted in, series**
3-game series
AL—1—Texas vs New York, 1998
Texas vs New York, 1999
NL—4—Chicago vs Atlanta, 1998
4-game series
NL—7—Houston vs San Diego, 1998
AL—5—Minnesota vs New York, 2003
5-game series
NL—10—Arizona vs St. Louis, 2001
AL—13—Milwaukee vs New York, 1995

**Fewest runs batted in by both clubs, series**
3-game series
AL—9—New York 8, Texas 1, 1998

NL—15—Atlanta 10, Los Angeles 5, 1996
4-game series
NL—20—San Diego 13, Houston 7, 1998
AL—20—New York 15, Minnesota 5, 2003
5-game series
NL—22—St. Louis 12, Arizona 10, 2001
AL—27—New York 16, Oakland 11, 2001

**Most runs batted in by pinch-hitters, series**
NL—5—Cincinnati vs Los Angeles, 1995 (3-game series)
AL—2—Baltimore vs Seattle, 1997 (4-game series)
Boston vs Oakland, 2003 (5-game series)

**Most runs batted in by pinch-hitters on both clubs, series**
NL—5—Cincinnati 5, Los Angeles 0, 1995 (3-game series)
AL—3—Baltimore 2, Seattle 1, 1997 (4-game series)
Boston 2, Oakland 1, 2003 (5-game series)

**Most runs batted in, game**
AL—23—Boston vs Cleveland, Oct 10, 1999
NL—12—Houston vs Atlanta, Oct 11, 2004

**Most runs batted in by both clubs, game**
AL—30—Boston 23, Cleveland 7, Oct 10, 1999
NL—15—Houston 12, Atlanta 3, Oct 11, 2004

**Fewest runs batted in by both clubs, game**
NL—0—Atlanta 0, Houston 0, Oct 10, 2001
AL—1—New York 1, Texas 0, Sept 29, 1998
Oakland 1, New York 0, Oct 11, 2001
New York 1, Oakland 0, Oct 13, 2001

**Most runs batted in, inning**
AL—8—Anaheim vs New York, Oct 5, 2002, 5th
NL—6—New York vs Arizona, Oct 8, 1999, 6th

**Most runs batted in by both clubs, inning**
AL—9—Anaheim 8, New York 1, Oct 5, 2002, 5th
NL—7—Atlanta 4, Colorado 3, Oct 7, 1995, 3rd

**Most runs batted in by pinch-hitters, inning**
NL—4—Cincinnati vs Los Angeles, Oct 6, 1995, 6th
AL—2—Baltimore vs Seattle, Oct 1, 1997, 6th

## BASES ON BALLS

**Most bases on balls, total series**
AL—178—New York; 11 series, 47 G
NL—167—Atlanta; 11 series, 42 G

**Most bases on balls, series**
3-game series
AL—20—Boston vs Anaheim, 2004
NL—19—Florida vs San Francisco, 1997
4-game series
NL—21—New York vs Arizona, 1999
Atlanta vs Houston, 2005
AL—20—Texas vs New York, 1996
5-game series
AL—32—New York vs Seattle, 1995
NL—22—Atlanta vs San Francisco, 2002

**Most bases on balls by both clubs, series**
3-game series
AL—31—Boston 20, Anaheim 11, 2004
NL—25—Florida 19, San Francisco 6, 1997
4-game series
NL—40—Florida 20, San Francisco 20, 2003
Atlanta 21, Houston 19, 2005
AL—33—Texas 20, New York 13, 1996
5-game series
AL—57—New York 32, Seattle 25, 1995
NL—41—Atlanta 21, Chicago 20, 2003

**Fewest bases on balls, series**
3-game series
NL—4—San Diego vs St. Louis, 1996
Atlanta vs Houston, 2001
AL—4—Texas vs New York, 1998
4-game series
AL—7—Seattle vs Baltimore, 1997
Anaheim vs New York, 2002
Minnesota vs New York, 2004
NL—9—Colorado vs Atlanta, 1995
San Diego vs Houston, 1998
5-game series
AL—5—Los Angeles vs New York, 2005
NL—12—St. Louis vs Arizona, 2001

**Fewest bases on balls by both clubs, series**
3-game series
AL—11—New York 7, Texas 4, 1998
NL—12—Houston 8, Atlanta 4, 2001
4-game series
NL—20—Houston 11, San Diego 9, 1998
AL—22—New York 15, Minnesota 7, 2004
5-game series
AL—22—Milwaukee 13, New York 9, 1995
NL—26—Los Angeles 13, Houston 13, 1995

**Most bases on balls by pinch-hitters, series**
NL—3—Houston vs Atlanta, 1999 (4-game series)
AL—2—Seattle vs New York, 1995 (5-game series)

**Most bases on balls by pinch-hitters on both clubs, series**
AL—2—Seattle 2, New York 0, 1995 (5-game series)
Baltimore 1, Cleveland 1, 1996 (4-game series)
Baltimore 1, Seattle 1, 1997 (4-game series)
NL—3—Houston 2, San Diego 1, 1998 (4-game series)
New York 2, Arizona 1, 1999 (4-game series)
Houston 3, Atlanta 0, 1999 (4-game series)

**Most bases on balls, game**
NL—10—Atlanta vs Houston, Oct 1, 1997
AL—8—New York vs Seattle, Oct 7, 1995
New York vs Los Angeles, Oct 9, 2005
[10—New York vs Seattle, Oct 8, 1995, 11 inn]

**Most bases on balls by both clubs, game**
NL—16—Atlanta 10, Houston 6, Oct 1, 1997
[17—Atlanta 11, Houston 6, Oct 9, 2005, 18 inn]
AL—14—Cleveland 9, Boston 5, Oct 10, 1999
[17—Oakland 10, Boston 7, Oct 1, 2003, 12 inn]

**Fewest bases on balls, game**
AL-NL—0—many clubs

**Fewest bases on balls by both clubs, game**
NL—1—Atlanta 1, Los Angeles 0, Oct 3, 1996
AL—1—New York 1, Texas 0, Sept 30, 1998
Minnesota 1, New York, 1, Oct 8, 2004

**Most bases on balls by pinch-hitters, game**
AL—1—many clubs
[2—Seattle vs New York, Oct 8, 1995, 11 inn]
NL—1—many clubs
[1—many clubs in extra innings]

**Most bases on balls by pinch-hitters on both clubs, game**
NL—2—San Diego 1, Houston 1, Oct 3, 1998
AL—1—many clubs
[2—Seattle 2, New York 0, Oct 8, 1995, 11 inn]

**Most bases on balls, inning**
NL—5—Florida vs San Francisco, Oct 1, 1997, 4th
AL—5—Cleveland vs Boston, Oct 10, 1999, 5th

**Most bases on balls by both clubs, inning**
NL—6—Florida 5, San Francisco 1, Oct 1, 1997, 4th
AL—5—Baltimore 4, Cleveland 1, Oct 2, 1996, 8th
Cleveland 3, Baltimore 2, Oct 4, 1996, 7th
Cleveland 5, Boston 0, Oct 10, 1999, 5th
Oakland 3, Boston 2, Oct 1, 2003, 12th

**Most bases on balls by pinch-hitters, inning**
AL—2—Seattle vs New York, Oct 8, 1995, 8th
NL—1—many clubs

## STRIKEOUTS

**Most strikeouts, total series**
AL—312—New York; 11 series, 47 G
NL—317—Atlanta; 11 series, 42 G

**Most strikeouts, series**
3-game series
NL—29—Los Angeles vs Atlanta, 1996
AL—28—Anaheim vs Boston, 2004
4-game series
NL—49—Houston vs San Diego, 1998
AL—42—Seattle vs Baltimore, 1997
5-game series
AL—48—Seattle vs Cleveland, 2001
NL—45—San Francisco vs Atlanta, 2002
Atlanta vs Houston, 2004

**Most strikeouts by both clubs, series**
3-game series
NL—53—Los Angeles 29, Atlanta 24, 1996
AL—51—Texas 27, New York 24, 1998
Anaheim 28, Boston 23, 2004
4-game series
NL—81—Houston 49, San Diego 32, 1998
AL—72—Baltimore 40, Cleveland 32, 1996
5-game series
AL—91—Seattle 48, Cleveland 43, 2001
NL—80—Atlanta 42, Chicago 38, 2003

**Fewest strikeouts, series**
3-game series
AL—11—Chicago vs Boston, 2005
NL—16—Florida vs San Francisco, 1997
Houston vs Atlanta, 2001

4-game series
AL—18—Anaheim vs New York, 2002
NL—20—Los Angeles vs St. Louis, 2004
5-game series
AL—22—Cleveland vs New York, 1997
NL—29—Arizona vs St. Louis, 2001

**Fewest strikeouts by both clubs, series**
3-game series
AL—25—Boston 14, Chicago 11, 2005
NL—34—Atlanta 18, Houston 16, 2001
San Diego 17, St. Louis 17, 2005
4-game series
AL—43—New York 25, Anaheim 18, 2002
NL—46—St. Louis 26, Los Angeles 20, 2004
5-game series
AL—48—New York 26, Cleveland 22, 1997
NL—67—St. Louis 38, Arizona 29, 2002

**Most strikeouts by pinch-hitters, series**
NL—4—Los Angeles vs Atlanta, 1996 (3-game series)
Houston vs Atlanta, 1997 (3-game series)
San Francisco vs Atlanta, 2002 (5-game series)
AL—3—New York vs Seattle, 1995 (5-game series)
Seattle vs Baltimore, 1997 (4-game series)
Oakland vs Minnesota, 2002 (5-game series)
Oakland vs Boston, 2003 (5-game series)

**Most strikeouts by pinch-hitters on both clubs, series**
NL—6—Los Angeles 4, Atlanta 2, 1996 (3-game series)
AL—5—Oakland 3, Minnesota 2, 2002 (5-game series)
Oakland 3, Boston 2, 2003 (5-games series)

**Most strikeouts, game**
NL—17—Houston vs San Diego, Sept 29, 1998
[18—Atlanta vs Houston, Oct 8, 1999, 12 inn]
AL—13—Baltimore vs Seattle, Oct 4, 1997
Cleveland vs Seattle, Oct 9, 2001
Cleveland vs Seattle, Oct 15, 2001
[23—Baltimore vs Cleveland, Oct 5, 1996, 12 inn]

**Most strikeouts by both clubs, game**
NL—28—Houston 17, San Diego 11, Sept 29, 1998
[30—Atlanta 18, Houston 12, Oct 8, 1999, 12 inn
Atlanta 16, Houston 14, Oct 9, 2005, 18 inn]
AL—25—Cleveland 13, Seattle 12, Oct 9, 2001
[33—Baltimore 23, Cleveland 10, Oct 5, 1996, 12 inn]

**Fewest strikeouts, game**
NL—2—Atlanta vs Houston, Oct 5, 1999
Arizona vs New York, Oct 8, 1999
Arizona vs St. Louis, Oct 13, 2001
Houston vs Atlanta, Oct 11, 2004
AL—1—Cleveland vs New York, Oct 4, 1997
Los Angeles vs New York, Oct 5, 2005

**Fewest strikeouts by both clubs, game**
AL—3—New York 2, Cleveland 1, Oct 4, 1997
NL—7—New York 5, Arizona 2, Oct 8, 1999
St. Louis 5, Arizona 2, Oct 13, 2001

**Most strikeouts by pinch-hitters, game**
NL—3—Houston vs Atlanta, Oct 3, 1997
AL—2—Minnesota vs Oakland, Oct 5, 2002

**Most consecutive strikeouts, game**
AL—5—Seattle vs New York, Oct 8, 1995 (3 in 6th, 2 in 7th)
Chicago vs Seattle, Oct 4, 2000 (2 in 8th, 3 in 9th)
Boston vs Oakland, Oct 2, 2003 (3 in 4th, 2 in 5th)
NL—6—Chicago vs Atlanta, Oct 1, 2003 (3 in 1st, 3 in 2nd)

**Most strikeouts, inning**
AL-NL—3—many clubs

**Most strikeouts by both clubs, inning**
AL—6—Seattle 3, Chicago 3, Oct 4, 2000, 9th
NL—5—Atlanta 3, Houston 2, Oct 3, 1997, 2nd
San Francisco 3, Florida 2, Sept 30, 2003, 3rd
Chicago 3, Atlanta 2, Sept 30, 2003, 7th

**Most strikeouts by pinch-hitters, inning**
NL—2—Houston vs Atlanta, Oct 3, 1997, 8th
AL—1—many clubs

## SACRIFICE HITS

**Most sacrifice hits, total series**
NL—19—St. Louis; 6 series, 21 G
AL—17—New York; 11 series, 47 G

**Most sacrifice hits, series**
NL—8—St. Louis vs Arizona, 2001 (5-game series)
AL—5—Los Angeles vs New York, 2005 (5-game series)

**Most sacrifice hits by both clubs, series**
NL—14—St. Louis 8, Arizona 6, 2001 (5-game series)
AL—7—Texas 4, New York 3, 1996 (4-game series)

**Fewest sacrifice hits, series**
AL-NL—0—many clubs

**Fewest sacrifice hits by both clubs, series**
NL—0—Atlanta 0, Houston 0, 1997 (3-game series)
AL—1—Boston 1, Cleveland 0, 1998 (4-game series)
New York 1, Texas 0, 1999 (3-game series)
Cleveland 1, Boston 0, 1999 (5-game series)
Oakland 1, Boston 1, 2003 (5-game series)
Anaheim 1, Boston 0, 2004 (3-game series)

**Most sacrifice hits, game**
AL—3—Seattle vs Chicago, Oct 6, 2000
NL—4—Houston vs Atlanta, Oct 5, 2005

**Most sacrifice hits by both clubs, game**
AL—4—Seattle 3, Chicago 1, Oct 6, 2000
[4—Texas 2, New York 2, Oct 2, 1996, 12 inn]
NL—4—Houston 4, Atlanta 0, Oct 5, 2005
[5—Chicago 3, Atlanta 2, Oct 1, 1998, 10 inn]

**Most sacrifice hits, inning**
AL—2—Los Angeles vs New York, Oct 5, 2005, 7th
Chicago vs Boston, Oct 7, 2005, 9th
NL—1—many clubs

## SACRIFICE FLIES

**Most sacrifice flies, total series**
AL—18—New York; 11 series, 47 G
NL—11—Atlanta; 11 series, 42 G

**Most sacrifice flies, series**
AL—4—Cleveland vs Boston, 1999 (5-game series)
Minnesota vs New York, 2004 (4-game series)
NL—4—Houston vs Atlanta, 2005 (4-game series)

**Most sacrifice flies by both clubs, series**
AL—7—Cleveland 4, Boston 3, 1999 (5-game series)
NL—5—Houston 4, Atlanta 1, 2005 (4-game series)

**Most sacrifice flies, game**
AL—2—Cleveland vs Boston, Oct 10, 1999
New York vs Oakland, Oct 8, 2000
Oakland vs New York, Oct 8, 2000
Oakland vs New York, Oct 10, 2001
New York vs Anaheim, Oct 4, 2002
NL—2—Atlanta vs Houston, Oct 6, 1999
San Francisco vs Florida, Oct 4, 2003
Houston vs Atlanta, Oct 8, 2005

**Most sacrifice flies by both clubs, game**
AL—4—New York 2, Oakland 2, Oct 8, 2000
NL—2—Atlanta 2, Houston 0, Oct 6, 1999
San Francisco 2, Florida 0, Oct 4, 2003
Houston 2, Atlanta 0, Oct 8, 2005
[2—Houston 1, Atlanta 1, Oct 9, 2005, 18 inn]

**Most sacrifice flies, inning**
AL—2—New York vs Oakland, Oct 8, 2000, 1st
Oakland vs New York, Oct 8, 2000, 4th
NL—1—many clubs

## HIT BY PITCH

**Most hit by pitch, total series**
AL—22—New York; 11 series, 47 G
NL—12—Atlanta; 11 series; 42 G

**Most hit by pitch, series**
AL—5—Chicago vs Boston, 2005 (3-game series)
NL—4—Houston vs San Diego, 1998 (4-game series)
Atlanta vs Houston, 2005 (4-game series)

**Most hit by pitch by both clubs, series**
AL—7—New York 4, Oakland 3, 2001 (5-game series)
NL—7—Houston 4, Atlanta 3, 2005 (4-game series)

**Most hit by pitch, game**
AL—3—Chicago vs Boston, Oct 4, 2005
NL—3—San Diego vs St. Louis, Oct 6, 2005

**Most hit by pitch by both clubs, game**
AL—3—Baltimore 2, Cleveland 1, Oct 1, 1996
New York 2, Oakland 1, Oct 15, 2001
Anaheim 2, New York 1, Oct 4, 2002
Chicago 3, Boston 0, Oct 4, 2005
NL—3—Florida 2, San Francisco 1, Oct 4, 2003
Houston 2, Atlanta 1, Oct 5, 2005
San Diego 3, St. Louis 0, Oct 6, 2005

**Most hit by pitch, inning**
AL—2—Minnesota vs New York, Oct 8, 2004, 9th
Chicago vs Boston, Oct 4, 2005, 1st
NL—2—St. Louis vs Los Angeles, Oct 7, 2004, 5th

# INDIVIDUAL BASERUNNING

## STOLEN BASES

**Most stolen bases, career**
ML—13—Kenny Lofton, Cleveland AL, 1995, 1996; Atlanta NL, 1997; Cleveland AL, 1998, 1999, 2001; San Francisco NL, 2002; Chicago NL, 2003; New York AL, 2004; 9 series, 35G
AL—10—Omar Vizquel, Cleveland, 1995-1999, 2001; 6 series, 26 G
NL—9—Rafael Furcal, Atlanta, 2000, 2002-2005; 6 series, 22 G

**Most stolen bases, series**
3-game series
NL—4—Barry Larkin, Cincinnati, 1995
AL—3—Jose Valentin, Chicago, 2000
Johnny Damon, Boston, 2004
4-game series
NL—6—Rickey Henderson, New York, 1999
AL—5—Kenny Lofton, Cleveland, 1996
5-game series
AL—4—Omar Vizquel, Cleveland, 1997
NL—3—Kenny Lofton, Chicago, 2003
Rafael Furcal, Atlanta, 2004

**Most stolen bases, game**
AL—3—Kenny Lofton, Cleveland, Oct 4, 1995
NL—3—Rickey Henderson, New York, Oct 6, 1999

**Most stolen bases by pinch-runner, game**
AL—1—Chone Figgins, Anaheim, Oct 2, 2002, 8th
NL—none

**Most times stealing home, game**
AL-NL—none

**Most stolen bases, inning**
AL—2—Kenny Lofton, Cleveland, Oct 2, 1996, 6th
NL—2—Barry Larkin, Cincinnati, Oct 3, 1995, 9th
Reggie Sanders, Cincinnati, Oct 4, 1995, 9th
Barry Larkin, Cincinnati, Oct 6, 1995, 1st
Rafael Furcal, Atlanta, Oct 9, 2005, 11th

## CAUGHT STEALING

**Most caught stealing, career**
ML—3—Marquis Grissom, Atlanta NL, 1995; Cleveland AL, 1997; San Francisco NL, 2003; 4 series, 16 G
Kenny Lofton, Cleveland AL, 1995, 1996; Atlanta NL, 1997; Cleveland 1998, 1999, 2001; San Francisco NL, 2002; Chicago NL, 2003; New York AL, 2004; 9 series, 35 G
AL—3—Bernie Williams, New York, 1995-2005; 11 series, 42 G
NL—2—many players

**Most caught stealing, series**
NL—2—Luis Alicea, St. Louis, 1996 (0 SB; 3-game series)
Sammy Sosa, Chicago, 1998 (0 SB; 3-game series)
AL—2—Omar Vizquel, Cleveland, 1996 (4 SB; 4-game series)
Ichiro Suzuki, Seattle, 2001 (1 SB; 5-game series)
Scott Podsednik, Chicago, 2005 (1 SB; 3-game series)
Adam Kennedy, Los Angeles, 2005 (0 SB; 5-game series)

**Most caught stealing, game**
AL-NL—1—many players

**Most caught stealing by pinch-runner, game**
AL-NL—none

**Most caught stealing, inning**
AL-NL—1—many players

# CLUB BASERUNNING

## STOLEN BASES

**Most stolen bases, total series**
NL—32—Atlanta; 11 series, 42 G
AL—27—Cleveland; 6 series, 26 G

**Most stolen bases, series**
3-game series
NL—9—Cincinnati vs Los Angeles, 1995
AL—4—Chicago vs Seattle, 2000
4-game series
AL—11—Cleveland vs Baltimore, 1996
NL—8—New York vs Arizona, 1999
5-game series
NL—7—Atlanta vs Houston, 2004
AL—6—Cleveland vs New York, 1997

**Most stolen bases by both clubs, series**
3-game series
NL—9—Cincinnati 9, Los Angeles 0, 1995
AL—6—Chicago 4, Seattle 2, 2000
4-game series
AL—12—Cleveland 11, Baltimore 1, 1996
NL—8—New York 8, Arizona 0, 1999
5-game series
NL—10—Atlanta 7, Houston 3, 2004
AL—9—Cleveland 6, New York 3, 1997

**Fewest stolen bases, series**
AL-NL—0—many clubs

**Fewest stolen bases by both clubs, series**
3-game series
AL—1—Texas 1, New York 0, 1999
NL—1—Atlanta 1, Houston 0, 2001
4-game series
AL—2—New York 1, Texas 1, 1996
NL—1—Houston 1, San Diego 0, 1998
5-game series
AL—3—Minnesota 2, Oakland 1, 2002
NL—3—Atlanta 2, San Francisco 1, 2002

**Most stolen bases, game**
AL—5—Cleveland vs Baltimore, Oct 4, 1996
NL—4—Cincinnati vs Los Angeles, Oct 4, 1995
New York vs Arizona, Oct 6, 1999
Atlanta vs Houston, Oct 10, 2004

**Most stolen bases by both clubs, game**
AL—6—Cleveland 5, Baltimore 1, Oct 4, 1996
NL—4—Cincinnati 4, Los Angeles 0, Oct 4, 1995
St. Louis 2, San Diego 2, Oct 1, 1996
New York 4, Arizona 0, Oct 6, 1999
St. Louis 3, Atlanta 1, Oct 7, 2000
Atlanta 4, Houston 0, Oct 10, 2004

**Longest game with no stolen bases, one club**
AL—15 inn—New York vs Seattle, Oct 4, 1995
Seattle vs New York, Oct 4, 1995
NL—13 inn—San Francisco vs New York, Oct 7, 2000

**Longest game with no stolen bases, both clubs**
AL—15 inn—New York 0, Seattle 0, Oct 4, 1995
NL—10 inn—Arizona 0, New York 0, Oct 9, 1999

**Most stolen bases, inning**
NL—3—Cincinnati vs Los Angeles, Oct 4, 1995, 9th
AL—2—many clubs

## CAUGHT STEALING

**Most caught stealing, series**
3-game series
NL—3—many clubs
AL—2—New York vs Texas, 1998
Chicago vs Boston, 2005
4-game series
AL—4—Minnesota vs New York, 2004
NL—2—Atlanta vs Colorado, 1995
New York vs San Francisco, 2000
St. Louis vs Los Angeles, 2004
5-game series
AL—4—New York vs Oakland, 2001
Los Angeles vs New York, 2005
NL—2—Arizona vs St. Louis, 2001
Chicago vs Atlanta, 2003
Houston vs Atlanta, 2004

**Most caught stealing by both clubs, series**
3-game series
NL—4—Atlanta 3, Los Angeles 1, 1996
Atlanta 3, St. Louis 1, 2000
Atlanta 3, Houston 1, 2001
AL—3—New York 2, Texas 1, 1998
4-game series
AL—6—Minnesota 4, New York 2, 2004

NL—3—Houston 2, Atlanta 1, 2004
5-game series
AL—6—Los Angeles 4, New York 2, 2005
NL—3—Houston 2, Atlanta 1, 2004

**Fewest caught stealing, series**
AL-NL—0—many clubs

**Fewest caught stealing by both clubs, series**
3-game series
NL—0—Cincinnati 0, Los Angeles 0, 1995
San Diego 0, St. Louis 0, 2005
AL—0—New York 0, Texas 0, 1999
4-game series
AL—0—Anaheim 0, New York 0, 2002
NL—0—Atlanta 0, Houston 0, 2005
5-game series
AL—0—Minnesota 0, Oakland 0, 2002
NL—2—Arizona 2, St. Louis 0, 2001
San Francisco 1, Atlanta 1, 2002
Chicago 2, Atlanta 0, 2003

**Most caught stealing, game**
AL—2—many clubs
[3—Minnesota vs New York, Oct 9, 2004, 11 inn]
NL—2—Atlanta vs St. Louis, Oct 3, 2000
Atlanta vs Houston, Oct 9, 2001
St. Louis vs San Diego, Oct 1, 1996
[3—Atlanta vs Los Angeles, Oct 2, 1996, 10 inn]

**Most caught stealing by both clubs, game**
AL—2—many games
[3—Minnesota 3, New York 0, Oct 9, 2004, 11 inn]
NL—2—St. Louis 2, San Diego 0, Oct 1, 1996
Atlanta 2, St. Louis 0, Oct 3, 2000
Atlanta 1, St. Louis 1, Oct 7, 2000
Atlanta 2, Houston 0, Oct 9, 2001
[4—Atlanta 3, Los Angeles 1, Oct 2, 1996, 10 inn]

**Most caught stealing, inning**
AL—2—New York vs Texas, Oct 4, 1996, 4th
NL—1—many clubs

## LEFT ON BASE

**Most left on base, total series**
AL—357—New York; 11 series, 47 G
NL—311—Atlanta; 11 series, 42 G

**Most left on base, series**
3-game series
AL—31—Boston vs Anaheim, 2004
NL—30—Los Angeles vs Cincinnati, 1995
4-game series
AL—45—Baltimore vs Cleveland, 1996
NL—38—Atlanta vs Houston, 2005
5-game series
AL—49—Seattle vs New York, 1995
NL—43—Atlanta vs Houston, 2004

**Most left on base by both clubs, series**
3-game series
AL—55—Boston 28, Cleveland 27, 1995
Boston 31, Anaheim 24, 2004
NL—51—San Diego 28, St. Louis 23, 2005
4-game series
NL—71—San Francisco 36, Florida 35, 2003
AL—65—Baltimore 36, Cleveland 29, 1996
5-game series
AL—94—Seattle 49, New York 45, 1995
NL—78—Atlanta 41, Chicago 37, 2003

**Fewest left on base, series**
3-game series
AL—11—Chicago vs Boston, 2005
NL—14—Atlanta vs Los Angeles, 1996
Los Angeles vs Atlanta, 1996
Atlanta vs Houston, 1997
Atlanta vs Houston, 2001
4-game series
NL—20—Arizona vs New York, 1999
AL—21—Seattle vs Baltimore, 1997
5-game series
AL—25—Boston vs Cleveland, 1999
NL—30—St. Louis vs Arizona, 2001

**Fewest left on base by both clubs, series**
3-game series
NL—28—Atlanta 14, Los Angeles 14, 1996
AL—31—New York 16, Texas 15, 1998
4-game series
AL—46—Baltimore 25, Seattle 21, 1997
NL—48—Houston 25, San Diego 23, 1998
5-game series
AL—61—Cleveland 36, Boston 25, 1999
NL—69—Atlanta 36, San Francisco 33, 2002

**Most left on bases, game**
NL—12—Atlanta vs Colorado, Oct 4, 1995
Atlanta vs San Francisco, Oct 7, 2002
Atlanta vs Chicago, Oct 4, 2003
Atlanta vs Houston, Oct 6, 2004
[18—San Francisco vs Florida, Oct 3, 2003, 11 inn
Atlanta vs Houston, Oct 9, 2005, 18 inn]
AL—12—Boston vs Cleveland, Oct 6, 1995
New York vs Seattle, Oct 7, 1995
Oakland vs Minnesota, Oct 1, 2002
[13—Seattle vs New York, Oct 8, 1995, 11 inn
Baltimore vs Cleveland, Oct 5, 1996, 12 inn
Boston vs Oakland, Oct 1, 2003, 12 inn]

**Most left on base by both clubs, game**
AL—22—Boston 12, Cleveland 10, Oct 6, 1995
New York 12, Seattle 10, Oct 7, 1995
[25—Boston 13, Oakland 12, Oct 1, 2003, 12 inn]
NL—22—Atlanta 11, St. Louis 11, Oct 3, 2000
[30—San Francisco 18, Florida 12, Oct 3, 2003, 11 inn]

**Fewest left on base, game**
AL—0—New York vs Anaheim, Oct 1, 2002
NL—1—Los Angeles vs Atlanta, Oct 3, 1996
Houston vs Atlanta, Oct 6, 1999

**Fewest left on base by both clubs, game**
NL—3—Atlanta 2, Los Angeles 1, Oct 3, 1996
AL—6—Cleveland 3, Boston 3, Oct 2, 1998

**Most left on base, shutout defeat**
AL—8—New York vs Oakland, Oct 11, 2001 (lost 2-0)
NL—5—St. Louis vs Arizona, Oct 9, 2001 (lost 1-0)
Houston vs Atlanta, Oct 10, 2001 (lost 1-0)
St. Louis vs Los Angeles, Oct 9, 2004 (lost 4-0)

# INDIVIDUAL PITCHING

## GAMES

**Most games, career**
AL—27—Mariano Rivera, New York, 1995-2005; 11 series
NL—15—John Smoltz, Atlanta, 1995-1999, 2001-2005; 10 series

**Most games, series**
3-game series
AL-NL—3—many pitchers
4-game series
AL—4—Jesse Orosco, Baltimore, 1996
Steve Karsay, New York, 2002
Mariano Rivera, New York, 2004
NL—4—Mike Munoz, Colorado, 1995
Bruce Ruffin, Colorado, 1995
Trevor Hoffman, San Diego, 1998
Chris Reitsma, Atlanta, 2005
5-game series
AL—5—Scott Williamson, Boston, 2003
NL—5—Kevin Gryboski, Atlanta, 2003, 2004

**Most consecutive games, series**
AL—5—Scott Williamson, Boston, 2003
NL—5—Kevin Gryboski, Atlanta, 2003, 2004

## GAMES STARTED

**Most games started, career**
ML—12—Andy Pettitte, New York AL, 1995-2003; Houston NL, 2005; 10 series
AL—11—Andy Pettitte, New York, 1995-2003; 9 series
NL—10—Greg Maddux, Atlanta, 1995-2003; 9 series

**Most opening games started, career**
NL—5—Greg Maddux, Atlanta, 1995, 1997, 1999-2001
AL—3—David Cone, New York, 1995-1997

Roger Clemens, Boston, 1995; New York, 2000, 2001
Pedro Martinez, Boston, 1998, 1999, 2003

**Most games started, series**
AL-NL—2—many pitchers

## GAMES RELIEVED

**Most games as relief pitcher, career**
AL—27—Mariano Rivera, New York, 1995-2005; 11 series
NL—13—Kevin Gryboski, Atlanta, 2002-2004; 3 series

**Most games as relief pitcher, seriesr**
AL—5—Scott Williamson, Boston, 2003 (5-game series)
NL—5—Kevin Gryboski, Atlanta, 2003, 2004 (both 5-game series)

## COMPLETE GAMES

**Most complete games, career**
NL—2—Curt Schilling, Arizona, 2001, 2002; 2 series
AL—1—many pitchers

**Most complete games, series**
NL—2—Curt Schilling, Arizona, 2001 (5-game series)
AL—1—many pitchers

## INNINGS

**Most innings pitched, career**
ML—74.0—Andy Pettitte, New York AL, 1995-2003; Houston NL, 2005; 10 series, 12 G
AL—67.0—Andy Pettitte, New York, 1995-2003; 9 series, 11 G
NL—66.0—Greg Maddux, Atlanta, 1995-2003; 9 series, 11 G

**Most innings pitched, series**
3-game series
AL—8.0—Erik Hanson, Boston, 1995
Orlando Hernandez, New York, 1999
Todd Stottlemyre, Texas, 1998
David Wells, New York, 1998
NL—9.0—John Smoltz, Atlanta, 1996, 1997
Greg Maddux, Atlanta, 1997
Kevin Tapani, Chicago, 1998
4-game series
NL—14.2—Kevin Brown, San Diego, 1998
AL—14.0—Mike Mussina, Baltimore, 1997
5-game series
NL—18.0—Curt Schilling, Arizona, 2001
AL—15.2—David Cone, New York, 1995

**Most innings pitched, game**
AL-NL—9.0—many pitchers

## GAMES WON

**Most games won, career**
NL—7—John Smoltz, Atlanta, 1995-1999, 2001-2005; 10 series, 15 G
AL—4—David Wells, Baltimore, 1996; New York, 1997, 1998, 2002, 2003; Boston, 2005; 6 series, 7 G
Andy Pettitte, New York, 1995-2003; 9 series, 11 G
Pedro Martinez, Boston, 1998-2000, 2003; 4 series, 6 G
Mike Mussina, Baltimore, 1996, 1997; New York, 2001-2005; 7 series, 9 G

**For a complete list of pitchers with three or more victories, see page 297.**

**Most games won without a defeat, career**
NL—7—John Smoltz, Atlanta, 1995-1999, 2001-2005; 10 series, 15 G
AL—4—Pedro Martinez, Boston, 1998, 1999, 2003, 2004; 4 series, 6 G

**Most opening games won, career**
AL—2—David Wells, Baltimore, 1996; New York, 1998
NL—2—John Smoltz, Atlanta, 1996, 1998

**Most consecutive games won, career**
ML—4—David Wells, Cincinnati NL, Oct 6, 1995; Baltimore AL, Oct 1, 1996; New York AL, Oct 4, 1997; Sept 29, 1998
NL—4—Greg Maddux, Atlanta, Oct 7, 1995; Oct 3, 1996; Sept 30, 1997; Oct 3, 1998
John Smoltz, Atlanta, Oct 2, 1996; Oct 3, 1997; Sept 30, 1998; Oct 9, 1999
AL—3—David Wells, Baltimore, Oct 1, 1996; New York, Oct 4, 1997; Sept 29, 1998
Mike Mussina, Baltimore, Oct 1, 5, 1997; New York, Oct 13, 2001

**Most consecutive complete games won, career**
NL—2—Curt Schilling, Arizona, Oct 9, 14, 2001
AL—none more than one

**Most games won, series**
AL-NL—2—many pitchers

**Most games won by relief pitcher, series**
NL—2—Alejandro Pena, Atlanta, 1995 (4-game series)
Jeff Fassero, St. Louis, 2002 (3-game series)
AL—2—Armando Benitez, Baltimore, 1996 (4-game series)
Francisco Rodriguez, Anaheim, 2002 (4-game series)

## SAVES

**Most saves, career**
AL—15—Mariano Rivera, New York, 1995-2005; 11 series, 27 G
NL—5—Mark Wohlers, Atlanta, 1995-1997; 3 series, 7 G

**Most saves, series**
3-game series
NL—3—Dennis Eckersley, St. Louis, 1996
Mark Wohlers, Atlanta, 1996
AL—2—Mariano Rivera, New York, 1998, 1999
Kazuhiro Sasaki, Seattle, 2000
Bobby Jenks, Chicago, 2005
4-game series
AL—3—Mike Jackson, Cleveland, 1998
NL—2—Mark Wohlers, Atlanta, 1995
Trevor Hoffman, San Diego, 1998
5-game series
AL—3—Mariano Rivera, New York, 2000
NL—2—Steve Kline, St. Louis, 2001
Robb Nen, San Francisco, 2002

## GAMES LOST

**Most games lost, career**
ML—7—Randy Johnson, Seattle AL, 1995, 1997; Houston NL, 1998; Arizona NL, 1999, 2001, 2002; New York, 2005 (2 in AL, 5 in NL); 7 series, 11 G
NL—5—Randy Johnson, Houston, 1998; Arizona, 1999, 2001, 2002; 4 series, 5 G
AL—4—Tim Wakefield, Boston, 1995, 1998, 1999, 2003, 2005; 5 series, 7 G

**Most games lost without a win, career**
ML—3—Bret Saberhagen, Colorado NL, 1995; Boston, 1998, 1999 (2 in AL, 1 in NL); 3 series, 4 G
AL—4—Tim Wakefield, Boston, 1995, 1998, 1999, 2003, 2005; 5 series, 7 G
NL—3—Mike Hampton, Houston, 1997-1999; New York, 2000; Atlanta, 2003; 5 series, 6 G

**Most consecutive games lost, career**
ML—7—Randy Johnson, Seattle AL, Oct 1, 5, 1997; Houston NL, Sept 29, Oct 5, 1998; Arizona NL, Oct 5, 2000, Oct 10, 2001, Oct 1, 2002
AL—3—Roger Clemens, New York, Oct 3, 7, 2000, Oct 10, 2001
Aaron Sele, Texas, Oct 2, 1998, Oct 5, 1999; Seattle, Oct 13, 2001
NL—2—many pitchers

**Most games lost, series**
NL—2—Randy Johnson, Houston, 1998 (4-game series)
Tom Glavine, Atlanta, 2002 (5-game series)
Jaret Wright, Atlanta, 2004 (5-game series)
AL—2—many pitchers

## RUNS

**Most runs allowed, career**
ML—36—Randy Johnson, Seattle AL, 1995, 1997; Houston NL, 1998; Arizona NL, 1999, 2001, 2002; New York, 2005; 7 series, 11 G
AL—32—Andy Pettitte, New York, 1995-2003; 9 series, 11 G
NL—30—Tom Glavine, Atlanta, 1995-2002; 8 series, 9 G

**Most runs allowed, series**
3-game series
AL—8—Jarrod Washburn, Anaheim, 2004
Matt Clement, Boston, 2005
NL—8—Jake Peavy, San Diego, 2005
4-game series
AL—9—Charles Nagy, Cleveland, 1996
NL—8—Odalis Perez, Los Angeles, 2004
Tim Hudson, Atlanta, 2005
5-game series
NL—13—Tom Glavine, Atlanta, 2002
AL—11—Andy Pettitte, New York, 1997
Bret Saberhagen, Boston, 1999
Tim Hudson, Oakland, 2002

**Most runs allowed, game**
AL—8—Steve Reed, Cleveland, Oct 10, 1999
Charles Nagy, Cleveland, Oct 11, 1999
Paul Abbott, Seattle, Oct 13, 2001
David Wells, New York, Oct 5, 2002
Matt Clement, Boston, Oct 4, 2005
NL—8—Jake Peavy, San Diego, Oct 4, 2005

**Most runs allowed, inning**
AL—7—David Wells, New York, Oct 5, 2002, 5th
NL—6—Greg Maddux, Atlanta, Oct 3, 2000, 1st

## EARNED RUNS

**Most earned runs allowed, career**
ML—34—Randy Johnson, Seattle AL, 1995, 1997; Houston NL, 1998; Arizona NL, 1999, 2001, 2002; New York, 2005; 7 series, 11 G
AL—32—Andy Pettitte, New York, 1995-2003; 9 series, 11 G
NL—29—Tom Glavine, Atlanta, 1995-2002; 8 series, 9 G

**Most earned runs allowed, series**
3-game series
AL—8—Matt Clement, Boston, 2005
NL—8—Jake Peavy, San Diego, 2005

4-game series
AL—9—Charles Nagy, Cleveland, 1996
NL—8—Odalis Perez, Los Angeles, 2004
Tim Hudson, Atlanta, 2005
5-game series
NL—13—Tom Glavine, Atlanta, 2002
AL—11—Andy Pettitte, New York, 1997
Bret Saberhagen, Boston, 1999

**Most earned runs allowed, game**
AL—8—Steve Reed, Cleveland, Oct 10, 1999
Paul Abbott, Seattle, Oct 13, 2001
David Wells, New York, Oct 5, 2002
Matt Clement, Boston, Oct 4, 2005
NL—8—Jake Peavy, San Diego, Oct 4, 2005

**Most earned runs allowed, inning**
AL—7—David Wells, New York, Oct 5, 2002, 5th
NL—5—Odalis Perez, Los Angeles, Oct 5, 2004, 3rd
Russ Ortiz, Atlanta, Oct 10, 2004, 2nd

## EARNED-RUN AVERAGE

**Lowest earned-run average, career (30 or more IP)**
AL—0.43—Mariano Rivera, New York, 1995-2005; 11 series, 27 G (42 IP)
NL—2.19—Matt Morris, St. Louis, 2000-2002, 2004, 2005; 5 series, 7 G (37 IP)

## SHUTOUTS AND SCORELESS INNINGS

**Most shutouts, series**
NL—1—Bobby J. Jones, New York, 2000
Curt Schilling, Arizona, 2001
Jason Schmidt, San Francisco, 2003
AL—none

**For a complete list of shutouts, see page 295.**

**Most consecutive scoreless innings, career**
AL—17—David Wells, New York, Oct 4 (7), 1997; Sept 29 (8), 1998; Oct 5 (2), 2002
NL—16—Curt Schilling, Arizona, Oct 9 (9), Oct 14 (7), 2001

**Most consecutive scoreless innings, series**
NL—16—Curt Schilling, Arizona, Oct 9 (9), Oct 14 (7), 2001
AL—14—Bartolo Colon, Cleveland, Oct 9 (8), Oct 14 (6), 2001

## HITS

**Most hits allowed, career**
ML—76—Andy Pettitte, New York AL, 1995-2003; Houston NL, 2005; 10 series, 12 G
AL—72—Andy Pettitte, New York, 1995-2003; 9 series, 11 G
NL—70—Greg Maddux, Atlanta, 1995-2003; 9 series, 11 G

**Most consecutive hitless innings, career**
AL—8—Mike Mussina, Baltimore, Oct 5, 1997 (5 inn); New York, Oct 13, 2001 (3 inn)
Pedro Martinez, Oct 6 (1), Oct 11 (6), 1999; Oct 1 (1), 2003
NL—7—Kevin Millwood, Atlanta, Oct 6, 1999

**Most hits allowed, series**
3-game series
AL—9—Curt Schilling, Boston, 2004
NL—10—Ramon Martinez, Los Angeles, 1995
Randy Johnson, Arizona, 2002
4-game series
NL—19—Greg Maddux, Atlanta, 1995
AL—15—David Wells, Baltimore, 1996
Charles Nagy, Cleveland, 1996
5-game series
NL—17—Tom Glavine, Atlanta, 2002
AL—15—David Cone, New York, 1995
Andy Pettitte, New York, 1997, 2000

**Most hits allowed, game**
AL—10—John Burkett, Texas, Oct 1, 1996
Andy Pettitte, New York, Oct 8, 2000
David Wells, New York, Oct 5, 2002
Tim Hudson, Oakland, Oct 1, 2003
Carlos Silva, Minnesota, Oct 8, 2004
NL—11—Carlos Zambrano, Chicago, Oct 1, 2003

**Most consecutive hitless innings, game**
NL—7—Kevin Millwood, Atlanta, Oct 6, 1999 (3rd-9th inn)
AL—6—Pedro Martinez, Boston, Oct 11, 1999 (4th-9th inn)

**Fewest hits allowed, game**
NL—1—Kevin Millwood, Atlanta, Oct 6, 1999
Bobby J. Jones, New York, Oct 8, 2000
AL—4—Erik Hanson, Boston, Oct 4, 1995

**Most hits allowed, inning**
AL—7—David Wells, New York, Oct 5, 2002, 5th
NL—5—Greg Maddux, Atlanta, Oct 3, 2000, 1st
Randy Johnson, Arizona, Oct 1, 2002, 4th
Russ Ortiz, Atlanta, Oct 10, 2004, 2nd

**Most consecutive hits allowed, inning (consecutive at-bats)**
AL—5—Bartolo Colon, Cleveland, Oct 10, 1999, 2nd
Freddy Garcia, Seattle, Oct 9, 2001, 4th
David Wells, New York, Oct 5, 2002, 5th
NL—4—Bret Saberhagen, Colorado, Oct 7, 1995, 3rd
Greg Maddux, Atlanta, Oct 3, 2000, 1st
Tom Glavine, Atlanta, Oct 2, 2002, 2nd
Tom Glavine, Atlanta, Oct 2, 2002, 4th
Kirk Rueter, San Francisco, Oct 3, 2002, 2nd (includes SH)

**Most consecutive hits allowed, inning (consecutive plate appearances)**
AL—5—Bartolo Colon, Cleveland, Oct 10, 1999, 2nd
David Wells, New York, Oct 5, 2002, 5th
NL—4—Bret Saberhagen, Colorado, Oct 7, 1995, 3rd
Greg Maddux, Atlanta, Oct 3, 2000, 1st
Tom Glavine, Atlanta, Oct 2, 2002, 2nd
Tom Glavine, Atlanta, Oct 2, 2002, 4th

## DOUBLES, TRIPLES AND HOME RUNS

**Most doubles allowed, game**
NL—5—Jorge Sosa, Atlanta, Oct 8, 2005
AL—4—many pitchers

**Most triples allowed, game**
AL—2—Freddy Garcia, Seattle, Oct 3, 2000
NL—1—many pitchers

**Most home runs allowed, career**
ML—13—Randy Johnson, Seattle AL, 1995, 1997; Houston NL, 1998; Arizona NL, 1999, 2001, 2002; New York AL, 2005 (6 in AL, 7 in NL); 7 series, 11 G
AL—9—Andy Pettitte, New York, 1995-2003; 9 series, 11 G
NL—8—John Smoltz, Atlanta, 1995-1999, 2001-2005; 10 series, 15 G

**Most home runs allowed, series**
3-game series
NL—3—Ismael Valdes, Los Angeles, 1996
AL—3—Matt Clement, Boston, 2005
Freddy Garcia, Chicago, 2005
4-game series
AL—4—Charles Nagy, Cleveland, 1996
NL—4—Odalis Perez, Los Angeles, 2004
5-game series
NL—5—Jaret Wright, Atlanta, 2004
AL—4—David Cone, New York, 1995
Rick Reed, Minnesota, 2002

**Most home runs allowed, game**
AL—4—Rick Reed, Minnesota, Oct 4, 2002
NL—3—Ismael Valdes, Los Angeles, Oct 3, 1996
Odalis Perez, Los Angeles, Oct 5, 2004
Jaret Wright, Atlanta, Oct 6, 2004
Jason Marquis, St. Louis, Oct 7, 2004

**Most grand slams allowed, game**
NL—1—Mark Guthrie, Los Angeles, Oct 6, 1995, 6th
Wilson Alvarez, San Francisco, Oct 3, 1997, 6th
Matt Karchner, Chicago, Sept 30, 1998, 7th
Rod Beck, Chicago, Oct 3, 1998, 8th
Bobby Chouinard, Arizona, Oct 5, 1999, 9th
Jake Peavy, San Diego, Oct 4, 2005, 5th
Brandon Backe, Houston, Oct 9, 2005, 3rd
Kyle Farnsworth, Atlanta, Oct 9, 2005, 8th
AL—1—John Wetteland, New York, Oct 7, 1995, 8th
Paul Shuey, Cleveland, Oct 1, 1996, 6th
Armando Benitez, Baltimore, Oct 4, 1996, 7th
Chad Ogea, Cleveland, Oct 4, 1997, 4th
John Wasdin, Boston, Oct 7, 1999, 4th
Charles Nagy, Cleveland, Oct 11, 1999, 3rd

**Most home runs allowed, inning**
AL-NL—2—many pitchers

## TOTAL BASES

**Most total bases allowed, career**
ML—126—Andy Pettitte, New York AL, 1995-2003; Houston NL, 2005; 10 series, 12 G
AL—114—Andy Pettitte, New York, 1995-2003; 9 series, 11 G
NL—96—Greg Maddux, Atlanta, 1995-2003; 9 series, 11 G

**Most total bases allowed, series**
3-game series
NL—19—Randy Johnson, Arizona, 2002
AL—17—Curt Schilling, Boston, 2004
Matt Clement, Boston, 2005
4-game series
NL—30—Greg Maddux, Atlanta, 1995
AL—28—Charles Nagy, Cleveland, 1996
5-game series
NL—31—Jaret Wright, Atlanta, 2004
AL—29—David Cone, New York, 1995

**Most total bases allowed, game**
AL—19—Paul Abbott, Seattle, Oct 13, 2001
Brad Radke, Minnesota, Oct 6, 2004
Randy Johnson, New York, Oct 7, 2005
NL—19—Randy Johnson, Arizona, Oct 1, 2002

## BASES ON BALLS

**Most bases on balls, career**
ML—30—Roger Clemens, Boston AL, 1995; New York AL, 1999-2003; Houston NL, 2004, 2005; 8 series, 12 G
NL—23—Tom Glavine, Atlanta, 1995-2002; 8 series, 9 G
Mike Hampton, Houston, 1997-1999; New York, 2000; Atlanta, 2003, 2004; 6 series, 8 G
AL—19—Roger Clemens, Boston, 1995; New York, 1999-2003; 6 series, 8 G

**Most bases on balls, series**
3-game series
NL—8—Mike Hampton, Houston, 1997
AL—6—Orlando Hernandez, New York, 1999
4-game series
NL—7—Kevin Brown, San Diego, 1998
Odalis Perez, Los Angeles, 2004
AL—6—Andy Pettitte, New York, 1996
Randy Johnson, Seattle, 1997
5-game series
AL—9—Andy Benes, Seattle, 1995
David Cone, New York, 1995
John Lackey, Los Angeles, 2005
NL—8—Russ Ortiz, San Francisco, 2002
Roger Clemens, Houston, 2004

**Most bases on balls, game**
NL—8—Mike Hampton, Houston, Oct 1, 1997
AL—6—David Cone, New York, Oct 3, 1995
Andy Benes, Seattle, Oct 8, 1995
Andy Pettitte, New York, Oct 2, 1996
Charles Nagy, Cleveland, Oct 4, 1997
Orlando Hernandez, New York, Oct 5, 1999

**Most bases on balls, inning**
AL—4—Andy Benes, Seattle, Oct 8, 1995, 6th
NL—4—Mike Hampton, Houston, Oct 1, 1997, 5th
Rick Ankiel, St. Louis, Oct 3, 2000, 3rd

**Most consecutive bases on balls, inning**
NL—4—Mike Hampton, Houston, Oct 1, 1997, 5th
AL—3—Tim Wakefield, Boston, Oct 6, 1995, 3rd
Andy Benes, Seattle, Oct 8, 1995, 6th

## STRIKEOUTS

**Most strikeouts, career**
ML—77—Randy Johnson, Seattle AL, 1995, 1997; Houston NL, 1998; Arizona NL, 1999, 2001, 2002; New York AL (36 in AL, 41 in NL); 7 series, 11 G
NL—53—John Smoltz, Atlanta, 1995-1999, 2001-2005; 10 series, 15 G
AL—43—Andy Pettitte, New York, 1995-2003; 9 series, 11 G

**Most strikeouts, series**
3-game series
NL—11—John Smoltz, Atlanta, 1997
AL—9—Rick Helling, Texas, 1998
David Wells, New York, 1998
4-game series
NL—21—Kevin Brown, San Diego, 1998
AL—16—Randy Johnson, Seattle, 1997
Mike Mussina, Baltimore, 1997
5-game series
NL—18—Curt Schilling, Arizona, 2001
Kerry Wood, Chicago, 2003
AL—16—Randy Johnson, Seattle, 1995

**Most strikeouts, game**
NL—16—Kevin Brown, San Diego, Sept 29, 1998
AL—13—Randy Johnson, Seattle, Oct 5, 1997

**For a complete list of pitchers with 10 or more strikeouts in a game, see page 297.**

**Most strikeouts by relief pitcher, game**
AL—8—Pedro Martinez, Boston, Oct 11, 1999; 6 IP
NL—6—Jose Cabrera, Houston, Oct 8, 1999; 2 IP

**Most consecutive strikeouts, game**
AL—5—David Cone, New York, Oct 8, 1995 (3 in 6th, 2 in 7th)
Barry Zito, Oakland, Oct 2, 2003 (3 in 4th, 2 in 5th)
NL—6—Mike Hampton, Atlanta, Oct 1, 2003 (3 in 1st, but not first batter, 3 in 2nd)

**Most consecutive strikeouts from start of game**
NL—2—Hideo Nomo, Los Angeles, Oct 5, 1996
Livan Hernandez, San Francisco, Oct 4, 2002
AL—2—Andy Benes, Seattle, Oct 8, 1995

**Most strikeouts, inning**
AL-NL—3—many pitchers

## HIT BATTERS, WILD PITCHES AND BALKS

**Most hit batters, career**
ML—4—Steve Reed, Colorado NL, 1995; Cleveland AL, 1998, 1999; Atlanta NL, 2001; 4 series, 8 G
AL—6—Tim Wakefield, Boston, 1995, 1998, 1999, 2003, 2005; 5 series, 7 G
NL—3—Kevin Brown, Florida, 1997; San Diego, 1998; 2 series, 3 G

**Most hit batters, series**
NL—3—Kevin Brown, San Diego, 1998
AL—2—many pitchers

**Most hit batters, game**
NL—2—Kevin Brown, San Diego, Oct 3, 1998
Jeff Weaver, Los Angeles, Oct 7, 2004
Mark Mulder, St. Louis, Oct 6, 2005
AL—2—many pitchers

**Most hit batters, inning**
AL—2—Felix Heredia, New York, Oct 8, 2004, 9th
Matt Clement, Boston, Oct 4, 2005, 1st
NL—2—Jeff Weaver, Los Angeles, Oct 7, 2004, 5th

**Most wild pitches, career**
ML—5—Roger Clemens, Boston AL, 1995; New York AL, 1999-2003; Houston NL, 2004, 2005; 8 series, 12 G
NL—5—Rick Ankiel, St. Louis, 2000; 1 series, 1 G
AL—3—David Cone, New York, 1995, 1996, 1997, 1998; 4 series, 5 G
Francisco Rodriguez, Anaheim, 2002, 2004; 2 series, 5 G

**Most wild pitches, series**
NL—5—Rick Ankiel, St. Louis, 2000 (3-game series)
AL—2—David Cone, New York, 1995 (5-game series)
Steve Karsay, Cleveland, 1999 (5-game series)
Francisco Rodriguez, Anaheim, 2004 (3-game series)

**Most wild pitches, game**
NL—5—Rick Ankiel, St. Louis, Oct 3, 2000, 2.2 IP
AL—2—Steve Karsay, Cleveland, Oct 10, 1999, 2 IP
Francisco Rodriguez, Anaheim, Oct 6, 2004, 2 IP
Kelvim Escobar, Los Angeles, Oct 9, 2005, 1.2 IP
[David Cone, New York, Oct 8, 1995, pitched 7.2 inn of 11-inn game]

**Most wild pitches, inning**
NL—5—Rick Ankiel, St. Louis, Oct 3, 2000, 3rd
AL—2—Kelvim Escobar, Los Angeles, Oct 9, 2005, 8th

**Most balks, game**
NL—1—Kevin Millwood, Atlanta, Oct 7, 2000
Andy Benes, St. Louis, Oct 5, 2002
[1—Kevin Tapani, Chicago, Oct 1, 1998, pitched 9 inn of 10-inn game]
AL—none

# CLUB PITCHING

## APPEARANCES

**Most appearances by pitchers, series**
3-game series
NL—16—Los Angeles vs Cincinnati, 1995
Atlanta vs St. Louis, 2000
AL—15—Chicago vs Seattle, 2000
4-game series
NL—24—Colorado vs Atlanta, 1995
AL—21—Cleveland vs Baltimore, 1996
5-game series
NL—27—Atlanta vs Houston, 2004
AL—22—Seattle vs New York, 1995

**Most appearances by pitchers of both clubs, series**
3-game series
NL—30—Atlanta 16, St. Louis 14, 2000
AL—28—Chicago 15, Seattle 13, 2000
4-game series
AL—40—Cleveland 21, Baltimore 19, 1996
NL—40—Colorado 24, Atlanta 16, 1995
Atlanta 20, Houston 20, 2005
5-game series
NL—49—Atlanta 27, Houston 22, 2004
AL—41—Seattle 22, New York 19, 1995
Boston 21, Cleveland 20, 1999
Oakland 21, Boston 20, 2003

## COMPLETE GAMES

**Most complete games, series**
NL—2—Atlanta vs Houston, 1997 (3-game series)
Arizona vs St. Louis, 2001 (5-game series)
AL—1—many teams

**Most complete games by both clubs, series**
NL—2—Atlanta 2, Houston 0, 1997 (3-game series)
Arizona 2, St. Louis 0, 2001 (5-game series)
AL—1—many series

## SAVES

**Most saves, series**
3-game series
NL—3—St. Louis vs San Diego, 1996
Atlanta vs Los Angeles, 1996
AL—2—New York vs Texas, 1998
New York vs Texas, 1999
Seattle vs Chicago, 2000
Chicago vs Boston, 2005
4-game series
AL—3—Cleveland vs Boston, 1998
NL—2—Atlanta vs Colorado, 1995
San Diego vs Houston, 1998
Atlanta vs Houston, 1999
5-game series
AL—3—New York vs Oakland, 2000
NL—2—St. Louis vs Arizona, 2001
San Francisco vs Atlanta, 2002

**Most saves by both clubs, series**
3-game series
NL—3—St. Louis 3, San Diego 0, 1996
Atlanta 3, Los Angeles 0, 1996
AL—2—New York 2, Texas 0, 1998
New York 2, Texas 0, 1999
Seattle 2, Chicago 0, 2000
Chicago 2, Boston 0, 2005
4-game series
NL—3—Atlanta 2, Colorado 1, 1995
AL—3—Cleveland 3, Boston 0, 1998
Anaheim 2, New York 1, 2002
New York 2, Minnesota 1, 2003
5-game series
AL—4—New York 3, Oakland 1, 2000
Oakland 2, New York 2, 2001
Los Angeles 2, New York 2, 2005
NL—3—St. Louis 2, Arizona 1, 2001

**Fewest saves by one and both clubs, series**
AL-NL—0—many clubs

## RUNS AND SHUTOUTS

**Most runs allowed, total series**
AL—188—New York; 11 series, 47 G
NL—182—Atlanta; 11 series, 42 G

**Most shutouts won, total series**
AL—7—New York; 11 series, 47 G
NL—1—many clubs

**For a complete list of shutouts, see page 295.**

**Most shutouts, series**
AL—2—New York vs Texas, 1998 (3-game series)
New York vs Texas, 1999 (3-game series)
NL—1—New York vs San Francisco, 2000 (4-game series)
Atlanta vs Houston, 2001 (3-game series)
Arizona vs St. Louis, 2001 (5-game series)
San Francisco vs Florida, 2003 (4-game series)
Los Angeles vs St. Louis, 2004 (4-game series)

**Most shutouts by both clubs, series**
AL—2—New York 2, Texas 0, 1998 (3-game series)
New York 2, Texas 0, 1999 (3-game series)
Oakland 1, New York 1, 2001 (5-game series)
NL—1—New York 1, San Francisco 0, 2000 (4-game series)
Atlanta 1, Houston 0, 2001 (3-game series)
Arizona 1, St. Louis 0, 2001 (5-game series)
San Francisco 1, Florida 0, 2003 (4-game series)
Los Angeles 1, St. Louis 0, 2004 (4-game series)

**Most consecutive shutouts won, series**
AL-NL—1—many clubs

**Largest score, shutout game**
AL—8-0—New York 8, Texas 0, Oct 5, 1999
NL—4-0—New York 4, San Francisco 0, Oct 8, 2000
Los Angeles 4, St. Louis 0, Oct 9, 2004

**Longest shutout game**
AL-NL—none more than 9 inn

**Most consecutive innings shutting out opponent, total series**
AL—25—New York vs Texas, Sept 30 (6th), 1998-Oct 7 (3rd), 1999
NL—18—New York vs San Francisco, Oct 7 (5th inn of 13-inn game)-Oct 8 (9th), 2000

**Most consecutive innings shutting out opponent, series**
AL—14—Boston vs Cleveland, Oct 3 (12th inn of 13-inn game)-Oct 6 (3rd), 1995
New York vs Texas, Oct 7 (5th)-Oct 9, (9th), 1999
Oakland vs New York, Oct 10 (9th)-Oct 13 (4th), 2001
NL—18—New York vs San Francisco, Oct 7 (5th inn of 13-inn game)-Oct 8 (9th), 2000

## WILD PITCHES AND BALKS

**Most wild pitches, series**
NL—5—St. Louis vs Atlanta, 2000 (3-game series)
AL—4—Oakland vs Minnesota, 2002 (5-game series)
Anaheim vs Boston, 2004 (3-game series)
Los Angeles vs New York, 2005 (5-game series)

**Most wild pitches by both clubs, series**
NL—6—St. Louis 5, Atlanta 1, 2000 (3-game series)
Chicago 4, Atlanta 2, 2003 (5-games series)
AL—5—Oakland 4, Minnesota 1, 2002 (5-game series)
Los Angeles 4, New York 1, 2005 (5-game series)

**Most balks, series**
NL—1—Chicago vs Atlanta, 1998 (3-game series)
Atlanta vs St. Louis, 2000 (3-game series)
St. Louis vs Arizona, 2002 (3-game series)
AL—none

# INDIVIDUAL FIELDING

## FIRST BASEMEN

### GAMES

**Most games, career**
ML—37—Tino Martinez, Seattle AL, 1995; New York AL, 1996-2001, 2005; St. Louis NL, 2002; 9 series
AL—34—Tino Martinez, Seattle, 1995; New York, 1996-2001, 2005; 8 series
NL—19—Jeff Bagwell, Houston, 1997-1999, 2001, 2004; 5 series

### PUTOUTS, ASSISTS AND CHANCES

**Most putouts, career**
ML—318—Tino Martinez, Seattle AL, 1995; New York AL, 1996-2001, 2005; St. Louis NL, 2002; 9 series, 37 G
AL—296—Tino Martinez, Seattle, 1995; New York, 1996-2001, 2005; 8 series, 34 G
NL—153—Jeff Bagwell, Houston, 1997-1999, 2001, 2004; 5 series, 19 G

**Most putouts, series**
NL—31—Albert Pujols, St. Louis, 2005
AL—30—Paul Konerko, Chicago, 2005
4-game series
NL—43—Albert Pujols, St. Louis, 2004
AL—42—Nick Johnson, New York, 2003
5-game series
AL—53—Jason Giambi, Oakland, 2001
NL—48—Jeff Bagwell, Houston, 2004

**Most putouts, game**
AL—16—Tino Martinez, New York, Oct 4, 2000
NL—14—Fred McGriff, Atlanta, Oct 3, 1995
Jeff Kent, San Francisco, Oct 1, 1997
Jeff Bagwell, Houston, Oct 5, 1999
Albert Pujols, St. Louis, Oct 6, 2005

**Most putouts, inning**
AL-NL—3—many first basemen

**Most assists, career**
ML—26—Tino Martinez, Seattle AL, 1995; New York AL, 1996-2001, 2005; St. Louis NL, 2002; 9 series, 37 G
AL—25—Tino Martinez, Seattle, 1995; New York, 1996-2001, 2005; 8 series, 34 G
NL—18—Jeff Bagwell, Houston, 1997-1999, 2001, 2004; 5 series, 19 G

**Most assists, series**

3-game series
NL—6—Jeff Bagwell, Houston, 1997
AL—5—Paul Sorrento, Cleveland, 1995

4-game series
AL—6—John Olerud, New York, 2004
NL—4—Jeff Bagwell, Houston, 1998
John Olerud, New York, 1999
Todd Zeile, New York, 2000

5-game series
AL—10—Kevin Millar, Boston, 2003
NL—7—J.T. Snow, San Francisco, 2002

**Most assists, game**

NL—3—Jeff Bagwell, Houston, Oct 1, 1997
Andres Galarraga, Atlanta, Oct 3, 1998
John Olerud, New York, Oct 8, 1999
AL—4—Jim Thome, Cleveland, Oct 7, 1999
[5—Kevin Millar, Boston, Oct 4, 2003, 11 inn]

**Most assists, inning**

AL-NL—2—many first basemen

**Most chances accepted, career**

ML—344—Tino Martinez, Seattle AL, 1995; New York AL, 1996-2001, 2005; St. Louis NL, 2002; 9 series, 37 G
AL—321—Tino Martinez, Seattle, 1995; New York, 1996-2001, 2005; 8 series, 34 G
NL—171—Jeff Bagwell, Houston, 1997-1999, 2001, 2004; 5 series, 19 G

**Most chances accepted, series**

3-game series
AL—33—Paul Konerko, Chicago, 2005
NL—32—Albert Pujols, St. Louis, 2005

4-game series
NL—44—Albert Pujols, St. Louis, 2004
AL—43—Nick Johnson, New York, 2003

5-game series
AL—55—Jason Giambi, Oakland, 2001
NL—51—Jeff Bagwell, Houston, 2004

**Most chances accepted, game**

AL—17—Tino Martinez, New York, Oct 4, 2000 (16 PO, 1 A)
NL—15—Fred McGriff, Atlanta, Oct 3, 1995 (14 PO, 1 A)
Jeff Kent, San Francisco, Oct 1, 1997 (14 PO, 1 A)
Jeff Bagwell, Houston, Oct 5, 1999 (14 PO, 1 A)
Albert Pujols, St. Louis, Oct 6, 2005 (14 PO, 1 A)

**Fewest chances offered, game**

NL—3—Eric Karros, Los Angeles, Oct 6, 1995 (3 PO)
J.T. Snow, San Francisco, Sept 30, 1997 (3 PO)
AL—3—Mike Stanley, Boston, Oct 7, 1999 (2 PO, 1 A)

**Most chances accepted, inning**

AL-NL—3—many first basemen

## ERRORS AND DOUBLE PLAYS

**Most errors, career**

AL—3—Paul Sorrento, Cleveland, 1995; Seattle, 1997; 2 series, 7 G
NL—3—Jeff Bagwell, Houston, 1997-1999, 2001, 2004; 5 series, 19 G

**Most consecutive errorless games, career**

ML—18—Julio Franco, Cleveland AL, Atlanta NL, Oct 1, 1996-Oct 9, 2005
AL—18—Tino Martinez, Seattle, New York, Oct 3, 1995-Oct 5, 1999
NL—15—Jeff Bagwell, Houston, Sept 29, 1998-Oct 10, 2004

**Most errors, series**

AL—2—Paul Sorrento, Cleveland, 1995 (3-game series)
NL—2—Jeff Bagwell, Houston, 1997 (3-game series)
J.T. Snow, San Francisco, 2003 (4-game series)

**Most chances accepted, errorless series**

AL—54—Tino Martinez, New York, 1997 (5-game series)
NL—49—J.T. Snow, San Francisco, 2002 (5-game series)

**Most errors, game**

AL-NL—1—many first basemen

**Most errors, inning**

AL-NL—1—many first basemen

**Most double plays, career**

AL—26—Tino Martinez, Seattle, 1995; New York, 1996-2001, 2005; 8 series, 34 G
NL—16—Jeff Bagwell, Houston, 1997-1999, 2001, 2004; 5 series, 19 G

**Most double plays, series**

AL—7—Justin Morneau, Minnesota, 2004 (4-game series)
NL—7—Albert Pujols, St. Louis (3-game series)

**Most double plays started, series**

AL—3—Tino Martinez, New York, 2001 (5-game series)
NL—2—J.T. Snow, San Francisco, 2002 (5-game series)

**Most double plays, game**

NL—4—Fred McGriff, Atlanta, Oct 3, 1995
Albert Pujols, St. Louis, Oct 6, 2005
AL—4—Scott Spiezio, Anaheim, Oct 1, 2002

**Most double plays started, game**

AL-NL—1—many first basemen

**Most unassisted double plays, game**

AL—1—Tino Martinez, New York, Oct 5, 1999, 6th
Tino Martinez, New York, Oct 10, 2001, 7th
Kevin Millar, Boston, Oct 5, 2003, 6th
Kevin Millar, Boston, Oct 6, 2004, 3rd
NL—none

# SECOND BASEMEN

## GAMES

**Most games, career**

ML—18—Jeff Kent, Cleveland AL, 1996; San Francisco NL, 1997, 2000, 2002; Houston NL, 2004, 5 series
AL—18—Roberto Alomar, Baltimore, 1996, 1997; Cleveland, 1999, 2001; 4 series
NL—18—Craig Biggio, Houston, 1997-1999, 2001, 2005; 5 series

## PUTOUTS, ASSISTS AND CHANCES ACCEPTED

**Most putouts, career**

AL—35—Roberto Alomar, Baltimore, 1996, 1997; Cleveland, 1999, 2001; 4 series, 18 G
NL—45—Marcus Giles, Atlanta, 2001, 2003-2005; 4 series, 16 G

**Most putouts, series**

3-game series
AL—10—Ray Durham, Chicago, 2000
Tony Graffanino, Boston, 2005
NL—9—Keith Lockhart, Atlanta, 1998

4-game series
NL—14—Craig Biggio, Houston, 1999
AL—12—Mike Benjamin, Boston, 1998

5-game series
NL—17—Marcus Giles, Atlanta, 2004
AL—15—Rey Sanchez, New York, 1997

**Most putouts, game**

AL—8—Rey Sanchez, New York, Oct 4, 1997
NL—6—Craig Biggio, Houston, Oct 3, 1998
Jeff Kent, San Francisco, Oct 2, 2002
Marcus Giles, Atlanta, Oct 5, 2005
[6—Luis Castillo, Florida, Oct 3, 2003, 11 inn]

**Most putouts, inning**

AL-NL—2—many second basemen

**Most assists, career**

NL—54—Marcus Giles, Atlanta, 2001, 2003-2005; 4 series, 16 G
AL—46—Mark McLemore, Texas, 1996, 1998, 1999; Seattle, 2000; 4 series, 13 G

**Most assists, series**

3-games series
NL—13—Fernando Vina, St. Louis, 2000
AL—12—Mark McLemore, Texas, 1998

4-game series
AL—16—Mark McLemore, Texas, 1996
NL—16—Mark Lemke, Atlanta, 1995
Craig Biggio, Houston, 2005

5-game series
NL—25—Marcus Giles, Atlanta, 2004
AL—22—Luis Sojo, New York, 2000

**Most assists, game**

NL—8—Mark Lemke, Atlanta, Oct 3, 1995
AL—8—Robinson Cano, New York, Oct 5, 2005

**Most assists, inning**

NL—3—Tony Womack, St. Louis, Oct 9, 2004, 8th
AL—2—many second basemen

**Most chances accepted, career**

NL—99—Marcus Giles, Atlanta, 2001, 2003-2005; 4 series, 16 G
AL—70—Roberto Alomar, Baltimore, 1996, 1997; Cleveland, 1999, 2001; 4 series, 18 G

**Most chances accepted, series**

3-game series
NL—20—Fernando Vina, St. Louis, 2000
Junior Spivey, Arizona, 2002
AL—19—Tony Graffanino, Boston, 2005

4-game series
AL—26—Mark McLemore, Texas, 1996
NL—26—Bret Boone, Atlanta, 1999

5-game series
NL—42—Marcus Giles, Atlanta, 2004
AL—32—Robinson Cano, New York, 2005

**Most chances accepted, game**

NL—11—Mark Lemke, Atlanta, Oct 3, 1995 (3 PO, 8 A)
Jeff Kent, San Francisco, Oct 2, 2002 (6 PO, 5 A)
AL—11—Luis Sojo, New York, Oct 7, 2000 (4 PO, 7 A)
[11—Randy Velarde, New York, Oct 4, 1995 (6 PO, 5 A), 15 inn]

**Fewest chances offered, game**

AL—0—Mark McLemore, Texas, Oct 7, 1999
NL—0—Marcus Giles, Atlanta, Oct 8, 2005

**Most chances accepted, inning**

AL-NL—3—many second basemen

## ERRORS AND DOUBLE PLAYS

**Most errors, career**
NL—3—Eric Young, Colorado, 1995; 1 series, 4 G
AL—2—many players

**Most consecutive errorless games, career**
AL—13—Mark McLemore, Texas, Seattle, Oct 1, 1996-Oct 6, 2000
NL—13—Keith Lockhart, Atlanta, Sept 30, 1998-Oct 7, 2002
Craig Biggio, Houston, Oct 3, 1998-Oct 9, 2005

**Most errors, series**
NL—3—Eric Young, Colorado, 1995 (4-game series)
AL—2—Randy Velarde, Oakland, 2000 (5-game series)
Todd Walker, Boston, 2003 (5-game series)
Robinson Cano, New York, 2005 (5-game series)

**Most chances accepted, errorless series**
NL—42—Marcus Giles, Atlanta, 2004 (5-game series)
AL—29—Rey Sanchez, New York, 1997 (5-game series)

**Most errors, game**
NL—2—Eric Young, Colorado, Oct 4, 1995
AL—1—many second basemen

**Most errors, inning**
AL-NL—1—many second basemen

**Most double plays, career**
NL—18—Marcus Giles, Atlanta, 2001, 2003-2005; 4 series, 16 G
AL—11—Mark McLemore, Texas, 1996, 1998, 1999; New York, 2000; 4 series, 13 G

**Most double plays, series**
AL—6—Luis Sojo, New York, 2000 (5-game series)
NL—6—Marcus Giles, Atlanta, 2004 (5-game series)

**Most double plays started, series**
NL—4—Quilvio Veras, San Diego, 1998 (4-game series)
AL—3—Mark McLemore, Seattle, 2000 (3-game series)
Luis Sojo, New York, 2000 (5-game series)

**Most double plays, game**
NL—3—Mark Lemke, Atlanta, Oct 3, 1995
Jeff Kent, San Francisco, Oct 2, 2002
Mark Grudzielanek, St. Louis, Oct 6, 2005
AL—3—Bip Roberts, Cleveland, Sept 30, 1997
Adam Kennedy, Anaheim, Oct 1, 2002

**Most double plays started, game**
NL—2—Mark Lemke, Atlanta, Oct 3, 1995
Quilvio Veras, San Diego, Oct 3, 1998
[2—Bret Boone, Atlanta, Oct 8, 1999, 12 inn]
AL—2—Mark McLemore, Seattle, Oct 6, 2000
Robinson Cano, New York, Oct 7, 2005
[2—Ray Durham, Chicago, Oct 3, 2000, 10 inn]

**Most unassisted double plays, game**
AL—1—Robinson Cano, New York, Oct 7, 2005
NL—none

# THIRD BASEMEN

## GAMES

**Most games, career**
NL—32—Chipper Jones, Atlanta, 1995-2001, 2004, 2005; 9 series
AL—20—Eric Chavez, Oakland, 2000-2003; 4 series

## PUTOUTS, ASSISTS AND CHANCES

**Most putouts, career**
AL—22—Eric Chavez, Oakland, 2000-2003; 4 series, 20 G
NL—20—Chipper Jones, Atlanta, 1995-2001, 2004, 2005; 9 series, 32 G

**Most putouts, series**
3-game series
AL—6—Jim Thome, Cleveland, 1995
NL—5—Vinny Castilla, Houston, 2001
4-game series
NL—7—Robin Ventura, New York, 2000
AL—5—John Valentin, Boston, 1998
Travis Fryman, Cleveland, 1998
Alex Rodriguez, New York, 2004
5-game series
AL—9—Bill Mueller, Boston, 2003
NL—4—Aramis Ramirez, Chicago, 2003

**Most putouts, game**
NL—4—Vinny Castilla, Houston, Oct 10, 2001
[5—Robin Ventura, New York, Oct 5, 2000, 10 inn]
AL—5—Bill Mueller, Boston, Oct 5, 2003
[5—Eric Chavez, Oakland, Oct 4, 2003, 11 inn]

**Most putouts, inning**
AL-NL—2—many third basemen

**Most assists, career**
NL—46—Vinny Castilla, Colorado, 1995; Houston, 2001; Atlanta, 2002, 2003; 4 series, 17 G
AL—34—Eric Chavez, Oakland, 2000-2003; 4 series, 20 G

**Most assists, series**
3-game series
AL—11—Joe Crede, Chicago, 2005
NL—9—Bill Mueller, San Francisco, 1997
4-game series
NL—13—Vinny Castilla, Colorado, 1995
AL—11—Troy Glaus, Anaheim, 2002
Alex Rodriguez, New York, 2004
5-game series
NL—15—Placido Polanco, St. Louis, 2001
Matt Williams, Arizona, 2001
AL—11—John Valentin, Boston, 1999
Eric Chavez, Oakland, 2001

**Most assists, game**
NL—7—Matt Williams, Arizona, Oct 12, 2001
David Bell, San Francisco, Oct 3, 2002
Vinny Castilla, Atlanta, Oct 5, 2003
AL—5—Scott Brosius, New York, Oct 4, 2000
Chone Figgins, Los Angeles, Oct 5, 2005
[6—Todd Zeile, Baltimore, Oct 5, 1996, 12 inn]

**Most assists, inning**
NL—3—Vinny Castilla, Colorado, Oct 4, 1995, 4th
AL—3—Travis Fryman, Cleveland, Oct 11, 2001, 3rd

**Most chances accepted, career**
NL—64—Chipper Jones, Atlanta, 1995-2001, 2004, 2005; 9 series, 32 G
AL—56—Eric Chavez, Oakland, 2000-2003; 4 series, 20 G

**Most chances accepted, series**
3-game series
AL—15—Joe Crede, Chicago, 2005
NL—12—Vinny Castilla, Houston, 2001
4-game series
NL—16—Vinny Castilla, Colorado, 1995
Morgan Ensberg, Houston, 2005
AL—16—Alex Rodriguez, New York, 2004
5-game series
AL—19—Bill Mueller, Boston, 2003
NL—17—Matt Williams, Arizona, 2001
David Bell, San Francisco, 2002
Vinny Castilla, Atlanta, 2003

**Most chances accepted, game**
NL—9—Vinny Castilla, Houston, Oct 10, 2001 (4 PO, 5 A)
AL—7—Eric Chavez, Oakland, Oct 4, 2002 (4 PO, 3 A)
Bill Mueller, Boston, Oct 5, 2003 (5 PO, 2 A)
Joe Crede, Chicago, Oct 7, 2005 (3 PO, 4 A)
[7—Todd Zeile, Baltimore, Oct 5, 1996 (1 PO, 6 A), 12 inn]

**Fewest chances offered, game**
AL-NL—0—many third basemen

**Most chances accepted, inning**
AL-NL—3—many third basemen

## ERRORS AND DOUBLE PLAYS

**Most errors, career**
AL—4—Todd Zeile, Texas, 1996, 1998, 1999; 3 series, 10 G
NL—4—Ken Caminiti, San Diego, 1996, 1998, 1999; 3 series, 11 G
Chipper Jones, Atlanta, 1995-2001, 2004, 2005; 9 series, 32 G

**Most consecutive errorless games, career**
ML—18—Bill Mueller, San Francisco NL, Boston AL, Sept 30, 1997-Oct 7, 2005
AL—14—Travis Fryman, Cleveland, Sept 29, 1998-Oct 15, 2001
NL—13—Vinny Castilla, Colorado, Houston, Atlanta, Oct 4, 1995-Oct 1, 2003

**Most errors, series**
NL—3—Ken Caminiti, San Diego, 1996 (3-game series)
AL—3—Charlie Hayes, New York, 1997 (5-game series)
Scott Brosius, New York, 2001 (5-game series)

**Most chances accepted, errorless series**
AL—19—Bill Mueller, Boston, 2003 (5-game series)
NL—14—Vinny Castilla, Atlanta, 2002 (5-game series)
Aramis Ramirez, Chicago, 2003 (5-games series)

**Most errors, game**
NL—2—Ken Caminiti, San Diego, Oct 5, 1996
AL—1—many third basemen
[2—Eric Chavez, Oakland, Oct 4, 2003, 11 inn]

**Most errors, inning**
AL-NL—1—many third basemen

**Most double plays, career**
NL—8—Vinny Castilla, Colorado, 1995; Houston, 2001; Atlanta, 2002, 2003; 4 series, 17 G
AL—6—Eric Chavez, Oakland, 2000-2003; 4 series, 20 G

**Most double plays, series**
AL—3—John Valentin, Boston, 1998 (4-game series)

Scott Brosius, New York, 2000 (5-game series)
Eric Chavez, Oakland, 2003 (5-game series)
NL—3—Vinny Castilla, Houston, 2001 (3-game series)
Matt Williams, Arizona, 2001 (5-game series)
Vinny Castilla, Atlanta, 2003 (5-game series)
Chipper Jones, Atlanta, 2004 (5-game series)

**Most double plays started, series**
AL—3—John Valentin, Boston, 1998 (4-game series)
Scott Brosius, New York, 2000 (5-game series)
Eric Chavez, Oakland, 2003 (5-game series)
NL—3—Vinny Castilla, Houston, 2001 (3-game series)
Matt Williams, Arizona, 2001 (5-game series)
Chipper Jones, Atlanta, 2004 (5-game series)

**Most double plays, game**
NL—3—Vinny Castilla, Houston, Oct 10, 2001
AL—2—Scott Brosius, New York, Oct 4, 2000
Troy Glaus, Anaheim, Oct 1, 2002

**Most double plays started, game**
NL—3—Vinny Castilla, Houston, Oct 10, 2001
AL—2—Scott Brosius, New York, Oct 4, 2000
[2—Eric Chavez, Oakland, Oct 4, 2003, 11 inn]

**Most unassisted double plays, game**
AL—1—Scott Brosius, New York, Oct 3, 2000
Joe Crede, Chicago, Oct 7, 2005
NL—none

## SHORTSTOPS

### GAMES

**Most games, career**
AL—42—Derek Jeter, New York, 1996-2005; 10 series
NL—22—Rafael Furcal, Atlanta, 2000, 2002-2005; 5 series

### PUTOUTS, ASSISTS AND CHANCES

**Most putouts, career**
AL—73—Derek Jeter, New York, 1996-2005; 10 series, 42 G
NL—38—Edgar Renteria, Florida, 1997; St. Louis, 2000-2002, 2004; 5 series, 18 G

**Most putouts, series**
3-game series
AL—10—Jose Valentin, Chicago, 2000
NL—9—Edgar Renteria, Florida, 1997
4-game series
AL—15—Derek Jeter, New York, 2004
NL—10—Rich Aurilia, San Francisco, 2000
Edgar Renteria, St. Louis, 2004
5-game series
AL—12—Derek Jeter, New York, 1997
Omar Vizquel, Cleveland, 1997
NL—9—Rafael Furcal, Atlanta, 2004

**Most putouts, game**
NL—6—Rey Sanchez, Atlanta, Oct 10, 2001
AL—5—Alex Rodriguez, Seattle, Oct 2, 1997
Omar Vizquel, Cleveland, Oct 6, 1997
Orlando Cabrera, Los Angeles, Oct 5, 2005
[7—Derek Jeter, New York, Oct 9, 2004, 11 inn]

**Most putouts, inning**
AL-NL—2—many shortstops

**Most assists, career**
AL—110—Derek Jeter, New York, 1996-2005; 10 series, 42 G
NL—79—Rafael Furcal, Atlanta, 2000, 2002-2005; 5 series, 22 G

**Most assists, series**
3-game series
AL—17—Jose Valentin, Chicago, 2000
NL—12—Khalil Greene, San Diego, 2005
4-game series
NL—17—Rich Aurilia, San Francisco, 2003
AL—21—Cristian Guzman, Minnesota, 2004
5-game series
NL—22—Rafael Furcal, Atlanta, 2003
AL—21—Omar Vizquel, Cleveland, 2001

**Most assists, game**
AL—9—Nomar Garciaparra, Boston, Oct 6, 2003
NL—7—Ricky Gutierrez, Houston, Oct 3, 1998
Alex S. Gonzalez, Chicago, Oct 3, 2003
Rafael Furcal, Atlanta, Oct 9, 2004
[7—Rafael Furcal, Atlanta, Oct 9, 2005, 18 inn]

**Most assists, inning**
NL—3—Jeff Blauser, Atlanta, Oct 4, 1995, 7th
AL—3—Derek Jeter, New York, Oct 2, 2002, 4th

**Most chances accepted, career**
AL—183—Derek Jeter, New York, 1996-2005; 10 series, 42 G
NL—110—Rafael Furcal, Atlanta, 2000, 2002-2005; 5 series, 22 G

**Most chances accepted, series**
3-game series
AL—27—Jose Valentin, Chicago, 2000
NL—20—Edgar Renteria, Florida, 1997
4-game series
AL—27—Cristian Guzman, Minnesota, 2004
NL—25—Rich Aurilia, San Francisco, 2003
5-game series
NL—30—Rafael Furcal, Atlanta, 2003
AL—27—Derek Jeter, New York, 1997
Omar Vizquel, Cleveland, 2001

**Most chances accepted, game**
AL—11—Jose Valentin, Chicago, Oct 4, 2000 (4 PO, 7 A)
Cristian Guzman, Minnesota, Oct 8, 2004 (4 PO, 7 A)
[11—Luis Sojo, Seattle, Oct 4, 1995 (3 PO, 8 A), 15 inn
Jose Valentin, Chicago, Oct 3, 2000 (5 PO, 6 A), 10 inn]
NL—9—Ricky Gutierrez, Houston, Oct 3, 1998 (2 PO, 7 A)
Rey Sanchez, Atlanta, Oct 10, 2001 (6 PO, 3 A)
Alex S. Gonzalez, Chicago, Oct 3, 2003 (2 PO, 7 A)
Rafael Furcal, Atlanta, Oct 9, 2004 (2 PO, 7 A)
David Eckstein, St. Louis, Oct 6, 2005 (3 PO, 6 A)

**Fewest chances offered, game**
NL—0—Chris Gomez, San Diego, Oct 3, 1996
Jose Vizcaino, San Francisco, Sept 30, 1997
Hanley Frias, Arizona, Oct 5, 1999
AL—1—Alex Rodriguez, Seattle, Oct 5, 1997
Derek Jeter, New York, Sept 30, 1998
Nomar Garciaparra, Boston, Oct 6, 1999
Derek Jeter, New York, Oct 4, 2002

**Most chances accepted, inning**
AL-NL—3—many shortstops

### ERRORS AND DOUBLE PLAYS

**Most errors, career**
NL—5—Edgar Renteria, Florida, 1997; St. Louis, 2000-2002, 2004; 5 series, 18 G
AL—5—Derek Jeter, New York, 1996-2005; 10 series, 42 G

**Most consecutive errorless games, career**
AL—24—Omar Vizquel, Cleveland, Oct 3, 1995-Oct 13, 2001
NL—11—Walt Weiss, Colorado, Atlanta, Oct 3, 1995-Oct 3, 2000
Rafael Furcal, Atlanta, Oct 4, 2003-Oct 9, 2005

**Most errors, series**
NL—3—Julio Lugo, Houston, 2001 (3-game series)
AL—1—many shortstops

**Most chances accepted, errorless series**
AL—27—Derek Jeter, New York, 1997 (5-game series)
Derek Jeter, New York, 2003 (4-game series)
NL—29—Rafael Furcal, Atlanta, 2004 (5-game series)

**Most errors, game**
NL—2—Edgar Renteria, Florida, Oct 3, 1997
Julio Lugo, Houston, Oct 10, 2001
AL—1—many shortstops

**Most errors, inning**
AL-NL—1—many shortstops

**Most double plays, career**
AL—27—Derek Jeter, New York, 1996-2005; 10 series, 42 G
NL—15—Rafael Furcal, Atlanta, 2000, 2002-2005; 5 series, 22 G

**Most double plays, series**
AL—6—Cristian Guzman, Minnesota, 2004 (4-game series)
NL—6—David Eckstein, St. Louis, 2005 (3-game series)
Rafael Furcal, Atlanta, 2005 (4-game series)

**Most double plays started, series**
AL—5—Christian Guzman, Minnesota, 2004 (4-game series)
NL—4—Rafael Furcal, Atlanta, 2003 (5-game series)

**Most double plays, game**
NL—4—David Eckstein, St. Louis, Oct 6, 2005
AL—3—Kevin Elster, Texas, Oct 4, 1996
Jose Valentin, Chicago, Oct 4, 2000
Cristian Guzman, Minnesota, Oct 5, 2004

**Most double plays started, game**
AL—3—Cristian Guzman, Minnesota, Oct 5, 2004
NL—2—many shortstops

**Most unassisted double plays, game**
AL-NL—none

## OUTFIELDERS

### GAMES

**Most games, career**
AL—45—Bernie Williams, New York, 1995-2005; 11 series
NL—38—Andruw Jones, Atlanta, 1996-2005; 10 series

### PUTOUTS, ASSISTS AND CHANCES

**Most putouts, career**
AL—110—Bernie Williams, New York, 1995-2005; 11 series, 45 G
NL—99—Andruw Jones, Atlanta, 1996-2005; 10 series, 38 G

**Most putouts, series**
3-game series
AL—15—Bernie Williams, New York, 1999
NL—13—Luis Gonzalez, Houston, 1997
4-game series
NL—19—Andruw Jones, Atlanta, 2005
AL—16—Darryl Hamilton, Texas, 1996
5-game series
AL—20—Jacque Jones, Minnesota, 2002
NL—13—Andruw Jones, Atlanta, 2003
Carlos Beltran, Houston, 2004

**Most putouts by left fielder, game**
NL—6—Luis Gonzalez, Houston, Sept 30, 1997
[7—Ryan Langerhans, Atlanta, Oct 9, 2005, 18 inn]
AL—6—Garret Anderson, Los Angeles, Oct 4, 2005
[6—Vince Coleman, Seattle, Oct 8, 1995, 11 inn]

**Most putouts by center fielder, game**
NL—8—Andruw Jones, Atlanta, Oct 8, 2005
AL—7—Bernie Williams, New York, Oct 5, 1999
Johnny Damon, Oakland, Oct 13, 2001
Johnny Damon, Boston, Oct 5, 2005

**Most putouts by right fielder, game**
NL—8—Jose Cruz Jr., Sept 20, 2003
AL—6—Ichiro Suzuki, Seattle, Oct 11, 2001
[6—Paul O'Neill, New York, Oct 2, 1996, 12 inn]

**Most consecutive putouts, game**
AL—3—Johnny Damon, Oakland, Oct 13, 2001; 2 in 5th inn, 1 in 6th inn
NL—2—many outfielders

**Most putouts, inning**
AL—3—Bernie Williams, New York, Oct 5, 1999, 3rd (CF)
Adam Piatt, Oakland, Oct 4, 2000, 1st (RF)
Mike Cameron, Seattle, Oct 6, 2000, 2nd (CF)
Johnny Damon, Oakland, Oct 13, 2001, 5th (CF)
Garret Anderson, Los Angeles, Oct 4, 2005, 9th (LF)
NL—2—many outfielders

**Most assists, career**
AL—4—David Justice, Cleveland, 1998, 1999; New York, 2000, 2001; Oakland, 2002; 5 series, 17 G
Manny Ramirez, Cleveland, 1995-1999; Boston, 2003-2005; 8 series, 32 G
NL—2—Albert Pujols, St. Louis, 2001, 2002, 2004; 3 series, 10 G
Kenny Lofton, Atlanta, 1997; San Francisco, 2002; Chicago, 2003; 3 series, 18 G
Andruw Jones, Atlanta, 1996-2005; 10 series, 38 G
Jason Lane, Houston, 2004, 2005; 2 series, 9 G

**Most assists, series**
AL—2—Manny Ramirez, Cleveland, 1996 (4-game series)
David Justice, Cleveland, 1999 (5-game series)
Johnny Damon, Boston, 2003 (5-game series)
NL—2—Albert Pujols, St. Louis, 2002 (3-game series)
Jason Lane, Houston, 2005 (4-game series)

**Most assists, game**
NL—2—Jason Lane, Houston, Oct 6, 2005
AL—1—many outfielders

**Most assists, inning**
NL—2—Jason Lane, Houston, Oct 6, 2005, 7th
AL—1—many outfielders

**Most chances accepted, career**
AL—111—Bernie Williams, New York, 1995-2005; 11 series, 45 G
NL—101—Andruw Jones, Atlanta, 1996-2005; 10 series, 38 G

**Most chances accepted, series**
3-game series
AL—15—Bernie Williams, New York, 1999
NL—14—Luis Gonzalez, Houston, 1997
4-game series
NL—19—Andruw Jones, Atlanta, 2005
AL—17—Darryl Hamilton, Texas, 1996
5-game series
AL—20—Jacque Jones, Minnesota, 2002
NL—13—Andruw Jones, Atlanta, 2002
Carlos Beltran, Houston, 2004

**Most chances accepted by left fielder, game**
NL—6—Luis Gonzalez, Houston, Sept 30, 1997 (6 PO)
[7—Ryan Langerhans, Atlanta, Oct 9, 2005, 18 inn]
AL—6—Garret Anderson, Los Angeles, Oct 4, 2005 (6 PO)
[6—Vince Coleman, Seattle, Oct 8, 1995 (6 PO), 11 inn]

**Most chances accepted by center fielder, game**
NL—8—Andruw Jones, Atlanta, Oct 8, 2005 (8 PO)
AL—7—Bernie Williams, New York, Oct 5, 1999 (7 PO)
Johnny Damon, Oakland, Oct 13, 2001 (7 PO)
Johnny Damon, Boston, Oct 5, 2005 (7 PO)
[7—Darryl Hamilton, Texas, Oct 2, 1996 (6 PO, 1 A), 12 inn]

**Most chances accepted by right fielder, game**
NL—8—Jose Cruz, Jr., San Francisco, Sept 20, 2003 (8 PO)
AL—6—Ichiro Suzuki, Seattle, Oct 11, 2001 (6 PO)
[6—Paul O'Neill, New York, Oct 2, 1996 (6 PO), 12 inn]

**Longest game with no chances offered to outfielder**
AL—13 inn—Albert Belle, Cleveland, Oct 3, 1995
NL—12 inn—Carl Everett, Houston, Oct 8, 1999

**Most chances accepted, inning**
AL-NL—3—many outfielders

## ERRORS AND DOUBLE PLAYS

**Most errors, career**
AL—3—Kenny Lofton, Cleveland, 1995, 1996, 1998, 1999, 2001; 5 series, 21 G
NL—2—Ryan Klesko, Atlanta, 1995-1998; 4 series, 13 G
Tony Womack, Arizona, 1999; 1 series, 4 G
Marquis Grissom, Atlanta, 1995, 1996; San Francisco, 2003; 3 series, 11 G

**Most consecutive errorless games, career**
AL—36—Bernie Williams, New York, Oct 3, 1995-Oct 2, 2003
NL—26—Andruw Jones, Atlanta, Oct 2, 1996-Oct 1, 2003

**Most errors, series**
AL—2—Kenny Lofton, Cleveland, 1995 (3-game series)
NL—2—Tony Womack, Arizona, 1999 (4-game series)

**Most chances accepted, errorless series**
NL—19—Andruw Jones, Atlanta, 2005 (4-game series)
AL—18—Johnny Damon, Boston, 2003 (5-game series)
Garret Anderson, Los Angeles, 2005 (5-game series)

**Most errors, game**
AL-NL—1—many outfielders

**Most errors, inning**
AL-NL—1—many outfielders

**Most double plays, career**
AL-NL—1—many outfielders

**Most double plays, series**
AL-NL—1—many outfielders

**Most double plays, game**
AL-NL—1—many outfielders

**Most unassisted double plays, game**
AL-NL—none

# CATCHERS

## GAMES

**Most games, career**
AL—31—Jorge Posada, New York, 1997-2005; 9 series
NL—21—Javy Lopez, Atlanta, 1995-1998, 2000, 2002, 2003; 7 series

## PUTOUTS, ASSISTS AND CHANCES

**Most putouts, career**
AL—184—Jorge Posada, New York, 1997-2005; 9 series, 31 G
NL—171—Javy Lopez, Atlanta, 1995-1998, 2000, 2002, 2003; 7 series, 21 G

**Most putouts, series**
3-game series
NL—31—Mike Piazza, Los Angeles, 1995
AL—29—Jason Varitek, Boston, 2004
4-game series
AL—40—Sandy Alomar Jr., Cleveland, 1995
NL—35—Eddie Perez, Atlanta, 1999
Brad Ausmus, Houston, 2005
5-game series
AL—51—Einar Diaz, Cleveland, 2001
NL—39—Damian Miller, Arizona, 2001
Javy Lopez, Atlanta, 2003

**Most putouts, game**
AL—13—Einar Diaz, Cleveland, Oct 9, 2001
[22—Sandy Alomar Jr., Cleveland, Oct 5, 1996, 12 inn]
NL—15—Carlos Hernandez, San Diego, Sept 29, 1998
[18—Tony Eusebio, Houston, Oct 8, 1999, 12 inn]

**Most putouts, inning**
AL-NL—3—many catchers

**Most assists, career**
AL—20—Jorge Posada, New York, 1995-2005; 9 series, 31 G
NL—14—Javy Lopez, Atlanta, 1995-1998, 2000, 2002, 2003; 7 series, 21 G

**Most assists, series**
3-game series
NL—4—Mike Piazza, Los Angeles, 1996
Carlos Hernandez, St. Louis, 2000
AL—3—Ivan Rodriguez, Texas, 1998
4-game series
NL—6—Carlos Hernandez, San Diego, 1998

AL—5—Jorge Posada, New York, 2004
5-game series
NL—4—Javy Lopez, Atlanta, 2003
Raul Chavez, Houston, 2004
AL—5—Bengie Molina, Los Angeles, 2005
Jorge Posada, New York, 2005

**Most assists, game**
NL—4—Raul Chavez, Houston, Oct 7, 2004
AL—3—Bengie Molina, Los Angeles, Oct 10, 2005
[3—Jorge Posada, New York, Oct 9, 2004, 11 inn]

**Most assists, inning**
AL-NL—1—many catchers

**Most chances accepted, career**
AL—204—Jorge Posada, New York, 1997-2005; 9 series, 31 G
NL—185—Javy Lopez, Atlanta, 1995-1998, 2000, 2002, 2003; 7 series, 21 G

**Most chances accepted, series**
3-game series
NL—31—Mike Piazza, Los Angeles, 1995
AL—31—Jason Varitek, Boston, 2004
4-game series
AL—44—Sandy Alomar Jr., Cleveland, 1996
NL—40—Carlos Hernandez, San Diego, 1998
5-game series
AL—55—Einar Diaz, Cleveland, 2001
NL—43—Javy Lopez, Atlanta, 2003

**Most chances accepted, game**
NL—17—Carlos Hernandez, San Diego, Sept 29, 1998 (15 PO, 2 A, 17 K)
[18—Tony Eusebio, Houston, Oct 8, 1999 (18 PO, 18 K), 12 inn]
AL—16—Einar Diaz, Cleveland, Oct 15, 2001 (14 PO, 2 A, 13 K)
[24—Sandy Alomar, Jr., Cleveland, Oct 5, 1996 (22 PO, 2 A, 23 K), 12 inn]

**Fewest chances offered, game**
AL—1—Joe Girardi, New York, Oct 4, 1997
NL—2—Eli Marrero, St. Louis, Oct 13, 2001

**Most chances accepted, inning**
AL-NL—3—many catchers

## ERRORS AND PASSED BALLS

**Most errors, career**
AL—4—Sandy Alomar Jr., Cleveland, 1995-1999; 5 series, 21 G
NL—2—Javy Lopez, Atlanta, 1995-1998, 2000, 2002, 2003; 7 series, 21 G

**Most consecutive errorless games, career**
NL—17—Brad Ausmus, Houston, Oct 1, 1997-Oct 9, 2005
AL—16—Jorge Posada, New York, Oct 2, 2002-Oct 1, 2005
Jason Varitek, Boston, Sept 30, 1998-Oct 7, 2005

**Most errors, series**
AL—2—Mike Macfarlane, Boston, 1995 (3-game series)
NL—1—many catchers

**Most chances accepted, errorless series**
NL—42—Damian Miller, Arizona, 2001 (5-game series)
AL—41—Dan Wilson, Seattle, 2001 (5-game series)

**Most errors, game**
AL-NL—1—many catchers

**Most errors, inning**
AL-NL—1—many catchers

**Most passed balls, career**
AL—5—Jason Varitek, Boston, 1998, 1999, 2003-2005; 5 series, 16 G
NL—2—Carlos Hernandez, San Diego, 1998; St. Louis, 2000; 2 series, 7 G

**Most passed balls, series**
AL—3—Jason Varitek, Boston, 1999 (5-game series)
NL—2—Carlos Hernandez, San Diego, 1998 (4-game series)

**Most passed balls, game**
NL—2—Carlos Hernandez, San Diego, Sept 29, 1998
AL—2—Jason Varitek, Boston, Sept 30, 1998
Jason Varitek, Boston, Oct 10, 1999

**Most passed balls, inning**
NL—2—Carlos Hernandez, San Diego, Sept 29, 1998, 3rd
AL—2—Jason Varitek, Boston, Sept 30, 1998, 1st

## DOUBLE PLAYS AND RUNNERS CAUGHT STEALING

**Most double plays, career**
ML—4—Joe Girardi, Colorado NL, 1995; New York AL, 1996-1999; 5 series, 17 G (2 in AL, 2 in NL)
NL—3—Javy Lopez, Atlanta, 1995-1998, 2000, 2002, 2003; 7 series, 21 G
AL—2—Ivan Rodriguez, Texas, 1996, 1998, 1999; 3 series, 10 G
Jorge Posada, New York, 1997-2005; 9 series, 31 G
Jason Varitek, Boston, 1998, 1999, 2003-2005; 5 series, 16 G
Henry Blanco, Minnesota, 2004; 1 series, 4 G

**Most double plays, series**
NL—2—Joe Girardi, Colorado, 1995 (4-game series)
Brian Johnson, San Diego, 1996 (3-game series)
Mike Piazza, Los Angeles, 1996 (3-game series)
Javy Lopez, Atlanta, 1998 (3-game series)
Bobby Estalella, San Francisco, 2000 (4-game series)
AL—2—Henry Blanco, Minnesota, 2004 (4-game series)

**Most double plays started, series**
NL—2—Joe Girardi, Colorado, 1995 (4-game series)
Mike Piazza, Los Angeles, 1996 (3-game series)
Javy Lopez, Atlanta, 1998 (3-game series)
Bobby Estalella, San Francisco, 2000 (4-game series)
AL—1—many catchers

**Most double plays, game**
NL—2—Mike Piazza, Los Angeles, Oct 5, 1996
[2—Joe Girardi, Colorado, Oct 6, 1995, 10 inn
Javy Lopez, Atlanta, Oct 1, 1998, 10 inn]
AL—2—Henry Blanco, Minnesota, Oct 5, 2004

**Most double plays started, game**
NL—2—Mike Piazza, Los Angeles, Oct 5, 1996
[2—Joe Girardi, Colorado, Oct 6, 1995, 10 inn
Javy Lopez, Atlanta, Oct 1, 1998, 10 inn]
AL—1—many catchers

**Most unassisted double plays, game**
AL—1—Jason Varitek, Boston, Oct 1, 2003, 2nd
NL—none

**Most runners caught stealing, career**
AL—9—Jorge Posada, New York, 1997-2005; 9 series, 31 G
NL—7—Javy Lopez, Atlanta, 1995-1998, 2000, 2002, 2003; 7 series, 21 G

**Most runners caught stealing, series**
AL—3—Chris Hoiles, Baltimore, 1996 (4-game series)
Jorge Posada, New York, 2004 (4-game series)
Jorge Posada, New York, 2005 (5-game series)
NL—3—Mike Piazza, Los Angeles, 1996 (3-game series)
Javy Lopez, Atlanta, 1998 (3-game series)
Carlos Hernandez, St. Louis, 2000 (3-game series)

**Most runners caught stealing, game**
AL—2—Ivan Rodriguez, Texas, Sept 29, 1998
Jorge Posada, New York, Oct 9, 2004
[2—Chris Hoiles, Baltimore, Oct 5, 1996, 12 inn]
NL—2—Brian Johnson, San Diego, Oct 1, 1996
Carlos Hernandez, St. Louis, Oct 3, 2000
Brad Ausmus, Houston, Oct 9, 2001
[3—Mike Piazza, Los Angeles, Oct 2, 1996, 10 inn]

**Most runners caught stealing, inning**
AL-NL—1—many catchers

# PITCHERS

## GAMES

**Most games, career**
AL—27—Mariano Rivera, New York, 1995-2005; 11 series
NL—15—John Smoltz, Atlanta, 1995-1999, 2001-2005; 10 series

**Most games, series**
3-game series
AL-NL—3—many pitchers
4-game series
AL—4—Jesse Orosco, Baltimore, 1996
Steve Karsay, New York, 2002
Mariano Rivera, New York, 2004
NL—4—Mike Munoz, Colorado, 1995
Bruce Ruffin, Colorado, 1995
Trevor Hoffman, San Diego, 1998
Chris Reitsma, Atlanta, 2005
5-game series
AL—5—Scott Williamson, Boston, 2003
NL—5—Kevin Gryboski, Atlanta, 2003, 2004

## PUTOUTS, ASSISTS AND CHANCES ACCEPTED

**Most putouts, career**
NL—7—Mike Hampton, Houston, 1997-1999; New York, 2000; Atlanta, 2003, 2004; 6 series, 8 G
AL—6—Derek Lowe, Boston, 1998, 1999, 2003, 2004; 4 series, 9 G
Mariano Rivera, New York, 1995-2005; 11 series, 27 G

**Most putouts, series**
3-game series
NL—3—Mike Hampton, Houston, 1997
AL—2—Charles Nagy, Cleveland, 1995

Pedro Martinez, Boston, 2004
Curt Schilling, Boston, 2004

4-game series
AL—2—Jamie Moyer, Seattle, 1997
Mike Mussina, Baltimore, 1997
Pete Schourek, Boston, 1998
Mariano Rivera, New York, 2003, 2004
Jon Lieber, New York, 2004
NL—2—Mike Hampton, New York, 2000

5-game series
AL—6—Derek Lowe, Boston, 2003
NL—2—Woody Williams, St. Louis, 2001
Livan Hernandez, San Francisco, 2002
John Smoltz, Atlanta, 2004

**Most putouts, game**
NL—3—Mike Hampton, Houston, Oct 1, 1997
Mike Hampton, New York, Oct 4, 2000
AL—3—Charles Nagy, Cleveland, Oct 7, 1999
[6—Derek Lowe, Boston, Oct 4, 2003, pitched 7 inn of 11-inn game]

**Most putouts, inning**
AL—2—Charles Nagy, Cleveland, Oct 6, 1995, 4th
NL—2—Jay Powell, Houston, Oct 1, 1998, 8th

**Most assists, career**
ML—18—Andy Pettitte, New York AL, 1995-2003; Houston NL, 2005; 10 series, 12 G
AL—16—Andy Pettitte, New York, 1995-2003; 9 series, 11 G
NL—12—Greg Maddux, Atlanta, 1995-2003; 9 series, 11 G

**Most assists, series**
3-game series
AL—3—Roger Clemens, New York, 1999
NL—3—Tom Glavine, Atlanta, 2001
Shane Reynolds, Houston, 2001
Mark Mulder, St. Louis, 2005

4-game series
NL—5—Greg Maddux, Atlanta, 1995
AL—4—Charles Nagy, Cleveland, 1996
Jeff Fassero, Seattle, 1997
Mike Mussina, Baltimore, 1997

5-game series
AL—5—Andy Pettitte, New York, 1997
John Lackey, Los Angeles, 2005
NL—4—Mike Hampton, Atlanta, 2003

**Most assists, game**
AL—4—Charles Nagy, Cleveland, Oct 1, 1996
Jeff Fassero, Seattle, Oct 4, 1997
Andy Pettitte, New York, Oct 6, 1997
Tim Hudson, Oakland, Oct 11, 2001
Mark Mulder, Oakland, Oct 2, 2002
NL—4—Greg Maddux, Atlanta, Oct 3, 1995
Kevin Millwood, Atlanta, Oct 6, 1999

**Most assists, inning**
AL—2—many pitchers
NL—2—Kevin Millwood, Atlanta, Oct 6, 1999, 3rd
Mark Mulder, St. Louis, Oct 6, 2005, 2nd

**Most chances accepted, career**
AL—18—Andy Pettitte, New York, 1995-2003; 9 series, 11 G
NL—17—Greg Maddux, Atlanta, 1995-2003; 9 series, 11 G

**Most chances accepted, series**
3-game series
AL—4—Erik Hanson, Boston, 1995
Roger Clemens, New York, 1999
NL—4—Greg Maddux, Atlanta, 1996
Tom Glavine, Atlanta, 2001

4-game series
NL—6—Greg Maddux, Atlanta, 1995
AL—6—Mike Mussina, Baltimore, 1997

5-game series
AL—8—Derek Lowe, Boston, 2003
NL—5—Mike Hampton, Atlanta, 2003

**Most chances accepted, game**
NL—5—Greg Maddux, Atlanta, Oct 3, 1995
Kevin Millwood, Atlanta, Oct 6, 1999
AL—5—Jeff Fassero, Seattle, Oct 4, 1997
Andy Pettitte, New York, Oct 6, 1997
Tim Hudson, Oakland, Oct 11, 2001
[8—Derek Lowe, Boston, Oct 4, 2003, pitched 7 inn of 11-inn game]

**Most chances accepted, inning**
AL-NL—2—many pitchers

## ERRORS AND DOUBLE PLAYS

**Most errors, career**
AL—2—LaTroy Hawkins, Minnesota, 2002, 2003; 2 series, 6 G
NL—1—many pitchers

**Most consecutive errorless games, career**
AL—27—Mariano Rivera, New York, Oct 4, 1995-Oct 9, 2005
NL—14—John Smoltz, Atlanta, Oct 6, 1995-Oct 10, 2004

**Most errors, series**
AL—2—LaTroy Hawkins, Minnesota, 2003 (4-game series)
NL—1—many pitchers

**Most chances accepted, errorless series**
NL—6—Greg Maddux, Atlanta, 1995 (4-game series)
AL—6—Mike Mussina, Baltimore, 1997 (4-game series)
Andy Pettitte, New York, 1997 (5-game series)

**Most errors, game**
AL-NL—1—many pitchers

**Most double plays, career**
AL—2—Darren Oliver, Texas, 1996; 1 series, 1 G
Freddy Garcia, Seattle, 2000, 2001; Chicago, 2005; 3 series, 4 G
NL—1—many pitchers

**Most double plays, series**
AL—2—Darren Oliver, Texas, 1996 (4-game series)
NL—1—many pitchers

**Most double plays started, series**
AL-NL—1—many pitchers

**Most double plays, game**
AL—2—Darren Oliver, Texas, Oct 4, 1996
NL—1—many pitchers

**Most double plays started, game**
AL-NL—1—many pitchers

**Most unassisted double plays, game**
AL-NL—none

# CLUB FIELDING

## AVERAGE

**Highest fielding average, series**
3-game series
NL—1.000—San Francisco vs Florida, 1997
Atlanta vs Chicago, 1998
AL—.991—New York vs Texas, 1998
Texas vs New York, 1998
Seattle vs Chicago, 2000
Boston vs Anaheim, 2004
Chicago vs Boston, 2005

4-game series
AL—1.000—Baltimore vs Seattle, 1997
Boston vs Cleveland, 1998
NL—1.000—New York vs Arizona, 1999
New York vs San Francisco, 2000
St. Louis vs Los Angeles, 2004
Atlanta vs. Houston, 2005

5-game series
NL—1.000—Atlanta vs San Francisco, 2002
Chicago vs Atlanta, 2003
AL—.994—Los Angeles vs New York, 2005

**For a list of fielding statistics by teams each series, see page 298.**

**Highest fielding average by both clubs, series**
3-game series
AL—.991—New York .991, Texas .991, 1998
NL—.983—Los Angeles .991, Atlanta .974, 1996

4-game series
AL—.997—Baltimore 1.000, Seattle .993, 1997
Boston 1.000, Cleveland .993, 1998
NL—.997—New York 1.000, San Francisco .994, 2000

5-game series
NL—.989—Atlanta 1.000, San Francisco .979, 2002
AL—.988—Seattle .990, New York .985, 1995

**Lowest fielding average, series**
3-game series
NL—.954—Atlanta vs St. Louis, 2000
AL—.955—Cleveland vs Boston, 1995

4-game series
NL—.955—San Francisco vs Florida, 2003

AL—.972—New York vs Anaheim, 2002
5-game series
AL—.968—New York vs Los Angeles, 2005
NL—.971—Atlanta vs Chicago, 2003

**Lowest fielding average by both clubs, series**
3-game series
AL—.961—Boston .967, Cleveland .955, 1995
NL—.969—Atlanta .974, Houston .962, 1997
4-game series
NL—.970—Florida .986, San Francisco .955, 2003
AL—.975—Cleveland .980, Baltimore .975, 1996
5-game series
AL—.974—New York .978, Oakland .970, 2001
NL—.981—St. Louis .984, Arizona .979, 2001

## PUTOUTS

**Most putouts, total series**
AL—1,288—New York; 11 series, 47 G
NL—1,165—Atlanta; 11 series, 42 G

**Most putouts, series**
3-game series
AL—93—Cleveland vs Boston, 1995
NL—84—Atlanta vs Los Angeles, 1996
Atlanta vs Chicago, 1998
4-game series
NL—132—Houston vs Atlanta, 2005
AL—123—New York vs Minnesota, 2004
5-game series
AL—154—Seattle vs New York, 1995
NL—140—Houston vs Atlanta, 2004

**Most putouts by both clubs, series**
3-game series
AL—182—Cleveland 93, Boston 89, 1995
NL—165—Atlanta 84, Los Angeles 81, 1996
4-game series
NL—262—Houston 132, Atlanta 130, 2005
AL—245—New York 123, Minnesota 122, 2004
5-game series
AL—304—Seattle 154, New York 150, 1995
NL—278—Houston 140, Atlanta 138, 2004

**Fewest putouts, series**
3-game series
NL—75—San Diego vs St. Louis, 1996
Houston vs Atlanta, 1997
Atlanta vs St. Louis, 2000
San Diego vs St. Louis, 2005
AL—75—Texas vs New York, 1998
Texas vs New York, 1999
Boston vs Chicago, 2005
4-game series
NL—102—Houston vs San Diego, 1998
Los Angeles vs St. Louis, 2004
AL—102—New York vs Anaheim, 2002
5-game series
AL—129—Cleveland vs Boston, 1999
Cleveland vs Seattle, 2001
New York vs Los Angeles, 2005
NL—131—St. Louis vs Arizona, 2001

**Fewest putouts by both clubs, series**
3-game series
NL—156—St. Louis 81, San Diego 75, 1996
Atlanta 81, Houston 75, 1997
St. Louis 81, Atlanta 75, 2000
St. Louis 81, San Diego 75, 2005
AL—156—New York 81, Texas 75, 1998
New York 81, Texas 75, 1999
Chicago 81, Boston 75, 2005
4-game series
AL—207—Anaheim 105, New York 102, 2002
NL—207—St. Louis 105, Los Angeles 102, 2004
5-game series
AL—259—Boston 130, Cleveland 129, 1999
NL—263—Arizona 132, St. Louis 131, 2001

**Most putouts by outfield, game**
AL—13—New York vs Texas, Oct 5, 1999
NL—12—San Francisco vs Florida, Sept 30, 1997
[17—Atlanta vs Houston, Oct 9, 2005, 18 inn]

**Most putouts by outfield of both clubs, game**
AL—22—New York 12, Seattle 10, Oct 3, 1995
NL—19—Cincinnati 11, Los Angeles 8, Oct 4, 1995
Los Angeles 10, St. Louis 9, Oct 7, 2004
Atlanta 11, Houston 8, Oct 8, 2005
[29—Atlanta 17, Houston 12, Oct 9, 2005, 18 inn]

**Fewest putouts by outfield, game**
NL—2—Houston vs San Diego, Oct 3, 1998 (fielded 8 inn)
Atlanta vs Chicago, Sept 30, 2003
Atlanta vs Chicago, Oct 5, 2003
Los Angeles vs St. Louis, Oct 5, 2004 (fielded 8 inn)
[3—Los Angeles vs Atlanta, Oct 2, 1996, 10 inn]
AL—2—many teams
[4—Oakland vs Boston, Oct 4, 2003, 11 inn
Anaheim vs Boston, Oct 8, 2004, 10 inn
New York vs Minnesota, Oct 6, 2004, 12 inn]

**Fewest putouts by outfield of both clubs, game**
NL—7—many games
[8—Atlanta 4, Houston 4, Oct 7, 2004, 10 inn]
AL—5—Seattle 3, Cleveland 2, Oct 15, 2001 (Cleveland fielded 8 inn)
[9—Boston 5, Oakland 4, Oct 4, 2003, 11 inn]

**Most putouts by outfield, inning**
AL-NL—3—many clubs

**Most putouts by outfield of both clubs, inning**
AL-NL—5—many times

**Most putouts by catchers of both clubs, inning**
AL—6—Chicago 3, Seattle 3, Oct 4, 2000, 9th
NL—5—Houston 3, Atlanta 2, Oct 3, 1997, 2nd

## ASSISTS

**Most assists, total series**
AL—491—New York; 11 series, 47 G
NL—459—Atlanta; 11 series, 42 G

**Most assists, series**
3-game series
AL—38—Chicago vs Seattle, 2000
NL—36—St. Louis vs San Diego, 2005
4-game series
NL—57—Houston vs Atlanta, 2005
AL—55—New York vs Minnesota, 2004
5-game series
NL—68—Atlanta vs Chicago, 2003
AL—60—Oakland vs New York, 2001

**Most assists by both clubs, series**
3-game series
AL—69—Chicago 35, Boston 34, 2005
NL—67—St. Louis 36, San Diego 31, 2005
4-game series
AL—105—New York 55, Minnesota 50, 2004
NL—102—Houston 57, Atlanta 45, 2005
5-game series
NL—122—Atlanta 64, Houston 58, 2004
AL—113—Cleveland 58, New York 55, 1997

**Fewest assists, series**
3-game series
NL—18—St. Louis vs San Diego, 1996
AL—25—Anaheim vs Boston, 2004
Boston vs Anaheim, 2004
4-game series
NL—31—Los Angeles vs St. Louis, 2004
AL—33—Boston vs Cleveland, 1998
Anaheim vs New York, 2002
5-game series
AL—36—Minnesota vs Oakland, 2002
NL—40—Atlanta vs San Francisco, 2002

**Fewest assists by both clubs, series**
3-game series
NL—45—Atlanta 25, Chicago 20, 1998
AL—50—Anaheim 25, Boston 25, 2004
4-game series
NL—65—St. Louis 34, Los Angeles 31, 2004
AL—72—New York 39, Anaheim 33, 2002
5-game series
AL—84—Oakland 48, Minnesota 36, 2002
NL—96—San Francisco 56, Atlanta 40, 2002

**Most assists, game**
NL—21—Atlanta vs Colorado, Oct 3, 1995
AL—17—New York vs Cleveland, Oct 6, 1997
New York vs Oakland, Oct 4, 2000
[21—New York vs Seattle, Oct 4, 1995, 15 inn]

**Most assists by both clubs, game**
NL—35—Atlanta 21, Colorado 14, Oct 3, 1995
AL—32—New York 17, Cleveland 15, Oct 6, 1997
Los Angeles 16, New York 16, Oct 5, 2005
[38—New York 21, Seattle 17, Oct 4, 1995, 15 inn]

**Fewest assists, game**
AL—4—Boston vs Cleveland, Oct 2, 1998 (fielded 8 inn)
Minnesota vs Oakland, Oct 5, 2002
[4—Cleveland vs Baltimore, Oct 5, 1996, 12 inn]
NL—2—Los Angeles vs St. Louis, Oct 7, 2004 (fielded 8 inn)

**Fewest assists by both clubs, game**
AL—15—Baltimore 10, Cleveland 5, Oct 4, 1996
[10—New York 5, Seattle 5, Oct 8, 1995, 11 inn]
NL—10—St. Louis 8, Los Angeles 2, Oct 7, 2004

**Most assists by outfield, game**
AL—2—Cleveland vs Baltimore, Oct 2, 1996
Seattle vs Baltimore, Oct 2, 1997
New York vs Minnesota, Oct 8, 2004
[2—Seattle vs New York, Oct 4, 1995, 15 inn]
NL—2—Houston vs Atlanta, Oct 6, 2005

**Most assists by outfield of both clubs, game**
AL—3—Seattle 2, Baltimore 1, Oct 2, 1997
[3—Seattle 2, New York 1, Oct 4, 1995, 15 inn]
NL—2—Houston 2, Atlanta 0, Oct 6, 2005

**Most assists by outfield, inning**
NL—2—Houston vs Atlanta, Oct 6, 2005, 7th
AL—1—many clubs

## CHANCES OFFERED

**Fewest chances offered to outfield, game**
NL—2—Houston vs San Diego, Oct 3, 1998 (fielded 8 inn)
Atlanta vs Chicago, Oct 5, 2003
Los Angeles vs St. Louis, Oct 5, 2004 (fielded 8 inn)
[3—Los Angeles vs Atlanta, Oct 2, 1996, 10 inn]
AL—2—Boston vs Cleveland, Oct 11, 1999
[4—Anaheim vs Boston, Oct 8, 2004, 10 inn]

**Fewest chances offered to outfield of both clubs, game**
NL—7—Florida 4, San Francisco 3, Oct 1, 1997
Houston 4, San Diego 3, Oct 4, 1998
New York 4, Arizona 3, Oct 6, 1999
St. Louis 5, Los Angeles 2, Oct 5, 2004 (Los Angeles fielded 8 inn)
[8—Atlanta 4, Houston 4, Oct 7, 2004, 11 inn]
AL—7—Boston 4, Cleveland 3, Sept 30, 1998 (Boston fielded 8 inn)
[11—Minnesota 6, New York 5, Oct 9, 2004, 11 inn]

## ERRORS

**Most errors, total series**
AL—32—New York; 11 series, 47 G
NL—23—Atlanta; 11 series, 42 G

**Most errors, series**
3-game series
AL—6—Cleveland vs Boston, 1995
NL—5—Atlanta vs St. Louis, 2000
4-game series
NL—7—Colorado vs Atlanta, 1995
San Francisco vs Florida, 2003
AL—4—Baltimore vs Cleveland, 1996
New York vs Anaheim, 2002
5-game series
NL—6—Atlanta vs Chicago, 2003
AL—6—Oakland vs New York, 2001
New York vs Los Angeles, 2005

**Most errors by both clubs, series**
3-game series
AL—10—Cleveland 6, Boston 4, 1995
NL—7—Houston 4, Atlanta 3, 1997
4-game series
NL—9—Colorado 7, Atlanta 2, 1995
San Francisco 7, Florida 2, 2003
AL—7—Baltimore 4, Cleveland 3, 1996
5-game series
AL—10—Oakland 6, New York 4, 2001
Boston 5, Oakland 5, 2003
NL—7—Arizona 4, St. Louis 3, 2001

**Fewest errors, series**
3-game series
NL—0—San Francisco vs Florida, 1997
Atlanta vs Chicago, 1998
AL—1—New York vs Texas, 1998
Texas vs New York, 1998
Seattle vs Chicago, 1999
Boston vs Anaheim, 2004
Chicago vs Boston, 2005
4-game series
AL—0—Baltimore vs Seattle, 1997
Boston vs Cleveland, 1998
NL—0—New York vs Arizona, 1999
New York vs San Francisco, 2000
St. Louis vs Los Angeles, 2004
Atlanta vs Houston, 2005
5-game series
NL—0—Atlanta vs San Francisco, 2002
Chicago vs Atlanta, 2003
AL—1—Los Angeles vs New York, 2005

**Fewest errors by both clubs, series**
3-game series
AL—1—Cleveland 1, Boston 0, 1998
NL—4—Atlanta 3, Los Angeles 1, 1996
Florida 4, San Francisco 0, 1997
Chicago 4, Atlanta 0, 1998
Houston 3, Atlanta 1, 2001
St. Louis 2, Arizona 2, 2002
San Diego 2, St. Louis 2, 2005
4-game series
AL—1—Seattle 1, Baltimore 0, 1997
NL—1—San Francisco 1, New York 0, 2000
5-game series
NL—4—San Francisco 4, Atlanta 0, 2002
Houston 3, Atlanta 1, 2004
AL—5—New York 3, Seattle 2, 1995

**Most errors, game**
NL—4—Colorado vs Atlanta, Oct 3, 1995
Atlanta vs Chicago, Oct 3, 2003
AL—3—Oakland vs New York, Oct 15, 2001
Seattle vs Cleveland, Oct 13, 2001
Minnesota vs Oakland, Oct 1, 2003
New York vs Los Angeles, Oct 5, 2005
[4—Oakland vs Boston, Oct 4, 2003, 11 inn]

**Most errors by both clubs, game**
AL—4—Oakland 3, New York 1, Oct 15, 2001
[6—Oakland 4, Boston 2, Oct 4, 2003, 11 inn]
NL—5—Colorado 4, Atlanta 1, Oct 3, 1995

**Most errors by infield, game**
NL—3—many clubs
AL—2—many clubs
[3—Oakland vs Boston, Oct 4, 2003, 11 inn]

**Most errors by infields of both clubs, game**
NL—3—Colorado 2, Atlanta 1, Oct 4, 1995
Atlanta 2, Houston 1, Oct 3, 1997
San Francisco 2, Florida 1, Sept 30, 2003
AL—3—Oakland 2, New York 1, Oct 15, 2001
[4—Oakland 3, Boston 1, Oct 4, 2003, 11 inn]

**Most errors by outfield, game**
NL—2—Atlanta vs Los Angeles, Oct 3, 1996
AL—2—Seattle vs Cleveland, Oct 13, 2001

**Most errors by outfields of both clubs, game**
NL—2—Atlanta 1, Colorado 1, Oct 3, 1995
Cincinnati 1, Los Angeles 1, Oct 6, 1995
Houston 1, Atlanta 1, Oct 1, 1997
Atlanta 2, Los Angeles 0, Oct 3, 1996
AL—2—Seattle 2, Cleveland 0, Oct 13, 2001

**Longest errorless game**
NL—18 inn—Houston vs Atlanta, Oct 9, 2005
AL—15 inn—New York vs Seattle, Oct 4, 1995

**Longest errorless game by both clubs**
NL—13 inn—New York 0, San Francisco 0, Oct 7, 2000
AL—11 inn—New York 0, Seattle 0, Oct 8, 1995

**Most errors, inning**
AL—3—Oakland vs Boston, Oct 4, 2003, 2nd
NL—2—Colorado vs Atlanta, Oct 3, 1995, 6th
Florida vs San Francisco, Oct 1, 1997, 9th
Atlanta vs St. Louis, Oct 3, 2000, 1st
Atlanta vs Chicago, Oct 6, 2003, 5th

## PASSED BALLS

**Most passed balls, total series**
AL—8—Boston; 6 series, 23 G
NL—2—San Diego; 3 series, 10 G

**Most passed balls, series**
AL—3—Boston vs Cleveland, 1999 (5-game series)
NL—2—San Diego vs Houston, 1998 (4-game series)

**Most passed balls by both clubs, series**
AL—3—Boston 3, Cleveland 0, 1999 (5-game series)
NL—2—San Diego 2, Houston 0, 1998 (4-game series)

**Most passed balls, game**
NL—2—San Diego vs Houston, Sept 29, 1998
AL—2—Boston vs Cleveland, Sept 30, 1998
Boston vs Cleveland, Oct 10, 1999

## DOUBLE AND TRIPLE PLAYS

**Most double plays, total series**
AL—43—New York; 11 series, 47 G
NL—41—Atlanta; 11 series, 42 G

**Most double plays, series**
3-game series
NL—7—Houston vs Atlanta, 2001
St. Louis vs San Diego, 2005
AL—5—New York vs Texas, 1999
Seattle vs Chicago, 2000
Chicago vs Seattle, 2000
4-game series
AL—9—Minnesota vs New York, 2004
NL—7—Atlanta vs Houston, 2005
5-game series
NL—8—Atlanta vs Chicago, 2003
AL—7—New York vs Oakland, 2000

**Most double plays by both clubs, series**
3-game series
NL—12—Houston 7, Atlanta 5, 2001
AL—10—Seattle 5, Chicago 5, 2000
4-game series
AL—13—Minnesota 9, New York 4, 2004
NL—13—Atlanta 7, Houston 6, 2005
5-game series
NL—11—Atlanta 7, Houston 4, 2004
AL—10—New York 7, Oakland 3, 2000

**Fewest double plays, series**
3-game series
AL—0—Boston vs Cleveland, 1995
NL—0—St. Louis vs San Diego, 1996
Atlanta vs St. Louis, 2000
St. Louis vs Arizona, 2002
4-game series
AL—1—Cleveland vs Baltimore, 1996
Baltimore vs Seattle, 1997
NL—1—Houston vs San Diego, 1998
New York vs San Francisco, 2000
5-game series
AL—2—New York vs Cleveland, 1997
Oakland vs Minnesota, 2002
Boston vs Oakland, 2003
NL—2—Atlanta vs San Francisco, 2002
Chicago vs Atlanta, 2003

**Fewest double plays by both clubs, series**
3-game series
AL—1—Cleveland 1, Boston 0, 1995
NL—1—Arizona 1, St. Louis 0, 2002
4-game series
AL—3—Baltimore 2, Cleveland 1, 1996
NL—3—San Francisco 3, Florida 0, 2003
5-game series
NL—8—Arizona 4, St. Louis 4, 2001
San Francisco 6, Atlanta 2, 2002
AL—6—Oakland 4, Minnesota 2, 2002
Oakland 4, Boston 2, 2003

**Most double plays, game**
AL—5—Minnesota vs New York, Oct 5, 2004
NL—4—Atlanta vs Colorado, Oct 3, 1995
Houston vs Atlanta, Oct 10, 2001
St. Louis vs San Diego, Oct 6, 2005

**Most double plays by both clubs, game**
NL—7—Houston 4, Atlanta 3, Oct 10, 2001
AL—6—Anaheim 4, New York 2, Oct 1, 2002

**Most triple plays, series**
AL-NL—none

# MISCELLANEOUS

## CLUB AND DIVISION

### ONE-RUN DECISIONS

**Most one-run games won, series**
AL—2—New York vs Texas, 1996 (4-game series)
Cleveland vs New York, 1997 (5-game series)
Cleveland vs Boston, 1998 (4-game series)
Boston vs Oakland, 2003 (5-game series)
New York vs Minnesota, 2004 (4-game series)
NL—2—Atlanta vs Los Angeles, 1996 (3-game series)
Florida vs San Francisco, 1997 (3-game series)
San Diego vs Houston, 1998 (4-game series)
New York vs San Francisco, 2000 (4-game series)
Arizona vs St. Louis, 2001 (5-game series)
Florida vs San Francisco, 2003 (5-game series)

**Most one-run games by both clubs, series**
NL—3—San Diego (won 2) vs Houston (won 1), 1998 (4-game series)
AL—3—Boston (won 2) vs Oakland (won 1), 2003 (5-game series)

### LENGTH OF GAMES

#### BY INNINGS

**Longest game**
NL—18 inn—Houston 7, Atlanta 6, Oct 9, 2005
AL—15 inn—Seattle 5 at New York 7, Oct 4, 1995

**For a complete list of extra-inning games, see page 295.**

**Most extra-inning games, total series**
AL—5—New York; 11 series, 47 G; won 4, lost 1
NL—5—Atlanta; 11 series, 42 G; won 3, lost 2

**Most extra-inning games won, total series**
AL—4—New York; 11 series, 47 G; lost 1
NL—3—Atlanta; 11 series, 42 G; lost 2

**Most extra-inning games lost, total series**
NL—2—San Francisco; 3 series, 12 G; won 0
AL—2—Boston; 5 series, 23 G; won 2
Minnesota; 3 series, 13 G; won 0

**Most extra-inning games, series**
AL—2—New York vs Seattle, 1995 (5-game series)
Oakland vs Boston, 2003 (5-game series)
New York vs, Minnesota, 2004 (4-game series)
NL—2—New York vs San Francisco, 2000 (4-game series)

#### BY TIME

**Longest 9-inning game**
AL—4 hrs, 13 min—New York 9 at Oakland 2, Oct 14, 2001
NL—3 hrs, 47 min—San Francisco 3 at Atlanta 1, Oct 7, 2002

**Longest extra-inning game**
NL—5 hrs, 50 min—Houston 7, Atlanta 6, Oct 9, 2005, 18 inn
AL—5 hrs, 13 min—Seattle 5 at New York 7, Oct 4, 1995, 15 inn

**Shortest game**
NL—2 hrs, 8 min—Atlanta 3 at Los Angeles 2, Oct 3, 1996
AL—2 hrs, 27 min—Cleveland 4 at Boston 3, Oct 2, 1998

### SERIES STARTING AND FINISHING DATES

**Earliest date for series game**
NL—Sept 29, 1998—San Diego at Houston
AL—Sept 29, 1998—Texas at New York
Sept 29, 1998—Boston at Cleveland

**Earliest date for series final game**
AL—Oct 2, 1998—New York at Texas (3-game series)
NL—Oct 3, 1997—Florida at San Francisco (3-game series)
Oct 3, 1997—Atlanta at Houston (3-game series)
Oct 3, 1998—Atlanta at Chicago (3-game series)

**Latest date for series start**
AL—Oct 10, 2001—Oakland at New York
NL—Oct 9, 2001—Atlanta at Houston
Oct 9, 2001—St. Louis at Arizona

**Latest date for series finish**
AL—Oct 15, 2001—Oakland at New York (5-game series)
Oct 15, 2001—Cleveland at Seattle (5-game series)
NL—Oct 14, 2001—St. Louis at Arizona (5-game series)

### SERIES AND GAMES WON

**Most series won**
NL—6—Atlanta, 1995-1999, 2001 (lost 5)
AL—7—New York, 1996, 1998-2001, 2003, 2004 (lost 4)

**For complete lists of results, and series played by all teams, see page 295.**

**Most times winning series in three consecutive games**
NL—4—Atlanta, 1996-1998, 2001
AL—2—New York, 1998, 1999

**Winning series after winning first game**
NL—accomplished 19 times
AL—accomplished 9 times

**Winning series after losing first game**
AL—accomplished 13 times
NL—accomplished 3 times

**Winning series after trailing two games to one**
NL—San Francisco vs Atlanta, 2002
AL—Seattle vs New York, 1995
Cleveland vs New York, 1997
Boston vs Cleveland, 1999
New York vs Oakland, 2001

Seattle vs Cleveland, 2001
Minnesota vs Oakland, 2002
Boston vs Oakland, 2003

**Winning series after losing first two games**

AL—Seattle vs New York, 1995
Boston vs Cleveland, 1999
New York vs Oakland, 2001
Boston vs Oakland, 2003
NL—none

**Most games won, total series**

AL—28—New York; 11 series; lost 19
NL—25—Atlanta; 11 series; lost 17

**For complete lists of results, and games played by all teams, see page 295.**

**Most consecutive games won, total series**

NL—10—Atlanta, 1995 (last 1), 1996 (all 3), 1997 (all 3), 1998 (all 3)
AL—6—New York, 1998 (all 3), 1999 (all 3)

## SERIES AND GAMES LOST

**Most series lost**

NL—5—Atlanta, 2000, 2002, 2003, 2004, 2005 (won 6)
AL—4—Oakland, 2000, 2001, 2002, 2003 (won 0)
New York, 1995, 1997, 2002, 2005 (won 7)

**For complete lists of results, and games played by all teams, see page 295.**

**Most games lost, total series**

AL—19—New York; 11 series; won 28
NL—17—Atlanta; 11 series; won 25

**Most consecutive games lost, total series**

AL—9—Texas, 1996 (last 3), 1998 (all 3), 1999 (all 3)
NL—8—Los Angeles, 1995 (all 3), 1996 (all 3), 2004 (first 2)

## ATTENDANCE

**Largest attendance, series**

3-game series
AL—164,853—New York vs Texas, 1999
NL—164,844—St. Louis vs San Diego, 1996
4-game series
NL—225,763—San Diego vs Houston, 1998
AL—224,561—New York vs Minnesota, 2003
5-game series
AL—286,839—New York vs Seattle, 1995
NL—239,108—Chicago vs Atlanta, 2003

**For a list of attendance each series, see page 296.**

**Smallest attendance, series**

3-game series
NL—111,180—Atlanta vs Houston, 2001
AL—117,072—Boston vs Chicago, 2005
4-game series
AL—157,065—Cleveland vs Boston, 1998
NL—173,943—Atlanta vs Houston, 2005
5-game series
AL—202,917—Boston vs Cleveland, 1999
NL—220,386—San Francisco vs Atlanta, 2002

**Largest attendance, game**

NL—65,464—At Florida, Oct 4, 2003 (Florida 7, San Francisco 6)
AL—59,579—At Seattle, Oct 1, 1997 (Baltimore 9, Seattle 3)

**Smallest attendance, game**

AL—31,953—At Oakland, Oct 2, 2002 (Oakland 9, Minnesota 1)
NL—35,553—At Houston, Oct 9, 2001 (Atlanta 7, Houston 4)

**Largest attendance by each club, game**

### AMERICAN LEAGUE

| Club | Attendance | Date |
|---|---|---|
| Anaheim | 45,150 | Oct 5, 2005 |
| Baltimore | 49,137 | Oct 4, 1997 |
| Boston | 35,547 | Oct 8, 2004 |
| Chicago | 45,383 | Oct 4, 2000 |
| Cleveland | 45,274 | Oct 4, 1997 |
| Minnesota | 55,960 | Oct 5, 2002 |
| New York | 57,485 | Oct 7, 1999 |
| Oakland | 55,861 | Oct 13, 2001 |
| Seattle | 59,579 | Oct 1, 1997 |
| Texas | 50,860 | Oct 4, 1996 |

### NATIONAL LEAGUE

| Club | Attendance | Date |
|---|---|---|
| Arizona | 49,584 | Oct 5, 1999 |
| Atlanta | 54,357 | Oct 5, 2003 |
| Chicago | 39,983 | Oct 4, 2003 |
| Cincinnati | 53,276 | Oct 6, 1995 |
| Colorado | 50,063 | Oct 4, 1995 |
| Florida | 65,464 | Oct 4, 2003 |
| Houston | 53,688 | Oct 3, 1997 |
| Los Angeles | 56,268 | Oct 10, 2004 |
| New York | 56,270 | Oct 7, 2000 |
| St. Louis | 56,752 | Oct 3, 1996 |
| San Diego | 65,235 | Oct 3, 1998 |
| San Francisco | 57,188 | Oct 3, 1997 |

**Smallest attendance by each club, game**

### AMERICAN LEAGUE

| Club | Attendance | Date |
|---|---|---|
| Anaheim | 44,608 | Oct 5, 2004 |
| Baltimore | 47,644 | Oct 1, 1996 |
| Boston | 33,114 | Oct 2, 1998 |
| Chicago | 40,717 | Oct 4, 2005 |
| Cleveland | 44,218 | Oct 3, 1995 |
| Minnesota | 52,498 | Oct 9, 2004 |
| New York | 55,749 | Oct 5, 2004 |
| Oakland | 31,953 | Oct 2, 2002 |
| Seattle | 47,867 | Oct 15, 2001 |
| Texas | 49,950 | Oct 2, 1998 |

### NATIONAL LEAGUE

| Club | Attendance | Date |
|---|---|---|
| Arizona | 41,793 | Oct 10, 2001 |
| Atlanta | 39,119 | Oct 5, 1999 |
| Chicago | 39,597 | Oct 3, 1998 |
| Cincinnati | 53,276 | Oct 6, 1995 |
| Colorado | 50,040 | Oct 3, 1995 |
| Florida | 41,283 | Oct 1, 1997 |
| Houston | 35,553 | Oct 9, 2001 |
| Los Angeles | 44,199 | Oct 3, 1995 |
| New York | 52,888 | Oct 8, 2000 |
| St. Louis | 52,127 | Oct 5, 2004 |
| San Diego | 45,093 | Oct 8, 2005 |
| San Francisco | 40,430 | Oct 4, 2000 |
| San Francisco | 40,430 | Oct 5, 2000 |

# NON-PLAYING PERSONNEL

## MANAGERS

**Most series by manager**

NL—11—Bobby Cox, Atlanta, 1995-2005 (won 6, lost 5)
AL—10—Joe Torre, New York, 1996-2005 (won 7, lost 3)

**For a complete list of managers and their records, see page 300.**

**Most division series winners managed**

NL—6—Bobby Cox, Atlanta, 1995-1999, 2001 (lost 5)
AL—7—Joe Torre, New York, 1996, 1998-2001, 2003, 2004 (lost 3)

**Most division series losers managed**

NL—5—Bobby Cox, Atlanta, 2000, 2002-2005 (won 6)
AL—3—Johnny Oates, Texas, 1996, 1998, 1999 (won 0)
Art Howe, Oakland, 2000, 2001, 2002 (won 0)
Joe Torre, New York, 1997, 2002, 2005 (won 7)

**Most different clubs managed, league**

NL—2—Dusty Baker, San Francisco, 1997, 2000, 2002; Chicago, 2003
AL—1—many managers

**Most different clubs managed, both leagues**

2—Dave Johnson, Cincinnati NL, 1995; Baltimore AL, 1996, 1997
Buck Showalter, New York AL, 1995; Arizona NL, 1999
Dusty Baker, San Francisco NL, 1997, 2000, 2002; Chicago NL, 2003

## UMPIRES

**Most years umpired**

7—Bruce Froemming, 1995, 1996, 1998, 1999, 2001-2003; 28 G

**Most games umpired**

28—Bruce Froemming, 7 seasons

# CAREER MILESTONES

(Players active in the major leagues in 2005 are in boldface.)



## SERVICE

### SERIES PLAYED

| | Player | Series |
|---|---|---|
| 1. | **Chipper Jones** | 11 |
| | **Mariano Rivera** | 11 |
| | **Bernie Williams** | 11 |
| 4. | **Derek Jeter** | 10 |
| | **Andruw Jones** | 10 |
| | **Andy Pettitte** | 10 |
| | **Jorge Posada** | 10 |
| | **John Smoltz** | 10 |
| 9. | **Kenny Lofton** | 9 |
| | **Greg Maddux** | 9 |
| | **Tino Martinez** | 9 |
| 12. | **Roger Clemens** | 8 |
| | **Tom Glavine** | 8 |
| | **Jeff Nelson** | 8 |
| | **Manny Ramirez** | 8 |
| 16. | **Steve Finley** | 7 |
| | **Randy Johnson** | 7 |
| | **Javy Lopez** | 7 |
| | **Mike Mussina** | 7 |
| | **David Wells** | 7 |
| | David Justice | 7 |
| | Paul O'Neill | 7 |

### SERIES PITCHED

| | Player | Series |
|---|---|---|
| 1. | **Mariano Rivera** | 11 |
| 2. | **Andy Pettitte** | 10 |
| | **John Smoltz** | 10 |
| 4. | **Greg Maddux** | 9 |
| | **Roger Clemens** | 9 |
| 6. | **Tom Glavine** | 8 |
| | **Jeff Nelson** | 8 |
| 8. | **Randy Johnson** | 7 |
| | **Mike Mussina** | 7 |
| | **David Wells** | 7 |
| 11. | **Mike Hampton** | 6 |
| | **Mike Stanton** | 6 |
| | **Mike Timlin** | 6 |
| | Mike Jackson | 6 |
| 15. | **Chad Bradford** | 5 |
| | **Bartolo Colon** | 5 |
| | **Orlando Hernandez** | 5 |
| | **Tim Hudson** | 5 |
| | **Jason Isringhausen** | 5 |
| | **Matt Morris** | 5 |
| | **Mike Remlinger** | 5 |
| | **Julian Tavarez** | 5 |
| | **Jaret Wright** | 5 |
| | Paul Assenmacher | 5 |
| | Charles Nagy | 5 |

## BATTING

### GAMES

| | Player | Games |
|---|---|---|
| 1. | **Bernie Williams** | 47 |
| 2. | **Derek Jeter** | 42 |
| | **Chipper Jones** | 42 |
| 4. | **Andruw Jones** | 38 |
| 5. | **Tino Martinez** | 37 |
| 6. | **Kenny Lofton** | 35 |
| 7. | **Jorge Posada** | 32 |
| | **Manny Ramirez** | 32 |
| 9. | David Justice | 30 |
| 10. | **Steve Finley** | 28 |
| 11. | **Mariano Rivera** | 27 |
| | Paul O'Neill | 27 |
| 13. | **Omar Vizquel** | 26 |
| 14. | **Jim Thome** | 25 |

### BATTING AVERAGE

(minimum 50 AB)

| | Player | Avg. |
|---|---|---|
| 1. | MIke Stanley | .400 |
| 2. | Edgar Martinez | .375 |
| 3. | **Johnny Damon** | .362 |
| 4. | **Derek Jeter** | .358 |
| 5. | **Torii Hunter** | .353 |
| | **Edgardo Alfonzo** | .353 |
| 7. | **Vinny Castilla** | .350 |
| 8. | **Brian Jordan** | .339 |
| 9. | **Jim Edmonds** | .338 |
| | **Jason Giambi** | .338 |
| 11. | **Omar Vizquel** | .314 |
| | **J.T. Snow** | .314 |

### AT-BATS

| | Player | AB |
|---|---|---|
| 1. | **Bernie Williams** | 180 |
| 2. | **Derek Jeter** | 165 |
| 3. | **Chipper Jones** | 151 |
| 4. | **Kenny Lofton** | 140 |
| 5. | **Tino Martinez** | 133 |
| 6. | **Andruw Jones** | 125 |
| 7. | **Manny Ramirez** | 124 |
| 8. | **David Justice** | 108 |
| | **Jorge Posada** | 108 |
| 10. | **Omar Vizquel** | 102 |
| 11. | Paul O'Neill | 101 |

### RUNS

| | Player | R |
|---|---|---|
| 1. | **Bernie Williams** | 36 |
| 2. | **Chipper Jones** | 30 |
| 3. | **Derek Jeter** | 29 |
| 4. | **Kenny Lofton** | 26 |
| 5. | **Andruw Jones** | 23 |
| 6. | **Manny Ramirez** | 21 |

### HITS

| | Player | H |
|---|---|---|
| 1. | **Derek Jeter** | 59 |
| 2. | **Bernie Williams** | 51 |
| 3. | **Chipper Jones** | 41 |
| 4. | **Andruw Jones** | 36 |
| 5. | **Tino Martinez** | 32 |
| | **Omar Vizquel** | 32 |
| 7. | **Kenny Lofton** | 31 |
| 8. | **Jason Giambi** | 27 |
| | **Jorge Posada** | 27 |
| | **Manny Ramirez** | 27 |
| | Paul O'Neill | 27 |
| 12. | **Johnny Damon** | 25 |
| | David Justice | 25 |

### SINGLES

| | Player | Singles |
|---|---|---|
| 1. | **Derek Jeter** | 45 |
| 2. | **Chipper Jones** | 27 |
| | **Bernie Williams** | 27 |
| 4. | **Omar Vizquel** | 26 |
| 5. | **Andruw Jones** | 24 |
| 6. | **Kenny Lofton** | 23 |
| 7. | **Tino Martinez** | 21 |
| 8. | **Jason Giambi** | 20 |
| 9. | **Jorge Posada** | 18 |
| 10. | **Johnny Damon** | 17 |
| | **Rafael Furcal** | 17 |
| | **Fernando Vina** | 17 |
| | Mike Stanley | 17 |
| 14. | **Moises Alou** | 15 |
| | **Vinny Castilla** | 15 |
| | **Steve Finley** | 15 |
| | Paul O'Neill | 15 |

### DOUBLES

| | Player | Doubles |
|---|---|---|
| 1. | **Bernie Williams** | 16 |
| 2. | Roberto Alomar | 9 |
| 3. | **Tino Martinez** | 8 |
| | **Manny Ramirez** | 8 |
| 5. | **Edgardo Alfonzo** | 7 |
| | **Craig Biggio** | 7 |
| | **Jim Edmonds** | 7 |
| | **Andruw Jones** | 7 |
| | **Jeff Kent** | 7 |
| | **David Ortiz** | 7 |
| | **Miguel Tejada** | 7 |
| | David Justice | 7 |
| 13. | **Johnny Damon** | 6 |
| | **Jorge Posada** | 6 |
| | Paul O'Neill | 6 |

### TRIPLES

| | Player | Triples |
|---|---|---|
| 1. | **Rafael Furcal** | 2 |
| | **Omar Vizquel** | 2 |
| | **Tony Womack** | 2 |
| | David Justice | 2 |
| 5. | many tied with 1 | |

## HOME RUNS

| | Player | HR |
|---|---|---|
| 1. | Chipper Jones | 9 |
| 2. | Juan Gonzalez | 8 |
| | Derek Jeter | 8 |
| | Manny Ramirez | 8 |
| | Jim Thome | 8 |
| | Bernie Williams | 8 |
| 7. | Jim Edmonds | 7 |
| | Edgar Martinez | 7 |
| 9. | Ken Caminiti | 6 |
| | Paul O'Neill | 6 |
| 11. | Vinny Castilla | 5 |
| | Nomar Garciaparra | 5 |
| | Troy Glaus | 5 |
| | Ken Griffey Jr. | 5 |
| | Andruw Jones | 5 |

## TOTAL BASES

| | Player | TB |
|---|---|---|
| 1. | Bernie Williams | 91 |
| 2. | Derek Jeter | 90 |
| 3. | Chipper Jones | 73 |
| 4. | Manny Ramirez | 59 |
| 5. | Andruw Jones | 58 |
| 6. | Jim Edmonds | 51 |
| | Paul O'Neill | 51 |
| 8. | Edgar Martinez | 50 |
| 9. | Tino Martinez | 49 |
| 10. | David Justice | 48 |
| 11. | Juan Gonzalez | 46 |
| 12. | Kenny Lofton | 45 |
| 13. | Jim Thome | 43 |
| 14. | Jorge Posada | 42 |
| 15. | Javy Lopez | 40 |
| | Omar Vizquel | 40 |
| 17. | Jason Giambi | 38 |
| 18. | Edgardo Alfonzo | 37 |
| | Vinny Castilla | 37 |
| 20. | Johnny Damon | 36 |
| | Reggie Sanders | 36 |

## SLUGGING PERCENTAGE

(Minimum 50 at-bats)

| | Player | SLG |
|---|---|---|
| 1. | Edgar Martinez | .781 |
| 2. | Jim Edmonds | .750 |
| 3. | Juan Gonzalez | .742 |
| 4. | Edgardo Alfonzo | .725 |
| 5. | Vinny Castilla | .617 |
| 6. | Torii Hunter | .608 |
| 7. | Brian Jordan | .554 |
| 8. | Derek Jeter | .545 |
| | Mike Stanley | .545 |
| 10. | Garret Anderson | .540 |
| 11. | Albert Pujols | .539 |
| 12. | Johnny Damon | .522 |
| 13. | Javy Lopez | .520 |
| 14. | Hideki Matsui | .519 |
| 15. | Barry Bonds | .509 |
| 16. | Bernie Williams | .506 |
| 17. | Paul O'Neill | .505 |

## EXTRA-BASE HITS

| | Player | EHB |
|---|---|---|
| 1. | Bernie Williams | 24 |
| 2. | Manny Ramirez | 16 |
| 3. | Jim Edmonds | 14 |
| | Derek Jeter | 14 |
| | Chipper Jones | 14 |
| 6. | David Justice | 13 |
| 7. | Juan Gonzalez | 12 |
| | Andruw Jones | 12 |
| | Edgar Martinez | 12 |
| | Paul O'Neill | 12 |
| 11. | Edgardo Alfonzo | 11 |
| | Tino Martinez | 11 |
| 13. | Roberto Alomar | 10 |

## RUNS BATTED IN

| | Player | RBI |
|---|---|---|
| 1. | Bernie Williams | 33 |
| 2. | Chipper Jones | 26 |
| 3. | Manny Ramirez | 23 |
| 4. | Edgar Martinez | 20 |
| 5. | Derek Jeter | 19 |
| | Andruw Jones | 19 |
| 7. | Edgardo Alfonzo | 17 |
| | Jim Thome | 17 |
| 9. | Brian Jordan | 16 |
| | Omar Vizquel | 16 |
| 11. | Jim Edmonds | 15 |
| | Nomar Garciaparra | 15 |
| | Juan Gonzalez | 15 |
| | Tino Martinez | 15 |
| | Reggie Sanders | 15 |
| | David Justice | 15 |

## WALKS

| | Player | BB |
|---|---|---|
| 1. | Chipper Jones | 36 |
| 2. | Bernie Williams | 26 |
| 3. | Jason Giambi | 20 |
| | Andruw Jones | 20 |
| 5. | Derek Jeter | 18 |
| | Gary Sheffield | 18 |
| 7. | Kenny Lofton | 17 |
| 8. | Jeff Bagwell | 15 |
| | Barry Bonds | 15 |
| | Tino Martinez | 15 |
| 11. | David Justice | 14 |
| 12. | Manny Ramirez | 13 |
| | Edgar Renteria | 13 |
| | Edgar Martinez | 13 |

## STRIKEOUTS

| | Player | K |
|---|---|---|
| 1. | Jim Thome | 34 |
| 2. | Manny Ramirez | 32 |
| 3. | Chipper Jones | 30 |
| 4. | Derek Jeter | 29 |
| | Bernie Williams | 29 |
| 6. | Jorge Posada | 27 |
| 7. | Andruw Jones | 26 |
| | Kenny Lofton | 26 |
| | Reggie Sanders | 26 |
| 10. | Jim Edmonds | 23 |
| 11. | Dan Wilson | 22 |
| 12. | David Justice | 21 |
| 13. | Ryan Klesko | 20 |

## STOLEN BASES

| | Player | SB |
|---|---|---|
| 1. | Kenny Lofton | 13 |
| 2. | Omar Vizquel | 10 |
| 3. | Rafael Furcal | 9 |
| | Rickey Henderson | 9 |
| 5. | Johnny Damon | 7 |
| 6. | Edgar Renteria | 5 |
| | Alfonso Soriano | 5 |
| 8. | Derek Jeter | 4 |
| | Reggie Sanders | 4 |
| | Barry Larkin | 4 |

# PITCHING

## GAMES

| | Player | Games |
|---|---|---|
| 1. | Mariano Rivera | 27 |
| 2. | Jeff Nelson | 20 |
| 3. | Mike Stanton | 16 |
| 4. | John Smoltz | 15 |
| | Mike Jackson | 15 |
| 6. | Paul Assenmacher | 14 |
| 7. | Kevin Gryboski | 13 |
| 8. | Roger Clemens | 12 |
| | Andy Pettitte | 12 |
| | Julian Tavarez | 12 |
| 11. | Jason Isringhausen | 11 |
| | Randy Johnson | 11 |
| | Greg Maddux | 11 |
| | Mike Remlinger | 11 |
| | Paul Shuey | 11 |
| | Mike Timlin | 11 |
| 17. | Armando Benitez | 10 |
| | Chad Bradford | 10 |
| | Alan Embree | 10 |
| | Tom Gordon | 10 |
| | Ricardo Rincon | 10 |
| | Jaret Wright | 10 |

## GAMES STARTED

| | Player | Games |
|---|---|---|
| 1. | Andy Pettitte | 12 |
| 2. | Roger Clemens | 11 |
| 3. | Greg Maddux | 10 |
| 4. | Tom Glavine | 9 |
| | Randy Johnson | 9 |
| | Mike Mussina | 9 |
| 7. | Bartolo Colon | 8 |

| | Player | Games |
|---|---|---|
| | Tim Hudson | 8 |
| | David Wells | 8 |
| 10. | Mike Hampton | 7 |
| | Charles Nagy | 7 |
| 12. | Russ Ortiz | 6 |
| | John Smoltz | 6 |
| 14. | Pedro Martinez | 5 |
| | Matt Morris | 5 |
| | Mark Mulder | 5 |
| | Jaret Wright | 5 |
| | Barry Zito | 5 |
| | David Cone | 5 |
| | Shane Reynolds | 5 |

## GAMES RELIEVED

| | Player | Games |
|---|---|---|
| 1. | Mariano Rivera | 27 |
| 2. | Jeff Nelson | 20 |
| 3. | Mike Stanton | 16 |
| 4. | Mike Jackson | 15 |
| 5. | Paul Assenmacher | 14 |
| 6. | Kevin Gryboski | 13 |
| 7. | Julian Tavarez | 12 |
| 8. | Jason Isringhausen | 11 |
| | Mike Remlinger | 11 |
| | Mike Timlin | 11 |
| | Paul Shuey | 11 |
| 12. | Armando Benitez | 10 |
| | Chad Bradford | 10 |
| | Alan Embree | 10 |
| | Tom Gordon | 10 |
| | Ricardo Rincon | 10 |

## COMPLETE GAMES

| | Player | CG |
|---|---|---|
| 1. | Curt Schilling | 2 |
| 2. | many tied with 1 | |

## INNINGS PITCHED

| | Player | IP |
|---|---|---|
| 1. | Andy Pettitte | 74.0 |
| 2. | Randy Johnson | 66.2 |
| 3. | Roger Clemens | 66.0 |
| | Greg Maddux | 66.0 |
| 5. | John Smoltz | 60.2 |
| 6. | David Wells | 56.0 |
| 7. | Mike Mussina | 53.1 |
| 8. | Tom Glavine | 50.2 |
| 9. | Tim Hudson | 47.2 |
| 10. | Bartolo Colon | 43.1 |
| 11. | Mike Hampton | 43.0 |
| 12. | Mariano Rivera | 42.0 |
| 13. | Charles Nagy | 40.0 |

## EARNED RUN AVERAGE

(minimum 30 IP)

| | Player | ERA |
|---|---|---|
| 1. | Mariano Rivera | 0.43 |
| 2. | Curt Schilling | 1.14 |
| 3. | Orlando Hernandez | 1.78 |
| 4. | Mark Mulder | 2.05 |
| 5. | Matt Morris | 2.19 |
| 6. | John Smoltz | 2.52 |
| 7. | Barry Zito | 2.76 |
| 8. | Pedro Martinez | 2.84 |
| 9. | David Wells | 3.05 |
| 10. | Greg Maddux | 3.14 |
| 11. | Mike Mussina | 3.38 |
| 12. | Tim Hudson | 3.97 |

## WINS

| | Player | W |
|---|---|---|
| 1. | John Smoltz | 7 |
| 2. | Greg Maddux | 5 |
| | Andy Pettitte | 5 |
| | David Wells | 5 |
| 5. | Roger Clemens | 4 |
| | Pedro Martinez | 4 |
| | Mike Mussina | 4 |
| 8. | many tied with 3 | |

## LOSSES

| | Player | L |
|---|---|---|
| 1. | Randy Johnson | 7 |
| 2. | Roger Clemens | 4 |
| | Tim Wakefield | 4 |
| | Jaret Wright | 4 |
| 5. | many tied with 3 | |

## SAVES

| | Player | SV |
|---|---|---|
| 1. | Mariano Rivera | 15 |
| 2. | Jason Isringhausen | 6 |
| 3. | Mark Wohlers | 5 |
| 4. | Kazuhiro Sasaki | 3 |
| | John Smoltz | 3 |
| | Rich Gossage | 3 |
| | Dennis Eckersley | 3 |
| | Mike Jackson | 3 |
| | Randy Myers | 3 |
| 10. | many tied with 2 | |

## RUNS

| | Player | R |
|---|---|---|
| 1. | Randy Johnson | 36 |
| 2. | Andy Pettitte | 35 |
| 3. | Roger Clemens | 33 |
| 4. | Tom Glavine | 30 |
| 5. | Greg Maddux | 28 |
| 6. | Tim Hudson | 27 |
| | Jaret Wright | 27 |
| 8. | Charles Nagy | 25 |
| 9. | Tim Wakefield | 24 |
| 10. | Mike Hampton | 23 |
| | David Wells | 23 |
| 12. | Mike Mussina | 21 |
| 13. | Bartolo Colon | 20 |
| | David Cone | 20 |
| | Bret Saberhagen | 20 |

## HITS

| | Player | H |
|---|---|---|
| 1. | Andy Pettitte | 76 |
| 2. | Greg Maddux | 70 |
| 3. | Randy Johnson | 67 |
| 4. | Roger Clemens | 62 |
| 5. | David Wells | 56 |
| 6. | Tom Glavine | 52 |
| 7. | Tim Hudson | 50 |
| 8. | Mike Mussina | 49 |
| 9. | Bartolo Colon | 45 |
| 10. | John Smoltz | 43 |

## HOME RUNS

| | Player | HR |
|---|---|---|
| 1. | Randy Johnson | 13 |
| 2. | Andy Pettitte | 11 |
| 3. | John Smoltz | 8 |
| | Jaret Wright | 8 |
| 5. | Mike Hampton | 7 |
| | Greg Maddux | 7 |
| | Mike Mussina | 7 |
| | David Cone | 7 |
| | Bret Saberhagen | 7 |
| 10. | Roger Clemens | 6 |
| | Kevin Millwood | 6 |
| | Andy Benes | 6 |
| | Charles Nagy | 6 |
| 14. | Bartolo Colon | 5 |
| | Freddy Garcia | 5 |
| | Tim Hudson | 5 |
| | Rick Reed | 5 |
| | Jarrod Washburn | 5 |

## TOTAL BASES

| | Player | TB |
|---|---|---|
| 1. | Andy Pettitte | 126 |
| 2. | Randy Johnson | 120 |
| 3. | Greg Maddux | 96 |
| 4. | Roger Clemens | 90 |
| 5. | Mike Mussina | 84 |
| 6. | Tim Hudson | 74 |
| | David Wells | 74 |
| 8. | Tom Glavine | 73 |
| | John Smoltz | 73 |
| 10. | Greg Maddux | 125 |
| | John Smoltz | 125 |

## STRIKEOUTS

| | Player | K |
|---|---|---|
| 1. | Randy Johnson | 77 |
| 2. | John Smoltz | 53 |
| 3. | Roger Clemens | 52 |
| 4. | Andy Pettitte | 49 |
| 5. | Mike Mussina | 48 |
| 6. | Greg Maddux | 40 |
| 7. | Bartolo Colon | 38 |
| 8. | Tom Glavine | 37 |
| | Mike Hampton | 37 |
| 10. | Pedro Martinez | 34 |

| Player | K |
|---|---|
| 11. Tim Hudson | 32 |
| Barry Zito | 32 |
| 13. David Wells | 31 |
| 14. David Cone | 30 |

## WALKS

| Player | BB |
|---|---|
| 1. Roger Clemens | 30 |
| 2. Tom Glavine | 23 |
| Mike Hampton | 23 |
| 4. Randy Johnson | 22 |
| 5. Russ Ortiz | 20 |
| Andy Pettitte | 20 |
| 7. Charles Nagy | 18 |
| 8. Bartolo Colon | 17 |
| 9. Tim Hudson | 16 |
| Greg Maddux | 16 |
| 11. Tim Wakefield | 15 |
| 12. Andy Benes | 14 |
| David Cone | 14 |
| 14. Orlando Hernandez | 13 |
| Matt Morris | 13 |
| Jaret Wright | 13 |
| 17. John Smoltz | 12 |
| 18. many tied with 11 | |

# GENERAL REFERENCE

## SERIES WON AND LOST BY TEAMS

### AMERICAN LEAGUE

| | W | L | Pct. |
|---|---|---|---|
| Baltimore | 2 | 0 | 1.000 |
| Seattle | 3 | 1 | .750 |
| Anaheim/Los Angeles | 2 | 1 | .667 |
| New York | 7 | 4 | .636 |
| Boston | 3 | 3 | .500 |
| Cleveland | 3 | 3 | .500 |
| Chicago | 1 | 1 | .500 |
| Minnesota | 1 | 2 | .333 |
| Texas | 0 | 3 | .000 |
| Oakland | 0 | 4 | .000 |

**Total Series: 22**

### NATIONAL LEAGUE

| | W | L | Pct. |
|---|---|---|---|
| Florida | 2 | 0 | 1.000 |
| New York | 2 | 0 | 1.000 |
| Cincinnati | 1 | 0 | 1.000 |
| St. Louis | 5 | 1 | .833 |
| Atlanta | 6 | 5 | .545 |
| Chicago | 1 | 1 | .500 |
| Houston | 2 | 4 | .333 |
| Arizona | 1 | 2 | .333 |
| San Diego | 1 | 2 | .333 |
| San Francisco | 1 | 3 | .250 |
| Colorado | 0 | 1 | .000 |
| Los Angeles | 0 | 3 | .000 |

**Total Series: 22**

## GAMES WON AND LOST BY TEAMS

### AMERICAN LEAGUE

| | W | L | Pct. |
|---|---|---|---|
| Baltimore | 6 | 2 | .750 |
| New York | 28 | 19 | .596 |
| Seattle | 10 | 7 | .588 |
| Cleveland | 14 | 12 | .538 |
| Anaheim | 6 | 6 | .500 |
| Chicago | 3 | 3 | .500 |
| Boston | 10 | 13 | .435 |
| Oakland | 8 | 12 | .400 |
| Minnesota | 5 | 8 | .385 |
| Texas | 1 | 9 | .100 |

**Total Games: 91**

### NATIONAL LEAGUE

| | W | L | Pct. |
|---|---|---|---|
| Cincinnati | 3 | 0 | 1.000 |
| Florida | 6 | 1 | .857 |
| St. Louis | 17 | 4 | .810 |
| New York | 6 | 2 | .750 |
| Atlanta | 25 | 17 | .595 |
| Chicago | 3 | 5 | .375 |
| Houston | 8 | 15 | .348 |
| Arizona | 4 | 8 | .333 |
| San Francisco | 5 | 11 | .313 |
| San Diego | 3 | 7 | .300 |
| Colorado | 1 | 3 | .250 |
| Los Angeles | 1 | 9 | .100 |

**Total Games: 82**

## HOME AND ROAD GAMES BY TEAMS

### AMERICAN LEAGUE

| | Series | Games | Home | Away |
|---|---|---|---|---|
| New York | 11 | 47 | 23 | 24 |
| Cleveland | 6 | 26 | 14 | 12 |
| Boston | 6 | 23 | 9 | 14 |
| Oakland | 4 | 20 | 11 | 9 |
| Seattle | 4 | 17 | 9 | 8 |
| Minnesota | 3 | 13 | 6 | 7 |
| Anaheim | 3 | 12 | 7 | 5 |
| Texas | 3 | 10 | 4 | 6 |
| Baltimore | 2 | 8 | 4 | 4 |
| Chicago | 2 | 6 | 4 | 2 |
| **Totals** | **22** | **91** | | |

### NATIONAL LEAGUE

| | Series | Games | Home | Away |
|---|---|---|---|---|
| Atlanta | 11 | 42 | 22 | 20 |
| Houston | 6 | 23 | 11 | 12 |
| St. Louis | 6 | 21 | 11 | 10 |
| San Francisco | 4 | 16 | 7 | 9 |
| Arizona | 3 | 12 | 7 | 5 |
| Los Angeles | 3 | 10 | 6 | 4 |
| San Diego | 3 | 10 | 4 | 6 |
| New York | 2 | 8 | 4 | 4 |
| Chicago | 2 | 8 | 3 | 5 |
| Florida | 2 | 7 | 4 | 3 |
| Colorado | 1 | 4 | 2 | 2 |
| Cincinnati | 1 | 3 | 1 | 2 |
| **Totals** | **22** | **82** | | |

## SHUTOUTS

### AMERICAN LEAGUE

| | |
|---|---|
| Oct 4, 1995 | Orel Hershiser, Julian Tavarez, Paul Assenmacher and Jose Mesa, Cleveland 4, Boston 0 (3 H) |
| Sept 29, 1998 | David Wells and Mariano Rivera, New York 2, Texas 0 (5 H) |
| Oct 2, 1998 | David Cone, Graeme Lloyd, Jeff Nelson and Mariano Rivera, New York 4, Texas 0 (3 H) |
| Oct 5, 1999 | Orlando Hernandez and Jeff Nelson, New York 8, Texas 0 (2 H) |
| Oct 9, 1999 | Roger Clemens, Jeff Nelson and Mariano Rivera, New York 3, Texas 0 (5 H) |
| Oct 4, 2000 | Andy Pettitte and Mariano Rivera, New York 4, Oakland 0 (6 H) |
| Oct 9, 2001 | Bartolo Colon and Bob Wickman, Cleveland 5, Seattle 0 (6 H) |
| Oct 11, 2001 | Tim Hudson and Jason Isringhausen, Oakland 2, New York 0 (7 H) |
| Oct 13, 2001 | Mike Mussina and Mariano Rivera, New York 1, Oakland 0 (6 H) |
| Oct 5, 2004 | Mike Mussina, Tom Gordon, Mariano Rivera, New York 2, Minnesota 0 (7 H) |

**Total number of shutouts: 10**

### NATIONAL LEAGUE

| | |
|---|---|
| Oct 8, 2000 | Bobby J. Jones, New York 4, San Francisco 0 (1 H) |
| Oct 9, 2001 | Curt Schilling, Arizona 1, St. Louis 0 (3 H) |
| Oct 10, 2001 | Tom Glavine and John Smoltz, Atlanta 1, Houston 0 (7 H) |
| Sept 30, 2003 | Jason Schmidt, San Francisco 2, Florida 0 (3 H) |
| Oct 9, 2004 | Jose Lima, Los Angeles 4, St. Louis 0 (5 H) |

**Total number of shutouts: 5**

## EXTRA-INNING GAMES

### AMERICAN LEAGUE

| | |
|---|---|
| Oct 3, 1995 | 13 inn, Cleveland 5, Boston 4 |
| Oct 4, 1995 | 15 inn, New York 7, Seattle 5 |
| Oct 8, 1995 | 11 inn, Seattle 6, New York 5 |
| Oct 2, 1996 | 12 inn, New York 5, Texas 4 |
| Oct 5, 1996 | 12 inn, Baltimore 4, Cleveland 3 |
| Oct 3, 2000 | 10 inn, Seattle 7, Chicago 4 |
| Oct 1, 2003 | 12 inn, Oakland 5, Boston 4 |
| Oct 4, 2003 | 11 inn, Boston 3, Oakland 1 |
| Oct 6, 2004 | 12 inn, New York 7, Minnesota 6 |
| Oct 8, 2004 | 10 inn, Boston 8, Anaheim 6 |
| Oct 9, 2004 | 11 inn, New York 6, Minnesota 5 |

**Total number of extra-inning games: 11**

### NATIONAL LEAGUE

| | |
|---|---|
| Oct 6, 1995 | 10 inn, Colorado 7, Atlanta 5 |
| Oct 2, 1996 | 10 inn, Atlanta 2, Los Angeles 1 |
| Oct 1, 1998 | 10 inn, Atlanta 2, Chicago 1 |
| Oct 8, 1999 | 12 inn, Atlanta 5, Houston 3 |
| Oct 9, 1999 | 10 inn, New York 4, Arizona 3 |

Oct 5, 2000 — 10 inn, New York 5, San Francisco 4
Oct 7, 2000 — 13 inn, New York 3, San Francisco 2
Oct 3, 2003 — 11 inn, Florida 4, San Francisco 3
Oct 7, 2004 — 11 inn, Atlanta 4, Houston 2
Oct 9, 2005 — 18 inn, Houston 7, Atlanta 6
**Total number of extra-inning games: 10**

## ATTENDANCE

### AMERICAN LEAGUE

| Year | Series | Games | Total | Series | Games | Total |
|---|---|---|---|---|---|---|
| 1995 | Cle-Bos | 3 | 122,693 | Sea-NY | 5 | 286,839 |
| 1996 | Bal-Cle | 4 | 185,144 | NY-Tex | 4 | 215,287 |
| 1997 | Bal-Sea | 4 | 216,791 | Cle-NY | 5 | 250,466 |
| 1998 | Cle-Bos | 4 | 157,005 | NY-Tex | 3 | 164,672 |
| 1999 | Bos-Cle | 5 | 202,917 | NY-Tex | 3 | 164,853 |
| 2000 | Sea-Chi | 3 | 138,683 | NY-Oak | 5 | 249,911 |
| 2001 | Sea-Cle | 5 | 234,046 | NY-Oak | 5 | 269,565 |
| 2002 | Min-Oak | 5 | 210,844 | Ana-N.Y | 4 | 203,544 |
| 2003 | NY-Min | 4 | 224,561 | Oak-Bos | 5 | 206,816 |
| 2004 | NY-Min | 4 | 219,404 | Bos-Ana | 3 | 125,273 |
| 2005 | Chi-Bos | 3 | 117,012 | LA-NY | 5 | 247,928 |

### NATIONAL LEAGUE

| Year | Series | Games | Total | Series | Games | Total |
|---|---|---|---|---|---|---|
| 1995 | Cin-LA | 3 | 143,526 | Atl-Col | 4 | 201,430 |
| 1996 | Atl-LA | 3 | 151,873 | St.L-SD | 3 | 164,844 |
| 1997 | Fla-SF | 3 | 140,638 | Atl-Hou | 3 | 149,355 |
| 1998 | SD-Hou | 4 | 225,763 | Atl-Chi | 3 | 136,908 |
| 1999 | NY-Ari | 4 | 211,269 | Atl-Hou | 4 | 178,210 |
| 2000 | NY-SF | 4 | 190,018 | St.L-Atl | 3 | 154,665 |
| 2001 | Atl-Hou | 3 | 111,180 | Ari-St.L | 5 | 231,321 |
| 2002 | St.L-Ari | 3 | 150,199 | SF-Atl | 5 | 220,386 |
| 2003 | Atl-Chi | 5 | 239,108 | SF-Fla | 4 | 214,422 |
| 2004 | St.L-LA | 4 | 216,615 | Atl-Hou | 5 | 222,490 |
| 2005 | St.L-SD | 3 | 150,041 | Atl-Hou | 4 | 173,943 |

## INDIVIDUAL BATTING

## LEADING BATTERS

**(Playing in all games, each series, with four or more hits)**

### AMERICAN LEAGUE

| Year | Player, Club | AB | H | TB | Avg. |
|---|---|---|---|---|---|
| 1995 | Luis Alicea, Boston | 10 | 6 | 10 | .600 |
| 1996 | Bernie Williams, New York | 15 | 7 | 16 | .467 |
| 1997 | Omar Vizquel, Cleveland | 18 | 9 | 9 | .500 |
| 1998 | John Valentin, Boston | 15 | 7 | 8 | .467 |
| 1999 | Mike Stanley, Boston | 20 | 10 | 14 | .500 |
| 2000 | Herbert Perry, Chicago | 9 | 4 | 5 | .444 |
| 2001 | Ichiro Suzuki, Seattle | 20 | 12 | 13 | .600 |
| 2002 | Benji Gil, Anaheim | 5 | 4 | 4 | .800 |
| 2003 | Eric Byrnes, Oakland | 13 | 6 | 7 | .462 |
| 2004 | David Ortiz, Boston | 11 | 6 | 11 | .545 |
| 2005 | Bengie Molina, Los Angeles | 18 | 8 | 17 | .444 |
| | A.J. Pierzynski, Chicago | 9 | 4 | 12 | .444 |

### NATIONAL LEAGUE

| Year | Player, Club | AB | H | TB | Avg. |
|---|---|---|---|---|---|
| 1995 | Dante Bichette, Colorado | 17 | 10 | 16 | .588 |
| 1996 | Ron Gant, St. Louis | 10 | 4 | 8 | .400 |
| 1997 | Gary Sheffield, Florida | 9 | 5 | 9 | .556 |
| 1998 | Carlos Hernandez, San Diego | 12 | 5 | 5 | .417 |
| 1999 | Bret Boone, Atlanta | 19 | 9 | 10 | .474 |
| 2000 | Jim Edmonds, St. Louis | 14 | 8 | 18 | .571 |
| 2001 | Andruw Jones, Atlanta | 12 | 6 | 9 | .500 |
| 2002 | Miguel Cairo, St. Louis | 4 | 4 | 5 | 1.000 |
| 2003 | Edgardo Alfonzo, San Francisco | 17 | 9 | 13 | .529 |
| 2004 | Andruw Jones, Atlanta | 19 | 10 | 18 | .526 |
| 2005 | Albert Pujols, St. Louis | 9 | 5 | 7 | .556 |

## .500 HITTERS

**(Playing in all games and having nine or more at-bats)**

### AMERICAN LEAGUE

| Player, Club | Year | AB | H | TB | Avg. |
|---|---|---|---|---|---|
| Shawn Wooten, Anaheim | 2002 | 9 | 6 | 9 | .667 |
| Luis Alicea, Boston | 1995 | 10 | 6 | 10 | .600 |
| Ichiro Suzuki, Seattle | 2001 | 20 | 12 | 13 | .600 |
| Edgar Martinez, Seattle | 1995 | 21 | 12 | 21 | .571 |
| David Ortiz, Boston | 2004 | 11 | 6 | 11 | .545 |
| Omar Vizquel, Cleveland | 1997 | 18 | 9 | 9 | .500 |
| Mike Stanley, Boston | 1999 | 20 | 10 | 14 | .500 |
| Derek Jeter, New York | 2002 | 16 | 8 | 14 | .500 |
| Scott Hatteberg, Oakland | 2002 | 14 | 7 | 12 | .500 |
| Darin Erstad, Anaheim | 2004 | 10 | 5 | 9 | .500 |

**Total number of occurrences: 10**

### NATIONAL LEAGUE

| Player, Club | Year | AB | H | TB | Avg. |
|---|---|---|---|---|---|
| Fernando Vina, St. Louis | 2002 | 15 | 9 | 9 | .600 |
| Dante Bichette, Colorado | 1995 | 17 | 10 | 16 | .588 |
| Jim Edmonds, St. Louis | 2000 | 14 | 8 | 18 | .571 |
| Gary Sheffield, Florida | 1997 | 9 | 5 | 9 | .556 |
| Edgardo Alfonzo, San Francisco | 2003 | 17 | 9 | 13 | .529 |
| Andruw Jones, Atlanta | 2004 | 19 | 10 | 18 | .526 |
| Marquis Grissom, Atlanta | 1995 | 21 | 11 | 22 | .524 |
| Chad Fonville, Los Angeles | 1995 | 12 | 6 | 6 | .500 |
| Eric Karros, Los Angeles | 1995 | 12 | 6 | 13 | .500 |
| Hal Morris, Cincinnati | 1995 | 10 | 5 | 6 | .500 |
| Andruw Jones, Atlanta | 2001 | 12 | 6 | 9 | .500 |
| Moises Alou, Chicago | 2003 | 20 | 10 | 20 | .500 |
| Albert Pujols, St. Louis | 2005 | 9 | 5 | 7 | .556 |

**Total number of occurrences: 13**

## HOME RUNS

### AMERICAN LEAGUE

1995—11—Seattle (West), Ken Griffey Jr. 5, Edgar Martinez 2, Jay Buhner, Vince Coleman, Joey Cora, Tino Martinez
11—New York (East), Paul O'Neill 3, Ruben Sierra 2, Bernie Williams 2, Wade Boggs, Jim Leyritz, Don Mattingly, Mike Stanley
4—Cleveland (Central), Albert Belle, Eddie Murray, Tony Pena, Jim Thome
3—Boston (East), Luis Alicea, Tim Naehring, John Valentin
1996—9—Baltimore (East), B.J. Surhoff 3, Brady Anderson 2, Bobby Bonilla 2, Roberto Alomar, Rafael Palmeiro
4—Cleveland (Central), Albert Belle 2, Manny Ramirez 2
6—Texas (West), Juan Gonzalez 5, Dean Palmer
4—New York (East), Bernie Williams 3, Cecil Fielder
1997—4—Cleveland (Central), Sandy Alomar 2, David Justice, Matt Williams
6—New York (East), Derek Jeter 2, Paul O'Neill 2, Tino Martinez, Tim Raines Sr.
6—Baltimore (East), German Berroa 2, Brady Anderson, Harold Baines, Chris Hoiles, Jeff Reboulet
6—Seattle (West), Jay Buhner 2, Edgar Martinez 2, Alex Rodriguez, Paul Sorrento
1998—4—New York (East), Shane Spencer 2, Scott Brosius, Paul O'Neill
0—Texas (West)
7—Cleveland (Central), Kenny Lofton 2, Manny Ramirez 2, Jim Thome 2, David Justice
5—Boston (East), Nomar Garciaparra 3, Mo Vaughn 2
1999—2—New York (East), Darryl Strawberry, Bernie Williams
1—Texas (West), Juan Gonzalez
10—Boston (East), John Valentin 3, Nomar Garciaparra 2, Troy O'Leary 2, Brian Daubach, Jose Offerman, Jason Varitek
7—Cleveland (Central), Jim Thome 4, Harold Baines, Wil Cordero, Travis Fryman
2000—1—New York (East), David Justice
2—Oakland (West), Terrence Long, Olmedo Saenz
4—Seattle (West), Jay Buhner, Edgar Martinez, John Olerud, Joe Oliver
1—Chicago (Central), Ray Durham
2001—4—Seattle (West), Edgar Martinez 2, David Bell, Mike Cameron
5—Cleveland (Central), Juan Gonzalez 2, Ellis Burks, Kenny Lofton, Jim Thome
3—New York (East), David Justice, Tino Martinez, Jorge Posada
4—Oakland (West), Terrence Long 2, Ron Gant, Jason Giambi
2002—9—Anaheim (West), Troy Glaus 3, Tim Salmon 2, Garret Anderson, Adam Kennedy, Scott Spiezio, Shawn Wooten
7—New York (East), Derek Jeter 2, Jason Giambi, Jorge Posada, Alfonso Soriano, Rondell White, Bernie Williams
5—Minnesota (Central), Doug Mientkiewicz 2, Cristian Guzman, Corey Koskie, A.J. Pierzynski
8—Oakland (West), Ray Durham 2, Eric Chavez, Jermaine Dye, Mark Ellis, Scott Hatteberg, Terrence Long, Miguel Tejada
2003—6—Boston (East), Todd Walker 3, Jason Varitek 2, Johnny Damon, Trot Nixon, Manny Ramirez
2—New York (East), Derek Jeter, Hideki Matsui
2—Minnesota (Central), Torii Hunter, A.J. Pierzynski
1—Oakland (West), Jermaine Dye
2004—4—Anaheim (West), Troy Glaus 2, Darin Erstad, Vlad Guerrero
4—Boston (East), Kevin Millar, David Ortiz, Manny Ramirez, Jason Varitek
4—Minnesota (Central), Jacque Jones 2, Henry Blanco, Torii Hunter
6—New York (East), Derek Jeter, Hideki Matsui, Alex Rodriguez, Gary Sheffield, Ruben Sierra, Bernie Williams
2005—3—Boston (East), Manny Ramirez 2, David Ortiz
7—Chicago (Central), Paul Konerko 2, A.J. Pierzynski 2, Tadahito Iguchi, Scott Podsednik, Juan Uribe
6—Los Angeles (West), Bengie Molina 3, Garret Anderson 2, Juan Rivera
4—New York (East), Derek Jeter 2, Hideki Matsui, Jorge Posada

**Total number of home runs: 214**

### NATIONAL LEAGUE

1995—7—Atlanta (East), Marquis Grissom 3, Chipper Jones 2, Fred McGriff 2
6—Colorado (West), Vinny Castilla 3, Dante Bichette, Larry Walker, Eric Young
5—Cincinnati (Central), Bret Boone, Ron Gant, Mark Lewis, Reggie Sanders, Benito Santiago
3—Los Angeles (West), Eric Karros 2, Mike Piazza
1996—5—Atlanta (East), Jermaine Dye, Chipper Jones, Ryan Klesko, Javy Lopez, Fred McGriff
0—Los Angeles (West)
4—San Diego (West), Ken Caminiti 3, Rickey Henderson
3—St. Louis (Central), Gary Gaetti, Ron Gant, Brian Jordan
1997—3—Atlanta (East), Jeff Blauser, Chipper Jones, Ryan Klesko
1—Houston (Central), Chuck Carr
4—Florida (East), Bobby Bonilla, Charles Johnson, Gary Sheffield, Devon White
4—San Francisco (West), Jeff Kent 2, Brian Johnson, Bill Mueller
1998—5—San Diego (West), Jim Leyritz 3, Wally Joyner, Greg Vaughn
1—Houston (Central), Derek Bell
4—Atlanta (East), Ryan Klesko, Javy Lopez, Eddie Perez, Michael Tucker
1—Chicago (Central), Tyler Houston
1999—1—Atlanta (East), Brian Jordan
5—Houston (Central), Ken Caminiti 3, Tony Eusebio, Daryle Ward
5—New York (East), Edgardo Alfonzo 3, John Olerud, Todd Pratt
4—Arizona (West), Greg Colbrunn, Erubiel Durazo, Luis Gonzalez, Turner Ward
2000—3—New York (East), Benny Agbayani, Edgardo Alfonzo, Robin Ventura

2—San Francisco (West), Ellis Burks, J.T. Snow
6—St. Louis (Central), Jim Edmonds 2, Will Clark, Carlos Hernandez, Mark McGwire, Fernando Vina
1—Atlanta (East), Andruw Jones
2001—6—Atlanta (East), Chipper Jones 2, Paul Bako, Julio Franco, Andruw Jones, Brian Jordan
3—Houston (Central), Brad Ausmus, Vinny Castilla, Daryle Ward
3—Arizona (West), Craig Counsell, Luis Gonzalez, Reggie Sanders
6—St. Louis (Central), Jim Edmonds 2, J.D. Drew, Albert Pujols, Edgar Renteria, Fernando Vina
2002—3—St. Louis (Central), J.D. Drew, Jim Edmonds, Scott Rolen
2—Arizona (West), Rod Barajas, David Dellucci
6—San Francisco (West), Barry Bonds 3, Rich Aurilia 2, J.T. Snow
5—Atlanta (East), Javy Lopez 2, Vinny Castilla, Keith Lockhart, Gary Sheffield
2003—4—Chicago (Central), Eric Karros 2, Alex S. Gonzalez, Aramis Ramirez
3—Atlanta (East), Chipper Jones 2, Marcus Giles
2—Florida (East), Juan Encarnacion, Ivan Rodriguez
0—San Francisco (West)
2004—7—Atlanta (East), Johnny Estrada 2, Rafael Furcal 2, Andruw Jones 2, Adam LaRoche
11—Houston (Central), Carlos Beltran 4, Jeff Bagwell 2, Brad Ausmus, Lance Berkman, Craig Biggio, Raul Chavez, Jason Lane
7—Los Angeles (West), Shawn Green 3, Jayson Werth 2, Milton Bradley, Tom Wilson
7—St. Louis (Central), Albert Pujols 2, Larry Walker 2, Jim Edmonds, Mike Matheny, Reggie Sanders
2005—5—Atlanta (East), Brian McCann 2, Andruw Jones, Chipper Jones, Adam LaRoche
4—Houston (Central), Brad Ausmus, Lance Berkman, Chris Burke, Mike Lamb
3—St. Louis (Central), David Eckstein, Jim Edmonds, Reggie Sanders
3—San Diego (West), Ramon Hernandez, Dave Roberts, Eric Young

**Total number of home runs: 173**

## PLAYERS WITH FOUR HOME RUNS

### BOTH LEAGUES

| Player | Series | HR |
|---|---|---|
| Jim Leyritz | 4 | 4 |

**Total number of players: 1**

### AMERICAN LEAGUE

| Player | Series | HR |
|---|---|---|
| Juan Gonzalez | 4 | 8 |
| Jim Thome | 6 | 8 |
| Manny Ramirez | 8 | 8 |
| Derek Jeter | 10 | 8 |
| Bernie Williams | 11 | 8 |
| Edgar Martinez | 4 | 7 |
| Paul O'Neill | 7 | 6 |
| Troy Glaus | 2 | 5 |
| Ken Griffey Jr. | 2 | 5 |
| Nomar Garciaparra | 3 | 5 |
| A.J. Pierzynski | 3 | 4 |
| John Valentin | 3 | 4 |
| Jay Buhner | 4 | 4 |
| Terrence Long | 4 | 4 |
| Jason Varitek | 5 | 4 |
| David Justice | 7 | 4 |

**Total number of players: 16**

### NATIONAL LEAGUE

| Player | Series | HR |
|---|---|---|
| Chipper Jones | 11 | 9 |
| Jim Edmonds | 5 | 7 |
| Ken Caminiti | 4 | 6 |
| Vinny Castilla | 4 | 5 |
| Andruw Jones | 10 | 5 |
| Carlos Beltran | 1 | 4 |
| Edgardo Alfonzo | 3 | 4 |
| Eric Karros | 3 | 4 |
| Reggie Sanders | 6 | 4 |
| Javy Lopez | 7 | 4 |

**Total number of players: 10**

## INDIVIDUAL PITCHING

## PITCHERS WITH THREE VICTORIES

### BOTH LEAGUES

| Pitcher, Club | Series | W | L |
|---|---|---|---|
| David Wells, Cin NL, Bal AL, NY AL, Bos AL | 7 | 5 | 2 |
| Andy Pettitte, NY AL, Hou NL | 10 | 5 | 3 |
| Roger Clemens, NY AL, Hou NL | 8 | 4 | 4 |
| Jeff Fassero, Sea AL, Tex AL, St. L NL | 3 | 3 | 0 |
| Curt Schilling, Ari NL, Bos AL | 3 | 3 | 0 |
| Armando Benitez, Bal AL, NY NL | 4 | 3 | 0 |
| Mark Mulder, Oak AL, St. L NL | 3 | 3 | 2 |

**Total number of pitchers: 7**

### AMERICAN LEAGUE

| Pitcher, Club | Yrs. | W | L |
|---|---|---|---|
| Pedro Martinez, Boston | 4 | 4 | 0 |
| David Wells, Baltimore, New York, Boston | 5 | 4 | 2 |
| Mike Mussina, Baltimore, New York | 7 | 4 | 3 |
| Andy Pettitte, New York | 9 | 4 | 3 |
| Orlando Hernandez, New York, Chicago | 5 | 3 | 1 |
| Barry Zito, Oakland | 4 | 3 | 2 |
| Charles Nagy, Cleveland | 5 | 3 | 2 |

**Total number of pitchers: 7**

### NATIONAL LEAGUE

| Pitcher, Club | Yrs. | W | L |
|---|---|---|---|
| John Smoltz, Atlanta | 10 | 7 | 0 |
| Greg Maddux, Atlanta | 9 | 5 | 3 |
| Russ Ortiz, San Francisco, Atlanta | 4 | 3 | 1 |
| Tom Glavine, Atlanta | 8 | 3 | 3 |

**Total number of pitchers: 4**

## 10-STRIKEOUT GAMES BY PITCHERS

### AMERICAN LEAGUE

| Date | Pitcher, Club | K |
|---|---|---|
| Oct 6, 1995 | Randy Johnson, Sea vs NY | 10 |
| Oct 5, 1996 | Charles Nagy, Cle vs Bal | 12 |
| Oct 5, 1997 | Randy Johnson, Sea vs Bal | 13 |
| Oct 6, 1999 | Bartolo Colon, Cle vs Bos | 11 |
| Oct 9, 2001 | Bartolo Colon, Cle vs Sea | 10 |
| Oct 2, 2003 | Andy Pettitte, NY vs Min | 10 |

**Total number of occurrences: 6**

### NATIONAL LEAGUE

| Date | Pitcher, Club | K |
|---|---|---|
| Oct 3, 1997 | John Smoltz, Atl vs Hou | 11 |
| Sept 29, 1998 | Kevin Brown, SD vs Hou | 16 |
| Oct 4, 1998 | Sterling Hitchcock, SD vs Hou | 11 |
| Oct 5, 1999 | Randy Johnson, Ari vs NY | 11 |
| Sept 30, 2003 | Kerry Wood, Chi vs Atl | 11 |

**Total number of occurrences: 5**

## CLUB BATTING

### AMERICAN LEAGUE

| Year | Team, Division | G | AB | R | H | TB | 2B | 3B | HR | SH | SF | SB | BB | SO | RBI | Avg. | LOB |
|---|---|---|---|---|---|---|---|---|---|---|---|---|---|---|---|---|---|
| 1995 | Boston, East | 3 | 114 | 6 | 21 | 32 | 2 | 0 | 3 | 1 | 1 | 2 | 11 | 26 | 6 | .184 | 28 |
| | Cleveland, Central | 3 | 114 | 17 | 25 | 43 | 4 | 1 | 4 | 2 | 0 | 1 | 13 | 22 | 17 | .219 | 27 |
| | New York, East* | 5 | 193 | 33 | 50 | 95 | 12 | 0 | 11 | 2 | 3 | 1 | 32 | 43 | 32 | .259 | 45 |
| | Seattle, West | 5 | 200 | 35 | 63 | 104 | 6 | 1 | 11 | 4 | 3 | 3 | 25 | 41 | 33 | .315 | 49 |
| 1996 | Baltimore, East* | 4 | 149 | 25 | 43 | 76 | 6 | 0 | 9 | 0 | 2 | 1 | 17 | 40 | 23 | .289 | 36 |
| | Cleveland, Central | 4 | 143 | 20 | 35 | 54 | 7 | 0 | 4 | 2 | 2 | 11 | 15 | 32 | 20 | .245 | 29 |
| | New York, East | 4 | 140 | 16 | 37 | 53 | 4 | 0 | 4 | 3 | 2 | 1 | 13 | 20 | 15 | .264 | 30 |
| | Texas, West | 4 | 142 | 16 | 31 | 53 | 4 | 0 | 6 | 4 | 0 | 1 | 20 | 30 | 16 | .218 | 33 |
| 1997 | Baltimore, East | 4 | 135 | 23 | 39 | 68 | 11 | 0 | 6 | 2 | 0 | 2 | 16 | 27 | 23 | .289 | 25 |
| | Seattle, West | 4 | 133 | 11 | 29 | 52 | 5 | 0 | 6 | 0 | 0 | 2 | 7 | 42 | 11 | .218 | 21 |
| | Cleveland, Central | 5 | 167 | 21 | 43 | 63 | 6 | 1 | 4 | 4 | 1 | 6 | 10 | 22 | 20 | .257 | 32 |
| | New York, East* | 5 | 166 | 24 | 43 | 68 | 7 | 0 | 6 | 2 | 2 | 3 | 20 | 26 | 23 | .259 | 37 |
| 1998 | Cleveland, Central | 4 | 126 | 18 | 26 | 59 | 12 | 0 | 7 | 0 | 1 | 3 | 15 | 26 | 17 | .206 | 22 |
| | Boston, East* | 4 | 135 | 20 | 34 | 55 | 6 | 0 | 5 | 1 | 2 | 1 | 14 | 28 | 19 | .252 | 26 |
| | New York, East | 3 | 91 | 9 | 23 | 41 | 6 | 0 | 4 | 1 | 0 | 2 | 7 | 24 | 8 | .253 | 16 |
| | Texas, West | 3 | 92 | 1 | 13 | 16 | 3 | 0 | 0 | 1 | 0 | 0 | 4 | 27 | 1 | .141 | 15 |
| 1999 | Boston, East* | 5 | 176 | 47 | 56 | 105 | 17 | 1 | 10 | 0 | 3 | 1 | 19 | 35 | 47 | .318 | 25 |
| | Cleveland, Central | 5 | 163 | 32 | 38 | 68 | 7 | 1 | 7 | 1 | 4 | 5 | 28 | 43 | 31 | .233 | 36 |
| | New York, East | 3 | 98 | 14 | 23 | 37 | 6 | 1 | 2 | 1 | 0 | 0 | 10 | 19 | 13 | .235 | 21 |

| Year | Team, Division | G | AB | R | H | TB | 2B | 3B | HR | SH | SF | SB | BB | SO | RBI | Avg. | LOB |
|---|---|---|---|---|---|---|---|---|---|---|---|---|---|---|---|---|---|
| | Texas, West | 3 | 92 | 1 | 14 | 19 | 2 | 0 | 1 | 0 | 0 | 1 | 9 | 17 | 1 | .152 | 19 |
| 2000 | New York, East | 5 | 168 | 19 | 41 | 56 | 12 | 0 | 1 | 1 | 3 | 1 | 16 | 35 | 19 | .244 | 38 |
| | Oakland, West | 5 | 167 | 23 | 44 | 59 | 9 | 0 | 2 | 1 | 2 | 3 | 19 | 31 | 22 | .263 | 36 |
| | Seattle, West* | 3 | 99 | 14 | 28 | 42 | 2 | 0 | 4 | 4 | 1 | 2 | 12 | 13 | 14 | .283 | 22 |
| | Chicago, Central | 3 | 92 | 7 | 17 | 30 | 6 | 2 | 1 | 2 | 2 | 4 | 15 | 16 | 6 | .185 | 21 |
| 2001 | New York, East | 5 | 166 | 18 | 40 | 59 | 8 | 1 | 3 | 2 | 1 | 4 | 11 | 29 | 16 | .241 | 34 |
| | Oakland, West* | 5 | 174 | 12 | 43 | 70 | 13 | 1 | 4 | 0 | 2 | 3 | 11 | 31 | 11 | .247 | 43 |
| | Seattle, West | 5 | 158 | 16 | 39 | 59 | 8 | 0 | 4 | 2 | 1 | 3 | 18 | 48 | 16 | .247 | 35 |
| | Cleveland, Central | 5 | 173 | 26 | 45 | 71 | 9 | 1 | 5 | 0 | 1 | 1 | 13 | 43 | 25 | .260 | 30 |
| 2002 | Anaheim, West* | 4 | 149 | 31 | 56 | 93 | 10 | 0 | 9 | 4 | 2 | 4 | 7 | 18 | 31 | .376 | 31 |
| | New York, East | 4 | 135 | 25 | 38 | 63 | 4 | 0 | 7 | 0 | 3 | 1 | 16 | 25 | 24 | .281 | 28 |
| | Minnesota, Central | 5 | 179 | 27 | 52 | 86 | 15 | 2 | 5 | 2 | 0 | 2 | 14 | 42 | 23 | .291 | 38 |
| | Oakland, West | 5 | 184 | 26 | 53 | 92 | 13 | 1 | 8 | 0 | 1 | 1 | 12 | 34 | 25 | .288 | 40 |
| 2003 | New York, East | 4 | 138 | 16 | 38 | 53 | 9 | 0 | 2 | 2 | 1 | 4 | 14 | 29 | 15 | .275 | 35 |
| | Minnesota, Central | 4 | 131 | 6 | 26 | 37 | 3 | 1 | 2 | 1 | 1 | 1 | 9 | 33 | 5 | .198 | 28 |
| | Boston, East* | 5 | 180 | 17 | 38 | 68 | 6 | 0 | 8 | 0 | 0 | 3 | 18 | 39 | 16 | .211 | 38 |
| | Oakland, West | 5 | 178 | 18 | 38 | 51 | 8 | 1 | 1 | 1 | 0 | 3 | 21 | 37 | 15 | .213 | 40 |
| 2004 | Boston, East* | 3 | 116 | 25 | 35 | 53 | 6 | 0 | 4 | 0 | 2 | 3 | 20 | 23 | 23 | .302 | 31 |
| | Anaheim, West | 3 | 106 | 12 | 24 | 39 | 3 | 0 | 4 | 1 | 0 | 1 | 11 | 28 | 12 | .226 | 24 |
| | New York, East | 4 | 154 | 21 | 43 | 71 | 10 | 0 | 6 | 2 | 1 | 4 | 15 | 30 | 20 | .279 | 30 |
| | Minnesota, Central | 4 | 152 | 12 | 43 | 62 | 7 | 0 | 4 | 1 | 4 | 4 | 7 | 28 | 17 | .283 | 28 |
| 2005 | Boston, East* | 3 | 104 | 9 | 25 | 43 | 9 | 0 | 3 | 0 | 0 | 0 | 8 | 14 | 8 | .240 | 22 |
| | Chicago, Central | 3 | 97 | 24 | 28 | 55 | 6 | 0 | 7 | 3 | 0 | 3 | 5 | 11 | 24 | .289 | 11 |
| | Los Angeles, West | 5 | 167 | 25 | 46 | 77 | 7 | 3 | 6 | 5 | 1 | 1 | 5 | 26 | 25 | .275 | 26 |
| | New York, East | 5 | 166 | 20 | 42 | 65 | 11 | 0 | 4 | 1 | 2 | 3 | 24 | 32 | 20 | .253 | 43 |

*wild-card team

## NATIONAL LEAGUE

| Year | Team, Division | G | AB | R | H | TB | 2B | 3B | HR | SH | SF | SB | BB | SO | RBI | Avg. | LOB |
|---|---|---|---|---|---|---|---|---|---|---|---|---|---|---|---|---|---|
| 1995 | Cincinnati, Central | 3 | 104 | 22 | 29 | 50 | 6 | 0 | 5 | 1 | 1 | 9 | 13 | 28 | 22 | .279 | 19 |
| | Los Angeles, West | 3 | 111 | 7 | 31 | 42 | 2 | 0 | 3 | 1 | 0 | 0 | 5 | 17 | 7 | .279 | 30 |
| | Atlanta, East | 4 | 154 | 27 | 51 | 80 | 8 | 0 | 7 | 0 | 1 | 3 | 12 | 27 | 24 | .331 | 33 |
| | Colorado, West* | 4 | 143 | 19 | 41 | 66 | 7 | 0 | 6 | 3 | 1 | 3 | 9 | 29 | 18 | .287 | 29 |
| 1996 | Atlanta, East | 3 | 89 | 10 | 16 | 34 | 3 | 0 | 5 | 2 | 1 | 5 | 12 | 24 | 10 | .180 | 14 |
| | Los Angeles, West* | 3 | 95 | 5 | 14 | 21 | 7 | 0 | 0 | 0 | 1 | 0 | 7 | 29 | 5 | .147 | 14 |
| | St. Louis, Central | 3 | 94 | 15 | 24 | 38 | 3 | 1 | 3 | 2 | 0 | 3 | 13 | 23 | 14 | .255 | 20 |
| | San Diego, West | 3 | 105 | 10 | 25 | 40 | 3 | 0 | 4 | 2 | 0 | 2 | 4 | 28 | 9 | .238 | 21 |
| 1997 | Florida, East* | 3 | 99 | 15 | 27 | 44 | 5 | 0 | 4 | 1 | 0 | 1 | 19 | 16 | 14 | .273 | 27 |
| | San Fran., West | 3 | 98 | 9 | 22 | 38 | 4 | 0 | 4 | 2 | 1 | 2 | 6 | 21 | 8 | .224 | 17 |
| | Atlanta, East | 3 | 92 | 19 | 20 | 33 | 4 | 0 | 3 | 0 | 1 | 1 | 15 | 20 | 15 | .217 | 14 |
| | Houston, Central | 3 | 96 | 5 | 16 | 20 | 1 | 0 | 1 | 0 | 0 | 2 | 8 | 24 | 5 | .167 | 18 |
| 1998 | San Diego, West | 4 | 125 | 14 | 27 | 48 | 4 | 1 | 5 | 2 | 1 | 0 | 9 | 32 | 13 | .216 | 23 |
| | Houston, Central | 4 | 121 | 8 | 22 | 30 | 5 | 0 | 1 | 2 | 0 | 1 | 11 | 49 | 7 | .182 | 25 |
| | Atlanta, East | 3 | 101 | 15 | 23 | 37 | 2 | 0 | 4 | 2 | 1 | 3 | 14 | 20 | 14 | .228 | 24 |
| | Chicago, Central* | 3 | 94 | 4 | 17 | 22 | 2 | 0 | 1 | 3 | 1 | 1 | 5 | 24 | 4 | .181 | 15 |
| 1999 | New York, East* | 4 | 134 | 22 | 34 | 54 | 5 | 0 | 5 | 4 | 1 | 8 | 21 | 28 | 22 | .254 | 32 |
| | Arizona, West | 4 | 126 | 16 | 26 | 47 | 7 | 1 | 4 | 0 | 1 | 0 | 14 | 22 | 16 | .206 | 20 |
| | Atlanta, East | 4 | 148 | 18 | 45 | 53 | 5 | 0 | 1 | 3 | 3 | 4 | 11 | 35 | 18 | .304 | 33 |
| | Houston, Central | 4 | 141 | 15 | 31 | 48 | 2 | 0 | 5 | 2 | 1 | 3 | 17 | 33 | 15 | .220 | 31 |
| 2000 | New York, East* | 4 | 143 | 13 | 30 | 46 | 7 | 0 | 3 | 0 | 1 | 3 | 20 | 30 | 13 | .210 | 36 |
| | San Fran., West | 4 | 146 | 11 | 30 | 44 | 6 | 1 | 2 | 2 | 0 | 2 | 16 | 36 | 11 | .205 | 33 |
| | St. Louis, Central | 3 | 102 | 24 | 28 | 51 | 5 | 0 | 6 | 2 | 1 | 6 | 14 | 19 | 23 | .275 | 22 |
| | Atlanta, East | 3 | 95 | 10 | 18 | 26 | 5 | 0 | 1 | 0 | 0 | 1 | 16 | 20 | 9 | .189 | 21 |
| 2001 | Atlanta, East | 3 | 99 | 14 | 30 | 54 | 6 | 0 | 6 | 1 | 1 | 1 | 4 | 18 | 13 | .303 | 14 |
| | Houston, Central | 3 | 95 | 6 | 19 | 30 | 2 | 0 | 3 | 0 | 0 | 0 | 8 | 16 | 6 | .200 | 16 |
| | Arizona, West | 5 | 156 | 10 | 37 | 51 | 5 | 0 | 3 | 6 | 0 | 1 | 18 | 29 | 10 | .237 | 40 |
| | St. Louis, Central* | 5 | 152 | 12 | 29 | 50 | 3 | 0 | 6 | 8 | 1 | 3 | 12 | 38 | 12 | .191 | 30 |
| 2002 | St. Louis, Central | 3 | 105 | 20 | 33 | 46 | 2 | 1 | 3 | 3 | 1 | 2 | 12 | 17 | 19 | .314 | 25 |
| | Arizona, West | 3 | 98 | 6 | 18 | 26 | 2 | 0 | 2 | 0 | 1 | 1 | 11 | 21 | 6 | .184 | 23 |
| | San Fran., West* | 5 | 166 | 24 | 41 | 68 | 9 | 0 | 6 | 2 | 2 | 1 | 18 | 45 | 24 | .247 | 33 |
| | Atlanta, East | 5 | 170 | 26 | 44 | 67 | 4 | 2 | 5 | 1 | 0 | 2 | 22 | 30 | 25 | .259 | 36 |
| 2003 | Florida, East* | 4 | 146 | 20 | 37 | 53 | 8 | 1 | 2 | 3 | 0 | 2 | 14 | 25 | 18 | .253 | 35 |
| | San Fran., West | 4 | 136 | 16 | 32 | 41 | 7 | 1 | 0 | 3 | 2 | 1 | 20 | 28 | 15 | .235 | 36 |
| | Chicago, Central | 5 | 167 | 19 | 43 | 63 | 8 | 0 | 4 | 0 | 1 | 5 | 20 | 38 | 19 | .257 | 37 |
| | Atlanta, East | 5 | 163 | 15 | 35 | 49 | 5 | 0 | 3 | 2 | 1 | 1 | 21 | 42 | 15 | .215 | 41 |
| 2004 | St. Louis, Central | 4 | 130 | 22 | 33 | 59 | 3 | 1 | 7 | 1 | 0 | 4 | 15 | 26 | 21 | .254 | 25 |
| | Los Angeles, West | 4 | 126 | 12 | 25 | 52 | 4 | 1 | 7 | 1 | 1 | 2 | 15 | 20 | 12 | .198 | 26 |
| | Houston, Central* | 5 | 180 | 36 | 58 | 103 | 12 | 0 | 11 | 3 | 3 | 3 | 21 | 30 | 36 | .322 | 34 |
| | Atlanta, East | 5 | 180 | 21 | 48 | 75 | 4 | 1 | 7 | 2 | 1 | 7 | 19 | 45 | 20 | .267 | 43 |
| 2005 | Atlanta, East | 4 | 161 | 21 | 41 | 69 | 11 | 1 | 5 | 4 | 1 | 4 | 21 | 36 | 21 | .255 | 38 |
| | Houston, Central* | 4 | 155 | 25 | 41 | 65 | 12 | 0 | 4 | 5 | 4 | 2 | 19 | 30 | 24 | .265 | 31 |
| | St. Louis, Central | 3 | 102 | 21 | 29 | 45 | 7 | 0 | 3 | 3 | 0 | 1 | 13 | 17 | 20 | .284 | 23 |
| | San Diego, West | 3 | 106 | 11 | 32 | 45 | 4 | 0 | 3 | 0 | 1 | 2 | 10 | 17 | 11 | .302 | 28 |

*wild-card team

# CLUB FIELDING AND PLAYERS USED

## AMERICAN LEAGUE

| Year | Team, Division | G | PO | A | E | DP | PB | Fielding Avg. | Players Used | Pitchers Used |
|---|---|---|---|---|---|---|---|---|---|---|
| 1995 | Boston, East | 3 | 89 | 29 | 4 | 0 | 2 | .967 | 23 | 10 |
| | Cleveland, Central | 3 | 93 | 34 | 6 | 1 | 0 | .955 | 22 | 9 |
| | New York, East* | 5 | 150 | 49 | 3 | 4 | 0 | .985 | 24 | 9 |
| | Seattle, West | 5 | 154 | 47 | 2 | 5 | 0 | .990 | 24 | 9 |
| 1996 | Baltimore, East* | 4 | 114 | 43 | 4 | 2 | 0 | .975 | 21 | 8 |
| | Cleveland, Central | 4 | 111 | 34 | 3 | 1 | 0 | .980 | 24 | 10 |

DIVISION SERIES *General reference*

| Year | Team, Division | G | PO | A | E | DP | PB | Fielding Avg. | Players Used | Pitchers Used |
|---|---|---|---|---|---|---|---|---|---|---|
| | New York, East | 4 | 117 | 38 | 2 | 3 | 0 | .987 | 25 | 10 |
| 1997 | Baltimore, East | 4 | 108 | 38 | 0 | 1 | 1 | 1.000 | 23 | 9 |
| | Seattle, West | 4 | 105 | 42 | 1 | 3 | 0 | .993 | 23 | 9 |
| | Cleveland, Central | 5 | 132 | 58 | 4 | 6 | 0 | .979 | 20 | 9 |
| | New York, East* | 5 | 130 | 55 | 4 | 2 | 0 | .979 | 25 | 10 |
| 1998 | Cleveland, Central | 4 | 108 | 43 | 1 | 3 | 0 | .993 | 22 | 11 |
| | Boston, East* | 4 | 105 | 33 | 0 | 4 | 2 | 1.000 | 24 | 10 |
| | New York, East | 3 | 81 | 28 | 1 | 2 | 0 | .991 | 19 | 6 |
| | Texas, West | 3 | 75 | 31 | 1 | 4 | 1 | .991 | 17 | 5 |
| 1999 | Boston, East* | 5 | 130 | 45 | 3 | 3 | 3 | .983 | 25 | 11 |
| | Cleveland, Central | 5 | 129 | 48 | 2 | 4 | 0 | .983 | 25 | 11 |
| | New York, East | 3 | 81 | 29 | 2 | 5 | 0 | .982 | 19 | 5 |
| | Texas, West | 3 | 75 | 27 | 3 | 1 | 0 | .981 | 19 | 9 |
| 2000 | New York, East | 5 | 132 | 56 | 2 | 7 | 0 | .989 | 21 | 8 |
| | Oakland, West | 5 | 132 | 42 | 5 | 3 | 0 | .972 | 24 | 9 |
| | Seattle, West* | 3 | 84 | 28 | 1 | 5 | 0 | .991 | 22 | 8 |
| | Chicago, Central | 3 | 82 | 38 | 2 | 5 | 0 | .984 | 24 | 10 |
| 2001 | New York, East | 5 | 135 | 42 | 4 | 4 | 0 | .978 | 21 | 9 |
| | Oakland, West* | 5 | 132 | 60 | 6 | 4 | 0 | .970 | 25 | 11 |
| | Seattle, West | 5 | 132 | 43 | 5 | 5 | 1 | .972 | 25 | 10 |
| | Cleveland, Central | 5 | 129 | 53 | 3 | 4 | 0 | .984 | 22 | 10 |
| 2002 | Anaheim, West*. | 4 | 105 | 33 | 2 | 6 | 0 | .986 | 22 | 9 |
| | New York, East | 4 | 102 | 39 | 4 | 5 | 0 | .972 | 24 | 10 |
| | Minnesota, Central | 5 | 132 | 36 | 4 | 2 | 0 | .977 | 25 | 11 |
| | Oakland, West | 5 | 132 | 48 | 3 | 4 | 0 | .963 | 25 | 10 |
| | Texas, West | 4 | 114 | 47 | 2 | 5 | 0 | .988 | 23 | 11 |
| 2003 | New York, East | 4 | 108 | 44 | 3 | 2 | 0 | .981 | 19 | 8 |
| | Minnesota, Central | 4 | 105 | 40 | 2 | 3 | 1 | .986 | 24 | 10 |
| | Boston, East* | 5 | 146 | 56 | 5 | 2 | 1 | .976 | 22 | 8 |
| | Oakland, West | 5 | 145 | 44 | 5 | 4 | 0 | .974 | 23 | 9 |
| 2004 | Boston, East* | 3 | 84 | 25 | 1 | 2 | 0 | .991 | 22 | 8 |
| | Anaheim, West | 3 | 83 | 25 | 3 | 2 | 0 | .973 | 14 | 8 |
| | New York, East | 4 | 123 | 55 | 1 | 4 | 1 | .994 | 22 | 10 |
| | Minnesota, Central | 4 | 122 | 50 | 2 | 9 | 1 | .989 | 24 | 10 |
| 2005 | Boston, East* | 3 | 75 | 34 | 2 | 3 | 0 | .982 | 23 | 9 |
| | Chicago, Central | 3 | 81 | 35 | 1 | 2 | 0 | .991 | 20 | 8 |
| | Los Angeles, West | 5 | 132 | 48 | 1 | 4 | 0 | .994 | 22 | 8 |
| | New York, East | 5 | 129 | 55 | 6 | 3 | 0 | .968 | 24 | 10 |

*wild-card team

## NATIONAL LEAGUE

| Year | Team, Division | G | PO | A | E | DP | PB | Fielding Avg. | Players Used | Pitchers Used |
|---|---|---|---|---|---|---|---|---|---|---|
| 1995 | Cincinnati, Central | 3 | 81 | 30 | 2 | 1 | 0 | .982 | 18 | 6 |
| | Los Angeles, West | 3 | 78 | 19 | 3 | 2 | 0 | .970 | 22 | 8 |
| | Atlanta, East | 4 | 111 | 49 | 2 | 5 | 0 | .988 | 24 | 10 |
| | Colorado, West* | 4 | 108 | 50 | 7 | 5 | 0 | .958 | 24 | 11 |
| 1996 | Atlanta, East | 3 | 84 | 28 | 3 | 1 | 0 | .974 | 19 | 6 |
| | Los Angeles, West* | 3 | 81 | 32 | 1 | 4 | 0 | .991 | 23 | 10 |
| | St. Louis, Central | 3 | 81 | 18 | 2 | 0 | 0 | .980 | 20 | 7 |
| | San Diego, West | 3 | 75 | 28 | 2 | 3 | 0 | .972 | 23 | 9 |
| 1997 | Florida, East* | 3 | 81 | 33 | 4 | 3 | 0 | .966 | 19 | 6 |
| | San Francisco, West | 3 | 77 | 31 | 0 | 4 | 0 | 1.000 | 21 | 8 |
| | Atlanta, East | 3 | 81 | 33 | 3 | 2 | 0 | .974 | 18 | 5 |
| | Houston, Central | 3 | 75 | 27 | 4 | 2 | 1 | .962 | 24 | 9 |
| 1998 | San Diego, West | 4 | 104 | 37 | 3 | 5 | 2 | .979 | 22 | 7 |
| | Houston, Central | 4 | 102 | 41 | 2 | 1 | 0 | .986 | 21 | 8 |
| | Atlanta, East | 3 | 84 | 25 | 0 | 2 | 0 | 1.000 | 21 | 7 |
| | Chicago, Central* | 3 | 79 | 20 | 4 | 1 | 1 | .961 | 22 | 8 |
| 1999 | New York, East* | 4 | 108 | 41 | 0 | 5 | 0 | 1.000 | 25 | 11 |
| | Arizona, West | 4 | 106 | 37 | 5 | 2 | 0 | .966 | 23 | 10 |
| | Atlanta, East | 4 | 117 | 46 | 2 | 4 | 0 | .988 | 23 | 9 |
| | Houston, Central | 4 | 114 | 50 | 4 | 4 | 0 | .976 | 24 | 10 |
| 2000 | New York, East* | 4 | 120 | 33 | 0 | 1 | 0 | 1.000 | 24 | 10 |
| | San Francisco, West | 4 | 118 | 40 | 1 | 4 | 0 | .994 | 25 | 11 |
| | St. Louis, Central | 3 | 81 | 29 | 1 | 2 | 0 | .991 | 21 | 9 |
| | Atlanta, East | 3 | 75 | 28 | 5 | 0 | 0 | .954 | 22 | 9 |
| 2001 | Atlanta, East | 3 | 81 | 32 | 1 | 5 | 0 | .991 | 21 | 8 |
| | Houston, Central | 3 | 78 | 30 | 3 | 7 | 0 | .973 | 22 | 9 |
| | Arizona, West | 5 | 132 | 54 | 4 | 4 | 0 | .979 | 23 | 8 |
| | St. Louis, Central* | 5 | 131 | 50 | 3 | 4 | 0 | .984 | 22 | 10 |
| 2002 | St. Louis, Central | 3 | 81 | 26 | 2 | 0 | 0 | .982 | 20 | 8 |
| | Arizona, West | 3 | 78 | 34 | 2 | 1 | 0 | .982 | 25 | 10 |
| | San Francisco, West* | 5 | 132 | 56 | 4 | 6 | 1 | .979 | 23 | 11 |
| | Atlanta, East | 5 | 132 | 40 | 0 | 2 | 0 | 1.000 | 24 | 10 |
| 2003 | Florida, East* | 4 | 111 | 33 | 2 | 0 | 0 | .986 | 21 | 9 |
| | San Francisco, West | 4 | 110 | 40 | 7 | 3 | 0 | .955 | 25 | 12 |
| | Chicago, Central | 5 | 132 | 52 | 0 | 2 | 0 | 1.000 | 25 | 11 |
| | Atlanta, East | 5 | 132 | 68 | 6 | 8 | 0 | .971 | 23 | 10 |
| 2004 | St. Louis, Central | 4 | 105 | 34 | 0 | 3 | 0 | 1.000 | 23 | 11 |
| | Los Angeles, West | 4 | 102 | 31 | 3 | 3 | 1 | .978 | 24 | 10 |
| | Houston, Central* | 5 | 140 | 58 | 3 | 4 | 0 | .985 | 24 | 10 |
| | Atlanta, East | 5 | 138 | 64 | 1 | 7 | 0 | .995 | 25 | 11 |
| 2005 | Atlanta, East | 4 | 130 | 45 | 0 | 7 | 0 | 1.000 | 24 | 10 |
| | Houston, Central* | 4 | 132 | 57 | 4 | 6 | 0 | .979 | 25 | 10 |
| | St. Louis, Central | 3 | 81 | 36 | 2 | 7 | 0 | .983 | 20 | 8 |
| | San Diego, West | 3 | 75 | 31 | 2 | 3 | 0 | .981 | 24 | 9 |

*wild-card team

## MANAGERIAL RECORDS

### AMERICAN LEAGUE

| Manager, Team | Series W | Series L | Games W | Games L |
|---|---|---|---|---|
| Terry Francona, Boston | 1 | 1 | 3 | 3 |
| Ron Gardenhire, Minnesota | 1 | 2 | 5 | 8 |
| Ozzie Guillen, Chicago | 1 | 0 | 3 | 0 |
| Mike Hargrove, Cleveland | 3 | 2 | 12 | 9 |
| Art Howe, Oakland | 0 | 3 | 6 | 9 |
| Dave Johnson, Baltimore | 2 | 0 | 6 | 2 |
| Kevin Kennedy, Boston | 0 | 1 | 0 | 0 |
| Grady Little, Boston | 1 | 0 | 3 | 2 |
| Ken Macha, Oakland | 0 | 1 | 2 | 3 |
| Charlie Manuel, Cleveland | 0 | 1 | 2 | 3 |
| Jerry Manuel, Chicago | 0 | 1 | 0 | 3 |
| John Oates, Texas | 0 | 3 | 1 | 9 |
| Lou Piniella, Seattle | 3 | 1 | 10 | 7 |
| Mike Scioscia, Anaheim | 2 | 1 | 6 | 6 |
| Buck Showalter, New York | 0 | 1 | 2 | 3 |
| Joe Torre, New York | 7 | 3 | 26 | 16 |
| Jimy Williams, Boston | 1 | 1 | 4 | 5 |

**Total number of managers: 17**

### NATIONAL LEAGUE

| Manager, Team | Series W | Series L | Games W | Games L |
|---|---|---|---|---|
| Felipe Alou, San Francisco | 0 | 1 | 1 | 3 |
| Dusty Baker, San Francisco, Chicago | 2 | 2 | 7 | 10 |
| Don Baylor, Colorado | 0 | 1 | 1 | 3 |
| Bruce Bochy, San Diego | 1 | 2 | 3 | 7 |
| Bob Brenly, Arizona | 1 | 1 | 3 | 5 |
| Bobby Cox, Atlanta | 6 | 5 | 25 | 17 |
| Larry Dierker, Houston | 0 | 4 | 2 | 12 |
| Phil Garner, Houston | 2 | 0 | 6 | 2 |
| Dave Johnson, Cincinnati | 1 | 0 | 3 | 0 |
| Tony LaRussa, St. Louis | 3 | 1 | 7 | 4 |
| Tom Lasorda, Los Angeles | 0 | 1 | 0 | 3 |
| Jim Leyland, Florida | 1 | 0 | 3 | 0 |
| Jack McKeon, Florida | 1 | 0 | 3 | 1 |
| Jim Riggleman, Chicago | 0 | 1 | 0 | 3 |
| Bill Russell, Los Angeles | 0 | 1 | 0 | 3 |
| Buck Showalter, Arizona | 0 | 1 | 1 | 3 |
| Jim Tracy, Los Angeles | 0 | 1 | 1 | 3 |
| Bobby Valentine, New York | 2 | 0 | 6 | 2 |

**Total number of managers: 18**

### COMBINED RECORDS FOR BOTH LEAGUES

| Manager, Team | Series W | Series L | Games W | Games L |
|---|---|---|---|---|
| Dave Johnson, Cin NL, Bal AL | 3 | 0 | 9 | 2 |
| Buck Showalter, NY AL, Ari NL | 0 | 2 | 3 | 6 |

**Total number of managers: 2**

# ADDENDUM - 1981

Major league baseball played a split season in 1981 because of a mid-season strike by the Major League Baseball Players Association. Following the regular season, the teams that finished first in each division during the first half of the season played the teams that finished first during the second half of the season in best-of-five series for the right to advance to the League Championship Series. These four intra-divisional playoffs (AL East: New York 3, Milwaukee 2; AL West: Oakland 3, Kansas City 0; NL East: Montreal 3, Philadelphia 2; and NL West: Los Angeles 3, Houston 2) were called division series at the time. But they are not the same as the Division Series played since 1995.

The 1997 edition of the Complete Baseball Record Book added a section for the Division Series. Included in this section were records set in 1981. Beginning with the 2004 edition, we removed the 1981 records from the Division Series section. We will continue to list Service, Batting, Baserunning, Pitching and Fielding records in this addendum so long as they have not been surpassed in Division Series play since 1995.

## CLUB SERVICE

**Fewest players, series**
AL—16—Kansas City vs. Oakland (3-game series)

**Fewest players used by both clubs, series**
AL—36—Oakland 20, Kansas City 16 (3-game series)

**Fewest pinch-hitters, series**
AL—0—Kansas City vs. Oakland (3-game series)

**Fewest pinch-hitters used by both clubs, series**
AL—1—Oakland 1, Kansas City 0 (3-game series)

**Most second basemen, series**
AL—3—Milwaukee vs. New York (5-game series)

**Most shortstops, series**
NL—3—Houston vs. Los Angeles (5-game series)

**Most shortstops used by both clubs, series**
NL—4—Houston 3, Los Angeles 1 (5-game series)

**Most right fielders, series**
NL—4—Philadelphia vs. Montreal (5-games series)

**Most right fielders used by both clubs, series**
NL—6—Philadelphia 4, Montreal 2 (5-game series)

**Fewest pitchers, series**
AL—5—Kansas City vs. Oakland (3-game series)
Oakland vs. Kansas City (3-game series)

**Fewest pitchers used by both clubs, series**
AL—10—Kansas City 5, Oakland 5 (3-game series)

## INDIVIDUAL BATTING

**Most games by pinch-hitter, series**
AL—3—Roy Howell, Milwaukee (5-game series))

**Highest slugging average, series (10 or more PA)**
AL—1.333—Oscar Gamble, New York (5-game series)

**Most hits by pinch-hitter, career**
NL—3—George Vukovich, Philadelphia; 4 G

**Most hits by pinch-hitter, series**
NL—3—George Vukovich, Philadelphia; 4 G

**Most consecutive hits, career**
AL—5—Tony Armas, Oakland, Oct 7 (4), 9 (1)

**Most consecutive hits by pinch-hitter, career**
NL—2—George Vukovich, Philadelphia, Oct 9, 10

**Most consecutive hits, series**
AL—5—Tony Armas, Oakland, Oct 7 (4), 9 (1)

**Most singles by pinch-hitter, series**
NL—2—George Vukovich, Philadelphia (5-game series)

**Most doubles, series**
NL—3—Gary Carter, Montreal (5-game series)

**Home runs by pinch-hitter**
NL—1—George Vukovich, Philadelphia, Oct 16, 10th inn

**Hitting home run in first series at-bat**
NL—Keith Moreland, Philadelphia, Oct 7, 2nd inn

**Most total bases by pinch-hitter, career**
NL—6—George Vukovich, Philadelphia; 4 G

**Most total bases by pinch-hitter, series**
NL—6—George Vuckovich, Philadelphia; 4 G

**Most game-winning RBIs, career and series**
AL—2—Tony Armas, Oakland (3-game series)
NL—2—Chris Speier, Montreal (5-game series)

**Most consecutive bases on balls, series**
NL—3—Chris Speier, Montreal, Oct 7

**Most bases on balls, game**
NL—3—Bill Russell, Los Angeles, Oct 7, 11 inn

**Most strikeouts, series**
NL—9—Warren Cromartie, Montreal (5-game series)

**Most consecutive strikeouts, series (consecutive at-bats)**
NL—8—Jerry Reuss, Los Angeles, Oct 7 (4 in 11 inn), Oct 11 (4)

**Most sacrifice flies, series**
AL—2—Cecil Cooper, Milwaukee (5-game series)

## CLUB BATTING

**Highest batting average by both clubs, series**
NL—.260—Philadelphia .265, Montreal .255 (5-game series)

**Lowest batting average, series**
NL—.179—Houston vs. Los Angeles (5-game series)

**Lowest batting average by both clubs, series**
NL—.188—Los Angeles .198, Houston .179 (5-game series)

**Lowest slugging average, series**
NL—.235—Houston vs. Los Angeles (5-game series)

**Lowest slugging average by both clubs, series**
NL—.269—Los Angeles .302, Houston .235 (5-game series)

**Fewest runs, series**
NL—6—Houston vs. Los Angeles (5-game series)

**Fewest runs by both clubs, series**
NL—19—Los Angeles 13, Houston 6 (5-game series)

**Largest score, shutout game**
NL—Los Angeles 4, Houston 0, Oct 11

**Fewest hits, series**
NL—29—Houston vs. Los Angeles (5-game series)
AL—36—Milwaukee vs. New York (5-game series)

**Fewest hits by both clubs, series**
NL—61—Los Angeles 32, Houston 29 (5-game series)

**Most hits by pinch-hitters, game**
NL—2—Montreal vs. Philadelphia, Oct 10, 10 inn

**Most hits by pinch-hitters on both clubs, game**
NL—3—Montreal 2, Philadelphia 1, Oct 10, 10 inn

**Most hits by pinch-hitters, inning**
NL—2—Montreal vs. Philadelphia, Oct 10, 6th

**Fewest singles by both clubs, series**
NL—46—Houston 24, Los Angeles 22 (5-game series)

**Fewest doubles, series**
3-game series
AL—1—Kansas City vs. Oakland
5-game series
NL—3—Houston vs. Los Angeles
AL—6—Milwaukee vs. New York

**Fewest doubles by both clubs, series**
AL—6—Oakland 5, Kansas City 1 (3-game series)

**Most triples by both clubs, series**
NL —2—Montreal 1, Philadelphia 1 (5-game series)

**Most triples by both clubs, game**
NL—2—Montreal 1, Philadelphia 1, Oct 7

**Fewest home runs, series**
3-game series
AL—0—Kansas City vs. Oakland
5-game series
NL—2—Houston vs. Los Angeles
Montreal vs. Philadelphia

**Fewest home runs by both clubs, series**
AL—3—Oakland 3, Kansas City 0 (3-game series)
NL—5—Los Angeles 3, Houston 2 (5-game series)

**Most home runs by pinch-hitters, series**
NL—1—Philadelphia vs. Montreal (5-game series)

**Fewest total bases, series**
NL—38—Houston vs. Los Angeles (5-game series)

**Fewest total bases by both clubs, series**
NL—87—Los Angeles 49, Houston 38 (5-game series)

**Fewest extra base hits, series**
3-game series
AL—1—Kansas City vs. Oakland
5-game series
NL—5—Houston vs. Los Angeles
AL—10—Milwaukee vs. New York

**Fewest extra base hits by both clubs, series**
3-game series
AL—9—Oakland 8, Kansas City 1
5-game series
NL—15—Los Angeles 10, Houston 5
AL—24—New York 14, Milwaukee 10

**Fewest runs batted in, series**
NL—6—Houston vs. Los Angeles (5-game series)

**Fewest runs batted in by both clubs, series**
NL—18—Los Angeles 12, Houston 6 (5-game series)

**Most bases on balls by pinch-hitters, series**
AL—2—Milwaukee vs. New York (5-game series)

**Most bases on balls by pinch-hitters on both clubs, series**
AL—3—Milwaukee 2, New York 1 (5-game series)

**Fewest strikeouts, series**
3-game series
AL—10—Oakland vs. Kansas City
5-game series
NL—19—Philadelphia vs. Montreal
AL—22—New York vs. Milwaukee

**Fewest strikeouts by both clubs, series**
AL—21—Kansas City 11, Oakland 10 (3-game series)
NL—55—Montreal 36, Philadelphia 19 (5-game series)

**Most strikeouts, game**
AL—14—Milwaukee vs. New York, Oct 8

**Fewest strikeouts, game**
NL—1—Los Angeles vs. Houston, Oct 10
AL—1—Milwaukee vs. New York, Oct 9
New York vs. Milwaukee, Oct 11

**Fewest strikeouts by both clubs, game**
NL—5—Houston 4, Los Angeles 1, Oct 10

**Most sacrifice hits, game**
AL—3—Oakland vs. Kansas City, Oct 7

## INDIVIDUAL BASERUNNING

**Most stolen bases, series**
NL—3—Jerry White, Montreal (5-game series)

**Most caught stealing, career**
NL—2—Cesar Cedeno, Houston; 4 G

**Most caught stealing, series**
NL—2—Cesar Cedeno, Houston; 2 SB (5-game series)

## CLUB BASERUNNING

**Most stolen bases, series**
NL—7—Montreal vs. Philadelphia (5-game series)

**Fewest stolen bases by both clubs, series**
AL—2—Milwaukee 1, New York 1 (5-game series)

**Most stolen bases, game**
NL—4—Montreal vs. Philadelphia, Oct 7

**Most caught stealing, series**
AL—3—Oakland vs. Kansas City (3-game series)
NL—5—Montreal vs Philadelphia (5-game series)

**Most caught stealing by both clubs, series**
AL—4—Milwaukee 2, New York 2 (5-game series)

**Most caught stealing, game**
NL—2—Montreal vs. Philadelphia, Oct 6
Montreal vs. Philadelphia, Oct 7

**Most caught stealing by both clubs, game**
NL—3—Montreal 2, Philadelphia 1, Oct 6

**Most caught stealing, inning**
AL—2—Oakland vs. Kansas City, Oct 9, 3rd

**Fewest left on base by both clubs, series**
NL—67—Los Angeles 35, Houston 32 (5-game series)

**Fewest left on base, game**
NL—1—Los Angeles vs. Houston, Oct 6

**Most left on base, shutout defeat**
AL—11—Milwaukee vs. New York, Oct 8 (lost 3-0)
NL—9—Houston vs. Los Angeles, Oct 11 (lost 4-0)
[13—Los Angeles vs. Houston, Oct 7 (lost 1-0), 11 inn]

## INDIVIDUAL PITCHING

**Most innings pitched, series**
3-game series
AL—9.0—Steve McCatty, Oakland
Mike Norris, Oakland
5-game series
NL—18.0—Jerry Reuss, Los Angeles

**Most saves, series**
AL—3—Rich Gossage, New York (5-game series)
NL—2—Jeff Reardon, Montreal (5-game series)

**Most games lost, series**
NL—2—Dave Stewart, Los Angeles (5-game series)
Steve Carlton, Philadelphia (5-game series)
AL—2—Moose Haas, Milwaukee (5-game series)

**Most shutouts, series**
AL—1—Mike Norris, Oakland
NL—1—Jerry Reuss, Los Angeles
Steve Rogers, Montreal

**Most consecutive scoreless innings, career**
NL—18—Jerry Reuss, Los Angeles, Oct 7 (9), 11 (9)

**Most consecutive scoreless innings, series**
NL—18—Jerry Reuss, Los Angeles, Oct 7 (9), 11 (9)

**Most hits allowed, series**
AL—10—Rick Langford, Oakland (3-game series)

**Most hits allowed, game**
AL—10—Rick Langford, Oakland, Oct 9

**Fewest hits allowed, game**
AL—4—Mike Norris, Oakland, Oct 6

**Most home runs allowed, inning**
AL—2—Moose Haas, Milwaukee, Oct 11, 4th (consec)

**Most bases on balls, series**
NL—8—Steve Carlton, Philadelphia (5-game series)

**Most consecutive strikeouts from start of game**
NL—3—Steve Carlton, Philadelphia, Oct 11
AL—2—Dave Righetti, New York, Oct 8

## CLUB PITCHING

**Most complete games, series**
3-game series
AL—2—Oakland vs. Kansas City
5-game series
NL—2—Houston vs. Los Angeles
Los Angeles vs. Houston

**Most complete games by both clubs, series**
NL—4—Houston 2, Los Angeles 2
AL—2—Oakland 2, Kansas City 0

**Most saves, series**
AL—3—New York vs. Milwaukee (5-game series)
NL—2—Montreal vs. Philadelphia (5-game series)

**Most saves by both clubs, series**
AL—4—New York 3, Milwaukee 1 (5-game series)

**Most shutouts by both clubs, series**
NL—2—Houston 1, Los Angeles 1 (5-game series)

**Longest shutout game**
NL—11 inn—Houston 1, Los Angeles 0, Oct 7

## INDIVIDUAL FIELDING

**Most putouts, series, first basemen**
NL—49—Steve Garvey, Los Angeles (5-game series)

**Most putouts, game, first basemen**
NL—15—Steve Garvey, Los Angeles, Oct 7, 11 inn

**Most assists, series, first basemen**
NL—8—Pete Rose, Philadelphia (5-game series)

**Most assists, game, first basemen**
NL—4—Pete Rose, Philadelphia, Oct 7

**Most chances accepted, series, first basemen**
NL—54—Steve Garvey, Los Angeles (5-game series)

**Most chances accepted, game, first basemen**
NL—16—Steve Garvey, Los Angeles, Oct 7, 11 inn (15 PO, 1 A)

**Fewest chances offered, game, first basemen**
AL—3—Bob Watson, New York, Oct 7 (3 PO)

**Most chances accepted, errorless series, first basemen**
NL—54—Steve Garvey (5-game series)

**Most assists, game, second basemen**
NL—8—Jerry Manuel, Montreal, Oct 7

**Fewest chances offered, game, second basemen**
NL—0—Phil Garner, Houston, Oct 7, 11 inn

**Most errors, career, second basemen**
NL—3—Jerry Manuel, Montreal; 1 series, 5 G
AL—2—Jim Gantner, Milwaukee; 1 series, 4 G

**Most errors, series, second basemen**
NL—3—Jerry Manuel, Montreal (5-game series)
AL—2—Jim Gantner, Milwaukee (5-game series)

**Most putouts, series, third basemen**
NL—8—Larry Parrish, Montreal (5-game series)

**Most assists, series, third basemen**
NL—15—Pedro Guerrero, Los Angeles (5-game series)

**Most chances accepted, errorless series, third basemen**
NL—14—Larry Parrish, Montreal (5-game series)

**Most double plays, game, third basemen**
AL—2—Wayne Gross, Oakland, Oct 6

**Most double plays started, game, third basemen**
AL—2—Wayne Gross, Oakland, Oct 6

**Most putouts, series, shortstops**
NL—17—Chris Speier, Montreal (5-game series)

**Most putouts, game, shortstops**
NL—7—Larry Bowa, Philadelphia, Oct 7
AL—5—Fred Stanley, Oakland, Oct 9

**Most assists, series, shortstops**
AL—23—Robin Yount, Milwaukee (5-game series)

**Most chances accepted, series, shortstops**
NL—32—Chris Speier, Montreal (5-game series)
AL—30—Robin Yount, Milwaukee (5-game series)

**Most chances accepted, game, shortstops**
NL—9—Dickie Thon, Houston, Oct 7, 11 inn (3 PO, 6 A)

**Most chances accepted, errorless series, shortstops**
NL—32—Chris Speier, Montreal (5-game series)

**Most putouts, series, outfielders**
NL—16—Ken Landreaux, Los Angeles (5-game series)

**Most putouts by center fielder, game**
AL—7—Dwayne Murphy, Oakland, Oct 6
Amos Otis, Kansas City, Oct 7

**Most putouts, inning, outfielders**
NL—3—Jerry White, Montreal, Oct 8, 2nd (RF)

**Most chances accepted, series, outfielders**
NL—16—Ken Landreaux, Los Angeles (5-game series)

**Most chances accepted by center fielder, game**
AL—7—Dwayne Murphy, Oakland, Oct 6 (7 PO)
Amos Otis, Kansas City, Oct 7 (7 PO)

**Most putouts, game, catchers**
AL—15—Rick Cerone, New York, Oct 8

**Most assists, series, catchers**
3-game series
AL—3—John Wathan, Kansas City
5-game series
NL—4—Gary Carter, Montreal
Mike Scioscia, Los Angeles

**Fewest chances offered, game, catchers**
AL—1—Rick Cerone, New York, Oct 9

**Most runners caught stealing, game, catchers**
AL—2—John Wathan, Kansas City, Oct 9

**Most runners caught stealing, inning, catchers**
AL—2—John Wathan, Kansas City, Oct 9, 3rd

**Most putouts, series, pitchers**
AL—3—Rick Langford, Oakland (3-game series)
Mike Norris, Oakland (3-game series)

**Most putouts, inning, pitchers**
AL—2—Rick Langford, Oakland, Oct 9, 1st
Moose Haas, Milwaukee, Oct 11, 1st

**Most assists, series, pitchers**
AL—4—Steve McCatty, Oakland (3-game series)
NL—5—Fernando Valenzuela, Los Angeles (5-game series)

**Most assists, game, pitchers**
AL—4—Steve McCatty, Oakland, Oct 7
NL—4—Nolan Ryan, Houston, Oct 6

**Most assists, inning, pitchers**
AL—2—Steve McCatty, Oakland, Oct 7, 1st
Tommy John, New York, Oct 9, 7th

**Most chances accepted, series, pitchers**
AL—4—Steve McCatty, Oakland (3-game series)

**Most chances accepted, game, pitchers**
NL—5—Verne Ruhle, Houston, Oct 10

## CLUB FIELDING

**Lowest fielding average by both clubs, series**
N.L.—.976—Philadelphia .984, Montreal .969 (5-game series)

**Most putouts by outfield of both clubs, game**
NL—19—Philadelphia 11, Montreal 8, Oct 9

**Fewest putouts by outfield, game**
NL—0—Philadelphia vs. Montreal, Oct 8 (fielded 8 inn)

**Fewest putouts by outfield of both clubs, game**
NL—6—Montreal 4, Philadelphia 2, Oct 7 (Montreal fielded 8 inn)

**Most assists, game**
AL—18—New York vs. Milwaukee, Oct 9

**Fewest assists, game**
AL—4—New York vs. Milwaukee, Oct 7
New York vs. Milwaukee, Oct 11

**Fewest chances offered to outfield, game**
NL—0—Philadelphia vs. Montreal, Oct 8 (fielded 8 inn)

**Most errors, series**
NL—6—Montreal vs. Philadelphia (5-game series)

**Most errors by both clubs, series**
NL—9—Montreal 6, Philadelphia 3 (5-game series)

**Most errors, game**
NL—4—Montreal vs. Philadelphia, Oct 9

**Most errors by infield, game**
NL—3—Houston vs. Los Angeles, Oct 11

**Most errors by infields of both clubs, game**
NL—5—Houston 3, Los Angeles 2, Oct 11

**Most errors, inning**
AL—3—Kansas City vs. Oakland, Oct 9, 3rd
NL—2—Montreal vs. Philadelphia, Oct 9, 8th

**Fewest double plays, series**
AL—1—New York vs. Milwaukee (5-game series)
NL—1—Houston vs. Los Angeles (5-game series)

**Fewest double plays by both clubs, series**
NL—3—Los Angeles 2, Houston 1 (5-game series)

# CHAMPIONSHIP SERIES

McCovey

# SERIES WINNERS

## AMERICAN LEAGUE

| Year | Winner | Loser | Games |
|---|---|---|---|
| 1969 | Baltimore (East) | Minnesota (West) | 3-0 |
| 1970 | Baltimore (East) | Minnesota (West) | 3-0 |
| 1971 | Baltimore (East) | Oakland (West) | 3-0 |
| 1972 | Oakland (West) | Detroit (East) | 3-2 |
| 1973 | Oakland (West) | Baltimore (East) | 3-2 |
| 1974 | Oakland (West) | Baltimore (East) | 3-1 |
| 1975 | Boston (East) | Oakland (West) | 3-0 |
| 1976 | New York (East) | Kansas City (West) | 3-2 |
| 1977 | New York (East) | Kansas City (West) | 3-2 |
| 1978 | New York (East) | Kansas City (West) | 3-1 |
| 1979 | Baltimore (East) | California (West) | 3-1 |
| 1980 | Kansas City (West) | New York (East) | 3-0 |
| 1981 | New York (East) | Oakland (West) | 3-0 |
| 1982 | Milwaukee (East) | California (West) | 3-2 |
| 1983 | Baltimore (East) | Chicago (West) | 3-1 |
| 1984 | Detroit (East) | Kansas City (West) | 3-0 |
| 1985 | Kansas City (West) | Toronto (East) | 4-3 |
| 1986 | Boston (East) | California (West) | 4-3 |
| 1987 | Minnesota (West) | Detroit (East) | 4-1 |
| 1988 | Oakland (West) | Boston (East) | 4-0 |
| 1989 | Oakland (West) | Toronto (East) | 4-1 |
| 1990 | Oakland (West) | Boston (East) | 4-0 |
| 1991 | Minnesota (West) | Toronto (East) | 4-1 |
| 1992 | Toronto (East) | Oakland (West) | 4-2 |
| 1993 | Toronto (East) | Chicago (West) | 4-2 |
| 1994 | no series played | | |
| 1995 | Cleveland (Central) | Seattle (West) | 4-2 |
| 1996 | New York (East) | Baltimore (East)* | 4-1 |
| 1997 | Cleveland (Central) | Baltimore (East) | 4-2 |
| 1998 | New York (East) | Cleveland (Central) | 4-2 |
| 1999 | New York (East) | Boston (East)* | 4-1 |
| 2000 | New York (East) | Seattle (West)* | 4-2 |
| 2001 | New York (East) | Seattle (West) | 4-1 |
| 2002 | Anaheim (West)* | Minnesota (Central) | 4-1 |
| 2003 | New York (East) | Boston (East)* | 4-3 |
| 2004 | Boston (East)* | New York (East) | 4-3 |
| 2005 | Chicago (Central) | Los Angeles (West) | 4-1 |

***wild-card team**

## NATIONAL LEAGUE

| Year | Winner | Loser | Games |
|---|---|---|---|
| 1969 | New York (East) | Atlanta (West) | 3-0 |
| 1970 | Cincinnati (West) | Pittsburgh (East) | 3-0 |
| 1971 | Pittsburgh (East) | San Francisco (West) | 3-1 |
| 1972 | Cincinnati (West) | Pittsburgh (East) | 3-2 |
| 1973 | New York (East) | Cincinnati (West) | 3-2 |
| 1974 | Los Angeles (West) | Pittsburgh (East) | 3-1 |
| 1975 | Cincinnati (West) | Pittsburgh (East) | 3-0 |
| 1976 | Cincinnati (West) | Philadelphia (East) | 3-0 |
| 1977 | Los Angeles (West) | Philadelphia (East) | 3-1 |
| 1978 | Los Angeles (West) | Philadelphia (East) | 3-1 |
| 1979 | Pittsburgh (East) | Cincinnati (West) | 3-0 |
| 1980 | Philadelphia (East) | Houston (West) | 3-2 |
| 1981 | Los Angeles (West) | Montreal (East) | 3-2 |
| 1982 | St. Louis (East) | Atlanta (West) | 3-0 |
| 1983 | Philadelphia (East) | Los Angeles (West) | 3-1 |
| 1984 | San Diego (West) | Chicago (East) | 3-2 |
| 1985 | St. Louis (East) | Los Angeles (West) | 4-2 |
| 1986 | New York (East) | Houston (West) | 4-2 |
| 1987 | St. Louis (East) | San Francisco (West) | 4-3 |
| 1988 | Los Angeles (West) | New York (East) | 4-3 |
| 1989 | San Francisco (West) | Chicago (East) | 4-1 |
| 1990 | Cincinnati (West) | Pittsburgh (East) | 4-2 |
| 1991 | Atlanta (West) | Pittsburgh (East) | 4-3 |
| 1992 | Atlanta (West) | Pittsburgh (East) | 4-3 |
| 1993 | Philadelphia (East) | Atlanta (West) | 4-2 |
| 1994 | no series played | | |
| 1995 | Atlanta (East) | Cincinnati (Central) | 4-0 |
| 1996 | Atlanta (East) | St. Louis (Central) | 4-3 |
| 1997 | Florida (East)* | Atlanta (East) | 4-2 |
| 1998 | San Diego (West) | Atlanta (East) | 4-2 |
| 1999 | Atlanta (East) | New York (East)* | 4-2 |
| 2000 | New York (East)* | St. Louis (Central) | 4-1 |
| 2001 | Arizona (West) | Atlanta (East) | 4-1 |
| 2002 | San Francisco (West)* | St. Louis (Central) | 4-1 |
| 2003 | Florida (East)* | Chicago (Central) | 4-3 |
| 2004 | St. Louis (Central) | Houston (Central)* | 4-3 |
| 2005 | Houston (Central)* | St. Louis (Central) | 4-2 |

# INDIVIDUAL SERVICE

## ALL PLAYERS

### SERIES AND CLUBS

**Most series played**

AL—11—Reggie Jackson, Oakland, 1971-1975; New York, 1977, 1978, 1980, 1981; California, 1982, 1986
NL—9—Tom Glavine, Atlanta, 1991-1993, 1995-1999, 2001
John Smoltz, Atlanta, 1991-1993, 1995-1999, 2001

**Most consecutive years played in series**

ML—5—Tino Martinez, New York AL, 1998-2001; St. Louis NL, 2002
AL—5—Sal Bando, Vida Blue, Bert Campaneris, Rollie Fingers, Reggie Jackson, Joe Rudi, Gene Tenace, Oakland, 1971-1975
NL—5—Tom Glavine, Chipper Jones, Ryan Klesko, Greg Maddux, John Smoltz, Atlanta, 1995-1999

**Most series playing in all games**

AL—9—Reggie Jackson, Oakland, 1971-1975; New York, 1977, 1978, 1980; California, 1982; 37 G
NL—7—Pete Rose, Cincinnati, 1970, 1972, 1973, 1975, 1976; Philadelphia, 1980, 1983; 28 G

**Most series played with one club**

NL—9—Tom Glavine, Atlanta, 1991-1993, 1995-1999, 2001
John Smoltz, Atlanta, 1991-1993, 1995-1999, 2001
AL—7—Jim Palmer, Baltimore, 1969-1971, 1973, 1974, 1979, 1983
Derek Jeter, New York, 1996, 1998-2001, 2003, 2004
Bernie Williams, New York, 1996, 1998-2001, 2003, 2004

**Most series appeared in as pinch-hitter**

ML—4—Vic Davalillo, Pittsburgh NL, 1971, 1972; Oakland AL, 1973; Los Angeles NL, 1977; 5 G
Danny Heep, Houston NL, 1980; New York NL, 1986; Los Angeles NL, 1988; Boston AL, 1990; 10 G
NL—4—Rick Monday, Los Angeles, 1977, 1978, 1981, 1983; 4 G
Richie Hebner, Pittsburgh, 1971; Philadelphia, 1977, 1978; Chicago, 1984; 5 G
Keith Lockhart, Atlanta, 1997-1999, 2001; 6 G
AL—3—Curt Motton, Baltimore, 1969, 1971, 1974; 4 G
Jim Holt, Minnesota, 1970; Oakland, 1974, 1975; 4 G
Cliff Johnson, New York, 1977, 1978; Toronto, 1985; 5 G
Jamie Quirk, Kansas City, 1976, 1985; Oakland, 1990; 4 G

**Most times on series-winning club (playing one or more game each series)**

ML—6—David Justice, Atlanta NL, 1991, 1992, 1995; Cleveland AL, 1997; New York AL, 2000, 2001
Paul O'Neill, Cincinnati NL, 1990; New York AL, 1996, 1998-2001
Mike Stanton, Atlanta NL, 1991, 1992; New York AL, 1998-2001
AL—6—Reggie Jackson, Oakland, 1972-1974; New York, 1977, 1978, 1981
NL—6—Pete Rose, Cincinnati, 1970, 1972, 1975, 1976; Philadelphia, 1980, 1983

**Most times on series-losing club (playing one or more game each series)**

NL—7—Richie Hebner, Pittsburgh, 1970, 1972, 1974, 1975; Philadelphia, 1977, 1978; Chicago, 1984
AL—5—Bobby Grich, Baltimore, 1973, 1974; California, 1979, 1982, 1986
Reggie Jackson, Oakland, 1971, 1975; New York, 1980; California, 1982, 1986

**Most clubs, career**

AL—5—Don Baylor, Baltimore, 1973, 1974; California, 1979, 1982; Boston, 1986; Minnesota, 1987; Oakland, 1988
NL—4—Shawon Dunston, Chicago, 1989; New York, 1999; St. Louis, 2000; San Francisco, 2002

### BY POSITION (EXCEPT PITCHERS)

**Most series by first baseman**

ML—7—Tino Martinez, Seattle AL, 1995; New York AL, 1996, 1998-2001; St. Louis NL, 2002; 37 G
John Olerud, Toronto AL, 1991-1993; New York NL, 1999; Seattle AL, 2000, 2001; New York AL, 2004; 38 G
AL—6—Tino Martinez, Seattle, 1995; New York, 1996, 1998-2001; 33 G
John Olerud, Toronto, 1991-1993; Seattle, 2000, 2001; New York, 2004; 32 G

NL—5—Tony Perez, Cincinnati, 1970, 1972, 1973, 1975, 1976; 17 G
Bob Robertson, Pittsburgh, 1970-1972, 1974, 1975; 11 G
Steve Garvey, Los Angeles, 1974, 1977, 1978, 1981; San Diego, 1984; 22 G

**Most series by second baseman**

NL—7—Joe Morgan, Cincinnati, 1972, 1973, 1975, 1976, 1979; Houston, 1980; Philadelphia, 1983; 27 G
AL—6—Frank White, Kansas City, 1976-1978, 1980, 1984, 1985; 26 G

**Most series by third baseman**

ML—6—Graig Nettles, New York AL, 1976-1978, 1980, 1981; San Diego NL, 1984; 23 G
AL—6—George Brett, Kansas City, 1976-1978, 1980, 1984, 1985; 27 G
NL—6—Terry Pendleton, St. Louis, 1985, 1987; Atlanta, 1991-1993, 1996; 34 G
Chipper Jones, Atlanta, 1995-2001, except 2000; 34 G

**Most series by shortstop**

AL—7—Derek Jeter, New York, 1996, 1998-2001, 2003, 2004; 41 G
NL—6—Jeff Blauser, Atlanta, 1991-1993, 1995, 1996, 1997; 29 G

**Most series by outfielder**

AL—10—Reggie Jackson, Oakland, 1971-1974, 1975; New York, 1977, 1978, 1980, 1981; California, 1982; 32 G
NL—5—Cesar Geronimo, Cincinnati, 1972, 1973, 1975, 1976, 1979; 17 G
Garry Maddox, Philadelphia, 1976-1978, 1980, 1983; 17 G
Ron Gant, Atlanta, 1991-1993; Cincinnati, 1995; St. Louis, 1996; 31 G
Andruw Jones, Atlanta, 1996-2001, except 2000; 27 G
Reggie Sanders, Cincinnati, 1995; Arizona, 2001; San Francisco, 2002; St. Louis, 2004, 2005; 24 G

**Most series by catcher**

ML—6—Bob Boone, Philadelphia NL, 1976-1978, 1980; California AL, 1982, 1986; 27 G
NL—6—Johnny Bench, Cincinnati, 1970, 1972, 1973, 1975, 1976, 1979; 22 G
Steve Yeager, Los Angeles, 1974, 1977, 1978, 1981, 1983, 1985; 15 G
Javy Lopez, Atlanta, 1992, 1995-1998, 2001; 27 G
AL—6—Jorge Posada, New York, 1998-2001, 2003, 2004; 33 G

## YOUNGEST AND OLDEST NON-PITCHERS

**Youngest championship series non-pitcher**

NL—19 years, 5 months, 16 days—Andruw Jones, Atlanta, Oct 9, 1996
AL—20 years, 1 month, 5 days—Claudell Washington, Oakland, Oct 5, 1974

**Oldest championship series non-pitcher**

NL—42 years, 5 months, 24 days—Pete Rose, Philadelphia, Oct 8, 1983
AL—41 years, 10 months, 21 days—Rickey Henderson, Seattle, Oct 15, 2000

## YEARS BETWEEN SERIES (INCLUDES PITCHERS)

**Most years between first and second series**

ML—16—Chuck Finley, California AL, 1986; St. Louis NL, 2002
NL—14—Tony Gwynn, San Diego, 1984, 1998
AL—12—Doyle Alexander, Baltimore, 1973; Toronto, 1985
(Bert Blyleven went 17 years between ALCS appearances with Minnesota in 1970 and 1987, but that span was interrupted by a 1979 NLCS appearance with Pittsburgh.)

**Most years between first and last series**

ML—19—Dennis Martinez, Baltimore AL, 1979; Atlanta NL, 1998
AL—19—Rickey Henderson, Oakland, 1981; Seattle, 2000
NL—17—Nolan Ryan, New York, 1969; Houston, 1986

## POSITIONS

**Most positions played, career**

NL—4—Pete Rose, Cincinnati, 1970, 1972, 1973, 1975, 1976; Philadelphia, 1980 (RF, LF, 3B, 1B); 24 G
Pedro Guerrero, Los Angeles, 1981, 1983, 1985 (RF, CF, 3B LF); 15 G
Lloyd McClendon, Chicago, 1989; Pittsburgh, 1991, 1992 (C, LF, 1B, RF); 11 G
AL—3—many players

**Most positions played, series**

AL—3—Cesar Tovar, Minnesota, 1970 (CF, 2B, LF); 3-game series, 3 G
Stan Javier, Seattle, 2000 (RF, CF, LF); 6-game series, 4 G
Mark McLemore, Seattle, 2001 (SS, LF, 2B); 5-game series; 5 G
NL—3—Melvin Mora, New York, 1999 (LF, CF, RF); 6-game series, 6 G
Joe McEwing, New York, 2000 (LF, 3B RF); 5-game series, 4 G
Craig Paquette, St. Louis, 2000 (3B, LF, RF); 5-game series, 4 G
Albert Pujols, St. Louis, 2002 (LF, 3B 1B); 5-game series, 5 G
Miquel Cabrera, Florida, 2003 (RF, 3B SS); 7-game series, 7 G

## SERIES

**Most series pitched**

NL—9—Tom Glavine, Atlanta, 1991-1993, 1995-1999, 2001; 15 G
John Smoltz, Atlanta, 1991-1993, 1995-1999, 2001; 17 G
AL—7—Roger Clemens, Boston, 1986, 1988, 1990; New York, 1999-2001, 2003; 11 G
Jeff Nelson, Seattle, 1995, 2001; New York, 1996, 1998-2000, 2003; 19 G
Mariano Rivera, New York, 1996, 1998-2001, 2003, 2004; 25 G

**Most series pitched by relief pitcher**

ML—7—Rick Honeycutt, Los Angeles NL, 1983, 1985; Oakland AL, 1988-1990, 1992; St. Louis, 1996; 20 G
Mark Wohlers, Atlanta NL, 1991-1993, 1995-1997; New York AL, 2001; 19 G
NL—6—Tug McGraw, New York, 1969, 1973; Philadelphia, 1976-1978, 1980; 15 G
Mark Wohlers, Atlanta, 1991-1993, 1995-1997; 18 G
AL—7—Jeff Nelson, Seattle, 1995, 2001; New York, 1996, 1998-2000, 2003; 19 G
Mariano Rivera, New York, 1996, 1998-2001, 2003, 2004; 25 G

## YOUNGEST AND OLDEST PITCHERS

**Youngest championship series pitcher**

AL—19 years, 5 months, 29 days—Bert Blyleven, Minnesota, Oct 5, 1970
NL—19 years, 8 months, 28 days—Don Gullett, Cincinnati, Oct 4, 1970

**Oldest championship series pitcher**

NL—43 years, 6 months, 8 days—Phil Niekro, Atlanta, Oct 9, 1982
AL—41 years, 6 months, 13 days—Don Sutton, California, Oct 15, 1986

# CLUB SERVICE

## PLAYERS USED

**Most players, series**

AL-NL—25—many clubs

**For a list of players and pitchers used each series, see page 355.**

**Most players used by both clubs, series**

3-game series
AL—46—Oakland 24, New York 22, 1981
NL—42—Pittsburgh 24, Cincinnati 18, 1975
4-game series
NL—46—Cincinnati 24, Atlanta 22, 1995
AL—45—Chicago 23, Baltimore 22, 1983
5-game series
AL—49—Oakland 25, Detroit 24, 1972
New York 25, Boston 24, 1999
Seattle 25, New York 24, 2001
Minnesota 25, Anaheim 24, 2002
NL—49—St. Louis 25, New York 24, 2000
6-game series
AL—50—Cleveland 25, Seattle 25, 1995
NL—50—Atlanta 25, New York 25, 1999
7-game series
NL—50—Pittsburgh 25, Atlanta 25, 1992
AL—46—Toronto 24, Kansas City 22, 1985

**Fewest players, series**

3-game series
AL—14—Baltimore vs Minnesota, 1970
Boston vs Oakland, 1975
NL—15—St. Louis vs Atlanta, 1982
4-game series
AL—20—Oakland vs Baltimore, 1974
Kansas City vs New York, 1978
Baltimore vs California, 1979
Boston vs Oakland, 1988.
NL—20—Philadelphia vs Los Angeles, 1983
5-game series
NL—17—New York vs Cincinnati, 1973
AL—18—New York vs Kansas City, 1977
6-game series
AL—19—Toronto vs Chicago, 1993
NL—21—Houston vs New York, 1986
Pittsburgh vs Cincinnati, 1990
7-game series
AL—20—Boston vs California, 1986
NL—22—New York vs Los Angeles, 1988

**Fewest players used by both clubs, series**

3-game series
AL—35—Oakland 20, Baltimore 15, 1971
New York 20, Kansas City 15, 1980
NL—35—Atlanta 20, St. Louis 15, 1982
4-game series
AL—41—New York 21, Kansas City 20, 1978
NL—42—Los Angeles 22, Philadelphia 20, 1983

5-game series
AL—40—Kansas City 22, New York 18, 1977
Milwaukee 20, California 20, 1982
NL—41—Cincinnati 24, New York 17, 1973
6-game series
AL—41—Chicago 22, Toronto 19, 1993
NL—43—New York 22, Houston 21, 1986
7-game series
AL—44—California 24, Boston 20, 1986
NL—46—St. Louis 23, San Francisco 23, 1987
Los Angeles 24, New York 22, 1988

**Most times one club using only nine players in game, series**
NL—3—New York vs Cincinnati, 1973 (5-game series)
AL—2—Baltimore vs Minnesota, 1970 (3-game series)

**Most players, game**
NL—21—St. Louis vs New York, Oct 16, 2000
[23—New York vs Atlanta, Oct 17, 1999, 15 inn]
AL—20—Oakland vs Detroit, Oct 10, 1972
[20—Oakland vs Detroit, Oct 11, 1972, 10 inn]

**Most players used by both clubs, game**
NL—37—Pittsburgh 20, Atlanta 17, Oct 7, 1992
St. Louis 19, Atlanta 18, Oct 14, 1996
[45—New York 23, Atlanta 22, Oct 17, 1999, 15 inn]
AL—37—Minnesota 19, Anaheim 18, Oct 13, 2002
[37—Baltimore 19, Cleveland 18, Oct 11, 1997, 12 inn]

## PINCH-HITTERS

**Most pinch-hitters, series**
NL—20—New York vs Atlanta, 1999 (6-game series)
AL—14—Oakland vs Detroit, 1972 (5-game series)

**Most pinch-hitters used by both clubs, series**
NL—32—New York 20, Atlanta 12, 1999 (6-game series)
AL—22—Oakland 14, Detroit 8, 1972 (5-game series)

**Fewest pinch-hitters, series**
AL-NL—0—many clubs

**Fewest pinch-hitters used by both clubs, series**
AL—2—California 2, Milwaukee 0, 1982 (5-game series)
Chicago 2, Toronto 0, 1993 (6-game series)
NL—5—Atlanta 4, St. Louis 1, 1982 (7-games series)

**Most pinch-hitters, game**
AL—6—Oakland vs Detroit, Oct 10, 1972
NL—5—many clubs
[6—Los Angeles vs New York, Oct 9, 1988, 12 inn
Atlanta vs New York, Oct 19, 1999, 11 inn]

**Most pinch-hitters used by both clubs, game**
AL—7—Oakland 6, Detroit 1, Oct 10, 1972
NL—7—Chicago 4, San Francisco 3, Oct 4, 1989
Florida 4, Chicago 3, Oct 8, 2003
[11—Atlanta 6, New York 5, Oct 19, 1999, 11 inn]

**Most pinch-hitters, inning**
AL—4—Baltimore vs Chicago, Oct 7, 1983, 9th
NL—4—Philadelphia vs Los Angeles, Oct 5, 1983, 9th

## PINCH-RUNNERS

**Most pinch-runners, series**
AL—5—Oakland vs Baltimore, 1974 (4-game series)
Oakland vs Boston, 1990 (4-game series)
NL—4—New York vs St. Louis, 2000 (5-game series)

**Most pinch-runners used by both clubs, series**
AL—8—Oakland 5, Baltimore 3, 1974 (4-game series)
NL—7—New York 4, St. Louis 3, 2000 (5-game series)

**Fewest pinch-runners used, series**
AL-NL—0—many clubs

**Fewest pinch-runners used by both clubs, series**
NL—0—Philadelphia 0, Los Angeles 0, 1978 (4-game series)
Florida 0, Atlanta 0, 1997 (6-game series)
San Francisco 0, St. Louis 0, 2002 (5-game series)
AL—0—Baltimore 0, Minnesota 0, 1969 (3-game series)
Kansas City 0, New York 0, 1980 (3-game series)

**Most pinch-runners, game**
AL—2—many clubs
[3—Kansas City vs Detroit, Oct 3, 1984, 11 inn]
NL—2—many clubs
[2—many clubs in extra innings]

**Most pinch-runners used by both clubs, game**
AL—3—many games
[4—Boston 2, California 2, Oct 12, 1986, 11 inn]
NL—3—many games
[3—Philadelphia 2, Houston 1, Oct 12, 1980, 10 inn
Atlanta 2, New York 1, Oct 17, 1999, 15 inn]

**Most pinch-runners, inning**
AL—2—Oakland vs Detroit, Oct 7, 1972, 11th
Baltimore vs Oakland, Oct 9, 1974, 9th
New York vs Seattle, Oct 13, 2000, 9th
NL—2—New York vs St. Louis, Oct 11, 2000, 9th

## NUMBER OF PLAYERS USED BY POSITION

### FIRST BASEMEN

**Most first basemen, series**
AL-NL—3—many clubs

**Most first basemen used by both clubs, series**
AL—5—Oakland 3, Baltimore 2, 1973 (5-game series)
California 3, Boston 2, 1986 (7-game series)
NL—5—Pittsburgh 3, Cincinnati 2, 1990 (6-game series)
Pittsburgh 3, Atlanta 2, 1991 (7-game series)

**Most first basemen, game**
NL—3—Los Angeles vs St. Louis, Oct 14, 1985
Atlanta vs New York, Oct 12, 1999
AL—2—many games

**Most first basemen used by both clubs, game**
NL—4—Los Angeles 3, St. Louis 1, Oct 14, 1985
Atlanta 2, Pittsburgh 2, Oct 7, 1992
Atlanta 2, Pittsburgh 2, Oct 10, 1992
Atlanta 3, New York 1, Oct 12, 1999
AL—4—Boston 2, New York 2, Oct 20, 2004

### SECOND BASEMEN

**Most second basemen, series**
AL—4—Oakland vs Detroit, 1972 (5-game series)
NL—3—Atlanta vs Pittsburgh, 1992 (7-game series)
Atlanta vs St. Louis, 1996 (7-game series)
Atlanta vs San Diego, 1998 (6-game series)
St. Louis vs Houston, 2004 (7-game series)

**Most second basemen used by both clubs, series**
AL—6—Oakland 4, Detroit 2, 1972 (5-game series)
NL—5—Atlanta 3, Pittsburgh 2, 1992 (7-game series)
Atlanta 3, St. Louis 2, 1996 (7-game series)
St. Louis 3, Houston 2, 2004 (7-game series)

**Most second basemen, game**
AL—3—Minnesota vs Baltimore, Oct 3, 1970
Oakland vs Detroit, Oct 10, 1972
Oakland vs Boston, Oct 7, 1975
New York vs Kansas City, Oct 4, 1978
[3—Oakland vs Detroit, Oct 7, 1972, 11 inn]
NL—2—many games
[3—St. Louis vs Houston, Oct 20, 2004, 12 inn]

**Most second basemen used by both clubs, game**
AL—4—Minnesota 3, Baltimore 1, Oct 3, 1970
Oakland 3, Detroit 1, Oct 10, 1972
Oakland 3, Boston 1, Oct 7, 1975
New York 3, Kansas City 1, Oct 4, 1978
[4—Oakland 3, Detroit 1, Oct 7, 1972, 11 inn]
NL—3—many games
[4—St. Louis 3, Houston 1, Oct 20, 2004, 12 inn]

### THIRD BASEMEN

**Most third basemen, series**
AL-NL—3—Held by many clubs

**Most third basemen used by both clubs, series**
NL—6—San Francisco 3, Chicago 3, 1989 (5-game series)
AL—5—Detroit 3, Kansas City 2, 1984 (3-game series)

**Most third basemen, game**
AL—3—Minnesota vs Toronto, Oct 8, 1991
[3—Detroit vs Kansas City, Oct 3, 1984, 11 inn]
NL—2—many clubs

**Most third basemen used by both clubs, game**
AL—4—New York 2, Oakland 2, Oct 14, 1981
Minnesota 3, Toronto 1, Oct 8, 1991
Cleveland 2, Seattle 2, Oct 15, 1995
[5—Detroit 3, Kansas City 2, Oct 3, 1984, 11 inn]
NL—4—Atlanta 2, St. Louis 2, Oct 14, 1996
St. Louis 2, New York 2, Oct 12, 2000

### SHORTSTOPS

**Most shortstops, series**
AL—4—Oakland vs Detroit, 1972 (5-game series)
NL—3—Cincinnati vs New York, 1973 (5-game series)
Pittsburgh vs Los Angeles, 1974 (4-game series)
Pittsburgh vs Cincinnati, 1975 (3-game series)

Florida vs Chicago, 2003 (7-game series)
Houston vs St. Louis, 2004 (7-game series)

**Most shortstops used by both clubs, series**

AL—6—Oakland 4, Detroit 2, 1972 (5-game series)
NL—5—Florida 3, Chicago 2, 2003 (7-game series)
Houston 3, St. Louis 2, 2004 (7-game series)

**Most shortstops, game**

NL—3—Pittsburgh vs Los Angeles, Oct 6, 1974
[3—Cincinnati vs New York, Oct 9, 1973, 12 inn
Pittsburgh vs Cincinnati, Oct 7, 1975, 10 inn]
AL—2—many clubs
[3—Oakland vs Detroit, Oct 11, 1972, 10 inn]

**Most shortstops used by both clubs, game**

AL-NL—4—many games

## LEFT FIELDERS

**Most left fielders, series**

NL—5—Philadelphia vs Houston, 1980 (5-game series)
AL—5—Seattle vs New York, 2000 (6-game series)
Seattle vs New York, 2001 (5-game series)

**Most left fielders used by both clubs, series**

AL—7—Seattle 5, New York 2, 2000 (6-game series)
Seattle 5, New York 2, 2001 (5-game series)
NL—7—St. Louis 4, Houston 3, 2004 (7-game series)

**Most left fielders, game**

AL-NL—3—many clubs

**Most left fielders used by both clubs, game**

NL—5—Atlanta 3, San Diego 2, Oct 12, 1998
St. Louis 3, Houston 2, Oct 17, 2004
AL—4—many games

## CENTER FIELDERS

**Most center fielders, series**

NL—4—St. Louis vs Atlanta, 1996 (7-game series)
AL—3—Oakland vs Baltimore, 1973 (5-game series)
New York vs Kansas City, 1978 (4-game series)
Los Angeles vs Chicago, 2005 (5-game series)

**Most center fielders used by both clubs, series**

AL—5—Oakland 3, Baltimore 2, 1973 (5-game series)
NL—5—St. Louis 4, Atlanta 1, 1996 (7-game series)

**Most center fielders, game**

NL—3—New York vs Atlanta, Oct 17, 1999
AL—2—many clubs

**Most center fielders used by both clubs, game**

AL—3—many games
NL—3—many games
[4—Houston 2, St. Louis 2, Oct 16, 2005]

## RIGHT FIELDERS

**Most right fielders, series**

NL—5—St. Louis vs San Francisco, 1987 (7-game series)
AL—4—New York vs Oakland, 1981 (3-game series)
Seattle vs New York, 2000 (6-game series)
New York vs Boston, 2003 (7-game series)

**Most right fielders used by both clubs, series**

NL—7—St. Louis 5, San Francisco 2, 1987 (7-game series)
San Francisco 4, St. Louis 3 (5-game series)
AL—6—Seattle 4, New York 2, 2000 (6-game series)
Anaheim 3, Minnesota 3, 2002 (5-game series)

**Most right fielders, game**

NL—4—St. Louis vs San Francisco, Oct 11, 1987
AL—3—New York vs Oakland, Oct 14, 1981
Seattle vs New York, Oct 20, 2001
Anaheim vs Minnesota, Oct 9, 2002

**Most right fielders used by both clubs, game**

NL—5—St. Louis 4, San Francisco 1, Oct 11, 1987
St. Louis 3, San Francisco 2, Oct 13, 1987
AL—5—Seattle 3, New York 2, Oct 20, 2001
Anaheim 3, Minnesota 2, Oct 9, 2002

## CATCHERS

**Most catchers, series**

AL—3—Kansas City vs New York, 1976 (5-game series)
Los Angeles vs Chicago, 2005 (5-game series)
NL—3—Philadelphia vs Cincinnati, 1976 (3-game series)
Houston vs Philadelphia, 1980 (5-game series)
Chicago vs San Francisco, 1989 (5-game series)
Atlanta vs Philadelphia, 1993 (6-game series)

**Most catchers used by both clubs, series**

NL—5—Houston 3, Philadelphia 2, 1980 (5-game series)
Chicago 3, San Francisco 2, 1989 (5-game series)
Atlanta 3, Philadelphia 2, 1993 (6-game series)
AL—4—many series

**Most catchers, game**

AL-NL—2—many clubs

**Most catchers used by both clubs, game**

NL—4—Chicago 2, San Francisco 2, Oct 8, 1989
Atlanta 2, St. Louis 2, Oct 14, 1996
Atlanta 2, San Diego 2, Oct 10, 1998
Houston 2, St. Louis 2, Oct 17, 2004
[4—New York 2, Los Angeles 2, Oct 9, 1988, 12 inn
Atlanta 2, New York 2, Oct 17, 1999, 15 inn
Atlanta 2, New York 2, Oct 19, 1999, 11 inn]
AL—4—New York 2, Boston 2, Oct 16, 1999
Seattle 2, New York 2, Oct 20, 2001
Anaheim 2, Minnesota 2, Oct 13, 2002
[4—Baltimore 2, Minnesota 2, Oct 4, 1969, 12 inn]

## PITCHERS

**Most pitchers, series**

3-game series
NL—10—Pittsburgh vs Cincinnati, 1975
AL—9—Minnesota vs Baltimore, 1969, 1970
4-game series
AL—10—Boston vs Oakland, 1990
NL—9—San Francisco vs Pittsburgh, 1971
Los Angeles vs Philadelphia, 1977, 1978
Cincinnati vs Atlanta, 1995
5-game series
AL—11—Seattle vs New York, 2001
Minnesota vs Anaheim, 2002
NL—10—Pittsburgh vs Cincinnati, 1972
San Diego vs Chicago, 1984
St. Louis vs New York, 2000
New York vs St. Louis, 2000
Atlanta vs Arizona, 2001
San Francisco vs St. Louis, 2002
St. Louis vs San Francisco, 2002
6-game series
AL—11—Oakland vs Toronto, 1992
Cleveland vs Seattle, 1995
Cleveland vs Baltimore, 1997
Cleveland vs New York, 1998
NL—11—New York vs Atlanta, 1999
7-game series
NL—11—Pittsburgh vs Atlanta, 1991
Florida vs Chicago, 2003
St. Louis vs Houston, 2004
AL—11—Boston vs New York, 2004
New York vs Boston, 2004

**For a list of players and pitchers used each series, see page 355.**

**Most pitchers used by both clubs, series**

3-game series
NL—17—Pittsburgh 10, Cincinnati 7, 1975
Cincinnati 9, Pittsburgh 8, 1979
AL—16—Minnesota 9, Baltimore 7, 1969
4-game series
NL—17—Los Angeles 9, Philadelphia 8, 1978
Cincinnati 9, Atlanta 8, 1995
AL—16—Oakland 9, Boston 7, 1988
Boston 10, Oakland 6, 1990
5-game series
NL—20—New York 10, Atlanta 10, 1999
St. Louis 10, New York 10, 2000
San Francisco 10, St. Louis 10, 2002
AL—20—Seattle 11, New York 9, 2001
Minnesota 11, Anaheim 9, 2002
6-game series
AL—21—Cleveland 11, Seattle 10, 1995
NL—19—San Diego 10, Atlanta 9, 1998
Houston 10, St. Louis 9, 2005
7-game series
AL—22—Boston 11, New York 11, 2004
NL—21—Florida 11, Chicago 10, 2003

**Fewest pitchers, series**

AL—4—Baltimore vs Minnesota, 1970 (3-game series)
Baltimore vs Oakland, 1971 (3-game series)
Kansas City vs New York, 1980 (3-game series)
NL—5—Pittsburgh vs Cincinnati, 1970 (3-game series)
St. Louis vs Atlanta, 1982 (3-game series)
Philadelphia vs Los Angeles, 1983 (4-game series)

**Fewest pitchers used by both clubs, series**

AL—10—New York 6, Kansas City 4, 1980 (3-game series)

NL—12—Cincinnati 7, Pittsburgh 5, 1970 (3-game series)

**Most pitchers, game**

AL—7—Minnesota vs Baltimore, Oct 6, 1969
Boston vs New York, Oct 12, 2004
[7—Cleveland vs Baltimore, Oct 11, 1997, 12 inn
Cleveland vs New York, Oct 7, 1998, 12 inn
Boston vs New York, Oct 18, 2004, 14 inn
New York vs Boston, Oct 18, 2004, 14 inn]
NL—7—San Francisco vs St. Louis, Oct 14, 1987
Pittsburgh vs Atlanta, Oct 7, 1992
Atlanta vs Arizona, Oct 19, 2001
[9—New York vs Atlanta, Oct 17, 1999, 15 inn]

**Most pitchers used by winning club, game**

NL—6—Los Angeles vs Philadelphia, Oct 7, 1977
St. Louis vs Atlanta, Oct 13, 1996
Arizona vs Atlanta, Oct 20, 2001
[9—New York vs Atlanta, Oct 17, 1999, 15 inn]
AL—6—Oakland vs Boston, Oct 8, 1988
Cleveland vs Baltimore, Oct 12, 1997
New York vs Boston, Oct 14, 1999
[7—Cleveland vs Baltimore, Oct 11, 1997, 12 inn
Cleveland vs New York, Oct 7, 1998, 12 inn
Boston vs New York, Oct 18, 2004, 14 inn]

**Most pitchers used by losing club, game**

AL—7—Minnesota vs Baltimore, Oct 6, 1969
NL—7—San Francisco vs St. Louis, Oct 14, 1987
Pittsburgh vs Atlanta, Oct 7, 1992
Atlanta vs Arizona, Oct 19, 2001
[8—New York vs Atlanta, Oct 19, 1999, 11 inn]

**Most pitchers used by both clubs, game**

NL—12—Pittsburgh 7, Atlanta 5, Oct 7, 1992
Arizona 6, Atlanta 6, Oct 20, 2001
[15—New York 9, Atlanta 6, Oct 17, 1999, 15 inn]
AL—11—Baltimore 6, New York 5, Oct 12, 1996
Cleveland 6, Baltimore 5, Oct 12, 1997
Minnesota 6, Anaheim 5, Oct 13, 2002
Boston 6, New York 5, Oct 15, 2003

**Most pitcher, inning**

AL—5—Kansas City vs New York, Oct 12, 1976, 6th
New York vs Boston, Oct 18, 1999, 8th
Minnesota vs Anaheim, Oc 12, 2002, 8th
NL—4—Los Angeles vs New York, Oct 8, 1988, 8th
New York vs Atlanta, Oct 17, 1999, 7th

## SERIES

**Most series played**

AL—12—New York, 1976-1978, 1980, 1981, 1996, 1998-2001, 2003, 2004 (won 10, lost 2)
NL—11—Atlanta, 1969, 1982, 1991-1993, 1995-1999, 2001 (won 5, lost 6)

**For a complete list of results and a complete list of series won and lost by teams, see page 348.**

# INDIVIDUAL BATTING



## GAMES

**Most games, career**

ML—46—David Justice, Atlanta NL, 1991-1993, 1995; Cleveland AL, 1997, 1998; New York AL, 2000, 2001; 8 series (23 in NL, 23 in AL)
AL—45—Reggie Jackson, Oakland, 1971-1975; New York, 1977, 1978, 1980, 1981; California, 1982, 1986; 11 series
NL—38—Terry Pendleton, St. Louis, 1985, 1987; Atlanta, 1991-1993, 1996; 6 series

**Most games with one club, career**

AL—41—Derek Jeter, New York, 1996, 1998-2001, 2003, 2004; 7 series
Bernie Williams, New York, 1996, 1998-2001, 2003, 2004; 7 series
NL—34—Chipper Jones, Atlanta, 1995-1999, 2001; 6 series

**Most games by pinch-hitter, career**

NL—10—Greg Colbrunn, Atlanta, 1997 (3), 1998 (6), Arizona, 2001 (1) (10 PA, 10 AB)
AL—6—Dane Iorg, Kansas City, 1984 (2), 1985 (4) (6 PA, 4 AB)

**Most games by pinch-hitter, series**

NL—6—Lonnie Smith, Atlanta, 1992 (7-game series)
Greg Colbrunn, Atlanta, 1998 (6-game series)
Roger Cedeno, St. Louis, 2004 (7-game series)
AL—4—George Hendrick, Oakland, 1972 (5-game series)
Dane Iorg, Kansas City, 1985 (7-game series)
Bobby Kielty, Minnesota, 2002 (5-game series)

**Most games by pinch-runner, career**

AL—4—Lance Blankenship, Oakland, 1990, 1992; 2 series
NL—3—Dave Concepcion, Cincinnati, 1970, 1972; 2 series

**Most games by pinch-runner, series**

AL—3—Dave Stapleton, Boston, 1986
Lance Blankenship, Oakland, 1990
Eric Fox, Oakland, 1992
Ruben Amaro Jr., Cleveland, 1995
Jose Vizcaino, New York, 2000
Chone Figgins, Anaheim, 2002
NL—3—Marty Malloy, Atlanta, 1998
Joe McEwing, New York, 2000

## BATTING AVERAGE

**Highest batting average, career (50 or more at-bats)**

NL—.468—Will Clark, San Francisco, 1987, 1989; St. Louis, 2000; 3 series, 17 G, 62 AB, 29 H
AL—.392—Devon White, California, 1986; Toronto, 1991-1993; 4 series, 21 G, 74 AB, 29 H

**For a list of batting leaders each series and a complete list of .500 hitters, see page 350.**

**Highest batting average, series (10 or more at-bats)**

3-game series
NL—.538—Art Shamsky, New York, 1969
(Jay Johnstone, Philadelphia, 1976, batted .778, 9 AB, 7 H, 1 BB)
AL—.583—Brooks Robinson, Baltimore, 1970
4-game series
NL—.467—Dusty Baker, Los Angeles, 1978
Mike Schmidt, Philadelphia, 1983
AL—.462—Reggie Jackson, New York, 1978
5-game series
NL—.650—Will Clark, San Francisco, 1989
AL—.611—Fred Lynn, California, 1982
6-game series
NL—.500—Keith Lockhart, Atlanta, 1997 (played 5 G)
Roger Cedeno, New York, 1999 (played 5 G)
Eddie Perez, Atlanta, 1999
AL—.458—Kenny Lofton, Cleveland, 1995
7-game series
NL—.772—Lloyd McClendon, Pittsburgh, 1992 (played 5 G)
AL—.455—Bob Boone, California, 1986

## ON-BASE PERCENTAGE

(official statistic since 1984; calculated from official statistics, 1969-1983)

**Highest percentage, career (50 or more plate appearances)**

NL—.529—Will Clark, San Francisco, 1987, 1989; St. Louis, 2000; 3 series, 17 G, 62 AB, 29 H, 7 BB, 1 HP
AL—.446—Devon White, California, 1986; Toronto, 1991, 1992, 1993; 4 series, 21 G, 74 AB, 29 H, 8 BB, 1 SF

**Highest percentage, series (10 or more plate appearances)**

3-game series
NL—.800—Jay Johnstone, Philadelphia, 1976
AL—.600—Jerry Mumphrey, New York, 1981
4-game series
AL—.588—Eddie Murray, Baltimore, 1979
NL—.579—Jimmy Wynn, Los Angeles, 1974
5-game series
NL—.682—Will Clark, San Francisco, 1989
AL—.650—Fred Lynn, California, 1982
6-game series
NL—.600—Sid Bream, Pittsburgh, 1990
AL—.593—Frank Thomas, Chicago, 1993
7-game series
NL—.750—Lloyd McClendon, Pittsburgh, 1992
AL—.500—George Brett, Kansas City, 1985
Bob Boone, California, 1986

## SLUGGING AVERAGE

**Highest average, career (50 or more PA)**

NL—.806—Will Clark, San Francisco, 1987, 1989; St. Louis, 2000; 3 series, 17 G, 62 AB, 29 H, 7 doubles, 1 triple, 4 HR, 50 TB
AL—.728—George Brett, Kansas City, 1976-1978, 1980, 1984, 1985; 6 series, 27 G, 103 AB, 35 H, 5 doubles, 4 triples, 9 HR, 75 TB

**Highest average, series (10 or more PA)**

3-game series
NL—1.182—Willie Stargell, Pittsburgh, 1979
AL—.917—Tony Oliva, Minnesota, 1970

Reggie Jackson, Oakland, 1971
Bob Watson, New York, 1980
4-game series
NL—1.250—Bob Robertson, Pittsburgh, 1971
AL—1.056—George Brett, Kansas City, 1978
5-game series
NL—1.200—Will Clark, San Francisco, 1989
AL—1.167—Darryl Strawberry, New York, 1996
6-game series
NL—.900—Eddie Perez, Atlanta, 1999
AL—.826—Jim Thome, Cleveland, 1998
7-game series
NL—1.182—Lloyd McClendon, Pittsburgh, 1992
AL—.826—George Brett, Kansas City, 1985

## AT-BATS AND PLATE APPEARANCES

**Most plate appearances, career**
AL—194—Derek Jeter, New York, 1996, 1998-2001, 2003, 2004; 7 series, 41 G
NL—154—Chipper Jones, Atlanta, 1995-1999, 2001; 6 series, 34 G

**Most plate appearances by pinch-hitter, career**
NL—10—Greg Colbrunn, Atlanta, 1997 (3), 1998 (6), Arizona, 2001 (1)
AL—6—Dane Iorg, Kansas City, 1984 (2), 1985 (4)

**Most plate appearances, series**
3-game series
AL—17—Paul Blair, Baltimore, 1969
Don Buford, Baltimore, 1969
NL—17—Tommie Agee, New York, 1969
4-game series
NL—20—Davey Lopes, Los Angeles, 1974
Marquis Grissom, Atlanta, 1995
AL—20—Al Bumbry, Baltimore, 1979
5-game series
NL—25—Enos Cabell, Houston, 1980
Pete Rose, Philadelphia, 1980
Mike Schmidt, Philadelphia, 1980
Ryne Sandberg, Chicago, 1989
AL—25—Jose Offerman, Boston, 1999
John Valentin, Boston, 1999
6-game series
NL—31—Gerald Williams, Atlanta, 1999
AL—30—Chuck Knoblauch, New York, 1998
7-game series
AL—38—Derek Jeter, New York, 2004
NL—36—Juan Pierre, Florida, 2003

**Most plate appearances, inning**
AL-NL—2—many players

**Most at-bats, career**
AL—168—Derek Jeter, New York, 1996, 1998-2001, 2003, 2004; 7 series, 41 G
NL—135—Terry Pendleton, St. Louis, 1985, 1987; Atlanta, 1991-1993, 1996; 6 series, 38 G

**Most at-bats by pinch-hitter, career**
NL—10—Greg Colbrunn, Atlanta, 1997 (3), 1998 (6), Arizona, 2001 (1)
AL—5—Cliff Johnson, New York, 1977 (1), 1978 (1), Toronto, 1985 (3)

**Most at-bats, series**
3-game series
AL—15—Mark Belanger, Baltimore, 1969
Paul Blair, Baltimore, 1969
NL—15—Ken Oberkfell, St. Louis, 1982
4-game series
NL—19—Dave Cash, Pittsburgh, 1971
Garry Maddox, Philadelphia, 1978
Marquis Grissom, Atlanta, 1995
AL—18—George Brett, Kansas City, 1978
Thurman Munson, New York, 1978
Rudy Law, Chicago, 1983
5-game series
NL—24—Mike Schmidt, Philadelphia, 1980
AL—24—Kirby Puckett, Minnesota, 1987
Derek Jeter, New York, 1996
Jose Offerman, Boston, 1999
6-game series
NL—28—Gerald Williams, Atlanta, 1999
AL—27—Joe Carter, Toronto, 1993
Tim Raines Sr., Chicago, 1993
Devon White, Toronto, 1993
Kenny Lofton, Cleveland, 1998
7-game series
AL—36—Bernie Williams, New York, 2004
NL—35—Marquis Grissom, Atlanta, 1996

**Most at-bats by pinch-hitter, series**
NL—6—Lonnie Smith, Atlanta, 1992
Greg Colbrunn, Atlanta, 1998
Roger Cedeno, St. Louis, 2004
AL—4—George Hendrick, Oakland, 1972

**Most consecutive at-bats without a hit, career**
ML—31—Billy North, Oakland AL, 1974 (last 13 AB), 1975 (all 10 AB); Los Angeles NL, 1978 (all 8 AB)
NL—30—Cesar Geronimo, Cincinnati, 1973 (last 13 AB), 1975 (all 10 AB), 1976 (first 7 AB)
AL—24—Bert Campaneris, Oakland, 1974 (last 13 AB), 1975 (all 11 AB)

**Most at-bats by player with no hits, career**
AL—16—John Wathan, Kansas City, 1977 (6), 1978 (3), 1980 (6), 1984 (1)
NL—11—Bob Didier, Atlanta, 1969
Ed Kirkpatrick, Pittsburgh, 1974 (9), 1975 (2)
Bob Walk, Pittsburgh, 1990 (4), 1991 (2), 1992 (5)

**Most at-bats, game**
AL—6—many players
[7—Tony Clark, New York, Oct 18, 2004, 14 inn
Derek Jeter, New York, Oct 18, 2004, 14 inn
Hideki Matsui, New York, Oct 18, 2004, 14 inn
Bernie Williams, New York, Oct 18, 2004, 14 inn]
NL—6—many players
[7—many players in extra innings]

**Most at-bats by player with no hits, game**
AL—6—Rickey Henderson, Toronto, Oct 5, 1993
[6—Don Buford, Baltimore, Oct 4, 1969, 12 inn
Chuck Knoblauch, New York, Oct 7, 1998, 12 inn]
NL—5—many players
[6—Alan Ashby, Houston, Oct 15, 1986, 16 inn]

**Most at-bats, inning**
AL-NL—2—many players

## RUNS

**Most runs, career**
AL—31—Bernie Williams, New York, 1996, 1998-2001, 2003, 2004; 7 series, 41 G
NL—20—Chipper Jones, Atlanta, 1995-1999, 2001; 6 series, 34 G

**Most runs by pinch-hitter, career**
NL—2—many players
AL—1—many players

**Most runs by pinch-runner, career**
AL—2—Marshall Edwards, Milwaukee, 1982; 1 series, 2 G
Devon White, California, 1986; 1 series, 2 G
NL—2—Gene Clines, Pittsburgh, 1972, 1974; 2 series, 2 G
Rafael Landestoy, Houston, 1980; 1 series, 2 G
Jose Gonzalez, Los Angeles, 1988; 1 series, 2 G
Joe McEwing, New York, 2000; 1 series, 3 G

**Most runs, series**
3-game series
AL—5—Mark Belanger, Baltimore, 1970
NL—4—many players
4-game series
AL—7—George Brett, Kansas City, 1978
NL—6—Steve Garvey, Los Angeles, 1978
5-game series
AL—8—Rickey Henderson, Oakland, 1989
NL—8—Will Clark, San Francisco, 1989
Timo Perez, New York, 2000
6-game series
AL—7—Dave Winfield, Toronto, 1992
Paul Molitor, Toronto, 1993
NL—6—Willie McGee, St. Louis, 1985
Fred McGriff, Atlanta, 1993
Gary Sheffield, Florida, 1997
7-game series
NL—12—Carlos Beltran, Houston, 2004
AL—9—Hideki Matsui, New York, 2004

**Most runs by pinch-hitter, series**
NL—2—Ty Cline, Cincinnati, 1970; 2 G
Tim Flannery, San Diego, 1984, 3 G
Todd Hollandsworth, Florida, 2003, 4 G
AL—1—many players

**Most runs by pinch-runner, series**
NL—2—Rafael Landestoy, Houston, 1980; 2 G
Jose Gonzalez, Los Angeles, 1988; 2 G
Joe McEwing, New York, 2000; 3 G
AL—2—Marshall Edwards, Milwaukee, 1982; 2 G
Devon White, California, 1986; 2 G

**Most runs, game**
NL—4—Bob Robertson, Pittsburgh, Oct 3, 1971
Steve Garvey, Los Angeles, Oct 9, 1974
Will Clark, San Francisco, Oct 4, 1989
Javy Lopez, Atlanta, Oct 14, 1996
Fred McGriff, Atlanta, Oct 17, 1996
AL—5—Alex Rodriguez, New York, Oct 16, 2004

**Most runs, inning**
AL—2—Scott Spiezio, Anaheim, Oct 13, 2002, 7th
Chone Figgins, Anaheim, Oct 13, 2002, 7th
NL—2—Cesar Cedeno, St. Louis, Oct 13, 1985, 2nd
Jack Clark, St. Louis, Oct 13, 1985, 2nd

# HITS

## CAREER AND SERIES

**Most hits, career**
AL—52—Bernie Williams, New York, 1996, 1998-2001, 2003, 2004; 7 series, 41 G
NL—45—Pete Rose, Cincinnati, 1970, 1972, 1973, 1975, 1976; Philadelphia, 1980, 1983; 7 series, 28 G

**Most hits by pinch-hitter, career**
NL—4—Greg Colbrunn, Atlanta, 1997, 1998; Arizona, 2001; 3 series, 10 G
AL—2—many players

**Most hits, series**
3-game series
AL—7—Brooks Robinson, Baltimore, 1969, 1970
NL—7—Art Shamsky, New York, 1969
Jay Johnstone, Philadelphia, 1976
4-game series
NL—8—Dave Cash, Pittsburgh, 1971
AL—7—George Brett, Kansas City, 1978
Rod Carew, California, 1979
Rudy Law, Chicago, 1983
Wade Boggs, Boston, 1990
Carney Lansford, Oakland, 1990
5-game series
NL—13—Will Clark, San Francisco, 1989
AL—11—Chris Chambliss, New York, 1976
Fred Lynn, California, 1982
Jose Offerman, Boston, 1999
6-game series
AL—12—Tim Raines Sr., Chicago, 1993
Devon White, Toronto, 1993
NL—10—Ozzie Smith, St. Louis, 1985
Fred McGriff, Atlanta, 1993
Eddie Perez, Atlanta, 1999
7-game series
NL—14—Albert Pujols, St. Louis, 2004
AL—14—Hideki Matsui, New York, 2004

**Most hits by pinch-hitter, series**
NL—3—Paul Popovich, Pittsburgh, 1974; 3 G
Todd Hollandsworth, Florida, 2003; 4 G
AL—2—many players

**Most series with one or more hits**
AL—10—Reggie Jackson, Oakland, 1971-1975; New York, 1977, 1978, 1980; California, 1982, 1986
NL—7—Richie Hebner, Pittsburgh, 1970-1972, 1974, 1975; Philadelphia, 1977, 1978
Pete Rose, Cincinnati, 1970, 1972, 1973, 1975, 1976; Philadelphia, 1980, 1983

**Most consecutive hits, career**
NL—6—Steve Garvey, Los Angeles, Oct 9, 1974 (4), Oct 4, 1977 (2)
Kenny Lofton, Chicago, Oct 9 (4), 10 (2), 2003
AL—6—Paul Molitor, Toronto, Oct 5 (4), 6 (2), 1993

**Most consecutive hits by pinch-hitter, career**
NL—3—Paul Popovich, Pittsburgh, Oct 5, 6, 9, 1974
AL—2—many players

**Most consecutive hits, series**
AL—6—Paul Molitor, Toronto, Oct 5 (4), 6 (2), 1993
NL—6—Kenny Lofton, Chicago, Oct 9 (4), 10 (2), 2003

## GAME AND INNING

**Most hits, game**
AL—5—Paul Blair, Baltimore, Oct 6, 1969
Hideki Matsui, New York, Oct 16, 2004
NL—4—many players

**Most times reached base safely, game (batting 1.000)**
AL—5—many players
NL—5—Felix Millan, Atlanta, Oct 5, 1969 (2 singles, 3 BB)
Will Clark, San Francisco, Oct 4, 1989 (1 single, 1 double, 2 HR, 1 BB)

**Most hits accounting for all of club's hits, game**
NL—2—Roberto Clemente, Pittsburgh, Oct 10, 1972
Andy Kosco, Cincinnati, Oct 7, 1973
AL—2—Willie Wilson, Kansas City, Oct 12, 1985

**Most consecutive games with one or more hits, career**
NL—15—Pete Rose, Cincinnati, 1973 (last 3), 1975 (3), 1976 (3); Philadelphia, 1980 (5), 1983 (first 1)
AL—12—Don Baylor, California, 1982 (last 3); Boston, 1986 (7); Minnesota, 1987 (2)

**Most hits, inning**
AL—2—Graig Nettles, New York, Oct 14, 1981, 4th
Rickey Henderson, Oakland, Oct 6, 1990, 9th
Scott Spiezio, Anaheim, Oct 13, 2002, 7th
Adam Kennedy, Anaheim, Oct 13, 2002, 7th
NL—2—Jack Clark, St. Louis, Oct 13, 1985, 2nd
Tito Landrum, St. Louis, Oct 13, 1985, 2nd
Jerome Walton, Chicago, Oct 5, 1989, 1st
Barry Bonds, Pittsburgh, Oct 13, 1992, 2nd
Lloyd McClendon, Pittsburgh, Oct 13, 1992, 2nd

# SINGLES

**Most singles, career**
NL—34—Pete Rose, Cincinnati, 1970, 1972, 1973, 1975, 1976; Philadelphia, 1980, 1983; 7 series, 28 G
AL—33—Bernie Williams, 1996, 1998-2001, 2003, 2004; 7 series, 41 G

**Most singles by pinch-hitter, career**
NL—4—Greg Colbrunn, Atlanta, 1997, 1998; Arizona, 2001; 3 series, 10 G
AL—2—many players

**Most singles, series**
3-game series
NL—7—Art Shamsky, New York, 1969
AL—6—Brooks Robinson, Baltimore, 1969
Larry Milbourne, New York, 1981
4-game series
NL—7—Bill Russell, Los Angeles, 1974
AL—6—Chris Chambliss, New York, 1978
Rudy Law, Chicago, 1983
Carney Lansford, Oakland, 1990
5-game series
AL—10—Jose Offerman, Boston, 1999
NL—8—Pete Rose, Philadelphia, 1980
Terry Puhl, Houston, 1980
Jerome Walton, Chicago, 1989
6-game series
AL—10—Tim Raines Sr., Chicago, 1993
Omar Vizquel, Cleveland, 1998
NL—8—Craig Biggio, Houston, 2005
7-game series
AL—9—Marty Barrett, Boston, 1986
Bob Boone, California, 1986
Orlando Cabrera, Boston, 2004
NL—9—Jay Bell, Pittsburgh, 1991
Mark Lemke, Atlanta, 1996
Chipper Jones, Atlanta, 1996
Kenny Lofton, Chicago, 2003

**Most singles by pinch-hitter, series**
NL—3—Paul Popovich, Pittsburgh, 1974 (3 G)
AL—2—many players

**Most singles, game**
AL—4—Chris Chambliss, New York, Oct 4, 1978
Kelly Gruber, Toronto, Oct 7, 1989
Jerry Browne, Oakland, Oct 12, 1992
[4—Brooks Robinson, Baltimore, Oct 4, 1969, 12 inn]
NL—4—Tito Landrum, St. Louis, Oct 13, 1985
Chipper Jones, Atlanta, Oct 9, 1996
Keith Lockhart, Atlanta, Oct 14, 1997
Kenny Lofton, Chicago, Oct 8, 2003
[4—Terry Puhl, Houston, Oct 12, 1980, 10 inn]

**Most singles, inning**
AL—2—Graig Nettles, New York, Oct 14, 1981, 4th
Rickey Henderson, Oakland, Oct 6, 1990, 9th
Scott Spiezio, Anaheim, Oct 13, 2002, 7th
NL—2—Jack Clark, St. Louis, Oct 13, 1985, 2nd
Tito Landrum, St. Louis, Oct 13, 1985, 2nd
Jerome Walton, Chicago, Oct 5, 1989, 1st
Lloyd McClendon, Pittsburgh, Oct 13, 1992, 2nd

# DOUBLES

**Most doubles, career**
AL—10—Bernie Williams, New York, 1996, 1998-2001, 2003, 2004; 7 series, 41 G
NL—7—Pete Rose, Cincinnati, 1970, 1972, 1973, 1975, 1976; Philadelphia, 1980, 1983; 7 series, 28 G
Richie Hebner, Pittsburgh, 1970-1972, 1974, 1975; Philadelphia, 1977, 1978; Chicago, 1984; 8 series, 27 G
Mike Schmidt, Philadelphia, 1976-1978, 1980, 1983; 5 series, 20 G
Ron Cey, Los Angeles, 1974, 1977, 1978, 1981; Chicago, 1984; 5 series, 22 G
Fred McGriff, Atlanta, 1993, 1995-1997; 4 series, 23 G
Javy Lopez, Atlanta, 1992, 1995-1998; 5 series, 22 G
Will Clark, San Francisco, 1987, 1989; St. Louis, 2000; 3 series, 17 G
Chipper Jones, Atlanta, 1995-2001, except 2000; 6 series, 34 G

**Most doubles by pinch-hitter, career**
NL—2—Manny Mota, Los Angeles, 1974, 1977, 1978; 3 series, 6 G
AL—1—many players

**Most doubles, series**
3-game series
NL—3—Joe Morgan, Cincinnati, 1975
Darrell Porter, St. Louis, 1982
AL—3—Bob Watson, New York, 1980
4-game series
NL—4—Fred McGriff, Atlanta, 1995
AL—3—Rod Carew, California, 1979
5-game series
AL—4—Matty Alou, Oakland, 1972
Tom Brunansky, Minnesota, 1987
NL—4—Pete Rose, Cincinnati, 1972
6-game series
NL—4—Tom Herr, St. Louis, 1985
Edgardo Alfonzo, New York, 1999
AL—3—Brian Giles, Cleveland, 1997
Mark McLemore, Seattle, 2000
John Olerud, Seattle, 2000

7-game series
AL—6—Hideki Matsui, New York, 2004
NL—5—Javy Lopez, Atlanta, 1996

**Most doubles, game**

NL—2—many players
[3—Fred McGriff, Atlanta, Oct 11, 1995, 10 inn]
AL—2—many players

**Most doubles, inning**

AL-NL—1—many players

## TRIPLES

**Most triples, career**

AL—4—George Brett, Kansas City, 1976-1978, 1980, 1984, 1985; 6 series, 27 G
NL—3—Willie McGee, St. Louis, 1982, 1985, 1987, 1996; 4 series, 22 G
Mariano Duncan, Los Angeles, Cincinnati, Philadelphia, 1985, 1990, 1993, 1995; 4 series, 17 G
Keith Lockhart, Atlanta, 1997-1999, 2001; 4 series, 16 G

**Most triples by pinch-hitter, career**

NL—1—Ty Cline, Cincinnati, 1970; 1 series, 2 G
Lenny Dykstra, New York, 1986; 1 series, 2 G
Lonnie Smith, Atlanta, 1992; 1 series, 6 G
Dmitri Young, St. Louis, 1996; 1 series, 3 G
Doug Glanville, Chicago, 2003; 1 series, 1 G
AL—1—Al Martin, Seattle, 2001; 1 series, 2 G

**Most triples, series**

AL—2—George Brett, Kansas City, 1977 (5-game series)
Kenny Lofton, Cleveland, 1995 (6-game series)
NL—2—Willie McGee, St. Louis, 1982 (3-game series)
Mariano Duncan, Philadelphia, 1993 (6-game series)
Juan Pierre, Florida, 2003 (7-game series)

**Most triples, game**

NL—2—Mariano Duncan, Oct 9, 1993
AL—1—many players

**Most triples with bases filled, game**

AL—1—Jim Sundberg, Kansas City, Oct 16, 1985
Mark McLemore, Seattle, Oct 20, 2001
NL—1—Tom Glavine, Atlanta, Oct 17, 1996

## HOME RUNS

### CAREER AND SERIES

**Most home runs, career**

AL—9—George Brett, Kansas City, 1976-1978, 1980, 1984, 1985; 6 series, 27 G
Bernie Williams, New York, 1996, 1998-2001, 2003, 2004; 7 series, 41 G
NL—8—Steve Garvey, Los Angeles, 1974, 1977, 1978, 1981; San Diego, 1984; 5 series, 22 G

**For a list of all home runs each series and a complete list of players with four or more career home runs, see page 350.**

**Most home runs, series**

3-game series
NL—3—Hank Aaron, Atlanta, 1969
AL—2—many players
4-game series
NL—4—Bob Robertson, Pittsburgh, 1971
Steve Garvey, Los Angeles, 1978
AL—3—George Brett, Kansas City, 1978
Jose Canseco, Oakland, 1988
5-game series
NL—3—Rusty Staub, New York, 1973
AL—3—Darryl Strawberry, New York, 1996
Todd Zeile, Baltimore, 1996
Bernie Williams, New York, 2001
Adam Kennedy, Anaheim, 2002
6-game series
AL—4—Jim Thome, Cleveland, 1998
NL—3—Bill Madlock, Los Angeles, 1985
7-game series
NL—4—Jeffrey Leonard, San Francisco, 1987
Carlos Beltran, Houston, 2004
Albert Pujols, St. Louis, 2004
AL—3—George Brett, Kansas City, 1985
Jason Giambi, New York, 2003
Trot Nixon, Boston, 2003
David Ortiz, Boston, 2004

**Most series with one or more home runs**

NL—5—Johnny Bench, Cincinnati, 1970 (1), 1972 (1), 1973 (1), 1976 (1), 1979 (1)
AL—4—Graig Nettles, New York, 1976 (2), 1978 (1), 1980 (1), 1981 (1)
Reggie Jackson, Oakland, 1971 (2), 1975 (1); New York, 1978 (2); California, 1982 (1)
George Brett, Kansas City, 1976 (1), 1978 (3), 1980 (2), 1985 (3)
Eddie Murray, Baltimore, 1979 (1), 1983 (1), 1996 (1); Cleveland, 1995 (1)
Bernie Williams, New York, 1996 (2), 1999 (1), 2000 (1), 2001 (3)

**Most series with two or more home runs**

AL—3—George Brett, Kansas City, 1978 (3), 1980 (2), 1985 (3)
Manny Ramirez, Cleveland, 1995 (2), 1996 (2), 1998 (2)
NL—2—Steve Garvey, Los Angeles, 1974 (2), 1978 (4)
Willie Stargell, Pittsburgh, 1974 (2), 1979 (2)
Gary Matthews, Philadelphia, 1983 (3); Chicago, 1984 (2)
Ron Gant, Atlanta, 1992 (2); St. Louis, 1996 (1)

### GAME AND INNING

**Most home runs, game**

NL—3—Bob Robertson, Pittsburgh, Oct 3, 1971
AL—3—George Brett, Kansas City, Oct 6, 1978
Adam Kennedy, Anaheim, Oct 13, 2002

**Most grand slams, game**

AL—1—Mike Cuellar, Baltimore, Oct 3, 1970, 4th
Don Baylor, California, Oct 9, 1982, 8th
Jim Thome, Cleveland, Oct 13, 1998, 5th
Ricky Ledee, New York, Oct 17, 1999, 9th
Johnny Damon, Boston, Oct 20, 2004, 2nd
NL—1—Ron Cey, Los Angeles, Oct 4, 1977, 7th
Dusty Baker, Los Angeles, Oct 5, 1977, 4th
Will Clark, San Francisco, Oct 4, 1989, 4th
Ron Gant, Atlanta, Oct 7, 1992, 5th
Gary Gaetti, St. Louis, Oct 10, 1996, 7th
Andres Galarraga, Atlanta, Oct 11, 1998, 7th
Aramis Ramirez, Chicago, Oct 11, 2003, 1st

**Inside-the-park home runs**

AL—Graig Nettles, New York, Oct 9, 1980, 5th (none on base)
Paul Molitor, Milwaukee, Oct 6, 1982, 5th (1 on base)
NL—none

**Home runs by pinch-hitter, game**

NL—Jerry Martin, Philadelphia, Oct 4, 1978, 9th
Bake McBride, Philadelphia, Oct 7, 1978, 7th
Harry Spilman, San Francisco, Oct 9, 1987, 9th
Greg Myers, San Diego, Oct 12, 1998, 9th
Erubiel Durazo, Arizona, Oct 21, 2001, 5th
J.D. Drew, St. Louis, Oct 9, 2002, 8th
Eduardo Perez, St. Louis, Oct 10, 2002, 8th
Chris Burke, Houston, Oct 12, 2005, 7th
AL—John Lowenstein, Baltimore, Oct 3, 1979, 10th
Pat Sheridan, Kansas City, Oct 9, 1985, 9th
Mike Pagliarulo, Minnesota, Oct 11, 1991, 10th
Eric Davis, Baltimore, Oct 13, 1997, 9th
Ricky Ledee, New York, Oct 17, 1999, 9th
Jay Buhner, Seattle, Oct 20, 2001, 9th

**Home runs by leadoff batter, start of game**

AL—Bert Campaneris, Oakland, Oct 7, 1973 (at Baltimore)
George Brett, Kansas City, Oct 6, 1978 (at New York)
Brady Anderson, Baltimore, Oct 8, 1997 (at Baltimore)
Kenny Lofton, Cleveland, Oct 11, 1998 (at Cleveland)
NL—Bob Dernier, Chicago, Oct 2, 1984 (at Chicago)
Orlando Merced, Pittsburgh, Oct 12, 1991 (at Atlanta)
Marcus Giles, Atlanta, Oct 17, 2001 (at Arizona)

**Home runs winning 1-0 games**

AL—Sal Bando, Oakland, Oct 8, 1974, 4th
Tony Fernandez, Cleveland, Oct 15, 1997, 11th
NL—Mike Schmidt, Philadelphia, Oct 4, 1983, 1st
Glenn Davis, Houston, Oct 8, 1986, 2nd

**Most home runs by pitcher, game**

AL—1—Mike Cuellar, Baltimore, Oct 3, 1970 (3 on base)
NL—1—Don Gullett, Cincinnati, Oct 4, 1975 (1 on base)
Steve Carlton, Philadelphia, Oct 6, 1978 (2 on base)
Rick Sutcliffe, Chicago, Oct 2, 1984 (none on base)

**Most home runs by rookie, game**

AL-NL—1—many players

**Most consecutive games hitting one or more home runs, career**

NL—4—Garry Mathews, Philadelphia, Oct 5, 7, 8, 1983; Chicago, Oct 2, 1984
Jeffrey Leonard, San Francisco, Oct 6, 7, 9, 10, 1987
Carlos Beltran, Houston, Oct 13, 14, 16, 17, 2004
AL—3—Bernie Williams, New York, Oct 20, 21, 22, 2001

**Most consecutive games hitting one or more home runs, series**

NL—4—Jeffrey Leonard, San Francisco, Oct 6, 7, 9, 10, 1987
Carlos Beltran, Houston, Oct 13, 14, 16, 17, 2004
AL—3—Bernie Williams, New York, Oct 20, 21, 22, 2001

**Most home runs in two consecutive games, series (homering each game)**

NL—4—Bob Robertson, Pittsburgh, Oct 3 (3), Oct 5 (1), 1971
AL—3—Jay Buhner, Seattle, Oct 11 (1), Oct 13 (2 in 11 inn), 1995
Darryl Strawberry, New York, Oct 12 (2), Oct 13 (1), 1996
Jason Giambi, New York, Oct 15 (1), Oct 16 (2), 2003

**Hitting home run in first championship series at-bat (*not first plate appearance)**

AL—Frank Robinson, Baltimore, Oct 4, 1969, 4th*
Norm Cash, Detroit, Oct 7, 1972, 2nd
Dan Ford, California, Oct 3, 1979, 1st
John Lowenstein, Baltimore, Oct 3, 1979, 10th (pinch-hit)
Rich Cerone, New York, Oct 8, 1980, 1st
Gorman Thomas, Milwaukee, Oct 5, 1982, 2nd
Gary Gaetti, Minnesota, Oct 7, 1987, 2nd
Mike Blowers, Seattle, Oct 10, 1995, 2nd
Rafael Palmeiro, Baltimore, Oct 9, 1996, 4th*
Joe Crede, Chicago, Oct 11, 2005, 3rd
NL—Joe Morgan, Cincinnati, Oct 7, 1972, 1st

Bob Dernier, Chicago, Oct 2, 1984, 1st
Rick Sutcliffe, Chicago, Oct 2, 1984, 3rd
Glenn Davis, Houston, Oct 8, 1986, 2nd
Mark Grace, Chicago, Oct 4, 1989, 1st
Orlando Merced, Pittsburgh, Oct 12, 1991, 1st
Mike Lowell, Florida, Oct 7, 2003, 11th
Chris Burke, Houston, Oct 12, 2005, 7th

**Hitting home runs in first two championship series at-bats**
AL—Gary Gaetti, Minnesota, Oct 7, 1987, 2nd and 5th
NL—none

**Most home runs, inning**
AL-NL—1—many players

**Most home runs, two consecutive innings**
NL—2—Rusty Staub, New York, Oct 8, 1973, 1st and 2nd
Will Clark, San Francisco, Oct 4, 1989, 3rd and 4th
AL—none

## TOTAL BASES

**Most total bases, career**
AL—89—Bernie Williams, 1996, 1998-2001, 2003, 2004; 7 series, 41 G
NL—63—Pete Rose, Cincinnati, 1970, 1972, 1973, 1975, 1976; Philadelphia, 1980, 1983; 7 series, 28 G

**Most total bases by pinch-hitter, career**
NL—6—Jerry Martin, Philadelphia, 1977, 1978; 2 series, 3 G
J.D. Drew, St. Louis, 2000, 2002; 2 series, 2 G
AL—4—John Lowenstein, Baltimore, 1979; 1 series, 2 G
Pat Sheridan, Kansas City, 1985; 1 series, 2 G
Mike Pagliarulo, Minnesota, 1991; 1 series, 1 G
Eric Davis, Baltimore, 1997; 1 series, 3 G
Ricky Ledee, New York, 1998, 1999; 2 series, 2 G
Jay Buhner, Seattle, 2000, 2001; 2 series, 2 G

**Most total bases, series**
3-game series
NL—16—Hank Aaron, Atlanta, 1969
AL—11—many players
4-game series
NL—22—Steve Garvey, Los Angeles, 1978
AL—19—George Brett, Kansas City, 1978
5-game series
NL—24—Will Clark, San Francisco, 1989
AL—20—Chris Chambliss, New York, 1976
6-game series
AL—19—Jim Thome, Cleveland, 1998
NL—18—Bill Madlock, Los Angeles, 1985
Eddie Perez, Atlanta, 1999
7-game series
NL—28—Albert Pujols, St. Louis, 2004
AL—28—Hideki Matsui, New York, 2004

**Most total bases by pinch-hitter, series**
NL—6—Jerry Martin, Philadelphia, 1978; 2 G
AL—4—John Lowenstein, Baltimore, 1979; 2 G
Pat Sheridan, Kansas City, 1985; 2 G
Mike Pagliarulo, Minnesota, 1991; 2 G
Eric Davis, Baltimore, 1997; 3 G
Ricky Ledee, New York, 1999; 1 G
Jay Buhner, Seattle, 2001; 1 G

**Most total bases, game**
NL—14—Bob Robertson, Pittsburgh, Oct 3, 1971 (1 double, 3 HR)
AL—13—Adam Kennedy, Anaheim, Oct 13, 2002 (1 single, 3 HR)
Hideki Matsui, New York, Oct 16, 2004 (1 single, 2 doubles, 2 HR)

**Most total bases, inning**
AL—5—Adam Kennedy, Anaheim, Oct 13, 2002, 7th (1 single, 1 HR)
NL—5—Barry Bonds, Pittsburgh, Oct 13, 1992, 2nd (1 single, 1 HR)

## EXTRA-BASE HITS

**Most extra-base hits, career**
AL—19—Bernie Williams, New York, 1996, 1998-2001, 2003, 2004; 7 series, 41 G
NL—12—Steve Garvey, Los Angeles, 1974, 1977, 1978, 1981; San Diego, 1984; 5 series, 22 G
Will Clark, San Francisco, 1987, 1989; St. Louis, 2000; 3 series, 17 G
Javy Lopez, Atlanta, 1992, 1995-1998, 2001; 6 series, 27 G

**Most extra-base hits, series**
3-game series
NL—5—Hank Aaron, Atlanta, 1969
AL—4—Bob Watson, New York, 1980
4-game series
NL—6—Steve Garvey, Los Angeles, 1978
AL—5—George Brett, Kansas City, 1978
5-game series
AL—6—Tom Brunansky, Minnesota, 1987
NL—6—Will Clark, San Francisco, 1989
6-game series
NL—5—Tom Herr, St. Louis, 1985
AL—5—Jay Buhner, Seattle, 1995
7-game series
AL—9—Hideki Matsui, New York, 2004
NL—7—Javy Lopez, Atlanta, 1996

**Most extra-base hits, game**
NL—4—Bob Robertson, Pittsburgh, Oct 3, 1971 (1 double, 3 HR)
AL—4—Hideki Matsui, New York, Oct 16, 2004 (2 doubles, 2 HR)

**Most extra-base hits, inning**
AL-NL—1—many players

## RUNS BATTED IN

**Most runs batted in, career**
AL—33—Bernie Williams, New York, 1996, 1998-2001, 2003, 2004; 7 series, 41 G
NL—21—Steve Garvey, Los Angeles, 1974, 1977, 1978, 1981; San Diego, 1984; 5 series, 22 G

**Most runs batted in by pinch-hitter, career**
AL—4—Ricky Ledee, New York, 1998, 1999; 2 series, 2 G
NL—2—J.C. Martin, New York, 1969; 1 series, 2 G
Jerry Martin, Philadelphia, 1977, 1978; 2 series, 3 G
Luis Quinones, Cincinnati, 1990; 1 series, 3 G
Francisco Cabrera, Atlanta, 1992, 1993; 2 series, 5 G
Dmitri Young, St. Louis, 1996; 1 series, 3 G
Greg Myers, San Diego, 1998; 1 series, 2 G
Erubiel Durazo, Arizona, 2001; 1 series, 2 G

**Most runs batted in, series**
3-game series
AL—9—Graig Nettles, New York, 1981
NL—7—Hank Aaron, Atlanta, 1969
4-game series
NL—8—Dusty Baker, Los Angeles, 1977
Gary Matthews, Philadelphia, 1983
AL—6—Reggie Jackson, New York, 1978
5-game series
AL—10—Don Baylor, California, 1982
NL—9—Matt Williams, San Francisco, 1989
6-game series
AL—8—Jim Thome, Cleveland, 1998
David Justice, New York, 2000
NL—7—Bill Madlock, Los Angeles, 1985
7-game series
AL—11—David Ortiz, Boston, 2004
NL—10—Ivan Rodriguez, Florida, 2003

**Most runs batted in by pinch-hitter, series**
AL—4—Ricky Ledee, New York, 1999; 1 G
NL—2—J.C. Martin, New York, 1969; 2 G
Jerry Martin, Philadelphia, 1978; 2 G
Luis Quinones, Cincinnati, 1990; 3 G
Dmitri Young, St. Louis, 1996; 3 G
Greg Myers, San Diego, 1998; 2 G
Jose Hernandez, Atlanta, 1999; 2 G
Erubiel Durazo, Arizona, 2001; 2 G
Todd Hollandsworth, Florida, 2003; 4 G
Chris Burke, Houston, 2005; 1 G

**Most runs batted in, game**
NL—6—Will Clark, San Francisco, Oct 4, 1989
Aramis Ramirez, Chicago, Oct 11, 2003
AL—6—Johnny Damon, Boston, Oct 20, 2004

**Most runs batted in by pinch-hitter, game**
AL—4—Ricky Ledee, New York, Oct 17, 1999, 9th
NL—2—J.C. Martin, New York, Oct 4, 1969, 8th
Dmitri Young, St. Louis, Oct 13, 1996, 7th
Greg Myers, San Diego, Oct 12, 1998, 9th
Jose Hernandez, Atlanta, Oct 19, 1999, 6th
Erubiel Durazo, Arizona, Oct 21, 2001, 5th
Chris Burke, Houston, Oct 12, 2005, 7th

**Most consecutive games with one or more runs batted in, career**
AL—6—Mark McGwire, Oakland, Oct 6, 8, 9, 1988; Oct 3, 4, 6, 1989
NL—5—Gary Matthews, Philadelphia, Oct 5, 7, 8, 1983; Chicago, Oct 2, 3, 1984
Ivan Rodriguez, Florida, Oct 10, 11, 12, 14, 15, 2003

**Most runs batted in accounting for all club's runs, game**
AL—3—Bert Campaneris, Oakland, Oct 5, 1974
Graig Nettles, New York, Oct 13, 1981
NL—3—Keith Hernandez, New York, Oct 5, 1988
Jeff Blauser, Atlanta, Oct 13, 1993
Ron Gant, St. Louis, Oct 12, 1996
John Olerud, New York, Oct 16, 1999
Steve Finley, Arizona, Oct 19, 2001
Jeff Kent, Houston, Oct 18, 2004

**Most runs batted in, inning**
AL—4—Mike Cuellar, Baltimore, Oct 3, 1970, 4th
Don Baylor, California, Oct 9, 1982, 8th
Jim Thome, Cleveland, Oct 13, 1998, 5th
Ricky Ledee, New York, Oct 17, 1999, 9th
Johnny Damon, Boston, Oct 20, 2004, 2nd
NL—4—Ron Cey, Los Angeles, Oct 4, 1977, 7th
Dusty Baker, Los Angeles, Oct 5, 1977, 4th
Will Clark, San Francisco, Oct 4, 1989, 4th
Ron Gant, Atlanta, Oct 7, 1992, 5th
Gary Gaetti, St. Louis, Oct 10, 1996, 7th
Andres Galarraga, Atlanta, Oct 11, 1998, 7th

## GAME-WINNING RBIs (1980-1988)

**Most game-winning RBIs, career (1980-88)**
AL—3—George Brett, Kansas City, 1980, 1985 (2)
NL—3—Gary Carter, Montreal, 1981; New York, 1986, 1988

**Most game-winning RBIs, series (1980-88)**
NL—2—Greg Luzinski, Philadelphia, 1980
Gary Carter, New York, 1986
Kirk Gibson, Los Angeles, 1988
AL—2—Cecil Cooper, Milwaukee, 1982
Al Oliver, Toronto, 1985

George Brett, Kansas City, 1985

## BASES ON BALLS

**Most bases on balls, career**
AL—26—Jorge Posada, New York, 1998-2001, 2003, 2004; 6 series, 33 G
NL—24—Chipper Jones, Atlanta, 1995-1999, 2001; 6 series, 34 G
Barry Bonds, Pittsburgh, 1990-1992; San Francisco, 2002; 4 series, 25 G

**Most bases on balls, series**
3-game series
AL—6—Harmon Killebrew, Minnesota, 1969
NL—6—Joe Morgan, Cincinnati, 1976
4-game series
NL—9—Jim Wynn, Los Angeles, 1974
AL—5—Reggie Jackson, Oakland, 1974
Eddie Murray, Baltimore, 1979
Gary Roenicke, Baltimore, 1983
Jose Canseco, Oakland, 1990
5-game series
NL—10—Barry Bonds, San Francisco, 2002
AL—7—Lou Whitaker, Detroit, 1987
Rickey Henderson, Oakland, 1989
6-game series
AL—10—Frank Thomas, Chicago, 1993
NL—9—Chipper Jones, Atlanta, 1999
7-game series
NL—8—Carlos Beltran, Houston, 2004
AL—7—George Brett, Kansas City, 1985
Jorge Posada, New York, 2004

**Most consecutive bases on balls, series**
AL—4—Harmon Killebrew, Minnesota, Oct 4 (3), 5 (1), 1969
Gary Roenicke, Baltimore, Oct 6 (1), 7 (1), 8 (2), 1983
Bernie Williams, New York, Oct 10 (3), 11 (1), 1998
NL—4—Darren Daulton, Philadelphia, Oct 10 (3), 11 (1), 1993

**Most bases on balls, game**
NL—4—Darren Daulton, Philadelphia, Oct 10, 1993
Ken Caminiti, San Diego, Oct 8, 1998
AL—4—Frank Thomas, Chicago, Oct 5, 1993
[4—Ruppert Jones, California, Oct 11, 1986, 11 inn]

**Most bases on balls with bases filled, game**
AL-NL—1—many players

**Bases on balls with bases filled by pinch-hitters, game**
NL—Duffy Dyer, Pittsburgh, Oct 7, 1975, 9th
Mike Sharperson, Los Angeles, Oct 8, 1988, 8th
AL—Bobby Kielty, Minnesota, Oct 13, 2002, 7th

**Most bases on balls, inning**
AL-NL—1—many players

## STRIKEOUTS

**Most strikeouts, career**
AL—41—Reggie Jackson, Oakland, 1971-1975; New York, 1977, 1978, 1980, 1981; California, 1982, 1986; 11 series, 45 G
NL—32—Reggie Sanders, Cincinnati, 1995; Arizona, 2001; San Francisco, 2002; St. Louis, 2004, 2005; 5 series, 24 G

**Most strikeouts, series**
3-game series
AL—7—Leo Cardenas, Minnesota, 1969
NL—7—Cesar Geronimo, Cincinnati, 1975
4-game series
NL—10—Reggie Sanders, Cincinnati, 1995
AL—7—Dave Henderson, Oakland, 1988
5-game series
NL—9—Jim Edmonds, St. Louis, 2000
AL—8—Kirk Gibson, Detroit, 1987
Chili Davis, Minnesota, 1991
Corey Koskie, Minnesota, 2002
6-game series
NL—12—Darryl Strawberry, New York, 1986
AL—10—Omar Vizquel, Cleveland, 1997
Rafael Palmeiro, Baltimore, 1997
7-game series
NL—12—John Shelby, Los Angeles, 1988
AL—11—Alfonso Soriano, New York, 2003
Mark Bellhorn, Boston, 2004

**Most strikeouts by pinch-hitter, series**
NL—3—Lee Mazzilli, New York, 1986; 5 G
Curtis Wilkerson, Pittsburgh, 1991; 4 G
Tom Goodwin, Chicago, 2003; 4 G
John Mabry, St. Louis, 2004; 4 G
AL—2—Matt Nokes, Detroit, 1987; 2 G
Larry Parrish, Boston, 1988; 3 G
Glenallen Hill, New York, 2000; 2 G
Bobby Kielty, Minnesota, 2002; 4 G
Shawn Wooten, Anaheim, 2002; 2 G

**Most consecutive strikeouts, series (consecutive at-bats)**
NL—7—Cesar Geronimo, Cincinnati, Oct 4 (1 in 10 inn), 5 (3), 7 (3), 1975
(one BB during streak)
AL—6—Corey Koskie, Minnesota, Oct 9 (1), 11 (4), 12 (1), 2002

**Most consecutive strikeouts, series (consecutive plate appearances)**
AL—6—Corey Koskie, Minnesota, Oct 9 (1), 11 (4), 12 (1), 2002
NL—5—Cesar Geronimo, Cincinnati, Oct 6 (1), 7 (3), 9 (1 in 12 inn), 1973
Reggie Sanders, Cincinnati, Oct 11 (2 in 10 inn), 13 (3), 1995

**Most strikeouts, game**
AL—4—Bobby Bonilla, Baltimore, Oct 10, 1996 (consec)
Corey Koskie, Minnesota, Oct 11, 2002 (consec)
Johnny Damon, Boston, Oct 12, 2004 (consec)
Mark Bellhorn, Boston, Oct 16, 2004 (consec)
[4—many players in extra inn]
NL—4—John Kruk, Philadelphia, Oct 10, 1993
Gerald Williams, Atlanta, Oct 10, 1998 (consec)
[4—Reggie Sanders, Cincinnati, Oct 11, 1995, 10 inn]

**Most strikeouts, inning**
AL—2—Ron Karkovice, Chicago, Oct 8, 1993, 3rd
NL—1—many players

## SACRIFICE HITS

**Most sacrifice hits, career**
NL—6—Greg Maddux, Chicago, 1989; Atlanta, 1993, 1995-1999, 2001; 8 series; 15 G
AL—5—Derek Jeter, New York, 1996, 1998-2001, 2003, 2004; 6 series, 41 G

**Most sacrifice hits, series**
AL—3—Enos Cabell, Houston, 1980 (5-game series)
NL—3—Rich Aurilia, San Francisco, 2002 (5-game series)
Mark Prior, Chicago, 2003 (7-game series)

**Most sacrifice hits, game**
AL-NL—2—many players

## SACRIFICE FLIES

**Most sacrifice flies, career**
ML—3—Robin Ventura, Chicago AL, 1993; New York NL, 1999, 2000; 3 series, 17 G
AL-NL—2—many players

**Most sacrifice flies, series**
AL-NL—2—many players

**Most sacrifice flies, game**
AL-NL—1—many players

## HIT BY PITCH

**Most hit by pitch, career**
NL—4—Richie Hebner, Pittsburgh, 1971 (1), 1972 (1), 1974 (1); Chicago, 1984 (1)
AL—4—Miguel Cairo, New York, 2004

**Most hit by pitch, series**
NL—2—Lenny Dykstra, New York, 1988 (7-game series)
Jeff Blauser, Atlanta, 1996 (7-game series)
Morgan Ensberg, Houston, 2004 (7-game series)
Jeff Kent, Houston, 2004 (7-game series)
David Eckstein, St. Louis, 2005 (6-game series)
AL—4—Miguel Cairo, New York, 2004 (7-game series)

**Most hit by pitch, game**
AL—2—Dan Gladden, Minnesota, Oct 11, 1987
Pat Sheridan, Detroit, Oct 12, 1987
NL—1—many players

## GROUNDING INTO DOUBLE PLAYS

**Most grounding into double play, career**
AL—6—Manny Ramirez, Cleveland, 1995-1999; Boston, 2003, 2004; 7 series, 35 G
NL—5—Pedro Guerrero, Los Angeles, 1981, 1983, 1985; 3 series, 15 G

**Most grounding into double play, series**
NL—4—Pedro Guerrero, Los Angeles, 1981 (5-game series)
AL—3—Tony Taylor, Detroit, 1972 (5-game series)
Doug DeCinces, California, 1986 (7-game series)
Paul Sorrento, Cleveland, 1995 (6-game series)
German Berroa, Baltimore, 1997 (6-game series)

**Most grounding into double play, game**
AL—3—Tony Taylor, Detroit, Oct 10, 1972
NL—2—Cleon Jones, New York, Oct 4, 1969
Pedro Guerrero, Los Angeles, Oct 16, 1981
Jerry Royster, Atlanta, Oct 10, 1982
Chris Gomez, San Diego, Oct 7, 1998
Gerald Williams, Atlanta, Oct 13, 1999
Damian Miller, Arizona, Oct 20, 2001
[2—Garry Maddox, Philadelphia, Oct 12, 1980, 10 inn
Bret Boone, Cincinnati, Oct 10, 1995, 11 inn]

## REACHING BASE ON INTERFERENCE

**Most times awarded first base on catcher's interference, game**
NL—1—Richie Hebner, Pittsburgh, Oct 8, 1974, 5th
Mike Scioscia, Los Angeles, Oct 14, 1985, 4th
AL—none

# CLUB BATTING

## GAMES

**Most games played, total series**
AL—61—New York; 12 series (won 39, lost 22)
NL—60—Atlanta; 11 series (won 27, lost 33)

**For summaries of series won and lost, games won and lost, and home and road games played, see page 348. For a list of batting statistics by teams each series, see page 353.**

## BATTING AVERAGE

**Highest average, series**
3-game series
AL—.336—New York vs Oakland, 1981
NL—.330—St. Louis vs Atlanta, 1982
4-game series
AL—.300—New York vs Kansas City, 1978
NL—.286—Los Angeles vs Philadelphia, 1978
5-game series
AL—.316—New York vs Kansas City, 1976
NL—.303—Chicago vs San Francisco, 1989
6-game series
AL—.301—Toronto vs Chicago, 1993
NL—.279—St. Louis vs Los Angeles, 1985
7-game series
NL—.309—Atlanta vs St. Louis, 1996
AL—.282—New York vs Boston, 2004

**Highest average, both clubs, series**
3-game series
NL—.292—New York .327, Atlanta .255, 1969
AL—.286—Baltimore .330, Minnesota .238, 1970
4-game series
AL—.282—New York .300, Kansas City .263, 1978
NL—.268—Los Angeles .286, Philadelphia .250, 1978
5-game series
NL—.285—Chicago .303, San Francisco .267, 1989
AL—.283—New York .316, Kansas City .247, 1976
6-game series
AL—.271—Toronto .301, Chicago .237, 1993
NL—.256—St. Louis .279, Los Angeles .234, 1985
7-game series
AL—.279—New York .282, Boston .277, 2004
NL—.262—Florida .266, Chicago .258, 2003

**Highest average, losing club, series**
NL—.303—Chicago vs San Francisco, 1989 (5-game series)
AL—.293—Boston vs New York, 1999 (5-game series)

**Lowest average, series**
3-game series
AL—.155—Minnesota vs Baltimore, 1969
NL—.169—Atlanta vs St. Louis, 1982
4-game series
AL—.177—Baltimore vs Oakland, 1974
NL—.194—Pittsburgh vs Los Angeles, 1974
5-game series
AL—.175—Los Angeles vs Chicago, 2005
NL—.186—Cincinnati vs New York, 1973
6-game series
AL—.184—Seattle vs Cleveland, 1995
NL—.189—New York vs Houston, 1986
7-game series
NL—.204—St. Louis vs Atlanta, 1996
AL—.225—Kansas City vs Toronto, 1985

**Lowest average, both clubs, series**
3-game series
AL—.202—Detroit .234, Kansas City .170, 1984
NL—.223—Pittsburgh .225, Cincinnati .220, 1970
4-game series
AL—.180—Oakland .183, Baltimore .177, 1974
NL—.232—Los Angeles .268, Pittsburgh .194, 1974
5-game series
NL—.203—New York .220, Cincinnati .186, 1973
AL—.205—Baltimore .211, Oakland .200, 1973
6-game series
NL—.204—Houston .218, New York .189, 1986
AL—.219—Cleveland .220, New York .218, 1998
7-game series
NL—.228—New York .242, Los Angeles .214, 1988
Atlanta .231, Pittsburgh .224, 1991
AL—.247—Toronto .269, Kansas City .225, 1985

**Lowest average, winning club, series**
AL—.183—Oakland vs Baltimore, 1974 (4-game series)
NL—.189—New York vs Houston, 1986 (6-game series)

## ON-BASE PERCENTAGE

(official statistic since 1984; calculated from official statistics, 1969-1983)

**Highest percentage, series**
3-game series
AL—.415—New York vs Oakland, 1981
NL—.395—St. Louis vs Atlanta, 1982
4-game series
NL—.399—Los Angeles vs Pittsburgh, 1974
AL—.399—Oakland vs Boston, 1990
5-game series
AL—.372—New York vs Kansas City, 1976
NL—.371—New York vs St. Louis, 2000
6-game series
NL—.371—St. Louis vs Los Angeles, 1985
AL—.367—Toronto vs Chicago, 1993
7-game series
NL—.375—Atlanta vs St. Louis, 1996
AL—.371—New York vs Boston, 2004

**Highest percentage, both clubs, series**
3-game series
NL—.355—New York .382, Atlanta .328, 1969
AL—.350—Baltimore .395, Minnesota .300, 1970
4-game series
NL—.332—Los Angeles .399, Pittsburgh .252, 1974
AL—.330—New York .331, Kansas City .329, 1978
5-game series
NL—.349—Chicago .361, San Francisco .337, 1989
AL—.340—Minnesota .359, Detroit .321, 1987
6-game series
AL—.360—Toronto .367, Chicago .352, 1993
NL—.336—St. Louis .371, Los Angeles .300, 1985
7-game series
AL—.358—New York, .371, Boston .344, 2004
NL—.332—Florida .340, Chicago .324, 2003

**Lowest percentage, series**
3-game series
AL—.214—Kansas City vs Detroit, 1984
NL—.219—Atlanta vs St. Louis, 1982
4-game series
AL—.209—Baltimore vs Oakland, 1974
NL—.252—Pittsburgh vs Los Angeles, 1974
5-game series
AL—.200—Los Angeles vs Chicago, 2005
NL—.243—Pittsburgh vs Cincinnati, 1972
6-game series
NL—.234—New York vs Houston, 1986
AL—.251—Seattle vs Cleveland, 1995
7-game series
NL—.244—St. Louis vs Atlanta, 1996
AL—.294—Kansas City vs Toronto, 1985

**Lowest percentage, both clubs, series**
3-game series
AL—.250—Detroit .284, Kansas City .214, 1984
NL—.293—Pittsburgh .307, Cincinnati .278, 1970
4-game series
AL—.264—Oakland .313, Baltimore .209, 1974
NL—.309—Philadelphia .336, Los Angeles .282, 1983
5-game series
AL—.268—Chicago .326, Los Angeles .200, 2005
NL—.269—Cincinnati .294, Pittsburgh .243, 1972
6-game series
NL—.255—Houston .276, New York .234, 1986
AL—.296—Cleveland .338, Seattle .251, 1995
7-game series
NL—.297—Atlanta .303, Pittsburgh .291, 1991
AL—.307—Toronto .319, Kansas City .294, 1985

## SLUGGING AVERAGE

**Highest average, series**
3-game series
NL—.575—New York vs Atlanta, 1969
AL—.560—Baltimore vs Minnesota, 1970
4-game series
NL—.544—Los Angeles vs Philadelphia, 1978
AL—.511—Oakland vs Boston, 1988
5-game series
AL—.497—Minnesota vs Detroit, 1987
New York vs Baltimore, 1996
NL—.494—Chicago vs San Diego, 1984
6-game series
AL—.471—Toronto vs Oakland, 1992
NL—.420—Philadelphia vs Atlanta, 1993
7-game series
NL—.484—Chicago vs Florida, 2003
AL—.469—New York vs Boston, 2004

**Highest average, both clubs, series**
3-game series
NL—.530—New York .575, Atlanta .481, 1969
AL—.476—Baltimore .560, Minnesota .386, 1970
4-game series
NL—.477—Los Angeles .544, Philadelphia .407, 1978
AL—.443—Kansas City .444, New York .443, 1978
5-game series
NL—.456—San Francisco .473, Chicago .440, 1989
AL—.448—New York .497, Baltimore .398, 1996
6-game series
NL—.415—Philadelphia .420, Atlanta .409, 1993
AL—.408—Toronto .471, Oakland .343, 1992
7-game series
NL—.469—Chicago .484, Florida .453, 2003
AL—.454—New York, .469, Boston .439, 2004

**Lowest average, series**
3-game series
NL—.180—Atlanta vs St. Louis, 1982
AL—.198—Kansas City vs Detroit, 1984
4-game series
AL—.241—Chicago vs Baltimore, 1983
NL—.261—Cincinnati vs Atlanta, 1995
5-game series
AL—.266—Los Angeles vs Chicago, 2005
NL—.278—Montreal vs Los Angeles, 1981
6-game series
NL—.260—Florida vs Atlanta, 1997
AL—.299—Seattle vs Cleveland, 1995
7-game series
NL—.288—Los Angeles vs New York, 1988
AL—.366—Kansas City vs Toronto, 1985

**Lowest average, both clubs, series**
3-game series
AL—.300—Detroit .402, Kansas City .198, 1984
NL—.318—St. Louis .437, Atlanta .180, 1982
4-game series
AL—.283—Oakland .308, Baltimore .258, 1974
NL—.339—Los Angeles .391, Philadelphia .290, 1977
5-game series
AL—.304—Detroit .321, Oakland .288, 1972
NL—.307—Cincinnati .311, New York .304, 1973
6-game series
NL—.288—Houston .311, New York .264, 1986
AL—.351—Baltimore .394, Cleveland .304, 1997
7-game series
NL—.325—New York .363, Los Angeles .288, 1988
AL—.369—Toronto .372, Kansas City .366, 1985

## AT-BATS AND PLATE APPEARANCES

**Most at-bats, total series**
AL—2,132—New York; 12 series, 61 G
NL—2,040—Atlanta; 11 series, 60 G

**Most at-bats, series**
3-game series
AL—123—Baltimore vs Minnesota, 1969
NL—113—New York vs Atlanta, 1969
4-game series
NL—149—Atlanta vs Cincinnati, 1995
AL—140—New York vs Kansas City, 1978
5-game series
NL—190—Philadelphia vs Houston, 1980
AL—184—Boston vs New York, 1999
6-game series
NL—227—New York vs Houston, 1986
AL—218—Baltimore vs Cleveland, 1997
7-game series
AL—277—New York vs Boston, 2004
NL—256—Florida vs Chicago, 2003

**Most at-bats by both clubs, series**
3-game series
AL—233—Baltimore 123, Minnesota 110, 1969
NL—219—New York 113, Atlanta 106, 1969
4-game series
NL—287—Los Angeles 147, Philadelphia 140, 1978
AL—273—New York 140, Kansas City 133, 1978
5-game series
NL—362—Philadelphia 190, Houston 172, 1980
AL—360—Boston 184, New York 176, 1999
6-game series
NL—452—New York 227, Houston 225, 1986
AL—425—Baltimore 218, Cleveland 207, 1997
7-game series
AL—548—Boston 277, New York 271, 2004
NL—508—Florida 256, Chicago 252, 2003

**Most at-bats by pinch-hitters, series**
NL—15—Atlanta vs Pittsburgh, 1992 (7-game series)
New York vs Atlanta, 1999 (6-game series)
St. Louis vs New York, 2000 (5-game series)
AL—13—Oakland vs Detroit, 1972 (5-game series)
Toronto vs Kansas City, 1985 (7-game series)

**Most at-bats by pinch-hitters on both clubs, series**
NL—25—Atlanta 15, Pittsburgh 10, 1992 (7-game series)
AL—20—Oakland 13, Detroit 7, 1972 (5-game series)

**Most plate appearances by pinch-hitters, series**
NL—18—New York vs Atlanta, 1999 (6-game series)
AL—14—Oakland vs Detroit, 1972 (5-game series)

**Most plate appearances by pinch-hitters on both clubs, series**
NL—29—New York 18, Atlanta 11, 1999 (6-game series)
AL—22—Oakland 14, Detroit 8, 1972 (5-game series)

**Fewest at-bats, series**
3-game series
NL—89—Atlanta vs St. Louis, 1982
AL—95—Baltimore vs Oakland, 1971
4-game series
AL—120—Oakland vs Baltimore, 1974
NL—129—Pittsburgh vs Los Angeles, 1974
Los Angeles vs Philadelphia, 1983
5-game series
AL—151—Milwaukee vs California, 1982
NL—155—San Diego vs Chicago, 1984
6-game series
NL—181—Florida vs Atlanta, 1997
AL—191—Seattle vs New York, 2000
7-game series
NL—215—St. Louis vs San Francisco, 1987
AL—227—Kansas City vs Toronto, 1985

**Fewest at-bats by both clubs, series**
3-game series
AL—191—Oakland 96, Baltimore 95, 1971
NL—192—St. Louis 103, Atlanta 89, 1982
4-game series
AL—244—Baltimore 124, Oakland 120, 1974
NL—259—Philadelphia 130, Los Angeles 129, 1983
5-game series
AL—308—California 157, Milwaukee 151, 1982
NL—317—Chicago 162, San Diego 155, 1984
6-game series
NL—375—Atlanta 194, Florida 181, 1997
AL—395—New York 204, Seattle 191, 2000
7-game series
NL—441—San Francisco 226, St. Louis 215, 1987
AL—469—Toronto 242, Kansas City 227, 1985

**Most at-bats, game**
NL—47—Atlanta vs St. Louis, Oct 14, 1996
[56—Houston vs New York, Oct 15, 1986, 16 inn]
AL—47—New York vs Boston, Oct 16, 2004
[49—Toronto vs Oakland, Oct 11, 1992, 11 inn]

**Most at-bats by both clubs, game**
AL—87—New York 47, Boston 40, Oct 16, 2004
[91—Toronto 49, Oakland 42, Oct 11, 1992, 11 inn]
NL—80—Atlanta 47, St. Louis 33, Oct 14, 1996
Arizona 42, Atlanta 38, Oct 20, 2001
[110—Houston 56, New York 54, Oct 15, 1986, 16 inn]

**Most at-bats by pinch-hitters, game**
AL—6—Oakland vs Detroit, Oct 10, 1972
NL—5—Atlanta vs Pittsburgh, Oct 14, 1992
St. Louis vs New York, Oct 16, 2000

**Most at-bats by pinch-hitters on both clubs, game**
AL—7—Oakland 6, Detroit 1, Oct 10, 1972
NL—6—Pittsburgh 3, Cincinnati 3, Oct 4, 1990
Atlanta 3, St. Louis 3, Oct 14, 1996
New York 4, St. Louis 2, Oct 14, 2000
[8—New York 4, Houston 4, Oct 15, 1986, 16 inn
New York 4, Atlanta 4, Oct 19, 1999, 11 inn]

**Most plate appearances by pinch-hitters, game**
AL—6—Oakland vs Detroit, Oct 10, 1972
NL—6—Pittsburgh vs Cincinnati, Oct 4, 1990

**Most plate appearances by pinch-hitters on both clubs, game**
AL—7—Oakland 6, Detroit 1, Oct 10, 1972
NL—6—many games
[10—New York 5, Houston 5, Oct 15, 1986, 16 inn
New York 5, Atlanta 5, Oct 19, 1999, 11 inn]

**Fewest at-bats, game**
NL—26—St. Louis vs San Francisco, Oct 7, 1987
Florida vs Atlanta, Oct 12, 1997 (batted 8 inn)
AL—25—California vs Milwaukee, Oct 6, 1982 (batted 8 inn)
Toronto vs Oakland, Oct 8, 1992 (batted 8 inn)
New York vs Seattle, Oct 21, 2001

**Fewest at-bats by both clubs, game**
AL—54—Seattle 29, New York 25, Oct 21, 2001
NL—56—Houston 28, St. Louis 28, Oct 18, 2004

**Most at-bats, inning**
AL—13—Anaheim vs Minnesota, Oct 13, 2002, 7th
NL—12—St. Louis vs Los Angeles, Oct 13, 1985, 2nd

**Most at-bats by both clubs, inning**
AL—18—Anaheim 13, Minnesota 5, Oct 13, 2002, 7th
NL—15—Philadelphia 8, Houston 7, Oct 12, 1980, 8th
St. Louis 12, Los Angeles 3, Oct 13, 1985, 2nd
Pittsburgh 8, Atlanta 7, Oct 7, 1992, 7th

**Most plate appearances, inning**
AL—15—Anaheim vs Minnesota, Oct 13, 2002, 7th
NL—14—St. Louis vs Los Angeles, Oct 13, 1985, 2nd

**Most plate appearances by both clubs, inning**
AL—22—Anaheim 15, Minnesota 7, Oct 13, 2002, 7th
NL—19—Atlanta 10, Pittsburgh 9, Oct 7, 1992, 7th

## RUNS

### SERIES AND GAMES

**Most runs, total series**
AL—297—New York; 12 series, 61 G
NL—247—Atlanta; 11 series, 60 G

**Most runs, series**
3-game series
AL—27—Baltimore vs Minnesota, 1970
NL—27—New York vs Atlanta, 1969
4-game series
AL—26—Baltimore vs California, 1979
NL—24—Pittsburgh vs San Francisco, 1971
5-game series
AL—34—Minnesota vs Detroit, 1987
NL—31—New York vs St. Louis, 2000
6-game series
NL—33—Atlanta vs Philadelphia, 1993
AL—31—Toronto vs Oakland, 1992
New York vs Seattle, 2000
7-game series
AL—45—New York vs Boston, 2004
NL—44—Atlanta vs St. Louis, 1996

**Most runs by both clubs, series**
3-game series
NL—42—New York 27, Atlanta 15, 1969
AL—37—Baltimore 27, Minnesota 10, 1970
4-game series
AL—41—Baltimore 26, California 15, 1979
NL—39—Pittsburgh 24, San Francisco 15, 1971
5-game series
AL—57—Minnesota 34, Detroit 23, 1987
NL—52—San Francisco 30, Chicago 22, 1989
New York 31, St. Louis 21, 2000
6-game series
NL—56—Atlanta 33, Philadelphia 23, 1993
AL—55—Toronto 31, Oakland 24, 1992
7-game series
AL—86—New York 45, Boston 41, 2004
NL—82—Chicago 42, Florida 40, 2003

**Most runs by losing club, series**
AL—45—New York vs Boston, 2004 (7-game series)
NL—42—Chicago vs Florida, 2003 (7-game series)

**Fewest runs, series**
3-game series
NL—3—Pittsburgh vs Cincinnati, 1970
AL—4—Oakland vs New York, 1981
Kansas City vs Detroit, 1984
4-game series
AL—3—Chicago vs Baltimore, 1983
NL—5—Cincinnati vs Atlanta, 1995
5-game series
NL—8—Cincinnati vs New York, 1973
AL—10—Detroit vs Oakland, 1972
6-game series
AL—12—Seattle vs Cleveland, 1995
NL—15—Pittsburgh vs Cincinnati, 1990
7-game series
NL—12—Pittsburgh vs Atlanta, 1991
AL—25—Toronto vs Kansas Ctiy, 1985

**Fewest runs by both clubs, series**
3-game series
NL—12—Cincinnati 9, Pittsburgh 3, 1970
AL—18—Detroit 14, Kansas City 4, 1984
4-game series
AL—18—Oakland 11, Baltimore 7, 1974
NL—24—Atlanta 19, Cincinnati 5, 1995
5-game series
AL—23—Oakland 13, Detroit 10, 1972
NL—25—Los Angeles 15, Montreal 10, 1981
6-game series
NL—35—Cincinnati 20, Pittsburgh 15, 1990
AL—35—Cleveland 23, Seattle 12, 1995
7-game series
NL—31—Atlanta 19, Pittsburgh 12, 1991
AL—51—Kansas City 26, Toronto 25, 1985

**Most runs, game**
AL—19—New York vs Boston, Oct 16, 2004
NL—15—Atlanta vs St. Louis, Oct 17, 1996

**Most earned runs, game**
AL—19—New York vs Boston, Oct 16, 2004
NL—15—Atlanta vs St. Louis, Oct 17, 1996

**Most runs by both clubs, game**
AL—27—New York 19, Boston 8, Oct 16, 2004
NL—18—Atlanta 13, Pittsburgh 5, Oct 7, 1992
[19—Atlanta 10, New York 9, Oct 19, 1999, 11 inn]

**Largest score, shutout game**
NL—Atlanta 15, St. Louis 0, Oct 17, 1996
AL—Baltimore 8, California 0, Oct 6, 1979

**Most players scoring one or more runs, game**
NL—11—Atlanta vs Philadelphia, Oct 7, 1993
AL—11—Seattle vs New York, Oct 20, 2001

**Most players from both clubs scoring one or more runs, game**
AL—14—Baltimore 9, Minnesota 5, Oct 3, 1970
Baltimore 7, California 7, Oct 4, 1979
Seattle 11, New York 3, Oct 20, 2001
New York 8, Boston 6, Oct 16, 2004
NL—14—Atlanta 10, Pittsburgh 4, Oct 7, 1992
Atlanta 11, Philadelphia 3, Oct 7, 1993
[14—New York 7, Atlanta 7, Oct 19, 1999, 11 inn
Chicago 7, Florida 7, Oct 7, 2003, 11 inn]

### INNING

**Most runs, inning**
AL—10—Anaheim vs Minnesota, Oct 13, 2002, 7th
NL—9—St. Louis vs Los Angeles, Oct 13, 1985, 2nd

**Most runs by both clubs, inning**
AL—13—Anaheim 10, Minnesota 3, Oct 13, 2002, 7th
NL—9—St. Louis 9, Los Angeles 0, Oct 13, 1985, 2nd
Atlanta 5, Pittsburgh 4, Oct 7, 1992, 7th

**Most runs, extra inning**
NL—4—Houston vs Philadelphia, Oct 8, 1980, 10th
Atlanta vs Cincinnati, Oct 11, 1995, 10th
AL—3—Detroit vs Oakland, Oct 11, 1972, 10th
Baltimore vs California, Oct 3, 1979, 10th
Baltimore vs Chicago, Oct 8, 1983, 10th
Seattle vs Cleveland, Oct 13, 1995, 11th
Cleveland vs New York, Oct 7, 1998, 12th

**Most runs by both clubs, extra inning**
AL—5—Detroit 3, Oakland 2, Oct 11, 1972, 10th
NL—5—Houston 4, Philadelphia 1, Oct 8, 1980, 10th
New York 3, Houston 2, Oct 15, 1986, 16th

**Most innings scored, game**
NL—6—New York vs Atlanta, Oct 5, 1969
Los Angeles vs Pittsburgh, Oct 9, 1974
Atlanta vs St. Louis, Oct 14, 1996
AL—6—Detroit vs Kansas City, Oct 2, 1984
Boston vs New York, Oct 16, 1999
New York vs Boston, Oct 16, 2004

**Most innings scored by both clubs, game**
NL—9—San Francisco 5, St. Louis 4, Oct 9, 2002
[9—Atlanta 5, New York 4, Oct 19, 1999, 11 inn]
AL—9—New York 6, Boston 3, Oct 16, 2004
[9—New York 5, Baltimore 4, Oct 9, 1996, 11 inn]

**Most runs, 1st inning**
NL—6—Chicago vs San Francisco, Oct 5, 1989
Atlanta vs St. Louis, Oct 17, 1996
AL—5—New York vs Cleveland, Oct 6, 1998

**Most runs, 2nd inning**
NL—9—St. Louis vs Los Angeles, Oct 13, 1985
AL—4—many clubs

**Most runs, 3rd inning**
NL—6—Atlanta vs Philadelphia, Oct 7, 1993
AL—6—New York vs Baltimore, Oct 13, 1996

**Most runs, 4th inning**
AL—7—Baltimore vs Minnesota, Oct 3, 1970
New York vs Oakland, Oct 14, 1981
NL—4—Los Angeles vs Philadelphia, Oct 5, 1977
San Francisco vs St. Louis, Oct 11, 1987
San Francisco vs Chicago, Oct 4, 1989
Atlanta vs St. Louis, Oct 17, 1996

**Most runs, 5th inning**
NL—6—Chicago vs San Diego, Oct 2, 1984
AL—5—Toronto vs Kansas City, Oct 11, 1985
Cleveland vs New York, Oct 13, 1998

Seattle vs New York, Oct 15, 2000

**Most runs, 6th inning**
AL—7—Seattle vs New York, Oct 20, 2001
NL—6—St. Louis vs Houston, Oct 13, 2004

**Most runs, 7th inning**
AL—10—Anaheim vs Minnesota, Oct 13, 2002
NL—6—Atlanta vs San Diego, Oct 11, 1998

**Most runs, 8th inning**
AL—7—New York vs Seattle, Oct 11, 2000
NL—8—Florida vs Chicago, Oct 14, 2003

**Most runs, 9th inning**
AL—7—Baltimore vs Minnesota, Oct 4, 1970
Oakland vs Boston, Oct 6, 1990
NL—4—New York vs Cincinnati, Oct 7, 1973
Los Angeles vs Montreal, Oct 17, 1981
Arizona vs Atlanta, Oct 20, 2001

**Most runs, 10th inning**
NL—4—Houston vs Philadelphia, Oct 8, 1980
Atlanta vs Cincinnati, Oct 11, 1995
AL—3—Detroit vs Oakland, Oct 11, 1972
Baltimore vs California, Oct 3, 1979
Baltimore vs Chicago, Oct 8, 1983

**Most runs, 11th inning**
NL—3—Pittsburgh vs Cincinnati, Oct 2, 1979
AL—3—Seattle vs Cleveland, Oct 13, 1995

**Most runs, 12th inning**
AL—3—Cleveland vs New York, Oct 7, 1998
NL—2—St. Louis vs Houston, Oct 20, 2004

**Most runs, 14th inning**
NL—1—Houston vs New York, Oct 15, 1986
New York vs Houston, Oct 15, 1986
AL—1—Boston vs New York, Oct 18, 2004

**Most runs, 15th inning**
NL—2—New York vs Atlanta, Oct 17, 1999
AL—none

**Most runs, 16th inning**
NL—3—New York vs Houston, Oct 15, 1986
AL—none

## GAMES BEING SHUT OUT

**Most times being shut out, total series**
NL—5—Pittsburgh, 1970, 1974, 1991 (3)
Atlanta, 1982, 1991, 1998 (2), 2001
AL—4—Baltimore, 1973, 1974 (2), 1997

**Most consecutive games without being shut out, total series**
NL—33—Atlanta, Oct 16, 1991-Oct 7, 1998
AL—36—New York, Oct 9, 1976-Oct 18, 1999

## HITS

### SERIES

**Most hits, total series**
AL—571—New York; 12 series, 61 G
NL—507—Atlanta; 11 series, 60 G

**Most hits, series**
3-game series
NL—37—New York vs Atlanta, 1969
AL—36—Baltimore vs Minnesota, 1969, 1970
New York vs Oakland, 1981
4-game series
NL—42—Los Angeles vs Philadelphia, 1978
Atlanta vs Cincinnati, 1995
AL—42—New York vs Kansas City, 1978
5-game series
AL—55—New York vs Kansas City, 1976
NL—55—Philadelphia vs Houston, 1980
6-game series
AL—65—Toronto vs Chicago, 1993
NL—59—Atlanta vs Philadelphia, 1993
7-game series
AL—78—New York vs Boston, 2004
NL—77—Atlanta vs St. Louis, 1996

**Most hits by both clubs, series**
3-game series
NL—64—New York 37, Atlanta 27, 1969
AL—60—Baltimore 36, Minnesota 24, 1970
4-game series
NL—77—Los Angeles 42, Philadelphia 35, 1978
AL—77—New York 42, Kansas City 35, 1978
5-game series
NL—97—Chicago 53, San Francisco 44, 1989
AL—96—Boston 54, New York 42, 1999
6-game series
AL—111—Toronto 59, Oakland 52, 1992
Toronto 65, Chicago 46, 1993
NL—106—Atlanta 59, Philadelphia 47, 1993
7-game series
AL—153—New York 78, Boston 75, 2004
NL—133—Florida 68, Chicago 65, 2003

**Fewest hits, series**
3-game series
NL—15—Atlanta vs St. Louis, 1982
AL—17—Minnesota vs Baltimore, 1969
4-game series
AL—22—Baltimore vs Oakland, 1974
Oakland vs Baltimore, 1974
NL—25—Pittsburgh vs Los Angeles, 1974
5-game series
AL—27—Los Angeles vs Chicago, 2005
NL—30—Pittsburgh vs Cincinnati, 1972
6-game series
NL—36—Florida vs Atlanta, 1997
AL—37—Seattle vs Cleveland, 1995
7-game series
NL—45—St. Louis vs Atlanta, 1996
AL—51—Kansas City vs Toronto, 1985

**Fewest hits by both clubs, series**
3-game series
AL—43—Detroit 25, Kansas City 18, 1984
NL—45—Pittsburgh 23, Cincinnati 22, 1970
4-game series
AL—44—Baltimore 22, Oakland 22, 1974
NL—62—Los Angeles 37, Pittsburgh 25, 1974
5-game series
AL—68—Baltimore 36, Oakland 32, 1973
Chicago 41, Los Angeles 27, 2005
NL—68—New York 37, Cincinnati 31, 1973
6-game series
NL—85—Atlanta 49, Florida 36, 1997
AL—88—Cleveland 45, New York 43, 1998
7-game series
NL—104—Atlanta 53, Pittsburgh 51, 1991
AL—116—Toronto 65, Kansas City 51, 1985

**Most hits by pinch-hitters, series**
AL—6—Toronto vs Kansas City, 1985 (7-game series)
NL—4—many series

**Most hits by pinch-hitters on both clubs, series**
NL—8—Pittsburgh 4, Los Angeles 4, 1974 (4-game series)
Chicago 4, Florida 4, 2003 (7-game series)
AL—8—Toronto 6, Kansas City 2, 1985 (7-game series)

### GAME AND INNING

**Most hits, game**
NL—22—Atlanta vs St. Louis, Oct 14, 1996
AL—22—New York vs Boston, Oct 16, 2004

**Most hits by both clubs, game**
AL—37—New York 22, Boston 15, Oct 16, 2004
NL—29—Atlanta 22, St. Louis 7, Oct 14, 1996

**Most hits by pinch-hitters, game**
AL—2—many teams
[3—Kansas City vs Detroit, Oct 3, 1984, 11 inn]
NL—2—many teams
[3—New York vs Atlanta, Oct 19, 1999, 11 inn]

**Most hits by pinch-hitters on both clubs, game**
NL—4—Los Angeles 2, Pittsburgh 2, Oct 6, 1974
[5—New York 3, Atlanta 2, Oct 19, 1999, 11 inn]
AL—3—Detroit 2, Minnesota 1, Oct 11, 1987
[3—Kansas City 3, Detroit 0, Oct 3, 1984, 11 inn]

**Fewest hits, game**
AL—1—Oakland vs Baltimore, Oct 9, 1974
Seattle vs New York, Oct 14, 2000
NL—1—Pittsburgh vs Cincinnati, Oct 12, 1990
St. Louis vs Houston, Oct 18, 2004

**Fewest hits by both clubs, game**
AL—6—Oakland 4, Baltimore 2, Oct 8, 1974
Baltimore 5, Oakland 1, Oct 9, 1974
Detroit 3, Kansas City 3, Oct 5, 1984
New York 5, Seattle 1, Oct 14, 2000
New York 4, Seattle 2, Oct 21, 2001
NL—4—Houston 3, St. Louis 1, Oct 18, 2004

**Most players with one or more hits, game**
NL—11—Chicago vs San Diego, Oct 2, 1984
Atlanta vs St. Louis, Oct 14, 1996
AL—10—New York vs Oakland, Oct 14, 1981
Toronto vs Kansas City, Oct 11, 1985
Seattle vs New York, Oct 20, 2001
Boston vs New York, Oct 20, 2004

**Most players with one or more hits by both clubs, game**
AL—18—New York 10, Oakland 8, Oct 14, 1981
[18—Boston 9, California 9, Oct 12, 1986, 11 inn]

NL—17—Atlanta 11, St. Louis 6, Oct 14, 1996
Atlanta 9, Arizona 8, Oct 20, 2001
[18—New York 10, Atlanta 8, Oct 19, 1999, 11 inn]

**Most hits, inning**
AL—10—Anaheim vs Minnesota, Oct 13, 2002, 7th
NL—8—St. Louis vs Los Angeles, Oct 13, 1985, 2nd
Pittsburgh vs Atlanta, Oct 13, 1992, 2nd

**Most hits by pinch-hitters, inning**
A.L.-NL—2—many times

**Most hits by both clubs, inning**
AL—13—Anaheim 10, Minnesota 3, Oct 13, 2002, 7th
NL—9—Philadelphia 5, Houston 4, Oct 12, 1980, 8th
Atlanta 6, St. Louis 3, Oct 14, 1996, 1st

**Most consecutive hits, inning (consecutive at-bats)**
AL—7—Baltimore vs Minnesota, Oct 3, 1970, 4th (1 SF during streak)
NL—6—Atlanta vs Arizona, Oct 17, 2001, 8th (1 BB during streak)
San Francisco vs St. Louis, Oct 9, 2002. 2nd

**Most consecutive hits, inning (consecutive plate appearances)**
NL—6—San Francisco vs St. Louis, Oct 9, 2002, 2nd
AL—6—Anaheim vs Minnesota, Oct 13, 2002, 7th

## SINGLES

**Most singles, total series**
AL—383—New York; 12 series, 61 G
NL—357—Atlanta; 11 series, 60 G

**Most singles, series**
3-game series
AL—29—New York vs Oakland, 1981
NL—27—St. Louis vs Atlanta, 1982
4-game series
AL—34—Oakland vs Boston, 1990
NL—31—Atlanta vs Cincinnati, 1995
5-game series
NL—45—Philadelphia vs Houston, 1980
AL—37—Minnesota vs Toronto, 1991
6-game series
AL—52—Toronto vs Chicago, 1993
NL—42—St. Louis vs Los Angeles, 1985
7-game series
NL—55—Atlanta vs St. Louis, 1996
AL—53—California vs Boston, 1986

**Most singles by both clubs, series**
3-game series
AL—46—New York 29, Oakland 17, 1981
NL—41—St. Louis 27, Atlanta 14, 1982
4-game series
AL—55—New York 33, Kansas City 22, 1978
NL—53—Atlanta 31, Cincinnati 22, 1995
5-game series
NL—73—Philadelphia 45, Houston 28, 1980
AL—73—Minnesota 37, Toronto 36, 1991
6-game series
AL—87—Toronto 52, Chicago 35, 1993
NL—79—San Diego 41, Atlanta 38, 1998
7-game series
AL—103—California 53, Boston 50, 1986
NL—90—Atlanta 55, St. Louis 35, 1996

**Fewest singles, series**
3-game series
AL—10—Oakland vs Baltimore, 1971
NL—13—Atlanta vs New York, 1969
4-game series
AL—14—Oakland vs Baltimore, 1974
NL—19—Los Angeles vs Philadelphia, 1983
5-game series
AL—19—Los Angeles vs Chicago, 2005
NL—20—Pittsburgh vs Cincinnati, 1972
Cincinnati vs New York, 1973
6-game series
AL—24—Seattle vs Cleveland, 1995
Seattle vs New York, 2000
NL—25—Philadelphia vs Atlanta, 1993
7-game series
NL—29—Houston vs St. Louis, 2004
AL—34—Kansas City vs Toronto, 1985
New York vs Boston, 2003

**Fewest singles by both clubs, series**
3-game series
AL—24—Baltimore 14, Oakland 10, 1971
NL—31—Philadelphia 17, Cincinnati 14, 1976
4-game series
AL—32—Baltimore 18, Oakland 14, 1974
NL—44—Philadelphia 25, Los Angeles 19, 1983
5-game series
AL—44—Chicago 25, Los Angeles 19, 2005
NL—47—Cincinnati 27, Pittsburgh 20, 1972
6-game series
AL—61—Cleveland 37, Seattle 24, 1995
NL—63—Atlanta 36, Florida 27, 1997
7-game series
NL—65—St. Louis 36, Houston 29, 2004
AL—78—Toronto 44, Kansas City 34, 1985

**Most singles by pinch-hitters, series**
NL—4—Pittsburgh vs Los Angeles, 1974 (4-game series)
Cincinnati vs Pittsburgh, 1990 (6-game series)
Atlanta vs Philadelphia, 1993 (6-game series)
AL—4—Toronto vs Kansas City, 1985 (7-game series)

**Most singles by pinch-hitters on both clubs, series**
NL—7—Pittsburgh 4, Los Angeles 3, 1974 (4-game series)
AL—4—Oakland 3, Detroit 1, 1972 (5-game series)
Toronto 4, Kansas City 0, 1985 (7-game series)
Detroit 3, Minnesota 1, 1987 (5-game series)

**Most singles, game**
AL—15—New York vs Oakland, Oct 14, 1981
NL—15—Atlanta vs St. Louis, Oct 14, 1996

**Most singles by both clubs, game**
AL—25—Kansas City 13, New York 12, Oct 4, 1978
NL—22—Atlanta 15, St. Louis 7, Oct 14, 1996

**Fewest singles, game**
AL—0—Oakland vs Baltimore, Oct 9, 1974
Seattle vs New York, Oct 14, 2000
NL—0—Pittsburgh vs Cincinnati, Oct 12, 1990

**Fewest singles by both clubs, game**
AL—2—Seattle 1, New York 1, Oct 21, 2001
NL—3—Houston 2, St. Louis 1, Oct 18, 2004

**Most singles, inning**
AL—9—Anaheim vs Minnesota, Oct 13, 2002, 7th
NL—8—St. Louis vs Los Angeles, Oct 13, 1985, 2nd

**Most singles by both clubs, inning**
AL—12—Anaheim 9, Minnesota 3, Oct 13, 2002, 7th
NL—8—Philadelphia 4, Houston 4, Oct 12, 1980, 8th
St. Louis 8, Los Angeles 0, Oct 13, 1985, 2nd

## DOUBLES

**Most doubles, total series**
AL—110—New York; 12 series, 61 G
NL—86—Atlanta; 11 series, 60 G

**Most doubles, series**
3-game series
NL—9—Atlanta vs New York, 1969
AL—8—Baltimore vs Minnesota, 1969
Oakland vs Baltimore, 1971
Boston vs Oakland, 1975
4-game series
AL—9—Baltimore vs Chicago, 1983
NL—8—Los Angeles vs Pittsburgh, 1974
Los Angeles vs Philadelphia, 1978
5-game series
AL—13—New York vs Kansas City, 1976
Minnesota vs Detroit, 1987
Boston vs New York, 1999
NL—12—New York vs St. Louis, 2000
6-game series
NL—14—Atlanta vs Philadelphia, 1993
AL—12—Seattle vs New York, 2000
7-game series
AL—21—New York vs Boston, 2004
NL—20—Pittsburgh vs Atlanta, 1992

**Most doubles by both clubs, series**
3-game series
NL—17—Atlanta 9, New York 8, 1969
AL—15—Oakland 8, Baltimore 7, 1971
4-game series
AL—13—Baltimore 9, Chicago 4, 1983
NL—11—Los Angeles 8, Philadelphia 3, 1978
Atlanta 6, Cincinnati 5, 1995
5-game series
NL—23—New York 12, St. Louis 11, 2000
AL—21—New York 12, Kansas City 9, 1977
6-game series
NL—25—Atlanta 14, Philadelphia 11, 1993
AL—22—Seattle 12, New York 10, 2000
7-game series
AL—33—New York 21, Boston 12, 2004
NL—31—Pittsburgh 20, Atlanta 11, 1992

**Fewest doubles, series**
3-game series
NL—1—Atlanta vs St. Louis, 1982
AL—1—Kansas City vs Detroit, 1984
4-game series
AL—1—Baltimore vs Oakland, 1974

NL—1—Pittsburgh vs Los Angeles, 1974
5-game series
NL—3—Los Angeles vs Montreal, 1981
San Francisco vs St. Louis, 2002
AL—4—Milwaukee vs California, 1982
Detroit vs Minnesota, 1987
Baltimore vs New York, 1996
New York vs Boston, 1999
Seattle vs New York, 2001
6-game series
AL—3—Cleveland vs New York, 1998
NL—4—New York vs Houston, 1986
Atlanta vs San Diego, 1998
7-game series
NL—4—St. Louis vs San Francisco, 1987
St. Louis vs Atlanta, 1996
AL—9—Kansas City vs Toronto, 1985
Boston vs New York, 2003

**Fewest doubles by both clubs, series**
3-game series
NL—5—St. Louis 4, Atlanta 1, 1982
AL—5—Detroit 4, Kansas City 1, 1984
4-game series
AL—5—Oakland 4, Baltimore 1, 1974
NL—9—San Francisco 5, Pittsburgh 4, 1971
Los Angeles 8, Pittsburgh 1, 1974
Los Angeles 6, Philadelphia 3, 1977
Los Angeles 5, Philadelphia 4, 1983
5-game series
NL—10—Montreal 7, Los Angeles 3, 1981
AL—11—New York 7, Seattle 4, 2001
6-game series
NL—10—Houston 6, New York 4, 1986
AL—11—New York 8, Cleveland 3, 1998
7-game series
NL—11—San Francisco 7, St. Louis 4, 1987
AL—21—New York 12, Boston 9, 2003

**Most doubles by pinch-hitters, series**
NL—3—St. Louis vs New York, 2000 (5-game series)
AL—2—Toronto vs Kansas City, 1985 (7-game series)

**Most doubles by pinch-hitters on both clubs, series**
AL—3—Toronto 2, Kansas City 1, 1985 (7-game series)
NL—3—St. Louis 3, New York 0, 2000 (5-game series)

**Most doubles, game**
AL—8—New York vs Boston, Oct 16, 2004
NL—6—Philadelphia vs Cincinnati, Oct 12, 1976
New York vs St. Louis, Oct 15, 2000

**Most doubles by both clubs, game**
AL—13—New York 8, Boston 5, Oct 16, 2004
NL—8—Los Angeles 5, St. Louis 3, Oct 12, 1985
Atlanta 5, Philadelphia 3, Oct 9, 1993
New York 6, St. Louis 2, Oct 15, 2000
[8—Philadelphia 5, Atlanta 3, Oct 6, 1993, 10 inn]

**Most doubles, inning**
NL—5—New York vs St. Louis, Oct 15, 2000, 1st
AL—3—Oakland vs Baltimore, Oct 10, 1973, 2nd
Boston vs Oakland, Oct 4, 1975, 7th
Minnesota vs Detroit, Oct 8, 1987, 2nd
New York vs Boston, Oct 16, 2003, 8th

## TRIPLES

**Most triples, total series**
AL—13—Kansas City; 6 series, 27 G
NL—11—Atlanta; 11 series, 60 G

**Most triples, series**
3-game series
NL—3—Cincinnati vs Philadelphia, 1976
AL—1—many clubs
4-game series
AL—3—Kansas City vs New York, 1978
NL—3—Los Angeles vs Philadelphia, 1978
5-game series
NL—5—Houston vs Philadelphia, 1980
AL—4—Kansas City vs New York, 1976
6-game series
NL—4—Philadelphia vs Atlanta, 1993
AL—3—Toronto vs Chicago, 1993
Cleveland 3, Seattle 0, 1995
7-game series
NL—4—St. Louis vs San Francisco, 1987
Chicago vs Florida, 2003
AL—2—Boston vs California, 1986
Boston vs New York, 2003
New York vs Boston, 2004

**Most triples by both clubs, series**
3-game series
NL—4—Cincinnati 3, Philadelphia 1, 1976
AL—2—Baltimore 1, Minnesota 1, 1969
Baltimore 1, Oakland 1, 1971
Kansas City 1, New York 1, 1980
4-game series
NL—5—Los Angeles 3, Philadelphia 2, 1978
AL—4—Kansas City 3, New York 1, 1978
5-game series
AL—6—Kansas City 4, New York 2, 1976
NL—6—Houston 5, Philadelphia 1, 1980
6-game series
NL—4—Philadelphia 4, Atlanta 0, 1993
AL—4—Toronto 3, Chicago 1, 1993
7-game series
NL—7—Chicago 4, Florida 3, 2003
AL—3—Boston 2, New York 1, 2004

**Fewest triples, series**
AL-NL—0—many clubs

**Fewest triples by both clubs, series**
AL-NL—0—many times

**Most triples by pinch-hitters, series**
NL—1—Cincinnati vs Pittsburgh, 1970 (3-game series)
New York vs Houston, 1986 (6-game series)
Atlanta vs Pittsburgh, 1992 (7-game series)
St. Louis vs Atlanta, 1996 (7-game series)
AL—1—Seattle vs New York, 2001 (5-game series)

**Most triples, game**
NL—3—Philadelphia vs Atlanta, Oct 9, 1993
AL—2—Kansas City vs New York, Oct 13, 1976
Kansas City vs New York, Oct 8, 1977
Seattle vs New York, Oct 20, 2001

**Most triples by both clubs, game**
NL—3—Los Angeles 2, Philadelphia 1, Oct 4, 1978
Philadelphia 3, Atlanta 0, Oct 9, 1993
AL—2—Baltimore 1, Minnesota 1, Oct 6, 1969
Kansas City 1, New York 1, Oct 9, 1976
Kansas City 2, New York 0, Oct 13, 1976
Kansas City 2, New York 0, Oct 8, 1977
Detroit 1, Kansas City 1, Oct 2, 1984
Toronto 1, Chicago 1, Oct 9, 1993
Seattle 2, New York 0, Oct 20, 2001

**Most triples, inning**
AL—2—Kansas City vs New York, Oct 8, 1977, 3rd
NL—2—Philadelphia vs Atlanta, Oct 9, 1993, 4th
Chicago vs Florida, Oct 7, 2003, 1st

## HOME RUNS

### SERIES

**Most home runs, total series**
AL—69—New York; 12 series, 61 G
NL—53—Atlanta; 11 series, 60 G

**Most grand slams, total series**
NL—2—Los Angeles, 1977 (2)
Atlanta, 1992, 1997
AL—1—Baltimore, 1970
California, 1982
Cleveland, 1998
New York, 1999
Boston, 2004

**Most home runs, series**
3-game series
NL—6—New York vs Atlanta, 1969
AL—6—Baltimore vs Minnesota, 1970
4-game series
NL—8—Pittsburgh vs San Francisco, 1971
Los Angeles vs Philadelphia, 1978
AL—7—Oakland vs Boston, 1988
5-game series
AL—10—New York vs Baltimore, 1996
NL—9—Chicago vs San Diego, 1984
6-game series
AL—10—Toronto vs Oakland, 1992
NL—7—Philadelphia vs Atlanta, 1993
7-game series
NL—14—Houston vs St. Louis, 2004
AL—12—Boston vs New York, 2003

**Most home runs by both clubs, series**
3-game series
NL—11—New York 6, Atlanta 5, 1969
AL—9—Baltimore 6, Minnesota 3, 1970
4-game series
NL—13—Pittsburgh 8, San Francisco 5, 1971
Los Angeles 8, Philadelphia 5, 197
AL—9—New York 5, Kansas City 4, 1978
Oakland 7, Boston 2, 1988
5-game series
AL—19—New York 10, Baltimore 9, 1996
NL—14—San Francisco 7, St. Louis 7, 2002

6-game series
AL—14—Toronto 10, Oakland 4, 1992
NL—12—Philadelphia 7, Atlanta 5, 1993
7-game series
NL—25—Houston 14, St. Louis 11, 2004
AL—20—Boston 12, New York 8, 2003

**Fewest home runs, series**
3-game series
NL—0—Pittsburgh vs Cincinnati, 1970
Atlanta vs St. Louis, 1982
AL—0—Oakland vs New York, 1981
Kansas City vs Detroit, 1984
4-game series
NL—0—Cincinnati vs Atlanta, 1995
AL—0—Chicago vs Baltimore, 1983
Oakland vs Boston, 1990
5-game series
NL—0—Houston vs Philadelphia, 1980
AL—0—Minnesota vs Anaheim, 2002
6-game series
NL—1—Florida vs Atlanta, 1997
AL—2—Toronto vs Chicago, 1993
7-game series
AL—2—Toronto vs Kansas City, 1985
NL—2—St. Louis vs San Francisco, 1987

**Fewest home runs by both clubs, series**
3-game series
NL—1—St. Louis 1, Atlanta 0, 1982
AL—2—New York 2, Oakland 0, 1981
4-game series
AL—1—Boston 1, Oakland 0, 1990
NL—4—Atlanta 4, Cincinnati 0, 1995
5-game series
NL—1—Philadelphia 1, Houston 0, 1980
AL—4—Minnesota 3, Toronto 1, 1991
6-game series
AL—7—Chicago 5, Toronto 2, 1993
NL—7—Atlanta 6, Florida 1, 1997
7-game series
NL—8—New York 5, Los Angeles 3, 1988
Atlanta 5, Pittsburgh 3, 1991
AL—9—Kansas City 7, Toronto 2, 1985

**Most grand slams, series**
NL—2—Los Angeles vs Philadelphia, 1977
AL—1—Baltimore vs Minnesota, 1970
California vs Milwaukee, 1982
Cleveland vs New York, 1998
New York vs Boston, 1999
Boston vs New York, 2004

**Most home runs by pinch-hitters, series**
NL—2—Philadelphia vs Los Angeles, 1978 (4-game series)
St. Louis vs San Francisco, 2002 (5-game series)
AL—1—Baltimore vs California, 1979 (4-game series)
Kansas City vs Toronto, 1985 (7-game series)
Minnesota vs Toronto, 1991 (5-game series)
New York vs Boston, 1999 (5-game series)
Seattle vs New York, 2001 (5-game series)
New York vs Boston, 2003 (7-game series)

## GAME AND INNING

**Most home runs, game**
NL—5—Chicago vs San Diego, Oct 2, 1984
AL—4—Baltimore vs Oakland, Oct 4, 1971
Oakland vs Baltimore, Oct 7, 1973
Oakland vs Boston, Oct 8, 1988
New York vs Baltimore, Oct 12, 1996
Cleveland vs New York, Oct 9, 1998
Anaheim vs Minnesota, Oct 13, 2002

**Most home runs by both clubs, game**
NL—7—Florida 4, Chicago 3, Oct 7, 2003
AL—6—New York 3, Baltimore 3, Oct 13, 1996
New York 4, Boston 2, Oct 16, 2004

**Most consecutive games with one or more home runs, total series**
AL—10—Baltimore, last 3 G vs Chicago, 1983 (3 HR), all 5 G vs New York, 1996 (9 HR), first 2 G vs Cleveland, 1997 (3 HR)
NL—8—Houston, last G vs New York, 1986 (1 HR), all 7 G vs St. Louis, 2004 (8 HR)

**Most consecutive games with one or more home runs, series**
AL—6—Toronto vs Oakland, Oct 7, 8, 10, 11, 12, 14, 1992 (10 HR)
NL—7—Houston vs St. Louis, Oct 13, 14, 16, 17, 18, 20, 21, 2004 (14 HR)

**Most home runs, inning**
AL—3—Baltimore vs Minnesota, Oct 3, 1970, 4th (first 2 consec)
New York vs Baltimore, Oct 13, 1996, 3rd (first 2 consec)
Baltimore vs Cleveland, Oct 12, 1997, 3rd (last 2 consec)
Cleveland vs New York, Oct 9, 1998, 5th (last 2 consec)
NL—3—Florida vs Chicago, Oct 7, 2003, 3rd (last 2 consec)

**Most home runs by both clubs, inning**
AL—3—Baltimore 3, Minnesota 0, Oct 3, 1970, 4th
Toronto 2, Kansas City 1, Oct 11, 1985, 5th
Oakland 2, Boston 1, Oct 8, 1988, 2nd
New York 3, Baltimore 0, Oct 13, 1996, 3rd
Baltimore 3, Cleveland 0, Oct 12, 1997, 3rd
Cleveland 3, New York 0, Oct 9, 1998, 5th
NL—3—San Francisco 2, Pittsburgh 1, Oct 6, 1971, 2nd
Florida 3, Chicago 0, Oct 7, 2003, 3rd
Florida 2, Chicago 1, Oct 9, 2003, 6th

**Most consecutive home runs, inning**
AL—2—Baltimore (Cuellar, Buford) vs Minnesota, Oct 3, 1970, 4th
Minnesota (Killebrew, Oliva) vs Baltimore, Oct 4, 1970, 4th
Oakland (Rudi, Bando) vs Baltimore, Oct 7, 1973, 6th
New York (Cerone, Piniella) vs Kansas City, Oct 8, 1980, 2nd
Oakland (McGwire, Steinbach) vs Toronto, Oct 7, 1992, 2nd
New York (Fielder, Strawberry) vs Baltimore, Oct 13, 1996, 3rd
Baltimore (Baines, Palmeiro) vs Cleveland, Oct 12, 1997, 3rd
Cleveland (Thome, Whiten) vs New York, Oct 9, 1998, 5th
New York (Williams, T. Martinez) vs Seattle, Oct 13, 2000, 2nd
Seattle (E. Martinez, Olerud) vs New York, Oct 15, 2000, 5th
NL—2—Cincinnati (Perez, Bench) vs Pittsburgh, Oct 5, 1970, 1st
Cincinnati (Foster, Bench) vs Philadelphia, Oct 12, 1976, 9th
Los Angeles (Guerrero, Scioscia) vs Montreal, Oct 13, 1981, 8th
Chicago (Davis, Durham) vs San Diego, Oct 6, 1984, 4th
New York (Strawberry, McReynolds) vs Los Angeles, Oct 9, 1988, 4th
Atlanta (Jordan, Klesko) vs New York, Oct 16, 1999, 8th
Florida (Cabrera, Encarnacion) vs Chicago, Oct 7, 2003, 3rd
Florida (Lee, Cabrera) vs Chicago, Oct 8, 2003, 6th
St. Louis (Pujols, Rolen) vs Houston, Oct 14, 2004, 8th

## TOTAL BASES

**Most total bases, total series**
AL—906—New York; 12 series, 61 G
NL—774—Atlanta; 11 series, 60 G

**Most total bases, series**
3-game series
NL—65—New York vs Atlanta, 1969
AL—61—Baltimore vs Minnesota, 1970
4-game series
NL—80—Los Angeles vs Philadelphia, 1978
AL—70—Oakland vs Boston, 1988
5-game series
AL—91—New York vs Baltimore, 1996
NL—80—Chicago vs San Diego, 1984
6-game series
AL—99—Toronto vs Oakland, 1992
NL—88—Atlanta vs Philadelphia, 1993
7-game series
AL—130—New York vs Boston, 2004
NL—122—Chicago vs Florida, 2003

**Most total bases by both clubs, series**
3-game series
NL—116—New York 65, Atlanta 51, 1969
AL—100—Baltimore 61, Minnesota 39, 1970
4-game series
NL—137—Los Angeles 80, Philadelphia 57, 1978
AL—121—New York 62, Kansas City 59, 1978
5-game series
AL—161—New York 91, Baltimore 70, 1996
NL—155—San Francisco 78, Chicago 77, 1989
6-game series
NL—175—Atlanta 88, Philadelphia 87, 1993
AL—170—Toronto 99, Oakland 71, 1992
7-game series
NL—238—Chicago 122, Florida 116, 2003
AL—249—New York 130, Boston 119, 2004

**Fewest total bases, series**
3-game series
NL—16—Atlanta vs St. Louis, 1982
AL—21—Kansas City vs Detroit, 1984
4-game series
AL—31—Boston vs Oakland, 1990
NL—35—Pittsburgh vs Los Angeles, 1974
Cincinnati vs Atlanta, 1995
5-game series
AL—41—Los Angeles vs Chicago, 2005
NL—44—Montreal vs Los Angeles, 1981
6-game series
NL—47—Florida vs Atlanta, 1997
AL—60—Seattle vs Cleveland, 1995
7-game series
NL—65—St. Louis vs Atlanta, 1996
AL—83—Kansas City vs Toronto, 1985

**Fewest total bases by both clubs, series**
3-game series
NL—61—St. Louis 45, Atlanta 16, 1982
AL—64—Detroit 43, Kansas City 21, 1984

4-game series
AL—69—Oakland 37, Baltimore 32, 1974
NL—91—Los Angeles 56, Pittsburgh 35, 1974
5-game series
NL—99—Los Angeles 55, Montreal 44, 1981
AL—101—Detroit 52, Oakland 49, 1972
6-game series
NL—123—Atlanta 76, Florida 47, 1997
AL—142—Cleveland 77, New York 65, 1998
7-game series
NL—150—Atlanta 80, Pittsburgh 70, 1991
AL—173—Toronto 90, Kansas City 83, 1985

**Most total bases, game**
AL—44—New York vs Boston, Oct 16, 2004
NL—34—Chicago vs San Diego, Oct 2, 1984
Atlanta vs St. Louis, Oct 14, 1996

**Most total bases by both clubs, game**
NL—48—Chicago 31, Florida 17, Oct 8, 2003
AL—70—New York 44, Boston 26, Oct 16, 2004

**Fewest total bases, game**
NL—1—St. Louis vs Houston, Oct 18, 2004
AL—2—Baltimore vs Oakland, Oct 8, 1974
Oakland vs Baltimore, Oct 9, 1974
Kansas City vs Toronto, Oct 12, 1985
Seattle vs New York, Oct 14, 2000

**Fewest total bases by both clubs, game**
AL—6—Detroit 3, Kansas City 3, Oct 5, 1984
NL—7—Houston 6, St. Louis 1, Oct 18, 2004

**Most total bases, inning**
AL—16—Baltimore vs Minnesota, Oct 3, 1970, 4th
NL—16—Pittsburgh vs Atlanta, Oct 13, 1992, 2nd

**Most total bases by both clubs, inning**
AL—18—Baltimore 16, Minnesota 2, Oct 3, 1970, 4th
NL—17—San Francisco 11, Pittsburgh 6, Oct 6, 1971, 2nd

## EXTRA-BASE HITS

**Most extra-base hits, total series**
AL—188—New York; 12 series, 61 G
NL—150—Atlanta; 11 series, 60 G

**Most extra-base hits, series**
3-game series
NL—15—New York vs Atlanta, 1969
AL—13—Baltimore vs Minnesota, 1969, 1970
4-game series
NL—19—Los Angeles vs Philadelphia, 1978
AL—15—Oakland vs Boston, 1988
5-game series
AL—22—Minnesota vs Detroit, 1987
NL—20—Chicago vs San Diego, 1984
6-game series
NL—22—Philadelphia vs Atlanta, 1993
AL—19—Toronto vs Oakland, 1992
7-game series
AL—32—New York vs Boston, 2004
NL—28—Pittsburgh vs Atlanta, 1992

**Most extra-base hits by both clubs, series**
3-game series
NL—29—New York 15, Atlanta 14, 1969
AL—24—Baltimore 12, Oakland 12, 1971
4-game series
NL—29—Los Angeles 19, Philadelphia 10, 1978
AL—22—Kansas City 13, New York 9, 1978
5-game series
AL—33—Minnesota 22, Detroit 11, 1987
New York 20, Baltimore 13, 1996
Boston 20, New York 13, 1999
NL—30—New York 17, St. Louis 13, 2000
6-game series
NL—41—Philadelphia 22, Atlanta 19, 1993
AL—33—Seattle 17, New York 16, 2000
7-game series
NL—52—Chicago 27, Florida 25, 2003
AL—55—New York 32, Boston 23, 2004

**Fewest extra-base hits, series**
3-game series
NL—1—Atlanta vs St. Louis, 1982
AL—2—Kansas City vs Detroit, 1984
4-game series
NL—4—Pittsburgh vs Los Angeles, 1974
AL—4—Baltimore vs Oakland, 1974
Chicago vs Baltimore, 1983
Oakland vs Boston, 1990
5-game series
NL—8—New York vs Cincinnati, 1973
Los Angeles vs Montreal, 1981
Montreal vs Los Angeles, 1981
San Diego vs Chicago, 1984
Arizona vs Atlanta, 2001
AL—7—Toronto vs Minnesota, 1991
6-game series
NL—9—New York vs Houston, 1986
Florida vs Atlanta, 1997
Atlanta vs San Diego, 1998
St. Louis vs Houston, 2005
AL—10—Oakland vs Toronto, 1992
7-game series
NL—10—St. Louis vs San Francisco, 1987
St. Louis vs Atlanta, 1996
AL—17—Kansas City vs Toronto, 1985

**Fewest extra-base hits by both clubs, series**
3-game series
NL—8—St. Louis 7, Atlanta 1, 1982
AL—11—Detroit 9, Kansas City 2, 1984
4-game series
AL—10—Boston 6, Oakland 4, 1990
NL—15—Los Angeles 10, Philadelphia 5, 1977
5-game series
NL—16—Los Angeles 8, Montreal 8, 1981
AL—20—Detroit 11, Oakland 9, 1972
Minnesota 13, Toronto 7, 1991
6-game series
NL—20—Houston 11, New York 9, 1986
AL—24—Toronto 13, Chicago 11, 1993
7-game series
NL—27—San Francisco 17, St. Louis 10, 1987
AL—37—Boston 19, California 18, 1986

**Most extra-base hits, game**
AL—13—New York vs Boston, Oct 16, 2004 (8 doubles, 1 triple, 4 HR)
NL—8—Cincinnati vs Philadelphia, Oct 9, 1976 (5 doubles, 2 triples, 1 HR)
Chicago vs San Diego, Oct 2, 1984 (3 doubles, 5 HR)

**Most extra-base hits by both clubs, game**
AL—20—New York 13 (8 doubles, 1 triple, 4 HR), Boston 7 (5 doubles, 2 HR), Oct 16, 2004
NL—12—Philadelphia 7 (3 doubles, 3 triples, 1 HR), Atlanta 5 (5 doubles), Oct 9, 1993

## RUNS BATTED IN

**Most runs batted in, total series**
AL—279—New York; 12 series, 61 G
NL—235—Atlanta; 11 series, 60 G

**Most runs batted in, series**
3-game series
AL—24—Baltimore vs Minnesota, 1970
NL—24—New York vs Atlanta, 1969
4-game series
AL—25—Baltimore vs California, 1979
NL—23—Pittsburgh vs San Francisco, 1971
5-game series
AL—33—Minnesota vs Detroit, 1987
NL—29—San Francisco vs Chicago, 1989
6-game series
NL—32—Atlanta vs Philadelphia, 1993
AL—30—Toronto vs Oakland, 1992
7-game series
AL—44—New York vs Boston, 2004
NL—43—Atlanta vs St. Louis, 1996

**Most runs batted in by both clubs, series**
3-game series
NL—39—New York 24, Atlanta 15, 1969
AL—34—Baltimore 24, Minnesota 10, 1970
4-game series
AL—39—Baltimore 25, California 14, 1979
NL—37—Pittsburgh 23, San Francisco 14, 1971
Los Angeles 21, Philadelphia 16, 1978
5-game series
AL—54—Minnesota 33, Detroit 21, 1987
NL—50—San Francisco 29, Chicago 21, 1989
6-game series
NL—54—Atlanta 32, Philadelphia 22, 1993
AL—53—Toronto 30, Oakland 23, 1992
7-game series
AL—84—New York 44, Boston 40, 2004
NL—80—Chicago 41, Florida 39, 2003

**Fewest runs batted in, series**
3-game series
NL—3—Pittsburgh vs Cincinnati, 1970
Atlanta vs St. Louis, 1982
AL—4—Oakland vs New York, 1981
Kansas City vs Detroit, 1984
4-game series
AL—2—Chicago vs Baltimore, 1983
NL—4—Cincinnati vs Atlanta, 1995
5-game series
NL—8—Cincinnati vs New York, 1973

Montreal vs Los Angeles, 1981
AL—10—Oakland vs Detroit, 1972
Detroit vs Oakland, 1972
6-game series
AL—10—Seattle vs Cleveland, 1995
NL—16—St. Louis vs Houston, 2005
7-game series
NL—11—Pittsburgh vs Atlanta, 1991
AL—23—Toronto vs Kansas City, 1985.

**Fewest runs batted in by both clubs, series**
3-game series
NL—11—Cincinnati 8, Pittsburgh 3, 1970
AL—18—Detroit 14, Kansas City 4, 1984
4-game series
AL—18—Oakland 11, Baltimore 7, 1974
NL—22—Philadelphia 15, Los Angeles 7, 1983
5-game series
AL—20—Oakland 10, Detroit 10, 1972
NL—23—Los Angeles 15, Montreal 8, 1981
6-game series
AL—31—Cleveland 21, Seattle 10, 1995
NL—35—Houston 19, St. Louis 16, 2005
7-game series
NL—30—Atlanta 19, Pittsburgh 11, 1991
AL—49—Kansas City 26, Toronto 23, 1985

**Most runs batted in by pinch-hitters, series**
AL—4—Baltimore vs California, 1979 (4-game series)
Toronto vs Kansas City, 1985 (7-game series)
Detroit vs Minnesota, 1987 (5-game series)
New York vs Boston, 1999 (5-game series)
NL—4—Philadelphia vs Houston, 1980 (5-game series)

**Most runs batted in by pinch-hitters on both clubs, series**
AL—6—Detroit 4, Minnesota 2, 1987 (5-game series)
NL—5—Philadelphia 4, Houston 1, 1980 (5-game series)

**Most runs batted in, game**
AL—18—New York vs Boston, Oct 16, 2004
NL—14—Atlanta vs Philadelphia, Oct 7, 1993
Atlanta vs St. Louis, Oct 14, 1996
Atlanta vs St. Louis, Oct 17, 1996

**Most runs batted in by both clubs, game**
AL—25—New York 18, Boston 7, Oct 16, 2004
NL—17—New York 11, Atlanta 6, Oct 5, 1969
Atlanta 13, Pittsburgh 4, Oct 7, 1992
Atlanta 14, Philadelphia 3, Oct 7, 1993
[18—New York 9, Atlanta 9, Oct 19, 1999, 11 inn]

**Fewest runs batted in by both clubs, game**
NL—0—Atlanta 0, New York 0, Oct 15, 1999
AL—1—many clubs

**Most runs batted in, inning**
AL—9—Anaheim vs Minnesota, Oct 13, 2002, 7th
NL—8—St. Louis vs Los Angeles, Oct 13, 1985, 2nd
Florida vs Chicago, Oct 14, 2003, 8th

**Most runs batted in by both clubs, inning**
AL—11—Anaheim 9, Minnesota 2, Oct 13, 2002, 7th
NL—8—St. Louis 8, Los Angeles 0, Oct 13, 1985, 2nd
Florida 8, Chicago 0, Oct 14, 2003, 8th

**Most runs batted in by pinch-hitters, inning**
AL—4—New York vs Boston, Oct 17, 1999, 9th
NL—2—many clubs

## BASES ON BALLS

**Most bases on balls, total series**
AL—226—New York; 12 series, 61 G
NL—215—Atlanta; 11 series, 60 G

**Most bases on balls, series**
3-game series
NL—15—Cincinnati vs Philadelphia, 1976
AL—13—Baltimore vs Minnesota, 1969
Baltimore vs Oakland, 1971
4-game series
NL—30—Los Angeles vs Pittsburgh, 1974
AL—22—Oakland vs Baltimore, 1974
5-game series
NL—31—Houston vs Philadelphia, 1980
AL—27—New York vs Seattle, 2000
6-game series
AL—35—New York vs Cleveland, 1998
NL—31—Atlanta vs New York, 1999
7-game series
AL—33—New York vs Boston, 2004
NL—29—Atlanta vs Pittsburgh, 1992
Pittsburgh vs Atlanta, 1992

**Most bases on balls by both clubs, series**
3-game series
NL—27—Cincinnati 15, Philadelphia 12, 1976
AL—25—Baltimore 13, Minnesota 12, 1969
4-game series
NL—38—Los Angeles 30, Pittsburgh 8, 1974
AL—28—Baltimore 16, Chicago 12, 1983
Boston 18, Oakland 10, 1988
5-game series
NL—44—Houston 31, Philadelphia 13, 1980
AL—41—New York 23, Seattle 18, 2001
6-game series
AL—53—Chicago 32, Toronto 21, 1993
NL—53—San Diego 27, Atlanta 26, 1998
7-game series
AL—61—New York 33, Boston 28, 2004
NL—58—Atlanta 29, Pittsburgh 29, 1992

**Fewest bases on balls, series**
3-game series
AL—3—Boston vs Oakland, 1975
NL—6—Atlanta vs St. Louis, 1982
4-game series
AL—5—Baltimore vs Oakland, 1974
NL—5—Pittsburgh vs San Francisco, 1971
5-game series
AL—4—Los Angeles vs Chicago, 2005
NL—9—Pittsburgh vs Cincinnati, 1972
6-game series
NL—10—Cincinnati vs Pittsburgh, 1990
AL—15—Seattle vs Cleveland, 1995
7-game series
NL—11—St. Louis vs Atlanta, 1996
AL—16—Toronto vs Kansas City, 1985

**Fewest bases on balls by both clubs, series**
3-game series
AL—12—Oakland 9, Boston 3, 1975
NL—18—St. Louis 12, Atlanta 6, 1982
4-game series
NL—18—Los Angeles 9, Philadelphia 9, 1978
AL—21—Kansas City 14, New York 7, 1978
5-game series
AL—16—Anaheim 9, Minnesota 7, 2002
NL—19—Cincinnati 10, Pittsburgh 9, 1972
6-game series
NL—31—Houston 17, New York 14, 1986
St. Louis 16, Houston 15, 2005
AL—40—Cleveland 25, Seattle 15, 1995
7-game series
NL—33—San Francisco 17, St. Louis 16, 1987
AL—38—Kansas City 22, Toronto 16, 1985
New York 21, Boston 17, 2003

**Most bases on balls by pinch-hitters, series**
NL—4—Los Angeles vs New York, 1988 (7-game series)
AL—2—many clubs

**Most bases on balls by pinch-hitters on both clubs, series**
NL—6—Los Angeles 4, New York 2, 1988 (7-game series)
AL—3—California 2, Baltimore 1, 1979 (4-game series)
Toronto 2, Minnesota 1, 1991 (5-game series)
Boston 2, New York 1, 1999 (5-game series)

**Most bases on balls, game**
AL—11—Oakland vs Baltimore, Oct 9, 1974
New York vs Cleveland, Oct 11, 1998
NL—11—Los Angeles vs Pittsburgh, Oct 9, 1974

**Most bases on balls by both clubs, game**
AL—15—New York 10, Seattle 5, Oct 21, 2001
NL—13—St. Louis 8, Los Angeles 5, Oct 12, 1985
Atlanta 8, Pittsburgh 5, Oct 7, 1992

**Fewest bases on balls, game**
AL-NL—0—many clubs

**Fewest bases on balls by both clubs, game**
AL—1—Oakland 1, Baltimore 0, Oct 8, 1974
New York 1, Kansas City 0, Oct 9, 1976
Chicago 1, Los Angeles, Oct 11, 2005
Chicago 1, Los Angeles, Oct 12, 2005
NL—1—New York 1, Atlanta 0, Oct 16, 1999

**Most bases on balls by pinch-hitters, game**
NL—2—Los Angeles vs New York, Oct 8, 1988
[2—Pittsburgh vs Cincinnati, Oct 7, 1975, 10 inn
Los Angeles vs New York, Oct 9, 1988, 12 inn]
AL—2—California vs Baltimore, Oct 4, 1979
Baltimore vs Chicago, Oct 7, 1983

**Most bases on balls by pinch-hitters on both clubs, game**
NL—3—Los Angeles 2, New York 1, Oct 8, 1988
[3—Pittsburgh 2, Cincinnati 1, Oct 7, 1975, 10 inn]
AL—2—California 2, Baltimore 0, Oct 4, 1979
Baltimore 2, Chicago 0, Oct 7, 1983
Baltimore 1, Cleveland 1, Oct 9, 1997
[2—Detroit 1, Oakland 1, Oct 11, 1972, 10 inn]

**Most bases on balls, inning**
AL—4—Oakland vs Baltimore, Oct 9, 1974, 5th (consec)
NL—4—Philadelphia vs Los Angeles, Oct 7, 1977, 2nd (consec)

St. Louis vs Los Angeles, Oct 12, 1985, 1st
San Francisco vs Chicago, Oct 9, 1989, 8th

**Most bases on balls by both clubs, inning**
NL—6—St. Louis 4, Los Angeles 2, Oct 12, 1985, 1st
AL—4—many innings

**Most bases on balls by pinch-hitters, inning**
NL—2—Pittsburgh vs Cincinnati, Oct 7, 1975, 9th
Los Angeles vs New York, Oct 8, 1988, 8th
AL—2—Baltimore vs Chicago, Oct 7, 1983, 9th

## STRIKEOUTS

**Most strikeouts, total series**
NL—421—Atlanta; 11 series, 60 G
AL—370—New York; 12 series, 61 G

**Most strikeouts, series**
3-game series
NL—28—Cincinnati vs Pittsburgh, 1975
AL—27—Minnesota vs Baltimore, 1969
4-game series
AL—35—Oakland vs Boston, 1988
NL—33—Pittsburgh vs San Francisco, 1971
5-game series
AL—44—New York vs Boston, 1999
NL—42—Cincinnati vs New York, 1973
6-game series
AL—62—Cleveland vs Baltimore, 1997
NL—57—New York vs Houston, 1986
7-game series
NL—57—Pittsburgh vs Atlanta, 1991
Chicago vs Florida, 2003
AL—60—Boston vs New York, 2003

**Most strikeouts by both clubs, series**
3-game series
NL—46—Cincinnati 28, Pittsburgh 18, 1975
AL—41—Minnesota 27, Baltimore 14, 1969
Minnesota 22, Baltimore 19, 1970
4-game series
NL—61—Pittsburgh 33, San Francisco 28, 1971
AL—58—Oakland 35, Boston 23, 1988
5-game series
AL—82—New York 44, Boston 38, 1999
NL—71—Atlanta 39, Arizona 32, 2001
6-game series
AL—109—Cleveland 62, Baltimore 47, 1997
NL—105—Atlanta 54, Philadelphia 51, 1993
7-game series
AL—109—Boston 60, New York 49, 2003
NL—104—St. Louis 53, Atlanta 51, 1996

**Fewest strikeouts, series**
3-game series
NL—9—Philadelphia vs Cincinnati, 1976
AL—10—New York vs Oakland, 1981
4-game series
AL—13—California vs Baltimore, 1979
NL—16—Los Angeles vs Pittsburgh, 1974
5-game series
AL—15—New York vs Kansas City, 1976
NL—19—Houston vs Philadelphia, 1980
6-game series
AL—29—Toronto vs Oakland, 1992
NL—31—Los Angeles vs St. Louis, 1985
7-game series
NL—28—Atlanta vs Pittsburgh, 1992
AL—31—Boston vs California, 1986

**Fewest strikeouts by both clubs, series**
3-game series
NL—25—Cincinnati 16, Philadelphia 9, 1976
AL—26—Oakland 14, Boston 12, 1975
4-game series
NL—33—Pittsburgh 17, Los Angeles 16, 1974
AL—36—Baltimore 20, Oakland 16, 1974
5-game series
AL—33—Kansas City 18, New York 15, 1976
NL—48—Montreal 25, Los Angeles 23, 1981
6-game series
AL—62—Oakland 33, Toronto 29, 1992
NL—65—St. Louis 34, Los Angeles 31, 1985
7-game series
NL—70—Pittsburgh 42, Atlanta 28, 1992
AL—75—California 44, Boston 31, 1986

**Most strikeouts by pinch-hitters, series**
NL—7—Cincinnati vs New York, 1973 (5-game series)
AL—4—Minnesota vs Baltimore, 1970 (3-game series)
Oakland vs Detroit, 1972 (5-game series)
Anaheim vs Minnesota, 2002 (5-game series)
Minnesota vs Anaheim, 2002 (5-game series)

**Most strikeouts by pinch-hitters on both clubs, series**
NL—11—New York 6, Atlanta 5, 1999 (6-game series)
AL—8—Anaheim 4, Minnesota 4, 2002 (5-game series)

**Most strikeouts, game**
NL—15—Philadelphia vs Atlanta, Oct 10, 1993
Atlanta vs Florida, Oct 12, 1997
[15—Cincinnati vs Pittsburgh, Oct 7, 1975, 10 inn
New York vs Houston, Oct 14, 1986, 12 inn]
AL—15—Seattle vs New York, Oct 14, 2000
[21—Cleveland vs Baltimore, Oct 11, 1997, 12 inn]

**Most strikeouts by both clubs, game**
NL—25—Atlanta 15, Florida 10, Oct 12, 1997
[32—Atlanta 19, New York 13, Oct 17, 1999, 15 inn]
AL—22—New York 13, Seattle 9, Oct 10, 2000
New York 12, Boston 10, Oct 13, 2003
[33—Cleveland 21, Baltimore 12, Oct 11, 1997, 12 inn]

**Most strikeouts by pinch-hitters, game**
AL—4—Oakland vs Detroit, Oct 10, 1972
NL—4—Pittsburgh vs Atlanta, Oct 10, 1992

**Fewest strikeouts, game**
NL—0—Pittsburgh vs Los Angeles, Oct 6, 1974
AL—1—Baltimore vs Oakland, Oct 11, 1973
New York vs Kansas City, Oct 13, 1976
Kansas City vs New York, Oct 4, 1978
Toronto vs Kansas City, Oct 12, 1985
Boston vs Oakland, Oct 10, 1990

**Fewest strikeouts by both clubs, game**
AL—3—Oakland 2, Baltimore 1, Oct 11, 1973
Kansas City 2, New York 1, Oct 13, 1976
NL—4—Philadelphia 2, Cincinnati 2, Oct 12, 1976

**Most consecutive strikeouts, game**
AL—5—Cleveland vs Baltimore, Oct 11, 1997 (1 in 5th, 3 in 6th, 1 in 7th)
Boston vs New York, Oct 12, 2004 (3 in 4th, 2 in 5th)
NL—5—Atlanta vs Philadelphia, Oct 6, 1993 (3 in 1st, 2 in 2nd)
Arizona vs Atlanta, Oct 11, 2003 (3 in 8th, 2 in 9th)

**Most strikeouts, inning**
AL-NL—3—many clubs

**Most strikeouts by both clubs, inning**
AL-NL—5—many innings

**Most strikeouts by pinch-hitters, inning**
AL—2—Oakland vs Baltimore, Oct 5, 1971, 9th (consec)
NL—2—Cincinnati vs New York, Oct 7, 1973, 8th (consec)
Pittsburgh vs Atlanta, Oct 10, 1992, 8th
Cincinnati vs Atlanta, Oct 10, 1995, 10th (consec)
Atlanta vs San Diego, Oct 10, 1998, 6th (consec)
New York vs St. Louis, Oct 14, 2000, 9th (consec)

## SACRIFICE HITS

**Most sacrifice hits, total series**
NL—31—Atlanta; 11 series, 60 G
St. Louis; 8 series, 46 G
AL—22—Oakland; 10 series, 42 G

**Most sacrifice hits, series**
NL—8—San Francisco vs St. Louis, 2002 (5-game series)
Houston vs St. Louis, 2005 (6-game series)
AL—5—Boston vs Oakland, 1975 (3-game series)
California vs Milwaukee, 1982 (5-game series)
Chicago vs Toronto, 1993 (6-game series)

**Most sacrifice hits by both clubs, series**
NL—13—San Francisco 8, St. Louis 5, 2002 (5-game series)
AL—7—Oakland 4, Detroit 3, 1972 (5-game series)
California 5, Milwaukee 2, 1982 (5-game series)
California 4, Boston 3, 1986 (7-game series)

**Fewest sacrifice hits, series**
AL-NL—0—many clubs

**Fewest sacrifice hits by both clubs, series**
NL—0—Cincinnati 0, Pittsburgh 0, 1975 (3-game series)
AL—0—Baltimore 0, New York 0, 1996 (5-game series)

**Most sacrifice hits, game**
NL—3—Los Angeles vs Montreal, Oct 17, 1981
St. Louis vs Atlanta, Oct 10, 1982
San Francisco vs St. Louis, Oct 12, 2002
St. Louis vs Houston, Oct 21, 2004
Houston vs St. Louis, Oct 19, 2005
[3—Pittsburgh vs Cincinnati, Oct 3, 1979, 10 inn
Philadelphia vs Houston, Oct 8, 1980, 10 inn
Atlanta vs New York, Oct 19, 1999, 11 inn]

AL—3—California vs Milwaukee, Oct 10, 1982
[3—California vs Boston, Oct 12, 1986, 11 inn]

**Most sacrifice hits by both clubs, game**
NL—4—Los Angeles 3, Montreal 1, Oct 17, 1981
St. Louis 2, Atlanta 2, Oct 9, 1982
Atlanta 2, Philadelphia 2, Oct 13, 1993
[4—Pittsburgh 3, Cincinnati 1, Oct 3, 1979, 10 inn
Atlanta 3, New York 1, Oct 19, 1999, 11 inn]
AL—3—California 3, Milwaukee 0, Oct 10, 1982
Oakland 2, Boston 1, Oct 6, 1990
[3—Boston 2, California 1, Oct 11, 1986, 11 inn
California 3, Boston 0, Oct 12, 1986, 11 inn]

**Most sacrifice hits, inning**
NL—2—Philadelphia vs Cincinnati, Oct 10, 1976, 4th
AL—1—many clubs

## SACRIFICE FLIES

**Most sacrifice flies, total series**
NL—18—St. Louis; 8 series, 46 G
AL—14—New York; 12 series, 61 G

**Most sacrifice flies, series**
AL—4—Kansas City vs New York, 1976 (5-game series)
Toronto vs Oakland, 1992 (6-game series)
NL—4—San Diego vs Chicago, 1984 (5-game series)
St. Louis vs San Francisco, 1987 (7-game series)
St. Louis vs Houston, 2005 (6-game series)

**Most sacrifice flies by both clubs, series**
NL—6—San Diego 4, Chicago 2, 1984 (5-game series)
St. Louis 4, Houston 2, 2005 (6-game series)
AL—6—Toronto 4, Oakland 2, 1992 (6-game series)

**Most sacrifice flies, game**
NL—3—St. Louis vs Atlanta, Oct 7, 1982
AL—2—many clubs

**Most sacrifice flies by both clubs, game**
NL—3—St. Louis 3, Atlanta 0, Oct 7, 1982
St. Louis 2, San Francisco 1, Oct 11, 1987
AL—3—Chicago 2, Los Angeles 1, Oct 16, 2005

**Most sacrifice flies, inning**
AL—2—Baltimore vs Chicago, Oct 7, 1983, 9th
Detroit vs Minnesota, Oct 7, 1987, 8th
NL—2—San Diego vs Chicago, Oct 7, 1984, 6th

## HIT BY PITCH

**Most hit by pitch, total series**
AL—23—New York; 12 series, 61 G
NL—13—Atlanta; 11 series, 60 G

**Most hit by pitch, series**
AL—7—New York vs Boston, 2004 (7-game series)
NL—5—Houston vs St. Louis, 2004 (7-game series)

**Most hit by pitch by both clubs, series**
AL—8—Minnesota 5, Detroit 3, 1987 (5-game series)
New York 7, Boston 1, 2004 (7-game series)
NL—7—Houston 5, St. Louis 2, 2004 (7-game series)

**Most hit by pitch, game**
AL—3—Minnesota vs Detroit, Oct 11, 1987
Cleveland vs Baltimore, Oct 9, 1997
NL—3—San Francisco vs St. Louis, Oct 14, 2002
[3—Atlanta vs New York, Oct 19, 1999, 11 inn]

**Most hit by pitch by both clubs, game**
AL—4—Detroit 2, Minnesota 2, Oct 12, 1987
Cleveland 2, New York 2, Oct 11, 1998
NL—3—Atlanta 2, Florida 1, Oct 7, 1997
San Francisco 3, St. Louis 0, Oct 14, 2002
[3—Atlanta 3, New York 0, Oct 19, 1999, 11 inn]

**Most hit by pitch, inning**
AL—3—Cleveland vs Baltimore, Oct 9, 1997, 1st
NL—2—Atlanta vs New York, Oct 19, 1999, 1st

# INDIVIDUAL BASERUNNING

## STOLEN BASES

**Most stolen bases, career**
ML—17—Rickey Henderson, Oakland AL, 1981, 1989, 1990, 1992; Toronto AL, 1993; New York NL, 1999; Seattle AL; 2000; 7 series, 33 G
AL—16—Rickey Henderson, Oakland, 1981, 1989, 1990, 1992; Toronto, 1993; Seattle, 2000; 6 series, 27 G
NL—9—Davey Lopes, Los Angeles, 1974, 1977, 1978, 1981; Chicago, 1984; Houston, 1986; 6 series, 22 G

**Most stolen bases, series**
3-game series
NL—4—Joe Morgan, Cincinnati, 1975
AL—2—Juan Beniquez, Boston, 1975
Amos Otis, Kansas City, 1980
Rickey Henderson, Oakland, 1981
4-game series
AL—4—Amos Otis, Kansas City, 1978
NL—3—Davey Lopes, Los Angeles, 1974
5-game series
AL—8—Rickey Henderson, Oakland, 1989
NL—5—Davey Lopes, Los Angeles, 1981
6-game series
AL—7—Willie Wilson, Oakland, 1992
NL—3—Billy Hatcher, Houston, 1986
Barry Larkin, Cincinnati, 1990
Chipper Jones, Atlanta, 1999
Gerald Williams, Atlanta, 1999
7-game series
NL—7—Ron Gant, Atlanta, 1991
AL—2—Johnny Damon, Boston, 2004

**Most stolen bases, game**
AL—4—Rickey Henderson, Oakland, Oct 4, 1989
NL—3—Joe Morgan, Cincinnati, Oct 4, 1975
Ken Griffey Sr., Cincinnati, Oct 5, 1975
Ron Gant, Atlanta, Oct 10, 1991
Edgar Renteria, St. Louis, Oct 12, 2000
[3—Steve Sax, Los Angeles, Oct 9, 1988, 12 inn]

**Most stolen bases by pinch-runner, game**
AL-NL—1—many players

**Most times stealing home, game**
AL—1—Reggie Jackson, Oakland, Oct 12, 1972, 2nd (part of double steal)
Marquis Grissom, Cleveland, Oct 11, 1997, 12th
NL—1—Jeff Branson, Cincinnati, Oct 11, 1995, 5th

**Most stolen bases, inning**
AL-NL—2—many players

## CAUGHT STEALING

**Most caught stealing, career**
AL—6—Hal McRae, Kansas City, 1976, 1977, 1978, 1980, 1984, 1985; 6 series, 28 G
NL—4—Willie McGee, St. Louis, 1982, 1985, 1987, 1996; 4 series, 22 G
Vince Coleman, St. Louis, 1985, 1987; 2 series, 10 G

**Most caught stealing by pinch-runner, career**
AL—2—Herb Washington, Oakland, 1974; 1 series, 2 G
NL—none

**Most caught stealing, series**
AL—4—Devon White, Toronto, 1992 (0 SB; 6-game series)
NL—3—Willie McGee, St. Louis, 1985 (2 SB; 6-game series)
Kevin Bass, Houston, 1986 (2 SB; 6-game series)
Juan Pierre, Florida, 2003 (1 SB; 7-game series)

**Most caught stealing by pinch-runner, series**
AL—2—Herb Washington, Oakland, 1974; 2 G
NL—none

**Most caught stealing, game**
AL—2—Trot Nixon, Boston, Oct 13, 2003
[2—Brooks Robinson, Baltimore, Oct 4, 1969, 12 inn]
NL—1—many players
[2—Kevin Bass, Houston, Oct 15, 1986, 16 inn]

**Most caught stealing by pinch-runner, game**
AL—1—Herb Washington, Oakland, Oct 6, 8, 1974
Sandy Alomar Sr., New York, Oct 14, 1976
Onix Concepcion, Kansas City, Oct 9, 1985
NL—none

**Most caught stealing, inning**
AL-NL—1—many players

# CLUB BASERUNNING

## STOLEN BASES

**Most stolen bases, total series**
AL—54—Oakland; 10 series, 42 G
NL—41—Atlanta; 11 series, 60 G

**Most stolen bases, series**
3-game series
NL—11—Cincinnati vs Pittsburgh, 1975
AL—4—Detroit vs Kansas City, 1984
4-game series
AL—9—Oakland vs Boston, 1990
NL—5—Los Angeles vs Pittsburgh, 1974
5-game series
AL—13—Oakland vs Toronto, 1989
NL—7—Philadelphia vs Houston, 1980
6-game series
AL—16—Oakland vs Toronto, 1992
NL—14—Atlanta vs New York, 1999
7-game series
NL—10—Atlanta vs Pittsburgh, 1991
AL—5—New York vs Boston, 2003

**Most stolen bases by both clubs, series**
3-game series
NL—11—Cincinnati 11, Pittsburgh 0, 1975
AL—4—New York 2, Oakland 2, 1981
Detroit 4, Kansas City 0, 1984
4-game series
AL—10—Oakland 9, Boston 1, 1990
NL—6—Los Angeles 5, Pittsburgh 1, 1974
Cincinnati 4, Atlanta 2, 1995
5-game series
AL—24—Oakland 13, Toronto 11, 1989
NL—11—Philadelphia 7, Houston 4, 1980
6-game series
AL—23—Oakland 16, Toronto 7, 1992
NL—21—Atlanta 14, New York 7, 1999
7-game series
NL—16—Atlanta 10, Pittsburgh 6, 1991
AL—7—New York 5, Boston 2, 2003
Boston 4, New York 3, 2004

**Fewest stolen bases, series**
AL-NL—0—many clubs

**Fewest stolen bases by both clubs, series**
3-game series
AL—0—Baltimore 0, Oakland 0, 1971
NL—1—Cincinnati 1, Pittsburgh 0, 1970
4-game series
NL—2—Los Angeles 2, Philadelphia 0, 1978
AL—1—Oakland 1, Boston 0, 1988
5-game series
NL—0—Cincinnati 0, New York 0, 1973
AL—3—Milwaukee 2, California 1, 1982
New York 3, Baltimore 0, 1996
6-game series
NL—2—Philadelphia 2, Atlanta 0, 1993
AL—7—New York 4, Seattle 3, 2000
7-game series
AL—2—Boston 1, California 1, 1986
NL—5—Atlanta 4, St. Louis 1, 1996
Florida 4, Chicago 1, 2003

**Most stolen bases, game**
NL—7—Cincinnati vs Pittsburgh, Oct 5, 1975
AL—6—Oakland vs Toronto, Oct 4, 1989
Oakland vs Toronto, Oct 8, 1992

**Most stolen bases by both clubs, game**
AL—8—Oakland 6, Toronto 2, Oct 4, 1989
Oakland 6, Toronto 2, Oct 8, 1992
NL—7—Cincinnati 7, Pittsburgh 0, Oct 5, 1975
[8—Atlanta 6, New York 2, Oct 19, 1999, 11 inn]

**Longest game with no stolen bases**
NL—16 inn—New York vs Houston, Oct 15, 1986
AL—14 inn—Boston vs New York, Oct 18, 2004
New York vs Boston, Oct 18, 2004

**Longest game with no stolen bases by either club**
NL—12 inn—New York 0, Cincinnati 0, Oct 9, 1973
AL—14 inn—Boston 0, New York 0, Oct 18, 2004

**Most stolen bases, inning**
AL—3—Oakland vs Detroit, Oct 12, 1972, 2nd
Oakland vs Toronto, Oct 8, 1992, 5th
NL—2—many clubs

## CAUGHT STEALING

**Most caught stealing, total series**
AL—22—Kansas City; 6 series, 24 G
NL—18—Atlanta; 11 series, 60 G

**Most caught stealing, series**
3-game series
AL—5—Kansas City vs New York, 1980
NL—2—Pittsburgh vs Cincinnati, 1970
Cincinnati vs Pittsburgh, 1979
Atlanta vs St. Louis, 1982
4-game series
AL—3—Oakland vs Baltimore, 1974
Baltimore vs Oakland, 1974
Kansas City vs New York, 1978
Oakland vs Boston, 1988, 1990
NL—3—Cincinnati vs Atlanta, 1995
5-game series
AL—5—Kansas City vs New York, 1976
NL—3—Philadelphia vs Houston, 1980
Chicago vs San Diego, 1984
6-game series
NL—6—St. Louis vs Los Angeles, 1985
AL—5—Toronto vs Oakland, 1992
7-game series
AL—5—Boston vs New York, 2003
NL—4—San Francisco vs St. Louis, 1987
St. Louis vs San Francisco, 1987
Atlanta vs Pittsburgh, 1991
Houston vs St. Louis, 2004

**Most caught stealing by both clubs, series**
3-game series
AL—5—Kansas City 5, New York 0, 1980
NL—3—Pittsburgh 2, Cincinnati 1, 1970
4-game series
AL—6—Oakland 3, Baltimore 3, 1974
NL—4—Cincinnati 3, Atlanta 1, 1995
5-game series
AL—8—Kansas City 5, New York 3, 1976
NL—5—Chicago 3, San Diego 2, 1984
6-game series
NL—7—St. Louis 6, Los Angeles 1, 1985
AL—7—Toronto 5, Oakland 2, 1992
7-game series
NL—8—San Francisco 4, St. Louis 4, 1987
AL—6—Kansas City 4, Toronto 2, 1985
Boston 5, New York 1, 2003

**Fewest caught stealing, series**
AL-NL—0—many clubs

**Fewest caught stealing by both clubs, series**
AL-NL—0—many clubs

**Most caught stealing, game**
AL-NL—2—many clubs

**Most caught stealing by both clubs, game**
AL—3—Baltimore 2, Oakland 1, Oct 10, 1973
Kansas City 2, New York 1, Oct 12, 1976
Milwaukee 2, California 1, Oct 9, 1982
NL—3—Chicago 2, San Diego 1, Oct 7, 1984
St. Louis 2, Los Angeles 1, Oct 12, 1985
San Francisco 2, St. Louis 1, Oct 7, 1987

**Most caught stealing, inning**
NL—2—St. Louis vs Los Angeles, Oct 10, 1985, 1st
St. Louis vs Los Angeles, Oct 12, 1985, 2nd
AL—1—many clubs

## LEFT ON BASE

**Most left on base, total series**
AL—481—New York; 12 series, 61 G
NL—441—Atlanta; 11 series, 60 G

**Most left on base, series**
3-game series
NL—31—St. Louis vs Atlanta, 1982
AL—30—New York vs Oakland, 1981
4-game series
NL—44—Los Angeles vs Pittsburgh, 1974
AL—35—Chicago vs Baltimore, 1983
Oakland vs Boston, 1990
5-game series
NL—45—Houston vs Philadelphia, 1980
AL—45—Boston vs New York, 1999
6-game series
AL—56—Toronto vs Chicago, 1993
NL—52—Philadelphia vs Atlanta, 1993
San Diego vs Atlanta, 1998
7-game series
AL—69—New York vs Boston, 2004
NL—58—Atlanta vs St. Louis, 1996

**Most left on base by both clubs, series**
3-game series
AL—50—Baltimore 28, Minnesota 22, 1969
New York 30, Oakland 20, 1981
NL—49—Cincinnati 25, Pittsburgh 24, 1979
4-game series
NL—68—Los Angeles 44, Pittsburgh 24, 1974

AL—59—Chicago 35, Baltimore 24, 1983
5-game series
NL—88—Houston 45, Philadelphia 43, 1980
AL—87—Boston 45, New York 42, 1999
6-game series
AL—106—Toronto 56, Chicago 50, 1993
NL—99—Philadelphia 52, Atlanta 47, 1993
7-game series
AL—122—New York 69, Boston 53, 2004
NL—105—Pittsburgh 54, Atlanta 51, 1991

**Fewest left on base, series**
3-game series
NL—12—Atlanta vs St. Louis, 1982
AL—14—Boston vs Oakland, 1975
4-game series
AL—16—Baltimore vs Oakland, 1974
NL—22—Los Angeles vs Philadelphia, 1977
5-game series
AL—17—Los Angeles vs Chicago, 2005
NL—24—Pittsburgh vs Cincinnati, 1972
6-game series
NL—33—Cincinnati vs Pittsburgh, 1990
AL—38—Seattle vs New York, 2000
7-game series
NL—34—St. Louis vs Atlanta, 1996
AL—44—Kansas City vs Toronto, 1985

**Fewest left on base by both clubs, series**
3-game series
AL—33—Oakland 19, Boston 14, 1975
NL—38—Pittsburgh 21, Cincinnati 17, 1975
4-game series
AL—45—Baltimore 23, California 22, 1979
NL—52—Los Angeles 28, Philadelphia 24, 1978
5-game series
AL—50—Chicago 33, Los Angeles 17, 2005
NL—54—Cincinnati 30, Pittsburgh 24, 1972
6-game series
NL—74—Pittsburgh 41, Cincinnati 33, 1990
AL—87—New York 48, Cleveland 39, 1998
New York 49, Seattle 38, 2000
7-game series
NL—80—San Francisco 43, St. Louis 37, 1987
AL—94—Toronto 50, Kansas City 44, 1985
Boston 49, New York 45, 2003

**Most left on bases, game**
NL—15—Philadelphia vs Atlanta, Oct 10, 1993
[19—Atlanta vs New York, Oct 17, 1999; 15 inn]
AL—15—New York vs Seattle, Oct 15, 2000.
[18—New York vs Boston, Oct 18, 2004, 14 inn]

**Most left on base, shutout defeat**
AL—10—Oakland vs Detroit, Oct 10, 1972 (lost 3-0)
[14—Baltimore vs Cleveland, Oct 15, 1997 (lost 1-0), 11 inn]
NL—10—Los Angeles vs Pittsburgh, Oct 8, 1974 (lost 7-0)
San Diego vs Chicago, Oct 2, 1984 (lost 13-0)
[11—Philadelphia vs Houston, Oct 10, 1980 (lost 1-0), 11 inn]

**Most left on base by both clubs, game**
NL—26—Philadelphia 15, Atlanta 11, Oct 10, 1993
[31—Atlanta 19, New York 12, Oct 17, 1999, 15 inn]
AL—25—Chicago 13, Toronto 12, Oct 5, 1993
[30—New York 18, Boston 12, Oct 18, 2004, 14 inn]

**Fewest left on base, game**
NL—0—Atlanta vs New York, Oct 16, 1999
AL—1—Baltimore vs New York, Oct 11, 1996
Los Angeles vs Chicago, Oct 14, 2005

**Fewest left on base by both clubs, game**
NL—3—New York 3, Atlanta 0, Oct 16, 1999
AL—6—Oakland 4, Detroit 2, Oct 8, 1972
New York 5, Baltimore 1, Oct 11, 1996
Boston 3, New York 3, Oct 11, 2003

# INDIVIDUAL PITCHING

## GAMES

**Most games, career**
AL—25—Mariano Rivera, New York, 1996, 1998-2001, 2003, 2004; 7 series
NL—18—Mark Wohlers, Atlanta, 1991-1993, 1995-1997; 6 series

**Most games, series**
3-game series
AL—3—Ron Perranoski, Minnesota, 1969
Jim Todd, Oakland, 1975
Willie Hernandez, Detroit, 1984
NL—3—Cecil Upshaw, Atlanta, 1969
Tom Hume, Cincinnati, 1979
Dave Tomlin, Cincinnati, 1979
4-game series
NL—4—Dave Giusti, Pittsburgh, 1971
Mark Wohlers, Atlanta, 1995
AL—4—Dennis Eckersley, Oakland, 1988
5-game series
NL—5—Tug McGraw, Philadelphia, 1980
AL—5—Jim Acker, Toronto, 1989
6-game series
NL—6—John Rocker, Atlanta, 1998, 1999
AL—5—Paul Assenmacher, Cleveland, 1997
Mike Jackson, Cleveland, 1997
Paul Shuey, Cleveland, 1998
Jose Paniagua, Seattle, 2000
7-game series
NL—6—Mark Petkovsek, St. Louis, 1996
Jason Isringhausen, St. Louis, 2004
AL—6—Alan Embree, Boston, 2004
Tom Gordon, New York, 2004

**Most consecutive games, series**
NL—6—John Rocker, Atlanta, Oct 7, 8, 10, 11, 12, 14, 1998
John Rocker, Atlanta, Oct 12, 13, 15, 16, 17, 19, 1999
AL—5—Jim Acker, Toronto, Oct 3, 4, 6, 7, 8, 1989
Paul Assenmacher, Cleveland, Oct 9, 11, 12, 13, 15, 1997
Mike Jackson, Cleveland, Oct 9, 11, 12, 13, 15, 1997
Alan Embree, Boston, Oct 12, 13, 16, 17, 18, 2004
Tom Gordon, New York, Oct 12, 13, 16, 17, 18, 2004

## GAMES STARTED

**Most games started, career**
NL—15—Tom Glavine, Atlanta, 1991-1993, 1995-1999, 2001; 9 series
AL—11—Roger Clemens, Boston, 1986, 1988, 1990; New York, 1999-2001, 2003; 7 series

**Most opening games started, career**
ML—4—Don Gullett, Cincinnati NL, 1972, 1975, 1976; New York AL, 1977 (won 2, lost 2)
NL—4—Steve Carlton, Philadelphia, 1976, 1977, 1980, 1983 (won 2, lost 1)
Greg Maddux, Chicago, 1989; Atlanta, 1997, 1999, 2001 (won 1, lost 3)
AL—4—Dave Stewart, Oakland, 1988-1990, 1992 (won 2, lost 0)

**Most games started, series**
AL—3—Dave Stieb, Toronto, 1985 (7-game series)
Roger Clemens, Boston, 1986 (7-game series)
NL—3—Orel Hershiser, Los Angeles, 1988 (7-games series)
Doug Drabek, Pittsburgh, 1992 (7-game series)
John Smoltz, Atlanta, 1992 (7-game series)

## GAMES RELIEVED

**Most games as relief pitcher, career**
AL—25—Mariano Rivera, New York, 1996, 1998-2001, 2003, 2004 (38.2 inn)
NL—18—Mark Wohlers, Atlanta, 1991-1993, 1995-1997 (19 inn)

**Most games as relief pitcher, series**
NL—6—Mark Petkovsek, St. Louis, 1996 (7-game series)
John Rocker, Atlanta, 1998 (6-game series)
John Rocker, Atlanta, 1999 (6-game series)
Jason Isringhausen, St. Louis, 2004 (7-game series)
AL—6—Alan Embree, Boston, 2004 (7-game series)
Tom Gordon, New York, 2004 (7-game series)

## COMPLETE GAMES

**Most complete games, career**
AL—5—Jim Palmer, Baltimore, 1969-1971, 1973, 1974
NL—2—many pitchers

**Most consecutive complete games, career**
AL—4—Jim Palmer, Baltimore, 1969 (1), 1970 (1), 1971 (1), 1973 (1); won 4, lost 0
NL—2—Tommy John, Los Angeles, 1977 (1), 1978 (1); won 2, lost 0
Mike Scott, Houston, 1986 (2); won 2, lost 0
Danny Cox, St. Louis, 1987 (2); won 1, lost 1
Tim Wakefield, Pittsburgh, 1992 (2); won 2, lost 0

**Most complete games, series**
NL—2—Mike Scott, Houston, 1986 (6-game series)
Danny Cox, St. Louis, 1987 (7-game series)
Tim Wakefield, Pittsburgh, 1992 (7-game series)
AL—1—many pitchers

## INNINGS

**Most innings pitched, career**
NL—95.1—John Smoltz, Atlanta, 1991-1993, 1995-1999, 2001; 9 series, 17 G
AL—75.1—Dave Stewart, Oakland, 1988-1990, 1992; Toronto, 1993; 5 series, 10 G

**Most innings pitched, series**
3-game series
AL—11—Dave McNally, Baltimore, 1969
Ken Holtzman, Oakland, 1975
NL—9.2—Dock Ellis, Pittsburgh, 1970
4-game series
NL—17—Don Sutton, Los Angeles, 1974
AL—16—Dave Stewart, Oakland, 1990
5-game series
AL—19—Mickey Lolich, Detroit, 1972
NL—17—Ray Burris, Montreal, 1981
6-game series
NL—18—Mike Scott, Houston, 1986
AL—16.2—Dave Stewart, Oakland, 1992
7-game series
NL—24.2—Orel Hershiser, Los Angeles, 1988
AL—22.2—Roger Clemens, Boston, 1986

**Most innings pitched, game**
AL—11—Dave McNally, Baltimore, Oct 5, 1969 (CG, won 1-0)
Ken Holtzman, Oakland, Oct 9, 1973 (CG, won 2-1)
NL—10—Joe Niekro, Houston, Oct 10, 1980 (no decision)
Dwight Gooden, New York, Oct 14, 1986 (no decision)

## GAMES WON

**Most games won, career**
AL—8—Dave Stewart, Oakland, 1988-1990, 1992; Toronto, 1993; 5 series, 10 G (lost 0)
NL—6—John Smoltz, Atlanta, 1991-1993, 1995-1999; 8 series, 15 G (lost 2)

**For a complete list of pitchers with four or more victories, see page 352.**

**Most games won without a defeat, career**
AL—8—Dave Stewart, Oakland, 1988-1990, 1992; Toronto, 1993
NL—3—Bruce Kison, Pittsburgh, 1971, 1972, 1974, 1975
Jesse Orosco, New York, 1986; Los Angeles, 1988

**Most opening games won, career**
NL—2—Don Gullett, Cincinnati, 1975, 1976
Steve Carlton, Philadelphia, 1980, 1983
John Smoltz, Atlanta, 1992, 1996
AL—2—Dick Hall, Baltimore, 1969, 1970
Tommy John, New York, 1981; California, 1982
Dave Stewart, Oakland, 1989, 1990
Jack Morris, Detroit, 1984; Minnesota, 1991
Mariano Rivera, New York, 1996, 1999

**Most consecutive games won, career**
AL—8—Dave Stewart, Oakland, Oct 9, 1988; Oct 3, 8, 1989; Oct 6, 10, 1990; Oct 12, 1992; Toronto, Oct 6, 12, 1993
NL—4—Steve Carlton, Philadelphia, Oct 6, 1978; Oct 7, 1980; Oct 4, 8, 1983
John Smoltz, Atlanta, Oct 6, 10, 1991; Oct 6, 10, 1992

**Most consecutive complete games won, career**
AL—4—Jim Palmer, Baltimore, Oct 6, 1969; Oct 5, 1970; Oct 5, 1971; Oct 6, 1973
NL—2—Tommy John, Los Angeles, Oct 8, 1977; Oct 5, 1978
Mike Scott, Houston, Oct 8, 12, 1986
Tim Wakefield, Pittsburgh, Oct 9, 13, 1992

**Most games won, series**
NL—3—Jesse Orosco, New York, 1986 (6-game series)
AL—2—many pitchers

**Most games won by relief pitcher, series**
NL—3—Jesse Orosco, New York, 1986 (6-game series)
AL—2—Sparky Lyle, New York, 1977 (5-game series)
Tom Henke, Toronto, 1985 (7-game series)
Jeff Reardon, Minnesota, 1987 (5-game series)
Francisco Rodriguez, Anaheim, 2002 (5-game series)

## SAVES

**Most saves, career**
ML—11—Dennis Eckersley, Oakland AL, 1988-1990, 1992; St. Louis NL, 1996
AL—10—Dennis Eckersley, Oakland, 1988-1990, 1992
Mariano Rivera, New York, 1996, 1998-2001, 2003, 2004
NL—5—Tug McGraw, New York, 1969, 1973; Philadelphia, 1977, 1980
Robb Nen, Florida, 1997; San Francisco, 2002
Brad Lidge, Houston, 2004, 2005

**Most saves, series**
3-game series
AL—2—Dick Drago, Boston, 1975
NL—2—Don Gullett, Cincinnati, 1970
4-game series
AL—4—Dennis Eckersley, Oakland, 1988
NL—3—Dave Giusti, Pittsburgh, 1971
5-game series
NL—3—Steve Bedrosian, San Francisco, 1989
Robb Nen, San Francisco, 2002
AL—3—Dennis Eckersley, Oakland, 1989
Rick Aguilera, Minnesota, 1991
6-game series
NL—3—Randy Myers, Cincinnati, 1990
Brad Lidge, Houston, 2005
AL—3—Tom Henke, Toronto, 1992
7-game series
NL—3—Alejandro Pena, Atlanta, 1991
Jason Isringhausen, St. Louis, 2004
AL—3—Scott Williamson, Boston, 2003

## GAMES LOST

**Most games lost, career**
NL—9—Tom Glavine, Atlanta, 1991-1993, 1995-1999, 2001; 9 series, 15 G
AL—4—Doyle Alexander, Baltimore, 1973; Toronto, 1985; Detroit, 1987; 3 series, 5 G

**Most games lost without a win, career**
NL—7—Jerry Reuss, Pittsburgh, 1974 (2), 1975; Los Angeles, 1981, 1983 (2), 1985
AL—4—Doyle Alexander, Baltimore, 1973; Toronto, 1985; Detroit, 1987 (2)

**Most consecutive games lost, career**
NL—7—Jerry Reuss, Pittsburgh, 1974 (2), 1975; Los Angeles, 1981, 1983 (2), 1985
AL—4—Doyle Alexander, Baltimore, 1973; Toronto, 1985; Detroit, 1987 (2)

**Most games lost, series**
NL—3—Doug Drabek, Pittsburgh, 1992
AL—2—many pitchers

## RUNS

**Most runs allowed, career**
NL—50—Greg Maddux, Chicago, 1989; Atlanta, 1993, 1995-1999, 2001; 8 series, 15 G
AL—29—Roger Clemens, Boston, 1986, 1988, 1990; New York, 1999-2001, 2003; 7 series, 11 G

**Most runs allowed, series**
3-game series
AL—9—Jim Perry, Minnesota, 1970
NL—9—Phil Niekro, Atlanta, 1969
4-game series
NL—11—Gaylord Perry, San Francisco, 1971
AL—10—Dave Frost, California, 1979
5-game series
NL—12—Greg Maddux, Chicago, 1989
AL—10—Doyle Alexander, Detroit, 1987
6-game series
NL—10—Joaquin Andujar, St. Louis, 1985
Tommy Greene, Philadelphia, 1993
AL—10—Jack McDowell, Chicago, 1993
7-game series
AL—13—Kirk McCaskill, California, 1986
NL—11—Doug Drabek, Pittsburgh, 1992
Tom Glavine, Atlanta, 1992
Todd Stottlemyre, St. Louis, 1996

**Most runs allowed, game**
NL—9—Phil Niekro, Atlanta, Oct 4, 1969
AL—8—Jim Perry, Minnesota, Oct 3, 1970
Roger Clemens, Boston, Oct 7, 1986
Hideki Irabu, New York, Oct 16, 1999

**Most runs allowed, inning**
NL—8—Tom Glavine, Atlanta, Oct 13, 1992, 2nd
AL—6—Jim Perry, Minnesota, Oct 3, 1970, 4th
Scott Erickson, Baltimore, Oct 13, 1996, 3rd

## EARNED RUNS

**Most earned runs allowed, career**
NL—36—Greg Maddux, Chicago, 1989; Atlanta, 1993, 1995-1999, 2001; 8 series, 15 G
AL—27—Roger Clemens, Boston, 1986, 1988, 1990; New York, 1999, 2000, 2001, 2003; 7 series, 11 G

**Most earned runs allowed, series**
3-game series
AL—8—Jim Perry, Minnesota, 1970
NL—6—Jerry Koosman, New York, 1969
Pat Jarvis, Atlanta, 1969
4-game series
NL—10—Gaylord Perry, San Francisco, 1971
AL— 9—Dave Frost, California, 1979
5-game series
NL—11—Greg Maddux, Chicago, 1989
AL—10—Doyle Alexander, Detroit, 1987
6-game series
NL—10—Tommy Greene, Philadelphia, 1993

AL—10—Jack McDowell, Chicago, 1993
7-game series
AL—11—Roger Clemens, Boston, 1986
NL—11—Todd Stottlemyre, St. Louis, 1996

**Most earned runs allowed, game**
AL—7—Jim Perry, Minnesota, Oct 3, 1970
Roger Clemens, Boston, Oct 7, 1986
Jack McDowell, Chicago, Oct 5, 1993
Hideki Irabu, New York, Oct 16, 1999
NL—8—Greg Maddux, Chicago, Oct 4, 1989

**Most earned runs allowed, inning**
NL—7—Tom Glavine, Atlanta, Oct 13, 1992, 2nd
AL—6—Jim Perry, Minnesota, Oct 3, 1970, 4th

## EARNED-RUN AVERAGE

**Lowest earned-run average, career (30 or more IP)**
AL—0.93—Mariano Rivera, New York, 1996, 1998-2001, 2003, 2004; 7 series, 25 G (38.2 IP)
NL—1.71—Don Sutton, Los Angeles, 1974, 1977, 1978; 3 series, 4 G (31.2 IP)

## SHUTOUTS AND SCORELESS INNINGS

**Most shutouts, series**
AL-NL—1—many pitchers

**For a complete list of shutouts, see page 348.**

**Most consecutive scoreless innings, career**
NL—22.1—Steve Avery, Atlanta, Oct 10 (8.1), Oct 16 (8), 1991; Oct 7 (6), 1992
AL—18—Ken Holtzman, Oakland, Oct 9 (9), 1973; Oct 6 (9), 1974

**Most consecutive scoreless innings, series**
NL—16.1—Steve Avery, Atlanta, Oct 10, 16, 1991
AL—11—Dave McNally, Baltimore, Oct 5, 1969

## HITS

**Most hits allowed, career**
NL—91—Tom Glavine, Atlanta, 1991-1993, 1995-1999, 2001; 9 series, 15 G
AL—63—Andy Pettitte, New York, 1996, 1998-2001, 2003; 6 series, 9 G

**Most consecutive hitless innings, career**
AL—10—Dave McNally, Baltimore, Oct 5 (7 inn), 1969; Oct 4 (3 inn), 1970
NL—7—Randy Johnson, Arizona, Oct 16 (7 inn), 2001

**Most hits allowed, series**
3-game series
AL—12—Ken Holtzman, Oakland, 1975
NL—10—Pat Jarvis, Atlanta, 1969
Pascual Perez, Atlanta, 1982
4-game series
NL—19—Gaylord Perry, San Francisco, 1971
AL—13—Dennis Leonard, Kansas City, 1978
5-game series
AL—18—Larry Gura, Kansas City, 1976
NL—16—Nolan Ryan, Houston, 1980
Scott Garrelts, San Francisco, 1989
Matt Morris, St. Louis, 2002
6-game series
AL—18—Jack McDowell, Chicago, 1993
NL—17—Orel Hershiser, Los Angeles, 1985
7-game series
AL—22—Roger Clemens, Boston, 1986
NL—19—Andy Benes, St. Louis, 1996

**Most hits allowed, game**
AL—13—Jack McDowell, Chicago, Oct 5, 1993
Hideki Irabu, New York, Oct 16, 1999
NL—11—Kevin Brown, Florida, Oct 14, 1997

**Most consecutive hitless innings, game**
AL—7—Dave McNally, Baltimore, Oct 5, 1969 (pitched all of an 11-inn game)
NL—7—Randy Johnson, Arizona, Oct 16, 2001

**Fewest hits allowed, game**
AL—1—Roger Clemens, New York, Oct 14, 2000
NL—2—Ross Grimsley, Cincinnati, Oct 10, 1972
Jon Matlack, New York, Oct 7, 1973
Dave Dravecky, San Francisco, Oct 7, 1987

**Most hits allowed, inning**
AL—6—Jim Perry, Minnesota, Oct 3, 1970, 4th
Kirk McCaskill, California, Oct 14, 1966, 3rd
NL—6—Greg A. Harris, San Diego, Oct 2, 1984, 5th
Tom Glavine, Atlanta, Oct 13, 1992, 2nd
Todd Stottlemyre, St. Louis, Oct 14, 1996, 1st
Matt Morris, St. Louis, Oct 9, 2002, 2nd

**Most consecutive hits allowed, inning (consecutive at-bats)**
AL—6—Jim Perry, Minnesota, Oct 3, 1970, 4th (includes SF)
NL—6—Matt Morris, St. Louis, Oct 9, 2002, 2nd

**Most consecutive hits allowed, inning (consecutive plate appearances)**
NL—6—Matt Morris, St. Louis, Oct 9, 2002, 2nd
AL—5—Dave Beard, Oakland, Oct 14, 1981, 4th
Jack Morris, Minnesota, Oct 8, 1991, 6th

## DOUBLES, TRIPLES AND HOME RUNS

**Most doubles allowed, game**
NL—6—Darryl Kile, St. Louis, Oct 15, 2000
AL—4—Dave McNally, Baltimore, Oct 3, 1971
Vida Blue, Oakland, Oct 3, 1971
Charlie Leibrandt, Kansas City, Oct 12, 1985
Hideki Irabu, New York, Oct 16, 1999
Orlando Hernandez, New York, Oct 17, 2000
Pedro Martinez, Boston, Oct 16, 2003

**Most triples allowed, game**
AL—2—Ed Figueroa, New York, Oct 8, 1977
NL—2—Steve Carlton, Philadelphia, Oct 9, 1976
Larry Christenson, Philadelphia, Oct 4, 1978
Tom Glavine, Atlanta, Oct 9, 1993
Josh Beckett, Florida, Oct 7, 2003
Carlos Zambrano, Chicago, Oct 7, 2003

**Most home runs allowed, career**
AL—12—Catfish Hunter, Oakland, 1971 (4), 1972 (2), 1974 (3); New York, 1978 (3)
NL—8—John Smoltz, Atlanta, 1991 (2), 1992, 1997, 1998 (2), 1999 (2)
Tom Glavine, Atlanta, 1991, 1992 (3), 1993, 1996 (2), 2001

**Most home runs allowed, series**
3-game series
AL—4—Catfish Hunter, Oakland, 1971
NL—3—Pat Jarvis, Atlanta, 1969
4-game series
NL—4—Steve Blass, Pittsburgh, 1971
AL—3—Catfish Hunter, Oakland, 1974
Catfish Hunter, New York, 1978
Mike Boddicker, Boston, 1988
5-game series
NL—5—Eric Show, San Diego, 1984
AL—4—Dave McNally, Baltimore, 1973
Andy Pettitte, New York, 1996
6-game series
AL—4—Andy Pettitte, New York, 1998
NL—3—Tommy Greene, Philadelphia, 1993
7-game series
AL—4—Mike Mussina, New York, 2003
NL—4—Tim Wakefield, Pittsburgh, 1992
Carlos Zambrano, Chicago, 2003

**Most home runs allowed, game**
AL—4—Catfish Hunter, Oakland, Oct 4, 1971
Dave McNally, Baltimore, Oct 7, 1973
Andy Pettitte, New York, Oct 9, 1998
NL—3—Pat Jarvis, Atlanta, Oct 6, 1969
Eric Show, San Diego, Oct 2, 1984
Danny Cox, St. Louis, Oct 10, 1987
Carlos Zambrano, Chicago, Oct 7, 2003

**Most grand slams allowed, game**
AL—1—Jim Perry, Minnesota, Oct 3, 1970, 4th
Moose Haas, Milwaukee, Oct 9, 1982, 8th
David Cone, New York, Oct 13, 1998, 5th
Rod Beck, Boston, Oct 17, 1999, 9th
Javier Vasquez, New York, Oct 20, 2004, 2nd
NL—1—Steve Carlton, Philadelphia, Oct 4, 1977, 7th
Jim Lonborg, Philadelphia, Oct 5, 1977, 4th
Greg Maddux, Chicago, Oct 4, 1989, 4th.
Bob Walk, Pittsburgh, Oct 7, 1992, 5th
Greg Maddux, Atlanta, Oct 10, 1996, 7th
Dan Miceli, San Diego, Oct 11, 1998, 7th

**Most home runs allowed, inning**
AL—3—Scott Erickson, Baltimore, Oct 13, 1996, 3rd
Jaret Wright, Cleveland, Oct 12, 1997, 3rd
Andy Pettitte, New York, Oct 9, 1998, 5th
NL—3—Carlos Zambrano, Chicago, Oct 7, 2003, 3rd

**Most consecutive home runs allowed, inning**
AL-NL—2—many pitchers

## TOTAL BASES

**Most total bases allowed, career**

NL—142—Tom Glavine, Atlanta, 1991-1993, 1995-1999, 2001; 9 series, 15 G
AL—112—Catfish Hunter, Oakland, 1971-1974; New York, 1976, 1978; 6 series, 10 G

**Most total bases allowed, series**

3-game series
NL—22—Pat Jarvis, Atlanta, 1969
AL—19—Jim Perry, Minnesota, 1969
Catfish Hunter, Oakland, 1971
Larry Gura, Kansas City, 1980
4-game series
NL—27—Steve Blass, Pittsburgh, 1971
AL—22—Dennis Leonard, Kansas City, 1978
5-game series
NL—32—Scott Garrelts, San Francisco, 1989
AL—26—Doyle Alexander, Detroit, 1987
6-game series
AL—26—Orlando Hernandez, New York, 2000
NL—23—Joaquin Andujar, St. Louis, 1985
7-game series
AL—32—Mike Mussina, New York, 2003
NL—31—Carlos Zambrano, Chicago, 2003

**Most total bases allowed, game**

AL—23—Hideki Irabu, New York, Oct 16, 1999
NL—23—Carlos Zambrano, Chicago, Oct 7, 2003

## BASES ON BALLS

**Most bases on balls, career**

NL—37—Tom Glavine, Atlanta, 1991-1993, 1995-1999, 2001; 9 series, 15 G
AL—26—Orlando Hernandez, New York, 1998-2001, 2004; 5 series, 7 G

**Most bases on balls, series**

3-game series
AL—7—Dave Boswell, Minnesota, 1969
NL—5—Fred Norman, Cincinnati, 1975
Steve Carlton, Philadelphia, 1976
4-game series
AL—13—Mike Cuellar, Baltimore, 1974
NL— 8—Jerry Reuss, Pittsburgh, 1974
Steve Carlton, Philadelphia, 1977
5-game series
AL—8—Jim Palmer, Baltimore, 1973
Paul Abbott, Seattle, 2001
NL—8—Steve Carlton, Philadelphia, 1980
Rick Sutcliffe, Chicago, 1984
6-game series
NL—11—Tom Glavine, Atlanta, 1997
AL— 9—Jack Morris, Toronto, 1992
Juan Guzman, Toronto, 1993
7-game series
AL—10—Dave Stieb, Toronto, 1985
NL—10—John Smoltz, Atlanta, 1992

**Most bases on balls, game**

AL—9—Mike Cuellar, Baltimore, Oct 9, 1974
NL—8—Fernando Valenzuela, Los Angeles, Oct 14, 1985

**Most bases on balls, inning**

AL—4—Mike Cuellar, Baltimore, Oct 9, 1974, 5th
NL—4—Burt Hooton, Los Angeles, Oct 7, 1977, 2nd
Bob Welch, Los Angeles, Oct 12, 1985, 1st

**Most consecutive bases on balls, inning**

AL—4—Mike Cuellar, Baltimore, Oct 9, 1974, 5th
NL—4—Burt Hooton, Los Angeles, Oct 7, 1977, 2nd

## STRIKEOUTS

**Most strikeouts, career**

NL—89—John Smoltz, Atlanta, 1991-1993, 1995-1999, 2001; 9 series, 17 G
AL—66—Mike Mussina, Baltimore, 1996, 1997; New York, 2001, 2003, 2004; 5 series, 9 G

**Most strikeouts, series**

3-game series
NL—14—John Candelaria, Pittsburgh, 1975
AL—12—Jim Palmer, Baltimore, 1970
4-game series
AL—14—Mike Boddicker, Baltimore, 1983
NL—13—Don Sutton, Los Angeles, 1974
Steve Carlton, Philadelphia, 1983
Pete Schourek, Cincinnati, 1995
5-game series
NL—19—Randy Johnson, Arizona, 2001
AL—15—Jim Palmer, Baltimore, 1973
6-game series
AL—25—Mike Mussina, Baltimore, 1997
NL—19—Mike Scott, Houston, 1986
Curt Schilling, Philadelphia, 1993
7-game series
NL—20—Dwight Gooden, New York, 1988
AL—18—Dave Stieb, Toronto, 1985

**Most strikeouts, game**

AL—15—Mike Mussina, Baltimore, Oct 11, 1997 (pitched first 7 inn of 9-inn game)
Roger Clemens, New York, Oct 14, 2000
NL—15—Livan Hernandez, Florida, Oct 12, 1997

**For a complete list of pitchers with 10 or more strikeouts in a game, see page 352.**

**Most strikeouts by relief pitcher, game**

AL—8—Wes Gardner, Boston, Oct 8, 1988, 4.2 IP
NL—7—Nolan Ryan, New York, Oct 6, 1969, 7 IP

**Most consecutive strikeouts, game**

NL—5—Curt Schilling, Philadelphia, Oct 6, 1993 (3 in 1st, 2 in 2nd)
AL—5—Mike Mussina, Baltimore, Oct 11, 1997 (1 in 5th, 3 in 6th, 1 in 7th)
Mike Mussina, New York, Oct 12, 2004 (3 in 4th, 2 in 5th)

**Most consecutive strikeouts from start of game**

NL—5—Curt Schilling, Philadelphia, Oct 6, 1993
AL—4—Nolan Ryan, California, Oct 3, 1979

**Most strikeouts, inning**

AL-NL—3—many pitchers

## HIT BATTERS, WILD PITCHES AND BALKS

**Most hit batters, career**

NL—5—Tom Glavine, Atlanta, 1992 (2), 1995-1997
Greg Maddux, Chicago, 1989; Atlanta, 1995, 1997, 1998, 2001
AL—4—Frank Tanana, California, 1979; Detroit, 1987 (3)
Mike Boddicker, Baltimore, 1983 (2); Boston, 1990 (2)
David Wells, Baltimore, 1996; New York, 1998 (2), 2003
Jeff Nelson, New York, 1998 (2), 1999, 2003
Pedro Martinez, Boston, 2003 (1), 2004 (3)

**Most hit batters, series**

AL—3—Frank Tanana, Detroit, 1987 (5-game series)
Jimmy Key, Baltimore, 1997 (6-game series)
Pedro Martinez, Boston, 2004 (7-game series)
NL—3—Matt Morris, St. Louis, 2002 (5-game series)

**Most hit batters, game**

AL—3—Frank Tanana, Detroit, Oct 11, 1987
Jimmy Key, Baltimore, Oct 9, 1997
NL—3—Matt Morris, St. Louis, Oct 14, 2002

**Most hit batters, inning**

AL—3—Jimmy Key, Baltimore, Oct 9, 1997, 1st
NL—2—Al Leiter, New York, Oct 19, 1999, 1st

**Most wild pitches, career**

ML—4—Orel Hershiser, Los Angeles NL, 1985, 1988 (2); Cleveland AL, 1995
Roger Clemens, Boston AL, 1988, 1990; New York AL, 2001; Houston NL, 2004
AL—4—Tommy John, New York, 1980; California, 1982
Juan Guzman, Toronto, 1991, 1992, 1993
NL—4—Alejandro Pena, Los Angeles, 1983; Atlanta 1991
Rick Ankiel, St. Louis, 2000

**Most wild pitches, series**

NL—4—Rick Ankiel, St. Louis, 2000 (5-game series)
AL—3—Tommy John, California, 1982 (5-game series)
Juan Guzman, Toronto, 1993 (6-game series)

**Most wild pitches, game**

AL—3—Tommy John, California, Oct 9, 1982
Juan Guzman, Toronto, Oct 5, 1993
NL—2—many pitchers

**Most wild pitches, inning**

AL—2—Chris Zachary, Detroit, Oct 8, 1972, 5th
Tommy John, California, Oct 9, 1982, 4th
David West, Minnesota, Oct 11, 1991, 5th
Juan Guzman, Toronto, Oct 5, 1993, 1st
Mariano Rivera, New York, Oct 17, 2001, 9th
NL—2—Jeff Calhoun, Houston, Oct 15, 1986, 16th
Sterling Hitchcock, San Diego, Oct 14, 1998, 2nd
Rick Ankiel, St. Louis, Oct 12, 2000, 1st
Rick Ankiel, St. Louis, Oct 16, 2000, 7th

**Most balks, game**

AL-NL—1—many pitchers

# CLUB PITCHING

## APPEARANCES

**Most appearances by pitchers, series**
3-game series
AL—14—Minnesota vs Baltimore, 1970
NL—13—Cincinnati vs Pittsburgh, 1979
4-game series
AL—16—Oakland vs Boston, 1988
NL—16—Atlanta vs Cincinnati, 1995
5-game series
AL—21—Baltimore vs New York, 1996
NL—22—St. Louis vs New York, 2000
San Francisco vs St. Louis, 2002
6-game series
NL—30—New York vs Atlanta, 1999
AL—29—Cleveland vs Baltimore, 1997
7-game series
NL—32—St. Louis vs Atlanta, 1996
AL—28—New York vs Boston, 2003

**Most appearances by pitchers of both clubs, series**
3-game series
NL—25—Cincinnati 13, Pittsburgh 12, 1979
AL—18—Minnesota 11, Baltimore 7, 1969
Minnesota 14, Baltimore 4, 1970
4-game series
NL—30—Atlanta 16, Cincinnati 14, 1995
AL—26—Oakland 16, Boston 10, 1988
Boston 15, Oakland 11, 1990
5-game series
AL—41—Baltimore 24, New York 17, 1996
NL—40—San Francisco 22, St. Louis 18, 2002
6-game series
NL—55—Atlanta 28, San Diego 27, 1998
AL—52—Cleveland 29, Baltimore 23, 1997
7-game series
NL—56—Florida 28, Chicago 28, 2003
AL—54—New York 28, Boston 26, 2003

## COMPLETE GAMES

**Most complete games, series**
3-game series
AL—2—Baltimore vs Minnesota, 1969
Baltimore vs Minnesota, 1970
Baltimore vs Oakland, 1971
NL—1—Cincinnati vs Pittsburgh, 1975
Pittsburgh vs Cincinnati, 1979
St. Louis vs Atlanta, 1982
4-game series
AL—2—Oakland vs Baltimore, 1974
NL—2—San Francisco vs Pittsburgh, 1971
Los Angeles vs Philadelphia, 1977
5-game series
AL—4—Chicago vs Los Angeles, 2005
NL—3—New York vs Cincinnati, 1973
6-game series
NL—2—Florida vs Atlanta, 1997
Houston vs New York, 1986
AL—1—Oakland vs Toronto, 1992
Toronto vs Oakland, 1992
Chicago vs Toronto, 1993
Cleveland vs New York, 1998
New York vs Seattle, 2000
7-game series
NL—3—Pittsburgh vs Atlanta, 1992
AL—1—Kansas City vs Toronto, 1985
Boston vs California, 1986
California vs Boston, 1986

**Most complete games by both clubs, series**
3-game series
AL—3—Baltimore 2, Oakland 1, 1971
NL—1—Cincinnati 1, Pittsburgh 0, 1975
Pittsburgh 1, Cincinnati 0, 1979
St. Louis 1, Atlanta 0, 1982
4-game series
AL—3—Oakland 2, Baltimore 1, 1974
NL—2—San Francisco 2, Pittsburgh 0, 1971
Los Angeles 2, Philadelphia 0, 1977
Los Angeles 1, Philadelphia 1, 1978
5-game series
AL—4—Baltimore 2, Oakland 2, 1973
Chicago 3, Los Angeles 0, 2005
NL—3—New York 3, Cincinnati 0, 1973
6-game series
NL—3—Houston 2, New York 1, 1986
Florida 2, Atlanta 1, 1997
AL—2—Oakland 1, Toronto 1, 1992
7-game series
NL—4—St. Louis 2, San Francisco 2, 1987
AL—2—Boston 1, California 1, 1986

## SAVES

**Most saves, series**
3-game series
NL—3—Cincinnati vs Pittsburgh, 1970
AL—2—Boston vs Oakland, 1975
4-game series
AL—4—Oakland vs Boston, 1988
NL—3—Pittsburgh vs San Francisco, 1971
5-game series
AL—3—Milwaukee vs California, 1982
Minnesota vs Detroit, 1987
Oakland vs Toronto, 1989
Minnesota vs Toronto, 1991
New York vs Boston, 1999
NL—3—San Francisco vs Chicago, 1989
San Francisco vs St. Louis, 2002
6-game series
NL—4—Cincinnati vs Pittsburgh, 1990
AL—3—Toronto vs Oakland, 1992
7-game series
NL—3—St. Louis vs San Francisco, 1987
Los Angeles vs New York, 1988
Atlanta vs Pittsburgh, 1991
St. Louis vs Houston, 2004
AL—3—Boston vs New York, 2003

**Most saves by both clubs, series**
3-game series
NL—3—Cincinnati 3, Pittsburgh 0, 1970
AL—2—Boston 2, Oakland 0, 1975
4-game series
AL—4—Oakland 4, Boston 0, 1988
NL—3—Pittsburgh 3, San Francisco 0, 1971
5-game series
NL—5—Houston 3, Philadelphia 2, 1980
AL—4—Minnesota 3, Toronto 1, 1991
6-game series
NL—6—Cincinnati 4, Pittsburgh 2, 1990
AL—4—Toronto 3, Oakland 1, 1992
7-game series
NL—5—Atlanta 3, Pittsburgh 2, 1991
St. Louis 3, Houston 2, 2004
AL—5—Boston 3, New York 2, 2003

**Fewest saves by one and both clubs, series**
AL-NL—0—many clubs

## RUNS AND SHUTOUTS

**Most runs allowed, total series**
AL—251—New York; 12 series, 61 G
NL—224—Atlanta; 11 series, 60 G

**Most shutouts won, total series**
NL—9—Atlanta, 1991 (3), 1995, 1996 (2), 1997, 1999, 2001
AL—6—Baltimore, 1969, 1973, 1979, 1983 (2), 1997

**For a complete list of shutouts, see page 348.**

**Most shutouts won, series**
NL—3—Atlanta vs Pittsburgh, 1991 (7-game series)
AL—2—Oakland vs Baltimore, 1974 (4-game series)
Baltimore vs Chicago, 1983 (4-game series)
Cleveland vs Seattle, 1995 (6-game series)

**Most consecutive shutouts won, series**
AL—2—Oakland vs Baltimore, Oct 6, 8, 1974
NL—2—St. Louis vs San Francisco, Oct 13, 14, 1987
Atlanta vs Pittsburgh, Oct 16, 17, 1991

**Most shutouts by both clubs, series**
NL—4—Atlanta 3, Pittsburgh 1, 1991 (7-game series)
AL—2—Oakland 1, Detroit 1, 1972 (5-game series)
Oakland 1, Baltimore 1, 1973 (5-game series)
Oakland 2, Baltimore 0, 1974 (4-game series)
Baltimore 2, Chicago 0, 1983 (4-game series)
Cleveland 2, Seattle 0, 1995 (6-game series)
Seattle 1, New York 1, 2000 (6-game series)

**Largest score, shutout game**
NL—15-0—Atlanta 15, St. Louis 0, Oct 17, 1996

AL—8-0—Baltimore 8, California 0, Oct 6, 1979

**Longest shutout game**

AL—11 inn—Baltimore 1, Minnesota 0, Oct 5, 1969
Cleveland 1, Baltimore 0, Oct 15, 1997
NL—11 inn—Houston 1, Philadelphia 0, Oct 10, 1980

**Most consecutive innings shutting out opponent, total series**

AL—30—Oakland vs Baltimore, Oct 5 (6th)-Oct 9 (8th), 1974
NL—26—Pittsburgh vs Atlanta, Oct 13 (2nd)-Oct 16 (8th), 1991

**Most consecutive innings shutting out opponent, series**

AL—30—Oakland vs Baltimore, Oct 5 (6th)-Oct 9 (8th), 1974
NL—26—Pittsburgh vs Atlanta, Oct 13 (2nd)-Oct 16 (8th), 1991

## WILD PITCHES AND BALKS

**Most wild pitches, series**

AL—5—Toronto vs Chicago, 1993 (6-game series)
NL—5—St. Louis vs New York, 2000 (5-game series)

**Most wild pitches by both clubs, series**

AL—7—Toronto 5, Chicago 2, 1993 (6-game series)
Anaheim 4, Minnesota 3, 2002 (5-game series)
NL—7—St. Louis 5, New York 2, 2000 (5-game series)
Florida 4, Chicago 3, 2003 (7-game series)

**Most balks, series**

AL—2—Baltimore vs Chicago, 1983 (4-game series)
NL—2—Pittsburgh vs Cincinnati, 1975 (3-game series)
New York vs Los Angeles, 1988 (7-game series)

**Most balks by both clubs, series**

NL—2—Pittsburgh 2, Cincinnati 0, 1975 (3-game series)
Philadelphia 1, Los Angeles 1, 1977 (4-game series)
New York 2, Los Angeles 0, 1988 (7-game series)
AL—2—Baltimore 2, Chicago 0, 1983 (4-game series)
Boston 1, Oakland 1, 1988 (4-game series)

# INDIVIDUAL FIELDING

## FIRST BASEMEN

### GAMES

**Most games, career**

ML—38—John Olerud, Toronto AL, 1991-1993; New York NL, 1999; Seattle AL, 2000, 2001; New York AL, 2004; 7 series (32 G in AL, 6 in NL)
AL—33—Tino Martinez, Seattle, 1995; New York, 1996, 1998-2001; 6 series
NL—23—Fred McGriff, Atlanta, 1993, 1995-1997; 4 series

### PUTOUTS, ASSISTS AND CHANCES

**Most putouts, career**

ML—313—John Olerud, Toronto AL, 1991-1993; New York NL, 1999; Seattle AL, 2000, 2001; New York AL, 2004; 7 series, 38 G (254 in AL, 59 in NL)
Tino Martinez, Seattle AL, 1995; New York AL, 1996, 1998-2001; St. Louis NL, 2002; 7 series, 37 G (256 in AL, 32 in NL)
AL—256—Tino Martinez, Seattle, 1995; New York, 1996, 1998-2001; 6 series, 33 G
NL—208—Steve Garvey, Los Angeles, 1974, 1977, 1978, 1981; San Diego, 1984; 5 series, 22 G

**Most putouts, series**

3-game series
NL—35—Keith Hernandez, St. Louis, 1982
AL—34—Boog Powell, Baltimore, 1969
4-game series
NL—44—Steve Garvey, Los Angeles, 1978
AL—44—Eddie Murray, Baltimore, 1979
5-game series
AL—57—Paul Konerko, Chicago, 2005
NL—53—Pete Rose, Philadelphia, 1980
6-game series
NL—67—Keith Hernandez, New York, 1986
AL—55—Rafael Palmeiro, Baltimore, 1997
7-game series
AL—72—Steve Balboni, Kansas City, 1985
NL—66—Derrek Lee, Florida, 2003

**Most putouts, game**

NL—17—Andres Galarraga, Atlanta, Oct 14, 1998
Albert Pujols, St. Louis, Oct 12, 2005
[21—Glenn Davis, Houston, Oct 15, 1986, 16 inn]
AL—15—Chris Chambliss, New York, Oct 14, 1976
Mark McGwire, Oakland, Oct 4, 1989
[16—John Olerud, Toronto, Oct 11, 1991, 10 inn
Herb Perry, Cleveland, Oct 13, 1995, 11 inn]

**Most putouts, inning**

AL-NL—3—many first basemen

**Most assists, career**

ML—33—Tino Martinez, Seattle AL, 1995; New York AL, 1996, 1998-2001; St. Louis NL, 2002; 7 series, 37 G (27 in AL, 6 in NL)
AL—27—Tino Martinez, Seattle, 1995; New York, 1996, 1998- 2001; 6 series, 33 G
NL—17—Keith Hernandez, St. Louis, 1982; New York, 1986, 1988; 3 series, 16 G

**Most assists, series**

3-game series
AL—5—Rich Reese, Minnesota, 1969
Bob Watson, New York, 1980
NL—5—Tony Perez, Cincinnati, 1975
Chris Chambliss, Atlanta, 1982
4-game series
NL—5—Steve Garvey, Los Angeles, 1978
AL—3—Eddie Murray, Baltimore, 1979, 1983
Tom Paciorek, Chicago, 1983
5-game series
AL—8—Kent Hrbek, Minnesota, 1991
NL—7—Pete Rose, Philadelphia, 1980
Julio Franco, Atlanta, 2001
6-game series
NL—12—Keith Hernandez, New York, 1986
AL—9—John Olerud, Toronto, 1993
7-game series
AL—8—Kevin Millar, Boston, 2003
NL—8—Albert Pujols, St. Louis, 2004

**Most assists, game**

NL—5—Tino Martinez, St. Louis, Oct 12, 2002
[7—Keith Hernandez, New York, Oct 15, 1986, 16 inn]
AL—4—Steve Balboni, Kansas City, Oct 12, 1985

**Most assists, inning**

AL-NL—2—many first basemen

**Most chances accepted, career**

ML—343—John Olerud, Toronto AL, 1991-1993; New York NL, 1999; Seattle AL, 2000, 2001; New York AL, 2004; 7 series, 38 G (280 in AL, 63 in NL)
AL—283—Tino Martinez, Seattle, 1995; New York, 1996, 1998-2001; 6 series; 33 G
NL—221—Steve Garvey, Los Angeles, 1974, 1977, 1978, 1981; San Diego, 1984; 5 series, 22 G

**Most chances accepted, series**

3-game series
NL—36—Keith Hernandez, St. Louis, 1982
AL—34—Boog Powell, Baltimore, 1969
4-game series
NL—49—Steve Garvey, Los Angeles, 1978
AL—47—Eddie Murray, Baltimore, 1979
5-game series
NL—60—Pete Rose, Philadelphia, 1980
AL—58—Paul Konerko, Chicago, 2005
6-game series
NL—79—Keith Hernandez, New York, 1986
AL—57—John Olerud, Toronto, 1993
Rafael Palmeiro, Baltimore, 1997
7-game series
AL—79—Steve Balboni, Kansas City, 1985
NL—72—Derrek Lee, Florida, 2003

**Most chances accepted, game**

NL—18—Steve Garvey, Los Angeles, Oct 6, 1978 (16 PO, 2 A)
[27—Keith Hernandez, New York, Oct 15, 1986 (20 PO, 7 A), 16 inn
AL—16—Steve Balboni, Kansas City, Oct 12, 1985 (12 PO, 4 A)
Kevin Millar, Boston, Oct 9, 2003 (12 PO, 4 A)
[16—George Hendrick, California, Oct 11, 1986 (14 PO, 2 A), 11 inn
John Olerud, Toronto, Oct 11, 1991 (16 PO), 10 inn
Herbert Perry, Cleveland, Oct 13, 1995 (16 PO), 11 inn]

**Fewest chances offered, game**

NL—2—Bob Robertson, Pittsburgh, Oct 2, 1971 (1 PO, 1 A)
AL—2—Carlos Quintana, Boston, Oct 6, 1990 (2 PO)

**Most chances accepted, inning**

AL-NL—3—many first basemen

### ERRORS AND DOUBLE PLAYS

**Most errors, career**

NL—4—Andres Galarraga, Atlanta, 1998; 1 series, 6 G
AL—3—Cecil Cooper, Boston, 1975; Milwaukee, 1982; 2 series, 8 G

Eddie Murray, Baltimore, 1979, 1983; 2 series, 8 G
Steve Balboni, Kansas City, 1984, 1985; 2 series, 10 G

**Most consecutive errorless games, career**
ML—24—Tino Martinez, New York AL, St. Louis NL, Oct 9, 1998-Oct 13, 2002 (20 in AL, 4 in NL)
AL—20—Tino Martinez, New York, Oct 9, 1998-Oct 22, 2001
NL—19—Steve Garvey, Los Angeles, San Diego, Oct 9, 1974-Oct 7, 1984

**Most errors, series**
NL—4—Andres Galarraga, Atlanta, 1998 (6-game series)
AL—2—many first basemen

**Most chances accepted, errorless series**
NL—79—Keith Hernandez, New York, 1986 (6-game series)
AL—64—Nick Johnson, New York, 2003 (7-game series)

**Most errors, game**
NL—1—many first basemen
[2—Andres Galarraga, Atlanta, Oct 7, 1998, 10 inn
Ryan Klesko, Atlanta, Oct 17, 1999, 15 inn]
AL—1—many first basemen
[1—many first basemen in extra innings]

**Most errors, inning**
NL—2—Andres Galarraga, Atlanta, Oct 7, 1998, 8th
Ryan Klesko, Atlanta, Oct 17, 1999, 6th
AL—1—many first basemen

**Most double plays, career**
ML—31—John Olerud, Toronto AL, 1991-1993; New York NL, 1999; Seattle AL, 2000, 2001; New York AL, 2004; 7 series, 38 G (26 in AL, 5 in NL)
AL—27—Tino Martinez, Seattle, 1995; New York, 1996, 1998-2001; 6 series, 33 G
NL—21—Steve Garvey, Los Angeles, 1974, 1977, 1978, 1981; San Diego, 1984; 5 series, 22 G

**Most double plays, series**
NL—10—Will Clark, San Francisco, 1987 (7-game series)
AL—9—Nick Johnson, New York, 2003 (7-game series)

**Most double plays started, series**
NL—2—Tino Martinez, St. Louis, Oct 12, 2002
AL—1—many first basemen

**Most double plays, game**
NL—4—Will Clark, San Francisco, Oct 10, 1987
AL—3—many first basemen

**Most double plays started, game**
NL—2—Tino Martinez, St. Louis, 2002 (5-game series)
AL—1—many first basemen

**Most unassisted double plays, game**
AL—1—Tino Martinez, New York, Oct 11, 1996
Tino Martinez, New York, Oct 22, 2001
Kevin Millar, Boston, Oct 13, 2003
John Olerud, New York, Oct 16, 2004
NL—1—John Mabry, St. Louis, Oct 14, 1996



## SECOND BASEMEN

### GAMES

**Most games, career**
NL—31—Mark Lemke, Atlanta, 1991-1993, 1995, 1996; 5 series
AL—28—Roberto Alomar, Toronto, 1991-1993; Baltimore, 1996, 1997; 5 series

### PUTOUTS, ASSISTS AND CHANCES

**Most putouts, career**
AL—69—Roberto Alomar, Toronto, 1991-1993; Baltimore, 1996, 1997; 5 series, 28 G
NL—63—Joe Morgan, Cincinnati, 1972, 1973, 1975, 1976, 1979; Houston, 1980; Philadelphia, 1983; 7 series, 27 G

**Most putouts, series**
3-game series
NL—12—Joe Morgan, Cincinnati, 1979
AL—12—Willie Randolph, New York, 1981
4-game series
AL—13—Bobby Grich, Baltimore, 1974
NL—13—Mark Lemke, Atlanta, 1995
5-game series
NL—18—Manny Trillo, Philadelphia, 1980
AL—16—Bobby Grich, Baltimore, 1973
6-game series
NL—19—Jose Lind, Pittsburgh, 1990
AL—18—Joey Cora, Chicago, 1993
7-game series
AL—19—Marty Barrett, Boston, 1986
NL—20—Mark Grudzielanek, Chicago, 2003

**Most putouts, game**
AL—7—Bobby Grich, Baltimore, Oct 6, 1974
[8—Roberto Alomar, Toronto, Oct 11, 1992, 11 inn]
NL—6—Dave Cash, Philadelphia, Oct 12, 1976
Dave Lopes, Los Angeles, Oct 13, 1981
Jose Lind, Pittsburgh, Oct 12, 1990
[7—Steve Sax, Los Angeles, Oct 9, 1988, 12 inn]

**Most putouts, inning**
NL—3—Joe Morgan, Cincinnati, Oct 10, 1976, 8th
Ryne Sandberg, Chicago, Oct 4, 1984, 5th
AL—3—Bobby Grich, Baltimore, Oct 11, 1973, 3rd
Dick Green, Oakland, Oct 8, 1974, 7th

**Most assists, career**
AL—86—Roberto Alomar, Toronto, 1991-1993; Baltimore, 1996, 1997; 5 series, 28 G
NL—85—Joe Morgan, Cincinnati, 1972, 1973, 1975, 1976, 1979; Houston, 1980; Philadelphia, 1983; 7 series, 27 G

**Most assists, series**
3-games series
NL—12—Tommy Helms, Cincinnati, 1970
AL—12—Willie Randolph, New York, 1981
4-game series
NL—18—Dave Lopes, Los Angeles, 1974
AL—14—Julio Cruz, Chicago, 1983
5-game series
NL—27—Joe Morgan, Cincinnati, 1973
AL—25—Roberto Alomar, Baltimore, 1996
6-game series
NL—21—Steve Sax, Los Angeles, 1985
AL—22—Carlos Baerga, Cleveland, 1995
7-game series
AL—28—Frank White, Kansas City, 1985
NL—24—Jose Lind, Pittsburgh, 1991

**Most assists, game**
AL—9—Joey Cora, Chicago, Oct 6, 1993
NL—8—Manny Trillo, Philadelphia, Oct 7, 1980
Mark Grudzielanek, Chicago, Oct 8, 2003
Mark Grudzielanek, St. Louis, Oct 12, 2005
[9—Wally Backman, Oct 14, 1986, 12 inn]

**Most assists, inning**
AL—3—Tony Phillips, Oakland, Oct 4, 1989, 5th
Joey Cora, Chicago, Oct 6, 1993, 6th
NL—3—Mark Lemke, Atlanta, Oct 13, 1993, 1st
Edgardo Alfonzo, New York, Oct 11, 2000, 1st

**Most chances accepted, career**
AL—155—Roberto Alomar, Toronto, 1991-1993; Baltimore, 1996, 1997; 5 series, 28 G
NL—148—Joe Morgan, Cincinnati, 1972, 1973, 1975, 1976, 1979; Houston, 1980; Philadelphia, 1983; 7 series, 27 G

**Most chances accepted, series**
3-game series
AL—24—Willie Randolph, New York, 1981
NL—23—Tommy Helms, Cincinnati, 1970
Joe Morgan, Cincinnati, 1979
4-game series
NL—29—Mark Lemke, Atlanta, 1995
AL—25—Bobby Grich, Baltimore, 1974
5-game series
NL—43—Manny Trillo, Philadelphia, 1980
AL—40—Roberto Alomar, Baltimore, 1996
6-game series
NL—38—Jose Lind, Pittsburgh, 1990
AL—38—Joey Cora, Chicago, 1993
7-game series
NL—43—Mark Grudzielanek, Chicago, 2003
AL—40—Marty Barrett, Boston, 1986

**Most chances accepted, game**
NL—13—Manny Trillo, Philadelphia, Oct 7, 1980 (5 PO, 8 A)
AL—12—Bobby Grich, Baltimore, Oct 6, 1974 (7 PO, 5 A, 1 E)
[13—Roberto Alomar, Toronto, Oct 11, 1992 (8 PO, 5 A), 11 inn]

**Fewest chances offered, game**
AL—0—Danny Thompson, Minnesota, Oct 4, 1970
Bobby Grich, California, Oct 10, 1986
Adam Kennedy, Anaheim, Oct 8, 2002
NL—0—Ryne Sandberg, Chicago, Oct 9, 1989

**Most chances accepted, inning**
AL-NL—3—many second basemen

### ERRORS AND DOUBLE PLAYS

**Most errors, career**
AL—5—Bobby Grich, Baltimore, 1973, 1974; California, 1979, 1982, 1986; 5 series, 21 G
NL—4—Dave Lopes, Los Angeles, 1974, 1977, 1978, 1981; 4 series, 17 G

**Most consecutive errorless games, career**
NL—27—Joe Morgan, Cincinnati, Houston, Philadelphia, Oct 7, 1972-Oct 8, 1983
AL—20—Willie Randolph, New York, Oakland, Oct 9, 1976-Oct 10, 1990

**Most errors, series**
AL—3—Joey Cora, Chicago, 1993 (6-game series)
NL—2—many second basemen

**Most chances accepted, errorless series**
AL—40—Marty Barrett, Boston, 1986 (7-game series)
NL—39—Joe Morgan, Cincinnati, 1973 (5-game series)

**Most errors, game**
AL—2—Dick Green, Oakland, Oct 8, 1974
Lance Blankenship, Oakland, Oct 10, 1992
[2—Dick Green, Oakland, Oct 9, 1973, 11 inn]
NL—1—many second basemen

**Most errors, inning**
AL-NL—1—many second basemen

**Most double plays, career**
AL—20—Roberto Alomar, Toronto, 1991-1993; Baltimore, 1996, 1997; 5 series, 28 G
NL—15—Joe Morgan, Cincinnati, 1972, 1973, 1975, 1976, 1979; Houston, 1980; Philadelphia, 1983; 7 series, 27 G

**Most double plays, series**
AL—9—Alfonso Soriano, New York, 2003 (7-game series)
NL—7—Rodney Scott, Montreal, 1981 (5-game series)

**Most double plays started, series**
NL—5—Steve Sax, Los Angeles, 1988 (7-game series)
AL—4—Alfonso Soriano, New York, 2003 (7-game series)

**Most double plays, game**
NL—4—Dave Lopes, Los Angeles, Oct 13, 1981
AL—3—Rob Wilfong, California, Oct 14, 1986
Bip Roberts, Cleveland, Oct 11, 1997
Alfonso Soriano, New York, Oct 13, 2003

**Most double plays started, game**
NL—2—many second basemen
AL—1—many second basemen

**Most unassisted double plays, game**
NL—1—Joe Morgan, Cincinnati, Oct 10, 1976
AL—none

## THIRD BASEMEN

### GAMES

**Most games, career**
NL—34—Terry Pendleton, St. Louis, 1985, 1987; Atlanta, 1991-1993, 1996; 6 series
Chipper Jones, Atlanta, 1995-2001, except 2000; 6 series
AL—27—George Brett, Kansas City, 1976-1978, 1980, 1984, 1985; 6 series

### PUTOUTS, ASSISTS AND CHANCES

**Most putouts, career**
AL—25—Sal Bando, Oakland, 1971-1975; 5 series, 20 G
NL—25—Terry Pendleton, St. Louis, 1985, 1987; Atlanta, 1991-1993, 1996; 6 series, 34 G

**Most putouts, series**
3-game series
AL—6—Brooks Robinson, Baltimore, 1969
Harmon Killebrew, Minnesota, 1969
Sal Bando, Oakland, 1971
NL—5—Tony Perez, Cincinnati, 1970
4-game series
NL—7—Ron Cey, Los Angeles, 1977
AL—7—Carney Lansford, Oakland, 1988
5-game series
AL—9—Doug DeCinces, California, 1982
NL—5—Richie Hebner, Pittsburgh, 1972
Ron Cey, Los Angeles, 1981
Graig Nettles, San Diego, 1984
Matt Williams, San Francisco, 1989
6-game series
NL—7—Chris Sabo, Cincinnati, 1990
Terry Pendleton, Atlanta, 1993
AL—6—Robin Ventura, Chicago, 1993
Matt Williams, Cleveland, 1997
7-game series
NL—11—Jeff King, Pittsburgh, 1992
AL—7—George Brett, Kansas City, 1985
Wade Boggs, Boston, 1986
Bill Mueller, Boston, 2004

**Most putouts, game**
AL—4—Carney Lansford, California, Oct 6, 1979
Wade Boggs, Boston, Oct 10, 1990
NL—3—many third basemen

**Most putouts, inning**
AL-NL—2—many third basemen

**Most assists, career**
NL—66—Mike Schmidt, Philadelphia, 1976-1978, 1980, 1983; 5 series, 20 G
AL—49—Brooks Robinson, Baltimore, 1969-1971, 1973, 1974; 5 series, 18 G
George Brett, Kansas City, 1976-1978, 1980, 1984, 1985; 6 series, 27 G

**Most assists, series**
3-game series
AL—11—Sal Bando, Oakland, 1975
NL—9—Mike Schmidt, Philadelphia, 1976
4-game series
NL—18—Mike Schmidt, Philadelphia, 1978
AL—13—Brooks Robinson, Baltimore, 1974
Todd Cruz, Baltimore, 1983
5-game series
NL—17—Mike Schmidt, Philadelphia, 1980
AL—16—Sal Bando, Oakland, 1972
6-game series
NL—19—Ray Knight, New York, 1986
AL—18—Matt Williams, Cleveland, 1997
7-game series
NL—19—Jeff King, Pittsburgh, 1992
AL—18—Doug DeCinces, California, 1986

**Most assists, game**
NL—8—Ron Cey, Los Angeles, Oct 16, 1981
AL—6—Sal Bando, Oakland, Oct 8, 1972
Todd Cruz, Baltimore, Oct 5, 1983
Tom Brookens, Detroit, Oct 11, 1987
Wade Boggs, New York, Oct 13, 1996
Cal Ripken, Baltimore, Oct 8, 1997
[7—Aurelio Rodriguez, Detroit, Oct 11, 1972, 10 inn]

**Most assists, inning**
NL—3—Ron Cey, Los Angeles, Oct 4, 1977, 4th
Ron Cey, Los Angeles, Oct 16, 1981, 8th
AL—3—Todd Cruz, Baltimore, Oct 5, 1983, 5th

**Most chances accepted, career**
NL—89—Terry Pendleton, St. Louis, 1985, 1987; Atlanta, 1991-1993, 1996; 6 series, 34 G
AL—72—Sal Bando, Oakland, 1971-1975; 5 series, 20 G

**Most chances accepted, series**
3-game series
AL—16—Brooks Robinson, Baltimore, 1969
NL—13—Mike Schmidt, Philadelphia, 1976
4-game series
NL—21—Ron Cey, Los Angeles, 1977
Mike Schmidt, Philadelphia, 1978
AL—19—Todd Cruz, Baltimore, 1983
5-game series
AL—22—Sal Bando, Oakland, 1972
NL—21—Ron Cey, Los Angeles, 1981
6-game series
NL—24—Terry Pendleton, St. Louis, 1985
Ray Knight, New York, 1986
AL—24—Matt Williams, Cleveland, 1997
7-game series
NL—30—Jeff King, Pittsburgh, 1992
AL—24—Doug DeCinces, California, 1986

**Most chances accepted, game**
NL—10—Ron Cey, Los Angeles, Oct 16, 1981 (2 PO, 8 A)
AL—9—Todd Cruz, Baltimore, Oct 5, 1983 (3 PO, 6 A)
Wade Boggs, Boston, Oct 10, 1990 (4 PO, 5 A)

**Fewest chances offered, game**
AL-NL—0—many players

**Most chances accepted, inning**
AL-NL—3—many third basemen

### ERRORS AND DOUBLE PLAYS

**Most errors, career**
AL—8—George Brett, Kansas City, 1976-1978, 1980, 1984, 1985; 6 series, 27 G
NL—5—Mike Schmidt, Philadelphia, 1976-1978, 1980, 1983; 5 series, 20 G

**Most consecutive errorless games, career**
NL—33—Terry Pendleton, St. Louis, Atlanta, Oct 10, 1985-Oct 17, 1996
AL—17—Sal Bando, Oakland, Oct 3, 1971-Oct 9, 1974
Carney Lansford, California, Oakland, Oct 3, 1979-Oct 8, 1992

**Most errors, series**
AL—3—George Brett, Kansas City, 1976 (5-game series)
Doug DeCinces, California, 1982 (5-game series)
Kelly Gruber, Toronto, 1991 (5-game series)
NL—3—Matt Williams, Arizona, 2001 (5-game series)

**Most chances accepted, errorless series**
NL—23—Scott Rolen, St. Louis, 2004 (7-game series)
AL—22—Sal Bando, Oakland, 1972 (5-game series)

**Most errors, game**
AL—2—George Brett, Kansas City, Oct 9, 1976
Doug DeCinces, California, Oct 9, 1982
Darrell Evans, Detroit, Oct 11, 1987
Kelly Gruber, Toronto, Oct 8, 1991
NL—2—Ron Cey, Los Angeles, Oct 5, 1974
Fernando Tatis, St. Louis, Oct 15, 2000

**Most errors, inning**
AL—2—George Brett, Kansas City, Oct 9, 1976, 1st
NL—2—Fernando Tatis, St. Louis, Oct 15, 2000, 6th

**Most double plays, career**
NL—8—Terry Pendleton, St. Louis, 1985, 1987; Atlanta, 1991-1993, 1996; 6 series, 34 G
AL—7—Doug DeCinces, Baltimore, 1979; California, 1982, 1986; 3 series, 16 G

**Most double plays, series**
NL—5—Jeff King, Pittsburgh, 1992 (7-game series)
AL—3—Carney Lansford, California, 1979 (4-game series)
Doug DeCinces, California, 1982 (5-game series)
Doug DeCinces, California, 1986 (7-game series)
Cal Ripken Jr., Baltimore, 1997 (6-game series)
Matt Williams, Cleveland, 1997 (6-game series)

**Most double plays started, series**
NL—5—Jeff King, Pittsburgh, 1992 (7-game series)
AL—3—Carney Lansford, California, 1979 (4-game series)
Doug DeCinces, California, 1986 (7-game series)
Cal Ripken Jr., Baltimore, 1997 (6-game series)
Matt Williams, Cleveland, 1997 (6-game series)

**Most double plays, game**
AL-NL—2—many third basemen

**Most double plays started, game**
AL-NL—2—many third basemen

**Most unassisted double plays, game**
NL—1—Mike Schmidt, Philadelphia, Oct 9, 1976
Jeff King, Pittsburgh, Oct 14, 1992
AL—none

## SHORTSTOPS

### GAMES

**Most games, career**
AL—41—Derek Jeter, New York, 1996, 1998-2001, 2003, 2004; 7 series
NL—29—Jeff Blauser, Atlanta, 1991-1993, 1995-1997; 6 series

### PUTOUTS, ASSISTS AND CHANCES

**Most putouts, career**
AL—83—Derek Jeter, New York, 1996, 1998-2001, 2003, 2004; 7 series, 41 G
NL—42—Bill Russell, Los Angeles, 1974, 1977, 1978, 1981, 1983; 5 series, 21 G

**Most putouts, series**
3-game series
AL—13—Leo Cardenas, Minnesota, 1969
NL—6—many shortstops
4-game series
NL—13—Bill Russell, Los Angeles, 1974
AL—9—Fred Patek, Kansas City, 1978
5-game series
NL—19—Garry Templeton, San Diego, 1984
AL—13—Fred Patek, Kansas City, 1976
6-game series
NL—21—Barry Larkin, Cincinnati, 1990
AL—16—Omar Vizquel, Cleveland, 1997
7-game series
AL—23—Derek Jeter, New York, 2004
NL—19—Edgar Renteria, St. Louis, 2004

**Most putouts, game**
NL—7—Garry Templeton, San Diego, Oct 4, 1984
AL—6—Mark Belanger, Baltimore, Oct 5, 1974
Bucky Dent, New York, Oct 5, 1977
Fred Patek, Kansas City, Oct 5, 1977
Manny Lee, Toronto, Oct 8, 1992
[7—Leo Cardenas, Minnesota, Oct 5, 1969, 11 inn]

**Most putouts, inning**
AL—3—Mark Belanger, Baltimore, Oct 5, 1974, 3rd
Fred Patek, Kansas City, Oct 5, 1977, 2nd
NL—3—Chris Speier, Montreal, Oct 14, 1981, 5th

**Most assists, career**
AL—104—Derek Jeter, New York, 1996, 1998-2001, 2003, 2004; 7 series, 41 G
NL—70—Larry Bowa, Philadelphia, 1976-1978, 1980; Chicago, 1984; 5 series, 21 G

**Most assists, series**
3-game series
AL—14—Mark Belanger, Baltimore, 1970
NL—14—Dave Concepcion, Cincinnati, 1979
4-game series
AL—17—Bert Campaneris, Oakland, 1974
NL—17—Larry Bowa, Philadelphia, 1977
5-game series
AL—26—Juan Uribe, Chicago, 2005
NL—16—Darrel Chaney, Cincinnati, 1972
Chris Speier, Montreal, 1981
6-game series
AL—26—Omar Vizquel, Cleveland, 1998
NL—24—Rey Ordonez, New York, 1999
7-game series
NL—26—Alex Gonzalez, Florida, 2003
AL—25—Derek Jeter, New York, 2003

**Most assists, game**
NL—9—Bill Russell, Los Angeles, Oct 5, 1978
AL—9—Kiko Garcia, Baltimore, Oct 4, 1979

**Most assists, inning**
AL-NL—3—many shortstops

**Most chances accepted, career**
AL—187—Derek Jeter, New York, 1996, 1998-2001, 2003, 2004; 7 series, 41 G
NL—107—Bill Russell, Los Angeles, 1974, 1977, 1978, 1981, 1983; 5 series, 21 G

**Most chances accepted, series**
3-game series
AL—25—Leo Cardenas, Minnesota, 1969
NL—17—Dave Concepcion, Cincinnati, 1979
4-game series
NL—29—Bill Russell, Los Angeles, 1974
AL—22—Kiko Garcia, Baltimore, 1979
Luis Rivera, Boston, 1990
5-game series
AL—33—Juan Uribe, Chicago, 2005
NL—31—Chris Speier, Montreal, 1981
6-game series
AL—37—Omar Vizquel, Cleveland, 1998
NL—36—Barry Larkin, Cincinnati, 1990
7-game series
AL—44—Derek Jeter, New York, 2003
NL—33—Edgar Renteria, St. Louis, 2004

**Most chances accepted, game**
NL—13—Bill Russell, Los Angeles, Oct 8, 1974 (6 PO, 7 A)
AL—11—Kiko Garcia, Baltimore, Oct 4, 1979 (2 PO, 9 A)
Omar Vizquel, Cleveland, Oct 9, 1998 (4 PO, 7 A)
[11—Leo Cardenas, Minnesota, Oct 5, 1969 (6 PO, 5 A), 11 inn]

**Fewest chances offered, game**
AL-NL—0—many shortstops

**Most chances accepted, inning**
AL-NL—3—many shortstops

### ERRORS AND DOUBLE PLAYS

**Most errors, career**
AL—5—Spike Owen, Boston, 1986; 1 series, 7 G
Nomar Garciaparra, Boston, 1999, 2003; 2 series, 12 G
NL—5—Jeff Blauser, Atlanta, 1991-1993, 1995-1997; 6 series, 29 G

**Most consecutive errorless games, career**
AL—20—Derek Jeter, New York, Oct 10, 2000-Oct 13, 2004
NL—13—Bill Russell, Los Angeles, Oct 5, 1977-Oct 4, 1983
Rafael Belliard, Atlanta, Oct 10, 1991-Oct 13, 1995
Edgar Renteria, Florida, St. Louis, Oct 7, 1997-Oct 10, 2002

**Most errors, series**
AL—5—Spike Owen, Boston, 1986 (7-game series)
NL—3—Darrel Chaney, Cincinnati, 1972 (5-game series)

**Most chances accepted, errorless series**
AL—44—Derek Jeter, New York, 2003, (7-game series)
NL—33—Edgar Renteria, St. Louis, 2004 (7-game series)

**Most errors, game**
AL—2—Leo Cardenas, Minnesota, Oct 4, 1970
[2—Manny Lee, Toronto, Oct 11, 1992, 11 inn
Nomar Garciaparra, Boston, Oct 13, 1999, 10 inn]
NL—2—Gene Alley, Pittsburgh, Oct 10, 1972
Bill Russell, Los Angeles, Oct 4, 1977
Rey Sanchez, Atlanta, Oct 20, 2001
[2—Kevin Elster, New York, Oct 9, 1988, 12 inn]

**Most errors, inning**
NL—2—Gene Alley, Pittsburgh, Oct 10, 1972, 4th
Kevin Elster, New York, Oct 9, 1988, 5th
AL—1—many shortstops

**Most double plays, career**
AL—30—Derek Jeter, New York, 1996, 1998-2001, 2003, 2004; 7 series, 41 G
NL—18—Bill Russell, Los Angeles, 1974, 1977, 1978, 1981, 1983; 5 series, 21 G

**Most double plays, series**
AL—9—Derek Jeter, New York, 2003 (7-game series)
NL—7—Jose Uribe, San Francisco, 1987 (7-game series)
Alfredo Griffin, Los Angeles, 1988 (7-game series)

**Most double plays started, series**
AL—5—Omar Vizquel, Cleveland, 1997 (6-game series)
NL—3—many shortstops

**Most double plays, game**
AL—3—Bert Campaneris, Oakland, Oct 5, 1975
Omar Vizquel, Cleveland, Oct 13, 1997
Omar Vizquel, Cleveland, Oct 9, 1998
Derek Jeter, New York, Oct 11, 2003
[3—Omar Vizquel, Cleveland, Oct 11, 1997, 12 inn]
NL—3—Bill Russell, Los Angeles, Oct 8, 1974
Bill Russell, Los Angeles, Oct 5, 1983
Jose Uribe, San Francisco, Oct 10, 1987
Ozzie Smith, St. Louis, Oct 14, 1987
[3—Jeff Blauser, Atlanta, Oct 10, 1995, 11 inn]

**Most double plays started, game**
NL—3—Bill Russell, Los Angeles, Oct 5, 1983

AL—3—Omar Vizquel, Cleveland, Oct 13, 1997

**Most unassisted double plays, game**
AL-NL—1—many shortstops

# OUTFIELDERS

## GAMES

**Most games, career**
AL—41—Bernie Williams, New York, 1996, 1998-2001, 2003, 2004; 7 series
NL—31—Ron Gant, Atlanta, 1991-1993; Cincinnati, 1995; St. Louis, 1996; 5 series

## PUTOUTS, ASSISTS AND CHANCES

**Most putouts, career**
AL—103—Bernie Williams, New York, 1996, 1998-2001, 2003, 2004; 7 series, 41 G
NL—62—Garry Maddox, Philadelphia, 1976-1978, 1980, 1983; 5 series, 17 G
Ron Gant, Atlanta, 1991, 1992, 1993; Cincinnati, 1995; St. Louis, 1996; 5 series, 31 G
Andruw Jones, Atlanta, 1996-2001, except 2000; 5 series, 27 G

**Most putouts, series**
3-game series
NL—13—Cesar Geronimo, Cincinnati, 1975
Dave Parker, Pittsburgh, 1975
AL—12—Fred Lynn, Boston, 1975
4-game series
NL—16—Garry Maddox, Philadelphia, 1978
AL—14—Bill North, Oakland, 1974
Rick Miller, California, 1979
Jose Canseco, Oakland, 1990
5-game series
NL—23—Garry Maddox, Philadelphia, 1980
AL—22—Dave Henderson, Oakland, 1989
6-game series
NL—18—Willie McGee, St. Louis, 1985
AL—16—Devon White, Toronto, 1992
Kenny Lofton, Cleveland, 1995
Mike Cameron, Seattle, 2000
7-game series
AL—28—Gary Pettis, California, 1986
NL—26—Kenny Lofton, Chicago, 2003

**Most putouts by left fielder, game**
AL—7—Roy White, New York, Oct 13, 1976
NL—7—Rennie Stennett, Pittsburgh, Oct 7, 1972
[7—Jose Cruz, Houston, Oct 10, 1980, 11 inn]

**Most putouts by center fielder, game**
AL—9—Gary Pettis, California, Oct 10, 1986
Darin Erstad, Anaheim, Oct 13, 2002
NL—8—Al Oliver, Pittsburgh, Oct 7, 1972
Don Hahn, New York, Oct 8, 1973

**Most putouts by right fielder, game**
AL—9—Jesse Barfield, Toronto, Oct 11, 1985
NL—8—Brian Jordan, Atlanta, Oct 21, 2001

**Most consecutive putouts, game**
AL—4—Oscar Gamble, New York, Oct 15, 1981, 3 in 6th, 1 in 7th (RF)
Dan Gladden, Minnesota, Oct 9, 1991, 3 in 8th, 1 in 9th (LF)
Darin Erstad, Anaheim, Oct 13, 2002, 2 in 3rd, 2 in 4th (CF)
NL—4—Andre Dawson, Montreal, Oct 19, 1981, 1 in 6th, 3 in 7th (CF)

**Most putouts, inning**
AL-NL—3—many outfielders

**Most assists, career**
ML—6—Lonnie Smith, Philadelphia NL, 1980; St. Louis NL, 1982; Kansas City AL, 1985; Atlanta NL, 1991; 4 series, 19 G
NL—5—Bake McBride, Philadelphia, 1977, 1978, 1980; 3 series, 11 G
AL—3—Tony Oliva, Minnesota, 1969, 1970; 2 series, 6 G
Reggie Jackson, Oakland, 1971-1975; New York, 1977, 1978, 1980, 1981; 9 series, 27 G
Lonnie Smith, Kansas City, 1985; 1 series, 7 G

**Most games played with no assists, career**
AL—25—Manny Ramirez, Cleveland, 1995, 1997, 1998; Boston, 2003; 4 series
NL—21—Willie McGee, St. Louis, 1982, 1985, 1987, 1996; 4 series

**Most assists, series**
3-game series
NL—2—George Foster, Cincinnati, 1979
AL—2—Tony Oliva, Minnesota, 1970
Carl Yastrzemski, Boston, 1975
Tony Armas, Oakland, 1981
4-game series
NL—2—Bake McBride, Philadelphia, 1977
AL—2—Rick Miller, California, 1979
5-game series
NL—3—Bake McBride, Philadelphia, 1980
AL—1—many outfielders
6-game series
NL—3—Melvin Mora, New York, 1999
AL—2—Tim Raines Sr., Chicago, 1993
7-game series
AL—3—Lonnie Smith, Kansas City, 1985
NL—3—David Justice, Atlanta, 1992

**Most assists, game**
AL—2—Tony Oliva, Minnesota, Oct 4, 1970
NL—2—Rickey Henderson, New York, Oct 15, 1999
[2—George Foster, Cincinnati, Oct 3, 1979, 10 inn
Bake McBride, Philadelphia, Oct 11, 1980, 10 inn]

**Most chances accepted, career**
AL—105—Bernie Williams, New York, 1996, 1998-2001, 2003, 2004; 7 series, 41 G
NL—65—Ron Gant, Atlanta, 1991-1993; Cincinnati, 1995; St. Louis, 1996; 5 series, 31 G

**Most chances accepted, series**
3-game series
NL—14—Dave Parker, Pittsburgh, 1975
AL—13—Fred Lynn, Boston, 1975
4-game series
NL—16—Garry Maddox, Philadelphia, 1978
AL—16—Rick Miller, California, 1979
5-game series
NL—23—Garry Maddox, Philadelphia, 1980
AL—22—Dave Henderson, Oakland, 1989
6-game series
NL—18—Willie McGee, St. Louis, 1985
AL—16—Devon White, Toronto, 1992
Willie Wilson, Oakland, 1992
Kenny Lofton, Cleveland, 1995
Mike Cameron, Seattle, 2000
7-game series
AL—28—Gary Pettis, California, 1986
NL—27—Kenny Lofton, Chicago, 2003

**Most chances accepted by left fielder, game**
AL—7—Roy White, New York, Oct 13, 1976 (7 PO)
Clint Hurdle, Kansas City, Oct 6, 1978 (6 PO, 1 A)
NL—7—Rennie Stennett, Pittsburgh, Oct 7, 1972 (7 PO)
Jose Cruz, Houston, Oct 10, 1980 (7 PO)
Kevin Mitchell, San Francisco, Oct 7, 1989 (6 PO, 1 A)

**Most chances accepted by center fielder, game**
AL—9—Gary Pettis, California, Oct 10, 1986 (9 PO)
Darin Erstad, Anaheim, Oct 13, 2002 (9 PO)
NL—8—Al Oliver, Pittsburgh, Oct 7, 1972 (8 PO)
Don Hahn, New York, Oct 8, 1973 (8 PO)

**Most chances accepted by right fielder, game**
AL—9—Jesse Barfield, Toronto, Oct 11, 1985 (9 PO)
NL—8—Brian Jordan, Atlanta, Oct 21, 2001 (8 PO)

**Longest game with no chances offered to outfielder**
NL—12 inn—Don Hahn, New York, Oct 9, 1973
Billy Hatcher, Houston, Oct 14, 1986
AL—12 inn—Brian Giles, Cleveland, Oct 11, 1997

**Most chances accepted, inning**
AL-NL—3—many players

## ERRORS AND DOUBLE PLAYS

**Most errors, career**
ML—7—Rickey Henderson, Oakland AL, 1981, 1989, 1990, 1992; Toronto AL, 1993; New York NL, 1999; Seattle AL, 2000; 7 series, 33 G (6 in AL, 1 in NL)
AL—6—Rickey Henderson, Oakland, 1981, 1989, 1990, 1992; Toronto, 1993; Seattle, 2000; 6 series, 27 G
NL—2—Reggie Smith, Los Angeles, 1977, 1978; 2 series, 8 G
Garry Maddox, Philadelphia, 1976-1978, 1980, 1983; 5 series, 17 G
David Justice, Atlanta, 1991-1993, 1995; 4 series, 23 G
Willie McGee, St. Louis, 1982, 1985, 1987, 1996; 4 series, 21 G
Marquis Grissom, Atlanta, 1995, 1996; 2 series, 11 G
Kenny Lofton, Atlanta, 1997; San Francisco, 2002; 2 series, 11 G
Jim Edmonds, St. Louis, 2000, 2002, 2004; 3 series, 17 G

**Most consecutive errorless games, career**
ML—31—Paul O'Neill, Cincinnati NL, New York AL, Oct 4, 1990-Oct 22, 2001
AL—26—Paul O'Neill, New York, Oct 9, 1996-Oct 22, 2001
NL—27—Andruw Jones, Atlanta, Oct 9, 1996-Oct 21, 2001

**Most errors, series**
AL—3—Rickey Henderson, Oakland, 1992 (6-game series)
NL—2—Kenny Lofton, Atlanta, 1997 (6-game series)

**Most chances accepted, errorless series**
NL—27—Kenny Lofton, Chicago, 2003 (7-game series)
AL—22—Dave Henderson, Oakland, 1989 (5-game series)

**Most errors, game**
AL—2—Tony Oliva, Minnesota, Oct 6, 1969
Ben Oglivie, Milwaukee, Oct 10, 1982
Albert Belle, Cleveland, Oct 15, 1995
NL—2—Wes Chamberlain, Philadelphia, Oct 11, 1993

**Most errors, inning**
AL-NL—1—many outfielders

**Most double plays, career**
NL—3—Bake McBride, Philadelphia, 1977, 1978, 1980; 3 series, 11 G
AL—2—Rick Miller, California, 1979; 1 series, 4 G

**Most double plays, series**
AL—2—Rick Miller, California, 1979 (4-game series)
NL—1—many outfielders

**Most double plays, game**
AL—1—many outfielders
NL—1—many outfielders
[2—Bake McBride, Philadelphia, Oct 11, 1980, 10 inn]

**Most unassisted double plays, game**
AL-NL—none

## CATCHERS

### GAMES

**Most games, career**
AL—33—Jorge Posada, New York, 1998-2001, 2003, 2004; 6 series
NL—27—Javy Lopez, Atlanta, 1992, 1995-1998, 2001; 6 series

### PUTOUTS, ASSISTS AND CHANCES

**Most putouts, career**
AL—255—Jorge Posada, New York, 1998-2001, 2003, 2004; 6 series, 33 G
NL—183—Javy Lopez, Atlanta, 1992, 1995-1998, 2001; 6 series, 27 G

**Most putouts, series**
3-game series
NL—29—Manny Sanguillen, Pittsburgh, 1975
AL—23—Rick Cerone, New York, 1981
4-game series
NL—34—Dick Dietz, San Francisco, 1971
AL—34—Rich Gedman, Boston, 1988
5-game series
AL—44—Jason Varitek, Boston, 1999
NL—42—Jerry Grote, New York, 1973
6-game series
NL—59—Alan Ashby, Houston, 1986
AL—51—Jorge Posada, New York, 2000
7-game series
NL—62—Greg Olson, Atlanta, 1991
AL—60—Jorge Posada, New York, 2003

**Most putouts, game**
AL—15—Rick Dempsey, Baltimore, Oct 6, 1983
Jorge Posada, New York, Oct 14, 2000
Jason Varitek, Boston, Oct 18, 2004
[15—Chris Hoiles, Baltimore, Oct 11, 1997, caught first 8 inn of 12-inn game]
NL—15—Charles Johnson, Florida, Oct 12, 1997
[16—Mike Piazza, New York, Oct 17, 1999, 15 inn]

**Most putouts, inning**
AL-NL—3—many catchers

**Most assists, career**
AL—19—Jorge Posada, New York, 1998-2001, 2003, 2004; 6 series, 33 G
NL—18—Johnny Bench, Cincinnati, 1970, 1972, 1973, 1975, 1976, 1979; 6 series, 22 G

**Most assists, series**
3-game series
AL—4—George Mitterwald, Minnesota, 1969
Rick Cerone, New York, 1980
NL—4—Johnny Bench, Cincinnati, 1975, 1976
4-game series
AL—5—Rick Dempsey, Baltimore, 1983
Rich Gedman, Boston, 1988
NL—2—many catchers
5-game series
AL—7—Bengie Molina, Los Angeles, 2005
NL—4—Terry Kennedy, San Diego, 1984
Mike Matheny, St. Louis, 2002
6-game series
AL—7—Terry Steinbach, Oakland, 1992
NL—7—Brad Ausmus, Houston, 2005
7-game series
AL—6—Jorge Posada, New York, 2003
NL—5—Tony Pena, St. Louis, 1987
Don Slaught, Pittsburgh, 1991
Damon Berryhill, Atlanta, 1992
Mike Matheny, St. Louis, 2004

**Most assists, game**
NL—3—Johnny Bench, Cincinnati, Oct 5, 1975
Mike Matheny, St. Louis, Oct 12, 2002
Brad Ausmus, Houston, Oct 16, 2005
[3—Johnny Bench, Cincinnati, Oct 3, 1970, 10 inn
Gary Carter, New York, Oct 15, 1986, 16 inn]
AL—4—Bengie Molina, Los Angeles, Oct 16, 2005

**Most assists, inning**
AL—3—Bengie Molina, Los Angeles, Oct 16, 2005, 9th
NL—2—Johnny Bench, Cincinnati, Oct 7, 1973, 8th
Mike Scioscia, Los Angeles, Oct 10, 1985, 1st
Gary Carter, New York, Oct 15, 1986, 12th

**Most chances accepted, career**
AL—274—Jorge Posada, New York, 1998-2001, 2003, 2004; 6 series, 33 G
NL—193—Javy Lopez, Atlanta, 1992, 1995-1998, 2001; 6 series, 27 G

**Most chances accepted, series**
3-game series
NL—30—Manny Sanguillen, Pittsburgh, 1975
AL—25—Rick Cerone, New York, 1981
4-game series
AL—39—Rich Gedman, Boston, 1988
NL—36—Dick Dietz, San Francisco, 1971
5-game series
AL—45—Jason Varitek, Boston, 1999
NL—43—Jerry Grote, New York, 1973
6-game series
NL—60—Alan Ashby, Houston, 1986
AL—54—Jorge Posada, New York, 2000
7-game series
AL—66—Jorge Posada, New York, 2003
NL—63—Greg Olson, Atlanta, 1991

**Most chances accepted, game**
AL—16—Rick Dempsey, Baltimore, Oct 6, 1983 (15 PO, 1 A, 14 K)
[16—Chris Hoiles, Baltimore, Oct 11, 1997 (15 PO, 1 A, 16 K),
caught first 8 inn of 12-inn game
Jorge Posada, New York, Oct 18, 2004 (13 PO, 3 A,12 K), 14 inn]
NL—16—Charles Johnson, Florida, Oct 12, 1997 (15 PO, 1 A, 15 K)
[18—Mike Piazza, New York, Oct 17, 1999 (17 PO, 1 A, 15 K),
caught first 13 inn of 15-inn game]

**Fewest chances offered, game**
AL-NL—2—many catchers

**Most chances accepted, inning**
AL-NL—3—many catchers

### ERRORS AND PASSED BALLS

**Most errors, career**
NL—5—Manny Sanguillen, Pittsburgh, 1970-1972, 1974, 1975; 5 series, 19 G
AL—3—Don Slaught, Kansas City, 1984; 1 series, 3 G
Pat Borders, Toronto, 1989, 1991-1993; 4 series, 18 G
Sandy Alomar, Cleveland, 1995, 1997, 1998; 3 series, 16 G

**Most consecutive errorless games, career**
AL—26—Jorge Posada, Oct 19, 1999-Oct 20, 2004
NL—18—Gary Carter, Montreal, New York, Oct 13, 1981-Oct 12, 1988

**Most errors, series**
AL—3—Don Slaught, Kansas City, 1984 (3-game series)
NL—3—Mike Piazza, New York, 1999 (6-game series)

**Most chances accepted, errorless series**
NL—63—Greg Olson, Atlanta, 1991 (7-game series)
AL—66—Jorge Posada, New York, 2003 (7-game series)

**Most errors, game**
AL—2—Thurman Munson, New York, Oct 10, 1976
Don Slaught, Kansas City, Oct 5, 1984
Sandy Alomar, Cleveland, Oct 10, 1998
NL—2—Manny Sanguillen, Pittsburgh, Oct 6, 1974
[2—Mike Piazza, New York, Oct 19, 1999, 11 inn]

**Most errors, inning**
AL-NL—1—many catchers

**Most passed balls, career**
NL—4—Manny Sanguillen, Pittsburgh, 1970-1972, 1974, 1975; 5 series, 19 G
AL—5—Pat Borders, Toronto, 1989, 1991-1993; 4 series, 18 G
Jason Varitek, Boston, 1999, 2003, 2004; 3 series, 18 G

**Most passed balls, series**
AL—3—Pat Borders, Toronto, 1992 (6-game series)
NL—2—Manny Sanguillen, Pittsburgh, 1975 (3-game series)
Alan Ashby, Houston, 1986 (6-game series)
Don Slaught, Pittsburgh, 1992 (7-game series)
Darren Daulton, Philadelphia, 1993 (6-game series)
Paul Bako, Chicago, 2003 (7-game series)

**Most passed balls, game**
NL—2—Manny Sanguillen, Pittsburgh, Oct 4, 1975
Alan Ashby, Houston, Oct 11, 1986
Don Slaught, Pittsburgh, Oct 13, 1992
AL—2—Pat Borders, Toronto, Oct 13, 1991
Pat Borders, Toronto, Oct 14, 1992
[3—Jason Varitek, Boston, Oct 18, 2004, 14 inn]

**Most passed balls, inning**
AL—3—Jason Varitek, Boston, Oct 18, 2004, 13th
NL—1—many catchers

### DOUBLE PLAYS AND RUNNERS CAUGHT STEALING

**Most double plays, career**
AL—5—Jorge Posada, New York, 1998-2001, 2003, 2004; 6 series, 33 G
NL—3—Manny Sanguillen, Pittsburgh, 1970-1972, 1974, 1975; 5 series, 19 G

Terry Kennedy, San Diego, 1984; San Francisco, 1989; 2 series, 10 G

**Most double plays, series**
AL—3—Jorge Posada, New York, 2003 (7-game series)
NL—2—Terry Kennedy, San Francisco, 1989 (5-game series)
Greg Olson, Atlanta, 1991 (7-game series)
Javy Lopez, Atlanta, 1997 (6-game series)
Mike Piazza, New York, 1999 (6-game series)
Mike Matheny, St. Louis, 2004 (7-game series)

**Most double plays started, series**
AL—3—Jorge Posada, New York, 2003 (7-game series)
NL—2—Mike Matheny, St. Louis, 2004 (7-game series)

**Most double plays, game**
AL-NL—1—many catchers

**Most double plays started, game**
AL-NL—1—many catchers

**Most unassisted double plays, game**
AL-NL—none

**Most runners caught stealing, career**
AL—12—Thurman Munson, New York, 1976-1978; 3 series, 14 G
NL—6—Mike Scioscia, Los Angeles, 1981, 1985, 1988; 3 series, 18 G

**Most runners caught stealing, series**
AL—5—Thurman Munson, New York, 1976 (5-game series)
Terry Steinbach, Oakland, 1992 (6-game series)
NL—4—Mike Scioscia, Los Angeles, 1985 (6-game series)
Mike Matheny, St. Louis, 2004 (7-game series)

**Most runners caught stealing, game**
AL-NL—2—many catchers

**Most runners caught stealing, inning**
NL—2—Mike Scioscia, Los Angeles, Oct 10, 1985, 1st
AL—1—many catchers

## PITCHERS

### GAMES

**Most games, career**
AL—25—Mariano Rivera, New York, 1996, 1998-2001, 2003, 2004; 7 series
NL—18—Mark Wohlers, Atlanta, 1991-1993, 1995-1997; 6 series

**Most games, series**
3-game series
AL-NL—3—many pitchers
4-game series
NL—4—Dave Giusti, Pittsburgh, 1971
Mark Wohlers, Atlanta, 1995
AL—4—Dennis Eckersley, Oakland, 1988
5-game series
NL—5—Tug McGraw, Philadelphia, 1980
AL—5—Jim Acker, Toronto, 1989
6-game series
NL—6—John Rocker, Atlanta, 1998
John Rocker, Atlanta, 1999
AL—5—Paul Assenmacher, Cleveland, 1997
Mike Jackson, Cleveland, 1997
Paul Shuey, Cleveland, 1998
Jose Paniagua, Seattle, 2000
7-game series
NL—6—Mark Petkovsek, St. Louis, 1996
Jason Isringhausen, St. Louis, 2004
AL—6—Alan Embree, Boston, 2004
Tom Gordon, New York, 2004

### PUTOUTS, ASSISTS AND CHANCES

**Most putouts, career**
AL—12—Mariano Rivera, New York, 1996, 1998-2001, 2003, 2004; 7 series, 24 G
NL—11—Greg Maddux, Chicago, 1989; Atlanta, 1993, 1995-1999, 2001; 8 series, 15 G

**Most putouts, series**
3-game series
NL—4—Don Gullett, Cincinnati, 1975
AL—2—Rick Wise, Boston, 1975
Rudy May, New York, 1980
Milt Wilcox, Detroit, 1984
4-game series
AL—3—Catfish Hunter, Oakland, 1974
NL—2—Juan Marichal, San Francisco, 1971
Don Sutton, Los Angeles, 1974
Jeff Brantley, Cincinnati, 1995
5-game series
AL—4—Mariano Rivera, 2001
NL—2—Tug McGraw, New York, 1973
Dick Ruthven, Philadelphia, 1980
Miguel Batista, Arizona, 2001
Tom Glavine, Atlanta, 2001
Greg Maddux, Atlanta, 2001
Kirk Rueter, San Francisco, 2002
6-game series
NL—4—Greg Maddux, Atlanta, 1993
Andy Ashby, San Diego, 1998
Roy Oswalt, Houston, 2005
AL—4—Brett Tomko, Seattle, 2000
7-game series
NL—4—Danny Cox, St. Louis, 1987
AL—4—Derek Lowe, Boston, 2004

**Most putouts, game**
NL—4—Don Gullett, Cincinnati, Oct 4, 1975
AL—3—Tommy John, California, Oct 5, 1982
Charlie Leibrandt, Kansas City, Oct 12, 1985
Charles Nagy, Cleveland, Oct 7, 1998
Derek Lowe, Boston, Oct 20, 2004

**Most putouts, inning**
AL—2—Mike Torrez, New York, Oct 7, 1977, 2nd
Charlie Leibrandt, Kansas City, Oct 12, 1985, 5th
Mike Witt, California, Oct 12, 1986, 1st
Mariano Rivera, New York, Oct 17, 2001, 9th
NL—2—Don Gullett, Cincinnati, Oct 4, 1975, 3rd
Roger McDowell, New York, Oct 15, 1986, 10th

**Most assists, career**
NL—25—Greg Maddux, Chicago, 1989; Atlanta, 1993, 1995-1999, 2001; 8 series, 15 G
AL—12—Mike Cuellar, Baltimore, 1969-1971, 1973, 1974; 5 series, 6 G

**Most assists, series**
3-game series
AL—4—Dave Boswell, Minnesota, 1969
Paul Lindblad, Oakland, 1975
NL—3—Phil Niekro, Atlanta, 1969
Dock Ellis, Pittsburgh, 1970
Pat Zachry, Cincinnati, 1976
4-game series
AL—5—Mike Cuellar, Baltimore, 1974
NL—5—Steve Carlton, Philadelphia, 1983
5-game series
NL—4—Darryl Kile, St. Louis, 2000
AL—4—Jose Contreras, Chicago, 2005
6-game series
NL—7—Greg Maddux, Atlanta, 1997
AL—5—Scott Erickson, Baltimore, 1997
7-game series
AL—7—Charlie Leibrandt, Kansas City, 1985
NL—5—Danny Cox, St. Louis, 1987

**Most assists, game**
AL—5—Charlie Leibrandt, Kansas City, Oct 12, 1985
NL—4—Juan Marichal, San Francisco, Oct 5, 1971
Greg Maddux, Atlanta, Oct 7, 1997
Andy Ashby, San Diego, Oct 7, 1998
Greg Maddux, Atlanta, Oct 12, 1999
Kenny Rogers, New York, Oct 13, 1999
Chris Carpenter, St. Louis, Oct 12, 2005
Chris Carpenter, St. Louis, Oct 17, 2005

**Most assists, inning**
NL—3—Pat Zachry, Cincinnati, Oct 10, 1976, 4th
AL—2—many pitchers

**Most chances accepted, career**
NL—35—Greg Maddux, Chicago, 1989; Atlanta, 1993, 1995-1999, 2001; 8 series, 15 G
AL—22—Mariano Rivera, New York, 1996, 1998-2001, 2003, 2004; 7 series, 24 G

**Most chances accepted, series**
3-game series
NL—5—Don Gullett, Cincinnati, 1975
AL—5—Dave Boswell, Minnesota, 1969
Rick Wise, Boston, 1975
Paul Lindblad, Oakland, 1975
4-game series
NL—6—Juan Marichal, San Francisco, 1971
Steve Carlton, Philadelphia, 1983
AL—5—Catfish Hunter, Oakland, 1974
Mike Cuellar, Baltimore, 1974
Larry Gura, Kansas City, 1978
5-game series
NL—5—Darryl Kile, St. Louis, 2000
Tom Glavine, Atlanta, 2001
Greg Maddux, Atlanta, 2001
Kirk Rueter, San Francisco, 2002
AL—5—Mike Flanagan, Toronto, 1989
Jack Morris, Minnesota, 1991
Mariano Rivera, New York, 2001
Jose Contreras, Chicago, 2005
6-game series
NL—9—Greg Maddux, Atlanta, 1993
Roy Oswalt, Houston, 2005
AL—5—Scott Erickson, Baltimore, 1997
7-game series
AL—10—Charlie Leibrandt, Kansas City, 1985
NL—9—Danny Cox, St. Louis, 1987

**Most chances accepted, game**
AL—8—Charlie Leibrandt, Kansas City, Oct 12, 1985
NL—6—Juan Marichal, San Francisco, Oct 5, 1971

**Most chances accepted, inning**
NL—3—Pat Zachry, Cincinnati, Oct 10, 1976, 4th
AL—3—Mariano Rivera, New York, Oct 17, 2001, 9th

## ERRORS AND DOUBLE PLAYS

**Most errors, career**
NL—3—Greg Maddux, Chicago, 1989; Atlanta, 1993, 1995-1998, 1999, 2001; 8 series, 15 G
AL—1—many pitchers

**Most consecutive errorless games, career**
AL—25—Mariano Rivera, New York, Oct 9, 1996-Oct 20, 2004
NL—18—Mark Wohlers, Atlanta, Oct 9, 1991-Oct 8, 1997

**Most errors, series**
NL—2—Joaquin Andujar, St. Louis, 1985
AL—1—many pitchers

**Most chances accepted, errorless series**
AL—10—Charlie Leibrandt, Kansas City, 1985 (7-game series)
NL—9—Danny Cox, St. Louis, 1987 (7-game series)

**Most errors, game**
AL-NL—1—many pitchers

**Most double plays, career**
NL—3—Greg Maddux, Chicago, 1989; Atlanta, 1993-2001, except 1994 and 2000; 8 series, 15 G
AL—2—Mike Flanagan, Baltimore, 1979, 1983; Toronto, 1989; 3 series, 3 G
Jeff Nelson, Seattle, 1995, 2001; New York, 1997-2000; 6 series, 15 G
Mariano Rivera, New York, 1996, 1998-2001, 2003, 2004; 7 series, 24 G

**Most double plays, series**
AL—2—Mike Flanagan, Toronto, 1989 (5-game series)
Jeff Nelson, Seattle, 1995 (6-game series)
NL—2—Danny Cox, St. Louis, 1987 (7-game series)
Pat Mahomes, New York, 1999 (6-game series)
Greg Maddux, Atlanta, 2001 (5-game series)

**Most double plays started, series**
AL—2—Mike Flanagan, Toronto, 1989 (5-game series)
Jeff Nelson, Seattle, 1995 (6-game series)
NL—2—Pat Mahomes, New York, 1999 (6-game series)
Greg Maddux, Atlanta, 2001 (5-game series)

**Most double plays, game**
AL—2—Mike Flanagan, Toronto, Oct 7, 1989
Jeff Nelson, Seattle, Oct 14, 1995
NL—2—Danny Cox, St. Louis, Oct 14, 1987
Greg Maddux, Atlanta, Oct 16, 2001

**Most unassisted double plays, game**
AL-NL—none

# CLUB FIELDING



## AVERAGE

**Highest fielding average, series**
3-game series
AL—1.000—Baltimore vs Minnesota, 1970
Oakland vs Baltimore, 1971
NL—1.000—Pittsburgh vs Cincinnati, 1979
4-game series
AL—.993—New York vs Kansas City, 1978
Boston vs Oakland, 1988
Oakland vs Boston, 1990
NL—.993—Los Angeles vs Philadelphia, 1983
5-game series
AL—.995—New York vs Baltimore, 1996
NL—.995—San Francisco vs St. Louis, 2002
6-game series
NL—.996—New York vs Houston, 1986
San Diego vs Atlanta, 1998
AL—.995—New York vs Seattle, 2000
7-game series
NL—.996—St. Louis vs Houston, 2004
AL—.996—Boston vs New York, 2004

**For a list of fielding statistics by teams each series, see page 355.**

**Highest fielding average by both clubs, series**
3-game series
NL—.996—Pittsburgh 1.000, Cincinnati .992, 1979
AL—.995—Oakland 1.000, Baltimore .991, 1971
4-game series
AL—.986—Boston .993, Oakland .979, 1988
NL—.985—Cincinnati .987, Atlanta .983, 1995
5-game series
NL—.994—San Francisco .995, St. Louis .994, 2002
AL—.987—New York .995, Baltimore .980, 1996
6-game series
AL—.991—New York .995, Seattle .986, 2000
NL—.985—New York .996, Houston .973, 1986
7-game series
NL—.994—St. Louis .996, Houston .992, 2004
AL—.991—Boston .996, New York .986, 2004

**Lowest fielding average, series**
3-game series
AL—.940—Kansas City vs Detroit, 1984
NL—.950—Atlanta vs New York, 1969
4-game series
NL—.957—Los Angeles vs Pittsburgh, 1974
AL—.968—Boston vs Oakland, 1990
5-game series
AL—.945—Boston vs New York, 1999
NL—.962—St. Louis vs New York, 2000
6-game series
AL—.966—Toronto vs Oakland, 1992
NL—.968—Philadelphia vs Atlanta, 1993
7-game series
NL—.969—New York vs Los Angeles, 1988
AL—.971—California vs Boston, 1986

**Lowest fielding average by both clubs, series**
3-game series
AL—.958—Boston .966, Oakland .950, 1975
NL—.965—New York .981, Atlanta .950, 1969
4-game series
NL—.964—Pittsburgh .973, Los Angeles .957, 1974
AL—.978—California .986, Baltimore .970, 1979
5-game series
AL—.961—New York .977, Boston .945, 1999
NL—.970—New York .978, St. Louis .962, 2000
6-game series
AL—.967—Oakland .969, Toronto .966, 1992
NL—.971—Atlanta .971, New York .970, 1999
7-game series
AL—.973—Boston .975, California .971, 1986
NL—.975—New York .969, Los Angeles .981, 1988

## PUTOUTS

**Most putouts, total series**
AL—1,664—New York; 12 series, 61 G
NL—1,620—Atlanta; 11 series, 60 G

**Most putouts, series**
3-game series
AL—96—Baltimore vs Minnesota, 1969
NL—90—Pittsburgh vs Cincinnati, 1979
4-game series
NL—117—Atlanta vs Cincinnati, 1995
AL—111—Baltimore vs Chicago, 1983
5-game series
NL—148—Philadelphia vs Houston, 1980
AL—141—New York vs Baltimore, 1996
6-game series
NL—189—New York vs Houston, 1986
AL—174—Baltimore vs Cleveland, 1997
Cleveland vs Baltimore, 1997
7-game series
AL—209—New York vs Boston, 2004
NL—198— Florida vs Chicago, 2003
Chicago vs Florida, 2003

**Most putouts by both clubs, series**
3-game series
AL—190—Baltimore 96, Minnesota 94, 1969
NL—177—Pittsburgh 90, Cincinnati 87, 1979
4-game series
NL—228—Atlanta 117, Cincinnati 111, 1995
AL—219—Baltimore 111, Chicago 108, 1983
5-game series
NL—295—Philadelphia 148, Houston 147, 1980

AL—279—New York 141, Baltimore 138, 1996
6-game series
NL—377—New York 189, Houston 188, 1986
AL—348—Baltimore 174, Cleveland 174, 1997
7-game series
AL—416—New York 209, Boston 207, 2004
NL—396—Florida 198, Chicago 198, 2003

**Fewest putouts, series**
3-game series
AL—75—Oakland vs Baltimore, 1971
Oakland vs Boston, 1975
New York vs Kansas City, 1980
Oakland vs New York, 1981
NL—76—Atlanta vs St. Louis, 1982
4-game series
AL—102—Kansas City vs New York, 1978
Boston vs Oakland, 1988, 1990
NL—102—San Francisco vs Pittsburgh, 1971
Los Angeles vs Philadelphia, 1983
5-game series
AL—126—California vs Milwaukee, 1982
NL—126—Chicago vs San Francisco, 1989
6-game series
NL—154—Los Angeles vs St. Louis, 1985
AL—156—Seattle vs New York, 2000
7-game series
NL—180—San Francisco vs St. Louis, 1987
St. Louis vs Atlanta, 1996
AL—186—Toronto vs Kansas City, 1985

**Fewest putouts by both clubs, series**
3-game series
AL—156—Baltimore 81, Oakland 75, 1971
Boston 81, Oakland 75, 1975
Kansas City 81, New York 75, 1980
New York 81, Oakland 75, 1981
NL—157—St. Louis 81, Atlanta 76, 1982
4-game series
AL—207—New York 105, Kansas City 102, 1978
NL—207—Pittsburgh 105, San Francisco 102, 1971
Philadelphia 105, Los Angeles 102, 1983
5-game series
AL—255—Milwaukee 129, California 126, 1982
NL—256—Chicago 129, San Diego 127, 1984
6-game series
NL—310—St. Louis 156, Los Angeles 154, 1985
AL—315—New York 159, Seattle 156, 2000
7-game series
NL—363—St. Louis 183, San Francisco 180, 1987
Atlanta 183, St. Louis 180, 1996
AL—374—Kansas City 188, Toronto 186, 1985

**Most putouts by outfield, game**
NL—18—Pittsburgh vs Cincinnati, Oct 7, 1972
AL—14—Boston vs Oakland, Oct 4, 1975
New York vs Kansas City, Oct 13, 1976
Anaheim vs Minnesota, Oct 13, 2002

**Most putouts by outfield of both clubs, game**
AL—26—New York 14, Kansas City 12, Oct 13, 1976
NL—25—Pittsburgh 18, Cincinnati 7, Oct 7, 1972

**Fewest putouts by outfield, game**
NL—1—Atlanta vs New York, Oct 4, 1969
Cincinnati vs Pittsburgh, Oct 5, 1970
Montreal vs Los Angeles, Oct 16, 1981
[3—Cincinnati vs Pittsburgh, Oct 3, 1970, 10 inn
Florida vs Chicago, Oct 7, 2003, 11 inn]
AL—1—Minnesota vs Anaheim, Oct 13, 2002 (fielded 8 inn)
[3—Baltimore vs Cleveland, Oct 11, 1997 (fielded 11.1 inn of 12-inn game)]

**Fewest putouts by outfield of both clubs, game**
NL—5—Pittsburgh 4, Cincinnati 1, Oct 5, 1970
[10—Chicago 7, Florida 3, Oct 7, 2003, 11 inn]
AL—6—New York 4, Boston 2, Oct 9, 2003
[9—Cleveland 6, Baltimore 3, Oct 11, 1997, 12 inn]

**Most putouts by outfield, inning**
AL-NL—3—many clubs

**Most putouts by outfield of both clubs, inning**
AL—6—Baltimore 3, Oakland 3, Oct 11, 1973, 7th
NL—5—New York 3, Atlanta 2, Oct 5, 1969, 7th
Pittsburgh 3, Cincinnati 2, Oct 7, 1972, 3rd
Los Angeles 3, Philadelphia 2, Oct 7, 1978, 3rd
St. Louis 3, Atlanta 2, Oct 9, 1996, 6th
New York 3, St. Louis 2, Oct 15, 2000, 2nd

**Most putouts by catchers of both clubs, inning**
AL-NL—5—many innings

## ASSISTS

**Most assists, total series**
NL—614—Atlanta; 11 series, 60 G
AL—598—New York; 12 series, 61 G

**Most assists, series**
3-game series
AL—41—New York vs Kansas City, 1980
NL—39—Cincinnati vs Pittsburgh, 1970, 1979
Atlanta vs St. Louis, 1982
4-game series
NL—54—Atlanta vs Cincinnati, 1995
AL—52—Baltimore vs California, 1979
5-game series
NL—71—Philadelphia vs Houston, 1980
AL—66—Chicago vs Los Angeles, 2005
6-game series
NL—94—New York vs Houston, 1986
AL—77—Cleveland vs New York, 1998
7-game series
AL—87—Kansas City vs Toronto, 1985
NL—81—Chicago vs Florida, 2003

**Most assists by both clubs, series**
3-game series
NL—76—Cincinnati 39, Pittsburgh 37, 1970
AL—73—Oakland 40, Boston 33, 1975
4-game series
AL—100—Chicago 51, Baltimore 49, 1983
NL—97—Atlanta 54, Cincinnati 43, 1995
5-game series
NL—123—Philadelphia 71, Houston 52, 1980
AL—113—Chicago 66, Los Angeles 47, 2005
6-game series
NL—160—New York 94, Houston 66, 1986
AL—131—Cleveland 77, New York 54, 1998
7-game series
AL—151—California 78, Boston 73, 1986
NL—151—Chicago 81, Florida 70, 2003

**Fewest assists, series**
3-game series
AL—15—Oakland vs Baltimore, 1971
NL—20—Pittsburgh vs Cincinnati, 1975
4-game series
AL—30—Oakland vs Boston, 1988
NL—32—Pittsburgh vs San Francisco, 1971
5-game series
NL—38—Pittsburgh vs Cincinnati, 1972
AL—38—New York vs Boston, 1999
Anaheim vs Minnesota, 2002
6-game series
NL—45—Cincinnati vs Pittsburgh, 1980
AL—54—New York vs Cleveland, 1998
New York vs Seattle, 2000
7-game series
NL—55—Atlanta vs St. Louis, 1996
AL—61—Toronto vs Kansas City, 1985

**Fewest assists by both clubs, series**
3-game series
AL—46—Baltimore 31, Oakland 15, 1971
NL—51—Cincinnati 31, Pittsburgh 20, 1975
4-game series
AL—64—Boston 34, Oakland 30, 1988
NL—69—San Francisco 37, Pittsburgh 32, 1971
5-game series
AL—78—New York 40, Boston 38, 1999
NL—88—St. Louis 49, New York 39, 2000
6-game series
NL—101—Atlanta 54, Philadelphia 47, 1993
AL—112—Seattle 58, New York 54, 2000
7-game series
NL—117—St. Louis 62, Atlanta 55, 1996
AL—140—New York 73, Boston 67, 2003
Boston 66, New York 74, 2004

**Most assists, game**
NL—21—Los Angeles vs Philadelphia, Oct 5, 1978
[31—New York vs Houston, Oct 15, 1986, 16 inn]
AL—19—Boston vs New York, Oct 9, 2003
[18—Toronto vs Oakland, Oct 11, 1992, 11 inn]

**Most assists by both clubs, game**
AL—33—Boston 18, Oakland 15, Oct 7, 1975
NL—30—Los Angeles 21, Philadelphia 9, Oct 5, 1978
[56—New York 31, Houston 25, Oct 15, 1986, 16 inn]

**Fewest assists, game**
AL—2—Boston vs Oakland, Oct 4, 1975
Boston vs New York, Oct 13, 2003
NL—2—Pittsburgh vs Cincinnati, Oct 7, 1972
[2—Pittsburgh vs Cincinnati, Oct 7, 1975, 10 inn]

**Fewest assists by both clubs, game**
AL—6—Anaheim 5, Minnesota 1, Oct 11, 2002
NL—7—Atlanta 4, St. Louis 3, Oct 9, 1996

**Most assists by outfield, game**
NL—3—New York vs Atlanta, Oct 15, 1999

[3—Philadelphia vs Houston, Oct 11, 1980, 10 inn]
AL—2—Minnesota vs Baltimore, Oct 4, 1970
Boston vs Oakland, Oct 5, 1975
Baltimore vs California, Oct 5, 1979
New York vs Boston, Oct 16, 2004

**Most assists by outfield of both clubs, game**
NL—3—Pittsburgh 2, Cincinnati 1, Oct 9, 1972
New York 3, Atlanta 0, Oct 15, 1999
[4—Philadelphia 3, Houston 1, Oct 11, 1980, 10 inn]
AL—3—Minnesota 2, Baltimore 1, Oct 4, 1970
Boston 2, Oakland 1, Oct 5, 1975
Baltimore 2, California 1, Oct 5, 1979

**Most assists by outfield, inning**
NL—2—Cincinnati vs New York, Oct 10, 1973, 5th
AL—1—many clubs

## CHANCES OFFERED

**Fewest chances offered to outfield, game**
NL—1—Cincinnati vs Pittsburgh, Oct 5, 1970
Montreal vs Los Angeles, Oct 16, 1981
[3—Cincinnati vs Pittsburgh, Oct 3, 1970, 10 inn
Florida vs Chicago, Oct 7, 2003, 11 inn]
AL—1—Minnesota vs Anaheim, Oct 13, 2002 (fielded 8 inn)
[3—Baltimore vs Cleveland, Oct 11, 1997 (fielded 11.1 inn of 12-inn game)]

**Fewest chances offered to outfields of both clubs, game**
NL—5—Pittsburgh 4, Cincinnati 1, Oct 5, 1970
[10—Chicago 7, Florida 3, Oct 7, 2003, 11 inn]
AL—7—Minnesota 4, Baltimore 3, Oct 3, 1970
New York 4, Boston 3, Oct 9, 2003
Boston 5, New York 2, Oct 14, 2003
[9—Cleveland 6, Baltimore 3, Oct 11, 1997, 12 inn]

## ERRORS

**Most errors, total series**
NL—51—Atlanta; 11 series, 60 G
AL—33—Oakland; 10 series, 42 G
New York, 12 series, 61 G

**Most errors, series**
3-game series
AL—7—Kansas City vs Detroit, 1984
NL—6—Atlanta vs New York, 1969
4-game series
NL—7—Los Angeles vs Pittsburgh, 1974
AL—5—Baltimore vs California, 1979
Boston vs Oakland, 1990
5-game series
AL—10—Boston vs New York, 1999
NL—7—St. Louis vs New York, 2000
Atlanta vs Arizona, 2001
6-game series
AL—8—Toronto vs Oakland, 1992
NL—8—Atlanta vs San Diego, 1998
New York vs Atlanta, 1999
7-game series
AL—8—California vs Boston, 1986
NL—8—New York vs Los Angeles, 1988

**Most errors by both clubs, series**
3-game series
AL—10—Oakland 6, Boston 4, 1975
NL—8—Atlanta 6, New York 2, 1969
4-game series
NL—11—Los Angeles 7, Pittsburgh 4, 1974
AL—7—Baltimore 5, California 2, 1979
5-game series
AL—14—Boston 10, New York 4, 1999
NL—11—St. Louis 7, New York 4, 2000
6-game series
AL—15—Toronto 8, Oakland 7, 1992
NL—15—New York 8, Atlanta 7, 1999
7-game series
AL—15—California 8, Boston 7, 1986
NL—13—New York 8, Los Angeles 5, 1988

**Fewest errors, series**
3-game series
AL—0—Baltimore vs Minnesota, 1970
Oakland vs Baltimore, 1971
NL—0—Pittsburgh vs Cincinnati, 1970
4-game series
AL—1—New York vs Kansas City, 1978
Boston vs Oakland, 1988
Oakland vs Boston, 1990
NL—1—Los Angeles vs Philadelphia, 1983
5-game series
NL—1—San Diego vs Chicago, 1984
San Francisco vs St. Louis, 2002
St. Louis vs San Francisco, 2002
AL—1—New York vs Baltimore, 1996
Seattle vs New York, 2001
6-game series
NL—1—New York vs Houston, 1986
San Diego vs Atlanta, 1998
AL—1—New York vs Seattle, 2000
7-game series
NL—1—St. Louis vs Houston, 2004
AL—1—Boston vs New York, 2004

**Fewest errors by both clubs, series**
3-game series
AL—1—Baltimore 1, Oakland 0, 1971
NL—1—Cincinnati 1, Pittsburgh 0, 1970
4-game series
AL—4—Oakland 3, Boston 1, 1988
NL—5—Atlanta 3, Philadelphia 2, 1995
5-game series
NL—2—San Francisco 1, St. Louis 1, 2002
AL—5—Oakland 3, Toronto 2, 1989
Baltimore 4, New York 1, 1996
New York 4, Seattle 1, 2001
6-game series
AL—4—Seattle 3, New York 1, 2000
NL—7—Pittsburgh 5, Cincinnati 2, 1990
Atlanta 4, Florida 3, 1997
7-game series
NL—3—Houston 2, St. Louis 1, 2004
AL—5—New York 4, Boston 1, 2004

**Most errors, game**
AL—5—New York vs Kansas City, Oct 10, 1976
NL—5—Los Angeles vs Pittsburgh, Oct 8, 1974

**Most errors by both clubs, game**
AL—7—Oakland 4, Boston 3, Oct 4, 1975
NL—5—Los Angeles 5, Pittsburgh 0, Oct 8, 1974

**Most errors by infield, game**
AL—3—California vs Boston, Oct 8, 1986
Oakland vs Toronto, Oct 10, 1992
[3—Oakland vs Baltimore, Oct 9, 1973, 11 inn]
NL—3—Atlanta vs Arizona, Oct 20, 2001

**Most errors by infields of both clubs, game**
AL—5—California 3, Boston 2, Oct 8, 1986
NL—3—Atlanta 2, New York 1, Oct 5, 1969
Pittsburgh 2, Cincinnati 1, Oct 10, 1972
Pittsburgh 2, Atlanta 1, Oct 14, 1991
St. Louis 2, Atlanta 1, Oct 10, 1996
Atlanta 3, Arizona 0, Oct 20, 2001
[3—New York 2, Los Angeles 1, Oct 9, 1988, 12 inn
Atlanta 2, New York 1, Oct 17, 1999, 15 inn]

**Most errors by outfield, game**
AL—2—Minnesota vs Baltimore, Oct 6, 1969
Oakland vs Boston, Oct 4, 1975
Milwaukee vs California, Oct 10, 1982
Cleveland vs Seattle, Oct 15, 1995
Cleveland vs Baltimore, Oct 9, 1997
New York vs St. Louis, Oct 11, 2000
NL—1—many clubs

**Most errors by outfields of both clubs, game**
AL—3—Oakland 2, Boston 1, Oct 4, 1975
Cleveland 2, Seattle 1, Oct 15, 1995
NL—2—Philadelphia 1, Atlanta 1, Oct 13, 1993
New York 1, Atlanta 1, Oct 12, 1999
New York 2, St. Louis 0, Oct 11, 2000
[2—Atlanta 1, Pittsburgh 1, Oct 13, 1991, 10 inn]

**Longest errorless game**
NL—16 inn—New York vs Houston, Oct 15, 1986
AL—12 inn—Cleveland vs Baltimore, Oct 11, 1997

**Longest errorless game by both clubs**
NL—12 inn—Houston vs St. Louis, Oct 20, 2004
AL—11 inn—California vs Boston, Oct 12, 1986
Cleveland vs Baltimore, Oct 15, 1997

**Most errors, inning**
AL—3—Oakland vs Boston, Oct 4, 1975, 1st
California vs Boston, Oct 8, 1986, 7th
NL—3—Atlanta vs Arizona, Oct 20, 2001, 3rd

## PASSED BALLS

**Most passed balls, total series**
AL—8—Boston; 7 series, 37 G
NL—6—Pittsburgh; 9 series, 42 G
Atlanta; 11 series, 60 G

**Most passed balls, series**
AL—3—Toronto vs Oakland, 1992 (6-game series)
Boston vs New York, 2003 (7-game series)

Boston vs New York, 2004 (7-game series)
NL—2—many clubs

**Most passed balls by both clubs, series**
AL—4—Boston 3, New York 1, 2004 (7-game series)
NL—3—Chicago 2, San Francisco 1, 1989 (5-game series)
Pittsburgh 2, Atlanta 1, 1992 (7-game series)

**Most passed balls, game**
NL—2—Pittsburgh vs Cincinnati, Oct 4, 1975
Houston vs New York, Oct 11, 1986
Pittsburgh vs Atlanta, Oct 13, 1992
AL—2—Toronto vs Oakland, Oct 14, 1992
[3—Boston vs New York, Oct 18, 2004, 14 inn]

**Most passed balls, inning**
AL—3—Boston vs New York, Oct 18, 2004, 13th
NL—1—many clubs

## DOUBLE AND TRIPLE PLAYS

**Most double plays, total series**
AL—59—New York; 12 series, 61 G
NL—49—Atlanta; 11 series, 60 G

**Most double plays, series**
3-game series
AL—6—New York vs Oakland, 1981
NL—4—Atlanta vs New York, 1969
4-game series
NL—8—Los Angeles vs Pittsburgh, 1974
AL—7—California vs Baltimore, 1979
5-game series
NL—8—Montreal vs Los Angeles, 1981
AL—7—Baltimore vs New York, 1996
New York vs Boston, 1999
6-game series
AL—11—Cleveland vs Baltimore, 1997
NL—9—New York vs Atlanta, 1999
7-game series
NL—10—San Francisco vs St. Louis, 1987
AL—12—New York vs Boston, 2003

**Most double plays by both clubs, series**
3-game series
AL—8—Minnesota 5, Baltimore 3, 1970
NL—6—Atlanta 4, New York 2, 1969
Cincinnati 3, Philadelphia 3, 1976
4-game series
AL—12—California 7, Baltimore 5, 1979
NL—11—Atlanta 7, Cincinnati 4, 1995
5-game series
NL—13—Montreal 8, Los Angeles 5, 1981
AL—9—Oakland 5, Detroit 4, 1972
Toronto 5, Oakland 4, 1989
Seattle 5, New York 4, 2001
Los Angeles 5, Chicago 4, 2005
6-game series
AL—15—Cleveland 11, Baltimore 4, 1997
NL—13—New York 9, Atlanta 4, 1999
7-game series
NL—15—San Francisco 10, St. Louis 5, 1987
AL—17—New York 12, Boston 5, 2003

**Fewest double plays, series**
3-game series
NL—0—Atlanta vs St. Louis, 1982
AL—0—Detroit vs Kansas City, 1984
4-game series
NL—0—Philadelphia vs Los Angeles, 1983
AL—2—New York vs Kansas City, 1978
Boston vs Oakland, 1988
5-game series
AL—0—Boston vs New York, 1999
NL—1—Chicago vs San Francisco, 1989
New York vs St. Louis, 2000
6-game series
NL—1—Atlanta vs Philadelphia, 1993
AL—4—Cleveland vs Seattle, 1995
Baltimore vs Cleveland, 1997
Seattle vs New York, 2000
7-game series
NL—2—New York vs Los Angeles, 1988
Houston vs St. Louis, 2004
AL—4—Toronto vs Kansas City, 1985
Boston vs New York, 2004

**Fewest double plays by both clubs, series**
3-game series
AL—2—Kansas City 2, Detroit 0, 1984
NL—3—St. Louis 3, Atlanta 0, 1982
4-game series
NL—3—Los Angeles 3, Philadelphia 0, 1983
AL—6—Kansas City 4, New York 2, 1978
5-game series
AL—4—Kansas City 2, New York 2, 1977
Minnesota 3, Detroit 1, 1987
NL—4—St. Louis 3, New York 1, 2000
6-game series
NL—3—Philadelphia 2, Atlanta 1, 1993
AL—9—New York 5, Seattle 4, 2000
7-game series
NL—7—St. Louis 5, Houston 2, 2004
AL—10—Boston 5, California 5, 1986

**Most double plays, game**
NL—4—Los Angeles vs Montreal, Oct 13, 1981
San Francisco vs St. Louis, Oct 10, 1987
[5—Atlanta vs Cincinnati, Oct 10, 1995, 11 inn]
AL—4—Oakland vs Boston, Oct 5, 1975
[4—Cleveland vs Baltimore, Oct 11, 1997, 12 inn]

**Most double plays by both clubs, game**
AL—6—Oakland 4, Boston 2, Oct 5, 1975
NL—5—Pittsburgh 3, Cincinnati 2, Oct 5, 1975
[6—Atlanta 5, Cincinnati 1, Oct 10, 1995, 11 inn]

**Most triple plays, series**
AL-NL—none

# MISCELLANEOUS

## CLUB AND DIVISION

### ONE-RUN DECISIONS

**Most one-run games won, series**
NL—3—New York vs Houston, 1986 (6-game series)
Atlanta vs New York, 1999 (6-game series)
AL—4—Cleveland vs Baltimore, 1997 (6-game series)

**Most one-run games by both clubs, series**
NL—5—Atlanta (won 3) vs New York (won 2), 1999 (6-game series)
AL—4—Cleveland (won 4) vs Baltimore, 1997 (6-game series)

### LENGTH OF GAMES

#### BY INNINGS

**Longest game**
NL—16 inn—New York 7, Houston 6, Oct 15, 1986 (at Houston)
AL—14 inn—Boston 5, New York 4, Oct 18, 2004 (at Boston)

**For a complete list of extra-inning games, see page 349.**

**Most extra-inning games, total series**
AL—8—Baltimore; 9 series, 37 games (won 4, lost 4)
NL—8—Atlanta; 11 series, 60 games (won 3, lost 5)

**Most extra-inning games won, total series**
AL—4—Baltimore; 9 series, 37 games (lost 4)
NL—4—Philadelphia; 6 series, 26 games (lost 0)

**Most extra-inning games lost, total series**
NL—5—Atlanta; 11 series, 60 games (won 3)
AL—4—Baltimore; 9 series, 37 games (won 4)

**Most extra-inning games, series**
NL—4—Philadelphia vs Houston, 1980 (5-game series)
AL—2—many games

#### BY TIME

**Longest 9-inning game**
AL—4 hrs, 20 min—New York 19, Boston 8, Oct 16, 2004 (at Boston)
NL—3 hrs, 59 min—New York 6, St. Louis 5, Oct 12, 2000 (at St. Louis)

**Longest extra-inning game**
AL—5 hrs, 49 min—Boston 5, New York 4, Oct 18, 2004, 14 inn (at Boston)
NL—5 hrs, 46 min—New York 4, Atlanta 3, Oct 17, 1999, 15 inn (at New York)

**Shortest game**
AL—1 hr, 57 min—Oakland 1, Baltimore 0, Oct 8, 1974 (at Baltimore)
NL—1 hr, 57 min—Pittsburgh 5, Cincinnati 1, Oct 7, 1972 (at Pittsburgh)

## SERIES STARTING AND FINISHING DATES

**Earliest date for series game**
NL—Oct 2, 1971—Pittsburgh at San Francisco
Oct 2, 1979—Pittsburgh at Cincinnati
Oct 2, 1984—San Diego at Chicago
AL—Oct 2, 1984—Detroit at Kansas City

**Earliest date for series final game**
NL—Oct 5, 1970—Pittsburgh at Cincinnati (3-game series)
Oct 5, 1979—Cincinnati at Pittsburgh (3-game series)
AL—Oct 5, 1970—Minnesota at Baltimore (3-game series)
Oct 5, 1971—Baltimore at Oakland (3-game series)
Oct 5, 1984—Kansas City at Detroit (3-game series)

**Latest date for series start**
AL—Oct 17, 2001—New York at Seattle
NL—Oct 16, 2001—Atlanta at Arizona

**Latest date for series finish**
AL—Oct 22, 2001—Seattle at New York (5-game series)
NL—Oct 21, 2001—Arizona at Atlanta (5-game series)
Oct 21, 2004—Houston at St. Louis (7-game series)

## SERIES AND GAMES WON

**Most series won**
AL—10—New York, 1976-1978, 1981, 1996, 1998-2001, 2003 (lost 2)
NL—5—Los Angeles, 1974, 1977, 1978, 1981, 1988 (lost 2)
Cincinnati, 1970, 1972, 1975, 1976, 1990 (lost 3)
Atlanta, 1991, 1992, 1995, 1996, 1999 (lost 6)

**For complete lists of results, and series played by all teams, see page 348.**

**Most consecutive years winning series**
AL—4—New York, 1998-2001
NL—2—Cincinnati, 1975, 1976
Los Angeles, 1977, 1978
Atlanta, 1991, 1992; 1995, 1996

**Most times winning series in four consecutive games (since 1985)**
AL—2—Oakland, 1988, 1990
NL—1—Atlanta, 1995

**Most times winning series in three consecutive games (1969-1984)**
AL—3—Baltimore, 1969-1971
NL—3—Cincinnati, 1970-1976

**Winning series after winning first game**
AL—accomplished 21 times
NL—accomplished 25 times

**Winning series after losing first game**
AL—accomplished 15 times
NL—accomplished 11 times

**Winning series after trailing two games to one**
NL—Cincinnati vs Pittsburgh, 1972 (5-game series)
Philadelphia vs Houston, 1980 (5-game series)
Los Angeles vs Montreal, 1981 (5-game series)
San Diego vs Chicago, 1984 (5-game series)
St. Louis vs Los Angeles, 1985 (6-game series)
Los Angeles vs New York, 1988 (7-game series)
Philadelphia vs Atlanta, 1993 (6-game series)
Atlanta vs St. Louis, 1996 (7-game series)
Florida vs Chicago, 2003 (7-game series)
AL—New York vs Kansas City, 1977 (5-game series)
Milwaukee vs California, 1982 (5-game series)
Kansas City vs Toronto, 1985 (7-game series)
Boston vs California, 1986 (7-game series)
Cleveland vs Seattle, 1995 (6-game series)
New York vs Cleveland, 1998 (6-game series)

**Winning series after trailing three games to one**
AL—Kansas City vs Toronto, 1985
Boston vs California, 1986
Boston vs New York, 2004
NL—Atlanta vs St. Louis, 1996
Florida vs Chicago, 2003

**Winning series after losing first two games**
AL—Milwaukee vs California, 1982 (5-game series)
Kansas City vs Toronto, 1985 (7-game series)
Boston vs New York, 2004 (7-game series)
NL—San Diego vs Chicago, 1984 (5-game series)
St. Louis vs Los Angeles, 1985 (6-game series)

**Winning series after losing first three games**
AL—Boston vs New York, 2004 (7-game series)
NL—none

**Most games won, total series**
AL—39—New York; 12 series; won 39, lost 22
NL—27—Atlanta; 11 series; won 27, lost 33

**For complete lists of results, and games played by all teams, see page 348.**

**Most consecutive games won, total series**
AL—10—Baltimore, 1969 (3), 1970 (3), 1971 (3), 1973 (first 1)
NL—6—Cincinnati, 1975 (3), 1976 (3)

## SERIES AND GAMES LOST

**Most series lost**
NL—7—Pittsburgh, 1970, 1972, 1974, 1975, 1990, 1991, 1992 (won 2)
AL—4—Kansas City, 1976, 1977, 1978, 1984 (won 2)
Oakland, 1971, 1975, 1981, 1992 (won 6)
Baltimore, 1973, 1974, 1996, 1997 (won 5)
Boston, 1988, 1990, 1999, 2003 (won 2)

**For complete lists of results, and series played by all teams, see page 348.**

**Most consecutive years losing series**
AL—3—Kansas City, 1976-1978
NL—3—Philadelphia, 1976-1978
Pittsburgh, 1990-1992

**Most games lost, total series**
NL—33—Atlanta; 11 series; won 27, lost 33
AL—22—New York; 12 series; won 39, lost 22

**For complete lists of results, and games played by all teams, see page 348.**

**Most consecutive games lost, total series**
AL—10—Boston, 1988 (4), 1990 (4), 1999 (2)
NL—7—Atlanta, 1969 (3), 1982 (3), 1991 (1)

## ATTENDANCE

**Largest attendance, series**
3-game series
NL—180,338—Cincinnati vs Philadelphia, 1976
AL—151,539—Oakland vs New York, 1981
4-game series
NL—240,584—Philadelphia vs Los Angeles, 1977
AL—195,748—Baltimore vs Chicago, 1983
5-game series
AL—284,691—California vs Milwaukee, 1982
NL—271,558—New York vs St. Louis, 2000
6-game series
NL—343,046—Philadelphia vs Atlanta, 1993
AL—309,828—New York vs Seattle, 2000
7-game series
NL—396,597—St. Louis vs San Francisco, 1987
AL—329,600—New York vs Boston, 2004

**For a list of attendance each series, see page 349.**

**Smallest attendance, series**
3-game series
AL—81,945—Baltimore vs Minnesota, 1970
NL—112,943—Pittsburgh vs Cincinnati, 1970
4-game series
AL—144,615—Baltimore vs Oakland, 1974
NL—157,348—San Francisco vs Pittsburgh, 1971
5-game series
AL—175,833—Baltimore vs Oakland, 1973
NL—206,630—Arizona vs Atlanta, 2001
6-game series
AL—282,431—Cleveland vs Baltimore, 1997
NL—286,431—St. Louis vs Houston, 2005
7-game series
AL—264,167—Kansas City vs Toronto, 1985
NL—337,655—Houston vs St. Louis, 2004

**Largest attendance, game**
NL—65,829—At Florida, Oct 11, 2003 (Chicago 8, Florida 3)
AL—64,406—At California, Oct 5, 1982 (California 8, Milwaukee 3)

**Smallest attendance, game**
AL—24,265—At Oakland, Oct 11, 1973 (Oakland 3, Baltimore 0)
NL—33,088—At Pittsburgh, Oct 3, 1970 (Cincinnati 3, Pittsburgh 0)

**Largest attendance by each club, game**

### AMERICAN LEAGUE

| Club | Attendance | Date |
|---|---|---|
| Baltimore | 52,787 | Oct 3,1979 |
| Boston | 35,578 | Oct 4, 1975 |
| | 35,578 | Oct 5, 1975 |
| California/Anaheim/Los Angeles | 64,406 | Oct 5, 1982 |
| Chicago | 46,635 | Oct 7, 1983 |
| Cleveland | 45,081 | Oct 12, 1997 |
| Detroit | 52,168 | Oct 5, 1984 |
| Kansas City | 42,633 | Oct 9, 1980 |
| Milwaukee | 54,968 | Oct 10, 1982 |
| Minnesota | 55,990 | Oct 9, 2002 |
| New York | 57,181 | Oct 13, 1999 |

| Club | Attendance | Date |
|---|---|---|
| Oakland | 49,444 | Oct 4, 1989 |
| Seattle | 58,489 | Oct 17, 1995 |
| Toronto | 51,889 | Oct 9, 1993 |

### NATIONAL LEAGUE

| Club | Attendance | Date |
|---|---|---|
| Arizona | 49,334 | Oct 17, 2001 |
| Atlanta | 52,335 | Oct 19, 1999 |
| Chicago | 39,577 | Oct 14, 2003 |
| Cincinnati | 56,079 | Oct 12, 1990 |
| Florida | 65,829 | Oct 11, 2003 |
| Houston | 45,718 | Oct 15, 1986 |
| Los Angeles | 55,973 | Oct 5, 1977 |
| Montreal | 54,499 | Oct 17, 1981 |
| New York | 55,911 | Oct 15, 1999 |
| Philadelphia | 65,476 | Oct 8, 1980 |
| Pittsburgh | 57,533 | Oct 10, 1991 |
| St. Louis | 56,782 | Oct 14, 1996 |
| San Diego | 65,042 | Oct 11, 1998 |
| San Francisco | 62,084 | Oct 9, 1989 |

**Smallest attendance by each club, game**

### AMERICAN LEAGUE

| Club | Attendance | Date |
|---|---|---|
| Baltimore | 27,608 | Oct 5, 1970 |
| Boston | 32,786 | Oct 8, 1986 |
| California/Anaheim/Los Angeles | 43,199 | Oct 5, 1979 |
| | 43,199 | Oct 6, 1979 |
| Chicago | 40,659 | Oct 11, 2005 |
| Cleveland | 43,607 | Oct 15, 1995 |
| Detroit | 37,615 | Oct 11, 1972 |
| Kansas City | 40,046 | Oct 13, 1985 |
| Milwaukee | 50,135 | Oct 8, 1982 |
| Minnesota | 26,847 | Oct 3, 1970 |
| New York | 48,497 | Oct 14, 1981 |
| Oakland | 24,265 | Oct 11, 1973 |
| Seattle | 47,644 | Oct 17, 2001 |
| Toronto | 32,084 | Oct 16, 1985 |

### NATIONAL LEAGUE

| Club | Attendance | Date |
|---|---|---|
| Arizona | 37,729 | Oct 16, 2001 |
| Atlanta | 35,652 | Oct 21, 2001 |
| Chicago | 36,282 | Oct 2, 1984 |
| | 36,282 | Oct 3, 1984 |
| Cincinnati | 39,447 | Oct 10, 1972 |
| Florida | 51,982 | Oct 12, 1997 |
| Houston | 42,760 | Oct 17, 2004 |
| Los Angeles | 49,963 | Oct 4, 1983 |
| Montreal | 36,491 | Oct 19, 1981 |
| New York | 44,672 | Oct 8, 1988 |
| Philadelphia | 53,490 | Oct 7, 1983 |
| Pittsburgh | 33,088 | Oct 3, 1970 |
| St. Louis | 52,140 | Oct 21, 2004 |
| San Diego | 58,346 | Oct 4, 1984 |
| San Francisco | 40,977 | Oct 2, 1971 |

# NON-PLAYING PERSONNEL

## MANAGERS

**Most series by manager**

ML—10—Bobby Cox, Toronto AL, 1985; Atlanta NL, 1991-2001, except 1994 and 2000 (won 5, lost 5)
NL—9—Bobby Cox, Atlanta, 1991-2001, except 1994 and 2000 (won 5, lost 4)
AL—7—Joe Torre, New York, 1996, 1998-2001, 2003, 2004 (won 6, lost 1)

**For a complete list of managers and their records, see page 357.**

**Most championship series winners managed**

ML—5—Sparky Anderson, Cincinnati NL, 1970, 1972, 1975, 1976; Detroit AL, 1984
NL—5—Bobby Cox, Atlanta, 1991, 1992, 1995, 1996, 1999
AL—6—Joe Torre, New York, 1996, 1998-2001, 2003

**Most championship series losers managed**

ML—5—Bobby Cox, Toronto AL, 1985; Atlanta NL, 1993, 1997, 1998, 2001
Tony La Russa, Chicago AL, 1983; Oakland AL, 1992; St. Louis NL, 1996, 2000, 2002
AL—3—Whitey Herzog, Kansas City, 1976, 1977, 1978
Billy Martin, Minnesota, 1969; Detroit, 1972; Oakland, 1981
Lou Piniella, Seattle, 1995, 2000, 2001
NL—4—Bobby Cox, Atlanta, 1993, 1997, 1998, 2001

**Most different clubs managed, league**

AL—4—Billy Martin, Minnesota 1970; Detroit 1972; New York 1976, 1977; Oakland 1981
NL—2—Bill Virdon, Pittsburgh 1972; Houston 1980
Dave Johnson, New York 1986, 1988; Cincinnati 1995

## UMPIRES

**Most series umpired**

11—Jerry Crawford; 60 G

**Most games umpired**

60—Jerry Crawford; 11 series

# CAREER MILESTONES

**(Players active in the major leagues in 2005 are in boldface.)**

## SERVICE

### SERIES PLAYED

| | Player | Series |
|---|---|---|
| 1. | Reggie Jackson | 11 |
| 2. | **Roger Clemens** | **9** |
| | **Tom Glavine** | **9** |
| | **John Smoltz** | **9** |
| 5. | **Greg Maddux** | **8** |
| | Richie Hebner | 8 |
| | David Justice | 8 |
| | Hal McRae | 8 |
| | Bob Welch | 8 |
| 10. | **Derek Jeter** | **7** |
| | **Tino Martinez** | **7** |
| | **Jeff Nelson** | **7** |
| | **John Olerud** | **7** |
| | **Andy Pettitte** | **7** |
| | **Mariano Rivera** | **7** |
| | **Bernie Williams** | **7** |
| | Don Baylor | 7 |
| | Paul Blair | 7 |
| | Rickey Henderson | 7 |
| | Rick Honeycutt | 7 |
| | Joe Morgan | 7 |
| | Graig Nettles | 7 |
| | Jim Palmer | 7 |
| | Pete Rose | 7 |
| | Mark Wohlers | 7 |

### SERIES PITCHED

| | Player | Series |
|---|---|---|
| 1. | **Roger Clemens** | **9** |
| | **Tom Glavine** | **9** |
| | **John Smoltz** | **9** |
| 4. | **Greg Maddux** | **8** |
| | Bob Welch | 8 |
| 6. | **Jeff Nelson** | **7** |
| | **Andy Pettitte** | **7** |
| | **Mariano Rivera** | 7 |
| | Rick Honeycutt | 7 |
| | Mark Wohlers | 7 |
| 11. | **Mike Stanton** | **6** |
| | **Mike Timlin** | **6** |
| | **David Wells** | **6** |
| | David Cone | 6 |
| | Dennis Eckersley | 6 |
| | Don Gullett | 6 |
| | Catfish Hunter | 6 |
| | Jimmy Key | 6 |

| Player | Series |
|---|---|
| Tug McGraw | 6 |
| Jim Palmer | 6 |
| Ron Reed | 6 |

# BATTING

## GAMES

| | Player | Games |
|---|---|---|
| 1. | David Justice | 46 |
| 2. | Reggie Jackson | 45 |
| **3.** | **Derek Jeter** | **41** |
| | **Bernie Williams** | **41** |
| **5.** | **John Olerud** | **38** |
| | Terry Pendleton | 38 |
| **7.** | **Tino Martinez** | **37** |
| **8.** | **Chipper Jones** | **34** |
| **9.** | **Kenny Lofton** | **33** |
| | **Jorge Posada** | **33** |
| | Rickey Henderson | 33 |
| **12.** | **Manny Ramirez** | **32** |
| 13. | Ron Gant | 31 |
| | Mark Lemke | 31 |
| | Paul O'Neill | 31 |
| 16. | Jeff Blauser | 29 |
| 17. | Roberto Alomar | 28 |
| | Don Baylor | 28 |
| | Fred McGriff | 28 |
| | Hal McRae | 28 |
| | Pete Rose | 28 |

## BATTING AVERAGE

(minimum 50 AB)

| | Player | BA |
|---|---|---|
| 1. | Will Clark | .468 |
| 2. | Mickey Rivers | .386 |
| 3. | Pete Rose | .381 |
| **4.** | **Albert Pujols** | **.371** |
| | Dusty Baker | .371 |
| **6.** | **Hideki Matsui** | **.367** |
| 7. | Steve Garvey | .356 |
| 8. | Brooks Robinson | .348 |
| 9. | Devon White | .347 |
| 10. | George Brett | .340 |
| 11. | Thurman Munson | .339 |
| 12. | Tony Fernandez | .338 |
| 13. | Bill Russell | .337 |
| 14. | Harold Baines | .333 |
| **15.** | **David Ortiz** | **.329** |
| 16. | Cal Ripken Jr. | .328 |
| 17. | Lenny Dykstra | .323 |
| **18.** | **Bernie Williams** | **.321** |
| | Paul O'Neill | .321 |
| 20. | Darrell Porter | .317 |

## AT-BATS

| | Player | AB |
|---|---|---|
| **1.** | **Derek Jeter** | **168** |
| 2. | David Justice | 166 |
| 3. | Reggie Jackson | 163 |
| **4.** | **Bernie Williams** | **162** |
| **5.** | **John Olerud** | **143** |
| **6.** | **Tino Martinez** | **141** |
| **7.** | **Kenny Lofton** | **140** |
| 8. | Terry Pendleton | 135 |
| **9.** | **Chipper Jones** | **127** |
| 10. | Rickey Henderson | 123 |
| **11.** | **Manny Ramirez** | **122** |
| 12. | Pete Rose | 118 |
| 13. | Ron Gant | 117 |
| 14. | Roberto Alomar | 114 |
| 15. | Mark Lemke | 110 |
| 16. | Fred McGriff | 109 |
| **17.** | **Jorge Posada** | **108** |
| 18. | Paul O'Neill | 106 |
| 19. | Chuck Knoblauch | 104 |
| 20. | George Brett | 103 |

## RUNS

| | Player | R |
|---|---|---|
| **1.** | **Bernie Williams** | **31** |
| **2.** | **Derek Jeter** | **25** |
| 3. | David Justice | 24 |
| **4.** | **Kenny Lofton** | **22** |
| | George Brett | 22 |
| | Rickey Henderson | 22 |
| **7.** | **Chipper Jones** | **20** |
| **8.** | **John Olerud** | **19** |
| 9. | Jeff Blauser | 18 |
| | Fred McGriff | 18 |
| **11.** | **Tino Martinez** | **17** |
| | **Jorge Posada** | **17** |
| | Ron Gant | 17 |
| | Pete Rose | 17 |
| **15.** | **Manny Ramirez** | **16** |
| | Reggie Jackson | 16 |
| | Devon White | 16 |
| **18.** | **Albert Pujols** | **15** |
| | **Barry Bonds** | **15** |
| | **Andruw Jones** | **15** |
| | Steve Garvey | 15 |
| | Chuck Knoblauch | 15 |
| | Willie McGee | 15 |

## HITS

| | Player | H |
|---|---|---|
| **1.** | **Bernie Williams** | **52** |
| 2. | Pete Rose | 45 |
| **3.** | **Derek Jeter** | **44** |
| **4.** | **Chipper Jones** | **40** |
| | **John Olerud** | **40** |
| **6.** | **Kenny Lofton** | **39** |
| | David Justice | 39 |
| **8.** | **Manny Ramirez** | **37** |
| | Reggie Jackson | 37 |
| 10. | Roberto Alomar | 36 |
| 11. | George Brett | 35 |
| 12. | Fred McGriff | 34 |
| | Paul O'Neill | 34 |
| 14. | Devon White | 33 |
| 15. | Steve Garvey | 32 |
| 16. | Mark Lemke | 31 |
| 17. | Rickey Henderson | 30 |
| | Chuck Knoblauch | 30 |
| | Terry Pendleton | 30 |
| **20.** | **Tino Martinez** | **29** |
| | Will Clark | 29 |

## SINGLES

| | Player | Singles |
|---|---|---|
| 1. | Pete Rose | 34 |
| **2.** | **Bernie Williams** | **33** |
| **3.** | **Derek Jeter** | **31** |
| | **Kenny Lofton** | **31** |
| **5.** | **Chipper Jones** | **30** |
| 6. | Roberto Alomar | 29 |
| **7.** | **John Olerud** | **28** |
| 8. | David Justice | 26 |
| | Devon White | 26 |
| **10.** | **Manny Ramirez** | **25** |
| | Bill Russell | 25 |
| 12. | Bob Boone | 24 |
| | Reggie Jackson | 24 |
| | Mark Lemke | 24 |
| | Paul O'Neill | 24 |
| 16. | Chuck Knoblauch | 23 |
| | Fred McGriff | 23 |
| 18. | Carney Lansford | 22 |
| | Terry Pendleton | 22 |
| **20.** | **Tino Martinez** | **20** |
| | Tony Fernandez | 20 |
| | Steve Garvey | 20 |

## DOUBLES

| | Player | Doubles |
|---|---|---|
| **1.** | **Bernie Williams** | **10** |
| **2.** | **Hideki Matsui** | **9** |
| **3.** | **Derek Jeter** | **7** |
| | **Chipper Jones** | **7** |
| | **Javy Lopez** | **7** |
| | **Jorge Posada** | **7** |
| | Ron Cey | 7 |
| | Will Clark | 7 |
| | Richie Hebner | 7 |
| | Rickey Henderson | 7 |
| | Reggie Jackson | 7 |
| | David Justice | 7 |
| | Chuck Knoblauch | 7 |
| | Fred McGriff | 7 |
| | Hal McRae | 7 |
| | Pete Rose | 7 |
| | Mike Schmidt | 7 |
| 18. | many with 6 | |

## TRIPLES

| | Player | Triples |
|---|---|---|
| 1. | George Brett | 4 |
| **2.** | **Kenny Lofton** | **3** |
| | Mariano Duncan | 3 |
| | Keith Lockhart | 3 |
| | Willie McGee | 3 |
| 6. | many tied with 2 | |

## HOME RUNS

| | Player | HR |
|---|---|---|
| 1. | **Bernie Williams** | **9** |
| | George Brett | 9 |
| 3. | **Manny Ramirez** | **8** |
| | Steve Garvey | 8 |
| 5. | **Albert Pujols** | **7** |
| | Darryl Strawberry | 7 |
| 7. | **John Olerud** | **6** |
| | **Jim Thome** | **6** |
| | Reggie Jackson | 6 |
| | David Justice | 6 |
| 11. | **Derek Jeter** | **5** |
| | **Javy Lopez** | **5** |
| | **David Ortiz** | **5** |
| | **Jason Varitek** | **5** |
| | Sal Bando | 5 |
| | Johnny Bench | 5 |
| | Ron Gant | 5 |
| | Greg Luzinski | 5 |
| | Gary Matthews | 5 |
| | Graig Nettles | 5 |
| | Paul O'Neill | 5 |

## TOTAL BASES

| | Player | TB |
|---|---|---|
| 1. | **Bernie Williams** | **89** |
| 2. | George Brett | 75 |
| 3. | **Derek Jeter** | **68** |
| 4. | **Manny Ramirez** | **65** |
| 5. | **John Olerud** | **64** |
| | David Justice | 64 |
| 7. | Pete Rose | 63 |
| 8. | Reggie Jackson | 62 |
| 9. | Steve Garvey | 61 |
| 10. | **Chipper Jones** | **56** |
| | **Kenny Lofton** | **56** |
| 12. | Paul O'Neill | 54 |
| 13. | Fred McGriff | 52 |
| 14. | **Albert Pujols** | **50** |
| | Will Clark | 50 |
| 16. | **Javy Lopez** | **49** |
| | Roberto Alomar | 49 |
| 18. | Rickey Henderson | 47 |
| 19. | Ron Gant | 45 |
| | Darryl Strawberry | 45 |

## SLUGGING PERCENTAGE

(Minimum 50 at-bats)

| | Player | SLG |
|---|---|---|
| 1. | Will Clark | .806 |
| 2. | George Brett | .728 |
| 3. | **Albert Pujols** | **.714** |
| 4. | Steve Garvey | .678 |
| 5. | **Hideki Matsui** | **.650** |
| 6. | Darryl Strawberry | .643 |
| 7. | Lenny Dykstra | .629 |
| 8. | **Alex Rodriguez** | **.611** |
| 9. | Dusty Baker | .597 |
| 10. | **David Ortiz** | **.589** |
| | Greg Luzinski | .589 |
| 12. | **Jason Varitek** | **.588** |
| 13. | **Jim Thome** | **.577** |
| 14. | **Jim Edmonds** | **.561** |
| 15. | **Bernie Williams** | **.549** |
| 16. | **Javy Lopez** | **.544** |
| 17. | Pete Rose | .534 |
| 18. | **Manny Ramirez** | **.533** |
| 19. | Johnny Bench | .530 |
| 20. | Sal Bando | .527 |

## EXTRA-BASE HITS

| | Player | EBH |
|---|---|---|
| 1. | **Bernie Williams** | **19** |
| 2. | George Brett | 18 |
| 3. | **Derek Jeter** | **13** |
| | Reggie Jackson | 13 |
| | David Justice | 13 |
| 6. | **Javy Lopez** | **12** |
| | **Hideki Matsui** | **12** |
| | **John Olerud** | **12** |
| | **Manny Ramirez** | **12** |
| | Will Clark | 12 |
| | Steve Garvey | 12 |
| | Greg Luzinski | 12 |
| 13. | Johnny Bench | 11 |
| | Ron Cey | 11 |
| | Rickey Henderson | 11 |
| | Fred McGriff | 11 |
| | Pete Rose | 11 |
| 18. | many tied with 10 | |

## RUNS BATTED IN

| | Player | RBI |
|---|---|---|
| 1. | **Bernie Williams** | **33** |
| 2. | David Justice | 27 |
| 3. | **John Olerud** | **23** |
| 4. | Steve Garvey | 21 |
| 5. | **Derek Jeter** | **20** |
| | Reggie Jackson | 20 |
| 7. | **David Ortiz** | **19** |
| | George Brett | 19 |
| | Graig Nettles | 19 |
| 10. | Fred McGriff | 18 |
| | Paul O'Neill | 18 |
| 12. | **Albert Pujols** | **17** |
| | Don Baylor | 17 |
| | Ron Gant | 17 |
| | Darryl Strawberry | 17 |
| 16. | **Jim Edmonds** | **16** |
| 17. | **Chipper Jones** | **15** |
| | **Jorge Posada** | **15** |
| | Roberto Alomar | 15 |
| | Al Oliver | 15 |

## WALKS

| | Player | BB |
|---|---|---|
| 1. | **Jorge Posada** | **26** |
| 2. | **Bernie Williams** | **25** |
| 3. | **Barry Bonds** | **24** |
| | **Chipper Jones** | **24** |
| | David Justice | 24 |
| 6. | Joe Morgan | 23 |
| 7. | **Derek Jeter** | **20** |
| 8. | Rickey Henderson | 19 |
| 9. | **Manny Ramirez** | **17** |
| | Reggie Jackson | 17 |
| 11. | **John Olerud** | **16** |
| | Darrell Porter | 16 |
| 13. | **Tino Martinez** | **15** |
| | Roberto Alomar | 15 |
| | Jeff Blauser | 15 |
| | Ryan Klesko | 15 |
| | Chuck Knoblauch | 15 |
| | Mark Lemke | 15 |

## STRIKEOUTS

| | Player | K |
|---|---|---|
| 1. | Reggie Jackson | 41 |
| 2. | **Reggie Sanders** | **32** |
| 3. | **Kenny Lofton** | **31** |
| 4. | **Tino Martinez** | **30** |
| 5. | **Derek Jeter** | **28** |
| | **Bernie Williams** | **28** |
| | David Justice | 28 |
| 8. | **Manny Ramirez** | **27** |
| 9. | Ron Gant | 26 |
| 10. | **Jim Edmonds** | **25** |
| 11. | Cesar Geronimo | 24 |
| 12. | **Chipper Jones** | **23** |
| | Jeff Blauser | 23 |
| | Fred McGriff | 23 |
| 15. | Bobby Grich | 22 |
| | Devon White | 22 |
| 17. | **Marquis Grissom** | **21** |
| | **Jorge Posada** | **21** |
| | Willie McGee | 21 |
| | Darryl Strawberry | 21 |
| 21. | **Javy Lopez** | **20** |
| | **David Ortiz** | **20** |
| | Mariano Duncan | 20 |
| | Rickey Henderson | 20 |
| | Greg Luzinski | 20 |

## STOLEN BASES

| | Player | SB |
|---|---|---|
| 1. | Rickey Henderson | 17 |
| 2. | Roberto Alomar | 11 |
| 3. | **Kenny Lofton** | **10** |
| 4. | Davey Lopes | 9 |
| 5. | **Derek Jeter** | **8** |
| | Ron Gant | 8 |
| | Joe Morgan | 8 |
| | Amos Otis | 8 |
| | Willie Wilson | 8 |
| 10. | **Omar Vizquel** | **7** |
| 11. | **Barry Bonds** | **6** |
| | Bert Campaneris | 6 |
| | Vince Coleman | 6 |
| | Kirk Gibson | 6 |
| | Steve Sax | 6 |
| | Walt Weiss | 6 |
| 17. | **Ken Griffey** | **5** |
| | **Marquis Grissom** | **5** |

| Player | SB |
|---|---|
| **Chipper Jones** | **5** |
| Tony Fernandez | 5 |
| Otis Nixon | 5 |

# PITCHING

## GAMES

| Player | Games |
|---|---|
| **1. Mariano Rivera** | **25** |
| **2. Mike Timlin** | **20** |
| Rick Honeycutt | 20 |
| **4. Jeff Nelson** | **19** |
| Mark Wohlers | 19 |
| 6. Dennis Eckersley | 18 |
| Randy Myers | 18 |
| **8. John Smoltz** | **17** |
| **Mike Stanton** | **17** |
| **10. Armando Benitez** | **15** |
| **Tom Glavine** | **15** |
| **Greg Maddux** | **15** |
| Tug McGraw | 15 |
| **14. Roger Clemens** | **14** |
| Jesse Orosco | 14 |
| **16. Alan Embree** | **13** |
| Paul Assenmacher | 13 |
| Dave Giusti | 13 |
| Alejandro Pena | 13 |
| Ron Reed | 13 |
| Mike Remlinger | 13 |

## GAMES STARTED

| Player | Games |
|---|---|
| **1. Tom Glavine** | **15** |
| **2. Roger Clemens** | **14** |
| **Greg Maddux** | **14** |
| **4. John Smoltz** | **13** |
| **5. Andy Pettitte** | **11** |
| 6. Catfish Hunter | 10 |
| Dave Stewart | 10 |
| **8. Mike Mussina** | **8** |
| Steve Carlton | 8 |
| David Cone | 8 |
| Orel Hershiser | 8 |
| **12. Orlando Hernandez** | **7** |
| Steve Avery | 7 |
| Doug Drabek | 7 |
| Tommy John | 7 |
| Jim Palmer | 7 |
| Jerry Reuss | 7 |
| 18. many tied with 6 | |

## GAMES RELIEVED

| Player | Games |
|---|---|
| **1. Mariano Rivera** | **25** |
| **2. Mike Timlin** | **20** |
| Rick Honeycutt | 20 |
| **4. Jeff Nelson** | **19** |
| Mark Wohlers | 19 |
| 6. Randy Myers | 18 |
| **7. Mike Stanton** | **17** |
| Dennis Eckersley | 17 |
| **9. Armando Benitez** | **15** |
| Tug McGraw | 15 |
| 11. Jesse Orosco | 14 |
| **12. Alan Embree** | **13** |
| **Mike Remlinger** | **13** |
| Paul Assenmacher | 13 |
| Dave Giusti | 13 |
| Alejandro Pena | 13 |
| 17. many tied with 12 | |

## COMPLETE GAMES

| Player | CG |
|---|---|
| 1. Jim Palmer | 5 |
| 2. Catfish Hunter | 3 |
| Tommy John | 3 |
| 4. many tied with 2 | |

## INNINGS PITCHED

| Player | IP |
|---|---|
| **1. John Smoltz** | **95.1** |
| **2. Tom Glavine** | **92.1** |
| **3. Greg Maddux** | **85.1** |
| **4. Roger Clemens** | **81.1** |
| 5. Dave Stewart | 75.1 |
| **6. Andy Pettitte** | **72.0** |
| 7. Catfish Hunter | 69.1 |
| 8. Orel Hershiser | 65.1 |
| 9. Jim Palmer | 59.2 |
| **10. Mike Mussina** | **56.2** |
| 11. Steve Carlton | 53.2 |
| 12. David Cone | 51.0 |
| 13. Don Sutton | 49.0 |
| 14. Doug Drabek | 48.1 |
| 15. Tommy John | 47.2 |
| **16. Orlando Hernandez** | **47.0** |
| 17. Steve Avery | 45.1 |
| **18. David Wells** | **44.2** |
| 19. Mike Cuellar | 44.0 |
| 20. Dwight Gooden | 42.1 |

## EARNED RUN AVERAGE

(minimum 30 IP)

| Player | ERA |
|---|---|
| **1. Mariano Rivera** | **0.93** |
| 2. Orel Hershiser | 1.52 |
| **3. Randy Johnson** | **1.72** |
| 4. Fernando Valenzuela | 1.95 |
| 5. Jim Palmer | 1.96 |
| 6. Don Sutton | 2.02 |
| 7. Dave Stewart | 2.03 |
| 8. Doug Drabek | 2.05 |
| 9. Ken Holtzman | 2.06 |
| 10. Tommy John | 2.08 |
| 11. Juan Guzman | 2.27 |
| 12. Dwight Gooden | 2.34 |
| 13. Steve Avery | 2.38 |
| 14. Charles Nagy | 2.64 |
| 15. Paul Splittorff | 2.68 |
| Dave McNally | 2.68 |
| **17. Tim Wakefield** | **2.81** |
| **18. Curt Schilling** | **2.83** |
| **John Smoltz** | **2.83** |
| 19. Tom Seaver | 2.84 |
| 20. Danny Jackson | 2.94 |

## WINS

| Player | W |
|---|---|
| 1. Dave Stewart | 8 |
| **2. Andy Pettitte** | **6** |
| **John Smoltz** | **6** |
| **4. Roger Clemens** | **5** |
| **Tom Glavine** | **5** |
| **Tim Wakefield** | **5** |
| Juan Guzman | 5 |
| **8. Orlando Hernandez** | **4** |
| **Greg Maddux** | **4** |
| **Mariano Rivera** | **4** |
| **Tim Wakefield** | **4** |
| **David Wells** | **4** |
| Steve Avery | 4 |
| Steve Carlton | 4 |
| David Cone | 4 |
| Orel Hershiser | 4 |
| Catfish Hunter | 4 |
| Tommy John | 4 |
| Bruce Kison | 4 |
| Jim Palmer | 4 |
| Don Sutton | 4 |

## LOSSES

| Player | L |
|---|---|
| **1. Tom Glavine** | **9** |
| **2. Greg Maddux** | **8** |
| 3. Jerry Reuss | 7 |
| 4. Doug Drabek | 5 |
| **5. Roger Clemens** | **4** |
| Doyle Alexander | 4 |
| Todd Stottlemyre | 4 |
| **8. Matt Morris** | **3** |
| **Mike Mussina** | **3** |
| **Aaron Sele** | **3** |
| Alex Fernandez | 3 |
| Gene Garber | 3 |
| Don Gullett | 3 |
| Ken Holtzman | 3 |
| Catfish Hunter | 3 |
| Charlie Leibrandt | 3 |
| Dennis Leonard | 3 |
| Chad Ogea | 3 |
| Zane Smith | 3 |
| Dave Stieb | 3 |

## SAVES

| | Player | SV |
|---|---|---|
| 1. | Dennis Eckersley | 11 |
| **2.** | **Mariano Rivera** | **10** |
| **3.** | **Jason Isringhausen** | **5** |
| | **Brad Lidge** | **5** |
| | Tug McGraw | 5 |
| | Robb Nen | 5 |
| 7. | Ken Dayley | 4 |
| | Dave Giusti | 4 |
| | Randy Myers | 4 |
| | Alejandro Pena | 4 |

## RUNS

| | Player | R |
|---|---|---|
| **1.** | **Greg Maddux** | **50** |
| **2.** | **Tom Glavine** | **40** |
| **3.** | **Roger Clemens** | **37** |
| **4.** | **John Smoltz** | **33** |
| **5.** | **Andy Pettitte** | **26** |
| 6. | Catfish Hunter | 25 |
| | Jerry Reuss | 25 |
| | Todd Stottlemyre | 25 |
| 9. | Doyle Alexander | 23 |
| | David Cone | 23 |
| 11. | Steve Carlton | 22 |
| | Jack Morris | 22 |
| **13.** | **Matt Morris** | **21** |
| | **Mike Mussina** | **21** |
| **15.** | **Kevin Brown** | **19** |
| | **Orlando Hernandez** | **19** |
| | Andy Benes | 19 |
| | Nolan Ryan | 19 |
| **19.** | **Pedro Martinez** | **18** |
| | **Scott Erickson** | **18** |
| | Don Gullett | 18 |
| | Bob Welch | 18 |

## HITS

| | Player | H |
|---|---|---|
| **1.** | **Tom Glavine** | **91** |
| **2.** | **Greg Maddux** | **86** |
| **3.** | **John Smoltz** | **81** |
| **4.** | **Andy Pettitte** | **78** |
| **5.** | **Roger Clemens** | **70** |
| 6. | Catfish Hunter | 57 |
| 7. | Steve Carlton | 53 |
| 8. | Dave Stewart | 52 |
| 9. | Orel Hershiser | 49 |
| 10. | Jim Palmer | 46 |
| 11. | David Cone | 45 |
| 12. | Larry Gura | 43 |
| **13.** | **Mike Mussina** | **42** |
| 14. | Doug Drabek | 40 |
| | Tommy John | 40 |
| **16.** | **David Wells** | **39** |
| | Jack Morris | 39 |
| **18.** | **Matt Morris** | **38** |
| | Danny Jackson | 38 |
| | Todd Stottlemyre | 38 |

## HOME RUNS

| | Player | HR |
|---|---|---|
| 1. | Catfish Hunter | 12 |
| **2.** | **Andy Pettitte** | **11** |
| **3.** | **Roger Clemens** | **8** |
| | **Tom Glavine** | **8** |
| | **John Smoltz** | **8** |
| **6.** | **Mike Musina** | **7** |
| | Dave McNally | 7 |
| | Dave Stewart | 7 |
| **9.** | **Scott Erickson** | **6** |
| | **Greg Maddux** | **6** |
| | **Tim Wakefield** | **6** |
| | **David Wells** | **6** |
| | Doyle Alexander | 6 |
| | Steve Blass | 6 |
| | Jim Perry | 6 |
| 16. | many tied with 5 | |

## TOTAL BASES

| | Player | TB |
|---|---|---|
| **1.** | **Tom Glavine** | **142** |
| **2.** | **Greg Maddux** | **125** |
| | **John Smoltz** | **125** |
| **4.** | **Andy Pettitte** | **121** |
| 5. | Catfish Hunter | 112 |
| **6.** | **Roger Clemens** | **107** |
| 7. | Steve Carlton | 85 |
| 8. | Dave Stewart | 80 |
| 9. | Jim Palmer | 75 |
| **10.** | **Mike Mussina** | **70** |
| 11. | David Cone | 69 |
| **12.** | **David Wells** | **64** |
| **13.** | **Matt Morris** | **63** |
| | Doyle Alexander | 63 |
| | Larry Gura | 63 |
| | Todd Stottlemyre | 63 |
| 17. | Orel Hershiser | 60 |
| | Jack Morris | 60 |
| 19. | Dave McNally | 59 |
| | Don Sutton | 59 |

## STRIKEOUTS

| | Player | K |
|---|---|---|
| **1.** | **John Smoltz** | **89** |
| **2.** | **Roger Clemens** | **71** |
| **3.** | **Mike Mussina** | **66** |
| **4.** | **Greg Maddux** | **64** |
| **5.** | **Tom Glavine** | **62** |
| 6. | Orel Hershiser | 47 |
| **7.** | **Orlando Hernandez** | **46** |
| | Jim Palmer | 46 |
| | Nolan Ryan | 46 |
| 10. | David Cone | 45 |
| **11.** | **David Wells** | **42** |
| **12.** | **Pedro Martinez** | **40** |
| **13.** | **Andy Pettitte** | **39** |
| | Steve Carlton | 39 |
| | Dave Stewart | 39 |
| 16. | Steve Avery | 37 |
| | Catfish Hunter | 37 |
| **18.** | **Curt Schilling** | **36** |
| 19. | Doug Drabek | 33 |
| | Dwight Gooden | 33 |
| | Denny Neagle | 33 |

## WALKS

| | Player | BB |
|---|---|---|
| **1.** | **Tom Glavine** | **37** |
| **2.** | **John Smoltz** | **34** |
| 3. | Steve Carlton | 28 |
| **4.** | **Roger Clemens** | **26** |
| | **Orlando Hernandez** | **26** |
| **6.** | **Greg Maddux** | **25** |
| | Dave Stewart | 25 |
| 8. | David Cone | 24 |
| **9.** | **Andy Pettitte** | **20** |
| | Orel Hershiser | 20 |
| 11. | Mike Cuellar | 19 |
| | Jim Palmer | 19 |
| | Fernando Valenzuela | 19 |
| 14. | Juan Guzman | 18 |
| | Catfish Hunter | 18 |
| **16.** | **Matt Morris** | **17** |
| | Steve Avery | 17 |
| | Jerry Reuss | 17 |
| 19. | Dwight Gooden | 16 |
| | Tug McGraw | 16 |
| | Denny Neagle | 16 |
| | Dave Stieb | 16 |

# GENERAL REFERENCE



## SERIES WON AND LOST BY TEAMS

### AMERICAN LEAGUE

| | W | L | Pct. |
|---|---|---|---|
| Milwaukee | 1 | 0 | 1.000 |
| New York | 10 | 2 | .833 |
| Cleveland | 2 | 1 | .667 |
| Oakland | 6 | 4 | .600 |
| Baltimore | 5 | 4 | .556 |
| Boston | 3 | 4 | .429 |
| Minnesota | 2 | 3 | .400 |
| Toronto | 2 | 3 | .400 |
| Kansas City | 2 | 4 | .333 |
| Chicago | 1 | 2 | .333 |
| Detroit | 1 | 2 | .333 |
| California/Anaheim/Los Angeles | 1 | 4 | .200 |
| Seattle | 0 | 3 | .000 |

**Total Series: 36**

### NATIONAL LEAGUE

| | W | L | Pct. |
|---|---|---|---|
| Florida | 2 | 0 | 1.000 |
| San Diego | 2 | 0 | 1.000 |
| Arizona | 1 | 0 | 1.000 |
| Los Angeles | 5 | 2 | .714 |
| New York | 4 | 2 | .667 |
| Cincinnati | 5 | 3 | .625 |
| St. Louis | 4 | 4 | .500 |
| Philadelphia | 3 | 3 | .500 |
| San Francisco | 2 | 2 | .500 |
| Atlanta | 5 | 6 | .455 |
| Houston | 1 | 3 | .250 |
| Pittsburgh | 2 | 7 | .222 |
| Montreal | 0 | 1 | .000 |
| Chicago | 0 | 3 | .000 |

**Total series: 36**

## GAMES WON AND LOST BY TEAMS

### AMERICAN LEAGUE

| | W | L | Pct. |
|---|---|---|---|
| New York | 39 | 22 | .639 |
| Milwaukee | 3 | 2 | .600 |
| Baltimore | 21 | 16 | .568 |
| Cleveland | 10 | 8 | .556 |
| Oakland | 23 | 19 | .548 |
| Chicago | 7 | 8 | .467 |
| Detroit | 6 | 7 | .462 |
| Toronto | 13 | 16 | .448 |
| Kansas City | 12 | 15 | .444 |
| Minnesota | 9 | 12 | .429 |
| California/Anaheim/Los Angeles | 11 | 15 | .423 |
| Boston | 15 | 22 | .405 |
| Seattle | 5 | 12 | .294 |

**Total games: 174**

### NATIONAL LEAGUE

| | W | L | Pct. |
|---|---|---|---|
| Arizona | 4 | 1 | .800 |
| San Diego | 7 | 4 | .636 |
| Florida | 8 | 5 | .615 |
| New York | 19 | 13 | .594 |
| San Francisco | 12 | 9 | .571 |
| Cincinnati | 18 | 14 | .563 |
| Los Angeles | 19 | 15 | .559 |
| St. Louis | 22 | 24 | .478 |
| Houston | 11 | 13 | .458 |
| Philadelphia | 12 | 14 | .462 |
| Atlanta | 27 | 33 | .450 |
| Pittsburgh | 17 | 25 | .405 |
| Montreal | 2 | 3 | .400 |
| Chicago | 6 | 11 | .353 |

**Total games: 184**

## HOME AND ROAD GAMES BY TEAMS

### AMERICAN LEAGUE

| | Series | Games | Home | Away |
|---|---|---|---|---|
| New York | 12 | 61 | 31 | 30 |
| Oakland | 10 | 42 | 19 | 23 |
| Baltimore | 9 | 37 | 19 | 18 |
| Boston | 7 | 37 | 19 | 18 |
| Toronto | 5 | 29 | 16 | 13 |
| Kansas City | 6 | 27 | 14 | 13 |
| California/Anaheim/Los Angeles | 5 | 26 | 13 | 13 |
| Minnesota | 5 | 21 | 9 | 12 |
| Cleveland | 3 | 18 | 9 | 9 |
| Seattle | 3 | 17 | 8 | 9 |
| Chicago | 3 | 15 | 7 | 8 |
| Detroit | 3 | 13 | 7 | 6 |
| Milwaukee | 1 | 5 | 3 | 2 |

### NATIONAL LEAGUE

| | Series | Games | Home | Away |
|---|---|---|---|---|
| Atlanta | 11 | 60 | 30 | 30 |
| St. Louis | 8 | 46 | 23 | 23 |
| Pittsburgh | 9 | 42 | 20 | 22 |
| Los Angeles | 7 | 34 | 17 | 17 |
| Cincinnati | 8 | 32 | 16 | 16 |
| New York | 6 | 32 | 16 | 16 |
| Philadelphia | 6 | 26 | 13 | 13 |
| Houston | 4 | 24 | 12 | 12 |
| San Francisco | 4 | 21 | 11 | 10 |
| Chicago | 3 | 17 | 8 | 9 |
| Florida | 2 | 13 | 6 | 7 |
| San Diego | 2 | 11 | 6 | 5 |
| Arizona | 1 | 5 | 2 | 3 |
| Montreal | 1 | 5 | 3 | 2 |

## SHUTOUTS

### AMERICAN LEAGUE

| | |
|---|---|
| Oct 5, 1969 | Dave McNally, Baltimore 1, Minnesota 0, 11 inn (3 H) |
| Oct 8, 1972 | Blue Moon Odom, Oakland 5, Detroit 0 (3 H) |
| Oct 10, 1972 | Joe Coleman, Detroit 3, Oakland 0 (7 H) |
| Oct 6, 1973 | Jim Palmer, Baltimore 6, Oakland 0 (5 H) |
| Oct 11, 1973 | Catfish Hunter, Oakland 3, Baltimore 0 (5 H) |
| Oct 6, 1974 | Ken Holtzman, Oakland 5, Baltimore 0 (5 H) |
| Oct 8, 1974 | Vida Blue, Oakland 1, Baltimore 0 (2 H) |
| Oct 6, 1979 | Scott McGregor, Baltimore 8, California 0 (6 H) |
| Oct 15, 1981 | Dave Righetti, Ron Davis, Rich Gossage, New York 4, Oakland 0 (5 H) |
| Oct 6, 1983 | Mike Boddicker, Baltimore 4, Chicago 0 (5 H) |
| Oct 8, 1983 | Storm Davis and Tippy Martinez, Baltimore 3, Chicago 0, 10 inn (10 H) |
| Oct 5, 1984 | Milt Wilcox and Willie Hernandez, Detroit 1, Kansas City 0 (3 H) |
| Oct 13, 1985 | Danny Jackson, Kansas City 2, Toronto 0 (8 H) |
| Oct 14, 1995 | Ken Hill, Jim Poole, Chad Ogea, Alan Embree, Cleveland 7, Seattle 0 (6 H) |
| Oct 17, 1995 | Dennis Martinez, Julian Tavares, Jose Mesa, Cleveland 4, Seattle 0 (4 H) |
| Oct 8, 1997 | Scott Erickson and Randy Myers, Baltimore 3, Cleveland 0 (4 H) |
| Oct 15, 1997 | Charles Nagy, Paul Assenmacher, Mike Jackson, Brian Anderson, Jose Mesa, Cleveland 1, Baltimore 0, 11 innings (10 H) |
| Oct 10, 1998 | Orlando Hernandez, New York 4, Cleveland 0 (4 H) |
| Oct 10, 2000 | Freddy Garcia, Jose Paniagua, Arthur Rhodes, Kazuhiro Sasaki, Seattle 2, New York 0 (6 H) |
| Oct 14, 2000 | Roger Clemens, New York 5, Seattle 0 (1 H) |

**Total number of shutouts: 20**

### NATIONAL LEAGUE

| | |
|---|---|
| Oct 3, 1970 | Gary Nolan, Clay Carroll, Cincinnati 3, Pittsburgh 0, 10 inn (8 H) |
| Oct 7, 1973 | Jon Matlack, New York 5, Cincinnati 0 (2 H) |
| Oct 5, 1974 | Don Sutton, Los Angeles 3, Pittsburgh 0 (4 H) |
| Oct 8, 1974 | Bruce Kison, Ramon Hernandez, Pittsburgh 7, Los Angeles 0 (4 H) |
| Oct 4, 1978 | Tommy John, Los Angeles 4, Philadelphia 0 (4 H) |
| Oct 10, 1980 | Joe Niekro, Dave Smith, Houston 1, Philadelphia 0, 11 inn (7 H) |
| Oct 14, 1981 | Ray Burris, Montreal 3, Los Angeles 0 (5 H) |
| Oct 7, 1982 | Bob Forsch, St. Louis 7, Atlanta 0 (3 H) |

Oct 4, 1983 Steve Carlton, Al Holland, Philadelphia 1, Los Angeles 0 (7 H)
Oct 2, 1984 Rick Sutcliffe, Warren Brusstar, Chicago 13, San Diego 0 (6 H)
Oct 8, 1986 Mike Scott, Houston 1, New York 0 (5 H)
Oct 7, 1987 Dave Dravecky, San Francisco 5, St. Louis 0 (2 H)
Oct 13, 1987 John Tudor, Todd Worrell, Ken Dayley, St. Louis 1, San Francisco 0 (6 H)
Oct 14, 1987 Danny Cox, St. Louis 6, San Francisco 0 (8 H)
Oct 12, 1988 Orel Hershiser, Los Angeles 6, New York 0 (5 H)
Oct 10, 1991 Steve Avery, Alejandro Pena, Atlanta 1, Pittsburgh 0 (6 H)
Oct 14, 1991 Zane Smith, Roger Mason, Pittsburgh 1, Atlanta 0 (9 H)
Oct 16, 1991 Steve Avery, Alejandro Pena, Atlanta 1, Pittsburgh 0 (4 H)
Oct 17, 1991 John Smoltz, Atlanta 4, Pittsburgh 0 (6 H)
Oct 14, 1995 Steve Avery, Greg McMichael, Alejandro Pena, Mark Wohlers, Atlanta 6, Cincinnati 0 (3 H)
Oct 14, 1996 John Smoltz, Mike Bielecki, Terrell Wade, Brad Clontz, Atlanta 14, St. L 0 (7 H)
Oct 17, 1996 Tom Glavine, Mike Bielecki, Steve Avery, Atlanta, 15, St. Louis 0 (4 H)
Oct 11, 1997 Denny Neagle, Atlanta 4, Florida 0 (4 H)
Oct 8, 1998 Kevin Brown, San Diego 3, Atlanta 0 (3 H)
Oct 14, 1998 Sterling Hitchcock, Brian Boehringer, Mark Langston, Joey Hamilton, Trevor Hoffman, San Diego 5, Atlanta 0 (2 H)
Oct 15, 1999 Tom Glavine, Mike Remlinger, John Rocker, Atlanta 1, New York 0 (7 H)
Oct 16, 2000 Mike Hampton, New York 7, St. Louis 0 (3 H)
Oct 16, 2001 Randy Johnson, Arizona 2, Atlanta 0 (3 H)
Oct 12, 2003 Josh Beckett, Florida 4, Chicago 0 (2 H)
Oct 18, 2004 Brandon Backe, Brad Lidge, Houston 3, St. Louis 0 (1 H)

**Total number of shutouts: 30**

## EXTRA-INNING GAMES

### AMERICAN LEAGUE

Oct 4, 1969 12 inn, Baltimore 4, Minnesota 3
Oct 5, 1969 11 inn, Baltimore 1, Minnesota 0
Oct 7, 1972 11 inn, Oakland 3, Detroit 2
Oct 11, 1972 10 inn, Detroit 4, Oakland 3
Oct 9, 1973 11 inn, Oakland 2, Baltimore 1
Oct 3, 1979 10 inn, Baltimore 6, California 2
Oct 8, 1983 10 inn, Baltimore 3, Chicago 0
Oct 3, 1984 11 inn, Detroit 5, Kansas City 3
Oct 9, 1985 10 inn, Toronto 6, Kansas City 5
Oct 11, 1986 11 inn, California 4, Boston 3
Oct 12, 1986 11 inn, Boston 7, California 6
Oct 11, 1991 10 inn, Minnesota 3, Toronto 2
Oct 11, 1992 11 inn, Toronto 7, Oakland 6
Oct 13, 1995 11 inn, Seattle 5, Cleveland 2
Oct 9, 1996 11 inn, New York 5, Baltimore 4
Oct 11, 1997 12 inn, Cleveland 2, Baltimore 1
Oct 15, 1997 11 inn, Cleveland 1, Baltimore 0
Oct 7, 1998 12 inn, Cleveland 4, New York 1
Oct 13, 1999 10 inn, New York 4, Boston 3
Oct 16, 2003 11 inn, New York 6, Boston 5
Oct 17, 2004 12 inn, Boston 6, New York 4
Oct 18, 2004 14 inn, Boston 5, New York 4

**Total number of extra-inning games: 22**

### NATIONAL LEAGUE

Oct 3, 1970 10 inn, Cincinnati 3, Pittsburgh 0
Oct 9, 1973 12 inn, Cincinnati 2, New York 1
Oct 7, 1975 10 inn, Cincinnati 5, Pittsburgh 3
Oct 7, 1978 10 inn, Los Angeles 4, Philadelphia 3
Oct 2, 1979 11 inn, Pittsburgh 5, Cincinnati 2
Oct 3, 1979 10 inn, Pittsburgh 3, Cincinnati 2
Oct 8, 1980 10 inn, Houston 7, Philadelphia 4
Oct 10, 1980 11 inn, Houston 1, Philadelphia 0
Oct 11, 1980 10 inn, Philadelphia 5, Houston 3
Oct 12, 1980 10 inn, Philadelphia 8, Houston 7
Oct 14, 1986 12 inn, New York 2, Houston 1
Oct 15, 1986 16 inn, New York 7, Houston 6
Oct 9, 1988 12 inn, Los Angeles 5, New York 4
Oct 13, 1991 10 inn, Pittsburgh 3, Atlanta 2
Oct 6, 1993 10 inn, Philadelphia 4, Atlanta 3
Oct 11, 1993 10 inn, Philadelphia 4, Atlanta 3
Oct 10, 1995 11 inn, Atlanta 2, Cincinnati 1
Oct 11, 1995 10 inn, Atlanta 6, Cincinnati 2
Oct 7, 1998 10 inn, San Diego 3, Atlanta 2
Oct 17, 1999 15 inn, New York 4, Atlanta 3
Oct 19, 1999 11 inn, Atlanta 10, New York 9
Oct 7, 2003 11 inn, Florida 9, Chicago 8
Oct 10, 2003 11 inn, Chicago 5, Florida 4
Oct 20, 2004 12 inn, St. Louis 6, Houston 4

**Total number of extra-inning games: 24**

## ATTENDANCE

### AMERICAN LEAGUE

| Year | Games | Total |
|---|---|---|
| 1969 | 3 | 113,763 |
| 1970 | 3 | 81,945 |
| 1971 | 3 | 110,800 |
| 1972 | 5 | 189,671 |
| 1973 | 5 | 175,833 |
| 1974 | 4 | 144,615 |
| 1975 | 3 | 120,514 |
| 1976 | 5 | 252,152 |
| 1977 | 5 | 234,713 |
| 1978 | 4 | 194,192 |
| 1979 | 4 | 191,293 |
| 1980 | 3 | 141,819 |
| 1981 | 3 | 151,539 |
| 1982 | 5 | 284,691 |
| 1983 | 4 | 195,748 |
| 1984 | 3 | 136,160 |
| 1985 | 7 | 264,167 |
| 1986 | 7 | 324,430 |
| 1987 | 5 | 257,631 |
| 1988 | 4 | 167,376 |
| 1989 | 5 | 249,247 |
| 1990 | 4 | 168,340 |
| 1991 | 5 | 263,987 |
| 1992 | 6 | 293,086 |
| 1993 | 6 | 292,921 |
| 1995 | 6 | 304,634 |
| 1996 | 5 | 259,254 |
| 1997 | 6 | 282,431 |
| 1998 | 6 | 323,007 |
| 1999 | 5 | 214,726 |
| 2000 | 6 | 309,828 |
| 2001 | 5 | 264,697 |
| 2002 | 5 | 245,451 |
| 2003 | 7 | 328,559 |
| 2004 | 7 | 329,600 |
| 2005 | 5 | 215,966 |

### NATIONAL LEAGUE

| Year | Games | Total |
|---|---|---|
| 1969 | 3 | 153,587 |
| 1970 | 3 | 112,943 |
| 1971 | 4 | 157,348 |
| 1972 | 5 | 234,814 |
| 1973 | 5 | 262,548 |
| 1974 | 4 | 200,262 |
| 1975 | 3 | 155,740 |
| 1976 | 3 | 180,338 |
| 1977 | 4 | 240,584 |
| 1978 | 4 | 234,269 |
| 1979 | 3 | 152,246 |
| 1980 | 5 | 264,950 |
| 1981 | 5 | 250,098 |
| 1982 | 3 | 158,589 |
| 1983 | 4 | 223,914 |
| 1984 | 5 | 247,623 |
| 1985 | 6 | 326,824 |
| 1986 | 6 | 299,316 |
| 1987 | 7 | 396,597 |
| 1988 | 7 | 373,695 |
| 1989 | 5 | 264,617 |
| 1990 | 6 | 310,528 |
| 1991 | 7 | 369,443 |

| Year | Games | Total |
|---|---|---|
| 1992 | 7 | 374,599 |
| 1993 | 6 | 343,046 |
| 1995 | 4 | 188,497 |
| 1996 | 7 | 375,202 |
| 1997 | 6 | 309,352 |
| 1998 | 6 | 306,259 |
| 1999 | 6 | 308,637 |
| 2000 | 5 | 271,558 |
| 2001 | 5 | 206,630 |
| 2002 | 5 | 231,896 |
| 2003 | 7 | 354,503 |
| 2004 | 7 | 337,655 |
| 2005 | 6 | 286,431 |

# INDIVIDUAL BATTING

## LEADING BATTERS

**(Playing in all games, each series, with four or more hits)**

### AMERICAN LEAGUE

| Year | Player, Club | AB | H | TB | Avg. |
|---|---|---|---|---|---|
| 1969 | Brooks Robinson, Baltimore | 14 | 7 | 8 | .500 |
| 1970 | Brooks Robinson, Baltimore | 12 | 7 | 9 | .583 |
| 1971 | Brooks Robinson, Baltimore | 11 | 4 | 8 | .364 |
| | Sal Bando, Oakland | 11 | 4 | 9 | .364 |
| 1972 | Matty Alou, Oakland | 21 | 8 | 12 | .381 |
| 1973 | Bert Campaneris, Oakland | 21 | 7 | 14 | .333 |
| 1974 | Ray Fosse, Oakland | 12 | 4 | 8 | .333 |
| 1975 | Sal Bando, Oakland | 12 | 6 | 8 | .500 |
| 1976 | Chris Chambliss, New York | 21 | 11 | 20 | .524 |
| 1977 | Hal McRae, Kansas City | 18 | 8 | 14 | .444 |
| 1978 | Reggie Jackson, New York | 13 | 6 | 13 | .462 |
| 1979 | Eddie Murray, Baltimore | 12 | 5 | 8 | .417 |
| 1980 | Frank White, Kansas City | 11 | 6 | 10 | .545 |
| 1981 | Graig Nettles, New York | 12 | 6 | 11 | .500 |
| | Jerry Mumphrey, New York | 12 | 6 | 7 | .500 |
| 1982 | Fred Lynn, California | 18 | 11 | 16 | .611 |
| 1983 | Cal Ripken Jr., Baltimore | 15 | 6 | 8 | .400 |
| 1984 | Kirk Gibson, Detroit | 12 | 5 | 9 | .417 |
| 1985 | Cliff Johnson, Toronto | 19 | 7 | 9 | .368 |
| 1986 | Bob Boone, California | 22 | 10 | 13 | .455 |
| 1987 | Tom Brunansky, Minnesota | 17 | 7 | 17 | .412 |
| 1988 | Ron Hassey, Oakland | 8 | 4 | 8 | .500 |
| 1989 | Rickey Henderson, Oakland | 15 | 6 | 15 | .400 |
| 1990 | Wade Boggs, Boston | 16 | 7 | 11 | .438 |
| | Carney Lansford, Oakland | 16 | 7 | 8 | .438 |
| 1991 | Roberto Alomar, Toronto | 19 | 9 | 9 | .474 |
| 1992 | Harold Baines, Oakland | 25 | 11 | 16 | .440 |
| 1993 | Tim Raines Sr., Chicago | 27 | 12 | 14 | .444 |
| | Devon White, Toronto | 27 | 12 | 18 | .444 |
| 1994 | no series | | | | |
| 1995 | Kenny Lofton, Cleveland | 24 | 11 | 15 | .458 |
| 1996 | Bernie Williams, New York | 19 | 9 | 18 | .474 |
| 1997 | Brady Anderson, Baltimore | 25 | 9 | 17 | .360 |
| 1998 | Omar Vizquel, Cleveland | 25 | 11 | 13 | .440 |
| 1999 | Jose Offerman, Boston | 24 | 11 | 13 | .458 |
| 2000 | Bernie Williams, New York | 23 | 10 | 14 | .435 |
| 2001 | Paul O'Neill, New York | 12 | 5 | 11 | .417 |
| 2002 | Dustan Mohr, Minnesota | 12 | 5 | 6 | .417 |
| 2003 | Todd Walker, Boston | 27 | 10 | 19 | .370 |
| 2004 | Hideki Matsui, New York | 34 | 14 | 28 | .412 |
| 2005 | Joe Crede, Chicago | 19 | 7 | 15 | .368 |

### NATIONAL LEAGUE

| Year | Player, Club | AB | H | TB | Avg. |
|---|---|---|---|---|---|
| 1969 | Art Shamsky, New York | 13 | 7 | 7 | .538 |
| 1970 | Willie Stargell, Pittsburgh | 12 | 6 | 7 | .500 |
| 1971 | Bob Robertson, Pittsburgh | 16 | 7 | 20 | .438 |
| 1972 | Pete Rose, Cincinnati | 20 | 9 | 13 | .450 |
| 1973 | Pete Rose, Cincinnati | 21 | 8 | 15 | .381 |
| 1974 | Willie Stargell, Pittsburgh | 15 | 6 | 12 | .400 |
| 1975 | Richie Zisk, Pittsburgh | 10 | 5 | 6 | .500 |
| 1976 | Jay Johnstone, Philadelphia | 9 | 7 | 10 | .778 |
| 1977 | Bob Boone, Philadelphia | 10 | 4 | 4 | .400 |
| 1978 | Dusty Baker, Los Angeles | 15 | 7 | 9 | .467 |
| 1979 | Willie Stargell, Pittsburgh | 11 | 5 | 13 | .455 |
| 1980 | Terry Puhl, Houston | 19 | 10 | 12 | .526 |
| 1981 | Gary Carter, Montreal | 16 | 7 | 8 | .438 |
| 1982 | Darrell Porter, St. Louis | 9 | 5 | 8 | .556 |
| | Ozzie Smith, St. Louis | 9 | 5 | 5 | .556 |
| 1983 | Mike Schmidt, Philadelphia | 15 | 7 | 12 | .467 |
| 1984 | Steve Garvey, San Diego | 20 | 8 | 12 | .400 |
| 1985 | Ozzie Smith, St. Louis | 23 | 10 | 16 | .435 |
| 1986 | Lenny Dykstra, New York | 23 | 7 | 13 | .304 |
| 1987 | Jeffrey Leonard, San Francisco | 24 | 10 | 22 | .417 |
| 1988 | Lenny Dykstra, New York | 14 | 6 | 12 | .439 |
| 1989 | Will Clark, San Francisco | 20 | 13 | 24 | .650 |
| 1990 | Mariano Duncan, Cincinnati | 20 | 6 | 9 | .300 |
| 1991 | Jay Bell, Pittsburgh | 29 | 12 | 17 | .414 |
| 1992 | Mark Lemke, Atlanta | 21 | 7 | 8 | .333 |
| 1993 | Fred McGriff, Atlanta | 23 | 10 | 15 | .435 |
| 1994 | no series | | | | |
| 1995 | Chipper Jones, Atlanta | 16 | 7 | 10 | .438 |
| | Fred McGriff, Atlanta | 16 | 7 | 11 | .438 |
| 1996 | Javy Lopez, Atlanta | 24 | 13 | 24 | .542 |
| 1997 | Keith Lockhart, Atlanta | 16 | 8 | 11 | .500 |
| 1998 | Michael Tucker, Atlanta | 13 | 5 | 9 | .385 |
| 1999 | Eddie Perez, Atlanta | 20 | 10 | 18 | .500 |
| | Roger Cedeno, New York | 12 | 6 | 7 | .500 |
| 2000 | Edgardo Alfonzo, New York | 18 | 8 | 11 | .444 |
| 2001 | Craig Counsell, Arizona | 21 | 8 | 11 | .381 |
| 2002 | David Bell, San Francisco | 17 | 7 | 11 | .412 |
| 2003 | Jeff Conine, Florida | 24 | 11 | 17 | .458 |
| 2004 | Albert Pujols, St. Louis | 28 | 14 | 28 | .500 |
| 2005 | Willy Taveras, Houston | 14 | 5 | 5 | .357 |

## .500 HITTERS

**(Playing in all games and having nine or more at-bats)**

### AMERICAN LEAGUE

| Player, Club | Year | AB | H | TB | Avg. |
|---|---|---|---|---|---|
| Fred Lynn, California | 1982 | 18 | 11 | 16 | .611 |
| Brooks Robinson, Baltimore | 1970 | 12 | 7 | 9 | .583 |
| Frank White, Kansas City | 1980 | 11 | 6 | 10 | .545 |
| Chris Chambliss, New York | 1976 | 21 | 11 | 20 | .524 |
| Brooks Robinson, Baltimore | 1969 | 14 | 7 | 8 | .500 |
| Tony Oliva, Minnesota | 1970 | 12 | 6 | 11 | .500 |
| Sal Bando, Oakland | 1975 | 12 | 6 | 8 | .500 |
| Bob Watson, New York | 1980 | 12 | 6 | 11 | .500 |
| Graig Nettles, New York | 1981 | 12 | 6 | 11 | .500 |
| Jerry Mumphrey, New York | 1981 | 12 | 6 | 7 | .500 |

**Total number of occurrences: 10**

### NATIONAL LEAGUE

| Player, Club | Year | AB | H | TB | Avg. |
|---|---|---|---|---|---|
| Jay Johnstone, Philadelphia | 1976 | 9 | 7 | 10 | .778 |
| Will Clark, San Francisco | 1989 | 20 | 13 | 24 | .650 |
| Mark Grace, Chicago | 1989 | 17 | 11 | 19 | .647 |
| Darrell Porter, St. Louis | 1982 | 9 | 5 | 8 | .556 |
| Ozzie Smith, St. Louis | 1982 | 9 | 5 | 5 | .556 |
| Javy Lopez, Atlanta | 1996 | 24 | 13 | 24 | .542 |
| Art Shamsky, New York | 1969 | 13 | 7 | 7 | .538 |
| Terry Puhl, Houston | 1980 | 19 | 10 | 12 | .526 |
| Albert Pujols, St. Louis | 2004 | 28 | 14 | 28 | .500 |
| Keith Lockhart, Atlanta | 1997 | 16 | 8 | 11 | .500 |
| Eddie Perez, Atlanta | 1999 | 20 | 10 | 18 | .500 |
| Willie Stargell, Pittsburgh | 1970 | 12 | 6 | 7 | .500 |
| Roger Cedeno, New York | 1999 | 12 | 6 | 7 | .500 |
| Richie Zisk, Pittsburgh | 1975 | 10 | 5 | 6 | .500 |

**Total number of occurrences: 14**

## HOME RUNS

### AMERICAN LEAGUE

1969—4—Baltimore (East), Frank Robinson, Mark Belanger, Boog Powell, Paul Blair
1—Minnesota (West), Tony Oliva

1970—6—Baltimore (East), Dave Johnson 2, Mike Cuellar, Don Buford, Boog Powell, Frank Robinson

3—Minnesota (West), Harmon Killebrew 2, Tony Oliva
1971—4—Baltimore (East), Boog Powell 2, Brooks Robinson, Elrod Hendricks
3—Oakland (West), Reggie Jackson 2, Sal Bando
1972—4—Detroit (East), Norm Cash, Al Kaline, Bill Freehan, Dick McAuliffe
1—Oakland (West), Mike Epstein
1973—5—Oakland (West), Sal Bando 2, Bert Campaneris 2, Joe Rudi
3—Baltimore (East), Earl Williams, Andy Etchebarren, Bobby Grich
1974—3—Baltimore (East), Paul Blair, Brooks Robinson, Bobby Grich
3—Oakland (West), Sal Bando 2, Ray Fosse
1975—2—Boston (East), Carl Yastrzemski, Rico Petrocelli
1—Oakland (West), Reggie Jackson
1976—4—New York (East), Graig Nettles 2, Chris Chambliss 2
2—Kansas City (West), John Mayberry, George Brett
1977—3—Kansas City (West), Hal McRae, John Mayberry, Al Cowens
2—New York (East), Thurman Munson, Cliff Johnson
1978—5—New York (East), Reggie Jackson 2, Thurman Munson, Graig Nettles, Roy White
4—Kansas City (West), George Brett 3, Fred Patek
1979—3—Baltimore (East), John Lowenstein, Eddie Murray, Pat Kelly
3—California (West), Dan Ford 2, Don Baylor
1980—3—New York (East), Rick Cerone, Lou Piniella, Graig Nettles
3—Kansas City (West), George Brett 2, Frank White
1981—3—New York (East), Lou Piniella, Graig Nettles, Willie Randolph
0—Oakland (West)
1982—5—Milwaukee (East), Paul Molitor 2, Gorman Thomas, Mark Brouhard, Ben Oglivie
4—California (West), Fred Lynn, Reggie Jackson, Bob Boone, Don Baylor
1983—3—Baltimore (East), Gary Roenicke, Eddie Murray, Tito Landrum
0—Chicago (West)
1984—4—Detroit (East), Kirk Gibson, Larry Herndon, Lance Parrish, Alan Trammell
0—Kansas City (West)
1985—7—Kansas City (West), George Brett 3, Pat Sheridan 2, Willie Wilson, Jim Sundberg
2—Toronto (East), Jesse Barfield, Rance Mulliniks
1986—7—California (West), Bob Boone, Doug DeCinces, Brian Downing, Bobby Grich, Wally Joyner, Gary Pettis, Dick Schofield
6—Boston (East), Jim Rice 2, Don Baylor, Dwight Evans, Rich Gedman, Dave Henderson
1987—8—Minnesota (West), Tom Brunansky 2, Gary Gaetti 2, Greg Gagne 2, Kent Hrbek, Kirby Puckett
7—Detroit (East), Chet Lemon 2, Kirk Gibson, Mike Heath, Matt Nokes, Pat Sheridan, Lou Whitaker
1988—7—Oakland (West), Jose Canseco 3, Ron Hassey, Dave Henderson, Carney Lansford, Mark McGwire
2—Boston (East), Rich Gedman, Mike Greenwell
1989—7—Oakland (West), Rickey Henderson 2, Dave Parker 2, Jose Canseco, Dave Henderson, Mark McGwire
3—Toronto (East), George Bell, Lloyd Moseby, Ernie Whitt
1990—1—Boston (East), Wade Boggs
0—Oakland (West)
1991—3—Minnesota (West), Kirby Puckett 2, Mike Pagliarulo
1—Toronto (East), Joe Carter
1992—10—Toronto (East), Roberto Alomar 2, Candy Maldonado 2, Dave Winfield 2, Pat Borders, Joe Carter, Kelly Gruber, John Olerud
4—Oakland (West), Harold Baines, Mark McGwire, Ruben Sierra, Terry Steinbach
1993—5—Chicago (West), Ellis Burks, Lance Johnson, Warren Newson, Frank Thomas, Robin Ventura
2—Toronto (East), Paul Molitor, Devon White
1994—no series
1995—7—Cleveland (Central), Manny Ramirez 2, Jim Thome 2, Carlos Baerga, Albert Belle, Eddie Murray
5—Seattle (West), Jay Buhner 3, Mike Blowers, Ken Griffey Jr.
1996—10—New York (East), Darryl Strawberry 3, Cecil Fielder 2, Bernie Williams 2, Derek Jeter 2, Jim Leyritz, Paul O'Neill
9—Baltimore (East), Todd Zeile 3, Rafael Palmeiro 2, Brady Anderson, Bobby Bonilla, Chris Hoiles, Eddie Murray
1997—7—Baltimore (East), Brady Anderson 2, Roberto Alomar, Harold Baines, Eric Davis, Rafael Palmeiro, Cal Ripken Jr.
5—Cleveland (Central), Manny Ramirez 2, Sandy Alomar Jr., Tony Fernandez, Marquis Grissom
1998—9—Cleveland (Central), Jim Thome 4, Manny Ramirez 2, David Justice, Kenny Lofton, Mark Whiten
4—New York (East), Scott Brosius, Chili Davis, Paul O'Neill, Jorge Posada
1999—8—New York (East), Scott Brosius 2, Derek Jeter, Ricky Ledee, Tino Martinez, Jorge Posada, Darryl Strawberry, Bernie Williams
5—Boston (East), Nomar Garciaparra 2, Brian Daubach, John Valentin, Jason Varitek
2000—6—New York (East), Derek Jeter 2, David Justice 2, Tino Martinez, Bernie Williams
5—Seattle (West), Alex Rodriguez 2, Carlos Guillen, Edgar Martinez, John Olerud
2001—7—New York (East), Bernie Williams 3, Paul O'Neill 2, Tino Martinez, Alfonso Soriano
5—Seattle (West), Bret Boone 2, Jay Buhner, Stan Javier, John Olerud
2002—8—Anaheim (West), Adam Kennedy 3, Garret Anderson, Darin Erstad, Brad Fullmer, Troy Glaus, Scott Spiezio
0—Minnesota (Central)
2003—12—Boston (East), Trot Nixon 3, David Ortiz 2, Manny Ramirez 2, Jason Varitek 2, Todd Walker 2, Kevin Millar
8—New York (East), Jason Giambi 3, Aaron Boone, Derek Jeter, Nick Johnson, Jorge Posada, Ruben Sierra
2004—10—Boston (East), David Ortiz 3, Mark Bellhorn 2, Johnny Damon 2, Jason Varitek 2, Trot Nixon
9—New York (East), Hideki Matsui 2, Alex Rodriguez 2, Bernie Williams 2, Kenny Lofton, John Olerud, Gary Sheffield
2005—5—Chicago (Central), Joe Crede 2, Paul Konerko 2, A.J. Pierzynski
3—Los Angeles (West), Garret Anderson, Orlando Cabrera, Robb Quinlan

**Total number of home runs: 323**

## NATIONAL LEAGUE

1969—6—New York (East), Tommie Agee 2, Ken Boswell 2, Cleon Jones, Wayne Garrett
5—Atlanta (West), Hank Aaron 3, Tony Gonzalez, Orlando Cepeda
1970—3—Cincinnati (West), Bobby Tolan, Tony Perez, Johnny Bench
0—Pittsburgh (East)
1971—8—Pittsburgh (East), Bob Robertson 4, Richie Hebner 2, Gene Clines, Al Oliver
5—San Francisco (West), Willie McCovey 2, Tito Fuentes, Willie Mays, Chris Speier
1972—4—Cincinnati (West), Joe Morgan 2, Cesar Geronimo, Johnny Bench
3—Pittsburgh (East), Al Oliver, Manny Sanguillen, Roberto Clemente
1973—5—Cincinnati (West), Pete Rose 2, Johnny Bench, Denis Menke, Tony Perez
3—New York (East), Rusty Staub 3
1974—3—Los Angeles (West), Steve Garvey 2, Ron Cey
3—Pittsburgh (East), Willie Stargell 2, Richie Hebner
1975—4—Cincinnati (West), Don Gullett, Tony Perez, Dave Concepcion, Pete Rose
1—Pittsburgh (East), Al Oliver
1976—3—Cincinnati (West), George Foster 2, Johnny Bench
1—Philadelphia (East), Greg Luzinski
1977—3—Los Angeles (West), Dusty Baker 2, Ron Cey
2—Philadelphia (East), Greg Luzinski, Bake McBride
1978—8—Los Angeles (West), Steve Garvey 4, Dave Lopes 2, Steve Yeager, Ron Cey
5—Philadelphia (East), Greg Luzinski 2, Jerry Martin, Steve Carlton, Bake McBride
1979—4—Pittsburgh (East), Willie Stargell 2, Phil Garner, Bill Madlock
2—Cincinnati (West), George Foster, Johnny Bench
1980—1—Philadelphia (East), Greg Luzinski
0—Houston (West)
1981—4—Los Angeles (West), Pedro Guerrero, Mike Scioscia, Steve Garvey, Rick Monday
1—Montreal (East), Jerry White
1982—1—St. Louis (East), Willie McGee
0—Atlanta (West)
1983—5—Philadelphia (East), Gary Matthews 3, Mike Schmidt, Sixto Lezcano
2—Los Angeles (West), Mike A. Marshall, Dusty Baker
1984—9—Chicago (East), Jody Davis 2, Leon Durham 2, Gary Matthews 2, Ron Cey, Bob Dernier, Rick Sutcliffe
2—San Diego (West), Steve Garvey, Kevin McReynolds
1985—5—Los Angeles (West), Bill Madlock 3, Greg Brock, Mike A. Marshall
3—St. Louis (East), Jack Clark, Tom Herr, Ozzie Smith
1986—5—Houston (West), Alan Ashby, Glenn Davis, Bill Doran, Billy Hatcher, Dickie Thon
3—New York (East), Darryl Strawberry 2, Lenny Dykstra
1987—9—San Francisco (West), Jeffrey Leonard 4, Bob Brenly, Will Clark, Kevin Mitchell, Harry Spilman, Robby Thompson
2—St. Louis (East), Jim Lindeman, Jose Oquendo
1988—5—New York (East), Kevin McReynolds 2, Lenny Dykstra, Keith Hernandez, Darryl Strawberry
3—Los Angeles (West), Kirk Gibson 2, Mike Scioscia
1989—8—San Francisco (West), Will Clark 2, Kevin Mitchell 2, Robby Thompson 2, Matt Williams 2
3—Chicago (East), Mark Grace, Luis Salazar, Ryne Sandberg
1990—4—Cincinnati (West), Mariano Duncan, Billy Hatcher, Paul O'Neill, Chris Sabo
3—Pittsburgh (East), Jay Bell, Sid Bream, Jose Lind
1991—5—Atlanta (West), Sid Bream, Ron Gant, Brian Hunter, David Justice, Greg Olson
3—Pittsburgh (East), Jay Bell, Orlando Merced, Andy Van Slyke
1992—6—Atlanta (West), Ron Gant 2, David Justice 2, Jeff Blauser, Sid Bream
5—Pittsburgh (East), Jay Bell, Barry Bonds, Jose Lind, Lloyd McClendon, Don Slaught
1993—7—Philadelphia (East), Lenny Dykstra 2, Dave Hollins 2, Darren Daulton, Pete Incaviglia, John Kruk
5—Atlanta (West), Jeff Blauser 2, Damon Berryhill, Fred McGriff, Terry Pendleton
1994—no series
1995—4—Atlanta (East), Mike Devereaux, Chipper Jones, Javy Lopez, Charlie O'Brien

0—Cincinnati (Central)
1996—8—Atlanta (East), Javy Lopez 2, Fred McGriff 2, Marquis Grissom, Andruw Jones, Ryan Klesko, Mark Lemke
4—St. Louis (Central), Ron Gant 2, Gary Gaetti, Brian Jordan
1997—6—Atlanta (East), Chipper Jones 2, Ryan Klesko 2, Jeff Blauser, Michael Tucker
1—Florida (East), Gary Sheffield
1998—5—San Diego (West), Ken Caminiti 2, Jim Leyritz, Greg Myers, John Vander Wal
4—Atlanta (East), Andres Galarraga, Andruw Jones, Javy Lopez, Michael Tucker
1999—5—Atlanta (East), Brian Jordan 2, Eddie Perez 2, Ryan Klesko
4—New York (East), John Olerud 2, Melvin Mora, Mike Piazza
2000—4—New York (East), Mike Piazza 2, Jay Payton, Todd Zeile
2—St. Louis (Central), Will Clark, Jim Edmonds
2001—5—Atlanta (East), Julio Franco, Marcus Giles, Andruw Jones, Javy Lopez, B.J. Surhoff
2—Arizona (West), Erubiel Durazo, Luis Gonzalez
2002—7—San Francisco (West), Rich Aurilia 2, Benito Santiago 2, David Bell, Barry Bonds, Kenny Lofton
7—St. Louis (Central), Miguel Cairo, J.D. Drew, Jim Edmonds, Eli Marrero, Mike Matheny, Eduardo Perez, Albert Pujols
2003—13—Chicago (Central), Alex S. Gonzalez 3, Aramis Ramirez 3, Moises Alou 2, Sammy Sosa 2, Troy O'Leary, Randall Simon, Kerry Wood
10—Florida (East), Miguel Cabrera 3, Mike Lowell 2, Ivan Rodriguez 2, Jeff Conine, Juan Encarnacion, Derrek Lee
2004—14—Houston (Central), Carlos Beltran 4, Lance Berkman 3, Jeff Kent 3, Mike Lamb 2, Craig Biggio, Morgan Ensberg
11—St. Louis (Central), Albert Pujols 4, Scott Rolen 3, Jim Edmonds 2, Larry Walker 2
2005—5—Houston (Central), Jason Lane 2, Lance Berkman, Chris Burke, Mike Lamb
3—St. Louis (Central), Albert Pujols 2, Reggie Sanders

**Total number of home runs: 314**

## PLAYERS WITH FOUR HOME RUNS

### BOTH LEAGUES

| Player | Series | HR |
|---|---|---|
| Darryl Strawberry | 4 | 7 |
| David Justice | 8 | 6 |
| John Olerud | 7 | 6 |
| Paul O'Neill | 6 | 5 |
| Kirk Gibson | 3 | 4 |
| Todd Zeile | 2 | 4 |

**Total number of players: 6**

### AMERICAN LEAGUE

| Player | Series | HR |
|---|---|---|
| George Brett | 6 | 9 |
| Bernie Williams | 7 | 9 |
| Manny Ramirez | 5 | 8 |
| Jim Thome | 3 | 6 |
| Reggie Jackson | 11 | 6 |
| David Ortiz | 3 | 5 |
| Jason Varitek | 3 | 5 |
| Sal Bando | 5 | 5 |
| Graig Nettles | 6 | 5 |
| Derek Jeter | 7 | 5 |
| Darryl Strawberry | 2 | 4 |
| Jay Buhner | 3 | 4 |
| Jose Canseco | 3 | 4 |
| Trot Nixon | 3 | 4 |
| Alex Rodriguez | 3 | 4 |
| Eddie Murray | 4 | 4 |
| Paul O'Neill | 5 | 4 |
| Boog Powell | 5 | 4 |
| John Olerud | 6 | 4 |

**Total number of players: 19**

### NATIONAL LEAGUE

| Player | Series | HR |
|---|---|---|
| Steve Garvey | 5 | 8 |
| Albert Pujols | 3 | 7 |
| Gary Matthews | 2 | 5 |
| Greg Luzinski | 4 | 5 |
| Ron Gant | 5 | 5 |
| Johnny Bench | 6 | 5 |
| Javy Lopez | 6 | 5 |
| Carlos Beltran | 1 | 4 |
| Lance Berkman | 2 | 4 |
| Jeffrey Leonard | 2 | 4 |
| Bill Madlock | 2 | 4 |
| Will Clark | 3 | 4 |
| Lenny Dykstra | 3 | 4 |
| Jim Edmonds | 4 | 4 |
| Ron Cey | 5 | 4 |
| Ryan Klesko | 5 | 4 |
| Bob Robertson | 5 | 4 |
| Jeff Blauser | 6 | 4 |
| Willie Stargell | 6 | 4 |

**Total number of players: 19**

# INDIVIDUAL PITCHING

## PITCHERS WITH FOUR VICTORIES

### BOTH LEAGUES

| Pitcher, Club | Series | W | L |
|---|---|---|---|
| Andy Pettitte, NY AL, Hou NL | 7 | 6 | 2 |
| Tim Wakefield, Pit NL, Bos AL | 3 | 5 | 1 |
| Roger Clemens, Bos AL, NY AL, Hou NL | 9 | 5 | 4 |
| Bruce Kison, Pit NL, Cal AL | 5 | 4 | 0 |
| Orel Hershiser, LA NL, Cle AL, NY NL | 5 | 4 | 0 |
| Tommy John, LA NL, NY AL, Cal AL | 5 | 4 | 1 |
| Don Sutton, LA NL, Mil AL, Cal AL | 5 | 4 | 1 |
| David Wells, Tor AL, Cin NL, Bal AL, NY AL | 6 | 4 | 1 |
| David Cone, NY NL, Tor AL, NY AL | 6 | 4 | 2 |

**Total number of pitchers: 9**

### AMERICAN LEAGUE

| Pitcher, Club | Yrs. | W | L |
|---|---|---|---|
| Dave Stewart, Oakland, Toronto | 5 | 8 | 0 |
| Juan Guzman, Toronto | 3 | 5 | 0 |
| Mariano Rivera, New York | 6 | 4 | 0 |
| David Wells, Toronto, Baltimore, New York | 5 | 4 | 0 |
| Andy Pettitte, New York | 6 | 6 | 1 |
| Orlando Hernandez, New York | 4 | 4 | 1 |
| Jim Palmer, Baltimore | 6 | 4 | 1 |
| Catfish Hunter, Oakland, New York | 6 | 4 | 3 |

**Total number of pitchers: 8**

### NATIONAL LEAGUE

| Pitcher, Club | Yrs. | W | L |
|---|---|---|---|
| Steve Avery, Atlanta | 5 | 4 | 1 |
| John Smoltz, Atlanta | 9 | 6 | 2 |
| Steve Carlton, Philadelphia | 5 | 4 | 2 |
| Tom Glavine, Atlanta | 9 | 5 | 9 |
| Greg Maddux, Chicago, Atlanta | 8 | 4 | 8 |

**Total number of pitchers: 5**

## 10-STRIKEOUT GAMES BY PITCHERS

### AMERICAN LEAGUE

| Date | Pitcher, Club | K |
|---|---|---|
| Oct 5, 1969 | Dave McNally, Bal vs Min (11 inn) | 11 |
| Oct 5, 1970 | Jim Palmer, Bal vs Min | 12 |
| Oct 10, 1972 | Joe Coleman, Det vs Oak | 14 |
| Oct 6, 1973 | Jim Palmer, Bal vs Oak | 12 |
| Oct 9, 1973 | Mike Cuellar, Bal vs Oak (10 inn) | 11 |
| Oct 6, 1983 | Mike Boddicker, Bal vs Chi | 14 |
| Oct 11, 1997 | Mike Mussina, Bal vs Cle (7 inn) | 15 |
| Oct 15, 1997 | Mike Mussina, Bal vs Cle (8 inn) | 10 |
| Oct 11, 1998 | David Wells, NY vs Cle (7.1 inn) | 11 |
| Oct 16, 1999 | Pedro Martinez, Bos vs NY (7 inn) | 12 |
| Oct 14, 2000 | Roger Clemens, NY vs Sea | 15 |
| Oct 13, 2003 | Mike Mussina, NY vs Bos | 10 |

**Total number of occurrences: 12**

### NATIONAL LEAGUE

| Date | Pitcher, Club | K |
|---|---|---|
| Oct 6, 1973 | Tom Seaver, NY vs Cin (8.1 inn) | 13 |
| Oct 7, 1975 | John Candelaria, Pit vs Cin (7.2 inn) | 14 |
| Oct 8, 1986 | Mike Scott, Hou vs NY | 14 |
| Oct 14, 1986 | Nolan Ryan, Hou vs NY | 12 |
| Oct 4, 1988 | Dwight Gooden, NY vs LA | 10 |
| Oct 5, 1988 | Tim Belcher, LA vs NY | 10 |
| Oct 6, 1993 | Curt Schilling, Phi vs Atl (8 inn) | 10 |
| Oct 10, 1993 | John Smoltz, Atl vs Phi (6.1 inn) | 10 |
| Oct 12, 1997 | Livan Hernandez, Fla vs Atl | 15 |
| Oct 8, 1998 | Kevin Brown, SD vs Atl | 11 |
| Oct 16, 2001 | Randy Johnson, Ari vs Atl | 11 |
| Oct 19, 2001 | Curt Schilling, Ari vs Atl | 12 |
| Oct 12, 2003 | Josh Beckett, Fla vs Chi | 11 |

**Total number of occurrences: 13**

## CLUB BATTING

### AMERICAN LEAGUE

| Year | Team, Division | G | AB | R | H | TB | 2B | 3B | HR | SH | SF | SB | BB | SO | RBI | Avg. | LOB |
|---|---|---|---|---|---|---|---|---|---|---|---|---|---|---|---|---|---|
| 1969 | Baltimore, East | 3 | 123 | 16 | 36 | 58 | 8 | 1 | 4 | 2 | 0 | 0 | 13 | 14 | 15 | .293 | 28 |
| | Minnesota, West | 3 | 110 | 5 | 17 | 25 | 3 | 1 | 1 | 0 | 1 | 2 | 12 | 27 | 5 | .155 | 22 |
| 1970 | Baltimore, East | 3 | 109 | 27 | 36 | 61 | 7 | 0 | 6 | 1 | 2 | 1 | 12 | 19 | 24 | .330 | 20 |
| | Minnesota, West | 3 | 101 | 10 | 24 | 39 | 4 | 1 | 3 | 1 | 0 | 0 | 9 | 22 | 10 | .238 | 20 |
| 1971 | Baltimore, East | 3 | 95 | 15 | 26 | 47 | 7 | 1 | 4 | 0 | 1 | 0 | 13 | 22 | 14 | .274 | 19 |
| | Oakland, West | 3 | 96 | 7 | 22 | 41 | 8 | 1 | 3 | 2 | 0 | 0 | 5 | 16 | 7 | .229 | 15 |
| 1972 | Detroit, East | 5 | 162 | 10 | 32 | 52 | 6 | 1 | 4 | 3 | 0 | 0 | 13 | 25 | 10 | .198 | 30 |
| | Oakland, West | 5 | 170 | 13 | 38 | 49 | 8 | 0 | 1 | 4 | 1 | 7 | 12 | 35 | 10 | .224 | 38 |
| 1973 | Baltimore, East | 5 | 171 | 15 | 36 | 52 | 7 | 0 | 3 | 0 | 0 | 1 | 16 | 25 | 15 | .211 | 36 |
| | Oakland, West | 5 | 160 | 15 | 32 | 54 | 5 | 1 | 5 | 4 | 1 | 3 | 17 | 39 | 15 | .200 | 34 |
| 1974 | Baltimore, East | 4 | 124 | 7 | 22 | 32 | 1 | 0 | 3 | 2 | 0 | 0 | 5 | 20 | 7 | .177 | 16 |
| | Oakland, West | 4 | 120 | 11 | 22 | 37 | 4 | 1 | 3 | 2 | 1 | 3 | 22 | 16 | 11 | .183 | 30 |
| 1975 | Boston, East | 3 | 98 | 18 | 31 | 45 | 8 | 0 | 2 | 5 | 1 | 3 | 3 | 12 | 14 | .316 | 14 |
| | Oakland, West | 3 | 98 | 7 | 19 | 28 | 6 | 0 | 1 | 0 | 0 | 0 | 9 | 14 | 7 | .194 | 19 |
| 1976 | New York, East | 5 | 174 | 23 | 55 | 84 | 13 | 2 | 4 | 2 | 1 | 4 | 16 | 15 | 21 | .316 | 41 |
| | Kansas City, West | 5 | 162 | 24 | 40 | 60 | 6 | 4 | 2 | 0 | 4 | 5 | 11 | 18 | 24 | .247 | 22 |
| 1977 | New York, East | 5 | 175 | 21 | 46 | 64 | 12 | 0 | 2 | 1 | 2 | 2 | 9 | 16 | 17 | .263 | 34 |
| | Kansas City, West | 5 | 163 | 22 | 42 | 66 | 9 | 3 | 3 | 2 | 2 | 5 | 15 | 22 | 21 | .258 | 28 |
| 1978 | New York, East | 4 | 140 | 19 | 42 | 62 | 3 | 1 | 5 | 0 | 1 | 0 | 7 | 18 | 18 | .300 | 27 |
| | Kansas City, West | 4 | 133 | 17 | 35 | 59 | 6 | 3 | 4 | 1 | 2 | 6 | 14 | 21 | 16 | .263 | 28 |
| 1979 | Baltimore, East | 4 | 133 | 26 | 37 | 53 | 5 | 1 | 3 | 1 | 3 | 5 | 18 | 24 | 25 | .278 | 23 |
| | California, West | 4 | 137 | 15 | 32 | 48 | 7 | 0 | 3 | 0 | 2 | 2 | 7 | 13 | 14 | .234 | 22 |
| 1980 | New York, East | 3 | 102 | 6 | 26 | 44 | 7 | 1 | 3 | 1 | 0 | 0 | 6 | 16 | 5 | .255 | 22 |
| | Kansas City, West | 3 | 97 | 14 | 28 | 45 | 6 | 1 | 3 | 0 | 0 | 3 | 9 | 15 | 14 | .289 | 18 |
| 1981 | New York, East | 3 | 107 | 20 | 36 | 49 | 4 | 0 | 3 | 2 | 1 | 2 | 13 | 10 | 20 | .336 | 30 |
| | Oakland, West | 3 | 99 | 4 | 22 | 28 | 4 | 1 | 0 | 0 | 0 | 2 | 6 | 23 | 4 | .222 | 20 |
| 1982 | Milwaukee, East | 5 | 151 | 23 | 33 | 52 | 4 | 0 | 5 | 2 | 3 | 2 | 15 | 28 | 20 | .219 | 24 |
| | California, West | 5 | 157 | 23 | 40 | 62 | 8 | 1 | 4 | 5 | 2 | 1 | 16 | 34 | 23 | .255 | 29 |
| 1983 | Baltimore, East | 4 | 129 | 19 | 28 | 46 | 9 | 0 | 3 | 1 | 3 | 2 | 16 | 24 | 17 | .217 | 24 |
| | Chicago, West | 4 | 133 | 3 | 28 | 32 | 4 | 0 | 0 | 1 | 0 | 4 | 12 | 26 | 2 | .211 | 35 |
| 1984 | Detroit, East | 3 | 107 | 14 | 25 | 43 | 4 | 1 | 4 | 2 | 1 | 4 | 8 | 17 | 14 | .234 | 20 |
| | Kansas City, West | 3 | 106 | 4 | 18 | 21 | 1 | 1 | 0 | 0 | 0 | 0 | 6 | 21 | 4 | .170 | 21 |
| 1985 | Toronto, East | 7 | 242 | 25 | 65 | 90 | 19 | 0 | 2 | 0 | 2 | 2 | 16 | 37 | 23 | .269 | 50 |
| | Kansas City, West | 7 | 227 | 26 | 51 | 83 | 9 | 1 | 7 | 4 | 2 | 2 | 22 | 51 | 26 | .225 | 44 |
| 1986 | Boston, East | 7 | 254 | 41 | 69 | 102 | 11 | 2 | 6 | 3 | 2 | 1 | 19 | 31 | 35 | .272 | 48 |
| | California, West | 7 | 256 | 30 | 71 | 103 | 11 | 0 | 7 | 4 | 2 | 1 | 20 | 44 | 29 | .277 | 60 |
| 1987 | Detroit, East | 5 | 167 | 23 | 40 | 65 | 4 | 0 | 7 | 2 | 2 | 5 | 18 | 35 | 21 | .240 | 37 |
| | Minnesota, West | 5 | 171 | 34 | 46 | 85 | 13 | 1 | 8 | 2 | 2 | 4 | 20 | 25 | 33 | .269 | 37 |
| 1988 | Boston, East | 4 | 126 | 11 | 26 | 36 | 4 | 0 | 2 | 2 | 2 | 0 | 18 | 23 | 10 | .206 | 30 |
| | Oakland, West | 4 | 137 | 20 | 41 | 70 | 8 | 0 | 7 | 0 | 1 | 1 | 10 | 35 | 20 | .299 | 26 |
| 1989 | Toronto, East | 5 | 165 | 21 | 40 | 54 | 5 | 0 | 3 | 0 | 3 | 11 | 15 | 24 | 19 | .242 | 30 |
| | Oakland, West | 5 | 158 | 26 | 43 | 75 | 9 | 1 | 7 | 3 | 2 | 13 | 20 | 32 | 23 | .272 | 29 |
| 1990 | Boston, East | 4 | 126 | 4 | 23 | 31 | 5 | 0 | 1 | 1 | 2 | 1 | 6 | 16 | 4 | .183 | 23 |
| | Oakland, West | 4 | 127 | 20 | 38 | 42 | 4 | 0 | 0 | 4 | 3 | 9 | 19 | 21 | 18 | .299 | 35 |
| 1991 | Toronto, East | 5 | 173 | 19 | 43 | 52 | 6 | 0 | 1 | 3 | 1 | 7 | 15 | 30 | 18 | .249 | 35 |
| | Minnesota, West | 5 | 181 | 27 | 50 | 70 | 9 | 1 | 3 | 1 | 2 | 8 | 15 | 37 | 25 | .276 | 38 |
| 1992 | Toronto, East | 6 | 210 | 31 | 59 | 99 | 8 | 1 | 10 | 1 | 4 | 7 | 23 | 29 | 30 | .281 | 45 |
| | Oakland, West | 6 | 207 | 24 | 52 | 71 | 5 | 1 | 4 | 3 | 2 | 16 | 24 | 33 | 23 | .251 | 48 |
| 1993 | Toronto, East | 6 | 216 | 26 | 65 | 85 | 8 | 3 | 2 | 1 | 1 | 7 | 21 | 36 | 24 | .301 | 56 |
| | Chicago, West | 6 | 194 | 23 | 46 | 68 | 5 | 1 | 5 | 5 | 1 | 3 | 32 | 43 | 22 | .237 | 50 |
| 1994 | no series | | | | | | | | | | | | | | | | |
| 1995 | Cleveland, East | 6 | 206 | 23 | 53 | 86 | 6 | 3 | 7 | 1 | 2 | 9 | 25 | 37 | 21 | .257 | 50 |
| | Seattle, West | 6 | 201 | 12 | 37 | 60 | 8 | 0 | 5 | 1 | 0 | 9 | 15 | 46 | 10 | .184 | 43 |
| 1996 | New York, East | 5 | 183 | 27 | 50 | 91 | 9 | 1 | 10 | 0 | 0 | 3 | 20 | 37 | 24 | .273 | 40 |
| | Baltimore, East | 5 | 176 | 19 | 39 | 70 | 4 | 0 | 9 | 0 | 3 | 0 | 15 | 33 | 19 | .222 | 34 |
| 1997 | Baltimore, East | 6 | 218 | 19 | 54 | 86 | 11 | 0 | 7 | 1 | 0 | 3 | 23 | 47 | 19 | .248 | 50 |
| | Cleveland, Central | 6 | 207 | 18 | 40 | 63 | 8 | 0 | 5 | 2 | 0 | 5 | 23 | 62 | 15 | .193 | 44 |
| 1998 | New York, East | 6 | 197 | 27 | 43 | 65 | 8 | 1 | 4 | 3 | 3 | 9 | 35 | 42 | 25 | .218 | 48 |
| | Cleveland, Central | 6 | 205 | 20 | 45 | 77 | 3 | 1 | 9 | 0 | 1 | 6 | 16 | 51 | 19 | .220 | 39 |
| 1999 | New York, East | 5 | 176 | 23 | 42 | 72 | 4 | 1 | 8 | 2 | 0 | 3 | 18 | 44 | 21 | .239 | 42 |
| | Boston, East | 5 | 184 | 21 | 54 | 86 | 13 | 2 | 5 | 1 | 0 | 4 | 15 | 38 | 19 | .293 | 45 |
| 2000 | New York, East | 6 | 204 | 31 | 57 | 85 | 10 | 0 | 6 | 1 | 3 | 4 | 25 | 41 | 31 | .279 | 49 |
| | Seattle, West | 6 | 191 | 18 | 41 | 68 | 12 | 0 | 5 | 2 | 1 | 3 | 21 | 48 | 18 | .215 | 38 |
| 2001 | New York, East | 5 | 159 | 25 | 42 | 70 | 7 | 0 | 7 | 4 | 1 | 3 | 23 | 31 | 24 | .264 | 34 |
| | Seattle, West | 5 | 171 | 22 | 36 | 59 | 4 | 2 | 5 | 1 | 0 | 3 | 18 | 35 | 20 | .211 | 34 |
| 2002 | Anaheim, West | 5 | 171 | 29 | 49 | 82 | 5 | 2 | 8 | 2 | 0 | 3 | 9 | 26 | 26 | .287 | 29 |
| | Minnesota, Central | 5 | 160 | 12 | 37 | 46 | 9 | 0 | 0 | 2 | 2 | 1 | 7 | 38 | 11 | .231 | 28 |
| 2003 | New York, East | 7 | 238 | 30 | 54 | 90 | 12 | 0 | 8 | 0 | 1 | 5 | 21 | 49 | 29 | .227 | 45 |
| | Boston, East | 7 | 250 | 29 | 68 | 117 | 9 | 2 | 12 | 0 | 0 | 2 | 17 | 60 | 26 | .272 | 49 |

| Year | Team, Division | G | AB | R | H | TB | 2B | 3B | HR | SH | SF | SB | BB | SO | RBI | Avg. | LOB |
|---|---|---|---|---|---|---|---|---|---|---|---|---|---|---|---|---|---|
| 2004 | Boston, East | 7 | 271 | 41 | 75 | 119 | 12 | 1 | 10 | 1 | 2 | 4 | 28 | 53 | 40 | .277 | 53 |
| | New York, East | 7 | 277 | 45 | 78 | 131 | 20 | 3 | 9 | 3 | 1 | 3 | 33 | 51 | 44 | .282 | 69 |
| 2005 | Chicago, Central | 5 | 165 | 23 | 41 | 68 | 10 | 1 | 5 | 3 | 2 | 5 | 16 | 36 | 23 | .248 | 33 |
| | Los Angeles, West | 5 | 154 | 11 | 27 | 41 | 5 | 0 | 3 | 3 | 1 | 2 | 4 | 22 | 11 | .175 | 17 |

## NATIONAL LEAGUE

| Year | Team, Division | G | AB | R | H | TB | 2B | 3B | HR | SH | SF | SB | BB | SO | RBI | Avg. | LOB |
|---|---|---|---|---|---|---|---|---|---|---|---|---|---|---|---|---|---|
| 1969 | New York, East | 3 | 113 | 27 | 37 | 65 | 8 | 1 | 6 | 1 | 0 | 5 | 10 | 25 | 24 | .327 | 19 |
| | Atlanta, West | 3 | 106 | 15 | 27 | 51 | 9 | 0 | 5 | 0 | 1 | 1 | 11 | 20 | 15 | .255 | 23 |
| 1970 | Pittsburgh, East | 3 | 102 | 3 | 23 | 29 | 6 | 0 | 0 | 2 | 0 | 0 | 12 | 19 | 3 | .225 | 29 |
| | Cincinnati, West | 3 | 100 | 9 | 22 | 36 | 3 | 1 | 3 | 0 | 0 | 1 | 8 | 12 | 8 | .220 | 18 |
| 1971 | Pittsburgh, East | 4 | 144 | 24 | 39 | 67 | 4 | 0 | 8 | 1 | 0 | 2 | 5 | 33 | 23 | .271 | 26 |
| | San Francisco, West | 4 | 132 | 15 | 31 | 51 | 5 | 0 | 5 | 4 | 0 | 2 | 16 | 28 | 14 | .235 | 33 |
| 1972 | Pittsburgh, East | 5 | 158 | 15 | 30 | 47 | 6 | 1 | 3 | 2 | 0 | 0 | 9 | 27 | 14 | .190 | 24 |
| | Cincinnati, West | 5 | 166 | 19 | 42 | 67 | 9 | 2 | 4 | 3 | 1 | 4 | 10 | 28 | 16 | .253 | 30 |
| 1973 | New York, East | 5 | 168 | 23 | 37 | 51 | 5 | 0 | 3 | 3 | 1 | 0 | 19 | 28 | 22 | .220 | 30 |
| | Cincinnati, West | 5 | 167 | 8 | 31 | 52 | 6 | 0 | 5 | 3 | 1 | 0 | 13 | 42 | 8 | .186 | 35 |
| 1974 | Pittsburgh, East | 4 | 129 | 10 | 25 | 35 | 1 | 0 | 3 | 2 | 0 | 1 | 8 | 17 | 10 | .194 | 24 |
| | Los Angeles, West | 4 | 138 | 20 | 37 | 56 | 8 | 1 | 3 | 1 | 0 | 5 | 30 | 16 | 19 | .268 | 44 |
| 1975 | Pittsburgh, East | 3 | 101 | 7 | 20 | 26 | 3 | 0 | 1 | 0 | 0 | 0 | 10 | 18 | 7 | .198 | 21 |
| | Cincinnati, West | 3 | 102 | 19 | 29 | 45 | 4 | 0 | 4 | 0 | 3 | 11 | 9 | 28 | 18 | .284 | 17 |
| 1976 | Philadelphia, East | 3 | 100 | 11 | 27 | 40 | 8 | 1 | 1 | 3 | 2 | 0 | 12 | 9 | 11 | .270 | 25 |
| | Cincinnati, West | 3 | 99 | 19 | 25 | 45 | 5 | 3 | 3 | 1 | 3 | 5 | 15 | 16 | 17 | .253 | 20 |
| 1977 | Philadelphia, East | 4 | 138 | 14 | 31 | 40 | 3 | 0 | 2 | 2 | 0 | 1 | 11 | 21 | 12 | .225 | 32 |
| | Los Angeles, West | 4 | 133 | 22 | 35 | 52 | 6 | 1 | 3 | 2 | 0 | 3 | 14 | 22 | 20 | .263 | 22 |
| 1978 | Philadelphia, East | 4 | 140 | 17 | 35 | 37 | 3 | 2 | 5 | 2 | 1 | 0 | 9 | 21 | 16 | .250 | 24 |
| | Los Angeles, West | 4 | 147 | 21 | 42 | 80 | 8 | 3 | 8 | 2 | 0 | 2 | 9 | 22 | 21 | .286 | 28 |
| 1979 | Pittsburgh, East | 3 | 105 | 15 | 28 | 47 | 3 | 2 | 4 | 5 | 3 | 4 | 13 | 13 | 14 | .267 | 24 |
| | Cincinnati, West | 3 | 107 | 5 | 23 | 35 | 4 | 1 | 2 | 1 | 1 | 4 | 11 | 26 | 5 | .215 | 25 |
| 1980 | Philadelphia, East | 5 | 190 | 20 | 55 | 68 | 8 | 1 | 1 | 5 | 1 | 7 | 13 | 37 | 19 | .291 | 43 |
| | Houston, West | 5 | 172 | 19 | 40 | 57 | 7 | 5 | 0 | 7 | 2 | 4 | 31 | 19 | 18 | .233 | 45 |
| 1981 | Montreal, East | 5 | 158 | 10 | 34 | 44 | 7 | 0 | 1 | 3 | 0 | 2 | 12 | 25 | 8 | .215 | 31 |
| | Los Angeles, West | 5 | 163 | 15 | 38 | 55 | 3 | 1 | 4 | 4 | 0 | 5 | 12 | 23 | 15 | .233 | 33 |
| 1982 | St. Louis, East | 3 | 103 | 17 | 34 | 45 | 4 | 2 | 1 | 5 | 3 | 1 | 12 | 16 | 16 | .330 | 31 |
| | Atlanta, West | 3 | 89 | 5 | 15 | 16 | 1 | 0 | 0 | 2 | 1 | 1 | 6 | 15 | 3 | .169 | 12 |
| 1983 | Philadelphia, East | 4 | 130 | 16 | 34 | 53 | 4 | 0 | 5 | 3 | 1 | 2 | 15 | 22 | 15 | .262 | 31 |
| | Los Angeles, West | 4 | 129 | 8 | 27 | 40 | 5 | 1 | 2 | 2 | 0 | 3 | 11 | 31 | 7 | .209 | 31 |
| 1984 | Chicago, East | 5 | 162 | 26 | 42 | 80 | 11 | 0 | 9 | 1 | 2 | 6 | 20 | 28 | 25 | .259 | 32 |
| | San Diego, West | 5 | 155 | 22 | 41 | 54 | 5 | 1 | 2 | 2 | 4 | 2 | 14 | 22 | 20 | .265 | 27 |
| 1985 | St. Louis, East | 6 | 201 | 29 | 56 | 77 | 10 | 1 | 3 | 2 | 1 | 6 | 30 | 34 | 26 | .279 | 51 |
| | Los Angeles, West | 6 | 197 | 23 | 46 | 75 | 12 | 1 | 5 | 1 | 1 | 4 | 19 | 31 | 23 | .234 | 40 |
| 1986 | New York, East | 6 | 227 | 21 | 43 | 60 | 4 | 2 | 3 | 1 | 3 | 4 | 14 | 57 | 19 | .189 | 36 |
| | Houston, West | 6 | 225 | 17 | 49 | 70 | 6 | 0 | 5 | 2 | 0 | 8 | 17 | 40 | 17 | .218 | 39 |
| 1987 | St. Louis, East | 7 | 215 | 23 | 56 | 74 | 4 | 4 | 2 | 5 | 4 | 4 | 16 | 42 | 22 | .260 | 37 |
| | San Francisco, West | 7 | 226 | 23 | 54 | 90 | 7 | 1 | 9 | 3 | 1 | 5 | 17 | 51 | 20 | .239 | 43 |
| 1988 | New York, East | 7 | 240 | 27 | 58 | 87 | 12 | 1 | 5 | 3 | 1 | 6 | 28 | 42 | 27 | .242 | 54 |
| | Los Angeles, West | 7 | 243 | 31 | 52 | 70 | 7 | 1 | 3 | 1 | 2 | 9 | 25 | 54 | 30 | .214 | 50 |
| 1989 | Chicago, East | 5 | 175 | 22 | 53 | 77 | 9 | 3 | 3 | 3 | 2 | 3 | 16 | 27 | 21 | .303 | 43 |
| | San Francisco, West | 5 | 165 | 30 | 44 | 78 | 6 | 2 | 8 | 2 | 1 | 2 | 17 | 29 | 29 | .267 | 30 |
| 1990 | Pittsburgh, East | 6 | 186 | 15 | 36 | 58 | 9 | 2 | 3 | 0 | 1 | 6 | 27 | 49 | 14 | .194 | 41 |
| | Cincinnati, West | 6 | 192 | 20 | 49 | 70 | 9 | 0 | 4 | 3 | 3 | 6 | 10 | 37 | 20 | .255 | 33 |
| 1991 | Pittsburgh, East | 7 | 228 | 12 | 51 | 70 | 10 | 0 | 3 | 4 | 1 | 6 | 22 | 57 | 11 | .224 | 54 |
| | Atlanta, West | 7 | 229 | 19 | 53 | 80 | 10 | 1 | 5 | 5 | 1 | 10 | 22 | 42 | 19 | .231 | 51 |
| 1992 | Pittsburgh, East | 7 | 231 | 35 | 59 | 100 | 20 | 3 | 5 | 3 | 3 | 1 | 29 | 42 | 32 | .255 | 50 |
| | Atlanta, West | 7 | 234 | 34 | 57 | 90 | 11 | 2 | 6 | 2 | 2 | 5 | 29 | 28 | 32 | .244 | 51 |
| 1993 | Philadelphia, East | 6 | 207 | 23 | 47 | 87 | 11 | 4 | 7 | 3 | 2 | 2 | 26 | 51 | 22 | .227 | 52 |
| | Atlanta, West | 6 | 215 | 33 | 59 | 88 | 14 | 0 | 5 | 5 | 2 | 0 | 22 | 54 | 32 | .274 | 47 |
| 1994 | no series | | | | | | | | | | | | | | | | |
| 1995 | Atlanta, East | 4 | 149 | 19 | 42 | 62 | 6 | 1 | 4 | 1 | 0 | 2 | 16 | 22 | 17 | .282 | 36 |
| | Cincinnati, Central | 4 | 134 | 5 | 28 | 35 | 5 | 1 | 0 | 1 | 1 | 4 | 12 | 31 | 4 | .209 | 28 |
| 1996 | Atlanta, East | 7 | 249 | 44 | 77 | 118 | 11 | 3 | 8 | 2 | 3 | 4 | 25 | 51 | 43 | .309 | 58 |
| | St. Louis, Central | 7 | 221 | 18 | 45 | 65 | 4 | 2 | 4 | 1 | 1 | 1 | 11 | 53 | 15 | .204 | 34 |
| 1997 | Atlanta, East | 6 | 194 | 21 | 49 | 76 | 5 | 2 | 6 | 5 | 3 | 1 | 16 | 49 | 21 | .253 | 40 |
| | Florida, East | 6 | 181 | 20 | 36 | 47 | 8 | 0 | 1 | 5 | 0 | 2 | 23 | 52 | 20 | .199 | 36 |
| 1998 | San Diego, West | 6 | 208 | 24 | 53 | 75 | 7 | 0 | 5 | 2 | 0 | 2 | 27 | 48 | 20 | .255 | 52 |
| | Atlanta, East | 6 | 200 | 18 | 47 | 65 | 4 | 1 | 4 | 2 | 1 | 3 | 26 | 54 | 17 | .235 | 46 |
| 1999 | Atlanta, East | 6 | 206 | 24 | 46 | 72 | 9 | 1 | 5 | 7 | 1 | 14 | 31 | 47 | 22 | .223 | 47 |
| | New York, East | 6 | 225 | 21 | 49 | 70 | 9 | 0 | 4 | 3 | 2 | 7 | 14 | 49 | 21 | .218 | 42 |
| 2000 | New York, East | 5 | 164 | 31 | 43 | 69 | 12 | 1 | 4 | 3 | 3 | 2 | 27 | 24 | 27 | .262 | 40 |
| | St. Louis, Central | 5 | 177 | 21 | 47 | 64 | 11 | 0 | 2 | 4 | 2 | 3 | 11 | 39 | 18 | .266 | 39 |
| 2001 | Atlanta, East | 5 | 169 | 15 | 35 | 56 | 6 | 0 | 5 | 0 | 0 | 0 | 11 | 39 | 14 | .207 | 30 |
| | Arizona, West | 5 | 172 | 22 | 40 | 52 | 6 | 0 | 2 | 2 | 0 | 3 | 18 | 32 | 19 | .233 | 39 |

| Year | Team, Division | G | AB | R | H | TB | 2B | 3B | HR | SH | SF | SB | BB | SO | RBI | Avg. | LOB |
|---|---|---|---|---|---|---|---|---|---|---|---|---|---|---|---|---|---|
| 2002 | San Fran., West | 5 | 158 | 23 | 39 | 67 | 3 | 2 | 7 | 8 | 2 | 1 | 21 | 36 | 23 | .247 | 38 |
| | St. Louis, Central | 5 | 171 | 16 | 44 | 73 | 8 | 0 | 7 | 5 | 2 | 1 | 10 | 23 | 16 | .257 | 39 |
| 2003 | Florida, East | 7 | 256 | 40 | 68 | 116 | 12 | 3 | 10 | 3 | 2 | 4 | 28 | 45 | 39 | .266 | 53 |
| | Chicago, Central | 7 | 252 | 42 | 65 | 122 | 10 | 4 | 13 | 7 | 1 | 1 | 23 | 57 | 41 | .258 | 45 |
| 2004 | St. Louis, Central | 7 | 235 | 34 | 60 | 107 | 12 | 1 | 11 | 6 | 1 | 2 | 17 | 56 | 33 | .255 | 40 |
| | Houston, Central | 7 | 233 | 31 | 53 | 105 | 10 | 0 | 14 | 1 | 1 | 6 | 25 | 42 | 30 | .227 | 44 |
| 2005 | Houston, Central | 6 | 198 | 22 | 55 | 81 | 7 | 2 | 5 | 8 | 3 | 1 | 15 | 33 | 19 | .278 | 46 |
| | St. Louis, Central | 6 | 187 | 16 | 39 | 54 | 6 | 0 | 3 | 3 | 4 | 3 | 16 | 42 | 16 | .209 | 38 |

## CLUB FIELDING AND PLAYERS USED

### AMERICAN LEAGUE

| Year | Team, Division | G | PO | A | E | DP | PB | Fielding Avg. | Players Used | Pitchers Used |
|---|---|---|---|---|---|---|---|---|---|---|
| 1969 | Baltimore, East | 3 | 96 | 31 | 1 | 2 | 0 | .992 | 20 | 7 |
| | Minnesota, West | 3 | 94 | 34 | 5 | 3 | 0 | .962 | 22 | 9 |
| 1970 | Baltimore, East | 3 | 81 | 29 | 0 | 3 | 0 | 1.000 | 14 | 4 |
| | Minnesota, West | 3 | 78 | 28 | 6 | 5 | 0 | .946 | 24 | 9 |
| 1971 | Baltimore, East | 3 | 81 | 31 | 1 | 3 | 0 | .991 | 15 | 4 |
| | Oakland, West | 3 | 75 | 15 | 0 | 4 | 0 | 1.000 | 20 | 7 |
| 1972 | Detroit, East | 5 | 139 | 48 | 7 | 4 | 0 | .964 | 24 | 8 |
| | Oakland, West | 5 | 138 | 59 | 3 | 5 | 1 | .985 | 25 | 8 |
| 1973 | Baltimore, East | 5 | 135 | 51 | 2 | 2 | 1 | .989 | 23 | 7 |
| | Oakland, West | 5 | 138 | 47 | 4 | 4 | 0 | .979 | 22 | 6 |
| 1974 | Baltimore, East | 4 | 105 | 50 | 4 | 4 | 0 | .975 | 22 | 7 |
| | Oakland, West | 4 | 108 | 43 | 2 | 4 | 1 | .987 | 20 | 5 |
| 1975 | Boston, East | 3 | 81 | 33 | 4 | 3 | 0 | .966 | 14 | 5 |
| | Oakland, West | 3 | 75 | 40 | 6 | 4 | 0 | .950 | 22 | 7 |
| 1976 | New York, East | 5 | 132 | 60 | 6 | 3 | 1 | .970 | 22 | 6 |
| | Kansas City, West | 5 | 129 | 51 | 4 | 5 | 0 | .978 | 24 | 9 |
| 1977 | New York, East | 5 | 132 | 51 | 2 | 2 | 0 | .989 | 18 | 6 |
| | Kansas City, West | 5 | 132 | 54 | 5 | 2 | 0 | .974 | 22 | 8 |
| 1978 | New York, East | 4 | 105 | 35 | 1 | 2 | 1 | .993 | 21 | 8 |
| | Kansas City, West | 4 | 102 | 36 | 4 | 4 | 1 | .972 | 20 | 7 |
| 1979 | Baltimore, East | 4 | 109 | 52 | 5 | 5 | 1 | .970 | 20 | 5 |
| | California, West | 4 | 107 | 37 | 2 | 7 | 0 | .986 | 23 | 9 |
| 1980 | New York, East | 3 | 75 | 42 | 1 | 2 | 0 | .991 | 20 | 6 |
| | Kansas City, West | 3 | 81 | 29 | 1 | 3 | 0 | .991 | 15 | 4 |
| 1981 | New York, East | 3 | 81 | 30 | 1 | 6 | 1 | .991 | 22 | 6 |
| | Oakland, West | 3 | 75 | 33 | 4 | 1 | 0 | .964 | 24 | 8 |
| 1982 | Milwaukee, East | 5 | 129 | 45 | 8 | 5 | 0 | .956 | 20 | 8 |
| | California, West | 5 | 126 | 46 | 4 | 3 | 1 | .977 | 20 | 7 |
| 1983 | Baltimore, East | 4 | 111 | 49 | 2 | 4 | 0 | .988 | 22 | 6 |
| | Chicago, West | 4 | 108 | 51 | 3 | 5 | 0 | .981 | 23 | 9 |
| 1984 | Detroit, East | 3 | 87 | 27 | 1 | 0 | 0 | .991 | 20 | 5 |
| | Kansas City, West | 3 | 84 | 26 | 7 | 2 | 0 | .940 | 22 | 6 |
| 1985 | Toronto, East | 7 | 186 | 61 | 4 | 4 | 0 | .984 | 24 | 8 |
| | Kansas City, West | 7 | 188 | 87 | 6 | 7 | 0 | .979 | 22 | 7 |
| 1986 | Boston, East | 7 | 196 | 73 | 7 | 5 | 0 | .975 | 20 | 7 |
| | California, West | 7 | 192 | 78 | 8 | 5 | 2 | .971 | 24 | 9 |
| 1987 | Detroit, East | 5 | 129 | 56 | 5 | 1 | 1 | .974 | 24 | 10 |
| | Minnesota, West | 5 | 132 | 41 | 3 | 3 | 0 | .983 | 21 | 7 |
| 1988 | Boston, East | 4 | 102 | 34 | 1 | 2 | 1 | .993 | 20 | 7 |
| | Oakland, West | 4 | 108 | 30 | 3 | 5 | 1 | .979 | 22 | 9 |
| 1989 | Toronto, East | 5 | 129 | 40 | 2 | 5 | 1 | .988 | 22 | 9 |
| | Oakland, West | 5 | 132 | 45 | 3 | 4 | 1 | .983 | 22 | 8 |
| 1990 | Boston, East | 4 | 102 | 47 | 5 | 6 | 1 | .968 | 23 | 10 |
| | Oakland, West | 4 | 108 | 43 | 1 | 3 | 0 | .993 | 21 | 6 |
| 1991 | Toronto, East | 5 | 135 | 49 | 7 | 4 | 0 | .963 | 23 | 10 |
| | Minnesota, West | 5 | 138 | 51 | 4 | 3 | 0 | .979 | 23 | 8 |
| 1992 | Toronto, East | 6 | 165 | 60 | 8 | 7 | 3 | .966 | 21 | 9 |
| | Oakland, West | 6 | 162 | 55 | 7 | 5 | 0 | .969 | 25 | 11 |
| 1993 | Toronto, East | 6 | 162 | 57 | 2 | 7 | 0 | .991 | 19 | 10 |
| | Chicago, West | 6 | 159 | 56 | 7 | 5 | 0 | .968 | 22 | 9 |
| 1994 | no series | | | | | | | | | |
| 1995 | Cleveland, East | 6 | 165 | 66 | 7 | 4 | 0 | .971 | 25 | 11 |
| | Seattle, West | 6 | 162 | 59 | 6 | 7 | 1 | .974 | 25 | 10 |
| 1996 | New York, East | 5 | 141 | 44 | 1 | 1 | 0 | .995 | 24 | 9 |
| | Baltimore, East | 5 | 138 | 58 | 4 | 7 | 0 | .980 | 23 | 10 |
| 1997 | Baltimore, East | 6 | 174 | 60 | 5 | 4 | 0 | .979 | 23 | 9 |
| | Cleveland, Central | 6 | 174 | 61 | 5 | 11 | 0 | .979 | 23 | 11 |
| 1998 | New York, East | 6 | 168 | 54 | 2 | 5 | 0 | .991 | 24 | 9 |
| | Cleveland, Central | 6 | 165 | 77 | 7 | 7 | 0 | .972 | 25 | 11 |

| Year | Team, Division | G | PO | A | E | DP | PB | Fielding Avg. | Players Used | Pitchers Used |
|---|---|---|---|---|---|---|---|---|---|---|
| 1999 | New York, East | 5 | 135 | 38 | 4 | 7 | 1 | .977 | 25 | 10 |
| | Boston, East | 5 | 132 | 40 | 10 | 0 | 0 | .945 | 24 | 10 |
| 2000 | New York, East | 6 | 159 | 54 | 1 | 5 | 0 | .995 | 22 | 10 |
| | Seattle, West | 6 | 156 | 58 | 3 | 4 | 1 | .986 | 25 | 10 |
| 2001 | New York, East | 5 | 135 | 47 | 4 | 4 | 0 | .978 | 24 | 9 |
| | Seattle, West | 5 | 130 | 45 | 1 | 5 | 0 | .994 | 25 | 11 |
| 2002 | Anaheim, West | 5 | 132 | 38 | 2 | 4 | 0 | .988 | 24 | 9 |
| | Minnesota, Central | 5 | 126 | 43 | 4 | 4 | 0 | .977 | 25 | 11 |
| 2003 | New York, East | 7 | 192 | 73 | 5 | 12 | 0 | .981 | 22 | 9 |
| | Boston, East | 7 | 189 | 67 | 3 | 5 | 3 | .988 | 23 | 10 |
| 2004 | Boston, East | 7 | 207 | 66 | 1 | 4 | 3 | .996 | 25 | 11 |
| | New York, East | 7 | 209 | 74 | 4 | 9 | 1 | .986 | 23 | 11 |
| 2005 | Chicago, Central | 5 | 135 | 66 | 3 | 4 | 2 | .985 | 15 | 5 |
| | Los Angeles, West | 5 | 134 | 47 | 7 | 5 | 0 | .963 | 25 | 10 |

## NATIONAL LEAGUE

| Year | Team, Division | G | PO | A | E | DP | PB | Fielding Avg. | Players Used | Pitchers Used |
|---|---|---|---|---|---|---|---|---|---|---|
| 1969 | New York, East | 3 | 81 | 23 | 2 | 2 | 1 | .981 | 17 | 6 |
| | Atlanta, West | 3 | 78 | 37 | 6 | 4 | 1 | .950 | 23 | 9 |
| 1970 | Pittsburgh, East | 3 | 81 | 37 | 2 | 3 | 0 | .983 | 18 | 5 |
| | Cincinnati, West | 3 | 84 | 39 | 1 | 1 | 0 | .992 | 20 | 7 |
| 1971 | Pittsburgh, East | 4 | 105 | 32 | 3 | 3 | 1 | .979 | 21 | 7 |
| | San Francisco, West | 4 | 102 | 37 | 4 | 1 | 1 | .972 | 22 | 9 |
| 1972 | Pittsburgh, East | 5 | 131 | 38 | 4 | 3 | 0 | .977 | 23 | 10 |
| | Cincinnati, West | 5 | 132 | 53 | 4 | 3 | 1 | .979 | 21 | 8 |
| 1973 | New York, East | 5 | 142 | 44 | 4 | 3 | 0 | .979 | 17 | 6 |
| | Cincinnati, West | 5 | 138 | 59 | 2 | 3 | 0 | .990 | 24 | 9 |
| 1974 | Pittsburgh, East | 4 | 105 | 37 | 4 | 2 | 1 | .973 | 22 | 8 |
| | Los Angeles, West | 4 | 108 | 46 | 7 | 8 | 1 | .957 | 22 | 7 |
| 1975 | Pittsburgh, East | 3 | 78 | 20 | 2 | 3 | 2 | .980 | 24 | 10 |
| | Cincinnati, West | 3 | 84 | 31 | 1 | 2 | 0 | .991 | 18 | 7 |
| 1976 | Philadelphia, East | 3 | 79 | 34 | 2 | 3 | 0 | .983 | 22 | 7 |
| | Cincinnati, West | 3 | 81 | 32 | 2 | 3 | 0 | .983 | 18 | 6 |
| 1977 | Philadelphia, East | 4 | 105 | 49 | 3 | 3 | 1 | .981 | 21 | 7 |
| | Los Angeles, West | 4 | 108 | 44 | 5 | 3 | 0 | .968 | 23 | 9 |
| 1978 | Philadelphia, East | 4 | 110 | 46 | 4 | 4 | 0 | .975 | 22 | 8 |
| | Los Angeles, West | 4 | 111 | 50 | 3 | 4 | 0 | .982 | 22 | 9 |
| 1979 | Pittsburgh, East | 3 | 90 | 34 | 0 | 2 | 0 | 1.000 | 20 | 8 |
| | Cincinnati, West | 3 | 87 | 39 | 1 | 2 | 0 | .992 | 20 | 9 |
| 1980 | Philadelphia, East | 5 | 148 | 71 | 6 | 7 | 0 | .973 | 23 | 9 |
| | Houston, West | 5 | 147 | 52 | 3 | 4 | 1 | .985 | 24 | 7 |
| 1981 | Montreal, East | 5 | 132 | 52 | 4 | 8 | 0 | .979 | 19 | 7 |
| | Los Angeles, West | 5 | 132 | 53 | 2 | 5 | 1 | .989 | 23 | 9 |
| 1982 | St. Louis, East | 3 | 81 | 35 | 2 | 3 | 0 | .983 | 15 | 5 |
| | Atlanta, West | 3 | 76 | 39 | 1 | 0 | 1 | .991 | 20 | 8 |
| 1983 | Philadelphia, East | 4 | 105 | 36 | 5 | 0 | 0 | .966 | 20 | 5 |
| | Los Angeles, West | 4 | 102 | 38 | 1 | 3 | 1 | .993 | 22 | 8 |
| 1984 | Chicago, East | 5 | 127 | 49 | 3 | 6 | 1 | .983 | 23 | 8 |
| | San Diego, West | 5 | 129 | 43 | 1 | 4 | 0 | .994 | 24 | 10 |
| 1985 | St. Louis, East | 6 | 156 | 54 | 4 | 4 | 1 | .981 | 23 | 9 |
| | Los Angeles, West | 6 | 154 | 72 | 6 | 3 | 0 | .974 | 25 | 9 |
| 1986 | New York, East | 6 | 189 | 94 | 1 | 6 | 0 | .996 | 22 | 8 |
| | Houston, West | 6 | 188 | 66 | 7 | 3 | 2 | .973 | 21 | 8 |
| 1987 | St. Louis, East | 7 | 183 | 67 | 3 | 5 | 0 | .988 | 23 | 8 |
| | San Francisco, West | 7 | 180 | 77 | 6 | 10 | 1 | .977 | 23 | 10 |
| 1988 | New York, East | 7 | 192 | 62 | 8 | 2 | 0 | .969 | 22 | 8 |
| | Los Angeles, West | 7 | 195 | 61 | 5 | 9 | 1 | .981 | 24 | 9 |
| 1989 | Chicago, East | 5 | 126 | 40 | 3 | 1 | 2 | .982 | 24 | 9 |
| | San Francisco, West | 5 | 132 | 49 | 5 | 7 | 1 | .973 | 24 | 9 |
| 1990 | Pittsburgh, East | 6 | 156 | 71 | 5 | 4 | 0 | .978 | 21 | 8 |
| | Cincinnati, West | 6 | 159 | 45 | 2 | 3 | 0 | .990 | 23 | 8 |
| 1991 | Pittsburgh, East | 7 | 189 | 75 | 6 | 3 | 0 | .978 | 25 | 11 |
| | Atlanta, West | 7 | 189 | 62 | 4 | 6 | 0 | .984 | 23 | 9 |
| 1992 | Pittsburgh, East | 7 | 182 | 63 | 5 | 6 | 2 | .980 | 25 | 10 |
| | Atlanta, West | 7 | 183 | 74 | 2 | 3 | 1 | .992 | 25 | 10 |
| 1993 | Philadelphia, East | 6 | 165 | 47 | 7 | 2 | 2 | .968 | 25 | 10 |
| | Atlanta, West | 6 | 163 | 54 | 5 | 1 | 0 | .977 | 23 | 8 |
| 1994 | no series | | | | | | | | | |
| 1995 | Atlanta, East | 4 | 117 | 54 | 3 | 7 | 0 | .983 | 22 | 8 |
| | Cincinnati, West | 4 | 111 | 43 | 2 | 4 | 1 | .987 | 25 | 10 |
| 1996 | Atlanta, East | 7 | 183 | 55 | 4 | 6 | 0 | .983 | 24 | 10 |
| | St. Louis, Central | 7 | 180 | 61 | 6 | 4 | 0 | .976 | 25 | 10 |
| 1997 | Atlanta, East | 6 | 156 | 57 | 4 | 7 | 0 | .982 | 22 | 8 |
| | Florida, East | 6 | 159 | 57 | 3 | 4 | 0 | .986 | 24 | 10 |
| 1998 | San Diego, West | 6 | 165 | 60 | 1 | 6 | 0 | .996 | 24 | 10 |
| | Atlanta, East | 6 | 162 | 74 | 8 | 6 | 1 | .967 | 24 | 9 |

| | | | | | | | | | | |
|---|---|---|---|---|---|---|---|---|---|---|
| 1999 | Atlanta, East | 6 | 181 | 55 | 7 | 4 | 1 | .971 | 25 | 9 |
| | New York, East | 6 | 178 | 82 | 8 | 9 | 0 | .970 | 25 | 11 |
| 2000 | New York, East | 5 | 135 | 39 | 4 | 1 | 0 | .978 | 24 | 10 |
| | St. Louis, Central | 5 | 129 | 49 | 7 | 3 | 1 | .962 | 25 | 10 |
| 2001 | Atlanta, East | 5 | 132 | 52 | 7 | 5 | 1 | .963 | 24 | 10 |
| | Arizona, West | 5 | 135 | 43 | 3 | 3 | 0 | .983 | 23 | 9 |
| 2002 | San Francisco, West | 5 | 135 | 49 | 1 | 4 | 0 | .995 | 23 | 10 |
| | St. Louis, Central | 5 | 131 | 40 | 1 | 4 | 0 | .994 | 22 | 10 |
| 2003 | Florida, East | 7 | 198 | 70 | 3 | 4 | 0 | .989 | 25 | 11 |
| | Chicago, Central | 7 | 198 | 81 | 4 | 6 | 2 | .986 | 24 | 10 |
| 2004 | St. Louis, Central | 7 | 190 | 66 | 1 | 5 | 0 | .996 | 25 | 11 |
| | Houston, Central | 7 | 187 | 71 | 2 | 2 | 1 | .992 | 23 | 9 |
| 2005 | Houston, Central | 6 | 159 | 77 | 3 | 4 | 0 | .987 | 23 | 10 |
| | St. Louis, Central | 6 | 156 | 73 | 5 | 3 | 1 | .979 | 21 | 9 |

## MANAGERIAL RECORDS

### AMERICAN LEAGUE

| Manager, Team | Series W | Series L | Games W | Games L |
|---|---|---|---|---|
| Joe Altobelli, Baltimore | 1 | 0 | 3 | 1 |
| Sparky Anderson, Detroit | 1 | 1 | 4 | 4 |
| Bobby Cox, Toronto | 0 | 1 | 3 | 4 |
| Alvin Dark, Oakland | 1 | 1 | 3 | 4 |
| Terry Francona, Boston | 1 | 0 | 4 | 3 |
| Jim Fregosi, California | 0 | 1 | 1 | 3 |
| Jim Frey, Kansas City | 1 | 0 | 3 | 0 |
| Ron Gardenhire, Minnesota | 0 | 1 | 1 | 4 |
| Cito Gaston, Toronto | 2 | 2 | 10 | 12 |
| Ozzie Guillen, Chicago | 1 | 0 | 4 | 1 |
| Mike Hargrove, Cleveland | 2 | 1 | 10 | 8 |
| Whitey Herzog, Kansas City | 0 | 3 | 5 | 9 |
| Dick Howser, New York, Kansas City | 1 | 2 | 4 | 9 |
| Darrell Johnson, Boston | 1 | 0 | 3 | 0 |
| Dave Johnson, Baltimore | 0 | 2 | 3 | 8 |
| Tom Kelly, Minnesota | 2 | 0 | 8 | 2 |
| Harvey Kuenn, Milwaukee | 1 | 0 | 3 | 2 |
| Gene Lamont, Chicago | 0 | 1 | 2 | 4 |
| Tony La Russa, Chicago, Oakland | 3 | 2 | 15 | 8 |
| Bob Lemon, New York | 2 | 0 | 6 | 1 |
| Grady Little, Boston | 0 | 1 | 3 | 4 |
| Billy Martin, Minnesota, Detroit, New York, Oakland | 2 | 3 | 8 | 13 |
| Gene Mauch, California | 0 | 2 | 5 | 7 |
| John McNamara, Boston | 1 | 0 | 4 | 3 |
| Joe Morgan, Boston | 0 | 2 | 0 | 8 |
| Lou Piniella, Seattle | 0 | 3 | 5 | 12 |
| Bill Rigney, Minnesota | 0 | 1 | 0 | 3 |
| Mike Scioscia, Anaheim/Los Angeles | 1 | 1 | 5 | 5 |
| Joe Torre, New York | 6 | 1 | 27 | 14 |
| Earl Weaver, Baltimore | 4 | 2 | 15 | 7 |
| Dick Williams, Oakland | 2 | 1 | 6 | 7 |
| Jimy Williams, Boston | 0 | 1 | 1 | 4 |

**Total number of managers: 32**

### NATIONAL LEAGUE

| Manager, Team | Series W | Series L | Games W | Games L |
|---|---|---|---|---|
| Walter Alston, Los Angeles | 1 | 0 | 3 | 1 |
| Sparky Anderson, Cincinnati | 4 | 1 | 14 | 5 |
| Dusty Baker, San Francisco, Chicago | 1 | 1 | 7 | 5 |
| Yogi Berra, New York | 1 | 0 | 3 | 2 |
| Bruce Bochy, San Diego | 1 | 0 | 4 | 2 |
| Bob Brenly, Arizona | 1 | 0 | 4 | 1 |
| Bobby Cox, Atlanta | 5 | 4 | 27 | 27 |
| Roger Craig, San Francisco | 1 | 1 | 7 | 5 |
| Jim Fanning, Montreal | 0 | 1 | 2 | 3 |
| Jim Fregosi, Philadelphia | 1 | 0 | 4 | 2 |
| Jim Frey, Chicago | 0 | 1 | 2 | 3 |
| Charlie Fox, San Francisco | 0 | 1 | 1 | 3 |
| Phil Garner, Houston | 1 | 1 | 7 | 6 |
| Dallas Green, Philadelphia | 1 | 0 | 3 | 2 |
| Lum Harris, Atlanta | 0 | 1 | 0 | 3 |
| Whitey Herzog, St. Louis | 3 | 0 | 11 | 5 |
| Gil Hodges, New York | 1 | 0 | 3 | 0 |
| Dave Johnson, New York, Cincinnati | 1 | 2 | 7 | 10 |
| Hal Lanier, Houston | 0 | 1 | 2 | 4 |
| Tony La Russa, St. Louis | 1 | 4 | 11 | 19 |
| Tom Lasorda, Los Angeles | 4 | 2 | 16 | 14 |
| Jim Leyland, Pittsburgh, Florida | 1 | 3 | 12 | 14 |
| Jack McKeon, Florida | 1 | 0 | 4 | 3 |
| John McNamara, Cincinnati | 0 | 1 | 0 | 3 |
| Danny Murtaugh, Pittsburgh | 1 | 3 | 4 | 10 |
| Paul Owens, Philadelphia | 1 | 0 | 3 | 1 |
| Danny Ozark, Philadelphia | 0 | 3 | 2 | 9 |
| Lou Piniella, Cincinnati | 1 | 0 | 4 | 2 |
| Chuck Tanner, Pittsburgh | 1 | 0 | 3 | 0 |
| Joe Torre, Atlanta | 0 | 1 | 0 | 3 |
| Bobby Valentine, New York | 1 | 1 | 6 | 5 |
| Bill Virdon, Pittsburgh, Houston | 0 | 2 | 4 | 6 |
| Dick Williams, San Diego | 1 | 0 | 3 | 2 |
| Don Zimmer, Chicago | 0 | 1 | 1 | 4 |

**Total number of managers: 34**

### COMBINED RECORDS FOR BOTH LEAGUES

| Manager, Team | Series W | Series L | Games W | Games L |
|---|---|---|---|---|
| Sparky Anderson, Cin NL, Det AL | 5 | 2 | 18 | 9 |
| Bobby Cox, Tor AL, Atl NL | 5 | 5 | 30 | 31 |
| Jim Fregosi, Cal AL, Phi NL | 1 | 1 | 5 | 5 |
| Jim Frey, KC AL, Chi NL | 1 | 1 | 5 | 3 |
| Whitey Herzog, KC AL, St. L NL | 3 | 3 | 16 | 14 |
| Dave Johnson, NY NL, Cin NL, Bal AL | 1 | 4 | 10 | 18 |
| Tony La Russa, Chi AL, Oak AL, St. L NL | 4 | 7 | 26 | 27 |
| John McNamara, Cin NL, Bos AL | 1 | 1 | 4 | 6 |
| Lou Piniella, Cin NL, Sea AL | 1 | 3 | 9 | 14 |
| Joe Torre, Atl NL, NY AL | 6 | 2 | 27 | 17 |
| Dick Williams, Oak AL, SD NL | 3 | 1 | 9 | 9 |

**Total number of managers: 11**

Roger Clemens

# WORLD SERIES

2006 MLB RECORD & FACT BOOK



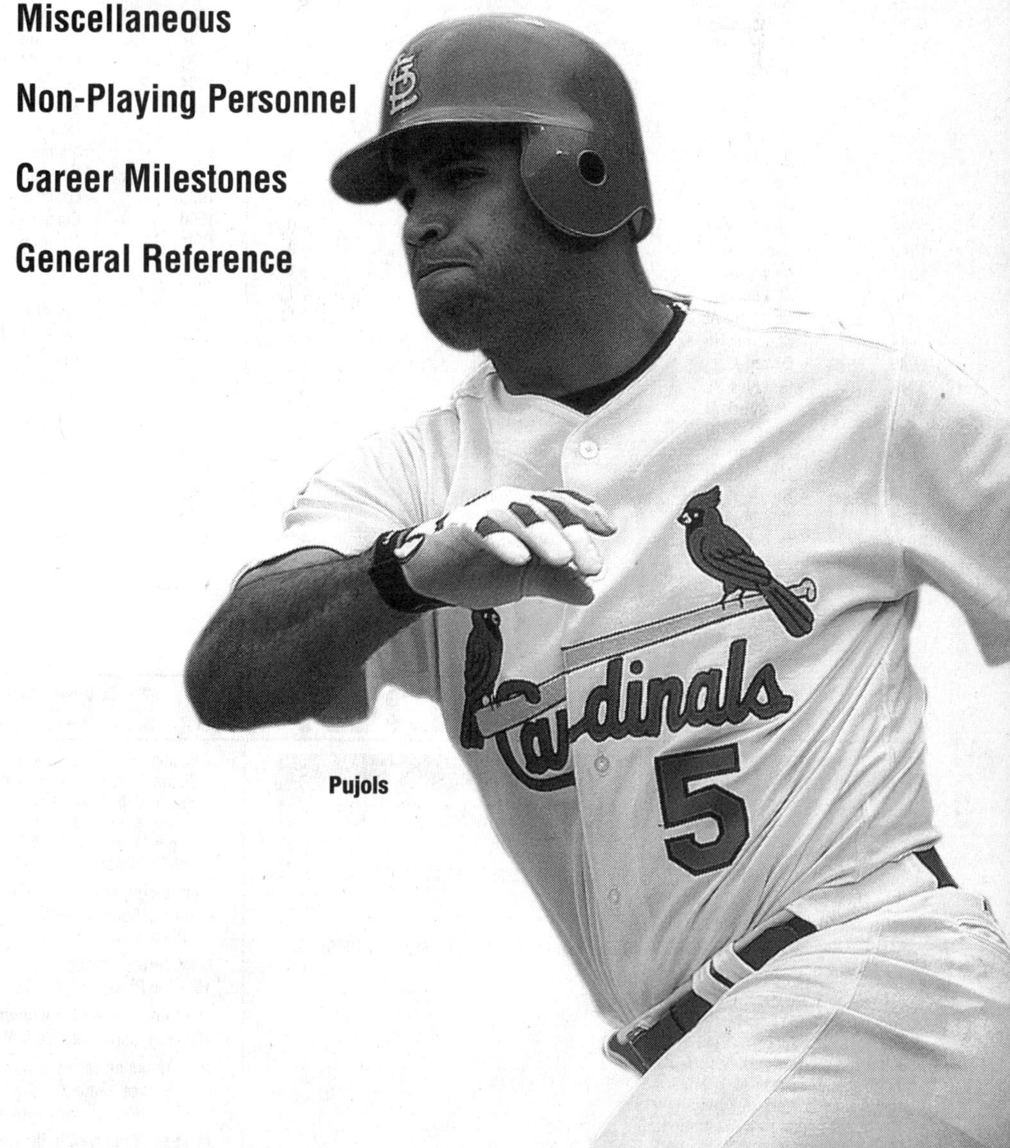


Pujols

# WORLD SERIES CHAMPIONS

| Year | Winner | Loser | Games |
|---|---|---|---|
| 1903 | Boston AL | Pittsburgh NL | 5-3 |
| 1904 | no series played | | |
| 1905 | New York NL | Philadelphia AL | 4-1 |
| 1906 | Chicago AL | Chicago NL | 4-2 |
| 1907 | Chicago NL | Detroit AL | *4-0 |
| 1908 | Chicago NL | Detroit AL | 4-1 |
| 1909 | Pittsburgh NL | Detroit AL | 4-3 |
| 1910 | Philadelphia AL | Chicago NL | 4-1 |
| 1911 | Philadelphia AL | New York NL | 4-2 |
| 1912 | Boston AL | New York NL | *4-3 |
| 1913 | Philadelphia AL | New York NL | 4-1 |
| 1914 | Boston NL | Philadelphia AL | 4-0 |
| 1915 | Boston AL | Philadelphia NL | 4-1 |
| 1916 | Boston AL | Brooklyn NL | 4-1 |
| 1917 | Chicago AL | New York NL | 4-2 |
| 1918 | Boston AL | Chicago NL | 4-2 |
| 1919 | Cincinnati NL | Chicago AL | 5-3 |
| 1920 | Cleveland AL | Brooklyn NL | 5-2 |
| 1921 | New York NL | New York AL | 5-3 |
| 1922 | New York NL | New York AL | *4-0 |
| 1923 | New York AL | New York NL | 4-2 |
| 1924 | Washington AL | New York NL | 4-3 |
| 1925 | Pittsburgh NL | Washington AL | 4-3 |
| 1926 | St. Louis NL | New York AL | 4-3 |
| 1927 | New York AL | Pittsburgh NL | 4-0 |
| 1928 | New York AL | St. Louis NL | 4-0 |
| 1929 | Philadelphia AL | Chicago NL | 4-1 |
| 1930 | Philadelphia AL | St. Louis NL | 4-2 |
| 1931 | St. Louis NL | Philadelphia AL | 4-3 |
| 1932 | New York AL | Chicago NL | 4-0 |
| 1933 | New York NL | Washington AL | 4-1 |
| 1934 | St. Louis NL | Detroit AL | 4-3 |
| 1935 | Detroit AL | Chicago NL | 4-2 |
| 1936 | New York AL | New York NL | 4-2 |
| 1937 | New York AL | New York NL | 4-1 |
| 1938 | New York AL | Chicago NL | 4-0 |
| 1939 | New York AL | Cincinnati NL | 4-0 |
| 1940 | Cincinnati NL | Detroit AL | 4-3 |
| 1941 | New York AL | Brooklyn NL | 4-1 |
| 1942 | St. Louis NL | New York AL | 4-1 |
| 1943 | New York AL | St. Louis NL | 4-1 |
| 1944 | St. Louis NL | St. Louis AL | 4-2 |
| 1945 | Detroit AL | Chicago NL | 4-3 |
| 1946 | St. Louis NL | Boston AL | 4-3 |
| 1947 | New York AL | Brooklyn NL | 4-3 |
| 1948 | Cleveland AL | Boston NL | 4-2 |
| 1949 | New York AL | Brooklyn NL | 4-1 |
| 1950 | New York AL | Philadelphia NL | 4-0 |
| 1951 | New York AL | New York NL | 4-2 |
| 1952 | New York AL | Brooklyn NL | 4-3 |
| 1953 | New York AL | Brooklyn NL | 4-2 |
| 1954 | New York NL | Cleveland AL | 4-0 |
| 1955 | Brooklyn NL | New York AL | 4-3 |
| 1956 | New York AL | Brooklyn NL | 4-3 |
| 1957 | Milwaukee NL | New York AL | 4-3 |
| 1958 | New York AL | Milwaukee NL | 4-3 |
| 1959 | Los Angeles NL | Chicago AL | 4-2 |
| 1960 | Pittsburgh NL | New York AL | 4-3 |
| 1961 | New York AL | Cincinnati NL | 4-1 |
| 1962 | New York AL | San Francisco NL | 4-3 |
| 1963 | Los Angeles NL | New York AL | 4-0 |
| 1964 | St. Louis NL | New York AL | 4-3 |
| 1965 | Los Angeles NL | Minnesota AL | 4-3 |
| 1966 | Baltimore AL | Los Angeles NL | 4-0 |
| 1967 | St. Louis NL | Boston AL | 4-3 |
| 1968 | Detroit AL | St. Louis NL | 4-3 |
| 1969 | New York NL | Baltimore AL | 4-1 |
| 1970 | Baltimore AL | Cincinnati NL | 4-1 |
| 1971 | Pittsburgh NL | Baltimore AL | 4-3 |
| 1972 | Oakland AL | Cincinnati NL | 4-3 |
| 1973 | Oakland AL | New York NL | 4-3 |
| 1974 | Oakland AL | Los Angeles NL | 4-1 |
| 1975 | Cincinnati NL | Boston AL | 4-3 |
| 1976 | Cincinnati NL | New York AL | 4-0 |
| 1977 | New York AL | Los Angeles NL | 4-2 |
| 1978 | New York AL | Los Angeles NL | 4-2 |
| 1979 | Pittsburgh NL | Baltimore AL | 4-3 |
| 1980 | Philadelphia NL | Kansas City AL | 4-2 |
| 1981 | Los Angeles NL | New York AL | 4-2 |
| 1982 | St. Louis NL | Milwaukee AL | 4-3 |
| 1983 | Baltimore AL | Philadelphia NL | 4-1 |
| 1984 | Detroit AL | San Diego NL | 4-1 |
| 1985 | Kansas City AL | St. Louis NL | 4-3 |
| 1986 | New York NL | Boston AL | 4-3 |
| 1987 | Minnesota AL | St. Louis NL | 4-3 |
| 1988 | Los Angeles NL | Oakland AL | 4-1 |
| 1989 | Oakland AL | San Francisco NL | 4-0 |
| 1990 | Cincinnati NL | Oakland AL | 4-0 |
| 1991 | Minnesota AL | Atlanta NL | 4-3 |
| 1992 | Toronto AL | Atlanta NL | 4-2 |
| 1993 | Toronto AL | Philadelphia NL | 4-2 |
| 1994 | no series played | | |
| 1995 | Atlanta NL | Cleveland AL | 4-2 |
| 1996 | New York AL | Atlanta NL | 4-2 |
| 1997 | Florida NL | Cleveland AL | 4-3 |
| 1998 | New York AL | San Diego NL | 4-0 |
| 1999 | New York AL | Atlanta NL | 4-0 |
| 2000 | New York AL | New York NL | 4-1 |
| 2001 | Arizona NL | New York AL | 4-3 |
| 2002 | Anaheim AL | San Francisco NL | 4-3 |
| 2003 | Florida NL | New York AL | 4-2 |
| 2004 | Boston AL | St. Louis NL | 4-0 |
| 2005 | Chicago AL | Houston NL | 4-0 |

* includes tie game

# INDIVIDUAL SERVICE

## ALL PLAYERS

### SERIES AND CLUBS

**Most series played**
14—Yogi Berra, New York AL, 1947, 1949-1953, 1955-1958, 1960-1963, 75 G (65 consec)

**Most series eligible, but did not play**
6—Charlie Silvera, New York AL, 1950-1953, 1955, 1956, 37 G (played 1 G in 1949)

**Most consecutive series played (17 times)**
5—Hank Bauer, New York AL, 1949-1953
Yogi Berra, New York AL, 1949-1953
Ed Lopat, New York AL, 1949-1953
Johnny Mize, New York AL, 1949-1953
Vic Raschi, New York AL, 1949-1953
Allie Reynolds, New York AL, 1949-1953
Phil Rizzuto, New York AL, 1949-1953
Gene Woodling, New York AL, 1949-1953
Johnny Blanchard, New York AL, 1960-1964
Clete Boyer, New York AL, 1960-1964
Ralph Terry, New York AL, 1960-1964
Whitey Ford, New York AL, 1960-1964
Elston Howard, New York AL, 1960-1964
Hector Lopez, New York AL, 1960-1964
Mickey Mantle, New York AL, 1960-1964
Roger Maris, New York AL, 1960-1964
Bobby Richardson, New York AL, 1960-1964

**Most series played with one club**
14—Yogi Berra, New York AL, 1947, 1949-1953, 1955-1958, 1960-1963, 75 G (65 consec)

**Most series playing in all games**
10—Joe DiMaggio, New York AL, 1936-1939, 1941, 1942, 1947, 1949-1951, 51 G

**Most times on series-winning club (playing at least one game each series)**
10—Yogi Berra, New York AL, 1947, 1949-1953, 1956, 1958, 1961, 1962

**Most times on series-losing club (playing at least one game each series)**
6—Pee Wee Reese, Brooklyn NL, 1941, 1947, 1949, 1952, 1953, 1956
Elston Howard, New York AL, 1955, 1957, 1960, 1963, 1964; Boston AL, 1967

**Most series played in first four major league seasons**
4—Joe DiMaggio, New York AL, 1936-1939
Elston Howard, New York AL, 1955-1958
Johnny Kucks, New York AL, 1955-1958

Orlando Hernandez, New York AL, 1998-2001

**Most clubs, career**

4—Lonnie Smith, Philadelphia NL, 1980; St. Louis NL, 1982; Kansas City AL, 1985; Atlanta NL, 1991, 1992

### BY POSITION (EXCEPT PITCHERS)

**Most series by first baseman**

8—Bill Skowron, New York AL, 1955-1958, 1960, 1961, 1962; Los Angeles NL, 1963, 37 G

**Most series by second baseman**

7—Frank Frisch, New York NL, 1922-1924; St. Louis NL, 1928, 1930, 1931, 1934, 42 G

**Most series by third baseman**

6—Red Rolfe, New York AL, 1936-1939, 1941, 1942, 28 G

**Most series by shortstop**

9—Phil Rizzuto, New York AL, 1941, 1942, 1947, 1949-1953, 1955, 52 G

**Most series by outfielder**

12—Mickey Mantle, New York AL, 1951-1953, 1955-1958, 1960-1964, 63 G

**Most series by catcher**

12—Yogi Berra, New York AL, 1947, 1949, 1950-1953, 1955-1958, 1960, 1962, 63 G

### YOUNGEST AND OLDEST NON-PITCHERS

**Youngest World Series non-pitcher**

18 years, 10 months, 13 days—Fred Lindstrom, New York NL, Oct 4, 1924

**Oldest World Series non-pitcher**

43 years, 7 months, 12 days—Sam Rice, Washington AL, Oct 4, 1933

### YEARS BETWEEN SERIES (INCLUDES PITCHERS)

**Most years between first and second series**

17—Jim Kaat, Minnesota AL, 1965; St. Louis NL, 1982

**Most years between first and last series**

22—Willie Mays, New York Giants NL, 1951; New York Mets NL, 1973

**Most years played in majors before playing in series**

21—Joe Niekro, Minnesota AL, Oct 21, 1987
Mike Morgan, Arizona NL, Oct 27, 2001

### POSITIONS

**Most positions played, career**

4—Babe Ruth, Boston AL, 1915, 1916, 1918; New York AL, 1921-1923, 1926-1928, 1932, 41 G (P, LF, RF, 1B)
Jackie Robinson, Brooklyn NL, 1947, 1949, 1952, 1953, 1955, 1956, 38 G (1B, 2B, LF, 3B)
Elston Howard, New York AL, 1955-1958, 1960-1964; Boston AL, 1967, 54 G (LF, RF, 1B, C)
Tony Kubek, New York AL, 1957, 1958, 1960-1963, 37 G (LF, 3B, CF, SS)
Pete Rose, Cincinnati NL, 1970, 1972, 1975, 1976; Philadelphia NL, 1980, 1983, 34 G (RF, LF, 3B, 1B)

**Most positions played, series**

3—many players

## PITCHERS

### SERIES

**Most series pitched**

11—Whitey Ford, New York AL, 1950, 1953, 1955-1958, 1960-1964, 22 G

**Most series pitched by relief pitcher**

6—Johnny Murphy, New York AL, 1936-1939, 1941, 1943, 8 G
Mike Stanton, Atlanta NL, 1991, 1992; New York AL, 1998-2001, 20 G
Mariano Rivera, New York AL, 1996, 1998-2001, 2003, 20 G

### YOUNGEST AND OLDEST PITCHERS

**Youngest World Series pitcher**

19 years, 20 days—Ken Brett, Boston AL, Oct 8, 1967

**Oldest World Series pitcher**

46 years, 2 months, 29 days—Jack Quinn, Philadelphia AL, Oct 4, 1930

# CLUB SERVICE

## PLAYERS USED

**Most players, series**

4-game series
25—Oakland AL vs Cincinnati NL, 1990
Atlanta NL vs New York AL, 1999
St. Louis NL vs Boston AL, 2004

5-game series
25—Brooklyn NL vs New York AL, 1949
New York NL vs New York AL, 2000

6-game series
25—Los Angeles NL vs New York AL, 1977
New York AL vs Atlanta NL, 1996

7-game series
26—Detroit AL vs Chicago NL, 1945
Boston AL vs St. Louis NL, 1946
Florida NL vs Cleveland AL, 1997
Anaheim AL vs San Francisco NL, 2002

8-game series
19—Chicago AL vs Cincinnati NL, 1919
New York AL vs New York NL, 1921

**For a list of players and pitchers used each series, see page 404.**

**Most players used by both clubs, series**

4-game series
48—Atlanta NL 25, New York AL 23, 1999
Chicago AL 24, Houston NL 24, 2005

5-game series
47—New York NL 25, New York AL 22, 2000

6-game series
49—New York AL 25, Atlanta NL 24, 1996

7-game series
51—Detroit AL 26, Chicago NL 25, 1945

8-game series
36—Chicago AL 19, Cincinnati NL 17, 1919

**Fewest players, series**

4-game series
13—Los Angeles NL vs New York AL, 1963
Baltimore AL vs Los Angeles NL, 1966

5-game series
12—New York NL vs Philadelphia AL, 1905
Philadelphia AL vs Chicago NL, 1910
Philadelphia AL vs New York NL, 1913

6-game series
14—Chicago NL vs Chicago AL, 1906
Philadelphia AL vs New York NL, 1911

7-game series
16—Detroit AL vs Pittsburgh NL, 1909

8-game series
13—Boston AL vs Pittsburgh NL, 1903
New York NL vs New York AL, 1921

**Fewest players used by both clubs, series**

4-game series
31—Philadelphia AL 16, Boston NL 15, 1914

5-game series
25—Philadelphia AL 13, New York NL 12, 1905

6-game series
29—New York NL 15, Philadelphia AL 14, 1911

7-game series
33—Pittsburgh NL 17, Detroit AL 16, 1909

8-game series
27—Pittsburgh NL 14, Boston AL 13, 1903

**Most times one club using only nine players in game, series**

5-game series
5—Philadelphia AL vs Chicago NL, 1910
Philadelphia AL vs New York NL, 1913

7-game series
5—New York AL vs Brooklyn NL, 1956

8-game series
6—Pittsburgh NL vs Boston AL, 1903

**Most times both clubs using only nine players in game, series**

7-game series
7—New York AL 5, Brooklyn NL 2, 1956

8-game series
11—Pittsburgh NL 6, Boston AL 5, 1903

**Most players, game**

21—New York AL vs Brooklyn NL, Oct 5, 1947
Cincinnati NL vs New York AL, Oct 9, 1961
[23—Minnesota AL vs Atlanta NL, Oct 22, 1991, 12 inn]

**Most players used by both clubs, game**
38—New York AL 21, Brooklyn NL 17, Oct 5, 1947
[43—Chicago AL 22, Houston NL 21, Oct 25, 2005, 14 inn]

## PINCH-HITTERS

**Most times pinch-hitters used, series**
23—Baltimore AL vs Pittsburgh NL, 1979 (7-game series)

**Most pinch-hitters used by both clubs, series**
37—Minnesota AL 21, Atlanta NL 16, 1991 (7-game series)

**Fewest times pinch-hitters used, series**
0—many clubs; last—Cincinnati NL vs New York AL, 1976 (4-game series)

**Fewest pinch-hitters used by both clubs, series**
2—New York NL 1, Philadelphia AL 1, 1905 (5-game series)

**Most pinch-hitters, game**
6—Los Angeles NL vs Chicago AL, Oct 6, 1959
[8—Minnesota AL vs Atlanta NL, Oct 22, 1991, 12 inn]

**Most pinch-hitters used by both clubs, game**
8—Oakland AL 5, New York NL 3, Oct 14, 1973
Baltimore AL 4, Philadelphia NL 4, Oct 15, 1983
[12—Minnesota AL 8, Atlanta NL 4, Oct 22, 1991, 12 inn]

**Most pinch-hitters, inning**
4—New York NL vs Oakland AL Oct 13, 1973, 9th
Baltimore AL vs Philadelphia NL, Oct 15, 1983, 6th
Minnesota AL vs St. Louis NL, Oct 22, 1987, 9th
Atlanta NL vs New York AL, Oct 23, 1999, 8th
New York NL vs New York AL, Oct 25, 2000, 7th

## PINCH-RUNNERS

**Most pinch-runners, series**
8—Oakland AL vs Cincinnati NL, 1972 (7-game series)

**Most pinch-runners used by both clubs, series**
10—Oakland AL 8, Cincinnati NL 2, 1972 (7-game series)

**Fewest pinch-runners, series**
0—many clubs

**Most pinch-runners, game**
2—many games

**Most pinch-runners used by both clubs, game**
4—St. Louis NL 2, Kansas City AL 2, Oct 26, 1985

**Most pinch-runners, inning**
2—many clubs

**Most pinch-runners used by both clubs, inning**
2—many games

## NUMBER OF PLAYERS USED BY POSITION

### FIRST BASEMEN

**Most first basemen, series**
4—New York AL vs Milwaukee NL, 1957 (7-game series)
Oakland AL vs New York NL, 1973 (7-game series)

**Most first basemen used by both clubs, series**
6—New York AL 4, Milwaukee NL 2, 1957 (7-game series)

**Most first basemen, game**
3—New York AL vs Milwaukee NL, Oct 2, 1957
New York AL vs Milwaukee NL, Oct 5, 1957
[3—Florida NL vs Cleveland AL, Oct 26, 1997, 11 inn]

**Most first basemen used by both clubs, game**
5—New York AL 3, Milwaukee NL 2, Oct 2, 1957
New York AL 3, Milwaukee NL 2, Oct 5, 1957

### SECOND BASEMEN

**Most second basemen, series**
4—Houston NL vs Chicago AL, 2005 (4-game series)

**Most second basemen used by both clubs, series**
7—Houston NL 4, Chicago AL 3, 2005 (4-game series)

**Most second basemen, game**
3—many clubs; last—Houston NL vs Chicago AL, Oct 23, 2005
[3—Oakland AL vs New York NL, Oct 14, 1973, 12 inn]

**Most second basemen used by both clubs, game**
4—many games; last—Houston NL 3, Chicago AL 1, Oct 23, 2005
[4—Houston NL 2, Chicago AL 2, Oct 25, 2005, 14 inn]

### THIRD BASEMEN

**Most third basemen, series**
3—many clubs; last—New York AL vs Atlanta NL, 1996 (6-game series)

**Most third basemen used by both clubs, series**
6—Oakland AL 3, San Francisco NL 3, 1989 (4-game series)

**Most third basemen, game**
3—many clubs; last—Minnesota AL vs Atlanta NL, Oct 23, 1991
[3—many clubs; last—New York AL vs Atlanta NL, Oct 23, 1996, 10 inn]

**Most third basemen used by both clubs, game**
4—many games
[5—New York AL 3, Atlanta NL 2, Oct 23, 1996, 10 inn]

### SHORTSTOPS

**Most shortstops, series**
3—many clubs; last—Atlanta NL vs New York AL, 1999 (4-game series)

**Most shortstops used by both clubs, series**
5—Chicago NL 3, Detroit AL 2, 1945 (7-game series)
New York AL 3, Pittsburgh NL 2, 1960 (7-game series)
Minnesota AL 3, Atlanta NL 2, 1991 (7-game series)

**Most shortstops, game**
3—New York AL vs Pittsburgh NL, Oct 13, 1960
Cincinnati NL vs Baltimore AL, Oct 14, 1970
[3—Minnesota AL vs Atlanta NL Oct 27, 1991, 10 inn
Atlanta NL vs New York AL, Oct 23, 1996, 10 inn]

**Most shortstops used by both clubs, game**
4—many games
[5—Minnesota AL 3, Atlanta NL 2, Oct 27, 1991, 10 inn]

### LEFT FIELDERS

**Most left fielders, series**
4—many clubs; last—Houston NL vs Chicago AL, 2005 (4-game series)

**Most left fielders used by both clubs, series**
7—Oakland AL 4, Los Angeles NL 3, 1988 (5-game series)
New York AL 4, Arizona NL 3, 2001 (7-game series)

**Most left fielders, game**
3—many clubs; last—Atlanta NL vs Cleveland AL, Oct 22, 1995
[4—Houston NL vs Chicago AL, Oct 25, 2005, 14 inn]

**Most left fielders used by both clubs, game**
5—Brooklyn NL 3, New York AL 2, Oct 5, 1947
[5—New York AL 3, New York NL 2, Oct 21, 2000, 12 inn
Houston NL 4, Chicago AL 1, Oct 25, 2005, 14 inn]

### CENTER FIELDERS

**Most center fielders, series**
4—Los Angeles NL vs Chicago AL, 1959 (6-game series)

**Most center fielders used by both clubs, series**
6—New York AL 3, Los Angeles NL 3, 1981 (6-game series)

**Most center fielders, game**
2—many clubs
[3—New York NL vs New York AL, Oct 5, 1922, 10 inn]

**Most center fielders used by both clubs, game**
4—many games; last—New York AL 2, Los Angeles NL 2, Oct 25, 1981

### RIGHT FIELDERS

**Most right fielders, series**
5—Los Angeles NL vs Chicago AL, 1959 (6-game series)
New York AL vs Florida NL, 2003 (6-game series)

**Most right fielders used by both clubs, series**
9—Los Angeles NL 5, Chicago AL 4, 1959 (6-game series)

**Most right fielders, game**
3—many clubs

**Most right fielders used by both clubs, game**
5—Los Angeles NL 3, Chicago AL 2, Oct 8, 1959
San Francisco NL 3, Anaheim AL 2, Oct 24, 2002

### CATCHERS

**Most catchers, series**
4—Los Angeles NL vs New York AL, 1978 (6-game series)

**Most catchers used by both clubs, series**
6—New York AL 3, Pittsburgh NL 3, 1927 (4-game series)
Los Angeles NL 4, New York AL 2, 1978 (6-game series)
New York AL 3, Pittsburgh NL 3, 1960 (7-game series)

**Most catchers, game**
3—Los Angeles NL vs New York AL, Oct 13, 1978
[3—Philadelphia NL vs New York AL, Oct 5, 1950, 10 inn]

**Most catchers used by both clubs, game**
4—many games

### PITCHERS

**Most pitchers, series**
4-game series
11—St. Louis NL vs Boston AL, 2004
Chicago AL vs Houston NL, 2005
Houston NL vs Chicago AL, 2005
5-game series
10—San Diego NL vs Detroit AL, 1984
Oakland AL vs Los Angeles NL, 1988
New York NL vs New York AL, 2000
6-game series
10—many clubs; last—Atlanta NL vs New York AL, 1996; New York AL vs Atlanta NL, 1996

7-game series
11—Boston AL vs St. Louis NL, 1946
Cleveland AL vs Florida NL, 1997
San Francisco NL vs Anaheim AL, 2002
8-game series
8—New York AL vs New York NL, 1921

**For a list of players and pitchers used each series, see page 407.**

**Most pitchers used by both clubs, series**
4-game series
22—Houston NL 11, Chicago AL 11, 2005
5-game series
18—Baltimore AL 9, Cincinnati NL 9, 1970
New York NL 10, New York AL 8, 2000
6-game series
20—Toronto AL 10, Philadelphia NL 10, 1993
Atlanta NL 10, New York AL 10, 1996
7-game series
21—Cleveland AL 11, Florida NL 10, 1997
San Francisco NL 11, Anaheim AL 10, 2002
8-game series
12—New York AL 8, New York NL 4, 1921
**Fewest pitchers, series**
2—Philadelphia AL vs Chicago NL 1910 (5-game series)
**Fewest pitchers used by both clubs, series**
6—Philadelphia AL 3, New York NL 3, 1905 (5-game series)
**Most different starting pitchers, series**
6—Brooklyn NL vs New York AL, 1947
Brooklyn NL vs New York AL, 1955
Pittsburgh NL vs Baltimore AL, 1971
**Most different starting pitchers used by both clubs, series**
11—Brooklyn NL 6, New York AL 5, 1955
**Most pitchers, game**
8—Cincinnati NL vs New York AL, Oct 9, 1961
St. Louis NL vs Boston AL, Oct 11, 1967
[9—Chicago AL vs Houston NL, Oct 25, 2005, 14 inn]
**Most pitchers used by winning club, game**
6—Cincinnati NL vs Oakland AL, Oct 20, 1972 (won 5-4)
[9—Chicago AL vs Houston NL, Oct 25, 2005 (won 7-5), 14 inn]
**Most pitchers used by losing club, game**
8—Cincinnati NL vs New York AL, Oct 9, 1961 (lost 13-5)
St. Louis NL vs Boston AL, Oct 11, 1967 (lost 8-4)
[8—Cincinnati NL vs Boston AL, Oct 21, 1975 (lost 7-6), 12 inn
Houston NL vs Chicago AL, Oct 25, 2005 (lost 7-5), 14 inn]
**Most pitchers used by both clubs, game**
11—St. Louis NL 8, Boston AL 3, Oct 11, 1967
San Francisco NL 6, Oakland AL 5, Oct 28, 1989
St. Louis NL 6, Boston AL 5, Oct 23, 2004
[17—Chicago AL 9, Houston NL 8, Oct 25, 2005, 14 inn]
**Most pitchers, inning**
5—Baltimore AL vs Pittsburgh NL, Oct 17, 1979, 9th
St. Louis NL vs Kansas City AL, Oct 27, 1985, 5th

## SERIES

**Most series played**
39—New York AL, 1921-1923, 1926-1928, 1932, 1936-1939, 1941-1943, 1947, 1949, 1953, 1955-1958, 1960-1964, 1976-1978, 1981, 1996, 1998-2001, 2003 (won 26, lost 13)
18—Brooklyn/Los Angeles NL, 1916, 1920, 1941, 1947, 1949, 1952, 1953, 1955, 1956, 1959, 1963, 1965, 1966, 1974, 1977, 1978, 1981, 1988 (won 6, lost 12)

**For a complete list of series won and lost by teams, see page 396.**

**Most consecutive series played between same clubs**
3—New York NL vs New York AL, 1921-1923

# INDIVIDUAL BATTING

## GAMES

**Most games, career**
75—Yogi Berra, New York AL, 1947, 1949-1953, 1955-1958, 1960-1963 (14 series, 65 consec games)

**Most games with one club, career**
75—Yogi Berra, New York AL, 1947, 1949-1953, 1955-1958, 1960-1963 (14 series, 65 consec games)

**Most consecutive games played, consecutive years**
30—Bobby Richardson, New York AL, Oct 5, 1960-Oct 15, 1964

**Most games by pinch-hitter, career**
12—Luis Polonia, Oakland AL, 1988 (2); Atlanta NL, 1995 (2), 1996 (6); New York AL, 2000 (2)

**Most games by pinch-hitter, series**
6—Luis Polonia, Atlanta NL, 1996

**Most games by pinch-runner, career**
9—Allan Lewis, Oakland AL, 1972, 1973; 2 series (scored 3 R)

**Most games by pinch-runner, series**
6—Allan Lewis, Oakland AL, 1972 (scored 2 R)

## BATTING AVERAGE

**Highest batting average, career (50 or more at-bats)**
.418—Pepper Martin, St. Louis NL, 1928, 1931, 1934; 3 series, 15 G, 55 AB, 23 H
Paul Molitor, Milwaukee AL, 1982; Toronto AL, 1993; 2 series, 13 G, 55 AB, 23 H

**For a yearly list of batting leaders and a complete list of .500 hitters, see page 398.**

**Highest batting average, series (10 or more at-bats)**
4-game series—.750—Billy Hatcher, Cincinnati NL, 1990
5-game series—.500—Larry McLean, New York NL, 1913
Joe Gordon, New York AL, 1941
6-game series—.500—Dave Robertson, New York NL, 1917
Billy Martin, New York AL, 1953
Paul Molitor, Toronto AL, 1993
7-game series—.583—Danny Bautista, Arizona NL, 2001 (played 5 G)
8-game series—.400—Buck Herzog, New York NL, 1912

**Most series leading club in batting average**
3—Home Run Baker, Philadelphia AL, 1911, 1913, 1914
Pee Wee Reese, Brooklyn NL, 1947, 1949, 1952 (tied)
Duke Snider, Brooklyn NL, 1952 (tied), 1955, 1956 (tied).
Gil Hodges, Brooklyn NL, Los Angeles NL, 1953, 1956 (tied), 1959
Steve Garvey, Los Angeles NL, 1974, 1977, 1981

**Most series batting .300 or over**
6—Babe Ruth, New York AL, 1921, 1923, 1926, 1927, 1928, 1932

## ON-BASE PERCENTAGE

(official statistic since 1984; calculated from official statistics, 1931-1983, except for 1939 for which there is no official tabulation of sacrifice flies)

**Highest percentage, career (50 or more plate appearances)**
.475—Paul Molitor, Milwaukee AL, 1982; Toronto AL, 1993; 2 series, 13 G, 55 AB, 23 H, 5 BB, 1 HP

**Highest on-base percentage, series**
4-game series—.800—Billy Hatcher, Cincinnati NL, 1990
5-game series—.667—Joe Gordon, New York AL, 1941
6-game series—.609—George McQuinn, St. Louis AL, 1944
7-game series—.700—Barry Bonds, San Francisco NL, 2002

## SLUGGING AVERAGE

**Highest average, career (50 or more PA)**
.755—Reggie Jackson, Oakland AL, 1973, 1974; New York AL, 1977, 1978, 1981; 5 series, 30 G, 98 AB, 35 H, 7 doubles, 1 triple, 10 HR, 74 TB

**Highest average, series**
4-game series—1.727—Lou Gehrig, New York AL, 1928
5-game series—1.071—Donn Clendenon, New York NL, 1969
6-game series—1.250—Reggie Jackson, New York AL, 1977
7-game series—1.294—Barry Bonds, San Francisco NL, 2002
8-game series—.600—Buck Herzog, New York NL, 1912

## PLATE APPEARANCES AND AT-BATS

**Most plate appearances, career**
295—Yogi Berra, New York AL, 1947, 1949-1953, 1955-1958, 1960-1963; 14 series, 75 G

**Most plate appearances by pinch-hitter, career**
12—Luis Polonia, Oakland AL (2), 1988; Atlanta NL (8), 1995, 1996; New York AL (2), 2000

**Most plate appearances, series**
4-game series—22—Scott Podsednik, Chicago AL, 2005
5-game series—25—Derek Jeter, New York AL, 2000
6-game series—30—Willie Wilson, Kansas City AL, 1980
Mariano Duncan, Philadelphia NL, 1993
Lenny Dykstra, Philadelphia NL, 1993
John Kruk, Philadelphia NL, 1993

7-game series—36—Wayne Garrett, New York NL, 1973
Devon White, Florida NL, 1997
8-game series—37—many players; last—George J. Burns, New York NL, 1921

**Most plate appearances, game**
6—many players; last—Johnny Damon, Boston AL, Oct 23, 2004
[8—Scott Podsednik, Chicago AL, Oct 25, 2005, 14 inn]

**Most plate appearances with no at-bats, game**
5—Fred Clarke, Pittsburgh NL, Oct 16, 1909 (4 BB, 1 SH)

**Most plate appearances, inning**
2—many players; last—Joe Crede, Chicago AL, Oct 25, 2005, 5th; Juan Uribe, Chicago AL, Oct 25, 2005, 5th

**Most times two plate appearances in an inning, career**
3—Joe DiMaggio, New York AL, Oct 6, 1936, 9th; Oct 6, 1937, 6th; Sept 30, 1947, 5th

**Most times two plate appearances in an inning, series**
2—Stan Musial, St. Louis NL, Sept 30, 9th; Oct 4, 1942, 4th

**Most at-bats, career**
259—Yogi Berra, New York AL, 1947, 1949-1953, 1955-1958, 1960-1963; 14 series, 75 G

**Most at-bats by pinch-hitter, career**
11—Luis Polonia, Oakland AL (2), 1988; Atlanta NL (7), 1995, 1996; New York AL (2), 2000

**Most at-bats, series**
4-game series—21—Johnny Damon, Boston AL, 2004
Scott Podsednik, Chicago AL, 2005
5-game series—23—Hal Janvrin, Boston AL, 1916
Joe Moore, New York NL, 1937
Bobby Richardson, New York AL, 1961
6-game series—29—Mariano Duncan, Philadelphia NL, 1993
7-game series—33—Bucky Harris, Washington AL, 1924
Sam Rice, Washington AL, 1925
Omar Moreno, Pittsburgh NL, 1979
Devon White, Florida NL, 1997
8-game series—36—Jimmy Collins, Boston AL, 1903

**Most at-bats by pinch-hitter, series**
5—Frank Secory, Chicago NL, 1945 (7-game series)
Cookie Lavagetto, Brooklyn NL, 1947 (7-game series)
Gonzalo Marquez, Oakland AL, 1972 (7-game series)
Angel Mangual, Oakland AL, 1973 (7-game series)
Luis Polonia, Atlanta NL, 1996 (6-game series)

**Most consecutive at-bats without a hit, career**
31—Marv Owen, Detroit AL, 1934 (last 12), 1935 (first 19)

**Most at-bats by player without a hit, career**
22—George Earnshaw, Philadelphia AL, 1929 (5), 1930 (9), 1931 (8)

**Most at-bats without a hit, series**
22—Dal Maxvill, St. Louis NL, 1968 (7-game series)

**Most at-bats, game**
6—many players; last—Johnny Damon, Boston AL, Oct 23, 2004
[8—Scott Podsednik, Chicago AL, Oct 25, 2005, 14 inn]

**Most at-bats by player without a hit, game**
5—many players; last—Orlando Cabrera, Boston AL, Oct 27, 2004
[6—many players; last—Brad Ausmus, Houston NL, Oct 25, 2005, 14 inn; Willie Taveras, Houston NL, Oct 25, 2005, 14 inn]

**Most at-bats, inning**
2—many players; last—Juan Uribe, Chicago AL, Oct 25, 2005, 5th

## RUNS

**Most runs, career**
42—Mickey Mantle, New York AL, 1951-1953, 1955-1958, 1960-1964; 12 series, 65 G

**Most runs, series**
4-game series—9—Babe Ruth, New York AL, 1928
Lou Gehrig, New York AL, 1932
5-game series—6—Home Run Baker, Philadelphia AL, 1910
Dan Murphy, Philadelphia AL, 1910
Harry Hooper, Boston AL, 1916
Al Simmons, Philadelphia AL, 1929
Lee May, Cincinnati NL, 1970
Boog Powell, Baltimore AL, 1970
Lou Whitaker, Detroit AL, 1984
Derek Jeter, New York AL, 2000
6-game series—10—Reggie Jackson, New York AL, 1977
Paul Molitor, Toronto AL, 1993
7-game series—8—Tommy Leach, Pittsburgh NL, 1909
Pepper Martin, St. Louis NL, 1934
Billy Johnson, New York AL, 1947
Mickey Mantle, New York AL, 1960
Bobby Richardson, New York AL, 1960
Mickey Mantle, New York AL, 1964
Lou Brock, St. Louis NL, 1967
Jim Thome, Cleveland AL, 1997
Matt Williams, Cleveland AL, 1997
Barry Bonds, San Francisco NL, 2002
8-game series—8—Fred Parent, Boston AL, 1903

**Most series scoring one or more runs**
12—Yogi Berra, New York AL, 1947, 1949-1953, 1955-1958, 1960, 1961

**Most at-bats without scoring a run, series**
33—Devon White, Florida NL, 1997 (7-game series)

**Most runs, game**
4—Babe Ruth, New York AL, Oct 6, 1926
Earle Combs, New York AL, Oct 2, 1932
Frank Crosetti, New York AL, Oct 2, 1936
Enos Slaughter, St. Louis NL, Oct 10, 1946
Reggie Jackson, New York AL, Oct 18, 1977
Kirby Puckett, Minnesota AL, Oct 24, 1987
Carney Lansford, Oakland AL, Oct 27, 1989
Lenny Dykstra, Philadelphia NL, Oct 20, 1993
Jeff Kent, San Francisco NL, Oct 24, 2002

**Most consecutive games scoring one or more runs, career**
9—Babe Ruth, New York AL, 1927 (last 2), 1928 (4), 1932 (first 3)

**Most runs, inning**
2—Frankie Frisch, New York NL, Oct 7, 1921, 7th
Al Simmons, Philadelphia AL, Oct 12, 1929, 7th
Jimmie Foxx, Philadelphia AL, Oct 12, 1929, 7th
Dick McAuliffe, Detroit AL, Oct 9, 1968, 3rd
Mickey Stanley, Detroit AL, Oct 9, 1968, 3rd
Al Kaline, Detroit AL, Oct 9, 1968, 3rd
Greg Colbrunn, Arizona NL, Nov 3, 2001, 3rd

## HITS

### CAREER AND SERIES

**Most hits, career**
71—Yogi Berra, New York AL, 1947, 1949-1953, 1955-1958, 1960-1963; 14 series, 75 G

**Most hits by pinch-hitter, career**
3—Ken O'Dea, Chicago NL, 1935 (1), 1938 (0); St. Louis NL, 1942 (1), 1943 (0), 1944 (1), 5 series, 8 G
Bobby Brown, New York AL, 1947 (3), 1949 (0), 1950 (0), 1951 (0), 4 series, 7 G
Johnny Mize, New York AL, 1949 (2), 1950 (0), 1951 (0), 1952 (1), 1953 (0), 5 series, 8 G
Dusty Rhodes, New York NL, 1954 (3), 1 series, 3 G
Carl Furillo, Brooklyn NL, 1947 (2), 1949 (0); Los Angeles NL, 1959 (1), 3 series, 7 G
Bob Cerv, New York AL, 1955 (1), 1956 (1), 1960 (1), 3 series, 3 G
John Blanchard, New York AL, 1960 (1), 1961 (1), 1962 (0), 1964 (1), 4 series, 10 G
Carl Warwick, St. Louis NL, 1964 (3), 1 series, 5 G
Gonzalo Marquez, Oakland AL, 1972 (3), 1 series, 5 G
Ken Boswell, New York NL, 1973 (3), 1 series, 3 G

**Most hits, series**
4-game series—10—Babe Ruth, New York AL, 1928
5-game series— 9—Home Run Baker, Philadelphia AL, 1910
Eddie Collins, Philadelphia AL, 1910
Home Run Baker, Philadelphia AL, 1913
Heinie Groh, New York NL, 1922
Joe Moore, New York NL, 1937
Bobby Richardson, New York AL, 1961
Paul Blair, Baltimore AL, 1970
Brooks Robinson, Baltimore AL, 1970
Alan Trammell, Detroit AL, 1984
Derek Jeter, New York AL, 2000
Paul O'Neill, New York AL, 2000
6-game series—12—Billy Martin, New York AL, 1953
Paul Molitor, Toronto AL, 1993
Roberto Alomar, Toronto AL, 1993
Marquis Grissom, Atlanta NL, 1996
7-game series—13—Bobby Richardson, New York AL, 1964
Lou Brock, St. Louis NL, 1968
Marty Barrett, Boston AL, 1986
8-game series—12—Buck Herzog, New York NL, 1912
Joe Jackson, Chicago AL, 1919

**Most hits by pinch-hitter, series**
3—Bobby Brown, New York AL, 1947 (consec; 4 G; 1 single, 2 doubles, 1 BB, 3 RBI)
Dusty Rhodes, New York NL, 1954 (consec; 3 G; 1 HR, 2 singles, 6 RBI)
Carl Warwick, St. Louis NL, 1964 (consec; 5 G; 3 singles, 1 BB, 1 RBI)
Gonzalo Marquez, Oakland AL, 1972 (consec; 3 G; 3 singles, 1 RBI)
Ken Boswell, New York NL, 1973 (consec; 3 G; 3 singles)

**Most series with one or more hits**
12—Yogi Berra, New York AL, 1947, 1949-1953, 1955-1958, 1960, 1961
Mickey Mantle, New York AL, 1951-1953, 1955-1958, 1960-1964

**Most consecutive hits, career**
7—Thurman Munson, New York AL, Oct 19 (2), 21 (4), 1976, Oct 11 (1), 1977
Billy Hatcher, Cincinnati NL, Oct 16 (3), 17 (4), 1990

**Most consecutive hits, series**
7—Billy Hatcher, Cincinnati NL, Oct 16 (3), 17 (4), 1990

**Most games with four or more hits, series**
2—Robin Yount, Milwaukee AL, Oct 12 (4), 16 (4), 1982

## GAME AND INNING

**Most hits, game**

5—Paul Molitor, Milwaukee AL, Oct 12, 1982

**Most times reached first base safely, game (batting 1.000)**

5—Babe Ruth, New York AL, Oct 6, 1926 (3 HR, 2 BB)
Babe Ruth, New York AL, Oct 10, 1926 (1 HR, 4 BB)
Lou Brock, St. Louis NL, Oct 4, 1967 (4 singles, 1 BB)
Brooks Robinson, Baltimore AL, Oct 11, 1971 (3 singles, 2 BB)
Rusty Staub, New York NL, Oct 17, 1973 (3 singles, 1 HR, 1 BB)
Kiko Garcia, Baltimore AL, Oct 12, 1979 (2 singles, 1 double, 1 triple, 1 BB)
Reggie Jackson, New York AL, Oct 24, 1981 (2 singles, 1 HR, 2 BB)
George Brett, Kansas City AL, Oct 22, 1985 (2 singles, 3 BB)
Kirby Puckett, Minnesota AL, Oct 24, 1987 (4 singles, 1 BB)
Billy Hatcher, Cincinnati NL, Oct 17, 1990 (1 single, 2 doubles, 1 triple, 1 BB)
Matt Williams, Cleveland AL, Oct 22, 1997 (2 singles, 1 HR, 2 BB)
Tim Salmon, Anaheim AL, Oct 20, 2002 (2 singles, 2 HR, 1 BB)
Bengie Molina, Anaheim AL, Oct 22, 2002 (2 singles, 3 BB)

**Most hits accounting for all club's hits, game**

3—Irish Meusel, New York NL, Oct 14, 1923 (1 single, 1 double, 1 triple)
Dave Parker, Oakland AL, Oct 16, 1988 (3 singles)

**Most at-bats with no hits, game**

5—many players; last—Orlando Cabrera, Boston AL, Oct 27, 2004
[6—Travis Jackson, New York NL, Oct 10, 1924, 12 inn
Hughie Critz, New York NL, Oct 6, 1933, 11 inn
Felix Millan, New York NL, Oct 14, 1973, 12 inn
Mickey Rivers, New York AL, Oct 11, 1977, 12 inn
Ron Gant, Atlanta NL, Oct 22, 1991, 12 inn
Devon White, Florida NL, Oct 26, 1997, 11 inn
Craig Counsell, Arizona NL, Nov 1, 2001, 12 inn
Brad Ausmus, Houston NL, Oct 25, 2005, 14 inn
Willy Taveras, Houston NL, Oct 25, 2005, 14 inn]

**Most consecutive games with one or more hits, career**

17—Hank Bauer, New York AL, 1956 (7), 1957 (7), 1958 (first 3)

**Most hits in two consecutive games, series**

7—Frank Isbell, Chicago AL, Oct 13 (4), 14 (3), 1906
Fred Lindstrom, New York NL, Oct 7 (3), 8 (4), 1924
Monte Irvin, New York NL, Oct 4 (4), 5 (3), 1951
Thurman Munson, New York AL, Oct 19 (3), 21 (4), 1976
Paul Molitor, Milwaukee AL, Oct 12 (5), 13 (2), 1982
Billy Hatcher, Cincinnati NL, Oct 16 (3), 17 (4), 1990

**Most hits, inning (18 times)**

2—Ross Youngs, New York NL, Oct 7, 1921, 7th
Al Simmons, Philadelphia AL, Oct 12, 1929, 7th
Jimmie Foxx, Philadelphia AL, Oct 12, 1929, 7th
Jimmie Dykes, Philadelphia AL, Oct 12, 1929, 7th
Joe Moore, New York NL, Oct 4, 1933, 6th
Dizzy Dean, St. Louis NL, Oct 9, 1934, 3rd
Joe DiMaggio, New York AL, Oct 6, 1936, 9th
Hank Leiber, New York NL, Oct 9, 1937, 2nd
Stan Musial, St. Louis NL, Oct 4, 1942, 4th
Elston Howard, New York AL, Oct 6, 1960, 6th
Bobby Richardson, New York AL, Oct 6, 1960, 6th
Bob Cerv, New York AL, Oct 8, 1960, 1st
Frank Quilici, Minnesota AL, Oct 6, 1965, 3rd
Al Kaline, Detroit AL, Oct 9, 1968, 3rd
Norm Cash, Detroit AL, Oct 9, 1968, 3rd
Merv Rettenmund, Baltimore AL, Oct 11, 1971, 5th
Gary Gaetti, Minnesota AL, Oct 17, 1987, 4th
Matt Williams, Arizona NL, Nov 3, 2001, 3rd

## SINGLES

**Most singles, career**

49—Yogi Berra, New York AL, 1947, 1949-1953, 1955-1958, 1960-1963; 14 series, 75 G

**Most singles, series**

4-game series—9—Thurman Munson, New York AL, 1976
5-game series—8—Frank Chance, Chicago NL, 1908
Home Run Baker, Philadelphia AL, 1913
Heinie Groh, New York NL, 1922
Joe Moore, New York NL, 1937
Bobby Richardson, New York AL, 1961
Paul Blair, Baltimore AL, 1970
Steve Garvey, Los Angeles NL, 1974.
6-game series—10—Red Rolfe, New York AL, 1936
Monte Irvin, New York NL, 1951
7-game series—12—Sam Rice, Washington AL, 1925
8-game series—9—Jimmy Sebring, Pittsburgh NL, 1903
Chief Meyers, New York NL, 1912

**Most singles, game**

5—Paul Molitor, Milwaukee AL, Oct 12, 1982

**Most singles, inning**

2—Jimmie Foxx, Philadelphia AL, Oct 12, 1929, 7th
Joe Moore, New York NL, Oct 4, 1933, 6th
Joe DiMaggio, New York AL, Oct 6, 1936, 9th
Hank Leiber, New York NL, Oct 9, 1937, 2nd
Bob Cerv, New York AL, Oct 8, 1960, 1st
Al Kaline, Detroit AL, Oct 9, 1968, 3rd
Norm Cash, Detroit AL, Oct 9, 1968, 3rd
Merv Rettenmund, Baltimore AL, Oct 11, 1971, 5th

## DOUBLES

**Most doubles, career**

10—Frank Frisch, New York NL (5), 1921-1924; St. Louis NL (5), 1928, 1930, 1931, 1934; 8 series, 50 G
Yogi Berra, New York AL, 1947, 1949-1953, 1955-1958, 1960-1963; 14 series, 75 G

**Most doubles, series**

4-game series—4—Billy Hatcher, Cincinnati, NL, 1990
Bret Boone, Atlanta NL, 1999
5-game series—4—Eddie Collins, Philadelphia AL, 1910
Rick Dempsey, Baltimore AL, 1983
6-game series—5—Chick Hafey, St. Louis NL, 1930
7-game series—6—Pete Fox, Detroit AL, 1934
8-game series—4—Red Murray, New York NL, 1912
Buck Herzog, New York NL, 1912
Buck Weaver, Chicago AL, 1919
George J. Burns, New York NL, 1921

**Most doubles, game**

4—Frank Isbell, Chicago AL, Oct 13, 1906

**Most doubles batting in three runs, game**

1—Frank Frisch, St. Louis NL, Oct 9, 1934, 3rd
Paul Richards, Detroit AL, Oct 10, 1945, 1st
Lou Brock, St. Louis NL, Oct 6, 1968, 8th
Terry Pendleton, St. Louis NL, Oct 20, 1985, 9th
Garret Anderson, Anaheim AL, Oct 27, 2002, 3rd

**Most doubles, inning**

2—Matt Williams, Arizona NL, Nov 3, 2001, 3rd

## TRIPLES

**Most triples, career**

4—Tommy Leach, Pittsburgh NL, 1903, 1909; 2 series, 15 G
Tris Speaker, Boston AL (3), 1912, 1915; Cleveland AL (1), 1920; 3 series, 20 G
Billy Johnson, New York AL, 1943, 1947, 1949, 1950; 4 series, 18 G

**Most games without a triple, career**

75—Yogi Berra, New York AL; 14 series, 259 AB

**Most triples, series**

4-game series—2—Lou Gehrig, New York AL, 1927
Tommy Davis, Los Angeles NL, 1963
Rickey Henderson, Oakland AL, 1989
Scott Podsednik, Chicago AL, 2005
5-game series—2—Eddie Collins, Philadelphia AL, 1913
Bobby Brown, New York AL, 1949
Paul O'Neill, New York AL, 2000
6-game series—2—George Rohe, Chicago AL, 1906
Bob Meusel, New York AL, 1923
Billy Martin, New York AL, 1953
Paul Molitor, Toronto AL, 1993
Devon White, Toronto AL, 1993
7-game series—3—Billy Johnson, New York AL, 1947
Mark Lemke, Atlanta NL, 1991
8-game series—4—Tommy Leach, Pittsburgh NL, 1903

**Most triples, game**

2—Tommy Leach, Pittsburgh NL, Oct 1, 1903
Patsy Dougherty, Boston AL, Oct 7, 1903
Dutch Ruether, Cincinnati NL, Oct 1, 1919
Bobby Richardson, New York AL, Oct 12, 1960
Tommy Davis, Los Angeles NL, Oct 3, 1963
Mark Lemke, Atlanta NL, Oct 24, 1991

**Most triples with bases filled, game**

1—George Rohe, Chicago AL, Oct 11, 1906, 6th
Ross Youngs, New York NL, Oct 7, 1921, 7th
Billy Johnson, New York AL, Oct 7, 1943, 8th
Bobby Brown, New York AL, Oct 8, 1949, 5th
Hank Bauer, New York AL, Oct 10, 1951, 6th
Billy Martin, New York AL, Sept 30, 1953, 1st
Kiko Garcia, Baltimore AL, Oct 12, 1979, 4th
Milt Thompson, Philadelphia NL, Oct 20, 1993, 1st

**Most triples, inning**

1—many players

## HOME RUNS

### CAREER AND SERIES

**Most home runs, career**

18—Mickey Mantle, New York AL, 1951-1953, 1955-1958, 1960-1964; 12 series, 65 G

For a list of all home runs each series and a complete list of players with five or more career home runs, see page 399.

**Most home runs by pitcher, career**
2—Bob Gibson, St. Louis NL, 1964 (0), 1967 (1), 1968 (1); 3 series, 9 G
Dave McNally, Baltimore AL, 1966 (0), 1969 (1), 1970 (1), 1971 (0); 4 series, 9 G

**Most games without a home run, career**
50—Frank Frisch, New York NL, St. Louis NL; 8 series, 197 AB

**Hitting home runs for teams in both leagues**
Enos Slaughter, NL (2), AL (1)
Bill Skowron, AL (7), NL (1)
Frank Robinson, NL (1), AL (7)
Roger Maris, AL (5), NL (1)
Reggie Smith, AL (2), NL (4)
Kirk Gibson, AL (2), NL (1)
Matt Williams, NL (2), AL (1)

**Most home runs, series**
4-game series—4—Lou Gehrig, New York AL, 1928
5-game series—3—Donn Clendenon, New York NL, 1969
6-game series—5—Reggie Jackson, New York, 1977
7-game series—4—Babe Ruth, New York AL, 1926
Duke Snider, Brooklyn NL, 1952
Duke Snider, Brooklyn NL, 1955
Hank Bauer, New York AL, 1958
Gene Tenace, Oakland AL, 1972
Barry Bonds, San Francisco NL, 2002
8-game series—2—Patsy Dougherty, Boston AL, 1903

**Most home runs by pinch-hitter, series**
2—Chuck Essegian, Los Angeles NL, 4 G, 1959
Bernie Carbo, Boston AL, 2 G, 1975

**Most home runs by rookie, series**
3—Charlie Keller, New York AL, 1939

**Most series with one or more home runs**
9—Yogi Berra, New York AL, 1947 (1), 1950 (1), 1952 (2), 1953 (1), 1955 (1), 1956 (3), 1957 (1), 1960 (1), 1961 (1)
Mickey Mantle, New York AL, 1952 (2), 1953 (2), 1955 (1), 1956 (3), 1957 (1), 1958 (2), 1960 (3), 1963 (1), 1964 (3)

**Most series with two or more home runs**
6—Mickey Mantle, New York AL, 1952 (2), 1953 (2), 1956 (3), 1958 (2), 1960 (3), 1964 (3)

**Most series with three or more home runs**
3—Babe Ruth, New York AL, 1923 (3), 1926 (4), 1928 (3)
Mickey Mantle, New York AL, 1956 (3), 1960 (3), 1964 (3)

**Most series with four or more home runs**
2—Duke Snider, Brooklyn NL, 1952 (4), 1955 (4)

**Most series with two or more home runs in a game**
4—Babe Ruth, New York AL, 1923, 1926, 1928, 1932 (2 HR in 1 game twice, 3 HR In 1 game twice)

**Most home runs, two consecutive series (two consecutive years)**
7—Reggie Jackson, New York AL, 1977 (5), 1978 (2)

**Most home runs, three consecutive series (three consecutive years)**
9—Babe Ruth, New York AL, 1926 (4), 1927 (2), 1928 (3)

## GAME AND INNING

**Most home runs, game (3 HR, 3 times; 2 HR, 39 times; *consecutive)**
3—Babe Ruth, New York AL, Oct 6, 1926 (2 consec)
Babe Ruth, New York AL, Oct 9, 1928, (2 consec)
Reggie Jackson, New York AL, Oct 18, 1977 (each on 1st pitch)*
2—Patsy Dougherty, Boston AL, Oct 2, 1903
Harry Hooper, Boston AL, Oct 13, 1915
Benny Kauff, New York NL, Oct 11, 1917
Babe Ruth, New York AL, Oct 11, 1923*
Lou Gehrig, New York AL, Oct 7, 1928*
Lou Gehrig, New York AL, Oct 1, 1932*
Babe Ruth, New York AL, Oct 1, 1932
Tony Lazzeri, New York AL, Oct 2, 1932
Charlie Keller, New York AL, Oct 7, 1939
Bob Elliott, Boston NL, Oct 10, 1948*
Duke Snider, Brooklyn NL, Oct 6, 1952*
Joe Collins, New York AL, Sept 28, 1955*
Duke Snider, Brooklyn NL, Oct 2, 1955*
Yogi Berra, New York AL, Oct 10, 1956*
Tony Kubek, New York AL, Oct 5, 1957
Mickey Mantle, New York AL, Oct 2, 1958
Ted Kluszewski, Chicago AL, Oct 1, 1959*
Charlie Neal, Los Angeles NL, Oct 2, 1959*
Mickey Mantle, New York AL, Oct 6, 1960
Carl Yastrzemski, Boston AL, Oct 5, 1967
Rico Petrocelli, Boston AL, Oct 11, 1967*
Gene Tenace, Oakland AL, Oct 14, 1972*
Tony Perez, Cincinnati NL, Oct 16, 1975*
Johnny Bench, Cincinnati NL, Oct 21, 1976
Dave Lopes, Los Angeles NL, Oct 10, 1978*
Willie Aikens, Kansas City AL, Oct 14, 1980
Willie Aikens, Kansas City AL, Oct 18, 1980
Willie McGee, St. Louis NL, Oct 15, 1982*
Eddie Murray, Baltimore AL, Oct 16, 1983*
Alan Trammell, Detroit AL, Oct 13, 1984*
Kirk Gibson, Detroit AL, Oct 14, 1984
Gary Carter, New York NL, Oct 22, 1986
Dave Henderson, Oakland AL, Oct 27, 1989*
Chris Sabo, Cincinnati NL, Oct 19, 1990*
Andruw Jones, Atlanta NL, Oct 20, 1996*
Scott Brosius, New York AL, Oct 20, 1998*
Chad Curtis, New York AL, Oct 26, 1999 (10 inn)
Troy Glaus, Anaheim AL, Oct 19, 2002
Jeff Kent, San Francisco NL, Oct 24, 2002*

**Home runs by pitcher, game (14)**
Jim Bagby Sr., Cleveland AL, Oct 10, 1920 (2 on base)
Rosy Ryan, New York NL, Oct 6, 1924 (none on base)
Jack Bentley, New York NL, Oct 8, 1924 (1 on base)
Jesse Haines, St. Louis NL, Oct 5, 1926 (1 on base)
Bucky Walters, Cincinnati NL, Oct 7, 1940 (none on base)
Lew Burdette, Milwaukee NL, Oct 2, 1958 (2 on base)
Mudcat Grant, Minnesota AL, Oct 13, 1965 (2 on base)
Jose R. Santiago, Boston AL, Oct 4, 1967 (none on base)
Bob Gibson, St. Louis NL, Oct 12, 1967 (none on base)
Mickey Lolich, Detroit AL, Oct 3, 1968 (none on base)
Bob Gibson, St. Louis NL, Oct 6, 1968 (none on base)
Dave McNally, Baltimore AL, Oct 16, 1969 (1 on base)
Dave McNally, Baltimore AL, Oct 13, 1970 (3 on base)
Ken Holtzman, Oakland AL, Oct 16, 1974 (none on base)

**Home runs by pinch-hitter, game (17)**
Yogi Berra, New York AL, Oct 2, 1947, 7th (none on base)
Johnny Mize, New York AL, Oct 3, 1952, 9th (none on base)
George Shuba, Brooklyn NL, Sept 30, 1953, 6th (1 on base)
Dusty Rhodes, New York NL, Sept 29, 1954, 10th (2 on base)
Hank Majeski, Cleveland AL, Oct 2, 1954, 5th (2 on base)
Bob Cerv, New York AL, Oct 2, 1955, 7th (none on base)
Chuck Essegian, Los Angeles NL, Oct 2, 1959, 7th (none on base)
Chuck Essegian, Los Angeles NL, Oct 8, 1959, 9th (none on base)
Elston Howard, New York AL, Oct 5, 1960, 9th (1 on base)
John Blanchard, New York AL, Oct 7, 1961, 8th (none on base)
Bernie Carbo, Boston AL, Oct 14, 1975, 7th (none on base)
Bernie Carbo, Boston AL, Oct 21, 1975, 8th (2 on base)
Jay Johnstone, Los Angeles NL, Oct 24, 1981, 6th (1 on base)
Kirk Gibson, Los Angeles NL, Oct 15, 1988, 9th (1 on base)
Bill Bathe, San Francisco NL, Oct 27, 1989, 9th (2 on base)
Chili Davis, Minnesota AL, Oct 22, 1991, 8th (1 on base)
Ed Sprague Jr., Toronto AL, Oct 18, 1992, 9th (1 on base)
Jim Leyritz, New York AL, Oct 27, 1999, 8th (none on base)

**Most home runs by rookie, game**
2—Charlie Keller, New York AL, Oct 7, 1939
Tony Kubek, New York AL, Oct 5, 1957
Willie McGee, St. Louis NL, Oct 15, 1982
Andruw Jones, Atlanta NL, Oct 20, 1996

**Hitting home run in first World Series at-bat (27 times; *not first plate appearance)**
Joe Harris, Washington AL, Oct 7, 1925, 2nd
George Watkins, St. Louis NL, Oct 2, 1930, 2nd
Mel Ott, New York NL, Oct 3, 1933, 1st
George Selkirk, New York AL, Sept 30, 1936, 3rd
Dusty Rhodes, New York NL, Sept 29, 1954, 10th
Elston Howard, New York AL, Sept 28, 1955, 2nd
Roger Maris, New York AL, Oct 5, 1960, 1st
Don Mincher, Minnesota AL, Oct 6, 1965, 2nd
Brooks Robinson, Baltimore AL, Oct 5, 1966, 1st
Jose R. Santiago, Boston AL, Oct 4, 1967, 3rd
Mickey Lolich, Detroit AL, Oct 3, 1968, 3rd
Don Buford, Baltimore AL, Oct 11, 1969, 1st
Gene Tenace, Oakland AL, Oct 14, 1972, 2nd
Jim Mason, New York AL Oct 19, 1976, 7th
Doug DeCinces, Baltimore AL, Oct 10, 1979, 1st
Amos Otis, Kansas City AL, Oct 14, 1980, 2nd
Bob Watson, New York AL, Oct 20, 1981, 1st
Jim Dwyer, Baltimore AL, Oct 11, 1983, 1st
Mickey Hatcher, Los Angeles NL, Oct 15, 1988, 1st
Jose Canseco, Oakland AL, Oct 15, 1988, 2nd*
Bill Bathe, San Francisco NL, Oct 27, 1989, 9th
Eric Davis, Cincinnati NL, Oct 16, 1990, 1st
Ed Sprague Jr., Toronto AL, Oct 18, 1992, 9th
Fred McGriff, Atlanta NL, Oct 21, 1995, 2nd
Andruw Jones, Atlanta NL, Oct 20, 1996, 2nd
Barry Bonds, San Francisco NL, Oct 19, 2002, 2nd
Troy Glaus, Anaheim AL, Oct 19, 2002, 2nd
Mike Lamb, Houston NL, Oct 22, 2005, 2nd
Geoff Blum, Chicago AL, Oct 25, 2005, 14th

**Hitting home runs in first two World Series at-bats (2)**
Gene Tenace, Oakland AL, Oct 14, 1972, 2nd and 5th
Andruw Jones, Atlanta NL, Oct 20, 1996, 2nd and 3rd

**Homering as leadoff batter at start of game (16)**
Patsy Dougherty, Boston AL, Oct 2, 1903
Davy Jones, Detroit AL, Oct 13, 1909

Phil Rizzuto, New York AL, Oct 5, 1942
Dale Mitchell, Cleveland AL, Oct 10, 1948
Gene Woodling, New York AL, Oct 4, 1953
Al Smith, Cleveland AL, Sept 30, 1954
Billy Bruton, Milwaukee NL, Oct 2, 1958
Lou Brock, St. Louis NL, Oct 6, 1968
Don Buford, Baltimore AL, Oct 11, 1969
Tommie Agee, New York NL, Oct 14, 1969
Pete Rose, Cincinnati NL, Oct 20, 1972
Wayne Garrett, New York NL, Oct 16, 1973
Dave Lopes, Los Angeles NL, Oct 17, 1978
Lenny Dykstra, New York NL, Oct 21, 1986
Rickey Henderson, Oakland AL, Oct 28, 1989
Derek Jeter, New York AL, Oct 25, 2000

**Hitting a home run to win a 1-0 game (5)**
Casey Stengel, New York NL, Oct 12, 1923, 7th
Tommy Henrich, New York AL, Oct 5, 1949, 9th
Paul Blair, Baltimore AL, Oct 8, 1966, 5th
Frank Robinson, Baltimore AL, Oct 9, 1966, 4th
David Justice, Atlanta NL, Oct 28, 1995, 6th

**Hitting a home run in extra innings (15)**
Hank Gowdy, Boston NL, Oct 12, 1914, 10th
Mel Ott, New York NL, Oct 7, 1933, 10th
Rudy York, Boston AL, Oct 6, 1946, 10th
Joe DiMaggio, New York AL, Oct 5, 1950, 10th
Dusty Rhodes, New York NL, Sept 29, 1954, 10th
Eddie Mathews, Milwaukee NL, Oct 6, 1957, 10th
Gil McDougald, New York AL, Oct 8, 1958, 10th
Tim McCarver, St. Louis NL, Oct 12, 1964, 10th
Carlton Fisk, Boston AL, Oct 21, 1975, 10th
Dave Henderson, Boston AL, Oct 25, 1986, 10th
Kirby Puckett, Minnesota AL, Oct 26, 1991, 11th
Chad Curtis, New York AL, Oct 26, 1999, 10th
Derek Jeter, New York AL, Oct 31, 2001, 10th
Alex Gonzalez, Florida NL, Oct 22, 2003, 12th
Geoff Blum, Chicago AL, Oct 25, 2005, 14th

**Grand slams (18)**
Elmer Smith, Cleveland AL, Oct 10, 1920, 1st
Tony Lazzeri, New York AL, Oct 2, 1936, 3rd
Gil McDougald, New York AL, Oct 9, 1951, 3rd
Mickey Mantle, New York AL, Oct 4, 1953, 3rd
Yogi Berra, New York AL, Oct 5, 1956, 2nd
Bill Skowron, New York AL, Oct 10, 1956, 7th
Bobby Richardson, New York AL, Oct 8, 1960, 1st
Chuck Hiller, San Francisco NL, Oct 8, 1962, 7th
Ken Boyer, St. Louis NL, Oct 11, 1964, 6th
Joe Pepitone, New York AL, Oct 14, 1964, 8th
Jim Northrup, Detroit AL, Oct 9, 1968, 3rd
Dave McNally, Baltimore AL, Oct 13, 1970, 6th
Dan Gladden, Minnesota AL, Oct 17, 1987, 4th
Kent Hrbek, Minnesota AL, Oct 24, 1987, 6th
Jose Canseco, Oakland AL, Oct 15, 1988, 2nd
Lonnie Smith, Atlanta NL, Oct 22, 1992, 5th
Tino Martinez, New York AL, Oct 17, 1998, 7th
Paul Konerko, Chicago AL, Oct 23, 2005, 7th

**Most home runs in two consecutive games, series (homering each game)**
4—Reggie Jackson, New York AL, Oct 16 (1), 18 (3), 1977

**Most home runs in three consecutive games, series (homering each game)**
5—Reggie Jackson, New York AL, Oct 15 (1), 16 (1), 18 (3), 1977

**Most home runs, four consecutive games (homering in each game)**
6—Reggie Jackson, New York AL, 1977 (5), last 3 G; 1978 (1), 1st G

**Most consecutive home runs in two consecutive games, series**
4—Reggie Jackson, New York AL, Oct 16 (1), 18 (3), 1977 (inc. 1 BB)

**Most home runs, inning**
1—many players

**Most home runs, two consecutive innings (10)**
2—Babe Ruth, New York AL, Oct 11, 1923, 4th and 5th
Babe Ruth, New York AL, Oct 9, 1928, 7th and 8th
Ted Kluszewski, Chicago AL, Oct 1, 1959, 3rd and 4th
Reggie Jackson, New York AL, Oct 18, 1977, 4th and 5th
Willie Aikens, Kansas City AL, Oct 18, 1980, 1st and 2nd
Dave Henderson, Oakland AL, Oct 27, 1989, 4th and 5th
Chris Sabo, Cincinnati NL, Oct 19, 1990, 2nd and 3rd
Andruw Jones, Atlanta NL, Oct 20, 1996, 2nd and 3rd
Scott Brosius, New York AL, Oct 20, 1998, 7th and 8th
Jeff Kent, San Francisco NL, Oct 24, 2002, 6th and 7th

## TOTAL BASES

**Most total bases, career**
123—Mickey Mantle, New York AL, 1951-1953, 1955-1958, 1960-1964; 12 series, 65 G

**Most total bases, series**
4-game series—22—Babe Ruth, New York AL, 1928
5-game series—19—Derek Jeter, New York AL, 2000
6-game series—25—Reggie Jackson, New York AL, 1977
7-game series—25—Willie Stargell, Pittsburgh NL, 1979
8-game series—18—Buck Herzog, New York NL, 1912
Joe Jackson, Chicago AL, 1919

**Most total bases by pinch-hitter, series**
8—Chuck Essegian, Los Angeles NL, 1959; 4 G (2 HR)
Bernie Carbo, Boston AL, 1975; 3 G (2 HR)

**Most total bases, game**
12—Babe Ruth, New York AL, Oct 6, 1926 (3 HR)
Babe Ruth, New York AL, Oct 9, 1928 (3 HR)
Reggie Jackson, New York AL, Oct 18, 1977 (3 HR)

**Most total bases, inning**
5—Ross Youngs, New York NL, Oct 7, 1921, 7th (1 double, 1 triple)
Al Simmons, Philadelphia AL, Oct 12, 1929, 7th (1 single, 1 HR)

## EXTRA-BASE HITS

**Most extra-base hits, career**
26—Mickey Mantle, New York AL, 1951-1953, 1955-1958, 1960-1964; 12 series, 65 G

**Most extra-base hits, series**
4-game series—6—Babe Ruth, New York AL, 1928
5-game series—5—Rick Dempsey, Baltimore AL, 1983
Derek Jeter, New York AL, 2000
6-game series—6—Reggie Jackson, New York AL, 1977
Paul Molitor, Toronto AL, 1993
Devon White, Toronto AL, 1993
7-game series—7—Willie Stargell, Pittsburgh NL, 1979
8-game series—5—Red Murray, New York NL, 1912
Buck Herzog, New York NL, 1912
Buck Weaver, Chicago AL, 1919
George J. Burns, New York NL, 1921

**Most extra-base hits, game**
4—Frank Isbell, Chicago AL, Oct 13, 1906 (4 doubles)

**Most extra-base hits, inning**
2—Ross Youngs, New York NL, Oct 7, 1921, 7th (1 double, 1 triple)
Matt Williams, Arizona NL, Nov 3, 2001, 3rd (2 doubles)

## RUNS BATTED IN

**Most runs batted in, career**
40—Mickey Mantle, New York AL, 1951-1953, 1955-1958, 1960-1964; 12 series, 65 G

**Most runs batted in, series**
4-game series—9—Lou Gehrig, New York AL, 1928
5-game series—9—Dan Murphy, Philadelphia AL, 1910
6-game series—10—Ted Kluszewski, Chicago AL, 1959
7-game series—12—Bobby Richardson, New York AL, 1960
8-game series—8—Tommy Leach, Pittsburgh NL, 1903
Pat Duncan, Cincinnati NL, 1919

**Most runs batted in by pinch-hitter, series**
6—Dusty Rhodes, New York NL, 1954; 3 G

**Most series with one or more runs batted in**
11—Yogi Berra, New York AL, 1947, 1949, 1950, 1952, 1953, 1955-1958, 1960, 1961

**Most at-bats without a run batted in, series**
34—Fred Clarke, Pittsburgh NL, 1903; 8 G
Buck Weaver, Chicago AL, 1919; 8 G

**Most runs batted in, game**
6—Bobby Richardson, New York AL, Oct 8, 1960

**Most consecutive games with one or more RBIs, career**
8—Lou Gehrig, New York AL, 1928 (4), 1932 (4); 17 RBI
Reggie Jackson, New York AL, 1977 (4), 1978 (4); 14 RBI

**Most runs batted in accounting for all club's runs, game**
4—Hank Bauer, New York AL, Oct 4, 1958 (won 4-0)
Ken Boyer, St. Louis NL, Oct 11, 1964 (won 4-3)
Ron Cey, Los Angeles NL, Oct 11, 1978 (won 4-3)
Alan Trammell, Detroit AL, Oct 13, 1984 (won 4-2)
Jose Canseco, Oakland AL, Oct 15, 1988 (lost 5-4)

**Most runs batted in, inning (18 times)**
4—Elmer Smith, Cleveland AL, Oct 10, 1920, 1st
Tony Lazzeri, New York AL, Oct 2, 1936, 3rd
Gil McDougald, New York AL, Oct 9, 1951, 3rd
Mickey Mantle, New York AL, Oct 4, 1953, 3rd
Yogi Berra, New York AL, Oct 5, 1956, 2nd
Bill Skowron, New York AL, Oct 10, 1956, 7th
Bobby Richardson, New York AL, Oct 8, 1960, 1st
Chuck Hiller, San Francisco NL, Oct 8, 1962, 7th
Ken Boyer, St. Louis NL, Oct 11, 1964, 6th
Joe Pepitone, New York AL, Oct 14, 1964, 8th
Jim Northrup, Detroit AL, Oct 9, 1968, 3rd
Dave McNally, Baltimore AL, Oct 13, 1970, 6th
Dan Gladden, Minnesota AL, Oct 17, 1987, 4th
Kent Hrbek, Minnesota AL, Oct 24, 1987, 6th
Jose Canseco, Oakland AL, Oct 15, 1988, 2nd
Lonnie Smith, Atlanta NL, Oct 22, 1992, 5th
Tino Martinez, New York AL, Oct 17, 1998, 7th
Paul Konerko, Chicago AL, Oct 23, 2005, 7th

## BASES ON BALLS

**Most bases on balls, career**
43—Mickey Mantle, New York AL, 1951-1953, 1956-1958, 1960-1964; 12 series, 65 G

**Most bases on balls, series**
4-game series—7—Hank Thompson, New York NL, 1954
5-game series—7—Jimmy Sheckard, Chicago NL, 1910
Mickey Cochrane, Philadelphia AL, 1929
Joe Gordon, New York AL, 1941
6-game series—9—Willie Randolph, New York AL, 1981
7-game series—13—Barry Bonds, San Francisco NL, 2002
8-game series—7—Josh Devore, New York NL, 1912
Ross Youngs, New York NL, 1921

**Most bases on balls by pinch-hitter, series**
3—Bennie Tate, Washington AL, 1924; 3 G

**Most series with one or more bases on balls, career**
13—Yogi Berra, New York AL, 1947, 1949, 1950-1953, 1955-1958, 1960-1962

**Most at-bats without a base on balls, series**
34—Buck Weaver, Chicago AL, 1919 (8-game series)

**Most consecutive bases on balls, series**
5—Lou Gehrig, New York AL, Oct 7 (2), Oct 9 (3), 1928

**Most bases on balls, game**
4—Fred Clarke, Pittsburgh NL, Oct 16, 1909
Babe Ruth, New York AL, Oct 10, 1926
Doug DeCinces, Baltimore AL, Oct 13, 1979
[4—Dick Hoblitzell, Boston AL, Oct 9, 1916, 14 inn
Ross Youngs, New York NL, Oct 10, 1924, 12 inn
Jackie Robinson, Brooklyn NL, Oct 5, 1952, 11 inn]

**Most bases on balls with bases filled, game**
2—Jim Palmer, Baltimore AL, Oct 11, 1971, 4th and 5th

**Most bases on balls, inning**
2—Lefty Gomez, New York AL, Oct 6, 1937, 6th
Dick McAuliffe, Detroit AL, Oct 9, 1968, 3rd

## STRIKEOUTS

**Most strikeouts, career**
54—Mickey Mantle, New York AL, 1951-1953, 1955-1958, 1960-1964; 12 series, 65 G

**Most strikeouts, series**
4-game series—7—Bob Meusel, New York AL, 1927
Ken Caminiti, San Diego NL, 1998
Morgan Ensberg, Houston NL, 2005
5-game series—9—Carmelo Martinez, San Diego NL, 1984
6-game series—12—Willie Wilson, Kansas City AL, 1980
7-game series—11—Eddie Mathews, Milwaukee NL, 1958
Wayne Garrett, New York NL, 1973
Luis Gonzalez, Arizona NL, 2001
Damian Miller, Arizona NL, 2001
8-game series—10—George Kelly, New York NL, 1921

**Most strikeouts by pinch-hitter, series**
3—Gabby Hartnett, Chicago NL, 1929; 3 G
Rollie Hemsley, Chicago NL, 1932; 3 G
Otto Velez, New York AL, 1976; 3 G
Luis Polonia, Atlanta NL, 1996; 6 G

**Most series with one or more strikeouts**
12—Mickey Mantle, New York AL, 1951-1953, 1955-1958, 1960, 1961, 1963, 1964

**Most at-bats without a strikeout, series**
30—Tim Foli, Pittsburgh NL, 1979 (7-game series)

**Most consecutive strikeouts, career**
8—Vida Blue, Oakland AL, Oct 14 (2), 18 (2), 1973; Oct 13 (2), 17 (2), 1974
David Justice, New York AL, Oct 27 (3), 30, (2), 31 (3), 2001

**Most consecutive strikeouts, series**
8—David Justice, New York AL, Oct 27 (3), 30, (2), 31 (3), 2001

**Most strikeouts, game**
5—George Pipgras, New York AL, Oct 1, 1932 (consec)

**Most strikeouts, inning**
2—Edgar Renteria, Florida NL, Oct 23, 1997, 6th

## SACRIFICE HITS

**Most sacrifice hits, career**
6—Eddie Collins, Philadelphia AL (5), 1910, 1911, 1913, 1914; Chicago AL (1), 1917, 1919; 6 series, 34 G
Wally Schang, Philadelphia AL (0), 1913, 1914; Boston AL (0), 1918; New York AL (6), 1921-1923; 6 series, 32 G

**Most sacrifice hits, series**
4-game series—2—Rube Oldring, Philadelphia AL, 1914
Joe Dugan, New York AL, 1927
Andy Seminick, Philadelphia NL, 1950
Davey Williams, New York NL, 1954
Willie Davis, Los Angeles NL, 1963
Willy Taveras, Houston NL, 2005
5-game series—4—Duffy Lewis, Boston AL, 1916
6-game series—3—Jimmy Sheckard, Chicago NL, 1906
Harry Steinfeldt, Chicago NL, 1906
Joe Tinker, Chicago NL, 1906
Bill Lee, Chicago NL, 1935
7-game series—4—Fred Clarke, Pittsburgh NL, 1909
Bucky Harris, Washington AL, 1925
Don Johnson, Chicago NL, 1945
8-game series—5—Jake Daubert, Cincinnati NL, 1919

**Most sacrifice hits, game**
3—Joe Tinker, Chicago NL, Oct 12, 1906
Craig Counsell, Arizona NL, Oct 31, 2001

**Most sacrifice hits, inning**
1—many players

## SACRIFICE FLIES

**Most sacrifice flies, career**
4—Joe Carter, Toronto AL, 1992 (1), 1993 (3); 2 series, 12 G

**Most sacrifice flies, series**
3—Joe Carter, Toronto AL, 1993 (6-game series)

**Most sacrifice flies, game**
2—Glenn Wright, Pittsburgh NL, Oct 5, 1927
Wes Westrum, New York NL, Oct 2, 1954
Manny Ramirez, Cleveland AL, Oct 25, 1997
Mike Matheny, St. Louis NL, Oct 23, 2004

**Most sacrifice flies, inning**
1—many players

**Most runs batted in on sacrifice fly**
2—Tommy Herr, St. Louis NL, Oct 16, 1982, 2nd

## HIT BY PITCH

**Most hit by pitch, career**
3—Frank Chance, Chicago NL, 1906 (2), 1907 (1)
Honus Wagner, Pittsburgh NL, 1903 (1), 1909 (2)
Fred Snodgrass, New York NL, 1911 (2), 1912 (1)
Max Carey, Pittsburgh NL, 1925 (3)
Yogi Berra, New York AL, 1953 (2), 1955 (1)
Elston Howard, New York AL, 1960 (1), 1962 (1), 1964 (1)
Frank Robinson, Cincinnati NL, 1961 (2); Baltimore AL, 1971 (1)
Bert Campaneris, Oakland AL, 1973 (2), 1974 (1)
Reggie Jackson, New York AL, 1977 (1), 1978 (2)
Derek Jeter, New York AL, 1996 (1), 2001 (1), 2003 (1)

**Most hit by pitch, series**
3—Max Carey, Pittsburgh NL, 1925 (7-game series)

**Most hit by pitch, game**
2—Max Carey, Pittsburgh NL, Oct 7, 1925
Yogi Berra, New York AL, Oct 2, 1953
Frank Robinson, Cincinnati NL, Oct 8, 1961
Jeff Bagwell, Houston NL, Oct 22, 2005
[2—Todd Pratt, New York NL, Oct 21, 2000, 12 inn]

**Most hit by pitch, inning**
1—many players

## GROUNDING INTO DOUBLE PLAYS

**Most grounding into double play, career**
7—Joe DiMaggio, New York AL, 1936-1939, 1941, 1942, 1947, 1949-1951; 10 series, 51 G
Paul O'Neill, Cincinnati NL, 1990; New York AL, 1996, 1998-2001; 6 series, 27 G

**Most grounding into double play, series**
5—Irv Noren, New York AL, 1955 (7-game series)

**Most grounding into double play, game**
3—Willie Mays, New York NL, Oct 8, 1951

## REACHING ON ERRORS OR INTERFERENCE

**Most times reaching first base on error, game**
3—Fred Clarke, Pittsburgh NL, Oct 10, 1903

**Most times awarded first base on catcher's interference, game**
1—Roger Peckinpaugh, Washington AL, Oct 15, 1925, 1st
Bud Metheny, New York AL, Oct 6, 1943, 6th
Ken Boyer, St. Louis NL, Oct 12, 1964, 1st
Pete Rose, Cincinnati NL, Oct 10, 1970, 5th
George Hendrick, St. Louis NL, Oct 15, 1982, 9th

# CLUB BATTING

## GAMES

**Most games played, total series**
219—New York AL; 39 series (won 130, lost 88, tied 1)

**For summaries of series won and lost, games won and lost, and home and road games played, see page 396. For a list of batting statistics by teams each series, see page 401.**

## BATTING AVERAGE

**Highest average, series**
4-game series
.317—Cincinnati NL vs Oakland AL, 1990
5-game series
.316—Philadelphia AL vs Chicago NL, 1910
6-game series
.311—Toronto AL vs Philadelphia NL, 1993
7-game series
.338—New York AL vs Pittsburgh NL, 1960
8-game series
.270—New York NL vs Boston AL, 1912

**Highest average, both clubs, series**
4-game series
.283—New York AL .313, Chicago NL .253, 1932
5-game series
.272—Philadelphia AL .316, Chicago NL .222, 1910
6-game series
.292—Philadelphia NL .294, Kansas City AL .290, 1980
Toronto AL .311, Philadelphia NL .274, 1993
7-game series
.300—New York AL .338, Pittsburgh NL .256, 1960
8-game series
.245—New York NL .270, Boston AL .220, 1912

**Highest average, losing club, series**
.338—New York AL vs Pittsburgh NL, 1960 (7-game series)

**Lowest average, series**
4-game series
.142—Los Angeles NL vs Baltimore AL, 1966
5-game series
.146—Baltimore AL vs New York NL, 1969
6-game series
.175—New York NL vs Philadelphia AL, 1911
7-game series
.183—New York AL vs Arizona NL, 2001
8-game series
.207—New York AL vs New York NL, 1921

**Lowest average, both clubs, series**
4-game series
.171—Baltimore AL .200, Los Angeles NL .142, 1966
5-game series
.184—New York NL .220, Baltimore AL .146, 1969
6-game series
.197—Chicago AL .198, Chicago NL .196, 1906
7-game series
.209—Oakland AL .209, Cincinnati NL .209, 1972
8-game series
.239—Cincinnati NL .255, Chicago AL .224, 1919

**Lowest average, winning club, series**
.186—Boston AL vs Chicago NL, 1918 (6-game series)

## ON-BASE PERCENTAGE

(official statistic since 1984; calculated from official statistics, 1931-1983, except for 1939 for which there is no official tabulation of sacrifice flies)

**Highest percentage, series**
4-game series
.421—New York AL vs Chicago NL, 1932
5-game series
.366—Baltimore AL vs Cincinnati NL, 1970
6-game series
.382—Toronto AL vs Philadelphia NL, 1993
7-game series
.386—Cleveland AL vs Florida NL, 1997

**Highest percentage, both clubs, series**
4-game series
.366—New York AL .421, Chicago NL .306, 1932
5-game series
.331—Detroit AL .355, San Diego NL .306, 1984
6-game series
.378—Toronto AL .382, Philadelphia NL .375, 1993
7-game series
.375—Cleveland AL .386, Florida NL .363, 1997

**Lowest percentage, series**
4-game series
.207—New York AL vs Los Angeles NL, 1963
5-game series
.220—Baltimore AL vs New York NL, 1969
6-game series
.250—Cleveland AL vs Boston NL, 1948
7-game series
.240—New York AL vs Arizona NL, 2001

**Lowest percentage, both clubs, series**
4-game series
.242—Los Angeles NL .279, New York AL .207, 1963
5-game series
.243—Baltimore AL .258, Philadelphia NL .228, 1983
6-game series
.270—Boston NL .291, Cleveland AL .250, 1948
7-game series
.271—New York AL .273, San Francisco NL .268, 1962

## SLUGGING AVERAGE

**Highest average, series**
4-game series
.582—Oakland AL vs San Francisco NL, 1989
5-game series
.509—Baltimore AL vs Cincinnati NL, 1970
6-game series
.510—Toronto AL vs Philadelphia NL, 1993
7-game series
.528—New York AL vs Pittsburgh NL, 1960
8-game series
.401—Boston AL vs Pittsburgh NL, 1903

**Highest average, both clubs, series**
4-game series
.468—Oakland AL .582, San Francisco NL .343, 1989
5-game series
.433—Baltimore AL .509, Cincinnati NL .354, 1970
6-game series
.467—Toronto AL .510, Philadelphia NL .425, 1993
7-game series
.481—San Francisco NL .498, Anaheim AL .465, 2002
8-game series
.344—New York NL .361, Boston AL .326, 1912

**Lowest average, series**
4-game series
.192—Los Angeles NL vs Baltimore AL, 1966
5-game series
.194—Philadelphia AL vs New York NL, 1905
6-game series
.233—Boston AL vs Chicago NL, 1918
7-game series
.237—Brooklyn NL vs Cleveland AL, 1920
8-game series
.270—New York AL vs New York NL, 1921

**Lowest average, both clubs, series**
4-game series
.267—Baltimore AL .342, Los Angeles NL .192, 1966
5-game series
.224—New York NL .255, Philadelphia AL .194, 1905
6-game series
.241—Chicago NL .250, Boston AL .233, 1918
7-game series
.285—Cleveland AL .332, Brooklyn NL .237, 1920
8-game series
.323—New York NL .371, New York AL .270, 1921

## AT-BATS AND PLATE APPEARANCES

**Most at-bats, total series**
7,345—New York AL; 39 series, 219 G

**Most at-bats, series**
4-game series
154—Chicago AL vs Houston NL, 2005
5-game series
179—New York AL vs New York NL, 2000
6-game series
222—New York AL vs Los Angeles NL, 1978
7-game series
269—New York AL vs Pittsburgh NL, 1960

8-game series
282—Boston AL vs Pittsburgh NL, 1903

**Most at-bats by both clubs, series**

4-game series
297—Chicago AL 154, Houston NL 143, 2005
5-game series
354—New York AL 179, New York NL 175, 2000
6-game series
421—New York AL 222, Los Angeles NL 199, 1978
7-game series
512—St. Louis NL 262, Detroit AL 250, 1934
8-game series
552—Boston AL 282, Pittsburgh NL 270, 1903

**Fewest at-bats, series**

4-game series
117—Los Angeles NL vs New York AL, 1963
5-game series
142—Oakland AL vs Los Angeles NL, 1974
6-game series
172—Boston AL vs Chicago NL, 1918
7-game series
215—Brooklyn NL vs Cleveland AL, 1920
Brooklyn NL vs New York AL, 1956
Minnesota AL vs Los Angeles NL, 1965
8-game series
241—New York AL vs New York NL, 1921

**Fewest at-bats by both clubs, series**

4-game series
240—Baltimore AL 120, Los Angeles NL 120, 1966
5-game series
300—Los Angeles NL 158, Oakland AL 142, 1974
6-game series
348—Chicago NL 176, Boston AL 172, 1918
7-game series
432—Cleveland AL 217, Brooklyn NL 215, 1920
8-game series
505—New York NL 264, New York AL 241, 1921

**Most at-bats, game**

46—Arizona NL vs New York AL, Nov 3, 2001
[54—New York NL vs Oakland AL, Oct 14, 1973, 12 inn]

**Most at-bats by both clubs, game**

85—Toronto AL 44, Philadelphia 41, Oct 20, 1993
[101—New York NL 54, Oakland AL 47, Oct 14, 1973, 12 inn]

**Fewest at-bats, game**

25—Philadelphia AL vs Boston NL, Oct 10, 1914
Atlanta NL vs Cleveland AL, Oct 21, 1995 (batted 8 inn)

**Fewest at-bats by both clubs, game**

54—Chicago NL 27, Chicago AL 27, Oct 12, 1906

**Most at-bats, inning**

13—Philadelphia AL vs Chicago NL, Oct 12, 1929, 7th

**Most at-bats by both clubs, inning**

17—Philadelphia AL 13, Chicago NL 4, Oct 12, 1929, 7th

**Most plate appearances, inning**

15—Philadelphia AL vs Chicago NL, Oct 12, 1929, 7th
Detroit AL vs St. Louis NL, Oct 9, 1968, 3rd

**Most plate appearances by both clubs, inning**

20—Philadelphia AL 15, Chicago NL 5, Oct 12, 1929, 7th

## RUNS

### SERIES AND GAME

**Most runs, total series**

957—New York AL; 39 series, 219 G

**Most runs, series**

4-game series
37—New York AL vs Chicago NL, 1932
5-game series
35—Philadelphia AL vs Chicago NL, 1910
6-game series
45—Toronto AL vs Philadelphia NL, 1993
7-game series
55—New York AL vs Pittsburgh NL, 1960
8-game series
39—Boston AL vs Pittsburgh NL, 1903

**Most runs by both clubs, series**

4-game series
56—New York AL 37, Chicago NL 19, 1932
5-game series
53—Baltimore AL 33, Cincinnati NL 20, 1970
6-game series
81—Toronto AL 45, Philadelphia NL 36, 1993
7-game series
85—San Francisco NL 44, Anaheim AL 41, 2002
8-game series
63—Boston AL 39, Pittsburgh NL 24, 1903

**Most runs by losing club, series**

55—New York AL vs Pittsburgh NL, 1960 (7-game series)

**Fewest runs, series**

4-game series
2—Los Angeles NL vs Baltimore AL, 1966
5-game series
3—Philadelphia AL vs New York NL, 1905
6-game series
9—Boston AL vs Chicago NL, 1918
7-game series
8—Brooklyn NL vs Cleveland AL, 1920
8-game series
20—Chicago AL vs Cincinnati NL, 1919

**Fewest runs by both clubs, series**

4-game series
15—Baltimore AL 13, Los Angeles NL 2, 1966
5-game series
18—New York NL 15, Philadelphia AL 3, 1905
6-game series
19—Chicago NL 10, Boston AL 9, 1918
7-game series
29—Cleveland AL 21, Brooklyn NL 8, 1920
8-game series
51—New York NL 29, New York AL 22, 1921

**Most runs, game**

18—New York AL vs New York NL, Oct 2, 1936 (won 18-4)

**Most earned runs, game**

17—New York AL vs New York NL, Oct 2, 1936 (won 18-4)

**Most runs by both clubs, game**

29—Toronto AL 15, Philadelphia NL 14, Oct 20, 1993

**Largest score, shutout game**

12-0—New York AL 12, Pittsburgh NL 0, Oct 12, 1960

**Most players scoring one or more runs, game**

9—St. Louis NL vs Detroit AL, Oct 9, 1934
New York AL vs New York NL, Oct 2, 1936
Milwaukee NL vs New York AL, Oct 2, 1958
New York AL vs Pittsburgh NL, Oct 6, 1960
Pittsburgh NL vs New York AL, Oct 13, 1960
St. Louis NL vs Milwaukee AL, Oct 19, 1982
Toronto AL vs Philadelphia NL, Oct 20, 1993

**Most players from both clubs scoring one or more runs, game**

16—Toronto AL 9, Philadelphia NL 7, Oct 20, 1993
Boston AL 8, St. Louis NL 8, Oct 23, 2004

### INNING

**Most runs, inning**

10—Philadelphia AL vs Chicago NL, Oct 12, 1929, 7th
Detroit AL vs St. Louis NL, Oct 9, 1968, 3rd

**Most runs by both clubs, inning**

11—Philadelphia AL 10, Chicago NL 1, Oct 12, 1929, 7th
Brooklyn NL 6, New York AL 5, Oct 5, 1956, 2nd

**Most runs, extra inning**

4—New York NL vs Oakland AL, Oct 14, 1973, 12th

**Most runs by both clubs, extra inning**

5—New York NL 4, Oakland AL 1, Oct 14, 1973, 12th
New York NL 3, Boston AL 2, Oct 25, 1986, 10th

**Most innings scored, game**

6—New York AL vs St. Louis NL, Oct 6, 1926
New York AL vs Brooklyn NL, Oct 1, 1947
New York AL vs Pittsburgh NL, Oct 6, 1960
Philadelphia NL vs Toronto AL, Oct 20, 1993

**Most innings scored by both clubs, game**

10—Philadelphia NL 6, Toronto AL 4, Oct 20, 1993

**Most runs, 1st inning**

7—Milwaukee NL vs New York AL, Oct 2, 1958

**Most runs, 2nd inning**

6—New York AL vs New York NL, Oct 13, 1923
New York NL vs New York AL, Oct 9, 1937
Brooklyn NL vs New York AL, Oct 2, 1947
Brooklyn NL vs New York AL, Oct 5, 1956

**Most runs,3rd inning**

10—Detroit AL vs St. Louis NL, Oct 9, 1968

**Most runs, 4th inning**

7—Minnesota AL vs St. Louis NL, Oct 17, 1987

**Most runs, 5th inning**

6—Baltimore AL vs Pittsburgh NL, Oct 11, 1971
Kansas City AL vs St. Louis NL, Oct 27, 1985

**Most runs, 6th inning**
7—New York AL vs New York NL, Oct 6, 1937
New York AL vs Pittsburgh NL, Oct 6, 1960

**Most runs, 7th inning**
10—Philadelphia AL vs Chicago NL, Oct 12, 1929

**Most runs, 8th inning**
6—Chicago NL vs Detroit AL, Oct 11, 1908
Baltimore AL vs Pittsburgh NL, Oct 13, 1979
Toronto AL vs Philadelphia NL, Oct 20, 1993

**Most runs, 9th inning**
7—New York AL vs New York NL, Oct 6, 1936

**Most runs in 9th inning with none on base and two out**
4—New York AL vs Brooklyn NL, Oct 5, 1941

**Most runs, 10th inning**
3—New York NL vs Philadelphia AL, Oct 8, 1913
New York AL vs Cincinnati NL, Oct 8, 1939
New York NL vs Cleveland AL, Sept 29, 1954
Milwaukee NL vs New York AL, Oct 6, 1957
St. Louis NL vs New York AL, Oct 12, 1964
New York NL vs Boston AL, Oct 25, 1986

**Most runs, 11th inning**
2—Philadelphia AL vs New York NL, Oct 17, 1911
Toronto AL vs Atlanta NL, Oct 24, 1992

**Most runs, 12th inning**
4—New York NL vs Oakland AL, Oct 14, 1973

**Most runs, 13th inning**
none

**Most runs, 14th inning**
2—Chicago AL vs Houston NL, Oct 25, 2005

## GAMES BEING SHUT OUT

**Most times shut out, total series**
15—New York AL; 39 series, 219 G

**Most times shut out, series**
4—Philadelphia AL vs New York NL, 1905

**Most consecutive times shut out, series**
3—Philadelphia AL vs New York NL, Oct 12, 13, 14, 1905
Los Angeles NL vs Baltimore AL, Oct 6, 8, 9, 1966

**Most consecutive games without being shut out, total series**
42—New York AL, Oct 6, 1926-Oct 1, 1942

## HITS

### SERIES

**Most hits, total series**
1,834—New York AL; 39 series, 219 G

**Most hits, series**
4-game series
45—New York AL vs Chicago NL, 1932
Cincinnati NL vs Oakland AL, 1990
5-game series
56—Philadelphia AL vs Chicago NL, 1910
6-game series
68—New York AL vs Los Angeles NL, 1978
7-game series
91—New York AL vs Pittsburgh NL, 1960
8-game series
74—New York NL vs Boston AL, 1912

**Most hits by both clubs, series**
4-game series
82—New York AL 45, Chicago NL 37, 1932
5-game series
91—Philadelphia AL 56, Chicago NL 35, 1910
6-game series
122—Toronto AL 64, Philadelphia NL 58, 1993
7-game series
151—New York AL 91, Pittsburgh NL 60, 1960
8-game series
135—Boston AL 71, Pittsburgh NL 64, 1903

**Fewest hits, series**
4-game series
17—Los Angeles NL vs Baltimore AL, 1966
5-game series
23—Baltimore AL vs New York NL, 1969
6-game series
32—Boston AL vs Chicago NL, 1918
7-game series
40—St. Louis NL vs Kansas City AL, 1985
8-game series
50—New York AL vs New York NL, 1921

**Fewest hits by both clubs, series**
4-game series
41—Baltimore AL 24, Los Angeles NL 17, 1966
5-game series
57—New York NL 32, Philadelphia AL 25, 1905
6-game series
69—Chicago NL 37, Boston AL 32, 1918
7-game series
92—Oakland AL 46, Cincinnati NL 46, 1972
8-game series
121—New York NL 71, New York AL 50, 1921

**Most hits by pinch-hitters, series**
6—New York AL vs Brooklyn NL, 1947 (7-game series)
New York AL vs Pittsburgh NL, 1960 (7-game series)
Oakland AL vs Cincinnati NL, 1972 (7-game series)
Baltimore AL vs Pittsburgh NL, 1979 (7-game series)

**Most hits by pinch-hitters on both clubs, series**
11—New York AL 6, Brooklyn NL 5, 1947 (7-game series)

**Most players with one or more hits in each game, series**
4—New York AL vs Los Angeles NL, 1978 (6-game series)

**Most consecutive hitless innings, series**
9—Brooklyn NL vs New York AL, Oct 8, 1956 (all 27 batters)

### GAME AND INNING

**Most hits, game**
22—Arizona NL vs New York AL, Nov 3, 2001

**Most hits by losing club, game**
17—Pittsburgh NL vs Baltimore AL, Oct 13, 1979

**Most hits by both clubs, game**
32—New York AL 19, Pittsburgh NL 13, Oct 6, 1960
Toronto AL 18, Philadelphia 14, Oct 20, 1993

**Most hits by pinch-hitters, game**
3—Oakland AL vs Cincinnati NL, Oct 19, 1972
Baltimore AL vs Pittsburgh NL, Oct 13, 1979

**Fewest hits, game**
0—Brooklyn NL vs New York AL, Oct 8, 1956

**Fewest hits by both clubs, game**
5—New York AL 3, New York NL 2, Oct 6, 1921
New York AL 5, Brooklyn NL 0, Oct 8, 1956
Atlanta NL 3, Cleveland AL 2, Oct 21, 1995

**Most players with one or more hits, game**
11—New York AL vs St. Louis NL, Oct 9, 1928
New York AL vs Pittsburgh NL, Oct 6, 1960

**Most players on both clubs with one or more hits, game**
19—New York AL 11, Pittsburgh NL 8, Oct 6, 1960

**Most hits, inning**
10—Philadelphia AL vs Chicago NL, Oct 12, 1929, 7th

**Most hits by both clubs, inning**
12—Philadelphia AL 10, Chicago NL 2, Oct 12, 1929, 7th

**Most hits by pinch-hitters, inning**
3—Oakland AL vs Cincinnati NL, Oct 19, 1972, 9th

**Most consecutive hits, inning (consecutive at-bats)**
8—New York NL vs New York AL, Oct 7, 1921, 7th (1 BB and 1 SH during streak)

**Most consecutive hits, inning (consecutive plate appearances)**
6—Chicago NL vs Detroit AL, Oct 10, 1908, 9th (6 singles)

## SINGLES

**Most singles, total series**
1,308—New York AL; 39 series, 219 G

**Most singles, series**
4-game series
32—New York AL vs San Diego NL, 1998
5-game series
46—New York NL vs New York AL, 1922
6-game series
57—New York AL vs Los Angeles NL, 1978
7-game series
64—New York AL vs Pittsburgh NL, 1960
8-game series
55—New York NL vs Boston AL, 1912

**Most singles by both clubs, series**
4-game series
55—New York AL 31, Chicago NL 24, 1932
5-game series
70—New York NL 39, Washington AL 31, 1933
6-game series
95—New York AL 57, Los Angeles NL 38, 1978
7-game series
109—New York AL 64, Pittsburgh NL 45, 1960

8-game series
96—Boston AL 49, Pittsburgh NL 47, 1903

**Fewest singles, series**

4-game series
13—Philadelphia AL vs Boston NL, 1914
Los Angeles NL vs Baltimore AL, 1966
5-game series
19—Brooklyn NL vs New York AL, 1941
Baltimore AL vs New York NL, 1969
6-game series
17—Philadelphia AL vs St. Louis NL, 1930
7-game series
27—Minnesota AL vs Los Angeles NL, 1965
St. Louis NL vs Kansas City AL, 1985
8-game series
39—Boston AL vs New York NL, 1912

**Fewest singles by both clubs, series**

4-game series
29—Baltimore AL 16, Los Angeles NL 13, 1966
5-game series
40—New York NL 21, Baltimore AL 19, 1969
6-game series
42—St. Louis NL 25, Philadelphia AL 17, 1930
7-game series
66—St. Louis NL 33, Boston AL 33, 1967
8-game series
92—Cincinnati NL 47, Chicago AL 45, 1919
New York NL 52, New York AL 40, 1921

**Most singles, game**

16—New York AL vs Los Angeles NL, Oct 15, 1978
Arizona NL vs New York AL, Nov 3, 2001

**Most singles by both clubs, game**

24—New York AL 16, Los Angeles NL 8, Oct 15, 1978

**Fewest singles, game**

0—Philadelphia AL vs St. Louis NL, Oct 1, 1930 (batted 8 inn)
Philadelphia AL vs St. Louis NL, Oct 8, 1930 (batted 8 inn)
Brooklyn NL vs New York AL, Oct 3, 1947 (batted 8.2 inn)
New York AL vs Brooklyn NL, Oct 4, 1952 (batted 8 inn)
Brooklyn NL vs New York AL, Oct 8, 1956
St. Louis NL vs Boston AL, Oct 5, 1967

**Fewest singles by both clubs, game**

2—St. Louis NL 2, Philadelphia AL 0, Oct 8, 1930

**Most singles, inning**

7—Philadelphia AL vs Chicago NL, Oct 12, 1929, 7th
New York NL vs Washington AL, Oct 4, 1933, 6th
Brooklyn NL vs New York AL, Oct 8, 1949, 6th

**Most singles by both clubs, inning**

8—Philadelphia AL 7, Chicago NL 1, Oct 12, 1929, 7th
New York NL 7, Washington AL 1, Oct 4, 1933, 6th
Brooklyn NL 7, New York AL 1, Oct 8, 1949, 6th

## DOUBLES

**Most doubles, total series**

264—New York AL; 39 series, 219 G

**Most doubles, series**

4-game series
11—Boston AL vs St. Louis NL, 2004
5-game series
19—Philadelphia AL vs Chicago NL, 1910
6-game series
15—Philadelphia AL vs New York NL, 1911
7-game series
19—St. Louis NL vs Boston AL, 1946
8-game series
14—Boston AL vs New York NL, 1912
New York NL vs Boston AL, 1912

**Most doubles by both clubs, series**

4-game series
19—Boston AL 11, St. Louis 8, 2004
5-game series
30—Philadelphia AL 19, Chicago NL 11, 1910
6-game series
26—Philadelphia AL 15, New York NL 11, 1911
7-game series
29—Detroit AL 16, Pittsburgh NL 13, 1909
8-game series
28—Boston AL 14, New York NL 14, 1912

**Fewest doubles, series**

4-game series
3—Cincinnati NL vs New York AL, 1939
New York AL vs Philadelphia NL, 1950
New York NL vs Cleveland AL, 1954
Los Angeles NL vs New York AL, 1963
New York AL vs Los Angeles NL, 1963
Baltimore AL vs Los Angeles NL, 1966
Los Angeles NL vs Baltimore AL, 1966
New York AL vs Cincinnati NL, 1976
5-game series
1—Detroit AL vs Chicago NL, 1907
Baltimore AL vs New York NL, 1969
6-game series
2—Boston AL vs Chicago NL, 1918
New York NL vs New York AL, 1923
7-game series
3—Baltimore AL vs Pittsburgh NL, 1971
8-game series
4—Boston AL vs Pittsburgh NL, 1903

**Fewest doubles by both clubs, series**

4-game series
6—Los Angeles NL 3, New York AL 3, 1963
Baltimore AL 3, Los Angeles NL 3, 1966
5-game series
6—Philadelphia NL 4, Boston AL 2, 1915
6-game series
7—Chicago NL 5, Boston AL 2, 1918
7-game series
11—St. Louis NL 7, Detroit AL 4, 1968
8-game series
11—Pittsburgh NL 7, Boston AL 4, 1903

**Most doubles, game**

8—Chicago AL vs Chicago NL, Oct 13, 1906
Pittsburgh NL vs Washington AL, Oct 15, 1925

**Most doubles by both clubs, game**

11—Chicago AL 8, Chicago NL 3, Oct 13, 1906

**Most doubles, inning**

3—Chicago AL vs Chicago NL, Oct 13, 1906, 4th
Philadelphia AL vs Chicago NL, Oct 18, 1910, 7th
Philadelphia AL vs New York NL, Oct 24, 1911, 4th (consec)
Pittsburgh NL vs Washington AL, Oct 15, 1925, 8th
St. Louis NL vs Detroit AL, Oct 9, 1934, 3rd
Brooklyn NL vs New York AL, Oct 2, 1947, 2nd
Brooklyn NL vs New York AL, Oct 5, 1947, 3rd (consec)
New York AL vs Brooklyn NL, Oct 8, 1949, 4th
Chicago AL vs Los Angeles NL, Oct 1, 1959, 3rd
Arizona NL vs New York AL, Nov 3, 2001, 3rd

## TRIPLES

**Most triples, total series**

52—New York AL; 39 series, 219 G

**Most triples, series**

4-game series
3—Cincinnati NL vs New York AL, 1976
Oakland AL vs San Francisco NL, 1989
5-game series
6—Boston AL vs Brooklyn NL, 1916
6-game series
5—Toronto AL vs Philadelphia NL, 1993
7-game series
5—St. Louis NL vs Detroit AL, 1934
New York AL vs Brooklyn NL, 1947
8-game series
16—Boston AL vs Pittsburgh NL, 1903

**Most triples by both clubs, series**

4-game series
4—Cincinnati NL 3, New York AL 1, 1976
Oakland AL 3, San Francisco NL 1, 1989
5-game series
11—Boston AL 6, Brooklyn NL 5, 1916
6-game series
7—New York AL 4, New York NL 3, 1923
Toronto AL 5, Philadelphia NL 2, 1993
7-game series
8—Atlanta NL 4, Minnesota AL 4, 1991
8-game series
25—Boston AL 16, Pittsburgh NL 9, 1903

**Fewest triples, series**

4-game series
0—many clubs; last—St. Louis NL, 2004
5-game series
0—many clubs; last—Oakland AL, 1988
6-game series
0—many clubs; last—Florida NL, 2003
7-game series
0—many clubs; last—Arizona NL, 2001; New York AL, 2001
8-game series
1—New York AL vs New York NL, 1921

**Fewest triples by both clubs, series**

4-game series
1—St. Louis NL 1, New York AL 0, 1928
Cleveland AL 1, New York NL 0, 1954
Baltimore AL 1, Los Angeles NL 0, 1966
San Diego NL 1, New York AL 0, 1998
Atlanta NL 1, New York AL 0, 1999

5-game series
0—New York NL 0, Philadelphia AL 0, 1905
New York NL 0, Washington AL 0, 1933
New York NL 0, Baltimore AL 0, 1969
Detroit AL 0, San Diego NL 0, 1984
6-game series
0—Cleveland AL 0, Boston NL 0, 1948
New York AL 0, Los Angeles NL 0, 1978
Toronto AL 0, Atlanta NL 0, 1992
7-game series
0—St. Louis NL 0, Philadelphia AL 0, 1931
Arizona NL 0, New York AL 0, 2001
8-game series
5—New York NL 4, New York AL 1, 1921

**Most triples, game**
5—Boston AL vs Pittsburgh NL, Oct 7, 1903
Boston AL vs Pittsburgh NL, Oct 10, 1903

**Most triples by both clubs, game**
7—Boston AL 5, Pittsburgh NL 2, Oct 10, 1903

**Most triples, inning**
2—Boston AL vs Pittsburgh NL, Oct 7, 1903, 8th
Boston AL vs Pittsburgh NL, Oct 10, 1903, 1st and 4th
Boston AL vs New York NL, Oct 12, 1912, 3rd
Philadelphia AL vs New York NL, Oct 7, 1913, 4th
Boston AL vs Chicago NL, Sept 6, 1918, 9th
New York AL vs Brooklyn NL, Oct 1, 1947, 3rd
New York AL vs Brooklyn NL, Sept 30, 1953, 1st
Detroit AL vs St. Louis NL, Oct 7, 1968, 4th

## HOME RUNS

### SERIES

**Most home runs, total series**
210—New York AL; 39 series, 219 G

**Most grand slams, total series**
8—New York AL; 39 series, 219 G

**Most home runs by pinch-hitters, total series**
7—New York AL; 39 series, 219 G

**Most home runs, series**
4-game series
9—New York AL vs St. Louis NL, 1928
Oakland AL vs San Francisco NL, 1989
5-game series
10—Baltimore AL vs Cincinnati NL, 1970
6-game series
9—New York AL vs Brooklyn NL, 1953
Los Angeles NL vs New York AL, 1977
7-game series
14—San Francisco NL vs Anaheim AL, 2002
8-game series
2—Boston AL vs Pittsburgh NL, 1903
New York AL vs New York NL, 1921
New York NL vs New York AL, 1921

**Most home runs by both clubs, series**
4-game series
13—Oakland AL 9, San Francisco NL 4, 1989
5-game series
15—Baltimore AL 10, Cincinnati NL 5, 1970
6-game series
17—New York AL 9, Brooklyn NL 8, 1953
Los Angeles NL 9, New York AL 8, 1977
7-game series
21—San Francisco NL 14, Anaheim AL 7, 2002
8-game series
4—New York NL 2, New York AL 2, 1921

**Fewest home runs, series**
4-game series
0—many clubs
5-game series
0—many clubs
6-game series
0—Chicago NL vs Chicago AL, 1906
Chicago AL vs Chicago NL, 1906
New York NL vs Philadelphia AL, 1911
Boston AL vs Chicago NL, 1918
Chicago NL vs Boston AL, 1918
7-game series
0—Brooklyn NL vs Cleveland AL, 1920
8-game series
0—Cincinnati NL vs Chicago AL, 1919

**Fewest home runs by both clubs, series**
4-game series
1—Boston NL 1, Philadelphia AL 0, 1914
5-game series
0—New York NL 0, Philadelphia AL 0, 1905
Chicago NL 0, Detroit AL 0, 1907
6-game series
0—Chicago AL 0, Chicago NL 0, 1906
Boston AL 0, Chicago NL 0, 1918
7-game series
2—Cleveland AL 2, Brooklyn NL 0, 1920
8-game series
1—Chicago AL 1, Cincinnati NL 0, 1919

**Most grand slams, series**
2—New York AL vs Brooklyn NL, 1956
Minnesota AL vs St. Louis NL, 1987

**Most grand slams by both clubs, series**
2—New York AL 2, Brooklyn NL 0, 1956
St. Louis NL 1, New York AL 1, 1964
Minnesota AL 2, St. Louis NL 0, 1987

**Most home runs by pinch-hitters, series**
2—Los Angeles NL vs Chicago AL, 1959
Boston AL vs Cincinnati NL, 1975

**Most home runs by pinch-hitters for both clubs, series**
2—New York NL 1, Cleveland AL 1, 1954
Los Angeles NL 2, Chicago AL 0, 1959
Boston AL 2, Cincinnati NL 0, 1975

**Most home runs by pitchers, series**
2—New York NL vs Washington AL, 1924

**Most home runs by pitchers for both clubs, series**
2—New York NL 2, Washington AL 0, 1924
Boston AL 1, St. Louis NL 1, 1967
Detroit AL 1, St. Louis NL 1, 1968

### GAME

**Most home runs, game**
5—New York AL vs St. Louis NL, Oct 9, 1928
Oakland AL vs San Francisco NL, Oct 27, 1989

**Most home runs by both clubs, game**
7—Oakland AL 5, San Francisco NL 2, Oct 27, 1989

**Most consecutive games with one or more home runs, total series**
9—New York AL, last 2 G vs Chicago NL, 1932 (7 HR), all 6 G vs New York NL, 1936 (7 HR), first G vs New York NL, 1937 (1 HR); total 15 HR
New York AL, all 7 G vs Brooklyn NL in 1952 (10 HR) and first 2 G vs Brooklyn NL, 1953 (4 HR); total 14 HR

**Most consecutive games with one or more home runs, series**
7—Washington AL vs Pittsburgh NL, Oct 7-15, 1925 (8 HR)
New York AL vs Brooklyn NL, Oct 1-7, 1952 (10 HR)

### INNING

**Most home runs, inning (two or more home runs, 38 times)**
3—Boston AL vs St. Louis NL, Oct 11, 1967, 4th, Yastrzemski, Smith, Petrocelli (2 consec)
2—New York NL vs New York AL, Oct 11, 1921, 2nd
Washington AL vs Pittsburgh NL, Oct 11, 1925, 3rd
New York AL vs St. Louis NL, Oct 9, 1928, 7th
New York AL vs St. Louis NL, Oct 9, 1928, 8th
Philadelphia AL vs Chicago NL, Oct 12, 1929, 7th
New York AL vs Chicago NL, Oct 1, 1932, 5th
New York AL vs Chicago NL, Oct 2, 1932, 9th
New York AL vs Cincinnati NL, Oct 7, 1939, 5th
New York AL vs Cincinnati NL, Oct 8, 1939, 7th
Detroit AL vs Cincinnati NL, Oct 4, 1940, 7th
Brooklyn NL vs New York AL, Oct 7, 1949, 9th
Brooklyn NL vs New York AL, Sept 30, 1953, 6th
Brooklyn NL vs New York AL, Oct 1, 1955, 4th
Milwaukee NL vs New York AL, Oct 6, 1957, 4th
Milwaukee NL vs New York AL, Oct 2, 1958, 1st
New York AL vs Milwaukee NL, Oct 2, 1958, 9th
Los Angeles NL vs Chicago AL, Oct 2, 1959, 7th
New York AL vs St. Louis NL, Oct 14, 1964, 6th
New York AL vs St. Louis NL, Oct 15, 1964, 9th
Baltimore AL vs Los Angeles NL, Oct 5, 1966, 1st
Baltimore AL vs New York NL, Oct 16, 1969, 3rd
Oakland AL vs New York NL, Oct 21, 1973, 3rd
Cincinnati NL vs Boston AL, Oct 14, 1975, 5th
New York AL vs Los Angeles NL, Oct 16, 1977, 8th
Los Angeles NL vs New York AL, Oct 10, 1978, 2nd
Los Angeles NL vs New York AL, Oct 25, 1981, 7th
Boston AL vs New York NL, Oct 27, 1986, 2nd
Oakland AL vs San Francisco NL, Oct 27, 1989, 4th and 5th
Philadelphia NL vs Toronto AL, Oct 20, 1993, 5th
Florida NL vs Cleveland AL, Oct 18, 1997, 4th
San Diego NL vs New York AL, Oct 17, 1998, 5th
New York AL vs San Diego NL, Oct 17, 1998, 7th
New York NL vs New York AL, Oct 22, 2000, 9th
Arizona NL vs New York AL, Nov 1, 2001, 5th
San Francisco NL vs Anaheim AL, Oct 19, 2002, 2nd
San Francisco NL vs Anaheim AL, Oct 20, 2002, 2nd

San Francisco NL vs Anaheim AL, Oct 22, 2002, 5th
New York AL vs Florida NL, Oct 21, 2003, 9th

**Most home runs by both clubs, inning**
3—New York NL 2, New York AL 1, Oct 11, 1921, 2nd
Boston AL 3, St. Louis NL 0, Oct 11, 1967, 4th
San Francisco NL 2, Anaheim AL 1, Oct 19, 2002, 2nd
San Francisco NL 2, Anaheim AL 1, Oct 20, 2002, 2nd

**Most consecutive home runs, inning (13 times)**
2—Washington AL vs Pittsburgh NL, Oct 11, 1925, 3rd
New York AL vs St. Louis NL, Oct9, 1928, 7th
New York AL vs Chicago NL, Oct 1, 1932, 5th
New York AL vs St. Louis NL, Oct 14, 1964, 6th
Baltimore AL vs Los Angeles NL, Oct 5, 1966, 1st
Boston AL vs St. Louis NL, Oct 11, 1967, 4th
Cincinnati NL vs Boston AL, Oct 14, 1975, 5th
New York AL vs Los Angeles NL, Oct 16, 1977, 8th
Los Angeles NL vs New York AL, Oct 25, 1981, 7th
Boston AL vs New York NL, Oct 27, 1986, 2nd
Florida NL vs Cleveland AL, Oct 18, 1997, 4th
San Diego NL vs New York AL, Oct 17, 1998, 5th
San Francisco NL vs Anaheim AL, Oct 20, 2002, 2nd

**Most times hitting two home runs in an inning, total series**
12—New York AL, 1928 (2), 1932 (2), 1939 (2), 1958 (1), 1964 (2), 1977 (1), 1998 (1), 2003 (1)

**Most times hitting two home runs in an inning, series**
3—San Francisco NL, 2002

**Most times hitting two home runs in an inning, game**
2—New York AL vs St. Louis NL, Oct 9, 1928, 7th and 8th
Oakland AL vs San Francisco NL, Oct 27, 1989, 4th and 5th

## TOTAL BASES

**Most total bases, total series**
2,832—New York AL; 39 series, 219 G

**Most total bases, series**
4-game series
85—Oakland AL vs San Francisco NL, 1989
5-game series
87—Baltimore AL vs Cincinnati NL, 1970
6-game series
105—Toronto AL vs Philadelphia NL, 1993
7-game series
142—New York AL vs Pittsburgh NL, 1960
8-game series
113—Boston AL vs Pittsburgh NL, 1903

**Most total bases by both clubs, series**
4-game series
133—New York AL 75, Chicago NL 58, 1932
5-game series
145—Baltimore AL 87, Cincinnati NL 58, 1970
6-game series
200—Brooklyn NL 103, New York AL 97, 1953
7-game series
231—San Francisco NL 117, Anaheim AL 114, 2002
8-game series
205—Boston AL 113, Pittsburgh NL 92, 1903

**Fewest total bases, series**
4-game series
23—Los Angeles NL vs Baltimore AL, 1966
5-game series
30—Philadelphia AL vs New York NL, 1905
6-game series
40—Boston AL vs Chicago NL, 1918
7-game series
51—Brooklyn NL vs Cleveland AL, 1920
8-game series
65—New York AL vs New York NL, 1921

**Fewest total bases by both clubs, series**
4-game series
64—Baltimore AL 41, Los Angeles NL 23, 1966
5-game series
69—New York NL 39, Philadelphia AL 30, 1905
6-game series
84—Chicago NL 44, Boston AL 40, 1918
7-game series
123—Cleveland AL 72, Brooklyn NL 51, 1920
8-game series
163—New York NL 98, New York AL 65, 1921

**Most total bases, game**
34—Atlanta NL vs Minnesota AL, Oct 24, 1991

**Most total bases by both clubs, game**
50—San Francisco NL 25, Anaheim AL 25, Oct 20, 2002

**Fewest total bases, game**
0—Brooklyn NL vs New York AL, Oct 8, 1956

**Fewest total bases by both clubs, game**
5—New York AL 3, New York NL 2, Oct 6, 1921

**Most total bases, inning**
17—Philadelphia AL vs Chicago NL, Oct 12, 1929, 7th

**Most total bases by both clubs, inning**
21—Philadelphia AL 17, Chicago NL 4, Oct 12, 1929, 7th

## EXTRA-BASE HITS

**Most extra-base hits, total series**
526—New York AL; 39 series, 219 G

**Most extra-base hits, series**
4-game series
20—Oakland AL vs San Francisco NL, 1989
5-game series
21—Philadelphia AL vs Chicago NL, 1910
6-game series
24—Toronto AL vs Philadelphia NL, 1993
7-game series
27—New York AL vs Pittsburgh NL, 1960
8-game series
22—Boston AL vs Pittsburgh NL, 1903

**Most extra-base hits by both clubs, series**
4-game series
29—Oakland AL 20, San Francisco NL 9, 1989
Chicago AL 17, Houston 12, 2005
5-game series
33—Philadelphia AL 21, Chicago NL 12, 1910
6-game series
41—Brooklyn NL 22, New York AL 19, 1953
7-game series
45—Anaheim AL 23, San Francisco NL 22, 2002
8-game series
40—Boston AL 21, New York NL 19, 1912

**Fewest extra-base hits, series**
4-game series
4—Cincinnati NL vs New York AL, 1939
Los Angeles NL vs Baltimore AL, 1966
5-game series
3—Detroit AL vs Chicago NL, 1907
6-game series
5—Boston AL vs Chicago NL, 1918
7-game series
6—Brooklyn NL vs Cleveland AL, 1920
8-game series
10—New York AL vs New York NL, 1921

**Fewest extra-base hits by both clubs, series**
4-game series
12—Baltimore AL 8, Los Angeles NL 4, 1966
5-game series
10—Chicago NL 7, Detroit AL 3, 1907
6-game series
11—Chicago NL 6, Boston AL 5, 1918
7-game series
19—Cleveland AL 13, Brooklyn NL 6, 1920
8-game series
29—New York NL 19, New York AL 10, 1921

**Most extra-base hits, game**
9—Pittsburgh NL vs Washington AL, Oct 15, 1925 (8 doubles, 1 triple)

**Most extra-base hits by both clubs, game**
11—Chicago AL 8 (eight doubles), Chicago NL 3 (3 doubles), Oct 13, 1906
Pittsburgh NL 9 (8 doubles, 1 triple), Washington AL 2 (1 double, 1 HR), Oct 15, 1925
New York AL 7 (4 doubles, 1 triple, 2 HR), Cincinnati NL 4 (2 doubles, 2 HR), Oct 9, 1961
Oakland AL 7 (2 doubles, 5 HR), San Francisco NL 4 (2 doubles, 2 HR), Oct 27, 1989
[11—Atlanta NL 8 (2 doubles, 3 triples, 3 HR), Minnesota AL 3 (1 double, 2 triples), Oct 24, 1991, 12 inn]

**Longest extra-inning game without an extra base hit**
12 inn—Chicago NL vs Detroit AL, Oct 8, 1907
Detroit AL vs Chicago NL, Oct 8, 1907

**Longest extra-inning game without an extra base hit by either club**
12 inn—Chicago NL 0, Detroit AL 0, Oct 8, 1907

## RUNS BATTED IN

**Most runs batted in, total series**
905—New York AL; 39 series, 219 G

**Most runs batted in, series**
4-game series
36—New York AL vs Chicago NL, 1932
5-game series
32—Baltimore AL vs Cincinnati NL, 1970
6-game series
45—Toronto AL vs Philadelphia NL, 1993
7-game series
54—New York AL vs Pittsburgh NL, 1960
8-game series
35—Boston AL vs Pittsburgh NL, 1903

**Most runs batted in by both clubs, series**
4-game series
52—New York AL 36, Chicago NL 16, 1932
5-game series
52—Baltimore AL 32, Cincinnati NL 20, 1970
6-game series
80—Toronto AL 45, Philadelphia NL 35, 1993
7-game series
80—New York AL 54, Pittsburgh NL 26, 1960
San Francisco NL 42, Anaheim AL 38, 2002
8-game series
58—Boston AL 35, Pittsburgh NL 23, 1903

**Fewest runs batted in, series**
4-game series
2—Los Angeles NL vs Baltimore AL, 1966
5-game series
2—Philadelphia AL vs New York NL, 1905
6-game series
6—Boston AL vs Chicago NL, 1918
7-game series
8—Brooklyn NL vs Cleveland AL, 1920
8-game series
17—Chicago AL vs Cincinnati NL, 1919

**Fewest runs batted in by both clubs, series**
4-game series
12—Los Angeles NL 2, Baltimore AL 10, 1966
5-game series
15—Philadelphia AL 2, New York NL 13, 1905
6-game series
16—Boston AL 6, Chicago NL 10, 1918
7-game series
26—Brooklyn NL 8, Cleveland AL 18, 1920
8-game series
46—Boston AL 21, New York NL 25, 1912

**Most runs batted in, game**
18—New York AL vs New York NL, Oct 2, 1936

**Most runs batted in by both clubs, game**
29—Toronto AL 15, Philadelphia NL 14, Oct 20, 1993

**Fewest runs batted in, game**
0—many clubs

**Most runs batted in, inning**
10—Philadelphia AL vs Chicago NL, Oct 12, 1929, 7th
Detroit AL vs St. Louis NL, Oct 9, 1968, 3rd

**Most runs batted in by both clubs, inning**
11—Philadelphia AL 10, Chicago NL 1, Oct 12, 1929, 7th
Brooklyn NL 6, New York AL 5, Oct 5, 1956, 2nd

**Fewest runs batted in by both clubs, game**
0—New York NL 0, Philadelphia AL 0, Oct 13, 1905
New York NL 0, New York AL 0, Oct 13, 1921
Chicago AL 0, Los Angeles NL 0, Oct 6, 1959
New York AL 0, San Francisco NL 0, Oct 16, 1962

## BASES ON BALLS

**Most bases on balls, total series**
769—New York AL; 39 series, 219 G

**Most bases on balls, series**
4-game series
24—Boston AL vs St. Louis NL, 2004
5-game series
25—New York AL vs New York NL, 2000
6-game series
34—Philadelphia NL vs Toronto AL, 1993
7-game series
40—Cleveland AL vs Florida NL, 1997
8-game series
27—New York AL vs New York NL, 1921

**Most bases on balls by both clubs, series**
4-game series
36—Boston AL 24, St. Louis NL 12, 2004
5-game series
37—New York AL 23, Brooklyn NL 14, 1941
6-game series
59—Philadelphia NL 34, Toronto AL 25, 1993
7-game series
76—Cleveland AL 40, Florida NL 36, 1997
8-game series
49—New York AL 27, New York NL 22, 1921

**Fewest bases on balls, series**
4-game series
4—Pittsburgh NL vs New York AL, 1927
5-game series
5—Philadelphia AL vs New York NL, 1905
6-game series
4—Philadelphia AL vs New York NL, 1911
7-game series
9—St. Louis NL vs Philadelphia AL, 1931
8-game series
13—Boston AL vs Pittsburgh NL, 1903

**Fewest bases on balls by both clubs, series**
4-game series
15—New York AL 9, Cincinnati NL 6, 1939
5-game series
15—New York NL 8, Philadelphia AL 7, 1913
6-game series
17—Chicago AL 11, New York NL 6, 1917
7-game series
30—New York AL 18, Pittsburgh NL 12, 1960
8-game series
27—Pittsburgh NL 14, Boston AL 13, 1903

**Most bases on balls, game**
11—Brooklyn NL vs New York AL, Oct 5, 1956
New York AL vs Milwaukee NL, Oct 5, 1957
Detroit AL vs San Diego NL, Oct 12, 1984

**Most bases on balls by both clubs, game**
19—New York AL 11, Milwaukee NL 8, Oct 5, 1957

**Longest game with no bases on balls, team**
12 inn—St. Louis NL vs Detroit AL, Oct 4, 1934

**Fewest bases on balls by both clubs, game**
0—Philadelphia AL 0, New York NL 0, Oct 16, 1911
New York NL 0, Chicago AL 0, Oct 10, 1917
New York NL 0, New York AL 0, Oct 9, 1921
Boston AL 0, St. Louis NL 0, Oct 7, 1967
Philadelphia NL 0, Baltimore AL 0, Oct 11, 1983

**Most bases on balls, inning**
5—New York AL vs St. Louis NL, Oct 6, 1926, 5th

**Most bases on balls by both clubs, inning**
6—New York AL 3, New York NL 3, Oct 7, 1921, 3rd
New York AL 5, St. Louis NL 1, Oct 6, 1926, 5th
St. Louis NL 4, Boston AL 2, Oct 23, 2004, 4th

**Most bases on balls by pinch-hitters, inning**
2—New York AL vs New York NL, Oct 15, 1923, 8th
Baltimore AL vs Philadelphia NL, Oct 15, 1983, 6th

## STRIKEOUTS

**Most strikeouts, total series**
1,242—New York AL; 39 series, 219 G

**Most strikeouts, series**
4-game series
37—New York AL vs Los Angeles NL, 1963
5-game series
50—Chicago NL vs Philadelphia AL, 1929
6-game series
50—Philadelphia NL vs Toronto AL, 1993
7-game series
70—Arizona NL vs New York AL, 2001
8-game series
45—Pittsburgh NL vs Boston AL, 1903

**Most strikeouts by both clubs, series**
4-game series
66—Houston 36, Chicago AL 30, 2005
5-game series
88—New York NL 48, New York AL, 40, 2000
6-game series
97—New York AL 49, Florida NL 48, 2003
7-game series
133—Arizona NL 70, New York AL 63, 2001
8-game series
82—New York AL 44, New York NL 38, 1921

**Fewest strikeouts, series**
4-game series
7—Pittsburgh NL vs New York AL, 1927
5-game series
15—New York NL vs New York AL, 1922
6-game series
14—Chicago NL vs Boston AL, 1918
7-game series
20—Brooklyn NL vs Cleveland AL, 1920
8-game series
22—Cincinnati NL vs Chicago AL, 1919

**Fewest strikeouts by both clubs, series**
4-game series
32—New York AL 25, Pittsburgh NL 7, 1927
Cincinnati NL 16, New York AL 16, 1976
5-game series
35—New York NL 19, Philadelphia AL 16, 1913
New York AL 20, New York NL 15, 1922
6-game series
35—Boston AL 21, Chicago NL 14, 1918
7-game series
41—Cleveland AL 21, Brooklyn NL 20, 1920

8-game series
52—Chicago AL 30, Cincinnati NL 22, 1919

**Most strikeouts, game**
17—Detroit AL vs St. Louis NL, Oct 2, 1968

**Most strikeouts by both clubs, game**
25—New York AL 15, Los Angeles NL 10, Oct 2, 1963
New York NL 13, New York AL 12, Oct 24, 2000
[25—Oakland AL 15, New York NL 10, Oct 14, 1973, 12 inn
Houston NL 14, Chicago AL 11, Oct 25, 2005, 14 inn]

**Most strikeouts by pinch-hitters, game**
4—St. Louis AL vs St. Louis NL, Oct 8, 1944 (consec)
St. Louis AL vs St. Louis NL, Oct 9, 1944 (consec)

**Most consecutive strikeouts, game**
6—Chicago AL vs Cincinnati NL, Oct 6, 1919 (3 in 2nd, 3 in 3rd)
Los Angeles NL vs Baltimore AL, Oct 5, 1966 (3 in 4th, 3 in 5th)
Kansas City AL vs St. Louis NL, Oct 24, 1985 (3 in 6th, 3 in 7th)

**Fewest strikeouts, game**
0—Chicago NL vs Boston AL, Sept 6, 1918 (batted 8 inn)
Chicago NL vs Boston AL, Sept 9, 1918
New York AL vs New York NL, Oct 6, 1921 (batted 8 inn)
New York AL vs Philadelphia NL, Oct 4, 1950
Brooklyn NL vs New York AL, Oct 3, 1952
Pittsburgh NL vs New York AL, Oct 6, 1960
Pittsburgh NL vs New York AL, Oct 13, 1960
New York AL vs Pittsburgh NL, Oct 13, 1960
Anaheim AL vs San Francisco NL, Oct 20, 2002 (batted 8 inn)

**Fewest strikeouts by both clubs, game**
0—Pittsburgh NL 0, New York AL 0, Oct 13, 1960

**Most strikeouts, inning**
4—Detroit AL vs Chicago NL, Oct 14, 1908, 1st

**Most strikeouts by pinch-hitters, inning**
3—St. Louis AL vs St. Louis NL, Oct 8, 1944, 9th

**Most strikeouts by both clubs, inning**
6—Cincinnati NL 3, Oakland AL 3, Oct 18, 1972, 5th
Kansas City AL 3, St. Louis NL 3, Oct 24, 1985, 7th
New York AL 3, New York NL 3, Oct 24, 2000, 2nd

## SACRIFICE HITS

**Most sacrifice hits, total series**
93—New York AL; 39 series, 219 G

**Most sacrifice hits, series**
13—Chicago NL vs Chicago AL, 1906 (6-game series)

**Most sacrifice hits by both clubs, series**
19—Chicago NL 13, Chicago AL 6, 1906 (6-game series)

**Fewest sacrifice hits, series**
0—many clubs; last—Atlanta NL vs New York AL, 1999

**Fewest sacrifice hits by both clubs, series**
0—New York AL 0, Brooklyn NL 0, 1941 (5-game series)
Cincinnati NL 0, New York AL 0, 1976 (4-game series)
Baltimore AL 0, Philadelphia NL 0, 1983 (5-game series)
Oakland AL 0, San Francisco NL 0, 1989 (4-game series)

**Most sacrifice hits, game**
5—Chicago NL vs Chicago AL, Oct 12, 1906

**Most sacrifice hits by both clubs, game**
6—Chicago NL 5, Chicago AL 1, Oct 12, 1906
Chicago NL 4, Detroit AL 2, Oct 10, 1908

**Most sacrifice hits, inning**
2—many teams

## SACRIFICE FLIES

**Most sacrifice flies, total series**
35—New York AL; 26 series, 150 G

**Most sacrifice flies, series**
7—Toronto AL vs Philadelphia NL, 1993 (6-game series)

**Most sacrifice flies by both clubs, series**
8—Toronto AL 7, Philadelphia NL 1, 1993 (6-game series)

**Most sacrifice flies, game**
3—New York AL vs Pittsburgh NL, Oct 6, 1927
Toronto AL vs Philadelphia NL, Oct 19, 1993

**Most sacrifice flies by both clubs, game**
5—New York AL 3, Pittsburgh NL 2, Oct 6, 1927

**Most sacrifice flies, inning**
2—Baltimore AL vs Pittsburgh NL, Oct 13, 1971, 1st

## HIT BY PITCH

**Most hit by pitch, total series**
49—New York AL; 39 series, 219 G

**Most hit by pitch, series**
6—Pittsburgh NL vs Detroit AL, 1909 (7-game series)
Arizona NL vs New York AL, 2001 (7-game series)

**Most hit by pitch by both clubs, series**
10—Pittsburgh NL 6, Detroit AL 4, 1909 (7-game series)

**Fewest hit by pitch, series**
0—many clubs

**Most hit by pitch, game**
3—Detroit AL vs St. Louis NL, Oct 9, 1968
Baltimore AL vs Pittsburgh NL, Oct 13, 1971
Houston NL vs Chicago AL, Oct 22, 2005

**Most hit by pitch by both clubs, game**
3—Philadelphia NL 2, Boston AL 1, Oct 13, 1915
Cincinnati NL 2, Chicago AL 1, Oct 9, 1919
Pittsburgh NL 2, Washington AL 1, Oct 7, 1925
Detroit AL 3, St. Louis NL 0, Oct 9, 1968
Baltimore AL 3, Pittsburgh NL 0, Oct 13, 1971
New York NL 2, Oakland AL 1, Oct 14, 1973
Minnesota AL 2, St. Louis NL 1, Oct 21, 1987
Houston NL 3, Chicago AL 0, Oct 22, 2005

**Most hit by pitch, inning**
2—Pittsburgh NL vs Detroit AL, Oct 11, 1909, 2nd (consec)
Detroit AL vs St. Louis NL, Oct 9, 1968, 8th
Pittsburgh NL vs Baltimore AL, Oct 17, 1979, 9th (consec)
Houston NL vs Chicago AL, Oct 22, 2005, 7th

## REACHING BASE ON ERRORS

**Most times reaching first base on error, game**
5—Chicago NL vs Chicago AL, Oct 13, 1906

**Most times reaching first base on error by both clubs, game**
6—Pittsburgh NL 4, Boston AL 2, Oct 10, 1903
Chicago NL 4, Philadelphia AL 2, Oct 18, 1910
New York NL 4, Philadelphia AL 2, Oct 26, 1911

# INDIVIDUAL BASERUNNING

## STOLEN BASES

**Most stolen bases, career**
14—Eddie Collins, Philadelphia AL (10), 1910, 1911, 1913, 1914; Chicago AL (4), 1917, 1919; 6 series, 34 G
Lou Brock, St. Louis NL, 1964 (0), 1967 (7), 1968 (7); 3 series, 21 G

**Most stolen bases, series**
4-game series—3—Rickey Henderson, Oakland AL, 1989, 1990
Derek Jeter, New York AL, 1999
5-game series—6—Jimmy Slagle, Chicago NL, 1907
6-game series—6—Kenny Lofton, Cleveland AL, 1995
7-game series—7—Lou Brock, St. Louis NL, 1967
Lou Brock, St. Louis NL, 1968
8-game series—4—Josh Devore, New York NL, 1912

**Most stolen bases, game**
3—Honus Wagner, Pittsburgh NL, Oct 11, 1909
Willie Davis, Los Angeles NL, Oct 11, 1965
Lou Brock, St. Louis NL, Oct 12, 1967
Lou Brock, St. Louis NL, Oct 5, 1968

**Most times stealing home, game (14 times; *part of double steal)**
1—Bill Dahlen, New York NL, Oct 12, 1905, 5th*

George Davis, Chicago AL, Oct 13, 1906, 3rd*
Jimmy Slagle, Chicago NL, Oct 11, 1907, 7th
Ty Cobb, Detroit AL, Oct 9, 1909, 3rd
Buck Herzog, New York NL, Oct 14, 1912, 1st*
Butch Schmidt, Boston NL, Oct 9, 1914, 8th*
Mike McNally, New York AL, Oct 5, 1921, 5th
Bob Meusel, New York AL, Oct 6, 1921, 8th
Bob Meusel, New York AL, Oct 7, 1928, 6th*
Hank Greenberg, Detroit AL, Oct 6, 1934, 8th*
Monte Irvin, New York NL, Oct 4, 1951, 1st
Jackie Robinson, Brooklyn NL, Sept 28, 1955, 8th
Tim McCarver, St. Louis NL, Oct 15, 1964, 4th*
Brad Fullmer, Anaheim AL, Oct 20, 2002, 1st*

**Most stolen bases, inning (9 times)**

2—Jimmy Slagle, Chicago NL, Oct 8, 1907, 10th
George Browne, New York NL, Oct 12, 1905, 9th
Ty Cobb, Detroit AL, Oct 12, 1908, 9th
Eddie Collins, Chicago AL, Oct 7, 1917, 6th
Babe Ruth, New York AL, Oct 6, 1921, 5th
Lou Brock, St. Louis NL, Oct 12, 1967, 5th
Dave Lopes, Los Angeles NL, Oct 15, 1974, 1st
Kenny Lofton, Cleveland AL, Oct 21, 1995, 1st
Omar Vizquel, Cleveland AL, Oct 26, 1997, 5th

### CAUGHT STEALING

**Most caught stealing, career**

9—Frank Schulte, Chicago NL, 1906, 1907, 1908, 1910; four series, 21 G

**Most caught stealing, series**

5—Frank Schulte, Chicago NL, 1910 (5-game series)

**Most caught stealing, game**

2—Frank Schulte, Chicago NL, Oct 17, 1910
Frank Schulte, Chicago NL, Oct 23, 1910
Fred Luderus, Philadelphia NL, Oct 8, 1915
Jimmy Johnston, Brooklyn NL, Oct 9, 1916
Mickey Livingston, Chicago NL, Oct 3, 1945
Billy Martin, New York AL, Sept 28, 1955

**Most caught stealing, inning**

1—many players

**Most times picked off base, game**

2—Max Flack, Chicago NL, Sept 9, 1918 (first base in 1st, second base in 3rd)

# CLUB BASERUNNING

## STOLEN BASES

**Most stolen bases, total series**

74—New York AL; 39 series, 219 G

**Most stolen bases, series**

4-game series—9—Boston NL vs Philadelphia AL, 1914
5-game series—18—Chicago NL vs Detroit AL, 1907
6-game series—15—Atlanta NL vs Toronto AL, 1992
7-game series—18—Pittsburgh NL vs Detroit AL, 1909
8-game series—12—New York NL vs Boston AL, 1912

**Most stolen bases by both clubs, series**

4-game series—11—Boston NL 9, Philadelphia AL 2, 1914
5-game series—25—Chicago NL 18, Detroit AL 7, 1907
6-game series—20—Atlanta NL 15, Toronto AL 5, 1992
7-game series—24—Pittsburgh NL 18, Detroit AL 6, 1909
8-game series—18—New York NL 12, Boston AL 6, 1912

**Fewest stolen bases, series**

4-game series—0—many clubs
5-game series—0—many clubs
6-game series—0—many clubs
7-game series—0—Philadelphia AL vs St. Louis NL, 1931
Detroit AL vs Cincinnati NL, 1940
New York AL vs Pittsburgh NL, 1960
Detroit AL vs St. Louis NL, 1968
New York NL vs Oakland AL, 1973
Boston AL vs Cincinnati NL, 1975
Pittsburgh NL vs Baltimore AL, 1979
Boston AL vs New York NL, 1986
8-game series—5—Boston AL vs Pittsburgh NL, 1903
Chicago AL vs Cincinnati NL, 1919

**Fewest stolen bases by both clubs, series**

4-game series—1—Cincinnati NL 1, New York AL 0, 1939
New York NL 1, Cleveland AL 0, 1954
Los Angeles NL 1, Baltimore AL 0, 1966
St. Louis NL 1, Boston AL 0, 2004
5-game series—1—Chicago NL 1, Philadelphia AL 0, 1929
Washington AL 1, New York NL 0, 1933
New York NL 1, New York AL 0, 1937
New York AL 1, Cincinnati NL 0, 1961
Cincinnati NL 1, Baltimore AL 0, 1970
New York AL 1, New York NL 0, 2000
6-game series—0—St. Louis NL 0, St. Louis AL 0, 1944
7-game series—1—Cincinnati NL 1, Detroit AL 0, 1940
8-game series—12—Pittsburgh NL 7, Boston AL 5, 1903
Cincinnati NL 7, Chicago AL 5, 1919

**Most stolen bases, game**

5—New York NL vs Philadelphia AL, Oct 12, 1905
Chicago NL vs Chicago AL, Oct 10, 1906
Chicago NL vs Detroit AL, Oct 9, 1907
St. Louis NL vs Minnesota AL, Oct 22, 1987
Atlanta NL vs Toronto AL, Oct 18, 1992
[7—Chicago NL vs Detroit AL, Oct 8, 1907, 12 inn]

**Most stolen bases by both clubs, game**

6—New York NL 5, Philadelphia AL 1, Oct 12, 1905
Pittsburgh NL 4, Detroit AL 2, Oct 13, 1909
New York NL 3, Philadelphia AL 3, Oct 9, 1913
St. Louis NL 5, Minnesota AL 1, Oct 22, 1987
[11—Chicago NL 7, Detroit AL 4, Oct 8, 1907, 12 inn]

**Longest game with no stolen bases, team**

14 inn—Boston AL vs Brooklyn NL, Oct 9, 1916
Brooklyn NL vs Boston AL, Oct 9, 1916

**Longest game with no stolen bases by either club**

14 inn—Boston AL vs Brooklyn NL, Oct 9, 1916

**Most stolen bases, inning**

3—Pittsburgh NL vs Boston AL, Oct 1, 1903, 1st
New York NL vs Philadelphia AL, Oct 12, 1905, 9th
Chicago NL vs Detroit AL, Oct 8, 1907, 10th
Chicago NL vs Detroit AL, Oct 11, 1908, 8th
New York NL vs Boston AL, Oct 14, 1912, 1st
Chicago AL vs New York NL, Oct 7, 1917, 6th

## CAUGHT STEALING

**Most caught stealing, series**

4-game series—5—Boston NL vs Philadelphia AL, 1914
Cincinnati NL vs New York, AL, 1976
5-game series—8—Chicago NL vs Philadelphia, AL, 1910
6-game series—13—New York NL vs Philadelphia, AL, 1911
7-game series—8—St. Louis NL vs Detroit AL, 1968
8-game series—11—New York NL vs Boston AL, 1912

**Most caught stealing by both clubs, series**

4-game series—7—Cincinnati NL 5, New York AL 2, 1976
5-game series—15—Chicago NL 8, Philadelphia AL 7, 1910
6-game series—19—New York NL 13, Philadelphia AL 6, 1911
7-game series—11—Pittsburgh NL 6, Detroit AL 5, 1909
8-game series—16—New York NL 11, Boston AL 5, 1912

**Fewest caught stealing, series**

0—many clubs

**Fewest caught stealing by both clubs, series**

4-game series—0—Boston AL 0, St. Louis NL 0, 2004
5-game series—0—New York AL 0, Brooklyn NL 0, 1949
6-game series—1—St. Louis NL 1, St. Louis AL 0, 1944
Cleveland AL 1, Boston NL 0, 1948

7-game series—0—St. Louis NL 0, New York AL 0, 1964
8-game series—6—Pittsburgh NL 4, Boston AL 2, 1903

**Most caught stealing, game**

3—many clubs; last—Los Angeles NL vs Oakland AL, Oct 19, 1988
[5—New York NL vs Philadelphia AL, Oct 17, 1911, 11 inn]

**Most caught stealing by both clubs, game**

5—Philadelphia AL 3, Chicago NL 2, Oct 17, 1910

**Most caught stealing, inning**

2—many innings

## LEFT ON BASE

**Most left on base, total series**

1,518—New York AL; 39 series, 219 G

**Most left on base, series**

4-game series—41—Boston AL vs St. Louis NL, 2004
5-game series—52—New York AL vs New York NL, 2000
6-game series—55—New York AL vs Los Angeles NL, 1981
7-game series—72—New York NL vs Oakland AL, 1973
8-game series—55—Boston AL vs Pittsburgh NL, 1903
Boston AL vs New York NL, 1912

**Most left on base by both clubs, series**

4-game series—70—Chicago AL 36, Houston NL 34, 2005
5-game series—88—New York AL 52, New York NL 36, 2000
6-game series—101—New York AL 55, Los Angeles NL 46, 1981
7-game series—130—New York NL 72, Oakland AL 58, 1973
8-game series—108—Boston AL 55, New York NL 53, 1912

**Fewest left on base, series**

4-game series—16—New York AL vs Cincinnati NL, 1939
5-game series—23—Philadelphia NL vs Boston AL, 1915
Philadelphia NL vs Baltimore AL, 1983
6-game series—29—Philadelphia AL vs New York NL, 1911
7-game series—36—Minnesota AL vs Los Angeles NL, 1965
8-game series—43—New York AL vs New York NL, 1921

**Fewest left on base by both clubs, series**

4-game series—39—Cincinnati NL 23, New York AL 16, 1939
5-game series—51—Baltimore AL 28, Philadelphia NL 23, 1983
6-game series—60—New York NL 31, Philadelphia AL 29, 1911
7-game series—82—Cleveland AL 43, Brooklyn NL 39, 1920
Brooklyn NL 42, New York AL 40, 1956
New York AL 43, San Francisco NL 39, 1962
8-game series—97—New York NL 54, New York AL 43, 1921

**Most left on base, game**

15—Anaheim AL vs San Francisco NL, Oct 22, 2002
[15—New York NL vs Oakland AL, Oct 14, 1973, 12 inn
Philadelphia NL vs Kansas City AL, Oct 17, 1980, 10 inn
New York AL vs New York NL, Oct 21, 2000, 12 inn
Chicago AL vs Houston NL, Oct 25, 2005, 14 inn
Houston NL vs Chicago AL, Oc 25, 2005, 14 inn]

**Most left on base, shutout defeat**

11—Philadelphia AL vs St. Louis NL, Oct 4, 1930 (lost 5-0)
St. Louis NL vs New York AL, Oct 11, 1943 (lost 2-0)
Los Angeles NL vs Chicago AL, Oct 6, 1959 (lost 1-0)
Baltimore AL vs New York NL, Oct 14, 1969 (lost 5-0)

**Most left on base by both clubs, game**

24—Detroit AL 14, San Diego NL 10, Oct 12, 1984
[30—Houston NL 15, Chicago AL 12, Oct 25, 2005, 14 inn]

**Fewest left on base, game**

0—Brooklyn NL vs New York AL, Oct 8, 1956
Los Angeles NL vs New York AL, Oct 6, 1963 (batted 8 inn)

**Fewest left on base by both clubs, game**

3—New York AL 3, Brooklyn NL 0, Oct 8, 1956

# INDIVIDUAL PITCHING

## GAMES

**Most games, career**

22—Whitey Ford, New York AL, 1950, 1953, 1955-1958, 1960-1964; 11 series

**Most games, series**

4-game series—4—Jeff Nelson, New York AL, 1999 (2.2 IP)
Keith Foulke, Boston AL, 2004 (5.0 IP)
Neal Cotts, Chicago AL, 2005 (1.1 IP)
Bobby Jenks, Chicago AL, 2005 (5.0 IP)
5-game series—5—Mike G. Marshall, Los Angeles NL, 1974 (9.0 IP)
6-game series—6—Dan Quisenberry, Kansas City AL, 1980 (10.1 IP)
7-game series—7—Darold Knowles, Oakland AL, 1973 (6.1 IP)
8-game series—5—Deacon Phillippe, Pittsburgh NL, 1903 (44 IP)

**Most consecutive games, series**

7—Darold Knowles, Oakland AL, Oct 13, 14, 16, 17, 18, 20, 21, 1973

## GAMES STARTED

**Most games started, career**

22—Whitey Ford, New York AL, 1950, 1953, 1955-1958, 1960-1964; 11 series

**Most opening games started, career**

8—Whitey Ford, New York AL, 1955-1958, 1961-1964 (won 4, lost 3)

**Most games started, series**

5—Deacon Phillippe, Pittsburgh NL, 1903 (8-game series)

**Most consecutive games started, series**

2—Deacon Phillippe, Pittsburgh NL, Oct 3, 6, 1903
Deacon Phillippe, Pittsburgh NL, Oct 10, 13, 1903
Jack Coombs, Philadelphia AL, Oct 18, 20, 1910
Christy Mathewson, New York NL, Oct 17, 24, 1911
George Earnshaw, Philadelphia AL, Oct 9, 11, 1929
George Earnshaw, Philadelphia AL, Oct 6, 8, 1930

**Most series with three games started, career**

3—Bob Gibson, St. Louis NL, 1964, 1967, 1968

**Oldest pitcher to start a game**

45 years, 3 months, 7 days—Jack Quinn, Philadelphia AL, Oct 12, 1929 (5 IP)

## GAMES RELIEVED

**Most games as relief pitcher, career**

20—Mike Stanton, Atlanta NL, 1991, 1992; New York AL, 1998-2001 (23.1 IP)
Mariano Rivera, New York AL, 1996, 1998-2001, 2003 (31.0 IP)

**Most games as relief pitcher, series**

7—Darold Knowles, Oakland AL, 1973 (7-game series)

## COMPLETE GAMES

**Most complete games, career**

10—Christy Mathewson, New York NL 1905, 1911-1913

**Most consecutive complete games, career**

8—Bob Gibson, St. Louis NL, 1964, 1967, 1968 (won 7, lost 1)

**Most consecutive complete games won, career**

7—Bob Gibson, St. Louis NL, Oct 12, 15, 1964; Oct 4, 8, 12, 1967; Oct 2, 6, 1968

**Most complete games, series**

5—Deacon Phillippe, Pittsburgh NL, 1903 (8-game series)

**Youngest pitcher to pitch a complete game**

20 years, 10 months, 12 days—Joe Bush, Philadelphia AL, Oct 9, 1913
(beat New York NL, 8-2)

**Oldest pitcher to pitch a complete game**

39 years, 7 months, 13 days—Grover Alexander, St. Louis NL, Oct 9, 1926
(beat New York AL, 10-2)

## INNINGS

**Most innings pitched, career**

146—Whitey Ford, New York AL, 1950, 1953, 1955-1958, 1960-1964; 11 series, 22 G

**Most innings pitched, series**

4-game series—18—Dick Rudolph, Boston NL, 1914
Waite Hoyt, New York AL, 1928
Red Ruffing, New York AL, 1938
Sandy Koufax, Los Angeles NL, 1963
5-game series—27—Christy Mathewson, New York NL, 1905
Jack Coombs, Philadelphia AL, 1910
6-game series—27—Christy Mathewson, New York NL, 1911
Red Faber, Chicago AL, 1917

Hippo Vaughn, Chicago NL, 1918
7-game series—32—George Mullin, Detroit AL, 1909
8-game series—44—Deacon Phillippe, Pittsburgh NL, 1903

**Most innings pitched, game**
14—Babe Ruth, Boston AL, Oct 9, 1916 (CG, won 2-1)

## GAMES WON

**Most games won, career**
10—Whitey Ford, New York AL, 1950, 1953, 1955-1958, 1960-1964; 11 series, 22 G (lost 8)

**For a complete list of pitchers with five or more victories, see page 401.**

**Most games won without a defeat, career**
6—Lefty Gomez, New York AL, 1932, 1936-1938

**Most opening games won, career**
5—Red Ruffing, New York AL, 1932, 1938, 1939, 1941, 1942, (4 CG)

**Most consecutive games won, career**
7—Bob Gibson, St. Louis NL, Oct 12, 15, 1964; Oct 4, 8, 12, 1967; Oct 2, 6, 1968 (7 CG)

**Most games won, series**
4-game series—2—8 pitchers; last—Mike Moore, Oakland AL, 1989; Dave Stewart, Oakland AL, 1989
5-game series—3—Christy Mathewson, New York NL, 1905
Jack Coombs, Philadelphia AL, 1910
6-game series—3—Red Faber, Chicago AL, 1917
7-game series—3—Babe Adams, Pittsburgh NL, 1909
Stan Coveleski, Cleveland AL, 1920
Harry Brecheen, St. Louis NL, 1946
Lew Burdette, Milwaukee NL, 1957
Bob Gibson, St. Louis NL, 1967
Mickey Lolich, Detroit AL, 1968
Randy Johnson, Arizona NL, 2001
8-game series—3—Bill Dinneen, Boston AL, 1903
Deacon Phillippe, Pittsburgh NL, 1903
Joe Wood, Boston AL, 1912

**Most games won without a defeat, series**
4-game series—2—many pitchers
5-game series—3—Christy Mathewson, New York NL, 1905
Jack Coombs, Philadelphia AL, 1910
6-game series—2—many pitchers
7-game series—3—Babe Adams, Pittsburgh NL, 1909
Stan Coveleski, Cleveland AL, 1920
Harry Brecheen, St. Louis NL, 1946
Lew Burdette, Milwaukee NL, 1957
Bob Gibson, St. Louis NL, 1967
Mickey Lolich, Detroit AL, 1968
Randy Johnson, Arizona NL, 2001
8-game series—2—Rube Marquard, New York NL, 1912
Hod Eller, Cincinnati NL, 1919
Dickie Kerr, Chicago AL, 1919
Jesse Barnes, New York NL, 1921

**Most games won by relief pitcher, series**
2—Jesse Barnes, New York NL, 1921 (8-game series)
Hugh Casey, Brooklyn NL, 1947 (7-game series)
Larry Sherry, Los Angeles NL, 1959 (6-game series)
Ross Grimsley, Cincinnati NL, 1972 (6-game series)
Rawly Eastwick, Cincinnati NL, 1975 (7-game series)
Duane Ward, Toronto AL, 1992 (6-game series)
Mike Stanton, New York AL, 2000 (5-game series)

## SAVES (SINCE 1969)

**Most saves, career**
9—Mariano Rivera, New York AL, 1996, 1998-2001, 2003

**Most saves, series**
4—John Wetteland, New York AL, 1996 (6-game series)

## GAMES LOST

**Most games lost, career**
8—Whitey Ford, New York AL, 1950, 1953, 1955-1958, 1960-1964; 11 series, 22 G (won 10)

**Most games lost without a win, career**
4—Ed Summers, Detroit AL, 1908 (2), 1909 (2)
Willie Sherdel, St. Louis NL, 1926 (2), 1928 (2)
Don Newcombe, Brooklyn NL, 1949 (2), 1955 (1), 1956 (1)
Charlie Leibrandt, Kansas City AL, 1985 (1); Atlanta NL, 1991 (2), 1992 (1)

**Most consecutive games lost, career**
5—Joe Bush, Philadelphia AL, 1914 (1), Boston AL, 1918 (1), New York AL, 1922 (2), 1923 (1)

**Most games lost, series**
4-game series—2—many pitchers
5-game series—2—many pitchers
6-game series—3—George Frazier, New York AL, 1981
7-game series—2—many pitchers
8-game series—3—Lefty Williams, Chicago AL, 1919

## RUNS, EARNED RUNS AND ERA

**Most runs allowed, career**
51—Whitey Ford, New York AL, 1950, 1953, 1955-1958, 1960-1964; 11 series; 22 G

**Most runs allowed, series**
4-game series—11—Grover Alexander, St. Louis NL, 1928
Bob Lemon, Cleveland AL, 1954
5-game series—16—Mordecai Brown, Chicago NL, 1910
6-game series—10—Slim Sallee, New York NL, 1917
Red Ruffing, New York AL, 1936
Don Gullett, New York AL, 1977
Don Sutton, Los Angeles NL, 1978
Jack Morris, Toronto AL, 1992
7-game series—17—Lew Burdette, Milwaukee NL, 1958
8-game series—19—Deacon Phillippe, Pittsburgh NL, 1903

**Most runs allowed, game**
10—Bill Kennedy, Pittsburgh NL, Oct 7, 1903

**Most runs allowed, inning**
7—Hooks Wiltse, New York NL, Oct 26, 1911, 7th
Carl Hubbell, New York NL, Oct 6, 1937, 6th

**Most earned runs allowed, career**
44—Whitey Ford, New York AL, 1950, 1953, 1955-1958, 1960-1964; 11 series; 22 G

**Most earned runs allowed, game**
8—Grover Alexander, St. Louis NL, Oct 5, 1928
Jay Witasick, New York AL, Nov 3, 2001

**Most earned runs allowed, inning**
6—Hooks Wiltse, New York NL, Oct 26, 1911, 7th
Danny Cox, St. Louis NL, Oct 18, 1987, 4th
Jay Witasick, New York AL, Nov 3, 2001, 3rd

**Lowest earned-run average, career (30 or more IP)**
0.83—Harry Breechen, St. Louis NL, 1943, 1944, 1946; 3 series; 3 G (32.2 IP)

**Lowest earned-run average, series (14 or more IP)**
0.00—Christy Mathewson, New York NL, 1905 (27 IP)
Waite Hoyt, New York AL, 1921 (27 IP)
Carl Hubbell, New York NL, 1933 (20 IP)
Whitey Ford, New York AL, 1960 (18 IP)
Joe McGinnity, New York NL, 1905 (17 IP)
Duster Mails, Cleveland AL, 1920 (15.2 IP)
Rube Benton, New York NL, 1917 (14 IP)
Whitey Ford, New York AL, 1961 (14 IP)

## SHUTOUTS AND SCORELESS INNINGS

**Most shutouts won, career**
4—Christy Mathewson, New York NL, 1905 (3), 1913 (1)

**For a complete list of shutouts, see page 396.**

**Most shutouts won, series**
3—Christy Mathewson, New York NL, Oct 9, 12, 14, 1905 (consec)

**Most 1-0 shutouts won, career**
2—Art Nehf, New York NL, Oct 13, 1921, Oct 12, 1923

**Most shutouts lost, career**
3—Eddie Plank, Philadelphia AL, 1905 (2), 1914 (1)

**Most 1-0 shutouts lost, career**
2—Eddie Plank, Philadelphia AL, Oct 13, 1905, Oct 10, 1914

**Youngest pitcher to win a complete game shutout**
20 years, 11 months, 21 days—Jim Palmer, Baltimore AL, vs Los Angeles, Oct 6, 1966 (won 6-0)

**Oldest pitcher to win a complete game shutout**
38 years, 1 month, 18 days—Randy Johnson, Arizona NL, vs New York AL, Oct 28, 2001 (won 4-0)

**Most consecutive scoreless innings, career**
33—Whitey Ford, New York AL, Oct 8, 1960 (9); Oct 12, 1960 (9); Oct 4, 1961 (9); Oct 8, 1961 (5); Oct 4, 1962 (1)

**Most consecutive scoreless innings, series**
27—Christy Mathewson, New York NL, Oct 9, 12, 14, 1905

**Retiring side on three pitched balls**
Christy Mathewson, New York NL, Oct 9, 1912, 11th
Christy Mathewson, New York NL, Oct 16, 1912, 5th
Rube Walberg, Philadelphia AL, Oct 14, 1929, 7th
Tiny Bonham, New York AL, Oct 6, 1941, 7th

## HITS

**Most hits allowed, career**
132—Whitey Ford, New York AL, 1950, 1953, 1955-1958, 1960-1964; 11 series, 22 G

**Most consecutive hitless innings, career**
11—Don Larsen, New York AL, Oct 8, 1956 (9), Oct 5, 1957 (2)

**Most consecutive hitless innings with no one reaching first base, career**
11—Don Larsen, New York AL, Oct 8, 1956 (9), Oct 5, 1957 (2)

**Most hits allowed, series**
4-game series—17—Red Ruffing, New York AL, 1938
5-game series—23—Jack Coombs, Philadelphia AL, 1910
Mordecai Brown, Chicago NL, 1910
6-game series—25—Christy Mathewson, New York NL, 1911
7-game series—30—Walter Johnson, Washington AL, 1924
8-game series—38—Deacon Phillippe, Pittsburgh NL, 1903

**Most consecutive hitless innings with no one reaching first base, series**
9—Don Larsen, New York AL, Oct 8, 1956

**Most hits allowed, game**
15—Walter Johnson, Washington AL, Oct 15, 1925

**Most consecutive hitless innings, game**
9—Don Larsen, New York AL, Oct 8, 1956

**Most consecutive hitless innings with no one reaching first base, game**
9—Don Larsen, New York AL, Oct 8, 1956 (perfect game)

**Fewest hits allowed, game**
0—Don Larsen, New York AL, Oct 8, 1956 (perfect game)

**One and two-hit games (9-inn complete games)**
1 hit—Ed Reulbach, Chicago NL, Oct 10, 1906 (hit came with 0 out in 7th)
Claude Passeau, Chicago NL, Oct 5, 1945 (hit came with 2 out in 2nd)
Bill Bevens, New York AL, Oct 3, 1947 (hit came with 2 out in 9th)
Jim Lonborg, Boston AL, Oct 5, 1967 (hit came with 2 out in 8th)
2 hits—Ed Walsh, Chicago AL, Oct 11, 1906
Mordecai Brown, Chicago NL, Oct 12, 1906
Eddie Plank, Philadelphia AL, Oct 11, 1913
Bill James, Boston NL, Oct 10, 1914
Waite Hoyt, New York AL, Oct 6, 1921
Burleigh Grimes, St. Louis NL, Oct 5, 1931
George Earnshaw, Philadelphia AL, Oct 6, 1931
Monte Pearson, New York AL, Oct 5, 1939
Mort Cooper, St. Louis NL, Oct 4, 1944
Bob Feller, Cleveland AL, Oct 6, 1948
Allie Reynolds, New York AL, Oct 5, 1949
Vic Raschi, New York AL, Oct 4, 1950
Warren Spahn, Milwaukee NL, Oct 5, 1958
Whitey Ford, New York AL, Oct 4, 1961
Nelson Briles, Pittsburgh NL, Oct 14, 1971
Greg Maddux, Atlanta NL, Oct 21, 1995

**Fewest hits allowed, two consecutive complete games**
4—Jim Lonborg, Boston AL, Oct 5 (1), Oct 9 (3), 1967

**Fewest hits allowed, three consecutive complete games**
14—Christy Mathewson, New York NL, Oct 5 (4), Oct 12 (4), Oct 14 (6), 1905
Bob Gibson, St. Louis NL, Oct 4 (6), Oct 8 (5), Oct 12 (3), 1967

**Most hits allowed, inning**
8—Jay Witasick, New York AL, November 3, 2001, 3rd

**Most consecutive hits allowed, inning (consecutive plate appearances)**
6—Ed Summers, Detroit AL, Oct 10, 1908, 9th (6 singles)

## DOUBLES, TRIPLES AND HOME RUNS

**Most doubles allowed, game**
8—Walter Johnson, Washington AL, Oct 15, 1925

**Most triples allowed, game**
5—Deacon Phillippe, Pittsburgh NL, Oct 10, 1903

**Most home runs allowed, career**
9—Catfish Hunter, Oakland AL, 1972-1974; New York AL, 1976-1978; 6 series, 12 G

**Most home runs allowed, series**
4-game series—4—Willie Sherdel, St. Louis NL, 1928
Charlie Root, Chicago NL, 1932
Junior Thompson, Cincinnati NL, 1939
Scott Garrelts, San Francisco NL, 1989
5-game series—4—Gary Nolan, Cincinnati NL, 1970
Charles Hudson, Philadelphia NL, 1983
6-game series—4—Allie Reynolds, New York AL, 1953
7-game series—5—Lew Burdette, Milwaukee NL, 1958
Dick Hughes, St. Louis NL, 1967
8-game series—2—Babe Adams, Pittsburgh NL, 1909
Harry Harper, New York AL, 1921

**Most home runs allowed, game**
4—Charlie Root, Chicago NL, Oct 1, 1932
Junior Thompson, Cincinnati NL, Oct 7, 1939
Dick Hughes, St. Louis NL, Oct 11, 1967

**Most home runs allowed, inning**
3—Dick Hughes, St. Louis NL, Oct 11, 1967, 4th

**Most consecutive home runs allowed, inning (13 times)**
2—Emil Yde, Pittsburgh NL, Oct 11, 1925, 3rd
Bill Sherdel, St. Louis NL, Oct 9, 1928, 7th
Charlie Root, Chicago NL, Oct 1, 1932, 5th
Curt Simmons, St. Louis NL, Oct 14, 1964, 6th
Don Drysdale, Los Angeles NL, Oct 5, 1966, 1st
Dick Hughes, St. Louis NL, Oct 11, 1967, 4th
Rick Wise, Boston AL, Oct 14, 1975, 5th
Don Sutton, Los Angeles NL, Oct 16, 1977, 8th.
Ron Guidry, New York AL, Oct 25, 1981, 7th
Ron Darling, New York NL, Oct 27, 1986, 2nd
Orel Hershiser, Cleveland AL, Oct 18, 1997, 4th
David Wells, New York AL, Oct 17, 1998, 5th
Kevin Appier, Anaheim AL, Oct 20, 2002, 2nd

## TOTAL BASES

**Most total bases allowed, career**
184—Whitey Ford, New York AL, 1950, 1953, 1955-1958, 1960-1964; 11 series, 22 G

**Most total bases allowed, series**
4-game series—30—Bill Sherdel, St. Louis NL, 1928
5-game series—33—Jack Coombs, Philadelphia AL, 1910
6-game series—37—Christy Mathewson, New York NL, 1911
7-game series—46—Walter Johnson, Washington AL, 1924
8-game series—58—Deacon Phillippe, Pittsburgh NL, 1903

**Most total bases allowed, game**
25—Walter Johnson, Washington AL, Oct 15, 1925

## BASES ON BALLS

**Most bases on balls, career**
34—Whitey Ford, New York AL, 1950, 1953, 1955-1958, 1960-1964; 11 series, 22 G

**Most innings pitched without allowing a base on balls, series**
26—Carl Mays, New York AL, 1921

**Most bases on balls, series**
4-game series—8—Bob Lemon, Cleveland AL, 1954
5-game series—14—Jack Coombs, Philadelphia AL, 1910
6-game series—11—Lefty Tyler, Chicago NL, 1918
Lefty Gomez, New York AL, 1936
Allie Reynolds, New York AL, 1951
7-game series—11—Walter Johnson, Washington AL, 1924
Bill Bevens, New York AL, 1947
8-game series—13—Art Nehf, New York NL, 1921

**Most bases on balls, game**
10—Bill Bevens, New York AL, Oct 3, 1947

**Longest game without allowing base on balls**
12 innings—Schoolboy Rowe, Detroit AL, Oct 4, 1934

**Most bases on balls, inning**
4—Bill Donovan, Detroit AL, Oct 16, 1909, 2nd
Art Reinhart, St. Louis NL, Oct 6, 1926, 5th (1 BB with bases full)
Guy Bush, Chicago NL, September 28, 1932, 6th
Don Gullett, Cincinnati NL, Oct 22, 1975, 3rd (2 BB with bases full)
Tom Glavine, Atlanta NL, Oct 24, 1991, 6th (2 BB with bases full)
Todd Stottlemyre, Toronto AL, Oct 20, 1993, 1st (1 BB with bases full)
Al Leiter, Florida NL, Oct 21, 1997, 4th (1 BB with bases full)
Tim Wakefield, Boston AL, Oct 23, 2004, 4th

**Most consecutive bases on balls, inning**
3—Bob Shawkey, New York AL, Oct 7, 1921, 4th (2 BB with bases full)
Art Reinhart, St. Louis NL, Oct 6, 1926, 5th (1 BB with bases full)
Guy Bush, Chicago NL, September 28, 1932, 6th
Joe Hoerner, St. Louis NL, Oct 3, 1968, 9th (2 BB with bases full)
Tom Glavine, Atlanta NL, Oct 24, 1991, 6th (2 BB with bases full)
Todd Stottlemyre, Toronto AL, Oct 20, 1993, 1st (1 BB with bases full)
Charles Nagy, Cleveland AL, Oct 21, 1997, 3rd (1 BB with bases full)
Jarrod Washburn, Anaheim AL, Oct 24, 2002, 1st (1 BB with bases full)
Tim Wakefield, Boston AL, Oct 23, 2004, 4th

## STRIKEOUTS

**Most strikeouts, career**
94—Whitey Ford, New York AL, 1950, 1953, 1955-1958, 1960-1964; 11 series, 22 G

**Most strikeouts, series**
4-game series—23—Sandy Koufax, Los Angeles NL, 1963
5-game series—18—Christy Mathewson, New York NL, 1905
6-game series—20—Chief Bender, Philadelphia AL, 1911
7-game series—35—Bob Gibson, St. Louis NL, 1968
8-game series—28—Bill Dinneen, Boston AL, 1903

**Most strikeouts, game**
17—Bob Gibson, St. Louis NL, Oct 2, 1968

**For a complete list of pitchers with 10 or more strikeouts in a game, see page 401.**

**Most games with 10 or more strikeouts, career**
5—Bob Gibson, St. Louis NL, 1964 (1), 1967 (2), 1968 (2)

**Most strikeouts by losing pitcher, game**
12—Orlando Hernandez, New York AL, Oct 24, 2000, 7.1 IP
[12—Walter Johnson, Washington AL, Oct 4, 1924, 12 IP]

**Most strikeouts by relief pitcher, game**
11—Moe Drabowsky, Baltimore AL, Oct 5, 1966, 6.2 IP

**Most consecutive strikeouts, game**
6—Hod Eller, Cincinnati NL, Oct 6, 1919 (3 in 2nd, 3 in 3rd)
Moe Drabowsky, Baltimore AL, Oct 5, 1966 (3 in 4th, 3 in 5th)
Todd Worrell, St. Louis NL, Oct 24, 1985 (3 in 6th, 3 in 7th)

**Most consecutive strikeouts from start of game**
5—Mort Cooper, St. Louis NL, Oct 11, 1943
Sandy Koufax, Los Angeles NL, Oct 23, 1963

**Most innings with one or more strikeouts, game**
9—Ed Walsh, Chicago AL, Oct 11, 1906 (12 K)
Bob Gibson, St. Louis NL, Oct 2, 1968 (17 K)

**Most strikeouts, inning**
4—Orval Overall, Chicago NL, Oct 14, 1908, 1st

## HIT BATTERS, WILD PITCHES AND BALKS

**Most hit batters, career**
4—Bill Donovan, Detroit AL, 1907 (3), 1909
Eddie Plank, Philadelphia AL, 1905, 1911, 1913, 1914

**Most hit batters, series**
3—Bill Donovan, Detroit AL, 1907 (5-game series)
Bruce Kison, Pittsburgh NL, 1971 (7-game series)
Jose Contreras, Chicago AL, 2005 (4-game series)

**Most hit batters, game**
3—Bruce Kison, Pittsburgh NL, Oct 13, 1971 (6.1 IP)
Jose Contreras, Chicago AL, Oct 22, 2005 (7.0 IP)

**Most hit batters, inning**
2—Ed Willett, Detroit AL, Oct 11, 1909, 2nd (consec)

Wayne Granger, St. Louis NL, Oct 9, 1968, 8th
Jose Contreras, Chicago AL, Oct 22, 2005, 7th

**Most wild pitches, career**
5—Hal Schumacher, New York NL, 1933 (2), 1936 (2), 1937
Jack Morris, Detroit AL, 1984 (2); Minnesota AL, 1991 (2); Toronto AL, 1992

**Most wild pitches, series**
3—Jeff Tesreau, New York NL, 1912
John Stuper, St. Louis NL, 1982

**Most wild pitches, game**
2—Jeff Tesreau, New York NL, Oct 15, 1912
Jeff Pfeffer, Brooklyn NL, Oct 12, 1916
Bob Shawkey, New York AL, Oct 5, 1922
Vic Aldridge, Pittsburgh NL, Oct 15, 1925
Johnny Miljus, Pittsburgh NL, Oct 8, 1927
Tex Carleton, Chicago NL, Oct 9, 1938
Jim Bouton, New York AL, Oct 5, 1963
John Stuper, St. Louis NL, Oct 13, 1982
George Medich, Milwaukee AL, Oct 19, 1982
Jack Morris, Detroit AL, Oct 13, 1984
Ron Darling, New York NL, Oct 18, 1986
Mike Moore, Oakland AL, Oct 15, 1989
John Smoltz, Atlanta NL, Oct 18, 1992
Glendon Rusch, New York NL, Oct 21, 2000

**Most wild pitches, inning**
2—Bob Shawkey, New York AL, Oct 5, 1922, 5th
Vic Aldridge, Pittsburgh NL, Oct 15, 1925, 1st
Johnny Miljus, Pittsburgh NL, Oct 8, 1927, 9th
Tex Carleton, Chicago NL, Oct 9, 1938, 8th
Doc Medich, Milwaukee AL, Oct 19, 1982, 6th

**Most balks, career**
2—Dave Stewart, Oakland, 1988; Toronto, 1993

**Most balks, series, game or inning**
1—many pitchers

# CLUB PITCHING

## APPEARANCES

**Most appearances by pitchers, series**
4-game series—20—Chicago AL vs Houston NL, 2005
5-game series—21—New York NL vs New York AL, 2000
6-game series—27—New York AL vs Atlanta NL, 1996
7-game series—33—Cleveland AL vs Florida NL, 1997
San Francisco NL vs Anaheim AL, 2002
8-game series—14—Boston AL vs New York NL, 1912

**Most appearances by pitchers from both clubs, series**
4-game series—39—Chicago AL 20, Houston NL 19, 2005
5-game series—38—New York NL 21, New York AL 17, 2000
6-game series—48—New York AL 27, Atlanta NL 21, 1996
7-game series—60—Cleveland AL 33, Florida NL 27, 1997
San Francisco NL 33, Anaheim AL 27, 2002
8-game series—25—Chicago AL 13, Cincinnati NL 12, 1919

## COMPLETE GAMES

**Most complete games, series**
4-game series
4—New York AL vs St. Louis NL, 1928
5-game series
5—Philadelphia AL vs New York NL, 1905
Philadelphia AL vs Chicago NL, 1910
Philadelphia AL vs New York NL, 1913
Boston AL vs Philadelphia NL, 1915
6-game series
5—Philadelphia AL vs New York NL, 1911
Boston AL vs Chicago NL, 1918
Detroit AL vs Chicago NL, 1935
7-game series
5—New York AL vs Brooklyn NL, 1956
8-game series
7—Boston AL vs Pittsburgh NL, 1903

**Most complete games from both clubs, series**
4-game series
5—Boston NL 3, Philadelphia AL 2, 1914
5-game series
9—Philadelphia AL 5, New York NL 4, 1905
Boston AL 5, Philadelphia NL 4, 1915
6-game series
9—Boston AL 5, Chicago NL 4, 1918
7-game series
8—Pittsburgh NL 4, Detroit AL 4, 1909
Pittsburgh NL 4, Washington AL 4, 1925
St. Louis NL 4, Detroit AL 4, 1934
Cincinnati NL 4, Detroit AL 4, 1940
New York AL 5, Brooklyn 3, 1956
8-game series
13—Boston AL 7 vs Pittsburgh NL 6, 1903

**Fewest complete games, series**
0—many clubs

**Fewest complete games by both clubs, series**
0—many times; last—Chicago AL 0, Houston NL 0, 2005 (4-game series)

## SAVES (SINCE 1969)

**Most saves, series**
4-game series—3—New York AL vs San Diego NL, 1998
Chicago AL vs Houston NL, 2005
5-game series—3—Oakland AL vs Los Angeles NL, 1974
6-game series—4—New York AL vs Atlanta NL, 1996
7-game series—4—Oakland AL vs New York NL, 1973

**Most saves by both clubs, series**
4-game series—3—New York AL 3, San Diego NL 0, 1998
Chicago AL 3, Houston NL 0, 2005
5-game series—4—Oakland AL 3, Los Angeles NL 1, 1974
6-game series—4—Philadelphia NL 3, Kansas City AL 1, 1980
Toronto AL 3, Atlanta NL 1, 1992
Atlanta NL 3, Cleveland AL 1, 1995
New York AL 4, Atlanta NL 0, 1996
7-game series—7—Oakland AL 4, New York NL 3, 1973

**Fewest saves, series**
0—many clubs

**Fewest saves by both clubs, series**
0—New York AL 0, Los Angeles NL 0, 1977 (6-game series)

## RUNS AND SHUTOUTS

**Most runs allowed, total series**
769—New York AL; 39 series, 219 G

**Most shutouts won, total series**
17—New York AL

For a complete list of shutouts, see page 396.

**Most shutouts won, series**
4—New York NL vs Philadelphia AL, 1905

**Most consecutive shutouts won, series**
3—New York NL vs Philadelphia AL, Oct 12, 13, 14, 1905
Baltimore AL, vs Los Angeles NL, Oct 6, 8, 9, 1966

**Most shutouts by both clubs, series**
5—New York NL 4, Philadelphia AL 1, 1905

**Fewest shutouts, series**
0—many clubs

**Fewest shutouts by both clubs, series**
0—many series

**Longest shutout**
10 innings—New York NL 3, Philadelphia AL 0, Oct 8, 1913
Brooklyn NL 1, New York AL 0, Oct 9, 1956
Minnesota AL 1, Atlanta NL 0, Oct 27, 1991

**Largest score, shutout**
12-0—New York AL 12, Pittsburgh NL 0, Oct 12, 1960

**Most consecutive innings shut out opponents, total series**
39—Baltimore AL, Oct 5, 1966 (4th)-Oct 11, 1969 (6th)

**Most consecutive innings shut out opponent, series**
33—Baltimore AL vs Los Angeles NL, Oct 5 (6), 6 (9), 8 (9), 9 (9), 1966

## 1-0 GAMES

**Most 1-0 games won, total series**
4—New York AL; 39 series, 219 G

**Most 1-0 games won, series**
2—Baltimore AL vs Los Angeles NL, 1966

**Most 1-0 games won by both clubs, series**
2—New York AL 1, Brooklyn NL 1, 1949
Baltimore AL 2, Los Angeles NL 0, 1966

## WILD PITCHES AND BALKS

**Most wild pitches, series**
5—Pittsburgh NL vs New York AL, 1960

**Most wild pitches by both clubs, series**
8—New York AL 4, Brooklyn NL 4, 1947

**Fewest wild pitches by both clubs, series**
0—many series

**Most balks, series**
2—Cleveland AL vs Boston NL, 1948
Minnesota AL vs St. Louis NL, 1987

**Most balks by both clubs, series**
2—Cleveland AL 2, Boston NL 0, 1948
Minnesota AL 2, St. Louis NL 0, 1987
Los Angeles NL 1, Oakland AL 1, 1988

**Fewest balks by both clubs, series**
0—many series

# INDIVIDUAL FIELDING

## FIRST BASEMEN

### GAMES

**Most games, career**
38—Gil Hodges, Brooklyn NL, 1949, 1952, 1953, 1955, 1956; Los Angeles NL, 1959; 6 series

### PUTOUTS, ASSISTS AND CHANCES

**Most putouts, career**
326—Gil Hodges, Brooklyn NL, 1949, 1952, 1953, 1955, 1956; Los Angeles NL, 1959; 6 series, 38 G

**Most putouts, series**
4-game series—52—Butch Schmidt, Boston NL, 1914
5-game series—69—Dick Hoblitzel, Boston AL, 1916
6-game series—79—Jiggs Donahue, Chicago AL, 1906
7-game series—79—Jim Bottomley, St. Louis NL, 1926
8-game series—92—Wally Pipp, New York AL, 1921

**Most putouts, game**
19—George Kelly, New York NL, Oct 15, 1923
Fred McGriff, Atlanta NL, Oct 21, 1995

**Most putouts, inning**
3—many first basemen

**Most assists, career**
29—Bill Skowron, New York AL, 1955-1958, 1960-1962; Los Angeles NL, 1963; 8 series, 37 G

**Most assists, series**
4-game series—6—Vic Wertz, Cleveland AL, 1954
Joe Pepitone, New York AL, 1963
5-game series—5—Claude Rossman, Detroit AL, 1908
Dolph Camilli, Brooklyn NL, 1941
Ray Sanders, St. Louis NL, 1943
Bill Skowron, New York AL, 1961
6-game series—9—Fred Merkle, Chicago NL, 1918
7-game series—10—Cecil Cooper, Milwaukee AL, 1982
8-game series—7—George Kelly, New York NL, 1921

**Most assists, game**
4—Marv Owen, Detroit AL, Oct 6, 1935
Don Mincher, Minnesota AL, Oct 7, 1965

**Most assists, inning**
2—many first basemen

**Most chances accepted, career**
350—Gil Hodges, Brooklyn NL, 1949, 1952, 1953, 1955, 1956; Los Angeles NL, 1959; 6 series, 38 G

**Most chances accepted, series**
4-game series—55—Butch Schmidt, Boston NL, 1914
5-game series—73—Dick Hoblitzel, Boston AL, 1916
6-game series—87—Jiggs Donahue, Chicago AL, 1906
7-game series—81—Cecil Cooper, Milwaukee AL, 1982
8-game series—93—George Kelly, New York NL, 1921
Wally Pipp, New York AL, 1921

**Most chances accepted, game**
20—Fred McGriff, Atlanta NL, Oct 21, 1995 (19 PO, 1 A)

**Fewest chances offered, game**
2—Wally Pipp, New York AL, Oct 11, 1921 (2 PO)
Orlando Cepeda, St. Louis NL, Oct 2, 1968 (1 PO, 1 A)

**Most chances accepted, inning**
3—many first basemen

### ERRORS AND DOUBLE PLAYS

**Most errors, career**
8—Fred Merkle, New York NL, 1911-1913 (7); Brooklyn NL, 1916 (1), Chicago NL, 1918 (0); 5 series, 25 G

**Most consecutive errorless games, career**
32—Bill Skowron, New York AL, Los Angeles NL, Oct 10, 1956-Oct 6, 1963

**Most errors, series**
4-game series—2—Mark McGwire, Oakland AL, 1990
Brian R. Hunter, Atlanta NL, 1999
5-game series—3—Frank Chance, Chicago NL, 1908
Harry Davis, Philadelphia AL, 1910
6-game series—3—Hank Greenberg, Detroit AL, 1935
7-game series—5—Bill Abstein, Pittsburgh NL, 1909
8-game series—3—Fred Merkle, New York NL, 1912

**Most chances accepted, errorless series**
93—George Kelly, New York NL, 1921 (8-game series)

Wally Pipp, New York AL, 1921 (8-game series)

**Most errors, game**
2—many first basemen

**Most errors, inning**
2—Hank Greenberg, Detroit AL, Oct 3, 1935, 5th
Johnny McCarthy, New York NL, Oct 8, 1937, 5th
Frank Torre, Milwaukee NL, Oct 9, 1958, 2nd
Brian R. Hunter, Atlanta NL, Oct 23, 1999, 8th

**Most double plays, career**
31—Gil Hodges, Brooklyn NL, 1949, 1952, 1953, 1955, 1956; Los Angeles NL, 1959; 6 series, 38 G

**Most double plays, series**
11—Gil Hodges, Brooklyn NL, 1955 (7-game series)

**Most double plays started, series**
3—Gil Hodges, Brooklyn NL, 1955 (7-game series)

**Most double plays, game**
4—Stuffy McInnis, Philadelphia AL, Oct 9, 1914
Joe Collins, New York AL, Oct 8, 1951
Gene Tenace, Oakland AL, Oct 17, 1973
Pete Rose, Philadelphia NL, Oct 15, 1980

**Most double plays started, game**
2—Eddie Murray, Baltimore AL, Oct 11, 1979

**Most unassisted double plays, game**
1—many first basemen

## SECOND BASEMEN

### GAMES

**Most games, career**
42—Frankie Frisch, New York NL (18), 1922-1924; St. Louis NL (24), 1928, 1930, 1931, 1934; 7 series

### PUTOUTS, ASSISTS AND CHANCES

**Most putouts, career**
104—Frankie Frisch, New York NL, St. Louis NL, 1922-1924, 1928, 1930, 1931, 1934; 7 series, 42 G

**Most putouts, series**
4-game series—14—Willie Randolph, Oakland AL, 1990
5-game series—20—Joe Gordon, New York AL, 1943
6-game series—26—Dave Lopes, Los Angeles NL, 1981
7-game series—26—Bucky Harris, Washington AL, 1924
8-game series—22—Morrie Rath, Cincinnati NL, 1919

**Most putouts, game**
8—Bucky Harris, Washington AL, Oct 8, 1924
Dave Lopes, Los Angeles NL, Oct 16, 1974
[9—Hughie Critz, New York NL, Oct 6, 1933, 11 inn]

**Most putouts, inning**
3—Larry Doyle, New York NL, Oct 9, 1913, 7th
Bill Wambsganss, Cleveland AL, Oct 10, 1920, 5th
Johnny Rawlings, New York NL, Oct 11, 1921, 9th
Dave Lopes, Los Angeles NL, Oct 16, 1974, 6th
Dave Lopes, Los Angeles NL, Oct 21, 1981, 4th

**Most assists, career**
135—Frankie Frisch, New York NL, St. Louis NL, 1922-1924, 1928, 1930, 1931, 1934; 7 series, 42 G

**Most assists, series**
4-game series—18—Tony Lazzeri, New York AL, 1927
5-game series—23—Joe Gordon, New York AL, 1943
6-game series—27—Aaron Ward, New York AL, 1923
7-game series—33—Jim Gantner, Milwaukee AL, 1982
8-game series—34—Aaron Ward, New York AL, 1921

**Most assists, game**
8—Claude Ritchey, Pittsburgh, NL, Oct 10, 1903
Germany Schaefer, Detroit AL, Oct 12, 1907
Hal Janvrin, Boston AL, Oct 7, 1916
Eddie Collins, Chicago AL, Oct 15, 1917
Bucky Harris, Washington AL, Oct 7, 1924
Joe Gordon, New York AL, Oct 5, 1943
Bobby Doerr, Boston AL, Oct 9, 1946
Mark Lemke, Atlanta NL, Oct 21, 1995

**Most assists, inning**
3—Eddie Collins, Philadelphia AL, Oct 12, 1914, 4th
Pete Kilduff, Brooklyn NL, Oct 10, 1920, 3rd
Aaron Ward, New York AL, Oct 12, 1921, 6th
Joe Gordon, New York AL, Oct 11, 1943, 8th
Jackie Robinson, Brooklyn NL, Oct 8, 1949, 7th
Phil Garner, Pittsburgh NL, Oct 13, 1979, 9th
Marty Barrett, Boston AL, Oct 23, 1986; 1st

**Most chances accepted, career**
239—Frankie Frisch, New York NL, St. Louis NL, 1922-1924, 1928, 1930, 1931, 1934; 7 series, 42 G

**Most chances accepted, series**
4-game series—28—Tony Lazzeri, New York AL, 1927
5-game series—43—Joe Gordon, New York AL, 1943
6-game series—40—Dave Lopes, Los Angeles NL, 1981
7-game series—54—Bucky Harris, Washington AL, 1924
8-game series—52—Eddie Collins, Chicago AL, 1919
Aaron Ward, New York AL, 1921

**Most chances accepted, game**
13—Claude Ritchey, Pittsburgh NL, Oct 10, 1903 (5 PO, 8 A)
Bucky Harris, Washington AL, Oct 11, 1925 (6 PO, 7 A)
Dave Lopes, Los Angeles NL, Oct 16, 1974 (8 PO, 5 A)
[14—Hughie Critz, New York NL, Oct 6, 1933 (9 PO, 5 A), 11 inn]

**Fewest chances offered, game**
0—Charlie Pick, Chicago NL, Sept 7, 1918
Max Bishop, Philadelphia AL, Oct 6, 1931
Jerry Coleman, New York AL, Oct 8, 1949
Willie Randolph, New York AL, Oct 25, 1981
Frank White, Kansas City AL, Oct 20, 1985
Mariano Duncan, Cincinnati NL, Oct 19, 1990

**Most chances accepted, inning**
3—many second basemen

### ERRORS AND DOUBLE PLAYS

**Most errors, career**
8—Larry Doyle, New York NL, 1911-1913; 3 series, 19 G
Eddie Collins, Philadelphia AL, 1910, 1911, 1913, 1914, Chicago AL, 1917, 1919; 6 series, 34 G

**Most consecutive errorless games, career**
23—Billy Martin, New York AL, Oct 5, 1952-Oct 10, 1956

**Most errors, series**
4-game series—2—Tony Lazzeri, New York AL, 1928
Joe Gordon, New York AL, 1938
Billy Herman, Chicago NL, 1938
Joe Morgan, Cincinnati NL, 1976
5-game series—4—Danny Murphy, Philadelphia AL, 1905
6-game series—6—Dave Lopes, Los Angeles NL, 1981
7-game series—5—Jim Gantner, Milwaukee AL, 1982
8-game series—4—Larry Doyle, New York NL, 1912

**Most chances accepted, errorless series**
49—Bobby Doerr, Boston AL, 1946 (7-game series)

**Most errors, game**
3—Danny Murphy, Philadelphia AL, Oct 12, 1905
Buddy Myer, Washington AL, Oct 3, 1933
Dave Lopes, Los Angeles NL, Oct 25, 1981

**Most errors, inning**
2—Danny Murphy, Philadelphia AL, Oct 12, 1905, 5th
Mike Andrews, Oakland AL, Oct 14, 1973, 12th
Dave Lopes, Los Angeles NL, Oct 25, 1981, 4th

**Most double plays, career**
24—Frankie Frisch, New York NL, St. Louis NL, 1922-1924, 1928, 1930, 1931, 1934; 7 series, 42 G

**Most double plays, series**
9—Phil Garner, Pittsburgh NL, 1979 (7-game series)

**Most double plays started, series**
5—Billy Herman, Chicago NL, 1932 (4-game series)
Tom Herr, St. Louis NL, 1985 (7-game series)

**Most double plays, game**
3—many second basemen

**Most double plays started, game**
3—Dick Green, Oakland AL, Oct 15, 1974

**Most unassisted double plays, game**
1—Hobe Ferris, Boston AL, Oct 2, 1903
Larry Doyle, New York NL, Oct 9, 1913
Buck Herzog, New York NL, Oct 7, 1917
Frank White, Kansas City AL, Oct 17, 1980
[1—Mark Lemke, Atlanta NL, Oct 27, 1991, 10 inn]

**Unassisted triple play**
1—Bill Wambsganss, Cleveland AL, Oct 10, 1920

## THIRD BASEMEN

### GAMES

**Most games, career**
31—Gil McDougald, New York AL, 1951-1953, 1955, 1960; 5 series

### PUTOUTS, ASSISTS AND CHANCES

**Most putouts, career**
37—Home Run Baker, Philadelphia AL, New York AL, 1910, 1911, 1913, 1914, 1921; 5 series, 22 G

**Most putouts, series**
4-game series—10—Home Run Baker, Philadelphia AL, 1914
5-game series—10—Harry Steinfeldt, Chicago NL, 1907
6-game series—14—Red Rolfe, New York AL, 1936
7-game series—13—Whitey Kurowski, St. Louis NL, 1946
8-game series—13—Frankie Frisch, New York NL, 1921

**Most putouts, game**
4—Art Devlin, New York NL, Oct 13, 1905
Bill Coughlin, Detroit AL, Oct 10, 1907
Bobby Byrne, Pittsburgh NL, Oct 9, 1909
Tommy Leach, Pittsburgh NL, Oct 16, 1909
Home Run Baker, Philadelphia AL, Oct 24, 1911
Heinie Zimmerman, New York NL, Oct 7, 1917
Jimmie Dykes, Philadelphia AL, Oct 2, 1930
Bob Elliott, Boston NL, Oct 11, 1948
Willie Jones, Philadelphia NL Oct 4, 1950
Bill Mueller, Boston AL, Oct 24, 2004

**Most putouts, inning**
2—many third basemen

**Most assists, career**
68—Graig Nettles, New York AL, 1976-1978, 1981; San Diego NL, 1984; 5 series, 24 G

**Most assists, series**
4-game series—15—Home Run Baker, Philadelphia AL, 1914
5-game series—18—Larry Gardner, Boston AL, 1916
6-game series—20—Graig Nettles, New York AL, 1977
7-game series—30—Pinky Higgins, Detroit AL, 1940
8-game series—24—Frankie Frisch, New York NL, 1921

**Most assists, game**
9—Pinky Higgins, Detroit AL, Oct 5, 1940

**Most assists, inning**
3—Jose Pagan, Pittsburgh NL, Oct 14, 1971, 9th
Sal Bando, Oakland AL, Oct 16, 1974, 6th
Wade Boggs, Boston AL, Oct 19, 1986, 3rd
Terry Pendleton, Atlanta NL, Oct 27, 1991, 7th

**Most chances accepted, career**
96—Graig Nettles, New York AL, 1976-1978, 1981; San Diego NL, 1984; 5 series, 24 G

**Most chances accepted, series**
4-game series—25—Home Run Baker, Philadelphia AL, 1914
5-game series—25—Larry Gardner, Boston AL, 1916
6-game series—27—Bobby Thomson, New York NL, 1951
7-game series—34—Pinky Higgins, Detroit AL, 1940
8-game series—37—Frankie Frisch, New York NL, 1921

**Most chances accepted, game**
10—Pinky Higgins, Detroit AL, Oct 5, 1940 (1 PO, 9 A)
Chris Sabo, Cincinnati NL, Oct 19, 1990 (3 PO, 7 A)

**Fewest chances offered, game**
0—many third basemen

**Most chances accepted, inning**
4—Eddie Mathews, Milwaukee NL, Oct 5, 1957, 3rd

## ERRORS AND DOUBLE PLAYS

**Most errors, career**
8—Larry Gardner, Boston AL, 1912, 1915, 1916 (6); Cleveland AL, 1920 (2); 4 series, 25 G

**Most consecutive errorless games, career**
22—Ron Cey, Los Angeles NL, Oct 13, 1974-Oct 28, 1981

**Most errors, series**
4-game series—3—Bill Mueller, Boston AL, 2004
5-game series—4—Harry Steinfeldt, Chicago NL, 1910
6-game series—3—George Rohe, Chicago AL, 1906
Buck Herzog, New York NL, 1911
Travis Jackson, New York NL, 1936
Bob Elliott, Boston NL, 1948
Aaron Boone, New York AL, 2003
7-game series—4—Pepper Martin, St. Louis NL, 1934
Gil McDougald, New York AL, 1952
8-game series—4—Tommy Leach, Pittsburgh NL, 1903
Larry Gardner, Boston AL, 1912

**Most chances accepted, errorless series**
29—Denis Menke, Cincinnati NL, 1972 (7-game series)

**Most errors, game**
3—Pepper Martin, St. Louis NL, Oct 6, 1934
Bill Mueller, Boston AL, Oct 24, 2004

**Most errors, inning**
2—Harry Steinfeldt, Chicago NL, Oct 18, 1910, 3rd
Doug DeCinces, Baltimore AL, Oct 10, 1979, 6th

**Most double plays, career**
7—Graig Nettles, New York AL, 1976-1978, 1981; San Diego NL, 1984; 5 series, 24 G

**Most double plays, series**
4—Jim Davenport, San Francisco NL, 1962 (7-game series)
Bill Madlock, Pittsburgh NL, 1979 (7-game series)

**Most double plays started, series**
4—Jim Davenport, San Francisco NL, 1962 (7-game series)

**Most double plays, game**
2—many third basemen

**Most double plays started, game**
2—Fred McMullin, Chicago AL, Oct 13, 1917
Ossie Bluege, Washington AL, Oct 5, 1924
Whitey Kurowski, St. Louis NL, Oct 13, 1946
Clete Boyer, New York AL, Oct 12, 1960
Dalton Jones, Boston AL, Oct 4, 1967
Graig Nettles, New York AL, Oct 19, 1976
Bobby Bonilla, Florida NL, Oct 19, 1997
Bill Mueller, Boston AL, Oct 24, 2004

**Most unassisted double plays, game**
1—Bill Mueller, Boston AL, Oct 24, 2004

# SHORTSTOPS

## GAMES

**Most games, career**
52—Phil Rizzuto, New York AL, 1941, 1942, 1947, 1949-1953, 1955; 9 series

## PUTOUTS, ASSISTS AND CHANCES

**Most putouts, career**
107—Phil Rizzuto, New York AL, 1941, 1942, 1947, 1949, 1950-1953, 1955; 9 series, 52 G

**Most putouts, series**
4-game series—16—Frank Crosetti, New York AL, 1938
5-game series—15—Joe Tinker, Chicago NL, 1907
Phil Rizzuto, New York AL, 1942
6-game series—16—Billy Jurges, Chicago NL, 1935
7-game series—22—Ozzie Smith, St. Louis NL, 1982
8-game series—24—Heinie Wagner, Boston AL, 1912

**Most putouts, game**
7—Buck Weaver, Chicago AL, Oct 7, 1917
Phil Rizzuto, New York AL, Oct 5, 1942

**Most putouts, inning**
3—Mickey Stanley, Detroit AL, Oct 10, 1968, 6th

**Most assists, career**
143—Phil Rizzuto, New York AL, 1941, 1942, 1947, 1949, 1950-1953, 1955; 9 series, 52 G

**Most assists, series**
4-game series—21—Jack Barry, Philadelphia AL, 1914
5-game series—25—Everett Scott, Boston AL, 1916
6-game series—26—Bill Russell, Los Angeles NL, 1981
7-game series—32—Tim Foli, Pittsburgh NL, 1979
8-game series—30—Freddy Parent, Boston AL, 1903

**Most assists, game**
9—Roger Peckinpaugh, New York AL, Oct 5, 1921
[10—Johnny Logan, Milwaukee NL, Oct 6, 1957, 10 inn]

**Most assists, inning**
3—Dave Bancroft, New York NL, Oct 8, 1922, 3rd
Ossie Bluege, Washington, AL, Oct 7, 1924, 6th
Glenn Wright, Pittsburgh NL, Oct 8, 1927, 2nd
Blondy Ryan, New York NL, Oct 7, 1933, 3rd
Phil Rizzuto, New York AL, Oct 3, 1942, 2nd
Ernie Bowman, San Francisco NL, Oct 8, 1962, 9th
Bud Harrelson, New York NL, Oct 14, 1969, 5th
Mark Belanger, Baltimore AL, Oct 16, 1971, 7th
Bud Harrelson, New York NL, Oct 13, 1973, 7th
Tim Foli, Pittsburgh NL, Oct 12, 1979, 2nd

**Most chances accepted, career**
250—Phil Rizzuto, New York AL, 1941, 1942, 1947, 1949-1953, 1955; 9 series, 52 G

**Most chances accepted, series**
4-game series—27—Maury Wills, Los Angeles NL, 1966
5-game series—38—Joe Tinker, Chicago NL, 1907
6-game series—37—Phil Rizzuto, New York AL, 1951
7-game series—42—Charlie Gelbert, St. Louis NL, 1931
8-game series—51—Swede Risberg, Chicago AL, 1919

**Most chances accepted, game**
13—Buck Weaver, Chicago AL, Oct 7, 1917 (7 PO, 6 A)

**Fewest chances offered, game**
0—Dave Bancroft, Philadelphia NL, Oct 12, 1915 (fielded 8 inn)
Joe Boley, Philadelphia AL, Oct 8, 1929
Pee Wee Reese, Brooklyn NL, Oct 1, 1947 (fielded 8 inn)
Phil Rizzuto, New York AL, Oct 7, 1949
Zoilo Versalles, Minnesota AL, Oct 7, 1965 (fielded 8 inn)
Rico Petrocelli, Boston AL, Oct 4, 1967

Bert Campaneris, Oakland AL, Oct 18, 1972
Dave Concepcion, Cincinnati NL, Oct 16, 1975
Ozzie Smith, St. Louis NL, Oct 23, 1985
Omar Vizquel, Cleveland AL, Oct 19, 1997

**Most chances accepted, inning**
3—many shortstops

## ERRORS AND DOUBLE PLAYS

**Most errors, career**
12—Art Fletcher, New York NL, 1911-1913, 1917; 4 series, 25 G

**Most consecutive errorless games, career**
26—Derek Jeter, New York AL, Oct 26, 1996-Oct 23, 2003

**Most errors, series**
4-game series—4—Frank Crosetti, New York AL, 1932
5-game series—4—Ivy Olson, Brooklyn NL, 1916
Woody English, Chicago NL, 1929
6-game series—4—Art Fletcher, New York NL, 1911
Buck Weaver, Chicago AL, 1917
7-game series—8—Roger Peckinpaugh, Washington AL, 1925
8-game series—6—Honus Wagner, Pittsburgh NL, 1903

**Most chances accepted, errorless series**
42—Charlie Gelbert, St. Louis NL, 1931 (7-game series)

**Most errors, game**
3—Jack Barry, Philadelphia AL, Oct 26, 1911
Art Fletcher, New York NL, Oct 9, 1912
Buck Weaver, Chicago AL, Oct 13, 1917

**Most errors, inning**
2—Roger Peckinpaugh, Washington AL, Oct 8, 1925, 8th
Woody English, Chicago NL, Oct 8, 1929, 9th
Dick Bartell, New York NL, Oct 9, 1937, 3rd
Pee Wee Reese, Brooklyn NL, Oct 2, 1941, 8th

**Most double plays, career**
32—Phil Rizzuto, New York AL, 1941, 1942, 1947, 1949, 1950-1953, 1955; 9 series, 52 G

**Most double plays, series**
8—Phil Rizzuto, New York AL, 1951 (6-game series)

**Most double plays started, series**
7—Larry Bowa, Philadelphia NL, 1980 (6-game series)

**Most double plays, game**
4—Phil Rizzuto, New York AL, Oct 8, 1951

**Most double plays started, game**
3—Phil Rizzuto, New York AL, Oct 10, 1951
Maury Wills, Los Angeles NL, Oct 11, 1965
Larry Bowa, Philadelphia NL, Oct 15, 1980

**Most unassisted double plays, game**
1—Joe Tinker, Chicago NL, Oct 10, 1907
Joe Tinker, Chicago NL, Oct 11, 1907
Charlie Gelbert, St. Louis NL, Oct 2, 1930
Eddie Kasko, Cincinnati NL, Oct 7, 1961
[1—Greg Gagne, Minnesota AL, Oct 26, 1991, 11 inn]

# OUTFIELDERS

## GAMES

**Most games, career**
63—Mickey Mantle, New York AL, 1951-1953, 1955-1958, 1960-1964; 12 series

## PUTOUTS, ASSISTS AND CHANCES

**Most putouts, career**
150—Joe DiMaggio, New York AL, 1936-1939, 1941, 1942, 1947, 1949-1951; 10 series, 51 G

**Most putouts, series**
4-game series—16—Earle Combs, New York AL, 1927
5-game series—20—Joe DiMaggio, New York AL, 1942
6-game series—24—Mickey Rivers, New York AL, 1977
7-game series—25—Dan Gladden, Minnesota AL, 1991
8-game series—30—Edd Roush, Cincinnati NL, 1919

**Most putouts by left fielder, game**
8—George Foster, Cincinnati NL, Oct 21, 1976

**Most putouts by center fielder, game**
8—Edd Roush, Cincinnati NL, Oct 1, 1919
[9—Amos Otis, Kansas City AL, Oct 17, 1980, 10 inn]

**Most putouts by right fielder, game**
7—Red Murray, New York NL, Oct 14, 1912
Bing Miller, Philadelphia AL, Oct 5, 1930
Ray Blades, St. Louis NL, Oct 5, 1930
Tony Oliva, Minnesota AL, Oct 6, 1965
Al Kaline, Detroit AL, Oct 9, 1968
Frank Robinson, Baltimore AL, Oct 14, 1969

**Most consecutive putouts, game**
4—Mike Donlin, New York NL, Oct 13, 1905, 1 in 3rd, 3 in 4th, (CF)
Dode Paskert, Philadelphia NL, Oct 11, 1915, 3 in 4th, 1 in 5th (CF)
Charlie Keller, New York AL, Oct 1, 1941, 1 in 2nd, 3 in 3rd (LF)
Monte Irvin, New York NL, Sept 29, 1954, 1 in 8th, 3 in 9th (LF); dropped fly for error after second PO in 9th
Tommie Agee, New York NL, Oct 14, 1969, 3 in 7th, 1 in 8th (CF)
Ben Oglivie, Milwaukee AL, Oct 19, 1982, 1 in 6th, 3 in 7th (LF)

**Most putouts by left fielder, inning**
3—Charlie Keller, New York AL, Oct 1, 1941, 3rd
Monte Irvin, New York NL, September 29, 1954, 9th
Tommy Davis, Los Angeles NL, Oct 3, 1963, 7th
Ben Oglivie, Milwaukee AL, Oct 19, 1982, 7th
Deion Sanders, Atlanta NL, Oct 22, 1992, 5th

**Most putouts by center fielder, inning**
3—Mike Donlin, New York NL, Oct 13, 1905, 4th
Dode Paskert, Philadelphia NL, Oct 11, 1915, 4th
Ernie Orsatti, St. Louis NL, Oct 8, 1934, 5th
Joe DiMaggio, New York AL, Oct 2, 1936, 9th
Joe DiMaggio, New York AL, Oct 7, 1937, 6th
Roger Maris, New York AL, Oct 11, 1964, 3rd
Reggie Smith, Boston AL, Oct 11, 1967, 7th
Tommie Agee, New York NL, Oct 14, 1969, 7th
Willie McGee, St. Louis NL, Oct 22, 1987, 8th
Andruw Jones, Atlanta NL, Oct 24, 1999, 7th
Kenny Lofton, San Francisco NL, Oct 22, 2002, 7th

**Most putouts by right fielder, inning**
3—Mel Ott, New York NL, Oct 4, 1933, 7th
Bob Hazle, Milwaukee NL, Oct 10, 1957, 4th
Ron Swoboda, New York NL, Oct 15, 1969, 9th
Charlie Moore, Milwaukee AL, Oct 12, 1982, 8th

**Most assists, career**
5—Harry Hooper, Boston AL, 1912, 1915, 1916, 1918; 4 series, 24 G
Ross Youngs, New York NL, 1921, 1922, 1923, 1924; 4 series, 26 G

**Most games by outfielder with no assists, career**
51—Joe DiMaggio, New York AL, 1936-1939, 1941, 1942, 1947, 1949-1951; 10 series

**Most assists, series**
4-game series—2—Joe Connally, Boston, NL, 1914
5-game series—2—many outfielders
6-game series—2—many outfielders
7-game series—4—Edgar Rice, Washington AL, 1924
8-game series—3—Patsy Dougherty, Boston AL, 1903
Harry Hooper, Boston AL, 1912
Edd Roush, Cincinnati NL, 1919

**Most assists, game**
2—many outfielders

**Most chances accepted, career**
150—Joe DiMaggio, New York AL, 1936-1939, 1941, 1942, 1947, 1949, 1950, 1951; 10 series, 51 G

**Most chances accepted, series**
4-game series—16—Earle Combs, New York AL, 1927
5-game series—20—Joe DiMaggio, New York AL, 1942
6-game series—25—Mickey Rivers, New York AL, 1977
7-game series—26—Andy Pafko, Chicago NL, 1945
Dan Gladden, Minnesota AL, 1991
8-game series—33—Edd Roush, Cincinnati NL, 1919

**Most chances accepted by left fielder, game**
8—George Foster, Cincinnati NL, Oct 21, 1976 (8 PO)

**Most chances accepted by center fielder, game**
8—Edd Roush, Cincinnati NL, Oct 1, 1919 (8 PO)
Hank Leiber, New York NL, Oct 2, 1936 (7 PO, 1 A)
[9—Edd Roush, Cincinnati NL, Oct 7, 1919 (7 PO, 2 A), 10 inn
Amos Otis, Kansas City AL, Oct 17, 1980 (9 PO), 10 inn]

**Most chances accepted by right fielder, game**
7—Red Murray, New York NL, Oct 14, 1912 (7 PO)
Bing Miller, Philadelphia AL, Oct 5, 1930 (7 PO)
Ray Blades, St. Louis NL, Oct 5, 1930 (7 PO)
Tony Oliva, Minnesota AL, Oct 6, 1965 (7 PO)
Al Kaline, Detroit AL, Oct 9, 1968 (7 PO)
Frank Robinson, Baltimore AL, Oct 14, 1969 (7 PO)

**Longest game with no chances offered**
14 inn—Jermaine Dye, Chicago AL, Oct 25, 2005 (RF, 14 inn)

**Most chances accepted, inning**
3—many outfielders

## ERRORS AND DOUBLE PLAYS

**Most errors, career**
4—Ross Youngs, New York NL, 1921-1924; 4 series, 26 G

**Most consecutive errorless games, career**
45—Joe DiMaggio, New York AL, Oct 6, 1937-Oct 10, 1951

**Most errors, series**
4-game series—3—Willie Davis, Los Angeles NL, 1966
5-game series—2—many outfielders
6-game series—3—Red Murray, New York NL, 1911
Shano Collins, Chicago AL, 1917
7-game series—2—Zack Wheat, Brooklyn NL, 1920
Ernie Orsatti, St. Louis NL, 1934
Goose Goslin, Detroit AL, 1934
Mickey Mantle, New York AL, 1964
Jim Northrup, Detroit AL, 1968
8-game series—2—many outfielders

**Most chances accepted, errorless series**
25—Mickey Rivers, New York AL, 1977 (6-game series)

**Most errors, game**
3—Willie Davis, Los Angeles NL, Oct 6, 1966

**Most errors, inning**
3—Willie Davis, Los Angeles NL, Oct 6, 1966, 5th

**Most double plays, career**
2—many outfielders

**Most double plays, series**
2—Danny Murphy, Philadelphia AL, 1910 (5-game series)
Tris Speaker, Boston AL, 1912 (8-game series)
Edd Roush, Cincinnati NL, 1919 (8-game series)
Elston Howard, New York AL, 1958 (7-game series)

**Most double plays, game**
1—many outfielders
[2—Edd Roush, Cincinnati NL, Oct 7, 1919, 10 inn]

**Most unassisted double plays, game**
1—Tris Speaker, Boston AL, Oct 15, 1912

## CATCHERS

### GAMES

**Most games, career**
63—Yogi Berra, New York AL, 1947, 1949-1953, 1955-1958, 1960, 1962; 12 series

### PUTOUTS, ASSISTS AND CHANCES

**Most putouts, career**
421—Yogi Berra, New York AL, 1947, 1949-1953, 1955-1958, 1960, 1962; 12 series, 63 G

**Most putouts, series**
4-game series—43—John Roseboro, Los Angeles NL, 1963
5-game series—59—Mickey Cochrane, Philadelphia AL, 1929
6-game series—55—Walker Cooper, St. Louis NL, 1944
7-game series—69—Jorge Posada, New York AL, 2001
8-game series—54—Lou Criger, Boston AL, 1903

**Most putouts, game**
18—John Roseboro, Los Angeles NL, Oct 2, 1963 (15 K)

**Most putouts, inning**
3—many catchers

**Most assists, career**
36—Yogi Berra, New York AL, 1947, 1949-1953, 1955-1958, 1960, 1962;
12 series, 63 G

**Most assists, series**
4-game series—7—Thurman Munson, New York AL, 1976
5-game series—9—Boss Schmidt, Detroit AL, 1907
Johnny Kling, Chicago NL, 1907
Ed Burns, Philadelphia NL, 1915
6-game series—12—Chief Meyers, New York NL, 1911
7-game series—11—Boss Schmidt, Detroit AL, 1909
8-game series—15—Ray Schalk, Chicago AL, 1919

**Most assists, game**
4—Johnny Kling, Chicago NL, Oct 9, 1907
Boss Schmidt, Detroit AL, Oct 11, 1907
Boss Schmidt, Detroit AL, Oct 14, 1908
George Gibson, Pittsburgh NL, Oct 12, 1909
Bill Rariden, New York NL, Oct 10, 1917
Sam Agnew, Boston AL, Sept 6, 1918
Bill DeLancey, St. Louis NL, Oct 8, 1934
[6—Jack Lapp, Philadelphia AL, Oct 17, 1911, 11 inn]

**Most assists, inning**
2—many catchers

**Most chances accepted, career**
457—Yogi Berra, New York AL, 1947, 1949-1953, 1955-1960, 1962; 12 series, 63 G

**Most chances accepted, series**
4-game series—43—John Roseboro, Los Angeles NL, 1963
5-game series—61—Mickey Cochrane, Philadelphia AL, 1929
6-game series—56—Johnny Kling, Chicago NL, 1906
Roy Campanella, Brooklyn NL, 1953
7-game series—73—Jorge Posada, New York AL, 2001
8-game series—62—Lou Criger, Boston AL, 1903

**Most chances accepted, game**
18—John Roseboro, Los Angeles NL, Oct 2, 1963, (18 PO, 15 K)
Tim McCarver, St. Louis NL, Oct 2, 1968 (17 PO, 1 A, 17 K)

**Fewest chances offered, game**
1—Wally Schang, Philadelphia AL, Oct 11, 1913 (1 K)
Wally Schang, New York AL, Oct 11, 1923 (1 K)
Muddy Ruel, Washington AL, Oct 5, 1924 (1 K)
Mickey Cochrane, Detroit AL, Oct 6, 1934 (1 K)
Gabby Hartnett, Chicago NL, Oct 2, 1935 (1 K)
Sherm Lollar, Chicago AL, Oct 6, 1959 (1 K)
Elston Howard, New York AL, Oct 6, 1960
[0—Benito Santiago, San Francisco NL, Oct 20, 2002, caught 8 inn]

**Most chances accepted, inning**
4—Tim McCarver, St. Louis NL, Oct 9, 1967, 9th (3 PO, 1 A, 2 K)

### ERRORS AND PASSED BALLS

**Most errors, career**
7—Boss Schmidt, Detroit AL, 1907-1909; 3 series, 13 G

**Most consecutive errorless games, career**
30—Yogi Berra, New York AL, Oct 4, 1952-Oct 9, 1957

**Most errors, series**
4-game series—3—Joe Oliver, Cincinnati NL, 1990
5-game series—2—Boss Schmidt, Detroit AL, 1907
Walker Cooper, St. Louis NL, 1943
Joe Ferguson, Los Angeles NL, 1974
6-game series—2—Ray Schalk, Chicago AL, 1917
7-game series—5—Boss Schmidt, Detroit AL, 1909
8-game series—3—Lou Criger, Boston AL, 1903

**Most chances accepted, errorless series**
71—Jerry Grote, New York NL, 1973 (7-game series)

**Most errors, game**
2—Lou Criger, Boston AL, Oct 1, 1903
Jimmie Wilson, St. Louis NL, Oct 7, 1928
Joe Ferguson, Los Angeles NL, Oct 15, 1974
[2—Carlton Fisk, Boston AL, Oct 14, 1975, 9.1 inn]

**Most errors, inning**
2—Lou Criger, Boston AL, Oct 1, 1903, 1st
Jimmie Wilson, St. Louis NL, Oct 7, 1928, 6th

**Most passed balls, career**
5—Johnny Kling, Chicago NL, 1906 (3), 1907, 1908

**Most passed balls, series**
3—Johnny Kling, Chicago NL, 1906
Smoky Burgess, Pittsburgh NL, 1960
Elston Howard, New York AL, 1964

**Most passed balls, game**
2—Johnny Kling, Chicago NL, Oct 9, 1906
Bill Killefer, Chicago NL, Sept 9, 1918
Paul Richards, Detroit AL, Oct 3, 1945
Bruce Edwards, Brooklyn NL, Oct 4, 1947
Smoky Burgess, Pittsburgh NL, Oct 6, 1960
Elston Howard, New York AL, Oct 7, 1964

**Most passed balls, inning**
1—many catchers

### DOUBLE PLAYS, RUNNERS CAUGHT STEALING

**Most double plays, career**
6—Yogi Berra, New York AL, 1947, 1949-1953, 1955-1958, 1960, 1962; 12 series, 63 G
Johnny Bench, Cincinnati NL, 1970, 1972, 1975, 1976;
4 series, 23 G

**Most double plays, series**
3—Johnny Kling, Chicago NL, 1906 (6-game series)
Boss Schmidt, Detroit AL, 1909 (7-game series)
Wally Schang, New York AL, 1921 (8-game series)
Johnny Bench, Cincinnati NL, 1975 (7-game series)

**Most double plays started, series**
3—Wally Schang, New York AL, 1921 (8-game series)

**Most double plays, game**
2—Boss Schmidt, Detroit AL, Oct 14, 1909
Wally Schang, New York AL, Oct 11, 1921
Gabby Hartnett, Chicago NL, September 29, 1932
Del Rice, Milwaukee NL, Oct 9, 1957
Rich Gedman, Boston AL, Oct 22, 1986

**Most double plays started, game**
2—Boss Schmidt, Detroit AL, Oct 14, 1909
Wally Schang, New York AL, Oct 11, 1921

**Most unassisted double plays, game**
None

**Most runners caught stealing, career**
20—Wally Schang, Philadelphia AL, 1913, 1914; Boston AL, 1918; New York AL, 1921-1923, 6 series, 32 G

**Most runners caught stealing, series**
10—Ray Schalk, Chicago AL, 1919 (8-game series)

**Most runners caught stealing, game**
3—9 times by 8 catchers; last—Terry Steinbach, Oakland AL, Oct 19, 1988
[5—Jack Lapp, Philadelphia AL, Oct 17, 1911, 11 inn]

**Most runners caught stealing, inning**
2—Jack Lapp, Philadelphia AL, Oct 17, 1911, 10th
Aaron Robinson, New York AL, Oct 6, 1947, 1st
Bill Carrigan, Boston AL, Oct 9, 1912, 11th
Roy Campanella, Brooklyn NL, Oct 2, 1952, 1st

## PITCHERS

### GAMES

**Most games, career**
22—Whitey Ford, New York AL, 1950, 1953, 1955-1958, 1960-1964; 11 series

### PUTOUTS, ASSISTS AND CHANCES

**Most putouts, career**
11—Whitey Ford, New York AL, 1950, 1953, 1955-1958, 1960-1964; 11 series, 22 G

**Most putouts, series**
4-game series—3—Whitey Ford, New York AL, 1963
5-game series—5—Jack Morris, Detroit, AL, 1984
6-game series—6—Nick Altrock, Chicago AL, 1906
Hippo Vaughn, Chicago NL, 1918
7-game series—5—Jim Kaat, Minnesota AL, 1965
8-game series—2—Deacon Phillippe, Pittsburgh NL, 1903
Phil Douglas, New York NL, 1921

**Most putouts, game**
5—Jim Kaat, Minnesota AL, Oct 7, 1965

**Most putouts, inning**
2—Johnny Beazley, St. Louis NL, Oct 5, 1942, 8th
Bob Turley, New York AL, Oct 9, 1957, 7th
Whitey Ford, New York AL, Oct 8, 1960, 9th
Bob Purkey, Cincinnati NL, Oct 7, 1961, 9th
John Denny, Philadelphia NL, Oct 15, 1983, 5th
Dave Stewart, Oakland AL, Oct 16, 1990, 3rd

**Most assists, career**
34—Christy Mathewson, New York NL, 1905, 1911-1913; 4 series, 11 G

**Most assists, series**
4-game series—5—Joe Bush, Philadelphia AL, 1914
Lefty Tyler, Boston NL, 1914
Bill James, Boston NL, 1914
Wilcy Moore, New York AL, 1927
Monte Pearson, New York AL, 1939
5-game series—10—Mordecai Brown, Chicago NL, 1910
6-game series—12—Mordecai Brown, Chicago NL, 1906
7-game series—12—George Mullin, Detroit AL, 1909
8-game series—12—Christy Mathewson, New York NL, 1912

**Most assists, game**
8—Nick Altrock, Chicago AL, Oct 12, 1906
Lon Warneke, Chicago NL, Oct 2, 1935

**Most assists, inning**
3—Eddie Plank, Philadelphia AL, Oct 13, 1905, 8th
Rube Marquard, New York NL, Oct 7, 1913, 4th
Lon Warneke, Chicago NL, Oct 2, 1935, 3rd
Johnny Murphy, New York AL, Oct 8, 1939, 8th
Bob Rush, Milwaukee NL, Oct 4, 1958, 3rd

**Most chances accepted, career**
40—Christy Mathewson, New York NL, 1905, 1911, 1912, 1913; 4 series, 11 G

**Most chances accepted, series**
4-game series—6—Lefty Tyler, Boston NL, 1914
Red Ruffing, New York AL, 1938
5-game series—10—Christy Mathewson, New York NL, 1905
Mordecai Brown, Chicago NL, 1910
6-game series—17—Nick Altrock, Chicago AL, 1906
Hippo Vaughn, Chicago NL, 1918
7-game series—12—George Mullin, Detroit AL, 1909
8-game series—13—Christy Mathewson, New York NL, 1912

**Most chances accepted, game**
11—Nick Altrock, Chicago AL, Oct 12, 1906 (3 PO, 8 A)

**Most chances accepted, inning**
3—many pitchers

### ERRORS AND DOUBLE PLAYS

**Most errors, career**
3—Deacon Phillippe, Pittsburgh NL, 1903, 1909; 2 series, 7 G
Ed Cicotte, Chicago AL, 1917, 1919; 2 series, 6 G
Max Lanier, St. Louis NL, 1942, 1943, 1944; 3 series, 7 G

**Most consecutive errorless games, career**
20—Mike Stanton, Atlanta NL, New York AL, Oct 19, 1991-Nov 4, 2001

**Most errors, series**
4-game series—1—many pitchers
5-game series—2—Jack Coombs, Philadelphia AL, 1910
Max Lanier, St. Louis NL, 1942
6-game series—2—Nels Potter, St. Louis AL, 1944
7-game series—2—Deacon Phillippe, Pittsburgh NL, 1909
Allie Reynolds, New York AL, 1952
8-game series—2—Ed Cicotte, Chicago AL, 1919

**Most chances accepted, errorless series**
17—Nick Altrock, Chicago AL, 1906 (6-game series)
Hippo Vaughn, Chicago NL, 1918 (6-game series)

**Most errors, game**
2—Deacon Phillippe, Pittsburgh NL, Oct 12, 1909
Jack Coombs, Philadelphia AL, Oct 18, 1910
Ed Cicotte, Chicago AL, Oct 4, 1919
Max Lanier, St. Louis NL, Sept 30, 1942
Nels Potter, St. Louis AL, Oct 5, 1944

**Most errors, inning**
2—Jack Coombs, Philadelphia AL, Oct 18, 1910, 5th
Ed Cicotte, Chicago AL, Oct 4, 1919, 5th
Max Lanier, St. Louis NL, Sept 30, 1942, 9th
Nels Potter, St. Louis AL, Oct 5, 1944, 3rd

**Most double plays, career**
3—Chief Bender, Philadelphia AL, 1905, 1910, 1911, 1913, 1914; 5 series, 10 G
Joe Bush, Philadelphia AL, Boston AL, New York AL, 1913, 1914, 1918, 1922, 1923; 5 series, 9 G
Allie Reynolds, New York AL, 1947, 1949-1953; 6 series, 15 G

**Most double plays, series**
2—many pitchers

**Most double plays started, series**
2—many pitchers

**Most double plays, game**
2—Chief Bender, Philadelphia AL, Oct 9, 1914
Joe Bush, New York AL, Oct 8, 1922
Allie Reynolds, New York AL, Oct 8, 1951

**Most double plays started, game**
2—Chief Bender, Philadelphia AL, Oct 9, 1914
Joe Bush, New York AL, Oct 8, 1922
Allie Reynolds, New York AL, Oct 8, 1951

**Most unassisted double plays**
None

# CLUB FIELDING

## AVERAGE

**Highest fielding average, series**
4-game series—1.000—Baltimore AL vs Los Angeles NL, 1966
5-game series—1.000—New York AL vs New York NL, 1937
6-game series—.996—Boston AL vs Chicago NL, 1918
St. Louis NL vs St. Louis AL, 1944
Los Angeles NL vs New York AL, 1977
7-game series—.993—Cincinnati NL vs Boston AL, 1975
8-game series—.984—New York NL vs New York AL, 1921

**For a list of fielding statistics by teams each series, see page 404.**

**Highest fielding average by both clubs, series**
4-game series—.9864—New York AL .993, Los Angeles NL .979, 1963
.9856—Houston NL .988, Chicago AL .983, 2005
5-game series—.986—Oakland AL .989, Los Angeles NL .983, 1988
6-game series—.991—Los Angeles NL .996, New York AL .987, 1977

7-game series—.990—St. Louis NL .992, Kansas City AL .989, 1985
8-game series—.983—New York NL .984, New York AL .981, 1921

**Lowest fielding average, series**
4-game series—.949—New York AL vs Chicago NL, 1932
5-game series—.942—Brooklyn NL vs Boston AL, 1916
6-game series—.938—New York NL vs Philadelphia AL, 1911
7-game series—.934—Detroit AL vs Pittsburgh NL, 1909
8-game series—.944—Pittsburgh NL vs Boston AL, 1903

**Lowest fielding average by both clubs, series**
4-game series—.954—Chicago NL .959, New York AL .949, 1932
5-game series—.946—Philadelphia AL .947, Chicago NL .946, 1910
6-game series—.947—Philadelphia AL .956, New York NL .938, 1911
7-game series—.941—Pittsburgh NL .947, Detroit AL .934, 1909
8-game series—.951—Boston AL .957, Pittsburgh NL .944, 1903

## PUTOUTS

**Most putouts, total series**
5,763—New York AL; 39 series, 219 G

**Most putouts, series**
4-game series—123—Chicago AL vs Houston NL, 2005
5-game series—147—Boston AL vs Brooklyn NL, 1916
6-game series—168—New York AL vs Los Angeles NL, 1977
Florida NL vs New York AL, 2003
7-game series—202—Minnesota AL vs Atlanta NL, 1991
8-game series—222—Boston AL vs New York NL, 1912

**Most putouts by both clubs, series**
4-game series—241—Chicago AL 123, Houston NL 118, 2005
5-game series—289—Boston AL 147, Brooklyn NL 142, 1916
6-game series—333—New York AL 168, Los Angeles NL 165, 1977
Florida NL 168, New York AL 165, 2003
7-game series—401—Washington AL 201, New York NL 200, 1924
8-game series—443—Boston AL 222, New York NL 221, 1912

**Fewest putouts, series**
4-game series—102—St. Louis NL vs New York AL, 1928
Chicago NL vs New York AL, 1932
Chicago NL vs New York AL, 1938
New York AL vs Los Angeles NL, 1963
Los Angeles NL vs Baltimore AL, 1966
San Francisco NL vs Oakland AL, 1989
San Diego NL vs New York AL, 1998
St. Louis NL vs Boston AL, 2004
5-game series—126—Los Angeles NL vs Oakland AL, 1974
San Diego NL vs Detroit AL, 1984
6-game series—153—New York NL vs Chicago AL, 1917
St. Louis NL vs Philadelphia AL, 1930
New York AL vs Los Angeles NL, 1981
7-game series—177—Brooklyn NL vs Cleveland AL, 1920
St. Louis NL vs Minnesota AL, 1987
8-game series—210—Pittsburgh NL vs Boston AL, 1903
New York AL vs New York NL, 1921

**Fewest putouts by both clubs, series**
4-game series—210—New York AL 108, St. Louis NL 102, 1928
New York AL 108, Chicago NL 102, 1932
New York AL 108, Chicago NL 102, 1938
Los Angeles NL 108, New York AL 102, 1963
Baltimore AL 108, Los Angeles NL 102, 1966
Oakland AL 108, San Francisco NL 102, 1989
New York AL 108, San Diego NL 102, 1998
Boston AL 108, St. Louis NL 102, 2004
5-game series—258—Oakland AL 132, Los Angeles NL 126, 1974
Detroit AL 132, San Diego NL 126, 1984
6-game series—309—Chicago AL 156, New York NL 153, 1917
Philadelphia AL 156, St. Louis NL 153, 1930
Los Angeles NL 156, New York AL 153, 1981
7-game series—357—Minnesota AL 180, St. Louis N.L 177, 1987
8-game series—422—New York NL 212, New York AL 210, 1921

**Most putouts by outfield, game**
15—New York NL vs Boston AL, Oct 14, 1912
Boston NL vs Cleveland AL, Oct 6, 1948
[16—Brooklyn NL vs New York AL, Oct 5, 1952, 11 inn]

**Most putouts by outfields of both clubs, game**
23—Pittsburgh NL 13, New York AL 10, Oct 6, 1927
[23—Brooklyn NL 16, New York AL 7, Oct 5, 1952, 11 inn]

**Fewest putouts by outfield, game**
0—New York NL vs New York AL, Oct 5, 1921
New York NL vs New York AL, Sept 30, 1936
Cleveland AL vs Atlanta NL, Oct 21, 1995 (fielded 8 inn)
[1—New York NL vs Oakland AL, Oct 14, 1973, 12 inn]

**Fewest putouts by outfields of both clubs, game**
2—Atlanta NL 2, Cleveland AL 0, Oct 21, 1995 (Cleveland fielded 8 inn)
3—New York AL 2, Brooklyn NL 1, Oct 10, 1956

**Most putouts by outfield, inning**
3—many games

**Most putouts by outfields of both clubs, inning**
6—Kansas City AL 3, St. Louis NL 3, Oct 27, 1985, 7th

**Most putouts by catchers of both clubs, inning**
6—Chicago AL 3, Cincinnati NL 3, Oct 6, 1919, 2nd
Cincinnati NL 3, Oakland AL 3, Oct 18, 1972, 5th
St. Louis NL 3, Kansas City AL 3, Oct 24, 1985, 7th
New York NL 3, New York AL 3, Oct 24, 2000, 2nd

## ASSISTS

**Most assists, total series**
2,312—New York AL; 39 series, 219 G

**Most assists, series**
4-game series—67—Philadelphia AL vs Boston NL, 1914
5-game series—90—Boston AL vs Brooklyn NL, 1916
6-game series—99—Chicago AL vs Chicago NL, 1906
7-game series—99—Washington AL vs New York NL, 1924
St. Louis NL vs New York AL, 1926
8-game series—116—Chicago AL vs Cincinnati NL, 1919

**Most assists by both clubs, series**
4-game series—129—Philadelphia AL 67, Boston NL 62, 1914
5-game series—160—Boston AL 90, Brooklyn NL 70, 1916
6-game series—183—Chicago AL 99, Chicago NL 84, 1906
7-game series—193—Washington AL 99, New York NL 94, 1924
8-game series—212—Chicago AL 116, Cincinnati NL 96, 1919

**Fewest assists, series**
4-game series—28—New York AL vs St. Louis NL, 1928
5-game series—36—Los Angeles NL vs Oakland AL, 1988
6-game series—41—Philadelphia AL vs St. Louis NL, 1930
7-game series—48—St. Louis NL vs Detroit AL, 1968
8-game series—96—Pittsburgh NL vs Boston AL, 1903
Cincinnati NL vs Chicago AL, 1919

**Fewest assists by both clubs, series**
4-game series—64—St. Louis NL 36, New York AL 28, 1928
5-game series—79—Oakland AL 43, Los Angeles NL 36, 1988
6-game series—96—St. Louis NL 55, Philadelphia AL 41, 1930
7-game series—120—Detroit AL 72, St. Louis NL 48, 1968
8-game series—198—Boston AL 102, Pittsburgh NL 96, 1903

**Most assists, game**
21—Chicago AL vs New York NL, Oct 7, 1917
Boston AL vs Chicago NL, Sept 9, 1918

**Most assists by both clubs, game**
38—Chicago AL 20, Chicago NL 18, Oct 12, 1906

**Fewest assists, game**
2—St. Louis NL vs Detroit AL, Oct 2, 1968

**Fewest assists by both clubs, game**
8—Philadelphia AL 5, St. Louis NL 3, Oct 2, 1930
Boston AL 5, Cincinnati NL 3, Oct 16, 1975

**Fewest assists by infield, game**
1—St. Louis NL vs Detroit AL, Oct 2, 1968

**Most assists by outfield, game**
4—St. Louis NL vs New York AL, Oct 6, 1926

**Most assists by outfields of both clubs, game**
5—St. Louis NL 4, New York AL 1, Oct 6, 1926

**Most assists by outfield, inning**
2—Boston AL vs St. Louis NL, Oct 10, 1946, 5th

## CHANCES OFFERED

**Fewest chances offered to outfield, game**
0—New York NL vs New York AL, Sept 30, 1936
Cleveland AL vs Atlanta NL, Oct 21, 1995 (fielded 8 inn)
[1—New York NL vs Oakland AL, Oct 14, 1973, 12 inn]

**Fewest chances offered to outfield by both clubs, game**
2—Atlanta NL 2, Cleveland AL 0, Oct 21, 1995 (Cleveland fielded 8 inn)
3—New York AL, 2, Brooklyn NL, 1, Oct 10, 1956 (both teams fielded 9 inn)

**Fewest chances offered to infield, game (excluding first base)**
2—Philadelphia AL vs St. Louis NL, Oct 6, 1931

## ERRORS

**Most errors, total series**
163—New York AL; 39 series, 219 G

**Most errors, series**
4-game series—8—New York AL vs Chicago NL, 1932
Boston AL vs St. Louis NL, 2004
5-game series—13—Brooklyn NL vs Boston AL, 1916
6-game series—16—New York NL vs Philadelphia AL, 1911
7-game series—19—Detroit AL vs Pittsburgh NL, 1909
8-game series—18—Pittsburgh NL vs Boston AL, 1903

**Most errors by both clubs, series**
4-game series—14—New York AL 8, Chicago NL 6, 1932
5-game series—23—Chicago NL 12, Philadelphia AL 11, 1910
6-game series—27—New York NL 16, Philadelphia AL 11, 1911
7-game series—34—Detroit AL 19, Pittsburgh NL 15, 1909
8-game series—32—Pittsburgh NL 18, Boston AL 14, 1903

**Fewest errors, series**
4-game series—0—Baltimore AL vs Los Angeles NL, 1966
5-game series—0—New York AL vs New York NL, 1937
6-game series—1—Boston AL vs Chicago NL, 1918
St. Louis NL vs St. Louis AL, 1944
New York AL vs Brooklyn NL, 1953
Los Angeles NL vs New York AL, 1977
7-game series—2—many clubs
8-game series—5—New York NL vs New York AL, 1921

**Fewest errors by both clubs, series**
4-game series—4—Los Angeles NL 3, New York AL 1, 1963
5-game series—5—Los Angeles NL 3, Oakland AL 2, 1988
6-game series—4—New York AL 3, Los Angeles NL 1, 1977
7-game series—5—Kansas City AL 3, St. Louis NL 2, 1985
8-game series—11—New York AL 6, New York NL 5, 1921

**Most errors, game**
6—Chicago AL vs Chicago NL, Oct 13, 1906
Pittsburgh NL vs Detroit AL, Oct 12, 1909
Chicago AL vs New York NL, Oct 13, 1917
Los Angeles NL vs Baltimore AL, Oct 6, 1966

**Most errors by both clubs, game**
9—Chicago AL 6, New York NL 3, Oct 13, 1917

**Most errors by outfield, game**
4—Los Angeles NL vs Baltimore AL, Oct 6, 1966

**Most errors by outfields of both clubs, game**
4—Los Angeles NL 4, Baltimore AL 0, Oct 6, 1966

**Most errors by infield, game**
5—Chicago AL vs Chicago NL, Oct 13, 1906
Detroit AL vs St. Louis NL, Oct 3, 1934
[5—New York NL vs Philadelphia AL, Oct 17, 1911, 11 inn]

**Most errors by infields of both clubs, game**
7—Chicago AL 4, New York NL 3, Oct 13, 1917
[7—New York NL 5, Philadelphia AL 2, Oct 17, 1911, 11 inn]

**Most errors, inning**
3—Chicago AL, Oct 13, 1917, 4th
New York NL, Oct 8, 1937, 5th
New York NL, Oct 9, 1937, 3rd
Cincinnati NL, Oct 8, 1939, 10th
Los Angeles NL, Oct 1, 1959, 3rd
Los Angeles NL, Oct 6, 1966, 5th
Cleveland AL, Oct 21, 1997, 9th

**Most errorless games, total series**
102—New York A.L; 39 series, 219 G

**Most consecutive errorless games, total series**
7—Philadelphia AL vs St. Louis NL, Oct 6, 7, 1930; Oct 1, 2, 5, 6, 7, 1931

**Most errorless games, series**
4-game series—4—Baltimore AL vs Los Angeles NL, 1966
5-game series—5—New York AL vs New York NL, 1937
6-game series—5—Boston AL vs Chicago NL, 1918
St. Louis NL vs St. Louis AL, 1944
New York AL vs Brooklyn NL, 1953
Los Angeles NL vs New York AL, 1977
7-game series—6—Arizona NL vs New York AL, 2001
8-game series—5—New York NL vs New York AL, 1921

**Most consecutive errorless games, series**
5—Philadelphia AL vs St. Louis NL, Oct 1, 2, 5, 6, 7, 1931
New York AL vs New York NL, Oct 6, 7, 8, 9, 10, 1937.
New York AL vs Brooklyn NL, Sept 29, 30, Oct 1, 2, 3, 1955

**Most errorless games by both clubs, series**
4-game series—7—Baltimore AL 4, Los Angeles NL 3, 1966
5-game series—7—New York AL 5, New York NL 2, 1937
6-game series—9—Los Angeles NL 5, New York AL 4, 1977
7-game series—10—St. Louis NL 5, Kansas City AL 5, 1985
8-game series—8—New York NL 5, New York AL 3, 1921

**Fewest errorless games, series**
0—many clubs

**Longest errorless game, team**
12 inn—Detroit AL vs St. Louis NL, Oct 4, 1934
New York AL vs Los Angeles NL, Oct 11, 1977
New York AL vs New York NL, Oct 21, 2000
Arizona NL vs New York AL, Nov 1, 2001
Florida NL vs New York AL, Oct 23, 2003

**Longest errorless game by both clubs**
12 inn—New York AL vs Los Angeles NL, Oct 11, 1977 (Los Angeles fielded 11 inn)
New York AL vs New York NL, Oct 21, 2000 (New York NL fielded 11.2 inn)
Florida NL vs New York AL, Oct 23, 2003 (New York fielded 11 inn)

## PASSED BALLS

**Most passed balls, total series**
15—New York AL; 39 series, 219 G

**Most passed balls, series**
3—Chicago NL vs Chicago AL, 1906
Pittsburgh NL vs New York AL, 1960
New York AL vs St. Louis NL, 1964

**Most passed balls by both clubs, series**
4—Chicago NL 3, Chicago AL 1, 1906 (6-game series)
New York AL 2, Brooklyn NL 2, 1947 (7-game series)

**Fewest passed balls, series**
0—many clubs

**Fewest passed balls by both clubs, series**
0—many clubs

**Most passed balls, game**
2—Chicago NL vs Chicago AL, Oct 9, 1906
Detroit AL vs Chicago NL, Oct 3, 1945
Brooklyn NL vs New York AL, Oct 4, 1947
Pittsburgh NL vs New York AL, Oct 6, 1960
New York AL vs St. Louis NL, Oct 7, 1964

**Most passed balls by both clubs, game**
2—Chicago NL vs Chicago AL, Oct 9, 1906
Chicago NL 1, Detroit AL 1, Oct 13, 1908
Detroit AL 1, Chicago NL 1, Oct 3, 1945
Brooklyn NL 1, New York AL 1, Oct 4, 1947
Pittsburgh NL 1, New York AL 1, Oct 6, 1960
New York AL 1, St. Louis NL 1, Oct 7, 1964
Oakland AL 1, Los Angeles NL 1, Oct 19, 1988

## DOUBLE AND TRIPLE PLAYS

**Most double plays, total series**
193—New York AL; 39 series, 219 G

**Most double plays, series**
4-game series—7—Chicago NL vs New York AL, 1932
New York AL vs Los Angeles NL, 1963
5-game series—7—New York AL vs New York NL, 1922
New York AL vs Brooklyn NL, 1941
Cincinnati NL vs New York AL, 1961
6-game series—10—New York AL vs New York NL, 1951
7-game series—12—Brooklyn NL vs New York AL, 1955
8-game series—9—Chicago AL vs Cincinnati NL, 1919

**Most double plays by both clubs, series**
4-game series—10—New York AL 6, Cincinnati NL 4, 1976
Houston NL 6, Chicago AL 4, 2005
5-game series—12—New York AL 7, Brooklyn NL 5, 1941
6-game series—16—Philadelphia NL 8, Kansas City AL 8, 1980
7-game series—19—Brooklyn NL 12, New York AL 7, 1955
8-game series—16—Chicago AL 9, Cincinnati NL 7, 1919

**Fewest double plays, series**
4-game series—1—New York AL vs Chicago NL, 1932
Cincinnati NL vs New York AL, 1939
Philadelphia NL vs New York AL, 1950
Los Angeles NL vs New York AL, 1963
Oakland AL vs San Francisco NL, 1989
5-game series—0—New York NL vs Baltimore AL, 1969
6-game series—2—Chicago AL vs Chicago NL, 1906
New York NL vs Philadelphia AL, 1911
Philadelphia AL vs New York NL, 1911
Philadelphia AL vs St. Louis NL, 1930
New York AL vs New York NL, 1936
Chicago AL vs Los Angeles NL, 1959.
New York AL vs Los Angeles NL, 1977
New York AL vs Los Angeles NL, 1981
7-game series—2—St. Louis NL vs Detroit AL, 1934
Baltimore AL vs Pittsburgh NL, 1971
St. Louis NL vs Minnesota AL, 1987
8-game series—4—New York NL vs Boston AL, 1912

**Fewest double plays by both clubs, series**
4-game series—4—New York NL 2, Cleveland AL 2, 1954
San Francisco NL 3, Oakland AL 1, 1989
5-game series—4—New York NL 2, Philadelphia AL 2, 1905
Baltimore AL 4, New York NL 0, 1969
New York NL 3, New York AL 1, 2000
6-game series—4—Philadelphia AL 2, New York NL 2, 1911
7-game series—6—Minnesota AL 4, St. Louis NL 2, 1987
8-game series—9—Boston AL 5, New York NL 4, 1912

**Most double plays, game**
4—Philadelphia AL vs Boston NL, Oct 9, 1914
Boston AL vs Brooklyn NL, Oct 7, 1916
Chicago NL vs New York AL, Sept 29, 1932
Cleveland AL vs Boston NL, Oct 11, 1948
New York AL vs New York NL, Oct 8, 1951
Oakland AL vs New York NL, Oct 17, 1973
Philadelphia NL vs Kansas City AL, Oct 15, 1980
[4—Houston NL, Oct 25, 2005, 14 inn]

**Most double plays by both clubs, game**
6—New York AL 3, Brooklyn NL 3, Sept 29, 1955
Philadelphia NL 4, Kansas City AL 2, Oct 15, 1980
[6—Houston NL 4, Chicago AL 2, Oct 25, 2005, 14 inn]

**Most triple plays, series**
1—Cleveland AL vs Brooklyn NL, 1920

# MISCELLANEOUS

## CLUB

### ONE-RUN DECISIONS

**Most one-run games, total series**
69—New York AL; 39 series; won 36 lost 33

**Most one-run games won, total series**
36—New York AL; 39 series

**Most one-run games lost, total series**
33—New York AL; 39 series

**Most one-run games won, series**
4-game series—3—New York AL vs Philadelphia NL, 1950
5-game series—4—Boston AL vs Philadelphia NL, 1915
6-game series—4—Boston AL vs Chicago NL, 1918
Toronto AL vs Atlanta NL, 1992
7-game series—4—Oakland AL vs Cincinnati NL, 1972
8-game series—3—Boston AL vs New York NL, 1912

**Most one-run games by both clubs, series**
4-game series—3—New York AL (won 3) vs Philadelphia NL, 1950
5-game series—4—Boston AL (won 4) vs Philadelphia NL, 1915
Oakland AL (won 3) vs Los Angeles NL (won 1), 1974
6-game series—5—Atlanta NL (won 3) vs Cleveland AL (won 2), 1995
7-game series—6—Oakland AL (won 4) vs Cincinnati NL (won 2), 1972
8-game series—4—Boston AL (won 3) vs New York NL (won 1), 1912

**Most consecutive one-run games won, total series**
6—Boston AL, 1915 (last 4), 1916 (first 2)

**Most consecutive one-run games lost, total series**
7—Philadelphia NL, 1915 (last 4), 1950 (first 3)

### LENGTH OF GAMES

#### BY INNINGS

**Longest game**
14 inn—Boston AL 2, Brooklyn NL 1, Oct 9, 1916 (at Boston)
Chicago AL 7, Houston NL 5, Oct 25, 2005 (at Houston)

**For a complete list of extra-inning games, see page 397.**

**Longest tie game**
12 inn—Chicago NL 3, Detroit AL 3, Oct 8, 1907 (at Chicago)

**Most extra-inning games, total series**
19—New York AL; 39 series (won 11, lost 7, tied 1)

**Most extra-inning games won, total series**
11—New York AL; 39 series

**Most extra-inning games lost, total series**
7—New York AL; 39 series

**Most extra-inning games, series**
4-game series—1—Boston NL vs Philadelphia AL, 1914
New York AL vs Cincinnati NL, 1939
New York AL vs Philadelphia NL, 1950
New York NL vs Cleveland AL, 1954
Chicago AL vs Houston NL, 2005
5-game series—2—New York NL vs Washington AL, 1933
6-game series—2—Philadelphia AL vs New York NL, 1911
7-game series—3—Minnesota AL vs Atlanta NL, 1991
8-game series—2—Boston AL vs New York NL, 1912

#### BY TIME

**Longest average time per game, series**
4-game series—3 hrs, 51 min—Chicago AL vs Houston NL, 2005
5-game series—3 hrs, 46 min—New York AL vs New York NL, 2000
6-game series—3 hrs, 29 min—Toronto AL vs Philadelphia NL, 1993
7-game series—3 hrs, 37 min—Anaheim AL vs San Francisco NL, 2002
8-game series—2 hrs, 14 min—Boston AL vs New York NL, 1912

**Shortest average time per game, series**
4-game series—1 hr, 46 min—New York AL vs Cincinnati NL, 1939
5-game series—1 hr, 46 min—Detroit AL vs Chicago NL, 1908
6-game series—1 hr, 49 min—Philadelphia AL vs St. Louis NL, 1930
7-game series—1 hr, 47 min—Cleveland AL vs Brooklyn NL, 1920
8-game series—1 hr, 48 min—Boston AL vs Pittsburgh NL, 1903

**Shortest game**
1 hr, 25 min—Chicago NL, 2, Detroit AL, 0, Oct 14, 1908 (at Detroit)

**Longest 9-inning day game**
3 hrs, 48 min—Baltimore AL, 9, Pittsburgh NL, 6, Oct 13, 1979 (at Pittsburgh)

**Longest 9-inning night game**
4 hrs, 14 min—Toronto AL, 15, Philadelphia NL, 14, Oct 20, 1993 (at Philadelphia)

**Longest extra-inning day game**
4 hrs, 13 min—New York NL, 10, Oakland AL, 7, Oct 14, 1973, 12 inn (at Oakland)

**Longest extra-inning night game**
5 hrs, 41 min—Chicago AL 7, Houston NL 5, Oct 25, 2005, 14 inn (at Houston)

### SERIES STARTING AND FINISHING DATES

**Earliest date for series game (except 1918)**
Sept 28, 1932—Chicago NL at New York AL
Sept 28, 1955—Brooklyn NL at New York AL

**Earliest date for series final game (except 1918)**
Oct 2, 1932—New York AL at Chicago NL (4-game series)
Oct 2, 1954—New York NL at Cleveland AL (4-game series)

**Latest date for series start**
Oct 27, 2001—New York AL at Arizona NL

**Latest date for series finish**
Nov 4, 2001—New York AL at Arizona NL
(7-game series)

### NIGHT GAMES

**First night game**
Oct 13, 1971—Pittsburgh NL, 4, Baltimore AL, 3 (at Pittsburgh)

**First year the entire series played at night**
1985—St. Louis NL vs Kansas City AL (7-game series)

### SERIES AND GAMES WON

**Most series won**
26—New York AL, 1923, 1927, 1928, 1932, 1936-1939, 1941, 1943, 1947, 1949-1953, 1956, 1958, 1961, 1962, 1977, 1978, 1996, 1998-2000 (lost 13)

**For complete lists of results, and series played by all teams, see page 396.**

**Most consecutive series won**
8—New York AL, 1927, 1928, 1932, 1936-1939, 1941

**Most consecutive years winning series**
5—New York AL, 1949-1953

**Most times winning series without losing a game**
8—New York AL, 1927, 1928, 1932, 1938, 1939, 1950, 1998, 1999

**Winning series after winning first game**
Accomplished 62 times

**Winning series after losing first game**
Accomplished 39 times

**Winning series after winning one game and losing three**
Boston AL vs Pittsburgh NL, 1903 (5 wins in 8-game series)
Pittsburgh NL vs Washington AL, 1925 (7-game series)
New York AL vs Milwaukee NL, 1958 (7-game series)
Detroit AL vs St. Louis NL, 1968 (7-game series)
Pittsburgh NL vs Baltimore AL, 1979 (7-game series)
Kansas City AL vs St. Louis NL, 1985 (7-game series)

**Winning series after losing first two games**
New York NL vs New York AL, 1921 (5 wins in 8-game series)
Brooklyn NL vs New York AL, 1955 (7-game series)
New York AL vs Brooklyn NL, 1956 (7-game series)
New York AL vs Milwaukee NL, 1958 (7-game series)
Los Angeles NL vs Minnesota AL, 1965 (7-game series)
Pittsburgh NL vs Baltimore AL, 1971 (7-game series)
New York AL vs Los Angeles NL, 1978 (6-game series)
Los Angeles NL vs New York AL, 1981 (6-game series)
Kansas City AL vs St. Louis NL, 1985 (7-game series)
New York NL vs Boston AL, 1986 (7-game series)
New York AL vs Atlanta NL, 1996 (6-game series)

**Winning series after losing first three games**
Never accomplished

**Most games won, total series**
130—New York AL; 39 series; lost 88, tied 1

**For complete lists of results, and games played by all teams, see page 396.**

**Most consecutive games won, total series**
14—New York AL, 1996 (last 4), 1998 (4), 1999 (4), 2000 (first 2)

## SERIES AND GAMES LOST

**Most series lost**
13—New York AL, 1921, 1922, 1926, 1942, 1955, 1957, 1960, 1963, 1964, 1976, 1981, 2001, 2003 (won 26)

**Most consecutive series lost**
7—Chicago NL, 1910, 1918, 1929, 1932, 1935, 1938, 1945
Brooklyn NL, 1916, 1920, 1941, 1947, 1949, 1952, 1953

**Most consecutive years losing series**
3—Detroit AL, 1907-1909
New York NL, 1911-1913

**Most games lost, total series**
88—New York AL; 39 series

**For complete lists of results, and games played by all teams, see page 396.**

**Most consecutive games lost, total series**
8—New York AL, 1921 (last 3), 1922 (4; one tie during streak), 1923 (first 1)
Philadelphia NL, 1915 (last 4), 1950 (4)
Atlanta NL, 1996 (last 4), 1999 (4)

## ATTENDANCE

**Largest attendance, series**
4-game series—251,507—New York NL vs Cleveland AL, 1954
5-game series—304,139—Baltimore AL vs Philadelphia NL, 1983
6-game series—420,784—Los Angeles NL vs Chicago AL, 1959
7-game series—403,617—Florida NL vs Cleveland AL, 1997
8-game series—269,976—New York NL vs New York AL, 1921

**For list of attendance by series each series, see page 397.**

**Smallest attendance, series**
4-game series—111,009—Boston NL vs Philadelphia AL, 1914
5-game series—62,232—Chicago NL vs Detroit AL, 1908
6-game series—99,845—Chicago AL vs Chicago NL, 1906
7-game series—145,295—Pittsburgh NL vs Detroit AL, 1909
8-game series—100,429—Pittsburgh NL vs Boston AL, 1903

**Largest attendance, game**
92,706—At Los Angeles, Oct 6, 1959, Chicago AL 1, Los Angeles NL 0

**Smallest attendance, game**
6,210—At Detroit, Oct 14, 1908; Chicago NL 2, Detroit AL 0

## LEAGUE

### SERIES AND GAMES WON AND LOST

**Most consecutive series won**
7—AL, 1947-1953

**Most consecutive series lost**
7—NL, 1947-1953

**Most consecutive games won**
10—AL, 1927 (4) 1928 (4), 1929 (first 2)
AL, 1937 (last 1), 1938 (4), 1939 (4), 1940 (first 1)
AL, 1998 (4), 1999 (4), 2000 (first 2)

## SHUTOUTS

**Most consecutive series with shutouts**
9—1955-1963

**Most consecutive series ending in shutouts**
3—1907-1909
1955-1957
2003-2005

**Most consecutive series without shutouts**
3—1910-1912
1927-1929
1936-1938

# NON-PLAYING PERSONNEL

## MANAGERS AND COACHES

**Most series by manager**
10—Casey Stengel, New York AL, 1949-1953, 1955, 1956-1958, 1960 (won 7, lost 3)

**For a complete list of managers and their records, see page 406.**

**Most series by coach**
15—Frank Crosetti, New York AL, 1947, 1949-1953, 1955-1958, 1960-1964 (won 10, lost 5)

**Most series eligible as player and coach**
23—Frank Crosetti, New York AL, 1932, 1936-1939, 1941, 1942, 1943 (8 series as player, won 7); 1947, 1949-1953, 1955-1958, 1960-1964 (15 series as coach, won 10)

**Most series winners managed**
7—Joe McCarthy, New York AL, 1932, 1936-1939, 1941, 1943
Casey Stengel, New York AL, 1949-1953, 1956, 1958

**Most consecutive years managing series winners**
5—Casey Stengel, New York AL, 1949-1953 (1st 5 seasons as New York AL manager)

**Most consecutive series winners managed, career**
6—Joe McCarthy, New York AL, 1932, 1936-1939, 1941

**Most series losers managed**
6—John McGraw, New York NL, 1911-1913, 1917, 1923, 1924

**Most consecutive years managing series losers**
3—Hughey Jennings, Detroit AL, 1907-1909
John McGraw, New York NL, 1911-1913

**Most consecutive series losers managed, career**
4—John McGraw, New York NL, 1911-1913, 1917

**Most different series winners managed**
2—Bill McKechnie, Pittsburgh NL, 1925; Cincinnati NL, 1940
Bucky Harris, Washington AL, 1924; New York AL, 1947
Sparky Anderson, Cincinnati NL, 1975, 1976; Detroit AL, 1984

**Most teams managed**
3—Bill McKechnie, Pittsburgh NL, 1925; St. Louis NL, 1928; Cincinnati NL, 1939, 1940
Dick Williams, Boston AL, 1967; Oakland AL, 1972, 1973; San Diego NL, 1984

**Most games by manager**
63—Casey Stengel, New York AL, 10 series

**Most games won by manager**
37—Casey Stengel, New York AL, 10 series

**Most games lost by manager**
28—John McGraw, New York NL, 10 series

**Youngest manager**
26 years, 11 months, 21 days—Joe Cronin, Washington AL vs New York NL, Oct 3, 1933

**Youngest manager of a series winner**
27 years, 11 months, 2 days—Bucky Harris, Washington AL vs New York NL, Oct 10, 1924

## UMPIRES

**Most series umpired**
18—Bill Klem, 1908, 1909, 1911-1915, 1917, 1918, 1920, 1922, 1924, 1926, 1929, 1931, 1932, 1934, 1940

**Most consecutive series umpired**
5—Bill Klem, 1911-1915

**Most games umpired**
104—Bill Klem, 18 series

# CAREER MILESTONES

(Players active in the major leagues in 2005 are in boldface.)

## SERVICE

### SERIES PLAYED

| | Player | Series |
|---|---|---|
| 1. | Yogi Berra | 14 |
| 2. | Mickey Mantle | 12 |
| 3. | Whitey Ford | 11 |
| 4. | Joe DiMaggio | 10 |
| | Elston Howard | 10 |
| | Babe Ruth | 10 |
| 7. | Hank Bauer | 9 |
| | Phil Rizzuto | 9 |
| 9. | Bill Dickey | 8 |
| | Frank Frisch | 8 |
| | Gil McDougald | 8 |
| | Bill Skowron | 8 |
| 12. | many tied with 7 | |

### SERIES PITCHED

| | Player | Series |
|---|---|---|
| 1. | Whitey Ford | 11 |
| **2.** | **Andy Pettitte** | **7** |
| | Waite Hoyt | 7 |
| | Red Ruffing | 7 |
| **5.** | **Roger Clemens** | **6** |
| | **Mariano Rivera** | **6** |
| | **Mike Stanton** | **6** |
| | Catfish Hunter | 6 |
| | Johnny Murphy | 6 |
| | Jim Palmer | 6 |
| | Vic Raschi | 6 |
| | Allie Reynolds | 6 |
| 12. | many tied with 5 | |

## BATTING

### GAMES

| | Player | Games |
|---|---|---|
| 1. | Yogi Berra | 75 |
| 2. | Mickey Mantle | 65 |
| 3. | Elston Howard | 54 |
| 4. | Hank Bauer | 53 |
| | Gil McDougald | 53 |
| 5. | Phil Rizzuto | 52 |
| 6. | Joe DiMaggio | 51 |
| 7. | Frank Frisch | 50 |
| 8. | Pee Wee Reese | 44 |
| 9. | Roger Maris | 41 |
| | Babe Ruth | 41 |
| 11. | Carl Furillo | 40 |
| 12. | Jim Gilliam | 39 |
| | Gil Hodges | 39 |
| | Bill Skowron | 39 |
| 15. | Bill Dickey | 38 |
| | Jackie Robinson | 38 |
| 17. | Tony Kubek | 37 |
| 18. | Joe Collins | 36 |
| | David Justice | 36 |
| | Bobby Richardson | 36 |
| | Duke Snider | 36 |

### BATTING AVERAGE

(minimum 50 AB)

| | Player | BA |
|---|---|---|
| 1. | Pepper Martin | .418 |
| | Paul Molitor | .418 |
| 3. | Lou Brock | .391 |
| 4. | Marquis Grissom | .390 |
| 5. | Thurman Munson | .373 |
| | George Brett | .373 |
| 7. | Hank Aaron | .364 |
| 8. | Frank Baker | .363 |
| 9. | Roberto Clemente | .362 |
| 10. | Lou Gehrig | .361 |
| 11. | Reggie Jackson | .357 |
| 12. | Carl Yastrzemski | .352 |
| 13. | Earle Combs | .350 |
| 14. | Stan Hack | .348 |
| 15. | Joe Jackson | .345 |
| 16. | Jimmie Foxx | .344 |
| 17. | Rickey Henderson | .339 |
| 18. | Julian Javier | .333 |
| | Billy Martin | .333 |
| 20. | Al Simmons | .329 |

### AT-BATS

| | Player | AB |
|---|---|---|
| 1. | Yogi Berra | 259 |
| 2. | Mickey Mantle | 230 |
| 3. | Joe DiMaggio | 199 |
| 4. | Frank Frisch | 197 |
| 5. | Gil McDougald | 190 |
| 6. | Hank Bauer | 188 |
| 7. | Phil Rizzuto | 183 |
| 8. | Elston Howard | 171 |
| 9. | Pee Wee Reese | 169 |
| 10. | Roger Maris | 152 |
| 11. | Jim Gilliam | 147 |
| 12. | Tony Kubek | 146 |
| 13. | Bill Dickey | 145 |
| 14. | Jackie Robinson | 137 |
| 15. | Bill Skowron | 133 |
| | Duke Snider | 133 |
| 17. | Gil Hodges | 131 |
| | Bobby Richardson | 131 |
| 19. | Pete Rose | 130 |
| **20.** | **Derek Jeter** | **129** |
| | Goose Goslin | 129 |
| | Bob Meusel | 129 |
| | Babe Ruth | 129 |

### RUNS

| | Player | R |
|---|---|---|
| 1. | Mickey Mantle | 42 |
| 2. | Yogi Berra | 41 |
| 3. | Babe Ruth | 37 |
| 4. | Lou Gehrig | 30 |
| **5.** | **Derek Jeter** | **27** |
| | Joe DiMaggio | 27 |
| 7. | Roger Maris | 26 |
| 8. | Elston Howard | 25 |
| 9. | Gil McDougald | 23 |
| 10. | Jackie Robinson | 22 |
| 11. | Hank Bauer | 21 |
| | Reggie Jackson | 21 |
| | Phil Rizzuto | 21 |
| | Duke Snider | 21 |
| | Gene Woodling | 21 |
| 16. | Eddie Collins | 20 |
| | Pee Wee Reese | 20 |
| 18. | Bill Dickey | 19 |
| | Frank Robinson | 19 |
| | Bill Skowron | 19 |

### HITS

| | Player | H |
|---|---|---|
| 1. | Yogi Berra | 71 |
| 2. | Mickey Mantle | 59 |
| 3. | Frank Frisch | 58 |
| 4. | Joe DiMaggio | 54 |
| 5. | Hank Bauer | 46 |
| | Pee Wee Reese | 46 |
| 7. | Gil McDougald | 45 |
| | Phil Rizzuto | 45 |
| 9. | Lou Gehrig | 43 |
| 10. | Eddie Collins | 42 |
| | Elston Howard | 42 |
| | Babe Ruth | 42 |
| 13. | Bobby Richardson | 40 |
| **14.** | **Derek Jeter** | **39** |
| | Bill Skowron | 39 |
| 16. | Duke Snider | 38 |
| 17. | Bill Dickey | 37 |
| | Goose Goslin | 37 |
| 19. | Steve Garvey | 36 |
| 20. | Gil Hodges | 35 |
| | Reggie Jackson | 35 |
| | Tony Kubek | 35 |
| | Pete Rose | 35 |

### SINGLES

| | Player | Singles |
|---|---|---|
| 1. | Yogi Berra | 49 |
| 2. | Frank Frisch | 45 |
| 3. | Joe DiMaggio | 40 |
| | Phil Rizzuto | 40 |
| 5. | Pee Wee Reese | 39 |
| 6. | Hank Bauer | 34 |
| 7. | Eddie Collins | 33 |
| | Mickey Mantle | 33 |
| | Gil McDougald | 33 |
| 10. | Tony Kubek | 31 |
| | Bobby Richardson | 31 |
| 12. | Bill Dickey | 30 |
| **13.** | **Derek Jeter** | **29** |
| | Steve Garvey | 29 |

| Player | Singles |
|---|---|
| Elston Howard | 29 |
| 16. Red Rolfe | 28 |
| 17. Gil Hodges | 27 |
| Pete Rose | 27 |
| 19. Bill Skowron | 26 |
| **20. Marquis Grissom** | **25** |
| Goose Goslin | 25 |

## DOUBLES

| Player | Doubles |
|---|---|
| 1. Yogi Berra | 10 |
| Frank Frisch | 10 |
| 3. Jack Barry | 9 |
| Pete Fox | 9 |
| Carl Furillo | 9 |
| 6. Lou Gehrig | 8 |
| Lonnie Smith | 8 |
| Duke Snider | 8 |
| 9. many tied with 7 | |

## TRIPLES

| Player | Triples |
|---|---|
| 1. Billy Johnson | 4 |
| Tommy Leach | 4 |
| Tris Speaker | 4 |
| 4. many tied with 1 | |

## HOME RUNS

| Player | HR |
|---|---|
| 1. Mickey Mantle | 18 |
| 2. Babe Ruth | 15 |
| 3. Yogi Berra | 12 |
| 4. Duke Snider | 11 |
| 5. Lou Gehrig | 10 |
| Reggie Jackson | 10 |
| 7. Joe DiMaggio | 8 |
| Frank Robinson | 8 |
| Bill Skowron | 8 |
| 10. Hank Bauer | 7 |
| Goose Goslin | 7 |
| Gil McDougald | 7 |
| 13. Lenny Dykstra | 6 |
| Roger Maris | 6 |
| Al Simmons | 6 |
| Reggie Smith | 6 |
| 17. many tied with 5 | |

## TOTAL BASES

| Player | TB |
|---|---|
| 1. Mickey Mantle | 123 |
| 2. Yogi Berra | 117 |
| 3. Babe Ruth | 96 |
| 4. Lou Gehrig | 87 |
| 5. Joe DiMaggio | 84 |
| 6. Duke Snider | 79 |
| 7. Hank Bauer | 75 |
| 8. Frank Frisch | 74 |
| Reggie Jackson | 74 |
| 10. Gil McDougald | 72 |
| 11. Bill Skowron | 69 |
| 12. Elston Howard | 66 |
| 13. Goose Goslin | 63 |
| 14. Pee Wee Reese | 59 |
| 15. Lou Brock | 57 |
| **16. Derek Jeter** | **56** |
| Roger Maris | 56 |
| Billy Martin | 56 |
| 19. Bill Dickey | 55 |
| 20. Gil Hodges | 54 |
| Phil Rizzuto | 54 |

## SLUGGING PERCENTAGE

(Minimum 50 at-bats)

| Player | SLG |
|---|---|
| 1. Reggie Jackson | .755 |
| 2. Babe Ruth | .744 |
| 3. Lou Gehrig | .731 |
| 4. Lenny Dykstra | .700 |
| 5. Al Simmons | .658 |
| 6. Lou Brock | .655 |
| 7. Pepper Martin | .636 |
| Paul Molitor | .636 |
| 9. Hank Greenberg | .623 |
| 10. Charlie Keller | .611 |
| 11. Jimmie Foxx | .609 |
| 12. Rickey Henderson | .607 |
| 13. Dave Henderson | .606 |
| 14. Hank Aaron | .600 |
| 15. Duke Snider | .594 |
| 16. Dwight Evans | .580 |
| 17. Steve Yeager | .579 |
| 18. Willie Stargell | .574 |
| 19. Billy Martin | .566 |
| 20. Carl Yastrzemski | .556 |

## EXTRA-BASE HITS

| Player | EBH |
|---|---|
| 1. Mickey Mantle | 26 |
| 2. Yogi Berra | 22 |
| Babe Ruth | 22 |
| 4. Lou Gehrig | 21 |
| 5. Duke Snider | 19 |
| 6. Reggie Jackson | 18 |
| 7. Joe DiMaggio | 14 |
| Hank Greenberg | 14 |
| 9. Lou Brock | 13 |
| Frank Frisch | 13 |
| Elston Howard | 13 |
| Bill Skowron | 13 |
| Lonnie Smith | 13 |
| 14. Hank Bauer | 12 |
| Goose Goslin | 12 |
| Gil McDougald | 12 |
| Al Simmons | 12 |
| 18. Carl Furillo | 11 |
| Dave Henderson | 11 |
| Roger Maris | 11 |
| Frank Robinson | 11 |
| Devon White | 11 |

## RUNS BATTED IN

| Player | RBI |
|---|---|
| 1. Mickey Mantle | 40 |
| 2. Yogi Berra | 39 |
| 3. Lou Gehrig | 35 |
| 4. Babe Ruth | 33 |
| 5. Joe DiMaggio | 30 |
| 6. Bill Skowron | 29 |
| 7. Duke Snider | 26 |
| 8. Hank Bauer | 24 |
| Bill Dickey | 24 |
| Reggie Jackson | 24 |
| Gil McDougald | 24 |
| 12. Hank Greenberg | 22 |
| 13. Gil Hodges | 21 |
| David Justice | 21 |
| 15. Goose Goslin | 19 |
| Elston Howard | 19 |
| Tony Lazzeri | 19 |
| Billy Martin | 19 |
| 19. Frank Baker | 18 |
| Charlie Keller | 18 |
| Roger Maris | 18 |

## WALKS

| Player | BB |
|---|---|
| 1. Mickey Mantle | 43 |
| 2. Babe Ruth | 33 |
| 3. Yogi Berra | 32 |
| 4. Phil Rizzuto | 30 |
| 5. Lou Gehrig | 26 |
| David Justice | 26 |
| 7. Mickey Cochrane | 25 |
| 8. Jim Gilliam | 23 |
| 9. Jackie Robinson | 21 |
| **10. Bernie Williams** | **20** |
| Gil McDougald | 20 |
| 12. Joe DiMaggio | 19 |
| Gene Woodling | 19 |
| 14. Roger Maris | 18 |
| Pee Wee Reese | 18 |
| 16. Gil Hodges | 17 |
| Gene Tenace | 17 |
| Ross Youngs | 17 |
| 19. Paul O'Neill | 16 |
| Pete Rose | 16 |

## STRIKEOUTS

| Player | K |
|---|---|
| 1. Mickey Mantle | 54 |
| 2. Elston Howard | 37 |
| **3. Derek Jeter** | **33** |
| Duke Snider | 33 |
| 5. David Justice | 30 |
| Babe Ruth | 30 |
| 7. Gil McDougald | 29 |
| **8. Bernie Williams** | **26** |
| Bill Skowron | 26 |
| 10. Hank Bauer | 25 |
| **11. Jorge Posada** | **24** |

| | Player | K |
|---|---|---|
| | Reggie Jackson | 24 |
| | Bob Meusel | 24 |
| 14. | Joe DiMaggio | 23 |
| | George Kelly | 23 |
| | Tony Kubek | 23 |
| | Frank Robinson | 23 |
| | Devon White | 23 |
| 19. | Jim Bottomley | 22 |
| | Joe Collins | 22 |
| | Gil Hodges | 22 |
| | Lonnie Smith | 22 |

## STOLEN BASES

| | Player | SB |
|---|---|---|
| 1. | Lou Brock | 14 |
| | Eddie Collins | 14 |
| 3. | Frank Chance | 10 |
| | Davey Lopes | 10 |
| | Phil Rizzuto | 10 |
| **6.** | **Kenny Lofton** | **9** |
| | Frank Frisch | 9 |
| | Honus Wagner | 9 |
| 9. | Johnny Evers | 8 |
| 10. | Roberto Alomar | 7 |
| | Rickey Henderson | 7 |
| | Pepper Martin | 7 |
| | Joe Morgan | 7 |
| | Joe Tinker | 7 |
| 15. | many tied with 6 | |

# PITCHING

## GAMES

| | Player | Games |
|---|---|---|
| 1. | Whitey Ford | 22 |
| **2.** | **Mariano Rivera** | **20** |
| | **Mike Stanton** | **20** |
| **4.** | **Jeff Nelson** | **16** |
| | Rollie Fingers | 16 |
| 6. | Allie Reynolds | 15 |
| | Bob Turley | 15 |
| 8. | Clay Carroll | 14 |
| 9. | Clem Labine | 13 |
| | Mark Wohlers | 13 |
| 11. | Waite Hoyt | 12 |
| | Catfish Hunter | 12 |
| | Art Nehf | 12 |
| **14.** | **Andy Pettitte** | **11** |
| | Paul Derringer | 11 |
| | Carl Erskine | 11 |
| | Rube Marquard | 11 |
| | Christy Mathewson | 11 |
| | Vic Raschi | 11 |
| 20. | many tied with 10 | |

## GAMES STARTED

| | Player | Games |
|---|---|---|
| 1. | Whitey Ford | 22 |
| **2.** | **Andy Pettitte** | **11** |
| | Waite Hoyt | 11 |
| | Christy Mathewson | 11 |
| 5. | Chief Bender | 10 |
| | Red Ruffing | 10 |
| 7. | Bob Gibson | 9 |
| | Catfish Hunter | 9 |
| | Art Nehf | 9 |
| | Allie Reynolds | 9 |
| 11. | many tied with 8 | |

## GAMES RELIEVED

| | Player | Games |
|---|---|---|
| **1.** | **Mariano Rivera** | **20** |
| **2.** | **Mike Stanton** | **20** |
| **3.** | **Jeff Nelson** | **16** |
| | Rollie Fingers | 16 |
| 5. | Clay Carroll | 14 |
| 6. | Mark Wohlers | 13 |
| 7. | Clem Labine | 12 |
| 8. | Pedro Borbon | 10 |
| | Dan Quisenberry | 10 |
| 10. | Paul Assenmacher | 9 |
| | Hugh Casey | 9 |
| | Tug McGraw | 9 |
| 13. | Ken Dayley | 8 |
| | Rich Gossage | 8 |
| | Don McMahon | 8 |
| | Johnny Murphy | 8 |
| | Duane Ward | 8 |
| 18. | many tied with 7 | |

## COMPLETE GAMES

| | Player | CG |
|---|---|---|
| 1. | Christy Mathewson | 10 |
| 2. | Chief Bender | 9 |
| 3. | Bob Gibson | 8 |
| | Red Ruffing | 8 |
| 5. | Whitey Ford | 7 |
| 6. | Waite Hoyt | 6 |
| | George Mullin | 6 |
| | Art Nehf | 6 |
| | Eddie Plank | 6 |
| 10. | Mordecai Brown | 5 |
| | Joe Bush | 5 |
| | Bill Donovan | 5 |
| | George Earnshaw | 5 |
| | Walter Johnson | 5 |
| | Carl Mays | 5 |
| | Deacon Phillippe | 5 |
| | Allie Reynolds | 5 |
| 18. | many tied with 4 | |

## INNINGS PITCHED

| | Player | IP |
|---|---|---|
| 1. | Whitey Ford | 146.0 |
| 2. | Christy Mathewson | 101.2 |
| 3. | Red Ruffing | 85.2 |
| 4. | Chief Bender | 85.0 |
| 5. | Waite Hoyt | 83.2 |
| 6. | Bob Gibson | 81.0 |
| 7. | Art Nehf | 79.0 |
| 8. | Allie Reynolds | 77.1 |
| **9.** | **Andy Pettitte** | **66.0** |
| 10. | Jim Palmer | 64.2 |
| 11. | Catfish Hunter | 63.0 |
| 12. | George Earnshaw | 62.2 |
| 13. | Joe Bush | 60.2 |
| 14. | Vic Raschi | 60.1 |
| 15. | Rube Marquard | 58.2 |
| 16. | Tom Glavine | 58.1 |
| 17. | George Mullin | 58.0 |
| 18. | Mordecai Brown | 57.2 |
| 19. | Carl Mays | 57.1 |
| 20. | Sandy Koufax | 57.0 |
| | Dave Stewart | 57.0 |

## EARNED RUN AVERAGE

(minimum 30 IP)

| | Player | ERA |
|---|---|---|
| 1. | Harry Brecheen | 0.83 |
| 2. | Babe Ruth | 0.87 |
| 3. | Sherry Smith | 0.89 |
| 4. | Sandy Koufax | 0.95 |
| 5. | Monte Pearson | 1.01 |
| 6. | Christy Mathewson | 1.06 |
| **7.** | **Mariano Rivera** | **1.16** |
| 8. | Eddie Plank | 1.32 |
| 9. | Rollie Fingers | 1.35 |
| 10. | Bill Hallahan | 1.36 |
| 11. | George Earnshaw | 1.58 |
| 12. | Spud Chandler | 1.62 |
| 13. | Jesse Haines | 1.67 |
| 14. | Ron Guidry | 1.69 |
| 15. | Max Lanier | 1.71 |
| 16. | Stan Coveleski | 1.74 |
| 17. | Lefty Grove | 1.75 |
| | Orval Overall | 1.75 |
| 19. | Carl Hubbell | 1.79 |
| 20. | Ernie Shore | 1.82 |

## WINS

| | Player | W |
|---|---|---|
| 1. | Whitey Ford | 10 |
| 2. | Bob Gibson | 7 |
| | Allie Reynolds | 7 |
| | Red Ruffing | 7 |
| 5. | Chief Bender | 6 |
| | Lefty Gomez | 6 |
| | Waite Hoyt | 6 |
| 8. | Mordecai Brown | 5 |
| | Jack Coombs | 5 |
| | Catfish Hunter | 5 |
| | Christy Mathewson | 5 |
| | Herb Pennock | 5 |
| | Vic Raschi | 5 |
| 14. | many tied with 4 | |

## LOSSES

| Player | L |
|---|---|
| 1. Whitey Ford | 8 |
| 2. Joe Bush | 5 |
| Rube Marquard | 5 |
| Christy Mathewson | 5 |
| Eddie Plank | 5 |
| Schoolboy Rowe | 5 |
| **7. Andy Pettitte** | **4** |
| Chief Bender | 4 |
| Mordecai Brown | 4 |
| Paul Derringer | 4 |
| Bill Donovan | 4 |
| Burleigh Grimes | 4 |
| Waite Hoyt | 4 |
| Charlie Leibrandt | 4 |
| Carl Mays | 4 |
| Art Nehf | 4 |
| Don Newcombe | 4 |
| Bill Sherdel | 4 |
| Dave Stewart | 4 |
| Ed Summers | 4 |
| Ralph Terry | 4 |

## SAVES

| Player | SV |
|---|---|
| **1. Mariano Rivera** | **9** |
| 2. Rollie Fingers | 6 |
| 3. Johnny Murphy | 4 |
| Robb Nen | 4 |
| Allie Reynolds | 4 |
| John Wetteland | 4 |
| **7. Troy Percival** | **3** |
| Roy Face | 3 |
| Firpo Marberry | 3 |
| Will McEnaney | 3 |
| Tug McGraw | 3 |
| Herb Pennock | 3 |
| Kent Tekulve | 3 |
| Todd Worrell | 3 |
| 15. many tied with 2 | |

## RUNS

| Player | R |
|---|---|
| 1. Whitey Ford | 51 |
| **2. Andy Pettitte** | **32** |
| Red Ruffing | 32 |
| Don Sutton | 32 |
| 5. Chief Bender | 28 |
| Carl Erskine | 28 |
| Burleigh Grimes | 28 |
| Waite Hoyt | 28 |
| Rube Marquard | 28 |
| 10. Mordecai Brown | 26 |
| Paul Derringer | 26 |
| 12. Allie Reynolds | 25 |
| Bob Shawkey | 25 |
| Dave Stewart | 25 |
| 15. Catfish Hunter | 24 |
| 16. Don Gullett | 23 |
| Art Nehf | 23 |
| Jim Palmer | 23 |
| Schoolboy Rowe | 23 |
| 20. Tommy Bridges | 22 |
| Christy Mathewson | 22 |
| George Mullin | 22 |

## HITS

| Player | H |
|---|---|
| 1. Whitey Ford | 132 |
| 2. Waite Hoyt | 81 |
| 3. Christy Mathewson | 76 |
| **4. Andy Pettitte** | **74** |
| Red Ruffing | 74 |
| 6. Chief Bender | 64 |
| 7. Allie Reynolds | 61 |
| 8. Catfish Hunter | 57 |
| 9. Walter Johnson | 56 |
| 10. Bob Gibson | 55 |
| Jim Palmer | 55 |
| Don Sutton | 55 |
| 13. Tommy Bridges | 52 |
| Rube Marquard | 52 |
| Vic Raschi | 52 |
| 16. Lefty Gomez | 51 |
| Ed Lopat | 51 |
| 18. Mordecai Brown | 50 |
| Art Nehf | 50 |
| Schoolboy Rowe | 50 |

## HOME RUNS

| Player | HR |
|---|---|
| 1. Catfish Hunter | 9 |
| 2. Don Drysdale | 8 |
| Whitey Ford | 8 |
| Tom Glavine | 8 |
| Burleigh Grimes | 8 |
| Don Newcombe | 8 |
| Gary Nolan | 8 |
| Allie Reynolds | 8 |
| Charlie Root | 8 |
| 10. Don Sutton | 7 |
| 11. Lew Burdette | 6 |
| Roger Craig | 6 |
| Bob Gibson | 6 |
| Bob Turley | 6 |
| 15. many tied with 5 | |

## TOTAL BASES

| Player | TB |
|---|---|
| 1. Whitey Ford | 184 |
| 2. Christy Mathewson | 105 |
| Allie Reynolds | 105 |
| 4. Red Ruffing | 104 |
| 5. Waite Hoyt | 102 |
| **6. Andy Pettitte** | **98** |
| 7. Catfish Hunter | 94 |
| 8. Chief Bender | 91 |
| Don Sutton | 88 |
| 10. Burleigh Grimes | 87 |
| 11. Bob Gibson | 86 |
| Rube Marquard | 86 |
| 13. Walter Johnson | 85 |
| 14. Jim Palmer | 82 |
| 15. Vic Raschi | 79 |
| 16. Tommy Bridges | 78 |
| 17. Schoolboy Rowe | 73 |
| Warren Spahn | 73 |
| 19. Jack Morris | 70 |
| 20. Ralph Terry | 69 |

## STRIKEOUTS

| Player | K |
|---|---|
| 1. Whitey Ford | 94 |
| 2. Bob Gibson | 92 |
| 3. Allie Reynolds | 62 |
| 4. Sandy Koufax | 61 |
| Red Ruffing | 61 |
| 6. Chief Bender | 59 |
| 7. George Earnshaw | 56 |
| **8. John Smoltz** | **52** |
| **9. Roger Clemens** | **49** |
| Waite Hoyt | 49 |
| 11. Christy Mathewson | 48 |
| **12. Andy Pettitte** | **46** |
| 13. Bob Turley | 46 |
| 14. Jim Palmer | 44 |
| 15. Vic Raschi | 43 |
| 16. Jack Morris | 40 |
| 17. Curt Schilling | 39 |
| **18. Tom Glavine** | **38** |
| 19. Don Gullett | 37 |
| **20. Orlando Hernandez** | **36** |
| Don Drysdale | 36 |
| Lefty Grove | 36 |
| George Mullin | 36 |

## WALKS

| Player | BB |
|---|---|
| 1. Whitey Ford | 34 |
| 2. Art Nehf | 32 |
| Allie Reynolds | 32 |
| 4. Jim Palmer | 31 |
| 5. Bob Turley | 29 |
| 6. Paul Derringer | 27 |
| Red Ruffing | 27 |
| 8 .Burleigh Grimes | 26 |
| Don Gullett | 26 |
| 10. Vic Raschi | 25 |
| 11. Carl Erskine | 24 |
| 12. Bill Hallahan | 23 |
| Dave Stewart | 23 |
| 14. Waite Hoyt | 22 |
| **15. John Smoltz** | **21** |
| Chief Bender | 21 |
| Jack Coombs | 21 |
| **18. Tom Glavine** | **20** |
| Joe Bush | 20 |
| David Cone | 20 |

# GENERAL REFERENCE

## SERIES WON AND LOST BY TEAMS

### AMERICAN LEAGUE

| | W | L | Pct. |
|---|---|---|---|
| Toronto | 2 | 0 | 1.000 |
| Anaheim | 1 | 0 | 1.000 |
| New York | 26 | 13 | .667 |
| Oakland | 4 | 2 | .667 |
| Minnesota | 2 | 1 | .667 |
| Philadelphia | 5 | 3 | .625 |
| Boston | 6 | 4 | .600 |
| Chicago | 3 | 2 | .600 |
| Baltimore | 3 | 3 | .500 |
| Kansas City | 1 | 1 | .500 |
| Detroit | 4 | 5 | .444 |
| Cleveland | 2 | 3 | .400 |
| Washington | 1 | 2 | .333 |
| Milwaukee | 0 | 1 | .000 |
| St. Louis | 0 | 1 | .000 |
| **Totals** | **60** | **41** | **.594** |

### NATIONAL LEAGUE

| | W | L | Pct. |
|---|---|---|---|
| Florida | 2 | 0 | 1.000 |
| Arizona | 1 | 0 | 1.000 |
| Pittsburgh | 5 | 2 | .714 |
| St. Louis | 9 | 7 | .563 |
| Cincinnati | 5 | 4 | .556 |
| Los Angeles | 5 | 4 | .555 |
| New York Mets | 2 | 2 | .500 |
| Boston | 1 | 1 | .500 |
| Milwaukee | 1 | 1 | .500 |
| New York Giants | 5 | 9 | .357 |
| Atlanta | 1 | 4 | .200 |
| Philadelphia | 1 | 4 | .200 |
| Chicago | 2 | 8 | .200 |
| Brooklyn | 1 | 8 | .111 |
| Houston | 0 | 1 | .000 |
| San Diego | 0 | 2 | .000 |
| San Francisco | 0 | 3 | .000 |
| **Totals** | **41** | **60** | **.406** |

## GAMES WON AND LOST BY TEAMS

*includes one tie per asterisk

### AMERICAN LEAGUE

| | W | L | Pct. |
|---|---|---|---|
| Toronto | 8 | 4 | .667 |
| New York* | 130 | 88 | .596 |
| Boston* | 37 | 26 | .587 |
| Baltimore | 19 | 14 | .576 |
| Anaheim | 4 | 3 | .571 |
| Chicago | 17 | 13 | .567 |
| Philadelphia | 24 | 19 | .558 |
| Oakland | 17 | 15 | .531 |
| Minnesota | 11 | 10 | .524 |
| Detroit* | 26 | 29 | .473 |
| Cleveland | 14 | 16 | .467 |
| Kansas City | 6 | 7 | .462 |
| Milwaukee | 3 | 4 | .429 |
| Washington | 8 | 11 | .421 |
| St. Louis | 2 | 4 | .333 |
| **Totals** | **326** | **263** | **.553** |

### NATIONAL LEAGUE

| | W | L | Pct. |
|---|---|---|---|
| Boston | 6 | 4 | .600 |
| Florida | 8 | 5 | .615 |
| Arizona | 4 | 3 | .571 |
| Los Angeles | 25 | 24 | .510 |
| Cincinnati | 26 | 25 | .510 |
| New York Mets | 12 | 12 | .500 |
| Milwaukee | 7 | 7 | .500 |
| Pittsburgh | 23 | 24 | .489 |
| New York Giants** | 39 | 41 | .488 |
| St. Louis | 48 | 52 | .480 |
| Atlanta | 11 | 18 | .379 |
| Chicago* | 19 | 33 | .365 |
| Brooklyn | 20 | 36 | .357 |
| San Francisco | 6 | 12 | .333 |
| Philadelphia | 8 | 18 | .308 |
| San Diego | 1 | 8 | .111 |
| Houston | 0 | 4 | .000 |
| **Totals** | **263** | **326** | **.447** |

## HOME AND ROAD GAMES BY TEAMS

### AMERICAN LEAGUE

| | Series | Games | Home | Away |
|---|---|---|---|---|
| New York | 39 | 219 | 106 | 113 |
| Boston | 10 | 64 | 33 | 31 |
| Detroit | 9 | 56 | 28 | 28 |
| Philadelphia | 8 | 43 | 20 | 23 |
| Baltimore | 6 | 33 | 17 | 16 |
| Oakland | 6 | 32 | 17 | 15 |
| Cleveland | 5 | 30 | 15 | 15 |
| Chicago | 5 | 30 | 15 | 15 |
| Minnesota | 3 | 21 | 12 | 9 |
| Washington | 3 | 19 | 10 | 9 |
| Kansas City | 2 | 13 | 7 | 6 |
| Toronto | 2 | 12 | 6 | 6 |
| Anaheim | 1 | 7 | 4 | 3 |
| Milwaukee | 1 | 7 | 3 | 4 |
| St. Louis | 1 | 6 | 3 | 3 |
| **Totals** | **101** | **592** | **296** | **296** |

### NATIONAL LEAGUE

| | Series | Games | Home | Away |
|---|---|---|---|---|
| St. Louis | 16 | 100 | 49 | 51 |
| New York Giants | 14 | 82 | 41 | 41 |
| Chicago | 10 | 53 | 27 | 26 |
| Brooklyn | 9 | 56 | 28 | 28 |
| Cincinnati | 9 | 51 | 26 | 25 |
| Los Angeles | 9 | 49 | 23 | 26 |
| Pittsburgh | 7 | 47 | 23 | 24 |
| Philadelphia | 5 | 26 | 14 | 12 |
| Atlanta | 5 | 29 | 14 | 15 |
| New York Mets | 4 | 24 | 13 | 11 |
| San Francisco | 3 | 18 | 9 | 9 |
| Milwaukee | 2 | 14 | 7 | 7 |
| Florida | 2 | 13 | 7 | 6 |
| Boston | 2 | 10 | 5 | 5 |
| San Diego | 2 | 9 | 4 | 5 |
| Arizona | 1 | 7 | 4 | 3 |
| Houston | 1 | 4 | 2 | 2 |
| **Totals** | **101** | **592** | **296** | **296** |

## TIE GAMES

Oct 8, 1907—12 inn, Chicago NL 3, Detroit AL 3
Oct 9, 1912—11 inn, Boston AL 6, New York NL 6
Oct 5, 1922—10 inn, New York AL 3, New York NL 3
**Total number of ties: 3**

## SHUTOUTS

| | |
|---|---|
| Oct 2, 1903 | Bill Dinneen, Boston AL 3, Pittsburgh NL 0 (3 H) |
| Oct 13, 1903 | Bill Dinneen, Boston AL 3, Pittsburgh NL 0 (4 H) |
| Oct 9, 1905 | Christy Mathewson, New York NL 3, Philadelphia AL 0 (4 H) |
| Oct 10, 1905 | Chief Bender, Philadelphia AL 3, New York NL 0 (4 H) |
| Oct 12, 1905 | Christy Mathewson, New York NL 9, Philadelphia AL 0 (4 H) |
| Oct 13, 1905 | Joe McGinnity, New York NL 1, Philadelphia AL 0 (5 H) |
| Oct 14, 1905 | Christy Mathewson, New York NL 2, Philadelphia AL 0 (6 H) |
| Oct 11, 1906 | Ed Walsh, Chicago AL 3, Chicago NL 0 (2 H) |
| Oct 12, 1906 | Mordecai Brown, Chicago NL 1, Chicago AL 0 (2 H) |
| Oct 12, 1907 | Mordecai Brown, Chicago NL 2, Detroit AL 0 (7 H) |
| Oct 13, 1908 | Mordecai Brown, Chicago NL 3, Detroit AL 0 (4 H) |
| Oct 14, 1908 | Orval Overall, Chicago NL 2, Detroit AL 0 (3 H) |
| Oct 12, 1909 | George Mullin, Detroit AL 5, Pittsburgh NL 0 (5 H) |
| Oct 16, 1909 | Babe Adams, Pittsburgh NL 8, Detroit AL 0 (6 H) |
| Oct 8, 1913 | Christy Mathewson, New York NL 3, Philadelphia AL 0, 10 inn (8 H) |
| Oct 10, 1914 | Bill James, Boston NL 1, Philadelphia AL 0 (2 H) |
| Oct 10, 1917 | Rube Benton, New York NL 2, Chicago AL 0 (5 H) |
| Oct 11, 1917 | Ferdie Schupp, New York NL 5, Chicago AL 0 (7 H) |
| Sept 5, 1918 | Babe Ruth, Boston AL 1, Chicago NL 0 (6 H) |
| Sept 10, 1918 | Hippo Vaughn, Chicago NL 3, Boston AL 0 (5 H) |
| Oct 3, 1919 | Dickie Kerr, Chicago AL 3, Cincinnati NL 0 (3 H) |
| Oct 4, 1919 | Jimmy Ring, Cincinnati NL 2, Chicago AL 0 (3 H) |
| Oct 6, 1919 | Hod Eller, Cincinnati NL 5, Chicago AL 0 (3 H) |
| Oct 6, 1920 | Burleigh Grimes, Brooklyn NL 3, Cleveland AL 0 (7 H) |
| Oct 11, 1920 | Duster Mails, Cleveland AL 1, Brooklyn NL 0 (3 H) |
| Oct 12, 1920 | Stan Coveleski, Cleveland AL 3, Brooklyn NL 0 (5 H) |
| Oct 5, 1921 | Carl Mays, New York AL 3, New York NL 0 (5 H) |
| Oct 6, 1921 | Waite Hoyt, New York AL 3, New York NL 0 (2 H) |
| Oct 13, 1921 | Art Nehf, New York NL 1, New York AL 0 (4 H) |
| Oct 6, 1922 | Jack Scott, New York NL 3, New York AL 0 (4 H) |
| Oct 12, 1923 | Art Nehf, New York NL 1, New York AL 0 (6 H) |
| Oct 11, 1925 | Walter Johnson, Washington AL 4, Pittsburgh NL 0 (6 H) |
| Oct 5, 1926 | Jesse Haines, St. Louis NL 4, New York AL 0 (5 H) |
| Oct 4, 1930 | Bill Hallahan, St. Louis NL 5, Philadelphia AL 0 (7 H) |
| Oct 6, 1930 | George Earnshaw, Lefty Grove, Philadelphia AL 2, St. Louis NL 0 (3 H) |
| Oct 2, 1931 | Bill Hallahan, St. Louis NL 2, Philadelphia AL 0 (3 H) |

Oct 6, 1931 George Earnshaw, Philadelphia AL 3, St. Louis NL 0 (2 H)
Oct 5, 1933 Earl Whitehill, Washington AL 4, New York NL 0 (5 H)
Oct 9, 1934 Dizzy Dean, St. Louis NL 11, Detroit AL 0 (6 H)
Oct 2, 1935 Lon Warneke, Chicago NL 3, Detroit AL 0 (4 H)
Oct 5, 1939 Monte Pearson, New York AL 4, Cincinnati NL 0 (2 H)
Oct 6, 1940 Bobo Newsom, Detroit AL 8, Cincinnati NL 0 (3 H)
Oct 7, 1940 Bucky Walters, Cincinnati NL 4, Detroit AL 0 (5 H)
Oct 3, 1942 Ernie White, St. Louis NL 2, New York AL 0 (6 H)
Oct 11, 1943 Spud Chandler, New York AL 2, St. Louis NL 0 (10 H)
Oct 8, 1944 Mort Cooper, St. Louis NL 2, St. Louis AL 0 (7 H)
Oct 3, 1945 Hank Borowy, Chicago NL 9, Detroit AL 0 (6 H)
Oct 5, 1945 Claude Passeau, Chicago NL 3, Detroit AL 0 (1 hit)
Oct 7, 1946 Harry Brecheen, St. Louis NL 3, Boston AL 0 (4 H)
Oct 9, 1946 Boo Ferriss, Boston AL 4, St. Louis NL 0 (6 H)
Oct 6, 1948 Johnny Sain, Boston NL 1, Cleveland AL 0 (4 H)
Oct 8, 1948 Gene Bearden, Cleveland AL 2, Boston NL 0 (5 H)
Oct 5, 1949 Allie Reynolds, New York AL 1, Brooklyn NL 0 (2 H)
Oct 6, 1949 Preacher Roe, Brooklyn NL 1, New York AL 0 (6 H)
Oct 4, 1950 Vic Raschi, New York AL 1, Philadelphia NL 0 (2 H)
Oct 4, 1952 Allie Reynolds, New York AL 2, Brooklyn NL 0 (4 H)
Oct 4, 1955 Johnny Podres, Brooklyn NL 2, New York AL 0 (8 H)
Oct 8, 1956 Don Larsen, New York AL 2, Brooklyn NL 0 (0 H)
Oct 9, 1956 Clem Labine, Brooklyn NL 1, New York AL 0, 10 inn (7 H)
Oct 10, 1956 Johnny Kucks, New York AL 9, Brooklyn NL 0 (3 H)
Oct 7, 1957 Lew Burdette, Milwaukee NL 1, New York AL 0 (7 H)
Oct 10, 1957 Lew Burdette, Milwaukee NL 5, New York AL 0 (7 H)
Oct 4, 1958 Don Larsen, Ryne Duren, New York AL 4, Milwaukee NL 0 (6 H)
Oct 5, 1958 Warren Spahn, Milwaukee NL 3, New York AL, 0 (2 H)
Oct 6, 1958 Bob Turley, New York AL 7, Milwaukee NL 0 (5 H)
Oct 1, 1959 Early Wynn, Gerry Staley, Chicago AL 11, Los Angeles NL 0 (8 H)
Oct 6, 1959 Bob Shaw, Billy Pierce, Dick Donovan, Chi AL 1, Los Angeles NL 0 (9 H)
Oct 8, 1960 Whitey Ford, New York AL 10, Pittsburgh NL 0 (4 H)
Oct 12, 1960 Whitey Ford, New York AL 12, Pittsburgh NL 0 (7 H)
Oct 4, 1961 Whitey Ford, New York AL 2, Cincinnati NL 0 (2 H)
Oct 8, 1961 Whitey Ford, Jim Coates, New York AL 7, Cincinnati NL 0 (5 H)
Oct 5, 1962 Jack Sanford, San Francisco NL 2, New York AL 0 (3 H)
Oct 16, 1962 Ralph Terry, New York AL 1, San Francisco NL 0 (4 H)
Oct 5, 1963 Don Drysdale, Los Angeles NL 1, New York AL 0 (3 H)
Oct 9, 1965 Claude Osteen, Los Angeles NL 4, Minnesota AL 0 (5 H)
Oct 11, 1965 Sandy Koufax, Los Angeles NL 7, Minnesota AL 0 (4 H)
Oct 14, 1965 Sandy Koufax, Los Angeles NL 2, Minnesota AL 0 (3 H)
Oct 6, 1966 Jim Palmer, Baltimore AL 6, Los Angeles NL 0 (4 H)
Oct 8, 1966 Wally Bunker, Baltimore AL 1, Los Angeles NL 0 (6 H)
Oct 9, 1966 Dave McNally, Baltimore AL 1, Los Angeles NL 0 (4 H)
Oct 5, 1967 Jim Lonborg, Boston AL 5, St. Louis NL 0 (1 H)
Oct 8, 1967 Bob Gibson, St. Louis NL 6, Boston AL 0 (5 H)
Oct 2, 1968 Bob Gibson, St. Louis NL 4, Detroit AL 0 (5 H)
Oct 14, 1969 Gary Gentry, Nolan Ryan, New York NL 5, Baltimore AL 0 (4 H)
Oct 14, 1971 Nelson Briles, Pittsburgh NL 4, Baltimore AL 0 (2 H)
Oct 18, 1972 Jack Billingham, Clay Carroll, Cincinnati NL 1, Oakland AL 0 (3 H)
Oct 18, 1973 Jerry Koosman, Tug McGraw, New York NL 2, Oakland AL 0 (3 H)
Oct 11, 1975 Luis Tiant, Boston AL 6, Cincinnati NL 0 (5 H)
Oct 16, 1979 John Candelaria, Kent Tekulve, Pittsburgh NL 4, Baltimore AL 0 (7 H)
Oct 21, 1981 Tommy John, Rich Gossage, New York AL, 3 Los Angeles NL 0 (4 H)
Oct 12, 1982 Mike Caldwell, Milwaukee AL 10, St. Louis NL 0 (3 H)
Oct 16, 1983 Scott McGregor, Baltimore AL 5, Philadelphia NL 0 (5 H)
Oct 23, 1985 John Tudor, St. Louis NL 3, Kansas City AL 0 (5 H)
Oct 27, 1985 Bret Saberhagen, Kansas City AL 11, St. Louis NL 0 (5 H)
Oct 18, 1986 Bruce Hurst, Calvin Schiraldi, Boston AL 1, New York NL 0 (5 H)
Oct 16, 1988 Orel Hershiser, Los Angeles NL 6, Oakland AL 0 (3 H)
Oct 14, 1989 Dave Stewart, Oakland AL 5, San Francisco NL 0 (5 H)
Oct 16, 1990 Jose Rijo, Rob Dibble, Randy Myers, Cincinnati NL 7, Oakland AL 0 (9 H)
Oct 27, 1991 Jack Morris, Minnesota AL 1, Atlanta NL 0, 10 inn (7 H)
Oct 21, 1993 Curt Schilling, Philadelphia NL 2, Toronto AL 0 (5 H)
Oct 28, 1995 Tom Glavine, Atlanta NL 1, Cleveland AL 0 (1 hit)
Oct 21, 1996 Greg Maddux, Atlanta NL 4, New York AL 0 (7 H)
Oct 24, 1996 Andy Pettitte, John Wetteland, New York AL 1, Atlanta NL 0 (5 H)
Oct 21, 1998 Andy Pettitte, Jeff Nelson, Mariano Rivera, NY AL 3, San Diego NL 0 (7 H)
Oct 28, 2001 Randy Johnson, Arizona NL 4, New York AL 0 (3 H)
Oct 25, 2003 Josh Beckett, Florida NL 2, New York AL 0 (2 H)
Oct 27, 2004 Derek Lowe, Bronson Arroyo, Alan Embree, Keith Foulke, Boston AL 3, St. Louis NL 0 (4 H)
Oct 26, 2005 Freddy Garcia, Cliff Politte, Neal Cotts, Bobby Jenks, Chi AL 1, Hou NL 0 (5 H)
**Total number of shutouts: 108**

## EXTRA-INNING GAMES

Oct 8, 1907 12 inn, Chicago NL 3, Detroit AL 3 (tie)
Oct 22, 1910 10 inn, Chicago NL 4, Philadelphia AL 3
Oct 17, 1911 11 inn, Philadelphia AL 3, New York NL 2
Oct 25, 1911 10 inn, New York NL 4, Philadelphia AL 3
Oct 9, 1912 11 inn, Boston AL, 6, New York NL 6 (tie)
Oct 16, 1912 10 inn, Boston AL 3, New York NL 2
Oct 8, 1913 10 inn, New York NL 3, Philadelphia AL 0
Oct 12, 1914 12 inn, Boston NL 5, Philadelphia AL 4
Oct 9, 1916 14 inn, Boston AL 2, Brooklyn NL 1
Oct 7, 1919 10 inn, Chicago AL 5, Cincinnati NL 4
Oct 5, 1922 10 inn, New York NL 3, New York AL 3 (tie)
Oct 4, 1924 12 inn, New York NL 4, Washington AL 3
Oct 10, 1924 12 inn, Washington AL 4, New York NL 3
Oct 7, 1926 10 inn, New York AL 3, St. Louis NL 2
Oct 6, 1933 11 inn, New York NL 2, Washington AL 1
Oct 7, 1933 10 inn, New York NL 4, Washington AL 3
Oct 4, 1934 12 inn, Detroit AL 3, St. Louis NL 2
Oct 4, 1935 11 inn, Detroit AL 6, Chicago NL 5
Oct 5, 1936 10 inn, New York NL 5, New York AL 4
Oct 8, 1939 10 inn, New York AL 7, Cincinnati NL 4
Oct 5, 1944 11 inn, St. Louis NL 3, St. Louis AL 2
Oct 8, 1945 12 inn, Chicago NL 8, Detroit AL 7
Oct 6, 1946 10 inn, Boston AL 3, St. Louis NL 2
Oct 5, 1950 10 inn, New York AL 2, Philadelphia NL 1
Oct 5, 1952 11 inn, Brooklyn NL 6, New York AL 5
Sept 29, 1954 10 inn, New York NL 5, Cleveland AL 2
Oct 9, 1956 10 inn, Brooklyn NL 1, New York AL 0
Oct 6, 1957 10 inn, Milwaukee NL 7, New York AL 5
Oct 1, 1958 10 inn, Milwaukee NL 4, New York AL 3
Oct 8, 1958 10 inn, New York AL 4, Milwaukee NL 3
Oct 12, 1964 10 inn, St. Louis NL 5, New York AL 2
Oct 15, 1969 10 inn, New York NL 2, Baltimore AL 1
Oct 16, 1971 10 inn, Baltimore AL 3, Pittsburgh NL 2
Oct 14, 1973 12 inn, New York NL 10, Oakland AL 7
Oct 16, 1973 11 inn, Oakland AL 3, New York NL 2
Oct 14, 1975 10 inn, Cincinnati NL 6, Boston AL 5
Oct 21, 1975 12 inn, Boston AL 7, Cincinnati NL 6
Oct 11, 1977 12 inn, New York AL 4, Los Angeles NL 3
Oct 14, 1978 10 inn, New York AL 4, Los Angeles NL 3
Oct 17, 1980 10 inn, Kansas City AL 4, Philadelphia NL 3
Oct 25, 1986 10 inn, New York NL 6, Boston AL 5
Oct 17, 1990 10 inn, Cincinnati NL 5, Oakland AL 4
Oct 22, 1991 12 inn, Atlanta NL 5, Minnesota AL 4
Oct 26, 1991 11 inn, Minnesota AL 4, Atlanta NL 3
Oct 27, 1991 10 inn, Minnesota AL 1, Atlanta NL 0
Oct 24, 1992 11 inn, Toronto AL 4, Atlanta NL 3
Oct 24, 1995 11 inn, Cleveland AL 7, Atlanta NL 6
Oct 23, 1996 10 inn, New York AL 8, Atlanta NL 6
Oct 26, 1997 11 inn, Florida NL 3, Cleveland AL 2
Oct 26, 1999 10 inn, New York AL 6, Atlanta NL 5
Oct 21, 2000 12 inn, New York AL 4, New York NL 3
Oct 31, 2001 10 inn, New York AL 4, Arizona NL 3
Nov 1, 2001 12 inn, New York AL 3, Arizona NL 2
Oct 22, 2003 12 inn, Florida NL 4, New York AL 3
Oct 25, 2005 14 inn, Chicago AL 7, Houston NL 5
**Total number of occurrences: 54**

## ATTENDANCE

| Year | Games | Total |
|---|---|---|
| 1903 | 8 | 100,429 |
| 1904 | no series | |
| 1905 | 5 | 91,723 |
| 1906 | 6 | 99,845 |
| 1907 | 5 | 78,068 |
| 1908 | 5 | 62,232 |
| 1909 | 7 | 145,295 |
| 1910 | 5 | 124,222 |
| 1911 | 6 | 179,851 |
| 1912 | 8 | 252,037 |
| 1913 | 5 | 151,000 |
| 1914 | 4 | 111,009 |
| 1915 | 5 | 143,351 |
| 1916 | 5 | 162,859 |
| 1917 | 6 | 186,654 |
| 1918 | 6 | 128,483 |
| 1919 | 8 | 236,928 |
| 1920 | 7 | 178,737 |
| 1921 | 8 | 269,976 |
| 1922 | 5 | 185,947 |
| 1923 | 6 | 301,430 |
| 1924 | 7 | 283,665 |
| 1925 | 7 | 282,848 |
| 1926 | 7 | 328,051 |
| 1927 | 4 | 201,705 |
| 1928 | 4 | 199,072 |
| 1929 | 5 | 190,490 |
| 1930 | 6 | 212,619 |
| 1931 | 7 | 231,567 |
| 1932 | 4 | 191,998 |
| 1933 | 5 | 163,076 |
| 1934 | 7 | 281,510 |
| 1935 | 6 | 286,672 |
| 1936 | 6 | 302,924 |
| 1937 | 5 | 238,142 |
| 1938 | 4 | 200,833 |
| 1939 | 4 | 183,849 |
| 1940 | 7 | 281,927 |
| 1941 | 5 | 235,773 |
| 1942 | 5 | 277,101 |
| 1943 | 5 | 277,312 |
| 1944 | 6 | 206,708 |
| 1945 | 7 | 333,457 |
| 1946 | 7 | 250,071 |
| 1947 | 7 | 389,763 |
| 1948 | 6 | 358,362 |
| 1949 | 5 | 236,716 |
| 1950 | 4 | 196,009 |

| Year | Games | Total |
|---|---|---|
| 1951 | 6 | 341,977 |
| 1952 | 7 | 340,706 |
| 1953 | 6 | 307,350 |
| 1954 | 4 | 251,507 |
| 1955 | 7 | 362,310 |
| 1956 | 7 | 345,903 |
| 1957 | 7 | 394,712 |
| 1958 | 7 | 393,909 |
| 1959 | 6 | 420,784 |
| 1960 | 7 | 349,813 |
| 1961 | 5 | 223,247 |
| 1962 | 7 | 376,864 |
| 1963 | 4 | 247,279 |
| 1964 | 7 | 321,807 |
| 1965 | 7 | 364,326 |
| 1966 | 4 | 220,791 |
| 1967 | 7 | 304,085 |
| 1968 | 7 | 379,670 |
| 1969 | 5 | 272,378 |
| 1970 | 5 | 253,183 |
| 1971 | 7 | 351,091 |
| 1972 | 7 | 363,149 |
| 1973 | 7 | 358,289 |
| 1974 | 5 | 260,004 |
| 1975 | 7 | 308,272 |
| 1976 | 4 | 223,009 |
| 1977 | 6 | 337,708 |
| 1978 | 6 | 337,304 |
| 1979 | 7 | 367,597 |
| 1980 | 6 | 324,516 |
| 1981 | 6 | 338,081 |
| 1982 | 7 | 384,570 |
| 1983 | 5 | 304,139 |
| 1984 | 5 | 271,820 |
| 1985 | 7 | 327,494 |
| 1986 | 7 | 321,774 |
| 1987 | 7 | 387,138 |
| 1988 | 5 | 259,984 |
| 1989 | 4 | 222,843 |
| 1990 | 4 | 208,544 |
| 1991 | 7 | 373,160 |
| 1992 | 6 | 311,460 |
| 1993 | 6 | 344,394 |
| 1994 | no series | |
| 1995 | 6 | 286,385 |
| 1996 | 6 | 324,685 |
| 1997 | 7 | 403,617 |
| 1998 | 4 | 243,498 |
| 1999 | 4 | 216,114 |
| 2000 | 5 | 277,853 |
| 2001 | 7 | 366,289 |
| 2002 | 7 | 306,414 |
| 2003 | 7 | 364,932 |
| 2004 | 4 | 174,088 |
| 2005 | 4 | 168,422 |



## INDIVIDUAL BATTING

### LEADING BATTERS

**(Playing in all games, each series; capitalized name denotes leader or tied for series lead, both teams)**

### AMERICAN LEAGUE

| Year | Player, Club | AB | H | TB | Avg. |
|---|---|---|---|---|---|
| 1903 | Chick Stahl, Boston | 33 | 10 | 17 | .303 |
| 1904 | no series | | | | |
| 1905 | Topsy Hartsel, Philadelphia | 17 | 5 | 6 | .294 |
| 1906 | GEORGE ROHE, Chicago | 21 | 7 | 12 | .333 |
| | JIGGS DONAHUE, Chicago | 18 | 6 | 10 | .333 |
| 1907 | Claude Rossman, Detroit | 20 | 8 | 10 | .400 |
| 1908 | Ty Cobb, Detroit | 19 | 7 | 8 | .368 |
| 1909 | Jim Delahanty, Detroit | 26 | 9 | 13 | .346 |
| 1910 | EDDIE COLLINS, Philadelphia | 21 | 9 | 13 | .429 |
| 1911 | HOME RUN BAKER, Philadelphia | 24 | 9 | 17 | .375 |
| 1912 | Tris Speaker, Boston | 30 | 9 | 14 | .300 |
| 1913 | Home Run Baker, Philadelphia | 20 | 9 | 12 | .450 |
| 1914 | Home Run Baker, Philadelphia | 16 | 4 | 6 | .250 |
| 1915 | DUFFY LEWIS, Boston | 18 | 8 | 12 | .444 |
| 1916 | DUFFY LEWIS, Boston | 17 | 6 | 10 | .353 |
| 1917 | Eddie Collins, Chicago | 22 | 9 | 10 | .409 |
| 1918 | Stuffy McInnis, Boston | 20 | 5 | 5 | .250 |
| | George Whiteman, Boston | 20 | 5 | 7 | .250 |
| 1919 | JOE JACKSON, Chicago | 32 | 12 | 18 | .375 |
| 1920 | STEVE O'NEILL, Cleveland | 21 | 7 | 10 | .333 |
| 1921 | Wally Schang, New York | 21 | 6 | 9 | .296 |
| 1922 | Bob Meusel, New York | 20 | 6 | 7 | .300 |
| 1923 | AARON WARD, New York | 24 | 10 | 13 | .417 |
| 1924 | JOE JUDGE, Washington | 26 | 10 | 11 | .385 |
| 1925 | Bucky Harris, Washington | 25 | 11 | 22 | .440 |
| 1926 | Earle Combs, New York | 28 | 10 | 12 | .357 |
| 1927 | MARK KOENIG, New York | 18 | 9 | 11 | .500 |
| 1928 | BABE RUTH, New York | 16 | 10 | 22 | .625 |
| 1929 | Jimmie Dykes, Philadelphia | 19 | 8 | 9 | .421 |
| 1930 | AL SIMMONS, Philadelphia | 22 | 8 | 16 | .364 |
| 1931 | Jimmie Foxx, Philadelphia | 23 | 8 | 11 | .348 |
| 1932 | LOU GEHRIG, New York | 17 | 9 | 19 | .529 |
| 1933 | Fred Schulte, Washington | 21 | 7 | 21 | .333 |
| 1934 | CHARLIE GEHRINGER, Detroit | 29 | 11 | 15 | .379 |
| 1935 | PETE FOX, Detroit | 26 | 10 | 15 | .385 |
| 1936 | JAKE POWELL, New York | 22 | 10 | 14 | .455 |
| 1937 | TONY LAZZERI, New York | 15 | 6 | 11 | .400 |
| 1938 | Bill Dickey, New York | 15 | 6 | 9 | .400 |
| | Joe Gordon, New York | 15 | 6 | 11 | .400 |
| 1939 | CHARLIE KELLER, New York | 16 | 7 | 19 | .438 |
| 1940 | Bruce Campbell, Detroit | 25 | 9 | 13 | .360 |
| 1941 | JOE GORDON, New York | 14 | 7 | 13 | .500 |
| 1942 | PHIL RIZZUTO, New York | 21 | 8 | 11 | .381 |
| 1943 | Billy Johnson, New York | 20 | 6 | 9 | .300 |
| 1944 | GEORGE McQUINN, St. Louis | 16 | 7 | 12 | .438 |
| 1945 | Roger Cramer, Detroit | 29 | 11 | 11 | .379 |
| 1946 | Rudy York, Boston | 23 | 6 | 15 | .261 |
| 1947 | TOMMY HENRICH, New York | 31 | 10 | 15 | .323 |
| 1948 | Larry Doby, Cleveland | 22 | 7 | 11 | .318 |
| 1949 | Tommy Henrich, New York | 19 | 5 | 8 | .263 |
| 1950 | GENE WOODLING, New York | 14 | 6 | 6 | .429 |
| 1951 | Phil Rizzuto, New York | 25 | 8 | 11 | .320 |
| 1952 | GENE WOODLING, New York | 23 | 8 | 14 | .348 |
| 1953 | BILLY MARTIN, New York | 24 | 12 | 23 | .500 |
| 1954 | VIC WERTZ, Cleveland | 16 | 8 | 15 | .500 |
| 1955 | YOGI BERRA, New York | 24 | 10 | 14 | .417 |
| 1956 | YOGI BERRA, New York | 25 | 9 | 20 | .360 |
| 1957 | Jerry Coleman, New York | 22 | 8 | 10 | .364 |
| 1958 | Hank Bauer, New York | 31 | 10 | 22 | .323 |
| 1959 | TED KLUSZEWSKI, Chicago | 23 | 9 | 19 | .391 |
| 1960 | MICKEY MANTLE, New York | 25 | 10 | 20 | .400 |
| 1961 | BOBBY RICHARDSON, New York | 23 | 9 | 10 | .391 |
| 1962 | Tom Tresh, New York | 28 | 9 | 13 | .321 |
| 1963 | Elston Howard, New York | 15 | 5 | 5 | .333 |
| 1964 | Bobby Richardson, New York | 32 | 13 | 15 | .406 |
| 1965 | Zoilo Versalles, Minnesota | 28 | 8 | 14 | .286 |
| | Harmon Killebrew, Minnesota | 21 | 6 | 9 | .286 |
| 1966 | BOOG POWELL, Baltimore | 14 | 5 | 6 | .357 |
| 1967 | Carl Yastrzemski, Boston | 25 | 10 | 21 | .400 |
| 1968 | Norm Cash, Detroit | 26 | 10 | 13 | .385 |
| 1969 | Boog Powell, Baltimore | 19 | 5 | 5 | .263 |
| 1970 | PAUL BLAIR, Baltimore | 19 | 9 | 10 | .474 |
| 1971 | Brooks Robinson, Baltimore | 22 | 7 | 7 | .318 |
| 1972 | Gene Tenace, Oakland | 23 | 8 | 21 | .348 |
| 1973 | Joe Rudi, Oakland | 27 | 9 | 11 | .333 |
| 1974 | Bert Campaneris, Oakland | 17 | 6 | 8 | .353 |
| 1975 | Carl Yastrzemski, Boston | 29 | 9 | 9 | .310 |
| 1976 | Thurman Munson, New York | 17 | 9 | 9 | .529 |
| 1977 | REGGIE JACKSON, New York | 20 | 9 | 25 | .450 |
| 1978 | BRIAN DOYLE, New York | 16 | 7 | 8 | .438 |
| 1979 | Ken Singleton, Baltimore | 28 | 10 | 11 | .357 |
| 1980 | AMOS OTIS, Kansas City | 23 | 11 | 22 | .478 |
| 1981 | LOU PINIELLA, New York | 16 | 7 | 8 | .438 |
| 1982 | ROBIN YOUNT, Milwaukee | 29 | 12 | 18 | .414 |
| 1983 | JOHN SHELBY, Baltimore | 9 | 4 | 4 | .444 |
| 1984 | ALAN TRAMMELL, Detroit | 20 | 9 | 16 | .450 |
| 1985 | GEORGE BRETT, Kansas City | 27 | 10 | 11 | .370 |
| 1986 | MARTY BARRETT, Boston | 30 | 13 | 15 | .433 |
| 1987 | Kirby Puckett, Minnesota | 28 | 10 | 13 | .357 |
| 1988 | Dave Henderson, Oakland | 20 | 6 | 8 | .300 |
| 1989 | RICKEY HENDERSON, Oakland | 19 | 9 | 17 | .474 |
| 1990 | Rickey Henderson, Oakland | 15 | 5 | 10 | .333 |
| 1991 | BRIAN HARPER, Minnesota | 21 | 8 | 10 | .381 |
| 1992 | PAT BORDERS, Toronto | 20 | 9 | 15 | .450 |
| 1993 | PAUL MOLITOR, Toronto | 24 | 12 | 24 | .500 |
| 1994 | no series | | | | |
| 1995 | Albert Belle, Cleveland | 17 | 4 | 10 | .235 |
| 1996 | Cecil Fielder, New York | 23 | 9 | 11 | .391 |
| 1997 | Matt Williams, Cleveland | 26 | 10 | 14 | .385 |
| 1998 | RICKY LEDEE, New York | 10 | 6 | 9 | .600 |
| 1999 | Scott Brosius, New York | 16 | 6 | 7 | .375 |
| 2000 | PAUL O'NEILL, New York | 19 | 9 | 15 | .474 |
| 2001 | Alfonso Soriano, New York | 25 | 6 | 9 | .240 |
| 2002 | Troy Glaus, Anaheim | 26 | 10 | 22 | .385 |
| 2003 | BERNIE WILLIAMS, New York | 25 | 10 | 18 | .400 |
| 2004 | BILL MUELLER, Boston | 14 | 6 | 8 | .429 |
| 2005 | CARL EVERETT, Chicago | 9 | 4 | 4 | .444 |

### NATIONAL LEAGUE

| Year | Player, Club | AB | H | TB | Avg. |
|---|---|---|---|---|---|
| 1903 | JIMMY SEBRING, Pittsburgh | 30 | 11 | 16 | .367 |
| 1904 | no series | | | | |
| 1905 | MIKE DONLIN, New York | 19 | 6 | 7 | .316 |
| 1906 | Solly Hofman, Chicago | 23 | 7 | 8 | .304 |
| 1907 | HARRY STEINFELDT, Chicago | 17 | 8 | 11 | .471 |
| 1908 | FRANK CHANCE, Chicago | 19 | 8 | 8 | .421 |
| 1909 | TOMMY LEACH, Pittsburgh | 25 | 9 | 14 | .360 |
| 1910 | Frank Schulte, Chicago | 17 | 6 | 9 | .353 |
| | Frank Chance, Chicago | 17 | 6 | 9 | .353 |

| Year | Player, Club | AB | H | TB | Avg. |
|---|---|---|---|---|---|
| 1911 | Larry Doyle, New York | 23 | 7 | 12 | .304 |
| 1912 | BUCK HERZOG, New York | 30 | 12 | 18 | .400 |
| 1913 | LARRY McLEAN, New York | 12 | 6 | 6 | .500 |
| 1914 | HANK GOWDY, Boston | 11 | 6 | 14 | .545 |
| 1915 | Fred Luderus, Philadelphia | 16 | 7 | 12 | .438 |
| 1916 | Ivy Olson, Brooklyn | 16 | 4 | 6 | .250 |
| 1917 | DAVE ROBERTSON, New York | 22 | 11 | 14 | .500 |
| 1918 | CHARLIE PICK, Chicago | 18 | 7 | 8 | .389 |
| 1919 | Greasy Neale, Cincinnati | 28 | 10 | 13 | .357 |
| 1920 | ZACH WHEAT, Brooklyn | 27 | 9 | 11 | .333 |
| 1921 | IRISH MEUSEL, New York | 29 | 10 | 17 | .345 |
| 1922 | HEINIE GROH, New York | 19 | 9 | 11 | .474 |
| 1923 | CASEY STENGEL, New York | 12 | 5 | 11 | .417 |
| 1924 | Frankie Frisch, New York | 30 | 10 | 16 | .333 |
| | Fred Lindstrom, New York | 30 | 10 | 12 | .333 |
| 1925 | MAX CAREY, Pittsburgh | 24 | 11 | 15 | .458 |
| 1926 | TOMMY THEVENOW, St. Louis | 24 | 10 | 14 | .417 |
| 1927 | Lloyd Waner, Pittsburgh | 15 | 6 | 9 | .400 |
| 1928 | Rabbit Maranville, St. Louis | 13 | 4 | 5 | .308 |
| 1929 | Hack Wilson, Chicago | 17 | 8 | 10 | .471 |
| 1930 | Charlie Gelbert, St. Louis | 17 | 6 | 8 | .353 |
| 1931 | PEPPER MARTIN, St. Louis | 24 | 12 | 19 | .500 |
| 1932 | Riggs Stephenson, Chicago | 18 | 8 | 9 | .444 |
| 1933 | MEL OTT, New York | 18 | 7 | 13 | .389 |
| 1934 | JOE MEDWICK, St. Louis | 29 | 11 | 16 | .379 |
| 1935 | Billy Herman, Chicago | 24 | 8 | 15 | .333 |
| 1936 | Dick Bartell, New York | 21 | 8 | 14 | .381 |
| 1937 | Joe Moore, New York | 23 | 9 | 10 | .391 |
| 1938 | STAN HACK, Chicago | 17 | 8 | 9 | .471 |
| 1939 | Frank McCormick, Cincinnati | 15 | 6 | 7 | .400 |
| 1940 | BILL WERBER, Cincinnati | 27 | 10 | 14 | .370 |
| 1941 | Joe Medwick, Brooklyn | 17 | 4 | 5 | .235 |
| 1942 | Jimmy Brown, St. Louis | 20 | 6 | 6 | .300 |
| 1943 | MARTY MARION, St. Louis | 14 | 5 | 10 | .357 |
| 1944 | Emil Verban, St. Louis | 17 | 7 | 7 | .412 |
| 1945 | PHIL CAVARRETTA, Chicago | 26 | 11 | 16 | .423 |
| 1946 | HARRY WALKER, St. Louis | 17 | 7 | 9 | .412 |
| 1947 | Pee Wee Reese, Brooklyn | 23 | 7 | 8 | .304 |
| 1948 | BOB ELLIOTT, Boston | 21 | 7 | 13 | .333 |
| 1949 | PEE WEE REESE, Brooklyn | 19 | 6 | 10 | .316 |
| 1950 | GRANNY HAMNER, Philadelphia | 14 | 6 | 10 | .429 |
| 1951 | MONTE IRVIN, New York | 24 | 11 | 13 | .458 |
| 1952 | Duke Snider, Brooklyn | 29 | 10 | 24 | .345 |
| | Pee Wee Reese, Brooklyn | 29 | 10 | 13 | .345 |
| 1953 | Gil Hodges, Brooklyn | 22 | 8 | 11 | .364 |
| 1954 | Alvin Dark, New York | 17 | 7 | 7 | .412 |
| 1955 | Duke Snider, Brooklyn | 25 | 8 | 21 | .320 |
| 1956 | Duke Snider, Brooklyn | 23 | 7 | 11 | .304 |
| | Gil Hodges, Brooklyn | 23 | 7 | 12 | .304 |
| 1957 | HANK AARON, Milwaukee | 28 | 11 | 22 | .393 |
| 1958 | BILL BRUTON, Milwaukee | 17 | 7 | 10 | .412 |
| 1959 | GIL HODGES, Los Angeles | 23 | 9 | 14 | .391 |
| 1960 | Bill Mazeroski, Pittsburgh | 25 | 8 | 16 | .320 |
| 1961 | Wally Post, Cincinnati | 18 | 6 | 10 | .333 |
| 1962 | JOSE PAGAN, San Francisco | 19 | 7 | 10 | .368 |
| 1963 | TOMMY DAVIS, Los Angeles | 15 | 6 | 10 | .400 |
| 1964 | TIM McCARVER, St. Louis | 23 | 11 | 17 | .478 |
| 1965 | RON FAIRLY, Los Angeles | 29 | 11 | 20 | .379 |
| 1966 | Lou Johnson, Los Angeles | 15 | 4 | 5 | .267 |
| 1967 | LOU BROCK, St. Louis | 29 | 12 | 19 | .414 |
| 1968 | LOU BROCK, St. Louis | 28 | 13 | 24 | .464 |
| 1969 | AL WEIS, New York | 11 | 5 | 8 | .455 |
| 1970 | Lee May, Cincinnati | 18 | 7 | 15 | .389 |
| 1971 | ROBERTO CLEMENTE, Pittsburgh | 29 | 12 | 22 | .414 |
| 1972 | TONY PEREZ, Cincinnati | 23 | 10 | 12 | .435 |
| 1973 | RUSTY STAUB, New York | 26 | 11 | 16 | .423 |
| 1974 | STEVE GARVEY, Los Angeles | 21 | 8 | 8 | .381 |
| 1975 | PETE ROSE, Cincinnati | 27 | 10 | 13 | .370 |
| 1976 | JOHNNY BENCH, Cincinnati | 15 | 8 | 17 | .533 |
| 1977 | Steve Garvey, Los Angeles | 24 | 9 | 15 | .375 |
| 1978 | Bill Russell, Los Angeles | 26 | 11 | 13 | .423 |
| 1979 | PHIL GARNER, Pittsburgh | 24 | 12 | 16 | .500 |
| 1980 | Bob Boone, Philadelphia | 17 | 7 | 9 | .412 |
| 1981 | Steve Garvey, Los Angeles | 24 | 10 | 11 | .417 |
| 1982 | George Hendrick, St. Louis | 28 | 9 | 9 | .321 |
| | Lonnie Smith, St. Louis | 28 | 9 | 15 | .321 |
| 1983 | Bo Diaz, Philadelphia | 15 | 5 | 6 | .333 |
| 1984 | Kurt Bevacqua, San Diego | 17 | 7 | 15 | .412 |
| 1985 | Tito Landrum, St. Louis | 25 | 9 | 14 | .360 |
| 1986 | Lenny Dykstra, New York | 27 | 8 | 14 | .296 |
| 1987 | TONY PENA, St. Louis | 22 | 9 | 10 | .409 |
| 1988 | MICKEY HATCHER, Los Angeles | 19 | 7 | 14 | .368 |
| 1989 | Ken Oberkfell, San Francisco | 6 | 2 | 2 | .333 |
| 1990 | BILLY HATCHER, Cincinnati | 12 | 9 | 15 | .750 |
| 1991 | Rafael Belliard, Atlanta | 16 | 6 | 7 | .375 |
| 1992 | Otis Nixon, Atlanta | 27 | 8 | 9 | .296 |
| 1993 | Lenny Dykstra, Philadelphia | 23 | 8 | 21 | .348 |
| | John Kruk, Philadelphia | 23 | 8 | 9 | .348 |
| 1994 | no series | | | | |
| 1995 | MARQUIS GRISSOM, Atlanta | 25 | 9 | 10 | .360 |
| 1996 | MARQUIS GRISSOM, Atlanta | 27 | 12 | 16 | .444 |
| 1997 | DARREN DAULTON, Florida | 18 | 7 | 12 | .389 |
| 1998 | Tony Gwynn, San Diego | 16 | 8 | 11 | .500 |
| 1999 | BRET BOONE, Atlanta | 13 | 7 | 11 | .538 |
| 2000 | Todd Zeile, New York | 20 | 8 | 10 | .400 |
| 2001 | STEVE FINLEY, Arizona | 19 | 7 | 10 | .368 |
| 2002 | BARRY BONDS, San Francisco | 17 | 8 | 22 | .471 |
| 2003 | Jeff Conine, Florida | 21 | 7 | 8 | .333 |
| 2004 | Larry Walker, St. Louis | 14 | 5 | 13 | .357 |
| 2005 | Lance Berkman, Houston | 13 | 5 | 7 | .385 |

## .500 HITTERS

(Playing in all games and having 10 or more at-bats)

| Player, Club | Year | AB | H | TB | Avg. |
|---|---|---|---|---|---|
| Billy Hatcher, Cincinnati NL | 1990 | 12 | 9 | 15 | .750 |
| Babe Ruth, New York AL | 1928 | 16 | 10 | 22 | .625 |
| Ricky Ledee, New York AL | 1998 | 10 | 6 | 9 | .600 |
| Chris Sabo, Cincinnati NL | 1990 | 16 | 9 | 16 | .563 |
| Hank Gowdy, Boston NL | 1914 | 11 | 6 | 14 | .545 |
| Lou Gehrig, New York AL | 1928 | 11 | 6 | 19 | .545 |
| Bret Boone, Atlanta NL | 1999 | 13 | 7 | 11 | .538 |
| Johnny Bench, Cincinnati NL | 1976 | 15 | 8 | 17 | .533 |
| Lou Gehrig, New York AL | 1932 | 17 | 9 | 19 | .529 |
| Thurman Munson, New York AL | 1976 | 17 | 9 | 9 | .529 |
| Larry McLean, New York NL | 1913 | 12 | 6 | 6 | .500 |
| Dave Robertson, New York NL | 1917 | 22 | 11 | 14 | .500 |
| Mark Koenig, New York AL | 1927 | 18 | 9 | 11 | .500 |
| Pepper Martin, St. Louis NL | 1931 | 24 | 12 | 19 | .500 |
| Joe Gordon, New York AL | 1941 | 14 | 7 | 13 | .500 |
| Billy Martin, New York AL | 1953 | 24 | 12 | 23 | .500 |
| Vic Wertz, Cleveland AL | 1954 | 16 | 8 | 15 | .500 |
| Phil Garner, Pittsburgh NL | 1979 | 24 | 12 | 16 | .500 |
| Paul Molitor, Toronto AL | 1993 | 24 | 12 | 24 | .500 |
| Tony Gwynn, San Diego NL | 1998 | 16 | 8 | 11 | .500 |

**Total number of occurrences: 20**

## HOME RUNS

### AMERICAN LEAGUE

1903—2—Boston, Patsy Dougherty 2
1904—no series
1905—0—Philadelphia
1906—0—Chicago
1907—0—Detroit
1908—0—Detroit
1909—2—Detroit, Davy Jones, Sam Crawford
1910—1—Philadelphia, Danny Murphy
1911—3—Philadelphia, Home Run Baker 2, Rube Oldring
1912—1—Boston, Larry Gardner
1913—2—Philadelphia, Home Run Baker, Wally Schang
1914—0—Philadelphia
1915—3—Boston, Harry Hooper 2, Duffy Lewis
1916—2—Boston, Larry Gardner 2
1917—1—Chicago, Happy Felsch
1918—0—Boston
1919—1—Chicago, Joe Jackson
1920—2—Cleveland, Elmer Smith, Jim Bagby
1921—2—New York, Babe Ruth, Chick Fewster
1922—2—New York, Aaron Ward 2
1923—5—New York, Babe Ruth 3, Aaron Ward, Joe Dugan
1924—5—Washington, Goose Goslin 3, Bucky Harris 2
1925—8—Washington, Bucky Harris 3, Goose Goslin 3, Joe Judge, Roger Peckinpaugh
1926—4—New York, Babe Ruth 4
1927—2—New York, Babe Ruth 2
1928—9—New York, Lou Gehrig 4, Babe Ruth 3, Bob Meusel, Cedric Durst
1929—6—Philadelphia, Jimmie Foxx 2, Al Simmons 2, Mule Haas 2
1930—6—Philadelphia, Mickey Cochrane 2, Al Simmons 2, Jimmie Foxx, Jimmie Dykes
1931—3—Philadelphia, Al Simmons 2, Jimmie Foxx
1932—8—New York, Lou Gehrig 3, Babe Ruth 2, Tony Lazzeri 2, Earle Combs
1933—2—Washington, Goose Goslin, Fred Schulte
1934—2—Detroit, Hank Greenberg, Charlie Gehringer
1935—1—Detroit, Hank Greenberg
1936—7—New York, Lou Gehrig 2, George Selkirk 2, Tony Lazzeri, Bill Dickey, Jake Powell
1937—4—New York, Tony Lazzeri, Lou Gehrig, Myril Hoag, Joe DiMaggio
1938—5—New York, Frank Crosetti, Joe DiMaggio, Joe Gordon, Bill Dickey, Tommy Henrich
1939—7—New York, Charlie Keller 3, Bill Dickey 2, Babe Dahlgren, Joe DiMaggio
1940—4—Detroit, Bruce Campbell, Rudy York, Pinky Higgins, Hank Greenberg
1941—2—New York, Joe Gordon, Tommy Henrich
1942—3—New York, Charlie Keller 2, Phil Rizzuto
1943—2—New York, Joe Gordon, Bill Dickey
1944—1—St. Louis, George McQuinn
1945—2—Detroit, Hank Greenberg 2
1946—4—Boston, Rudy York 2, Bobby Doerr, Leon Culberson
1947—4—New York, Joe DiMaggio 2, Tommy Henrich, Yogi Berra
1948—4—Cleveland, Larry Doby, Dale Mitchell, Jim Hegan, Joe Gordon
1949—2—New York, Tommy Henrich, Joe DiMaggio
1950—2—New York, Joe DiMaggio, Yogi Berra
1951—5—New York, Joe Collins, Gene Woodling, Joe DiMaggio, Gil McDougald, Phil Rizzuto

1952—10—New York, Johnny Mize 3, Mickey Mantle 2, Yogi Berra 2, Gil McDougald, Billy Martin, Gene Woodling
1953—9—New York, Mickey Mantle 2, Gil McDougald 2, Billy Martin 2, Yogi Berra, Joe Collins, Gene Woodling
1954—3—Cleveland, Al Smith, Vic Wertz, Hank Majeski
1955—8—New York, Joe Collins 2, Yogi Berra, Bob Cerv, Elston Howard, Mickey Mantle, Gil McDougald, Bill Skowron
1956—12—New York, Mickey Mantle 3, Yogi Berra 3, Billy Martin 2, Enos Slaughter, Hank Bauer, Elston Howard, Bill Skowron
1957—7—New York, Hank Bauer 2, Tony Kubek 2, Mickey Mantle, Yogi Berra, Elston Howard
1958—10—New York, Hank Bauer 4, Gil McDougald 2, Mickey Mantle 2, Bill Skowron 2
1959—4—Chicago, Ted Kluszewski 3, Sherm Lollar
1960—10—New York, Mickey Mantle 3, Roger Maris 2, Bill Skowron 2, Yogi Berra, Elston Howard, Bobby Richardson
1961—7—New York, Johnny Blanchard 2, Yogi Berra, Elston Howard, Hector Lopez, Roger Maris, Bill Skowron
1962—3—New York, Tom Tresh, Roger Maris, Clete Boyer
1963—2—New York, Tom Tresh, Mickey Mantle
1964—10—New York, Mickey Mantle 3, Phil Linz 2, Tom Tresh 2, Roger Maris, Joe Pepitone, Clete Boyer
1965—6—Minnesota, Zoilo Versalles, Tony Oliva, Harmon Killebrew, Don Mincher, Bob Allison, Mudcat Grant
1966—4—Baltimore, Frank Robinson 2, Brooks Robinson, Paul Blair
1967—8—Boston, Carl Yastrzemski 3, Reggie Smith 2, Rico Petrocelli 2, Jose Santiago
1968—8—Detroit, Al Kaline 2, Jim Northrup 2, Norm Cash, Willie Horton, Mickey Lolich, Dick McAuliffe
1969—3—Baltimore, Don Buford, Dave McNally, Frank Robinson
1970—10—Baltimore, Boog Powell 2, Frank Robinson 2, Brooks Robinson 2, Don Buford, Elrod Hendricks, Dave McNally, Merv Rettenmund
1971—5—Baltimore, Don Buford 2, Frank Robinson 2, Merv Rettenmund
1972—5—Oakland, Gene Tenace 4, Joe Rudi
1973—2—Oakland, Bert Campaneris, Reggie Jackson
1974—4—Oakland, Ray Fosse, Ken Holtzman, Reggie Jackson, Joe Rudi
1975—6—Boston, Bernie Carbo 2, Carlton Fisk 2, Dwight Evans, Fred Lynn
1976—1—New York, Jim Mason
1977—8—New York, Reggie Jackson 5, Chris Chambliss, Thurman Munson, Willie Randolph
1978—3—New York, Reggie Jackson 2, Roy White
1979—4—Baltimore, Doug DeCinces, Eddie Murray, Benny Ayala, Rich Dauer
1980—8—Kansas City, Willie Aikens 4, Amos Otis 3, George Brett
1981—6—New York, Willie Randolph 2, Bob Watson 2, Rich Cerone, Reggie Jackson
1982—5—Milwaukee, Ted Simmons 2, Cecil Cooper, Ben Oglivie, Robin Yount
1983—6—Baltimore, Eddie Murray 2, Jim Dwyer, John Lowenstein, Dan Ford, Rick Dempsey
1984—7—Detroit, Kirk Gibson 2, Alan Trammell 2, Marty Castillo, Larry Herndon, Lance Parrish
1985—2—Kansas City, Frank White, Darryl Motley
1986—5—Boston, Dwight Evans 2, Dave Henderson 2, Rich Gedman
1987—7—Minnesota, Don Baylor, Gary Gaetti, Greg Gagne, Dan Gladden, Kent Hrbek, Tim Laudner, Steve Lombardozzi
1988—2—Oakland, Jose Canseco, Mark McGwire
1989—9—Oakland, Dave Henderson 2, Jose Canseco, Rickey Henderson, Carney Lansford, Dave Parker, Tony Phillips, Terry St.einbach, Walt Weiss
1990—3—Oakland, Harold Baines, Jose Canseco, Rickey Henderson
1991—8—Minnesota, Chili Davis 2, Kirby Puckett 2, Greg Gagne, Kent Hrbek, Scott Leius, Mike Pagliarulo
1992—6—Toronto, Joe Carter 2, Pat Borders, Kelly Gruber, Candy Maldonado, Ed Sprague
1993—6—Toronto, Joe Carter 2, Paul Molitor 2, John Olerud, Devon White
1994—no series
1995—5—Cleveland, Albert Belle 2, Eddie Murray, Manny Ramirez, Jim Thome
1996—2—New York, Jim Leyritz, Bernie Williams
1997—7—Cleveland, Sandy Alomar Jr 2, Manny Ramirez 2, Jim Thome 2, Matt Williams
1998—6—New York, Scott Brosius 2, Chuck Knoblauch, Tino Martinez, Jorge Posada, Bernie Williams
1999—5—New York, Chad Curtis 2, Chuck Knoblauch, Jim Leyritz, Tino Martinez
2000—4—New York, Derek Jeter 2, Scott Brosius, Bernie Williams
2001—6—New York, Scott Brosius, Derek Jeter, Tino Martinez, Jorge Posada, Alfonso Soriano, Shane Spencer
2002—7—Anaheim, Troy Glaus 3, Tim Salmon 2, Darin Erstad, Scott Spiezio
2003—6—New York, Bernie Williams 2, Aaron Boone, Jason Giambi, Hideki Matsui, Alfonso Soriano
2004—4—Boston, Mark Bellhorn, Johnny Damon, David Ortiz, Manny Ramirez
2005—6—Joe Crede 2, Jermaine Dye, Paul Konerko, Scott Podsednik, Geoff Blum

**Total number of home runs: 453**

## NATIONAL LEAGUE

1903—1—Pittsburgh, Jimmy Sebring
1904—no series
1905—0—New York
1906—0—Chicago
1907—0—Chicago
1908—1—Chicago, Joe Tinker
1909—2—Pittsburgh, Fred Clarke 2
1910—0—Chicago
1911—0—New York
1912—1—New York, Larry Doyle
1913—1—New York, Fred Merkle
1914—1—Boston, Hank Gowdy
1915—1—Philadelphia, Fred Luderus
1916—1—Brooklyn, Hy Myers
1917—2—New York, Benny Kauff 2
1918—0—Chicago
1919—0—Cincinnati
1920—0—Brooklyn
1921—2—New York, Frank Snyder, Irish Meusel
1922—1—New York, Irish Meusel
1923—5—New York, Casey St.engel 2, Irish Meusel, Ross Youngs, Frank Snyder
1924—4—New York, George Kelly, Bill Terry, Rosy Ryan, Jack Bentley
1925—4—Pittsburgh, Pie Traynor, Glenn Wright, Kiki Cuyler, Eddie Moore
1926—4—St. Louis, Billy Southworth, Tommy Thevenow, Jesse Haines, Les Bell
1927—0—Pittsburgh
1928—1—St. Louis, Jim Bottomley
1929—1—Chicago, Charlie Grimm
1930—2—St. Louis, George Watkins, Taylor Douthit
1931—2—St. Louis, Pepper Martin, George Watkins
1932—3—Chicago, Kiki Cuyler, Gabby Hartnett, Frank Demaree
1933—3—New York, Mel Ott 2, Bill Terry
1934—2—St. Louis, Joe Medwick, Bill DeLancey
1935—5—Chicago, Frank Demaree 2, Gabby Hartnett, Chuck Klein, Billy Herman
1936—4—New York, Dick Bartell, Jimmy Ripple, Mel Ott, Joe Moore
1937—1—New York, Mel Ott
1938—2—Chicago, Joe Marty, Ken O'Dea
1939—0—Cincinnati
1940—2—Cincinnati, Jimmy Ripple, Bucky Walters
1941—1—Brooklyn, Pete Reiser
1942—2—St. Louis, Enos Slaughter, Whitey Kurowski
1943—2—St. Louis, Marty Marion, Ray Sanders
1944—3—St. Louis, Stan Musial, Ray Sanders, Danny Litwhiler
1945—1—Chicago, Phil Cavarretta
1946—1—St. Louis, Enos Slaughter
1947—1—Brooklyn, Dixie Walker
1948—4—Boston, Bob Elliott 2, Marv Rickert, Bill Salkeld
1949—4—Brooklyn, Pee Wee Reese, Luis Olmo, Roy Campanella, Gil Hodges
1950—0—Philadelphia
1951—2—New York, Alvin Dark, Whitey Lockman
1952—6—Brooklyn, Duke Snider 4, Jackie Robinson, Pee Wee Reese
1953—8—Brooklyn, Jim Gilliam 2, Roy Campanella, Billy Cox, Carl Furillo, Gil Hodges, George Shuba, Duke Snider
1954—2—New York, Dusty Rhodes 2
1955—9—Brooklyn, Duke Snider 4, Roy Campanella 2, Sandy Amoros, Carl Furillo, Gil Hodges
1956—3—Brooklyn, Duke Snider, Jackie Robinson, Gil Hodges
1957—8—Milwaukee, Hank Aaron 3, Frank Torre 2, Eddie Mathews, Johnny Logan, Del Crandall
1958—3—Milwaukee, Del Crandall, Bill Bruton, Lew Burdette
1959—7—Los Angeles, Charlie Neal 2, Chuck Essegian 2, Wally Moon, Duke Snider, Gil Hodges
1960—4—Pittsburgh, Bill Mazeroski 2, Rocky Nelson, Hal Smith
1961—3—Cincinnati, Gordy Coleman, Wally Post, Frank Robinson
1962—5—San Francisco, Chuck Hiller, Willie McCovey, Tom Haller, Ed Bailey, Jose Pagan
1963—3—Los Angeles, John Roseboro, Bill Skowron, Frank Howard
1964—5—St. Louis, Ken Boyer 2, Lou Brock, Mike Shannon, Tim McCarver
1965—5—Los Angeles, Ron Fairly 2, Lou Johnson 2, Wes Parker
1966—1—Los Angeles, Jim Lefebvre
1967—5—St. Louis, Lou Brock, Bob Gibson, Julian Javier, Roger Maris, Mike Shannon
1968—7—St. Louis, Lou Brock 2, Orlando Cepeda 2, Bob Gibson, Tim McCarver, Mike Shannon
1969—6—New York, Donn Clendenon 3, Tommie Agee, Ed Kranepool, Al Weis
1970—5—Cincinnati, Lee May 2, Johnny Bench, Pete Rose, Bobby Tolan
1971—5—Pittsburgh, Bob Robertson 2, Roberto Clemente 2, Richie Hebner
1972—3—Cincinnati, Johnny Bench, Denis Menke, Pete Rose
1973—4—New York, Wayne Garrett 2, Cleon Jones, Rusty Staub
1974—4—Los Angeles, Bill Buckner, Willie Crawford, Joe Ferguson, Jim Wynn
1975—7—Cincinnati, Tony Perez 3, Cesar Geronimo 2, Johnny Bench, David Concepcion
1976—4—Cincinnati, Johnny Bench 2, Dan Driessen, Joe Morgan
1977—9—Los Angeles, Reggie Smith 3, Steve Yeager 2, Dusty Baker, Ron Cey, Steve Garvey, Dave Lopes
1978—6—Los Angeles, Dave Lopes 3, Dusty Baker, Ron Cey, Reggie Smith
1979—3—Pittsburgh, Willie Stargell 3
1980—3—Philadelphia, Mike Schmidt 2, Bake McBride
1981—6—Los Angeles, Pedro Guerrero 2, Steve Yeager 2, Ron Cey, Jay Johnstone
1982—4—St. Louis, Willie McGee 2, Keith Hernandez, Darrell Porter
1983—4—Philadelphia, Joe Morgan, Garry Maddox, Gary Matthews
1984—3—San Diego, Kurt Bevacqua 2, Terry Kennedy
1985—2—St. Louis, Tito Landrum, Willie McGee
1986—7—New York, Gary Carter 2, Lenny Dykstra 2, Ray Knight, Darryl Strawberry, Tim Teufel
1987—2—St. Louis, Tom Herr, Tom Lawless
1988—5—Los Angeles, Mickey Hatcher 2, Mike Davis, Kirk Gibson, Mike A. Marshall
1989—4—San Francisco, Bill Bathe, Greg Litton, Kevin Mitchell, Matt Williams
1990—3—Cincinnati, Chris Sabo 2, Eric Davis
1991—8—Atlanta, Lonnie Smith 3, David Justice 2, Terry Pendleton 2, Brian Hunter
1992—3—Atlanta, Damon Berryhill, David Justice, Lonnie Smith
1993—7—Philadelphia, Lenny Dykstra 4, Darren Daulton, Jim Eisenreich, Milt Thompson
1994—no series
1995—8—Atlanta, Ryan Klesko 3, Fred McGriff 2, David Justice, Javier Lopez, Luis Polonia
1996—4—Atlanta, Andruw Jones 2, Fred McGriff 2
1997—8—Florida, Moises Alou 3, Bobby Bonilla, Darren Daulton, Jim Eisenreich, Charles Johnson, Gary Sheffield
1998—3—San Diego, Greg Vaughn 2, Tony Gwynn
1999—1—Atlanta, Chipper Jones
2000—4—New York, Mike Piazza 2, Jay Payton, Robin Ventura
2001—6—Arizona, Rod Barajas, Craig Counsell, Steve Finley, Luis Gonzalez, Mark Grace, Matt Williams
2002—14—San Francisco, Barry Bonds 4, Jeff Kent 3, Rich Aurilia 2, Reggie Sanders 2, David Bell, Shawon Dunston, J.T. Snow
2003—2—Florida, Miguel Cabrera, Alex Gonzalez

2004—2—St. Louis, Larry Walker 2
2005—3—Morgan Ensberg, Mike Lamb, Jason Lane
**Total number of home runs: 337**

## PLAYERS WITH FIVE HOME RUNS

| Player | Series | HR |
|---|---|---|
| Mickey Mantle | 12 | 18 |
| Babe Ruth | 10 | 15 |
| Yogi Berra | 14 | 12 |
| Duke Snider | 6 | 11 |
| Reggie Jackson | 5 | 10 |
| Lou Gehrig | 7 | 10 |
| Frank Robinson | 5 | 8 |
| Bill Skowron | 8 | 8 |
| Joe DiMaggio | 10 | 8 |
| Goose Goslin | 5 | 7 |
| Gil McDougald | 8 | 7 |
| Hank Bauer | 9 | 7 |
| Lenny Dykstra | 2 | 6 |
| Al Simmons | 4 | 6 |
| Reggie Smith | 4 | 6 |
| Roger Maris | 7 | 6 |
| Charlie Keller | 4 | 5 |
| Hank Greenberg | 4 | 5 |
| Johnny Bench | 4 | 5 |
| Billy Martin | 5 | 5 |
| Bernie Williams | 6 | 5 |
| Gil Hodges | 7 | 5 |
| Bill Dickey | 8 | 5 |
| Elston Howard | 9 | 5 |

**Total number of players: 24**

# INDIVIDUAL PITCHING

## PITCHERS WITH FIVE VICTORIES

| Pitcher, Club | Series | W | L |
|---|---|---|---|
| Whitey Ford, New York AL | 11 | 10 | 8 |
| Red Ruffing, New York AL | 7 | 7 | 2 |
| Allie Reynolds, New York AL | 6 | 7 | 2 |
| Bob Gibson, St. Louis NL | 3 | 7 | 2 |
| Lefty Gomez, New York AL | 4 | 6 | 0 |
| Chief Bender, Philadelphia AL | 5 | 6 | 4 |
| Waite Hoyt, New York AL, Philadelphia AL | 6 | 6 | 4 |
| Jack Coombs, Philadelphia AL, Brooklyn NL | 3 | 5 | 0 |
| Herb Pennock, New York AL | 3 | 5 | 0 |
| Vic Raschi, New York AL | 5 | 5 | 3 |
| Catfish Hunter, Oakland AL, New York AL | 6 | 5 | 3 |
| Mordecai Brown, Chicago NL | 4 | 5 | 4 |
| Christy Mathewson, New York NL | 4 | 5 | 5 |

**Total number of pitchers: 13**

## 10-STRIKEOUT GAMES BY PITCHERS

| Date | Pitcher, Club | K |
|---|---|---|
| Oct 1, 1903 | Deacon Phillippe, Pit NL vs Bos AL | 10 |
| Oct 2, 1903 | Bill Dinneen, Bos AL vs Pit NL | 11 |
| Oct 11, 1906 | Ed Walsh, Chi AL vs Chi NL | 12 |
| Oct 8, 1907 | Bill Donovan, Det AL vs Chi NL (12 inn) | 12 |
| Oct 14, 1908 | Orval Overall, Chi NL vs Det AL | 10 |
| Oct 12, 1909 | George Mullin, Det AL vs Pit NL | 10 |
| Oct 14, 1911 | Chief Bender, Phi AL vs NY NL (8 inn) | 11 |
| Oct 8, 1912 | Joe Wood, Bos AL vs NY NL | 11 |
| Oct 11, 1921 | Jesse Barnes, NY NL vs NY AL | 10 |
| Oct 24, 1924 | Walter Johnson, Was AL vs NY NL (12 inn) | 12 |
| Oct 7, 1925 | Walter Johnson, Was AL vs Pit NL | 10 |
| Oct 3, 1926 | Grover Alexander, St.L NL vs NY AL | 10 |
| Oct 8, 1929 | Howard Ehmke, Phi AL vs Chi NL | 13 |
| Oct 11, 1929 | George Earnshaw, Phi AL vs Chi NL | 10 |
| Sept 28, 1932 | Red Ruffing, NY AL vs Chi NL | 10 |
| Oct 3, 1933 | Carl Hubbell, NY NL vs Was AL | 10 |
| Oct 5, 1936 | Hal Schmuacher, NY NL vs NY AL (10 inn) | 10 |
| Oct 6, 1944 | Jack Kramer, St.L AL vs St.L NL | 10 |
| Oct 8, 1944 | Denny Galehouse, St.L AL vs St.L NL | 10 |
| Oct 8, 1944 | Mort Cooper, St.L NL vs St.L AL | 12 |
| Oct 10, 1945 | Hal Newhouser, Det AL vs Chi NL | 10 |
| Oct 5, 1949 | Don Newcombe, Bkn NL vs NY AL (8 inn) | 11 |
| Oct 4, 1952 | Allie Reynolds, NY AL vs Bkn NL | 10 |
| Oct 2, 1953 | Carl Erskine, Bkn NL vs NY AL | 14 |
| Oct 3, 1956 | Sal Maglie, Bkn NL vs NY AL | 10 |
| Oct 9, 1956 | Bob Turley, NY AL vs Bkn NL | 11 |
| Oct 6, 1958 | Bob Turley, NY AL vs Mil NL | 10 |
| Oct 10, 1962 | Jack Sanford, SF NL vs NY AL | 10 |
| Oct 2, 1963 | Sandy Koufax, LA NL vs NY AL | 15 |
| Oct 12, 1964 | Bob Gibson, St.L NL vs NY AL (10 inn) | 13 |
| Oct 10, 1965 | Don Drysdale, LA NL vs Min AL | 11 |
| Oct 11, 1965 | Sandy Koufax, LA NL vs Min AL | 10 |
| Oct 14, 1965 | Sandy Koufax, LA NL vs Min AL | 10 |
| Oct 5, 1966 | Moe Drabowsky, Bal AL vs LA NL | 11 |
| Oct 4, 1967 | Bob Gibson, St.L NL vs Bos AL | 10 |
| Oct 12, 1967 | Bob Gibson, St.L NL vs Bos AL | 10 |
| Oct 2, 1968 | Bob Gibson, St.L NL vs Det AL | 17 |
| Oct 6, 1968 | Bob Gibson, St.L NL vs Det AL | 10 |
| Oct 11, 1971 | Jim Palmer, Bal AL vs Pit NL | 10 |
| Oct 18, 1972 | Blue Moon Odom, Oak AL vs Cin NL (7 inn) | 11 |
| Oct 16, 1973 | Tom Seaver, NY NL vs Oak AL (8 inn) | 12 |
| Oct 15, 1980 | Steve Carlton, Phi NL vs KC AL (8 inn) | 10 |
| Oct 24, 1996 | John Smoltz, Atl NL vs NY AL (8 inn) | 10 |
| Oct 23, 1999 | Orlando Hernandez, NY AL vs Atl NL (7 inn) | 10 |
| Oct 27, 1999 | John Smoltz, Atl NL vs NY AL (7 inn) | 11 |
| Oct 24, 2000 | Orlando Hernandez, NY AL vs NY NL | 12 |
| Oct 28, 2001 | Randy Johnson, Ariz NL vs NY AL | 11 |
| Nov 1, 2001 | Mike Mussina, NY AL vs Ariz NL (8 inn) | 10 |
| Nov 3, 2001 | Roger Clemens, NY AL vs Ariz NL (6.1 inn) | 10 |
| Oct 21, 2003 | Josh Beckett, Fla NL vs NY AL (7. 1 inn) | 10 |

**Total number of performances: 50**

# INDIVIDUAL FIELDING

## UNASSISTED TRIPLE PLAYS

Bill Wambsganss, second baseman, Cleveland AL vs Brooklyn NL at Cleveland, Oct 10, 1920, 5th inn - Wambsganss caught Clarence Mitchell's line drive, stepped on second to retire Pete Kilduff, then tagged Otto Miller coming from first (This unassisted triple play was made with runners on first and second bases only)

**Total number of occurrences: 1**

# CLUB BATTING

| Year | Team, League | G | AB | R | H | TB | 2B | 3B | HR | SB | BB | SO | RBI | Avg. | LOB |
|---|---|---|---|---|---|---|---|---|---|---|---|---|---|---|---|
| 1903 | Pittsburgh NL | 8 | 270 | 24 | 64 | 92 | 7 | 9 | 1 | 7 | 14 | 45 | 23 | .237 | 51 |
| | Boston AL | 8 | 282 | 39 | 71 | 113 | 4 | 16 | 2 | 5 | 13 | 27 | 35 | .252 | 55 |
| 1904 | no series played | | | | | | | | | | | | | | |
| 1905 | New York NL | 5 | 153 | 15 | 32 | 39 | 7 | 0 | 0 | 11 | 15 | 26 | 13 | .209 | 31 |
| | Philadelphia AL | 5 | 155 | 3 | 25 | 30 | 5 | 0 | 0 | 2 | 5 | 25 | 2 | .161 | 26 |
| 1906 | Chicago NL | 6 | 184 | 18 | 36 | 45 | 9 | 0 | 0 | 8 | 18 | 27 | 11 | .196 | 37 |
| | Chicago AL | 6 | 187 | 22 | 37 | 53 | 10 | 3 | 0 | 6 | 18 | 35 | 19 | .198 | 33 |
| 1907 | Chicago NL | 5 | 167 | 19 | 43 | 51 | 6 | 1 | 0 | 18 | 12 | 25 | 16 | .257 | 35 |
| | Detroit AL | 5 | 173 | 6 | 36 | 41 | 1 | 2 | 0 | 7 | 9 | 21 | 6 | .208 | |
| 36 | | | | | | | | | | | | | | | |
| 1908 | Chicago NL | 5 | 164 | 24 | 48 | 59 | 4 | 2 | 1 | 13 | 13 | 26 | 21 | .293 | 30 |
| | Detroit AL | 5 | 158 | 15 | 32 | 37 | 5 | 0 | 0 | 5 | 12 | 26 | 14 | .203 | 27 |
| 1909 | Pittsburgh NL | 7 | 223 | 34 | 49 | 70 | 12 | 1 | 2 | 18 | 20 | 34 | 26 | .220 | 44 |
| | Detroit AL | 7 | 234 | 28 | 55 | 77 | 16 | 0 | 2 | 6 | 20 | 22 | 25 | .235 | 50 |
| 1910 | Chicago NL | 5 | 158 | 15 | 35 | 48 | 11 | 1 | 0 | 3 | 18 | 31 | 13 | .222 | 31 |
| | Philadelphia AL | 5 | 177 | 35 | 56 | 80 | 19 | 1 | 1 | 7 | 17 | 24 | 29 | .316 | 36 |
| 1911 | New York NL | 6 | 189 | 13 | 33 | 46 | 11 | 1 | 0 | 4 | 14 | 44 | 10 | .175 | 31 |
| | Philadelphia AL | 6 | 205 | 27 | 50 | 74 | 15 | 0 | 3 | 4 | 4 | 31 | 21 | .244 | 29 |
| 1912 | New York NL | 8 | 274 | 31 | 74 | 99 | 14 | 4 | 1 | 12 | 22 | 39 | 25 | .270 | 53 |
| | Boston AL | 8 | 273 | 25 | 60 | 89 | 14 | 6 | 1 | 6 | 19 | 36 | 21 | .220 | 55 |
| 1913 | New York NL | 5 | 164 | 15 | 33 | 41 | 3 | 1 | 1 | 5 | 8 | 19 | 15 | .201 | 24 |
| | Philadelphia AL | 5 | 174 | 23 | 46 | 64 | 4 | 4 | 2 | 5 | 7 | 16 | 21 | .264 | 30 |
| 1914 | Boston NL | 4 | 135 | 16 | 33 | 46 | 6 | 2 | 1 | 9 | 15 | 18 | 14 | .244 | 27 |
| | Philadelphia AL | 4 | 128 | 6 | 22 | 31 | 9 | 0 | 0 | 2 | 13 | 28 | 5 | .172 | 21 |

| Year | Team, League | G | AB | R | H | TB | 2B | 3B | HR | SB | BB | SO | RBI | Avg. | LOB |
|---|---|---|---|---|---|---|---|---|---|---|---|---|---|---|---|
| 1915 | Philadelphia NL | 5 | 148 | 10 | 27 | 36 | 4 | 1 | 1 | 2 | 10 | 25 | 9 | .182 | 23 |
| | Boston AL | 5 | 159 | 12 | 42 | 57 | 2 | 2 | 3 | 1 | 11 | 25 | 11 | .264 | 35 |
| 1916 | Brooklyn NL | 5 | 170 | 13 | 34 | 49 | 2 | 5 | 1 | 1 | 14 | 19 | 11 | .200 | 32 |
| | Boston AL | 5 | 164 | 21 | 39 | 64 | 7 | 6 | 2 | 1 | 18 | 25 | 18 | .238 | 31 |
| 1917 | New York NL | 6 | 199 | 17 | 51 | 70 | 5 | 4 | 2 | 4 | 6 | 27 | 16 | .256 | 37 |
| | Chicago AL | 6 | 197 | 21 | 54 | 63 | 6 | 0 | 1 | 6 | 11 | 28 | 18 | .274 | 37 |
| 1918 | Chicago NL | 6 | 176 | 10 | 37 | 44 | 5 | 1 | 0 | 3 | 18 | 14 | 10 | .210 | 31 |
| | Boston AL | 6 | 172 | 9 | 32 | 40 | 2 | 3 | 0 | 3 | 16 | 21 | 6 | .186 | 32 |
| 1919 | Cincinnati NL | 8 | 251 | 35 | 64 | 88 | 10 | 7 | 0 | 7 | 25 | 22 | 34 | .255 | 46 |
| | Chicago AL | 8 | 263 | 20 | 59 | 78 | 10 | 3 | 1 | 5 | 15 | 30 | 17 | .224 | 52 |
| 1920 | Brooklyn NL | 7 | 215 | 8 | 44 | 51 | 5 | 1 | 0 | 1 | 10 | 20 | 8 | .205 | 39 |
| | Cleveland AL | 7 | 217 | 21 | 53 | 72 | 9 | 2 | 2 | 2 | 21 | 21 | 18 | .244 | 43 |
| 1921 | New York NL | 8 | 264 | 29 | 71 | 98 | 13 | 4 | 2 | 7 | 22 | 38 | 28 | .269 | 54 |
| | New York AL | 8 | 241 | 22 | 60 | 65 | 7 | 1 | 2 | 6 | 27 | 44 | 20 | .207 | 43 |
| 1922 | New York NL | 5 | 162 | 18 | 50 | 57 | 2 | 1 | 1 | 1 | 12 | 15 | 18 | .309 | 32 |
| | New York AL | 5 | 158 | 11 | 32 | 46 | 6 | 1 | 2 | 2 | 8 | 20 | 11 | .203 | 25 |
| 1923 | New York NL | 6 | 201 | 17 | 47 | 70 | 2 | 3 | 5 | 1 | 12 | 18 | 17 | .234 | 35 |
| | New York AL | 6 | 205 | 30 | 60 | 91 | 8 | 4 | 5 | 1 | 20 | 22 | 29 | .293 | 43 |
| 1924 | New York NL | 7 | 253 | 27 | 66 | 91 | 9 | 2 | 4 | 3 | 25 | 40 | 22 | .261 | 59 |
| | Washington AL | 7 | 248 | 26 | 61 | 85 | 9 | 0 | 5 | 5 | 29 | 34 | 23 | .246 | 57 |
| 1925 | Pittsburgh NL | 7 | 230 | 25 | 61 | 89 | 12 | 2 | 4 | 7 | 17 | 32 | 25 | .265 | 54 |
| | Washington AL | 7 | 225 | 26 | 59 | 91 | 8 | 0 | 8 | 2 | 17 | 32 | 25 | .262 | 46 |
| 1926 | St. Louis NL | 7 | 239 | 31 | 65 | 91 | 12 | 1 | 4 | 2 | 11 | 30 | 30 | .272 | 43 |
| | New York AL | 7 | 223 | 21 | 54 | 78 | 10 | 1 | 4 | 1 | 31 | 31 | 19 | .242 | 55 |
| 1927 | Pittsburgh NL | 4 | 130 | 10 | 29 | 37 | 6 | 1 | 0 | 0 | 4 | 7 | 10 | .223 | 23 |
| | New York AL | 4 | 136 | 23 | 38 | 54 | 6 | 2 | 2 | 2 | 13 | 25 | 19 | .279 | 29 |
| 1928 | St. Louis NL | 4 | 131 | 10 | 27 | 37 | 5 | 1 | 1 | 3 | 11 | 29 | 9 | .206 | 27 |
| | New York AL | 4 | 134 | 27 | 37 | 71 | 7 | 0 | 9 | 4 | 13 | 12 | 25 | .276 | 24 |
| 1929 | Chicago NL | 5 | 173 | 17 | 43 | 56 | 6 | 2 | 1 | 1 | 13 | 50 | 15 | .249 | 36 |
| | Philadelphia AL | 5 | 171 | 26 | 48 | 71 | 5 | 0 | 6 | 0 | 13 | 27 | 26 | .281 | 35 |
| 1930 | St. Louis NL | 6 | 190 | 12 | 38 | 56 | 10 | 1 | 2 | 1 | 11 | 33 | 11 | .200 | 37 |
| | Philadelphia AL | 6 | 178 | 21 | 35 | 67 | 10 | 2 | 6 | 0 | 24 | 32 | 21 | .197 | 36 |
| 1931 | St. Louis NL | 7 | 229 | 19 | 54 | 71 | 11 | 0 | 2 | 8 | 9 | 41 | 17 | .236 | 40 |
| | Philadelphia AL | 7 | 227 | 22 | 50 | 64 | 5 | 0 | 3 | 0 | 28 | 46 | 20 | .220 | 52 |
| 1932 | Chicago NL | 4 | 146 | 19 | 37 | 58 | 8 | 2 | 3 | 2 | 11 | 24 | 16 | .253 | 31 |
| | New York AL | 4 | 144 | 37 | 45 | 75 | 6 | 0 | 8 | 0 | 23 | 26 | 36 | .313 | 33 |
| 1933 | New York NL | 5 | 176 | 16 | 47 | 61 | 5 | 0 | 3 | 0 | 11 | 21 | 16 | .267 | 39 |
| | Washington AL | 5 | 173 | 11 | 37 | 47 | 4 | 0 | 2 | 1 | 13 | 25 | 11 | .214 | 37 |
| 1934 | St. Louis NL | 7 | 262 | 34 | 73 | 103 | 14 | 5 | 2 | 2 | 11 | 31 | 32 | .279 | 49 |
| | Detroit AL | 7 | 250 | 23 | 56 | 76 | 12 | 1 | 2 | 4 | 25 | 43 | 20 | .224 | 64 |
| 1935 | Chicago NL | 6 | 202 | 18 | 48 | 73 | 6 | 2 | 5 | 1 | 11 | 29 | 17 | .238 | 33 |
| | Detroit AL | 6 | 206 | 21 | 51 | 67 | 11 | 1 | 1 | 1 | 25 | 27 | 18 | .248 | 51 |
| 1936 | New York NL | 6 | 203 | 23 | 50 | 71 | 9 | 0 | 4 | 0 | 21 | 33 | 20 | .246 | 46 |
| | New York AL | 6 | 215 | 43 | 65 | 96 | 8 | 1 | 7 | 1 | 26 | 35 | 41 | .302 | 43 |
| 1937 | New York NL | 5 | 169 | 12 | 40 | 49 | 6 | 0 | 1 | 1 | 11 | 21 | 12 | .237 | 36 |
| | New York AL | 5 | 169 | 28 | 42 | 68 | 6 | 4 | 4 | 0 | 21 | 21 | 25 | .249 | 36 |
| 1938 | Chicago NL | 4 | 136 | 9 | 33 | 45 | 4 | 1 | 2 | 0 | 6 | 26 | 8 | .243 | 26 |
| | New York AL | 4 | 135 | 22 | 37 | 60 | 6 | 1 | 5 | 3 | 11 | 16 | 21 | .274 | 24 |
| 1939 | Cincinnati NL | 4 | 133 | 8 | 27 | 32 | 3 | 1 | 0 | 1 | 6 | 22 | 8 | .203 | 23 |
| | New York AL | 4 | 131 | 20 | 27 | 54 | 4 | 1 | 7 | 0 | 9 | 20 | 18 | .206 | 16 |
| 1940 | Cincinnati NL | 7 | 232 | 22 | 58 | 78 | 14 | 0 | 2 | 1 | 15 | 30 | 21 | .250 | 49 |
| | Detroit AL | 7 | 228 | 28 | 56 | 83 | 9 | 3 | 4 | 0 | 30 | 30 | 24 | .246 | 50 |
| 1941 | Brooklyn NL | 5 | 159 | 11 | 29 | 43 | 7 | 2 | 1 | 0 | 14 | 21 | 11 | .182 | 27 |
| | New York AL | 5 | 166 | 17 | 41 | 54 | 5 | 1 | 2 | 2 | 23 | 18 | 16 | .247 | 42 |
| 1942 | St. Louis NL | 5 | 163 | 23 | 39 | 53 | 4 | 2 | 2 | 0 | 17 | 19 | 23 | .239 | 32 |
| | New York AL | 5 | 178 | 18 | 44 | 59 | 6 | 0 | 3 | 3 | 8 | 22 | 14 | .247 | 34 |
| 1943 | St. Louis NL | 5 | 165 | 9 | 37 | 48 | 5 | 0 | 2 | 1 | 11 | 26 | 8 | .224 | 37 |
| | New York AL | 5 | 159 | 17 | 35 | 50 | 5 | 2 | 2 | 2 | 12 | 30 | 14 | .220 | 29 |
| 1944 | St. Louis NL | 6 | 204 | 16 | 49 | 69 | 9 | 1 | 3 | 0 | 19 | 43 | 15 | .240 | 51 |
| | St. Louis AL | 6 | 197 | 12 | 36 | 50 | 9 | 1 | 1 | 0 | 23 | 49 | 9 | .183 | 44 |
| 1945 | Chicago NL | 7 | 247 | 29 | 65 | 90 | 16 | 3 | 1 | 2 | 19 | 48 | 27 | .263 | 50 |
| | Detroit AL | 7 | 242 | 32 | 54 | 70 | 10 | 0 | 2 | 3 | 33 | 22 | 32 | .223 | 53 |
| 1946 | St. Louis NL | 7 | 232 | 28 | 60 | 86 | 19 | 2 | 1 | 3 | 19 | 30 | 27 | .259 | 50 |
| | Boston AL | 7 | 233 | 20 | 56 | 77 | 7 | 1 | 4 | 2 | 22 | 28 | 18 | .240 | 53 |
| 1947 | Brooklyn NL | 7 | 226 | 29 | 52 | 70 | 13 | 1 | 1 | 7 | 30 | 32 | 26 | .230 | 46 |
| | New York AL | 7 | 238 | 38 | 67 | 100 | 11 | 5 | 4 | 2 | 38 | 37 | 36 | .282 | 63 |
| 1948 | Boston NL | 6 | 187 | 17 | 43 | 61 | 6 | 0 | 4 | 1 | 16 | 19 | 16 | .230 | 34 |
| | Cleveland AL | 6 | 191 | 17 | 38 | 57 | 7 | 0 | 4 | 2 | 12 | 26 | 16 | .199 | 34 |
| 1949 | Brooklyn NL | 5 | 162 | 14 | 34 | 55 | 7 | 1 | 4 | 1 | 15 | 38 | 14 | .210 | 31 |
| | New York AL | 5 | 164 | 21 | 37 | 57 | 10 | 2 | 2 | 2 | 18 | 27 | 20 | .226 | 32 |
| 1950 | Philadelphia NL | 4 | 128 | 5 | 26 | 34 | 6 | 1 | 0 | 1 | 7 | 24 | 3 | .203 | 26 |
| | New York AL | 4 | 135 | 11 | 30 | 41 | 3 | 1 | 2 | 1 | 13 | 12 | 10 | .222 | 33 |
| 1951 | New York NL | 6 | 194 | 18 | 46 | 61 | 7 | 1 | 2 | 2 | 25 | 22 | 15 | .237 | 45 |
| | New York AL | 6 | 199 | 29 | 49 | 75 | 7 | 2 | 5 | 0 | 26 | 23 | 25 | .246 | 41 |
| 1952 | Brooklyn NL | 7 | 233 | 20 | 50 | 75 | 7 | 0 | 6 | 5 | 24 | 49 | 18 | .215 | 52 |
| | New York AL | 7 | 232 | 26 | 50 | 89 | 5 | 2 | 10 | 1 | 31 | 32 | 24 | .216 | 48 |
| 1953 | Brooklyn NL | 6 | 213 | 27 | 64 | 103 | 13 | 1 | 8 | 2 | 15 | 30 | 26 | .300 | 49 |
| | New York AL | 6 | 201 | 33 | 56 | 97 | 6 | 4 | 9 | 2 | 25 | 43 | 32 | .279 | 47 |
| 1954 | New York NL | 4 | 130 | 21 | 33 | 42 | 3 | 0 | 2 | 1 | 17 | 24 | 20 | .254 | 28 |
| | Cleveland AL | 4 | 137 | 9 | 26 | 42 | 5 | 1 | 3 | 0 | 16 | 23 | 9 | .190 | 37 |
| 1955 | Brooklyn NL | 7 | 223 | 31 | 58 | 95 | 8 | 1 | 9 | 2 | 33 | 38 | 30 | .260 | 55 |
| | New York AL | 7 | 222 | 26 | 55 | 87 | 4 | 2 | 8 | 3 | 22 | 39 | 25 | .248 | 41 |
| 1956 | Brooklyn NL | 7 | 215 | 25 | 42 | 61 | 8 | 1 | 3 | 1 | 32 | 47 | 24 | .195 | 42 |
| | New York AL | 7 | 229 | 33 | 58 | 100 | 6 | 0 | 12 | 2 | 21 | 43 | 33 | .253 | 40 |
| 1957 | Milwaukee NL | 7 | 225 | 23 | 47 | 79 | 6 | 1 | 8 | 1 | 22 | 40 | 22 | .209 | 46 |
| | New York AL | 7 | 230 | 25 | 57 | 87 | 7 | 1 | 7 | 1 | 22 | 34 | 25 | .248 | 45 |
| 1958 | Milwaukee NL | 7 | 240 | 25 | 60 | 81 | 10 | 1 | 3 | 1 | 27 | 56 | 24 | .250 | 58 |
| | New York AL | 7 | 233 | 29 | 49 | 86 | 5 | 1 | 10 | 1 | 21 | 42 | 29 | .210 | 40 |
| 1959 | Los Angeles NL | 6 | 203 | 21 | 53 | 79 | 3 | 1 | 7 | 5 | 12 | 27 | 19 | .261 | 42 |
| | Chicago AL | 6 | 199 | 23 | 52 | 74 | 10 | 0 | 4 | 2 | 20 | 33 | 19 | .261 | 43 |
| 1960 | Pittsburgh NL | 7 | 234 | 27 | 60 | 83 | 11 | 0 | 4 | 2 | 12 | 26 | 26 | .256 | 42 |

| Year | Team, League | G | AB | R | H | TB | 2B | 3B | HR | SB | BB | SO | RBI | Avg. | LOB |
|---|---|---|---|---|---|---|---|---|---|---|---|---|---|---|---|
| | New York AL | 7 | 269 | 55 | 91 | 142 | 13 | 4 | 10 | 0 | 18 | 40 | 54 | .338 | 51 |
| 1961 | Cincinnati NL | 5 | 170 | 13 | 35 | 52 | 8 | 0 | 3 | 0 | 8 | 27 | 11 | .206 | 33 |
| | New York AL | 5 | 165 | 27 | 42 | 73 | 8 | 1 | 7 | 1 | 24 | 25 | 26 | .255 | 34 |
| 1962 | San Francisco NL | 7 | 226 | 21 | 51 | 80 | 10 | 2 | 5 | 1 | 12 | 39 | 19 | .226 | 39 |
| | New York AL | 7 | 221 | 20 | 44 | 61 | 6 | 1 | 3 | 4 | 21 | 39 | 17 | .199 | 43 |
| 1963 | Los Angeles NL | 4 | 117 | 12 | 25 | 41 | 3 | 2 | 3 | 2 | 11 | 25 | 12 | .214 | 17 |
| | New York AL | 4 | 129 | 4 | 22 | 31 | 3 | 0 | 2 | 0 | 5 | 37 | 4 | .171 | 24 |
| 1964 | St. Louis NL | 7 | 240 | 32 | 61 | 90 | 8 | 3 | 5 | 3 | 18 | 39 | 29 | .254 | 47 |
| | New York AL | 7 | 239 | 33 | 60 | 101 | 11 | 0 | 10 | 2 | 25 | 54 | 33 | .251 | 47 |
| 1965 | Los Angeles NL | 7 | 234 | 24 | 64 | 91 | 10 | 1 | 5 | 9 | 13 | 31 | 21 | .274 | 52 |
| | Minnesota AL | 7 | 215 | 20 | 42 | 71 | 7 | 2 | 6 | 2 | 19 | 54 | 19 | .195 | 36 |
| 1966 | Los Angeles NL | 4 | 120 | 2 | 17 | 23 | 3 | 0 | 1 | 1 | 13 | 28 | 2 | .142 | 24 |
| | Baltimore AL | 4 | 120 | 13 | 24 | 41 | 3 | 1 | 4 | 0 | 11 | 17 | 10 | .200 | 18 |
| 1967 | St. Louis NL | 7 | 229 | 25 | 51 | 81 | 11 | 2 | 5 | 7 | 17 | 30 | 24 | .223 | 40 |
| | Boston AL | 7 | 222 | 21 | 48 | 80 | 6 | 1 | 8 | 1 | 17 | 49 | 19 | .216 | 43 |
| 1968 | St. Louis NL | 7 | 239 | 27 | 61 | 95 | 7 | 3 | 7 | 11 | 21 | 40 | 27 | .255 | 49 |
| | Detroit AL | 7 | 231 | 34 | 56 | 90 | 4 | 3 | 8 | 0 | 27 | 59 | 33 | .242 | 44 |
| 1969 | New York NL | 5 | 159 | 15 | 35 | 61 | 8 | 0 | 6 | 1 | 15 | 35 | 13 | .220 | 34 |
| | Baltimore AL | 5 | 157 | 9 | 23 | 33 | 1 | 0 | 3 | 1 | 15 | 28 | 9 | .146 | 29 |
| 1970 | Cincinnati NL | 5 | 164 | 20 | 35 | 58 | 6 | 1 | 5 | 1 | 15 | 23 | 20 | .213 | 28 |
| | Baltimore AL | 5 | 171 | 33 | 50 | 87 | 7 | 0 | 10 | 0 | 20 | 33 | 32 | .292 | 31 |
| 1971 | Pittsburgh NL | 7 | 238 | 23 | 56 | 84 | 9 | 2 | 5 | 5 | 26 | 47 | 21 | .235 | 63 |
| | Baltimore AL | 7 | 219 | 24 | 45 | 65 | 3 | 1 | 5 | 1 | 20 | 35 | 22 | .205 | 39 |
| 1972 | Cincinnati NL | 7 | 220 | 21 | 46 | 65 | 8 | 1 | 3 | 12 | 27 | 46 | 21 | .209 | 49 |
| | Oakland AL | 7 | 220 | 16 | 46 | 65 | 4 | 0 | 5 | 1 | 21 | 37 | 16 | .209 | 45 |
| 1973 | New York NL | 7 | 261 | 24 | 66 | 89 | 7 | 2 | 4 | 0 | 26 | 36 | 16 | .253 | 72 |
| | Oakland AL | 7 | 241 | 21 | 51 | 75 | 12 | 3 | 2 | 3 | 28 | 62 | 20 | .212 | 58 |
| 1974 | Los Angeles NL | 5 | 158 | 11 | 36 | 54 | 4 | 1 | 4 | 3 | 16 | 32 | 10 | .228 | 36 |
| | Oakland AL | 5 | 142 | 16 | 30 | 46 | 4 | 0 | 4 | 3 | 16 | 42 | 14 | .211 | 26 |
| 1975 | Cincinnati NL | 7 | 244 | 29 | 59 | 95 | 9 | 3 | 7 | 9 | 25 | 30 | 29 | .242 | 50 |
| | Boston AL | 7 | 239 | 30 | 60 | 89 | 7 | 2 | 6 | 0 | 30 | 40 | 30 | .251 | 52 |
| 1976 | Cincinnati NL | 4 | 134 | 22 | 42 | 70 | 10 | 3 | 4 | 7 | 12 | 16 | 21 | .313 | 22 |
| | New York AL | 4 | 135 | 8 | 30 | 38 | 3 | 1 | 1 | 1 | 12 | 16 | 8 | .222 | 33 |
| 1977 | Los Angeles NL | 6 | 208 | 28 | 48 | 86 | 5 | 3 | 9 | 2 | 16 | 36 | 28 | .231 | 31 |
| | New York AL | 6 | 205 | 26 | 50 | 84 | 10 | 0 | 8 | 1 | 11 | 37 | 25 | .244 | 32 |
| 1978 | Los Angeles NL | 6 | 199 | 23 | 52 | 78 | 8 | 0 | 6 | 5 | 20 | 31 | 22 | .261 | 38 |
| | New York AL | 6 | 222 | 36 | 68 | 85 | 8 | 0 | 3 | 5 | 16 | 40 | 34 | .306 | 47 |
| 1979 | Pittsburgh NL | 7 | 251 | 32 | 81 | 110 | 18 | 1 | 3 | 0 | 16 | 35 | 32 | .323 | 60 |
| | Baltimore AL | 7 | 233 | 26 | 54 | 78 | 10 | 1 | 4 | 2 | 26 | 41 | 23 | .232 | 49 |
| 1980 | Philadelphia NL | 6 | 201 | 27 | 59 | 81 | 13 | 0 | 3 | 3 | 15 | 17 | 26 | .294 | 41 |
| | Kansas City AL | 6 | 207 | 23 | 60 | 97 | 9 | 2 | 8 | 6 | 26 | 49 | 22 | .290 | 54 |
| 1981 | Los Angeles NL | 6 | 198 | 27 | 51 | 77 | 6 | 1 | 6 | 6 | 20 | 44 | 26 | .258 | 46 |
| | New York AL | 6 | 193 | 22 | 46 | 74 | 8 | 1 | 6 | 4 | 33 | 24 | 22 | .238 | 55 |
| 1982 | St. Louis NL | 7 | 245 | 39 | 67 | 101 | 16 | 3 | 4 | 7 | 20 | 26 | 34 | .273 | 49 |
| | Milwaukee AL | 7 | 238 | 33 | 64 | 95 | 12 | 2 | 5 | 1 | 19 | 28 | 29 | .269 | 44 |
| 1983 | Philadelphia NL | 5 | 159 | 9 | 31 | 49 | 4 | 1 | 4 | 1 | 7 | 29 | 9 | .195 | 23 |
| | Baltimore AL | 5 | 164 | 18 | 35 | 61 | 8 | 0 | 6 | 1 | 10 | 37 | 17 | .213 | 28 |
| 1984 | San Diego NL | 5 | 166 | 15 | 44 | 60 | 7 | 0 | 3 | 2 | 11 | 26 | 14 | .265 | 34 |
| | Detroit AL | 5 | 158 | 23 | 40 | 65 | 4 | 0 | 7 | 7 | 24 | 27 | 23 | .253 | 39 |
| 1985 | St. Louis NL | 7 | 216 | 13 | 40 | 58 | 10 | 1 | 2 | 2 | 28 | 42 | 13 | .185 | 38 |
| | Kansas City AL | 7 | 236 | 28 | 68 | 90 | 12 | 2 | 2 | 7 | 18 | 56 | 26 | .288 | 56 |
| 1986 | New York NL | 7 | 240 | 32 | 65 | 92 | 6 | 0 | 7 | 7 | 21 | 43 | 29 | .271 | 50 |
| | Boston AL | 7 | 248 | 27 | 69 | 99 | 11 | 2 | 5 | 0 | 28 | 53 | 26 | .278 | 69 |
| 1987 | St. Louis NL | 7 | 232 | 26 | 60 | 74 | 8 | 0 | 2 | 12 | 13 | 44 | 25 | .259 | 43 |
| | Minnesota AL | 7 | 238 | 38 | 64 | 101 | 10 | 3 | 7 | 6 | 29 | 36 | 38 | .269 | 56 |
| 1988 | Los Angeles NL | 5 | 167 | 21 | 41 | 66 | 8 | 1 | 5 | 4 | 13 | 36 | 19 | .246 | 30 |
| | Oakland AL | 5 | 158 | 11 | 28 | 37 | 3 | 0 | 2 | 3 | 17 | 41 | 11 | .177 | 34 |
| 1989 | San Francisco NL | 4 | 134 | 14 | 28 | 46 | 4 | 1 | 4 | 2 | 8 | 27 | 14 | .209 | 21 |
| | Oakland AL | 4 | 146 | 32 | 44 | 85 | 8 | 3 | 9 | 4 | 18 | 22 | 30 | .301 | 31 |
| 1990 | Cincinnati NL | 4 | 142 | 22 | 45 | 67 | 9 | 2 | 3 | 2 | 15 | 9 | 22 | .317 | 32 |
| | Oakland AL | 4 | 135 | 8 | 28 | 41 | 4 | 0 | 3 | 7 | 12 | 28 | 8 | .207 | 31 |
| 1991 | Atlanta NL | 7 | 249 | 29 | 63 | 105 | 10 | 4 | 8 | 5 | 26 | 39 | 29 | .253 | 52 |
| | Minnesota AL | 7 | 241 | 24 | 56 | 96 | 8 | 4 | 8 | 7 | 21 | 48 | 24 | .232 | 47 |
| 1992 | Atlanta NL | 6 | 200 | 20 | 44 | 59 | 6 | 0 | 3 | 15 | 20 | 48 | 19 | .220 | 40 |
| | Toronto AL | 6 | 196 | 17 | 45 | 71 | 8 | 0 | 6 | 5 | 18 | 33 | 17 | .230 | 38 |
| 1993 | Philadelphia NL | 6 | 212 | 36 | 58 | 90 | 7 | 2 | 7 | 7 | 34 | 50 | 35 | .274 | 54 |
| | Toronto AL | 6 | 206 | 45 | 64 | 105 | 13 | 5 | 6 | 7 | 25 | 30 | 45 | .311 | 39 |
| 1994 | no series played | | | | | | | | | | | | | | |
| 1995 | Atlanta NL | 6 | 193 | 23 | 47 | 81 | 10 | 0 | 8 | 5 | 25 | 34 | 23 | .244 | 44 |
| | Cleveland AL | 6 | 195 | 19 | 35 | 59 | 7 | 1 | 5 | 8 | 25 | 37 | 17 | .179 | 39 |
| 1996 | Atlanta NL | 6 | 201 | 26 | 51 | 74 | 9 | 1 | 4 | 3 | 23 | 36 | 26 | .254 | 41 |
| | New York AL | 6 | 199 | 18 | 43 | 57 | 6 | 1 | 2 | 4 | 26 | 43 | 16 | .216 | 48 |
| 1997 | Florida NL | 7 | 250 | 37 | 68 | 106 | 12 | 1 | 8 | 4 | 36 | 48 | 34 | .272 | 62 |
| | Cleveland AL | 7 | 247 | 44 | 72 | 107 | 12 | 1 | 7 | 5 | 40 | 51 | 42 | .291 | 59 |
| 1998 | San Diego NL | 4 | 134 | 13 | 32 | 50 | 7 | 1 | 3 | 1 | 12 | 29 | 11 | .239 | 27 |
| | New York AL | 4 | 139 | 26 | 43 | 66 | 5 | 0 | 6 | 1 | 20 | 29 | 25 | .309 | 34 |
| 1999 | Atlanta NL | 4 | 130 | 9 | 26 | 36 | 5 | 1 | 1 | 1 | 15 | 26 | 9 | .200 | 25 |
| | New York AL | 4 | 137 | 21 | 37 | 57 | 5 | 0 | 5 | 5 | 13 | 31 | 20 | .270 | 27 |
| 2000 | New York NL | 5 | 175 | 16 | 40 | 60 | 8 | 0 | 4 | 0 | 11 | 48 | 15 | .229 | 36 |
| | New York AL | 5 | 179 | 19 | 47 | 73 | 8 | 3 | 4 | 1 | 25 | 40 | 18 | .263 | 52 |
| 2001 | Arizona NL | 7 | 246 | 37 | 65 | 97 | 14 | 0 | 6 | 2 | 17 | 70 | 36 | .264 | 49 |
| | New York AL | 7 | 229 | 14 | 42 | 66 | 6 | 0 | 6 | 1 | 16 | 63 | 14 | .183 | 38 |
| 2002 | San Francisco NL | 7 | 235 | 44 | 66 | 117 | 7 | 1 | 14 | 5 | 30 | 50 | 42 | .281 | 47 |
| | Anaheim AL | 7 | 245 | 41 | 76 | 114 | 15 | 1 | 7 | 6 | 23 | 38 | 38 | .310 | 54 |
| 2003 | Florida NL | 6 | 203 | 17 | 47 | 61 | 8 | 0 | 2 | 2 | 14 | 48 | 17 | .232 | 43 |
| | New York AL | 6 | 207 | 21 | 54 | 84 | 10 | 1 | 6 | 2 | 22 | 49 | 21 | .261 | 47 |
| 2004 | Boston AL | 4 | 138 | 24 | 39 | 66 | 1 | 2 | 4 | 0 | 24 | 20 | 24 | .283 | 41 |
| | St. Louis NL | 4 | 126 | 12 | 24 | 38 | 8 | 0 | 2 | 1 | 12 | 32 | 8 | .190 | 24 |

| Year | Team, League | G | AB | R | H | TB | 2B | 3B | HR | SB | BB | SO | RBI | Avg. | LOB |
|---|---|---|---|---|---|---|---|---|---|---|---|---|---|---|---|
| 2005 | Chicago AL | 4 | 154 | 20 | 44 | 75 | 9 | 2 | 6 | 5 | 15 | 30 | 20 | .286 | 36 |
| | Houston NL | 4 | 143 | 14 | 29 | 48 | 8 | 1 | 3 | 5 | 17 | 36 | 14 | .203 | 34 |

## CLUB FIELDING AND PLAYERS USED

| Year | Team, League | G | PO | A | E | DP | PB | Fielding Avg. | Players Used | Pitchers Used | PH | PR |
|---|---|---|---|---|---|---|---|---|---|---|---|---|
| 1903 | Pittsburgh NL | 8 | 210 | 96 | 18 | 5 | 0 | .944 | 14 | 5 | 1 | 0 |
| | Boston AL | 8 | 213 | 102 | 14 | 6 | 2 | .957 | 13 | 3 | 4 | 0 |
| 1904 | no series | | | | | | | | | | | |
| 1905 | New York NL | 5 | 135 | 78 | 6 | 2 | 0 | .973 | 12 | 3 | 1 | 0 |
| | Philadelphia AL | 5 | 129 | 56 | 9 | 2 | 0 | .954 | 13 | 3 | 1 | 0 |
| 1906 | Chicago NL | 6 | 159 | 84 | 7 | 4 | 3 | .972 | 14 | 4 | 4 | 0 |
| | Chicago AL | 6 | 162 | 99 | 14 | 2 | 1 | .949 | 16 | 4 | 2 | 1 |
| 1907 | Chicago NL | 5 | 144 | 65 | 10 | 6 | 1 | .954 | 15 | 4 | 2 | 0 |
| | Detroit AL | 5 | 138 | 70 | 9 | 2 | 0 | .959 | 14 | 4 | 1 | 1 |
| 1908 | Chicago NL | 5 | 135 | 74 | 5 | 4 | 1 | .977 | 13 | 4 | 1 | 0 |
| | Detroit AL | 5 | 131 | 63 | 10 | 5 | 1 | .951 | 16 | 5 | 4 | 1 |
| 1909 | Pittsburgh NL | 7 | 182 | 88 | 15 | 3 | 0 | .947 | 17 | 6 | 3 | 0 |
| | Detroit AL | 7 | 183 | 87 | 19 | 4 | 1 | .934 | 16 | 5 | 5 | 0 |
| 1910 | Chicago NL | 5 | 132 | 77 | 12 | 3 | 0 | .946 | 18 | 7 | 6 | 1 |
| | Philadelphia AL | 5 | 136 | 59 | 11 | 6 | 0 | .947 | 12 | 2 | 0 | 0 |
| 1911 | New York NL | 6 | 162 | 79 | 16 | 2 | 1 | .938 | 15 | 5 | 4 | 0 |
| | Philadelphia AL | 6 | 167 | 72 | 11 | 2 | 0 | .956 | 14 | 3 | 0 | 1 |
| 1912 | New York NL | 8 | 221 | 108 | 17 | 4 | 0 | .951 | 17 | 5 | 5 | 3 |
| | Boston AL | 8 | 222 | 101 | 14 | 5 | 0 | .958 | 17 | 5 | 5 | 1 |
| 1913 | New York NL | 5 | 135 | 67 | 7 | 1 | 1 | .967 | 20 | 5 | 6 | 5 |
| | Philadelphia AL | 5 | 138 | 54 | 5 | 6 | 0 | .975 | 12 | 3 | 0 | 0 |
| 1914 | Boston NL | 4 | 117 | 62 | 4 | 4 | 0 | .978 | 15 | 3 | 3 | 1 |
| | Philadelphia AL | 4 | 111 | 66 | 3 | 4 | 1 | .983 | 16 | 6 | 1 | 0 |
| 1915 | Philadelphia NL | 5 | 131 | 54 | 3 | 3 | 0 | .984 | 16 | 4 | 2 | 2 |
| | Boston AL | 5 | 132 | 58 | 4 | 2 | 0 | .979 | 17 | 3 | 3 | 1 |
| 1916 | Brooklyn NL | 5 | 142 | 70 | 13 | 2 | 2 | .942 | 20 | 7 | 6 | 1 |
| | Boston AL | 5 | 147 | 90 | 6 | 5 | 1 | .975 | 20 | 5 | 3 | 1 |
| 1917 | New York NL | 6 | 153 | 72 | 11 | 3 | 1 | .953 | 17 | 6 | 3 | 0 |
| | Chicago AL | 6 | 156 | 82 | 12 | 7 | 1 | .952 | 16 | 5 | 5 | 0 |
| 1918 | Chicago NL | 6 | 156 | 76 | 5 | 7 | 2 | .979 | 17 | 4 | 8 | 2 |
| | Boston AL | 6 | 159 | 88 | 1 | 4 | 1 | .996 | 15 | 4 | 5 | 0 |
| 1919 | Cincinnati NL | 8 | 216 | 96 | 12 | 7 | 0 | .963 | 17 | 6 | 3 | 1 |
| | Chicago AL | 8 | 213 | 116 | 12 | 9 | 1 | .965 | 19 | 7 | 6 | 0 |
| 1920 | Brooklyn NL | 7 | 177 | 91 | 6 | 5 | 2 | .978 | 21 | 7 | 7 | 3 |
| | Cleveland AL | 7 | 182 | 89 | 12 | 8 | 0 | .958 | 20 | 5 | 12 | 1 |
| 1921 | New York NL | 8 | 212 | 102 | 5 | 5 | 2 | .984 | 13 | 4 | 2 | 0 |
| | New York AL | 8 | 210 | 106 | 6 | 8 | 0 | .981 | 19 | 8 | 3 | 2 |
| 1922 | New York NL | 5 | 138 | 70 | 6 | 4 | 0 | .972 | 16 | 5 | 3 | 1 |
| | New York AL | 5 | 129 | 62 | 1 | 7 | 1 | .995 | 17 | 5 | 4 | 0 |
| 1923 | New York NL | 6 | 159 | 80 | 6 | 8 | 0 | .976 | 22 | 8 | 9 | 3 |
| | New York AL | 6 | 162 | 77 | 3 | 6 | 0 | .988 | 17 | 5 | 4 | 2 |
| 1924 | New York NL | 7 | 200 | 94 | 6 | 4 | 0 | .980 | 21 | 9 | 7 | 3 |
| | Washington AL | 7 | 201 | 99 | 12 | 10 | 1 | .962 | 21 | 8 | 8 | 2 |
| 1925 | Pittsburgh NL | 7 | 182 | 89 | 7 | 4 | 0 | .980 | 18 | 7 | 5 | 2 |
| | Washington AL | 7 | 180 | 75 | 9 | 8 | 1 | .966 | 21 | 6 | 7 | 4 |
| 1926 | St. Louis NL | 7 | 189 | 99 | 5 | 6 | 0 | .983 | 19 | 8 | 6 | 0 |
| | New York AL | 7 | 189 | 82 | 7 | 3 | 1 | .975 | 19 | 7 | 7 | 2 |
| 1927 | Pittsburgh NL | 4 | 104 | 46 | 6 | 2 | 0 | .962 | 21 | 7 | 5 | 1 |
| | New York AL | 4 | 108 | 44 | 3 | 4 | 0 | .981 | 15 | 4 | 1 | 0 |
| 1928 | St. Louis NL | 4 | 102 | 36 | 5 | 3 | 0 | .965 | 20 | 6 | 6 | 1 |
| | New York AL | 4 | 108 | 28 | 6 | 3 | 0 | .958 | 16 | 3 | 4 | 0 |
| 1929 | Chicago NL | 5 | 131 | 44 | 7 | 4 | 0 | .962 | 19 | 6 | 8 | 0 |
| | Philadelphia AL | 5 | 135 | 40 | 4 | 2 | 6 | .978 | 17 | 6 | 3 | 0 |
| 1930 | St. Louis NL | 6 | 153 | 55 | 5 | 4 | 1 | .977 | 21 | 7 | 7 | 0 |
| | Philadelphia AL | 6 | 156 | 41 | 3 | 2 | 0 | .985 | 15 | 5 | 3 | 0 |
| 1931 | St. Louis NL | 7 | 186 | 73 | 4 | 7 | 0 | .985 | 21 | 6 | 6 | 1 |
| | Philadelphia AL | 7 | 183 | 69 | 2 | 4 | 0 | .992 | 20 | 6 | 8 | 1 |
| 1932 | Chicago NL | 4 | 102 | 40 | 6 | 7 | 0 | .959 | 22 | 8 | 6 | 1 |
| | New York AL | 4 | 108 | 41 | 8 | 1 | 0 | .949 | 16 | 6 | 6 | 1 |
| 1933 | New York NL | 5 | 141 | 67 | 4 | 5 | 0 | .981 | 15 | 5 | 2 | 0 |
| | Washington AL | 5 | 138 | 65 | 4 | 4 | 0 | .981 | 10 | 7 | 5 | 1 |
| 1934 | St. Louis NL | 7 | 196 | 73 | 15 | 2 | 0 | .947 | 20 | 8 | 5 | 2 |
| | Detroit AL | 7 | 195 | 70 | 12 | 6 | 0 | .957 | 17 | 6 | 4 | 0 |
| 1935 | Chicago NL | 6 | 164 | 74 | 6 | 5 | 0 | .975 | 18 | 7 | 5 | 0 |
| | Detroit AL | 6 | 165 | 72 | 9 | 7 | 1 | .963 | 15 | 5 | 2 | 0 |
| 1936 | New York NL | 6 | 159 | 62 | 7 | 7 | 0 | .969 | 22 | 8 | 10 | 2 |
| | New York AL | 6 | 162 | 57 | 6 | 2 | 0 | .973 | 16 | 6 | 2 | 2 |
| 1937 | New York NL | 5 | 129 | 46 | 9 | 5 | 0 | .951 | 20 | 7 | 7 | 0 |
| | New York AL | 5 | 132 | 47 | 0 | 2 | 0 | 1.000 | 17 | 7 | 1 | 0 |
| 1938 | Chicago NL | 4 | 102 | 35 | 3 | 3 | 0 | .979 | 20 | 8 | 8 | 0 |
| | New York AL | 4 | 108 | 39 | 6 | 4 | 0 | .961 | 14 | 4 | 1 | 0 |
| 1939 | Cincinnati NL | 4 | 106 | 34 | 4 | 1 | 0 | .972 | 18 | 5 | 3 | 2 |
| | New York AL | 4 | 111 | 50 | 2 | 5 | 0 | .988 | 15 | 7 | 0 | 0 |
| 1940 | Cincinnati NL | 7 | 183 | 67 | 8 | 9 | 1 | .969 | 23 | 9 | 9 | 1 |
| | Detroit AL | 7 | 180 | 80 | 4 | 4 | 0 | .985 | 20 | 8 | 6 | 0 |
| 1941 | Brooklyn NL | 5 | 132 | 60 | 4 | 5 | 0 | .980 | 20 | 7 | 6 | 0 |

| Year | Team, League | G | PO | A | E | DP | PB | Fielding Avg. | Players Used | Pitchers Used | PH | PR |
|---|---|---|---|---|---|---|---|---|---|---|---|---|
| | New York AL | 5 | 135 | 55 | 2 | 7 | 0 | .990 | 18 | 7 | 2 | 1 |
| 1942 | St. Louis NL | 5 | 135 | 45 | 10 | 3 | 0 | .947 | 18 | 6 | 4 | 1 |
| | New York AL | 5 | 132 | 45 | 5 | 2 | 0 | .973 | 20 | 7 | 4 | 2 |
| 1943 | St. Louis NL | 5 | 129 | 53 | 10 | 4 | 0 | .948 | 20 | 6 | 6 | 1 |
| | New York AL | 5 | 135 | 63 | 5 | 3 | 0 | .975 | 16 | 5 | 2 | 0 |
| 1944 | St. Louis NL | 6 | 165 | 59 | 1 | 3 | 1 | .996 | 20 | 8 | 7 | 0 |
| | St. Louis AL | 6 | 163 | 60 | 10 | 4 | 0 | .957 | 22 | 7 | 13 | 1 |
| 1945 | Chicago NL | 7 | 195 | 78 | 6 | 5 | 1 | .978 | 25 | 8 | 14 | 3 |
| | Detroit AL | 7 | 197 | 85 | 5 | 4 | 2 | .983 | 26 | 9 | 11 | 1 |
| 1946 | St. Louis NL | 7 | 186 | 68 | 4 | 7 | 1 | .984 | 19 | 7 | 5 | 0 |
| | Boston AL | 7 | 183 | 76 | 10 | 5 | 0 | .963 | 26 | 11 | 10 | 3 |
| 1947 | Brooklyn NL | 7 | 180 | 71 | 8 | 8 | 2 | .969 | 24 | 8 | 19 | 5 |
| | New York AL | 7 | 185 | 70 | 4 | 4 | 2 | .985 | 24 | 9 | 11 | 0 |
| 1948 | Boston NL | 6 | 156 | 54 | 6 | 3 | 0 | .972 | 20 | 6 | 8 | 4 |
| | Cleveland AL | 6 | 159 | 72 | 3 | 9 | 0 | .987 | 23 | 8 | 3 | 0 |
| 1949 | Brooklyn NL | 5 | 132 | 40 | 5 | 1 | 0 | .972 | 25 | 9 | 11 | 0 |
| | New York AL | 5 | 135 | 44 | 3 | 5 | 0 | .984 | 20 | 5 | 4 | 2 |
| 1950 | Philadelphia NL | 4 | 107 | 35 | 4 | 1 | 0 | .973 | 20 | 5 | 6 | 4 |
| | New York AL | 4 | 111 | 41 | 2 | 4 | 0 | .987 | 18 | 5 | 2 | 2 |
| 1951 | New York NL | 6 | 156 | 65 | 10 | 4 | 0 | .957 | 24 | 9 | 10 | 2 |
| | New York AL | 6 | 159 | 67 | 4 | 10 | 1 | .982 | 21 | 8 | 5 | 2 |
| 1952 | Brooklyn NL | 7 | 192 | 71 | 4 | 4 | 0 | .985 | 19 | 6 | 8 | 1 |
| | New York AL | 7 | 192 | 66 | 10 | 7 | 1 | .963 | 19 | 8 | 6 | 1 |
| 1953 | Brooklyn NL | 6 | 154 | 62 | 7 | 3 | 0 | .969 | 23 | 10 | 8 | 0 |
| | New York AL | 6 | 156 | 60 | 1 | 5 | 0 | .995 | 20 | 9 | 7 | 0 |
| 1954 | New York NL | 4 | 111 | 40 | 7 | 2 | 0 | .955 | 15 | 6 | 3 | 0 |
| | Cleveland AL | 4 | 106 | 40 | 4 | 2 | 0 | .973 | 24 | 7 | 16 | 2 |
| 1955 | Brooklyn NL | 7 | 180 | 84 | 6 | 12 | 0 | .978 | 22 | 10 | 6 | 1 |
| | New York AL | 7 | 180 | 72 | 2 | 7 | 0 | .992 | 24 | 9 | 12 | 3 |
| 1956 | Brooklyn NL | 7 | 183 | 69 | 2 | 8 | 0 | .992 | 21 | 8 | 9 | 0 |
| | New York AL | 7 | 185 | 66 | 6 | 7 | 0 | .977 | 22 | 8 | 6 | 0 |
| 1957 | Milwaukee NL | 7 | 186 | 93 | 3 | 10 | 1 | .989 | 23 | 8 | 9 | 2 |
| | New York AL | 7 | 187 | 72 | 6 | 5 | 0 | .977 | 23 | 9 | 10 | 2 |
| 1958 | Milwaukee NL | 7 | 189 | 78 | 7 | 5 | 0 | .974 | 19 | 6 | 8 | 5 |
| | New York AL | 7 | 191 | 65 | 3 | 5 | 1 | .988 | 22 | 9 | 9 | 0 |
| 1959 | Los Angeles NL | 6 | 159 | 69 | 4 | 7 | 0 | .983 | 24 | 9 | 13 | 4 |
| | Chicago AL | 6 | 156 | 62 | 4 | 2 | 1 | .982 | 21 | 7 | 9 | 2 |
| 1960 | Pittsburgh NL | 7 | 186 | 67 | 4 | 7 | 3 | .984 | 25 | 10 | 9 | 2 |
| | New York AL | 7 | 183 | 93 | 8 | 9 | 0 | .972 | 25 | 10 | 11 | 3 |
| 1961 | Cincinnati NL | 5 | 132 | 42 | 4 | 7 | 1 | .978 | 24 | 9 | 15 | 1 |
| | New York AL | 5 | 135 | 50 | 5 | 1 | 1 | .974 | 18 | 6 | 4 | 1 |
| 1962 | San Francisco NL | 7 | 183 | 67 | 8 | 9 | 1 | .969 | 21 | 7 | 7 | 1 |
| | New York AL | 7 | 183 | 67 | 5 | 5 | 0 | .980 | 18 | 6 | 4 | 0 |
| 1963 | Los Angeles NL | 4 | 108 | 31 | 3 | 1 | 0 | .979 | 13 | 4 | 1 | 0 |
| | New York AL | 4 | 102 | 49 | 1 | 7 | 0 | .993 | 20 | 7 | 7 | 0 |
| 1964 | St. Louis NL | 7 | 189 | 64 | 4 | 6 | 0 | .984 | 21 | 8 | 12 | 3 |
| | New York AL | 7 | 186 | 82 | 9 | 6 | 3 | .968 | 21 | 9 | 8 | 1 |
| 1965 | Los Angeles NL | 7 | 180 | 72 | 6 | 7 | 0 | .977 | 20 | 7 | 7 | 1 |
| | Minnesota AL | 7 | 180 | 58 | 5 | 3 | 0 | .979 | 21 | 9 | 7 | 0 |
| 1966 | Los Angeles NL | 4 | 102 | 44 | 6 | 4 | 0 | .961 | 23 | 8 | 8 | 1 |
| | Baltimore AL | 4 | 108 | 33 | 0 | 4 | 0 | 1.000 | 13 | 4 | 0 | 0 |
| 1967 | St. Louis NL | 7 | 183 | 66 | 4 | 3 | 0 | .984 | 23 | 10 | 8 | 0 |
| | Boston AL | 7 | 183 | 66 | 4 | 4 | 1 | .984 | 25 | 10 | 13 | 1 |
| 1968 | St. Louis NL | 7 | 186 | 48 | 2 | 7 | 0 | .992 | 25 | 10 | 8 | 1 |
| | Detroit AL | 7 | 186 | 72 | 11 | 4 | 0 | .959 | 24 | 9 | 8 | 1 |
| 1969 | New York NL | 5 | 135 | 42 | 2 | 0 | 0 | .989 | 21 | 6 | 4 | 1 |
| | Baltimore AL | 5 | 129 | 51 | 4 | 4 | 0 | .978 | 21 | 7 | 5 | 3 |
| 1970 | Cincinnati NL | 5 | 129 | 50 | 3 | 4 | 0 | .984 | 24 | 9 | 13 | 0 |
| | Baltimore AL | 5 | 135 | 43 | 5 | 3 | 0 | .973 | 21 | 9 | 3 | 0 |
| 1971 | Pittsburgh NL | 7 | 185 | 70 | 3 | 7 | 1 | .988 | 25 | 10 | 8 | 1 |
| | Baltimore AL | 7 | 183 | 69 | 9 | 2 | 0 | .966 | 21 | 10 | 6 | 1 |
| 1972 | Cincinnati NL | 7 | 187 | 89 | 5 | 5 | 0 | .982 | 22 | 8 | 16 | 2 |
| | Oakland AL | 7 | 186 | 65 | 9 | 4 | 0 | .965 | 23 | 8 | 13 | 8 |
| 1973 | New York NL | 7 | 195 | 72 | 10 | 3 | 1 | .964 | 22 | 7 | 15 | 3 |
| | Oakland AL | 7 | 198 | 79 | 9 | 8 | 1 | .969 | 24 | 8 | 20 | 4 |
| 1974 | Los Angeles NL | 5 | 126 | 50 | 6 | 5 | 0 | .967 | 19 | 6 | 9 | 2 |
| | Oakland AL | 5 | 132 | 51 | 5 | 6 | 0 | .973 | 20 | 5 | 6 | 4 |
| 1975 | Cincinnati NL | 7 | 195 | 76 | 2 | 8 | 0 | .993 | 22 | 9 | 8 | 0 |
| | Boston AL | 7 | 196 | 72 | 6 | 6 | 0 | .978 | 23 | 10 | 13 | 0 |
| 1976 | Cincinnati NL | 4 | 108 | 36 | 5 | 4 | 0 | .966 | 16 | 7 | 0 | 0 |
| | New York AL | 4 | 104 | 41 | 2 | 6 | 0 | .986 | 21 | 7 | 9 | 0 |
| 1977 | Los Angeles NL | 6 | 165 | 69 | 1 | 4 | 0 | .996 | 25 | 9 | 10 | 1 |
| | New York AL | 6 | 168 | 68 | 3 | 2 | 1 | .987 | 20 | 7 | 6 | 0 |
| 1978 | Los Angeles NL | 6 | 158 | 64 | 7 | 4 | 0 | .969 | 23 | 8 | 4 | 0 |
| | New York AL | 6 | 159 | 54 | 2 | 9 | 1 | .991 | 24 | 8 | 5 | 2 |
| 1979 | Pittsburgh NL | 7 | 186 | 79 | 9 | 11 | 0 | .967 | 24 | 9 | 11 | 1 |
| | Baltimore AL | 7 | 186 | 85 | 9 | 5 | 0 | .968 | 25 | 9 | 23 | 2 |
| 1980 | Philadelphia NL | 6 | 161 | 68 | 2 | 8 | 0 | .991 | 22 | 10 | 4 | 1 |
| | Kansas City AL | 6 | 156 | 72 | 7 | 8 | 0 | .970 | 21 | 7 | 3 | 3 |
| 1981 | Los Angeles NL | 6 | 156 | 65 | 9 | 6 | 0 | .961 | 24 | 10 | 14 | 2 |
| | New York AL | 6 | 153 | 55 | 4 | 2 | 1 | .981 | 24 | 9 | 10 | 5 |

| Year | Team, League | G | PO | A | E | DP | PB | Fielding Avg. | Players Used | Pitchers Used | PH | PR |
|---|---|---|---|---|---|---|---|---|---|---|---|---|
| 1982 | St. Louis NL | 7 | 183 | 74 | 7 | 9 | 0 | .973 | 22 | 8 | 8 | 3 |
| | Milwaukee AL | 7 | 180 | 81 | 11 | 3 | 0 | .960 | 21 | 9 | 2 | 1 |
| 1983 | Philadelphia NL | 5 | 132 | 42 | 3 | 3 | 0 | .983 | 23 | 8 | 12 | 3 |
| | Baltimore AL | 5 | 135 | 51 | 4 | 5 | 0 | .979 | 23 | 7 | 13 | 2 |
| 1984 | San Diego NL | 5 | 126 | 40 | 4 | 5 | 0 | .976 | 24 | 10 | 4 | 3 |
| | Detroit AL | 5 | 132 | 52 | 4 | 2 | 0 | .979 | 22 | 7 | 10 | 1 |
| 1985 | St. Louis NL | 7 | 184 | 60 | 2 | 9 | 1 | .992 | 24 | 9 | 8 | 2 |
| | Kansas City AL | 7 | 186 | 80 | 3 | 3 | 1 | .989 | 22 | 6 | 13 | 3 |
| 1986 | New York NL | 7 | 189 | 63 | 5 | 4 | 0 | .981 | 22 | 8 | 11 | 2 |
| | Boston AL | 7 | 188 | 79 | 4 | 7 | 1 | .985 | 21 | 8 | 6 | 3 |
| 1987 | St. Louis NL | 7 | 177 | 69 | 6 | 2 | 1 | .976 | 24 | 9 | 4 | 1 |
| | Minnesota AL | 7 | 180 | 74 | 3 | 4 | 0 | .988 | 24 | 9 | 15 | 2 |
| 1988 | Los Angeles NL | 5 | 133 | 36 | 3 | 3 | 1 | .983 | 22 | 7 | 11 | 0 |
| | Oakland AL | 5 | 131 | 43 | 2 | 2 | 1 | .989 | 24 | 10 | 4 | 3 |
| 1989 | San Francisco NL | 4 | 102 | 40 | 4 | 3 | 0 | .973 | 24 | 9 | 10 | 0 |
| | Oakland AL | 4 | 108 | 35 | 1 | 1 | 1 | .993 | 19 | 6 | 4 | 0 |
| 1990 | Cincinnati NL | 4 | 111 | 42 | 4 | 2 | 0 | .975 | 21 | 8 | 6 | 0 |
| | Oakland AL | 4 | 106 | 46 | 5 | 5 | 0 | .968 | 25 | 10 | 8 | 1 |
| 1991 | Atlanta NL | 7 | 196 | 86 | 5 | 9 | 0 | .983 | 25 | 10 | 16 | 1 |
| | Minnesota AL | 7 | 202 | 75 | 5 | 6 | 1 | .982 | 25 | 9 | 21 | 2 |
| 1992 | Atlanta NL | 6 | 163 | 68 | 2 | 7 | 0 | .991 | 22 | 8 | 7 | 3 |
| | Toronto AL | 6 | 165 | 47 | 4 | 5 | 0 | .981 | 23 | 10 | 8 | 0 |
| 1993 | Philadelphia NL | 6 | 157 | 54 | 2 | 5 | 1 | .991 | 23 | 10 | 7 | 1 |
| | Toronto AL | 6 | 159 | 45 | 7 | 5 | 0 | .967 | 23 | 10 | 3 | 3 |
| 1994 | no series | | | | | | | | | | | |
| 1995 | Atlanta NL | 6 | 162 | 69 | 6 | 2 | 0 | .975 | 23 | 10 | 9 | 0 |
| | Cleveland AL | 6 | 159 | 73 | 6 | 8 | 1 | .975 | 23 | 9 | 6 | 2 |
| 1996 | Atlanta NL | 6 | 162 | 73 | 4 | 6 | 0 | .983 | 24 | 10 | 10 | 3 |
| | New York AL | 6 | 165 | 63 | 5 | 7 | 0 | .979 | 25 | 10 | 8 | 1 |
| 1997 | Florida NL | 7 | 192 | 82 | 8 | 9 | 0 | .972 | 25 | 10 | 17 | 2 |
| | Cleveland AL | 7 | 191 | 64 | 5 | 8 | 0 | .981 | 23 | 11 | 5 | 0 |
| 1998 | San Diego NL | 4 | 102 | 41 | 3 | 5 | 0 | .979 | 24 | 10 | 9 | 2 |
| | New York AL | 4 | 108 | 36 | 2 | 4 | 1 | .986 | 21 | 9 | 3 | 2 |
| 1999 | Atlanta NL | 4 | 105 | 31 | 4 | 4 | 0 | .971 | 25 | 9 | 11 | 1 |
| | New York AL | 4 | 111 | 48 | 1 | 5 | 0 | .994 | 23 | 9 | 4 | 1 |
| 2000 | New York NL | 5 | 140 | 47 | 5 | 3 | 0 | .974 | 25 | 10 | 11 | 2 |
| | New York AL | 5 | 141 | 46 | 2 | 1 | 1 | .989 | 22 | 8 | 8 | 1 |
| 2001 | Arizona NL | 7 | 195 | 61 | 3 | 6 | 0 | .988 | 25 | 10 | 5 | 4 |
| | New York AL | 7 | 190 | 75 | 8 | 7 | 0 | .971 | 25 | 10 | 8 | 2 |
| 2002 | San Francisco NL | 7 | 180 | 70 | 5 | 7 | 1 | .980 | 24 | 11 | 11 | 0 |
| | Anaheim AL | 7 | 183 | 56 | 5 | 6 | 1 | .980 | 25 | 10 | 9 | 2 |
| 2003 | Florida NL | 6 | 168 | 57 | 2 | 8 | 0 | .991 | 20 | 9 | 3 | 0 |
| | New York AL | 6 | 165 | 66 | 5 | 6 | 0 | .979 | 23 | 9 | 12 | 3 |
| 2004 | St. Louis NL | 4 | 102 | 37 | 1 | 3 | 0 | .993 | 25 | 11 | 5 | 1 |
| | Boston AL | 4 | 108 | 32 | 8 | 5 | 1 | .946 | 21 | 8 | 5 | 3 |
| 2005 | Houston NL | 4 | 118 | 53 | 2 | 6 | 0 | .988 | 24 | 11 | 9 | 2 |
| | Chicago AL | 4 | 123 | 49 | 3 | 4 | 0 | .983 | 24 | 11 | 4 | 1 |

## MANAGERIAL RECORDS

### AMERICAN LEAGUE

| Manager, Team | Series W | Series L | Games W | Games L |
|---|---|---|---|---|
| Joe Altobelli, Baltimore | 1 | 0 | 4 | 1 |
| Sparky Anderson, Detroit | 1 | 0 | 4 | 1 |
| Del Baker, Detroit | 0 | 1 | 3 | 4 |
| Ed Barrow, Boston | 1 | 0 | 4 | 2 |
| Hank Bauer, Baltimore | 1 | 0 | 4 | 0 |
| Yogi Berra, New York | 0 | 1 | 3 | 4 |
| Lou Boudreau, Cleveland | 1 | 0 | 4 | 2 |
| Bill Carrigan, Boston | 2 | 0 | 8 | 2 |
| Mickey Cochrane, Detroit | 1 | 1 | 7 | 6 |
| Jimmy Collins, Boston | 1 | 0 | 5 | 3 |
| Joe Cronin, Washington, Boston | 0 | 2 | 4 | 8 |
| Alvin Dark, Oakland | 1 | 0 | 4 | 1 |
| Terry Francona, Boston | 1 | 0 | 4 | 0 |
| Jim Frey, Kansas City | 0 | 1 | 2 | 4 |
| Cito Gaston, Toronto | 2 | 0 | 8 | 4 |
| Kid Gleason, Chicago | 0 | 1 | 3 | 5 |
| Ozzie Guillen, Chicago | 1 | 0 | 4 | 0 |
| Mike Hargrove, Cleveland | 0 | 2 | 5 | 8 |
| Bucky Harris, Washington, New York | 2 | 1 | 11 | 10 |
| Ralph Houk, New York | 2 | 1 | 8 | 8 |
| Dick Howser, Kansas City | 1 | 0 | 4 | 3 |
| Miller Huggins, New York* | 3 | 3 | 18 | 15 |
| Hughey Jennings, Detroit* | 0 | 3 | 4 | 12 |
| Darrell Johnson, Boston | 0 | 1 | 3 | 4 |
| Fielder Jones, Chicago | 1 | 0 | 4 | 2 |
| Tom Kelly, Minnesota | 2 | 0 | 8 | 6 |
| Harvey Kuenn, Milwaukee | 0 | 1 | 3 | 4 |
| Tony La Russa, Oakland | 1 | 2 | 5 | 8 |
| Bob Lemon, New York | 1 | 1 | 6 | 6 |
| Al Lopez, Cleveland, Chicago | 0 | 2 | 2 | 8 |
| Connie Mack, Philadelphia | 5 | 3 | 24 | 19 |
| Billy Martin, New York | 1 | 1 | 4 | 6 |
| Joe McCarthy, New York | 7 | 1 | 29 | 9 |
| John McNamara, Boston | 0 | 1 | 3 | 4 |
| Sam Mele, Minnesota | 0 | 1 | 3 | 4 |
| Steve O'Neill, Detroit | 1 | 0 | 4 | 3 |
| Pants Rowland, Chicago | 1 | 0 | 4 | 2 |
| Mike Scioscia, Anaheim | 1 | 0 | 4 | 3 |
| Luke Sewell, St. Louis | 0 | 1 | 2 | 4 |
| Mayo Smith, Detroit | 1 | 0 | 4 | 3 |
| Tris Speaker, Cleveland | 1 | 0 | 5 | 2 |
| Jake Stahl, Boston* | 1 | 0 | 4 | 3 |
| Joe Torre, New York | 4 | 2 | 21 | 11 |
| Casey St.engel, New York | 7 | 3 | 37 | 26 |
| Earl Weaver, Baltimore | 1 | 3 | 11 | 13 |
| Dick Williams, Boston, Oakland | 2 | 1 | 11 | 10 |

**Total number of managers: 46**

*includes one tie per asterisk

### NATIONAL LEAGUE

| Manager, Team | Series W | Series L | Games W | Games L |
|---|---|---|---|---|
| Walter Alston, Brooklyn, Los Angeles | 4 | 3 | 20 | 20 |
| Sparky Anderson, Cincinnati | 2 | 2 | 12 | 11 |
| Dusty Baker, San Francisco | 0 | 1 | 3 | 4 |
| Yogi Berra, New York | 0 | 1 | 3 | 4 |

| Manager, Team | Series W | Series L | Games W | Games L |
|---|---|---|---|---|
| Bruce Bochy, San Diego | 0 | 1 | 0 | 4 |
| Bob Brenly, Arizona | 1 | 0 | 4 | 3 |
| Donie Bush, Pittsburgh | 0 | 1 | 0 | 4 |
| Frank Chance, Chicago* | 2 | 2 | 11 | 9 |
| Fred Clarke, Pittsburgh | 1 | 1 | 7 | 8 |
| Bobby Cox, Atlanta | 1 | 4 | 11 | 18 |
| Roger Craig, San Francisco | 0 | 1 | 0 | 4 |
| Alvin Dark, San Francisco | 0 | 1 | 3 | 4 |
| Charlie Dressen, Brooklyn | 0 | 2 | 5 | 8 |
| Leo Durocher, Brooklyn, New York | 1 | 2 | 7 | 8 |
| Eddie Dyer, St. Louis | 1 | 0 | 4 | 3 |
| Jim Fregosi, Philadelphia | 0 | 1 | 2 | 4 |
| Frank Frisch, St. Louis | 1 | 0 | 4 | 3 |
| Phil Garner, Houston | 0 | 1 | 0 | 4 |
| Dallas Green, Philadelphia | 1 | 0 | 4 | 2 |
| Chuck Grimm, Chicago | 0 | 3 | 5 | 12 |
| Fred Haney, Milwaukee | 1 | 1 | 7 | 7 |
| Gabby Hartnett, Chicago | 0 | 1 | 0 | 4 |
| Whitey Herzog, St. Louis | 1 | 2 | 10 | 11 |
| Gil Hodges, New York | 1 | 0 | 4 | 1 |
| Rogers Hornsby, St. Louis | 1 | 0 | 4 | 3 |
| Fred Hutchinson, Cincinnati | 0 | 1 | 1 | 4 |
| Dave Johnson, New York | 1 | 0 | 4 | 3 |
| Johnny Keane, St. Louis | 1 | 0 | 4 | 3 |
| Tony La Russa, St. Louis | 0 | 1 | 0 | 4 |
| Tom Lasorda, Los Angeles | 2 | 2 | 12 | 11 |
| Jim Leyland, Florida | 1 | 0 | 4 | 3 |
| Joe McCarthy, Chicago | 0 | 1 | 1 | 4 |
| John McGraw, New York** | 3 | 6 | 26 | 28 |
| Bill McKechnie, Pit, St. L, Cin | 2 | 2 | 8 | 14 |
| Jack McKeon, Florida | 1 | 0 | 4 | 2 |
| Fred Mitchell, Chicago | 0 | 1 | 2 | 4 |
| Pat Moran, Philadelphia, Cincinnati | 1 | 1 | 6 | 7 |
| Danny Murtaugh, Pittsburgh | 2 | 0 | 8 | 6 |
| Paul Owens, Philadelphia | 0 | 1 | 1 | 4 |
| Lou Piniella, Cincinnati | 1 | 0 | 4 | 0 |
| Wilbert Robinson, Brooklyn | 0 | 2 | 3 | 9 |
| Eddie Sawyer, Philadelphia | 0 | 1 | 0 | 4 |
| Red Schoendienst, St. Louis | 1 | 1 | 7 | 7 |
| Burt Shotton, Brooklyn | 0 | 2 | 4 | 8 |
| Billy Southworth, St. Louis, Boston | 2 | 2 | 11 | 11 |
| George Stallings, Boston | 1 | 0 | 4 | 0 |
| Gabby Street, St. Louis | 1 | 1 | 6 | 7 |
| Chuck Tanner, Pittsburgh | 1 | 0 | 4 | 3 |
| Bill Terry, New York | 1 | 2 | 7 | 9 |
| Bobby Valentine, New York | 0 | 1 | 1 | 4 |
| Dick Williams, San Diego | 0 | 1 | 1 | 4 |

**Total number of managers: 50**

## COMBINED RECORDS FOR BOTH LEAGUES

| Manager, Team | Series W | Series L | Games W | Games L |
|---|---|---|---|---|
| Sparky Anderson, Cin NL, Det AL | 3 | 2 | 16 | 12 |
| Yogi Berra, NY AL, NY NL | 0 | 2 | 6 | 8 |
| Alvin Dark, SF NL, Oak AL | 1 | 1 | 7 | 5 |
| Tony La Russa, Oak AL, St. L NL | 1 | 3 | 5 | 12 |
| Joe McCarthy, Chi NL, NY AL | 7 | 2 | 30 | 13 |
| Dick Williams, Bos AL, Oak AL, SD NL | 2 | 2 | 12 | 14 |

**Total number of managers: 6**

Mark McGwire

# ALL-STAR GAME

2006 MLB RECORD & FACT BOOK

Maris
Williams
Mantle

# RESULTS

| Year | Date | Site | Winner | Manager | Loser | Manager | Score |
|---|---|---|---|---|---|---|---|
| 1933 | July 6 | Comiskey Park, Chicago | AL | Connie Mack, Philadelphia | NL | John McGraw, New York | 4-2 |
| 1934 | July 10 | Polo Grounds, New York | AL | Joe Cronin, Washington | NL | Bill Terry, New York | 9-7 |
| 1935 | July 8 | Cleveland Stadium, Cleveland | AL | Mickey Cochrane, Detroit | NL | Frankie Frisch, St. Louis | 4-1 |
| 1936 | July 7 | Braves Field, Boston | NL | Charley Grimm, Chicago | AL | Joe McCarthy, New York | 4-3 |
| 1937 | July 7 | Griffith Stadium, Washington | AL | Joe McCarthy, New York | NL | Bill Terry, New York | 8-3 |
| 1938 | July 6 | Crosley Field, Cincinnati | NL | Bill Terry, New York | AL | Joe McCarthy, New York | 4-1 |
| 1939 | July 11 | Yankee Stadium, New York | AL | Joe McCarthy, New York | NL | Gabby Hartnett, Chicago | 3-1 |
| 1940 | July 9 | Sportsman's Park, St. Louis | NL | Bill McKechnie, Cincinnati | AL | Joe Cronin, Boston | 4-0 |
| 1941 | July 8 | Briggs Stadium, Detroit | AL | Del Baker, Detroit | NL | Bill McKechnie, Cincinnati | 7-5 |
| 1942 | July 6 | Polo Grounds, New York | AL | Joe McCarthy, New York | NL | Leo Durocher, Brooklyn | 3-1 |
| 1943 | July 13 | Shibe Park, Philadelphia | AL | Joe McCarthy, New York | NL | Billy Southworth, St. Louis | 5-3 |
| 1944 | July 11 | Forbes Field, Pittsburgh | NL | Billy Southworth, St. Louis | AL | Joe McCarthy, New York | 7-1 |
| 1945 | | GAME CANCELED BECAUSE OF TRAVEL RESTRICTIONS DURING WORLD WAR II | | | | | |
| 1946 | July 9 | Fenway Park, Boston | AL | Steve O'Neill, Detroit | NL | Charley Grimm, Chicago | 12-0 |
| 1947 | July 8 | Wrigley Field, Chicago | AL | Joe Cronin, Boston | NL | Eddie Dyer, St. Louis | 2-1 |
| 1948 | July 13 | Sportsman's Park, St. Louis | AL | Bucky Harris, New York | NL | Leo Durocher, Brooklyn | 5-2 |
| 1949 | July 12 | Ebbets Field, Brooklyn | AL | Lou Boudreau, Cleveland | NL | Billy Southworth, Boston | 11-7 |
| 1950 | July 11 | Comiskey Park, Chicago | NL | Burt Shotton, Brooklyn | AL | Casey Stengel, New York | 4-3, 14 inn |
| 1951 | July 10 | Briggs Stadium, Detroit | NL | Eddie Sawyer, Philadelphia | AL | Casey Stengel, New York | 8-3 |
| 1952 | July 8 | Shibe Park, Philadelphia | NL | Leo Durocher, New York | AL | Casey Stengel, New York | 3-2, 5 inn |
| 1953 | July 14 | Crosley Field, Cincinnati | NL | Charlie Dressen, Brooklyn | AL | Casey Stengel, New York | 5-1 |
| 1954 | July 13 | Cleveland Stadium, Cleveland | AL | Casey Stengel, New York | NL | Walter Alston, Brooklyn | 11-9 |
| 1955 | July 12 | County Stadium, Milwaukee | NL | Leo Durocher, New York | AL | Al Lopez, Cleveland | 6-5, 12 inn |
| 1956 | July 10 | Griffith Stadium, Washington | NL | Walter Alston, Brooklyn | AL | Casey Stengel, New York | 7-3 |
| 1957 | July 9 | Busch Stadium, St. Louis | AL | Casey Stengel, New York. | NL | Walter Alston, Brooklyn | 6-5 |
| 1958 | July 8 | Memorial Stadium, Baltimore | AL | Casey Stengel, New York | NL | Fred Haney, Milwaukee | 4-3 |
| 1959 | July 7 | Forbes Field, Pittsburgh | NL | Fred Haney, Milwaukee | AL | Casey Stengel, New York | 5-4 |
| | Aug 3 | Memorial Coliseum, Los Angeles | AL | Casey Stengel, New York | NL | Fred Haney, Milwaukee | 5-3 |
| 1960 | July 11 | Municipal Stadium, Kansas City | NL | Walter Alston, Los Angeles | AL | Al Lopez, Chicago | 5-3 |
| | July 13 | Yankee Stadium, New York | NL | Walter Alston, Los Angeles | AL | Al Lopez, Chicago | 6-0 |
| 1961 | July 11 | Candlestick Park, San Francisco | NL | Danny Murtaugh, Pittsburgh | AL | Paul Richards, Baltimore | 5-4, 10 inn |
| | July 31 | Fenway Park, Boston | — | Paul Richards, Baltimore | — | Danny Murtaugh, Pittsburgh | 1-1, tie |
| 1962 | July 10 | District of Columbia Stadium, Washington | NL | Fred Hutchinson, Cincinnati | AL | Ralph Houk, New York | 3-1 |
| | July 30 | Wrigley Field, Chicago | AL | Ralph Houk, New York | NL | Fred Hutchinson, Cincinnati | 9-4 |
| 1963 | July 9 | Cleveland Stadium, Cleveland | NL | Alvin Dark, San Francisco | AL | Ralph Houk, New York | 5-3 |
| 1964 | July 7 | Shea Stadium, New York | NL | Walter Alston, Los Angeles | AL | Al Lopez, Chicago | 7-4 |
| 1965 | July 13 | Metropolitan Stadium, Bloomington | NL | Gene Mauch, Philadelphia | AL | Al Lopez, Chicago | 6-5 |
| 1966 | July 12 | Busch Memorial Stadium, St. Louis | NL | Walter Alston, Los Angeles | AL | Sam Mele, Minnesota | 2-1, 10 inn |
| 1967 | July 11 | Anaheim Stadium, Anaheim | NL | Walter Alston, Los Angeles | AL | Hank Bauer, Baltimore | 2-1, 15 inn |
| 1968 | July 9 | Astrodome, Houston | NL | Red Schoendienst, St. Louis | AL | Dick Williams, Boston | 1-0 |
| 1969 | July 23 | Robert F. Kennedy Memorial Stadium, Washington | NL | Red Schoendienst, St. Louis | AL | Mayo Smith, Detroit | 9-3 |
| 1970 | July 14 | Riverfront Stadium, Cincinnati | NL | Gil Hodges, New York | AL | Earl Weaver, Baltimore | 5-4, 12 inn |
| 1971 | July 13 | Tiger Stadium, Detroit | AL | Earl Weaver, Baltimore | NL | Sparky Anderson, Cincinnati | 6-4 |
| 1972 | July 25 | Atlanta Stadium, Atlanta | NL | Danny Murtaugh, Pittsburgh | AL | Earl Weaver, Baltimore | 4-3, 10 inn |
| 1973 | July 24 | Royals Stadium, Kansas City | NL | Sparky Anderson, Cincinnati | AL | Dick Williams, Oakland | 7-1 |
| 1974 | July 23 | Three Rivers Stadium, Pittsburgh | NL | Yogi Berra, New York | AL | Dick Williams, Cal | 7-2 |
| 1975 | July 15 | County Stadium, Milwaukee | NL | Walter Alston, Los Angeles | AL | Alvin Dark, Oakland | 6-3 |
| 1976 | July 13 | Veterans Stadium, Philadelphia | NL | Sparky Anderson, Cincinnati | AL | Darrell Johnson, Boston | 7-1 |
| 1977 | July 19 | Yankee Stadium, New York | NL | Sparky Anderson, Cincinnati | AL | Billy Martin, New York | 7-5 |
| 1978 | July 11 | San Diego Stadium, San Diego | NL | Tom Lasorda, Los Angeles | AL | Billy Martin, New York | 7-3 |
| 1979 | July 17 | Kingdome, Seattle | NL | Tom Lasorda, Los Angeles | AL | Bob Lemon, New York | 7-6 |
| 1980 | July 8 | Dodger Stadium, Los Angeles | NL | Chuck Tanner, Pittsburgh | AL | Earl Weaver, Baltimore | 4-2 |
| 1981 | Aug 9 | Cleveland Stadium, Cleveland | NL | Dallas Green, Philadelphia | AL | Jim Frey, Kansas City | 5-4 |
| 1982 | July 13 | Olympic Stadium, Montreal | NL | Tom Lasorda, Los Angeles | AL | Billy Martin, New York | 4-1 |
| 1983 | July 6 | Comiskey Park, Chicago | AL | Harvey Kuenn, Milwaukee | NL | Whitey Herzog, St. Louis | 13-3 |
| 1984 | July 10 | Candlestick Park, San Francisco | NL | Paul Owens, Philadelphia | AL | Joe Altobelli, Baltimore | 3-1 |
| 1985 | July 16 | Metrodome, Minneapolis | NL | Dick Williams, San Diego | AL | Sparky Anderson, Detroit | 6-1 |
| 1986 | July 15 | Astrodome, Houston | AL | Dick Howser, Kansas City | NL | Whitey Herzog, St. Louis | 3-2 |
| 1987 | July 14 | Oakland Coliseum, Oakland | NL | Dave Johnson, New York | AL | John McNamara, Boston | 2-0, 13 inn |
| 1988 | July 12 | Riverfront Stadium, Cincinnati | AL | Tom Kelly, Minnesota | NL | Whitey Herzog, St. Louis | 2-1 |
| 1989 | July 11 | Anaheim Stadium, Anaheim | AL | Tony La Russa, Oakland | NL | Tom Lasorda, Los Angeles | 5-3 |
| 1990 | July 10 | Wrigley Field, Chicago | AL | Tony La Russa, Oakland | NL | Roger Craig, San Francisco | 2-0 |
| 1991 | July 9 | SkyDome, Toronto | AL | Tony La Russa, Oakland | NL | Lou Piniella, Cincinnati | 4-2 |
| 1992 | July 14 | Jack Murphy Stadium, San Diego | AL | Tom Kelly, Minnesota | NL | Bobby Cox, Atlanta | 13-6 |
| 1993 | July 13 | Oriole Park at Camden Yards, Baltimore | AL | Cito Gaston, Toronto | NL | Bobby Cox, Atlanta | 9-3 |
| 1994 | July 12 | Three Rivers Stadium, Pittsburgh | NL | Jim Fregosi, Philadelphia | AL | Cito Gaston, Toronto | 8-7, 10 inn |
| 1995 | July 11 | The Ballpark in Arlington, Texas | NL | Felipe Alou, Montreal | AL | Buck Showalter, New York | 3-2 |
| 1996 | July 9 | Veterans Stadium, Philadelphia | NL | Bobby Cox, Atlanta | AL | Mike Hargrove, Cleveland | 6-0 |
| 1997 | July 8 | Jacobs Field, Cleveland | AL | Joe Torre, New York | NL | Bobby Cox, Atlanta | 3-1 |
| 1998 | July 7 | Coors Field, Colorado | AL | Mike Hargrove, Cleveland | NL | Jim Leyland, Florida | 13-8 |
| 1999 | July 13 | Fenway Park, Boston | AL | Joe Torre, New York | NL | Bruce Bochy, San Diego | 4-1 |
| 2000 | July 11 | Turner Field, Atlanta | AL | Joe Torre, New York | NL | Bobby Cox, Atlanta | 6-3 |
| 2001 | July 10 | Safeco Field, Seattle | AL | Joe Torre, New York | NL | Bobby Valentine, New York | 4-1 |
| 2002 | July 9 | Miller Park, Milwaukee | — | Joe Torre, New York | — | Bob Brenly, Arizona | 7-7, tie, 11 inn |
| 2003 | July 15 | U.S. Cellular Field, Chicago | AL | Mike Scioscia, Anaheim | NL | Dusty Baker, Chicago | 7-6 |
| 2004 | July 13 | Minute Maid Park, Houston | AL | Joe Torre, New York | NL | Jack McKeon, Florida | 9-4 |
| 2005 | July 12 | Comerica Park, Detroit | AL | Terry Francona, Boston | NL | Tony La Russa, St. Louis | 7-5 |

**Overall record: NL wins, 40; AL wins, 34; 2 ties**

# SERVICE

## INDIVIDUAL

### CLUBS

**Most clubs represented, career**

5—Gary Sheffield, San Diego NL, 1992; Florida NL, 1993, 1996; Los Angeles NL, 1998-2000; Atlanta NL, 2003; New York AL, 2004, 2005 (9 G)
Moises Alou, Montreal NL, 1994; Florida NL, 1997; Houston NL, 1998, 2001; Chicago NL, 2004; San Francisco NL, 2005 (6 G)

### PLAYING ON WINNING AND LOSING CLUBS

**Most times playing on winning club**

17—Willie Mays, NL, 1955, 1956, 1959 (1st), 1960 (both), 1961 (1st), 1962 (1st), 1963-1970, 1972, 1973 (1 tie—1961, 2nd)
Hank Aaron, NL, 1955, 1956, 1959 (1st), 1960, 1960, 1961 (1st), 1963-1970, 1972-1974 (1 tie—1961, 2nd)

**Most times playing on losing club**

15—Brooks Robinson, AL, 1960, 1960, 1961 (1st), 1962 (1st), 1963-1970, 1972-1974 (1 tie—1961, 2nd)

### YOUNGEST AND OLDEST PLAYERS

**Youngest player**

19 years, 7 months, 24 days—Dwight Gooden, NL, 1984

**Oldest player**

47 years, 7 days—Satchel Paige, AL, 1953

### POSITIONS

**Most fielding positions played, career**

5—Pete Rose, NL (2B, LF, RF, 3B, 1B); 16 G

**Most fielding positions played, game**

2—many players

## CLUB

### PLAYERS USED

**Most players, game**

30—AL, July 12, 2005
[30—AL, July 9, 2002, 11 inn
NL, July 9, 2002, 11 inn]

**Most players by both clubs, game**

58—NL 29, AL 29, July 10, 2001
AL 30, NL 28, July 12, 2005
[60—AL 30, NL 30, July 9, 2002, 11 inn]

**Fewest players, game**

11—AL, July 6, 1942

**Fewest players by both clubs, game**

27—AL 15, NL 12, July 1, 1938

### PINCH-HITTERS

**Most pinch-hitters, game**

8—NL, July 9, 1957

**Most pinch-hitters by both clubs, game**

11—NL 7, AL 4, July 24, 1973
NL 7, AL 4, Aug 9, 1981
[11—NL 6, AL 5, July 11, 1967, 15 inn]

**Fewest pinch-hitters, game**

0—AL, July 8, 1935
NL, July 9, 1940
AL, July 8, 1980

**Fewest pinch-hitters by both clubs, game**

1—AL 1, NL 0, July 9, 1940

# INDIVIDUAL BATTING

### GAMES

**Most games played**

24—Stan Musial, NL, 1943, 1944, 1946-1958, 1959 (both), 1960 (both), 1961 (both), 1962 (both), 1963 (consec)
Willie Mays, NL, 1954-1958, 1959 (both), 1960 (both), 1961 (both), 1962 (both), 1963-1973 (consec)
Hank Aaron, NL, 1955-1958, 1959 (both), 1960 (both), 1961 (both), 1962 (2nd), 1963-1974 (23 G); AL, 1975 (1 G)

**Most games by pinch-hitter**

10—Stan Musial, 1947, 1955, 1959 (1st), 1960 (both), 1961 (both), 1962 (both) 1963 (10 PH AB)

### BATTING AVERAGE AND AT-BATS

**Highest batting average, career (5 or more games)**

.700—Derek Jeter, AL, 1998-2002, 2004 (6 G, 10 AB, 7 H)

**Most at-bats, career**

75—Willie Mays, NL, 1954-1958, 1959 (both), 1960 (both), 1961 (both), 1962 (both), 1963-1973 (24 G)

**Most at-bats, game**

5—many players; last—Cal Ripken, AL, July 12, 1994; Ivan Rodriguez, AL, July 12, 1994; Tony Gwynn, NL, July 12, 1994
[7—Willie Jones, NL, July 11, 1950, 14 inn]

**Most at-bats, inning**

2—Jim Rice, AL, July 6, 1983, 3rd

**Most times faced pitcher, inning**

2—Babe Ruth, AL, July 10, 1934, 5th
Lou Gehrig, AL, July 10, 1934, 5th
Jim Rice, AL, July 6, 1983, 3rd

### RUNS

**Most runs, career**

20—Willie Mays, NL, 1954-1958, 1959 (both), 1960 (both), 1961 (both), 1962 (both), 1963-1973 (24 G)

**Most runs, game**

4—Ted Williams, AL, July 9, 1946

**Most runs, inning**

1—many players

### HITS

**Most hits, career**

23—Willie Mays, NL, 1954-1958, 1959 (both), 1960 (both), 1961 (both), 1962 (both), 1963-1973 (24 G)

**Most hits by pinch-hitter, career**

3—Stan Musial, NL, 1943, 1944, 1946-1958, 1959 (both), 1960 (both), 1961 (both), 1962 (both), 1963 (24 G)

**Most consecutive games batted safely**

7—Mickey Mantle, AL, 1954-1958, 1959 (2nd), 1960, (2nd); PR in 1959 (1st); 2 BB in 1960 (1st)
Joe Morgan, NL, 1970, 1972-1977 (not on team in 1971)
Dave Winfield, AL, 1982-1988

**Most at-bats without a hit, career**

10—Terry Moore, NL, 1939-1942 (4 G)

**Most hits, game**

4—Joe Medwick, NL, July 7, 1937 (2 singles, 2 doubles; consec)
Ted Williams, AL, July 9, 1946 (2 singles, 2 HR, also 1 BB; consec)
[4—Carl Yastrzemski, AL, July 14, 1970 (3 singles, 1 double), 12 inn]

**Most times reached first base safely, game**

5—Charlie Gehringer, AL, July 10, 1934 (3 BB, 2 singles)

Phil Cavarretta, NL, July 11, 1944 (3 BB, 1 single, 1 triple)
Ted Williams, AL, July 9, 1946 (2 singles, 2 HR, 1 BB)

**Most hits, inning**
1—many players

## SINGLES

**Most singles, career**
15—Willie Mays, NL, 1954-1958, 1959 (both), 1960 (both), 1961 (both), 1962 (both), 1963-1973 (24 G)

**Most singles, game**
3—Charlie Gehringer, AL, July 7, 1937
Billy Herman, NL, July 9, 1940
Stan Hack, NL, July 13, 1943
Bobby Avila, AL, July 13, 1954
Ken Boyer, NL, July 10, 1956
Harmon Killebrew, AL, July 7, 1964
Rickey Henderson, AL, July 13, 1982
Ivan Rodriguez, AL, July 7, 1998
Derek Jeter, AL, July 13, 2004
[3—Carl Yastrzemski, AL, July 14, 1970, 12 inn]

**Most singles, inning**
1—many players

## DOUBLES

**Most doubles, career**
7—Dave Winfield, NL, 1977-1980; AL, 1981-1988 (12 G)

**Most doubles, game**
2—Joe Medwick, NL, July 7, 1937
Al Simmons, AL, July 10, 1934
Ted Kluszewski, NL, July 10, 1956
Ernie Banks, NL, July 7, 1959
Barry Bonds, NL, July 13, 1993
Paul Konerko, AL, July 9, 2002
Damian Miller, AL, July 9, 2002
Albert Pujols, NL, July 13, 2004

**Most doubles, inning**
1—many players

**Most doubles driving in three runs, inning**
none

## TRIPLES

**Most triples, career**
3—Willie Mays, NL, 1954-1958, 1959 (both), 1960 (both), 1961 (both), 1962 (both), 1963-1973 (24 G)
Brooks Robinson, AL, 1960 (both), 1961 (both), 1962 (both), 1963-1974 (18 G)

**Most triples, game**
2—Rod Carew, AL, July 11, 1978

**Most triples, inning**
1—many players

**Most triples driving in three runs, inning**
none

## HOME RUNS

**Most home runs, career**
6—Stan Musial, NL, 1943, 1944, 1946-1958, 1959 (both), 1960 (both), 1961 (both), 1962 (both), 1963 (24 G)

**For a complete list of All-Star Game home runs, see page 422.**

**Most home runs, game**
2—Arky Vaughan, NL, July 8, 1941 (consec)
Ted Williams, AL, July 9, 1946
Al Rosen, AL, July 13, 1954 (consec)
Willie McCovey, NL, July 23, 1969 (consec)
Gary Carter, NL, August 9, 1981 (consec)

**Home runs by pinch-hitter, game (17)**
Mickey Owen, NL, July 6, 1942, 8th
Gus Bell, NL, July 13, 1954, 8th
Larry Doby, AL, July 14, 1954, 8th
Willie Mays, NL, July 10, 1956, 4th
Stan Musial, NL, July 13, 1960, 7th
Harmon Killebrew, AL, July 11, 1961, 6th
George Altman, NL, July 11, 1961, 8th
Pete Runnels, AL, July 30, 1962, 3rd
Reggie Jackson, AL, July 13, 1971, 3rd
Cookie Rojas, AL, July 25, 1972, 8th
Willie Davis, NL, July 24, 1973, 6th
Carl Yastrzemski, AL, July 15, 1975, 6th
Lee Mazzilli, NL, July 17, 1979, 8th
Frank White, AL, July 15, 1986, 7th
Fred McGriff, NL, July 12, 1994, 9th
Jeff Conine, NL, July 11, 1995, 8th
Hank Blalock, AL, July 15, 2003, 8th

**Home runs as leadoff batter, start of game (5)**
Frankie Frisch, NL, July 10, 1934
Lou Boudreau, AL, July 6, 1942
Willie Mays, NL, July 13, 1965
Joe Morgan, NL, July 19, 1977
Bo Jackson, AL, July 11, 1989

**Hitting home run in first at-bat (12)**
Max West, NL, July 9, 1940, 1st
Hoot Evers, AL, July 13, 1948, 2nd
Jim Gilliam, NL, Aug 3, 1959, 7th
George Altman, NL, July 11, 1961, 8th
Johnny Bench, NL, July 23, 1969, 2nd
Dick Dietz, NL, July 14, 1970, 9th
Lee Mazzilli, NL, July 17, 1979, 8th
Terry Steinbach, AL, July 12, 1988, 3rd
Bo Jackson, AL, July 11, 1989, 1st
Jeff Conine, NL, July 11, 1995, 8th
Javy Lopez, NL, July 8, 1997, 7th
Hank Blalock, AL, July 15, 2003, 8th

**Most grand slams, game**
1—Fred Lynn, AL, July 6, 1983, 3rd

**Most home runs, inning**
1—many players

## TOTAL BASES

**Most total bases, career**
40—Stan Musial, NL, 1943, 1944, 1946-1958, 1959 (both), 1960 (both), 1961 (both), 1962 (both), 1963 (24 G)
Willie Mays, NL, 1954-1958, 1959 (both), 1960 (both), 1961 (both), 1962 (both), 1963-1973 (24 G)

**Most total bases, game**
10—Ted Williams, AL, July 9, 1946

**Most total bases, inning**
4—many players

## EXTRA-BASE HITS

**Most extra-base hits, career**
8—Stan Musial, NL, 1943, 1944, 1946-1958, 1959 (both), 1960 (both), 1961 (both), 1962 (both), 1963 (24 G; 2 doubles, 6 HR)
Willie Mays, NL, 1954-1958, 1959 (both), 1960 (both), 1961 (both), 1962 (both), 1963-1973 (24 G; 2 doubles, 3 triples, 3 HR)

**Most extra-base hits, game**
2—many players

**Most extra-base hits, inning**
1—many players

## RUNS BATTED IN

**Most runs batted in, career**
12—Ted Williams, AL, 1940-1942, 1946-1951, 1954-1958, 1959 (both), 1960 (both) (18 G)

**Most runs batted in, game**
5—Ted Williams AL, July 9, 1946
Al Rosen, AL, July 13, 1954

**Most runs batted in, inning**
4—Fred Lynn, AL, July 6, 1983, 3rd

## BASES ON BALLS

**Most bases on balls, career**
11—Ted Williams, AL, 1940-1942, 1946-1951, 1954-1958, 1959 (both), 1960 (both) (18 G)

**Most bases on balls, game**
3—Charlie Gehringer, AL, July 10, 1934
Phil Cavarretta, NL, July 11, 1944 (also 1 single, 1 triple)

**Most bases on balls, inning**
1—many players

## STRIKEOUTS

**Most strikeouts, career**
17—Mickey Mantle, AL, 1953-1958, 1959 (both), 1960 (both), 1961 (both), 1962 (1st), 1964, 1967, 1968 (16 G)

**Most strikeouts, game**
3—Lou Gehrig, AL, July 10, 1934
Bob L. Johnson, AL, July 8, 1935
Stan Hack, NL, July 11, 1939
Joe Gordon, AL, July 6, 1942

Ken Keltner, AL, July 13, 1943
Jim Hegan, AL, July 11, 1950
Mickey Mantle, AL, July 10, 1956
Johnny Roseboro, NL, July 31, 1961
Willie McCovey, NL, July 9, 1968
Johnny Bench, NL, July 14, 1970
Albert Belle, AL, July 9, 1996
Craig Biggio, NL, July 7, 1998
[4—Roberto Clemente, NL (consec), July 11, 1967]

**Most strikeouts, inning**
1—many players

## SACRIFICE HITS AND FLIES

**Most sacrifice hits, career**
1—many players

**Most sacrifice hits, game or inning**
1—many players

**Most sacrifice flies, career**
3—George Brett, AL, 1976-1979, 1981-1985, 1988 (10 G)

**Most sacrifice flies, game or inning**
1—many players

## HIT BY PITCH, GROUNDING INTO DOUBLE PLAYS

**Most hit by pitch, career**
1—many players

**Most grounding into double plays, career**
3—Joe DiMaggio, AL, 1936-1942, 1947-1950 (11 G)
Pete Rose NL, 1965, 1967, 1969-1971, 1973-1982, 1985 (16 G)

**Most grounding into double plays, game**
2—Bobby Richardson, AL, July 9, 1963

## REACHING ON ERRORS OR INTERFERENCE

**Most times reaching base on catcher's interference, game**
1—Paul Molitor, AL, July 9, 1991

# CLUB BATTING

## BATTING AVERAGE

**Highest batting average, game**
.442—AL, July 7, 1998 (43 AB, 19 H)

**Lowest batting average, game**
.069—NL, July 10, 1990 (29 AB, 2 H)

## AT-BATS AND PLATE APPEARANCES

**Most at-bats, game**
44—AL, July 14, 1992

**Most at-bats by both clubs, game**
83—AL 44, NL 39, July 14, 1992

**Fewest at-bats, game**
27—NL, July 9, 1968 (batted 8 inn)
29—many clubs; last—NL, July 10, 2001

**Fewest at-bats by both clubs, game**
57—AL 30, NL 27, July 9, 1968

**Most consecutive batters facing pitcher with none reaching base, game**
20—AL, July 9, 1968 (Jim Fregosi doubled to start game, then 20 consecutive batters were retired before Tony Oliva doubled in 7th.)

**Most batters facing pitcher, inning**
11—AL, July 10, 1934, 5th

**Most batters facing pitcher by both clubs, inning**
19—AL 11, NL 8, July 10, 1934, 5th

## RUNS

**Most runs, game**
13—AL, July 6, 1983
AL, July 14, 1992
AL, July 7, 1998

**Most runs by both clubs, game**
21—AL 13, NL 8, July 7, 1998

**Most runs, inning**
7—AL, July 6, 1983, 3rd

**Most runs by both clubs, inning**
9—AL 6, NL 3, July 10, 1934, 5th

**Most innings scored, game**
6—AL, July 7, 1998

**Most innings scored by both clubs, game**
10—AL 6, NL 4, July 7, 1998

**Most consecutive scoreless innings by one league, total games**
19—AL, 1967 (last 9 inn), 1968 (all 9 inn), 1969 (1st inn)

## EARNED RUNS

**Most earned runs, game**
13—AL, July 14, 1992

**Most earned runs by both clubs, game**
20—AL 11, NL 9, July 13, 1954

**Fewest earned runs, game**
0—many games; last—AL, July 9, 1996

**Fewest earned runs by both clubs, game**
0— AL 0, NL 0, July 9, 1968

## HITS

**Most hits, game**
19—AL, July 14, 1992

**Most hits by both clubs, game**
31—AL 17, NL 14, July 13, 1954
AL 19, NL 12, July 14, 1992
AL 19, NL 12, July 7, 1998

**Fewest hits, game**
2—NL, July 10, 1990

**Fewest hits by both clubs, game**
8—NL 5, AL 3, July 9, 1968

## SINGLES

**Most singles, game**
16—AL, July 7, 1998

**Most singles by both clubs, game**
26—AL 16, NL 10, July 7, 1998

**Fewest singles, game**
0—AL, July 9, 1968
NL, July 11, 1995

**Fewest singles by both clubs, game**
4—NL 4, AL 0, July 9, 1968

## DOUBLES

**Most doubles, game**
5—AL, July 10, 1934
AL, July 12, 1949

**Most doubles by both clubs, game**
7—AL 5, NL 2, July 12, 1949
AL 4, NL 3, July 13, 1993

**Fewest doubles, game**
0—many games

**Fewest doubles by both clubs, game**
0—many games; last—July 13, 1976

## TRIPLES

**Most triples, game**
2—AL, July 10, 1934
AL, July 10, 1951
NL, July 13, 1976
AL, July 11, 1978
AL, July 6, 1983

**Most triples by both clubs, game**
3—AL 2, NL 1, July 11, 1978

**Fewest triples, game**
0—many games

**Fewest triples by both clubs, game**
0—many games

## HOME RUNS

**Most home runs, game**
4—NL, July 10, 1951
AL, July 13, 1954
NL, July 10, 1960
NL, August 9, 1981

**Most home runs by both clubs, game**
6—NL 4, AL 2, July 10, 1951
AL 4, NL 2, July 13, 1954
AL 3, NL 3, July 13, 1971

**Most home runs accounting for all runs by both clubs, game**
3—NL 2, AL 1, July 11, 1967, 15 inn

**Fewest home runs, game**
0—many games

**Fewest home runs by both clubs, game**
0—many games

**Most consecutive games, one or more home runs**
9—NL, 1969-1977

**Most consecutive home runs from start of game**
2—AL, July 11, 1989 (Jackson, Boggs)

**Most home runs, inning (13 times; *consecutive)**
2—AL, July 6, 1942, 1st (Boudreau, York)
NL, July 10, 1951, 4th (Musial, Elliott)
AL, July 13, 1954, 3rd* (Rosen, Boone)
AL, July 10, 1956, 6th* (Williams, Mantle)
NL, July 7, 1964, 4th (Williams, Boyer)
NL, July 13, 1965, 1st (Mays, Torre)
AL, July 13, 1965, 5th (McAuliffe, Killebrew)
AL, July 13, 1971, 3rd (Jackson, F. Robinson)
NL, July 15, 1975, 2nd* (Garvey, Wynn)
NL, July 19, 1977, 1st (Morgan, Luzinski)
AL, July 6, 1983, 3rd (Rice, Lynn)
AL, July 11, 1989, 1st* (Jackson, Boggs)
AL, July 10, 2001, 6th* (Jeter, Ordonez)

**Most home runs by both clubs, inning**
3—NL 2 (Musial, Elliott), AL 1 (Wertz), July 10, 1951, 4th
AL 2 (Jackson, F. Robinson), NL 1 (Aaron), July 13, 1971, 3rd

## TOTAL BASES

**Most total bases, game**
29—AL, July 13, 1954

**Most total bases by both clubs, game**
52—AL 29, NL 23, July 13, 1954

**Fewest total bases, game**
2—NL, July 10, 1990

**Fewest total bases by both clubs, game**
12—AL 6, NL 6, 1968

## EXTRA-BASE HITS

**Most extra-base hits, game**
7—AL, July 10, 1934 (5 doubles, 2 triples)
AL, July 6, 1983 (3 doubles, 2 triples, 2 HR)

**Most extra-base hits by both clubs, game**
10—NL 5 (1 double, 4 HR); AL 5 (1 double, 2 triples, 2 HR), July 10, 1951
AL 6 (4 doubles, 2 HR); NL 4 (3 doubles, 1 HR), July 13, 1993

**Fewest extra base hits, game**
0—many games; last—AL, July 13, 1999

**Fewest extra base hits by both clubs, game**
0—July 8, 1958

## RUNS BATTED IN

**Most runs batted in, game**
13—AL, July 6, 1983
AL, July 14, 1992

**Most runs batted in by both clubs, game**
20—AL 11, NL 9, July 13, 1954

**Fewest runs batted in, game**
0—many games; last—AL, July 9, 1996

**Fewest runs batted in, game, both clubs**
0—AL 0, NL 0, July 9, 1968

## BASES ON BALLS

**Most bases on balls, game**
9—AL, July 10, 1934

**Most bases on balls by both clubs, game**
13—NL 8, AL 5, July 12, 1949

**Fewest bases on balls, game**
0—many games; last—AL, July 10, 2001

**Fewest bases on balls by both clubs, ame**
0—AL 0, NL 0, July 9, 1996
[2—AL 2, NL 0, July 11, 1967, 15 inn]

## STRIKEOUTS

**Most strikeouts, game**
12—AL, July 10, 1934
NL, July 10, 1956
AL, Aug 3, 1959
AL, July 15, 1986
NL, July 13, 1999
[17—AL, July 11, 1967, 15 inn]

**Most strikeouts by both clubs, game**
22—NL 12, AL 10, July 13, 1999
[30—AL 17, NL 13, July 11, 1967, 15 inn]

**Fewest strikeouts, game**
0—NL, July 7, 1937

**Fewest strikeouts by both clubs, game**
6—AL 4, NL 2, July 8, 1958

## SACRIFICE HITS

**Most sacrifice hits, game**
3—NL, July 11, 1944
[3—NL 3, AL 0, July 11, 1944]

**Fewest sacrifice hits, game**
0—many games

**Fewest sacrifice hits by both clubs, game**
0—many games

## HIT BY PITCH

**Most hit by pitch, game**
2—AL, July 10, 1962

**Most hit by pitch by both clubs, game**
2—AL 2, NL 0, July 10, 1962
AL 1, NL 1, July 15, 1975
AL 1, NL 1, July 19, 1977

# BASERUNNING

## INDIVIDUAL

**Most stolen bases, career**
6—Willie Mays, NL, 1954-1958, 1959 (both), 1960 (both), 1961 (both), 1962 (both), 1963-1973 (24 G)

**Most stolen bases, game**
2—Willie Mays, NL, July 9, 1963
Kelly Gruber, AL, July 10, 1990
Roberto Alomar, AL, July 14, 1992
Kenny Lofton, AL, July 9, 1996

**Stealing home, game**
Pie Traynor, NL, July 10, 1934, 5th (front end of a double steal with Mel Ott)

**Most times caught stealing, game**
1—many players

[2—Tony Oliva, AL, July 11, 1967, 15 inn]

### CLUB

**Most stolen bases, game**
5—AL, July 7, 1998

**Most stolen bases by both clubs, game**
5—AL 3, NL 2, July 16, 1985
AL 4, NL 1, July 10, 1990
AL 5, NL 0, July 7, 1998
AL 3, NL 2, July 9, 2002

**Fewest stolen bases, game**
0—many games

**Fewest stolen bases by both clubs, game**
0—many games

**Most left on base, game**
12—AL, July 10, 1934
NL, July 12, 1949
AL, July 13, 1960

**Most left on base by both clubs, game**
20—NL 12, AL 8, July 12, 1949

**Fewest left on bases, game**
0—NL, July 11, 1995

**Fewest left on base by both clubs, game**
4—NL 2, AL 2, July 13, 1971

# PITCHING

### GAMES

**Most games pitched**
10—Roger Clemens, AL, 1986, 1988, 1991, 1992, 1997, 1998, 2001, 2003; NL, 2004, 2005

**Most consecutive games pitched**
6—Ewell Blackwell, NL, 1946-1951
Early Wynn, AL, 1955-1958, 1959 (both)

### GAMES STARTED

**Most games started**
5—Lefty Gomez, AL, 1933-1935, 1937, 1938
Robin Roberts, NL, 1950, 1951, 1953-1955
Don Drysdale, NL 1959 (both), 1962 (1st), 1964, 1968

### GAMES RELIEVED

**Most games as relief pitcher**
7—Tom Seaver, NL, 1967, 1968, 1973, 1975-1977, 1981
Roger Clemens, AL, 1988, 1991, 1992, 1997, 1998, 2003; NL, 2005

### INNINGS

**Most innings pitched, career**
19.1—Don Drysdale, NL, 1959 (both), 1962 (1st), 1963-1965, 1967, 1968 (8 G)

**Most innings, game**
6—Lefty Gomez, AL, July 8, 1935

### GAMES WON AND LOST

**Most games won**
3—Lefty Gomez, AL, 1933, 1935, 1937

**Most games lost**
2—Mort Cooper, NL, 1942, 1943
Claude Passeau, NL, 1941, 1946
Whitey Ford, AL, 1959 (1st), 1960 (2nd)
Luis Tiant, AL, 1968, 1974
Catfish Hunter, AL, 1967, 1975
Dwight Gooden, NL, 1986, 1988
John Smoltz, NL, 1989, 2005

### SAVES (SINCE 1969)

**Most saves**
3—Dennis Eckersley, AL, 1988, 1990, 1991

### RUNS, EARNED RUNS AND ERA

**Most runs allowed, career**
13—Whitey Ford, AL, 1954-1956, 1959 (1st), 1960 (2nd), 1961 (1st)

**Most earned runs allowed, career**
11—Whitey Ford, AL, 1954-1956, 1959 (1st), 1960 (2nd), 1961 (1st)

**Most runs allowed, game**
7—Atlee Hammaker, NL, July 6, 1983

**Most earned runs allowed, game**
7—Atlee Hammaker, NL, July 6, 1983

**Most runs allowed, inning**
7—Atlee Hammaker, NL, July 6, 1983, 3rd

**Most earned runs allowed, inning**
7—Atlee Hammaker, NL, July 6, 1983, 3rdd

**Lowest earned run average (at least 9.0 IP)**
0.00—Mel Harder, AL, 1934-1937 (13.0 IP)

### HITS

**Most hits allowed, total games**
19—Whitey Ford, AL, 1954-1956, 1959 (1st), 1960 (2nd), 1961 (1st)

**Most hits allowed, game**
9—Tom Glavine, NL, July 14, 1992

**Most hits allowed, inning**
7—Tom Glavine, NL, July 14, 1992, 1st (consec)

### HOME RUNS

**Most home runs allowed, career**
4—Vida Blue, AL, 1971, 1975
Catfish Hunter, AL, 1967, 1970, 1973-1976

**Most home runs allowed, game**
3—Jim Palmer, AL, July 19, 1977

**Most home runs allowed, inning (12 times; *consecutive)**
2—Mort Cooper, NL, July 6, 1942, 1st
Eddie Lopat, AL, July 10, 1951, 4th
Robin Roberts, NL, July 13, 1954, 3rd*
Warren Spahn, NL, July 10, 1956, 6th*
John Wyatt, AL, July 7, 1964, 4th
Milt Pappas, AL, July 13, 1965, 1st
Jim Maloney, NL, July 13, 1965, 5th
Dock Ellis, NL, July 13, 1971, 3rd
Vida Blue, AL, July 15, 1975, 2nd*
Jim Palmer, AL, July 19, 1977, 1st
Atlee Hammaker, AL, July 6, 1983, 3rd
Rick Reuschel, NL, July 11, 1989, 1st*
Jon Lieber, NL, July 10, 2001, 6th*

### BASES ON BALLS

**Most bases on balls, career**
7—Jim Palmer, AL, 1970-1972, 1977, 1978

**Most bases on balls, game**
5—Bill Hallahan, NL, July 6, 1933 (2 IP)

**Most bases on balls, inning (*consecutive)**
3—Early Wynn, AL, Aug 3, 1959, 5th
Jim Palmer, AL, July 11, 1978, 3rd*
Jim Kern, AL, July 17, 1979, 9th
Dan Petry, AL, July 16, 1985, 9th
Kevin Brown, NL, July 11, 2000, 3rd

### STRIKEOUTS

**Most strikeouts, career**
19—Don Drysdale, NL, 1959 (both), 1962 (1st), 1963-1965, 1967, 1968 (8 G)

**Most strikeouts, game**
6—Carl Hubbell, NL, July 10, 1934 (3 IP)
Johnny Vander Meer, NL, July 13, 1943 (2.2 IP)
Larry Jansen, NL, July 11, 1950 (5 IP)
Ferguson Jenkins, NL, July 11, 1967 (3 IP)

**Most consecutive strikeouts, game**
5—Carl Hubbell, NL, July 10, 1934 (Ruth, Gehrig, Foxx in 1st, Simmons, Cronin in 2nd)
Fernando Valenzuela, NL, July 15, 1986 (Mattingly, Ripken, Barfield in 4th, Whitaker, Higuera in 5th)

**Most consecutive strikeouts from start of game**
4—Pedro Martinez, AL, July 13, 1999 (Larkin, Walker, Sosa in 1st, McGwire in 2nd)

### HIT BATSMEN, WILD PITCHES AND BALKS

**Most hit batsmen, inning or game**
1—many pitchers

**Most wild pitches, career**
2—Ewell Blackwell, NL, 1946-1951
Robin Roberts, NL, 1950, 1951, 1953-1955
Tom Brewer, AL, 1956
Juan Marichal, NL, 1962 (both), 1964-1968, 1971
Dave Stieb, AL, 1980, 1981
Steve Rogers, NL, 1978, 1979, 1982
John Smoltz, NL, 1989, 1992, 1993, 1996, 2002, 2005

**Most wild pitches, game**
2—Tom Brewer, AL, July 10, 1956, 6th and 7th
Juan Marichal, NL, July 30, 1962, 9th
Dave Stieb, AL, July 8, 1980, 7th
John Smoltz, NL, July 13, 1993, 6th

**Most wild pitches, inning**
2—Juan Marichal, NL, July 30, 1962, 9th
Dave Stieb, AL, July 8, 1980, 7th
John Smoltz, NL, July 13, 1993, 6th

**Most balks, career**
2—Dwight Gooden, NL, 1986, 1988

**Most balks, inning or game**
1—Bob Friend, NL, July 11, 1960
Stu Miller, NL, July 11, 1961
Steve Busby, AL, July 15, 1975
Jim Kern, AL, July 17, 1979
Dwight Gooden, NL, July 15, 1986; July 12, 1988
Charlie Hough, AL, July 15, 1986

# INDIVIDUAL FIELDING

## FIRST BASEMEN

**Most games**
10—Steve Garvey, NL, 1974-1981, 1984, 1985

**Most putouts, career**
53—Lou Gehrig, AL, 1933-1938

**Most putouts, game**
14—George McQuinn, AL, July 13, 1948
[14—Harmon Killebrew, AL, July 11, 1967, 15 inn]

**Most assists, career**
6—Steve Garvey, NL, 1974-1981, 1984, 1985

**Most assists, game**
3—Rudy York, AL, July 6, 1942
Bill White, NL, July 9, 1963

**Most chances accepted, career**
55—Lou Gehrig, AL, 1933-1938
Steve Garvey, NL, 1974-1981, 1984, 1985

**Most chances accepted, game**
14—Rudy York, AL, July 6, 1942
George McQuinn, AL, July 13, 1948
[15—Harmon Killebrew, AL, July 11, 1967, 15 inn]

**Most errors, career**
2—Lou Gehrig, AL, 1933-1938

**Most errors, game and inning**
1—many players

**Most double plays, career**
6—Bill White, NL, 1960 (both), 1961 (both), 1963
Harmon Killebrew, AL, 1965, 1967, 1968, 1971

**Most double plays, game**
3—Stan Musial, NL, July 8, 1958

**Most unassisted double plays, game**
1—Pete Runnels, AL, Aug 3, 1959, 2nd
Lee May, NL, July 25, 1972, 3rd

## SECOND BASEMEN

**Most games**
13—Nellie Fox, AL, 1951, 1953-1958, 1959 (both), 1960 (both), 1961 (1st), 1963

**Most putouts, career**
25—Nellie Fox, AL, 1951, 1953-1958, 1959 (both), 1960 (both), 1961 (1st), 1963

**Most putouts, game**
5—Frankie Frisch, NL, July 6, 1933
[7—Juan Samuel, NL, July 14, 1987, 13 inn]

**Most assists, career**
23—Billy Herman, NL, 1934-1938, 1940-1943

**Most assists, game**
6—Willie Randolph, AL, July 19, 1977

**Most chances accepted, career**
39—Nellie Fox, AL, 1951, 1953-1958, 1959 (both), 1960 (both), 1961 (1st), 1963

**Most chances accepted, game**
9—Bill Mazeroski, NL, July 8, 1958
[9—Juan Samuel, NL, July 14, 1987, 13 inn]

**Most errors, career**
2—Billy Herman, NL, 1934-1938, 1940-1943
Nellie Fox, AL, 1951, 1953-1958, 1959 (both), 1960 (both), 1961, 1963
Willie Randolph, AL, 1977, 1980, 1981, 1987, 1989
Steve Sax, NL, 1982, 1983, 1986, 1989, 1990

**Most errors, game**
2—Billy Herman, NL, July 13, 1943
Willie Randolph, AL, July 8, 1980

**Most double plays, career**
5—Roberto Alomar, NL, 1990; AL 1991-2001

**Most double plays, game**
3—Billy Herman, NL, July 13, 1943
Bill Mazeroski, NL, July 8, 1958

**Most unassisted double plays, game**
none

## THIRD BASEMEN

**Most games**
18—Brooks Robinson, AL, 1960 (both), 1961 (both), 1962 (both), 1963-1974 (consec)

**Most putouts, career**
11—Brooks Robinson, AL, 1960 (both), 1961 (both), 1962 (both), 1963-1974

**Most putouts, game**
4—George Kell, AL, July 10, 1951
[4—Brooks Robinson, AL, July 12, 1966, 9.1 inn]

**Most assists, career**
32—Brooks Robinson, AL, 1960 (both), 1961 (both), 1962 (both), 1963-1974

**Most assists, game**
6—Ken Keltner, AL, July 13, 1948
Frank Malzone, AL, Aug 3, 1959

**Most chances accepted, career**
43—Brooks Robinson, AL, 1960 (both), 1961 (both), 1962 (both), 1963-1974

**Most chances accepted, game**
7—Ken Keltner, AL, July 13, 1948
Frank Malzone, AL, Aug 3, 1959
[8—Brooks Robinson, AL, July 12, 1966, 9.1 inn]

**Most errors, career**
6—Eddie Mathews, NL, 1953, 1955, 1957, 1959 (1st), 1960 (both), 1961 (both), 1962 (2nd)

**Most errors, game**
2—Red Rolfe, AL, July 7, 1937
Eddie Mathews, NL, July 11, 1960; July 30, 1962
(2—Ken Boyer, NL, July 11, 1961, 10 inn]

**Most errors, inning**
2—Eddie Mathews, NL, July 30, 1962, 9th

**Most double plays, career**
3—Frank Malzone, AL, 1957, 1958, 1959 (both), 1960 (both), 1963
Brooks Robinson, AL, 1960 (both), 1961 (both), 1962 (both), 1963-1974
George Brett, AL, 1976-1979, 1981-1983

**Most double plays, game**
1—many players

**Most unassisted double plays, game**
none

## SHORTSTOPS

**Most games**
15—Cal Ripken Jr., AL, 1983-1996, 2001

**Most putouts, career**
16—Ozzie Smith, NL, 1981-1992, 1994, 1996

**Most putouts, game**
5—Chico Carrasquel, AL, July 13, 1954

**Most assists, career**
24—Joe Cronin, AL, 1933-1935, 1937-1939, 1941

**Most assists, game**
8—Joe Cronin, AL, July 10, 1934

**Most chances accepted, career**
39—Ozzie Smith, NL, 1981-1992, 1994, 1996

**Most chances accepted, game**
10—Joe Cronin, AL, July 10, 1934
Marty Marion, NL, July 9, 1946

**Most errors, career**
2—Joe Cronin, AL, 1933-1935, 1937-1939, 1941
Ernie Banks, NL, 1955, 1957, 1958, 1959 (both), 1960 (both), 1961 (2nd)
Nomar Garciaparra, AL, 1997, 1999, 2000

**Most errors, game**
2—Nomar Garciaparra, AL, July 11, 2000

**Most double plays, career**
6—Ernie Banks, NL, 1955, 1957, 1958, 1959 (both), 1960 (both), 1961 (2nd)

**Most double plays, game**
2—many players; last—Miguel Tejada, AL, July 12, 2005

**Most unassisted double plays, game**
none

## OUTFIELDERS

**Most games**
22—Willie Mays, NL, 1954-1958, 1959 (both), 1960 (both), 1961 (both), 1962 (both), 1963-1972

**Most putouts, career**
55—Willie Mays, NL, 1954-1958, 1959 (both), 1960 (both), 1961 (both), 1962 (both), 1963-1972

**Most putouts, left fielder, game**
5—Sammy West, AL, July 7, 1937
Frank Robinson, NL, July 9, 1957
Joe Rudi, AL, July 15, 1975

**Most putouts, center fielder, game**
7—Chet Laabs, AL, July 13, 1943
Willie Mays, NL, July 7, 1964
[9—Larry Doby, AL, July 11, 1950, 14 inn]

**Most putouts, right fielder, game**
4—Charlie Keller, AL, July 9, 1940
Enos Slaughter, NL, July 14, 1953
Darryl Strawberry, NL, July 12, 1988
[6—Roberto Clemente, NL, July 11, 1967, 15 inn]

**Most assists, career**
3—Stan Musial, NL, 1943, 1944, 1946, 1948, 1949, 1951-1956, 1962 (2nd)

**Most assists, left fielder, game**
1—many players

**Most assists, center fielder, game**
1—many players

**Most assists, right fielder, game**
2—Dave Parker, NL, July 17, 1979
Tony Gwynn, NL, July 14, 1992

**Most chances accepted, career**
55—Willie Mays, NL, 1954-1958, 1959 (both), 1960 (both), 1961 (both), 1962 (both), 1963-1972

**Most chances accepted, left fielder, game**
5—Samny West, AL, July 7, 1937
Joe Rudi, AL, July 15, 1975

**Most chances accepted, center fielder, game**
7—Chet Laabs, AL, July 13, 1943
Willie Mays, NL, July 7, 1964
[9—Larry Doby, AL, July 11, 1950, 14 inn]

**Most chances accepted, right fielder, game**
4—Charlie Keller, AL, July 9, 1940
Enos Slaughter, NL, July 14, 1953
Darryl Strawberry, NL, July 12, 1988

**Most errors, career**
2—Pete Reiser, NL, 1941, 1942
Joe DiMaggio, AL, 1936-1942, 1947, 1949, 1950

**Most errors, left fielder, game**
1—many players

**Most errors, center fielder, game**
2—Pete Reiser, NL, July 8, 1941

**Most errors, right fielder, game**
1—many players

**Most double plays, career**
1—Stan Spence, AL, 1944, 1946, 1947
Tommy Davis, NL, 1962, 1962, 1963
Darryl Strawberry, NL, 1984-1988, 1990

**Most double plays, left fielder, game**
1—Tommy Davis, NL, July 9, 1963

**Most double plays, center fielder, game**
none

**Most double plays, right fielder, game**
1—Stan Spence, AL, July 11, 1944
Darryl Strawberry, NL, July 10, 1990

**Most unassisted double plays, game**
none

## CATCHERS

**Most games**
14—Yogi Berra, AL, 1949-1958, 1959 (2nd), 1960 (both), 1961 (1st)

**Most innings, game**
15—Bill Freehan, AL, July 11, 1967 (complete game)

**Most putouts, career**
61—Yogi Berra, AL, 1949-1958, 1959 (2nd), 1960 (both), 1961 (1st)

**Most putouts, game**
10—Bill Dickey, AL, July 11, 1939
Yogi Berra, AL, July 10, 1956
Del Crandall, NL, July 7, 1959
Johnny Bench, NL, July 15, 1975
Ivan Rodriguez, AL, July 13, 1999
[13—Roy Campanella, NL, July 11, 1950, 14 inn
Smoky Burgess, NL, July 11, 1961, 10 inn
Bill Freehan, AL, July 11, 1967, 15 inn]

**Most assists, career**
7—Yogi Berra, AL, 1949-1958, 1959 (2nd), 1960 (both), 1961 (1st)

**Most assists, game**
3—Lance Parrish, AL, July 13, 1982

**Most chances accepted, career**
68—Yogi Berra, AL, 1949-1958, 1959, 1960, 1960 (both), 1961 (1st)

**Most chances accepted, game**
11—Yogi Berra, AL, July 10, 1956
Johnny Bench, NL, July 15, 1975
Ivan Rodriguez, AL, July 13, 1999
[15—Roy Campanella, NL, July 11, 1950, 14 inn]

**Most errors, career**
2—Smoky Burgess, NL, 1954, 1955, 1960 (both), 1961 (both)

**Most errors, game**
1—many players

**Most passed balls, career and game**
1—many catchers

**Most double plays, career**
2—Ivan Rodriguez, AL, 1992-2001, 2004, 2005

**Most double plays, game**
1—many catchers

**Most unassisted double plays, game**
none

## PITCHERS

**Most putouts, career**
3—Spud Chandler, AL, 1942

**Most putouts, game**
3—Spud Chandler, AL, July 6, 1942

**Most assists, career**
5—Johnny Vander Meer, NL, 1938, 1942, 1943

**Most assists, game**
3—Johnny Vander Meer, NL, July 6, 1938
Don Drysdale, NL, July 7, 1964
Mickey Lolich, AL, July 13, 1971

**Most chances accepted, career**
5—Mel Harder, AL, 1934-1937
Johnny Vander Meer, NL, 1938, 1942, 1943
Don Drysdale, NL, 1959 (both), 1962 (1st), 1963-1965, 1967, 1968

**Most chances accepted, game**
4—Spud Chandler, AL, July 6, 1942

**Most errors, career and game**
1—many pitchers

**Most double plays, career and game**
1—many pitchers

**Most unassisted double plays, game**
none

# CLUB FIELDING

## NUMBER OF PLAYERS AT POSITIONS

### INFIELDERS

**Most infielders, game**
10—NL, July 13, 1960
NL, July 13, 1976
AL, July 11, 2000
AL, July 10, 2001

**Most infielders by both clubs, game**
19—AL 10, NL 9, July 11, 2000

**Most first basemen, game**
3—NL, July 9, 1946
NL, July 13, 1960
NL, July 24, 1973
AL, July 11, 2000
AL, July 10, 2001

**Most first basemen by both clubs, game**
5—NL 3, AL 2, July 9, 1946
NL 3, AL 2, July 13, 1960
AL 3, NL 2, July 11, 2000
NL 3, AL 2, July 10, 2001

**Most second basemen, game**
3—NL, July 13, 1960
NL, Aug 9, 1981
AL, July 14, 1992
AL, July 8, 1997
NL, July 11, 2000

**Most second basemen by both clubs, game**
5—NL 3, AL 2, July 13, 1960
NL 3, AL 2, Aug 9, 1981
AL 3, NL 2, July 14, 1992
AL 3, NL 2, July 8, 1997
NL 3, AL 2, July 11, 2000

**Most third basemen, game**
3—many clubs

**Most third basemen by both clubs, game**
6—AL 3, NL 3, July 10, 2001

**Most shortstops, game**
3—many clubs

**Most shortstops by both clubs, game**
6—AL 3, NL 3, July 13, 1976

### OUTFIELDERS

**Most outfielders, game**
8—NL, July 24, 1973

**Most outfielders by both clubs, game**
14—NL 7, AL 7, July 8, 1980

**Most right fielders, game**
4—NL, July 13, 1976

**Most right fielders by both clubs, game**
6—NL 4, AL 2, July 13, 1976

**Most center fielders, game**
3—many times

**Most center fielders by both clubs, game**
5—many times

**Most left fielders, game**
3—many times

**Most left fielders by both clubs, game**
5—many times
[6—NL 3, AL 3, July 14, 1970, 12 inn]

### BATTERY

**Most catchers, game**
3—many times

**Most catchers by both clubs, game**
6—many times

**Most pitchers, game**
10—AL, July 14, 1992
AL, July 12, 2005

**Most pitchers by both clubs, game**
19—AL 10, NL 9, July 12, 2005

**Fewest pitchers, game**
2—AL, July 8, 1935
AL, July 6, 1942

**Fewest pitchers by both clubs, game**
6—many times

## PUTOUTS, ASSISTS

**Most players with one or more putouts, game**
14—NL, July 13, 1976
AL, July 6, 1983
AL, July 14, 1992
AL, July 10, 2001

**Most players with one or more putouts by both clubs, game**
25—NL 14, AL 11, July 13, 1976
AL 13, NL 12, July 16, 1985
AL 14, NL 11, July 14, 1992

**Most assists, game**
16—AL, July 6, 1942
AL, Aug 9, 1981

**Most assists by both clubs, game**
26—AL 15, NL 11, July 12, 1949
AL 16, NL 10, Aug 9, 1981
AL 14, NL 12, July 8, 1997

**Fewest assists, game**
5—NL, July 10, 1934
NL, July 9, 1957
NL, July 23, 1969
NL, July 13, 1999
AL, July 15, 2003
[3—NL, July 15, 2003, fielded 8 inn]

**Fewest assists by both clubs, game**
8—AL 5, NL 3, July 15, 2003

**Most players one or more assists, game**
10—NL, July 24, 1973

**Most players one or more assists by both clubs, game**
19—NL 10, AL 9, July 24, 1973

## ERRORS, DOUBLE PLAYS

**Most errors, game**
5—NL, July 12, 1949
NL, July 11, 1961

**Most errors by both clubs, game**
6—NL 5, AL 1, July 12, 1949
[7—NL 5, AL 2, July 11, 1961, 10 inn]

**Fewest errors, game**
0—many times

**Fewest errors by both clubs, game**
0—many times

**Most consecutive errorless games**
11—NL, 1963-1973

**Most double plays, game**
3—many times

**Most double plays by both clubs, game**
4—many times

**Fewest double plays, game**
0—many times

**Fewest double plays by both clubs, game**
0—many times

# MISCELLANEOUS

## EARLIEST AND LATEST GAME DATES

**Earliest date for All-Star Game**
July 6, 1933 at Comiskey Park, Chicago
July 6, 1938 at Crosley Field, Cincinnati
July 6, 1942 at Polo Grounds, New York
July 6, 1983 at Comiskey Park, Chicago

**Latest date for All-Star Game**
Aug 9, 1981 at Municipal Stadium, Cleveland

## NIGHT GAMES

**First night game**
July 13, 1943 at Shibe Park, Philadelphia

## LENGTH OF GAMES

**Longest game, by innings**
15 inn—at Anaheim Stadium, California, July 11, 1967

**Shortest game, by innings**
5 inn—at Shibe Park, Philadelphia, July 8, 1952 (rain)

**Longest 9-inning game, by time**
3:38—at Coors Field, Colorado, July 7, 1998

**Shortest 9-inning game, by time**
1:53—at Sportsman's Park, St. Louis, July 9, 1940

**Longest extra-inning game, by time**
3:41—at Anaheim Stadium, California, July 11, 1967, 15 inn

## GAMES WON AND LOST

**All-Star games won**
40—National League (lost 34, tied 2)
34—American League (lost 40, tied 2)

**For a complete list of All-Star Game results, see page 410.**

**Most consecutive All-Star games won**
11—National League, 1972-1982

**Most consecutive All-Star games lost**
11—American League, 1972-1982

## ATTENDANCE

**Largest attendance, game**
72,086—at Municipal Stadium, Cleveland, Aug 9, 1981

**Smallest attendance, game**
25,556—at Braves Field, Boston, July 7, 1936

# NON-PLAYING PERSONNEL

## MANAGERS

### GAMES

**Most All-Star games managed**
10—Casey Stengel, AL, 1950-1954, 1956, 1957, 1958, 1959 (both), (won 4, lost 6)

**Most consecutive All-Star games managed**
5—Casey Stengel, AL, 1950-1954; also 1956, 1957, 1958, 1959 (both)

### GAMES WON

**Most All-Star games won as manager**
7—Walter Alston, NL, 1956, 1960 (both), 1964, 1966, 1967, 1975 (lost 2)

**Most All-Star games won as undefeated manager**
5—Joe Torre, AL, 1997, 1999 through 2001, 2004 (tie in 2003)

**Most consecutive victories as All-Star manager**
6—Walter Alston, NL, 1960 (both), 1964, 1966, 1967, 1975

**Most consecutive years managing All-Star winners**
3—Tony La Russa, AL, 1989-1991
Joe Torre, AL, 1999-2001

**Most All-Star games won as manager, one season**
2—Walter Alston, NL, July 11, July 13, 1960

### GAMES LOST

**Most All-Star games lost as manager**
6—Casey Stengel, AL, 1950-1953, 1956, 1959 (1st), (won 4)

**Most All-Star games lost as winless manager**
5—Al Lopez, AL, 1955, 1960 (both), 1964, 1965

**Most consecutive defeats as All-Star manager**
5—Al Lopez, AL, 1955, 1960 (both), 1964, 1965

**Most consecutive years managing All-Star losers**
4—Casey Stengel, AL, 1950-1953

**Most All-Star games lost as manager, one season**
2—Al Lopez, AL, July 11, July 13, 1960

## UMPIRES

**Most games umpired**
7—Bill Summers, AL, 1936, 1941, 1946, 1949, 1952, 1955, 1959 (2nd)
Al Barlick, NL, 1942, 1949, 1952, 1955, 1959 (1st), 1966, 1970

**Most consecutive games umpired**
2—many umpires

# CAREER MILESTONES

(Players active in the major leagues in 2005 are in boldface.)

## SERVICE

### GAMES PLAYED

| Player | Games |
|---|---|
| 1. Hank Aaron | 24 |
| 2. Willie Mays | 24 |
| Stan Musial | 24 |
| 4. Cal Ripken Jr. | 18 |
| Brooks Robinson | 18 |
| Ted Williams | 18 |
| 7. Al Kaline | 16 |
| Mickey Mantle | 16 |
| Pete Rose | 16 |
| 10. Yogi Berra | 15 |
| Rod Carew | 15 |
| 12. Roberto Clemente | 14 |
| Ozzie Smith | 14 |
| Carl Yastrzemski | 14 |
| 15. Ernie Banks | 13 |
| Nellie Fox | 13 |
| Tony Gwynn | 13 |
| **18. Barry Bonds** | **12** |
| **Ivan Rodriguez** | **12** |
| Roberto Alomar | 12 |
| Johnny Bench | 12 |
| Wade Boggs | 12 |
| Barry Bonds | 12 |
| Reggie Jackson | 12 |
| Dave Winfield | 12 |

### GAMES PITCHED

| Player | Games |
|---|---|
| **1. Roger Clemens** | **10** |
| **2. Randy Johnson** | **8** |
| Jim Bunning | 8 |
| Don Drysdale | 8 |
| Juan Marichal | 8 |
| Tom Seaver | 8 |
| 7. Dave Stieb | 7 |
| Early Wynn | 7 |
| **9. Tom Glavine** | **6** |
| **John Smoltz** | **6** |
| Ewell Blackwell | 6 |
| Dennis Eckersley | 6 |
| Whitey Ford | 6 |
| Bob Gibson | 6 |
| Rich Gossage | 6 |
| Catfish Hunter | 6 |
| 17. many tied with 5 | |

## BATTING

### BATTING AVERAGE

(minimum 10 AB)

| Player | BA |
|---|---|
| **1. Derek Jeter** | **.700** |
| 2. Richie Ashburn | .600 |
| **3. Moises Alou** | **.500** |
| Charlie Gehringer | .500 |
| Ted Klusewski | .500 |
| 6. Al Simmons | .461 |
| 7. Joe Carter | .454 |
| Leon Wagner | .454 |
| **9. Ken Griffey Jr.** | **.435** |
| 10. Billy Herman | .433 |
| 11. Bill Skowron | .429 |
| **12. Sandy Alomar Jr.** | **.417** |
| **13. Chipper Jones** | **.400** |
| Stan Hack | .400 |
| Andy Pafko | .400 |
| Bill Terry | .400 |
| 17. Steve Garvey | .393 |
| 18. Bobby Bonilla | .385 |
| Will Clark | .385 |
| Ernie Lombardi | .385 |

### AT-BATS

| Player | AB |
|---|---|
| 1. Willie Mays | 75 |
| 2. Hank Aaron | 67 |
| 3. Stan Musial | 63 |
| 4. Cal Ripken Jr. | 49 |
| 5. Ted Williams | 46 |
| 6. Brooks Robinson | 45 |
| 7. Mickey Mantle | 43 |
| 8. Yogi Berra | 41 |
| Rod Carew | 41 |
| 10. Joe DiMaggio | 40 |
| 11. Nellie Fox | 38 |
| 12. Al Kaline | 37 |
| 13. Dave Winfield | 36 |
| 14. Carl Yastrzemski | 34 |
| 15. Ernie Banks | 33 |
| Pete Rose | 33 |
| **17. Ivan Rodriguez** | **32** |
| 18. Roberto Clemente | 31 |
| 19. Roberto Alomar | 30 |
| Billy Herman | 30 |

### RUNS

| Player | R |
|---|---|
| 1. Willie Mays | 20 |
| 2. Stan Musial | 11 |
| 3. Ted Williams | 10 |
| 4. Rod Carew | 8 |
| 5. Hank Aaron | 7 |
| Joe DiMaggio | 7 |
| Nellie Fox | 7 |
| Steve Garvey | 7 |
| Al Kaline | 7 |
| Joe Morgan | 7 |
| Jackie Robinson | 7 |
| 12. Dave Winfield | 6 |
| 13. many tied with 5 | |

### HITS

| Player | H |
|---|---|
| 1. Willie Mays | 23 |
| 2. Stan Musial | 20 |
| 3. Nellie Fox | 14 |
| Ted Williams | 14 |
| 5. Hank Aaron | 13 |
| Billy Herman | 13 |
| Cal Ripken Jr. | 13 |
| Brooks Robinson | 13 |
| Dave Winfield | 13 |
| 10. Al Kaline | 12 |
| 11. Steve Garvey | 11 |
| 12. many tied with 10 | |

### SINGLES

| Player | Singles |
|---|---|
| 1. Willie Mays | 15 |
| 2. Nellie Fox | 14 |
| 3. Stan Musial | 12 |
| 4. Hank Aaron | 11 |
| Billy Herman | 11 |
| 6. Al Kaline | 9 |
| Brooks Robinson | 9 |
| **8. Ivan Rodriguez** | **8** |
| 8. Wade Boggs | 8 |
| Charlie Gehringer | 8 |
| Mickey Mantle | 8 |
| Cal Ripken Jr. | 8 |
| 12. many tied with 7 | |

### DOUBLES

| Player | Doubles |
|---|---|
| 1. Dave Winfield | 7 |
| 2. many tied with 3 | |

### TRIPLES

| Player | Triples |
|---|---|
| 1. Willie Mays | 3 |
| Brooks Robinson | 3 |
| 3. Rod Carew | 2 |
| Steve Garvey | 2 |
| 5. many tied with 1 | |

### HOME RUNS

| Player | HR |
|---|---|
| 1. Stan Musial | 6 |
| 2. Fred Lynn | 4 |
| Ted Williams | 4 |
| 4. Johnny Bench | 3 |
| Gary Carter | 3 |
| Rocky Colavito | 3 |
| Harmon Killebrew | 3 |
| Ralph Kiner | 3 |
| Willie Mays | 3 |
| 10. many tied with 2 | |

## TOTAL BASES

| | Player | TB |
|---|---|---|
| 1. | Willie Mays | 40 |
| | Stan Musial | 40 |
| 3. | Ted Williams | 30 |
| 4. | Steve Garvey | 23 |
| 5. | Cal Ripken Jr. | 22 |
| | Brooks Robinson | 22 |
| 7. | Dave Winfield | 20 |
| 8. | Hank Aaron | 19 |
| | Johnny Bench | 19 |
| | Al Kaline | 19 |
| 11. | Ernie Banks | 18 |
| | Fred Lynn | 18 |
| 13. | Roberto Clemente | 17 |
| | Harmon Killebrew | 17 |
| 15. | Rocky Colavito | 16 |
| | Mickey Mantle | 16 |
| **17.** | **Barry Bonds** | **15** |
| | **Ken Griffey Jr.** | **15** |
| | Rod Carew | 15 |
| | Gary Carter | 15 |
| | Billy Herman | 15 |
| | Arky Vaughan | 15 |
| | Carl Yastrzemski | 15 |

## SLUGGING PERCENTAGE

(Minimum 50 at-bats)

| | Player | SLG |
|---|---|---|
| **1.** | **Derek Jeter** | **1.100** |
| 2. | Ralph Kiner | .933 |
| 3. | Ted Kluszewski | .929 |
| 4. | Fred Lynn | .900 |
| 5. | Steve Garvey | .821 |
| 6. | Al Rosen | .818 |
| 7. | Gary Carter | .750 |
| 8. | George Foster | .727 |
| | Leon Wagner | .727 |
| **10.** | **Moises Alou** | **.700** |
| | **Garret Anderson** | **.700** |
| | **Chipper Jones** | **.700** |
| | Richie Ashburn | .700 |
| | Larry Doby | .700 |
| 15. | Al Simmons | .692 |
| 16. | Arky Vaughan | .682 |
| 17. | Johnny Bench | .679 |
| **18.** | **Sandy Alomar** | **.667** |
| | Mike Schmidt | .667 |
| 20. | Harmon Killebrew | .654 |

## EXTRA-BASE HITS

| | Player | EBH |
|---|---|---|
| 1. | Willie Mays | 8 |
| | Stan Musial | 8 |
| 3. | Ted Williams | 7 |
| | Dave Winfield | 7 |
| 5. | Steve Garvey | 6 |
| **6.** | **Barry Bonds** | **5** |
| | Ernie Banks | 5 |
| | Cal Ripken Jr. | 5 |
| 9. | many tied with 4 | |

## RUNS BATTED IN

| | Player | RBI |
|---|---|---|
| 1. | Ted Williams | 12 |
| 2. | Fred Lynn | 10 |
| | Stan Musial | 10 |
| 4. | Willie Mays | 9 |
| 5. | Hank Aaron | 8 |
| | Rocky Colavito | 8 |
| | Cal Ripken Jr. | 8 |
| **8.** | **Barry Bonds** | **7** |
| | Steve Garvey | 7 |
| **10.** | **Andruw Jones** | **6** |
| | Johnny Bench | 6 |
| | Joe DiMaggio | 6 |
| | Al Kaline | 6 |
| | Harmon Killebrew | 6 |
| | Joe Medwick | 6 |
| 16. | many tied with 5 | |

## WALKS

| | Player | BB |
|---|---|---|
| 1. | Ted Williams | 11 |
| 2. | Charlie Gehringer | 9 |
| | Mickey Mantle | 9 |
| 4. | Rod Carew | 7 |
| | Willie Mays | 7 |
| | Stan Musial | 7 |
| 7. | Lou Gehrig | 6 |
| 8. | Ron Santo | 5 |
| 9. | many tied with 4 | |

## STRIKEOUTS

| | Player | K |
|---|---|---|
| 1. | Mickey Mantle | 17 |
| 2. | Willie Mays | 14 |
| 3. | Ted Williams | 10 |
| **4.** | **Alex Rodriguez** | **9** |
| | Roberto Clemente | 9 |
| | Reggie Jackson | 9 |
| | Mark McGwire | 9 |
| | Ryne Sandberg | 9 |
| 9. | Hank Aaron | 8 |
| | Ernie Banks | 8 |
| | Joe Gordon | 8 |
| | Jim Rice | 8 |
| | Carl Yastrzemski | 8 |

## STOLEN BASES

| | Player | SB |
|---|---|---|
| 1. | Willie Mays | 6 |
| **2.** | **Kenny Lofton** | **5** |
| | Roberto Alomar | 5 |
| 4. | Rod Carew | 3 |
| | Steve Sax | 3 |
| 6. | many tied with 2 | |

# PITCHING

## GAMES STARTED

| | Player | Games |
|---|---|---|
| 1. | Don Drysdale | 5 |
| | Lefty Gomez | 5 |
| | Robin Roberts | 5 |
| **4.** | **Randy Johnson** | **4** |
| | Jim Palmer | 4 |
| 6. | many tied with 3 | |

## GAMES RELIEVED

| | Player | Games |
|---|---|---|
| **1.** | **Roger Clemens** | **7** |
| | Tom Seaver | 7 |
| 3. | Rich Gossage | 6 |
| | Juan Marichal | 6 |
| | Early Wynn | 6 |
| 6. | many tied with 5 | |

## INNINGS PITCHED

| | Player | IP |
|---|---|---|
| 1. | Don Drysdale | 19.1 |
| 2. | Jim Bunning | 18.0 |
| | Lefty Gomez | 18.0 |
| | Juan Marichal | 18.0 |
| 5. | Robin Roberts | 14.0 |
| | Warren Spahn | 14.0 |
| 7. | Ewell Blackwell | 13.2 |
| **8.** | **Roger Clemens** | **13.0** |
| | Mel Harder | 13.0 |
| | Tom Seaver | 13.0 |
| 11. | Catfish Hunter | 12.2 |
| | Jim Palmer | 12.2 |
| 13. | Bob Feller | 12.1 |
| | Early Wynn | 12.1 |
| **15.** | **Randy Johnson** | **12.0** |
| | Whitey Ford | 12.0 |
| 17. | Dave Stieb | 11.2 |
| 18. | Bob Gibson | 11.0 |
| | Vic Raschi | 11.0 |

## EARNED RUN AVERAGE

(minimum 30 IP)

| | Player | ERA |
|---|---|---|
| 1. | Mel Harder | 0.00 |
| 2. | Juan Marichal | 0.50 |
| 3. | Bob Feller | 0.73 |
| **4.** | **Randy Johnson** | **0.75** |
| 5. | Dave Stieb | 0.77 |
| 6. | Jim Bunning | 1.00 |
| 7. | Ewell Blackwell | 1.32 |
| 8. | Don Drysdale | 1.40 |
| 9. | Hal Newshouser | 1.69 |
| 10. | Bucky Walters | 2.00 |
| 11. | Vic Raschi | 2.45 |
| 12. | Lefty Gomez | 2.50 |
| 13. | Jack Morris | 2.53 |
| 14. | Dizzy Dean | 2.70 |
| 15. | Carl Hubbell | 2.79 |

| | Player | ERA |
|---|---|---|
| 16. | Early Wynn | 2.92 |
| 17. | Warren Spahn | 3.21 |
| 18. | Bob Gibson | 3.27 |
| 19. | Billy Pierce | 3.38 |
| **20.** | **Roger Clemens** | **4.15** |

## WINS

| | Player | W |
|---|---|---|
| 1. | Lefty Gomez | 3 |
| 2. | Vida Blue | 2 |
| | Don Drysdale | 2 |
| | Bob Friend | 2 |
| | Juan Marichal | 2 |
| | Bruce Sutter | 2 |
| 7. | many tied with 1 | |

## LOSSES

| | Player | L |
|---|---|---|
| **1.** | **John Smoltz** | **2** |
| | Mort Cooper | 2 |
| | Whitey Ford | 2 |
| | Dwight Gooden | 2 |
| | Catfish Hunter | 2 |
| | Claude Passeau | 2 |
| | Luis Tiant | 2 |
| 8. | many tied with 1 | |

## SAVES (SINCE 1969)

| | Player | SV |
|---|---|---|
| 1. | Dennis Eckersley | 3 |
| **2.** | **Mariano Rivera** | **2** |
| 3. | many tied with 1 | |

## RUNS

| | Player | R |
|---|---|---|
| 1. | Whitey Ford | 13 |
| 2. | Robin Roberts | 10 |
| | Warren Spahn | 10 |
| **4.** | **Roger Clemens** | **9** |
| | **Tom Glavine** | **9** |
| | Catfish Hunter | 9 |
| 7. | Vida Blue | 8 |
| | Jim Palmer | 8 |
| | Tom Seaver | 8 |
| 10. | Mort Cooper | 7 |
| | Rich Gossage | 7 |
| | Atlee Hammaker | 7 |
| | Claude Passeau | 7 |
| 14. | Roy Face | 6 |
| | Lefty Gomez | 6 |
| | Tex Hughson | 6 |
| | Van Mungo | 6 |
| | Gaylord Perry | 6 |
| | Red Ruffing | 6 |
| 20. | many tied with 5 | |

## HITS

| | Player | H |
|---|---|---|
| 1. | Whitey Ford | 19 |
| 2. | Robin Roberts | 17 |
| | Warren Spahn | 17 |
| **4.** | **Tom Glavine** | **16** |
| 5. | Catfish Hunter | 15 |
| 6. | Jack Morris | 14 |

| | Player | ERA |
|---|---|---|
| | Gaylord Perry | 14 |
| | Tom Seaver | 14 |
| 9. | Red Ruffing | 13 |
| 10. | Vida Blue | 12 |
| **11.** | **Roger Clemens** | **11** |
| | Bob Gibson | 11 |
| | Lefty Gomez | 11 |
| | Jim Palmer | 11 |
| 15. | Dizzy Dean | 10 |
| | Don Drysdale | 10 |
| | Lefty Grove | 10 |
| | Tex Hughson | 10 |
| | Nolan Ryan | 10 |
| | Bucky Walters | 10 |
| | Lon Warneke | 10 |

## HOME RUNS

| | Player | HR |
|---|---|---|
| 1. | Vida Blue | 4 |
| | Catfish Hunter | 4 |
| **3.** | **Roger Clemens** | **3** |
| | Steve Carlton | 3 |
| | Mort Cooper | 3 |
| | Whitey Ford | 3 |
| | Jim Palmer | 3 |
| | Milt Pappas | 3 |
| | Robin Roberts | 3 |
| | Tom Seaver | 3 |
| 11. | many tied with 2 | |

## STRIKEOUTS

| | Player | K |
|---|---|---|
| 1. | Don Drysdale | 19 |
| 2. | Tom Seaver | 16 |
| 3. | Jim Palmer | 14 |
| 4. | Jim Bunning | 13 |
| | Bob Feller | 13 |
| | Catfish Hunter | 13 |
| | Ewell Blackwell | 13 |
| **8.** | **Randy Johnson** | **12** |
| | Juan Marichal | 12 |
| | Sam McDowell | 12 |
| | Billy Pierce | 12 |
| 12. | Carl Hubbell | 11 |
| | Johnny Vander Meer | 11 |
| 13. | Dizzy Dean | 10 |
| | Bob Gibson | 10 |
| | Dick Radatz | 10 |
| | Nolan Ryan | 10 |
| | Warren Spahn | 10 |
| | Dave Stieb | 10 |

## WALKS

| | Player | BB |
|---|---|---|
| 1. | Jim Palmer | 7 |
| 2. | Carl Hubbell | 6 |
| | Robin Roberts | 6 |
| | Dave Stieb | 6 |
| | Lon Warneke | 6 |
| 6. | Ewell Blackwell | 5 |
| | Steve Carlton | 5 |
| | Dizzy Dean | 5 |
| | Bob Gibson | 5 |
| | Bill Hallahan | 5 |
| | Nolan Ryan | 5 |
| | Warren Spahn | 5 |
| 13. | many tied with 4 | |

# GENERAL REFERENCE



## HOME RUNS (161)

**(Numbers in parentheses indicate cumulative totals by batters or pitchers)**

| Player | Date | Inning | On | Pitcher |
|---|---|---|---|---|
| Babe Ruth, AL | July 6, 1933 | 3 | 1 | Bill Hallahan |
| Frankie Frisch, NL | July 6, 1933 | 6 | 0 | Alvin Crowder |
| Frankie Frisch, NL (2) | July 10, 1934 | 1 | 0 | Lefty Gomez |
| Joe Medwick, NL | July 10, 1934 | 3 | 2 | Lefty Gomez (2) |
| Jimmie Foxx, AL | July 8, 1935 | 1 | 1 | Bill Walker |
| Augie Galan, NL | July 7, 1936 | 5 | 0 | Schoolboy Rowe |
| Lou Gehrig, AL | July 7, 1936 | 7 | 0 | Curt Davis |
| Lou Gehrig, AL (2) | July 7, 1937 | 3 | 1 | Dizzy Dean |
| Joe DiMaggio, AL | July 11, 1939 | 5 | 0 | Bill C. Lee |
| Max West, NL | July 9, 1940 | 1 | 2 | Red Ruffing |
| Arky Vaughan, NL | July 8, 1941 | 7 | 1 | Sid Hudson |
| Arky Vaughan, NL (2) | July 8, 1941 | 8 | 1 | Eddie Smith |
| Ted Williams, AL | July 8, 1941 | 9 | 2 | Claude Passeau |
| Lou Boudreau, AL | July 6, 1942 | 1 | 0 | Mort Cooper |
| Rudy York, AL | July 6, 1942 | 1 | 1 | Mort Cooper (2) |
| Mickey Owen, NL | July 6, 1942 | 8 | 0 | Al Benton |
| Bobby Doerr, AL | July 13, 1943 | 2 | 2 | Mort Cooper (3) |
| Vince DiMaggio, NL | July 13, 1943 | 9 | 0 | Cecil Hughson |
| Charlie Keller, AL | July 9, 1946 | 1 | 1 | Claude Passeau |
| Ted Williams, AL (2) | July 9, 1946 | 4 | 0 | Kirby Higbe |
| Ted Williams, AL (3) | July 9, 1946 | 8 | 2 | Rip Sewell |
| Johnny Mize, NL | July 8, 1947 | 4 | 0 | Spec Shea |
| Stan Musial, NL | July 13, 1948 | 1 | 1 | Walt Masterson |
| Hoot Evers, AL | July 13, 1948 | 2 | 0 | Ralph Branca |

| Player | Date | Inning | On | Pitcher |
|---|---|---|---|---|
| Stan Musial, NL (2) | July 12, 1949 | 1 | 1 | Mel Parnell |
| Ralph Kiner, NL | July 12, 1949 | 6 | 1 | Lou Brissie |
| Ralph Kiner, NL (2) | July 11, 1950 | 9 | 0 | Art Houtteman |
| Red Schoendienst, NL | July 11, 1950 | 14 | 0 | Ted Gray |
| Stan Musial, NL (3) | July 10, 1951 | 4 | 0 | Eddie Lopat |
| Bob Elliott, NL | July 10, 1951 | 4 | 1 | Eddie Lopat (2) |
| Vic Wertz, AL | July 10, 1951 | 4 | 0 | Sal Maglie |
| George Kell, AL | July 10, 1951 | 5 | 0 | Sal Maglie (2) |
| Gil Hodges, NL | July 10, 1951 | 6 | 1 | Fred Hutchinson |
| Ralph Kiner, NL (3) | July 10, 1951 | 8 | 0 | Mel Parnell (2) |
| Jackie Robinson, NL | July 8, 1952 | 1 | 0 | Vic Raschi |
| Hank Sauer, NL | July 8, 1952 | 4 | 1 | Bob Lemon |
| Al Rosen, AL | July 13, 1954 | 3 | 2 | Robin Roberts |
| Ray Boone, AL | July 13, 1954 | 3 | 0 | Robin Roberts (2) |
| Ted Kluszewski, NL | July 13, 1954 | 5 | 1 | Bob Porterfield |
| Al Rosen, AL (2) | July 13, 1954 | 5 | 1 | Johnny Antonelli |
| Gus Bell, NL | July 13, 1954 | 8 | 1 | Bob Keegan |
| Larry Doby, AL | July 13, 1954 | 8 | 0 | Gene Conley |
| Mickey Mantle, AL | July 12, 1955 | 1 | 2 | Robin Roberts (3) |
| Stan Musial, NL (4) | July 12, 1955 | 12 | 0 | Frank Sullivan |
| Willie Mays, NL | July 10, 1956 | 4 | 1 | Whitey Ford |
| Ted Williams, AL (4) | July 10, 1956 | 6 | 1 | Warren Spahn |
| Mickey Mantle, AL (2) | July 10, 1956 | 6 | 0 | Warren Spahn (2) |
| Stan Musial, NL (5) | July 10, 1956 | 7 | 0 | Tom Brewer |
| Eddie Mathews, NL | July 7, 1959 | 1 | 0 | Early Wynn |
| Al Kaline, AL | July 7, 1959 | 4 | 0 | Lew Burdette |
| Frank Malzone, AL | Aug 3, 1959 | 2 | 0 | Don Drysdale |
| Yogi Berra, AL | Aug 3, 1959 | 3 | 1 | Don Drysdale (2) |
| Frank Robinson, NL | Aug 3, 1959 | 5 | 0 | Early Wynn (2) |
| Jim Gilliam, NL | Aug 3, 1959 | 7 | 0 | Billy O'Dell |
| Rocky Colavito, AL | Aug 3, 1959 | 8 | 0 | Roy Face |
| Ernie Banks, NL | July 11, 1960 | 1 | 1 | Bill Monbouquette |
| Del Crandall, NL | July 11, 1960 | 2 | 0 | Bill Monbouquette (2) |
| Al Kaline, AL (2) | July 11, 1960 | 8 | 0 | Bob Buhl |
| Eddie Mathews, NL (2) | July 13, 1960 | 2 | 1 | Whitey Ford (2) |
| Willie Mays, NL (2) | July 13, 1960 | 3 | 0 | Whitey Ford (3) |
| Stan Musial, NL (6) | July 13, 1960 | 7 | 0 | Gerry Staley |
| Ken Boyer, NL | July 13, 1960 | 9 | 1 | Gary Bell |
| Harmon Killebrew, AL | July 11, 1961 | 6 | 0 | Mike McCormick |
| George Altman, NL | July 11, 1961 | 8 | 0 | Mike Fornieles |
| Rocky Colavito, AL (2) | July 31, 1961 | 1 | 0 | Bob Purkey |
| Pete Runnels, AL | July 30, 1962 | 3 | 0 | Art Mahaffey |
| Leon Wagner, AL | July 30, 1962 | 4 | 1 | Art Mahaffey (2) |
| Rocky Colavito, AL (3) | July 30, 1962 | 7 | 2 | Dick Farrell |
| Johnny Roseboro, NL | July 30, 1962 | 9 | 0 | Milt Pappas |
| Billy Williams, NL | July 7, 1964 | 4 | 0 | John Wyatt |
| Ken Boyer, NL (2) | July 7, 1964 | 4 | 0 | John Wyatt (2) |
| Johnny Callison, NL | July 7, 1964 | 9 | 2 | Dick Radatz |
| Willie Mays, NL (3) | July 13, 1965 | 1 | 0 | Milt Pappas (2) |
| Joe Torre, NL | July 13, 1965 | 1 | 1 | Milt Pappas (3) |
| Willie Stargell, NL | July 13, 1965 | 2 | 1 | Mudcat Grant |
| Dick McAuliffe, AL | July 13, 1965 | 5 | 1 | Jim Maloney |
| Harmon Killebrew, AL (2) | July 13, 1965 | 5 | 1 | Jim Maloney (2) |
| Dick Allen, NL | July 11, 1967 | 2 | 0 | Dean Chance |
| Brooks Robinson, AL | July 11, 1967 | 6 | 0 | Ferguson Jenkins |
| Tony Perez, NL | July 11, 1967 | 15 | 0 | Catfish Hunter |
| Johnny Bench, NL | July 23, 1969 | 2 | 1 | Mel Stottlemyre |
| Frank Howard, AL | July 23, 1969 | 2 | 0 | Steve Carlton |
| Willie McCovey, NL | July 23, 1969 | 3 | 1 | Blue Moon Odom |
| Bill Freehan, AL | July 23, 1969 | 3 | 0 | Steve Carlton (2) |
| Willie McCovey, NL (2) | July 23, 1969 | 4 | 0 | Denny McLain |
| Dick Dietz, NL | July 14, 1970 | 9 | 0 | Catfish Hunter (2) |
| Johnny Bench, NL (2) | July 13, 1971 | 2 | 1 | Vida Blue |
| Hank Aaron, NL | July 13, 1971 | 3 | 0 | Vida Blue (2) |
| Reggie Jackson, AL | July 13, 1971 | 3 | 1 | Dock Ellis |
| Frank Robinson, AL (2) | July 13, 1971 | 3 | 1 | Dock Ellis (2) |
| Harmon Killebrew, AL (3) | July 13, 1971 | 6 | 1 | Ferguson Jenkins |
| Roberto Clemente, NL | July 13, 1971 | 8 | 0 | Mickey Lolich |
| Hank Aaron, NL (2) | July 25, 1972 | 6 | 1 | Gaylord Perry |
| Cookie Rojas, AL | July 25, 1972 | 8 | 1 | Bill Stoneman |
| Johnny Bench, NL (3) | July 24, 1973 | 4 | 0 | Bill Singer |
| Bobby Bonds, NL | July 24, 1973 | 5 | 1 | Bill Singer (2) |
| Willie Davis, NL | July 24, 1973 | 6 | 1 | Nolan Ryan |
| Reggie Smith, NL | July 23, 1974 | 7 | 0 | Catfish Hunter (3) |
| Steve Garvey, NL | July 15, 1975 | 2 | 0 | Vida Blue (3) |
| Jimmy Wynn, NL | July 15, 1975 | 2 | 0 | Vida Blue (4) |
| Carl Yastrzemski, AL | July 15, 1975 | 6 | 2 | Tom Seaver |
| George Foster, NL | July 13, 1976 | 3 | 1 | Catfish Hunter (4) |
| Fred Lynn, AL | July 13, 1976 | 4 | 0 | Tom Seaver (2) |
| Cesar Cedeno, NL | July 13, 1976 | 8 | 1 | Frank Tanana |
| Joe Morgan, NL | July 19, 1977 | 1 | 0 | Jim Palmer |
| Greg Luzinski, NL | July 19, 1977 | 1 | 1 | Jim Palmer (2) |
| Steve Garvey, NL (2) | July 19, 1977 | 3 | 0 | Jim Palmer (3) |
| George Scott, AL | July 19, 1977 | 9 | 1 | Rich Gossage |
| Fred Lynn, AL (2) | July 17, 1979 | 1 | 1 | Steve Carlton (3) |
| Lee Mazzilli, NL | July 17, 1979 | 8 | 0 | Jim Kern |
| Fred Lynn, AL (3) | July 8, 1980 | 5 | 1 | Bob Welch |
| Ken Griffey Sr., NL | July 8, 1980 | 5 | 0 | Tommy John |
| Ken Singleton, AL | Aug 9, 1981 | 2 | 0 | Tom Seaver (3) |
| Gary Carter, NL | Aug 9, 1981 | 5 | 0 | Ken Forsch |
| Dave Parker, NL | Aug 9, 1981 | 6 | 0 | Mike Norris |
| Gary Carter, NL (2) | Aug 9, 1981 | 7 | 0 | Ron Davis |
| Mike Schmidt, NL | Aug 9, 1981 | 8 | 1 | Rollie Fingers |
| Dave Concepcion, NL | July 13, 1982 | 2 | 1 | Dennis Eckersley |
| Jim Rice, AL | July 6, 1983 | 3 | 0 | Atlee Hammaker |
| Fred Lynn, AL (4) | July 6, 1983 | 3 | 3 | Atlee Hammaker (2) |
| George Brett, AL | July 10, 1984 | 2 | 0 | Charlie Lea |
| Gary Carter, NL (3) | July 10, 1984 | 2 | 0 | Dave Stieb |
| Dale Murphy, NL | July 10, 1984 | 8 | 0 | Guillermo Hernandez |
| Lou Whitaker, AL | July 15, 1986 | 2 | 1 | Dwight Gooden |
| Frank White, AL | July 15, 1986 | 7 | 0 | Mike Scott |
| Terry Steinbach, AL | July 12, 1988 | 3 | 0 | Dwight Gooden (2) |
| Bo Jackson, AL | July 11, 1989 | 1 | 0 | Rick Reuschel |
| Wade Boggs, AL | July 11, 1989 | 1 | 0 | Rick Reuschel (2) |
| Cal Ripken Jr., AL | July 9, 1991 | 3 | 2 | Dennis Martinez |
| Andre Dawson, NL | July 9, 1991 | 4 | 0 | Roger Clemens |
| Ken Griffey Jr., AL | July 14, 1992 | 3 | 0 | Greg Maddux |
| Ruben Sierra, AL | July 14, 1992 | 6 | 1 | Bob Tewksbury |
| Will Clark, NL | July 14, 1992 | 8 | 2 | Rick Aguilera |
| Gary Sheffield, NL | July 13, 1993 | 1 | 1 | Mark Langston |
| Kirby Puckett, AL | July 13, 1993 | 2 | 0 | Terry Mulholland |
| Roberto Alomar, AL | July 13, 1993 | 3 | 0 | Andy Benes |
| Marquis Grissom, NL | July 12, 1994 | 6 | 0 | Randy Johnson |
| Fred McGriff, NL | July 12, 1994 | 9 | 1 | Lee Smith |
| Frank Thomas, AL | July 11, 1995 | 4 | 1 | John Smiley |
| Craig Biggio, NL | July 11, 1995 | 6 | 0 | Dennis Martinez (2) |
| Mike Piazza, NL | July 11, 1995 | 7 | 0 | Kenny Rogers |
| Jeff Conine, NL | July 11, 1995 | 8 | 0 | Steve Ontiveros |
| Mike Piazza, NL (2) | July 9, 1996 | 2 | 0 | Charles Nagy |
| Ken Caminiti, NL | July 9, 1996 | 6 | 0 | Roger Pavlik |
| Edgar Martinez, AL | July 8, 1997 | 2 | 0 | Greg Maddux (2) |
| Javy Lopez, NL | July 8, 1997 | 7 | 0 | Jose Rosado |
| Sandy Alomar Jr., AL | July 8, 1997 | 7 | 1 | Shawn Estes |
| Alex Rodriguez, AL | July 7, 1998 | 5 | 0 | Andy Ashby |
| Barry Bonds, NL | July 7, 1998 | 5 | 2 | Bartolo Colon |
| Roberto Alomar, AL (2) | July 7, 1998 | 7 | 0 | Trevor Hoffman |
| Chipper Jones, NL | July 11, 2000 | 3 | 0 | James Baldwin |
| Cal Ripken Jr., AL (2) | July 10, 2001 | 3 | 0 | Chan Ho Park |
| Derek Jeter, AL | July 10, 2001 | 6 | 0 | Jon Lieber |
| Magglio Ordonez, AL | July 10, 2001 | 6 | 0 | Jon Lieber (2) |
| Barry Bonds, NL (2) | July 9, 2002 | 3 | 1 | Roy Halladay |
| Alfonso Soriano, AL | July 9, 2002 | 5 | 0 | Eric Gagne |
| Todd Helton, NL | July 15, 2003 | 5 | 1 | Shigetoshi Hasegawa |
| Garrett Anderson, AL | July 15, 2003 | 6 | 1 | Woody Williams |
| Andruw Jones, AL | July 15, 2003 | 7 | 0 | Mark Mulder |
| Jason Giambi, AL | July 15, 2003 | 7 | 0 | Billy Wagner |
| Hank Blalock, AL | July 15, 2003 | 8 | 1 | Eric Gagne (2) |
| Manny Ramirez, AL | July 13, 2004 | 1 | 1 | Roger Clemens (2, 1st in NL) |
| Alfonso Soriano, AL | July 13, 2004 | 1 | 2 | Roger Clemens (3, 2nd in NL) |
| David Ortiz, AL | July 13, 2004 | 6 | 1 | Carl Pavano |
| Miguel Tejada, AL | July 12, 2005 | 2 | 0 | John Smoltz |
| Mark Teixeira, AL | July 12, 2005 | 6 | 1 | Dontrelle Willis |
| Andruw Jones, NL | July 12, 2005 | 7 | 1 | Kenny Rogers |

## MANAGERIAL RECORDS

### AMERICAN LEAGUE

| | Games W | Games L |
|---|---|---|
| Joe Altobelli, Baltimore | 0 | 1 |
| Sparky Anderson, Detroit | 0 | 1 |
| Del Baker, Detroit | 1 | 0 |
| Hank Bauer, Baltimore | 0 | 1 |
| Lou Boudreau, Cleveland | 1 | 0 |
| Mickey Cochrane, Detroit | 1 | 0 |
| Joe Cronin, Boston, Washington | 2 | 1 |
| Alvin Dark, Oakland | 0 | 1 |
| Terry Francona, Boston | 1 | 0 |
| Jim Frey, Kansas City | 0 | 1 |
| Cito Gaston, Toronto | 1 | 1 |
| Mike Hargrove, Cleveland | 1 | 1 |
| Bucky Harris, New York | 1 | 0 |
| Ralph Houk, New York | 1 | 2 |
| Dick Howser, Kansas City | 1 | 0 |
| Darrell Johnson, Boston | 0 | 1 |
| Tom Kelly, Minnesota | 2 | 0 |
| Harvey Kuenn, Milwaukee | 1 | 0 |
| Tony La Russa, Oakland | 3 | 0 |

| Manager | W | L |
|---|---|---|
| Bob Lemon, New York | 0 | 1 |
| Al Lopez, Cleveland-Chicago | 0 | 5 |
| Connie Mack, Philadelphia | 1 | 0 |
| Billy Martin, New York | 0 | 3 |
| Joe McCarthy, New York | 4 | 3 |
| John McNamara, Boston | 0 | 1 |
| Sam Mele, Minnesota | 0 | 1 |
| Steve O'Neill, Detroit | 1 | 0 |
| Paul Richards, Baltimore* | 0 | 1 |
| Mike Scioscia, Anaheim | 1 | 0 |
| Buck Showalter, New York | 0 | 1 |
| Mayo Smith, Detroit | 0 | 1 |
| Casey Stengel, New York | 4 | 6 |
| Joe Torre, New York* | 5 | 0 |
| Earl Weaver, Baltimore | 1 | 2 |
| Dick Williams, Boston, Oakland, California | 0 | 3 |

**Total number of managers: 35**

*includes one tie per asterisk

## NATIONAL LEAGUE

| | Games | |
|---|---|---|
| Manager | W | L |
| Felipe Alou, Montreal | 1 | 0 |
| Walter Alston, Brooklyn, Los Angeles | 7 | 2 |
| Sparky Anderson, Cincinnati | 3 | 1 |
| Dusty Baker, Chicago | 0 | 1 |
| Yogi Berra, New York | 1 | 0 |
| Bruce Bochy, San Diego | 0 | 1 |
| Bob Brenly, Arizona* | 0 | 0 |
| Bobby Cox, Atlanta | 1 | 4 |
| Roger Craig, San Francisco | 0 | 1 |
| Alvin Dark, San Francisco | 1 | 0 |
| Charlie Dressen, Brooklyn | 1 | 0 |
| Leo Durocher, Brooklyn | 2 | 2 |
| Eddie Dyer, St. Louis | 0 | 1 |
| Jim Fregosi, Philadelphia | 1 | 0 |
| Frankie Frisch, St. Louis | 0 | 1 |
| Dallas Green, Philadelphia | 1 | 0 |
| Charley Grimm, Chicago | 1 | 1 |
| Fred Haney, Milwaukee | 1 | 2 |
| Gabby Hartnett, Chicago | 0 | 1 |
| Whitey Herzog, St. Louis | 0 | 3 |
| Gil Hodges, New York | 1 | 0 |
| Fred Hutchinson, Cincinnati | 1 | 1 |
| Dave Johnson, New York | 1 | 0 |
| Tony La Russa, St. Louis | 0 | 1 |
| Tom Lasorda, Los Angeles | 3 | 1 |
| Jim Leyland, Florida | 0 | 1 |
| Gene Mauch, Philadelphia | 1 | 0 |
| John McGraw, New York | 0 | 1 |
| Bill McKechnie, Cincinnati | 1 | 1 |
| Jack McKeon, Florida | 0 | 1 |
| Danny Murtaugh, Pittsburgh* | 2 | 0 |
| Paul Owens, Philadelphia | 1 | 0 |
| Lou Piniella, Cincinnati | 0 | 1 |
| Eddie Sawyer, Philadelphia | 1 | 0 |
| Red Schoendienst, St. Louis | 2 | 0 |
| Burt Shotton, Brooklyn | 1 | 0 |
| Billy Southworth, St. Louis | 1 | 2 |
| Chuck Tanner, Pittsburgh | 1 | 0 |
| Bill Terry, New York | 1 | 2 |
| Bobby Valentine, New York | 0 | 1 |
| Dick Williams, San Diego | 1 | 0 |

**Total number of managers: 41**

## COMBINED RECORDS FOR BOTH LEAGUES

| | Games | |
|---|---|---|
| Manager | W | L |
| Sparky Anderson, Cincinnati NL, Detroit AL | 3 | 2 |
| Tony La Russa, Oakland AL, St. Louis NL | 3 | 1 |
| Alvin Dark, San Francisco NL, Oakland AL | 1 | 1 |
| Dick Williams, Boston AL , Oakland AL, California AL, San Diego NL | 1 | 3 |

**Total number of managers: 4**

# SEASON BY SEASON RECAPS

Robinson

Mickey Mantle

## 1876

### FINAL STANDINGS

**National League**

| Team | W | L | Pct. | GB |
|---|---|---|---|---|
| Chicago | 52 | 14 | .788 | ... |
| St. Louis | 45 | 19 | .703 | 6 |
| Hartford | 47 | 21 | .691 | 6 |
| Boston | 39 | 31 | .557 | 15 |
| Louisville | 30 | 36 | .455 | 22 |
| New York | 21 | 35 | .375 | 26 |
| Philadelphia | 14 | 45 | .237 | 34.5 |
| Cincinnati | 9 | 56 | .138 | 42.5 |

### SIGNIFICANT EVENTS

■ William Hulbert, president of the National Association's Chicago franchise, presided over a February meeting that signaled the official beginning of a new National League. Morgan Bulkeley was selected as the new circuit's first president.

■ The New York Mutuals, following the lead of the Philadelphia Athletics, announced they would not make their season-ending Western trip, forcing cancellation of a major chunk of the N.L.'s September schedule.

■ During a December meeting in Cleveland, the Athletics and Mutuals were expelled from the N.L. lineup and William Hulbert was elected president.

### MEMORABLE MOMENTS

■ Boston 6, Philadelphia 5 in the first N.L. game. Jim O'Rourke entered the record books as the first player to get a hit in the April 22 battle at Athletic Park.

■ Chicago's Ross Barnes became the first N.L. player to hit a home run—an inside-the-park drive in a game at Cincinnati.

■ St. Louis' George Bradley pitched the first no-hitter in N.L. history, defeating Hartford, 2-0.

■ Hartford 14-8, Cincinnati 4-1 in baseball's first doubleheader.

■ Chicago clinched the N.L.'s first pennant with a victory over Hartford.

### LEADERS

**BA:** Ross Barnes, Chi., .403.
**Runs:** Ross Barnes, Chi., 126.
**Hits:** Ross Barnes, Chi., 138.
**TB:** Ross Barnes, Chi., 190.
**HR:** George Hall, Phil., 5.
**RBI:** Deacon White, Chi., 60.
**Wins:** Al Spalding, Chi., 47.
**ERA:** George Bradley, St.L., 1.23.
**CG:** Jim Devlin, Lou., 66.
**IP:** Jim Devlin, Lou., 622.
**SO:** Jim Devlin, Lou., 122.

**20-game winners**

Al Spalding, Chi., 47-12
George Bradley, St.L., 45-19
Tommy Bond, Hart., 31-13
Jim Devlin, Lou., 30-35
Bobby Mathews, N.Y., 21-34

### THE RULES

■ The new National League adopted a detailed rule book that included these interesting variations to the rules we use today:

■ The Strike Zone: The batter, upon stepping into position, had to call for a high or low pitch and the umpire notified the pitcher to deliver the ball as requested, making his calls accordingly.

■ The Strikeout: When a batter with two strikes failed to swing at the next good pitch, the umpire warned him by calling "good ball." If the batter swung and missed or failed to swing at the next "good ball", the umpire called "three strikes" and the batter was expected to run to first as if he had hit a fair ball.

■ Substitutions: No player could be replaced after the fourth inning, except those giving way temporarily for a pinch runner.

■ Batter/Position: When batters stepped outside the box while striking at the ball, the umpire would call "foul balk and out," allowing all runners to return to their bases.

■ Pitchers threw underhanded from a box with a front line that was 45 feet from the center of home base.

## 1877

### FINAL STANDINGS

**National League**

| Team | W | L | Pct. | GB |
|---|---|---|---|---|
| Boston | 42 | 18 | .700 | ... |
| Louisville | 35 | 25 | .583 | 7 |
| Hartford | 31 | 27 | .534 | 10 |
| St. Louis | 28 | 32 | .467 | 14 |
| Chicago | 26 | 33 | .441 | 15.5 |
| Cincinnati | 15 | 42 | .263 | 25.5 |

### SIGNIFICANT EVENTS

■ The Hartford club announced in March that it would play its 1877 "home games" in Brooklyn while retaining its base of Hartford.

■ Without enough money to finance a mid-season trip, the Cincinnati club disbanded. It was reorganized three days later under new ownership.

■ The Louisville team expelled players George Hall, Jim Devlin, Al Nichols and Bill Craver for fixing games, a move that later would be supported by league officials.

■ At its December meeting, the N.L. dropped franchises in Hartford and St. Louis and admitted teams in Indianapolis and Milwaukee.

### MEMORABLE MOMENTS

■ Boston and Hartford opened the N.L.'s second season with an 11-inning 1-1 tie at Brooklyn.

■ Boston clinched the N.L. pennant with a victory over Hartford.

### LEADERS

**BA:** Deacon White, Bos., .387.
**Runs:** Jim O'Rourke, Bos., 68.
**Hits:** Deacon White, Bos., 103.
**TB:** Deacon White, Bos., 145.
**HR:** Lip Pike, Cin., 4.
**RBI:** Deacon White, Bos., 49.
**Wins:** Tommy Bond, Bos., 40.
**ERA:** Tommy Bond, Bos., 2.11.
**CG:** Jim Devlin, Lou., 61.
**IP:** Jim Devlin, Lou., 559.
**SO:** Tommy Bond, Bos., 170.

**20-game winners**

Tommy Bond, Bos., 40-17
Jim Devlin, Lou., 35-25
Terry Larkin, Hart., 29-25

### MAJOR RULES CHANGES

■ Any batted ball that bounced into foul territory before passing first or third base became a "foul" ball instead of a "fair" ball.

■ Home base was repositioned entirely in fair territory, two sides laying flush with the foul lines. The 17-inch move forward forced a corresponding move back of the pitcher's box.

■ The batter's box was changed to 6 feet in length—3 feet in front and 3 feet in back of the home-base line.

■ The size of bases was enlarged to 15 square inches, with their sides positioned parallel to the base lines.

■ An at-bat was not charged when a batter drew a base on balls.

## 1878

### FINAL STANDINGS

**National League**

| Team | W | L | Pct. | GB |
|---|---|---|---|---|
| Boston | 41 | 19 | .683 | ... |
| Cincinnati | 37 | 23 | .617 | 4 |
| Providence | 33 | 27 | .550 | 8 |
| Chicago | 30 | 30 | .500 | 11 |
| Indianapolis | 24 | 36 | .400 | 17 |
| Milwaukee | 15 | 45 | .250 | 26 |

### SIGNIFICANT EVENTS

■ The N.L. increased its membership to seven with the addition of the Grays, a new franchise in Providence, R.I., but the field was reduced back to six when Louisville, unable to put together a competitive roster, resigned from the league.

■ At its winter meetings, the N.L. admitted new members Syracuse, Buffalo and Cleveland while dropping Indianapolis and Milwaukee.

### MEMORABLE MOMENTS

■ Defending-champion Boston spoiled the Major League debut of the Grays, 1-0, in an opening day game at Providence's new Messer Street Park.

■ Tommy Bond defeated Providence for his 40th victory and brought Boston within range of its second consecutive pennant.

### LEADERS

**BA:** Abner Dalrymple, Mil., .354.
**Runs:** Dick Higham, Pro., 60.
**Hits:** Joe Start, Chi., 100.
**TB:** Paul Hines, Pro.; Joe Start, Chi.; Tom York, Pro., 125.
**HR:** Paul Hines, Pro., 4.
**RBI:** Paul Hines, Pro., 50.
**Wins:** Tommy Bond, Bos., 40.
**ERA:** Monte Ward, Pro., 1.51.
**CG:** Tommy Bond, Bos., 57.
**IP:** Tommy Bond, Bos., 532.2.
**SO:** Tommy Bond, Bos., 182.

**20-game winners**

Tommy Bond, Bos., 40-19
Will White, Cin., 30-21
Terry Larkin, Chi. 29-26
Monte Ward, Pro., 22-13

### MAJOR RULES CHANGES

■ Captains were required to position their players and after one at-bat, the batting order could no longer be changed.

■ Pinch runners were not allowed except in cases of illness or injury. The emergency substitute could enter the game only after the original player had reached base.

## 1879

### FINAL STANDINGS

**National League**

| Team | W | L | Pct. | GB |
|---|---|---|---|---|
| Providence | 59 | 25 | .702 | ... |
| Boston | 54 | 30 | .643 | 5 |
| Buffalo | 46 | 32 | .590 | 10 |
| Chicago | 46 | 33 | .582 | 10.5 |
| Cincinnati | 43 | 37 | .538 | 14 |
| Cleveland | 27 | 55 | .329 | 31 |
| Syracuse | 22 | 48 | .314 | 30 |
| Troy | 19 | 56 | .253 | 35.5 |

### SIGNIFICANT EVENTS

■ The N.L. beefed up its preseason roster by admitting a new Troy franchise.

■ The Syracuse Stars, facing bankruptcy in mid-September, resigned from the N.L., leaving the league with an incomplete schedule.

■ The financially strapped Cincinnati club ended the season and folded operation, refusing to pay its players their final month's salary.

■ A new Cincinnati club gained quick N.L. acceptance during the annual winter meetings.

### MEMORABLE MOMENTS

■ John Montgomery Ward's streak of having pitched every inning of 73 consecutive Providence games ended in mid-July when he was relieved in the fourth inning of a 9-0 loss to Cincinnati.

■ The Providence Grays scored a ninth-inning run and claimed a pennant-clinching victory over Boston.

■ Cincinnati pitcher Will White completed the season with 75 complete games and 680 innings—still-standing Major League records.

### LEADERS

**BA:** Cap Anson, Chi., .317.
**Runs:** Charley Jones, Bos., 85.
**Hits:** Paul Hines, Pro., 146.
**TB:** Paul Hines, Pro., 197.
**HR:** Charley Jones, Bos., 9.
**RBI:** Charley Jones, Bos.; Jim O'Rourke, Bos., 62.
**Wins:** Monte Ward, Pro., 47.
**ERA:** Tommy Bond, Bos., 1.96.
**CG:** Will White, Cin., 75.
**IP:** Will White, Cin., 680.
**SO:** Monte Ward, Pro., 239.

**20-game winners**

Monte Ward, Pro., 47-19
Tommy Bond, Bos., 43-19
Will White, Cin., 43-31
Pud Galvin, Buf., 37-27
Terry Larkin, Chi., 31-23
Jim McCormick, Cle., 20-40

### MAJOR RULES CHANGES

■ The size of the pitcher's box was enlarged to 4-by-6 feet.

■ A batter was declared out after three strikes if the pitch was caught before touching the ground.

■ Any pitcher who, in the opinion of the umpire, intentionally hit a batter with a pitch was fined from $10 to $50.

■ The "Spalding League Ball" was adopted as the official ball.

# 1880

## FINAL STANDINGS

**National League**

| Team | W | L | Pct. | GB |
|---|---|---|---|---|
| Chicago | 67 | 17 | .798 | ... |
| Providence | 52 | 32 | .619 | 15 |
| Cleveland | 47 | 37 | .560 | 20 |
| Troy | 41 | 42 | .494 | 25.5 |
| Worcester | 40 | 43 | .482 | 26.5 |
| Boston | 40 | 44 | .476 | 27 |
| Buffalo | 24 | 58 | .293 | 42 |
| Cincinnati | 21 | 59 | .263 | 44 |

## SIGNIFICANT EVENTS

- The preseason addition of a team in Worcester brought the N.L. field back to eight.
- After kicking Cincinnati out of the league for rules violations, the N.L. admitted a new franchise from Detroit.

## MEMORABLE MOMENTS

- A Major League first—Worcester's Lee Richmond was perfect in a 1-0 victory over Cleveland.
- Providence ace John Montgomery Ward matched the perfect-game feat of Lee Richmond five days earlier, retiring all 27 Buffalo batters he faced in a 5-0 victory.
- Fred Dunlap's ninth-inning home run broke a scoreless tie and gave Cleveland a victory over Chicago, snapping the White Stockings' record 21-game winning streak.
- Chicago completed its season with a 67-17 record and a 15-game bulge over second-place Providence.

## LEADERS

**BA:** George Gore, Chi., .360.
**Runs:** Abner Dalrymple, Chi., 91.
**Hits:** Abner Dalrymple, Chi., 126.
**TB:** Abner Dalrymple, Chi., 175.
**HR:** Jim O'Rourke, Bos.; Harry Stovey, Wor., 6.
**RBI:** Cap Anson, Chi., 74.
**Wins:** Jim McCormick, Cle., 45.
**ERA:** Tim Keefe, Troy, 0.86.
**CG:** Jim McCormick, Cle., 72.
**IP:** Jim McCormick, Cle., 657.2.
**SO:** Larry Corcoran, Chi., 268.

**20-game winners**

Jim McCormick, Cle., 45-28
Larry Corcoran, Chi., 43-14
Monte Ward, Pro., 39-24
Mickey Welch, Troy, 34-30
Lee Richmond, Wor., 32-32
Tommy Bond, Bos., 26-29
Fred Goldsmith, Chi., 21-3
Pud Galvin, Buf., 20-35

## MAJOR RULES CHANGES

- A walk was awarded after eight balls instead of nine.
- A runner was declared out if hit by a batted ball, and no run was allowed to score on the play.
- The batter was required to run for first base immediately after "strike three" was called by the umpire.

# 1881

## FINAL STANDINGS

**National League**

| Team | W | L | Pct. | GB |
|---|---|---|---|---|
| Chicago | 56 | 28 | .667 | ... |
| Providence | 47 | 37 | .560 | 9 |
| Buffalo | 45 | 38 | .542 | 10.5 |
| Detroit | 41 | 43 | .488 | 15 |
| Troy | 39 | 45 | .464 | 17 |
| Boston | 38 | 45 | .458 | 17.5 |
| Cleveland | 36 | 48 | .429 | 20 |
| Worcester | 32 | 50 | .390 | 23 |

## SIGNIFICANT EVENTS

- One month after the 1881 season had ended, officials announced the formation of the American Association, a rival Major League with franchises in St. Louis, Cincinnati, Louisville, Philadelphia, Pittsburgh and Brooklyn.
- American Association officials voted to ignore N.L. rules against Sunday games, liquor sales and 25-cent ticket prices. They also announced their decision not to abide by the N.L.'s restrictive reserve clause in player contracts.

## MEMORABLE MOMENTS

- Troy's Roger Connor hit the first grand slam in N.L. history—a bottom-of-the-ninth blow that handed Worcester an 8-7 defeat.
- Chicago clinched its second straight pennant with a victory over Boston and White Stockings star Cap Anson put the finishing touches on his league-leading .399 average.

## LEADERS

**BA:** Cap Anson, Chi., .399.
**Runs:** George Gore, Chi., 86.
**Hits:** Cap Anson, Chi., 137.
**TB:** Cap Anson, Chi., 175.
**HR:** Dan Brouthers, Buf., 8.
**RBI:** Cap Anson, Chi., 82.
**Wins:** Larry Corcoran, Chi.; Jim Whitney, Bos., 31.
**ERA:** Stump Weidman, Det., 1.80.
**CG:** Jim McCormick, Cle.; Jim Whitney, Bos., 57.
**IP:** Jim Whitney, Bos., 552.1.
**SO:** George Derby, Det., 212.

**20-game winners**

Larry Corcoran, Chi., 31-14
Jim Whitney, Bos., 31-33
George Derby, Det., 29-26
Pud Galvin, Buf., 28-24
Jim McCormick, Cle., 26-30
Hoss Radbourn, Pro., 25-11
Lee Richmond, Wor., 25-26
Fred Goldsmith, Chi., 24-13
Mickey Welch, Troy, 21-18

## MAJOR RULES CHANGES

- The front line of the pitcher's box was moved from 45 to 50 feet from the center of home base.
- A batter was awarded first base after seven balls.
- No substitutes were permitted except in the cases of illness or injury.
- Umpires no longer gave players the "good ball" warning on called third strikes.

# 1882

## FINAL STANDINGS

**American Association**

| Team | W | L | Pct. | GB |
|---|---|---|---|---|
| Cincinnati | 55 | 25 | .688 | ... |
| Philadelphia | 41 | 34 | .547 | 11.5 |
| Louisville | 42 | 38 | .525 | 13 |
| Pittsburgh | 39 | 39 | .500 | 15 |
| St. Louis | 37 | 43 | .463 | 18 |
| Baltimore | 19 | 54 | .260 | 32.5 |

## SIGNIFICANT EVENTS

- After completing its first season as a six-team circuit, the American Association added franchises in Columbus and New York.
- A baseball first: The Association formed the first permanent staff of umpires.

## MEMORABLE MOMENTS

- Opening day for the new American Association: St. Louis 9, Louisville 7; Philadelphia 10, Baltimore 7; Allegheny 10, Cincinnati 9.
- Louisville ace Tony Mullane recorded the league's first no-hitter, beating the Red Stockings 2-0 at Cincinnati.
- Cincinnati clinched the first A.A. pennant with a 6-1 mid-September victory over Louisville as the second-place Athletics dropped a game at Pittsburgh.
- In the first post-season matchup of Major League champions, the Red Stockings split a two-game series with N.L. pennant winner Chicago.

## LEADERS

**BA:** Pete Browning, Lou., .378.
**Runs:** Ed Swartwood, Pit., 86.
**Hits:** Hick Carpenter, Cin., 120.
**TB:** Ed Swartwood, Pit., 159.
**HR:** Oscar Walker, St.L., 7.
**Wins:** Will White, Cin., 40.
**ERA:** Denny Driscoll, Pit., 1.21.
**CG:** Will White, Cin., 52.
**IP:** Will White, Cin., 480.
**SO:** Tony Mullane, Lou., 170.

**20-game winners**

Will White, Cin., 40-12
Tony Mullane, Lou., 30-24
Sam Weaver, Phil., 26-15
George McGinnis, St.L., 25-18
Harry Salisbury, Pit., 20-18

## THE RULES

- The new American Association began its first season with several modifications to the existing rules book. Among the variations:
- Sunday games were allowed.
- Teams could charge 25 cents for admission rather than the N.L. price of 50 cents.
- Liquor could be sold at the ballparks.
- Pitchers judged to be intentionally throwing at batters were not subject to immediate fines.

## FINAL STANDINGS

**National League**

| Team | W | L | Pct. | GB |
|---|---|---|---|---|
| Chicago | 55 | 29 | .655 | ... |
| Providence | 52 | 32 | .619 | 3 |
| Boston | 45 | 39 | .536 | 10 |
| Buffalo | 45 | 39 | .536 | 10 |
| Cleveland | 42 | 40 | .512 | 12 |
| Detroit | 42 | 41 | .506 | 12.5 |
| Troy | 35 | 48 | .422 | 19.5 |
| Worcester | 18 | 66 | .214 | 37 |

## SIGNIFICANT EVENTS

- When N.L. President William Hulbert died of a heart attack in April, Boston team president A.H. Soden was named as his replacement.
- At the winter meetings, N.L. officials replaced the Troy and Worcester franchises with teams from New York and Philadelphia, keeping the league roster at eight.

## MEMORABLE MOMENTS

- Chicago 35, Cleveland 4: a record rout in which seven White Stockings got four or more hits.
- Chicago ace Larry Corcoran pitched his second career no-hitter, beating Worcester, 5-0.
- Chicago finished with a 55-29 record and claimed its third straight N.L. pennant by three games over Providence.

## LEADERS

**BA:** Dan Brouthers, Buf., .368.
**Runs:** George Gore, Chi., 99.
**Hits:** Dan Brouthers, Buf., 129.
**TB:** Dan Brouthers, Buf., 192.
**HR:** George Wood, Det., 7.
**RBI:** Cap Anson, Chi., 83.
**Wins:** Jim McCormick, Cle., 36.
**ERA:** Larry Corcoran, Chi., 1.95.
**CG:** Jim McCormick, Cle., 65.
**IP:** Jim McCormick, Cle., 595.2.
**SO:** Hoss Radbourn, Pro., 201.

**20-game winners**

Jim McCormick, Cle., 36-30
Hoss Radbourn, Pro., 33-20
Fred Goldsmith, Chi., 28-17
Pud Galvin, Buf., 28-23
Larry Corcoran, Chi., 27-12
George Weidman, Det., 25-20
Jim Whitney, Bos., 24-21

## MAJOR RULES CHANGES

- Umpires could call for a new ball at the end of even innings, provided the old ball was unfit for fair use.
- The home team was required to provide a players' bench, 12 feet in length and fastened to the ground. Racks that held at least 20 bats became mandatory.
- A baserunner obstructing a player attempting to field a batted ball was called out for interference.
- Spectators caught hissing or hooting at the umpire were ejected from the park.

# 1883

## FINAL STANDINGS

**American Association**

| Team | W | L | Pct. | GB |
|---|---|---|---|---|
| Philadelphia | 66 | 32 | .673 | ... |
| St. Louis | 65 | 33 | .663 | 1 |
| Cincinnati | 61 | 37 | .622 | 5 |
| New York | 54 | 42 | .563 | 11 |
| Louisville | 52 | 45 | .536 | 13.5 |
| Columbus | 32 | 65 | .330 | 33.5 |
| Pittsburgh | 31 | 67 | .316 | 35 |
| Baltimore | 28 | 68 | .292 | 37 |

## SIGNIFICANT EVENTS

■ In a significant February meeting, baseball officials drafted the first National Agreement, ensuring peaceful co-existence and respect for player contracts between the N.L. and American Association. Both leagues embraced the controversial reserve clause.

■ The Association announced post-season plans to expand to 12 teams with new franchises in Brooklyn, Washington, Indianapolis and Toledo.

## MEMORABLE MOMENTS

■ New York's Tim Keefe celebrated Independence Day by winning both ends of a doubleheader against Columbus. Keefe allowed only three total hits.

■ The Athletics posted a late-September victory over Louisville and claimed the American Association's second pennant.

## LEADERS

**BA:** Ed Swartwood, Pit., .357.
**Runs:** Harry Stovey, Phil., 110.
**Hits:** Ed Swartwood, Pit., 147.
**TB:** Harry Stovey, Phil., 213.
**HR:** Harry Stovey, Phil., 14.
**Wins:** Will White, Cin., 43.
**ERA:** Will White, Cin., 2.09.
**CG:** Tim Keefe, N.Y., 68.
**IP:** Tim Keefe, N.Y., 619.
**SO:** Tim Keefe, N.Y., 359.

**20-game winners**

Will White, Cin., 43-22
Tim Keefe, N.Y., 41-27
Tony Mullane, St.L., 35-15
Bobby Mathews, Phil., 30-13
George McGinnis, St.L., 28-16
Sam Weaver, Lou., 26-22
Guy Hecker, Lou., 26-23
Frank Mountain, Col., 26-33

## MAJOR RULES CHANGES

■ Pitchers were allowed to deliver the ball from a shoulder-length position instead of the former below-the-waist position.

■ A runner touching and overrunning first base put himself at risk of being tagged out if he turned to his left while returning to the bag.

■ Pinch runners were allowed in cases of illness and injury.

## FINAL STANDINGS

**National League**

| Team | W | L | Pct. | GB |
|---|---|---|---|---|
| Boston | 63 | 35 | .643 | ... |
| Chicago | 59 | 39 | .602 | 4 |
| Providence | 58 | 40 | .592 | 5 |
| Cleveland | 55 | 42 | .567 | 7.5 |
| Buffalo | 52 | 45 | .536 | 10.5 |
| New York | 46 | 50 | .479 | 16 |
| Detroit | 40 | 58 | .408 | 23 |
| Philadelphia | 17 | 81 | .173 | 46 |

## SIGNIFICANT EVENTS

■ Peace prevails: The N.L. and American Association signed a new National Agreement, ensuring respect for player contracts under the controversial reserve system.

## MEMORABLE MOMENTS

■ Philadelphia 28, Providence 0—the most lopsided shutout in Major League history.

■ The White Stockings exploded for a record 18 runs in the seventh inning of a victory over Detroit.

■ Boston broke Chicago's three-year stranglehold on the N.L. pennant with a clinching victory over Cleveland.

## LEADERS

**BA:** Dan Brouthers, Buf., .374.
**Runs:** Joe Hornung, Bos., 107.
**Hits:** Dan Brouthers, Buf., 159.
**TB:** Dan Brouthers, Buf., 243.
**HR:** Buck Ewing, N.Y., 10.
**RBI:** Dan Brouthers, Buf., 97.
**Wins:** Hoss Radbourn, Pro., 48.
**ERA:** Jim McCormick, Cle., 1.84.
**CG:** Pud Galvin, Buf., 72.
**IP:** Pud Galvin, Buf., 656.1.
**SO:** Jim Whitney, Bos., 345.

**20-game winners**

Hoss Radbourn, Pro., 48-25
Pud Galvin, Buf., 46-29
Jim Whitney, Bos., 37-21
Larry Corcoran, Chi., 34-20
Jim McCormick, Cle., 28-12
Charlie Buffinton, Bos., 25-14
Fred Goldsmith, Chi., 25-19
Mickey Welch, N.Y., 25-23
Hugh Daily, Cle., 23-19

## MAJOR RULES CHANGES

■ Pitchers working within the confines of the box and facing the batter could deliver the ball with more forceful motion. The ball, on delivery, had to pass below the line of the pitcher's shoulder instead of below his waist.

■ A batted ball caught in foul territory was declared an out. Previously, balls caught on one bounce in foul territory were outs.

■ A player batting out of order was declared out.

■ Umpires became salaried employees.

# 1884

## FINAL STANDINGS

**Union Association**

| Team | W | L | Pct. | GB |
|---|---|---|---|---|
| St. Louis | 94 | 19 | .832 | ... |
| Milwaukee | 8 | 4 | .667 | 35.5 |
| Cincinnati | 69 | 36 | .657 | 21 |
| Baltimore | 58 | 47 | .552 | 32 |
| Boston | 58 | 51 | .532 | 34 |
| Chicago-Pitt. | 41 | 50 | .451 | 42 |
| Washington | 47 | 65 | .420 | 46.5 |
| Philadelphia | 21 | 46 | .313 | 50 |
| St. Paul | 2 | 6 | .250 | 39.5 |
| Altoona | 6 | 19 | .240 | 44 |
| Kansas City | 16 | 63 | .203 | 61 |
| Wilmington | 2 | 16 | .111 | 44.5 |

## SIGNIFICANT EVENTS

■ The new Union Association, organized the previous September as a third Major League, added a Boston team to its roster while preparing for its first season.

■ U.A. casualties: Altoona (6-19) ceased operations in May, Philadelphia (21-46) disbanded in August and Chicago transferred operations in late August to Pittsburgh. Wilmington and Pittsburgh later were replaced by Milwaukee and Omaha—a franchise that lasted eight days and was replaced by St. Paul.

■ Only five teams attended the U.A.'s winter meetings, setting the stage for the league to disband in January.

## MEMORABLE MOMENTS

■ Boston defeated St. Louis and ended the Maroons' 20-game winning streak.

■ Boston's Fred Shaw held St. Louis to one hit and struck out 18, but he still lost a 1-0 decision to the pennant-bound Maroons.

## LEADERS

**BA:** Fred Dunlap, St.L., .412.
**Runs:** Fred Dunlap, St.L., 160.
**Hits:** Fred Dunlap, St.L., 185.
**TB:** Fred Dunlap, St.L., 279.
**HR:** Fred Dunlap, St.L., 13.
**Wins:** Bill Sweeney, Bal., 40.
**ERA:** Jim McCormick, Cin., 1.54.
**CG:** Bill Sweeney, Bal., 58.
**IP:** Bill Sweeney, Bal., 538.
**SO:** Hugh Daily, CP-Wash., 483.

**20-game winners**

Bill Sweeney, Bal., 40-21
Hugh Daily, C-W-P, 28-28
Billy Taylor, St.L., 25-4
George Bradley, Cin., 25-15
Charlie Sweeney, St.L., 24-7
Dick Burns, Cin., 23-15
Bill Wise, Wash., 23-18
Jim McCormick, Cin., 21-3
Fred Shaw, Bos., 21-15

## THE RULES

■ The Union Association, in its only Major League season, adopted the American Association rules book, which still included the shoulder-length restriction on pitching deliveries and seven-ball walks. The U.A., however, did adopt the N.L. rule on foul flies. The A.A.'s new hit-by-pitch rule was not adopted by the U.A.

## FINAL STANDINGS

**American Association**

| Team | W | L | Pct. | GB |
|---|---|---|---|---|
| New York | 75 | 32 | .701 | ... |
| Columbus | 69 | 39 | .639 | 6.5 |
| Louisville | 68 | 40 | .630 | 7.5 |
| St. Louis | 67 | 40 | .626 | 8 |
| Cincinnati | 68 | 41 | .624 | 8 |
| Baltimore | 63 | 43 | .594 | 11.5 |
| Philadelphia | 61 | 46 | .570 | 14 |
| Toledo | 46 | 58 | .442 | 27.5 |
| Brooklyn | 40 | 64 | .385 | 33.5 |
| Richmond | 12 | 30 | .286 | 30.5 |
| Pittsburgh | 30 | 78 | .278 | 45.5 |
| Indianapolis | 29 | 78 | .271 | 46 |
| Washington | 12 | 51 | .190 | 41 |

## SIGNIFICANT EVENTS

■ Toledo's Fleetwood Walker became the Major League's first black player when he went 0-for-3 in an opening day loss to Louisville.

■ Columbus, a second-place finisher in its only season, sold its players and dropped out of the league.

## MEMORABLE MOMENTS

■ Louisville ace Guy Hecker, en route to Association season-high totals of 52 wins and 72 complete games, pitched both ends of a Fourth of July doubleheader sweep of Brooklyn.

■ The Metropolitans captured their first A.A. pennant with a 4-1 victory over Columbus.

■ The N.L.'s Providence Grays posted a 6-0 victory over New York in a post-season matchup of pennant winners. The Grays would go on to win three straight games and an unofficial world championship.

## LEADERS

**BA:** Dude Esterbrook, N.Y., .314.
**Runs:** Harry Stovey, Phil., 124.
**Hits:** Dave Orr, N.Y., 162.
**TB:** Dave Orr, N.Y.; John Reilly, Cin., 247.
**HR:** John Reilly, Cin., 11.
**Wins:** Guy Hecker, Lou., 52.
**ERA:** Guy Hecker, Lou., 1.80.
**CG:** Guy Hecker, Lou., 72.
**IP:** Guy Hecker, Lou., 670.2.
**SO:** Guy Hecker, Lou., 385.

**20-game winners**

Guy Hecker, Lou., 52-20
Jack Lynch, N.Y., 37-15
Tim Keefe, N.Y., 37-17
Tony Mullane, Tol., 36-26
Ed Morris, Col., 34-13
Will White, Cin., 34-18
Bob Emslie, Bal., 32-17
Bobby Mathews, Phil., 30-18
Hardie Henderson, Bal., 27-23
George McGinnis, St.L., 24-16
Frank Mountain, Col., 23-17

## MAJOR RULES CHANGES

■ Any batter hit by a pitch after trying to avoid the ball was awarded first base.

■ Each team was allowed an extra person on the field to take charge of bats—the equivalent of a modern-day bat boy.

# 1884

## FINAL STANDINGS

**National League**

| Team | W | L | Pct. | GB |
|---|---|---|---|---|
| Providence | 84 | 28 | .750 | ... |
| Boston | 73 | 38 | .658 | 10.5 |
| Buffalo | 64 | 47 | .577 | 19.5 |
| Chicago | 62 | 50 | .554 | 22 |
| New York | 62 | 50 | .554 | 22 |
| Philadelphia | 39 | 73 | .348 | 45 |
| Cleveland | 35 | 77 | .313 | 49 |
| Detroit | 28 | 84 | .250 | 56 |

## SIGNIFICANT EVENTS

■ N.L. officials legalized overhand pitching, stipulating that pitchers must keep both feet on the ground through their delivery.

## MEMORABLE MOMENTS

■ Providence pitcher Charlie Sweeney struck out a record 19 Boston batters in a 2-1 victory over the Red Stockings.

■ Chicago ace Larry Corcoran pitched his record third career no-hitter, ending a 10-game Providence winning streak with a 6-0 victory.

■ New York's Mickey Welch opened a game against Philadelphia with a record nine consecutive strikeouts.

■ September 11: Hoss Radbourn, who would finish the season with a record 59 wins, pitched pennant-bound Providence to a victory over Cleveland—the Grays' 20th consecutive triumph.

■ Providence completed a three-game sweep of the American Association's New York Metropolitans with an 12-2 victory, punctuating baseball's second post-season matchup between pennant winners.

## LEADERS

**BA:** Jim O'Rourke, Buf., .347.
**Runs:** King Kelly, Chi., 120.
**Hits:** Jim O'Rourke, Buf.; Ezra Sutton, Bos., 162.
**TB:** Abner Dalrymple, Chi., 263.
**HR:** Ned Williamson, Chi., 27.
**RBI:** Cap Anson, Chi., 102.
**Wins:** Hoss Radbourn, Pro., 59.
**ERA:** Hoss Radbourn, Pro., 1.38.
**CG:** Hoss Radbourn, Pro., 73.
**IP:** Hoss Radbourn, Pro., 678.2.
**SO:** Hoss Radbourn, Pro., 441.

**20-game winners**

Hoss Radbourn, Pro., 59-12
Charlie Buffinton, Bos., 48-16
Pud Galvin, Buf., 46-22
Mickey Welch, N.Y., 39-21
Larry Corcoran, Chi., 35-23
Jim Whitney, Bos., 23-14
Charlie Ferguson, Phil., 21-25

## POST-SEASON PLAYOFF

(Providence N.L. 3, New York A.A. 0)

**Game 1**—Providence 6, New York 0

**Game 2**—Providence 3, New York 1

**Game 3**—Providence 12, New York 2 (6 innings, darkness)

## MAJOR RULES CHANGES

■ All restrictions against pitching deliveries were lifted, meaning pitchers could throw overhand for the first time.

■ Batters were awarded first base after six balls.

■ Any ball leaving the park was declared either fair or foul, depending on its position within the foul lines.

# 1885

## FINAL STANDINGS

**American Association**

| Team | W | L | Pct. | GB |
|---|---|---|---|---|
| St. Louis | 79 | 33 | .705 | ... |
| Cincinnati | 63 | 49 | .563 | 16 |
| Pittsburgh | 56 | 55 | .505 | 22.5 |
| Philadelphia | 55 | 57 | .491 | 24 |
| Louisville | 53 | 59 | .473 | 26 |
| Brooklyn | 53 | 59 | .473 | 26 |
| New York | 44 | 64 | .407 | 33 |
| Baltimore | 41 | 68 | .376 | 36.5 |

## SIGNIFICANT EVENTS

■ The reorganized American Association began play with teams located in St. Louis, Philadelphia, Cincinnati, Pittsburgh, Brooklyn, Louisville, New York and Baltimore.

## MEMORABLE MOMENTS

■ St. Louis jumped into first place with an early May victory over Philadelphia—a position the Browns would hold the remainder of the season.

■ Baltimore snapped St. Louis' A.A.-record 17-game winning streak with a 7-1 victory.

■ The Browns, refusing to acknowledge a controversial Game 2 forfeit loss to N.L.-champion Chicago, "claimed" status as baseball world champions after beating the White Stockings and knotting the post-season series at three games apiece.

## LEADERS

**BA:** Pete Browning, Lou., .362.
**Runs:** Harry Stovey, Phil., 130.
**Hits:** Pete Browning, Phil., 174.
**TB:** Pete Browning, Lou., 255.
**HR:** Harry Stovey, Phil., 13.
**Wins:** Bob Caruthers, St.L., 40.
**ERA:** Bob Caruthers, St.L., 2.07.
**CG:** Ed Morris, Pit., 63.
**IP:** Ed Morris, Pit., 581.
**SO:** Ed Morris, Pit., 298.

**20-game winners**

Bob Caruthers, St.L., 40-13
Ed Morris, Pit., 39-24
Dave Foutz, St.L., 33-14
Henry Porter, Brk., 33-21
Bobby Mathews, Phil., 30-17
Guy Hecker, Lou., 30-23
Hardie Henderson, Bal., 25-35
Jack Lynch, N.Y., 23-21
Larry McKeon, Cin., 20-13

## MAJOR RULES CHANGES

■ The one-bounce rule was dropped and fielders were required to catch foul balls on the fly to record an out.

■ Home-team captains were given the option of batting first or second.

■ The overhand delivery was permitted, bringing league pitchers in line with their N.L. counterparts.

■ Every team was required to wear a neat and attractive uniform.

## FINAL STANDINGS

**National League**

| Team | W | L | Pct. | GB |
|---|---|---|---|---|
| Chicago | 87 | 25 | .777 | ... |
| New York | 85 | 27 | .759 | 2 |
| Philadelphia | 56 | 54 | .509 | 30 |
| Providence | 53 | 57 | .482 | 33 |
| Boston | 46 | 66 | .411 | 41 |
| Detroit | 41 | 67 | .380 | 44 |
| Buffalo | 38 | 74 | .339 | 49 |
| St. Louis | 36 | 72 | .333 | 49 |

## SIGNIFICANT EVENTS

■ Providence ace Hoss Radbourn, the N.L.'s highest paid player, was suspended for poor pitching after a lopsided loss to New York.

■ The Washington Nationals were accepted into the league, replacing Providence.

## MEMORABLE MOMENTS

■ Philadelphia snapped Chicago's 18-game winning streak—the White Stockings' first loss at new West Side Park.

■ John Clarkson, en route to a Major League-high 53 wins, held Providence hitless in an 4-0 victory.

■ Game 2 of a post-season "World's Series" between Chicago and American Association-champion St. Louis ended in controversy when the Browns refused to continue the game in the sixth inning because of umpiring decisions. The White Stockings were declared forfeit winners.

■ The Browns defeated the White Stockings 13-4 in the championship finale, tying the series at 3-3. The Browns claimed victory, refusing to accept the forfeit decision.

## LEADERS

**BA:** Roger Connor, N.Y., .371.
**Runs:** King Kelly, Chi., 124.
**Hits:** Roger Connor, N.Y., 169.
**TB:** Roger Connor, N.Y., 225.
**HR:** Abner Dalrymple, Chi., 11.
**RBI:** Cap Anson, Chi., 108.
**Wins:** John Clarkson, Chi., 53.
**ERA:** Tim Keefe, N.Y., 1.58.
**CG:** John Clarkson, Chi., 68.
**IP:** John Clarkson, Chi., 623.
**SO:** John Clarkson, Chi., 308.

**20-game winners**

John Clarkson, Chi., 53-16
Mickey Welch, N.Y., 44-11
Tim Keefe, N.Y., 32-13
Hoss Radbourn, Pro., 28-21
Charlie Ferguson, Phil., 26-20
Ed Daily, Phil., 26-23
Fred Shaw, Pro., 23-26
Charlie Buffinton, Bos., 22-27
Jim McCormick, Pro.-Chi., 21-7

## POST-SEASON PLAYOFF

(Chicago N.L. 3, St. Louis A.A. 3; 1 tie)

**Game 1**—Chicago 5, St. Louis 5 (8 innings, darkness)

**Game 2**—Chicago awarded 5-4 forfeit victory

**Game 3**—St. Louis 7, Chicago 4

**Game 4**—St. Louis 3, Chicago 2

**Game 5**—Chicago 9, St. Louis 2 (7 innings, darkness)

**Game 6**—Chicago 9, St. Louis 2

**Game 7**—St. Louis 13, Chicago 4 (8 innings, darkness)

## MAJOR RULES CHANGES

■ The batter's box was resized to 4 feet wide by 6 feet long and moved a foot closer to home base.

■ Pitchers were required to keep both feet in contact with the ground during delivery. Batters were awarded first base after two "foul balks," a rule that was eliminated at midseason.

■ Players were permitted to use bats with one flat side.

■ Any ball leaving the park at a distance of less than 210 feet was declared an automatic double.

# 1886

## FINAL STANDINGS

**American Association**

| Team | W | L | Pct. | GB |
|---|---|---|---|---|
| St. Louis | 93 | 46 | .669 | ... |
| Pittsburgh | 80 | 57 | .584 | 12 |
| Brooklyn | 76 | 61 | .555 | 16 |
| Louisville | 66 | 70 | .485 | 25.5 |
| Cincinnati | 65 | 73 | .471 | 27.5 |
| Philadelphia | 63 | 72 | .467 | 28 |
| New York | 53 | 82 | .393 | 38 |
| Baltimore | 48 | 83 | .366 | 41 |

## SIGNIFICANT EVENTS

■ When Pittsburgh defected to the rival N.L. in November, the American Association filled the void with a new Cleveland franchise.

## MEMORABLE MOMENTS

■ Louisville pitcher Guy Hecker belted a record-tying three home runs and scored a Major League-record seven times in a victory over Brooklyn.

■ The St. Louis Browns posted a 4-3 victory over the N.L.'s Chicago White Stockings in Game 6 of the "World's Series," staking their undisputed claim as king of baseball.

## LEADERS

**BA:** Dave Orr, N.Y., .338.
**Runs:** Arlie Latham, St.L., 152.
**Hits:** Dave Orr, N.Y., 193.
**TB:** Dave Orr, N.Y., 301.
**HR:** Bid McPhee, Cin., 8.
**SB:** Harry Stovey, Phil., 68.
**Wins:** Dave Foutz, St.L.; Ed Morris, Pit., 41.
**ERA:** Dave Foutz, St.L., 2.11.
**CG:** Matt Kilroy, Bal.; Toad Ramsey, Lou., 66.
**IP:** Toad Ramsey, Lou., 588.2.
**SO:** Matt Kilroy, Bal., 513.

**20-game winners**

Dave Foutz, St.L., 41-16
Ed Morris, Pit., 41-20
Tom Ramsey, Lou., 38-27
Tony Mullane, Cin., 33-27
Bob Caruthers, St.L., 30-14
Pud Galvin, Pit., 29-21
Matt Kilroy, Bal., 29-34
Henry Porter, Brk., 27-19
Guy Hecker, Lou., 26-23
Al Atkinson, Phil., 25-17
Jack Lynch, N.Y., 20-30

## MAJOR RULES CHANGES

■ A 4-by-1 foot smooth stone slab was placed at the front end of the pitcher's box, helping umpires determine if the pitcher had stepped beyond the front line.

■ The number of balls required for a walk was decreased from seven to six.

■ The A.A. adopted the reshaped 6-by-3 foot batter's box and 4-by-7 foot pitcher's box.

■ Stolen bases were credited for any base a runner was able to gain on his own volition, such as a first-to-third dash on a single.

# 1886

## FINAL STANDINGS

**National League**

| Team | W | L | Pct. | GB |
|---|---|---|---|---|
| Chicago | 90 | 34 | .726 | ... |
| Detroit | 87 | 36 | .707 | 2.5 |
| New York | 75 | 44 | .630 | 12.5 |
| Philadelphia | 71 | 43 | .623 | 14 |
| Boston | 56 | 61 | .479 | 30.5 |
| St. Louis | 43 | 79 | .352 | 46 |
| Kansas City | 30 | 91 | .248 | 58.5 |
| Washington | 28 | 92 | .233 | 60 |

## SIGNIFICANT EVENTS

■ The N.L. increased its preseason roster to eight with the addition of a Kansas City team on a one-year trial basis.

■ The N.L. adopted the stolen base as an official statistic and reshaped the pitcher's box to 4-by-7 feet.

■ New rules: 4 strikes for an out; 5 balls for a walk; a standardized strike zone from the knees to the shoulders, and a 55½-foot pitching distance.

■ Pittsburgh made a November jump from the American Association to the N.L., replacing Kansas City.

## MEMORABLE MOMENTS

■ The White Stockings clinched another N.L. pennant with a final-day victory over Boston. The final lead was 2½ games over Detroit.

■ Chicago dropped a 4-3 decision to the American Association-champion Browns and lost the best-of-seven "World's Series" in six games.

## LEADERS

**BA:** King Kelly, Chi., .388.
**Runs:** King Kelly, Chi., 155.
**Hits:** Hardy Richardson, Det., 189.
**TB:** Dan Brouthers, Det., 284.
**HR:** Dan Brouthers, Det.;
Hardy Richardson, Det., 11.
**RBI:** Cap Anson, Chi., 147.
**SB:** Ed Andrews, Phil., 56.
**Wins:** Lady Baldwin, Det.; Tim Keefe, N.Y., 42.
**ERA:** Henry Boyle, St.L., 1.76.
**CG:** Tim Keefe, N.Y., 62.
**IP:** Tim Keefe, N.Y., 535.
**SO:** Lady Baldwin, Det., 323.

**20-game winners**

Lady Baldwin, Det., 42-13
Tim Keefe, N.Y., 42-20
John Clarkson, Chi., 36-17]
Mickey Welch, N.Y., 33-22
Charlie Ferguson, Phil., 30-9
Charlie Getzien, Det., 30-11
Jim McCormick, Chi., 31-11
Hoss Radbourn, Bos., 27-31
Dan Casey, Phil., 24-18
Jocko Flynn, Chi., 23-6
Bill Stemmeyer, Bos., 22-18

## POST-SEASON PLAYOFF

(St. Louis A.A. 4, Chicago N.L. 2)
**Game 1**—Chicago 6, St. Louis 0
**Game 2**—St. Louis 12, Chicago 0 (8 innings, darkness)
**Game 3**—Chicago 11, St. Louis 4 (8 innings, darkness)
**Game 4**—St. Louis 8, Chicago 5 (7 innings, darkness)
**Game 5**—St. Louis 10, Chicago 3 (8 innings, darkness)
**Game 6**—St. Louis 4, Chicago 3 (10 innings)

## MAJOR RULES CHANGES

■ The number of balls required for a walk was increased from six to seven.

■ The shape of the pitcher's box was changed from 6-by-6 to 4-by-7 feet.

■ Pitchers no longer were required to keep both feet on the ground during delivery. "Foul balks" were eliminated.

■ The batter's box was reshaped to its 6-by-3 shape, 12 inches from home base.

■ Stolen bases were credited for any base a runner was able to gain on his own volition, such as a first-to-third dash on a single.

# 1887

## FINAL STANDINGS

**American Association**

| Team | W | L | Pct. | GB |
|---|---|---|---|---|
| St. Louis | 95 | 40 | .704 | ... |
| Cincinnati | 81 | 54 | .600 | 14 |
| Baltimore | 77 | 58 | .570 | 18 |
| Louisville | 76 | 60 | .559 | 19.5 |
| Philadelphia | 64 | 69 | .481 | 30 |
| Brooklyn | 60 | 74 | .448 | 34.5 |
| New York | 44 | 89 | .331 | 50 |
| Cleveland | 39 | 92 | .298 | 54 |

## SIGNIFICANT EVENTS

■ The 4-strike rule was eliminated in a November meeting and officials reversed their preseason decision to count walks as "hits."

## MEMORABLE MOMENTS

■ St. Louis, en route to 95 victories and its third straight A.A. pennant, defeated the Athletics for its 15th consecutive victory.

■ The 52-game hitting streak of Athletics star Denny Lyons came to an end in late August. Lyons' streak included two games in which he managed only walks, which were counted as hits in the 1887 season.

■ The Browns defeated New York for their 12th straight victory and increased their lead over second-place Cincinnati to a whopping 19½ games.

■ The Browns closed their best-of-15 "World's Series" battle against Detroit with a 9-2 victory, but they still lost the war, 10 games to 5.

## LEADERS

**BA:** Tip O'Neill, St.L., .485.
**Runs:** Tip O'Neill, St.L., 167.
**Hits:** Tip O'Neill, St.L., 275.
**TB:** Tip O'Neill, St.L., 407.
**HR:** Tip O'Neill, St.L., 14.
**SB:** Hugh Nicol, Cin., 138.
**Wins:** Matt Kilroy, Bal., 46.
**ERA:** Elmer Smith, Cin., 2.94.
**CG:** Matt Kilroy, Bal., 66.
**IP:** Matt Kilroy, Bal., 589.1.
**SO:** Toad Ramsey, Lou., 355.

**20-game winners**

Matt Kilroy, Bal., 46-19
Toad Ramsey, Lou., 37-27
Silver King, St.L., 32-12
Elmer Smith, Cin., 34-17
Tony Mullane, Cin., 31-17
Bob Caruthers, St.L., 29-9
John Smith, Bal., 25-30
Gus Weyhing, Phil., 26-28
Ed Seward, Phil., 25-25
Dave Foutz, St.L., 25-12

## MAJOR RULES CHANGES

■ The National League and American Association agreed to abide by a uniform rules book and several rules were rewritten. Here are some of the more significant changes:

■ Batters no longer were allowed to call for high or low pitches and the strike zone was defined as the area between the top of the shoulder and the bottom of the knees.

■ The pitcher's box was reshaped to 4-by-5½ feet.

■ Batters hit by a pitch were awarded first base and not charged with an at-bat.

■ The number of balls required for a walk was dropped to five.

■ The batter was declared out after four strikes.

■ Batters drawing a base on balls were credited with a hit and charged with a time at-bat.

## FINAL STANDINGS

**National League**

| Team | W | L | Pct. | GB |
|---|---|---|---|---|
| Detroit | 79 | 45 | .637 | ... |
| Philadelphia | 75 | 48 | .610 | 3.5 |
| Chicago | 71 | 50 | .587 | 6.5 |
| New York | 68 | 55 | .553 | 10.5 |
| Boston | 61 | 60 | .504 | 16.5 |
| Pittsburgh | 55 | 69 | .444 | 24 |
| Washington | 46 | 76 | .377 | 32 |
| Indianapolis | 37 | 89 | .294 | 43 |

## SIGNIFICANT EVENTS

■ The N.L.'s St. Louis franchise was sold to Indianapolis interests.

■ The Phillies christened their new ballpark, which would remain in use as the "Baker Bowl" until 1938.

■ N.L. officials held a November meeting with the Brotherhood of Professional Base Ball Players, an organization set up to protect players' contract interests.

## MEMORABLE MOMENTS

■ Detroit posted a doubleheader sweep of Chicago, increasing its N.L. lead to seven games and putting the city on the verge of its first pennant.

■ The best-of-15 "World's Series" opened with the Browns posting a 6-1 victory over Detroit.

■ The post-season title series ended with Detroit holding a commanding 10 games to 5 advantage.

## LEADERS

**BA:** Cap Anson, Chi., .421.
**Runs:** Dan Brouthers, Det., 153.
**Hits:** Sam Thompson, Det., 235.
**TB:** Sam Thompson, Det., 340.
**HR:** Billy O'Brien, Wash., 19.
**RBI:** Sam Thompson, Det., 166.
**SB:** Monte Ward, N.Y., 111.
**Wins:** John Clarkson, Chi., 38.
**ERA:** Dan Casey, Phil., 2.86.
**CG:** John Clarkson, Chi., 56.
**IP:** John Clarkson, Chi., 523.
**SO:** John Clarkson, Chi., 237.

**20-game winners**

John Clarkson, Chi., 38-21
Tim Keefe, N.Y., 35-19
Charlie Getzien, Det., 29-13
Dan Casey, Phil., 28-13
Pud Galvin, Pit., 28-21
Jim Whitney, Wash., 24-21
Hoss Radbourn, Bos., 24-23
Charlie Ferguson, Phil., 22-10
Mickey Welch, N.Y., 22-15
Kid Madden, Bos., 21-14
Charlie Buffinton, Phil., 21-17

## POST-SEASON PLAYOFF

(Detroit N.L. 10, St. Louis A.A. 5)
**Game 1**—St. Louis 6, Detroit 1
**Game 2**—Detroit 5, St. Louis 3
**Game 3**—Detroit 2, St. Louis 1(13 innings)
**Game 4**—Detroit 8, St. Louis 0
**Game 5**—St. Louis 5, Detroit 2
**Game 6**—Detroit 9, St. Louis 0
**Game 7**—Detroit 3, St. Louis 1
**Game 8**—Detroit 9, St. Louis 2
**Game 9**—Detroit 4, St. Louis 2
**Game 10**—St. Louis 11, Detroit 4
**Game 11**—Detroit 13, St. Louis 3
**Game 12**—St. Louis 5, Detroit 1 (7 innings, darkness)
**Game 13**—Detroit 6, St. Louis 3
**Game 14**—Detroit 4, St. Louis 3
**Game 15**—St. Louis 9, Detroit 2 (6 innings, cold)

## MAJOR RULES CHANGES

■ The National League and American Association agreed to abide by a uniform rules book and several rules were rewritten. Here are some of the more significant changes:

■ Batters no longer were allowed to call for high or low pitches and the strike zone was defined as the area between the top of the shoulder and the bottom of the knees.

■ The pitcher's box was reshaped to 4-by-5½ feet.

■ Batters hit by a pitch were awarded first base and not charged with an at-bat.

■ The number of balls required for a walk was dropped to five.

■ The batter was declared out after four strikes.

■ Batters drawing a base on balls were credited with a hit and charged with a time at-bat.

# 1888

## FINAL STANDINGS

**American Association**

| Team | W | L | Pct. | GB |
|---|---|---|---|---|
| St. Louis | 92 | 43 | .681 | ... |
| Brooklyn | 88 | 52 | .629 | 6.5 |
| Philadelphia | 81 | 52 | .609 | 10 |
| Cincinnati | 80 | 54 | .597 | 11.5 |
| Baltimore | 57 | 80 | .416 | 36 |
| Cleveland | 50 | 82 | .379 | 40.5 |
| Louisville | 48 | 87 | .356 | 44 |
| Kansas City | 43 | 89 | .326 | 47.5 |

## SIGNIFICANT EVENTS

■ Columbus became a member of the American Association roster in December, replacing Cleveland.

## MEMORABLE MOMENTS

■ The St. Louis Browns, seeking their fourth straight A.A. pennant, moved into first place with a mid-July victory over Kansas City—a position they would not relinquish the rest of the season.

■ St. Louis ace Silver King posted his 45th victory and raised his league-leading totals in games (66), innings (585⅔), complete games (64) and ERA (1.64).

■ The Browns fell to N.L.-champion New York in a best-of-10 "World's Series," despite winning the finale, 18-7.

## LEADERS

**BA:** Tip O'Neill, St.L., .335.
**Runs:** George Pinkney, Brk., 134.
**Hits:** Tip O'Neill, St.L., 177.
**TB:** John Reilly, Cin., 264.
**HR:** John Reilly, Cin., 13.
**RBI:** John Reilly, Cin., 103.
**SB:** Arlie Latham, St.L., 109.
**Wins:** Silver King, St.L., 45.
**ERA:** Silver King, St.L., 1.64.
**CG:** Silver King, St.L., 64.
**IP:** Silver King, St.L., 585.2.
**SO:** Ed Seward, Phil., 272.

**20-game winners**

Silver King, St.L., 45-21
Ed Seward, Phil., 35-19
Bob Caruthers, Brk., 29-15
Gus Weyhing, Phil., 28-18
Lee Viau, Cin., 27-14
Tony Mullane, Cin., 26-16
Nat Hudson, St.L., 25-10
Elton Chamberlain, Lou.-St.L., 25-11
Mickey Hughes, Brk., 25-13
Ed Bakely, Cle., 25-33
Elmer Smith, Cin., 22-17
Bert Cunningham, Bal., 22-29

## MAJOR RULES CHANGES

■ The rule awarding the batter a hit on a base on balls was reversed.

■ The batter was credited with a "hit" on any batted ball that struck a baserunner, even though the runner was declared out.

■ The number of strikes required for a strikeout was reduced to three.

■ Pitchers were charged with an error for walks, wild pitches, hit batters and balks.

## 1888

### FINAL STANDINGS

**National League**

| Team | W | L | Pct. | GB |
|---|---|---|---|---|
| New York | 84 | 47 | .641 | ... |
| Chicago | 77 | 58 | .570 | 9 |
| Philadelphia | 69 | 61 | .531 | 14.5 |
| Boston | 70 | 64 | .522 | 15.5 |
| Detroit | 68 | 63 | .519 | 16 |
| Pittsburgh | 66 | 68 | .493 | 19.5 |
| Indianapolis | 50 | 85 | .370 | 36 |
| Washington | 48 | 86 | .358 | 37.5 |

### SIGNIFICANT EVENTS

■ Rules changes: 4 balls for a walk and 3 strikes for a strikeout—standards that would hold up for more than a century.

■ Cleveland, a former American Association franchise, was admitted to the N.L., replacing Detroit.

### MEMORABLE MOMENTS

■ With more than 10,000 fans watching at New York's Polo Grounds, Giants pitcher Tim Keefe dropped a 4-2 decision to Pittsburgh, snapping his record 19-game winning streak.

■ Pittsburgh ace Ed Morris pitched his record fourth consecutive shutout—a 1-0 victory over New York.

■ The Giants clinched the first of many N.L. pennants.

■ The Giants clinched their best-of-10 "World's Series" against St. Louis in Game 8 with an 11-3 victory.

### LEADERS

**BA:** Cap Anson, Chi., .344.
**Runs:** Dan Brouthers, Det., 118.
**Hits:** Jimmy Ryan, Chi., 182.
**TB:** Jimmy Ryan, Chi., 283.
**HR:** Jimmy Ryan, Chi., 16.
**RBI:** Cap Anson, Chi., 84.
**SB:** Dummy Hoy, Wash., 82.
**Wins:** Tim Keefe, N.Y., 35.
**ERA:** Tim Keefe, N.Y., 1.74.
**CG:** Ed Morris, Pit., 54.
**IP:** John Clarkson, Bos., 483.1.
**SO:** Tim Keefe, N.Y., 333.

**20-game winners**

Tim Keefe, N.Y., 35-12
John Clarkson, Bos., 33-20
Pete Conway, Det., 30-14
Ed Morris, Pit., 29-23
Charlie Buffinton, Phil., 28-17
Mickey Welch, N.Y., 26-19
Gus Krock, Chi., 25-14
Pud Galvin, Pit., 23-25

### POST-SEASON PLAYOFF

(New York N.L. 6, St. Louis A.A. 4)
**Game 1**—New York 2, St. Louis 1
**Game 2**—St. Louis 3, New York 0
**Game 3**—New York 4, St. Louis 2
**Game 4**—New York 6, St. Louis 3
**Game 5**—St. Louis 6, New York 4 (8 innings, darkness)
**Game 6**—New York 12, St. Louis 5 (8 innings, darkness)
**Game 7**—St. Louis 7, New York 5 (8 innings, darkness)
**Game 8**—New York 11, St. Louis 3
**Game 9**—St. Louis 14, New York 11 (10 innings)
**Game 10**—St. Louis 18, New York 7

### MAJOR RULES CHANGES

■ The rule awarding the batter a hit on a base on balls was reversed.

■ The batter was credited with a "hit" on any batted ball that struck a baserunner, even though the runner was declared out.

■ Pitchers were charged with an error for walks, wild pitches, hit batters and balks.

## 1889

### FINAL STANDINGS

**American Association**

| Team | W | L | Pct. | GB |
|---|---|---|---|---|
| Brooklyn | 93 | 44 | .679 | ... |
| St. Louis | 90 | 45 | .667 | 2 |
| Philadelphia | 75 | 58 | .564 | 16 |
| Cincinnati | 76 | 63 | .547 | 18 |
| Baltimore | 70 | 65 | .519 | 22 |
| Columbus | 60 | 78 | .435 | 33.5 |
| Kansas City | 55 | 82 | .401 | 38 |
| Louisville | 27 | 111 | .196 | 66.5 |

**National League**

| Team | W | L | Pct. | GB |
|---|---|---|---|---|
| New York | 83 | 43 | .659 | ... |
| Boston | 83 | 45 | .648 | 1 |
| Chicago | 67 | 65 | .508 | 19 |
| Philadelphia | 63 | 64 | .496 | 20.5 |
| Pittsburgh | 61 | 71 | .462 | 25 |
| Cleveland | 61 | 72 | .459 | 25.5 |
| Indianapolis | 59 | 75 | .440 | 28 |
| Washington | 41 | 83 | .331 | 41 |

### SIGNIFICANT EVENTS

■ A record Association crowd of 22,122 showed up for a May 30 game in Brooklyn to watch the Bridegrooms play the Browns.

■ Baltimore, following the lead of Brooklyn, Cincinnati and Kansas City, dropped out of the American Association.

### MEMORABLE MOMENTS

■ Toad Ramsey pitched Louisville to a victory over St. Louis, snapping the Colonels' Major League-record losing streak at 26 games.

■ The Browns, leading 4-2 in the ninth inning of a September 7 game, walked off the field in Brooklyn, claiming it was too dark to continue. The Bridegrooms were declared forfeit winners, a ruling that later would be reversed.

■ The Browns, claiming they feared for the personal safety amid unruly Brooklyn fans, forfeited their September 8 game to the Bridegrooms—a defeat that would help Brooklyn claim the A.A. pennant.

■ The Bridegrooms dropped a 3-2 decision to the N.L.-champion Giants in the decisive Game 9 of the "World's Series."

### LEADERS

**BA:** Tommy Tucker, Bal., .372.
**Runs:** Mike Griffin, Bal.; Harry Stovey, Phil., 152.
**Hits:** Tommy Tucker, Bal., 196.
**TB:** Harry Stovey, Phil., 292.
**HR:** Bug Holliday, Cin.; Harry Stovey, Phil., 19.
**RBI:** Harry Stovey, Phil., 119.
**SB:** Billy Hamilton, K.C., 111.
**Wins:** Bob Caruthers, Brk., 40.
**ERA:** Jack Stivetts, St.L., 2.25.
**CG:** Matt Kilroy, Bal., 55.
**IP:** Mark Baldwin, Col., 513.2.
**SO:** Mark Baldwin, Col., 368.

**20-game winners**

Bob Caruthers, Brk., 40-11
Silver King, St.L., 35-16
Elton Chamberlain, St.L., 32-15
Jesse Duryea, Cin., 32-19
Gus Weyhing, Phil., 30-21
Matt Kilroy, Bal., 29-25
Mark Baldwin, Col., 27-34
Frank Foreman, Bal., 23-21
Adonis Terry, Brk., 22-15
Lee Viau, Cin., 22-20
Ed Seward, Phil., 21-15

### MAJOR RULES CHANGES

■ The number of balls required for a walk was reduced to four.

■ A foul tip was defined as a foul hit that did not rise above the batter's head and was caught within 10 feet of home base. Batters could not be declared out on a caught foul tip and runners were permitted to return safely to their bases.

■ Pitchers were required to get into pitching position by placing one foot on the back line of the pitching box and only one step was allowed during delivery.

■ One "extra player" could be substituted at the end of any complete inning, but the player leaving the game could not return. Substitutions could be made at any time for a disabled player.

■ Pitchers no longer were charged with errors for walks, wild pitches, hit batsmen and balks.

■ The sacrifice bunt was recognized for the first time, although the hitter still was charged with an at-bat.

### SIGNIFICANT EVENTS

■ Brooklyn and Cincinnati made a November jump from the American Association to the N.L., creating a 10-team circuit.

■ A threat becomes official: The Brotherhood of Professional Base Ball Players formally organized the Players League, a third major circuit partially operated by the players themselves.

### MEMORABLE MOMENTS

■ The Giants christened their new Polo Grounds with a victory over Pittsburgh.

■ The New York Giants captured their second straight pennant on the final day of the season, beating Cleveland while Boston was losing to Pittsburgh.

■ The Giants reigned as world champions again, thanks to a 6 games to 3 post-season victory over the American Association's Brooklyn Bridegrooms. New York won Game 9, 3-2.

### LEADERS

**BA:** Dan Brouthers, Bos., .373.
**Runs:** Mike Tiernan, N.Y., 147.
**Hits:** Jack Glasscock, Ind., 205.
**TB:** Jimmy Ryan, Chi., 287.
**HR:** Sam Thompson, Phil., 20.
**RBI:** Roger Connor, N.Y., 130.
**SB:** Jim Fogarty, Phil., 99.
**Wins:** John Clarkson, Bos., 49.
**ERA:** John Clarkson, Bos., 2.73.
**CG:** John Clarkson, Bos., 68.
**IP:** John Clarkson, Bos., 620.
**SO:** John Clarkson, Bos., 284.

**20-game winners**

John Clarkson, Bos., 49-19
Tim Keefe, N.Y., 28-13
Charlie Buffinton, Phil., 28-16
Mickey Welch, N.Y., 27-12
Pud Galvin, Pit., 23-16
Darby O'Brien, Cle., 22-17
Henry Boyle, Ind., 21-23
Harry Staley, Pit., 21-26
Hoss Radbourn, Bos., 20-11
Ed Beatin, Cle., 20-15

### POST-SEASON PLAYOFF

(New York N.L. 6, Brooklyn A.A. 3)
**Game 1**—Brooklyn 12, New York 10 (8 innings, darkness)
**Game 2**—New York 6, Brooklyn 2
**Game 3**—Brooklyn 8, New York 7 (8 innings, darkness)
**Game 4**—Brooklyn 10, New York 7 (6 innings, darkness)
**Game 5**—New York 11, Brooklyn 3
**Game 6**—New York 2, Brooklyn 1 (11 innings)
**Game 7**—New York 11, Brooklyn 7
**Game 8**—New York 16, Brooklyn 7
**Game 9**—New York 3, Brooklyn 2

### MAJOR RULES CHANGES

■ The number of balls required for a walk was reduced to four.

■ A foul tip was defined as a foul hit that did not rise above the batter's head and was caught within 10 feet of home base. Batters could not be declared out on a caught foul tip and runners were permitted to return safely to their bases.

■ Pitchers were required to get into pitching position by placing one foot on the back line of the pitching box and only one step was allowed during delivery.

■ One "extra player" could be substituted at the end of any complete inning, but the player leaving the game could not return. Substitutions could be made at any time for a disabled player.

■ Pitchers no longer were charged with errors for walks, wild pitches, hit batsmen and balks.

■ The sacrifice bunt was recognized for the first time, although the hitter still was charged with an at-bat.

## 1890

### FINAL STANDINGS

**Players League**

| Team | W | L | Pct. | GB |
|---|---|---|---|---|
| Boston | 81 | 48 | .628 | ... |
| Brooklyn | 76 | 56 | .576 | 6.5 |
| New York | 74 | 57 | .565 | 8 |
| Chicago | 75 | 62 | .547 | 10 |
| Philadelphia | 68 | 63 | .519 | 14 |
| Pittsburgh | 60 | 68 | .469 | 20.5 |
| Cleveland | 55 | 75 | .423 | 26.5 |
| Buffalo | 36 | 96 | .273 | 46.5 |

### SIGNIFICANT EVENTS

■ The new Players League won the first of many lawsuits it would have to endure when a judge refused to grant a January injunction against Brotherhood president John Montgomery Ward.

■ The Players League began its inaugural season in a war-like atmosphere, thanks to the league-jumping antics of many big-name stars from the National League and American Association.

■ The New York and Pittsburgh teams combined with the same-city franchises from the N.L., pronouncing last rites for the one-year circuit. The December defections would prompt Players League backers to seek their own deals in a scramble to remain solvent.

### MEMORABLE MOMENTS

■ Willie McGill, a 16-year-old Cleveland hurler, became the youngest Major League pitcher to throw a complete game when he defeated Buffalo.

■ Boston closed out the first and last Players League season with an 81-48 record, capturing the pennant by 6½ games over Brooklyn.

### LEADERS

**BA:** Pete Browning, Cle., .373.
**Runs:** Hugh Duffy, Chi., 161.
**Hits:** Hugh Duffy, Chi., 191.
**TB:** Billy Shindle, Phil., 281.
**HR:** Roger Connor, N.Y., 14.
**RBI:** Hardy Richardson, Bos., 146.
**SB:** Harry Stovey, Bos., 97.
**Wins:** Mark Baldwin, Chi., 34.
**ERA:** Silver King, Chi., 2.69.
**CG:** Mark Baldwin, Chi., 54.
**IP:** Mark Baldwin, Chi., 501.
**SO:** Mark Baldwin, Chi., 211.

**20-game winners**

Mark Baldwin, Chi., 34-24
Gus Weyhing, Brk., 30-16
Silver King, Chi., 30-22
Hoss Radbourn, Bos., 27-12
Addison Gumbert, Bos., 23-12
Phil Knell, Phil., 22-11
Hank O'Day, N.Y., 22-13
Henry Gruber, Cle., 22-23
Harry Staley, Pit., 21-25

### THE RULES

■ The one-season Players League adopted its own rules book with only slight variations to the ones used by the American Association and National League. The most significant was a resized pitcher's box that reverted to the 6-by-4 foot rectangle last used in 1885 with a front line 51 feet from the center of home base. Other key variations:

■ If a team failed to begin play within one minute after the umpire called "play" at the start of a game, a forfeit was declared.

■ Each corner of the reshaped pitcher's box was marked by a wooden peg, a variation from the flat rubber plates used by the other leagues.

■ Two umpires were required for each championship game, one behind the plate and the other standing in the field.

# 1890

## FINAL STANDINGS

### American Association

| Team | W | L | Pct. | GB |
|---|---|---|---|---|
| Louisville | 88 | 44 | .667 | ... |
| Columbus | 79 | 55 | .590 | 10 |
| St. Louis | 78 | 58 | .574 | 12 |
| Toledo | 68 | 64 | .515 | 20 |
| Rochester | 63 | 63 | .500 | 22 |
| Baltimore | 15 | 19 | .441 | 24 |
| Syracuse | 55 | 72 | .433 | 30.5 |
| Philadelphia | 54 | 78 | .409 | 34 |
| Brooklyn | 26 | 73 | .263 | 45.5 |

## SIGNIFICANT EVENTS

■ Brooklyn joined Syracuse, Rochester and Toledo as new American Association cities.

■ The bankrupt Athletics disbanded, releasing and selling their players. A patchwork Philadelphia club would close the season with 22 consecutive losses.

■ The Athletics were expelled, a new Philadelphia franchise was admitted and new teams from Boston, Washington and Chicago replaced Syracuse, Rochester and Toledo in action at the winter meetings.

## MEMORABLE MOMENT

■ Louisville defeated N.L.-champion Brooklyn 6-2 to salvage a "World's Series" split. Each team won three games and one ended in a tie.

## LEADERS

**BA:** Jimmy Wolf, Lou., .363.
**Runs:** Jim McTamany, Col., 140.
**Hits:** Jimmy Wolf, Lou., 197.
**TB:** Jimmy Wolf, Lou., 260.
**HR:** Count Campau, St.L., 9.
**SB:** Tommy McCarthy, St.L., 83.
**Wins:** Sadie McMahon, Phil.-Bal., 36.
**ERA:** Scott Stratton, Lou., 2.36.
**CG:** Sadie McMahon, Phil.-Bal., 55.
**IP:** Sadie McMahon, Phil.-Bal., 509.
**SO:** Sadie McMahon, Phil.-Bal., 291.

**20-game winners**

Sadie McMahon, Phil.-Bal., 36-21
Scott Stratton, Lou., 34-14
Hank Gastright, Col., 30-14
Bob Barr, Rch., 28-24
Jack Stivetts, St.L., 27-21
Red Ehret, Lou., 25-14
Toad Ramsey, St.L., 24-17
John Healy, Tol., 22-21

## MAJOR RULES CHANGES

■ Pitchers and other players were no longer allowed to discolor the ball by rubbing it with soil or other foreign substances.

■ Each team was allowed a second "extra player" and substitutions could be made at any time with retiring players unable to return.

## FINAL STANDINGS

### National League

| Team | W | L | Pct. | GB |
|---|---|---|---|---|
| Brooklyn | 86 | 43 | .667 | ... |
| Chicago | 84 | 53 | .613 | 6 |
| Philadelphia | 78 | 54 | .591 | 9.5 |
| Cincinnati | 77 | 55 | .583 | 10.5 |
| Boston | 76 | 57 | .571 | 12 |
| New York | 63 | 68 | .481 | 24 |
| Cleveland | 44 | 88 | .333 | 43.5 |
| Pittsburgh | 23 | 113 | .169 | 66.5 |

## SIGNIFICANT EVENTS

■ Committees from the three rival Major Leagues began October peace negotiations that eventually would signal the end of the Players League.

## MEMORABLE MOMENTS

■ N.L. newcomer Brooklyn moved into first place with a victory over Cincinnati. The Bridegrooms would win the pennant with a six-game edge over Chicago.

■ Brooklyn swept a tripleheader from hapless Pittsburgh and stretched its losing streak to 22 games. Pittsburgh would finish the season with a record 113 losses.

■ Brooklyn (N.L.) and Louisville (A.A.) began play in a "World's Series" that did not include Players League champion Boston. The Bridegrooms won the opener, 9-0, but the series would end in a 3-3 deadlock with one tie.

## LEADERS

**BA:** Jack Glasscock, N.Y., .336.
**Runs:** Hub Collins, Brk., 148.
**Hits:** Jack Glasscock, N.Y.; Sam Thompson, Phil., 172.
**TB:** Mike Tiernan, N.Y., 274.
**HR:** Oyster Burns, Brk.; Mike Tiernan, N.Y.; Walt Wilmot, Chi., 13.
**RBI:** Oyster Burns, Brk., 128.
**SB:** Billy Hamilton, Phil., 102.
**Wins:** Bill Hutchinson, Chi., 42.
**ERA:** Billy Rhines, Cin., 1.95.
**CG:** Bill Hutchinson, Chi., 65.
**IP:** Bill Hutchinson, Chi., 603.
**SO:** Amos Rusie, N.Y., 341.

**20-game winners**

Bill Hutchinson, Chi., 42-25
Kid Gleason, Phil., 38-17
Tom Lovett, Brk., 30-11
Amos Rusie, N.Y., 29-34
Billy Rhines, Cin., 28-17
Kid Nichols, Bos., 27-19
Adonis Terry, Brk., 26-16
John Clarkson, Bos., 26-18
Tom Vickery, Phil., 24-22
Bob Caruthers, Brk., 23-11
Charlie Getzien, Bos., 23-17
Ed Beatin, Cle., 22-30
Pat Luby, Chi., 20-9

## POST-SEASON PLAYOFF

(Brooklyn N.L. 3, Louisville A.A. 3; 1 tie)

**Game 1**—Brooklyn 9, Louisville 0 (8 innings, darkness)

**Game 2**—Brooklyn 5, Louisville 3

**Game 3**—Brooklyn 7, Louisville 7 (8 innings, darkness)

**Game 4**—Louisville 5, Brooklyn 4

**Game 5**—Brooklyn 7, Louisville 2

**Game 6**—Louisville 9, Brooklyn 8

**Game 7**—Louisville 6, Brooklyn 2

## MAJOR RULES CHANGES

■ Pitchers and other players were no longer allowed to discolor the ball by rubbing it with soil or other foreign substances.

■ Each team was allowed a second "extra player" and substitutions could be made at any time with retiring players unable to return.

# 1891

## FINAL STANDINGS

### American Association

| Team | W | L | Pct. | GB |
|---|---|---|---|---|
| Boston | 93 | 42 | .689 | ... |
| St. Louis | 86 | 52 | .623 | 8.5 |
| Milwaukee | 21 | 15 | .583 | 22.5 |
| Baltimore | 71 | 64 | .526 | 22 |
| Philadelphia | 73 | 66 | .525 | 22 |
| Columbus | 61 | 76 | .445 | 33 |
| Cincinnati | 43 | 57 | .430 | 32.5 |
| Louisville | 55 | 84 | .396 | 40 |
| Washington | 44 | 91 | .326 | 49 |

## SIGNIFICANT EVENTS

■ In a February declaration of war, the American Association withdrew from the National Agreement and moved its Chicago franchise to Cincinnati to compete with the N.L.'s Reds.

■ The Association's Cincinnati franchise folded in mid-August and was replaced by the Western Association's Milwaukee Brewers.

■ The Boston Reds, en route to the A.A. pennant, were shocked by the August defection of star King Kelly to their Boston N.L. rival.

■ A "World's Series" challenge by Reds owners was turned down by the the N.L.-champion Boston team. N.L. officials cited the A.A.'s withdrawal from the National Agreement.

■ After 10 Major League seasons, the Association died when four of its eight teams joined the N.L. and the other four accepted buyouts.

## MEMORABLE MOMENTS

■ The Boston Reds defeated Baltimore and clinched the final A.A. pennant.

■ Browns rookie Ted Breitenstein, making his first Major League start on the final day of the season, pitched an 8-0 no-hitter against Louisville.

## LEADERS

**BA:** Dan Brouthers, Bos., .350.
**Runs:** Tom Brown, Bos., 177.
**Hits:** Tom Brown, Bos., 189.
**TB:** Tom Brown, Bos., 276.
**HR:** Duke Farrell, Bos., 12.
**RBI:** Hugh Duffy, Bos.; Duke Farrell, Bos., 110.
**SB:** Tom Brown, Bos., 106.
**Wins:** Sadie McMahon, Bal., 35.
**ERA:** Ed Crane, Cin., 2.45.
**CG:** Sadie McMahon, Bal., 53.
**IP:** Sadie McMahon, Bal., 503.
**SO:** Jack Stivetts, St.L., 259.

**20-game winners**

Sadie McMahon, Bal., 35-24
George Haddock, Bos., 34-11
Jack Stivetts, St.L., 33-22
Gus Weyhing, Phil., 31-20
Charlie Buffinton, Bos., 29-9
Phil Knell, Col., 28-27
Elton Chamberlain, Phil., 22-23
Willie McGill, Cin.-St.L., 21-15

## MAJOR RULES CHANGE

■ All teams were required to have one or more substitutes available for each game.

## FINAL STANDINGS

### National League

| Team | W | L | Pct. | GB |
|---|---|---|---|---|
| Boston | 87 | 51 | .630 | ... |
| Chicago | 82 | 53 | .607 | 3.5 |
| New York | 71 | 61 | .538 | 13 |
| Philadelphia | 68 | 69 | .496 | 18.5 |
| Cleveland | 65 | 74 | .468 | 22.5 |
| Brooklyn | 61 | 76 | .445 | 25.5 |
| Cincinnati | 56 | 81 | .409 | 30.5 |
| Pittsburgh | 55 | 80 | .407 | 30.5 |

## SIGNIFICANT EVENTS

■ The American Association withdrew from the National Agreement in February and declared war, moving its Chicago franchise to Cincinnati to compete with the N.L.'s Reds.

■ Pittsburgh secured its nickname as "Pirates" when it lured stars Pete Browning and Scott Stratton away from the A.A.'s Louisville team.

■ With August peace talks between the National League and American Association in progress, the N.L. Boston team shattered the calm by pirating King Kelly away from its A.A. Boston rival.

■ The American Association ceased operations in December when four A.A. clubs (St. Louis, Louisville, Washington and Baltimore) joined the N.L., creating "The National League and American Association of Professional Base Ball Clubs."

## MEMORABLE MOMENTS

■ Cy Young christened Cleveland's new League Park, pitching the Spiders to an easy victory over the Reds.

■ Chicago's Wild Bill Hutchison defeated Boston for his 40th victory en route to a Major League-high 44.

■ Boston clinched the N.L. pennant with a victory over Philadelphia—its 17th in a row.

## LEADERS

**BA:** Billy Hamilton, Phil., .340.
**Runs:** Billy Hamilton, Phil., 141.
**Hits:** Billy Hamilton, Phil., 179.
**TB:** Harry Stovey, Bos., 271.
**HR:** Harry Stovey, Bos.; Mike Tiernan, N.Y., 16.
**RBI:** Cap Anson, Chi., 120.
**SB:** Billy Hamilton, Phil., 111.
**Wins:** Bill Hutchinson, Chi., 44.
**ERA:** John Ewing, N.Y., 2.27.
**CG:** Bill Hutchinson, Chi., 56.
**IP:** Bill Hutchinson, Chi., 561.
**SO:** Amos Rusie, N.Y., 337.

**20-game winners**

Bill Hutchison, Chi., 44-19
John Clarkson, Bos., 33-19
Amos Rusie, N.Y., 33-20
Kid Nichols, Bos., 30-17
Cy Young, Cle., 27-22
Harry Staley, Pit.-Bos., 24-13
Kid Gleason, Phil., 24-22
Tom Lovett, Brk., 23-19
Tony Mullane, Cin., 23-26
Mark Baldwin, Pit., 22-28
John Ewing, N.Y., 21-8
Duke Esper, Phil., 20-15

## MAJOR RULES CHANGE

■ All teams were required to have one or more substitutes available for each game.

# 1892

## FINAL STANDINGS

### National League

| Team | W | L | Pct. | GB |
|---|---|---|---|---|
| Boston | 102 | 48 | .680 | ... |
| Cleveland | 93 | 56 | .624 | 8.5 |
| Brooklyn | 95 | 59 | .617 | 9 |
| Philadelphia | 87 | 66 | .569 | 16.5 |
| Cincinnati | 82 | 68 | .547 | 20 |
| Pittsburgh | 80 | 73 | .523 | 23.5 |
| Chicago | 70 | 76 | .479 | 30 |
| New York | 71 | 80 | .470 | 31.5 |
| Louisville | 63 | 89 | .414 | 40 |
| Washington | 58 | 93 | .384 | 44.5 |
| St. Louis | 56 | 94 | .373 | 46 |
| Baltimore | 46 | 101 | .313 | 54.5 |

## SIGNIFICANT EVENTS

■ The new 12-team N.L. adopted a 154-game split schedule featuring first-half and second-half champions.
■ Cincinnati, playing host to the first Sunday game in N.L. history, defeated the Browns, 5-1.
■ N.L. owners, holding a mid-November meeting in Chicago, shortened the 1893 schedule to 132 games and dropped the split-season format.

## MEMORABLE MOMENTS

■ Baltimore catcher Wilbert Robinson collected a record seven hits during a 25-7 victory over the Browns.
■ Cincinnati's Bumpus Jones made his Major League debut a spectacular one, holding Pittsburgh hitless in a 7-1 victory.
■ First-half champion Boston swept aside second-half champion Cleveland in a post-season playoff. The Beaneaters won five of the six games and the other ended in a tie.

## LEADERS

**BA:** Dan Brouthers, Brk., .335.
**Runs:** Cupid Childs, Cle., 136.
**Hits:** Dan Brouthers, Brk., 197.
**TB:** Dan Brouthers, Brk., 282.
**HR:** Bug Holliday, Cin., 13.
**RBI:** Dan Brouthers, Brk., 124.
**SB:** Monte Ward, Brk., 88.
**Wins:** Bill Hutchinson, Chi.; Cy Young, Cle., 36.
**ERA:** Cy Young, Cle., 1.93.
**CG:** Bill Hutchinson, Chi., 67.
**IP:** Bill Hutchinson, Chi., 627.
**SO:** Bill Hutchinson, Chi., 316.

**20-game winners**

Bill Hutchinson, Chi., 36-36
Cy Young, Cle., 36-12
Kid Nichols, Bos., 35-16
Jack Stivetts, Bos., 35-16
Gus Weyhing, Phil., 32-21
Amos Rusie, N.Y., 31-31
George Haddock, Brk., 29-13
Frank Killen, Wash., 29-26
George Cuppy, Cle., 28-13
Ed Stein, Brk., 27-16
Mark Baldwin, Pit., 26-27
John Clarkson, Bos.-Cle., 25-16
Silver King, N.Y., 23-24
Harry Staley, Bos., 22-10
Ad Gumbert, Chi., 22-19
Tony Mullane, Cin., 21-13
Frank Dwyer, St.L.-Cin., 21-18
Scott Stratton, Lou., 21-19
Kid Gleason, St.L., 20-24

## POST-SEASON PLAYOFF

(Boston 5, Cleveland 0; 1 tie)
**Game 1**—Boston 0, Cleveland 0 (11 innings, darkness)
**Game 2**—Boston 4, Cleveland 3
**Game 3**—Boston 3, Cleveland 2
**Game 4**—Boston 4, Cleveland 0
**Game 5**—Boston 12, Cleveland 7
**Game 6**—Boston 8, Cleveland 3

## MAJOR RULES CHANGES

■ Games were declared "official" after five full innings or 4½ if the home team was leading.

■ An umpire was given authority to declare a forfeit when he believed players were using delay tactics to gain suspension of a game.

■ Any ball hit over an outfield fence was declared a home run, except in cases where the distance was less than 235 feet from home base. Such drives were called ground-rule doubles.

■ Any batter obstructing or interfering with a catcher's throw was declared out.

# 1893

## FINAL STANDINGS

### National League

| Team | W | L | Pct. | GB |
|---|---|---|---|---|
| Boston | 86 | 43 | .667 | ... |
| Pittsburgh | 81 | 48 | .628 | 5 |
| Cleveland | 73 | 55 | .570 | 12.5 |
| Philadelphia | 72 | 57 | .558 | 14 |
| New York | 68 | 64 | .515 | 19.5 |
| Brooklyn | 65 | 63 | .508 | 20.5 |
| Cincinnati | 65 | 63 | .508 | 20.5 |
| Baltimore | 60 | 70 | .462 | 26.5 |
| Chicago | 56 | 71 | .441 | 29 |
| St. Louis | 57 | 75 | .432 | 30.5 |
| Louisville | 50 | 75 | .400 | 34 |
| Washington | 40 | 89 | .310 | 46 |

## SIGNIFICANT EVENT

■ A revolutionary rules change: The pitching box was eliminated and a pitcher's rubber was placed 5 feet behind the back line of the box—60 feet, 6 inches from home plate.

## MEMORABLE MOMENTS

■ Boston defeated Baltimore 6-2 in a late July game and took over permanent posession of first place en route to its third consecutive pennant.
■ Cleveland ended the 33-game hitting streak of George Davis during an 8-6 victory over the Giants.

## LEADERS

**BA:** Hugh Duffy, Bos., .363.
**Runs:** Herman Long, Bos., 149.
**Hits:** Sam Thompson, Phil., 222.
**TB:** Ed Delahanty, Phil., 347.
**HR:** Ed Delahanty, Phil., 19.
**RBI:** Ed Delahanty, Phil., 146.
**SB:** Tom Brown, Lou., 66.
**Wins:** Frank Killen, Pit., 36.
**ERA:** Ted Breitenstein, St.L., 3.18.
**CG:** Amos Rusie, N.Y., 50.
**IP:** Amos Rusie, N.Y., 482.
**SO:** Amos Rusie, N.Y., 208.

**20-game winners**

Frank Killen, Pit., 36-14
Kid Nichols, Bos., 34-14
Cy Young, Cle., 34-16
Amos Rusie, N.Y., 33-21
Brickyard Kennedy, Brk., 25-20
Gus Weyhing, Phil., 23-16
Sadie McMahon, Bal., 23-18
Kid Gleason, St.L., 21-22
Jack Stivetts, Bos., 20-12

## MAJOR RULES CHANGES

■ The pitcher's box was eliminated and the pitching distance was lengthened to 60 feet, 6 inches from the outer corner of home base. The distance was marked by a rubber slab (a pitching rubber) 12 inches long and 4 inches wide.

■ Pitchers were required to deliver the ball with one foot remaining in contact with the rubber.

■ Bats with a flat surface were outlawed. Bats were required to be completely round.

■ Lineups were submitted before each game and the batting order was followed throughout the contest. Each new inning started with the batter whose name followed the man who had made the final out of the previous inning.

# 1894

## FINAL STANDINGS

### National League

| Team | W | L | Pct. | GB |
|---|---|---|---|---|
| Baltimore | 89 | 39 | .695 | ... |
| New York | 88 | 44 | .667 | 3 |
| Boston | 83 | 49 | .629 | 8 |
| Philadelphia | 71 | 57 | .555 | 18 |
| Brooklyn | 70 | 61 | .534 | 20.5 |
| Cleveland | 68 | 61 | .527 | 21.5 |
| Pittsburgh | 65 | 65 | .500 | 25 |
| Chicago | 57 | 75 | .432 | 34 |
| St. Louis | 56 | 76 | .424 | 35 |
| Cincinnati | 55 | 75 | .423 | 35 |
| Washington | 45 | 87 | .341 | 46 |
| Louisville | 36 | 94 | .277 | 54 |

## SIGNIFICANT EVENT

■ Rules changes: Foul bunts became strikes and the infield fly rule was entered into the books.

## MEMORABLE MOMENTS

■ Boston second baseman Bobby Lowe became baseball's first four-homer man when he connected in consecutive at-bats during a rout of Cincinnati.
■ Chicago shortstop Bill Dahlen failed to get a hit in six at-bats against Cincinnati, ending his 42-game hitting streak.
■ Philadelphia star Billy Hamilton tied a Major League record with seven stolen bases in a victory over Washington.
■ The Orioles clinched the first of three consecutive pennants with a victory over Cleveland.
■ Second-place New York defeated regular-season champion Baltimore 16-3 and concluded its sweep of the best-of-seven Temple Cup series—a new post-season playoff.

## LEADERS

**BA:** Hugh Duffy, Bos., .440.
**Runs:** Billy Hamilton, Phil., 192.
**Hits:** Hugh Duffy, Bos., 237.
**TB:** Hugh Duffy, Bos., 374.
**HR:** Hugh Duffy, Bos., 18.
**RBI:** Hugh Duffy, Bos., 145.
**SB:** Billy Hamilton, Phil., 98.
**Wins:** Amos Rusie, N.Y., 36.
**ERA:** Amos Rusie, N.Y., 2.78.
**CG:** Ted Breitenstein, St.L., 46.
**IP:** Ted Breitenstein, St.L., 447.1.
**SO:** Amos Rusie, N.Y., 195.

**20-game winners**

Amos Rusie, N.Y., 36-13
Jouett Meekin, N.Y., 33-9
Kid Nichols, Bos., 32-13
Ted Breitenstein, St.L., 27-23
Ed Stein, Brk., 26-14
Jack Stivetts, Bos., 26-14
Cy Young, Cle., 26-21
Sadie McMahon, Bal., 25-8
George Cuppy, Cle., 24-15
Brickyard Kennedy, Brk., 24-20
Jack Taylor, Phil., 23-13
Clark Griffith, Chi., 21-14

## TEMPLE CUP

(New York 4, Baltimore 0)
**Game 1**—New York 4, Baltimore 1
**Game 2**—New York 9, Baltimore 6
**Game 3**—New York 4, Baltimore 1
**Game 4**—New York 16, Baltimore 3

## MAJOR RULES CHANGES

■ Batters were charged with a strike when bunting the ball into foul territory.

■ Batters who advanced a runner with a bunt while being put out were credited with a sacrifice and not charged with an at-bat.

# 1895

## FINAL STANDINGS

### National League

| Team | W | L | Pct. | GB |
|---|---|---|---|---|
| Baltimore | 87 | 43 | .669 | ... |
| Cleveland | 84 | 46 | .646 | 3 |
| Philadelphia | 78 | 53 | .595 | 9.5 |
| Chicago | 72 | 58 | .554 | 15 |
| Boston | 71 | 60 | .542 | 16.5 |
| Brooklyn | 71 | 60 | .542 | 16.5 |
| Pittsburgh | 71 | 61 | .538 | 17 |
| Cincinnati | 66 | 64 | .508 | 21 |
| New York | 66 | 65 | .504 | 21.5 |
| Washington | 43 | 85 | .336 | 43 |
| St. Louis | 39 | 92 | .298 | 48.5 |
| Louisville | 35 | 96 | .267 | 52.5 |

## SIGNIFICANT EVENT

■ N.L. officials, reacting to player complaints, restricted the size of gloves for everybody but first basemen and catchers to 10 ounces and 14 inches in circumference around the palm.

## MEMORABLE MOMENTS

■ Louisville defeated Washington, but Colonels star Fred Clarke saw his 35-game hitting streak come to an end.
■ Baltimore clinched its second straight pennant with a victory over New York—two days before the regular season ended.
■ Cleveland captured the Temple Cup with a fifth-game, 5-2 victory over Baltimore.

## LEADERS

**BA:** Jesse Burkett, Cle., .409.
**Runs:** Billy Hamilton, Phil., 166.
**Hits:** Jesse Burkett, Cle., 225.
**TB:** Sam Thompson, Phil., 352.
**HR:** Sam Thompson, Phil., 18.
**RBI:** Sam Thompson, Phil., 165.
**SB:** Billy Hamilton, Phil., 97.
**Wins:** Cy Young, Cle., 35.
**ERA:** Al Maul, Wash., 2.45.
**CG:** Ted Breitenstein, St.L., 46.
**IP:** Pink Hawley, Pit., 444.1.
**SO:** Amos Rusie, N.Y., 201.

**20-game winners**

Cy Young, Cle., 35-10
Bill Hoffer, Bal., 31-6
Pink Hawley, Pit., 31-22
George Cuppy, Cle., 26-14
Clark Griffith, Chi., 26-14
Jack Taylor, Phil., 26-14
Kid Nichols, Bos., 26-16
Kid Carsey, Phil., 24-16
Amos Rusie, N.Y., 23-23
Adonis Terry, Chi., 21-14
George Hemming, Bal., 20-13

## TEMPLE CUP

(Cleveland 4, Baltimore 1)
**Game 1**—Cleveland 5, Baltimore 4
**Game 2**—Cleveland 7, Baltimore 2
**Game 3**—Cleveland 7, Baltimore 1
**Game 4**—Baltimore 5, Cleveland 0
**Game 5**—Cleveland 5, Baltimore 2

## MAJOR RULES CHANGES

■ The pitching rubber was enlarged to 24-by-6 inches, its current size.

■ A foul tip caught by the catcher became a strike.

■ The infield fly rule became official.

■ Bats were limited to 2¾ inches in diameter.

■ Catchers and first basemen were given permission to use oversized gloves. Other fielders still were restricted to gloves weighing 10 ounces with a hand size not more than 14 inches.

## 1896

### FINAL STANDINGS

**National League**

| Team | W | L | Pct. | GB |
|---|---|---|---|---|
| Baltimore | 90 | 39 | .698 | ... |
| Cleveland | 80 | 48 | .625 | 9.5 |
| Cincinnati | 77 | 50 | .606 | 12 |
| Boston | 74 | 57 | .565 | 17 |
| Chicago | 71 | 57 | .555 | 18.5 |
| Pittsburgh | 66 | 63 | .512 | 24 |
| New York | 64 | 67 | .489 | 27 |
| Philadelphia | 62 | 68 | .477 | 28.5 |
| Brooklyn | 58 | 73 | .443 | 33 |
| Washington | 58 | 73 | .443 | 33 |
| St. Louis | 40 | 90 | .308 | 50.5 |
| Louisville | 38 | 93 | .290 | 53 |

### SIGNIFICANT EVENT

■ Cleveland's Jesse Burkett collected three final-day hits and finished with a league-leading .410 average—his record second consecutive .400 season.

### MEMORABLE MOMENTS

■ Philadelphia star Ed Delahanty matched Bobby Lowe's 1894 record of four home runs in a game—all inside-the-park shots in a loss to Chicago.
■ Baltimore clinched its third straight pennant with a victory over Brooklyn.
■ Regular-season champion Baltimore defeated Cleveland 5-0 and capped its four-game sweep of the Temple Cup series.

### LEADERS

**BA:** Jesse Burkett, Cle., .410.
**Runs:** Jesse Burkett, Cle., 160.
**Hits:** Jesse Burkett, Cle., 240.
**TB:** Jesse Burkett, Cle., 317.
**HR:** Ed Delahanty, Phil.;
Bill Joyce, Wash.-N.Y., 13.
**RBI:** Ed Delahanty, Phil., 126.
**SB:** Joe Kelley, Bal., 87.
**Wins:** Frank Killen, Pit.; Kid Nichols, Bos., 30.
**ERA:** Billy Rhines, Cin., 2.45.
**CG:** Frank Killen, Pit., 44.
**IP:** Frank Killen, Pit., 432.1.
**SO:** Cy Young, Cle., 140.

**20-game winners**

Kid Nichols, Bos., 30-14
Frank Killen, Pit., 30-18
Cy Young, Cle., 28-15
Jouett Meekin, N.Y., 26-14
Bill Hoffer, Bal., 25-7
George Cuppy, Cle., 25-14
George Mercer, Wash., 25-18
Frank Dwyer, Cin., 24-11
Clark Griffith, Chi., 23-11
Jack Stivetts, Bos., 22-14
Pink Hawley, Pit., 22-21
Jack Taylor, Phil., 20-21

### TEMPLE CUP

(Baltimore 4, Cleveland 0)
**Game 1**—Baltimore 7, Cleveland 1
**Game 2**—Baltimore 7, Cleveland 2 (8 innings, darkness)
**Game 3**—Baltimore 6, Cleveland 2
**Game 4**—Baltimore 5, Cleveland 0

### MAJOR RULES CHANGES

■ Pitchers were no longer required to hold the ball in full sight of the umpire up to delivery.
■ Umpires were given authority to eject players using vulgar language and fine them $25. Umpires also were allowed to fine players $5 to $10 for specified misconduct.
■ Home teams were required to have at least 12 regulation balls available for each game.

## 1897

### FINAL STANDINGS

**National League**

| Team | W | L | Pct. | GB |
|---|---|---|---|---|
| Boston | 93 | 39 | .705 | ... |
| Baltimore | 90 | 40 | .692 | 2 |
| New York | 83 | 48 | .634 | 9.5 |
| Cincinnati | 76 | 56 | .576 | 17 |
| Cleveland | 69 | 62 | .527 | 23.5 |
| Brooklyn | 61 | 71 | .462 | 32 |
| Washington | 61 | 71 | .462 | 32 |
| Pittsburgh | 60 | 71 | .458 | 32.5 |
| Chicago | 59 | 73 | .447 | 34 |
| Philadelphia | 55 | 77 | .417 | 38 |
| Louisville | 52 | 78 | .400 | 40 |
| St. Louis | 29 | 102 | .221 | 63.5 |

### SIGNIFICANT EVENT

■ The 4-year-old Temple Cup series, which failed to attract fan interest, died a quiet death after regular-season champion Boston lost a five-game series to second-place Baltimore.

### MEMORABLE MOMENTS

■ Pittsburgh pitcher Frank Killen defeated Baltimore and ended Willie Keeler's 44-game hitting streak.
■ Chicago set an N.L. single-game scoring record during a 36-7 demolition of Louisville.
■ Boston's victory over Brooklyn, coupled with Baltimore's same-day loss to Washington, gave the Beaneaters the N.L. pennant.

### LEADERS

**BA:** Willie Keeler, Bal., .424.
**Runs:** Billy Hamilton, Bos., 152.
**Hits:** Willie Keeler, Bal., 239.
**TB:** Nap Lajoie, Phil., 310.
**HR:** Hugh Duffy, Bos., 11.
**RBI:** George Davis, N.Y., 136.
**SB:** Bill Lange, Chi., 73.
**Wins:** Kid Nichols, Bos., 31.
**ERA:** Amos Rusie, N.Y., 2.54.
**CG:** Red Donahue, St.L.; Clark Griffith, Chi.;
Frank Killen, Pit., 38.
**IP:** Kid Nichols, Bos., 368.
**SO:** Doc McJames, Wash., 156.

**20-game winners**

Kid Nichols, Bos., 31-11
Amos Rusie, N.Y., 28-10
Fred Klobedanz, Bos., 26-7
Joe Corbett, Bal., 24-8
Ted Breitenstein, Cin., 23-12
Bill Hoffer, Bal., 22-11
Ted Lewis, Bos., 21-12
Bill Rhines, Cin., 21-15
Clark Griffith, Chi., 21-18
Cy Young, Cle., 21-19
Jerry Nops, Bal., 20-6
Jouett Meekin, N.Y., 20-11
George Mercer, Wash., 20-20

### TEMPLE CUP

(Baltimore 4, Boston 1)
**Game 1**—Boston 13, Baltimore 12
**Game 2**—Baltimore 13, Boston 11
**Game 3**—Baltimore 8, Boston 3 (7 innings, rain)
**Game 4**—Baltimore 12, Boston 11
**Game 5**—Baltimore 9, Boston 3

### MAJOR RULES CHANGES

■ Runners who were held or obstructed by fielders without the ball were given the base they were trying to reach. Any fielder stopping a ball in any way other than with his hands was guilty of obstruction and runners were allowed to advance.
■ Runners returning to their original base after a caught fly ball were required to retouch all bases they had passed in reverse order.
■ Any judgement call by the umpire was final and could not be reversed.
■ Earned runs were defined as runs scored without the aid of errors.

## 1898

### FINAL STANDINGS

**National League**

| Team | W | L | Pct. | GB |
|---|---|---|---|---|
| Boston | 102 | 47 | .685 | ... |
| Baltimore | 96 | 53 | .644 | 6 |
| Cincinnati | 92 | 60 | .605 | 11.5 |
| Chicago | 85 | 65 | .567 | 17.5 |
| Cleveland | 81 | 68 | .544 | 21 |
| Philadelphia | 78 | 71 | .523 | 24 |
| New York | 77 | 73 | .513 | 25.5 |
| Pittsburgh | 72 | 76 | .486 | 29.5 |
| Louisville | 70 | 81 | .464 | 33 |
| Brooklyn | 54 | 91 | .372 | 46 |
| Washington | 51 | 101 | .336 | 52.5 |
| St. Louis | 39 | 111 | .260 | 63.5 |

### SIGNIFICANT EVENT

■ Cap Anson, who compiled a 1,293-932 record over 19 seasons as a Chicago manager, was fired.

### MEMORABLE MOMENTS

■ A Major League first: Baltimore's Jim Hughes and Cincinnati's Ted Breitenstein pitched nine-inning no-hitters on the same day.
■ Philadelphia pitcher Bill Duggleby hit a grand slam in his first Major League at-bat—a feat never since duplicated.
■ Boston, en route to a record-tying 102 wins, clinched its second straight pennant with a victory over Washington.

### LEADERS

**BA:** Willie Keeler, Bal., .385.
**Runs:** John McGraw, Bal., 143.
**Hits:** Willie Keeler, Bal., 216.
**TB:** Jimmy Collins, Bos., 286.
**HR:** Jimmy Collins, Bos., 15.
**RBI:** Nap Lajoie, Phil., 127.
**SB:** Ed Delahanty, Phil., 58.
**Wins:** Kid Nichols, Bos., 31.
**ERA:** Clark Griffith, Chi., 1.88.
**CG:** Jack Taylor, St.L., 42.
**IP:** Jack Taylor, St.L., 397.1.
**SO:** Cy Seymour, N.Y., 239.

**20-game winners**

Kid Nichols, Bos., 31-12
Bert Cunningham, Lou., 28-15
Pink Hawley, Cin., 27-11
Doc McJames, Bal., 27-15
Ted Lewis, Bos., 26-8
Jesse Tannehill, Pit., 25-13
Vic Willis, Bos., 25-13
Cy Young, Cle., 25-13
Cy Seymour, N.Y., 25-19
Clark Griffith, Chi., 24-10
Wiley Piatt, Phil., 24-14
Jim Hughes, Bal., 23-12
Jack Powell, Cle., 23-15
Al Maul, Bal., 20-7
Jim Callahan, Chi., 20-10
Amos Rusie, N.Y., 20-11
Ted Breitenstein, Cin., 20-14

### MAJOR RULES CHANGES

■ Penalties were specified for teams batting out of order.
■ Detailed definitions were provided for pitchers committing balks, including illegal motions to home base and to the bases.
■ Stolen bases were awarded for bases attained without the aid of batted balls or errors.

## 1899

### FINAL STANDINGS

**National League**

| Team | W | L | Pct. | GB |
|---|---|---|---|---|
| Brooklyn | 101 | 47 | .682 | ... |
| Boston | 95 | 57 | .625 | 8 |
| Philadelphia | 94 | 58 | .618 | 9 |
| Baltimore | 86 | 62 | .581 | 15 |
| St. Louis | 84 | 67 | .556 | 18.5 |
| Cincinnati | 83 | 67 | .553 | 19 |
| Pittsburgh | 76 | 73 | .510 | 25.5 |
| Chicago | 75 | 73 | .507 | 26 |
| Louisville | 75 | 77 | .493 | 28 |
| New York | 60 | 90 | .400 | 42 |
| Washington | 54 | 98 | .355 | 49 |
| Cleveland | 20 | 134 | .130 | 84 |

### SIGNIFICANT EVENTS

■ John McGraw made his managerial debut a successful one, leading Baltimore to a victory over New York.
■ The Western League changed its name to the American Baseball League, setting the stage for Ban Johnson's circuit to gain "Major League" credibility.

### MEMORABLE MOMENTS

■ Cleveland defeated Washington and snapped its 24-game losing streak.
■ The Brooklyn Superbas, en route to 101 victories, clinched the pennant with a win over New York.
■ Cincinnati posted a season-closing sweep of Cleveland, handing the Spiders their 133rd and 134th losses.

### LEADERS

**BA:** Ed Delahanty, Phil., .410.
**Runs:** Willie Keeler, Brk.;
John McGraw, Bal., 140.
**Hits:** Ed Delahanty, Phil., 238.
**TB:** Ed Delahanty, Phil., 338.
**HR:** Buck Freeman, Wash., 25.
**RBI:** Ed Delahanty, Phil., 137.
**SB:** Jimmy Sheckard, Bal., 77.
**Wins:** Jim Hughes, Brk.; Joe McGinnity, Bal., 28.
**ERA:** Vic Willis, Bos., 2.50.
**CG:** Bill Carrick, N.Y.; Jack Powell, St.L.;
Cy Young, St.L., 40.
**IP:** Sam Leever, Pit., 379.
**SO:** Noodles Hahn, Cin., 145.

**20-game winners**

Jim Hughes, Brk., 28-6
Joe McGinnity, Bal., 28-16
Vic Willis, Bos., 27-8
Cy Young, St.L., 26-16
Jesse Tannehill, Pit., 24-14
Noodles Hahn, Cin., 23-8
Jack Dunn, Brk., 23-13
Wiley Piatt, Phil., 23-15
Jack Powell, St.L., 23-19
Brickyard Kennedy, Brk., 22-9
Clark Griffith, Chi., 22-14
Frank Kitson, Bal., 22-16
Red Donahue, Phil., 21-8
Jim Callahan, Chi., 21-12
Chick Fraser, Phil., 21-12
Deacon Phillippe, Lou., 21-17
Kid Nichols, Bos., 21-19
Sam Leever, Pit., 21-23

### MAJOR RULES CHANGES

■ The score of any game suspended or called before the full nine innings had been played reverted back to the last full inning completed.
■ Batters were awarded first base for catcher's interference.
■ The 1898 balk rules were further defined.
■ Each team was required to wear uniforms that conformed in color and style.

## 1900

### FINAL STANDINGS

**National League**

| Team | W | L | Pct. | GB |
|---|---|---|---|---|
| Brooklyn | 82 | 54 | .603 | ... |
| Pittsburgh | 79 | 60 | .568 | 4.5 |
| Philadelphia | 75 | 63 | .543 | 8 |
| Boston | 66 | 72 | .478 | 17 |
| Chicago | 65 | 75 | .464 | 19 |
| St. Louis | 65 | 75 | .464 | 19 |
| Cincinnati | 62 | 77 | .446 | 21.5 |
| New York | 60 | 78 | .435 | 23 |

### SIGNIFICANT EVENTS

■ **March 8:** The National League streamlined its product, reducing from 12 to eight teams.
■ **March 9:** N.L. officials expanded the strike zone by reshaping home plate from a 12-inch square to a 17-inch-wide, five-sided figure.
■ **March 16:** Ban Johnson announced formation of a franchise in Chicago, giving his young American League teams in eight cities. The others were Kansas City, Minneapolis, Milwaukee, Indianapolis, Detroit, Cleveland and Buffalo.
■ **October 11:** Ban Johnson's new American League, claiming status as an equal to the National League, announced plans to locate franchises in Baltimore and Washington.
■ **November 14:** The N.L. declared war when it rejected the A.L. as an equal and pronounced it an "outlaw league" outside the National Agreement.
■ **December 15:** The Giants traded aging Amos Rusie to the Reds for a young pitcher named Christy Mathewson.

### MEMORABLE MOMENTS

■ **April 19:** Ban Johnson's new American League opened with a bang when Buffalo's Doc Amole pitched an 8-0 no-hitter against the Tigers.
■ **July 7:** Boston's Kid Nichols defeated the Cubs 11-4 for his 300th career victory.
■ **October 3:** Brooklyn clinched the N.L. pennant with a 6-4, 5-4 sweep at Boston, giving manager Ned Hanlon his fifth championship in seven years.

### LEADERS

**BA:** Honus Wagner, Pit., .381.
**Runs:** Roy Thomas, Phil., 132.
**Hits:** Willie Keeler, Brk., 204.
**TB:** Honus Wagner, Pit., 302.
**HR:** Herman Long, Bos., 12.
**RBI:** Elmer Flick, Phil., 110.
**SB:** Patsy Donovan, St.L.; George Van Haltren, N.Y., 45.
**Wins:** Joe McGinnity, Brk., 28.
**ERA:** Rube Waddell, Pit., 2.37.
**CG:** Pink Hawley, N.Y., 34.
**IP:** Joe McGinnity, Brk., 343.
**SO:** Noodles Hahn, Cin., 132.

**20-game winners**
Joe McGinnity, Brk., 28-8
Jesse Tannehill, Pit., 20-6
Brickyard Kennedy, Brk., 20-13
Deacon Phillippe, Pit., 20-13
Bill Dinneen, Bos., 20-14

**100 RBIs**
Elmer Flick, Phil., 110
Ed Delahanty, Phil., 109
Honus Wagner, Pit., 100

### CHRONICLE-TELEGRAPH CUP

(Brooklyn 3, Pittsburgh 1)
**Game 1**—Brooklyn 5, Pittsburgh 2
**Game 2**—Brooklyn 4, Pittsburgh 2
**Game 3**—Pittsburgh 10, Brooklyn 0
**Game 4**—Brooklyn 6, Pittsburgh 1

### MAJOR RULES CHANGES

■ Home "base" became home "plate" when its shape was changed from a 12-inch square to a five-sided flat surface 17 inches wide.
■ A batter was not awarded first base on a pitcher's balk.

## 1901

### FINAL STANDINGS

**American League**

| Team | W | L | Pct. | GB |
|---|---|---|---|---|
| Chicago | 83 | 53 | .610 | ... |
| Boston | 79 | 57 | .581 | 4 |
| Detroit | 74 | 61 | .548 | 8.5 |
| Philadelphia | 74 | 62 | .544 | 9 |
| Baltimore | 68 | 65 | .511 | 13.5 |
| Washington | 61 | 72 | .459 | 20.5 |
| Cleveland | 54 | 82 | .397 | 29 |
| Milwaukee | 48 | 89 | .350 | 35.5 |

**National League**

| Team | W | L | Pct. | GB |
|---|---|---|---|---|
| Pittsburgh | 90 | 49 | .647 | ... |
| Philadelphia | 83 | 57 | .593 | 7.5 |
| Brooklyn | 79 | 57 | .581 | 9.5 |
| St. Louis | 76 | 64 | .543 | 14.5 |
| Boston | 69 | 69 | .500 | 20.5 |
| Chicago | 53 | 86 | .381 | 37 |
| New York | 52 | 85 | .380 | 37 |
| Cincinnati | 52 | 87 | .374 | 38 |

### SIGNIFICANT EVENTS

■ **January 28:** When the A.L. formally organized as an eight-team "Major League," it placed franchises in Chicago, Philadelphia and Boston—N.L. strongholds.
■ **February 27:** Among a series of N.L. rules changes was the declaration that all foul balls will count as strikes, except when the batter already has two.
■ **March 28:** In a move to keep Napoleon Lajoie from jumping to the A.L.'s Athletics, the Phillies filed for an injunction to keep him from playing for any other team.
■ **September 19:** The baseball schedule was canceled because of the funeral of President William McKinley, who was killed by an assassin's bullet.
■ **October 20:** Seven Cardinals, including top hitters Jesse Burkett and Bobby Wallace, jumped to the American League's new St. Louis franchise.
■ **November 20:** A.L. President Ban Johnson shifted his Milwaukee franchise to St. Louis for a head-to-head battle with the N.L.'s Cardinals.

### MEMORABLE MOMENTS

■ **April 24:** Chicago played host to the A.L.'s first Major League game, defeating Cleveland, 8-2.
■ **April 25:** Detroit celebrated its A.L. debut by scoring 10 ninth-inning runs and beating Milwaukee, 14-13.
■ **July 15:** Christy Mathewson, the Giants' 21-year-old rookie righthander, held the Cardinals hitless in a 5-0 New York victory at St. Louis.
■ **September 29:** The White Stockings captured the first A.L. pennant, but Philadelphia's Napoleon Lajoie compiled Triple Crown totals of .426, 14 homers and 125 RBI.

### LEADERS

**American League**
**BA:** Nap Lajoie, Phil., .420.
**Runs:** Nap Lajoie, Phil., 145.
**Hits:** Lajoie, Phil., 232.
**TB:** Nap Lajoie, Phil., 350.
**HR:** Nap Lajoie, Phil., 14.
**RBI:** Nap Lajoie, Phil., 125.
**SB:** Frank Isbell, Chi., 52.
**Wins:** Cy Young, Bos., 33
**ERA:** Cy Young, Bos., 1.62
**CG:** Joe McGinnity, Balt., 39.
**IP:** Joe McGinnity, Balt., 382.
**SO:** Cy Young, Bos., 158.

**National League**
**BA:** Jesse Burkett, St.L., .376.
**Runs:** Jesse Burkett, St.L., 142.
**Hits:** Jesse Burkett, St.L., 226.
**TB:** Jesse Burkett, St.L., 306.
**HR:** Sam Crawford, Cin., 16.
**RBI:** Honus Wagner, Pit., 126.
**SB:** Honus Wagner, Pit., 49.
**Wins:** Bill Donovan, Brk., 25.
**ERA:** Jesse Tannehill, Pit., 2.18.
**CG:** Noodles Hahn, Cin., 41.
**IP:** Noodles Hahn, Cin., 375.1.
**SO:** Noodles Hahn, Cin., 239.

**A.L. 20-game winners**
Cy Young, Bos., 33-10
Joe McGinnity, Bal., 26-20
Clark Griffith, Chi., 24-7
Roscoe Miller, Det., 23-13
Chick Fraser, Phil., 22-16
Roy Patterson, Chi., 20-15
Red Donahue, Phil., 21-13
Al Orth, Phil., 20-12
Christy Mathewson, N.Y., 20-17
Vic Willis, Bos., 20-17

**N.L. 20-game winners**
Bill Donovan, Brk., 25-15
Jack Harper, St.L., 23-13
Deacon Phillippe, Pit., 22-12
Noodles Hahn, Cin., 22-19
Jack Chesbro, Pit., 21-10

**A.L. 100 RBIs**
Nap Lajoie, Phil., 125
Buck Freeman, Bos., 114

**N.L. 100 RBIs**
Honus Wagner, Pit., 126
Ed Delahanty, Phil., 108
Jimmy Sheckard, Brk., 104
Sam Crawford, Cin., 104

## 1902

### FINAL STANDINGS

**American League**

| Team | W | L | Pct. | GB |
|---|---|---|---|---|
| Philadelphia | 83 | 53 | .610 | ... |
| St. Louis | 78 | 58 | .574 | 5 |
| Boston | 77 | 60 | .562 | 6.5 |
| Chicago | 74 | 60 | .552 | 8 |
| Cleveland | 69 | 67 | .507 | 14 |
| Washington | 61 | 75 | .449 | 22 |
| Detroit | 52 | 83 | .385 | 30.5 |
| Baltimore | 50 | 88 | .362 | 34 |

**National League**

| Team | W | L | Pct. | GB |
|---|---|---|---|---|
| Pittsburgh | 103 | 36 | .741 | ... |
| Brooklyn | 75 | 63 | .543 | 27.5 |
| Boston | 73 | 64 | .533 | 29 |
| Cincinnati | 70 | 70 | .500 | 33.5 |
| Chicago | 68 | 69 | .496 | 34 |
| St. Louis | 56 | 78 | .418 | 44.5 |
| Philadelphia | 56 | 81 | .409 | 46 |
| New York | 48 | 88 | .353 | 53.5 |

### SIGNIFICANT EVENTS

■ **April 21:** The Pennsylvania Supreme Court granted an injunction barring league-jumper Napoleon Lajoie from playing for any team but the Phillies.
■ **May 27:** To keep Lajoie from returning to the N.L., A.L. president Ban Johnson shifted his contract from the Athletics to the Indians, getting him out of Pennsylvania.
■ **July 8:** The A.L. lost Baltimore manager John McGraw, who jumped to the N.L. as manager of the Giants and took five players with him.
■ **September 28:** Philadelphia Athletics star Socks Seybold completed the American League season with a Major League single-season record 16 home runs.
■ **December 9:** The A.L. announced plans to locate a franchise in New York for the 1903 season.
■ **December 12:** Owners elected Harry Pulliam as N.L. president.

### MEMORABLE MOMENTS

■ **April 26:** In a stirring Major League debut, Cleveland's Addie Joss fired a one-hitter and beat the Browns, 3-0.
■ **July 19:** The New York Giants, en route to a last-place finish in the N.L., dropped a 5-3 decision to Philadelphia in the managerial debut of John McGraw.
■ **October 4:** The Pirates completed their 103-36 season with a 27½-game lead over second-place Brooklyn in the N.L.

### LEADERS

**American League**
**BA:** Ed Delahanty, Was., .376.
**Runs:** Dave Fultz, Phil.; Topsy Hartsel, Phil., 109.
**Hits:** Charlie Hickman, Bos.-Cle., 193.
**TB:** Charlie Hickman, Bos.-Cle., 288.
**HR:** Socks Seybold, Phil., 16.
**RBI:** Buck Freeman, Bos., 121.
**SB:** Topsy Hartsel, Phil., 47.
**Wins:** Cy Young, Bos., 32.
**ERA:** Ed Siever, Det., 1.91.
**CG:** Cy Young, Bos., 41.
**IP:** Cy Young, Bos., 384.2
**SO:** Rube Waddell, Phil., 210.

**National League**
**BA:** Ginger Beaumont, Pit., .357.
**Runs:** Honus Wagner, Pit., 105.
**Hits:** Ginger Beaumont, Pit., 193.
**TB:** Sam Crawford, Cin., 256.
**HR:** Tommy Leach, Pit., 6.
**RBI:** Honus Wagner, Pit., 91.
**SB:** Honus Wagner, Pit., 42.
**Wins:** Jack Chesbro, Pit., 28.
**ERA:** Jack Taylor, Chi., 1.33.
**CG:** Vic Willis, Bos., 45
**IP:** Vic Willis, Bos., 410.
**SO:** Vic Willis, Bos., 225.

**A.L. 20-game winners**
Cy Young, Bos., 32-11
Rube Waddell, Phil., 24-7
Red Donahue, St.L., 22-11
Jack Powell, St.L., 22-17
Bill Dinneen, Bos., 21-21
Eddie Plank, Phil., 20-15

**N.L. 20-game winners**
Jack Chesbro, Pit., 28-6
Togie Pittinger, Bos., 27-16
Vic Willis, Bos., 27-20
Jack Taylor, Chi., 23-11
Noodles Hahn, Cin., 23-12
Jesse Tannehill, Pit., 20-6
Deacon Phillippe, Pit., 20-9

**A.L./N.L. 20-game winner**
Joe McGinnity, Bal.-Pit., 21

**A.L. 100 RBIs**
Buck Freeman, Bos., 121
Charlie Hickman, Bos.-Cle., 110
Lave Cross, Phil., 108

# 1903

## FINAL STANDINGS

**American League**

| Team | W | L | Pct. | GB |
|---|---|---|---|---|
| Boston | 91 | 47 | .659 | ... |
| Philadelphia | 75 | 60 | .556 | 14.5 |
| Cleveland | 77 | 63 | .550 | 15 |
| New York | 72 | 62 | .537 | 17 |
| Detroit | 65 | 71 | .478 | 25 |
| St. Louis | 65 | 74 | .468 | 26.5 |
| Chicago | 60 | 77 | .438 | 30.5 |
| Washington | 43 | 94 | .314 | 47.5 |

**National League**

| Team | W | L | Pct. | GB |
|---|---|---|---|---|
| Pittsburgh | 91 | 49 | .650 | ... |
| New York | 84 | 55 | .604 | 6.5 |
| Chicago | 82 | 56 | .594 | 8 |
| Cincinnati | 74 | 65 | .532 | 16.5 |
| Brooklyn | 70 | 66 | .515 | 19 |
| Boston | 58 | 80 | .420 | 32 |
| Philadelphia | 49 | 86 | .363 | 39.5 |
| St. Louis | 43 | 94 | .314 | 46.5 |

## SIGNIFICANT EVENTS

■ **January 9:** A peace treaty was signed with the N.L. agreeing to recognize the A.L. as a Major League and both parties agreeing to honor the reserve clause in player contracts.

■ **July 2:** Washington star Ed Delahanty died when he fell off a railroad bridge spanning the Niagara River at Fort Erie, Ontario.

■ **August 8:** A bleacher overhang at Philadelphia's N.L. park collapsed, killing 12 and injuring 282.

■ **September 16:** The presidents of the A.L. Boston and N.L. Pittsburgh teams agreed to a best-of-nine championship playoff—baseball's first World Series.

## MEMORABLE MOMENTS

■ **April 22:** The A.L.'s new New York team officially opened play, but the Highlanders dropped a 3-1 decision at Washington.

■ **April 30:** The A.L.'s New York team opened new Hilltop Park with a 6-2 victory over Washington.

■ **September 17:** Boston clinched the A.L. pennant with a victory over Cleveland and set up a championship showdown with N.L.-winner Pittsburgh.

## LEADERS

**American League**

**BA:** Nap Lajoie, Cle., .344.
**Runs:** Patsy Dougherty, Bos., 107.
**Hits:** Patsy Dougherty, Bos., 195.
**TB:** Buck Freeman, Bos., 281.
**HR:** Buck Freeman, Bos., 13.
**RBI:** Buck Freeman, Bos., 104.
**SB:** Harry Bay, Cle., 45.
**Wins:** Cy Young, Bos., 28.
**ERA:** Earl Moore, Cle., 1.74.
**CG:** Bill Donovan, Det.; Rube Waddell, Phil.; Cy Young, Bos., 34.
**IP:** Cy Young, Bos., 341.2.
**SO:** Rube Waddell, Phil., 302.

**National League**

**BA:** Honus Wagner, Pit., .355.
**Runs:** Ginger Beaumont, Pit., 137.
**Hits:** Ginger Beaumont, Pit., 209.
**TB:** Ginger Beaumont, Pit., 272.
**HR:** Jimmy Sheckard, Brk., 9.
**RBI:** Sam Mertes, N.Y., 104.
**SB:** Frank Chance, Chi.; Jimmy Sheckard, Brk., 67.
**Wins:** Joe McGinnity, N.Y., 31.
**ERA:** Sam Leever, Pit., 2.06.
**CG:** Joe McGinnity, N.Y., 44.
**IP:** Joe McGinnity, N.Y., 434.
**SO:** Christy Mathewson, N.Y., 267.

**A.L. 20-game winners**
Cy Young, Bos., 28-9
Eddie Plank, Phil., 23-16
Bill Dinneen, Bos., 21-13
Jack Chesbro, N.Y., 21-15
Willie Sudhoff, St.L., 21-15
Rube Waddell, Phil., 21-16
Tom Hughes, Bos., 20-7
Earl Moore, Cle., 20-8

**N.L. 20-game winners**
Joe McGinnity, N.Y., 31-20
Christy Mathewson, N.Y., 30-13
Sam Leever, Pit., 25-7
Deacon Phillippe, Pit., 25-9
Noodles Hahn, Cin., 22-12
Henry Schmidt, Brk., 22-13
Jack Taylor, Chi., 21-14
Jake Weimer, Chi., 20-8
Bob Wicker, St.L.-Chi., 20-9

**A.L. 100 RBIs**
Buck Freeman, Bos., 104

**N.L. 100 RBIs**
Sam Mertes, N.Y., 104
Honus Wagner, Pit., 101

## WORLD SERIES

■ **Winner:** The Red Sox captured the first modern World Series with a five-games-to-three victory over the N.L.-champion Pirates.

■ **Turning point:** A 7-3 Game 7 victory in which the Red Sox claimed a 4-3 Series lead and finally showed they could beat Pirates starter Deacon Phillippe.

■ **Memorable moments:** Pirates right fielder Jimmy Sebring's Game 1 home run—the first in World Series history.

■ **Top guns:** Bill Dinneen (35 IP, 3-1, 2.06 ERA), Cy Young (34 IP, 2-1, 1.59), Red Sox; Phillippe (44 IP, 3-2), Pirates.

**Linescores**

**Game 1**—October 1, at Boston
Pittsburgh...... 4 0 1 1 0 0 1 0 0 — 7 12 2
Boston........... 0 0 0 0 0 0 2 0 1 — 3 6 4
Phillippe; Young. W—Phillippe. L—Young.
HR—Sebring (Pit.).

**Game 2**—October 2, at Boston
Pittsburgh...... 0 0 0 0 0 0 0 0 0 — 0 3 2
Boston........... 2 0 0 0 0 1 0 0 x — 3 9 0
Leever, Veil (2); Dinneen. W—Dinneen. L—Leever.
HR—Dougherty 2 (Bos.).

**Game 3**—October 3, at Boston
Pittsburgh...... 0 1 2 0 0 0 0 1 0 — 4 7 0
Boston........... 0 0 0 1 0 0 0 1 0 — 2 4 2
Phillippe; Hughes, Young (3). W—Phillippe. L—Hughes.

**Game 4**—October 6, at Pittsburgh
Boston........... 0 0 0 0 1 0 0 0 3 — 4 9 1
Pittsburgh...... 1 0 0 0 1 0 3 0 x — 5 12 1
Dinneen; Phillippe. W—Phillippe. L—Dinneen.

**Game 5**—October 7, at Pittsburgh
Boston........... 0 0 0 0 0 6 4 1 0 — 11 14 2
Pittsburgh...... 0 0 0 0 0 0 0 2 0 — 2 6 4
Young; Kennedy, Thompson (8). W—Young. L—Kennedy.

**Game 6**—October 8, at Pittsburgh
Boston........... 0 0 3 0 2 0 1 0 0 — 6 10 1
Pittsburgh...... 0 0 0 0 0 0 3 0 0 — 3 10 3
Dinneen; Leever. W—Dinneen. L—Leever.

**Game 7**—October 10, at Pittsburgh
Boston........... 2 0 0 2 0 2 0 1 0 — 7 11 4
Pittsburgh...... 0 0 0 1 0 1 0 0 1 — 3 10 3
Young; Phillippe. W—Young. L—Phillippe.

**Game 8**—October 13, at Boston
Pittsburgh...... 0 0 0 0 0 0 0 0 0 — 0 4 3
Boston........... 0 0 0 2 0 1 0 0 x — 3 8 0
Phillippe; Dinneen. W—Dinneen. L—Phillippe.

# 1904

## FINAL STANDINGS

**American League**

| Team | W | L | Pct. | GB |
|---|---|---|---|---|
| Boston | 95 | 59 | .617 | ... |
| New York | 92 | 59 | .609 | 1.5 |
| Chicago | 89 | 65 | .578 | 6 |
| Cleveland | 86 | 65 | .570 | 7.5 |
| Philadelphia | 81 | 70 | .536 | 12.5 |
| St. Louis | 65 | 87 | .428 | 29 |
| Detroit | 62 | 90 | .408 | 32 |
| Washington | 38 | 113 | .252 | 55.5 |

**National League**

| Team | W | L | Pct. | GB |
|---|---|---|---|---|
| New York | 106 | 47 | .693 | ... |
| Chicago | 93 | 60 | .608 | 13 |
| Cincinnati | 88 | 65 | .575 | 18 |
| Pittsburgh | 87 | 66 | .569 | 19 |
| St. Louis | 75 | 79 | .487 | 31.5 |
| Brooklyn | 56 | 97 | .366 | 50 |
| Boston | 55 | 98 | .359 | 51 |
| Philadelphia | 52 | 100 | .342 | 53.5 |

## SIGNIFICANT EVENT

■ **October 10:** Chastising the A.L. as a "minor circuit," Giants owner John T. Brush and manager John McGraw refused to meet the A.L.-champion Red Sox in a second "World Series."

## MEMORABLE MOMENTS

■ **May 5:** Boston great Cy Young pitched the century's first perfect game, retiring all 27 Athletics he faced in a 3-0 victory.

■ **July 5:** The Phillies defeated the Giants 6-5 in 10 innings, ending New York's winning streak at 18 games.

■ **October 6:** Cardinals pitcher Jack Taylor pitched his Major League-record 39th consecutive complete game, but dropped a 6-3 decision to Pittsburgh.

■ **October 10:** The Red Sox captured their second straight A.L. pennant when New York's Jack Chesbro uncorked a final-day wild pitch that allowed the winning run to score in a 3-2 victory.

## LEADERS

**American League**

**BA:** Nap Lajoie, Cle., .376.
**Runs:** Patsy Dougherty, Bos.-N.Y., 113.
**Hits:** Nap Lajoie, Cle., 208.
**TB:** Nap Lajoie, Cle., 305.
**HR:** Harry Davis, Phil., 10.
**RBI:** Nap Lajoie, Cle., 102.
**SB:** Harry Bay, Cle.; Elmer Flick, Cle., 38.
**Wins:** Jack Chesbro, N.Y., 41.
**ERA:** Addie Joss, Cle., 1.59.
**CG:** Jack Chesbro, N.Y., 48.
**IP:** Jack Chesbro, N.Y., 454.2.
**SO:** Rube Waddell, Phil., 349.

**National League**

**BA:** Honus Wagner, Pit., .349.
**Runs:** George Browne, N.Y., 99.
**Hits:** Ginger Beaumont, Pit., 185.
**TB:** Honus Wagner, Pit., 255.
**HR:** Harry Lumley, Brk., 9.
**RBI:** Bill Dahlen, N.Y., 80.
**SB:** Honus Wagner, Pit., 53.
**Wins:** Joe McGinnity, N.Y., 35.
**ERA:** Joe McGinnity, N.Y., 1.61.
**CG:** Jack Taylor, St.L.; Vic Willis, Bos., 39.
**IP:** Joe McGinnity, N.Y., 408.
**SO:** Christy Mathewson, N.Y., 212.

**A.L. 20-game winners**
Jack Chesbro, N.Y., 41-12
Cy Young, Bos., 26-16
Eddie Plank, Phil., 26-17
Rube Waddell, Phil., 25-19
Bill Bernhard, Cle., 23-13
Bill Dinneen, Bos., 23-14
Jack Powell, N.Y., 23-19
Jesse Tannehill, Bos., 21-11
Frank Owen, Chi., 21-15

**N.L. 20-game winners**
Joe McGinnity, N.Y., 35-8
Christy Mathewson, N.Y., 33-12
Jack Harper, Cin., 23-9
Kid Nichols, St.L., 21-13
Dummy Taylor, N.Y., 21-15
Jake Weimer, Chi., 20-14
Jack Taylor, St.L., 20-19

**A.L./N.L. 20-game winner**
Patsy Flaherty, Chi.-Pit., 20

**A.L. 100 RBIs**
Nap Lajoie, Cle., 102

No World Series in 1904.

**Nap Lajoie was the leading hitter in the majors in 1904.**

# 1905

## FINAL STANDINGS

**American League**

| Team | W | L | Pct. | GB |
|---|---|---|---|---|
| Philadelphia | 92 | 56 | .622 | ... |
| Chicago | 92 | 60 | .605 | 2 |
| Detroit | 79 | 74 | .516 | 15.5 |
| Boston | 78 | 74 | .513 | 16 |
| Cleveland | 76 | 78 | .494 | 19 |
| New York | 71 | 78 | .477 | 21.5 |
| Washington | 64 | 87 | .424 | 29.5 |
| St. Louis | 54 | 99 | .353 | 40.5 |

**National League**

| Team | W | L | Pct. | GB |
|---|---|---|---|---|
| New York | 105 | 48 | .686 | ... |
| Pittsburgh | 96 | 57 | .627 | 9 |
| Chicago | 92 | 61 | .601 | 13 |
| Philadelphia | 83 | 69 | .546 | 21.5 |
| Cincinnati | 79 | 74 | .516 | 26 |
| St. Louis | 58 | 96 | .377 | 47.5 |
| Boston | 51 | 103 | .331 | 54.5 |
| Brooklyn | 48 | 104 | .316 | 56.5 |

## SIGNIFICANT EVENTS

■ **October 3:** The National Commission adopted the John T. Brush rules for World Series play: a seven-game format, four umpires, two from each league, to work the Series and a revenue-sharing formula for the teams involved.

## MEMORABLE MOMENTS

■ **June 13:** New York's Christy Mathewson pitched his second career no-hitter, but the Giants needed a ninth-inning run off Chicago's Mordecai Brown to post a 1-0 victory.
■ **August 30:** Detroit's Ty Cobb made his Major League debut, doubling off New York's Jack Chesbro in a 5-3 Tigers victory.
■ **September 27:** Boston's Bill Dinneen pitched the fourth no-hitter of the season, beating Chicago 2-0 in the first game of a doubleheader.
■ **October 6:** Despite losing to Washington 10-4, the Athletics clinched the A.L. pennant when the Browns defeated the White Sox 6-2 on the next-to-last day of the season.

## LEADERS

**American League**
**BA:** Elmer Flick, Cle., .308
**Runs:** Harry Davis, Phil., 93.
**Hits:** George Stone, St.L., 187.
**TB:** George Stone, St.L., 259.
**HR:** Harry Davis, Phil., 8.
**RBI:** Harry Davis, Phil., 83.
**SB:** Danny Hoffman, Phil., 46.
**Wins:** Rube Waddell, Phil., 27.
**ERA:** Rube Waddell, Phil., 1.48.
**CG:** Harry Howell, St.L.; George Mullin, Det.; Eddie Plank, Phil., 35.
**IP:** George Mullin, Det., 347.2.
**SO:** Rube Waddell, Phil., 287.

**National League**
**BA:** Cy Seymour, Cin., .377.
**Runs:** Mike Donlin, N.Y., 124.
**Hits:** Cy Seymour, Cin., 219.
**TB:** Cy Seymour, Cin., 325.
**HR:** Fred Odwell, Cin., 9.
**RBI:** Cy Seymour, Cin., 121.
**SB:** Art Devlin, N.Y.; Billy Maloney, Chi., 59.
**Wins:** Christy Mathewson, N.Y., 31.
**ERA:** Christy Mathewson, N.Y., 1.28.
**CG:** Irv Young, Bos., 41.
**IP:** Irv Young, Bos., 378.
**SO:** Christy Mathewson, N.Y., 206.

**A.L. 20-game winners**
Rube Waddell, Phil., 27-10
Eddie Plank, Phil., 24-12
Nick Altrock, Chi., 23-12
Ed Killian, Det., 23-14
Jesse Tannehill, Bos., 22-9
Frank Owen, Chi., 21-13
George Mullin, Det., 21-21
Addie Joss, Cle., 20-12
Frank Smith, Chi., 20-14

**N.L. 20-game winners**
Christy Mathewson, N.Y., 31-9
Togie Pittinger, Phil., 23-14
Red Ames, N.Y., 22-8
Joe McGinnity, N.Y., 21-15
Sam Leever, Pit., 20-5
Bob Ewing, Cin., 20-11
Deacon Phillippe, Pit., 20-13
Irv Young, Bos., 20-21

**N.L. 100 RBIs**
Cy Seymour, Cin., 121
Sam Mertes, N.Y., 108
Honus Wagner, Pit., 101

## WORLD SERIES

■ **Winner:** The Giants prevailed over the Athletics in an all-shutout fall classic.
■ **Turning point:** Joe McGinnity's five-hit, 1-0 victory over Athletics lefthander Eddie Plank in Game 4. Plank allowed only four hits.
■ **Memorable moment:** New York's John McGraw and Philadelphia's Connie Mack exchanging lineups before Game 1. The two managers would dominate baseball for more than three decades.
■ **Top guns:** Christy Mathewson (3 shutouts, 0.00 ERA), Joe McGinnity, (17 IP, 0.00), Giants; Chief Bender (17 IP, 1.06), Athletics.

**Linescores**

**Game 1**—October 9, at Philadelphia
New York........ 0 0 0 0 2 0 0 0 1 — 3 10 1
Philadelphia.... 0 0 0 0 0 0 0 0 0 — 0 4 0
Mathewson; Plank. W—Mathewson. L—Plank.

**Game 2**—October 10, at New York
Philadelphia.... 0 0 1 0 0 0 0 2 0 — 3 6 2
New York........ 0 0 0 0 0 0 0 0 0 — 0 4 2
Bender; McGinnity, Ames (9). W—Bender. L—McGinnity.

**Game 3**—October 12, at Philadelphia
New York........ 2 0 0 0 5 0 0 0 2 — 9 9 1
Philadelphia.... 0 0 0 0 0 0 0 0 0 — 0 4 5
Mathewson; Coakley. W—Mathewson. L—Coakley.

**Game 4**—October 13, at New York
Philadelphia.... 0 0 0 0 0 0 0 0 0 — 0 5 2
New York........ 0 0 0 1 0 0 0 0 x — 1 4 1
Plank; McGinnity. W—McGinnity. L—Plank.

**Game 5**—October 14, at New York
Philadelphia.... 0 0 0 0 0 0 0 0 0 — 0 6 0
New York........ 0 0 0 0 1 0 0 1 x — 2 5 1
Bender; Mathewson. W—Mathewson. L—Bender.

# 1906

## FINAL STANDINGS

**American League**

| Team | W | L | Pct. | GB |
|---|---|---|---|---|
| Chicago | 93 | 58 | .616 | ... |
| New York | 90 | 61 | .596 | 3 |
| Cleveland | 89 | 64 | .582 | 5 |
| Philadelphia | 78 | 67 | .538 | 12 |
| St. Louis | 76 | 73 | .510 | 16 |
| Detroit | 71 | 78 | .477 | 21 |
| Washington | 55 | 95 | .367 | 37.5 |
| Boston | 49 | 105 | .318 | 45.5 |

**National League**

| Team | W | L | Pct. | GB |
|---|---|---|---|---|
| Chicago | 116 | 36 | .763 | ... |
| New York | 96 | 56 | .632 | 20 |
| Pittsburgh | 93 | 60 | .608 | 23.5 |
| Philadelphia | 71 | 82 | .464 | 45.5 |
| Brooklyn | 66 | 86 | .434 | 50 |
| Cincinnati | 64 | 87 | .424 | 51.5 |
| St. Louis | 52 | 98 | .347 | 63 |
| Boston | 49 | 102 | .325 | 66.5 |

## SIGNIFICANT EVENTS

■ **August 13:** When Chicago's Jack Taylor failed to last through the third inning of a game against Brooklyn, it ended his record complete-game streak at 187.
■ **October 7:** The Cubs ended an amazing regular season with a Major League-record 116 victories and a team ERA of 1.76.

## MEMORABLE MOMENTS

■ **May 25:** Jesse Tannehill snapped Boston's A.L.-record 20-game losing streak with a 3-0 victory over the White Sox.
■ **June 9:** The Boston Beaneaters ended their 19-game losing streak with a 6-3 victory over the Cardinals.
■ **August 23:** Washington ended the Chicago White Stockings' A.L.-record winning streak at 19 games.
■ **September 1:** The Athletics scored three times in the top of the 24th inning and claimed a 4-1 victory over Boston in the longest game in Major League history.
■ **October 3:** Chicago's "Hitless Wonders" clinched the A.L. pennant when the Athletics posted a 3-0 victory over New York in the second game of a doubleheader.

## LEADERS

**American League**
**BA:** George Stone, St.L., .358.
**Runs:** Elmer Flick, Cle., 98.
**Hits:** Nap Lajoie, Cle., 214.
**TB:** George Stone, St.L., 291.
**HR:** Harry Davis, Phil., 12.
**RBI:** Harry Davis, Phil., 96.
**SB:** John Anderson, Wash.; Elmer Flick, Cle., 39.
**Wins:** Al Orth, N.Y., 27.
**ERA:** Doc White, Chi., 1.52.
**CG:** Al Orth, N.Y., 36.
**IP:** Al Orth, N.Y., 338.2.
**SO:** Rube Waddell, Phil., 196.

**National League**
**BA:** Honus Wagner, Pit., .339.
**Runs:** Frank Chance, Chi.; Honus Wagner, Pit., 103.
**Hits:** Harry Steinfeldt, Chi., 176.
**TB:** Honus Wagner, Pit., 237.
**HR:** Tim Jordan, Brk., 12.
**RBI:** Jim Nealon, Pit.; Harry Steinfeldt, Chi., 83.
**SB:** Frank Chance, Chi., 57.
**Wins:** Joe McGinnity, N.Y., 27.
**ERA:** Mordecai Brown, Chi., 1.04.
**CG:** Irv Young, Bos., 37.
**IP:** Irv Young, Bos., 358.1.
**SO:** Fred Beebe, Chi.-St.L., 171.

**A.L. 20-game winners**
Al Orth, N.Y., 27-17
Jack Chesbro, N.Y., 23-17
Bob Rhoades, Cle., 22-10
Frank Owen, Chi., 22-13
Addie Joss, Cle., 21-9
George Mullin, Det., 21-18
Nick Altrock, Chi., 20-13
Otto Hess, Cle., 20-17

**N.L. 20-game winners**
Joe McGinnity, N.Y., 27-12
Mordecai Brown, Chi., 26-6
Vic Willis, Pit., 23-13
Sam Leever, Pit., 22-7
Christy Mathewson, N.Y., 22-12
Jack Pfiester, Chi., 20-8
Jack Taylor, St.L.-Chi., 20-12
Jake Weimer, Cin., 20-14

## WORLD SERIES

■ **Winner:** Chicago's "Hitless Wonders" pulled an intra-city shocker with a six-game victory over the powerful Cubs.
■ **Turning point:** An eight-run Game 5 explosion by the light-hitting White Sox, which was spiced by Frank Isbell's four doubles and two RBIs.
■ **Memorable moment:** Big Ed Walsh's two-hit Game 3 shutout. The Cubs were held hitless after getting a first-inning single and double.
■ **Top guns:** Walsh (2-0, 1.80 ERA), George Rohe (.333, 4 RBIs), White Sox; Ed Reulbach (Game 2 1-hitter), Cubs.

**Linescores**

**Game 1**—October 9, at Chicago Cubs
White Sox....... 0 0 0 0 1 1 0 0 0 — 2 4 1
Cubs.............. 0 0 0 0 0 1 0 0 0 — 1 4 2
Altrock; Brown. W—Altrock. L—Brown.

**Game 2**—October 10, at Chicago White Sox
Cubs.............. 0 3 1 0 0 1 0 2 0 — 7 10 2
White Sox....... 0 0 0 0 1 0 0 0 0 — 1 1 2
Reulbach; White, Owen (4). W—Reulbach. L—White.

**Game 3**—October 11, at Chicago Cubs
White Sox....... 0 0 0 0 0 3 0 0 0 — 3 4 1
Cubs.............. 0 0 0 0 0 0 0 0 0 — 0 2 2
Walsh; Pfiester. W—Walsh. L—Pfiester.

**Game 4**—October 12, at Chicago White Sox
Cubs.............. 0 0 0 0 0 0 1 0 0 — 1 7 1
White Sox....... 0 0 0 0 0 0 0 0 0 — 0 2 1
Brown; Altrock. W—Brown. L—Altrock.

**Game 5**—October 13, at Chicago Cubs
White Sox....... 1 0 2 4 0 1 0 0 0 — 8 12 6
Cubs.............. 3 0 0 1 0 2 0 0 0 — 6 6 0
Walsh, White (7); Reulbach, Pfiester (3), Overall (4). W—Walsh. L—Pfiester.

**Game 6**—October 14, at Chicago White Sox
Cubs.............. 1 0 0 0 1 0 0 0 1 — 3 7 0
White Sox....... 3 4 0 0 0 0 0 1 x — 8 14 3
Brown, Overall (2); White. W—White. L—Brown.

# 1907

## FINAL STANDINGS

**American League**

| Team | W | L | Pct. | GB |
|---|---|---|---|---|
| Detroit | 92 | 58 | .613 | ... |
| Philadelphia | 88 | 57 | .607 | 1.5 |
| Chicago | 87 | 64 | .576 | 5.5 |
| Cleveland | 85 | 67 | .559 | 8 |
| New York | 70 | 78 | .473 | 21 |
| St. Louis | 69 | 83 | .454 | 24 |
| Boston | 59 | 90 | .396 | 32.5 |
| Washington | 49 | 102 | .325 | 43.5 |

**National League**

| Team | W | L | Pct. | GB |
|---|---|---|---|---|
| Chicago | 107 | 45 | .704 | ... |
| Pittsburgh | 91 | 63 | .591 | 17 |
| Philadelphia | 83 | 64 | .565 | 21.5 |
| New York | 82 | 71 | .536 | 25.5 |
| Brooklyn | 65 | 83 | .439 | 40 |
| Cincinnati | 66 | 87 | .431 | 41.5 |
| Boston | 58 | 90 | .392 | 47 |
| St. Louis | 52 | 101 | .340 | 55.5 |

## SIGNIFICANT EVENTS

- **April 11:** Giants catcher Roger Bresnahan introduced his newest innovation in a game against the Phillies: wooden shinguards to protect his legs and knees.
- **August 2:** Washington fireballer Walter Johnson dropped a 3-2 decision to Detroit in his Major League debut.

## MEMORABLE MOMENTS

- **May 20:** The Cardinals ended New York's 17-game winning streak with a 6-4 victory at the Polo Grounds.
- **October 3:** The seventh-place Boston Red Sox edged sixth-place St. Louis 1-0 and ended their 16-game losing streak.
- **October 5:** The Tigers, locked in a tight A.L. pennant race with Philadelphia, clinched the title with a 10-2 victory over St. Louis.

## LEADERS

**American League**

**BA:** Ty Cobb, Det., .350.
**Runs:** Sam Crawford, Det., 102.
**Hits:** Ty Cobb, Det., 212.
**TB:** Ty Cobb, Det., 283.
**HR:** Harry Davis, Phil., 8.
**RBI:** Ty Cobb, Det., 119.
**SB:** Ty Cobb, Det., 49.
**Wins:** Addie Joss, Cle.; Doc White, Chi., 27.
**ERA:** Ed Walsh, Chi., 1.60.
**CG:** Ed Walsh, Chi., 37.
**IP:** Ed Walsh, Chi., 422.1.
**SO:** Rube Waddell, Phil., 232.

**National League**

**BA:** Honus Wagner, Pit., .350.
**Runs:** Spike Shannon, N.Y., 104.
**Hits:** Ginger Beaumont, Bos., 187.
**TB:** Honus Wagner, Pit., 264.
**HR:** Dave Brain, Bos., 10.
**RBI:** Sherry Magee, Phil., 85.
**SB:** Honus Wagner, Pit., 61.
**Wins:** Christy Mathewson, N.Y., 24.
**ERA:** Jack Pfiester, Chi., 1.15.
**CG:** Stoney McGlynn, St.L., 33.
**IP:** Stoney McGlynn, St.L., 352.1.
**SO:** Christy Mathewson, N.Y., 178.

**A.L. 20-game winners**

Addie Joss, Cle., 27-11
Doc White, Chi., 27-13
Bill Donovan, Det., 25-4
Ed Killian, Det., 25-13
Eddie Plank, Phil., 24-16
Ed Walsh, Chi., 24-18
Frank Smith, Chi., 23-10
Jimmy Dygert, Phil., 21-8
Cy Young, Bos., 21-15
George Mullin, Det., 20-20

**N.L. 20-game winners**

Christy Mathewson, N.Y., 24-12
Orval Overall, Chi., 23-7
Tully Sparks, Phil., 22-8
Vic Willis, Pit., 21-11
Mordecai Brown, Chi., 20-6
Lefty Leifield, Pit., 20-16

**A.L. 100 RBIs**

Ty Cobb, Det., 119

## WORLD SERIES

- **Winner:** The powerful Cubs, atoning for their shocking loss to the White Sox in 1906, made short work of the A.L.-champion Tigers.
- **Turning point:** A ninth-inning passed ball by Tigers catcher Charlie Schmidt that allowed the Cubs to score the tying run in a Game 1 battle that would end in a 3-3 deadlock.
- **Memorable moment:** Schmidt's passed ball, which awoke the Cubs and set the stage for their sweeping finish.
- **Top guns:** Harry Steinfeldt (.471), Johnny Evers (.350), Cubs; Claude Rossman (.400), Tigers.

### Linescores

**Game 1**—October 8, at Chicago
Detroit...0 0 0 000 030 000—3 9 3
Chicago.0 0 0 100 002 000—3 10 5
Donovan; Overall, Reulbach (10). Game called after 12 innings because of darkness.

**Game 2**—October 9, at Chicago
Detroit........... 010 000 000 — 1 9 1
Chicago.......... 010 200 00x — 3 9 1
Mullin; Pfiester. W—Pfiester. L—Mullin.

**Game 3**—October 10, at Chicago
Detroit........... 000 001 000 — 1 6 1
Chicago.......... 010 310 00x — 5 10 1
Siever, Killian (5); Reulbach. W—Reulbach. L—Siever.

**Game 4**—October 11, at Detroit
Chicago.......... 000 020 301 — 6 7 2
Detroit........... 000 100 000 — 1 5 2
Overall; Donovan. W—Overall. L—Donovan.

**Game 5**—October 12, at Detroit
Chicago.......... 110 000 000 — 2 7 1
Detroit........... 000 000 000 — 0 7 2
Brown; Mullin. W—Brown. L—Mullin.

# 1908

## FINAL STANDINGS

**American League**

| Team | W | L | Pct. | GB |
|---|---|---|---|---|
| Detroit | 90 | 63 | .588 | ... |
| Cleveland | 90 | 64 | .584 | .5 |
| Chicago | 88 | 64 | .579 | 1.5 |
| St. Louis | 83 | 69 | .546 | 6.5 |
| Boston | 75 | 79 | .487 | 15.5 |
| Philadelphia | 68 | 85 | .444 | 22 |
| Washington | 67 | 85 | .441 | 22.5 |
| New York | 51 | 103 | .331 | 39.5 |

**National League**

| Team | W | L | Pct. | GB |
|---|---|---|---|---|
| Chicago | 99 | 55 | .643 | ... |
| New York | 98 | 56 | .636 | 1 |
| Pittsburgh | 98 | 56 | .636 | 1 |
| Philadelphia | 83 | 71 | .539 | 16 |
| Cincinnati | 73 | 81 | .474 | 26 |
| Boston | 63 | 91 | .409 | 36 |
| Brooklyn | 53 | 101 | .344 | 46 |
| St. Louis | 49 | 105 | .318 | 50 |

## SIGNIFICANT EVENTS

- **February 27:** Baseball adopted the sacrifice fly rule, stating that a batter will not be charged with an at-bat if a runner tags up and scores after the catch of his fly ball.

## MEMORABLE MOMENTS

- **June 30:** Boston's 41-year-old Cy Young became the first pitcher to notch three career no-hitters when he defeated New York, 8-0.
- **September 23:** The outcome of an important Giants-Cubs game was thrown into confusion when New York baserunner Fred Merkle failed to touch second base on an apparent game-ending hit, prompting the Cubs' claims of a game-prolonging forceout.
- **September 24:** N.L. President Harry Pulliam declared the September 23 Cubs-Giants game a tie.
- **September 26:** Chicago's Ed Reulbach made baseball history when he shut out Brooklyn twice—5-0 and 3-0—on the same day.
- **October 2:** Cleveland's Addie Joss became the second modern-era pitcher to throw a perfect game, retiring all 27 Chicago batters he faced in a 1-0 victory.
- **October 6:** The Tigers defeated the White Sox, 7-0, and claimed the A.L. pennant on the season's final day.
- **October 8:** In an N.L. pennant-deciding matchup dictated by the controversial September 23 tie game, Chicago defeated the Giants, 4-2.

## LEADERS

**American League**

**BA:** Ty Cobb, Det., .324.
**Runs:** Matty McIntyre, Det., 105.
**Hits:** Ty Cobb, Det., 188.
**TB:** Ty Cobb, Det., 276.
**HR:** Sam Crawford, Det., 7.
**RBI:** Ty Cobb, Det., 108.
**SB:** Patsy Dougherty, Chi., 47.
**Wins:** Ed Walsh, Chi., 40.
**ERA:** Addie Joss, Cle., 1.16.
**CG:** Ed Walsh, Chi., 42.
**IP:** Ed Walsh, Chi., 464.
**SO:** Ed Walsh, Chi., 269.

**National League**

**BA:** Honus Wagner, Pit., .354.
**Runs:** Fred Tenney, N.Y., 101.
**Hits:** Honus Wagner, Pit., 201.
**TB:** Honus Wagner, Pit., 308.
**HR:** Tim Jordan, Brk., 12.
**RBI:** Honus Wagner, Pit., 109.
**SB:** Honus Wagner, Pit., 53.
**Wins:** Christy Mathewson, N.Y., 37.
**ERA:** Christy Mathewson, N.Y., 1.43.
**CG:** Christy Mathewson, N.Y., 34.
**IP:** Christy Mathewson, N.Y., 390.2.
**SO:** Christy Mathewson, N.Y., 259.

**A.L. 20-game winners**

Ed Walsh, Chi., 40-15
Addie Joss, Cle., 24-11
Ed Summers, Det., 24-12
Cy Young, Bos., 21-11

**N.L. 20-game winners**

Christy Mathewson, N.Y., 37-11
Mordecai Brown, Chi., 29-9
Ed Reulbach, Chi., 24-7
Nick Maddox, Pit., 23-8
Vic Willis, Pit. 23-11
Hooks Wiltse, N.Y., 23-14
George McQuillan, Phil., 23-17

**A.L. 100 RBIs**

Ty Cobb, Det., 108

**N.L. 100 RBIs**

Honus Wagner, Pit., 109
Mike Donlin, N.Y., 106

## WORLD SERIES

- **Winner:** The Cubs became the first two-time Series champs by defeating Detroit for the second consecutive year.
- **Turning point:** A five-run ninth-inning rally that turned a 6-5 Game 1 deficit into a 10-6 Cubs victory.
- **Memorable moment:** A two-run eighth-inning home run by Chicago's Joe Tinker that broke up a scoreless Game 2 pitching duel and gave Orval Overall a 6-1 victory over Bill Donovan.
- **Top guns:** Overall (2-0, 0.98 ERA), Frank Chance (.421), Cubs; Ty Cobb (.368), Tigers.

### Linescores

**Game 1**—October 10, at Detroit
Chicago.......... 004 000 105 —10 14 2
Detroit........... 100 000 320 — 6 10 4
Reulbach, Overall (7), Brown (8); Killian, Summers (3). W—Brown. L—Summers.

**Game 2**—October 11, at Chicago
Detroit........... 000 000 001 — 1 4 1
Chicago.......... 000 000 06x — 6 7 1
Donovan; Overall. W—Overall. L—Donovan. HR—Tinker (Chi.).

**Game 3**—October 12, at Chicago
Detroit........... 100 005 020 — 8 11 4
Chicago.......... 000 300 000 — 3 7 2
Mullin; Pfiester, Reulbach (9). W—Mullin. L—Pfiester.

**Game 4**—October 13, at Detroit
Chicago.......... 002 000 001 — 3 10 0
Detroit........... 000 000 000 — 0 4 1
Brown; Summers, Winter (9). W—Brown. L—Summers.

**Game 5**—October 14, at Detroit
Chicago.......... 100 010 000 — 2 10 0
Detroit........... 000 000 000 — 0 3 0
Overall; Donovan. W—Overall. L—Donovan.

# 1909

## FINAL STANDINGS

**American League**

| Team | W | L | Pct. | GB |
|---|---|---|---|---|
| Detroit | 98 | 54 | .645 | ... |
| Philadelphia | 95 | 58 | .621 | 3.5 |
| Boston | 88 | 63 | .583 | 9.5 |
| Chicago | 78 | 74 | .513 | 20 |
| New York | 74 | 77 | .490 | 23.5 |
| Cleveland | 71 | 82 | .464 | 27.5 |
| St. Louis | 61 | 89 | .407 | 36 |
| Washington | 42 | 110 | .276 | 56 |

**National League**

| Team | W | L | Pct. | GB |
|---|---|---|---|---|
| Pittsburgh | 110 | 42 | .724 | ... |
| Chicago | 104 | 49 | .680 | 6.5 |
| New York | 92 | 61 | .601 | 18.5 |
| Cincinnati | 77 | 76 | .503 | 33.5 |
| Philadelphia | 74 | 79 | .484 | 36.5 |
| Brooklyn | 55 | 98 | .359 | 55.5 |
| St. Louis | 54 | 98 | .355 | 56 |
| Boston | 45 | 108 | .294 | 65.5 |

## SIGNIFICANT EVENTS

- **April 12:** The Athletics and pitcher Eddie Plank christened Philadelphia's new Shibe Park with an 8-1 victory over Boston.
- **June 30:** The Cubs spoiled Pittsburgh's opening of new Forbes Field, posting a 3-2 victory over the Pirates.
- **July 29:** N.L. President Harry Pulliam shocked the baseball world when he shot himself to death.
- **October 5:** Detroit's Ty Cobb finished his Triple Crown season with a .377 average, 9 home runs and 107 RBIs.

## MEMORABLE MOMENTS

- **April 15:** New York's Red Ames lost his Opening Day no-hit bid in the 10th inning and the game in the 13th when Brooklyn scored a 3-0 victory.
- **July 16:** A Detroit-Washington game ended 0-0 after 18 innings—the longest scoreless tie in A.L. history.
- **July 19:** Cleveland shortstop Neal Ball pulled off the first unassisted triple play of the century in a game against the Red Sox.

## LEADERS

**American League**

**BA:** Ty Cobb, Det., .377.
**Runs:** Ty Cobb, Det., 116.
**Hits:** Ty Cobb, Det., 216.
**TB:** Ty Cobb, Det., 296.
**HR:** Ty Cobb, Det., 9.
**RBI:** Ty Cobb, Det., 107.
**SB:** Ty Cobb, Det., 76.
**Wins:** George Mullin, Det., 29.
**ERA:** Harry Krause, Phil., 1.39.
**CG:** Frank Smith, Chi., 37.
**IP:** Frank Smith, Chi., 365.
**SO:** Frank Smith, Chi., 177.

**National League**

**BA:** Honus Wagner, Pit., .339.
**Runs:** Tommy Leach, Pit., 126.
**Hits:** Larry Doyle, N.Y., 172.
**TB:** Honus Wagner, Pit., 242.
**HR:** Red Murray, N.Y., 7.
**RBI:** Honus Wagner, Pit., 100.
**SB:** Bob Bescher, Cin., 54.
**Wins:** Mordecai Brown, Chi., 27.
**ERA:** Christy Mathewson, N.Y., 1.14.
**CG:** Mordecai Brown, Chi., 32.
**IP:** Mordecai Brown, Chi., 342.2.
**SO:** Orval Overall, Chi., 205.

**A.L. 20-game winners**

George Mullin, Det., 29-8
Frank Smith, Chi., 25-17
Ed Willett, Det., 21-10

**N.L. 20-game winners**

Mordecai Brown, Chi., 27-9
Howie Camnitz, Pit., 25-6
Christy Mathewson, N.Y., 25-6
Vic Willis, Pit., 22-11
Orval Overall, Chi., 20-11
Hooks Wiltse, N.Y., 20-11

**A.L. 100 RBIs**

Ty Cobb, Det., 107

**N.L. 100 RBIs**

Honus Wagner, Pit., 100

## WORLD SERIES

- **Winner:** The Pirates, losers in baseball's first World Series, bounced back to hand the Tigers their third straight post-season loss.
- **Turning point:** A tie-breaking three-run homer by Pirates player/manager Fred Clarke that keyed an 8-4 victory in the pivotal fifth game.
- **Memorable moment:** When Pirates pitcher Babe Adams retired the final Tiger in Game 7 and ended the first Series to go the distance.
- **Top guns:** Adams (3-0, 1.33 ERA), Honus Wagner (.333, 7 RBIs, 6 SB), Pirates; Jim Delahanty (.346), Tigers.

**Linescores**

**Game 1**—October 8, at Pittsburgh

Detroit........... 1 0 0  0 0 0  0 0 0 — 1 6 4
Pittsburgh...... 0 0 0  1 2 1  0 0 x — 4 5 0
Mullin; Adams. W—Adams. L—Mullin.
HR—Clarke (Pit.).

**Game 2**—October 9, at Pittsburgh

Detroit........... 0 2 3  0 2 0  0 0 0 — 7 9 3
Pittsburgh...... 2 0 0  0 0 0  0 0 0 — 2 5 1
Donovan; Camnitz, Willis (3). W—Donovan.
L—Camnitz.

**Game 3**—October 11, at Detroit

Pittsburgh...... 5 1 0  0 0 0  0 0 2 — 8 10 3
Detroit........... 0 0 0  0 0 0  4 0 2 — 6 10 5
Maddox; Summers, Willett (1), Works (8).
W—Maddox. L—Summers.

**Game 4**—October 12, at Detroit

Pittsburgh...... 0 0 0  0 0 0  0 0 0 — 0 5 6
Detroit........... 0 2 0  3 0 0  0 0 x — 5 8 0
Leifield, Phillippe (5); Mullin. W—Mullin.
L—Leifield.

**Game 5**—October 13, at Pittsburgh

Detroit........... 1 0 0  0 0 2  0 1 0 — 4 6 1
Pittsburgh...... 1 1 1  0 0 0  4 1 x — 8 10 1
Summers, Willett (8); Adams. W—Adams.
L—Summers. HR—D. Jones, Crawford (Det.); Clarke (Pit.).

**Game 6**—October 14, at Detroit

Pittsburgh...... 3 0 0  0 0 0  0 0 1 — 4 7 3
Detroit........... 1 0 0  2 1 1  0 0 x — 5 10 3
Willis, Camnitz (6), Phillippe (7); Mullin.
W—Mullin. L—Willis.

**Game 7**—October 16, at Detroit

Pittsburgh...... 0 2 0  2 0 3  0 1 0 — 8 7 0
Detroit........... 0 0 0  0 0 0  0 0 0 — 0 6 3
Adams; Donovan, Mullin (4). W—Adams.
L—Donovan.

# 1910

## FINAL STANDINGS

**American League**

| Team | W | L | Pct. | GB |
|---|---|---|---|---|
| Philadelphia | 102 | 48 | .680 | ... |
| New York | 88 | 63 | .583 | 14.5 |
| Detroit | 86 | 68 | .558 | 18 |
| Boston | 81 | 72 | .529 | 22.5 |
| Cleveland | 71 | 81 | .467 | 32 |
| Chicago | 68 | 85 | .444 | 35.5 |
| Washington | 66 | 85 | .437 | 36.5 |
| St. Louis | 47 | 107 | .305 | 57 |

**National League**

| Team | W | L | Pct. | GB |
|---|---|---|---|---|
| Chicago | 104 | 50 | .675 | ... |
| New York | 91 | 63 | .591 | 13 |
| Pittsburgh | 86 | 67 | .562 | 17.5 |
| Philadelphia | 78 | 75 | .510 | 25.5 |
| Cincinnati | 75 | 79 | .487 | 29 |
| Brooklyn | 64 | 90 | .416 | 40 |
| St. Louis | 63 | 90 | .412 | 40.5 |
| Boston | 53 | 100 | .346 | 50.5 |

## SIGNIFICANT EVENTS

- **February 18:** The N.L. approved a 154-game schedule, a plan already adopted by the A.L.
- **April 14:** William Howard Taft became the first U.S. President to throw out the first ball at a season opener in Washington.
- **April 21:** Detroit spoiled the opening of Cleveland's League Park with a 5-0 victory over the Indians.
- **July 1:** Chicago unveiled White Sox Park (Comiskey Park), but the Browns spoiled the occasion with a 2-0 victory.

## MEMORABLE MOMENTS

- **July 19:** The incredible Cy Young earned his 500th career victory when he pitched Cleveland to an 11-inning, 5-2 win over Washington.
- **August 30:** The Highlanders' Tom Hughes lost his no-hit bid against Cleveland with one out in the 10th and lost the game, 5-0, in the 11th.
- **September 25:** The scoreless streak of Philadelphia's Jack Coombs ended at 53 innings in a darkness-shortened 5-2 loss to Chicago in the second game of a doubleheader.
- **October 9:** Cleveland's Napoleon Lajoie collected eight final-day hits, seven of them bunt singles, in a doubleheader against the Browns and lifted his final average to .384—one point ahead of Detroit's Ty Cobb.
- **October 15:** A.L. President Ban Johnson adjusted Cobb's final average to .385 and declared him winner of the A.L. batting title.

## LEADERS

**American League**

**BA:** Ty Cobb, Det., .383.
**Runs:** Ty Cobb, Det., 106.
**Hits:** Nap Lajoie, Cle., 227.
**TB:** Nap Lajoie, Cle., 304.
**HR:** Jake Stahl, Bos., 10.
**RBI:** Sam Crawford, Det., 120.
**SB:** Eddie Collins, Phil., 81.
**Wins:** Jack Coombs, Phil., 31.
**ERA:** Ed Walsh, Chi., 1.27.
**CG:** Walter Johnson, Wash., 38.
**IP:** Walter Johnson, Wash., 370.
**SO:** Walter Johnson, Wash., 313.

**National League**

**BA:** Sherry Magee, Phil., .331.
**Runs:** Sherry Magee, Phil., 110.
**Hits:** Bobby Byrne, Pit.; Honus Wagner, Pit., 178.
**TB:** Sherry Magee, Phil., 263.
**HR:** Fred Beck, Bos.; Frank Schulte, Chi., 10.
**RBI:** Sherry Magee, Phil., 123.
**SB:** Bob Bescher, Cin., 70.
**Wins:** Christy Mathewson, N.Y., 27.
**ERA:** King Cole, Chi., 1.80.
**CG:** Mordecai Brown, Chi.; Christy Mathewson, N.Y.; Nap Rucker, Brk., 27
**IP:** Nap Rucker, Brk., 320.1.
**SO:** Earl Moore, Phil., 185.

**A.L. 20-game winners**

Jack Coombs, Phil., 31-9
Russ Ford, N.Y., 26-6
Walter Johnson, Wash., 25-17
Chief Bender, Phil., 23-5
George Mullin, Det., 21-12

**N.L. 20-game winners**

Christy Mathewson, N.Y., 27-9
Mordecai Brown, Chi., 25-14
Earl Moore, Phil., 22-15
King Cole, Chi., 20-4
George Suggs, Cin., 20-12

**A.L. 100 RBIs**

Sam Crawford, Det., 120

**N.L. 100 RBIs**

Sherry Magee, Phil., 123

## WORLD SERIES

- **Winner:** Philadelphia won their first Series championship and thwarted the Cubs' bid to become a three-time winner.
- **Turning point:** The Cubs' failure to take advantage of the less-than-artistic Jack Coombs in Game 2. Coombs allowed eight hits and nine walks but still won, 9-3.
- **Memorable moment:** A three-run homer by Danny Murphy that broke up a tight Game 3 and helped Philadelphia to a 12-5 victory.
- **Top guns:** Eddie Collins (.429), Murphy (.350, 8 RBIs), Frank Baker (.409), Athletics; Frank Chance (.353), Frank Schulte (.353), Cubs.

**Linescores**

**Game 1**—October 17, at Philadelphia

Chicago.......... 0 0 0  0 0 0  0 0 1 — 1 3 1
Philadelphia.... 0 2 1  0 0 0  0 1 x — 4 7 2
Overall, McIntire (4); Bender. W—Bender.
L—Overall.

**Game 2**—October 18, at Philadelphia

Chicago.......... 1 0 0  0 0 0  1 0 1 — 3 8 3
Philadelphia.... 0 0 2  0 1 0  6 0 x — 9 14 4
Brown, Richie (8); Coombs. W—Coombs.
L—Brown.

**Game 3**—October 20, at Chicago

Philadelphia.... 1 2 5  0 0 0  4 0 0 — 12 15 1
Chicago.......... 1 2 0  0 0 0  0 2 0 — 5 6 5
Coombs; Reulbach, McIntire (3), Pfiester (3).
W—Coombs. L—McIntire. HR—Murphy (Phil.).

**Game 4**—October 22, at Chicago

Philadelphia 0 0 1  2 0 0  0 0 0  0 — 3 11 3
Chicago 1 0 0  1 0 0  0 0 1  1 — 4 9 1
Bender; Cole, Brown (9). W—Brown. L—Bender.

**Game 5**—October 23, at Chicago

Philadelphia.... 1 0 0  0 1 0  0 5 0 — 7 9 1
Chicago.......... 0 1 0  0 0 0  0 1 0 — 2 9 2
Coombs; Brown. W—Coombs. L—Brown.

# 1911

## FINAL STANDINGS

**American League**

| Team | W | L | Pct. | GB |
|---|---|---|---|---|
| Philadelphia | 101 | 50 | .669 | ... |
| Detroit | 89 | 65 | .578 | 13.5 |
| Cleveland | 80 | 73 | .523 | 22 |
| Chicago | 77 | 74 | .510 | 24 |
| Boston | 78 | 75 | .510 | 24 |
| New York | 76 | 76 | .500 | 25.5 |
| Washington | 64 | 90 | .416 | 38.5 |
| St. Louis | 45 | 107 | .296 | 56.5 |

**National League**

| Team | W | L | Pct. | GB |
|---|---|---|---|---|
| New York | 99 | 54 | .647 | ... |
| Chicago | 92 | 62 | .597 | 7.5 |
| Pittsburgh | 85 | 69 | .552 | 14.5 |
| Philadelphia | 79 | 73 | .520 | 19.5 |
| St. Louis | 75 | 74 | .503 | 22 |
| Cincinnati | 70 | 83 | .458 | 29 |
| Brooklyn | 64 | 86 | .427 | 33.5 |
| Boston | 44 | 107 | .291 | 54 |

## SIGNIFICANT EVENTS

■ **April 14:** New York's Polo Grounds burned down, forcing the Giants to play a big stretch of their schedule at the Highlanders' Hilltop Park.
■ **June 28:** The Giants defeated the Braves, 3-0, in the first game at the new Polo Grounds.
■ **October 11:** Chalmers automobile recipients as baseball's first MVPs: Detroit's Ty Cobb in the A.L. and Chicago's Frank Schulte in the N.L.

## MEMORABLE MOMENTS

■ **May 13:** The Giants exploded for a record 13 first-inning runs, 10 before the first out was recorded, in a 19-5 victory over St. Louis.
■ **July 4:** Chicago ace Ed Walsh stopped Detroit, 7-3, and ended Ty Cobb's hitting streak at 40 games.
■ **September 29:** Phillies righthander Grover Cleveland Alexander defeated Pittsburgh 7-4 and claimed his rookie-record 28th victory.
■ **September 22:** Cy Young, ending his career with the Braves, won his 511th and final game, beating Pittsburgh 1-0.

## LEADERS

**American League**

**BA:** Ty Cobb, Det., .420.
**Runs:** Ty Cobb, Det., 147.
**Hits:** Ty Cobb, Det., 248.
**TB:** Ty Cobb, Det., 367.
**HR:** Frank Baker, Phil., 11.
**RBI:** Ty Cobb, Det., 127.
**SB:** Ty Cobb, Det., 83.
**Wins:** Jack Coombs, Phil., 28.
**ERA:** Vean Gregg, Cle., 1.80.
**CG:** Walter Johnson, Wash., 36.
**IP:** Ed Walsh, Chi., 368.2.
**SO:** Ed Walsh, Chi., 255.

**National League**

**BA:** Honus Wagner, Pit., .334.
**Runs:** Jimmy Sheckard, Chi., 121.
**Hits:** Doc Miller, Bos., 192.
**TB:** Frank Schulte, Chi., 308.
**HR:** Frank Schulte, Chi., 21.
**RBI:** Frank Schulte, Chi.; Chief Wilson, Pit., 107.
**SB:** Bob Bescher, Cin., 80.
**Wins:** Grover Alexander, Phil., 28.
**ERA:** Christy Mathewson, N.Y., 1.99.
**CG:** Grover Alexander, Phil., 31.
**IP:** Grover Alexander, Phil., 367.
**SO:** Rube Marquard, N.Y., 237.

**A.L. 20-game winners**

Jack Coombs, Phil., 28-12
Ed Walsh, Chi., 27-18
Walter Johnson, Wash., 25-13
Vean Gregg, Cle., 23-7
Eddie Plank, Phil., 23-8
Joe Wood, Bos., 23-17
Russ Ford, N.Y., 22-11

**N.L. 20-game winners**

Grover Alexander, Phil., 28-13
Christy Mathewson, N.Y., 26-13
Rube Marquard, N.Y., 24-7
Bob Harmon, St.L., 23-16
Babe Adams, Pit., 22-12
Nap Rucker, Brk., 22-18
Mordecai Brown, Chi., 21-11
Howie Camnitz, Pit., 20-15

**A.L. 100 RBIs**

Ty Cobb, Det., 127
Frank Baker, Phil., 115
Sam Crawford, Det., 115

**N.L. 100 RBIs**

Frank Schulte, Chi., 107
Chief Wilson, Pit., 107

**Chalmers MVP**

A.L.: Ty Cobb, OF, Det.
N.L.: Frank Schulte, OF, Chi.

## WORLD SERIES

■ **Winner:** The Athletics became baseball's second back-to-back winners and gained revenge for their 1905 loss to the Giants.

■ **Turning point:** A ninth-inning Game 3 homer by Frank Baker off Christy Mathewson. The solo shot tied the game at 1-1 and the A's won in 11 innings, 3-2.

■ **Memorable moment:** Baker's homer off Mathewson.

■ **Top guns:** Chief Bender (2-1, 1.04 ERA), Baker (.375, 2 HR), Jack Barry (.368), Athletics; Mathewson (27 IP, 2.00), Giants.

### Linescores

**Game 1**—October 14, at New York
Philadelphia.... 0 1 0 000 000 — 1 6 2
New York........ 0 0 0 100 10x — 2 5 0
Bender; Mathewson. W—Mathewson. L—Bender.

**Game 2**—October 16, at Philadelphia
New York........ 0 1 0 000 000 — 1 5 3
Philadelphia.... 1 0 0 002 00x — 3 4 0
Marquard, Crandall (8); Plank. W—Plank. L—Marquard. HR—Baker (Phil.).

**Game 3**—October 17, at New York
Philadelphia ....0 0 0 000 001 02—3 9 2
New York ........0 0 1 000 000 01—2 3 5
Coombs; Mathewson. W—Coombs. L—Mathewson. HR—Baker (Phil.).

**Game 4**—October 24, at Philadelphia
New York........ 2 0 0 000 000 — 2 7 3
Philadelphia.... 0 0 0 310 00x — 4 1 1
Mathewson, Wiltse (8); Bender. W—Bender. L—Mathewson.

**Game 5**—October 25, at New York
Philadelphia.... 0 0 3 000 000 0 — 3 7 1
New York........ 0 0 0 000 102 1 — 4 9 2
Coombs, Plank (10); Marquard, Ames (4), Crandall (8). W—Crandall. L—Plank. HR—Oldring (Phil.).

**Game 6**—October 26, at Philadelphia
New York........ 1 0 0 000 001 — 2 4 3
Philadelphia.... 0 0 1 401 70x — 13 3 5
Ames, Wiltse (5), Marquard (7); Bender. W—Bender. L—Ames.

# 1912

## FINAL STANDINGS

**American League**

| Team | W | L | Pct. | GB |
|---|---|---|---|---|
| Boston | 105 | 47 | .691 | ... |
| Washington | 91 | 61 | .599 | 14 |
| Philadelphia | 90 | 62 | .592 | 15 |
| Chicago | 78 | 76 | .506 | 28 |
| Cleveland | 75 | 78 | .490 | 30.5 |
| Detroit | 69 | 84 | .451 | 36.5 |
| St. Louis | 53 | 101 | .344 | 53 |
| New York | 50 | 102 | .329 | 55 |

**National League**

| Team | W | L | Pct. | GB |
|---|---|---|---|---|
| New York | 103 | 48 | .682 | ... |
| Pittsburgh | 93 | 58 | .616 | 10 |
| Chicago | 91 | 59 | .607 | 11.5 |
| Cincinnati | 75 | 78 | .490 | 29 |
| Philadelphia | 73 | 79 | .480 | 30.5 |
| St. Louis | 63 | 90 | .412 | 41 |
| Brooklyn | 58 | 95 | .379 | 46 |
| Boston | 52 | 101 | .340 | 52 |

## SIGNIFICANT EVENTS

■ **April 11:** Cincinnati celebrated the opening of new Redland Field with a 10-6 victory over the Cubs.
■ **April 20:** The Red Sox christened Fenway Park with an 11-inning 7-6 victory over New York and the Tigers opened Navin Field with an 11-inning 6-5 victory over Cleveland.
■ **May 16:** A.L. President Ban Johnson handed Detroit's Ty Cobb an indefinite suspension after Cobb entered the stands at New York's Hilltop Park to fight a heckler.
■ **May 18:** A team of amateur Tigers dropped a 24-2 decision to the Athletics when the regular Tigers went on strike to protest Cobb's suspension.
■ **May 20:** The Tigers, facing the threat of lifetime suspensions from Johnson, returned to uniform.

## MEMORABLE MOMENTS

■ **June 13:** New York's Christy Mathewson earned his 300th career victory and 20th win of the season when he defeated the Cubs, 3-2.
■ **July 3:** Giants lefty Rube Marquard earned his record 19th consecutive victory of the season and 21st straight over two years, stopping Brooklyn, 2-1.
■ **August 26:** The Browns handed Washington's Walter Johnson a 3-2 loss and ended his A.L.-record winning streak at 16 games.
■ **September 20:** Joe Wood's record-tying 16-game winning streak ended when Detroit handed Boston a 6-4 loss.
■ **September 22:** For the second time in 11 days, Athletics star Eddie Collins stole a modern-record six bases in a game—an 8-2 victory over the Browns.

## LEADERS

**American League**

**BA:** Ty Cobb, Det., .409.
**Runs:** Eddie Collins, Phil., 137.
**Hits:** Ty Cobb, Det.; Joe Jackson, Cle., 226.
**TB:** Joe Jackson, Cle., 331.
**HR:** Frank Baker, Phil.; Tris Speaker, Bos., 10.
**RBI:** Frank Baker, Phil., 130.
**SB:** Clyde Milan, Wash., 88.
**Wins:** Joe Wood, Bos., 34.
**ERA:** Walter Johnson, Wash., 1.39.
**CG:** Joe Wood, Bos., 35.
**IP:** Ed Walsh, Chi., 393.
**SO:** Walter Johnson, Wash., 303.

**National League**

**BA:** Heinie Zimmerman, Chi., .372.
**Runs:** Bob Bescher, Cin., 120.
**Hits:** Heinie Zimmerman, Chi., 207.
**TB:** Heinie Zimmerman, Chi., 318.
**HR:** Heinie Zimmerman, Chi., 14.
**RBI:** Honus Wagner, Pit., 102.
**SB:** Bob Bescher, Cin., 67.
**Wins:** Larry Cheney, Chi.; Rube Marquard, N.Y., 26.
**ERA:** Jeff Tesreau, N.Y., 1.96.
**CG:** Larry Cheney, Chi., 28.
**IP:** Grover Alexander, Phil., 310.1.
**SO:** Grover Alexander, Phil., 195.

**A.L. 20-game winners**

Joe Wood, Bos., 34-5
Walter Johnson, Wash., 33-12
Ed Walsh, Chi., 27-17
Eddie Plank, Phil., 26-6
Bob Groom, Wash., 24-13
Jack Coombs, Phil., 21-10
Hugh Bedient, Bos., 20-9
Vean Gregg, Cle., 20-13
Buck O'Brien, Bos., 20-13

**N.L. 20-game winners**

Larry Cheney, Chi., 26-10
Rube Marquard, N.Y., 26-11
Claude Hendrix, Pit., 24-9
Christy Mathewson, N.Y., 23-12
Howie Camnitz, Pit., 22-12

**A.L. 100 RBIs**

Frank Baker, Phil., 130
Sam Crawford, Det., 109
Duffy Lewis, Bos., 109
Stuffy McInnis, Phil., 101

**N.L. 100 RBIs**

Honus Wagner, Pit., 102
Bill Sweeney, Bos., 100

**Chalmers MVP**

A.L.: Tris Speaker, OF, Bos.
N.L.: Larry Doyle, 2B, N.Y.

## WORLD SERIES

■ **Winners:** The Red Sox, who had not made a Series appearance since beating Pittsburgh in the 1903 inaugural, made it two for two with a victory over the Giants.

■ **Turning point:** A dropped fly ball by Giants center fielder Fred Snodgrass in the Series-deciding eighth game. The Red Sox wiped out a 2-1 deficit against Christy Mathewson and claimed a 3-2 victory.

■ **Memorable moment:** Snodgrass' muff and the failure of catcher Chief Meyers and first baseman Fred Merkle to catch a foul pop in the same inning.

■ **Top guns:** Joe Wood (3-1), Red Sox; Buck Herzog (.400), Meyers (.357), Giants.

### Linescores

**Game 1**—October 8, at New York
Boston....................0 0 0 001 300 — 4 6 1
New York................0 0 2 000 001 — 3 8 1
Wood; Tesreau, Crandall (8). W—Wood. L—Tesreau.

**Game 2**—October 9, at Boston
New York......0 1 0 100 030 10 — 6 11 5
Boston..........3 0 0 010 010 10 — 6 10 1
Mathewson; Collins, Hall (8), Bedient (11). Game called after 11 innings because of darkness.

**Game 3**—October 10, at Boston
New York................0 1 0 010 000 — 2 7 1
Boston....................0 0 0 000 001 — 1 7 0
Marquard; O'Brien, Bedient (9). W—Marquard. L—O'Brien.

**Game 4**—October 11, at New York
Boston....................0 1 0 100 001 — 3 8 1
New York................0 0 0 000 100 — 1 9 1
Wood; Tesreau, Ames (8). W—Wood. L—Tesreau.

**Game 5**—October 12, at Boston
New York.............0 0 0 000 100 — 1 3 11
Boston..................0 0 2 000 00x — 2 5 1
Mathewson; Bedient. W—Bedient. L—Mathewson.

**Game 6**—October 14, at New York
Boston..................0 2 0 000 000 — 2 7 2
New York.............5 0 0 000 00x — 5 11 2
O'Brien, Collins (2); Marquard. W—Marquard. L—O'Brien.

**Game 7**—October 15, at Boston
New York...........6 1 0 002 101 — 11 16 4
Boston...............0 1 0 000 210 — 4 9 3
Tesreau; Wood, Hall (2). W—Tesreau. L—Wood. HR—Doyle (N.Y.); Gardner (Bos.).

**Game 8**—October 16, at Boston
New York.........0 0 1 000 000 1 — 2 9 2
Boston.............0 0 0 000 100 2 — 3 8 5
Mathewson; Bedient, Wood (8). W—Wood. L—Mathewson.

# 1913

## FINAL STANDINGS

**American League**

| Team | W | L | Pct. | GB |
|---|---|---|---|---|
| Philadelphia | 96 | 57 | .627 | ... |
| Washington | 90 | 64 | .584 | 6.5 |
| Cleveland | 86 | 66 | .566 | 9.5 |
| Boston | 79 | 71 | .527 | 15.5 |
| Chicago | 78 | 74 | .513 | 17.5 |
| Detroit | 66 | 87 | .431 | 30 |
| New York | 57 | 94 | .377 | 38 |
| St. Louis | 57 | 96 | .373 | 39 |

**National League**

| Team | W | L | Pct. | GB |
|---|---|---|---|---|
| New York | 101 | 51 | .664 | ... |
| Philadelphia | 88 | 63 | .583 | 12.5 |
| Chicago | 88 | 65 | .575 | 13.5 |
| Pittsburgh | 78 | 71 | .523 | 21.5 |
| Boston | 69 | 82 | .457 | 31.5 |
| Brooklyn | 65 | 84 | .436 | 34.5 |
| Cincinnati | 64 | 89 | .418 | 37.5 |
| St. Louis | 51 | 99 | .340 | 49 |

## SIGNIFICANT EVENTS

■ **January 22:** The Yankees, no longer tenants of Hilltop Park, received permission from the New York Giants to use the Polo Grounds as co-tenants.
■ **April 9:** The Dodgers lost their Ebbets Field debut to the Phillies, 1-0.
■ **April 10:** The A.L.'s New York team began life anew as the "Yankees," losing to Washington, 2-1, in the season opener.
■ **November 2:** The outlaw Federal League began its challenge as a third Major League when its Kansas City entry enticed Browns manager George Stovall to jump.
■ **December 9:** N.L. owners elected Pennsylvania Governor John K. Tener as their new president.

## MEMORABLE MOMENTS

■ **May 14:** Walter Johnson's Major League-record 56-inning scoreless streak ended when the Washington righthander yielded a fourth-inning run to the Browns.
■ **August 28:** Johnson's 14-game winning streak came to an end when the Senators fell to Boston, 1-0, in 11 innings.
■ **September 29:** Johnson defeated the Athletics, 1-0, and closed his incredible season with a 36-7 record, 11 shutouts and a 1.14 ERA.

## LEADERS

**American League**
**BA:** Ty Cobb, Det., .390.
**Runs:** Eddie Collins, Phil., 125.
**Hits:** Joe Jackson, Cle., 197.
**TB:** Sam Crawford, Det., 298.
**HR:** Frank Baker, Phil., 12.
**RBI:** Frank Baker, Phil., 117.
**SB:** Clyde Milan, Wash., 75.
**Wins:** Walter Johnson, Wash., 36.
**ERA:** Walter Johnson, Wash., 1.14.
**CG:** Walter Johnson, Wash., 29.
**IP:** Walter Johnson, Wash., 346.
**SO:** Walter Johnson, Wash., 243.

**National League**
**BA:** Jake Daubert, Brk., .350.
**Runs:** Max Carey, Pit.; Tommy Leach, Chi., 99.
**Hits:** Gavvy Cravath, Phil., 179.
**TB:** Gavvy Cravath, Phil., 298.
**HR:** Gavvy Cravath, Phil., 19.
**RBI:** Gavvy Cravath, Phil., 128.
**SB:** Max Carey, Pit., 61.
**Wins:** Tom Seaton, Phil., 27.
**ERA:** Christy Mathewson, N.Y., 2.06.
**CG:** Lefty Tyler, Bos., 28.
**IP:** Tom Seaton, Phil., 322.1.
**SO:** Tom Seaton, Phil., 168.

**A.L. 20-game winners**
Walter Johnson, Wash., 36-7
Cy Falkenberg, Cle., 23-10
Reb Russell, Chi., 22-16
Chief Bender, Phil., 21-10
Vean Gregg, Cle., 20-13
Jim Scott, Chi., 20-21

**N.L. 20-game winners**
Tom Seaton, Phil., 27-12
Christy Mathewson, N.Y., 25-11
Rube Marquard, N.Y., 23-10
Grover Alexander, Phil., 22-8
Jeff Tesreau, N.Y., 22-13
Babe Adams, Pit., 21-10
Larry Cheney, Chi., 21-14

**A.L. 100 RBIs**
Frank Baker, Phil., 117

**N.L. 100 RBIs**
Gavvy Cravath, Phil., 128

**Chalmers MVP**
A.L.: Walter Johnson, P, Wash.
N.L.: Jake Daubert, 1B, Brk.

## WORLD SERIES

■ **Winner:** The Athletics needed only five games to win their third Series in four years and hand the Giants their third straight loss.

■ **Turning point:** Complete-game victories by A's pitchers Joe Bush and Chief Bender in Games 3 and 4, setting up Eddie Plank for the kill.

■ **Memorable moment:** A Game 2 pitching duel between Plank and Christy Mathewson. The Giants scored three runs in the 10th for a 3-0 win.

■ **Top guns:** Frank Baker (.450, 7 RBIs), Eddie Collins (.421), Athletics; Mathewson (19 IP, 0.95 ERA), Giants.

**Linescores**

**Game 1**—October 7, at New York
Philadelphia........ 0 0 0 3 2 0 0 1 0 — 6 11 1
New York............ 0 0 1 0 3 0 0 0 0 — 4 11 0
Bender; Marquard, Crandall (6), Tesreau (8). W—Bender. L—Marquard. HR—Baker (Phil.).

**Game 2**—October 8, at Philadelphia
New York.......... 0 0 0 0 0 0 0 0 0 3 — 3 7 2
Philadelphia...... 0 0 0 0 0 0 0 0 0 0 — 0 8 2
Mathewson; Plank. W—Mathewson. L—Plank.

**Game 3**—October 9, at New York
Philadelphia........ 3 2 0 0 0 0 2 1 0 — 8 12 1
New York............ 0 0 0 0 1 0 1 0 0 — 2 5 1
Bush; Tesreau, Crandall (7). W—Bush. L—Tesreau. HR—Schang (Phil.).

**Game 4**—October 10, at Philadelphia
New York.............. 0 0 0 0 0 0 3 2 0 — 5 8 2
Philadelphia.......... 0 1 0 3 2 0 0 0 x — 6 9 0
Demaree, Marquard (5); Bender. W—Bender. L—Demaree. HR—Merkle (N.Y.).

**Game 5**—-October 11, at New York
Philadelphia.......... 1 0 2 0 0 0 0 0 0 — 3 6 1
New York.............. 0 0 0 0 1 0 0 0 0 — 1 2 2
Plank; Mathewson. W—Plank. L—Mathewson.

# 1914

## FINAL STANDINGS

**American League**

| Team | W | L | Pct. | GB |
|---|---|---|---|---|
| Philadelphia | 99 | 53 | .651 | ... |
| Boston | 91 | 62 | .595 | 8.5 |
| Washington | 81 | 73 | .526 | 19 |
| Detroit | 80 | 73 | .523 | 19.5 |
| St. Louis | 71 | 82 | .464 | 28.5 |
| Chicago | 70 | 84 | .455 | 30 |
| New York | 70 | 84 | .455 | 30 |
| Cleveland | 51 | 102 | .333 | 48.5 |

**National League**

| Team | W | L | Pct. | GB |
|---|---|---|---|---|
| Boston | 94 | 59 | .614 | ... |
| New York | 84 | 70 | .545 | 10.5 |
| St. Louis | 81 | 72 | .529 | 13 |
| Chicago | 78 | 76 | .506 | 16.5 |
| Brooklyn | 75 | 79 | .487 | 19.5 |
| Philadelphia | 74 | 80 | .481 | 20.5 |
| Pittsburgh | 69 | 85 | .448 | 25.5 |
| Cincinnati | 60 | 94 | .390 | 34.5 |

## SIGNIFICANT EVENTS

■ **April 13:** The outlaw Federal League, claiming to be a Major League equal, opened play with Baltimore defeating Buffalo, 3-2.
■ **November 1:** Philadelphia's Connie Mack began dismantling his powerful Athletics team by asking waivers on Jack Coombs, Eddie Plank and Chief Bender.
■ **December 8:** Connie Mack continued his housecleaning by selling star second baseman Eddie Collins to the White Sox for $50,000.

## MEMORABLE MOMENTS

■ **May 14:** Chicago's Jim Scott lost his no-hit bid and the game when the Senators scored on two 10th-inning hits for a 1-0 victory.
■ **July 11:** Young Babe Ruth pitched the Red Sox to a 4-3 victory over Cleveland in his Major League debut.
■ **July 17:** Giants 3, Pirates 1 as Rube Marquard outpitched Babe Adams in a 21-inning marathon.
■ **September 23:** The Reds snapped their team-record 19-game losing streak with a 3-0 victory over the Braves.
■ **September 27:** Cleveland's Napoleon Lajoie collected career hit No. 3,000, a double, and the Indians defeated the Yankees, 5-3.
■ **September 29:** The Miracle Braves, who would finish with an incredible 68-19 rush, clinched their first N.L. pennant with a 3-2 victory over the Cubs.
■ **October 7:** The Indianapolis Hoosiers defeated St. Louis, 4-0, and claimed the Federal League pennant.

## LEADERS

**American League**
**BA:** Ty Cobb, Det., .368.
**Runs:** Eddie Collins, Phil., 122.
**Hits:** Tris Speaker, Bos., 193.
**TB:** Tris Speaker, Bos., 287.
**HR:** Frank Baker, Phil., 9.
**RBI:** Sam Crawford, Det., 104.
**SB:** Fritz Maisel, N.Y., 74.
**Wins:** Walter Johnson, Wash., 28.
**ERA:** Dutch Leonard, Bos., 0.96.
**CG:** Walter Johnson, Wash., 33.
**IP:** Walter Johnson, Wash., 371.2.
**SO:** Walter Johnson, Wash., 225.

**National League**
**BA:** Jake Daubert, Brk., .329.
**Runs:** George Burns, N.Y., 100.
**Hits:** Sherry Magee, Phil., 171.
**TB:** Sherry Magee, Phil., 277.
**HR:** Gavvy Cravath, Phil., 19.
**RBI:** Sherry Magee, Phil., 103.
**SB:** George Burns, N.Y., 62.
**Wins:** Grover Alexander, Phil., 27.
**ERA:** Bill Doak, St.L., 1.72.
**CG:** Grover Alexander, Phil., 32.
**IP:** Grover Alexander, Phil., 355.
**SO:** Grover Alexander, Phil., 214.

**A.L. 20-game winners**
Walter Johnson, Wash., 28-18
Harry Coveleski, Det., 22-12
Ray Collins, Bos., 20-13

**N.L. 20-game winners**
Grover Alexander, Phil., 27-15
Bill James, Bos., 26-7
Dick Rudolph, Bos., 26-10
Jeff Tesreau, N.Y., 26-10
Christy Mathewson, N.Y., 24-13
Jeff Pfeffer, Brk., 23-12
Hippo Vaughn, Chi., 21-13
Erskine Mayer, Phil., 21-19
Larry Cheney, Chi., 20-18

**A.L. 100 RBIs**
Sam Crawford, Det., 104

**N.L. 100 RBIs**
Sherry Magee, Phil., 103
Gavvy Cravath, Phil., 100

**Chalmers MVP**
A.L.: Eddie Collins, 2B, Phil.
N.L.: Johnny Evers, 2B, Bos.

## WORLD SERIES

■ **Winner:** The Braves, playing their Series home games in Fenway Park because it was deemed a more attractive facility than their South End Grounds venue, punctuated their miracle pennant run with a shocking four-game sweep of the powerful Athletics.

■ **Turning point:** Boston's come-from-behind effort in Game 3 that produced a 5-4 victory in 12 innings. The Braves stayed alive by scoring two 10th-inning runs after falling behind in the top of the inning.

■ **Memorable moment:** A dramatic Game 2 pitching duel between Boston's Bill James and Eddie Plank. James won 1-0 on Les Mann's ninth-inning single.

■ **Top guns:** James (2-0, 0.00 ERA), Dick Rudolph (2-0, 0-50), Hank Gowdy (.545), Johnny Evers (.438), Braves.

**Linescores**

**Game 1**—October 9, at Philadelphia
Boston............ 0 2 0 0 1 3 0 1 0 — 7 11 2
Phil................ 0 1 0 0 0 0 0 0 0 —.1 5 0
Rudolph; Bender, Wyckoff (6). W—Rudolph. L—Bender.

**Game 2**—October 10, at Philadelphia
Boston............ 0 0 0 0 0 0 0 0 1 — 1 7 1
Phil................ 0 0 0 0 0 0 0 0 0 — 0 2 1
James; Plank. W—James. L—Plank.

**Game 3**—October 12, at Boston
Phil..........1 0 0 1 0 0 0 0 0 2 0 0 — 4 8 2
Boston......0 1 0 1 0 0 0 0 0 2 0 1 — 5 9 1
Bush; Tyler, James (11). W—James. L—Bush. HR—Gowdy (Bos.).

**Game 4**—October 13, at Boston
Phil. ......................0 0 0 0 1 0 0 0 0 — 1 7 0
Boston ...................0 0 0 1 2 0 0 0 x — 3 6 0
Shawkey, Pennock (6); Rudolph. W—Rudolph. L—Shawkey.

## 1914—Federal League

### FINAL STANDINGS

| Team | W | L | Pct. | GB |
|---|---|---|---|---|
| Indianapolis | 88 | 65 | .575 | ... |
| Chicago | 87 | 67 | .565 | 1.5 |
| Baltimore | 84 | 70 | .545 | 4.5 |
| Buffalo | 80 | 71 | .530 | 7 |
| Brooklyn | 77 | 77 | .500 | 11.5 |
| Kansas City | 67 | 84 | .444 | 20 |
| Pittsburgh | 64 | 86 | .427 | 22.5 |
| St. Louis | 62 | 89 | .411 | 25 |

### SIGNIFICANT EVENT

■ **November 1:** After being released by A's boss Connie Mack, pitchers Eddie Plank (St. Louis) and Chief Bender (Baltimore) signed contracts to play in the second-year Federal League.

### MEMORABLE MOMENTS

■ **April 13:** Baltimore pitcher Jack Quinn, working before an estimated crowd of 28,000 at new Terrapin Park, posted a 3-2 victory over Buffalo in the Federal League inaugural.

■ **April 23:** The Chicago Whales christened new Weeghman Park—the future Wrigley Field—with a 9-1 victory over the Kansas City Packers.

■ **September 19:** Brooklyn's Ed Lafitte pitched the Federal League's first no-hitter, beating the Packers 6-2.

■ **October 6:** An Indianapolis victory over St. Louis combined with a Chicago loss to Kansas City clinched the first Federal League pennant for the Hoosiers, who finished with an 88-65 record.

### LEADERS

**BA:** Benny Kauff, Ind., .370
**Runs:** Benny Kauff, Ind., 120
**Hits:** Benny Kauff, Ind., 211
**TB:** Benny Kauff, Ind., 305
**HR:** Dutch Zwilling, Chi., 16
**RBI:** Frank LaPorte, Ind., 107
**SB:** Benny Kauff, Ind., 75
**Wins:** Claude Hendrix, Chi., 29
**ERA:** Claude Hendrix, Chi., 1.69
**CG:** Claude Hendrix, Chi., 34
**IP:** Cy Falkenberg, Ind., 377.1
**SO:** Cy Falkenberg, Ind., 236

**20-game winners**
Claude Hendrix, Chi., 29-10
Jack Quinn, Bal., 26-14
Tom Seaton, Brk., 25-14
Cy Falkenberg, Ind., 25-16
George Suggs, Bal., 24-14
Russ Ford, Buf., 21-6
Elmer Knetzer, Pit., 20-12
Gene Packard, K.C., 20-14

**100 RBIs**
Frank LaPorte, Ind., 107

## 1915—Federal League

### FINAL STANDINGS

| Team | W | L | Pct. | GB |
|---|---|---|---|---|
| Chicago | 86 | 66 | .566 | ... |
| St. Louis | 87 | 67 | .565 | ... |
| Pittsburgh | 86 | 67 | .562 | 0.5 |
| Kansas City | 81 | 72 | .529 | 5.5 |
| Newark | 80 | 72 | .526 | 6 |
| Buffalo | 74 | 78 | .487 | 12 |
| Brooklyn | 70 | 82 | .461 | 16 |
| Baltimore | 47 | 107 | .305 | 40 |

### SIGNIFICANT EVENTS

■ **January 5:** The Federal League filed a lawsuit challenging Organized Baseball as an illegal trust that should be dissolved.
■ **December 22:** Organized Baseball's costly two-year battle against the Federal League ended when a peace treaty was arranged and the outlaw circuit was disbanded.

### MEMORABLE MOMENTS

■ **April 24:** Pittsburgh's Frank Allen held St. Louis hitless in the Rebels' 2-0 victory.
■ **May 15:** Chicago's Claude Hendrix pitched a Whale of a game—a 10-0 no-hitter against Pittsburgh.
■ **July 31:** St. Louis' Dave Davenport pitched a pair of 1-0 games on the same day against Buffalo, winning the opener and dropping the nightcap.
■ **August 16, September 7:** Kansas City's Miles Main and St. Louis' Dave Davenport joined the no-hit fraternity. Main stopped Buffalo 5-0 and Davenport beat Chicago 3-0.
■ **October 3:** Chicago's season-ending victory over Pittsburgh clinched the second Federal League pennant—by an incredible .001 over St. Louis and a half game over the Rebels.

### LEADERS

**BA:** Benny Kauff, Brk., .342
**Runs:** Babe Borton, St.L., 97
**Hits:** Jack Tobin, St.L., 184
**TB:** Ed Konetchy, Pit., 278
**HR:** Hal Chase, Buf., 17
**RBI:** Dutch Zwilling, Chi., 94
**SB:** Benny Kauff, Brk., 55
**Wins:** George McConnell, Chi., 25
**ERA:** Earl Moseley, New., 1.91
**CG:** Dave Davenport, St.L., 30
**IP:** Dave Davenport, St.L., 392.2
**SO:** Dave Davenport, St.L., 229

**20-game winners**
George McConnell, Chi., 25-10
Frank Allen, Pit., 23-13
Nick Cullop, K.C., 22-11
Dave Davenport, St.L., 22-18
Ed Reulbach, New., 21-10
Eddie Plank, St.L., 21-11
Al Schulz, Buf., 21-14
Doc Crandall, St.L., 21-15
Gene Packard, K.C., 20-12

## 1915

### FINAL STANDINGS

**American League**

| Team | W | L | Pct. | GB |
|---|---|---|---|---|
| Boston | 101 | 50 | .669 | ... |
| Detroit | 100 | 54 | .649 | 2.5 |
| Chicago | 93 | 61 | .604 | 9.5 |
| Washington | 85 | 68 | .556 | 17 |
| New York | 69 | 83 | .454 | 32.5 |
| St. Louis | 63 | 91 | .409 | 39.5 |
| Cleveland | 57 | 95 | .375 | 44.5 |
| Philadelphia | 43 | 109 | .283 | 58.5 |

**National League**

| Team | W | L | Pct. | GB |
|---|---|---|---|---|
| Philadelphia | 90 | 62 | .592 | ... |
| Boston | 83 | 69 | .546 | 7 |
| Brooklyn | 80 | 72 | .526 | 10 |
| Chicago | 73 | 80 | .477 | 17.5 |
| Pittsburgh | 73 | 81 | .474 | 18 |
| St. Louis | 72 | 81 | .471 | 18.5 |
| Cincinnati | 71 | 83 | .461 | 20 |
| New York | 69 | 83 | .454 | 21 |

### SIGNIFICANT EVENTS

■ **August 18:** Boston defeated St. Louis, 3-1, in the first game at new Braves Field.
■ **December 22:** Organized Baseball's costly two-year battle against the Federal League ended when a peace treaty was arranged and the outlaw circuit was disbanded.

### MEMORABLE MOMENTS

■ **September 29:** Grover Cleveland Alexander pitched a one-hitter and his 12th shutout of the season as the Phillies clinched their first N.L. pennant with a 5-0 victory over the Braves.
■ **September 30:** The Red Sox clinched the A.L. pennant when the St. Louis Browns handed the Tigers an 8-2 loss in a game at Detroit.
■ **October 3:** Detroit's Ty Cobb, on his way to a record ninth consecutive A.L. batting title, stole his record 96th base in a 6-5 victory over Cleveland.

### LEADERS

**American League**
**BA:** Ty Cobb, Det., .369.
**Runs:** Ty Cobb, Det., 144.
**Hits:** Ty Cobb, Det., 208.
**TB:** Ty Cobb, Det., 274.
**HR:** Braggo Roth, Chi.-Cle., 7.
**RBI:** Sam Crawford, Det.; Bobby Veach, Det., 112.
**SB:** Ty Cobb, Det., 96.
**Wins:** Walter Johnson, Wash., 27.
**ERA:** Joe Wood, Bos., 1.49.
**CG:** Walter Johnson, Wash., 35.
**IP:** Walter Johnson, Wash., 336.2.
**SO:** Walter Johnson, Wash., 203.

**National League**
**BA:** Larry Doyle, N.Y., .320.
**Runs:** Gavvy Cravath, Phil., 89.
**Hits:** Larry Doyle, N.Y., 189.
**TB:** Gavvy Cravath, Phil., 266.
**HR:** Gavvy Cravath, Phil., 24.
**RBI:** Gavvy Cravath, Phil., 115.
**SB:** Max Carey, Pit., 36.
**Wins:** Grover Alexander, Phil., 31.
**ERA:** Grover Alexander, Phil., 1.22.
**CG:** Grover Alexander, Phil., 36.
**IP:** Grover Alexander, Phil, 376.1
**SO:** Grover Alexander, Phil., 241.

**A.L. 20-game winners**
Walter Johnson, Wash., 27-13
Jim Scott, Chi., 24-11
Hooks Dauss, Det., 24-13
Red Faber, Chi., 24-14
Harry Coveleski, Det., 22-13

**N.L. 20-game winners**
Grover Alexander, Phil., 31-10
Dick Rudolph, Bos., 22-19
Al Mamaux, Pit., 21-8
Erskine Mayer, Phil., 21-15
Hippo Vaughn, Chi., 20-12

**A.L. 100 RBIs**
Sam Crawford, Det., 112
Bobby Veach, Det., 112

**N.L. 100 RBIs**
Gavvy Cravath, Phil., 115

### WORLD SERIES

■ **Winner:** The Red Sox, playing their Series home games in new Braves Field because of its large capacity, matched the Athletics as three-time Series winners with a five-game romp past another Philadelphia team — the Phillies.

■ **Turning point:** Dutch Leonard's 2-1 Game 3 victory over Phillies ace Grover Cleveland Alexander. The game was decided in the ninth inning on Duffy Lewis' RBI single.

■ **Memorable moment:** Harry Hooper's Series-deciding ninth-inning home run in Game 5 off Philadelphia reliever Eppa Rixey.

■ **Top guns:** Rube Foster (2-0, 2.00 ERA), Lewis (.444), Red Sox; Fred Luderus (.438), Phillies.

**Linescores**

**Game 1**—October 8, at Philadelphia
Boston........... 0 0 0 0 0 0 0 1 0 — 1 8 1
Philadelphia... 0 0 0 1 0 0 0 2 x — 3 5 1
Shore; Alexander. W—Alexander. L—Shore.

**Game 2**—October 9, at Philadelphia
Boston........... 1 0 0 0 0 0 0 0 1 — 2 10 0
Philadelphia... 0 0 0 0 1 0 0 0 0 — 1 3 1
Foster; Mayer. W—Foster. L—Mayer.

**Game 3**—October 11, at Boston
Philadelphia... 0 0 1 0 0 0 0 0 0 — 1 3 0
Boston........... 0 0 0 1 0 0 0 0 1 — 2 6 1
Alexander; Leonard. W—Leonard. L—Alexander.

**Game 4**—October 12, at Boston
Philadelphia... 0 0 0 0 0 0 0 1 0 — 1 7 0
Boston........... 0 0 1 0 0 1 0 0 x — 2 8 1
Chalmers; Shore. W—Shore. L—Chalmers.

**Game 5**—October 13, at Philadelphia
Boston........... 0 1 1 0 0 0 0 2 1 — 5 10 1
Philadelphia... 2 0 0 2 0 0 0 0 0 — 4 9 1
Foster; Mayer, Rixey (3). W—Foster. L—Rixey. HR—Hooper 2, Lewis (Bos.); Luderus (Phil.).

## 1916

### FINAL STANDINGS

**American League**

| Team | W | L | Pct. | GB |
|---|---|---|---|---|
| Boston | 91 | 63 | .591 | ... |
| Chicago | 89 | 65 | .578 | 2 |
| Detroit | 87 | 67 | .565 | 4 |
| New York | 80 | 74 | .519 | 11 |
| St. Louis | 79 | 75 | .513 | 12 |
| Cleveland | 77 | 77 | .500 | 14 |
| Washington | 76 | 77 | .497 | 14.5 |
| Philadelphia | 36 | 117 | .235 | 54.5 |

**National League**

| Team | W | L | Pct. | GB |
|---|---|---|---|---|
| Brooklyn | 94 | 60 | .610 | ... |
| Philadelphia | 91 | 62 | .595 | 2.5 |
| Boston | 89 | 63 | .586 | 4 |
| New York | 86 | 66 | .566 | 7 |
| Chicago | 67 | 86 | .438 | 26.5 |
| Pittsburgh | 65 | 89 | .422 | 29 |
| Cincinnati | 60 | 93 | .392 | 33.5 |
| St. Louis | 60 | 93 | .392 | 33.5 |

### SIGNIFICANT EVENTS

■ **July 20:** Giants great Christy Mathewson was traded to Cincinnati in a career-prolonging deal that allowed him to become manager of the Reds.
■ **November 1:** Harry Frazee, a New York theater owner and producer, bought the Red Sox for $675,000.

### MEMORABLE MOMENTS

■ **August 9:** The Athletics' 20-game losing streak came to a merciful end when they defeated the Tigers, 7-1.
■ **September 30:** The Braves ended New York's winning streak at a Major League-record 26 games with an 8-3 victory in the second game of a doubleheader.
■ **October 2:** Grover Cleveland Alexander pitched the Phillies to a 2-0 victory over the Braves—his modern record 16th shutout of the season.

### LEADERS

**American League**
**BA:** Tris Speaker, Cle., .386.
**Runs:** Ty Cobb, Det., 113.
**Hits:** Tris Speaker, Cle., 211.
**TB:** Joe Jackson, Chi., 293.
**HR:** Wally Pipp, N.Y., 12.
**RBI:** Del Pratt, St.L., 103.
**SB:** Ty Cobb, Det., 68.
**Wins:** Walter Johnson, Wash., 25.
**ERA:** Babe Ruth, Bos., 1.75.
**CG:** Walter Johnson, Wash., 36.
**IP:** Walter Johnson, Wash., 369.2.
**SO:** Walter Johnson, Wash., 228.

**National League**
**BA:** Hal Chase, Cin., .339.
**Runs:** George Burns, N.Y., 105.
**Hits:** Hal Chase, Cin., 184.
**TB:** Zack Wheat, Brk., 262.
**HR:** Dave Robertson, N.Y.; Cy Williams, Chi., 12.
**RBI:** Heinie Zimmerman, Chi.-N.Y., 83.
**SB:** Max Carey, Pit., 63.
**Wins:** Grover Alexander, Phil., 33.
**ERA:** Grover Alexander, Phil., 1.55.
**CG:** Grover Alexander, Phil., 38.
**IP:** Grover Alexander, Phil., 389.
**SO:** Grover Alexander, Phil., 167.

**A.L. 20-game winners**
Walter Johnson, Wash., 25-20
Bob Shawkey, N.Y., 24-14
Babe Ruth, Bos., 23-12
Harry Coveleski, Det., 21-11

**N.L. 20-game winners**
Grover Alexander, Phil., 33-12
Jeff Pfeffer, Brk., 25-11
Eppa Rixey, Phil., 22-10
Al Mamaux, Pit., 21-15

**A.L. 100 RBIs**
Del Pratt, St.L., 103

### WORLD SERIES

■ **Winner:** Stingy Boston pitchers allowed only eight earned runs and the Red Sox closed down the Dodgers to become the first four-time Series winners.

■ **Turning point:** Larry Gardner's three-run Game 4 homer propelled Dutch Leonard to a 6-2 victory and the Red Sox to a 3-1 Series advantage.

■ **Memorable moment:** A 14-inning Game 2 pitching duel between Boston's Babe Ruth and Brooklyn's Sherry Smith. Ruth won 2-1 on Del Gainor's pinch-hit single.

■ **Top guns:** Ernie Shore (2-0, 1.53 ERA), Duffy Lewis (.353), Red Sox; Casey Stengel (.364), Dodgers.

**Linescores**

**Game 1**—October 7, at Boston
Brooklyn ..........................0 0 0 1 0 0 0 0 4 — 5 10 4
Boston .............................0 0 1 0 1 0 3 1 x — 6 8 1
Marquard, Pfeffer (8); Shore, Mays (9). W—Shore. L—Marquard.

**Game 2**—October 9, at Boston
Brooklyn........1 0 0 0 0 0 0 0 0 0 0 0 0 0 — 1 6 2
Boston...........0 0 1 0 0 0 0 0 0 0 0 0 0 1 — 2 7 1
Smith; Ruth. W—Ruth. L—Smith. HR—Myers (Brk.).

**Game 3**—October 10, at Brooklyn
Boston .............................0 0 0 0 0 2 1 0 0 — 3 7 1
Brooklyn...........................0 0 1 1 2 0 0 0 x — 4 10 0
Mays, Foster (6); Coombs, Pfeffer (7). W—Coombs. L—Mays. HR—Gardner (Bos.).

**Game 4**—October 11, at Brooklyn
Boston .............................0 3 0 1 1 0 1 0 0 — 6 10 1
Brooklyn ..........................2 0 0 0 0 0 0 0 0 — 2 5 4
Leonard; Marquard, Cheney (5), Rucker (8). W—Leonard. L—Marquard. HR—Gardner (Bos.).

**Game 5**—October 12, at Boston
Brooklyn ............................0 1 0 0 0 0 0 0 0 — 1 3 3
Boston ...............................0 1 2 0 1 0 0 0 x — 4 7 2
Pfeffer, Dell (8); Shore. W—Shore. L—Pfeffer.

# 1917

## FINAL STANDINGS

**American League**

| Team | W | L | Pct. | GB |
|---|---|---|---|---|
| Chicago | 100 | 54 | .649 | ... |
| Boston | 90 | 62 | .592 | 9 |
| Cleveland | 88 | 66 | .571 | 12 |
| Detroit | 78 | 75 | .510 | 21.5 |
| Washington | 74 | 79 | .484 | 25.5 |
| New York | 71 | 82 | .464 | 28.5 |
| St. Louis | 57 | 97 | .370 | 43 |
| Philadelphia | 55 | 98 | .359 | 44.5 |

**National League**

| Team | W | L | Pct. | GB |
|---|---|---|---|---|
| New York | 98 | 56 | .636 | ... |
| Philadelphia | 87 | 65 | .572 | 10 |
| St. Louis | 82 | 70 | .539 | 15 |
| Cincinnati | 78 | 76 | .506 | 20 |
| Chicago | 74 | 80 | .481 | 24 |
| Boston | 72 | 81 | .471 | 25.5 |
| Brooklyn | 70 | 81 | .464 | 26.5 |
| Pittsburgh | 51 | 103 | .331 | 47 |

## SIGNIFICANT EVENTS

- **October 26:** New York owner Jacob Ruppert took a dynastic step when he signed former Cardinals manager Miller Huggins to manage the Yankees.

## MEMORABLE MOMENTS

- **April 14:** Chicago ace Eddie Cicotte kicked off the season's no-hitter parade with an 11-0 victory over St. Louis. Cicotte's no-hitter was the first of five in the American League.
- **May 2:** Cincinnati's Fred Toney and Chicago's Hippo Vaughn matched no-hitters for an unprecedented nine innings before Vaughn wilted in the 10th and the Reds scored a 1-0 victory.
- **May 6:** Browns pitcher Bob Groom pitched a 3-0 no-hitter against the White Sox, matching the previous-day feat of teammate Ernie Koob in a 1-0 victory over Chicago.
- **June 23:** Boston's Ernie Shore retired 27 consecutive Senators after replacing starter Babe Ruth, who was ejected after walking the first batter of the game. The runner was thrown out trying to steal and Shore went on to claim a 4-0 victory.
- **September 3:** Grover Alexander, en route to a Major League-leading 30 victories, pitched both ends of the Phillies' 6-0 and 9-3 doubleheader sweep of Brooklyn.

## LEADERS

**American League**

**BA:** Ty Cobb, Det., .383.
**Runs:** Donie Bush, Det., 112.
**Hits:** Ty Cobb, Det., 225.
**TB:** Ty Cobb, Det., 335.
**HR:** Wally Pipp, N.Y., 9.
**RBI:** Bobby Veach, Det., 103.
**SB:** Ty Cobb, Det., 55.
**Wins:** Eddie Cicotte, Chi., 28.
**ERA:** Eddie Cicotte, Chi., 1.53.
**CG:** Babe Ruth, Bos., 35.
**IP:** Eddie Cicotte, Chi., 346.2.
**SO:** Walter Johnson, Wash., 188.

**National League**

**BA:** Edd Roush, Cin., .341.
**Runs:** George Burns, N.Y., 103.
**Hits:** Heinie Groh, Cin., 182.
**TB:** Rogers Hornsby, St.L., 253.
**HR:** Gavvy Cravath, Phil.; Dave Robertson, N.Y., 12.
**RBI:** Heinie Zimmerman, N.Y., 102.
**SB:** Max Carey, Pit., 46.
**Wins:** Grover Alexander, Phil., 30.
**ERA:** Fred Anderson, N.Y., 1.44.
**CG:** Grover Alexander, Phil., 34.
**IP:** Grover Alexander, Phil., 388.
**SO:** Grover Alexander, Phil., 200.

**A.L. 20-game winners**
Ed Cicotte, Chi., 28-12
Babe Ruth, Bos., 24-13
Jim Bagby, Cle., 23-13
Walter Johnson, Wash., 23-16
Carl Mays, Bos., 22-9

**N.L. 20-game winners**
Grover Alexander, Phil., 30-13
Fred Toney, Cin., 24-16
Hippo Vaughn, Chi., 23-13
Ferdie Schupp, N.Y., 21-7
Pete Schneider, Cin., 20-19

**A.L. 100 RBIs**
Bobby Veach, Det., 103
Ty Cobb, Det., 102
Happy Felsch, Chi., 102

**N.L. 100 RBIs**
Heinie Zimmerman, N.Y., 102

## WORLD SERIES

- **Winner:** The White Sox, making their first Series appearance since 1906, took advantage of the Giants' sloppy play for a six-game victory.
- **Turning point:** The White Sox rallied for six seventh and eighth-inning runs to claim an 8-5 victory in the pivotal fifth game.
- **Memorable moment:** Third baseman Heinie Zimmerman giving futile chase to Chicago's Eddie Collins as he bolted toward the uncovered plate on one of several Game 6 fielding gaffes by the Giants. The White Sox closed out the Series with a 4-2 victory.
- **Top guns:** Red Faber (3-1), Collins (.409), White Sox; Dave Robertson (.500), Giants.

**Linescores**

**Game 1**—October 6, at Chicago
New York........ 0 0 0 0 1 0 0 0 0 — 1 7 1
Chicago.......... 0 0 1 1 0 0 0 0 x — 2 7 1
Sallee; Cicotte. W—Cicotte. L—Sallee.
HR—Felsch (Chi.).

**Game 2**—October 7, at Chicago
New York........ 0 2 0 0 0 0 0 0 0 — 2 8 1
Chicago.......... 0 2 0 5 0 0 0 0 x — 7 14 1
Schupp, Anderson (2), Perritt (4), Tesreau (8); Faber. W—Faber. L—Anderson.

**Game 3**—October 10, at New York
Chicago.......... 0 0 0 0 0 0 0 0 0 — 0 5 3
New York........ 0 0 0 2 0 0 0 0 x — 2 8 2
Cicotte; Benton. W—Benton. L—Cicotte.

**Game 4**—October 11, at New York
Chicago.......... 0 0 0 0 0 0 0 0 0 — 0 7 0
New York........ 0 0 0 1 1 0 1 2 x — 5 10 1
Faber, Danforth (8); Schupp. W—Schupp. L—Faber. HR—Kauff 2 (N.Y.).

**Game 5**—October 13, at Chicago
New York........ 2 0 0 2 0 0 1 0 0 — 5 12 3
Chicago.......... 0 0 1 0 0 1 3 3 x — 8 14 6
Sallee, Perritt (8); Russell, Cicotte (1), Williams (7), Faber (8). W—Faber. L—Sallee.

**Game 6**—October 15, at New York
Chicago.......... 0 0 0 3 0 0 0 0 1 — 4 7 1
New York........ 0 0 0 0 2 0 0 0 0 — 2 6 3
Faber; Benton, Perritt (6). W—Faber. L—Benton.

# 1918

## FINAL STANDINGS

**American League**

| Team | W | L | Pct. | GB |
|---|---|---|---|---|
| Boston | 75 | 51 | .595 | ... |
| Cleveland | 73 | 54 | .575 | 2.5 |
| Washington | 72 | 56 | .563 | 4 |
| New York | 60 | 63 | .488 | 13.5 |
| St. Louis | 58 | 64 | .475 | 15 |
| Chicago | 57 | 67 | .460 | 17 |
| Detroit | 55 | 71 | .437 | 20 |
| Philadelphia | 52 | 76 | .406 | 24 |

**National League**

| Team | W | L | Pct. | GB |
|---|---|---|---|---|
| Chicago | 84 | 45 | .651 | ... |
| New York | 71 | 53 | .573 | 10.5 |
| Cincinnati | 68 | 60 | .531 | 15.5 |
| Pittsburgh | 65 | 60 | .520 | 17 |
| Brooklyn | 57 | 69 | .452 | 25.5 |
| Philadelphia | 55 | 68 | .447 | 26 |
| Boston | 53 | 71 | .427 | 28.5 |
| St. Louis | 51 | 78 | .395 | 33 |

## SIGNIFICANT EVENTS

- **April 30:** Cubs great Grover Cleveland Alexander answered the draft call and reported for World War I duty with the Army.
- **May 14:** Washington D.C. officials repealed the ban against night baseball in the nation's capital, citing the need for more wartime recreational outlets.
- **July 19:** U.S. Secretary of War Newton Baker issued a "Work or Fight" order forcing all able-bodied Americans into jobs considered essential to the war.
- **August 2:** A.L. and N.L. officials voted to close down the regular season by September 2 (Labor Day) with the World Series to follow immediately.
- **October 5:** Infielder Eddie Grant became baseball's first war casualty when he was killed during action in France.
- **December 10:** N.L. secretary John Heydler was selected to replace John K. Tener as the league's new president.

## MEMORABLE MOMENTS

- **April 15:** Babe Ruth got the Red Sox' s season off to a rousing start with an opening day 7-1 victory over the A's.
- **June 3:** Boston's Dutch Leonard pitched the season's only no-hitter, beating the Tigers 5-0 with the aide of a Babe Ruth home run.
- **August 31:** Babe Ruth pitched the Red Sox to an A.L. pennant-clinching 6-1 victory over the Athletics.

## LEADERS

**American League**

**BA:** Ty Cobb, Det., .382.
**Runs:** Ray Chapman, Cle., 84.
**Hits:** George Burns, Phil., 178.
**TB:** George Burns, Phil., 236.
**HR:** Babe Ruth, Bos.; Tilly Walker, Phil., 11.
**RBI:** Bobby Veach, Det., 78.
**SB:** George Sisler, St.L., 45.
**Wins:** Walter Johnson, Wash., 23.
**ERA:** Walter Johnson, Wash., 1.27.
**CG:** Carl Mays, Bos.; Scott Perry, Phil., 30.
**IP:** Scott Perry, Phil., 332.1.
**SO:** Walter Johnson, Wash., 162.

**National League**

**BA:** Zack Wheat, Brk., .335.
**Runs:** Heinie Groh, Cin., 86.
**Hits:** Charlie Hollocher, Chi., 161.
**TB:** Charlie Hollocher, Chi., 202.
**HR:** Gavvy Cravath, Phil., 8.
**RBI:** Sherry Magee, Cin., 76.
**SB:** Max Carey, Pit., 58.
**Wins:** Hippo Vaughn, Chi., 22.
**ERA:** Hippo Vaughn, Chi., 1.74.
**CG:** Art Nehf, Bos., 28.
**IP:** Hippo Vaughn, Chi., 290.1.
**SO:** Hippo Vaughn, Chi., 148.

**A.L. 20-game winners**
Walter Johnson, Wash., 23-13
Stan Coveleski, Cle., 22-13
Carl Mays, Bos., 21-13
Scott Perry, Phil., 20-19

**N.L. 20-game winners**
Hippo Vaughn, Chi., 22-10
Claude Hendrix, Chi., 20-7

## WORLD SERIES

- **Winner:** The Red Sox ended baseball's war-depleted season by defeating the Cubs and winning their fifth Series in as many tries.
- **Turning point:** Babe Ruth's second victory, a 3-2 Game 4 decision that gave the Red Sox a three games to one advantage.
- **Memorable moment:** A Game 6 delay while players haggled with the owners over gate receipts. The Red Sox closed out the Cubs with a 2-1 victory.
- **Top guns:** Carl Mays (2-0, 1.00 ERA), Ruth (2-0, 1.06), Red Sox; Charlie Pick (.389), Cubs.

**Linescores**

**Game 1**—September 5, at Chicago
Boston ..........0 0 0 1 0 0 0 0 0 — 1 5 0
Chicago..........0 0 0 0 0 0 0 0 0 — 0 6 0
Ruth; Vaughn. W—Ruth. L—Vaughn.

**Game 2**—September 6, at Chicago
Boston ..........0 0 0 0 0 0 0 0 1 — 1 6 1
Chicago..........0 3 0 0 0 0 0 0 x — 3 7 1
Bush; Tyler. W—Tyler. L—Bush.

**Game 3**—September 7, at Chicago
Boston ..........0 0 0 2 0 0 0 0 0 — 2 7 0
Chicago..........0 0 0 0 1 0 0 0 0 — 1 7 1
Mays; Vaughn. W—Mays. L—Vaughn.

**Game 4**—September 9, at Boston
Chicago..........0 0 0 0 0 0 0 2 0 — 2 7 1
Boston............0 0 0 2 0 0 0 1 x — 3 4 0
Tyler, Douglas (8); Ruth, Bush (9). W—Ruth. L—Douglas.

**Game 5**—September 10, at Boston
Chicago..........0 0 1 0 0 0 0 2 0 — 3 7 0
Boston ...........0 0 0 0 0 0 0 0 0 — 0 5 0
Vaughn; Jones. W—Vaughn. L—Jones.

**Game 6**—September 11, at Boston
Chicago..........0 0 0 1 0 0 0 0 0 — 1 3 2
Boston............0 0 2 0 0 0 0 0 x — 2 5 0
Tyler, Hendrix (8); Mays. W—Mays. L—Tyler.

# 1919

## FINAL STANDINGS

**American League**

| Team | W | L | Pct. | GB |
|---|---|---|---|---|
| Chicago | 88 | 52 | .629 | ... |
| Cleveland | 84 | 55 | .604 | 3.5 |
| New York | 80 | 59 | .576 | 7.5 |
| Detroit | 80 | 60 | .571 | 8 |
| St. Louis | 67 | 72 | .482 | 20.5 |
| Boston | 66 | 71 | .482 | 20.5 |
| Washington | 56 | 84 | .400 | 32 |
| Philadelphia | 36 | 104 | .257 | 52 |

**National League**

| Team | W | L | Pct. | GB |
|---|---|---|---|---|
| Cincinnati | 96 | 44 | .686 | ... |
| New York | 87 | 53 | .621 | 9 |
| Chicago | 75 | 65 | .536 | 21 |
| Pittsburgh | 71 | 68 | .511 | 24.5 |
| Brooklyn | 69 | 71 | .493 | 27 |
| Boston | 57 | 82 | .410 | 38.5 |
| St. Louis | 54 | 83 | .394 | 40.5 |
| Philadelphia | 47 | 90 | .343 | 47.5 |

## SIGNIFICANT EVENTS

■ **April 19:** New York Governor Al Smith signed a bill permitting Sunday baseball throughout the state.
■ **April 23:** The slimmed-down 140-game Major League schedule opened in Washington, where Walter Johnson shut out the A's, 1-0.
■ **September 2:** Major League officials approved a best-of-nine World Series format, replacing the long-running seven-game format.

## MEMORABLE MOMENTS

■ **September 16:** The Reds defeated the Giants, 4-3, and clinched their first N.L. pennant of the century.
■ **September 24:** The White Sox captured their second A.L. pennant in three years when they defeated St. Louis, 6-5.
■ **September 27:** Boston's Babe Ruth stretched his one-season home run record to 29 in a game at Washington.

## LEADERS

**American League**

**BA:** Ty Cobb, Det., .384.
**Runs:** Babe Ruth, Bos., 103.
**Hits:** Ty Cobb, Det.; Bobby Veach, Det., 191.
**TB:** Babe Ruth, Bos., 284.
**HR:** Babe Ruth, Bos., 29.
**RBI:** Babe Ruth, Bos., 114.
**SB:** Eddie Collins, Chi., 33.
**Wins:** Eddie Cicotte, Chi., 29.
**ERA:** Walter Johnson, Wash., 1.49.
**CG:** Eddie Cicotte, Chi., 30.
**IP:** Eddie Cicotte, Chi.; Jim Shaw, Wash., 306.2.
**SO:** Walter Johnson, Wash., 147.

**National League**

**BA:** Gavvy Cravath, Phil., .341.
**Runs:** George Burns, N.Y., 86.
**Hits:** Ivy Olson, Brk., 164.
**TB:** Hy Myers, Brk., 223.
**HR:** Gavvy Cravath, Phil., 12.
**RBI:** Hy Myers, Brk., 73.
**SB:** George Burns, N.Y., 40.
**Wins:** Jesse Barnes, N.Y., 25.
**ERA:** Grover Alexander, Chi., 1.72.
**CG:** Wilbur Cooper, Pit., 27.
**IP:** Hippo Vaughn, Chi., 306.2.
**SO:** Hippo Vaughn, Chi., 141.

**A.L. 20-game winners**
Ed Cicotte, Chi., 29-7
Stan Coveleski, Cle., 24-12
Lefty Williams, Chi., 23-11
Hooks Dauss, Det., 21-9
Allen Sothoron, St.L., 20-12
Bob Shawkey, N.Y., 20-11
Walter Johnson, Wash., 20-14

**N.L. 20-game winners**
Jess Barnes, N.Y., 25-9
Slim Sallee, Cin., 21-7
Hippo Vaughn, Chi., 21-14

**A.L. 100 RBIs**
Babe Ruth, Bos., 114
Bobby Veach, Det., 101

## WORLD SERIES

■ **Winner:** The Reds earned their first Series victory amid suspicions the White Sox were consorting with gamblers in a fall classic fix.

■ **Turning point:** The Series' first pitch, when Chicago starter Eddie Cicotte hit Cincinnati leadoff man Morrie Rath, reportedly signaling to bettors the fix was on.

■ **Memorable moment:** White Sox lefthander Dickey Kerr, suspecting something was brewing among his teammates, fired a heroic three-hit shutout in Game 3.

■ **Top guns:** Hod Eller (2-0, 2.00 ERA), Greasy Neale (.357), Reds; Kerr (2-0, 1.42), White Sox.

### Linescores

**Game 1**—October 1, at Cincinnati
Chicago.......... 0 1 0 0 0 0 0 0 0 — 1 6 1
Cincinnati....... 1 0 0 5 0 0 2 1 x — 9 14 1
Cicotte, Wilkinson (4), Lowdermilk (8); Ruether. W—Ruether. L—Cicotte.

**Game 2**—October 2, at Cincinnati
Chicago.......... 0 0 0 0 0 0 2 0 0 — 2 10 1
Cincinnati....... 0 0 0 3 0 1 0 0 x — 4 4 2
Williams; Sallee. W—Sallee. L—Williams.

**Game 3**—October 3, at Chicago
Cincinnati....... 0 0 0 0 0 0 0 0 0 — 0 3 1
Chicago.......... 0 2 0 1 0 0 0 0 x — 3 7 0
Fisher, Luque (8); Kerr. W—Kerr. L—Fisher.

**Game 4**—October 4, at Chicago
Cincinnati....... 0 0 0 0 2 0 0 0 0—2 5 2
Chicago.......... 0 0 0 0 0 0 0 0 0—0 3 2
Ring; Cicotte. W—Ring. L—Cicotte.

**Game 5**—October 6, at Chicago
Cincinnati....... 0 0 0 0 0 4 0 0 1 — 5 4 0
Chicago.......... 0 0 0 0 0 0 0 0 0 — 0 3 3
Eller; Williams, Mayer (9). W—Eller. L—Williams.

**Game 6**—October 7, at Cincinnati
Chicago.......... 0 0 0 0 1 3 0 0 0 1—5 10 3
Cincinnati....... 0 0 2 2 0 0 0 0 0 0—4 11 0
Kerr; Ruether, Ring (6). W—Kerr. L—Ring.

**Game 7**—October 8, at Cincinnati
Chicago.......... 1 0 1 0 2 0 0 0 0 — 4 10 1
Cincinnati....... 0 0 0 0 0 1 0 0 0 — 1 7 4
Cicotte; Sallee, Fisher (5), Luque (6). W—Cicotte. L—Sallee.

**Game 8**—October 9, at Chicago
Cincinnati....... 4 1 0 0 1 3 0 1 0 — 10 16 2
Chicago.......... 0 0 1 0 0 0 0 4 0 — 5 10 1
Eller; Williams, James (1), Wilkinson (6). W—Eller. L—Williams. HR—Jackson (Chi.).

# 1920

## FINAL STANDINGS

**American League**

| Team | W | L | Pct. | GB |
|---|---|---|---|---|
| Cleveland | 98 | 56 | .636 | ... |
| Chicago | 96 | 58 | .623 | 2 |
| New York | 95 | 59 | .617 | 3 |
| St. Louis | 76 | 77 | .497 | 21.5 |
| Boston | 72 | 81 | .471 | 25.5 |
| Washington | 68 | 84 | .447 | 29 |
| Detroit | 61 | 93 | .396 | 37 |
| Philadelphia | 48 | 106 | .312 | 50 |

**National League**

| Team | W | L | Pct. | GB |
|---|---|---|---|---|
| Brooklyn | 93 | 61 | .604 | ... |
| New York | 86 | 68 | .558 | 7 |
| Cincinnati | 82 | 71 | .536 | 10.5 |
| Pittsburgh | 79 | 75 | .513 | 14 |
| Chicago | 75 | 79 | .487 | 18 |
| St. Louis | 75 | 79 | .487 | 18 |
| Boston | 62 | 90 | .408 | 30 |
| Philadelphia | 62 | 91 | .405 | 30.5 |

## SIGNIFICANT EVENTS

■ **January 5:** The New York Yankees acquired pitcher-outfielder Babe Ruth from Boston Red Sox owner Harry Frazee for the incredible price of $125,000.
■ **February 9:** Baseball's joint rules committee banned the use of all foreign substances and ball-doctoring methods used by pitchers.
■ **September 28:** A Chicago grand jury indicted eight White Sox players, including star center fielder Joe Jackson, for conspiring to fix the 1919 World Series. All eight were immediately suspended by Chicago owner Charles Comiskey.

## MEMORABLE MOMENTS

■ **May 1:** Boston's Joe Oeschger and Brooklyn's Leon Cadore traded pitches for a Major League-record 26 innings in a game that ended in a 1-1 tie at Braves Field.
■ **May 14:** Washington great Walter Johnson defeated Detroit for his 300th career victory.
■ **August 17:** Cleveland shortstop Ray Chapman died a day after he was hit on the head by a pitch from Yankee righthander Carl Mays.
■ **October 2:** Pittsburgh and Cincinnati played the century's only tripleheader.
■ **October 3:** Browns first baseman George Sisler collected his record-setting 257th hit of the season.

## LEADERS

**American League**

**BA:** George Sisler, St.L., .407.
**Runs:** Babe Ruth, N.Y., 158.
**Hits:** George Sisler, St.L., 257.
**TB:** George Sisler, St.L., 399.
**HR:** Babe Ruth, N.Y., 54.
**RBI:** Babe Ruth, N.Y., 137.
**SB:** Sam Rice, Wash., 63.
**Wins:** Jim Bagby, Cle., 31.
**ERA:** Bob Shawkey, N.Y., 2.45.
**CG:** Jim Bagby, Cle., 30.
**IP:** Jim Bagby, Cle., 339.2.
**SO:** Stan Coveleski, Cle., 133.

**National League**

**BA:** Rogers Hornsby, St.L., .370.
**Runs:** George Burns, N.Y., 115.
**Hits:** Rogers Hornsby, St.L., 218.
**TB:** Rogers Hornsby, St.L., 329.
**HR:** Cy Williams, Phil., 15.
**RBI:** Rogers Hornsby, St.L.; George Kelly, N.Y., 94.
**SB:** Max Carey, Pit., 52.
**Wins:** Grover Alexander, Chi., 27.
**ERA:** Grover Alexander, Chi., 1.91.
**CG:** Grover Alexander, Chi., 33.
**IP:** Grover Alexander, Chi., 363.1.
**SO:** Grover Alexander, Chi., 173.

**A.L. 20-game winners**
Jim Bagby, Cle., 31-12
Carl Mays, N.Y., 26-11
Stan Coveleski, Cle., 24-14
Red Faber, Chi., 23-13
Lefty Williams, Chi., 22-14
Dickie Kerr, Chi., 21-9
Ed Cicotte, Chi., 21-10
Ray Caldwell, Cle., 20-10
Urban Shocker, St.L., 20-10
Bob Shawkey, N.Y., 20-13

**N.L. 20-game winners**
Grover Alexander, Chi., 27-14
Wilbur Cooper, Pit., 24-15
Burleigh Grimes, Brk., 23-11
Fred Toney, N.Y., 21-11
Art Nehf, N.Y., 21-12
Bill Doak, St.L., 20-12
Jess Barnes, N.Y., 20-15

**A.L. 100 RBIs**
Babe Ruth, N.Y., 137
Bill Jacobson, St.L., 122
George Sisler, St.L., 122
Joe Jackson, Chi., 121
Larry Gardner, Cle., 118
Happy Felsch, Chi., 115
Bobby Veach, Det., 113
Tris Speaker, Cle., 107
Elmer Smith, Cle., 103

**A.L. 40 homers**
Babe Ruth, N.Y., 54

## WORLD SERIES

■ **Winner:** The Indians, Series newcomers, held off the Dodgers in a seven-game fall classic filled with memorable firsts.

■ **Turning point:** Stan Coveleski's second win, a 5-1 Game 4 decision, that knotted the Series at two and set up a dramatic Game 5.

■ **Memorable moments:** There were several for the Indians in Game 5. Elmer Smith hit the first grand slam in Series history, Jim Bagby became the first pitcher to hit a Series homer and second baseman Bill Wambsganss pulled off the first Series triple play — unassisted.

■ **Top guns:** Coveleski (3-0, 0.67 ERA), Smith (.308, 5 RBIs), Indians; Zack Wheat (.333), Dodgers.

### Linescores

**Game 1**—October 5, at Brooklyn
Cleveland........ 0 2 0 1 0 0 0 0 0 — 3 5 0
Brooklyn......... 0 0 0 0 0 0 1 0 0 — 1 5 1
Coveleski; Marquard, Mamaux (7), Cadore (9). W—Coveleski. L—Marquard.

**Game 2**—October 6, at Brooklyn
Cleveland........ 0 0 0 0 0 0 0 0 0 — 0 7 1
Brooklyn......... 1 0 1 0 1 0 0 0 x — 3 7 0
Bagby, Uhle (7); Grimes. W—Grimes. L—Bagby.

**Game 3**—October 7, at Brooklyn
Cleveland........ 0 0 0 1 0 0 0 0 0 — 1 3 1
Brooklyn......... 2 0 0 0 0 0 0 0 x — 2 6 1
Caldwell, Mails (1), Uhle (8); S. Smith. W—S. Smith. L—Caldwell.

**Game 4**—October 9, at Cleveland
Brooklyn......... 0 0 0 1 0 0 0 0 0 — 1 5 1
Cleveland........ 2 0 2 0 0 1 0 0 x — 5 12 2
Cadore, Mamaux (2), Marquard (3), Pfeffer (6); Coveleski. W—Coveleski. L—Cadore.

**Game 5**—October 10, at Cleveland
Brooklyn......... 0 0 0 0 0 0 0 0 1 — 1 13 1
Cleveland........ 4 0 0 3 1 0 0 0 x — 8 12 2
Grimes, Mitchell (4); Bagby. W—Bagby. L—Grimes. HR—E. Smith, Bagby (Cle.).

**Game 6**—October 11, at Cleveland
Brooklyn......... 0 0 0 0 0 0 0 0 0 — 0 3 0
Cleveland........ 0 0 0 0 0 1 0 0 x — 1 7 3
S. Smith; Mails. W—Mails. L—S. Smith.

**Game 7**—October 12, at Cleveland
Brooklyn......... 0 0 0 0 0 0 0 0 0 — 0 5 2
Cleveland........ 0 0 0 1 1 0 1 0 x — 3 7 3
Grimes, Mamaux (8); Coveleski. W—Coveleski. L—Grimes.

# 1921

## FINAL STANDINGS

**American League**

| Team | W | L | Pct. | GB |
|---|---|---|---|---|
| New York | 98 | 55 | .641 | ... |
| Cleveland | 94 | 60 | .610 | 4.5 |
| St. Louis | 81 | 73 | .526 | 17.5 |
| Washington | 80 | 73 | .523 | 18 |
| Boston | 75 | 79 | .487 | 23.5 |
| Detroit | 71 | 82 | .464 | 27 |
| Chicago | 62 | 92 | .403 | 36.5 |
| Philadelphia | 53 | 100 | .346 | 45 |

**National League**

| Team | W | L | Pct. | GB |
|---|---|---|---|---|
| New York | 94 | 59 | .614 | ... |
| Pittsburgh | 90 | 63 | .588 | 4 |
| St. Louis | 87 | 66 | .569 | 7 |
| Boston | 79 | 74 | .516 | 15 |
| Brooklyn | 77 | 75 | .507 | 16.5 |
| Cincinnati | 70 | 83 | .458 | 24 |
| Chicago | 64 | 89 | .418 | 30 |
| Philadelphia | 51 | 103 | .331 | 43.5 |

## SIGNIFICANT EVENTS

■ **January 21:** Federal Judge Kenesaw Mountain Landis began his seven-year contract as baseball's first commissioner.
■ **August 3:** Commissioner Landis banned eight Chicago White Sox players from baseball for life, even though a Chicago jury had cleared them of charges that they conspired to fix the 1919 World Series.
■ **August 5:** Pittsburgh radio station KDKA did the first Major League baseball broadcast—a Pirates-Phillies game at Forbes Field.
■ **October 5:** Pittsburgh radio station KDKA broadcast the opening game of the Yankees-Giants World Series.
■ **October 21:** Commissioner Landis suspended Babe Ruth and Yankee teammates Bob Meusel and Bill Piercy for their illegal barnstorming tour after the 1921 World Series.

## MEMORABLE MOMENTS

■ **August 19:** Detroit's Ty Cobb collected career hit No. 3,000 off Boston pitcher Elmer Myers.
■ **October 2:** Babe Ruth connected for record home run No. 59 off Boston's Curt Fullerton.

## LEADERS

**American League**

**BA:** Harry Heilmann, Det., .394.
**Runs:** Babe Ruth, N.Y., 177.
**Hits:** Harry Heilmann, Det., 237.
**TB:** Babe Ruth, N.Y., 457.
**HR:** Babe Ruth, N.Y., 59.
**RBI:** Babe Ruth, N.Y., 171.
**SB:** George Sisler, St.L., 35.
**Wins:** Carl Mays, N.Y.; Urban Shocker, St.L., 27.
**ERA:** Red Faber, Chi., 2.48.
**CG:** Red Faber, Chi., 32.
**IP:** Carl Mays, N.Y., 336.2.
**SO:** Walter Johnson, Wash., 143.

**National League**

**BA:** Rogers Hornsby, St.L., .397.
**Runs:** Rogers Hornsby, St.L., 131.
**Hits:** Rogers Hornsby, St.L., 235.
**TB:** Rogers Hornsby, St.L., 378.
**HR:** George Kelly, N.Y., 23.
**RBI:** Rogers Hornsby, St.L., 126.
**SB:** Frank Frisch, N.Y., 49.
**Wins:** Wilbur Cooper, Pit.; Burleigh Grimes, Brk., 22.
**ERA:** Bill Doak, St.L., 2.59.
**CG:** Burleigh Grimes, Brk., 30.
**IP:** Wilbur Cooper, Pit., 327.
**SO:** Burleigh Grimes, Brk., 136.

**A.L. 20-game winners**
Carl Mays, N.Y., 27-9
Urban Shocker, St.L., 27-12
Red Faber, Chi., 25-15
Stan Coveleski, Cle., 23-13
Sam Jones, Bos., 23-16

**N.L. 20-game winners**
Burleigh Grimes, Brk., 22-13
Wilbur Cooper, Pit., 22-14
Art Nehf, N.Y., 20-10
Joe Oeschger, Bos., 20-14

**A.L. 100 RBIs**
Babe Ruth, N.Y., 170
Harry Heilmann, Det., 139
Bob Meusel, N.Y., 135
Bobby Veach, Det., 128
Ken Williams, St.L., 117
Larry Gardner, Cle., 115
George Sisler, St.L., 104
Ty Cobb, Det., 101
Tilly Walker, Phil., 101
Del Pratt, Bos., 100

**N.L. 100 RBIs**
Rogers Hornsby, St.L., 126
George Kelly, N.Y., 122
Austin McHenry, St.L., 102
Ross Youngs, N.Y., 102
Frank Frisch, N.Y., 100

**A.L. 40 homers**
Babe Ruth, N.Y., 59

## WORLD SERIES

■ **Winner:** The Giants shook the ghosts of Series past and rallied for an eight-game victory in the battle of New York.

■ **Turning point:** Down two games to none and trailing 4-0 in the third inning of Game 3, the Giants rallied for a 13-5 victory.

■ **Memorable moment:** An unusual 4-3-5 double play that finished off Art Nehf's 1-0 Game 8 victory over Yankee Waite Hoyt and provided a dramatic conclusion to the Series.

■ **Top guns:** Jesse Barnes (2-0, 1.65 ERA), Frank Snyder (.364), Irish Meusel (.345, 7 RBIs), Giants; Hoyt (2-1, 0.00), Yankees.

**Linescores**

**Game 1**—October 5, at Polo Grounds
Yankees.......... 1 0 0 0 1 1 0 0 0 — 3 7 0
Giants............ 0 0 0 0 0 0 0 0 0 — 0 5 0
Mays; Douglas, Barnes (9). W—Mays. L—Douglas.

**Game 2**—October 6, at Polo Grounds
Giants............ 0 0 0 0 0 0 0 0 0 — 0 2 3
Yankees.......... 0 0 0 1 0 0 0 2 x — 3 3 0
Nehf; Hoyt. W—Hoyt. L—Nehf.

**Game 3**—October 7, at Polo Grounds
Yankees.......... 0 0 4 0 0 0 0 1 0 — 5 8 0
Giants............ 0 0 4 0 0 0 8 1 x — 13 20 0
Shawkey, Quinn (3), Collins (7), Rogers (7); Toney, Barnes (3). W—Barnes. L—Quinn.

**Game 4**—October 9, at Polo Grounds
Giants............ 0 0 0 0 0 0 0 3 1 — 4 9 1
Yankees.......... 0 0 0 0 1 0 0 0 1 — 2 7 1
Douglas; Mays. W—Douglas. L—Mays. HR—Ruth (NYY).

**Game 5**—October 10, at Polo Grounds
Yankees.......... 0 0 1 2 0 0 0 0 0 — 3 6 1
Giants............ 1 0 0 0 0 0 0 0 0 — 1 10 1
Hoyt; Nehf. W—Hoyt. L—Nehf.

**Game 6**—October 11, at Polo Grounds
Giants............ 0 3 0 4 0 1 0 0 0 — 8 13 0
Yankees.......... 3 2 0 0 0 0 0 0 0 — 5 7 2
Toney, Barnes (1); Harper, Shawkey (2), Piercy (9). W—Barnes. L—Shawkey. HR—E. Meusel, Snyder (NYG); Fewster (NYY).

**Game 7**—October 12, at Polo Grounds
Yankees.......... 0 1 0 0 0 0 0 0 0 — 1 8 1
Giants............ 0 0 0 1 0 0 1 0 x — 2 6 0
Mays; Douglas. W—Douglas. L—Mays.

**Game 8**—October 13, at Polo Grounds
Giants............ 1 0 0 0 0 0 0 0 0 — 1 6 0
Yankees.......... 0 0 0 0 0 0 0 0 0 — 0 4 1
Nehf; Hoyt. W—Nehf. L—Hoyt.

# 1922

## FINAL STANDINGS

**American League**

| Team | W | L | Pct. | GB |
|---|---|---|---|---|
| New York | 94 | 60 | .610 | ... |
| St. Louis | 93 | 61 | .604 | 1 |
| Detroit | 79 | 75 | .513 | 15 |
| Cleveland | 78 | 76 | .506 | 16 |
| Chicago | 77 | 77 | .500 | 17 |
| Washington | 69 | 85 | .448 | 25 |
| Philadelphia | 65 | 89 | .422 | 29 |
| Boston | 61 | 93 | .396 | 33 |

**National League**

| Team | W | L | Pct. | GB |
|---|---|---|---|---|
| New York | 93 | 61 | .604 | ... |
| Cincinnati | 86 | 68 | .558 | 7 |
| Pittsburgh | 85 | 69 | .552 | 8 |
| St. Louis | 85 | 69 | .552 | 8 |
| Chicago | 80 | 74 | .519 | 13 |
| Brooklyn | 76 | 78 | .494 | 17 |
| Philadelphia | 57 | 96 | .373 | 35.5 |
| Boston | 53 | 100 | .346 | 39.5 |

## SIGNIFICANT EVENTS

■ **March 5:** Babe Ruth signed a three-year Yankee contract for a record $52,000 per season.
■ **September 21:** Browns first baseman George Sisler, a .420 hitter, was the choice of A.L. baseball writers for the first MVP award presented since 1914.
■ **October:** The World Series returned to a best-of-seven format and the entire Series was broadcast over the radio.

## MEMORABLE MOMENTS

■ **April 30:** Chicago rookie Charlie Robertson became the third modern-era pitcher to throw a perfect game, retiring all 27 Tigers he faced in a 2-0 victory at Detroit.
■ **May 7:** Giants righthander Jesse Barnes pitched a 6-0 no-hitter against Philadelphia, an effort blemished only by a fifth-inning walk.
■ **June 28:** Washington fireballer Walter Johnson outdueled New York ace Waite Hoyt and recorded his 95th career shutout with a 1-0 victory at Griffith Stadium.
■ **August 25:** Chicago and Philadelphia combined for a record 49 runs and 51 hits in the Cubs' 26-23 victory at Wrigley Field.
■ **September 18:** The New York Yankees ended George Sisler's modern-era record hitting streak at 41 games during a 3-2 victory over the Browns.
■ **October 1:** Cardinals second baseman Rogers Hornsby became baseball's third Triple Crown winner when he finished the season at .401 with 42 homers and 152 RBI.

## LEADERS

**American League**

**BA:** George Sisler, St.L., .420.
**Runs:** George Sisler, St.L., 134.
**Hits:** George Sisler, St.L., 246.
**TB:** Ken Williams, St.L., 367.
**HR:** Ken Williams, St.L., 39.
**RBI:** Ken Williams, St.L., 155.
**SB:** George Sisler, St.L., 51.
**Wins:** Eddie Rommel, Phil., 27.
**ERA:** Red Faber, Chi., 2.81.
**CG:** Red Faber, Chi., 31.
**IP:** Red Faber, Chi., 352.
**SO:** Urban Shocker, St.L., 149.

**National League**

**BA:** Rogers Hornsby, St.L., .401.
**Runs:** Rogers Hornsby, St.L., 141.
**Hits:** Rogers Hornsby, St.L., 250.
**TB:** Rogers Hornsby, St.L., 450.
**HR:** Rogers Hornsby, St.L., 42.
**RBI:** Rogers Hornsby, St.L., 152.
**SB:** Max Carey, Pit., 51.
**Wins:** Eppa Rixey, Cin., 25.
**ERA:** Phil Douglas, N.Y., 2.63.
**CG:** Wilbur Cooper, Pit., 27.
**IP:** Eppa Rixey, Cin., 313.1.
**SO:** Dazzy Vance, Brk., 134.

**A.L. 20-game winners**
Eddie Rommel, Phil., 27-13
Joe Bush, N.Y., 26-7
Urban Shocker, St.L., 24-17
George Uhle, Cle., 22-16
Red Faber, Chi., 21-17
Bob Shawkey, N.Y., 20-12

**N.L. 20-game winners**
Eppa Rixey, Cin., 25-13
Wilbur Cooper, Pit., 23-14
Dutch Ruether, Brk., 21-12

**A.L. 100 RBIs**
Ken Williams, St.L., 155
Bobby Veach, Det., 126
Marty McManus, St.L., 109
George Sisler, St.L., 105
Bill Jacobson, St.L., 102

**N.L. 100 RBIs**
Rogers Hornsby, St.L., 152
Irish Meusel, N.Y., 132
Zack Wheat, Brk., 112
George Kelly, N.Y., 107

**N.L 40 homers**
Rogers Hornsby, St.L., 42

**League MVP**
A.L.: George Sisler, 1B, St.L.
N.L.: No selection.

## WORLD SERIES

■ **Winner:** The all-New York rematch had the same result, the Giants winning this time in five games.

■ **Turning point:** A 3-3 Game 2 tie that took away the Yankees' best hope for a victory.

■ **Memorable moment:** Giants lefthander Art Nehf closing out the Yankees in the Series finale for the second straight year.

■ **Top guns:** Heinie Groh (.474), Frankie Frisch (.471), Irish Meusel (7 RBIs), Giants.

**Linescores**

**Game 1**—October 4, at Polo Grounds
Yankees.......... 0 0 0 0 0 1 1 0 0 — 2 7 0
Giants............ 0 0 0 0 0 0 0 3 x — 3 11 3
Bush, Hoyt (8); Nehf, Ryan (8). W—Ryan. L—Bush.

**Game 2**—October 5, at Polo Grounds
Giants............ 3 0 0 0 0 0 0 0 0 0 — 3 8 1
Yankees.......... 1 0 0 1 0 0 0 1 0 0 — 3 8 0
J. Barnes; Shawkey. HR—E. Meusel (NYG); Ward (NYY). Game called after 10 innings because of darkness.

**Game 3**—October 6, at Polo Grounds
Yankees.......... 0 0 0 0 0 0 0 0 0 — 0 4 1
Giants............ 0 0 2 0 0 0 1 0 x — 3 12 1
Hoyt, Jones (8); J. Scott. W—J. Scott. L—Hoyt.

**Game 4**—October 7, at Polo Grounds
Giants............ 0 0 0 0 4 0 0 0 0 — 4 9 1
Yankees.......... 2 0 0 0 0 0 1 0 0 — 3 8 0
McQuillan; Mays, Jones (9). W—McQuillan. L—Mays. HR—Ward (NYY).

**Game 5**—October 8, at Polo Grounds
Yankees.......... 1 0 0 0 1 0 1 0 0 — 3 5 0
Giants............ 0 2 0 0 0 0 0 3 x — 5 10 0
Bush; Nehf. W—Nehf. L—Bush.

# 1923

## FINAL STANDINGS

**American League**

| Team | W | L | Pct. | GB |
|---|---|---|---|---|
| New York | 98 | 54 | .645 | ... |
| Detroit | 83 | 71 | .539 | 16 |
| Cleveland | 82 | 71 | .536 | 16.5 |
| Washington | 75 | 78 | .490 | 23.5 |
| St. Louis | 74 | 78 | .487 | 24 |
| Philadelphia | 69 | 83 | .454 | 29 |
| Chicago | 69 | 85 | .448 | 30 |
| Boston | 61 | 91 | .401 | 37 |

**National League**

| Team | W | L | Pct. | GB |
|---|---|---|---|---|
| New York | 95 | 58 | .621 | ... |
| Cincinnati | 91 | 63 | .591 | 4.5 |
| Pittsburgh | 87 | 67 | .565 | 8.5 |
| Chicago | 83 | 71 | .539 | 12.5 |
| St. Louis | 79 | 74 | .516 | 16 |
| Brooklyn | 76 | 78 | .494 | 19.5 |
| Boston | 54 | 100 | .351 | 41.5 |
| Philadelphia | 50 | 104 | .325 | 45.5 |

## SIGNIFICANT EVENTS

■ **April 18:** A Major League-record 74,217 fans watched Babe Ruth christen new Yankee Stadium with a three-run homer that sparked a 4-1 victory over Boston.

## MEMORABLE MOMENTS

■ **May 2:** New York Yankee shortstop Everett Scott was honored when his ironman streak reached 1,000 games.

■ **May 11:** The Phillies defeated the Cardinals 20-14 in a game that featured 10 homers—three by Philadelphia's Cy Williams.

■ **July 7:** Cleveland, scoring in each of its eight at-bats, set an A.L. record for runs in a 27-3 victory over Boston.

■ **July 22:** Washington's Walter Johnson fanned five Indians and became the first pitcher to record 3,000 career strikeouts.

■ **September 7:** Boston's Howard Ehmke, duplicating the no-hit feat of New York Yankee Sam Jones three days earlier in the same stadium, stopped the Athletics 4-0 at Philadelphia.

■ **October 7:** St. Louis ended the regular season with a doubleheader split against the Cubs and Cardinals star Rogers Hornsby captured his fourth straight batting title with a .384 average.

## LEADERS

**American League**

**BA:** Harry Heilmann, Det., .403.
**Runs:** Babe Ruth, N.Y., 151.
**Hits:** Charlie Jamieson, Cle., 222.
**TB:** Babe Ruth, N.Y., 399.
**HR:** Babe Ruth, N.Y., 41.
**RBI:** Babe Ruth, N.Y., 131.
**SB:** Eddie Collins, Chi., 49.
**Wins:** George Uhle, Cle., 26.
**ERA:** Stan Coveleski, Cle., 2.76.
**CG:** George Uhle, Cle., 29.
**IP:** George Uhle, Cle., 357.2.
**SO:** Walter Johnson, Wash., 130.

**National League**

**BA:** Rogers Hornsby, St.L., .384.
**Runs:** Ross Youngs, N.Y., 121.
**Hits:** Frank Frisch, N.Y., 223.
**TB:** Frank Frisch, N.Y., 311.
**HR:** Cy Williams, Phil., 41.
**RBI:** Irish Meusel, N.Y., 125.
**SB:** Max Carey, Pit., 51.
**Wins:** Dolf Luque, Cin., 27.
**ERA:** Dolf Luque, Cin., 1.93.
**CG:** Burleigh Grimes, Brk., 33.
**IP:** Burleigh Grimes, Brk., 327.
**SO:** Dazzy Vance, Brk., 197.

**A.L. 20-game winners**

George Uhle, Cle., 26-16
Sam Jones, N.Y., 21-8
Hooks Dauss, Det., 21-13
Urban Shocker, St.L., 20-12
Howard Ehmke, Bos., 20-17

**N.L. 20-game winners**

Dolf Luque, Cin., 27-8
Johnny Morrison, Pit., 25-13
Grover Alexander, Chi., 22-12
Pete Donohue, Cin., 21-15
Burleigh Grimes, Brk., 21-18
Jesse Haines, St.L., 20-13
Eppa Rixey, Cin., 20-15

**A.L. 100 RBIs**

Babe Ruth, N.Y., 130
Tris Speaker, Cle., 130
Harry Heilmann, Det., 115
Joe Sewell, Cle., 109
Wally Pipp, N.Y., 108

**N.L. 100 RBIs**

Irish Meusel, N.Y., 125
Cy Williams, Phil., 114
Frank Frisch, N.Y., 111
George Kelly, N.Y., 103
Jack Fournier, Brk., 102
Pie Traynor, Pit., 101

**A.L. 40 homers**

Babe Ruth, N.Y., 41

**N.L. 40 homers**

Cy Williams, Phil., 41

**League MVP**

A.L.: Babe Ruth, OF, N.Y.
N.L.: No selection.

## WORLD SERIES

■ **Winner:** The third Series was a charm for the Yankees, who ascended to baseball's throne with a six-game victory over the Giants.

■ **Turning point:** A three-hit Game 5 performance by Joe Bush that helped the Yankees claim an 8-1 victory and a 3-2 Series lead.

■ **Memorable moment:** Veteran Casey Stengel chugging around the bases on a ninth-inning inside-the-park home run that gave the Giants a 5-4 Game 1 victory in the first Series contest at new Yankee Stadium.

■ **Top guns:** Aaron Ward (.417), Babe Ruth (.368, 3 HR), Yankees; Stengel (.417, 2 HR), Giants.

### Linescores

**Game 1**—October 10, at Yankee Stadium
Giants............. 0 0 4 0 0 0 0 0 1 — 5 8 0
Yankees.......... 1 2 0 0 0 0 1 0 0 — 4 12 1
Watson, Ryan (3); Hoyt, Bush (3). W—Ryan. L—Bush. HR—Stengel (NYG).

**Game 2**—October 11, at Polo Grounds
Yankees.......... 0 1 0 2 1 0 0 0 0 — 4 10 0
Giants............. 0 1 0 0 0 1 0 0 0 — 2 9 2
Pennock; McQuillan, Bentley (4). W—Pennock. L—McQuillan. HR—Ward, Ruth 2 (NYY); E. Meusel (NYG).

**Game 3**—October 12, at Yankee Stadium
Giants............. 0 0 0 0 0 0 1 0 0 — 1 4 0
Yankees.......... 0 0 0 0 0 0 0 0 0 — 0 6 1
Nehf; Jones, Bush (9). W—Nehf. L—Jones. HR—Stengel (NYG).

**Game 4**—October 13, at Polo Grounds
Yankees.......... 0 6 1 1 0 0 0 0 0 — 8 13 1
Giants............. 0 0 0 0 0 0 0 3 1 — 4 13 1
Shawkey, Pennock (8); J. Scott, Ryan (2), McQuillan (2), Jonnard (8), Barnes (9). W—Shawkey. L—J. Scott. HR—Youngs (NYG).

**Game 5**—October 14, at Yankee Stadium
Giants............. 0 1 0 0 0 0 0 0 0 — 1 3 2
Yankees.......... 3 4 0 1 0 0 0 0 x — 8 14 0
Bentley, J. Scott (2), Barnes (4), Jonnard (8); Bush. W—Bush. L—Bentley. HR—Dugan (NYY).

**Game 6**—October 15, at Polo Grounds
Yankees.......... 1 0 0 0 0 0 0 5 0 — 6 5 0
Giants............. 1 0 0 1 1 1 0 0 0 — 4 10 1
Pennock, Jones (8); Nehf, Ryan (8). W—Pennock. L—Nehf. HR—Ruth (NYY); Snyder (NYG).

# 1924

## FINAL STANDINGS

**American League**

| Team | W | L | Pct. | GB |
|---|---|---|---|---|
| Washington | 92 | 62 | .597 | ... |
| New York | 89 | 63 | .586 | 2 |
| Detroit | 86 | 68 | .558 | 6 |
| St. Louis | 74 | 78 | .487 | 17 |
| Philadelphia | 71 | 81 | .467 | 20 |
| Cleveland | 67 | 86 | .438 | 24.5 |
| Boston | 67 | 87 | .435 | 25 |
| Chicago | 66 | 87 | .431 | 25.5 |

**National League**

| Team | W | L | Pct. | GB |
|---|---|---|---|---|
| New York | 93 | 60 | .608 | ... |
| Brooklyn | 92 | 62 | .597 | 1.5 |
| Pittsburgh | 90 | 63 | .588 | 3 |
| Cincinnati | 83 | 70 | .542 | 10 |
| Chicago | 81 | 72 | .529 | 12 |
| St. Louis | 65 | 89 | .422 | 28.5 |
| Philadelphia | 55 | 96 | .364 | 37 |
| Boston | 53 | 100 | .346 | 40 |

## SIGNIFICANT EVENTS

■ **March 7:** Reds manager Pat Moran died of Bright's disease at a hospital in Orlando, Fla., the team's spring training home.

■ **December 10:** National League owners accepted a proposal to go to a 2-3-2 World Series format.

## MEMORABLE MOMENTS

■ **June 13:** The Yankees were awarded a 9-0 forfeit victory over the Tigers when a ninth-inning players' fight escalated into a full-scale fan riot at Detroit's Navin Field, creating a life-threatening situation for players, umpires and police.

■ **July 16:** Giants first baseman George Kelly set a Major League record when he homered in his sixth consecutive game—an 8-7 victory over the Pirates.

■ **September 16:** Jim Bottomley collected six hits, belted two homers and drove in a single-game record 12 runs in St. Louis' 17-3 victory over Brooklyn.

■ **September 28:** Cardinals second baseman Rogers Hornsby finished the season with the highest average in baseball history—.424.

## LEADERS

**American League**

**BA:** Babe Ruth, N.Y., .378.
**Runs:** Babe Ruth, N.Y., 143.
**Hits:** Sam Rice, Wash., 216.
**TB:** Babe Ruth, N.Y., 391.
**HR:** Babe Ruth, N.Y., 46.
**RBI:** Goose Goslin, Wash., 129.
**SB:** Eddie Collins, Chi., 42.
**Wins:** Walter Johnson, Wash., 23.
**ERA:** Walter Johnson, Wash., 2.72.
**CG:** Sloppy Thurston, Chi., 28.
**IP:** Howard Ehmke, Bos., 315.
**SO:** Walter Johnson, Wash., 158.

**National League**

**BA:** Rogers Hornsby, St.L., .424.
**Runs:** Frank Frisch, N.Y.; Rogers Hornsby, St.L., 121.
**Hits:** Rogers Hornsby, St.L., 227.
**TB:** Rogers Hornsby, St.L., 373.
**HR:** Jack Fournier, Brk., 27.
**RBI:** George Kelly, N.Y., 136.
**SB:** Max Carey, Pit., 49.
**Wins:** Dazzy Vance, Brk., 28.
**ERA:** Dazzy Vance, Brk., 2.16.
**CG:** Burleigh Grimes, Brk.; Dazzy Vance, Brk., 30.
**IP:** Burleigh Grimes, Brk., 310.2.
**SO:** Dazzy Vance, Brk., 262.

**A.L. 20-game winners**

Walter Johnson, Wash., 23-7
Herb Pennock, N.Y., 21-9
Sloppy Thurston, Chi., 20-14
Joe Shaute, Cle., 20-17

**N.L. 20-game winners**

Dazzy Vance, Brk., 28-6
Burleigh Grimes, Brk., 22-13
Carl Mays, Cin., 20-9
Wilbur Cooper, Pit., 20-14

**A.L. 100 RBIs**

Goose Goslin, Wash., 129
Babe Ruth, N.Y., 121
Bob Meusel, N.Y., 120
Joe Hauser, Phil., 115
Harry Heilmann, Det., 113
Wally Pipp, N.Y., 113
Joe Sewell, Cle., 104
Earl Sheely, Chi., 103
Al Simmons, Phil., 102

**N.L. 100 RBIs**

George Kelly, N.Y., 136
Jack Fournier, Brk., 116
Jim Bottomley, St.L., 111
Glenn Wright, Pit., 111
Irish Meusel, N.Y., 102

**A.L. 40 homers**

Babe Ruth, N.Y., 46

**League MVP**

A.L.: Walter Johnson, P, Wash.
N.L.: Dazzy Vance, P, Brk.

## WORLD SERIES

■ **Winner:** The Senators made their first appearance in baseball's fall classic a successful one.

■ **Turning point:** A dramatic 2-1 Game 6 victory that kept Washington's hopes alive. Tom Zachary allowed seven hits and player/manager Bucky Harris drove in both runs with a fifth-inning single.

■ **Memorable moment:** Earl McNeely's 12th-inning Game 7 ground ball that took an inexplicable hop over third baseman Fred Lindstrom's head and gave the Senators a Series-ending 4-3 victory.

■ **Top guns:** Zachary (2-0, 2.04 ERA), Goose Goslin (.344, 3 HR, 7 RBIs), Harris (.333, 7 RBIs), Senators; Bill Terry (.429), Giants.

### Linescores

**Game 1**—October 4, at Washington
N,Y,........0 1 0 1 0 0 0 0 0 0 0 2 — 4 14 1
Wash.....0 0 0 0 0 1 0 0 1 0 0 1 — 3 10 1
Nehf; Johnson. W—Nehf. L—Johnson. HR—Kelly, Terry (N.Y.).

**Game 2**—October 5, at Washington
N.Y. ............... 0 0 0 0 0 0 1 0 2 — 3 6 0
Wash............. 2 0 0 0 1 0 0 0 1 — 4 6 1
Bentley; Zachary, Marberry (9). W—Zachary. L—Bentley. HR—Goslin, Harris (Wash.).

**Game 3**—October 6, at New York
Wash............. 0 0 0 2 0 0 0 1 1 — 4 9 2
N.Y. ............... 0 2 1 1 0 1 0 1 x — 6 12 0
Marberry, Russell (4), Martina (7), Speece (8); McQuillan, Ryan (4), Jonnard (9), Watson (9). W—McQuillan. L—Marberry. HR—Ryan (N.Y.).

**Game 4**—October 7, at New York
Wash............. 0 0 3 0 2 0 0 2 0 — 7 13 3
N.Y. ............... 1 0 0 0 0 1 0 1 1 — 4 6 1
Mogridge, Marberry (8); Barnes, Baldwin (6), Dean (8). W—Mogridge. L—Barnes. HR—Goslin (Wash.).

**Game 5**—October 8, at New York
Wash............. 0 0 0 1 0 0 0 1 0 — 2 9 1
N.Y. ............... 0 0 1 0 2 0 0 3 x — 6 13 0
Johnson; Bentley, McQuillan (8). W—Bentley. L—Johnson. HR—Bentley (N.Y.); Goslin (Wash.).

**Game 6**—October 9, at Washington
N.Y. ............... 1 0 0 0 0 0 0 0 0 — 1 7 1
Wash............. 0 0 0 0 2 0 0 0 x — 2 4 0
Nehf, Ryan (8); Zachary. W—Zachary. L—Nehf.

**Game 7**—October 10, at Washington
N.Y.........0 0 0 0 0 3 0 0 0 0 0 0 — 3 8 3
Wash.....0 0 0 1 0 0 0 2 0 0 0 1 — 4 10 4
Barnes, Nehf (8), McQuillan (9), Bentley (11); Ogden, Mogridge (1), Marberry (6), Johnson (9). W—Johnson. L—Bentley. HR—Harris (Wash.).

# 1925

## FINAL STANDINGS

**American League**

| Team | W | L | Pct. | GB |
|---|---|---|---|---|
| Washington | 96 | 55 | .636 | ... |
| Philadelphia | 88 | 64 | .579 | 8.5 |
| St. Louis | 82 | 71 | .536 | 15 |
| Detroit | 81 | 73 | .526 | 16.5 |
| Chicago | 79 | 75 | .513 | 18.5 |
| Cleveland | 70 | 84 | .455 | 27.5 |
| New York | 69 | 85 | .448 | 28.5 |
| Boston | 47 | 105 | .309 | 49.5 |

**National League**

| Team | W | L | Pct. | GB |
|---|---|---|---|---|
| Pittsburgh | 95 | 58 | .621 | ... |
| New York | 86 | 66 | .566 | 8.5 |
| Cincinnati | 80 | 73 | .523 | 15 |
| St. Louis | 77 | 76 | .503 | 18 |
| Boston | 70 | 83 | .458 | 25 |
| Brooklyn | 68 | 85 | .444 | 27 |
| Philadelphia | 68 | 85 | .444 | 27 |
| Chicago | 68 | 86 | .442 | 27.5 |

## SIGNIFICANT EVENTS

■ **April 17:** Yankee slugger Babe Ruth underwent surgery for an intestinal abscess, an injury that would sideline him until June 1.

■ **April 18:** Brooklyn owner Charles Ebbets died on the morning of his Dodgers' home opener against the Giants at Ebbets Field.

■ **October 7:** Christy Mathewson, considered by many the greatest pitcher in history, died after a five-year bout with tuberculosis at age 45.

## MEMORABLE MOMENTS

■ **May 5:** Detroit's Ty Cobb enjoyed a six-hit, three-homer game against the Browns, setting a modern Major League record with 16 total bases.

■ **May 6:** Yankee manager Miller Huggins benched shortstop Everett Scott, ending his record consecutive-games streak at 1,307.

■ **May 17:** Cleveland's Tris Speaker collected career hit No. 3,000 off Washington lefthander Tom Zachary.

■ **June 3:** White Sox manager Eddie Collins joined baseball's select 3,000-hit circle in a game against Detroit.

■ **June 15:** The Philadelphia Athletics, trailing 15-4 in the eighth inning, exploded for 13 runs and a 17-15 victory over the Indians.

■ **October 4:** St. Louis manager Rogers Hornsby matched his 1922 Triple Crown feat when he finished with a .403 average, 39 home runs and 143 RBIs.

## LEADERS

**American League**

**BA:** Harry Heilmann, Det., .393.
**Runs:** Johnny Mostil, Chi., 135.
**Hits:** Al Simmons, Phil., 253.
**TB:** Al Simmons, Phil., 392.
**HR:** Bob Meusel, N.Y., 33.
**RBI:** Bob Meusel, N.Y., 138.
**SB:** Johnny Mostil, Chi., 43.
**Wins:** Ted Lyons, Chi.; Eddie Rommel, Phil., 21.
**ERA:** Stan Coveleski, Wash., 2.84.
**CG:** Howard Ehmke, Bos.; Sherry Smith, Cle., 22.
**IP:** Herb Pennock, N.Y., 277.
**SO:** Lefty Grove, Phil., 116.

**National League**

**BA:** Rogers Hornsby, St.L., .403.
**Runs:** Kiki Cuyler, Pit., 144.
**Hits:** Jim Bottomley, St.L., 227.
**TB:** Rogers Hornsby, St.L., 381.
**HR:** Rogers Hornsby, St.L., 39.
**RBI:** Rogers Hornsby, St.L., 143.
**SB:** Max Carey, Pit., 46.
**Wins:** Dazzy Vance, Brk., 22.
**ERA:** Dolf Luque, Cin., 2.63.
**CG:** Pete Donohue, Cin., 27.
**IP:** Pete Donohue, Cin., 301.
**SO:** Dazzy Vance, Brk., 221.

**A.L. 20-game winners**

Eddie Rommel, Phil., 21-10
Ted Lyons, Chi., 21-11
Stan Coveleski, Wash., 20-5
Walter Johnson, Wash., 20-7

**N.L. 20-game winners**

Dazzy Vance, Brk., 22-9
Eppa Rixey, Cin., 21-11
Pete Donohue, Cin., 21-14

**A.L. 100 RBIs**

Bob Meusel, N.Y., 138
Harry Heilmann, Det., 133
Al Simmons, Phil., 129
Goose Goslin, Wash., 113
Earl Sheely, Chi., 111
George Sisler, St.L., 105
Ken Williams, St.L., 105
Ty Cobb, Det., 102

**N.L. 100 RBIs**

Rogers Hornsby, St.L., 143
Jack Fournier, Brk., 130
Jim Bottomley, St.L., 128
Glenn Wright, Pit., 121
Clyde Barnhart, Pit., 114
Irish Meusel, N.Y., 111
Pie Traynor, Pit., 106
Zack Wheat, Brk., 103
Kiki Cuyler, Pit., 102

**League MVP**

A.L.: Roger Peckinpaugh, SS, Wash.
N.L.: Rogers Hornsby, 2B, St.L.

## WORLD SERIES

■ **Winner:** The Pirates became the first team to rally from a three-games-to-one Series deficit and ruined Washington's hopes for a repeat victory.

■ **Turning point:** A Game 6 home run by Eddie Moore that gave Pittsburgh a 3-2 victory and knotted the Series at three games apiece.

■ **Memorable moment:** Washington's 37-year-old Walter Johnson battling valiantly but coming up short in Pittsburgh's 9-7 Game 7 victory.

■ **Top guns:** Max Carey (.458), Pirates; Joe Harris (.440, 3 HR, 6 RBIs), Goose Goslin (3 HR, 6 RBIs), Senators.

### Linescores

**Game 1**—October 7, at Pittsburgh
Washington.... 0 1 0 0 2 0 0 0 1 — 4 8 1
Pittsburgh...... 0 0 0 0 1 0 0 0 0 — 1 5 0
Johnson; Meadows, Morrison (9). W—Johnson. L—Meadows. HR—J. Harris (Wash.); Traynor (Pit.).

**Game 2**—October 8, at Pittsburgh
Washington.... 0 1 0 0 0 0 0 0 1 — 2 8 2
Pittsburgh...... 0 0 0 1 0 0 0 2 x — 3 7 0
Coveleski; Aldridge. W—Aldridge. L—Coveleski.. HR—Judge (Wash.); Wright, Cuyler (Pit.).

**Game 3**—October 10, at Washington
Pittsburgh...... 0 1 0 1 0 1 0 0 0 — 3 8 3
Washington.... 0 0 1 0 0 1 2 0 x — 4 10 1
Kremer; Ferguson, Marberry (8). W—Ferguson. L—Kremer. HR—Goslin (Wash.).

**Game 4**—October 11, at Washington
Pittsburgh...... 0 0 0 0 0 0 0 0 0 — 0 6 1
Washington.... 0 0 4 0 0 0 0 0 x — 4 12 0
Yde, Morrison (3), C. Adams (8); Johnson. W—Johnson. L—Yde. HR—Goslin, J. Harris (Wash.).

**Game 5**—October 12, at Washington
Pittsburgh...... 0 0 2 0 0 0 2 1 1 — 6 13 0
Washington.... 1 0 0 1 0 0 1 0 0 — 3 8 1
Aldridge; Coveleski, Ballou (7), Zachary (8), Marberry (9). W—Aldridge. L—Coveleski. HR—J. Harris (Wash.).

**Game 6**——October 13, at Pittsburgh
Washington.... 1 1 0 0 0 0 0 0 0 — 2 6 2
Pittsburgh...... 0 0 2 0 1 0 0 0 x — 3 7 1
Ferguson, Ballou (8); Kremer. W—Kremer. L—Ferguson. HR—Goslin (Wash.); Moore (Pit.).

**Game 7**—October 15, at Pittsburgh
Washington.... 4 0 0 2 0 0 0 1 0 — 7 7 2
Pittsburgh...... 0 0 3 0 1 0 2 3 x — 9 15 2
Johnson; Aldridge, Morrison (1), Kremer (5), Oldham (9). W—Kremer. L—Johnson. HR—Peckinpaugh (Wash.).

# 1926

## FINAL STANDINGS

**American League**

| Team | W | L | Pct. | GB |
|---|---|---|---|---|
| New York | 91 | 63 | .591 | ... |
| Cleveland | 88 | 66 | .571 | 3 |
| Philadelphia | 83 | 67 | .553 | 6 |
| Washington | 81 | 69 | .540 | 8 |
| Chicago | 81 | 72 | .529 | 9.5 |
| Detroit | 79 | 75 | .513 | 12 |
| St. Louis | 62 | 92 | .403 | 29 |
| Boston | 46 | 107 | .301 | 44.5 |

**National League**

| Team | W | L | Pct. | GB |
|---|---|---|---|---|
| St. Louis | 89 | 65 | .578 | ... |
| Cincinnati | 87 | 67 | .565 | 2 |
| Pittsburgh | 84 | 69 | .549 | 4.5 |
| Chicago | 82 | 72 | .532 | 7 |
| New York | 74 | 77 | .490 | 13.5 |
| Brooklyn | 71 | 82 | .464 | 17.5 |
| Boston | 66 | 86 | .434 | 22 |
| Philadelphia | 58 | 93 | .384 | 29.5 |

## SIGNIFICANT EVENTS

■ **January 30:** The Major League rules committee granted pitchers permission to use a resin bag during the course of games.

■ **October 13:** Cleveland first baseman George Burns, who batted .358 with a record 64 doubles, captured A.L. MVP honors, even though the Yankees' Babe Ruth batted .372 with 47 homers and 146 RBIs.

■ **December 16:** Commissioner Kenesaw Mountain Landis was elected to a second seven-year term.

■ **December 20:** In a trade billed as the biggest in baseball history, Cardinals manager Rogers Hornsby was dealt to the Giants for second baseman Frank Frisch and pitcher Jimmy Ring.

■ **December 22:** Baseball greats Ty Cobb and Tris Speaker denied accusations by former Detroit pitcher Dutch Leonard that they had conspired to throw 1919 Tigers-Indians games and had bet on their outcome. The charges would be investigated by Commissioner Kenesaw Mountain Landis and later dismissed for lack of evidence.

## MEMORABLE MOMENTS

■ **May 12:** Washington fireballer Walter Johnson defeated St. Louis, 7-4, and became baseball's second 400-game winner.

■ **May 21:** Chicago's Earl Sheely belted a home run and three doubles in a game against Boston, giving him a record seven consecutive extra-base hits.

## LEADERS

**American League**

**BA:** Heinie Manush, Det., .378.
**Runs:** Babe Ruth, N.Y., 139.
**Hits:** George Burns, Cle.; Sam Rice, Wash., 216.
**TB:** Babe Ruth, N.Y., 365.
**HR:** Babe Ruth, N.Y., 47.
**RBI:** Babe Ruth, N.Y., 146.
**SB:** Johnny Mostil, Chi., 35.
**Wins:** George Uhle, Cle., 27.
**ERA:** Lefty Grove, Phil., 2.51.
**CG:** George Uhle, Cle., 32.
**IP:** George Uhle, Cle., 318.1.
**SO:** Lefty Grove, Phil., 194.

**National League**

**BA:** Bubbles Hargrave, Cin., .353.
**Runs:** Kiki Cuyler, Pit., 113.
**Hits:** Eddie Brown, Bos., 201.
**TB:** Jim Bottomley, St.L., 305.
**HR:** Hack Wilson, Chi., 21.
**RBI:** Jim Bottomley, St.L., 120.
**SB:** Kiki Cuyler, Pit., 35.
**Wins:** Pete Donohue, Cin.; Ray Kremer, Pit.; Lee Meadows, Pit.; Flint Rhem, St.L., 20.
**ERA:** Ray Kremer, Pit., 2.61.
**CG:** Carl Mays, Cin., 24.
**IP:** Pete Donohue, Cin., 285.2.
**SO:** Dazzy Vance, Brk., 140.

**A.L. 20-game winners**

George Uhle, Cle., 27-11
Herb Pennock, N.Y., 23-11

**N.L. 20-game winners**

Remy Kremer, Pit., 20-6
Flint Rhem, St.L., 20-7
Lee Meadows, Pit., 20-9
Pete Donohue, Cin., 20-14

**A.L. 100 RBIs**

Babe Ruth, N.Y., 146
George Burns, Cle., 114
Tony Lazzeri, N.Y., 114
Al Simmons, Phil., 109
Bibb Falk, Chi., 108
Goose Goslin, Wash., 108
Lou Gehrig, N.Y., 107
Harry Heilmann, Det., 103

**N.L. 100 RBIs**

Jim Bottomley, St.L., 120
Hack Wilson, Chi., 109
Les Bell, St.L., 100

**A.L. 40 homers**

Babe Ruth, N.Y., 47

**League MVP**

A.L.: George Burns, 1B, Cle.
N.L.: Bob O'Farrell, C, St.L.

## WORLD SERIES

■ **Winner:** The Cardinals, making their first Series appearance, outlasted the Yankees in a seven-game classic.

■ **Turning point:** A Series-squaring 10-2 Cardinals victory in Game 6. Lester Bell homered and drove in four runs.

■ **Memorable moment:** The aging Grover Cleveland Alexander striking out Yankee slugger Tony Lazzeri with the bases loaded in the seventh inning of Game 7, saving the Cardinals.

■ **Top guns:** Jesse Haines (2-0, 1.08 ERA), Alexander (2-0, 1.33), Tommy Thevenow (.417), Cardinals; Babe Ruth (4 HR), Yankees.

### Linescores

**Game 1**—October 2, at New York
St. Louis......... 1 0 0 0 0 0 0 0 0 — 1 3 1
New York........ 1 0 0 0 0 1 0 0 x — 2 6 0
Sherdel, Haines (8); Pennock. W—Pennock. L—Sherdel.

**Game 2**—October 3, at New York
St. Louis......... 0 0 2 0 0 0 3 0 1 — 6 12 1
New York........ 0 2 0 0 0 0 0 0 0 — 2 4 0
Alexander; Shocker, Shawkey (8), Jones (9). W—Alexander. L—Shawkey. HR—Southworth, Thevenow (St.L.).

**Game 3**—October 5, at St. Louis
New York........ 0 0 0 0 0 0 0 0 0 — 0 5 1
St. Louis......... 0 0 0 3 1 0 0 0 x — 4 8 0
Ruether, Shawkey (5), Thomas (8); Haines. W—Haines. L—Ruether. HR—Haines (St.L.).

**Game 4**—October 6, at St. Louis
New York........ 1 0 1 1 4 2 1 0 0 —10 14 1
St. Louis......... 1 0 0 3 0 0 0 0 1 — 5 14 0
Hoyt; Rhem, Reinhart (5), H. Bell (5), Hallahan (7), Keen (9). W—Hoyt. L—Reinhart. HR—Ruth 3 (N.Y.).

**Game 5**—October 7, at St. Louis
New York........ 0 0 0 0 0 10 0 1 1—3 9 1
St. Louis......... 0 0 0 1 0 01 0 0 0—2 7 1
Pennock; Sherdel. W—Pennock. L—Sherdel.

**Game 6**—October 9, at New York
St. Louis......... 3 0 0 0 1 0 5 0 1 —10 13 2
New York........ 0 0 0 1 0 0 1 0 0 — 2 8 1
Alexander; Shawkey, Shocker (7), Thomas (8). W—Alexander. L—Shawkey. HR—L. Bell (St.L.).

**Game 7**—October 10, at New York
St. Louis......... 0 0 0 3 0 0 0 0 0 — 3 8 0
New York........ 0 0 1 0 0 1 0 0 0 — 2 8 3
Haines, Alexander (7); Hoyt, Pennock (7). W—Haines. L—Hoyt. HR—Ruth (N.Y.).

# 1927

## FINAL STANDINGS

**American League**

| Team | W | L | Pct. | GB |
|---|---|---|---|---|
| New York | 110 | 44 | .714 | ... |
| Philadelphia | 91 | 63 | .591 | 19 |
| Washington | 85 | 69 | .552 | 25 |
| Detroit | 82 | 71 | .536 | 27.5 |
| Chicago | 70 | 83 | .458 | 39.5 |
| Cleveland | 66 | 87 | .431 | 43.5 |
| St. Louis | 59 | 94 | .386 | 50.5 |
| Boston | 51 | 103 | .331 | 59 |

**National League**

| Team | W | L | Pct. | GB |
|---|---|---|---|---|
| Pittsburgh | 94 | 60 | .610 | ... |
| St. Louis | 92 | 61 | .601 | 1.5 |
| New York | 92 | 62 | .597 | 2 |
| Chicago | 85 | 68 | .556 | 8.5 |
| Cincinnati | 75 | 78 | .490 | 18.5 |
| Brooklyn | 65 | 88 | .425 | 28.5 |
| Boston | 60 | 94 | .390 | 34 |
| Philadelphia | 51 | 103 | .331 | 43 |

## SIGNIFICANT EVENTS

■ **March 3:** The Yankees made slugger Babe Ruth the highest paid player in baseball history, signing him for three years at a reported $70,000 per season.
■ **October 17:** A.L. founder and 28-year president Ban Johnson retired, three days after 416-game winner Walter Johnson called it quits after 21 seasons with Washington.
■ **October 22:** Ross Youngs, a .322 hitter over 10 seasons with the Giants, died of Bright's disease at age 30.
■ **November 2:** E.S. Barnard was named new A.L. president, replacing Ban Johnson.

## MEMORABLE MOMENTS

■ **May 30-31:** Cubs shortstop Jimmy Cooney and Detroit first baseman Johnny Neun pulled off rare unassisted triple plays on consecutive days.
■ **July 18:** Philadelphia's Ty Cobb opened a new club when he doubled against his former Detroit teammates for hit No. 4,000.
■ **July 19:** The Cubs spoiled John McGraw Day at the Polo Grounds by beating the Giants. But fans enjoyed festivities honoring McGraw for his 25 years as New York manager.
■ **September 30:** Yankee slugger Babe Ruth broke his own one-season record when he blasted home run No. 60 off Washington lefty Tom Zachary.

## LEADERS

**American League**
**BA:** Harry Heilmann, Det., .398.
**Runs:** Babe Ruth, N.Y., 158.
**Hits:** Earle Combs, N.Y., 231.
**TB:** Lou Gehrig, N.Y., 447.
**HR:** Babe Ruth, N.Y., 60.
**RBI:** Lou Gehrig, N.Y., 175.
**SB:** George Sisler, St.L., 27.
**Wins:** Waite Hoyt, N.Y.; Ted Lyons, Chi., 22.
**ERA:** Wilcy Moore, N.Y., 2.28.
**CG:** Ted Lyons, Chi., 30.
**IP:** Ted Lyons, Chi.; Tommy Thomas, Chi., 307.2
**SO:** Lefty Grove, Phil., 174.

**National League**
**BA:** Paul Waner, Pit., .380.
**Runs:** Rogers Hornsby, N.Y.; Lloyd Waner, Pit., 133.
**Hits:** Paul Waner, Pit., 237.
**TB:** Paul Waner, Pit., 342.
**HR:** Cy Williams, Phil.; Hack Wilson, Chi., 30.
**RBI:** Paul Waner, Pit., 131.
**SB:** Frank Frisch, St.L., 48.
**Wins:** Charlie Root, Chi., 26.
**ERA:** Ray Kremer, Pit., 2.47.
**CG:** Jesse Haines, St.L.; Lee Meadows, Pit.; Dazzy Vance, Brk., 25.
**IP:** Charlie Root, Chi., 309.
**SO:** Dazzy Vance, Brk., 184.

**A.L. 20-game winners**
Waite Hoyt, N.Y., 22-7
Ted Lyons, Chi., 22-14
Lefty Grove, Phil., 20-13

**N.L. 20-game winners**
Charlie Root, Chi., 26-15
Jesse Haines, St.L., 24-10
Carmen Hill, Pit., 22-11
Grover Alexander, St.L., 21-10

**A.L. 100 RBIs**
Lou Gehrig, N.Y., 175
Babe Ruth, N.Y., 164
Goose Goslin, Wash., 120
Harry Heilmann, Det., 120
Bob Fothergill, Det., 114
Al Simmons, Phil., 108
Bob Meusel, N.Y., 103
Tony Lazzeri, N.Y., 102

**N.L. 100 RBIs**
Paul Waner, Pit., 131
Hack Wilson, Chi., 129
Rogers Hornsby, N.Y., 125
Jim Bottomley, St.L., 124
Bill Terry, N.Y., 121
Pie Traynor, Pit., 106
Glenn Wright, Pit., 105

**A.L. 40 homers**
Babe Ruth, N.Y., 60
Lou Gehrig, N.Y., 47

**League MVP**
A.L.: Lou Gehrig, 1B, N.Y.
N.L.: Paul Waner, OF, Pit.

## WORLD SERIES

■ **Winner:** The powerful Yankees made short work of the overmatched Pirates.
■ **Turning point:** When the Pirates watched the Yankees take batting practice before Game 1.
■ **Memorable moment:** Yankee Earle Combs dancing across the plate with the Series-ending run after a John Miljus wild pitch.
■ **Top guns:** Wilcy Moore (1-0, 0.84 ERA), Herb Pennock (1-0, 1.00), Mark Koenig (.500), Babe Ruth (.400, 2 HR, 7 RBIs), Yankees; Lloyd Waner (.400), Pirates.

**Linescores**

**Game 1**—October 5, at Pittsburgh
New York........ 1 0 3 0 1 0 0 0 0 — 5 6 1
Pittsburgh...... 1 0 1 0 1 0 0 1 0 — 4 9 2
Hoyt, Moore (8); Kremer, Miljus (6). W—Hoyt. L—Kremer.

**Game 2**—October 6, at Pittsburgh
New York........ 0 0 3 0 0 0 0 3 0 — 6 11 0
Pittsburgh...... 1 0 0 0 0 0 0 1 0 — 2 7 2
Pipgras; Aldridge, Cvengros (8), Dawson (9). W—Pipgras. L—Aldridge.

**Game 3**—October 7, at New York
Pittsburgh...... 0 0 0 0 0 0 0 1 0 — 1 3 1
New York........ 2 0 0 0 0 0 6 0 x — 8 9 0
Meadows, Cvengros (7); Pennock. W—Pennock. L—Meadows. HR—Ruth (N.Y.).

**Game 4**—October 8, at New York
Pittsburgh...... 1 0 0 0 0 0 2 0 0 — 3 10 1
New York........ 1 0 0 0 2 0 0 0 1 — 4 12 2
Hill, Miljus (7); Moore. W—Moore. L—Miljus. HR—Ruth (N.Y.).

# 1928

## FINAL STANDINGS

**American League**

| Team | W | L | Pct. | GB |
|---|---|---|---|---|
| New York | 101 | 53 | .656 | ... |
| Philadelphia | 98 | 55 | .641 | 2.5 |
| St. Louis | 82 | 72 | .532 | 19 |
| Washington | 75 | 79 | .487 | 26 |
| Chicago | 72 | 82 | .468 | 29 |
| Detroit | 68 | 86 | .442 | 33 |
| Cleveland | 62 | 92 | .403 | 39 |
| Boston | 57 | 96 | .373 | 43.5 |

**National League**

| Team | W | L | Pct. | GB |
|---|---|---|---|---|
| St. Louis | 95 | 59 | .617 | ... |
| New York | 93 | 61 | .604 | 2 |
| Chicago | 91 | 63 | .591 | 4 |
| Pittsburgh | 85 | 67 | .559 | 9 |
| Cincinnati | 78 | 74 | .513 | 16 |
| Brooklyn | 77 | 76 | .503 | 17.5 |
| Boston | 50 | 103 | .327 | 44.5 |
| Philadelphia | 43 | 109 | .283 | 51 |

## SIGNIFICANT EVENTS

■ **May 14:** Giants manager John McGraw was hit by a car while crossing a street outside Chicago's Wrigley Field, an injury that would sideline him for six weeks.
■ **September 9:** Urban Shocker, a 187-game winner for the Yankees and Browns, died of pneumonia at age 38.
■ **November 7:** Massachusetts voters cleared the way for Sunday baseball in Boston, leaving Pennsylvania as the only state still enforcing the blue law.
■ **December 13:** National League President John Heydler, contending fans were tired of watching weak-hitting pitchers try to bat, proposed a designated hitter rule that was voted down at the annual winter meetings.

## MEMORABLE MOMENTS

■ **July 21:** Philadelphia's Jimmie Foxx became the first player to hit a ball over the double-decked left-field stands of Shibe Park during a game against St. Louis.
■ **September 3:** Athletics pinch-hitter Ty Cobb stroked his 724th career double and final career hit—No. 4,191—in a game against Washington.
■ **September 28-29:** The New York Yankees clinched the A.L. pennant with a victory over the Tigers and the Cardinals closed out a tight N.L. race with a next-day win over the Braves.

## LEADERS

**American League**
**BA:** Goose Goslin, Wash., .379.
**Runs:** Babe Ruth, N.Y., 163.
**Hits:** Heinie Manush, St.L., 241.
**TB:** Babe Ruth, N.Y., 380.
**HR:** Babe Ruth, N.Y., 54.
**RBI:** Lou Gehrig, N.Y.; Babe Ruth, N.Y., 142.
**SB:** Buddy Myer, Bos., 30.
**Wins:** Lefty Grove, Phil.; George Pipgras, N.Y., 24.
**ERA:** Garland Braxton, Wash., 2.51.
**CG:** Red Ruffing, Bos., 25.
**IP:** George Pipgras, N.Y., 300.2.
**SO:** Lefty Grove, Phil., 183.

**National League**
**BA:** Rogers Hornsby, Bos., .387.
**Runs:** Paul Waner, Pit., 142.
**Hits:** Fred Lindstrom, N.Y., 231.
**TB:** Jim Bottomley, St.L., 362.
**HR:** Jim Bottomley, St.L.; Hack Wilson, Chi., 31.
**RBI:** Jim Bottomley, St.L., 136.
**SB:** Kiki Cuyler, Chi., 37.
**Wins:** Larry Benton, N.Y.; Burleigh Grimes, Pit., 25.
**ERA:** Dazzy Vance, Brk., 2.09.
**CG:** Larry Benton, N.Y.; Burleigh Grimes, Pit., 28.
**IP:** Burleigh Grimes, Pit., 330.2.
**SO:** Dazzy Vance, Brk., 200.

**A.L. 20-game winners**
Lefty Grove, Phil., 24-8
George Pipgras, N.Y., 24-13
Waite Hoyt, N.Y., 23-7
General Crowder, St.L., 21-5
Sam Gray, St.L., 20-12

**N.L. 20-game winners**
Larry Benton, N.Y., 25-9
Burleigh Grimes, Pit., 25-14
Dazzy Vance, Brk., 22-10
Bill Sherdel, St.L., 21-10
Jesse Haines, St.L., 20-8
Fred Fitzsimmons, N.Y., 20-9

**A.L. 100 RBIs**
Lou Gehrig, N.Y., 142
Babe Ruth, N.Y., 142
Bob Meusel, N.Y., 113
Heinie Manush, St.L., 108
Harry Heilmann, Det., 107
Al Simmons, Phil., 107
Goose Goslin, Wash., 102

**N.L. 100 RBIs**
Jim Bottomley, St.L., 136
Pie Traynor, Pit., 124
Hack Wilson, Chi., 120
Chick Hafey, St.L., 111
Fred Lindstrom, N.Y., 107
Del Bissonette, Brk., 106
Pinky Whitney, Phil., 103
Bill Terry, N.Y., 101

**A.L. 40 homers**
Babe Ruth, N.Y., 54

**League MVP**
A.L.: Mickey Cochrane, C, Phil.
N.L.: Jim Bottomley, 1B, St.L.

## WORLD SERIES

■ **Winner:** The muscular Yankees swept aside St. Louis for their third Series victory of the decade.
■ **Turning point:** A 9-3 second-game romp that made it clear the Cardinals were overmatched.
■ **Memorable moment:** Babe Ruth's show-stealing three-home run performance in Game 4 at St. Louis' Sportsman's Park.
■ **Top guns:** Waite Hoyt (2-0, 1.50 ERA), Ruth (.625, 3 HR), Lou Gehrig, (.545, 4 HR, 9 RBIs).

**Linescores**

**Game 1**—October 4, at New York
St. Louis......... 0 0 0 0 0 0 1 0 0 — 1 3 1
New York........ 1 0 0 2 0 0 0 1 x — 4 7 0
Sherdel, Johnson (8); Hoyt. W—Hoyt. L—Sherdel. HR—Meusel (N.Y.); Bottomley (St.L.).

**Game 2**—October 5, at New York
St. Louis......... 0 3 0 0 0 0 0 0 0 — 3 4 1
New York........ 3 1 4 0 0 0 1 0 x — 9 8 2
Alexander, Mitchell (3); Pipgras. W—Pipgras. L—Alexander. HR—Gehrig (N.Y.).

**Game 3**—October 7, at St. Louis
New York........ 0 1 0 2 0 3 1 0 0 — 7 7 2
St. Louis......... 2 0 0 0 1 0 0 0 0 — 3 9 3
Zachary; Haines, Johnson (7), Rhem (8). W—Zachary. L—Haines. HR—Gehrig 2 (N.Y.).

**Game 4**—October 9, at St. Louis
New York........ 0 0 0 1 0 0 4 2 0 — 7 15 2
St. Louis......... 0 0 1 1 0 0 0 0 1 — 3 11 0
Hoyt; Sherdel, Alexander (7). W—Hoyt. L—Sherdel. HR—Ruth 3, Durst, Gehrig (N.Y.).

# 1929

## FINAL STANDINGS

**American League**

| Team | W | L | Pct. | GB |
|---|---|---|---|---|
| Philadelphia | 104 | 46 | .693 | ... |
| New York | 88 | 66 | .571 | 18 |
| Cleveland | 81 | 71 | .533 | 24 |
| St. Louis | 79 | 73 | .520 | 26 |
| Washington | 71 | 81 | .467 | 34 |
| Detroit | 70 | 84 | .455 | 36 |
| Chicago | 59 | 93 | .388 | 46 |
| Boston | 58 | 96 | .377 | 48 |

**National League**

| Team | W | L | Pct. | GB |
|---|---|---|---|---|
| Chicago | 98 | 54 | .645 | ... |
| Pittsburgh | 88 | 65 | .575 | 10.5 |
| New York | 84 | 67 | .556 | 13.5 |
| St. Louis | 78 | 74 | .513 | 20 |
| Philadelphia | 71 | 82 | .464 | 27.5 |
| Brooklyn | 70 | 83 | .458 | 28.5 |
| Cincinnati | 66 | 88 | .429 | 33 |
| Boston | 56 | 98 | .364 | 43 |

## SIGNIFICANT EVENTS

■ **January 22:** The Yankees announced an innovation: permanent numbers on the backs of uniforms corresponding to players' positions in the batting order.

■ **September 25:** New York manager Miller Huggins, who led the Yankees to six pennants and three World Series championships in 12 seasons, died suddenly of blood poisoning at age 49.

## MEMORABLE MOMENTS

■ **July 6:** The Cardinals set a modern Major League record for runs and an N.L. record for hits (28) when they pounded the Phillies, 28-6.

■ **August 10:** Cardinals great Grover Cleveland Alexander shut out Philadelphia in four innings of relief and was credited with an 11-9 victory—the 373rd and last of his career.

■ **August 11:** Yankee Babe Ruth drove a Willis Hudlin pitch out of Cleveland's League Park for career homer No. 500.

■ **October 5:** Philadelphia slugger Chuck Klein hit home run No. 43 in a final-day doubleheader against New York, setting a one-season N.L. record and edging Giants outfielder Mel Ott by one.

■ **October 6:** Cleveland third baseman Joe Sewell finished the season with an amazing four strikeouts in 578 official at-bats.

## LEADERS

**American League**

**BA:** Lew Fonseca, Cle., .369.
**Runs:** Charley Gehringer, Det., 131.
**Hits:** Dale Alexander, Det.; Charley Gehringer, Det., 215.
**TB:** Al Simmons, Phil., 373.
**HR:** Babe Ruth, N.Y., 46.
**RBI:** Al Simmons, Phil., 157.
**SB:** Charley Gehringer, Det., 27.
**Wins:** George Earnshaw, Phil., 24.
**ERA:** Lefty Grove, Phil., 2.81.
**CG:** Tommy Thomas, Chi., 24.
**IP:** Sam Gray, St.L., 305.
**SO:** Lefty Grove, Phil., 170.

**National League**

**BA:** Lefty O'Doul, Phil., .398.
**Runs:** Rogers Hornsby, Chi., 156.
**Hits:** Lefty O'Doul, Phil., 254.
**TB:** Rogers Hornsby, Chi., 409.
**HR:** Chuck Klein, Phil., 43.
**RBI:** Hack Wilson, Chi., 159.
**SB:** Kiki Cuyler, Chi., 43.
**Wins:** Pat Malone, Chi., 22.
**ERA:** Bill Walker, N.Y., 3.09.
**CG:** Red Lucas, Cin., 28.
**IP:** Watty Clark, Brk., 279.
**SO:** Pat Malone, Chi., 166.

**A.L. 20-game winners**
George Earnshaw, Phil., 24-8
Wes Ferrell, Cle., 21-10
Lefty Grove, Phil., 20-6

**N.L. 20-game winners**
Pat Malone, Chi., 22-10

**A.L. 100 RBIs**
Al Simmons, Phil., 157
Babe Ruth, N.Y., 154
Dale Alexander, Det., 137
Lou Gehrig, N.Y., 126
Harry Heilmann, Det., 120
Jimmie Foxx, Phil., 117
Red Kress, St.L., 107
Charlie Gehringer, Det., 106
Tony Lazzeri, N.Y., 106
Lew Fonseca, Cle., 103

**N.L. 100 RBIs**
Hack Wilson, Chi., 159
Mel Ott, N.Y., 151
Rogers Hornsby, Chi., 149
Chuck Klein, Phil., 145
Jim Bottomley, St.L., 137
Chick Hafey, St.L., 125
Don Hurst, Phil., 125
Lefty O'Doul, Phil., 122
Bill Terry, N.Y., 117
Pinky Whitney, Phil., 115
Babe Herman, Brk., 113
Riggs Stephenson, Chi., 110
Pie Traynor, Pit., 108
George Kelly, Cin., 103
Kiki Cuyler, Chi., 102
Paul Waner, Pit., 100

**A.L. 40 homers**
Babe Ruth, N.Y., 46

**N.L. 40 homers**
Chuck Klein, Phil., 43
Mel Ott, N.Y., 42

**League MVP**
A.L.: No selection.
N.L.: Rogers Hornsby, 2B, Chi.

## WORLD SERIES

■ **Winner:** The Athletics, an A.L. doormat since their last Series appearance in 1914, re-emerged as baseball's dominant team.

■ **Turning point:** The seventh inning of Game 4. Leading the Series two games to one but trailing the Cubs 8-0, the A's exploded for an incredible 10 runs.

■ **Memorable moments:** Mule Haas' three-run inside-the-park home run in the 10-run seventh inning and his ninth-inning game-tying homer in the Series-ending fifth game; surprise starter Howard Ehmke's record 13 strikeouts in Game 1.

■ **Top guns:** Jimmie Dykes (.421), Jimmie Foxx (.350, 2 HR, 5 RBIs), Haas (2 HR, 6 RBIs), Athletics; Hack Wilson (.471), Cubs.

**Linescores**

**Game 1**—October 8, at Chicago
Philadelphia.... 0 0 0 0 0 0 1 0 2 — 3 6 1
Chicago.......... 0 0 0 0 0 0 0 0 1 — 1 8 2
Ehmke; Root, Bush (8). W—Ehmke. L—Root. HR—Foxx (Phil.).

**Game 2**—October 9, at Chicago
Philadelphia.... 0 0 3 3 0 0 1 2 0 — 9 12 0
Chicago.......... 0 0 0 0 3 0 0 0 0 — 3 11 1
Earnshaw, Grove (5); Malone, Blake (4), Carlson (6), Nehf (9). W—Earnshaw. L—Malone. HR—Simmons, Foxx (Phil.).

**Game 3**—October 11, at Philadelphia
Chicago.......... 0 0 0 0 0 3 0 0 0 — 3 6 1
Philadelphia..... 0 0 0 0 1 0 0 0 0 — 1 9 1
Bush; Earnshaw. W—Bush. L—Earnshaw.

**Game 4**—October 12, at Philadelphia
Chicago.......... 0 0 0 2 0 5 1 0 0 — 8 10 2
Philadelphia..... 0 0 0 0 0 0 10 0 x — 10 15 2
Root, Nehf (7), Blake (7), Malone (7), Carlson (8); Quinn, Walberg (6), Rommel (7), Grove (8). W—Rommel. L—Blake. HR—Grimm (Chi.); Haas, Simmons (Phil.).

**Game 5**—October 14, at Philadelphia
Chicago.......... 0 0 0 2 0 0 0 0 0 — 2 8 1
Philadelphia..... 0 0 0 0 0 0 0 0 3 — 3 6 0
Malone; Ehmke, Walberg (4). W—Walberg. L—Malone. HR—Haas (Phil.).

# 1930

## FINAL STANDINGS

**American League**

| Team | W | L | Pct. | GB |
|---|---|---|---|---|
| Philadelphia | 102 | 52 | .662 | ... |
| Washington | 94 | 60 | .610 | 8 |
| New York | 86 | 68 | .558 | 16 |
| Cleveland | 81 | 73 | .526 | 21 |
| Detroit | 75 | 79 | .487 | 27 |
| St. Louis | 64 | 90 | .416 | 38 |
| Chicago | 62 | 92 | .403 | 40 |
| Boston | 52 | 102 | .338 | 50 |

**National League**

| Team | W | L | Pct. | GB |
|---|---|---|---|---|
| St. Louis | 92 | 62 | .597 | ... |
| Chicago | 90 | 64 | .584 | 2 |
| New York | 87 | 67 | .565 | 5 |
| Brooklyn | 86 | 68 | .558 | 6 |
| Pittsburgh | 80 | 74 | .519 | 12 |
| Boston | 70 | 84 | .455 | 22 |
| Cincinnati | 59 | 95 | .383 | 33 |
| Philadelphia | 52 | 102 | .338 | 40 |

## SIGNIFICANT EVENTS

■ **March 8:** Yankee slugger Babe Ruth signed a record two-year contract at $80,000 per season.

■ **December 11:** Major League officials granted the Baseball Writers Association of America permission to conduct future MVP balloting—a practice that would continue without interruption.

■ **December 12:** Rules changes: The sacrifice fly was eliminated and balls bouncing into the stands were classified as ground-rule doubles instead of home runs.

## MEMORABLE MOMENTS

■ **May 2:** Commissioner Kenesaw Mountain Landis attended Organized Baseball's first game under permanently installed lights at Des Moines (Iowa) of the Western League.

■ **September 27:** Chicago's Hack Wilson hit home runs 55 and 56—an N.L. record—in a game against the Reds.

■ **September 28:** Wilson drove in his Major League-record 190th and 191st runs in Chicago's season-finale victory over the Reds.

■ **September 28:** New York's Bill Terry finished with a .401 average and N.L. hitters closed with a composite .303 mark.

## LEADERS

**American League**

**BA:** Al Simmons, Phil., .381.
**Runs:** Al Simmons, Phil., 152.
**Hits:** Johnny Hodapp, Cle., 225.
**TB:** Lou Gehrig, N.Y., 419.
**HR:** Babe Ruth, N.Y., 49.
**RBI:** Lou Gehrig, N.Y., 174.
**SB:** Marty McManus, Det., 23.
**Wins:** Lefty Grove, Phil., 28.
**ERA:** Lefty Grove, Phil., 2.54.
**CG:** Ted Lyons, Chi., 29.
**IP:** Lyons, Chi., 297.2.
**SO:** Lefty Grove, Phil., 209.

**National League**

**BA:** Bill Terry, N.Y., .401.
**Runs:** Chuck Klein, Phil., 158.
**Hits:** Bill Terry, N.Y., 254.
**TB:** Chuck Klein, Phil., 445.
**HR:** Hack Wilson, Chi., 56.
**RBI:** Hack Wilson, Chi., 191.
**SB:** Kiki Cuyler, Chi., 37.
**Wins:** Ray Kremer, Pit.; Pat Malone, Chi., 20.
**ERA:** Dazzy Vance, Brk., 2.61.
**CG:** Erv Brame, Pit.; Pat Malone, Chi., 22.
**IP:** Ray Kremer, Pit., 276.
**SO:** Bill Hallahan, St.L., 177.

**A.L. 20-game winners**
Lefty Grove, Phil., 28-5
Wes Ferrell, Cle., 25-13
George Earnshaw, Phil., 22-13
Ted Lyons, Chi., 22-15
Lefty Stewart, St.L., 20-12

**N.L. 20-game winners**
Pat Malone, Chi., 20-9
Remy Kremer, Pit., 20-12

**A.L. 100 RBIs**
Lou Gehrig, N.Y., 174
Al Simmons, Phil., 165
Jimmie Foxx, Phil., 156
Babe Ruth, N.Y., 153
Goose Goslin, Wash.-St.L., 138
Ed Morgan, Cle., 136
Dale Alexander, Det., 135
Joe Cronin, Wash., 126
Johnny Hodapp, Cle., 121
Tony Lazzeri, N.Y., 121
Earl Averill, Cle., 119
Smead Jolley, Chi., 114
Red Kress, St.L., 112
Carl Reynolds, Chi., 104
Bing Miller, Phil., 100

**N.L. 100 RBIs**
Hack Wilson, Chi., 190
Chuck Klein, Phil., 170
Kiki Cuyler, Chi., 134
Babe Herman, Brk., 130
Bill Terry, N.Y., 129
Glenn Wright, Brk., 126
Gabby Hartnett, Chi., 122
Wally Berger, Bos., 119
Adam Comorosky, Pit., 119
Mel Ott, N.Y., 119
Pie Traynor, Pit., 119
Pinky Whitney, Pit., 117
Frank Frisch, St.L., 114
Del Bissonette, Brk., 113
Chick Hafey, St.L., 107
Gus Suhr, Pit., 107
Fred Lindstrom, N.Y., 106

**A.L. 40 homers**
Babe Ruth, N.Y., 49
Lou Gehrig, N.Y., 41

**N.L. 40 homers**
Hack Wilson, Chi., 56
Chuck Klein, Phil., 40

## WORLD SERIES

■ **Winner:** The Athletics became the first team to win back-to-back Series twice.

■ **Turning point:** Jimmie Foxx's two-run ninth-inning home run off Burleigh Grimes, which broke open a scoreless Game 5 and put Philadelphia in the driver's seat.

■ **Memorable moment:** Foxx's Game 5-winning home run.

■ **Top guns:** George Earnshaw (2-0, 0.72 ERA), Al Simmons (.364, 2 HR, 4 RBIs), Athletics; Jesse Haines (1-0, 1.00), Cardinals.

**Linescores**

**Game 1**—October 1, at Philadelphia
St. Louis ..........0 0 2 0 0 0 0 0 0—2 9 0
Philadelphia........0 1 0 1 0 1 1 1 x—5 5 0
Grimes; Grove. W—Grove. L—Grimes. HR—Cochrane, Simmons (Phil.).

**Game 2**—October 2, at Philadelphia
St. Louis ............0 1 0 0 0 0 0 0 0—1 6 2
Philadelphia........2 0 2 2 0 0 0 0 x—6 7 2
Rhem, Lindsey (4), Johnson (7); Earnshaw. W—Earnshaw. L—Rhem. HR—Cochrane (Phil.); Watkins (St.L.).

**Game 3**—October 4, at St. Louis
Philadelphia......0 0 0 0 0 0 0 0 0—0 7 0
St. Louis ..........0 0 0 1 1 0 2 1 x—5 10 0
Walberg, Shores (5), Quinn (7); Hallahan. W—Hallahan. L—Walberg. HR—Douthit (St.L.).

**Game 4**—October 5, at St. Louis
Philadelphia........1 0 0 0 0 0 0 0 0—1 4 1
St. Louis ............0 0 1 2 0 0 0 0 x—3 5 1
Grove; Haines. W—Haines. L—Grove.

**Game 5**—October 6, at St. Louis
Philadelphia........0 0 0 0 0 0 0 0 2—2 5 0
St. Louis ............0 0 0 0 0 0 0 0 0—0 3 1
Earnshaw, Grove (8); Grimes. W—Grove. L—Grimes. HR—Foxx (Phil.).

**Game 6**—October 8, at Philadelphia
St. Louis ............0 0 0 0 0 0 0 0 1—1 5 1
Philadelphia........2 0 1 2 1 1 0 0 x—7 7 0
Hallahan, Johnson (3), Lindsey (6), Bell (8); Earnshaw. W—Earnshaw. L—Hallahan. HR—Dykes, Simmons (Phil.).

## 1931

### FINAL STANDINGS

**American League**

| Team | W | L | Pct. | GB |
|---|---|---|---|---|
| Philadelphia | 107 | 45 | .704 | ... |
| New York | 94 | 59 | .614 | 13.5 |
| Washington | 92 | 62 | .597 | 16 |
| Cleveland | 78 | 76 | .506 | 30 |
| St. Louis | 63 | 91 | .409 | 45 |
| Boston | 62 | 90 | .408 | 45 |
| Detroit | 61 | 93 | .396 | 47 |
| Chicago | 56 | 97 | .366 | 51.5 |

**National League**

| Team | W | L | Pct. | GB |
|---|---|---|---|---|
| St. Louis | 101 | 53 | .656 | ... |
| New York | 87 | 65 | .572 | 13 |
| Chicago | 84 | 70 | .545 | 17 |
| Brooklyn | 79 | 73 | .520 | 21 |
| Pittsburgh | 75 | 79 | .487 | 26 |
| Philadelphia | 66 | 88 | .429 | 35 |
| Boston | 64 | 90 | .416 | 37 |
| Cincinnati | 58 | 96 | .377 | 43 |

### SIGNIFICANT EVENTS

■ **March 27-28:** Former A.L. president and founder Ban Johnson died at age 67, 16 hours after E.S. Barnard, the man who succeeded him, died of a heart attack at age 56.

■ **October 20, 28:** The Baseball Writers Association of America named its first MVPs: Cardinals infielder Frank Frisch and Athletics 31-game winner Lefty Grove.

■ **October 26:** Charles Comiskey, one of the A.L.'s founding fathers and longtime owner of the White Sox, died at age 72.

### MEMORABLE MOMENTS

■ **May 26:** The Yankees ended Philadelphia's winning streak at 17 games with a 6-2 victory.

■ **August 21:** Yankee Babe Ruth belted his historic 600th career home run off Browns righthander George Blaeholder.

■ **August 23:** Philadelphia's Lefty Grove, bidding to break the A.L. record of 16 straight victories, dropped a 1-0 decision to the Browns.

■ **September 1:** Yankee Lou Gehrig, en route to an A.L.-record 184 RBIs, became the third player to hit home runs in six straight games —a streak that included three grand slams in five days.

### LEADERS

**American League**

**BA:** Al Simmons, Phil., .390.
**Runs:** Lou Gehrig, N.Y., 163.
**Hits:** Lou Gehrig, N.Y., 211.
**TB:** Lou Gehrig, N.Y., 410.
**HR:** Lou Gehrig, N.Y.; Babe Ruth, N.Y., 46.
**RBI:** Lou Gehrig, N.Y., 184.
**SB:** Ben Chapman, N.Y., 61.
**Wins:** Lefty Grove, Phil., 31.
**ERA:** Lefty Grove, Phil., 2.06.
**CG:** Wes Ferrell, Cle.; Lefty Grove, Phil., 27.
**IP:** Rube Walberg, Phil., 291.
**SO:** Lefty Grove, Phil., 175.

**National League**

**BA:** Chick Hafey, St.L., .349.
**Runs:** Chuck Klein, Phil.; Bill Terry, N.Y., 121.
**Hits:** Lloyd Waner, Pit., 214.
**TB:** Chuck Klein, Phil., 347.
**HR:** Chuck Klein, Phil., 31.
**RBI:** Chuck Klein, Phil., 121.
**SB:** Frank Frisch, St.L., 28.
**Wins:** Jumbo Elliott, Phil.; Bill Hallahan, St.L.; Heinie Meine, Pit., 19.
**ERA:** Bill Walker, N.Y., 2.26.
**CG:** Red Lucas, Cin., 24.
**IP:** Heinie Meine, Pit., 284.
**SO:** Bill Hallahan, St.L., 159.

**A.L. 20-game winners**
Lefty Grove, Phil., 31-4
Wes Ferrell, Cle., 22-12
George Earnshaw, Phil., 21-7
Lefty Gomez, N.Y., 21-9
Rube Walberg, Phil., 20-12

**A.L. 100 RBIs**
Lou Gehrig, N.Y., 184
Babe Ruth, N.Y., 163
Earl Averill, Cle., 143
Al Simmons, Phil., 128
Joe Cronin, Wash., 126
Ben Chapman, N.Y., 122
Jimmie Foxx, Phil., 120
Joe Vosmik, Cle., 117
Red Kress, St.L., 114
Lyn Lary, N.Y., 107
Goose Goslin, St.L., 105
Earl Webb, Bos., 103

**N.L. 100 RBIs**
Chuck Klein, Phil., 121
Mel Ott, N.Y., 115
Bill Terry, N.Y., 112
Pie Traynor, Pit., 103

**A.L. 40 homers**
Lou Gehrig, N.Y., 46
Babe Ruth, N.Y., 46

**Most Valuable Player**
A.L.: Lefty Grove, P, Phil.
N.L.: Frank Frisch, 2B, St.L.

### WORLD SERIES

■ **Winner:** The Cardinals spoiled Philadelphia's bid to win a record third consecutive Series.

■ **Turning point:** A pair of two-run innings that staked Cardinals spitballer Burleigh Grimes to a 4-0 lead in Game 7.

■ **Memorable moment:** The Series-long do-everything performance of exciting Cardinals center fielder Pepper Martin.

■ **Top guns:** Grimes (2-0, 2.04 ERA), Bill Hallahan (2-0, 0.49), Martin (.500, 12 hits, 5 RBIs, 5 SB), Cardinals; Al Simmons (.333, 2 HR, 8 RBIs), Athletics.

**Linescores**

**Game 1**—October 1, at St. Louis
Philadelphia......0 0 4 0 0 0 2 0 0—6 11 0
St. Louis ..........2 0 0 0 0 0 0 0 0—2 12 0
Grove; Derringer, Johnson (8). W—Grove. L—Derringer. HR—Simmons (Phil.).

**Game 2**—October 2, at St. Louis
Philadelphia........0 0 0 0 0 0 0 0 0—0 3 0
St. Louis ............0 1 0 0 0 0 1 0 x—2 6 1
Earnshaw; Hallahan. W—Hallahan. L—Earnshaw.

**Game 3**—October 5, at Philadelphia
St. Louis ..........0 2 0 2 0 0 0 0 1—5 12 0
Philadelphia......0 0 0 0 0 0 0 0 2—2 2 0
Grimes; Grove, Mahaffey (9). W—Grimes. L—Grove. HR—Simmons (Phil).

**Game 4**—October 6, at Philadelphia
St. Louis ..........0 0 0 0 0 0 0 0 0—0 2 1
Philadelphia......1 0 0 0 0 2 0 0 x—3 10 0
Johnson, Lindsey (6), Derringer (8); Earnshaw. W—Earnshaw. L—Johnson. HR—Foxx (Phil.).

**Game 5**—October 7, at Philadelphia
St. Louis ..........1 0 0 0 0 2 0 1 1—5 12 0
Philadelphia......0 0 0 0 0 0 1 0 0—1 9 0
Hallahan; Hoyt, Walberg (7), Rommel (9). W—Hallahan. L—Hoyt. HR—Martin (St.L.).

**Game 6**—October 9, at St. Louis
Philadelphia........0 0 0 0 4 0 4 0 0—8 8 1
St. Louis ...........0 0 0 0 0 1 0 0 0—1 5 2
Grove; Derringer, Johnson (5), Lindsey (7), Rhem (9). W—Grove. L—Derringer.

**Game 7**—October 10, at St. Louis
Philadelphia........0 0 0 0 0 0 0 0 2—2 7 1
St. Louis ...........2 0 2 0 0 0 0 0 x—4 5 0
Earnshaw, Walberg (8); Grimes, Hallahan (9). W—Grimes. L—Earnshaw. HR—Watkins (St.L.).

## 1932

### FINAL STANDINGS

**American League**

| Team | W | L | Pct. | GB |
|---|---|---|---|---|
| New York | 107 | 47 | .695 | ... |
| Philadelphia | 94 | 60 | .610 | 13 |
| Washington | 93 | 61 | .604 | 14 |
| Cleveland | 87 | 65 | .572 | 19 |
| Detroit | 76 | 75 | .503 | 29.5 |
| St. Louis | 63 | 91 | .409 | 44 |
| Chicago | 49 | 102 | .325 | 56.5 |
| Boston | 43 | 111 | .279 | 64 |

**National League**

| Team | W | L | Pct. | GB |
|---|---|---|---|---|
| Chicago | 90 | 64 | .584 | ... |
| Pittsburgh | 86 | 68 | .558 | 4 |
| Brooklyn | 81 | 73 | .526 | 9 |
| Philadelphia | 78 | 76 | .506 | 12 |
| Boston | 77 | 77 | .500 | 13 |
| New York | 72 | 82 | .468 | 18 |
| St. Louis | 72 | 82 | .468 | 18 |
| Cincinnati | 60 | 94 | .390 | 30 |

### SIGNIFICANT EVENTS

■ **June 22:** N.L. officials, after a long holdout, approved the use of numbers to identify their players.

■ **July 31:** The 76,979 fans who turned out for Cleveland's unveiling of Municipal Stadium watched the Indians lose a 1-0 decision to the Athletics and Lefty Grove.

■ **September 28:** Connie Mack began dismantling his powerful Athletics with the sale of Al Simmons, Jimmie Dykes and Mule Haas to the White Sox for $150,000.

■ **October 19:** A Philadelphia double: Athletics slugger Jimmie Foxx earned A.L. MVP honors and Phillies slugger Chuck Klein captured the N.L. award.

### MEMORABLE MOMENTS

■ **June 3:** An historic day: Yankee Lou Gehrig belted four home runs in a game at Philadelphia and John McGraw retired after 31 seasons as manager of the Giants.

■ **July 4:** In a Fourth of July battle between the Yankees and Senators, New York catcher Bill Dickey punched Washington outfielder Carl Reynolds and broke his jaw, a tantrum that would cost him a 30-day suspension and $1,000.

■ **September 25:** Athletics slugger Jimmie Foxx hit home run No. 58 in the season finale against Washington, falling two short of Babe Ruth's single-season record.

### LEADERS

**American League**

**BA:** Dale Alexander, Det.-Bos., .367.
**Runs:** Jimmie Foxx, Phil., 151.
**Hits:** Al Simmons, Phil., 216.
**TB:** Jimmie Foxx, Phil., 438.
**HR:** Jimmie Foxx, Phil., 58.
**RBI:** Jimmie Foxx, Phil., 169.
**SB:** Ben Chapman, N.Y., 38.
**Wins:** General Crowder, Wash., 26.
**ERA:** Lefty Grove, Phil., 2.84.
**CG:** Lefty Grove, Phil., 27.
**IP:** General Crowder, Wash., 327.
**SO:** Red Ruffing, N.Y., 190.

**National League**

**BA:** Lefty O'Doul, Brk., .368.
**Runs:** Chuck Klein, Phil., 152.
**Hits:** Chuck Klein, Phil., 226.
**TB:** Chuck Klein, Phil., 420.
**HR:** Chuck Klein, Phil.; Mel Ott, N.Y., 38.
**RBI:** Don Hurst, Phil., 143.
**SB:** Chuck Klein, Phil., 20.
**Wins:** Lon Warneke, Chi., 22.
**ERA:** Lon Warneke, Chi., 2.37.
**CG:** Red Lucas, Cin., 28.
**IP:** Dizzy Dean, St.L., 286.
**SO:** Dizzy Dean, St.L., 191.

**A.L. 20-game winners**
General Crowder, Wash., 26-13
Lefty Grove, Phil., 25-10
Lefty Gomez, N.Y., 24-7
Wes Ferrell, Cle., 23-13
Monte Weaver, Wash., 22-10

**N.L. 20-game winners**
Lon Warneke, Chi., 22-6
Watty Clark, Brk., 20-12

**A.L. 100 RBIs**
Jimmie Foxx, Phil., 169
Lou Gehrig, N.Y., 151
Al Simmons, Phil., 151
Babe Ruth, N.Y., 137
Earl Averill, Cle., 124
Joe Cronin, Wash., 116
Heinie Manush, Wash., 116
Tony Lazzeri, N.Y., 113
Mickey Cochrane, Phil., 112
John Stone, Det., 108
Ben Chapman, N.Y., 107
Charlie Gehringer, Det., 107
Smead Jolley, Chi.-St.L., 106
Goose Goslin, St.L., 104

**N.L. 100 RBIs**
Don Hurst, Phil., 143
Chuck Klein, Phil., 137
Pinky Whitney, Phil., 124
Mel Ott, N.Y., 123
Hack Wilson, Brk., 123
Bill Terry, N.Y., 117

**A.L. 40 homers**
Jimmie Foxx, Phil., 58
Babe Ruth, N.Y., 41

**Most Valuable Player**
A.L.: Jimmie Foxx, 1B, Phil.
N.L.: Chuck Klein, OF, Phil.

### WORLD SERIES

■ **Winner:** The Yankees played long ball in their sweep of the Cubs.

■ **Turning point:** A fourth-inning Game 1 homer by Lou Gehrig that gave the Yankees a 3-2 lead and propelled them to their sweep.

■ **Memorable moment:** Babe Ruth's second homer in Game 3 off Cubs righthander Charlie Root — whether it was a "called shot" or not.

■ **Top guns:** Gehrig (.529, 3 HR, 8 RBIs), Ruth (.333, 2 HR, 6 RBIs), Yankees; Riggs Stephenson (.444), Cubs.

**Linescores**

**Game 1**—September 28, at New York
Chicago..........2 0 0 0 0 0 2 2 0— 6 10 1
New York........0 0 0 3 0 5 3 1 x—12 8 2
Bush, Grimes (6), Smith (8); Ruffing. W—Ruffing. L—Bush. HR—Gehrig (N.Y.).

**Game 2**—September 29, at New York
Chicago...........1 0 1 0 0 0 0 0 0—2 9 0
New York..........2 0 2 0 1 0 0 0 x—5 10 1
Warneke; Gomez. W—Gomez. L—Warneke.

**Game 3**—October 1, at Chicago
New York ..........3 0 1 0 2 0 0 0 1—7 8 1
Chicago..............1 0 2 1 0 0 0 0 1—5 9 4
Pipgras, Pennock (9); Root, Malone (5), May (8), Tinning (9). W—Pipgras. L—Root. HR—Ruth 2, Gehrig 2 (N.Y.); Cuyler, Hartnett (Chi.).

**Game 4**—October 2, at Chicago
New York ......1 0 2 0 0 2 4 0 4—13 19 4
Chicago..........4 0 0 0 0 1 0 0 1— 6 9 1
Allen, W. Moore (1), Pennock (7); Bush, Warneke (1), May (4), Tinning (7), Grimes (9). W—W. Moore. L—May. HR—Demaree (Chi.); Lazzeri 2, Combs (N.Y.).

# 1933

## FINAL STANDINGS

**American League**

| Team | W | L | Pct. | GB |
|---|---|---|---|---|
| Washington | 99 | 53 | .651 | ... |
| New York | 91 | 59 | .607 | 7 |
| Philadelphia | 79 | 72 | .523 | 19.5 |
| Cleveland | 75 | 76 | .497 | 23.5 |
| Detroit | 75 | 79 | .487 | 25 |
| Chicago | 67 | 83 | .447 | 31 |
| Boston | 63 | 86 | .423 | 34.5 |
| St. Louis | 55 | 96 | .364 | 43.5 |

**National League**

| Team | W | L | Pct. | GB |
|---|---|---|---|---|
| New York | 91 | 61 | .599 | ... |
| Pittsburgh | 87 | 67 | .565 | 5 |
| Chicago | 86 | 68 | .558 | 6 |
| Boston | 83 | 71 | .539 | 9 |
| St. Louis | 82 | 71 | .536 | 9.5 |
| Brooklyn | 65 | 88 | .425 | 26.5 |
| Philadelphia | 60 | 92 | .395 | 31 |
| Cincinnati | 58 | 94 | .382 | 33 |

## SIGNIFICANT EVENTS

- **January 7:** Commissioner Kenesaw Mountain Landis, sending a Depression-era message to owners and players, took a voluntary $25,000 cut in salary.
- **November 7:** A referendum was passed by Pennsylvania voters legalizing Sunday baseball for Pittsburgh and Philadelphia — the only Major League cities still observing the blue law.

## MEMORABLE MOMENTS

- **July 30:** Cardinals ace Dizzy Dean set a modern record with 17 strikeouts in an 8-2 victory over Chicago.
- **July 2:** Giants pitchers Carl Hubbell (18) and Roy Parmelee (9) combined for 27 scoreless innings in a doubleheader shutout of the St. Louis Cardinals. Both games ended 1-0.
- **August 1:** Giants lefty Carl Hubbell extended his N.L.-record scoreless-innings streak to 45 in a game eventually won by Boston, 3-1.
- **August 17:** Yankee Lou Gehrig broke Everett Scott's Major League record when he played in his 1,308th consecutive game — a 7-6 loss at St. Louis.
- **October 1:** Philadelphia stars Jimmie Foxx (.356, 48 homers, 163 RBIs) and Chuck Klein (.368, 28, 120) completed an unprecedented one-season double, becoming the fifth and sixth Triple Crown winners of the century.

## LEADERS

**American League**

**BA:** Jimmie Foxx, Phil., .356.
**Runs:** Lou Gehrig, N.Y., 138.
**Hits:** Heinie Manush, Wash., 221.
**TB:** Jimmie Foxx, Phil., 403.
**HR:** Jimmie Foxx, Phil., 48.
**RBI:** Jimmie Foxx, Phil., 163.
**SB:** Ben Chapman, N.Y., 27.
**Wins:** General Crowder, Wash.; Lefty Grove, Phil., 24.
**ERA:** Mel Harder, Cle., 2.95.
**CG:** Lefty Grove, Phil., 21.
**IP.** Bump Hadley, St.L., 316.2.
**SO:** Lefty Gomez, N.Y., 163.

**National League**

**BA:** Chuck Klein, Phil., .368.
**Runs:** Pepper Martin, St.L., 122.
**Hits:** Chuck Klein, Phil., 223.
**TB:** Chuck Klein, Phil., 365.
**HR:** Chuck Klein, Phil., 28.
**RBI:** Chuck Klein, Phil., 120.
**SB:** Pepper Martin, St.L., 26.
**Wins:** Carl Hubbell, N.Y., 23.
**ERA:** Carl Hubbell, N.Y., 1.66.
**CG:** Dizzy Dean, St.L.; Lon Warneke, Chi., 26.
**IP:** Carl Hubbell, N.Y., 308.2.
**SO:** Dizzy Dean, St.L., 199.

**A.L. 20-game winners**

Lefty Grove, Phil., 24-8
General Crowder, Wash., 24-15
Earl Whitehill, Wash., 22-8

**N.L. 20-game winners**

Carl Hubbell, N.Y., 23-12
Ben Cantwell, Bos., 20-10
Guy Bush, Chi., 20-12
Dizzy Dean, St.L., 20-18

**A.L. 100 RBIs**

Jimmie Foxx, Phil., 163
Lou Gehrig, N.Y., 139
Al Simmons, Chi., 119
Joe Cronin, Wash., 118
Joe Kuhel, Wash., 107
Bruce Campbell, St.L., 106
Charlie Gehringer, Det., 105
Tony Lazzeri, N.Y., 104
Babe Ruth, N.Y., 103

**N.L. 100 RBIs**

Chuck Klein, Phil., 120
Wally Berger, Bos., 106
Mel Ott, N.Y., 103

**A.L. 40 homers**

Jimmie Foxx, Phil., 48

**Most Valuable Player**

A.L.: Jimmie Foxx, 1B, Phil.
N.L.: Carl Hubbell, P, N.Y.

## ALL-STAR GAME

- **Winner:** The American League prevailed 4-2 in baseball's "Game of the Century," which gathered the biggest stars from both leagues for an unprecedented meeting at Chicago's Comiskey Park.
- **Key inning:** The third, when Yankee slugger Babe Ruth pounded a two-run homer and gave the A.L. a 3-0 lead.
- **Memorable moment:** The star-studded pregame introductions for baseball's first All-Star classic.
- **Top guns:** Lefty Gomez (Yankees), Ruth (Yankees), Jimmie Dykes (White Sox), A.L.; Frank Frisch (Cardinals), Bill Terry (Giants), N.L.
- **MVP:** Ruth.

### Linescore

July 6, at Chicago's Comiskey Park
N.L. ............................0 0 0  0 0 2  0 0 0—2 8 0
A.L. ............................0 1 2  0 0 1  0 0 x—4 9 1
Hallahan (Cardinals), Warneke (Cubs) 3, Hubbell (Giants) 7; Gomez (Yankees), Crowder (Senators) 4, Grove (Athletics) 7. W—Gomez. L—Hallahan. HR—Ruth, A.L.; Frisch (N.L.).

## WORLD SERIES

- **Winner:** The pitching-rich Giants, now under the direction of player/manager Bill Terry, captured their first Series without John McGraw at the helm.
- **Turning point:** Carl Hubbell's 2-1, 11-inning victory that gave the Giants a three-games-to-one edge.
- **Memorable moment:** A 10th-inning home run by Mel Ott that gave the Giants a Series-ending 4-3 victory.
- **Top guns:** Hubbell (2-0, 0.00 ERA), Ott (.389, 2 HR, 4 RBIs), Giants; Fred Schulte (.333), Senators.

### Linescores

**Game 1**—October 3, at New York
Washington.............0 0 0  1 0 0  0 0 1—2  5 3
New York..................2 0 2  0 0 0  0 0 x—4 10 2
Stewart, Russell (3), Thomas (8); Hubbell. W—Hubbell. L—Stewart. HR—Ott (N.Y.).

**Game 2**—October 4, at New York
Washington.............0 0 1  0 0 0  0 0 0—1  5 0
New York..................0 0 0  0 0 6  0 0 x—6 10 0
Crowder, Thomas (6), McColl (7); Schumacher. W—Schumacher. L—Crowder. HR—Goslin (Wash.).

**Game 3**—October 5, at Washington
New York...................0 0 0  0 0 0  0 0 0—0 5 0
Washington...............2 1 0  0 0 0  1 0 x—4 9 1
Fitzsimmons, Bell (8); Whitehill. W—Whitehill. L—Fitzsimmons.

**Game 4**—October 6, at Washington
New York........0 0 0  1 0 0  0 0 0  0 1—2 11 1
Washington....0 0 0  0 0 0  1 0 0  0 0—1  8 0
Hubbell; Weaver, Russell (11). W—Hubbell. L—Weaver. HR—Terry (N.Y.).

**Game 5**—October 7, at Washington
New York...........0 2 0  0 0 1  0 0 0  1—4 11 1
Washington........0 0 0  0 0 3  0 0 0  0—3 10 0
Schumacher, Luque (6); Crowder, Russell (6). W—Luque. L—Russell. HR—Schulte (Wash.); Ott (N.Y.).

# 1934

## FINAL STANDINGS

**American League**

| Team | W | L | Pct. | GB |
|---|---|---|---|---|
| Detroit | 101 | 53 | .656 | ... |
| New York | 94 | 60 | .610 | 7 |
| Cleveland | 85 | 69 | .552 | 16 |
| Boston | 76 | 76 | .500 | 24 |
| Philadelphia | 68 | 82 | .453 | 31 |
| St. Louis | 67 | 85 | .441 | 33 |
| Washington | 66 | 86 | .434 | 34 |
| Chicago | 53 | 99 | .349 | 47 |

**National League**

| Team | W | L | Pct. | GB |
|---|---|---|---|---|
| St. Louis | 95 | 58 | .621 | ... |
| New York | 93 | 60 | .608 | 2 |
| Chicago | 86 | 65 | .570 | 8 |
| Boston | 78 | 73 | .517 | 16 |
| Pittsburgh | 74 | 76 | .493 | 19.5 |
| Brooklyn | 71 | 81 | .467 | 23.5 |
| Philadelphia | 56 | 93 | .376 | 37 |
| Cincinnati | 52 | 99 | .344 | 42 |

## SIGNIFICANT EVENTS

- **February 25:** John McGraw, considered by many the greatest manager of all time, died of cancer at age 60.
- **November 9:** N.L. officials selected Ford Frick as league president, six days after John Heydler resigned for health reasons.
- **December 12:** The N.L., acting independently of the A.L., voted to allow night baseball on a limited basis.

## MEMORABLE MOMENTS

- **July 13:** Yankee outfielder Babe Ruth opened the 700-homer club when he connected off righthander Tommy Bridges in a game at Detroit.
- **August 25:** Detroit rookie Schoolboy Rowe defeated Washington 4-2 for his A.L. record-tying 16th consecutive victory.
- **September 21:** Cardinals ace Dizzy Dean shut out Brooklyn on three hits in the first game of a doubleheader and brother Paul pitched a no-hitter against the Dodgers in the nightcap.

## LEADERS

**American League**

**BA:** Lou Gehrig, N.Y., .363.
**Runs:** Charley Gehringer, Det., 134.
**Hits:** Charley Gehringer, Det., 214.
**TB:** Lou Gehrig, N.Y., 409.
**HR:** Lou Gehrig, N.Y., 49.
**RBI:** Lou Gehrig, N.Y., 165.
**SB:** Billy Werber, Bos., 40.
**Wins:** Lefty Gomez, N.Y., 26.
**ERA:** Lefty Gomez, N.Y., 2.33.
**CG:** Lefty Gomez, N.Y., 25.
**IP:** Lefty Gomez, N.Y., 281.2.
**SO:** Lefty Gomez, N.Y., 158.

**National League**

**BA:** Paul Waner, Pit., .362.
**Runs:** Paul Waner, Pit., 122.
**Hits:** Paul Waner, Pit., 217.
**TB:** Ripper Collins, St.L., 369.
**HR:** Ripper Collins, St.L.; Mel Ott, N.Y., 35.
**RBI:** Mel Ott, N.Y., 135.
**SB:** Pepper Martin, St.L., 23.
**Wins:** Dizzy Dean, St.L., 30.
**ERA:** Carl Hubbell, N.Y., 2.30.
**CG:** Carl Hubbell, N.Y., 25.
**IP:** Van Lingle Mungo, Brk., 315.1.
**SO:** Dizzy Dean, St.L., 195.

**A.L. 20-game winners**

Lefty Gomez, N.Y., 26-5
Schoolboy Rowe, Det., 24-8
Tommy Bridges, Det., 22-11
Mel Harder, Cle., 20-12

**N.L. 20-game winners**

Dizzy Dean, St.L., 30-7
Hal Schumacher, N.Y., 23-10
Lon Warneke, Chi., 22-10
Carl Hubbell, N.Y., 21-12

**A.L. 100 RBIs**

Lou Gehrig, N.Y., 165
Hal Trosky, Cle., 142
Hank Greenberg, Det., 139
Jimmie Foxx, Phil., 130
Charlie Gehringer, Det., 127
Roy Johnson, Bos., 119
Earl Averill, Cle., 113
Zeke Bonura, Chi., 110
Al Simmons, Chi., 104
Joe Cronin, Wash., 101
Odell Hale, Cle., 101
Roy Pepper, St.L., 101
Goose Goslin, Det., 100
Billy Rogell, Det., 100

**N.L. 100 RBIs**

Mel Ott, N.Y., 135
Ripper Collins, St.L., 128
Wally Berger, Bos., 121
Joe Medwick, St.L., 106
Gus Suhr, Pit., 103
Sam Leslie, Brk., 102
Travis Jackson, N.Y., 101

**A.L. 40 homers**

Lou Gehrig, N.Y., 49
Jimmie Foxx, Phil., 44

**Most Valuable Player**

A.L.: Mickey Cochrane, C, Det.
N.L.: Dizzy Dean, P, St.L.

## ALL-STAR GAME

- **Winner:** The A.L. made it two in a row by roaring back from a 4-0 deficit for a 9-7 victory.
- **Key inning:** The fifth, when the A.L. scored six times to take command. Cleveland's Earl Averill doubled home two runs and Yankee pitcher Red Ruffing singled in two more.
- **Memorable moment:** The first- and second-inning performance of Giants lefthander Carl Hubbell, who struck out A.L. bashers Babe Ruth (Yankees), Lou Gehrig (Yankees), Jimmie Foxx (Athletics), Al Simmons (White Sox) and Joe Cronin (Senators) consecutively.
- **Top guns:** Mel Harder (Indians), Averill (Indians), Cronin (Senators), Simmons (White Sox), A.L.; Hubbell (Giants), Joe Medwick (Cardinals), Frank Frisch (Cardinals), N.L.
- **MVP:** Averill.

### Linescore

July 10, at New York's Polo Grounds
A.L. ...........................0 0 0  2 6 1  0 0 0—9 14 1
N.L. ...........................1 0 3  0 3 0  0 0 0—7  8 1
Gomez (Yankees), Ruffing (Yankees) 4, Harder (Indians) 5, A.L.; Hubbell (Giants), Warneke (Cubs) 4, Mungo (Dodgers) 5, Dean (Cardinals) 6, Frankhouse (Braves) 9. W—Harder. L—Mungo. HR—Frisch, Medwick, N.L.

## WORLD SERIES

- **Winner:** St. Louis' Gas House Gang defeated the Tigers in the infamous "Garbage" World Series.
- **Turning point:** Paul Dean's pitching and hitting gave the Cardinals a 4-3 Game 6 victory that set up a winner-take-all seventh game.
- **Memorable moment:** A seventh-game outburst by frustrated Tigers fans who pelted Cardinals left fielder Joe Medwick with garbage and other debris, forcing a long delay. The Cardinals were leading 9-0 en route to an 11-0 victory.
- **Top guns:** Paul Dean (2-0, 1.00 ERA), Dizzy Dean (2-1, 1.73), Medwick (.379, 5 RBIs), Cardinals; Charley Gehringer (.379), Tigers.

### Linescores

**Game 1**—October 3, at Detroit
St. Louis .................0 2 1  0 1 4  0 0 0—8 13 2
Detroit......................0 0 1  0 0 1  0 1 0—3  8 5
D. Dean; Crowder, Marberry (6), Hogsett (6). W—D. Dean. L—Crowder. HR—Medwick (St.L.); Greenberg (Det.).

**Game 2**—October 4, at Detroit
St. Louis ......0 1 1  0 0 0  0 0 0  0 0 0—2 7 3
Detroit.........0 0 0  1 0 0  0 0 1  0 0 1—3 7 0
Hallahan, W. Walker (9); Rowe. W—Rowe. L—W. Walker.

**Game 3**—October 5, at St. Louis
Detroit.......................0 0 0  0 0 0  0 0 1—1 8 2
St. Louis ...................1 1 0  0 2 0  0 0 x—4 9 1
Bridges, Hogsett (5); P. Dean. W—P. Dean. L—Bridges.

**Game 4**—October 6, at St. Louis
Detroit....................0 0 3  1 0 0  1 5 0—10 13 1
St. Louis ................0 1 1  2 0 0  0 0 0— 4 10 5
Auker; Carleton, Vance (3), W. Walker (5), Haines (8), Mooney (9). W—Auker. L—W. Walker.

**Game 5**—October 7, at St. Louis
Detroit.......................0 1 0  0 0 2  0 0 0—3 7 0
St. Louis ...................0 0 0  0 0 0  1 0 0—1 7 1
Bridges; D. Dean, Carleton (9). W—Bridges. L—D. Dean. HR—Gehringer (Det.); DeLancey (St.L.).

**Game 6**—October 8, at Detroit
St. Louis .................1 0 0  0 2 0  1 0 0—4 10 2
Detroit.....................0 0 1  0 0 2  0 0 0—3  7 1
P. Dean; Rowe. W—P. Dean. L—Rowe.

**Game 7**—October 9, at Detroit
St. Louis ................0 0 7  0 0 2  2 0 0—11 17 1
Detroit....................0 0 0  0 0 0  0 0 0— 0  6 3
D. Dean; Auker, Rowe (3), Hogsett (3), Bridges (3), Marberry (8), Crowder (9). W—D. Dean. L—Auker.

# 1935

## FINAL STANDINGS

**American League**

| Team | W | L | Pct. | GB |
|---|---|---|---|---|
| Detroit | 93 | 58 | .616 | ... |
| New York | 89 | 60 | .597 | 3 |
| Cleveland | 82 | 71 | .536 | 12 |
| Boston | 78 | 75 | .510 | 16 |
| Chicago | 74 | 78 | .487 | 19.5 |
| Washington | 67 | 86 | .438 | 27 |
| St. Louis | 65 | 87 | .428 | 28.5 |
| Philadelphia | 58 | 91 | .389 | 34 |

**National League**

| Team | W | L | Pct. | GB |
|---|---|---|---|---|
| Chicago | 100 | 54 | .649 | ... |
| St. Louis | 96 | 58 | .623 | 4 |
| New York | 91 | 62 | .595 | 8.5 |
| Pittsburgh | 86 | 67 | .562 | 13.5 |
| Brooklyn | 70 | 83 | .458 | 29.5 |
| Cincinnati | 68 | 85 | .444 | 31.5 |
| Philadelphia | 64 | 89 | .418 | 35.5 |
| Boston | 38 | 115 | .248 | 61.5 |

## SIGNIFICANT EVENTS

■ **February 26:** Babe Ruth ended his long love affair with New York fans when the Yankees granted him a release to sign with the Braves.

■ **December 10:** A.L. owners attending the winter meetings voted not to sanction night baseball.

## MEMORABLE MOMENTS

■ **May 24:** Larry MacPhail's Reds staged the first night game in Major League history and defeated the Phillies, 2-1, at Crosley Field.

■ **June 2:** Braves slugger Babe Ruth retired, eight days after a three-homer game at Pittsburgh had raised his career total to 714.

■ **August 31:** Chicago pitcher Vern Kennedy pitched the first no-hitter in Comiskey Park history and punctuated his 5-0 victory over Cleveland with a bases-loaded triple.

■ **September 22:** The lowly Braves lost their Major League-record 110th game en route to 115 losses.

■ **September 27:** The Cubs clinched the N.L. pennant with a 6-2 victory over St. Louis — their 20th straight win in a streak that would end at 21.

## LEADERS

**American League**

**BA:** Buddy Myer, Wash., .349.
**Runs:** Lou Gehrig, N.Y., 125.
**Hits:** Joe Vosmik, Cle., 216.
**TB:** Hank Greenberg, Det., 389.
**HR:** Jimmie Foxx, Phil.; Hank Greenberg, Det., 36.
**RBI:** Hank Greenberg, Det., 170.
**SB:** Billy Werber, Bos., 29.
**Wins:** Wes Ferrell, Bos., 25.
**ERA:** Lefty Grove, Bos., 2.70.
**CG:** Wes Ferrell, Bos., 31.
**IP:** Wes Ferrell, Bos., 322.1.
**SO:** Tommy Bridges, Det., 163.

**National League**

**BA:** Arky Vaughan, Pit., .385.
**Runs:** Augie Galan, Chi., 133.
**Hits:** Billy Herman, Chi., 227.
**TB:** Joe Medwick, St.L., 365.
**HR:** Wally Berger, Bos., 34.
**RBI:** Wally Berger, Bos., 130.
**SB:** Augie Galan, Chi., 22.
**Wins:** Dizzy Dean, St.L., 28.
**ERA:** Cy Blanton, Pit., 2.58.
**CG:** Dizzy Dean, St.L., 29.
**IP:** Dizzy Dean, St.L., 325.1
**SO:** Dizzy Dean, St.L., 190.

**A.L. 20-game winners**

Wes Ferrell, Bos., 25-14
Mel Harder, Cle., 22-11
Tommy Bridges, Det., 21-10
Lefty Grove, Bos., 20-12

**N.L. 20-game winners**

Dizzy Dean, St.L., 28-12
Carl Hubbell, N.Y., 23-12
Paul Derringer, Cin., 22-13
Bill Lee, Chi., 20-6
Lon Warneke, Chi., 20-13

**A.L. 100 RBIs**

Hank Greenberg, Det., 170
Lou Gehrig, N.Y., 119
Jimmie Foxx, Phil., 115
Hal Trosky, Cle., 113
Moose Solters, Bos.-St.L., 112
Joe Vosmik, Cle., 110
Goose Goslin, Det., 109
Bob Johnson, Phil., 109
Charlie Gehringer, Det., 108
Odell Hale, Cle., 101
Buddy Myer, Wash., 100

**N.L. 100 RBIs**

Wally Berger, Bos., 130
Joe Medwick, St.L., 126
Ripper Collins, St.L., 122
Mel Ott, N.Y., 114
Hank Leiber, N.Y., 107

**Most Valuable Player**

A.L.: Hank Greenberg, 1B, Det.
N.L.: Gabby Hartnett, C, Chi.

## ALL-STAR GAME

■ **Winner:** New York's Lefty Gomez and Cleveland's Mel Harder combined on a four-hitter and the A.L. recorded its third straight All-Star victory, 4-1.

■ **Key inning:** The first, when Athletics slugger Jimmie Foxx belted a two-run homer off Bill Walker, giving Gomez and Harder all the runs they would need.

■ **Memorable moment:** The ovation for hometown favorite Harder after his three-inning, one-hit pitching to close out the N.L.

■ **Top guns:** Gomez (Yankees), Harder (Indians), Foxx (Athletics), Charley Gehringer (Tigers), A.L.; Bill Terry (Giants), N.L.

■ **MVP:** Foxx.

**Linescore**

July 8, at Cleveland Stadium
N.L.............................0 0 0 1 0 0 0 0 0—1 4 1
A.L. ...........................2 1 0 0 1 0 0 0 x—4 8 0
Walker (Cardinals), Schumacher (Giants) 3, Derringer (Reds) 7, Dean (Cardinals) 8; Gomez (Yankees), Harder (Indians) 7. W—Gomez. L—Walker. HR—Foxx, A.L.

## WORLD SERIES

■ **Winner:** The Tigers, four-time Series losers, won their first in a six-game battle with the Cubs.

■ **Turning point:** Detroit's 6-5 Game 3 victory. Jo Jo White drove in the game-winner with an 11th-inning single, giving the Tigers a two-games-to-one edge.

■ **Memorable moment:** Detroit pitcher Tommy Bridges' dramatic ninth-inning escape in Game 7 after giving up a leadoff triple to Stan Hack with the game tied, 3-3. The Tigers ended the Series in the bottom of the inning.

■ **Top guns:** Bridges (2-0, 2.50 ERA), Pete Fox (.385), Tigers; Lon Warneke (2-0, 0.54), Billy Herman (.333, 6 RBIs), Cubs.

**Linescores**

**Game 1**—October 2, at Detroit
Chicago.....................2 0 0 0 0 0 0 0 1—3 7 0
Detroit.......................0 0 0 0 0 0 0 0 0—0 4 3
Warneke; Rowe. W—Warneke. L—Rowe. HR—Demaree (Chi.).

**Game 2**—October 3, at Detroit
Chicago.....................0 0 0 0 1 0 2 0 0—3 6 1
Detroit.......................4 0 0 3 0 0 1 0 x—8 9 2
Root, Henshaw (1), Kowalik (4); Bridges. W—Bridges. L—Root. HR—Greenberg (Det.).

**Game 3**—October 4, at Chicago
Detroit............0 0 0 0 0 1 0 4 0 0 1—6 12 2
Chicago..........0 2 0 0 1 0 0 0 2 0 0—5 10 3
Auker, Hogsett (7), Rowe (8); Lee, Warneke (8), French (10). W—Rowe. L—French. HR—Demaree (Chi.).

**Game 4**—October 5, at Chicago
Detroit.......................0 0 1 0 0 1 0 0 0—2 7 0
Chicago.....................0 1 0 0 0 0 0 0 0—1 5 2
Crowder; Carleton, Root (8). W—Crowder. L—Carleton. HR—Hartnett (Chi.).

**Game 5**—October 6, at Chicago
Detroit.......................0 0 0 0 0 0 0 0 1—1 7 1
Chicago.....................0 0 2 0 0 0 1 0 x—3 8 0
Rowe; Warneke, Lee (7). W—Warneke. L—Rowe. HR—Klein (Chi.).

**Game 6**—October 7, at Detroit
Chicago...................0 0 1 0 2 0 0 0 0—3 12 0
Detroit.....................1 0 0 1 0 1 0 0 1—4 12 1
French; Bridges. W—Bridges. L—French. HR—Herman (Chi.).

# 1936

## FINAL STANDINGS

**American League**

| Team | W | L | Pct. | GB |
|---|---|---|---|---|
| New York | 102 | 51 | .667 | ... |
| Detroit | 83 | 71 | .539 | 19.5 |
| Chicago | 81 | 70 | .536 | 20 |
| Washington | 82 | 71 | .536 | 20 |
| Cleveland | 80 | 74 | .519 | 22.5 |
| Boston | 74 | 80 | .481 | 28.5 |
| St. Louis | 57 | 95 | .375 | 44.5 |
| Philadelphia | 53 | 100 | .346 | 49 |

**National League**

| Team | W | L | Pct. | GB |
|---|---|---|---|---|
| New York | 92 | 62 | .597 | ... |
| Chicago | 87 | 67 | .565 | 5 |
| St. Louis | 87 | 67 | .565 | 5 |
| Pittsburgh | 84 | 70 | .545 | 8 |
| Cincinnati | 74 | 80 | .481 | 18 |
| Boston | 71 | 83 | .461 | 21 |
| Brooklyn | 67 | 87 | .435 | 25 |
| Philadelphia | 54 | 100 | .351 | 38 |

## SIGNIFICANT EVENTS

■ **February 2:** Ty Cobb, Babe Ruth, Honus Wagner, Walter Johnson and Christy Mathewson were named charter members of baseball's new Hall of Fame.

■ **June 4:** Detroit player/manager Mickey Cochrane collapsed in a Shibe Park dugout and was hospitalized on the threshold of a career-threatening nervous breakdown.

■ **December 9:** A.L. owners granted the Browns permission to play night baseball in St. Louis and ruled that players must have at least 400 at-bats to qualify for a batting championship.

## MEMORABLE MOMENTS

■ **May 24:** Tony Lazzeri drilled three home runs, including a single-game record two grand slams, and drove in an A.L.-record 11 runs in the Yankees' 25-2 pounding of the Athletics.

■ **July 10:** Philadelphia's Chuck Klein became the fourth Major Leaguer to hit four homers in one game, completing his big day with a solo blast leading off the 10th inning of a 9-6 victory over Pittsburgh.

■ **September 13:** Cleveland 17-year-old Bob Feller tied a Major League record when he struck out 17 Athletics in a 5-2 victory.

## LEADERS

**American League**

**BA:** Luke Appling, Chi., .388.
**Runs:** Lou Gehrig, N.Y., 167.
**Hits:** Earl Averill, Cle., 232.
**TB:** Hal Trosky, Cle., 405.
**HR:** Lou Gehrig, N.Y., 49.
**RBI:** Hal Trosky, Cle., 162.
**SB:** Lyn Lary, St.L., 37.
**Wins:** Tommy Bridges, Det., 23.
**ERA:** Lefty Grove, Bos., 2.81.
**CG:** Wes Ferrell, Bos., 28.
**IP:** Wes Ferrell, Bos., 301.
**SO:** Tommy Bridges, Det., 175.

**National League**

**BA:** Paul Waner, Pit., .373.
**Runs:** Arky Vaughan, Pit., 122.
**Hits:** Joe Medwick, St.L., 223.
**TB:** Joe Medwick, St.L., 367.
**HR:** Mel Ott, N.Y., 33.
**RBI:** Joe Medwick, St.L., 138.
**SB:** Pepper Martin, St.L., 23.
**Wins:** Carl Hubbell, N.Y., 26.
**ERA:** Carl Hubbell, N.Y., 2.31.
**CG:** Dizzy Dean, St.L., 28.
**IP:** Dizzy Dean, St.L., 315.
**SO:** Van Lingle Mungo, Brk., 238.

**A.L. 20-game winners**

Tommy Bridges, Det., 23-11
Vern Kennedy, Chi., 21-9
Johnny Allen, Cle., 20-10
Red Ruffing, N.Y., 20-12
Wes Ferrell, Bos., 20-15

**N.L. 20-game winners**

Carl Hubbell, N.Y., 26-6
Dizzy Dean, St.L., 24-13

**A.L. 100 RBIs**

Hal Trosky, Cle., 162
Lou Gehrig, N.Y., 152
Jimmie Foxx, Bos., 143
Zeke Bonura, Chi., 138
Moose Solters, St.L., 134
Luke Appling, Chi., 128
Earl Averill, Cle., 126
Joe DiMaggio, N.Y., 125
Goose Goslin, Det., 125
Beau Bell, St.L., 123
Bob Johnson, Phil., 121
Joe Kuhel, Wash., 118
Charlie Gehringer, Det., 116
Al Simmons, Det., 112
Tony Lazzeri, N.Y., 109
Bill Dickey, N.Y., 107
George Selkirk, N.Y., 107
Marv Owen, Det., 105

**N.L. 100 RBIs**

Joe Medwick, St.L., 138
Mel Ott, N.Y., 135
Gus Suhr, Pit., 118
Chuck Klein, Chi.-Phil., 104
Bill Brubaker, Pit., 102
Dolph Camilli, Phil., 102

**A.L. 40 homers**

Lou Gehrig, N.Y., 49
Hal Trosky, Cle., 42
Jimmie Foxx, Bos., 41

**Most Valuable Player**

A.L.: Lou Gehrig, 1B, N.Y.
N.L.: Carl Hubbell, P, N.Y.

**Hall of Fame additions**

**Charter Class**

Ty Cobb, OF, 1905-28
Walter Johnson, P, 1907-27
Christy Mathewson, P, 1900-16
Babe Ruth, P/OF, 1914-35
Honus Wagner, SS, 1897-1917

## ALL-STAR GAME

■ **Winner:** The N.L. recorded its first All-Star victory, thanks to the work of three Cubs — Gabby Hartnett (a run-scoring triple), Augie Galan (a solo home run) and pitcher Lon Warneke.

■ **Key inning:** After the A.L. had cut its deficit to 4-3 in the seventh, Warneke retired Yankee slugger Joe DiMaggio on a line drive with the bases loaded.

■ **Memorable moment:** Galan's fifth-inning blast into the right-field bleachers. It drew a vehement protest from A.L. manager Joe McCarthy, who thought it was foul.

■ **Top guns:** Dizzy Dean (Cardinals), Warneke (Cubs), Galan (Cubs), Hartnett (Cubs), N.L.; Lou Gehrig (Yankees), Luke Appling (White Sox), A.L.

■ **MVP:** Warneke.

**Linescore**

July 7, at Boston's Braves Field
A.L.............................0 0 0 0 0 0 3 0 0—3 7 1
N.L. ...........................0 2 0 0 2 0 0 0 x—4 9 0
Grove (Red Sox), Rowe (Tigers) 4, Harder (Indians) 7; D. Dean (Cardinals), Hubbell (Giants) 4, Davis (Cubs) 7, Warneke (Cubs) 7. W—D. Dean. L—Grove. HR—Galan, N.L.; Gehrig, A.L.

## WORLD SERIES

■ **Winner:** Renewing an old New York rivalry, the Yankees prevailed in their first Series without Babe Ruth.

■ **Turning point:** Lou Gehrig's two-run Game 4 homer off Giants ace Carl Hubbell propelled the Yankees to a 5-2 victory and a three-games-to-one Series lead.

■ **Memorable moment:** Yankee slugger Tony Lazzeri's Game 2 grand slam, only the second in Series history.

■ **Top guns:** Jake Powell (.455), Gehrig (2 HR, 7 RBIs), Red Rolfe (.400), Yankees; Dick Bartell (.381), Giants.

**Linescores**

**Game 1**—September 30, at Polo Grounds
Yankees......................0 0 1 0 0 0 0 0 0—1 7 2
Giants ........................0 0 0 0 1 1 0 4 x—6 9 1
Ruffing; Hubbell. W—Hubbell. L—Ruffing. HR—Bartell (NYG); Selkirk (NYY).

**Game 2**—October 2, at Polo Grounds
Yankees.................2 0 7 0 0 1 2 0 6—18 17 0
Giants ..................0 1 0 3 0 0 0 0 0— 4 6 1
Gomez; Schumacher, Smith (3), Coffman (3), Gabler (5), Gumbert (9). W—Gomez. L—Schumacher. HR—Dickey, Lazzeri (NYY).

**Game 3**—October 3, at Yankee Stadium
Giants .....................0 0 0 0 1 0 0 0 0—1 11 0
Yankees...................0 1 0 0 0 0 0 1 x—2 4 0
Fitzsimmons; Hadley, Malone (9). W—Hadley. L—Fitzsimmons. HR—Gehrig (NYY); Ripple (NYG).

**Game 4**—October 4, at Yankee Stadium
Giants .....................0 0 0 1 0 0 0 1 0—2 7 1
Yankees...................0 1 3 0 0 0 0 1 x—5 10 1
Hubbell, Gabler (8); Pearson. W—Pearson. L—Hubbell. HR—Gehrig (NYY).

**Game 5**—October 5, at Yankee Stadium
Giants ................3 0 0 0 0 1 0 0 0 1—5 8 3
Yankees..............0 1 1 0 0 2 0 0 0 0—4 10 1
Schumacher; Ruffing, Malone (7). W—Schumacher. L—Malone. HR—Selkirk (NYY).

**Game 6**—October 6, at Polo Grounds
Yankees..................0 2 1 2 0 0 0 1 7—13 17 2
Giants ...................2 0 0 0 1 0 1 1 0— 5 9 1
Gomez, Murphy (7); Fitzsimmons, Castleman (4), Coffman (9), Gumbert (9). W—Gomez. L—Fitzsimmons. HR—Moore, Ott (NYG); Powell (NYY).

# 1937

## FINAL STANDINGS

**American League**

| Team | W | L | Pct. | GB |
|---|---|---|---|---|
| New York | 102 | 52 | .662 | ... |
| Detroit | 89 | 65 | .578 | 13 |
| Chicago | 86 | 68 | .558 | 16 |
| Cleveland | 83 | 71 | .539 | 19 |
| Boston | 80 | 72 | .526 | 21 |
| Washington | 73 | 80 | .477 | 28.5 |
| Philadelphia | 54 | 97 | .358 | 46.5 |
| St. Louis | 46 | 108 | .299 | 56 |

**National League**

| Team | W | L | Pct. | GB |
|---|---|---|---|---|
| New York | 95 | 57 | .625 | ... |
| Chicago | 93 | 61 | .604 | 3 |
| Pittsburgh | 86 | 68 | .558 | 10 |
| St. Louis | 81 | 73 | .526 | 15 |
| Boston | 79 | 73 | .520 | 16 |
| Brooklyn | 62 | 91 | .405 | 33.5 |
| Philadelphia | 61 | 92 | .399 | 34.5 |
| Cincinnati | 56 | 98 | .364 | 40 |

## SIGNIFICANT EVENTS

■ **May 25:** Detroit player/manager Mickey Cochrane suffered a career-ending skull fracture when he was struck by a pitch from Yankee Bump Hadley.

■ **May 26:** Commissioner Kenesaw Mountain Landis took the All-Star vote away from the fans and decreed that the two managers would select future teams.

## MEMORABLE MOMENTS

■ **April 20:** Detroit outfielder Gee Walker carved out his own piece of the Major League record book when he hit a single, double, triple and home run in a season-opening victory over Cleveland—the first player to hit for the cycle on Opening Day.

■ **May 27:** Giants lefty Carl Hubbell, asked to make a rare relief appearance, pitched two scoreless innings and earned a 3-2 victory over the Reds, his record 24th straight over two seasons.

■ **August 31:** Detroit rookie Rudy York hit two home runs against Washington, capping the biggest home run-hitting month in baseball history with 18.

■ **October 3:** Cleveland's Johnny Allen, 15-0 and one win from tying the A.L. record for consecutive victories, dropped a 1-0 final-day decision to Detroit.

■ **October 3:** St. Louis' Joe Medwick captured an N.L. Triple Crown, batting .374, driving in 154 runs and tying New York's Mel Ott with 31 homers.

## LEADERS

**American League**

**BA:** Charley Gehringer, Det., .371.
**Runs:** Joe DiMaggio, N.Y., 151.
**Hits:** Beau Bell, St.L., 218.
**TB:** Joe DiMaggio, N.Y., 418.
**HR:** Joe DiMaggio, N.Y., 46.
**RBI:** Hank Greenberg, Det., 183.
**SB:** Ben Chapman, Wash.-Bos.; Billy Werber, Phil., 35.
**Wins:** Lefty Gomez, N.Y., 21.
**ERA:** Lefty Gomez, N.Y., 2.33.
**CG:** Wes Ferrell, Wash.-Bos., 26.
**IP:** Wes Ferrell, Wash.-Bos., 281.
**SO:** Lefty Gomez, N.Y., 194.

**National League**

**BA:** Joe Medwick, St.L., .374.
**Runs:** Joe Medwick, St.L., 111.
**Hits:** Joe Medwick, St.L., 237.
**TB:** Joe Medwick, St.L., 406.
**HR:** Joe Medwick, St.L.; Mel Ott, N.Y., 31.
**RBI:** Joe Medwick, St.L., 154.
**SB:** Augie Galan, Chi., 23.
**Wins:** Carl Hubbell, N.Y., 22.
**ERA:** Jim Turner, Bos., 2.38.
**CG:** Jim Turner, Bos., 24.
**IP:** Claude Passeau, Phil., 292.1.
**SO:** Carl Hubbell, N.Y., 159.

**A.L. 20-game winners**

Lefty Gomez, N.Y., 21-11
Red Ruffing, N.Y., 20-7

**N.L. 20-game winners**

Carl Hubbell, N.Y., 22-8
Cliff Melton, N.Y., 20-9
Lou Fette, Bos., 20-10
Jim Turner, Bos., 20-11

**A.L. 100 RBIs**

Hank Greenberg, Det., 183
Joe DiMaggio, N.Y., 167
Lou Gehrig, N.Y., 159
Bill Dickey, N.Y., 133
Hal Trosky, Cle., 128
Jimmie Foxx, Bos., 127
Harlond Clift, St.L., 118
Beau Bell, St.L., 117
Gee Walker, Det., 113
Joe Cronin, Bos., 110
Moose Solters, Cle., 109
Bob Johnson, Phil., 108
Pinky Higgins, Bos., 106
Rudy York, Det., 103
Zeke Bonura, Chi., 100

**N.L. 100 RBIs**

Joe Medwick, St.L., 154
Frank Demaree, Chi., 115
Johnny Mize, St.L., 113

**A.L. 40 homers**

Joe DiMaggio, N.Y., 46
Hank Greenberg, Det., 40

**Most Valuable Player**

A.L.: Charley Gehringer, 2B, Det.
N.L.: Joe Medwick, OF, St.L.

**Hall of Fame additions**

Morgan Bulkeley, executive
Ban Johnson, executive
Napoleon Lajoie, 2B, 1896-1916
Connie Mack, manager/owner
John McGraw, manager
Tris Speaker, OF, 1907-28
George Wright, player/manager
Cy Young, P, 1890-1911

## ALL-STAR GAME

■ **Winner:** Yankees Lou Gehrig, Red Rolfe and Bill Dickey combined for seven RBIs and teammate Lefty Gomez claimed his third All-Star victory as the A.L. won for the fourth time in five years.

■ **Key inning:** The third, when Gehrig blasted a Dizzy Dean pitch for a two-run homer. The Yankee first baseman later added a two-run double.

■ **Memorable moment:** A third-inning Earl Averill line drive that deflected off the foot of Dean. The Cardinals' righthander suffered a broken toe that would begin to unravel his outstanding career.

■ **Top guns:** Gomez (Yankees), Gehrig (Yankees), Rolfe (Yankees), Dickey (Yankees), Charley Gehringer (Tigers), A.L.; Joe Medwick (Cardinals), Billy Herman (Cubs), N.L.

■ **MVP:** Gehrig.

**Linescore**

July 7, at Washington's Griffith Stadium
N.L. ..........................0 0 0 1 1 1 0 0 0—3 13 0
A.L. ..........................0 0 2 3 1 2 0 0 x—8 13 2
D. Dean (Cardinals), Hubbell (Giants) 4, Blanton (Pirates) 4, Grissom (Reds) 5, Mungo (Dodgers) 6, Walters (Phillies) 8; Gomez (Yankees), Bridges (Tigers) 4, Harder (Indians) 7. W—Gomez. L—D. Dean. HR—Gehrig, A.L.

## WORLD SERIES

■ **Winner:** Two in a row. The first of several big Yankee World Series runs began to take shape.

■ **Turning point:** The Yankees' 8-1 pounding of Giants ace Carl Hubbell in Game 1.

■ **Memorable moment:** Yankee pitcher Lefty Gomez, a notoriously poor hitter, driving in the Game 5 winner with a fifth-inning single.

■ **Top guns:** Gomez (2-0, 1.50 ERA), Tony Lazzeri (.400), Yankees; Joe Moore (.391), Giants.

**Linescores**

**Game 1**—October 6, at Yankee Stadium
Giants ........................0 0 0 0 1 0 0 0 0—1 6 2
Yankees ......................0 0 0 0 0 7 0 1 x—8 7 0
Hubbell, Gumbert (6), Coffman (6), Smith (8); Gomez. W—Gomez. L—Hubbell. HR—Lazzeri (NYY).

**Game 2**—October 7, at Yankee Stadium
Giants ......................1 0 0 0 0 0 0 0 0—1 7 0
Yankees ....................0 0 0 0 2 4 2 0 x—8 12 0
Melton, Gumbert (5), Coffman (6); Ruffing. W—Ruffing. L—Melton.

**Game 3**—October 8, at Polo Grounds
Yankees.....................0 1 2 1 1 0 0 0 0—5 9 0
Giants ......................0 0 0 0 0 0 1 0 0—1 5 4
Pearson, Murphy (9); Schumacher, Melton (7), Brennan (9). W—Pearson. L—Schumacher.

**Game 4**—October 9, at Polo Grounds
Yankees....................1 0 1 0 0 0 0 0 1—3 6 0
Giants .....................0 6 0 0 0 0 1 0 x—7 12 3
Hadley, Andrews (2), Wicker (8); Hubbell. W—Hubbell. L—Hadley. HR—Gehrig (NYY).

**Game 5**—October 10, at Polo Grounds
Yankees...................0 1 1 0 2 0 0 0 0—4 8 0
Giants .....................0 0 2 0 0 0 0 0 0—2 10 0
Gomez; Melton, Smith (6), Brennan (8). W—Gomez. L—Melton. HR—DiMaggio, Hoag (NYY); Ott (NYG).

# 1938

## FINAL STANDINGS

**American League**

| Team | W | L | Pct. | GB |
|---|---|---|---|---|
| New York | 99 | 53 | .651 | ... |
| Boston | 88 | 61 | .591 | 9.5 |
| Cleveland | 86 | 66 | .566 | 13 |
| Detroit | 84 | 70 | .545 | 16 |
| Washington | 75 | 76 | .497 | 23.5 |
| Chicago | 65 | 83 | .439 | 32 |
| St. Louis | 55 | 97 | .362 | 44 |
| Philadelphia | 53 | 99 | .349 | 46 |

**National League**

| Team | W | L | Pct. | GB |
|---|---|---|---|---|
| Chicago | 89 | 63 | .586 | ... |
| Pittsburgh | 86 | 64 | .573 | 2 |
| New York | 83 | 67 | .553 | 5 |
| Cincinnati | 82 | 68 | .547 | 6 |
| Boston | 77 | 75 | .507 | 12 |
| St. Louis | 71 | 80 | .470 | 17.5 |
| Brooklyn | 69 | 80 | .463 | 18.5 |
| Philadelphia | 45 | 105 | .300 | 43 |

## SIGNIFICANT EVENTS

■ **April 16:** The Cardinals sent shockwaves through baseball when they traded ace Dizzy Dean to the Cubs for two pitchers and an outfielder.

■ **May 31:** Yankee Lou Gehrig stretched his ironman streak to an incredible 2,000 games during a victory over Boston.

■ **December 14:** The N.L. granted Cincinnati, baseball's first professional team, permission to play its traditional season opener.

## MEMORABLE MOMENTS

■ **June 15:** Cincinnati's Johnny Vander Meer pitched his record second consecutive no-hitter, a 6-0 victory that stole the spotlight from the Dodgers in the first night game at Brooklyn's Ebbets Field.

■ **June 21:** Boston third baseman Pinky Higgins etched his name in the record books when he collected 12 consecutive hits over a two-day, four-game stretch against Chicago and Detroit.

■ **September 28:** Moments away from a suspended game, Chicago catcher Gabby Hartnett stroked a ninth-inning homer into the thickening darkness of Wrigley Field, giving the Cubs a crucial 6-5 victory over Pittsburgh and half-game lead in the tense N.L. pennant race.

■ **October 2:** Cleveland's Bob Feller struck out a Major League-record 18 batters while losing a 4-1 decision to the Tigers.

## LEADERS

**American League**

**BA:** Jimmie Foxx, Bos., .349.
**Runs:** Hank Greenberg, Det., 144.
**Hits:** Joe Vosmik, Bos., 201.
**TB:** Jimmie Foxx, Bos., 398.
**HR:** Hank Greenberg, Det., 58.
**RBI:** Jimmie Foxx, Bos., 175.
**SB:** Frank Crosetti, N.Y., 27.
**Wins:** Red Ruffing, N.Y., 21.
**ERA:** Lefty Grove, Bos., 3.08.
**CG:** Bobo Newsom, St.L., 31.
**IP:** Bobo Newsom, St.L., 329.2.
**SO:** Bob Feller, Cle., 240.

**National League**

**BA:** Ernie Lombardi, Cin., .342.
**Runs:** Mel Ott, N.Y., 116.
**Hits:** Frank McCormick, Cin., 209.
**TB:** Johnny Mize, St.L., 326.
**HR:** Mel Ott, N.Y., 36.
**RBI:** Joe Medwick, St.L., 122.
**SB:** Stan Hack, Chi., 16.
**Wins:** Bill Lee, Chi., 22.
**ERA:** Bill Lee, Chi., 2.66.
**CG:** Paul Derringer, Cin., 26.
**IP:** Paul Derringer, Cin., 307.
**SO:** Clay Bryant, Chi., 135.

**A.L. 20-game winners**

Red Ruffing, N.Y., 21-7
Bobo Newsom, St.L., 20-16

**N.L. 20-game winners**

Bill Lee, Chi., 22-9
Paul Derringer, Cin., 21-14

**A.L. 100 RBIs**

Jimmie Foxx, Bos., 175
Hank Greenberg, Det., 146
Joe DiMaggio, N.Y., 140
Rudy York, Det., 127
Harlond Clift, St.L., 118
Bill Dickey, N.Y., 115
Zeke Bonura, Wash., 114
Lou Gehrig, N.Y., 114
Bob Johnson, Phil., 113
Ken Keltner, Cle., 113
Jeff Heath, Cle., 112
Hal Trosky, Cle., 110
Charlie Gehringer, Det., 107
Pinky Higgins, Bos., 106

**N.L. 100 RBIs**

Joe Medwick, St.L., 122
Mel Ott, N.Y., 116
Johnny Rizzo, Pit., 111
Frank McCormick, Cin., 106
Johnny Mize, St.L., 102
Dolph Camilli, Brk., 100

**A.L. 40 homers**

Hank Greenberg, Det., 58
Jimmie Foxx, Bos., 50

**Most Valuable Player**

A.L.: Jimmie Foxx, 1B, Bos.
N.L.: Ernie Lombardi, C, Cin.

**Hall of Fame additions**

Grover Alexander, P, 1911-30
Alexander Cartwright, executive
Henry Chadwick, historian, executive

## ALL-STAR GAME

■ **Winner:** Cincinnati's Johnny Vander Meer, Chicago's Bill Lee and Pittsburgh's Mace Brown held the A.L. to seven hits as the N.L. claimed its second All-Star victory.

■ **Key inning:** The first, when the N.L. took a lead it never surrendered on Red Sox shortstop Joe Cronin's error.

■ **Memorable moment:** A seventh-inning sacrifice bunt by Brooklyn's Leo Durocher that resulted in two N.L. runs. Durocher circled the bases when third baseman Jimmie Foxx and right fielder Joe DiMaggio made wild throws on the play.

■ **Top guns:** Vander Meer (Reds), Lee (Cubs), Ernie Lombardi (Reds), N.L.; Cronin (Red Sox), A.L.

■ **MVP:** Vander Meer.

**Linescore**

July 6, at Cincinnati's Crosley Field
A.L. ............................0 0 0 0 0 0 0 0 1—1 7 4
N.L. ............................1 0 0 1 0 0 2 0 x—4 8 0
Gomez (Yankees), Allen (Indians) 4, Grove (Red Sox) 7; Vander Meer (Reds), Lee (Cubs) 4, Brown (Pirates) 7. W—Vander Meer. L—Gomez.

## WORLD SERIES

■ **Winner:** Three in a row. Another Series first for the vaunted Yankee machine of Joe McCarthy.

■ **Turning point:** Light-hitting Frankie Crosetti hit an eighth-inning Game 2 homer, helping the Yankees rally to a 6-3 victory over Chicago veteran Dizzy Dean.

■ **Memorable moment:** Lou Gehrig's fourth-game single — his last hit in World Series competition.

■ **Top guns:** Red Ruffing (2-0, 1.50 ERA), Bill Dickey (.400), Joe Gordon (.400, 6 RBIs), Crosetti (6 RBIs), Yankees; Stan Hack (.471), Cubs.

**Linescores**

**Game 1**—October 5, at Chicago
New York ................0 2 0 0 0 0 1 0 0—3 12 1
Chicago ..................0 0 1 0 0 0 0 0 0—1 9 1
Ruffing; Lee, Russell (9). W—Ruffing. L—Lee.

**Game 2**—October 6, at Chicago
New York ................0 2 0 0 0 0 0 2 2—6 7 2
Chicago ..................1 0 2 0 0 0 0 0 0—3 11 0
Gomez, Murphy (8); Dean, French (9). W—Gomez. L—Dean. HR—Crosetti, DiMaggio (N.Y.).

**Game 3**—October 8, at New York
Chicago ....................0 0 0 0 1 0 0 1 0—2 5 1
New York ..................0 0 0 0 2 2 0 1 x—5 7 2
Bryant, Russell (6), French (7); Pearson. W—Pearson. L—Bryant. HR—Dickey, Gordon (N.Y.); Marty (Chi.).

**Game 4**—October 9, at New York
Chicago ..................0 0 0 1 0 0 0 2 0—3 8 1
New York ................0 3 0 0 0 1 0 4 x—8 11 1
Lee, Root (4), Page (7), French (8), Carleton (8), Dean (8); Ruffing. W—Ruffing. L—Lee. HR—Henrich (N.Y.); O'Dea (Chi.).

# 1939

## FINAL STANDINGS

**American League**

| Team | W | L | Pct. | GB |
|---|---|---|---|---|
| New York | 106 | 45 | .702 | ... |
| Boston | 89 | 62 | .589 | 17 |
| Cleveland | 87 | 67 | .565 | 20.5 |
| Chicago | 85 | 69 | .552 | 22.5 |
| Detroit | 81 | 73 | .526 | 26.5 |
| Washington | 65 | 87 | .428 | 41.5 |
| Philadelphia | 55 | 97 | .362 | 51.5 |
| St. Louis | 43 | 111 | .279 | 64.5 |

**National League**

| Team | W | L | Pct. | GB |
|---|---|---|---|---|
| Cincinnati | 97 | 57 | .630 | ... |
| St. Louis | 92 | 61 | .601 | 4.5 |
| Brooklyn | 84 | 69 | .549 | 12.5 |
| Chicago | 84 | 70 | .545 | 13 |
| New York | 77 | 74 | .510 | 18.5 |
| Pittsburgh | 68 | 85 | .444 | 28.5 |
| Boston | 63 | 88 | .417 | 32.5 |
| Philadelphia | 45 | 106 | .298 | 50.5 |

## SIGNIFICANT EVENTS

- **June 12:** Baseball dignitaries, gathering in Cooperstown, N.Y., for a centennial celebration, dedicated the sport's new Hall of Fame museum and inducted its first four classes of Hall of Famers.
- **August 26:** Red Barber handled the play-by-play as experimental station W2XBS presented Major League baseball's first telecast, a game between the Dodgers and Reds at Ebbets Field.

## MEMORABLE MOMENTS

- **May 16:** The visiting Indians recorded a 10-inning 8-3 victory in the A.L.'s first night game at Philadelphia's Shibe Park.
- **June 27:** Brooklyn and Boston battled for 23 innings and more than five hours before settling for a 2-2 tie in a marathon game at Braves Field.
- **June 28:** The New York Yankees rocketed a doubleheader-record 13 home runs out of Shibe Park in a 23-2 and 10-0 sweep of the Athletics.
- **July 4:** Lou Gehrig, forced to end his incredible ironman streak at 2,130 games and retire because of a life-threatening disease, was honored in an emotional farewell at Yankee Stadium.
- **July 4:** Boston's Jim Tabor tied a Major League record with two grand slams during an 18-12 victory over the Athletics.

## LEADERS

**American League**

**BA:** Joe DiMaggio, N.Y., .381.
**Runs:** Red Rolfe, N.Y., 139.
**Hits:** Red Rolfe, N.Y., 213.
**TB:** Ted Williams, Bos., 344.
**HR:** Jimmie Foxx, Bos., 35.
**RBI:** Ted Williams, Bos., 145.
**SB:** George Case, Wash., 51.
**Wins:** Bob Feller, Cle., 24.
**ERA:** Lefty Grove, Bos., 2.54.
**CG:** Bob Feller, Cle.; Bobo Newsom, St.L.-Det., 24.
**IP:** Bob Feller, Cle., 296.2.
**SO:** Bob Feller, Cle., 246.

**National League**

**BA:** Johnny Mize, St.L., .349.
**Runs:** Billy Werber, Cin., 115.
**Hits:** Frank McCormick, Cin., 209.
**TB:** Johnny Mize, St.L., 353.
**HR:** Johnny Mize, St.L., 28.
**RBI:** Frank McCormick, Cin., 128.
**SB:** Stan Hack, Chi.; Lee Handley, Pit., 17.
**Wins:** Bucky Walters, Cin., 27.
**ERA:** Bucky Walters, Cin., 2.29.
**CG:** Bucky Walters, Cin., 31.
**IP:** Bucky Walters, Cin., 319.
**SO:** Claude Passeau, Phil.-Chi.; Bucky Walters, Cin., 137.

**A.L. 20-game winners**

Bob Feller, Cle., 24-9
Red Ruffing, N.Y., 21-7
Dutch Leonard, Wash., 20-8
Bobo Newsom, St.L.-Det., 20-11

**N.L. 20-game winners**

Bucky Walters, Cin., 27-11
Paul Derringer, Cin., 25-7
Curt Davis, St.L., 22-16
Luke Hamlin, Brk., 20-13

**A.L. 100 RBIs**

Ted Williams, Bos., 145
Joe DiMaggio, N.Y., 126
Bob Johnson, Phil., 114
Hank Greenberg, Det., 112
Joe Gordon, N.Y., 111
Gee Walker, Chi., 111
Joe Cronin, Bos., 107
Bill Dickey, N.Y., 105
Jimmie Foxx, Bos., 105
Hal Trosky, Cle., 104
George Selkirk, N.Y., 101

**N.L. 100 RBIs**

Frank McCormick, Cin., 128
Joe Medwick, St.L., 117
Johnny Mize, St.L., 108
Dolph Camilli, Brk., 104

**Most Valuable Player**

A.L.: Joe DiMaggio, OF, N.Y.
N.L.: Bucky Walters, P, Cin.

**Hall of Fame additions**

Cap Anson, 1B, 1876-97
Eddie Collins, 2B, 1906-30
Charles Comiskey, manager/exec.
Candy Cummings, P, 1872-77
Buck Ewing, C, 1880-97
Lou Gehrig, 1B, 1923-39
Willie Keeler, OF, 1892-1910
Hoss Radbourn, P, 1880-91
George Sisler, 1B, 1915-30
Al Spalding, pitcher/executive

## ALL-STAR GAME

- **Winner:** The A.L.'s Yankee-studded lineup posted a ho-hum 3-1 victory before 62,892 fans at Yankee Stadium.
- **Key inning:** The sixth, when the N.L. loaded the bases with one out. Indians fireballer Bob Feller was summoned and got Pittsburgh's Arky Vaughan to hit into a first-pitch double play. Feller allowed one hit the rest of the way.
- **Memorable moment:** Joe DiMaggio's fifth-inning home run, which touched off a celebration among ecstatic Yankee fans.
- **Top guns:** Tommy Bridges (Tigers), Feller (Indians), George Selkirk (Yankees), DiMaggio (Yankees), A.L.; Paul Derringer (Reds), Lonny Frey (Reds), N.L.
- **MVP:** Feller.

**Linescore**

July 11, at New York's Yankee Stadium
N.L. ......................0 0 1 000 000—1 7 1
A.L. ......................0 0 0 210 00x—3 6 1
Derringer (Reds), Lee (Cubs) 4, Fette (Braves) 7; Ruffing (Yankees), Bridges (Tigers) 4, Feller (Indians) 6. W—Bridges. L—Lee. HR—DiMaggio, A.L.

## WORLD SERIES

- **Winner:** Four in a row. The Yankees recorded their second straight sweep and 13th victory in 14 Series games.
- **Turning point:** Bill Dickey's ninth-inning single gave New York a 2-1 victory in Game 1 and momentum the Reds could not stop.
- **Memorable moment:** A strange Game 4 play that helped produce three 10th-inning Yankee runs. Joe DiMaggio singled to right with two runners aboard and circled the bases when Reds catcher Ernie Lombardi lay dazed after a home-plate collision with Yankee runner Charlie Keller. "Lombardi's Snooze."
- **Top guns:** Keller (.438, 3 HR, 6 RBIs), Dickey (2 HR, 5 RBIs), Yankees; Frank McCormick (.400), Reds.

**Linescores**

**Game 1**—October 4, at New York
Cincinnati 0 0 0 1 0 0 0 0 0 — 1 4 0
New York 0 0 0 0 1 0 0 0 1 — 2 6 0
Derringer; Ruffing. W—Ruffing. L—Derringer.

**Game 2**—October 5, at New York
Cincinnati 0 0 0 0 0 0 0 0 0 — 0 2 0
New York 0 0 3 1 0 0 0 0 x — 4 9 0
Walters; Pearson. W—Pearson. L—Walters. HR—Dahlgren (N.Y.).

**Game 3**—October 7, at Cincinnati
New York 2 0 2 0 3 0 0 0 0 — 7 5 1
Cincinnati 1 2 0 0 0 0 0 0 0 — 3 10 0
Gomez, Hadley (2); Thompson, Grissom (5), Moore (7). W—Hadley. L—Thompson. HR—Keller 2, DiMaggio, Dickey (N.Y.).

**Game 4**—October 8, at Cincinnati
New York 0 0 0 0 0 0 2 0 2 3—7 7 1
Cincinnati 0 0 0 0 0 0 3 1 0 0—4 11 4
Hildebrand, Sundra (5), Murphy (7); Derringer, Walters (8). W—Murphy. L—Walters. HR—Keller, Dickey (N.Y.).

# 1940

## FINAL STANDINGS

**American League**

| Team | W | L | Pct. | GB |
|---|---|---|---|---|
| Detroit | 90 | 64 | .584 | ... |
| Cleveland | 89 | 65 | .578 | 1 |
| New York | 88 | 66 | .571 | 2 |
| Boston | 82 | 72 | .532 | 8 |
| Chicago | 82 | 72 | .532 | 8 |
| St. Louis | 67 | 87 | .435 | 23 |
| Washington | 64 | 90 | .416 | 26 |
| Philadelphia | 54 | 100 | .351 | 36 |

**National League**

| Team | W | L | Pct. | GB |
|---|---|---|---|---|
| Cincinnati | 100 | 53 | .654 | ... |
| Brooklyn | 88 | 65 | .575 | 12 |
| St. Louis | 84 | 69 | .549 | 16 |
| Pittsburgh | 78 | 76 | .506 | 22.5 |
| Chicago | 75 | 79 | .487 | 25.5 |
| New York | 72 | 80 | .474 | 27.5 |
| Boston | 65 | 87 | .428 | 34.5 |
| Philadelphia | 50 | 103 | .327 | 50 |

## SIGNIFICANT EVENTS

- **January 14:** In the biggest free-agency ruling ever handed down, Commissioner Kenesaw Mountain Landis freed 91 members of the Tigers organization, citing player-movement coverup.
- **May 7:** The Dodgers became the first N.L. team to travel by air, flying in two planes from St. Louis to Chicago.
- **May 24, June 4:** The first night games were played at New York's Polo Grounds, St. Louis' Sportsman's Park and Pittsburgh's Forbes Field.
- **August 3:** Reds catcher Willard Hershberger, despondent over what he considered inadequate play, committed suicide in his Boston hotel room.

## MEMORABLE MOMENTS

- **April 16:** Cleveland's Bob Feller fired the first Opening Day no-hitter in baseball history, beating the White Sox, 1-0, at Chicago's Comiskey Park.
- **September 24:** Jimmie Foxx became baseball's second 500-homer man when he hit one of Boston's four sixth-inning blasts in a 16-8 victory over the Athletics.
- **September 27:** Detroit rookie Floyd Giebell ignored near-riotous Cleveland fans and outpitched Bob Feller in an A.L. pennant-clinching 2-0 Tigers victory.

## LEADERS

**American League**

**BA:** Joe DiMaggio, N.Y., .352.
**Runs:** Ted Williams, Bos., 134.
**Hits:** Doc Cramer, Bos.; Barney McCosky, Det.; Rip Radcliff, St.L., 200.
**TB:** Hank Greenberg, Det., 384.
**HR:** Hank Greenberg, Det., 41.
**RBI:** Hank Greenberg, Det., 150.
**SB:** George Case, Wash., 35.
**Wins:** Bob Feller, Cle., 27.
**ERA:** Bob Feller, Cle., 2.61.
**CG:** Bob Feller, Cle., 31.
**IP:** Bob Feller, Cle., 320.1.
**SO:** Bob Feller, Cle., 261.

**National League**

**BA:** Debs Garms, Pit., .355.
**Runs:** Arky Vaughan, Pit., 113.
**Hits:** Stan Hack, Chi.; Frank McCormick, Cin., 191.
**TB:** Johnny Mize, St.L., 368.
**HR:** Johnny Mize, St.L., 43.
**RBI:** Johnny Mize, St.L., 137.
**SB:** Lonny Frey, Cin., 22.
**Wins:** Bucky Walters, Cin., 22.
**ERA:** Bucky Walters, Cin., 2.48.
**CG:** Bucky Walters, Cin., 29.
**IP:** Bucky Walters, Cin., 305.
**SO:** Kirby Higbe, Phil., 137.

**A.L. 20-game winners**

Bob Feller, Cle., 27-11
Bobo Newsom, Det., 21-5

**N.L. 20-game winners**

Bucky Walters, Cin., 22-10
Paul Derringer, Cin., 20-12
Claude Passeau, Chi., 20-13

**A.L. 100 RBIs**

Hank Greenberg, Det., 150
Rudy York, Det., 134
Joe DiMaggio, N.Y., 133
Jimmie Foxx, Bos., 119
Ted Williams, Bos., 113
Joe Cronin, Bos, 111
Bobby Doerr, Bos., 105
Joe Gordon, N.Y., 103
Bob Johnson, Phil., 103
Lou Boudreau, Cle., 101

**N.L. 100 RBIs**

Johnny Mize, St.L., 137
Frank McCormick, Cin., 127
Maurice Van Robays, Pit., 116
Elbie Fletcher, Pit., 104
Babe Young, N.Y., 101

**A.L. 40 homers**

Hank Greenberg, Det., 41

**N.L. 40 homers**

Johnny Mize, St.L., 43

**Most Valuable Player**

A.L.: Hank Greenberg, OF, Det.
N.L.: Frank McCormick, 1B, Cin.

## ALL-STAR GAME

- **Winner:** Five N.L. pitchers shut down the A.L. on three hits and recorded the first shutout in All-Star Game history.
- **Key inning:** The first, when Boston's Max West connected with a Red Ruffing delivery for a three-run homer.
- **Memorable moment:** An inning after his home run, West crashed into the outfield wall while chasing a fly ball and had to be helped off the field.
- **Top guns:** Paul Derringer (Reds), Bucky Walters (Reds), Whitlow Wyatt (Dodgers), Larry French (Cubs), Carl Hubbell (Giants), West (Braves), Billy Herman (Cubs), N.L.; Luke Appling (White Sox), A.L.
- **MVP:** West.

**Linescore**

July 9, at St. Louis' Sportsman's Park
A.L. ............................0 0 0 000 000—0 3 1
N.L. ............................3 0 0 000 01x—4 7 0
Ruffing (Yankees), Newsom (Tigers) 4, Feller (Indians) 7; Derringer (Reds), Walters (Reds) 3, Wyatt (Dodgers) 5, French (Cubs) 7, Hubbell (Giants) 9. W—Derringer. L—Ruffing. HR—West, N.L.

## WORLD SERIES

- **Winner:** The Reds needed seven games to dispatch the Tigers and capture their first non-tainted World Series.
- **Turning point:** The Reds' Game 6 victory in which Bucky Walters pitched a 4-0 shutout and also hit a home run.
- **Memorable moment:** Reds pitcher Paul Derringer retiring Detroit in order in a tense ninth inning of Game 7.
- **Top guns:** Walters (2-0, 1.50 ERA), Jimmy Ripple (.333, 6 RBIs), Reds; Hank Greenberg (.357, 6 RBIs), Pinky Higgins (.333, 6 RBIs), Tigers.

**Linescores**

**Game 1**—October 2, at Cincinnati
Detroit ....................0 5 0 0 2 0 0 0 0—7 10 1
Cincinnati................0 0 0 1 0 0 0 1 0—2 8 3
Newsom; Derringer, Moore (2), Riddle (9). W—Newsom. L—Derringer. HR—Campbell (Det.).

**Game 2**—October 3, at Cincinnati
Detroit ......................2 0 0 0 0 1 0 0 0—3 3 1
Cincinnati..................0 2 2 1 0 0 0 0 x—5 9 0
Rowe, Gorsica (4); Walters. W—Walters. L—Rowe. HR—Ripple (Cin.).

**Game 3**—October 4, at Detroit
Cincinnati................1 0 0 0 0 0 0 1 2—4 10 1
Detroit ....................0 0 0 1 0 0 4 2 x—7 13 1
Turner, Moore (7), Beggs (8); Bridges. W—Bridges. L—Turner. HR—York, Higgins (Det.).

**Game 4**—October 5, at Detroit
Cincinnati................2 0 1 1 0 0 0 1 0—5 11 1
Detroit ....................0 0 1 0 0 1 0 0 0—2 5 1
Derringer; Trout, Smith (3), McKain (7). W—Derringer. L—Trout.

**Game 5**—October 6, at Detroit
Cincinnati................0 0 0 0 0 0 0 0 0—0 3 0
Detroit ....................0 0 3 4 0 0 0 1 x—8 13 0
Thompson, Moore (4), Vander Meer (5), Hutchings (8); Newsom. W—Newsom. L—Thompson. HR—Greenberg (Det.).

**Game 6**—October 7, at Cincinnati
Detroit ....................0 0 0 0 0 0 0 0 0—0 5 0
Cincinnati................2 0 0 0 0 1 0 1 x—4 10 2
Rowe, Gorsica (1), Hutchinson (8); Walters. W—Walters. L—Rowe. HR—Walters (Cin.).

**Game 7**—October 8, at Cincinnati
Detroit ....................0 0 1 0 0 0 0 0 0—1 7 0
Cincinnati................0 0 0 0 0 0 2 0 x—2 7 1
Newsom; Derringer. W—Derringer. L—Newsom.

# 1941

## FINAL STANDINGS

**American League**

| Team | W | L | Pct. | GB |
|---|---|---|---|---|
| New York | 101 | 53 | .656 | ... |
| Boston | 84 | 70 | .545 | 17 |
| Chicago | 77 | 77 | .500 | 24 |
| Cleveland | 75 | 79 | .487 | 26 |
| Detroit | 75 | 79 | .487 | 26 |
| St. Louis | 70 | 84 | .455 | 31 |
| Washington | 70 | 84 | .455 | 31 |
| Philadelphia | 64 | 90 | .416 | 37 |

**National League**

| Team | W | L | Pct. | GB |
|---|---|---|---|---|
| Brooklyn | 100 | 54 | .649 | ... |
| St. Louis | 97 | 56 | .634 | 2.5 |
| Cincinnati | 88 | 66 | .571 | 12 |
| Pittsburgh | 81 | 73 | .526 | 19 |
| New York | 74 | 79 | .484 | 25.5 |
| Chicago | 70 | 84 | .455 | 30 |
| Boston | 62 | 92 | .403 | 38 |
| Philadelphia | 43 | 111 | .279 | 57 |

## SIGNIFICANT EVENTS

■ **May 1:** Dodgers President Larry MacPhail submitted a patent application on the "Brooklyn Safety Cap," a hat lined with plastic to protect players from bean balls.

■ **May 7:** Detroit slugger Hank Greenberg reported for duty in the U.S. Army—one of many Major Leaguers who would leave baseball to fight in World War II.

■ **June 2:** Former Yankee great Lou Gehrig died at age 37 from the incurable disease that had forced his retirement two years earlier.

■ **May 28:** The Senators dropped a 6-5 decision to the Yankees in the first night game at Washington's Griffith Stadium.

## MEMORABLE MOMENTS

■ **July 17:** Yankee center fielder Joe DiMaggio's record 56-game hitting streak was stopped by pitchers Al Smith and Jim Bagby Jr. at Cleveland Stadium.

■ **July 25:** Boston's Lefty Grove joined the 300-victory club when he staggered to a 10-6 victory over Cleveland at Fenway Park.

■ **September 4:** The Yankees recorded the earliest pennant-clinching date in history when they defeated Boston, 6-3.

■ **November 27:** Yankee Joe DiMaggio won the A.L. MVP by a slim 37-point margin over Boston's Ted Williams, baseball's first .400 hitter (.406) since 1930.

## LEADERS

**American League**

**BA:** Ted Williams, Bos., .406.
**Runs:** Ted Williams, Bos., 135.
**Hits:** Cecil Travis, Wash., 218.
**TB:** Joe DiMaggio, N.Y., 348.
**HR:** Ted Williams, Bos., 37.
**RBI:** Joe DiMaggio, N.Y., 125.
**SB:** George Case, Wash., 33.
**Wins:** Bob Feller, Cle., 25.
**ERA:** Thornton Lee, Chi., 2.37.
**CG:** Thornton Lee, Chi., 30.
**IP:** Bob Feller, Cle., 343.
**SO:** Bob Feller, Cle., 260.

**National League**

**BA:** Pete Reiser, Brk., .343.
**Runs:** Pete Reiser, Brk., 117.
**Hits:** Stan Hack, Chi., 186.
**TB:** Pete Reiser, Brk., 299.
**HR:** Dolph Camilli, Brk., 34.
**RBI:** Dolph Camilli, Brk., 120.
**SB:** Danny Murtaugh, Phil., 18.
**Wins:** Kirby Higbe, Brk.; Whitlow Wyatt, Brk., 22.
**ERA:** Elmer Riddle, Cin., 2.24.
**CG:** Bucky Walters, Cin., 27.
**IP:** Bucky Walters, Cin., 302.
**SO:** Johnny Vander Meer, Cin., 202.

**A.L. 20-game winners**
Bob Feller, Cle., 25-13
Thornton Lee, Chi., 22-11

**N.L. 20-game winners**
Kirby Higbe, Brk., 22-9
Whitlow Wyatt, Brk., 22-10

**A.L. 100 RBIs**
Joe DiMaggio, N.Y., 125
Jeff Heath, Cle., 123
Charlie Keller, N.Y., 122
Ted Williams, Bos., 120
Rudy York, Det., 111
Bob Johnson, Phil., 107
Sam Chapman, Phil., 106
Jimmie Foxx, Bos., 105
Jim Tabor, Bos., 101
Cecil Travis, Wash., 101

**N.L. 100 RBIs**
Dolph Camilli, Brk., 120
Babe Young, N.Y., 104
Vince DiMaggio, Pit., 100
Johnny Mize, St.L., 100

**Most Valuable Player**
A.L.: Joe DiMaggio, OF, N.Y.
N.L.: Dolf Camilli, 1B, Brk.

## ALL-STAR GAME

■ **Winner:** The A.L. scored four ninth-inning runs and overcame a pair of home runs by Pittsburgh's Arky Vaughan for a 7-5 victory in the most exciting All-Star Game in the classic's nine-year history.

■ **Key inning:** The ninth, when the A.L. overcame a 5-3 deficit to claim its sixth victory in nine All-Star Games.

■ **Memorable moment:** A dramatic game-ending, three-run homer by Boston slugger Ted Williams with two out in the ninth. Williams connected off Chicago's Claude Passeau after the N.L. had botched what could have been a game-ending double play.

■ **Top guns:** Bob Feller (Indians), Williams (Red Sox), Lou Boudreau (Indians), A.L.; Vaughan (Pirates), N.L.

■ **MVP:** Williams.

### Linescore

July 8, at Detroit's Briggs Stadium
N.L. ..........................0 0 0 0 0 1 2 2 0—5 10 2
A.L. ..........................0 0 0 1 0 1 0 1 4—7 11 3
Wyatt (Dodgers), Derringer (Reds) 3, Walters (Reds) 5, Passeau (Cubs) 7; Feller (Indians), Lee (White Sox) 4, Hudson (Senators) 7, Smith (White Sox) 8. W—Smith. L—Passeau. HR—Vaughan 2, N.L.; Williams, A.L.

## WORLD SERIES

■ **Winner:** The Yankees returned to the top and won the first of many memorable meetings with the Dodgers.

■ **Turning point:** A two-out, ninth-inning passed ball by Dodgers catcher Mickey Owen that could have finished off a 4-3 Brooklyn victory in Game 4. Given new life, the Yanks scored four times and took a three-games-to-one Series lead.

■ **Memorable moment:** Owen's passed ball.

■ **Top guns:** Joe Gordon (.500, 5 RBIs), Charlie Keller (.389, 5 RBIs), Yankees.

### Linescores

**Game 1**—October 1, at New York
Brooklyn ....................0 0 0 0 1 0 1 0 0—2 6 0
New York....................0 1 0 1 0 1 0 0 x—3 6 1
Davis, Casey (6), Allen (7); Ruffing. W—Ruffing. L—Davis. HR—Gordon (N.Y.).

**Game 2**—October 2, at New York
Brooklyn ....................0 0 0 0 2 1 0 0 0—3 6 2
New York....................0 1 1 0 0 0 0 0 0—2 9 1
Wyatt; Chandler, Murphy (6). W—Wyatt. L—Chandler.

**Game 3**—October 4, at Brooklyn
New York....................0 0 0 0 0 0 0 2 0—2 8 0
Brooklyn ....................0 0 0 0 0 0 0 1 0—1 4 0
Russo; Fitzsimmons, Casey (8), French (8), Allen (9). W—Russo. L—Casey.

**Game 4**—October 5, at Brooklyn
New York..................1 0 0 2 0 0 0 0 4—7 12 0
Brooklyn ..................0 0 0 2 2 0 0 0 0—4 9 1
Donald, Breuer (5), Murphy (8); Higbe, French (4), Allen (5), Casey (5). W—Murphy. L—Casey. HR—Reiser (Brk.).

**Game 5**—October 6, at Brooklyn
New York....................0 2 0 0 1 0 0 0 0—3 6 0
Brooklyn ....................0 0 1 0 0 0 0 0 0—1 4 1
Bonham; Wyatt. W—Bonham. L—Wyatt. HR—Henrich (N.Y.).

# 1942

## FINAL STANDINGS

**American League**

| Team | W | L | Pct. | GB |
|---|---|---|---|---|
| New York | 103 | 51 | .669 | ... |
| Boston | 93 | 59 | .612 | 9 |
| St. Louis | 82 | 69 | .543 | 19.5 |
| Cleveland | 75 | 79 | .487 | 28 |
| Detroit | 73 | 81 | .474 | 30 |
| Chicago | 66 | 82 | .446 | 34 |
| Washington | 62 | 89 | .411 | 39.5 |
| Philadelphia | 55 | 99 | .357 | 48 |

**National League**

| Team | W | L | Pct. | GB |
|---|---|---|---|---|
| St. Louis | 106 | 48 | .688 | ... |
| Brooklyn | 104 | 50 | .675 | 2 |
| New York | 85 | 67 | .559 | 20 |
| Cincinnati | 76 | 76 | .500 | 29 |
| Pittsburgh | 66 | 81 | .449 | 36.5 |
| Chicago | 68 | 86 | .442 | 38 |
| Boston | 59 | 89 | .399 | 44 |
| Philadelphia | 42 | 109 | .278 | 62.5 |

## SIGNIFICANT EVENTS

■ **January 6:** Cleveland ace Bob Feller became the second high-profile star to leave baseball for the armed services when he enlisted in the Navy and reported for duty.

■ **January 16:** U.S. President Franklin D. Roosevelt gave baseball the "green light" to continue wartime play as a needed diversion for hard-working Americans.

■ **February 3:** In response to President Roosevelt's request for more night games, baseball owners softened restrictions and more than doubled the nocturnal schedule.

■ **October 29:** Cardinals Vice President Branch Rickey resigned to become president of the Dodgers.

■ **November 4:** Yankee second baseman Joe Gordon edged out Boston Triple Crown winner Ted Williams by 21 votes for A.L. MVP.

## MEMORABLE MOMENTS

■ **June 19:** Boston's Paul Waner became baseball's seventh 3,000-hit man when he singled off Pittsburgh's Rip Sewell.

■ **July 7:** One day after defeating the N.L. in the annual All-Star Game, the A.L. beat Mickey Cochrane's Armed Service All-Stars, 5-0, in a game to raise money for the war effort.

■ **September 27:** The Cardinals recorded a final-day sweep of the Cubs and finished with 106 victories, two more than the Dodgers in an amazing N.L. pennant battle.

## LEADERS

**American League**

**BA:** Ted Williams, Bos., .356.
**Runs:** Ted Williams, Bos., 141.
**Hits:** Johnny Pesky, Bos., 205.
**TB:** Ted Williams, Bos., 338.
**HR:** Ted Williams, Bos., 36.
**RBI:** Ted Williams, Bos., 137.
**SB:** George Case, Wash., 44.
**Wins:** Tex Hughson, Bos., 22.
**ERA:** Ted Lyons, Chi., 2.10.
**CG:** Tiny Bonham, N.Y.; Tex Hughson, Bos., 22.
**IP:** Tex Hughson, Bos., 281.
**SO:** Tex Hughson, Bos.;
Bobo Newsom, Wash., 113.

**National League**

**BA:** Ernie Lombardi, Cin., .330.
**Runs:** Mel Ott, N.Y., 118.
**Hits:** Enos Slaughter, St.L., 188.
**TB:** Enos Slaughter, St.L., 292.
**HR:** Mel Ott, N.Y., 30.
**RBI:** Johnny Mize, N.Y., 110.
**SB:** Pete Reiser, Brk., 20.
**Wins:** Mort Cooper, St.L., 22.
**ERA:** Mort Cooper, St.L., 1.78.
**CG:** Jim Tobin, Bos., 28.
**IP:** Jim Tobin, Bos., 287.2.
**SO:** Johnny Vander Meer, Cin., 186.

**A.L. 20-game winners**
Tex Hughson, Bos., 22-6
Tiny Bonham, N.Y., 21-5

**N.L. 20-game winners**
Mort Cooper, St.L., 22-7
Johnny Beazley, St.L., 21-6

**A.L. 100 RBIs**
Ted Williams, Bos., 137
Joe DiMaggio, N.Y., 114
Charlie Keller, N.Y., 108
Joe Gordon, N.Y., 103
Bobby Doerr, Bos., 102

**N.L. 100 RBIs**
Johnny Mize, N.Y., 110
Dolph Camilli, Brk., 109

**Most Valuable Player**
A.L.: Joe Gordon, 2B, N.Y.
N.L.: Mort Cooper, P, St.L.

**Hall of Fame addition**
Rogers Hornsby, 2B, 1915-37

## ALL-STAR GAME

■ **Winner:** Spud Chandler and Al Benton combined on a six-hitter and the A.L. made it 7 for 10 with a rainy-day victory in an All-Star Game played with war-depleted rosters.

■ **Key inning:** The first, when the A.L. scored all of its runs, one coming on a leadoff home run by Cleveland's Lou Boudreau.

■ **Memorable moment:** After New York's Tommy Henrich had followed Boudreau's home run with a double, Detroit slugger Rudy York lined an opposite-field shot that settled into the right-field bleachers for a two-run homer.

■ **Top guns:** Chandler (Yankees), Benton (Tigers), Boudreau (Indians), York (Tigers), A.L.; Johnny Vander Meer (Reds), Mickey Owen (Dodgers), N.L.

■ **MVP:** York.

### Linescore

July 7, at New York's Polo Grounds
A.L. ..........................3 0 0 0 0 0 0 0 0—3 7 0
N.L. ..........................0 0 0 0 0 0 0 1 0—1 6 1
Chandler (Yankees), Benton (Tigers) 5; M. Cooper (Cardinals), Vander Meer (Reds) 4, Passeau (Cubs) 7, Walters (Reds) 9. W—Chandler. L—M. Cooper. HR—Boudreau, York, A.L.; Owen, N.L.

## WORLD SERIES

■ **Winner:** After losing the opener, the Cardinals tamed the powerful Yankees with four consecutive victories.

■ **Turning point:** The ninth inning of Game 1. Although the Cardinals' four-run rally fell short in a 7-4 Yankee victory, they delivered a message that would become more clear as the Series progressed.

■ **Memorable moment:** A two-run, ninth-inning home run by Whitey Kurowski that gave St. Louis a Series-ending 4-2 victory.

■ **Top guns:** Johnny Beazley (2-0, 2.50 ERA), Kurowski (5 RBIs), Cardinals; Phil Rizzuto (.381), Yankees.

### Linescores

**Game 1**—September 30, at St. Louis
New York..................0 0 0 1 1 0 0 3 2—7 11 0
St. Louis ..................0 0 0 0 0 0 0 0 4—4 7 4
Ruffing, Chandler (9); M. Cooper, Gumbert (8), Lanier (9). W—Ruffing. L—M. Cooper.

**Game 2**—October 1, at St. Louis
New York..................0 0 0 0 0 0 0 3 0—3 10 2
St. Louis ..................2 0 0 0 0 0 1 1 x—4 6 0
Bonham; Beazley. W—Beazley. L—Bonham. HR—Keller (N.Y.).

**Game 3**—October 3, at New York
St. Louis ....................0 0 1 0 0 0 0 0 1—2 5 1
New York....................0 0 0 0 0 0 0 0 0—0 6 1
White; Chandler, Breuer (9), Turner (9). W—White. L—Chandler.

**Game 4**—October 4, at New York
St. Louis ..................0 0 0 6 0 0 2 0 1—9 12 1
New York..................1 0 0 0 0 5 0 0 0—6 10 1
M. Cooper, Gumbert (6), Pollet (6), Lanier (7); Borowy, Donald (4), Bonham (7). W—Lanier. L—Donald. HR—Keller (N.Y.).

**Game 5**—October 5, at New York
St. Louis ....................0 0 0 1 0 1 0 0 2—4 9 4
New York....................1 0 0 1 0 0 0 0 0—2 7 1
Beazley; Ruffing. W—Beazley. L—Ruffing. HR—Rizzuto (N.Y.); Slaughter, Kurowski (St.L.).

# 1943

## FINAL STANDINGS

**American League**

| Team | W | L | Pct. | GB |
|---|---|---|---|---|
| New York | 98 | 56 | .636 | ... |
| Washington | 84 | 69 | .549 | 13.5 |
| Cleveland | 82 | 71 | .536 | 15.5 |
| Chicago | 82 | 72 | .532 | 16 |
| Detroit | 78 | 76 | .506 | 20 |
| St. Louis | 72 | 80 | .474 | 25 |
| Boston | 68 | 84 | .447 | 29 |
| Philadelphia | 49 | 105 | .318 | 49 |

**National League**

| Team | W | L | Pct. | GB |
|---|---|---|---|---|
| St. Louis | 105 | 49 | .682 | ... |
| Cincinnati | 87 | 67 | .565 | 18 |
| Brooklyn | 81 | 72 | .529 | 23.5 |
| Pittsburgh | 80 | 74 | .519 | 25 |
| Chicago | 74 | 79 | .484 | 30.5 |
| Boston | 68 | 85 | .444 | 36.5 |
| Philadelphia | 64 | 90 | .416 | 41 |
| New York | 55 | 98 | .359 | 49.5 |

## SIGNIFICANT EVENTS

■ **January 5:** In concessions to the war and travel restrictions, Major League owners agreed to open the season a week late and to conduct spring training in northern cities.

■ **February 28:** The Texas League suspended operations, cutting the minor league ranks to nine circuits—down from the 41 that operated in 1941.

■ **April 20:** Boston Braves manager Casey Stengel suffered a broken leg when he was hit by a Boston taxicab—an injury that would sideline him for much of the season.

■ **May 8:** Baseball's two-week "dead ball" era came to an end when A.G. Spalding's "war ball" was replaced with a more lively ball.

## MEMORABLE MOMENTS

■ **June 4:** Cardinals ace Mort Cooper stopped Philadelphia 5-0 at Sportsman's Park—his second consecutive one-hit shutout.

■ **June 17:** Boston player-manager Joe Cronin made history when he blasted three-run pinch-hit homers in both ends of a doubleheader against Philadelphia at Fenway Park.

■ **August 24:** The Athletics ended their A.L. record-tying losing streak at 20 with an 8-1 victory in the second game of a doubleheader at Chicago.

## LEADERS

**American League**

**BA:** Luke Appling, Chi., .328.
**Runs:** George Case, Wash., 102.
**Hits:** Dick Wakefield, Det., 200.
**TB:** Rudy York, Det., 301.
**HR:** Rudy York, Det., 34.
**RBI:** Rudy York, Det., 118.
**SB:** George Case, Wash., 61.
**Wins:** Spud Chandler, N.Y.; Dizzy Trout, Det., 20.
**ERA:** Spud Chandler, N.Y., 1.64.
**CG:** Spud Chandler, N.Y.; Tex Hughson, Bos., 20.
**IP:** Jim Bagby, Cle., 273.
**SO:** Allie Reynolds, Cle., 151.

**National League**

**BA:** Stan Musial, St.L., .357.
**Runs:** Arky Vaughan, Brk., 112.
**Hits:** Stan Musial, St.L., 220.
**TB:** Stan Musial, St.L., 347.
**HR:** Bill Nicholson, Chi., 29.
**RBI:** Bill Nicholson, Chi., 128.
**SB:** Arky Vaughan, Brk., 20.
**Wins:** Mort Cooper, St.L.; Elmer Riddle, Cin.; Rip Sewell, Pit., 21.
**ERA:** Max Lanier, St.L., 1.90.
**CG:** Rip Sewell, Pit., 25.
**IP:** Al Javery, Bos., 303.
**SO:** Johnny Vander Meer, Cin., 174.

**A.L. 20-game winners**
Spud Chandler, N.Y., 20-4
Dizzy Trout, Det., 20-12

**N.L. 20-game winners**
Mort Cooper, St.L., 21-8
Rip Sewell, Pit., 21-9
Elmer Riddle, Cin., 21-11

**A.L. 100 RBIs**
Rudy York, Det., 118
Nick Etten, N.Y., 107

**N.L. 100 RBIs**
Bill Nicholson, Chi., 128
Bob Elliott, Pit., 101
Billy Herman, Brk., 100

**Most Valuable Player**
A.L.: Spud Chandler, P, N.Y.
N.L.: Stan Musial, OF, St.L.

## ALL-STAR GAME

■ **Winner:** A.L. manager Joe McCarthy, tired of complaints that he favored his own Yankee players in All-Star competition, guided his team to a Yankeeless victory.

■ **Key inning:** The second, when Boston's Bobby Doerr belted a three-run homer that gave the A.L. a lead it never relinquished.

■ **Memorable moments:** A seventh-inning run-scoring triple and a ninth-inning home run by Pittsburgh's Vince DiMaggio, brother of Yankee great Joe DiMaggio.

■ **Top guns:** Hal Newhouser (Tigers), Doerr (Red Sox), Dick Wakefield (Tigers), A.L.; V. DiMaggio (Pirates), Stan Hack (Cubs), N.L.

■ **MVP:** Doerr.

### Linescore

July 13, at Philadelphia's Shibe Park
N.L.........................1 0 0 0 0 0 1 0 1—3 10 3
A.L.........................0 3 1 0 1 0 0 0 x—5 8 1
M. Cooper (Cardinals), Vander Meer (Reds) 3, Sewell (Pirates) 6, Javery (Braves) 7; Leonard (Senators), Newhouser (Tigers) 4, Hughson (Red Sox) 7. W—Leonard. L—M. Cooper. HR—Doerr, A.L.; DiMaggio, N.L.

## WORLD SERIES

■ **Winner:** Joe McCarthy managed his seventh and final Series champion as the Yankees avenged their 1942 loss to the Cardinals.

■ **Turning point:** Billy Johnson's bases-loaded triple that keyed a five-run eighth inning and helped the Yankees to a 6-2 victory in Game 3.

■ **Memorable moment:** Bill Dickey's two-run, sixth-inning home run in New York's 2-0 Series-ending victory.

■ **Top guns:** Spud Chandler (2-0, 0.50 ERA), Dickey (4 RBIs), Yankees; Marty Marion (.357), Cardinals.

### Linescores

**Game 1**—October 5, at New York
St. Louis...................0 1 0 0 1 0 0 0 0—2 7 2
New York .................0 0 0 2 0 2 0 0 x—4 8 2
Lanier, Brecheen (8); Chandler. W—Chandler. L—Lanier. HR—Gordon (N.Y.).

**Game 2**—October 6, at New York
St. Louis...................0 0 1 3 0 0 0 0 0—4 7 2
New York .................0 0 0 1 0 0 0 0 2—3 6 0
M. Cooper; Bonham, Murphy (9). W—M. Cooper. L—Bonham. HR—Marion, Sanders (St.L.).

**Game 3**—October 7, at New York
St. Louis...................0 0 0 2 0 0 0 0 0—2 6 4
New York .................0 0 0 0 0 1 0 5 x—6 8 0
Brazle, Krist (8), Brecheen (8); Borowy, Murphy (9). W—Borowy. L—Brazle.

**Game 4**—October 10, at St. Louis
New York .................0 0 0 1 0 0 0 1 0—2 6 2
St. Louis...................0 0 0 0 0 0 1 0 0—1 7 1
Russo; Lanier, Brecheen (8). W—Russo. L—Brecheen.

**Game 5**—October 11, at St. Louis
New York ...............0 0 0 0 0 2 0 0 0—2 7 1
St. Louis.................0 0 0 0 0 0 0 0 0—0 10 1
Chandler; M. Cooper, Lanier (8), Dickson (9). W—Chandler. L—M. Cooper. HR—Dickey (N.Y.).

# 1944

## FINAL STANDINGS

**American League**

| Team | W | L | Pct. | GB |
|---|---|---|---|---|
| St. Louis | 89 | 65 | .578 | ... |
| Detroit | 88 | 66 | .571 | 1 |
| New York | 83 | 71 | .539 | 6 |
| Boston | 77 | 77 | .500 | 12 |
| Cleveland | 72 | 82 | .468 | 17 |
| Philadelphia | 72 | 82 | .468 | 17 |
| Chicago | 71 | 83 | .461 | 18 |
| Washington | 64 | 90 | .416 | 25 |

**National League**

| Team | W | L | Pct. | GB |
|---|---|---|---|---|
| St. Louis | 105 | 49 | .682 | ... |
| Pittsburgh | 90 | 63 | .588 | 14.5 |
| Cincinnati | 89 | 65 | .578 | 16 |
| Chicago | 75 | 79 | .487 | 30 |
| New York | 67 | 87 | .435 | 38 |
| Boston | 65 | 89 | .422 | 40 |
| Brooklyn | 63 | 91 | .409 | 42 |
| Philadelphia | 61 | 92 | .399 | 43.5 |

## SIGNIFICANT EVENTS

■ **June 6:** Baseball canceled its schedule as Americans braced for D-day—the invasion of Europe on the beaches of Normandy, France.

■ **October:** Major League baseball raised $329,555 for the National War Fund Inc. and the American Red Cross through its 16 war relief games.

■ **November 25:** Kenesaw Mountain Landis, baseball's first commissioner, died of a heart attack at age 78.

## MEMORABLE MOMENTS

■ **April 30:** Giants first baseman Phil Weintraub drove in 11 runs, one short of the Major League record, in a 26-8 victory over the Dodgers.

■ **June 10:** Reds pitcher Joe Nuxhall, at 15 years and 10 months, became the youngest player to compete in a Major League game when he worked 2/3 of an inning against the Cardinals.

■ **August 10:** Braves righthander Red Barrett threw a record-low 58 pitches in a 2-0 victory over the Reds.

■ **October 1:** The Browns recorded a final-day 5-2 victory over the Yankees and clinched the first pennant of their frustrating 44-year history.

## LEADERS

**American League**

**BA:** Lou Boudreau, Cle., .327.
**Runs:** Snuffy Stirnweiss, N.Y., 125.
**Hits:** Snuffy Stirnweiss, N.Y., 205.
**TB:** Johnny Lindell, N.Y., 297.
**HR:** Nick Etten, N.Y., 22.
**RBI:** Vern Stephens, St.L., 109.
**SB:** Snuffy Stirnweiss, N.Y., 55.
**Wins:** Hal Newhouser, Det., 29.
**ERA:** Dizzy Trout, Det., 2.12.
**CG:** Dizzy Trout, Det., 33.
**IP:** Dizzy Trout, Det., 352.1.
**SO:** Hal Newhouser, Det., 187.

**National League**

**BA:** Dixie Walker, Brk., .357.
**Runs:** Bill Nicholson, Chi., 116.
**Hits:** Phil Cavarretta, Chi.; Stan Musial, St.L., 197.
**TB:** Bill Nicholson, Chi., 317.
**HR:** Bill Nicholson, Chi., 33.
**RBI:** Bill Nicholson, Chi., 122.
**SB:** Johnny Barrett, Pit., 28.
**Wins:** Bucky Walters, Cin., 23.
**ERA:** Ed Heusser, Cin., 2.38.
**CG:** Jim Tobin, Bos., 28.
**IP:** Bill Voiselle, N.Y., 312.2.
**SO:** Bill Voiselle, N.Y., 161.

**A.L. 20-game winners**
Hal Newhouser, Det., 29-9
Dizzy Trout, Det., 27-14

**N.L. 20-game winners**
Bucky Walters, Cin., 23-8
Mort Cooper, St.L., 22-7
Rip Sewell, Pit., 21-12
Bill Voiselle, N.Y., 21-16

**A.L. 100 RBIs**
Vern Stephens, St.L., 109
Bob Johnson, Bos., 106
Johnny Lindell, N.Y., 103
Stan Spence, Wash., 100

**N.L. 100 RBIs**
Bill Nicholson, Chi., 122
Bob Elliott, Pit., 108
Ron Northey, Phil., 104
Frank McCormick, Cin., 102
Ray Sanders, St.L., 102
Babe Dahlgren, Pit., 101

**Most Valuable Player**
A.L.: Hal Newhouser, P, Det.
N.L.: Marty Marion, SS, St.L.

**Hall of Fame addition**
Kenesaw M. Landis, commissioner

## ALL-STAR GAME

■ **Winner:** With many of baseball's stars serving their country in World War II, four pitchers held the A.L. to six hits and the N.L. claimed a 7-1 victory.

■ **Key inning:** The fifth, when the N.L. scored four times on RBI hits by Chicago's Bill Nicholson, St. Louis' Walker Cooper and Dodgers' Augie Galan and Dixie Walker.

■ **Memorable moment:** Pittsburgh's Rip Sewell threw two "ephus pitches" to Browns first baseman George McQuinn, who took one for a called strike and bunted the other for an out.

■ **Top guns:** Sewell (Pirates), Phil Cavarretta (Cubs), Cooper (Cardinals), Walker (Dodgers), Whitey Kurowski (Cardinals), Nicholson (Cubs), N.L.; Hank Borowy (Yankees), A.L.

■ **MVP:** Sewell.

### Linescore

July 11, at Pittsburgh's Forbes Field
A.L.........................0 1 0 0 0 0 0 0 0—1 6 3
N.L.........................0 0 0 0 4 0 2 1 x—7 12 1
Borowy (Yankees), Hughson (Red Sox) 4, Muncrief (Browns) 5, Newhouser (Tigers) 7, Newsom (Athletics) 8; Walters (Reds), Raffensberger (Phillies) 4, Sewell (Pirates) 6, Tobin (Braves) 9. W—Raffensberger. L—Hughson.

## WORLD SERIES

■ **Winner:** Playing with a war-depleted roster, the Cardinals won the all-Sportsman's Park Series and the Battle of St. Louis.

■ **Turning point:** Game 5 homers by Ray Sanders and Danny Litwhiler that gave the Cardinals a 2-0 victory and a three-games-to-two edge.

■ **Memorable moment:** A two-run George McQuinn homer that gave the long-suffering Browns a 2-1 victory in their first-ever Series game.

■ **Top guns:** Emil Verban (.412), Walker Cooper (.318), Cardinals; McQuinn (.438, 5 RBIs), Browns.

### Linescores

**Game 1**—October 4, at St. Louis
Browns.......................0 0 0 2 0 0 0 0 0—2 2 0
Cardinals....................0 0 0 0 0 0 0 0 1—1 7 0
Galehouse; M. Cooper, Donnelly (8). W—Galehouse. L—M. Cooper. HR—McQuinn (Browns).

**Game 2**—October 5, at St. Louis
Browns............0 0 0 0 0 0 2 0 0 0 0—2 7 4
Cardinals..........0 0 1 1 0 0 0 0 0 0 1—3 7 0
Potter, Muncrief (7); Lanier, Donnelly (8). W—Donnelly. L—Muncrief.

**Game 3**—October 6, at St. Louis
Cardinals...................1 0 0 0 0 0 1 0 0—2 7 0
Browns.......................0 0 4 0 0 0 2 0 x—6 8 2
Wilks, Schmidt (3), Jurisich (7), Byerly (7); Kramer. W—Kramer. L—Wilks.

**Game 4**—October 7, at St. Louis
Cardinals.................2 0 2 0 0 1 0 0 0—5 12 0
Browns.....................0 0 0 0 0 0 0 1 0—1 9 1
Brecheen; Jakucki, Hollingsworth (4), Shirley (8). W—Brecheen. L—Jakucki. HR—Musial (Cardinals).

**Game 5**—October 8, at St. Louis
Cardinals...................0 0 0 0 0 1 0 1 0—2 6 1
Browns.......................0 0 0 0 0 0 0 0 0—0 7 1
M. Cooper; Galehouse. W—M. Cooper. L—Galehouse. HR—Sanders, Litwhiler (Cardinals).

**Game 6**—October 9, at St. Louis
Browns.....................0 1 0 0 0 0 0 0 0—1 3 2
Cardinals.................0 0 0 3 0 0 0 0 0—3 10 0
Potter, Muncrief (4), Kramer (7); Lanier, Wilks (6). W—Lanier. L—Potter.

# 1945

## FINAL STANDINGS

**American League**

| Team | W | L | Pct. | GB |
|---|---|---|---|---|
| Detroit | 88 | 65 | .575 | ... |
| Washington | 87 | 67 | .565 | 1.5 |
| St. Louis | 81 | 70 | .536 | 6 |
| New York | 81 | 71 | .533 | 6.5 |
| Cleveland | 73 | 72 | .503 | 11 |
| Chicago | 71 | 78 | .477 | 15 |
| Boston | 71 | 83 | .461 | 17.5 |
| Philadelphia | 52 | 98 | .347 | 34.5 |

**National League**

| Team | W | L | Pct. | GB |
|---|---|---|---|---|
| Chicago | 98 | 56 | .636 | ... |
| St. Louis | 95 | 59 | .617 | 3 |
| Brooklyn | 87 | 67 | .565 | 11 |
| Pittsburgh | 82 | 72 | .532 | 16 |
| New York | 78 | 74 | .513 | 19 |
| Boston | 67 | 85 | .441 | 30 |
| Cincinnati | 61 | 93 | .396 | 37 |
| Philadelphia | 46 | 108 | .299 | 52 |

## SIGNIFICANT EVENTS

■ **January 26:** The Yankees were sold to the triumvirate of Larry MacPhail, Dan Topping and Del Webb for $2.8 million.

■ **April 24:** Kentucky Senator Albert B. (Happy) Chandler was the unanimous selection as baseball's second commissioner.

■ **July 10:** The All-Star Game, a baseball fixture since 1933, was not played because of wartime travel restrictions.

■ **October 23:** Brooklyn President Branch Rickey signed Jackie Robinson to a minor league contract, giving Organized Baseball its first black player since the turn of the century.

## MEMORABLE MOMENTS

■ **April 18:** One-armed St. Louis outfielder Pete Gray collected one hit in his Major League debut—a 7-1 Browns victory over Detroit.

■ **July 12:** Boston's Tommy Holmes failed to get a hit during a 6-1 loss to the Cubs, ending his modern-era N.L.-record 37-game hitting streak.

■ **August 1:** Giants slugger Mel Ott became baseball's third 500-homer man when he connected off Boston's Johnny Hutchings.

■ **September 9:** Philadelphia's Dick Fowler, released from military duty nine days earlier, pitched a 1-0 no-hitter against the Browns in his first post-war appearance.

## LEADERS

**American League**

**BA:** Snuffy Stirnweiss, N.Y., .309.
**Runs:** Snuffy Stirnweiss, N.Y., 107.
**Hits:** Snuffy Stirnweiss, N.Y., 195.
**TB:** Snuffy Stirnweiss, N.Y., 301.
**HR:** Vern Stephens, St.L., 24.
**RBI:** Nick Etten, N.Y., 111.
**SB:** Snuffy Stirnweiss, N.Y., 33.
**Wins:** Hal Newhouser, Det., 25.
**ERA:** Hal Newhouser, Det., 1.81.
**CG:** Hal Newhouser, Det., 29.
**IP:** Hal Newhouser, Det., 313.1.
**SO:** Hal Newhouser, Det., 212.

**National League**

**BA:** Phil Cavarretta, Chi., .355.
**Runs:** Eddie Stanky, Brk., 128.
**Hits:** Tommy Holmes, Bos., 224.
**TB:** Tommy Holmes, Bos., 367.
**HR:** Tommy Holmes, Bos., 28.
**RBI:** Dixie Walker, Brk., 124.
**SB:** Red Schoendienst, St.L., 26.
**Wins:** Red Barrett, Bos.-St.L., 23.
**ERA:** Ray Prim, Chi., 2.40.
**CG:** Red Barrett, Bos.-St.L., 24.
**IP:** Red Barrett, Bos.-St.L., 284.2.
**SO:** Preacher Roe, Pit., 148.

**A.L. 20-game winners**
Hal Newhouser, Det., 25-9
Boo Ferriss, Bos., 21-10
Roger Wolff, Wash., 20-10

**N.L. 20-game winners**
Red Barrett, Bos.-St.L., 23-12
Hank Wyse, Chi., 22-10

**A.L./N.L. 20-game winner**
Hank Borowy, N.Y.-Chi., 21

**A.L. 100 RBIs**
Nick Etten, N.Y., 111

**N.L. 100 RBIs**
Dixie Walker, Brk., 124
Tommy Holmes, Bos., 117
Luis Olmo, Brk., 110
Andy Pafko, Chi., 110
Buster Adams, Phil.-St.L., 109
Bob Elliott, Pit., 108
Whitey Kurowski, St.L., 102

**Most Valuable Player**
A.L.: Hal Newhouser, P, Det.
N.L.: Phil Cavarretta, 1B, Chi.

**Hall of Fame additions**
Roger Bresnahan, C, 1897-1915
Dan Brouthers, 1B, 1879-1904
Fred Clarke, OF, 1894-1915
Jimmy Collins, 3B, 1895-1908
Ed Delahanty, OF, 1888-1903
Hugh Duffy, OF, 1888-1906
Hugh Jennings, SS, 1891-1918
Mike (King) Kelly, C, 1878-93
Jim O'Rourke, OF, 1876-1904
Wilbert Robinson, manager

## ALL-STAR GAME

The scheduled 13th All-Star Game was called off because of wartime travel restrictions.

## WORLD SERIES

■ **Winner:** The Tigers won only their second Series and the Cubs lost their seventh straight in the last of the wartime fall classics.

■ **Turning point:** A four-run, sixth-inning explosion that broke a 1-1 tie and helped the Tigers to an 8-4 victory in the pivotal fifth game.

■ **Memorable moment:** Stan Hack's 12th-inning bad-hop double that gave the Cubs an 8-7 victory in a must-win sixth game.

■ **Top guns:** Roger Cramer (.379), Hank Greenberg (.304, 2 HR, 7 RBIs), Tigers; Phil Cavarretta (.423, 5 RBIs), Cubs.

### Linescores

**Game 1**—October 3, at Detroit
Chicago....................4 0 3 0 0 0 2 0 0—9 13 0
Detroit......................0 0 0 0 0 0 0 0 0—0 6 0
Borowy; Newhouser, Benton (3), Tobin (5), Mueller (8). W—Borowy. L—Newhouser. HR—Cavarretta (Chi.).

**Game 2**—October 4, at Detroit
Chicago......................0 0 0 1 0 0 0 0 0—1 7 0
Detroit.......................0 0 0 0 4 0 0 0 x—4 7 0
Wyse, Erickson (7); Trucks. W—Trucks. L—Wyse. HR—Greenberg (Det.).

**Game 3**—October 5, at Detroit
Chicago......................0 0 0 2 0 0 1 0 0—3 8 0
Detroit.......................0 0 0 0 0 0 0 0 0—0 1 2
Passeau; Overmire, Benton (7). W—Passeau. L—Overmire.

**Game 4**—October 6, at Chicago
Detroit.......................0 0 0 4 0 0 0 0 0—4 7 1
Chicago......................0 0 0 0 0 1 0 0 0—1 5 1
Trout; Prim, Derringer (4), Vandenberg (6), Erickson (8). W—Trout. L—Prim.

**Game 5**—October 7, at Chicago
Detroit.......................0 0 1 0 0 4 1 0 2—8 11 0
Chicago......................0 0 1 0 0 0 2 0 1—4 7 2
Newhouser; Borowy, Vandenberg (6), Chipman (6), Derringer (7), Erickson (9). W—Newhouser. L—Borowy.

**Game 6**—October 8, at Chicago
Detroit........0 1 0 0 0 0 2 4 0 0 0 0—7 13 1
Chicago......0 0 0 0 4 1 2 0 0 0 0 1—8 15 3
Trucks, Caster (5), Bridges (6), Benton (7), Trout (8); Passeau, Wyse (7), Prim (8), Borowy (9). W—Borowy. L—Trout. HR—Greenberg (Det.).

**Game 7**—October 10, at Chicago
Detroit.......................5 1 0 0 0 0 1 2 0—9 9 1
Chicago......................1 0 0 1 0 0 0 1 0—3 10 0
Newhouser; Borowy, Derringer (1), Vandenberg (2), Erickson (6), Passeau (8), Wyse (9). W—Newhouser. L—Borowy.

# 1946

## FINAL STANDINGS

**American League**

| Team | W | L | Pct. | GB |
|---|---|---|---|---|
| Boston | 104 | 50 | .675 | ... |
| Detroit | 92 | 62 | .597 | 12 |
| New York | 87 | 67 | .565 | 17 |
| Washington | 76 | 78 | .494 | 28 |
| Chicago | 74 | 80 | .481 | 30 |
| Cleveland | 68 | 86 | .442 | 36 |
| St. Louis | 66 | 88 | .429 | 38 |
| Philadelphia | 49 | 105 | .318 | 55 |

**National League**

| Team | W | L | Pct. | GB |
|---|---|---|---|---|
| *St. Louis | 98 | 58 | .628 | ... |
| Brooklyn | 96 | 60 | .615 | 2 |
| Chicago | 82 | 71 | .536 | 14.5 |
| Boston | 81 | 72 | .529 | 15.5 |
| Philadelphia | 69 | 85 | .448 | 28 |
| Cincinnati | 67 | 87 | .435 | 30 |
| Pittsburgh | 63 | 91 | .409 | 34 |
| New York | 61 | 93 | .396 | 36 |

*Defeated Brooklyn 2-0 in pennant playoff.

## SIGNIFICANT EVENTS

■ **February 19:** Giants outfielder Danny Gardella jumped to the outlaw Mexican League, the first in a group of Major Leaguers who would fall victim to big-money inducements.

■ **April 18:** Jackie Robinson broke Organized Baseball's color barrier with a four-hit debut for the International League's Montreal Royals.

■ **September 16:** Among the benefits awarded players in a history-making New York meeting were a $5,000 minimum salary, upgraded hospital and medical expenses and salary-cut guarantees.

■ **December 6:** Baseball owners decided to return the All-Star vote to the fans.

## MEMORABLE MOMENTS

■ **July 27:** Boston's Rudy York belted a record-tying two grand slams and drove in 10 runs in a 13-6 victory over the Browns.

■ **October 3:** The Cardinals capped their two-game sweep of the Dodgers with an 8-4 victory in baseball's first pennant playoff.

## LEADERS

**American League**

**BA:** Mickey Vernon, Wash., .353.
**Runs:** Ted Williams, Bos., 142.
**Hits:** Johnny Pesky, Bos., 208.
**TB:** Ted Williams, Bos., 343.
**HR:** Hank Greenberg, Det., 44.
**RBI:** Hank Greenberg, Det., 127.
**SB:** George Case, Cle., 28.
**Wins:** Bob Feller, Cle.; Hal Newhouser, Det., 26.
**ERA:** Hal Newhouser, Det., 1.94.
**CG:** Bob Feller, Cle., 36.
**IP:** Bob Feller, Cle., 371.1.
**SO:** Bob Feller, Cle., 348.

**National League**

**BA:** Stan Musial, St.L., .365.
**Runs:** Stan Musial, St.L., 124.
**Hits:** Stan Musial, St.L., 228.
**TB:** Stan Musial, St.L., 366.
**HR:** Ralph Kiner, Pit., 23.
**RBI:** Enos Slaughter, St.L., 130.
**SB:** Pete Reiser, Brk., 34.
**Wins:** Howie Pollet, St.L., 21.
**ERA:** Howie Pollet, St.L., 2.10.
**CG:** Johnny Sain, Bos., 24.
**IP:** Howie Pollet, St.L., 266.
**SO:** Johnny Schmitz, Chi., 135.

**A.L. 20-game winners**
Hal Newhouser, Det., 26-9
Bob Feller, Cle., 26-15
Boo Ferriss, Bos., 25-6
Spud Chandler, N.Y., 20-8
Tex Hughson, Bos., 20-11

**N.L. 20-game winners**
Howie Pollet, St.L., 21-10
Johnny Sain, Bos., 20-14

**A.L. 100 RBIs**
Hank Greenberg, Det., 127
Ted Williams, Bos., 123
Rudy York, Bos., 119
Bobby Doerr, Bos., 116
Charlie Keller, N.Y., 101

**N.L. 100 RBIs**
Enos Slaughter, St.L., 130
Dixie Walker, Brk., 116
Stan Musial, St.L., 103

**A.L. 40 homers**
Hank Greenberg, Det., 44

**Most Valuable Player**
A.L.: Ted Williams, OF, Bos.
N.L.: Stan Musial, 1B, St.L.

**Hall of Fame additions**
Jesse Burkett, OF, 1890-1905
Frank Chance, 1B, 1898-1914
Jack Chesbro, P, 1899-1909
Johnny Evers, 2B, 1902-29
Clark Griffith, P/Man./Exec.
Tommy McCarthy, OF, 1884-96
Joe McGinnity, P, 1899-1908
Eddie Plank, P, 1901-17
Joe Tinker, SS, 1902-16
Rube Waddell, P, 1897-1910
Ed Walsh, P, 1904-17

## ALL-STAR GAME

■ **Winner:** War hero Ted Williams rewarded his home fans with a four-hit, two-homer, five-RBI performance and three pitchers — Cleveland's Bob Feller, Detroit's Hal Newhouser and St. Louis' Jack Kramer — combined on a three-hitter that produced a 12-0 victory.

■ **Key inning:** The first, when Yankee Charlie Keller hit a two-run homer that ignited the A.L. charge.

■ **Memorable moment:** Williams' three-run, eighth-inning homer off Rip Sewell's famed "ephus pitch"—one of the All-Star Game's classic moments.

■ **Top guns:** Feller (Indians), Newhouser (Tigers), Kramer (Browns), Williams (Red Sox), Keller (Yankees), Vern Stephens (Browns), A.L.

■ **MVP:** Williams.

### Linescore

July 9, at Boston's Fenway Park
N.L.........................0 0 0 0 0 0 0 0 0— 0 3 0
A.L. .......................2 0 0 1 3 0 2 4 x—12 14 1
Passeau (Cubs), Higbe (Dodgers) 4, Blackwell (Reds) 5, Sewell (Pirates) 8; Feller (Indians), Newhouser (Tigers) 4, Kramer (Browns) 7. W—Feller. L—Passeau. HR—Keller, Williams 2, A.L.

## WORLD SERIES

■ **Winner:** The Cardinals celebrated the end of wartime baseball with seven-game victory over the Red Sox.

■ **Turning point:** Harry Brecheen's seven-hit pitching gave the Cardinals a 4-1 victory in a must-win sixth game.

■ **Memorable moments:** The eighth inning of Game 7, when Enos Slaughter made his game-winning "Mad Dash" around the bases on Harry Walker's double. The ninth inning of Game 7, when Brecheen pitched out of a two-on, nobody out jam to secure the victory.

■ **Top guns:** Brecheen (3-0, 0.45 ERA), Slaughter (.320), Walker (.412, 6 RBIs), Cardinals; Bobby Doerr (.409), Rudy York (2 HR, 5 RBIs), Red Sox.

### Linescores

**Game 1**—October 6, at St. Louis
Boston ................0 1 0 0 0 0 0 0 1 1—3 9 2
St. Louis .............0 0 0 0 0 1 0 1 0 0—2 7 0
Hughson, Johnson (9); Pollet. W—Johnson. L—Pollet. HR—York (Bos.).

**Game 2**—October 7, at St. Louis
Boston ......................0 0 0 0 0 0 0 0 0—0 4 1
St. Louis ...................0 0 1 0 2 0 0 0 x—3 6 0
Harris, Dobson (8); Brecheen. W—Brecheen. L—Harris.

**Game 3**—October 9, at Boston
St. Louis ...................0 0 0 0 0 0 0 0 0—0 6 1
Boston.......................3 0 0 0 0 0 0 1 x—4 8 0
Dickson, Wilks (8); Ferriss. W—Ferriss. L—Dickson. HR—York (Bos.).

**Game 4**—Ocotber 10, at Boston
St. Louis ................0 3 3 0 1 0 1 0 4—12 20 1
Boston ..................0 0 0 1 0 0 0 2 0— 3 9 4
Munger; Hughson, Bagby (3), Zuber (6), Brown (8), Ryba (9), Driesewerd (9). W—Munger. L—Hughson. HR—Slaughter (St.L.); Doerr (Bos.).

**Game 5**—October 11, at Boston
St. Louis ..................0 1 0 0 0 0 0 0 2—3 4 1
Boston.......................1 1 0 0 0 1 3 0 x—6 11 3
Pollet, Brazle (1), Beazley (8); Dobson. W—Dobson. L—Brazle. HR—Culberson (Bos.).

**Game 6**—October 13, at St. Louis
Boston ......................0 0 0 0 0 0 1 0 0—1 7 0
St. Louis ...................0 0 3 0 0 0 0 1 x—4 8 0
Harris, Hughson (3), Johnson (8); Brecheen. W—Brecheen. L—Harris.

**Game 7**—October 15, at St. Louis
Boston .....................1 0 0 0 0 0 0 2 0—3 8 0
St. Louis ..................0 1 0 0 2 0 0 1 x—4 9 1
Ferriss, Dobson (5), Klinger (8), Johnson (8); Dickson, Brecheen (8). W—Brecheen. L—Klinger.

# 1947

## FINAL STANDINGS

**American League**

| Team | W | L | Pct. | GB |
|---|---|---|---|---|
| New York | 97 | 57 | .630 | ... |
| Detroit | 85 | 69 | .552 | 12 |
| Boston | 83 | 71 | .539 | 14 |
| Cleveland | 80 | 74 | .519 | 17 |
| Philadelphia | 78 | 76 | .506 | 19 |
| Chicago | 70 | 84 | .455 | 27 |
| Washington | 64 | 90 | .416 | 33 |
| St. Louis | 59 | 95 | .383 | 38 |

**National League**

| Team | W | L | Pct. | GB |
|---|---|---|---|---|
| Brooklyn | 94 | 60 | .610 | ... |
| St. Louis | 89 | 65 | .578 | 5 |
| Boston | 86 | 68 | .558 | 8 |
| New York | 81 | 73 | .526 | 13 |
| Cincinnati | 73 | 81 | .474 | 21 |
| Chicago | 69 | 85 | .448 | 25 |
| Philadelphia | 62 | 92 | .403 | 32 |
| Pittsburgh | 62 | 92 | .403 | 32 |

## SIGNIFICANT EVENTS

■ **April 9:** Brooklyn manager Leo Durocher was suspended by Commissioner Happy Chandler for the entire 1947 season for "conduct detrimental to baseball."

■ **April 15:** The Major League color barrier came tumbling down when Jackie Robinson went hitless in the Dodgers' 5-3 Opening Day victory over the Braves at Ebbets Field.

■ **April 27:** Cancer-stricken Babe Ruth was honored throughout baseball on "Babe Ruth Day" and in special ceremonies at Yankee Stadium.

■ **July 5:** Cleveland's Larry Doby became the A.L.'s first black player when he struck out as a pinch-hitter in a 6-5 loss at Chicago.

■ **November 12:** Dodgers first baseman Jackie Robinson capped his historic season by capturing the first Rookie of the Year award.

## MEMORABLE MOMENTS

■ **June 22:** Cincinnati's Ewell Blackwell fell two outs short of matching Johnny Vander Meer's back-to-back no-hitter feat when Brooklyn's Eddie Stanky stroked a ninth-inning single.

■ **September 28:** The greatest home run battle in history ended with neither Pittsburgh's Ralph Kiner nor New York's Johnny Mize adding to their 51-homer totals.

## LEADERS

**American League**

**BA:** Ted Williams, Bos., .343.
**Runs:** Ted Williams, Bos., 125.
**Hits:** Johnny Pesky, Bos., 207.
**TB:** Ted Williams, Bos., 335.
**HR:** Ted Williams, Bos., 32.
**RBI:** Ted Williams, Bos., 114.
**SB:** Bob Dillinger, St.L., 34.
**Wins:** Bob Feller, Cle., 20.
**ERA:** Joe Haynes, Chi., 2.42.
**CG:** Hal Newhouser, Det., 24.
**IP:** Bob Feller, Cle., 299.
**SO:** Bob Feller, Cle., 196.

**National League**

**BA:** Harry Walker, St.L.-Phil., .363.
**Runs:** Johnny Mize, N.Y., 137.
**Hits:** Tommy Holmes, Bos., 191.
**TB:** Ralph Kiner, Pit., 361.
**HR:** Ralph Kiner, Pit.; Johnny Mize, N.Y., 51.
**RBI:** Johnny Mize, N.Y., 138.
**SB:** Jackie Robinson, Brk., 29.
**Wins:** Ewell Blackwell, Cin., 22.
**ERA:** Warren Spahn, Bos., 2.33.
**CG:** Ewell Blackwell, Cin., 23.
**IP:** Warren Spahn, Bos., 289.2.
**SO:** Ewell Blackwell, Cin., 193.

### A.L. 20-game winners
Bob Feller, Cle., 20-11

### N.L. 20-game winners
Ewell Blackwell, Cin., 22-8
Larry Jansen, N.Y., 21-5
Warren Spahn, Bos., 21-10
Ralph Branca, Brk., 21-12
Johnny Sain, Bos., 21-12

### A.L. 100 RBIs
Ted Williams, Bos., 114

### N.L. 100 RBIs
Johnny Mize, N.Y., 138
Ralph Kiner, Pit., 127
Walker Cooper, N.Y., 122
Bob Elliott, Bos., 113
Willard Marshall, N.Y., 107
Whitey Kurowski, St.L., 104

### N.L. 40 homers
Ralph Kiner, Pit., 51
Johnny Mize, N.Y., 51

### Most Valuable Player
A.L.: Joe DiMaggio, OF, N.Y.
N.L.: Bob Elliott, 3B, Bos.

### Rookie of the Year
A.L.-N.L.: Jackie Robinson, 1B, Brk.

### Hall of Fame additions
Mickey Cochrane, C, 1925-37
Frank Frisch, 2B, 1919-37
Lefty Grove, P, 1925-41
Carl Hubbell, P, 1928-43

## ALL-STAR GAME

■ **Winner:** The A.L. won its 10th All-Star Game in 14 tries with a 2-1 decision at windswept Wrigley Field.

■ **Key inning:** The seventh, when Washington pinch-hitter Stan Spence singled home Boston's Bobby Doerr with the eventual winning run.

■ **Memorable moment:** A game-saving defensive play by Cleveland shortstop Lou Boudreau in the eighth inning on a ball hit by St. Louis' Enos Slaughter with two men on base.

■ **Top guns:** Hal Newhouser (Tigers), Spec Shea (Yankees), Ted Williams (Red Sox), Spence (Senators), A.L.; Ewell Blackwell (Reds), Johnny Mize (Giants), N.L.

■ **MVP:** Spence.

### Linescore

July 8, at Chicago's Wrigley Field
A.L. ............................0 0 0 0 0 1 1 0 0—2 8 0
N.L. ............................0 0 0 1 0 0 0 0 0—1 5 1
Newhouser (Tigers), Shea (Yankees) 4, Masterson (Senators) 7, Page (Yankees) 8; Blackwell (Reds), Brecheen (Cardinals) 4, Sain (Braves) 7, Spahn (Braves) 8. W—Shea. L—Sain. HR—Mize, N.L.

## WORLD SERIES

■ **Winner:** After a three-year drought, the Yankees returned to the top in a memorable seven-game battle against the Dodgers.

■ **Turning point:** Spec Shea's 2-1 Game 5 victory — the day after teammate Bill Bevens, one out away from victory and the first no-hitter in Series history, had surrendered a game-deciding two-run double to Dodgers pinch-hitter Cookie Lavagetto.

■ **Memorable moments:** Lavagetto's Game 4 hit and a spectacular Game 6 catch by Dodgers left fielder Al Gionfriddo that robbed Joe DiMaggio of a home run and helped secure an 8-6 must victory for Brooklyn.

■ **Top guns:** Shea (2-0, 2.35 ERA), Johnny Lindell (.500, 7 RBIs), Yankees; Hugh Casey (2-0, 0.87), Carl Furillo (.353), Dodgers.

### Linescores

**Game 1**—September 30, at New York
Brooklyn ....................1 0 0 0 0 1 1 0 0—3 6 0
New York....................0 0 0 0 5 0 0 0 x—5 4 0
Branca, Behrman (5), Casey (7); Shea, Page (6). W—Shea. L—Branca.

**Game 2**—October 1, at New York
Brooklyn ...............0 0 1 1 0 0 0 0 1— 3 9 2
New York...............1 0 1 1 2 1 4 0 x—10 15 1
Lombardi, Gregg (5), Behrman (7), Barney (7); Reynolds. W—Reynolds. L—Lombardi. HR—Walker (Brk.); Henrich (N.Y.).

**Game 3**—October 2, at Brooklyn
New York...................0 0 2 2 2 1 1 0 0—8 13 0
Brooklyn ..................0 6 1 2 0 0 0 0 x—9 13 1
Newsom, Raschi (2), Drews (3), Chandler (4), Page (6); Hatten, Branca (5), Casey (7). W—Casey. L—Newsom. HR—DiMaggio, Berra (N.Y.).

**Game 4**—October 3, at Brooklyn
New York...................1 0 0 1 0 0 0 0 0—2 8 1
Brooklyn ...................0 0 0 0 1 0 0 0 2—3 1 3
Bevens; Taylor, Gregg (1), Behrman (8), Casey (9). W—Casey. L—Bevens.

**Game 5**—October 4, at Brooklyn
New York...................0 0 0 1 1 0 0 0 0—2 5 0
Brooklyn ....................0 0 0 0 0 1 0 0 0—1 4 1
Shea; Barney, Hatten (5), Behrman (7), Casey (8). W—Shea. L—Barney. HR—DiMaggio (N.Y.).

**Game 6**—October 5, at New York
Brooklyn ..................2 0 2 0 0 4 0 0 0—8 12 1
New York.................0 0 4 1 0 0 0 0 1—6 15 2
Lombardi, Branca (3), Hatten (6), Casey (9); Reynolds, Drews (3), Page (5), Newsom (6), Raschi (7), Wensloff (8). W—Branca. L—Page.

**Game 7**—October 6, at New York
Brooklyn ...................0 2 0 0 0 0 0 0 0—2 7 0
New York...................0 1 0 2 0 1 1 0 x—5 7 0
Gregg, Behrman (4), Hatten (6), Barney (6), Casey (7); Shea, Bevens (2), Page (5). W—Page. L—Gregg.

# 1948

## FINAL STANDINGS

**American League**

| Team | W | L | Pct. | GB |
|---|---|---|---|---|
| *Cleveland | 97 | 58 | .626 | ... |
| Boston | 96 | 59 | .619 | 1 |
| New York | 94 | 60 | .610 | 2.5 |
| Philadelphia | 84 | 70 | .545 | 12.5 |
| Detroit | 78 | 76 | .506 | 18.5 |
| St. Louis | 59 | 94 | .386 | 37 |
| Washington | 56 | 97 | .366 | 40 |
| Chicago | 51 | 101 | .336 | 44.5 |

*Defeated Boston in one-game pennant playoff.

**National League**

| Team | W | L | Pct. | GB |
|---|---|---|---|---|
| Boston | 91 | 62 | .595 | ... |
| St. Louis | 85 | 69 | .552 | 6.5 |
| Brooklyn | 84 | 70 | .545 | 7.5 |
| Pittsburgh | 83 | 71 | .539 | 8.5 |
| New York | 78 | 76 | .506 | 13.5 |
| Philadelphia | 66 | 88 | .429 | 25.5 |
| Cincinnati | 64 | 89 | .418 | 27 |
| Chicago | 64 | 90 | .416 | 27.5 |

## SIGNIFICANT EVENTS

■ **June 15:** The Tigers became the final A.L. team to host a night game when they posted a 4-1 victory over the Athletics at Briggs Stadium.

■ **August 16:** Babe Ruth, whose uniform No. 3 had been retired by the Yankees two months earlier, died of throat cancer at age 53.

■ **October 3:** The Indians finished the season with a record attendance of 2,620,627.

■ **October 12:** Casey Stengel brought his colorful antics to New York when he signed a two-year contract to manage the Yankees.

## MEMORABLE MOMENTS

■ **July 18:** Chicago's Pat Seerey joined a select club when he pounded an 11th-inning home run, his fourth of the game, to give the White Sox a 12-11 victory over the Athletics.

■ **October 4:** Player-manager Lou Boudreau belted two home runs and the Indians posted an 8-3 victory over Boston in a one-game playoff to decide the A.L. pennant.

## LEADERS

**American League**

**BA:** Ted Williams, Bos., .369.
**Runs:** Tommy Henrich, N.Y., 138.
**Hits:** Bob Dillinger, St.L., 207.
**TB:** Joe DiMaggio, N.Y., 355.
**HR:** Joe DiMaggio, N.Y., 39.
**RBI:** Joe DiMaggio, N.Y., 155.
**SB:** Bob Dillinger, St.L., 28.
**Wins:** Hal Newhouser, Det., 21.
**ERA:** Gene Bearden, Cle., 2.43.
**CG:** Bob Lemon, Cle., 20.
**IP:** Bob Lemon, Cle., 293.2.
**SO:** Bob Feller, Cle., 164.

**National League**

**BA:** Stan Musial, St.L., .376.
**Runs:** Stan Musial, St.L., 135.
**Hits:** Stan Musial, St.L., 230.
**TB:** Stan Musial, St.L., 429.
**HR:** Ralph Kiner, Pit.; Johnny Mize, N.Y., 40.
**RBI:** Stan Musial, St.L., 131.
**SB:** Richie Ashburn, Phil., 32.
**Wins:** Johnny Sain, Bos., 24.
**ERA:** Harry Brecheen, St.L., 2.24.
**CG:** Johnny Sain, Bos., 28.
**IP:** Johnny Sain, Bos., 314.2.
**SO:** Harry Brecheen, St.L., 149.

### A.L. 20-game winners
Hal Newhouser, Det., 21-12
Gene Bearden, Cle., 20-7
Bob Lemon, Cle., 20-14

### N.L. 20-game winners
Johnny Sain, Bos., 24-15
Harry Brecheen, St.L., 20-7

### A.L. 100 RBIs
Joe DiMaggio, N.Y., 155
Vern Stephens, Bos., 137
Ted Williams, Bos., 127
Joe Gordon, Cle., 124
Hank Majeski, Phil., 120
Ken Keltner, Cle., 119
Bobby Doerr, Bos., 111
Lou Boudreau, Cle., 106
Hoot Evers, Det., 103
Tommy Henrich, N.Y., 100

### N.L. 100 RBIs
Stan Musial, St.L., 131
Johnny Mize, N.Y., 125
Ralph Kiner, Pit., 123
Sid Gordon, N.Y., 107
Andy Pafko, Chi., 101
Bob Elliott, Bos., 100

### N.L. 40 homers
Ralph Kiner, Pit., 40
Johnny Mize, N.Y., 40

### Most Valuable Player
A.L.: Lou Boudreau, SS, Cle.
N.L.: Stan Musial, OF, St.L.

### Rookie of the Year
A.L.-N.L.: Alvin Dark, SS, Bos. (N.L.).

### Hall of Fame additions
Herb Pennock, P, 1912-34
Pie Traynor, 3B, 1920-37

## ALL-STAR GAME

■ **Winner:** Yankee Vic Raschi and Philadelphia's Joe Coleman pitched six innings of shutout relief and the A.L. won for the 11th time in 15 All-Star classics.

■ **Key inning:** The fourth, when the A.L. broke a 2-2 tie with three runs. Two scored on a bases-loaded single by pitcher Raschi.

■ **Memorable moment:** A first-inning home run by hometown favorite Stan Musial — the first of a record six All-Star homers he would hit.

■ **Top guns:** Raschi (Yankees), Coleman (Athletics), Hoot Evers (Tigers), A.L.; Musial (Cardinals), Richie Ashburn (Phillies).

■ **MVP:** Raschi.

### Linescore

July 13, at St. Louis' Sportsman's Park
N.L. ............................2 0 0 0 0 0 0 0 0—2 8 0
A.L. ............................0 1 1 3 0 0 0 0 x—5 6 0
Branca (Dodgers), Schmitz (Cubs) 4, Sain (Braves) 4, Blackwell (Reds) 6; Masterson (Senators), Raschi (Yankees) 4, Coleman (Athletics) 7. W—Raschi. L—Schmitz. HR—Musial, N.L.; Evers, A.L.

## WORLD SERIES

■ **Winner:** The Indians, survivors of a pennant playoff against the Red Sox, needed six games to dispatch Boston's other team in the Series.

■ **Turning point:** Gene Bearden's 2-0 Game 3 shutout, which put the Indians in the driver's seat.

■ **Memorable moment:** The Game 5 appearance of Indians pitcher Satchel Paige, the 42-year-old former Negro Leagues legend. Paige became the first black pitcher in Series history.

■ **Top guns:** Bob Lemon (2-0, 1.65 ERA), Larry Doby (.318), Indians; Bob Elliott (.333, 2 HR, 5 RBIs), Braves.

### Linescores

**Game 1**—October 6, at Boston
Cleveland ..................0 0 0 0 0 0 0 0 0—0 4 0
Boston........................0 0 0 0 0 0 0 1 x—1 2 2
Feller; Sain. W—Sain. L—Feller.

**Game 2**—October 7, at Boston
Cleveland ..................0 0 0 2 1 0 0 0 1—4 8 1
Boston ........................1 0 0 0 0 0 0 0 0—1 8 3
Lemon; Spahn, Barrett (5), Potter (8). W—Lemon. L—Spahn.

**Game 3**—October 8, at Cleveland
Boston .......................0 0 0 0 0 0 0 0 0—0 5 1
Cleveland....................0 0 1 1 0 0 0 0 x—2 5 0
Bickford, Voiselle (4), Barrett (8); Bearden. W—Bearden. L—Bickford.

**Game 4**—October 9, at Cleveland
Boston .......................0 0 0 0 0 0 1 0 0—1 7 0
Cleveland....................1 0 1 0 0 0 0 0 x—2 5 0
Sain; Gromek. W—Gromek. L—Sain. HR—Doby (Cle.); Rickert (Bos.).

**Game 5**—October 10, at Cleveland
Boston ................3 0 1 0 0 1 6 0 0—11 12 0
Cleveland .............1 0 0 4 0 0 0 0 0— 5 6 2
Potter, Spahn (4); Feller, Klieman (7), Christopher (7), Paige (7), Muncrief (8). W—Spahn. L—Feller. HR—Elliott 2, Salkeld (Bos.); Mitchell, Hegan (Cle.).

**Game 6**—October 11, at Boston
Cleveland ...............0 0 1 0 0 2 0 1 0—4 10 0
Boston ...................0 0 0 1 0 0 0 2 0—3 9 0
Lemon, Bearden (8); Voiselle, Spahn (8). W—Lemon. L—Voiselle. HR—Gordon (Cle.).

# 1949

## FINAL STANDINGS

**American League**

| Team | W | L | Pct. | GB |
|---|---|---|---|---|
| New York | 97 | 57 | .630 | ... |
| Boston | 96 | 58 | .623 | 1 |
| Cleveland | 89 | 65 | .578 | 8 |
| Detroit | 87 | 67 | .565 | 10 |
| Philadelphia | 81 | 73 | .526 | 16 |
| Chicago | 63 | 91 | .409 | 34 |
| St. Louis | 53 | 101 | .344 | 44 |
| Washington | 50 | 104 | .325 | 47 |

**National League**

| Team | W | L | Pct. | GB |
|---|---|---|---|---|
| Brooklyn | 97 | 57 | .630 | ... |
| St. Louis | 96 | 58 | .623 | 1 |
| Philadelphia | 81 | 73 | .526 | 16 |
| Boston | 75 | 79 | .487 | 22 |
| New York | 73 | 81 | .474 | 24 |
| Pittsburgh | 71 | 83 | .461 | 26 |
| Cincinnati | 62 | 92 | .403 | 35 |
| Chicago | 61 | 93 | .396 | 36 |

## SIGNIFICANT EVENTS

■ **February 7:** Yankee star Joe DiMaggio signed baseball's first $100,000 contract.
■ **April 19:** In ceremonies at Yankee Stadium, the Yankees unveiled center-field granite monuments honoring Babe Ruth, Lou Gehrig and Miller Huggins.
■ **June 5:** Commissioner Happy Chandler lifted the five-year suspensions of the 18 players who jumped to the outlaw Mexican League in 1946.
■ **June 15:** Phillies star Eddie Waitkus was shot and seriously wounded in a Chicago hotel room by a 19-year-old woman who professed to having a secret crush on him.
■ **December 12:** Baseball's Rules Committee redefined the strike zone as the area over home plate between the batter's armpits and the top of his knees.

## MEMORABLE MOMENTS

■ **September 30:** Pittsburgh's Ralph Kiner, the first N.L. player to top the 50-homer plateau twice, blasted No. 54 in a 3-2 victory over the Reds.
■ **October 2:** The Yankees posted a 5-3 final-day victory over Boston in a pennant-deciding battle at Yankee Stadium.
■ **October 2:** The Dodgers held off the Cardinals and claimed the N.L. pennant with a 10-inning, 9-7 final-day victory over Philadelphia.

## LEADERS

**American League**
**BA:** George Kell, Det., .343.
**Runs:** Ted Williams, Bos., 150.
**Hits:** Dale Mitchell, Cle., 203.
**TB:** Ted Williams, Bos., 368.
**HR:** Ted Williams, Bos., 43.
**RBI:** Vern Stephens, Bos.; Ted Williams, Bos., 159.
**SB:** Bob Dillinger, St.L., 20.
**Wins:** Mel Parnell, Bos., 25.
**ERA:** Mike Garcia, Cle., 2.36.
**CG:** Mel Parnell, Bos., 27.
**IP:** Mel Parnell, Bos., 295.1.
**SO:** Virgil Trucks, Det., 153.

**National League**
**BA:** Jackie Robinson, Brk., .342.
**Runs:** Pee Wee Reese, Brk., 132.
**Hits:** Stan Musial, St.L., 207.
**TB:** Stan Musial, St.L., 382.
**HR:** Ralph Kiner, Pit., 54.
**RBI:** Ralph Kiner, Pit., 127.
**SB:** Jackie Robinson, Brk., 37.
**Wins:** Warren Spahn, Bos., 21.
**ERA:** Dave Koslo, N.Y., 2.50.
**CG:** Warren Spahn, Bos., 25.
**IP:** Warren Spahn, Bos., 302.1.
**SO:** Warren Spahn, Bos., 151.

**A.L. 20-game winners**
Mel Parnell, Bos., 25-7
Ellis Kinder, Bos., 23-6
Bob Lemon, Cle., 22-10
Vic Raschi, N.Y., 21-10
Alex Kellner, Phil., 20-12

**N.L. 20-game winners**
Warren Spahn, Bos., 21-14
Howie Pollet, St.L., 20-9

**A.L. 100 RBIs**
Vern Stephens, Bos., 159
Ted Williams, Bos., 159
Vic Wertz, Det., 133
Bobby Doerr, Bos., 109
Sam Chapman, Phil., 108

**N.L. 100 RBIs**
Ralph Kiner, Pit., 127
Jackie Robinson, Brk., 124
Stan Musial, St.L., 123
Gil Hodges, Brk., 115
Del Ennis, Phil., 110
Bobby Thomson, N.Y., 109
Carl Furillo, Brk., 106
Wally Westlake, Pit., 104

**A.L. 40 homers**
Ted Williams, Bos., 43

**N.L. 40 homers**
Ralph Kiner, Pit., 54

**Most Valuable Player**
A.L.: Ted Williams, OF, Bos.
N.L.: Jackie Robinson, 2B, Brk.

**Rookie of the Year**
A.L.: Roy Sievers, OF, St.L.
N.L.: Don Newcombe, P, Brk.

**Hall of Fame additions**
Three Finger Brown, P, 1903-16
Charley Gehringer, 2B, 1924-42
Kid Nichols, P, 1890-1906

## ALL-STAR GAME

■ **Winner:** The DiMaggios, Boston's Dom and New York's Joe, combined for four RBIs and Yankee pitcher Vic Raschi shut down the N.L. over the last three innings as the A.L. prevailed in a sloppy game at Brooklyn.

■ **Key inning:** The seventh, when the A.L. broke open a close game with a three-run rally.

■ **Memorable moment:** Jackie Robinson's first-inning double — the first hit by a black player in the first integrated All-Star Game.

■ **Top guns:** Raschi (Yankees), D. DiMaggio (Red Sox), J. DiMaggio (Yankees), George Kell (Tigers), A.L.; Stan Musial (Cardinals), Ralph Kiner (Pirates), N.L.

■ **MVP:** Joe DiMaggio.

### Linescore

July 12, at Brooklyn's Ebbets Field
A.L. ........................4 0 0 2 0 2 3 0 0—1 13 1
N.L. ........................2 1 2 0 0 2 0 0 0—7 12 5
Parnell (Red Sox), Trucks (Tigers) 2, Brissie (Athletics) 4, Raschi (Yankees) 7; Spahn (Braves), Newcombe (Dodgers) 2, Munger (Cardinals) 5, Bickford (Braves) 6, Pollet (Cardinals) 7, Blackwell (Reds) 8, Roe (Dodgers) 9. W—Trucks. L—Newcombe. HR—Musial, Kiner, N.L.

## WORLD SERIES

■ **Winner:** The Yankee machine was back, this time with a new driver. Casey Stengel made his Series managerial debut a successful one.

■ **Turning point:** A three-run ninth inning that produced a 4-3 Yankee victory in Game 3.

■ **Memorable moment:** Tommy Henrich's leadoff ninth-inning home run that decided a 1-0 pitching duel between Dodgers ace Don Newcombe and Yankee righthander Allie Reynolds in Game 1.

■ **Top guns:** Reynolds (12⅓ IP, 0.00 ERA), Bobby Brown (.500, 5 RBIs), Yankees; Pee Wee Reese (.316), Dodgers.

### Linescores

**Game 1**—Oct. 5, at New York
Brooklyn ....................0 0 0 0 0 0 0 0 0—0 2 0
New York....................0 0 0 0 0 0 0 0 1—1 5 1
Newcombe; Reynolds. W—Reynolds. L—Newcombe. HR—Henrich (N.Y.).

**Game 2**—October 6, at New York
Brooklyn ....................0 1 0 0 0 0 0 0 0—1 7 2
New York....................0 0 0 0 0 0 0 0 0—0 6 1
Roe; Raschi, Page (9). W—Roe. L—Raschi.

**Game 3**—October 7, at Brooklyn
New York....................0 0 1 0 0 0 0 0 3—4 5 0
Brooklyn ....................0 0 0 1 0 0 0 0 2—3 5 0
Byrne, Page (4); Branca, Banta (9). W—Page. L—Branca. HR—Reese, Olmo, Campanella (Brk.).

**Game 4**—October 8, at Brooklyn
New York..................0 0 0 3 3 0 0 0 0—6 10 0
Brooklyn ..................0 0 0 0 0 4 0 0 0—4 9 1
Lopat, Reynolds (6); Newcombe, Hatten (4), Erskine (6), Banta (7). W—Lopat. L—Newcombe.

**Game 5**—October 9, at Brooklyn
New York...............2 0 3 1 1 3 0 0 0—10 11 1
Brooklyn ...............0 0 1 0 0 1 4 0 0— 6 11 2
Raschi, Page (7); Barney, Banta (3), Erskine (6), Hatten (6), Palica (7), Minner (9). W—Raschi. L—Barney. HR—DiMaggio (N.Y.); Hodges (Brk.).

# 1950

## FINAL STANDINGS

**American League**

| Team | W | L | Pct. | GB |
|---|---|---|---|---|
| New York | 98 | 56 | .636 | ... |
| Detroit | 95 | 59 | .617 | 3 |
| Boston | 94 | 60 | .610 | 4 |
| Cleveland | 92 | 62 | .597 | 6 |
| Washington | 67 | 87 | .435 | 31 |
| Chicago | 60 | 94 | .390 | 38 |
| St. Louis | 58 | 96 | .377 | 40 |
| Philadelphia | 52 | 102 | .338 | 46 |

**National League**

| Team | W | L | Pct. | GB |
|---|---|---|---|---|
| Philadelphia | 91 | 63 | .591 | ... |
| Brooklyn | 89 | 65 | .578 | 2 |
| New York | 86 | 68 | .558 | 5 |
| Boston | 83 | 71 | .539 | 8 |
| St. Louis | 78 | 75 | .510 | 12.5 |
| Cincinnati | 66 | 87 | .431 | 24.5 |
| Chicago | 64 | 89 | .418 | 26.5 |
| Pittsburgh | 57 | 96 | .373 | 33.5 |

## SIGNIFICANT EVENTS

■ **January 31:** Pittsburgh made 18-year-old pitcher Paul Pettit baseball's first $100,000 bonus baby.
■ **October 18:** Connie Mack retired after 50 years as manager and owner of the Athletics, the team he built in 1901 when the American League was organized.
■ **December 11:** Major League owners pulled a shocker when they voted not to renew the contract of Commissioner Happy Chandler.
■ **December 26:** Chandler announced that the Gillette Safety Razor Company had agreed to pay a six-year fee of $6 million for rights to the World Series and All-Star Game.

## MEMORABLE MOMENTS

■ **June 8:** The Red Sox, in the biggest single-game explosion in history, defeated the Browns 29-4 at Boston's Fenway Park.
■ **August 31:** Brooklyn's Gil Hodges became the sixth player to hit four home runs in a game during a 19-3 rout of the Braves at Ebbets Field. Hodges also singled and tied the single-game record of 17 total bases.
■ **October 1:** Dick Sisier crashed a three-run 10th-inning home run to give the Phillies a 4-1 victory over the Dodgers and their first N.L. pennant in 35 years.

## LEADERS

**American League**
**BA:** Billy Goodman, Bos., .354.
**Runs:** Dom DiMaggio, Bos., 131.
**Hits:** George Kell, Det., 218.
**TB:** Walt Dropo, Bos., 326.
**HR:** Al Rosen, Cle., 37.
**RBI:** Walt Dropo, Bos.; Vern Stephens, Bos., 144.
**SB:** Dom DiMaggio, Bos., 15.
**Wins:** Bob Lemon, Cle., 23.
**ERA:** Early Wynn, Cle., 3.20.
**CG:** Ned Garver, St.L.; Bob Lemon, Cle., 22.
**IP:** Bob Lemon, Cle., 288.
**SO:** Bob Lemon, Cle., 170.

**National League**
**BA:** Stan Musial, St.L., .346.
**Runs:** Earl Torgeson, Bos., 120.
**Hits:** Duke Snider, Brk., 199.
**TB:** Duke Snider, Brk., 343.
**HR:** Ralph Kiner, Pit., 47.
**RBI:** Del Ennis, Phil., 126.
**SB:** Sam Jethroe, Bos., 35.
**Wins:** Warren Spahn, Bos., 21.
**ERA:** Sal Maglie, N.Y., 2.71.
**CG:** Vern Bickford, Bos., 27.
**IP:** Vern Bickford, Bos., 311.2.
**SO:** Warren Spahn, Bos., 191.

**A.L. 20-game winners**
Bob Lemon, Cle., 23-11
Vic Raschi, N.Y., 21-8

**N.L. 20-game winners**
Warren Spahn, Bos., 21-17
Robin Roberts, Phil., 20-11
Johnny Sain, Bos., 20-13

**A.L. 100 RBIs**
Walt Dropo, Bos., 144
Vern Stephens, Bos., 144
Yogi Berra, N.Y., 124
Vic Wertz, Det., 123
Joe DiMaggio, N.Y., 122
Bobby Doerr, Bos., 120
Al Rosen, Cle., 116
Luke Easter, Cle., 107
Hoot Evers, Det., 103
Larry Doby, Cle., 102
George Kell, Det., 101

**N.L. 100 RBIs**
Del Ennis, Phil., 126
Ralph Kiner, Pit., 118
Gil Hodges, Brk., 113
Ted Kluszewski, Cin., 111
Stan Musial, St.L., 109
Bob Elliott, Bos., 107
Duke Snider, Brk., 107
Carl Furillo, Brk., 106
Sid Gordon, Bos., 103
Hank Sauer, Chi., 103
Enos Slaughter, St.L., 101

**N.L. 40 homers**
Ralph Kiner, Pit., 47

**Most Valuable Player**
A.L.: Phil Rizzuto, SS, N.Y.
N.L.: Jim Konstanty, P, Phil.

**Rookie of the Year**
A.L.: Walt Dropo, 1B, Bos.
N.L.: Sam Jethroe, OF, Bos.

## ALL-STAR GAME

■ **Winner:** The N.L. broke a four-game losing streak with a 4-3 victory in the first extra-inning All-Star Game.

■ **Key inning:** The ninth, when Tigers pitcher Art Houtteman, trying to close out a 3-2 A.L. victory, surrendered a game-tying home run to Pirates slugger Ralph Kiner.

■ **Memorable moment:** A dramatic 14th-inning home run by Cardinals second baseman Red Schoendienst that gave the N.L. its first win since 1944. Schoendienst was an 11th-inning defensive replacement.

■ **Top guns:** Larry Jansen (Giants), Ewell Blackwell (Reds), Kiner (Pirates), Schoendienst (Cardinals), N.L.; Bob Lemon (Indians), Larry Doby (Indians), A.L.

■ **MVP:** Schoendienst.

### Linescore

July 11, at Chicago's Comiskey Park
N.L.......0 2 0 0 0 0 0 0 1 0 0 0 0 1—4 10 0
A.L.......0 0 1 0 2 0 0 0 0 0 0 0 0 0—3 8 1
Roberts (Phillies), Newcombe (Dodgers) 4, Konstanty (Phillies) 6, Jansen (Giants) 7, Blackwell (Reds) 12; Raschi (Yankees), Lemon (Indians) 4, Houtteman (Tigers) 7, Reynolds (Yankees) 10, Gray (Tigers) 13, Feller (Indians) 14. W—Blackwell. L—Gray. HR—Kiner, Schoendienst, N.L.

## WORLD SERIES

■ **Winner:** Rekindling memories of New York's 1936-39 machine, the Bronx Bombers captured their second straight Series with a sweep of the Phillies.

■ **Turning point:** Joe DiMaggio's 10th-inning homer that gave the Yankees and Allie Reynolds a 2-1 victory in Game 2.

■ **Memorable moment:** Rookie Whitey Ford's first Series victory — a 5-2 Game 4 decision.

■ **Top guns:** Gene Woodling (.429), Bobby Brown (.333), Yankees; Granny Hamner (.429), Phillies.

### Linescores

**Game 1**—October 4, at Philadelphia
New York ....................0 0 0 1 0 0 0 0 0—1 5 0
Philadelphia ................0 0 0 0 0 0 0 0 0—0 2 1
Raschi; Konstanty, Meyer (9). W—Raschi. L—Konstanty.

**Game 2**—October 5, at Philadelphia
New York ..............0 1 0 0 0 0 0 0 0 1—2 10 0
Philadelphia ..........0 0 0 0 1 0 0 0 0 0—1 7 0
Reynolds; Roberts. W—Reynolds. L—Roberts. HR—DiMaggio (N.Y.).

**Game 3**—October 6, at New York
Philadelphia .............0 0 0 0 0 1 1 0 0—2 10 2
New York .................0 0 1 0 0 0 0 1 1—3 7 0
Heintzelman, Konstanty (8), Meyer (9); Lopat, Ferrick (9). W—Ferrick. L—Meyer.

**Game 4**—October 7, at New York
Philadelphia ................0 0 0 0 0 0 0 0 2—2 7 1
New York ....................2 0 0 0 0 3 0 0 x—5 8 2
Miller, Konstanty (1), Roberts (8); Ford, Reynolds (9). W—Ford. L—Miller. HR—Berra (N.Y.).

# 1951

## FINAL STANDINGS

**American League**

| Team | W | L | Pct. | GB |
|---|---|---|---|---|
| New York | 98 | 56 | .636 | ... |
| Cleveland | 93 | 61 | .604 | 5 |
| Boston | 87 | 67 | .565 | 11 |
| Chicago | 81 | 73 | .526 | 17 |
| Detroit | 73 | 81 | .474 | 25 |
| Philadelphia | 70 | 84 | .455 | 28 |
| Washington | 62 | 92 | .403 | 36 |
| St. Louis | 52 | 102 | .338 | 46 |

**National League**

| Team | W | L | Pct. | GB |
|---|---|---|---|---|
| *New York | 98 | 59 | .624 | ... |
| Brooklyn | 97 | 60 | .618 | 1 |
| St. Louis | 81 | 73 | .526 | 15.5 |
| Boston | 76 | 78 | .494 | 20.5 |
| Philadelphia | 73 | 81 | .474 | 23.5 |
| Cincinnati | 68 | 86 | .442 | 28.5 |
| Pittsburgh | 64 | 90 | .416 | 32.5 |
| Chicago | 62 | 92 | .403 | 34.5 |

*Defeated Brooklyn 2-1 in pennant playoff.

## SIGNIFICANT EVENTS

■ **August 19:** Browns owner Bill Veeck pulled off a wild promotional stunt when he sent midget Eddie Gaedel to the plate as a surprise pinch-hitter in a Sportsman's Park game against the Tigers.

■ **September 20:** N.L. President Ford Frick was selected as baseball's third commissioner during a marathon meeting in Chicago.

■ **December 11:** Yankee center fielder Joe DiMaggio, a three-time A.L. MVP, announced his retirement.

## MEMORABLE MOMENTS

■ **September 14:** Browns outfielder Bob Nieman became the first player to hit home runs in his first two big-league at-bats. Both came off Mickey McDermott in a game at Boston.

■ **September 28:** New York's Allie Reynolds fired his record-tying second no-hitter of the season in the opener of a doubleheader against Boston, earning an 8-0 decision and clinching at least a tie for the A.L. pennant. The Yankees clinched their third straight flag with an 11-3 win in the nightcap.

■ **October 3:** Bobby Thomson smashed a three-run, ninth-inning homer—giving the Giants a dramatic 5-4 victory over the Dodgers in the decisive third game of an N.L. pennant playoff.

## LEADERS

**American League**

**BA:** Ferris Fain, Phil., .344.
**Runs:** Dom DiMaggio, Bos., 113.
**Hits:** George Kell, Det., 191.
**TB:** Ted Williams, Bos., 295.
**HR:** Gus Zernial, Chi.-Phil., 33.
**RBI:** Gus Zernial, Chi.-Phil., 129.
**SB:** Minnie Minoso, Cle.-Chi., 31.
**Wins:** Bob Feller, Cle., 22.
**ERA:** Saul Rogovin, Det.-Chi., 2.78.
**CG:** Ned Garver, St.L., 24.
**IP:** Early Wynn, Cle., 274.1.
**SO:** Vic Raschi, N.Y., 164.

**National League**

**BA:** Stan Musial, St.L., .355.
**Runs:** Ralph Kiner, Pit.; Stan Musial, St.L., 124.
**Hits:** Richie Ashburn, Phil., 221.
**TB:** Stan Musial, St.L., 355.
**HR:** Ralph Kiner, Pit., 42.
**RBI:** Monte Irvin, N.Y., 121.
**SB:** Sam Jethroe, Bos., 35.
**Wins:** Larry Jansen, N.Y.; Sal Maglie, N.Y., 23.
**ERA:** Chet Nichols, Bos., 2.88.
**CG:** Warren Spahn, Bos., 26.
**IP:** Robin Roberts, Phil., 315.
**SO:** Don Newcombe, Brk.; Warren Spahn, Bos., 164.

**A.L. 20-game winners**

Bob Feller, Cle., 22-8
Eddie Lopat, N.Y., 21-9
Vic Raschi, N.Y., 21-10
Ned Garver, St.L., 20-12
Mike Garcia, Cle., 20-13
Early Wynn, Cle., 20-13

**N.L. 20-game winners**

Sal Maglie, N.Y., 23-6
Larry Jansen, N.Y., 23-11
Preacher Roe, Brk., 22-3
Warren Spahn, Bos., 22-14
Robin Roberts, Phil., 21-15
Don Newcombe, Brk., 20-9
Murry Dickson, Pit., 20-16

**A.L. 100 RBIs**

Gus Zernial, Chi.-Phil., 129
Ted Williams, Bos., 126
Eddie Robinson, Chi., 117
Luke Easter, Cle., 103
Al Rosen, Cle., 102

**N.L. 100 RBIs**

Monte Irvin, N.Y., 121
Sid Gordon, Bos., 109
Ralph Kiner, Pit., 109
Roy Campanella, Brk., 108
Stan Musial, St.L., 108
Gil Hodges, Brk., 103
Duke Snider, Brk., 101
Bobby Thomson, N.Y., 101

**N.L. 40 homers**

Ralph Kiner, Pit., 42
Gil Hodges, Brk., 40

**Most Valuable Player**

A.L.: Yogi Berra, C, N.Y.
N.L.: Roy Campanella, C, Brk.

**Rookie of the Year**

A.L.: Gil McDougald, 3B, N.Y.
N.L.: Willie Mays, OF, N.Y.

**Hall of Fame additions**

Jimmie Foxx, 1B, 1925-45
Mel Ott, OF, 1926-47

## ALL-STAR GAME

■ **Winner:** The N.L. hit an All-Star Game-record four home runs in an 8-3 victory. It marked the first time the senior circuit had recorded back-to-back wins.

■ **Key inning:** A three-run fourth, when St. Louis' Stan Musial and Boston's Bob Elliott connected off Yankee lefty Eddie Lopat.

■ **Memorable moments:** A.L. home runs by Vic Wertz and George Kell before their home fans at Detroit's Briggs Stadium.

■ **Top guns:** Don Newcombe (Dodgers), Musial (Cardinals), Elliott (Braves), Jackie Robinson (Dodgers), Ralph Kiner (Pirates), Gil Hodges (Dodgers), N.L.; Wertz (Tigers), Kell (Tigers), A.L.

■ **MVP:** Elliott.

**Linescore**

July 10, at Detroit's Briggs Stadium
N.L. ..........................1 0 0 3 0 2 1 1 0—8 12 1
A.L. ..........................0 1 0 1 1 0 0 0 0—3 10 2
Roberts (Phillies), Maglie (Giant) 3, Newcombe (Dodgers) 6, Blackwell (Reds) 9; Garver (Browns), Lopat (Yankees) 4, Hutchinson (Tigers) 5, Parnell (Red Sox) 8, Lemon (Indians) 9. W—Maglie. L—Lopat. HR—Musial, Elliott, Hodges, Kiner, N.L.; Wertz, Kell, A.L.

## WORLD SERIES

■ **Winner:** The Yankees' third straight Series victory came at the expense of the torrid Giants, who had beaten Brooklyn in a memorable pennant playoff series.

■ **Turning point:** Infielder Gil McDougald's Game 5 grand slam, which sparked a momentum-turning 13-1 Yankee victory.

■ **Memorable moment:** Yankee right fielder Hank Bauer's Game 6 heroics: a bases-loaded triple and a spectacular Series-ending catch in a 4-3 victory.

■ **Top guns:** Eddie Lopat (2-0, 0.50 ERA), Bobby Brown (.357), McDougald (7 RBIs), Yankees; Monte Irvin (.458), Alvin Dark (.417), Giants.

**Linescores**

**Game 1**—October 4, at Yankee Stadium
Giants ......................2 0 0 0 0 3 0 0 0—5 10 1
Yankees ....................0 1 0 0 0 0 0 0 0—1 7 1
Koslo; Reynolds, Hogue (7), Morgan (8). W—Koslo. L—Reynolds. HR—Dark (Giants).

**Game 2**—October 5, at Yankee Stadium
Giants ........................0 0 0 0 0 0 1 0 0—1 5 1
Yankees ......................1 1 0 0 0 0 0 1 x—3 6 0
Jansen, Spencer (7); Lopat. W—Lopat. L—Jansen. HR—Collins (Yankees).

**Game 3**—October 6, at Polo Grounds
Yankees ......................0 0 0 0 0 0 0 1 1—2 5 2
Giants ........................0 1 0 0 5 0 0 0 x—6 7 2
Raschi, Hogue (5), Ostrowski (8); Hearn, Jones (8). W—Hearn. L—Raschi. HR—Lockman (Giants); Woodling (Yankees).

**Game 4**—October 8, at Polo Grounds
Yankees ....................0 1 0 1 2 0 2 0 0—6 12 0
Giants ......................1 0 0 0 0 0 0 0 1—2 8 2
Reynolds; Maglie, Jones (6), Kennedy (9). W—Reynolds. L—Maglie. HR—DiMaggio (Yankees).

**Game 5**—October 9, at Polo Grounds
Yankees .................0 0 5 2 0 2 4 0 0—13 12 1
Giants ...................1 0 0 0 0 0 0 0 0— 1 5 3
Lopat; Jansen, Kennedy (4), Spencer (6), Corwin (7), Konikowski (9). W—Lopat. L—Jansen. HR—McDougald, Rizzuto (Yankees).

**Game 6**—October 10, at Yankee Stadium
Giants ......................0 0 0 0 1 0 0 0 2—3 11 1
Yankees ....................1 0 0 0 0 3 0 0 x—4 7 0
Koslo, Hearn (7), Jansen (8); Raschi, Sain (7), Kuzava (9). W—Raschi. L—Koslo.

# 1952

## FINAL STANDINGS

**American League**

| Team | W | L | Pct. | GB |
|---|---|---|---|---|
| New York | 95 | 59 | .617 | ... |
| Cleveland | 93 | 61 | .604 | 2 |
| Chicago | 81 | 73 | .526 | 14 |
| Philadelphia | 79 | 75 | .513 | 16 |
| Washington | 78 | 76 | .506 | 17 |
| Boston | 76 | 78 | .494 | 19 |
| St. Louis | 64 | 90 | .416 | 31 |
| Detroit | 50 | 104 | .325 | 45 |

**National League**

| Team | W | L | Pct. | GB |
|---|---|---|---|---|
| Brooklyn | 96 | 57 | .627 | ... |
| New York | 92 | 62 | .597 | 4.5 |
| St. Louis | 88 | 66 | .571 | 8.5 |
| Philadelphia | 87 | 67 | .565 | 9.5 |
| Chicago | 77 | 77 | .500 | 19.5 |
| Cincinnati | 69 | 85 | .448 | 27.5 |
| Boston | 64 | 89 | .418 | 32 |
| Pittsburgh | 42 | 112 | .273 | 54.5 |

## SIGNIFICANT EVENTS

■ **May 2:** Boston's Ted Williams, who lost three years to military service in World War II, returned to a 17-month tour of duty with the U.S. Marines as a fighter pilot in Korea.

■ **May-June-July:** Joining Williams on the Korean front were such name players as Don Newcombe, Willie Mays, Jerry Coleman, Bob Kennedy, Bobby Brown and Tom Morgan.

## MEMORABLE MOMENTS

■ **April 23:** Browns lefty Bob Cain outdueled Cleveland ace Bob Feller, 1-0, in a record-tying battle of one-hitters at St. Louis' Sportsman's Park.

■ **May 21:** The Dodgers exploded for a Major League-record 15 first-inning runs and coasted to a 19-1 victory over the Reds at Ebbets Field.

■ **July 15:** Detroit first baseman Walt Dropo doubled in the second game of a doubleheader against Washington for his 12th consecutive hit, tying the 1938 record set by Boston's Pinky Higgins.

■ **August 25:** Detroit's Virgil Trucks became the third pitcher to throw two no-hitters in one season when he stopped New York, 1-0, at Yankee Stadium.

## LEADERS

**American League**

**BA:** Ferris Fain, Phil., .327.
**Runs:** Larry Doby, Cle., 104.
**Hits:** Nellie Fox, Chi., 192.
**TB:** Al Rosen, Cle., 297.
**HR:** Larry Doby, Cle., 32.
**RBI:** Al Rosen, Cle., 105.
**SB:** Minnie Minoso, Chi., 22.
**Wins:** Bobby Shantz, Phil., 24.
**ERA:** Allie Reynolds, N.Y., 2.06.
**CG:** Bob Lemon, Cle., 28.
**IP:** Bob Lemon, Cle., 309.2.
**SO:** Allie Reynolds, N.Y., 160.

**National League**

**BA:** Stan Musial, St.L., .336.
**Runs:** Solly Hemus, St.L.; Stan Musial, St.L., 105.
**Hits:** Stan Musial, St.L., 194.
**TB:** Stan Musial, St.L., 311.
**HR:** Ralph Kiner, Pit.; Hank Sauer, Chi., 37.
**RBI:** Hank Sauer, Chi., 121.
**SB:** Pee Wee Reese, Brk., 30.
**Wins:** Robin Roberts, Phil., 28.
**ERA:** Hoyt Wilhelm, N.Y., 2.43.
**CG:** Robin Roberts, Phil., 30.
**IP:** Robin Roberts, Phil., 330.
**SO:** Warren Spahn, Bos., 183.

**A.L. 20-game winners**

Bobby Shantz, Phil., 24-7
Early Wynn, Cle., 23-12
Mike Garcia, Cle., 22-11
Bob Lemon, Cle., 22-11
Allie Reynolds, N.Y., 20-8

**N.L. 20-Game Winner**

Robin Roberts, Phil., 28-7

**A.L. 100 RBIs**

Al Rosen, Cle., 105
Larry Doby, Cle., 104
Eddie Robinson, Chi., 104
Gus Zernial, Phil., 100

**N.L. 100 RBIs**

Hank Sauer, Chi., 121
Bobby Thomson, N.Y., 108
Del Ennis, Phil., 107
Gil Hodges, Brk., 102
Enos Slaughter, St.L., 101

**Most Valuable Player**

A.L.: Bobby Shantz, P, Phil.
N.L.: Hank Sauer, OF, Chi.

**Rookie of the Year**

A.L.: Harry Byrd, P, Phil.
N.L.: Joe Black, P, Brk.

**Hall of Fame additions**

Harry Heilmann, OF/1B, 1914-32
Paul Waner, OF, 1926-45

## ALL-STAR GAME

■ **Winner:** The N.L. recorded a rain-shortened 3-2 victory and closed its All-Star deficit to 12-7.

■ **Key inning:** The fourth, when the A.L. scored twice for a 2-1 lead and the N.L. answered with a two-run homer by the Cubs' Hank Sauer.

■ **Memorable moments:** The pitching of Philadelphia stars Curt Simmons (Phillies) and Bobby Shantz (Athletics) before their home fans. Simmons pitched three scoreless innings for the N.L. and Shantz struck out all three batters he faced in a scoreless fifth.

■ **Top guns:** Simmons (Phillies), Jackie Robinson (Dodgers), Sauer (Cubs), N.L.; Shantz (Athletics), Bobby Avila (Indians), A.L.

■ **MVP:** Sauer.

**Linescore**

July 8, at Philadelphia's Shibe Park
A.L. .............................................0 0 0 2 0—2 5 0
N.L. .............................................1 0 0 2 0—3 3 0
Raschi (Yankees), Lemon (Indians) 3, Shantz (Athletics) 5; Simmons (Phillies), Rush (Cubs) 4. W—Rush. L—Lemon. HR—J. Robinson, Sauer, N.L.

## WORLD SERIES

■ **Winner:** The Yankees tied their own previous best run of four consecutive Series championships with a seven-game thriller against the Dodgers.

■ **Turning point:** Game 6 home runs by Yogi Berra and Mickey Mantle that keyed a 3-2 victory and tied the Series at three games apiece.

■ **Memorable moment:** Yankee second baseman Billy Martin's Series-saving shoetop catch of Jackie Robinson's bases-loaded infield popup, which appeared destined to fall untouched. Martin's mad-dash catch saved a 4-2 victory.

■ **Top guns:** Vic Raschi (2-0, 1.59 ERA), Johnny Mize (.400, 3 HR, 6 RBIs), Mantle (.345, 2 HR), Yankees; Duke Snider (.345, 4 HR, 8 RBIs), Pee Wee Reese (.345), Dodgers.

**Linescores**

**Game 1**—October 1, at Brooklyn
New York ....................0 0 1 0 0 0 0 1 0—2 6 2
Brooklyn ....................0 1 0 0 0 2 0 1 x—4 6 0
Reynolds, Scarborough (8); Black. W—Black. L—Reynolds. HR—Robinson, Snider, Reese (Brk.); McDougald (N.Y.).

**Game 2**—October 2, at Brooklyn
New York ..................0 0 0 1 1 5 0 0 0—7 10 0
Brooklyn ..................0 0 1 0 0 0 0 0 0—1 3 1
Raschi; Erskine, Loes (6), Lehman (8). W—Raschi. L—Erskine. HR—Martin (N.Y.).

**Game 3**—October 3, at New York
Brooklyn ..................0 0 1 0 1 0 0 1 2—5 11 0
New York .................0 1 0 0 0 0 0 1 1—3 6 2
Roe; Lopat, Gorman (9). W—Roe. L—Lopat. HR—Berra, Mize (N.Y.).

**Game 4**—October 4, at New York
Brooklyn ....................0 0 0 0 0 0 0 0 0—0 4 1
New York ....................0 0 0 1 0 0 0 1 x—2 4 1
Black, Rutherford (8); Reynolds. W—Reynolds. L—Black. HR—Mize (N.Y.).

**Game 5**—October 5, at New York
Brooklyn ........0 1 0 0 3 0 1 0 0 0 1—6 10 0
New York ........0 0 0 0 5 0 0 0 0 0 0—5 5 1
Erskine; Blackwell, Sain (6). W—Erskine. L—Sain. HR—Snider (Brk.); Mize (N.Y.).

**Game 6**—October 6, at Brooklyn
New York ....................0 0 0 0 0 0 2 1 0—3 9 0
Brooklyn ....................0 0 0 0 0 1 0 1 0—2 8 1
Raschi, Reynolds (8); Loes, Roe (9). W—Raschi. L—Loes. HR—Mantle, Berra (N.Y.); Snider 2 (Brk.).

**Game 7**—October 7, at Brooklyn
New York ..................0 0 0 1 1 1 1 0 0—4 10 4
Brooklyn ..................0 0 0 1 1 0 0 0 0—2 8 1
Lopat, Reynolds (4), Raschi (7), Kuzava (7); Black, Roe (6), Erskine (8). W—Reynolds. L—Black. HR—Woodling, Mantle (N.Y.).

# 1953

## FINAL STANDINGS

**American League**

| Team | W | L | Pct. | GB |
|---|---|---|---|---|
| New York | 99 | 52 | .656 | ... |
| Cleveland | 92 | 62 | .597 | 8.5 |
| Chicago | 89 | 65 | .578 | 11.5 |
| Boston | 84 | 69 | .549 | 16 |
| Washington | 76 | 76 | .500 | 23.5 |
| Detroit | 60 | 94 | .390 | 40.5 |
| Philadelphia | 59 | 95 | .383 | 41.5 |
| St. Louis | 54 | 100 | .351 | 46.5 |

**National League**

| Team | W | L | Pct. | GB |
|---|---|---|---|---|
| Brooklyn | 105 | 49 | .682 | ... |
| Milwaukee | 92 | 62 | .597 | 13 |
| Philadelphia | 83 | 71 | .539 | 22 |
| St. Louis | 83 | 71 | .539 | 22 |
| New York | 70 | 84 | .455 | 35 |
| Cincinnati | 68 | 86 | .442 | 37 |
| Chicago | 65 | 89 | .422 | 40 |
| Pittsburgh | 50 | 104 | .325 | 55 |

## SIGNIFICANT EVENTS

■ **March 18:** The Braves, a fixture in Boston for 77 years, received unanimous approval for a move to Milwaukee—big-league baseball's first franchise shift since 1903.

■ **September 29:** Bill Veeck sold his St. Louis Browns to a syndicate that received quick approval to move the franchise to Baltimore.

■ **November 9:** Baseball won a major victory when the U.S. Supreme Court ruled that it is a sport, not an interstate business, and therefore not subject to federal antitrust laws.

## MEMORABLE MOMENTS

■ **May 6:** Browns rookie Bobo Holloman made baseball history when he pitched a no-hitter against Philadelphia in his first Major League start.

■ **May 25:** Milwaukee's Max Surkont struck out a modern-record eight consecutive Reds en route to a 10-3 victory.

■ **June 18:** The Red Sox scored a record 17 runs in the seventh inning of a 23-3 victory over the Tigers.

## LEADERS

**American League**

**BA:** Mickey Vernon, Wash., .337.
**Runs:** Al Rosen, Cle., 115.
**Hits:** Harvey Kuenn, Det., 209.
**TB:** Al Rosen, Cle., 367.
**HR:** Al Rosen, Cle., 43.
**RBI:** Al Rosen, Cle., 145.
**SB:** Minnie Minoso, Chi., 25.
**Wins:** Bob Porterfield, Wash., 22.
**ERA:** Eddie Lopat, N.Y., 2.42.
**CG:** Bob Porterfield, Wash., 24.
**IP:** Bob Lemon, Cle., 286.2.
**SO:** Billy Pierce, Chi., 186.

**National League**

**BA:** Carl Furillo, Brk., .344.
**Runs:** Duke Snider, Brk., 132.
**Hits:** Richie Ashburn, Phil., 205.
**TB:** Duke Snider, Brk., 370.
**HR:** Eddie Mathews, Mil., 47.
**RBI:** Roy Campanella, Brk., 142.
**SB:** Bill Bruton, Mil., 26.
**Wins:** Robin Roberts, Phil.; Warren Spahn, Mil., 23.
**ERA:** Warren Spahn, Mil., 2.10.
**CG:** Robin Roberts, Phil., 33.
**IP:** Robin Roberts, Phil., 346.2.
**SO:** Robin Roberts, Phil., 198.

**A.L. 20-game winners**

Bob Porterfield, Wash., 22-10
Mel Parnell, Bos., 21-8
Bob Lemon, Cle., 21-15
Virgil Trucks, St.L.-Chi., 20-10

**N.L. 20-game winners**

Warren Spahn, Mil., 23-7
Robin Roberts, Phil., 23-16
Carl Erskine, Brk., 20-6
Harvey Haddix, St.L., 20-9

**A.L. 100 RBIs**

Al Rosen, Cle., 145
Mickey Vernon, Wash., 115
Ray Boone, Cle.-Det., 114
Yogi Berra, N.Y., 108
Gus Zernial, Phil., 108
Minnie Minoso, Chi., 104
Larry Doby, Cle., 102
Eddie Robinson, Phil., 102

**N.L. 100 RBIs**

Roy Campanella, Brk., 142
Eddie Mathews, Mil., 135
Duke Snider, Brk., 126
Del Ennis, Phil., 125
Gil Hodges, Brk., 122
Ralph Kiner, Pit.-Chi., 116
Stan Musial, St.L., 113
Ray Jablonski, St.L., 112
Ted Kluszewski, Cin., 108
Bobby Thomson, N.Y., 106
Gus Bell, Cin., 105
Frank Thomas, Pit., 102
Jim Greengrass, Cin., 100

**A.L. 40 homers**

Al Rosen, Cle., 43
Gus Zernial, Phil., 42

**N.L. 40 homers**

Eddie Mathews, Mil., 47
Duke Snider, Brk., 42
Roy Campanella, Brk., 41
Ted Kluszewski, Cin., 40

**Most Valuable Player**

A.L.: Al Rosen, 3B, Cle.
N.L.: Roy Campanella, C, Brk.

**Rookie of the Year**

A.L.: Harvey Kuenn, SS, Det.
N.L.: Jim Gilliam, 2B, Brk.

**Hall of Fame additions**

Ed Barrow, manager/executive
Chief Bender, P, 1903-25
Tommy Connolly, umpire
Dizzy Dean, P, 1930-47
Bill Klem, umpire
Al Simmons, OF, 1924-44
Bobby Wallace, SS, 1894-1918
Harry Wright, manager

## ALL-STAR GAME

■ **Winner:** Robin Roberts (Phillies), Warren Spahn (Braves), Curt Simmons (Phillies) and Murry Dickson (Pirates) combined on a six-hitter and the N.L. rolled to its fourth consecutive victory.

■ **Key inning:** The N.L.'s two-run fifth, when Philadelphia's Richie Ashburn and Brooklyn's Pee Wee Reese singled home runs.

■ **Memorable moment:** The eighth-inning appearance of Browns righthander Satchel Paige, a former Negro leagues legend and the oldest man (47) ever to play in an All-Star Game.

■ **Top guns:** Roberts (Phillies), Spahn (Braves), Simmons (Phillies), Reese (Dodgers), N.L.; Billy Pierce (White Sox), Minnie Minoso (White Sox), A.L.

■ **MVP:** Reese.

**Linescore**

July 14, at Cincinnati's Crosley Field
A.L. ..........................0 0 0 0 0 0 0 0 1—1 5 0
N.L. ..........................0 0 0 0 2 0 1 2 x—5 10 0
Pierce (White Sox), Reynolds (Yankees) 4, Garcia (Indians) 6, Paige (Browns) 8; Roberts (Phillies), Spahn (Braves) 4, Simmons (Phillies) 6, Dickson (Pirates) 8. W—Spahn. L—Reynolds.

## WORLD SERIES

■ **Winner:** The Yankees earned their record fifth consecutive Series victory and remained perfect in post-season play under manager Casey Stengel.

■ **Turning point:** Billy Martin's two-run homer and Mickey Mantle's grand slam in the Yankees' 11-7 fifth-game Series-turning triumph.

■ **Memorable moment:** Martin's ninth-inning Series-ending single in Game 6 — his record-tying 12th hit of the fall classic.

■ **Top guns:** Martin (.500, 12 hits, 2 HR, 8 RBIs), Mantle (2 HR, 7 RBIs), Yankees; Gil Hodges (.364), Carl Furillo (.333), Dodgers.

**Linescores**

**Game 1**—September 30, at New York
Brooklyn ..................0 0 0 0 1 3 1 0 0—5 12 2
New York ..................4 0 0 0 1 0 1 3 x—9 12 0
Erskine, Hughes (2), Labine (6), Wade (7); Reynolds, Sain (6). W—Sain. L—Labine. HR—Berra, Collins (N.Y.); Gilliam, Hodges, Shuba (Brk.).

**Game 2**—October 1, at New York
Brooklyn ..................0 0 0 2 0 0 0 0 0—2 9 1
New York ..................1 0 0 0 0 0 1 2 x—4 5 0
Roe; Lopat. W—Lopat. L—Roe. HR—Martin, Mantle (N.Y.).

**Game 3**—October 2, at Brooklyn
New York ..................0 0 0 0 1 0 0 1 0—2 6 0
Brooklyn ..................0 0 0 0 1 1 0 1 x—3 9 0
Raschi; Erskine. W—Erskine. L—Raschi. HR—Campanella (Brk.).

**Game 4**—October 3, at Brooklyn
New York ..................0 0 0 0 2 0 0 0 1—3 9 0
Brooklyn ..................3 0 0 1 0 2 1 0 x—7 12 0
Ford, Gorman (2), Sain (5), Schallock (7); Loes, Labine (9). W—Loes. L—Ford. HR—McDougald (N.Y.); Snider (Brk.).

**Game 5**—October 4, at Brooklyn
New York ................1 0 5 0 0 0 3 1 1—11 11 1
Brooklyn ................0 1 0 0 1 0 0 4 1— 7 14 1
McDonald, Kuzava (8), Reynolds (9); Podres, Meyer (3), Wade (8), Black (9). W—McDonald. L—Podres. HR—Woodling, Mantle, Martin, McDougald (N.Y.); Cox, Gilliam (Brk.).

**Game 6**—October 5, at New York
Brooklyn ..................0 0 0 0 0 1 0 0 2—3 8 3
New York ..................2 1 0 0 0 0 0 0 1—4 13 0
Erskine, Milliken (5), Labine (7); Ford, Reynolds (8). W—Reynolds. L—Labine. HR—Furillo (Brk.).

# 1954

## FINAL STANDINGS

**American League**

| Team | W | L | Pct. | GB |
|---|---|---|---|---|
| Cleveland | 111 | 43 | .721 | ... |
| New York | 103 | 51 | .669 | 8 |
| Chicago | 94 | 60 | .610 | 17 |
| Boston | 69 | 85 | .448 | 42 |
| Detroit | 68 | 86 | .442 | 43 |
| Washington | 66 | 88 | .429 | 45 |
| Baltimore | 54 | 100 | .351 | 57 |
| Philadelphia | 51 | 103 | .331 | 60 |

**National League**

| Team | W | L | Pct. | GB |
|---|---|---|---|---|
| New York | 97 | 57 | .630 | ... |
| Brooklyn | 92 | 62 | .597 | 5 |
| Milwaukee | 89 | 65 | .578 | 8 |
| Philadelphia | 75 | 79 | .487 | 22 |
| Cincinnati | 74 | 80 | .481 | 23 |
| St. Louis | 72 | 82 | .468 | 25 |
| Chicago | 64 | 90 | .416 | 33 |
| Pittsburgh | 53 | 101 | .344 | 44 |

## SIGNIFICANT EVENTS

■ **July 12:** Big-league players organized into a group called the Major League Baseball Players Association and hired J. Norman Lewis to represent the association in negotiations with owners.

■ **November 8:** A.L. owners approved the sale of the Athletics to Chicago industrialist Arnold Johnson and transfer of the team to Kansas City.

■ **December 1:** The finishing touches were put on a record 17-player trade between the Orioles and Yankees.

## MEMORABLE MOMENTS

■ **April 15:** Baltimore welcomed its new Orioles with a huge celebration and the team responded with a 3-1 victory over Chicago at Memorial Stadium.

■ **May 2:** Cardinals slugger Stan Musial hit a doubleheader-record five home runs in a split with the Giants at Busch Stadium.

■ **July 31:** Milwaukee's Joe Adcock joined the exclusive four-homer club in a 15-7 victory over Brooklyn and set a record for total bases (18) when he added a double to his offensive explosion.

■ **September 25:** Early Wynn fired a two-hitter and the Indians defeated Detroit, 11-1, for their A.L.-record 111th victory of the season.

## LEADERS

**American League**

**BA:** Bobby Avila, Cle., .341.
**Runs:** Mickey Mantle, N.Y., 129.
**Hits:** Nellie Fox, Chi.; Harvey Kuenn, Det., 201.
**TB:** Minnie Minoso, Chi., 304.
**HR:** Larry Doby, Cle., 32.
**RBI:** Larry Doby, Cle., 126.
**SB:** Jackie Jensen, Bos., 22.
**Wins:** Bob Lemon, Cle.; Early Wynn, Cle., 23.
**ERA:** Mike Garcia, Cle., 2.64.
**CG:** Bob Lemon, Cle.; Bob Porterfield, Wash., 21.
**IP:** Early Wynn, Cle., 270.2.
**SO:** Bob Turley, Bal., 185.

**National League**

**BA:** Willie Mays, N.Y., .345.
**Runs:** Stan Musial, St.L.; Duke Snider, Brk., 120.
**Hits:** Don Mueller, N.Y., 212.
**TB:** Duke Snider, Brk., 378.
**HR:** Ted Kluszewski, Cin., 49.
**RBI:** Ted Kluszewski, Cin., 141.
**SB:** Bill Bruton, Mil., 34.
**Wins:** Robin Roberts, Phil., 23.
**ERA:** Johnny Antonelli, N.Y., 2.30.
**CG:** Robin Roberts, Phil., 29.
**IP:** Robin Roberts, Phil., 336.2.
**SO:** Robin Roberts, Phil., 185.

**A.L. 20-game winners**

Bob Lemon, Cle., 23-7
Early Wynn, Cle., 23-11
Bob Grim, N.Y., 20-6

**N.L. 20-game winners**

Robin Roberts, Phil., 23-15
Johnny Antonelli, N.Y., 21-7
Warren Spahn, Mil., 21-12

**A.L. 100 RBIs**

Larry Doby, Cle., 126
Yogi Berra, N.Y., 125
Jackie Jensen, Bos., 117
Minnie Minoso, Chi., 116
Mickey Mantle, N.Y., 102
Al Rosen, Cle., 102
Roy Sievers, Wash., 102

**N.L. 100 RBIs**

Ted Kluszewski, Cin., 141
Gil Hodges, Brk., 130
Duke Snider, Brk., 130
Stan Musial, St.L., 126
Del Ennis, Phil., 119
Willie Mays, N.Y., 110
Ray Jablonski, St.L., 104
Eddie Mathews, Mil., 103
Hank Sauer, Chi., 103
Gus Bell, Cin., 101

**N.L. 40 homers**

Ted Kluszewski, Cin., 49
Gil Hodges, Brk., 42
Willie Mays, N.Y., 41
Hank Sauer, Chi., 41
Eddie Mathews, Mil., 40
Duke Snider, Brk., 40

**Most Valuable Player**

A.L.: Yogi Berra, C, N.Y.
N.L.: Willie Mays, OF, N.Y.

**Rookie of the Year**

A.L.: Bob Grim, P, N.Y.
N.L.: Wally Moon, OF, St.L.

**Hall of Fame additions**

Bill Dickey, C, 1928-46
Rabbit Maranville, SS, 1912-35
Bill Terry, 1B, 1923-36

## ALL-STAR GAME

■ **Winner:** Chicago's Nellie Fox looped a two-run eighth-inning single to spark the A.L. in a game that featured two home runs and five RBIs by Cleveland fan favorite Al Rosen.

■ **Key inning:** The eighth. Before Fox's game-winning single, Cleveland's Larry Doby excited the home fans with a game-tying home run.

■ **Memorable moment:** Senators lefthander Dean Stone's no-pitch victory. Stone entered the game with two out in the eighth and retired St. Louis' Red Schoendienst trying to steal home.

■ **Top guns:** Rosen (Indians), Bobby Avila (Indians), Doby (Indians), Ray Boone (Tigers), Fox (White Sox), Yogi Berra (Yankees), A.L.; Duke Snider (Dodgers), Ted Kluszewski (Reds), Gus Bell (Reds), N.L.

■ **MVP:** Rosen.

**Linescore**

July 13, at Cleveland Stadium
N.L. ........................0 0 0 5 2 0 0 2 0— 9 14 0
A.L. ........................0 0 4 1 2 1 0 3 x—11 17 1
Roberts (Phillies), Antonelli (Giants) 4, Spahn (Braves) 6, Grissom (Giants) 6, Conley (Braves) 8, Erskine (Dodgers) 8; Ford (Yankees), Consuegra (White Sox) 4, Lemon (Indians) 4, Porterfield (Senators) 5, Keegan (White Sox) 8, Stone (Senators) 8, Trucks (White Sox) 9. W—Stone. L—Conley. HR—Rosen 2, Boone, Doby, A.L.; Kluszewski, Bell, N.L.

## WORLD SERIES

■ **Winner:** The Giants pulled off a surprising sweep of the Indians, who had won an A.L.-record 111 games.

■ **Turning point:** A three-run 10th-inning home run by pinch-hitter Dusty Rhodes that decided Game 1. Rhodes' pop-fly homer traveled 260 feet.

■ **Memorable moment:** Center fielder Willie Mays' over-the-shoulder catch of a Game 1 blast by Cleveland's Vic Wertz — perhaps the greatest defensive play in Series history.

■ **Top guns:** Rhodes (.667, 2 HR, 7 RBIs), Alvin Dark (.412), Don Mueller (.389), Giants; Wertz (.500), Indians.

**Linescores**

**Game 1**—September 29, at New York
Cleveland ............2 0 0 0 0 0 0 0 0 0—2 8 0
New York.............0 0 2 0 0 0 0 0 0 3—5 9 3
Lemon; Maglie, Liddle (8), Grissom (8). W—Grissom. L—Lemon. HR—Rhodes (N.Y.).

**Game 2**—September 30, at New York
Cleveland ..................1 0 0 0 0 0 0 0 0—1 8 0
New York...................0 0 0 0 2 0 1 0 x—3 4 0
Wynn, Mossi (8); Antonelli. W—Antonelli. L—Wynn. HR—Smith (Cle.); Rhodes (N.Y.).

**Game 3**—October 1, at Cleveland
New York.................1 0 3 0 1 1 0 0 0—6 10 1
Cleveland ................0 0 0 0 0 0 1 1 0—2 4 2
Gomez, Wilhelm (8); Garcia, Houtteman (4), Narleski (6), Mossi (9). W—Gomez. L—Garcia. HR—Wertz (Cle.).

**Game 4**—October 2, at Cleveland
New York.................0 2 1 0 4 0 0 0 0—7 10 3
Cleveland ................0 0 0 0 3 0 1 0 0—4 6 2
Liddle, Wilhelm (7), Antonelli (8); Lemon, Newhouser (5), Narleski (5), Mossi (6), Garcia (8). W—Liddle. L—Lemon. HR—Majeski (Cle.).

# 1955

## FINAL STANDINGS

**American League**

| Team | W | L | Pct. | GB |
|---|---|---|---|---|
| New York | 96 | 58 | .623 | ... |
| Cleveland | 93 | 61 | .604 | 3 |
| Chicago | 91 | 63 | .591 | 5 |
| Boston | 84 | 70 | .545 | 12 |
| Detroit | 79 | 75 | .513 | 17 |
| Kansas City | 63 | 91 | .409 | 33 |
| Baltimore | 57 | 97 | .370 | 39 |
| Washington | 53 | 101 | .344 | 43 |

**National League**

| Team | W | L | Pct. | GB |
|---|---|---|---|---|
| Brooklyn | 98 | 55 | .641 | ... |
| Milwaukee | 85 | 69 | .552 | 13.5 |
| New York | 80 | 74 | .519 | 18.5 |
| Philadelphia | 77 | 77 | .500 | 21.5 |
| Cincinnati | 75 | 79 | .487 | 23.5 |
| Chicago | 72 | 81 | .471 | 26 |
| St. Louis | 68 | 86 | .442 | 30.5 |
| Pittsburgh | 60 | 94 | .390 | 38.5 |

## SIGNIFICANT EVENT

■ **April 14:** The New York Yankees, one of four non-integrated teams, broke the color barrier when Elston Howard played at Boston. He singled in his first big-league at-bat.

## MEMORABLE MOMENTS

■ **April 12:** The Athletics made their Kansas City debut with a 6-2 victory over the Tigers.
■ **April 23:** The White Sox hit seven home runs and tied a modern run-scoring record with a 29-6 victory at Kansas City.
■ **September 25:** Giants slugger Willie Mays, baseball's seventh 50-homer man, belted No. 51 in a 5-2 victory over the Phillies.
■ **September 25:** Tigers outfielder Al Kaline, 20, became baseball's youngest batting champ when he finished with an A.L.-best .340 average.

## LEADERS

**American League**
**BA:** Al Kaline, Det., .340.
**Runs:** Al Smith, Cle., 123.
**Hits:** Al Kaline, Det., 200.
**TB:** Al Kaline, Det., 321.
**HR:** Mickey Mantle, N.Y., 37.
**RBI:** Ray Boone, Det.; Jackie Jensen, Bos., 116.
**SB:** Jim Rivera, Chi., 25.
**Wins:** Whitey Ford, N.Y.; Bob Lemon, Cle.; Frank Sullivan, Bos., 18.
**ERA:** Billy Pierce, Chi., 1.97.
**CG:** Whitey Ford, N.Y., 18.
**IP:** Frank Sullivan, Bos., 260.
**SO:** Herb Score, Cle., 245.

**National League**
**BA:** Richie Ashburn, Phil., .338.
**Runs:** Duke Snider, Brk., 126.
**Hits:** Ted Kluszewski, Cin., 192.
**TB:** Willie Mays, N.Y., 382.
**HR:** Willie Mays, N.Y., 51.
**RBI:** Duke Snider, Brk., 136.
**SB:** Bill Bruton, Mil., 25.
**Wins:** Robin Roberts, Phil., 23.
**ERA:** Bob Friend, Pit., 2.83.
**CG:** Robin Roberts, Phil., 26.
**IP:** Robin Roberts, Phil., 305.
**SO:** Sam Jones, Chi., 198.

**N.L. 20-game winners**
Robin Roberts, Phil., 23-14
Don Newcombe, Brk., 20-5

**A.L. 100 RBIs**
Ray Boone, Det., 116
Jackie Jensen, Bos., 116
Yogi Berra, N.Y., 108
Roy Sievers, Wash., 106
Al Kaline, Det., 102

**N.L. 100 RBIs**
Duke Snider, Brk., 136
Willie Mays, N.Y., 127
Del Ennis, Phil., 120
Ernie Banks, Chi., 117
Ted Kluszewski, Cin., 113
Wally Post, Cin., 109
Stan Musial, St.L., 108
Roy Campanella, Brk., 107
Hank Aaron, Mil., 106
Gus Bell, Cin., 104
Gil Hodges, Brk., 102
Eddie Mathews, Mil., 101

**N.L. 40 homers**
Willie Mays, N.Y., 51
Ted Kluszewski, Cin., 47
Ernie Banks, Chi., 44
Duke Snider, Brk., 42
Eddie Mathews, Mil., 41
Wally Post, Cin., 40

**Most Valuable Player**
A.L.: Yogi Berra, C, N.Y.
N.L.: Roy Campanella, C, Brk.

**Rookie of the Year**
A.L.: Herb Score, P, Cle.
N.L.: Bill Virdon, OF, St.L.

**Hall of Fame additions**
Home Run Baker, 3B, 1908-22
Joe DiMaggio, OF, 1936-51
Gabby Hartnett, C, 1922-41
Ted Lyons, P, 1923-46
Ray Schalk, C, 1912-29
Dazzy Vance, P, 1915-35

## ALL-STAR GAME

■ **Winner:** The N.L., down 5-0 entering the seventh inning, rallied for a 6-5 victory in 12 innings — the second longest All-Star Game.
■ **Key inning:** The N.L.'s three-run eighth, which tied the score and forced extra innings. The tying run scored on right fielder Al Kaline's wild throw.
■ **Memorable moment:** Stan Musial's first-pitch home run in the 12th off Boston's Frank Sullivan. It was Musial's record fourth All-Star homer.
■ **Top guns:** Joe Nuxhall (Reds), Gene Conley (Braves), Willie Mays (Giants), Hank Aaron (Braves), Musial (Cardinals), N.L.; Billy Pierce (White Sox), Chico Carrasquel (White Sox), Mickey Mantle (Yankees), A.L.
■ **MVP:** Musial.

**Linescore**

July 12, at Milwaukee's County Stadium
A.L. ..............4 0 0 0 0 1 0 0 0 0 0 0—5 10 2
N.L. ..............0 0 0 0 0 0 2 3 0 0 0 1—6 13 1
Pierce (White Sox), Wynn (Indians) 4, Ford (Yankees) 7, Sullivan (Red Sox) 8; Roberts (Phillies), Haddix (Cardinals) 4, Newcombe (Dodgers) 7, Jones (Cubs) 8, Nuxhall (Reds) 8, Conley (Braves) 12. W—Conley. L—Sullivan. HR—Mantle, A.L.; Musial, N.L.

## WORLD SERIES

■ **Winner:** Brooklyn's long wait finally ended as the Dodgers won a Series on their eighth try — beating the hated Yankees in the process.
■ **Turning point:** Hot-hitting Duke Snider's two home runs powered the Dodgers to within a game of their first championship in a 5-3 Game 5 victory.
■ **Memorable moment:** A spectacular Series-saving catch by Dodgers outfielder Sandy Amoros in the sixth inning of Game 7. The two-on, nobody-out catch of Yogi Berra's line drive resulted in a double play and preserved Johnny Podres' 2-0 shutout.
■ **Top guns:** Podres (2-0, 1.00 ERA), Snider (.320, 4 HR, 7 RBIs), Dodgers; Whitey Ford (2-0, 2.12), Hank Bauer (.429), Berra (.417), Yankees.
■ **MVP:** Podres.

**Linescores**

**Game 1**—September 28, at New York
Brooklyn ..................0 2 1 0 0 0 0 2 0—5 10 0
New York..................0 2 1 1 0 2 0 0 x—6 9 1
Newcombe, Bessent (6), Labine (8); Ford, Grim (9). W—Ford. L—Newcombe. HR—Collins 2, Howard (N.Y.); Furillo, Snider (Brk.).

**Game 2**—September 29, at New York
Brooklyn ..................0 0 0 1 1 0 0 0 0—2 5 2
New York..................0 0 0 4 0 0 0 0 x—4 8 0
Loes, Bessent (4), Spooner (5), Labine (8); Byrne. W—Byrne. L—Loes.

**Game 3**—September 30, at Brooklyn
New York..................0 2 0 0 0 0 1 0 0—3 7 0
Brooklyn ..................2 2 0 2 0 0 2 0 x—8 11 1
Turley, Morgan (2), Kucks (5), Sturdivant (7); Podres. W—Podres. L—Turley. HR—Campanella (Brk.); Mantle (N.Y.).

**Game 4**—October 1, at Brooklyn
New York..................1 1 0 1 0 2 0 0 0—5 9 0
Brooklyn ..................0 0 1 3 3 0 1 0 x—8 14 0
Larsen, Kucks (5), R. Coleman (6), Morgan (7), Sturdivant (8); Erskine, Bessent (4), Labine (5). W—Labine. L—Larsen. HR—McDougald (N.Y.); Campanella, Hodges, Snider (Brk).

**Game 5**—October 2, at Brooklyn
New York..................0 0 0 1 0 0 1 1 0—3 6 0
Brooklyn ..................0 2 1 0 1 0 0 1 x—5 9 2
Grim, Turley (7); Craig, Labine (7). W—Craig. L—Grim. HR—Snider 2, Amoros (Brk.); Cerv, Berra (N.Y.).

**Game 6**—October 3, at New York
Brooklyn ..................0 0 0 1 0 0 0 0 0—1 4 1
New York..................5 0 0 0 0 0 0 0 x—5 8 0
Spooner, Meyer (1), Roebuck (7); Ford. W—Ford. L—Spooner. HR—Skowron (N.Y.).

**Game 7**—October 4, at New York
Brooklyn ..................0 0 0 1 0 1 0 0 0—2 5 0
New York..................0 0 0 0 0 0 0 0 0—0 8 1
Podres; Byrne, Grim (6), Turley (8). W—Podres. L—Byrne.

# 1956

## FINAL STANDINGS

**American League**

| Team | W | L | Pct. | GB |
|---|---|---|---|---|
| New York | 97 | 57 | .630 | ... |
| Cleveland | 88 | 66 | .571 | 9 |
| Chicago | 85 | 69 | .552 | 12 |
| Boston | 84 | 70 | .545 | 13 |
| Detroit | 82 | 72 | .532 | 15 |
| Baltimore | 69 | 85 | .448 | 28 |
| Washington | 59 | 95 | .383 | 38 |
| Kansas City | 52 | 102 | .338 | 45 |

**National League**

| Team | W | L | Pct. | GB |
|---|---|---|---|---|
| Brooklyn | 93 | 61 | .604 | ... |
| Milwaukee | 92 | 62 | .597 | 1 |
| Cincinnati | 91 | 63 | .591 | 2 |
| St. Louis | 76 | 78 | .494 | 17 |
| Philadelphia | 71 | 83 | .461 | 22 |
| New York | 67 | 87 | .435 | 26 |
| Pittsburgh | 66 | 88 | .429 | 27 |
| Chicago | 60 | 94 | .390 | 33 |

## SIGNIFICANT EVENTS

■ **April 19:** The Dodgers played the first of seven "home-away-from-home" games at Jersey City's Roosevelt Stadium and posted a 10-inning, 5-4 victory over the Phillies.
■ **September 30:** Yankee slugger Mickey Mantle finished his Triple Crown journey with a .353 average, 52 home runs and 130 RBIs.
■ **November 21:** N.L. MVP Don Newcombe, who finished 27-7 for the Dodgers, captured the inaugural Cy Young Award as baseball's top pitcher.

## MEMORABLE MOMENTS

■ **May 28:** Pittsburgh first baseman Dale Long hit a home run in his record eighth consecutive game as the Pirates defeated Brooklyn, 3-2.
■ **September 11:** Cincinnati's Frank Robinson tied the rookie home run record when he hit No. 38 in an 11-5 victory over the Giants.
■ **September 30:** The Dodgers posted a final-day 8-6 victory over Pittsburgh and captured their second straight N.L. pennant by one game over Milwaukee.

## LEADERS

**American League**
**BA:** Mickey Mantle, N.Y., .353.
**Runs:** Mickey Mantle, N.Y., 132.
**Hits:** Harvey Kuenn, Det., 196.
**TB:** Mickey Mantle, N.Y., 376.
**HR:** Mickey Mantle, N.Y., 52.
**RBI:** Mickey Mantle, N.Y., 130.
**SB:** Luis Aparicio, Chi., 21.
**Wins:** Frank Lary, Det., 21.
**ERA:** Whitey Ford, N.Y., 2.47.
**CG:** Bob Lemon, Cle.; Billy Pierce, Chi., 21.
**IP:** Frank Lary, Det., 294.
**SO:** Herb Score, Cle., 263.

**National League**
**BA:** Hank Aaron, Mil., .328.
**Runs:** Frank Robinson, Cin., 122.
**Hits:** Hank Aaron, Mil., 200.
**TB:** Hank Aaron, Mil., 340.
**HR:** Duke Snider, Brk., 43.
**RBI:** Stan Musial, St.L., 109.
**SB:** Willie Mays, N.Y., 40.
**Wins:** Don Newcombe, Brk., 27.
**ERA:** Lew Burdette, Mil., 2.70.
**CG:** Robin Roberts, Phil., 22.
**IP:** Bob Friend, Pit., 314.1
**SO:** Sam Jones, Chi., 176.

**A.L. 20-game winners**
Frank Lary, Det., 21-13
Herb Score, Cle., 20-9
Early Wynn, Cle., 20-9
Billy Pierce, Chi., 20-9
Bob Lemon, Cle., 20-14
Billy Hoeft, Det., 20-14

**N.L. 20-game winners**
Don Newcombe, Brk., 27-7
Warren Spahn, Mil., 20-11
Johnny Antonelli, N.Y., 20-13

**A.L. 100 RBIs**
Mickey Mantle, N.Y., 130
Al Kaline, Det., 128
Vic Wertz, Cle., 106
Yogi Berra, N.Y., 105
Harry Simpson, K.C., 105
Larry Doby, Chi., 102

**N.L. 100 RBIs**
Stan Musial, St.L., 109
Joe Adcock, Mil., 103
Ted Kluszewski, Cin., 102
Duke Snider, Brk., 101

**A.L. 40 homers**
Mickey Mantle, N.Y., 52

**N.L. 40 homers**
Duke Snider, Brk., 43

**Most Valuable Player**
A.L.: Mickey Mantle, OF, N.Y.
N.L.: Don Newcombe, P, Brk.

**Cy Young Award**
A.L.-N.L.: Don Newcombe, Brk.

**Rookie of the Year**
A.L.: Luis Aparicio, SS, Chi.
N.L.: Frank Robinson, OF, Cin.

**Hall of Fame additions**
Joe Cronin, SS/Man./Exec.
Hank Greenberg, 1B, 1930-47

## ALL-STAR GAME

■ **Winner:** Third baseman Ken Boyer singled three times and made three outstanding defensive plays to lead the N.L. to victory — its sixth in seven years.
■ **Key inning:** The fourth, when the N.L. stretched its 1-0 lead on a two-run pinch-hit homer by Willie Mays.
■ **Memorable moment:** Stan Musial's fifth All-Star home run, a seventh-inning shot that offset sixth-inning blasts by A.L. stars Ted Williams and Mickey Mantle.
■ **Top guns:** Bob Friend (Pirates), Boyer (Cardinals), Mays (Giants), Ted Kluszewski (Reds), Musial (Cardinals), N.L.; Williams (Red Sox), Mantle (Yankees), Yogi Berra (Yankees), A.L.
■ **MVP:** Boyer.

**Linescore**

July 10, at Washington's Griffith Stadium
N.L. ..........................0 0 1 2 1 1 2 0 0—7 11 0
A.L. ..........................0 0 0 0 0 3 0 0 0—3 11 0
Friend (Pirates), Spahn (Braves) 4, Antonelli (Giants) 6; Pierce (White Sox), Ford (Yankees) 4, Wilson (White Sox) 5, Brewer (Red Sox) 6, Score (Indians) 8, Wynn (Indians) 9. W—Friend. L—Pierce. HR—Mays, Musial, N.L.; Williams, Mantle, A.L.

## WORLD SERIES

■ **Winner:** The Yankees turned the tables on the Dodgers in a Series featuring one of baseball's most incredible pitching performances.
■ **Turning point:** 5-3 and 6-2 Yankee victories in Games 3 and 4 after the Dodgers had won the first two games.
■ **Memorable moment:** The final pitch of Yankee righthander Don Larsen's Game 5 perfect game — the first no-hitter in Series history. Larsen struck out pinch-hitter Dale Mitchell to complete his 2-0 shutout.
■ **Top guns:** Larsen (1-0, 0.00 ERA), Yogi Berra (.360, 3 HR, 10 RBIs), Enos Slaughter (.350), Yankees; Gil Hodges (.304, 8 RBIs), Dodgers.
■ **MVP:** Larsen.

**Linescores**

**Game 1**—October 3, at Brooklyn
New York.....................2 0 0 1 0 0 0 0 0—3 9 1
Brooklyn .....................0 2 3 1 0 0 0 0 x—6 9 0
Ford, Kucks (4), Morgan (6), Turley (8); Maglie. W—Maglie. L—Ford. HR—Mantle, Martin (N.Y.); Robinson, Hodges (Brk.).

**Game 2**—October 5, at Brooklyn
New York..........1 5 0 1 0 0 0 0 1— 8 12 2
Brooklyn ................0 6 1 2 2 0 0 2 x—13 12 0
Larsen, Kucks (2), Byrne (2), Sturdivant (3), Morgan (3), Turley (5), McDermott (6); Newcombe, Roebuck (2), Bessent (3). W—Bessent. L—Morgan. HR—Berra (N.Y.); Snider (Brk.).

**Game 3**—October 6, at New York
Brooklyn .....................0 1 0 0 0 1 1 0 0—3 8 1
New York.....................0 1 0 0 0 3 0 1 x—5 8 1
Craig, Labine (7); Ford. W—Ford. L—Craig. HR—Martin, Slaughter (N.Y.).

**Game 4**—October 7, at New York
Brooklyn .....................0 0 0 1 0 0 0 0 1—2 6 0
New York.....................1 0 0 2 0 1 2 0 x—6 7 2
Erskine, Roebuck (5), Drysdale (7); Sturdivant. W—Sturdivant. L—Erskine. HR—Mantle, Bauer (N.Y.).

**Game 5**—October 8, at New York
Brooklyn .....................0 0 0 0 0 0 0 0 0—0 0 0
New York.....................0 0 0 1 0 1 0 0 x—2 5 0
Maglie; Larsen. W—Larsen. L—Maglie. HR—Mantle (N.Y.).

**Game 6**—October 9, at Brooklyn
New York...............0 0 0 0 0 0 0 0 0 0—0 7 0
Brooklyn ..............0 0 0 0 0 0 0 0 0 1—1 4 0
Turley; Labine. W—Labine. L—Turley.

**Game 7**—October 10, at Brooklyn
New York...................2 0 2 1 0 0 4 0 0—9 10 0
Brooklyn ...................0 0 0 0 0 0 0 0 0—0 3 1
Kucks; Newcombe, Bessent (4), Craig (7), Roebuck (7), Erskine (9). W—Kucks. L—Newcombe. HR—Berra 2, Howard, Skowron (N.Y.).

# 1957

## FINAL STANDINGS

**American League**

| Team | W | L | Pct. | GB |
|---|---|---|---|---|
| New York | 98 | 56 | .636 | ... |
| Chicago | 90 | 64 | .584 | 8 |
| Boston | 82 | 72 | .532 | 16 |
| Detroit | 78 | 76 | .506 | 20 |
| Baltimore | 76 | 76 | .500 | 21 |
| Cleveland | 76 | 77 | .497 | 21.5 |
| Kansas City | 59 | 94 | .386 | 38.5 |
| Washington | 55 | 99 | .357 | 43 |

**National League**

| Team | W | L | Pct. | GB |
|---|---|---|---|---|
| Milwaukee | 95 | 59 | .617 | ... |
| St. Louis | 87 | 67 | .565 | 8 |
| Brooklyn | 84 | 70 | .545 | 11 |
| Cincinnati | 80 | 74 | .519 | 15 |
| Philadelphia | 77 | 77 | .500 | 18 |
| New York | 69 | 85 | .448 | 26 |
| Chicago | 62 | 92 | .403 | 33 |
| Pittsburgh | 62 | 92 | .403 | 33 |

## SIGNIFICANT EVENTS

■ **February 2:** Baseball owners approved a five-year pension plan offering more liberal benefits to players, coaches and trainers.

■ **April 22:** The Phillies became the final N.L. team to break the color barrier when John Kennedy was inserted as a pinch-runner in a 5-1 loss to Brooklyn.

■ **May 28:** N.L. owners approved the proposed moves of the Dodgers and Giants to the West Coast, opening the door for relocations that would become official in the fall.

■ **June 28:** Commissioner Ford Frick infuriated ballot-stuffing Cincinnati fans when he replaced three members of an all-Reds starting lineup for the All-Star Game.

## MEMORABLE MOMENTS

■ **May 7:** Young Cleveland ace Herb Score suffered a career-threatening injury when he was hit in the eye by Yankee Gil McDougald's line drive.

■ **September 23:** Hank Aaron belted a two-run, 11th-inning homer to give the Braves a 4-2 victory over St. Louis and their first pennant since moving to Milwaukee.

## LEADERS

**American League**

**BA:** Ted Williams, Bos., .388.
**Runs:** Mickey Mantle, N.Y., 121.
**Hits:** Nellie Fox, Chi., 196.
**TB:** Roy Sievers, Wash., 331.
**HR:** Roy Sievers, Wash., 42.
**RBI:** Roy Sievers, Wash., 114.
**SB:** Luis Aparicio, Chi., 28.
**Wins:** Jim Bunning, Det.; Billy Pierce, Chi., 20.
**ERA:** Bobby Shantz, N.Y., 2.45.
**CG:** Dick Donovan, Chi.; Billy Pierce, Chi., 16.
**IP:** Jim Bunning, Det., 267.1.
**SO:** Early Wynn, Cle., 184.

**National League**

**BA:** Stan Musial, St.L., .351.
**Runs:** Hank Aaron, Mil., 118.
**Hits:** Red Schoendienst, N.Y.-Mil., 200.
**TB:** Hank Aaron, Mil., 369.
**HR:** Hank Aaron, Mil., 44.
**RBI:** Hank Aaron, Mil., 132.
**SB:** Willie Mays, N.Y., 38.
**Wins:** Warren Spahn, Mil., 21.
**ERA:** Johnny Podres, Brk., 2.66.
**CG:** Warren Spahn, Mil., 18.
**IP:** Bob Friend, Pit., 277.
**SO:** Jack Sanford, Phil., 188.

**A.L. 20-game winners**
Jim Bunning, Det., 20-8
Billy Pierce, Chi., 20-12

**N.L. 20-game winners**
Warren Spahn, Mil., 21-11

**A.L. 100 RBIs**
Roy Sievers, Wash., 114
Vic Wertz, Cle., 105
Jackie Jensen, Bos., 103
Frank Malzone, Bos., 103
Minnie Minoso, Chi., 103

**N.L. 100 RBIs**
Hank Aaron, Mil., 132
Del Ennis, St.L., 105
Ernie Banks, Chi., 102
Stan Musial, St.L., 102

**A.L. 40 homers**
Roy Sievers, Wash., 42

**N.L. 40 homers**
Hank Aaron, Mil., 44
Ernie Banks, Chi., 43
Duke Snider, Brk., 40

**Most Valuable Player**
A.L.: Mickey Mantle, OF, N.Y.
N.L.: Hank Aaron, OF, Mil.

**Cy Young Award**
A.L.-N.L.: Warren Spahn, Mil.

**Rookie of the Year**
A.L.: Tony Kubek, IF/OF, N.Y.
N.L.: Jack Sanford, P, Phil.

**Hall of Fame additions**
Sam Crawford, OF, 1899-1917
Joe McCarthy, manager

## ALL-STAR GAME

■ **Winner:** Minnie Minoso, who had doubled home a run in the top of the ninth, made two outstanding defensive plays in the bottom of the inning to preserve the A.L.'s victory.

■ **Key inning:** The ninth. After the A.L. had scored three times in the top of the frame for a 6-2 lead, the N.L. answered with three runs and had the tying run on second when the game ended.

■ **Memorable moment:** Left fielder Minoso, who had just thrown out a runner trying to advance to third, made an outstanding game-ending catch of a Gil Hodges drive into left-center field.

■ **Top guns:** Jim Bunning (Tigers), Al Kaline (Tigers), Bill Skowron (Yankees), Minoso (White Sox), A.L.; Lew Burdette (Braves), Willie Mays (Giants), Gus Bell (Reds), N.L.

■ **MVP:** Minoso.

**Linescore**

July 9, at St. Louis' Busch Stadium
A.L. ..........................0 2 0 0 0 1 0 0 3—6 10 0
N.L. ..........................0 0 0 0 0 0 2 0 3—5 9 1
Bunning (Tigers), Loes (Orioles) 4, Wynn (Indians) 7, Pierce (White Sox) 7, Mossi (Indians) 9, Grim (Yankees) 9; Simmons (Phillies), Burdette (Braves) 2, Sanford (Phillies) 6, Jackson (Cardinals) 7, Labine (Dodgers) 9. W—Bunning. L—Simmons.

## WORLD SERIES

■ **Winner:** The Braves' fifth Milwaukee season produced the franchise's first Series winner since the miracle of 1914.

■ **Turning point:** A two-run 10th-inning home run by Eddie Mathews that gave Milwaukee a 7-5 victory in Game 4 and evened the Series at two games apiece.

■ **Memorable moment:** The final pitch of Milwaukee righthander Lew Burdette's 5-0 seventh-game shutout, giving Milwaukee its first Series championship.

■ **Top guns:** Burdette (3-0, 0.67 ERA), Hank Aaron (.393, 3 HR, 7 RBIs), Frank Torre (.300, 2 HR), Braves; Jerry Coleman (.364), Yankees.

■ **MVP:** Burdette.

**Linescores**

**Game 1**—October 2, at New York
Milwaukee..................0 0 0 0 0 0 1 0 0—1 5 0
New York....................0 0 0 0 1 2 0 0 x—3 9 1
Spahn, Johnson (6), McMahon (7); Ford. W—Ford. L—Spahn.

**Game 2**—October 3, at New York
Milwaukee..................0 1 1 2 0 0 0 0 0—4 8 0
New York....................0 1 1 0 0 0 0 0 0—2 7 2
Burdette; Shantz, Ditmar (4), Grim (8). W—Burdette. L—Shantz. HR—Logan (Mil.); Bauer (N.Y.).

**Game 3**—October 5, at Milwaukee
New York..................3 0 2 2 0 0 5 0 0—12 9 0
Milwaukee................0 1 0 0 2 0 0 0 0— 3 8 1
Turley, Larsen (2); Buhl, Pizarro (1), Conley (3), Johnson (5), Trowbridge (7), McMahon (8). W—Larsen. L—Buhl. HR—Kubek 2, Mantle (N.Y.); Aaron (Mil.).

**Game 4**—October 6, at Milwaukee
New York...........1 0 0 0 0 0 0 0 3 1—5 11 0
Milwaukee..........0 0 0 4 0 0 0 0 0 3—7 7 0
Sturdivant, Shantz (5), Kucks (8), Byrne (8), Grim (10); Spahn. W—Spahn. L—Grim. HR—Aaron, Torre, Mathews (Mil.); Howard (N.Y.).

**Game 5**—October 7, at Milwaukee
New York....................0 0 0 0 0 0 0 0 0—0 7 0
Milwaukee..................0 0 0 0 0 1 0 0 x—1 6 1
Ford, Turley (8); Burdette. W—Burdette. L—Ford.

**Game 6**—October 9, at New York
Milwaukee..................0 0 0 0 1 0 1 0 0—2 4 0
New York....................0 0 2 0 0 0 1 0 x—3 7 0
Buhl, Johnson (3), McMahon (8); Turley. W—Turley. L—Johnson. HR—Berra, Bauer (N.Y.); Torre, Aaron (Mil.).

**Game 7**—October 10, at New York
Milwaukee..................0 0 4 0 0 0 0 1 0—5 9 1
New York....................0 0 0 0 0 0 0 0 0—0 7 3
Burdette; Larsen, Shantz (3), Ditmar (4), Sturdivant (6), Byrne (8). W—Burdette. L—Larsen. HR—Crandall (Mil.).

# 1958

## FINAL STANDINGS

**American League**

| Team | W | L | Pct. | GB |
|---|---|---|---|---|
| New York | 92 | 62 | .597 | ... |
| Chicago | 82 | 72 | .532 | 10 |
| Boston | 79 | 75 | .513 | 13 |
| Cleveland | 77 | 76 | .503 | 14.5 |
| Detroit | 77 | 77 | .500 | 15 |
| Baltimore | 74 | 79 | .484 | 17.5 |
| Kansas City | 73 | 81 | .474 | 19 |
| Washington | 61 | 93 | .396 | 31 |

**National League**

| Team | W | L | Pct. | GB |
|---|---|---|---|---|
| Milwaukee | 92 | 62 | .597 | ... |
| Pittsburgh | 84 | 70 | .545 | 8 |
| San Francisco | 80 | 74 | .519 | 12 |
| Cincinnati | 76 | 78 | .494 | 16 |
| Chicago | 72 | 82 | .468 | 20 |
| St. Louis | 72 | 82 | .468 | 20 |
| Los Angeles | 71 | 83 | .461 | 21 |
| Philadelphia | 69 | 85 | .448 | 23 |

## SIGNIFICANT EVENTS

■ **January 28:** Dodgers catcher Roy Campanella suffered a broken neck and paralysis from his shoulders down when the car he was driving overturned on a slippery road in Glen Cove, N.Y.

■ **January 29:** Stan Musial became the N.L.'s first six-figure star when he signed with the Cardinals for $100,000.

■ **January 30:** Commissioner Ford Frick took the All-Star vote away from the fans, handing it back to the players, coaches and managers.

■ **September 28:** Boston's 40-year-old Ted Williams used a 7-for-11 closing surge to win his sixth A.L. batting title with a .328 average.

■ **December 3:** Will Harridge, who served as A.L. president for more than 27 years, retired at age 72.

## MEMORABLE MOMENTS

■ **April 15:** The Giants rolled to an 8-0 victory over the Dodgers at San Francisco's Seals Stadium in the first Major League game on the West Coast.

■ **April 18:** The Dodgers rewarded a record Los Angeles Coliseum crowd of 78,672 with a 6-5 victory over the Giants in their West Coast home debut.

■ **May 13:** Stan Musial became the eighth member of baseball's 3,000-hit club when he stroked a pinch-hit double off Moe Drabowsky in a 5-3 Cardinals victory at Chicago.

## LEADERS

**American League**

**BA:** Ted Williams, Bos., .328.
**Runs:** Mickey Mantle, N.Y., 127.
**Hits:** Nellie Fox, Chi., 187.
**TB:** Mickey Mantle, N.Y., 307.
**HR:** Mickey Mantle, N.Y., 42.
**RBI:** Jackie Jensen, Bos., 122.
**SB:** Luis Aparicio, Chi., 29.
**Wins:** Bob Turley, N.Y., 21.
**ERA:** Whitey Ford, N.Y., 2.01.
**CG:** Frank Lary, Det.; Billy Pierce, Chi.; Bob Turley, N.Y., 19.
**IP:** Frank Lary, Det., 260.1.
**SO:** Early Wynn, Chi., 179.

**National League**

**BA:** Richie Ashburn, Phil., .350.
**Runs:** Willie Mays, S.F., 121.
**Hits:** Richie Ashburn, Phil., 215.
**TB:** Ernie Banks, Chi., 379.
**HR:** Ernie Banks, Chi., 47.
**RBI:** Ernie Banks, Chi., 129.
**SB:** Willie Mays, S.F., 31.
**Wins:** Bob Friend, Pit.; Warren Spahn, Mil., 22.
**ERA:** Stu Miller, S.F., 2.47.
**CG:** Warren Spahn, Mil., 23.
**IP:** Warren Spahn, Mil., 290.
**SO:** Sam Jones, St.L., 225.

**A.L. 20-game winners**
Bob Turley, N.Y., 21-7

**N.L. 20-game winners**
Warren Spahn, Mil., 22-11
Bob Friend, Pit., 22-14
Lew Burdette, Mil., 20-10

**A.L. 100 RBIs**
Jackie Jensen, Bos., 122
Rocky Colavito, Cle., 113
Roy Sievers, Wash., 108
Bob Cerv, K.C., 104

**N.L. 100 RBIs**
Ernie Banks, Chi., 129
Frank Thomas, Pit., 109

**A.L. 40 homers**
Mickey Mantle, N.Y., 42
Rocky Colavito, Cle., 41

**N.L. 40 homers**
Ernie Banks, Chi., 47

**Most Valuable Player**
A.L.: Jackie Jensen, OF, Bos.
N.L.: Ernie Banks, SS, Chi.

**Cy Young Award**
A.L.-N.L.: Bob Turley, N.Y. (AL).

**Rookie of the Year**
A.L.: Albie Pearson, OF, Wash.
N.L.: Orlando Cepeda, 1B, S.F.

## ALL-STAR GAME

■ **Winner:** After spotting the N.L. a 3-1 lead, the A.L. rallied for a 4-3 victory in the first All-Star Game without an extra-base hit. Ray Narleski, Early Wynn and Billy O'Dell allowed one hit over the final 7 1/3 innings.

■ **Key inning:** The sixth, when the A.L. scored the go-ahead run on a single by Gil McDougald.

■ **Memorable moment:** The last out of the game — the ninth consecutive batter retired by hometown favorite O'Dell.

■ **Top guns:** Narleski (Indians), Wynn (White Sox), O'Dell (Orioles), Nellie Fox (White Sox), McDougald (Yankees), A.L.; Willie Mays (Giants), N.L.

■ **MVP:** O'Dell.

**Linescore**

July 8, at Baltimore's Memorial Stadium
N.L. ..........................2 1 0 0 0 0 0 0 0—3 4 2
A.L. ..........................1 1 0 0 1 1 0 0 x—4 9 2
Spahn (Braves), Friend (Pirates) 4, Jackson (Cardinals) 6, Farrell (Phillies) 7; Turley (Yankees), Narleski (Indians) 2, Wynn (White Sox) 6, O'Dell (Orioles) 7. W—Wynn. L—Friend.

## WORLD SERIES

■ **Winner:** The Yankees became only the second team to recover from a three-games-to-one deficit en route to their seventh Series victory in 10 years under manager Casey Stengel.

■ **Turning point:** Bob Turley's five-hit 7-0 victory in Game 5 with his Yankees on the brink of elimination.

■ **Memorable moment:** A 10th-inning Game 6 home run by Gil McDougald that lifted the Yankees to a 4-3 victory and forced a seventh game.

■ **Top guns:** Turley (2-1, 2.76 ERA), Hank Bauer (.323, 4 HR, 8 RBIs), McDougald (.321, 2 HR, 4 RBIs), Yankees; Bill Bruton (.412), Braves.

■ **MVP:** Turley.

**Linescores**

**Game 1**—October 1, at Milwaukee
New York............0 0 0 1 2 0 0 0 0 0—3 8 1
Milwaukee..........0 0 0 2 0 0 0 1 0 1—4 10 0
Ford, Duren (8); Spahn. W—Spahn. L—Duren. HR—Skowron, Bauer (N.Y.).

**Game 2**—October 2, at Milwaukee
New York................1 0 0 1 0 0 0 0 3— 5 7 0
Milwaukee..............7 1 0 0 0 0 2 3 x—13 15 1
Turley, Maas (1), Kucks (1), Dickson (5), Monroe (8); Burdette. W—Burdette. L—Turley. HR—Bruton, Burdette (Mil.); Mantle 2, Bauer (N.Y.).

**Game 3**—October 4, at New York
Milwaukee..................0 0 0 0 0 0 0 0 0—0 6 0
New York....................0 0 0 0 2 0 2 0 x—4 4 0
Rush, McMahon (7); Larsen, Duren (8). W—Larsen. L—Rush. HR—Bauer (N.Y.).

**Game 4**—October 5, at New York
Milwaukee..................0 0 0 0 0 1 1 1 0—3 9 0
New York....................0 0 0 0 0 0 0 0 0—0 2 1
Spahn; Ford, Kucks (8), Dickson (9). W—Spahn. L—Ford.

**Game 5**—October 6, at New York
Milwaukee................0 0 0 0 0 0 0 0 0—0 5 0
New York..................0 0 1 0 0 6 0 0 x—7 10 0
Burdette, Pizarro (6), Willey (8); Turley. W—Turley. L—Burdette. HR—McDougald (N.Y.).

**Game 6**——October 8, at Milwaukee
New York............1 0 0 0 0 1 0 0 0 2—4 10 1
Milwaukee..........1 1 0 0 0 0 0 0 0 1—3 10 4
Ford, Ditmar (2), Duren (6), Turley (10); Spahn, McMahon (10). W—Duren. L—Spahn. HR—Bauer, McDougald (N.Y.).

**Game 7**—October 9, at Milwaukee
New York...................0 2 0 0 0 0 0 4 0—6 8 0
Milwaukee.................1 0 0 0 0 1 0 0 0—2 5 2
Larsen, Turley (3); Burdette, McMahon (9). W—Turley. L—Burdette. HR—Crandall (Mil.); Skowron (N.Y.).

# 1959

## FINAL STANDINGS

**American League**

| Team | W | L | Pct. | GB |
|---|---|---|---|---|
| Chicago | 94 | 60 | .610 | ... |
| Cleveland | 89 | 65 | .578 | 5 |
| New York | 79 | 75 | .513 | 15 |
| Detroit | 76 | 78 | .494 | 18 |
| Boston | 75 | 79 | .487 | 19 |
| Baltimore | 74 | 80 | .481 | 20 |
| Kansas City | 66 | 88 | .429 | 28 |
| Washington | 63 | 91 | .409 | 31 |

**National League**

| Team | W | L | Pct. | GB |
|---|---|---|---|---|
| *Los Angeles | 88 | 68 | .564 | ... |
| Milwaukee | 86 | 70 | .551 | 2 |
| San Francisco | 83 | 71 | .539 | 4 |
| Pittsburgh | 78 | 76 | .506 | 9 |
| Chicago | 74 | 80 | .481 | 13 |
| Cincinnati | 74 | 80 | .481 | 13 |
| St. Louis | 71 | 83 | .461 | 16 |
| Philadelphia | 64 | 90 | .416 | 23 |

*Defeated Milwaukee 2-0 in pennant playoff.

## SIGNIFICANT EVENT

■ **July 21:** The Red Sox became the last Major League team to break the color barrier when infielder Pumpsie Green played briefly in a game at Chicago.

## MEMORABLE MOMENTS

■ **May 26:** In an amazing pitching performance, Pittsburgh's Harvey Haddix worked 12 perfect innings before losing to the Braves, 1-0, in the 13th.
■ **June 10:** Cleveland's Rocky Colavito became the eighth member of an exclusive club when he belted four home runs during the Indians' 11-8 victory over Baltimore.
■ **September 11:** The Dodgers ended the two-year, 22-game winning streak of Pittsburgh reliever Elroy Face when they scored two ninth-inning runs for a 5-4 victory.
■ **September 29:** The Dodgers completed their two-game sweep of a pennant-playoff series against Milwaukee with a 12-inning, 6-5 victory at Los Angeles.

## LEADERS

**American League**
**BA:** Harvey Kuenn, Det., .353.
**Runs:** Eddie Yost, Det., 115.
**Hits:** Harvey Kuenn, Det., 198.
**TB:** Rocky Colavito, Cle., 301.
**HR:** Rocky Colavito, Cle.; Harmon Killebrew, Wash., 42.
**RBI:** Jackie Jensen, Bos., 112.
**SB:** Luis Aparicio, Chi., 56.
**Wins:** Early Wynn, Chi., 22.
**ERA:** Hoyt Wilhelm, Bal., 2.19.
**CG:** Camilo Pascual, Wash., 17.
**IP:** Early Wynn, Chi., 255.2.
**SO:** Jim Bunning, Det., 201.

**National League**
**BA:** Hank Aaron, Mil., .355.
**Runs:** Vada Pinson, Cin., 131.
**Hits:** Hank Aaron, Mil., 223.
**TB:** Hank Aaron, Mil., 400.
**HR:** Eddie Mathews, Mil., 46.
**RBI:** Ernie Banks, Chi., 143.
**SB:** Willie Mays, S.F., 27.
**Wins:** Lew Burdette, Mil.; Sam Jones, S.F.; Warren Spahn, Mil., 21.
**ERA:** Sam Jones, S.F., 2.83.
**CG:** Warren Spahn, Mil., 21.
**IP:** Warren Spahn, Mil., 292.
**SO:** Don Drysdale, L.A., 242.

**A.L. 20-game winners**
Early Wynn, Chi., 22-10

**N.L. 20-game winners**
Lew Burdette, Mil., 21-15
Warren Spahn, Mil., 21-15
Sam Jones, S.F., 21-15

**A.L. 100 RBIs**
Jackie Jensen, Bos., 112
Rocky Colavito, Cle., 111
Harmon Killebrew, Wash., 105
Jim Lemon, Wash., 100

**N.L. 100 RBIs**
Ernie Banks, Chi., 143
Frank Robinson, Cin., 125
Hank Aaron, Mil., 123
Gus Bell, Cin., 115
Eddie Mathews, Mil., 114
Orlando Cepeda, S.F., 105
Willie Mays, S.F., 104

**A.L. 40 homers**
Rocky Colavito, Cle., 42
Harmon Killebrew, Wash., 42

**N.L. 40 homers**
Eddie Mathews, Mil., 46
Ernie Banks, Chi., 45

**Most Valuable Player**
A.L.: Nellie Fox, 2B, Chi.
N.L.: Ernie Banks, SS, Chi.

**Cy Young Award**
A.L.-N.L.: Early Wynn, Chi. (AL)

**Rookie of the Year**
A.L.: Bob Allison, OF, Wash.
N.L.: Willie McCovey, 1B, S.F.

**Hall of Fame addition**
Zack Wheat, OF, 1909-27

## ALL-STAR GAMES

■ **Winner:** Home runs by Frank Malzone, Yogi Berra and Rocky Colavito helped the A.L. to a 5-3 victory and a split of the first All-Star doubleheader. The N.L. had won the first game four weeks earlier, 5-4.

■ **Key Innings:** The eighth in Game 1, when San Francisco's Willie Mays tripled home the winning run. The third in Game 2, when Berra pounded a two-run homer to give the A.L. a lead it never relinquished.

■ **Memorable moment:** The final out of Game 2. With hometown favorite Jim Gilliam at bat and the potential tying runs on second and third, Los Angeles fans roared. But Gilliam grounded out.

■ **Top guns:** Game 1: Don Drysdale (Dodgers), Eddie Mathews (Braves), Hank Aaron (Braves), N.L.; Al Kaline (Tigers), Gus Triandos (Orioles), A.L.; Game 2: Berra (Yankees), Malzone (Red Sox), Colavito (Indians), A.L.; Frank Robinson (Reds), Gilliam (Dodgers), N.L.

■ **MVPs:** Game 1: Drysdale. Game 2: Berra.

### Linescores

**Game 1,** July 7, at Pittsburgh's Forbes Field
A.L. ............0 0 0 1 0 0 0 3 0—4 8 0
N.L. ............1 0 0 0 0 0 2 2 x—5 9 1
Wynn (White Sox), Duren (Yankees) 4, Bunning (Tigers) 7, Ford (Yankees) 8, Daley (Athletics) 8; Drysdale (Dodgers), Burdette (Braves) 4, Face (Pirates) 7, Antonelli (Giants) 8, Elston (Cubs) 9. W—Antonelli. L—Ford. HR—Mathews, N.L.; Kaline, A.L.

**Game 2,** August 3, at Los Angeles Coliseum
A.L. ............0 1 2 0 0 0 1 1 0—5 6 0
N.L. ............1 0 0 0 1 0 1 0 0—3 6 3
Walker (Orioles), Wynn (White Sox) 4, Wilhelm (Orioles) 6, O'Dell (Orioles) 7, McLish (Indians) 8; Drysdale (Dodgers), Conley (Phillies) 4, Jones (Giants) 6, Face (Pirates) 8. W—Walker. L—Drysdale. HR—Malzone, Berra, Colavito, A.L.; Robinson, Gilliam, N.L.

## WORLD SERIES

■ **Winner:** The Dodgers, winners of a pennant playoff against Milwaukee, defeated the "Go-Go" White Sox for their first Series victory in Los Angeles.

■ **Turning point:** The Dodgers' 5-4 fourth-game victory, which was decided by Gil Hodges' home run.

■ **Memorable moment:** The first West Coast World Series contest — a 3-1 Dodger victory in Game 3.

■ **Top guns:** Larry Sherry (2-0, 0.71 ERA), Charlie Neal (.370, 2 HR, 6 RBIs), Chuck Essegian (2 PH HR), Dodgers; Ted Kluszewski (.391, 3 HR, 10 RBIs), Nellie Fox (.375), White Sox.

■ **MVP:** Sherry.

### Linescores

**Game 1**—October 1, at Chicago
Los Angeles ..........0 0 0 0 0 0 0 0 0— 0 8 3
Chicago..................2 0 7 2 0 0 0 0 x—11 11 0
Craig, Churn (3), Labine (4), Koufax (5), Klippstein (7); Wynn, Staley (8). W—Wynn. L—Craig. HR—Kluszewski 2 (Chi.).

**Game 2**—October 2, at Chicago
Los Angeles ............0 0 0 0 1 0 3 0 0—4 9 1
Chicago...................2 0 0 0 0 0 0 1 0—3 8 0
Podres, Sherry (7); Shaw, Lown (7). W—Podres. L—Shaw. HR—Neal 2, Essegian (L.A.).

**Game 3**—October 4, at Los Angeles.
Chicago...................0 0 0 0 0 0 0 1 0—1 12 0
Los Angeles ...........0 0 0 0 0 0 2 1 x—3 5 0
Donovan, Staley (7); Drysdale, Sherry (8). W—Drysdale. L—Donovan.

**Game 4**—October 5, at Los Angeles
Chicago...................0 0 0 0 0 0 4 0 0—4 10 3
Los Angeles ............0 0 4 0 0 0 0 1 x—5 9 0
Wynn, Lown (3), Pierce (4), Staley (7); Craig, Sherry (8). W—Sherry. L—Staley. HR—Lollar (Chi.); Hodges (L.A.).

**Game 5**—October 6, at Los Angels
Chicago....................0 0 0 1 0 0 0 0 0—1 5 0
Los Angeles .............0 0 0 0 0 0 0 0 0—0 9 0
Shaw, Pierce (8), Donovan (8); Koufax, Williams (8). W—Shaw. L—Koufax.

**Game 6**—October 8, at Chicago
Los Angeles ............0 0 2 6 0 0 0 0 1—9 13 0
Chicago...................0 0 0 3 0 0 0 0 0—3 6 1
Podres, Sherry (4); Wynn, Donovan (4), Lown (4), Staley (5), Pierce (8), Moore (9). W—Sherry. L—Wynn. HR—Snider, Moon, Essegian (L.A.); Kluszewski (Chi.).

# 1960

## FINAL STANDINGS

**American League**

| Team | W | L | Pct. | GB |
|---|---|---|---|---|
| New York | 97 | 57 | .630 | ... |
| Baltimore | 89 | 65 | .578 | 8 |
| Chicago | 87 | 67 | .565 | 10 |
| Cleveland | 76 | 78 | .494 | 21 |
| Washington | 73 | 81 | .474 | 24 |
| Detroit | 71 | 83 | .461 | 26 |
| Boston | 65 | 89 | .422 | 32 |
| Kansas City | 58 | 96 | .377 | 39 |

**National League**

| Team | W | L | Pct. | GB |
|---|---|---|---|---|
| Pittsburgh | 95 | 59 | .617 | ... |
| Milwaukee | 88 | 66 | .571 | 7 |
| St. Louis | 86 | 68 | .558 | 9 |
| Los Angeles | 82 | 72 | .532 | 13 |
| San Francisco | 79 | 75 | .513 | 16 |
| Cincinnati | 67 | 87 | .435 | 28 |
| Chicago | 60 | 94 | .390 | 35 |
| Philadelphia | 59 | 95 | .383 | 36 |

## SIGNIFICANT EVENTS

■ **August 3:** In baseball's most bizarre trade, the Indians swapped manager Joe Gordon to Detroit for manager Jimmie Dykes.
■ **October 18:** Casey Stengel, who managed the Yankees to 10 pennants and seven World Series titles in 12 years, was fired.
■ **October 26:** The A.L. announced relocation of the Senators to Minneapolis-St. Paul and 1961 expansion to Los Angeles and Washington.

## MEMORABLE MOMENTS

■ **June 17:** Ted Williams became the fourth member of the 500-homer fraternity when he connected off Cleveland's Wynn Hawkins in a 3-1 Boston victory.
■ **September 28:** Williams belted career homer No. 521 in Boston's 5-4 victory over Baltimore and promptly retired.

## LEADERS

**American League**
**BA:** Pete Runnels, Bos., .320.
**Runs:** Mickey Mantle, N.Y., 119.
**Hits:** Minnie Minoso, Chi., 184.
**TB:** Mickey Mantle, N.Y., 294.
**HR:** Mickey Mantle, N.Y., 40.
**RBI:** Roger Maris, N.Y., 112.
**SB:** Luis Aparicio, Chi., 51.
**Wins:** Chuck Estrada, Bal.; Jim Perry, Cle., 18.
**ERA:** Frank Baumann, Chi., 2.67.
**CG:** Frank Lary, Det., 15.
**IP:** Frank Lary, Det., 274.1.
**SO:** Jim Bunning, Det., 201.

**National League**
**BA:** Dick Groat, Pit., .325.
**Runs:** Bill Bruton, Mil., 112.
**Hits:** Willie Mays, S.F., 190.
**TB:** Hank Aaron, Mil., 334.
**HR:** Ernie Banks, Chi., 41.
**RBI:** Hank Aaron, Mil., 126.
**SB:** Maury Wills, L.A., 50.
**Wins:** Ernie Broglio, St.L.; Warren Spahn, Mil., 21.
**ERA:** Mike McCormick, S.F., 2.70.
**CG:** Lew Burdette, Mil.; Vernon Law, Pit.; Warren Spahn, Mil., 18.
**IP:** Larry Jackson, St.L., 282.
**SO:** Don Drysdale, L.A., 246.

**N.L. 20-game winners**
Ernie Broglio, St.L., 21-9
Warren Spahn, Mil., 21-10
Vernon Law, Pit., 20-9

**A.L. 100 RBIs**
Roger Maris, N.Y., 112
Minnie Minoso, Chi., 105
Vic Wertz, Bos., 103
Jim Lemon, Wash., 100

**N.L. 100 RBIs**
Hank Aaron, Mil., 126
Eddie Mathews, Mil., 124
Ernie Banks, Chi., 117
Willie Mays, S.F., 103

**A.L. 40 homers**
Mickey Mantle, N.Y., 40

**N.L. 40 homers**
Ernie Banks, Chi., 41
Hank Aaron, Mil., 40

**Most Valuable Player**
A.L.: Roger Maris, OF, N.Y.
N.L.: Dick Groat, SS, Pit.

**Cy Young Award**
A.L.-N.L.: Vernon Law, Pit.

**Rookie of the Year**
A.L.: Ron Hansen, SS, Bal.
N.L.: Frank Howard, OF, L.A.

## ALL-STAR GAMES

■ **Winner:** In a three-day All-Star doubleheader, the N.L. pulled off a 5-3 and 6-0 sweep and narrowed its once-embarrassing overall deficit to 16-13.

■ **Key Innings:** The first in Game 1, when a Willie Mays triple and an Ernie Banks homer sparked the N.L. to a 3-0 lead; the second in Game 2, when Eddie Mathews opened the N.L. scoring with a two-run homer.

■ **Memorable moment:** A third-inning Game 2 home run by Mays, who was 6 for 8 in the two games. The homer gave Mays a perfect 6-for-6 All-Star ledger against Yankee great Whitey Ford.

■ **Top guns:** Game 1: Bob Friend (Pirates), Mays (Giants), Banks (Cubs), N.L.; Al Kaline (Tigers), A.L.; Game 2: Vernon Law (Pirates), Mays (Giants), Mathews (Braves), Ken Boyer (Cardinals), N.L.

■ **MVPs:** Games 1 and 2 : Mays.

### Linescores

**Game 1,** July 11, at Kansas City's Municipal Stadium
N.L. ............3 1 1 0 0 0 0 0 0—5 12 4
A.L. ............0 0 0 0 0 1 0 2 0—3 6 1
Friend (Pirates), McCormick (Giants) 4, Face (Pirates) 6, Buhl (Braves) 8, Law (Pirates) 9; Monbouquette (Red Sox), Estrada (Orioles) 3, Coates (Yankees) 4, Bell (Indians) 6, Lary (Tigers) 8, Daley (Athletics) 9. W—Friend. L—Monbouquette. HR—Banks, Crandall, N.L.; Kaline, A.L.

**Game 2,** July 13, at New York's Yankee Stadium
N.L. ............0 2 1 0 0 0 1 0 2—6 10 0
A.L. ............0 0 0 0 0 0 0 0 0—0 8 0
Law (Pirates), Podres (Dodgers) 3, S. Williams (Dodgers) 5, Jackson (Cardinals) 7, Henry (Reds) 8, McDaniel (Cardinals) 9; Ford (Yankees), Wynn (White Sox) 4, Staley (White Sox) 6, Lary (Tigers) 8, Bell (Indians) 9. W—Law. L—Ford. HR—Mathews, Mays, Musial, Boyer, N.L.

## WORLD SERIES

■ **Winner:** Despite being outscored 55-27, the Pirates edged the Yankees in a seven-game Series that will be long remembered for its classic ending.

■ **Turning point:** The Pirates' 3-2 fourth-game victory after suffering successive 16-3 and 10-0 losses to the hard-hitting Yankees.

■ **Memorable moment:** Bill Mazeroski's Series-ending ninth-inning home run that broke a 9-9 tie after the Yankees had rallied for two runs in the top of the frame. One of the classic moments in Series history.

■ **Top guns:** Vernon Law (2-0), Mazeroski (.320, 2 HR, 5 RBIs), Pirates; Whitey Ford (2-0, 0.00 ERA), Mickey Mantle (.400, 3 HR, 11 RBIs), Bobby Richardson (.367, 12 RBIs), Yankees.

■ **MVP:** Richardson.

### Linescores

**Game 1**—October 5, at Pittsburgh
New York...............1 0 0 1 0 0 0 0 2—4 13 2
Pittsburgh ..............3 0 0 2 0 1 0 0 x—6 8 0
Ditmar, Coates (1), Maas (5), Duren (7); Law, Face (8). W—Law. L—Ditmar. HR—Maris, Howard (N.Y.); Mazeroski (Pit.).

**Game 2**—October 6, at Pittsburgh
New York...............0 0 2 1 2 7 3 0 1—16 19 1
Pittsburgh .............0 0 0 1 0 0 0 0 2— 3 13 1
Turley, Shantz (9); Friend, Green (5), Labine (6), Witt (6), Gibbon (7), Cheney (9). W—Turley. L—Friend. HR—Mantle 2 (N.Y.).

**Game 3**—October 8, at New York
Pittsburgh .............0 0 0 0 0 0 0 0 0— 0 4 0
New York...............6 0 0 4 0 0 0 0 x—10 16 1
Mizell, Labine (1), Green (1), Witt (4), Cheney (6), Gibbon (8); Ford. W—Ford. L—Mizell. HR—Richardson, Mantle (N.Y.).

**Game 4**—October 9, at New York
Pittsburgh .................0 0 0 0 3 0 0 0 0—3 7 0
New York...................0 0 0 1 0 0 1 0 0—2 8 0
Law, Face (7); Terry, Shantz (7), Coates (8). W—Law. L—Terry. HR—Skowron (N.Y.).

**Game 5**—October 10, at New York
Pittsburgh ...............0 3 1 0 0 0 0 0 1—5 10 2
New York.................0 1 1 0 0 0 0 0 0—2 5 2
Haddix, Face (7); Ditmar, Arroyo (2), Stafford (3), Duren (8). W—Haddix. L—Ditmar. HR—Maris (N.Y.).

**Game 6**—October 12, at Pittsburgh
New York...............0 1 5 0 0 2 2 2 0—12 17 1
Pittsburgh .............0 0 0 0 0 0 0 0 0— 0 7 1
Ford; Friend, Cheney (3), Mizell (4), Green (6), Labine (6), Witt (9). W—Ford. L—Friend.

**Game 7**—October 13, at Pittsburgh
New York...............0 0 0 0 1 4 0 2 2— 9 13 1
Pittsburgh .............2 2 0 0 0 0 0 5 1—10 11 0
Turley, Stafford (2), Shantz (3), Coates (8), Terry (8); Law, Face (6), Friend (9), Haddix (9). W—Haddix. L—Terry. HR—Skowron, Berra (N.Y.); Nelson, Smith, Mazeroski (Pit.).

# 1961

## FINAL STANDINGS

**American League**

| Team | W | L | Pct. | GB |
|---|---|---|---|---|
| New York | 109 | 53 | .673 | ... |
| Detroit | 101 | 61 | .623 | 8 |
| Baltimore | 95 | 67 | .586 | 14 |
| Chicago | 86 | 76 | .531 | 23 |
| Cleveland | 78 | 83 | .484 | 30.5 |
| Boston | 76 | 86 | .469 | 33 |
| Minnesota | 70 | 90 | .438 | 38 |
| Los Angeles | 70 | 91 | .435 | 38.5 |
| Kansas City | 61 | 100 | .379 | 47.5 |
| Washington | 61 | 100 | .379 | 47.5 |

**National League**

| Team | W | L | Pct. | GB |
|---|---|---|---|---|
| Cincinnati | 93 | 61 | .604 | ... |
| Los Angeles | 89 | 65 | .578 | 4 |
| San Francisco | 85 | 69 | .552 | 8 |
| Milwaukee | 83 | 71 | .539 | 10 |
| St. Louis | 80 | 74 | .519 | 13 |
| Pittsburgh | 75 | 79 | .487 | 18 |
| Chicago | 64 | 90 | .416 | 29 |
| Philadelphia | 47 | 107 | .305 | 46 |

## SIGNIFICANT EVENTS

- **April 6:** The Cubs designated Vedie Himsl as the first of nine coaches who would rotate as the team's manager during the season.
- **July 17:** Commissioner Ford Frick ruled that nobody could be credited with breaking Babe Ruth's 60-homer record unless he did it in the first 154 games of a season.
- **October 10:** The Mets and Colt .45s combined to pick 45 players in the N.L.'s first expansion draft.

## MEMORABLE MOMENTS

- **April 30:** Willie Mays became the ninth player to hit four homers in a game during the Giants' 14-4 victory at Milwaukee.
- **August 11:** Warren Spahn pitched Milwaukee to a 2-1 victory over Chicago and claimed his 300th career victory.
- **August 20:** The Phillies defeated Milwaukee, 7-4, and ended their modern-era record losing streak at 23.
- **October 1:** Roger Maris drove a pitch from Boston's Tracy Stallard for his record-setting 61st home run, giving New York a 1-0 victory at Yankee Stadium.

## LEADERS

**American League**

**BA:** Norm Cash, Det., .361.
**Runs:** Mickey Mantle, N.Y.; Roger Maris, N.Y., 132.
**Hits:** Norm Cash, Det., 193.
**TB:** Roger Maris, N.Y., 366.
**HR:** Roger Maris, N.Y., 61.
**RBI:** Roger Maris, N.Y., 142.
**SB:** Luis Aparicio, Chi., 53.
**Wins:** Whitey Ford, N.Y., 25.
**ERA:** Dick Donovan, Wash., 2.40.
**CG:** Frank Lary, Det., 22.
**IP:** Whitey Ford, N.Y., 283.
**SO:** Camilo Pascual, Min., 221.

**National League**

**BA:** Roberto Clemente, Pit., .351.
**Runs:** Willie Mays, S.F., 129.
**Hits:** Vada Pinson, Cin., 208.
**TB:** Hank Aaron, Mil., 358.
**HR:** Orlando Cepeda, S.F., 46.
**RBI:** Orlando Cepeda, S.F., 142.
**SB:** Maury Wills, L.A., 35.
**Wins:** Joey Jay, Cin.; Warren Spahn, Mil., 21.
**ERA:** Warren Spahn, Mil., 3.02.
**CG:** Warren Spahn, Mil., 21.
**IP:** Lew Burdette, Mil., 272.1.
**SO:** Sandy Koufax, L.A., 269.

**A.L. 20-game winners**
Whitey Ford, N.Y., 25-4
Frank Lary, Det., 23-9

**N.L. 20-game winners**
Joey Jay, Cin., 21-10
Warren Spahn, Mil., 21-13

**A.L. 100 RBIs**
Roger Maris, N.Y., 142
Jim Gentile, Bal., 141
Rocky Colavito, Det., 140
Norm Cash, Det., 132
Mickey Mantle, N.Y., 128
Harmon Killebrew, Min., 122
Bob Allison, Min., 105

**N.L. 100 RBIs**
Orlando Cepeda, S.F., 142
Frank Robinson, Cin., 124
Willie Mays, S.F., 123
Hank Aaron, Mil., 120
Dick Stuart, Pit., 117
Joe Adcock, Mil., 108

**A.L. 40 homers**
Roger Maris, N.Y., 61
Mickey Mantle, N.Y., 54
Jim Gentile, Bal., 46
Harmon Killebrew, Min., 46
Rocky Colavito, Det., 45
Norm Cash, Det., 41

**N.L. 40 homers**
Orlando Cepeda, S.F., 46
Willie Mays, S.F., 40

**Most Valuable Player**
A.L.: Roger Maris, OF, N.Y.
N.L.: Frank Robinson, OF, Cin.

**Cy Young Award**
A.L.-N.L.: Whitey Ford, N.Y. (AL)

**Rookie of the Year**
A.L.: Don Schwall, P, Bos.
N.L.: Billy Williams, OF, Chi.

**Hall of Fame additions**
Max Carey, OF, 1910-29
Billy Hamilton, OF, 1888-1901

## ALL-STAR GAMES

- **Winner:** The N.L. captured a wind-blown 5-4 victory in the All-Star opener at Candlestick Park and played to a 1-1 tie in a second game that was halted by a Boston rainstorm after nine innings.
- **Key inning:** The 10th in Game 1, when the A.L. took a 4-3 lead and the N.L. answered with two runs. The winner was driven home by a Roberto Clemente single.
- **Memorable moment:** The ninth inning of Game 1 when the A.L.'s two-run, game-tying rally received a big assist from a gust of wind that blew Giants reliever Stu Miller off the mound in mid delivery for a balk.
- **Top guns:** Game 1: Warren Spahn (Braves), Willie Mays (Giants), Clemente (Pirates), N.L.; Harmon Killebrew (Twins), A.L.; Game 2: Jim Bunning (Tigers), Camilo Pascual (Twins), Rocky Colavito (Tigers), A.L.; Miller (Giants), Bill White (Cardinals), N.L.
- **MVPs:** Game 1: Clemente; Game 2: Bunning.

### Linescores

**Game 1**, July 11, at San Francisco's Candlestick Park
A.L. ....................0 0 0 0 0 1 0 0 2 1—4 4 2
N.L. ....................0 1 0 1 0 0 0 1 0 2—5 11 5
Ford (Yankees), Lary (Tigers) 4, Donovan (Senators) 4, Bunning (Tigers) 6, Fornieles (Red Sox) 8, Wilhelm (Orioles) 8; Spahn (Braves), Purkey (Reds) 4, McCormick (Giants) 6, Face (Pirates) 9, Koufax (Dodgers) 9, Miller (Giants) 9. W—Miller. L—Wilhelm. HR—Killebrew, A.L.; Altman, N.L.

**Game 2**, July 31, at Boston's Fenway Park
N.L. ..........................0 0 0 0 0 1 0 0 0—1 5 1
A.L. ..........................1 0 0 0 0 0 0 0 0—1 4 0
Purkey (Reds), Mahaffey (Phillies) 3, Koufax (Dodgers) 5, Miller (Giants) 7; Bunning (Tigers), Schwall (Red Sox) 4, Pascual (Twins) 7. HR—Colavito, A.L.

## WORLD SERIES

- **Winner:** The Yankee machine, powered by 61-homer man Roger Maris, earned its first Series championship since 1947 without Casey Stengel at the helm.
- **Turning point:** A ninth-inning Maris home run that lifted the Yankees to a 3-2 victory in Game 3.
- **Memorable moment:** Yankee lefthander Whitey Ford's five shutout innings in Game 4, which lifted his consecutive-inning scoreless streak to a Series-record 32.
- **Top guns:** Ford (2-0, 0.00 ERA), John Blanchard (.400, 2 HR), Bill Skowron (.353, 5 RBIs), Hector Lopez (.333, 7 RBIs), Yankees; Wally Post (.333), Reds.
- **MVP:** Ford.

### Linescores

**Game 1**—October 4, at New York
Cincinnati..................0 0 0 0 0 0 0 0 0—0 2 0
New York ..................0 0 0 1 0 1 0 0 x—2 6 0
O'Toole, Brosnan (8); Ford. W—Ford. L—O'Toole. HR—Howard, Skowron (N.Y.).

**Game 2**—October 5, at New York
Cincinnati..................0 0 0 2 1 1 0 2 0—6 9 0
New York ..................0 0 0 2 0 0 0 0 0—2 4 3
Jay; Terry, Arroyo (8). W—Jay. L—Terry. HR—Coleman (Cin.); Berra (N.Y.).

**Game 3**—October 7, at Cincinnati
New York ..................0 0 0 0 0 0 1 1 1—3 6 1
Cincinnati..................0 0 1 0 0 0 1 0 0—2 8 0
Stafford, Daley (7), Arroyo (8); Purkey. W—Arroyo. L—Purkey. HR—Blanchard, Maris (N.Y.).

**Game 4**—October 8, at Cincinnati
New York ................0 0 0 1 1 2 3 0 0—7 11 0
Cincinnati................0 0 0 0 0 0 0 0 0—0 5 1
Ford, Coates (6); O'Toole, Brosnan (6), Henry (9). W—Ford. L—O'Toole.

**Game 5**—October 9, at Cincinnati
New York ..............5 1 0 5 0 2 0 0 0—13 15 1
Cincinnati..............0 0 3 0 2 0 0 0 0— 5 11 3
Terry, Daley (3); Jay, Maloney (1), K. Johnson (2), Henry (3), Jones (4), Purkey (5), Brosnan (7), Hunt (9). W—Daley. L—Jay. HR—Blanchard, Lopez (N.Y.); Robinson, Post (Cin.).

# 1962

## FINAL STANDINGS

**American League**

| Team | W | L | Pct. | GB |
|---|---|---|---|---|
| New York | 96 | 66 | .593 | ... |
| Minnesota | 91 | 71 | .562 | 5 |
| Los Angeles | 86 | 76 | .531 | 10 |
| Detroit | 85 | 76 | .528 | 10.5 |
| Chicago | 85 | 77 | .525 | 11 |
| Cleveland | 80 | 82 | .494 | 16 |
| Baltimore | 77 | 85 | .475 | 19 |
| Boston | 76 | 84 | .475 | 19 |
| Kansas City | 72 | 90 | .444 | 24 |
| Washington | 60 | 101 | .373 | 35.5 |

**National League**

| Team | W | L | Pct. | GB |
|---|---|---|---|---|
| *San Francisco | 103 | 62 | .624 | ... |
| Los Angeles | 102 | 63 | .618 | 1 |
| Cincinnati | 98 | 64 | .605 | 3.5 |
| Pittsburgh | 93 | 68 | .578 | 8 |
| Milwaukee | 86 | 76 | .531 | 15.5 |
| St. Louis | 84 | 78 | .519 | 17.5 |
| Philadelphia | 81 | 80 | .503 | 20 |
| Houston | 64 | 96 | .400 | 36.5 |
| Chicago | 59 | 103 | .364 | 42.5 |
| New York | 40 | 120 | .250 | 60.5 |

*Defeated Los Angeles 2-1 in pennant playoff.

## SIGNIFICANT EVENTS

- **April 9-10:** The Senators christened their $20-million D.C. Stadium with a 4-1 victory over Detroit, but Cincinnati beat Los Angeles 6-3 in the first game at Dodger Stadium.
- **November 23:** Dodgers shortstop Maury Wills, who ran his way to a record 104 stolen bases, walked away with the N.L. MVP.

## MEMORABLE MOMENTS

- **September 12:** Washington's Tom Cheney set a single-game record when he struck out 21 batters in a 16-inning 2-1 victory over the Orioles.
- **October 3:** The Giants captured the N.L. pennant with a 6-4 victory over the Dodgers in the third game of a three-game playoff.

## LEADERS

**American League**

**BA:** Pete Runnels, Bos., .326.
**Runs:** Albie Pearson, L.A., 115.
**Hits:** Bobby Richardson, N.Y., 209.
**TB:** Rocky Colavito, Det., 309.
**HR:** Harmon Killebrew, Min., 48.
**RBI:** Harmon Killebrew, Min., 126.
**SB:** Luis Aparicio, Chi., 31.
**Wins:** Ralph Terry, N.Y., 23.
**ERA:** Hank Aguirre, Det., 2.21.
**CG:** Camilo Pascual, Min., 18.
**IP:** Ralph Terry, N.Y., 298.2.
**SO:** Camilo Pascual, Min., 206.

**National League**

**BA:** Tommy Davis, L.A., .346.
**Runs:** Frank Robinson, Cin., 134.
**Hits:** Tommy Davis, L.A., 230.
**TB:** Willie Mays, S.F., 382.
**HR:** Willie Mays, S.F., 49.
**RBI:** Tommy Davis, L.A., 153.
**SB:** Maury Wills, L.A., 104.
**Wins:** Don Drysdale, L.A., 25.
**ERA:** Sandy Koufax, L.A., 2.54.
**CG:** Warren Spahn, Mil., 22.
**IP:** Don Drysdale, L.A., 314.1.
**SO:** Don Drysdale, L.A., 232.

**A.L. 20-game winners**
Ralph Terry, N.Y., 23-12
Ray Herbert, Chi., 20-9
Dick Donovan, Cle., 20-10
Camilo Pascual, Min., 20-11

**N.L. 20-game winners**
Don Drysdale, L.A., 25-9
Jack Sanford, S.F., 24-7
Bob Purkey, Cin., 23-5
Joey Jay, Cin., 21-14

**A.L. 100 RBIs**
Harmon Killebrew, Min., 126
Norm Siebern, K.C., 117
Rocky Colavito, Det., 112
Floyd Robinson, Chi., 109
Leon Wagner, L.A., 107
Lee Thomas, L.A., 104
Bob Allison, Min., 102
Roger Maris, N.Y., 100

**N.L. 100 RBIs**
Tommy Davis, L.A., 153
Willie Mays, S.F., 141
Frank Robinson, Cin., 136
Hank Aaron, Mil., 128
Frank Howard, L.A., 119
Orlando Cepeda, S.F., 114
Don Demeter, Phil., 107
Ernie Banks, Chi., 104
Bill White, St.L., 102
Vada Pinson, Cin., 100

**N.L. 40 homers**
Willie Mays, S.F., 49
Hank Aaron, Mil., 45

**A.L. 40 homers**
Harmon Killebrew, Min., 48

**Most Valuable Player**
A.L.: Mickey Mantle, OF, N.Y.
N.L.: Maury Wills, SS, L.A.

**Cy Young Award**
A.L.-N.L.: Don Drysdale, L.A. (NL)

**Rookie of the Year**
A.L.: Tom Tresh, SS, N.Y.
N.L.: Ken Hubbs, 2B, Chi.

**Hall of Fame additions**
Bob Feller, P, 1936-56
Bill McKechnie, manager
Jackie Robinson, 2B, 1947-56
Edd Roush, OF, 1913-31

## ALL-STAR GAMES

- **Winner:** The N.L. narrowed its series deficit to 16-15 with a 3-1 victory in the All-Star opener, but the A.L. pulled out its heavy artillery in a 9-4 second-game rout.
- **Key Innings:** The sixth in Game 1, when pinch-runner Maury Wills sparked a two-run rally with a stolen base; the seventh in Game 2, when Rocky Colavito belted a three-run homer.
- **Memorable moment:** The final out of the second game. The A.L. would not win again in the 1960s.
- **Top guns:** Game 1: Don Drysdale (Dodgers), Juan Marichal (Giants), Roberto Clemente (Pirates), Wills (Dodgers), N.L.; Game 2: Leon Wagner (Angels), Pete Runnels (Red Sox), Colavito (Tigers), A.L.
- **MVPs:** Game 1: Wills; Game 2: Wagner.

### Linescores

**Game 1**, July 10, at Washington's D.C. Stadium
N.L. ..........................0 0 0 0 0 2 0 1 0—3 8 0
A.L. ..........................0 0 0 0 0 1 0 0 0—1 4 0
Drysdale (Dodgers), Marichal (Giants) 4, Purkey (Reds) 6, Shaw (Braves) 8; Bunning (Tigers), Pascual (Twins) 4, Donovan (Indians) 7, Pappas (Orioles) 9. W—Marichal. L—Pascual.

**Game 2**, July 30, at Chicago's Wrigley Field
A.L. .........................0 0 1 2 0 1 3 0 2—9 10 0
N.L. .........................0 1 0 0 0 0 1 1 1—4 10 4
Stenhouse (Senators), Herbert (White Sox) 3, Aguirre (Tigers) 6, Pappas (Orioles) 9; Podres (Dodgers), Mahaffey (Phillies) 3, Gibson (Cardinals) 5, Farrell (Colts) 7, Marichal (Giants) 8. W—Herbert. L—Mahaffey. HR—Runnels, Wagner, Colavito, A.L.; Roseboro, N.L.

## WORLD SERIES

- **Winner:** The Yankees prevailed over the Giants, who were making their first Series appearance since moving from New York to San Francisco.
- **Turning point:** A three-run eighth-inning homer by rookie Tom Tresh that lifted Ralph Terry and the Yankees to a 5-3 Game 5 victory.
- **Memorable moment:** Yankee second baseman Bobby Richardson snagging Willie McCovey's vicious seventh-game line drive with runners on second and third base, preserving Terry's 1-0 shutout and ending the Series. A slight variation in the path of McCovey's shot would have given the Giants a championship.
- **Top guns:** Terry (2-1, 1.80 ERA), Tresh (.321, 4 RBIs), Yankees; Jose Pagan (.368), Giants.
- **MVP:** Terry.

### Linescores

**Game 1**—October 4, at San Francisco
New York..................2 0 0 0 0 0 1 2 1—6 11 0
San Francisco ..........0 1 1 0 0 0 0 0 0—2 10 0
Ford; O'Dell, Larsen (8), Miller (9). W—Ford. L—O'Dell. HR—Boyer (N.Y.).

**Game 2**—October 5, at San Francisco
New York....................0 0 0 0 0 0 0 0 0—0 3 1
San Francisco ............1 0 0 0 0 0 1 0 x—2 6 0
Terry, Daley (8); Sanford. W—Sanford. L—Terry. HR—McCovey (S.F.).

**Game 3**—October 7, at New York
San Francisco ............0 0 0 0 0 0 0 0 2—2 4 3
New York....................0 0 0 0 0 0 3 0 x—3 5 1
Pierce, Larsen (7), Bolin (8); Stafford. W—Stafford. L—Pierce. HR—Bailey (S.F.).

**Game 4**—October 8, at New York
San Francisco ..:..........0 2 0 0 0 0 4 0 1—7 9 1
New York....................0 0 0 0 0 2 0 0 1—3 9 1
Marichal, Bolin (5), Larsen (6), O'Dell (7); Ford, Coates (7), Bridges (7). W—Larsen. L—Coates. HR—Haller, Hiller (S.F.).

**Game 5**—October 10, at New York
San Francisco ............0 0 1 0 1 0 0 0 1—3 8 2
New York....................0 0 0 1 0 1 0 3 x—5 6 0
Sanford, Miller (8); Terry. W—Terry. L—Sanford. HR—Pagan (S.F.); Tresh (N.Y.).

**Game 6**—October 15, at San Francisco
New York..................0 0 0 0 1 0 0 1 0—2 3 2
San Francisco ..........0 0 0 3 2 0 0 0 x—5 10 1
Ford, Coates (5), Bridges (8); Pierce. W—Pierce. L—Ford. HR—Maris (N.Y.).

**Game 7**—October 16, at San Francisco
New York....................0 0 0 0 1 0 0 0 0—1 7 0
San Francisco ............0 0 0 0 0 0 0 0 0—0 4 1
Terry; Sanford, O'Dell (8). W—Terry. L—Sanford.

# 1963

## FINAL STANDINGS

**American League**

| Team | W | L | Pct. | GB |
|---|---|---|---|---|
| New York | 104 | 57 | .646 | ... |
| Chicago | 94 | 68 | .580 | 10.5 |
| Minnesota | 91 | 70 | .565 | 13 |
| Baltimore | 86 | 76 | .531 | 18.5 |
| Cleveland | 79 | 83 | .488 | 25.5 |
| Detroit | 79 | 83 | .488 | 25.5 |
| Boston | 76 | 85 | .472 | 28 |
| Kansas City | 73 | 89 | .451 | 31.5 |
| Los Angeles | 70 | 91 | .435 | 34 |
| Washington | 56 | 106 | .346 | 48.5 |

**National League**

| Team | W | L | Pct. | GB |
|---|---|---|---|---|
| Los Angeles | 99 | 63 | .611 | ... |
| St. Louis | 93 | 69 | .574 | 6 |
| San Francisco | 88 | 74 | .543 | 11 |
| Philadelphia | 87 | 75 | .537 | 12 |
| Cincinnati | 86 | 76 | .531 | 13 |
| Milwaukee | 84 | 78 | .519 | 15 |
| Chicago | 82 | 80 | .506 | 17 |
| Pittsburgh | 74 | 88 | .457 | 25 |
| Houston | 66 | 96 | .407 | 33 |
| New York | 51 | 111 | .315 | 48 |

## SIGNIFICANT EVENTS

- **January 26:** Baseball's Rules Committee expanded the strike zone—from the top of the shoulders to the bottom of the knees.
- **September 29:** Cardinals great Stan Musial retired with N.L. records for hits (3,630) and RBIs (1,951).
- **November 7:** Yankee catcher Elston Howard became the first black MVP in A.L. history.

## MEMORABLE MOMENTS

- **July 13:** Cleveland's Early Wynn struggled through five rocky innings but still won his 300th career game, a 7-4 victory over Kansas City.
- **August 21:** Pittsburgh's Jerry Lynch hit his record-setting 15th career pinch-hit homer in a 7-6 victory at Chicago.
- **September 8:** 42-year-old Braves lefty Warren Spahn tied the N.L. record when he stopped Philadelphia 3-2, becoming a 20-game winner for the 13th time.

## LEADERS

**American League**

**BA:** Carl Yastrzemski, Bos., .321.
**Runs:** Bob Allison, Min., 99.
**Hits:** Carl Yastrzemski, Bos., 183.
**TB:** Dick Stuart, Bos., 319.
**HR:** Harmon Killebrew, Min., 45.
**RBI:** Dick Stuart, Bos., 118.
**SB:** Luis Aparicio, Bal., 40.
**Wins:** Whitey Ford, N.Y., 24.
**ERA:** Gary Peters, Chi., 2.33.
**CG:** Camilo Pascual, Min.; Ralph Terry, N.Y., 18.
**IP:** Whitey Ford, N.Y., 269.1.
**SO:** Camilo Pascual, Min., 202.

**National League**

**BA:** Tommy Davis, L.A., .326.
**Runs:** Hank Aaron, Mil., 121.
**Hits:** Vada Pinson, Cin., 204.
**TB:** Hank Aaron, Mil., 370.
**HR:** Hank Aaron, Mil.; Willie McCovey, S.F., 44.
**RBI:** Hank Aaron, Mil., 130.
**SB:** Maury Wills, L.A., 40.
**Wins:** Sandy Koufax, L.A.; Juan Marichal, S.F., 25.
**ERA:** Sandy Koufax, L.A., 1.88.
**CG:** Warren Spahn, Mil., 22.
**IP:** Juan Marichal, S.F., 321.1.
**SO:** Sandy Koufax, L.A., 306.

**A.L. 20-game winners**

Whitey Ford, N.Y., 24-7
Jim Bouton, N.Y., 21-7
Camilo Pascual, Min., 21-9
Bill Monbouquette, Bos., 20-10
Steve Barber, Bal., 20-13

**N.L. 20-game winners**

Sandy Koufax, L.A., 25-5
Juan Marichal, S.F., 25-8
Jim Maloney, Cin., 23-7
Warren Spahn, Mil., 23-7
Dick Ellsworth, Chi., 22-10

**A.L. 100 RBIs**

Dick Stuart, Bos., 118
Al Kaline, Det., 101

**N.L. 100 RBIs**

Hank Aaron, Mil., 130
Ken Boyer, St.L., 111
Bill White, St.L., 109
Vada Pinson, Cin., 106
Willie Mays, S.F., 103
Willie McCovey, S.F., 102

**A.L. 40 homers**

Harmon Killebrew, Min., 45
Dick Stuart, Bos., 42

**N.L. 40 homers**

Hank Aaron, Mil., 44
Willie McCovey, S.F., 44

**Most Valuable Player**

A.L.: Elston Howard, C, N.Y.
N.L.: Sandy Koufax, P, L.A.

**Cy Young Award**

A.L.-N.L.: Sandy Koufax, L.A. (NL)

**Rookie of the Year**

A.L.: Gary Peters, P, Chi.
N.L.: Pete Rose, 2B, Cin.

**Hall of Fame additions**

John Clarkson, P, 1882-94
Elmer Flick, OF, 1898-1910
Sam Rice, OF, 1915-35
Eppa Rixey, P, 1912-33

## ALL-STAR GAME

- **Winner:** The N.L. unleashed secret weapon Willie Mays on the A.L. again and claimed a 5-3 victory in a return to the single All-Star Game format.
- **Key inning:** The third, when Mays singled home a run, stole his second base and scored on a single by Dick Groat. Mays scored two runs, drove in two and made an outstanding catch.
- **Memorable moment:** Pinch-hitter Stan Musial lining out to right field in his 24th, and last, All-Star appearance. Musial batted .317 and hit a record six home runs.
- **Top guns:** Mays (Giants), Ron Santo (Cubs), N.L.; Albie Pearson (Angels), Leon Wagner (Angels), A.L.
- **MVP:** Mays.

**Linescore**

July 9, at Cleveland Stadium
N.L. ..........................0 1 2 0 1 0 0 1 0—5 6 0
A.L. ..........................0 1 2 0 0 0 0 0 0—3 11 1
O'Toole (Reds), Jackson (Cubs) 3, Culp (Phillies) 5, Woodeshick (Colts) 6, Drysdale (Dodgers) 8; McBride (Angels), Bunning (Tigers) 4, Bouton (Yankees) 6, Pizarro (White Sox) 7, Radatz (Red Sox) 8. W—Jackson. L—Bunning.

## WORLD SERIES

- **Winner:** The Dodgers cut down their old nemesis in an impressive pitching-dominated sweep.
- **Turning point:** The first two innings of Game 1. Dodgers lefthander Sandy Koufax set the tone for the Series when he struck out the first five Yankees he faced en route to a record-setting 15-strikeout performance.
- **Memorable moment:** The first World Series game at new Dodger Stadium — a three-hit 1-0 victory for Los Angeles righthander Don Drysdale in Game 3.
- **Top guns:** Koufax (2-0, 1.50 ERA), Tommy Davis (.400), Bill Skowron (.385), Dodgers; Elston Howard (.333), Yankees.
- **MVP:** Koufax.

**Linescores**

**Game 1**—October 2, at New York
Los Angeles ..............0 4 1 0 0 0 0 0 0—5 9 0
New York....................0 0 0 0 0 0 0 2 0—2 6 0
Koufax; Ford, Williams (6), Hamilton (9). W—Koufax. L—Ford. HR—Roseboro (L.A.); Tresh (N.Y.).

**Game 2**—October 3, at New York
Los Angeles ............2 0 0 1 0 0 0 1 0—4 10 1
New York..................0 0 0 0 0 0 0 0 1—1 7 0
Podres, Perranoski (9); Downing, Terry (6), Reniff (9). W—Podres. L—Downing. HR—Skowron (L.A.).

**Game 3**—October 5, at Los Angeles
New York....................0 0 0 0 0 0 0 0 0—0 3 0
Los Angeles ..............1 0 0 0 0 0 0 0 0—1 4 1
Bouton, Reniff (8); Drysdale. W—Drysdale. L—Bouton.

**Game 4**—October 6, at Los Angeles
New York....................0 0 0 0 0 0 1 0 0—1 6 1
Los Angeles................0 0 0 0 1 0 1 0 x—2 2 1
Ford, Reniff (8); Koufax. W—Koufax. L—Ford. HR—F. Howard (L.A.); Mantle (N.Y.).

# 1964

## FINAL STANDINGS

**American League**

| Team | W | L | Pct. | GB |
|---|---|---|---|---|
| New York | 99 | 63 | .611 | ... |
| Chicago | 98 | 64 | .605 | 1 |
| Baltimore | 97 | 65 | .599 | 2 |
| Detroit | 85 | 77 | .525 | 14 |
| Los Angeles | 82 | 80 | .506 | 17 |
| Cleveland | 79 | 83 | .488 | 20 |
| Minnesota | 79 | 83 | .488 | 20 |
| Boston | 72 | 90 | .444 | 27 |
| Washington | 62 | 100 | .383 | 37 |
| Kansas City | 57 | 105 | .352 | 42 |

**National League**

| Team | W | L | Pct. | GB |
|---|---|---|---|---|
| St. Louis | 93 | 69 | .574 | ... |
| Cincinnati | 92 | 70 | .568 | 1 |
| Philadelphia | 92 | 70 | .568 | 1 |
| San Francisco | 90 | 72 | .556 | 3 |
| Milwaukee | 88 | 74 | .543 | 5 |
| Los Angeles | 80 | 82 | .494 | 13 |
| Pittsburgh | 80 | 82 | .494 | 13 |
| Chicago | 76 | 86 | .469 | 17 |
| Houston | 66 | 96 | .407 | 27 |
| New York | 53 | 109 | .327 | 40 |

## SIGNIFICANT EVENTS

- **February 13:** Ken Hubbs, the Cubs' 22-year-old second baseman, died when the single-engine plane he was flying crashed near Provo, Utah.
- **April 17:** The Mets opened $25-million Shea Stadium with a 4-3 loss to the Pirates.
- **November 7:** The Braves received N.L. permission to move their sagging franchise from Milwaukee to Atlanta after the 1965 season.

## MEMORABLE MOMENTS

- **April 23:** Houston's Ken Johnson became the first pitcher to lose a game in which he had thrown a complete-game no-hitter. Johnson dropped a 1-0 decision to the Reds.
- **June 4:** Dodgers lefty Sandy Koufax joined Bob Feller as the only three-time no-hit pitchers of the 20th Century when he stopped the Phillies, 3-0.
- **June 21:** Philadelphia's Jim Bunning fired baseball's first regular-season perfect game in 42 years, beating the Mets, 6-0.

## LEADERS

**American League**

**BA:** Tony Oliva, Min., .323.
**Runs:** Tony Oliva, Min., 109.
**Hits:** Tony Oliva, Min., 217.
**TB:** Tony Oliva, Min., 374.
**HR:** Harmon Killebrew, Min., 49.
**RBI:** Brooks Robinson, Bal., 118.
**SB:** Luis Aparicio, Bal., 57.
**Wins:** Dean Chance, L.A.; Gary Peters, Chi., 20.
**ERA:** Dean Chance, L.A., 1.65.
**CG:** Dean Chance, L.A., 15.
**IP:** Dean Chance, L.A., 278.1.
**SO:** Al Downing, N.Y., 217.

**National League**

**BA:** Roberto Clemente, Pit., .339.
**Runs:** Dick Allen, Phil., 125.
**Hits:** Roberto Clemente, Pit.; Curt Flood, St.L., 211.
**TB:** Dick Allen, Phil., 352.
**HR:** Willie Mays, S.F., 47.
**RBI:** Ken Boyer, St.L., 119.
**SB:** Maury Wills, L.A., 53.
**Wins:** Larry Jackson, Chi., 24.
**ERA:** Sandy Koufax, L.A., 1.74.
**CG:** Juan Marichal, S.F., 22.
**IP:** Don Drysdale, L.A., 321.1.
**SO:** Bob Veale, Pit., 250.

**A.L. 20-game winners**

Dean Chance, L.A., 20-9
Gary Peters, Chi., 20-8

**N.L. 20-game winners**

Larry Jackson, Chi., 24-11
Juan Marichal, S.F., 21-8
Ray Sadecki, St.L., 20-11

**A.L. 100 RBIs**

Brooks Robinson, Bal., 118
Dick Stuart, Bos., 114
Harmon Killebrew, Min., 111
Mickey Mantle, N.Y., 111
Rocky Colavito, K.C., 102
Joe Pepitone, N.Y., 100
Leon Wagner, Cle., 100

**N.L. 100 RBIs**

Ken Boyer, St.L., 119
Ron Santo, Chi., 114
Willie Mays, S.F., 111
Joe Torre, Mil., 109
Johnny Callison, Phil., 104
Bill White, St.L., 102

**A.L. 40 homers**

Harmon Killebrew, Min., 49

**N.L. 40 homers**

Willie Mays, S.F., 47

**Most Valuable Player**

A.L.: Brooks Robinson, 3B, Bal.
N.L.: Ken Boyer, 3B, St.L.

**Cy Young Award**

A.L.-N.L.: Dean Chance, L.A. (AL)

**Rookie of the Year**

A.L.: Tony Oliva, OF, Min.
N.L.: Dick Allen, 3B, Phil.

**Hall of Fame additions**

Luke Appling, SS, 1930-50
Red Faber, P, 1914-33
Burleigh Grimes, P, 1916-34
Miller Huggins, manager
Tim Keefe, P, 1880-93
Heinie Manush, OF, 1923-39
Monte Ward, IF/P, 1878-94

## ALL-STAR GAME

- **Winner:** In a game that rekindled memories of 1941, the N.L. struck for four ninth-inning runs and escaped with a stunning 7-4 victory.
- **Key inning:** The ninth, when Willie Mays walked, stole second moved to third on Orlando Cepeda's bloop single and scored the tying run on a wild throw. But the N.L. was far from finished.
- **Memorable moment:** Johnny Callison's stunning three-run homer that finished off the A.L. in the ninth. The blast was hit off Boston relief ace Dick Radatz.
- **Top guns:** Billy Williams (Cubs), Ken Boyer (Cardinals), Callison (Phillies), N.L.; Dean Chance (Angels), Harmon Killebrew (Twins), A.L.
- **MVP:** Callison.

**Linescore**

July 7, at New York's Shea Stadium
A.L. ..............................1 0 0 0 0 2 1 0 0—4 9 1
N.L. ..............................0 0 0 2 1 0 0 0 4—7 8 0
Chance (Angels), Wyatt (Athletics) 4, Pascual (Twins) 5, Radatz (Red Sox) 7; Drysdale (Dodgers), Bunning (Phillies) 4, Short (Phillies) 6, Farrell (Colts) 7, Marichal (Giants) 9. W—Marichal. L—Radatz. HR—Williams, Boyer, Callison, N.L.

## WORLD SERIES

- **Winner:** The Cardinals brought down the curtain on the Yankee dynasty with a seven-game triumph.
- **Turning point:** Trailing two games to one and 3-0 in the sixth inning of Game 4, the Cardinals rallied to a 4-3 victory when Ken Boyer connected for a grand slam.
- **Memorable moment:** A dramatic Game 3-ending homer by Mickey Mantle on the first ninth-inning pitch by St. Louis reliever Barney Schultz.
- **Top guns:** Bob Gibson (2-1, 3.00 ERA), Tim McCarver (.478, 5 RBIs), Boyer (2 HR, 6 RBIs), Lou Brock (.300, 5 RBIs), Cardinals; Bobby Richardson (13 hits, .406), Mantle (.333, 3 HR, 8 RBIs), Yankees.
- **MVP:** Gibson.

**Linescores**

**Game 1**—October 7, at St. Louis
New York..................0 3 0 0 1 0 0 1 0—5 12 2
St. Louis ..................1 1 0 0 0 4 0 3 x—9 12 0
Ford, Downing (6), Sheldon (8), Mikkelsen (8); Sadecki, Schultz (7). W—Sadecki. L—Ford. HR—Tresh (N.Y.); Shannon (St.L.).

**Game 2**—October 8, at St. Louis
New York..................0 0 0 1 0 1 2 0 4—8 12 0
St. Louis ..................0 0 1 0 0 0 0 1 1—3 7 0
Stottlemyre; Gibson, Schultz (9); G. Richardson (9); Craig (9). W—Stottlemyre. L—Gibson. HR—Linz (N.Y.).

**Game 3**—October 10, at New York
St. Louis ....................0 0 0 0 1 0 0 0 0—1 6 0
New York....................0 1 0 0 0 0 0 0 1—2 5 2
Simmons, Schultz (9); Bouton. W—Bouton. L—Schultz. HR—Mantle (N.Y.).

**Game 4**—October 11, at New York
St. Louis ....................0 0 0 0 0 4 0 0 0—4 6 1
New York....................3 0 0 0 0 0 0 0 0—3 6 1
Sadecki, Craig (1), Taylor (6); Downing, Mikkelsen (7), Terry (8). W—Craig. L—Downing. HR—K. Boyer (St.L.).

**Game 5**—October 12, at New York
St. Louis ............0 0 0 0 2 0 0 0 0 3—5 10 1
New York............0 0 0 0 0 0 0 0 2 0—2 6 2
Gibson; Stottlemyre, Reniff (8), Mikkelsen (8). W—Gibson. L—Mikkelsen. HR—Tresh (N.Y.); McCarver (St.L.).

**Game 6**—October 14, at St. Louis
New York..................0 0 0 0 1 2 0 5 0—8 10 0
St. Louis ..................1 0 0 0 0 0 0 1 1—3 10 1
Bouton, Hamilton (9); Simmons, Taylor (7), Schultz (8), G. Richardson (8), Humphreys (9). W—Bouton. L—Simmons. HR—Maris, Mantle, Pepitone (N.Y.).

**Game 7**—October 15, at St. Louis
New York..................0 0 0 0 0 3 0 0 2—5 9 2
St. Louis ..................0 0 0 3 3 0 1 0 x—7 10 1
Stottlemyre, Downing (5), Sheldon (5), Hamilton (7), Mikkelsen (8); Gibson. W—Gibson. L—Stottlemyre. HR—Brock, K. Boyer (St.L.); Mantle, C. Boyer, Linz (N.Y.).

# 1965

## FINAL STANDINGS

**American League**

| Team | W | L | Pct. | GB |
|---|---|---|---|---|
| Minnesota | 102 | 60 | .630 | ... |
| Chicago | 95 | 67 | .586 | 7 |
| Baltimore | 94 | 68 | .580 | 8 |
| Detroit | 89 | 73 | .549 | 13 |
| Cleveland | 87 | 75 | .537 | 15 |
| New York | 77 | 85 | .475 | 25 |
| California | 75 | 87 | .463 | 27 |
| Washington | 70 | 92 | .432 | 32 |
| Boston | 62 | 100 | .383 | 40 |
| Kansas City | 59 | 103 | .364 | 43 |

**National League**

| Team | W | L | Pct. | GB |
|---|---|---|---|---|
| Los Angeles | 97 | 65 | .599 | ... |
| San Francisco | 95 | 67 | .586 | 2 |
| Pittsburgh | 90 | 72 | .556 | 7 |
| Cincinnati | 89 | 73 | .549 | 8 |
| Milwaukee | 86 | 76 | .531 | 11 |
| Philadelphia | 85 | 76 | .528 | 11.5 |
| St. Louis | 80 | 81 | .497 | 16.5 |
| Chicago | 72 | 90 | .444 | 25 |
| Houston | 65 | 97 | .401 | 32 |
| New York | 50 | 112 | .309 | 47 |

## SIGNIFICANT EVENTS

■ **April 9:** The Houston Astrodome, baseball's first domed stadium, was unveiled for an exhibition game between the Astros and Yankees.

■ **August 22:** Giants pitcher Juan Marichal touched off a wild 14-minute brawl when he attacked Dodgers catcher John Roseboro with a bat.

■ **August 29:** Citing poor health, Casey Stengel stepped down as Mets manager and ended his 56-year baseball career.

■ **September 2:** The Los Angeles Angels, preparing to move to Anaheim, changed their name to the California Angels.

## MEMORABLE MOMENTS

■ **August 19:** Cincinnati's Jim Maloney, who had no-hit the Mets two months earlier only to lose in the 11th, fired another 10-inning no-hitter and beat the Cubs, 1-0.

■ **September 13:** San Francisco's Willie Mays, en route to his second 50-homer season, became the fifth member of the 500 club when he connected off Houston's Don Nottebart in a game at the Astrodome.

■ **September 29:** Dodgers ace Sandy Koufax reached perfection when he retired all 27 Cubs he faced in a 1-0 victory—his record fourth career no-hitter.

## LEADERS

**American League**

**BA:** Tony Oliva, Min., .321.
**Runs:** Zoilo Versalles, Min., 126.
**Hits:** Tony Oliva, Min., 185.
**TB:** Zoilo Versalles, Min., 308.
**HR:** Tony Conigliaro, Bos., 32.
**RBI:** Rocky Colavito, Cle., 108.
**SB:** Campy Campaneris, K.C., 51.
**Wins:** Jim (Mudcat) Grant, Min., 21.
**ERA:** Sam McDowell, Cle., 2.18.
**CG:** Mel Stottlemyre, N.Y., 18.
**IP:** Mel Stottlemyre, N.Y., 291.
**SO:** Sam McDowell, Cle., 325.

**National League**

**BA:** Roberto Clemente, Pit., .329.
**Runs:** Tommy Harper, Cin., 126.
**Hits:** Pete Rose, Cin., 209.
**TB:** Willie Mays, S.F., 360.
**HR:** Willie Mays, S.F., 52.
**RBI:** Deron Johnson, Cin., 130.
**SB:** Maury Wills, L.A., 94.
**Wins:** Sandy Koufax, L.A., 26.
**ERA:** Sandy Koufax, L.A., 2.04.
**CG:** Sandy Koufax, L.A., 27.
**IP:** Sandy Koufax, L.A., 335.2.
**SO:** Sandy Koufax, L.A., 382.

**A.L. 20-game winners**

Jim (Mudcat) Grant, Min., 21-7
Mel Stottlemyre, N.Y., 20-9

**N.L. 20-game winners**

Sandy Koufax, L.A., 26-8
Tony Cloninger, Mil., 24-11
Don Drysdale, L.A., 23-12
Sammy Ellis, Cin., 22-10
Juan Marichal, S.F., 22-13
Jim Maloney, Cin., 20-9
Bob Gibson, St.L., 20-12

**A.L. 100 RBIs**

Rocky Colavito, Cle., 108
Willie Horton, Det., 104

**N.L. 100 RBIs**

Deron Johnson, Cin., 130
Frank Robinson, Cin., 113
Willie Mays, S.F., 112
Billy Williams, Chi., 108
Willie Stargell, Pit., 107
Ernie Banks, Chi., 106
Johnny Callison, Phil., 101
Ron Santo, Chi., 101

**N.L. 40 homers**

Willie Mays, S.F., 52

**Most Valuable Player**

A.L.: Zoilo Versalles, SS, Min.
N.L.: Willie Mays, OF, S.F.

**Cy Young Award**

A.L.-N.L.: Sandy Koufax, L.A. (NL)

**Rookie of the Year**

A.L.: Curt Blefary, OF, Bal.
N.L.: Jim Lefebvre, 2B, L.A.

**Hall of Fame addition**

Pud Galvin, P, 1879-92

## ALL-STAR GAME

■ **Winner:** The N.L. took its first All-Star lead when Ron Santo drove home Willie Mays with a seventh-inning infield single that produced the winning run.

■ **Key Innings:** An N.L. first that featured home runs by Mays and Joe Torre and an A.L. fifth that featured Dick McAuliffe and Harmon Killebrew homers.

■ **Memorable moment:** Bob Gibson striking out Killebrew and New York's Joe Pepitone in the ninth inning with the tying run on second base.

■ **Top guns:** Juan Marichal (Giants), Mays (Giants), Willie Stargell (Pirates), Joe Torre (Braves), N.L.; McAuliffe (Tigers), Killebrew (Twins), A.L.

■ **MVP:** Marichal.

### Linescore

July 13, at Minnesota's Metropolitan Stadium
N.L. ..........................3 2 0 0 0 0 1 0 0—6 11 0
A.L. ..........................0 0 0 1 4 0 0 0 0—5 8 0
Marichal (Giants), Maloney (Reds) 4, Drysdale (Dodgers) 5, Koufax (Dodgers) 6, Farrell (Astros) 7, Gibson (Cardinals) 8; Pappas (Orioles), Grant (Twins) 2, Richert (Senators) 4, McDowell (Indians) 6, Fisher (White Sox) 8. W—Koufax. L—McDowell. HR—Mays, Torre, Stargell, N.L.; McAuliffe, Killebrew, A.L.

## WORLD SERIES

■ **Winner:** The pitching-rich Dodgers prevailed after dropping the first two games to the Twins — Minnesota's first World Series representative.

■ **Turning point:** A 4-0 shutout by Dodgers lefthander Claude Osteen in Game 3, after the Twins had beaten Don Drysdale and Sandy Koufax in Games 1 and 2.

■ **Memorable moment:** A three-hit seventh-game shutout by Koufax, who struck out 10 in his 2-0 victory.

■ **Top guns:** Koufax (2-1, 0.38 ERA), Ron Fairly (2 HR, 6 RBIs), Dodgers; Jim Grant (2-1, 2.74), Twins.

■ **MVP:** Koufax.

### Linescores

**Game 1**—October 6, at Minnesota
Los Angeles ............0 1 0 0 0 0 0 0 1—2 10 1
Minnesota ................0 1 6 0 0 1 0 0 x—8 10 0
Drysdale, Reed (3), Brewer (5), Perranoski (7); Grant. W—Grant. L—Drysdale. HR—Fairly (L.A.); Mincher, Versalles (Min.).

**Game 2**—October 7, at Minnesota
Los Angeles ..............0 0 0 0 0 0 1 0 0—1 7 3
Minnesota ..................0 0 0 0 0 2 1 2 x—5 9 0
Koufax, Perranoski (7), Miller (8); Kaat. W—Kaat. L—Koufax.

**Game 3**—October 9, at Los Angeles
Minnesota ................0 0 0 0 0 0 0 0 0—0 5 0
Los Angeles..............0 0 0 2 1 1 0 0 x—4 10 1
Pascual, Merritt (6), Klippstein (8); Osteen. W—Osteen. L—Pascual.

**Game 4**—October 10, at Los Angeles
Minnesota ................0 0 0 1 0 1 0 0 0—2 5 2
Los Angeles..............1 1 0 1 0 3 0 1 x—7 10 0
Grant, Worthington (6), Pleis (8); Drysdale. W—Drysdale. L—Grant. HR—Killebrew, Oliva (Min.); Parker, Johnson (L.A.).

**Game 5**—October 11, at Los Angeles
Minnesota ................0 0 0 0 0 0 0 0 0—0 4 1
Los Angeles..............2 0 2 1 0 0 2 0 x—7 14 0
Kaat, Boswell (3), Perry (6); Koufax. W—Koufax. L—Kaat.

**Game 6**—October 13, at Minnesota
Los Angeles ..............0 0 0 0 0 0 1 0 0—1 6 1
Minnesota ..................0 0 0 2 0 3 0 0 x—5 6 1
Osteen, Reed (6), Miller (8); Grant. W—Grant. L—Osteen. HR—Fairly (L.A.); Allison, Grant (Min.).

**Game 7**—October 14, at Minnesota
Los Angeles ..............0 0 0 2 0 0 0 0 0—2 7 0
Minnesota ..................0 0 0 0 0 0 0 0 0—0 3 1
Koufax; Kaat, Worthington (4), Klippstein (6), Merritt (7), Perry (9). W—Koufax. L—Kaat. HR—Johnson (L.A.).

# 1966

## FINAL STANDINGS

**American League**

| Team | W | L | Pct. | GB |
|---|---|---|---|---|
| Baltimore | 97 | 63 | .606 | ... |
| Minnesota | 89 | 73 | .549 | 9 |
| Detroit | 88 | 74 | .543 | 10 |
| Chicago | 83 | 79 | .512 | 15 |
| Cleveland | 81 | 81 | .500 | 17 |
| California | 80 | 82 | .494 | 18 |
| Kansas City | 74 | 86 | .463 | 23 |
| Washington | 71 | 88 | .447 | 25.5 |
| Boston | 72 | 90 | .444 | 26 |
| New York | 70 | 89 | .440 | 26.5 |

**National League**

| Team | W | L | Pct. | GB |
|---|---|---|---|---|
| Los Angeles | 95 | 67 | .586 | ... |
| San Francisco | 93 | 68 | .578 | 1.5 |
| Pittsburgh | 92 | 70 | .568 | 3 |
| Philadelphia | 87 | 75 | .537 | 8 |
| Atlanta | 85 | 77 | .525 | 10 |
| St. Louis | 83 | 79 | .512 | 12 |
| Cincinnati | 76 | 84 | .475 | 18 |
| Houston | 72 | 90 | .444 | 23 |
| New York | 66 | 95 | .410 | 28.5 |
| Chicago | 59 | 103 | .364 | 36 |

## SIGNIFICANT EVENTS

■ **March 30:** The joint 32-day holdout of Dodger pitchers Sandy Koufax and Don Drysdale ended when they agreed to a combined package worth more than $210,000.

■ **April 11:** Another barrier fell when Emmett Ashford, baseball's first black umpire, worked the season opener at Washington.

■ **April 12:** The Braves dropped a 3-2 verdict to the Pirates in their debut at the new $18-million Atlanta Stadium.

■ **November 18:** Sandy Koufax, baseball's only three-time Cy Young Award winner, stunned the Dodgers when he announced his retirement at age 30 because of an arthritic elbow.

## MEMORABLE MOMENTS

■ **June 9:** Rich Rollins, Zoilo Versalles, Tony Oliva, Don Mincher and Harmon Killebrew hit home runs in a seventh-inning explosion against Kansas City, matching a Major League record.

■ **August 17:** San Francisco's Willie Mays belted career homer No. 535 off St. Louis' Ray Washburn and moved into second place on the all-time list.

■ **September 22:** The Orioles clinched their first A.L. pennant with a 6-1 victory over Kansas City.

■ **October 2:** Sandy Koufax, working on two days rest, beat Philadelphia 6-3 for his 27th victory and clinched the Dodgers' third pennant in four years.

■ **November 8:** Baltimore's Frank Robinson, baseball's 13th Triple Crown winner, became the first player to win MVP honors in both leagues.

## LEADERS

**American League**

**BA:** Frank Robinson, Bal., .316.
**Runs:** Frank Robinson, Bal., 122.
**Hits:** Tony Oliva, Min., 191.
**TB:** Frank Robinson, Bal., 367.
**HR:** Frank Robinson, Bal., 49.
**RBI:** Frank Robinson, Bal., 122.
**SB:** Campy Campaneris, K.C., 52.
**Wins:** Jim Kaat, Min., 25.
**ERA:** Gary Peters, Chi., 1.98.
**CG:** Jim Kaat, Min., 19.
**IP:** Jim Kaat, Min., 304.2.
**SO:** Sam McDowell, Cle., 225.

**National League**

**BA:** Matty Alou, Pit., .342.
**Runs:** Felipe Alou, Atl., 122.
**Hits:** Felipe Alou, Atl., 218.
**TB:** Felipe Alou, Atl., 355.
**HR:** Hank Aaron, Atl., 44.
**RBI:** Hank Aaron, Atl., 127.
**SB:** Lou Brock, St.L., 74.
**Wins:** Sandy Koufax, L.A., 27.
**ERA:** Sandy Koufax, L.A., 1.73.
**CG:** Sandy Koufax, L.A., 27.
**IP:** Sandy Koufax, L.A., 323.
**SO:** Sandy Koufax, L.A., 317.

**A.L. 20-game winners**

Jim Kaat, Min., 25-13
Denny McLain, Det., 20-14

**N.L. 20-game winners**

Sandy Koufax, L.A., 27-9
Juan Marichal, S.F., 25-6
Gaylord Perry, S.F., 21-8
Bob Gibson, St.L., 21-12
Chris Short, Phil., 20-10

**A.L. 100 RBIs**

Frank Robinson, Bal., 122
Harmon Killebrew, Min., 110
Boog Powell, Bal., 109
Willie Horton, Det., 100
Brooks Robinson, Bal., 100

**N.L. 100 RBIs**

Hank Aaron, Atl., 127
Roberto Clemente, Pit., 119
Dick Allen, Phil., 110
Willie Mays, S.F., 103
Bill White, Phil., 103
Willie Stargell, Pit., 102
Joe Torre, Atl., 101

**A.L. 40 homers**

Frank Robinson, Bal., 49

**N.L. 40 homers**

Hank Aaron, Atl., 44
Dick Allen, Phil., 40

**Most Valuable Player**

A.L.: Frank Robinson, OF, Bal.
N.L.: Roberto Clemente, OF, Pit.

**Cy Young Award**

A.L.-N.L.: Sandy Koufax, L.A. (NL)

**Rookie of the Year**

A.L.: Tommie Agee, OF, Chi.
N.L.: Tommy Helms, 3B, Cin.

**Hall of Fame additions**

Casey Stengel, manager
Ted Williams, OF, 1939-60

## ALL-STAR GAME

■ **Winner:** The N.L. needed 10 innings to win its fourth consecutive All-Star Game in the blistering 105-degree heat of St. Louis.

■ **Key inning:** The 10th, when Maury Wills singled home Tim McCarver with the game-ending run.

■ **Memorable moment:** The almost-constant sight of fans being helped in the stands after passing out because of the heat.

■ **Top guns:** Gaylord Perry (Giants), Roberto Clemente (Pirates), Wills (Dodgers), N.L.; Denny McLain (Tigers), Brooks Robinson (Orioles), A.L.

■ **MVP:** Robinson.

### Linescore

July 12, at St. Louis' Busch Stadium
A.L. ......................0 1 0 0 0 0 0 0 0 0—1 6 0
N.L. ......................0 0 0 1 0 0 0 0 0 1—2 6 0
McLain (Tigers), Kaat (Twins) 4, Stottlemyre (Yankees) 6, Siebert (Indians) 8, Richert (Senators) 10; Koufax (Dodgers), Bunning (Phillies) 4, Marichal (Giants) 6, Perry (Giants) 9. W—Perry. L—Richert.

## WORLD SERIES

■ **Winner:** The Orioles, making only the second Series appearance in franchise history and first since moving from St. Louis to Baltimore, allowed only two Dodger runs — none after the third inning of Game 1.

■ **Turning point:** Game 1, when Moe Drabowsky relieved Baltimore lefty Dave McNally with the bases loaded in the third inning. Drabowsky worked 6⅔ innings of shutout relief and struck out 11 Dodgers in a 5-2 victory.

■ **Memorable moments:** Series-ending 1-0 victories by Wally Bunker (six-hitter) and McNally (four-hitter).

■ **Top guns:** Boog Powell (.357), Frank Robinson (2 HR, 3 RBIs), Orioles.

■ **MVP:** Frank Robinson.

### Linescores

**Game 1**—October 5, at Los Angeles
Baltimore ..................3 1 0 1 0 0 0 0 0—5 9 0
Los Angeles .............0 1 1 0 0 0 0 0 0—2 3 0
McNally, Drabowsky (3); Drysdale, Moeller (3), R. Miller (5), Perranoski (8). W—Drabowsky. L—Drysdale. HR—F. Robinson, B. Robinson (Bal.); Lefebvre (L.A.).

**Game 2**—October 6, at Los Angeles
Baltimore ..................0 0 0 0 3 1 0 2 0—6 8 0
Los Angeles .............0 0 0 0 0 0 0 0 0—0 4 6
Palmer; Koufax, Perranoski (7), Regan (8), Brewer (9). W—Palmer. L—Koufax.

**Game 3**—October 8, at Baltimore
Los Angeles .............0 0 0 0 0 0 0 0 0—0 6 0
Baltimore....................0 0 0 0 1 0 0 0 x—1 3 0
Osteen, Regan (8); Bunker. W—Bunker. L—Osteen. HR—Blair (Bal.).

**Game 4**—October 9, at Baltimore
Los Angeles .............0 0 0 0 0 0 0 0 0—0 4 0
Baltimore....................0 0 0 1 0 0 0 0 x—1 4 0
Drysdale; McNally. W—McNally. L—Drysdale. HR—F. Robinson.

# 1967

## FINAL STANDINGS

**American League**

| Team | W | L | Pct. | GB |
|---|---|---|---|---|
| Boston | 92 | 70 | .568 | ... |
| Detroit | 91 | 71 | .562 | 1 |
| Minnesota | 91 | 71 | .562 | 1 |
| Chicago | 89 | 73 | .549 | 3 |
| California | 84 | 77 | .522 | 7.5 |
| Baltimore | 76 | 85 | .472 | 15.5 |
| Washington | 76 | 85 | .472 | 15.5 |
| Cleveland | 75 | 87 | .463 | 17 |
| New York | 72 | 90 | .444 | 20 |
| Kansas City | 62 | 99 | .385 | 29.5 |

**National League**

| Team | W | L | Pct. | GB |
|---|---|---|---|---|
| St. Louis | 101 | 60 | .627 | ... |
| San Francisco | 91 | 71 | .562 | 10.5 |
| Chicago | 87 | 74 | .540 | 14 |
| Cincinnati | 87 | 75 | .537 | 14.5 |
| Philadelphia | 82 | 80 | .506 | 19.5 |
| Pittsburgh | 81 | 81 | .500 | 20.5 |
| Atlanta | 77 | 85 | .475 | 24.5 |
| Los Angeles | 73 | 89 | .451 | 28.5 |
| Houston | 69 | 93 | .426 | 32.5 |
| New York | 61 | 101 | .377 | 40.5 |

## SIGNIFICANT EVENT

■ **October 18:** The A.L. approved the Athletics' move to Oakland and 1969 expansion to Kansas City and Seattle.

## MEMORABLE MOMENTS

■ **April 14:** Boston lefthander Bill Rohr, making his Major League debut, lost a no-hit bid when Yankee Elston Howard singled with two out in the ninth inning of a 3-0 Red Sox victory.

■ **April 30:** Baltimore's Steve Barber and Stu Miller combined to pitch a no-hitter, but the Orioles lost, 2-1, when Detroit scored two ninth-inning runs.

■ **May 14, July 14:** New York's Mickey Mantle and Houston's Eddie Mathews became the sixth and seventh members of the 500-homer club exactly two months apart.

## LEADERS

**American League**

**BA:** Carl Yastrzemski, Bos., .326.
**Runs:** Carl Yastrzemski, Bos., 112.
**Hits:** Carl Yastrzemski, Bos., 189.
**TB:** Carl Yastrzemski, Bos., 360.
**HR:** Harmon Killebrew, Min.; Carl Yastrzemski, Bos., 44.
**RBI:** Carl Yastrzemski, Bos., 121.
**SB:** Campy Campaneris, K.C., 55.
**Wins:** Jim Lonborg, Bos.; Earl Wilson, Det., 22.
**ERA:** Joel Horlen, Chi., 2.06.
**CG:** Dean Chance, Min., 18.
**IP:** Dean Chance, Min., 283.2.
**SO:** Jim Lonborg, Bos., 246.

**National League**

**BA:** Roberto Clemente, Pit., .357.
**Runs:** Hank Aaron, Atl.; Lou Brock, St.L., 113.
**Hits:** Roberto Clemente, Pit., 209.
**TB:** Hank Aaron, Atl., 344.
**HR:** Hank Aaron, Atl., 39.
**RBI:** Orlando Cepeda, St.L., 111.
**SB:** Lou Brock, St.L., 52.
**Wins:** Mike McCormick, S.F., 22.
**ERA:** Phil Niekro, Atl., 1.87.
**CG:** Ferguson Jenkins, Chi., 20.
**IP:** Jim Bunning, Phil., 302.1.
**SO:** Jim Bunning, Phil., 253.

**A.L. 20-game winners**
Jim Lonborg, Bos., 22-9
Earl Wilson, Det., 22-11
Dean Chance, Min., 20-14

**N.L. 20-game winners**
Mike McCormick, S.F., 22-10
Ferguson Jenkins, Chi., 20-13

**A.L. 100 RBIs**
Carl Yastrzemski, Bos., 121
Harmon Killebrew, Min., 113

**N.L. 100 RBIs**
Orlando Cepeda, St.L., 111
Roberto Clemente, Pit., 110
Hank Aaron, Atl., 109
Jim Wynn, Hou., 107
Tony Perez, Cin., 102

**A.L. 40 homers**
Harmon Killebrew, Min., 44
Carl Yastrzemski, Bos., 44

**Most Valuable Player**
A.L.: Carl Yastrzemski, OF, Bos.
N.L.: Orlando Cepeda, 1B, St.L.

**Cy Young Award**
A.L.: Jim Lonborg, Bos.
N.L.: Mike McCormick, S.F.

**Rookie of the Year**
A.L.: Rod Carew, 2B, Min.
N.L.: Tom Seaver, P, N.Y.

**Hall of Fame additions**
Branch Rickey, executive
Red Ruffing, P, 1924-47
Lloyd Waner, OF, 1927-45

## ALL-STAR GAME

■ **Winner:** The N.L. continued its All-Star hex with a pulsating 15-inning 2-1 victory — the longest game in the classic's 35-year history.

■ **Key inning:** The 15th, when Cincinnati's Tony Perez deposited a Catfish Hunter pitch over the left-field fence, ending the N.L.'s 12-inning scoreless run.

■ **Memorable moment:** The overall performance of 12 pitchers, who gave up only 17 hits and two bases on balls while recording 30 strikeouts.

■ **Top guns:** Juan Marichal (Giants), Don Drysdale (Dodgers), Richie Allen (Phillies), Perez (Reds), N.L.; Gary Peters (White Sox), Hunter (Athletics), Carl Yastrzemski (Red Sox), Brooks Robinson (Orioles), A.L.

■ **MVP:** Perez.

**Linescore**

July 11, at California's Anaheim Stadium
N.L. ..0 1 0 000 000 000 001—2 9 0
A.L. ..0 0 0 001 000 000 000—1 8 0
Marichal (Giants), Jenkins (Cubs) 4, Gibson (Cardinals) 7, Short (Phillies) 9, Cuellar (Astros) 11, Drysdale (Dodgers) 13, Seaver (Mets) 15; Chance (Twins), McGlothlin (Angels) 4, Peters (White Sox) 6, Downing (Yankees) 9, Hunter (Athletics) 11. W—Drysdale. L—Hunter. HR—Allen, Perez, N.L.; Robinson, A.L.

## WORLD SERIES

■ **Winner:** It took seven games for the Cardinals to ruin Boston's "impossible dream" of winning its first Series championship since 1918.

■ **Turning point:** The seventh-game heroics of Bob Gibson, who belted a home run and pitched the Cardinals to a 7-2 victory.

■ **Memorable moment:** A two-out eighth-inning double by St. Louis' Julian Javier in Game 2, ending Boston righthander Jim Lonborg's no-hit bid. Lonborg finished with a one-hit 5-0 victory.

■ **Top guns:** Gibson (3-0, 1.00 ERA), Lou Brock (.414), Roger Maris (.385, 7 RBIs), Cardinals; Lonborg (2-1), Carl Yastrzemski (.400, 3 HR, 5 RBIs), Red Sox.

■ **MVP:** Gibson.

**Linescores**

**Game 1**—October 4, at Boston
St. Louis ..................0 0 1 0 0 0 1 0 0—2 10 0
Boston ....................0 0 1 0 0 0 0 0 0—1 6 0
Gibson; Santiago, Wyatt (8). W—Gibson. L—Santiago. HR—Santiago (Bos.).

**Game 2**—October 5, at Boston
St. Louis ..................0 0 0 0 0 0 0 0 0—0 1 1
Boston.......................0 0 0 1 0 1 3 0 x—5 9 0
Hughes, Willis (6), Hoerner (7), Lamabe (7); Lonborg. W—Lonborg. L—Hughes. HR—Yastrzemski 2 (Bos.).

**Game 3**—Ocotber 7, at St. Louis
Boston ....................0 0 0 0 0 1 1 0 0—2 7 1
St. Louis ..................1 2 0 0 0 1 0 1 x—5 10 0
Bell, Waslewski (3), Stange (6), Osinski (8); Briles. W—Briles. L—Bell. HR—Shannon (St.L.); Smith (Bos.).

**Game 4**—October 8, at St. Louis
Boston ......................0 0 0 0 0 0 0 0 0—0 5 0
St. Louis ..................4 0 2 0 0 0 0 0 x—6 9 0
Santiago, Bell (1), Stephenson (3), Morehead (5), Brett (8); Gibson. W—Gibson. L—Santiago.

**Game 5**—October 9, at St. Louis
Boston ......................0 0 1 0 0 0 0 0 2—3 6 1
St. Louis ..................0 0 0 0 0 0 0 0 1—1 3 2
Lonborg; Carlton, Washburn (7), Willis (9), Lamabe (9). W—Lonborg. L—Carlton. HR—Maris.

**Game 6**—October 11, at Boston
St. Louis ..................0 0 2 0 0 0 2 0 0— 4 8 0
Boston......................0 1 0 3 0 0 4 0 x—8 12 1
Hughes, Willis (4), Briles (5), Lamabe (7), Hoerner (7), Jaster (7), Washburn (7), Woodeshick (8); Waslewski, Wyatt (6), Bell (8). W—Wyatt. L—Lamabe. HR—Petrocelli 2, Yastrzemski, Smith (Bos.); Brock (St.L.).

**Game 7**—October 12, at Boston
St. Louis ..................0 0 2 0 2 3 0 0 0—7 10 1
Boston ....................0 0 0 0 1 0 0 1 0—2 3 1
Gibson; Lonborg, Santiago (7), Morehead (9), Osinski (9), Brett (9). W—Gibson. L—Lonborg. HR—Gibson, Javier (St.L.).

# 1968

## FINAL STANDINGS

**American League**

| Team | W | L | Pct. | GB |
|---|---|---|---|---|
| Detroit | 103 | 59 | .636 | ... |
| Baltimore | 91 | 71 | .562 | 12 |
| Cleveland | 86 | 75 | .534 | 16.5 |
| Boston | 86 | 76 | .531 | 17 |
| New York | 83 | 79 | .512 | 20 |
| Oakland | 82 | 80 | .506 | 21 |
| Minnesota | 79 | 83 | .488 | 24 |
| California | 67 | 95 | .414 | 36 |
| Chicago | 67 | 95 | .414 | 36 |
| Washington | 65 | 96 | .404 | 37.5 |

**National League**

| Team | W | L | Pct. | GB |
|---|---|---|---|---|
| St. Louis | 97 | 65 | .599 | ... |
| San Francisco | 88 | 74 | .543 | 9 |
| Chicago | 84 | 78 | .519 | 13 |
| Cincinnati | 83 | 79 | .512 | 14 |
| Atlanta | 81 | 81 | .500 | 16 |
| Pittsburgh | 80 | 82 | .494 | 17 |
| Los Angeles | 76 | 86 | .469 | 21 |
| Philadelphia | 76 | 86 | .469 | 21 |
| New York | 73 | 89 | .451 | 24 |
| Houston | 72 | 90 | .444 | 25 |

## SIGNIFICANT EVENTS

■ **May 27:** The N.L. crossed the Canadian border when it awarded 1969 expansion franchises to Montreal and San Diego.

■ **July 10:** A.L. and N.L. officials agreed to uniformity in their 1969 expansions: two-division formats, 162-game schedules and best-of-five League Championship Series.

■ **December 3:** The Rules Committee lowered the mound, shrunk the strike zone and cracked down on illegal pitches in an effort to increase offense.

■ **December 6:** Baseball owners forced William Eckert to resign as commissioner.

## MEMORABLE MOMENTS

■ **May 8:** A's righthander Catfish Hunter fired baseball's ninth perfect game, retiring all 27 Twins he faced in a 4-0 victory at Oakland.

■ **July 30:** Washington shortstop Ron Hansen pulled off baseball's eighth unassisted triple play in the first inning of a 10-1 loss at Cleveland.

■ **September 14:** The Tigers rallied for two ninth-inning runs and defeated Oakland 5-4, allowing Denny McLain to become baseball's first 30-game winner since 1934.

## LEADERS

**American League**

**BA:** Carl Yastrzemski, Bos., .301.
**Runs:** Dick McAuliffe, Det., 95.
**Hits:** Campy Campaneris, Oak., 177.
**TB:** Frank Howard, Wash., 330.
**HR:** Frank Howard, Wash., 44.
**RBI:** Ken Harrelson, Bos., 109.
**SB:** Campy Campaneris, Oak., 62.
**Wins:** Denny McLain, Det., 31.
**ERA:** Luis Tiant, Cle., 1.60.
**CG:** Denny McLain, Det., 28.
**IP:** Denny McLain, Det., 336.
**SO:** Sam McDowell, Cle., 283.

**National League**

**BA:** Pete Rose, Cin., .335.
**Runs:** Glenn Beckert, Chi., 98.
**Hits:** Felipe Alou, Atl.; Pete Rose, Cin., 210.
**TB:** Billy Williams, Chi., 321.
**HR:** Willie McCovey, S.F., 36.
**RBI:** Willie McCovey, S.F., 105.
**SB:** Lou Brock, St.L., 62.
**Wins:** Juan Marichal, S.F., 26.
**ERA:** Bob Gibson, St.L., 1.12.
**CG:** Juan Marichal, S.F., 30.
**IP:** Juan Marichal, S.F., 326.
**SO:** Bob Gibson, St.L., 268.

**A.L. 20-game winners**
Denny McLain, Det., 31-6
Dave McNally, Bal., 22-10
Luis Tiant, Cle., 21-9
Mel Stottlemyre, N.Y., 21-12

**N.L. 20-game winners**
Juan Marichal, S.F., 26-9
Bob Gibson, St.L., 22-9
Ferguson Jenkins, Chi., 20-15

**A.L. 100 RBIs**
Ken Harrelson, Bos., 109
Frank Howard, Wash., 106

**N.L. 100 RBIs**
Willie McCovey, S.F., 105

**A.L. 40 homers**
Frank Howard, Wash., 44

**Most Valuable Player**
A.L.: Denny McLain, P, Det.
N.L.: Bob Gibson, P, St.L.

**Cy Young Award**
A.L.: Denny McLain, Det.
N.L.: Bob Gibson, St.L.

**Rookie of the Year**
A.L.: Stan Bahnsen, P, N.Y.
N.L.: Johnny Bench, C, Cin.

**Hall of Fame additions**
Kiki Cuyler, OF, 1921-38
Goose Goslin, OF, 1921-38
Joe Medwick, OF, 1932-48

## ALL-STAR GAME

■ **Winner:** The N.L. stretched its winning streak to six with the first 1-0 game in All-Star history. It also was the first played indoors and on an artificial surface.

■ **Key inning:** The first, when the N.L. scored the game's only run on a double-play grounder.

■ **Memorable moment:** The performance of a six-man N.L. staff that held the A.L. to three hits.

■ **Top guns:** Don Drysdale (Dodgers), Juan Marichal (Giants), Steve Carlton (Cardinals), Tom Seaver (Mets), Willie Mays (Giants), N.L.; Blue Moon Odom (Athletics), Denny McLain (Tigers), A.L.

■ **MVP:** Mays.

**Linescore**

July 9, at Houston's Astrodome
A.L. ..............................0 0 0 0 0 0 0 0 0—0 3 1
N.L. ..............................1 0 0 0 0 0 0 0 x—1 5 0
Tiant (Indians), Odom (Athletics) 3, McLain (Tigers) 5, McDowell (Indians) 7, Stottlemyre (Yankees) 8, John (White Sox) 8; Drysdale (Dodgers), Marichal (Giants) 4, Carlton (Cardinals) 6, Seaver (Mets) 7, Reed (Braves) 9, Koosman (Mets) 9. W—Drysdale. L—Tiant.

## WORLD SERIES

■ **Winner:** The Tigers, down three games to one, rallied to win their first World Series since 1945.

■ **Turning point:** With the Tigers on the brink of elimination entering Game 5, lefthander Mickey Lolich pitched them to a 5-3 victory.

■ **Memorable moments:** Bob Gibson striking out 17 Tigers in Game 1. Cardinals center fielder Curt Flood misjudging Jim Northrup's seventh-game fly ball, which became a Series-deciding two-run triple.

■ **Top guns:** Lolich (3-0, 1.67 ERA), Norm Cash (.385, 5 RBIs); Al Kaline (.379, 2 HR, 8 RBIs), Tigers; Gibson (2-1, 1.67), Lou Brock (.464, 2 HR, 5 RBIs), Cardinals.

■ **MVP:** Lolich.

**Linescores**

**Game 1**—October 2, at St. Louis
Detroit.........................0 0 0 0 0 0 0 0 0—0 5 3
St. Louis ....................0 0 0 3 0 0 1 0 x—4 6 0
McLain, Dobson (6), McMahon (8); Gibson. W—Gibson. L—McLain. HR—Brock (St.L.).

**Game 2**—October 3, at St. Louis
Detroit.......................0 1 1 0 0 3 1 0 2—8 13 1
St. Louis ..................0 0 0 0 0 1 0 0 0—1 6 1
Lolich; Briles, Carlton (6), Willis (7), Hoerner (9). W—Lolich. L—Briles. HR—Horton, Lolich, Cash (Det.).

**Game 3**—October 5, at Detroit
St. Louis ..................0 0 0 0 4 0 3 0 0—7 13 0
Detroit.......................0 0 2 0 1 0 0 0 0—3 4 0
Washburn, Hoerner (6); Wilson, Dobson (5), McMahon (6), Patterson (7), Hiller (8). W—Washburn. L—Wilson. HR—Kaline, McAuliffe (Det.); McCarver, Cepeda (St.L.).

**Game 4**—October 6, at Detroit
St. Louis ...............2 0 2 2 0 0 0 4 0—10 13 0
Detroit.....................0 0 0 1 0 0 0 0 0— 1 5 4
Gibson; McLain, Sparma (3), Patterson (4), Lasher (6), Hiller (8), Dobson (8). W—Gibson. L—McLain. HR—Brock, Gibson (St.L.); Northrup (Det.).

**Game 5**—October 7, at Detroit
St. Louis ...................3 0 0 0 0 0 0 0 0—3 9 0
Detroit.......................0 0 0 2 0 0 3 0 x—5 9 1
Briles, Hoerner (7), Willis (7); Lolich. W—Lolich. L—Hoerner. HR—Cepeda (St.L.).

**Game 6**—October 9, at St. Louis
Detroit.................0 2 10 0 1 0 0 0 0—13 12 1
St. Louis .............0 0 0 0 0 0 0 0 1— 1 9 1
McLain; Washburn, Jaster (3), Willis (3), Hughes (3), Carlton (4), Granger (7), Nelson (9). W—McLain. L—Washburn. HR—Northrup, Kaline (Det.).

**Game 7**—October 10, at St. Louis
Detroit.........................0 0 0 0 0 0 3 0 1—4 8 1
St. Louis ....................0 0 0 0 0 0 0 0 1—1 5 0
Lolich; Gibson. W—Lolich. L—Gibson. HR—Shannon (St.L.).

# 1969

## FINAL STANDINGS

### American League

**East Division**

| Team | Bal. | Det. | Bos. | Wash. | N.Y. | Cle. | Min. | Oak. | Cal. | K.C. | Chi. | Sea. | W | L | Pct. | GB |
|---|---|---|---|---|---|---|---|---|---|---|---|---|---|---|---|---|
| Baltimore | ... | 11 | 10 | 13 | 11 | 13 | 8 | 8 | 6 | 11 | 9 | 9 | 109 | 53 | .673 | ... |
| Detroit | 7 | ... | 8 | 7 | 10 | 11 | 6 | 7 | 7 | 8 | 9 | 10 | 90 | 72 | .556 | 19 |
| Boston | 8 | 10 | ... | 6 | 11 | 12 | 7 | 4 | 8 | 10 | 5 | 6 | 87 | 75 | .537 | 22 |
| Washington | 5 | 11 | 12 | ... | 8 | 15 | 6 | 4 | 7 | 5 | 8 | 5 | 86 | 76 | .531 | 23 |
| New York | 7 | 8 | 7 | 10 | ... | 8 | 2 | 6 | 9 | 7 | 9 | 7 | 80 | 81 | .497 | 28.5 |
| Cleveland | 5 | 7 | 6 | 3 | 9 | ... | 5 | 5 | 4 | 7 | 4 | 7 | 62 | 99 | .385 | 46.5 |

**West Division**

| Team | Min. | Oak. | Cal. | K.C. | Chi. | Sea. | Bal. | Det. | Bos. | Wash. | N.Y. | Cle. | W | L | Pct. | GB |
|---|---|---|---|---|---|---|---|---|---|---|---|---|---|---|---|---|
| Minnesota | ... | 13 | 11 | 10 | 13 | 12 | 4 | 6 | 5 | 6 | 10 | 7 | 97 | 65 | .599 | ... |
| Oakland | 5 | ... | 10 | 10 | 10 | 12 | 4 | 5 | 8 | 8 | 6 | 7 | 88 | 74 | .543 | 9 |
| California | 7 | 6 | ... | 9 | 9 | 9 | 6 | 5 | 4 | 5 | 3 | 8 | 71 | 91 | .438 | 26 |
| Kansas City | 8 | 8 | 9 | ... | 10 | 10 | 1 | 4 | 2 | 7 | 5 | 5 | 69 | 93 | .426 | 28 |
| Chicago | 5 | 8 | 9 | 8 | ... | 10 | 3 | 3 | 7 | 4 | 3 | 8 | 68 | 94 | .420 | 29 |
| Seattle | 6 | 5 | 9 | 8 | 8 | ... | 3 | 2 | 6 | 7 | 5 | 5 | 64 | 98 | .395 | 33 |

### National League

**East Division**

| Team | N.Y. | Chi. | Pit. | St.L. | Phi. | Mon. | Atl. | S.F. | Cin. | L.A. | Hou. | S.D. | W | L | Pct. | GB |
|---|---|---|---|---|---|---|---|---|---|---|---|---|---|---|---|---|
| New York | ... | 10 | 10 | 12 | 12 | 13 | 8 | 8 | 6 | 8 | 2 | 11 | 100 | 62 | .617 | ... |
| Chicago | 8 | ... | 7 | 9 | 12 | 10 | 9 | 6 | 6 | 6 | 8 | 11 | 92 | 70 | .568 | 8 |
| Pittsburgh | 8 | 11 | ... | 9 | 8 | 13 | 4 | 5 | 7 | 4 | 9 | 10 | 88 | 74 | .543 | 12 |
| St. Louis | 6 | 9 | 9 | ... | 11 | 11 | 6 | 9 | 4 | 9 | 5 | 8 | 87 | 75 | .537 | 13 |
| Philadelphia | 6 | 6 | 10 | 7 | ... | 7 | 6 | 3 | 2 | 4 | 4 | 8 | 63 | 99 | .389 | 37 |
| Montreal | 5 | 8 | 5 | 7 | 11 | ... | 4 | 1 | 4 | 2 | 1 | 4 | 52 | 110 | .321 | 48 |

**West Division**

| Team | Atl. | S.F. | Cin. | L.A. | Hou. | S.D. | N.Y. | Chi. | Pit. | St.L | Phi. | Mon. | W | L | Pct. | GB |
|---|---|---|---|---|---|---|---|---|---|---|---|---|---|---|---|---|
| Atlanta | ... | 9 | 12 | 9 | 15 | 13 | 4 | 3 | 8 | 6 | 6 | 8 | 93 | 69 | .574 | ... |
| San Fran. | 9 | ... | 8 | 13 | 8 | 12 | 4 | 6 | 7 | 3 | 9 | 11 | 90 | 72 | .556 | 3 |
| Cincinnati | 6 | 10 | ... | 10 | 9 | 11 | 6 | 6 | 5 | 8 | 10 | 8 | 89 | 73 | .549 | 4 |
| Los Angeles | 9 | 5 | 8 | ... | 12 | 12 | 4 | 6 | 8 | 3 | 8 | 10 | 85 | 77 | .525 | 8 |
| Houston | 3 | 10 | 9 | 6 | ... | 10 | 10 | 4 | 3 | 7 | 8 | 11 | 81 | 81 | .500 | 12 |
| San Diego | 5 | 6 | 7 | 6 | 8 | ... | 1 | 1 | 2 | 4 | 4 | 8 | 52 | 110 | .321 | 41 |

## SIGNIFICANT EVENTS

■ **February 4:** Bowie Kuhn, a little-known attorney, was handed a one-year term as a compromise choice to succeed William Eckert as commissioner.

■ **February 25:** Baseball owners avoided a strike by increasing player pension plan contributions and granting improvements in other important benefits.

■ **April 8:** The four expansion teams—Kansas City, Seattle, Montreal and San Diego—recorded Opening Day victories.

■ **April 14:** The first Major League game on foreign soil: Montreal defeated the Cardinals, 8-7, at Jarry Park.

■ **December 4:** Chub Feeney was named to succeed Warren Giles as N.L. president.

## MEMORABLE MOMENTS

■ **April 30-May 1:** Cincinnati's Jim Maloney and Houston's Don Wilson fired back-to-back no-hitters at Crosley Field, matching the Gaylord Perry-Ray Washburn feat of 1968.

■ **September 15:** Cardinals lefty Steve Carlton struck out a record 19 batters, but the Mets won the game 4-3 on a pair of two-run homers by Ron Swoboda.

■ **September 22:** San Francisco's Willie Mays became the second batter to hit 600 home runs when he connected off Mike Corkins in a 4-2 victory over San Diego.

## LEADERS

**American League**
**BA:** Rod Carew, Min., .332.
**Runs:** Reggie Jackson, Oak., 123.
**Hits:** Tony Oliva, Min., 197.
**TB:** Frank Howard, Wash., 340.
**HR:** Harmon Killebrew, Min., 49.
**RBI:** Harmon Killebrew, Min., 140.
**SB:** Tommy Harper, Sea., 73.
**Wins:** Denny McLain, Det., 24.
**ERA:** Dick Bosman, Wash., 2.19.
**CG:** Mel Stottlemyre, N.Y., 24.
**IP:** Denny McLain, Det., 325.
**SO:** Sam McDowell, Cle., 279.
**SV:** Ron Perranoski, Min., 31.

**National League**
**BA:** Pete Rose, Cin., .348.
**Runs:** Bobby Bonds, S.F.; Pete Rose, Cin., 120.
**Hits:** Matty Alou, Pit., 231.
**TB:** Hank Aaron, Atl., 332.
**HR:** Willie McCovey, S.F., 45.
**RBI:** Willie McCovey, S.F., 126.
**SB:** Lou Brock, St.L., 53.
**Wins:** Tom Seaver, N.Y., 25.
**ERA:** Juan Marichal, S.F., 2.10.
**CG:** Bob Gibson, St.L., 28.
**IP:** Gaylord Perry, S.F., 325.1.
**SO:** Ferguson Jenkins, Chi., 273.
**SV:** Fred Gladding, Hou., 29.

**A.L. 20-game winners**
Denny McLain, Det., 24-9
Mike Cuellar, Bal., 23-11
Jim Perry, Min., 20-6
Dave McNally, Bal., 20-7
Dave Boswell, Min., 20-12
Mel Stottlemyre, N.Y., 20-14

**N.L. 20-game winners**
Tom Seaver, N.Y., 25-7
Phil Niekro, Atl., 23-13
Juan Marichal, S.F., 21-11
Ferguson Jenkins, Chi., 21-15
Bill Singer, L.A., 20-12
Larry Dierker, Hou., 20-13
Bob Gibson, St.L., 20-13
Bill Hands, Chi., 20-14
Claude Osteen, L.A., 20-15

**A.L. 100 RBIs**
Harmon Killebrew, Min., 140
Boog Powell, Bal., 121
Reggie Jackson, Oak., 118
Sal Bando, Oak., 113
Frank Howard, Wash., 111
Carl Yastrzemski, Bos., 111
Tony Oliva, Min., 101
Frank Robinson, Bal., 100

**N.L. 100 RBIs**
Willie McCovey, S.F., 126
Ron Santo, Chi., 123
Tony Perez, Cin., 122
Lee May, Cin., 110
Ernie Banks, Chi., 106
Joe Torre, St.L., 101

**A.L. 40 homers**
Harmon Killebrew, Min., 49
Frank Howard, Wash., 48
Reggie Jackson, Oak., 47
Rico Petrocelli, Bos., 40
Carl Yastrzemski, Bos., 40

**N.L. 40 homers**
Willie McCovey, S.F., 45
Hank Aaron, Atl., 44

**Most Valuable Player**
A.L.: Harmon Killebrew, 3B, Min.
N.L.: Willie McCovey, 1B, S.F.

**Cy Young Award**
A.L.: Denny McLain, Det.
Mike Cuellar, Bal.
N.L.: Tom Seaver, N.Y.

**Rookie of the Year**
A.L.: Lou Piniella, OF, K.C.
N.L.: Ted Sizemore, 2B, L.A.

**Hall of Fame additions**
Roy Campanella, C, 1948-57
Stan Coveleski, P, 1912-28
Waite Hoyt, P, 1918-38
Stan Musial, OF/1B, 1941-63

## ALL-STAR GAME

■ **Winner:** Willie McCovey belted a pair of home runs and Johnny Bench hit another as the N.L. stretched its winning streak to seven.

■ **Key inning:** A five-run N.L. third, fueled by the first of McCovey's two blasts. The explosion broke open a 3-1 contest.

■ **Memorable moment:** A sensational leaping catch by A.L. left fielder Carl Yastrzemski in the sixth inning, robbing Bench of another home run.

■ **Top guns:** McCovey (Giants), Bench (Reds), Cleon Jones (Mets), Felix Millan (Braves), N.L.; Frank Howard (Senators), Bill Freehan (Tigers), A.L.

■ **MVP:** McCovey.

**Linescore**
July 22, at Washington's RFK Stadium
N.L.............1 2 5 1 0 0 0 0 0—9 11 0
A.L.............0 1 1 1 0 0 0 0 0—3 6 2
Carlton (Cardinals), Gibson (Cardinals) 4, Singer (Dodgers) 5, Koosman (Mets) 7, Dierker (Astros) 8, Niekro (Braves) 9; Stottlemyre (Yankees), Odom (Athletics) 3, Knowles (Senators) 3, McLain (Tigers) 4, McNally (Orioles) 5, McDowell (Indians) 7, Culp (Red Sox) 9. W—Carlton. L—Stottlemyre. HR—McCovey 2, Bench, N.L.; Howard, Freehan, A.L.

## ALCS

■ **Winner:** The Baltimore Orioles, hailed by many as the best A.L. team since the Yankee pennant-winning machines of yesteryear, swept past Minnesota in baseball's first season of League Championship Series play.

■ **Turning point:** Paul Blair's 12th-inning squeeze bunt gave the Orioles a 4-3 Game 1 victory after Boog Powell had tied the contest with a ninth-inning home run.

■ **Memorable moment:** An 11th-inning Curt Motton pinch-hit single that put the capper on a second-game, three-hit, 1-0 shutout by Orioles lefthander Dave McNally.

■ **Top guns:** McNally (1-0, 0.00 ERA), Brooks Robinson (.500), Blair (.400, 6 RBIs), Orioles; Tony Oliva (.385), Twins.

■ **MVP:** McNally.

**Linescores**
**Game 1**—October 4, at Baltimore
Minn. 0 0 0 0 1 0 2 0 0 0 0 0—3 4 2
Balt. ..0 0 0 1 1 0 0 0 1 0 0 1—4 10 1
Perry, Perranoski (9); Cuellar, Richert (9), Watt (10), Lopez (12), Hall (12). W—Hall. L—Perranoski. HR—F. Robinson, Belanger, Powell (Bal.); Oliva (Min.).

**Game 2**—October 5, at Baltimore
Minn. ....0 0 0 0 0 0 0 0 0 0 0—0 3 1
Balt. ......0 0 0 0 0 0 0 0 0 0 1—1 8 0
Boswell, Perranoski (11); McNally. W—McNally. L—Boswell.

**Game 3**—October 6, at Minnesota
Balt. ........0 3 0 2 0 1 0 2 3—11 18 0
Minn. ......1 0 0 0 1 0 0 0 0— 2 10 2
Palmer; Miller, Woodson (2), Hall (4), Worthington (5), Grzenda (6), Chance (7), Perranoski (9). W—Palmer. L—Miller. HR—Blair (Bal.).

## NLCS

■ **Winner:** The Mets completed their stunning pennant run by sweeping the Braves in the N.L.'s first League Championship Series.

■ **Turning point:** A five-run eighth-inning rally that produced a 9-5 Mets victory in Game 1 and set the tone for the rest of the series.

■ **Memorable moment:** Young Nolan Ryan's Game 3 heroics. Ryan took over for starter Gary Gentry in the third inning with runners on second and third, none out and the Braves leading 2-0. He pitched out of the jam and recorded the series-ending victory with seven innings of three-hit pitching.

■ **Top guns:** Art Shamsky (.538), Cleon Jones (.429), Ken Boswell (.333, 2 HR, 5 RBIs), Mets; Orlando Cepeda (.455), Hank Aaron (.357, 3 HR, 7 RBIs), Braves.

■ **MVP:** Boswell.

**Linescores**
**Game 1**—October 4, at Atlanta
New York ..0 2 0 2 0 0 0 5 0—9 10 1
Atlanta ......0 1 2 0 1 0 1 0 0—5 10 2
Seaver, Taylor (8); Niekro, Upshaw (9). W—Seaver. L—Niekro. S—Taylor. HR—Gonzalez, H. Aaron (Atl.).

**Game 2**—October 5, at Atlanta
New York 1 3 2 2 1 0 2 0 0—11 13 1
Atlanta ....0 0 0 1 5 0 0 0 0— 6 9 3
Koosman, Taylor (5), McGraw (7); Reed, Doyle (2), Pappas (3), Britton (6), Upshaw (6), Neibauer (9). W—Taylor. L—Reed. S—McGraw. HR—Agee, Boswell, Jones (N.Y.); H. Aaron (Atl.).

**Game 3**—October 6, at New York
Atlanta ......2 0 0 0 2 0 0 0 0—4 8 1
New York ..0 0 1 2 3 1 0 0 x—7 14 0
Jarvis, Stone (5), Upshaw (6); Gentry, Ryan (3). W—Ryan. L—Jarvis. HR—H. Aaron, Cepeda (Atl.); Agee, Boswell, Garrett (N.Y.).

## WORLD SERIES

■ **Winner:** The Amazing Mets completed their Cinderella season with a shocking five-game victory over the powerful Orioles.

■ **Turning point:** A ninth-inning RBI single by light-hitting Al Weis that gave the Mets and Jerry Koosman a Series-evening 2-1 victory in Game 2.

■ **Memorable moments:** Tommie Agee's Game 3 performance. Center fielder Agee hit a first-inning home run and made two spectacular catches that saved five runs and preserved a 5-0 victory.

■ **Top guns:** Koosman (2-0, 2.04 ERA), Weis (.455), Donn Clendenon (.357, 3 HR, 4 RBIs), Mets.

■ **MVP:** Clendenon.

**Linescores**
**Game 1**—October 11, at Baltimore
NY................0 0 0 0 0 0 1 0 0—1 6 1
Balt. ............1 0 0 3 0 0 0 0 x—4 6 0
Seaver, Cardwell (6), Taylor (7); Cuellar. W—Cuellar. L—Seaver. HR—Buford (Bal.).

**Game 2**—October 12, at Baltimore
NY................0 0 0 1 0 0 0 0 1—2 6 0
Balt. ............0 0 0 0 0 0 1 0 0—1 2 0
Koosman, Taylor (9); McNally. W—Koosman. L—McNally. HR—Clendenon (N.Y.).

**Game 3**—October 14, at New York
Balt. ............0 0 0 0 0 0 0 0 0—0 4 1
NY................1 2 0 0 0 1 0 1 x—5 6 0
Palmer, Leonhard (7); Gentry, Ryan (7). W—Gentry. L—Palmer. S—Ryan. HR—Agee, Kranepool (N.Y.).

**Game 4**—Ocotber 15, at New York
Balt. ........0 0 0 0 0 0 0 0 1 0—1 6 1
NY ..........0 1 0 0 0 0 0 0 0 1—2 10 1
Cuellar, Watt (8), Hall (10), Richert (10); Seaver. W—Seaver. L—Hall. HR—Clendenon (N.Y.).

**Game 5**—October 16, at New York
Balt. ............0 0 3 0 0 0 0 0 0—3 5 2
NY................0 0 0 0 0 2 1 2 x—5 7 0
McNally, Watt (8); Koosman. W—Koosman. L—Watt. HR—McNally, F. Robinson (Bal.); Clendenon, Weis (N.Y.).

# 1970

## FINAL STANDINGS

### American League

**East Division**

| Team | Bal. | N.Y. | Bos. | Det. | Cle. | Wsh. | Min. | Oak. | Cal. | K.C. | Mil. | Chi. | W | L | Pct. | GB |
|---|---|---|---|---|---|---|---|---|---|---|---|---|---|---|---|---|
| Baltimore | ... | 11 | 13 | 11 | 14 | 12 | 5 | 7 | 7 | 12 | 7 | 9 | 108 | 54 | .667 | ... |
| New York | 7 | ... | 8 | 11 | 10 | 10 | 7 | 6 | 7 | 11 | 9 | 7 | 93 | 69 | .574 | 15 |
| Boston | 5 | 10 | ... | 9 | 12 | 12 | 7 | 7 | 5 | 7 | 5 | 8 | 87 | 75 | .537 | 21 |
| Detroit | 7 | 7 | 9 | ... | 11 | 9 | 4 | 6 | 6 | 6 | 8 | 6 | 79 | 83 | .488 | 29 |
| Cleveland | 4 | 8 | 6 | 7 | ... | 11 | 6 | 7 | 6 | 8 | 7 | 6 | 76 | 86 | .469 | 32 |
| Washington | 6 | 8 | 6 | 9 | 7 | ... | 6 | 2 | 5 | 6 | 7 | 8 | 70 | 92 | .432 | 38 |

**West Division**

| Team | Min. | Oak. | Cal. | K.C. | Mil. | Chi. | Bal. | N.Y. | Bos. | Det. | Cle. | Wsh. | W | L | Pct. | GB |
|---|---|---|---|---|---|---|---|---|---|---|---|---|---|---|---|---|
| Minnesota | ... | 13 | 10 | 13 | 13 | 12 | 7 | 5 | 5 | 8 | 6 | 6 | 98 | 64 | .605 | ... |
| Oakland | 5 | ... | 10 | 11 | 10 | 16 | 5 | 6 | 5 | 6 | 5 | 10 | 89 | 73 | .549 | 9 |
| California | 8 | 8 | ... | 10 | 12 | 12 | 5 | 5 | 7 | 6 | 6 | 7 | 86 | 76 | .531 | 12 |
| Kansas City | 5 | 7 | 8 | ... | 12 | 11 | 0 | 1 | 5 | 6 | 4 | 6 | 65 | 97 | .401 | 33 |
| Milwaukee | 5 | 8 | 6 | 6 | ... | 11 | 5 | 3 | 7 | 4 | 5 | 5 | 65 | 97 | .401 | 33 |
| Chicago | 6 | 2 | 6 | 7 | 7 | ... | 3 | 5 | 4 | 6 | 6 | 4 | 56 | 106 | .346 | 42 |

### National League

**East Division**

| Team | Pit. | Chi. | N.Y. | St.L. | Phi. | Mon. | Cin. | L.A. | S.F. | Hou. | Atl. | S.D. | W | L | Pct. | GB |
|---|---|---|---|---|---|---|---|---|---|---|---|---|---|---|---|---|
| Pittsburgh | ... | 10 | 12 | 12 | 14 | 9 | 4 | 6 | 4 | 6 | 6 | 6 | 89 | 73 | .549 | ... |
| Chicago | 8 | ... | 7 | 7 | 9 | 13 | 7 | 6 | 7 | 7 | 4 | 9 | 84 | 78 | .519 | 5 |
| New York | 6 | 11 | ... | 12 | 13 | 8 | 4 | 5 | 6 | 6 | 6 | 6 | 83 | 79 | .512 | 6 |
| St. Louis | 6 | 11 | 6 | ... | 10 | 11 | 3 | 5 | 5 | 6 | 5 | 8 | 76 | 86 | .469 | 13 |
| Philadelphia | 4 | 9 | 5 | 8 | ... | 7 | 5 | 5 | 8 | 8 | 5 | 9 | 73 | 88 | .453 | 15.5 |
| Montreal | 9 | 5 | 10 | 7 | 11 | ... | 5 | 4 | 6 | 4 | 6 | 6 | 73 | 89 | .451 | 16 |

**West Division**

| Team | Cin. | L.A. | S.F. | Hou. | Atl. | S.D. | Pit. | Chi. | N.Y. | St.L. | Phi. | Mon. | W | L | Pct. | GB |
|---|---|---|---|---|---|---|---|---|---|---|---|---|---|---|---|---|
| Cincinnati | ... | 13 | 9 | 15 | 13 | 8 | 8 | 5 | 8 | 9 | 7 | 7 | 102 | 60 | .630 | ... |
| Los Angeles | 5 | ... | 9 | 10 | 12 | 11 | 6 | 6 | 7 | 7 | 6 | 8 | 87 | 74 | .540 | 14.5 |
| San Fran. | 9 | 9 | ... | 8 | 11 | 13 | 8 | 5 | 6 | 7 | 4 | 6 | 86 | 76 | .531 | 16 |
| Houston | 3 | 8 | 10 | ... | 9 | 14 | 6 | 5 | 6 | 6 | 4 | 8 | 79 | 83 | .488 | 23 |
| Atlanta | 5 | 6 | 7 | 9 | ... | 9 | 6 | 8 | 6 | 7 | 7 | 6 | 76 | 86 | .469 | 26 |
| San Diego | 10 | 7 | 5 | 4 | 9 | ... | 6 | 3 | 6 | 4 | 3 | 6 | 63 | 99 | .389 | 39 |

## LEADERS

**American League**
**BA:** Alex Johnson, Cal., .329.
**Runs:** Carl Yastrzemski, Bos., 125.
**Hits:** Tony Oliva, Min., 204.
**TB:** Carl Yastrzemski, Bos., 335.
**HR:** Frank Howard, Wash., 44.
**RBI:** Frank Howard, Wash., 126.
**SB:** Campy Campaneris, Oak., 42.
**Wins:** Mike Cuellar, Bal.; Dave McNally, Bal.; Jim Perry, Min., 24.
**ERA:** Diego Segui, Oak., 2.56.
**CG:** Mike Cuellar, Bal., 21.
**IP:** Sam McDowell, Cle.; Jim Palmer, Bal., 305.
**SO:** Sam McDowell, Cle., 304.
**SV:** Ron Perranoski, Min., 34.

**National League**
**BA:** Rico Carty, Atl., .366.
**Runs:** Billy Williams, Chi., 137.
**Hits:** Pete Rose, Cin.; Billy Williams, Chi., 205.
**TB:** Billy Williams, Chi., 373.
**HR:** Johnny Bench, Cin., 45.
**RBI:** Johnny Bench, Cin., 148.
**SB:** Bobby Tolan, Cin., 57.
**Wins:** Bob Gibson, St.L.; Gaylord Perry, S.F., 23.
**ERA:** Tom Seaver, N.Y., 2.82.
**CG:** Ferguson Jenkins, Chi., 24.
**IP:** Gaylord Perry, S.F., 328.2.
**SO:** Tom Seaver, N.Y., 283.
**SV:** Wayne Granger, Cin., 35.

**A.L. 20-game winners**
Mike Cuellar, Bal., 24-8
Dave McNally, Bal., 24-9
Jim Perry, Min., 24-12
Clyde Wright, Cal., 22-12
Jim Palmer, Bal., 20-10
Fritz Peterson, N.Y., 20-11
Sam McDowell, Cle., 20-12

**N.L. 20-game winners**
Bob Gibson, St.L., 23-7
Gaylord Perry, S.F., 23-13
Ferguson Jenkins, Chi., 22-16
Jim Merritt, Cin., 20-12

**A.L. 100 RBIs**
Frank Howard, Wash., 126
Tony Conigliaro, Bos., 116
Boog Powell, Bal., 114
Harmon Killebrew, Min., 113
Tony Oliva, Min., 107
Rico Petrocelli, Bos., 103
Carl Yastrzemski, Bos., 102

**N.L. 100 RBIs**
Johnny Bench, Cin., 148
Tony Perez, Cin., 129
Billy Williams, Chi., 129
Willie McCovey, S.F., 126
Hank Aaron, Atl., 118
Jim Hickman, Chi., 115
Ron Santo, Chi., 114
Orlando Cepeda, Atl., 111
Wes Parker, L.A., 111
Dick Dietz, S.F., 107
Dick Allen, St.L., 101
Rico Carty, Atl., 101
Joe Torre, St.L., 100

**A.L. 40 homers**
Frank Howard, Wash., 44
Harmon Killebrew, Min., 41
Carl Yastrzemski, Bos., 40

**N.L. 40 homers**
Johnny Bench, Cin., 45
Billy Williams, Chi., 42
Tony Perez, Cin., 40

**Most Valuable Player**
A.L.: Boog Powell, 1B, Bal.
N.L.: Johnny Bench, C, Cin.

**Cy Young Award**
A.L.: Jim Perry, Min.
N.L.: Bob Gibson, St.L.

**Rookie of the Year**
A.L.: Thurman Munson, C, N.Y.
N.L.: Carl Morton, P, Mon.

**Hall of Fame additions**
Lou Boudreau, SS, 1938-52
Earle Combs, OF, 1924-35
Ford Frick, exec./commissioner
Jesse Haines, P, 1918-37

## SIGNIFICANT EVENTS

■ **January 16:** Outfielder Curt Flood, who refused to report to Philadelphia after being traded by the Cardinals, filed a federal lawsuit challenging baseball's reserve clause.

■ **March 28:** Commissioner Bowie Kuhn returned the All-Star selection to the fans, with voting to be done on punch cards and processed by computer.

■ **March 31:** The financially strapped Pilots ended their one-year Seattle existence when the team was sold and moved to Milwaukee.

■ **June 30, July 16:** The Reds lost in their Riverfront Stadium debut to Atlanta, 8-2, but spoiled the Pirates' Three Rivers Stadium inaugural, 3-2.

■ **September 3:** Exhausted Cubs star Billy Williams ended his N.L.-record ironman streak at 1,117 games.

■ **October 4:** Umpires ended their unprecedented one-day strike when they accepted a four-year contract and returned to work for the second games of the League Championship Series.

## MEMORABLE MOMENTS

■ **April 22:** Mets righthander Tom Seaver tied the Major League record when he struck out 19 Padres, including a record 10 in succession, during a 2-1 victory at Shea Stadium.

■ **May 10:** Atlanta knuckleballer Hoyt Wilhelm became the first pitcher to appear in 1,000 Major League games.

■ **May 12:** Cubs shortstop Ernie Banks hit his 500th career home run off Atlanta's Pat Jarvis in a 4-3 victory at Wrigley Field.

■ **May 17, July 18:** Two new members of baseball's 3,000-hit club: Atlanta's Hank Aaron and San Francisco's Willie Mays.

■ **June 21:** Detroit's Cesar Gutierrez performed a 20th Century first when he collected seven hits (six singles and a double) in a 12-inning 9-8 victory over Cleveland.

■ **June 26:** Baltimore's Frank Robinson belted a record-tying two grand slams in the Orioles' 12-2 victory over the Senators.

■ **October 1:** California's Alex Johnson collected two final-day hits and edged Boston's Carl Yastrzemski, .3289 to .3286, in the tightest A.L. batting race since 1946.

## ALL-STAR GAME

■ **Winner:** Chicago's Jim Hickman singled home Pete Rose in the 12th inning, giving the N.L. a come-from-behind victory that pushed its All-Star winning streak to eight games.

■ **Key inning:** The bottom of the ninth, when a Dick Dietz home run, an RBI single by Willie McCovey and Roberto Clemente's sacrifice fly brought the N.L. back from a 4-1 deficit and forced extra innings.

■ **Memorable moment:** A game-ending collision between Rose and A.L. catcher Ray Fosse. Rose, playing before his home fans, jarred the ball free and sent Fosse sprawling with a nasty body block.

■ **Top guns:** Tom Seaver (Mets), Bud Harrelson (Mets), Dietz (Giants), McCovey (Giants), Rose (Reds), Hickman (Cubs), N.L.; Jim Palmer (Orioles), Sam McDowell (Indians), Carl Yastrzemski (Red Sox), Brooks Robinson (Orioles), A.L.

■ **MVP:** Yastrzemski

**Linescore**

July 14, at Cincinnati's Riverfront Stadium
A.L....0 0 0  0 0 1  1 2 0  0 0 0—4 12 0
N.L. 0 0 0  0 0 0  1 0 3  0 0 1—5 10 0
Palmer (Orioles), McDowell (Indians) 4, J. Perry (Twins) 7, Hunter (Athletics) 9, Peterson (Yankees) 9, Stottlemyre (Yankees) 9, Wright (Angels) 11; Seaver (Mets), Merritt (Reds) 4, G. Perry (Giants) 6, Gibson (Cardinals) 8, Osteen (Dodgers) 10. W—Osteen. L—Wright. HR—Dietz, N.L.

## ALCS

■ **Winner:** Powerful Baltimore made it two straight over the Twins, who were outscored by an average of almost six runs per game.

■ **Turning point:** The fourth inning of Game 1. The Orioles scored seven times and broke the only tie the Twins could manage in the entire series.

■ **Memorable moment:** A fourth-inning Game 1 grand slam homer by light-hitting pitcher Mike Cuellar. He pulled the pitch down the right-field line, clearly foul, but a gusty wind brought the ball back inside the foul pole.

■ **Top guns:** Jim Palmer (1-0, 1.00 ERA), Brooks Robinson (.583), Boog Powell (.429, 6 RBIs), Don Buford (.429), Orioles; Tony Oliva (.500), Twins.

■ **MVP:** Powell.

**Linescores**

**Game 1**—October 3, at Minnesota
Balt. ........0 2 0  7 0 1  0 0 0—10 13 0
Minn. ......1 1 0  1 3 0  0 0 0— 6 11 2
Cuellar, Hall (5); Perry, Zepp (4), Woodson (5), Williams (6), Perranoski (9). W—Hall. L—Perry. HR—Cuellar, Buford, Powell (Bal.); Killebrew (Min.).

**Game 2**—October 4, at Minnesota
Balt. ........1 0 2  1 0 0  0 0 7—11 13 0
Minn. ......0 0 0  3 0 0  0 0 0— 3 6 2
McNally; Hall, Zepp (4), Williams (5), Perranoski (8), Tiant (9). W—McNally. L—Hall. HR—F. Robinson, Johnson (Bal.); Killebrew, Oliva (Min.).

**Game 3**—October 5, at Baltimore
Minn. ........0 0 0  0 1 0  0 0 0—1 7 2
Balt. ..........1 1 3  0 0 0  1 0 x—6 10 0
Kaat, Blyleven (3), Hall (5), Perry (7); Palmer. W—Palmer. L—Kaat. HR—Johnson (Bal.).

## NLCS

■ **Winner:** Power-packed Cincinnati's sweep of Pittsburgh was orchestrated by an oft-maligned pitching staff that recorded a 0.96 series ERA.

■ **Turning point:** Don Gullett's 3⅓ innings of hitless relief in Game 2. He secured a 3-1 Cincinnati victory and struck out the side in an impressive seventh inning.

■ **Memorable moment:** Back-to-back Game 3 homers by Tony Perez and Johnny Bench — the Reds' only power display of the series.

■ **Top guns:** Gary Nolan (1-0, 0-00 ERA), Bobby Tolan (.417), Reds; Richie Hebner (.667), Willie Stargell (.500), Pirates.

■ **MVP:** Reds' pitching staff (0.96 ERA).

**Linescores**

**Game 1**—October 3, at Pittsburgh
Cin. ..........0 0 0  0 0 0  0 0 0 3—3 9 0
Pitt. ..........0 0 0  0 0 0  0 0 0 0—0 8 0
Nolan, Carroll (10); Ellis, Gibbon (10). W—Nolan. L—Ellis S—Carroll.

**Game 2**—October 4, at Pittsburgh
Cincinnati ....0 0 1  0 1 0  0 1 0—3 8 1
Pittsburgh....0 0 0  0 0 1  0 0 0—1 5 2
Merritt, Carroll (6), Gullett (6); Walker, Giusti (8). W—Merritt. L—Walker. HR—Tolan (Cin.).

**Game 3**—October 5, at Cincinnati
Pittsburgh..1 0 0  0 1 0  0 0 0—2 10 0
Cincinnati ..2 0 0  0 0 0  0 1 x—3 5 0
Moose, Gibbon (8), Giusti (8); Cloninger, Wilcox (6), Granger (9), Gullett (9). W—Wilcox. L—Moose. S—Gullett. HR—Perez, Bench (Cin.).

## WORLD SERIES

■ **Winner:** The Orioles, still reeling from their five-game 1969 loss to the Mets, turned the tables on the young Reds.

■ **Turning point:** Game 1. The Orioles, down 3-0 in the first Series game at new Riverfront Stadium, rallied on home runs by Boog Powell, Brooks Robinson and Elrod Hendricks for a 4-3 victory.

■ **Memorable moments:** The incredible fielding artistry of Orioles third baseman Brooks Robinson, who constantly foiled the Reds with big plays, and Baltimore pitcher Dave McNally's third-game grand slam.

■ **Top guns:** Brooks Robinson (.429, 6 RBIs), Paul Blair (.474), Orioles; Hal McRae (.455), Lee May (.389, 2 HR, 8 RBIs), Reds.

■ **MVP:** Brooks Robinson.

**Linescores**

**Game 1**—October 10, at Cincinnati
Balt. ..............0 0 0  2 1 0  1 0 0—4 7 2
Cin. ...............1 0 2  0 0 0  0 0 0—3 5 0
Palmer, Richert (9); Nolan, Carroll (7). W—Palmer. L—Nolan. S—Richert. HR—May (Cin.); Powell, Hendricks, B. Robinson (Bal.).

**Game 2**—October 11, at Cincinnati
Balt. ..........0 0 0  1 5 0  0 0 0—6 10 2
Cin. .............3 0 1  0 0 1  0 0 0—5 7 0
Cuellar, Phoebus (3), Drabowsky (5), Lopez (7), Hall (7); McGlothlin, Wilcox (5), Carroll (5), Gullett (8). W—Phoebus. L—Wilcox. S—Hall. HR—Tolan, Bench (Cin.); Powell (Bal.).

**Game 3**—October 13, at Baltimore
Cin. ..............0 1 0  0 0 0  2 0 0—3 9 0
Balt. ..........2 0 1  0 1 4  1 0 x—9 10 1
Cloninger, Granger (6), Gullett (7); McNally. W—McNally. L—Cloninger. HR—F. Robinson, Buford, McNally (Bal.).

**Game 4**—October 14, at Baltimore
Cin. ...............0 1 1  0 1 0  0 3 0—6 8 3
Balt. ..............0 1 3  0 0 1  0 0 0—5 8 0
Nolan, Gullett (3), Carroll (6); Palmer, Watt (8), Drabowsky (9). W—Carroll. L—Watt. HR—B. Robinson (Bal.); Rose, May (Cin.).

**Game 5**—October 15, at Baltimore
Cin. ..............3 0 0  0 0 0  0 0 0—3 6 0
Balt. ..........2 2 2  0 1 0  0 2 x—9 15 0
Merritt, Granger (2), Wilcox (3), Cloninger (5), Washburn (7), Carroll (8); Cuellar. W—Cuellar. L—Merritt. HR—F. Robinson, Rettenmund (Bal.).

# 1971

## FINAL STANDINGS

### American League

**East Division**

| Team | Bal. | Det. | Bos. | N.Y. | Wash. | Cle. | Oak. | K.C. | Chi. | Cal. | Min. | Mil. | W | L | Pct. | GB |
|---|---|---|---|---|---|---|---|---|---|---|---|---|---|---|---|---|
| Baltimore | ... | 8 | 9 | 11 | 13 | 13 | 7 | 6 | 8 | 7 | 10 | 9 | 101 | 57 | .639 | ... |
| Detroit | 10 | ... | 6 | 10 | 14 | 12 | 4 | 8 | 5 | 6 | 6 | 10 | 91 | 71 | .562 | 12 |
| Boston | 9 | 12 | ... | 7 | 12 | 11 | 3 | 1 | 10 | 6 | 8 | 6 | 85 | 77 | .525 | 18 |
| New York | 7 | 8 | 11 | ... | 7 | 10 | 5 | 7 | 7 | 6 | 4 | 10 | 82 | 80 | .506 | 21 |
| Washington | 3 | 4 | 6 | 11 | ... | 11 | 3 | 3 | 2 | 8 | 6 | 6 | 63 | 96 | .396 | 38.5 |
| Cleveland | 5 | 6 | 7 | 8 | 7 | ... | 4 | 2 | 9 | 4 | 4 | 4 | 60 | 102 | .370 | 43 |

**West Division**

| Team | Oak. | K.C. | Chi. | Cal. | Min. | Mil. | Bal. | Det. | Bos. | N.Y. | Wash. | Cle. | W | L | Pct. | GB |
|---|---|---|---|---|---|---|---|---|---|---|---|---|---|---|---|---|
| Oakland | ... | 13 | 7 | 11 | 10 | 15 | 4 | 8 | 9 | 7 | 9 | 8 | 101 | 60 | .627 | ... |
| Kansas City | 5 | ... | 9 | 10 | 9 | 8 | 5 | 4 | 11 | 5 | 9 | 10 | 85 | 76 | .528 | 16 |
| Chicago | 11 | 9 | ... | 10 | 7 | 11 | 4 | 7 | 2 | 5 | 10 | 3 | 79 | 83 | .488 | 22.5 |
| California | 7 | 8 | 8 | ... | 12 | 6 | 5 | 6 | 6 | 6 | 4 | 8 | 76 | 86 | .469 | 25.5 |
| Minnesota | 8 | 9 | 11 | 6 | ... | 7 | 2 | 6 | 4 | 8 | 5 | 8 | 74 | 86 | .463 | 26.5 |
| Milwaukee | 3 | 10 | 7 | 12 | 10 | ... | 3 | 2 | 6 | 2 | 6 | 8 | 69 | 92 | .429 | 32 |

### National League

**East Division**

| Team | Pit. | St.L. | Chi. | N.Y. | Mon. | Phi. | S.F. | L.A. | Atl. | Cin. | Hou. | S.D. | W | L | Pct. | GB |
|---|---|---|---|---|---|---|---|---|---|---|---|---|---|---|---|---|
| Pittsburgh | ... | 11 | 12 | 8 | 11 | 12 | 3 | 8 | 8 | 7 | 8 | 9 | 97 | 65 | .599 | ... |
| St. Louis | 7 | ... | 9 | 8 | 14 | 11 | 7 | 6 | 6 | 4 | 10 | 8 | 90 | 72 | .556 | 7 |
| Chicago | 6 | 9 | ... | 11 | 8 | 11 | 3 | 8 | 7 | 6 | 5 | 9 | 83 | 79 | .512 | 14 |
| New York | 10 | 10 | 7 | ... | 9 | 13 | 4 | 7 | 5 | 4 | 7 | 7 | 83 | 79 | .512 | 14 |
| Montreal | 7 | 4 | 10 | 9 | ... | 6 | 7 | 4 | 5 | 5 | 8 | 6 | 71 | 90 | .441 | 25.5 |
| Philadelphia | 6 | 7 | 7 | 5 | 12 | ... | 6 | 5 | 4 | 7 | 4 | 4 | 67 | 95 | .414 | 30 |

**West Division**

| Team | S.F. | L.A. | Atl. | Cin. | Hou. | S.D. | Pit. | St.L. | Chi. | N.Y. | Mon. | Phi. | W | L | Pct. | GB |
|---|---|---|---|---|---|---|---|---|---|---|---|---|---|---|---|---|
| San Fran. | ... | 6 | 11 | 9 | 9 | 13 | 9 | 5 | 9 | 8 | 5 | 6 | 90 | 72 | .556 | ... |
| L.A. | 12 | ... | 9 | 11 | 10 | 13 | 4 | 6 | 4 | 5 | 8 | 7 | 89 | 73 | .549 | 1 |
| Atlanta | 7 | 9 | ... | 9 | 9 | 11 | 4 | 6 | 5 | 7 | 7 | 8 | 82 | 80 | .506 | 8 |
| Cincinnati | 9 | 7 | 9 | ... | 5 | 10 | 5 | 8 | 6 | 8 | 7 | 5 | 79 | 83 | .488 | 11 |
| Houston | 9 | 8 | 9 | 13 | ... | 10 | 4 | 2 | 7 | 5 | 4 | 8 | 79 | 83 | .488 | 11 |
| San Diego | 5 | 5 | 7 | 8 | 8 | ... | 3 | 4 | 3 | 5 | 5 | 8 | 61 | 100 | .379 | 28.5 |

## SIGNIFICANT EVENTS

■ **April 10:** The Phillies made their Veterans Stadium debut a successful one, defeating Montreal, 4-1.

■ **May 6:** Commissioner Bowie Kuhn closed a deal with NBC-TV that would net the 24 teams $72 million over four years.

■ **September 21:** Baseball ended its 71-year association with the nation's capital when owners approved the Senators' transfer to the Dallas-Fort Worth area.

## MEMORABLE MOMENTS

■ **April 27:** The 600-homer club welcomed its third member when Atlanta's Hank Aaron connected off Gaylord Perry in a 10-inning 6-5 loss to the Giants.

■ **June 23:** Philadelphia's Rick Wise pitched a no-hitter and spiced his 4-0 victory over Cincinnati with two home runs.

■ **August 10, September 13:** Minnesota's Harmon Killebrew and Baltimore's Frank Robinson became the 10th and 11th players to hit 500 career home runs.

■ **September 26:** When Jim Palmer blanked Cleveland 5-0 for his 20th victory, the Orioles joined the 1920 White Sox as the only teams to boast four 20-game winners in one season. Palmer joined Dave McNally, Mike Cuellar and Pat Dobson in the select circle.

■ **September 30:** The Senators had to forfeit their final game in Washington to the Yankees when fans swarmed out of the stands in the ninth inning and began tearing up RFK Stadium.

## LEADERS

**American League**
**BA:** Tony Oliva, Min., .337.
**Runs:** Don Buford, Bal., 99.
**Hits:** Cesar Tovar, Min., 204.
**TB:** Reggie Smith, Bos., 302.
**HR:** Bill Melton, Chi., 33.
**RBI:** Harmon Killebrew, Min., 119.
**SB:** Amos Otis, K.C., 52.
**Wins:** Mickey Lolich, Det., 25.
**ERA:** Vida Blue, Oak., 1.82.
**CG:** Mickey Lolich, Det., 29.
**IP:** Mickey Lolich, Det., 376.
**SO:** Mickey Lolich, Det., 308.
**SV:** Ken Sanders, Mil., 31.

**National League**
**BA:** Joe Torre, St.L., .363.
**Runs:** Lou Brock, St.L., 126.
**Hits:** Joe Torre, St.L., 230.
**TB:** Joe Torre, St.L., 352.
**HR:** Willie Stargell, Pit., 48.
**RBI:** Joe Torre, St.L., 137.
**SB:** Lou Brock, St.L., 64.
**Wins:** Ferguson Jenkins, Chi., 24.
**ERA:** Tom Seaver, N.Y., 1.76.
**CG:** Ferguson Jenkins, Chi., 30.
**IP:** Ferguson Jenkins, Chi., 325.
**SO:** Tom Seaver, N.Y., 289.
**SV:** Dave Giusti, Pit., 30.

**A.L. 20-game winners**
Mickey Lolich, Det., 25-14
Vida Blue, Oak., 24-8
Wilbur Wood, Chi., 22-13
Dave McNally, Bal., 21-5
Catfish Hunter, Oak., 21-11
Pat Dobson, Bal., 20-8
Jim Palmer, Bal., 20-9
Mike Cuellar, Bal., 20-9
Joe Coleman, Det., 20-9
Andy Messersmith, Cal., 20-13

**N.L. 20-game winners**
Ferguson Jenkins, Chi., 24-13
Al Downing, L.A., 20-9
Steve Carlton, St.L., 20-9
Tom Seaver, N.Y., 20-10

**A.L. 100 RBIs**
Harmon Killebrew, Min., 119

**N.L. 100 RBIs**
Joe Torre, St.L., 137
Willie Stargell, Pit., 125
Hank Aaron, Mil., 118
Bobby Bonds, S.F., 102

**N.L. 40 homers**
Willie Stargell, Pit., 48
Hank Aaron, Atl., 47

**Most Valuable Player**
A.L.: Vida Blue, P, Oak.
N.L.: Joe Torre, 3B, St.L.

**Cy Young Award**
A.L.: Vida Blue, Oak.
N.L.: Ferguson Jenkins, Chi.

**Rookie of the Year**
A.L.: Chris Chambliss, 1B, Cle.
N.L.: Earl Williams, C, Atl.

**Hall of Fame additions**
Dave Bancroft, SS, 1915-30
Jake Beckley, 1B, 1888-1907
Chick Hafey, OF, 1924-37
Harry Hooper, OF, 1909-25
Joe Kelley, OF, 1891-1908
Rube Marquard, P, 1908-25
Satchel Paige, P, 1948-65
George Weiss, executive

## ALL-STAR GAME

■ **Winner:** The A.L. ended its eight-year All-Star drought with a three-homer barrage that produced a 6-4 victory.

■ **Key inning:** After falling behind 3-0 on Johnny Bench and Hank Aaron home runs, the A.L. struck for four third-inning runs on two-run homers by Reggie Jackson and Frank Robinson.

■ **Memorable moment:** The titanic third-inning blast by Jackson, which struck a light tower on the roof of Tiger Stadium, 520 feet from home plate in right-center field.

■ **Top guns:** Jackson (Athletics), F. Robinson (Orioles), Harmon Killebrew (Twins), A.L.; Bench (Reds), Aaron (Braves), Roberto Clemente (Pirates), N.L.

■ **MVP:** F. Robinson.

**Linescore**
July 13, at Detroit's Tiger Stadium
N.L...............0 2 1  0 0 0  0 1 0—4 5 0
A.L. ..............0 0 4  0 0 2  0 0 x—6 7 0
Ellis (Pirates), Marichal (Giants) 4, Jenkins (Cubs) 6, Wilson (Astros) 7; Blue (Athletics), Palmer (Orioles) 4, Cuellar (Orioles) 6, Lolich (Tigers) 8. W—Blue. L—Ellis. HR—Bench, Aaron, Clemente, N.L.; Jackson, F. Robinson, Killebrew, A.L.

## ALCS

■ **Winner:** The Orioles recorded their third consecutive Championship Series sweep, turning aside the up-and-coming Oakland Athletics.

■ **Turning point:** A four-run seventh-inning Game 1 rally that wiped out a 3-1 deficit and marked the last time Baltimore trailed in the series.

■ **Memorable moments:** A four-homer Game 2 salvo and Mike Cuellar's six-hit pitching added up to a 5-1 Orioles' victory.

■ **Top guns:** Cuellar (1-0, 1.00 ERA), Brooks Robinson (.364, 3 RBIs), Boog Powell (2 HR, 3 RBIs), Orioles; Sal Bando (.364), Reggie Jackson (.333, 2 HR), Athletics.

■ **MVP:** Cuellar.

**Linescores**

**Game 1**—October 3, at Baltimore
Oakland........0 2 0  1 0 0  0 0 0—3 9 0
Baltimore .....0 0 0  1 0 0  4 0 x—5 7 1
Blue, Fingers (8); McNally, Watt (8). W—McNally. L—Blue. S—Watt.

**Game 2**—October 4, at Baltimore
Oakland........0 0 0  1 0 0  0 0 0—1 6 0
Baltimore .....0 1 1  0 0 0  1 2 x—5 7 0
Hunter; Cuellar. W—Cuellar. L—Hunter. HR—B. Robinson, Powell 2, Hendricks (Bal.).

**Game 3**—October 5, at Oakland
Baltimore ..1 0 0  0 2 0  2 0 0—5 12 0
Oakland......0 0 1  0 0 1  0 1 0—3 7 0
Palmer; Segui, Fingers (5), Knowles (7), Locker (7), Grant (8). W—Palmer. L—Segui. HR—Jackson 2, Bando (Oak.).

## NLCS

■ **Winner:** Pittsburgh defeated San Francisco to claim its first pennant since 1960. The Pirates needed four games to win the first LCS not decided by a sweep.

■ **Turning point:** Richie Hebner's eighth-inning Game 3 home run, which gave substitute starter Bob Johnson a 2-1 victory and the Pirates a 2-1 series edge.

■ **Memorable moment:** Pittsburgh first baseman Bob Robertson's ninth-inning Game 2 home run — his record-setting third of the game — capping a 9-4 Pirates victory.

■ **Top guns:** Robertson (.438, 4 HR, 6 RBIs), Dave Cash (.421), Hebner (2 HR, 4 RBIs), Pirates; Willie McCovey (.429, 2 HR, 6 RBIs), Chris Speier (.357), Giants.

■ **MVP:** Robertson.

**Linescores**

**Game 1**—October 2, at San Francisco
Pitt..............0 0 2  0 0 0  2 0 0—4 9 0
San Fran.......0 0 1  0 4 0  0 0 x—5 7 2
Blass, Moose (6), Giusti (8); Perry. W—Perry. L—Blass. HR—Fuentes, McCovey (S.F.).

**Game 2**—October 3, at San Francisco
Pitt............0 1 0  2 1 0  4 0 1—9 15 0
San Fran. ..1 1 0  0 0 0  0 0 2—4 9 0
Ellis, Miller (6), Giusti (9); Cumberland, Barr (4), McMahon (5), Carrithers (7), Bryant (7), Hamilton (9). W—Ellis. L—Cumberland. S—Giusti. HR—Robertson 3, Clines (Pit.); Mays (S.F.).

**Game 3**—October 5, at Pittsburgh
San Fran. ....0 0 0  0 0 1  0 0 0—1 5 2
Pitt...............0 1 0  0 0 0  0 1 x—2 4 1
Marichal; Johnson, Giusti (9). W—Johnson. L—Marichal. S—Giusti. HR—Robertson, Hebner (Pit.).

**Game 4**—October 6, at Pittsburgh
San Fran. ..1 4 0  0 0 0  0 0 0—5 10 0
Pitt.............2 3 0  0 0 4  0 0 x—9 11 2
Perry, Johnson (6), McMahon (8); Blass, Kison (3), Giusti (7). W—Kison. L—Perry. S—Giusti. HR—Speier, McCovey (S.F.); Hebner, Oliver (Pit.).

## WORLD SERIES

■ **Winner:** The Pirates, absent from Series competition for a decade, rebounded after losing the first two games.

■ **Turning point:** After Pittsburgh starter Luke Walker surrendered three first-inning runs in Game 4, Bruce Kison and Dave Giusti pitched 8⅓ scoreless innings and the Pirates rallied for a 4-3 victory.

■ **Memorable moments:** The Game 7 performances of Roberto Clemente, who homered, and Steve Blass, who shut down the Orioles 2-1 on a gritty four-hitter.

■ **Top guns:** Blass (2-0, 1.00 ERA), Clemente (.414, 12 hits, 2 HR, 4 RBIs), Manny Sanguillen (.379), Pirates; Dave McNally (2-1, 1.98), Orioles.

■ **MVP:** Clemente.

**Linescores**

**Game 1**—October 9, at Baltimore
Pitt.............0 3 0  0 0 0  0 0 0—3 3 0
Balt. ..........0 1 3  0 1 0  0 0 x—5 10 3
Ellis, Moose (3), Miller (7); McNally. W—McNally. L—Ellis. HR—F. Robinson, Rettenmund, Buford (Bal.).

**Game 2**—October 11, at Baltimore
Pitt...........0 0 0  0 0 0  0 3 0— 3 8 1
Balt. ........0 1 0  3 6 1  0 0 x—11 14 1
R. Johnson, Kison (4), Moose (4), Veale (5), Miller (6), Giusti (8); Palmer, Hall (9). W—Palmer. L—R. Johnson. S—Hall. HR—Hebner (Pit.).

**Game 3**—October 12, at Pittsburgh
Balt. ...........0 0 0  0 0 0  1 0 0—1 3 3
Pitt...............1 0 0  0 0 1  3 0 x—5 7 0
Cuellar, Dukes (7), Watt (8); Blass. W—Blass. L—Cuellar. HR—F. Robinson (Bal.); Robertson (Pit.).

**Game 4**—October 13, at Pittsburgh
Balt. ..........3 0 0  0 0 0  0 0 0—3 4 1
Pitt.............2 0 1  0 0 0  1 0 x—4 14 0
Dobson, Jackson (6), Watt (7), Richert (8); Walker, Kison (1), Giusti (8). W—Kison. L—Watt. S—Giusti.

**Game 5**—October 14, at Pittsburgh
Balt. ...........0 0 0  0 0 0  0 0 0—0 2 1
Pitt. ..............0 2 1  0 1 0  0 0 x—4 9 0
McNally, Leonhard (5), Dukes (6); Briles. W—Briles. L—McNally. HR—Robertson (Pit.).

**Game 6**—October 16, at Baltimore
Pitt..........0 1 1  0 0 0  0 0 0 0—2 9 1
Balt. ........0 0 0  0 0 1  1 0 0 1—3 8 0
Moose, R. Johnson (6), Giusti (7), Miller (10); Palmer, Dobson (10), McNally (10). W—McNally. L—Miller. HR—Clemente (Pit.); Buford (Bal.).

**Game 7**—October 17, at Baltimore
Pitt..............0 0 0  1 0 0  0 1 0—2 6 1
Balt. .............0 0 0  0 0 0  0 1 0—1 4 0
Blass; Cuellar, Dobson (9), McNally (9). W—Blass. L—Cuellar. HR—Clemente (Pit.).

## FINAL STANDINGS

### American League

#### East Division

| Team | Det. | Bos. | Bal. | N.Y. | Cle. | Mil. | Oak. | Chi. | Min. | K.C. | Cal. | Tex. | W | L | Pct. | GB |
|---|---|---|---|---|---|---|---|---|---|---|---|---|---|---|---|---|
| Detroit | ... | 9 | 8 | 7 | 8 | 10 | 4 | 7 | 9 | 7 | 7 | 10 | 86 | 70 | .551 | ... |
| Boston | 5 | ... | 11 | 9 | 8 | 11 | 9 | 6 | 4 | 6 | 8 | 8 | 85 | 70 | .548 | .5 |
| Baltimore | 10 | 7 | ... | 7 | 8 | 10 | 6 | 8 | 6 | 6 | 6 | 6 | 80 | 74 | .519 | 5 |
| New York | 9 | 9 | 6 | ... | 11 | 9 | 3 | 5 | 6 | 5 | 8 | 8 | 79 | 76 | .510 | 6.5 |
| Cleveland | 10 | 7 | 10 | 7 | ... | 5 | 2 | 4 | 8 | 6 | 4 | 9 | 72 | 84 | .462 | 14 |
| Milwaukee | 8 | 7 | 5 | 9 | 10 | ... | 4 | 3 | 4 | 5 | 5 | 5 | 65 | 91 | .417 | 21 |

#### West Division

| Team | Oak. | Chi. | Min. | K.C. | Cal. | Tex. | Det. | Bos. | Bal. | N.Y. | Cle. | Mil | W | L | Pct. | GB |
|---|---|---|---|---|---|---|---|---|---|---|---|---|---|---|---|---|
| Oakland | ... | 8 | 9 | 11 | 10 | 11 | 8 | 3 | 6 | 9 | 10 | 8 | 93 | 62 | .600 | ... |
| Chicago | 7 | ... | 8 | 8 | 11 | 14 | 5 | 6 | 4 | 7 | 8 | 9 | 87 | 67 | .565 | 5.5 |
| Minnesota | 8 | 6 | ... | 9 | 8 | 11 | 3 | 8 | 6 | 6 | 4 | 8 | 77 | 77 | .500 | 15.5 |
| Kansas City | 7 | 9 | 9 | ... | 6 | 8 | 5 | 6 | 6 | 7 | 6 | 7 | 76 | 78 | .494 | 16.5 |
| California | 8 | 7 | 7 | 9 | ... | 10 | 5 | 4 | 6 | 4 | 8 | 7 | 75 | 80 | .484 | 18 |
| Texas | 4 | 4 | 7 | 6 | 7 | ... | 2 | 4 | 6 | 4 | 3 | 7 | 54 | 100 | .351 | 38.5 |

### National League

#### East Division

| Team | Pit. | Chi. | N.Y. | St.L. | Mon. | Phi. | Cin. | Hou. | L.A. | Atl. | S.F. | S.D. | W | L | Pct. | GB |
|---|---|---|---|---|---|---|---|---|---|---|---|---|---|---|---|---|
| Pittsburgh | ... | 12 | 6 | 10 | 12 | 13 | 4 | 9 | 5 | 6 | 9 | 10 | 96 | 59 | .619 | ... |
| Chicago | 3 | ... | 10 | 10 | 10 | 10 | 8 | 3 | 8 | 7 | 7 | 9 | 85 | 70 | .548 | 11 |
| New York | 8 | 8 | ... | 7 | 12 | 13 | 4 | 6 | 5 | 5 | 8 | 7 | 83 | 73 | .532 | 13.5 |
| St. Louis | 8 | 8 | 9 | ... | 8 | 7 | 2 | 8 | 4 | 6 | 7 | 8 | 75 | 81 | .481 | 21.5 |
| Montreal | 6 | 5 | 6 | 9 | ... | 10 | 4 | 4 | 6 | 8 | 6 | 6 | 70 | 86 | .449 | 26.5 |
| Philadelphia | 5 | 7 | 5 | 8 | 6 | ... | 2 | 3 | 5 | 6 | 6 | 6 | 59 | 97 | .378 | 37.5 |

#### West Division

| Team | Cin. | Hou. | L.A. | Atl. | S.F. | S.D. | Pit. | Chi. | N.Y. | St.L. | Mon. | Phi. | W | L | Pct. | GB |
|---|---|---|---|---|---|---|---|---|---|---|---|---|---|---|---|---|
| Cincinnati | ... | 11 | 9 | 9 | 10 | 8 | 8 | 4 | 8 | 10 | 8 | 10 | 95 | 59 | .617 | ... |
| Houston | 6 | ... | 7 | 7 | 13 | 12 | 3 | 9 | 6 | 4 | 8 | 9 | 84 | 69 | .549 | 10.5 |
| Los Angeles | 5 | 11 | ... | 8 | 9 | 13 | 7 | 4 | 7 | 8 | 6 | 7 | 85 | 70 | .548 | 10.5 |
| Atlanta | 9 | 7 | 7 | ... | 7 | 6 | 6 | 5 | 7 | 6 | 4 | 6 | 70 | 84 | .455 | 25 |
| San Fran. | 5 | 5 | 9 | 11 | ... | 10 | 3 | 5 | 4 | 5 | 6 | 6 | 69 | 86 | .445 | 26.5 |
| San Diego | 10 | 2 | 5 | 11 | 4 | ... | 2 | 3 | 5 | 4 | 6 | 6 | 58 | 95 | .379 | 36.5 |

## SIGNIFICANT EVENTS

■ **April 2:** Gil Hodges, completing spring training preparations for his fifth season as Mets manager, died from a heart attack at West Palm Beach, Fla., at age 47.

■ **April 13:** The first players' strike in baseball history was settled after 13 days and 86 cancelled games.

■ **April 21:** The Rangers celebrated their Texas debut with a 7-6 victory over California at Arlington Stadium.

■ **June 19:** The U.S. Supreme Court upheld baseball's antitrust exemption and ended Curt Flood's long, frustrating challenge to the sport's reserve clause.

■ **November 2:** Steve Carlton, who posted 27 of the last-place Phillies' 59 victories, captured the N.L. Cy Young Award.

■ **December 31:** Pirates outfielder Roberto Clemente, the newest member of baseball's 3,000-hit club, died when a cargo plane carrying supplies to Nicaraguan earthquake victims crashed near San Juan, Puerto Rico.

## MEMORABLE MOMENTS

■ **May 14:** Willie Mays, returning to New York after more than 14 seasons in San Francisco, belted a game-winning solo home run against the Giants in his first game with the Mets.

■ **June 10:** Atlanta's Hank Aaron hit his N.L. record-tying 14th grand slam in a 15-3 victory over the Phillies and moved into second place on the all-time home run list.

■ **August 1:** San Diego's Nate Colbert belted a record-tying five homers and drove in a doubleheader-record 13 runs in a 9-0 and 11-7 sweep of the Braves.

## LEADERS

**American League**
**BA:** Rod Carew, Min., .318.
**Runs:** Bobby Murcer, N.Y., 102.
**Hits:** Joe Rudi, Oak., 181.
**TB:** Bobby Murcer, N.Y., 314.
**HR:** Dick Allen, Chi., 37.
**RBI:** Dick Allen, Chi., 113.
**SB:** Campy Campaneris, Oak., 52.
**Wins:** Gaylord Perry, Cle.; Wilbur Wood, Chi., 24.
**ERA:** Luis Tiant, Bos., 1.91.
**CG:** Gaylord Perry, Cle., 29.
**IP:** Wilbur Wood, Chi., 376.2.
**SO:** Nolan Ryan, Cal., 329.
**SV:** Sparky Lyle, N.Y., 35.

**National League**
**BA:** Billy Williams, Chi., .333.
**Runs:** Joe Morgan, Cin., 122.
**Hits:** Pete Rose, Cin., 198.
**TB:** Billy Williams, Chi., 348.
**HR:** Johnny Bench, Cin., 40.
**RBI:** Johnny Bench, Cin., 125.
**SB:** Lou Brock, St.L., 63.
**Wins:** Steve Carlton, Phil., 27.
**ERA:** Steve Carlton, Phil., 1.97.
**CG:** Steve Carlton, Phil., 30.
**IP:** Steve Carlton, Phil., 346.1.
**SO:** Steve Carlton, Phil., 310.
**SV:** Clay Carroll, Cin., 37.

**A.L. 20-game winners**
Gaylord Perry, Cle., 24-16
Wilbur Wood, Chi., 24-17
Mickey Lolich, Det., 22-14
Catfish Hunter, Oak., 21-7
Jim Palmer, Bal., 21-10
Stan Bahnsen, Chi., 21-16

**N.L. 20-game winners**
Steve Carlton, Phil., 27-10
Tom Seaver, N.Y., 21-12
Claude Osteen, L.A., 20-11
Ferguson Jenkins, Chi., 20-12

**A.L. 100 RBIs**
Dick Allen, Chi., 113
John Mayberry, K.C., 100

**N.L. 100 RBIs**
Johnny Bench, Cin., 125
Billy Williams, Chi., 122
Willie Stargell, Pit., 112
Nate Colbert, S.D., 111

**N.L. 40 homers**
Johnny Bench, Cin., 40

**Most Valuable Player**
A.L.: Dick Allen, 1B, Chi.
N.L.: Johnny Bench, C, Cin.

**Cy Young Award**
A.L.: Gaylord Perry, Cle.
N.L.: Steve Carlton, Phil.

**Rookie of the Year**
A.L.: Carlton Fisk, C, Bos.
N.L.: Jon Matlack, P, N.Y.

**Hall of Fame additions**
Yogi Berra, C, 1946-65
Josh Gibson, C, Negro Leagues
Lefty Gomez, P, 1930-43
Will Harridge, executive
Sandy Koufax, P, 1955-66
Buck Leonard, 1B, Negro Leagues
Early Wynn, P, 1939-63
Ross Youngs, OF, 1917-26

## ALL-STAR GAME

■ **Winner:** Joe Morgan's 10th-inning single capped another N.L. comeback that produced a 4-3 victory — the senior circuit's seventh consecutive extra-inning All-Star decision.
■ **Key inning:** The ninth, when the N.L. tied the game 3-3 on a pair of singles and Lee May's ground-ball out.
■ **Memorable moment:** Hank Aaron, who entered the game with 659 career home runs, sent the Atlanta crowd into a frenzy when he hit a two-run shot in the sixth inning.
■ **Top guns:** Tug McGraw (Mets), Aaron (Braves), Morgan (Reds), N.L.; Jim Palmer (Orioles), Cookie Rojas (Royals), Rod Carew (Twins), A.L.
■ **MVP:** Morgan.

**Linescore**
July 25, at Atlanta Stadium
A.L..........0 0 1 0 0 0 2 0 0 0—3 6 0
N.L...........0 0 0 0 0 2 0 0 1 1—4 8 0
Palmer (Orioles), Lolich (Tigers) 4, Perry (Indians) 6, Wood (White Sox) 8, McNally (Orioles) 10; Gibson (Cardinals), Blass (Pirates) 3, Sutton (Dodgers) 4, Carlton (Phillies) 6, Stoneman (Expos) 7, McGraw (Mets) 9. W—McGraw. L—McNally. HR—Aaron, N.L.; Rojas, A.L.

## ALCS

■ **Winner:** The Athletics claimed their first pennant in 41 years and first since moving to Oakland. The A's victory over Detroit marked the first ALCS to go beyond three games.
■ **Turning point:** The Game 5 pitching of left-hander Vida Blue, who worked four scoreless innings in relief of Blue Moon Odom to secure the A's series-ending 2-1 victory.
■ **Memorable moment:** A seventh-inning melee triggered by A's shortstop Bert Campaneris in Game 2. When Campaneris was hit by a Lerrin LaGrow pitch, he threw his bat at the pitcher and both benches emptied. Campaneris was suspended for the remainder of the series.
■ **Top guns:** Odom (2-0, 0.00 ERA), Blue (0.00), Matty Alou (.381), Athletics; Joe Coleman (1-0, 0-00 ERA), Jim Northrup (.357), Tigers.
■ **MVP:** Odom.

**Linescores**

**Game 1**—October 7, at Oakland
Det...0 1 0 0 0 0 0 0 0 0 1—2 6 2
Oak. 0 0 1 0 0 0 0 0 0 0 2—3 10 1
Lolich, Seelbach (11); Hunter, Blue (9), Fingers (9). W—Fingers. L—Lolich. HR—Cash, Kaline (Det.).

**Game 2**—October 8, at Oakland
Det...............0 0 0 0 0 0 0 0 0—0 3 1
Oak. ............1 0 0 0 4 0 0 0 x—5 8 0
Fryman, Zachary (5), Scherman (5), LaGrow (6), Hiller (7); Odom. W—Odom. L—Fryman.

**Game 3**—October 10, at Detroit
Oak. ............0 0 0 0 0 0 0 0 0—0 7 0
Det...............0 0 0 2 0 0 0 1 x—3 8 1
Holtzman, Fingers (5), Blue (6), Locker (7); Coleman. W—Coleman. L—Holtzman. HR—Freehan (Det.).

**Game 4**—October 11, at Detroit
Oak. ......0 0 0 0 0 0 1 0 0 2—3 9 2
Det.........0 0 1 0 0 0 0 0 0 3—4 10 1
Hunter, Fingers (8), Blue (9), Locker (10), Horlen (10), Hamilton (10); Lolich, Seelbach (10), Hiller (10). W—Hiller. L—Horlen. HR—McAuliffe (Det.); Epstein (Oak.).

**Game 5**—October 12, at Detroit
Oak. ............0 1 0 1 0 0 0 0 0—2 4 0
Det...............1 0 0 0 0 0 0 0 0—1 5 2
Odom, Blue (6); Fryman, Hiller (9). W—Odom. L—Fryman. S—Blue.

## NLCS

■ **Winner:** Cincinnati needed an N.L.-record five games to get past Pittsburgh and claim its second pennant in three years.
■ **Turning point:** Down two games to one and facing elimination, the Reds got two-hit pitching from Ross Grimsley and forged a 7-1 victory that forced a decisive fifth game.
■ **Memorable moment:** Cincinnati's George Foster racing across the plate with the series-ending run on a Bob Moose wild pitch with two out in the ninth inning of Game 5. The Reds had tied the game moments earlier on a Johnny Bench home run.
■ **Top guns:** Pete Rose (.450), Bench (.333), Reds; Manny Sanguillen (.313), Pirates.
■ **MVP:** Rose.

**Linescores**

**Game 1**—October 7, at Pittsburgh
Cin...............1 0 0 0 0 0 0 0 0—1 8 0
Pitt...............3 0 0 0 2 0 0 0 x—5 6 0
Gullett, Borbon (7); Blass, R. Hernandez (9). W—Blass. L—Gullett. S—R. Hernandez. HR—Morgan (Cin.); Oliver (Pit.).

**Game 2**—October 8, at Pittsburgh
Cin...............4 0 0 0 0 0 0 1 0—5 8 1
Pitt...............0 0 0 1 1 1 0 0 0—3 7 1
Billingham, Hall (5); Moose, Johnson (1), Kison (6), R. Hernandez (7), Giusti (9). W—Hall. L—Moose. HR—Morgan (Cin.).

**Game 3**—October 9, at Cincinnati
Pitt...............0 0 0 0 1 0 1 1 0—3 7 0
Cin...............0 0 2 0 0 0 0 0 0—2 8 1
Briles, Kison (7), Giusti (8); Nolan, Borbon (7), Carroll (7), McGlothlin (9). W—Kison. L—Carroll. S—Giusti. HR—Sanguillen (Pit.).

**Game 4**—October 10, at Cincinnati
Pitt.............0 0 0 0 0 0 1 0 0—1 2 3
Cin. ............1 0 0 2 0 2 2 0 x—7 11 1
Ellis, Johnson (6), Walker (7), Miller (8); Grimsley. W—Grimsley. L—Ellis. HR—Clemente (Pit.).

**Game 5**—October 11, at Cincinnati
Pitt...............0 2 0 1 0 0 0 0 0—3 8 0
Cin...............0 0 1 0 1 0 0 0 2—4 7 1
Blass, R. Hernandez (8), Giusti (9), Moose (9); Gullett, Borbon (4), Hall (6), Carroll (9). W—Carroll. L—Giusti. HR—Geronimo, Bench (Cin.).

## WORLD SERIES

■ **Winner:** The Athletics, who had not played in a World Series since 1931 when the franchise was located in Philadelphia, began a run that would put them in select company.
■ **Turning point:** A Game 4 ninth-inning rally that gave Oakland a three games to one lead. Down 2-1 with one out, the A's scored two runs on four consecutive singles.
■ **Memorable moment:** A's catcher Gene Tenace blasting home runs in his first two Series at-bats — and a record-tying four overall.
■ **Top guns:** Catfish Hunter (2-0, 2.81 ERA), Tenace (.348, 4 HR, 9 RBIs), Athletics; Tony Perez (.435), Bobby Tolan (6 RBIs), Reds.
■ **MVP:** Tenace.

**Linescores**

**Game 1**—October 14, at Cincinnati
Oakland........0 2 0 0 1 0 0 0 0—3 4 0
Cincinnati ....0 1 0 1 0 0 0 0 0—2 7 0
Holtzman, Fingers (6), Blue (7); Nolan, Borbon (7), Carroll (8). W—Holtzman. L—Nolan. S—Blue. HR—Tenace 2 (Oak.).

**Game 2**—October 15, at Cincinnati
Oakland........0 1 1 0 0 0 0 0 0—2 9 2
Cincinnati ....0 0 0 0 0 0 0 0 1—1 6 0
Hunter, Fingers (9); Grimsley, Borbon (6), Hall (8). W—Hunter. L—Grimsley. S—Fingers. HR—Rudi (Oak.).

**Game 3**—October 18, at Oakland
Cincinnati ....0 0 0 0 0 0 1 0 0—1 4 2
Oakland........0 0 0 0 0 0 0 0 0—0 3 2
Billingham, Carroll (9); Odom, Blue (8), Fingers (8). W—Billingham. L—Odom. S—Carroll.

**Game 4**—October 19, at Oakland
Cincinnati ..0 0 0 0 0 0 0 2 0—2 7 1
Oakland......0 0 0 0 1 0 0 0 2—3 10 1
Gullett, Borbon (8), Carroll (9); Holtzman, Blue (8), Fingers (9). W—Fingers. L—Carroll. HR—Tenace (Oak.).

**Game 5**—October 20, at Oakland
Cincinnati ....1 0 0 1 1 0 0 1 1—5 8 0
Oakland........0 3 0 1 0 0 0 0 0—4 7 2
McGlothlin, Borbon (4), Hall (5), Carroll (7), Grimsley (8), Billingham (9); Hunter, Fingers (5), Hamilton (9). W—Grimsley. L—Fingers. S—Billingham. HR—Rose, Menke (Cin.); Tenace (Oak.).

**Game 6**—October 21, at Cincinnati
Oakland......0 0 0 0 1 0 0 0 0—1 7 1
Cincinnati ..0 0 0 1 1 1 5 0 x—8 10 0
Blue, Locker (6), Hamilton (7), Horlen (7); Nolan, Grimsley (5), Borbon (6), Hall (7). W—Grimsley. L—Blue. S—Hall. HR—Bench (Cin.).

**Game 7**—October 22, at Cincinnati
Oakland........1 0 0 0 0 2 0 0 0—3 6 1
Cincinnati ....0 0 0 0 1 0 0 1 0—2 4 2
Odom, Hunter (5), Holtzman (8), Fingers (8); Billingham, Borbon (6), Carroll (6), Grimsley (7), Hall (8). W—Hunter. L—Borbon. S—Fingers.

# 1973

## FINAL STANDINGS

### American League

**East Division**

| Team | Bal. | Bos. | Det. | N.Y. | Mil. | Cle. | Cal. | Chi. | K.C. | Min. | Oak. | Tex. | W | L | Pct. | GB |
|---|---|---|---|---|---|---|---|---|---|---|---|---|---|---|---|---|
| Baltimore | ... | 7 | 9 | 9 | 15 | 12 | 6 | 8 | 8 | 8 | 5 | 10 | 97 | 65 | .599 | ... |
| Boston | 11 | ... | 3 | 14 | 12 | 9 | 7 | 6 | 8 | 6 | 4 | 9 | 89 | 73 | .549 | 8 |
| Detroit | 9 | 15 | ... | 7 | 12 | 9 | 5 | 7 | 4 | 5 | 7 | 5 | 85 | 77 | .525 | 12 |
| New York | 9 | 4 | 11 | ... | 8 | 11 | 6 | 4 | 6 | 9 | 4 | 8 | 80 | 82 | .494 | 17 |
| Milwaukee | 3 | 6 | 6 | 10 | ... | 9 | 7 | 9 | 4 | 8 | 4 | 8 | 74 | 88 | .457 | 23 |
| Cleveland | 6 | 9 | 9 | 7 | 9 | ... | 7 | 5 | 2 | 7 | 3 | 7 | 71 | 91 | .438 | 26 |

**West Division**

| Team | Oak. | K.C. | Min. | Cal. | Chi. | Tex. | Bal. | Bos. | Cle. | Det. | Mil. | N.Y. | W | L | Pct. | GB |
|---|---|---|---|---|---|---|---|---|---|---|---|---|---|---|---|---|
| Oakland | ... | 10 | 4 | 12 | 12 | 11 | 7 | 8 | 9 | 5 | 8 | 8 | 94 | 68 | .580 | ... |
| Kansas City | 8 | ... | 9 | [illegible] | 12 | 11 | 4 | 4 | 10 | [illegible] | [illegible] | [illegible] | [illegible] | 71 | [illegible] | 6 |
| Minnesota | 14 | 9 | ... | 8 | 9 | 12 | 4 | 6 | 5 | 7 | 4 | 3 | 81 | 81 | .500 | 13 |
| California | 6 | 10 | 10 | ... | 8 | 11 | 6 | 5 | 5 | 7 | 5 | 6 | 79 | 83 | .488 | 15 |
| Chicago | 6 | 6 | 9 | 10 | ... | 13 | 4 | 6 | 7 | 5 | 3 | 8 | 77 | 85 | .475 | 17 |
| Texas | 7 | 7 | 6 | 7 | 5 | ... | 2 | 3 | 5 | 7 | 4 | 4 | 57 | 105 | .352 | 37 |

### National League

**East Division**

| Team | N.Y. | St.L. | Pit. | Mon. | Chi. | Phi. | Atl. | Cin. | Hou. | L.A. | S.D. | S.F. | W | L | Pct. | GB |
|---|---|---|---|---|---|---|---|---|---|---|---|---|---|---|---|---|
| New York | ... | 10 | 13 | 9 | 7 | 9 | 6 | 4 | 6 | 5 | 8 | 5 | 82 | 79 | .509 | ... |
| St. Louis | 8 | ... | 8 | 10 | 9 | 9 | 6 | 6 | 7 | 4 | 8 | 6 | 81 | 81 | .500 | 1.5 |
| Pittsburgh | 5 | 10 | ... | 12 | 12 | 10 | 5 | 5 | 6 | 2 | 8 | 5 | 80 | 82 | .494 | 2.5 |
| Montreal | 9 | 8 | 6 | ... | 9 | 13 | 6 | 4 | 6 | 5 | 7 | 6 | 79 | 83 | .488 | 3.5 |
| Chicago | 10 | 9 | 6 | 9 | ... | 10 | 5 | 8 | 6 | 5 | 7 | 2 | 77 | 84 | .478 | 5 |
| Philadelphia | 9 | 9 | 8 | 5 | 8 | ... | 6 | 4 | 5 | 3 | 9 | 5 | 71 | 91 | .438 | 11.5 |

**West Division**

| Team | Cin. | L.A. | S.F. | Hou. | Atl. | S.D. | Chi. | Mon. | N.Y. | Phi. | Pit. | St.L. | W | L | Pct. | GB |
|---|---|---|---|---|---|---|---|---|---|---|---|---|---|---|---|---|
| Cincinnati | ... | 11 | 10 | 11 | 13 | 13 | 4 | 8 | 8 | 8 | 7 | 6 | 99 | 63 | .611 | ... |
| Los Angeles | 7 | ... | 9 | 7 | 15 | 9 | 7 | 7 | 7 | 9 | 10 | 8 | 95 | 66 | .590 | 3.5 |
| San Fran. | 8 | 9 | ... | 7 | 10 | 11 | 10 | 6 | 7 | 7 | 7 | 6 | 88 | 74 | .543 | 11 |
| Houston | 7 | 11 | 11 | ... | 7 | 10 | 6 | 6 | 6 | 7 | 6 | 5 | 82 | 80 | .506 | 17 |
| Atlanta | 5 | 2 | 8 | 11 | ... | 12 | 7 | 6 | 6 | 6 | 7 | 6 | 76 | 85 | .472 | 22.5 |
| San Diego | 5 | 9 | 7 | 8 | 6 | ... | 5 | 5 | 4 | 3 | 4 | 4 | 60 | 102 | .370 | 39 |

## SIGNIFICANT EVENTS

■ **January 3:** An investment group headed by shipbuilder George Steinbrenner purchased the Yankees from CBS for $10 million.

■ **February 25:** Owners and players approved a three-year Basic Agreement that included binding arbitration and modifications of the controversial reserve clause.

■ **April 6:** The A.L. began its designated hitter experiment when Yankee Ron Blomberg drew a first-inning walk in a game at Boston's Fenway Park.

■ **April 10:** New Royals Stadium received a rousing welcome when Kansas City pounded Texas, 12-1.

## MEMORABLE MOMENTS

■ **July 15:** Angels ace Nolan Ryan held Detroit hitless in a 6-0 victory, becoming the fourth pitcher to throw two no-hitters in one season.

■ **July 21:** Atlanta's Hank Aaron inched closer to Babe Ruth's all-time record when he belted homer No. 700 off Philadelphia's Ken Brett in an 8-4 loss.

■ **September 28:** Ryan struck out 16 Twins in his final start, raising his record season strikeout total to 383.

■ **October 1:** The Mets posted a final-day 6-4 victory over Chicago and clinched the N.L. East championship with an 82-79 record.

## LEADERS

**American League**
**BA:** Rod Carew, Min., .350.
**Runs:** Reggie Jackson, Oak., 99.
**Hits:** Rod Carew, Min., 203.
**TB:** Sal Bando, Oak.; Dave May, Mil.; George Scott, Mil., 295.
**HR:** Reggie Jackson, Oak., 32.
**RBI:** Reggie Jackson, Oak., 117.
**SB:** Tommy Harper, Bos., 54.
**Wins:** Wilbur Wood, Chi., 24.
**ERA:** Jim Palmer, Bal., 2.40.
**CG:** Gaylord Perry, Cle., 29.
**IP:** Wilbur Wood, Chi., 359.1.
**SO:** Nolan Ryan, Cal., 383.
**SV:** John Hiller, Det., 38.

**National League**
**BA:** Pete Rose, Cin., .338.
**Runs:** Bobby Bonds, S.F., 131.
**Hits:** Pete Rose, Cin., 230.
**TB:** Bobby Bonds, S.F., 341.
**HR:** Willie Stargell, Pit., 44.
**RBI:** Willie Stargell, Pit., 119.
**SB:** Lou Brock, St.L., 70.
**Wins:** Ron Bryant, S.F., 24.
**ERA:** Tom Seaver, N.Y., 2.08.
**CG:** Steve Carlton, Phil.; Tom Seaver, N.Y., 18.
**IP:** Jack Billingham, Cin.; Steve Carlton, Phil., 293.1.
**SO:** Tom Seaver, N.Y., 251.
**SV:** Mike Marshall, Mon., 31.

**A.L. 20-game winners**
Wilbur Wood, Chi., 24-20
Joe Coleman, Det., 23-15
Jim Palmer, Bal., 22-9
Catfish Hunter, Oak., 21-5
Ken Holtzman, Oak., 21-13
Nolan Ryan, Cal., 21-16
Vida Blue, Oak., 20-9
Paul Splittorff, K.C., 20-11
Jim Colborn, Mil., 20-12
Luis Tiant, Bos., 20-13
Bill Singer, Cal., 20-14
Bert Blyleven, Min., 20-17

**N.L. 20-game winners**
Ron Bryant, S.F., 24-12

**A.L. 100 RBIs**
Reggie Jackson, Oak., 117
George Scott, Mil., 107
John Mayberry, K.C., 100

**N.L. 100 RBIs**
Willie Stargell, Pit., 119
Lee May, Hou., 105
Johnny Bench, Cin., 104
Darrell Evans, Atl., 104
Ken Singleton, Mon., 103
Tony Perez, Cin., 101

**N.L. 40 homers**
Willie Stargell, Pit., 44
Dave Johnson, Atl., 43
Darrell Evans, Atl., 41
Hank Aaron, Atl., 40

**Most Valuable Player**
A.L.: Reggie Jackson, OF, Oak.
N.L.: Pete Rose, OF, Cin.

**Cy Young Award**
A.L.: Jim Palmer, Bal.
N.L.: Tom Seaver, N.Y.

**Rookie of the Year**
A.L.: Al Bumbry, OF, Bal.
N.L.: Gary Matthews, OF, S.F.

**Hall of Fame additions**
Roberto Clemente, OF, 1955-72
Billy Evans, umpire
Monte Irvin, OF, 1949-56
George Kelly, 1B, 1915-32
Warren Spahn, P, 1942-65
Mickey Welch, P, 1880-92

## ALL-STAR GAME

■ **Winners:** Johnny Bench, Bobby Bonds and Willie Davis powered the N.L. to its 10th All-Star victory in 11 years in the 40th anniversary of the midsummer classic.
■ **Key innings:** The fourth, fifth and sixth, when the N.L.'s Big Three hit home runs that accounted for five runs.
■ **Memorable moment:** An eighth-inning strikeout by pinch-hitter Willie Mays, who was making his 24th and final appearance in the baseball classic he had dominated like no other player.
■ **Top guns:** Bonds (Giants), Bench (Reds), Davis (Dodgers), N.L.; Amos Otis (Royals), A.L.
■ **MVP:** Bonds.

**Linescore**
July 24, at Kansas City's Royals Stadium
N.L.............0 0 2 1 2 2 0 0 0—7 10 0
A.L.............0 1 0 0 0 0 0 0 0—1 5 0
Wise (Cardinals), Osteen (Dodgers) 3, Sutton (Dodgers) 5, Twitchell (Phillies) 6, Giusti (Pirates) 7, Seaver (Mets) 8, Brewer (Dodgers) 9; Hunter (Athletics), Holtzman (Athletics) 2, Blyleven (Twins) 3, Singer (Angels) 4, Ryan (Angels) 6, Lyle (Yankees) 8, Fingers (Athletics) 9. W—Wise. L—Blyleven. HR—Bench, Bonds, Davis, N.L.

## ALCS

■ **Winner:** The Athletics earned their second consecutive pennant and the Orioles lost their first ALCS after three previous sweeps.
■ **Turning point:** An 11th-inning Game 3 home run by Bert Campaneris that broke up a pitching duel between Oakland's Ken Holtzman and Baltimore's Mike Cuellar. The 2-1 victory gave the A's a 2-1 series advantage.
■ **Memorable moment:** A game-tying three-run seventh-inning home run by catcher Andy Etchebarren that kept Baltimore's hopes alive in Game 4. The Orioles won, 5-4, and forced a fifth game.
■ **Top guns:** Catfish Hunter (2-0, 1.65 ERA), Vic Davalillo (.625), Campaneris (.333, 2 HR), Athletics; Etchebarren (.357, 4 RBIs), Orioles.
■ **MVP:** Hunter.

**Linescores**

**Game 1**—October 6, at Baltimore
Oak. ..........0 0 0 0 0 0 0 0 0—0 5 1
Balt. ..........4 0 0 0 0 0 1 1 x—6 12 0
Blue, Pina (1), Odom (3), Fingers (8); Palmer. W—Palmer. L—Blue.

**Game 2**—October 7, at Baltimore
Oak. ...........1 0 0 0 0 2 0 2 1—6 9 0
Balt. ...........1 0 0 0 0 1 0 1 0—3 8 0
Hunter, Fingers (8); McNally, Reynolds (8), G. Jackson (9). W—Hunter. L—McNally. S—Fingers. HR—Campaneris, Rudi, Bando 2 (Oak.).

**Game 3**—October 9, at Oakland
Balt. .......0 1 0 0 0 0 0 0 0 0 0—1 3 0
Oak. .......0 0 0 0 0 0 0 1 0 0 1—2 4 3
Cuellar; Holtzman. W—Holtzman. L—Cuellar. HR—Williams (Bal.); Campaneris (Oak.).

**Game 4**—October 10, at Oakland
Balt. ...........0 0 0 0 0 0 4 1 0—5 8 0
Oak. ...........0 3 0 0 0 1 0 0 0—4 7 0
Palmer, Reynolds (2), Watt (7), G. Jackson (7); Blue, Fingers (7). W—G. Jackson. L—Fingers. HR—Etchebarren, Grich (Bal.).

**Game 5**—October 11, at Oakland
Balt. ...........0 0 0 0 0 0 0 0 0—0 5 2
Oak. ...........0 0 1 2 0 0 0 0 x—3 7 0
Alexander, Palmer (4); Hunter. W—Hunter. L—Alexander.

## NLCS

■ **Winner:** The New York Mets captured their second pennant in five years and kept Cincinnati from repeating as N.L. champion.
■ **Turning point:** New York's 9-2 Game 3 victory that was spiced by a fifth-inning fight between Mets shortstop Bud Harrelson and Cincinnati leftfielder Pete Rose. Reds manager Sparky Anderson had to temporarily pull his team from the field in the next half inning when fans began pelting Rose with garbage and other debris.
■ **Memorable moment:** Rose's 12th-inning Game 4 home run that kept the Reds alive and forced a fifth game.
■ **Top guns:** Jon Matlack (1-0, 0.00 ERA), Felix Millan (.316), Rusty Staub (3 HR, 5 RBIs), Mets; Rose (.381, 2 HR), Reds.
■ **MVP:** Staub.

**Linescores**

**Game 1**—October 6, at Cincinnati
N.Y. ..............0 1 0 0 0 0 0 0 0—1 3 0
Cin. ..............0 0 0 0 0 0 0 1 1—2 6 0
Seaver; Billingham, Hall (9), Borbon (9). W—Borbon. L—Seaver. HR—Rose, Bench (Cin.).

**Game 2**—October 7, at Cincinnati
N.Y. ..............0 0 0 1 0 0 0 0 4—5 7 0
Cin. ..............0 0 0 0 0 0 0 0 0—0 2 0
Matlack; Gullett, Carroll (6), Hall (9), Borbon (9). W—Matlack. L—Gullett. HR—Staub (N.Y.).

**Game 3**—October 8, at New York
Cin. ............0 0 2 0 0 0 0 0 0—2 8 1
N.Y. ............1 5 1 2 0 0 0 0 x—9 11 1
Grimsley, Hall (2), Tomlin (3), Nelson (4), Borbon (7); Koosman. W—Koosman. L—Grimsley. HR—Staub 2 (N.Y.); Menke (Cin.).

**Game 4**—October 9, at New York
Cin.......0 0 0 0 0 0 1 0 0 0 0 1—2 8 0
N.Y.......0 0 1 0 0 0 0 0 0 0 0 0—1 3 2
Norman, Gullett (6), Carroll (10), Borbon (12); Stone, McGraw (7), Parker (12). W—Carroll. L—Parker. S—Borbon. HR—Perez, Rose (Cin.).

**Game 5**—October 10, at New York
Cin. ............0 0 1 0 1 0 0 0 0—2 7 1
N.Y. ............2 0 0 0 4 1 0 0 x—7 13 1
Billingham, Gullett (5), Carroll (5), Grimsley (7); Seaver, McGraw (9). W—Seaver. L—Billingham. S—McGraw.

## WORLD SERIES

■ **Winner:** The Athletics made it two in a row with a seven-game scramble against the resilient Mets.
■ **Turning point:** In a valiant Game 6 performance that staved off elimination, the A's prevailed 3-1 behind Catfish Hunter's pitching and the two-RBI hitting of Reggie Jackson.
■ **Memorable moment:** The "firing" of A's second baseman Mike Andrews by owner Charles O. Finley. Andrews' two 12th-inning errors in Game 2 enabled the Mets to post a 10-7 victory.
■ **Top guns:** Joe Rudi (.333), Jackson (.310, 6 RBIs), Athletics; Rusty Staub (.423, 6 RBIs), Mets.
■ **MVP:** Jackson.

**Linescores**

**Game 1**—October 13, at Oakland
N.Y. ..............0 0 0 1 0 0 0 0 0—1 7 2
Oak. ............0 0 2 0 0 0 0 0 x—2 4 0
Matlack, McGraw (7); Holtzman, Fingers (6), Knowles (9). W—Holtzman. L—Matlack. S—Knowles.

**Game 2**—October 14, at Oakland
N.Y.........011 004 000 004—10 15 1
Oak. ........210 000 102 001— 7 13 5
Koosman, Sadecki (3), Parker (5), McGraw (6), Stone (12); Blue, Pina (6), Knowles (6), Odom (8), Fingers (10), Lindblad (12). W—McGraw. L—Fingers. S—Stone. HR—Jones, Garrett (N.Y.).

**Game 3**—October 16, at New York
Oak. ........000 001 010 01—3 10 1
N.Y. ........200 000 000 00—2 10 2
Hunter, Knowles (7), Lindblad (9), Fingers (11); Seaver, Sadecki (9), McGraw (9), Parker (11). W—Lindblad. L—Parker. S—Fingers. HR—Garrett (N.Y.).

**Game 4**—October 17, at New York
Oak. ....................000 100 000—1 5 1
N.Y. ....................300 300 00x—6 13 1
Holtzman, Odom (1), Knowles (4), Pina (5), Lindblad (8); Matlack, Sadecki (9). W—Matlack. L—Holtzman. S—Sadecki. HR—Staub (N.Y.).

**Game 5**—October 18, at New York
Oak. ...........0 0 0 0 0 0 0 0 0—0 3 1
N.Y. ...........0 1 0 0 0 1 0 0 x—2 7 1
Blue, Knowles (6), Fingers (7); Koosman, McGraw (7). W—Koosman. L—Blue. S—McGraw.

**Game 6**—October 20, at Oakland
N.Y. ..............0 0 0 0 0 0 0 1 0—1 6 2
Oak. ...........1 0 1 0 0 0 0 1 x—3 7 0
Seaver, McGraw (8); Hunter, Knowles (8), Fingers (8). W—Hunter. L—Seaver. S—Fingers.

**Game 7**—October 21, at Oakland
N.Y. ..............0 0 0 0 0 1 0 0 1—2 8 1
Oak. ...........0 0 4 0 1 0 0 0 x—5 9 1
Matlack, Parker (3), Sadecki (5), Stone (7); Holtzman, Fingers (6), Knowles (9). W—Holtzman. L—Matlack. S—Knowles. HR—Campaneris, Jackson (Oak.).

# 1974

## FINAL STANDINGS

### American League

**East Division**

| Team | Bal. | N.Y. | Bos. | Cle. | Mil. | Det. | Cal. | Chi. | K.C. | Min. | Oak. | Tex. | W | L | Pct. | GB |
|---|---|---|---|---|---|---|---|---|---|---|---|---|---|---|---|---|
| Baltimore | ... | 11 | 10 | 12 | 8 | 14 | 7 | 5 | 8 | 6 | 6 | 4 | 91 | 71 | .562 | ... |
| New York | 7 | ... | 7 | 11 | 9 | 7 | 9 | 8 | 8 | 8 | 7 | 8 | 89 | 73 | .549 | 2 |
| Boston | 8 | 11 | ... | 9 | 10 | 11 | 4 | 8 | 4 | 6 | 8 | 5 | 84 | 78 | .519 | 7 |
| Cleveland | 6 | 7 | 9 | ... | 10 | 9 | 9 | 4 | 8 | 6 | 5 | 4 | 77 | 85 | .475 | 14 |
| Milwaukee | 10 | 9 | 8 | 8 | .. | 9 | 9 | 4 | 1 | 6 | 5 | 7 | 76 | 86 | .469 | 15 |
| Detroit | 4 | 11 | 7 | 9 | 9 | ... | 7 | 5 | 7 | 3 | 5 | 5 | 72 | 90 | .444 | 19 |

**West Division**

| Team | Oak. | Tex. | Min. | Chi. | K.C. | Cal. | Bal. | Bos. | Cle. | Det. | Mil. | N.Y. | W | L | Pct. | GB |
|---|---|---|---|---|---|---|---|---|---|---|---|---|---|---|---|---|
| Oakland | ... | 8 | 13 | 11 | 10 | 12 | 6 | 4 | 7 | 7 | 7 | 5 | 90 | 72 | .556 | ... |
| Texas | 10 | ... | 9 | 7 | 10 | 9 | 8 | 7 | 8 | 7 | 5 | 4 | 84 | 76 | .525 | 5 |
| Minnesota | 5 | 9 | ... | 11 | 10 | 10 | 6 | 6 | 6 | 9 | 6 | 4 | 82 | 80 | .506 | 8 |
| Chicago | 7 | 9 | 7 | ... | 11 | 8 | 7 | 4 | 8 | 7 | 8 | 4 | 80 | 80 | .500 | 9 |
| Kansas City | 8 | 8 | 8 | 7 | ... | 10 | 4 | 8 | 4 | 5 | 11 | 4 | 77 | 85 | .475 | 13 |
| California | 6 | 9 | 8 | 10 | 8 | ... | 5 | 8 | 3 | 5 | 3 | 3 | 68 | 94 | .420 | 22 |

### National League

**East Division**

| Team | Pit. | St.L. | Phi. | Mon. | N.Y. | Chi. | Atl. | Cin. | Hou. | L.A. | S.D. | S.F. | W | L | Pct. | GB |
|---|---|---|---|---|---|---|---|---|---|---|---|---|---|---|---|---|
| Pittsburgh | ... | 7 | 8 | 9 | 11 | 9 | 8 | 4 | 7 | 8 | 9 | 8 | 88 | 74 | .543 | ... |
| St. Louis | 11 | ... | 9 | 9 | 12 | 13 | 3 | 6 | 4 | 6 | 7 | 6 | 86 | 75 | .534 | 1.5 |
| Philadelphia | 10 | 9 | ... | 7 | 11 | 10 | 4 | 4 | 6 | 6 | 5 | 8 | 80 | 82 | .494 | 8 |
| Montreal | 9 | 8 | 11 | ... | 9 | 13 | 3 | 6 | 6 | 4 | 6 | 4 | 79 | 82 | .491 | 8.5 |
| New York | 7 | 6 | 7 | 9 | ... | 10 | 4 | 3 | 6 | 7 | 6 | 6 | 71 | 91 | .438 | 17 |
| Chicago | 9 | 5 | 8 | 5 | 8 | ... | 8 | 5 | 4 | 2 | 6 | 6 | 66 | 96 | .407 | 22 |

**West Division**

| Team | L.A. | Cin. | Atl. | Hou. | S.F. | S.D. | Chi. | Mon. | N.Y. | Phi. | Pit. | St.L. | W | L | Pct. | GB |
|---|---|---|---|---|---|---|---|---|---|---|---|---|---|---|---|---|
| Los Angeles | ... | 12 | 10 | 13 | 12 | 16 | 10 | 8 | 5 | 6 | 4 | 6 | 102 | 60 | .630 | ... |
| Cincinnati | 6 | ... | 11 | 14 | 11 | 12 | 7 | 6 | 9 | 8 | 8 | 6 | 98 | 64 | .605 | 4 |
| Atlanta | 8 | 7 | ... | 6 | 8 | 17 | 4 | 9 | 8 | 8 | 4 | 9 | 88 | 74 | .543 | 14 |
| Houston | 5 | 4 | 12 | ... | 10 | 11 | 8 | 6 | 6 | 6 | 5 | 8 | 81 | 81 | .500 | 21 |
| San Fran. | 6 | 7 | 10 | 8 | ... | 7 | 6 | 8 | 6 | 4 | 4 | 6 | 72 | 90 | .444 | 30 |
| San Diego | 2 | 6 | 1 | 7 | 11 | ... | 6 | 6 | 6 | 7 | 3 | 5 | 60 | 102 | .370 | 42 |

## SIGNIFICANT EVENTS

■ **January 1:** Lee MacPhail took the reins as A.L. president, succeeding retiring Joe Cronin.

■ **February 11:** Baseball's first arbitration hearing was decided in favor of Twins pitcher Dick Woodson.

■ **October 3:** The Indians crossed another color barrier when they named Frank Robinson as baseball's first black manager and the game's first player-manager since 1959.

■ **November 2:** The Braves honored the request of home run king Hank Aaron when they traded him to Milwaukee, the city where he started his career in 1954.

■ **November 6:** Mike Marshall, who appeared in a record 106 games for the Dodgers, became the first relief pitcher to earn a Cy Young Award.

■ **December 31:** The Yankees won the most celebrated free-agent chase in history when they signed former Oakland ace Catfish Hunter to a five-year, $3.75-million contract.

## MEMORABLE MOMENTS

■ **April 8:** Atlanta's Hank Aaron overtook Babe Ruth as baseball's all-time greatest slugger when he connected off Al Downing for record home run No. 715 in a 7-4 victory over the Dodgers.

■ **July 17:** Bob Gibson became the second pitcher to reach 3,000 strikeouts when he fanned Cincinnati's Cesar Geronimo in a game at St. Louis.

■ **August 12:** California's Nolan Ryan tied the single-game record when he struck out 19 Red Sox in a 4-2 victory.

■ **September 24:** Al Kaline doubled off Baltimore's Dave McNally for hit No. 3,000 in Detroit's 5-4 loss.

■ **September 29:** St. Louis speedster Lou Brock swiped his record 118th base in a 7-3 victory over the Cubs.

■ **October 1:** The Orioles, who finished the season on a 28-6 run, clinched the A.L. East with a 7-6 victory over the Tigers.

## LEADERS

**American League**
**BA:** Rod Carew, Min., .364.
**Runs:** Carl Yastrzemski, Bos., 93.
**Hits:** Rod Carew, Min., 218.
**TB:** Joe Rudi, Oak., 287.
**HR:** Dick Allen, Chi., 32.
**RBI:** Jeff Burroughs, Tex., 118.
**SB:** Bill North, Oak., 54.
**Wins:** Catfish Hunter, Oak.; Ferguson Jenkins, Tex., 25.
**ERA:** Catfish Hunter, Oak., 2.49.
**CG:** Ferguson Jenkins, Tex., 29.
**IP:** Nolan Ryan, Cal., 332.2.
**SO:** Nolan Ryan, Cal., 367.
**SV:** Terry Forster, Chi., 24.

**National League**
**BA:** Ralph Garr, Atl., .353.
**Runs:** Pete Rose, Cin., 110.
**Hits:** Ralph Garr, Atl., 214.
**TB:** Johnny Bench, Cin., 315.
**HR:** Mike Schmidt, Phil., 36.
**RBI:** Johnny Bench, Cin., 129.
**SB:** Lou Brock, St.L., 118.
**Wins:** Andy Messersmith, L.A.; Phil Niekro, Atl., 20.
**ERA:** Buzz Capra, Atl., 2.28.
**CG:** Phil Niekro, Atl., 18.
**IP:** Phil Niekro, Atl., 302.1.
**SO:** Steve Carlton, Phil., 240.
**SV:** Mike Marshall, L.A., 21.

**A.L. 20-game winners**
Catfish Hunter, Oak., 25-12
Ferguson Jenkins, Tex., 25-12
Mike Cuellar, Bal., 22-10
Luis Tiant, Bos., 22-13
Steve Busby, K.C., 22-14
Nolan Ryan, Cal., 22-16
Jim Kaat, Chi., 21-13
Gaylord Perry, Cle., 21-13
Wilbur Wood, Chi., 20-19

**N.L. 20-game winners**
Andy Messersmith, L.A., 20-6
Phil Niekro, Atl., 20-13

**A.L. 100 RBIs**
Jeff Burroughs, Tex., 118
Sal Bando, Oak., 103

**N.L. 100 RBIs**
Johnny Bench, Cin., 129
Mike Schmidt, Phil., 116
Steve Garvey, L.A., 111
Jim Wynn, L.A., 108
Ted Simmons, St.L., 103
Cesar Cedeno, Hou., 102
Tony Perez, Cin., 101
Reggie Smith, St.L., 100
Richie Zisk, Pit., 100

**Most Valuable Player**
A.L.: Jeff Burroughs, OF, Tex.
N.L.: Steve Garvey, 1B, L.A.

**Cy Young Award**
A.L.: Catfish Hunter, Oak.
N.L.: Mike Marshall, L.A.

**Rookie of the Year**
A.L.: Mike Hargrove, 1B, Tex.
N.L.: Bake McBride, OF, St.L.

**Hall of Fame additions**
Cool Papa Bell, OF, Negro Leagues
Jim Bottomley, 1B, 1922-37
Jocko Conlan, umpire
Whitey Ford, P, 1950-67
Mickey Mantle, OF, 1951-68
Sam Thompson, OF, 1885-1906

## ALL-STAR GAME

■ **Winner:** The N.L. continued its amazing All-Star run with a 7-2 victory fashioned by five pitchers who had never worked in a mid-summer classic.

■ **Key inning:** A two-run N.L. fourth, when Steve Garvey doubled home the tying run and the lead run scored on Ron Cey's groundout.

■ **Memorable moment:** A third-inning diving stop by N.L. first baseman Garvey on a smash by Bobby Murcer. The play saved at least two A.L. runs and possibly the game.

■ **Top guns:** Mike Marshall (Dodgers), Reggie Smith (Cardinals), Garvey (Dodgers), Cey (Dodgers), N.L.; Dick Allen (White Sox), A.L.

■ **MVP:** Garvey.

**Linescore**
July 23, at Pittsburgh's Three Rivers Stadium
A.L. ............0 0 2 0 0 0 0 0 0—2 4 1
N.L. ............0 1 0 2 1 0 1 2 x—7 10 1
Perry (Indians), Tiant (Red Sox) 4, Hunter (Athletics) 6, Fingers (Athletics) 8; Messersmith (Dodgers), Brett (Pirates) 4, Matlack (Mets) 6, McGlothen (Cardinals) 7, Marshall (Dodgers) 8. W—Brett. L—Tiant. HR—Smith, N.L.

## ALCS

■ **Winner:** The Athletics needed only four games to earn their third consecutive A.L. pennant and second straight ALCS victory over Baltimore.

■ **Turning point:** Oakland's 1-0 Game 3 victory, which was decided by a fourth-inning Sal Bando home run. A's lefty Vida Blue allowed only two hits and gave his team a 2-1 series advantage.

■ **Memorable moment:** Reggie Jackson's seventh-inning double in Game 4. The A's only hit in a 2-1 series-ending victory drove in the winning run.

■ **Top guns:** Blue (1-0, 0-00 ERA), Ken Holtzman (1-0, 0.00), Bando (2 HR), Athletics; Andy Etchebarren (.333), Orioles.

■ **MVP:** Blue.

**Linescores**

**Game 1**—October 5, at Oakland
Baltimore ..1 0 0 1 4 0 0 0 0—6 10 0
Oakland......0 0 1 0 1 0 0 0 1—3 9 0
Cuellar, Grimsley (9); Hunter, Odom (5), Fingers (9). W—Cuellar. L—Hunter. HR—Blair, Robinson, Grich (Bal.).

**Game 2**—October 6, at Oakland
Baltimore ....0 0 0 0 0 0 0 0 0—0 5 2
Oakland........0 0 0 1 0 1 0 3 x—5 8 0
McNally, Garland (6), Reynolds (7), G. Jackson (8); Holtzman. W—Holtzman. L—McNally. HR—Bando, Fosse (Oak.).

**Game 3**—October 8, at Baltimore
Oakland........0 0 0 1 0 0 0 0 0—1 4 2
Baltimore ....0 0 0 0 0 0 0 0 0—0 2 1
Blue; Palmer. W—Blue. L—Palmer. HR—Bando (Oak.).

**Game 4**—October 9, at Baltimore
Oakland........0 0 0 0 1 0 1 0 0—2 1 0
Baltimore ....0 0 0 0 0 0 0 0 1—1 5 1
Hunter, Fingers (8); Cuellar, Grimsley (5). W—Hunter. L—Cuellar. S—Fingers.

## NLCS

■ **Winner:** Los Angeles, making its first Championship Series appearance, overpowered Pittsburgh and claimed its first pennant since 1966.

■ **Turning point:** Pitchers Don Sutton, Andy Messersmith and Mike Marshall held the Pirates scoreless in 17 of the first 18 innings as the Dodgers forged a 2-0 series advantage.

■ **Memorable moment:** The Game 4 performance of Los Angeles first baseman Steve Garvey, who collected four hits, belted two home runs and drove in four runs in a 12-1 series-ending victory.

■ **Top guns:** Sutton (2-0, 0.53 ERA), Garvey (.389, 2 HR, 5 RBIs), Bill Russell (.389), Dodgers; Bruce Kison (1-0, 0.00), Willie Stargell (.400, 2 HR, 4 RBIs), Pirates.

■ **MVP:** Sutton.

**Linescores**

**Game 1**—October 5, at Pittsburgh
L.A. ..............0 1 0 0 0 0 0 0 2—3 9 2
Pitt. ..............0 0 0 0 0 0 0 0 0—0 4 0
Sutton; Reuss, Giusti (8). W—Sutton. L—Reuss.

**Game 2**—October 6, at Pittsburgh
L.A. ............1 0 0 1 0 0 0 3 0—5 12 0
Pitt. ............0 0 0 0 0 0 2 0 0—2 8 3
Messersmith, Marshall (8); Rooker, Giusti (8), Demery (8), Hernandez (8). W—Messersmith. L—Giusti. HR—Cey (L.A.).

**Game 3**—October 8, at Los Angeles
Pitt. ............5 0 2 0 0 0 0 0 0—7 10 0
L.A. ............0 0 0 0 0 0 0 0 0—0 4 5
Kison, Hernandez (7); Rau, Hough (1), Downing (4), Solomon (8). W—Kison. L—Rau. HR—Stargell, Hebner (Pit.).

**Game 4**—October 9, at Los Angeles
Pitt. ..........0 0 0 0 0 0 1 0 0— 1 3 1
L.A. ..........1 0 2 0 2 2 2 3 x—12 12 0
Reuss, Brett (3), Demery (6), Giusti (7), Pizarro (8); Sutton, Marshall (9). W—Sutton. L—Reuss. HR—Garvey 2 (L.A.); Stargell (Pit.).

## WORLD SERIES

■ **Winner:** Manager Alvin Dark's Athletics, who had won the previous two years under Dick Williams, became only the second team to win three consecutive World Series.

■ **Turning point:** The A's 5-2 Game 4 victory, which featured a home run by pitcher Ken Holtzman, who had not batted all season because of the A.L.'s designated hitter rule.

■ **Memorable moment:** Joe Rudi's tie-breaking solo home run off Dodger ironman reliever Mike Marshall in the seventh inning of Game 5.

■ **Top guns:** Rollie Fingers (1-0, 2 saves, 1.93 ERA), Holtzman (1-0, 1.50, 1 HR), Rudi (.333, 4 RBIs), A's; Steve Garvey (.381), Dodgers.

■ **MVP:** Fingers.

**Linescores**

**Game 1**—October 12, at Los Angeles
Oakland......0 1 0 0 1 0 0 1 0—3 6 2
L.A. ............0 0 0 0 1 0 0 0 1—2 11 1
Holtzman, Fingers (5), Hunter (9); Messersmith, Marshall (9). W—Fingers. L—Messersmith. S—Hunter. HR—Jackson (Oak.); Wynn (L.A.).

**Game 2**—October 13, at Los Angeles
Oakland........0 0 0 0 0 0 0 0 2—2 6 0
L.A. ..............0 1 0 0 0 2 0 0 x—3 6 1
Blue, Odom (8); Sutton, Marshall (9). W—Sutton. L—Blue. S—Marshall. HR—Ferguson (L.A.).

**Game 3**—October 15, at Oakland
L.A. ..............0 0 0 0 0 0 0 1 1—2 7 2
Oakland........0 0 2 1 0 0 0 0 x—3 5 2
Downing, Brewer (4), Hough (5), Marshall (7); Hunter, Fingers (8). W—Hunter. L—Downing. S—Fingers. HR—Buckner, Crawford (L.A.).

**Game 4**—October 16, at Oakland
L.A. ..............0 0 0 2 0 0 0 0 0—2 7 1
Oakland........0 0 1 0 0 4 0 0 x—5 7 0
Messersmith, Marshall (7); Holtzman, Fingers (8). W—Holtzman. L—Messersmith. S—Fingers. HR—Holtzman.

**Game 5**—October 17, at Oakland
L.A. ..............0 0 0 0 0 2 0 0 0—2 5 1
Oakland........1 1 0 0 0 0 1 0 x—3 6 1
Sutton, Marshall (6); Blue, Odom (7), Fingers (8). W—Odom. L—Marshall. S—Fingers. HR—Fosse, Rudi (Oak.).

# 1975

## FINAL STANDINGS

### American League

**East Division**

| Team | Bos. | Bal. | N.Y. | Cle. | Mil. | Det. | Cal. | Chi. | K.C. | Min. | Oak. | Tex. | W | L | Pct. | GB |
|---|---|---|---|---|---|---|---|---|---|---|---|---|---|---|---|---|
| Boston | ... | 9 | 11 | 7 | 10 | 13 | 6 | 8 | 7 | 10 | 6 | 8 | 95 | 65 | .594 | ... |
| Baltimore | 9 | ... | 8 | 10 | 14 | 12 | 6 | 7 | 7 | 6 | 4 | 7 | 90 | 69 | .566 | 4.5 |
| New York | 5 | 10 | ... | 9 | 9 | 12 | 5 | 6 | 5 | 8 | 6 | 8 | 83 | 77 | .519 | 12 |
| Cleveland | 11 | 8 | 9 | ... | 9 | 12 | 9 | 5 | 6 | 3 | 2 | 5 | 79 | 80 | .497 | 15.5 |
| Milwaukee | 8 | 4 | 9 | 9 | ... | 11 | 5 | 4 | 5 | 2 | 5 | 6 | 68 | 94 | .420 | 28 |
| Detroit | 5 | 4 | 6 | 6 | 7 | ... | 5 | 7 | 6 | 4 | 6 | 1 | 57 | 102 | .358 | 37.5 |

**West Division**

| Team | Oak. | K.C. | Tex. | Min. | Chi. | Cal. | Bal. | Bos. | Cle. | Det. | Mil. | N.Y. | W | L | Pct. | GB |
|---|---|---|---|---|---|---|---|---|---|---|---|---|---|---|---|---|
| Oakland | ... | 11 | 12 | 12 | 9 | 11 | 8 | 6 | 10 | 6 | 7 | 6 | 98 | 64 | .605 | ... |
| Kansas City | 7 | ... | 14 | 11 | 9 | 14 | 5 | 5 | 6 | 6 | 7 | 7 | 91 | 71 | .562 | 7 |
| Texas | 6 | 4 | ... | 10 | 13 | 9 | 5 | 4 | 7 | 11 | 6 | 4 | 79 | 83 | .488 | 19 |
| Minnesota | 6 | 7 | 8 | ... | 9 | 10 | 6 | 2 | 6 | 8 | 10 | 4 | 76 | 83 | .478 | 20.5 |
| Chicago | 9 | 9 | 5 | 9 | ... | 9 | 4 | 4 | 7 | 5 | 8 | 6 | 75 | 86 | .466 | 22.5 |
| California | 7 | 4 | 9 | 8 | 9 | ... | 6 | 6 | 3 | 6 | 7 | 7 | 72 | 89 | .447 | 25.5 |

### National League

**East Division**

| Team | Pit. | Phi. | N.Y. | St.L. | Chi. | Mon. | Atl. | Cin. | Hou. | L.A. | S.D. | S.F. | W | L | Pct. | GB |
|---|---|---|---|---|---|---|---|---|---|---|---|---|---|---|---|---|
| Pittsburgh | ... | 7 | 13 | 10 | 12 | 11 | 8 | 6 | 5 | 7 | 8 | 5 | 92 | 69 | .571 | ... |
| Philadelphia | 11 | ... | 11 | 10 | 6 | 11 | 7 | 5 | 6 | 5 | 7 | 7 | 86 | 76 | .531 | 6.5 |
| New York | 5 | 7 | ... | 9 | 11 | 8 | 8 | 4 | 8 | 6 | 8 | 8 | 82 | 80 | .506 | 10.5 |
| St. Louis | 8 | 8 | 9 | ... | 7 | 7 | 9 | 4 | 8 | 7 | 8 | 7 | 82 | 80 | .506 | 10.5 |
| Chicago | 6 | 12 | 7 | 11 | ... | 9 | 7 | 1 | 7 | 5 | 5 | 5 | 75 | 87 | .463 | 17.5 |
| Montreal | 7 | 7 | 10 | 11 | 9 | ... | 4 | 4 | 4 | 7 | 7 | 5 | 75 | 87 | .463 | 17.5 |

**West Division**

| Team | Cin. | L.A. | S.F. | S.D. | Atl. | Hou. | Chi. | Mon. | N.Y. | Phi. | Pit. | St.L. | W | L | Pct. | GB |
|---|---|---|---|---|---|---|---|---|---|---|---|---|---|---|---|---|
| Cincinnati | ... | 8 | 13 | 11 | 15 | 13 | 11 | 8 | 8 | 7 | 6 | 8 | 108 | 54 | .667 | ... |
| L.A. | 10 | ... | 10 | 11 | 10 | 12 | 7 | 5 | 6 | 7 | 5 | 5 | 88 | 74 | .543 | 20 |
| San Fran. | 5 | 8 | ... | 10 | 9 | 13 | 7 | 7 | 4 | 5 | 7 | 5 | 80 | 81 | .497 | 27.5 |
| San Diego | 7 | 7 | 8 | ... | 11 | 9 | 7 | 5 | 4 | 5 | 4 | 4 | 71 | 91 | .438 | 37 |
| Atlanta | 3 | 8 | 8 | 7 | ... | 12 | 5 | 8 | 4 | 5 | 4 | 3 | 67 | 94 | .416 | 40.5 |
| Houston | 5 | 6 | 5 | 9 | 6 | ... | 5 | 8 | 4 | 6 | 6 | 4 | 64 | 97 | .398 | 43.5 |

## SIGNIFICANT EVENTS

■ **January 5:** Houston righthander Don Wilson died of carbon monoxide poisoning in the garage of his Houston home, an apparent suicide victim at age 29.

■ **November 26:** Boston's Fred Lynn became the first rookie MVP winner in baseball history.

■ **December 23:** Baseball's reserve system was shattered when labor arbitrator Peter Seitz handed pitchers Andy Messersmith and Dave McNally their unqualified free agency.

## MEMORABLE MOMENTS

■ **April 8:** Frank Robinson belted a dramatic home run and led the Indians to a 5-3 Opening Day victory over the Yankees in his historic debut as baseball's first black manager.

■ **May 1:** Milwaukee's Hank Aaron drove in two runs in a 17-3 victory over Detroit and became baseball's all-time RBI leader with 2,211.

■ **June 1:** California's Nolan Ryan tied Sandy Koufax's record when he pitched his fourth career no-hitter, a 1-0 victory over the Orioles.

■ **June 18:** Boston rookie Fred Lynn drove in 10 runs with three home runs, a triple and a single in a 15-1 victory over the Tigers.

■ **September 16:** Pirates second baseman Rennie Stennett became the first modern-era player to collect seven hits in a nine-inning game—a 22-0 victory over the Cubs.

■ **September 28:** Oakland's Vida Blue, Glenn Abbott, Paul Lindblad and Rollie Fingers combined for the first multi-pitcher no-hitter in baseball history—a final-day 5-0 victory over the Angels.

## LEADERS

**American League**
**BA:** Rod Carew, Min., .359.
**Runs:** Fred Lynn, Bos., 103.
**Hits:** George Brett, K.C., 195.
**TB:** George Scott, Mil., 318.
**HR:** Reggie Jackson, Oak.; George Scott, Mil., 36.
**RBI:** George Scott, Mil., 109.
**SB:** Mickey Rivers, Cal., 70.
**Wins:** Catfish Hunter, N.Y.; Jim Palmer, Bal., 23.
**ERA:** Jim Palmer, Bal., 2.09.
**CG:** Catfish Hunter, N.Y., 30.
**IP:** Catfish Hunter, N.Y., 328.
**SO:** Frank Tanana, Cal., 269.
**SV:** Goose Gossage, Chi., 26.

**National League**
**BA:** Bill Madlock, Chi., .354.
**Runs:** Pete Rose, Cin., 112.
**Hits:** Dave Cash, Phil., 213.
**TB:** Greg Luzinski, Phil., 322.
**HR:** Mike Schmidt, Phil., 38.
**RBI:** Greg Luzinski, Phil., 120.
**SB:** Dave Lopes, L.A., 77.
**Wins:** Tom Seaver, N.Y., 22.
**ERA:** Randy Jones, S.D., 2.24.
**CG:** Andy Messersmith, L.A., 19.
**IP:** Andy Messersmith, L.A., 321.2.
**SO:** Tom Seaver, N.Y., 243.
**SV:** Rawly Eastwick, Cin.; Al Hrabosky, St.L., 22.

**A.L. 20-game winners**
Jim Palmer, Bal., 23-11
Catfish Hunter, N.Y., 23-14
Vida Blue, Oak., 22-11
Mike Torrez, Bal., 20-9
Jim Kaat, Chi., 20-14

**N.L. 20-game winners**
Tom Seaver, N.Y., 22-9
Randy Jones, S.D., 20-12

**A.L. 100 RBIs**
George Scott, Mil., 109
John Mayberry, K.C., 106
Fred Lynn, Bos., 105
Reggie Jackson, Oak., 104
Thurman Munson, N.Y., 102
Jim Rice, Bos., 102

**N.L. 100 RBIs**
Greg Luzinski, Phil., 120
Johnny Bench, Cin., 110
Tony Perez, Cin., 109
Rusty Staub, N.Y., 105
Ron Cey, L.A., 101
Willie Montanez, Phil.-S.F., 101
Dave Parker, Pit., 101
Ted Simmons, St.L., 100

**Most Valuable Player**
A.L.: Fred Lynn, OF, Bos.
N.L.: Joe Morgan, 2B, Cin.

**Cy Young Award**
A.L.: Jim Palmer, Bal.
N.L.: Tom Seaver, N.Y.

**Rookie of the Year**
A.L.: Fred Lynn, OF, Bos.
N.L.: John Montefusco, P, S.F.

**Hall of Fame additions**
Earl Averill, OF, 1929-41
Bucky Harris, manager
Billy Herman, 2B, 1931-47
Judy Johnson, 3B, Negro Leagues
Ralph Kiner, OF, 1946-55

## ALL-STAR GAME

■ **Winner:** The N.L., having uncharacteristically squandered a 3-0 lead, scored three ninth-inning runs and escaped with a 6-3 victory, its 12th in 13 years.

■ **Key inning:** The ninth, when Bill Madlock delivered the big blow with a two-run single and Pete Rose added an insurance run with a sacrifice fly.

■ **Memorable moment:** A long sixth-inning three-run homer by Carl Yastrzemski that wiped away the 3-0 deficit and gave the A.L. brief hope for a victory.

■ **Top guns:** Steve Garvey (Dodgers), Jim Wynn (Dodgers), Rose (Reds), Madlock (Cubs), N.L.; Yastrzemski (Red Sox), Bert Campaneris (Athletics), A.L.

■ **MVP:** Madlock.

**Linescore**
July 15, at Milwaukee's County Stadium
N.L. ............0 2 1 0 0 0 0 0 3—6 13 1
A.L. ............0 0 0 0 0 3 0 0 0—3 10 1
Reuss (Pirates), Sutton (Dodgers) 4, Seaver (Mets) 6, Matlack (Mets) 7, Jones (Padres) 9; Blue (Athletics), Busby (Royals) 3, Kaat (White Sox) 5, Hunter (Yankees) 7, Gossage (White Sox) 9. W—Matlack. L—Hunter. HR—Garvey, Wynn, N.L.; Yastrzemski, A.L.

## ALCS

■ **Winner:** The Boston Red Sox brought a surprising end to Oakland's three-year championship reign and made it look as easy as 1-2-3.

■ **Turning point:** Oakland's four-error first-game performance that helped Boston to a 7-1 victory and set the tone for the series.

■ **Memorable moment:** Reggie Jackson's first-inning Game 2 home run, which gave Oakland its only lead of the series.

■ **Top guns:** Luis Tiant (1-0, 0.00 ERA), Carl Yastrzemski (.455), Rick Burleson (.444), Carlton Fisk (.417), Red Sox; Sal Bando (.500), Jackson (.417), Athletics.

■ **MVP:** Yastrzemski.

**Linescores**

**Game 1**—October 4, at Boston
Oakland........0 0 0 0 0 0 0 1 0—1 3 4
Boston ........2 0 0 0 0 0 5 0 x—7 8 3
Holtzman, Todd (7), Lindblad (7), Bosman (7), Abbott (8); Tiant. W—Tiant. L—Holtzman.

**Game 2**—October 5, at Boston
Oakland......2 0 0 1 0 0 0 0 0—3 10 0
Boston ......0 0 0 3 0 1 1 1 x—6 12 0
Blue, Todd (4), Fingers (5); Cleveland, Moret (6), Drago (7). W—Moret. L—Fingers. S—Drago. HR—Jackson (Oak.); Yastrzemski, Petrocelli (Bos.)

**Game 3**—October 7, at Oakland
Boston ......0 0 0 1 3 0 0 1 0—5 11 1
Oakland......0 0 0 0 0 1 0 2 0—3 6 2
Wise, Drago (8); Holtzman, Todd (5), Lindblad (5). W—Wise. L—Holtzman. S—Drago.

## NLCS

■ **Winner:** Cincinnati's Big Red Machine rolled over Pittsburgh in a quick and easy Championship Series.

■ **Turning point:** Reds pitcher Don Gullett hit a homer, drove in three runs and pitched an eight-hit, first-game victory.

■ **Memorable moment:** A two-run eighth-inning home run by Cincinnati's Pete Rose erased a 2-1, Game 3 deficit in a contest eventually won by the Reds in 10 innings, 5-3.

■ **Top guns:** Gullett (1-0, 1 HR, 3 RBIs), Dave Concepcion (.455), Tony Perez (.417, 4 RBIs), Reds; Richie Zisk (.500), Pirates.

■ **MVP:** Gullett.

**Linescores**

**Game 1**—October 4, at Cincinnati
Pitt.............0 2 0 0 0 0 0 0 1—3 8 0
Cin. ............0 1 3 0 4 0 0 0 x—8 11 0
Reuss, Brett (3), Demery (5), Ellis (7); Gullett. W—Gullett. L—Reuss. HR—Gullett (Cin.).

**Game 2**—October 5, at Cincinnati
Pitt.............0 0 0 1 0 0 0 0 0—1 5 0
Cin. ............2 0 0 2 0 1 1 0 x—6 12 1
Rooker, Tekulve (5), Brett (6), Kison (7); Norman, Eastwick (7). W—Norman. L—Rooker. S—Eastwick. HR—Perez (Cin.).

**Game 3**—October 7, at Pittsburgh
Cin. ..........0 1 0 0 0 0 0 2 0 2—5 6 0
Pitt. ..........0 0 0 0 0 2 0 0 1 0—3 7 2
Nolan, Carroll (7), McEnaney (8), Eastwick (9), Borbon (10); Candelaria, Giusti (8), Hernandez (10), Tekulve (10). W—Eastwick. L—Hernandez. S—Borbon. HR—Concepcion, Rose (Cin.); Oliver (Pit.).

## WORLD SERIES

■ **Winner:** Cincinnati's Big Red Machine held off the gritty Red Sox in one of the most exciting Series in baseball history.

■ **Turning point:** Reds second baseman Joe Morgan's Series-deciding single in the ninth inning of Game 7. The Series was that close.

■ **Memorable moments:** In the Red Sox's 7-6 Game 6 victory: Boston pinch-hitter Bernie Carbo's game-tying, three-run homer in the eighth inning; Boston right fielder Dwight Evans' spectacular, leaping, 11th-inning catch that he turned into a rally-killing double play; Boston catcher Carlton Fisk's dramatic, game-ending, "fair-or-foul" home run in the 12th inning.

■ **Top guns:** Pete Rose (.370), Tony Perez (3 HR, 7 RBIs), Reds; Carbo (2 PH HR), Carl Yastrzemski (.310, 4 RBIs), Rico Petrocelli (.308, 4 RBIs), Red Sox.

■ **MVP:** Rose.

**Linescores**

**Game 1**—October 11, at Boston
Cin. ............0 0 0 0 0 0 0 0 0—0 5 0
Bos. ...........0 0 0 0 0 0 6 0 x—6 12 0
Gullett, Carroll (7), McEnaney (7); Tiant. W—Tiant. L—Gullett.

**Game 2**—October 12, at Boston
Cin. .............0 0 0 1 0 0 0 0 2—3 7 1
Bos. ...........1 0 0 0 0 1 0 0 0—2 7 0
Billingham, Borbon (6), McEnaney (7), Eastwick (8); Lee, Drago (9). W—Eastwick. L—Drago.

**Game 3**—October 14, at Cincinnati
Bos. ......0 1 0 0 0 1 1 0 2 0—5 10 2
Cin. .......0 0 0 2 3 0 0 0 0 1—6 7 0
Wise, Burton (5), Cleveland (5), Willoughby (7), Moret (10); Nolan, Darcy (5), Carroll (7), McEnaney (7), Eastwick (9). W—Eastwick. L—Willoughby. HR—Fisk, Carbo, Evans (Bos.); Bench, Concepcion, Geronimo (Cin.).

**Game 4**—October 15, at Cincinnati
Bos. ..........0 0 0 5 0 0 0 0 0—5 11 1
Cin. ............2 0 0 2 0 0 0 0 0—4 9 1
Tiant; Norman, Borbon (4), Carroll (5), Eastwick (7). W—Tiant. L—Norman.

**Game 5**—October 16, at Cincinnati
Bos. ...........1 0 0 0 0 0 0 0 1—2 5 0
Cin. .............0 0 0 1 1 3 0 1 x—6 8 0
Cleveland, Willoughby (6), Pole (8), Segui (8); Gullett, Eastwick (9). W—Gullett. L—Cleveland. S—Eastwick. HR—Perez 2 (Cin.).

**Game 6**—October 21, at Boston
Cin.....0 0 0 0 3 0 2 1 0 0 0 0—6 14 0
Bos. ..3 0 0 0 0 0 0 3 0 0 0 1—7 10 1
Nolan, Norman (3), Billingham (3), Carroll (5), Borbon (6), Eastwick (8), McEnaney (9), Darcy (10); Tiant, Moret (8), Drago (9), Wise (12). W—Wise. L—Darcy. HR—Lynn, Carbo, Fisk (Bos.); Geronimo (Cin.).

**Game 7**—October 22, at Boston
Cin. .............0 0 0 0 0 2 1 0 1—4 9 0
Bos. ...........0 0 3 0 0 0 0 0 0—3 5 2
Gullett, Billingham (5), Carroll (7), McEnaney (9); Lee, Moret (7), Willoughby (7), Burton (9), Cleveland (9). W—Carroll. L—Burton. S—McEnaney. HR—Perez (Cin.).

# 1976

## FINAL STANDINGS

### American League

**East Division**

| Team | N.Y. | Bal. | Bos. | Cle. | Det. | Mil. | Cal. | Chi. | K.C. | Min. | Oak. | Tex. | W | L | Pct. | GB |
|---|---|---|---|---|---|---|---|---|---|---|---|---|---|---|---|---|
| New York | ... | 5 | 11 | 12 | 8 | 13 | 7 | 11 | 5 | 10 | 6 | 9 | 97 | 62 | .610 | ... |
| Baltimore | 13 | ... | 7 | 7 | 12 | 11 | 8 | 8 | 6 | 4 | 4 | 8 | 88 | 74 | .543 | 10.5 |
| Boston | 7 | 11 | ... | 9 | 14 | 12 | 7 | 6 | 3 | 7 | 4 | 3 | 83 | 79 | .512 | 15.5 |
| Cleveland | 4 | 11 | 9 | ... | 6 | 11 | 5 | 9 | 6 | 9 | 4 | 7 | 81 | 78 | .509 | 16 |
| Detroit | 9 | 6 | 4 | 12 | ... | 12 | 6 | 6 | 4 | 4 | 6 | 5 | 74 | 87 | .460 | 24 |
| Milwaukee | 5 | 7 | 6 | 6 | 6 | ... | 8 | 5 | 4 | 4 | 5 | 10 | 66 | 95 | .410 | 32 |

**West Division**

| Team | K.C. | Oak. | Min. | Cal. | Tex. | Chi. | Bal. | Bos. | Cle. | Det. | Mil. | N.Y. | W | L | Pct. | GB |
|---|---|---|---|---|---|---|---|---|---|---|---|---|---|---|---|---|
| Kansas City | ... | 9 | 10 | 10 | 7 | 10 | 6 | 9 | 6 | 8 | 8 | 7 | 90 | 72 | .556 | ... |
| Oakland | 9 | ... | 7 | 12 | 7 | 9 | 8 | 8 | 8 | 6 | 7 | 6 | 87 | 74 | .540 | 2.5 |
| Minnesota | 8 | 11 | ... | 10 | 11 | 11 | 8 | 5 | 3 | 8 | 8 | 2 | 85 | 77 | .525 | 5 |
| California | 8 | 6 | 8 | ... | 12 | 11 | 4 | 5 | 7 | 6 | 4 | 5 | 76 | 86 | .469 | 14 |
| Texas | 11 | 11 | 7 | 6 | ... | 11 | 4 | 9 | 5 | 7 | 2 | 3 | 76 | 86 | .469 | 14 |
| Chicago | 8 | 8 | 7 | 7 | 7 | ... | 4 | 6 | 3 | 6 | 7 | 1 | 64 | 97 | .398 | 25.5 |

### National League

**East Division**

| Team | Phi. | Pit. | N.Y. | Chi. | St.L. | Mon. | Atl. | Cin. | Hou. | L.A. | S.D. | S.F. | W | L | Pct. | GB |
|---|---|---|---|---|---|---|---|---|---|---|---|---|---|---|---|---|
| Philadelphia | ... | 8 | 13 | 10 | 12 | 15 | 7 | 7 | 8 | 7 | 8 | 6 | 101 | 61 | .623 | ... |
| Pittsburgh | 10 | ... | 8 | 10 | 12 | 10 | 9 | 4 | 10 | 3 | 7 | 9 | 92 | 70 | .568 | 9 |
| New York | 5 | 10 | ... | 13 | 9 | 10 | 8 | 6 | 6 | 5 | 7 | 7 | 86 | 76 | .531 | 15 |
| Chicago | 8 | 8 | 5 | ... | 12 | 11 | 6 | 3 | 5 | 3 | 6 | 8 | 75 | 87 | .463 | 26 |
| St. Louis | 6 | 6 | 9 | 6 | ... | 11 | 8 | 6 | 3 | 2 | 8 | 7 | 72 | 90 | .444 | 29 |
| Montreal | 3 | 8 | 8 | 7 | 7 | ... | 4 | 3 | 2 | 2 | 4 | 7 | 55 | 107 | .340 | 46 |

**West Division**

| Team | Cin. | L.A. | Hou. | S.F. | S.D. | Atl. | Chi. | Mon. | N.Y. | Phi. | Pit. | St.L. | W | L | Pct. | GB |
|---|---|---|---|---|---|---|---|---|---|---|---|---|---|---|---|---|
| Cincinnati | ... | 13 | 12 | 9 | 13 | 12 | 9 | 9 | 6 | 5 | 8 | 6 | 102 | 60 | .630 | ... |
| L.A. | 5 | ... | 13 | 8 | 6 | 10 | 9 | 10 | 7 | 5 | 9 | 10 | 92 | 70 | .568 | 10 |
| Houston | 6 | 5 | ... | 10 | 10 | 11 | 7 | 10 | 6 | 4 | 2 | 9 | 80 | 82 | .494 | 22 |
| San Fran. | 9 | 10 | 8 | ... | 10 | 9 | 4 | 5 | 5 | 6 | 3 | 5 | 74 | 88 | .457 | 28 |
| San Diego | 5 | 12 | 8 | 8 | ... | 8 | 6 | 8 | 5 | 4 | 5 | 4 | 73 | 89 | .451 | 29 |
| Atlanta | 6 | 8 | 7 | 9 | 10 | ... | 6 | 8 | 4 | 5 | 3 | 4 | 70 | 92 | .432 | 32 |

## SIGNIFICANT EVENTS

■ **January 14:** N.L. owners approved the sale of the Braves to Ted Turner, head of Turner Communications, for $12 million.

■ **April 10:** Free-agent pitcher Andy Messersmith signed a "lifetime contract" to pitch for new Braves owner Turner.

■ **April 25:** Cubs center fielder Rick Monday dashed into left field at Dodger Stadium and snatched an American flag away from two protestors who were trying to set it on fire.

■ **June 18:** Commissioner Bowie Kuhn voided Oakland owner Charles O. Finley's sale of Vida Blue to the Yankees and Joe Rudi and Rollie Fingers to the Red Sox.

■ **September 29:** Walter Alston, who compiled 2,040 victories over 23 seasons as manager of the Dodgers, retired at age 64.

■ **November 5:** The A.L. conducted its third expansion draft to fill rosters of new teams in Seattle and Toronto.

■ **November 6:** Reliever Bill Campbell, one of the plums of baseball's first free-agent reentry draft, signed a four-year, $1 million contract with the Red Sox.

## MEMORABLE MOMENTS

■ **April 17:** Mike Schmidt's two-run, 10th-inning home run, his record-tying fourth of the game, gave the Phillies an 18-16 victory over the Cubs at Wrigley Field.

■ **October 3:** George Brett collected three final-day hits and edged Kansas City teammate Hal McRae, .3333 to .3326, for the A.L. batting title.

## LEADERS

**American League**
**BA:** George Brett, K.C., .333.
**Runs:** Roy White, N.Y., 104.
**Hits:** George Brett, K.C., 215.
**TB:** George Brett, K.C., 298.
**HR:** Graig Nettles, N.Y., 32.
**RBI:** Lee May, Bal., 109.
**SB:** Bill North, Oak., 75.
**Wins:** Jim Palmer, Bal., 22.
**ERA:** Mark Fidrych, Det., 2.34.
**CG:** Mark Fidrych, Det., 24.
**IP:** Jim Palmer, Bal., 315.
**SO:** Nolan Ryan, Cal., 327.
**SV:** Sparky Lyle, N.Y., 23.

**National League**
**BA:** Bill Madlock, Chi., .339.
**Runs:** Pete Rose, Cin., 130.
**Hits:** Pete Rose, Cin., 215.
**TB:** Mike Schmidt, Phil., 306.
**HR:** Mike Schmidt, Phil., 38.
**RBI:** George Foster, Cin., 121.
**SB:** Dave Lopes, L.A., 63.
**Wins:** Randy Jones, S.D., 22.
**ERA:** John Denny, St.L., 2.52.
**CG:** Randy Jones, S.D., 25.
**IP:** Randy Jones, S.D., 315.1.
**SO:** Tom Seaver, N.Y., 235.
**SV:** Rawly Eastwick, Cin., 26.

**A.L. 20-game winners**
Jim Palmer, Bal., 22-13
Luis Tiant, Bos., 21-12
Wayne Garland, Bal., 20-7

**N.L. 20-game winners**
Randy Jones, S.D., 22-14
Jerry Koosman, N.Y., 21-10
Don Sutton, L.A., 21-10
Steve Carlton, Phil., 20-7
J.R. Richard, Hou., 20-15

**A.L. 100 RBIs**
Lee May, Bal., 109
Thurman Munson, N.Y., 105
Carl Yastrzemski, Bos., 102

**N.L. 100 RBIs**
George Foster, Cin., 121
Joe Morgan, Cin., 111
Mike Schmidt, Phil., 107
Bob Watson, Hou., 102

**Most Valuable Player**
A.L.: Thurman Munson, C, N.Y.
N.L.: Joe Morgan, 2B, Cin.

**Cy Young Award**
A.L.: Jim Palmer, Bal.
N.L.: Randy Jones, S.D.

**Rookie of the Year**
A.L.: Mark Fidrych, P, Det.
N.L.: Butch Metzger, P, S.D.
Pat Zachry, P, Cin.

**Hall of Fame additions**
Oscar Charleston, OF, Negro Leagues
Roger Connor, 1B, 1880-97
Cal Hubbard, umpire
Bob Lemon, P, 1946-58
Fred Lindstrom, 3B, 1924-36
Robin Roberts, P, 1948-66

## ALL-STAR GAME

■ **Winner:** Baseball celebrated the nation's Bicentennial with another N.L. All-Star victory — a 7-1 rout sparked by George Foster and Cesar Cedeno.

■ **Key innings:** The third, when Foster blasted a two-run homer, and the eighth, when Cedeno secured the outcome with another two-run shot.

■ **Memorable moment:** The five-hit pitching of an N.L. staff that surrendered the A.L.'s lone run on a homer by Fred Lynn.

■ **Top guns:** Randy Jones (Padres), Foster (Reds), Cedeno (Astros), Pete Rose (Reds), N.L.; Lynn (Red Sox), Rusty Staub (Tigers), A.L.

■ **MVP:** Foster.

**Linescore**

July 13, at Philadelphia's Veterans Stadium
A.L.............0 0 0 1 0 0 0 0 0—1 5 0
N.L.............2 0 2 0 0 0 0 3 x—7 10 0
Fidrych (Tigers), Hunter (Yankees) 3, Tiant (Red Sox) 5, Tanana (Angels) 7; Jones (Padres), Seaver (Mets) 4, Montefusco (Giants) 6, Rhoden (Dodgers) 8, Forsch (Astros) 9. W—Jones. L—Fidrych. HR—Foster, Cedeno, N.L.; Lynn, A.L.

## ALCS

■ **Winner:** The New York Yankees, absent from post-season play since 1964, qualified for their 30th World Series with a riveting five-game victory over postseason newcomer Kansas City.

■ **Turning point:** The Yankees' 5-3 Game 3 victory, which was fueled by a homer and three RBIs by first baseman Chris Chambliss.

■ **Memorable moment:** Chambliss' dramatic series-ending home run leading off the ninth inning of Game 5. The blast off Royals reliever Mark Littell gave the Yankees a 7-6 victory and touched off a wild mob scene at Yankee Stadium.

■ **Top guns:** Chambliss (.524, 2 HR, 8 RBIs), Thurman Munson (.435), Mickey Rivers (.348), Yankees; Paul Splittorff (1-0, 1.93 ERA), George Brett (.444, 5 RBIs), Royals.

■ **MVP:** Chambliss.

**Linescores**

**Game 1**—October 9, at Kansas City
N.Y.............2 0 0 0 0 0 0 0 2—4 12 0
K.C.............0 0 0 0 0 0 0 1 0—1 5 2
Hunter; Gura, Littell (9). W—Hunter. L—Gura.

**Game 2**—October 10, at Kansas City
N.Y ............0 1 2 0 0 0 0 0 0—3 12 5
K.C. ............2 0 0 0 0 2 0 3 x—7 9 0
Figueroa, Tidrow (6); Leonard, Splittorff (3), Mingori (9). W—Splittorff. L—Figueroa.

**Game 3**—October 12, at New York
K.C. ..............3 0 0 0 0 0 0 0 0—3 6 0
N.Y. ..............0 0 0 2 0 3 0 0 x—5 9 0
Hassler, Pattin (6), Hall (6), Mingori (6), Littell (6); Ellis, Lyle (9). W—Ellis. L—Hassler. S—Lyle. HR—Chambliss (N.Y.).

**Game 4**—October 13, at New York
K.C.............0 3 0 2 0 1 0 1 0—7 9 1
N.Y.............0 2 0 0 0 0 1 0 1—4 11 0
Gura, Bird (3), Mingori (7); Hunter, Tidrow (4), Jackson (7). W—Bird. L—Hunter. S—Mingori. HR—Nettles 2 (N.Y.).

**Game 5**—October 14, at New York
K.C.............2 1 0 0 0 0 0 3 0—6 11 1
N.Y.............2 0 2 0 0 2 0 0 1—7 11 1
Leonard, Splittorff (1), Pattin (4), Hassler (5), Littell (7); Figueroa, Jackson (8), Tidrow (9). W—Tidrow. L—Littell. HR—Mayberry, Brett (K.C.); Chambliss (N.Y.).

## NLCS

■ **Winner:** Philadelphia was no match for the powerful Reds, who were being hailed as one of the great teams in baseball history.

■ **Turning point:** The Reds took quick control with a 6-3 first-game victory over the Phillies and ace lefthander Steve Carlton.

■ **Memorable moment:** The ninth inning of Game 3. After tying the game with consecutive home runs by George Foster and Johnny Bench, the Reds claimed a 7-6 victory when Ken Griffey singled with the bases loaded off reliever Tom Underwood.

■ **Top guns:** Don Gullett (1-0, 1.13 ERA), Pete Rose (.429), Griffey (.385), Foster (2 HR, 4 RBIs), Reds; Jay Johnstone (.778), Phillies.

■ **MVP:** Griffey.

**Linescores**

**Game 1**—October 9, at Philadelphia
Cin. ............0 0 1 0 0 2 0 3 0—6 10 0
Phil. ...........1 0 0 0 0 0 0 0 2—3 6 1
Gullett, Eastwick (9); Carlton, McGraw (8). W—Gullett. L—Carlton. HR—Foster (Cin.).

**Game 2**—October 10, at Philadelphia
Cin. ............0 0 0 0 0 4 2 0 0—6 6 0
Phil. ...........0 1 0 0 1 0 0 0 0—2 10 1
Zachry, Borbon (6); Lonborg, Garber (6), McGraw (7), Reed (7). W—Zachry. L—Lonborg. S—Borbon. HR—Luzinski (Phil.).

**Game 3**—October 12, at Cincinnati
Phil. ...........0 0 0 1 0 0 2 2 1—6 11 0
Cin. ............0 0 0 0 0 0 4 0 3—7 9 2
Kaat, Reed (7), Garber (9), Underwood (9); Nolan, Sarmiento (6), Borbon (7), Eastwick (8). W—Eastwick. L—Garber. HR—Foster, Bench (Cin.).

## WORLD SERIES

■ **Winner:** Cincinnati's Big Red Machine was in full gear as it rolled over the Yankees, who were making their first Series appearance since 1964.

■ **Turning point:** Joe Morgan's first-inning home run in Game 1. The Reds never looked back.

■ **Memorable moment:** Game 3 at refurbished Yankee Stadium. Despite a 6-2 New York loss, the atmosphere was electric and baseball's most revered ballpark was the stately host for its 28th World Series.

■ **Top guns:** Johnny Bench (.533, 2 HR, 6 RBIs), George Foster (.429), Dave Concepcion (.357), Dan Driessen (.357), Reds; Thurman Munson (.529), Yankees.

■ **MVP:** Bench.

**Linescores**

**Game 1**—October 16, at Cincinnati
N.Y.............0 1 0 0 0 0 0 0 0—1 5 1
Cin. ............1 0 1 0 0 1 2 0 x—5 10 1
Alexander, Lyle (7); Gullett, Borbon (8). W—Gullett. L—Alexander. HR—Morgan (Cin.).

**Game 2**—October 17, at Cincinnati
N.Y.............0 0 0 1 0 0 2 0 0—3 9 1
Cin. ............0 3 0 0 0 0 0 0 1—4 10 0
Hunter; Norman, Billingham (7). W—Billingham. L—Hunter.

**Game 3**—October 19, at New York
Cin. ............0 3 0 1 0 0 0 2 0—6 13 2
N.Y. .............0 0 0 1 0 0 1 0 0—2 8 0
Zachry, McEnaney (7); Ellis, Jackson (4), Tidrow (8). W—Zachry. L—Ellis. S—McEnaney. HR—Driessen (Cin.); Mason (N.Y.).

**Game 4**—October 21, at New York
Cin. ............0 0 0 3 0 0 0 0 4—7 9 2
N.Y. ..............1 0 0 0 1 0 0 0 0—2 8 0
Nolan, McEnaney (7); Figueroa, Tidrow (9), Lyle (9). W—Nolan. L—Figueroa. S—McEnaney. HR—Bench 2 (Cin.).

# 1977

## FINAL STANDINGS

### American League

**East Division**

| Team | N.Y. | Bos. | Bal. | Det. | Cle. | Mil. | Tor. | Cal. | Chi. | K.C. | Min. | Oak. | Sea. | Tex. | W | L | Pct. | GB |
|---|---|---|---|---|---|---|---|---|---|---|---|---|---|---|---|---|---|---|
| New York | ... | 7 | 7 | 9 | 12 | 7 | 9 | 7 | 7 | 5 | 8 | 9 | 6 | 7 | 100 | 62 | .617 | ... |
| Boston | 8 | ... | 8 | 9 | 8 | 9 | 12 | 7 | 3 | 5 | 4 | 8 | 10 | 6 | 97 | 64 | .602 | 2.5 |
| Baltimore | 8 | 6 | ... | 12 | 11 | 11 | 10 | 5 | 5 | 4 | 6 | 8 | 7 | 4 | 97 | 64 | .602 | 2.5 |
| Detroit | 6 | 6 | 3 | ... | 7 | 10 | 10 | 6 | 6 | 3 | 5 | 5 | 5 | 2 | 74 | 88 | .457 | 26 |
| Cleveland | 3 | 7 | 4 | 8 | ... | 11 | 9 | 4 | 4 | 3 | 2 | 7 | 7 | 2 | 71 | 90 | .441 | 28.5 |
| Milwaukee | 8 | 6 | 4 | 5 | 4 | ... | 8 | 5 | 5 | 2 | 3 | 5 | 7 | 5 | 67 | 95 | .414 | 33 |
| Toronto | 6 | 3 | 5 | 5 | 5 | 7 | ... | 4 | 3 | 2 | 1 | 3 | 6 | 4 | 54 | 107 | .335 | 45.5 |

**West Division**

| Team | K.C. | Tex. | Chi. | Min. | Cal. | Sea. | Oak. | Bal. | Bos. | Cle. | Det. | Mil. | N.Y. | Tor. | W | L | Pct. | GB |
|---|---|---|---|---|---|---|---|---|---|---|---|---|---|---|---|---|---|---|
| Kansas City | ... | 8 | 7 | 10 | 9 | 11 | 9 | 7 | 5 | 7 | 8 | 8 | 5 | 8 | 102 | 60 | .630 | ... |
| Texas | 7 | ... | 9 | 7 | 10 | 6 | 13 | 6 | 4 | 9 | 8 | 5 | 3 | 7 | 94 | 68 | .580 | 8 |
| Chicago | 8 | 6 | ... | 10 | 7 | 10 | 10 | 5 | 7 | 6 | 4 | 6 | 3 | 8 | 90 | 72 | .556 | 12 |
| Minnesota | 5 | 8 | 5 | ... | 8 | 7 | 8 | 4 | 6 | 9 | 5 | 8 | 2 | 9 | 84 | 77 | .522 | 17.5 |
| California | 6 | 5 | 8 | 7 | ... | 9 | 5 | 6 | 3 | 6 | 4 | 5 | 4 | 6 | 74 | 88 | .457 | 28 |
| Seattle | 4 | 9 | 5 | 8 | 6 | ... | 8 | 3 | 1 | 3 | 6 | 3 | 4 | 4 | 64 | 98 | .395 | 38 |
| Oakland | 6 | 2 | 5 | 6 | 10 | 7 | ... | 2 | 3 | 3 | 5 | 5 | 2 | 7 | 63 | 98 | .391 | 38.5 |

### National League

**East Division**

| Team | Phi. | Pit. | St.L. | Chi. | Mon. | N.Y. | Atl. | Cin. | Hou. | L.A. | S.D. | S.F. | W | L | Pct. | GB |
|---|---|---|---|---|---|---|---|---|---|---|---|---|---|---|---|---|
| Philadelphia | ... | 8 | 11 | 12 | 11 | 13 | 10 | 4 | 8 | 6 | 9 | 9 | 101 | 61 | .623 | ... |
| Pittsburgh | 10 | ... | 9 | 11 | 11 | 14 | 9 | 9 | 8 | 3 | 10 | 2 | 96 | 66 | .593 | 5 |
| St.Louis | 7 | 9 | ... | 11 | 6 | 10 | 11 | 7 | 7 | 6 | 4 | 5 | 83 | 79 | .512 | 18 |
| Chicago | 6 | 7 | 7 | ... | 10 | 9 | 7 | 7 | 6 | 6 | 7 | 9 | 81 | 81 | .500 | 20 |
| Montreal | 7 | 7 | 12 | 8 | ... | 10 | 6 | 5 | 4 | 5 | 5 | 6 | 75 | 87 | .463 | 26 |
| New York | 5 | 4 | 8 | 9 | 8 | ... | 5 | 2 | 6 | 4 | 6 | 7 | 64 | 98 | .395 | 37 |

**West Division**

| Team | L.A. | Cin. | Hou. | S.F. | S.D. | Atl. | Chi. | Mon. | N.Y. | Phi. | Pit. | St.L. | W | L | Pct. | GB |
|---|---|---|---|---|---|---|---|---|---|---|---|---|---|---|---|---|
| Los Angeles | ... | 8 | 9 | 14 | 12 | 13 | 6 | 7 | 8 | 6 | 9 | 6 | 98 | 64 | .605 | ... |
| Cincinnati | 10 | ... | 5 | 10 | 11 | 14 | 5 | 7 | 10 | 8 | 3 | 5 | 88 | 74 | .543 | 10 |
| Houston | 9 | 13 | ... | 9 | 8 | 9 | 6 | 8 | 6 | 4 | 4 | 5 | 81 | 81 | .500 | 17 |
| San Fran. | 4 | 8 | 9 | .. | 10 | 10 | 3 | 6 | 5 | 3 | 10 | 7 | 75 | 87 | .463 | 23 |
| San Diego | 6 | 7 | 10 | 8 | ... | 7 | 5 | 7 | 6 | 3 | 2 | 8 | 69 | 93 | .426 | 29 |
| Atlanta | 5 | 4 | 9 | 8 | 11 | ... | 5 | 6 | 7 | 2 | 3 | 1 | 61 | 101 | .377 | 37 |

## SIGNIFICANT EVENTS

■ **January 2:** Commissioner Bowie Kuhn suspended Braves owner Ted Turner for a year and fined him $10,000 for "tampering" with free-agent outfielder Gary Matthews.

■ **April 6-7:** The expansion Mariners lost their debut, 7-0, to the Angels, but the Blue Jays won their Toronto inaugural, 9-5, over the White Sox.

■ **April 15:** The Expos opened new Olympic Stadium, but the Phillies spoiled the occasion with a 7-2 victory.

■ **March 28:** Texas second baseman Lenny Randle, frustrated over losing his starting job, sent 50-year-old manager Frank Lucchesi to the hospital with a vicious beating before a spring training game.

■ **October 25:** Yankees lefty Sparky Lyle became the first A.L. reliever to win a Cy Young Award.

■ **November 8:** Cincinnati's George Foster, the first player to top the 50-homer barrier since 1965, earned N.L. MVP honors.

## MEMORABLE MOMENTS

■ **June 8:** California's Nolan Ryan struck out 19 Blue Jays in a 10-inning performance, reaching that single-game plateau for the fourth time.

■ **August 29:** St. Louis' Lou Brock swiped two bases in a game against San Diego, lifting his career total to 893 and passing Ty Cobb as baseball's greatest modern-era basestealer.

## LEADERS

**American League**
**BA:** Rod Carew, Min., .388.
**Runs:** Rod Carew, Min., 128.
**Hits:** Rod Carew, Min., 239.
**TB:** Jim Rice, Bos., 382.
**HR:** Jim Rice, Bos., 39.
**RBI:** Larry Hisle, Min., 119.
**SB:** Fred Patek, K.C., 53.
**Wins:** Dave Goltz, Min.; Dennis Leonard, K.C.; Jim Palmer, Bal., 20.
**ERA:** Frank Tanana, Cal., 2.54.
**CG:** Jim Palmer, Bal.; Nolan Ryan, Cal., 22.
**IP:** Jim Palmer, Bal., 319.
**SO:** Nolan Ryan, Cal., 341.
**SV:** Bill Campbell, Bos., 31.

**National League**
**BA:** Dave Parker, Pit., .338.
**Runs:** George Foster, Cin., 124.
**Hits:** Dave Parker, Pit., 215.
**TB:** George Foster, Cin., 388.
**HR:** George Foster, Cin., 52.
**RBI:** George Foster, Cin., 149.
**SB:** Frank Taveras, Pit., 70.
**Wins:** Steve Carlton, Phil., 23.
**ERA:** John Candelaria, Pit., 2.34.
**CG:** Phil Niekro, Atl., 20.
**IP:** Phil Niekro, Atl., 330.1.
**SO:** Phil Niekro, Atl., 262.
**SV:** Rollie Fingers, S.D., 35.

**A.L. 20-game winners**
Jim Palmer, Bal., 20-11
Dave Goltz, Min., 20-11
Dennis Leonard, K.C., 20-12

**N.L. 20-game winners**
Steve Carlton, Phil., 23-10
Tom Seaver, N.Y.-Cin., 21-6
John Candelaria, Pit., 20-5
Bob Forsch, St.L., 20-7
Tommy John, L.A., 20-7
Rick Reuschel, Chi., 20-10

**A.L. 100 RBIs**
Larry Hisle, Min., 119
Bobby Bonds, Cal., 115
Jim Rice, Bos., 114
Al Cowens, K.C., 112
Butch Hobson, Bos., 112
Reggie Jackson, N.Y., 110
Graig Nettles, N.Y., 107
Jason Thompson, Det., 105
Carlton Fisk, Bos., 102
Carl Yastrzemski, Bos., 102
Rusty Staub, Det., 101
Richie Zisk, Chi., 101
Rod Carew, Min., 100
Thurman Munson, N.Y., 100

**N.L. 100 RBIs**
George Foster, Cin., 149
Greg Luzinski, Phil., 130
Steve Garvey, L.A., 115
Jeff Burroughs, Atl., 114
Ron Cey, L.A., 110
Bob Watson, Hou., 110
Johnny Bench, Cin., 109
Bill Robinson, Pit., 104
Mike Schmidt, Phil., 101

**N.L. 40 homers**
George Foster, Cin., 52
Jeff Burroughs, Atl., 41

**Most Valuable Player**
A.L.: Rod Carew, 1B, Min.
N.L.: George Foster, OF, Cin.

**Cy Young Award**
A.L.: Sparky Lyle, N.Y.
N.L.: Steve Carlton, Phil.

**Rookie of the Year**
A.L.: Eddie Murray, 1B, Bal.
N.L.: Andre Dawson, OF, Mon.

**Hall of Fame additions**
Ernie Banks, SS, 1953-71
Martin Dihigo, P/IF, Negro Leagues
John Henry Lloyd, SS, Negro Leagues
Al Lopez, manager
Amos Rusie, P, 1889-1901
Joe Sewell, SS, 1920-33

## ALL-STAR GAME

■ **Winner:** The N.L. continued its All-Star mastery with a 7-5 victory — its sixth in a row and 14th in 15 contests.

■ **Key inning:** The first, when the N.L. struck for four quick runs. A leadoff homer by Joe Morgan and a two-run shot by Greg Luzinski were the big blows.

■ **Memorable moment:** Watching the N.L. close out another All-Star victory at venerable Yankee Stadium, where so much A.L. glory had been achieved.

■ **Top guns:** Don Sutton (Dodgers), Morgan (Reds), Luzinski (Phillies), Dave Winfield (Padres), Steve Garvey (Dodgers), N.L.; Dennis Eckersley (Indians), Richie Zisk (White Sox), George Scott (Red Sox), A.L.

■ **MVP:** Sutton.

**Linescore**
July 19, at New York's Yankee Stadium
N.L..............4 0 1 0 0 0 0 2 0—7 9 1
A.L..............0 0 0 0 0 2 1 0 2—5 8 0
Sutton (Dodgers), Lavelle (Giants) 4, Seaver (Reds) 6, R. Reuschel (Cubs) 8, Gossage (Pirates) 9; Palmer (Orioles), Kern (Indians) 3, Eckersley (Indians) 4, LaRoche (Angels) 6, Campbell (Red Sox) 7, Lyle (Yankees) 8. W—Sutton. L—Palmer. HR—Morgan, Luzinski, Garvey, N.L.; Scott, A.L.

## ALCS

■ **Winner:** The Yankees, bidding to return to the World Series for a second consecutive season, needed a three-run ninth-inning rally to defeat Kansas City in the decisive fifth game.

■ **Turning point:** Sparky Lyle's 5⅓ innings of scoreless Game 4 relief after the Royals, bidding to close out the series, had cut a 4-0 Yankee lead to 5-4. The Yanks evened the series with a 6-4 win.

■ **Memorable moment:** A bloop single by light-hitting Yankee Paul Blair leading off the ninth inning of Game 5. Blair's hit off Royals ace Dennis Leonard set up the Yankees' series-winning rally.

■ **Top guns:** Lyle (2-0, 0.96 ERA), Cliff Johnson (.400), Mickey Rivers (.391), Yankees; Hal McRae (.444), Fred Patek (.389), Royals.

■ **MVP:** Lyle.

**Linescores**

**Game 1**—October 5, at New York
K.C..............2 2 2 0 0 0 0 1 0—7 9 0
N.Y..............0 0 2 0 0 0 0 0 0—2 9 0
Splittorff, Bird (9); Gullett, Tidrow (3), Lyle (9). W—Splittorff. L—Gullett. HR—McRae, Mayberry, Cowens (K.C.); Munson (N.Y.).

**Game 2**—October 6, at New York
K.C............0 0 1 0 0 1 0 0 0—2 3 1
N.Y............0 0 0 0 2 3 0 1 x—6 10 1
Hassler, Littell (6), Mingori (8); Guidry. W—Guidry. L—Hassler. HR—Johnson (N.Y.).

**Game 3**—October 7, at Kansas City
N.Y............0 0 0 0 1 0 0 0 1—2 4 1
K.C............0 1 1 0 1 2 1 0 x—6 12 1
Torrez, Lyle (6); Leonard. W—Leonard. L—Torrez.

**Game 4**—October 8, at Kansas City
N.Y............1 2 1 1 0 0 0 0 1—6 13 0
K.C............0 0 2 2 0 0 0 0 0—4 8 2
Figueroa, Tidrow (4), Lyle (4); Gura, Pattin (3), Mingori (9), Bird (9). W—Lyle. L—Gura.

**Game 5**—October 9, at Kansas City
N.Y............0 0 1 0 0 0 0 1 3—5 10 0
K.C............2 0 1 0 0 0 0 0 0—3 10 1
Guidry, Torrez (3), Lyle (8); Splittorff, Bird (8), Mingori (8), Leonard (9), Gura (9), Littell (9). W—Lyle. L—Leonard.

## NLCS

■ **Winner:** The Dodgers returned to the World Series for the second time in four years and denied Philadelphia its first pennant since 1950.

■ **Turning point:** The ninth inning of Game 3. With the series tied at a game apiece and the Phillies holding a 5-3 lead with two out and nobody on base in the final inning, the Dodgers collected four straight hits, scored three runs and escaped with a 6-5 victory.

■ **Memorable moment:** Dusty Baker's two-run fourth-game homer that helped Dodgers lefty Tommy John record a 4-1 series-ending victory in a steady rain.

■ **Top guns:** John (1-0, 0.66 ERA), Baker (.357, 2 HR, 8 RBIs), Ron Cey (.308, 4 RBIs), Dodgers; Bob Boone (.400), Richie Hebner (.357), Phillies.

■ **MVP:** Baker.

**Linescores**

**Game 1**—October 4, at Los Angeles
Phil. ...........2 0 0 0 2 1 0 0 2—7 9 0
L.A..............0 0 0 0 1 0 4 0 0—5 9 2
Carlton, Garber (7), McGraw (9); John, Garman (5), Hough (6), Sosa (8). W—Garber. L—Sosa. S—McGraw. HR—Luzinski (Phil.); Cey (L.A.).

**Game 2**—October 5, at Los Angeles
Phil. ...........0 0 1 0 0 0 0 0 0—1 9 1
L.A..............0 0 1 4 0 1 1 0 x—7 9 1
Lonborg, Reed (5), Brusstar (7); Sutton. W—Sutton. L—Lonborg. HR—McBride (Phil.); Baker (L.A.).

**Game 3**—October 7, at Philadelphia
L.A............0 2 0 1 0 0 0 0 3—6 12 2
Phil. ..........0 3 0 0 0 0 0 2 0—5 6 2
Hooton, Rhoden (2), Rau (7), Sosa (8), Rautzhan (8), Garman (9); Christenson, Brusstar (4), Reed (5), Garber (7). W—Rautzhan. L—Garber. S—Garman.

**Game 4**—October 8, at Philadelphia
L.A..............0 2 0 0 2 0 0 0 0—4 5 0
Phil. ...........0 0 0 1 0 0 0 0 0—1 7 0
John; Carlton, Reed (6), McGraw (7), Garber (9). W—John. L—Carlton. HR—Baker (L.A.).

## WORLD SERIES

■ **Winner:** The Yankees won their record 21st World Series — but first since 1962.

■ **Turning point:** Ron Guidry's four-hit pitching in Game 4 — a 4-2 victory that gave the Yankees a three-games-to-one edge.

■ **Memorable moment:** Reggie Jackson's eighth-inning Game 6 blast into the center field bleachers — his record-tying third home run of the contest. The Yankees ended the classic with an 8-4 victory and Jackson finished with a Series-record five homers.

■ **Top guns:** Mike Torrez (2-0, 2.50 ERA), Jackson (.450, 5 HR, 8 RBIs), Yankees; Steve Garvey (.375), Steve Yeager (.316, 2 HR, 5 RBIs), Dodgers.

■ **MVP:** Jackson.

**Linescores**

**Game 1**—October 11, at New York
L.A.....2 0 0 0 0 0 0 0 1 0 0 0—3 6 0
N.Y.....1 0 0 0 0 1 0 1 0 0 0 1—4 11 0
Sutton, Rautzhan (8), Sosa (8), Garman (9), Rhoden (12); Gullett, Lyle (9). W—Lyle. L—Rhoden. HR—Randolph (N.Y.).

**Game 2**—October 12, at New York
L.A..............2 1 2 0 0 0 0 0 1—6 9 0
N.Y..............0 0 0 1 0 0 0 0 0—1 5 0
Hooton; Hunter, Tidrow (3), Clay (6), Lyle (9). W—Hooton. L—Hunter. HR—Cey, Yeager, Smith, Garvey (L.A.).

**Game 3**—October 14, at Los Angeles
N.Y............3 0 0 1 1 0 0 0 0—5 10 0
L.A............0 0 3 0 0 0 0 0 0—3 7 1
Torrez; John, Hough (7). W—Torrez. L—John. HR—Baker (L.A.).

**Game 4**—October 15, at Los Angeles
N.Y..............0 3 0 0 0 1 0 0 0—4 7 0
L.A..............0 0 2 0 0 0 0 0 0—2 4 0
Guidry; Rau, Rhoden (2), Garman (9). W—Guidry. L—Rau. HR—Lopes (L.A.); Jackson (N.Y.).

**Game 5**—October 16, at Los Angeles
N.Y..........0 0 0 0 0 0 2 2 0— 4 9 2
L.A. ..........1 0 0 4 3 2 0 0 x—10 13 0
Gullett, Clay (5), Tidrow (6), Hunter (7); Sutton. W—Sutton. L—Gullett. HR—Yeager, Smith (L.A.); Munson, Jackson (N.Y.).

**Game 6**—October 18, at New York
L.A..............2 0 1 0 0 0 0 0 1—4 9 0
N.Y. .............0 2 0 3 2 0 0 1 x—8 8 1
Hooton, Sosa (4), Rau (5), Hough (7); Torrez. W—Torrez. L—Hooton. HR—Chambliss, Jackson 3 (N.Y.); Smith (L.A.).

## FINAL STANDINGS

### American League

#### East Division

| Team | N.Y. | Bos. | Mil. | Bal. | Det. | Cle. | Tor. | Cal. | Chi. | K.C. | Min. | Oak. | Sea. | Tex. | W | L | Pct. | GB |
|---|---|---|---|---|---|---|---|---|---|---|---|---|---|---|---|---|---|---|
| New York | ... | 9 | 5 | 9 | 11 | 9 | 11 | 5 | 9 | 5 | 7 | 8 | 6 | 6 | 100 | 63 | .613 | ... |
| Boston | 7 | ... | 10 | 8 | 12 | 7 | 11 | 9 | 7 | 4 | 9 | 5 | 7 | 3 | 99 | 64 | .607 | 1 |
| Milwaukee | 10 | 5 | ... | 8 | 8 | 10 | 12 | 5 | 7 | 4 | 4 | 9 | 5 | 6 | 93 | 69 | .574 | 6.5 |
| Baltimore | 6 | 7 | 7 | ... | 7 | 9 | 8 | 4 | 8 | 2 | 5 | 11 | 9 | 7 | 90 | 71 | .559 | 9 |
| Detroit | 4 | 3 | 7 | 8 | ... | 10 | 9 | 7 | 9 | 4 | 4 | 6 | 8 | 7 | 86 | 76 | .531 | 13.5 |
| Cleveland | 6 | 8 | 5 | 6 | 5 | ... | 10 | 4 | 2 | 5 | 5 | 4 | 8 | 1 | 69 | 90 | .434 | 29 |
| Toronto | 4 | 4 | 3 | 7 | 6 | 4 | ... | 3 | 6 | 5 | 4 | 4 | 2 | 7 | 59 | 102 | .366 | 40 |

#### West Division

| Team | K.C. | Cal. | Tex. | Min. | Chi. | Oak. | Sea. | Bal. | Bos. | Cle. | Det. | Mil. | N.Y. | Tor. | W | L | Pct. | GB |
|---|---|---|---|---|---|---|---|---|---|---|---|---|---|---|---|---|---|---|
| Kansas City | ... | 6 | 7 | 7 | 7 | 10 | 12 | 8 | 6 | 6 | 6 | 6 | 6 | 5 | 92 | 70 | .568 | ... |
| California | 9 | ... | 5 | 12 | 8 | 9 | 9 | 6 | 2 | 6 | 4 | 5 | 5 | 7 | 87 | 75 | .537 | 5 |
| Texas | 8 | 10 | ... | 9 | 4 | 9 | 12 | 4 | 7 | 9 | 3 | 4 | 4 | 4 | 87 | 75 | .537 | 5 |
| Minnesota | 8 | 3 | 6 | ... | 7 | 9 | 6 | 5 | 2 | 5 | 6 | 7 | 3 | 6 | 73 | 89 | .451 | 19 |
| Chicago | 8 | 7 | 11 | 8 | ... | 7 | 7 | 1 | 3 | 8 | 2 | 4 | 1 | 4 | 71 | 90 | .441 | 20.5 |
| Oakland | 5 | 6 | 6 | 6 | 8 | ... | 13 | 0 | 5 | 6 | 4 | 1 | 2 | 7 | 69 | 93 | .426 | 23 |
| Seattle | 3 | 6 | 3 | 9 | 8 | 2 | ... | 1 | 3 | 1 | 2 | 5 | 5 | 8 | 56 | 104 | .350 | 35 |

### National League

#### East Division

| Team | Phi. | Pit. | Chi. | Mon. | St.L. | N.Y. | Atl. | Cin. | Hou. | L.A. | S.D. | S.F. | W | L | Pct. | GB |
|---|---|---|---|---|---|---|---|---|---|---|---|---|---|---|---|---|
| Philadelphia | ... | 11 | 14 | 9 | 10 | 12 | 4 | 5 | 6 | 5 | 8 | 6 | 90 | 72 | .556 | ... |
| Pittsburgh | 7 | ... | 11 | 11 | 9 | 11 | 10 | 7 | 8 | 5 | 5 | 4 | 88 | 73 | .547 | 1.5 |
| Chicago | 4 | 7 | ... | 7 | 15 | 11 | 7 | 7 | 6 | 4 | 7 | 4 | 79 | 83 | .488 | 11 |
| Montreal | 9 | 7 | 11 | ... | 9 | 8 | 7 | 4 | 6 | 4 | 6 | 5 | 76 | 86 | .469 | 14 |
| St. Louis | 8 | 9 | 3 | 9 | ... | 11 | 7 | 4 | 5 | 7 | 3 | 3 | 69 | 93 | .426 | 21 |
| New York | 6 | 7 | 7 | 10 | 7 | ... | 6 | 5 | 5 | 5 | 5 | 3 | 66 | 96 | .407 | 24 |

#### West Division

| Team | L.A. | Cin. | S.F. | S.D. | Hou. | Atl. | Chi. | Mon. | N.Y. | Phi. | Pit. | St.L. | W | L | Pct. | GB |
|---|---|---|---|---|---|---|---|---|---|---|---|---|---|---|---|---|
| Los Angeles | ... | 9 | 11 | 9 | 11 | 13 | 8 | 8 | 7 | 7 | 7 | 5 | 95 | 67 | .586 | ... |
| Cincinnati | 9 | ... | 12 | 9 | 11 | 12 | 5 | 8 | 7 | 7 | 4 | 8 | 92 | 69 | .571 | 2.5 |
| San Fran. | 7 | 6 | ... | 10 | 12 | 7 | 8 | 7 | 9 | 6 | 8 | 9 | 89 | 73 | .549 | 6 |
| San Diego | 9 | 9 | 8 | ... | 10 | 10 | 5 | 6 | 7 | 4 | 7 | 9 | 84 | 78 | .519 | 11 |
| Houston | 7 | 7 | 6 | 8 | ... | 10 | 6 | 6 | 7 | 6 | 4 | 7 | 74 | 88 | .457 | 21 |
| Atlanta | 5 | 6 | 11 | 8 | 8 | ... | 5 | 5 | 6 | 8 | 2 | 5 | 69 | 93 | .426 | 26 |

## SIGNIFICANT EVENTS

■ **June 31:** Larry Doby, baseball's second black player in 1947, became the game's second black manager when he took the White Sox reins from Bob Lemon.

■ **August 26:** Major League umpires were forced back to work by a restraining order after a one-day strike.

■ **September 23:** Angels outfielder Lyman Bostock, a .311 career hitter, was killed by an errant shotgun blast while riding in a car in Gary, Ind.

■ **October 24:** Padres ace Gaylord Perry became the first pitcher to win a Cy Young Award in both leagues.

■ **December 5:** Pete Rose completed his high-profile free-agency showcase by signing with the Phillies for $3.2 million over four years.

## MEMORABLE MOMENTS

■ **May 5:** Cincinnati's Pete Rose collected career hit No. 3,000 in a 4-3 loss to the Expos.

■ **June 30:** Giants first baseman Willie McCovey crashed his 500th career home run off Jamie Easterly in a 10-9 loss to the Braves.

■ **August 1:** Atlanta pitchers Larry McWilliams and Gene Garber stopped Rose's N.L. record-tying hitting streak at 44 games in a 16-4 victory over the Reds.

■ **October 2:** The Yankees capped their incredible comeback from a 14-game A.L. East Division deficit with a 5-4 victory over Boston in a one-game playoff to decide the A.L. East Division title.

## LEADERS

**American League**
**BA:** Rod Carew, Min., .333.
**Runs:** Ron LeFlore, Det., 126.
**Hits:** Jim Rice, Bos., 213.
**TB:** Jim Rice, Bos., 406.
**HR:** Jim Rice, Bos., 46.
**RBI:** Jim Rice, Bos., 139.
**SB:** Ron LeFlore, Det., 68.
**Wins:** Ron Guidry, N.Y., 25.
**ERA:** Ron Guidry, N.Y., 1.74.
**CG:** Mike Caldwell, Mil., 23.
**IP:** Jim Palmer, Bal., 296.
**SO:** Nolan Ryan, Cal., 260.
**SV:** Goose Gossage, N.Y., 27.

**National League**
**BA:** Dave Parker, Pit., .334.
**Runs:** Ivan DeJesus, Chi., 104.
**Hits:** Steve Garvey, L.A., 202.
**TB:** Dave Parker, Pit., 340.
**HR:** George Foster, Cin., 40.
**RBI:** George Foster, Cin., 120.
**SB:** Omar Moreno, Pit., 71.
**Wins:** Gaylord Perry, S.D., 21.
**ERA:** Craig Swan, N.Y., 2.43.
**CG:** Phil Niekro, Atl., 22.
**IP:** Phil Niekro, Atl., 334.1.
**SO:** J.R. Richard, Hou., 303.
**SV:** Rollie Fingers, S.D., 37.

**A.L. 20-game winners**
Ron Guidry, N.Y., 25-3
Mike Caldwell, Mil., 22-9
Jim Palmer, Bal., 21-12
Dennis Leonard, K.C., 21-17
Dennis Eckersley, Bos., 20-8
Ed Figueroa, N.Y., 20-9

**N.L. 20-game winners**
Gaylord Perry, S.D., 21-6
Ross Grimsley, Mon., 20-11

**A.L. 100 RBIs**
Jim Rice, Bos., 139
Rusty Staub, Det., 121
Larry Hisle, Mil., 115
Andre Thornton, Cle., 105

**N.L. 100 RBIs**
George Foster, Cin., 120
Dave Parker, Pit., 117
Steve Garvey, L.A., 113
Greg Luzinski, Phil., 101

**A.L. 40 homers**
Jim Rice, Bos., 46

**N.L. 40 homers**
George Foster, Cin., 40

**Most Valuable Player**
A.L.: Jim Rice, OF, Bos.
N.L.: Dave Parker, OF, Pit.

**Cy Young Award**
A.L.: Ron Guidry, N.Y.
N.L.: Gaylord Perry, S.D.

**Rookie of the Year**
A.L.: Lou Whitaker, 2B, Det.
N.L.: Bob Horner, 3B, Atl.

**Hall of Fame additions**
Addie Joss, P, 1902-10
Larry MacPhail, executive
Eddie Mathews, 3B, 1952-68

## ALL-STAR GAME

■ **Winner:** The N.L. varied its approach, spotting the A.L. a 3-0 lead before roaring to its seventh straight All-Star victory.

■ **Key inning:** The eighth, when the N.L. broke a 3-3 deadlock with four runs. The tie-breaker scored on a Goose Gossage wild pitch and two more came home on Bob Boone's single.

■ **Memorable moment:** A stunning third-inning collapse by A.L. starting pitcher Jim Palmer, who issued consecutive two-out walks to Joe Morgan, George Foster and Greg Luzinski to force in a run and then gave up a game-tying, two-run single to Steve Garvey.

■ **Top guns:** Bruce Sutter (Cubs), Garvey (Dodgers), Boone (Phillies), N.L.; Lary Sorensen (Brewers), George Brett (Royals), Rod Carew (Twins), A.L.

■ **MVP:** Garvey.

**Linescore**
July 11, at San Diego Stadium
A.L. ............2 0 1 0 0 0 0 0 0—3 8 1
N.L. ............0 0 3 0 0 0 0 4 x—7 10 0
Palmer (Orioles), Keough (Athletics) 3, Sorensen (Brewers) 4, Kern (Indians) 7, Guidry (Yankees) 7, Gossage (Yankees) 8; Blue (Giants), Rogers (Expos) 4, Fingers (Padres) 6, Sutter (Cubs) 8, Niekro (Braves) 9. W—Sutter. L—Gossage.

## ALCS

■ **Winner:** The Yankees, extended to the limit by the Royals in 1976 and '77, needed only four games to claim their third consecutive A.L. pennant.

■ **Turning point:** Yankee catcher Thurman Munson's two-run, eighth-inning home run off Royals reliever Doug Bird in Game 3. The shot turned a 5-4 New York deficit into a 6-5 victory.

■ **Memorable moment:** The three-home run performance of Kansas City's George Brett in the pivotal third game. Brett's three solo shots off Yankee ace Catfish Hunter were wasted.

■ **Top guns:** Reggie Jackson (.462, 2 HR, 6 RBIs), Mickey Rivers (.455), Chris Chambliss (.400), Yankees; Amos Otis (.429), Brett (.389, 3 HR), Royals.

■ **MVP:** Munson.

**Linescores**

**Game 1**—October 3, at Kansas City
N.Y. ............0 1 1 0 2 0 0 3 0—7 16 0
K.C. ............0 0 0 0 0 1 0 0 0—1 2 2
Beattie, Clay (6); Leonard, Mingori (5), Hrabosky (8), Bird (9). W—Beattie. L—Leonard. S—Clay. HR—Jackson (N.Y.).

**Game 2**—October 4, at Kansas City
N.Y. ..........0 0 0 0 0 0 2 2 0— 4 12 1
K.C. ..........1 4 0 0 0 0 3 2 0—10 16 1
Figueroa, Tidrow (2), Lyle (7); Gura, Pattin (7), Hrabosky (8). W—Gura. L—Figueroa. HR—Patek (K.C.).

**Game 3**—October 6, at New York
K.C. ............1 0 1 0 1 0 0 2 0—5 10 1
N.Y. ............0 1 0 2 0 1 0 2 x—6 10 0
Splittorff, Bird (8), Hrabosky (8); Hunter, Gossage (7). W—Gossage. L—Bird. \HR—Brett 3 (K.C.); Jackson, Munson (N.Y.).

**Game 4**—October 7, at New York
K.C. ..............1 0 0 0 0 0 0 0 0—1 7 0
N.Y. ..............0 1 0 0 0 1 0 0 x—2 4 0
Leonard; Guidry, Gossage (9). W—Guidry. L—Leonard. S—Gossage. HR—Nettles, R. White (N.Y.).

## NLCS

■ **Winner:** Los Angeles earned its second consecutive pennant and handed Philadelphia its third straight NLCS defeat.

■ **Turning point:** The first inning of Game 4, when the Phillies loaded the bases against Dodgers starter Doug Rau with nobody out—and failed to score.

■ **Memorable moment:** The two-out, 10th-inning line drive that sure-handed Phillies center fielder Garry Maddox dropped. Dodger shortstop Bill Russell followed with a game- and series-winning single.

■ **Top guns:** Tommy John (1-0, 0.00 ERA), Dusty Baker (.467), Russell (.412), Steve Garvey (.389, 4 HR, 7 RBIs), Dodgers; Ted Sizemore (.385), Greg Luzinski (.375, 2 HR), Phillies.

■ **MVP:** Garvey.

**Linescores**

**Game 1**—October 4, at Philadelphia
L.A. ............0 0 4 2 1 1 0 0 1—9 13 1
Phil. ..........0 1 0 0 3 0 0 0 1—5 12 1
Hooton, Welch (5); Christenson, Brusstar (5), Eastwick (6), McGraw (7). W—Welch. L—Christenson. HR—Garvey 2, Lopes, Yeager (L.A.); Martin (Phil.).

**Game 2**—October 5, at Philadelphia
L.A. ..............0 0 0 1 2 0 1 0 0—4 8 0
Phil. ............0 0 0 0 0 0 0 0 0—0 4 0
John; Ruthven, Brusstar (5), Reed (7), McGraw (9). W—John. L—Ruthven. HR—Lopes (L.A.).

**Game 3**—October 6, at Los Angeles
Phil. ..........0 4 0 0 0 3 1 0 1—9 11 1
L.A. ............0 1 2 0 0 0 0 1 0—4 8 2
Carlton; Sutton, Rautzhan (6), Hough (8). W—Carlton. L—Sutton. HR—Carlton, Luzinski (Phil.); Garvey (L.A.).

**Game 4**—October 7, at Los Angeles
Phil. ......0 0 2 0 0 0 1 0 0 0—3 8 2
L.A. .........0 1 0 1 0 1 0 0 0 1—4 13 0
Lerch, Brusstar (6), Reed (7), McGraw (9); Rau, Rhoden (6), Forster (10). W—Forster. L—McGraw. HR—Luzinski, McBride (Phil.); Cey, Garvey (L.A.).

## WORLD SERIES

■ **Winner:** The Yankees became the first team to win a six-game Series after losing the first two games. The Dodgers became their Series victim for the eighth time.

■ **Turning point:** A 10th-inning RBI single by Lou Piniella that gave the Yankees a 4-3 Game 4 victory and tied the Series at two games.

■ **Memorable moment:** A Bob Welch-Reggie Jackson battle in Game 2. With the Dodgers leading 4-3 and two out in the ninth, Dodger rookie Welch needed nine pitches to strike out Yankee slugger Jackson in a classic duel with two men on base.

■ **Top guns:** Denny Doyle (.438), Bucky Dent (.417, 7 RBIs), Jackson (.391, 2 HR, 8 RBIs), Yankees; Bill Russell (.423), Dave Lopes (3 HR, 7 RBIs), Dodgers.

■ **MVP:** Dent.

**Linescores**

**Game 1**—October 10, at Los Angeles
N.Y. ..........0 0 0 0 0 0 3 2 0— 5 9 1
L.A. ..........0 3 0 3 1 0 3 1 x—11 15 2
Figueroa, Clay (2), Lindblad (5), Tidrow (7); John, Forster (8). W—John. L—Figueroa. HR—Jackson (N.Y.); Baker, Lopes 2 (L.A.).

**Game 2**—October 11, at Los Angeles
N.Y. ............0 0 2 0 0 0 1 0 0—3 11 0
L.A. ............0 0 0 1 0 3 0 0 x—4 7 0
Hunter, Gossage (7); Hooton, Forster (7), Welch (9). W—Hooton. L—Hunter. S—Welch. HR—Cey (L.A.).

**Game 3**—October 13, at New York
L.A. ............0 0 1 0 0 0 0 0 0—1 8 0
N.Y. ............1 1 0 0 0 0 3 0 x—5 10 1
Sutton, Rautzhan (7), Hough (8); Guidry. W—Guidry. L—Sutton. HR—White (N.Y.).

**Game 4**—October 14, at New York
L.A. ..........0 0 0 0 3 0 0 0 0 0—3 6 1
N.Y. ..........0 0 0 0 0 2 0 1 0 1—4 9 0
John, Forster (8), Welch (8); Figueroa, Tidrow (6), Gossage (9). W—Gossage. L—Welch. HR—Smith (L.A.).

**Game 5**—October 15, at New York
L.A. ..........1 0 1 0 0 0 0 0 0— 2 9 3
N.Y. ..........0 0 4 3 0 0 4 1 x—12 18 0
Hooton, Rautzhan (3), Hough (4); Beattie. W—Beattie. L—Hooton.

**Game 6**—October 17, at Los Angeles
N.Y. ............0 3 0 0 0 2 2 0 0—7 11 0
L.A. ............1 0 1 0 0 0 0 0 0—2 7 1
Hunter, Gossage (8); Sutton, Welch (6), Rau (8). W—Hunter. L—Sutton. HR—Lopes (L.A.); Jackson (N.Y.).

# 1979

## FINAL STANDINGS

### American League

**East Division**

| Team | Bal. | Mil. | Bos. | N.Y. | Det. | Cle. | Tor. | Cal. | Chi. | K.C. | Min. | Oak. | Sea. | Tex. | W | L | Pct. | GB |
|---|---|---|---|---|---|---|---|---|---|---|---|---|---|---|---|---|---|---|
| Baltimore | ... | 8 | 8 | 5 | 7 | 8 | 11 | 9 | 8 | 6 | 8 | 8 | 10 | 6 | 102 | 57 | .642 | ... |
| Milwaukee | 5 | ... | 4 | 9 | 7 | 9 | 10 | 5 | 7 | 7 | 8 | 6 | 9 | 9 | 95 | 66 | .590 | 8 |
| Boston | 5 | 8 | ... | 5 | 8 | 6 | 9 | 5 | 5 | 8 | 9 | 9 | 8 | 6 | 91 | 69 | .569 | 11.5 |
| New York | 6 | 4 | 8 | ... | 6 | 8 | 9 | 5 | 8 | 7 | 5 | 9 | 6 | 8 | 89 | 71 | .556 | 13.5 |
| Detroit | 6 | 6 | 5 | 7 | ... | 6 | 9 | 8 | 9 | 5 | 4 | 7 | 7 | 6 | 85 | 76 | .528 | 18 |
| Cleveland | 5 | 4 | 7 | 5 | 6 | ... | 8 | 6 | 6 | 6 | 8 | 8 | 7 | 5 | 81 | 80 | .503 | 22 |
| Toronto | 2 | 3 | 4 | 4 | 4 | 5 | ... | 5 | 5 | 3 | 1 | 8 | 4 | 5 | 53 | 109 | .327 | 50.5 |

**West Division**

| Team | Cal. | K.C. | Tex. | Min. | Chi. | Sea. | Oak. | Bal. | Bos. | Cle. | Det. | Mil. | N.Y. | Tor. | W | L | Pct. | GB |
|---|---|---|---|---|---|---|---|---|---|---|---|---|---|---|---|---|---|---|
| California | | 7 | 5 | 9 | 9 | 7 | 10 | 3 | 7 | 6 | 4 | 7 | 7 | 7 | 88 | 74 | .543 | |
| Kansas City | 6 | ... | 6 | 7 | 8 | 7 | 9 | 6 | 4 | 6 | 7 | 5 | 5 | 9 | 85 | 77 | .525 | 3 |
| Texas | 8 | 7 | ... | 9 | 2 | 7 | 11 | 6 | 6 | 7 | 6 | 3 | 4 | 7 | 83 | 79 | .512 | 5 |
| Minnesota | 4 | 6 | 4 | ... | 8 | 10 | 9 | 4 | 3 | 4 | 8 | 4 | 7 | 11 | 82 | 80 | .506 | 6 |
| Chicago | 4 | 5 | 11 | 5 | ... | 5 | 9 | 3 | 6 | 6 | 3 | 5 | 4 | 7 | 73 | 87 | .456 | 14 |
| Seattle | 6 | 6 | 6 | 3 | 8 | ... | 5 | 2 | 4 | 5 | 5 | 3 | 6 | 8 | 67 | 95 | .414 | 21 |
| Oakland | 3 | 4 | 2 | 4 | 4 | 8 | ... | 4 | 3 | 4 | 5 | 6 | 3 | 4 | 54 | 108 | .333 | 34 |

### National League

**East Division**

| Team | Pit. | Mon. | St.L. | Phi. | Chi. | N.Y. | Atl. | Cin. | Hou. | L.A. | S.D. | S.F. | W | L | Pct. | GB |
|---|---|---|---|---|---|---|---|---|---|---|---|---|---|---|---|---|
| Pittsburgh | ... | 11 | 11 | 10 | 12 | 10 | 8 | 4 | 8 | 8 | 7 | 9 | 98 | 64 | .605 | ... |
| Montreal | 7 | ... | 10 | 11 | 12 | 15 | 9 | 6 | 5 | 6 | 7 | 7 | 95 | 65 | .594 | 2 |
| St. Louis | 7 | 8 | ... | 11 | 10 | 11 | 8 | 4 | 6 | 6 | 8 | 7 | 86 | 76 | .531 | 12 |
| Philadelphia | 8 | 7 | 7 | ... | 9 | 13 | 5 | 4 | 7 | 9 | 9 | 6 | 84 | 78 | .519 | 14 |
| Chicago | 6 | 6 | 8 | 9 | ... | 8 | 8 | 7 | 6 | 5 | 9 | 8 | 80 | 82 | .494 | 18 |
| New York | 8 | 3 | 7 | 5 | 10 | ... | 8 | 4 | 3 | 3 | 4 | 8 | 63 | 99 | .389 | 35 |

**West Division**

| Team | Cin. | Hou. | L.A. | S.F. | S.D. | Atl. | Chi. | Mon. | N.Y. | Phi. | Pit. | St.L. | W | L | Pct. | GB |
|---|---|---|---|---|---|---|---|---|---|---|---|---|---|---|---|---|
| Cincinnati | ... | 8 | 11 | 6 | 10 | 12 | 5 | 6 | 8 | 8 | 8 | 8 | 90 | 71 | .559 | ... |
| Houston | 10 | ... | 10 | 7 | 14 | 11 | 6 | 7 | 9 | 5 | 4 | 6 | 89 | 73 | .549 | 1.5 |
| Los Angeles | 7 | 8 | ... | 14 | 9 | 6 | 7 | 6 | 9 | 3 | 4 | 6 | 79 | 83 | .488 | 11.5 |
| San Fran. | 12 | 11 | 4 | ... | 10 | 7 | 4 | 5 | 4 | 6 | 3 | 5 | 71 | 91 | .438 | 19.5 |
| San Diego | 7 | 4 | 9 | 8 | ... | 12 | 3 | 5 | 8 | 3 | 5 | 4 | 68 | 93 | .422 | 22 |
| Atlanta | 6 | 7 | 12 | 11 | 6 | ... | 4 | 1 | 4 | 7 | 4 | 4 | 66 | 94 | .413 | 23.5 |

## SIGNIFICANT EVENTS

■ **May 19:** Major League umpires returned to work after a six-week strike that forced baseball to play its games with amateur and minor league arbiters.

■ **July 12:** Bill Veeck's "Disco Demolition Night" promotion turned into Comiskey Park bedlam when fans refused to leave the field, and the White Sox were forced to forfeit the second game of a doubleheader to Detroit.

■ **August 2:** Yankee catcher Thurman Munson, the 1976 A.L. MVP, died at age 32 when the plane he was flying crashed short of the runway at the Akron-Canton Airport in Ohio.

■ **October 29:** Willie Mays was banned from baseball after accepting a job with a corporation that operates gambling casinos.

■ **November 13:** The N.L. crowned baseball's first co-MVPs—Pittsburgh's Willie Stargell and St. Louis' Keith Hernandez.

## MEMORABLE MOMENTS

■ **May 17:** The Phillies beat the Cubs, 23-22, in an 11-homer, 50-hit slugfest at wind-swept Wrigley Field.

■ **August 13, September 12:** St. Louis' Lou Brock and Boston's Carl Yastrzemski became baseball's 14th and 15th 3,000-hit men in games against the Cubs and Yankees.

■ **September 23:** Brock stole his 938th and final base in a 7-4 victory over the Mets, moving past Billy Hamilton into first place on the all-time list.

## LEADERS

**American League**
**BA:** Fred Lynn, Bos., .333.
**Runs:** Don Baylor, Cal., 120.
**Hits:** George Brett, K.C., 212.
**TB:** Jim Rice, Bos., 369.
**HR:** Gorman Thomas, Mil., 45.
**RBI:** Don Baylor, Cal., 139.
**SB:** Willie Wilson, K.C., 83.
**Wins:** Mike Flanagan, Bal., 23.
**ERA:** Ron Guidry, N.Y., 2.78.
**CG:** Dennis Martinez, Bal., 18.
**IP:** Dennis Martinez, Bal., 292.1.
**SO:** Nolan Ryan, Cal., 223.
**SV:** Mike Marshall, Min., 32.

**National League**
**BA:** Keith Hernandez, St.L., .344.
**Runs:** Keith Hernandez, St.L., 116.
**Hits:** Garry Templeton, St.L., 211.
**TB:** Dave Winfield, S.D., 333.
**HR:** Dave Kingman, Chi., 48.
**RBI:** Dave Winfield, S.D., 118.
**SB:** Omar Moreno, Pit., 77.
**Wins:** Joe Niekro, Hou.; Phil Niekro, Atl., 21.
**ERA:** J.R. Richard, Hou., 2.71.
**CG:** Phil Niekro, Atl., 23.
**IP:** Phil Niekro, Atl., 342.
**SO:** J.R. Richard, Hou., 313.
**SV:** Bruce Sutter, Chi., 37.

**A.L. 20-game winners**
Mike Flanagan, Bal., 23-9
Tommy John, N.Y., 21-9
Jerry Koosman, Min., 20-13

**N.L. 20-game winners**
Joe Niekro, Hou., 21-11
Phil Niekro, Atl., 21-20

**A.L. 100 RBIs**
Don Baylor, Cal., 139
Jim Rice, Bos., 130
Gorman Thomas, Mil., 123
Fred Lynn, Bos., 122
Darrell Porter, K.C., 112
Ken Singleton, Bal., 111
George Brett, K.C., 107
Cecil Cooper, Mil., 106
Willie Horton, Sea., 106
Steve Kemp, Det., 105
Buddy Bell, Tex., 101
Dan Ford, Cal., 101
Bobby Grich, Cal., 101
Sixto Lezcano, Mil., 101
Bruce Bochte, Sea., 100

**N.L. 100 RBIs**
Dave Winfield, S.D., 118
Dave Kingman, Chi., 115
Mike Schmidt, Phil., 114
Steve Garvey, L.A., 110
Keith Hernandez, St.L., 105

**A.L. 40 homers**
Gorman Thomas, Mil., 45

**N.L. 40 homers**
Dave Kingman, Chi., 48
Mike Schmidt, Phil., 45

**Most Valuable Player**
A.L.: Don Baylor, OF, Cal.
N.L.: Willie Stargell, 1B, Pit.
Keith Hernandez, 1B, St.L.

**Cy Young Award**
A.L.: Mike Flanagan, Bal.
N.L.: Bruce Sutter, Chi.

**Rookie of the Year**
A.L.: John Castino, 3B, Min.
Alfredo Griffin, SS, Tor.
N.L.: Rick Sutcliffe, P, L.A.

**Hall of Fame additions**
Warren Giles, executive
Willie Mays, OF, 1951-73
Hack Wilson, OF, 1923-34

## ALL-STAR GAME

■ **Winner:** Lee Mazzilli tied the game with an eighth-inning homer and drove in the winner in the ninth with a bases-loaded walk as the N.L. recorded a 7-6 victory in the 50th All-Star Game.

■ **Key innings:** The eighth, when Mazzilli erased a 6-5 deficit with an opposite-field blast, and the ninth, when he drew a base on balls off Ron Guidry after Jim Kern had walked the bases loaded.

■ **Memorable moments:** Game-saving seventh- and eighth-inning throws by right fielder Dave Parker that cut down A.L. runners at third base and home plate.

■ **Top guns:** Steve Rogers (Expos), Mazzilli (Mets), Mike Schmidt (Phillies), Parker (Pirates), N.L.; Fred Lynn (Red Sox), Don Baylor (Angels), Carl Yastrzemski (Red Sox), A.L.

■ **MVP:** Parker.

**Linescore**
July 17, at Seattle's Kingdome
N.L. ............2 1 1 0 0 1 0 1 1—7 10 1
A.L. ............3 0 2 0 0 1 0 0 0—6 10 0
Carlton (Phillies), Andujar (Astros) 2, Rogers (Expos) 4, Perry (Padres) 6, Sambito (Astros) 6, LaCoss (Reds) 6, Sutter (Cubs) 8; Ryan (Angels), Stanley (Red Sox) 3, Clear (Angels) 5, Kern (Rangers) 7, Guidry (Yankees) 9. W—Sutter. L—Kern. HR—Lynn, A.L.; Mazzilli, N.L.

## ALCS

■ **Winner:** Baltimore, winner of the first three A.L. Championship Series, ruined California's first experience in the post-season spotlight.

■ **Turning point:** A dramatic three-run homer by Baltimore pinch-hitter John Lowenstein in the 10th inning of Game 1. Lowenstein's opposite-field shot broke a 3-3 deadlock and propelled the Orioles to their first pennant since 1971.

■ **Memorable moment:** A dramatic defensive play by Orioles third baseman Doug DeCinces. With one out and the bases loaded in the fifth inning of Game 4, DeCinces made a diving stop of Jim Anderson's shot down the third-base line, stepped on third and fired to first for a rally-killing double play that preserved a 3-0 lead.

■ **Top guns:** Scott McGregor (1-0, 0.00 ERA), Eddie Murray (.417, 5 RBIs), Rick Dempsey (.400), Orioles; Rod Carew (.412), Dan Ford (2 HR, 4 RBIs), Angels.

■ **MVP:** Murray.

**Linescores**

**Game 1**—October 3, at Baltimore
Cal. ..........1 0 1 0 0 1 0 0 0 0—3 7 1
Balt. .........0 0 2 1 0 0 0 0 0 3—6 6 0
Ryan, Montague (8); Palmer, Stanhouse (10). W—Stanhouse. L—Montague. HR—Ford (Cal.); Lowenstein (Bal.).

**Game 2**—October 4, at Baltimore
Cal. ..................1 0 0 0 0 1 1 3 2—8 10 1
Balt. .................4 4 1 0 0 0 0 0 x—9 11 1
Frost, Clear (2), Aase (8); Flanagan, Stanhouse (8). W—Flanagan. L—Frost. HR—Ford (Cal.); Murray (Bal.).

**Game 3**—October 5, at California
Balt. ............0 0 0 1 0 1 1 0 0—3 8 3
Cal. .............1 0 0 1 0 0 0 0 2—4 9 0
D. Martinez, Stanhouse (9); Tanana, Aase (6). W—Aase. L—Stanhouse. HR—Baylor (Cal.).

**Game 4**—October 6, at California
Balt. ..........0 0 2 1 0 0 5 0 0—8 12 1
Cal. ...........0 0 0 0 0 0 0 0 0—0 6 0
McGregor; Knapp, LaRoche (3), Frost (4), Montague (7), Barlow (9). W—McGregor. L—Knapp. HR—Kelly (Bal.).

## NLCS

■ **Winner:** Pittsburgh, which had been swept by Cincinnati in the 1970 and '75 NLCS, turned the tables on the Reds and earned its first World Series berth since 1971.

■ **Turning point:** A 10th-inning single by Dave Parker that gave the Pirates a 3-2 victory in Game 2.

■ **Memorable moment:** Willie Stargell's three-run, 11th-inning home run, which gave the Pirates a 5-2 Game 1 victory and all the momentum they needed.

■ **Top guns:** Stargell (.455, 2 HR, 6 RBIs), Phil Garner (.417), Pirates; Dave Concepcion (.429), Reds.

■ **MVP:** Stargell.

**Linescores**

**Game 1**—October 2, at Cincinnati
Pitt. ..........0 0 2 0 0 0 0 0 0 0 3—5 10 0
Cin. ..........0 0 0 2 0 0 0 0 0 0 0—2 7 0
Candelaria, Romo (8), Tekulve (8), Jackson (10), D. Robinson (11); Seaver, Hume (9), Tomlin (11). W—Jackson. L—Hume. S—D. Robinson. HR—Garner, Stargell (Pit); Foster (Cin.).

**Game 2**—October 3, at Cincinnati
Pitt.........0 0 0 1 1 0 0 0 0 1—3 11 0
Cin. .........0 1 0 0 0 0 0 0 1 0—2 8 0
Bibby, Jackson (8), Romo (8), Tekulve (8), Roberts (9), D. Robinson (9); Pastore, Tomlin (8), Hume (8), Bair (10). W—D. Robinson. L—Bair.

**Game 3**—October 5, at Pittsburgh
Cin. ..............0 0 0 0 0 1 0 0 0—1 8 1
Pitt. ..............1 1 2 2 0 0 0 1 x—7 7 0
LaCoss, Norman (2), Leibrandt (4), Soto (5), Tomlin (7), Hume (8); Blyleven. W—Blyleven. L—LaCoss. HR—Stargell, Madlock (Pit.); Bench (Cin.).

## WORLD SERIES

■ **Winner:** Pittsburgh's "Family" beat the Orioles and became the fourth team to recover from a three-games-to-one deficit.

■ **Turning point:** After blowing a 6-3, eighth-inning lead in Game 4 to fall within a game of elimination, the Pirates regrouped to win Game 5, 7-1, behind the six-hit pitching of Jim Rooker and Bert Blyleven.

■ **Memorable moment:** Willie Stargell's two-run, sixth-inning homer that put the Pirates ahead to stay in a 4-1 Series-ending victory.

■ **Top guns:** Phil Garner (.500, 12 hits), Stargell (.400, 12 hits, 3 HR, 7 RBIs), Bill Madlock (.375), Pirates; Kiko Garcia (.400, 6 RBIs), Orioles.

■ **MVP:** Stargell.

**Linescores**

**Game 1**—October 10, at Baltimore
Pitt. ............0 0 0 1 0 2 0 1 0—4 11 3
Balt. ..........5 0 0 0 0 0 0 0 x—5 6 3
Kison, Rooker (1), Romo (5), D. Robinson (6), Jackson (8); Flanagan. W—Flanagan. L—Kison. HR—DeCinces (Bal.); Stargell (Pit.).

**Game 2**—October 11, at Baltimore
Pitt. ............0 2 0 0 0 0 0 0 1—3 11 2
Balt. ..........0 1 0 0 0 1 0 0 0—2 6 1
Blyleven, D. Robinson (7), Tekulve (9); Palmer, T. Martinez (8), Stanhouse (9). W—D. Robinson. L—Stanhouse. S—Tekulve. HR—Murray (Bal.).

**Game 3**—October 12, at Pittsburgh
Balt. ..........0 0 2 5 0 0 1 0 0—8 13 0
Pitt. ............1 2 0 0 0 1 0 0 0—4 9 2
McGregor; Candelaria, Romo (4), Jackson (7), Tekulve (8). W—McGregor. L—Candelaria. HR—Ayala (Bal.).

**Game 4**—October 13, at Pittsburgh
Balt. ..........0 0 3 0 0 0 0 6 0—9 12 0
Pitt. ............0 4 0 0 1 1 0 0 0—6 17 1
D. Martinez, Stewart (2), Stone (5), Stoddard (7); Bibby, Jackson (7), D. Robinson (8), Tekulve (8). W—Stoddard. L—Tekulve. HR—Stargell (Pit.).

**Game 5**—October 14, at Pittsburgh
Balt. ..........0 0 0 0 1 0 0 0 0—1 6 2
Pitt. ............0 0 0 0 0 2 2 3 x—7 13 1
Flanagan, Stoddard (7), T. Martinez (7), Stanhouse (8); Rooker, Blyleven (6). W—Blyleven. L—Flanagan.

**Game 6**—October 16, at Baltimore
Pitt. ............0 0 0 0 0 0 2 2 0—4 10 0
Balt. ..........0 0 0 0 0 0 0 0 0—0 7 1
Candelaria, Tekulve (7); Palmer, Stoddard (9). W—Candelaria. L—Palmer. S—Tekulve.

**Game 7**—October 17, at Baltimore
Pitt. ............0 0 0 0 0 2 0 0 2—4 10 0
Balt. ..........0 0 1 0 0 0 0 0 0—1 4 2
Bibby, D. Robinson (5), Jackson (5), Tekulve (8); McGregor, Stoddard (9), Flanagan (9), Stanhouse (9), T. Martinez (9), D. Martinez (9). W—Jackson. L—McGregor. S—Tekulve. HR—Dauer (Bal.); Stargell (Pit.).

# 1980

## FINAL STANDINGS

### American League

**East Division**

| Team | N.Y. | Bal. | Mil. | Bos. | Det. | Cle. | Tor. | Cal. | Chi. | K.C. | Min. | Oak. | Sea. | Tex. | W | L | Pct. | GB |
|---|---|---|---|---|---|---|---|---|---|---|---|---|---|---|---|---|---|---|
| New York | ... | 6 | 8 | 10 | 8 | 8 | 10 | 10 | 7 | 4 | 8 | 8 | 9 | 7 | 103 | 59 | .636 | ... |
| Baltimore | 7 | ... | 7 | 8 | 10 | 6 | 11 | 10 | 6 | 6 | 10 | 7 | 6 | 6 | 100 | 62 | .617 | 3 |
| Milwaukee | 5 | 6 | ... | 7 | 6 | 10 | 5 | 6 | 7 | 6 | 7 | 7 | 9 | 5 | 86 | 76 | .531 | 17 |
| Boston | 3 | 5 | 6 | ... | 8 | 7 | 7 | 9 | 6 | 5 | 6 | 9 | 7 | 5 | 83 | 77 | .519 | 19 |
| Detroit | 5 | 3 | 7 | 5 | ... | 10 | 9 | 7 | 10 | 2 | 6 | 6 | 10 | 4 | 84 | 78 | .519 | 19 |
| Cleveland | 5 | 7 | 3 | 6 | 3 | ... | 8 | 6 | 7 | 5 | 9 | 6 | 8 | 6 | 79 | 81 | .494 | 23 |
| Toronto | 3 | 2 | 8 | 6 | 4 | 5 | ... | 9 | 7 | 3 | 5 | 4 | 6 | 5 | 67 | 95 | .414 | 36 |

**West Division**

| Team | K.C. | Oak. | Min. | Tex. | Chi. | Cal. | Sea. | Bal. | Bos. | Cle. | Det. | Mil. | N.Y. | Tor. | W | L | Pct. | GB |
|---|---|---|---|---|---|---|---|---|---|---|---|---|---|---|---|---|---|---|
| Kansas City | ... | 6 | 5 | 10 | 8 | 8 | 7 | 6 | 7 | 7 | 10 | 6 | 8 | 9 | 97 | 65 | .599 | ... |
| Oakland | 7 | ... | 7 | 7 | 7 | 10 | 8 | 5 | 3 | 6 | 6 | 5 | 4 | 8 | 83 | 79 | .512 | 14 |
| Minnesota | 8 | 6 | ... | 9 | 8 | 6 | 7 | 2 | 6 | 3 | 6 | 5 | 4 | 7 | 77 | 84 | .478 | 19.5 |
| Texas | 3 | 6 | 3 | ... | 7 | 2 | 9 | 6 | 7 | 6 | 8 | 7 | 5 | 7 | 76 | 85 | .472 | 20.5 |
| Chicago | 5 | 6 | 5 | 6 | ... | 10 | 6 | 6 | 4 | 5 | 2 | 5 | 5 | 5 | 70 | 90 | .438 | 26 |
| California | 5 | 3 | 7 | 11 | 3 | ... | 11 | 2 | 3 | 4 | 5 | 6 | 2 | 3 | 65 | 95 | .406 | 31 |
| Seattle | 6 | 5 | 6 | 4 | 7 | 2 | ... | 6 | 5 | 4 | 2 | 3 | 3 | 6 | 59 | 103 | .364 | 38 |

### National League

**East Division**

| Team | Phi. | Mon. | Pit. | St.L. | N.Y. | Chi. | Atl. | Cin. | Hou. | L.A. | S.D. | S.F. | W | L | Pct. | GB |
|---|---|---|---|---|---|---|---|---|---|---|---|---|---|---|---|---|
| Philadelphia | ... | 9 | 7 | 9 | 12 | 13 | 7 | 5 | 9 | 6 | 8 | 6 | 91 | 71 | .562 | ... |
| Montreal | 9 | ... | 6 | 12 | 10 | 12 | 7 | 9 | 7 | 1 | 10 | 7 | 90 | 72 | .556 | 1 |
| Pittsburgh | 11 | 12 | ... | 10 | 8 | 10 | 1 | 6 | 5 | 6 | 6 | 8 | 83 | 79 | .512 | 8 |
| St. Louis | 9 | 6 | 8 | ... | 9 | 9 | 6 | 7 | 5 | 5 | 5 | 5 | 74 | 88 | .457 | 17 |
| New York | 6 | 8 | 10 | 9 | ... | 8 | 9 | 4 | 4 | 5 | 1 | 3 | 67 | 95 | .414 | 24 |
| Chicago | 5 | 6 | 8 | 9 | 10 | ... | 4 | 7 | 1 | 5 | 4 | 5 | 64 | 98 | .395 | 27 |

**West Division**

| Team | Hou. | L.A. | Cin. | Atl. | S.F. | S.D. | Chi. | Mon. | N.Y. | Phi. | Pit. | St.L. | W | L | Pct. | GB |
|---|---|---|---|---|---|---|---|---|---|---|---|---|---|---|---|---|
| Houston | ... | 9 | 10 | 11 | 11 | 11 | 11 | 5 | 8 | 3 | 7 | 7 | 93 | 70 | .571 | ... |
| Los Angeles | 10 | ... | 9 | 7 | 13 | 9 | 7 | 11 | 7 | 6 | 6 | 7 | 92 | 71 | .564 | 1 |
| Cincinnati | 8 | 9 | ... | 16 | 7 | 15 | 5 | 3 | 8 | 7 | 6 | 5 | 89 | 73 | .549 | 3.5 |
| Atlanta | 7 | 11 | 2 | ... | 11 | 12 | 8 | 5 | 3 | 5 | 11 | 6 | 81 | 80 | .503 | 11 |
| San Fran. | 7 | 5 | 11 | 6 | ... | 8 | 7 | 5 | 9 | 6 | 4 | 7 | 75 | 86 | .466 | 17 |
| San Diego | 7 | 9 | 3 | 6 | 10 | ... | 8 | 2 | 11 | 4 | 6 | 7 | 73 | 89 | .451 | 19.5 |

## SIGNIFICANT EVENTS

■ **January 24:** Nelson Doubleday and Fred Wilpon headed a group that bought the New York Mets for a reported $21.1 million.

■ **May 23:** The owners and players agreed to defer settlement of the free-agent compensation issue, thus avoiding the first in-season player walkout in baseball history.

■ **July 30:** Houston ace J.R. Richard was rushed to the hospital after suffering a career-ending stroke during a light workout at the Astrodome.

■ **November 18:** Kansas City's George Brett, who finished the season with the highest average (.390) since 1941, captured A.L. MVP honors.

## MEMORABLE MOMENTS

■ **September 30:** Oakland's Rickey Henderson, en route to the A.L.'s first 100-steal season, passed Ty Cobb's A.L. record of 96 in a 5-1 victory over Chicago.

■ **October 6:** The Astros, who allowed the Dodgers to force a division playoff with a three-game season-closing sweep, rebounded to win their first N.L. West title with a 7-1 victory.

## LEADERS

**American League**
**BA:** George Brett, K.C., .390.
**Runs:** Willie Wilson, K.C., 133.
**Hits:** Willie Wilson, K.C., 230.
**TB:** Cecil Cooper, Mil., 335.
**HR:** Reggie Jackson, N.Y.; Ben Oglivie, Mil., 41.
**RBI:** Cecil Cooper, Mil., 122.
**SB:** Rickey Henderson, Oak., 100.
**Wins:** Steve Stone, Bal., 25.
**ERA:** Rudy May, N.Y., 2.46.
**CG:** Rick Langford, Oak., 28.
**IP:** Rick Langford, Oak., 290.
**SO:** Len Barker, Cle., 187.
**SV:** Goose Gossage, N.Y.; Dan Quisenberry, K.C., 33.

**National League**
**BA:** Bill Buckner, Chi., .324.
**Runs:** Keith Hernandez, St.L., 111.
**Hits:** Steve Garvey, L.A., 200.
**TB:** Mike Schmidt, Phil., 342.
**HR:** Mike Schmidt, Phil., 48.
**RBI:** Mike Schmidt, Phil., 121.
**SB:** Ron LeFlore, Mon., 97.
**Wins:** Steve Carlton, Phil., 24.
**ERA:** Don Sutton, L.A., 2.20.
**CG:** Steve Rogers, Mon., 14.
**IP:** Steve Carlton, Phil., 304.
**SO:** Steve Carlton, Phil., 286.
**SV:** Bruce Sutter, Chi., 28.

**A.L. 20-game winners**
Steve Stone, Bal., 25-7
Tommy John, N.Y., 22-9
Mike Norris, Oak., 22-9
Scott McGregor, Bal., 20-8
Dennis Leonard, K.C., 20-11

**N.L. 20-game winners**
Steve Carlton, Phil., 24-9
Joe Niekro, Hou., 20-12

**A.L. 100 RBIs**
Cecil Cooper, Mil., 122
George Brett, K.C., 118
Ben Oglivie, Mil., 118
Al Oliver, Tex., 117
Eddie Murray, Bal., 116
Reggie Jackson, N.Y., 111
Tony Armas, Oak., 109
Tony Perez, Bos., 105
Gorman Thomas, Mil., 105
Ken Singleton, Bal., 104
Steve Kemp, Det., 101

**N.L. 100 RBIs**
Mike Schmidt, Phil., 121
George Hendrick, St.L., 109
Steve Garvey, L.A., 106
Gary Carter, Mon., 101

**A.L. 40 homers**
Reggie Jackson, N.Y., 41
Ben Oglivie, Mil., 41

**N.L. 40 homers**
Mike Schmidt, Phil., 48

**Most Valuable Player**
A.L.: George Brett, 3B, K.C.
N.L.: Mike Schmidt, 3B, Phil.

**Cy Young Award**
A.L.: Steve Stone, Bal.
N.L.: Steve Carlton, Phil.

**Rookie of the Year**
A.L.: Joe Charboneau, OF, Cle.
N.L.: Steve Howe, P, L.A.

**Hall of Fame additions**
Al Kaline, OF, 1953-74
Chuck Klein, OF, 1928-44
Duke Snider, OF, 1947-64
Tom Yawkey, executive/owner

## ALL-STAR GAME

■ **Winner:** The N.L., held hitless for 4⅔ innings, scored the go-ahead run on a sixth-inning error and started the new decade with a 4-2 victory, its ninth straight in All-Star competition.

■ **Key inning:** The sixth, when the N.L. took a 3-2 lead on George Hendrick's single and second baseman Willie Randolph's error on a smash hit by Dave Winfield.

■ **Memorable moment:** Ken Griffey's two-out homer in the fifth. Before the solo blast, the N.L. had not even managed a baserunner against A.L. hurlers Steve Stone and Tommy John.

■ **Top guns:** J.R. Richard (Astros), Griffey (Reds), Hendrick (Cardinals), N.L.; Stone (Orioles), Rod Carew (Angels), Fred Lynn (Red Sox), A.L.

■ **MVP:** Griffey.

**Linescore**
July 8, at Los Angeles' Dodger Stadium
A.L. ..............0 0 0 0 2 0 0 0 0—2 7 2
N.L. ..............0 0 0 0 1 2 1 0 x—4 7 0
Stone (Orioles), John (Yankees) 4, Farmer (White Sox) 6, Stieb (Blue Jays) 7, Gossage (Yankees) 8; Richard (Astros), Welch (Dodgers) 3, Reuss (Dodgers) 6, Bibby (Pirates) 7, Sutter (Cubs) 8. W—Reuss. L—John. S—Sutter. HR—Lynn, A.L.; Griffey, N.L.

## ALCS

■ **Winner:** Kansas City, a Championship Series loser to the Yankees in 1976, '77 and '78, qualified for its first World Series with an impressive sweep.

■ **Turning point:** The eighth inning of Game 2, when the Royals threw out Yankee Willie Randolph at the plate, preserving a 3-2 victory. Randolph was trying to score on a two-out double by Bob Watson.

■ **Memorable moment:** A titanic three-run homer by George Brett that produced a 4-2 series-ending victory. Brett's seventh-inning blast off relief ace Goose Gossage landed in the third deck at Yankee Stadium.

■ **Top guns:** Dan Quisenberry (1-0, 1 save, 0.00 ERA), Frank White (.545), Brett (2 HR, 4 RBIs), Royals; Watson (.500), Randolph (.385), Yankees.

■ **MVP:** White.

**Linescores**

**Game 1**—October 8, at Kansas City
N.Y. ............0 2 0 0 0 0 0 0 0—2 10 1
K.C. ............0 2 2 0 0 0 1 2 x—7 10 0
Guidry, Davis (4), Underwood (8); Gura. W—Gura. L—Guidry. HR—Cerone, Piniella (N.Y.); Brett (K.C.).

**Game 2**—October 9, at Kansas City
N.Y. ..............0 0 0 0 2 0 0 0 0—2 8 0
K.C. ..............0 0 3 0 0 0 0 0 x—3 6 0
May; Leonard, Quisenberry (9). W—Leonard. L—May. S—Quisenberry. HR—Nettles (N.Y.).

**Game 3**—October 10, at New York
K.C. ............0 0 0 0 1 0 3 0 0—4 12 1
N.Y. ............0 0 0 0 0 2 0 0 0—2 8 0
Splittorff, Quisenberry (6); John, Gossage (7), Underwood (8). W—Quisenberry. L—Gossage. HR—White, Brett (K.C.).

## NLCS

■ **Winner:** Philadelphia scored in the 10th inning of Game 5 to dispatch Houston, 8-7, and qualify for its first World Series since 1950.

■ **Turning point:** A Game 4 collision in which Pete Rose bowled over Houston catcher Bruce Bochy. Rose scored the winning run on the 10th-inning play, giving the Phillies a series-tying victory.

■ **Memorable moment:** A fourth-game controversy that wiped out Houston claims of a triple play and sparked protests by both teams. The fourth-inning confusion revolved around the "catch" or "trap" of a line drive by Astros pitcher Vern Ruhle and stopped play for 20 minutes.

■ **Top guns:** Rose (.400), Manny Trillo (.381), Phillies; Joe Niekro (10 IP, 0.00 ERA), Terry Puhl (.526), Jose Cruz (.400), Astros.

■ **MVP:** Trillo.

**Linescores**

**Game 1**—October 7, at Philadelphia
Hou. ............0 0 1 0 0 0 0 0 0—1 7 0
Phil. ............0 0 0 0 0 2 1 0 x—3 8 1
Forsch; Carlton, McGraw (8). W—Carlton. L—Forsch. S—McGraw. HR—Luzinski (Phil.).

**Game 2**—October 8, at Philadelphia
Hou. ......0 0 1 0 0 0 1 1 0 4—7 8 1
Phil. ......0 0 0 2 0 0 0 1 0 1—4 14 2
Ryan, Sambito (7), D. Smith (7), LaCorte (9), Andujar (10); Ruthven, McGraw (8), Reed (9), Saucier (10). W—LaCorte. L—Reed. S—Andujar.

**Game 3**—October 10, at Houston
Phil. ..0 0 0 0 0 0 0 0 0 0 0—0 7 1
Hou. ..0 0 0 0 0 0 0 0 0 0 1—1 6 1
Christenson, Noles (7), McGraw (8); Niekro, D. Smith (11). W—D. Smith. L—McGraw.

**Game 4**—October 11, at Houston
Phil. ......0 0 0 0 0 0 0 3 0 2—5 13 0
Hou. ......0 0 0 1 1 0 0 0 1 0—3 5 1
Carlton, Noles (6), Saucier (7), Reed (7), Brusstar (8), McGraw (10); Ruhle, D. Smith (8), Sambito (8). W—Brusstar. L—Sambito. S—McGraw.

**Game 5**—October 12, at Houston
Phil. ......0 2 0 0 0 0 0 5 0 1—8 13 2
Hou. ......1 0 0 0 0 1 3 2 0 0—7 14 0
Bystrom, Brusstar (6), Christenson (7), Reed (7), McGraw (8), Ruthven (9); Ryan, Sambito (8), Forsch (8), LaCorte (9). W—Ruthven. L—LaCorte.

## WORLD SERIES

■ **Winner:** The Phillies, two-time Series qualifiers in their 97-year history, won their first fall classic with a six-game victory over the Royals — first-time Series participants.

■ **Turning point:** A two-run, ninth-inning rally that gave the Phillies a 4-3 victory in Game 5 and a three-games-to-two Series lead.

■ **Memorable moments:** The clutch pitching of Phillies reliever Tug McGraw, who recorded bases-loaded, game-ending strikeouts in Games 5 and 6.

■ **Top guns:** Steve Carlton (2-0, 2.40 ERA), McGraw (2 saves, 1.17), Mike Schmidt (.381, 2 HR, 7 RBIs), Phillies; Amos Otis (.478, 3 HR, 7 RBIs), Willie Aikens (.400, 4 HR, 8 RBIs), Royals.

■ **MVP:** Schmidt.

**Linescores**

**Game 1**—October 14, at Philadelphia
K.C. ............0 2 2 0 0 0 0 2 0—6 9 1
Phil. ..........0 0 5 1 1 0 0 0 x—7 11 0
Leonard, Martin (4), Quisenberry (8); Walk, McGraw (8). W—Walk. L—Leonard. S—McGraw. HR—Otis, Aikens 2 (K.C.); McBride (Phil.).

**Game 2**—October 15, at Philadelphia
K.C. ............0 0 0 0 0 1 3 0 0—4 11 0
Phil. ..........0 0 0 0 2 0 0 4 x—6 8 1
Gura, Quisenberry (7); Carlton, Reed (9). W—Carlton. L—Quisenberry. S—Reed.

**Game 3**—October 17, at Kansas City
Phil. ......0 1 0 0 1 0 0 1 0 0—3 14 0
K.C. ........1 0 0 1 0 0 1 0 0 1—4 11 0
Ruthven, McGraw (10); Gale, Martin (5), Quisenberry (8). W—Quisenberry. L—McGraw. HR—Brett, Otis (K.C.); Schmidt (Phil.).

**Game 4**—October 18, at Kansas City
Phil. ..........0 1 0 0 0 0 1 1 0—3 10 1
K.C. ............4 1 0 0 0 0 0 0 x—5 10 2
Christenson, Noles (1), Saucier (6), Brusstar (6); Leonard, Quisenberry (8). W—Leonard. L—Christenson. S—Quisenberry. HR—Aikens 2 (K.C.).

**Game 5**—October 19, at Kansas City
Phil. ..........0 0 0 2 0 0 0 0 2—4 7 0
K.C. ............0 0 0 0 1 2 0 0 0—3 12 2
Bystrom, Reed (6), McGraw (7); Gura, Quisenberry (7). W—McGraw. L—Quisenberry. HR—Schmidt (Phil.); Otis (K.C.).

**Game 6**—October 21, at Philadelphia
K.C. ..............0 0 0 0 0 0 0 1 0—1 7 2
Phil. ............0 0 2 0 1 1 0 0 x—4 9 0
Gale, Martin (3), Splittorff (5), Pattin (7), Quisenberry (8); Carlton, McGraw (8). W—Carlton. L—Gale. S—McGraw.

# 1981

## FINAL STANDINGS

### American League

**East Division**

| Team | Mil. | Bal. | N.Y. | Det. | Bos. | Cle. | Tor. | Oak. | Tex. | Chi. | K.C. | Cal. | Sea. | Min. | W | L | Pct. | GB |
|---|---|---|---|---|---|---|---|---|---|---|---|---|---|---|---|---|---|---|
| Milwaukee† | ... | 4 | 3 | 8 | 7 | 6 | 6 | 4 | 4 | 1 | 5 | 3 | 2 | 9 | 62 | 47 | .569 | ... |
| Baltimore | 2 | ... | 7 | 6 | 2 | 4 | 5 | 7 | 2 | 3 | 5 | 6 | 4 | 6 | 59 | 46 | .562 | 1 |
| New York* | 3 | 6 | ... | 7 | 3 | 5 | 2 | 4 | 5 | 7 | 10 | 2 | 2 | 3 | 59 | 48 | .551 | 2 |
| Detroit | 5 | 7 | 3 | ... | 1 | 5 | 6 | 1 | 9 | 3 | 3 | 3 | 5 | 9 | 60 | 49 | .550 | 2 |
| Boston | 6 | 2 | 3 | 6 | ... | 7 | 4 | 7 | 3 | 5 | 3 | 2 | 9 | 2 | 59 | 49 | .546 | 2.5 |
| Cleveland | 3 | 2 | 7 | 1 | 6 | ... | 4 | 3 | 2 | 5 | 4 | 5 | 8 | 2 | 52 | 51 | .505 | 7 |
| Toronto | 4 | 2 | 3 | 4 | 0 | 2 | ... | 2 | 2 | 5 | 3 | 6 | 3 | 1 | 37 | 69 | .349 | 23.5 |

**West Division**

| Team | Oak. | Tex. | Chi. | K.C. | Cal. | Sea. | Min. | Mil. | Bal. | N.Y. | Det. | Bos. | Cle. | Tor. | W | L | Pct. | GB |
|---|---|---|---|---|---|---|---|---|---|---|---|---|---|---|---|---|---|---|
| Oakland* | ... | 4 | 6 | 3 | 8 | 6 | 8 | 2 | 5 | 3 | 2 | 5 | 2 | 10 | 64 | 45 | .587 | ... |
| Texas | 2 | ... | 4 | 4 | 4 | 8 | 8 | 5 | 1 | 4 | 3 | 6 | 2 | 6 | 57 | 48 | .543 | 5 |
| Chicago | 7 | 2 | ... | 2 | 7 | 3 | 2 | 4 | 6 | 5 | 3 | 4 | 2 | 7 | 54 | 52 | .509 | 8.5 |
| Kansas City† | 3 | 3 | 0 | ... | 6 | 6 | 9 | 4 | 3 | 2 | 2 | 3 | 4 | 5 | 50 | 53 | .485 | 11 |
| California | 2 | 2 | 6 | 0 | ... | 6 | 3 | 4 | 6 | 2 | 3 | 4 | 7 | 6 | 51 | 59 | .464 | 13.5 |
| Seattle | 1 | 5 | 3 | 7 | 4 | ... | 6 | 2 | 2 | 3 | 1 | 3 | 4 | 3 | 44 | 65 | .404 | 20 |
| Minnesota | 2 | 5 | 4 | 4 | 3 | 3 | ... | 3 | 0 | 3 | 3 | 5 | 1 | 5 | 41 | 68 | .376 | 23 |

### National League

**East Division**

| Team | St.L. | Mon. | Phi. | Pit. | N.Y. | Chi. | Cin. | L.A. | Hou. | S.F. | Atl. | S.D. | W | L | Pct. | GB |
|---|---|---|---|---|---|---|---|---|---|---|---|---|---|---|---|---|
| St.Louis | ... | 9 | 6 | 8 | 5 | 4 | 5 | 5 | 4 | 3 | 3 | 7 | 59 | 43 | .578 | ... |
| Montreal† | 6 | ... | 7 | 10 | 9 | 7 | 4 | 2 | 2 | 2 | 7 | 4 | 60 | 48 | .556 | 2 |
| Philadelphia* | 7 | 4 | ... | 7 | 7 | 10 | 2 | 3 | 6 | 4 | 5 | 4 | 59 | 48 | .551 | 2.5 |
| Pittsburgh | 3 | 3 | 5 | ... | 6 | 10 | 2 | 1 | 4 | 3 | 3 | 6 | 46 | 56 | .451 | 13 |
| New York | 6 | 3 | 7 | 3 | ... | 8 | 3 | 1 | 3 | 2 | 3 | 2 | 41 | 62 | .398 | 18.5 |
| Chicago | 5 | 4 | 2 | 4 | 5 | ... | 1 | 6 | 1 | 5 | 2 | 3 | 38 | 65 | .369 | 21.5 |

**West Division**

| Team | Cin. | L.A. | Hou. | S.F. | Atl. | S.D. | St.L. | Mon. | Phi. | Pit. | N.Y. | Chi. | W | L | Pct. | GB |
|---|---|---|---|---|---|---|---|---|---|---|---|---|---|---|---|---|
| Cincinnati | ... | 8 | 8 | 9 | 5 | 10 | 0 | 5 | 5 | 4 | 7 | 5 | 66 | 42 | .611 | ... |
| Los Angeles* | 8 | ... | 8 | 7 | 7 | 6 | 5 | 5 | 3 | 5 | 5 | 4 | 63 | 47 | .573 | 4 |
| Houston† | 4 | 4 | ... | 9 | 8 | 11 | 2 | 5 | 4 | 2 | 6 | 6 | 61 | 49 | .555 | 6 |
| San Fran. | 5 | 5 | 6 | ... | 7 | 7 | 2 | 5 | 3 | 7 | 4 | 5 | 56 | 55 | .505 | 11.5 |
| Atlanta | 6 | 7 | 4 | 5 | ... | 9 | 4 | 3 | 4 | 2 | 3 | 3 | 50 | 56 | .472 | 15 |
| San Diego | 2 | 5 | 3 | 6 | 6 | ... | 3 | 2 | 2 | 4 | 5 | 3 | 41 | 69 | .373 | 26 |

* Won first-half division title † Won second-half division title

## SIGNIFICANT EVENTS

■ **February 12:** Boston catcher Carlton Fisk was declared a free agent because the Red Sox violated the Basic Agreement by mailing his contract two days beyond the deadline.

■ **July 31:** Baseball's 50-day strike, the longest in American sports history, ended when owners and players reached agreement on the free-agent compensation issue.

■ **November 11:** Dodgers lefty Fernando Valenzuela became the first rookie to win a Cy Young when he outpointed the Reds' Tom Seaver for N.L. honors.

■ **November 25:** Milwaukee's Rollie Fingers, who earlier was named A.L. Cy Young winner, became the first relief pitcher to win an A.L. MVP.

## MEMORABLE MOMENTS

■ **May 15:** Cleveland's Len Barker retired 27 consecutive Blue Jays in a 3-0 victory and pitched the first Major League perfect game in 13 years.

■ **August 10:** Philadelphia's Pete Rose collected career hit No. 3,631 in a 6-2 loss to St. Louis and moved into third place on the all-time list.

■ **September 26:** Houston's Nolan Ryan stepped into uncharted territory when he fired his record-setting fifth no-hitter, beating the Dodgers, 5-0.

■ **October 11:** The Dodgers, Expos and Yankees won decisive fifth games of special post-season series set up to determine division champions because of the 50-day baseball strike.

## LEADERS

**American League**
**BA:** Carney Lansford, Bos., .336.
**Runs:** Rickey Henderson, Oak., 89.
**Hits:** Rickey Henderson, Oak., 135.
**TB:** Dwight Evans, Bos., 215.
**HR:** Tony Armas, Oak.; Dwight Evans, Bos.; Bobby Grich, Cal.; Eddie Murray, Bal., 22.
**RBI:** Eddie Murray, Bal., 78.
**SB:** Rickey Henderson, Oak., 56.
**Wins:** Dennis Martinez, Bal.; Steve McCatty, Oak.; Jack Morris, Det.; Pete Vuckovich, Mil., 14.
**ERA:** Dave Righetti, N.Y., 2.05
**CG:** Rick Langford, Oak., 18.
**IP:** Dennis Leonard, K.C., 201.2.
**SO:** Len Barker, Cle., 127.
**SV:** Rollie Fingers, Mil., 28.

**National League**
**BA:** Bill Madlock, Pit., .341.
**Runs:** Mike Schmidt, Phil., 78.
**Hits:** Pete Rose, Phil., 140.
**TB:** Mike Schmidt, Phil., 228.
**HR:** Mike Schmidt, Phil., 31.
**RBI:** Mike Schmidt, Phil., 91.
**SB:** Tim Raines, Mon., 71.
**Wins:** Tom Seaver, Cin., 14.
**ERA:** Nolan Ryan, Hou., 1.69.
**CG:** Fernando Valenzuela, L.A., 11.
**IP:** Fernando Valenzuela, L.A., 192.1.
**SO:** Fernando Valenzuela, L.A., 180.
**SV:** Bruce Sutter, St.L., 25.

**Most Valuable Player**
A.L.: Rollie Fingers, P, Mil.
N.L.: Mike Schmidt, 3B, Phil.

**Cy Young Award**
A.L.: Rollie Fingers, Mil.
N.L.: Fernando Valenzuela, L.A.

**Rookie of the Year**
A.L.: Dave Righetti, P, N.Y.
N.L.: Fernando Valenzuela, P, L.A.

**Hall of Fame additions**
Rube Foster, manager/executive, Negro Leagues
Bob Gibson, P, 1959-75
Johnny Mize, 1B, 1936-53

## ALL-STAR GAME

■ **Winner:** With the All-Star Game serving as the official resumption of the season after a 50-day players' strike, the N.L. continued its winning ways by belting four home runs and stretching its winning streak to 10.

■ **Key inning:** The eighth, when Mike Schmidt drilled a two-run homer off Rollie Fingers, giving the N.L. its tying and winning runs.

■ **Memorable moment:** Gary Carter's solo blast in the seventh inning, his second home run of the game. Carter became the fifth All-Star performer to homer twice.

■ **Top guns:** Schmidt (Phillies), Carter (Expos), Dave Parker (Pirates), N.L.; Len Barker (Indians), Fred Lynn (Angels), Ken Singleton (Orioles), A.L.

■ **MVP:** Carter.

**Linescore**
August 9, at Cleveland Stadium
N.L.............0 0 0 0 1 1 1 2 0—5 9 1
A.L. ............0 1 0 0 0 3 0 0 0—4 11 1
Valenzuela (Dodgers), Seaver (Reds) 2, Knepper (Astros) 3, Hooton (Dodgers) 5, Ruthven (Phillies) 6, Blue (Giants) 7, Ryan (Astros) 8, Sutter (Cardinals) 9; Morris (Tigers), Barker (Indians) 3, Forsch (Angels) 5, Norris (Athletics) 6, Davis (Yankees) 7, Fingers (Brewers) 8, Stieb (Blue Jays) 8. W—Blue. L—Fingers. S—Sutter. HR—Singleton, A.L.; Carter 2, Parker, Schmidt, N.L.

## DIVISIONAL PLAYOFFS

Los Angeles defeated Houston, 3 games to 2
Montreal defeated Philadelphia, 3 games to 2
NY Yankees defeated Milwaukee, 3 games to 2
Oakland defeated Kansas City, 3 games to 0

## ALCS

■ **Winner:** The New York Yankees captured their 33rd pennant with a 1-2-3 Championship Series victory over Oakland.

■ **Turning point:** The first inning of Game 1, when Yankee third baseman Graig Nettles drilled a three-run double, giving lefty Tommy John and two relievers all the runs they needed for a 3-1 victory.

■ **Memorable moment:** The ninth inning of Game 3, when Nettles drilled another three-run double, putting the wraps on a 4-0 series-ending victory.

■ **Top guns:** Nettles (.500, 1 HR, 9 RBIs), Jerry Mumphrey (.500), Larry Milbourne (.462), Yankees; Rickey Henderson (.364), Athletics.

■ **MVP:** Nettles.

**Linescores**

**Game 1**—October 13 at New York
Oakland........0 0 0 0 1 0 0 0 0—1 6 1
N.Y. ..............3 0 0 0 0 0 0 0 x—3 7 1
Norris, Underwood (8); John, Davis (7), Gossage (8). W—John. L—Norris. S—Gossage.

**Game 2**—October 14, at New York
Oakland....0 0 1 2 0 0 0 0 0— 3 11 1
N.Y. ..........1 0 0 7 0 1 4 0 x—13 19 0
McCatty, Beard (4), Jones (5), Kingman (7), Owchinko (7); May, Frazier (4). W—Frazier. L—McCatty. HR—Piniella, Nettles (N.Y.).

**Game 3**—October 15, at Oakland
N.Y. ............0 0 0 0 0 1 0 0 3—4 10 0
Oakland......0 0 0 0 0 0 0 0 0—0 5 2
Righetti, Davis (7), Gossage (9); Keough, Underwood (9). W—Righetti. L—Keough. HR—Randolph (N.Y.).

## NLCS

■ **Winner:** The Los Angeles Dodgers ruined Montreal's bid to become the first Canadian qualifier for a World Series with a dramatic ninth-inning home run in the fifth game.

■ **Turning point:** An eighth-inning Game 4 home run by Steve Garvey that broke a 1-1 tie and propelled the Dodgers to an elimination-saving 7-1 victory.

■ **Memorable moment:** A ninth-inning series-winning home run by Dodgers outfielder Rick Monday off Expos ace Steve Rogers in Game 5 at frigid Montreal.

■ **Top guns:** Burt Hooton (2-0, 0.00 ERA), Monday (.333), Dusty Baker (.316), Dodgers; Ray Burris (1-0, 0.53 ERA), Gary Carter (.438), Expos.

■ **MVP:** Hooton.

**Linescores**

**Game 1**—October 13, at Los Angeles
Montreal......0 0 0 0 0 0 0 0 1—1 9 0
L.A. ..............0 2 0 0 0 0 0 3 x—5 8 0
Gullickson, Reardon (8); Hooton, Welch (8), Howe (9). W—Hooton. L—Gullickson. HR—Guerrero, Scioscia (L.A.).

**Game 2**—October 14, at Los Angeles
Montreal ....0 2 0 0 0 1 0 0 0—3 10 1
L.A. ............0 0 0 0 0 0 0 0 0—0 5 1
Burris; Valenzuela, Niedenfuer (7), Forster (7), Pena (7), Castillo (9). W—Burris. L—Valenzuela.

**Game 3**—October 16, at Montreal
L.A. ..............0 0 0 1 0 0 0 0 0—1 7 0
Montreal ......0 0 0 0 0 4 0 0 x—4 7 1
Reuss, Pena (8); Rogers. W—Rogers. L—Reuss. HR—White (Mon.).

**Game 4**—October 17, at Montreal
L.A. ............0 0 1 0 0 0 0 2 4—7 12 1
Montreal ....0 0 0 1 0 0 0 0 0—1 5 1
Hooton, Welch (8), Howe (9); Gullickson, Fryman (8), Sosa (9), Lee (9). W—Hooton. L—Gullickson. HR—Garvey (L.A.).

**Game 5**—October 19, at Montreal
L.A. ..............0 0 0 0 1 0 0 0 1—2 6 0
Montreal ......1 0 0 0 0 0 0 0 0—1 3 1
Valenzuela, Welch (9); Burris, Rogers (9). W—Valenzuela. L—Rogers. S—Welch. HR—Monday (L.A.).

## WORLD SERIES

■ **Winner:** The Dodgers brought the strike-shortened season to an end by duplicating the Yankees' 1978 feat against them—four straight victories after two opening losses.

■ **Turning point:** After falling behind 4-0 and 6-3 in Game 4, the Dodgers rallied for an 8-7 victory that squared the Series at two games.

■ **Memorable moment:** Back-to-back, seventh-inning home runs by Pedro Guerrero and Steve Yeager that gave Jerry Reuss a 2-1 victory over Ron Guidry and the Yankees in the pivotal fifth game.

■ **Top guns:** Steve Garvey (.417), Ron Cey (.350, 6 RBIs), Guerrero (.333, 2 HR, 7 RBIs), Dodgers; Bob Watson (.318, 2 HR, 7 RBIs), Yankees.

■ **Co-MVPs:** Guerrero, Yeager, Cey.

**Linescores**

**Game 1**—October 20, at New York
L.A. ..............0 0 0 0 1 0 0 2 0—3 5 0
N.Y. ..............3 0 1 1 0 0 0 0 x—5 6 0
Reuss, Castillo (3), Goltz (4), Niedenfuer (5), Stewart (8); Guidry, Davis (8), Gossage (8). W—Guidry. L—Reuss. S—Gossage. HR—Yeager (L.A.); Watson (N.Y.).

**Game 2**—October 21, at New York
L.A. ..............0 0 0 0 0 0 0 0 0—0 4 2
N.Y. ..............0 0 0 0 1 0 0 2 x—3 6 1
Hooton, Forster (7), Howe (8), Stewart (8); John, Gossage (8). W—John. L—Hooton. S—Gossage.

**Game 3**—October 23, at Los Angeles
N.Y. ............0 2 2 0 0 0 0 0 0—4 9 0
L.A. ............3 0 0 0 2 0 0 0 x—5 11 1
Righetti, Frazier (3), May (5), Davis (8); Valenzuela. W—Valenzuela. L—Frazier. HR—Cey (L.A.); Watson, Cerone (N.Y.).

**Game 4**—October 24, at Los Angeles
N.Y. ............2 1 1 0 0 2 0 1 0—7 13 1
L.A. ............0 0 2 0 1 3 2 0 x—8 14 2
Reuschel, May (4), Davis (5), Frazier (6), John (7); Welch, Goltz (1), Forster (4), Niedenfuer (5), Howe (7). W—Howe. L—Frazier. HR—Randolph, Jackson (N.Y.); Johnstone (L.A.).

**Game 5**—October 25, at Los Angeles
N.Y. ..............0 1 0 0 0 0 0 0 0—1 5 0
L.A. ..............0 0 0 0 0 0 2 0 x—2 4 3
Guidry, Gossage (8); Reuss. W—Reuss. L—Guidry. HR—Guerrero, Yeager (L.A.).

**Game 6**—October 28, at New York
L.A. ............0 0 0 1 3 4 0 1 0—9 13 1
N.Y. ............0 0 1 0 0 1 0 0 0—2 7 2
Hooton, Howe (6); John, Frazier (5), Davis (6), Reuschel (6), May (7), LaRoche (9). W—Hooton. L—Frazier. S—Howe. HR—Randolph (N.Y.); Guerrero (L.A.).

# 1982

## FINAL STANDINGS

### American League

**East Division**

| Team | Mil. | Bal. | Bos. | Det. | N.Y. | Tor. | Cle. | Cal. | Chi. | K.C. | Min. | Oak. | Sea. | Tex. | W | L | Pct. | GB |
|---|---|---|---|---|---|---|---|---|---|---|---|---|---|---|---|---|---|---|
| Milwaukee | ... | 4 | 9 | 10 | 8 | 9 | 6 | 6 | 9 | 5 | 7 | 7 | 8 | 7 | 95 | 67 | .586 | ... |
| Baltimore | 9 | ... | 4 | 7 | 11 | 10 | 6 | 7 | 5 | 4 | 8 | 7 | 7 | 9 | 94 | 68 | .580 | 1 |
| Boston | 4 | 9 | ... | 8 | 7 | 7 | 6 | 7 | 4 | 6 | 6 | 8 | 7 | 10 | 89 | 73 | .549 | 6 |
| Detroit | 3 | 6 | 5 | ... | 8 | 6 | 7 | 7 | 3 | 6 | 9 | 9 | 6 | 8 | 83 | 79 | .512 | 12 |
| New York | 5 | 2 | 6 | 5 | ... | 6 | 9 | 5 | 4 | 7 | 10 | 7 | 6 | 7 | 79 | 83 | .488 | 16 |
| Toronto | 4 | 3 | 6 | 7 | 7 | ... | 6 | 4 | 4 | 8 | 7 | 9 | 5 | 8 | 78 | 84 | .481 | 17 |
| Cleveland | 7 | 7 | 7 | 6 | 4 | 7 | ... | 4 | 6 | 2 | 8 | 4 | 9 | 7 | 78 | 84 | .481 | 17 |

**West Division**

| Team | Cal. | K.C. | Chi. | Sea. | Oak. | Tex. | Min. | Bal. | Bos. | Cle. | Det. | Mil. | N.Y. | Tor. | W | L | Pct. | GB |
|---|---|---|---|---|---|---|---|---|---|---|---|---|---|---|---|---|---|---|
| California | ... | 7 | 8 | 10 | 9 | 8 | 7 | 5 | 5 | 8 | 5 | 6 | 7 | 8 | 93 | 69 | .574 | ... |
| Kansas City | 6 | ... | 10 | 7 | 7 | 7 | 7 | 8 | 6 | 10 | 6 | 7 | 5 | 4 | 90 | 72 | .556 | 3 |
| Chicago | 5 | 3 | ... | 6 | 9 | 8 | 7 | 7 | 8 | 6 | 9 | 3 | 8 | 8 | 87 | 75 | .537 | 6 |
| Seattle | 3 | 6 | 7 | ... | 7 | 9 | 8 | 5 | 5 | 3 | 6 | 4 | 6 | 7 | 76 | 86 | .469 | 17 |
| Oakland | 4 | 6 | 4 | 6 | ... | 5 | 10 | 5 | 4 | 8 | 3 | 5 | 5 | 3 | 68 | 94 | .420 | 25 |
| Texas | 5 | 6 | 5 | 4 | 8 | ... | 8 | 3 | 2 | 5 | 4 | 5 | 5 | 4 | 64 | 98 | .395 | 29 |
| Minnesota | 6 | 6 | 6 | 5 | 3 | 5 | ... | 4 | 6 | 4 | 3 | 5 | 2 | 5 | 60 | 102 | .370 | 33 |

### National League

**East Division**

| Team | St.L. | Phi. | Mon. | Pit. | Chi. | N.Y. | Atl. | Cin. | Hou. | L.A. | S.D. | S.F. | W | L | Pct | .GB |
|---|---|---|---|---|---|---|---|---|---|---|---|---|---|---|---|---|
| St. Louis | ... | 11 | 8 | 11 | 12 | 12 | 5 | 7 | 6 | 5 | 8 | 7 | 92 | 70 | .568 | ... |
| Philadelphia | 7 | ... | 10 | 9 | 9 | 11 | 6 | 7 | 5 | 8 | 7 | 10 | 89 | 73 | .549 | 3 |
| Montreal | 10 | 8 | ... | 7 | 12 | 11 | 7 | 8 | 8 | 4 | 7 | 4 | 86 | 76 | .531 | 6 |
| Pittsburgh | 7 | 9 | 11 | ... | 9 | 10 | 8 | 8 | 3 | 7 | 6 | 6 | 84 | 78 | .519 | 8 |
| Chicago | 6 | 9 | 6 | 9 | ... | 9 | 4 | 6 | 9 | 5 | 4 | 6 | 73 | 89 | .451 | 19 |
| New York | 6 | 7 | 7 | 8 | 9 | ... | 3 | 5 | 4 | 6 | 6 | 4 | 65 | 97 | .401 | 27 |

**West Division**

| Team | Atl. | L.A. | S.F. | S.D. | Hou. | Cin. | Chi. | Mon. | N.Y. | Phi. | Pit. | St.L. | W | L | Pct. | GB |
|---|---|---|---|---|---|---|---|---|---|---|---|---|---|---|---|---|
| Atlanta | ... | 7 | 8 | 11 | 10 | 14 | 8 | 5 | 9 | 6 | 4 | 7 | 89 | 73 | .549 | ... |
| Los Angeles | 11 | .. | 9 | 9 | 11 | 11 | 7 | 8 | 6 | 4 | 5 | 7 | 88 | 74 | .543 | 1 |
| San Fran. | 10 | 9 | ... | 8 | 13 | 12 | 6 | 8 | 8 | 2 | 6 | 5 | 87 | 75 | .537 | 2 |
| San Diego | 7 | 9 | 10 | ... | 9 | 12 | 8 | 5 | 6 | 5 | 6 | 4 | 81 | 81 | .500 | 8 |
| Houston | 8 | 7 | 5 | 9 | ... | 11 | 3 | 4 | 8 | 7 | 9 | 6 | 77 | 85 | .475 | 12 |
| Cincinnati | 4 | 7 | 6 | 6 | 7 | ... | 6 | 4 | 7 | 5 | 4 | 5 | 61 | 101 | .377 | 28 |

## SIGNIFICANT EVENTS

■ **April 6:** Seattle spoiled the Metrodome inaugural for Minnesota fans with an 11-7 Opening Day victory over the Twins.

■ **April 22:** The Reds defeated Atlanta, 2-1, handing the Braves their first loss after a season-opening record 13 consecutive victories.

■ **October 3:** The Brewers captured their first A.L. East title when they defeated Baltimore, 10-2, in a winner-take-all final-day battle.

■ **October 3:** The Braves, final-day losers to San Diego, clinched their first division title since 1969 when San Francisco defeated the Dodgers, 5-3, on Joe Morgan's three-run homer.

■ **October 26:** Phillies ace Steve Carlton captured his record fourth N.L. Cy Young Award.

■ **November 1:** Owners ended the 14-year reign of commissioner Bowie Kuhn when they voted not to renew his contract at a meeting in Chicago.

## MEMORABLE MOMENTS

■ **May 6:** Gaylord Perry pitched the Mariners to a 7-3 victory over the Yankees and became the 15th member of baseball's 300-win club.

■ **June 22:** Philadelphia's Pete Rose doubled off the Cardinals' John Stuper and moved into second place on the all-time hit list with 3,772.

■ **August 27:** Oakland's Rickey Henderson claimed the one-season basestealing record when he swiped four in a game at Milwaukee, giving him 122 en route to a final total of 130.

## LEADERS

**American League**
**BA:** Willie Wilson, K.C., .332.
**Runs:** Paul Molitor, Mil., 136.
**Hits:** Robin Yount, Mil., 210.
**TB:** Robin Yount, Mil., 367.
**HR:** Reggie Jackson, Cal.; Gorman Thomas, Mil., 39.
**RBI:** Hal McRae, K.C., 133.
**SB:** Rickey Henderson, Oak., 130.
**Wins:** LaMarr Hoyt, Chi., 19.
**ERA:** Rick Sutcliffe, Cle., 2.96.
**CG:** Dave Stieb, Tor., 19.
**IP:** Dave Stieb, Tor., 288.1.
**SO:** Floyd Bannister, Sea., 209.
**SV:** Dan Quisenberry, K.C., 35.

**National League**
**BA:** Al Oliver, Mon., .331.
**Runs:** Lonnie Smith, St.L., 120.
**Hits:** Al Oliver, Mon., 204.
**TB:** Al Oliver, Mon., 317.
**HR:** Dave Kingman, N.Y., 37.
**RBI:** Dale Murphy, Atl.; Al Oliver, Mon., 109.
**SB:** Tim Raines, Mon., 78.
**Wins:** Steve Carlton, Phil., 23.
**ERA:** Steve Rogers, Mon., 2.40.
**CG:** Steve Carlton, Phil., 19.
**IP:** Steve Carlton, Phil., 295.2.
**SO:** Steve Carlton, Phil., 286.
**SV:** Bruce Sutter, St.L., 36.

**N.L. 20-game winner**
Steve Carlton, Phil., 23-11

**A.L. 100 RBIs**
Hal McRae, K.C., 133
Cecil Cooper, Mil., 121
Andre Thornton, Cle., 116
Robin Yount, Mil., 114
Gorman Thomas, Mil., 112
Eddie Murray, Bal., 110
Dave Winfield, N.Y., 106
Harold Baines, Chi., 105
Greg Luzinski, Chi., 102
Ben Oglivie, Mil., 102
Reggie Jackson, Cal., 101

**N.L. 100 RBIs**
Dale Murphy, Atl., 109
Al Oliver, Mon., 109
Bill Buckner, Chi., 105
George Hendrick, St.L., 104
Jack Clark, S.F., 103
Jason Thompson, Pit., 101
Pedro Guerrero, L.A., 100

**Most Valuable Player**
A.L.: Robin Yount, SS, Mil.
N.L.: Dale Murphy, OF, Atl.

**Cy Young Award**
A.L.: Pete Vuckovich, Mil.
N.L.: Steve Carlton, Phil.

**Rookie of the Year**
A.L.: Cal Ripken, SS, Bal.
N.L.: Steve Sax, 2B, L.A.

**Hall of Fame additions**
Hank Aaron, OF, 1954-76
Happy Chandler, commissioner
Travis Jackson, SS, 1922-36
Frank Robinson, OF, 1956-76

## ALL-STAR GAME

■ **Winner:** The N.L. made it 11 in a row and 19 of 20 with a 4-1 victory at Montreal — the first midsummer classic played on foreign soil.

■ **Key inning:** The second, when Dave Concepcion pounded a two-run homer, giving N.L. pitchers all the runs they would need.

■ **Memorable moment:** A sixth-inning run manufactured by a pair of Expos. Al Oliver thrilled the home fans with a double and Gary Carter singled him home.

■ **Top guns:** Steve Carlton (Phillies), Oliver (Expos), Concepcion (Reds), N.L.; Rickey Henderson (Athletics), George Brett (Royals), A.L.

■ **MVP:** Concepcion.

**Linescore**
July 13, at Montreal's Olympic Stadium
A.L. ..............1 0 0  0 0 0  0 0 0—1 8 2
N.L. ..............0 2 1  0 0 1  0 0 x—4 8 1
Eckersley (Red Sox), Clancy (Blue Jays) 4, Bannister (Mariners) 5, Quisenberry (Royals) 6, Fingers (Brewers) 8; Rogers (Expos), Carlton (Phillies) 4, Soto (Reds) 6, Valenzuela (Dodgers) 8, Minton (Giants) 8, Howe (Dodgers) 9, Hume (Reds) 9. W—Rogers. L—Eckersley. S—Hume. HR—Concepcion, N.L.

## ALCS

■ **Winner:** In a battle of first-time pennant hopefuls, the Milwaukee Brewers defeated California and became the first team to recover from a two-games-to-none deficit in a League Championship Series.

■ **Turning point:** The unexpected Game 4 boost the Brewers received from substitute left fielder Mark Brouhard, who collected three hits, belted a home run and drove in three runs in Milwaukee's elimination-saving 9-5 victory.

■ **Memorable moment:** Cecil Cooper's two-run, seventh-inning single that wiped out a 3-2 Angels lead and gave the Brewers a 4-3 Game 5 victory and the franchise's first World Series berth.

■ **Top guns:** Charlie Moore (.462), Paul Molitor (.316, 2 HR, 5 RBIs), Brouhard (.750), Brewers; Bruce Kison (1-0, 1.93 ERA), Fred Lynn (.611, 5 RBIs), Don Baylor (10 RBIs), Angels.

■ **MVP:** Lynn.

**Linescores**
**Game 1**—October 5, at California
Mil. ............0 2 1  0 0 0  0 0 0—3  7 2
Cal. ............1 0 4  2 1 0  0 0 x—8 10 0
Caldwell, Slaton (4), Ladd (7), Bernard (8); John. W—John. L—Caldwell. HR—Thomas (Mil.); Lynn (Cal.).

**Game 2**—October 6, at California
Mil. ..............0 0 0  0 2 0  0 0 0—2 5 0
Cal. ..............0 2 1  1 0 0  0 0 x—4 6 0
Vuckovich; Kison. W—Kison. L—Vuckovich. HR—Re. Jackson (Cal.); Molitor (Mil.).

**Game 3**—October 8, at Milwaukee
Cal. ..............0 0 0  0 0 0  0 3 0—3 8 0
Mil. ..............0 0 0  3 0 0  2 0 x—5 6 0
Zahn, Witt (4), Hassler (7); Sutton, Ladd (8). W—Sutton. L—Zahn. S—Ladd. HR—Molitor (Mil.); Boone (Cal).

**Game 4**—October 9, at Milwaukee
Cal. ..............0 0 0  0 0 1  0 4 0—5 5 3
Mil. ..............0 3 0  3 0 1  0 2 x—9 9 2
John, Goltz (4), Sanchez (8); Haas, Slaton (8). W—Haas. L—John. S—Slaton. HR—Baylor (Cal.); Brouhard (Mil.).

**Game 5**—October 10, at Milwaukee
Cal. ............1 0 1  1 0 0  0 0 0—3 11 1
Mil. ............1 0 0  1 0 0  2 0 x—4  6 4
Kison, Sanchez (6), Hassler (7); Vuckovich, McClure (7), Ladd (9). W—McClure. L—Sanchez. S—Ladd. HR—Oglivie (Mil.).

## NLCS

■ **Winner:** The Atlanta Braves, who were swept by the New York Mets in the first NLCS in 1969, suffered the same fate against St. Louis in the franchise's second post-season appearance.

■ **Turning point:** A Game 1 rainstorm that wiped out a 1-0 Braves lead after 4½ innings and forced Atlanta to bypass ace Phil Niekro in the rescheduled opener.

■ **Memorable moment:** Ken Oberkfell's ninth-inning line drive that eluded Braves center fielder Brett Butler and drove home David Green, giving the Cardinals a 4-3 Game 2 victory.

■ **Top guns:** Bob Forsch (1-0, 0.00 ERA), Darrell Porter (.556), Ozzie Smith (.556), Cardinals; Claudell Washington (.333), Braves.

■ **MVP:** Porter.

**Linescores**
**Game 1**—October 7, at St. Louis
Atlanta ............0 0 0  0 0 0  0 0 0—0  3 0
St. Louis ..........0 0 1  0 0 5  0 1 x—7 13 1
Perez, Bedrosian (6), Moore (6), Walk (8); Forsch. W—Forsch. L—Perez.

**Game 2**—October 9, at St. Louis
Atlanta ........0 0 2  0 1 0  0 0 0—3 6 0
St. Louis ......1 0 0  0 0 1  0 1 1—4 9 1
Niekro, Garber (7); Stuper, Bair (7), Sutter (8). W—Sutter. L—Garber.

**Game 3**—October 10, at Atlanta
St. Louis ....0 4 0  0 1 0  0 0 1—6 12 0
Atlanta ......0 0 0  0 0 0  2 0 0—2  6 1
Andujar, Sutter (7); Camp, Perez (2), Moore (5), Mahler (7), Bedrosian (8), Garber (9). W—Andujar. L—Camp. S—Sutter. HR—McGee (St.L.).

## WORLD SERIES

■ **Winner:** The resilient Cardinals tamed "Harvey's Wallbangers" and spoiled the Brewers' first World Series.

■ **Turning point:** A special Game 3 performance by center fielder Willie McGee, who stepped out of character to hit two home runs and added two spectacular catches in a 6-2 victory that gave the Cardinals their first Series lead.

■ **Memorable moment:** A two-run single by Keith Hernandez and a run-scoring single by George Hendrick in a three-run sixth inning that rallied the Cardinals to a seventh-game 6-3 victory.

■ **Top guns:** Joaquin Andujar (2-0, 1.35 ERA), Dane Iorg (.529), Darrell Porter (5 RBIs), Hernandez (8 RBIs), Cardinals; Mike Caldwell (2-0, 2.04), Robin Yount (.414, 12 hits, 6 RBIs), Paul Molitor (.355), Brewers.

■ **MVP:** Porter.

**Linescores**
**Game 1**—October 12, at St. Louis
Mil. ..........2 0 0  1 1 2  0 0 4—10 17 0
St. Louis ..0 0 0  0 0 0  0 0 0— 0  3 1
Caldwell; Forsch, Kaat (6), LaPoint (8), Lahti (9). W—Caldwell. L—Forsch. HR—Simmons (Mil.).

**Game 2**—October 13, at St. Louis
Mil. ............0 1 2  0 1 0  0 0 0—4 10 1
St. Louis ....0 0 2  0 0 2  0 1 x—5  8 0
Sutton, McClure (7), Ladd (8); Stuper, Kaat (5), Bair (5), Sutter (7). W—Sutter. L—McClure. HR—Simmons (Mil.).

**Game 3**—October 15, at Milwaukee
St. Louis ......0 0 0  0 3 0  2 0 1—6 6 1
Mil. ..............0 0 0  0 0 0  0 2 0—2 5 3
Andujar, Kaat (7), Bair (7), Sutter (7); Vuckovich, McClure (9). W—Andujar. L—Vuckovich. S—Sutter. HR—McGee 2 (St.L.); Cooper (Mil.).

**Game 4**—October 16, at Milwaukee
St. Louis ....1 3 0  0 0 1  0 0 0—5  8 1
Mil. ............0 0 0  0 1 0  6 0 x—7 10 2
LaPoint, Bair (7), Kaat (7), Lahti (7); Haas, Slaton (6), McClure (8). W—Slaton. L—Bair. S—McClure.

**Game 5**—October 17, at Milwaukee
St. Louis ....0 0 1  0 0 0  1 0 2—4 15 2
Mil. ............1 0 1  0 1 0  1 2 x—6 11 1
Forsch, Sutter (8); Caldwell, McClure (9). W—Caldwell. L—Forsch. S—McClure. HR—Yount (Mil.).

**Game 6**—October 19, at St. Louis
Mil. ..........0 0 0  0 0 0  0 0 1— 1  4 4
St. Louis ..0 2 0  3 2 6  0 0 x—13 12 1
Sutton, Slaton (5), Medich (6), Bernard (8); Stuper. W—Stuper. L—Sutton. HR—Porter, Hernandez (St.L.).

**Game 7**—October 20, at St. Louis
Mil. ............0 0 0  0 1 2  0 0 0—3  7 0
St. Louis ....0 0 0  1 0 3  0 2 x—6 15 1
Vuckovich, McClure (6), Haas (6), Caldwell (8); Andujar, Sutter (8). W—Andujar. L—McClure. S—Sutter. HR—Oglivie (Mil.).

# 1983

## FINAL STANDINGS

### American League

**East Division**

| Team | Bal. | Det. | N.Y. | Tor. | Mil. | Bos. | Cle. | Cal. | Chi. | K.C. | Min. | Oak. | Sea. | Tex. | W | L | Pct. | GB |
|---|---|---|---|---|---|---|---|---|---|---|---|---|---|---|---|---|---|---|
| Baltimore | ... | 5 | 6 | 7 | 11 | 8 | 6 | 7 | 7 | 8 | 8 | 8 | 8 | 9 | 98 | 64 | .605 | ... |
| Detroit | 8 | ... | 5 | 6 | 6 | 9 | 8 | 8 | 4 | 7 | 9 | 6 | 8 | 8 | 92 | 70 | .568 | 6 |
| New York | 7 | 8 | ... | 7 | 9 | 6 | 7 | 7 | 4 | 6 | 8 | 8 | 7 | 7 | 91 | 71 | .562 | 7 |
| Toronto | 6 | 7 | 6 | ... | 5 | 6 | 9 | 8 | 7 | 6 | 7 | 6 | 8 | 8 | 89 | 73 | .549 | 9 |
| Milwaukee | 2 | 7 | 4 | 8 | ... | 9 | 10 | 6 | 8 | 6 | 8 | 6 | 5 | 8 | 87 | 75 | .537 | 11 |
| Boston | 5 | 4 | 7 | 7 | 4 | ... | 7 | 6 | 6 | 5 | 5 | 8 | 7 | 7 | 78 | 84 | .481 | 20 |
| Cleveland | 7 | 5 | 6 | 4 | 3 | 6 | ... | 4 | 4 | 7 | 6 | 7 | 8 | 3 | 70 | 92 | .432 | 28 |

**West Division**

| Team | Chi. | K.C. | Tex. | Oak. | Cal. | Min. | Sea. | Bal. | Bos. | Cle. | Det. | Mil. | N.Y. | Tor. | W | L | Pct. | GB |
|---|---|---|---|---|---|---|---|---|---|---|---|---|---|---|---|---|---|---|
| Chicago | ... | 9 | 8 | 8 | 10 | 8 | 12 | 5 | 6 | 8 | 8 | 4 | 8 | 5 | 99 | 63 | .611 | ... |
| Kansas City | 4 | ... | 8 | 7 | 7 | 6 | 8 | 4 | 7 | 5 | 5 | 6 | 6 | 6 | 79 | 83 | .488 | 20 |
| Texas | 5 | 5 | ... | 11 | 7 | 8 | 7 | 3 | 5 | 9 | 4 | 4 | 5 | 4 | 77 | 85 | .475 | 22 |
| Oakland | 5 | 6 | 2 | ... | 8 | 9 | 9 | 4 | 4 | 5 | 6 | 6 | 4 | 6 | 74 | 88 | .457 | 25 |
| California | 3 | 6 | 6 | 5 | ... | 6 | 6 | 5 | 6 | 8 | 4 | 6 | 5 | 4 | 70 | 92 | .432 | 29 |
| Minnesota | 5 | 7 | 5 | 4 | 7 | ... | 9 | 4 | 7 | 6 | 3 | 4 | 4 | 5 | 70 | 92 | .432 | 29 |
| Seattle | 1 | 5 | 6 | 4 | 7 | 4 | ... | 4 | 5 | 4 | 4 | 7 | 5 | 4 | 60 | 102 | .370 | 39 |

### National League

**East Division**

| Team | Phi. | Pit. | Mon. | St.L. | Chi. | N.Y. | Atl. | Cin. | Hou. | L.A. | S.D. | S.F. | W | L | Pct. | GB |
|---|---|---|---|---|---|---|---|---|---|---|---|---|---|---|---|---|
| Philadelphia | ... | 11 | 10 | 14 | 13 | 12 | 5 | 6 | 8 | 1 | 5 | 5 | 90 | 72 | .556 | ... |
| Pittsburgh | 7 | ... | 10 | 10 | 9 | 9 | 6 | 6 | 6 | 6 | 9 | 6 | 84 | 78 | .519 | 6 |
| Montreal | 8 | 8 | ... | 9 | 11 | 8 | 5 | 8 | 4 | 5 | 8 | 8 | 82 | 80 | .506 | 8 |
| St. Louis | 4 | 8 | 9 | ... | 8 | 12 | 5 | 6 | 10 | 3 | 6 | 8 | 79 | 83 | .488 | 11 |
| Chicago | 5 | 9 | 7 | 10 | ... | 9 | 7 | 4 | 5 | 6 | 5 | 4 | 71 | 91 | .438 | 19 |
| New York | 6 | 9 | 10 | 6 | 9 | ... | 4 | 5 | 3 | 5 | 6 | 5 | 68 | 94 | .420 | 22 |

**West Division**

| Team | L.A. | Atl. | Hou. | S.D. | S.F. | Cin. | Chi. | Mon. | N.Y. | Phi. | Pit. | St.L. | W | L | Pct. | GB |
|---|---|---|---|---|---|---|---|---|---|---|---|---|---|---|---|---|
| Los Angeles | ... | 11 | 12 | 6 | 5 | 11 | 6 | 7 | 7 | 11 | 6 | 9 | 91 | 71 | .562 | ... |
| Atlanta | 7 | ... | 11 | 9 | 9 | 12 | 5 | 7 | 8 | 7 | 6 | 7 | 88 | 74 | .543 | 3 |
| Houston | 6 | 7 | ... | 11 | 12 | 13 | 7 | 8 | 9 | 4 | 6 | 2 | 85 | 77 | .525 | 6 |
| San Diego | 12 | 9 | 7 | ... | 11 | 9 | 7 | 4 | 6 | 7 | 3 | 6 | 81 | 81 | .500 | 10 |
| San Fran. | 13 | 9 | 6 | 7 | ... | 8 | 8 | 4 | 7 | 7 | 6 | 4 | 79 | 83 | .488 | 12 |
| Cincinnati | 7 | 6 | 5 | 9 | 10 | ... | 8 | 4 | 7 | 6 | 6 | 6 | 74 | 88 | .457 | 17 |

## SIGNIFICANT EVENTS

■ **April 7:** ABC and NBC agreed to share a lucrative six-year television contract that would pay baseball $1.2 billion.

■ **February 8:** Former Yankee great Mickey Mantle was ordered to sever ties with baseball after taking a job with an Atlantic City hotel and casino.

■ **July 29:** The N.L.-record ironman streak of San Diego's Steve Garvey ended at 1,207 games when he dislocated his thumb in a home-plate collision against the Braves.

■ **November 17:** A U.S. magistrate handed three members of the 1983 Royals, Willie Wilson, Willie Aikens and Jerry Martin, three-month prison sentences for attempting to purchase cocaine.

■ **December 8:** Dr. Bobby Brown was elected as the successor to retiring A.L. president Lee MacPhail.

■ **December 19:** Former Cy Young winner Vida Blue became the fourth Kansas City player to receive a three-month prison sentence for attempting to purchase cocaine.

## MEMORABLE MOMENTS

■ **July 24:** A two-out, game-winning home run by Kansas City's George Brett off Yankee reliever Goose Gossage was nullified by umpires who said Brett's bat was illegally covered by pine tar—a controversial ruling that later would be overturned.

■ **June 26:** Mets veteran Rusty Staub collected his record-tying eighth consecutive pinch hit in an 8-4 loss to the Phillies.

■ **September 23:** Philadelphia lefty Steve Carlton became baseball's 16th 300-game winner when he defeated St. Louis, 6-2.

## LEADERS

**American League**
**BA:** Wade Boggs, Bos., .361.
**Runs:** Cal Ripken, Bal., 121.
**Hits:** Cal Ripken, Bal., 211.
**TB:** Jim Rice, Bos., 344.
**HR:** Jim Rice, Bos., 39.
**RBI:** Cecil Cooper, Mil.; Jim Rice, Bos., 126.
**SB:** Rickey Henderson, Oak., 108.
**Wins:** LaMarr Hoyt, Chi., 24.
**ERA:** Rick Honeycutt, Tex., 2.42.
**CG:** Ron Guidry, N.Y., 21.
**IP:** Jack Morris, Det., 293.2.
**SO:** Jack Morris, Det., 232.
**SV:** Dan Quisenberry, K.C., 45.

**National League**
**BA:** Bill Madlock, Pit., .323.
**Runs:** Tim Raines, Mon., 133.
**Hits:** Jose Cruz, Hou.; Andre Dawson, Mon., 189.
**TB:** Andre Dawson, Mon., 341.
**HR:** Mike Schmidt, Phil., 40.
**RBI:** Dale Murphy, Atl., 121.
**SB:** Tim Raines, Mon., 90.
**Wins:** John Denny, Phil., 19.
**ERA:** Atlee Hammaker, S.F., 2.25.
**CG:** Mario Soto, Cin., 18.
**IP:** Steve Carlton, Phil., 283.2.
**SO:** Steve Carlton, Phil., 275.
**SV:** Lee Smith, Chi., 29.

**A.L. 20-game winners**
LaMarr Hoyt, Chi., 24-10
Rich Dotson, Chi., 22-7
Ron Guidry, N.Y., 21-9
Jack Morris, Det., 20-13

**A.L. 100 RBIs**
Cecil Cooper, Mil., 126
Jim Rice, Bos., 126
Dave Winfield, N.Y., 116
Lance Parrish, Det., 114
Eddie Murray, Bal., 111
Ted Simmons, Mil., 108
Tony Armas, Bos., 107
Willie Upshaw, Tor., 104
Cal Ripken, Bal., 102
Ron Kittle, Chi., 100

**N.L. 100 RBIs**
Dale Murphy, Atl., 121
Andre Dawson, Mon., 113
Mike Schmidt, Phil., 109
Pedro Guerrero, L.A., 103

**N.L. 40 homers**
Mike Schmidt, Phil., 40

**Most Valuable Player**
A.L.: Cal Ripken, SS, Bal.
N.L.: Dale Murphy, OF, Atl.

**Cy Young Award**
A.L.: LaMarr Hoyt, Chi.
N.L.: John Denny, Phil.

**Rookie of the Year**
A.L.: Ron Kittle, OF, Chi.
N.L.: Darryl Strawberry, OF, N.Y.

**Manager of the Year**
A.L.: Tony La Russa, Chi.
N.L.: Tommy Lasorda, L.A.

**Hall of Fame additions**
Walter Alston, manager
George Kell, 3B, 1943-57
Juan Marichal, P, 1960-75
Brooks Robinson, 3B, 1955-77

## ALL-STAR GAME

■ **Winner:** The A.L. snapped its frustrating 11-game All-Star losing streak with a 13-3 rout in a special 50th-anniversary celebration of the midsummer classic at Chicago's Comiskey Park.

■ **Key inning:** A record seven-run third that gave the A.L. a 9-1 lead and set the course for its first victory since 1971.

■ **Memorable moment:** Fred Lynn's third-inning bases-loaded homer off Atlee Hammaker — the first grand slam in 54 All-Star Games.

■ **Top guns:** Dave Stieb (Blue Jays), Lynn (Angels), Jim Rice (Red Sox), George Brett (Royals), Dave Winfield (Yankees), A.L.; Steve Sax (Dodgers), N.L.

■ **MVP:** Lynn.

**Linescore**
July 6, Chicago's Comiskey Park
N.L..........1 0 0 1 1 0 0 0 0— 3 8 3
A.L. .........1 1 7 0 0 0 2 2 x—13 15 2
Soto (Reds), Hammaker (Giants) 3, Dawley (Astros) 3, Dravecky (Padres) 5, Perez (Braves) 7, Orosco (Mets) 7, L. Smith (Cubs) 8; Stieb (Blue Jays), Honeycutt (Rangers) 4, Stanley (Red Sox) 6, Young (Mariners) 8, Quisenberry (Royals) 9. W—Stieb. L—Soto. HR—Rice, Lynn, A.L.

## ALCS

■ **Winner:** Baltimore, a 2-1 loser to the Chicago White Sox in the opener, roared to three consecutive victories and claimed its fifth pennant since LCS play began in 1969.

■ **Turning point:** Mike Boddicker's five-hit, 4-0 shutout in Game 2. Orioles pitchers would finish the series with a 0.49 ERA.

■ **Memorable moment:** A 10th-inning home run by unlikely Baltimore hero Tito Landrum off Chicago lefty Britt Burns in Game 4. The blast broke up a scoreless battle and propelled the Orioles to a series-ending 3-0 victory.

■ **Top guns:** Boddicker (1-0, 0.00 ERA), Tippy Martinez (1-0, 0.00), Cal Ripken (.400), Orioles; LaMarr Hoyt (1-0, 1.00), Rudy Law (.389), White Sox.

■ **MVP:** Boddicker.

**Linescores**

**Game 1**—October 5, at Baltimore
Chi. ..............0 0 1 0 0 1 0 0 0—2 7 0
Balt. ..............0 0 0 0 0 0 0 0 1—1 5 1
Hoyt; McGregor, Stewart (7), T. Martinez (8). W—Hoyt. L—McGregor.

**Game 2**—October 6, at Baltimore
Chi. ..............0 0 0 0 0 0 0 0 0—0 5 2
Balt. ..............0 1 0 1 0 2 0 0 x—4 6 0
Bannister, Barojas (7), Lamp (8); Boddicker. W—Boddicker. L—Bannister. HR—Roenicke (Bal.).

**Game 3**—October 7, at Chicago
Balt. ..........3 1 0 0 2 0 0 1 4—11 8 1
Chi. ..............0 1 0 0 0 0 0 0 0— 1 6 1
Flanagan, Stewart (6); Dotson, Tidrow (6), Koosman (9), Lamp (9). W—Flanagan. L—Dotson. S—Stewart. HR—Murray (Bal.).

**Game 4**—October 8, at Chicago
Balt. ....0 0 0 0 0 0 0 0 0 3—3 9 0
Chi. ....0 0 0 0 0 0 0 0 0 0—0 10 0
Davis, T. Martinez (7); Burns, Barojas (10), Agosto (10), Lamp (10). W—T. Martinez. L—Burns. HR—Landrum (Bal.).

## NLCS

■ **Winner:** The Philadelphia Phillies advanced to their second World Series in four years and settled an old NLCS score with the Dodgers, who had defeated them in 1977 and '78.

■ **Turning point:** The Game 3 performance of veteran outfielder Gary Matthews: three hits, a home run and four RBIs in a 7-2 Phillies victory.

■ **Memorable moment:** A three-run, first-inning home run by Matthews in Game 4. Matthews' third homer in as many games propelled the Phillies to a series-ending 7-2 victory.

■ **Top guns:** Steve Carlton (2-0, 0.66 ERA), Mike Schmidt (.467), Matthews (.429, 3 HR, 8 RBIs), Phillies; Fernando Valenzuela (1-0, 1.13), Dusty Baker (.357), Dodgers.

■ **MVP:** Matthews.

**Linescores**

**Game 1**—October 4, at Los Angeles
Phil. ............1 0 0 0 0 0 0 0 0—1 5 1
L.A. ..............0 0 0 0 0 0 0 0 0—0 7 0
Carlton, Holland (8); Reuss, Niedenfuer (9). W—Carlton. L—Reuss. S—Holland. HR—Schmidt (Phil.).

**Game 2**—October 5, at Los Angeles
Phil. ............0 1 0 0 0 0 0 0 0—1 7 2
L.A. ..............1 0 0 0 2 0 0 1 x—4 6 1
Denny, Reed (7); Valenzuela, Niedenfuer (9). W—Valenzuela. L—Denny. S—Niedenfuer. HR—Matthews (Phil.).

**Game 3**—October 7, at Philadelphia
L.A. ..............0 0 0 2 0 0 0 0 0—2 4 0
Phil. ............0 2 1 1 2 0 1 0 x—7 9 1
Welch, Pena (2), Honeycutt (5), Beckwith (5), Zachry (7); Hudson. W—Hudson. L—Welch. HR—Marshall (L.A.); Matthews (Phil.).

**Game 4**—October 8, at Philadelphia
L.A. ............0 0 0 1 0 0 0 1 0—2 10 0
Phil. ..........3 0 0 0 2 2 0 0 x—7 13 1
Reuss, Beckwith (5), Honeycutt (5), Zachry (7); Carlton, Reed (7), Holland (8). W—Carlton. L—Reuss. HR—Matthews, Lezcano (Phil.); Baker (L.A.).

## WORLD SERIES

■ **Winner:** The Orioles lost the opener and then sprinted past the Phillies for their first championship since 1970.

■ **Turning point:** When Phillies manager Paul Owens let starting pitcher Steve Carlton bat with two runners on base in the sixth inning of Game 3. Carlton struck out and then yielded two seventh-inning runs that vaulted the Orioles to a 3-2 victory.

■ **Memorable moment:** Garry Maddox's game-deciding eighth-inning homer in Game 1. Maddox connected on the first pitch from Scott McGregor, who stood on the mound for about five minutes while President Ronald Reagan was being interviewed for television.

■ **Top guns:** Rick Dempsey (.385), John Lowenstein (.385), Orioles; Bo Diaz (.333), Phillies.

■ **MVP:** Dempsey.

**Linescores**

**Game 1**—October 11, at Baltimore
Phil. ............0 0 0 0 0 1 0 1 0—2 5 0
Baltimore ....1 0 0 0 0 0 0 0 0—1 5 1
Denny, Holland (8); McGregor, Stewart (9), T. Martinez (9). W—Denny. L—McGregor. S—Holland. HR—Dwyer (Bal.); Morgan, Maddox (Phil.).

**Game 2**—October 12, at Baltimore
Phil. ............0 0 0 1 0 0 0 0 0—1 3 0
Baltimore ....0 0 0 0 3 0 1 0 x—4 9 1
Hudson, Hernandez (5), Andersen (6), Reed (8); Boddicker. W—Boddicker. L—Hudson. HR—Lowenstein (Bal.).

**Game 3**—October 14, at Philadelphia
Baltimore ....0 0 0 0 0 1 2 0 0—3 6 1
Phil. ............0 1 1 0 0 0 0 0 0—2 8 2
Flanagan, Palmer (5), Stewart (7), T. Martinez (9); Carlton, Holland (7). W—Palmer. L—Carlton. S—T. Martinez. HR—Matthews, Morgan (Phil.); Ford (Bal.).

**Game 4**—October 15, at Philadelphia
Baltimore ..0 0 0 2 0 2 1 0 0—5 10 1
Phil. ..........0 0 0 1 2 0 0 0 1—4 10 0
Davis, Stewart (6), T. Martinez (8); Denny, Hernandez (6), Reed (6), Andersen (8). W—Davis. L—Denny. S—T. Martinez.

**Game 5**—October 16, at Philadelphia
Baltimore ....0 1 1 2 1 0 0 0 0—5 5 0
Phil. ............0 0 0 0 0 0 0 0 0—0 5 1
McGregor; Hudson, Bystrom (5), Hernandez (6), Reed (9). W—McGregor. L—Hudson. HR—Murray 2, Dempsey (Bal.).

# 1984

## FINAL STANDINGS

### American League

**East Division**

| Team | Det. | Tor. | N.Y. | Bos. | Bal. | Cle. | Mil. | Cal. | Chi. | K.C. | Min. | Oak. | Sea. | Tex. | W | L | Pct. | GB |
|---|---|---|---|---|---|---|---|---|---|---|---|---|---|---|---|---|---|---|
| Detroit | ... | 8 | 7 | 6 | 6 | 9 | 11 | 8 | 8 | 7 | 9 | 9 | 6 | 10 | 104 | 58 | .642 | ... |
| Toronto | 5 | ... | 5 | 8 | 9 | 7 | 3 | 5 | 8 | 7 | 11 | 8 | 7 | 6 | 89 | 73 | .549 | 15 |
| New York | 6 | 8 | ... | 6 | 8 | 11 | 7 | 4 | 5 | 7 | 4 | 8 | 7 | 6 | 87 | 75 | .537 | 17 |
| Boston | 7 | 5 | 7 | ... | 7 | 10 | 9 | 9 | 7 | 3 | 6 | 7 | 4 | 5 | 86 | 76 | .531 | 18 |
| Baltimore | 7 | 4 | 5 | 6 | ... | 7 | 7 | 8 | 7 | 5 | 5 | 6 | 9 | 9 | 85 | 77 | .525 | 19 |
| Cleveland | 4 | 6 | 2 | 3 | 6 | ... | 9 | 4 | 4 | 6 | 7 | 7 | 8 | 9 | 75 | 87 | .463 | 29 |
| Milwaukee | 2 | 10 | 6 | 4 | 6 | 4 | ... | 4 | 5 | 6 | 5 | 4 | 6 | 5 | 67 | 94 | .416 | 36.5 |

**West Division**

| Team | K.C. | Cal. | Min. | Oak. | Chi. | Sea. | Tex. | Bal. | Bos. | Cle. | Det. | Mil. | N.Y. | Tor. | W | L | Pct. | GB |
|---|---|---|---|---|---|---|---|---|---|---|---|---|---|---|---|---|---|---|
| Kansas City | ... | 7 | 6 | 5 | 8 | 9 | 6 | 7 | 9 | 6 | 5 | 6 | 5 | 5 | 84 | 78 | .519 | ... |
| California | 6 | ... | 4 | 7 | 8 | 9 | 5 | 4 | 3 | 8 | 4 | 8 | 8 | 7 | 81 | 81 | .500 | 3 |
| Minnesota | 7 | 9 | ... | 8 | 5 | 7 | 8 | 7 | 6 | 5 | 3 | 7 | 8 | 1 | 81 | 81 | .500 | 3 |
| Oakland | 8 | 6 | 5 | ... | 7 | 8 | 8 | 6 | 5 | 5 | 3 | 8 | 4 | 4 | 77 | 85 | .475 | 7 |
| Chicago | 5 | 5 | 8 | 6 | ... | 5 | 5 | 5 | 5 | 8 | 4 | 7 | 7 | 4 | 74 | 88 | .457 | 10 |
| Seattle | 4 | 4 | 6 | 5 | 8 | ... | 10 | 3 | 8 | 4 | 6 | 6 | 5 | 5 | 74 | 88 | .457 | 10 |
| Texas | 7 | 8 | 5 | 5 | 8 | 3 | ... | 3 | 7 | 3 | 2 | 6 | 6 | 6 | 69 | 92 | .429 | 14.5 |

### National League

**East Division**

| Team | Chi. | N.Y. | St.L. | Phi. | Mon. | Pit. | Atl. | Cin. | Hou. | L.A. | S.D. | S.F. | W | L | Pct. | GB |
|---|---|---|---|---|---|---|---|---|---|---|---|---|---|---|---|---|
| Chicago | ... | 12 | 13 | 9 | 10 | 8 | 9 | 7 | 6 | 7 | 6 | 9 | 96 | 65 | .596 | ... |
| New York | 6 | ... | 7 | 10 | 11 | 12 | 8 | 9 | 8 | 9 | 6 | 4 | 90 | 72 | .556 | 6.5 |
| St. Louis | 5 | 11 | ... | 10 | 9 | 14 | 7 | 8 | 4 | 6 | 5 | 5 | 84 | 78 | .519 | 12.5 |
| Philadelphia | 9 | 8 | 8 | ... | 7 | 7 | 5 | 7 | 6 | 9 | 7 | 8 | 81 | 81 | .500 | 15.5 |
| Montreal | 7 | 7 | 9 | 11 | ... | 7 | 7 | 5 | 5 | 6 | 7 | 7 | 78 | 83 | .484 | 18 |
| Pittsburgh | 10 | 6 | 4 | 11 | 11 | ... | 4 | 5 | 6 | 8 | 4 | 6 | 75 | 87 | .463 | 21.5 |

**West Division**

| Team | S.D. | Atl. | Hou. | L.A. | Cin. | S.F. | Chi. | Mon. | N.Y. | Phi. | Pit. | St.L. | W | L | Pct. | GB |
|---|---|---|---|---|---|---|---|---|---|---|---|---|---|---|---|---|
| San Diego | ... | 11 | 12 | 8 | 11 | 13 | 6 | 5 | 6 | 5 | 8 | 7 | 92 | 70 | .568 | ... |
| Atlanta | 7 | ... | 12 | 6 | 13 | 10 | 3 | 5 | 4 | 7 | 8 | 5 | 80 | 82 | .494 | 12 |
| Houston | 6 | 6 | ... | 9 | 10 | 12 | 6 | 7 | 4 | 6 | 6 | 8 | 80 | 82 | .494 | 12 |
| L.A. | 10 | 12 | 9 | ... | 11 | 10 | 5 | 6 | 3 | 3 | 4 | 6 | 79 | 83 | .488 | 13 |
| Cincinnati | 7 | 5 | 8 | 7 | ... | 12 | 5 | 7 | 3 | 5 | 7 | 4 | 70 | 92 | .432 | 22 |
| San Fran. | 5 | 8 | 6 | 8 | 6 | ... | 3 | 5 | 8 | 4 | 6 | 7 | 66 | 96 | .407 | 26 |

## SIGNIFICANT EVENTS

■ **March 3:** Baseball's owners selected businessman Peter V. Ueberroth as the sixth commissioner, succeeding Bowie Kuhn.

■ **August 16:** Pete Rose, who joined the select 4,000-hit circle early in the season as a member of the Expos, returned to his hometown Cincinnati as the Reds' player-manager.

■ **September 20, 24:** The Padres clinched their first-ever division title and the Cubs clinched their first post-season appearance since 1945.

■ **October 7:** Major League umpires, agreeing to let Commissioner Ueberroth arbitrate their dispute over post-season pay, ended a one-week strike and returned for the final game of the NLCS.

■ **November 6:** Detroit reliever Willie Hernandez capped his big season with an A.L. Cy Young-MVP sweep.

## MEMORABLE MOMENTS

■ **September 17:** Kansas City posted a 10-1 victory, but the night belonged to Angels slugger Reggie Jackson, who belted his 500th homer off lefty Bud Black.

■ **September 28:** Cardinals reliever Bruce Sutter notched his 45th save in a 4-1 victory over the Cubs, matching the 1-year-old record of Kansas City's Dan Quisenberry.

■ **September 30:** California's Mike Witt brought a dramatic end to the regular season when he fired baseball's 11th perfect game, beating Texas, 1-0.

## LEADERS

**American League**
**BA:** Don Mattingly, N.Y., .343.
**Runs:** Dwight Evans, Bos., 121.
**Hits:** Don Mattingly, N.Y., 207.
**TB:** Tony Armas, Bos., 339.
**HR:** Tony Armas, Bos., 43.
**RBI:** Tony Armas, Bos., 123.
**SB:** Rickey Henderson, Oak., 66.
**Wins:** Mike Boddicker, Bal., 20.
**ERA:** Mike Boddicker, Bal., 2.79.
**CG:** Charlie Hough, Tex., 17.
**IP:** Dave Stieb, Tor., 267.
**SO:** Mark Langston, Sea., 204.
**SV:** Dan Quisenberry, K.C., 44.

**National League**
**BA:** Tony Gwynn, S.D., .351.
**Runs:** Ryne Sandberg, Chi., 114.
**Hits:** Tony Gwynn, S.D., 213.
**TB:** Dale Murphy, Atl., 332.
**HR:** Dale Murphy, Atl.; Mike Schmidt, Phil., 36.
**RBI:** Gary Carter, Mon.; Mike Schmidt, Phil., 106.
**SB:** Tim Raines, Mon., 75.
**Wins:** Joaquin Andujar, St.L., 20.
**ERA:** Alejandro Pena, L.A., 2.48.
**CG:** Mario Soto, Cin., 13.
**IP:** Joaquin Andujar, St.L., 261.1.
**SO:** Dwight Gooden, N.Y., 276.
**SV:** Bruce Sutter, St.L., 45.

**A.L. 20-game winner**
Mike Boddicker, Bal., 20-11

**N.L. 20-game winner**
Joaquin Andujar, St.L., 20-14

**A.L./N.L. 20-game winner**
Rick Sutcliffe, Cle.-Chi., 20

**A.L. 100 RBIs**
Tony Armas, Bos., 123
Jim Rice, Bos., 122
Dave Kingman, Oak., 118
Alvin Davis, Sea., 116
Don Mattingly, N.Y., 110
Eddie Murray, Bal., 110
Kent Hrbek, Min., 107
Dwight Evans, Bos., 104
Larry Parrish, Tex., 101
Dave Winfield, N.Y., 100

**N.L. 100 RBIs**
Gary Carter, Mon., 106
Mike Schmidt, Phil., 106
Dale Murphy, Atl., 100

**A.L. 40 homers**
Tony Armas, Bos., 43

**Most Valuable Player**
A.L.: Willie Hernandez, P, Det.
N.L.: Ryne Sandberg, 2B, Chi.

**Cy Young Award**
A.L.: Willie Hernandez, Det.
N.L.: Rick Sutcliffe, Chi.

**Rookie of the Year**
A.L.: Alvin Davis, 1B, Sea.
N.L.: Dwight Gooden, P, N.Y.

**Manager of the Year**
A.L.: Sparky Anderson, Det.
N.L.: Jim Frey, Chi.

**Hall of Fame additions**
Luis Aparicio, SS, 1956-73
Don Drysdale, P, 1956-69
Rick Ferrell, C, 1929-47
Harmon Killebrew, 1B/3B, 1954-75
Pee Wee Reese, SS, 1940-58

## ALL-STAR GAME

■ **Winner:** After a one-year lull, it was business as usual for the N.L., which used home runs by Gary Carter and Dale Murphy to post a 3-1 All-Star victory.

■ **Key inning:** The second, when Carter belted a solo shot to give the N.L. a 2-1 lead after the A.L. had tied in the top of the inning on George Brett's home run.

■ **Memorable moment:** A fourth and fifth-inning strikeout flurry by the N.L.'s Fernando Valenzuela and Dwight Gooden. Consecutive victims Dave Winfield, Reggie Jackson, Brett, Lance Parrish, Chet Lemon and Alvin Davis broke the 50-year-old record of five straight.

■ **Top guns:** Valenzuela (Dodgers), Gooden (Mets), Carter (Expos), Murphy (Braves), N.L.; Brett (Royals), Lou Whitaker (Tigers), A.L.

■ **MVP:** Carter.

**Linescore**
July 10, at San Francisco's Candlestick Park
A.L. ..............0 1 0 0 0 0 0 0 0—1 7 2
N.L. ..............1 1 0 0 0 0 0 1 x—3 8 0
Stieb (Blue Jays), Morris (Tigers) 3, Dotson (White Sox) 5, Caudill (Athletics) 7, W. Hernandez (Tigers) 8; Lea (Expos), Valenzuela (Dodgers) 3, Gooden (Mets) 5, Soto (Reds) 7, Gossage (Padres) 9. W—Lea. L—Steib. S—Gossage. HR—Brett, A.L.; Carter, Murphy, N.L.

## ALCS

■ **Winner:** The Detroit Tigers capped their 104-victory regular season with a sweep of Kansas City and claimed their first pennant since 1968.

■ **Turning point:** The 11th inning of Game 2, when Johnny Grubb's one-out double off Royals relief ace Dan Quisenberry drove in two runs and gave the Tigers a 5-3 victory and a two-games-to-none series edge.

■ **Memorable moment:** The Game 3 pitching performance of Tigers veteran Milt Wilcox, who allowed only two hits in eight innings of a series-clinching 1-0 victory.

■ **Top guns:** Wilcox (1-0, 0.00 ERA), Jack Morris (1-0, 1.29), Kirk Gibson (.417), Alan Trammell (.364), Tigers; Don Slaught (.364), Royals.

■ **MVP:** Gibson.

**Linescores**

**Game 1**—October 2, at Kansas City
Det.............2 0 0 1 1 0 1 2 1—8 14 0
K.C.............0 0 0 0 0 0 1 0 0—1 5 1
Morris, Hernandez (8); Black, Huismann (6), M. Jones (8). W—Morris. L—Black. HR—Herndon, Trammell, Parrish (Det.).

**Game 2**—October 3, at Kansas City
Det...2 0 1 0 0 0 0 0 0 0 2—5 8 1
K.C...0 0 0 1 0 0 1 1 0 0 0—3 10 3
Petry, Hernandez (8), Lopez (9); Saberhagen, Quisenberry (9). W—Lopez. L—Quisenberry. HR—Gibson (Det.).

**Game 3**—October 5, at Detroit
K.C..............0 0 0 0 0 0 0 0 0—0 3 3
Det. ..............0 1 0 0 0 0 0 0 x—1 3 0
Leibrandt; Wilcox, Hernandez (9). W—Wilcox. L—Leibrandt. S—Hernandez.

## NLCS

■ **Winner:** The San Diego Padres became the first N.L. team to recover from a two-game deficit and captured their first-ever pennant, denying the Cubs their first World Series appearance since 1945.

■ **Turning point:** The seventh inning of Game 5. The key blows in San Diego's four-run series-deciding rally were an error by Cubs first baseman Leon Durham and a bad-hop double by Tony Gwynn that drove in two runs and broke a 3-3 tie.

■ **Memorable moment:** Steve Garvey's two-run ninth-inning home run that gave the Padres an elimination-saving 7-5 victory in Game 4.

■ **Top guns:** Craig Lefferts (2-0, 0.00 ERA), Garvey (.400, 7 RBIs), Gwynn (.368), Padres; Jody Davis (.389, 2 HR, 6 RBIs), Gary Matthews (2 HR, 5 RBIs), Cubs.

■ **MVP:** Garvey.

**Linescores**

**Game 1**—October 2, at Chicago
S.D...........0 0 0 0 0 0 0 0 0— 0 6 1
Chicago....2 0 3 0 6 2 0 0 x—13 16 0
Show, Harris (5), Booker (7); Sutcliffe, Brusstar (8). W—Sutcliffe. L—Show. HR—Dernier, Matthews 2, Sutcliffe, Cey (Chi.).

**Game 2**—October 3, at Chicago
S.D...............0 0 0 1 0 1 0 0 0—2 5 0
Chicago........1 0 2 1 0 0 0 0 x—4 8 1
Thurmond, Hawkins (4), Dravecky (6), Lefferts (8); Trout, Smith (9). W—Trout. L—Thurmond. S—Smith.

**Game 3**—October 4, at San Diego
Chicago......0 1 0 0 0 0 0 0 0—1 5 0
S.D............0 0 0 0 3 4 0 0 x—7 11 0
Eckersley, Frazier (6), Stoddard (8); Whitson, Gossage (9). W—Whitson. L—Eckersley. HR—McReynolds (S.D.).

**Game 4**—October 6, at San Diego
Chicago......0 0 0 3 0 0 0 2 0—5 8 1
S.D............0 0 2 0 1 0 2 0 2—7 11 0
Sanderson, Brusstar (5), Stoddard (7), Smith (8); Lollar, Hawkins (5), Dravecky (6), Gossage (8), Lefferts (9). W—Lefferts. L—Smith. HR—Davis, Durham (Chi.); Garvey (S.D.).

**Game 5**—October 7, at San Diego
Chicago ........2 1 0 0 0 0 0 0 0—3 5 1
S.D...............0 0 0 0 0 2 4 0 x—6 8 0
Sutcliffe, Trout (7), Brusstar (8); Show, Hawkins (2), Dravecky (4), Lefferts (6), Gossage (8). W—Lefferts. L—Sutcliffe. S—Gossage. HR—Durham, Davis (Chi.).

## WORLD SERIES

■ **Winner:** The Tigers made short work of first-time Series qualifier San Diego and Sparky Anderson became the first man to manage champions in both leagues.

■ **Turning point:** Jack Morris pitched a five-hitter and Alan Trammell drove in all of Detroit's runs with two homers in a 4-2 Game 4 victory.

■ **Memorable moment:** The ever-intense Kirk Gibson stomping on home plate after an eighth-inning upper-deck home run in the Series finale — his second of the game. Gibson also drove in five runs and scored three times in the Tigers' 8-4 victory.

■ **Top guns:** Morris (2-0, 2.00 ERA), Trammell (.450, 2 HR, 6 RBIs), Gibson (.333, 2 HR, 7 RBIs), Tigers; Kurt Bevacqua (.412), Alan Wiggins (.364), Padres.

■ **MVP:** Trammell.

**Linescores**

**Game 1**—October 9, at San Diego
Detroit..........1 0 0 0 2 0 0 0 0—3 8 0
San Diego ....2 0 0 0 0 0 0 0 0—2 8 1
Morris; Thurmond, Hawkins (6), Dravecky (8). W—Morris. L—Thurmond. HR—Herndon (Det.).

**Game 2**—October 10, at San Diego
Detroit........3 0 0 0 0 0 0 0 0—3 7 3
San Diego ..1 0 0 1 3 0 0 0 x—5 11 0
Petry, Lopez (5), Scherrer (6), Bair (7), Hernandez (8); Whitson, Hawkins (1), Lefferts (7). W—Hawkins. L—Petry. S—Lefferts. HR—Bevacqua (S.D.).

**Game 3**—October 12, at Detroit
San Diego ..0 0 1 0 0 0 1 0 0—2 10 0
Detroit........0 4 1 0 0 0 0 0 x—5 7 0
Lollar, Booker (2), Harris (3); Wilcox, Scherrer (7), Hernandez (7). W—Wilcox. L—Lollar. S—Hernandez. HR—Castillo (Det.).

**Game 4**—October 13, at Detroit
San Diego ....0 1 0 0 0 0 0 0 1—2 5 2
Detroit..........2 0 2 0 0 0 0 0 x—4 7 0
Show, Dravecky (3), Lefferts (7), Gossage (8); Morris. W—Morris. L—Show. HR—Trammell 2 (Det.); Kennedy (S.D.).

**Game 5**—October 14, at Detroit
San Diego ..0 0 1 2 0 0 0 1 0—4 10 1
Detroit........3 0 0 0 1 0 1 3 x—8 11 1
Thurmond, Hawkins (1), Lefferts (5), Gossage (7); Petry, Scherrer (4), Lopez (5), Hernandez (8). W—Lopez. L—Hawkins. S—Hernandez. HR—Gibson 2, Parrish (Det.); Bevacqua (S.D.).

# 1985

## FINAL STANDINGS

### American League

**East Division**

| Team | Tor. | N.Y. | Det. | Bal. | Bos. | Mil. | Cle. | K.C. | Cal. | Chi. | Min. | Oak. | Sea. | Tex. | W | L | Pct. | GB |
|---|---|---|---|---|---|---|---|---|---|---|---|---|---|---|---|---|---|---|
| Toronto | ... | 7 | 7 | 8 | 4 | 9 | 9 | 5 | 7 | 9 | 8 | 7 | 10 | 9 | 99 | 62 | .615 | ... |
| New York | 6 | ... | 3 | 12 | 8 | 6 | 7 | 7 | 9 | 6 | 9 | 7 | 9 | 8 | 97 | 64 | .602 | 2 |
| Detroit | 6 | 9 | ... | 7 | 7 | 9 | 8 | 5 | 4 | 6 | 3 | 8 | 5 | 7 | 84 | 77 | .522 | 15 |
| Baltimore | 4 | 1 | 6 | ... | 5 | 9 | 8 | 6 | 7 | 8 | 6 | 7 | 6 | 10 | 83 | 78 | .516 | 16 |
| Boston | 9 | 5 | 6 | 8 | ... | 5 | 8 | 5 | 5 | 4 | 7 | 8 | 6 | 5 | 81 | 81 | .500 | 18.5 |
| Milwaukee | 4 | 7 | 4 | 4 | 8 | ... | 6 | 4 | 3 | 7 | 9 | 3 | 4 | 8 | 71 | 90 | .441 | 28 |
| Cleveland | 4 | 6 | 5 | 5 | 5 | 7 | ... | 2 | 4 | 2 | 4 | 3 | 6 | 7 | 60 | 102 | .370 | 39.5 |

**West Division**

| Team | K.C. | Cal. | Chi. | Min. | Oak. | Sea. | Tex. | Tor. | N.Y. | Det. | Bal. | Bos. | Mil. | Cle. | W | L | Pct. | GB |
|---|---|---|---|---|---|---|---|---|---|---|---|---|---|---|---|---|---|---|
| Kansas City | ... | 9 | 8 | 7 | 8 | 3 | 6 | 7 | 5 | 7 | 6 | 7 | 8 | 10 | 91 | 71 | .562 | ... |
| California | 4 | ... | 8 | 9 | 6 | 9 | 9 | 5 | 3 | 8 | 5 | 7 | 9 | 8 | 90 | 72 | .556 | 1 |
| Chicago | 5 | 5 | ... | 6 | 8 | 9 | 10 | 3 | 6 | 6 | 4 | 8 | 5 | 10 | 85 | 77 | .525 | 6 |
| Minnesota | 6 | 4 | 7 | ... | 8 | 6 | 8 | 4 | 3 | 9 | 6 | 5 | 3 | 8 | 77 | 85 | .475 | 14 |
| Oakland | 5 | 7 | 5 | 5 | ... | 8 | 6 | 5 | 5 | 4 | 5 | 4 | 9 | 9 | 77 | 85 | .475 | 14 |
| Seattle | 10 | 4 | 4 | 7 | 5 | ... | 6 | 2 | 3 | 7 | 6 | 6 | 8 | 6 | 74 | 88 | .457 | 17 |
| Texas | 7 | 4 | 3 | 5 | 7 | 7 | ... | 3 | 4 | 5 | 2 | 7 | 3 | 5 | 62 | 99 | .385 | 28.5 |

### National League

**East Division**

| Team | St.L. | N.Y. | Mon. | Chi. | Phi. | Pit. | L.A. | Cin. | Hou. | S.D. | Atl. | S.F. | W | L | Pct. | GB |
|---|---|---|---|---|---|---|---|---|---|---|---|---|---|---|---|---|
| St. Louis | ... | 10 | 7 | 14 | 10 | 15 | 5 | 7 | 6 | 8 | 9 | 10 | 101 | 61 | .623 | ... |
| New York | 8 | ... | 9 | 14 | 11 | 10 | 5 | 8 | 8 | 7 | 10 | 8 | 98 | 64 | .605 | 3 |
| Montreal | 11 | 9 | ... | 11 | 8 | 9 | 5 | 4 | 6 | 5 | 9 | 7 | 84 | 77 | .522 | 16.5 |
| Chicago | 4 | 4 | 7 | ... | 13 | 13 | 5 | 5 | 5 | 8 | 7 | 6 | 77 | 84 | .478 | 23.5 |
| Philadelphia | 8 | 7 | 10 | 5 | ... | 11 | 8 | 5 | 8 | 5 | 2 | 6 | 75 | 87 | .463 | 26 |
| Pittsburgh | 3 | 8 | 8 | 5 | 7 | ... | 4 | 3 | 6 | 4 | 6 | 3 | 57 | 104 | .354 | 43.5 |

**West Division**

| Team | L.A. | Cin. | Hou. | S.D. | Atl. | S.F. | St.L. | N.Y. | Mon. | Chi. | Phi. | Pit. | W | L | Pct. | GB |
|---|---|---|---|---|---|---|---|---|---|---|---|---|---|---|---|---|
| Los Angeles | ... | 11 | 12 | 8 | 13 | 11 | 7 | 7 | 7 | 7 | 4 | 8 | 95 | 67 | .586 | ... |
| Cincinnati | 7 | ... | 11 | 9 | 11 | 12 | 5 | 4 | 8 | 6 | 7 | 9 | 89 | 72 | .553 | 5.5 |
| Houston | 6 | 7 | ... | 12 | 10 | 15 | 6 | 4 | 6 | 7 | 4 | 6 | 83 | 79 | .512 | 12 |
| San Diego | 10 | 9 | 6 | ... | 11 | 12 | 4 | 5 | 7 | 4 | 7 | 8 | 83 | 79 | .512 | 12 |
| Atlanta | 5 | 7 | 8 | 7 | ... | 10 | 3 | 2 | 3 | 5 | 10 | 6 | 66 | 96 | .407 | 29 |
| San Fran. | 7 | 6 | 3 | 6 | 8 | ... | 2 | 4 | 5 | 6 | 6 | 9 | 62 | 100 | .383 | 33 |

## LEADERS

**American League**
**BA:** Wade Boggs, Bos., .368.
**Runs:** Rickey Henderson, N.Y., 146.
**Hits:** Wade Boggs, Bos., 240.
**TB:** Don Mattingly, N.Y., 370.
**HR:** Darrell Evans, Det., 40.
**RBI:** Don Mattingly, N.Y., 145.
**SB:** Rickey Henderson, N.Y., 80.
**Wins:** Ron Guidry, N.Y., 22.
**ERA:** Dave Stieb, Tor., 2.48.
**CG:** Bert Blyleven, Cle.-Min., 24.
**IP:** Bert Blyleven, Cle.-Min., 293.2.
**SO:** Bert Blyleven, Cle.-Min., 206.
**SV:** Dan Quisenberry, K.C., 37.

**National League**
**BA:** Willie McGee, St.L., .353.
**Runs:** Dale Murphy, Atl., 118.
**Hits:** Willie McGee, St.L., 216.
**TB:** Dave Parker, Cin., 350.
**HR:** Dale Murphy, Atl., 37.
**RBI:** Dave Parker, Cin., 125.
**SB:** Vince Coleman, St.L., 110.
**Wins:** Dwight Gooden, N.Y., 24.
**ERA:** Dwight Gooden, N.Y., 1.53.
**CG:** Dwight Gooden, N.Y., 16.
**IP:** Dwight Gooden, N.Y., 276.2.
**SO:** Dwight Gooden, N.Y., 268.
**SV:** Jeff Reardon, Mon., 41.

**A.L. 20-game winners**
Ron Guidry, N.Y., 22-6
Bret Saberhagen, K.C., 20-6

**N.L. 20-game winners**
Dwight Gooden, N.Y., 24-4
John Tudor, St.L., 21-8
Joaquin Andujar, St.L., 21-12
Tom Browning, Cin., 20-9

**A.L. 100 RBIs**
Don Mattingly, N.Y., 145
Eddie Murray, Bal., 124
Dave Winfield, N.Y., 114
Harold Baines, Chi., 113
George Brett, K.C., 112
Bill Buckner, Bos., 110
Cal Ripken, Bal., 110
Carlton Fisk, Chi., 107
Jim Rice, Bos., 103

**N.L. 100 RBIs**
Dave Parker, Cin., 125
Dale Murphy, Atl., 111
Tommy Herr, St.L., 110
Keith Moreland, Chi., 106
Glenn Wilson, Phil., 102
Hubie Brooks, Mon., 100
Gary Carter, N.Y., 100

**A.L. 40 homers**
Darrell Evans, Det., 40

**Most Valuable Player**
A.L.: Don Mattingly, 1B, N.Y.
N.L.: Willie McGee, OF, St.L.

**Cy Young Award**
A.L.: Bret Saberhagen, K.C.
N.L.: Dwight Gooden, N.Y.

**Rookie of the Year**
A.L.: Ozzie Guillen, SS, Chi.
N.L.: Vince Coleman, OF, St.L.

**Manager of the Year**
A.L.: Bobby Cox, Tor.
N.L.: Whitey Herzog, St.L.

**Hall of Fame additions**
Lou Brock, OF, 1961-79
Enos Slaughter, OF, 1938-59
Arky Vaughan, IF, 1932-48
Hoyt Wilhelm, P, 1952-72

## SIGNIFICANT EVENTS

■ **April 25:** Denny McLain, a 31-game winner in 1968, was sentenced to 23 years in prison after his conviction on racketeering, extortion and cocaine-possession charges in Tampa, Fla.
■ **March 18:** The baseball bans against former greats Mickey Mantle and Willie Mays were lifted by Commissioner Peter V. Ueberroth.
■ **April 3:** The owners and players agreed to expand the League Championship Series from a best-of-five to best-of-seven format.
■ **August 7:** Major League players ended their two-day, 25-game strike when owners dropped their demand for an arbitration salary cap.

## MEMORABLE MOMENTS

■ **July 11:** Houston's Nolan Ryan became the first pitcher to record 4,000 career strikeouts when he fanned Danny Heep in a 4-3 victory over the Mets.
■ **August 4:** Chicago's Tom Seaver earned career win No. 300 against the Yankees and California's Rod Carew got hit No. 3,000 against the Twins in games played a continent apart on the same day.
■ **September 11:** Reds player-manager Pete Rose overtook all-time hit leader Ty Cobb when he singled off San Diego's Eric Show for career hit No. 4,192.
■ **October 6:** Yankee knuckleballer Phil Niekro fired a final-day 8-0 shutout at the Blue Jays and joined baseball's 300-win club.

## ALL-STAR GAME

■ **Winner:** The N.L. made it 21 of 23 and two in a row as five pitchers shut down the A.L. on five hits.
■ **Key inning:** The third, when the N.L. took the lead on a double by Tommy Herr and Steve Garvey's single.
■ **Memorable moment:** The performance of the N.L. pitchers, who did not even allow an extra-base hit.
■ **Top guns:** LaMarr Hoyt (Padres), Nolan Ryan (Astros), Garvey (Dodgers), Willie McGee (Cardinals), Ozzie Virgil (Phillies), N.L.; Rickey Henderson (Yankees), A.L.
■ **MVP:** Hoyt.

**Linescore**
July 16, at Minnesota's Metrodome
N.L. ..............0 1 1 0 2 0 0 0 2—6 9 1
A.L. ..............1 0 0 0 0 0 0 0 0—1 5 0
Hoyt (Padres), Ryan (Astros) 4, Valenzuela (Dodgers) 7, Reardon (Expos) 8, Gossage (Padres) 9; Morris (Tigers), Key (Blue Jays) 3, Blyleven (Indians) 4, Stieb (Blue Jays) 6, Moore (Angels) 7, Petry (Tigers) 9, Hernandez (Tigers) 9. W—Hoyt. L—Morris.

## ALCS

■ **Winner:** The Kansas City Royals, taking advantage of baseball's expanded seven-game playoff format, rallied from a three-games-to-one deficit to deny Toronto's bid for a first Canadian pennant.
■ **Turning point:** One day after the Blue Jays had rallied for three ninth-inning runs and a 3-1 series edge, Danny Jackson steadied the Royals with an eight-hit, 2-0 shutout at Royals Stadium.
■ **Memorable moment:** A bases-loaded, opposite-field Jim Sundberg blast that bounded high off the wall and resulted in a three-run, sixth-inning triple — the big blow in Kansas City's seventh-game 6-2 victory.
■ **Top guns:** Jackson (1-0, 0.00 ERA), George Brett (.348, 3 HR, 5 RBIs), Willie Wilson (.310), Royals; Al Oliver (.375), Cliff Johnson (.368), Blue Jays.
■ **MVP:** Brett.

**Linescores**

**Game 1**—October 8, at Toronto
K.C. ............0 0 0 0 0 0 0 0 1—1 5 1
Tor. ............0 2 3 1 0 0 0 0 x—6 11 0
Leibrandt, Farr (3), Gubicza (5), Jackson (8); Stieb, Henke (9). W—Stieb. L—Leibrandt.

**Game 2**—October 9, at Toronto
K.C. .........0 0 2 1 0 0 0 0 1 1—5 10 3
Tor. ........0 0 0 1 0 2 0 1 0 2—6 10 0
Black, Quisenberry (8); Key, Lamp (4), Lavelle (8), Henke (8). W—Henke. L—Quisenberry. HR—Wilson, Sheridan (K.C.).

**Game 3**—October 11, at Kansas City
Tor. ............0 0 0 0 5 0 0 0 0—5 13 1
K.C. ............1 0 0 1 1 2 0 1 x—6 10 1
Alexander, Lamp (6), Clancy (8); Saberhagen, Black (5), Farr (5). W—Farr. L—Clancy. HR—Brett 2, Sundberg (K.C.); Barfield, Mulliniks (Tor.)

**Game 4**—October 12, at Kansas City
Tor. ..............0 0 0 0 0 0 0 0 3—3 7 0
K.C. ..............0 0 0 0 0 1 0 0 0—1 2 0
Stieb, Henke (7); Leibrandt, Quisenberry (9). W—Henke. L—Leibrandt.

**Game 5**—October 13, at Kansas City
Tor. ..............0 0 0 0 0 0 0 0 0—0 8 0
K.C. ..............1 1 0 0 0 0 0 0 x—2 8 0
Key, Acker (6); Jackson. W—Jackson. L—Key.

**Game 6**—October 15, at Toronto
K.C. ..............1 0 1 0 1 2 0 0 0—5 8 1
Tor. ..............1 0 1 0 0 1 0 0 0—3 8 2
Gubicza, Black (6), Quisenberry (9); Alexander, Lamp (6). W—Gubicza. L—Alexander. S—Quisenberry. HR—Brett (K.C.).

**Game 7**—October 16, at Toronto
K.C. ..............0 1 0 1 0 4 0 0 0—6 8 0
Tor. ..............0 0 0 0 1 0 0 0 1—2 8 1
Saberhagen, Leibrandt (4), Quisenberry (9); Stieb, Acker (6). W—Leibrandt. L—Stieb. HR—Sheridan (K.C.).

## NLCS

■ **Winner:** The speed-and-pitching oriented St. Louis Cardinals used a new weapon — the dramatic home run — to post a six-game NLCS victory over Los Angeles.
■ **Turning point:** The ninth inning of Game 5 when light-hitting Ozzie Smith, who had hit only 14 career home runs, stunned the Dodgers with a shot down the right-field line against Tom Niedenfuer that produced a 3-2 Cardinals victory and a 3-2 series edge.
■ **Memorable moment:** A three-run, series-clinching home run by Cardinals first baseman Jack Clark in the ninth inning of Game 6. The shot off Niedenfuer gave St. Louis a 7-5 victory — its fourth straight after the Dodgers had won Games 1 and 2.
■ **Top guns:** Ken Dayley (6 IP, 2 saves, 0.00 ERA), Smith (.435), Clark (.381), Cardinals; Fernando Valenzuela (1-0, 1.88), Bill Madlock (.333, 3 HR, 7 RBIs), Dodgers.
■ **MVP:** Smith.

**Linescores**

**Game 1**—October 9, at Los Angeles
St. Louis ......0 0 0 0 0 0 1 0 0—1 8 1
L.A. ..............0 0 0 1 0 3 0 0 x—4 8 0
Tudor, Dayley (6), Campbell (7), Worrell (8); Valenzuela, Niedenfuer (7). W—Valenzuela. L—Tudor. S—Niedenfuer.

**Game 2**—October 10, at Los Angeles
St. Louis ....0 0 1 0 0 0 0 0 1—2 8 1
L.A. ............0 0 3 2 1 2 0 0 x—8 13 1
Andujar, Horton (5), Campbell (6), Dayley (7), Lahti (8); Hershiser. W—Hershiser. L—Andujar. HR—Brock (L.A.).

**Game 3**—October 12, at St. Louis
L.A. ..............0 0 0 1 0 0 1 0 0—2 7 2
St. Louis ......2 2 0 0 0 0 0 0 x—4 8 0
Welch, Honeycutt (3), Diaz (5), Howell (7); Cox, Horton (7), Worrell (7), Dayley (9). W—Cox. L—Welch. S—Dayley. HR—Herr (St.L.).

**Game 4**—October 13, at St. Louis
L.A. ..........0 0 0 0 0 0 1 1 0— 2 5 2
St. Louis ..0 9 0 1 1 0 0 1 x—12 15 0
Reuss, Honeycutt (2), Castillo (2), Diaz (8); Tudor, Horton (8), Campbell (9). W—Tudor. L—Reuss. HR—Madlock (L.A.).

**Game 5**—October 14, at St. Louis
L.A. ..............0 0 0 2 0 0 0 0 0—2 5 1
St. Louis ......2 0 0 0 0 0 0 0 1—3 5 1
Valenzuela, Niedenfuer (9); Forsch, Dayley (4), Worrell (7), Lahti (9). W—Lahti. L—Niedenfuer. HR—Madlock (L.A.); Smith (St.L.).

**Game 6**—October 16, at Los Angeles
St. Louis ....0 0 1 0 0 0 3 0 3—7 12 1
L.A. ............1 1 0 0 2 0 0 1 0—5 8 0
Andujar, Worrell (7), Dayley (9); Hershiser, Niedenfuer (7). W—Worrell. L—Niedenfuer. S—Dayley. HR—Madlock, Marshall (L.A.); Clark (St.L.).

## WORLD SERIES

■ **Winner:** The Royals needed three consecutive victories and a controversial sixth-game decision to claim their first Series triumph in an all-Missouri fall classic.
■ **Turning point:** A blown call at first base by umpire Don Denkinger in the Royals' ninth inning of Game 6. After arguing vehemently, the Cardinals unraveled and the Royals scored twice, claiming a 2-1 victory and forcing a seventh game.
■ **Memorable moment:** Royals catcher Jim Sundberg sliding around the tag of Cardinals catcher Darrell Porter with the winning run in Game 6. Sundberg and Onix Concepcion scored on Dane Iorg's one-out single.
■ **Top guns:** Bret Saberhagen (2-0, 0.50 ERA), George Brett (.370), Willie Wilson (.367), Royals; Tito Landrum (.360), Cardinals.
■ **MVP:** Saberhagen.

**Linescores**

**Game 1**—October 19, at Kansas City
St. Louis ......0 0 1 1 0 0 0 0 1—3 7 1
K.C. ..............0 1 0 0 0 0 0 0 0—1 8 0
Tudor, Worrell (7); Jackson, Quisenberry (8), Black (9). W—Tudor. L—Jackson. S—Worrell.

**Game 2**—October 20, at Kansas City
St. Louis ......0 0 0 0 0 0 0 0 4—4 6 0
K.C. ..............0 0 0 2 0 0 0 0 0—2 9 0
Cox, Dayley (8), Lahti (9); Leibrandt, Quisenberry (9). W—Dayley. L—Leibrandt. S—Lahti.

**Game 3**—October 22; at St. Louis
K.C. ............0 0 0 2 2 0 2 0 0—6 11 0
St. Louis ....0 0 0 0 0 1 0 0 0—1 6 0
Saberhagen; Andujar, Campbell (5), Horton (6), Dayley (8). W—Saberhagen. L—Andujar. HR—White (K.C.).

**Game 4**—October 23, at St. Louis
K.C. ..............0 0 0 0 0 0 0 0 0—0 5 1
St. Louis ......0 1 1 0 1 0 0 0 x—3 6 0
Black, Beckwith (6), Quisenberry (8); Tudor. W—Tudor. L—Black. HR—Landrum, McGee (St.L.).

**Game 5**—October 24, at St. Louis
K.C. ............1 3 0 0 0 0 0 1 1—6 11 2
St. Louis ....1 0 0 0 0 0 0 0 0—1 5 1
Jackson; Forsch, Horton (2), Campbell (4), Worrell (6), Lahti (8). W—Jackson. L—Forsch.

**Game 6**—October 26, at Kansas City
St. Louis ....0 0 0 0 0 0 0 1 0—1 5 0
K.C. ............0 0 0 0 0 0 0 0 2—2 10 0
Cox, Dayley (8), Worrell (9); Leibrandt, Quisenberry (8). W—Quisenberry. L—Worrell.

**Game 7**—October 27, at Kansas City
St. Louis ..0 0 0 0 0 0 0 0 0— 0 5 0
K.C. ..........0 2 3 0 6 0 0 0 x—11 14 0
Tudor, Campbell (3), Lahti (5), Horton (5), Andujar (5), Forsch (5), Dayley (7); Saberhagen. W—Saberhagen. L—Tudor. HR—Motley (K.C.).

# 1986

## FINAL STANDINGS

### American League

**East Division**

| Team | Bos. | N.Y. | Det. | Tor. | Cle. | Mil. | Bal. | Cal. | Tex. | K.C. | Oak. | Chi. | Min. | Sea. | W | L | Pct. | GB |
|---|---|---|---|---|---|---|---|---|---|---|---|---|---|---|---|---|---|---|
| Boston | ... | 5 | 7 | 7 | 10 | 6 | 9 | 5 | 8 | 6 | 7 | 7 | 10 | 8 | 95 | 66 | .590 | ... |
| New York | 8 | ... | 7 | 7 | 8 | 5 | 8 | 5 | 7 | 8 | 5 | 6 | 8 | 8 | 90 | 72 | .556 | 5.5 |
| Detroit | 6 | 6 | ... | 4 | 9 | 8 | 12 | 5 | 7 | 5 | 6 | 6 | 7 | 6 | 87 | 75 | .537 | 8.5 |
| Toronto | 6 | 6 | 9 | ... | 10 | 6 | 5 | 6 | 7 | 7 | 4 | 6 | 8 | 6 | 86 | 76 | .531 | 9.5 |
| Cleveland | 3 | 5 | 4 | 3 | ... | 8 | 9 | 6 | 6 | 8 | 10 | 7 | 6 | 9 | 84 | 78 | .519 | 11.5 |
| Milwaukee | 6 | 8 | 5 | 7 | 5 | ... | 7 | 7 | 4 | 6 | 5 | 7 | 4 | 6 | 77 | 84 | .478 | 18 |
| Baltimore | 4 | 5 | 1 | 8 | 4 | 6 | ... | 6 | 5 | 6 | 5 | 9 | 8 | 6 | 73 | 89 | .451 | 22.5 |

**West Division**

| Team | Cal. | Tex. | K.C. | Oak. | Chi. | Min. | Sea. | Bos. | N.Y. | Det. | Tor. | Cle. | Mil. | Bal. | W | L | Pct. | GB |
|---|---|---|---|---|---|---|---|---|---|---|---|---|---|---|---|---|---|---|
| California | ... | 8 | 8 | 10 | 7 | 7 | 8 | 7 | 7 | 7 | 6 | 6 | 5 | 6 | 92 | 70 | .568 | ... |
| Texas | 5 | ... | 5 | 10 | 11 | 7 | 9 | 4 | 5 | 5 | 5 | 6 | 8 | 7 | 87 | 75 | .537 | 5 |
| Kansas City | 5 | 8 | ... | 8 | 6 | 6 | 5 | 6 | 4 | 7 | 5 | 4 | 6 | 6 | 76 | 86 | .469 | 16 |
| Oakland | 3 | 3 | 5 | ... | 6 | 7 | 10 | 5 | 7 | 6 | 8 | 2 | 7 | 7 | 76 | 86 | .469 | 16 |
| Chicago | 6 | 2 | 7 | 7 | ... | 6 | 8 | 5 | 6 | 6 | 6 | 5 | 5 | 3 | 72 | 90 | .444 | 20 |
| Minnesota | 6 | 6 | 7 | 6 | 7 | ... | 6 | 2 | 4 | 5 | 4 | 6 | 8 | 4 | 71 | 91 | .438 | 21 |
| Seattle | 5 | 4 | 8 | 3 | 5 | 7 | ... | 4 | 4 | 6 | 6 | 3 | 6 | 6 | 67 | 95 | .414 | 25 |

### National League

**East Division**

| Team | N.Y. | Phi. | St.L. | Mon. | Chi. | Pit. | Hou. | Cin. | S.F. | S.D. | L.A. | Atl. | W | L | Pct. | GB |
|---|---|---|---|---|---|---|---|---|---|---|---|---|---|---|---|---|
| New York | ... | 8 | 12 | 10 | 12 | 17 | 7 | 8 | 7 | 10 | 9 | 8 | 108 | 54 | .667 | ... |
| Phil. | 10 | ... | 6 | 10 | 8 | 11 | 6 | 5 | 9 | 6 | 7 | 8 | 86 | 75 | .534 | 21.5 |
| St. Louis | 6 | 12 | ... | 9 | 7 | 11 | 5 | 5 | 7 | 7 | 4 | 6 | 79 | 82 | .491 | 28.5 |
| Montreal | 8 | 8 | 9 | ... | 10 | 11 | 4 | 5 | 5 | 4 | 7 | 7 | 78 | 83 | .484 | 29.5 |
| Chicago | 6 | 9 | 10 | 8 | ... | 7 | 4 | 5 | 6 | 6 | 6 | 3 | 70 | 90 | .438 | 37 |
| Pittsburgh | 1 | 7 | 7 | 7 | 11 | ... | 6 | 2 | 4 | 8 | 4 | 7 | 64 | 98 | .395 | 44 |

**West Division**

| Team | Hou. | Cin. | S.F. | S.D. | L.A. | Atl. | N.Y. | Phi. | St.L. | Mon. | Chi. | Pit. | W | L | Pct. | GB |
|---|---|---|---|---|---|---|---|---|---|---|---|---|---|---|---|---|
| Houston | ... | 14 | 9 | 10 | 10 | 13 | 5 | 6 | 7 | 8 | 8 | 6 | 96 | 66 | .593 | ... |
| Cincinnati | 4 | ... | 9 | 9 | 10 | 12 | 4 | 7 | 7 | 7 | 7 | 10 | 86 | 76 | .531 | 10 |
| San Fran. | 9 | 9 | ... | 10 | 10 | 11 | 5 | 3 | 5 | 7 | 6 | 8 | 83 | 79 | .512 | 13 |
| San Diego | 8 | 9 | 8 | ... | 12 | 6 | 2 | 6 | 5 | 8 | 6 | 4 | 74 | 88 | .457 | 22 |
| Los Angeles | 8 | 8 | 8 | 6 | ... | 8 | 3 | 5 | 8 | 5 | 6 | 8 | 73 | 89 | .451 | 23 |
| Atlanta | 5 | 6 | 7 | 12 | 10 | ... | 4 | 4 | 6 | 4 | 9 | 5 | 72 | 89 | .447 | 23.5 |

## LEADERS

**American League**
**BA:** Wade Boggs, Bos., .357.
**Runs:** Rickey Henderson, N.Y., 130.
**Hits:** Don Mattingly, N.Y., 238.
**TB:** Don Mattingly, N.Y., 388.
**HR:** Jesse Barfield, Tor., 40.
**RBI:** Joe Carter, Cle., 121.
**SB:** Rickey Henderson, N.Y., 87.
**Wins:** Roger Clemens, Bos., 24.
**ERA:** Roger Clemens, Bos., 2.48.
**CG:** Tom Candiotti, Cle., 17.
**IP:** Bert Blyleven, Min., 271.2.
**SO:** Mark Langston, Sea., 245.
**SV:** Dave Righetti, N.Y., 46.

**National League**
**BA:** Tim Raines, Mon., .334.
**Runs:** Tony Gwynn, S.D.;
Von Hayes, Phil., 107.
**Hits:** Tony Gwynn, S.D., 211.
**TB:** Dave Parker, Cin., 304.
**HR:** Mike Schmidt, Phil., 37.
**RBI:** Mike Schmidt, Phil., 119.
**SB:** Vince Coleman, St.L., 107.
**Wins:** Fernando Valenzuela, L.A., 21.
**ERA:** Mike Scott, Hou., 2.22.
**CG:** Fernando Valenzuela, L.A., 20.
**IP:** Mike Scott, Hou., 275.1.
**SO:** Mike Scott, Hou., 306.
**SV:** Todd Worrell, St.L., 36.

**A.L. 20-game winners**
Roger Clemens, Bos., 24-4
Jack Morris, Det., 21-8
Ted Higuera, Mil., 20-11

**N.L. 20-game winners**
Fernando Valenzuela, L.A., 21-11
Mike Krukow, S.F., 20-9

**A.L. 100 RBIs**
Joe Carter, Cle., 121
Jose Canseco, Oak., 117
Don Mattingly, N.Y., 113
Jim Rice, Bos., 110
Jesse Barfield, Tor., 108
George Bell, Tor., 108
Gary Gaetti, Min., 108
Jim Presley, Sea., 107
Dave Winfield, N.Y., 104
Bill Buckner, Bos., 102
Wally Joyner, Cal., 100

**N.L. 100 RBIs**
Mike Schmidt, Phil., 119
Dave Parker, Cin., 116
Gary Carter, N.Y., 105
Glenn Davis, Hou., 101

**A.L. 40 homers**
Jesse Barfield, Tor., 40

**Most Valuable Player**
A.L.: Roger Clemens, P, Bos.
N.L.: Mike Schmidt, 3B, Phil.

**Cy Young Award**
A.L.: Roger Clemens, Bos.
N.L.: Mike Scott, Hou.

**Rookie of the Year**
A.L.: Jose Canseco, OF, Oak.
N.L.: Todd Worrell, P, St.L.

**Manager of the Year**
A.L.: John McNamara, Bos.
N.L.: Hal Lanier, Hou.

**Hall of Fame additions**
Bobby Doerr, 2B, 1937-51
Ernie Lombardi, C, 1931-47
Willie McCovey, 1B, 1959-80

## SIGNIFICANT EVENTS

■ **February 28:** Commissioner Peter V. Ueberroth handed one-year suspensions to players Dave Parker, Keith Hernandez, Lonnie Smith, Dale Berra, Jeffrey Leonard, Enos Cabell and Joaquin Andujar for drug-related activities.
■ **June 20:** Bo Jackson, the 1985 Heisman Trophy winner from Auburn, stunningly signed with the Royals instead of the NFL's Tampa Bay Buccaneers.

## MEMORABLE MOMENTS

■ **April 29:** Boston's Roger Clemens broke a long-standing Major League record when he struck out 20 Mariners in a 3-1 victory at Fenway Park.
■ **June 18:** California's Don Sutton became a 300-game winner when he defeated the Rangers, 5-1.
■ **July 6:** Bob Horner became the 11th Major Leaguer to hit four homers in a game, but his Braves still dropped an 11-8 decision to the Expos.
■ **August 5:** Giants lefty Steve Carlton joined Nolan Ryan in the exclusive 4,000-strikeout club, but dropped an 11-6 decision to the Reds.
■ **September 25:** Houston righthander Mike Scott pitched the first pennant-clinching no-hitter in baseball history, beating the Giants, 2-0.
■ **October 4:** Yankee closer Dave Righetti set a one-season record when he recorded his 45th and 46th saves in a doubleheader sweep of the Red Sox.

## ALL-STAR GAME

■ **Winner:** The A.L., looking to break its one-win-per-decade streak, got home runs from second basemen Lou Whitaker and Frank White and scored a 3-2 victory — its second of the 1980s.
■ **Key inning:** The second, when Whitaker followed a Dave Winfield double with a two-run shot off Dwight Gooden.
■ **Memorable moment:** Fernando Valenzuela tied Carl Hubbell's 1934 All-Star record when he struck out, consecutively, Don Mattingly, Cal Ripken, Jesse Barfield, Whitaker and Ted Higuera.
■ **Top guns:** Roger Clemens (Red Sox), Higuera (Brewers), Whitaker (Tigers), White (Royals), A.L.; Valenzuela (Dodgers), Steve Sax (Dodgers), N.L.
■ **MVP:** Clemens.

**Linescore**
July 15, at Houston's Astrodome
A.L..............0 2 0 0 0 0 1 0 0—3 5 0
N.L..............0 0 0 0 0 0 0 2 0—2 5 1
Clemens (Red Sox), Higuera (Brewers) 4, Hough (Rangers) 7, Righetti (Yankees) 8, Aase (Orioles) 9; Gooden (Mets), Valenzuela (Dodgers) 4, Scott (Astros) 7, Fernandez (Mets) 8, Krukow (Giants) 9. W—Clemens. L—Gooden. HR—Whitaker, White, A.L.

## ALCS

■ **Winner:** Boston, on the verge of elimination in the ninth inning of Game 5, roared back to post a seven-game triumph over the stunned California Angels.
■ **Turning point:** Dave Henderson, one strike away from becoming the final out in the Angels' pennant-clinching victory, stroked a Donnie Moore pitch into the left-field bleachers for a two-run homer. The blast gave the Red Sox a 6-5 lead and they went on to post a series-turning 7-6 victory in 11 innings.
■ **Memorable moment:** Henderson dancing triumphantly around the bases as a crowd of 64,223 watched in stunned silence at Anaheim Stadium.
■ **Top guns:** Spike Owen (.429), Marty Barrett (.367, 5 RBIs), Rich Gedman (.357, 6 RBIs), Jim Rice (2 HR, 6 RBIs), Red Sox; Bob Boone (.455), Wally Joyner (.455), Angels.
■ **MVP:** Barrett.

**Linescores**
**Game 1**—October 7, at Boston
Cal. ............0 4 1 0 0 0 0 3 0—8 11 0
Boston ......0 0 0 0 0 1 0 0 0—1 5 1
Witt; Clemens, Sambito (8), Stanley (8). W—Witt. L—Clemens.
**Game 2**—October 8, at Boston
Cal. ............0 0 0 1 1 0 0 0 0—2 11 3
Boston ......1 1 0 0 1 0 3 3 x—9 13 2
McCaskill, Lucas (8), Corbett (8); Hurst. W—Hurst. L—McCaskill. HR—Joyner (Cal.); Rice (Bos.).
**Game 3**—October 10, at California
Boston ........0 1 0 0 0 0 0 2 0—3 9 1
Cal. .............0 0 0 0 0 1 3 1 x—5 8 0
Boyd, Sambito (7), Schiraldi (8); Candelaria, Moore (8). W—Candelaria. L—Boyd. S—Moore. HR—Schofield, Pettis (Cal.).
**Game 4**—October 11, at California
Boston....000 001 020 00—3 6 1
Cal. ........000 000 003 01—4 11 2
Clemens, Schiraldi (9); Sutton, Lucas (7), Ruhle (7), Finley (8), Corbett (8). W—Corbett. L—Schiraldi. HR—DeCinces (Cal.).
**Game 5**—October 12, at California
Boston....020 000 004 01—7 12 0
Cal. ........001 002 201 00—6 13 0
Hurst, Stanley (7), Sambito (9), Crawford (9), Schiraldi (11); Witt, Lucas (9), Moore (9), Finley (11). W—Crawford. L—Moore. S—Schiraldi. HR—Gedman, Baylor, Henderson (Bos.); Boone, Grich (Cal.).
**Game 6**—October 14, at Boston
Cal. ..........2 0 0 0 0 0 1 1 0— 4 11 1
Boston ....2 0 5 0 1 0 2 0 x—10 16 1
McCaskill, Lucas (3), Corbett (4), Finley (7); Boyd, Stanley (8). W—Boyd. L—McCaskill. HR—Downing (Cal.).
**Game 7**—October 15, at Boston
Cal. ...............0 0 0 0 0 0 0 1 0—1 6 2
Boston ........0 3 0 4 0 0 1 0 x—8 8 1
Candelaria, Sutton (4), Moore (8); Clemens, Schiraldi (8). W—Clemens. L—Candelaria. HR—Rice, Evans (Bos.).

## NLCS

■ **Winner:** The New York Mets overcame the outstanding pitching of Houston's Mike Scott and denied the Astros their first-ever pennant.
■ **Turning point:** The Mets claimed a 6-5 Game 3 victory when Lenny Dykstra stroked a two-run homer in the bottom of the ninth inning.
■ **Memorable moment:** Mets relief ace Jesse Orosco fired a pennant-winning third strike past Houston's Kevin Bass with two runners on base in the bottom of the 16th inning, preserving New York's 7-6 victory in the longest Championship Series game ever played.
■ **Top guns:** Orosco (3-0), Dykstra (.304), Darryl Strawberry (2 HR, 5 RBIs), Mets; Scott (2-0, 0.50 ERA), Craig Reynolds (.333), Astros.
■ **MVP:** Scott.

**Linescores**
**Game 1**—October 8, at Houston
N.Y..............0 0 0 0 0 0 0 0 0—0 5 0
Hou. ............0 1 0 0 0 0 0 0 x—1 7 1
Gooden, Orosco (8); Scott. W—Scott. L—Gooden. HR—Davis (Hou.).
**Game 2**—October 9, at Houston
N.Y............0 0 0 2 3 0 0 0 0—5 10 0
Hou. ..........0 0 0 0 0 0 1 0 0—1 10 2
Ojeda; Ryan, Andersen (6), Lopez (8), Kerfeld (9). W—Ojeda. L—Ryan.
**Game 3**—October 11, at New York
Hou. ..........2 2 0 0 0 0 1 0 0—5 8 1
N.Y............0 0 0 0 0 4 0 0 2—6 10 1
Knepper, Kerfeld (8), Smith (9); Darling, Aguilera (6), Orosco (8). W—Orosco. L—Smith. HR—Doran (Hou.); Strawberry, Dykstra (N.Y.).
**Game 4**—October 12, at New York
Hou. ............0 2 0 0 1 0 0 0 0—3 4 1
N.Y..............0 0 0 0 0 0 0 1 0—1 3 0
Scott; Fernandez, McDowell (7), Sisk (9). W—Scott. L—Fernandez. HR—Ashby, Thon (Hou.).
**Game 5**—October 14, at New York
Hou. ......000 010 000 000—1 9 1
N.Y........000 010 000 001—2 4 0
Ryan, Kerfeld (10); Gooden, Orosco (11). W—Orosco. L—Kerfeld. HR—Strawberry (N.Y.).
**Game 6**—October 15, at Houston
N.Y. ....000 000 003 000 0103—7 11 0
Hou.....300 000 000 000 0102—6 11 1
Ojeda, Aguilera (6), McDowell (9), Orosco (14); Knepper, Smith (9), Andersen (11), Lopez (14), Calhoun (16). W—Orosco. L—Lopez. HR—Hatcher (Hou.).

## WORLD SERIES

■ **Winner:** The Mets, on the brink of elimination, made a wild Game 6 recovery and kept the Red Sox without a Series victory since 1918.
■ **Turning point:** The bottom of the 10th inning of Game 6. One out away from elimination and trailing 5-3 with nobody on base, the Mets amazingly rallied for three runs and a 6-5, Game 7-forcing victory.
■ **Memorable moments:** A tense, 10-pitch battle between Mets batter Mookie Wilson and Boston pitcher Bob Stanley in the fateful 10th inning of Game 6. One Stanley pitch was wild, allowing the tying run to score, and Wilson slapped the final one to first baseman Bill Buckner, who let the ball dribble between his legs for a game-deciding error.
■ **Top guns:** Ray Knight (.391), Gary Carter (2 HR, 9 RBIs), Mets; Bruce Hurst (2-0, 1.96 ERA), Dwight Evans (2 HR, 9 RBIs), Red Sox.
■ **MVP:** Knight.

**Linescores**
**Game 1**—October 18, at New York
Boston ........0 0 0 0 0 0 1 0 0—1 5 0
N.Y..............0 0 0 0 0 0 0 0 0—0 4 1
Hurst, Schiraldi (9); Darling, McDowell (8). W—Hurst. L—Darling. S—Schiraldi.
**Game 2**—October 19, at New York
Boston ......0 0 3 1 2 0 2 0 1—9 18 0
N.Y............0 0 2 0 1 0 0 0 0—3 8 1
Clemens, Crawford (5), Stanley (7); Gooden, Aguilera (6), Orosco (7), Fernandez (9), Sisk (9). W—Crawford. L—Gooden. S—Stanley. HR—Henderson, Evans (Bos.).
**Game 3**—October 21, at Boston
N.Y............4 0 0 0 0 0 2 1 0—7 13 0
Boston ......0 0 1 0 0 0 0 0 0—1 5 0
Ojeda, McDowell (8); Boyd, Sambito (8), Stanley (8). W—Ojeda. L—Boyd. HR—Dykstra (N.Y.).
**Game 4**—October 22, at Boston
N.Y............0 0 0 3 0 0 2 1 0—6 12 0
Boston ......0 0 0 0 0 0 0 2 0—2 7 1
Darling, McDowell (8), Orosco (8); Nipper, Crawford (7), Stanley (9). W—Darling. L—Nipper. S—Orosco. HR—Carter 2, Dykstra (N.Y.).
**Game 5**—October 23, at Boston
N.Y............0 0 0 0 0 0 0 1 1—2 10 1
Boston ......0 1 1 0 2 0 0 0 x—4 12 0
Gooden, Fernandez (5); Hurst. W—Hurst. L—Gooden. HR—Teufel (N.Y.).
**Game 6**—October 25, at New York
Boston ..1 1 0 0 0 0 1 0 0 2—5 13 3
N.Y........0 0 0 0 2 0 0 1 0 3—6 8 2
Clemens, Schiraldi (8), Stanley (10); Ojeda, McDowell (7), Orosco (8), Aguilera (9). W—Aguilera. L—Schiraldi. HR—Henderson (Bos.).
**Game 7**—October 27, at New York
Boston ......0 3 0 0 0 0 0 2 0—5 9 0
N.Y............0 0 0 0 0 3 3 2 x—8 10 0
Hurst, Schiraldi (7), Sambito (7), Stanley (7), Nipper (8), Crawford (8); Darling, Fernandez (4), McDowell (7), Orosco (8). W—McDowell. L—Schiraldi. S—Orosco. HR—Evans, Gedman (Bos.); Knight, Strawberry (N.Y.).

# 1987

## FINAL STANDINGS

### American League

**East Division**

| Team | Det. | Tor. | Mil. | N.Y. | Bos. | Bal. | Cle. | Min. | K.C. | Oak. | Sea. | Chi. | Tex. | Cal. | W | L | Pct. | GB |
|---|---|---|---|---|---|---|---|---|---|---|---|---|---|---|---|---|---|---|
| Detroit | ... | 7 | 6 | 5 | 11 | 9 | 9 | 8 | 5 | 5 | 7 | 9 | 8 | 9 | 98 | 64 | .605 | ... |
| Toronto | 6 | ... | 4 | 7 | 7 | 12 | 8 | 9 | 4 | 5 | 10 | 8 | 9 | 7 | 96 | 66 | .593 | 2 |
| Milwaukee | 7 | 9 | ... | 7 | 7 | 11 | 9 | 3 | 8 | 6 | 4 | 6 | 9 | 5 | 91 | 71 | .562 | 7 |
| New York | 8 | 6 | 6 | ... | 6 | 10 | 7 | 6 | 7 | 5 | 7 | 7 | 5 | 9 | 89 | 73 | .549 | 9 |
| Boston | 2 | 6 | 6 | 7 | ... | 12 | 7 | 7 | 6 | 4 | 7 | 3 | 7 | 4 | 78 | 84 | .481 | 20 |
| Baltimore | 4 | 1 | 2 | 3 | 1 | ... | 7 | 5 | 9 | 7 | 4 | 8 | 7 | 9 | 67 | 95 | .414 | 31 |
| Cleveland | 4 | 5 | 4 | 6 | 6 | 6 | ... | 3 | 6 | 4 | 5 | 5 | 2 | 5 | 61 | 101 | .377 | 37 |

**West Division**

| Team | Min. | K.C. | Oak. | Sea. | Chi. | Tex. | Cal. | Det. | Tor. | Mil. | N.Y. | Bos. | Bal. | Cle. | W | L | Pct. | GB |
|---|---|---|---|---|---|---|---|---|---|---|---|---|---|---|---|---|---|---|
| Minnesota | ... | 5 | 10 | 9 | 7 | 6 | 5 | 4 | 3 | 9 | 6 | 5 | 7 | 9 | 85 | 77 | .525 | ... |
| Kansas City | 8 | ... | 5 | 9 | 7 | 7 | 8 | 7 | 8 | 4 | 5 | 6 | 3 | 6 | 83 | 79 | .512 | 2 |
| Oakland | 3 | 8 | ... | 5 | 4 | 6 | 7 | 7 | 7 | 6 | 7 | 8 | 5 | 8 | 81 | 81 | .500 | 4 |
| Seattle | 4 | 4 | 8 | ... | 7 | 9 | 6 | 5 | 2 | 8 | 5 | 5 | 8 | 7 | 78 | 84 | .481 | 7 |
| Chicago | 6 | 6 | 9 | 6 | ... | 7 | 5 | 3 | 4 | 6 | 5 | 9 | 4 | 7 | 77 | 85 | .475 | 8 |
| Texas | 7 | 6 | 7 | 4 | 6 | ... | 8 | 4 | 3 | 3 | 7 | 5 | 5 | 10 | 75 | 87 | .463 | 10 |
| California | 8 | 5 | 6 | 7 | 8 | 5 | ... | 3 | 5 | 7 | 3 | 8 | 3 | 7 | 75 | 87 | .463 | 10 |

### National League

**East Division**

| Team | St.L. | N.Y. | Mon. | Phi. | Pit. | Chi. | S.F. | Cin. | Hou. | L.A. | Atl. | S.D. | W | L | Pct. | GB |
|---|---|---|---|---|---|---|---|---|---|---|---|---|---|---|---|---|
| St. Louis | ... | 9 | 7 | 10 | 11 | 12 | 5 | 8 | 7 | 9 | 9 | 8 | 95 | 67 | .586 | ... |
| New York | 9 | ... | 10 | 13 | 12 | 9 | 9 | 5 | 6 | 6 | 5 | 8 | 92 | 70 | .568 | 3 |
| Montreal | 11 | 8 | ... | 10 | 11 | 8 | 5 | 6 | 5 | 9 | 9 | 9 | 91 | 71 | .562 | 4 |
| Philadelphia | 8 | 5 | 8 | ... | 11 | 10 | 2 | 7 | 6 | 10 | 5 | 8 | 80 | 82 | .494 | 15 |
| Pittsburgh | 7 | 6 | 7 | 7 | ... | 14 | 6 | 8 | 6 | 6 | 5 | 8 | 80 | 82 | .494 | 15 |
| Chicago | 6 | 9 | 10 | 8 | 4 | ... | 5 | 6 | 8 | 6 | 5 | 9 | 76 | 85 | .472 | 18.5 |

**West Division**

| Team | S.F. | Cin. | Hou. | L.A. | Atl. | S.D. | St.L. | N.Y. | Mon. | Phi. | Pit. | Chi. | W | L | Pct. | GB |
|---|---|---|---|---|---|---|---|---|---|---|---|---|---|---|---|---|
| San Fran. | ... | 11 | 8 | 8 | 10 | 13 | 7 | 3 | 7 | 10 | 6 | 7 | 90 | 72 | .556 | ... |
| Cincinnati | 7 | ... | 13 | 10 | 10 | 12 | 4 | 7 | 6 | 5 | 4 | 6 | 84 | 78 | .519 | 6 |
| Houston | 10 | 5 | ... | 12 | 10 | 5 | 5 | 6 | 7 | 6 | 6 | 4 | 76 | 86 | .469 | 14 |
| Los Angeles | 10 | 8 | 6 | ... | 12 | 11 | 3 | 6 | 3 | 2 | 6 | 6 | 73 | 89 | .451 | 17 |
| Atlanta | 8 | 8 | 8 | 6 | ... | 6 | 3 | 7 | 3 | 7 | 7 | 6 | 69 | 92 | .429 | 20.5 |
| San Diego | 5 | 6 | 13 | 7 | 12 | ... | 4 | 4 | 3 | 4 | 4 | 3 | 65 | 97 | .401 | 25 |

## SIGNIFICANT EVENTS

■ **April 8:** Dodgers vice president Al Campanis, reeling from criticism he had generated two days earlier with his nationally televised comments about the role of blacks in sports, resigned.

■ **July 14:** Kansas City's Bo Jackson became a two-sport star when he signed a five-year contract to play football for the Los Angeles Raiders.

## MEMORABLE MOMENTS

■ **April 18:** Mike Schmidt joined the 500-homer club with a dramatic three-run ninth-inning shot that gave the Phillies an 8-6 victory over the Pirates.

■ **July 18:** Yankee Don Mattingly tied a 31-year-old Major League record when he hit a home run in his eighth consecutive game—a 7-2 loss to the Rangers.

■ **August 26:** Cleveland pitcher John Farrell stopped Paul Molitor's 39-game hitting streak, but Milwaukee won in 10 innings, 1-0.

■ **September 14:** Catcher Ernie Whitt belted three home runs to lead a Toronto assault that produced a record 10 homers and an 18-3 rout of the Orioles.

■ **September 29:** Oakland's Mark McGwire pounded his 49th home run in a 5-4 victory over Cleveland, giving him 11 more than the previous rookie record.

■ **October 3:** Dodgers ace Orel Hershiser ended Padres catcher Benito Santiago's rookie-record 34-game hitting streak.

■ **October 4:** The Tigers defeated Toronto, 1-0, and completed a season-ending, A.L. East-deciding sweep of the Blue Jays.

## LEADERS

**American League**
**BA:** Wade Boggs, Bos., .363.
**Runs:** Paul Molitor, Mil., 114.
**Hits:** Kirby Puckett, Min.; Kevin Seitzer, K.C., 207.
**TB:** George Bell, Tor., 369.
**HR:** Mark McGwire, Oak., 49.
**RBI:** George Bell, Tor., 134.
**SB:** Harold Reynolds, Sea., 60.
**Wins:** Roger Clemens, Bos.; Dave Stewart, Oak., 20.
**ERA:** Jimmy Key, Tor., 2.76.
**CG:** Roger Clemens, Bos., 18.
**IP:** Charlie Hough, Tex., 285.1.
**SO:** Mark Langston, Sea., 262.
**SV:** Tom Henke, Tor., 34.

**National League**
**BA:** Tony Gwynn, S.D., .370.
**Runs:** Tim Raines, Mon., 123.
**Hits:** Tony Gwynn, S.D., 218.
**TB:** Andre Dawson, Chi., 353.
**HR:** Andre Dawson, Chi., 49.
**RBI:** Andre Dawson, Chi., 137.
**SB:** Vince Coleman, St.L., 109.
**Wins:** Rick Sutcliffe, Chi., 18.
**ERA:** Nolan Ryan, Hou., 2.76.
**CG:** Rick Reuschel, Pit.-S.F.; Fernando Valenzuela, L.A., 12.
**IP:** Orel Hershiser, L.A., 264.2.
**SO:** Nolan Ryan, Hou., 270.
**SV:** Steve Bedrosian, Phil., 40.

**A.L. 20-game winners**
Roger Clemens, Bos., 20-9
Dave Stewart, Oak., 20-13

**A.L. 100 RBIs**
George Bell, Tor., 134
Dwight Evans, Bos., 123
Mark McGwire, Oak., 118
Wally Joyner, Cal., 117
Don Mattingly, N.Y., 115
Jose Canseco, Oak., 113
Gary Gaetti, Min., 109
Ruben Sierra, Tex., 109
Joe Carter, Cle., 106
Alan Trammell, Det., 105
Robin Yount, Mil., 103
Danny Tartabull, K.C., 101
Alvin Davis, Sea., 100
Larry Parrish, Tex., 100

**N.L. 100 RBIs**
Andre Dawson, Chi., 137
Tim Wallach, Mon., 123
Mike Schmidt, Phil., 113
Jack Clark, St.L., 106
Willie McGee, St.L., 105
Dale Murphy, Atl., 105
Darryl Strawberry, N.Y., 104
Eric Davis, Cin., 100
Juan Samuel, Phil., 100

**A.L. 40 homers**
Mark McGwire, Oak., 49
George Bell, Tor., 47

**N.L. 40 homers**
Andre Dawson, Chi., 49
Dale Murphy, Atl., 44

**Most Valuable Player**
A.L.: George Bell, OF, Tor.
N.L.: Andre Dawson, OF, Chi.

**Cy Young Award**
A.L.: Roger Clemens, Bos.
N.L.: Steve Bedrosian, Phil.

**Rookie of the Year**
A.L.: Mark McGwire, 1B, Oak.
N.L.: Benito Santiago, C, S.D.

**Manager of the Year**
A.L.: Sparky Anderson, Det.
N.L.: Buck Rodgers, Mon.

**Hall of Fame additions**
Ray Dandridge, 3B, Negro Leagues
Catfish Hunter, P, 1965-79
Billy Williams, OF, 1959-76

## ALL-STAR GAME

■ **Winner:** The N.L. broke a scoreless deadlock in the 13th inning to claim a 2-0 victory.

■ **Key inning:** The 13th, when Tim Raines drilled a two-out Jay Howell pitch for a two-run triple, scoring Ozzie Virgil and Hubie Brooks.

■ **Memorable moment:** A violent collision between Dave Winfield and N.L. catcher Virgil in the ninth. Winfield, trying to score from second on a failed double-play attempt, was called out when Virgil held onto the ball.

■ **Top guns:** Mike Scott (Astros), Rick Sutcliffe (Cubs), Orel Hershiser (Dodgers), Raines (Expos), N.L.; Bret Saberhagen (Royals), Mark Langston (Mariners), A.L.

■ **MVP:** Raines.

**Linescore**
July 14, at the Oakland Coliseum
N.L. ..........000 000 000 0002—2 8 2
A.L. ..........000 000 000 0000—0 6 1
Scott (Astros), Sutcliffe (Cubs) 3, Hershiser (Dodgers) 5, Reuschel (Pirates) 7, Franco (Reds) 8, Bedrosian (Phillies) 9, L. Smith (Cubs) 10, S. Fernandez (Mets) 13; Saberhagen (Royals), Morris (Tigers) 4, Langston (Mariners) 6, Plesac (Brewers) 8, Righetti (Yankees) 9, Henke (Blue Jays) 9, Howell (Athletics) 12. W—L. Smith. L—Howell. S—S. Fernandez.

## ALCS

■ **Winner:** Minnesota, a loser in the A.L.'s first two LCS in 1969 and '70, surprised the favored Detroit Tigers in a five-game romp.

■ **Turning point:** The sixth inning of Game 4. With the Twins leading the series 2-1 and the game 4-3, Detroit's Darrell Evans let Minnesota catcher Tim Laudner pick him off third base — a mistake that doomed the Tigers' pennant hopes.

■ **Memorable moment:** The Game 5 hitting of Twins right fielder Tom Brunansky, who collected a single, double, homer and three RBIs in Minnesota's series-closing 9-5 victory.

■ **Top guns:** Brunansky (.412, 2 HR, 9 RBIs), Dan Gladden (.350), Gary Gaetti (.300, 2 HR, 5 RBIs), Twins; Johnny Grubb (.571), Chet Lemon (2 HR, 4 RBIs), Tigers.

■ **MVP:** Gaetti.

**Linescores**
**Game 1**—October 7, at Minnesota
Detroit........0 0 1 0 0 1 1 2 0—5 10 0
Minnesota..0 1 0 0 3 0 0 4 x—8 10 0
Alexander, Henneman (8), Hernandez (8), King (8); Viola, Reardon (8). W—Reardon. L—Alexander. HR—Gaetti 2 (Min.); Heath, Gibson (Det.).

**Game 2**—October 8, at Minnesota
Detroit..........0 2 0 0 0 0 0 1 0—3 7 1
Minnesota....0 3 0 2 1 0 0 0 x—6 6 0
Morris; Blyleven, Berenguer (8). W—Blyleven. L—Morris. S—Berenguer. HR—Lemon, Whitaker (Det.); Hrbek (Min.).

**Game 3**—October 10, at Detroit
Minnesota....0 0 0 2 0 2 2 0 0—6 8 1
Detroit..........0 0 5 0 0 0 0 2 x—7 7 0
Straker, Schatzeder (3), Berenguer (7), Reardon (8); Terrell, Henneman (7). W—Henneman. L—Reardon. HR—Gagne, Brunansky (Min.); Sheridan (Det.).

**Game 4**—October 11, at Detroit
Minnesota....0 0 1 1 1 1 0 1 0—5 7 1
Detroit..........1 0 0 0 1 1 0 0 0—3 7 3
Viola, Atherton (6), Berenguer (6), Reardon (9); Tanana, Petry (6), Thurmond (9). W—Viola. L—Tanana. S—Reardon. HR—Puckett, Gagne (Min.).

**Game 5**—October 12, at Detroit
Minnesota..0 4 0 0 0 0 1 1 3—9 15 1
Detroit........0 0 0 3 0 0 0 1 1—5 9 1
Blyleven, Schatzeder (7), Berenguer (8), Reardon (8); Alexander, King (2), Henneman (7), Robinson (9). W—Blyleven. L—Alexander. S—Reardon. HR—Nokes, Lemon (Det.); Brunansky (Min.).

## NLCS

■ **Winner:** The Cardinals had to overcome the lusty hitting of San Francisco's Jeffrey Leonard to claim their third pennant of the decade.

■ **Turning point:** The combined six-hit pitching of Cardinals John Tudor, Todd Worrell and Ken Dayley in a 1-0 Game 6 victory.

■ **Memorable moment:** Leonard's two-run homer in the fifth inning of Game 4—his record-tying fourth in the series.

■ **Top guns:** Tony Pena (.381), Willie McGee (.308), Cardinals; Dave Dravecky (1-1, 0.60 ERA), Leonard (.417, 4 HR, 5 RBIs), Giants.

■ **MVP:** Leonard.

**Linescores**
**Game 1**—October 6, at St. Louis
San Fran. ....1 0 0 1 0 0 0 1 0—3 7 1
St. Louis ......0 0 1 1 0 3 0 0 x—5 10 1
Reuschel, Lefferts (7), Garrelts (8); Mathews, Worrell (8), Dayley (8). W—Mathews. L—Reuschel. S—Dayley. HR—Leonard (S.F.).

**Game 2**—October 7, at St. Louis
San Fran. ....0 2 0 1 0 0 0 2 0—5 10 0
St. Louis ......0 0 0 0 0 0 0 0 0—0 2 1
Dravecky; Tudor, Forsch (9). W—Dravecky. L—Tudor. HR—W. Clark, Leonard (S.F.).

**Game 3**—October 9, at San Francisco
St. Louis ......0 0 0 0 0 2 4 0 0—6 11 1
San Fran. ....0 3 1 0 0 0 0 0 1—5 7 1
Magrane, Forsch (5), Worrell (7); Hammaker, D. Robinson (7), Lefferts (7), LaCoss (8). W—Forsch. L—D. Robinson. S—Worrell. HR—Leonard, Spilman (S.F.); Lindeman (St.L.).

**Game 4**—October 10, at San Francisco
St. Louis ........0 2 0 0 0 0 0 0 0—2 9 0
San Fran.........0 0 0 1 2 0 0 1 x—4 9 2
Cox; Krukow. W—Krukow. L—Cox. HR—Thompson, Leonard, Brenly (S.F.).

**Game 5**—October 11, at San Francisco
St. Louis ........1 0 1 1 0 0 0 0 0—3 7 0
San Fran. ......1 0 1 4 0 0 0 0 x—6 7 1
Mathews, Forsch (4), Horton (4), Dayley (7); Reuschel, Price (5). W—Price. L—Forsch. HR—Mitchell (S.F.).

**Game 6**—October 13, at St. Louis
San Fran. ......0 0 0 0 0 0 0 0 0—0 6 0
St. Louis ........0 1 0 0 0 0 0 0 x—1 5 0
Dravecky, D. Robinson (7); Tudor, Worrell (8), Dayley (9). W—Tudor. L—Dravecky. S—Dayley.

**Game 7**—October 14, at St. Louis
San Fran. ....0 0 0 0 0 0 0 0 0—0 8 1
St. Louis ......0 4 0 0 0 2 0 0 x—6 12 0
Hammaker, Price (3), Downs (3), Garrelts (5), Lefferts (6), LaCoss (6), D. Robinson (8); Cox. W—Cox. L—Hammaker. HR—Oquendo (St.L.).

## WORLD SERIES

■ **Winner:** The Twins held off the Cardinals and captured a Series in which the home team won every game.

■ **Turning point:** Don Baylor's two-run fifth-inning homer and Kent Hrbek's grand slam, blows that turned a 5-2 deficit into an 11-5 sixth-game victory for the Twins.

■ **Memorable moment:** Hrbek's arm-pumping jaunt around the bases after his Game 6 slam.

■ **Top guns:** Frank Viola (2-1), Steve Lombardozzi (.412), Twins; Tony Pena (.409), Willie McGee (.370), Cardinals.

■ **MVP:** Viola.

**Linescores**
**Game 1**—October 17, at Minnesota
St. Louis ..0 1 0 0 0 0 0 0 0— 1 5 1
Minn. ......0 0 0 7 2 0 1 0 x—10 11 0
Magrane, Forsch (4), Horton (7); Viola, Atherton (9). W—Viola. L—Magrane. HR—Gladden, Lombardozzi (Min.).

**Game 2**—October 18, at Minnesota
St. Louis ....0 0 0 0 1 0 1 2 0—4 9 0
Minn. ........0 1 0 6 0 1 0 0 x—8 10 0
Cox, Tunnell (4), Dayley (7), Worrell (8); Blyleven, Berenguer (8), Reardon (9). W—Blyleven. L—Cox. HR—Gaetti, Laudner (Min.).

**Game 3**—October 20, at St. Louis
Minn. ..........0 0 0 0 0 1 0 0 0—1 5 1
St. Louis ......0 0 0 0 0 0 3 0 x—3 9 1
Straker, Berenguer (7), Schatzeder (7); Tudor, Worrell (8). W—Tudor. L—Berenguer. S—Worrell.

**Game 4**—October 21, at St. Louis
Minn. ........0 0 1 0 1 0 0 0 0—2 7 1
St. Louis ....0 0 1 6 0 0 0 0 x—7 10 1
Viola, Schatzeder (4), Niekro (5), Frazier (7); Mathews, Forsch (4), Dayley (7). W—Forsch. L—Viola. S—Dayley. HR—Gagne (Min.); Lawless (St.L.).

**Game 5**—October 22, at St. Louis
Minn. ........0 0 0 0 0 0 0 2 0—2 6 1
St. Louis ....0 0 0 0 0 3 1 0 x—4 10 0
Blyleven, Atherton (7), Reardon (7); Cox, Dayley (8), Worrell (8). W—Cox. L—Blyleven. S—Worrell.

**Game 6**—October 24, at Minnesota
St. Louis ..1 1 0 2 1 0 0 0 0— 5 11 2
Minn. ......2 0 0 0 4 4 0 1 x—11 15 0
Tudor, Horton (5), Forsch (6), Dayley (6), Tunnell (7); Straker, Schatzeder (4), Berenguer (6), Reardon (9). W—Schatzeder. L—Tudor. HR—Herr (St.L.); Baylor, Hrbek (Min.).

**Game 7**—October 25, at Minnesota
St. Louis ....0 2 0 0 0 0 0 0 0—2 6 1
Minn. ........0 1 0 0 1 1 0 1 x—4 10 0
Magrane, Cox (5), Worrell (6); Viola, Reardon (9). W—Viola. L—Cox. S—Reardon.

# 1988

## FINAL STANDINGS

### American League

**East Division**

| Team | Bos. | Det. | Mil. | Tor. | N.Y. | Cle. | Bal. | Oak. | Min. | K.C. | Cal. | Chi. | Tex. | Sea. | W | L | Pct. | GB |
|---|---|---|---|---|---|---|---|---|---|---|---|---|---|---|---|---|---|---|
| Boston | ... | 6 | 10 | 2 | 9 | 8 | 9 | 3 | 7 | 6 | 8 | 7 | 8 | 6 | 89 | 73 | .549 | ... |
| Detroit | 7 | ... | 5 | 5 | 8 | 9 | 8 | 4 | 1 | 8 | 7 | 9 | 8 | 9 | 88 | 74 | .543 | 1 |
| Milwaukee | 3 | 8 | ... | 7 | 6 | 4 | 9 | 3 | 7 | 9 | 9 | 6 | 8 | 8 | 87 | 75 | .537 | 2 |
| Toronto | 11 | 8 | 6 | ... | 7 | 7 | 8 | 3 | 5 | 8 | 6 | 5 | 6 | 7 | 87 | 75 | .537 | 2 |
| New York | 4 | 5 | 7 | 6 | ... | 7 | 10 | 6 | 9 | 6 | 6 | 9 | 5 | 5 | 85 | 76 | .528 | 3.5 |
| Cleveland | 5 | 4 | 9 | 6 | 6 | ... | 9 | 4 | 5 | 6 | 4 | 9 | 6 | 5 | 78 | 84 | .481 | 11 |
| Baltimore | 4 | 5 | 4 | 5 | 3 | 4 | ... | 4 | 3 | 0 | 5 | 4 | 6 | 7 | 54 | 107 | .335 | 34.5 |

**West Division**

| Team | Oak. | Min. | K.C. | Cal. | Chi. | Tex. | Sea. | Bos. | Det. | Mil. | Tor. | N.Y. | Cle. | Bal. | W | L | Pct. | GB |
|---|---|---|---|---|---|---|---|---|---|---|---|---|---|---|---|---|---|---|
| Oakland | ... | 8 | 5 | 9 | 8 | 8 | 9 | 9 | 8 | 9 | 9 | 6 | 8 | 8 | 104 | 58 | .642 | ... |
| Minnesota | 5 | ... | 6 | 9 | 9 | 7 | 8 | 5 | 11 | 5 | 7 | 3 | 7 | 9 | 91 | 71 | .562 | 13 |
| Kansas City | 8 | 7 | ... | 8 | 6 | 7 | 7 | 6 | 4 | 3 | 4 | 6 | 6 | 12 | 84 | 77 | .522 | 19.5 |
| California | 4 | 4 | 5 | ... | 9 | 8 | 6 | 4 | 5 | 3 | 6 | 6 | 8 | 7 | 75 | 87 | .463 | 29 |
| Chicago | 5 | 4 | 7 | 4 | ... | 8 | 9 | 5 | 3 | 6 | 7 | 3 | 3 | 7 | 71 | 90 | .441 | 32.5 |
| Texas | 5 | 6 | 6 | 5 | 5 | ... | 7 | 4 | 4 | 4 | 6 | 6 | 6 | 6 | 70 | 91 | .435 | 33.5 |
| Seattle | 4 | 5 | 5 | 7 | 4 | 6 | ... | 6 | 3 | 4 | 5 | 7 | 7 | 5 | 68 | 93 | .422 | 35.5 |

### National League

**East Division**

| Team | N.Y. | Pit. | Mon. | Chi. | St.L. | Phi. | L.A. | Cin. | S.D. | S.F. | Hou. | Atl. | W | L | Pct. | GB |
|---|---|---|---|---|---|---|---|---|---|---|---|---|---|---|---|---|
| New York | ... | 12 | 12 | 9 | 14 | 10 | 10 | 7 | 7 | 4 | 7 | 8 | 100 | 60 | .625 | ... |
| Pittsburgh | 6 | ... | 10 | 11 | 11 | 11 | 6 | 5 | 8 | 8 | 4 | 5 | 85 | 75 | .531 | 15 |
| Montreal | 6 | 8 | ... | 9 | 13 | 9 | 4 | 7 | 4 | 7 | 6 | 8 | 81 | 81 | .500 | 20 |
| Chicago | 9 | 7 | 9 | ... | 7 | 8 | 4 | 6 | 8 | 5 | 7 | 7 | 77 | 85 | .475 | 24 |
| St. Louis | 4 | 7 | 5 | 11 | ... | 12 | 5 | 6 | 6 | 5 | 6 | 9 | 76 | 86 | .469 | 25 |
| Philadelphia | 8 | 7 | 9 | 10 | 6 | ... | 1 | 3 | 4 | 7 | 4 | 6 | 65 | 96 | .404 | 35.5 |

**West Division**

| Team | L.A. | Cin. | S.D. | S.F. | Hou. | Atl. | N.Y. | Pit. | Mon. | Chi. | St.L. | Phi. | W | L | Pct. | GB |
|---|---|---|---|---|---|---|---|---|---|---|---|---|---|---|---|---|
| Los Angeles | ... | 11 | 7 | 12 | 9 | 14 | 1 | 6 | 8 | 8 | 7 | 11 | 94 | 67 | .584 | ... |
| Cincinnati | 7 | ... | 10 | 11 | 9 | 13 | 4 | 7 | 5 | 6 | 6 | 9 | 87 | 74 | .540 | 7 |
| San Diego | 11 | 8 | ... | 8 | 12 | 10 | 5 | 4 | 8 | 4 | 6 | 7 | 83 | 78 | .516 | 11 |
| San Fran. | 6 | 7 | 10 | ... | 11 | 13 | 8 | 4 | 5 | 7 | 7 | 5 | 83 | 79 | .512 | 11.5 |
| Houston | 9 | 9 | 6 | 7 | ... | 13 | 5 | 8 | 6 | 5 | 6 | 8 | 82 | 80 | .506 | 12.5 |
| Atlanta | 4 | 5 | 8 | 5 | 5 | ... | 4 | 5 | 4 | 5 | 3 | 6 | 54 | 106 | .338 | 39.5 |

## LEADERS

**American League**
**BA:** Wade Boggs, Bos., .366.
**Runs:** Wade Boggs, Bos., 128.
**Hits:** Kirby Puckett, Min., 234.
**TB:** Kirby Puckett, Min., 358.
**HR:** Jose Canseco, Oak., 42.
**RBI:** Jose Canseco, Oak., 124.
**SB:** Rickey Henderson, N.Y., 93.
**Wins:** Frank Viola, Min., 24.
**ERA:** Allan Anderson, Min., 2.45.
**CG:** Roger Clemens, Bos.; Dave Stewart, Oak., 14.
**IP:** Dave Stewart, Oak., 275.2.
**SO:** Roger Clemens, Bos., 291.
**SV:** Dennis Eckersley, Oak., 45.

**National League**
**BA:** Tony Gwynn, S.D., .313.
**Runs:** Brett Butler, S.F., 109.
**Hits:** Andres Galarraga, Mon., 184.
**TB:** Andres Galarraga, Mon., 329.
**HR:** Darryl Strawberry, N.Y., 39.
**RBI:** Will Clark, S.F., 109.
**SB:** Vince Coleman, St.L., 81.
**Wins:** Orel Hershiser, L.A.; Danny Jackson, Cin., 23.
**ERA:** Joe Magrane, St.L., 2.18.
**CG:** Orel Hershiser, L.A.; Danny Jackson, Cin., 15.
**IP:** Orel Hershiser, L.A., 267.
**SO:** Nolan Ryan, Hou., 228.
**SV:** John Franco, Cin., 39.

**A.L. 20-game winners**
Frank Viola, Min., 24-7
Dave Stewart, Oak., 21-12
Mark Gubicza, K.C., 20-8

**N.L. 20-game winners**
Orel Hershiser, L.A., 23-8
Danny Jackson, Cin., 23-8
David Cone, N.Y., 20-3

**A.L. 100 RBIs**
Jose Canseco, Oak., 124
Kirby Puckett, Min., 121
Mike Greenwell, Bos., 119
Dwight Evans, Bos., 111
Dave Winfield, N.Y, 107
George Brett, K.C., 103
Danny Tartabull, K.C., 102

**N.L. 100 RBIs**
Will Clark, S.F., 109
Darryl Strawberry, N.Y., 101
Bobby Bonilla, Pit., 100
Andy Van Slyke, Pit., 100

**A.L. 40 homers**
Jose Canseco, Oak., 42

**Most Valuable Player**
A.L.: Jose Canseco, OF, Oak.
N.L.: Kirk Gibson, OF, L.A.

**Cy Young Award**
A.L.: Frank Viola, Min.
N.L.: Orel Hershiser, L.A.

**Rookie of the Year**
A.L.: Walt Weiss, SS, Oak.
N.L.: Chris Sabo, 3B, Cin.

**Manager of the Year**
A.L.: Tony La Russa, Oak.
N.L.: Tommy Lasorda, L.A.

**Hall of Fame addition**
Willie Stargell, OF/1B, 1962-82

## SIGNIFICANT EVENTS

■ **January 22:** Kirk Gibson and Carlton Fisk were among seven players declared free agents by an arbitrator who ruled that owners had acted in collusion against free agents after the 1985 season.

■ **June 23:** Yankee owner George Steinbrenner fired manager Billy Martin for a fifth time and replaced him with the man he had replaced—Lou Piniella.

■ **August 9:** The Cubs defeated the Mets, 6-4, in the first official night game at Chicago's 74-year-old Wrigley Field.

■ **August 31:** Major League owners were stunned when a labor arbitrator found them guilty of collusion for a second time—this time against the 1986 class of free agents.

■ **September 8:** N.L. President A. Bartlett Giamatti was elected to succeed Peter V. Ueberroth as baseball's seventh commissioner.

## MEMORABLE MOMENTS

■ **April 29:** The Orioles defeated Chicago, 9-0, and ended their record season-opening losing streak at 21 games.

■ **June 25:** Orioles shortstop Cal Ripken stretched his ironman streak to 1,000 games in a 10-3 loss to Boston.

■ **September 16:** Cincinnati's Tom Browning retired 27 consecutive Dodgers in a 1-0 victory—baseball's 12th perfect game.

■ **September 23:** Oakland's Jose Canseco swiped two bases in a victory over Milwaukee and became the first player to hit 40 homers and record 40 steals in the same season.

■ **September 28:** Dodgers righthander Orel Hershiser worked 10 shutout innings against the Padres in his final regular-season start and stretched his scoreless-innings streak to a record 59.

## ALL-STAR GAME

■ **Winner:** A.L. pitchers held the N.L. to five hits and catcher Terry Steinbach supplied all the offense they needed for a 2-1 All-Star Game victory.

■ **Key inning:** The third, when Steinbach drove a Dwight Gooden pitch over the right-field wall, giving the A.L. a lead it never relinquished.

■ **Memorable moment:** Steinbach, maligned by the media as an unworthy starter because of his .217 season average, drove in the winning run with a fourth-inning sacrifice fly and walked away with MVP honors.

■ **Top guns:** Frank Viola (Twins), Dennis Eckersley (Athletics), Steinbach (Athletics), A.L.; Vince Coleman (Cardinals), N.L.

■ **MVP:** Steinbach.

**Linescore**

July 12, at Cincinnati's Riverfront Stadium
A.L. ..............0 0 1 1 0 0 0 0 0—2 6 2
N.L. ..............0 0 0 1 0 0 0 0 0—1 5 0
Viola (Twins), Clemens (Red Sox) 3, Gubicza (Royals) 4, Stieb (Blue Jays) 6, Russell (Rangers) 7, Jones (Indians) 8, Plesac (Brewers) 8, Eckersley (Athletics) 9; Gooden (Mets), Knepper (Astros) 4, Cone (Mets) 5, Gross (Dodgers) 6, Davis (Padres) 7, Walk (Phillies) 7, Hershiser (Dodgers) 8, Worrell (Cardinals) 9. W—Viola. L—Gooden. S—Eckersley. HR—Steinbach, A.L.

## ALCS

■ **Winner:** The Oakland Athletics, making their first Championship Series appearance since 1975, recorded the first sweep in the best-of-seven format and claimed their first pennant since 1974.

■ **Turning point:** Amid a flurry of Oakland home runs, the Athletics actually took control on a ninth-inning Walt Weiss single that produced a 4-3 Game 2 victory over the Red Sox at Fenway Park.

■ **Memorable moment:** Jose Canseco's first-inning home run in the fourth game, his third of the series and Oakland's seventh. The A's went on to close out the Red Sox with a 4-1 victory.

■ **Top guns:** Dennis Eckersley (4 games, 4 saves, 0.00 ERA), Gene Nelson (2-0, 0.00), Rickey Henderson (.375), Canseco (.313, 3 HR, 4 RBIs), Athletics; Wade Boggs (.385), Rich Gedman (.357), Red Sox.

■ **MVP:** Eckersley.

**Linescores**

**Game 1**—October 5, at Boston
Oakland........0 0 0 1 0 0 0 1 0—2 6 0
Boston ........0 0 0 0 0 0 1 0 0—1 6 0
Stewart, Honeycutt (7), Eckersley (8); Hurst. W—Honeycutt. L—Hurst. S—Eckersley. HR—Canseco (Oak.).

**Game 2**—October 6, at Boston
Oakland......0 0 0 0 0 0 3 0 1—4 10 1
Boston .......0 0 0 0 0 2 1 0 0—3 4 1
Davis, Cadaret (7), Nelson (7), Eckersley (9); Clemens, Stanley (8), Smith (8). W—Nelson. L—Smith. S—Eckersley. HR—Canseco (Oak.); Gedman (Bos.).

**Game 3**—October 8, at Oakland
Boston ....3 2 0 0 0 0 1 0 0— 6 12 0
Oakland....0 4 2 0 1 0 1 2 x—10 15 1
Boddicker, Gardner (3), Stanley (8); Welch, Nelson (2), Young (6), Plunk (7), Honeycutt (7), Eckersley (8). W—Nelson. L—Boddicker. S—Eckersley. HR—Greenwell (Bos.); McGwire, Lansford, Hassey, Henderson (Oak.).

**Game 4**—October 9, at Oakland
Boston ......0 0 0 0 0 1 0 0 0—1 4 0
Oakland.......1 0 1 0 0 0 0 2 x—4 10 1
Hurst, Smithson (5), Smith (7); Stewart, Honeycutt (8), Eckersley (9). W—Stewart. L—Hurst. S—Eckersley. HR—Canseco (Oak.).

## NLCS

■ **Winner:** Los Angeles ace Orel Hershiser denied New York's bid for its second pennant in three years with a 6-0 shutout in Game 7.

■ **Turning point:** Game 4, when Dodgers catcher Mike Scioscia hit a game-tying two-run homer in the ninth inning and Kirk Gibson settled matters with a solo shot in the 12th, knotting the series at two games apiece.

■ **Memorable moment:** The eighth inning of Game 3, when Dodgers relief ace Jay Howell was thrown out of the game because a foreign substance was found in his glove. The Mets scored five runs in the inning and claimed an 8-4 victory.

■ **Top guns:** Hershiser (1-0, 1.09 ERA), Scioscia (.364), Gibson (2 HR, 6 RBIs), Dodgers; Randy Myers (2-0, 0.00), Lenny Dykstra (.429), Darryl Strawberry (.300, 6 RBIs), Mets.

■ **MVP:** Hershiser.

**Linescores**

**Game 1**—October 4, at Los Angeles
N.Y. ..............0 0 0 0 0 0 0 0 3—3 8 1
L.A. ..............1 0 0 0 0 0 1 0 0—2 4 0
Gooden, Myers (8); Hershiser, J. Howell (9). W—Myers. L—J. Howell.

**Game 2**—October 5, at Los Angeles
N.Y. ..............0 0 0 2 0 0 0 0 1—3 6 0
L.A. ..............1 4 0 0 1 0 0 0 x—6 7 0
Cone, Aguilera (3), Leach (6), McDowell (8); Belcher, Orosco (9), Pena (9). W—Belcher. L—Cone. S—Pena. HR—Hernandez (N.Y.).

**Game 3**—October 8, at New York
L.A. ..............0 2 1 0 0 0 0 1 0—4 7 2
N.Y. ..............0 0 1 0 0 2 0 5 x—8 9 2
Hershiser, J. Howell (8), Pena (8), Orosco (8), Horton (8); Darling, McDowell (7), Myers (8), Cone (9). W—Myers. L—Pena.

**Game 4**—October 9, at New York
L.A. ......200 000 002 001—5 7 1
N.Y. ......000 301 000 000—4 10 2
Tudor, Holton (6), Horton (7), Pena (9), Leary (12), Orosco (12), Hershiser (12); Gooden, Myers (9), McDowell (11). W—Pena. L—McDowell. S—Hershiser. HR—Strawberry, McReynolds (N.Y.); Scioscia, Gibson (L.A.).

**Game 5**—October 10, at New York
L.A. ............0 0 0 3 3 0 0 0 1—7 12 0
N.Y. ............0 0 0 0 3 0 0 1 0—4 9 1
Belcher, Horton (8), Holton (8); Fernandez, Leach (5), Aguilera (6), McDowell (8). W—Belcher. L—Fernandez. S—Holton. HR—Gibson (L.A.); Dykstra (N.Y.).

**Game 6**—October 11, at Los Angeles
N.Y. ...........1 0 1 0 2 1 0 0 0—5 11 0
L.A. ............0 0 0 0 1 0 0 0 0—1 5 2
Cone; Leary, Holton (5), Horton (6), Orosco (8). W—Cone. L—Leary. HR—McReynolds (N.Y.).

**Game 7**—October 12, at Los Angeles
N.Y. ...........0 0 0 0 0 0 0 0 0—0 5 2
L.A. ...........1 5 0 0 0 0 0 0 x—6 10 0
Darling, Gooden (2), Leach (5), Aguilera (7); Hershiser. W—Hershiser. L—Darling.

## WORLD SERIES

■ **Winner:** The Cinderella Dodgers pulled off a five-game surprise against the powerful Athletics.

■ **Turning point:** A two-out, ninth-inning, two-run, pinch-hit homer by Kirk Gibson that gave the Dodgers a shocking 5-4 victory in Game 1.

■ **Memorable moment:** The gimpy Gibson, wincing in pain with every swing, connecting with a Dennis Eckersley pitch and then limping triumphantly around the bases with the winning run in the Series opener.

■ **Top guns:** Orel Hershiser (2-0, 1.00 ERA), Gibson (1 AB, 1 hit, 1 HR, 2 RBIs), Mickey Hatcher (.368, 5 RBIs), Dodgers; Terry Steinbach (.364), Athletics.

■ **MVP:** Hershiser.

**Linescores**

**Game 1**—October 15, at Los Angeles
Oakland........0 4 0 0 0 0 0 0 0—4 7 0
L.A. ..............2 0 0 0 0 1 0 0 2—5 7 0
Stewart, Eckersley (9); Belcher, Leary (3), Holton (6), Pena (8). W—Pena. L—Eckersley. HR—Hatcher, Gibson (L.A.); Canseco (Oak.).

**Game 2**—October 16, at Los Angeles
Oakland......0 0 0 0 0 0 0 0 0—0 3 0
L.A. ..............0 0 5 1 0 0 0 0 x—6 10 1
S. Davis, Nelson (4), Young (6), Plunk (7), Honeycutt (8); Hershiser. W—Hershiser. L—S. Davis. HR—Marshall (L.A.).

**Game 3**—October 18, at Oakland
L.A. ..............0 0 0 0 1 0 0 0 0—1 8 1
Oakland........0 0 1 0 0 0 0 0 1—2 5 0
Tudor, Leary (2), Pena (6), J. Howell (9); Welch, Cadaret (6), Nelson (6), Honeycutt (8). W—Honeycutt. L—J. Howell. HR—McGwire (Oak.).

**Game 4**—October 19, at Oakland
L.A. ..............2 0 1 0 0 0 1 0 0—4 8 1
Oakland........1 0 0 0 0 1 1 0 0—3 9 2
Belcher, J. Howell (7); Stewart, Cadaret (7), Eckersley (9). W—Belcher. L—Stewart. S—J. Howell.

**Game 5**—October 20, at Oakland
L.A. ..............2 0 0 2 0 1 0 0 0—5 8 0
Oakland........0 0 1 0 0 0 0 1 0—2 4 0
Hershiser; S. Davis, Cadaret (5), Nelson (5), Honeycutt (8), Plunk (9), Burns (9). W—Hershiser. L—S. Davis. HR—Hatcher, M. Davis (L.A.).

# 1989

## FINAL STANDINGS

### American League

**East Division**

| Team | Tor. | Bal. | Bos. | Mil. | N.Y. | Cle. | Det. | Oak. | K.C. | Cal. | Tex. | Min. | Sea. | Chi. | W | L | Pct. | GB |
|---|---|---|---|---|---|---|---|---|---|---|---|---|---|---|---|---|---|---|
| Toronto | ... | 6 | 8 | 7 | 6 | 8 | 11 | 5 | 5 | 5 | 7 | 3 | 7 | 11 | 89 | 73 | .549 | ... |
| Baltimore | 7 | ... | 6 | 7 | 8 | 7 | 10 | 5 | 6 | 6 | 9 | 4 | 6 | 6 | 87 | 75 | .537 | 2 |
| Boston | 5 | 7 | ... | 6 | 7 | 8 | 11 | 7 | 4 | 4 | 6 | 6 | 5 | 7 | 83 | 79 | .512 | 6 |
| Milwaukee | 6 | 6 | 7 | ... | 8 | 10 | 7 | 5 | 4 | 5 | 5 | 9 | 7 | 2 | 81 | 81 | .500 | 8 |
| New York | 7 | 5 | 6 | 5 | ... | 4 | 7 | 3 | 6 | 6 | 5 | 6 | 8 | 6 | 74 | 87 | .460 | 14.5 |
| Cleveland | 5 | 6 | 5 | 3 | 9 | ... | 5 | 2 | 8 | 7 | 7 | 5 | 6 | 5 | 73 | 89 | .451 | 16 |
| Detroit | 2 | 3 | 2 | 6 | 6 | 8 | ... | 4 | 6 | 1 | 4 | 5 | 4 | 8 | 59 | 103 | .364 | 30 |

**West Division**

| Team | Oak. | K.C. | Cal. | Tex. | Min. | Sea. | Chi. | Tor. | Bal. | Bos. | Mil. | N.Y. | Cle. | Det. | W | L | Pct. | GB |
|---|---|---|---|---|---|---|---|---|---|---|---|---|---|---|---|---|---|---|
| Oakland | ... | 6 | 8 | 8 | 7 | 9 | 8 | 7 | 7 | 5 | 7 | 9 | 10 | 8 | 99 | 63 | .611 | ... |
| Kansas City | 7 | ... | 9 | 8 | 7 | 9 | 7 | 7 | 6 | 8 | 8 | 6 | 4 | 6 | 92 | 70 | .568 | 7 |
| California | 5 | 4 | ... | 6 | 11 | 7 | 8 | 7 | 6 | 8 | 7 | 6 | 5 | 11 | 91 | 71 | .562 | 8 |
| Texas | 5 | 5 | 7 | ... | 8 | 7 | 10 | 5 | 3 | 6 | 7 | 7 | 5 | 8 | 83 | 79 | .512 | 16 |
| Minnesota | 6 | 6 | 2 | 5 | ... | 7 | 8 | 9 | 8 | 6 | 3 | 6 | 7 | 7 | 80 | 82 | .494 | 19 |
| Seattle | 4 | 4 | 6 | 6 | 6 | ... | 6 | 5 | 6 | 7 | 5 | 4 | 6 | 8 | 73 | 89 | .451 | 26 |
| Chicago | 5 | 6 | 5 | 3 | 5 | 7 | ... | 1 | 6 | 5 | 10 | 5 | 7 | 4 | 69 | 92 | .429 | 29.5 |

### National League

**East Division**

| Team | Chi. | N.Y. | St.L. | Mon. | Pit. | Phi. | S.F. | S.D. | Hou. | L.A. | Cin. | Atl. | W | L | Pct. | GB |
|---|---|---|---|---|---|---|---|---|---|---|---|---|---|---|---|---|
| Chicago | ... | 10 | 11 | 10 | 12 | 10 | 6 | 8 | 5 | 7 | 7 | 7 | 93 | 69 | .574 | ... |
| New York | 8 | ... | 10 | 9 | 9 | 12 | 3 | 5 | 6 | 7 | 8 | 10 | 87 | 75 | .537 | 6 |
| St. Louis | 7 | 8 | ... | 13 | 5 | 11 | 5 | 10 | 5 | 9 | 4 | 9 | 86 | 76 | .531 | 7 |
| Montreal | 8 | 9 | 5 | ... | 11 | 9 | 7 | 5 | 8 | 5 | 8 | 6 | 81 | 81 | .500 | 12 |
| Pittsburgh | 6 | 9 | 13 | 7 | ... | 8 | 5 | 3 | 5 | 5 | 5 | 8 | 74 | 88 | .457 | 19 |
| Philadelphia | 8 | 6 | 7 | 9 | 10 | ... | 4 | 2 | 3 | 6 | 8 | 4 | 67 | 95 | .414 | 26 |

**West Division**

| Team | S.F. | S.D. | Hou. | L.A. | Cin. | Atl. | Chi. | N.Y. | St.L. | Mon. | Pit. | Phi. | W | L | Pct. | GB |
|---|---|---|---|---|---|---|---|---|---|---|---|---|---|---|---|---|
| San Fran. | ... | 10 | 10 | 8 | 10 | 12 | 6 | 9 | 7 | 5 | 7 | 8 | 92 | 70 | .568 | ... |
| San Diego | 8 | ... | 10 | 12 | 9 | 11 | 4 | 7 | 2 | 7 | 9 | 10 | 89 | 73 | .549 | 3 |
| Houston | 8 | 8 | ... | 10 | 10 | 10 | 7 | 6 | 7 | 4 | 7 | 9 | 86 | 76 | .531 | 6 |
| Los Angeles | 10 | 6 | 8 | ... | 10 | 10 | 5 | 5 | 3 | 7 | 7 | 6 | 77 | 83 | .481 | 14 |
| Cincinnati | 8 | 9 | 8 | 8 | ... | 10 | 5 | 4 | 8 | 4 | 7 | 4 | 75 | 87 | .463 | 17 |
| Atlanta | 6 | 7 | 8 | 6 | 8 | ... | 5 | 2 | 3 | 6 | 4 | 8 | 63 | 97 | .394 | 28 |

## SIGNIFICANT EVENTS

■ **January 5:** Commissioner Peter Ueberroth signed a $400-million cable television package with ESPN, a month after signing a four-year, $1.06-billion contract with CBS-TV.

■ **February 3:** Bill White became the highest ranking black executive in professional sports when he was tabbed to succeed A. Bartlett Giamatti as N.L. president.

■ **June 5:** The Blue Jays opened SkyDome with a 5-3 loss to the Brewers.

■ **August 24:** Commissioner A. Bartlett Giamatti handed all-time hits leader Pete Rose, who had been implicated in a gambling scandal, a lifetime ban from baseball.

■ **September 1:** Giamatti, 51, died of a heart attack at his Massachusetts summer cottage, eight days after handing Rose his lifetime ban.

■ **September 13:** Giamatti assistant Fay Vincent was elected as baseball's eighth commissioner.

■ **December 25:** Former player and manager Billy Martin died when a pickup truck in which he was riding crashed near his home in Binghamton, N.Y.

## MEMORABLE MOMENTS

■ **August 15:** Giants lefty Dave Dravecky, on the comeback trail from cancer surgery, broke his arm while throwing a pitch in a game at Montreal.

■ **August 22:** Nolan Ryan fired a fastball past Oakland's Rickey Henderson and became the first Major Leaguer to record 5,000 career strikeouts.

## LEADERS

**American League**
**BA:** Kirby Puckett, Min., .339.
**Runs:** Wade Boggs, Bos.;
Rickey Henderson, N.Y.-Oak., 113.
**Hits:** Kirby Puckett, Min., 215.
**TB:** Ruben Sierra, Tex., 344.
**HR:** Fred McGriff, Tor., 36.
**RBI:** Ruben Sierra, Tex., 119.
**SB:** Rickey Henderson, N.Y.-Oak., 77.
**Wins:** Bret Saberhagen, K.C., 23.
**ERA:** Bret Saberhagen, K.C., 2.16.
**CG:** Bret Saberhagen, K.C., 12.
**IP:** Bret Saberhagen, K.C., 262.1.
**SO:** Nolan Ryan, Tex., 301.
**SV:** Jeff Russell, Tex., 38.

**National League**
**BA:** Tony Gwynn, S.D., .336.
**Runs:** Will Clark, S.F.; Howard Johnson, N.Y.;
Ryne Sandberg, Chi., 104.
**Hits:** Tony Gwynn, S.D., 203.
**TB:** Kevin Mitchell, S.F., 345.
**HR:** Kevin Mitchell, S.F., 47.
**RBI:** Kevin Mitchell, S.F., 125.
**SB:** Vince Coleman, St.L., 65.
**Wins:** Mike Scott, Hou., 20.
**ERA:** Scott Garrelts, S.F., 2.28.
**CG:** Tim Belcher, L.A.; Bruce Hurst, S.D., 10.
**IP:** Orel Hershiser, L.A., 256.2.
**SO:** Jose DeLeon, St.L., 201.
**SV:** Mark Davis, S.D., 44.

**A.L. 20-game winners**
Bret Saberhagen, K.C., 23-6
Dave Stewart, Oak., 21-9

**N.L. 20-game winner**
Mike Scott, Hou., 20-10

**A.L. 100 RBIs**
Ruben Sierra, Tex., 119
Don Mattingly, N.Y., 113
Nick Esasky, Bos., 108
Joe Carter, Cle., 105
Bo Jackson, K.C., 105
George Bell, Tor., 104
Robin Yount, Mil., 103
Dwight Evans, Bos., 100

**N.L. 100 RBIs**
Kevin Mitchell, S.F., 125
Pedro Guerrero, St.L., 117
Will Clark, S.F., 111
Eric Davis, Cin., 101
Howard Johnson, N.Y., 101

**N.L. 40 homers**
Kevin Mitchell, S.F., 47

**Most Valuable Player**
A.L.: Robin Yount, OF, Mil.
N.L.: Kevin Mitchell, OF, S.F.

**Cy Young Award**
A.L.: Bret Saberhagen, K.C.
N.L.: Mark Davis, S.D.

**Rookie of the Year**
A.L.: Gregg Olson, P, Bal.
N.L.: Jerome Walton, OF, Chi.

**Manager of the Year**
A.L.: Frank Robinson, Bal.
N.L.: Don Zimmer, Chi.

**Hall of Fame additions**
Al Barlick, umpire
Johnny Bench, C, 1967-83
Red Schoendienst, 2B, 1945-63
Carl Yastrzemski, OF, 1961-83

## ALL-STAR GAME

■ **Winner:** The A.L.'s 5-3 victory marked its first back-to-back All-Star wins since 1957-58.
■ **Key inning:** The third, when the A.L. added to its 3-2 advantage with run-scoring singles by Harold Baines and Ruben Sierra.
■ **Memorable moment:** Consecutive home runs by Bo Jackson and Wade Boggs to lead off the A.L. first inning. That was an All-Star first.
■ **Top guns:** Nolan Ryan (Rangers), Jackson (Royals), Boggs (Red Sox), Sierra (Rangers), A.L.; Kevin Mitchell (Giants), Bobby Bonilla (Pirates), N.L.
■ **MVP:** Jackson.

**Linescore**
July 11, at California's Anaheim Stadium
N.L.............2 0 0 0 0 0 0 1 0—3 9 1
A.L. ............2 1 2 0 0 0 0 0 x—5 12 0
Reuschel (Giants), Smoltz (Braves) 2, Sutcliffe (Cubs) 3, Burke (Expos) 4, M. Davis (Padres) 6, Howell (Dodgers) 7, Williams (Cubs) 8; Stewart (Athletics), Ryan (Rangers) 2, Gubicza (Royals) 4, Moore (Athletics) 5, Swindell (Indians) 6, Russell (Rangers) 7, Plesac (Brewers) 8, Jones (Indians) 8. W—Ryan. L—Smoltz. S—Jones. HR—Jackson, Boggs, A.L.

## ALCS

■ **Winner:** The Oakland Athletics ran and muscled their way past Toronto in a series dominated by leadoff hitter Rickey Henderson.
■ **Turning point:** After killing the Blue Jays in Games 1 and 2 with his speed, Henderson muscled up for two home runs in a 6-5 Game 4 victory that gave Oakland a 3-1 series edge.
■ **Memorable moment:** A mammoth Game 4 home run by Oakland slugger Jose Canseco that landed in the fifth tier of the left-field bleachers at SkyDome. The ball officially was measured at 490 feet, but most observers claimed it traveled well beyond 500.
■ **Top guns:** Dennis Eckersley (4 games, 3 saves, 1.59 ERA), Carney Lansford (.455), Henderson (.400, 8 SB, 8 runs, 2 HR, 5 RBIs), Mark McGwire (.389), Athletics; Tony Fernandez (.350), Blue Jays.
■ **MVP:** Henderson.

**Linescores**
**Game 1**—October 3, at Oakland
Toronto ......0 2 0 1 0 0 0 0 0—3 5 1
Oakland......0 1 0 0 1 3 0 2 x—7 11 0
Stieb, Acker (6), Ward (8); Stewart, Eckersley (9). W—Stewart. L—Stieb. HR—D. Henderson, McGwire (Oak.); Whitt (Tor.).

**Game 2**—October 4, at Oakland
Toronto ........0 0 1 0 0 0 0 2 0—3 5 1
Oakland........0 0 0 2 0 3 1 0 x—6 9 1
Stottlemyre, Acker (6), Wells (6), Henke (7), Cerutti (8); Moore, Honeycutt (8), Eckersley (8). W—Moore. L—Stottlemyre. S—Eckersley. HR—Parker (Oak.).

**Game 3**—October 6, at Toronto
Oakland........1 0 1 1 0 0 0 0 0—3 8 1
Toronto ........0 0 0 4 0 0 3 0 x—7 8 0
Davis, Honeycutt (7), Nelson (7), M. Young (8); Key, Acker (7), Henke (9). W—Key. L—Davis. HR—Parker (Oak.).

**Game 4**—October 7, at Toronto
Oakland......0 0 3 0 2 0 1 0 0—6 11 1
Toronto ......0 0 0 1 0 1 1 2 0—5 13 0
Welch, Honeycutt (6), Eckersley (8); Flanagan, Ward (5), Cerutti (8), Acker (9). W—Welch. L—Flanagan. S—Eckersley. HR—R. Henderson 2, Canseco (Oak.).

**Game 5**—October 8, at Toronto
Oakland........1 0 1 0 0 0 2 0 0—4 4 0
Toronto ........0 0 0 0 0 0 0 1 2—3 9 0
Stewart, Eckersley (9); Stieb, Acker (7), Henke (9). W—Stewart. L—Stieb. S—Eckersley. HR—Moseby, Bell (Tor.).

## NLCS

■ **Winner:** First basemen Will Clark and Mark Grace took center stage as San Francisco won its first pennant since 1962 and stretched Chicago's pennant drought to 44 years.
■ **Turning point:** The seventh inning of Game 3 when Giants second baseman Robby Thompson belted a two-run homer off reliever Les Lancaster, giving San Francisco a 5-4 victory and a 2-1 series edge.
■ **Memorable moment:** Game 1 at Chicago — the first post-season game played under the lights of Wrigley Field. San Francisco's Clark stole the show with four hits, a grand slam and six RBIs in the Giants' 11-3 victory.
■ **Top guns:** Steve Bedrosian (3 saves), Clark (.650, 13 hits, 2 HR, 8 RBIs), Kevin Mitchell (.353, 2 HR, 7 RBIs), Matt Williams (2 HR, 9 RBIs), Giants; Grace (.647, 8 RBIs), Ryne Sandberg (.400), Cubs.
■ **MVP:** Clark.

**Linescores**
**Game 1**—October 4, at Chicago
S.F. ..........3 0 1 4 0 0 0 3 0—11 13 0
Chicago....2 0 1 0 0 0 0 0 0— 3 10 1
Garrelts, Brantley (8), Hammaker (9); Maddux, Kilgus (5), Wilson (8). W—Garrelts. L—Maddux. HR—Grace, Sandberg (Chi.); Clark 2, Mitchell (S.F.).

**Game 2**—October 5, at Chicago
S.F. ............0 0 0 2 0 0 0 2 1—5 10 0
Chicago......6 0 0 0 0 3 0 0 x—9 11 0
Reuschel, Downs (1), Lefferts (6), Brantley (7), Bedrosian (8); Bielecki, Assenmacher (5), Lancaster (6). W—Lancaster. L—Reuschel. HR—Mitchell, Ma. Williams, Thompson (S.F.).

**Game 3**—October 7, at San Francisco
Chicago......2 0 0 1 0 0 1 0 0—4 10 0
S.F. ...........3 0 0 0 0 0 2 0 x—5 8 3
Sutcliffe, Assenmacher (7), Lancaster (7); LaCoss, Brantley (4), Robinson (7), Lefferts (8), Bedrosian (9). W—Robinson. L—Lancaster. S—Bedrosian. HR—Thompson (S.F.).

**Game 4**—October 8, at San Francisco
Chicago......1 1 0 0 2 0 0 0 0—4 12 1
S.F. ...........1 0 2 1 2 0 0 0 x—6 9 1
Maddux, Wilson (4), Sanderson (6), Mi. Williams (8); Garrelts, Downs (5), Bedrosian (9). W—Downs. L—Wilson. S—Bedrosian. HR—Salazar (Chi.); Ma. Williams (S.F.).

**Game 5**—October 9, at San Francisco
Chicago......0 0 1 0 0 0 0 0 1—2 10 1
S.F. ...........0 0 0 0 0 0 1 2 x—3 4 1
Bielecki, Mi. Williams (8), Lancaster (8); Reuschel, Bedrosian (9). W—Reuschel. L—Bielecki. S—Bedrosian.

## WORLD SERIES

■ **Winner:** Oakland's four-game sweep of San Francisco in the first Bay Area Series was overshadowed by a massive earthquake that rocked parts of California, causing death and destruction and forcing postponement of the fall classic's final two games for 10 days.
■ **Turning point:** The second inning of Game 1, when Oakland jumped on the Giants for three runs en route to a 5-0 victory. That outburst set the pattern for the rest of the Series.
■ **Memorable moment:** The moments leading up to Game 3, when an earthquake measuring 7.1 on the Richter scale shook San Francisco and Candlestick Park. With the power out and incoming reports of mass destruction, Commissioner Fay Vincent ordered postponement of the game and told officials to clear the park.
■ **Top guns:** Dave Stewart (2-0, 1.69 ERA), Mike Moore (2-0, 2.08), Rickey Henderson (.474), Carney Lansford (.438), Athletics; Kevin Mitchell (.294), Giants.
■ **MVP:** Stewart.

**Linescores**
**Game 1**—October 14, at Oakland
S.F. ...........0 0 0 0 0 0 0 0 0—0 5 1
Oakland......0 3 1 1 0 0 0 0 x—5 11 1
Garrelts, Hammaker (5), Brantley (6), LaCoss (8); Stewart. W—Stewart. L—Garrelts. HR—Parker, Weiss (Oak.).

**Game 2**—October 15, at Oakland
S.F. .............0 0 1 0 0 0 0 0 0—1 4 0
Oakland........1 0 0 4 0 0 0 0 x—5 7 0
Reuschel, Downs (5), Lefferts (7), Bedrosian (8); Moore, Honeycutt (8), Eckersley (9). W—Moore. L—Reuschel. HR—Steinbach (Oak.).

**Game 3**—October 27, at San Francisco
Oakland....2 0 0 2 4 1 0 4 0—13 14 0
S.F. .........0 1 0 2 0 0 0 0 4— 7 10 3
Stewart, Honeycutt (8), Nelson (9), Burns (9); Garrelts, Downs (4), Brantley (5), Hammaker (8), Lefferts (8). W—Stewart. L—Garrelts. HR—Williams, Bathe (S.F.); D. Henderson 2, Phillips, Canseco, Lansford (Oak.).

**Game 4**—October 28, at San Francisco
Oakland......1 3 0 0 3 1 0 1 0—9 12 0
S.F. ...........0 0 0 0 0 2 4 0 0—6 9 0
Moore, Nelson (7), Honeycutt (7), Burns (7), Eckersley (9); Robinson, LaCoss (2), Brantley (6), Downs (6), Lefferts (8), Bedrosian (8). W—Moore. L—Robinson. S—Eckersley. HR—R. Henderson (Oak.); Mitchell, Litton (S.F.).

# 1990

## FINAL STANDINGS

### American League

#### East Division

| Team | Bos. | Tor. | Det. | Cle. | Bal. | Mil. | N.Y. | Oak. | Chi. | Tex. | Cal. | Sea. | K.C. | Min. | W | L | Pct. | GB |
|---|---|---|---|---|---|---|---|---|---|---|---|---|---|---|---|---|---|---|
| Boston | ... | 10 | 8 | 9 | 9 | 5 | 9 | 4 | 6 | 5 | 7 | 8 | 4 | 4 | 88 | 74 | .543 | ... |
| Toronto | 3 | ... | 8 | 9 | 8 | 6 | 8 | 5 | 7 | 5 | 5 | 6 | 7 | 9 | 86 | 76 | .531 | 2 |
| Detroit | 5 | 5 | ... | 8 | 7 | 3 | 7 | 6 | 7 | 6 | 7 | 7 | 5 | 6 | 79 | 83 | .488 | 9 |
| Cleveland | 4 | 4 | 5 | ... | 7 | 9 | 5 | 4 | 7 | 7 | 5 | 7 | 6 | 7 | 77 | 85 | .475 | 11 |
| Baltimore | 4 | 5 | 6 | 6 | ... | 7 | 6 | 4 | 6 | 8 | 7 | 3 | 8 | 6 | 76 | 85 | .472 | 11.5 |
| Milwaukee | 8 | 7 | 10 | 4 | 6 | ... | 6 | 5 | 2 | 5 | 5 | 4 | 8 | 4 | 74 | 88 | .457 | 14 |
| New York | 4 | 5 | 6 | 8 | 7 | 7 | ... | 0 | 2 | 3 | 6 | 9 | 4 | 6 | 67 | 95 | .414 | 21 |

#### West Division

| Team | Oak. | Chi. | Tex. | Cal. | Sea. | K.C. | Min. | Bos. | Tor. | Det. | Cle. | Bal. | Mil. | N.Y. | W | L | Pct. | GB |
|---|---|---|---|---|---|---|---|---|---|---|---|---|---|---|---|---|---|---|
| Oakland | ... | 5 | 8 | 9 | 9 | 9 | 7 | 8 | 7 | 6 | 8 | 8 | 7 | 12 | 103 | 59 | .636 | ... |
| Chicago | 8 | ... | 7 | 8 | 8 | 9 | 7 | 6 | 5 | 5 | 5 | 6 | 10 | 10 | 94 | 68 | .580 | 9 |
| Texas | 5 | 6 | ... | 5 | 6 | 8 | 8 | 7 | 7 | 6 | 5 | 4 | 7 | 9 | 83 | 79 | .512 | 20 |
| California | 4 | 5 | 8 | ... | 5 | 7 | 9 | 5 | 7 | 5 | 7 | 5 | 7 | 6 | 80 | 82 | .494 | 23 |
| Seattle | 4 | 5 | 7 | 8 | ... | 6 | 7 | 4 | 6 | 5 | 5 | 9 | 8 | 3 | 77 | 85 | .475 | 26 |
| Kansas City | 4 | 4 | 5 | 6 | 7 | ... | 8 | 8 | 5 | 7 | 6 | 3 | 4 | 8 | 75 | 86 | .466 | 27.5 |
| Minnesota | 6 | 6 | 5 | 4 | 6 | 5 | ... | 8 | 3 | 6 | 5 | 6 | 8 | 6 | 74 | 88 | .457 | 29 |

### National League

#### East Division

| Team | Pit. | N.Y. | Mon. | Chi. | Phi. | St.L. | Cin. | L.A. | S.F. | Hou. | S.D. | Atl. | W | L | Pct. | GB |
|---|---|---|---|---|---|---|---|---|---|---|---|---|---|---|---|---|
| Pittsburgh | ... | 8 | 5 | 14 | 12 | 10 | 6 | 8 | 8 | 7 | 10 | 7 | 95 | 67 | .586 | ... |
| New York | 10 | ... | 10 | 9 | 10 | 12 | 6 | 7 | 7 | 7 | 5 | 8 | 91 | 71 | .562 | 4 |
| Montreal | 13 | 8 | ... | 7 | 10 | 11 | 3 | 6 | 7 | 7 | 7 | 6 | 85 | 77 | .525 | 10 |
| Chicago | 4 | 9 | 11 | ... | 11 | 8 | 4 | 3 | 7 | 6 | 8 | 6 | 77 | 85 | .475 | 18 |
| Philadelphia | 6 | 8 | 8 | 7 | ... | 10 | 5 | 4 | 8 | 7 | 7 | 7 | 77 | 85 | .475 | 18 |
| St. Louis | 8 | 6 | 7 | 10 | 8 | ... | 3 | 5 | 3 | 6 | 9 | 5 | 70 | 92 | .432 | 25 |

#### West Division

| Team | Cin. | L.A. | S.F. | Hou. | S.D. | Atl. | Pit. | N.Y. | Mon. | Chi. | Phi. | St.L. | W | L | Pct. | GB |
|---|---|---|---|---|---|---|---|---|---|---|---|---|---|---|---|---|
| Cincinnati | ... | 9 | 7 | 11 | 9 | 10 | 6 | 6 | 9 | 8 | 7 | 9 | 91 | 71 | .562 | ... |
| Los Angeles | 9 | ... | 8 | 9 | 9 | 12 | 4 | 5 | 6 | 9 | 8 | 7 | 86 | 76 | .531 | 5 |
| San Fran. | 11 | 10 | ... | 8 | 11 | 13 | 4 | 5 | 5 | 5 | 4 | 9 | 85 | 77 | .525 | 6 |
| Houston | 7 | 9 | 10 | ... | 4 | 13 | 5 | 5 | 5 | 6 | 5 | 6 | 75 | 87 | .463 | 16 |
| San Diego | 9 | 9 | 7 | 14 | ... | 10 | 2 | 7 | 5 | 4 | 5 | 3 | 75 | 87 | .463 | 16 |
| Atlanta | 8 | 6 | 5 | 5 | 8 | ... | 5 | 4 | 6 | 6 | 5 | 7 | 65 | 97 | .401 | 26 |

## SIGNIFICANT EVENTS

■ **March 18:** Players and owners reached agreement on a four-year contract that ended a 32-day lockout and cleared the way for spring training camps to open.
■ **June 14:** The N.L. announced plans to expand from 12 to 14 teams for the 1993 season.
■ **July 30:** Commissioner Fay Vincent banned George Steinbrenner from involvement with the Yankees for actions "not in the best interests of baseball."
■ **August 8:** Former baseball great Pete Rose reported to a federal work camp at Marion, Ill., to begin serving his five-month sentence for income tax evasion.

## MEMORABLE MOMENTS

■ **June 11:** Rangers ace Nolan Ryan fired his record sixth no-hitter, defeating Oakland 5-0.
■ **June 12:** Baltimore's Cal Ripken Jr. moved into second place on the all-time ironman list when he pushed his consecutive-games streak to 1,308 in a 4-3 victory over Milwaukee.
■ **June 29:** A baseball first: Oakland's Dave Stewart and Dodgers lefthander Fernando Valenzuela threw no-hitters on the same day.
■ **July 1:** Yankees righthander Andy Hawkins became the second Major League pitcher to throw a complete-game no-hitter and lose when the White Sox stumbled to a 4-0 victory.
■ **July 31:** Ryan became baseball's 20th 300-game winner when the Rangers pounded the Brewers, 11-3.
■ **August 31:** The Griffeys, 20-year-old Ken Jr. and 40-year-old Ken Sr., became baseball's first father-son combination when both played for Seattle in a game against Kansas City.
■ **September 2:** Dave Stieb held Cleveland without a hit in a 3-0 victory—the first no-hitter in Blue Jays history and the record ninth of the season in the Major Leagues.
■ **October 3:** Detroit's Cecil Fielder became the first player in 13 years to break the 50-homer barrier when he crashed Nos. 50 and 51 in a final-day 10-3 victory over the Yankees.

## LEADERS

**American League**
**BA:** George Brett, K.C., .329.
**Runs:** Rickey Henderson, Oak., 119.
**Hits:** Rafael Palmeiro, Tex., 191.
**TB:** Cecil Fielder, Det., 339.
**HR:** Cecil Fielder, Det., 51.
**RBI:** Cecil Fielder, Det., 132.
**SB:** Rickey Henderson, Oak., 65.
**Wins:** Bob Welch, Oak., 27.
**ERA:** Roger Clemens, Bos., 1.93.
**CG:** Jack Morris, Det.; Dave Stewart, Oak., 11.
**IP:** Dave Stewart, Oak., 267.
**SO:** Nolan Ryan, Tex., 232.
**SV:** Bobby Thigpen, Chi., 57.

**National League**
**BA:** Willie McGee, St.L., .335.
**Runs:** Ryne Sandberg, Chi., 116.
**Hits:** Brett Butler, S.F.; Lenny Dykstra, Phil., 192.
**TB:** Ryne Sandberg, Chi., 344.
**HR:** Ryne Sandberg, Chi., 40.
**RBI:** Matt Williams, S.F., 122.
**SB:** Vince Coleman, St.L., 77.
**Wins:** Doug Drabek, Pit., 22.
**ERA:** Danny Darwin, Hou., 2.21.
**CG:** Ramon Martinez, L.A., 12.
**IP:** Frank Viola, N.Y., 249.2.
**SO:** David Cone, N.Y., 233.
**SV:** John Franco, N.Y., 33.

**A.L. 20-game winners**
Bob Welch, Oak., 27-6
Dave Stewart, Oak., 22-11
Roger Clemens, Bos., 21-6

**N.L. 20-game winners**
Doug Drabek, Pit., 22-6
Ramon Martinez, L.A., 20-6
Frank Viola, N.Y., 20-12

**A.L. 100 RBIs**
Cecil Fielder, Det., 132
Kelly Gruber, Tor., 118
Mark McGwire, Oak., 108
Jose Canseco, Oak., 101

**N.L. 100 RBIs**
Matt Williams, S.F., 122
Bobby Bonilla, Pit., 120
Joe Carter, S.D., 115
Barry Bonds, Pit., 114
Darryl Strawberry, N.Y., 108
Andre Dawson, Chi., 100
Ryne Sandberg, Chi., 100

**A.L. 40 homers**
Cecil Fielder, Det., 51

**N.L. 40 homers**
Ryne Sandberg, Chi., 40

**Most Valuable Player**
A.L.: Rickey Henderson, OF, Oak.
N.L.: Barry Bonds, OF, Pit.

**Cy Young Award**
A.L.: Bob Welch, Oak.
N.L.: Doug Drabek, Pit.

**Rookie of the Year**
A.L.: Sandy Alomar Jr., C, Cle.
N.L.: Dave Justice, OF, Atl.

**Manager of the Year**
A.L.: Jeff Torborg, Chi.
N.L.: Jim Leyland, Pit.

**Hall of Fame additions**
Joe Morgan, 2B, 1963-84
Jim Palmer, P, 1965-84

## ALL-STAR GAME

■ **Winner:** Six pitchers held the N.L. to an All-Star record-low two hits and the A.L. won for the third straight year, 2-0.
■ **Key inning:** The seventh, when the A.L. broke a scoreless deadlock on a two-run double by Julio Franco off fireballer Rob Dibble. Franco was the first batter after a 68-minute rain delay.
■ **Memorable moment:** The performance of an A.L. staff that allowed only a first-inning single by Will Clark and a ninth-inning single by Lenny Dykstra and retired 16 consecutive batters at one point.
■ **Top guns:** Bob Welch (Athletics), Dave Stieb (Blue Jays), Bret Saberhagen (Royals), Franco (Rangers), Wade Boggs (Red Sox), A.L.
■ **MVP:** Franco.

**Linescore**
July 10, at Chicago's Wrigley Field
A.L. ..............0 0 0 0 0 0 2 0 0—2 7 0
N.L. ..............0 0 0 0 0 0 0 0 0—0 2 1
Welch (Athletics), Stieb (Blue Jays) 3, Saberhagen (Royals) 5, Thigpen (White Sox) 7, Finley (Angels) 8, Eckersley (Athletics) 9; Armstrong (Reds), R. Martinez (Dodgers) 3, D. Martinez (Expos) 4, Viola (Mets) 5, D. Smith (Astros) 6, Brantley (Giants) 6, Dibble (Reds) 7, Myers (Reds) 8, Jo. Franco (Mets) 9. W—Saberhagen. L—Brantley. S—Eckersley.

## ALCS

■ **Winner:** The powerful Athletics swept to their third consecutive pennant without benefit of a home run — their trademark offensive weapon.
■ **Turning point:** The final three innings of Game 1. Trailing 1-0 when Boston starter Roger Clemens left the game, the A's pounded five Red Sox relievers for nine runs and set the pattern for the series.
■ **Memorable moment:** The second inning of Game 4 when Clemens, frustrated by his team's 3-0 series deficit and the calls of umpire Terry Cooney, was ejected during an angry exchange, killing any hopes for a Boston comeback.
■ **Top guns:** Dave Stewart (2-0, 1.13 ERA), Terry Steinbach (.455), Carney Lansford (.438), Athletics; Wade Boggs (.438), Red Sox.
■ **MVP:** Stewart.

**Linescores**

**Game 1**—October 6, at Boston
Oakland......0 0 0 0 0 0 1 1 7—9 13 0
Boston ......0 0 0 1 0 0 0 0 0—1 5 1
Stewart, Eckersley (9); Clemens, Andersen (7), Bolton (8), Gray (8), Lamp (9), Murphy (9). W—Stewart. L—Andersen. HR—Boggs (Bos.).

**Game 2**—October 7, at Boston
Oakland......0 0 0 1 0 0 1 0 2—4 13 1
Boston ......0 0 1 0 0 0 0 0 0—1 6 0
Welch, Honeycutt (8), Eckersley (8); Kiecker, Harris (6), Andersen (7), Reardon (8). W—Welch. L—Harris. S—Eckersley.

**Game 3**—October 9, at Oakland
Boston ........0 1 0 0 0 0 0 0 0—1 8 3
Oakland........0 0 0 2 0 2 0 0 x—4 6 0
Boddicker; Moore, Nelson (7), Honeycutt (8), Eckersley (9). W—Moore. L—Boddicker. S—Eckersley.

**Game 4**—October 10, at Oakland
Boston ........0 0 0 0 0 0 0 0 1—1 4 1
Oakland........0 3 0 0 0 0 0 0 x—3 6 0
Clemens, Bolton (2), Gray (5), Andersen (8); Stewart, Honeycutt (9). W—Stewart. L—Clemens. S—Honeycutt.

## NLCS

■ **Winner:** Cincinnati prevailed over Pittsburgh in a matchup of teams that dominated in the 1970s and failed to qualify for post-season play in the 1980s.
■ **Turning point:** The pivotal third game when the Reds got unlikely home runs from Billy Hatcher and Mariano Duncan and recorded a 6-3 victory.
■ **Memorable moment:** Glenn Braggs, a defensive replacement in right field, made a sensational over-the-wall catch in the ninth inning of Game 6, robbing Pittsburgh's Carmelo Martinez of a two-run homer and preserving the Reds' series-ending 2-1 victory.
■ **Top guns:** Randy Myers (3 saves, 7 SO, 0.00 ERA), Rob Dibble (1 save, 10 SO, 0.00), Paul O'Neill (.471), Hal Morris (.417), Reds; Doug Drabek (1-1, 1.65), Pirates.
■ **MVPs:** Dibble and Myers.

**Linescores**

**Game 1**—October 4, at Cincinnati
Pitt. ..............0 0 1 2 0 0 1 0 0—4 7 1
Cin. ..............3 0 0 0 0 0 0 0 0—3 5 0
Walk, Belinda (7), Patterson (9), Power (9); Rijo, Charlton (6), Dibble (9). W—Walk. L—Charlton. S—Power. HR—Bream (Pit.).

**Game 2**—October 5, at Cincinnati
Pitt. .............0 0 0 0 1 0 0 0 0—1 6 0
Cin. ..............1 0 0 0 1 0 0 0 x—2 5 0
Drabek; Browning, Dibble (7), Myers (8). W—Browning. L—Drabek. S—Myers. HR—Lind (Pit.).

**Game 3**—October 8, at Pittsburgh
Cin. ............0 2 0 0 3 0 0 0 1—6 13 1
Pitt. ............0 0 0 2 0 0 0 1 0—3 8 0
Jackson, Dibble (6), Charlton (8), Myers (9); Smith, Landrum (6), Smiley (7), Belinda (9). W—Jackson. L—Smith. S—Myers. HR—Hatcher, Duncan (Cin.).

**Game 4**—October 9, at Pittsburgh
Cin. ............0 0 0 2 0 0 2 0 1—5 10 1
Pitt. ............1 0 0 1 0 0 0 1 0—3 8 0
Rijo, Myers (8), Dibble (9); Walk, Power (8). W—Rijo. L—Walk. S—Dibble. HR—O'Neill, Sabo (Cin.); Bell (Pit.).

**Game 5**—October 10, at Pittsburgh
Cin. ..............1 0 0 0 0 0 0 1 0—2 7 0
Pitt. ..............2 0 0 1 0 0 0 0 x—3 6 1
Browning, Mahler (6), Charlton (7), Scudder (8); Drabek, Patterson (9). W—Drabek. L—Browning. S—Patterson.

**Game 6**—October 12, at Cincinnati
Pitt. ..............0 0 0 0 1 0 0 0 0—1 1 3
Cin. ..............1 0 0 0 0 0 1 0 x—2 9 0
Power, Smith (3), Belinda (7), Landrum (8); Jackson, Charlton (7), Myers (8). W—Charlton. L—Smith. S—Myers.

## WORLD SERIES

■ **Winner:** The Oakland Athletics' aura of invincibility was shattered by the Cincinnati Reds in a startling sweep. The A's, who were looking for a second straight championship, entered the Series with a 10-game post-season winning streak.
■ **Turning point:** Game 1. Eric Davis' first-inning home run and the combined nine-hit pitching of Jose Rijo, Rob Dibble and Randy Myers in a 7-0 victory served notice that the A's had their hands full.
■ **Memorable moment:** Relief ace Myers retiring Jose Canseco and Carney Lansford in the ninth inning of Game 4 to preserve a 2-1 victory for Rijo and complete the sweep.
■ **Top guns:** Rijo (2-0, 0.59 ERA), Myers (3 games, 0.00), Dibble (1-0, 0.00), Billy Hatcher (.750), Chris Sabo (.563, 2 HR, 5 RBIs), Reds; Rickey Henderson (.333), Athletics.
■ **MVP:** Rijo.

**Linescores**

**Game 1**—October 16, at Cincinnati
Oak. ..........0 0 0 0 0 0 0 0 0—0 9 1
Cin. ............2 0 2 0 3 0 0 0 x—7 10 0
Stewart, Burns (5), Nelson (5), Sanderson (7), Eckersley (8); Rijo, Dibble (8), Myers (9). W—Rijo. L—Stewart. HR—Davis (Cin.).

**Game 2**—October 17, at Cincinnati
Oak. ......1 0 3 0 0 0 0 0 0 0—4 10 2
Cin. ........2 0 0 1 0 0 0 1 0 1—5 14 2
Welch, Honeycutt (8), Eckersley (10); Jackson, Scudder (3), Armstrong (5), Charlton (8), Dibble (9). W—Dibble. L—Eckersley. HR—Canseco (Oak.).

**Game 3**—October 19, at Oakland
Cin. ...........0 1 7 0 0 0 0 0 0—8 14 1
Oak. ...........0 2 1 0 0 0 0 0 0—3 7 1
Browning, Dibble (7), Myers (8); Moore, Sanderson (3), Klink (4), Nelson (4), Burns (8), Young (9). W—Browning. L—Moore. HR—Sabo 2 (Cin.); Baines, R. Henderson (Oak.).

**Game 4**—October 20, at Oakland
Cin. ..............0 0 0 0 0 0 0 2 0—2 7 1
Oak. ............1 0 0 0 0 0 0 0 0—1 2 1
Rijo, Myers (9); Stewart. W—Rijo. L—Stewart. S—Myers.

# 1991

## FINAL STANDINGS

### American League

**East Division**

| Team | Tor. | Det. | Bos. | Mil. | N.Y. | Bal. | Cle. | Min. | Chi. | Tex. | Oak. | Sea. | K.C. | Cal. | W | L | Pct. | GB |
|---|---|---|---|---|---|---|---|---|---|---|---|---|---|---|---|---|---|---|
| Toronto | ... | 8 | 4 | 7 | 7 | 8 | 12 | 8 | 5 | 6 | 6 | 7 | 7 | 6 | 91 | 71 | .562 | ... |
| Detroit | 5 | ... | 8 | 4 | 8 | 8 | 6 | 4 | 8 | 6 | 4 | 8 | 8 | 7 | 84 | 78 | .519 | 7 |
| Boston | 9 | 5 | ... | 7 | 6 | 5 | 9 | 3 | 7 | 5 | 8 | 9 | 7 | 4 | 84 | 78 | .519 | 7 |
| Milwaukee | 6 | 9 | 6 | ... | 6 | 10 | 8 | 6 | 5 | 7 | 8 | 3 | 3 | 6 | 83 | 79 | .512 | 8 |
| New York | 6 | 5 | 7 | 7 | ... | 8 | 7 | 2 | 4 | 5 | 6 | 3 | 5 | 6 | 71 | 91 | .438 | 20 |
| Baltimore | 5 | 5 | 8 | 3 | 5 | ... | 7 | 4 | 4 | 9 | 3 | 4 | 4 | 6 | 67 | 95 | .414 | 24 |
| Cleveland | 1 | 7 | 4 | 5 | 6 | 6 | ... | 2 | 6 | 4 | 5 | 2 | 4 | 5 | 57 | 105 | .352 | 34 |

**West Division**

| Team | Min. | Chi. | Tex. | Oak. | Sea. | K.C. | Cal. | Tor. | Det. | Bos. | Mil. | N.Y. | Bal. | Cle. | W | L | Pct. | GB |
|---|---|---|---|---|---|---|---|---|---|---|---|---|---|---|---|---|---|---|
| Minnesota | ... | 5 | 6 | 8 | 9 | 7 | 5 | 4 | 8 | 9 | 6 | 10 | 8 | 10 | 95 | 67 | .586 | ... |
| Chicago | 8 | ... | 8 | 7 | 7 | 7 | 5 | 7 | 4 | 5 | 7 | 8 | 8 | 6 | 87 | 75 | .537 | 8 |
| Texas | 7 | 5 | ... | 9 | 8 | 6 | 8 | 6 | 6 | 7 | 5 | 7 | 3 | 8 | 85 | 77 | .525 | 10 |
| Oakland | 5 | 6 | 4 | ... | 6 | 7 | 12 | 6 | 8 | 4 | 4 | 6 | 9 | 7 | 84 | 78 | .519 | 11 |
| Seattle | 4 | 6 | 5 | 7 | ... | 6 | 7 | 5 | 4 | 3 | 9 | 9 | 8 | 10 | 83 | 79 | .512 | 12 |
| Kansas City | 6 | 6 | 7 | 6 | 7 | ... | 4 | 5 | 4 | 5 | 9 | 7 | 8 | 8 | 82 | 80 | .506 | 13 |
| California | 8 | 8 | 5 | 1 | 6 | 9 | ... | 6 | 5 | 8 | 6 | 6 | 6 | 7 | 81 | 81 | .500 | 14 |

### National League

**East Division**

| Team | Pit. | St.L. | Phi. | Chi. | N.Y. | Mon. | Atl. | L.A. | S.D. | S.F. | Cin. | Hou. | W | L | Pct. | GB |
|---|---|---|---|---|---|---|---|---|---|---|---|---|---|---|---|---|
| Pittsburgh | ... | 11 | 12 | 11 | 12 | 12 | 3 | 5 | 7 | 7 | 10 | 8 | 98 | 64 | .605 | ... |
| St. Louis | 7 | ... | 12 | 8 | 11 | 11 | 3 | 6 | 3 | 8 | 8 | 7 | 84 | 78 | .519 | 14 |
| Philadelphia | 6 | 6 | ... | 10 | 7 | 14 | 7 | 5 | 9 | 6 | 3 | 5 | 78 | 84 | .481 | 20 |
| Chicago | 7 | 10 | 8 | ... | 11 | 10 | 6 | 2 | 4 | 6 | 4 | 9 | 77 | 83 | .481 | 20 |
| New York | 6 | 7 | 11 | 6 | ... | 14 | 3 | 5 | 7 | 6 | 7 | 5 | 77 | 84 | .478 | 20.5 |
| Montreal | 6 | 7 | 4 | 7 | 4 | ... | 7 | 7 | 6 | 7 | 6 | 10 | 71 | 90 | .441 | 26.5 |

**West Division**

| Team | Atl. | L.A. | S.D. | S.F. | Cin. | Hou. | Pit. | St.L. | Phi. | Chi. | N.Y. | Mon. | W | L | Pct. | GB |
|---|---|---|---|---|---|---|---|---|---|---|---|---|---|---|---|---|
| Atlanta | ... | 7 | 11 | 9 | 11 | 13 | 9 | 9 | 5 | 6 | 9 | 5 | 94 | 68 | .580 | ... |
| Los Angeles | 11 | ... | 10 | 8 | 12 | 10 | 7 | 6 | 7 | 10 | 7 | 5 | 93 | 69 | .574 | 1 |
| San Diego | 7 | 8 | ... | 11 | 10 | 12 | 5 | 9 | 3 | 8 | 5 | 6 | 84 | 78 | .519 | 10 |
| San Fran. | 9 | 10 | 7 | ... | 8 | 9 | 5 | 4 | 6 | 6 | 6 | 5 | 75 | 87 | .463 | 19 |
| Cincinnati | 7 | 6 | 8 | 10 | ... | 9 | 2 | 4 | 9 | 8 | 5 | 6 | 74 | 88 | .457 | 20 |
| Houston | 5 | 8 | 6 | 9 | 9 | ... | 4 | 5 | 7 | 3 | 7 | 2 | 65 | 97 | .401 | 29 |

## LEADERS

**American League**
**BA:** Julio Franco, Tex., .341.
**Runs:** Paul Molitor, Mil., 133.
**Hits:** Paul Molitor, Mil., 216.
**TB:** Cal Ripken, Bal., 368.
**HR:** Jose Canseco, Oak.; Cecil Fielder, Det., 44.
**RBI:** Cecil Fielder, Det., 133.
**SB:** Rickey Henderson, Oak., 58.
**Wins:** Scott Erickson, Min.; Bill Gullickson, Det., 20.
**ERA:** Roger Clemens, Bos., 2.62.
**CG:** Jack McDowell, Chi., 15.
**IP:** Roger Clemens, Bos., 271.1.
**SO:** Roger Clemens, Bos., 241.
**SV:** Bryan Harvey, Cal., 46.

**National League**
**BA:** Terry Pendleton, Atl., .319.
**Runs:** Brett Butler, L.A., 112.
**Hits:** Terry Pendleton, Atl., 187.
**TB:** Will Clark, S.F.; Terry Pendleton, Atl., 303.
**HR:** Howard Johnson, N.Y., 38.
**RBI:** Howard Johnson, N.Y., 117.
**SB:** Marquis Grissom, Mon., 76.
**Wins:** Tom Glavine, Atl.; John Smiley, Pit., 20.
**ERA:** Dennis Martinez, Mon., 2.39.
**CG:** Tom Glavine, Atl.; Dennis Martinez, Mon., 9.
**IP:** Greg Maddux, Chi., 263.
**SO:** David Cone, N.Y., 241.
**SV:** Lee Smith, St.L., 47.

**A.L. 20-game winners**
Scott Erickson, Min., 20-8
Bill Gullickson, Det., 20-9

**N.L. 20-game winners**
John Smiley, Pit., 20-8
Tom Glavine, Atl., 20-11

**A.L. 100 RBIs**
Cecil Fielder, Det., 133
Jose Canseco, Oak., 122
Ruben Sierra, Tex., 116
Cal Ripken, Bal., 114
Frank Thomas, Chi., 109
Joe Carter, Tor., 108
Juan Gonzalez, Tex., 102
Ken Griffey Jr., Sea., 100
Danny Tartabull, K.C., 100
Robin Ventura, Chi., 100

**N.L. 100 RBIs**
Howard Johnson, N.Y., 117
Barry Bonds, Pit., 116
Will Clark, S.F., 116
Fred McGriff, S.D., 106
Ron Gant, Atl., 105
Andre Dawson, Chi., 104
Ryne Sandberg, Chi., 100
Bobby Bonilla, Pit., 100

**A.L. 40 homers**
Jose Canseco, Oak., 44
Cecil Fielder, Det., 44

**Most Valuable Player**
A.L.: Cal Ripken, SS, Bal.
N.L.: Terry Pendleton, 3B, Atl.

**Cy Young Award**
A.L.: Roger Clemens, Bos.
N.L.: Tom Glavine, Atl.

**Rookie of the Year**
A.L.: Chuck Knoblauch, 2B, Min.
N.L.: Jeff Bagwell, 1B, Hou.

**Manager of the Year**
A.L.: Tom Kelly, Min.
N.L.: Bobby Cox, Atl.

**Hall of Fame additions**
Rod Carew, 2B/1B, 1967-85
Ferguson Jenkins, P, 1965-83
Tony Lazzeri, 2B, 1926-39
Gaylord Perry, P, 1962-83
Bill Veeck, executive/owner

## SIGNIFICANT EVENTS

■ **April 18:** The Tigers spoiled the dedication of Chicago's new Comiskey Park when they routed the White Sox, 16-0.

■ **June 10:** Miami and Denver were declared winners by a four-man N.L. expansion committee.

## MEMORABLE MOMENTS

■ **May 1:** Oakland's Rickey Henderson swiped his 939th base in a game against the Yankees, passing Lou Brock as baseball's all-time greatest base stealer.

■ **May 1:** Nolan Ryan, stealing the day's headlines from Henderson, fired his seventh career no-hitter, striking out 16 Blue Jays in a 3-0 victory.

■ **July 28:** Montreal's Dennis Martinez became the 14th pitcher to throw a perfect game when he retired all 27 Dodgers he faced in a 2-0 victory.

■ **October 2:** Cardinals closer Lee Smith, who had notched his 300th career save earlier in the year, recorded his single-season N.L-record 47th in a 6-4 victory over Montreal.

■ **October 6:** Mets righthander David Cone tied the N.L. single-game record when he struck out 19 Phillies in a 7-0 victory.

## ALL-STAR GAME

■ **Winner:** The A.L. ran its winning streak to four with a 4-2 victory and the N.L. ran its four-year run total to a paltry six.

■ **Key inning:** The third, when Cal Ripken followed singles by Rickey Henderson and Wade Boggs with a home run.

■ **Memorable moment:** A first-inning line drive by Bobby Bonilla that struck A.L. starter Jack Morris on the ankle, reviving All-Star memories of the 1937 Earl Averill shot that broke Dizzy Dean's toe.

■ **Top guns:** Ripken (Orioles), Ken Griffey Jr. (Mariners), Henderson (Athletics), Boggs (Red Sox), A.L.; Tom Glavine (Braves), Bonilla (Pirates), Andre Dawson (Cubs), N.L.

■ **MVP:** Ripken.

**Linescore**

July 9, at Toronto's SkyDome
N.L............1 0 0 1 0 0 0 0 0—2 10 1
A.L. ...........0 0 3 0 0 0 1 0 x—4 8 0
Glavine (Braves), De. Martinez (Expos) 3, Viola (Mets) 5, Harnisch (Astros) 6, Smiley (Pirates) 7, Dibble (Reds) 7, Morgan (Dodgers) 8; Morris (Twins), Key (Blue Jays) 3, Clemens (Red Sox) 4, McDowell (White Sox) 5, Reardon (Red Sox) 7, Aguilera (Twins) 7, Eckersley (Athletics) 9. W—Key. L—De. Martinez. S—Eckersley. HR—Ripken, A.L.; Dawson, N.L.

## ALCS

■ **Winner:** Minnesota won an LCS-record three road games and its second pennant in five years while handing Toronto its third Championship Series defeat.

■ **Turning point:** The 10th inning of Game 3 when Minnesota's Mike Pagliarulo homered off Toronto reliever Mike Timlin, giving the Twins a 3-2 victory and a 2-1 series advantage.

■ **Memorable moment:** Minnesota first baseman Kent Hrbek delivered a two-run single off David Wells in the eighth inning of Game 5 to cap a series-ending 8-5 victory.

■ **Top guns:** Rick Aguilera (3 saves, 0.00 ERA), Kirby Puckett (.429, 2 HR, 6 RBIs), Twins; Roberto Alomar (.474), Blue Jays.

■ **MVP:** Puckett.

**Linescores**

**Game 1**—October 8, at Minnesota
Toronto......0 0 0 1 0 3 0 0 0—4 9 3
Minn. ........2 2 1 0 0 0 0 0 x—5 11 0
Candiotti, Wells (3), Timlin (6); Morris, Willis (6), Aguilera (8). W—Morris. L—Candiotti. S—Aguilera.

**Game 2**—October 9, at Minnesota
Toronto........1 0 2 0 0 0 2 0 0—5 9 0
Minn. ..........0 0 1 0 0 1 0 0 0—2 5 1
Guzman, Henke (6), Ward (8); Tapani, Bedrosian (7), Guthrie (7). W—Guzman. L—Tapani. S—Ward.

**Game 3**—October 11, at Toronto
Minn. ......0 0 0 0 1 1 0 0 0 1—3 7 0
Tor. ..........2 0 0 0 0 0 0 0 0 0—2 5 1
Erickson, West (5), Willis (7), Guthrie (9), Aguilera (10); Key, Wells (7), Henke (8), Timlin (10). W—Guthrie. L—Timlin. S—Aguilera. HR—Carter (Tor.); Pagliarulo (Min.).

**Game 4**—October 12, at Toronto
Minn. ........0 0 0 4 0 2 1 1 1—9 13 1
Toronto......0 1 0 0 0 1 0 0 1—3 11 2
Morris, Bedrosian (9); Stottlemyre, Wells (4), Acker (6), Timlin (7), MacDonald (9). W—Morris. L—Stottlemyre. HR—Puckett (Min.).

**Game 5**—October 13, at Toronto
Minn. ........1 1 0 0 0 3 0 3 0—8 14 2
Toronto......0 0 3 2 0 0 0 0 0—5 9 1
Tapani, West (5), Willis (8), Aguilera (9); Candiotti, Timlin (6), Ward (6), Wells (8). W—West. L—Ward. S—Aguilera. HR—Puckett (Min.).

## NLCS

■ **Winner:** The young Braves, last-place N.L. West finishers in 1990, defeated the Pirates and won their first pennant since moving to Atlanta.

■ **Turning point:** Greg Olson's run-scoring double in the ninth inning of Game 6, which gave Braves lefthander Steve Avery his second 1-0 victory.

■ **Memorable moment:** The final pitch of John Smoltz's 4-0 Game 7 victory. The shutout, the Braves' third, gave Atlanta fans their first World Series qualifier.

■ **Top guns:** Avery (2-0, 0.00 ERA), Smoltz (2-0, 1.76), Olson (.333), Brian Hunter (.333), Braves; Doug Drabek (1-1, 0.60), Zane Smith (1-1, 0.61), Jay Bell (.414), Pirates.

■ **MVP:** Avery.

**Linescores**

**Game 1**—October 9, at Pittsburgh
Atlanta ........0 0 0 0 0 0 0 0 1—1 5 1
Pit. .............1 0 2 0 0 1 0 1 x—5 8 1
Glavine, Wohlers (7), Stanton (8); Drabek, Walk (7). W—Drabek. L—Glavine. S—Walk. HR—Van Slyke (Pit.); Justice (Atl.).

**Game 2**—October 10, at Pittsburgh
Atlanta ........0 0 0 0 0 1 0 0 0—1 8 0
Pit. .............0 0 0 0 0 0 0 0 0—0 6 0
Avery, Pena (9); Z. Smith, Mason (8), Belinda (9). W—Avery. L—Z. Smith. S—Pena.

**Game 3**—October 12, at Atlanta
Pit. ..........1 0 0 1 0 0 1 0 0— 3 10 2
Atlanta......4 1 1 0 0 0 1 3 x—10 11 0
Smiley, Landrum (3), Patterson (4), Kipper (6), Rodriguez (8); Smoltz, Stanton (7), Wohlers (8), Pena (8). W—Smoltz. L—Smiley. S—Pena. HR—Gant, Olson, Bream (Atl.); Merced, Bell (Pit.).

**Game 4**—October 13, at Atlanta
Pit. ......0 1 0 0 1 0 0 0 0 1—3 11 1
Atlanta 2 0 0 0 0 0 0 0 0 0—2 7 1
Tomlin, Walk (7), Belinda (9); Leibrandt, Clancy (7), Stanton (8), Mercker (10), Wohlers (10). W—Belinda. L—Mercker.

**Game 5**—October 14, at Atlanta
Pit. .............0 0 0 0 1 0 0 0 0—1 6 2
Atlanta ........0 0 0 0 0 0 0 0 0—0 9 1
Z. Smith, Mason (8); Glavine, Pena (9). W—Z. Smith. L—Glavine. S—Mason.

**Game 6**—October 16, at Pittsburgh
Atlanta ........0 0 0 0 0 0 0 0 1—1 7 0
Pit. .............0 0 0 0 0 0 0 0 0—0 4 0
Avery, Pena (9); Drabek. W—Avery. L—Drabek. S—Pena.

**Game 7**—October 17, at Pittsburgh
Atlanta ........3 0 0 0 1 0 0 0 0—4 6 1
Pit. .............0 0 0 0 0 0 0 0 0—0 6 0
Smoltz; Smiley, Walk (1), Mason (6), Belinda (8). W—Smoltz. L—Smiley. HR—Hunter (Atl.).

## WORLD SERIES

■ **Winner:** Minnesota defeated Atlanta in the "worst-to-first" World Series, which featured teams that had risen from last-place 1990 finishes to win pennants.

■ **Turning point:** The 11th-inning of Game 6, when Kirby Puckett greeted Braves reliever Charlie Leibrandt with a game-ending home run, squaring the Series. Puckett had made an outstanding leaping catch earlier in the 4-3 victory.

■ **Memorable moment:** A seventh-game baserunning blunder by Atlanta's Lonnie Smith, who failed to score on Terry Pendleton's eighth-inning double. The Twins and Jack Morris went on to post a 1-0 Series-ending victory on Gene Larkin's 12th-inning single.

■ **Top guns:** Morris (2-0, 1.17 ERA), Brian Harper (.381), Puckett (2 HR, 4 RBIs), Twins; David Justice (2 HR, 6 RBIs), Braves.

■ **MVP:** Morris.

**Linescores**

**Game 1**—October 19, at Minnesota
Atlanta ........0 0 0 0 0 1 0 1 0—2 6 1
Minn. ..........0 0 1 0 3 1 0 0 x—5 9 1
Leibrandt, Clancy (5), Wohlers (7), Stanton (8); Morris, Guthrie (8), Aguilera (8). W—Morris. L—Leibrandt. S—Aguilera. HR—Gagne, Hrbek (Min.).

**Game 2**—October 20, at Minnesota
Atlanta ........0 1 0 0 1 0 0 0 0—2 8 1
Minn. ..........2 0 0 0 0 0 0 1 x—3 4 1
Glavine; Tapani, Aguilera (9). W—Tapani. L—Glavine. S—Aguilera. HR—Davis, Leius (Min.).

**Game 3**—October 22, at Atlanta
Minn. ........1 0 0 0 0 0 1 2 0 0 0 0—4 10 1
Atl. ...........0 1 0 1 2 0 0 0 0 0 0 1—5 8 2
Erickson, West (5), Leach (5), Bedrosian (6), Willis (8), Guthrie (10), Aguilera (12); Avery, Pena (8), Stanton (10), Wohlers (12), Mercker (12), Clancy (12). W—Clancy. L—Aguilera. HR—Justice, Smith (Atl.); Puckett, Davis (Min.).

**Game 4**—October 23, at Atlanta
Minn. ............0 1 0 0 0 0 1 0 0—2 7 0
Atlanta ..........0 0 1 0 0 0 1 0 1—3 8 0
Morris, Willis (7), Guthrie (8), Bedrosian (9); Smoltz, Wohlers (8), Stanton (8). W—Stanton. L—Guthrie. HR—Pendleton, Smith (Atl.); Pagliarulo (Min.).

**Game 5**—October 24, at Atlanta
Minn. ......0 0 0 0 0 3 0 1 1— 5 7 1
Atlanta......0 0 0 4 1 0 6 3 x—14 17 1
Tapani, Leach (5), West (7), Bedrosian (7), Willis (8); Glavine, Mercker (6), Clancy (7), St. Claire (9). W—Glavine. L—Tapani. HR—Justice, Smith, Hunter (Atl.).

**Game 6**—October 26, at Minnesota
Atl. ....0 0 0 0 2 0 1 0 0 0 0—3 9 0
Minn. 2 0 0 0 1 0 0 0 0 0 1—4 9 1
Avery, Stanton (7), Pena (9), Leibrandt (11); Erickson, Guthrie (7), Willis (7), Aguilera (10). W—Aguilera. L—Leibrandt. HR—Pendleton (Atl.); Puckett (Min.).

**Game 7**—October 27, at Minnesota
Atl. ........0 0 0 0 0 0 0 0 0 0—0 7 0
Minn. ....0 0 0 0 0 0 0 0 0 1—1 10 0
Smoltz, Stanton (8), Pena (9); Morris. W—Morris. L—Pena.

# 1992

## FINAL STANDINGS

### American League

**East Division**

| Team | Tor. | Mil. | Bal. | Cle. | N.Y. | Det. | Bos. | Oak. | Min. | Chi. | Tex. | Cal. | K.C. | Sea. | W | L | Pct. | GB |
|---|---|---|---|---|---|---|---|---|---|---|---|---|---|---|---|---|---|---|
| Toronto | ... | 5 | 8 | 7 | 11 | 8 | 6 | 6 | 7 | 7 | 9 | 7 | 7 | 8 | 96 | 66 | .593 | ... |
| Milwaukee | 8 | ... | 7 | 8 | 6 | 8 | 8 | 7 | 6 | 7 | 7 | 7 | 5 | 8 | 92 | 70 | .568 | 4 |
| Baltimore | 5 | 6 | ... | 7 | 5 | 10 | 8 | 6 | 6 | 6 | 7 | 8 | 8 | 7 | 89 | 73 | .549 | 7 |
| Cleveland | 6 | 5 | 6 | ... | 7 | 5 | 7 | 6 | 6 | 5 | 5 | 6 | 5 | 7 | 76 | 86 | .469 | 20 |
| New York | 2 | 7 | 8 | 6 | ... | 8 | 6 | 6 | 5 | 4 | 6 | 5 | 7 | 6 | 76 | 86 | .469 | 20 |
| Detroit | 5 | 5 | 3 | 8 | 5 | ... | 9 | 6 | 3 | 2 | 8 | 5 | 7 | 9 | 75 | 87 | .463 | 21 |
| Boston | 7 | 5 | 5 | 6 | 7 | 4 | ... | 5 | 3 | 6 | 4 | 8 | 7 | 6 | 73 | 89 | .451 | 23 |

**West Division**

| Team | Oak. | Min. | Chi. | Tex. | Cal. | K.C. | Sea. | Tor. | Mil. | Bal. | Cle. | N.Y. | Det. | Bos. | W | L | Pct. | GB |
|---|---|---|---|---|---|---|---|---|---|---|---|---|---|---|---|---|---|---|
| Oakland | ... | 8 | 8 | 9 | 8 | 9 | 12 | 6 | 5 | 6 | 6 | 6 | 6 | 7 | 96 | 66 | .593 | ... |
| Minnesota | 5 | ... | 5 | 6 | 11 | 7 | 8 | 5 | 6 | 6 | 6 | 7 | 9 | 9 | 90 | 72 | .556 | 6 |
| Chicago | 5 | 8 | ... | 5 | 10 | 7 | 4 | 5 | 5 | 6 | 7 | 8 | 10 | 6 | 86 | 76 | .531 | 10 |
| Texas | 4 | 7 | 8 | ... | 4 | 7 | 9 | 3 | 5 | 5 | 7 | 6 | 4 | 8 | 77 | 85 | .475 | 19 |
| California | 5 | 2 | 3 | 9 | ... | 8 | 7 | 5 | 5 | 4 | 6 | 7 | 7 | 4 | 72 | 90 | .444 | 24 |
| Kansas City | 4 | 6 | 6 | 6 | 5 | ... | 7 | 5 | 7 | 4 | 7 | 5 | 5 | 5 | 72 | 90 | .444 | 24 |
| Seattle | 1 | 5 | 9 | 4 | 6 | 6 | ... | 4 | 4 | 5 | 5 | 6 | 3 | 6 | 64 | 98 | .395 | 32 |

### National League

**East Division**

| Team | Pit. | Mon. | St.L. | Chi. | N.Y. | Phi. | Atl. | Cin. | S.D. | Hou. | S.F. | L.A. | W | L | Pct. | GB |
|---|---|---|---|---|---|---|---|---|---|---|---|---|---|---|---|---|
| Pittsburgh | ... | 9 | 15 | 10 | 14 | 13 | 5 | 6 | 5 | 6 | 6 | 7 | 96 | 66 | .593 | ... |
| Montreal | 9 | ... | 6 | 11 | 12 | 9 | 8 | 7 | 8 | 4 | 5 | 8 | 87 | 75 | .537 | 9 |
| St. Louis | 3 | 12 | ... | 7 | 9 | 11 | 6 | 5 | 8 | 7 | 7 | 8 | 83 | 79 | .512 | 13 |
| Chicago | 8 | 7 | 11 | ... | 9 | 9 | 2 | 5 | 5 | 8 | 8 | 6 | 78 | 84 | .481 | 18 |
| New York | 4 | 6 | 9 | 9 | ... | 6 | 5 | 5 | 4 | 7 | 10 | 7 | 72 | 90 | .444 | 24 |
| Philadelphia | 5 | 9 | 7 | 9 | 12 | ... | 6 | 5 | 3 | 4 | 3 | 7 | 70 | 92 | .432 | 26 |

**West Division**

| Team | Atl. | Cin. | S.D. | Hou. | S.F. | L.A. | Pit. | Mon. | St.L. | Chi. | N.Y. | Phi. | W | L | Pct. | GB |
|---|---|---|---|---|---|---|---|---|---|---|---|---|---|---|---|---|
| Atlanta | ... | 9 | 13 | 13 | 11 | 12 | 7 | 4 | 6 | 10 | 7 | 6 | 98 | 64 | .605 | ... |
| CIncinnati | 9 | ... | 11 | 10 | 10 | 11 | 6 | 5 | 7 | 7 | 7 | 7 | 90 | 72 | .556 | 8 |
| San Diego | 5 | 7 | ... | 11 | 11 | 9 | 7 | 4 | 4 | 7 | 8 | 9 | 82 | 80 | .506 | 16 |
| Houston | 5 | 8 | 7 | ... | 12 | 13 | 6 | 8 | 5 | 4 | 5 | 8 | 81 | 81 | .500 | 17 |
| San Fran. | 7 | 8 | 7 | 6 | ... | 11 | 6 | 7 | 5 | 4 | 2 | 9 | 72 | 90 | .444 | 26 |
| Los Angeles | 6 | 7 | 9 | 5 | 7 | ... | 5 | 4 | 4 | 6 | 5 | 5 | 63 | 99 | .389 | 35 |

## LEADERS

**American League**
**BA:** Edgar Martinez, Sea., .343.
**Runs:** Tony Phillips, Det., 114.
**Hits:** Kirby Puckett, Min., 210.
**TB:** Kirby Puckett, Min., 313.
**HR:** Juan Gonzalez, Tex., 43.
**RBI:** Cecil Fielder, Det., 124.
**SB:** Kenny Lofton, Cle., 66.
**Wins:** Kevin Brown, Tex.;
Jack Morris, Tor., 21.
**ERA:** Roger Clemens, Bos., 2.41.
**CG:** Jack McDowell, Chi., 13.
**IP:** Kevin Brown, Tex., 265.2.
**SO:** Randy Johnson, Sea., 241.
**SV:** Dennis Eckersley, Oak., 51.

**National League**
**BA:** Gary Sheffield, S.D., .330.
**Runs:** Barry Bonds, Pit., 109.
**Hits:** Terry Pendleton, Atl.;
Andy Van Slyke, Pit., 199.
**TB:** Gary Sheffield, S.D., 323.
**HR:** Fred McGriff, S.D., 35.
**RBI:** Darren Daulton, Phil., 109.
**SB:** Marquis Grissom, Mon., 78.
**Wins:** Tom Glavine, Atl.;
Greg Maddux, Chi., 20.
**ERA:** Bill Swift, S.F., 2.08.
**CG:** Terry Mulholland, Phil., 12.
**IP:** Greg Maddux, Chi., 268.
**SO:** John Smoltz, Atl., 215.
**SV:** Lee Smith, St.L., 43.

**A.L. 20-game winners**
Jack Morris, Tor., 21-6
Kevin Brown, Tex., 21-11
Jack McDowell, Chi., 20-10

**N.L. 20-game winners**
Tom Glavine, Atl., 20-8
Greg Maddux, Chi., 20-11

**A.L. 100 RBIs**
Cecil Fielder, Det., 124
Joe Carter, Tor., 119
Frank Thomas, Chi., 115
George Bell, Chi., 112
Albert Belle, Cle., 112
Kirby Puckett, Min., 110
Juan Gonzalez, Tex., 109
Dave Winfield, Tor., 108
Mike Devereaux, Bal., 107
Carlos Baerga, Cle., 105
Mark McGwire, Oak., 104
Ken Griffey Jr., Sea., 103

**N.L. 100 RBIs**
Darren Daulton, Phil., 109
Terry Pendleton, Atl., 105
Fred McGriff, S.D., 104
Barry Bonds, Pit., 103
Gary Sheffield, S.D., 100

**A.L. 40 homers**
Juan Gonzalez, Tex., 43
Mark McGwire, Oak., 42

**Most Valuable Player**
A.L.: Dennis Eckersley, P, Oak.
N.L.: Barry Bonds, OF, Pit.

**Cy Young Award**
A.L.: Dennis Eckersley, Oak.
N.L.: Greg Maddux, Chi.

**Rookie of the Year**
A.L.: Pat Listach, SS, Mil.
N.L.: Eric Karros, 1B, L.A.

**Manager of the Year**
A.L.: Tony La Russa, Oak.
N.L.: Jim Leyland, Pit.

**Hall of Fame additions**
Rollie Fingers, P, 1968-85
Bill McGowan, umpire
Hal Newhouser, P, 1939-55
Tom Seaver, P, 1967-86

## SIGNIFICANT EVENTS

■ **April 6:** The Orioles opened their new Camden Yards home with a 2-0 victory over Cleveland.
■ **September 7:** Fay Vincent, reacting to an 18-9 no-confidence vote by the owners, resigned his post as baseball's eighth commissioner.
■ **November 17:** The Florida Marlins and Colorado Rockies selected 36 players apiece in baseball's first expansion draft since 1976.

## MEMORABLE MOMENTS

■ **April 12:** Boston's Matt Young became the third pitcher in history to lose a complete-game no-hitter when he dropped a 2-1 decision to Cleveland.
■ **September 9, 30:** Milwaukee's Robin Yount and Kansas City's George Brett became the 17th and 18th members of baseball's 3,000-hit club.
■ **September 20:** Philadelphia second baseman Mickey Morandini pulled off baseball's ninth unassisted triple play and the N.L.'s first since 1927 in the sixth inning of a game against Pittsburgh.

## ALL-STAR GAME

■ **Winner:** Ken Griffey Jr. went 3 for 3 as the suddenly dominant A.L. pounded out 19 hits and romped to an easy 13-6 victory.
■ **Key inning:** The A.L. first, when N.L. starter Tom Glavine was touched for four runs on seven consecutive singles.
■ **Memorable moment:** Ruben Sierra's two-run sixth-inning homer, which lifted the A.L.'s lead to 10-0.
■ **Top guns:** Griffey Jr. (Mariners), Sierra (Rangers), Robin Ventura (White Sox), Joe Carter (Blue Jays), Will Clark (Giants), Fred McGriff (Padres), N.L.
■ **MVP:** Griffey Jr.

**Linescore**
July 14, at San Diego's Jack Murphy Stadium
A.L.............4 1 1  0 0 4  0 3 0—13 19 1
N.L.............0 0 0  0 0 1  0 3 2— 6 12 1
Brown (Rangers), McDowell (White Sox) 2, Guzman (Blue Jays) 3, Clemens (Red Sox) 4, Mussina (Orioles) 5, Langston (Angels) 6, Nagy (Indians) 7, Montgomery (Royals) 8, Aguilera (Twins) 8, Eckersley (Athletics) 9; Glavine (Braves), Maddux (Braves) 2, Cone (Mets) 4, Tewksbury (Cardinals) 5, Smoltz (Braves) 6, D. Martinez (Expos) 7, Jones (Astros) 8, Charlton (Reds) 9. W—Brown. L—Glavine. HR—Griffey, Sierra, A.L.; Clark, N.L.

## ALCS

■ **Winner:** The Toronto Blue Jays, three-time Championship Series losers, brought Canada its first pennant with a rousing six-game victory over Oakland.
■ **Turning point:** Down 6-1 entering the eighth inning of Game 4, the Blue Jays rallied to tie against A's relief ace Dennis Eckersley and won in the 11th on Pat Borders' sacrifice fly. Instead of a 2-2 series tie, Toronto was up 3-1.
■ **Memorable moment:** Roberto Alomar's stunning game-tying homer off Eckersley in the ninth inning of Game 4. The two-run shot forced extra innings.
■ **Top guns:** Juan Guzman (2-0, 2.08 ERA), Alomar (.423, 2 HR), Candy Maldonado (2 HR, 6 RBIs), Blue Jays; Harold Baines (.440), Ruben Sierra (.333, 7 RBIs), Athletics.
■ **MVP:** Alomar.

**Linescores**
**Game 1**—October 7, at Toronto
Oak. ............0 3 0  0 0 0  0 0 1—4 6 1
Tor. .............0 0 0  0 1 1  0 1 0—3 9 0
Stewart, Russell (8), Eckersley (9); Morris. W—Russell. L—Morris. S—Eckersley. HR—McGwire, Steinbach, Baines (Oak.); Borders, Winfield (Tor.).
**Game 2**—October 8, at Toronto
Oak. ............0 0 0  0 0 0  0 0 1—1 6 0
Tor. .............0 0 0  0 2 0  1 0 x—3 4 0
Moore, Corsi (8), Parrett (8); Cone, Henke (9). W—Cone. L—Moore. S—Henke. HR—Gruber (Tor.).
**Game 3**—October 10, at Oakland
Tor. ...............0 1 0 1 1 0 2 1 1—7 9 1
Oak. .............0 0 0 2 0 0 2 1 0—5 13 3
Guzman, Ward (7), Timlin (8), Henke (8); Darling, Downs (7), Corsi (8), Russell (8), Honeycutt (9), Eckersley (9). W—Guzman. L—Darling. S—Henke. HR—Alomar, Maldonado (Tor.).
**Game 4**—October 11, at Oakland
Tor. ........0 1 0  0 0 0  0 3 2  0 1—7 17 4
Oak. ........0 0 5  0 0 1  0 0 0  0 0—6 12 2
Morris, Stottlemyre (4), Timlin (8), Ward (9), Henke (11); Welch, Parrett (8), Eckersley (8), Corsi (9), Downs (10). W—Ward. L—Downs. S—Henke. HR—Olerud, Alomar (Tor.).
**Game 5**—October 12, at Oakland
Tor. ...............0 0 0  1 0 0  1 0 0—2 7 3
Oak. ...........2 0 1  0 3 0  0 0 x—6 8 0
Cone, Key (5), Eichhorn (8); Stewart. W—Stewart. L—Cone. HR—Sierra (Oak.); Winfield (Tor.).
**Game 6**—October 14, at Toronto
Oak. ..........0 0 0  0 0 1  0 1 0—2 7 1
Tor. ...........2 0 4  0 1 0  0 2 x—9 13 0
Moore, Parrett (3), Honeycutt (5), Russell (7), Witt (8); Guzman, Ward (8), Henke (9). W—Guzman. L—Moore. HR—Carter, Maldonado (Tor.).

## NLCS

■ **Winner:** Atlanta won its rematch with Pittsburgh and captured its second straight pennant in a stirring Championship Series that was decided on the final pitch.
■ **Turning point:** The incredible ninth inning of Game 7. Down 2-0 to Pirates ace Doug Drabek after eight innings and on the brink of blowing what had once been a three-games-to-one advantage, the Braves rallied for three runs.
■ **Memorable moment:** With two out and the bases loaded in the bottom of the ninth inning of Game 7, pinch-hitter Francisco Cabrera delivered a two-run, pennant-deciding single to left field off Stan Belinda.
■ **Top guns:** John Smoltz (2-0, 2.66 ERA), Mark Lemke (.333), David Justice (2 HR, 6 RBIs), Ron Gant (2 HR, 6 RBIs), Braves; Tim Wakefield (2-0, 3.00), Lloyd McClendon (.727), Gary Redus (.438), Pirates.
■ **MVP:** Smoltz.

**Linescores**
**Game 1**—October 6, at Atlanta
Pitt..............0 0 0  0 0 0  0 1 0—1 5 1
Atlanta..........0 1 0  2 1 0  1 0 x—5 8 0
Drabek, Patterson (5), Neagle (7), Cox (8); Smoltz, Stanton (9). W—Smoltz. L—Drabek. HR—Blauser (Atl.); Lind (Pit.).
**Game 2**—October 7, at Atlanta
Pitt...........0 0 0  0 0 0  4 1 0— 5 7 0
Atlanta......0 4 0  0 4 0  5 0 x—13 14 0
Jackson, Mason (2), Walk (3), Tomlin (5), Neagle (7), Patterson (7), Belinda (8); Avery, Freeman (7), Stanton (7), Wohlers (8), Reardon (9). W—Avery. L—Jackson. HR—Gant (Atl.).
**Game 3**—October 9, at Pittsburgh
Atlanta ........0 0 0  1 0 0  1 0 0—2 5 0
Pitt..............0 0 0  0 1 1  1 0 x—3 8 1
Glavine, Stanton (7), Wohlers (8); Wakefield. W—Wakefield. L—Glavine. HR—Slaught (Pit.); Bream, Gant (Atl.).
**Game 4**—October 10, at Pittsburgh
Atlanta ......0 2 0  0 2 2  0 0 0—6 11 1
Pitt.............0 2 1  0 0 0  1 0 0—4 6 1
Smoltz, Stanton (7), Reardon (9); Drabek, Tomlin (5), Cox (6), Mason (7). W—Smoltz. L—Drabek. S—Reardon.
**Game 5**—October 11, at Pittsburgh
Atlanta ......0 0 0  0 0 0  0 1 0—1 3 0
Pitt............4 0 1  0 0 1  1 0 x—7 13 0
Avery, P. Smith (1), Leibrandt (5), Freeman (6), Mercker (8); Walk. W—Walk. L—Avery.
**Game 6**—October 13, at Atlanta
Pitt...........0 8 0  0 4 1  0 0 0—13 13 1
Atlanta ....0 0 0  1 0 0  1 0 2— 4 9 1
Wakefield; Glavine, Leibrandt (2), Freeman (5), Mercker (7), Wohlers (9). W—Wakefield. L—Glavine. HR—Bonds, Bell, McClendon (Pit.); Justice 2 (Atl.).
**Game 7**—October 14, at Atlanta
Pitt..............1 0 0  0 0 1  0 0 0—2 7 1
Atlanta ........0 0 0  0 0 0  0 0 3—3 7 0
Drabek, Belinda (9); Smoltz, Stanton (7), P. Smith (7), Avery (7), Reardon (9). W—Reardon. L—Drabek.

## WORLD SERIES

■ **Winner:** Toronto brought a baseball championship to Canada and the Braves failed to give Atlanta its long-awaited title for the second year in a row.
■ **Turning point:** The Blue Jays took a three-games-to-one advantage with a 2-1 victory in Game 4, thanks to the combined five-hit pitching of Jimmy Key, Duane Ward and Tom Henke and a home run by Pat Borders.
■ **Memorable moment:** Dave Winfield's two-run double in the 11th inning of Game 6 , which gave Toronto a 4-3 Series-clinching win.
■ **Top guns:** Key (2-0, 1.00 ERA), Borders (.450), Joe Carter (2 HR), Blue Jays; Deion Sanders (.533), Braves.
■ **MVP:** Borders.

**Linescores**
**Game 1**—October 17, at Atlanta
Tor. .............0 0 0  1 0 0  0 0 0—1 4 0
Atl. .............0 0 0  0 0 3  0 0 x—3 4 0
Morris, Stottlemyre (7), Wells (8); Glavine. W—Glavine. L—Morris. HR—Carter (Tor.); Berryhill (Atl.).
**Game 2**—October 18, at Atlanta
Tor. .............0 0 0  0 2 0  0 1 2—5 9 2
Atl. .............0 1 0  1 2 0  0 0 0—4 5 1
Cone, Wells (5), Stottlemyre (7), Ward (8), Henke (9); Smoltz, Stanton (8), Reardon (8). W—Ward. L—Reardon. S—Henke. HR—Sprague (Tor.).
**Game 3**—October 20, at Toronto
Atl. .............0 0 0  0 0 1  0 1 0—2 9 0
Tor. .............0 0 0  1 0 0  0 1 1—3 6 1
Avery, Wohlers (9), Stanton (9), Reardon (9); Guzman, Ward (9). W—Ward. L—Avery. HR—Carter, Gruber (Tor.).
**Game 4**—October 21, at Toronto
Atl. .............0 0 0  0 0 0  0 1 0—1 5 0
Tor. .............0 0 1  0 0 0  1 0 x—2 6 0
Glavine; Key, Ward (8), Henke (9). W—Key. L—Glavine. S—Henke. HR—Borders (Tor.).
**Game 5**—October 22, at Toronto
Atl. ...........1 0 0  1 5 0  0 0 0—7 13 0
Tor. ...........0 1 0  1 0 0  0 0 0—2 6 0
Smoltz, Stanton (7); Morris, Wells (5), Timlin (7), Eichhorn (8), Stottlemyre (9). W—Smoltz. L—Morris. S—Stanton. HR—Justice, L. Smith (Atl.).
**Game 6**—October 24, at Atlanta
Tor. ..1 0 0  1 0 0  0 0 0  0 2—4 14 1
Atl. ..0 0 1  0 0 0  0 0 1  0 1—3 8 1
Cone, Stottlemyre (7), Wells (7), Ward (8), Henke (9), Key (10), Timlin (11); Avery, P. Smith (5), Stanton (8), Wohlers (9), Leibrandt (10). W—Key. L—Leibrandt. S—Timlin. HR—Maldonado (Tor.).

# 1993

## FINAL STANDINGS

### American League

**East Division**

| Team | Tor. | N.Y. | Det. | Bal. | Bos. | Cle. | Mil. | Chi. | Tex. | K.C. | Sea. | Min. | Cal. | Oak. | W | L | Pct. | GB |
|---|---|---|---|---|---|---|---|---|---|---|---|---|---|---|---|---|---|---|
| Toronto | ... | 8 | 7 | 8 | 10 | 9 | 8 | 6 | 5 | 4 | 5 | 10 | 8 | 7 | 95 | 67 | .586 | ... |
| New York | 5 | ... | 9 | 7 | 7 | 7 | 9 | 8 | 3 | 6 | 7 | 8 | 6 | 6 | 88 | 74 | .543 | 7 |
| Detroit | 6 | 4 | ... | 8 | 7 | 7 | 8 | 5 | 6 | 5 | 7 | 6 | 8 | 8 | 85 | 77 | .525 | 10 |
| Baltimore | 5 | 6 | 5 | ... | 6 | 8 | 8 | 4 | 4 | 7 | 7 | 8 | 7 | 10 | 85 | 77 | .525 | 10 |
| Boston | 3 | 6 | 6 | 7 | ... | 5 | 5 | 7 | 6 | 5 | 7 | 7 | 7 | 9 | 80 | 82 | .494 | 15 |
| Cleveland | 4 | 6 | 6 | 5 | 8 | ... | 8 | 3 | 7 | 7 | 3 | 4 | 7 | 8 | 76 | 86 | .469 | 19 |
| Milwaukee | 5 | 4 | 5 | 5 | 8 | 5 | ... | 3 | 4 | 7 | 4 | 7 | 5 | 7 | 69 | 93 | .426 | 26 |

**West Division**

| Team | Chi. | Tex. | K.C. | Sea. | Min. | Cal. | Oak. | Tor. | N.Y. | Det. | Bal. | Bos. | Cle. | Mil. | W | L | Pct. | GB |
|---|---|---|---|---|---|---|---|---|---|---|---|---|---|---|---|---|---|---|
| Chicago | ... | 8 | 6 | 9 | 10 | 6 | 7 | 6 | 4 | 7 | 8 | 5 | 9 | 9 | 94 | 68 | .580 | ... |
| Texas | 5 | ... | 6 | 5 | 6 | 7 | 8 | 7 | 9 | 6 | 8 | 6 | 5 | 8 | 86 | 76 | .531 | 8 |
| Kansas City | 7 | 7 | ... | 7 | 7 | 7 | 6 | 8 | 6 | 7 | 5 | 7 | 5 | 5 | 84 | 78 | .519 | 10 |
| Seattle | 4 | 8 | 6 | ... | 9 | 7 | 4 | 7 | 5 | 5 | 5 | 5 | 9 | 8 | 82 | 80 | .506 | 12 |
| Minnesota | 3 | 7 | 6 | 4 | ... | 9 | 8 | 2 | 4 | 6 | 4 | 5 | 8 | 5 | 71 | 91 | .438 | 23 |
| California | 7 | 6 | 6 | 6 | 4 | ... | 6 | 4 | 6 | 4 | 5 | 5 | 5 | 7 | 71 | 91 | .438 | 23 |
| Oakland | 6 | 5 | 7 | 9 | 5 | 7 | ... | 5 | 6 | 4 | 2 | 3 | 4 | 5 | 68 | 94 | .420 | 26 |

### National League

**East Division**

| Team | Phi. | Mon. | St.L. | Chi. | Pit. | Fla. | N.Y. | Atl. | S.F. | Hou. | L.A. | Cin. | Col. | S.D. | W | L | Pct. | GB |
|---|---|---|---|---|---|---|---|---|---|---|---|---|---|---|---|---|---|---|
| Philadelphia | ... | 7 | 8 | 6 | 7 | 9 | 10 | 6 | 4 | 7 | 10 | 8 | 9 | 6 | 97 | 65 | .599 | ... |
| Montreal | 6 | ... | 7 | 8 | 8 | 8 | 9 | 5 | 3 | 7 | 6 | 8 | 9 | 10 | 94 | 68 | .580 | 3 |
| St. Louis | 5 | 6 | ... | 5 | 9 | 9 | 8 | 6 | 8 | 6 | 6 | 7 | 7 | 5 | 87 | 75 | .537 | 10 |
| Chicago | 7 | 5 | 8 | ... | 5 | 6 | 8 | 5 | 6 | 4 | 7 | 7 | 8 | 8 | 84 | 78 | .519 | 13 |
| Pittsburgh | 6 | 5 | 4 | 8 | ... | 7 | 9 | 5 | 5 | 5 | 4 | 4 | 4 | 9 | 75 | 87 | .463 | 22 |
| Florida | 4 | 5 | 4 | 7 | 6 | ... | 4 | 5 | 4 | 3 | 5 | 5 | 5 | 7 | 64 | 98 | .395 | 33 |
| New York | 3 | 4 | 5 | 5 | 4 | 9 | ... | 3 | 4 | 1 | 4 | 6 | 6 | 5 | 59 | 103 | .364 | 38 |

**West Division**

| Team | Atl. | S.F. | Hou. | L.A. | Cin. | Col. | S.D. | Phi. | Mon. | St.L. | Chi. | Pit. | Fla. | N.Y. | W | L | Pct. | GB |
|---|---|---|---|---|---|---|---|---|---|---|---|---|---|---|---|---|---|---|
| Atlanta | ... | 7 | 8 | 8 | 10 | 13 | 9 | 6 | 7 | 6 | 7 | 7 | 7 | 9 | 104 | 58 | .642 | ... |
| San Fran. | 6 | ... | 10 | 6 | 11 | 10 | 10 | 8 | 9 | 4 | 6 | 7 | 8 | 8 | 103 | 59 | .636 | 1 |
| Houston | 5 | 3 | ... | 9 | 7 | 2 | 8 | 5 | 5 | 6 | 8 | 7 | 9 | 11 | 85 | 77 | .525 | 19 |
| Los Angeles | 5 | 7 | 4 | ... | 8 | 6 | 9 | 2 | 6 | 6 | 5 | 8 | 7 | 8 | 81 | 81 | .500 | 23 |
| Cincinnati | 3 | 2 | 6 | 5 | ... | 9 | 9 | 4 | 4 | 5 | 5 | 8 | 7 | 6 | 73 | 89 | .451 | 31 |
| Colorado | 0 | 3 | 11 | 7 | 4 | ... | 6 | 3 | 3 | 5 | 4 | 8 | 7 | 6 | 67 | 95 | .414 | 37 |
| San Diego | 4 | 3 | 5 | 4 | 4 | 7 | ... | 6 | 2 | 7 | 4 | 3 | 5 | 7 | 61 | 101 | .377 | 43 |

## LEADERS

**American League**
**BA:** John Olerud, Tor., .363.
**Runs:** Rafael Palmeiro, Tex., 124.
**Hits:** Paul Molitor, Tor., 211.
**TB:** Ken Griffey, Jr., Sea., 359.
**HR:** Juan Gonzalez, Tex., 46.
**RBI:** Albert Belle, Cle., 129.
**SB:** Kenny Lofton, Cle., 70.
**Wins:** Jack McDowell, Chi., 22.
**ERA:** Kevin Appier, K.C., 2.56.
**CG:** Chuck Finley, Cal., 13.
**IP:** Cal Eldred, Mil., 258.
**SO:** Randy Johnson, Sea., 308.
**SV:** Jeff Montgomery, K.C.; Duane Ward, Tor., 45.

**National League**
**BA:** Andres Galarraga, Col., .370.
**Runs:** Lenny Dykstra, Phil., 143.
**Hits:** Lenny Dykstra, Phil., 194.
**HR:** Barry Bonds, S.F., 46.
**RBI:** Barry Bonds, S.F., 123.
**SB:** Chuck Carr, Fla., 58.
**Wins:** John Burkett, S.F.; Tom Glavine, Atl., 22.
**ERA:** Greg Maddux, Atl., 2.36.
**CG:** Greg Maddux, Atl., 8.
**IP:** Greg Maddux, Atl., 267.
**SO:** Jose Rijo, Cin. 227.
**SV:** Randy Myers, Chi., 53.

**A.L. 20-game winner**
Jack McDowell, Chi., 22-10

**N.L. 20-game winners**
Tom Glavine, Atl., 22-6
John Burkett, S.F., 22-7
Bill Swift, S.F., 21-8
Greg Maddux, Atl., 20-10

**A.L. 100 RBIs**
Albert Belle, Cle., 129
Frank Thomas, Chi., 128
Joe Carter, Tor., 121
Juan Gonzalez, Tex., 118
Cecil Fielder, Det., 117
Carlos Baerga, Cle., 114
Chili Davis, Cal., 112
Paul Molitor, Tor., 111
Mickey Tettleton, Det., 110
Ken Griffey Jr., Sea., 109
John Olerud, Tor., 107
Rafael Palmeiro, Tex., 105
Danny Tartabull, N.Y., 102
Mo Vaughn, Bos., 101
Ruben Sierra, Oak., 101

**N.L. 100 RBIs**
Barry Bonds, S.F., 123
David Justice, Atl., 120
Ron Gant, Atl., 117
Mike Piazza, L.A., 112
Matt Williams, S.F., 110
Darren Daulton, Phil., 105
Todd Zeile, St.L., 103
Fred McGriff, S.D.-Atl., 101
Eddie Murray, N.Y., 100
Phil Plantier, S.D., 100

**A.L. 40 homers**
Juan Gonzalez, Tex., 46
Ken Griffey Jr., Sea., 45
Frank Thomas, Chi., 41

**N.L. 40 homers**
Barry Bonds, S.F., 46
David Justice, Atl., 40

**Most Valuable Player**
A.L.: Frank Thomas, 1B, Chi.
N.L.: Barry Bonds, OF, S.F.

**Cy Young Award**
A.L.: Jack McDowell, Chi.
N.L.: Greg Maddux, Atl.

**Rookie of the Year**
A.L.: Tim Salmon, OF, Cal.
N.L.: Mike Piazza, C, L.A.

**Manager of the Year**
A.L.: Gene Lamont, Chi.
N.L.: Dusty Baker, S.F.

**Hall of Fame addition**
Reggie Jackson, OF, 1967-87

## SIGNIFICANT EVENTS

■ **March 22:** Cleveland players Steve Olin and Tim Crews were killed and pitcher Bob Ojeda was seriously injured in a spring training boating accident near Orlando, Fla.
■ **September 9:** Owners and players agreed to split the A.L. and N.L. into three divisions and expand the number of playoff qualifiers from four to eight teams.
■ **October 3:** The Braves clinched the N.L. West Division title with a final-day 5-3 victory over Colorado while the Giants were losing to the Dodgers, 12-1.

## MEMORABLE MOMENTS

■ **July 28:** Seattle's Ken Griffey Jr. tied a long-standing record when he homered in his eighth consecutive game—a 5-1 loss to Minnesota.
■ **July 28:** The Mets scored two ninth-inning runs against Florida, handing Anthony Young a 5-4 victory and ending his record 27-game losing streak.
■ **September 7:** St. Louis' Mark Whiten tied a pair of records when he hit four homers and drove in 12 runs in a 15-2 victory over Cincinnati.
■ **September 16:** Minnesota's Dave Winfield joined baseball's exclusive 3,000-hit club in a game against Oakland.

## ALL-STAR GAME

■ **Winner:** Kirby Puckett fueled the high-powered A.L. offense to a 9-3 victory — its sixth straight.
■ **Key inning:** The fifth. After hitting a solo home run in the second, Puckett contributed a run-scoring double in a three-run fifth that broke a 2-2 tie.
■ **Memorable moment:** Hard-throwing A.L. lefty Randy Johnson striking out John Kruk, who bailed out on three straight pitches, swinging feebly at the third.
■ **Top guns:** Johnson (Mariners), Puckett (Twins), Roberto Alomar (Blue Jays), Albert Belle (Indians), A.L.; Gary Sheffield (Marlins), Barry Bonds (Giants), N.L.
■ **MVP:** Puckett.

**Linescore**
July 13, at Baltimore's Camden Yards
N.L. ............2 0 0  0 0 1  0 0 0—3 7 2
A.L. ............0 1 1  0 3 3  1 0 x—9 11 0
Mulholland (Phillies), Benes (Padres) 3, Burkett (Giants) 5, Avery (Braves) 5, Smoltz (Braves) 6, Beck (Giants) 7, Harvey (Marlins) 8; Langston (Angels), Johnson (Mariners) 3, McDowell (White Sox) 5, Key (Yankees) 6, Montgomery (Royals) 7, Aguilera (Twins) 8, Ward (Blue Jays) 9. W—McDowell. L—Burkett. HR—Sheffield, N.L.; Puckett, Alomar, A.L.

## ALCS

■ **Winner:** Toronto kept the A.L. pennant on Canadian soil and denied Chicago's bid for its first World Series appearance since 1959.
■ **Turning point:** The Blue Jays defeated the White Sox, 5-3, in the pivotal fifth game, which wasn't decided until reliever Duane Ward struck out Bo Jackson with a man on base in the ninth inning.
■ **Memorable moment:** A 6-3 finale in which Toronto's Dave Stewart lifted his LCS record to 8-0 and pitched his fourth pennant-clinching victory in six seasons.
■ **Top guns:** Stewart (2-0, 2.03 ERA), Juan Guzman (2-0, 2.08), Devon White (.444), Blue Jays; Tim Raines (.444), White Sox.
■ **MVP:** Stewart.

**Linescores**

**Game 1**—October 5, at Chicago
Toronto ......0 0 0  2 3 0  2 0 0—7 17 1
Chicago......0 0 0  3 0 0  0 0 0—3 6 1
Guzman, Cox (7), Ward (9); McDowell, DeLeon (7), Radinsky (8), McCaskill (9). W—Guzman. L—McDowell. HR—Molitor (Tor.).

**Game 2**—October 6, at Chicago
Toronto........1 0 0  2 0 0  0 0 0—3 8 0
Chicago........1 0 0  0 0 0  0 0 0—1 7 2
Stewart, Leiter (7), Ward (9); A. Fernandez, Hernandez (9). W—Stewart. L—A. Fernandez. S—Ward.

**Game 3**—October 8, at Toronto
Chicago......0 0 5  1 0 0  0 0 0—6 12 0
Toronto ......0 0 1  0 0 0  0 0 0—1 7 1
Alvarez; Hentgen, Cox (4), Eichhorn (7), Castillo (9). W—Alvarez. L—Hentgen.

**Game 4**—October 9, at Toronto
Chicago......0 2 0  0 0 3  1 0 1—7 11 0
Toronto ......0 0 3  0 0 1  0 0 0—4 9 0
Bere, Belcher (3), McCaskill (7), Radinsky (8), Hernandez (9); Stottlemyre, Leiter (7), Timlin (7). W—Belcher. L—Stottlemyre. S—Hernandez. HR—Thomas, Johnson (Chi.).

**Game 5**—October 10, at Toronto
Chicago......0 0 0  0 1 0  0 0 2—3 5 1
Toronto ......1 1 1  1 0 0  1 0 x—5 14 0
McDowell, DeLeon (3), Radinsky (7), Hernandez (7); Guzman, Castillo (8), Ward (9). W—Guzman. L—McDowell. HR—Burks, Ventura (Chi.).

**Game 6**—October 12, at Chicago
Toronto ......0 2 0  1 0 0  0 0 3—6 10 0
Chicago......0 0 2  0 0 0  0 0 1—3 5 3
Stewart, Ward (8); A. Fernandez, McCaskill (8), Radinsky (9), Hernandez (9). W—Stewart. L—A. Fernandez. S—Ward. HR—White (Tor.); Newson (Chi.).

## NLCS

■ **Winner:** Philadelphia needed six games to ruin Atlanta's bid for a third consecutive pennant.
■ **Turning point:** The pivotal fifth game, when Curt Schilling pitched eight innings of four-hit ball and Lenny Dykstra hit a game-winning 10th-inning home run.
■ **Memorable moment:** The ninth inning of Game 6. Phillies lefthander Mitch Williams, also known as "Wild Thing," pulled a shocker when he retired the Braves 1-2-3 for his second series save and a 6-3 pennant-clinching victory.
■ **Top guns:** Schilling (1.69 ERA), Williams (2-0, 2 saves, 1.69), Dykstra (2 HR), Phillies; Fred McGriff (.435), Otis Nixon (.348), Terry Pendleton (.346), Braves.
■ **MVP:** Schilling.

**Linescores**

**Game 1**—October 6, at Philadelphia
Atlanta ....0 0 1  1 0 0  0 0 1 0—3 9 0
Phil. ........1 0 0  1 0 1  0 0 0 1—4 9 1
Avery, Mercker (7), McMichael (9); Schilling, Williams (9). W—Williams. L—McMichael. HR—Incaviglia (Phil.).

**Game 2**—October 7, at Philadelphia
Atlanta ....2 0 6  0 1 0  0 4 1—14 16 0
Phil. ........0 0 0  2 0 0  0 0 1— 3 7 2
Maddux, Stanton (8), Wohlers (9); Greene, Thigpen (3), Rivera (4), Mason (6), West (8), Andersen (9). W—Maddux. L—Greene. HR—McGriff, Blauser, Berryhill, Pendleton (Atl.); Hollins, Dykstra (Phil.).

**Game 3**—October 9, at Atlanta
Phil. ..........0 0 0  1 0 1  0 1 1—4 10 1
Atlanta........0 0 0  0 0 5  4 0 x—9 12 0
Mulholland, Mason (6), Andersen (7), West (7), Thigpen (8); Glavine, Mercker (8), McMichael (9). W—Glavine. L—Mulholland. HR—Kruk (Phil.)

**Game 4**—October 10, at Atlanta
Phil. ..........0 0 0  2 0 0  0 0 0—2 8 1
Atlanta ......0 1 0  0 0 0  0 0 0—1 10 1
Jackson, Williams (8); Smoltz, Mercker (7), Wohlers (8). W—Jackson. L—Smoltz. S—Williams.

**Game 5**—October 11, at Atlanta
Phil. ........1 0 0  1 0 0  0 0 1 1—4 6 1
Atlanta ....0 0 0  0 0 0  0 0 3 0—3 7 1
Schilling, Williams (9), Andersen (10); Avery, Mercker (8), McMichael (9), Wohlers (10). W—Williams. L—Wohlers. S—Andersen. HR—Daulton, Dykstra (Phil.).

**Game 6**—October 13, at Philadelphia
Atlanta ........0 0 0  0 1 0  2 0 0—3 5 3
Phil. ............0 0 2  0 2 2  0 0 x—6 7 1
Maddux, Mercker (6), McMichael (7), Wohlers (7); Greene, West (8), Williams (9). W—Greene. L—Maddux. S—Williams. HR—Hollins (Phil.); Blauser (Atl.).

## WORLD SERIES

■ **Winner:** Toronto defeated Philadelphia to become the first back-to-back Series winner since the Yankees of 1977-78.
■ **Turning point:** The Blue Jays' six-run, eighth-inning rally that turned a 14-9 Game 4 deficit into a 15-14 victory and a 3-1 Series lead.
■ **Memorable moment:** Joe Carter's three-run, ninth-inning home run that turned a 6-5 Game 6 deficit into one of the most dramatic victories in World Series history.
■ **Top guns:** Paul Molitor (.500, 2 HR, 8 RBIs), Roberto Alomar (.480), Tony Fernandez (.333, 9 RBIs), Carter (2 HR, 8 RBIs), Blue Jays; Lenny Dykstra (.348, 4 HR, 8 RBIs), John Kruk (.348), Phillies.
■ **MVP:** Molitor.

**Linescores**

**Game 1**—October 16, at Toronto
Phil. ..........2 0 1  0 1 0  0 0 1—5 11 1
Toronto ......0 2 1  0 1 1  3 0 x—8 10 3
Schilling, West (7), Andersen (7), Mason (8); Guzman, Leiter (6), Ward (8). W—Leiter. L—Schilling. S—Ward. HR—White, Olerud (Tor.).

**Game 2**—October 17, at Toronto
Phil. ..........0 0 5  0 0 0  1 0 0—6 12 0
Toronto .......0 0 0  2 0 1  0 1 0—4 8 0
Mulholland, Mason (6), Williams (7); Stewart, Castillo (7), Eichhorn (8), Timlin (8). W—Mulholland. L—Stewart. S—Williams. HR—Carter (Tor.); Dykstra, Eisenreich (Phil.).

**Game 3**—October 19, at Philadelphia
Toronto ....3 0 1  0 0 1  3 0 2—10 13 1
Phil. ........0 0 0  0 1 0  1 0 1— 3 9 0
Hentgen, Cox (7), Ward (9); Jackson, Rivera (6), Thigpen (7), Andersen (9). W—Hentgen. L—Jackson. HR—Thompson (Phil.); Molitor (Tor.).

**Game 4**—October 20, at Philadelphia
Toronto ....3 0 4  0 0 2  0 6 0—15 18 0
Phil. ........4 2 0  1 5 1  1 0 0—14 14 0
Stottlemyre, Leiter (3), Castillo (5), Timlin (8), Ward (8); Greene, Mason (3), West (6), Andersen (7), Williams (8), Thigpen (9). W—Castillo. L—Williams. S—Ward. HR—Dykstra 2, Daulton (Phil.).

**Game 5**—October 21, at Philadelphia
Toronto ........0 0 0  0 0 0  0 0 0—0 5 1
Phil. ............1 1 0  0 0 0  0 0 x—2 5 1
Guzman, Cox (8); Schilling. W—Schilling. L—Guzman.

**Game 6**—October 23, at Toronto
Phil. ..........0 0 0  1 0 0  5 0 0—6 7 0
Toronto......3 0 0  1 1 0  0 0 3—8 10 2
Mulholland, Mason (6), West (8), Andersen (8), Williams (9); Stewart, Cox (7), Leiter (7), Ward (9). W—Ward. L—Williams. HR—Molitor, Carter (Tor.); Dykstra (Phil.).

## FINAL STANDINGS

### American League

**East Division**

| Team | N.Y. | Bal. | Tor. | Bos. | Det. | Chi. | Cle. | K.C. | Min. | Mil. | Tex. | Oak. | Sea. | Cal. | W | L | Pct. | GB |
|---|---|---|---|---|---|---|---|---|---|---|---|---|---|---|---|---|---|---|
| New York | ... | 6 | 3 | 7 | 3 | 2 | 9 | 2 | 5 | 7 | 3 | 7 | 8 | 8 | 70 | 43 | .619 | ... |
| Baltimore | 4 | ... | 7 | 4 | 3 | 2 | 4 | 4 | 4 | 7 | 3 | 7 | 6 | 8 | 63 | 49 | .563 | 6.5 |
| Toronto | 4 | 2 | ... | 3 | 4 | 3 | 4 | 6 | 8 | 3 | 8 | 1 | 5 | 4 | 55 | 60 | .478 | 16 |
| Boston | 3 | 2 | 7 | ... | 4 | 2 | 3 | 4 | 1 | 5 | 1 | 9 | 6 | 7 | 54 | 61 | .470 | 17 |
| Detroit | 3 | 4 | 5 | 2 | ... | 4 | 2 | 4 | 3 | 6 | 5 | 5 | 6 | 4 | 53 | 62 | .461 | 18 |

**Central Division**

| Team | Chi. | Cle. | K.C. | Min. | Mil. | N.Y. | Bal. | Tor. | Bos. | Det. | Tex. | Oak. | Sea. | Cal. | W | L | Pct. | GB |
|---|---|---|---|---|---|---|---|---|---|---|---|---|---|---|---|---|---|---|
| Chicago | ... | 7 | 3 | 2 | 9 | 4 | 4 | 2 | 4 | 8 | 4 | 6 | 9 | 5 | 67 | 46 | .593 | ... |
| Cleveland | 5 | ... | 1 | 9 | 5 | 0 | 6 | 6 | 7 | 8 | 5 | 6 | 3 | 5 | 66 | 47 | .584 | 1 |
| Kansas City | 7 | 4 | ... | 6 | 5 | 4 | 1 | 6 | 2 | 8 | 4 | 7 | 6 | 4 | 64 | 51 | .557 | 4 |
| Minnesota | 4 | 3 | 4 | ... | 6 | 4 | 5 | 4 | 8 | 3 | 4 | 2 | 3 | 3 | 53 | 60 | .469 | 14 |
| Milwaukee | 3 | 2 | 7 | 6 | ... | 2 | 3 | 7 | 5 | 4 | 3 | 4 | 4 | 3 | 53 | 62 | .461 | 15 |

**West Division**

| Team | Tex. | Oak. | Sea. | Cal. | N.Y. | Bal. | Tor. | Bos. | Det. | Chi. | Cle. | K.C. | Min. | Mil. | W | L | Pct. | GB |
|---|---|---|---|---|---|---|---|---|---|---|---|---|---|---|---|---|---|---|
| Texas | ... | 3 | 1 | 4 | 2 | 3 | 4 | 5 | 7 | 5 | 7 | 3 | 5 | 3 | 52 | 62 | .456 | ... |
| Oakland | 7 | ... | 4 | 6 | 5 | 5 | 5 | 3 | 4 | 3 | 0 | 3 | 5 | 1 | 51 | 63 | .447 | 1 |
| Seattle | 9 | 3 | ... | 7 | 4 | 4 | 1 | 6 | 3 | 1 | 2 | 4 | 3 | 2 | 49 | 63 | .438 | 2 |
| California | 6 | 3 | 2 | ... | 4 | 4 | 3 | 5 | 3 | 5 | 0 | 6 | 3 | 3 | 47 | 68 | .409 | 5.5 |

### National League

**East Division**

| Team | Mon. | Atl. | N.Y. | Phi. | Fla. | Cin. | Hou. | Pit. | St.L. | Chi. | L.A. | S.F. | Col. | S.D. | W | L | Pct. | GB |
|---|---|---|---|---|---|---|---|---|---|---|---|---|---|---|---|---|---|---|
| Montreal | ... | 5 | 4 | 5 | 7 | 2 | 4 | 8 | 7 | 4 | 9 | 5 | 2 | 12 | 74 | 40 | .649 | ... |
| Atlanta | 4 | ... | 5 | 6 | 8 | 5 | 3 | 3 | 5 | 4 | 6 | 5 | 8 | 6 | 68 | 46 | .596 | 6 |
| New York | 3 | 4 | ... | 4 | 4 | 4 | 3 | 4 | 6 | 4 | 6 | 6 | 1 | 6 | 55 | 58 | .487 | 18.5 |
| Philadelphia | 4 | 3 | 6 | ... | 6 | 2 | 1 | 5 | 4 | 6 | 5 | 4 | 4 | 4 | 54 | 61 | .470 | 20.5 |
| Florida | 2 | 4 | 6 | 4 | ... | 5 | 2 | 1 | 3 | 5 | 3 | 2 | 9 | 5 | 51 | 64 | .443 | 23.5 |

**Central Division**

| Team | Cin. | Hou. | Pit. | St.L. | Chi. | Mon. | Atl. | N.Y. | Phi. | Fla. | L.A. | S.F. | Col. | S.D. | W | L | Pct. | GB |
|---|---|---|---|---|---|---|---|---|---|---|---|---|---|---|---|---|---|---|
| Cincinnati | ... | 4 | 9 | 2 | 7 | 4 | 5 | 2 | 4 | 7 | 3 | 7 | 4 | 8 | 66 | 48 | .579 | ... |
| Houston | 6 | ... | 8 | 8 | 8 | 2 | 3 | 3 | 5 | 4 | 1 | 8 | 5 | 5 | 66 | 49 | .574 | .5 |
| Pittsburgh | 3 | 4 | ... | 5 | 5 | 2 | 9 | 5 | 4 | 6 | 3 | 1 | 3 | 3 | 53 | 61 | .465 | 13 |
| St. Louis | 2 | 4 | 5 | ... | 5 | 3 | 7 | 3 | 3 | 7 | 4 | 4 | 4 | 2 | 53 | 61 | .465 | 13 |
| Chicago | 5 | 4 | 5 | 5 | ... | 2 | 2 | 1 | 1 | 4 | 3 | 5 | 6 | 6 | 49 | 64 | .434 | 16.5 |

**West Division**

| Team | L.A. | S.F. | Col. | S.D. | Mon. | Atl. | N.Y. | Phi. | Fla. | Cin. | Hou. | Pit. | St.L. | Chi. | W | L | Pct. | GB |
|---|---|---|---|---|---|---|---|---|---|---|---|---|---|---|---|---|---|---|
| Los Angeles | ... | 5 | 6 | 6 | 3 | 0 | 6 | 7 | 3 | 6 | 8 | 3 | 2 | 3 | 58 | 56 | .509 | ... |
| San Fran. | 5 | ... | 7 | 2 | 7 | 1 | 6 | 8 | 4 | 2 | 2 | 5 | 2 | 4 | 55 | 60 | .478 | 3.5 |
| Colorado | 4 | 3 | ... | 5 | 4 | 2 | 5 | 2 | 3 | 4 | 5 | 2 | 8 | 6 | 53 | 64 | .453 | 6.5 |
| San Diego | 4 | 5 | 5 | ... | 0 | 1 | 6 | 8 | 1 | 2 | 5 | 3 | 4 | 3 | 47 | 70 | .402 | 12.5 |

## SIGNIFICANT EVENTS

- **March 1, June 7:** The N.L. elected Leonard Coleman as its new president and the A.L. opted for Gene Budig.
- **April 4, 11:** Two parks were dedicated: The Indians needed 11 innings to beat Seattle, 4-3, in their Jacobs Field opener and the Rangers lost their debut at The Ballpark in Arlington to Milwaukee, 4-3.
- **August 12:** Major League players brought the season to a skidding halt when they called a general strike—baseball's eighth work stoppage since 1972.
- **September 14:** Baseball owners announced cancellation of the regular season and Post Season, rubber-stamping the first uncompleted season in the game's long history.
- **December 28:** The Astros and Padres completed a 12-player trade, baseball's largest since 1957.

Despite the abbreviated season, Houston slugger Jeff Bagwell finished with 116 RBIs.

The Braves' Greg Maddux captured the third of his four consecutive Cy Young Awards in the strike-shortened 1994 season. He had a 1.56 ERA.

## MEMORABLE MOMENTS

- **April 4:** Tuffy Rhodes became the first player to homer in his first three Opening Day at-bats, but the Cubs still dropped a 12-8 decision to the Mets.
- **July 8:** Boston shortstop John Valentin pulled off baseball's 10th unassisted triple play and the Red Sox beat Seattle, 4-3.
- **July 28:** When Kenny Rogers retired all 27 Minnesota hitters in a 4-0 victory, he became the first A.L. lefthander to throw a perfect game.
- **August 1:** Cal Ripken stretched his ironman streak to 2,000 games and the Orioles celebrated with a 1-0 victory over Minnesota.
- **August 6:** The Mariners routed Kansas City, 11-2, and ended the Royals' winning streak at 14 games.

## LEADERS

**American League**
**BA:** Paul O'Neill, N.Y., .359.
**Runs:** Frank Thomas, Chi., 106.
**Hits:** Kenny Lofton, Cle., 160.
**TB:** Albert Belle, Cle., 294.
**HR:** Ken Griffey, Jr., Sea., 40.
**RBI:** Kirby Puckett, Min., 112.
**SB:** Lofton, Cle., 60.
**Wins:** Jimmy Key, N.Y., 17.
**ERA:** Steve Ontiveros, Oak., 2.65.
**CG:** Randy Johnson, Sea., 9.
**IP:** Chuck Finley, Cal., 183.1.
**SO:** Randy Johnson, Sea., 204.
**SV:** Lee Smith, Bal., 33.

**National League**
**BA:** Tony Gwynn, S.D., .394.
**Runs:** Jeff Bagwell, Hou., 104.
**Hits:** Gwynn, S.D., 165.
**TB:** Bagwell, Hou., 300.
**HR:** Matt Williams, S.F., 43.
**RBI:** Bagwell, Hou., 116.
**SB:** Craig Biggio, Hou., 39.
**Wins:** Ken Hill, Mon.; Greg Maddux, Atl., 16.
**ERA:** Greg Maddux, Atl., 1.56.
**CG:** Maddux, Atl., 10.
**IP:** Maddux, Atl., 202.
**SO:** Andy Benes, S.D., 189.
**SV:** John Franco, N.Y., 30.

**A.L. 100 RBIs**
Kirby Puckett, Min., 112
Joe Carter, Tor., 103
Albert Belle, Cle., 101
Frank Thomas, Chi., 101

**N.L. 100 RBIs**
Jeff Bagwell, Hou., 116

**A.L. 40 homers**
Ken Griffey Jr., Sea., 40

**N.L. 40 homers**
Matt Williams, S.F., 43

**Most Valuable Player**
A.L.: Frank Thomas, 1B, Chi.
N.L.: Jeff Bagwell, 1B, Hou.

**Cy Young Award**
A.L.: David Cone, K.C.
N.L.: Greg Maddux, Atl.

**Rookie of the Year**
A.L.: Bob Hamelin, DH, K.C.
N.L.: Raul Mondesi, OF, L.A.

**Manager of the Year**
A.L.: Buck Showalter, N.Y.
N.L.: Felipe Alou, Mon.

**Hall of Fame additions**
Steve Carlton, P, 1965-88
Leo Durocher, manager
Phil Rizzuto, SS, 1941-56

## ALL-STAR GAME

- **Winner:** The N.L. scored two runs in the ninth and one in the 10th to snap the A.L.'s six-game All-Star winning streak with an 8-7 victory.
- **Key inning:** The 10th, when the N.L. scored its winning run on a single by Tony Gwynn and a game-ending double by Moises Alou.
- **Memorable moment:** Fred McGriff's two-run, game-tying homer in the ninth off relief ace Lee Smith.
- **Top guns:** Ken Hill (Expos), Gwynn (Padres), Alou (Expos), Marquis Grissom (Expos), McGriff (Braves), Gregg Jefferies (Cardinals), N.L.; Ken Griffey Jr. (Mariners), Kenny Lofton (Indians), Frank Thomas (White Sox), A.L.
- **MVP:** McGriff.

**Linescore**

July 12, at Pittsburgh's Three Rivers Stadium
A.L.........1 0 0 0 0 3 3 0 0 0—7 15 0
N.L.........1 0 3 0 0 1 0 0 2 1—8 12 1
Key (Yankees), Cone (Royals) 3, Mussina (Orioles) 5, Johnson (Mariners) 6, Hentgen (Blue Jays) 7, Alvarez (White Sox) 8, L. Smith (Orioles) 9, Bere (White Sox) 10; Maddux (Braves), Hill (Expos) 4, Drabek (Astros) 6, Hudek (Astros) 6, Jackson (Phillies) 7, Beck (Giants) 7, Myers (Cubs) 9, Jones (Phillies) 10. W—Jones. L—Bere. HR—Grissom, McGriff, N.L.

# 1995

## FINAL STANDINGS

### American League

**East Division**

| Team | Bos. | N.Y. | Bal. | Det. | Tor. | Cle. | K.C. | Chi. | Mil. | Min. | Sea. | Cal. | Tex. | Oak. | W | L | Pct. | GB |
|---|---|---|---|---|---|---|---|---|---|---|---|---|---|---|---|---|---|---|
| Boston | ... | 5 | 9 | 8 | 8 | 6 | 3 | 5 | 8 | 5 | 7 | 11 | 3 | 8 | 86 | 58 | .597 | ... |
| New York | 8 | ... | 7 | 8 | 12 | 6 | 7 | 2 | 6 | 4 | 4 | 5 | 6 | 4 | 79 | 65 | .549 | 7 |
| Baltimore | 4 | 6 | ... | 8 | 7 | 2 | 4 | 6 | 7 | 3 | 6 | 9 | 4 | 5 | 71 | 73 | .493 | 15 |
| Detroit | 5 | 5 | 5 | ... | 7 | 3 | 3 | 4 | 8 | 7 | 5 | 2 | 4 | 2 | 60 | 84 | .417 | 26 |
| Toronto | 5 | 1 | 6 | 6 | ... | 3 | 5 | 5 | 5 | 4 | 4 | 2 | 3 | 7 | 56 | 88 | .389 | 30 |

**Central Division**

| Team | Cle. | K.C. | Chi. | Mil. | Min. | Bos. | N.Y. | Bal. | Det. | Tor. | Sea. | Cal. | Tex. | Oak. | W | L | Pct. | GB |
|---|---|---|---|---|---|---|---|---|---|---|---|---|---|---|---|---|---|---|
| Cleveland | ... | 11 | 8 | 9 | 9 | 7 | 6 | 10 | 10 | 10 | 5 | 2 | 6 | 7 | 100 | 44 | .694 | ... |
| Kansas City | 1 | ... | 5 | 10 | 6 | 2 | 3 | 5 | 4 | 7 | 7 | 7 | 8 | 5 | 70 | 74 | .486 | 30 |
| Chicago | 5 | 8 | ... | 6 | 10 | 3 | 3 | 1 | 8 | 6 | 4 | 2 | 5 | 7 | 68 | 76 | .472 | 32 |
| Milwaukee | 4 | 2 | 7 | ... | 9 | 4 | 5 | 5 | 5 | 7 | 3 | 2 | 5 | 7 | 65 | 79 | .451 | 35 |
| Minnesota | 4 | 7 | 3 | 4 | ... | 4 | 3 | 6 | 5 | 1 | 4 | 5 | 5 | 5 | 56 | 88 | .389 | 44 |

**West Division**

| Team | Sea. | Cal. | Tex. | Oak. | Bos. | N.Y. | Bal. | Det. | Tor. | Cle. | K.C. | Chi. | Mil. | Min. | W | L | Pct. | GB |
|---|---|---|---|---|---|---|---|---|---|---|---|---|---|---|---|---|---|---|
| Seattle | ... | 6 | 10 | 6 | 5 | 9 | 7 | 5 | 3 | 4 | 5 | 9 | 2 | 8 | 79 | 66 | .545 | ... |
| California | 7 | ... | 6 | 6 | 3 | 7 | 4 | 6 | 8 | 3 | 5 | 10 | 5 | 8 | 78 | 67 | .538 | 1 |
| Texas | 3 | 7 | ... | 8 | 4 | 3 | 1 | 8 | 9 | 3 | 6 | 7 | 7 | 8 | 74 | 70 | .514 | 4.5 |
| Oakland | 7 | 7 | 5 | ... | 4 | 9 | 7 | 3 | 3 | 0 | 8 | 5 | 2 | 7 | 67 | 77 | .465 | 11.5 |

### National League

**East Division**

| Team | Atl. | Phi. | N.Y. | Fla. | Mon. | Cin. | Hou. | Chi. | St.L. | Pit. | L.A. | Col. | S.D. | S.F. | W | L | Pct. | GB |
|---|---|---|---|---|---|---|---|---|---|---|---|---|---|---|---|---|---|---|
| Atlanta | ... | 7 | 5 | 10 | 9 | 8 | 6 | 8 | 7 | 4 | 5 | 9 | 5 | 7 | 90 | 54 | .625 | ... |
| Philadelphia | 6 | ... | 6 | 7 | 5 | 3 | 7 | 1 | 5 | 6 | 9 | 2 | 6 | 6 | 69 | 75 | .479 | 21 |
| New York | 8 | 7 | ... | 6 | 6 | 5 | 6 | 3 | 3 | 4 | 6 | 4 | 6 | 5 | 69 | 75 | .479 | 21 |
| Florida | 3 | 6 | 7 | ... | 6 | 6 | 8 | 4 | 4 | 5 | 3 | 7 | 3 | 5 | 67 | 76 | .469 | 22.5 |
| Montreal | 4 | 8 | 7 | 7 | ... | 4 | 3 | 5 | 4 | 4 | 5 | 1 | 7 | 7 | 66 | 78 | .458 | 24 |

**Central Division**

| Team | Cin. | Hou. | Chi. | St.L. | Pit. | Atl. | Phi. | N.Y. | Fla. | Mon. | L.A. | Col. | S.D. | S.F. | W | L | Pct. | GB |
|---|---|---|---|---|---|---|---|---|---|---|---|---|---|---|---|---|---|---|
| Cincinnati | ... | 12 | 7 | 8 | 8 | 5 | 9 | 7 | 6 | 8 | 4 | 5 | 3 | 3 | 85 | 59 | .590 | ... |
| Houston | 1 | ... | 8 | 9 | 9 | 6 | 5 | 6 | 4 | 9 | 3 | 4 | 7 | 5 | 76 | 68 | .528 | 9 |
| Chicago | 3 | 5 | ... | 9 | 8 | 4 | 6 | 4 | 8 | 3 | 7 | 6 | 5 | 5 | 73 | 71 | .507 | 12 |
| St. Louis | 5 | 4 | 4 | ... | 7 | 5 | 4 | 4 | 3 | 3 | 5 | 7 | 5 | 6 | 62 | 81 | .434 | 22.5 |
| Pittsburgh | 5 | 4 | 5 | 6 | ... | 2 | 3 | 3 | 8 | 4 | 4 | 4 | 4 | 6 | 58 | 86 | .403 | 27 |

**West Division**

| Team | L.A. | Col. | S.D. | S.F. | Atl. | Phi. | N.Y. | Fla. | Mon. | Cin. | Hou. | Chi. | St.L. | Pit. | W | L | Pct. | GB |
|---|---|---|---|---|---|---|---|---|---|---|---|---|---|---|---|---|---|---|
| Los Angeles | ... | 9 | 7 | 8 | 4 | 4 | 6 | 7 | 7 | 3 | 2 | 5 | 7 | 9 | 78 | 66 | .542 | ... |
| Colorado | 4 | ... | 9 | 8 | 4 | 4 | 5 | 5 | 7 | 7 | 4 | 7 | 5 | 8 | 77 | 67 | .535 | 1 |
| San Diego | 6 | 4 | ... | 6 | 2 | 6 | 7 | 2 | 5 | 6 | 4 | 7 | 7 | 8 | 70 | 74 | .486 | 8 |
| San Fran. | 5 | 5 | 7 | ... | 1 | 6 | 8 | 3 | 6 | 3 | 3 | 7 | 7 | 6 | 67 | 77 | .465 | 11 |

## LEADERS

**American League**
**BA:** Edgar Martinez, Sea., .356.
**Runs:** Albert Belle, Cle.; Edgar Martinez, Sea., 121.
**Hits:** Lance Johnson, Chi., 186.
**TB:** Albert Belle, Cle., 377.
**HR:** Albert Belle, Cle., 50.
**RBI:** Albert Belle, Cle.; Mo Vaughn, Bos., 126.
**SB:** Kenny Lofton, Cle., 54.
**Wins:** Mike Mussina, Bal., 19.
**ERA:** Randy Johnson, Sea., 2.48.
**CG:** Jack McDowell, N.Y., 8.
**IP:** David Cone, Tor.-N.Y., 229.1.
**SO:** Randy Johnson, Sea., 294.
**SV:** Jose Mesa, Cle., 46.

**National League**
**BA:** Tony Gwynn, S.D., .368.
**Runs:** Craig Biggio, Hou., 123.
**Hits:** Dante Bichette, Col.; Tony Gwynn, S.D., 197.
**TB:** Dante Bichette, Col., 359.
**HR:** Dante Bichette, Col., 40.
**RBI:** Dante Bichette, Col., 128.
**SB:** Quilvio Veras, Fla., 56.
**Wins:** Greg Maddux, Atl., 19.
**ERA:** Greg Maddux, Atl., 1.63.
**CG:** Greg Maddux, Atl., 10.
**IP:** Greg Maddux, Atl.; Denny Neagle, Pit., 209.2.
**SO:** Hideo Nomo, L.A., 236.
**SV:** Randy Myers, Chi., 38.

**A.L. 100 RBIs**
Albert Belle, Cle., 126
Mo Vaughn, Bos., 126
Jay Buhner, Sea., 121
Edgar Martinez, Sea., 113
Tino Martinez, Sea., 111
Frank Thomas, Chi., 111
Jim Edmonds, Cal., 107
Manny Ramirez, Cle., 107
Tim Salmon, Cal., 105
Rafael Palmeiro, Bal., 104
J.T. Snow, Cal., 102
John Valentin, Bos., 102

**N.L. 100 RBIs**
Dante Bichette, Col., 128
Sammy Sosa, Chi., 119
Andres Galarraga, Col., 106
Jeff Conine, Fla., 105
Eric Karros, L.A., 105
Barry Bonds, S.F., 104
Larry Walker, Col., 101

**A.L. 40 homers**
Albert Belle, Cle., 50
Jay Buhner, Sea., 40
Frank Thomas, Chi., 40

**N.L. 40 homers**
Dante Bichette, Col., 40

**Most Valuable Player**
A.L.: Mo Vaughn, 1B, Bos.
N.L.: Barry Larkin, SS, Cin.

**Cy Young Award**
A.L.: Randy Johnson, Sea.
N.L.: Greg Maddux, Atl.

**Rookie of the Year**
A.L.: Marty Cordova, OF, Min.
N.L.: Hideo Nomo, P, L.A.

**Manager of the Year**
A.L.: Lou Piniella, Sea.
N.L.: Don Baylor, Col.

**Hall of Fame additions**
Richie Ashburn, OF, 1948-62
Leon Day, P, Negro Leagues
William Hulbert, Executive
Mike Schmidt, 3B, 1972-89
Vic Willis, P, 1898-1910

## SIGNIFICANT EVENTS

■ **April 2:** Baseball owners, blocked by an injunction preventing them from imposing new work rules and using replacement players in the 1995 season, invited striking players to return to work, ending the 234-day work stoppage. Opening Day was pushed back to April 25 and the schedule was reduced to 144 games.

■ **April 30:** Major League Baseball agreed to a new contract with its umpires, ending a lockout that had extended a week into the regular season and forced use of replacement arbiters.

■ **March 9:** Major League owners approved expansion franchises for Tampa Bay (Devil Rays) and Phoenix (Arizona Diamondbacks), with play to begin in 1998.

■ **August 13:** Baseball was stung by the loss of former Yankee great Mickey Mantle, who died at age 63 of lung cancer.

■ **October 2:** Sparky Anderson, whose 2,194 managerial victories ranked third all-time to Connie Mack and John McGraw, retired after nine seasons with the Reds and 17 with the Tigers.

■ **November 13:** Atlanta righthander Greg Maddux won his record-setting fourth consecutive N.L. Cy Young after a 19-2, 1.63-ERA season. Maddux joined Steve Carlton as the only four-time Cy Young winners.

## MEMORABLE MOMENTS

■ **June 3:** Montreal's Pedro Martinez pitched nine perfect innings before giving up a 10th-inning double to San Diego's Bip Roberts after the Expos had scored in the top of the inning. Martinez did not finish his 1-0 victory.

■ **June 30:** Cleveland's Eddie Murray joined baseball's 3,000-hit club when he singled off Minnesota righthander Mike Trombley.

■ **September 6:** Baltimore shortstop Cal Ripken passed Lou Gehrig's ironman streak when he played in his 2,131st consecutive game — a 4-2 victory over California at Camden Yards.

■ **September 8:** Cleveland defeated Baltimore 3-2 and clinched the team's first title of any kind in 41 years. The Indians' final 30-game A.L. Central Division margin over Kansas City was the largest in modern baseball history.

■ **October 2:** The Mariners defeated California 9-1 in a one-game playoff, giving Seattle its first division title in the franchise's 19-year history.

## ALL-STAR GAME

■ **Winner:** The N.L. managed only three hits off seven A.L. pitchers, but all were solo home runs and produced an unlikely 3-2 victory.

■ **Key inning:** The seventh, when Los Angeles catcher Mike Piazza collected the N.L.'s second hit, a game-tying homer off Texas' Kenny Rogers, and Phillies reliever Heathcliff Slocumb pitched the N.L. out of a two-on, one-out jam.

■ **Memorable moment:** Pinch-hitter Jeff Conine's eighth-inning blast off Oakland's Steve Ontiveros, which broke the 2-2 tie and gave the N.L. its first lead. Conine became the 10th player to hit a homer in his first All-Star at-bat.

■ **Top guns:** Randy Johnson (Mariners), Kevin Appier (Royals), Frank Thomas (White Sox), Carlos Baerga (Indians), A.L.; Hideo Nomo (Dodgers), Slocumb (Phillies), Craig Biggio (Astros), Piazza (Dodgers), Conine (Marlins), N.L.

■ **MVP:** Conine.

**Linescore**

July 11, at Texas' The Ballpark in Arlington
N.L. ..............0 0 0  0 0 1  1 1 0—3 3 0
A.L. ..............0 0 0  2 0 0  0 0 0—2 8 0
Nomo (Dodgers), Smiley (Reds) 3, Green (Phillies) 5, Neagle (Pirates) 6, C. Perez (Expos) 7, Slocumb (Phillies) 7, Henke (Cardinals) 8, Myers (Cubs) 9; Johnson (Mariners), Appier (Royals) 3, Martinez (Indians) 5, Rogers (Rangers) 7, Ontiveros (A's) 8, Wells (Tigers) 8, Mesa (Indians) 9. W—Slocumb. L—Ontiveros. S—Myers. HR—Thomas, A.L.; Biggio, Piazza, Conine, N.L.

## A.L. DIVISION SERIES

■ **Winners:** Cleveland swept past Boston, but Seattle needed five games and extra innings to defeat New York in baseball's inaugural Division Series. The Mariners could not secure victory until the 11th inning of Game 5.

■ **Turning points:** For Cleveland, catcher Tony Pena's Game 1-ending home run in the bottom of the 13th inning. For Seattle, Edgar Martinez's two-homer, seven-RBI Game 4 effort that kept the Mariners' title hopes alive.

■ **Memorable moments:** Martinez's tie-breaking eighth-inning grand slam in Game 4 and his Series-ending two-run double in the 11th inning of Game 5.

■ **Memorable performances:** The playoff-record five-home run effort of Seattle outfielder Ken Griffey and Martinez's 10-RBI effort.

**Linescores**

Cleveland vs. Boston

**Game 1**—October 3, at Cleveland
Bos. ..........0 0 2  0 0 0  0 1 0  0 1 0  0—4 11 2
Cle. ............0 0 0  0 0 3  0 0 0  0 1 0  1—5 10 2
Clemens, Cormier (8), Belinda (8), Stanton (8), Aguilera (11), Maddux (11), Smith (13); Martinez, Tavarez (7), Assenmacher (8), Plunk (8), Mesa (10), Poole (11), Hill (12). W—Hill. L—Smith. HR—Valentin, Alicea, Naehring (Bos.); Belle, Pena (Cle.).

**Game 2**—October 4, at Cleveland
Bos. ............0 0 0  0 0 0  0 0 0—0 3 1
Cle. ..............0 0 0  0 2 0  0 2 x—4 4 2
Hanson; Hershiser, Tavarez (8), Assenmacher (8), Mesa (9). W—Hershiser. L—Hanson. HR—Murray (Cle.).

**Game 3**—October 6, at Boston
Cle. ............0 2 1  0 0 5  0 0 0—8 11 2
Bos. ..........0 0 0  1 0 0  0 1 0—2 7 1
Nagy, Tavarez (8), Assenmacher (9); Wakefield, Cormier (6), Maddux (6), Hudson (9). W—Nagy. L—Wakefield. HR—Thome (Cle.).

Seattle vs. New York

**Game 1**—October 3, at New York
Seattle........0 0 0  1 0 1  2 0 2—6 9 0
N.Y. ............0 0 2  0 0 2  4 1 x—9 13 0
Bosio, Nelson (6), Ayala (7), Risley (7), Wells (8); Cone, Wetteland (9). W—Cone. L—Nelson. HR—Griffey 2 (Sea.); Boggs, Sierra (N.Y.).

**Game 2**—October 4, at New York
Seattle......0 0 1  0 0 1  2 0 0  0 0 1  0 0 0—5 16 2
N.Y. ..........0 0 0  0 1 2  1 0 0  0 0 1  0 0 2—7 11 0
Benes, Risley (6), Charlton (7), Nelson (11), Belcher (12); Pettitte, Wickman (8), Wetteland (9), Rivera (12). W—Rivera. L—Belcher. HR—Coleman, Griffey (Sea.); Sierra, Mattingly, O'Neill, Leyritz (N.Y.).

**Game 3**—October 6, at Seattle
N.Y. ..............0 0 0  1 0 0  1 2 0—4 6 2
Seattle..........0 0 0  0 2 4  1 0 x—7 7 0
McDowell, Howe (6), Wickman (6), Hitchcock (7), Rivera (7); Johnson, Risley (8), Charlton (8). W—Johnson. L—McDowell. S—Charlton. HR—B. Williams 2, Stanley (N.Y.); T. Martinez (Sea.).

**Game 4**—October 7, at Seattle
N.Y. ..........3 0 2  0 0 0  0 1 2— 8 14 1
Seattle......0 0 4  0 1 1  0 5 x—11 16 0
Kamieniecki, Hitchcock (6), Wickman (7), Wetteland (8), Howe (8); Bosio, Nelson (3), Belcher (7), Charlton (8), Ayala (9), Risley (9). W—Charlton. L—Wetteland. S—Risley. HR—O'Neill (N.Y.); E. Martinez 2, Griffey, Buhner (Sea.).

**Game 5**—October 8, at Seattle
N.Y. ......0 0 0  2 0 2  0 0 0  0 1—5 6 0
Seattle 0 0 1  1 0 0  0 2 0  0 2—6 15 0
Cone, Rivera (8), McDowell (9); Benes, Charlton (7), Johnson (9). W—Johnson. L—McDowell. HR—O'Neill (N.Y.); Cora, Griffey (Sea.).

## N.L. DIVISION SERIES

■ **Winners:** Atlanta and Cincinnati powered past West Division opponents in the N.L.'s first Division Series.

■ **Turning points:** For the Braves, a four-run ninth-inning Game 2 rally that produced a 7-4 victory and a two-games-to-none edge over the Rockies. For the Reds, a 5-4 Game 2 victory, despite being outhit by the Dodgers, 14-6.

■ **Memorable moment:** Colorado pitcher Lance Painter striking out with the bases loaded in the ninth inning of a 5-4 Game 1 loss to the Braves. Painter was pinch-hitting because Colorado manager Don Baylor had no more position players on his bench.

■ **Top performances:** Atlanta third baseman Chipper Jones belted two Game 1 homers, including the game-winner in the top of the ninth inning; Braves first baseman Fred McGriff broke out of a slump with a two-homer, five-RBI Game 5 effort; Reds infielder Mark Lewis broke open Game 3 against the Dodgers with the first pinch-hit grand slam in playoff history.

**Linescores**

Atlanta vs. Colorado

**Game 1**—October 3, at Colorado
Atlanta ......0 0 1  0 0 2  0 1 1—5 12 1
Colorado....0 0 0  3 0 0  0 1 0—4 13 4
Maddux, McMichael (8), Pena (8), Wohlers (9); Ritz, Reed (6), Ruffin (7), Munoz (8), Holmes (8), Leskanic (9). W—Pena. L—Leskanic. S—Wohlers. HR—Jones 2, Grissom (Atl.); Castilla (Col.).

**Game 2**—October 4, at Colorado

Atlanta ......1 0 1 1 0 0 0 0 4—7 13 1
Colorado....0 0 0 0 0 3 0 1 0—4 8 2
Glavine, Avery (8), Pena (8), Wohlers (9); Painter, Reed (6), Ruffin (7), Leskanic (8), Munoz (9), Holmes (9). W—Pena. L—Munoz. S—Wohlers. HR—Grissom 2 (Atl.); Walker (Col.).

**Game 3**—October 6, at Atlanta
Colorado......1 0 2 0 0 2 0 0 0 2—7 9 0
Atlanta ........0 0 0 3 0 0 1 0 1 0—5 11 0
Swift, Reed (7), Munoz (7), Leskanic (7), Ruffin (8), Holmes (9), Thompson (10); Smoltz, Clontz (6), Borbon (8), McMichael (9), Wohlers (10), Mercker (10). W—Holmes. L—Wohlers. S—Thompson. HR—Young, Castilla (Col.).

**Game 4**— October 7, at Atlanta
Colorado..........0 0 3 0 0 1 0 0 0— 4 11 1
Atlanta ............0 0 4 2 1 3 0 0 x—10 15 0
Saberhagen, Ritz (5), Munoz (6), Reynoso (7), Ruffin (8); Maddux, Pena (8). W—Maddux. L—Saberhagen. HR—Bichette, Castilla (Col.); McGriff 2 (Atl.).

Cincinnati vs. Los Angeles

**Game 1**—October 3, at Los Angeles
Cincinnati ..........4 0 0 0 3 0 0 0 0—7 12 0
Los Angeles ......0 0 0 0 1 1 0 0 0—2 8 0
Schourek, Jackson (8), Brantley (9); Martinez, Cummings (5), Astacio (6), Guthrie (8), Osuna (9). W—Schourek. L—Martinez. HR—Santiago (Cin.); Piazza (L.A.).

**Game 2**—October 4, at Los Angeles
Cincinnati ..........0 0 0 2 0 0 0 1 2—5 6 0
Los Angeles ......1 0 0 1 0 0 0 0 2—4 14 2
Smiley, Burba (7), Jackson (8), Brantley (9); Valdes, Osuna (8), Tapani (9), Guthrie (9), Astacio (9). W—Burba. L—Osuna. S—Brantley. HR—Sanders (Cin.); Karros 2 (L.A.).

**Game 3**—October 6, at Cincinnati
Los Angeles ....0 0 0 1 0 0 0 0 0— 1 9 1
Cincinnati ........0 0 2 1 0 4 3 0 x—10 11 2
Nomo, Tapani (6), Guthrie (6), Astacio (6), Cummings (7), Osuna (7); Wells, Jackson (7), Brantley (9). W—Wells. L—Nomo. HR—Gant, Boone, M. Lewis (Cin.).

### ALCS

■ **Winner:** The Cleveland Indians needed six games and a hard-fought victory over Seattle ace lefthander Randy Johnson to secure their first World Series berth in 41 years.

■ **Turning point:** With the intimidating Johnson scheduled to pitch Game 6 in Seattle, the Indians won the pivotal fifth game, 3-2, on Jim Thome's two-run sixth-inning homer. The victory gave them a three-games-to-two advantage.

■ **Memorable moment:** A two-run passed ball in the eighth inning of Cleveland's 4-0 pennant-clinching victory. Ruben Amaro scored from third base and speedy Kenny Lofton surprised the Mariners with a mad dash from second, extending the Indians' lead to 3-0.

■ **Top guns:** Orel Hershiser (2-0, 1.29 ERA), Lofton (.458, 5 SB), Carlos Baerga (.400), Thome (2 HR, 5 RBI), Indians; Ken Griffey (.333), Jay Buhner (3 HR, 5 RBI), Norm Charlton (1-0, 0.00, 1 sv), Mariners.

■ **MVP:** Hershiser.

**Linescores**

**Game 1**—October 10, at Seattle
Cleveland ..........0 0 1 0 0 0 1 0 0—2 10 1
Seattle ..............0 2 0 0 0 0 1 0 x—3 7 0
D. Martinez, Tavarez (7), Assenmacher (8), Plunk (8); Wolcott, Nelson (8), Charlton (8). W—Wolcott. L—D. Martinez. S—Charlton. HR—Belle (Cle.); Blowers (Sea.).

**Game 2**—October 11, at Seattle
Cleveland ..........0 0 0 0 2 2 0 1 0—5 12 0
Seattle ..............0 0 0 0 0 1 0 0 1—2 6 1
Hershiser, Mesa (9); Belcher, Ayala (6), Risley (9). W—Hershiser. L—Belcher. HR—Ramirez 2 (Cle.); Griffey, Buhner (Sea.).

**Game 3**—October 13, at Cleveland
Seattle ......0 1 1 0 0 0 0 0 0 0 3—5 9 1
Cleveland ..0 0 0 1 0 0 0 1 0 0 0—2 4 2
Johnson, Charlton (9); Nagy, Mesa (9), Tavarez (10), Assenmacher (11), Plunk (11). W—Charlton. L—Tavarez. HR—Buhner 2 (Sea.).

**Game 4**—October 14, at Cleveland
Seattle ................0 0 0 0 0 0 0 0 0—0 6 1
Cleveland ............3 1 2 0 0 1 0 0 x—7 9 0
Benes, Wells (3), Ayala (6), Nelson (7), Risley (8); Hill, Poole (8), Ogea (9), Embree (9). W—Hill. L—Benes. HR—Murray, Thome (Cle.).

**Game 5**—October 15, at Cleveland
Seattle ..............0 0 1 0 1 0 0 0 0—2 5 2
Cleveland ..........1 0 0 0 0 2 0 0 x—3 10 4
Bosio, Nelson (6), Risley (7); Hershiser, Tavarez (7), Assenmacher (7), Plunk (8), Mesa (9). W—Hershiser. L—Bosio. S—Mesa. HR—Thome (Cle.).

**Game 6**—October 17, at Seattle
Cleveland ............0 0 0 0 1 0 0 3 0—4 8 0
Seattle ................0 0 0 0 0 0 0 0 0—0 4 1
D. Martinez, Tavarez (8), Mesa (9); Johnson, Charlton (8). W—D. Martinez. L—Johnson. HR—Baerga (Cle.).

### NLCS

■ **Winner:** Atlanta pitchers limited Cincinnati to five total runs and the Braves swept past the Reds and claimed their third World Series berth of the decade.

■ **Turning point:** It came early, in the 11th inning of Game 1. Mike Devereaux singled home the winner in a 2-1 victory and the Braves cruised the rest of the way.

■ **Memorable moment:** A three-run, 10th-inning blast off the left-field foul pole by Atlanta catcher Javier Lopez that secured Atlanta's 6-2 victory in Game 2.

■ **Top guns:** Greg Maddux (1-0, 1.13 ERA), Steve Avery (1-0, 0.00), Fred McGriff (.438), Chipper Jones (.438), Lopez (.357), Devereaux (5 RBI), Braves; Barry Larkin (.389), Reds.

■ **MVP:** Devereaux.

**Linescores**

**Game 1**—October 10, at Cincinnati
Atlanta ......0 0 0 0 0 0 0 0 1 0 1—2 7 0
Cincinnati ..0 0 0 1 0 0 0 0 0 0 0—1 8 0
Glavine, Pena (8), Wohlers (9), Clontz (11), Avery (11), McMichael (11); Schourek, Brantley (9), Jackson (11). W—Wohlers. L—Jackson. S—McMichael.

**Game 2**—October 11, at Cincinnati
Atlanta ........1 0 0 1 0 0 0 0 0 4—6 11 1
Cincinnati ....0 0 0 0 2 0 0 0 0 0—2 9 1
Smoltz, Pena (8), McMichael (9), Wohlers (10); Smiley, Burba (6), Jackson (8), Brantley (9), Portugal (10). W—McMichael. L—Portugal. HR—Lopez (Atl.)

**Game 3**—October 13, at Atlanta
Cincinnati ........0 0 0 0 0 0 0 1 1—2 8 0
Atlanta ............0 0 0 0 0 3 2 0 x—5 12 1
Wells, Hernandez (7), Carrasco (7); Maddux, Wohlers (9). W—Maddux. L—Wells. HR: O'Brien, Jones (Atl.).

**Game 4**—October 14, at Atlanta
Cincinnati ........0 0 0 0 0 0 0 0 0—0 3 1
Atlanta ............0 0 1 0 0 0 0 5 x—6 12 1
Schourek, Jackson (7), Burba (7); Avery, McMichael (7), Pena (8), Wohlers (9). W—Avery. L—Schourek. HR—Devereaux (Atl.).

### WORLD SERIES

■ **Winner:** The Braves needed six games to give Atlanta its first championship in any major sport and the franchise its first World Series title since 1957. The loss extended Cleveland's championship drought to 47 years.

■ **Turning point:** A two-run, sixth-inning homer by Javier Lopez in Game 2. It gave the Braves a 4-3 victory and put the Indians in a two-games-to-none hole.

■ **Memorable moment:** A Series-opening two-hitter by Braves ace Greg Maddux and a Series-closing combined one-hitter by Tom Glavine and Mark Wohlers. The 1-0 finale was decided by a Dave Justice home run.

■ **Top guns:** Glavine (2-0, 1.29 ERA), Wohlers (1.80, 2 sv), Marquis Grissom (.360), Ryan Klesko (.313, 3 HR), Braves; Albert Belle (2 HR), Indians.

■ **MVP:** Glavine.

**Linescores**

**Game 1**—October 21, at Atlanta
Cleveland ..........1 0 0 0 0 0 0 0 1—2 2 0
Atlanta ..............0 1 0 0 0 0 2 0 x—3 3 2
Hershiser, Assenmacher (7), Tavarez (7), Embree (8); Maddux. W—Maddux. L—Hershiser. HR—McGriff (Atl.).

**Game 2**—October 22, at Atlanta
Cleveland ..........0 2 0 0 0 0 1 0 0—3 6 2
Atlanta ..............0 0 2 0 0 2 0 0 x—4 8 2
Martinez, Embree (6), Poole (7), Tavarez (8); Glavine, McMichael (7), Pena (7), Wohlers (8). W—Glavine. L—Martinez. S—Wohlers. HR—Murray (Cle.), Lopez (Atl.).

**Game 3**—October 24, at Cleveland
Atlanta ............1 0 0 0 0 1 1 3 0 0 0—6 12 1
Cleveland .........2 0 2 0 0 0 1 1 0 0 1—7 12 2
Smoltz, Clontz (3), Mercker (5), McMichael (7), Wohlers (8), Pena (11); Nagy, Assenmacher (8), Tavarez (8), Mesa (9). W—Mesa. L—Pena. HR—McGriff, Klesko (Atl.).

**Game 4**—October 25, at Cleveland
Atlanta ............0 0 0 0 0 1 3 0 1—5 11 1
Cleveland ........0 0 0 0 0 1 0 0 1—2 6 0
Avery, McMichael (7), Wohlers (9), Borbon (9); Hill, Assenmacher (7), Tavarez (8), Embree (8). W—Avery. L—Hill. S—Borbon. HR—Klesko (Atl.); Belle, Ramirez (Cle.).

**Game 5**—October 26, at Cleveland
Atlanta ..............0 0 0 1 1 0 0 0 2—4 7 0
Cleveland ..........2 0 0 0 0 2 0 1 x—5 8 1
Maddux, Clontz (8); Hershiser, Mesa (8). W—Hershiser. L—Maddux. S—Mesa. HR—Polonia, Klesko (Atl.); Belle, Thome (Cle.).

**Game 6**—October 28, at Atlanta
Cleveland ........0 0 0 0 0 0 0 0 0—0 1 1
Atlanta ............0 0 0 0 0 1 0 0 x—1 6 0
Martinez, Poole (5), Hill (7), Embree (7), Tavarez (8), Assenmacher (8); Glavine, Wohlers (9). W—Glavine. L—Poole. S—Wohlers. HR—Justice (Atl.).

**The schedule was cut back to 144 games in 1995, but outfielder Albert Belle nonetheless reached the 50-homer mark for the A.L. pennant-winning Indians.**

# 1996

## FINAL STANDINGS

### American League

**East Division**

| Team | N.Y. | Bal. | Bos. | Tor. | Det. | Cle. | Chi. | Mil. | Min. | K.C. | Tex. | Sea. | Oak. | Cal. | W | L | Pct. | GB |
|---|---|---|---|---|---|---|---|---|---|---|---|---|---|---|---|---|---|---|
| New York | ... | 10 | 6 | 8 | 8 | 9 | 7 | 6 | 7 | 8 | 5 | 3 | 9 | 6 | 92 | 70 | .568 | ... |
| Baltimore | 3 | ... | 7 | 8 | 11 | 5 | 4 | 9 | 7 | 9 | 3 | 7 | 9 | 6 | 88 | 74 | .543 | 4.0 |
| Boston | 7 | 6 | ... | 8 | 12 | 1 | 6 | 7 | 6 | 3 | 6 | 7 | 8 | 8 | 85 | 77 | .525 | 7.0 |
| Toronto | 5 | 5 | 5 | ... | 7 | 5 | 5 | 7 | 5 | 8 | 2 | 7 | 8 | 5 | 74 | 88 | .457 | 18.0 |
| Detroit | 5 | 2 | 1 | 6 | ... | 3 | 4 | 6 | 6 | 0 | 4 | 6 | 4 | 6 | 53 | 109 | .327 | 39.0 |

**Central Division**

| Team | Cle. | Chi. | Mil. | Min. | K.C. | N.Y. | Bal. | Bos. | Tor. | Det. | Tex. | Sea. | Oak. | Cal. | W | L | Pct. | GB |
|---|---|---|---|---|---|---|---|---|---|---|---|---|---|---|---|---|---|---|
| Cleveland | ... | 8 | 7 | 10 | 7 | 3 | 7 | 11 | 7 | 12 | 4 | 8 | 6 | 9 | 99 | 62 | .615 | ... |
| Chicago | 5 | ... | 6 | 6 | 7 | 6 | 8 | 6 | 7 | 10 | 8 | 5 | 5 | 6 | 85 | 77 | .525 | 14.5 |
| Milwaukee | 0 | 7 | ... | 0 | 0 | 6 | 3 | 5 | 5 | 8 | 6 | 1 | 7 | 5 | 80 | 82 | .494 | 19.5 |
| Minnesota | 3 | 7 | 4 | ... | 7 | 5 | 5 | 6 | 8 | 6 | 7 | 6 | 6 | 8 | 78 | 84 | .481 | 21.5 |
| Kansas City | 6 | 6 | 4 | 6 | ... | 4 | 3 | 9 | 5 | 6 | 6 | 7 | 5 | 8 | 75 | 86 | .466 | 24 |

**West Division**

| Team | Tex. | Sea. | Oak. | Cal. | N.Y. | Bal. | Bos. | Tor. | Det. | Cle. | Chi. | Mil. | Min. | K.C. | W | L | Pct. | GB |
|---|---|---|---|---|---|---|---|---|---|---|---|---|---|---|---|---|---|---|
| Texas | ... | 3 | 6 | 9 | 7 | 10 | 6 | 10 | 9 | 8 | 4 | 7 | 5 | 6 | 90 | 72 | .556 | ... |
| Seattle | 10 | ... | 5 | 8 | 9 | 5 | 6 | 5 | 6 | 4 | 7 | 9 | 6 | 5 | 85 | 76 | .528 | 4.5 |
| Oakland | 7 | 8 | ... | 7 | 3 | 4 | 5 | 4 | 8 | 6 | 7 | 5 | 7 | 7 | 78 | 84 | .481 | 12 |
| California | 4 | 5 | 6 | ... | 7 | 6 | 4 | 7 | 6 | 4 | 6 | 7 | 4 | 4 | 70 | 91 | .435 | 19.5 |

### National League

**East Division**

| Team | Atl. | Mon. | Fla. | N.Y. | Phil. | St.L. | Hou. | Cin. | Chi. | Pit. | S.D. | L.A. | Col. | S.F. | W | L | Pct. | GB |
|---|---|---|---|---|---|---|---|---|---|---|---|---|---|---|---|---|---|---|
| Atlanta | ... | 10 | 6 | 7 | 9 | 9 | 6 | 7 | 7 | 9 | 9 | 5 | 5 | 7 | 96 | 66 | .593 | ... |
| Montreal | 3 | ... | 8 | 7 | 6 | 8 | 9 | 9 | 6 | 7 | 4 | 3 | 9 | 9 | 88 | 74 | .543 | 8 |
| Florida | 7 | 5 | ... | 7 | 6 | 6 | 7 | 9 | 6 | 5 | 3 | 6 | 8 | 5 | 80 | 82 | .494 | 16 |
| New York | 6 | 6 | 6 | ... | 7 | 5 | 4 | 6 | 5 | 8 | 3 | 4 | 5 | 6 | 71 | 91 | .438 | 25 |
| Philadelphia | 4 | 7 | 7 | 6 | ... | 4 | 2 | 2 | 6 | 7 | 4 | 6 | 6 | 6 | 67 | 95 | .414 | 29 |

**Central Division**

| Team | St.L. | Hou. | Cin. | Chi. | Pit. | Atl. | Mon. | Fla. | N.Y. | Phil. | S.D. | L.A. | Col. | S.F. | W | L | Pct. | GB |
|---|---|---|---|---|---|---|---|---|---|---|---|---|---|---|---|---|---|---|
| St. Louis | ... | 11 | 8 | 8 | 10 | 4 | 4 | 6 | 7 | 8 | 8 | 4 | 4 | 6 | 88 | 74 | .543 | ... |
| Houston | 2 | ... | 6 | 8 | 8 | 6 | 4 | 5 | 8 | 10 | 6 | 6 | 5 | 8 | 82 | 80 | .506 | 6 |
| Cincinnati | 5 | 7 | ... | 8 | 5 | 5 | 3 | 3 | 6 | 10 | 9 | 4 | 7 | 9 | 81 | 81 | .500 | 7 |
| Chicago | 5 | 5 | 5 | ... | 4 | 5 | 6 | 6 | 7 | 7 | 6 | 8 | 5 | 7 | 76 | 86 | .469 | 12 |
| Pittsburgh | 3 | 5 | 8 | 9 | ... | 3 | 5 | 7 | 5 | 5 | 4 | 6 | 5 | 8 | 73 | 89 | .451 | 15 |

**West Division**

| Team | S.D. | L.A. | Col. | S.F. | Atl. | Mon. | Fla. | N.Y. | Phil. | St.L. | Hou. | Cin. | Chi. | Pit. | W | L | Pct. | GB |
|---|---|---|---|---|---|---|---|---|---|---|---|---|---|---|---|---|---|---|
| San Diego | ... | 8 | 5 | 11 | 4 | 8 | 9 | 10 | 8 | 4 | 6 | 3 | 6 | 9 | 91 | 71 | .562 | ... |
| Los Angeles | 5 | ... | 7 | 7 | 7 | 9 | 7 | 8 | 7 | 8 | 6 | 8 | 5 | 6 | 90 | 72 | .556 | 1 |
| Colorado | 8 | 6 | ... | 5 | 7 | 3 | 5 | 7 | 6 | 8 | 8 | 6 | 7 | 7 | 83 | 79 | .512 | 8 |
| San Fran. | 2 | 6 | 8 | ... | 5 | 4 | 7 | 6 | 6 | 7 | 4 | 4 | 5 | 4 | 68 | 94 | .420 | 23 |

## LEADERS

**American League**
**BA:** Alex Rodriguez, Sea., .358.
**Runs:** Alex Rodriguez, Sea., .358.
**Hits:** Paul Molitor, Min., 225.
**TB:** Alex Rodriguez, Sea., 379.
**HR:** Mark McGwire, Oak., 52.
**RBI:** Albert Belle, Cle., 148.
**SB:** Kenny Lofton, Cle., 75.
**Wins:** Andy Pettitte, N.Y., 21.
**ERA:** Juan Guzman, Tor., 2.93.
**CG:** Pat Hentgen, Tor., 10.
**IP:** Pat Hentgen, Tor., 265.2.
**SO:** Roger Clemens, Bos., 257.
**SV:** John Wetteland, N.Y., 43.

**National League**
**BA:** Tony Gwynn, S.D., .353.
**Runs:** Ellis Burks, Col., 142.
**Hits:** Lance Johnson, N.Y., 227.
**TB:** Ellis Burks, Col., 392
**HR:** Andres Galarraga, Col., 47.
**RBI:** Andres Galarraga, Col., 150
**SB:** Eric Young, Col., 53.
**Wins:** John Smoltz, Atl., 24.
**ERA:** Kevin Brown, Fla., 1.89.
**CG:** Curt Schilling, Phi., 8.
**IP:** John Smoltz, Atl., 253.2
**SO:** John Smoltz, Atl., 276.
**SV.** Jeff Brantley, Cin.,
Todd Worrell, L.A., 44.

**A.L. 20-game winners**
Andy Pettitte, N.Y., 21
Pat Hentgen, Tor., 20

**N.L. 20-game winner**
John Smoltz, Atl., 24

**A.L. 100 RBIs**
Albert Belle, Cle., 148
Juan Gonzalez, Tex., 144
Mo Vaughn, Bos., 143
Rafael Palmeiro, Bal., 142
Ken Griffey Jr., Sea., 140
Jay Buhner, Sea., 138
Frank Thomas, Chi., 134
Alex Rodriguez, Sea., 123
John Jaha, Mil., 118
Cecil Fielder, Det.-N.Y., 117
Tino Martinez, N.Y., 117
Bobby Bonilla, Bal., 116
Jim Thome, Cle., 116
Mark McGwire, Oak., 113
Paul Molitor, Min., 113
Manny Ramirez, Cle., 112
Marty Cordova, Min., 111
Brady Anderson, Bal., 110
Joe Carter, Tor., 107
Dean Palmer, Tex., 107
Geronimo Berroa, Oak., 106
Robin Ventura, Chi., 105
Edgar Martinez, Sea., 103
Cal Ripken, Bal., 102
Bernie Williams, N.Y., 102
Ed Sprague, Tor., 101
Danny Tartabull, Chi., 101
Travis Fryman, Det., 100
Rusty Greer, Tex., 100
Terry Steinbach, Oak., 100

**N.L. 100 RBIs**
Andres Galarraga, Col., 150
Dante Bichette, Col., 141
Ken Caminiti, S.D., 130
Barry Bonds, S.F., 129
Ellis Burks, Col., 128
Jeff Bagwell, Hou., 120
Gary Sheffield, Fla., 120
Bernard Gilkey, N.Y., 117
Derek Bell, Hou., 113
Vinny Castilla, Col., 113
Todd Hundley, N.Y., 112
Eric Karros, L.A., 111
Jeff King, Pit., 111
Chipper Jones, Atl., 110
Fred McGriff, Atl., 107
Mike Piazza, L.A., 105
Brian Jordan, St.L., 104
Henry Rodriguez, Mon., 103
Sammy Sosa, Chi., 100

**A.L./N.L. 100 RBIs**
Greg Vaughn, Mil.-S.D., 117

**A.L. 40 homers**
Mark McGwire, Oak., 52
Brady Anderson, Bal., 50
Ken Griffey Jr., Sea., 49
Albert Belle, Cle., 48
Juan Gonzalez, Tex., 47
Jay Buhner, Sea., 44
Mo Vaughn, Bos., 44
Frank Thomas, Chi., 40

**N.L. 40 homers**
Andres Galarraga, Col., 47
Barry Bonds, S.F., 42
Gary Sheffield, Fla., 42
Todd Hundley, N.Y., 41
Ellis Burks, Col., 40
Ken Caminiti, S.D., 40
Vinny Castilla, Col., 40
Sammy Sosa, Chi., 40

**A.L./N.L. 40 homers**
Greg Vaughn, Mil.-S.D., 41

**Most Valuable Player**
A.L.: Juan Gonzalez, OF, Tex.
N.L.: Ken Caminiti, 3B, Hou.

**Cy Young Award**
A.L.: Pat Hentgen, Tor.
N.L.: John Smoltz, Atl.

**Rookie of the Year**
A.L.: Derek Jeter, SS, N.Y.
N.L.: Todd Hollandsworth, OF, L.A.

**Manager of the Year**
A.L.: Johnny Oates, Tex.; Joe Torre, N.Y.
N.L.: Bruce Bochy, S.D.

**Hall of Fame additions**
Jim Bunning, P, 1955-71
Bill Foster, P, Negro Leagues
Ned Hanlon, manager
Earl Weaver, manager

## SIGNIFICANT EVENTS

■ **January:** The Official Playing Rules Committee lowered the strike zone from "a line at the top of the knees" to "a line at the hollow beneath the kneecap."

■ **April 1:** Umpire John McSherry collapsed seven pitches into the opening day game between the Expos and Reds at Cincinnati and died about an hour later from a heart problem. The game was postponed.

■ **June 12:** Reds owner Marge Schott agreed to surrender day-to-day control of the team through the 1998 season as discipline for actions and statements detrimental to baseball.

■ **September 27:** In what would develop into one of the most controversial player-umpire disputes in baseball history, Baltimore second baseman Roberto Alomar spat in the face of umpire John Hirshbeck during a called-strike argument.

■ **November 19:** White Sox owner Jerry Reinsdorf signed Cleveland slugger Albert Belle to the richest contract in baseball history—$50 million over five years.

■ **November 26:** After completing the first full-schedule season since 1993, Major League Baseball and the players' association agreed on a contract that would run through October 31, 2000.

## MEMORABLE MOMENTS

■ **September 6:** Baltimore's Eddie Murray connected for his 500th career home run against Detroit and joined 14 other players in that exclusive circle.

■ **September 16:** Minnesota's Paul Molitor became the 21st player to record 3,000 career hits when he tripled in the fifth inning of a game at Kansas City.

■ **September 18:** Boston ace Roger Clemens matched his own major league record when he struck out 20 Tigers in a nine-inning game.

■ **September 29:** Giants slugger Barry Bonds completed the season with 42 homers and 40 stolen bases, joining Jose Canseco as the only members of the 40-40 club.

■ **September 29:** The Orioles, led by Brady Anderson's 50 home runs, finished the season with a one-season record 257.

■ **September 29:** San Diego's Tony Gwynn finished the season with a .353 average and won his seventh N.L. batting title.

## ALL-STAR GAME

■ **Winner:** Nine N.L. pitchers combined on a seven hitter as the A.L. lost its third consecutive midsummer classic and saw the N.L.'s All-Star domination grow to 40-26-1.

■ **Key inning:** The second, when the A.L. failed to score after putting its leadoff man on second base and the N.L. stretched its lead to 2-0 on Dodgers catcher Mike Piazza's solo home run.

■ **Memorable moment:** Piazza, who drove in two runs with his homer and a double, holding up the MVP trophy for a large hometown contingent at Philadelphia. Piazza was born in nearby Norristown, Pa., and once served as a bat boy at Veterans Stadium.

■ **Top guns:** Piazza (Dodgers), Lance Johnson (Mets), John Smoltz (Braves), Steve Trachsel (Cubs), N.L.; Kenny Lofton (Indians), A.L.

■ **MVP:** Piazza.

**Linescore**

July 9, at Philadelphia's Veterans Stadium
A.L. ..............0 0 0 0 0 0 0 0 0—0 7 0
N.L. ..............1 2 1 0 0 2 0 0 x—6 12 1
Smoltz (Braves), Brown (Marlins) 3, Glavine (Braves) 4, Bottalico (Phillies) 5, P. Martinez (Expos) 6, Trachsel (Cubs) 7, Worrell (Dodgers) 8, Wohlers (Braves) 9, Leiter (Marlins) 9; Nagy (Indians), Finley (Angels) 3, Pavlik (Rangers) 5, Percival (Angels) 7, Hernandez (White Sox) 8. W—Smoltz. L—Nagy. HR—Piazza, Caminiti, N.L.

## A.L. DIVISION SERIES

■ **Winners:** The Yankees, bidding for their 34th World Series appearance, ruined the Rangers' postseason debut with a four-game victory; the wild-card Orioles pulled off a surprising four-game upset of the Indians.

■ **Turning points:** Throwing errors turned the tide for both the Yankees and Orioles. New York took control in the 10th inning of Game 2 when the Rangers failed to score after loading the bases in the top of the inning and the Yankees won in the bottom of the frame on third baseman Dean Palmer's wild throw. The Orioles took control when Cleveland catcher Sandy Alomar fired wildly on an eighth-inning home-to-first double-play attempt in Game 2, allowing the winning run to score in an eventual 7-4 victory. The Indians argued that batter B.J. Surhoff ran out of the baseline, causing Alomar's miscue.

■ **Memorable moments:** The final out of Texas' 6-2 Game 1 victory over the Yankees—the first postseason win in Rangers history. The Game 4 heroics of Baltimore second baseman Roberto Alomar, who tied the game with a ninth-inning single and clinched the series victory with a 12th-inning home run. It was sweet vindication for Alomar, who had been the center of controversy since a late-season spitting incident involving umpire John Hirschbeck.

■ **Memorable performances:** Bernie Williams batted .467, hit three home runs, including two in the decisive fourth game, and drove in five runs for the Yankees; Yankee relievers Mariano Rivera, David Weathers, Jeff Nelson and John Wetteland combined for 17⅓ scoreless innings, allowing only five hits; Juan Gonzalez set a record pace for the Rangers, hitting .438 with five home runs and nine RBIs; B.J. Surhoff hit three home runs and Bobby Bonilla hit two, including a grand slam, for the Orioles; Albert Belle hit a Game 3 grand slam for the Indians.

**Linescores**

Baltimore vs. Cleveland

**Game 1**—October 1, at Baltimore
Cleveland ..0 1 0 2 0 0 1 0 0— 4 10 0
Baltimore....1 1 2 0 0 5 1 0 x—10 12 1
Nagy, Embree (6), Shuey (6), Tavarez (8); Wells, Orosco (7), Mathews (7), Rhodes (8), Myers (9). W—Wells. L—Nagy. HR—Ramirez (Cle.); Anderson, Bonilla, Surhoff 2 (Bal.).

**Game 2**—October 2, at Baltimore
Cleveland ......0 0 0 0 0 3 0 1 0—4 8 2
Baltimore........1 0 0 0 3 0 0 3 x—7 9 0
Hershiser, Plunk (6), Assenmacher (8), Tavaraz (8); Erickson, Orosco (7), Benitez (8), Myers (9). W—Benitez. L—Plunk. S—Myers. HR—Belle (Cle.); Anderson (Bal.).

**Game 3**—October 4, at Cleveland
Baltimore ....0 1 0 3 0 0 0 0 0—4 8 2
Cleveland......1 2 0 1 0 0 4 1 x—9 10 0
Mussina, Orosco (7), Benitez (7), Rhodes (8), Mathews (8); McDowell, Embree (6), Shuey (7), Assenmacher (7), Plunk (8), Mesa (9). W—Assenmacher. L—Orosco. HR—Surhoff (Bal.); Belle, Ramirez (Cle.).

**Game 4**—October 5, at Cleveland
Bal. 0 2 0 0 0 0 0 0 1 0 0 1—4 14 1
Cle. ..0 0 0 2 1 0 0 0 0 0 0 0—3 7 1
Wells, Mathews (8), Orosco (9), Benitez (10), Myers (12); Nagy, Embree (7), Shuey (7), Assenmacher (7), Plunk (8), Mesa (9), Ogea (12). W—Benitez. L—Mesa. S—Myers. HR—R. Alomar, Palmeiro, Bonilla (Bal.).

New York vs. Texas

**Game 1**—October 1, at New York
Texas............0 0 0 5 0 1 0 0 0—6 8 0
New York......1 0 0 1 0 0 0 0 0—2 10 0
Burkett; Cone, Lloyd (7), Weathers (8). W—Burkett. L—Cone. HR—Gonzalez, Palmer (Tex.).

**Game 2**—October 2, at New York
Texas 0 1 3 0 0 0 0 0 0 0 0 0—4 8 1
N.Y. ..0 1 0 1 0 0 1 1 0 0 0 1—5 8 0
Hill, Cook (7), Russell (8), Stanton (10), Henneman (12); Pettitte, M. Rivera (7), Wetteland (10), Lloyd (12), Nelson (12), Rogers (12), Boehringer (12). W—Boehringer. L—Stanton. HR—Gonzalez 2 (Tex.); Fielder (N.Y.).

**Game 3**—October 4, at Texas
New York........1 0 0 0 0 0 0 0 2—3 7 1
Texas............0 0 0 1 1 0 0 0 0—2 6 1
Key, Nelson (6), Wetteland (9); Oliver, Henneman (9), Stanton (9). W—Nelson. L—Oliver. S-Wetteland. HR—Williams (N.Y.); Gonzalez (Tex.).

**Game 4**—October 5, at Texas
New York......0 0 0 3 1 0 1 0 1—6 12 1
Texas............0 2 2 0 0 0 0 0 0—4 9 0
Rogers, Boehringer (3), Weathers (4), M. Rivera (7), Wetteland (9); Witt, Patterson (4), Cook (4), Pavlik (5), Vosberg (7), Russell (7), Stanton (8), Henneman (9). W—Weathers. L—Pavlik. S—Wetteland. HR—Williams 2 (N.Y.); Gonzalez (Tex.).

## N.L. DIVISION SERIES

■ **Winners:** The Braves continued their quest for back-to-back World Series titles with a sweep of the Dodgers; St. Louis matched that 1-

2-3 effort against San Diego.

■ **Turning points:** For the Braves, catcher Javy Lopez's Game 1-winning 10th-inning home run in a 2-1 victory. The Cardinals took control of their series in the opening inning of Game 1 when Gary Gaetti hit a three-run homer, giving pitcher Todd Stottlemyre all the runs he would need for a 3-1 victory.

■ **Memorable moments:** The Braves put the Dodgers away in the seventh inning of Game 2 when Fred McGriff and Jermaine Dye hit solo home runs, wiping out a 2-1 deficit and setting up Greg Maddux for a 3-2 victory. Cardinals right fielder Brian Jordan finished off the Padres in Game 3 with a great run-saving catch in the eighth inning and a game-winning two-run homer in the ninth.

■ **Top performances:** The Braves' pitching staff, with starters John Smoltz, Maddux and Tom Glavine working $22\frac{2}{3}$ innings, posted a sparkling 0.96 ERA against the Dodgers.
St. Louis' Ron Gant batted .400, hit a home run and drove in four runs against the Padres and closer Dennis Eckersley saved all three victories.

**Linescores**

St. Louis vs. San Diego

**Game 1**—October 1, at St. Louis
San Diego ......0 0 0 0 0 1 0 0 0—1 8 1
St. Louis ........3 0 0 0 0 0 0 0 x—3 6 0
Hamilton, Blair (7); Stottlemyre, Honeycutt (7), Eckersley (8). W—Stottlemyre. L—Hamilton. S—Eckersley. HR—Henderson (S.D.); Gaetti (St.L.).

**Game 2**—October 3, at St. Louis
San Diego .............0 0 0 0 1 2 0 1 0—4
St. Louis ...............0 0 1 0 3 0 0 1 x—5
Sanders, Veras (5), Worrell (6), Bochtler (8), Hoffman (8); An. Benes, Honeycutt (8), Eckersley (9). W—Honeycutt. L—Bochtler. S—Eckersley. HR—Caminiti (S.D.).

**Game 3**—October 5, at San Diego
St. Louis ...............1 0 0 0 0 3 1 0 2—7
San Diego .............0 2 1 1 0 0 0 1 0—5
Osborne, Petkovsek (5), Honeycutt (7), Mathews (8), Eckersley (9); Ashby, Worrell (6), Valenzuela (8), Veras (8), Hoffman (9). W—Mathews. L—Hoffman. S—Eckersley. HR—Gant, Jordan (St.L.); Caminiti 2 (S.D.).

Atlanta vs. Los Angeles

**Game 1**—October 2, at Los Angeles
Atlanta ...........0 0 0 1 0 0 0 0 0 1—2 4 1
Los Angeles....0 0 0 0 1 0 0 0 0 0—1 5 0
Smoltz, Wohlers (10); Martinez, Radinsky (9), Osuna (9). W—Smoltz. L—Osuna. S—Wohlers. HR—Lopez (Atl.).

**Game 2**—October 3, at Los Angeles
Atlanta...........0 1 0 0 0 0 2 0 0—3 5 2
Los Angeles...1 0 0 1 0 0 0 0 0—2 3 0
Maddux, McMichael (8), Wohlers (9); Valdes, Astacio (7), Worrell (9). W—Maddux. L—Valdes. S—Wohlers. HR—McGriff, Klesko, Dye (Atl.).

**Game 3**—October 5, at Atlanta
Los Angeles....0 0 0 0 0 0 1 1 0—2 6 1
Atlanta ...........1 0 0 4 0 0 0 0 x—5 7 0
Nomo, Guthrie (4), Candiotti (5), Radinsky (7), Osuna (8), Dreifort (8); Glavine, McMichael (7), Bielecki (8), Wohlers (8). W—Glavine. L—Nomo. S—Wohlers. HR—C. Jones (Atl.).

## ALCS

■ **Winner:** The Yankees overpowered Baltimore, the most prolific home run team in baseball history, and earned the franchise's 34th pennant. The five-game victory set up the Yankees' first World Series appearance since 1981.

■ **Turning point:** The eighth inning of Game 3, when the Yankees, trailing 2-1, struck for four two-out runs against Orioles ace Mike Mussina. The key plays were Bernie Williams' game-tying single, third baseman Todd Zeile's error and Cecil Fielder's two-run homer.

■ **Memorable moment:** The eighth inning of Game 1, when 12-year-old fan Jeff Maier reached over Yankee Stadium's right field wall and unwittingly set the course for the series. The Orioles held a 4-3 advantage when shortstop Derek Jeter hit a fly ball to deep right that backed Baltimore outfielder Tony Tarasco to the wall. As Tarasco reached up in an attempt to make the catch, Maier stuck his glove over the wall and pulled the ball into the stands. The Orioles argued vehemently for fan interference, but umpire Richie Garcia ruled it a game-tying home run and the Yankees won in the 11th on a Williams home run. Maier became an instant national celebrity.

■ **Top guns:** Williams (.474, 2 HR, 6 RBI), Jeter (.417), Darryl Strawberry (.417, 3 HR), Cecil Fielder (8 RBI), Mariano Rivera (0.00 ERA), Yankees; Zeile (3 HR, 5 RBI), Rafael Palmeiro (2 HR), Orioles.
MVP: Williams.

**Linescores**

**Game 1**—October 9, at New York
Bal. ....0 1 1 1 0 1 0 0 0 0 0—4 11 1
N.Y. ....1 1 0 0 0 0 1 1 0 0 1—5 11 0
Erickson, Orosco (7), Benitez (7), Rhodes (8), Mathews (9), Myers (9); Pettitte, Nelson (8), Wetteland (9), M. Rivera (10). W—M. Rivera. L—Myers. HR—Anderson, Palmeiro (Bal.); Jeter, Williams (N.Y.).

**Game 2**—October 10, at New York
Baltimore......0 0 2 0 0 0 2 1 0—5 10 0
New York......2 0 0 0 0 0 1 0 0—3 11 1
Wells, Mills (7), Orosco (7), Myers (9), Benitez (9); Cone, Nelson (7), Lloyd (8), Weathers (9). W—Wells. L—Nelson. S—Benitez. HR—Zeile, Palmeiro (Bal.).

**Game 3**—October 11, at Baltimore
New York........0 0 0 1 0 0 0 4 0—5 8 0
Baltimore.......2 0 0 0 0 0 0 0 0—2 3 2
Key, Wetteland (9); Mussina, Orosco (8), Mathews (9). W—Key. L—Mussina. S—Wetteland. HR—Fielder (N.Y.); Zeile (Bal.).

**Game 4**—October 12, at Baltimore
New York......2 1 0 2 0 0 0 3 0—8 9 0
Baltimore......1 0 1 2 0 0 0 0 0—4 11 0
Rogers, Weathers (4), Lloyd (6), M. Rivera (7), Wetteland (9); Coppinger, Rhodes (6), Mills (7), Orosco (8), Benitez (8), Mathews (9). W—Weathers. L—Coppinger. HR—Williams, Strawberry 2, O'Neill (N.Y.); Hoiles (Bal.).

**Game 5**—October 13, at Baltimore
New York......0 0 6 0 0 0 0 0 0—6 11 0
Baltimore......0 0 0 0 0 1 0 1 2—4 4 1
Pettitte, Wetteland (9); Erickson, Rhodes (6), Mills (7), Myers (8). W—Pettitte. L—Erickson. HR—Fielder, Strawberry, Leyritz (N.Y.); Zeile, Bonilla, Murray (Bal.).

## NLCS

■ **Winner:** The Braves, hoping to become the N.L.'s first repeat World Series champion in 20 years, recovered from a three-games-to-one deficit in a tense seven-game victory over the Cardinals. The Braves, on the brink of elimination, outscored St. Louis 32-1 over the final three games to earn their eighth fall classic appearance and fourth of the decade.

■ **Turning point:** The first inning of Game 5, when the Braves scored five runs off Cardinals starter Todd Stottlemyre. That 14-0 victory served notice that rumors of the Braves' demise were premature.

■ **Memorable moment:** An eighth-inning Game 4 home run by St. Louis' Brian Jordan, the blow that gave ecstatic home fans a 4-3 victory and put the Cardinals on the brink of a 16th World Series appearance.

■ **Top guns:** Javier Lopez (.542, 6 RBI), Mark Lemke (.444), Fred McGriff (2 HR, 7 RBI), John Smoltz (2-0, 1.20 ERA), Braves; Royce Clayton (.350), Ron Gant (2 HR, 4 RBI), Cardinals.

■ **MVP:** Lopez.

**Linescores**

**Game 1**—October 9, at Atlanta
St. Louis ........0 1 0 0 0 0 1 0 0—2 5 1
Atlanta ...........0 0 0 0 2 0 0 2 x—4 9 0
An. Benes, Petkovsek (7), Fossas (8), Mathews (8); Smoltz, Wohlers (9). W—Smoltz. L—Petkovsek. S—Wohlers.

**Game 2**—October 10, at Atlanta
St. Louis ......1 0 2 0 0 0 5 0 0—8 11 2
Atlanta..........0 0 2 0 0 1 0 0 0—3 5 2
Stottlemyre, Petkovsek (7), Honeycutt (8), Eckersley (8); Maddux, McMichael (7), Neagle (8), Avery (9). W—Stottlemyre. L—Maddux. HR—Gaetti (St.L.); Grissom (Atl.).

**Game 3**—October 12, at St. Louis
Atlanta...........1 0 0 0 0 0 0 1 0—2 8 1
St. Louis ........2 0 0 0 0 1 0 0 x—3 7 0
Glavine, Bielecki (7), McMichael (8); Osborne, Petkovsek (8), Honeycutt (9), Eckersley (9). W—Osborne. L—Glavine. S—Eckersley. HR—Gant 2 (St.L.).

**Game 4**—October 13, at St. Louis
Atlanta...........0 1 0 0 0 2 0 0 0—3 9 1
St. Louis ........0 0 0 0 0 0 3 1 x—4 5 0
Neagle, McMichael (7), Wohlers (8); An. Benes, Fossas (6), Mathews (6), Al. Benes (6), Honeycutt (8), Eckersley (8). W—Eckersley. L—McMichael. HR—Lemke, Klesko (Atl.); Jordan (St.L.).

**Game 5**—October 14, at St. Louis
Atlanta........5 2 0 3 1 0 0 1 2—14 22 0
St. Louis ....0 0 0 0 0 0 0 0 0— 0 7 0
Smoltz, Bielecki (8), Wade (9), Clontz (9); Stottlemyre, Jackson (2), Fossas (5), Petkovsek (7), Honeycutt (9). W—Smoltz. L—Stottlemyre. HR—McGriff, Lopez (Atl.).

**Game 6**—October16, at Atlanta
St. Louis ........0 0 0 0 0 0 0 1 0—1 6 1
Atlanta ............0 1 0 0 1 0 0 1 x—3 7 0
Al. Benes, Fossas (6), Petkovsek (6), Stottlemyre (8); Maddux, Wohlers (8). W—Maddux. L—Al. Benes. S—Wohlers.

**Game 7**—October 17, at Atlanta
St. Louis ....0 0 0 0 0 0 0 0 0— 0 4 2
Atlanta ........6 0 0 4 0 3 2 0 x—15 17 0
Osborne, An. Benes (1), Petkovsek (6), Honeycutt (6), Fossas (8); Glavine, Bielecki (8), Avery (9). W—Glavine. L—Osborne. HR—McGriff, Lopez, A. Jones (Atl.).

## WORLD SERIES

■ **Winner:** The Yankees, missing from the World Series scene since 1981, collected their franchise-record 23rd championship when they spotted Atlanta two wins and stormed back to post an impressive six-game victory. The New York triumph dashed the Braves' hope of becoming the N.L.'s first back-to-back fall classic winner in 20 years.

■ **Turning point:** The eighth inning of Game 4, when catcher Jim Leyritz rocked Braves closer Mark Wohlers for a three-run, game-tying homer that set up an eventual 8-6 Yankees victory. The Braves had led the game 6-0 and appeared on the verge of taking a three games-to-one series lead.

■ **Memorable moment:** Right fielder Paul O'Neill's over-the-shoulder Game 5-ending catch that saved a 1-0 victory for the Yankees and Andy Pettitte. The catch denied Braves' pinch-hitter Luis Polonia extra bases with runners on first and third.

■ **Top guns:** Cecil Fielder (.391), Jeff Nelson (3 games, 0.00 ERA), Mariano Rivera (4 games, 1.59 ERA), John Wetteland (4 saves, 2.08 ERA), Yankees; Grissom (.444), A. Jones (.400, 2 HR, 6 RBI), Fred McGriff (2 HR, 6 RBI), John Smoltz (1-1, 0.64 ERA), Braves.

■ **MVP:** Wetteland.

**Linescores**

**Game 1**—October 20, at New York
Atlanta........0 2 6 0 1 3 0 0 0—12 13 0
New York....0 0 0 0 1 0 0 0 0— 1 4 1
Smoltz, McMichael (7), Neagle (8), Wade (9), Clontz (9); Pettitte, Boehringer (3), Weathers (6), Nelson (8), Wetteland (9). W—Smoltz. L—Pettitte. HR—McGriff, A. Jones 2 (Atl.).

**Game 2**—October 21, at New York
Atlanta.........1 0 1 0 1 1 0 0 0—4 10 0
New York......0 0 0 0 0 0 0 0 0—0 7 1
Maddux, Wohlers (9); Key, Lloyd (7), Nelson (7), M. Rivera (9). W—Maddux. L—Key.

**Game 3**—October 22, at Atlanta
New York.......1 0 0 1 0 0 0 3 0—5 8 1
Atlanta............0 0 0 0 0 1 0 1 0—2 6 1
Cone, M. Rivera (7), Lloyd (8), Wetteland (9); Glavine, McMichael (8), Clontz (8), Bielecki (9). W—Cone. L—Glavine. S—Wetteland. HR—Williams (N.Y.).

**Game 4**—October 23, at Atlanta
N.Y. ........0 0 0 0 0 3 0 3 0 2—8 12 0
Atlanta....0 4 1 0 1 0 0 0 0 0—6 9 2
Rogers, Boehringer (3), Weathers (5), Nelson (6), M. Rivera (8), Lloyd (9), Wetteland (10); Neagle, Wade (6), Bielecki (6), Wohlers (8), Avery (10), Clontz (10). W—Lloyd. L—Avery. S—Wetteland. HR—Leyritz (N.Y.); McGriff (Atl.).

**Game 5**—October 24, at Atlanta
New York.......0 0 0 1 0 0 0 0 0—1 4 1
Atlanta............0 0 0 0 0 0 0 0 0—0 5 1
Pettitte, Wetteland (9); Smoltz, Wohlers (9). W—Pettitte. L—Smoltz. S—Wetteland.

**Game 6**—October 26, at New York
Atlanta............0 0 0 1 0 0 0 0 1—2 8 0
New York.......0 0 3 0 0 0 0 0 x—3 8 1
Maddux, Wohlers (8); Key, Weathers (6), Lloyd (6), M. Rivera (7), Wetteland (9). W—Key. L—Maddux. S—Wetteland.

**The Yankees' Andy Pettitte won an A.L.-leading 21 games and a World Series ring in 1996. The Series championship was the first for the Yankees since 1978.**

# 1997

## FINAL STANDINGS

### American League

**East Division**

| Team | Bal. | NYY | Det. | Bos. | Tor. | Cle. | ChW | Mil. | Min. | K.C. | Sea. | Ana. | Tex. | Oak. | Atl. | Fla. | NYM | Mtl. | Phi. | W | L | Pct. | GB |
|---|---|---|---|---|---|---|---|---|---|---|---|---|---|---|---|---|---|---|---|---|---|---|---|
| Baltimore | ... | 8 | 6 | 5 | 6 | 6 | 5 | 5 | 10 | 7 | 7 | 7 | 10 | 8 | 3 | 0 | 1 | 1 | 3 | 98 | 64 | .605 | ... |
| New York | 4 | ... | 10 | 8 | 7 | 6 | 9 | 7 | 8 | 8 | 4 | 7 | 7 | 6 | 1 | 1 | 2 | 1 | 0 | 96 | 66 | .593 | 2 |
| Detroit | 6 | 2 | ... | 7 | 6 | 5 | 7 | 4 | 4 | 6 | 4 | 6 | 7 | 7 | 2 | 1 | 3 | 0 | 2 | 79 | 83 | .488 | 19 |
| Boston | 7 | 4 | 5 | ... | 6 | 6 | 3 | 8 | 8 | 3 | 7 | 5 | 3 | 7 | 0 | 1 | 2 | 0 | 3 | 78 | 84 | .481 | 20 |
| Toronto | 6 | 5 | 6 | 6 | ... | 5 | 6 | 4 | 8 | 6 | 3 | 5 | 7 | 5 | 1 | 0 | 0 | 1 | 2 | 76 | 86 | .469 | 22 |

**Central Division**

| Team | Bal. | NYY | Det. | Bos. | Tor. | Cle. | ChW | Mil. | Min. | K.C. | Sea. | Ana. | Tex. | Oak. | Hou. | Pit. | Cin. | St.L. | ChC | W | L | Pct. | GB |
|---|---|---|---|---|---|---|---|---|---|---|---|---|---|---|---|---|---|---|---|---|---|---|---|
| Cleveland | 5 | 5 | 6 | 5 | 6 | ... | 7 | 8 | 8 | 8 | 3 | 4 | 5 | 7 | 2 | 2 | 1 | 2 | 2 | 86 | 75 | .534 | ... |
| Chicago | 6 | 2 | 4 | 8 | 5 | 5 | ... | 4 | 6 | 11 | 5 | 5 | 3 | 8 | 3 | 0 | 2 | 1 | 2 | 80 | 81 | .497 | 6 |
| Milwaukee | 6 | 4 | 7 | 3 | 7 | 4 | 7 | ... | 5 | 6 | 5 | 4 | 7 | 5 | 2 | 2 | 0 | 3 | 1 | 78 | 83 | .484 | 8 |
| Minnesota | 1 | 3 | 7 | 3 | 3 | 4 | 6 | 7 | ... | 5 | 5 | 7 | 3 | 7 | 2 | 2 | 2 | 0 | 1 | 68 | 94 | .420 | 18½ |
| Kansas City | 4 | 3 | 5 | 8 | 5 | 3 | 1 | 6 | 7 | ... | 5 | 5 | 6 | 3 | 2 | 2 | 1 | 1 | 0 | 67 | 94 | .416 | 19 |

**West Division**

| Team | Bal. | NYY | Det. | Bos. | Tor. | Cle. | ChW | Mil. | Min. | K.C. | Sea. | Ana. | Tex. | Oak. | S.F. | L.A. | Col. | S.D. | W | L | Pct. | GB |
|---|---|---|---|---|---|---|---|---|---|---|---|---|---|---|---|---|---|---|---|---|---|---|
| Seattle | 4 | 7 | 7 | 4 | 8 | 8 | 6 | 6 | 6 | 6 | ... | 6 | 8 | 7 | 1 | 3 | 2 | 1 | 90 | 72 | .556 | ... |
| Anaheim | 4 | 4 | 5 | 6 | 6 | 7 | 6 | 7 | 4 | 6 | 6 | ... | 8 | 11 | 1 | 0 | 1 | 2 | 84 | 78 | .519 | 6 |
| Texas | 1 | 4 | 4 | 8 | 4 | 6 | 8 | 4 | 8 | 5 | 4 | 4 | ... | 7 | 2 | 3 | 3 | 2 | 77 | 85 | .475 | 13 |
| Oakland | 3 | 5 | 4 | 4 | 6 | 4 | 3 | 6 | 4 | 8 | 5 | 1 | 5 | ... | 2 | 1 | 1 | 3 | 65 | 97 | .401 | 25 |

### National League

**East Division**

| Team | Atl. | Fla. | NYM | Mtl. | Phi. | Hou. | Pit. | Cin. | St.L. | ChC | S.F. | L.A. | Col. | S.D. | Bal. | NYY | Det. | Bos. | Tor. | W | L | Pct. | GB |
|---|---|---|---|---|---|---|---|---|---|---|---|---|---|---|---|---|---|---|---|---|---|---|---|
| Atlanta | ... | 4 | 5 | 10 | 10 | 7 | 5 | 9 | 8 | 9 | 7 | 6 | 5 | 8 | 0 | 2 | 1 | 3 | 2 | 101 | 61 | .623 | ... |
| Florida | 8 | ... | 4 | 7 | 6 | 7 | 7 | 6 | 5 | 9 | 5 | 7 | 4 | 5 | 3 | 2 | 2 | 2 | 3 | 92 | 70 | .568 | 9 |
| New York | 7 | 8 | ... | 7 | 7 | 4 | 7 | 9 | 9 | 5 | 3 | 5 | 5 | 5 | 2 | 1 | 0 | 1 | 3 | 88 | 74 | .543 | 13 |
| Montreal | 2 | 5 | 5 | ... | 6 | 3 | 5 | 5 | 6 | 7 | 6 | 4 | 4 | 8 | 2 | 2 | 3 | 3 | 2 | 78 | 84 | .481 | 23 |
| Philadelphia | 2 | 6 | 5 | 6 | ... | 7 | 5 | 3 | 6 | 5 | 3 | 1 | 7 | 7 | 0 | 3 | 1 | 0 | 1 | 68 | 94 | .420 | 33 |

**Central Division**

| Team | Atl. | Fla. | NYM | Mtl. | Phi. | Hou. | Pit. | Cin. | St.L. | ChC | S.F. | L.A. | Col. | S.D. | Cle. | ChW | Mil. | Min. | K.C. | W | L | Pct. | GB |
|---|---|---|---|---|---|---|---|---|---|---|---|---|---|---|---|---|---|---|---|---|---|---|---|
| Houston | 4 | 4 | 7 | 8 | 4 | ... | 6 | 7 | 9 | 9 | 3 | 7 | 6 | 6 | 1 | 0 | 1 | 1 | 1 | 84 | 78 | .519 | ... |
| Pittsburgh | 6 | 4 | 4 | 6 | 6 | 6 | ... | 4 | 9 | 5 | 8 | 2 | 7 | 5 | 1 | 3 | 1 | 1 | 1 | 79 | 83 | .488 | 5 |
| Cincinnati | 2 | 5 | 2 | 6 | 8 | 5 | 8 | ... | 6 | 5 | 4 | 6 | 5 | 5 | 2 | 1 | 3 | 1 | 2 | 76 | 86 | .469 | 8 |
| St. Louis | 3 | 6 | 2 | 5 | 5 | 3 | 3 | 6 | ... | 8 | 8 | 6 | 4 | 6 | 1 | 2 | 0 | 3 | 2 | 73 | 89 | .451 | 11 |
| Chicago | 2 | 2 | 6 | 4 | 6 | 3 | 7 | 7 | 4 | ... | 5 | 5 | 2 | 6 | 1 | 1 | 2 | 2 | 3 | 68 | 94 | .420 | 16 |

**West Division**

| Team | Atl. | Fla. | NYM | Mtl. | Phi. | Hou. | Pit. | Cin. | St.L. | ChC | S.F. | L.A. | Col. | S.D. | Sea. | Ana. | Tex. | Oak. | W | L | Pct. | GB |
|---|---|---|---|---|---|---|---|---|---|---|---|---|---|---|---|---|---|---|---|---|---|---|
| San Fran. | 4 | 6 | 8 | 5 | 8 | 8 | 3 | 7 | 3 | 6 | ... | 6 | 8 | 8 | 3 | 3 | 2 | 2 | 90 | 72 | .556 | ... |
| Los Angeles | 5 | 4 | 6 | 7 | 10 | 4 | 9 | 5 | 5 | 6 | 6 | ... | 7 | 5 | 1 | 4 | 1 | 3 | 88 | 74 | .543 | 2 |
| Colorado | 6 | 7 | 6 | 7 | 4 | 5 | 4 | 6 | 7 | 9 | 4 | 5 | ... | 4 | 2 | 3 | 1 | 3 | 83 | 79 | .512 | 7 |
| San Diego | 3 | 6 | 6 | 3 | 4 | 5 | 6 | 6 | 5 | 5 | 4 | 7 | 8 | ... | 3 | 2 | 2 | 1 | 76 | 86 | .469 | 14 |

## SIGNIFICANT EVENTS

- **April 4:** The Atlanta Braves christened new Turner Field with a 5-4 come-from-behind victory over Chicago.
- **April 15:** Celebrating the 50th anniversary of Jackie Robinson's debut as the first black Major League player of the century, baseball announced every team would retire Robinson's uniform No. 42.
- **April 19:** St. Louis recorded a 1-0 victory over San Diego in the opener of the three-game Paradise Series—the first Major League regular-season game ever played in Hawaii.
- **April 20:** The Chicago Cubs defeated the New York Mets in the second game of a doubleheader, ending their season-opening losing streak at 14 games.
- **June 12:** The San Francisco Giants posted a 4-3 victory at Texas in the first interleague game in baseball history.
- **November 5:** The Milwaukee Brewers agreed to move from the American League to the National League Central Division, completing a re-alignment that placed Tampa Bay in the A.L. East, moved Detroit to the A.L. Central and positioned Arizona in the N.L. West.
- **November 18:** Tampa Bay opened the expansion draft by selecting pitcher Tony Saunders off the Florida roster and Arizona followed by grabbing Cleveland pitcher Brian Anderson.

## MEMORABLE MOMENTS

- **June 30:** Texas' Bobby Witt became the first American League pitcher to hit a home run since October 1972 when he connected off Los Angeles' Ismael Valdes in an interleague contest.
- **August 8:** For the second time in six weeks, Seattle lefthander Randy Johnson struck out 19 batters in a game—the first time a pitcher had reached that plateau twice in a season. Johnson shut out Chicago, 5-0.
- **September 20:** Colorado's Larry Walker doubled during a victory over Los Angeles, becoming the first National League player to reach 400 total bases in a season since Hank Aaron in 1959.
- **September 26:** Philadelphia's Curt Schilling struck out six Marlins in a 5-3 victory over Florida, setting a National League record for most strikeouts by a righthander with 319.
- **September 27:** San Francisco clinched the N.L. West title with a 6-1 victory over San Diego, becoming the fourth last-to-first team of the century.
- **September 28:** St. Louis' Mark McGwire, the second player in history to record back-to-back 50-homer seasons, connected for No. 58 in a final-day victory over Chicago—matching Jimmie Foxx and Hank Greenberg for the single-season record by a righthanded hitter. The total topped Seattle's Ken Griffey Jr. by two and was the highest in one season since Roger Maris hit his record 61 in 1961.
- **September 28:** San Diego's Tony Gwynn completed a .372 season and captured his N.L.-record tying eighth batting championship.

## ALL-STAR GAME

- **Winner:** The A.L. snapped a three-year losing streak with a 3-1 victory behind the late-inning heroics of hometown Cleveland catcher Sandy Alomar and the three-hit work of an eight-man pitching parade.
- **Key inning:** The fourth, when the N.L. ran itself out of a potential big inning that opened with walks to San Francisco's Barry Bonds and Los Angeles' Mike Piazza. After Bonds had advanced to third on a fly ball by Houston's Jeff Bagwell, Piazza was caught trying to advance to second on a ball that momentarily eluded Rangers catcher Ivan Rodriguez. Larry Walker grounded out to end the N.L.'s only serious threat of the game.
- **Memorable moment:** Alomar, who entered the mid-summer classic with a 30-game hitting streak, broke a 1-1 tie with a seventh-inning two-run homer—in his only at-bat. The blow wiped out a game-tying solo homer in the top of the inning by Atlanta catcher Javy Lopez and earned Alomar home-field MVP honors.
- **Top guns:** S. Alomar (Indians), Edgar Martinez (Mariners), Brady Anderson (Orioles), Randy Johnson (Mariners), A.L.; Lopez (Braves), Curt Schilling (Phillies), N.L.
- **MVP:** S. Alomar.

**Linescore**

July 8 at Cleveland's Jacobs Field

N.L. ................0 0 0 0 0 0 1 0 0—1 3 0
A.L. ................0 1 0 0 0 0 2 0 x—3 7 0

Maddux (Braves), Schilling (Phillies) 3, Brown (Marlins) 5, P. Martinez (Expos) 6, Estes (Giants) 7, B. Jones (Mets) 8; R. Johnson (Mariners), Clemens (Blue Jays) 3, Cone (Yankees) 4, Thompson (Tigers) 5, Hentgen (Blue Jays) 6, Rosado (Royals) 7, Myers (Orioles) 8, Rivera (Yankees) 9. W—Rosado. L—Estes. HR—E. Martinez, S. Alomar, A.L.; Lopez, N.L.

## LEADERS

**American League**
**BA:** Frank Thomas, Chi., .347.
**Runs:** Ken Griffey Jr., Sea., 125.
**Hits:** Nomar Garciaparra, Bos., 209.
**TB:** Ken Griffey Jr., Sea., 393.
**HR:** Ken Griffey Jr., Sea., 56.
**RBI:** Ken Griffey Jr., Sea., 147.
**SB:** Brian Hunter, Det., 74.
**Wins:** Roger Clemens, Tor., 21.
**ERA:** Roger Clemens, Tor., 2.05.
**CG:** Roger Clemens, Tor.; Pat Hentgen, Tor., 9.
**IP:** Roger Clemens, Tor.; Pat Hentgen, Tor., 264.0.
**SO:** Roger Clemens, Tor., 292.
**SV:** Randy Myers, Bal., 45.

**National League**
**BA:** Tony Gwynn, S.D., .372.
**Runs:** Craig Biggio, Hou., 146.
**Hits:** Tony Gwynn, S.D., 220.
**TB:** Larry Walker, Col., 409.
**HR:** Larry Walker, Col., 49.
**RBI:** Larry Walker, Col., 140.
**SB:** Tony Womack, Pit., 60.
**Wins:** Denny Neagle, Atl., 20.
**ERA:** Pedro J. Martinez, Mon., 1.90.
**CG:** Pedro J. Martinez, Mon., 13.
**IP:** John Smoltz, Atl., 256.0.
**SO:** Curt Schilling, Phi., 319.
**SV:** Jeff Shaw, Cin., 42.

**A.L. 20-game winners**
Roger Clemens, Tor., 21
Randy Johnson, Sea., 20
Brad Radke, Min., 20

**N.L. 20-game winner**
Denny Neagle, Atl., 20

**A.L. 100 RBIs**
Ken Griffey Jr., Sea., 147
Tino Martinez, N.Y., 141
Juan Gonzalez, Tex., 131
Tim Salmon, Ana., 129
Frank Thomas, Chi., 125
Tony Clark, Det., 117
Paul O'Neill, N.Y., 117
Albert Belle, Chi., 116
Jeff King, K.C., 112
Rafael Palmeiro, Bal., 110
Jay Buhner, Sea., 109
Edgar Martinez, Sea., 108
Matt Williams, Cle., 105
Joe Carter, Tor., 102
Travis Fryman, Det., 102
Jim Thome, Cle., 102
Bobby Higginson, Det., 101
David Justice, Cle., 101
Bernie Williams, N.Y., 100

**N.L. 100 RBIs**
Andres Galarraga, Col., 140
Jeff Bagwell, Hou., 135
Larry Walker, Col., 130
Mike Piazza, L.A., 124
Jeff Kent, S.F., 121
Tony Gwynn, S.D., 119
Sammy Sosa, Chi., 119
Dante Bichette, Col., 118
Moises Alou, Fla., 115
Vinny Castilla, Col., 113
Chipper Jones, Atl., 111
Eric Karros, L.A., 104
J.T. Snow, S.F., 104
John Olerud, N.Y., 102
Barry Bonds, S.F., 101

**A.L./N.L. 100 RBIs**
Mark McGwire, Oak.-St.L., 123

**A.L. 40 homers**
Ken Griffey Jr., Sea., 56
Tino Martinez, N.Y., 44
Juan Gonzalez, Tex., 42
Jay Buhner, Sea., 40
Jim Thome, Cle., 40

**N.L. 40 homers**
Larry Walker, Col., 49
Jeff Bagwell, Hou., 43
Andres Galarraga, Col., 41
Barry Bonds, S.F., 40
Vinny Castilla, Col., 40
Mike Piazza, L.A., 40

**A.L./N.L. 40 homers**
Mark McGwire, Oak.-St.L., 58

**Most Valuable Player**
A.L.: Ken Griffey Jr., OF, Sea.
N.L.: Larry Walker, OF, Col.

**Cy Young Award**
A.L.: Roger Clemens, Tor.
N.L.: Pedro Martinez, Mon.

**Rookie of the Year**
A.L.: Nomar Garciaparra, SS, Bos.
N.L.: Scott Rolen, 3B, Phi.

**Manager of the Year**
A.L.: Davey Johnson, Bal.
N.L.: Dusty Baker, S.F.

**Hall of Fame additions**
Nellie Fox, 2B, 1947-65.
Tom Lasorda, manager
Phil Niekro, P, 1964-87.
Willie Wells, IF-P, Negro Leagues

## A.L. DIVISION SERIES

- **Winners:** Baltimore claimed a surprisingly easy four-game victory over Seattle and Cleveland survived a comeback-filled five-game battle against the wild-card New York Yankees. The Indians' victory set up a grudge match with the Orioles, who had eliminated them in a 1996 Division Series.
- **Turning points:** The Orioles claimed their second straight A.L. Championship Series berth because of their ability to beat Mariners ace Randy Johnson. Baltimore scored five earned runs in Johnson's five Game 1 innings en route to a 9-3 victory and then handed the big lefthander a 3-1 defeat in the Game 4 clincher. The Indians advanced because they finally were able to break the stranglehold of a powerful New York bullpen that had worked $11\frac{2}{3}$ scoreless innings entering Game 4. Cleveland scored single runs in the eighth and ninth innings off Mariano Rivera and Ramiro Mendoza to claim a 3-2 Game 4 win and prevailed in a 4-3 clincher behind the pitching of rookie Jaret Wright.
- **Memorable moments:** The Game 4 home run of light-hitting Baltimore second baseman Jeff Reboulet, who also hit two regular-season homers off the intimidating Johnson. The consecutive Game 1 home runs by Yankees Tim Raines, Derek Jeter and Paul O'Neill, a postseason record that helped the New Yorkers rally for an 8-6 victory. Omar Vizquel's ninth-inning single that completed the Indians' rally for a series-tying Game 4 victory.
- **Memorable performances:** Geronimo Berroa hit a pair of home runs, including one in the decisive 3-1 series-clinching victory, and batted .385 for the Orioles; Baltimore righthander Mike Mussina recorded two wins and a 1.93 ERA while outdueling Mariners ace Johnson; Yankees right fielder O'Neill batted .421 with two homers, including a Game 3 grand slam, and seven RBIs against the Indians; catcher Sandy Alomar hit a pair of home runs and the 21-year-old Wright won twice for Cleveland.

**Linescores**

Baltimore vs. Seattle

**Game 1**—October 1, at Seattle
Baltimore......0 0 1 0 4 4 0 0 0—9 13 0
Seattle..........0 0 0 1 0 0 1 0 1—3 7 1
Mussina, Orosco (8), Benitez (9); Johnson, Timlin (6), Spoljaric (6), Wells (7), Charlton (8). W—Mussina. L—Johnson. HR—Berroa, Hoiles (Bal.); Martinez, Buhner, Rodriguez (Sea.).

**Game 2**—October 2, at Seattle
Baltimore......0 1 0 0 2 0 2 4 0—9 14 0
Seattle..........2 0 0 0 0 0 1 0 0—3 9 0
Erickson, Benitez (7), Orosco (8), Myers (9); Moyer, Spoljaric (5), Ayala (7), Charlton (8), Slocumb (9). W—Erickson. L—Moyer. HR—Baines, Anderson (Bal.).

**Game 3**—October 4, at Baltimore
Seattle..........0 0 1 0 1 0 0 0 2—4 11 0
Baltimore......0 0 0 0 0 0 0 0 2—2 5 0
Fassero, Slocumb (9); Key, Mills (5), Rhodes (6), Mathews (9). W—Fassero. L—Key. HR—Buhner, Sorrento (Sea.).

**Game 4**—October 5, at Baltimore
Seattle............0 1 0 0 0 0 0 0 0—1 2 0
Baltimore........2 0 0 0 1 0 0 0 x—3 7 0
Johnson; Mussina, Benitez (8), Myers (9). W—Mussina. L—Johnson. S—Myers. HR—Reboulet, Berroa (Bal.); Martinez (Sea.).

Cleveland vs. New York

**Game 1**—September 30, at New York
Cleveland......5 0 0 1 0 0 0 0 0—6 11 0
New York......0 1 0 1 1 5 0 0 0—8 11 0
Hershiser, Morman (5), Plunk (5), Assenmacher (6), Jackson (7); Cone, Mendoza (4), Stanton (7), Nelson (7), Rivera (8). W—Mendoza. L—Plunk. S—Rivera. HR—Alomar (Cle.); Martinez, Raines, Jeter, O'Neill (N.Y.).

**Game 2**—October 2, at New York
Cleveland......0 0 0 5 2 0 0 0 0—7 11 1
New York......3 0 0 0 0 0 0 1 1—5 7 2
Wright, Jackson (7), Assenmacher (7), Mesa (8); Pettitte, Boehringer (6), Lloyd (7), Nelson (9). W—Wright. L—Pettitte. HR—M. Williams (Cle.); Jeter (N.Y.).

**Game 3**—October 4, at Cleveland
New York........1 0 1 4 0 0 0 0 0—6 4 1
Cleveland........0 1 0 0 0 0 0 0 0—1 5 1

Wells; Nagy, Ogea (4). W—Wells. L—Nagy. HR—O'Neill (N.Y.).

**Game 4**—October 5, at Cleveland
New York........2 0 0 000 0 0—2 9 1
Cleveland........0 1 0 000 0 1 1—3 9 0
Gooden, Lloyd (6), Nelson (6), Stanton (7), Rivera (8), Mendoza (8); Hershiser, Assenmacher (8), Jackson (8). W—Jackson. L—Mendoza. HR—Justice, Alomar (Cle.).

**Game 5**—October 6, at Cleveland
New York......0 0 0 0 2 1 0 0 0—3 12 0
Cleveland......0 0 3 1 0 0 0 0 x—4 7 2
Pettitte, Nelson (7), Stanton (8); Wright, Jackson (6), Assenmacher (7), Mesa (8). W—Wright. L—Pettitte. S—Mesa.

## N.L. DIVISION SERIES

■ **Winners:** The Atlanta Braves and the wild-card Florida Marlins set up an NLCS showdown of East Division teams with convincing sweeps of the Houston Astros and San Francisco Giants. The Braves earned a record sixth straight LCS appearance behind the outstanding pitching of Greg Maddux, John Smoltz and Tom Glavine. The 5-year-old Marlins became the youngest expansion team to win a playoff series behind the near-perfect combination of clutch hitting and pitching.
■ **Turning points:** Maddux set the tone for Atlanta's victory by throwing a Game 1 seven-hitter and outdueling Houston ace Darryl Kile for a 2-1 victory. Edgar Renteria gave the Marlins a 2-1 Game 1 victory with a bases-loaded, ninth-inning single and Moises Alou singled home the winning run in the ninth inning of a 7-6 Game 2 win—a two-games-to-none hole from which the Giants could not recover.
■ **Memorable moments:** Smoltz took Atlanta honors with an 11-strikeout three-hitter in a 4-1 Game 3 victory that completed the Braves' sweep of Houston. Florida's 6-2 third-game victory over the Giants was keyed by Devon White's sixth-inning grand slam, which erased a 1-0 deficit.
■ **Memorable performances:** Third baseman Chipper Jones batted .500 with a home run and Jeff Blauser had a home run and four RBIs for the Braves, who also got a victory from each of their Big Three—Maddux, Glavine and Smoltz. The Marlins rode the clutch hitting of Renteria, Alou and White and the outstanding pitching of Kevin Brown and Alex Fernandez. The Giants got two home runs from second baseman Jeff Kent and a nice pitching effort from Kirk Rueter, who failed to get a decision.

**Linescores**

Atlanta vs. Houston

**Game 1**—September 30, at Atlanta
Houston................0 0 0 0 1 0 0 0 0—1 7 1
Atlanta..................1 1 0 0 0 0 0 0 x—2 2 0
Kile, Springer (8), Martin (8); Maddux. W—Maddux. L—Kile. HR—Klesko (Atl.).

**Game 2**—October 1, at Atlanta
Houston...........0 0 0 3 0 0 0 0 0— 3 6 2
Atlanta .............0 0 3 0 3 5 0 2 x—13 10 1
Hampton, Magnante (5), Garcia (6), Lima (7), Wagner (8); Glavine, Cather (7), Wohlers (9). W—Glavine. L—Hampton. HR—Blauser (Atl.).

**Game 3**—October 3, at Houston
Atlanta .................1 1 0 0 0 0 1 1 0—4 8 2
Houston................0 0 0 0 0 0 1 0 0—1 3 1
Smoltz; Reynolds, Springer (7), Martin (8), Garcia (8), Magnante (9). W—Smoltz. L—Reynolds. HR—C. Jones (Atl.), Carr (Hou.).

Florida vs. San Francisco

**Game 1**—September 30, at Florida
San Francisco ......0 0 0 0 0 0 1 0 0—1 4 0
Florida .................0 0 0 0 0 0 1 0 1—2 7 0
Rueter, Tavarez (8), R. Hernandez (9); Brown, Cook (8). W—Cook. L—Tavarez. HR—Mueller (S.F.), C. Johnson (Fla.).

**Game 2**—October 1, at Florida
San Francisco ....1 1 1 1 0 0 1 0 1—6 11 0
Florida ...............2 0 1 2 0 1 0 0 1—7 10 2
Estes, Henry (3), Tavarez (6), Rodriguez (8), R. Hernandez (9); Leiter, L. Hernandez (5), Nen (9). W—Nen. L—R. Hernandez. HR—Bonilla, Sheffield (Fla.), B. Johnson (S.F.).

**Game 3**—October 3, at San Francisco
Florida .................0 0 0 0 0 4 0 2 0—6 10 2
San Francisco ....0 0 0 1 0 1 0 0 0—2 7 0
Fernandez, Cook (8), Nen (9); Alvarez, Tavarez (7), R. Hernandez (8), Rodriguez (8), Beck (8). W—Fernandez. L—Alvarez. HR—Kent 2 (S.F.), White (Fla.).

## ALCS

■ **Winner:** The Indians, looking for their first championship since 1948, earned their second World Series appearance in three years with a six-game victory over the Orioles. The Indians overcame a .193 team average to claim the franchise's fifth pennant behind clutch pitching and timely hitting that produced four one-run wins over the A.L.'s winningest regular-season team.
■ **Turning point:** The fifth inning of Game 4, when Indians catcher Sandy Alomar took center stage with a baserunning gamble. The bases were loaded and the score was tied when Alomar, stationed at second, alertly raced home after an Arthur Rhodes wild pitch led to a home-plate collision between lead runner Dave Justice and catcher Lenny Webster. The Orioles fought back for a 7-7 tie, but Alomar decided the game with a ninth-inning single off Baltimore closer Armando Benitez to give the Indians a three-games-to-one series advantage.
■ **Memorable moment:** The 11th inning of Game 6 when shortstop Tony Fernandez drove a Benitez pitch into the right field seats at Camden Yards and gave the Indians a 1-0 series-clinching win. The Indians had managed only one hit through eight innings off Orioles starter Mike Mussina while Baltimore stranded 14 baserunners and was 0-for-12 with men in scoring position against Cleveland starter Charles Nagy and four relievers.
■ **Top guns:** Manny Ramirez (2 HR, 3 RBI), Fernandez (.357, 1 HR, 2 RBI), Marquis Grissom (1 HR, 4 RBI), S. Alomar (1 HR, 4 RBI), Mike Jackson (5 games, 0.00 ERA), Indians; Brady Anderson (.360, 2 HR, 3 RBI), Cal Ripken (.348, 1 HR, 3 RBI), Harold Baines (.353, 1 HR), Mussina (15 IP, 0.60 ERA), Orioles.
■ **MVP:** Marquis Grissom.

**Linescores**

**Game 1**—October 8, at Baltimore
Cleveland........0 0 0 0 0 0 0 0 0—0 4 1
Baltimore........1 0 2 0 0 0 0 0 x—3 6 1
Ogea, Bri. Anderson (7); Erickson, Myers (9). W—Erickson. L—Ogea. S—Myers. HR—Bra. Anderson, R. Alomar (Bal.).

**Game 2**—October 9, at Baltimore
Cleveland........2 0 0 0 0 0 0 3 0—5 6 3
Baltimore........0 2 0 0 0 2 0 0 0—4 8 1
Nagy, Morman (6), Juden (7), Assenmacher (7), Jackson (8), Mesa (9); Key, Kamieniecki (5), Benitez (8), Mills (9). W—Assenmacher. L—Benitez. S—Mesa. HR—Ramirez, Grissom (Cle.); Ripken (Bal.).

**Game 3**—October 11, at Cleveland
Bal. ........0 0 0 0 0 0 0 0 1 0 0—1 8 1
Cle. ........0 0 0 0 0 0 1 0 0 0 1—2 6 0
Mussina, Benitez (8), Orosco (9), Mills (9), Rhodes (10), Myers (11); Hershiser, Assenmacher (8), Jackson (8), Mesa (9), Juden (11), Morman (11), Plunk (12). W—Plunk. L—Myers.

**Game 4**—October 12, at Cleveland
Baltimore ....0 1 4 0 0 0 1 0 1—7 12 2
Cleveland......0 2 0 1 4 0 0 0 1—8 13 0
Erickson, Rhodes (5), Mills (7), Orosco (9), Benitez (9); Wright, Bri. Anderson (4), Juden (7), Assenmacher (7), Jackson (7), Mesa (8). W—Mesa. L—Mills. HR—S. Alomar, Ramirez (Cle.); Bra. Anderson, Baines, Palmeiro (Bal.).

**Game 5**—October 13, at Cleveland
Baltimore......0 0 2 0 0 0 0 0 2—4 10 0
Cleveland......0 0 0 0 0 0 0 0 2—2 8 1
Kamieniecki, Key (6), Myers (9); Ogea, Assenmacher (9), Jackson (9). W—Kamieniecki. L—Ogea. HR—Davis (Bal.).

**Game 6**—October 15, at Baltimore
Cle. ..........0 0 0 0 0 0 0 0 0 0 1—1 3 0
Bal. ..........0 0 0 0 0 0 0 0 0 0 0—0 10 0
Nagy, Assenmacher (8), Jackson (8), Bri. Anderson (10), Mesa (11); Mussina, Myers (9), Benitez (11). W—Bri. Anderson. L—Benitez. S—Mesa. HR—Fernandez (Cle.).

## NLCS

■ **Winner:** The Marlins became the first wild-card team to reach the World Series when they upended the defending-N.L. champion Braves in a six-game NLCS. The 5-year-old Marlins also became the youngest expansion team to reach the fall classic while giving the spring training haven of South Florida its first World Series. The Marlins, who finished nine games behind Atlanta in the N.L. East, didn't even exist in 1991 when the Braves began their long playoff run.
■ **Turning point:** After righthander Livan Hernandez surrendered a Game 5-opening triple to Kenny Lofton and a walk to Keith Lockhart, he came back to strike out Chipper Jones, Fred McGriff and Ryan Klesko in a scoreless first inning. Bolstered by that great escape, Hernandez surrendered only two more hits and tied the LCS record with 15 strikeouts while outdueling Greg Maddux in a 2-1 victory at Pro Player Stadium.
■ **Memorable moment:** Kevin Brown's final pitch of Game 6, which extended the Marlins' Cinderella run and gave manager Jim Leyland his first World Series appearance in a career that spanned 33 years. Brown, the Game 1 winner, struggled through an 11-hit, complete-game 7-4 victory while fighting a stomach flu.
■ **Top guns:** Craig Counsell (.429), Bobby Bonilla (4 RBI), Charles Johnson (5 RBI), Jeff Conine (5 RBI), Hernandez (2-0, 0.84 ERA), Brown (2-0), Marlins; Lockhart (.500), Andruw Jones (.444), McGriff (.333, 4 RBI), Chipper Jones (2 HR, 4 RBI), Ryan Klesko (2 HR, 4 RBI), Denny Neagle (12 IP, 1-0, 0.00 ERA), Maddux (13 IP, 0-2, 1.38 ERA), Braves.
■ **MVP:** Hernandez.

**Linescores**

**Game 1**—October 7, at Atlanta
Florida ...........3 0 2 0 0 0 0 0 0—5 6 0
Atlanta............1 0 1 0 0 1 0 0 0—3 5 2
Brown, Cook (7), Powell (8), Nen (9); Maddux, Neagle (7). W—Brown. L—Maddux. S—Nen. HR—C. Jones, Klesko (Atl.).

**Game 2**—October 8, at Atlanta
Florida ..........0 0 0 0 0 0 0 1 0—1 3 1
Atlanta ..........3 0 2 0 0 0 2 0 x—7 13 0
Fernandez, Leiter (3), Heredia (6), Vosberg (7); Glavine, Cather (8), Wohlers (9). W—Glavine. L—Fernandez. HR—Klesko, C. Jones (Atl.).

**Game 3**—October 10, at Florida
Atlanta............0 0 0 1 0 1 0 0 0—2 6 1
Florida ............0 0 0 1 0 4 0 0 x—5 8 1
Smoltz, Cather (7), Ligtenberg (8); Saunders, Hernandez (6), Cook (8), Nen (9). W—Hernandez. L—Smoltz. S—Nen. HR—Sheffield (Fla.).

**Game 4**—October 11, at Florida
Atlanta..........1 0 1 0 2 0 0 0 0—4 11 0
Florida ..........0 0 0 0 0 0 0 0 0—0 4 0
Neagle; Leiter, Heredia (7), Vosberg (9). W—Neagle. L—Leiter. HR—Blauser (Atl.).

**Game 5**—October 12, at Florida
Atlanta............0 1 0 0 0 0 0 0 0—1 3 0
Florida ............1 0 0 0 0 0 1 0 x—2 5 0
Maddux, Cather (8); Hernandez. W—Hernandez. L—Maddux. HR—Tucker (Atl.).

**Game 6**—October 14, at Atlanta
Florida..........4 0 0 0 0 3 0 0 0—7 10 1
Atlanta..........1 2 0 0 0 0 0 0 1—4 11 1
Brown; Glavine, Cather (6), Ligtenberg (7), Embree (9). W—Brown. L—Glavine.

## WORLD SERIES

■ **Winner:** The expansion Marlins, who had undergone an $89 million offseason facelift, made the investment pay off when they outlasted the Indians in an exciting World Series that was decided in the 11th inning of Game 7 at Pro Player Stadium. The victory gave the 5-year-old Marlins distinction as the youngest team ever to win a fall classic and the only wild-card team to earn a championship. The Indians failed to win their first World Series since 1948 for the second time in three years.
■ **Turning point:** It didn't arrive until the ninth inning of Game 7, when the Indians were leading 2-1 and two outs away from an elusive championship. That's when the Marlins scored the tying run on Craig Counsell's sacrifice fly, setting the stage for a dramatic finish to a closely contested series in which the teams alternated victories.
■ **Memorable moment:** The bases-loaded, 11th-inning single by shortstop Edgar Renteria that gave the Marlins their unlikely victory and sent 67,204 fans at Pro Player Stadium into a frenzy. The two-out hit completed a gutsy comeback after the Marlins had been limited to two hits over eight innings by starter Jaret Wright and three Cleveland relievers. It also made a winner out of Jay Powell, who completed the six-pitcher six-hitter with a scoreless top of the 11th.
■ **Top guns:** Darren Daulton (.389), Charles Johnson (.357), Moises Alou (.321, 3 HR, 9 RBI), Livan Hernandez (2-0), Marlins; Matt Williams (.385), Sandy Alomar (.367, 2 HR, 10 RBI), Manny Ramirez (2 HR, 6 RBI); Chad Ogea (2-0, 1.54 ERA), Wright (1-0, 2.92), Indians.
■ **MVP:** Hernandez.

**Linescores**

**Game 1**—October 18, at Florida
Cleveland......1 0 0 0 1 1 0 1 0—4 11 0
Florida ..........0 0 1 4 2 0 0 0 x—7 7 1
Hershiser, Juden (5), Plunk (6), Assenmacher (8); Hernandez, Cook (6), Powell (8), Nen (9). W—Hernandez. L—Hershiser. S—Nen. HR—Alou, Johnson (Fla.), Ramirez, Thome (Cle.).

**Game 2**—October 19, at Florida
Cleveland......1 0 0 0 3 2 0 0 0—6 14 0
Florida..........1 0 0 0 0 0 0 0 0—1 8 0
Ogea, Jackson (7), Mesa (9); Brown, Heredia (7), Alfonseca (8). W—Ogea. L—Brown. HR—Alomar (Cle.).

**Game 3**—October 21, at Cleveland
Florida........1 0 1 1 0 2 2 0 7—14 16 3
Cleveland....2 0 0 3 2 0 0 0 4—11 10 3
Leiter, Heredia (5), Cook (8), Nen (9); Nagy, Anderson (7), Jackson (7), Assenmacher (8), Plunk (8), Morman (9), Mesa (9). W—Cook. L—Plunk. HR—Sheffield, Daulton, Eisenreich (Fla.), Thome (Cle.).

**Game 4**—October 22, at Cleveland
Florida..........0 0 0 1 0 2 0 0 0— 3 6 2
Cleveland....3 0 3 0 0 1 1 2 x—10 15 0
Saunders, Alfonseca (3), Vosberg (6), Powell (8); Wright, Anderson (7). W—Wright. L—Saunders. S—Anderson. HR—Ramirez, Williams (Cle.), Alou (Fla.).

**Game 5**—October 23, at Cleveland
Florida ..........0 2 0 0 0 4 0 1 1—8 15 2
Cleveland......0 1 3 0 0 0 0 0 3—7 9 0
Hernandez, Nen (9); Hershiser, Morman (6), Plunk (6), Juden (7), Assenmacher (8), Mesa (9). W—Hernandez. L—Hershiser. S—Nen. HR—Alomar (Cle.), Alou (Fla.).

**Game 6**—October 25, at Florida
Cleveland........0 2 1 0 1 0 0 0 0—4 8 0
Florida ............0 0 0 0 1 0 0 0 0—1 8 0
Ogea, Jackson (6), Assenmacher (8), Mesa (9); Brown, Heredia (6), Powell (8), Vosberg (9). W—Ogea. L—Brown. S—Mesa.

**Game 7**—October 26, at Florida
Cle. ......0 0 2 0 0 0 0 0 0 0 0—2 6 2
Fla. ......0 0 0 0 0 0 1 0 1 0 1—3 8 0
Wright, Assenmacher (7), Jackson (8), Anderson (8), Mesa (9), Nagy (10); Leiter, Cook (7), Alfonseca (8), Heredia (9), Nen (9), Powell (11). W—Powell. L—Nagy. HR—Bonilla (Fla.).

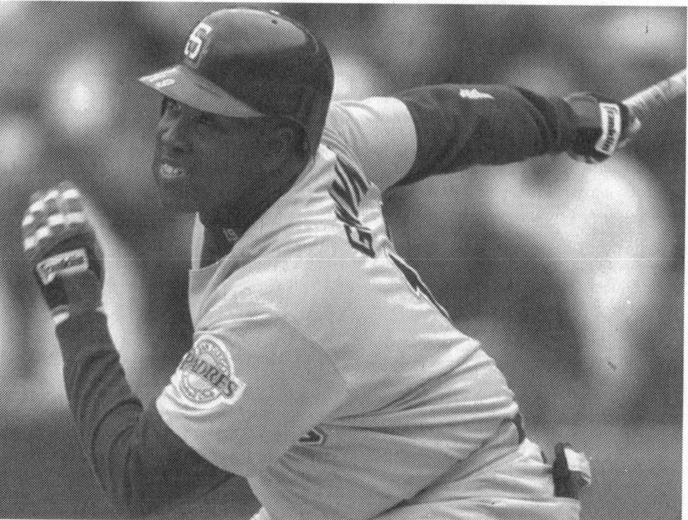

**San Diego's Tony Gwynn brought his total of National League batting crowns to eight in 1997, equaling the record number of N.L. titles won by Honus Wagner.**

# 1998

## FINAL STANDINGS

### American League

**East Division**

| Team | N.Y. | Bos. | Tor. | Bal. | T.B. | Cle. | Chi. | K.C. | Min. | Det. | Tex. | Ana. | Sea. | Oak. | Atl. | NYM | Phi. | Mtl. | Fla. | W | L | Pct. | GB |
|---|---|---|---|---|---|---|---|---|---|---|---|---|---|---|---|---|---|---|---|---|---|---|---|
| New York | ... | 7 | 6 | 9 | 11 | 7 | 7 | 10 | 7 | 8 | 8 | 5 | 8 | 8 | 3 | 2 | 3 | 2 | 3 | 114 | 48 | .704 | ... |
| Boston | 5 | ... | 5 | 6 | 9 | 8 | 5 | 8 | 5 | 5 | 6 | 5 | 7 | 9 | 2 | 1 | 1 | 3 | 2 | 92 | 70 | .568 | 22 |
| Toronto | 6 | 7 | ... | 7 | 7 | 4 | 6 | 5 | 7 | 6 | 4 | 7 | 7 | 6 | 1 | 2 | 1 | 4 | 1 | 88 | 74 | .543 | 26 |
| Baltimore | 3 | 6 | 5 | ... | 5 | 5 | 2 | 5 | 7 | 10 | 6 | 6 | 6 | 8 | 1 | 1 | 2 | 0 | 1 | 79 | 83 | .488 | 35 |
| Tampa Bay | 1 | 3 | 5 | 7 | ... | 3 | 6 | 3 | 4 | 6 | 4 | 5 | 5 | 6 | 0 | 1 | 2 | 1 | 1 | 63 | 99 | .389 | 51 |

**Central Division**

| Team | N.Y. | Bos. | Tor. | Bal. | T.B. | Cle. | Chi. | K.C. | Min. | Det. | Tex. | Ana. | Sea. | Oak. | Hou. | ChC | Stl. | Cin. | Mil. | Pit. | W | L | Pct. | GB |
|---|---|---|---|---|---|---|---|---|---|---|---|---|---|---|---|---|---|---|---|---|---|---|---|---|
| Cleveland | 4 | 3 | 7 | 6 | 7 | ... | 6 | 8 | 6 | 9 | 4 | 7 | 9 | 3 | 1 | 2 | 2 | 2 | 2 | 1 | 89 | 73 | .549 | ... |
| Chicago | 4 | 6 | 4 | 9 | 5 | 6 | ... | 8 | 6 | 6 | 5 | 6 | 4 | 4 | 1 | 0 | 2 | 1 | 1 | 2 | 80 | 82 | .494 | 9 |
| Kansas City | 0 | 3 | 6 | 6 | 8 | 4 | 4 | ... | 7 | 6 | 3 | 5 | 4 | 7 | 1 | 2 | 2 | 2 | 1 | 1 | 72 | 89 | .447 | 16.5 |
| Minnesota | 4 | 6 | 4 | 3 | 7 | 6 | 6 | 5 | ... | 4 | 7 | 5 | 2 | 4 | 1 | 2 | 2 | 1 | 0 | 1 | 70 | 92 | .432 | 19 |
| Detroit | 3 | 5 | 5 | 1 | 5 | 3 | 6 | 6 | 8 | ... | 3 | 3 | 3 | 7 | 0 | 2 | 1 | 0 | 2 | 2 | 65 | 97 | .401 | 24 |

**West Division**

| Team | N.Y. | Bos. | Tor. | Bal. | T.B. | Cle. | Chi. | K.C. | Min. | Det. | Tex. | Ana. | Sea. | Oak. | S.D. | S.F. | L.A. | Col. | Ari. | W | L | Pct. | GB |
|---|---|---|---|---|---|---|---|---|---|---|---|---|---|---|---|---|---|---|---|---|---|---|---|
| Texas | 3 | 5 | 7 | 5 | 7 | 7 | 6 | 8 | 4 | 8 | ... | 7 | 7 | 6 | 2 | 1 | 0 | 2 | 3 | 88 | 74 | .543 | ... |
| Anaheim | 6 | 6 | 4 | 5 | 6 | 4 | 5 | 6 | 6 | 8 | 5 | ... | 9 | 5 | 1 | 1 | 3 | 3 | 2 | 85 | 77 | .525 | 3 |
| Seattle | 3 | 4 | 4 | 5 | 6 | 2 | 7 | 6 | 9 | 8 | 5 | 3 | ... | 7 | 2 | 1 | 1 | 2 | 1 | 76 | 85 | .472 | 11.5 |
| Oakland | 3 | 2 | 5 | 3 | 5 | 8 | 7 | 4 | 7 | 4 | 6 | 7 | 5 | ... | 2 | 2 | 1 | 1 | 2 | 74 | 88 | .457 | 14 |

### National League

**East Division**

| Team | Atl. | N.Y. | Phi. | Mtl. | Fla. | Hou. | Chi. | Stl. | Cin. | Mil. | Pit. | S.D. | S.F. | L.A. | Col. | Ari. | NYY | Bos. | Tor. | Bal. | T.B. | W | L | Pct. | GB |
|---|---|---|---|---|---|---|---|---|---|---|---|---|---|---|---|---|---|---|---|---|---|---|---|---|---|
| Atlanta | ... | 9 | 8 | 6 | 7 | 4 | 3 | 6 | 7 | 7 | 7 | 5 | 7 | 8 | 5 | 8 | 1 | 1 | 2 | 2 | 3 | 106 | 56 | .654 | ... |
| New York | 3 | ... | 8 | 4 | 7 | 4 | 5 | 6 | 6 | 8 | 4 | 4 | 4 | 5 | 6 | 5 | 1 | 2 | 1 | 3 | 2 | 88 | 74 | .543 | 18 |
| Philadelphia | 4 | 4 | ... | 7 | 6 | 2 | 6 | 3 | 5 | 5 | 8 | 1 | 2 | 4 | 4 | 7 | 0 | 3 | 2 | 1 | 1 | 75 | 87 | .463 | 31 |
| Montreal | 6 | 8 | 5 | ... | 7 | 2 | 2 | 3 | 1 | 3 | 2 | 4 | 3 | 4 | 2 | 7 | 1 | 0 | 0 | 3 | 2 | 65 | 97 | .401 | 41 |
| Florida | 5 | 5 | 6 | 5 | ... | 3 | 2 | 4 | 0 | 0 | 3 | 4 | 0 | 4 | 3 | 2 | 0 | 1 | 2 | 2 | 3 | 54 | 108 | .333 | 52 |

**Central Division**

| Team | Atl. | N.Y. | Phi. | Mtl. | Fla. | Hou. | Chi. | Stl. | Cin. | Mil. | Pit. | S.D. | S.F. | L.A. | Col. | Ari. | Cle. | ChW | K.C. | Min. | Det. | W | L | Pct. | GB |
|---|---|---|---|---|---|---|---|---|---|---|---|---|---|---|---|---|---|---|---|---|---|---|---|---|---|
| Houston | 5 | 5 | 7 | 7 | 6 | ... | 7 | 5 | 8 | 9 | 9 | 5 | 6 | 3 | 5 | 5 | 2 | 2 | 2 | 1 | 3 | 102 | 60 | .630 | ... |
| Chicago | 6 | 4 | 3 | 7 | 7 | 4 | ... | 4 | 6 | 6 | 8 | 5 | 7 | 4 | 7 | 7 | 0 | 3 | 1 | 1 | 0 | 90 | 73 | .552 | 12.5 |
| St. Louis | 3 | 3 | 6 | 6 | 5 | 7 | 7 | ... | 3 | 8 | 5 | 3 | 5 | 5 | 6 | 7 | 0 | 1 | 1 | 1 | 1 | 83 | 79 | .512 | 19 |
| Cincinnati | 2 | 3 | 4 | 8 | 9 | 3 | 5 | 8 | ... | 6 | 5 | 1 | 2 | 5 | 4 | 5 | 1 | 1 | 0 | 2 | 3 | 77 | 85 | .475 | 25 |
| Milwaukee | 2 | 1 | 4 | 6 | 9 | 2 | 6 | 3 | 5 | ... | 6 | 3 | 5 | 4 | 7 | 3 | 1 | 2 | 2 | 2 | 1 | 74 | 88 | .457 | 28 |
| Pittsburgh | 2 | 5 | 1 | 7 | 6 | 2 | 3 | 6 | 7 | 5 | ... | 5 | 2 | 5 | 4 | 3 | 2 | 0 | 1 | 2 | 1 | 69 | 93 | .426 | 33 |

**West Division**

| Team | Atl. | N.Y. | Phi. | Mtl. | Fla. | Hou. | Chi. | Stl. | Cin. | Mil. | Pit. | S.D. | S.F. | L.A. | Col. | Ari. | Tex. | Ana. | Sea. | Oak. | W | L | Pct. | GB |
|---|---|---|---|---|---|---|---|---|---|---|---|---|---|---|---|---|---|---|---|---|---|---|---|---|
| San Diego | 4 | 5 | 8 | 4 | 5 | 4 | 4 | 6 | 11 | 6 | 4 | ... | 8 | 7 | 7 | 9 | 1 | 2 | 2 | 1 | 98 | 64 | .605 | ... |
| San Fran. | 2 | 5 | 6 | 6 | 9 | 3 | 3 | 7 | 7 | 4 | 7 | 4 | ... | 6 | 5 | 7 | 2 | 2 | 2 | 2 | 89 | 74 | .546 | 9.5 |
| Los Angeles | 1 | 3 | 5 | 5 | 5 | 6 | 5 | 4 | 4 | 5 | 7 | 5 | 6 | ... | 6 | 8 | 3 | 1 | 2 | 2 | 83 | 79 | .512 | 15 |
| Colorado | 3 | 3 | 5 | 7 | 6 | 6 | 2 | 3 | 5 | 4 | 5 | 5 | 7 | 6 | ... | 6 | 1 | 0 | 1 | 2 | 77 | 85 | .475 | 21 |
| Arizona | 1 | 4 | 2 | 2 | 6 | 4 | 5 | 2 | 4 | 6 | 6 | 3 | 5 | 4 | 6 | ... | 1 | 1 | 2 | 1 | 65 | 97 | .401 | 33 |

## LEADERS

**American League**
**BA:** Bernie Williams, N.Y., .339.
**Runs:** Derek Jeter, N.Y., 127.
**Hits:** Alex Rodriguez, Sea., 213.
**TB:** Albert Belle, Chi., 399.
**HR:** Ken Griffey Jr., Sea., 56.
**RBI:** Juan Gonzalez, Tex., 157.
**SB:** Rickey Henderson, Oak., 66.
**Wins:** Roger Clemens, Tor., David Cone, N.Y., Rick Helling, Tex., 20.
**ERA:** Roger Clemens, Tor., 2.65.
**CG:** Scott Erickson, Bal., 11.
**IP:** Scott Erickson, Bal., 251.1.
**SO:** Roger Clemens, Tor., 271.
**Sv.:** Tom Gordon, Bos., 46.

**National League**
**BA:** Larry Walker, Col., .363.
**Runs:** Sammy Sosa, Chi., 134.
**Hits:** Dante Bichette, Col., 219.
**TB:** Sammy Sosa, Chi., 416.
**HR:** Mark McGwire, St.L., 70.
**RBI:** Sammy Sosa, Chi., 158.
**SB:** Tony Womack, Pit., 58.
**Wins:** Tom Glavine, Atl., 20.
**ERA:** Greg Maddux, Atl., 2.22.
**CG:** Curt Schilling, Phi., 15.
**IP:** Curt Schilling, Phi., 268.2.
**SO:** Curt Schilling, Phi., 300.
**Sv.:** Trevor Hoffman, S.D., 53.

**A.L. 20-game winners**
Roger Clemens, Tor., 20
David Cone, N.Y., 20
Rick Helling, Tex., 20

**N.L. 20-game winner**
Tom Glavine, Atl., 20

**A.L. 100 RBIs**
Juan Gonzalez, Tex., 157
Albert Belle, Chi., 152
Ken Griffey Jr., Sea., 146
Manny Ramirez, Cle., 145
Alex Rodriguez, Sea., 124
Tino Martinez, N.Y., 123
Nomar Garciaparra, Bos., 122
Rafael Palmeiro, Bal., 121
Dean Palmer, K.C., 119
Paul O'Neill, N.Y., 116
Carlos Delgado, Tor., 115
Mo Vaughn, Bos., 115
Jason Giambi, Oak., 110
Frank Thomas, Chi., 109
Rusty Greer, Tex., 108
Jose Canseco, Tor., 107
Matt Stairs, Oak., 106
Tony Clark, Det., 103
Will Clark, Tex., 102
Edgar Martinez, Sea., 102
Damion Easley, Det., 100
Shawn Green, Tor., 100

**N.L. 100 RBIs**
Sammy Sosa, Chi., 158
Mark McGwire, St.L., 147
Vinny Castilla, Col., 144
Jeff Kent, S.F., 128
Jeromy Burnitz, Mil., 125
Moises Alou, Hou., 124
Dante Bichette, Col., 122
Barry Bonds, S.F., 122
Andres Galarraga, Atl., 121
Greg Vaughn, S.D., 119
Jeff Bagwell, Hou., 111
Mike Piazza, L.A., Fla., N.Y., 111
Scott Rolen, Phi., 110
Vladimir Guerrero, Mon., 109
Derek Bell, Hou., 108
Kevin Young, Pit., 108
Chipper Jones, Atl., 107
Javy Lopez, Atl., 106
Ray Lankford, St.L., 105
Rico Brogna, Phi., 104

**A.L. 40 homers**
Ken Griffey Jr., Sea., 56
Albert Belle, Chi., 49
Jose Canseco, Tor., 46
Juan Gonzalez, Tex., 45
Manny Ramirez, Cle., 45
Rafael Palmeiro, Bal., 43
Alex Rodriguez, Sea., 42
Mo Vaughn, Bos., 40

**N.L. 40 homers**
Mark McGwire, St.L., 70
Sammy Sosa, Chi., 66
Greg Vaughn, S.D., 50
Vinny Castilla, Col., 46
Andres Galarraga, Atl., 44

**Most Valuable Player**
A.L.: Juan Gonzalez, OF, Tex.
N.L.: Sammy Sosa, OF, Chi.

**Cy Young Award**
A.L.: Roger Clemens, Tor.
N.L.: Tom Glavine, Atl.

**Rookie of the Year**
A.L.: Ben Grieve, OF, Oak.
N.L.: Kerry Wood, P, Chi.

**Manager of the Year**
A.L.: Joe Torre, N.Y.
N.L.: Larry Dierker, Hou.

**Hall of Fame additions**
George Davis, SS, 1890-1909
Larry Doby, OF, 1947-59.
Lee MacPhail, Executive
Joe Rogan, P, Negro Leagues
Don Sutton, P, 1966-88

## SIGNIFICANT EVENTS

■ **March 31:** Two expansion teams made their major league debut, Arizona losing 9-2 to the Colorado Rockies at new Bank One Ballpark in Phoenix and Tampa Bay dropping an 11-6 decision to Detroit at new Tropicana Field.

■ **March 31:** The Milwaukee Brewers, transplanted to the National League because of expansion, lost their first N.L. game, 2-1, at Atlanta. The Brewers became the first modern-era team in baseball history to switch leagues.

■ **April 15:** The New York Yankees, forced to temporarily abandon Yankee Stadium when a steel beam fell from beneath the upper deck to the empty seats below, posted a 6-3 win over the Angels at Shea Stadium, home of the Mets. The Mets came back that night to beat the Cubs 2-1—the first time this century that two regular-season games involving four teams were played in the same stadium on the same day.

■ **July 9:** After serving as chairman of the Executive Committee and interim commissioner for almost six years, Allan (Bud) Selig, the Milwaukee Brewers' president and chief executive officer, accepted a five-year term as baseball's ninth commissioner.

■ **August 9:** Atlanta veteran Dennis Martinez posted his 244th career victory in a relief role against San Francisco, making him the winningest Latin pitcher in major league history.

■ **September 28:** Gary Gaetti's two-run homer lifted Chicago to a 5-3 win over San Francisco in the first-ever playoff to decide a league's wild-card representative.

■ **December 12:** The Los Angeles Dodgers broke new ground when they signed pitcher Kevin Brown to a seven-year contract worth \$105 million—the first \$100 million deal in baseball history.

## MEMORABLE MOMENTS

■ **May 6:** Chicago Cubs rookie Kerry Wood tied Roger Clemens' single-game strikeout record when he fanned 20 Houston batters in a one-hit, 2-0 shutout at Wrigley Field.

■ **May 17:** Lefthander David Wells fired the first regular-season perfect game in New York Yankees history and the 13th perfecto of the modern era when he retired all 27 Minnesota Twins he faced in a 4-0 win before 49,820 fans at Yankee Stadium.

■ **September 8:** St. Louis first baseman Mark McGwire broke Roger Maris' 37-year-old single-season home run record when he drove a pitch from Chicago righthander Steve Trachsel over the left field fence at Busch Stadium for homer No. 62.

■ **September 13:** Chicago right fielder Sammy Sosa, following McGwire's home run lead, hit Nos. 61 and 62 during a Sunday night victory over Milwaukee at Wrigley Field.

■ **September 20:** Baltimore third baseman Cal Ripken ended his record ironman streak at 2,632 consecutive games when he sat out against the New York Yankees in the Orioles' final home contest of the season.

■ **September 25:** The Yankees posted a 6-1 victory over Tampa Bay at Yankee Stadium for their 112th win, topping the American League record of 111 set by the 1954 Cleveland Indians. The Yanks would go on to win 114 times.

■ **September 27:** McGwire, who trailed Sosa briefly on the final Friday of the great 1998 home run race, capped a five-homer final weekend with two final-day shots against Montreal, bringing his record season total to 70.

## ALL-STAR GAME

■ **Winner:** The A.L. obliterated the N.L. with a 19-hit, five-stolen base barrage that resulted in a 13-8 victory. The A.L.'s second straight win featured home runs by Alex Rodriguez and Roberto Alomar and a surprising running attack.

■ **Key inning:** The sixth, when the A.L. broke out its ugly game and scored three times for an 8-6 lead. The rally off Montreal righthander Ugueth Urbina featured four stolen bases and runners crossing the plate on a wild pitch and a passed ball. The uprising wiped out a three-run fifth-inning homer by San Francisco's Barry Bonds.

■ **Memorable moment:** A towering two-run double to right by third baseman Cal Ripken in the fourth. The double was Ripken's 11th hit in his 16th All-Star Game.

■ **Top guns:** Rafael Palmeiro (Orioles), Alex Rodriguez (Mariners), Ken Griffey Jr. (Mariners), Roberto Alomar (Indians), Ripken (Orioles), David Wells (Yankees), A.L.; Bonds (Giants), Tony Gwynn (Padres), N.L.

■ **MVP:** Roberto Alomar.

**Linescore**

July 7 at Colorado's Coors Field
A.L. ............0 0 0 4 1 3 1 1 3—13 19 2
N.L. ............0 0 2 1 3 0 0 2 0— 8 12 1
Wells (Yankees), Clemens (Blue Jays) 3, Radke (Twins) 4, Colon (Indians) 5, Arrojo (Devil Rays) 6, Wetteland (Rangers) 7, Gordon (Red Sox) 8, Percival (Angels) 9 and I. Rodriguez (Rangers), S. Alomar (Indians); Maddux (Braves), Glavine (Braves) 3, Brown (Padres) 4, Ashby (Padres) 5, Urbina (Expos) 6, Hoffman (Padres) 7, Shaw (Dodgers) 8, Nen (Giants) 9 and Piazza (Mets), Lopez (Braves). W—Colon. L—Urbina. HR—A. Rodriguez, R. Alomar, A.L.; Bonds, N.L.

## A.L. DIVISION SERIES

■ **Winners:** The New York Yankees, who won an A.L.-record 114 regular-season games, carried that dominance into the postseason with a three-game Division Series sweep of the Texas Rangers, and the Cleveland Indians earned their third ALCS berth in four years with an exciting four-game victory over the wild-card Boston Red Sox. Yankee pitchers shut down the A.L.'s top-hitting team (a .141 average) en route to their second ALCS opportunity in three years and the Indians overcame an 11-3 series-opening loss while extending Boston's 80-year World Series championship drought.

■ **Turning points:** What little offense the Yankees needed in 2-0, 3-1 and 4-0 victories was provided by unlikely sources: Third baseman Scott Brosius singled in the go-ahead run in Game 1 and hit a lead-extending two-run homer in Game 2; backup outfielder Shane Spencer homered in Game 2 and hit a key three-run shot in Game 3. A Game 2 first-inning ejection of Cleveland manager Mike Hargrove and starting pitcher Dwight Gooden seemed to energize the lethargic Indians, who erupted for six runs in the first two innings and went on to a 9-5 series-squaring win.

■ **Memorable moments:** A Game 3 Texas-type downpour that forced a 3-hour, 16-minute rain delay in Game 3, but merely delayed the inevitable for the Rangers. The delay knocked Yankee starter David Cone out of the game, but three relievers came on to complete his shutout and Spencer delivered the big blow. Left fielder David Justice provided the big plays in Game 4 for the Indians, a sixth-inning throw that cut down Boston runner John Valentin at the plate and a two-run, eighth-inning double that secured a 2-1 victory.

■ **Memorable performances:** Brosius and Spencer combined for seven of the Yankees' eight RBIs in the series, but the real heroes were pitchers David Wells, Andy Pettitte, Cone, Mariano Rivera, Jeff Nelson and Graeme Lloyd, who combined for a 0.33 ERA—allowing only one run in three games. Texas starters—Todd Stottlemyre, Rick Helling, Aaron Sele—all pitched well, but got little run support. Kenny Lofton, Manny Ramirez, Jim Thome and Justice provided the bulk of Cleveland's offense and the Indians got good pitching from starters Charles Nagy and Bartolo Colon and three saves from Mike Jackson. First baseman Mo Vaughn (2 homers, 7 RBIs) and shortstop Nomar Garciaparra (3, 11) were prolific offensively for the losing Red Sox.

**Linescores**

New York vs. Texas

**Game 1**—September 29, at New York
Texas..............0 0 0 0 0 0 0 0 0—0 5 0
New York........0 2 0 0 0 0 0 0 x—2 6 0
Stottlemyre and Rodriguez; Wells, Rivera (9) and Posada. W—Wells. L—Stottlemyre. S—Rivera.

**Game 2**—September 30, at New York
Texas..............0 0 0 0 1 0 0 0 0—1 5 0
New York........0 1 0 2 0 0 0 0 x—3 8 0
Helling, Crabtree (7) and Rodriguez; Pettitte, Nelson (8), Rivera (8) and Girardi. W—Pettitte. L—Helling. S—Rivera. HR—Spencer, Brosius (N.Y.).

**Game 3**—October 2, at Texas
New York........0 0 0 0 0 4 0 0 0—4 9 1
Texas..............0 0 0 0 0 0 0 0 0—0 3 1
Cone, Lloyd (6), Nelson (7), Rivera (9) and Girardi; Sele, Crabtree (7), Wetteland (9) and Rodriguez. W—Cone. L—Sele. HR—O'Neill, Spencer (N.Y.).

Boston vs. Cleveland

**Game 1**—September 29, at Cleveland
Boston........3 0 0  0 3 2  0 3 0—11 12 0
Cleveland....0 0 0  0 0 2  1 0 0— 3  7  0
Martinez, Corsi (8) and Hatteberg; Wright, Jones (5), Reed (8), Poole (8), Shuey (8), Assenmacher (9) and Alomar. W—Martinez. L—Wright. HR—Vaughn 2, Garciaparra (Bos.); Lofton, Thome (Cle.).

**Game 2**—September 30, at Cleveland
Boston..........2 0 1  0 0 2  0 0 0—5 10 0
Cleveland......1 5 1  0 0 1  0 1 x—9  9  1
Wakefield, Wasdin (2), Lowe (4), Swindell (6), Gordon (8) and Varitek; Gooden, Burba (1), Shuey (6), Assenmacher (8), Jackson (8) and Alomar. W—Burba. L—Wakefield. S—Jackson. HR—Justice (Cle.).

**Game 3**—October 2, at Boston
Cleveland........0 0 0  0 1 1  1 0 1—4 5 0
Boston............0 0 0  1 0 0  0 0 2—3 6 0
Nagy, Jackson (9) and Alomar; Saberhagen, Corsi (8), Eckersley (9) and Hatteberg. W—Nagy. L—Saberhagen. S—Jackson. HR—Thome, Lofton, M. Ramirez 2 (Cle.); Garciaparra (Bos.).

**Game 4**—October 3, at Boston
Cleveland........0 0 0  0 0 0  0 2 0—2 5 0
Boston............0 0 0  1 0 0  0 0 0—1 6 0
Colon, Poole (6), Reed (7), Assenmacher (8), Shuey (8), Jackson (9) and Alomar; Schourek, Lowe (6), Gordon (8) and Hatteberg. W—Reed. L—Gordon. S—Jackson. HR—Garciaparra (Bos.).

## N.L. DIVISION SERIES

■ **Winners:** The Atlanta Braves earned their seventh straight N.L. Championship Series berth by sweeping past the wild-card Chicago Cubs, and the San Diego Padres reached the NLCS for the first time since 1984 by throttling the Houston Astros and their N.L.-leading offense. Braves pitchers simply were too much for the overmatched Cubs, who scored only four runs in the three games, and the Padres followed that lead by holding the high-powered Astros to a .182 average in a surprising four-game victory.
■ **Turning points:** The Braves took control of the series in Game 2 when they tied the game at 1-1 in the bottom of the ninth and then won in the 10th on a Chipper Jones single down the left field line. The Padres served notice to the Astros in Game 1 when starter Kevin Brown struck out 16 batters and allowed two hits over eight innings while outdueling Houston ace Randy Johnson, 2-1.
■ **Memorable moments:** The ninth inning of Game 2, when Atlanta catcher Javy Lopez connected off Chicago pitcher Kevin Tapani for a one-out home run that tied the game 1-1. The Padres got a dramatic Game 2-tying home run from Jim Leyritz off Houston closer Billy Wagner in the ninth inning, but the Astros rebounded in the bottom of the ninth to post a 5-4 victory—their only win of the series.
■ **Memorable performances:** Atlanta catchers Lopez and Eddie Perez combined for eight RBIs and Braves pitchers, led by starters John Smoltz, Tom Glavine and Greg Maddux, posted a 1.29 ERA. Tapani and rookie Kerry Wood had outstanding starting efforts for the Cubs, but there was too little offensive support. San Diego's biggest offensive gun was Leyritz, who came off the bench to hit three home runs, while pitchers Brown and Sterling Hitchcock led a staff that compiled a 1.78 ERA. Johnson allowed only three earned runs in two starts covering 14 innings for the Astros, but all he had to show for his efforts were two losses.

**Linescores**

Chicago vs. Atlanta

**Game 1**—September 30, at Atlanta
Chicago.........0 0 0  0 0 0  0 1 0—1 5 1
Atlanta .........0 2 0  0 0 1  4 0 x—7 8 0
Clark, Heredia (7), Karchner (7), Morgan (8) and Houston; Smoltz, Rocker (8), Ligtenberg (9) and Lopez. W—Smoltz. L—Clark. HR—Houston (Chi.); Tucker, Klesko (Atl.).

**Game 2**—October 1, at Atlanta
Chicago....0 0 0  0 0 1  0 0 0  0—1 4 1
Atlanta ....0 0 0  0 0 0  0 0 1  1—2 6 0
Tapani, Mulholland (10) and Servais, Houston; Glavine, Rocker (8), Seanez (9), O. Perez (10) and Lopez. W—O. Perez. L—Mulholland. HR—Lopez (Atl.).

**Game 3**—October 3, at Chicago
Atlanta...........0 0 1  0 0 0  0 5 0—6 9 0
Chicago..........0 0 0  0 0 0  0 2 0—2 8 2
Maddux, Ligtenberg (8) and E. Perez; Wood, Mulholland (6), Beck (8), Morgan (9) and Houston, Martinez. W—Maddux. L—Wood. HR—E. Perez (Atl.).

Houston vs. San Diego

**Game 1**—September 29, at Houston
San Diego ......0 0 0  0 0 1  0 1 0—2 9 1
Houston .........0 0 0  0 0 0  0 0 1—1 4 0
Brown, Hoffman (9) and Hernandez; Johnson, Powell (9), Henry (9) and Ausmus. W—Brown. L—Johnson. S—Hoffman. HR—Vaughn (S.D.).

**Game 2**—October 1, at Houston
San Diego ....0 0 0  0 0 2  0 0 2—4  8 1
Houston ......1 0 2  0 0 0  0 1 1—5 11 1
Ashby, Hamilton (5), Wall (8), Miceli (9), Hoffman (9) and Hernandez, Myers; Reynolds, Powell (8), Wagner (9) and Eusebio, Ausmus. W—Wagner. L—Miceli. HR—Leyritz (S.D.); Bell (Hou.).

**Game 3**—October 3, at San Diego
Houston ........0 0 0  0 0 0  1 0 0—1 4 0
San Diego ......0 0 0  0 0 1  1 0 x—2 3 0
Hampton, Elarton (7) and Ausmus; Brown, Miceli (7), Hoffman (9) and Hernandez. W—Miceli. L—Elarton. S—Hoffman. HR—Leyritz (S.D.).

**Game 4**—October 4, at San Diego
Houston ........0 0 0  1 0 0  0 0 0—1 3 1
San Diego ......0 1 0  0 0 1  0 4 x—6 7 1
Johnson, Miller (7), Henry (7), Powell (8) and Ausmus; Hitchcock, Hamilton (7), Miceli (7), Hoffman (9) and Leyritz, Hernandez. W—Hitchcock. L—Johnson. HR—Leyritz, Joyner (S.D.).

## ALCS

■ **Winner:** The New York Yankees raised their incredible 1998 season record to 121-50 with a surprisingly difficult six-game victory over Cleveland. After watching the Indians jump to a two-games-to-one advantage, the Yankees won three straight times and advanced to the franchise's record 35th World Series.
■ **Turning point:** Down two-games-to-one and in danger of watching an incredible season unravel, the Yankees tied the series at Cleveland's Jacobs Field behind the four-hit pitching of Orlando Hernandez, Mike Stanton and Mariano Rivera, who combined for a 4-0 shutout of the powerful Indians. Paul O'Neill provided all the offense the trio would need with a solo home run in the first inning.
■ **Memorable moment:** The 12th inning of Game 2 at New York, when a sacrifice bunt by Cleveland's Travis Fryman transformed a 1-1 tie into a 4-1 Indians victory. Yankees first baseman Tino Martinez fielded the bunt and fired to second baseman Chuck Knoblauch covering first. But the ball hit Fryman, who appeared to be running illegally inside the line, and caromed about 20 feet away. Instead of chasing the ball, Knoblauch argued the noncall of umpire Ted Hendry as pinch runner Enrique Wilson circled the bases to score the go-ahead run. Kenny Lofton's two-run single finished the Yankees in an ugly and controversial end to what had been a well-played game.
■ **Top guns:** Bernie Williams (.381, 5 RBIs), Scott Brosius (.300, 6 RBIs), Hernandez (1-0, 0.00 ERA), David Wells (2-0, 2.87), Rivera (4 games, 0.00), Yankees; Omar Vizquel (.440), Jim Thome (.304, 4 HRs, 8 RBIs), Manny Ramirez (.333, 2 HRs, 4 RBIs), Bartolo Colon (1-0, 1.00 ERA), Paul Shuey (5 games, 0.00), Indians.
■ **MVP:** Wells.

**Linescores**

**Game 1**—October 6, a New York
Cleveland......0 0 0  0 0 0  0 0 2—2  5 0
New York......5 0 0  0 0 1  1 0 x—7 11 0
Wright, Ogea (1), Poole (7), Reed (7), Shuey (8) and Alomar, Diaz; Wells, Nelson (9) and Posada. W—Wells. L—Wright. HR—Ramirez (Cle.); Posada (N.Y.).

**Game 2**—October 7, at New York
Cleveland0 0 0  1 0 0  0 0 0  0 0 3—4 7 1
New York0 0 0  0 0 0  1 0 0  0 0 0—1 7 1
Nagy, Reed (7), Poole (8), Shuey (8), Assenmacher (10), Burba (11), Jackson (12) and Alomar; Cone, Rivera (9), Stanton (11), Nelson (11), Lloyd (12) and Girardi. W—Burba. L—Nelson. S—Jackson. HR—Justice (Cle.).

**Game 3**—October 9, at Cleveland
New York......1 0 0  0 0 0  0 0 0—1 4 0
Cleveland......0 2 0  0 4 0  0 0 x—6 12 0
Pettitte, Mendoza (5), Stanton (7) and Girardi, Posada; Colon and Alomar. W—Colon. L—Pettitte. HR—Thome 2, Ramirez, Whiten (Cle.).

**Game 4**—October 10, at Cleveland
New York.......1 0 0  2 0 0  0 0 1—4 4 0
Cleveland........0 0 0  0 0 0  0 0 0—0 4 3
Hernandez, Stanton (8), Rivera (9) and Posada; Gooden, Poole (5), Burba (6), Shuey (9) and Alomar, Diaz. W—Hernandez. L—Gooden. HR—O'Neill (N.Y.).

**Game 5**—October 11, at Cleveland
New York........3 1 0  1 0 0  0 0 0—5 6 0
Cleveland........2 0 0  0 0 1  0 0 0—3 8 0
Wells, Nelson (8), Rivera (8) and Posada; Ogea, Wright (2), Reed (8), Assenmacher (8), Shuey (9) and Diaz. W—Wells. L—Ogea. S—Rivera. HR—Lofton, Thome (Cle.); Davis (N.Y.).

**Game 6**—October 13, at New York
Cleveland......0 0 0  0 5 0  0 0 0—5  8 3
New York......2 1 3  0 0 3  0 0 x—9 11 1
Nagy, Burba (4), Poole (6), Shuey (6), Assenmacher (8) and Alomar, Diaz; Cone, Mendoza (6), Rivera (9) and Girardi. W—Cone. L—Nagy. HR—Brosius (N.Y.); Thome (Cle.).

## NLCS

■ **Winner:** The San Diego Padres, the dark horse in National League playoffs that featured high-powered teams from Houston and Atlanta, claimed the second pennant of their 30-year existence with a six-game victory over the N.L. East Division-champion Braves, who had won a club-record 106 games during the regular season. The Padres, 98-game winners, beat the Braves at their own game—pitching and defense—and gave them the distinction of becoming the winningest team not to reach the World Series.
■ **Turning point:** Game 3, when the Braves loaded the bases three times—twice with less than two out—and failed to score. Starting pitcher Sterling Hitchcock worked out of the first jam, Dan Miceli came out of the bullpen in the sixth to strike out consecutive pinch hitters and Trevor Hoffman came on in the eighth to strike out catcher Javy Lopez, who represented the potential winning run. The Padres' 4-1 win over Greg Maddux gave them a shocking three-games-to-none advantage over an experienced Braves team appearing in its seventh straight NLCS.
■ **Memorable moment:** Michael Tucker's three-run, eighth-inning homer off Padres ace Kevin Brown in Game 5, a blow that temporarily rescued the Braves from elimination and gave them hope of becoming the first baseball team to come back and win a postseason series after losing the first three games. Brown, who was making a surprise relief appearance after throwing a three-hit shutout in Game 2, escaped a seventh-inning jam but coughed up a 4-2 San Diego lead in the eighth when he walked Ryan Klesko, gave up an infield single to Lopez and then surrendered the game-turning homer to Tucker.
■ **Top guns:** Ozzie Guillen (.417), Tucker (.385, 1 HR, 5 RBIs), John Rocker (6 games, 1-0, 0.00 ERA), Braves; John Vander Wal (.429), Steve Finley (.333), Ken Caminiti (2 HRs, 4 RBIs), Brown (1-1, 2.61 ERA), Hitchcock (2-0, 0-90), Padres.
■ **MVP:** Hitchcock.

**Game 1**—October 7, at Atlanta
San Diego....0 0 0  0 1 0  0 1 0  1—3 7 0
Atlanta ........0 0 1  0 0 0  0 0 1  0—2 8 3
Ashby, R. Myers (8), Miceli (8), Hoffman (8), Wall (10) and Hernandez; Smoltz, Rocker (8), Martinez (8), Ligtenberg (9) and Lopez, E. Perez. W—Hoffman. L—Ligtenberg. S—Wall. HR—A. Jones (Atl.); Caminiti (S.D.).

**Game 2**—October 8, at Atlanta
San Diego ....0 0 0  0 0 1  0 0 2—3 11 0
Atlanta.........0 0 0  0 0 0  0 0 0—0  3 1
Brown and Hernandez; Glavine, Rocker (7), Seanez (8), O. Perez (9), Ligtenberg (9) and Lopez. W—Brown. L—Glavine.

**Game 3**—October 10, at San Diego
Atlanta ..........0 0 1  0 0 0  0 0 0—1 8 2
San Diego ......0 0 0  0 2 0  0 2 x—4 7 0
Maddux, Martinez (6), Rocker (7), Seanez (8) and E. Perez, Lopez; Hitchcock, Wall (6), Miceli (8) R. Myers (8), Hoffman (8) and Leyritz, Hernandez. W—Hitchcock. L—Maddux. S—Hoffman.

**Game 4**—October 11, at San Diego
Atlanta..........0 0 0  1 0 1  6 0 0—8 12 0
San Diego ....0 0 2  0 0 1  0 0 0—3  8 0
Neagle, Martinez (6), Rocker (7), O. Perez (8), Seanez (8), Ligtenberg (9) and Lopez; Hamilton, R. Myers (7), Miceli (7), Boehringer (8), Langston (9) and Hernandez. W—Martinez. L—Hamilton. HR—Leyritz (S.D.); Lopez, Galarraga (Atl.).

**Game 5**—October 12, at San Diego
Atlanta..........0 0 0  1 0 1  0 5 0—7 14 1
San Diego ....2 0 0  0 0 2  0 0 2—6 10 1
Smoltz, Rocker (7), Seanez (8), Ligtenberg (9), Maddux (9) and Lopez, E. Perez; Ashby, Langston (7), Brown (7), Wall (8), Boehringer (9), R. Myers (9) and Hernandez. W—Rocker. L—Brown. S—Maddux. HR—Caminiti, Vander Wal (S.D.); Tucker (Atl.).

**Game 6**—October 14, at Atlanta
San Diego ....0 0 0  0 0 5  0 0 0—5 10 0
Atlanta..........0 0 0  0 0 0  0 0 0—0  2 1
Hitchcock, Boehringer (6), Langston (7), Hamilton (7), Hoffman (9) and Leyritz, Hernandez; Glavine, Rocker (6), Martinez (6), Neagle (8) and Lopez. W—Hitchcock. L—Glavine.

## WORLD SERIES

■ **Winner:** New York closed out its remarkable season with a four-game sweep of San Diego, giving the Yankees a shockingly efficient 125-50 final 1998 record, including regular season and playoffs. The World Series championship was New York's record 24th overall and second in three years. The sweep was the first in Series play since 1990.
■ **Turning point:** A second-inning Chili Davis smash in Game 1 that struck the left shin of Padres righthander Kevin Brown. San Diego's ace went on to pitch 61/3 innings before leaving with a sore leg and the Yankees exploded for seven runs in the seventh inning, turning a 5-2 deficit into a 9-5 advantage. New York's 9-6 win deflated the overmatched Padres.
■ **Memorable moment:** When Scott Brosius, the World Series MVP, hit a three-run, eighth-inning Game 3 home run off San Diego closer Trevor Hoffman, wiping away a 3-2 New York deficit and giving the Yankees a lead they never relinquished. It was Brosius' second homer of the game and he finished the 5-4 victory with four RBIs.
■ **Top guns:** Tony Gwynn (.500, 3 RBIs), Greg Vaughn (2 HR, 4 RBIs), Sterling Hitchcock (1.50 ERA), Padres; Ricky Ledee (.600, 4 RBIs), Brosius (.471, 2 HR, 6 RBIs), Tino Martinez (.385, 1 HR, 4 RBIs), Andy Pettitte (1-0, 0.00 ERA), Orlando Hernandez (1-0, 1.29 ERA), Mariano Rivera (3 games, 0.00 ERA, 3 saves), Yankees.
■ **MVP:** Brosius.

**Game 1**—October 17, at New York
San Diego ......0 0 2  0 3 0  0 1 0—6 8 1
New York........0 2 0  0 0 0  7 0 x—9 9 1
Brown, Wall (7), Langston (7), Boehringer (8), R. Myers (8) and C. Hernandez; Wells, Nelson (8), Rivera (8) and Posada. W—Wells. L—Wall. S—Rivera. HR—Vaughn 2, Gwynn (S.D.); Knoblauch, Martinez (N.Y.).

**Game 2**—October 18, at New York
San Diego ....0 0 0  0 1 0  0 2 0—3 10 1
New York......3 3 1  0 2 0  0 0 x—9 16 0
Ashby, Boehringer (3), Wall (5), Miceli (8) and G. Myers; O. Hernandez, Stanton (8), Nelson (8) and Posada. W—O. Hernandez. L—Ashby. HR—Williams, Posada (N.Y.).

**Game 3**—October 20, at San Diego
New York........0 0 0  0 0 0  2 3 0—5 9 1
San Diego ......0 0 0  0 0 3  0 1 0—4 7 1
Cone, Lloyd (7), Mendoza (7), Rivera (8) and Girardi; Hitchcock, Hamilton (7), R. Myers (8), Hoffman (8) and Leyritz, C. Hernandez. W—Mendoza. L—Hoffman. S—Rivera. HR—Brosius 2 (N.Y.).

**Game 4**—October 21, at San Diego
New York........0 0 0  0 0 1  0 2 0—3 9 0
San Diego ......0 0 0  0 0 0  0 0 0—0 7 0
Pettitte, Nelson (8), Rivera (8) and Girardi; Brown, Miceli (9), R. Myers (9) and C. Hernandez. W—Pettitte. L—Brown. S—Rivera.

**Roger Clemens made it two Cy Young Awards in his two years with Toronto.**

# 1999

## FINAL STANDINGS

### American League

#### East Division

| Team | N.Y. | Bos | Tor. | Bal. | T.B. | Cle. | Chi. | Det. | K.C. | Min. | Tex. | Oak. | Sea. | Ana. | Atl. | N.Y. | Phi. | Mon. | Fla. | W | L | Pct. | GB |
|---|---|---|---|---|---|---|---|---|---|---|---|---|---|---|---|---|---|---|---|---|---|---|---|
| New York | ... | 4 | 10 | 9 | 8 | 7 | 7 | 7 | 4 | 6 | 8 | 6 | 9 | 4 | 1 | 3 | 1 | 2 | 2 | 98 | 64 | .605 | ... |
| Boston | 8 | ... | 9 | 7 | 4 | 8 | 7 | 7 | 8 | 6 | 4 | 4 | 7 | 9 | 2 | 1 | 1 | 0 | 2 | 94 | 68 | .580 | 4 |
| Toronto | 2 | 3 | ... | 11 | 8 | 7 | 4 | 10 | 7 | 6 | 4 | 2 | 2 | 9 | 3 | 0 | 1 | 4 | 1 | 84 | 78 | .519 | 14 |
| Baltimore | 4 | 5 | 1 | ... | 5 | 1 | 7 | 5 | 6 | 8 | 6 | 5 | 5 | 9 | 3 | 1 | 3 | 3 | 1 | 78 | 84 | .481 | 20 |
| Tampa Bay | 4 | 9 | 5 | 7 | ... | 4 | 4 | 5 | 8 | 5 | 4 | 1 | 4 | 5 | 0 | 1 | 1 | 1 | 1 | 69 | 93 | .426 | 29 |

#### Central Division

| Team | Cle. | Chi. | Det. | K.C. | Min. | N.Y. | Bos. | Tor. | Bal. | T.B. | Tex. | Oak. | Sea. | Ana. | Hou. | Cin. | Pit. | St.L. | Mil. | Chi. | W | L | Pct. | GB |
|---|---|---|---|---|---|---|---|---|---|---|---|---|---|---|---|---|---|---|---|---|---|---|---|---|
| Cleveland | ... | 9 | 8 | 7 | 9 | 3 | 4 | 5 | 9 | 5 | 3 | 10 | 7 | 9 | 1 | 4 | 1 | ... | 1 | 2 | 97 | 65 | .599 | ... |
| Chicago | 2 | ... | 7 | 6 | 8 | 5 | 5 | 6 | 3 | 6 | 5 | 3 | 4 | 5 | 1 | ... | 2 | 1 | 1 | 4 | 75 | 86 | .466 | 21.5 |
| Detroit | 5 | 5 | ... | 7 | 6 | 5 | 5 | 2 | 5 | 4 | 5 | 4 | 3 | 5 | 0 | 2 | 2 | 3 | 1 | ... | 69 | 92 | .429 | 27.5 |
| Kansas City | 5 | 6 | 4 | ... | 5 | 5 | 2 | 3 | 4 | 2 | 4 | 6 | 7 | 5 | 0 | 0 | 1 | 2 | 1 | 2 | 64 | 97 | .398 | 32.5 |
| Minnesota | 3 | 3 | 6 | 8 | ... | 4 | 4 | 4 | 1 | 5 | 0 | 7 | 4 | 4 | 1 | 2 | 2 | 2 | 2 | 1 | 63 | 97 | .394 | 33 |

#### West Division

| Team | Tex. | Oak. | Sea. | Ana. | N.Y. | Bos. | Tor. | Bal. | T.B. | Cle. | Chi. | Det. | K.C. | Min. | Ari. | S.F. | L.A. | S.D. | Col. | W | L | PCT | GB |
|---|---|---|---|---|---|---|---|---|---|---|---|---|---|---|---|---|---|---|---|---|---|---|---|
| Texas | ... | 7 | 8 | 6 | 4 | 5 | 6 | 6 | 8 | 7 | 5 | 5 | 6 | 12 | 3 | 3 | 2 | 1 | 1 | 95 | 67 | .586 | ... |
| Oakland | 5 | ... | 6 | 4 | 4 | 6 | 8 | 7 | 9 | 2 | 7 | 6 | 6 | 5 | 2 | 3 | 3 | 1 | 3 | 87 | 75 | .537 | 8 |
| Seattle | 5 | 6 | ... | 6 | 1 | 3 | 7 | 5 | 8 | 3 | 8 | 7 | 5 | 8 | 2 | 1 | 0 | 2 | 2 | 79 | 83 | .488 | 16 |
| Anaheim | 6 | 8 | 6 | ... | 6 | 1 | 3 | 3 | 7 | 1 | 5 | 5 | 7 | 6 | 1 | 1 | 2 | 0 | 2 | 70 | 92 | .432 | 25 |

### National League

#### East Division

| Team | Atl. | N.Y. | Phi. | Mon. | Fla. | Hou. | Cin. | Pit. | St.L. | Mil. | Chi. | Ari. | S.F. | L.A. | S.D. | Col. | N.Y. | Bos. | Tor. | Bal. | T.B. | W | L | Pct. | GB |
|---|---|---|---|---|---|---|---|---|---|---|---|---|---|---|---|---|---|---|---|---|---|---|---|---|---|
| Atlanta | ... | 9 | 8 | 9 | 9 | 6 | 8 | 6 | 8 | 5 | 2 | 5 | 4 | 5 | 5 | 5 | 2 | 4 | 0 | 0 | 3 | 103 | 59 | .636 | ... |
| New York | 3 | ... | 6 | 8 | 10 | 5 | 5 | 7 | 5 | 5 | 6 | 2 | 7 | 4 | 7 | 5 | 3 | 2 | 3 | 2 | 2 | 97 | 66 | .595 | 6.5 |
| Philadelphia | 5 | 6 | ... | 6 | 11 | 1 | 3 | 3 | 4 | 4 | 7 | 1 | 2 | 3 | 6 | 4 | 2 | 2 | 2 | 3 | 2 | 77 | 85 | .475 | 26 |
| Montreal | 4 | 5 | 6 | ... | 4 | 2 | 3 | 3 | 5 | 4 | 5 | 3 | 4 | 4 | 5 | 3 | 1 | 3 | 2 | 0 | 2 | 68 | 94 | .420 | 35 |
| Florida | 4 | 3 | 2 | 8 | ... | 2 | 1 | 3 | 3 | 5 | 3 | 1 | 4 | 7 | 3 | 4 | 1 | 1 | 2 | 2 | 5 | 64 | 98 | .395 | 39 |

#### Central Division

| Team | Hou. | Cin. | Pit. | St.L. | Mil. | Chi. | Atl. | N.Y. | Phi. | Mon. | Fla. | Ari. | S.F. | L.A. | S.D. | Col. | Cle. | Chi. | Det. | K.C. | Min. | W | L | Pct. | GB |
|---|---|---|---|---|---|---|---|---|---|---|---|---|---|---|---|---|---|---|---|---|---|---|---|---|---|
| Houston | ... | 4 | 5 | 5 | 8 | 9 | 1 | 4 | 6 | 7 | 7 | 4 | 5 | 6 | 8 | 6 | 2 | 2 | 3 | 3 | 2 | 97 | 65 | .599 | ... |
| Cincinnati | 9 | ... | 7 | 8 | 6 | 8 | 1 | 5 | 6 | 4 | 6 | 8 | 4 | 4 | 6 | 7 | 2 | ... | 1 | 3 | 1 | 96 | 67 | .589 | 1.5 |
| Pittsburgh | 7 | 6 | ... | 7 | 4 | 6 | 3 | 2 | 4 | 6 | 4 | 2 | 4 | 6 | 3 | 7 | 2 | 1 | 1 | 2 | 1 | 78 | 83 | .484 | 18.5 |
| St. Louis | 7 | 4 | 5 | ... | 6 | 5 | 1 | 2 | 5 | 4 | 4 | 4 | 3 | 6 | 7 | 5 | ... | 2 | 3 | 1 | 1 | 75 | 86 | .466 | 21.5 |
| Milwaukee | 5 | 6 | 8 | 7 | ... | 6 | 2 | 2 | 5 | 5 | 4 | 4 | 4 | 2 | 3 | 3 | 2 | 2 | 2 | 2 | 0 | 74 | 87 | .460 | 22.5 |
| Chicago | 3 | 5 | 7 | 7 | 6 | ... | 5 | 3 | 2 | 2 | 6 | 2 | 1 | 2 | 6 | 4 | 1 | 2 | ... | 1 | 2 | 67 | 95 | .414 | 30 |

#### West Division

| Team | Ari. | S.F. | L.A. | S.D. | Col. | Atl. | N.Y. | Phi. | Mon. | Fla. | Hou. | Cin. | Pit. | St.L. | Mil. | Chi. | Tex. | Oak. | Sea. | Ana. | W | L | Pct. | GB |
|---|---|---|---|---|---|---|---|---|---|---|---|---|---|---|---|---|---|---|---|---|---|---|---|---|
| Arizona | ... | 9 | 7 | 11 | 6 | 4 | 7 | 8 | 6 | 8 | 5 | 1 | 5 | 4 | 5 | 7 | 3 | 1 | 1 | 2 | 100 | 62 | .617 | ... |
| San Fran. | 3 | ... | 5 | 7 | 9 | 5 | 2 | 6 | 5 | 5 | 4 | 5 | 5 | 6 | 5 | 7 | 0 | 3 | 2 | 2 | 86 | 76 | .531 | 14 |
| Los Angeles | 6 | 8 | ... | 3 | 5 | 4 | 4 | 6 | 5 | 2 | 3 | 3 | 3 | 3 | 7 | 7 | 1 | 0 | 3 | 4 | 77 | 85 | .475 | 23 |
| San Diego | 2 | 5 | 9 | ... | 9 | 4 | 2 | 3 | 3 | 6 | 1 | 3 | 6 | 2 | 5 | 3 | 2 | 2 | 4 | 3 | 74 | 88 | .457 | 26 |
| Colorado | 7 | 4 | 8 | 4 | ... | 4 | 4 | 5 | 6 | 5 | 2 | 2 | 2 | 4 | 6 | 5 | 2 | 0 | 1 | 1 | 72 | 90 | .444 | 28 |

## LEADERS

**American League**
**BA:** Nomar Garciaparra, Bos., .357.
**Runs:** Roberto Alomar, Cle., 138.
**Hits:** Derek Jeter, N.Y., 219.
**TB:** Shawn Green, Tor., 361.
**HR:** Ken Griffey Jr., Sea., 48.
**RBI:** Manny Ramirez, Cle., 165.
**SB:** Brian L. Hunter, Det.-Sea., 44.
**Wins:** Pedro Martinez, Bos., 23.
**ERA:** Pedro Martinez, Bos., 2.07.
**CG:** David Wells, Tor., 7.
**IP:** David Wells, Tor., 231.2.
**SO:** Pedro Martinez, Bos., 313.
**Sv.:** Mariano Rivera, N.Y., 45.

**National League**
**BA:** Larry Walker, Col., .379.
**Runs:** Jeff Bagwell, Hou., 143.
**Hits:** Luis Gonzalez, Ari., 206.
**TB:** Sammy Sosa, Chi., 397.
**HR:** Mark McGwire, St.L., 65.
**RBI:** Mark McGwire, St.L., 147.
**SB:** Tony Womack, Ari., 72.
**Wins:** Mike Hampton, Hou., 22.
**ERA:** Randy Johnson, Ari., 2.48.
**CG:** Randy Johnson, Ari., 12.
**IP:** Randy Johnson, Ari., 271.2.
**SO:** Randy Johnson, Ari., 364.
**Sv.:** Ugueth Urbina, Mon., 41.

**A.L. 20-game winner**
Pedro Martinez, Bos., 23
**N.L. 20-game winners**
Mike Hampton, Hou., 22
Jose Lima, Hou., 21
**A.L. 100 RBIs**
Manny Ramirez, Cle., 165
Rafael Palmeiro, Tex., 148
Ken Griffey Jr., Sea., 134
Carlos Delgado, Tor., 134
Juan Gonzalez, Tex., 128
Jason Giambi, Oak., 123
Shawn Green, Tor., 123
Roberto Alomar, Cle., 120
Jermaine Dye, K.C., 119
Albert Belle, Bal., 117
Magglio Ordonez, Chi., 117
Richie Sexson, Cle., 116
Bernie Williams, N.Y., 115
Ivan Rodriguez, Tex., 113
John Jaha, Oak., 111
Alex Rodriguez, Sea., 111
Paul O'Neill, N.Y., 110
Carlos Beltran, K.C., 108
Jim Thome, Cle., 108
Mo Vaughn, Ana., 108
B.J. Surhoff, Bal., 107
Tino Martinez, N.Y., 105
Nomar Garciaparra, Bos., 104
Fred McGriff, T.B., 104
Harold Baines, Bal.-Cle., 103
Troy O'Leary, Bos., 103
Derek Jeter, N.Y., 102
Matt Stairs, Oak., 102
Mike Sweeney, K.C., 102
Rusty Greer, Tex., 101
Dean Palmer, Det., 100
**N.L. 100 RBIs**
Mark McGwire, St.L., 147
Matt Williams, Ari., 142
Sammy Sosa, Chi., 141
Dante Bichette, Col, 133
Vladimir Guerrero, Mon., 131
Jeff Bagwell, Hou., 126
Mike Piazza, N.Y., 124
Robin Ventura, N.Y., 120
Greg Vaughn, Cin., 118
Brian Giles, Pit., 115
Brian Jordan, Atl., 115
Larry Walker, Col., 115
Todd Helton, Col., 113
Jay Bell, Ari., 112
Eric Karros, L.A., 112
Luis Gonzalez, Ari., 111
Chipper Jones, Atl., 110
Edgardo Alfonzo, N.Y., 108
Carl Everett, Hou., 108
Fernando Tatis, St.L., 107
Kevin Young, Pit., 106
Jeromy Burnitz, Mil., 103
Steve Finley, Ari., 103
Rico Brogna, Phi., 102
Vinny Castilla, Col., 102
Jeff Kent, S.F., 101
Gary Sheffield, L.A., 101
**N.L./A.L. 100 RBIs**
Tony Batista, Ari.-Tor., 100
**A.L. 40 homers**
Ken Griffey Jr., Sea., 48
Rafael Palmeiro, Tex., 47
Carlos Delgado, Tor., 44
Manny Ramirez, Cle., 44
Shawn Green, Tor., 42
Alex Rodriguez, Sea., 42
**N.L. 40 homers**
Mark McGwire, St.L., 65
Sammy Sosa, Chi., 63
Chipper Jones, Atl., 45
Greg Vaughn, Cin., 45
Jeff Bagwell, Hou., 42
Vladimir Guerrero, Mon., 42
Mike Piazza, N.Y., 40
**Most Valuable Player**
A.L.: Ivan Rodriguez, C, Tex.
N.L.: Chipper Jones, 3B, Atl.
**Cy Young Award**
A.L.: Pedro Martinez, Bos.
N.L.: Randy Johnson, Ari.
**Rookie of the Year**
A.L.: Carlos Beltran, OF, K.C.
N.L.: Scott Williamson, P, Cin.
**Manager of the Year**
A.L.: Jimy Williams, Bos.
N.L.: Jack McKeon, Cin.
**Hall of Fame additions**
George Brett, 3B, 1973-93
Orlando Cepeda, OF-1B, 1958-74
Nestor Chylak, umpire
Nolan Ryan, P, 1966-93
Frank Selee, manager
Smokey Joe Williams, P, Negro Leagues
Robin Yount, SS-OF, 1974-93

## SIGNIFICANT EVENTS

■ **March 28:** As part of a U.S. initiative to build ties with Cuba, the Baltimore Orioles played the first game of a two-game exhibition series against the Cuban National Team. The Orioles won the game, played in Havana, 3-2 in 11 innings. The second game was played on May 3 in Baltimore, and this time the Cubans won, 12-6.
■ **April 4:** The San Diego Padres opened their "home" season with a game in Monterrey, Mexico, losing before a capaticy crowd of 27,104 to the Colorado Rockies, 8-2.
■ **July 14:** A 567-foot crane lifting a 400-ton section of Miller Park, the Milwaukee Brewers' new home under construction, collapsed, killing three in the accident. The damage was estimated at $50 to $75 million and postponed the anticipated opening of the park until the 2001 season.
■ **July 14:** Richie Phillips, general counsel of the Major League Umpires Association, announced a mass resignation of umpires, effective September 2. This strategy, designed to force management to the bargaining table before December 31, the expiration date of the contract, backfired. Major League Baseball accepted the resignations of 22 umpires, and the union split in two. On November 30, dissidents won an NLRB election, decertifying the MLUA.
■ **July 15:** The Mariners opened their new park, Safeco Field, with a 3-2 loss to the San Diego Padres. The Mariners had played their final game at the Kingdome on June 27, defeating Texas, 5-2.
■ **September 27:** The Detroit Tigers played their final game at Tiger Stadium, beating Kansas City, 8-2.
■ **September 30:** The San Francisco Giants played their final game at 3Com Park (formerly Candlestick Park), losing a 9-4 contest to the Los Angeles Dodgers.
■ **October 9:** The Astros played their final game at the Houston Astrodome—baseball's first domed stadium—losing the fourth and final game of the N.L. Division Series to the Atlanta Braves, 7-5.

## MEMORABLE MOMENTS

■ **April 13:** Fernando Tatis of the St. Louis Cardinals became the first player in major league history to hit two grand slams in the same inning. Both came off Los Angeles Dodgers starter Chan Ho Park during an 11-run third inning in a 12-5 victory over the Dodgers.
■ **May 3:** Creighton Gubanich of the Boston Red Sox became the fourth player to hit a grand slam for his first big-league hit in a game at Oakland.
■ **May 20:** Robin Ventura of the New York Mets became the first player in major league history to belt grand slams in both games of a doubleheader against Milwaukee at Shea Stadium.
■ **July 18:** David Cone of the New York Yankees pitched the second perfect game at Yankee Stadium in two years and only the 14th perfecto of the modern era, when he retired all 27 Montreal Expos batters in a 6-0 victory.
■ **August 5:** Mark McGwire of St. Louis became the 17th member of the 500-home run club, and reached the milestone in his 5,487th career at-bat—the fewest at-bats ever needed to reach 500 homers. McGwire ended the season in 10th place on the all-time list with 522.
■ **August 6:** San Diego's Tony Gwynn singled off the Expos' Dan Smith at Montreal for his 3,000th major league hit.
■ **August 7:** Wade Boggs of the Devil Rays homered off Chris Haney of the Cleveland Indians for his 3,000th big-league hit.
■ **September 18:** Sammy Sosa became the first player to hit 60 homers twice when he hit his 60th at Wrigley Field against Milwaukee. Mark McGwire of the Cardinals joined Sosa eight days later, and hit five more thereafter to edge Sosa for the home run crown, 65-63.

## ALL-STAR GAME

■ **Winner:** The A.L. won the contest with pitching and timely hitting, extending its streak to four straight victories over the N.L. American League starting pitcher Pedro Martinez struck out the first four batters and five of the six he retired.
■ **Key inning:** The first, when Cleveland players provided most of the excitement. Kenny Lofton singled and two outs later stole second. Manny Ramirez walked and Jim Thome singled Lofton home with the game's first run. Baltimore's Cal Ripken followed with a single to drive in Ramirez.
■ **Memorable moment:** Mike Mussina struck out Sammy Sosa and Mark McGwire with runners on second and third to end the fifth inning. The strikeouts shut down the N.L.'s last big scoring threat of the game.
■ **Top guns:** Martinez (Red Sox), Lofton (Indians), Thome (Indians), Ripken (Orioles), Rafael Palmeiro (Rangers), A.L.; Jeromy Burnitz (Brewers), Barry Larkin (Reds), N.L.
■ **MVP:** Martinez.

**Linescore**
July 13 at Boston's Fenway Park
N.L. ............0 0 1 0 0 0 0 0 0—1 7 1
A.L. ...............2 0 0 2 0 0 0 0 x—4 6 2
Schilling (Phillies), Johnson (Diamondbacks) 3, Bottenfield (Cardinals) 4, Lima (Astros) 5, Millwood (Braves) 6, Ashby (Padres) 7, Hampton (Astros) 7, Hoffman (Padres) 8, Wagner (Astros) 8 and Piazza (Mets), Lieberthal (Phillies), Nilsson (Brewers); Martinez (Red Sox), Cone (Yankees) 3, Mussina (Orioles) 5, Rosado (Royals) 6, Zimmerman (Rangers) 7, Hernandez (Devil Rays) 8, Wetteland (Rangers) 9 and Rodriguez (Rangers), Ausmus (Tigers). W—Martinez. L—Schilling. S—Wetteland.

## A.L. DIVISION SERIES

■ **Winners:** For the second straight year the New York Yankees swept the Texas Rangers and held the Rangers to only one run in the series. The Boston Red Sox came back from a two-game deficit to defeat the Cleveland Indians in a high-scoring five-game series.
■ **Turning points:** The Yankees' Bernie Williams lined a two-run double in the fifth inning of the opener and finished the game with six RBIs in an 8-0 victory. Down 1-0 with runners on second and third and nobody out in the fifth inning of Game 2, Andy Pettitte settled down by striking out Mark McLemore, getting Royce Clayton to ground out and striking out Rusty Greer to end the inning. The Yankees scored three runs over the next four innings to win the game. A pair of 37-year-olds—pitcher Roger Clemens and slugger Darryl Strawberry— were the heroes of Game 3. Clemens pitched seven shutout innings after Strawberry gave the Yankees all their runs with a three-run homer in the first inning.
■ **Memorable moments:** Troy O'Leary, who had hit a grand slam earlier in the game, hit a two-run homer in the seventh inning to break an 8-8 tie in the deciding fifth game. O'Leary collected seven RBIs in the game, matching John Valentin's total a night earlier when the Red Sox tied the series with a 23-7 trouncing of the Indians. Valentin also contributed heavily in the Game 3 victory with a two-run double, and Brian Daubach chipped in a three-run homer in the 9-3 victory.
■ **Memorable performances:** Orlando Hernandez allowed only two hits in his series-opening victory. Clemens was unscored upon in his seven-inning Game 3 stint, and Pettitte allowed only a home run to Juan Gonzalez in his Game 2 victory. Derek Jeter led all batters with five hits, three runs scored and a .455 average during the series. Williams finished with a .364 average, four hits and six RBIs. The Red Sox had many offensive stars in their series. Mike Stanley led all batters with 10 hits, and batted .500. Nomar Garciaparra batted .417 with six runs, two doubles and two homers. Valentin hit three homers and collected 12 RBIs, and Jose Offerman added seven hits, six RBIs and batted .389. Much of the Red Sox's offense was provided in Game 4, when they exploded for 24 hits and slugged four home runs in a 23-7 thrashing of Cleveland. While the Indians were outhit, .318 to .233, they had some offensive stars, led by Jim Thome (four homers, seven runs, .353 average) and Roberto Alomar (four doubles, seven hits, .368 average).

**Linescores**

New York vs. Texas

**Game 1**—October 5, at New York
Texas............0 0 0 0 0 0 0 0 0—0 2 1
New York......0 1 0 0 2 4 0 1 x—8 10 0
Sele, Crabtree (6), Venafro (6), Patterson (7), Fassero (8) and Rodriguez; Hernandez, Nelson (9) and Posada. W—Hernandez. L—Crabtree. HR—Williams (N.Y.).

**Game 2**—October 7, at New York
Texas.............0 0 0 1 0 0 0 0 0—1 7 0
New York........0 0 0 0 1 0 1 1 x—3 7 2
Helling, Crabtree (7), Venafro (8) and Rodriguez; Pettitte, Nelson (8), Rivera (9) and Girardi. W—Pettitte. L—Helling. S—Rivera. HR—Gonzalez (Tex.).

**Game 3**—October 9, at Texas
New York........3 0 0 0 0 0 0 0 0—3 6 0
Texas.............0 0 0 0 0 0 0 0 0—0 5 1
Clemens, Nelson (8), Rivera (8) and Girardi; Loaiza, Zimmerman (8), Wetteland (9) and Rodriguez. W—Clemens. L—Loaiza. S—Rivera. HR—Strawberry (N.Y.).

Boston vs. Cleveland

**Game 1**—October 6, at Cleveland
Boston............0 1 0 1 0 0 0 0 0—2 5 1
Cleveland.......0 0 0 0 0 2 0 0 1—3 6 1
P. Martinez, Lowe (5), Cormier (9), Garces (9) and Varitek; Colon, Shuey (9) and S. Alomar. W—Shuey. L—Lowe. HR—Garciaparra (Bos.); Thome (Cle.).

**Game 2**—October 7, at Cleveland
Boston..........0 0 1 0 0 0 0 0 0— 1 6 0
Cleveland......0 0 6 5 0 0 0 0 x—11 8 0
Saberhagen, Wasdin (3), Wakefield (5), Gordon (7), Beck (8) and Varitek; Nagy, Karsay (8), Jackson (8) and S. Alomar. W—Nagy. L—Saberhagen. HR—Baines, Thome (Cle.).

**Game 3**—October 9, at Boston
Cleveland.......0 0 0 1 0 1 1 0 0—3 9 1
Boston...........0 0 0 0 2 1 6 0 x—9 11 2
Burba, Wright (5), Rincon (7), DePaula (7), Reed (8) and S. Alomar; R. Martinez, Lowe (6), Beck (9) and Varitek. W—Lowe. L—Wright. HR—Valentin, Daubach (Bos.).

**Game 4**—October 10, at Boston
Cleveland....1 1 0 0 4 0 0 0 1— 7 8 0
Boston.........2 5 3 5 3 0 3 2 x—23 24 0
Colon, Karsay (2), Reed (4), DePaula (5), Assenmacher (7), Shuey (8) and S. Alomar, Diaz; Mercker, Garces (2), Wakefield (5), Wasdin (5), Cormier (5), Gordon (9) and Varitek, Hatteberg. W—Garces. L—Colon. HR—Cordero (Cle.); Valentin 2, Offerman, Varitek (Bos.).

**Game 5**—October 11, at Cleveland
Boston........2 0 5 1 0 0 3 0 1—12 10 0
Cleveland....3 2 3 0 0 0 0 0 0— 8 7 1
Saberhagen, Lowe (2), P. Martinez (4) and Varitek; Nagy, DePaula (4), Shuey (7), Jackson (9) and S. Alomar. W—P. Martinez. L—Shuey. HR—O'Leary 2, Garciaparra (Bos.); Thome 2, Fryman (Cle.).

## N.L. DIVISION SERIES

■ **Winners:** Following an opening game loss, the Atlanta Braves earned their eighth straight N.L. Championship Series berth by defeating the Houston Astros in three straight games. The wild-card New York Mets, playing in their first postseason action since 1988, beat the second-year expansion Arizona Diamondbacks in four games.

■ **Turning points:** Atlanta starter Kevin Milwood pitched a one-hitter in Game 2, allowing only a home run to Ken Caminiti. John Rocker escaped a 10th inning jam with the bases loaded and no outs in Game 3. Two innings later, Brian Jordan's two-run double drove home the winning runs. The Braves jumped out to a 7-0 lead and held on to a 7-5 victory in Game 4. The Mets took the first game of their series on a ninth-inning grand slam by Edgardo Alfonzo to win the game, 8-4. A two-run single by John Olerud in the sixth inning helped the Mets win Game 3, 9-2, and Todd Pratt's homer in the 10th inning of Game 4 clinched the series for New York. A costly error by Diamondbacks outfielder Tony Womack in the eighth allowed the Mets to tie the game.

■ **Memorable moments:** After the Astros came back from a 7-0 deficit in Game 4, they were down 7-5 with a runner on and nobody out in the ninth. Rocker struck out Jeff Bagwell and Carl Everett, then retired Ken Caminiti, a .471 hitter during the series, for the final out. Olerud's Game 1 homer off Randy Johnson was the first homer by a lefthander off Johnson since September 23, 1997. The two-run third-inning shot gave the Mets a 3-0 lead in the game.

■ **Memorable performances:** Olerud led all hitters with seven hits and a .438 average. In addition, he collected six RBIs. Alfonzo clubbed three homers and also had six RBIs for the Mets. Bret Boone had nine hits and a .474 average to lead the Braves. Jordan chipped in eight hits and seven RBIs while batting .471 for Atlanta. Millwood pitched 10 innings, allowing only one hit, one run, and struck out nine for the Braves.

**Linescores**

New York vs. Arizona

**Game 1**—October 5, at Arizona
New York......1 0 2 1 0 0 0 0 4—8 10 0
Arizona ......0 0 1 1 0 2 0 0 0—4 7 0
Yoshii, Cook (6), Wendell (8), Benitez (9) and Piazza; Johnson, Chouinard (9) and Stinnett. W—Wendell. L—Johnson. HR—Alfonzo 2, Olerud (N.Y.); Durazo, Gonzalez (Ari.).

**Game 2**—October 6, at Arizona
New York........0 0 1 0 0 0 0 0 0—1 5 0
Arizona ........0 0 3 0 2 0 2 0 x—7 9 1
Rogers, Mahomes (5), Dotel (7), J. Franco (7) and Piazza; Stottlemyre, Olson (7), Swindell (8) and Stinnett. W—Stottlemyre. L—Rogers.

**Game 3**—October 8, at New York
Arizona ......0 0 0 0 2 0 0 0 0—2 5 3
New York......0 1 2 0 0 6 0 0 x—9 11 0
Daal, Holmes (5), Plesac (6), Chouinard (6), Swindell (8) and Stinnett; Reed, Wendell (7), J. Franco (8), Hershiser (9) and Pratt. W—Reed. L—Daal. HR—Ward (Ari.).

**Game 4**—October 9, at New York
Arizona ....0 0 0 0 1 0 0 2 0 0—3 5 1
New York ..0 0 0 1 0 1 0 1 0 1—4 8 0
Anderson, Olson (8), Swindell (8), Mantei (8) and Stinnett; Leiter, Benitez (8), J. Franco (9) and Pratt. W—J. Franco. L—Mantei. HR—Colbrunn (Ari.); Alfonzo, Pratt (N.Y.).

Atlanta vs. Houston

**Game 1**—October 5, at Atlanta
Houston ......0 1 0 0 0 1 0 0 4—6 13 0
Atlanta..........0 0 0 0 1 0 0 0 0—1 7 0
Reynolds, Miller (7), Henry (7), Wagner (9) and Eusebio; Maddux, Remlinger (8) and Perez. W—Reynolds. L—Maddux. HR—Ward, Caminiti (Hou.).

**Game 2**—October 6, at Atlanta
Houston ........0 1 0 0 0 0 0 0 0—1 1 1
Atlanta ..........1 0 0 0 0 1 3 0 x—5 11 1
Lima, Elarton (7), Powell (8) and Eusebio; Millwood and Perez. W—Millwood. L—Lima. HR—Caminiti (Hou.).

**Game 3**—October 8, at Houston
Atl. ....0 0 0 0 0 3 0 0 0 0 0 2—5 12 0
Hou. ..2 0 0 0 0 0 1 0 0 0 0 0—3 9 2
Glavine, Mulholland (7), Maddux (7), Remlinger (7), Springer (9), Rocker (10), Millwood (12) and Perez; Hampton, Cabrera (8), Henry (10), Powell (12) and Eusebio. W—Rocker. L—Powell. S—Millwood. HR—Jordan (Atl.).

**Game 4**—October 4, at San Diego
Atlanta ..........1 0 1 0 0 5 0 0 0—7 15 1
Houston ........0 0 0 0 0 0 1 4 0—5 8 1
Smoltz, Mulholland (8), McGlinchy (8), Rocker (8) and Perez; Reynolds, Holt (6), Elarton (6), Miller (8), Powell (9) and Eusebio. W—Smoltz. L—Reynolds. S—Rocker. HR—Eusebio, Caminiti (Hou.).

## ALCS

■ **Winner:** Despite being outhit, .293 to .239, the New York Yankees used timely hitting to defeat the Boston Red Sox in five games to advance to the franchise's record 36th World Series.

■ **Turning point:** Yankee center fielder Bernie Williams belted a home run in the bottom of the 10th inning to cap a 4-3 comeback win in the opening game. Down, 2-0 and then 3-2 early in the contest, the Yankees tied the score in the seventh when Derek Jeter singled home Scott Brosius.

■ **Memorable moment:** With his team trailing, 3-2 in the bottom of the eighth, Boston's Jose Offerman was declared out on a tag play that umpire Tim Tschida later admitted he called wrong. It was the second time in the series an umpire admitted making an incorrect call against the Red Sox. An inning later, the Red Sox allowed six runs in the top of the ninth and lost, 9-2. In that frame, Offerman made a bad throw on a double-play ball. The error kept the inning alive and Ricky Ledee followed with a grand slam.

■ **Top guns:** Derek Jeter (.350, 7 hits), Hernandez (1-0, 15 IP, 13 SO, 1.80 ERA), Chuck Knoblauch (.333, 6 hits), Scott Brosius (2 HRs), Yankees; Jose Offerman (.458, 11 hits), Nomar Garciaparra (.400, 8 hits, 2 HR, 5 RBIs), Troy O'Leary (.350, 7 hits, 3 doubles), John Valentin (.348, 8 hits, 5 RBIs), P. Martinez (1-0, 7 IP, 12 SO, 0.00 ERA), Red Sox.

■ **MVP:** Hernandez.

**Linescores**

**Game 1**—October 13, at New York
Boston ........2 1 0 0 0 0 0 0 0 0—3 8 3
New York.....0 2 0 0 0 0 1 0 0 1—4 10 0
Mercker, Garces (5), Lowe (7), Cormier (9), Beck (10) and Varitek; Hernandez, Rivera (9) and Posada. W—Rivera. L—Beck. HR—Brosius, Williams (N.Y.).

**Game 2**—October 14, at New York
Boston..........0 0 0 0 2 0 0 0 0—2 10 0
New York......0 0 0 1 0 0 2 0 x—3 7 0
R. Martinez, Gordon (7), Cormier (7) and Varitek; Cone, Stanton (8), Nelson (8), Watson (8), Mendoza (8), Rivera (9) and Girardi. W—Cone. L—R. Martinez. S—Rivera. HR—Garciaparra (Bos.); T. Martinez (N.Y.).

**Game 3**—October 16, at Boston
New York....0 0 0 0 0 0 0 1 0— 1 3 3
Boston........2 2 2 0 2 1 4 0 x—13 21 1
Clemens, Irabu (3), Stanton (7), Watson (8) and Girardi, Posada; P. Martinez, Gordon (8), Rapp (9) and Varitek, Hatteberg. W—P. Martinez. L—Clemens. HR—Brosius (N.Y.); Valentin, Daubach, Garciaparra (Bos.).

**Game 4**—October 10, at Boston
New York......0 1 0 2 0 0 0 0 6—9 11 0
Boston..........0 1 1 0 0 0 0 0 0—2 10 4
Pettitte, Rivera (8) and Girardi; Saberhagen, Lowe (7), Cormier (8), Garces (8), Beck (9) and Varitek. W—Pettitte. L—Saberhagen. S—Rivera. HR—Strawberry, Ledee (N.Y.).

**Game 5**—October 11, at Boston
New York......2 0 0 0 0 0 2 0 2—6 11 1
Boston..........0 0 0 0 0 0 0 1 0—1 5 2
Hernandez, Stanton (8), Nelson (8), Watson (8), Mendoza (8) and Posada; Mercker, Lowe (4), Cormier (7), Gordon (9) and Varitek. W—Hernandez. L—Mercker. S—Mendoza. HR—Jeter, Posada (N.Y.); Varitek (Bos.).

## NLCS

■ **Winner:** The Atlanta Braves jumped out to a three-game lead in the series, then held on to win their fifth National League pennant of the '90s in six games. The Braves dominated the Mets during the regular season, winning nine of 12 games. Atlanta compiled a 103-59 record and finished 6 1/2 games ahead of the wild-card Mets. New York, which had a major league low 68 errors during the regular season, didn't field as well in the series, committing eight errors.

■ **Turning point:** Game 2, when Mets manager Bobby Valentine decided to stay with starter Kenny Rogers over reliever Turk Wendell against Eddie Perez in the sixth inning. Rogers had just given up a two-run homer to Brian Jordan and a single to Andruw Jones, and the hot-hitting Perez was coming to bat. Valentine left Rogers in, and Perez belted a two-run homer giving the Braves a 4-2 lead.

■ **Memorable moment:** Robin Ventura belted a game-ending grand slam in the 15th inning in Game 5, but the hit was officially declared a single when he was mobbed by teammates after rounding first base and couldn't complete the trip around the bases. The hit enabled to Mets to win the game, 4-3, and kept New York in the series.

■ **Top guns:** Perez (.500, 10 hits, 2 doubles, 2 HRs, 5 RBIs), Jordan (2 HRs, 5 RBIs), Greg Maddux (1-0, 14 IP, 1.93 ERA), Braves; Roger Cedeno (.500, 6 hits), John Olerud (8 hits, 6 RBIs), Edgardo Alfonzo (4 doubles), Mets.

■ **MVP:** Perez.

**Game 1**—October 12, at Atlanta
New York..........0 0 0 1 0 0 0 0 1—2 6 2
Atlanta..............1 0 0 0 1 1 0 1 x—4 8 2
Yoshii, Mahomes (5), Cook (7), Wendell (8) and Piazza; Maddux, Remlinger (8), Rocker (8) and Perez. W—Maddux. L—Yoshii. S—Rocker. HR—Perez (Atl.).

**Game 2**—October 13, at Atlanta
New York........0 1 0 0 1 0 0 1 0—3 5 1
Atlanta.............0 0 0 0 0 4 0 0 0—4 9 1
Rogers, Wendell (6), Benitez (8) and Piazza; Millwood, Rocker (8), Smoltz (9) and Perez. W—Millwood. L—Rogers. S—Smoltz. HR—Mora (N.Y.); Jordan, Perez (Atl.).

**Game 3**—October 15, at New York
Atlanta ..........1 0 0 0 0 0 0 0 0—1 3 1
New York.........0 0 0 0 0 0 0 0 0—0 7 2
Glavine, Remlinger (8), Rocker (9) and Perez; Leiter, J. Franco (8), Benitez (8) and Piazza. W—Glavine. L—Leiter. S—Rocker.

**Game 4**—October 16, at New York
Atlanta............0 0 0 0 0 0 0 2 0—2 3 0
New York........0 0 0 0 0 1 0 2 x—3 5 0
Smoltz, Remlinger (8), Rocker (8) and Perez; Reed, Wendell (8), Benitez (9) and Piazza. W—Wendell. L—Remlinger. S—Benitez. HR—Jordan, Klesko (Atl.); Olerud (N.Y.).

**Game 5**—October 17, at New York
Atl. ..0 0 0 2 0 0 0 0 0 0 0 0 0 0 1—3 13 2
N.Y. ..2 0 0 0 0 0 0 0 0 0 0 0 0 0 2—4 11 1
Maddux, Mulholland (8), Remlinger (10), Springer (12), Rocker (13), McGlinchy (14) and Perez, Myers; Yoshii, Hershiser (4), Wendell (7), Cook (7), Mahomes (7), J. Franco (8), Benitez (10), Rogers (11), Dotel (13) and Piazza, Pratt. W—Dotel. L—McGlinchy. HR—Olerud (N.Y.).

**Game 6**—October 19, at Atlanta
N.Y. ........0 0 0 0 0 3 4 1 0 1 0— 9 15 2
Atlanta .....5 0 0 0 0 2 0 1 0 1 1—10 10 1
Leiter, Mahomes (1), Wendell (5), Cook (6), Hershiser (7), J. Franco (8), Benitez (9), Rogers (11) and Piazza, Pratt; Millwood, Mulholland (6), Smoltz (7), Remlinger (7), Rocker (9), Springer (11) and Perez, Myers. W—Springer. L—Rogers. HR—Piazza (N.Y.).

## WORLD SERIES

■ **Winner:** After sweeping San Diego in the 1999 World Series, the New York Yankees swept their second straight World Series, this time against Atlanta. The World Series championship was New York's record 25th overall and third in four years. The sweep was the eighth by the Yankees.

■ **Turning point:** Two errors by Brian Hunter, inserted into the lineup as a defensive replacement for Ryan Klesko at first base in the eighth inning, allowed the Yankees to turn a 1-0 deficit into a 4-1 victory in the opener. After Scott Brosius singled and Darryl Strawberry walked, Chad Curtis came in to pinch-run for Strawberry. Chuck Knoblauch sacrificed but was safe at first on Hunter's first error, which allowed the other runners to advance to third and second. Derek Jeter singled home Brosius to tie the game, 1-1, and John Rocker replaced starter Greg Maddux on the mound. Paul O'Neill singled and went to second on a wild throw by Hunter—his second error of the inning—as Curtis and Knoblauch scored and Jeter went to third. The Yankees scored one more run in the inning to take a 4-1 lead, which became the final score.

■ **Memorable moment:** When Knoblauch tied Game 3 in the eighth with a two-run homer off Braves starter Tom Glavine. Glavine, who had been pushed back from a Game 1 start because of the flu, had given his club seven strong innings. Atlanta manager Bobby Cox gambled and left Glavine in to pitch the eighth, but the Braves lefthander allowed a leadoff single to Joe Girardi, followed by Knoblauch's shot, which knotted the game, 5-5.

■ **Top guns:** Brosius (.375, 6 hits), Jeter (.353, 4 runs, 6 hits), Curtis (.333, 2 HR), Tino Martinez (5 RBIs), David Cone (1-0, 0.00 ERA), Roger Clemens (1-0, 1.17 ERA), Orlando Hernandez (1-0, 1.29 ERA, 10 SO), Mariano Rivera (1-0, 2 Saves, 0.00 ERA), Yankees; Bret Boone (.538, 7 hits, 4 doubles), Braves.

■ **MVP:** Rivera.

**Linescores**

**Game 1**—October 23, at Atlanta
New York........0 0 0 0 0 0 0 4 0—4 6 0
Atlanta............0 0 0 1 0 0 0 0 0—1 2 2
O. Hernandez, Nelson (8), Stanton (8), Rivera (8) and Posada; Maddux, Rocker (8), Remlinger (9) and Perez. W—O. Hernandez. L—Maddux. S—Rivera. HR—C. Jones (Atl.).

**Game 2**—October 24, at Atlanta
New York......3 0 2 1 1 0 0 0 0—7 14 1
Atlanta..........0 0 0 0 0 0 0 0 2—2 5 1
Cone, Mendoza (8), Nelson (9) and Girardi; Millwood, Mulholland (3), Springer (6), McGlinchy and Myers. W—Cone. L—Millwood.

**Game 3**—October 26, at New York
Atlanta ....1 0 3 1 0 0 0 0 0 0—5 14 1
New York..1 0 0 0 1 0 1 2 0 1—6 9 0
Glavine, Rocker (8), Remlinger (10) and Perez, Myers; Pettitte, Grimsley (4), Nelson (7), Rivera (9) and Girardi. W—Rivera. L—Remlinger. HR—Curtis 2, Knoblauch, Martinez (N.Y.).

**Game 4**—October 27, at New York
Atlanta............0 0 0 0 0 0 0 1 0—1 5 0
New York........0 0 3 0 0 0 0 1 x—4 8 0
Smoltz, Mulholland (8), Springer (8) and Perez, Myers; Clemens, Nelson (8), Rivera (8) and Posada. W—Clemens. L—Smoltz. S—Rivera.

# 2000

## FINAL STANDINGS

### American League

**East Division**

| Team | N.Y. | Bos. | Tor. | Bal. | T.B. | Chi. | Cle. | Det. | K.C. | Min. | Oak. | Sea. | Ana. | Tex. | Atl. | N.Y. | Fla. | Mon. | Phi. | W | L | Pct. | GB |
|---|---|---|---|---|---|---|---|---|---|---|---|---|---|---|---|---|---|---|---|---|---|---|---|
| New York | ... | 7 | 5 | 7 | 6 | 4 | 5 | 4 | 8 | 5 | 6 | 4 | 5 | 10 | 2-1 | 4-2 | 1-1 | 2-1 | 2-1 | 87 | 74 | .540 | ... |
| Boston | 6 | ... | 4 | 7 | 6 | 7 | 6 | 7 | 4 | 8 | 5 | 5 | 4 | 7 | 2-4 | 2-1 | 2-1 | 3-0 | 0-3 | 85 | 77 | .525 | 2.5 |
| Toronto | 7 | 8 | ... | 6 | 7 | 5 | 4 | 9 | 6 | 4 | 3 | 2 | 7 | 6 | 2-1 | 1-2 | 1-2 | 4-2 | 1-2 | 83 | 79 | .512 | 4.5 |
| Baltimore | 5 | 5 | 7 | ... | 8 | 4 | 5 | 6 | 3 | 6 | 4 | 3 | 5 | 6 | 0-3 | 1-2 | 2-1 | 0-3 | 4-2 | 74 | 88 | .457 | 13.5 |
| Tampa Bay | 6 | 6 | 5 | 5 | ... | 4 | 2 | 5 | 5 | 6 | 2 | 3 | 6 | 5 | 1-2 | 1-2 | 3-3 | 2-1 | 2-1 | 69 | 92 | .429 | 18.0 |

**Central Division**

| Team | Chi. | Cle. | Det. | K.C. | Min. | N.Y. | Bos. | Tor. | Bal. | T.B. | Oak. | Sea. | Ana. | Tex. | St.L. | Cin. | Mil. | Hou. | Pit. | Chi. | W | L | Pct. | GB |
|---|---|---|---|---|---|---|---|---|---|---|---|---|---|---|---|---|---|---|---|---|---|---|---|---|
| Chicago | ... | 8 | 9 | 5 | 7 | 8 | 5 | 5 | 6 | 6 | 6 | 7 | 6 | 5 | 1-2 | 3-0 | 3-0 | 2-1 | ... | 3-3 | 95 | 67 | .586 | ... |
| Cleveland | 6 | ... | 6 | 6 | 5 | 5 | 6 | 8 | 4 | 8 | 6 | 7 | 6 | 6 | 2-1 | 3-3 | 3-0 | 2-1 | 3-0 | ... | 90 | 72 | .556 | 5.0 |
| Detroit | 3 | 7 | ... | 5 | 7 | 8 | 5 | 3 | 4 | 4 | 6 | 7 | 5 | 5 | 2-1 | 2-1 | 1-2 | 2-1 | 1-2 | 2-1 | 79 | 83 | .488 | 16.0 |
| Kansas City | 7 | 7 | 7 | ... | 7 | 2 | 6 | 4 | 7 | 5 | 4 | 4 | 6 | 3 | 1-2 | ... | 1-2 | 1-2 | 4-2 | 1-2 | 77 | 85 | .475 | 18.0 |
| Minnesota | 5 | 8 | 6 | 5 | ... | 5 | 2 | 5 | 3 | 4 | 5 | 3 | 3 | 8 | 2-1 | 0-3 | 1-2 | 2-1 | 1-2 | 1-2 | 69 | 93 | .426 | 26.0 |

**West Division**

| Team | Oak. | Sea. | Ana. | Tex. | N.Y. | Bos. | Tor. | Bal. | T.B. | Chi. | Cle. | Det. | K.C. | Min. | S.F. | L.A. | Ari. | Col. | S.D. | W | L | Pct. | GB |
|---|---|---|---|---|---|---|---|---|---|---|---|---|---|---|---|---|---|---|---|---|---|---|---|
| Oakland | ... | 9 | 8 | 5 | 3 | 5 | 7 | 8 | 7 | 3 | 6 | 4 | 8 | 7 | 3-3 | 2-1 | 2-1 | 1-2 | 3-0 | 91 | 70 | .565 | ... |
| Seattle | 4 | ... | 8 | 7 | 6 | 5 | 8 | 7 | 9 | 5 | 2 | 2 | 8 | 9 | 2-1 | 2-1 | 2-1 | 2-1 | 3-3 | 91 | 71 | .562 | 0.5 |
| Anaheim | 5 | 5 | ... | 7 | 5 | 5 | 5 | 7 | 6 | 4 | 3 | 5 | 6 | 7 | 2-1 | 4-2 | 1-2 | 3-0 | 2-1 | 82 | 80 | .506 | 9.5 |
| Texas | 7 | 5 | 5 | ... | 2 | 3 | 4 | 6 | 7 | 5 | 4 | 5 | 7 | 4 | 0-3 | 1-2 | 4-2 | 0-3 | 2-1 | 71 | 91 | .438 | 20.5 |

Note: Read across for wins, down for losses.

Clinching dates: New York (East)—September 29; Chicago (Central)—September 24; Oakland (West)—October 1; Seattle (wild card)—October 1.

### National League

**East Division**

| Team | Atl. | N.Y. | Fla. | Mon. | Phi. | St.L. | Cin. | Mil. | Hou. | Pit. | Chi. | S.F. | L.A. | Ari. | Col. | S.D. | N.Y. | Bos. | Tor. | Bal. | T.B. | W | L | Pct. | GB |
|---|---|---|---|---|---|---|---|---|---|---|---|---|---|---|---|---|---|---|---|---|---|---|---|---|---|
| Atlanta | ... | 7 | 6 | 6 | 8 | 3 | 2 | 6 | 5 | 5 | 4 | 6 | 7 | 6 | 5 | 8 | 1-2 | 4-2 | 1-2 | 3-0 | 2-1 | 95 | 67 | .586 | ... |
| New York | 6 | ... | 6 | 9 | 6 | 6 | 4 | 7 | 5 | 7 | 5 | 3 | 5 | 7 | 6 | 3 | 2-4 | 1-2 | 2-1 | 2-1 | 2-1 | 94 | 68 | .580 | 1.0 |
| Florida | 6 | 6 | ... | 7 | 9 | 3 | 6 | 3 | 3 | 5 | 6 | 3 | 2 | 5 | 5 | 2 | 1-1 | 1-2 | 2-1 | 1-2 | 3-3 | 79 | 82 | .491 | 15.5 |
| Montreal | 7 | 3 | 6 | ... | 5 | 2 | 3 | 5 | 5 | 3 | 5 | 3 | 3 | 5 | 2 | 3 | 1-2 | 0-3 | 2-4 | 3-0 | 1-2 | 67 | 95 | .414 | 28.0 |
| Philadelphia | 5 | 7 | 4 | 7 | ... | 2 | 4 | 5 | 4 | 3 | 3 | 2 | 4 | 1 | 3 | 2 | 1-2 | 3-0 | 2-1 | 2-4 | 1-2 | 65 | 97 | .401 | 30.0 |

**Central Division**

| Team | St.L. | Cin. | Mil. | Hou. | Pit. | Chi. | Atl. | N.Y. | Fla. | Mon. | Phi. | S.F. | L.A. | Ari. | Col. | S.D. | Chi. | Cle. | Det. | K.C. | Min. | W | L | Pct. | GB |
|---|---|---|---|---|---|---|---|---|---|---|---|---|---|---|---|---|---|---|---|---|---|---|---|---|---|
| St. Louis | ... | 6 | 7 | 6 | 8 | 10 | 4 | 3 | 6 | 5 | 7 | 4 | 6 | 4 | 3 | 9 | 2-1 | 1-2 | 1-2 | 2-1 | 1-2 | 95 | 67 | .586 | ... |
| Cincinnati | 7 | ... | 5 | 7 | 7 | 8 | 5 | 5 | 3 | 6 | 3 | 3 | 4 | 5 | 6 | 4 | 0-3 | 3-3 | 1-2 | ... | 3-0 | 85 | 77 | .525 | 10.0 |
| Milwaukee | 5 | 8 | ... | 6 | 7 | 7 | 3 | 2 | 4 | 4 | 2 | 3 | 4 | 5 | 5 | 2 | 0-3 | 0-3 | 2-1 | 2-1 | 2-1 | 73 | 89 | .451 | 22.0 |
| Houston | 6 | 5 | 7 | ... | 10 | 7 | 4 | 2 | 5 | 4 | 5 | 1 | 3 | 1 | 4 | 2 | 1-2 | 1-2 | 1-2 | 2-1 | 1-2 | 72 | 90 | .444 | 23.0 |
| Pittsburgh | 4 | 6 | 5 | 3 | ... | 9 | 2 | 2 | 4 | 4 | 6 | 2 | 5 | 2 | 2 | 7 | ... | 0-3 | 2-1 | 2-4 | 2-1 | 69 | 93 | .426 | 26.0 |
| Chicago | 3 | 4 | 6 | 5 | 3 | ... | 5 | 2 | 1 | 4 | 6 | 4 | 3 | 4 | 4 | 3 | 3-3 | ... | 1-2 | 2-1 | 2-1 | 65 | 97 | .401 | 30.0 |

**West Division**

| Team | S.F. | L.A. | Ari. | Col. | S.D. | Atl. | N.Y. | Fla. | Mon. | Phi. | St.L. | Cin. | Mil. | Hou. | Pit. | Chi. | Oak. | Sea. | Ana. | Tex. | W | L | Pct. | GB |
|---|---|---|---|---|---|---|---|---|---|---|---|---|---|---|---|---|---|---|---|---|---|---|---|---|
| San Fran. | ... | 5 | 7 | 7 | 7 | 3 | 5 | 6 | 6 | 7 | 5 | 6 | 6 | 8 | 6 | 5 | 3-3 | 1-2 | 1-2 | 3-0 | 97 | 65 | .599 | ... |
| Los Angeles | 7 | ... | 6 | 9 | 8 | 2 | 4 | 7 | 5 | 5 | 3 | 5 | 3 | 6 | 4 | 6 | 1-2 | 1-2 | 2-4 | 2-1 | 86 | 76 | .531 | 11.0 |
| Arizona | 6 | 7 | ... | 7 | 9 | 3 | 2 | 4 | 4 | 8 | 5 | 2 | 4 | 6 | 7 | 5 | 1-2 | 1-2 | 2-1 | 2-4 | 85 | 77 | .525 | 12.0 |
| Colorado | 6 | 4 | 6 | ... | 7 | 4 | 3 | 4 | 7 | 6 | 5 | 3 | 4 | 5 | 7 | 5 | 2-1 | 1-2 | 0-3 | 3-0 | 82 | 80 | .506 | 15.0 |
| San Diego | 5 | 5 | 4 | 6 | ... | 1 | 6 | 7 | 6 | 5 | 0 | 5 | 7 | 7 | 2 | 5 | 0-3 | 3-3 | 1-2 | 1-2 | 76 | 86 | .469 | 21.0 |

Note: Read across for wins, down for losses.

Tie game—Milwaukee at Cincinnati, April 3 (5 innings).

Clinching dates: Atlanta (East)—September 26; St. Louis (Central)—September 20; San Francisco (West)—September 21; New York (wild card)—September 27.

## LEADERS

**American League**
**BA:** Nomar Garciaparra, Bos., .372.
**Runs:** Johnny Damon, K.C., 136.
**Hits:** Darin Erstad, Ana., 240.
**TB:** Carlos Delgado, Tor., 378.
**HR:** Troy Glaus, Ana., 47.
**RBI:** Edgar Martinez, Sea., 145.
**SB:** Johnny Damon, K.C., 46.
**Wins:** Tim Hudson, Oak.; David Wells, Tor., 20.
**ERA:** Pedro Martinez, Bos., 1.74.
**CG:** David Wells, Tor., 9.
**IP:** Mike Mussina, Bal., 237.2.
**SO:** Pedro Martinez, Bos., 284.
**Sv.:** Todd Jones, Det.; Derek Lowe, Bos., 42.

**National League**
**BA:** Todd Helton, Col., .372.
**Runs:** Jeff Bagwell, Hou., 152.
**Hits:** Todd Helton, Col., 216.
**TB:** Todd Helton, Col., 405.
**HR:** Sammy Sosa, Chi., 50.
**RBI:** Todd Helton, Col., 147.
**SB:** Luis Castillo, Fla., 62.
**Wins:** Tom Glavine, Atl., 21.
**ERA:** Kevin Brown, L.A., 2.58.
**CG:** Randy Johnson, Ari.; Curt Schilling, Phi.-Ari., 8.
**IP:** Jon Lieber, Chi., 251.0.
**SO:** Randy Johnson, Ari., 347.
**Sv.:** Antonio Alfonseca, Fla., 45.

**A.L. 20-game winners**
Tim Hudson, Oak., 20
David Wells, Tor., 20

**N.L. 20-game winners**
Tom Glavine, Atl., 21
Darryl Kile, St.L., 20

**A.L. 100 RBIs**
Edgar Martinez, Sea., 145
Mike Sweeney, K.C., 144
Frank Thomas, Chi., 143
Carlos Delgado, Tor., 137
Jason Giambi, Oak., 137
Alex Rodriguez, Sea., 132
Magglio Ordonez, Chi., 126
Manny Ramirez, Cle., 122
Bernie Williams, N.Y., 121
Rafael Palmeiro, Tex., 120
Jermaine Dye, K.C., 118
David Justice, Cle.-N.Y., 118
Garret Anderson, Ana., 117
Mo Vaughn, Ana., 117
Miguel Tejada, Oak., 115
Tony Batista, Tor., 114
Carl Everett, Bos., 108
Travis Fryman, Cle., 106
Fred McGriff, T.B., 106
Joe Randa, K.C., 106
Jim Thome, Cle., 106
Brad Fullmer, Tor., 104
Ben Grieve, Oak., 104
Albert Belle, Bal., 103
John Olerud, Sea., 103
David Segui, Tex.-Cle., 103
Troy Glaus, Ana., 102
Bobby Higginson, Det., 102
Dean Palmer, Det., 102
Darin Erstad, Ana., 100
Paul O'Neill, N.Y., 100

**N.L. 100 RBIs**
Todd Helton, Col., 147
Sammy Sosa, Chi., 138
Jeff Bagwell, Hou., 132
Jeff Kent, S.F., 125
Brian Giles, Pit., 123
Vladimir Guerrero, Mon., 123
Richard Hidalgo, Hou., 122
Preston Wilson, Fla., 121
Ken Griffey Jr., Cin., 118
Jeff Cirillo, Col., 115
Moises Alou, Hou., 114
Luis Gonzalez, Ari., 114
Mike Piazza, N.Y., 113
Chipper Jones, Atl., 111
Gary Sheffield, L.A., 109
Jim Edmonds, St.L., 108
Phil Nevin, S.D., 107
Barry Bonds, S.F., 106
Jeffrey Hammonds, Col., 106
Eric Karros, L.A., 106
Andruw Jones, Atl., 104
Andres Galarraga, Atl., 100

**A.L. 40 homers**
Troy Glaus, Ana., 47
Jason Giambi, Oak., 43
Frank Thomas, Chi., 43
Tony Batista, Tor., 41
Carlos Delgado, Tor., 41
David Justice, Cle.-N.Y., 41
Alex Rodriguez, Sea., 41

**N.L. 40 homers**
Sammy Sosa, Chi., 50
Barry Bonds, S.F., 49
Jeff Bagwell, Hou., 47
Vladimir Guerrero, Mon., 44
Richard Hidalgo, Hou., 44
Gary Sheffield, L.A., 43
Jim Edmonds, St.L., 42
Todd Helton, Col., 42
Ken Griffey Jr., Cin., 40

**Most Valuable Player**
A.L.: Jason Giambi, 1B, Oak.
N.L.: Jeff Kent, 2B, S.F.

**Cy Young Award**
A.L.: Pedro Martinez, Bos.
N.L.: Randy Johnson, Ari.

**Rookie of the Year**
A.L.: Kazuhiro Sasaki, P, Sea.
N.L.: Rafael Furcal, SS-2B, Atl.

**Manager of the Year**
A.L.: Jerry Manuel, Chi.
N.L.: Dusty Baker, S.F.

**Hall of Fame additions**
Sparky Anderson, manager
Carlton Fisk, C, 1969-93
John (Bid) McPhee, 2B, 1882-99
Tony Perez, 3B-1B, 1964-86
Norman (Turkey) Stearnes, OF-1B, Negro Leagues

## SIGNIFICANT EVENTS

■ **March 29:** As part of a Major League Baseball's desire to expand its international presence, the Cubs and Mets opened the season in Japan. The Cubs beat the Mets, 5-3 at the Tokyo Dome. The Mets beat the Cubs, 5-1 in 11 innings the next day.
■ **April 7:** The Houston Astros opened their new park, Enron Field, with a 4-1 loss to the Philadelphia Phillies.
■ **April 11:** The Detroit Tigers opened their new park, Comerica Park, by beating the Seattle Mariners, 5-2. The San Francisco Giants also opened their new park, Pacific Bell Park, with a 6-5 loss to the Los Angeles Dodgers. Kevin Elster of the Dodgers belted three home runs in the contest.
■ **September 28:** The Milwaukee Brewers played their final game at County Stadium, losing to Cincinnati, 8-1.
■ **October 1:** The Pirates played their final game at Three Rivers Stadium, losing to the Cubs, 10-9.

## MEMORABLE MOMENTS

■ **April 15:** Cal Ripken Jr. of the Baltimore Orioles collected his 3,000th career hit, a single off Twins pitcher Hector Carrasco in the seventh inning of a game at Minnesota.
■ **May 29:** Second baseman Randy Velarde of the Oakland Athletics became the 11th player to turn an unassisted triple play, retiring three New York Yankees on one play in the sixth inning.
■ **July 6:** Keith McDonald of the St. Louis Cardinals becomes only the second player in major league history to homer in his first two major league at-bats. McDonald, who hit his first home run two days earlier, joined Bob Nieman of the St. Louis Browns, who homered in his first two big-league at-bats on September 14, 1951.
■ **September 6:** Scott Sheldon of the Texas Rangers became the third player in big league history to play all nine positions in one game, performing his feat against the Chicago White Sox.
■ **October 1:** Shane Halter of the Detroit Tigers became the fourth player in major league history to play all nine positions in one game. Halter performed his feat on the last day of the regular season against the Minnesota Twins.

## ALL-STAR GAME

■ **Winner:** The A.L. used eight pitchers to hold the N.L. to only three runs, and Derek Jeter led the American Leaguers with three hits and two RBIs to pace the offense. It gave the A.L. its fourth straight victory and 10th in its last 13 games.
■ **Key inning:** The fourth, when Jeter singled home Jermaine Dye and Travis Fryman to give the A.L. a 3-1 lead. N.L. shortstop Barry Larkin made a costly error on a forceout attempt of Fryman at second base earlier in the inning.
■ **Memorable moment:** N.L. center fielder Jim Edmonds made a twisting, back-to-the-infield catch on Mike Bordick's drive leading off the third inning. Despite the great play, the A.L. managed to score a run off Kevin Brown, who walked three in the inning, including a bases-loaded walk to Carl Everett.
■ **Top guns:** Jeter (Yankees), Matt Lawton (Twins), Magglio Ordonez (White Sox), A.L.; Chipper Jones (Braves), Andruw Jones (Braves), Steve Finley (Diamondbacks), N.L.
■ **MVP:** Jeter.

**Linescore**

July 11 at Atlanta's Turner Field
A.L. ......................0 0 1 2 0 0 0 0 3—6
N.L. ......................0 0 1 0 1 0 0 0 1—3
Wells (Blue Jays), Baldwin (White Sox) 3, Sele (Mariners) 4, Isringhausen (Athletics) 5, Lowe (Red Sox) 6, T. Jones, (Tigers) 7, Hudson (Athletics) 8, Rivera (Yankees) 9; Johnson (Diamondbacks), Graves (Reds) 2, Brown (Dodgers) 3, Leiter (Mets) 4, Glavine (Braves) 5, Kile (Cardinals) 6, Wickman (Brewers) 8, Hoffman (Padres) 9. W—Baldwin. L—Leiter.

## A.L. DIVISION SERIES

■ **Winners:** Seattle completed a three-game sweep of Chicago, allowing the White Sox only seven runs. The Yankees edged Oakland in a five-game series victory.
■ **Turning points:** White Sox pitcher Keith Foulke surrendered a single to Mike Cameron leading off the 10th inning of the opener. Cameron proceeded to take long leads off first base and lured Foulke into throwing a number of pickoff attempts. After Cameron finally stole second, Foulke, obviously rattled, surrendered home runs to Edgar Martinez and John Olerud, giving the Mariners a 7-4 victory. In Game 2, the White Sox scored a run in the first and had Jose Valentin on third with none out, but failed to score. Mariners pitcher Paul Abbott retired Frank Thomas, Carlos Lee and Paul Konerko to keep the White Sox from scoring more. It shifted the momentum to the Mariners, who scored two runs the following inning to take the lead. For the White Sox, the first inning represented just one of a number of frustrating innings they endured during the series. Their trio of Thomas, Lee and Konerko hit a combined 1-for-29 during the three games. The Yankees received a big lift from Andy Pettitte in Game 2 of their series. Pettitte and Mariano Rivera combined to shut out Oakland 4-0 to tie the series and end an eight-game losing streak the Yankees had suffered ending the season and going through Game 1. Orlando Hernandez kept the momentum on the Yankees' side in Game 3 as he allowed four hits and combined with Rivera for a 4-2 victory.
■ **Memorable moments:** The Mariners won the series in the ninth inning of Game 3 when pinch-hitter Carlos Guillen squeezed home Rickey Henderson with the winning run. After the Yankees were blown out 11-1 in Game 4, they jumped on A's starter Gil Heredia for six runs in the first inning of the deciding Game 5. Tino Martinez highlighted the frame with a bases-loaded double.
■ **Memorable performances:** David Bell and Edgar Martinez each batted .364 for the Mariners. Game 3 starter Aaron Sele didn't get a decision, but allowed only one run and three hits in 7.1 innings of the Mariners' 2-1 series-clinching victory. A.L. Rookie of the Year Kazuhiro Sasaki struck out five batters and saved two games in his two innings of work during the series. Tino Martinez collected eight hits and four RBIs, and batted .421 for the Yankees. Luis Sojo had only three hits, but drove in a team-high five runs for New York. Rivera was unscored upon in three relief appearances, and saved all three Yankee victories. Catcher Ramon Hernandez led the Athletics with a .375 average, and Eric Chavez batted .350 for the A's in a losing cause.

**Linescores**

Seattle vs. Chicago

**Game 1**—October 3, at Chicago
Seattle.............2 1 0 0 0 0 1 0 0 3—7
Chicago.............0 2 2 0 0 0 0 0 0 0—4
Garcia, Tomko (4), Paniagua (7), Rhodes (9), Mesa (9), Sasaki (10) and Oliver, Wilson; Parque, Howry (7), Bradford (7), Wunsch (8), Simas (8), Foulke (9) and Johnson. W—Mesa. L—Foulke. S—Sasaki. HR—Olerud, Martinez, Oliver (Sea.); Durham (Chi.).

**Game 2**—October 4, at Chicago
Seattle ....................0 2 0 1 1 0 0 0 1—5
Chicago.....................1 0 1 0 0 0 0 0 0—2
P. Abbott, Rhodes (6), Mesa (6), Sasaki (9) and Oliver, Wilson; Sirotka, Barcelo (6), Wunsch (8),

Simas (8), Buehrle (9) and Johnson. W—P. Abbott, L—Sirotka. S—Sasaki. HR—Buhner (Sea.).

**Game 3**—October 6, at Seattle
Chicago..................0 1 0 0 0 0 0 0 0—1
Seattle...................0 0 0 1 0 0 0 0 1—2
One out when winning run scored.
Baldwin, Howry (7), Wunsch (9), Foulke (9) and Johnson; Sele, Rhodes (8), Paniagua (9) and Oliver. W—Paniagua. L—Wunsch.

New York vs. Oakland

**Game 1**—October 3, at Oakland
New York................0 2 0 0 0 1 0 0 0—3
Oakland..................0 0 0 0 3 1 0 1 x—5
Clemens, Stanton (7), Nelson (8) and Posada; Heredia, Tam (7), Mecir (7), Isringhausen (9) and R. Hernandez. W—Heredia. L—Clemens. S—Isringhausen.

**Game 2**—October 4, at Oakland
New York................0 0 0 0 0 3 0 0 1—4
Oakland..................0 0 0 0 0 0 0 0 0—0
Pettitte, Rivera (8) and Posada; Appier, Magnante (7), Tam (9), Jones (9) and R. Hernandez. W—Pettitte. L—Appier. S—Rivera.

**Game 3**—October 6, at New York
Oakland..................0 1 0 0 1 0 0 0 0—2
New York................0 2 0 1 0 0 0 1 x—4
Hudson and R. Hernandez; O. Hernandez, Rivera (8) and Posada. W—O. Hernandez. L—Hudson. S—Rivera. HR—Long (Oak.).

**Game 4**—October 7, at New York
Oakland................3 0 0 0 0 3 0 1 4—11
New York.............0 0 0 0 0 1 0 0 0— 1
Zito, Mecir (6), Magnante (7), Jones (9) and R. Hernandez; Clemens, Stanton (6), Choate (7), Gooden (8) and Posada. W—Zito. L—Clemens. HR—Saenz (Oak.).

**Game 5**—October 8, at Oakland
New York...............6 0 0 1 0 0 0 0 0—7
Oakland..................0 2 1 2 0 0 0 0 0—5
Pettitte, Stanton (4), Nelson (6), O. Hernandez (8), Rivera (8) and Posada; Heredia, Tam (1), Appier (2), Mecir (6), Isringhausen (9) and R. Hernandez, Fasano. HR—Justice (N.Y.).

## N.L. DIVISION SERIES

■ **Winners:** The Cardinals rocked the Braves for 24 runs to end the Braves' division series mastery during the '90s with a three-game sweep. Atlanta had been 15-2 in division series games prior to 2000. The wild-card Mets followed an opening game loss with three straight victories to beat the Giants, whose 97 victories represented the best record in baseball during the regular season.
■ **Turning points:** The Cardinals pounded Greg Maddux for six first-inning runs to take the opener, 7-5. The Cardinals' big lead was enough to offset the control troubles of their starter, rookie Rick Ankiel, who threw a record five wild pitches and allowed four runs in the first three innings. St. Louis struck early and often in the second game, too, as they erased a 2-0 deficit with three first-inning runs. They added one in the second and three in the third off Braves' 21-game winner Tom Glavine to coast to a 10-4 win. The Mets, after losing the first game, held a 4-1 lead going into the bottom of the ninth inning of Game 2, before J.T. Snow belted a game-tying home run. New York managed to grab the lead and the momentum in the 10th when Darryl Hamilton hit a two-out double and scored when Jay Payton singled him home with the winning run. The Mets took the series lead in Game 3 when Benny Agbayani smacked a 13th-inning home run to win an exhausting game that lasted 5 hours and 22 minutes.
■ **Memorable moments:** Mark McGwire, out of the lineup with a sore knee, thrilled the hometown fans in Game 2 with an eighth-inning pinch home run that gave the Cardinals a 10-4 lead. Fernando Vina started the Cardinals on their way to a 7-1 Game 3 victory with a leadoff home run in the first inning. The Braves tied the game with a run in their first, but St. Louis went ahead to stay in the third on a two-run home run by Jim Edmonds. The Giants had a chance to win Game 3 of their series, but Mets reliever Rick White induced Barry Bonds to pop out with two runners on base in the 13th inning. Agbayani ended the game a short time later with his home run.
■ **Memorable performances:** Edmonds led all hitters with two home runs, four doubles, eight hits , seven RBIs and a .571 batting average. Brian Jordan batted .364 to lead the Braves' meager offense (.189 team batting average). Agbayani led the Mets offense with a .333 average. He joined Edgardo Alfonso and Timo Perez as the Mets' leaders with five hits apiece. Snow led the Giants with a .400 average, while National League MVP Jeff Kent collected six hits and batted .375.

**Linescores**

New York vs. San Francisco

**Game 1**—October 4, at San Francisco
New York................0 0 1 0 0 0 0 0 0—1
San Francisco ........1 0 4 0 0 0 0 0 x—5
Hampton, Wendell (6), Cook (7), White (7), Rusch (8) and Piazza; Hernandez, Rodriguez (8), Nen (9) and Estalella. W—Hernandez. L—Hampton. HR—Burks (S.F.).

**Game 2**—October 5, at San Francisco
New York..........0 2 0 0 0 0 0 0 2 1—5
San Francisco ..0 1 0 0 0 0 0 0 3 0—4
Leiter, Benitez (9), J. Franco (10) and Piazza; Estes, Rueter (4), Henry (8), Rodriguez (9) and Estalella. W—Benitez. L—Rodriguez. S—J. Franco. HR—Alfonzo (N.Y.); Snow (S.F.).

**Game 3**—October 7, at New York
S.F. ....0 0 0 2 0 0 0 0 0 0 0 0—2
N.Y. ....0 0 0 0 0 1 0 1 0 0 0 1—3
One out when winning run scored.
Ortiz, Embree (6), Henry (7), Nen (8), Rodriguez (10), Fultz (12) and Estalella, Mirabelli; Reed, Cook (7), Wendell (7), J. Franco (9), Benitez (10), White (12) and Piazza, Pratt. W—White. L—Fultz. HR—Agbayani (N.Y.).

**Game 4**—October 8, at New York
San Francisco ........0 0 0 0 0 0 0 0 0—0
New York................2 0 0 0 2 0 0 0 x—4
Gardner, Henry (5), Embree (7), Del Toro (8) and Mirabelli, Estalella; B.J. Jones and Piazza. W—B.J. Jones. L—Gardner. HR—Ventura (N.Y.).

St. Louis vs. Atlanta

**Game 1**—October 3, at St. Louis
Atlanta....................0 0 4 0 0 0 0 0 1—5
St. Louis ...............6 0 0 1 0 0 0 0 x—7
Maddux, Remlinger (5), Mulholland (6), Rocker (7), Ligtenberg (8) and Bako, Lopez; Ankiel, James (3), Timlin (6), Reames (7), Veres (9) and Hernandez. W—James. L—Maddux. S—Veres. HR—Edmonds (St.L.).

**Game 2**—October 5, at St. Louis
Atlanta..................2 0 0 0 0 0 0 2 0— 4
St. Louis .............3 1 3 1 0 1 0 1 x—10
Glavine, Ashby (3), Burkett (5), Mulholland (6), Ligtenberg (7), Remlinger (8) and Lopez; Kile, Christiansen (8), Timlin (8), Morris (9) and Hernandez. W—Kile. L—Glavine. HR—McGwire, Hernandez, Clark (St.L.); A. Jones (Atl.).

**Game 3**—October 7, at Atlanta
St. Louis ...............1 0 2 0 1 3 0 0 0—7
Atlanta....................1 0 0 0 0 0 0 0 0—1
Stephenson, Reames (4), James (6), Morris (8), Veres (9) and Hernandez; Millwood, Mulholland (5), Ligtenberg (6), Remlinger (6), Ashby (8) and Lopez, Bako. W—Reames. L—Millwood. HR—Vina, Edmonds (St.L.).

## NLCS

■ **Winner:** The Mets' lefthanded pitchers led them to a relatively easy victory over the Cardinals despite the fact that St. Louis outhit New York, .266 to .262. Mike Hampton dominated the Cardinals with 16 innings of scoreless pitching, allowing a total of nine hits and four walks, and striking out 12 in his two victories. Their series victory made the Mets only the second wild-card team (Florida Marlins, 1997) to win a league pennant since the format was begun in 1995.
■ **Turning point:** Hampton shut the Cardinals down on six hits in seven innings in the opener. Mike Piazza's double keyed a two-run first inning, and ninth-inning homers by Todd Zeile and Jay Payton iced the victory. The next night, Payton hit a run-scoring ninth-inning single to give the Mets a 2-0 series lead.
■ **Memorable moments:** Will Clark, normally a sure-handed first baseman, booted a ground ball hit by Robin Ventura leading off the ninth inning of Game 2. Joe McEwing pinch-ran for Ventura later in the inning and scored the winning run on Payton's single. Cardinals rookie Rick Ankiel continued his postseason wildness problems in Game 2. The lefthander started and allowed three walks, two hits, two runs and threw two wild pitches before being relieved in the first inning. The Mets pounded St. Louis with a record five doubles in the first inning of Game 4, and built a 7-2 lead after two innings. The Cardinals fought back to make the score 8-6, but they couldn't catch the Mets.
■ **Top guns:** Edgardo Alfonso (.444, 8 hits), Piazza (.412, 7 runs, 7 hits, 2 HRs), Zeile (.368, 7 hits, 8 RBIs), Agbayani (.353, 6 hits), Perez (.304, 7 hits, 8 runs), Hampton (16 IP, 12 SO, 0.00 ERA), Mets; Clark (.412, 7 hits), J.D. Drew (.333, 4 hits), Ray Lankford (.333, 4 hits), Cardinals.
■ **MVP:** Hampton.

**Linescores**

**Game 1**—October 11, at St. Louis
New York....................2 0 0 0 1 0 0 0 3—6
St. Louis ...................0 0 0 0 0 0 0 0 2—2
Hampton, J. Franco (8), Benitez (9) and Piazza; Kile, James (8), Christiansen (8) and Hernandez, Marrero. W—Hampton. L—Kile. HR—Zeile, Payton (N.Y.).

**Game 2**—October 12, at St. Louis
New York...............2 0 1 0 0 0 0 2 1—6
St. Louis ...............0 1 0 0 2 0 0 2 0—5
Leiter, J. Franco (8), Wendell (8), Benitez (9) and Piazza; Ankiel, Reames (1), Morris (6), Veres (9), Timlin (9) and Marrero, Hernandez. W—Wendell. L—Timlin. S—Benitez. HR—Piazza (N.Y.).

**Game 3**—October 14, at New York
St. Louis ...............2 0 2 1 3 0 0 0 0—8
New York...............1 0 0 1 0 0 0 0 0—2
Benes, James (9), Veres (9) and Hernandez; Reed, Rusch (4), White (5), Cook (8), Wendell (9) and Piazza. W—Benes. L—Reed.

**Game 4**—October 15, at New York
St. Louis .............2 0 0 1 3 0 0 0 0— 6
New York.............4 3 0 1 0 2 0 0 x—10
Kile, James (4), Timlin (5), Morris (7), Christiansen (8) and Hernandez; B.J. Jones, Rusch (5), J. Franco (8), Benitez (9) and Piazza. W—Rusch. L—Kile. HR—Edmonds, Clark (St.L.); Piazza (N.Y.).

**Game 5**—October 16, at New York
St. Louis ...............0 0 0 0 0 0 0 0 0—0
New York...............3 0 0 3 0 0 1 0 x—7
Hentgen, Timlin (4), Reames (5), Ankiel (7), James (7), Veres (8) and Hernandez; Hampton and Piazza. W—Hampton. L—Hentgen.

## ALCS

■ **Winner:** The New York Yankees, after losing the first game, allowed Seattle only three runs over the next three games and beat the Mariners in a six-game series. The victory gave the Yankees their third straight A.L. title, making them the first team since the 1988-90 Oakland A's to win three straight pennants.
■ **Turning point:** Game 2, when the Yankees, trailing 1-0, rallied for seven runs in the eighth inning to win 7-1. Starter John Halama and reliever Jose Paniagua had held New York to six hits over the first seven innings. But David Justice greeted reliever Arthur Rhodes with a leadoff double in the eighth. Bernie Williams followed with a single to center and the Yankees went on to collect eight straight hits in the big inning. Williams and Tino Martinez hit back-to-back home runs in the second inning of Game 3 and the Yankees took control of the series, winning Games 3 and 4 by scores of 8-2 and 5-0. In the latter game, Roger Clemens overpowered the Mariners, striking out 15 in a one-hit shutout.
■ **Memorable moment:** Trailing 4-3 in the seventh inning of Game 6, David Justice slugged a dramatic three-run homer, and the Yankees went on to score six runs to win the series with a 9-7 victory.
■ **Top guns:** Williams (.435,10 hits), T. Martinez (.320, 8 hits), Jeter (.318, 6 runs, 7 hits, 2 HRs), Justice (2 HRs, 8 RBIs), Clemens, (9 IP, 1 H, 15 SO), Yankees; Alex Rodriguez (.409, 9 hits, 2 HRs), John Olerud (.350, 7 hits), Mariners.
■ **MVP:** Justice.

**Game 1**—October 10, at New York
Seattle.....................0 0 0 0 1 1 0 0 0—2
New York..................0 0 0 0 0 0 0 0 0—0
Garcia, Paniagua (7), Rhodes (8), Sasaki (9) and Oliver; Neagle, Nelson (6), Choate (9), Grimsley (9) and Posada. W—Garcia. L—Neagle. S—Sasaki. HR—Rodriguez (Sea.).

**Game 2**—October 11, at New York
Seattle....................0 0 1 0 0 0 0 0 0—1
New York................0 0 0 0 0 0 0 7 x—7
Halama, Paniagua (7), Rhodes (8), Mesa (8) and Wilson; Hernandez, Rivera (9) and Posada. W—Hernandez. L—Rhodes. HR—Jeter (N.Y.).

**Game 3**—October 13, at Seattle
New York...............0 2 1 0 0 1 0 0 4—8
Seattle...................1 0 0 0 1 0 0 0 0—2
Pettitte, Nelson (7), Rivera (8) and Posada; Sele, Tomko (7), Ramsay (9) and Oliver. W—Pettitte. L—Sele. S—Rivera. HR—Williams, T. Martinez (N.Y.).

**Game 4**—October 14, at Seattle
New York...............0 0 0 0 3 0 0 2 0—5
Seattle...................0 0 0 0 0 0 0 0 0—0
Clemens and Posada; Abbott, Ramsay (6), Mesa (7), Paniagua (9) and Wilson, Oliver. W—Clemens. L—Abbott. HR—Jeter, Justice (N.Y.).

**Game 5**—October 15, at Seattle
New York...............0 0 0 2 0 0 0 0 0—2
Seattle...................1 0 0 0 5 0 0 0 x—6
Neagle, Nelson (5), Grimsley (5), Gooden (5), Cone (8) and Posada; Garcia, Paniagua (6), Rhodes (7), Sasaki (8) and Wilson. W—Garcia. L—Neagle. HR—E. Martinez, Olerud (Sea.).

**Game 6**—October 17, at New York
Seattle...................2 0 0 2 0 0 0 3 0—7
New York...............0 0 0 3 0 0 6 0 x—9
Halama, Tomko (4), Paniagua (7), Rhodes (7), Mesa (7) and Wilson, Oliver; Hernandez, Rivera (8) and Posada. W—Hernandez. L—Paniagua. HR—Rodriguez, Guillen (Sea.); Justice (N.Y.).

## WORLD SERIES

■ **Winner:** The Yankees won their 26th World Series in 37 tries and won their third in a row, making them the first team since the 1972-74 Oakland A's to win three World Series.
■ **Turning point:** Jose Vizcaino, making his first start of the postseason, went 4-for-6 and drove in the winning run in the 12th inning to win Game 1, 4-3.
■ **Memorable moment:** When Clemens faced Piazza in the first inning of Game 2. Piazza shattered his bat hitting a foul ball and then ran toward first not realizing it was foul. Clemens tossed the barrel of the bat toward the Mets catcher, with the jagged end of the bat coming dangerously close to Piazza. Piazza glared at Clemens and the players exchanged words as the benches cleared. Clemens was later fined $50,000.
■ **Top guns:** O'Neill (.474, 9 hits), Jeter (.409, 6 runs, 9 hits, 2 HRs), Martinez (.364, 8 hits), Clemens (0.00 ERA, 8 IP, 2 hits, 9 SO), Yankees; Zeile (.400, 8 hits), Payton (.333, 7 hits), Piazza (2 HRs), Mets.
■ **MVP:** Jeter.

**Linescores**

**Game 1**—October 21, at Yankee Stadium
N.Y. Mets ......0 0 0 0 0 0 3 0 0 0 0 0—3
N.Y. Yankees ..0 0 0 0 0 2 0 0 1 0 0 1—4
Leiter, J. Franco (8), Benitez (9), Cook (10), Rusch (10), Wendell (11) and Pratt; Pettitte, Nelson (7), Rivera (9), Stanton (11) and Posada. W—Stanton. L—Wendell.

**Game 2**—October 22, at Yankee Stadium
New York Mets ......0 0 0 0 0 0 0 0 5—5
New York Yankees ..2 1 0 0 1 0 1 1 x—6
Hampton, Rusch (7), White (7), Cook (8) and Piazza; Clemens, Nelson (9), Rivera (9) and Posada. W—Clemens. L—Hampton. HR—Piazza, Payton (Mets); Brosius (Yankees).

**Game 3**—October 24, at Shea Stadium
New York Yankees ..0 0 1 1 0 0 0 0 0—2
New York Mets ......0 1 0 0 0 1 0 2 x—4
Hernandez, Stanton (8) and Posada; Reed, Wendell (7), Cook (7), J. Franco (8), Benitez (9) and Piazza. W—J. Franco. L—Hernandez. S—Benitez. HR—Ventura (Mets).

**Game 4**—October 25, at Shea Stadium
New York Yankees ..1 1 1 0 0 0 0 0 0—3
New York Mets ......0 0 2 0 0 0 0 0 0—2
Neagle, Cone (5), Nelson (6), Stanton (7), Rivera (8) and Posada; B.J. Jones, Rusch (6), J. Franco (8), Benitez (9) and Piazza. W—Nelson. L—B.J. Jones. S—Rivera. HR—Jeter (Yankees); Piazza (Mets).

**Game 5**—October 26, at Shea Stadium
New York Yankees ..0 1 0 0 0 1 0 0 2—4
New York Mets ......0 2 0 0 0 0 0 0 0—2
Pettitte, Stanton (8), Rivera (9) and Posada; Leiter, J. Franco (9) and Piazza. W—Stanton. L—Leiter. S—Rivera. HR—Jeter, Williams (Yankees).

# 2001

## FINAL STANDINGS

### American League

#### East Division

| Team | N.Y. | Bos. | Tor. | Bal. | T.B. | Cle. | Min. | Chi. | Det. | K.C. | Sea. | Oak. | Ana. | Tex. | Atl. | Phi. | N.Y. | Fla. | Mon. | W | L | Pct. | GB |
|---|---|---|---|---|---|---|---|---|---|---|---|---|---|---|---|---|---|---|---|---|---|---|---|
| New York | ... | 13 | 11 | 13 | 13 | 5 | 2 | 5 | 5 | 6 | 3 | 3 | 3 | 3 | 1-2 | 2-1 | 4-2 | 1-2 | 2-1 | 95 | 65 | .594 | ... |
| Boston | 5 | ... | 12 | 10 | 14 | 3 | 3 | 3 | 4 | 3 | 3 | 4 | 3 | 5 | 3-3 | 2-1 | 1-2 | 2-1 | 2-1 | 82 | 79 | .509 | 13.5 |
| Toronto | 8 | 7 | ... | 12 | 10 | 4 | 5 | 3 | 4 | 3 | 3 | 3 | 4 | 6 | 2-1 | 2-1 | 0-3 | 1-2 | 3-3 | 80 | 82 | .494 | 16.0 |
| Baltimore | 5 | 9 | 7 | ... | 10 | 1 | 3 | 3 | 4 | 5 | 1 | 2 | 5 | 2 | 1-2 | 2-4 | 1-2 | 0-3 | 2-1 | 63 | 98 | .391 | 32.5 |
| Tampa Bay | 6 | 5 | 9 | 9 | ... | 1 | 6 | 2 | 2 | 2 | 2 | 2 | 2 | 4 | 2-1 | 3-0 | 2-1 | 2-4 | 1-2 | 62 | 100 | .383 | 34.0 |

#### Central Division

| Team | Cle. | Min. | Chi. | Det. | K.C. | N.Y. | Bos. | Tor. | Bal. | T.B. | Sea. | Oak. | Ana. | Tex. | Hou. | St.L. | Chi. | Mil. | Cin. | Pit. | Ari. | W | L | Pct. | GB |
|---|---|---|---|---|---|---|---|---|---|---|---|---|---|---|---|---|---|---|---|---|---|---|---|---|---|
| Cleveland | ... | 14 | 9 | 13 | 11 | 4 | 6 | 2 | 5 | 5 | 2 | 4 | 4 | 5 | 1-2 | 2-1 | ... | 1-2 | 3-3 | 0-3 | ... | 91 | 71 | .562 | ... |
| Minnesota | 5 | ... | 11 | 10 | 10 | 1 | 3 | 2 | 3 | 1 | 1 | 5 | 6 | 4 | 2-1 | 0-3 | 0-3 | 2-1 | 3-0 | 2-1 | ... | 85 | 77 | .525 | 6.0 |
| Chicago | 10 | 5 | ... | 13 | 14 | 1 | 3 | 3 | 4 | 5 | 2 | 1 | 3 | 7 | ... | 0-3 | 4-2 | 3-0 | 3-0 | 2-1 | ... | 83 | 79 | .512 | 8.0 |
| Detroit | 6 | 4 | 6 | ... | 8 | 4 | 5 | 2 | 2 | 4 | 2 | 1 | 4 | 8 | ... | 2-1 | 1-2 | 2-1 | 2-1 | 2-1 | 1-2 | 66 | 96 | .407 | 25.0 |
| Kansas City | 8 | 6 | 5 | 11 | ... | 0 | 3 | 4 | 2 | 4 | 3 | 3 | 4 | 4 | 0-3 | 3-0 | 1-2 | 2-1 | ... | 1-2 | 1-2 | 65 | 97 | .401 | 26.0 |

#### West Division

| Team | Sea. | Oak. | Ana. | Tex. | N.Y. | Bos. | Tor. | Bal. | T.B. | Cle. | Min. | Chi. | Det. | K.C. | Ari. | S.F. | L.A. | S.D. | Col. | Hou. | W | L | Pct. | GB |
|---|---|---|---|---|---|---|---|---|---|---|---|---|---|---|---|---|---|---|---|---|---|---|---|---|
| Seattle | ... | 10 | 15 | 15 | 6 | 6 | 6 | 8 | 7 | 5 | 8 | 7 | 5 | 6 | 2-1 | 2-1 | 2-1 | 4-2 | 2-1 | ... | 116 | 46 | .716 | ... |
| Oakland | 9 | ... | 14 | 9 | 6 | 5 | 6 | 7 | 7 | 3 | 4 | 8 | 6 | 6 | 3-0 | 2-4 | 2-1 | 2-1 | 3-0 | ... | 102 | 60 | .630 | 14.0 |
| Anaheim | 4 | 6 | ... | 7 | 4 | 4 | 5 | 4 | 7 | 5 | 3 | 6 | 5 | 5 | 1-2 | 0-3 | 4-2 | 2-1 | 3-0 | ... | 75 | 87 | .463 | 41.0 |
| Texas | 5 | 10 | 12 | ... | 4 | 2 | 3 | 7 | 5 | 4 | 5 | 2 | 1 | 5 | ... | 1-2 | 1-2 | 1-2 | 2-1 | 3-3 | 73 | 89 | .451 | 43.0 |

NOTE: Read across for wins, down for losses.

Tie game—Baltimore at New York, September 30 (15 innings).

Clinching dates: New York (East)—September 25; Cleveland (Central)—September 30; Seattle (West)—September 19; Oakland (wild card)—September 23.

### National League

#### East Division

| Team | Atl. | Phi. | N.Y. | Fla. | Mon. | Hou. | St.L. | Chi. | Mil. | Cin. | Pit. | Ari. | S.F. | L.A. | S.D. | Col. | N.Y. | Bos. | Tor. | Bal. | T.B. | W | L | Pct. | GB |
|---|---|---|---|---|---|---|---|---|---|---|---|---|---|---|---|---|---|---|---|---|---|---|---|---|---|
| Atlanta | ... | 10 | 10 | 9 | 13 | 3 | 3 | 4 | 3 | 4 | 5 | 2 | 4 | 2 | 3 | 4 | 2-1 | 3-3 | 1-2 | 2-1 | 1-2 | 88 | 74 | .543 | ... |
| Philadelphia | 9 | ... | 8 | 14 | 10 | 3 | 2 | 2 | 3 | 4 | 5 | 4 | 3 | 3 | 5 | 4 | 1-2 | 1-2 | 1-2 | 4-2 | 0-3 | 86 | 76 | .531 | 2.0 |
| New York | 9 | 11 | ... | 12 | 11 | 3 | 1 | 2 | 3 | 2 | 4 | 3 | 3 | 4 | 1 | 3 | 2-4 | 2-1 | 3-0 | 2-1 | 1-2 | 82 | 80 | .506 | 6.0 |
| Florida | 10 | 5 | 7 | ... | 12 | 3 | 3 | 3 | 4 | 2 | 4 | 2 | 2 | 2 | 3 | 2 | 2-1 | 1-2 | 2-1 | 3-0 | 4-2 | 76 | 86 | .469 | 12.0 |
| Montreal | 6 | 9 | 8 | 7 | ... | 0 | 2 | 3 | 2 | 2 | 5 | 3 | 2 | 4 | 3 | 4 | 1-2 | 1-2 | 3-3 | 1-2 | 2-1 | 68 | 94 | .420 | 20.0 |

#### Central Division

| Team | Hou. | St.L. | Chi. | Mil. | Cin. | Pit. | Atl. | Phi. | N.Y. | Fla. | Mon. | Ari. | S.F. | L.A. | S.D. | Col. | Tex. | Cle. | Min. | Chi. | Det. | K.C. | W | L | Pct. | GB |
|---|---|---|---|---|---|---|---|---|---|---|---|---|---|---|---|---|---|---|---|---|---|---|---|---|---|---|
| Houston | ... | 9 | 9 | 12 | 11 | 9 | 3 | 3 | 3 | 3 | 6 | 4 | 3 | 2 | 3 | 4 | 3-3 | 2-1 | 1-2 | ... | ... | 3-0 | 93 | 69 | .574 | ... |
| St. Louis | 7 | ... | 8 | 10 | 10 | 14 | 3 | 4 | 5 | 3 | 4 | 4 | 2 | 3 | 5 | 3 | ... | 1-2 | 3-0 | 3-0 | 1-2 | 0-3 | 93 | 69 | .574 | ... |
| Chicago | 8 | 9 | ... | 8 | 13 | 10 | 2 | 4 | 4 | 3 | 3 | 3 | 3 | 4 | 2 | 3 | ... | ... | 3-0 | 2-4 | 2-1 | 2-1 | 88 | 74 | .543 | 5.0 |
| Milwaukee | 5 | 7 | 9 | ... | 10 | 6 | 3 | 3 | 3 | 2 | 4 | 3 | 5 | 1 | 1 | 1 | ... | 2-1 | 1-2 | 0-3 | 1-2 | 1-2 | 68 | 94 | .420 | 25.0 |
| Cincinnati | 6 | 7 | 4 | 6 | ... | 9 | 2 | 2 | 4 | 4 | 4 | 1 | 4 | 4 | 2 | 3 | ... | 3-3 | 0-3 | 0-3 | 1-2 | ... | 66 | 96 | .407 | 27.0 |
| Pittsburgh | 8 | 3 | 6 | 11 | 8 | ... | 1 | 1 | 2 | 2 | 1 | 2 | 1 | 2 | 2 | 4 | ... | 3-0 | 1-2 | 1-2 | 1-2 | 2-1 | 62 | 100 | .383 | 31.0 |

#### West Division

| Team | Ari. | S.F. | L.A. | S.D. | Col. | Atl. | Phi. | N.Y. | Fla. | Mon. | Hou. | St.L. | Chi. | Mil. | Cin. | Pit. | K.C. | Det. | Sea. | Oak. | Ana. | Tex. | W | L | Pct. | GB |
|---|---|---|---|---|---|---|---|---|---|---|---|---|---|---|---|---|---|---|---|---|---|---|---|---|---|---|
| Arizona | ... | 10 | 10 | 12 | 13 | 5 | 3 | 3 | 4 | 3 | 2 | 2 | 6 | 3 | 5 | 4 | 2-1 | 2-1 | 1-2 | 0-3 | 2-1 | ... | 92 | 70 | .568 | ... |
| San Fran. | 9 | ... | 8 | 14 | 10 | 2 | 3 | 4 | 4 | 5 | 3 | 4 | 3 | 4 | 2 | 5 | ... | ... | 1-2 | 4-2 | 3-0 | 2-1 | 90 | 72 | .556 | 2.0 |
| Los Ang. | 9 | 11 | ... | 9 | 11 | 5 | 3 | 2 | 5 | 2 | 4 | 3 | 2 | 5 | 2 | 7 | ... | ... | 1-2 | 1-2 | 2-4 | 2-1 | 86 | 76 | .531 | 6.0 |
| San Diego | 7 | 5 | 10 | ... | 10 | 3 | 2 | 5 | 4 | 3 | 6 | 1 | 4 | 5 | 4 | 4 | ... | ... | 2-4 | 1-2 | 1-2 | 2-1 | 79 | 83 | .488 | 13.0 |
| Colorado | 6 | 9 | 8 | 9 | ... | 2 | 2 | 4 | 4 | 3 | 2 | 6 | 3 | 5 | 6 | 2 | ... | ... | 1-2 | 0-3 | 0-3 | 1-2 | 73 | 89 | .451 | 19.0 |

NOTE: Read across for wins, down for losses; interleague games are shaded.

Clinching dates: Atlanta (East)—October 5; Houston (Central)—October 7; Arizona (West)—October 5; St. Louis (wild card)—October 7.

## LEADERS

**American League**
**BA:** Ichiro Suzuki, Sea., .350.
**Runs:** Alex Rodriguez, Tex., 133.
**Hits:** Ichiro Suzuki, Sea., 242.
**TB:** Alex Rodriguez, Tex., 393.
**HR:** Alex Rodriguez, Tex., 52.
**RBI:** Bret Boone, Sea., 141.
**SB:** Ichiro Suzuki, Sea., 56.
**Wins:** Mark Mulder, Oak., 21.
**ERA:** Freddy Garcia, Sea., 3.05.
**CG:** Steve W. Sparks, Det., 8.
**IP:** Freddy Garcia, Sea., .238.2.
**SO:** Hideo Nomo, Bos., 220.
**Sv.:** Mariano Rivera, N.Y., 50.

**National League**
**BA:** Larry Walker, Col., .350.
**Runs:** Sammy Sosa, Chi., 146.
**Hits:** Rich Aurilia, S.F., 206.
**TB:** Sammy Sosa, Chi., 425.
**HR:** Barry Bonds, S.F., 73.
**RBI:** Sammy Sosa, Chi., 160.
**SB:** Juan Pierre, Col.; Jimmy Rollins, Phi., 46.
**Wins:** Matt Morris, St.L.; Curt Schilling, Ari., 22.
**ERA:** Randy Johnson, Ari., 2.49.
**CG:** Curt Schilling, Ari., 6.
**IP:** Curt Schilling, Ari., 256.2.
**SO:** Randy Johnson, Ari., 372.
**Sv.:** Robb Nen, S.F., 45.

**A.L. 20-game winners**
Mark Mulder, Oak., 21
Roger Clemens, N.Y., 20
Jamie Moyer, Sea., 20

**N.L. 20-game winners**
Matt Morris, St.L., 22
Curt Schilling, Ari., 22
Randy Johnson, Ari., 21
Jon Lieber, Chi., 20

**A.L. 100 RBIs**
Bret Boone, Sea., 141
Juan Gonzalez, Cle., 140
Alex Rodriguez, Tex., 135
Manny Ramirez, Bos., 125
Jim Thome, Cle., 124
Garret Anderson, Ana., 123
Rafael Palmeiro, Tex., 123
Jason Giambi, Oak., 120
Edgar Martinez, Sea., 116
Eric Chavez, Oak., 114
Tino Martinez, N.Y., 113
Magglio Ordonez, Chi., 113
Miguel Tejada, Oak., 113
Mike Cameron, Sea., 110
Troy Glaus, Ana., 108
Jermaine Dye, K.C.-Oak., 106
Corey Koskie, Min., 103
Carlos Delgado, Tor., 102
Carlos Beltran, K.C., 101
Roberto Alomar, Cle., 100

**N.L. 100 RBIs**
Sammy Sosa, Chi., 160
Todd Helton, Col., 146
Luis Gonzalez, Ari., 142
Barry Bonds, S.F., 137
Jeff Bagwell, Hou., 130
Albert Pujols, St.L., 130
Lance Berkman, Hou., 126
Phil Nevin, S.D., 126
Shawn Green, L.A., 125
Richie Sexson, Mil., 125
Larry Walker, Col., 123
Ryan Klesko, S.D., 113
Aramis Ramirez, Pit., 112
Bobby Abreu, Phi., 110
Jim Edmonds, St.L., 110
Moises Alou, Hou., 108
Vladimir Guerrero, Mon., 108
Scott Rolen, Phi., 107
Jeff Kent, S.F., 106
Andruw Jones, Atl., 104
Cliff Floyd, Fla., 103
Chipper Jones, Atl., 102
Jeromy Burnitz, Mil., 100
Mike Lowell, Fla., 100
Gary Sheffield, L.A., 100

**A.L. 40 homers**
Alex Rodriguez, Tex., 52
Jim Thome, Cle., 49
Rafael Palmeiro, Tex., 47
Troy Glaus, Ana., 41
Manny Ramirez, Bos., 41

**N.L. 40 homers**
Barry Bonds, S.F., 73
Sammy Sosa, Chi., 64
Luis Gonzalez, Ari., 57
Shawn Green, L.A., 49
Todd Helton, Col., 49
Richie Sexson, Mil., 45
Phil Nevin, S.D., 41

**Most Valuable Player**
A.L.: Ichiro Suzuki, OF, Sea.
N.L.: Barry Bonds, OF, S.F.

**Cy Young Award**
A.L.: Roger Clemens, N.Y.
N.L.: Randy Johnson, Ari.

**Rookie of the Year**
A.L.: Ichiro Suzuki, OF, Sea.
N.L.: Albert Pujols, OF-3B-1B, St.L.

**Manager of the Year**
A.L.: Lou Piniella, Sea.
N.L.: Larry Bowa, Phi.

**Hall of Fame additions**
Bill Mazeroski, 2B, 1956-72
Kirby Puckett, OF, 1984-95
Hilton Smith, P-OF-1B, Negro Leagues
Dave Winfield, OF, 1973-95

## SIGNIFICANT EVENTS

■ **April 1:** As part of Major League Baseball's desire to expand its international presence, the Rangers and Blue Jays opened the season in Puerto Rico. The Blue Jays beat the Rangers, 8-1, at Hiram Bithorn Stadium.

■ **April 6:** The Milwaukee Brewers opened their new park, Miller Park, with a 5-4 victory over the Cincinnati Reds.

■ **April 9:** The Pittsburgh Pirates opened their new park, PNC Park, by losing to the Cincinnati Reds, 8-2.

■ **September 11:** Following terrorist attacks that saw hijacked airplanes crash into New York City's World Trade Center, the Pentagon and a field in western Pennsylvania, baseball postponed all games—a total of 91—until September 17. The games were made up at the end of the schedule by extending the season one week.

## MEMORABLE MOMENTS

■ **April 17:** Barry Bonds of the San Francisco Giants collected his 500th career home run, a two-run shot in the eighth inning off Los Angeles Dodgers reliever Terry Adams.

■ **September 19:** Roger Clemens of the New York Yankees won his 16th consecutive game to tie an American League record. Clemens' 6-3 victory over the White Sox in Chicago enabled him to join Walter Johnson (Washington, 1912), Joe Wood (Boston, 1912), Lefty Grove (Philadelphia, 1931) and Schoolboy Rowe (Detroit, 1934) as the only pitchers in A.L. history to win 16 straight games.

■ **October 5:** Barry Bonds belted his 71st homer of the season, breaking Mark McGwire's 1998 record. Bonds hit the record home run in the first inning off Los Angeles Dodgers starter Chan Ho Park, and two innings later clubbed another homer off Park. Two days later, Bonds hit his 73rd and final homer of the season off Dodgers starter Dennis Springer.

■ **October 6:** The Seattle Mariners defeated the Texas Rangers, 1-0, to win their 116th game of the season, tying the major league record set by the 1906 Chicago Cubs. The Mariners finished the season the next day with a record of 116-46.

## ALL-STAR GAME

■ **Winner:** The A.L. used nine pitchers to hold the N.L. to only three hits and one run, and Derek Jeter, Cal Ripken Jr. and Magglio Ordonez each hit solo home runs to lead the American Leaguers. It gave the A.L. its fourth straight victory and 10th in the last 13 All-Star Games.

■ **Key inning:** The sixth, when leading, 2-1, Jeter and Ordonez homered consecutively to give the A.L. a 4-1 lead.

■ **Memorable moment:** A.L. third baseman Ripken, playing in his 18th and final All-Star Game, led off the third inning with a home run off Chan Ho Park to give the A.L. a 1-0 lead. Ripken, who at age 40 became the oldest player to hit a home run in an All-Star Game, received a thunderous standing ovation and later was named the game's MVP. It was Ripken's second All-Star Game MVP performance, as he joined Ted Williams, Willie Mays, Steve Garvey and Gary Carter as two-time winners.

■ **Top guns:** Jeff Kent (Giants), Randy Johnson (Diamondbacks), N.L.; Ripken (Orioles), Jeter (Yankees), Ordonez (White Sox), Roger Clemens (Yankees), A.L.

■ **MVP:** Ripken.

**Linescore**

July 10 at Seattle's Safeco Field
N.L. ......................0 0 0 0 0 1 0 0 0—1
A.L. ......................0 0 1 0 1 2 0 0 x—4
R. Johnson (Diamondbacks), Park (Dodgers) 3, Burkett (Braves) 4, Hampton (Rockies) 5, Lieber (Cubs) 6, Morris (Cardinals) 7, Shaw (Dodgers) 8, Wagner (Astros) 8, Sheets (Brewers) 8; Clemens (Yankees), Garcia (Mariners) 3, Pettitte (Yankees) 4, Mays (Twins) 5, Quantrill (Blue Jays) 6, Stanton (Yankees) 6, Nelson (Mariners) 7, Percival (Angels) 8, Sasaki (Mariners) 9. W—Garcia. L—Park. S—Sasaki.

## A.L. DIVISION SERIES

■ **Winners:** Seattle, down 2-1 after the first three games, came back to beat Cleveland two straight. The Yankees came back from a 2-0 deficit with three straight wins to edge Oakland in a five-game series victory.

■ **Turning points:** The tide turned in favor of the Mariners in the seventh inning of Game 4. Bartolo Colon was enjoying a 1-0 lead and the Indians were nine outs away from a series victory when the roof caved in. John Olerud started the inning with a walk and advanced to second on single by Stan Javier. Colon tried to pick Olerud off second, but his throw sailed into center field, allowing the runner to go to third. Colon then walked Mike Cameron to load the bases. Al Martin reached on a forceout at the plate. David Bell followed by hitting a foul ball down the left field line which outfielder Marty Cordova caught, but the ball was hit deep enough to allow Javier to score the tying run after the catch. Ichiro Suzuki and Mark McLemore followed with RBI singles to give the Mariners the lead on their way to a 6-2 victory. The Yankees lost the first two games of their series, but managed to win the third game, 1-0, on a home run by catcher Jorge Posada. Posada was hitless in nine previous career at-bats against lefthander Barry Zito, but he managed to connect in the fifth inning. His hit was one of only two safeties by the Yankees in the game.

■ **Memorable moments:** The Mariners were leading, 2-1, in Game 5, when the Indians loaded the bases in the third inning. The Indians' next batter, switch-hitter Roberto Alomar, had not grounded into a double play from the right side all season. But Mariners lefty Jamie Moyer induced Alomar into hitting into his second double play from the right side in three innings and Seattle survived the threat. The Mariners bullpen, which had been pounded two days earlier in a 17-2 loss, pitched three scoreless innings to secure the victory. Yankees righthander Roger Clemens was trailing 2-0 in the fifth inning of the opener, when he appeared uncomfortable on the mound. After manager Joe Torre went to investigate, Clemens was removed from the game, having suffered a strained hamstring making a play in the field earlier in the game. The Yankee bullpen couldn't keep them in the game, and the A's took the first game. In Game 4, A's right fielder Jermaine Dye suffered a broken leg while fouling off a pitch, ending his participation in the series.

■ **Memorable performances:** American League Rookie of the Year Suzuki collected 12 hits and batted .600, while teammates Bell and Edgar Martinez each batted .313 for the Mariners. Omar Vizquel had nine hits, six RBIs and a .409 batting mark for the Indians. His teammate, Juan Gonzalez, batted .348 with two home runs and five RBIs. Shortstop Derek Jeter and Posada each collected eight hits and batted .444 for the Yankees. A's center fielder Johnny Damon batted .409, first baseman Jason Giambi hit .353 and Terrence Long homered twice while batting .389. Zito allowed only two hits in eight innings of Game 3, but the big blow was Posada's home run that won the game, 1-0. Mike Mussina allowed only four hits in seven innings in winning the game for the Yankees. Tim Hudson hurled eight shutout innings in a 2-0 Game 2 victory.

**Linescores**

Seattle vs. Cleveland

**Game 1**—October 9, at Seattle
Cleveland...............0 0 0 3 0 1 0 1 0—5
Seattle ...................0 0 0 0 0 0 0 0 0—0
Colon, Wickman (9); Garcia, Charlton (6), Paniagua (8), Halama. W—Colon. L—Garcia.

HR—Burks (Cle.).

**Game 2**—October 11, at Seattle
Cleveland...............0 0 0 0 0 0 1 0 0—1
Seattle...................4 0 0 0 1 0 0 0 x—5
Finley, Riske (5), Shuey (7), Baez (8); Moyer, Nelson (7), Rhodes (8), Sasaki (9). W—Moyer. L—Finley. HR—Cameron, Martinez, Bell (Sea.).

**Game 3**—October 13, at Cleveland
Seattle...................1 0 0 0 0 0 1 0 0— 2
Cleveland...............2 2 4 0 1 3 0 5 x—17
Sele, Abbott (3), Halama (6), Paniagua (8); Sabathia, Riske (7), Rincon (7), Burba (8), Rocker (9). W—Sabathia. L—Sele. HR—Gonzalez, Lofton, Thome (Cle.).

**Game 4**—October 14, at Cleveland
Seattle...................0 0 0 0 0 0 3 1 2—6
Cleveland...............0 1 0 0 0 0 1 0 0—2
Garcia, Nelson (7), Rhodes (7), Sasaki (9); Colon, Baez (7), Rincon (8), Shuey (8). W—Garcia. L—Colon. HR—Martinez (Sea.); Gonzalez (Sea.).

**Game 5**—October 15, at Seattle
Cleveland...............0 0 1 0 0 0 0 0 0—1
Seattle...................0 2 0 0 0 0 1 0 x—3
Finley, Riske (5), Rincon (6), Baez (7); Moyer, Nelson (7), Rhodes (8), Sasaki (9). W—Moyer. L—Finley. S—Sasaki.

New York vs. Oakland

**Game 1**—October 10, at New York
Oakland..................1 0 0 1 0 0 1 2 0—5
New York................0 0 0 0 1 0 0 2 0—3
Mulder, Mecir (7), Isringhausen (9); Clemens, Hitchcock (5), Witasick (8), Stanton (8). W—Mulder. L—Clemens. S—Isringhausen. HR—Long 2, Ja. Giambi (Oak.); Martinez (N.Y.).

**Game 2**—October 11, at New York
Oakland..................0 0 0 1 0 0 0 0 1—2
New York................0 0 0 0 0 0 0 0 0—0
Hudson, Isringhausen (9); Pettitte, Mendoza (7), Rivera (9). W—Hudson. L—Pettitte. S—Isringhausen. HR—Gant (Oak.).

**Game 3**—October 13, at Oakland
New York................0 0 0 0 1 0 0 0 0—1
Oakland..................0 0 0 0 0 0 0 0 0—0
Mussina, Rivera (8); Zito, Guthrie (9). W—Mussina. L—Zito. S—Rivera. HR—Posada (N.Y.).

**Game 4**—October 14, at Oakland
New York................0 2 2 3 0 0 0 0 2—9
Oakland..................0 0 2 0 0 0 0 0 0—2
O. Hernandez, Stanton (6), Mendoza (8); Lidle, Hiljus (4), Magnante (4), Guthrie (6), Bradford (8), Tam (9). W—O. Hernandez. L—Lidle.

**Game 5**—October 15, at New York
Oakland..................1 1 0 0 1 0 0 0 0—3
New York................0 2 1 1 0 1 0 0 x—5
Mulder, Hudson (5), Mecir (7); Clemens, Stanton (5), Mendoza (7), Rivera (8). W—Stanton. L—Mulder. S—Rivera. HR—Justice (N.Y.).

## N.L. DIVISION SERIES

■ **Winners:** The Braves swept the Astros, outscoring Houston 14-6 in the three games. The Astros batted only .200 during the series and went hitless with runners in scoring position. The Diamondbacks edged the Cardinals in five games in a low-scoring series in which St. Louis actually outscored Arizona, 12-10. Righthander Curt Schilling was the difference in the series, as he twice defeated the Cardinals, holding them to one run on nine hits in 18 innings.

■ **Turning points:** The Braves took control of the series in the eighth inning of Game 1, when Chipper Jones belted a three-run homer off Astros closer Billy Wagner, giving Atlanta a 6-3 lead in an eventual 7-4 win. Shortly after the Cardinals' J.D. Drew homered in the eighth inning of Game 5 to tie the score, 1-1, the Diamondbacks ended the series in dramatic fashion with a ninth-inning rally at home. Matt Williams doubled to lead off the inning. Midre Cummings pinch-ran for Williams and was sacrificed to third by Damian Miller. After the Cardinals brought in reliever Steve Kline, Greg Colbrunn was intentionally walked. The next batter, Tony Womack, missed the pitch trying to bunt and Cummings was tagged out trying to steal home while Colbrunn advanced to second. After Danny Bautista pinch-ran for Colbrunn at second, Womack slapped a single to left field, scoring Bautista with the series-winning run.

■ **Memorable moments:** Craig Counsell of the Diamondbacks, who had hit only four home runs in 458 at-bats during the regular season, connected for a three-run homer in the seventh inning of Game 3, breaking a 2-2 deadlock in a game Arizona would win, 5-3.

■ **Memorable performances:** The Braves' Andruw Jones led all regulars with six hits and a .500 batting average. Chipper Jones smacked two home runs, drove in five runs and batted .444, and Julio Franco batted .308. Tom Glavine pitched eight scoreless innings and John Burkett allowed only two runs in 6.1 innings for Atlanta. Jeff Bagwell batted .429 on three hits for Houston.

### Linescores

Atlanta vs. Houston

**Game 1**—October 9, at Houston
Atlanta....................1 0 0 1 0 0 0 4 1—7
Houston .................0 0 0 0 2 1 0 0 1—4
Maddux, Seanez (7), Smoltz (8); Miller, Jackson (8), Wagner (8), Williams (9). W—Seanez. L—Jackson. S—Smoltz. HR—C. Jones, Jordan, A. Jones, Castilla (Atl.); Ausmus (Hou.).

**Game 2**—October 10, at Houston
Atlanta....................0 1 0 0 0 0 0 0 0—1
Houston .................0 0 0 0 0 0 0 0 0—0
Glavine, Smoltz (9); Mlicki, Dotel (6), Jackson (8), Cruz (8), Wagner (9). W—Glavine. L—Mlicki. S—Smoltz.

**Game 3**—October 12, at Atlanta
Houston .................0 0 0 0 0 0 2 0 0—2
Atlanta....................0 2 1 1 0 0 0 2 x—6
Reynolds, Cruz (5), Dotel (7), Villone (8); Burkett, Reed (7), Remlinger (7), Karsay (8), Smoltz (9). W—Burkett. L—Reynolds. HR—Ward (Hou.); Franco, C. Jones, Bako (Atl.).

St. Louis vs. Atlanta

**Game 1**—October 9, at Arizona
St. Louis ................0 0 0 0 0 0 0 0 0—0
Arizona ..................0 0 0 0 1 0 0 0 x—1
Morris, Stechschulte (8), Veres (8); Schilling. W—Schilling. L—Morris.

**Game 2**—October 10, at Arizona
St. Louis ................2 0 1 0 0 0 0 0 1—4
Arizona ..................0 0 0 0 0 0 0 1 0—1
W. Williams, Kline (8); Johnson, Morgan (9), Swindell (9), Batista (9). W—W. Williams. L—Johnson. HR—Pujols (St.L.).

**Game 3**—October 12, at St. Louis
Arizona ..................0 0 0 0 0 1 4 0 0—5
St. Louis ................0 0 0 2 0 0 1 0 0—3
Batista, Anderson (7), Morgan (8), Kim (8); Kile, Matthews (7), Timlin (7), Stechschulte (9), Kline (9). W—Batista. L—Matthews. S—Kim. HR—Counsell, Gonzalez (Ari.); Edmonds, Renteria (St.L.).

**Game 4**—October 13, at St. Louis
Arizona ..................1 0 0 0 0 0 0 0 0—1
St. Louis ................1 1 2 0 0 0 0 0 x—4
Lopez, Anderson (4), Swindell (7), Morgan (8); Smith, Hermanson (6), Kline (9). W—Smith. L—Lopez. S—Kline. HR—Vina, Edmonds (St.L.).

**Game 5**—October 14, at Arizona
St. Louis ................0 0 0 0 0 0 0 1 0—1
Arizona ..................0 0 0 1 0 0 0 0 1—2
Morris, Veres (9), Kline (9); Schilling. W—Schilling. L—Kline. HR—Drew (St.L.); Sanders (Ari.).

## NLCS

■ **Winner:** The Diamondbacks, in only their fourth year of existence, became the fastest expansion team in major league history to reach the World Series. Led by dominating pitching performances by aces Randy Johnson and Curt Schilling, and helped by some costly Atlanta errors, Arizona defeated the Braves in five games.

■ **Turning point:** Johnson's three-hit shutout in the opener and Schilling's four-hit win in Game 3 gave the Diamondbacks all the momentum they needed.

■ **Memorable moments:** A pinch-homer by Erubiel Durazo in the fifth inning of Game 5 broke a 1-1 tie and sent the Diamondbacks toward their first World Series. Atlanta second baseman Marcus Giles started the inning by booting a grounder by Craig Counsell. Two outs later, Mark Grace was due to bat, but he left the game with a tight hamstring. Durazo replaced Grace and made the Braves pay for Giles' error with his two-run shot.

■ **Top guns:** Craig Counsell (.381, 8 hits, 5 runs, 3 2Bs), Mark Grace (.375, 6 hits), Randy Johnson (2-0, 16.0 IP, 10 hits, 19 SO, 1.13 ERA), Curt Schilling (1-0, 9 IP, 12 SO, 1.00 ERA), Byung-Hyun Kim (5.0 IP, 2 Sv., 0.00 ERA), Diamondbacks; Tom Glavine (1-1, 12.0 IP, 1.50 ERA), Braves.

■ **MVP:** Counsell.

### Linescores

**Game 1**—October 16, at Arizona
Atlanta....................0 0 0 0 0 0 0 0 0—0
Arizona ..................1 0 0 0 1 0 0 0 x—2
Maddux, Remlinger (8), Karsay (8); Johnson. W—Johnson. L—Maddux.

**Game 2**—October 17, at Arizona
Atlanta....................1 0 0 0 0 0 2 5 0—8
Arizona ..................0 0 0 0 0 1 0 0 0—1
Glavine, Karsay (8), Smoltz; Batista, Morgan (8), Swindell (8), Witt (8), Kim (9). W—Glavine. L—Batista. HR—Giles, Surhoff, J. Lopez (Atl.).

**Game 3**—October 19, at Atlanta
Arizona ..................0 0 2 0 3 0 0 0 0—5
Atlanta....................0 0 0 1 0 0 0 0 0—1
Schilling; Burkett, Reed (5), Remlinger (5), Ligtenberg (6), Seanez (7), Millwood (8), Marquis (9). W—Schilling. L—Burkett.

**Game 4**—October 20, at Atlanta
Arizona ..................0 0 4 2 0 0 0 1 4—11
Atlanta....................1 1 0 0 0 0 1 1 0— 4
A. Lopez, Anderson (4), Morgan (7), Swindell (7), Batista (8), Kim (8); Maddux, Remlinger (4), Ligtenberg (5), Seanez (7), Karsay (8), Marquis (9). W—Anderson. L—Maddux. S—Kim. HR—Gonzalez (Ari.); A. Jones (Atl.).

**Game 5**—October 21, at Atlanta
Arizona ..................0 0 0 1 2 0 0 0 0—3
Atlanta....................0 0 0 1 0 0 1 0 0—2
Johnson, Kim (8); Glavine, Karsay (6), Smoltz (8). W—Johnson. L—Glavine. S—Kim. HR—Durazo (Ari.); Franco (Atl.).

## ALCS

■ **Winner:** The New York Yankees won their fourth straight pennant by holding the Mariners to a .211 batting average. The Mariners romped, 14-3, in Game 3, but could score only eight runs in their other four games. Seattle's scoring drought represented quite a turnaround for a Seattle team which won a major league record-tying 116 games and led the big leagues with 927 runs scored during the regular season.

■ **Turning point:** The Yankees took control in Game 1, scoring on an RBI single by Chuck Knoblauch in the second and adding two runs in the fourth on a home run by Paul O'Neill. They scored three second-inning runs the next day and held on to a 3-2 victory and a two-game series lead.

■ **Memorable moments:** The Mariners not only trounced the Yankees, 14-3 in Game 3, but they turned in two great defensive plays. In the third inning, Stan Javier robbed Alfonso Soriano of a home run with a leaping catch in left field. The following inning, right fielder Ichiro Suzuki nabbed Bernie Williams' drive to the wall.

■ **Top guns:** Paul O'Neill (.417, 5 hits, 2 HRs), Alfonso Soriano (.400, 6 hits, 5 runs), Chuck Knoblauch (.333, 6 hits), Bernie Williams (3 HRs), Andy Pettitte, (2-0, 14.1 IP, 11 hits, 2.51 ERA), Yankees; Bret Boone (.316, 6 hits, 2 HRs, 6 RBIs), Mariners.

■ **MVP:** Pettitte.

**Game 1**—October 17, at Seattle
New York...............0 1 0 2 0 0 0 0 1—4
Seattle...................0 0 0 0 1 0 0 0 1—2
Pettitte, Rivera (9); Sele, Charlton (7), Paniagua (8). W—Pettitte. L—Sele. S—Rivera. HR—O'Neill (N.Y.).

**Game 2**—October 18, at Seattle
New York...............0 3 0 0 0 0 0 0 0—3
Seattle...................0 0 0 2 0 0 0 0 0—2
Mussina, Mendoza (7), Rivera (8); Garcia, Rhodes (8), Nelson (9). W—Mussina. L—Garcia. S—Rivera. HR—Javier (Sea.).

**Game 3**—October 20, at New York
Seattle...................0 0 0 0 2 7 2 1 2—14
New York...............2 0 0 0 0 0 0 1 0— 3
Moyer, Paniagua (8), Halama (9); Hernandez, Stanton (6), Wohlers (6), Witasick (7). W—Moyer. L—Hernandez. HR—Boone, Buhner, Olerud (Sea.); Williams (N.Y.).

**Game 4**—October 21, at New York
Seattle...................0 0 0 0 0 0 0 1 0—1
New York...............0 0 0 0 0 0 0 1 2—3
Abbott, Charlton (6), Nelson (6), Rhodes (8), Sasaki (9); Clemens, Mendoza (6), Rivera (9). W—Rivera. L—Sasaki. HR—Boone (Sea.); Williams, Soriano (N.Y.).

**Game 5**—October 22, at New York
Seattle...................0 0 0 0 0 0 3 0 0— 3
New York...............0 0 4 1 0 4 0 3 x—12
Sele, Halama (5), Pineiro (6), Paniagua (8); Pettitte, Mendoza (7), Stanton (8), Rivera (9). W—Pettitte. L—Sele. HR—Williams, T. Martinez, O'Neill (N.Y.).

## WORLD SERIES

■ **Winner:** The Diamondbacks won their first World Series in a drama-filled series. Trailing 3-2 in the series, Arizona enjoyed a 15-2 laugher in Game 6, but had to rally for two runs off Yankee closer Mariano Rivera in the bottom of the ninth in Game 7.

■ **Turning point:** Luis Gonzalez' one-out single in the bottom of the ninth inning of Game 7 drove in Jay Bell with the series-ending run. Trailing 2-1, Arizona opened the inning with a single by Mark Grace. After David Dellucci was sent in to run for Grace, Damian Miller bunted to Rivera, who threw wildly to second, putting runners at first and second. Bell tried bunting the runners over, but forced Dellucci at third. Tony Womack then doubled home the tying run and Craig Counsell was hit by a pitch to load the bases. Gonzalez was the next batter and, with the infield playing in, blooped a single over short that scored Bell.

■ **Memorable moments:** With the Yankees trailing 3-1 with two out in the bottom of the ninth and a runner on first in Game 4, Tino Martinez hit a dramatic home run to tie the game. One inning later, Derek Jeter homered to give New York a 4-3 win in 10 innings. The next night the Yankees were trailing 2-0 with two out in the bottom of the ninth and this time Scott Brosius provided the dramatics with a home run to tie the game. Alfonso Soriano drove in the winning run for New York in the bottom of the 12th.

■ **Top guns:** Johnson (3-0, 17.1 IP, 9 hits, 19 SO, 1.04 ERA), Schilling (1-0, 21.1 IP, 12 hits, 26 SO, 1.69 ERA), Danny Bautista (.583, 7 hits), Steve Finley (.368, 7 hits, 5 runs), Reggie Sanders (.304, 6 runs, 7 hits), Diamondbacks; Paul O'Neill (.333, 5 hits), Roger Clemens (1-0, 13.1 IP, 10 hits, 19 SO, 1.35 ERA), Yankees.

■ **MVPs:** Johnson, Schilling.

### Linescores

**Game 1**—October 27, at Arizona
New York...............1 0 0 0 0 0 0 0 0—1
Arizona ..................1 0 4 4 0 0 0 0 x—9
Mussina, Choate (4), Hitchcock (5), Stanton (8); Schilling, Morgan (8), Swindell (9). W—Schilling. L—Mussina. HR—Counsell, Gonzalez (Ari.).

**Game 2**—October 28, at Arizona
New York...............0 0 0 0 0 0 0 0 0—0
Arizona ..................0 1 0 0 0 0 3 0 x—4
Pettitte, Stanton (8); Johnson. W—Johnson. L—Pettitte. HR—M. Williams (Ari.).

**Game 3**—October 30, at New York
Arizona ..................0 0 0 1 0 0 0 0 0—1
New York...............0 1 0 0 0 1 0 0 x—2
Anderson, Morgan (6), Swindell (7); Clemens, Rivera (8). W—Clemens. L—Anderson. S—Rivera. HR—Posada (N.Y.).

**Game 4**—October 31, at New York
Arizona ...........0 0 0 1 0 0 0 2 0 0—3
New York...........0 0 1 0 0 0 0 0 2 1—4
Schilling, Kim (8); Hernandez, Stanton (7), Mendoza (8), Rivera (10). W—Rivera. L—Kim. HR—Grace (Ari.); Martinez, Jeter, Spencer (N.Y.).

**Game 5**—November 1, at New York
Arizona ....0 0 0 0 2 0 0 0 0 0 0—2
New York..0 0 0 0 0 0 0 0 2 0 1—3
Batista, Swindell (8), Kim (9), Morgan (9), Lopez (12); Mussina, Mendoza (9), Rivera (10), Hitchcock (12). W—Hitchcock. L—Lopez. HR—Finley, Barajas (Ari.); Brosius (N.Y.).

**Game 6**—November 3, at Arizona
New York...............0 0 0 0 0 2 0 0 0— 2
Arizona ..................1 3 8 3 0 0 0 0 x—15
Pettitte, Witasick (3), Choate (4), Stanton (7); Johnson, Witt (8), Brohawn (9). W—Johnson. L—Pettitte.

**Game 7**—November 4, at Arizona
New York...............0 0 0 0 0 0 1 1 0—2
Arizona ..................0 0 0 0 0 1 0 0 2—3
Clemens, Stanton (7), Rivera (8); Schilling, Batista (8), Johnson (8). W—Johnson. L—Rivera. HR—Soriano (N.Y.).

# 2002

## FINAL STANDINGS

### American League

**East Division**

| Team | N.Y. | Bos. | Tor. | Bal. | T.B. | Min. | Chi. | Cle. | K.C. | Det. | Oak. | Ana. | Sea. | Tex. | N.L. | W | L | Pct. | GB |
|---|---|---|---|---|---|---|---|---|---|---|---|---|---|---|---|---|---|---|---|
| New York | .... | 10 | 10 | 13 | 13 | 6 | 4 | 6 | 5 | 8 | 5 | 4 | 4 | 4 | 11-7 | 103 | 58 | .640 | .... |
| Boston | 9 | .... | 13 | 13 | 16 | 3 | 2 | 5 | 4 | 5 | 6 | 4 | 4 | 4 | 5-13 | 93 | 69 | .574 | 10.5 |
| Toronto | 9 | 6 | .... | 15 | 11 | 1 | 2 | 3 | 4 | 6 | 6 | 2 | 3 | 1 | 9-9 | 78 | 84 | .481 | 25.5 |
| Baltimore | 6 | 6 | 4 | .... | 10 | 5 | 3 | 1 | 7 | 2 | 4 | 2 | 5 | 3 | 9-9 | 67 | 95 | .414 | 36.5 |
| Tampa Bay | 5 | 3 | 8 | 9 | .... | 2 | 3 | 2 | 2 | 4 | 1 | 1 | 4 | 4 | 7-11 | 55 | 106 | .342 | 48.0 |

**Central Division**

| Team | Min. | Chi. | Cle. | K.C. | Det. | N.Y. | Bos. | Tor. | Bal. | T.B. | Oak. | Ana. | Sea. | Tex. | N.L. | W | L | Pct. | GB |
|---|---|---|---|---|---|---|---|---|---|---|---|---|---|---|---|---|---|---|---|
| Minnesota | .... | 11 | 11 | 14 | 14 | 0 | 3 | 6 | 1 | 5 | 3 | 5 | 5 | 6 | 10-8 | 94 | 67 | .584 | .... |
| Chicago | 8 | .... | 9 | 11 | 12 | 2 | 4 | 4 | 4 | 4 | 2 | 3 | 5 | 5 | 8-10 | 81 | 81 | .500 | 13.5 |
| Cleveland | 8 | 10 | .... | 9 | 10 | 3 | 4 | 3 | 5 | 4 | 2 | 3 | 3 | 4 | 6-12 | 74 | 88 | .457 | 20.5 |
| Kansas City | 5 | 8 | 10 | .... | 10 | 1 | 2 | 3 | 0 | 4 | 1 | 3 | 3 | 7 | 5-13 | 62 | 100 | .383 | 32.5 |
| Detroit | 4 | 7 | 9 | 9 | .... | 1 | 4 | 0 | 4 | 2 | 1 | 1 | 2 | 5 | 6-12 | 55 | 106 | .342 | 39.0 |

**West Division**

| Team | Oak. | Ana. | Sea. | Tex. | N.Y. | Bos. | Tor. | Bal. | T.B. | Min. | Chi. | Cle. | K.C. | Det. | N.L. | W | L | Pct. | GB |
|---|---|---|---|---|---|---|---|---|---|---|---|---|---|---|---|---|---|---|---|
| Oakland | .... | 11 | 8 | 13 | 4 | 3 | 3 | 5 | 8 | 6 | 7 | 5 | 8 | 6 | 16-2 | 103 | 59 | .636 | .... |
| Anaheim | 9 | .... | 9 | 12 | 3 | 3 | 7 | 7 | 8 | 4 | 6 | 6 | 6 | 8 | 11-7 | 99 | 63 | .611 | 4.0 |
| Seattle | 11 | 10 | .... | 13 | 5 | 5 | 6 | 4 | 5 | 4 | 4 | 4 | 6 | 5 | 11-7 | 93 | 69 | .574 | 10.0 |
| Texas | 6 | 7 | 7 | .... | 3 | 3 | 8 | 6 | 5 | 3 | 4 | 5 | 2 | 4 | 9-9 | 72 | 90 | .444 | 31.0 |

NOTE: Read across for wins, down for losses.

Clinching dates: New York (East)—September 21; Minnesota (Central)—September 15; Oakland (West)—September 26; Anaheim (wild card)—September 26.

### National League

**East Division**

| Team | Atl. | Mon. | Phi. | Fla. | N.Y. | St.L. | Hou. | Cin. | Pit. | Chi. | Mil. | Ari. | S.F. | L.A. | Col. | S.D. | A.L. | W | L | Pct. | GB |
|---|---|---|---|---|---|---|---|---|---|---|---|---|---|---|---|---|---|---|---|---|---|
| Atlanta | .... | 13 | 11 | 11 | 12 | 5 | 3 | 4 | 3 | 4 | 5 | 3 | 3 | 2 | 4 | 3 | 15-3 | 101 | 59 | .631 | .... |
| Montreal | 6 | .... | 11 | 9 | 11 | 3 | 3 | 5 | 3 | 3 | 4 | 2 | 4 | 2 | 2 | 3 | 12-6 | 83 | 79 | .512 | 19.0 |
| Philadelphia | 7 | 8 | .... | 9 | 10 | 4 | 3 | 4 | 2 | 4 | 5 | 3 | 3 | 3 | 3 | 2 | 10-8 | 80 | 81 | .497 | 21.5 |
| Florida | 8 | 10 | 10 | .... | 8 | 4 | 3 | 1 | 4 | 2 | 4 | 1 | 4 | 3 | 2 | 5 | 10-8 | 79 | 83 | .488 | 23.0 |
| New York | 7 | 8 | 9 | 11 | .... | 3 | 2 | 4 | 1 | 5 | 5 | 2 | 0 | 2 | 3 | 3 | 10-8 | 75 | 86 | .466 | 26.5 |

**Central Division**

| Team | St.L. | Hou. | Cin. | Pit. | Chi. | Mil. | Atl. | Mon. | Phi. | Fla. | N.Y. | Ari. | S.F. | L.A. | Col. | S.D. | A.L. | W | L | Pct. | GB |
|---|---|---|---|---|---|---|---|---|---|---|---|---|---|---|---|---|---|---|---|---|---|
| St. Louis | .... | 13 | 11 | 11 | 12 | 10 | 1 | 3 | 2 | 2 | 3 | 4 | 4 | 4 | 4 | 5 | 8-4 | 97 | 65 | .599 | .... |
| Houston | 6 | .... | 11 | 11 | 11 | 10 | 3 | 3 | 3 | 3 | 4 | 3 | 1 | 3 | 3 | 4 | 5-7 | 84 | 78 | .519 | 13.0 |
| Cincinnati | 8 | 6 | .... | 11 | 12 | 13 | 2 | 1 | 2 | 5 | 2 | 0 | 2 | 4 | 3 | 5 | 2-10 | 78 | 84 | .481 | 19.0 |
| Pittsburgh | 6 | 6 | 7 | .... | 9 | 15 | 3 | 3 | 4 | 2 | 4 | 2 | 2 | 2 | 2 | 2 | 3-9 | 72 | 89 | .447 | 24.5 |
| Chicago | 6 | 8 | 5 | 10 | .... | 7 | 2 | 3 | 2 | 4 | 1 | 2 | 3 | 2 | 4 | 2 | 6-6 | 67 | 95 | .414 | 30.0 |
| Milwaukee | 7 | 8 | 6 | 4 | 10 | .... | 1 | 2 | 1 | 2 | 1 | 2 | 1 | 1 | 3 | 5 | 2-10 | 56 | 106 | .346 | 41.0 |

**West Division**

| Team | Ari. | S.F. | L.A. | Col. | S.D. | Atl. | Mon. | Phi. | Fla. | N.Y. | St.L. | Hou. | Cin. | Pit. | Chi. | Mil. | A.L. | W | L | Pct. | GB |
|---|---|---|---|---|---|---|---|---|---|---|---|---|---|---|---|---|---|---|---|---|---|
| Arizona | .... | 8 | 9 | 14 | 12 | 3 | 4 | 4 | 5 | 5 | 2 | 3 | 6 | 4 | 4 | 4 | 11-7 | 98 | 64 | .605 | .... |
| San Fran. | 11 | .... | 11 | 11 | 14 | 3 | 2 | 3 | 3 | 6 | 2 | 5 | 4 | 4 | 3 | 5 | 8-10 | 95 | 66 | .590 | 2.5 |
| Los Angeles | 10 | 8 | .... | 12 | 10 | 4 | 5 | 4 | 3 | 4 | 2 | 3 | 2 | 4 | 4 | 5 | 12-6 | 92 | 70 | .568 | 6.0 |
| Colorado | 5 | 8 | 7 | .... | 11 | 3 | 4 | 3 | 5 | 3 | 2 | 3 | 3 | 4 | 2 | 3 | 7-11 | 73 | 89 | .451 | 25.0 |
| San Diego | 7 | 5 | 9 | 8 | .... | 3 | 4 | 4 | 1 | 4 | 1 | 2 | 1 | 4 | 4 | 1 | 8-10 | 66 | 96 | .407 | 32.0 |

NOTE: Read across for wins, down for losses; interleague games are shaded.

Tie game—San Francisco at Atlanta (3-3), August 15 (10 innings).

Clinching dates: Atlanta (East)—September 9; St. Louis (Central)—September 20; Arizona (West)—September 28; San Francisco (wild card)—September 28.

## LEADERS

**American League**
**BA:** Manny Ramirez, Bos., .349.
**Runs:** Alfonso Soriano, N.Y., 128.
**Hits:** Alfonso Soriano, N.Y., 209
**TB:** Alex Rodriguez, Tex., 389.
**HR:** Alex Rodriguez, Tex., 57.
**RBI:** Alex Rodriguez, Tex., 142.
**SB:** Alfonso Soriano, N.Y., 41.
**Wins:** Barry Zito, Oak., 23.
**ERA:** Pedro Martinez, Bos., 2.26.
**CG:** Paul Byrd, Kansas City, 7.
**IP:** Roy Halladay, Tor., 239.1.
**SO:** Pedro Martinez, 239.
**Sv.:** Eddie Guardado, Min., 45.

**National League**
**BA:** Barry Bonds, S.F., .370.
**Runs:** Sammy Sosa, Chi., 122.
**Hits:** Vladimir Guerrero, Mon., 206.
**TB:** Vladimir Guerrero, Mon., 364.
**HR:** Sammy Sosa, Chi., 49.
**RBI:** Lance Berkman, Hou., 128.
**SB:** Luis Castillo, Fla., 48.
**Wins:** Randy Johnson, Ari., 24.
**ERA:** Randy Johnson, Ari., 2.32.
**CG:** Randy Johnson, Ari., 8.
**IP:** Randy Johnson, Ari., 260.
**SO:** Randy Johnson, Ari., 334.
**Sv.:** John Smoltz., Atl., 55.

**A.L. 20-game winners**
Barry Zito, Oak., 23
Derek Lowe, Bos., 21
Pedro Martinez, Bos., 20

**N.L. 20-game winners**
Randy Johnson, Ari., 24
Curt Schilling, Ari., 23

**A.L. 100 RBIs**
Alex Rodriguez, Tex., 142
Maggio Ordonez, Chi., 135
Miguel Tejada, Oak., 131
Garret Anderson, Ana., 123
Jason Giambi, N.Y., 122
Nomar Garciaparra, Bos., 120
Jim Thome, Cle., 118
Troy Glaus, Ana, 111
Eric Chavez, Oak., 109
Carlos Delgado, Tor., 108
Manny Ramirez, Bos., 107
Bret Boone, Sea.,107
Carlos Beltran, K.C., 105
Rafael Palmeiro, Tex., 105
Paul Konerko, Chi., 104
Raul Ibanez., K.C., 103
John Olerud, Sea., 102
Bernie Williams, N.Y., 102
Alfonso Soriano, N.Y., 102
Vernon Wells, Tor., 100

**N.L. 100 RBIs**
Lance Berkman, Hou., 128
Albert Pujols, St.L., 127
Pat Burrell, Phi., 116
Shawn Green, L.A., 114
Valadimir Guerrero, Mon., 111
Barry Bonds, S.F., 110
Scott Rolen, Phi.-St.L., 110
Todd Helton, Col., 109
Jeff Kent, S.F., 108
Sammy Sosa, Chi., 108
Larry Walker, Col., 104
Brian Giles, Pit., 103
Tony Gonzalez, Ari., 103
Fred McGriff, Chi., 103
Richie Sexson, Mil., 102
Chipper Jones, Atl, 100

**A.L. 40 homers**
Alex Rodriguez, Tex., 57
Jim Thome, Cle., 52
Rafael Palmeiro, Tex., 43
Jason Giambi, N.Y., 41

**N.L. 40 homers**
Sammy Sosa, Chi., 49
Barry Bonds, S.F., 46
Lance Berkman, Hou., 42
Shawn Green, L.A., 42

**Most Valuable Player**
A.L.: Miguel Tejada, SS, Oak.
N.L.: Barry Bonds, OF, S.F.

**Cy Young Award**
A.L.: Barry Zito, Oak.
N.L.: Randy Johnson, Ari.

**Rookie of the Year**
A.L.: Eric Hinske, 3B, Tor.
N.L.: Jason Jennings, P, Col.

**Manager of the Year**
A.L.: Mike Scioscia, Ana.
N.L.: Tony La Russa, St.L.

**Hall of Fame additions**
Ozzie Smith, SS, 1978-1996

## SIGNIFICANT EVENTS

■ **February 12:** Major League Baseball took over ownership of the struggling Montreal Expos franchise.
■ **June 22:** Cardinals pitcher Darryl Kile was found dead in his Chicago hotel room. Longtime Cardinals broadcaster Jack Buck had died four days earlier in St. Louis.
■ **July 5:** Baseball was saddened again when former Red Sox great Ted Williams died in Inverness, Fla.
■ **August 30:** Just hours before baseball would have experienced another work stoppage, owners and players resolved their labor impasse. The new Basic Agreement will expire in December 2006.

## MEMORABLE MOMENTS

■ **April 27:** Boston's Derek Lowe tossed a no-hitter against Tampa Bay in a 10-0 Red Sox victory.
■ **May 2:** Mike Cameron became the 13th player in big-league history to hit four home runs in one game. The Seattle player accomplished the feat against the White Sox in a 15-4 Mariners romp.
■ **May 23:** Los Angeles' Shawn Green became the 14th man in the four-homer club. In addition to his home run outburst, he also hit a single and a double against Milwaukee and established a Major League total-bases record (19) in a 16-3 Dodgers triumph.
■ **August 9:** Barry Bonds became the fourth major leaguer to reach 600 homers. He joined Hank Aaron, Babe Ruth and Willie Mays when he connected against Pittsburgh's Kip Wells.
■ **September 4:** Oakland set an A.L. record with its 20th consecutive victory, a 12-11 win over Kansas City. The A's had an off-day September 5, then saw their streak end September 6 in a 6-0 loss to Minnesota.

## ALL-STAR GAME

■ **Winner:** What winner? With both teams' 30-man rosters depleted by the 11th inning, the managers, umpires and commissioner Bud Selig decided the 73rd All-Star game would end in a tie, 7-7.
■ **Key inning:** The 11th. The decision had been made before the bottom of the inning that if the National League could not push across a run, the game would end. Florida's Mike Lowell made it to second base with one out, but Seattle's Freddy Garcia struck out pitcher Vicente Padilla and catcher Benito Santiago. The sellout crowd at Miller Park was informed of the decision and let its displeasure be known.
■ **Memorable moment:** Offense ruled the day as the game had four lead changes. But Twins outfielder Torii Hunter provided a defensive gem in the first inning when he robbed Giants star Barry Bonds of a homer. Hunter ranged back and made a leaping grab to pull Bonds' drive back from the fence and into his glove for the out.
■ **Top guns:** Bonds (Giants), Lowell (Marlins), Jimmy Rollins (Phillies) Curt Schilling (Diamondbacks), N.L.; Alfonso Soriano (Yankees), Johnny Damon (Red Sox), Paul Konerko (White Sox), Garcia (Seattle), A.L.
■ **MVP:** None. There was no winner; there was no MVP.

**Linescore**

July 9 at Milwaukee's Miller Park
A.L. ....................................000 110 410 00—7
N.L. ....................................013 010 200 00—7
Lowe (Red Sox), Halladay (Blue Jays) 3, Buehrle (White Sox) 4, Zito (Athletics) 6, Guardado (Twins) 6, Sasaki (Mariners) 7, Urbina (Red Sox) 8, Rivera (Yankees) 9, Garcia (Mariners) 10; Schilling (Diamondbacks), Williams (Pirates) 3, Perez (Dodgers) 4, Gagne (Dodgers) 5, Hoffman (Padres) 6, Remlinger (Braves) 7, Kim (Diamondbacks) 7, Nen (Giants) 8, Smoltz (Braves) 9, Padilla (Philles) 10.

## A.L. DIVISION SERIES

■ **Winners:** Minnesota, down 2-1 after three games, shocked Oakland, which lost a Game 5 in a Division Series for the third consecutive year. In another shocker, Anaheim won its first postseason series ever by handling the Yankees in four games.
■ **Turning points:** The scrappy Twins, targeted for elimination before the season by commissioner Bud Selig, came out clawing and scratching in Game 1. They overcame a 5-1 deficit with two runs in the third, three in the sixth and one in the seventh to win 7-5. By Game 4, they were trailing in the series 2-1 and facing elimination when the A's jumped on top 2-0. The Twins went on to score 11 unanswered runs, aided by two A's fourth-inning throwing errors, to win the game. They closed it out the next day with a 5-4 victory. ... With the series tied at 1, the Angels took control of Game 3 in the eighth inning when, having overcome a 6-1 deficit with clutch hitting and clutch pitching to pull into a tie, they got an RBI double from Darin Erstad and a two-run homer from Tim Salmon. It was the third straight game in the series in which the eighth inning proved decisive. The Yankees were stunned and never fully recovered in the series. Another benchmark of the game: The Angels' bullpen shut out the Yankees in Game 3, allowing only three hits in 6⅔ innings.
■ **Memorable moments:** The Twins-A's series came down to the bottom of the ninth in Game 5 as the A's had rallied from a 5-1 deficit to get to within one. With two outs and the A's Randy Velarde on first, Twins closer Eddie Guardado got Ray Durham to pop up for the last out and the Twins won, 5-4. ... By wasting a five-run led in Game 3, the Yankees blew the second largest lead in their postseason history. In Game 2, the Angels set a club postseason record with 17 hits and four home runs. In the four games, the Angels' offense scored 31 runs and hit .376, a divisional postseason record. Jarrod Washburn's Game 4 victory snapped a streak of 15 consecutive winless starts made by postseason pitchers on three days' rest. Also in Game 4, the Angels set a Division Series record in the bottom of the fifth by scoring eight runs on 10 hits, breaking the game open.
■ **Memorable performances:** Twins catcher A.J. Pierzynski had a career-high four hits in Game 1. He hit .438 in the series with four RBIs. Twins rookie Michael Cuddyer hit .385. Teammate Doug Mientkiewicz had four RBIs and two home runs. Pitcher Brad Radke won two games in the series, including the deciding Game 5 in which he allowed only one run in 6⅔ innings. A's third baseman Eric Chavez hit .381 with five RBIs and a home run. A's pitcher Mark Mulder made Game 5 a pitching duel with a strong seven-inning performance in which he allowed two runs and struck out nine. ... Angels third baseman Troy Glaus hit two home runs in Game 1, becoming only the seventh major leaguer to accomplish that feat in his first playoff game. Glaus hit .313 for the series. Angels pitcher Francisco Rodriguez became the first pitcher in MLB history to win two postseason games without recording a regular-season win. Yankees shortstop Derek Jeter hit .500 in the series with eight hits (including two home runs) and three RBIs.

**Linescores**

Minnesota vs. Oakland

**Game 1**—October 1 at Oakland
Minnesota .............0 1 2 0 0 3 1 0 0—7
Oakland ..................3 2 0 0 0 0 0 0 0—5
Radke, Santana (6), Romero (7), Guardado (9); Hudson, Lilly (6), Lidle (7), Rincon (8), Mecir (9). W—Radke. L—Lilly. HR—Koskie, Mientkiewicz (Min.).

**Game 2**—October 2, at Oakland
Minnesota .............0 0 0 0 0 1 0 0 0—1
Oakland ..................3 0 0 5 1 0 0 0 x—9
Mays, Fiore (4), Lohse (6), Hawkins (8); Mulder, Bradford (7), Koch (9). W—Mulder. L—Mays. HR—Guzman (Min.); Chavez (Oak.).

**Game 3**—October 4, at Minnesota
Oakland .............2 0 0 1 0 1 2 0 0— 6
Minnesota .............0 0 0 1 2 0 0 0 0—3
Zito, Rincon (7), Koch (9); Reed, Santana (6), Jackson (7), Romero (8), Hawkins (9). W—Zito. L—Reed. S—Koch. HR—Dye, Hatteberg, Durham (Oak.).

**Game 4**—October 5, at Minnesota
Oakland ................0 0 2 0 0 0 0 0 0— 2
Minnesota ...........0 0 2 7 0 0 2 0 x—11
Hudson, Lilly (4), Bowie (8); Milton, Lohse (8). W—Milton. L—Hudson. HR—Tejada (Oak.); Mientkiewicz (Min.).

**Game 5**—October 6, at Oakland
Minnesota .............0 1 1 0 0 0 0 0 3—5
Oakland ..................0 0 1 0 0 0 0 0 3—4
Radke, Romero (7), Hawkins (8), Guardado (9); Mulder, Bradford (8), Koch (9). W—Radke. L—Mulder. HR—Pierzynski (Min.); Ellis (Oak.).

Anaheim vs. New York

**Game 1**—October 1, at New York
Anaheim ................0 0 1 0 2 1 0 1 0—5
New York................1 0 0 2 1 0 0 4 x—8
Washburn, Weber (8), Schoeneweis (8), Donnelly (8); Clemens, Mendoza (6), Karsay (8), Rivera (9). W—Karsay. L—Weber. S—Rivera. HR—Glaus 2 (Ana.); Williams, White, Giambi, Jeter (N.Y.).

**Game 2**—October 2, at New York
Anaheim ................1 2 1 0 0 0 0 3 1—8
New York................0 0 1 2 0 2 0 0 1—6
Appier, Rodriguez (6), Weber (8), Donnelly (8), Percival (8); Pettitte, Hernandez (4), Karsay (8), Stanton (8), Weaver (9). W—Rodriguez. L—Hernandez. S—Percival. HR—Salmon, Spiezio, Anderson, Glaus (Ana.); Jeter, Soriano (N.Y.).

**Game 3**—October 4, at Anaheim
New York................3 0 3 0 0 0 0 0 0—6
Anaheim ................0 1 2 1 0 1 1 3 x—9
Mussina, Weaver (5), Stanton (6), Karsay (8); Ra. Ortiz, Lackey (3), Schoeneweis (6), Rodriguez (7), Percival (9).W—Rodriguez. L—Stanton. S—Percival. HR—Salmon, Kennedy (Ana.).

**Game 4**—October 5, at Anaheim
New York................0 1 0 0 1 1 1 0 1—5
Anaheim ................0 0 1 0 8 0 0 0 x—9
Wells, Mendoza (5), Hernandez (5), Karsay (8), Stanton (8); Washburn, Donnelly (6), Schoeneweis (7), Rodriguez (7), Percival (9). W—Washburn. L—Wells. HR—Posada (N.Y.); Wooten (Ana.).

## N.L. DIVISION SERIES

■ **Winners:** The Cardinals' potent lineup neutralized the Diamondbacks' pitching and St. Louis won in three games. The Cards outscored Arizona, 20-6, and trailed in only one inning. The Giants defeated the Braves, who owned the N.L.'s best regular-season record, in five games.

■ **Turning points:** Game 1, when Arizona ace Randy Johnson was roughed up for 10 hits and two home runs in a 12-2 Cardinals romp. For the D-backs, the game got off to an ominous start with a first-inning throwing error by shortstop Tony Womack. In Game 5 of the Giants-Braves series, slugger Barry Bonds hit a leadoff home run in the fourth, giving his team a 2-0 lead it would not give up. It finally give Bonds a meaningful postseason dinger.

■ **Memorable moments:** After collecting two hits against Schilling and a two-run homer off Johnson, Cards third baseman Scott Rolen suffered a season-ending shoulder sprain in a fluke collision with baserunner Alex Cintron. Miguel Cairo delivered a tie-breaking single in the ninth inning of Game 2, then took over for Rolen in Game 3 and went 3-for-3 with two RBIs. ... Bonds got a playoff monkey off his back by breaking out in Game 2 with his second postseason home run. Braves pitcher Greg Maddux shook off past postseason disappointments in Game 3 and won. Giants pitcher Livan Hernandez boasted before Game 4 that he never lost in October, then went out and backed up his words with a stellar performance. After the Giants clinched the series with a game-ending double-play in Game 5, Bonds temporarily forgot there was already one out and it took a little longer for the victory to sink in.

■ **Memorable performances:** Cards lefthander Chuck Finley matched the D-backs' Curt Schilling pitch-for-pitch in a classic postseason duel. Left fielder Albert Pujols contributed two defensive gems in Game 3 by throwing out runners at home plate. Fernando Vina had nine hits in the series. ... Braves third baseman Vinny Castilla hit .389 in the series with seven hits, one homer and four RBIs. Pitcher Kevin Millwood had 14 strikeouts in two starts. Giants center fielder Kenny Lofton was a catalyst all series long as the leadoff man, hitting .350 with seven hits and two RBIs. Pitcher Russ Ortiz picked up two wins.

### Linescores

St. Louis vs. Arizona

**Game 1**—October 1, at Arizona
St. Louis ..............2 0 0 3 0 1 6 0 0—12
Arizona ................1 0 1 0 0 0 0 0 0— 2
Morris, Fassero (8), Crudale (9); Johnson, Mantei (7), Swindell (7), Fetters (7), Helling (8). W—Morris. L—Johnson. HR—Rolen, Edmonds (St.L.).

**Game 2**—October 3, at Arizona
St. Louis ...............0 0 1 0 0 0 0 0 1—2
Arizona .................0 0 0 0 0 0 0 1 0—1
C. Finley, Kline (7), White (7), Fassero (8), Isringhausen (9); Schilling, Koplove (8), Myers (9). W—Fassero. L—Koplove. S—Isringhausen. HR—Drew (St. L.).

**Game 3**—October 5, at St. Louis
Arizona .................0 2 0 0 1 0 0 0 0—3
St. Louis ...............0 1 1 2 0 0 0 2 x—6
Batista, Swindell (4), Helling (5), Myers (7), Kim (8); Benes, Fassero (5), White (7), Kline (8), Isringhausen (9). W—Fassero. L—Batista. S—Isringhausen. HR—Barajas, Dellucci (Ariz.).

San Francisco vs. Atlanta

**Game 1**—October 2, at Atlanta
San Francisco ........0 3 0 3 0 2 0 0 0—8
Atlanta....................0 2 0 0 0 0 0 3 0—5
Ortiz, Worrell (8), Eyre (8), Nen (9); Glavine, Hammond (6), Gryboski (6), Moss (8), Holmes (9). W—Ortiz. L—Glavine. S—Nen. HR—Lopez, Sheffield (Atl.).

**Game 2**—October 3, at Atlanta
San Francisco ........0 1 0 0 0 1 0 0 1—3
Atlanta....................1 3 0 3 0 0 0 0 x—7
Rueter, Aybar (4), Witasick (6), Rodriguez (8); Millwood, Remlinger (7), Holmes (8), Smoltz (8). W—Millwood. L—Rueter. HR—Bonds, Aurilia, Snow (S.F.); Castilla, Lopez (Atl.).

**Game 3**—October 5, at San Francisco
Atlanta..................0 0 1 0 0 5 0 0 4—10
San Francisco ......1 0 0 0 0 1 1 0 0— 2
Maddux, Hammond (7), Remlinger (8), Gryboski (9); Schmidt, Aybar (6), Rodriguez (7), Eyre (8), Worrell (9), Fultz (9), Nen (9), Witasick (9). W—Maddux. L—Schmidt. HR—Lockhart (Atl.); Bonds (S.F.).

**Game 4**—October 6, at San Francisco
Atlanta....................0 0 0 0 1 2 0 0 0—3
San Francisco ........2 2 3 0 1 0 0 0 x—8
Glavine, Gryboski (3), Moss (5), Ligtenberg (7); Hernandez, Eyre (9), Nen (9). W—Hernandez. L—Glavine. HR—Aurilia (S.F.).

**Game 5**—October 7, at Atlanta
San Francisco ........0 1 0 1 0 0 1 0 0—3
Atlanta....................0 0 0 0 0 1 0 0 0—1
Ortiz, Fultz (6), Rodriguez (6), Worrell (7), Nen (9); Millwood, Hammond (6), Remlinger (7), Holmes (7), Smoltz (8). W—Ortiz. L—Millwood. S—Nen. HR—Bonds (S.F.).

## NLCS

■ **Winner:** The Giants needed just five games to upend the Cardinals and their potent offense with timely pitching and a little offensive firepower of their own.

■ **Turning point:** In the eighth inning of Game 4 with the score tied and the Giants leading the series 2-1, Cardinals manager Tony La Russa opted to walk Giants slugger Barry Bonds. The strategy backfired when catcher Benito Santiago followed with a two-run shot that would become the game-winner. The Giants took command of the series and never looked back.

■ **Memorable moments:** In Game 1, Kenny Lofton provided an Oscar-worthy performance by looking indignant at Mike Crudale when the Cardinals reliever threw high and inside. It sparked a bench-clearing incident that included an exchange of words between managers. It gave an edge to the Giants, as Lofton seemed to pester and distract the Cardinals all series long—he got the pennant-clinching hit in the bottom of the ninth of Game 5. Little-used Shawon Dunston set up Lofton's decisive hit with a single.

■ **Top guns:** Bonds had just one home run in the series, but his presence rattled the Cardinals so much that La Russa seemed to overstrategize. Giants third baseman David Bell hit .412 in the series with seven hits. Shortstop Rich Aurilia hit .333 with two home runs and five RBIs. Jason Schmidt pitched seven shutout innings in a stellar Game 2 performance, limiting the Cards to four hits while striking out eight. Much was written in St. Louis about the absence of Scott Rolen, but Miguel Cairo more than pulled his weight by hitting .385 with five hits. Jim Edmonds hit .400 wtih eight hits and four RBIs.

■ **MVP:** Santiago

### Linescores

**Game 1**—October 9, at St. Louis
San Francisco ........1 4 1 0 1 2 0 0 0—9
St. Louis ...............0 1 0 0 2 2 0 1 0—6
Rueter, Rodriguez (6), Worrell (8), Nen (9); Morris, Crudale (5), Veres (7), Kline (9). W—Rueter. L—Morris. S—Nen. HR—Lofton, Bell, Santiago (S.F.); Pujols, Cairo, Drew (St. L.).

**Game 2**—October 10, at St. Louis
San Francisco ........1 0 0 0 2 0 0 0 1—4
St. Louis ...............0 0 0 0 0 0 0 1 0—1
Schmidt, Eyre (8), Nen (8); Williams, White (7), Fassero (8), Isringhausen (9). W—Schmidt. L—Williams. S—Nen. HR—Aurilia (S.F.); Perez (St.L.).

**Game 3**—October 12, at San Francisco
St. Louis ...............0 0 2 1 1 1 0 0 0—5
San Francisco ........0 1 0 0 3 0 0 0 0—4
Finley, Veres (6), Kline (7), White (8), Isringhausen (9); Ortiz, Fultz (5), Witasick (6), Rodriguez (7), Eyre (8), Worrell (9). W—Finley. L—Witasick. S—Isringhausen. HR—Matheny, Edmonds, Marrero (St.L.); Bonds (S.F.).

**Game 4**—October 13, at San Francisco
St. Louis ...............2 0 0 0 0 0 0 0 1—3
San Francisco ........0 0 0 0 0 2 0 2 x—4
Benes, White (6), Kline (8); Hernandez, Rodriguez (7), Eyre (8), Worrell (8), Nen (9). W—Worrell. L—White. S—Nen. HR—Santiago (S.F.).

**Game 5**—October 14, at San Francisco
St. Louis ...............0 0 0 0 0 0 1 0 0—1
San Francisco ........0 0 0 0 0 0 0 1 1—2
Morris, Kline (9); Rueter, Rodriguez (7), Eyre (8), Worrell (8). W—Worrell. L—Morris.

## ALCS

■ **Winner:** The Angels in four. After losing the first game in Minnesota, Anaheim took three straight and won the series. Angels pitchers did not allow a home run in the entire series.

■ **Turning point:** Darin Erstad's home run in the first inning of Game 2 gave notice the Angels' bats would not stay silenced as they were in Game 1. The one-run lead would turn into six before the Twins got on the board, and the Angels never looked back the rest of the series. The win snapped the Angels' four-game losing streak in ALCS competition.

■ **Memorable moments:** The 10-run seventh inning in Game 5 set LCS records for most runs, plate appearances and hits in an inning. Scott Spiezo and Adam Kennedy had two hits in the inning, another first. Kennedy had three home runs in the game and would be named MVP of the series based on his Game 5 performance. Angels pitcher Francisco Rodriguez's Game 3 victory in relief, added to his two wins in the divisional series against New York, made him the first pitcher in MLB history to get his first three Ws in the postseason. The Angels bullpen was a strength the entire season, allowing only four runs over 14-1/3 innings of work in the series and striking out 18. The Twins got a strong pitching performce in Game 3 from Eric Milton, who pitched six strong innings only to be matched by the Angels' Jarrod Washburn's seven strong innings.

■ **Top guns:** Darrin Erstad (.364, 8 hits, 2 RBIs), Adam Kennedy (.357, 5 hits, 3 HRs, 5 RBIs), Scott Spezio (.353, 6 hits, 1 HR, 5 RBIs), Francisco Rodriguez (0.00 ERA, 2 wins, 7 Ks); David Ortiz (.313, 5 hits, 2 RBIs), Eric Milton (1.50 ERA, 4 Ks).

■ **MVP:** Kennedy

**Game 1**—October 8, at Minnesota
Anaheim ................0 0 1 0 0 0 0 0 0—1
Minnesota .............0 1 0 0 1 0 0 0 x—2
Appier, Donnelly (6), Schoeneweis (7), Weber (8); Mays, Guardado (9). W—Mays. L—Appier. S—Guardado.

**Game 2**—October 9, at Minnesota
Anaheim ................1 3 0 0 0 2 0 0 0—6
Minnesota .............0 0 0 0 0 3 0 0 0—3
R. Ortiz, Donnelly (6), Rodriguez (7), Percival (8); Reed, Santana (6), Romero (8), Hawkins (8), Jackson (9). W—R. Ortiz. L—Reed. S—Percival. HR—Erstad, Fullmer (Ana.).

**Game 3**—October 11, at Anaheim
Minnesota .............0 0 0 0 0 0 1 0 0—1
Anaheim ................0 1 0 0 0 0 0 1 x—2
Milton, Hawkins (7), Santana (7), Jackson (7), Romero (7); Washburn, Rodriguez (8), Percival (9). W—Rodriguez. L—Romero. S—Percival. HR—Anderson, Glaus (Ana.).

**Game 4**—October 12, at Anaheim
Minnesota .............0 0 0 0 0 0 0 0 1—1
Anaheim ................0 0 0 0 0 0 2 5 x—7
Radke, Santana (7), Hawkins (8), Romero (8), Jackson (8), Wells (8); Lackey, Rodriguez (8), Weber (9). W—Lackey. L—Radke.

**Game 5**—October 13, at Anaheim
Minnesota ..........1 1 0 0 0 0 3 0 0— 5
Anaheim ............0 0 1 0 2 0 10 0 x—13
Mays, Santana (6), Hawkins (7), Romero (7), Wells (7), Lohse (8); Appier, Donnelly (6), Rodriguez (7), Weber (8), Percival (9). W—Rodriguez. L—Santana. HR—Kennedy 3, Spezio (Ana.).

## WORLD SERIES

■ **Winner:** The Angels over the Giants in seven games in a thrilling, back-and-forth all-California Fall Classic. The Angels won despite trailing at one point in all four of their victories. Offense was key: The two teams combined for 21 home runs and 85 runs, a Series-first in each category.

■ **Turning point:** The Angels came back to Anaheim for Game 6 trailing 3-2 in the series. Falling behind 5-0 and just eight outs from elimination, the team came alive. Scott Spezio sparked the comeback in the bottom of the seventh with a three-run homer. The Angels got three more in the bottom of the eighth with the help of a two-run double by Troy Glaus. Troy Percival retired the Giants in the ninth. The comeback was the biggest ever by a team facing World Series elimination.

■ **Memorable moments:** Game 2 was wild and wooly, with neither starters Russ Ortiz nor Kevin Appier pitching beyond the third inning. The game, won by the Angels 11-10, had six home runs, including two by Tim Salmon whose eighth-inning shot gave the Angels the lead for good. Salmon's prowess would make him the first player to have four hits and two homers in a World Series game. Rookie phenom reliever Francisco Rodriguez's three three innings of shutout work in Game 2. In Game 3's 10-4 win over the Giants, the Angels batted around in consecutive innings—another World Series first. The Giants scored 16 runs on 16 hits in a Game 5 rout sparked by Jeff Kent's two home runs. In Game 7, Darin Erstad caught Kenny Lofton's flyball with two on, two out to clinch the Angels' first World Series title.

■ **Top guns:** Barry Bonds (.471, 4 HRs, 6 RBIs), J.T. Snow, (.407, 11 hits, 4 RBIs), Jeff Kent (3 HRs, 7 RBIs); Troy Glaus (.385, 3 HRs, 10 hits, 8 RBIs), Tim Salmon (.346, 9 hits, 2 HRs, 5 RBIs), Scott Spezio (6 hits, 1 HR, 8 RBIs), Francisco Rodriguez (2.08 ERA, 13 Ks).

■ **MVP:** Glaus

### Linescores

**Game 1**—October 19, at Anaheim
San Francisco ........0 2 0 0 0 2 0 0 0—4
Anaheim ................0 1 0 0 0 2 0 0 0—3
Schmidt, Rodriguez (6), Worrell (8), Nen (9); Washburn, Donnelly (6), Schoeneweis (8), Weber (8). W— Schmidt. L—Washburn. S—Nen. HR—Bonds, Sanders, Snow (S.F.), Glaus 2 (Ana.).

**Game 2**—October 20, at Anaheim
San Francisco ......0 4 1 0 4 0 0 0 1—10
Anaheim ..............5 2 0 0 1 1 0 2 x—11
Ortiz, Zerber (2), Witasick (6), Fultz (6), Rodriguez (6), Worrell (8); Appier, Lackey (3), Weber (5), Rodriguez (6), Percival (9). W—Rodriguez. L—Rodriguez. S—Percival. HR—Sanders, Bell, Kent, Bonds (S.F.), Salmon 2 (Ana.).

**Game 3**—October 22, at San Francisco
Anaheim ..............0 0 4 4 0 1 0 1 0—10
San Francisco ......1 0 0 0 3 0 0 0 0— 4
Ortiz, Donnelly (6), Schoeneweis (8); Hernandez, Witasick (4), Fultz (5), Rodriguez (7), Eyre (8). W—Ortiz. L—Hernandez. HR— Aurilia, Bonds (S.F.).

**Game 4**—October 23, at San Francisco
Anaheim ................0 1 2 0 0 0 0 0 0—3
San Francisco ........0 0 0 0 3 0 0 1 x—4
Lackey, Weber (6), Rodriguez (7); Rueter, Rodriguez (7), Worrell (8), Nen (9). W—Worell. L—Rodriguez. S—Nen. HR—Glaus (Ana.).

**Game 5**—October 24, at San Francisco
Anaheim ..............0 0 0 0 3 1 0 0 0— 4
San Francisco ......3 3 0 0 0 2 4 4 x—16
Washburn, Donnelly (5), Weber (6), Shields (7); Schmidt, Zerbe (5), Rodriguez (7), Worrell (8). W—Zerbe. L—Washburn. HR—Kent 2, Aurilia (S.F.).

**Game 6**—October 26, at Anaheim
San Francisco ........0 0 0 0 3 1 1 0 0—5
Anaheim ................0 0 0 0 0 0 3 3 x—6
Ortiz, Rodriguez (7), Eyre (7), Worrell (7), Nen (8); Appier, Rodriguez (5), Donnelly (8), Percival (9). W—Donnelly. L—Worrell. HR—Dunston, Bonds (S.F.), Spiezio, Erstad (Ana.).

**Game 7**—October 27, at Anaheim
San Francisco ........0 1 0 0 0 0 0 0 0—1
Anaheim ................0 1 3 0 0 0 0 0 x—4
Hernandez, Zerbe (3), Rueter (4), Worrell (8); Lackey, Donnelly (6), Rodriguez (8), Percival (9). W—Lackey. L—Hernandez. S—Percival.

# 2003

## FINAL STANDINGS

### American League

#### East Division

| Team | N.Y. | Bos. | Tor. | Bal. | T.B. | Min. | Chi. | K.C. | Cle. | Det. | Oak. | Sea. | Ana. | Tex. | N.L. | W | L | Pct. | GB |
|---|---|---|---|---|---|---|---|---|---|---|---|---|---|---|---|---|---|---|---|
| New York | ... | 10 | 10 | 13 | 14 | 7 | 2 | 4 | 5 | 5 | 3 | 5 | 6 | 4 | 13-5 | 101 | 61 | .623 | ..... |
| Boston | 9 | ... | 10 | 10 | 12 | 2 | 5 | 5 | 4 | 8 | 3 | 5 | 6 | 5 | 11-7 | 95 | 67 | .586 | 6.0 |
| Toronto | 9 | 9 | ... | 11 | 8 | 3 | 3 | 5 | 4 | 7 | 2 | 4 | 7 | 4 | 10-8 | 86 | 76 | .531 | 15.0 |
| Baltimore | 6 | 9 | 8 | ... | 8 | 3 | 2 | 3 | 3 | 3 | 2 | 4 | 8 | 7 | 5-13 | 71 | 91 | .438 | 30.0 |
| Tampa Bay | 5 | 7 | 11 | 11 | ... | 0 | 3 | 3 | 2 | 4 | 3 | 5 | 3 | 3 | 3-15 | 63 | 99 | .389 | 38.0 |

#### Central Division

| Team | Min. | Chi. | K.C. | Cle. | Det. | N.Y. | Bos. | Tor. | Bal. | T.B. | Oak. | Sea. | Ana. | Tex. | N.L. | W | L | Pct. | GB |
|---|---|---|---|---|---|---|---|---|---|---|---|---|---|---|---|---|---|---|---|
| Minnesota | ... | 10 | 8 | 10 | 15 | 0 | 4 | 3 | 4 | 6 | 8 | 3 | 4 | 5 | 10-8 | 90 | 72 | .556 | ..... |
| Chicago | 9 | ... | 11 | 11 | 11 | 4 | 4 | 6 | 4 | 3 | 4 | 2 | 4 | 3 | 10-8 | 86 | 76 | .531 | 4.0 |
| Kansas City | 11 | 8 | ... | 13 | 14 | 2 | 1 | 1 | 4 | 4 | 2 | 4 | 3 | 7 | 9-9 | 83 | 79 | .512 | 7.0 |
| Cleveland | 9 | 8 | 6 | ... | 12 | 2 | 2 | 2 | 3 | 5 | 3 | 3 | 3 | 4 | 6-12 | 68 | 94 | .420 | 22.0 |
| Detroit | 4 | 8 | 5 | 7 | ... | 1 | 1 | 2 | 3 | 2 | 3 | 1 | 1 | 1 | 4-14 | 43 | 119 | .265 | 47.0 |

#### West Division

| Team | Oak. | Sea. | Ana. | Tex. | N.Y. | Bos. | Tor. | Bal. | T.B. | Min. | Chi. | K.C. | Cle. | Det. | N.L. | W | L | Pct. | GB |
|---|---|---|---|---|---|---|---|---|---|---|---|---|---|---|---|---|---|---|---|
| Oakland | ... | 7 | 12 | 15 | 6 | 4 | 5 | 7 | 6 | 1 | 5 | 7 | 6 | 6 | 9-9 | 96 | 66 | .593 | ..... |
| Seattle | 12 | ... | 11 | 10 | 4 | 2 | 3 | 5 | 4 | 6 | 7 | 5 | 6 | 8 | 10-8 | 93 | 69 | .574 | 3.0 |
| Anaheim | 8 | 8 | ... | 9 | 3 | 3 | 2 | 1 | 6 | 5 | 3 | 6 | 6 | 6 | 11-7 | 77 | 85 | .475 | 19.0 |
| Texas | 4 | 10 | 10 | ... | 5 | 4 | 5 | 2 | 6 | 4 | 4 | 2 | 5 | 6 | 4-14 | 71 | 91 | .438 | 25.0 |

NOTE: Read across for wins, down for losses.

Clinching dates: New York (East)—September 23; Minnesota (Central)—September 23; Oakland (West)—September 23; Boston (wild card)—September 25.

### National League

#### East Division

| Team | Atl. | Fla. | Phi. | Mon. | N.Y. | Chi. | Hou. | St.L. | Pit. | Cin. | Mil. | S.F. | L.A. | Ari. | Col. | S.D. | A.L. | W | L | Pct. | GB |
|---|---|---|---|---|---|---|---|---|---|---|---|---|---|---|---|---|---|---|---|---|---|
| Atlanta | ... | 9 | 9 | 12 | 11 | 4 | 5 | 4 | 7 | 3 | 4 | 2 | 4 | 5 | 6 | 6 | 10-5 | 101 | 61 | .623. | ... |
| Florida | 10 | ... | 13 | 13 | 12 | 2 | 1 | 3 | 2 | 4 | 7 | 1 | 2 | 5 | 2 | 5 | 9-6 | 91 | 71 | .562 | 10.0 |
| Phil. | 10 | 6 | ... | 11 | 12 | 5 | 4 | 4 | 2 | 4 | 2 | 3 | 5 | 2 | 4 | 4 | 8-7 | 86 | 76 | .531 | 15.0 |
| Montreal | 7 | 6 | 8 | ... | 14 | 3 | 3 | 1 | 3 | 4 | 6 | 7 | 2 | 2 | 4 | 4 | 9-9 | 83 | 79 | .512 | 18.0 |
| New York | 8 | 7 | 7 | 5 | ... | 1 | 4 | 1 | 4 | 4 | 3 | 4 | 3 | 2 | 5 | 3 | 5-10 | 66 | 95 | .410 | 34.5 |

#### Central Division

| Team | Chi. | Hou. | St.L. | Pit. | Cin. | Mil. | Atl. | Fla. | Phi. | Mon. | N.Y. | S.F. | L.A. | Ari. | Col. | S.D. | A.L. | W | L | Pct. | GB |
|---|---|---|---|---|---|---|---|---|---|---|---|---|---|---|---|---|---|---|---|---|---|
| Chicago | ... | 9 | 8 | 10 | 10 | 10 | 2 | 4 | 1 | 3 | 5 | 4 | 2 | 4 | 3 | 4 | 9-9 | 88 | 74. | 543 | ... |
| Houston | 7 | ... | 11 | 10 | 12 | 9 | 1 | 5 | 2 | 3 | 2 | 2 | 4 | 1 | 4 | 3 | 11-7 | 87 | 75 | .537 | 1.0 |
| St. Louis | 9 | 7 | ... | 10 | 7 | 13 | 2 | 3 | 2 | 5 | 5 | 1 | 2 | 3 | 2 | 4 | 10-8 | 85 | 77 | .525 | 3.0 |
| Pittsburgh | 8 | 6 | 7 | ... | 11 | 7 | 2 | 4 | 4 | 3 | 2 | 2 | 1 | 3 | 6 | 4 | 5-7 | 75 | 87 | .463 | 13.0 |
| Cincinnati | 7 | 5 | 9 | 5 | ... | 8 | 3 | 2 | 5 | 2 | 2 | 3 | 2 | 2 | 4 | 3 | 7-5 | 69 | 93 | .426 | 19.0 |
| Milw. | 6 | 8 | 3 | 10 | 10 | ... | 2 | 2 | 4 | 0 | 6 | 1 | 2 | 3 | 1 | 5 | 5-7 | 68 | 94 | .420 | 20.0 |

#### West Division

| Team | S.F. | L.A. | Ari. | Col. | S.D. | Atl. | Fla. | Phi. | Mon. | N.Y. | Chi. | Hou. | St.L. | Pit. | Cin. | Mil. | A.L. | W | L | Pct. | GB |
|---|---|---|---|---|---|---|---|---|---|---|---|---|---|---|---|---|---|---|---|---|---|
| San Fran. | ... | 13 | 14 | 12 | 14 | 4 | 5 | 3 | 0 | 2 | 2 | 4 | 5 | 4 | 3 | 5 | 10-8 | 100 | 61 | .621 | ... |
| Los Ang. | 6 | ... | 9 | 12 | 8 | 2 | 5 | 2 | 4 | 3 | 4 | 2 | 4 | 5 | 4 | 4 | 11-7 | 85 | 77 | .525 | 15.5 |
| Arizona | 5 | 10 | ... | 10 | 9 | 2 | 2 | 4 | 4 | 4 | 2 | 5 | 3 | 3 | 7 | 3 | 11-4 | 84 | 78 | .519 | 16.5 |
| Colorado | 7 | 7 | 9 | ... | 12 | 0 | 4 | 2 | 3 | 2 | 3 | 2 | 4 | 3 | 2 | 5 | 9-6 | 74 | 88 | .457 | 26.5 |
| San Diego | 5 | 11 | 10 | 7 | ... | 1 | 1 | 3 | 2 | 3 | 2 | 3 | 2 | 2 | 3 | 1 | 8-10 | 64 | 98 | .395 | 36.5 |

NOTE: Read across for wins, down for losses.

Clinching dates: Atlanta (East)—September 18; Chicago (Central)—September 27; San Francisco (West)—September 17; Florida (wild card)—September 26.

## SIGNIFICANT EVENTS

■ **February 19:** MLB proposed evaluating umpires with QuesTec Inc.'s Umpire Information System. The system was used in at least 10 parks in 2003, prompting backlash from the World Umpires Association.
■ **March 18:** Because of the impending war in Iraq, MLB canceled the season opener in Japan.
■ **May 15:** Major League Baseball approved the sale of the Angels to advertising businessman Arturo Moreno, who became the first Hispanic owner to hold a majority stake in a major league club.

## MEMORABLE MOMENTS

■ **April 2:** The Rangers' Alex Rodriguez became the youngest player to hit 300 home runs.
■ **April 4:** The Cubs' Sammy Sosa became the 18th player—and first Latin American—to hit 500 home runs.
■ **April 27:** Philadelphia's Kevin Millwood threw a no-hitter in a 1-0 win against the Giants.
■ **May 11:** The Rangers' Rafael Palmeiro became the 19th player to hit 500 home runs.
■ **June 3:** In a game at Wrigley Field, umpires found cork in Sammy Sosa's shattered bat. He was suspended for eight games.
■ **June 11:** A record six Astros pitchers combined for the first no-hitter against the Yankees since 1958.
■ **June 13:** In his fourth attempt, Yankees pitcher Roger Clemens got his 300th career victory. In the same game, against the Cardinals, he recorded his 4,000th career strikeout.
■ **June 23:** With a steal against the Dodgers, the Giants' Barry Bonds became the first player to steal 500 bases and hit 500 home runs.
■ **June 29:** Boston's Bill Mueller became the first major leaguer to hit grand slams from each side of the plate in the same game when he did it in a win against the Rangers.

## ALL-STAR GAME

■ **Winner:** American League, 7-6.
■ **Key inning:** The eighth. The A.L. trailed 6-4 heading into the inning, but Eric Gagne surrendered a one-out double to Garret Anderson. Anderson was removed for pinch runner Melvin Mora, who scored on a double by Vernon Wells, to make it 6-5. Pinch hitter Hank Blalock then hit a two-run homer to put the A.L. up for good.
■ **Memorable moments:** Blalock's home run came in his first All-Star at-bat. It won the game and also, for the first time, clinched home-field advantage in the World Series for the American League. Garret Anderson, who had won the Home Run Derby the night before, was 3-for-4 with a home run and two RBIs.
■ **Top guns:** Andruw Jones (Braves), Mike Lowell (Marlins), Todd Helton (Rockies), Jason Schmidt (Giants) N.L.; Anderson (Angels), Blalock (Rangers), Roger Clemens (Yankees), Jason Giambi (Yankees), Vernon Wells (Blue Jays), A.L.
■ **MVP:** Anderson.

**Linescore**

July 15 at Chicago's U.S. Cellular Field
A.L. ....................................000 050 100—7
N.L.......................................001 002 13x—6
Schmidt (Giants), Randy Wolf (Phillies) 3, Kerry Wood (Cubs) 4, Russ Ortiz (Braves) 5, Woody Williams (Cardinals) 6, Billy Wagner (Astros) 7, Gagne (Dodgers) 8, Esteban Loaiza (White Sox), Clemens (Yankees) 3, Jamie Moyer (Mariners) 4, Shigetoshi Hasegawa (Mariners) 5, Eddie Guardado (Twins) 5, Mark Mulder (A's) 6, Brendan Donnelly (Angels) 8, Keith Foulke (A's) 9. W—Donnelly. L—Gagne. S—Foulke. HR—A. Jones, Helton, N.L., Giambi, Anderson, Blalock, A.L.

## LEADERS

**American League**
**BA:** Bill Mueller, Bos., .326.
**Runs:** Alex Rodriguez, Tex., 124.
**Hits:** Vernon Wells, Tor., 215.
**TB:** Vernon Wells, Tor., 373.
**HR:** Alex Rodriguez, Tex., 47.
**RBI:** Carlos Delgado, Tor., 145.
**SB:** Carl Crawford, T.B., 55.
**Wins:** Roy Halladay, Tor., 22.
**ERA:** Pedro Martinez, Bos., 2.22.
**CG:** Paul Byrd, Kansas City, 7.
**IP:** Roy Halladay, Tor., 266.0.
**SO:** Esteban Loiaza, CWS., 207.
**Sv.:** Keith Foulke, Oak., 43.

**National League**
**BA:** Albert Pujols, St.L., .359.
**Runs:** Albert Pujols, St.L., 137.
**Hits:** Albert Pujols, St.L., 212.
**TB:** Albert Pujols, St.L., 394.
**HR:** Sammy Sosa, CHC, 49.
**RBI:** Preston Wilson, Col., 141.
**SB:** Juan Pierre, Fla., 65.
**Wins:** Russ Ortiz, Atl., 21.
**ERA:** Jason Schmidt, S.F., 2.34.
**CG:** Randy Johnson, Ari., 8.
**IP:** Livan Hernandez, Mon., 233.1.
**SO:** Kerry Wood, CHC., 266.
**Sv.:** Eric Gagne, L.A., 55.

**A.L. 20-game winners**
Roy Halladay, Tor., 22
Esteban Loaiza, Chi., 21
Jamie Moyer, Sea., 21
Andy Pettite, N.Y., 21

**N.L. 20-game winners**
Russ Ortiz, Atl., 21

**A.L. 100 RBIs**
Carlos Delgado, Tor., 145
Alex Rodriguez, Tex., 118
Bret Boone, Sea., 117
Vernon Wells, Tor., 117
Garret Anderson, Ana., 116
Carlos Lee, CWS, 113
Rafael Palmeiro, Tex., 112
Jason Giambi, NYY, 107
Aubrey Huff, T.B., 107
Hideki Matsui, NYY, 106
Miguel Tejada, Oak., 106
Nomar Garciaparra, Bos., 105
Frank Thomas, CWS, 105
Manny Ramirez, Bos., 104
Torii Hunter, Min., 103
Eric Chavez, Oak., 101
David Ortiz, Bos., 101
Jorge Posada, NYY, 101
Carlos Beltran, K.C., 100
Jay Gibbons, Bal., 100

**N.L. 100 RBIs**
Preston Wilson, Col., 141
Gary Sheffield, Atl., 132
Jim Thome, Phi., 131
Albert Pujols, St.L., 124
Richie Sexson, Mil., 124
Todd Helton, Col., 117
Andruw Jones, Atl., 116
Javy Lopez, Atl., 109
Chipper Jones, Atl., 106
Aramis Ramirez, Pit.-CHC, 106
Mike Lowell, Fla., 105
Luis Gonzalez, Ari., 104
Scott Rolen, St.L., 104
Sammy Sosa, CHC, 103
Bobby Abreu, Phi., 101
Jeff Bagwell, Hou., 100
Edgar Renteria, St.L., 100

**A.L. 40 homers**
Alex Rodriguez, Tex., 47
Carlos Delgado, Tor., 42
Frank Thomas, CWS, 42
Jason Giambi, NYY, 41

**N.L. 40 homers**
Jim Thome, Phi., 47
Barry Bonds, S.F., 45
Richie Sexson, Mil., 45
Javy Lopez, Atl., 43
Albert Pujols, St.L., 43
Sammy Sosa, CHC, 40

**Most Valuable Player**
A.L.: Alex Rodriguez, SS, Tex.
N.L.: Barry Bonds, OF, S.F.

**Cy Young Award**
A.L.: Roy Halladay, Tor.
N.L.: Eric Gagne, L.A.

**Rookie of the Year**
A.L.: Angel Berroa, SS, K.C.
N.L.: Dontrelle Willis, LHP, Fla.

**Manager of the Year**
A.L.: Tony Pena, K.C.
N.L.: Jack McKeon, Fla.

**Hall of Fame additions**
Eddie Murray, 1B, 1977-1997
Gary Carter, C, 1975-1992

## A.L. DIVISION SERIES

■ **Winners:** After losing the series opener, the Yankees bounced back to beat the Twins in four games. The Red Sox overcame an 0-2 deficit and edged the A's in Game 5.
■ **Turning points:** Alfonso Soriano's RBI single in the seventh inning of Game 2 broke a 1-1 tie and sparked a 3-run inning for the Yankees. They were down 0-1 in the series, and the win meant they headed to the Metrodome with the series even instead of down 0-2. They then pulled off back-to-back wins at the Metrodome—the first team ever to do so in the postseason. ... The Red Sox fell behind the A's 0-2 in the series and headed back to Boston in a must-win situation. In Game 3, the A's were down 1-0 when bats came alive in the sixth. But baserunning mistakes by Eric Byrnes and Miguel Tejada cost the A's. They left the sixth with a 1-1 tie instead of leading 3-1 and went on to lose the game, 3-1, on Trot Nixon's walkoff two-run homer in the 11th inning. They would go on to drop Games 4 and 5 and lose the series.
■ **Memorable moments:** In Game 4, the Twins' Johan Santana and the Yankees' David Wells engaged in a pitchers' duel for three innings before the Yankees struck in the fourth. Nick Johnson, who had been on an 0-for-26 skid, hit a single to left to score two runs after the Twins walked Juan Rivera in front of him. His hit put the Yankees up 6-0. ... Nixon's pinch-hit walkoff homer on a 1-1 pitch in the 11th staved off elimination for the Red Sox and allowed them to go on to win the series. Ramirez's game-turning three-run homer in the sixth inning of Game 5 powered the Red Sox to a series win and was especially memorable because those RBIs were his first of the series.
■ **Memorable performances:** The Yankees starters—Mike Mussina, Andy Pettitte, Roger Clemens and David Wells—went 3-1 with a 1.88 ERA in the series. In 2002, the same four pitchers went 0-1 with a 10.41 ERA in the Yankees Division Series loss to Anaheim. Derek Jeter hit a solo homer in the ninth inning, his 12th career playoff homer and major league-record 107th career postseason hit. Closer Mariano Rivera threw four perfect innings in two games, earning saves in both. ... The Boston bullpen performed well in the series, earning two of the team's three wins in the series and a save in the third.

**Linescores**

New York vs. Minnesota

**Game 1**—September 30, at New York
Minnesota...............0 0 1 0 0 2 0 0 0—3
New York................0 0 0 0 0 0 0 0 1—1
Santana, Reed (5), Romero (7), Hawkins (7) and Guardado (9); Mussina, Nelson (8) and Heredia (8). W—Hawkins. L—Mussina. S—Guardado.

**Game 2**—October 2, at New York
Minnesota ..............0 0 0 0 1 0 0 0 0—1
New York................1 0 0 0 0 0 3 0 x—4
Radke, Hawkins (7), Romero (7) and Rincon (8); Pettitte and Rivera (8). W—Pettitte. L—Radke. S—Rivera. HR—Hunter (Min.).

**Game 3**—October 4, at Minnesota
New York................0 2 1 0 0 0 0 0 0—3
Minnesota ..............0 0 1 0 0 0 0 0 0—1
Clemens and Rivera (8); Lohse, Rogers (6), Romero (7), Rincon (8). W—Clemens. L—Lohse. S—Rivera. HR—Matsui (N.Y.); Pierzynski (Min.).

**Game 4**—October 5, at Minnesota
New York................0 0 0 6 0 0 0 1 1—8
Minnesota ..............0 0 0 1 0 0 0 0 0—1
Wells and White (8); Santana, Rincon (4), Milton (4), Hawkins (8), Guardado (9). W—Wells. L—Santana. HR—Jeter (NYY).

Boston vs. Oakland

**Game 1**—October 1, at Oakland
Boston......1 0 0 0 1 0 2 0 0 0 0 0—4
Oakland ....0 0 3 0 0 0 0 0 1 0 0 1—5
Martinez, Timlin (8), Kim (9), Embree (9), Williamson (10), Lowe (11); Hudson, Rincon (7), Bradford (8), Foulke (9), Harden (12). W—Harden. L—Lowe. HR—Walker (2) and Varitek (Bos.).

**Game 2**—October 2, at Oakland
Boston ..................0 0 1 0 0 0 0 0 0—1
Oakland ..................0 5 0 0 0 0 0 0 x—5
Wakefield, Embree (7) and Williamson (8); Zito, Bradford (8) and Foulke (9). W—Zito. L—Wakefield.

**Game 3**—October 4, at Boston
Oakland ........0 0 0 0 0 1 0 0 0 0 0—1
Boston...........0 1 0 0 0 0 0 0 0 0 2—5
Lilly, Bradford (8), Rincon (9), Mecir (10) and Harden (11); Lowe, Timlin (8) and Williamson (11). W—Williamson. L—Harden. HR—Nixon (Bos.).

**Game 4**—October 5, at Boston
Oakland..................010 003 000—4
Boston...................002 001 02x—5
Hudson, Sparks (2), Rincon (6) and Foulke (8); Burkett, Wakefield (6) and Williamson (8). W—Williamson. L—Foulke. HR—Damon and Walker (Bos.); Dye (Oak.).

**Game 5**—October 6, at Oakland
Boston...................000 004 000—4
Oakland..................000 101 010—3
Martinez, Embree (8), Timlin (8), Williamson (9) and Lowe (9); Zito, Lilly (7), Bradford (9) and Rincon (9). W—Martinez. L—Zito. HR—Varitek and Ramirez (Bos.).

## N.L. DIVISION SERIES

■ **Winners:** The Marlins dropped the first game of the series but beat the Giants in three consecutive games to move on to the NLCS. With the series knotted at two games apiece, the Cubs beat the Braves, 5-1, in Game 5, to win the series.

■ **Turning points:** For the Cubs, Game 3 would be the key to the series. After they dropped Game 2, 23-year-old Mark Prior, in his first postseason start, threw a complete-game two-hitter. The 2-1 win broke a 1-1 series tie and fueled the Cubs to their first postseason series victory since 1908. ... In Game 3 of the Marlins-Giants series, with the series knotted 1-1 and with one out in the 11th inning, Giants right fielder Jose Cruz dropped a Jeff Conine fly ball. That set the stage for Miguel Cabrera's sacrifice bunt, which put runners in scoring position with two out. Ivan Rodriguez then hit a walkoff two-run single with two strikes and two out in the 11th inning. The hit won the game for Florida, 4-3, and put the Marlins up 2-1 in the series.

■ **Memorable moments:** With the Game 1 tied at 1 in the sixth, Cubs pitcher Kerry Wood hit a two-run double off Russ Ortiz, and the Cubs would go on to take the series opener. Chipper Jones had two two-run homers—one from each side of the plate—to stave off elimination for the Braves in Game 4. In Game 5, Wood forgot his glove, borrowed Mark Prior's and struck out seven on his way to a 5-1 victory to lead the Cubs to the NLCS. ... For Game 4, Marlins manager Jack McKeon decided to play 20-year-old Miguel Cabrera at third base instead of veteran Mike Lowell, and the decision paid off. Cabrera, who had previously been 0-for-9 with five strikeouts in the series, had four hits in the deciding game, including a two-run single in the eighth inning. The Marlins-Giants series ended when Rodriguez tagged J.T. Snow, the tying run, out at the plate.

■ **Memorable performances:** The Cubs pitchers were the story of the series. Wood won Games 1 and 5, and his 18 strikeouts were the second-highest in Division Series history. He also had two hits in Game 1, including a tiebreaking double. Prior's complete-game two-hitter in Game 3 kept the Cubs from falling behind in the series. ... The Braves Mike Hampton had six consecutive strikeouts to start the game—a postseason record. ... In a crucial Game 2, the Marlins' Juan Pierre went 4-for-5, scored three runs, drove in three runs and stole a base. His two-run double broke a 5-5 tie and keyed a three-run sixth inning that put the Marlins up for good. ... In Game 1, the Giants' Jason Schmidt threw a three-hit, complete-game shutout.

**Linescores**

Chicago vs. Atlanta

**Game 1**—September 30, at Atlanta
Chicago..................000 400 000—4
Atlanta..................001 000 010—2
Wood, Remlinger (8), Farnsworth (8) and Borowski (9); Ortiz, King (6), Gryboski (6), Wright (7), Mercker (8) and Hernandez (9). W—Wood. L—Ortiz. S—Borowski. HR—Giles (Atl.).

**Game 2**—October 1, at Atlanta
Chicago..................200 000 010—3
Atlanta..................100 101 02x—5
Zambrano, Farnsworth (6) and Veres (8); Hampton, King (7), Gryboski (7) and Smoltz (8). W—Smoltz. L—Veres.

**Game 3**—October 3, at Chicago
Atlanta..................000 000 010—1
Chicago..................200 001 01x—4
Maddux, Wright (7) and Gryboski (8); Prior. W—Prior. L—Maddux.

**Game 4**—October 4, at Chicago
Atlanta..................000 130 020—6
Chicago..................001 001 011—4
Ortiz, King (6), Gryboski (6), Wright (7), Cunnane (8) and Smoltz (9); Clement, Alfonseca (5), Remlinger (6), Veres (7), Farnsworth (7), Guthrie (8) and Cruz (9). W—Ortiz. L—Clement. S—Smoltz. HR—C. Jones (2) (Atl.).; E Karros (2) (Chi.).

**Game 5**—October 5, at Atlanta
Chicago..................110 002 001—5
Atlanta..................000 001 000—1
Wood and Borowski (9); Hampton, Gryboski (7), Wright (8), Cunnane (9) and King (9). W—Wood. L—Hampton. HR—Ramirez, Gonzalez (Chi.).

Florida vs. San Francisco

**Game 1**—September 30, at San Francisco
Florida..................000 000 000—0
San Francisco............000 100 01x—2
Beckett and Fox (8); Schmidt. W—Schmidt. L—Beckett.

**Game 2**—October 1, at San Francisco
Florida..................100 033 110—9
San Francisco............100 310 000—5
Penny, Helling (5), Pavano (5), Fox (6), Willis (8), Looper (8) and Urbina (9); Ponson, Nathan (6), Christiansen (6), Herges (6), Rodriguez (7), Brower (8), Worrell (9). W—Pavano. L—Nathan. HR—Encarnacion (Fla.).

**Game 3**—October 3, at Florida
San Francisco............000 002 000 01—3
Florida..................200 000 000 02—4
Rueter, Herges (6), Eyre (7), Nathan (8), F. Rodriguez (8) and Worrell (10); Redman, Fox (7), Urbina (9), Pavano (10) and Looper (11). W—Looper. L—Worrell. HR—I. Rodriguez (Fla.).

**Game 4**—October 4, at Florida
San Francisco............010 004 001—6
Florida..................012 200 02x—5
Williams, Brower (3), Hermanson (5), Herges (6) and F. Rodriguez (8); Willis, Penny (6), Pavano (8) and Urbina (9). W—Pavano. L—F. Rodriguez.

## ALCS

■ **Winner:** In a matchup true to the Yankees-Red Sox rivalry and one of the most exciting Championship Series finishes in history, the Yankees won the series on a walkoff homerun by Aaron Boone in the 11th inning of Game 7.

■ **Turning point:** In Game 7, with one out in the bottom of the eighth and a 5-2 lead, Red Sox starter Pedro Martinez began to struggle, and the Yankees strung together a series of hits and tied the game. Red Sox manager Grady Little conferenced with his starter but chose to leave him in—a decision that would cost the Red Sox the series and Little his job.

■ **Memorable moments:** With the series tied at 1-1, the Yankees and Red Sox headed to Boston for Game 3. Cy Young Award winners Martinez and Roger Clemens faced off, and the Fenway faithful jeered their former ace from the first pitch. In the fourth inning, with the Sox up 2-1, Martinez gave up a run-scoring double to Hideki Matsui, then hit Karim Garcia with the next pitch, and umpires warned both teams. Garcia was then forced out at second on a double play, slid hard into Boston second baseman Todd Walker, and the two players exchanged words. When Clemens brushed back Manny Ramirez with the first pitch of the next inning, the benches cleared. In the scuffle, Yankees bench coach Don Zimmer charged Martinez, who grabbed Zimmer by his head and threw him to the ground. The melee caused a 13-minute delay, but no players or managers were ejected.

■ **Top guns:** Walker was 10-for-27 (.370) for the series, and the Red Sox set a postseason-series record with 12 home runs in the ALCS. Mike Timlin threw 5 1/3 scoreless innings for the Red Sox, giving up just one hit. Yankees closer Mariano Rivera had a 1-0 record in the LCS, with a 1.13 ERA and two saves over eight innings in four appearances, including three scoreless innings in Game 7. Jason Giambi had three home runs in the series, including two in Game 7.

■ **MVP:** Rivera.

**Linescores**

**Game 1**—October 8, at New York
Boston...................000 220 100—5
New York.................000 000 200—2
Wakefield, Embree (7), Timlin (8) and Williamson (9); Mussina, Heredia (6), Nelson (7), White (7) and Contreras (9). W—Wakefield. L—Mussina. S—Williamson. HR—Walker, Ramirez, Ortiz (Bos.).

**Game 2**—October 9, at New York
Boston...................010 001 000—2
New York.................021 010 20x—6
Lowe, Sauerbeck (7) and Arroyo (8); Pettitte, Contreras (7) and Rivera (9). W—Pettitte. L—Lowe. HR—Varitek (Bos.) and Johnson (N.Y.).

**Game 3**—October 11, at Boston
New York.................011 200 000—4
Boston...................200 000 100—3
Clemens, Heredia (7), Contreras (7) and Rivera (8); Martinez, Timlin (8) and Embree (9). W—Clemens. L—Martinez. S—Rivera. HR—Jeter (N.Y.).

**Game 4**—October 13, at Boston
New York.................000 010 001—2
Boston...................000 110 10x—3
Mussina, Heredia (7) and Nelson (8); Wakefield, Timlin (8) and Williamson (9). W—Wakefield. L—Mussina. S—Williamson. HR—Sierra (N.Y.); Walker and Nixon (Bos.).

**Game 5**—October 14, at Boston
New York.................030 000 010—4
Boston...................000 100 010—2
Wells and Rivera (8); Lowe, Embree (8) and Arroyo (9). W—Wells. L—Lowe. S—Rivera. HR—Ramirez (Bos.).

**Game 6**—October 15, at New York
Boston...................004 000 302—9
New York.................100 410 000—6
Burkett, Arroyo (4), Jones (6), Embree (6), Timlin (8) and Williamson (9); Pettitte, Contreras (6), Heredia (7), Nelson (8) and White (9). W—Embree. L—Heredia. S—Williamson. HR—Nixon and Varitek (Bos.); Giambi and Posada (N.Y.).

**Game 7**—October 16, at New York
Boston...................030 100 010 00—5
New York.................000 010 130 01—6
Martinez, Embree (8), Timlin (8) and Wakefield (10); Clemens, Mussina (4), Heredia (7), Nelson (7), Wells (8) and Rivera (9). W—Rivera. L—Wakefield. HR—Ortiz, Millar and Nixon (Bos.); Giambi (2) and Boone (NY.).

## NLCS

■ **Winner:** The Marlins came back from a 3-1 series deficit to beat the Cubs in seven games.

■ **Turning point:** With one out and one on in the eighth inning of Game 6 and the Marlins down 3-0 in the game and 3-2 in the series, Luis Castillo hit a lazy foul ball near the left field wall. Moises Alou leaped for the ball, but a Chicago fan reached out and deflected it, and the umpire ruled the ball foul. Mark Prior then walked Castillo, and Ivan Rodriguez followed with an RBI single. The Marlins went on to score eight runs in the inning and won the game, 8-3. The next night, they would win the NLCS and move on to the World Series.

■ **Memorable moments:** In Game 1, after being down two runs in the ninth, Marlins veteran Mike Lowell had a pinch-hit home run in the 11th, and Florida won the opener in Chicago. ... In Game 3, with the series tied 1-1, pinch hitter Doug Glanville, the last position player on the Cubs postseason roster, hit an RBI triple in the 11th to win the game.

■ **Top guns:** Beckett, 23, threw a complete game two-hit shutout and struck out 11 in Game 5, tying an LCS record for fewest hits allowed. In Game 7, Cabrera, a 20-year-old rookie called up in July, had four RBIs. He was 10-for-30 in the series, with three home runs and six RBIs. Rodriguez set an NLCS record with 10 RBIs. In Game 4, the Cubs' Aramis Ramirez had six RBIs. The teams set an LCS series record for home runs with 23.

■ **MVP:** Rodriguez.

**Game 1**—October 7, at Chicago
Florida..................005 001 002 01—9
Chicago..................400 002 002 00—8
Beckett, Fox (7), Urbina (9) and Looper (11); Zambrano, Remlinger (7), Farnsworth (7), Borowski (9), Guthrie (11) and Alfonseca (11). W—Urbina. L—Guthrie. S—Looper. HR—I. Rodriguez, Cabrera, Encarnacion and Lowell (Fla.); Sosa, Alou and A. Gonzalez (Chi.).

**Game 2**—October 8, at Chicago
Florida..................000 002 010—3
Chicago..................233 031 00x—12
Penny, Bump (3), Helling (4), Pavano (7) and Tejera (8); Prior, Veres (8) and Guthrie (9). W—Prior. L—Penny. HR—D. Lee and Cabrera (Fla.); Sosa, A. Ramirez and A. Gonzalez (2) (Chi.).

**Game 3**—October 10, at Florida
Chicago..................110 000 020 1—5
Florida..................010 000 210 0—4
Wood, Farnsworth (7), Borowski (8) and Remlinger (11); Redman, Fox (7), Urbina (9), Tejera (11) and Looper (11). W—Borowski. L—Tejera. S—Remlinger. H—Simon (Chi.).

**Game 4**—October 11, at Florida
Chicago..................402 100 100—8
Florida..................000 020 010—3
Clement and Farnsworth (8); Willis, Helling (3), Bump (6), Penny (8) and Pavano (9). W—Clement. L—Willis. HR—A. Ramirez (2) (Chi.).

**Game 5**—October 12, at Florida
Chicago..................000 000 000—0
Florida..................000 020 11x—4
Zambrano, Veres (6), Alfonseca (7) and Remlinger (8); Beckett. W—Beckett. L—Zambrano. HR—I. Rodriguez, Lowell and Conine (Fla.).

**Game 6**—October 14, at Chicago
Florida..................000 000 080—8
Chicago..................100 001 100—3
Pavano, Willis (6), Fox (7) and Urbina (8); Prior, Farnsworth (8), Remlinger (8) and Alfonseca (9). W—Fox. L—Prior.

**Game 7**—October 15, at Chicago
Florida..................300 031 200—9
Chicago..................032 000 100—6
Redman, Penny (4), Beckett (5) and Urbina (9); Wood, Farnsworth (6), Veres (7), Remlinger (8), Borowski (8). W—Penny. L—Wood. S—Urbina. HR—Cabrera (Fla.); Alou, Wood and O'Leary (Chi.).

## WORLD SERIES

■ **Winner:** The Marlins won their second World Series title, beating an experienced Yankees squad with a young club. They won the championship in six games, the last coming at Yankee Stadium.

■ **Turning point:** In Game 4, the Marlins trailed 2-1 in the series and faced Roger Clemens. The Marlins lost their lead the ninth when Ruben Sierra hit a game-tying two-run triple off closer Ugueth Urbina. The game went into extra innings. To lead off the 12th, Marlins shortstop Alex Gonzalez, who was 1-for-14 before the at-bat, hit a walkoff home run off Jeff Weaver. The Marlins tied the series at two games apiece and rode the momentum to two consecutive wins and the World Series championship.

■ **Memorable moments:** In Game 4, in Miami, Clemens, thought to be starting his last game, received a standing ovation after striking out Luis Castillo to end the seventh. The Marlins players also clapped for Clemens, who came out for a curtain call. ... In Game 6 and with the score tied at zero, Luis Castillo, who was on an 0-for-14 skid, slapped a pitch to right field, and Alex Gonzalez slid past Yankees catcher Jorge Posada and got his hand on the plate just before Posada's tag. It would be the Marlins only earned run of the game—and enough for them to win the game and the series.

■ **Top guns:** Bernie Williams had a .400 average in the series, with two home runs and five RBIs. In Game 3, he set records for postseason home runs (19) and RBIs (65). Andy Pettitte threw 15.2 innings, gave up three runs and struck out 14. Josh Beckett, on three days' rest, threw a five-hit, nine-strikeout, complete-game shutout in Game 6. In the series, he threw 16.1 innings, struck out 19 and had a 1.10 ERA. Jeff Conine and Juan Pierre each had seven hits.

■ **MVP:** Beckett.

**Linescores**

**Game 1**—October 18, at New York
Florida..................100 020 000—3
New York.................001 002 001—2
Penny, Willis (6) and Urbina (8); Wells, Nelson (8) and Contreras (9). W—Penny. L—Wells. S—Urbina. HR—B. Williams (N.Y.)

**Game 2**—October 19, at New York
Florida..................000 000 001—1
New York.................310 200 00x—6
Redman, Helling (3), Fox (6), Pavano (7) and Looper (8); Pettitte and Contreras (9). W—Pettitte. L—Redman. HR—Soriano and Matsui (N.Y.)

**Game 3**—October 21, at Florida
New York.................000 100 014—6
Florida..................100 000 000—1
Mussina and Rivera (8); Beckett, Willis (8), Fox (8) and Looper (9). W—Mussina. L—Beckett. HR—B. Williams and A. Boone (N.Y.)

**Game 4**—October 22, at Florida
New York.................010 000 002 000—3
Florida..................300 000 000 001—4
Clemens, Nelson (8), Contreras (9) and Weaver (11); Pavano, Urbina (9), Fox (10) and Looper (11). W—Looper. L—Weaver. HR—Cabrera and A. Gonzalez (Fla.)

**Game 5**—October 23, at Florida
New York.................100 000 102—4
Florida..................030 120 00x—6
Wells, Contreras (2), Hammond (5) and Nelson (7); Penny, Willis (8), Looper (9) and Urbina (9). W—Penny. L—Contreras. S—Urbina. HR—Giambi.

**Game 6**—October 25, at New York
Florida..................000 011 000—2
New York.................000 000 00x—0
Beckett; Pettitte and Rivera (8). W—Beckett. L—Pettitte.

# 2004

## FINAL STANDINGS

### American League

#### East Division

| Team | N.Y. | Bos. | Bal. | T.B. | Tor. | Min. | Chi. | Cle. | Det. | K.C. | Ana. | Oak. | Tex. | Sea. | N.L. | W | L | Pct. | GB |
|---|---|---|---|---|---|---|---|---|---|---|---|---|---|---|---|---|---|---|---|
| New York | ... | 8 | 14 | 15 | 12 | 4 | 4 | 4 | 3 | 5 | 4 | 7 | 5 | 6 | 10-8 | 101 | 61 | .623 | ..... |
| Boston | 11 | ... | 9 | 14 | 14 | 2 | 4 | 3 | 6 | 4 | 5 | 8 | 4 | 5 | 9-9 | 98 | 64 | .605 | 3.0 |
| Baltimore | 5 | 10 | ... | 11 | 11 | 4 | 2 | 3 | 6 | 6 | 3 | 0 | 5 | 7 | 5-13 | 78 | 84 | .481 | 23.0 |
| Tampa Bay | 4 | 5 | 8 | ... | 9 | 5 | 2 | 3 | 3 | 6 | 1 | 2 | 2 | 5 | 15-3 | 70 | 91 | .435 | 30.5 |
| Toronto | 7 | 5 | 8 | 9 | ... | 2 | 4 | 2 | 2 | 3 | 5 | 3 | 2 | 7 | 8-10 | 67 | 94 | .416 | 33.5 |

#### Central Division

| Team | Min. | Chi. | Cle. | Det. | K.C. | N.Y. | Bos. | Bal. | T.B. | Tor. | Ana. | Oak. | Tex. | Sea. | N.L. | W | L | Pct. | GB |
|---|---|---|---|---|---|---|---|---|---|---|---|---|---|---|---|---|---|---|---|
| Minnesota | ... | 10 | 12 | 12 | 12 | 2 | 4 | 5 | 4 | 4 | 4 | 2 | 5 | 5 | 11-7 | 92 | 70 | .568 | ..... |
| Chicago | 9 | ... | 10 | 8 | 13 | 3 | 2 | 4 | 4 | 3 | 4 | 2 | 6 | 7 | 8-10 | 83 | 79 | .512 | 9.0 |
| Cleveland | 7 | 9 | ... | 9 | 11 | 2 | 4 | 3 | 3 | 5 | 5 | 6 | 1 | 5 | 10-8 | 80 | 82 | .494 | 12.0 |
| Detroit | 7 | 11 | 10 | ... | 8 | 4 | 1 | 0 | 3 | 4 | 2 | 4 | 4 | 5 | 9-9 | 72 | 90 | .444 | 20.0 |
| Kansas City | 7 | 6 | 8 | 11 | ... | 1 | 2 | 3 | 3 | 3 | 0 | 2 | 4 | 2 | 6-12 | 58 | 104 | .358 | 34.0 |

#### West Division

| Team | Ana. | Oak. | Tex. | Sea. | N.Y. | Bos. | Bal. | T.B. | Tor. | Min. | Chi. | Cle. | Det. | K.C. | N.L. | W | L | Pct. | GB |
|---|---|---|---|---|---|---|---|---|---|---|---|---|---|---|---|---|---|---|---|
| Anaheim | ... | 10 | 9 | 13 | 5 | 4 | 6 | 6 | 4 | 5 | 5 | 4 | 7 | 7 | 7-11 | 92 | 70 | .568 | ..... |
| Oakland | 9 | ... | 11 | 11 | 2 | 1 | 7 | 7 | 6 | 5 | 7 | 3 | 5 | 7 | 10-8 | 91 | 71 | .562 | 1.0 |
| Texas | 10 | 9 | ... | 12 | 4 | 5 | 2 | 7 | 7 | 2 | 3 | 8 | 5 | 5 | 10-8 | 89 | 73 | .549 | 3.0 |
| Seattle | 7 | 8 | 7 | ... | 3 | 4 | 2 | 2 | 2 | 4 | 2 | 4 | 4 | 5 | 9-9 | 63 | 99 | .389 | 29.0 |

NOTE: Read across for wins, down for losses.

Clinching dates: New York (East)—September 30; Minnesota (Central)—September 20; Anaheim (West)—October 2; Boston (wild card)—September 27.

### National League

#### East Division

| Team | Atl. | Phi. | Fla. | N.Y. | Mon. | St.L. | Hou. | Chi. | Cin. | Pit. | Mil. | L.A. | S.F. | S.D. | Col. | Ari. | A.L. | W | L | Pct. | GB |
|---|---|---|---|---|---|---|---|---|---|---|---|---|---|---|---|---|---|---|---|---|---|
| Atlanta | ... | 9 | 9 | 12 | 11 | 4 | 5 | 4 | 7 | 3 | 4 | 2 | 4 | 5 | 6 | 6 | 10-5 | 101 | 61 | .623 | ... |
| Florida | 10 | ... | 13 | 13 | 12 | 2 | 1 | 3 | 2 | 4 | 7 | 1 | 2 | 5 | 2 | 5 | 9-6 | 91 | 71 | .562 | 10.0 |
| Phil. | 10 | 6 | ... | 11 | 12 | 5 | 4 | 4 | 2 | 4 | 2 | 3 | 5 | 2 | 4 | 4 | 8-7 | 86 | 76 | .531 | 15.0 |
| Montreal | 7 | 6 | 8 | ... | 14 | 3 | 3 | 1 | 3 | 4 | 6 | 7 | 2 | 2 | 4 | 4 | 9-9 | 83 | 79 | .512 | 18.0 |
| New York | 8 | 7 | 7 | 5 | ... | 1 | 4 | 1 | 4 | 4 | 3 | 4 | 3 | 2 | 5 | 3 | 5-10 | 66 | 95 | .410 | 34.5 |

#### Central Division

| Team | St.L. | Hou. | Chi. | Cin. | Pit. | Mil. | Atl. | Phi. | Fla. | N.Y. | Mon. | L.A. | S.F. | S.D. | Col. | Ari. | A.L. | W | L | Pct. | GB |
|---|---|---|---|---|---|---|---|---|---|---|---|---|---|---|---|---|---|---|---|---|---|
| St. Louis | ... | 8 | 11 | 14 | 12 | 9 | 4 | 3 | 4 | 5 | 3 | 4 | 3 | 4 | 5 | 5 | 11-1 | 105 | 57 | .648 | ... |
| Houston | 10 | ... | 9 | 11 | 12 | 13 | 3 | 6 | 3 | 2 | 2 | 1 | 2 | 2 | 5 | 4 | 7-5 | 92 | 70 | .568 | 13.0 |
| Chicago | 8 | 10 | ... | 9 | 13 | 10 | 3 | 3 | 3 | 4 | 3 | 2 | 2 | 4 | 5 | 2 | 8-4 | 89 | 73 | .549 | 16.0 |
| Cincinnati | 5 | 6 | 8 | ... | 9 | 10 | 4 | 3 | 4 | 3 | 4 | 4 | 3 | 2 | 3 | 3 | 5-7 | 76 | 86 | .469 | 29.0 |
| Pittsburgh | 5 | 5 | 5 | 10 | ... | 12 | 2 | 3 | 5 | 5 | 2 | 0 | 5 | 3 | 4 | 4 | 2-10 | 72 | 89 | .447 | 32.5 |
| Milwaukee | 8 | 6 | 7 | 8 | 6 | ... | 2 | 0 | 2 | 2 | 5 | 3 | 1 | 2 | 4 | 3 | 8-4 | 67 | 94 | .416 | 37.5 |

#### West Division

| Team | L.A. | S.F. | S.D. | Col. | Ari. | Atl. | Phi. | Fla. | N.Y. | Mon. | St.L. | Hou. | Chi. | Cin. | Pit. | Mil. | A.L. | W | L | Pct. | GB |
|---|---|---|---|---|---|---|---|---|---|---|---|---|---|---|---|---|---|---|---|---|---|
| Los Ang. | ... | 10 | 10 | 11 | 16 | 3 | 1 | 3 | 3 | 4 | 2 | 5 | 4 | 2 | 6 | 3 | 10-8 | 93 | 69 | .574 | ... |
| San Fran. | 9 | ... | 7 | 11 | 14 | 3 | 4 | 5 | 2 | 5 | 3 | 4 | 4 | 3 | 1 | 5 | 11-7 | 91 | 71 | .562 | 2.0 |
| San Diego | 9 | 12 | ... | 9 | 12 | 3 | 1 | 2 | 6 | 6 | 2 | 4 | 2 | 4 | 3 | 4 | 8-10 | 87 | 75 | .537 | 6.0 |
| Colorado | 8 | 8 | 10 | ... | 13 | 2 | 5 | 1 | 1 | 2 | 1 | 1 | 1 | 3 | 2 | 2 | 8-10 | 68 | 94 | .420 | 25.0 |
| Arizona | 3 | 5 | 7 | 6 | ... | 2 | 1 | 3 | 3 | 0 | 1 | 2 | 4 | 3 | 2 | 3 | 6-12 | 51 | 111 | .315 | 42.0 |

NOTE: Read across for wins, down for losses.

Clinching dates: Atlanta (East)—September 24; St. Louis (Central)—September 18; Los Angeles (West)—October 2; Houston (wild card)—October 3.

## SIGNIFICANT EVENTS

■ **January 3:** Former player Pete Rose admitted that he did bet on baseball while managing the Reds.
■ **February 12:** U.S. Attorney General John Ashcroft announced a 42-count indictment against individuals connected to the Bay Area Laboratory Co-operative, widening the debate over the use of steroids in baseball.
■ **September 29:** Commissioner Selig announced an agreement to move the Montreal Expos to Washington in 2005 where they would be known as the Nationals.

## MEMORABLE MOMENTS

■ **April 4:** The San Diego Padres opened Petco Park, beating the Giants, 4-3 in 10 innings.
■ **April 12:** The Philadelphia Phillies opened Citizens Bank Park, losing to the Reds, 4-1.
■ **April 13:** The Giants' Barry Bonds hit his 661st home run, moving him into third place on the all-time list ahead of Willie Mays and behind only Henry Aaron and Babe Ruth.
■ **May 18:** The Yankees' Randy Johnson pitched the 17th perfect game, beating the Braves, 2-0.
■ **June 20:** The Reds' Ken Griffey Jr. became the 20th player and the sixth youngest to hit 500 homers, connecting off Matt Morris of the Cardinals.
■ **June 29:** The Yankees' Randy Johnson became the fourth pitcher to strike out 4,000 batters, fanning Jeff Cirillo of the Padres in the eighth inning.
■ **August 7:** The Cubs' Greg Maddux became the 20th pitcher to win 300 games, defeating the Giants, 8-4.
■ **October 1:** The Mariners' Ichiro Suzuki got his 257th and 258th hits of the season, tying and breaking George Sisler's record for most hits in a season, set in 1920.

## ALL-STAR GAME

■ **Winner:** American League, 9-4.
■ **Key inning:** The first. The A.L. jumped all over N.L. starter Roger Clemens, who was pitching in his home park, with six first-inning runs. Ichiro Suzuki doubled to start the game, and Ivan Rodriguez followed that with a triple. Then Manny Ramirez blasted a home run one out later. Alfonso Soriano did the rest of the damage with a three-run homer.
■ **Memorable moments:** The A.L. clinched home-field advantage for the second straight year and extended its unbeaten streak to eight games, including the controversial 2002 tie game. The N.L.'s Albert Pujols was the main offensive threat for the losing team, hitting two doubles and driving in two runs. The A.L.'s Derek Jeter finished 3-for-3.
■ **Top guns:** Pujols (Cardinals), Edgar Renteria (Cardinals), Jeff Kent (Houston), N.L.; Ramirez (Red Sox), David Ortiz (Red Sox), Soriano (Rangers), Jeter (Yankees), Rodriguez (Tigers), A.L.
■ **MVP:** Soriano.

**Linescore**

July 13 at Houston's Minute Maid Park
A.L. ....................................600 102 000—9
N.L. ....................................100 300 000—4
Clemens (Astros), Dan Kolb (Braves) 2, Randy Johnson (Diamondbacks) 3, Carlos Zambrano (Cubs) 4, Carl Pavano (Marlins) 5, Tom Glavine (Mets) 7, Ben Sheets (Brewers) 8, Eric Gagne (Dodgers) 9, Mark Mulder (A's), Esteban Loaiza (White Sox) 3, C.C. Sabathia (Indians) 4, Javier Vazquez (Yankees) 5, Ted Lilly (Blue Jays) 6, Joe Nathan (Twins) 7, Tom Gordon (Yankees) 8, Francisco Rodriguez (Angels) 8, Mariano Rivera (Yankees) 9. W—Mulder. L—Clemens. HR—Ramirez, Ortiz, Soriano, A.L.

**American League**
**BA:** Ichiro Suzuki, Sea., .372.
**Runs:** Vladimir Guerrero, Ana., 124.
**Hits:** Ichiro Suzuki, Sea., 262.
**TB:** Vladimir Guerrero, Ana., 366.
**HR:** Manny Ramirez, Bos., 43.
**RBI:** Miguel Tejada, Bal., 150.
**SB:** Carl Crawford, T.B., 59.
**Wins:** Curt Schilling, Bos., 21.
**ERA:** Johan Santana, Min., 2.61.
**CG:** Mark Mulder (Oak.), Sidney Ponson (Bal.), Jake Westbrook (Cle.), 5.
**IP:** Mark Buehrle, CWS, 245.1.
**SO:** Johan Santana, Min., 265.
**Sv.:** Keith Foulke, Oak., 40.

**National League**
**BA:** Barry Bonds, S.F., .362.
**Runs:** Albert Pujols, St.L., 133.
**Hits:** Juan Pierre, Fla., 221.
**TB:** Albert Pujols, St.L., 389.
**HR:** Adrian Beltre, LA, 48 .
**RBI:** Vinny Castilla, Col., 131.
**SB:** Scott Podsednik, Mil., 70.
**Wins:** Roy Oswalt, Hou., 20.
**ERA:** Jake Peavy, S.D., 2.27.
**CG:** Livan Hernandez, Mon., 9.
**IP:** Livan Hernandez, Mon., 255.0 .
**SO:** Randy Johnson, Ari., 290.
**Sv.:** Armando Benitez (Fla.), Jason Isringhausen (St.L.), 47.

**A.L. 20-game winners**
Curt Schilling, Bos., 21
Johan Santana, Min., 20

**N.L. 20-game winners**
Roy Oswalt, Hou., 20

**A.L. 100 RBIs**
Miguel Tejada, Bal., 150
David Ortiz, Bos., 139
Manny Ramirez, Bos., 130
Vladimir Guerrero, Ana., 126
Gary Sheffield, NYY, 121
Paul Konerko, CWS, 117
Mark Teixeira, Tex., 112
Hank Blalock, Tex., 110
Travis Hafner, Cle., 109
Victor Martinez, Cle., 108
Hideki Matsui, NYY, 108
Alex Rodriguez, NYY, 106
Jose Guillen, Ana., 104
Aubrey Huff, T.B., 104
Melvin Mora, Bal., 104

**N.L. 100 RBIs**
Vinny Castilla, Col., 131
Scott Rolen, St.L., 124
Albert Pujols, St.L., 123
Adrian Beltre, LA, 121
Miguel Cabrera, Fla., 112
Jim Edmonds, St.L., 111
Tony Batista, Mon., 110
Jeromy Burnitz, Col., 110
Jeff Kent, Hou., 107
Moises Alou, ChC., 106
Lance Berkman, Hou., 106
Bobby Abreu, Phi., 105
Phil Nevin, S.D., 105
Jim Thome, Phi., 105
Carlos Beltran, KC-Hou., 104
Aramis Ramirez, ChC., 103
Adam Dunn, Cin., 102
Barry Bonds, S.F., 101

**A.L. 40 homers**
Manny Ramirez, Bos., 43
Paul Konerko, CWS, 41
David Ortiz, Bos., 41

**N.L. 40 homers**
Adrian Beltre, LA, 48
Adam Dunn, Cin., 46
Albert Pujols, St.L., 46
Barry Bonds, S.F., 45
Jim Edmonds, St.L., 42
Jim Thome, Phi., 42

**Most Valuable Player**
A.L.: Vladimir Guerrero, OF, Ana.
N.L.: Barry Bonds, OF, S.F.

**Cy Young Award**
A.L.: Johan Santana, Min.
N.L.: Roger Clemens, Hou.

**Rookie of the Year**
A.L.: Bobby Crosby, SS, Oak.
N.L.: Jason Bay, OF, Pit.

**Manager of the Year**
A.L.: Buck Showalter, Tex.
N.L.: Bobby Cox, Atl.

**Hall of Fame additions**
Paul Molitor, IF/OF, 1978-1998
Dennis Eckersley, P, 1975-1997

## A.L. DIVISION SERIES

■ **Winners:** After dropping game one in New York, the Yankees beat the Twins three games to one. Boston swept Anaheim.
■ **Turning point:** The Yankees were shut down in game one, but in the bottom of the 12th, they put together two runs, with help from a double by Alex Rodriguez, and never looked back in the series. ... The Red Sox jumped all over Angels starter Jarrod Washburn in the top of the fourth inning. The seven runs scored in that inning led to an easy victory. The Angels took Game 3 to 10 innings, but the Sox prevailed and swept the Angels with a walkoff home run.
■ **Memorable moments:** The Yankees had to deal with 20-game winner Johan Santana, who was 13-0 in the regular season after the All-Star break and led the A.L. with a 2.61 ERA and 265 strikeouts. In Game 1, his secret to success in beating Mike Mussina was relying on his defense; the Bronx Bombers hit into a postseason-record five double plays. Kevin Brown, who had broken his glove hand late in the season in a fit of rage, vindicated himself with a solid start to get the decision in an 8-4 Game 3 victory. In Game 4, the Twins again were in position to change history, but they blew a 5-1 lead. Ruben Sierra's three-run homer in the eighth tied it, and again it was Rodriguez proving his worth, this time in the 11th inning by manufacturing the clincher all by himself. He doubled off Kyle Lohse, stole third base and scored on a wild pitch. ... Hoping to lead Anaheim back to the promised land it had visited in 2002, Vladimir Guerrero followed up a sensational first season (.337 batting average, 39 homers, 126 RBIs) by hushing Fenway Park with a game-tying grand slam off Boston reliever Mike Timlin in the seventh inning of Game 3. But Boston was a true team of destiny. With two out in the bottom of the 10th, David Ortiz hit a walkoff homer that sent Fenway into delirium and the Sox into the A.L. Championship Series.
■ **Top guns:** Johan Santana pitched seven shutout innings against the Yankees. Boston's David Ortiz hit .545 and slugged 1.000. The Yankee's Rodriguez hit .421 and scored the winning run in game 4.

**Linescores**

New York vs. Minnesota

**Game 1**—October 5, at New York
Minnesota ......................0 0 1 0 0 1 0 0 0—2
New York.........................0 0 0 0 0 0 0 0 0—0
Santana, J. Rincon (8), Nathan (9); Mussina, Gordon (8), Rivera (9). W—Santana. L—Mussina. S—Nathan. HR—J. Jones (Min).

**Game 2**—October 6, at New York
Minnesota ............1 2 0 0 0 0 0 2 0 0 0 1—6
New York..............1 0 2 0 1 0 1 0 0 0 0 2—7
Radke, Balfour (7), Rincon (8), Nathan (10), Romero (12); Lieber, Gordon (7), Rivera (8), Sturtze (9), Quantrill (12). W—Quantrill. L—Nathan. HR—Jeter (NYY), Sheffield (NYY), Rodriguez (NYY), Hunter (Min).

**Game 3**—October 8, at Minnesota
New York.........................0 3 0 0 0 4 1 0 0—8
Minnesota .......................1 0 0 0 0 0 0 0 3—4
Brown, Quantrill (7), Heredia (8), Sturtze (9) and Rivera (9); Silva, Romero (6) and Crain (6), Mulholland (7). W—Brown. L—Silva. HR—J. Jones (Min), Williams (NYY), Matsui (NYY).

**Game 4**—October 9, at Minnesota
New York ................0 0 1 0 0 0 0 4 0 0 1—6
Minnesota ..............1 0 0 1 3 0 0 0 0 0 0—5
Vazquez, Loaiza (6), Gordon (8), Rivera (10); Santana, Balfour (6), Rincon (8) and Nathan (7), Lohse (10). W—Rivera. L—Lohse. HR—Blanco (Min), Sierra (NYY).

Boston vs. Anaheim

**Game 1**—October 5, at Anaheim
Boston ..........................1 0 0 7 0 0 0 1 0—9
Anaheim.........................0 0 0 1 0 0 2 0 0—3
Schilling, Embree (7), Timlin (8); Washburn, Shields (4), Gregg (6), Ortiz (8) W—Schilling. L—Washburn. HR—Millar (Bos), Ramirez (Bos), Glaus (Ana), Erstad (Ana).

**Game 2**—October 6, at Anaheim
Boston ..........................0 1 0 0 0 2 1 0 4—8
Anaheim.........................0 1 0 0 2 0 0 0 0—3
Martinez, Timlin (8) and Myers (8) and Foulk (8); Colon, Rodriguez (7), Donnelly (9). W—Martinez. L—Rodriguez. HR—Varitek (Bos).

**Game 3**—October 8, at Boston
Anaheim ..............................000 100 500 0—6
Boston ................................002 310 200 2—8
Escobar, Shields (4), Donnelly (6), Rodriguez (8), Washburn (10); Arroyo, Myers (7) and Timlin (7) and Embree (7), Foulk (8), Lowe (10). W—Lowe. L—Rodriguez. HR—Glaus (Ana), Guerrero (Ana), Ortiz (Bos).

## N.L. DIVISION SERIES

■ **Winners:** The Cardinals were shut out in Game 3 but scored at least six runs every other game to win the series 3-1. ... The Astros and Braves battled back and forth, but the Astros won the decisive Game 5 in Atlanta, sending the Braves to another early postseason exit.
■ **Turning point:** Albert Pujols blasted a solo shot in the first inning of Game 1, which set the tone for five Cardinal home runs on the day. Two came from Larry Walker. The Dodger's Jose Lima pitched a complete game shutout in Game 3, but the Redbirds' big bats prevailed in Game 4, when Pujols crushed a three-run shot in the fourth inning. ... After a solid Game 3 win, 8-5, the Astros failed to clinch at home when Braves closer John Smoltz worked two clutch innings. But Game 5 was all Houston. A five-run seventh inning led to a 12-3 romp, and when it was over the Astros had shattered several playoff records, including the NLDS record for runs with 36. That was *nine* more than the old record.
■ **Memorable moments:** Lima worked his "Lima Time" magic against the Cards, constantly showing emotion on the mound. The Cards and Dodgers shook hands after the series, a highly uncommon practice in baseball. Carlos Beltran of the Astros showed why he was a big reason that the Astros caught fire in the second half of the season. He hit .455 with four home runs, nine RBIs and a 1.091 slugging average to help Houston finally beat the Braves and advance to the second round.
■ **Top guns:** Pujols and Walker each had two home runs to lead the powerful St. Louis lineup. Beltran worked some postseason magic of his own, and Lima's performance was the only shutout of the 2004 postseason.

### Linescores

Los Angeles vs. St. Louis

**Game 1**—October 5, at St. Louis
Los Angeles ..........................000 011 001—3
St. Louis ..............................105 100 10x—8
Perez, Dessens (3), Sanchez (5), Venafro (6), Carrara (7), Brazoban (8); Williams, Calero (7), King (8), Isringhausen (9). W—Williams. L—Perez. HR—Pujols, Walker 2, Edmonds, Matheny (St.L); Wilson (LA).

**Game 2**—October 7, at St. Louis
Los Angeles. ..........................100 200 000—3
St. Louis ..............................030 030 20x—8
Weaver, Sanchez (5), Alvarez (6), Carrara (7), Gagne (8); Marquis, Eldred (4), Haren (5), King (7), Tavarez (8), Kline (9). W—Haren. L—Weaver. HR—Werth, Green, Bradley (LA).

**Game 3**—October 9, at Los Angeles
St. Louis ..............................000 000 000—3
Los Angeles ..........................002 101 00x—8
Morris, Eldred (8) and Kline (8); Lima. W—Lima. L—Morris. HR—Green 2 (LA).

**Game 4**—October 10, at Los Angeles
St. Louis ..............................011 300 100—6
Los Angeles ..........................101 000 000—2
Suppan, Tavarez (8) and King (8), Isringhausen (9); Perez, Alvarez (3), Brazoban (5), Venafro (7) and Carrara (7), Gagne (8). W—Suppan. L—Alvarez. HR—Werth (LA); Sanders, Pujols (St.L).

Houston vs. Atlanta

**Game 1**—October 6, at Atlanta
Houston ................................004 030 101—9
Atlanta ................................100 011 000—3
Clemens, Qualls (8), Gallo (9); Wright, Gryboski (5), Cruz (6), Alfonseca (8), Reitsma (9). W—Clemens. L—Wright. HR—Ausmus, Berkman, Beltran, Lane (Hou); A. Jones (Atl).

**Game 2**—October 7, at Atlanta
Houston ..........................101 000 000 00—9
Atlanta..............................000 000 110 02—3
Oswalt, Lidge (7), Miceli (10); Hampton, Gryboski (7), Smoltz (8), Alfonseca (11). W—Alfonseca L—Miceli. HR—Bagwell, Chavez (Hou); Furcal (Atl).

**Game 3**—October 9, at Houston
Atlanta ..................................000 200 030—5
Houston ................................002 023 10x—8
Thomson and Paul Byrd (1), Gryboski (5), Alfonseca (6) and Martin (6) and Reitsma (6), Cruz (8); Backe, Qualls (7), Springer (8), Lidge (9). W—Backe. L—Byrd. S—Lidge. HR—Beltran (Hou); Estrada, A. Jones (Atl).

**Game 4**—October 10, at Houston
Atlanta ..................................020 003 001—6
Houston ................................050 000 000—8
Ortiz, Gryboski (4), Alfonseca (6), Hampton (7), Smoltz (8); Clemens, Qualls (6), Gallo (7) and Miceli (7), Lidge (8), Springer (9). W—Smoltz. L—Springer. HR—Biggio (Hou); LaRoche (Atl).

**Game 5**—October 11, at Atlanta
Houston ................................021 001 530—12
Atlanta ..................................000 020 100—3
Oswalt, Qualls (6), Gallo (7) and Harville (7), Miceli (8), Wheeler (9); Wright, Gryboski (6), Reitsma (7) and Martin (7), Cruz (8), Byrd (9). W—Oswalt. L—Wright. HR—Beltran 2, Bagwell (Hou); Estrada, Furcal (Atl).

## ALCS

■ **Winner:** The Red Sox did the unthinkable by coming back from a 3-0 series deficit to stun the Yankees and win the series.
■ **Turning point:** Although every moment after the Yankees' dominating Game 3 victory, 19-8, could count as the turning point, a little hope was gained by Red Sox nation at the end of Game 4. In a marathon at Boston which lasted five hours and two minutes, it was David Ortiz's two-run walkoff homer in the 12th inning that gave the Red Sox new life with a 6-4 victory. It had been pinch-runner Dave Roberts' steal of second base and then game-tying run in the ninth inning that typified the little things that it took to get there. In the even longer Game 5 at Boston (five hours, 49 minutes), it was again Ortiz winning the game—this time by singling home Johnny Damon in the 14th inning. It had been Roberts scoring the tying run again as a pinch-runner in the eighth inning to get it there. And the most amazing story of all during the comeback: Mariano Rivera, the ultimate October reliever, unbelievably blew consecutive save opportunities.
■ **Memorable moments:** Pitching with a bloody ankle—the result of loosened sutures that were necessary to mend ligament damage—righthander Curt Schilling threw seven strong innings in a 4-2 victory. Ortiz's walkoff hits and Johnny Damon's two homer performance in the decicive Game 7 in New York all will be remembered as the year that the Sox beat their nemesis. Red Sox starter Pedro Martinez gave Yankees fans plenty of fodder when he said the Yankees were his "Daddy," but he shut them up when he pitched in relief in Game 7, a 10-3 blowout.
■ **Top guns:** Ortiz hit .387 with three home runs and 11 RBIs. Yankees right fielder Gary Sheffield was hitting .692 and left fielder Hideki Matsui .600 after three games. It was indeed a series of big bats.
■ **MVP:** Ortiz.

### Linescores

**Game 1**—October 12, at New York
Boston ..................................000 000 520—7
New York ..............................204 002 02x—10
Schilling, Leskanic (4), Mendoza (5), Wakefield (6) Embree (7), Timlin (8) and Foulke (8); Mussina, Sturtze (7), Gordon (8) and Rivera (8). W—Mussina. L—Schilling. S—Rivera. HR—Lofton (NYY); Varitek (Bos).

**Game 2**—October 13, at New York
Boston ..................................000 000 010—1
New York ..............................100 002 00x—3
Martinez, Timlin (7) and Embree (7), Foulk (8); Lieber, Gordon (8) and Rivera (8). W—Lieber. L—Martinez. S—Rivera. HR—Olerud (NYY).

**Game 3**—October 16, at Boston
New York ..............................303 520 402—19
Boston ..................................042 000 200—8
Brown, Vazquez (3), Quantrill (7), Gordon (9); Arroyo, Mendoza (3), Leskanic (4) and Wakefield (4), Embree (7), Myers (8). W—Vazquez. L—Mendoza. HR—Matsui 2, Rodriguez, Sheffield (NYY), Varitek, Nixon (Bos.).

**Game 4**—October 17, at Boston
New York ....................002 002 000 000—4
Boston ........................000 030 001 002—6
Hernandez, Sturtze (6), Rivera (8), Gordon (10), Quantrill (12); Lowe, Timlin (6), Foulke (7), Embree (10), Myers (11) and Leskanic (11). W—Leskanic. L—Quantrill. HR—Rodriguez (NYY); Ortiz (Bos).

**Game 5**—October 18, at Boston
New York ............010 003 000 000 00—4
Boston ...............200 000 020 000 01—5
Mussina, Sturtze (7) and Gordon (7), Rivera (8), Heredia (10) and Quantrill (10), Loaiza (11); Martinez, Timlin (7), Foulke (8), Arroyo (10), Myers (11) and Embree (11), Wakefield (12). W—Wakefield. L—Loaiza. HR—Williams (NYY); Ortiz (Bos).

**Game 6**—October 19, at New York
Boston ..................................000 400 000—4
New York ..............................000 011 000—2
Schilling, Arroyo (8), Foulke (9); Lieber, Heredia (8) and Quantrill (8), Sturtze (9). W—Schilling L—Lieber S—Foulke. HR—Williams (NYY); Bellhorn (Bos).

**Game 7**—October 20, at New York
Boston ..................................240 200 011—10
New York ..............................001 000 200—3
Lowe, Martinez (7), Timlin (8), Embree (9); Brown, Vazquez (2), Loaiza (4), Heredia (7), Gordon (8), Rivera (9). W—Lowe L—Brown HR—Damon 2, Ortiz, Bellhorn (Bos).

## NLCS

■ **Winner:** In a series in which the home team won every game, the Cardinals climbed back from a 3-2 series deficit and won Games 6 and 7.
■ **Turning point:** After the Astros' Jeff Kent gave his team a 3-2 series lead with a three-run walkoff home run in Game 5, Jim Edmonds of the Cardinals returned the favor in Game 6 and ended a 12-inning battle with a walkoff of his own. In Game 7, the Cardinals scored three runs in the bottom of the sixth and one in the eighth to seal the deal and advance to the World Series for the first time since 1987.
■ **Memorable moments:** Astros midseason pickup Carlos Beltran and the Cardinals' Albert Pujols exchanged home runs and showed they were two of the game's best. Beltran homered in Games 1-4, and Pujols powered shots in Games 1,2,4 and 6. But Kent's three-run shot in the bottom of the ninth of a scoreless Game 5 sent Minute Maid Park into a frenzy. Jim Edmonds' two-run shot two nights later rocked Busch Stadium and sent the series to Game 7. Brandon Backe pitched eight scoreless innings of one-hit ball against the thunderous Cardinals' lineup in Game 5. St. Louis' Scott Rolen hit a line-drive home run off of a decent pitcher, one Roger Clemens, in the sixth inning with one on and two out to seal the NLCS for the Cards.
■ **Top guns:** Astros closer Brad Lidge allowed one hit in eight total innings, and he had 14 strikeouts in that time to lead all Astros pitchers in that category in the NLCS. Pujols and Beltran each had four home runs, but Pujols had nine RBIs to Beltran's five.
■ **MVP:** Pujols.

### Linescores

**Game 1**—October 13, at St. Louis
Houston ................200 200 021—7
St. Louis ..............200 026 00x—10
Backe, Qualls (5), Harville (6), Wheeler (7); Williams, Calero (7), Haren (8) and King (8) and Tavarez (8), Isringhausen (9). W—Williams. L—Qualls. S—Isringhausen. HR—Beltran, Kent, Berkmann, Lamb (Hou); Pujols (St.L).

**Game 2**—October 14, at St. Louis
Houston ................100 110 100—4
St. Louis ..............000 400 02x—6
Munro, Harville (5), Wheeler (6), Miceli (8); Morris, Kline (6) and Calero (6), Tavarez (8), Isringhausen (9). W—Tavarez. L—Miceli. S—Isringhausen. HR—Beltran, Ensberg (Hou); Rolen 2, Walker, Pujols (St.L).

**Game 3**—October 16, at Houston
St. Louis ................110 000 000—2
Houston..................300 000 02x—5
Suppan, Haren (7), King (8) and Eldred (8); Clemens, Lidge (8). W—Clemens L—Suppan. S—Lidge. HR—Beltran, Kent, Berkmann (Hou); Walker, Edmonds (St.L).

**Game 4**—October 17, at Houston
St. Louis ................301 100 000—5
Houston..................102 002 10x—6
Marquis, Calero (5), King (6), Tavarez (7), Isringhausen (8); Oswalt, Wheeler (7), Lidge (8). W—Wheeler L—Tavarez. S—Lidge. HR—Beltran, Berkmann (Hou); Pujols (St.L).

**Game 5**—October 18, at Houston
St. Louis ................000 000 000—0
Houston ................000 000 003—3
Williams, Isringhausen (8); Backe, Lidge (9). W—Lidge L—Isringhausen. HR—Kent (Hou).

**Game 6**—October 20, at St. Louis
Houston......101 100 001 000—4
St. Louis ......202 000 000 002—6
Munro, Harville (3), Qualls (4), Wheeler (7), Lidge (9), Miceli (12); Morris, King (6) and Calero (6), Isringhausen (8), Tavarez (11). W—Tavarez. L—Miceli. HR—Lamb (Hou); Pujols, Edmonds (St.L).

**Game 7**—October 21, at St. Louis
Houston ................101 000 000—2
St. Louis ..............001 003 01x—5
Clemens, Oswalt (7); Suppan, Calero (7), Tavarez (8), Isringhausen (9). W—Suppan L—Clemens S—Isringhausen. HR—Biggio (Hou); Rolen (St.L).

## WORLD SERIES

■ **Winner:** The Red Sox never trailed in their sweep of the Cardinals, winning the World Series for the first time since 1918.
■ **Turning point:** The Red Sox and Cardinals exchanged blows in Game 1, with Boston taking the lead for good in the bottom of the eighth on Mark Bellhorn's two-run home run. The Cardinals only mustered three runs in the final three games.
■ **Memorable moments:** Johnny Damon hit the fourth pitch of the fourth game over the right field wall to spark Boston, and four Red Sox pitchers combined to pitch a four-hit shutout in Game 4. The Cardinals offense slumped horribly, with Rolen and Edmonds going a combined 1-for-30. The Series itself wasn't very dramatic, but the fact the Red Sox broke the Curse and won after 86 years was truly memorable.
■ **Top guns:** St. Louis' Larry Walker hit .357 with two home runs, and Albert Pujols hit .333. But that was about it for the Redbirds. Manny Ramirez hit .412 with a home run, and pitchers Derek Lowe and Pedro Martinez each pitched seven scoreless innings of three-hit ball.
■ **MVP:** Ramirez.

### Linescores

**Game 1**—October 23, at Boston
St. Louis ..............................011 302 020—9
Boston...................................403 000 22x—11
Williams, Haren (3), Calero (7) and King (7) and Eldred (7), Tavarez (8); Wakefield, Arroyo (4), Timlin (7), Embree (8) and Fouke (8). W—Foulke L—Tavarez HR—Ortiz, Bellhorn (Bos); Walker (St.L).

**Game 2**—October 24, at Boston
St. Louis ..............................000 100 010—2
Boston...................................200 202 00x—6
Morris, Eldred (5), King (6), Marquis (7), Reyes (8); Schilling, Embree (7), Timlin (8) and Foulke (8). W—Schilling L—Morris.

**Game 3**—October 26, at St. Louis
Boston ..................................100 120 000—4
St. Louis ..............................000 000 001—1
Martinez, Timlin (8), Foulke (8); Suppan, Reyes (5), Calero (6), King (7), Tavarez (9). W—Martinez L—Suppan. HR—Ramirez (Bos); Walker (St.L).

**Game 4**—October 27, at St. Louis
Boston ..................................102 000 000—3
St. Louis ..............................000 000 000—0
Lowe, Arroyo (8) and Embree (8), Foulke (9); Marquis, Haren (7), Isringhausen (8). W—Lowe L—Marquis. HR—Damon (Bos).

# 2005

## FINAL STANDINGS

### American League

#### East Division

| Team | N.Y. | Bos. | Tor. | Bal. | T.B. | Chi. | Cle. | Min. | Det. | K.C. | LAA. | Oak. | Tex. | Sea. | N.L. | W | L | Pct. | GB |
|---|---|---|---|---|---|---|---|---|---|---|---|---|---|---|---|---|---|---|---|
| New York | ... | 10 | 12 | 11 | 8 | 3 | 4 | 3 | 5 | 3 | 4 | 7 | 7 | 7 | 11-7 | 95 | 67 | .586 | ... |
| Boston | 9 | ... | 7 | 10 | 13 | 4 | 4 | 4 | 6 | 4 | 6 | 6 | 7 | 3 | 12-6 | 95 | 67 | .586 | ... |
| Toronto | 6 | 11 | ... | 10 | 11 | 2 | 2 | 2 | 3 | 6 | 5 | 5 | 3 | 6 | 8-10 | 80 | 82 | .494 | 15.0 |
| Baltimore | 7 | 8 | 9 | ... | 12 | 2 | 1 | 3 | 3 | 4 | 2 | 4 | 4 | 7 | 8-10 | 74 | 88 | .457 | 21.0 |
| Tampa Bay | 11 | 6 | 8 | 6 | ... | 2 | 6 | 0 | 2 | 5 | 5 | 5 | 6 | 2 | 3-15 | 67 | 95 | .414 | 28.0 |

#### Central Division

| Team | Chi. | Cle. | Min. | Det. | K.C. | N.Y. | Bos. | Tor. | Bal. | T.B. | LAA. | Oak. | Tex. | Sea. | N.L. | W | L | Pct. | GB |
|---|---|---|---|---|---|---|---|---|---|---|---|---|---|---|---|---|---|---|---|
| Chicago | ... | 14 | 11 | 14 | 13 | 3 | 3 | 4 | 6 | 4 | 4 | 2 | 3 | 6 | 12-6 | 99 | 63 | .611 | ..... |
| Cleveland | 5 | ... | 10 | 12 | 10 | 0 | 2 | 4 | 0 | 4 | 0 | 0 | 0 | 7 | [illegible] | [illegible] | [illegible] | [illegible] | 6.0 |
| Minnesota | 7 | 9 | ... | 11 | 13 | 3 | 2 | 4 | 3 | 6 | 4 | 4 | 3 | 6 | 8-10 | 83 | 79 | .512 | 16.0 |
| Detroit | 5 | 6 | 8 | ... | 10 | 1 | 4 | 4 | 5 | 5 | 4 | 1 | 4 | 5 | 9-9 | 71 | 91 | .438 | 28.0 |
| Kansas City | 5 | 6 | 6 | 9 | ... | 3 | 2 | 3 | 2 | 3 | 2 | 2 | 2 | 2 | 9-9 | 56 | 106 | .346 | 43.0 |

#### West Division

| Team | LAA | Oak. | Tex. | Sea. | N.Y. | Bos. | Tor. | Bal. | T.B. | Chi. | Cle. | Min. | Det. | K.C. | N.L. | W | L | Pct. | GB |
|---|---|---|---|---|---|---|---|---|---|---|---|---|---|---|---|---|---|---|---|
| Los Angeles | ... | 10 | 15 | 9 | 6 | 4 | 1 | 4 | 4 | 6 | 5 | 6 | 6 | 7 | 12-6 | 95 | 67 | .586 | ..... |
| Oakland | 9 | ... | 11 | 12 | 2 | 4 | 5 | 6 | 4 | 7 | 3 | 6 | 5 | 4 | 10-8 | 88 | 74 | .543 | 7.0 |
| Texas | 4 | 8 | ... | 13 | 3 | 2 | 7 | 6 | 2 | 6 | 3 | 6 | 2 | 8 | 9-9 | 79 | 83 | .488 | 16.0 |
| Seattle | 9 | 6 | 6 | ... | 3 | 3 | 4 | 3 | 4 | 3 | 3 | 4 | 4 | 7 | 10-8 | 69 | 93 | .426 | 26.0 |

NOTE: Read across for wins, down for losses.

Clinching dates: New York (East)—October 1; Chicago (Central)—September 29; Los Angeles (West)—September 28; Boston (wild card)—October 2.

### National League

#### East Division

| Team | Atl. | Phi. | NY. | Fla. | Was. | St.L. | Hou. | Mil. | Chi. | Cin. | Pit. | S.D. | Ari. | S.F. | LAD. | Col. | A.L. | W | L | Pct. | GB |
|---|---|---|---|---|---|---|---|---|---|---|---|---|---|---|---|---|---|---|---|---|---|
| Atlanta | ... | 9 | 13 | 10 | 10 | 3 | 5 | 3 | 6 | 7 | 4 | 1 | 3 | 4 | 3 | 2 | 7-8 | 90 | 72 | .556 | ... |
| Phil. | 10 | ... | 7 | 10 | 11 | 4 | 0 | 5 | 4 | 4 | 4 | 6 | 4 | 5 | 3 | 4 | 7-8 | 88 | 74 | .543 | 2.0 |
| New York | 6 | 11 | ... | 10 | 11 | 2 | 5 | 3 | 4 | 3 | 3 | 4 | 6 | 3 | 3 | 4 | 5-10 | 83 | 79 | .512 | 7.0 |
| Florida | 8 | 9 | 8 | ... | 9 | 3 | 4 | 3 | 4 | 4 | 3 | 2 | 4 | 4 | 5 | 3 | 10-5 | 83 | 79 | .512 | 7.0 |
| Wash. | 9 | 8 | 8 | 9 | ... | 2 | 2 | 4 | 5 | 1 | 5 | 1 | 4 | 3 | 4 | 4 | 12-6 | 81 | 81 | .500 | 9.0 |

#### Central Division

| Team | St.L. | Hou. | Mil. | Chi. | Cin. | Pit. | Atl. | Phi. | NY. | Fla. | Was. | S.D. | Ari. | S.F. | LAD. | Col. | A.L. | W | L | Pct. | GB |
|---|---|---|---|---|---|---|---|---|---|---|---|---|---|---|---|---|---|---|---|---|---|
| St. Louis | ... | 11 | 11 | 6 | 11 | 12 | 3 | 2 | 5 | 4 | 4 | 3 | 5 | 4 | 5 | 4 | 10-5 | 100 | 62 | .617 | ... |
| Houston | 5 | ... | 10 | 7 | 12 | 9 | 1 | 6 | 5 | 3 | 5 | 4 | 3 | 3 | 4 | 5 | 7-8 | 89 | 73 | .549 | 11.0 |
| Milw. | 5 | 5 | ... | 9 | 10 | 9 | 3 | 4 | 3 | 4 | 4 | 3 | 4 | 4 | 1 | 5 | 8-7 | 81 | 81 | .500 | 19.0 |
| Chicago | 10 | 9 | 7 | ... | 6 | 11 | 1 | 2 | 2 | 5 | 1 | 4 | 2 | 5 | 4 | 4 | 6-9 | 79 | 83 | .488 | 21.0 |
| Cincinnati | 5 | 4 | 6 | 9 | ... | 9 | 3 | 3 | 3 | 2 | 5 | 4 | 4 | 3 | 3 | 3 | 7-8 | 73 | 89 | .451 | 27.0 |
| Pittsburgh | 4 | 7 | 7 | 5 | 7 | ... | 3 | 3 | 3 | 4 | 1 | 3 | 4 | 2 | 2 | 7 | 5-7 | 67 | 95 | .414 | 33.0 |

#### West Division

| Team | S.D. | Ari. | S.F. | LAD. | Col. | Atl. | Phi. | NY. | Fla. | Was. | St.L. | Hou. | Mil. | Chi. | Cin. | Pit. | A.L. | W | L | Pct. | GB |
|---|---|---|---|---|---|---|---|---|---|---|---|---|---|---|---|---|---|---|---|---|---|
| S.D. | ... | 9 | 12 | 7 | 11 | 5 | 0 | 2 | 4 | 5 | 4 | 3 | 4 | 3 | 2 | 4 | 7-11 | 82 | 80 | .506 | ... |
| Arizona | 10 | ... | 7 | 13 | 11 | 3 | 3 | 1 | 2 | 2 | 2 | 3 | 2 | 5 | 2 | 3 | 8-10 | 77 | 85 | .475 | 5.0 |
| San Fran. | 6 | 11 | ... | 10 | 11 | 2 | 1 | 3 | 2 | 3 | 2 | 4 | 3 | 2 | 5 | 4 | 6-12 | 75 | 87 | .463 | 7.0 |
| Los Ang. | 11 | 5 | 9 | ... | 8 | 3 | 3 | 3 | 2 | 2 | 2 | 2 | 5 | 2 | 4 | 5 | 5-13 | 71 | 91 | .438 | 11.0 |
| Colorado | 7 | 7 | 7 | 11 | ... | 4 | 2 | 3 | 3 | 2 | 4 | 1 | 1 | 3 | 3 | 3 | 6-9 | 67 | 95 | .414 | 15.0 |

NOTE: Read across for wins, down for losses.

Clinching dates: Atlanta (East)—September 27; St. Louis (Central)—September 15; San Diego (West)—September 28; Houston (wild card)—October 2.

## SIGNIFICANT EVENTS

■ **January 13:** MLB and MLBPA agree on new drug-testing policy and stiffer penalties beginning with 10-day suspension for a first postive test.
■ **March 17:** Commissioner Selig and several present and former players testify on steroids in baseball before House Committee on Government Reform.
■ **August 1:** Baltimore Orioles first baseman Rafael Palmeiro becomes seventh major-league player to test positive, drawing a 10-day suspension and lots of adverse publicity.
■ **November 15:** MLB and MLBPA announce a second revision to drug-testing policy, adding amphetamines and increasing length of suspension for first positive test to 50 days.

## MEMORABLE MOMENTS

■ **April 4:** Transposed Montreal Expos play first game as Washington Nationals, losing, 8-4, in Philadelphia.
■ **July 15:** The Orioles' Rafael Palmeiro becomes the 26th member of the 3,000-hit club.
■ **July 26:** The Cubs' Greg Maddux becomes the 13th pitcher to reach 3,000 strikeouts.
■ **August 31:** The Marlins' Jeremy Hermida becomes 2nd player to hit grand slam in first major-league at-bat.
■ **September 14:** The Braves' Andruw Jones becomes 12th player to hit 300 home runs before his 30th birthday.
■ **October 2:** Philadelphia's Jimmy Rollins hits in 36th consecutive game, longest streak since Paul Molitor hit in 39 straight games in 1987.
■ **October 2:** Cardinals defeat Cincinnati Reds, 7-5, in final regular season game at St. Louis' Busch Stadium.

## ALL-STAR GAME

■ **Winner:** American League, 7-5.
■ **Key inning:** The third. With a 1-0 lead going into the third, the A.L. sent Boston's David Ortiz to the dish. He singled home Red Sox teammate Johnny Damon. One out later, Baltimore's Miguel Tejada knocked in the Yankees' Alex Rodriguez. The A.L. added two runs in the fourth and sixth innings.
■ **Memorable moments:** The A.L. continued its dominance in the All-Star game by stretching its unbeaten streak to nine games, including the controversial 2002 tie game. St. Louis' Chris Carpenter started the game for the N.L. over Houston's Roger Clemens. Carpenter pitched one inning and gave up zero runs. Andruw Jones of the Braves homered for the N.L. off of Texas' Kenny Rogers, who was involved in an altercation with a cameraman a few weeks before the game. ■
**Top guns:** Jones (Braves), Brad Lidge (Astros), Luis Gonzalez (Diamondbacks), N.L.; Manny Ramirez (Red Sox), Ortiz (Red Sox),Tejada (Orioles), Mark Teixeira (Rangers) Mark Buehrle (White Sox), A.L.
■ **MVP:** Tejada.

**Linescore**

July 12 at Detroit's Comerica Park
N.L. ........................................000 000 212—5
A.L. ........................................012 202 00x—7

Carpenter (Cardinals), John Smoltz (Braves) 2, Roy Oswalt (Astros) 3, Livan Hernandez (Nationals) 4, Clemens (Astros) 5, Dontrelle Willis (Marlins) 6, Lidge (Astros) 7, Jake Peavy (Padres) 8 and Chad Cordero (Nationals) 8; Buehrle (White Sox), Bartolo Colon (Angels) 3, Johan Santana (Twins) 4, Matt Clement (Red Sox) 5, Jon Garland (White Sox) 6, Rogers (Rangers) 7, Joe Nathan (Twins) 8, Bob Wickman (Indians) 9, B.J. Ryan (Orioles) 9, and Mariano Rivera (Yankees) 9. W—Buehrle. L—Smoltz. S—Rivera. HR—Teixeira, Tejada, A.L.; A. Jones, N.L.

**American League**
**BA:** Michael Young, Tex., .331.
**Runs:** Alex Rodriguez, NYY, 124.
**Hits:** Michael Young, Tex., 221.
**TB:** Mark Teixeira, Tex., 370.
**HR:** Alex Rodriguez, NYY, 48.
**RBI:** David Ortiz, Bos., 148.
**SB:** Chone Figgins, LAA, 62.
**Wins:** Bartolo Colon, LAA., 21.
**ERA:** Kevin Millwood, Cle., 2.86.
**CG:** Roy Halladay, Tor., 5.
**IP:** Mark Buehrle, CWS, 236.2.
**SO:** Johan Santana, Min., 238.
**Sv.:** Francisco Rodriguez (LAA), Bob Wickman (Cle), 45.

**National League**
**BA:** Derrek Lee, ChC, .335.
**Runs:** Albert Pujols, St.L., 129.
**Hits:** Derrek Lee, ChC, 199.
**TB:** Derrek Lee, ChC, 393.
**HR:** Andruw Jones, Atl., 51.
**RBI:** Andruw Jones, Atl., 128.
**SB:** Jose Reyes, NYM, 60.
**Wins:** Dontrelle Willis, Fla., 22.
**ERA:** Roger Clemens, Hou., 1.87.
**CG:** Chris Carpenter (St.L), Dontrelle Willis (Fla.), 7.
**IP:** Livan Hernandez, Was., 246.1.
**SO:** Jake Peavy, S.D., 216.
**Sv.:** Chad Cordero, Was., 47.

**A.L. 20-game winners**
Bartolo Colon, LAA., 21

**N.L. 20-game winners**
Dontrelle Willis, Fla., 22
Chris Carpenter, St.L., 21
Roy Oswalt, Hou., 20

**A.L. 100 RBIs**
David Ortiz, Bos., 148
Manny Ramirez, Bos., 144
Mark Teixeira, Tex., 144
Alex Rodriguez, NYY, 130
Gary Sheffield, NYY, 123
Richie Sexson, Sea., 121
Jorge Cantu, T.B., 117
Hideki Matsui, NYY, 116
Vladimir Guerrero, LAA., 108
Travis Hafner, Cle., 108
Alfonso Soriano, Tex., 104
Eric Chavez, Oak., 101
Paul Konerko, CWS, 100

**N.L. 100 RBIs**
Andruw Jones, Atl., 128
Pat Burrell, Phi., 117
Albert Pujols, St.L., 117
Miguel Cabrera, Fla., 116
Carlos Delgado, Fla., 115
Cliff Lee, Mil., 114
Derrek Lee, ChC, 107
Jeff Kent, LAD, 105
Chase Utley, Phi., 105
Bobby Abreu, Phi., 102
David Wright, NYM, 102
Jason Bay, Pit., 101
Adam Dunn, Cin., 101
Morgan Ensberg, Hou., 101

**A.L. 40 homers**
Alex Rodriguez, NYY, 48
David Ortiz, Bos., 47
Manny Ramirez, Bos., 45
Mark Teixeira, Tex., 43
Paul Konerko, CWS, 40

**N.L. 40 homers**
Andruw Jones, Atl., 51
Derrek Lee, ChC, 46
Albert Pujols, St.L., 41
Adam Dunn, Cin., 40

**Most Valuable Player**
A.L.: Alex Rodriguez, 3B, NYY
N.L.: Albert Pujols, 1B, St.L.

**Cy Young Award**
A.L.: Bartolo Colon, LAA
N.L.: Chris Carpenter, St.L.

**Rookie of the Year**
A.L.: Huston Street, P, Oak.
N.L.: Ryan Howard, 1B, Phi.

**Manager of the Year**
A.L.: Ozzie Guillen, CWS
N.L.: Bobby Cox, Atl.

**Hall of Fame additions**
Wade Boggs, 3B, 1982-1999
Ryne Sandberg, 2B, 1981-1997

## A.L. DIVISION SERIES

■ **Winners:** The White Sox swept the Red Sox, showing that their shaky play at the end of the regular season was not a sign of things to come. Chicago held Boston to nine runs in three games. The Angels won two of the first three games and beat the Yankees in Game 5, roughing up starter Mike Mussina, who did not survive the third inning.
■ **Turning point:** Chicago blasted five home runs off the defending champions in Game 1 and scored five runs in the first inning to set the tone. A clutch three-run homer off the bat of Tadahito Iguchi gave Chicago the momentum in Game 2. Red Sox second baseman Tony Graffanino's error set up the shot that put Sox in the lead. Rookie Bobby Jenks recorded his first postseason save. The Red Sox could not muster another impressive comeback this year as the White Sox finished the sweep in Boston. Paul Konerko's two-run home run in the sixth gave Chicago the lead for good. … In Game 3, the Angels scored two runs in the sixth, seventh and eighth innings to grab the series lead. In Game 5, Los Angeles jumped on Yankee starter Mike Mussina, who had pitched 5.2 shutout innings in Game 1, for five runs in 2.2 innings. The Angels did not need any more help than that.
■ **Memorable moments:** For the first time since 2002, neither New York nor Boston advanced to the ALCS. In the sixth inning of Game 2, Orlando Hernandez pitched out of a bases-loaded jam to hold Red Sox at bay. LA's Ervin Santana pitched 5.1 clutch innings in Game 5 after an injury to Bartolo Colon.
■ **Top guns:** A.J. Pierzynski blasted two home runs in Game 1 for Chicago, and Konerko contributed two of his own. Bengie Molina, not known for power, hit home runs in the first three games against New York and batted .444.

**Linescores**

Boston vs. Chicago

**Game 1**—October 4, at Chicago
Boston........................000 200 000—2
Chicago......................501 204 02x—14
Clement, Bradford (4), Gonzalez (5), Arroyo (8); Contreras, Cotts (8), Politte (9). W—Contreras. L—Clement. HR—Podsednik, Konerko, Pierzynski 2, Uribe (Chi).

**Game 2**—October 5, at Chicago
Boston........................202 000 000—4
Chicago ......................000 050 00x—5
Wells, Papelbon (7); Buehrle, Jenks (8). W—Buehrle. L—Wells. S—Jenks. HR—Iguchi (Chi).

**Game 3**—October 7, at Boston
Chicago ......................002 002 001—5
Boston........................000 201 000—3
Garcia, Marte (6) and Hernandez (6), Jenks (9); Wakefield, Bradford (6) and Myers (6) and Papelbon (6), Timlin (9). W—Garcia. L—Wakefield. S—Jenks HR—Konerko (Chi); Ortiz, Ramirez 2 (Bos).

New York vs. Los Angeles

**Game 1**—October 4, at Los Angeles
New York ....................310 000 000—4
LAA ..........................000 000 101—2
Mussina, Leiter (6), Sturtze (7) and Gordon (7), Rivera (9); Colon, Shields (8). W—Mussina. L—Colon. S—Rivera. HR—B. Molina (LA).

**Game 2**—October 5, at Los Angeles
New York ....................010 010 001—3
LAA ..........................010 011 21x—5
Wang, Leiter (7), Proctor (8); Lackey, Shields (6), Escobar (7), F. Rodriguez (9). W—Escobar. L—Wang. HR—Posada (NY); B. Molina, Rivera (LA).

**Game 3**—October 7, at New York
LAA ..................302 002 220—11
New York ..........000 420 010—7
Byrd, Donnelly (4), Shields (5), Escobar (7), F. Rodriguez (9); Johnson, Small (4), Tanyon Sturtze (6), Gordon (7) and Leiter (7), Proctor (8). W—Shields L—Small. HR—B. Molina, Anderson (LA); Jeter, Matsui (NY).

**Game 4**—October 9, at New York
LAA ....................000 002 000—2
New York...........102 001 20x—3
Lackey, Shields (6), Escobar (7); Chacon, Leiter (7), Rivera (8). W—Leiter L—Shields. S—Rivera.

**Game 5**—October 10, at Los Angeles
New York ..........020 000 100—3
LAA ....................032 000 00x—5
Mussina, Johnson (3), Gordon (8); Colon, Santana (2), Escobar (7), F. Rodriguez (8). W—Santana L—Mussina. S—Rodriguez. HR—Jeter (NY); Anderson (LA).

## N.L. DIVISION SERIES

■ **Winners:** The Cardinals, who finished with the majors' best record, swept the Padres, who finished barely over .500, 82-80. Houston beat Atlanta three games to one with the Astros' final victory coming in an epic game.

■ **Turning point:** Reggie Sanders belted a fifth-inning grand slam off of Padres ace Jake Peavy in Game 1, and St. Louis never trailed in the series. ... Game 4 between the Astros and Braves, the longest game in postseason history, ended in the 18th inning with a walk-off home run off the bat of Chris Burke, who entered the game in the 11th inning. Roger Clemens, who had started Game 2, pitched three innings of relief and earned the win.

■ **Memorable moments:** Reggie Sanders was the hottest of the hot in the Cardinals lineup, totaling 10 RBIs in just three games. Braves starter-turned-closer-turned starter again John Smoltz dominated Houston's lineup in a Game 2 matchup pitting Smoltz and his one Cy Young award against Clemens and his seven Cy Young awards. The 18-inning marathon Game 4 went into extra innings when Brad Ausmus hit a solo shot in the bottom of the ninth with two outs to tie the score, 6-6. The shot just cleared the yellow line on the outfield wall.

■ **Top guns:** Reggie Sanders (Cardinals) hit .333 to go with his 10 RBIs, and teammate Albert Pujols scored four runs and hit .556. Lance Berkman led the Astros with a .357 average for regular players, but Burke, with only 3 at-bats, slugged 2.000, hitting a double and home run.

### Linescores

San Diego vs. St. Louis

**Game 1**—October 4, at St. Louis
San Diego........................0 0 0 0 0 0 1 1 3—5
St. Louis ..........................1 0 3 0 4 0 0 0 x—8
Peavy, Hensley (5), Lawrence (6), Otsuka (7), Linebrink (8); Carpenter, Thompson (7) and Flores (7), Eldred (8), Isringhausen (9). W—Carpenter. L—Peavy. HR—Edmonds, Sanders (St.L), Young (S.D.).

**Game 2**—October 6, at St. Louis
San Diego. ......................0 0 0 0 0 0 1 1 0—2
St. Louis ..........................0 0 2 2 0 0 2 0 x—6
Astacio, Hensley (5), Seanez (7), Otsuka (8); Mulder, Tavarez (7), Flores (8), Isringhausen (9) W—Mulder. L—Astacio.

**Game 3**—October 8, at San Diego
St. Louis..........................1 4 0 0 2 0 0 0 0—7
San Diego........................0 0 0 0 2 0 1 1 0—4
Morris, Thompson (7) and Fores (7), Tavarez (8) and Isringhausen (8); Williams, Lawrence (2), Hensley (4), Seanez (6), Otsuka (8), Hoffman (9). W—Morris. L—Williams. S—Isringhausen HR—Eckstein (St.L); Roberts, Hernandez (S.D.).

Houston vs. Atlanta

**Game 1**—October 5, at Atlanta
Houston ..........................1 0 2 1 0 0 1 5 0—10
Atlanta.............................1 0 0 2 0 0 0 1 1— 5
Pettitte, Wheeler (8), Springer (9) and Gallo (9); Hudson, Devine (7), Reitsma (8) and Foster (8) and Brower (8), McBride (9). W—Pettitte. L—Hudson. HR—C. Jones, A. Jones (Atl.).

**Game 2**—October 6, at Atlanta
Houston ..........................1 0 0 0 0 0 0 0 0—1
Atlanta.............................0 3 2 0 0 0 2 0 x—7
Clemens, Backe (6), Qualls (7), Lidge (8); Smoltz, Reitsma (8), Farnsworth (9). W—Smoltz L—Clemens. HR—McCann (Atl.).

**Game 3**—October 8, at Houston
Atlanta.............................0 2 0 0 0 0 0 1 0—3
Houston...........................2 0 1 0 0 0 4 0 x—7
Sosa, Reitsma (7) and Foster (7) and Devine (7) and Brower (7); Oswalt, Wheeler (8) and Gallo (8), Lidge (9). W—Oswalt. L—Sosa. HR—Lamb (Hou.).

**Game 4**—October 9, at Houston
Atlanta...0 0 4 0 1 0 0 1 0 0 0 0 0 0 0 0 0 0—6
Hous......0 0 0 0 1 0 0 4 1 0 0 0 0 0 0 0 0 1—7
Hudson, Farnsworth (8), Reitsma (10), Thomson (12), Brower (14), Devine (17); Backe, Gallo (5), Springer (6), Rodriguez (8), Qualls (9), Lidge (11), Wheeler (13), Clemens (16). W—Clemens. L—Devine. HR—LaRoche, McCann (Atl); Berkman, Burke, Ausmus (Hou.).

## ALCS

■ **Winner:** The Chicago White Sox stayed hot and beat the Angels four games to one.

■ **Turning point:** After the Angels took Game 1 in Chicago, the White Sox won Game 2 in dramatic and controversial fashion. With the score tied and two out in the bottom of the ninth, Sox catcher A.J. Pierzynski swung at strike three. Angels catcher Josh Paul thought he had caught the pitch and rolled the ball toward the mound. Pierzynski ran to first, and home plate umpire Doug Eddings, after giving a confusing signal, ruled that the pitch had hit the dirt. Pierzynski then scored the winning run on a Joe Crede double.

■ **Memorable moments:** Pierzynski was involved with three disputed calls: the dropped third strike, an uncalled catcher's interference that resulted in a double play against the Angels in Game 4 and a missed tag at first base in Game 5. Chicago's starting pitchers also chipped in. The Sox bullpen threw a total of seven pitches in the entire series, all in Game 1 after Jose Contreras went 8.1 inning. Chicago's starters then threw four straight complete games. 2004 A.L. MVP Vladimir Guerrero was a paltry 1-for-20 in the series. Angels ace and 2005 Cy Young winner Bartolo Colon did not pitch in the series because of inflammation in his right shoulder.

■ **Top guns:** Chicago's starting pitchers: Contreras, Mark Buehrle, Jon Garland and Freddy Garcia, all of whom threw complete games. Chicago's Crede and Paul Konerko each had two homers and seven RBIs; Crede hit .368 and Konerko hit .286.

■ **MVP:** Konerko.

### Linescores

Los Angeles vs. Chicago

**Game 1**—October 11, at Chicago
LAA ................................0 1 2 0 0 0 0 0 0— 3
Chicago ..........................0 0 1 1 0 0 0 0 0—2
Byrd, Shields (7), F. Rodriguez (9); Contreras, Cotts (9). W—Byrd. L—Contreras. S—Rodriguez. HR—Anderson (LA); Crede (Chi).

**Game 2**—October 12, at Chicago
LAA ................................0 0 0 0 1 0 0 0 0— 1
Chicago ..........................1 0 0 0 0 0 0 0 1—2
Washburn, Donnelly (5), Shields (6), Escobar (7); Buehrle. W—Buehrle. L—Escobar. HR—Quinlan (LA).

**Game 3**—October 14, at Los Angeles
Chicago ..........................3 0 1 0 1 0 4 0 2— 5
LAA ................................0 0 0 0 0 2 0 0 0— 2
Garland; Lackey, Gregg (6), Donnelly (8). W—Garland. L—Lackey. HR—Konerko (Chi); Cabrera (LA).

**Game 4**—October 15, at Los Angeles
Chicago ..........................3 0 1 1 1 0 0 2 0— 8
LAA ................................0 1 0 1 0 0 0 0 0— 2
Garcia; Santana, Shields (5), Donnelly (7), Yan (8). W—Garcia. L—Santana. HR—Konerko, Pierzynski (Chi).

**Game 5**—October 16, at Los Angeles
Chicago ..........................0 1 0 0 1 0 1 1 2— 6
LAA ................................0 0 1 0 2 0 0 0 0— 3
Contreras; Byrd, Shields (5), Escobar (7), F. Rodriguez (8). W—Contreras. L—Escobar. HR—Crede (Chi).

## NLCS

■ **Winner:** The Astros reversed the results of the 2004 NLCS by prevailing over St. Louis in six games. After Houston endured a disheartening loss in Game 5, Roy Oswalt won his second game of the series.

■ **Turning point:** When Oswalt took the mound for Game 6, the Cardinals had regained momentum. Albert Pujols had done the improbable in Game 5 by hitting a three-run homer off the generally unhittable Astros closer Brad Lidge, and the home crowd in St. Louis wanted to extend the life of Busch Stadium, which was torn down at season's end. But Oswalt shut down the Cardinals' offense, which had been struggling against Houston's impressive starting pitching, to lead his team to its first World Series appearance and the first for a team from Texas.

■ **Memorable moments:** After Oswalt yielded only 5 hits in 7 innings in Game 2, Lidge came in to close the door and allow Houston to tie the series. Roger Clemens pitched six strong innings in Game 3, with Lidge again earning the save, and Brandon Backe pitched equally well in Game 4. With the Cardinals on the brink of elimination in Game 5, Lidge came in to shut the door on the Redbirds yet again. Lidge struck out pinch hitter John Rodriguez, then John Mabry. Leadoff man David Eckstein hit a single and Jim Edmonds drew a walk. Pujols hit a ball that left fans in the Crawford Boxes looking skyward as he gave his team some breathing room and took the series back to St. Louis. Oswalt earned two wins in the series by pitching 14 innings and allowing only two runs. Both of his outings took place after an Astros loss. Yadier Molina lined out to right field for the final out at Busch Stadium.

■ **Top guns:** Oswalt. Pujols hit .304 with two home runs and six RBIs. Yadier Molina (Cardinals) hit .318 with three doubles. Chris Burke (Astros) hit .300 with a triple and home run. He also scored five runs. Jason Lane (Astros) hit two homers.

■ **MVP:** Oswalt.

### Linescores

Houston vs. St. Louis

**Game 1**—October 12, at St. Louis
Houston ............0 0 0 0 0 0 2 0 1—3
St. Louis ............2 1 0 0 2 0 0 0 x—5
Pettitte, Springer (7), Astacio (8); Carpenter, Isringhausen (9). W—Carpenter. L—Pettitte. S—Isringhausen. HR—Burke (Hou); Sanders (St.L).

**Game 2**—October 13, at St. Louis
Houston ............0 1 0 0 1 0 0 2 0—4
St. Louis ............0 0 0 0 0 1 0 0 0—1
Owalt, Lidge (8); Mulder, Tavarez (8), Isringhausen (9). W—Oswalt. L—Mulder. S—Lidge. HR—Pujols (St.L).

**Game 3**—October 15, at Houston
St. Louis ............0 0 0 0 1 1 0 0 1—3
Houston ............0 0 0 2 0 2 0 0 x—4
Morris, Thompson (6), Flores (7), Tavarez (8); Clemens, Qualls (7), Lidge (9). W—Clemens L—Morris. S—Lidge. HR—Lamb (Hou.).

**Game 4**—October 16, at Houston
St. Louis ............0 0 0 1 0 0 0 0 0—1
Houston ............0 0 0 1 0 0 1 0 x—2
Suppan, Marquis (6); Backe, Gallo (6), Qualls (7), Wheeler (8), Lidge (9). W—Qualls L—Marquis. S—Lidge. HR—Lane (Hou.).

**Game 5**—October 17, at Houston
St. Louis ............0 0 2 0 0 0 0 0 3—5
Houston ............0 1 0 0 0 0 3 0 0—4
Carpenter, Isringhausen (8); Pettitte, Qualls (7), Gallo (8) and Wheeler (8), Lidge (9). W—Isringhausen L—Lidge. HR—Pujols (St.L), Berkman (Hou.).

**Game 6**—October 19, at St. Louis
Houston ............0 0 2 1 0 1 1 0 0—5
St. Louis ............0 0 0 0 1 0 0 0 0—1
Oswalt, Qualls (8), Wheeler (9); Mulder, Thompson (5), Marquis (6), Flores (7) and Tavarez (7), Isringhausen (9). W—Oswalt. L—Mulder. HR—Lane (Hou.).

## WORLD SERIES

■ **Winner:** Appearing in the World Series for the first time since 1959, the White Sox swept the Astros. Doing something that a White Sox team has not done since 1917, they became world champions in convincing fashion.

■ **Turning point:** The White Sox did not dominate the Astros from a scoring standpoint. Houston was outscored by only six runs total, tying the record for the smallest margin of runs scored in a sweep, set in 1950 when the Yankees defeated the Phillies.The winner of Game 1 has won the World Series every year since 1997, except for 2002, and when White Sox closer Bobby Jenks came in with two outs in the top of the eighth and struck out future Hall of Famer Jeff Bagwell and then got three quick outs in the ninth, Houston knew it had a hill to climb.

■ **Memorable moments:** Jermaine Dye's solo home run in the first inning of Game 1 got Chicago off to a good start, and Joe Crede's homer in the fourth put them ahead to stay. Scott Podsednik's one-out blast in the bottom of the ninth off the once unhittable Lidge made for two dramatic home runs in Game 2. Earlier, teammate Paul Konerko belted a grand slam off reliever Chad Qualls to put his team up, 6-4. But the Astros tied the score on a two-run pinch-hit single by Jose Vizcaino in the top of the ninth. Roy Oswalt, the NLCS MVP, got roughed up for five runs in Game 3, all in the fifth inning.The Astros had scored four before then, and they got Oswalt off the hook by tying the score in the eighth on a double by Jason Lane. The Astros, who played in the longest postseason game in baseball history in the NLDS, then played 14 innings, tying the record for the longest World Series game. But it was a former Astro who ended it. Geoff Blum hit a solo shot in the top of the 14th, and Houston could not answer back. The White Sox snapped the second longest Series streak at 88 years with a 1-0 victory in Game 4. They also became the only team other than the 1999 Yankees to go 11-1 in the postseason. Roger Clemens became the second oldest pitcher to start a World Series game, but he left after two innings of a rough outing in Game 1 with a sore hamstring.

■ **Top guns:** Dye hit .438 with a homer and double, 3 RBIs and 3 runs scored. Teammate Joe Crede hit .294 with two homers and a Series-best .706 slugging average among regular players. Carl Everett (Chi) got four hits and batted .444. Freddy Garcia pitched 7 shutout innings in Game 4, giving up only four hits. Lance Berkman (Astros) hit .385 with 6 RBIs and proved to be the main offensive threat for Houston, though Willy Taveras hit .333 and slugged .600. Starter Brandon Backe continued a solid postseason with 7 shutout innings in Game 4, matching counterpart Garcia.

■ **MVP:** Dye.

### Linescores

Houston vs. Chicago

**Game 1**—October 22, at Chicago
Houston .........................0 1 2 0 0 0 0 0 0— 3
Chicago .........................1 2 0 1 0 0 0 1 x—5
Clemens, W. Rodriguez (3), Qualls (6), Springer (8); Contreras, Cotts (8) and Jenks (8). W—Contreras L—Rodriguez HR—Lamb (Hou.); Dye, Crede (Chi).

**Game 2**—October 23, at Chicago
Houston ...........................0 1 1 0 2 0 0 0 2—6
Chicago ...........................0 2 0 0 0 0 4 0 1—7
Pettitte, Wheeler (7) and Qualls (7), Gallo (8), Lidge (9); Buehrle, Politte (8), Jenks (9) and Cotts (9). W—Cotts L—Lidge. HR—Ensberg (Hou.); Podsednik, Konerko (Chi).

**Game 3**—October 25, at Houston
Chicago ........0 0 0 0 5 0 0 0 0 0 0 0 0 2—7
Houston ........1 0 2 1 0 0 0 1 0 0 0 0 0 0—5
Garland, Politte (8) and Cotts (8) and Hermanson (8), Hernandez (9), Vizcaino (10), Jenks (11), Marte (13), Buehrle (14); Oswalt, Springer (7), Wheeler (8), Gallo (9) and Lidge (9), Qualls (11), E. Astacio (14) and W. Rodriguez (14). W—Marte L—Astacio. S—Buehrle HR—Blum, Crede (Chi); Lane (Hou.).

**Game 4**—October 26, at Houston
Chicago ...........................0 0 0 0 0 0 0 1 0—1
Houston ...........................0 0 0 0 0 0 0 0 0—0
Garcia, Politte (8) and Cotts (8), Jenks (9); Backe, Lidge (8). W—Garcia L—Lidge. S—Jenks.

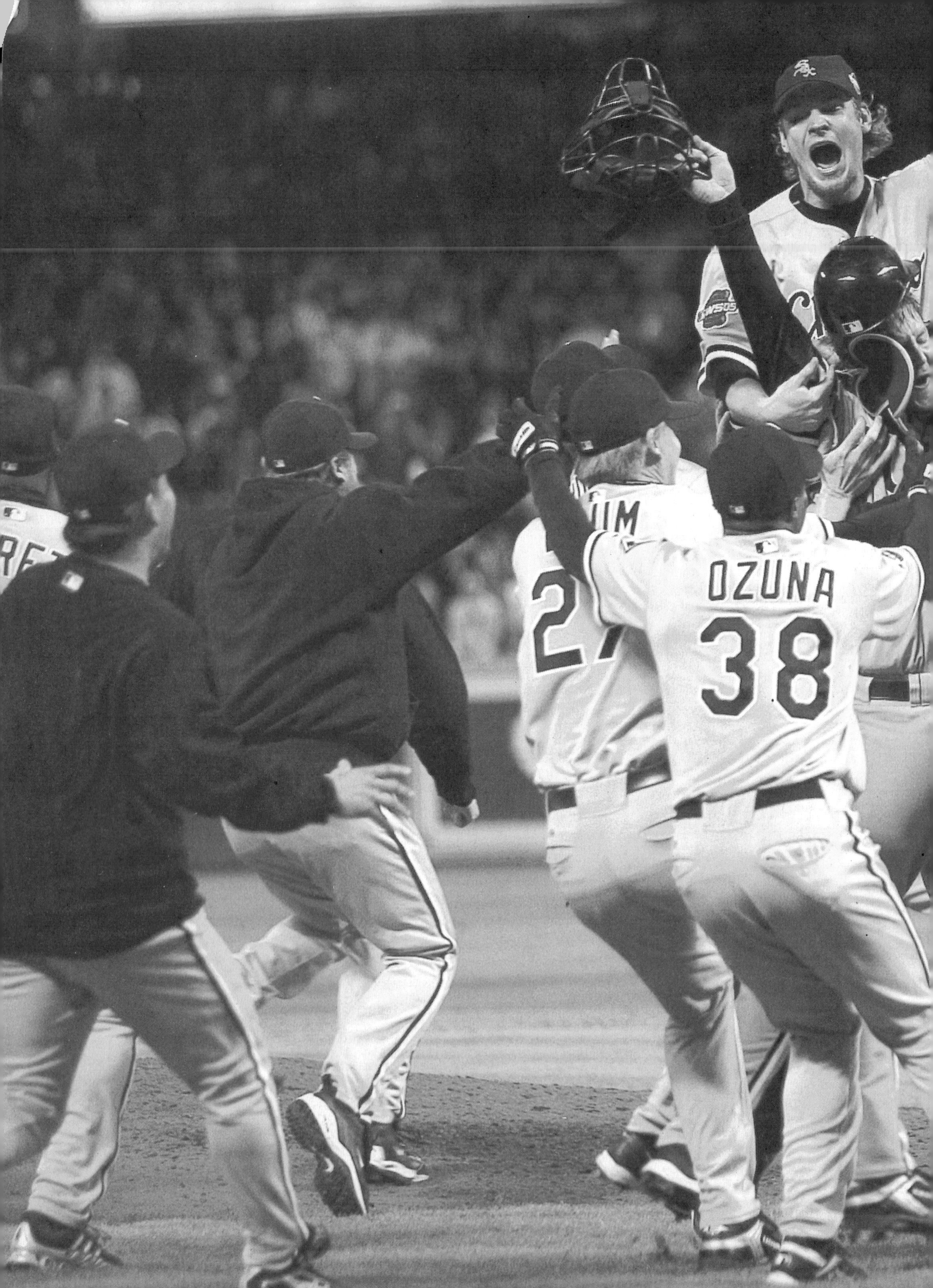
OZUNA
38

Members of the Chicago White Sox celebrate after winning the World Series on October 26, 2005. The White Sox defeated the Houston Astros, four games to none, to win the Series for the first time since 1917.